6
4–5
7
8–9
10–11
14–15
12
13
St. John's
Halifax
Québec
Montréal
Ottawa
Toronto
Hamilton

KEY TO MAPS OF CANADA

PROVINCES

Alberta	18–19
Alberta – South	22–23
British Columbia	18
British Columbia – South	24–25
Manitoba	19
Manitoba – South	21
New Brunswick	9
Newfoundland	3
Island	7
Labrador	6
Northwest Territories	26–27
Nova Scotia	9
Ontario	2–3
Ontario – Central	16–17
Ontario – South	14–15
Prince Edward Island	9
Québec	3
Québec – North	6
Québec – South	10–11
Saskatchewan	19
Saskatchewan – South	20–21
Yukon Territory	26

CITIES

Calgary	31
Edmonton	31
Halifax	9
Hamilton	30
Montréal	29
Ottawa	30
Québec	30
St. John's	7
Toronto	28
Vancouver	32
Victoria	25
Winnipeg	31

The page numbers refer to the Canadian map section.

1:8 000 000

1:5 600 000

1:2 000 000

1: 480 000

■ Town Plans

Philips' ATLAS OF CANADA & THE WORLD

Produced exclusively for W. H. Smith in Canada

Edited by
B. M. Willett Director and Cartographic Editor, George Philip Ltd.

David Gaylard, Joan Russell, Ray Smith and Amanda Wells

Maps prepared by George Philip Cartographic Services under the direction of A. G. Poynter, Director of Cartography

Printed in Hong Kong

ISBN 0-88665-488-2

Philips'

ATLAS OF CANADA & THE WORLD

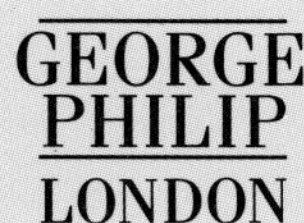
GEORGE
PHILIP
LONDON

CONTENTS

CANADA

		Map Scale
1	Canadian Map Symbols	
2–3	Canada	1:14M
4–5	Eastern Canada	1:5.6M
6	Labrador and Québec-North	1:5.6M
7	Newfoundland	1:2M
	St. John's	1:200 000
8–9	Atlantic Provinces	1:2M
	Halifax	1:200 000
10–11	Québec – South	1:2M
12	The Montréal Region	1:480 000
13	The Golden Horseshoe	1:480 000
14-15	Ontario – South	1:2M
16–17	Central Ontario – Lake Superior	1:2M
18–19	Western Canada	1:5.6M
20–21	Manitoba and Saskatchewan – South	1:2M
22–23	Alberta – South	1:2M
24–25	British Columbia – South	1:2M
	Victoria	1:200 000
26–27	Yukon and the Northwest Territories	1:8M
28	Toronto	1:200 000
29	Montréal	1:200 000
30	Québec, Ottawa, Hamilton	1:200 000
31	Winnipeg, Calgary, Edmonton	1:200 000
32	Vancouver	1:200 000
33–47	Index for Canada	

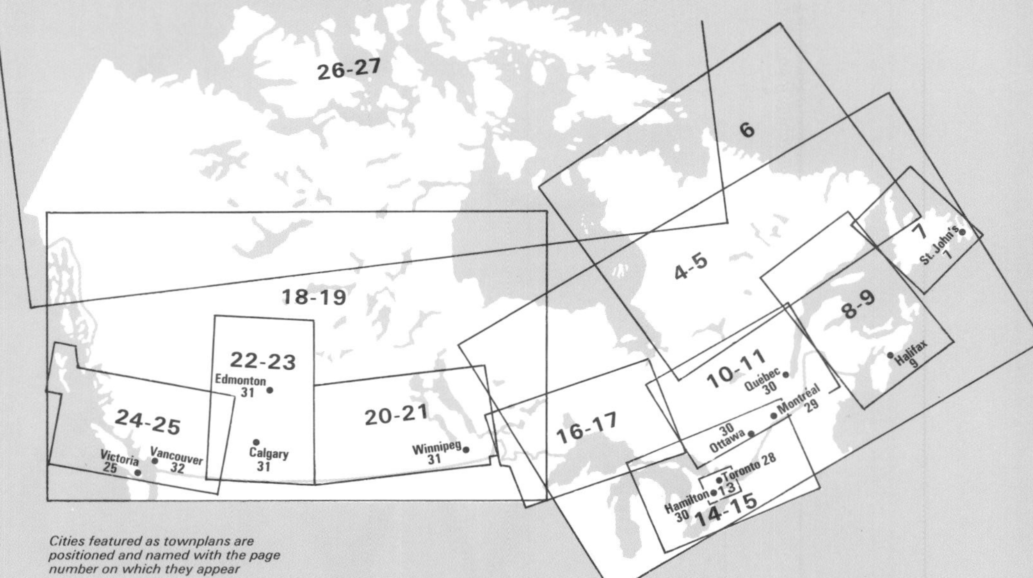

26-27
6
7
St. John's 7
4-5
18-19
8-9
Halifax 9
22-23
Edmonton 31
10-11
Québec 30
Montréal 29
24-25
Victoria 25
Vancouver 32
Calgary 31
20-21
Winnipeg 31
16-17
30 Ottawa
Toronto 28
Hamilton 30
13
14-15

Cities featured as townplans are positioned and named with the page number on which they appear

THE WORLD

1	General Reference	
2–3	The World: Physical	1:80M
4–5	The World: Political	1:64M

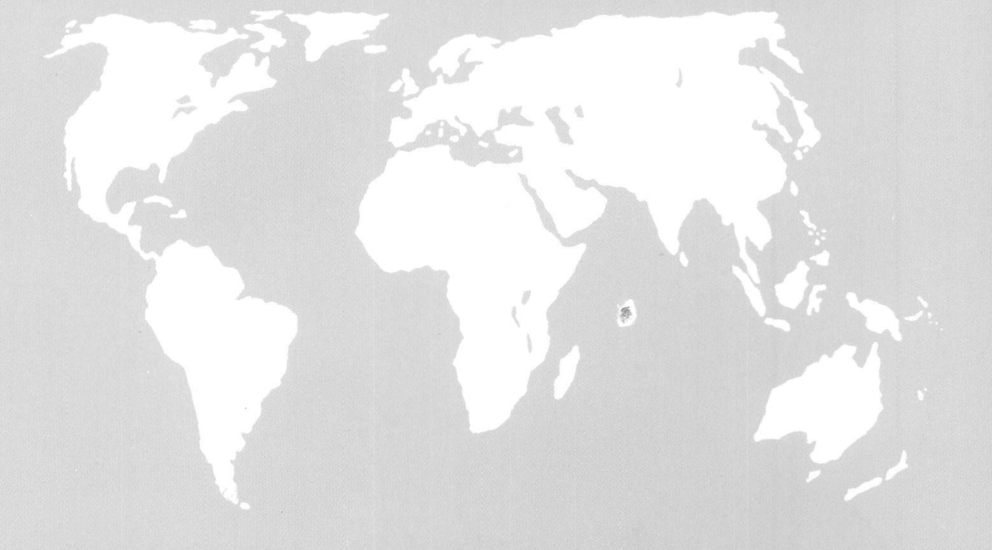

EUROPE

		Map Scale
6	Europe: Physical	1:16M
7	Europe: Political	1:16M
8–9	Scandinavia and the Baltic Lands	1:4M
	Iceland	1:4M
10–11	Denmark and Southern Sweden	1:2M
12–13	England and Wales	1:1.6M
14	Scotland	1:1.6M
15	Ireland	1:1.6M
16–17	Netherlands, Belgium and Luxembourg	1:1M
18–19	Northern France	1:2M
20–21	Southern France	1:2M
22–23	Western Spain and Portugal	1:2M
24–25	Eastern Spain	1:2M
	Canary Is.	1:1.6M
26–27	Northern Italy and Western Yugoslavia	1:2M
28–29	Southern Italy	1:2M
30–31	Germany and Switzerland	1:2M
32–33	Central Europe	1:2.8M
34–35	The Balkans	1:2.8M
36–37	European Russia – Central	1:4M
38–39	European Russia – South	1:4M
40–41	Union of Soviet Socialist Republics	1:16M

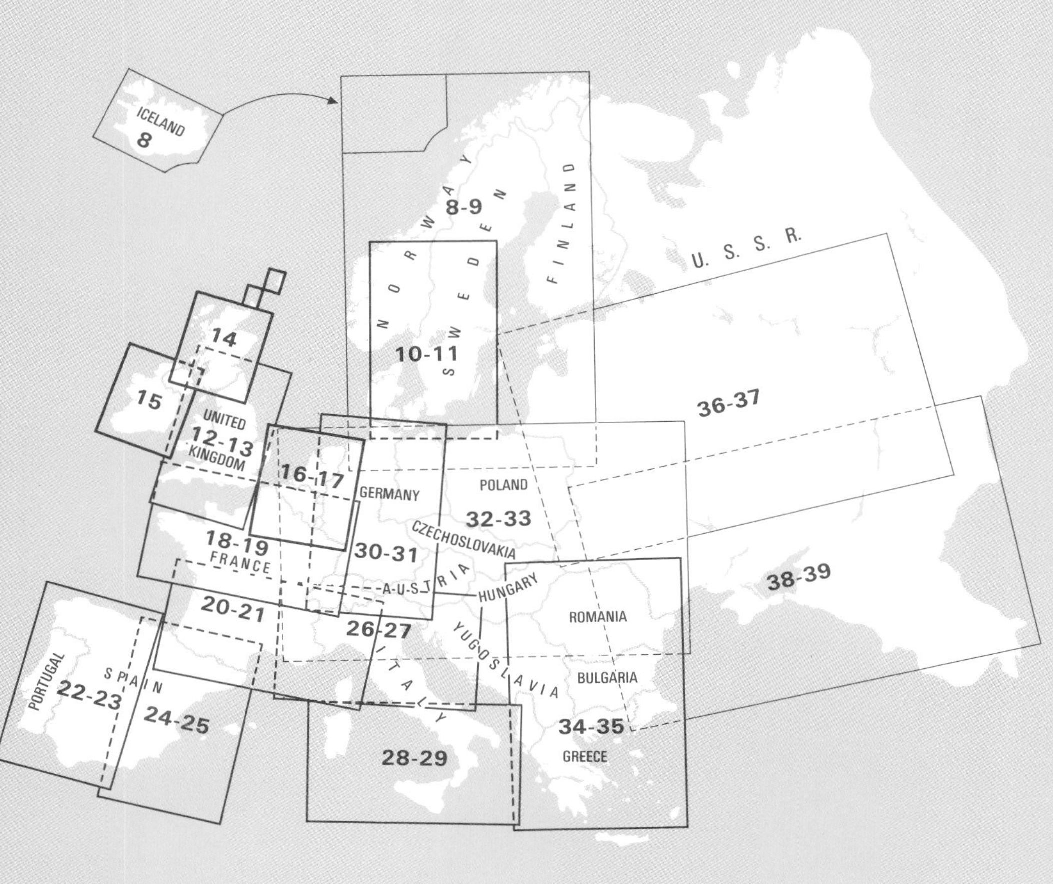

ICELAND
8
8-9
NORWAY
SWEDEN
FINLAND
U. S. S. R.
10-11
14
15
UNITED
12-13
KINGDOM
16-17
GERMANY
POLAND
32-33
36-37
18-19
FRANCE
30-31
CZECHOSLOVAKIA
AUSTRIA
HUNGARY
ROMANIA
38-39
20-21
26-27
YUGOSLAVIA
BULGARIA
PORTUGAL
SPAIN
22-23
24-25
ITALY
34-35
GREECE
28-29

ASIA

42	Asia: Physical	1:40M
43	Asia: Political	1:40M
44	Israel and West Jordan	1:800 000
45	Arabia and the Horn of Africa	1:12M
46–47	The Near and Middle East	1:8M
48–49	The Indo-Gangetic Plain	1:4.8M
50–51	Southern India and Sri Lanka	1:4.8M
52	Bangladesh, North-Eastern India and Burma	1:4.8M
53	Indian Ocean	1:40M
54–55	Mainland South-East Asia	1:4.8M
56–57	The East Indies	1:10M
	Java and Madura	1:6M
58–59	Southern China	1:4.8M
60–61	Northern China and Korea	1:4.8M
62	China	1:16M
63	Japan	1:6M
64–65	Southern Japan	1:2M

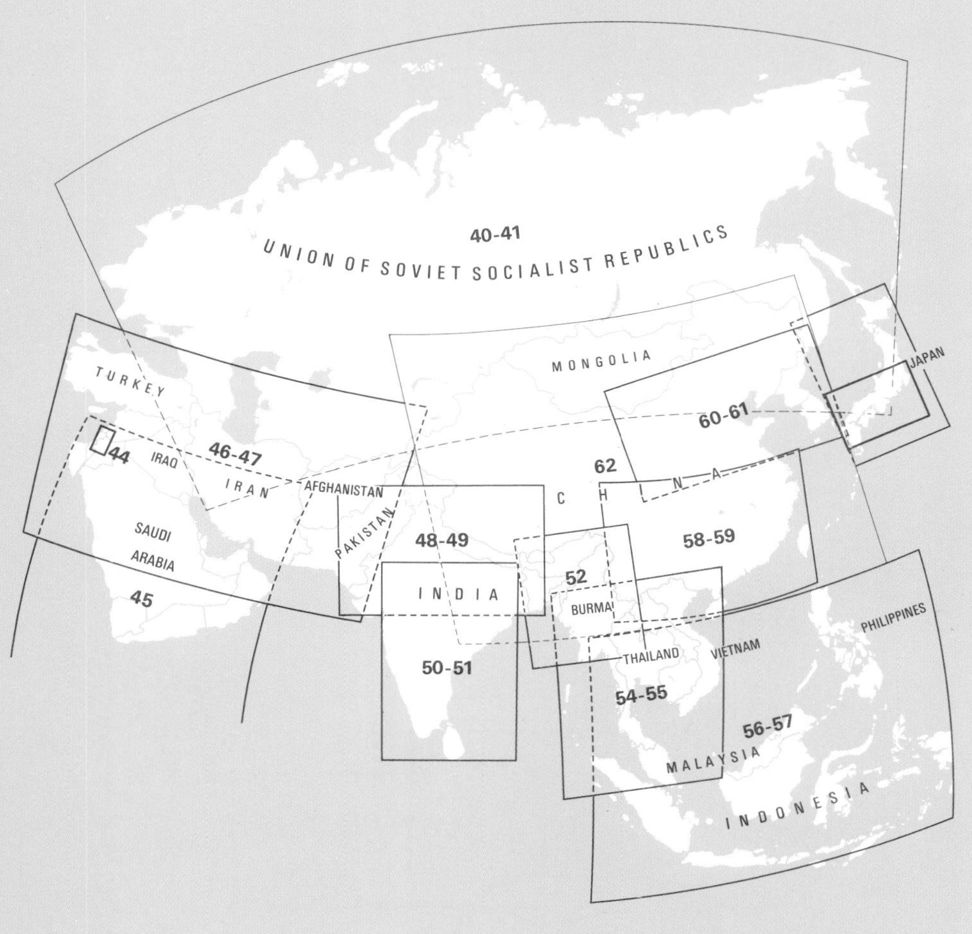

40-41
UNION OF SOVIET SOCIALIST REPUBLICS
MONGOLIA
TURKEY
JAPAN
60-61
44
IRAQ
46-47
IRAN
AFGHANISTAN
62
CHINA
SAUDI
ARABIA
PAKISTAN
48-49
58-59
45
52
INDIA
BURMA
PHILIPPINES
THAILAND
VIETNAM
50-51
54-55
56-57
MALAYSIA
INDONESIA

OCEANIA

		Map Scale
66–67	Pacific Ocean	1:43M
68	Islands of the South-West Pacific	1:4M
69	Papua New Guinea	1:5.2M
70–71	Australia	1:11.2M
72–73	Eastern Australia	1:6.4M
74–75	Victoria	1:2M
76	New South Wales – East	1:2M
77	Northern Rivers	1:2M
78–79	Western Australia	1:6.4M
80	New Zealand – North Island	1:2.8M
81	New Zealand – South Island	1:2.8M

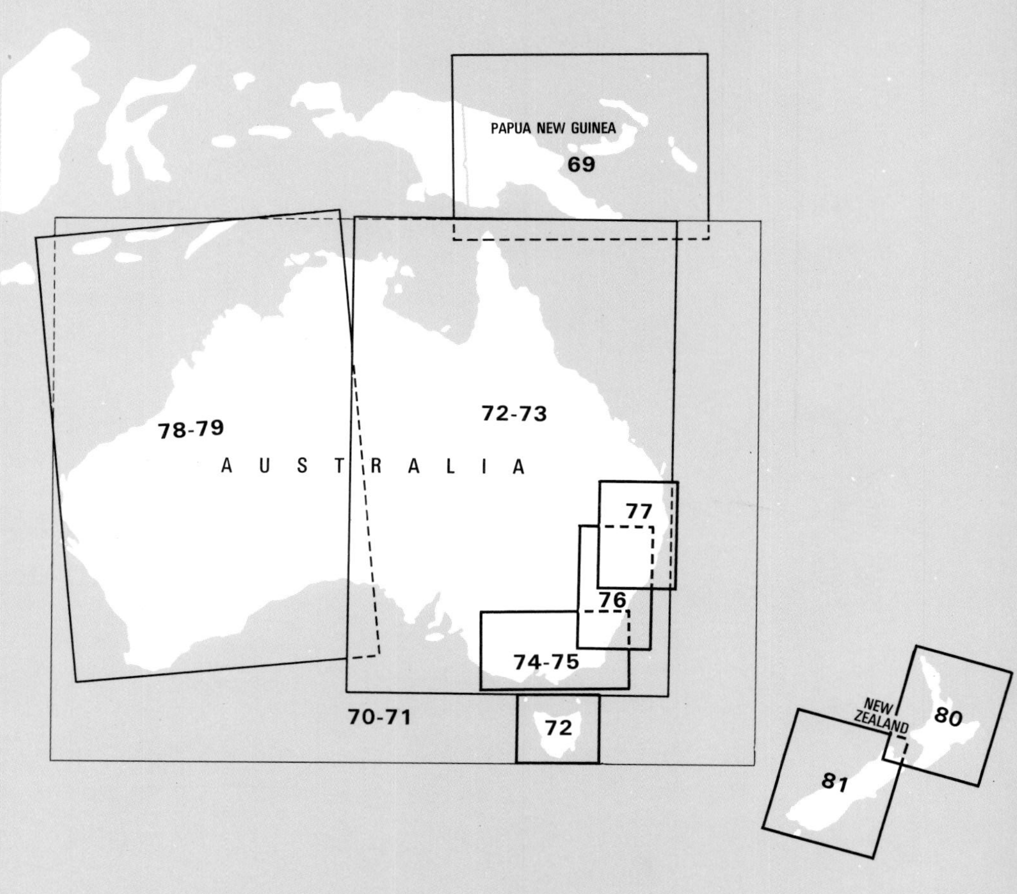

PAPUA NEW GUINEA
69
78-79
72-73
AUSTRALIA
77
76
74-75
70-71
72
NEW ZEALAND
80
81

AFRICA

82	Africa: Physical	1:32M
83	Africa: Political	1:32M
84–85	North-West Africa	1:6.4M
86–87	Central North Africa	1:6.4M
88–89	The Nile Valley	1:6.4M
	The Nile Delta	1:3.2M
90–91	West Africa	1:6.4M
92–93	East Africa	1:6.4M
94–95	Central Africa	1:6.4M
96–97	Southern Africa	1:6.4M
98	Horn of Africa	1:6.4M

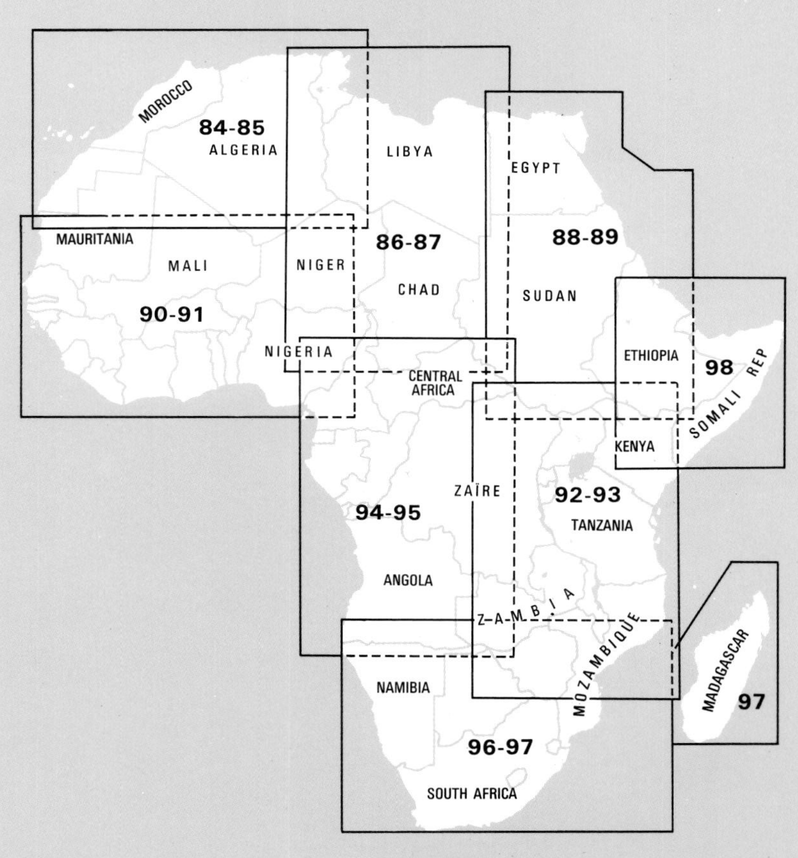

MOROCCO
84-85
ALGERIA
LIBYA
EGYPT
MAURITANIA
MALI
NIGER
86-87
88-89
CHAD
SUDAN
90-91
NIGERIA
CENTRAL AFRICA
ETHIOPIA
98
SOMALI REP
KENYA
ZAIRE
94-95
92-93
TANZANIA
ANGOLA
ZAMBIA
MOZAMBIQUE
NAMIBIA
MADAGASCAR
97
96-97
SOUTH AFRICA

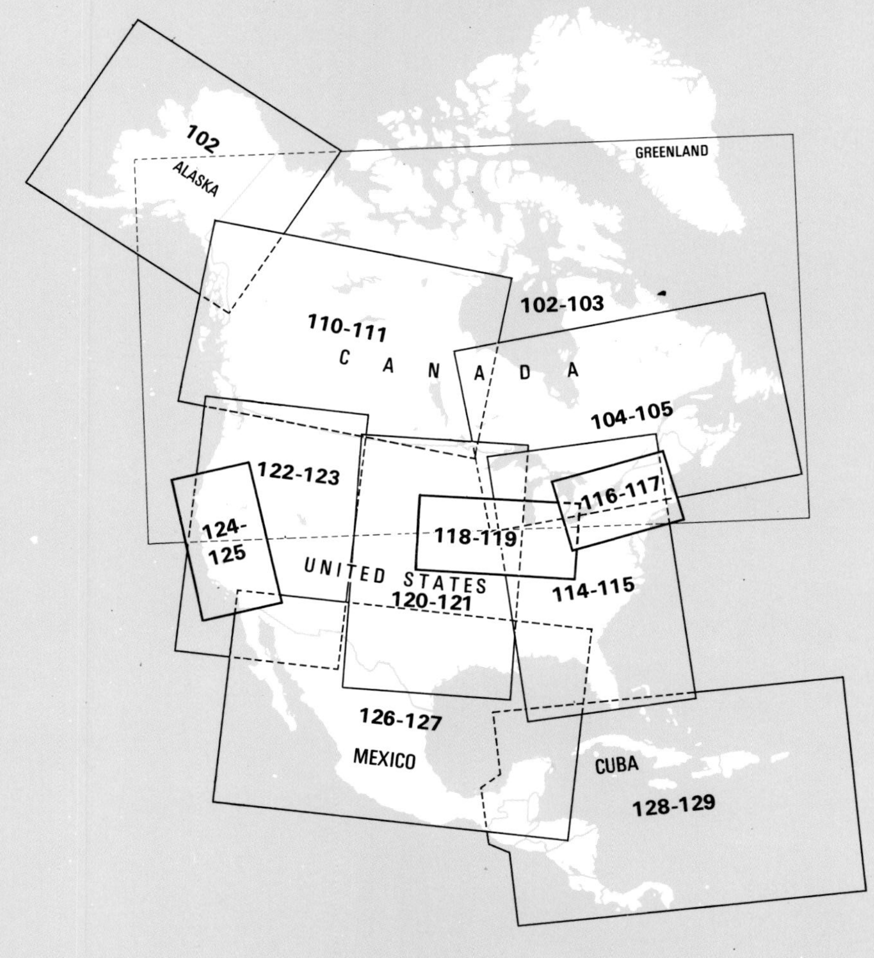
102
ALASKA
GREENLAND
102-103
110-111
C A N A D A
104-105
122-123
116-117
124-125
118-119
UNITED STATES
120-121
114-115
126-127
MEXICO
CUBA
128-129

NORTH AMERICA

		Map Scale
99	The Americas	1:48M
100	North America: Physical	1:28M
101	North America: Political	1:28M
102–103	Canada	1:12M
	Alaska	1:24M
104–105	Eastern Canada	1:5.6M
106–107	Québec – South	1:2M
108–109	Ontario – South	1:2M
110–111	Western Canada	1:5.6M
112–113	United States	1:9.6M
	Hawaii	1:8M
114–115	Eastern United States	1:4.8M
116–117	North-Eastern United States	1:2M
118–119	Chicago and the Midwest	1:2M
120–121	Middle United States	1:4.8M
122–123	Western United States	1:4.8M
124–125	Central and Southern California and Washington	1:2M
126–127	Mexico	1:6.4M
128–129	Central America and the Antilles	1:6.4M
130–131	The Atlantic Ocean	1:36M

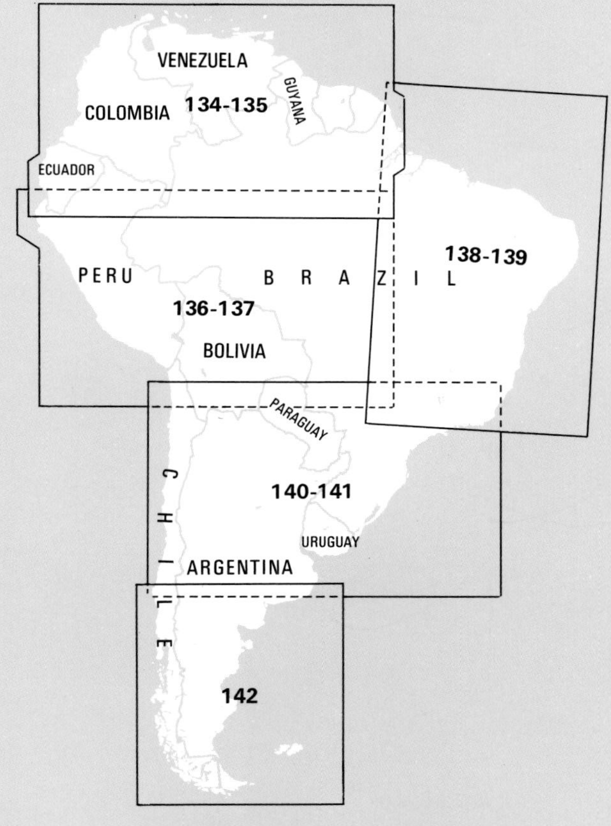
VENEZUELA
GUYANA
COLOMBIA
134-135
ECUADOR
138-139
PERU
B R A Z I L
136-137
BOLIVIA
PARAGUAY
C H I L E
140-141
URUGUAY
ARGENTINA
142

SOUTH AMERICA

132	South America: Physical	1:24M
133	South America: Political	1:24M
134–135	South America – North-West	1:6.4M
136–137	South America – West	1:6.4M
138–139	Eastern Brazil	1:6.4M
140–141	Central South America	1:6.4M
142	Southern Chile and Argentina	1:6.4M
143	South Polar Regions	1:28M
144	North Polar Regions	1:28M

INDEX

1-144

ATLAS OF CANADA

SETTLEMENTS AND BOUNDARIES

Settlements in order of size :-

MONTRÉAL **Hamilton** **Moose Jaw** **Prince Rupert** **Gaspé** Banff Miquelon

International Boundaries
Internal Boundaries
Internal Boundaries (Undemarcated or Undefined)

These show the de facto situation where there are rival claims to territory.

National and Provincial Parks

COMMUNICATIONS

Freeways
Under construction
Trans-Canada Highway
Principal Roads
Other Roads
Trails and Seasonal Roads
Principal Railroads
Other Railroads
Under construction
Railroad Tunnels
Road Tunnels
Principal Canals
Passes
Airports

PHYSICAL FEATURES

Perennial Streams
8848 Spot Height in meters
Seasonal Lakes, Salt Flats
Swamps, Marshes
8050 Sea Depths in meters
Permanent Ice
1134 Height of Lake Surface Above Sea Level, in meters

ARCTIC OCEAN
Beaufort Sea
PACIFIC OCEAN
ALASKA (U.S.A.)
YUKON TERRITORY
NORTHWEST TERRITORIES
BRITISH COLUMBIA
ALBERTA
SASKATCHEWAN
MANITOBA
INUVIK REGION
KITIKMEOT REGION
FORT SMITH REGION
KEEWATIN REGION
WASHINGTON
OREGON
IDAHO
MONTANA
WYOMING
NEVADA
CALIFORNIA
NORTH DAKOTA
SOUTH DAKOTA
MINNESOTA
WISCONSIN
NEBRASKA
UNITED STATES
Queen Elizabeth Islands
Sverdrup Islands
Banks Island
Victoria Island
Prince of Wales Island
Somerset Island
Devon I.
Axel Heiberg I.
Melville I.
Prince Patrick I.
Queen Charlotte Is.
Vancouver I.
Amundsen Gulf
Coronation Gulf
Queen Maud Gulf
Gulf of Boothia
Boothia Peninsula
M'Clure Strait
Viscount Melville Sound
M'Clintock Channel
Great Bear Lake
Great Slave L.
Lake Athabasca
Reindeer Lake
Lake Winnipeg
L. Manitoba
L. of the Woods
Arctic Circle
Rocky Mountains
Mackenzie Mountains
Coast Mountains
Fairbanks
Anchorage
Whitehorse
Dawson
Yellowknife
Edmonton
Calgary
Vancouver
Victoria
Seattle
Tacoma
Spokane
Portland
Saskatoon
Regina
Moose Jaw
Prince Albert
Lethbridge
Medicine Hat
Brandon
Winnipeg
St. Boniface
Minneapolis
St. Paul
Milwaukee
Salt Lake City
Sacramento
San Francisco
Oakland
Berkeley
Richmond
Stockton
Great Falls
Billings
Duluth
Churchill
Mt. McKinley 6194
Mt. Logan 6050
Mt. St. Elias 5489
Mt. Fairweather 4663
Mt. Robson 3954
Mt. Rainier 4392
Mt. Shasta 4317
m
4000
3000
2000
1500
1000
400
200
0
-200
m
Projection: Bonne
West from Greenwich
170
160
150
140
130
120
110
100
90
60
50
40

1 : 14 000 000
200 0 200 400 600 km
CANADA ADMINISTRATIVE
1 : 32 000 000
National Capital
Provincial or Territorial Capital
Undemarcated boundary
District boundary
GREENLAND
ALASKA
Inuvik Region
Kitikmeot Region
Baffin Region
NORTHWEST TERRITORIES
YUKON TERRITORY
Whitehorse
Fort Smith Region
Yellowknife
Keewatin Region
NEWFOUNDLAND
BRITISH COLUMBIA
ALBERTA
Edmonton
SASKATCHEWAN
Regina
MANITOBA
Winnipeg
ONTARIO
QUÉBEC
PRINCE EDWARD ISLAND
Charlottetown
NEW BRUNSWICK
Fredericton
NOVA SCOTIA
Halifax
St. John's
Quebec
Ottawa
Toronto
Victoria
UNITED STATES
West from Greenwich
Baffin Bay
Hudson Strait
Ungava Bay
Foxe Channel
Foxe Basin
Southampton I.
Coats I.
Mansel I.
James Bay
Gulf of St. Lawrence
ATLANTIC OCEAN
ST. PIERRE & MIQUELON (Fr.)
Sable I. (Nova Scotia)
PR. EDWARD I.
NEW BRUNSWICK
MONTRÉAL
Québec
Ottawa
Hull
Toronto
Hamilton
London
Buffalo
DETROIT
Windsor
Cleveland
Toledo
Boston
Providence
Halifax
Sydney
St. John's
Lake Huron
L. Michigan
L. Ontario
Lake Erie
NEW YORK
VERMONT
NEW HAMPSHIRE
MAINE
MASS.
CONN.
COPYRIGHT, GEORGE PHILIP & SON, LTD.

1 2 N. W. TERRITORIES 4

A

B

C

D

MANITOBA

HUDSON BAY

JAMES BAY

ONTARIO

Q

LAKE SUPERIOR

LAKE MICHIGAN

LAKE HURON

LAKE ONTARIO

LAKE ERIE

WISCONSIN

ILLINOIS

NEW YORK

m
1500
1000
400
200
0
0
200
2000
4000
m

Lambert's Equivalent Azimuthal

INDIANA OHIO PENNSYLVANIA

2 3 4

1 : 5 600 000
50 0 50 100 150 200 250 300 km
West from Greenwich
A
B
C
D
5
6
7
8
9
COAST OF LABRADOR
NEWFOUNDLAND
QUEBEC
NEW BRUNSWICK
NOVA SCOTIA
PRINCE EDWARD ISLAND
MAINE
GULF OF ST. LAWRENCE
ATLANTIC OCEAN
Cabot Strait
Str. of Belle Isle
St. Lawrence
Bay of Fundy
Northumberland Str.
Î. d'Anticosti
Dét. de Jacques-Cartier
Dét. d'Honguedo
Cape Breton Island
Avalon Peninsula
SAINT-PIERRE ET MIQUELON (Fr.)
Miquelon
Langlade
St. Pierre
Sable I. (Nova Scotia)
Îs. de la Madeleine (Quebec)
Pén. de Gaspé
Mts. Chic-Chocs
Long Range Mts.
Mealy Mts.
Rés. Manicouagan
Kaniapiskau Lake
Michikamau Lake
L. Melville
Happy Valley-Goose Bay
Churchill Falls
Labrador City
Schefferville
Sept-Îles
Hopedale
Nain
Battle Harbour
St. Anthony
Corner Brook
Gander
St. John's
Grand Falls
Stephenville
Port aux Basques
Charlottetown
Summerside
Sydney
Glace Bay
New Waterford
Halifax
Dartmouth
Truro
New Glasgow
Yarmouth
Moncton
Saint John
Fredericton
Bathurst
Campbellton
Edmundston
Chatham
Newcastle
Rimouski
Rivière-du-Loup
Chicoutimi
Jonquière
QUEBEC
Lévis
Sherbrooke
Bangor
Augusta
Portland
Manchester
BOSTON
COPYRIGHT, GEORGE PHILIP & SON, LTD.

1 : 5 600 000
50 0 50 100 150 200 250 300 km
ATLANTIC OCEAN
HUDSON STRAIT
UNGAVA BAY
HUDSON BAY
JAMES BAY
COAST OF LABRADOR
LABRADOR
NOUVEAU-QUÉBEC
QUÉBEC
Ungava Peninsula
Resolution I.
Hatton Headland
Edgell I.
Button Is.
C. Chidley
Killinek I.
Black Rock Pt.
North Aulatsivik I.
Ryans B.
Torngat Mts.
Seven Islands B.
Nachvak Fd.
Ramah B.
Ramah
Mt d'Iberville 1622
Saglek B.
Saglek Fd.
C. Uivuk
Hebron
Hebron Fd.
Napaktok B.
Cod I.
Okak Is.
Okak
Nutok
North
C. Kiglapait
South Aulatsivik I.
High I.
Paul I.
Nain
Voiseys B.
Tunungayualuk I.
Davis Inlet
Nunaksaluk I.
Hopedale
Kaipokok B.
Aillik
Makkovik
Adlavik Is.
C. Harrison
Holton
Indian Harbour
Groswater B.
Rigolet
Hamilton Inlet
L. Melville
Mealy Mts.
1128
Happy Valley
Goose Bay
North-West River
Grand L.
Cartwright
Sandwich B.
Table B.
Island of Ponds
Separation Point
Paradise River
Eagle
Paradise
Alexis
Square Islands
Battle Harbour
Mary's Harbour
St. Lewis
Belle I.
Str. of Belle Isle
Red Bay
L'Anse-au-Loup
Forteau
St. Lunaire-Griquet
Hare B.
Groais I.
Conche
Bell I.
Englee
Horse Is.
White B.
Baie Verte
Springdale
Seal Cove
Sop's Arm
Long Range Mts.
Great Harbour Deep
Roddickton
Flower's Cove
Port Saunders
Daniel's Harbour
Bradore Bay
Lourdes-de-Blanc-Sablon
Outer I.
St-Augustin
St-Augustin-Saguenay
St-Paul
I. du Petit-Mécatina
Little Mecatina
Minipi L.
NFLD.
QUÉBEC
Olomane
L. Musquaro
Natashquan
Aguanus
Nabisipi
Kegaska
Aguanish
Gethsémani
Romaine
Havre-St-Pierre
Lac Allard
Magpie L.
West Magpie
St-Jean
Mingan
Sheldrake
Dét. de Jacques-Cartier
Sept-Îles
Port-Cartier
Clarke City
Moisie
Nicman
L. Manitou
1048
Nipissis
Waco
Eric
Ste-Marguerite
Walker L.
Labrador City
Wabush
Mont Wright
Emeril
Lac Joseph
Ashuanipi
Ashuanipi L.
Esker
Schefferville
Menihek
Menihek Lakes
Attikamagen L.
Petitsikapau L.
Shabogamo L.
Opiskotish L.
Opiscoteo L.
Michikamau Lake (Smallwood Reservoir)
Nashaupi
Kanairiktok
Seal L.
Nipishish L.
Harp L.
Ossokmanuan L.
Winokapau L.
Atikonak L.
Churchill
Goose
Burnt L.
Kaniapiskau
Kaniapiskau L.
Petit Lac Manicouagan
Manicouagan
Rés. Manicouagan
Mts Groulx
Gagnon
Outardes
Mouchalagane
Betsiamites
L. Manouane
L. Plétipi
Mts. Otish
L. Péribonca
Péribonca
Mistassibi
Témiscamie
L. Albanei
L. Mistassini
372
Baie-du-Poste
Chibougamau
L. Chibougamau
L. Waconichi
Opémisca
556
Troilus
Lac Bienville
Grand Baleine
Petite Baleine
L. Guillaume-Delisle
L. à l'Eau Claire
Nastapoka
Nastapoka Is.
L. Minto
Mélèzes
Du Gué
Lac D'Iberville
Lacs des Loups-Marins
L. Gayot
L. Néret
L. Bermen
L. Naococane
Nitchequon
L. Châteauguay
L. Le Moyne
L. Nachikapau
Chakonipau L.
Otelnuk L.
Wheeler
L. Wakuach
Lac Champdoré
L. Tudor
610
L. de la Hutte Sauvage
Whitegull L.
Mistastin L.
Kogaluk
Fraser
Big Bay
Sandy
Sérigny
Fort McKenzie
Koksoak
Kuujjuaq
George
Tunulic
Port-Nouveau-Québec
Kangiqsualujjuaq (George River)
Qikirtajuaq
Pte. Cognarauya
Koroc
Payne B.
Dry B.
Akpatok I.
Diana B.
C. Hopes Advance
Koartac
Hopes Advance B.
Fj. Alluviaq
B. Keglo
I. Kikkertorsoak
Gyrfalcon Is.
B. aux Feuilles
375
Feuilles (Leaf)
Lac Faribault
Lac la Potherie
L. Tassialouc
Lepelle
Arnaud
L. Peters
Kangirsuk
Wales I.
C. Prince of Wales
Joy B.
Maricourt (Wakeham)
Douglas Hr.
Charles I.
Maiden I.
C. de Nlle-France
Fj. Deception
Saglouc
Mts. de Povungnituk
Povungnituk
Mts. St-Louis
Digges Is.
Ivujivik
C. Wolstenholme
Mansel I.
L. Nantais
L. Pélican
L. Klotz
L. Couture
L. Chavigny
L. Leroy
Kogaluk
B. Kogaluk
B. Povungnituk
Povungnituk
Pte Dufrost
Pte aux Écueils
Mosquito B.
Cape Smith
Smith I.
Pte Cusson
B. Kovic
Inoucdjouac
Hopewell Is.
Promontoire Portland
Farmer I.
Ottawa Is.
South Sleeper Is.
North Belcher Is.
Belcher Islands
Kugong I.
Flaherty I.
Qurlutuc
King George Is.
Baker's Dozen Is.
Tukarak I.
Innetalling I.
Merry I.
Kuujjuarapik
Long I.
Pte. Louis-XIV
L. Burton
Roggan River
Roggan
Roggan L.
Julian L.
Craven L.
Kanaaupscow
LA1
LG1
LG2
LG3
LG4
Fort George
Duncan L.
Castor
L. Sakami
Sakami
L. Yasinski
Boyd L.
Opinaca L.
Opinaca
Eastmain
EM1
Nouveau Comptoir
L. de la Corvette
Lac Rossignol
Frégate
Neoskweskau
Rupert
L. Mesgouez
L. Nemiscau
Némiscau
L. Evans
Broadback
Nottaway
Dana
L. Poncheville
L. au Goéland
Waswanipi
L. Waswanipi
L. Olga
Matagami
L. Matagami
L. Soscumica
Fort Rupert
Rupert B.
Missisicabi
Harricana
ONTARIO
QUÉBEC
North Twin I.
South Twin I.
Weston I.
Charlton I.
Trodely I.
Projection: Lambert's Equivalent Azimuthal
West from Greenwich
© COPYRIGHT, GEORGE PHILIP & SON, LTD.
m 1500 1000 400 200 0
0 200 2000 4000 m

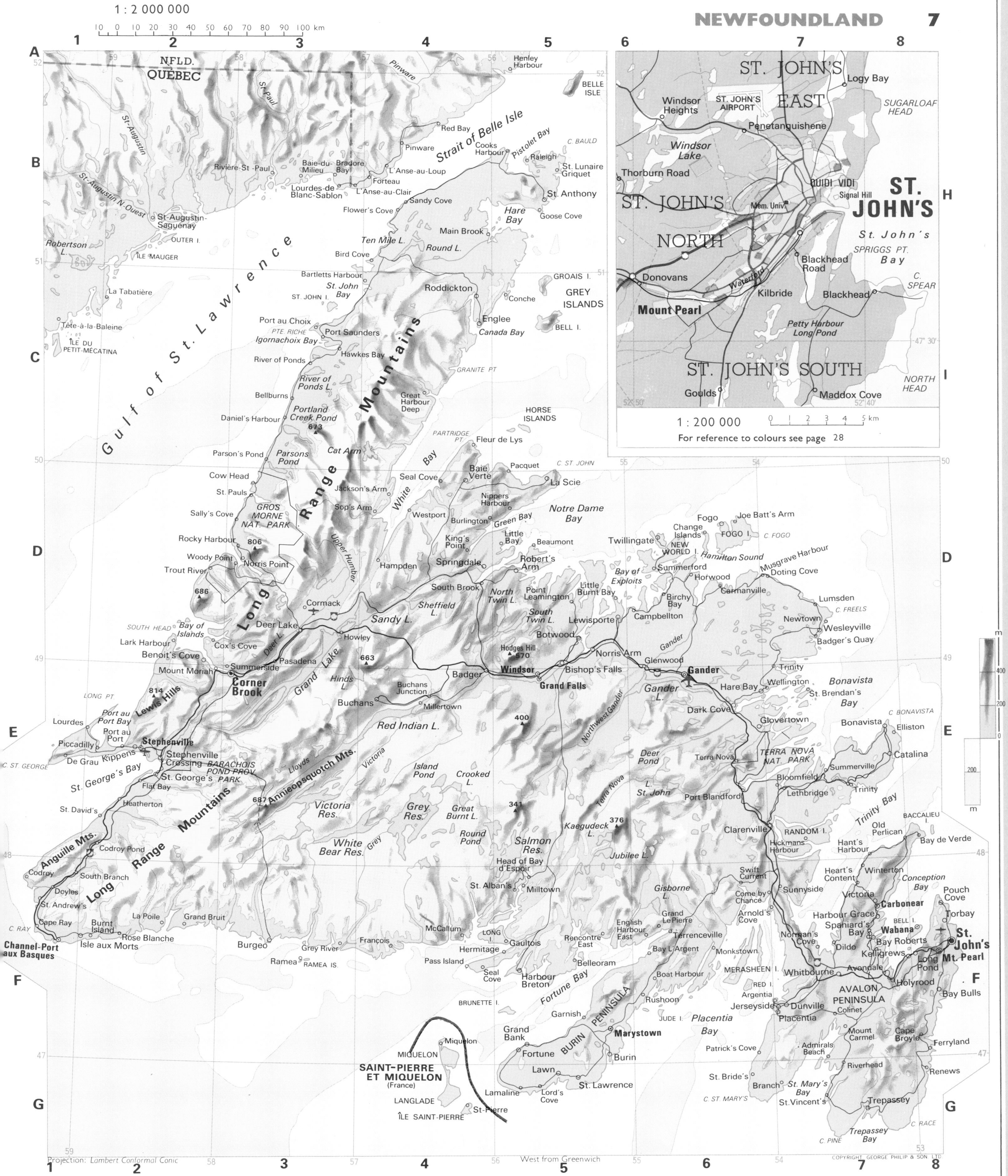

1 : 2 000 000

10 0 10 20 30 40 50 60 70 80 90 100 km

NFLD.
QUEBEC
St-Paul
St-Augustin
Rivière-St-Paul
St-Augustin N-Ouest
St-Augustin-Saguenay
OUTER I.
ÎLE MAUGER
Robertson L.
La Tabatière
Tête-à-la-Baleine
ÎLE DU PETIT-MÉCATINA
Baie-du-Milieu
Bradore Bay
Lourdes-de Blanc-Sablon
L'Anse-au-Clair
Forteau
L'Anse-au-Loup
Pinware
Red Bay
Henley Harbour
BELLE ISLE
Strait of Belle Isle
Cooks Harbour
Pistolet Bay
C. BAULD
Raleigh
St. Lunaire Griquet
St. Anthony
Goose Cove
Hare Bay
Sandy Cove
Flower's Cove
Main Brook
Ten Mile L.
Round L.
Bird Cove
Bartletts Harbour
St. John Bay
ST. JOHN I.
Roddickton
Conche
GROAIS I.
GREY ISLANDS
BELL I.
Englee
Canada Bay
Gulf of St. Lawrence
Port au Choix
PTE RICHE
Igornachoix Bay
Port Saunders
Hawkes Bay
River of Ponds
River of Ponds L.
GRANITE PT
Bellburns
Portland Creek Pond
Great Harbour Deep
HORSE ISLANDS
Daniel's Harbour
673
Long Range Mountains
Cat Arm
PARTRIDGE PT.
Fleur de Lys
Parson's Pond
Parsons Pond
White Bay
C. ST JOHN
Pacquet
Baie Verte
La Scie
Cow Head
Seal Cove
St. Pauls
Jackson's Arm
Nippers Harbour
Sally's Cove
GROS MORNE NAT. PARK
Sop's Arm
Westport
Burlington
Green Bay
Notre Dame Bay
Rocky Harbour
806
Upper Humber
King's Point
Little Bay
Beaumont
Twillingate
Change Islands
Fogo
FOGO I.
C. FOGO
Joe Batt's Arm
Woody Point
Norris Point
Trout River
Hampden
Springdale
Robert's Arm
NEW WORLD I.
Hamilton Sound
Summerford
Horwood
Musgrave Harbour
Doting Cove
686
South Brook
North Twin L.
Point Leamington
Little Burnt Bay
Bay of Exploits
Birchy Bay
Carmanville
Lumsden
C. FREELS
Cormack
Sheffield L.
South Twin L.
Lewisporte
Campbellton
Newtown
Wesleyville
Badger's Quay
SOUTH HEAD
Bay of Islands
Deer Lake
Sandy L.
Botwood
Lark Harbour
Cox's Cove
Howley
Deer L.
Hodges Hill 570
Norris Arm
Gander
Glenwood
Benoit's Cove
Pasadena
663
Mount Moriah
Summerside
Grand Lake
Windsor
Bishop's Falls
Badger
Grand Falls
Corner Brook
Gander
Trinity
LONG PT
Hinds L.
Buchans Junction
Gander L.
Hare Bay
Wellington
Bonavista Bay
St. Brendan's
814
Lewis Hills
Buchans
Millertown
Dark Cove
Lourdes
Port au Port Bay
Port au Port
400
Red Indian L.
Northwest Gander
Glovertown
C. BONAVISTA
Bonavista
Elliston
Piccadilly
Stephenville
Kippens
Catalina
C. ST GEORGE
De Grau
Stephenville Crossing
BARACHOIS POND PROV. PARK
Lloyds
Annieopsquotch Mts.
Victoria
Island Pond
Crooked L.
Deer Pond
Terra Nova
TERRA NOVA NAT. PARK
Summerville
St. George's Bay
St. George's
Flat Bay
Bloomfield
Trinity
Lethbridge
687
L. St. John
Port Blandford
Trinity Bay
Heatherton
St. David's
Mountains
Victoria Res.
Grey Res.
Great Burnt L.
341
Terra Nova
Kaegudeck L.
376
Clarenville
BACCALIEU I.
Old Perlican
RANDOM I.
Hickmans Harbour
Hant's Harbour
Bay de Verde
Round Pond
White Bear Res.
Grey
Salmon Res.
Jubilee L.
Anguille Mts.
Codroy Pond
Range
Head of Bay d'Espoir
Swift Current
Heart's Content
Winterton
Conception Bay
Codroy
South Branch
Long
Doyles
St. Andrew's
St. Alban's
Milltown
Gisborne L.
Sunnyside
Pouch Cove
Come by Chance
Victoria
Carbonear
Torbay
La Poile
Grand Bruit
Cape Ray
Burnt Islands
Grand Le Pierre
Arnold's Cove
Harbour Grace
BELL I.
C. RAY
McCallum
English Harbour East
Terrenceville
Spaniard's Bay
Wabana
St. John's
Channel-Port aux Basques
Rose Blanche
Isle aux Morts
Burgeo
François
LONG I.
Gaultois
Rencontre East
Norman's Cove
Bay Roberts
Dildo
Kelligrews
Mt. Pearl
Grey River
Hermitage
Bay L'Argent
Monkstown
Long Pond
Ramea
RAMEA IS.
Pass Island
Belleoram
MERASHEEN I.
Whitbourne
Avondale
Seal Cove
Harbour Breton
Fortune Bay
Boat Harbour
Holyrood
RED I.
Argentia
AVALON PENINSULA
Bay Bulls
BRUNETTE I.
Rushoon
Jerseyside
Dunville
Garnish
JUDE I.
Placentia
Colinet
BURIN PENINSULA
Placentia Bay
Grand Bank
Marystown
Mount Carmel
Cape Broyle
Miquelon
MIQUELON
Fortune
Patrick's Cove
Admirals Beach
Ferryland
Burin
SAINT-PIERRE ET MIQUELON (France)
Lawn
Riverhead
Renews
St. Bride's
Lamaline
Lord's Cove
St. Lawrence
Branch
St. Mary's Bay
LANGLADE
C. ST MARY'S
St. Vincent's
Trepassey
ÎLE SAINT-PIERRE
St-Pierre
C. RACE
C. PINE
Trepassey Bay

ST. JOHN'S EAST
Logy Bay
Windsor Heights
ST. JOHN'S AIRPORT
SUGARLOAF HEAD
Penetanguishene
Windsor Lake
Thorburn Road
BUIDI VIDI
ST. JOHN'S
Signal Hill
ST. JOHN'S NORTH
Mem. Univ.
St. John's
SPRIGGS PT.
Bay
Blackhead Road
Donovans
Waterford
Kilbride
Blackhead
C. SPEAR
Mount Pearl
Petty Harbour Long Pond
47° 30'
ST. JOHN'S SOUTH
NORTH HEAD
Goulds
Maddox Cove
52° 50'
52° 40'

1 : 200 000

0 1 2 3 4 5 km

For reference to colours see page 28

m
400
200
0
200
m

Projection: Lambert Conformal Conic

West from Greenwich

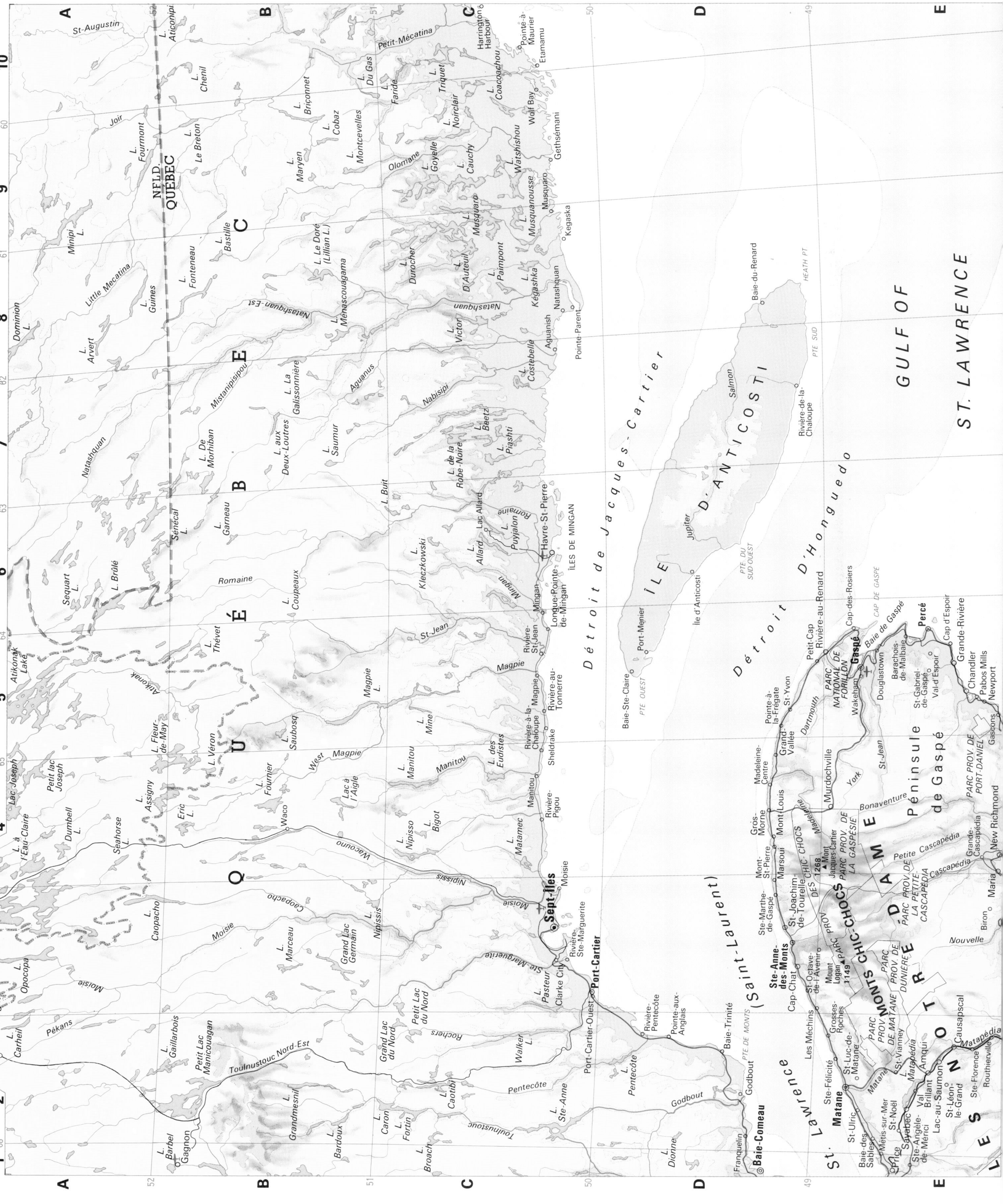

NFLD.
QUEBEC

GULF OF ST. LAWRENCE

ÎLE D'ANTICOSTI

Détroit de Jacques-Cartier

Détroit d'Honguedo

St. Lawrence (Saint-Laurent)

Péninsule de Gaspé

MONTS CHIC-CHOCS

Sept-Îles

Port-Cartier

Baie-Comeau

Matane

Gaspé

Percé

Labrador City

Havre-St-Pierre

9
1 : 2 000 000
NEW BRUNSWICK
PRINCE EDWARD ISLAND
NOVA SCOTIA
CAPE BRETON ISLAND
ÎLES DE LA MADELEINE (QUÉBEC)
MAINE
ATLANTIC OCEAN
Bay of Fundy
Northumberland Strait
Chaleur Bay
Minas Basin
Minas Channel
Chignecto Bay
Fredericton
Saint John
Moncton
Charlottetown
Summerside
Halifax
Dartmouth
Truro
Sydney
Yarmouth
Campbellton
Bathurst
Edmundston
Newcastle
Chatham
MOUNT CARLETON PROV. PARK
KOUCHIBOUGUAC NAT. PARK
FUNDY NAT. PARK
PRINCE EDWARD ISLAND NAT. PARK
KEJIMKUJIK NAT. PARK
CAPE BRETON HIGHLANDS NAT. PARK
LOUISBOURG NAT. HISTORIC PARK
1 : 200 000
For reference to colours see page 28
HALIFAX
DARTMOUTH
Bedford Basin
Projection: Bonne
West from Greenwich
COPYRIGHT. GEORGE PHILIP & SON. LTD.

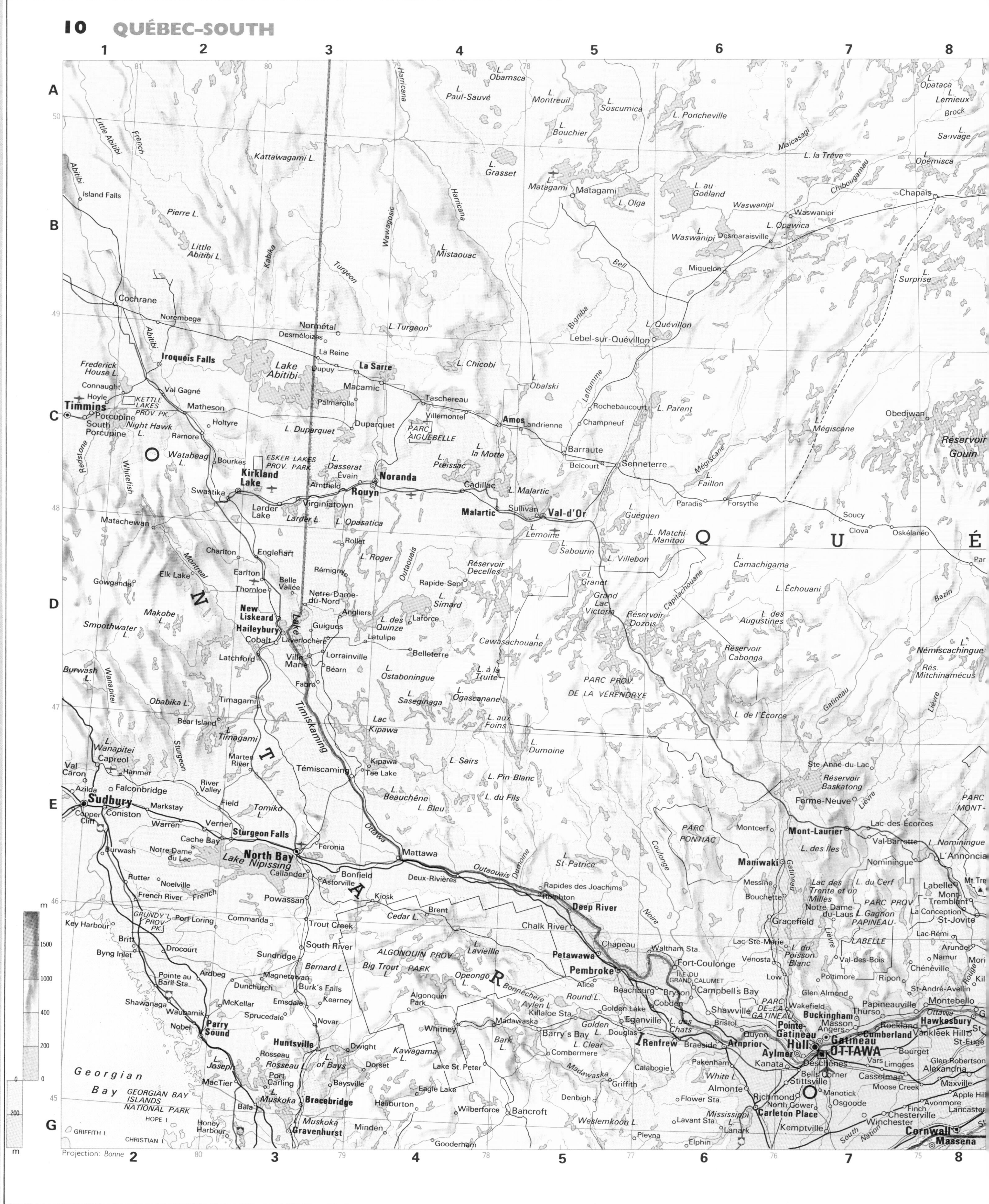
Projection: Bonne

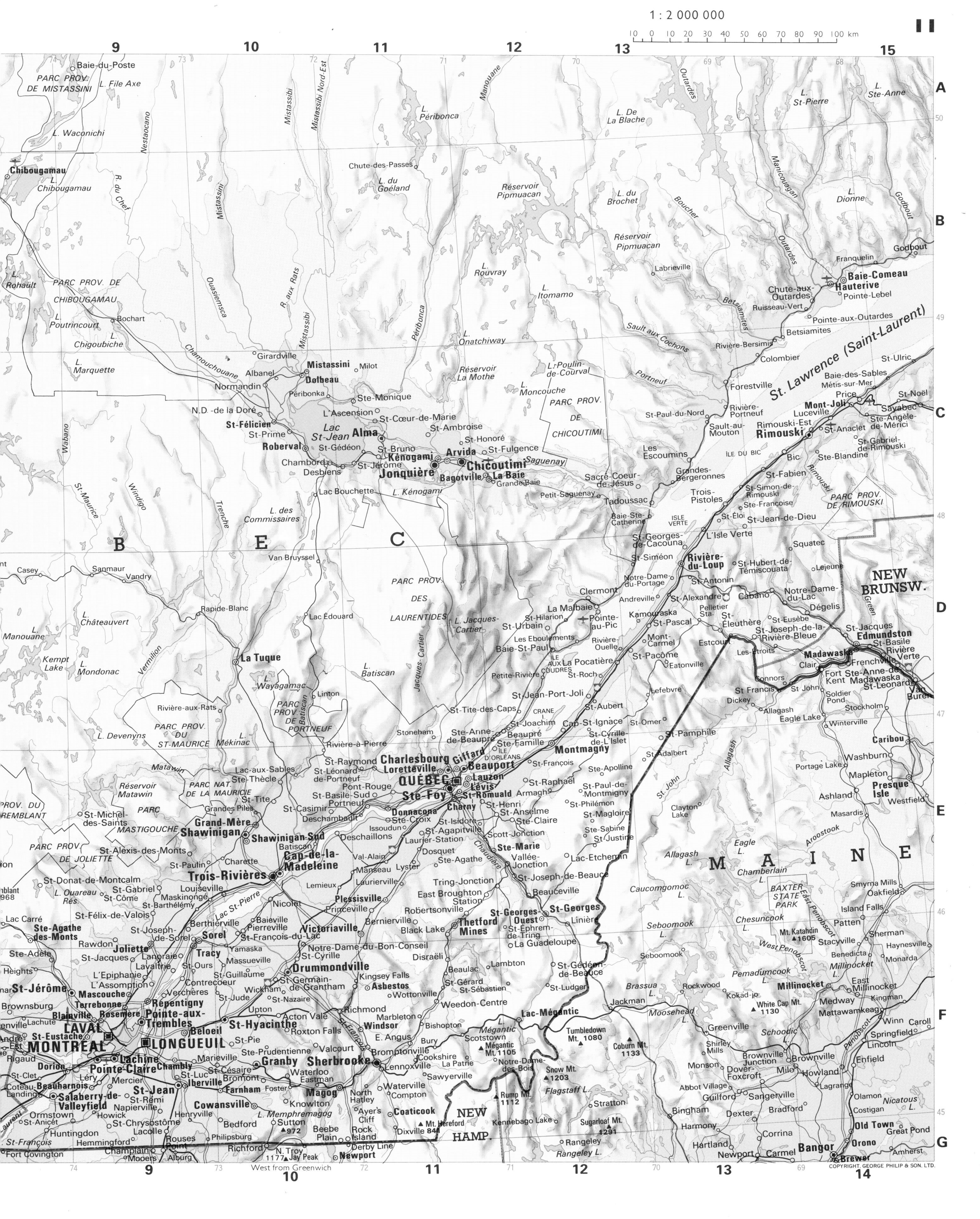
1 : 2 000 000
10 0 10 20 30 40 50 60 70 80 90 100 km
9
10
11
12
13
15
A
B
C
D
E
F
G
Baie-du-Poste
PARC PROV. DE MISTASSINI
L. File Axe
L. Waconichi
Nestaocano
Mistassibi
Mistassibi Nord-Est
Manouane
L. Péribonca
Outardes
L. De La Blache
L. St-Pierre
L. Ste-Anne
Chibougamau
L. Chibougamau
R. du Chef
Mistassini
Chute-des-Passes
L. du Goéland
Réservoir Pipmuacan
L. du Brochet
Boucher
Manicouagan
L. Dionne
Godbout
Réservoir Pipmuacan
Franquelin
Labrieville
L. Rouvray
Baie-Comeau
Hauterive
Pointe-Lebel
L. Rohault
PARC PROV. DE CHIBOUGAMAU
Ouasiemsca
R. aux Rats
Péribonca
L. Itomamo
Chute-aux-Outardes
Ruisseau-Vert
Betsiamites
L. Poutrincourt
Bochart
L. Chigoubiche
Pointe-aux-Outardes
Sault aux Cochons
Betsiamites
St Lawrence (Saint-Laurent)
L. Onatchiway
Girardville
Rivière-Bersimis
Colombier
St-Ulric
L. Marquette
Chamouchouane
Mistassini
Milot
Albanel
Dolbeau
Réservoir La Mothe
L. Poulin-de-Courval
L. Moncouche
Portneuf
Forestville
Baie-des-Sables
Métis-sur-Mer
Price
St-Noël
Normandin
Péribonka
Ste-Monique
PARC PROV. DE CHICOUTIMI
Rivière-Portneuf
Mont-Joli
Luceville
Sayabec
Ste-Angèle-de-Mérici
N.D.-de la Doré
St-Félicien
L'Ascension
St-Cœur-de-Marie
Lac St-Jean
St-Ambroise
St-Paul-du-Nord
Sault-au-Mouton
Rimouski-Est
Rimouski
St-Anaclet
St-Gabriel-de-Rimouski
St-Prime
Alma
St-Honoré
Wabano
Roberval
St-Gédéon
St-Bruno
Kénogami
Arvida
St-Fulgence
Saguenay
Les Escoumins
ÎLE DU BIC
Bic
Ste-Blandine
Chambord
Desbiens
St-Jérôme
Jonquière
Chicoutimi
Bagotville
La Baie
Grande-Baie
Sacré-Coeur-de-Jésus
Grandes-Bergeronnes
St-Fabien
Rimouski
St-Maurice
Windigo
Trenche
Lac Bouchette
L. Kénogami
Petit-Saguenay
Tadoussac
Trois-Pistoles
St-Simon-de-Rimouski
Ste-Françoise
PARC PROV. DE RIMOUSKI
L. des Commissaires
Baie-Ste-Catherine
ISLE VERTE
St-Éloi
St-Jean-de-Dieu
B
E
C
St-Georges-de-Cacouna
L'Isle Verte
Squatec
Van Bruyssel
St-Siméon
Rivière-du-Loup
St-Hubert-de-Témiscouata
Lejeune
NEW BRUNSW.
Casey
Sanmaur
Vandry
PARC PROV. DES LAURENTIDES
Notre-Dame-du-Portage
St-Antonin
Clermont
Notre-Dame-du-Lac
Green
Andreville
St-Alexandre
Cabano
Dégelis
Rapide-Blanc
Lac Édouard
La Malbaie
Kamouraska
Pelletier Sta.
L. Châteauvert
L. Jacques-Cartier
St-Hilarion
Pointe-au-Pic
St-Pascal
St-Éleuthère
St-Eusèbe
St-Jacques
Manouane
St-Urbain
St-Joseph-de-la-Rivière-Bleue
Edmundston
Les Eboulements
Rivière-Ouelle
Mont-Carmel
Estcourt
Les Étroits
St-Basile
Rivière Verte
Kempt Lake
Vermilion
La Tuque
Baie-St-Paul
ÎLE AUX COUDRES
Madawaska
L. Mondonac
Jacques-Cartier
La Pocatière
St-Pacôme
Clair
Frenchville
Eatonville
L. Batiscan
Petite-Rivière
St-Roch
Connors
Fort Kent
Ste-Anne-de-Madawaska
St-Leonard
Van Buren
L. Wayagamac
Linton
St-Jean-Port-Joli
Lefebvre
St Francis
St John
Soldier Pond
Rivière-aux-Rats
PARC PROV. DE PORTNEUF
St-Tite-des-Caps
St-Aubert
Dickey
Allagash
Eagle Lake
Stockholm
CRANE
St-Joachim
Cap-St-Ignace
St-Omer
L. Devenyns
PARC PROV. DU ST-MAURICE
L. Mékinac
Stoneham
Ste-Anne-de-Beaupré
Beaupré
Ste-Famille
ÎLE D'ORLÉANS
St-Cyrille-de-L'Islet
St-Pamphile
Winterville
Rivière-à-Pierre
Montmagny
Caribou
Charlesbourg
Giffard
St-Adalbert
Allagash
Washburn
Matawin
Lac-aux-Sables
St-Raymond
St-Léonard-de-Portneuf
Loretteville
Beauport
St-François
Ste-Apolline
Portage Lake
Ste-Thècle
QUÉBEC
Lauzon
Lévis
St-Raphaël
St-Paul-de-Montmigny
St John
Mapleton
Réservoir Matawin
PARC NAT. DE LA MAURICIE
Pont-Rouge
Portneuf
Presque Isle
St-Tite
St-Basile-Sud
Ste-Foy
St-Romuald
Armagh
St-Philémon
Clayton Lake
Ashland
Westfield
PROV. DU TREMBLANT
St-Michel-des-Saints
PARC
Grandes Piles
Grand-Mère
St-Casimir
Deschambault
Donnacona
Charny
St-Henri
St-Anselme
Ste-Claire
St-Magloire
Masardis
PARC MASTIGOUCHE
Shawinigan
Shawinigan-Sud
Ste-Croix
St-Isidore
Issoudun
St-Agapitville
Scott-Jonction
Ste-Sabine
St-Justine
Aroostook
Deschaillons
Batiscan
Laurier-Station
Chaudière
Ste-Marie
Eagle L.
PARC PROV. DE JOLIETTE
St-Alexis-des-Monts
St-Paulin
Charette
Cap-de-la-Madeleine
Val-Alain
Dosquet
Ste-Agathe
Vallée-Jonction
Lac-Etchemin
Allagash L.
M A I N E
Trois-Rivières
Manseau
Lyster
St-Joseph-de-Beauce
Chamberlain L.
St-Donat-de-Montcalm
Lemieux
Laurierville
Tring-Jonction
BAXTER STATE PARK
Smyrna Mills
St-Gabriel
Louiseville
East Broughton Station
Beauceville
Caucomgomoc L.
Oakfield
L. Ouareau Rés.
St-Côme
Maskinongé
Nicolet
Plessisville
Robertsonville
St-Barthélémy
Princeville
Lac Carré
St-Félix-de-Valois
Lac St-Pierre
Baieville
Pierreville
Bernierville
St-Georges-Ouest
St-Georges
Linière
Chesuncook L.
Island Falls
East Penobscot
Ste-Agathe-des-Monts
St-Joseph-de-Sorel
Berthierville
Victoriaville
Black Lake
Thetford Mines
St-Éphrem-de-Tring
Seboomook L.
Patten
Rawdon
Joliette
Sorel
St-François-du-Lac
La Guadeloupe
Mt. Katahdin 1605
Sherman
Yamaska
Notre-Dame-du-Bon-Conseil
West Penobscot
Stacyville
Ste-Adèle
St-Jacques
Lavaltrie
Tracy
Massueville
St-Cyrille
Disraëli
Benedicta
Haynesville
Seboomook
Millinocket
Monarda
St-Ours
Drummondville
L'Épiphanie
L'Assomption
St-Guillaume
Kingsey Falls
Beaulac
Lambton
St-Gédéon-de-Beauce
Pemadumcook L.
Contrecoeur
St-Germain-de-Grantham
Asbestos
St-Gérard
Brassua L.
Rockwood
East Millinocket
St-Jérôme
Mascouche
Verchères
Wickham
Wottonville
St-Sébastien
St-Ludger
Kokad-jo
Millinocket
Terrebonne
Repentigny
St-Jude
St-Nazaire
Weedon-Centre
White Cap Mt. 1130
Medway
Kingman
Brownsburg
Blainville
Rosemère
Pointe-aux-Trembles
Upton
Richmond
Lac-Mégantic
Jackman
Moosehead L.
Mattawamkeag
Lachute
Acton Vale
Marbleton
Winn
Caroll
LAVAL
Beloeil
St-Hyacinthe
Roxton Falls
Windsor
Bishopton
Mégantic
Tumbledown Mt. 1080
Greenville
Schoodic L.
Springfield
St-Eustache
MONTRÉAL
LONGUEUIL
St-Pie
E. Angus
Scotstown
Mégantic Mt. 1105
Coburn Mt. 1133
Shirley Mills
Lincoln
Rigaud
Lachine
Chambly
Ste-Prudentienne
Valcourt
Bury
Brompton ville
Penobscot
Dorion
Pointe-Claire
Marieville
Granby
Sherbrooke
Cookshire
La Patrie
Notre-Dame-des-Bois
Brownville Junction
Brownville
Enfield
St-Clet
Léry
Mercier
St-Luc
Ste-Césaire
Lennoxville
Snow Mt. 1203
Monson
Dover-Foxcroft
Milo
Howland
Coteau-Landing
Beauharnois
Iberville
Bromont
Waterloo
Eastman
Sawyerville
Flagstaff L.
Lagrange
Salaberry-de-Valleyfield
St-Jean
St-Rémi
Farnham
Foster
Magog
North Hatley
Waterville
Compton
Rump Mt. 1112
Abbot Village
Guilford
Sangerville
Olamon
Nicatous L.
Ormstown
Howick
Napierville
Cowansville
Knowlton
NEW HAMP.
Stratton
Bingham
Dexter
Bradford
Costigan
St-Anicet
St-Chrysostôme
Henryville
L. Memphremagog
Ayer's Cliff
Coaticook
Huntingdon
Lacolle
Bedford
Sutton 972
Beebe Plain
Rock Island
Mt. Hereford 840
Kennebago Lake
Sugarloaf Mt. 1291
Harmony
Corrina
Old Town
Great Pond
St-François
Hemmingford
Rouses Point
Philipsburg
Dixville
Derby Line
Rangeley
Hartland
Orono
Fort Covington
Champlain
Mooers
Alburg
Richford
N. Troy
Jay Peak 1177
Newport
Rangeley L.
Newport
Carmel
Bangor
Brewer
Amherst
74
73
72
71
70
69
68
50
49
48
47
46
45
West from Greenwich
COPYRIGHT GEORGE PHILIP & SON, LTD.

1 : 480 000

5 0 5 10 15 20 25 km

MONTRÉAL
LAVAL
ÎLE JÉSUS
Longueuil
St-Bruno-de-Montarville
Boucherville
Repentigny
St-Jérôme
St-Jean
St-Hyacinthe
Granby
Cowansville
Chambly
Châteauguay
Salaberry-de-Valleyfield
Lachute
Hawkesbury
Beloeil
Terrebonne
Ste-Thérèse
Pointe-Claire
Dorval
Beaconsfield
Pierrefonds
Dollard-des-Ormeaux
Lachine
Lasalle
Verdun
Westmount
Outremont
Mont-Royal
St-Laurent
Anjou
Montréal-Nord
St-Léonard
Brossard
Greenfield Park
St-Lambert
Lemoyne
St-Hubert
Laflèche
Delson
Candiac
La Prairie
Caughnawaga
Iberville
Farnham
Bedford
Huntingdon
Ormstown
Beauharnois
Vaudreuil
Dorion
Rigaud
Oka
Mascouche
Mirabel Airport
Lac des Deux Montagnes
Lake St. Francis
L. St-Louis
St-Laurent (St. Lawrence)
Richelieu
Yamaska
Châteauguay
Ottawa (Outaouais)

ARGENTEUIL
TERREBONNE
MONTCALM
L'ASSOMPTION
DEUX MONTAGNES
VAUDREUIL
SOULANGES
BEAUHARNOIS
CHÂTEAUGUAY
HUNTINGDON
LAPRAIRIE
NAPIERVILLE
SAINT-JEAN
IBERVILLE
ROUVILLE
CHAMBLY
VERCHÈRES
ST-HYACINTHE
RICHELIEU
YAMASKA
BAGOT
BROME
MISSISQUOI
PRESCOTT
GLENGARRY

QUÉBEC
ONTARIO
NEW YORK
VERMONT
CANADA
UNITED STATES

Projection: Transverse Mercator

1 : 480 000

5 0 5 10 15 20 25 km

Projection: Transverse Mercator

m: 500, 200, 100, 0

m Lake Depths: 0, 50, 100

1 2 3 4 5 6 7

A B C D E F

Sault Sainte Marie
Paradise
Whitefish Bay
Brimley
Sault Sainte Marie
Echo Bay
Mississagi
Wakomata L.
MISSISSAGI PROV. PARK
aux Sables
Benny
Onaping
Cartier
Levack
Val Caron
L. Wanapitei
Capreol
Hanmer
Sturgeon
Marten River
Témiscaming
Newberry
Hulbert
Dafter
Strongs Corners
Little White
Big Basswood L.
Elliot Lake
Spanish
Onaping
Chelmsford
Sudbury
Azilda
Lively
Copper Cliff
Falconbridge
Coniston
Markstay
River Valley
Field
Tomiko L.
Desbarats
Iron Bridge
Matinenda L.
Whitefish
Naughton
Warren
Verner
Sturgeon Falls
Rexton
Engadine
Trout Lake
Rudyard
Hilton Beach
Thessalon
Webbwood
Nairn
Cache Bay
Feronia
Pickford
ST. JOSEPH I.
Spragge
Espanola
L. Panache
Burwash
Wanapitei
Notre Dame du Lac
North Bay
Lake Nipissing
Bonfield
Callander
Naubinway
Blind River
Spanish
Massey
Brevort
Moran
Hessel
Goetzville
Drummond
North Channel
Whitefish Falls
KILLARNEY PROV. PARK
Rutter
Noelville
Astorville
Cedarville
COCKBURN ISLAND
MACKINAC I.
MARQUETTE I.
De Tour
CLAPPERTON I.
Little Current
French River
French
Powassan
GARDEN I.
HOG I.
Straits
St. Ignace
DRUMMOND ISLAND
Meldrum Bay
Gore Bay
Killarney
GRUNDY L. PROV. PK.
Port Loring
Commanda
Trout Creek
St. James
Mackinaw City
Mackinac
BOIS BLANC I.
Kagawong L.
Sheguiandah
Key Harbour
South River
BEAVER I.
Silver Water
WESTERN DUCK I.
Manitou L.
Wikwemikong
Britt
Drocourt
Sundridge
Levering
Cheboygan
MANITOULIN
Mindemoya
Manitowaning
Byng Inlet
Bernard L.
Good Hart
Pellston
Mullett L.
Hammond Bay
GREAT DUCK I.
Providence Bay
ISLAND
Ardbeg
Magnetawan
Burt L.
Alanson
Burk's Falls
Harbor Springs
Indian River
Black L.
Rogers City
South Baymouth
LONELY I.
Pointe au Baril Sta.
Dunchurch
Charlevoix
Petoskey
FITZWILLIAM I.
Shawanaga
McKellar
Emsdale
Kearney
Boyne City
Onaway
Millersburg
Waubamik
Sprucedale
Novar
L. Charlevoix
Wolverine
Grand L.
Georgian Bay
Parry Sound
Nobel
Posen
COVE I.
Huntsville
East Jordan
Tobermory
Rosseau
Central Lake
Vanderbilt
Rosseau L.
L. of Bays
Gaylord
Hillman
Alpena
L. Joseph
Port Carling
Bellaire
Atlanta
MacTier
Baysville
Elk Rapids
Mancelona
BRUCE PENINSULA
Stokes Bay
GEORGIAN BAY ISLANDS NATIONAL PARK
L. Muskoka
Bracebridge
Lewiston
Ossineke
GREENOUGH PT
Lion's Head
C CROKER
Bala
Rapid City
SOUTH PT
LYAL I.
HAY I.
Muskoka
Gravenhurst
Black River
HOPE I.
Honey Harbour
Kalkaska
Hubbard L.
GRIFFITH I.
CHRISTIAN I.
Port Severn
Black
Fairview
Curran
Victoria Harbour
Waubaushene
Grayling
Au Sable
LAKE HURON
Penetanguishene
Washago
Manistee
Mio
Lincoln
Harrisville
Wiarton
C. RICH
Midland
Coldwater
Walton
Mikado
CHIEFS PT
Hepworth
Nottawasaga
Greenbush
Glennie
Meaford
Bay
Orillia
Roscommon
Shallow Lake
Thornbury
Elmvale
Higgins L.
Manton
Owen Sound
Wasaga Beach
Brechin
Rose City
Long Lake
Southampton
Collingwood
L. Simcoe
Lake City
Oscoda-Au Sable
Tara
Chatsworth
Beaverton
Houghton L.
Hale
Port Elgin
Stayner
Barrie
Cadillac
West Branch
177
Houghton Lake Heights
AU SABLE PT
Markdale
Creemore
Angus
GEORGINA I.
MICHIGAN
East Tawas
DOUGLAS PT
Tiverton
Paisley
Chesley
Stroud
Lefroy
Sutton
Tawas City
Saugeen
Marion
Muskegon
Alabaster
Kincardine
Flesherton
Camp Borden
Keswick
Tittabawassee
Durham
Harrison
PTE AUX BARQUES
Walkerton
Dundalk
Hornings Mills
Mount Albert
Uxbridge
Port Austin
Hanover
Alliston
Bradford
Gladwin
Standish
Au Gres
CHARITY I.
Ripley
Neustadt
PT. CLARK
Shelburne
Beeton
Newmarket
Evart
Beaverton
Caseville
Kinde
Port Hope
Mildmay
Tottenham
Aurora
Stouffville
Farewell
SAND PT
Lucknow
Teeswater
Mount Forest
Clare
Pinconning
Saginaw Bay
Bay Port
Pigeon
Bad Axe
Harbor Beach
Orangeville
Richmond Hill
Whitby
Coleman
Elkton
Wingham
Harriston
ONTARIO
Dungannon
Palmerston
Arthur
Grand
Bolton
Markham
Mount Pleasant
FISH PT
Sebewaing
Alton
Erin
Remus
Midland
Ruth
Goderich
Blyth
Brussels
Listowel
Drayton
Fergus
Woodbridge
Brampton
Essexville
Unionville
Palms
Elora
Georgetown
Toronto
Shepherd
Bay City
Cass
Cass City
Clinton
Atwood
Monkton
Elmira
Rockwood
Acton
Mississauga
Lakeview
Zilwaukee
Fairgrove
Deckerville
Bayfield
Seaforth
Milverton
Linwood
Guelph
Streetsville
Port Credit
St. Louis
Carollton
Merrill
Reese
Caro
Black
Mitchell
Waterloo
Milton
Edmore
Alma
Breckenridge
Saginaw
Sandusky
Port Sanilac
Zurich
Hensall
KITCHENER
Cambridge
Oakville
Stanton
Ithaca
Bridgeport
Vassar
Kingston
Exeter
Sebringville
New Hamburg
BURLINGTON
Niagara-on-the-Lake
Sheridan
St. Charles
Millington
Croswell
Grand Bend
Stratford
Nith
Waterdown
Greenville
Carson City
Chesaning
Birch Run
Peck
Crediton
Tavistock
Ayr
Dundas
HAMILTON
Belding
Shiawassee
Montrose
Otter Lake
Brown City
Lexington
KETTLE PT
Thedford
Parkhill
Lucan
St. Marys
Drumbo
St. George
Grimsby
St. Catharines
Elsie
Mt. Morris
Columbiaville
Yale
Embro
Innerkip
Paris
Stoney Creek
Beamsville
Ionia
St. Johns
Ovid
Flushing
Davison
Lapeer
Lakeport
HARRIS PT
Ausable
Ailsa Craig
Woodstock
Brantford
Thorold
Fowler
Corunna
Imlay City
Point Edward
Forest
Thamesford
Burford
Smithville
Niagara Falls
Saranac
Portland
Owosso
Durand
Swartz Creek
FLINT
Emmett
Arkona
Ingersoll
Scotland
Caledonia
Grand Blanc
Capac
Port Huron
Sarnia
Strathroy
LONDON
Norwich
Welland
De Witt
Linden
Almont
Marysville
Wyoming
Watford
Otterville
Hagersville
Cayuga
Lake Odessa
Perry
Memphis
Corunna
Petrolia
Alvinston
Mount Brydges
Lambeth
Waterford
Dunnville
Port Colborne
LANSING
East Lansing
Fenton
Holly
Oxford
Richmond
Courtright
Tillsonburg
Delhi
Jarvis
Williamston
Lake Orion
St. Clair
Belmont
Springfield
Simcoe
Selkirk
Lackawanna
Nashville
Drayton Plains
New Haven
Marine City
Oil Springs
Sydenham
Glencoe
Thames
Courtland
Aylmer
Fowlerville
Rochester
Sombra
St. Thomas
Port Dover
Charlotte
Howell
Pontiac
Utica
New Baltimore
Bothwell
Dutton
Port Stanley
Vienna
Long Point Bay
Mason
Milford
Birmingham
Fraser
Mt. Clemens
Algonac
Wallaceburg
Port Burwell
Bellevue
Eaton Rapids
South Lyon
Royal Oak
Roseville
Dresden
Rodney
W. Lorne
Port Rowan
Leslie
Stockbridge
Ferndale
E. Detroit
Thamesville
LONG PT
Battle Creek
Chelsea
Dexter
LIVONIA
DETROIT
Lake St. Clair
Chatham
Ridgetown
Silver Creek
Marshall
Albion
Jackson
ANN ARBOR
Plymouth
DEARBORN
Tecumseh
Dunkirk
Fredonia
Van Buren Pt.
Concord
Michigan Center
Ypsilanti
Wayne
Ecorse
River Rouge
WINDSOR
Belle River
Tilbury
Blenheim
RONDEAU PROV. PARK
Brocton
Westfield
Cassadaga
Homer
Manchester
Saline
Wyandotte
Trenton
GROSSE I.
Essex
Comber
Erieau
PTE AUX PINS
Ripley
Mayville
Chautauqua L.
Sinclairville
Milan
Flat Rock
Cottam
174
PRESQUE I.
North East
Randolph
Coldwater
Jonesville
Tecumseh
Amherstburg
Wheatley
Leamington
LAKE ERIE
ERIE
Wesleyville
Sherman
Falconer
Hillsdale
Manitou Beach
Newport
Dundee
Harrow
Kingsville
Jamestown
Lakewood
Clymer
Adrian
Hudson
Petersburg
POINT PELEE NAT. PARK
Lake City
Wattsburg
Reading
South Monroe
Monroe
Conneaut
Girard
Sugar Grove
Waldron
Blissfield
N. Kingsville
Waterford
Corry
Warren
Morenci
Lambertville
Ashtabula
Albion
Union City
Youngsville
Fremont
Geneva
Edinboro
Angola
Sylvania
CEDAR PT
PELEE I.
Madison
Conneautville
Spartansburg
Sheffield
Fayette
Lyons
TOLEDO
N. BASS I.
MIDDLE BASS I.
Fairport
Jefferson
Cambridge Springs
Tidioute
Montpelier
West Unity
Rossford
Oregon
S. BASS I.
Mentor-on-the-Lake
Grand
Pierpont
Saegerstown
Hydetown
IND.
Bryan
Wauseon
Maumee
Port Clinton
KELLEYS I.
Willoughby
Painesville
Rock Creek
Dorset
Linesville
Titusville
Butler
Archbold
Liberty Center
Perrysburg
Portage
Oak Harbor
Lakeside
CLEVELAND
Wickliffe
Mentor
Andover
Meadville
Pleasantville
Edgerton
Napoleon
Maumee
Bowling Green
Luckey
Sandusky
Avon Lake
Lakewood
Euclid
Chardon
Pymatuning Res.
Conneaut Lake
Cochranton
Tionesta
OHIO
Woodville
Lorain
Rocky River
Cleveland Heights
Orwell
Hicksville
Sherwood
Gibsonburg
Fremont
Huron
Amherst
Berea
Shaker Hts.
Solon
Middlefield
Jamestown
Sugar Creek
Oil City
PENNSYLVANIA
Defiance
Holgate
Weston
Bradner
Clyde
Bellevue
Elyria
PARMA
Maple Hts.
Aurora
Cortland
Mosquito Creek Res.
Kinsman
Greenville
Franklin
Polk
Stoneboro
Leeper

85 84 83 82 81 80
46 45 44 43 42

m
1500
1000
400
200
0
-200
m

Projection: Bonne

2 3 4 5 6 7

1 : 2 000 000
10 0 10 20 30 40 50 60 70 80 90 100 km
8
9
10
11
12
14
13
A
B
C
D
E
F
QUÉBEC
ONTARIO
NEW YORK
PENNSYLVANIA
VERMONT
MASS.
CONN.
N. J.
LAKE ONTARIO
APPALACHIAN
Adirondack Mountains
Catskill Mts.
Réservoir Baskatong
PARC PROV. DU MONT-TREMBLANT
PARC PROV. DE JOLIETTE
PARC MASTIGOUCHE
PARC PONTIAC
PARC PROV. PAPINEAU-LABELLE
PARC DE LA GATINEAU
ALGONQUIN PROV. PARK
BON ECHO PROV. PARK
Kipawa
L. Sairs
L. Pin-Blanc
L. du Fils
L. Beauchûne
L. Bleu
Tree Lake
Ottawa
Mattawa
Outaouais
L. St-Patrice
Dumoine
Coulonge
Deux-Rivières
Rapides des Joachims
Rolphton
Deep River
Chalk River
Kiosk
Brent
Cedar L.
L. Lavieille
Petawawa
Pembroke
Chapeau
Waltham Sta.
Fort-Coulonge
Big Trout L.
Opeongo L.
Alice
Beachburg
Bryson
Campbell's Bay
Cobden
Shawville
Bristol
Golden Lake
Eganville
Killaloe Sta.
Round L.
Algonquin Park
Whitney
Madawaska
Barry's Bay
Golden L.
Douglas
Renfrew
Braeside
Arnprior
Combermere
Bark L.
L. Clear
Kawagama L.
Dwight
Dorset
Lake St. Peter
Eagle Lake
Haliburton
Wilberforce
Bancroft
Griffith
Denbigh
Calabogie
Pakenham
White L.
Almonte
Flower Sta.
Lavant Sta.
Mississippi L.
Lanark
Perth
Elphin
Plevna
Weslemkoon L.
Minden
Gooderham
Coe Hill
Gilmour
Cloyne
Maberly
Sharbot Lake
Kinmount
Apsley
Millbridge
Bannockburn
Arden
Parham
Westport
Burnt River
Fenelon Falls
Burleigh Falls
Kaladar
Eldorado
Madoc
Tweed
Stony L.
Kirkfield
Sturgeon L.
Bobcaygeon
Buckhorn L.
Lakefield
Pigeon L.
Marmora
Havelock
Marlbank
Tamworth
Verona
Lindsay
Bridgenorth
Hastings
Norwood
Campbellford
Stirling
Newburgh
Yarker
Odessa
Peterborough
Omemee
Keene
Trent
Frankford
Napanee
Kingston
Bath
Belleville
Deseronto
Rossmore
Trenton
Bayside
Brighton
Rice L.
Bethany
L. Scugog
Millbrook
Port Perry
Pontypool
Bewdley
Colborne
Consecon
Picton
Wellington
Bloomfield
Orono
Cobourg
Port Hope
Bowmanville
Oshawa
Ajax
Hampton
AMHERST I.
WOLFE I.
GRENADIER I.
PR EDWARD PT
GALLOO I.
STONY PT
WICKED PT
Montcerf
Mont-Laurier
Ferme-Neuve
Lièvre
Lac-des-Écorces
Val-Barrette
L. Nominingue
L'Annonciation
Nominingue
L. des Iles
Maniwaki
Messine
Bouchette
Gatineau
Lac des Trente et un Milles
L. de Cerf
Notre-Dame-du-Laus
L. Gagnon
Labelle
Mt. Tremblant 968
Mont-Tremblant
La Conception
St-Jovite
Lac Carré
Gracefield
Lac-Ste-Marie
L. du Poisson Blanc
Venosta
Low
Val-des-Bois
Poltimore
Ripon
Lac-Rémi
Arundel
Namur
Chénéville
Glen Almond
Wakefield
Papineauville
Thurso
Buckingham
Masson
Angers
Rockland
Cumberland
Pointe-Gatineau
Gatineau
Hull
OTTAWA
Quyon
Aylmer
Deschênes
Kanata
Bells Corner
Stittsville
Richmond
North Gower
Carleton Place
Manotick
Osgoode
Kemptville
Smiths Falls
Jasper
Big Rideau L.
Portland
Elgin
Newboro L.
Charleston L.
Mallorytown
Seeley's Bay
Lansdowne
Harrowsmith
Gananoque
Barriefield
HOWE I.
GRINDSTONE I.
Athens
Brockville
Prescott
Spencerville
Merrickville
Vars
Limoges
Casselman
Bourget
Moose Creek
Winchester
Chesterville
Finch
Morrisburg
Iroquois
Cardinal
South Nation
Montebello
Grenville
Hawkesbury
Vankleek Hill
St-Eugène
Alexandria
Glen Robertson
Maxville
Apple Hill
Avonmore
Lancaster
Cornwall
Ste-Agathe-des-Monts
Ste-Adèle
Morin Heights
St-Jérôme
Kilmar
St-André-Avellin
Brownsburg
Lachute
St-Andre Est
St-Eustache
Blainville
LAVAL
MONTREAL
Lachine
Pointe-Claire
Dorion
Rigaud
St-Clet
Coteau Landing
Beauharnois
Salaberry-de-Valleyfield
Léry
Ormstown
St-Anicet
Huntingdon
Hemmingford
L. St-François
Fort Covington
St-Michel-des-Saints
St-Alexis-des-Monts
Shawinigan
Shawinigan-Sud
Charette
St-Paulin
Trois-Rivières
St-Donat-de-Montcalm
St-Gabriel
St-Côme
L. Ouareau Rés.
Louiseville
Maskinongé
Nicolet
St-Félix-de-Valois
St-Barthélémy
Lac St-Pierre
Baieville
Pierreville
Berthierville
St-François-du-Lac
St-Joseph-de-Sorel
Sorel
Tracy
Yamaska
Massueville
Joliette
Lanoraie
Rawdon
St-Jacques
Lavaltrie
St-Ours
St-Guillaume
L'Epiphanie
L'Assomption
Contrecoeur
Wickham
Verchères
St-Jude
St-Nazaire
Mascouche
Repentigny
Terrebonne
Rosemère
Pointe-aux-Trembles
St-Hyacinthe
Beloeil
St-Pie
LONGUEUIL
Marieville
Granby
Chambly
St-Césaire
St-Luc
Bromont
Iberville
Farnham
St-Jean
Mercier
St-Rémi
Napierville
Cowansville
Sutton
Henryville
Bedford
Howick
St-Chrysostôme
Lacolle
Philipsburg
Rouses Point
Richford
Champlain
Alburg
Enosburg Falls
Mooers
Chazy
Swanton
St. Albans
West Chazy
Bakersfield
Grand Isle
Dannemora
Fairfax
Johnson
Plattsburgh
Milton
Mt. Mansfield 1339
Lake Champlain
Lyon Mtn. 1167
Redford
Winooski
Essex Junction
Stowe
Port Kent
Keeseville
Burlington
Richmond
Au Sable Forks
Shelburne
Waterbury
Willsboro
Charlotte
Essex
Vergennes
Westport
Mt. Ellen 1260
Port Henry
Middlebury
Otter Cr.
Crown Point
Brandon
Ticonderoga
Hague
Pittsford
Proctor
Rutland
Castleton
Fair Haven
West Rutland
Poultney
Whitehall
Granville
Fort Ann
Dorset Mt. 1159
Hudson Falls
Fort Edward
Manchester
Salem
Stratton Mt. 1176
Arlington
Cambridge
N. Bennington
Wilmington
Bennington
Readsboro
Williamstown
N. Adams
Adams
Dalton
Pittsfield
Lenox
Lee
Great Barrington
Sheffield
Canaan
Winsted
Winchester
Torrington
Bristol
Litchfield
Thomaston
New Milford
WATERBURY
Naugatuck
Seymour
Danbury
Ansonia
Shelton
Bethel
Milford
Ridgefield
BRIDGEPORT
Fairfield
Massena
Waddington
Brasher Falls
Madrid
Norwood
Potsdam
Brushton
Malone
Owls Head
Nicholville
St. Regis Falls
Ogdensburg
Heuvelton
Parishville
Canton
South Colton
Morristown
Black L.
Hammond
Hermon
Russell
Paul Smiths
Gabriels
Whiteface Mt. 1485
Saranac Lake
Lake Placid
Keene
Raquette
Oswegatchie
Gouverneur
Edwards
Piercefield
Tupper Lake
Alexandria Bay
Redwood
Theresa
Clayton
Newton Falls
Antwerp
Mt. Marcy 1629
Elizabethtown
Cape Vincent
Philadelphia
Harrisville
Sabattis
Chaumont
Natural Bridge
Evans Mills
Deferiet
Carthage
Dexter
Watertown
Long Lake
Newcomb
Schroon Lake
Sackets Harbor
Croghan
Copenhagen
Raquette Lake
Blue Mountain Lake
Indian Lake
Adams
Lowville
Black
Big Moose
Inlet
Snowy Mt. 1190
Pottersville
N. Creek
Belleville
Glenfield
Old Forge
Chestertown
Moose
Lyons Falls
Port Leyden
663
Bolton Landing
Lacona
Orwell
Pulaski
Speculator
Warrensburg
Lake George
Mexico Bay
Lake Pleasant
Boonville
Oswego
Mexico
Fernwood
Minetto
Parish
Williamstown
W. Canada Cr.
Wells
Hamilton Mt. 991
Glens Falls
Corinth
Hannibal
Fulton
Camden
Taberg
Remsen
Trenton
Prospect
Northville
Sacandaga Res.
Saratoga Springs
Schuylerville
Greenwich
Central Square
Constantia
Sylvan Beach
Red Creek
Phoenix
Brewerton
Rome
Newport
Mayfield
Baldwinsville
Oriskany
Whitesboro
Utica
Dolgeville
Little Falls
Gloversville
Broadalbin
Ballston Spa
Stillwater
Liverpool
N. Syracuse
Sodus
Williamson
Webster
Clyde
Lyons
Jordan
Solvay
SYRACUSE
Oneida
New Hartford
Frankfort
Herkimer
St. Johnsville
Johnstown
Fonda
Amsterdam
Mechanicville
Hoosick Falls
Newark
Weedsport
Seneca Falls
Auburn
Fairmount
Skaneateles
Cazenovia
Ilion
Mohawk
Ft. Plain
Canajoharie
Scotia
Schenectady
Cohoes
Troy
ALBANY
Rensselaer
Watervliet
Waterville
Bridgewater
Richfield Springs
Cherry Valley
Sharon Springs
Duanesburg
Sloansville
Altamont
Cobleskill
Schoharie
Delmar
Nassau
Cayuga
Union Springs
Owasco L.
Moravia
Aurora
Cayuga L.
Skaneateles L.
Tully
Truxton
Homer
Cortland
McGraw
Hamilton
Georgetown
Earlville
Morrisville
Sherburne
New Berlin
Edmeston
Cooperstown
Worcester
Schenevus
Middleburg
Ravena
Norwich
Morris
Oxford
Cincinnatus
Willet
Marathon
Mt. Upton
Oneonta
Stamford
Greenville
Stuyvesant
Chatham
Philmont
Unadilla
Grand Gorge
Cairo
Athens
Catskill
Hudson
Hillsdale
Copake
Greene
Bainbridge
Afton
Walton
Delhi
Andes
Lexington
Hunter
Margaretville
Downsville
Saugerties
Glasco
Pepacton Res.
Phoenicia
Slide Mt. 1281
W. Hurley
Red Hook
Millerton
Rhinebeck
Amenia
Millbrook
Kingston
Port Ewen
Hyde Park
Ashokan Res.
Roscoe
Livingston Manor
Grahamsville
Liberty
Napanoch
New Paltz
Arlington
Poughkeepsie
Callicoon
Woodbourne
Ellenville
Monticello
Woodridge
Wappingers Falls
Fishkill
Beacon
Wurtsboro
Walden
Newburgh
Middletown
Goshen
Monroe
Carmel
Brewster
Mahopac
Peekskill
Port Jervis
Florida
Warwick
Stony Point
Haverstraw
Sussex
Shawangunk Mts.
Lackawaxen
Hawley
Matamoras
Milford
Newfoundland
Dingmans Ferry
Hudson
Housatonic
Delaware
Susquehanna
Schoharie
Mohawk
Sodus
Hilton
Hamlin
Lyndonville
Barker
Albion
Brockport
Sea Breeze
Holley
Spencerport
Medina
Newfane
Wilson
Youngstown
Lewiston
Lockport
Niagara Falls
N. Tonawanda
Tonawanda
Erie Canal
Oakfield
Bergen
N. Chili
ROCHESTER
E. Rochester
Fairport
Pittsford
Batavia
Le Roy
Scottsville
Palmyra
Manchester
Depew
Lancaster
BUFFALO
Pavilion
Attica
Caledonia
Avon
Victor
Canandaigua
Phelps
Geneva
Livonia
Geneseo
Canandaigua L.
Stanley
Rushville
Waterloo
E. Aurora
Varysburg
Mt. Morris
Hamburg
Warsaw
Willard
Ovid
Genoa
Holland
Castile
Perry
Springwater
Naples
Penn Yan
Interlaken
Groton
Dryden
Trumansburg
Eden
N. Collins
Bliss
Nunda
Wayland
Keuka L.
Dundee
Springville
Arcade
Delevan
Dansville
Cohocton
657
Canaseraga
Avoca
Hammondsport
Ithaca
Gowanda
Houghton
Arkport
Bath
Watkins Glen
Newfield
Whitney Point
Machias
Franklinville
Belfast
Hornell
Canisteo
Montour Falls
Berkshire
Newark Valley
Cattaraugus
Ellicottville
Almond
Savona
Campbell
Spencer
Little Valley
Cuba
Belmont
Alfred
Salamanca
Friendship
Andover
Corning
Horseheads
Elmira Hts.
Owego
Endwell
Johnson City
Binghamton
Endicott
Windsor
Deposit
Cadosia
Hancock
Allegany
Olean
Wellsville
Jasper
Addison
Elmira
Southport
Waverly
Nichols
Sayre
Athens
Great Bend
Hallstead
Susquehanna Depot
Lanesboro
Bolivar
Whitesville
Elkland
Allegheny Res.
Limestone
Portville
Eldred
Bradford
Genesee
Shinglehouse
Westfield
Knoxville
Lawrenceville
Tioga
Gillett
Lewis Run
Port Allegany
Gold
Sabinsville
Mansfield
Wellsboro
Coudersport
Gaines
Troy
Rome
Montrose
New Milford
Thompson
Towanda
Monroeton
Camptown
Hop Bottom
821
Pleasant Mount
Forest City
Carbondale
Honesdale
Smethport
Mt. Jewett
Crosby
Ludlow
Mt. Brodhead 759
Galeton
Blossburg
Canton
Wyalusing
Meshoppen
Tunkhannock
Nicholson
Jermyn
Archbald
Kane
Austin
Morris
New Albany
Dushore
Liberty
Clarks Summit
Dickson City
Olyphant
Dunmore
Wilcox
Emporium
Wharton
Oleona
Pine Cr.
Ralston
Forksville
Mildred
Old Forge
Duryea
SCRANTON
Moscow
St. Marys
Ridgway
Driftwood
Renovo
North Bend
Cammal
Waterville
Trout Run
Eagles Mere
Noxen
Luzerne
Pittston
Kingston
Edwardsville
Brandy Camp
West from Greenwich
COPYRIGHT GEORGE PHILIP & SON. LTD.

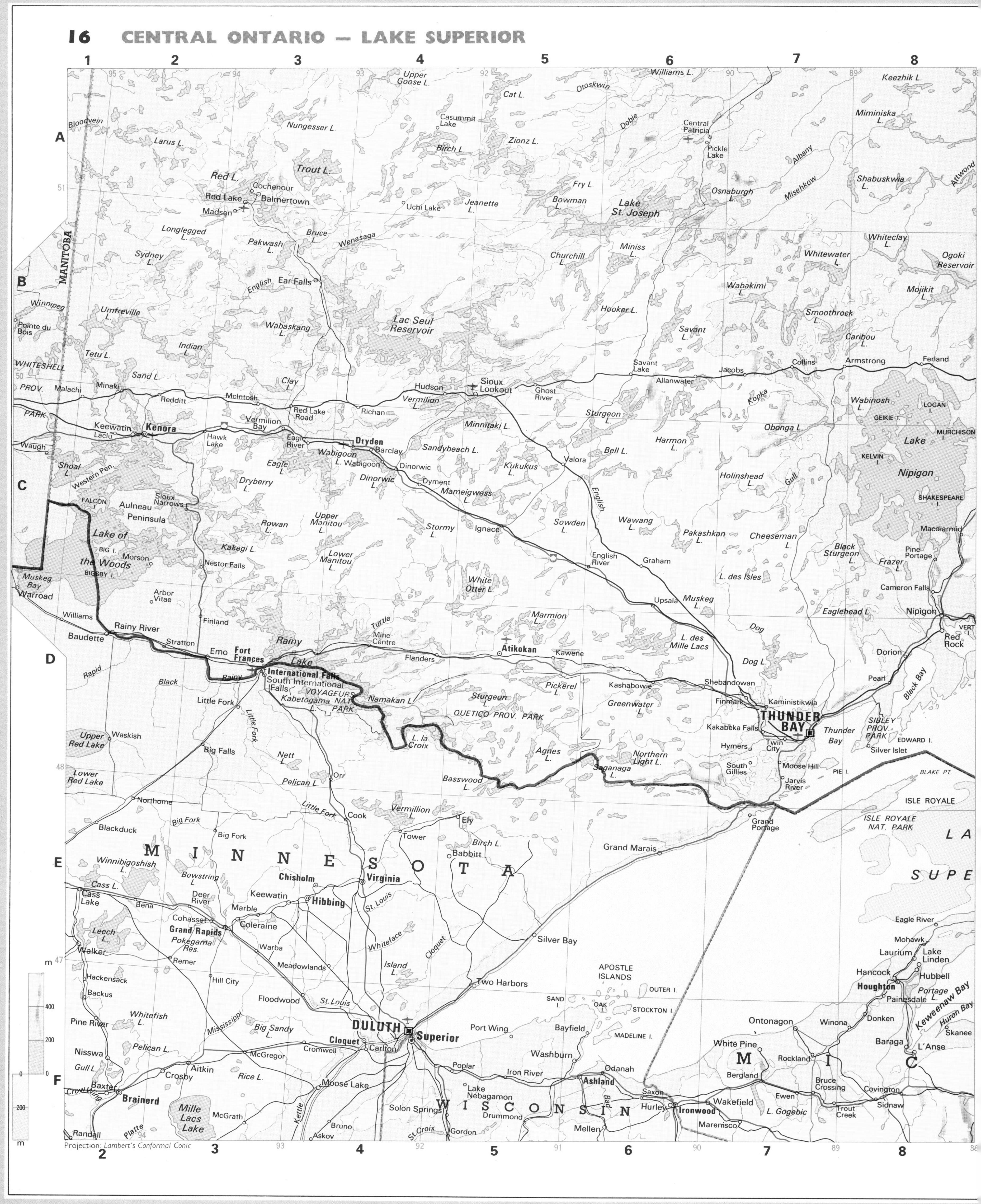

1
2
3
4
5
6
7
8
A
B
C
D
E
F
Upper Goose L.
Williams L.
Keezhik L.
Cat L.
Otoskwin
Bloodvein
Nungesser L.
Casummit Lake
Dobie
Central Patricia
Miminiska L.
Larus L.
Zionz L.
Birch L.
Pickle Lake
Albany
Attwood
Trout L.
Red L.
Fry L.
Misehkow
Shabuskwia L.
Cochenour
Red Lake
Balmertown
Osnaburgh L.
Madsen
Uchi Lake
Jeanette L.
Bowman L.
Lake St. Joseph
Longlegged L.
Bruce L.
Wenasaga
Pakwash L.
MANITOBA
Sydney L.
Churchill L.
Miniss L.
Whiteclay L.
Whitewater L.
Ogoki Reservoir
English
Ear Falls
Wabakimi L.
Mojikit L.
Winnipeg
Umfreville L.
Hooker L.
Smoothrock L.
Pointe du Bois
Wabaskang L.
Lac Seul Reservoir
Savant L.
Caribou L.
Indian L.
Tetu L.
WHITESHELL PROV. PARK
Sand L.
Clay L.
Savant Lake
Jacobs
Collins
Armstrong
Ferland
Malachi
Minaki
Hudson
Sioux Lookout
Allanwater
Ghost River
Reddit
McIntosh
Vermilion L.
Kopka
Wabinosh L.
LOGAN I.
GEIKIE I.
Richan
Red Lake Road
Sturgeon L.
Keewatin
Kenora
Laclu
Vermilion Bay
Minnitaki L.
Obonga L.
MURCHISON I.
Waugh
Hawk Lake
Eagle River
Dryden
Barclay
Sandybeach L.
Harmon L.
Lake Nipigon
Wabigoon
L. Wabigoon
Bell L.
Eagle L.
Dinorwic
Valora
KELVIN I.
Shoal L.
Kukukus L.
Holinshead L.
Gull
Western Pen.
Dryberry L.
Dinorwic L.
Dyment
Mameigwess L.
FALCON I.
Sioux Narrows
English
SHAKESPEARE I.
Aulneau Peninsula
Upper Manitou L.
Rowan L.
Stormy L.
Ignace
Sowden L.
Wawang L.
Pakashkan L.
Cheeseman L.
Macdiarmid
Lake of the Woods
BIG I.
Kakagi L.
Black Sturgeon L.
Pine Portage
Morson
Lower Manitou L.
English River
Graham
Frazer L.
BIGSBY I.
Nestor Falls
Muskeg Bay
White Otter L.
L. des Isles
Cameron Falls
Warroad
Arbor Vitae
Upsala
Muskeg L.
Williams
Finland
Marmion L.
Eaglehead L.
Nipigon
Baudette
Rainy River
Turtle
Dog
VERT I.
Red Rock
Stratton
Rainy Lake
Mine Centre
Atikokan
L. des Mille Lacs
Dorion
Emo
Fort Frances
Flanders
Kawene
Dog L.
Rapid
International Falls
Rainy
South International Falls
Pickerel L.
Kashabowie
Shebandowan
Pearl
Black Bay
Black
VOYAGEURS NAT. PARK
Kabetogama L.
Namakan L.
Sturgeon L.
Greenwater L.
Finmark
Kaministikwia
Little Fork
QUETICO PROV. PARK
THUNDER BAY
SIBLEY PROV. PARK
Upper Red Lake
Waskish
Kakabeka Falls
Thunder Bay
EDWARD I.
L. la Croix
Agnes L.
Northern Light L.
Hymers
Twin City
Silver Islet
Big Falls
Nett L.
Saganaga L.
South Gillies
Moose Hill
Lower Red Lake
PIE I.
BLAKE PT.
Orr
Basswood L.
Jarvis River
Pelican L.
Northome
ISLE ROYALE
Little Fork
Cook
Vermillion L.
Grand Portage
Big Fork
Big Fork
Ely
ISLE ROYALE NAT. PARK
Blackduck
Tower
Birch L.
LA
MINNESOTA
Grand Marais
Babbitt
Winnibigoshish L.
Bowstring L.
Chisholm
Virginia
SUPE
Cass L.
Cass Lake
Deer River
Keewatin
Hibbing
Bena
Marble
St. Louis
Cohasset
Coleraine
Grand Rapids
Eagle River
Leech L.
Pokegama Res.
Warba
Whiteface
Silver Bay
Mohawk
Walker
Cloquet
Laurium
Lake Linden
Remer
Meadowlands
Island L.
APOSTLE ISLANDS
Hancock
Hubbell
Hackensack
Hill City
Two Harbors
Houghton
Backus
Floodwood
St. Louis
SAND I.
OUTER I.
Portage L.
Painesdale
OAK I.
STOCKTON I.
Keweenaw Bay
Whitefish L.
Ontonagon
Winona
Pine River
Mississippi
Big Sandy L.
DULUTH
Superior
Port Wing
Bayfield
Donken
Huron Bay
MADELINE I.
Skanee
Cloquet
Baraga
Nisswa
Pelican L.
McGregor
Cromwell
Carlton
White Pine
L'Anse
Washburn
Gull L.
Aitkin
Poplar
Iron River
Rockland
MIC
Odanah
Crosby
Rice L.
Bergland
Baxter
Ashland
Moose Lake
Lake Nebagamon
Bruce Crossing
Crow Wing
Brainerd
Saxon
Ewen
Covington
Bad
Wakefield
Mille Lacs Lake
McGrath
Kettle
Solon Springs
WISCONSIN
Hurley
Ironwood
Trout Creek
Sidnaw
Drummond
L. Gogebic
Bruno
Marenisco
Mellen
Randall
Platte
Askov
St. Croix
Gordon
95
94
93
92
91
90
89
88
51
50
48
47
m
400
200
0
200
Projection: Lambert's Conformal Conic

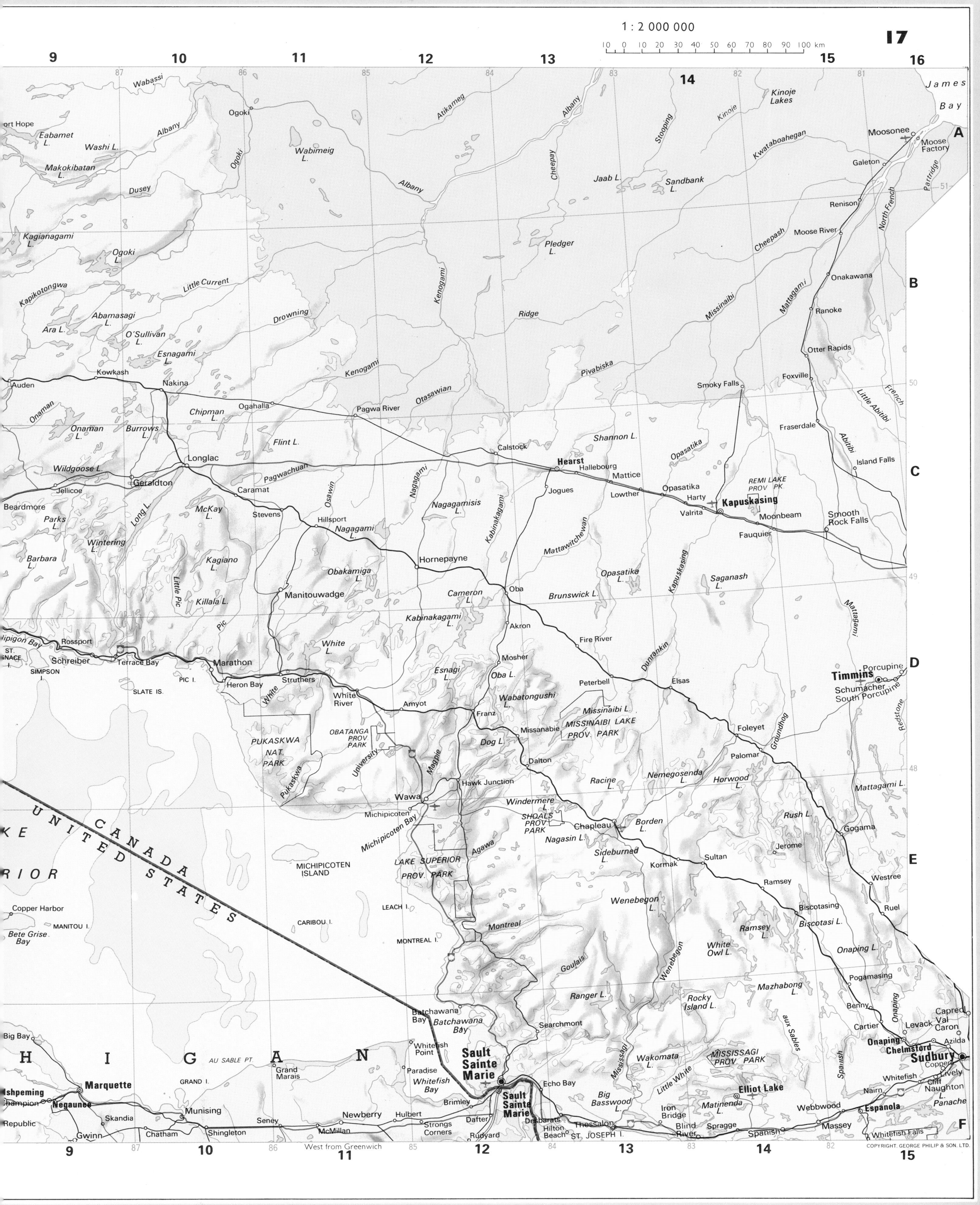
1 : 2 000 000
10 0 10 20 30 40 50 60 70 80 90 100 km
James Bay
Moosonee
Moose Factory
Galeton
Partridge
Renison
North French
Moose River
Onakawana
Ranoke
Otter Rapids
Foxville
Little Abitibi
French
Fraserdale
Abitibi
Island Falls
Smooth Rock Falls
Kinoje Lakes
Kinoje
Kwataboahegan
Stooping
Sandbank L.
Jaab L.
Cheepay
Albany
Atikameg
Ogoki
Wabassi
ort Hope
Eabamet L.
Washi L.
Makokibatan L.
Dusey
Wabimeig L.
Kagianagami L.
Ogoki L.
Little Current
Kapikotongwa
Abamasagi L.
Ara L.
O'Sullivan L.
Esnagami L.
Drowning
Kenogami
Ridge
Pledger L.
Cheepash
Missinaibi
Mattagami
Pivabiska
Smoky Falls
Otasawian
Pagwa River
Kowkash
Auden
Nakina
Ogahalla
Onaman
Onaman L.
Chipman L.
Burrows L.
Flint L.
Calstock
Shannon L.
Hearst
Hallebourg
Mattice
Opasatika
Lowther
Harty
Kapuskasing
REMI LAKE PROV. PK.
Valrita
Moonbeam
Fauquier
Jogues
Longlac
Wildgoose L.
Geraldton
Jellicoe
Beardmore
Caramat
Pagwachuan
Parks L.
McKay L.
Stevens
Osawin
Hillsport
Nagagami
Nagagami L.
Nagagamisis L.
Kabinakagami
Long L.
Wintering L.
Barbara L.
Kagiano L.
Little Pic
Killala L.
Manitouwadge
Obakamiga L.
Hornepayne
Mattawitchewan
Opasatika L.
Kapuskasing
Saganash L.
Cameron L.
Oba
Brunswick L.
Kabinakagami L.
Akron
Fire River
Pic
White L.
Dunrankin
Mattagami
Nipigon Bay
Rossport
ST. IGNACE I.
Schreiber
Terrace Bay
SIMPSON I.
Marathon
PIC I.
SLATE IS.
Heron Bay
Struthers
White
White River
Amyot
Esnagi L.
Mosher
Oba L.
Wabatongushi L.
Peterbell
Elsas
Missinaibi L.
MISSINAIBI LAKE PROV. PARK
Missanabie
Franz
Dog L.
Timmins
Porcupine
Schumacher
South Porcupine
Redstone
Foleyet
Groundhog
Palomar
PUKASKWA NAT. PARK
OBATANGA PROV. PARK
University
Magpie
Pukaskwa
Dalton
Hawk Junction
Racine L.
Nemegosenda L.
Horwood L.
Mattagami L.
Wawa
Michipicoten
Michipicoten Bay
Windermere L.
SHOALS PROV. PARK
Chapleau
Borden L.
Nagasin L.
Rush L.
Gogama
Jerome
Sideburned L.
Kormak
Sultan
LAKE SUPERIOR PROV. PARK
Agawa
MICHIPICOTEN ISLAND
CANADA
UNITED STATES
LAKE SUPERIOR
Westree
Ramsey
Wenebegon L.
Biscotasing
Biscotasi L.
Ruel
Copper Harbor
MANITOU I.
CARIBOU I.
LEACH I.
Montreal
Bete Grise Bay
MONTREAL I.
Ramsey L.
White Owl L.
Onaping L.
Goulais
Wenebegon
Pogamasing
Mazhabong L.
Ranger L.
Rocky Island L.
aux Sables
Benny
Onaping
Batchawana Bay
Batchawana Bay
Searchmont
Cartier
Levack
Capreol
Val Caron
Big Bay
Whitefish Point
Onaping
Azilda
Chelmsford
Sudbury
MICHIGAN
AU SABLE PT.
Grand Marais
Sault Sainte Marie
Wakomata L.
MISSISSAGI PROV. PARK
Mississagi
Spanish
Copper Cliff
Lively
Naughton
Ishpeming
Marquette
GRAND I.
Paradise
Whitefish Bay
Echo Bay
Little White
Elliot Lake
Whitefish
Champion
Negaunee
Munising
Brimley
Big Basswood L.
Matinenda L.
Nairn
Panache L.
Skandia
Newberry
Hulbert
Dafter
Sault Sainte Marie
Desbarats
Thessalon
Iron Bridge
Webbwood
Espanola
Republic
Gwinn
Chatham
Shingleton
Seney
McMillan
Strongs Corners
Rudyard
Hilton Beach
ST. JOSEPH I.
Blind River
Sprague
Spanish
Massey
Whitefish Falls
West from Greenwich
A B C D E F
9 10 11 12 13 14 15 16
87 86 85 84 83 82 81
51 50 49 48
COPYRIGHT. GEORGE PHILIP & SON, LTD.

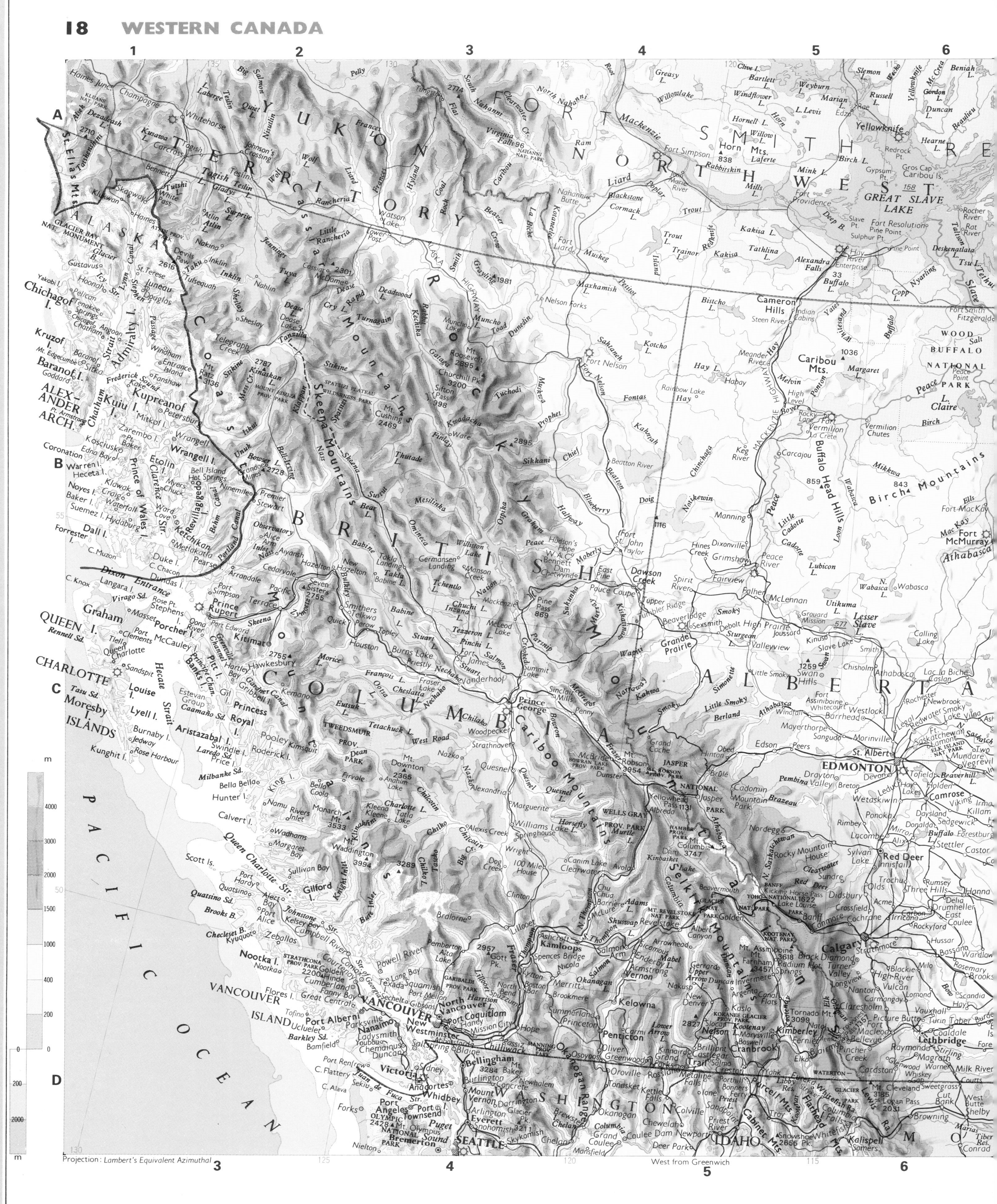

YUKON TERRITORY
NORTHWEST TERRITORIES
FORT SMITH
BRITISH COLUMBIA
ALBERTA
ALASKA
WASHINGTON
IDAHO
PACIFIC OCEAN
QUEEN CHARLOTTE ISLANDS
VANCOUVER ISLAND
ALEXANDER ARCH.
Whitehorse
Yellowknife
GREAT SLAVE LAKE
Fort Simpson
Fort Nelson
Fort St. John
Dawson Creek
Prince Rupert
Prince George
Grande Prairie
Peace River
EDMONTON
Calgary
Red Deer
Lethbridge
Kamloops
Kelowna
Penticton
VANCOUVER
Victoria
SEATTLE
Bellingham
Juneau
Skagway
Ketchikan
Coast Mountains
Skeena Mountains
Rocky Mountains
Cariboo Mountains
Selkirk Mountains
Birch Mountains
Caribou Mts.
Buffalo Head Hills
Cassiar Mountains
WOOD BUFFALO NATIONAL PARK
JASPER NATIONAL PARK
TWEEDSMUIR PROV. PARK
WELLS GRAY PROV. PARK
Mt. Robson 3954
Mt. Waddington 3994
Mt. Columbia 3747
Mt. Assiniboine 3618
Mt. Baker 3284
Dixon Entrance
Hecate Strait
Queen Charlotte Sd.
Queen Charlotte Str.
Str. of Georgia
Juan de Fuca Str.
Puget Sound
Projection: Lambert's Equivalent Azimuthal
West from Greenwich

1 : 5 600 000
50 0 50 100 150 200 250 300 km
7
8
9
10
11
A
B
C
D
KEEWATIN
REGION
HUDSON
BAY
MANITOBA
SASKATCHEWAN
ONTARIO
NORTH
DAKOTA
MINNESOTA
LAKE WINNIPEG
Lake Athabasca
Reindeer L.
Wollaston L.
Southern Indian L.
Lac la Ronge
Cedar Lake
Lake Winnipegosis
Lake Manitoba
Lake of the Woods
Churchill
C. Churchill
Port Nelson
Thompson
Flin Flon
The Pas
Prince Albert
North Battleford
Saskatoon
Regina
Moose Jaw
Swift Current
Medicine Hat
Brandon
Portage la Prairie
WINNIPEG
St. Boniface
Transcona
Selkirk
Kenora
Fort Frances
International Falls
Yorkton
Dauphin
Estevan
Weyburn
Minot
Grand Forks
Duluth
Cypress Hills
Uranium City
Eskimo Point
Whale Cove
Gillam
COPYRIGHT GEORGE PHILIP & SON LTD.

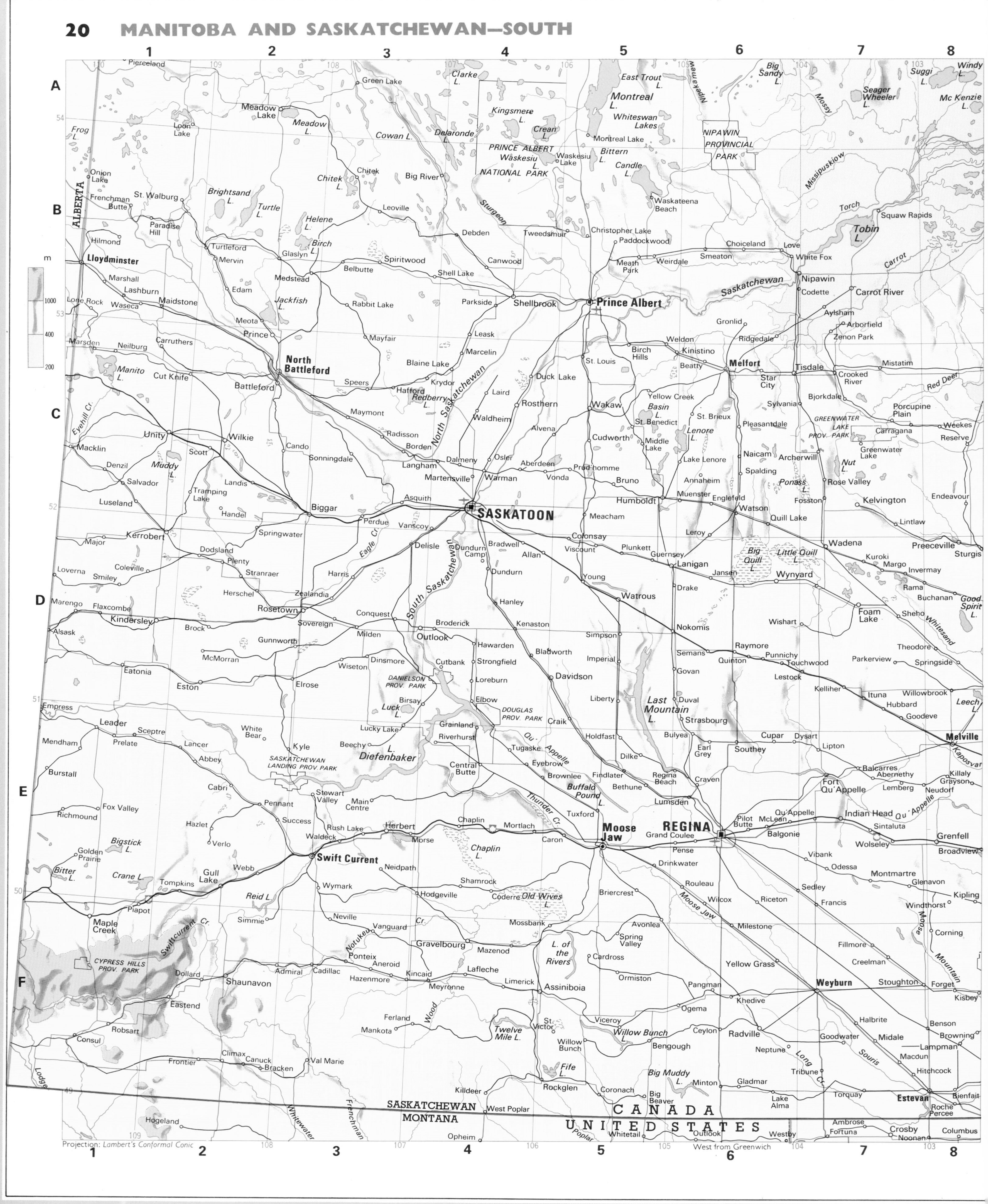
1
2
3
4
5
6
7
8
A
B
C
D
E
F
m
1000
400
200
Pierceland
Green Lake
Clarke L.
East Trout L.
Big Sandy L.
Suggi L.
Windy L.
Meadow Lake
Meadow L.
Kingsmere L.
Montreal L.
Seager Wheeler L.
Mc Kenzie L.
Frog L.
Loon Lake
Cowan L.
Delaronde L.
Crean L.
Whiteswan Lakes
Montreal Lake
NIPAWIN PROVINCIAL PARK
Nipekamew
Mossy
PRINCE ALBERT NATIONAL PARK
Waskesiu L.
Waskesiu Lake
Bittern L.
Candle L.
Onion Lake
Chitek L.
Chitek
Big River
Missipuskiow
ALBERTA
Frenchman Butte
St. Walburg
Brightsand L.
Turtle L.
Helene L.
Leoville
Sturgeon
Waskateena Beach
Torch
Squaw Rapids
Tobin L.
Paradise Hill
Hilmond
Birch L.
Debden
Tweedsmuir
Christopher Lake
Paddockwood
Choiceland
Love
White Fox
Carrot
Lloydminster
Turtleford
Mervin
Glaslyn
Spiritwood
Canwood
Meath Park
Weirdale
Smeaton
Nipawin
Codette
Carrot River
Marshall
Lashburn
Medstead
Belbutte
Shell Lake
Saskatchewan
Lone Rock
Waseca
Maidstone
Edam
Jackfish L.
Rabbit Lake
Parkside
Shellbrook
Prince Albert
Aylsham
Arborfield
Zenon Park
Meota
Prince
Leask
Gronlid
Ridgedale
Marsden
Neilburg
Carruthers
Mayfair
Marcelin
Birch Hills
Weldon
Kinistino
North Battleford
Blaine Lake
St. Louis
Beatty
Melfort
Tisdale
Mistatim
Manito L.
Cut Knife
Battleford
Speers
Krydor
Hafford
Redberry L.
Duck Lake
Laird
Star City
Crooked River
Red Deer
Eyehill Cr.
Maymont
North Saskatchewan
Rosthern
Yellow Creek
Basin L.
Bjorkdale
Porcupine Plain
Unity
Wilkie
Radisson
Waldheim
Wakaw
St. Benedict
St. Brieux
Sylvania
GREENWATER LAKE PROV. PARK
Weekes
Macklin
Scott
Borden
Alvena
Cudworth
Lenore L.
Pleasantdale
Carragana
Reserve
Denzil
Muddy L.
Cando
Sonningdale
Langham
Dalmeny
Osler
Aberdeen
Middle Lake
Lake Lenore
Naicam
Archerwill
Nut L.
Greenwater Lake
Salvador
Landis
Martensville
Warman
Vonda
Prud'homme
Bruno
Annaheim
Spalding
Ponass L.
Rose Valley
Tramping Lake
Asquith
Humboldt
Muenster
Englefeld
Fosston
Kelvington
Endeavour
Luseland
Handel
Biggar
SASKATOON
Meacham
Watson
Quill Lake
Lintlaw
Perdue
Vanscoy
Eagle Cr.
Leroy
Kerrobert
Springwater
Delisle
Dundurn Camp
Bradwell
Colonsay
Viscount
Plunkett
Guernsey
Big Quill L.
Little Quill L.
Wadena
Preeceville
Sturgis
Major
Dodsland
Plenty
Allan
Lanigan
Kuroki
Margo
Invermay
Loverna
Coleville
Smiley
Stranraer
Harris
South Saskatchewan
Dundurn
Young
Jansen
Wynyard
Rama
Herschel
Zealandia
Drake
Buchanan
Good Spirit L.
Marengo
Flaxcombe
Kindersley
Rosetown
Hanley
Watrous
Foam Lake
Sheho
Alsask
Brock
Sovereign
Conquest
Broderick
Kenaston
Nokomis
Wishart
Whitesand
Gunnworth
Milden
Outlook
Simpson
Raymore
Theodore
McMorran
Hawarden
Bladworth
Imperial
Semans
Punnichy
Quinton
Touchwood
Parkerview
Springside
Eatonia
Dinsmore
Cutbank
Strongfield
Govan
Lestock
Eston
Wiseton
Elrose
DANIELSON PROV. PARK
Loreburn
Davidson
Kelliher
Ituna
Willowbrook
Empress
Birsay
Elbow
Liberty
Last Mountain L.
Duval
Hubbard
Leech L.
Leader
Luck L.
DOUGLAS PROV. PARK
Craik
Strasbourg
Goodeve
Sceptre
White Bear
Lucky Lake
Grainland
Riverhurst
Qu' Appelle
Holdfast
Bulyea
Cupar
Dysart
Melville
Mendham
Prelate
Lancer
Kyle
Beechy
Diefenbaker L.
Tugaske
Dilke
Earl Grey
Southey
Lipton
Kaposvar
Abbey
SASKATCHEWAN LANDING PROV. PARK
Central Butte
Eyebrow
Findlater
Regina Beach
Balcarres
Killaly
Burstall
Cabri
Brownlee
Bethune
Craven
Abernethy
Grayson
Fort Qu'Appelle
Lemberg
Neudorf
Stewart Valley
Buffalo Pound
Lumsden
Pennant
Main Centre
Thunder Cr.
Tuxford
Fox Valley
Richmound
Success
Chaplin
Mortlach
Moose Jaw
REGINA
Pilot Butte
McLean
Qu'Appelle
Indian Head
Sintaluta
Hazlet
Rush Lake
Herbert
Caron
Grand Coulee
Balgonie
Grenfell
Waldeck
Morse
Wolseley
Bigstick L.
Verlo
Chaplin L.
Pense
Broadview
Golden Prairie
Swift Current
Vibank
Odessa
Gull Lake
Webb
Neidpath
Drinkwater
Bitter L.
Crane L.
Tompkins
Shamrock
Rouleau
Montmartre
Glenavon
Wymark
Sedley
Reid L.
Hodgeville
Coderre
Old Wives L.
Briercrest
Wilcox
Riceton
Kipling
Piapot
Moose Jaw
Francis
Windthorst
Maple Creek
Swiftcurrent Cr.
Simmie
Neville
Vanguard
Cr.
Mossbank
Avonlea
Milestone
Corning
Notukeu
Spring Valley
Moose Mountain
CYPRESS HILLS PROV. PARK
Gravelbourg
Mazenod
L. of the Rivers
Fillmore
Ponteix
Aneroid
Cardross
Creelman
Dollard
Admiral
Cadillac
Lafleche
Yellow Grass
Shaunavon
Hazenmore
Kincaid
Ormiston
Meyronne
Limerick
Assiniboia
Pangman
Weyburn
Stoughton
Forget
Eastend
Khedive
Kisbey
Ogema
Wood
Ferland
Viceroy
St. Victor
Halbrite
Benson
Robsart
Mankota
Twelve Mile L.
Willow Bunch L.
Ceylon
Radville
Goodwater
Midale
Browning
Consul
Willow Bunch
Bengough
Lampman
Neptune
Macklin
Souris
Climax
Canuck
Macoun
Frontier
Bracken
Val Marie
Fife L.
Long Cr.
Tribune
Hitchcock
Big Muddy L.
Lodge
Rockglen
Coronach
Minton
Gladmar
Lake Alma
Torquay
Estevan
Bienfait
Killdeer
Big Beaver
Roche Percee
SASKATCHEWAN
MONTANA
West Poplar
CANADA
UNITED STATES
Hogeland
Whitewater
Frenchman
Opheim
Poplar
Whitetail
Outlook
Westby
Ambrose
Fortuna
Crosby
Noonan
Columbus
110
109
108
107
106
105
104
103
54
53
52
51
50
49
Projection: Lambert's Conformal Conic
West from Greenwich

1 : 2 000 000
10 0 10 20 30 40 50 60 70 80 90 100 km
9
10
11
12
13
14
15
A
B
C
D
E
F
Goose L.
Simonhouse
Cormorant
Cormorant L.
Namew L.
Cumberland L.
Cumberland House
Wanless
CLEARWATER L. PROV. PARK
Talbot L.
Minago
Kiskitto L.
Kiskittogisu L.
Molson L.
Norway House
Playgreen L.
Stevenson L.
Moose L.
William L.
The Pas
Limestone Bay
EAGLE I.
Bigstone L.
Moose Lake
Gunisao
Gunisao L.
Contin L.
Westray
Belanger
Cedar L.
SELKIRK I.
LAKE WINNIPEG
Hudwin L.
Otosquen
253
Grand Rapids
Mukutawa
Overflowing
Easterville
Long Point
217
Elliot L.
Leaf L.
SPRUCE I.
Lake
Poplar
Red Deer L.
Dawson Bay
GRAND I.
Katimik L.
Kawinaw L.
Charron L.
Hudson Bay
Barrows
Pelican Rapids
ONTARIO
Mafeking
253
REINDEER I.
Poplar
Bellsite
Swan L.
Winnipegosis
BIRCH I.
Pelican L.
Chitek L.
Beren's River
BERENS I.
Berens
Birch River
Swan
COMMISSIONER I.
Little Grand Rapids
Fishing L.
Bowsman
Swan
Duck Bay
Waterhen L.
Sturgeon Bay
Family L.
Swan River
Minitonas
Cowan
Anama Bay
Kenville
Camperville
Skownan
Matheson Island
Hyas
Arran
Norquay
Pelly
Pine River
Gypsumville
MOOSE I.
Pine Dock
Sasaginnigak L.
DUCK MOUNTAIN PROV. PARKS
L. St. Martin
Fairford
Fisher Bay
Fisher Bay
Bloodvein
Canora
Winnipegosis
Crane River
Portage Bay
Kamsack
Veregin
Ethelbert
Fork River
Gammon
Steep Rock
Grahamdale
HECLA PROV. PARK
San Clara
Rorketon
BLACK I.
Togo
Sifton
Dauphin L.
Lake
Hodgson
Rhein
Ashern
Manigotan
Bissett
Roblin
HECLA I.
Yorkton
Wroxton
Dauphin
Fisher Branch
Riverton
Manigotagan L.
Grandview
Dog L.
Gilbert Plains
MacNutt
Ochre River
Ste. Rose du Lac
Vogar
Arborg
217
Saltcoats
Shellmouth
Laurier
Eriksdale
Poplarfield
Bredenbury
RIDING MOUNTAIN NATIONAL PARK
Silver Ridge
Manitoba
Victoria Beach
NOPIMING PROV. PARK
Churchbridge
McCreary
Langenburg
Russell
750
Lundar
Fraserwood
Gimli
Pine Falls
Angusville
Cr.
Dubuc
Stockholm
Rossburn
Onanole
Kelwood
Amaranth
L. du Bonnet
Binscarth
Inwood
Beaconia
Great Falls
Winnipeg
Esterhazy
Glenella
Oak Point
Winnipeg Beach
Assiniboine
Elphinstone
Teulon
Tantallon
Frikson
Plumas
Langruth
St. Laurent
Petersfield
Lac du Bonnet
Pointe du Bois
Shoal Lake
Eden
248
St. Lazare
Birtle
Balmoral
Rocanville
Clanwilliam
Arden
Delta Beach
Argyle
Seven Sisters Falls
Pinawa
WHITESHELL PROV. PARK
Whitewood
Wapella
Gladstone
Woodlands
Stonewall
Selkirk
Minnedosa
Neepawa
Grosse Isle
Stony Mountain
Tyndall
Beauséjour
McAuley
Hamiota
Rapid City
Westbourne
Poplar Point
Rivercrest
Oakbank
Whitemouth
Pipestone Cr.
Moosomin
Marquette
WINNIPEG
Transcona
Oak River
Brookdale
MacGregor
St. Eustache
Anola
Elma
Rennie
Fleming
Elkhorn
Rivers
Portage La Prairie
St. François Xavier
St. James
St. Boniface
Kennedy
Carberry
Sidney
Reynolds
Waugh
Virden
Starbuck
Grande Pointe
MOOSE MTN. PROV. PARK
Maryfield
Brandon
Shilo
Assiniboine
St. Norbert
Lorette
Ste. Anne
Oak Lake
SPRUCE WOODS PROV. PARK
St. Claude
Niverville
Whitemouth
Cromer
Treherne
Brunkild
La Broquerie
Morris
Ste. Agathe
Arcola
Carlyle
Wawanesa
Notre Dame de Lourdes
Steinbach
Cr.
Redvers
Souris
Sperling
Manor
Glenboro
Cypress River
Carman
St. Pierre
Grunthal
Antler
Reston
Roseisle
Souris
Lowe Farm
Whitemouth L.
Hartney
Elgin
Ninette
Belmont
Somerset
Roland
Morris
St. Malo
Rat
Woodridge
Alida
Tilston
Souris
Baldur
St. Jean Baptiste
Vassar
Napinka
Pilot Mound
Manitou
Thornhill
Plum Coulee
Sundown
Alameda
Oxbow
Antler
Melita
Boissevain
Killarney
Morden
Winkler
Altona
Red
Dominion City
Sprague
Pierson
Crystal City
Tolstoi
15
Frobisher
Glen Ewen
Carnduff
Deloraine
Reinland
Gretna
Emerson
MINNESOTA
Cartwright
Snowflake
Humboldt
TURTLE MT. PROV. PARK
Waskada
MANITOBA
NORTH DAKOTA
Neche
Pembina
Lancaster
Roseau
North Portal
Sarles
Hannah
Wales
Walhalla
Bathgate
Malung
766
Saint John
Cavalier
Hallock
Lake Bronson
Sherwood
Antler
Westhope
Flaxton
Bottineau
Rolla
Rocklake
Langdon
Greenbush
102
101
100
99
98
97
96
95
54
53
52
51
50
49
14
COPYRIGHT GEORGE PHILIP & SON, LTD.

1 : 2 000 000

10 0 10 20 30 40 50 60 70 80 90 100 km

SASKATCHEWAN

Fort McMurray
Fort MacKay
Athabasca
Clearwater
Christina
Firebag
Mc Clelland L.
Gordon L.
Garson L.
Winefred L.
Conklin
Sand
Ells
MacKay
Gardiner Lakes
Birch
Mikkwa
Wabasca
N. Wabasca L.
S. Wabasca L.
Desmarais
Muskwa
Muskwa L.
Peerless Lake
Peerless L.
Graham L.
Nipisi L.
Utikuma L.
Gift Lake
Lubicon Lake
Lubicon L.
Loon
Wadlin L.
Buffalo
Bison L.
Cadotte
Little Cadotte
Peace
Peace River
Smoky
Little Smoky
South Heart
Kimiwan L.
McLennan
Winagami L.
WINAGAMI LAKE PROV. PARK
Girouard Mission
Falher
Donnelly
Girouxville
High Prairie
Enilda
Joussard
Faust
Kinuso
Canyon Creek
Lesser Slave L.
LESSER SLAVE LAKE PROV. PARK
Slave Lake
Swan
Swan Hills
Freeman
Smith
Hondo
Chisholm
Flatbush
Fawcett
Calling Lake
Calling L.
Athabasca
Colinton
Rochester
Plamondon
Lac La Biche
North Buck L.
Caslan
Kikino
Long L.
Boyle
Newbrook
Cold L.
Cold Lake
Medley
Grand Centre
Marie L.
Ardmore
Bonnyville
Muriel L.
Frog L.
Glendon
Mallaig
Ashmont
Vilna
St. Paul
Elk Point
Smoky Lake
Saskatchewan
North Saskatchewan
Willingdon
Two Hills
Derwent
Dewberry
Marwayne
Kitscoty
Islay
Blackfoot
Vermilion
Clandonald
Mannville
Myrnam
Innisfree
Ranfurly
Lavoy
Birch L.
Mundare
Vegreville
Beaverhill L.
Holden
Ryley
Tofield
Cooking
Andrew
Chipman
Bruderheim
Lamont
ELK ISLAND NAT. PARK
Waskatenau
Radway
Redwater
Gibbons
Fort Saskatchewan
Sherwood Park
New Sarepta
Beaumont
Leduc
EDMONTON
St. Albert
Spruce Grove
Stony Plain
Devon
Calmar
Thorsby
Legal
Bon Accord
Morinville
Carbondale
Thorhild
Westlock
Clyde
Arvilla
Sandy L.
Onoway
Rich Valley
Highridge
Barrhead
Linaria
Fort Assiniboine
Cherhill
Lac Ste. Anne
Alberta Beach
Wabamun
Isle L.
Genesee
Seba Beach
Round Valley
Sangudo
Pembina
Evansburg
Drayton Valley
Mystery Lake
Lone Pine
Blue Ridge
Mayerthorpe
Hattonford
Chip L.
Wildwood
Cynthia
MacKay
Whitecourt
Windfall
Two Creeks
Fox Creek
McLeod
Peers
Edson
Robb
Mercoal
Obed
Hinton
WILLIAM A. SWITZER PROV. PARK
Wildhay
Miette Hotsprings
Brûlé
Berland
Simonette
Muskeg River
Grande Cache
WILLMORE WILDERNESS PARK
JASPER
Mt. Robson
MT. ROBSON
Kakwa
Cutbank
Narraway
Manning
North Star
Notikewin
Hotchkiss
Dixonville
Chinook Valley
Cardinal L.
Grimshaw
Berwyn
Fairview
Dunvegan
Eureka River
Hines Creek
Worsley
Chinchaga
Clear
Doig
Bonanza
Blueberry Mountain
Spirit River
Rycroft
Eaglesham
Wanham
Bad Heart
Teepee Creek
Debolt
Sturgeon L.
Valleyview
Snipe L.
Clairmont
Grande Prairie
Sexsmith
Homestead
Bear L.
Wapiti
Grovedale
Wembley
Hythe
Lymburn
Beaverlodge
Redwillow
Elmworth
Sylvester

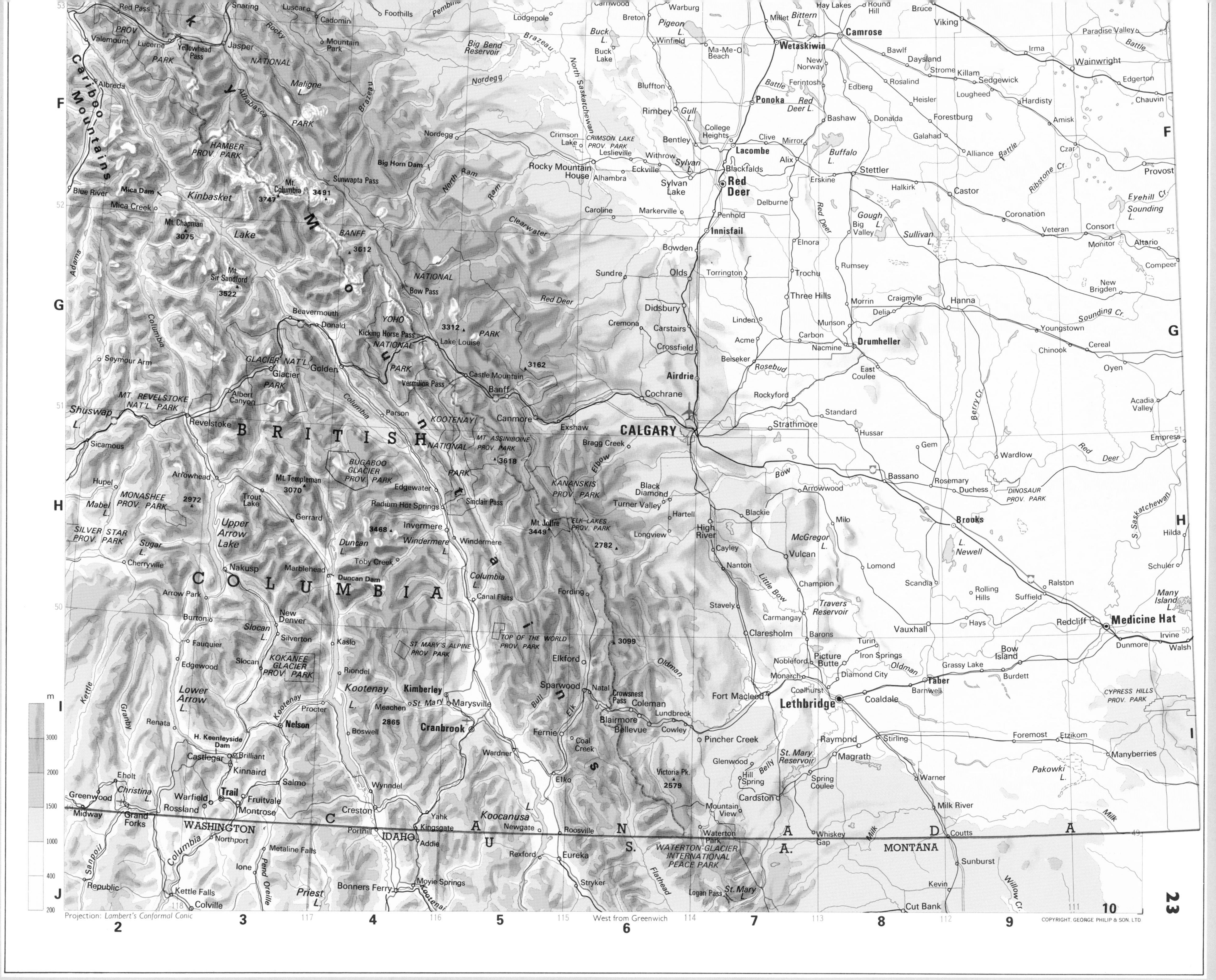

CALGARY
Red Deer
Lethbridge
Medicine Hat
Drumheller
Camrose
Wetaskiwin
Lacombe
Ponoka
Airdrie
Brooks
Innisfail
Banff
Canmore
Cochrane
Golden
Revelstoke
Nelson
Cranbrook
Kimberley
Trail
Castlegar
Fernie
Grand Forks
Nakusp
B R I T I S H
C O L U M B I A
Cariboo Mountains
MONTANA
IDAHO
WASHINGTON
U. S. A.
BANFF NATIONAL PARK
YOHO NATIONAL PARK
KOOTENAY NATIONAL PARK
GLACIER NAT'L PARK
MT. REVELSTOKE NAT'L PARK
WATERTON-GLACIER INTERNATIONAL PEACE PARK
DINOSAUR PROV. PARK
CYPRESS HILLS PROV. PARK
KANANSKIS PROV. PARK
North Saskatchewan
Red Deer
Bow
Oldman
Columbia
Kootenay
Upper Arrow Lake
Lower Arrow L.
Kootenay L.
Kinbasket Lake
Koocanusa L.
Mt. Columbia 3747
Mt. Assiniboine 3618
Projection: Lambert's Conformal Conic
West from Greenwich
COPYRIGHT, GEORGE PHILIP & SON, LTD
m
3000
2000
1500
1000
400
200

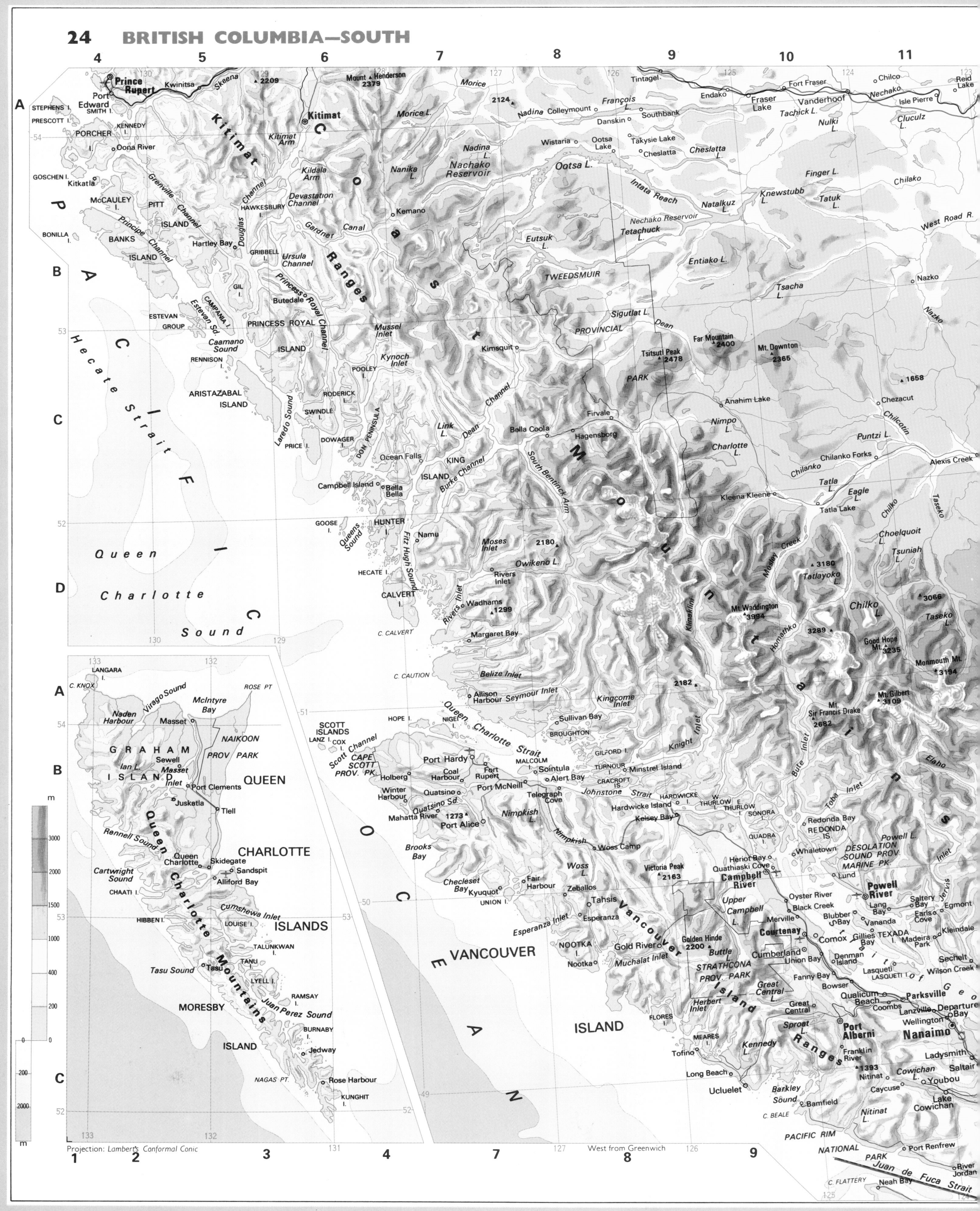

Projection: Lambert's Conformal Conic
West from Greenwich

1 : 2 000 000
10 0 10 20 30 40 50 60 70 80 90 100 km
12
13
14
15
16
17
18
19
20
H
D
E
F
G
Prince George
Shelley
Pineview
Red Rock
Stoner
Woodpecker
Hixon
Strathnaver
Dunkley
Moose Heights
Quesnel
Kersley
Alexandria
Castle Rock
Marguerite
Macalister
Williams Lake
150 Mile House
Meldrum Creek
Mt. Alex Graham 1665
Riske Creek
Hanceville
Chilcotin
Big Creek
Gang Ranch
Dog Creek
Fraser
Bowron
Cariboo Mountains
BOWRON LAKE PROV. PARK
Wells
Mitchell L.
Quesnel L.
Likely
Horsefly L.
Horsefly
Penny
Dome Creek
Crescent Spur
Lamming Mills
McBride
Dunster
Rocky Mountains
WILLMORE WILDERNESS PARK
ALTA. B.C.
Mt. Robson 3954
MT. ROBSON PROV. PARK
Red Pass
Lucerne
Yellowhead Pass
Valemount
Albreda
HAMBER PROV. PARK
Mt. Columbia 3747
3491
Kinbasket Lake
Mica Dam
Mica Creek
Mt. Chapman 3075
Mt. Sir Sandford 3522
BANFF NATIONAL PARK
3612
Bow Pass
3312
Lake Louise
YOHO NATIONAL PARK
Kicking Horse Pass
Vermilion Pass
Beavermouth
Donald
Golden
GLACIER NAT'L PARK
Glacier
Parson
Columbia
Albert Canyon
Revelstoke
MT. REVELSTOKE NAT'L. PARK
Seymour Arm
BUGABOO GLACIER PROV. PARK
Mt. Templeman 3070
3468
Hobson L.
Azure L.
WELLS GRAY PROVINCIAL PARK
Clearwater L.
Murtle L.
Blue River
North Thompson
Hendrix Lake
Mahood L.
Mahood Falls
Canim L.
Canim Lake
Clearwater
Avola
Vavenby
Birch Island
Lac la Hache
Forest Grove
Buffalo Creek
Wright
Tatton
Springhouse
100 Mile House
Lone Butte
Sheridan L.
Little Fort
Chu Chua
Adams L.
2303
Barrière
Louis Creek
McLure
Bonaparte L.
70 Mile House
Chasm
2243
Clinton
Big Bar Creek
Black Pines
Chase
Shuswap L.
Sicamous
Canoe
Salmon Arm
Rayleigh
Westsyde
Kamloops L.
Walhachin
Savona
Cherry Creek
Kamloops
South Thompson
Cache Creek
Ashcroft
Carpenter L.
2877
Bralorne
Shalalth
Seton Portage
Seton
Lillooet
2329
Anderson L.
Spences Bridge
Birken
Pemberton
Lillooet L.
Skihist Mt. 2944
Lytton
Thompson
Lower Nicola
Nicola L.
Nicola
Merritt
Quilchena
Valleyview
Enderby
Armstrong
SILVER STAR PROV. PARK
Vernon
Oyama
Hupel
Mabel L.
MONASHEE PROV. PARK
2972
Sugar L.
Cherryville
Arrowhead
Trout Lake
Gerrard
Upper Arrow Lake
Duncan L.
Toby Creek
Duncan Dam
Marblehead
Nakusp
Arrow Park
Burton
New Denver
Slocan L.
Silverton
Kaslo
Riondel
KOKANEE GLACIER PROV. PARK
Fauquier
Slocan
Edgewood
Wilson Landing
Kelowna
Okanagan L.
Okanagan Mission
OKANAGAN MOUNTAIN PROV. PARK
Peachland
Carmi
Kettle
Granby
Lower Arrow L.
Procter
Nelson
Kootenay L.
Boswell
Alta Lake
Squamish
GARIBALDI PROV. PARK
Mt. Garibaldi 2678
2385
North Bend
Boston Bar
Aspen Grove
Brookmere
Summerland
Penticton
Beaverdell
Renata
H. Keenleyside Dam
Brilliant
Castlegar
Kinnaird
Salmo
2602
Brackendale
Woodfibre
Britannia Beach
Howe
Port Mellon
GAMBIER I.
Roberts Creek
Bowen Island
Gibsons
GOLDEN EARS PROV. PARK
Harrison Lake
Pitt L.
Stave L.
Harrison Hot Springs
Spuzzum
Yale
Hope
Coalmont
Princeton
Similkameen
Hedley
Keremeos
Oliver
2304
Greenwood
Eholt
Christina L.
Rock Creek
Grand Forks
Warfield
Trail
Fruitvale
Montrose
Rossland
North Vancouver
Port Moody
Port Coquitlam
Haney
VANCOUVER
New Westminster
Fort Langley
Langley
Stave Falls
Deroche
Mission
City
Agassiz
Laidlaw
Cheam View
Rosedale
Chilliwack
Sardis
Yarrow
Silvertip Mt. 2606
MANNING PROV. PARK
Manning Park
CATHEDRAL PROV. PARK 2593
Osoyoos
Osoyoos L.
Oroville
Midway
WASHINGTON
Northport
Metaline Falls
IDAHO
Priest L.
Ione
Pend Oreille
CANADA
U. S. A.
GABRIOLA I.
VALDES I.
Abbotsford
Lindell Beach
White Rock
Blaine
Sumas
Lynden
Mount Baker
Ross L.
NORTH CASCADES NATIONAL PARK
Tonasket
Republic
Kettle Falls
Colville
Chewelah
Newport
ROBERTS
Chemainus
Crofton
Maple Bay
Mayne
Saturna
Fulford Harbour
Duncan
East Sound
ORCAS I.
Orcas
Sidney
Friday Harbor
SAN JUAN I.
LOPEZ I.
Haro Str.
Maple Falls
Ferndale
Bellingham
L. Whatcom
Mt. Baker 3284
Shannon L.
Newhalem
Concrete
Marblemount
2703
Rockport
Hamilton
LUMMI I.
Anacortes
Sedro Woolley
Burlington
Mount Vernon
Mazama
Methow
Winthrop
Chewack Creek
Conconully
Riverside
Omak
Omak L.
Okanogan
Malott
Carlton
Twisp
Sanpoil
Nespelem
Columbia
Springdale
Stehekin
L. Chelan
Holden
Lucerne
Darrington
Arlington
Glacier Peak 3211
Silverton
Oak Harbor
WHIDBEY I.
Coupeville
Stanwood
CAMANO I.
VICTORIA
Sooke
BEECHEY HEAD
120
119
118
116
117
121
122
123
49
50
51
53
48
1 : 200 000
0 1 2 3 4 5 km
For reference to colours see page 28.
Royal Oak
GORDON HEAD
Colquitz
Lake Hill
Mt. Tolmie
SAANICH
Cadboro Bay
Craigflower
Langford
Belmont Park
Colwood
ESQUIMALT
MACAULAY PT.
Victoria Harb.
Beacon Hill Park
OAK BAY
DISCOVERY I.
CLOVER PT.
48° 30'
123° 20'
COPYRIGHT. GEORGE PHILIP & SON. LTD.

ARCTIC OCEAN
Beaufort Sea
Permanent Polar Ice
Pt. Franklin
Barrow
Pt. Barrow
C. Halkett
Colville
Umiat
Prudhoe Bay
Kaktovik
Martin Pt.
Brooks Range
Mt. Doonerak 2320
Endicott Mts.
Mt. Isto 2761
Evansville
Wiseman
Allakaket
Arctic Village
Herschel I.
British Mts.
Mackenzie Bay
Richards I.
ALASKA (U.S.A.)
Stevens
Beaver
Fort Yukon
Porcupine
Old Crow
Livengood
Fairbanks
Tanana
Yukon
Delta Junction
Eagle
Clinton Creek
Tanacross
Ogilvie Mts.
Aklavik
Richardson Mts.
Tuktoyaktuk
Eskimo Lakes
Inuvik
Arctic Red River
McPherson
Peel
Mackenzie
Dawson
Klondike
Mt. Sanford 4949
Wrangell Mts.
Stewart River
Elsa
Keno Hill
Mayo
Mackenzie Mountains
Beaver Creek
Pelly Crossing
YUKON TERRITORY
Mt. Steele 5011
Mt. Logan 6051
Kluane L.
Burwash Landing
Destruction Bay
Carmacks
Faro
Mt. Kennedy 4236
KLUANE NAT. PARK
Haines Junc.
Whitehorse
Ross River
Pelly
2965
S. Nahanni
2743
Tungsten
St. Elias Mts.
Yakutat
Carcross
Bennett
Jakes Corner
Johnsons Crossing
Teslin
Mt. Fairweather 4663
Skagway
Atlin
NAHANNI NAT. PARK
Nahanni Butte
Upper Liard
Watson Lake
Cassiar Mts.
Cassiar
Cross Sd.
Chichagof I.
Douglas
Juneau
Admiralty
Sitka
Baranof I.
Dease
Dease Lake
Stikine
Telegraph Creek
B.C.
Fort Liard
ALASKA HIGHWAY
Ft. Nelson
Mt. Lloyd George 3292
Nelson
Petitot
Trout L.
Trout Lake
ALTA.
Meander River
Caribou Mts.
HAY RIVER HIGHWAY
WOOD BUFFALO NAT. PARK
Ft. Smith
SASK.
Liverpool Bay
C. Bathurst
Franklin Bay
Darnley Bay
Paulatuk
Anderson
INUVIK REGION
Horton
Hornaday
Bluenose L.
Aubry L.
Colville Lake
L. Maunoir
L. Belot
Ft. Good Hope
L. des Bois
NORTHWEST
Smith Arm
Dease Arm
Franklin Mts.
Norman Wells
Ft. Norman
Fort Franklin
Great Bear
Keith Arm
Gt. Bear Lake
157
Echo Bay (Port Radium)
Coppermine
Hottah L.
Point L.
Wrigley
L. la Martre
Lac la Martre
Rae Lakes
Snare Lakes
Yellowknife
Rae-Edzo
Detah
FORT SMITH REGION
Mackenzie
Ft. Simpson
Jean Marie River
Liard
Fort Providence
Great Slave L.
156
Hay River
Enterprise
Pine Point
Fort Resolution
Rocher River
Slave
Reliance
Snowdrift
Nonacho L.
Dubawnt
Wholdaia L.
Aylmer L.
Clinton Colden L.
L. de Gras
Contwoyto L.
Takiyuak L.
Burnside
Back
Pelly L.
Bathurst Inlet
Kent Pen.
Coronation Gulf
Queen
Cambridge Bay
Read Island
Dolphin & Union Str.
Wollaston Pen.
Prince Albert Sd.
C. Baring
Holman
Victoria Island
KITIK
RE
Amundsen Gulf
C. Lambton
750
Thesiger Bay
Sachs Harbour
C. Kellett
Banks Island
Storkerson B.
C. Prince Alfred
C. Wrottesley
M'Clure Strait
Prince of Wales Str.
Passage Pt.
Prince Albert Pen.
Wynniatt Bay
Hadley Bay
Stefansson I.
M'Clintock
Viscount Melville Sound
C. Hay
Dundas Pen.
Liddon Gulf
Melville I.
Byam Martin I.
Blue Hills 1067
Kellett Str.
Mould Bay
Eglinton I.
Prince Patrick I.
Parry Islands
Queen
Austin
Lougheed I.
Mackenzie King I.
Brock I.
Borden I.
Prince Gustav Adolf Sea
Maclean
Projection: Bonne

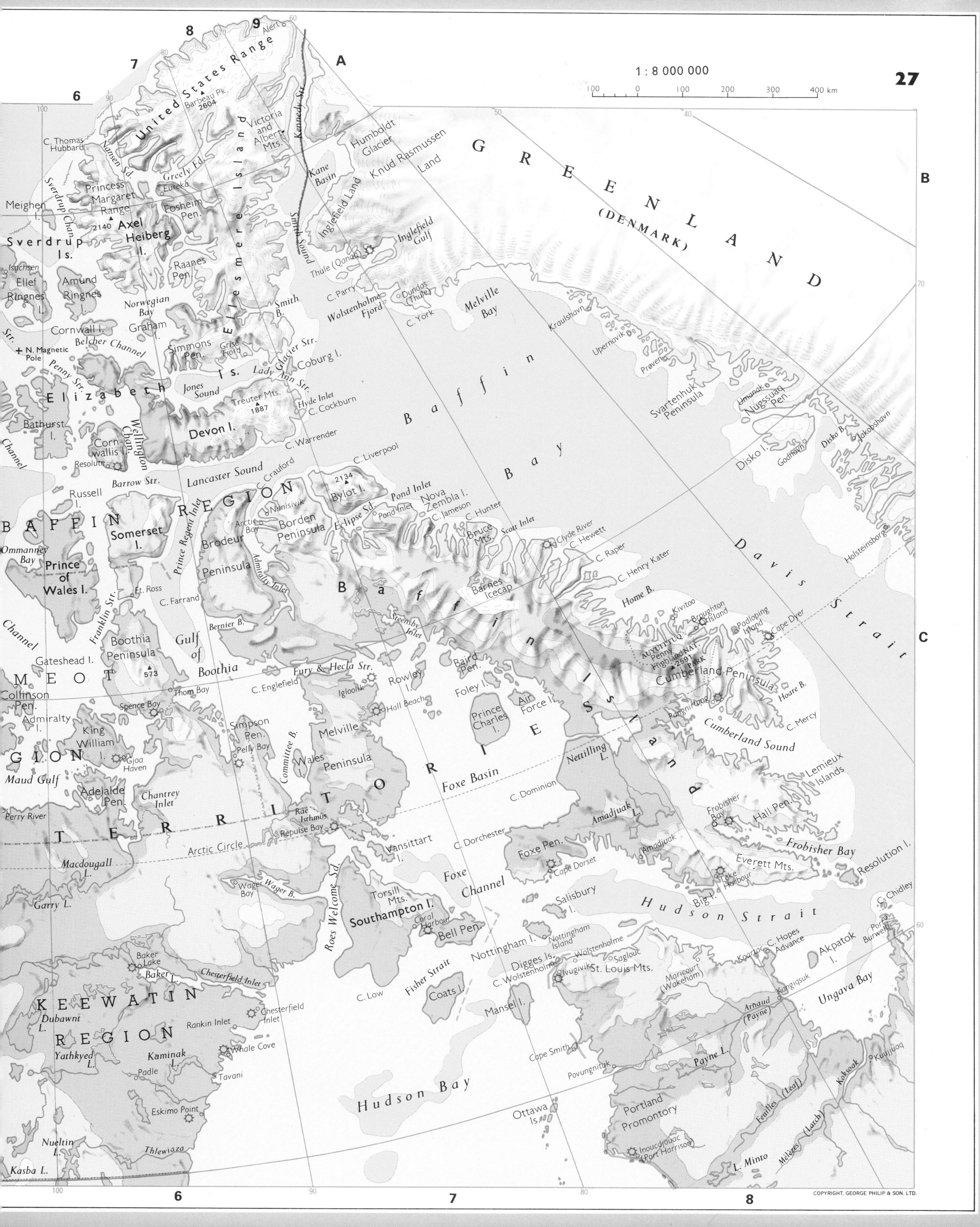
1 : 8 000 000
100 0 100 200 300 400 km
GREENLAND
(DENMARK)
United States Range
Barbeau Pk. 2604
Alert
Kennedy Str.
Victoria and Albert Mts.
Ellesmere Island
Humboldt Glacier
Knud Rasmussen Land
Kane Basin
Inglefield Land
Inglefield Gulf
Smith Sound
Thule (Qanaq)
C. Parry
Dundas (Thule)
Wolstenholme Fjord
C. York
Melville Bay
Kraulshavn
Upernavik
Prøven
Svartenhuk Peninsula
Umanak
Nugssuaq Pen.
Disko I.
Godhavn
Disko B.
Jakobshavn
Holsteinsborg
Davis Strait
C. Thomas Hubbard
Nansen Sd.
Greely Fd.
Eureka
Fosheim Pen.
Sverdrup Chan.
Princess Margaret Range
2140
Axel Heiberg I.
Meighen I.
Sverdrup Is.
Isachsen
Ellef Ringnes I.
Amund Ringnes I.
Raanes Pen.
Norwegian Bay
Smith B.
Graham I.
Cornwall I.
Belcher Channel
N. Magnetic Pole
Penny Str.
Simmons Pen.
Grise Fiord
Glacier Str.
Coburg I.
Lady Ann Str.
Elizabeth Is.
Jones Sound
Treuter Mts.
1887
Hyde Inlet
C. Cockburn
Devon I.
Bathurst I.
Cornwallis I.
Wellington Chan.
Resolute
C. Warrender
Baffin Bay
C. Liverpool
Lancaster Sound
C. Crauford
Barrow Str.
Russell I.
2134
Bylot I.
Pond Inlet
Nova Zembla I.
C. Jameson
C. Hunter
Nanisivik
Arctic Bay
Borden Peninsula
Eclipse Sd.
Bruce Mts.
Scott Inlet
Clyde River
C. Hewett
C. Raper
C. Henry Kater
BAFFIN REGION
Somerset I.
Prince Regent Inlet
Brodeur Peninsula
Admiralty Inlet
Ommanney Bay
Prince of Wales I.
Ft. Ross
C. Farrand
Barnes Icecap
Home B.
Kivitoo
Broughton Island
Padloping Island
Cape Dyer
Baffin Island
AUYUITTUQ NAT. PARK
Penny Highland
2591
Cumberland Peninsula
Hoare B.
Franklin Str.
Bernier B.
Steensby Inlet
Boothia Peninsula
573
Gulf of Boothia
Gateshead I.
Fury & Hecla Str.
C. Englefield
Igloolik
Rowley I.
Baird Pen.
Foley I.
Prince Charles I.
Air Force I.
Pangnirtung
Cumberland Sound
C. Mercy
Collinson Pen.
Thom Bay
Spence Bay
Admiralty I.
King William I.
Gjoa Haven
Simpson Pen.
Pelly Bay
Hall Beach
Melville Peninsula
Committee B.
Wales I.
Nettilling L.
Lemieux Islands
Maud Gulf
Adelaide Pen.
Chantrey Inlet
NORTHWEST TERRITORIES
Foxe Basin
C. Dominion
Amadjuak L.
Frobisher Bay
Hall Pen.
Perry River
Rae Isthmus
Repulse Bay
Vansittart I.
C. Dorchester
Foxe Pen.
Amadjuak
Frobisher Bay
Resolution I.
Arctic Circle
Macdougall L.
Wager Bay
Wager B.
Roes Welcome Sd.
Torsill Mts.
Foxe Channel
Cape Dorset
Everett Mts.
Lake Harbour
Big I.
Garry L.
Southampton I.
Coral Harbour
Bell Pen.
Salisbury I.
Hudson Strait
C. Chidley
Port Burwell
Baker Lake
Baker L.
Chesterfield Inlet
Nottingham I.
Nottingham Island
Digges Is.
Wolstenholme
C. Wolstenholme
Ivugivik
Saglouc
St. Louis Mts.
Maricourt (Wakeham)
Koartac
C. Hopes Advance
Akpatok I.
KEEWATIN REGION
Dubawnt L.
Chesterfield Inlet
C. Low
Fisher Strait
Coats I.
Mansel I.
Kangiqsuk
Arnaud (Payne)
Ungava Bay
Rankin Inlet
Yathkyed L.
Kaminak L.
Whale Cove
Padle
Tavani
Cape Smith
Payne L.
Koksoak
Kuujjuaq
Povungnituk
Hudson Bay
Eskimo Point
Ottawa Is.
Portland Promontory
Feuilles (Leaf)
Mélèzes (Larch)
Nueltin L.
Thlewiaza
Inoucdjouac (Port Harrison)
L. Minto
Kasba L.

1 : 200 000

5 4 3 2 1 0 5 10 km

Residential
Commercial
Industrial
Institutional
Recreational
Woodland
Transportation and utilities
Agricultural and other
Freeway with interchange
Trans-Canada Highway
County or Regional Municipality Boundary
Subway
Railway with station
Bolton
Humber
RICHMOND HILL
MARKHAM
Whitevale
Brock Road
West Duffin
Little Rouge
Y O R K
Maple
Unionville
Buttonville
Rouge
East Humber
Kleinburg
Tormore
Richvale
Cherrywood
Pickering
Ajax
Langstaff
Armadale
Dunbarton
Duffin
Coleraine
Wildfield
East Don
Milliken
Fairport
West Don
Thornhill
Rouge Hill
MOORE POINT
Humber
West Humber
Edgeley
Concord
NEWTON BROOK
Malvern
Tullamore
Pine Grove
AGINCOURT
HIGHLAND CREEK
Woodbridge
WILLOWDALE
York Univ.
NORTHMOUNT
401
WOBURN
WEST HILL
BENDALE
LANSING
YORK MILLS
NORTH YORK
WEXFORD
SCARBOROUGH
Woodhill
Mimico Cr.
THISTLETOWN
DON MILLS
SCARBOROUGH
DOWNSVIEW
REXDALE
T O R O N T O
DANFORTH
BRAMALEA
Malton
WESTON
LEASIDE
ETOBICOKE
FOREST HILL
BRAMPTON
LESTER B. PEARSON INTERNATIONAL AIRPORT
Humber
MOUNT DENNIS
YORK
EAST YORK
Don
BIRCH CLIFF
Etobicoke Cr.
PEEL
Mimico Cr.
LAMBTON MILLS
SWANSEA
Univ. of Toronto
City Hall
Kew Gardens
Hanlan
Eldorado Park
Etobicoke Cr.
ISLINGTON
High Park
C.N. Tower
TORONTO
HUMBER BAY
Humber Bay
Exhibition Park
Toronto Harbour
Credit
Burnhamthorpe
Summerville
TORONTO ISLAND
Centre Island Park
MIMICO
NEW TORONTO
Lake Ontario
LONG BRANCH
Cooksville
Streetsville
Lakeview
MISSISSAUGA
Credit
Port Credit
Erindale
Q.E.W.
Lorne Park
Clarkson
Sheridan
Trafalgar
HALTON
79° 40'
79° 30'
79° 20'
79° 10'
43° 50'
43° 40'
43° 30'
400
West from Greenwich

Projection: Transverse Mercator

1 : 200 000

5 4 3 2 1 0 5 10 km

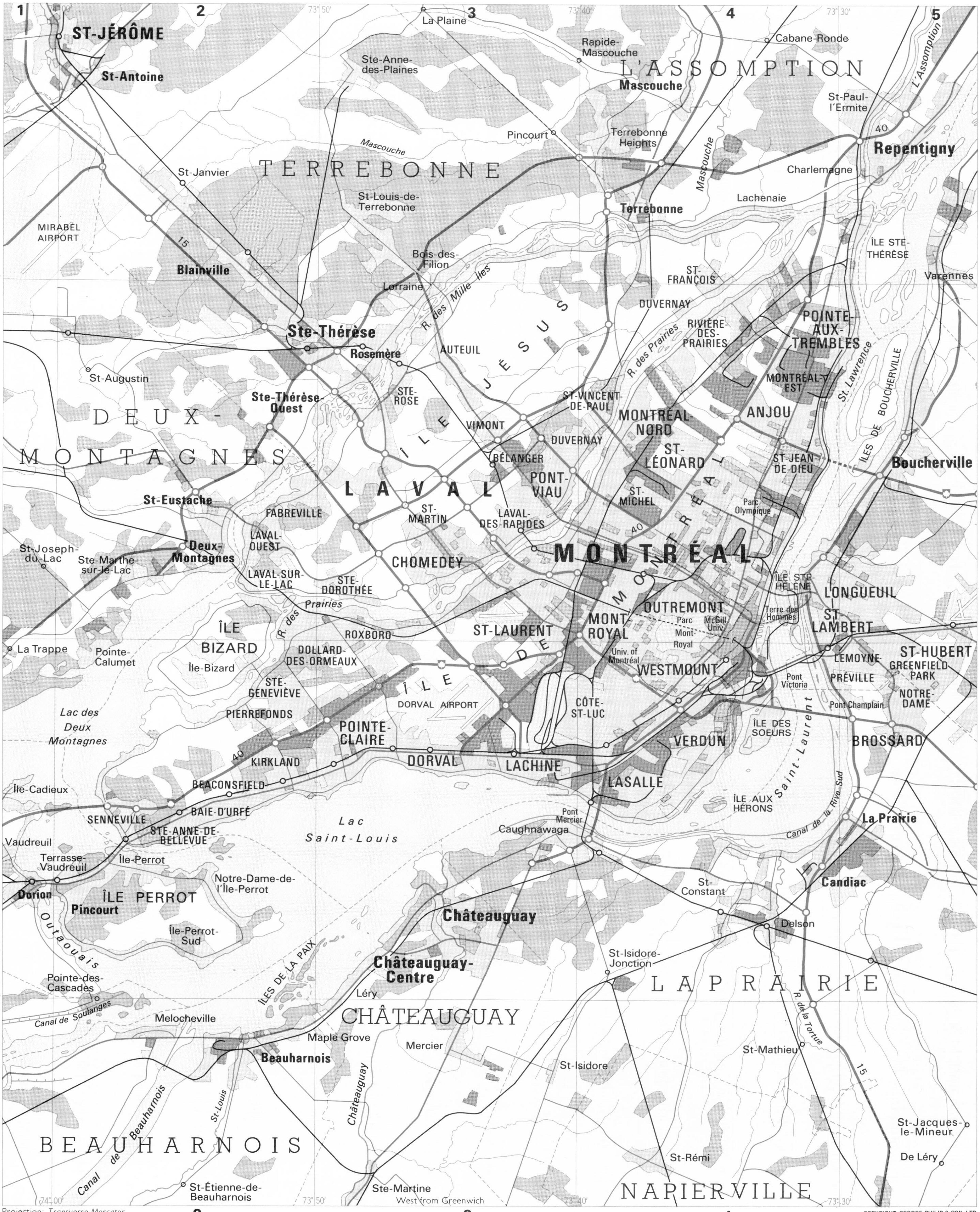

ST-JÉRÔME
St-Antoine
La Plaine
Rapide-Mascouche
Cabane-Ronde
L'ASSOMPTION
Ste-Anne-des-Plaines
Mascouche
St-Paul-l'Ermite
Pincourt
Terrebonne Heights
Repentigny
TERREBONNE
St-Janvier
Charlemagne
St-Louis-de-Terrebonne
Terrebonne
Lachenaie
MIRABEL AIRPORT
Blainville
Bois-des-Filion
ÎLE STE-THÉRÈSE
ST-FRANÇOIS
Varennes
Lorraine
DUVERNAY
Ste-Thérèse
Rosemère
AUTEUIL
RIVIÈRE-DES-PRAIRIES
POINTE-AUX-TREMBLES
St-Augustin
STE-ROSE
MONTRÉAL-EST
Ste-Thérèse-Ouest
ST-VINCENT-DE-PAUL
MONTRÉAL-NORD
ANJOU
DEUX-MONTAGNES
VIMONT
DUVERNAY
ST-LÉONARD
ST-JEAN-DE-DIEU
BÉLANGER
Boucherville
LAVAL
PONT-VIAU
St-Eustache
ST-MICHEL
Parc Olympique
FABREVILLE
ST-MARTIN
LAVAL-DES-RAPIDES
St-Joseph-du-Lac
Ste-Marthe-sur-le-Lac
Deux-Montagnes
LAVAL-OUEST
MONTRÉAL
CHOMEDEY
LAVAL-SUR-LE-LAC
STE-DOROTHÉE
ÎLE STE-HÉLÈNE
LONGUEUIL
OUTREMONT
ÎLE BIZARD
ROXBORO
MONT-ROYAL
Parc Mont-Royal
McGill Univ.
Terre des Hommes
ST-LAMBERT
ST-LAURENT
La Trappe
Pointe-Calumet
Île-Bizard
DOLLARD-DES-ORMEAUX
Univ. of Montréal
WESTMOUNT
LEMOYNE
ST-HUBERT
GREENFIELD PARK
STE-GENEVIÈVE
Pont Victoria
PRÉVILLE
DORVAL AIRPORT
CÔTE-ST-LUC
NOTRE-DAME
Lac des Deux Montagnes
PIERREFONDS
Pont Champlain
POINTE-CLAIRE
ÎLE DES SOEURS
VERDUN
BROSSARD
KIRKLAND
DORVAL
LACHINE
Île-Cadieux
BEACONSFIELD
LASALLE
ÎLE AUX HÉRONS
BAIE-D'URFÉ
SENNEVILLE
Lac Saint-Louis
Pont Mercier
La Prairie
STE-ANNE-DE-BELLEVUE
Caughnawaga
Vaudreuil
Terrasse-Vaudreuil
Île-Perrot
Notre-Dame-de-l'Île-Perrot
St-Constant
Candiac
Dorion
Pincourt
ÎLE PERROT
Châteauguay
Delson
Île-Perrot-Sud
Châteauguay-Centre
St-Isidore-Jonction
Pointe-des-Cascades
LAPRAIRIE
Léry
Melocheville
CHÂTEAUGUAY
Maple Grove
Mercier
St-Mathieu
Beauharnois
St-Isidore
St-Jacques-le-Mineur
BEAUHARNOIS
St-Rémi
De Léry
St-Étienne-de-Beauharnois
Ste-Martine
NAPIERVILLE

Canal de Soulanges
Canal de Beauharnois
Canal de la Rive Sud
Saint-Laurent
St. Lawrence
Outaouais
ÎLES DE LA PAIX
ÎLE JÉSUS
ÎLE DE MONTRÉAL
ÎLES DE BOUCHERVILLE
R. des Mille Îles
R. des Prairies
R. de la Tortue
Mascouche
L'Assomption
St-Louis
Châteauguay

Projection: *Transverse Mercator*
West from Greenwich

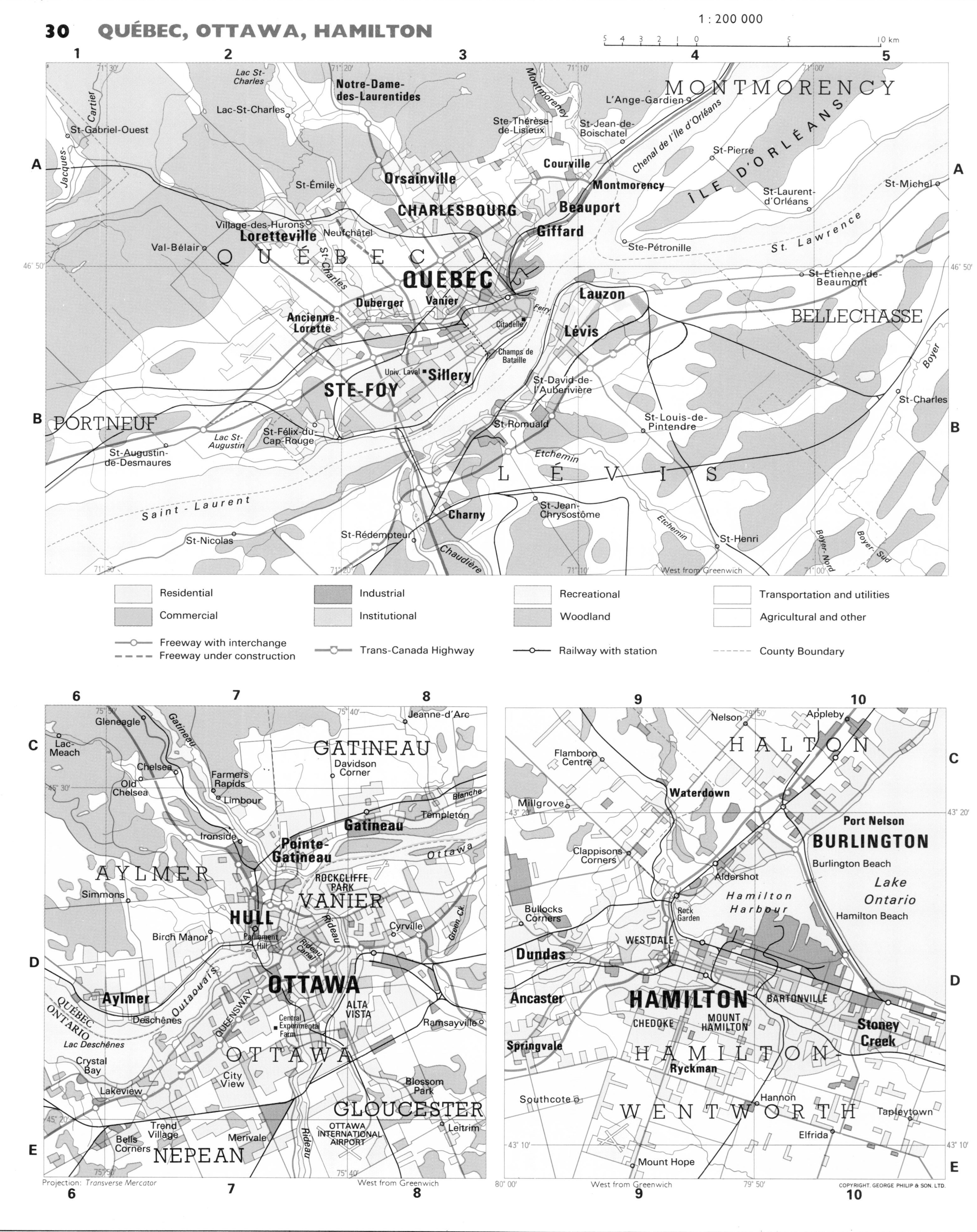
1 : 200 000
QUEBEC
STE-FOY
CHARLESBOURG
Loretteville
Sillery
Lévis
Lauzon
Beauport
Giffard
Charny
MONTMORENCY
ÎLE D'ORLÉANS
BELLECHASSE
PORTNEUF
Q U É B E C
L É V I S
Saint - Laurent
St. Lawrence
Residential
Commercial
Industrial
Institutional
Recreational
Woodland
Transportation and utilities
Agricultural and other
Freeway with interchange
Freeway under construction
Trans-Canada Highway
Railway with station
County Boundary
OTTAWA
HULL
VANIER
GATINEAU
AYLMER
NEPEAN
GLOUCESTER
Ottawa International Airport
HAMILTON
BURLINGTON
HALTON
HAMILTON-WENTWORTH
Lake Ontario
Hamilton Harbour
Dundas
Ancaster
Stoney Creek
Waterdown
Projection: Transverse Mercator
West from Greenwich
COPYRIGHT, GEORGE PHILIP & SON, LTD.

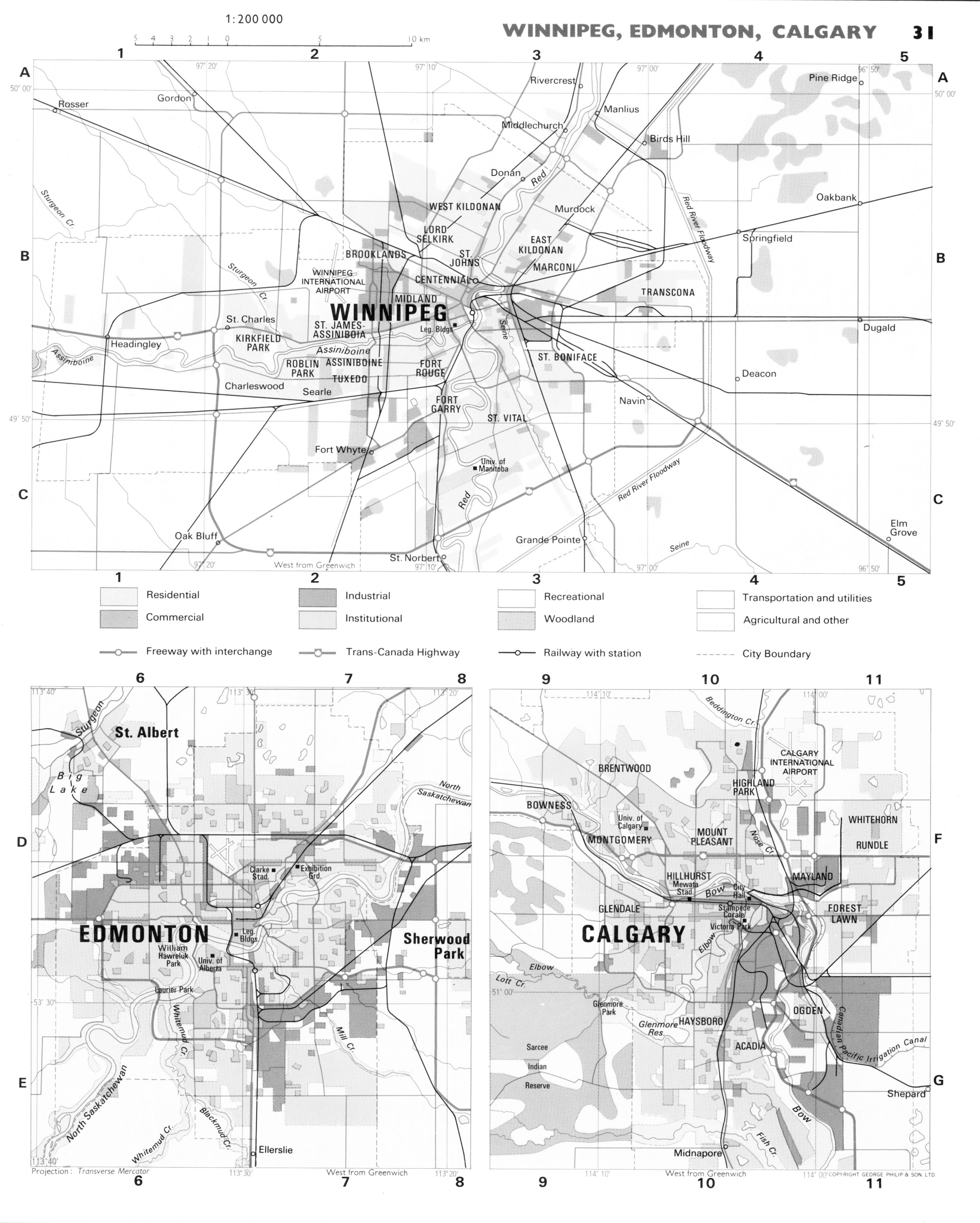
1:200 000
WINNIPEG
Rivercrest
Manlius
Middlechurch
Birds Hill
Pine Ridge
Rosser
Gordon
Donan
Oakbank
WEST KILDONAN
Murdock
LORD SELKIRK
EAST KILDONAN
Springfield
BROOKLANDS
ST. JOHNS
MARCONI
WINNIPEG INTERNATIONAL AIRPORT
CENTENNIAL
TRANSCONA
MIDLAND
St. Charles
ST. JAMES-ASSINIBOIA
Leg. Bldgs.
Dugald
Headingley
KIRKFIELD PARK
ST. BONIFACE
ROBLIN PARK
ASSINIBOINE
FORT ROUGE
Deacon
Charleswood
TUXEDO
Searle
Navin
FORT GARRY
ST. VITAL
Fort Whyte
Univ. of Manitoba
Red River Floodway
Oak Bluff
Grande Pointe
Elm Grove
St. Norbert
West from Greenwich
Residential
Commercial
Industrial
Institutional
Recreational
Woodland
Transportation and utilities
Agricultural and other
Freeway with interchange
Trans-Canada Highway
Railway with station
City Boundary
St. Albert
Big Lake
North Saskatchewan
Clarke Stad.
Exhibition Grd.
EDMONTON
Leg. Bldgs.
Sherwood Park
William Hawreluk Park
Univ. of Alberta
Laurier Park
Whitemud Cr.
Mill Cr.
Blackmud Cr.
Ellerslie
Projection: Transverse Mercator
BRENTWOOD
CALGARY INTERNATIONAL AIRPORT
HIGHLAND PARK
BOWNESS
Univ. of Calgary
MOUNT PLEASANT
WHITEHORN
MONTGOMERY
RUNDLE
HILLHURST
Mewata Stad.
City Hall
MAYLAND
GLENDALE
Stampede Corale
Victoria Park
FOREST LAWN
CALGARY
Glenmore Park
Glenmore Res.
HAYSBORO
OGDEN
Canadian Pacific Irrigation Canal
Sarcee Indian Reserve
ACADIA
Shepard
Midnapore
Fish Cr.
Bow
Elbow
COPYRIGHT GEORGE PHILIP & SON, LTD.

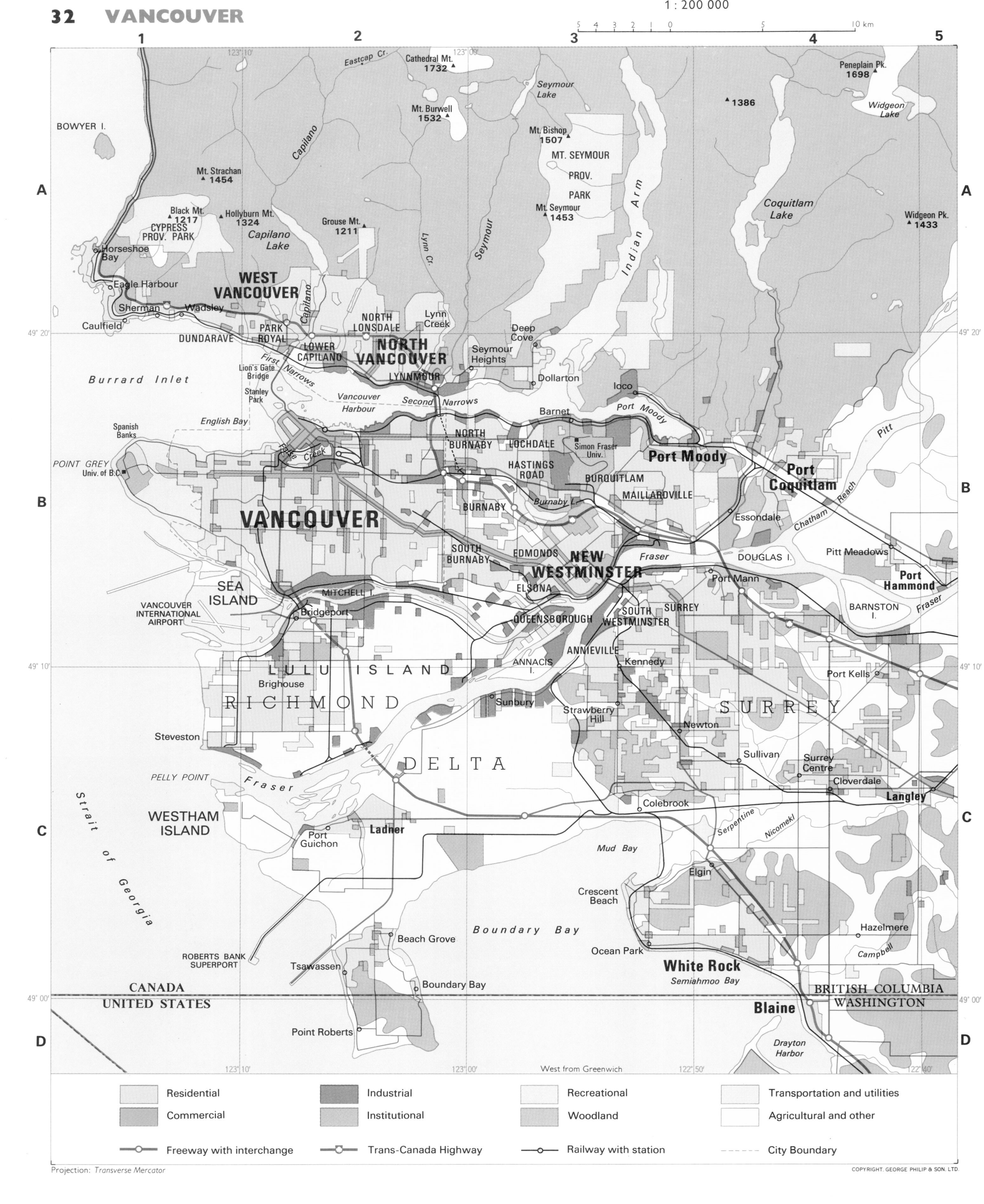
1 : 200 000
5 4 3 2 1 0 5 10 km
1
2
3
4
5
A
B
C
D
123° 10'
123° 00'
122° 50'
122° 40'
49° 20'
49° 10'
49° 00'
Eastcap Cr.
Cathedral Mt.
1732
Seymour Lake
Peneplain Pk.
1698
1386
Widgeon Lake
BOWYER I.
Mt. Burwell
1532
Mt. Bishop
1507
MT. SEYMOUR
PROV.
PARK
Capilano
Mt. Strachan
1454
Black Mt.
1217
Hollyburn Mt.
1324
CYPRESS
PROV. PARK
Capilano
Lake
Grouse Mt.
1211
Lynn Cr.
Seymour
Mt. Seymour
1453
Indian Arm
Coquitlam
Lake
Widgeon Pk.
1433
Horseshoe
Bay
Eagle Harbour
WEST
VANCOUVER
Sherman
Wadsley
Caulfield
DUNDARAVE
PARK
ROYAL
NORTH
LONSDALE
Lynn
Creek
Deep
Cove
LOWER
CAPILANO
NORTH
VANCOUVER
Seymour
Heights
Dollarton
Burrard Inlet
Lion's Gate
Bridge
First Narrows
Stanley
Park
LYNNMOUR
Vancouver
Harbour
Second Narrows
Ioco
Port Moody
Barnet
English Bay
Spanish
Banks
NORTH
BURNABY
LOCHDALE
Simon Fraser
Univ.
Port Moody
Pitt
POINT GREY
Univ. of B.C.
False Creek
HASTINGS
ROAD
BURQUITLAM
Port
Coquitlam
MAILLARDVILLE
BURNABY
Burnaby L.
Essondale
Chatham Reach
VANCOUVER
SOUTH
BURNABY
EDMONDS
NEW
WESTMINSTER
Fraser
DOUGLAS I.
Pitt Meadows
Port Mann
Port
Hammond
SEA
ISLAND
MITCHELL I.
ELSONA
VANCOUVER
INTERNATIONAL
AIRPORT
Bridgeport
QUEENSBOROUGH
SOUTH
WESTMINSTER
SURREY
BARNSTON
I.
Fraser
ANNIEVILLE
ANNACIS
I.
Kennedy
Port Kells
LULU ISLAND
Brighouse
RICHMOND
Sunbury
Strawberry
Hill
SURREY
Newton
Steveston
Sullivan
Surrey
Centre
DELTA
PELLY POINT
Fraser
Cloverdale
Langley
Strait of Georgia
WESTHAM
ISLAND
Colebrook
Serpentine
Nicomekl
Port
Guichon
Ladner
Mud Bay
Elgin
Crescent
Beach
Boundary Bay
Hazelmere
Beach Grove
Campbell
ROBERTS BANK
SUPERPORT
Ocean Park
Tsawassen
White Rock
Semiahmoo Bay
Boundary Bay
CANADA
UNITED STATES
BRITISH COLUMBIA
WASHINGTON
Blaine
Point Roberts
Drayton
Harbor
West from Greenwich
Residential
Commercial
Industrial
Institutional
Recreational
Woodland
Transportation and utilities
Agricultural and other
Freeway with interchange
Trans-Canada Highway
Railway with station
City Boundary
Projection: Transverse Mercator

Index of Canada

The first number in dark type after each name in the index refers to the page number in the Canadian map section. The letter and number which follow the page number indicate the section of the page where that place or feature can be found. These are followed by the geographical co-ordinates, in lighter type, which give the latitude and longitude of a particular place or feature.

The geographical co-ordinates which follow the name are sometimes only approximate but are close enough for the place or feature to be located. Rivers have been indexed to their mouth or confluence.

An open square □ signifies that the name is an administrative subdivision such as a province, county or district. An arrow → follows the name of a river. Each entry is followed by the name of the province in which that place or feature can be found.

The alphabetic order of names composed of two or more words is governed primarily by the first word and then by the second. This rule applies even when the second word is a description or its abbreviation, C., L., I. for example. Names composed of a proper name (St. Lawrence) and a description (Gulf of) are positioned alphabetically by the proper name.

Abbreviations used in the index

Alta. – Alberta
B. – Baie, Bay
B.C. – British Columbia
C. – Cap, Cape
Chan. – Channel
Cr. – Creek
E. – East
Fd. – Fiord
G. – Golfe, Gulf
I. – Ile, Island, Isle
L. – Lac, Lake
Man. – Manitoba
Mt. – Mont, Mount, Mountain
N. – North
N.Amer. – North America
N.B. – New Brunswick
N.S. – Nova Scotia
N.W.T. – Northwest Territories
Nat. – National
Newf. – Newfoundland
Ont. – Ontario
P. – Pass
P.E.I. – Prince Edward Island
Pen. – Péninsule, Peninsula
Pk. – Peak
Qué. – Québec
Res. – Reservoir
S. – South
Sask. – Saskatchewan
Sd. – Sound
St. – Saint
St. P. & M. – St Pierre & Miquelon
Ste. – Sainte
Str. – Strait
W. – West
Y. – Yukon

A

Abamasagi L., *Ont.* **17 B9** 50 28N 87 15W
Abbey, *Sask.* **20 E2** 50 44N 108 45W
Abbotsford, *B.C.* **25 F12** 49 5N 122 20W
Abbott Corners, *Qué.* **12 B5** 45 3N 72 48W
Aberdeen, *Sask.* **20 C4** 52 20N 106 8W
Aberfoyle, *Ont.* **13 B2** 43 28N 80 9W
Abernethy, *Sask.* **20 E7** 50 45N 103 25W
Abingdon, *Ont.* **13 B3** 43 5N 79 41W
Abitau →, *Sask.* **19 B7** 59 53N 109 3W
Abitau L., *N.W.T.* **19 A7** 60 27N 107 15W
Abitibi →, *Ont.* **17 A16** 51 3N 80 55W
Abitibi L., *Ont.* **4 C4** 48 40N 79 40W
Acadia, *Alta.* **31 G10** 50 58N 114 4W
Acadia Valley, *Alta.* **23 G10** 51 8N 110 13W
Acme, *Alta.* **23 G7** 51 33N 113 30W
Acton, *Ont.* **13 A2** 43 38N 80 3W
Acton Vale, *Qué.* **11 F10** 45 39N 72 34W
Adams →, *B.C.* **25 D15** 51 25N 119 27W
Adams L., *B.C.* **25 D15** 51 10N 119 40W
Adamsville, *Qué.* **12 B5** 45 17N 72 47W
Adelaide Pen., *N.W.T.* **27 C6** 68 15N 97 30W
Adlavik Is., *Nfld.* **6 B6** 55 2N 57 45W
Admiral, *Sask.* **20 F2** 49 43N 108 1W
Admiral's Beach, *Nfld.* **7 F7** 47 1N 53 39W
Admiralty I., *N.W.T.* **27 C5** 69 25N 101 10W
Admiralty Inlet, *N.W.T.* **27 B7** 72 30N 86 0W
Advocate Harbour, *N.S.* **9 H5** 45 20N 64 47W
Agassiz, *B.C.* **25 F13** 49 14N 121 46W
Agawa →, *Ont.* **17 E12** 47 23N 84 40W
Agincourt, *Ont.* **28 B4** 43 47N 79 17W
Agnes L., *Ont.* **16 D5** 48 15N 91 20W
Aguanish, *Qué.* **8 C7** 50 14N 62 2W
Aguanus →, *Qué.* **8 C7** 50 13N 62 5W
Aiguebelle, Parc, *Qué.* **10 C4** 48 30N 78 45W
Aillik, *Nfld.* **6 B6** 55 11N 59 18W
Ailsa Craig, *Ont.* **14 D5** 43 8N 81 33W
Ainslie, L., *N.S.* **9 G8** 46 8N 61 11W
Air Force I., *N.W.T.* **27 C8** 67 58N 74 5W
Airdrie, *Alta.* **23 G6** 51 18N 114 2W
Aiyansh, *B.C.* **18 B3** 55 17N 129 2W
Ajax, *Ont.* **15 D8** 43 50N 79 1W
Akimiski I., *N.W.T.* **4 B3** 52 50N 81 30W
Aklavik, *N.W.T.* **26 C2** 68 12N 135 0W
Akpatok I., *N.W.T.* **6 A4** 60 25N 68 8W
Akron, *Ont.* **17 D12** 48 55N 84 7W
Alameda, *Sask.* **21 F8** 49 16N 102 17W
Alaska Highway, *B.C.* **18 B3** 60 0N 130 0W
Albanel, *Qué.* **11 C10** 48 53N 72 27W
Albanel, L., *Qué.* **6 C3** 50 55N 73 12W
Albany →, *Ont.* **4 B3** 52 17N 81 31W
Albert Canyon, *B.C.* **25 D17** 51 8N 117 41W
Alberta □, *Alta.* **18 C6** 54 40N 115 0W
Alberta Beach, *Alta.* **22 E6** 53 40N 114 21W
Alberton, *Ont.* **13 B2** 43 11N 80 5W
Alberton, *P.E.I.* **9 G6** 46 50N 64 0W
Albreda, *B.C.* **25 C15** 52 35N 119 10W
Alcantara L., *N.W.T.* **19 A7** 60 57N 108 9W
Aldershot, *N.S.* **9 H5** 45 6N 64 31W
Aldershot, *Ont.* **30 D9** 43 18N 79 51W
Alert, *N.W.T.* **27 A9** 83 2N 60 0W
Alert Bay, *B.C.* **24 E8** 50 30N 126 55W
Alex Graham, Mt., *B.C.* **25 C12** 52 4N 122 52W
Alexandra Falls, *N.W.T.* **18 A5** 60 29N 116 18W
Alexandria, *B.C.* **25 C12** 52 35N 122 27W
Alexandria, *Ont.* **15 B12** 45 19N 74 38W
Alexis →, *Nfld.* **6 C6** 52 33N 56 8W
Alexis Creek, *B.C.* **24 C11** 52 10N 123 20W
Algonquin Prov. Park, *Ont.* **15 B8** 45 50N 78 30W
Alhambra, *Alta.* **23 F6** 52 20N 114 40W
Alice, *Ont.* **15 B9** 45 47N 77 14W
Alice Arm, *B.C.* **18 B3** 55 29N 129 31W
Alida, *Sask.* **21 F9** 49 25N 101 55W
Alix, *Alta.* **23 F7** 52 24N 113 11W
Allan, *Sask.* **20 D4** 51 53N 106 4W
Allanburg, *Ont.* **13 B4** 43 5N 79 12W
Allanwater, *Ont.* **16 B6** 50 14N 90 10W
Allard, L., *Qué.* **8 C6** 50 32N 63 31W
Allardville, *N.B.* **9 F4** 47 28N 65 29W
Alliance, *Alta.* **23 F9** 52 26N 111 47W
Alliford Bay, *B.C.* **24 B3** 53 12N 131 58W
Allison Harbour, *B.C.* **24 D7** 51 2N 127 29W
Alliston, *Ont.* **14 C7** 44 9N 79 52W
Alluviaq, Fj., *Qué.* **6 B4** 59 27N 65 10W
Alma, *N.B.* **9 H5** 45 36N 64 57W
Alma, *Ont.* **13 A2** 43 44N 80 30W
Alma, *Qué.* **11 C11** 48 35N 71 40W
Almonte, *Ont.* **10 F6** 45 14N 76 12W
Alsask, *Sask.* **20 D1** 51 21N 109 59W
Alta Lake, *B.C.* **25 E12** 50 10N 123 0W
Alta Vista, *Ont.* **30 D8** 45 23N 75 40W
Altario, *Alta.* **23 G10** 51 55N 110 9W
Alton, *Ont.* **13 A2** 43 54N 80 5W
Altona, *Man.* **21 F13** 49 6N 97 33W
Altona, *Ont.* **13 A4** 43 58N 79 12W
Alvena, *Sask.* **20 C4** 52 31N 106 1W
Alvinston, *Ont.* **14 E5** 42 49N 81 52W
Amadjuak, *N.W.T.* **27 C8** 64 0N 72 39W
Amadjuak L., *N.W.T.* **27 C8** 65 0N 71 8W
Amaranth, *Man.* **21 E12** 50 36N 98 43W
Amery, *Man.* **19 B10** 56 34N 94 3W
Amet Sound, *N.S.* **9 H6** 45 47N 63 10W
Amherst, *N.S.* **9 H5** 45 48N 64 8W
Amherst I., *Ont.* **15 C10** 44 8N 76 43W
Amherstburg, *Ont.* **14 E3** 42 6N 83 6W
Amisk, *Alta.* **23 F9** 52 33N 111 4W
Amisk L., *Sask.* **19 C8** 54 35N 102 15W
Amos, *Qué.* **10 C4** 48 35N 78 5W
Amqui, *Qué.* **8 E2** 48 28N 67 27W
Amund Ringnes I., *N.W.T.* **27 B6** 78 20N 96 25W
Amundsen Gulf, *N.W.T.* **26 B3** 71 0N 124 0W
Amyot, *Ont.* **17 D12** 48 29N 84 57W
Anahim Lake, *B.C.* **24 C9** 52 28N 125 18W
Anama Bay, *Man.* **21 D12** 51 58N 98 4W
Anaunethad L., *N.W.T.* **19 A8** 60 55N 104 25W
Ancaster, *Ont.* **30 D9** 43 13N 79 59W
Ancienne-Lorette, *Qué.* **30 B2** 46 48N 71 21W
Anderson →, *N.W.T.* **26 C3** 69 42N 129 0W
Anderson L., *B.C.* **25 E12** 50 37N 122 25W
Andover, *N.B.* **9 G2** 46 45N 67 42W
Andreville, *Qué.* **11 D13** 47 41N 69 44W
Andrew, *Alta.* **22 E8** 53 53N 112 21W
Aneroid, *Sask.* **20 F3** 49 43N 107 18W
Angers, *Qué.* **10 F7** 45 31N 75 29W
Angikuni L., *N.W.T.* **19 A9** 62 0N 100 0W
Angliers, *Qué.* **10 D3** 47 33N 79 14W
Anguille Mts., *Nfld.* **7 F1** 48 0N 59 11W
Angus, *Ont.* **14 C7** 44 19N 79 53W
Angusville, *Man.* **21 E9** 50 44N 101 1W
Anjou, *Qué.* **12 A3** 45 36N 73 33W
Annacis I., *B.C.* **32 C3** 49 10N 122 57W
Annaheim, *Sask.* **20 C6** 52 19N 104 49W
Annapolis Royal, *N.S.* **9 I4** 44 44N 65 32W
Annieopsquotch Mts., *Nfld.* **7 E3** 48 20N 57 30W
Annieville, *B.C.* **32 B3** 49 11N 122 55W
Annonciation, L', *Qué.* **10 E8** 46 25N 74 55W
Anola, *Man.* **21 F14** 49 53N 96 38W
Anse-au-Clair, L', *Nfld.* **7 B3** 51 25N 57 5W
Anse au Loup, L', *Nfld.* **7 B4** 51 32N 56 50W
Anticosti, I. d', *Qué.* **8 D7** 49 30N 63 0W
Antigonish, *N.S.* **9 H8** 45 38N 61 58W
Antler, *Sask.* **21 F9** 49 34N 101 27W
Antler →, *Man.* **21 F10** 49 8N 101 0W
Apohaqui, *N.B.* **9 H4** 45 42N 65 36W
Apple Hill, *Ont.* **15 B12** 45 13N 74 46W
Appleby, *Ont.* **30 C10** 43 23N 79 46W
Apsley, *Ont.* **15 C8** 44 45N 78 6W
Ara L., *Ont.* **17 B9** 50 33N 87 28W
Arbor Vitae, *Ont.* **16 D2** 48 54N 94 18W
Arborfield, *Sask.* **20 B7** 53 6N 103 39W
Arborg, *Man.* **21 E13** 50 54N 97 13W
Arcadia, *N.S.* **9 J3** 43 50N 66 4W
Archerwill, *Sask.* **20 C7** 52 26N 103 51W
Arcola, *Sask.* **21 F8** 49 40N 102 30W
Arctic Bay, *N.W.T.* **27 B7** 73 1N 85 7W
Arctic Red River, *Yukon* **26 C2** 67 15N 134 0W
Ardbeg, *Ont.* **14 B6** 45 38N 80 5W
Arden, *Man.* **21 E11** 50 17N 99 16W
Arden, *Ont.* **15 C10** 44 43N 76 56W
Ardmore, *Alta.* **22 D10** 54 20N 110 29W
Ardoise, L', *N.S.* **9 H9** 45 37N 60 45W
Argenteuil □, *Qué.* **12 A2** 45 50N 74 30W
Argentia, *Nfld.* **7 F7** 47 18N 53 58W
Argyle, *Man.* **21 E13** 50 11N 97 27W
Arichat, *N.S.* **9 H8** 45 31N 61 1W
Ariss, *Ont.* **13 A2** 43 35N 80 22W
Aristazabal I., *B.C.* **24 C5** 52 40N 129 10W
Arkell, *Ont.* **13 A2** 43 32N 80 10W
Arkona, *Ont.* **14 D5** 43 4N 81 50W
Armadale, *Ont.* **28 B4** 43 50N 79 15W
Armagh, *Qué.* **11 E12** 46 41N 70 32W
Armdale, *N.S.* **9 L11** 44 37N 63 38W
Armstrong, *B.C.* **25 E15** 50 25N 119 10W
Armstrong, *Ont.* **16 B7** 50 18N 89 4W
Arnaud →, *Qué.* **6 B4** 59 59N 69 46W
Arnot, *Man.* **19 B9** 55 56N 96 41W
Arnprior, *Ont.* **15 B10** 45 26N 76 21W
Arntfield, *Qué.* **10 C3** 48 12N 79 15W
Arran, *Sask.* **21 D9** 51 53N 101 43W
Arrandale, *B.C.* **18 C3** 54 57N 130 0W
Arrow Park, *B.C.* **25 E17** 50 6N 117 57W
Arrowhead, *B.C.* **25 E17** 50 40N 117 55W
Arrowwood, *Alta.* **23 H7** 50 44N 113 9W
Arsenault L., *Sask.* **19 B7** 55 6N 108 32W
Arthur, *Ont.* **13 A1** 43 50N 80 32W
Arthurette, *N.B.* **9 G2** 46 47N 67 29W
Artillery L., *N.W.T.* **19 A7** 63 9N 107 52W
Arundel, *Qué.* **10 F8** 45 58N 74 37W
Arvert, L., *Nfld.* **8 A8** 52 18N 61 45W
Arvida, *Qué.* **11 C11** 48 25N 71 14W
Arvilla, *Alta.* **22 E7** 53 59N 114 0W
Asbestos, *Qué.* **5 C5** 45 47N 71 58W
Ashcroft, *B.C.* **25 E13** 50 40N 121 20W
Ashern, *Man.* **21 D12** 51 11N 98 21W
Asheweig →, *Ont.* **4 B2** 54 17N 87 12W
Ashgrove, *Ont.* **13 A3** 43 36N 79 53W
Ashmont, *Alta.* **22 D9** 54 7N 111 35W
Ashuanipi, L., *Nfld.* **8 A3** 52 45N 66 15W
Aspen, *N.S.* **9 H7** 45 18N 62 3W
Aspen Grove, *B.C.* **25 F14** 49 57N 120 37W
Asquith, *Sask.* **20 C3** 52 8N 107 13W
Assigny, L., *Nfld.* **8 B4** 52 0N 65 20W
Assiniboia, *Sask.* **20 F5** 49 40N 105 59W
Assiniboine →, *Man.* **31 B3** 49 53N 97 8W
Assomption, L', *Qué.* **12 A4** 45 50N 73 25W
Assomption, L' □, *Qué.* **12 A4** 45 49N 73 30W
Assomption, L' →, *Qué.* **12 A4** 45 43N 73 29W
Astorville, *Ont.* **14 A7** 46 11N 79 17W
Athabasca, *Alta.* **22 D7** 54 45N 113 20W
Athabasca →, *Alta.* **19 B6** 58 40N 110 50W
Athabasca, L., *Sask.* **19 B7** 59 15N 109 15W
Athelstan, *Qué.* **12 B2** 45 2N 74 10W
Athens, *Ont.* **15 C11** 44 38N 75 57W
Atherley, *Ont.* **14 C7** 44 37N 79 20W
Atholville, *N.B.* **9 F3** 47 59N 66 43W
Aticonipi, L., *Qué.* **7 B2** 51 45N 59 22W
Atikokan, *Ont.* **16 D5** 48 45N 91 37W
Atikonak →, *Nfld.* **8 A4** 52 51N 65 16W
Atikonak L., *Nfld.* **8 A5** 52 40N 64 32W
Atlin, *B.C.* **18 B2** 59 31N 133 41W
Atlin, L., *B.C.* **18 B2** 59 26N 133 45W
Attawapiskat, *Ont.* **4 B3** 52 56N 82 24W
Attawapiskat →, *Ont.* **4 B3** 52 57N 82 18W
Attawapiskat, L., *Ont.* **4 B2** 52 18N 87 54W
Attercliffe, *Ont.* **13 C3** 42 59N 79 36W
Attikamagen L., *Nfld.* **6 C4** 55 0N 66 30W
Attwood →, *Ont.* **16 A8** 51 15N 88 30W
Atwood, *Ont.* **14 D5** 43 40N 81 1W
Aubry L., *N.W.T.* **26 C3** 67 23N 126 30W
Auden, *Ont.* **17 B9** 50 14N 87 53W
Audley, *Ont.* **13 A4** 43 54N 79 4W
Augustines, L. des, *Qué.* **10 D7** 47 37N 75 56W
Aulneau Pen., *Ont.* **16 C2** 49 23N 94 29W
Aurora, *Ont.* **13 A4** 44 0N 79 28W
Ausable →, *Ont.* **14 D5** 43 19N 81 46W
Austin Chan., *N.W.T.* **27 B5** 75 35N 103 25W
Auteuil, *Qué.* **29 B3** 45 38N 73 46W
Auteuil, L. d', *Qué.* **8 C8** 50 38N 61 17W
Avalon Pen., *Nfld.* **7 F7** 47 30N 53 20W
Avola, *B.C.* **25 D15** 51 45N 119 19W
Avondale, *Nfld.* **7 F7** 47 25N 53 12W
Avonlea, *Sask.* **20 F6** 50 0N 105 0W
Avonmore, *Ont.* **10 F8** 45 10N 74 58W
Axel Heiberg I., *N.W.T.* **27 B7** 80 0N 90 0W
Ayer's Cliff, *Qué.* **11 F10** 45 10N 72 3W
Aylen L., *Ont.* **15 B9** 45 37N 77 51W
Aylmer, *Ont.* **14 E6** 42 46N 80 59W
Aylmer, *Qué.* **30 D6** 45 24N 75 51W
Aylmer L., *N.W.T.* **26 C4** 64 0N 110 8W
Aylsham, *Sask.* **20 B7** 53 12N 103 49W
Ayr, *Ont.* **13 B2** 43 17N 80 27W
Azilda, *Ont.* **14 A5** 46 33N 81 6W
Azure L., *B.C.* **25 C14** 52 23N 120 3W

B

Babine, *B.C.* **18 B3** 55 22N 126 37W
Babine →, *B.C.* **18 B3** 55 45N 127 44W
Babine L., *B.C.* **18 C3** 54 48N 126 0W
Baccalieu I., *Nfld.* **7 E8** 48 8N 52 48W
Back →, *N.W.T.* **26 C5** 65 10N 104 0W
Back Bay, *N.B.* **9 H3** 45 3N 66 52W
Bad Heart, *Alta.* **22 C2** 55 30N 118 18W
Baddeck, *N.S.* **9 G9** 46 6N 60 45W
Badger, *Nfld.* **7 E4** 49 0N 56 4W
Badger's Quay, *Nfld.* **7 D7** 49 7N 53 35W
Baffin □, *N.W.T.* **27 C8** 70 0N 80 0W
Baffin B., *N.W.T.* **27 B9** 72 0N 64 0W
Baffin I., *N.W.T.* **27 C8** 68 0N 75 0W
Bagot □, *Qué.* **12 A5** 45 35N 72 45W
Bagotville, *Qué.* **11 C12** 48 22N 70 54W
Baie Comeau, *Qué.* **8 D1** 49 12N 68 10W
Baie-des-Sables, *Qué.* **8 E2** 48 43N 67 54W
Baie-du-Poste, *Qué.* **11 A9** 50 24N 73 56W
Baie-du-Renard, *Qué.* **8 D8** 49 17N 61 50W
Baie-St-Paul, *Qué.* **11 D12** 47 28N 70 32W
Baie-Ste-Anne, *N.B.* **9 F5** 47 3N 64 58W
Baie-Ste-Catherine, *Qué.* **11 C13** 48 6N 69 44W
Baie-Ste-Claire, *Qué.* **8 D5** 49 54N 64 30W
Baie Trinité, *Qué.* **8 D2** 49 25N 67 20W
Baie Verte, *N.B.* **9 G5** 46 1N 64 6W
Baie Verte, *Nfld.* **7 D4** 49 55N 56 12W
Baieville, *Qué.* **11 E10** 46 8N 72 43W
Bainsville, *Qué.* **12 B2** 45 10N 74 25W
Baird Pen., *N.W.T.* **27 C8** 68 55N 76 4W
Baker, L., *N.W.T.* **27 C6** 64 0N 96 0W
Baker Lake, *N.W.T.* **27 C6** 64 20N 96 3W
Baker's Dozen Is., *N.W.T.* **6 B2** 56 45N 78 45W
Bala, *Ont.* **14 B7** 45 1N 79 37W
Balcarres, *Sask.* **20 E7** 50 50N 103 35W
Baldock L., *Man.* **19 B9** 56 33N 97 57W
Baldur, *Man.* **21 F11** 49 23N 99 15W
Balgonie, *Sask.* **20 E6** 50 29N 104 16W
Ballinafad, *Ont.* **13 A2** 43 42N 80 1W
Balmertown, *Ont.* **16 A3** 51 4N 93 41W
Balmoral, *Man.* **21 E13** 50 15N 97 19W
Balsam, *Ont.* **13 A4** 43 59N 79 4W
Bamfield, *B.C.* **24 G9** 48 45N 125 10W
Bancroft, *Ont.* **15 B9** 45 3N 77 51W
Banff, *Alta.* **23 G5** 51 10N 115 34W
Banff Nat. Park, *Alta.* **23 G4** 51 30N 116 15W
Banks I., *B.C.* **24 B5** 53 20N 130 0W
Banks I., *N.W.T.* **26 B3** 73 15N 121 30W
Bannockburn, *Ont.* **15 C9** 44 39N 77 33W
Barachois-de-Malbaie, *Qué.* **8 E5** 48 37N 64 17W
Barachois Pond Prov. Park, *Nfld.* **7 E2** 48 28N 58 15W
Baralzon L., *Man.* **19 B9** 60 0N 98 3W
Barbara L., *Ont.* **17 C9** 49 20N 87 47W
Barbeau Pk., *N.W.T.* **27 A8** 81 54N 75 1W
Barbel, L., *Qué.* **8 B1** 51 55N 68 13W
Barclay, *Ont.* **16 C4** 49 47N 92 43W
Bardoux, L., *Qué.* **8 B2** 51 9N 67 50W
Baring, C., *N.W.T.* **26 C4** 70 0N 117 30W
Bark L., *Ont.* **10 F5** 45 27N 77 51W
Barkley Sound, *B.C.* **24 G9** 48 50N 125 10W
Barlow L., *N.W.T.* **19 A8** 62 0N 103 0W
Barnes Icecap, *N.W.T.* **27 C8** 70 0N 73 15W
Barnet, *B.C.* **32 B3** 49 17N 122 55W
Barnston I., *B.C.* **32 B4** 49 12N 122 42W
Barnwell, *Alta.* **23 I8** 49 46N 112 15W
Barons, *Alta.* **23 I7** 50 0N 113 5W
Barraute, *Qué.* **10 C5** 48 26N 77 38W
Barrhead, *Alta.* **22 D6** 54 10N 114 24W
Barrie, *Ont.* **14 C7** 44 24N 79 40W
Barriefield, *Ont.* **15 C10** 44 14N 76 28W
Barrière, *B.C.* **25 D14** 51 12N 120 7W
Barrington, *Qué.* **12 B3** 45 6N 73 35W
Barrington L., *Man.* **19 B8** 56 55N 100 15W
Barrington Passage, *N.S.* **9 J4** 43 30N 65 38W
Barrow Str., *N.W.T.* **27 B6** 74 20N 95 0W
Barrows, *Man.* **21 C9** 52 50N 101 27W
Barry's Bay, *Ont.* **15 B9** 45 29N 77 41W
Bartlett, L., *N.W.T.* **18 A5** 63 5N 118 20W
Bartletts Harbour, *Nfld.* **7 C4** 50 57N 57 0W
Bartonville, *Ont.* **30 D10** 43 14N 79 48W
Bashaw, *Alta.* **23 F8** 52 35N 112 58W
Basin L., *Sask.* **20 C5** 52 38N 105 17W
Baskatong, Rés., *Qué.* **10 E7** 46 46N 75 50W
Bass River, *N.S.* **9 H6** 45 25N 63 47W
Bassano, *Alta.* **23 H8** 50 48N 112 20W
Bastille, L., *Qué.* **8 B8** 51 46N 61 11W
Batchawana B., *Ont.* **17 F12** 46 53N 84 30W
Batchawana Bay, *Ont.* **17 F12** 46 55N 84 37W
Bath, *N.B.* **9 G2** 46 31N 67 36W
Bath, *Ont.* **15 C10** 44 11N 76 47W
Bathurst, *N.B.* **9 F4** 47 37N 65 43W
Bathurst, C., *N.W.T.* **26 B3** 70 34N 128 0W
Bathurst I., *N.W.T.* **27 B5** 76 0N 100 30W
Bathurst Inlet, *N.W.T.* **26 C5** 66 50N 108 1W
Batiscan, *Qué.* **11 E10** 46 30N 72 15W
Batiscan →, *Qué.* **11 E10** 46 16N 72 15W
Batiscan, L., *Qué.* **11 D11** 47 22N 71 55W
Battle →, *Sask.* **20 C2** 52 43N 108 15W
Battle Harbour, *Nfld.* **6 C6** 52 16N 55 35W
Battleford, *Sask.* **20 C2** 52 45N 108 15W
Bauld, C., *Nfld.* **7 B5** 51 38N 55 26W
Bawlf, *Alta.* **23 F8** 52 55N 112 28W
Bay Bulls, *Nfld.* **7 F8** 47 19N 52 50W
Bay de Verde, *Nfld.* **7 E8** 48 5N 52 54W
Bay L'Argent, *Nfld.* **7 F6** 47 33N 54 54W
Bay Roberts, *Nfld.* **7 F7** 47 36N 53 16W
Bayfield, *Ont.* **14 D5** 43 34N 81 42W
Bays, L. of, *Ont.* **14 B7** 45 15N 79 4W
Bayside, *Ont.* **15 C9** 44 7N 77 30W
Baysville, *Ont.* **14 B7** 45 9N 79 7W
Bazin →, *Qué.* **10 D7** 47 29N 75 22W
Beach Grove, *B.C.* **32 C2** 49 2N 123 3W
Beachburg, *Ont.* **15 B10** 45 44N 76 51W
Beachville, *Ont.* **14 D6** 43 5N 80 49W
Beaconia, *Man.* **21 E14** 50 25N 96 31W

Beaconsfield, *Qué.* **29 C3** 45 26N 73 50W
Beale, C., *B.C.* **24 G9** 48 47N 125 13W
Beamsville, *Ont.* **14 D7** 43 12N 79 28W
Bear L., *Alta.* **22 C1** 55 9N 119 4W
Bear L., *B.C.* **18 B3** 56 10N 126 52W
Bear L., *Man.* **19 B9** 55 8N 96 0W
Bear River, *N.S.* **9 I4** 44 34N 65 39W
Beardmore, *Ont.* **17 C9** 49 36N 87 57W
Béarn, *Qué.* **10 D3** 47 17N 79 20W
Bearskin Lake, *Ont.* **4 B1** 53 58N 91 2W
Beatton —►, *B.C.* **18 B4** 56 15N 120 45W
Beatton River, *B.C.* **18 B4** 57 26N 121 20W
Beatty, *Sask.* **20 C6** 52 54N 104 48W
Beauceville, *Qué.* **11 E12** 46 13N 70 46W
Beauchêne, L., *Qué.* **10 E4** 46 35N 78 55W
Beauharnois, *Qué.* **29 D2** 45 20N 73 52W
Beauharnois □, *Qué.* **29 D2** 45 15N 74 0W
Beauharnois, Canal de, *Qué.* **29 D2** 45 19N 73 54W
Beaulac, *Qué.* **11 F11** 45 50N 71 23W
Beaulieu —►, *N.W.T.* **18 A6** 62 3N 113 11W
Beaumont, *Alta.* **22 E7** 53 21N 113 25W
Beaumont, *Nfld.* **7 D5** 49 37N 55 41W
Beauport, *Qué.* **30 A3** 46 52N 71 11W
Beaupré, *Qué.* **11 D12** 47 3N 70 54W
Beauséjour, *Man.* **21 E14** 50 5N 96 35W
Beauval, *Sask.* **19 B7** 55 9N 107 37W
Beaver —►, *B.C.* **18 B4** 59 52N 124 20W
Beaver —►, *Ont.* **4 A2** 55 55N 87 48W
Beaver —►, *Sask.* **19 B7** 55 26N 107 45W
Beaver Brook Station, *N.B.* **9 F4** 47 8N 65 36W
Beaver Creek, *N.W.T.* **26 C1** 63 0N 141 0W
Beaver Hill L., *Man.* **19 C10** 54 5N 94 50W
Beaverdell, *B.C.* **25 F15** 49 27N 119 6W
Beaverhill L., *Alta.* **22 E8** 53 27N 112 32W
Beaverhill L., *N.W.T.* **19 A8** 63 2N 104 22W
Beaverlodge, *Alta.* **22 C1** 55 11N 119 29W
Beavermouth, *B.C.* **25 D17** 51 32N 117 23W
Beaverstone —►, *Ont.* **4 B2** 54 59N 89 25W
Beaverton, *Ont.* **14 C7** 44 26N 79 9W
Beddington Cr. —►, *Alta.* **31 F10** 51 9N 114 3W
Bedford, *N.S.* **9 I6** 44 44N 63 40W
Bedford, *Qué.* **12 B5** 45 7N 72 59W
Bedford Basin, *N.S.* **9 K11** 44 42N 63 38W
Beebe Plain, *Qué.* **11 F10** 45 1N 72 9W
Beechey Hd., *B.C.* **25 G11** 48 10N 123 30W
Beechy, *Sask.* **20 E3** 50 53N 107 24W
Beeton, *Ont.* **14 C7** 44 5N 79 47W
Beetz, L., *Qué.* **8 C7** 50 34N 62 42W
Beiseker, *Alta.* **23 G7** 51 23N 113 32W
Bélanger, *Qué.* **29 B3** 45 36N 73 43W
Belanger —►, *Man.* **21 B13** 53 27N 97 41W
Belbutte, *Sask.* **20 B3** 53 22N 107 49W
Belcher Chan., *N.W.T.* **27 B6** 77 15N 95 0W
Belcher Is., *N.W.T.* **6 B2** 56 15N 78 45W
Belcourt, *Qué.* **10 C5** 48 24N 77 21W
Belfountain, *Ont.* **13 A2** 43 48N 80 1W
Belize Inlet, *B.C.* **24 D7** 51 8N 127 20W
Bell —►, *Qué.* **10 B5** 49 48N 77 38W
Bell I., *Nfld.* **7 F8** 47 38N 52 58W
Bell I., *Nfld.* **7 C5** 50 46N 55 35W
Bell-Irving —►, *B.C.* **18 B3** 56 12N 129 5W
Bell L., *Ont.* **16 C6** 49 48N 90 58W
Bell Peninsula, *N.W.T.* **27 C7** 63 50N 82 0W
Bella Bella, *B.C.* **24 C6** 52 10N 128 10W
Bella Coola, *B.C.* **24 C8** 52 25N 126 40W
Bellburns, *Nfld.* **7 C3** 50 20N 57 32W
Belle Isle, *Nfld.* **7 B5** 51 57N 55 25W
Belle Isle, Str. of, *Nfld.* **7 B4** 51 30N 56 30W
Belle River, *Ont.* **14 E4** 42 18N 82 43W
Belle-Vallée, *Qué.* **12 B4** 45 4N 73 26W
Bellechasse □, *Qué.* **30 B5** 46 47N 71 14W
Belleoram, *Nfld.* **7 F5** 47 31N 55 25W
Bellerive, *Qué.* **12 B2** 45 15N 74 10W
Belleterre, *Qué.* **10 D4** 47 25N 78 41W
Belleville, *Ont.* **15 C9** 44 10N 77 23W
Bellevue, *Alta.* **23 I6** 49 35N 114 22W
Bellin, *Qué.* **6 B4** 60 0N 70 0W
Belliveau Cove, *N.S.* **9 I3** 44 23N 66 4W
Bells Corners, *Ont.* **30 E7** 45 19N 75 50W
Bellsite, *Man.* **21 C9** 52 35N 101 4W
Belly —►, *Alta.* **23 I7** 49 46N 113 2W
Belmont, *Man.* **21 F11** 49 25N 99 27W
Belmont, *N.S.* **9 H6** 45 25N 63 23W
Belmont, *Ont.* **14 E5** 42 53N 81 5W
Belmont Park, *B.C.* **25 H19** 48 27N 123 27W
Beloeil, *Qué.* **12 A4** 45 34N 73 12W
Belot, L., *N.W.T.* **26 C3** 66 53N 126 16W
Belwood, *Ont.* **13 A2** 43 47N 80 19W
Belwood, L., *Ont.* **13 A2** 43 46N 80 20W
Bendale, *Ont.* **28 B4** 43 46N 79 14W
Bengough, *Sask.* **20 F5** 49 25N 105 10W
Beniah L., *N.W.T.* **18 A6** 63 23N 112 17W
Bennett, *B.C.* **18 B2** 59 56N 134 53W
Benny, *Ont.* **14 A5** 46 47N 81 38W
Benoit's Cove, *Nfld.* **7 D2** 49 1N 58 7W
Benson, *Sask.* **20 F7** 49 27N 103 1W
Bentley, *Alta.* **23 F6** 52 28N 114 4W
Berens —►, *Man.* **21 C13** 52 25N 97 2W
Berens I., *Man.* **21 C13** 52 18N 97 18W
Berens River, *Man.* **21 C14** 52 25N 97 0W
Beresford, *N.B.* **9 F4** 47 42N 65 42W
Berland —►, *Alta.* **22 E4** 54 0N 116 50W
Bermen, L., *Qué.* **6 C4** 53 35N 68 55W
Bernard L., *Ont.* **14 B7** 45 45N 79 23W
Bernier B., *N.W.T.* **27 B7** 71 5N 88 15W
Bernierville, *Qué.* **11 E11** 46 6N 71 34W
Berry Cr. —►, *Alta.* **23 H9** 50 50N 111 37W
Berthierville, *Qué.* **11 E9** 46 5N 73 10W
Bertrand, *N.B.* **9 F4** 47 45N 65 4W
Berwick, *N.B.* **9 H4** 45 47N 65 36W
Berwick, *N.S.* **9 H5** 45 3N 64 44W
Berwyn, *Alta.* **22 B3** 56 9N 117 44W
Besnard L., *Sask.* **19 B7** 55 25N 106 0W
Bethany, *Ont.* **15 C8** 44 11N 78 34W
Bethesda, *Ont.* **13 A4** 43 58N 79 21W
Bethune, *Sask.* **20 E5** 50 43N 105 13W
Betsiamites, *Qué.* **11 C14** 48 56N 68 40W
Betsiamites —►, *Qué.* **11 C14** 48 56N 68 38W
Bevin, L., *Qué.* **12 A1** 45 57N 74 35W
Bewdley, *Ont.* **15 C8** 44 5N 78 19W
Bibby I., *N.W.T.* **19 A10** 61 55N 93 0W
Bic, *Qué.* **11 C14** 48 20N 68 41W
Bic, Île du, *Qué.* **11 C14** 48 24N 68 52W
Biche, L. la, *Alta.* **22 D8** 54 50N 112 3W
Biche, La —►, *B.C.* **18 B4** 59 57N 123 50W
Bickerton West, *N.S.* **9 H8** 45 6N 61 44W
Bienfait, *Sask.* **20 F8** 49 10N 102 50W
Bienville, L., *Qué.* **6 B3** 55 5N 72 40W
Big —►, *Nfld.* **6 C6** 54 50N 58 55W
Big B., *Nfld.* **6 B5** 55 43N 60 35W
Big Bar Creek, *B.C.* **25 D12** 51 12N 122 7W
Big Basswood L., *Ont.* **14 A3** 46 25N 83 23W
Big Beaver, *Sask.* **20 F5** 49 10N 105 10W
Big Bend Res., *Alta.* **23 F5** 52 59N 115 30W
Big Cr. —►, *B.C.* **25 D12** 51 42N 122 41W
Big Creek, *B.C.* **25 D11** 51 43N 123 2W
Big Horn Dam, *Alta.* **23 F4** 52 20N 116 20W
Big I., *N.W.T.* **27 C8** 62 43N 70 43W
Big I., *Ont.* **16 C2** 49 9N 94 40W
Big L., *Alta.* **31 D6** 53 37N 113 42W
Big Muddy L., *Sask.* **20 F6** 49 9N 104 51W
Big Pond, *N.S.* **9 H9** 45 57N 60 32W
Big Quill L., *Sask.* **20 D6** 51 55N 104 50W
Big Rideau L., *Ont.* **15 C10** 44 40N 76 15W
Big River, *Sask.* **20 B4** 53 50N 107 0W
Big Sand L., *Man.* **19 B9** 57 45N 99 45W
Big Sandy L., *Sask.* **20 A6** 54 27N 104 6W
Big Trout L., *Ont.* **15 B8** 45 46N 78 37W
Big Trout L., *Ont.* **4 B2** 53 40N 90 0W
Big Valley, *Alta.* **23 F8** 52 2N 112 46W
Biggar, *Sask.* **20 C3** 52 4N 108 0W
Bigniba —►, *Qué.* **10 B5** 49 18N 77 20W
Bigot, L., *Qué.* **8 C4** 50 50N 65 39W
Bigsby I, *Ont.* **16 C2** 49 4N 94 34W
Bigstick L., *Sask.* **20 E1** 50 16N 109 20W
Bigstone L., *Man.* **21 B15** 53 42N 95 44W
Binbrook, *Ont.* **13 B3** 43 7N 79 48W
Binscarth, *Man.* **21 E9** 50 37N 101 17W
Birch Cliff, *Ont.* **28 B4** 43 41N 79 17W
Birch Cove, *N.S.* **9 K10** 44 42N 63 41W
Birch Hills, *Sask.* **20 C5** 52 59N 105 25W
Birch I., *Man.* **21 C11** 52 26N 99 54W
Birch Island, *B.C.* **25 D15** 51 37N 119 54W
Birch L., *Alta.* **22 E9** 53 19N 111 35W
Birch L., *N.W.T.* **18 A5** 62 4N 116 33W
Birch L., *Ont.* **16 A4** 51 23N 92 18W
Birch L., *Sask.* **20 B2** 53 27N 108 10W
Birch Manor, *Ont.* **30 D7** 45 26N 75 46W
Birch Mts., *Alta.* **18 B6** 57 30N 113 10W
Birch River, *Man.* **21 C9** 52 24N 101 6W
Birchy Bay, *Nfld.* **7 D6** 49 21N 54 44W
Bird, *Man.* **19 B10** 56 30N 94 13W
Bird Cove, *Nfld.* **7 B4** 51 3N 56 56W
Birds Hill, *Man.* **31 B4** 49 59N 97 0W
Birken, *B.C.* **25 E12** 50 28N 122 37W
Biron, *Qué.* **8 E3** 48 12N 66 16W
Birsay, *Sask.* **20 D4** 51 6N 106 59W
Birtle, *Man.* **21 E9** 50 30N 101 5W
Biscostasing, *Ont.* **17 E14** 47 18N 82 9W
Biscotasi L., *Ont.* **17 E14** 47 22N 82 1W
Bishop, Mt., *B.C.* **32 A3** 49 26N 122 56W
Bishop's Falls, *Nfld.* **7 D5** 49 2N 55 30W
Bishopton, *Qué.* **11 F11** 45 35N 71 35W
Bismarck, *Ont.* **13 B4** 43 3N 79 30W
Bison L., *Alta.* **22 A4** 57 12N 116 8W
Bissett, *Man.* **21 D15** 51 2N 95 41W
Bistcho L., *Alta.* **18 B5** 59 45N 118 50W
Bitter L., *Sask.* **20 E1** 50 7N 109 48W
Bittern L., *Alta.* **23 E7** 53 3N 113 5W
Bittern L., *Sask.* **20 B5** 53 56N 105 45W
Bizard, Île, *Qué.* **29 C2** 45 29N 73 54W
Bjorkdale, *Sask.* **20 C7** 52 43N 103 39W
Blache, L. de la, *Qué.* **11 A13** 50 5N 69 29W
Black —►, *Ont.* **14 C7** 44 42N 79 19W
Black B., *Ont.* **16 D8** 48 40N 88 25W
Black Creek, *B.C.* **24 F9** 49 49N 125 7W
Black Diamond, *Alta.* **23 H6** 50 45N 114 14W
Black Horse, *Ont.* **13 A3** 43 59N 79 49W
Black I., *Man.* **21 D14** 51 12N 96 30W
Black L., *Sask.* **19 B7** 59 12N 105 15W
Black Lake, *Qué.* **11 E11** 46 1N 71 22W
Black Mt., *B.C.* **32 A1** 49 23N 123 13W
Black Pines, *B.C.* **25 E14** 50 57N 120 15W
Black Rock Pt., *Nfld.* **6 A5** 60 2N 64 10W
Black Sturgeon L., *Ont.* **16 C8** 49 20N 88 53W
Blackfalds, *Alta.* **23 F7** 52 23N 113 47W
Blackfoot, *Alta.* **22 E10** 53 17N 110 10W
Blackhead, *Nfld.* **7 H8** 47 32N 52 39W
Blackhead Road, *Nfld.* **7 H7** 47 33N 52 43W
Blackheath, *Ont.* **13 B3** 43 4N 79 49W
Blackie, *Alta.* **23 H7** 50 36N 113 37W
Blackmud Cr. —►, *Alta.* **31 E6** 53 27N 113 33W
Blackpool, *Qué.* **12 B4** 45 1N 73 28W
Blacks Harbour, *N.B.* **9 H3** 45 3N 66 49W
Blackstone —►, *N.W.T.* **18 A4** 61 5N 122 55W
Blackville, *N.B.* **9 G4** 46 44N 65 50W
Bladworth, *Sask.* **20 D4** 51 22N 106 8W
Blaine Lake, *Sask.* **20 C4** 52 51N 106 52W
Blainville, *Qué.* **29 B2** 45 40N 73 52W
Blair, *Ont.* **13 B2** 43 23N 80 23W
Blairmore, *Alta.* **23 I6** 49 40N 114 25W
Blanche —►, *Ont.* **30 D8** 45 30N 75 33W
Blenheim, *Ont.* **14 E5** 42 20N 82 0W
Bleu, L., *Qué.* **10 E4** 46 35N 78 24W
Blind River, *Ont.* **14 A4** 46 10N 82 58W
Blissfield, *N.B.* **9 G3** 46 36N 66 5W
Bloodvein —►, *Man.* **21 D14** 51 47N 96 43W
Bloomfield, *Nfld.* **7 E7** 48 23N 53 54W
Bloomfield, *Ont.* **15 D9** 43 59N 77 14W
Bloomingdale, *Ont.* **13 A2** 43 31N 80 27W
Blossom Park, *Ont.* **30 D8** 45 21N 75 37W
Blubber Bay, *B.C.* **24 F10** 49 47N 124 37W
Blue Hills, *N.W.T.* **26 B4** 75 34N 114 30W
Blue Ridge, *Alta.* **22 D5** 54 8N 115 22W
Blue River, *B.C.* **25 C15** 52 6N 119 18W
Blueberry —►, *B.C.* **18 B4** 56 45N 120 49W
Blueberry Mountain, *Alta.* **22 C1** 55 56N 119 9W
Bluenose L., *N.W.T.* **26 C4** 68 30N 119 35W
Bluffton, *Alta.* **23 F6** 52 45N 114 17W
Blyth, *Ont.* **14 D5** 43 44N 81 26W
Boat Harbour, *Nfld.* **7 F6** 47 24N 54 50W
Bobcaygeon, *Ont.* **15 C8** 44 33N 78 33W
Bochart, *Qué.* **11 B9** 49 10N 73 30W
Bogtown, *Qué.* **12 B3** 45 5N 73 53W
Bois, L. des, *N.W.T.* **26 C3** 66 50N 125 9W
Bois-des-Filion, *Qué.* **29 B3** 45 40N 73 45W
Boisdale, *N.S.* **9 G9** 46 6N 60 30W
Boissevain, *Man.* **21 F10** 49 15N 100 5W
Bolton, *Ont.* **28 A1** 43 54N 79 45W
Bon Accord, *Alta.* **22 E7** 53 50N 113 25W
Bon Echo Prov. Park, *Ont.* **15 C9** 45 0N 77 20W
Bonanza, *Alta.* **22 C1** 55 55N 119 49W
Bonaparte L., *B.C.* **25 D14** 51 15N 120 34W
Bonaventure, *N.B.* **9 E4** 48 5N 65 32W
Bonavista, *Nfld.* **7 E7** 48 40N 53 5W
Bonavista, C., *Nfld.* **7 E7** 48 42N 53 5W
Bonavista B., *Nfld.* **7 E7** 48 45N 53 25W
Bonfield, *Ont.* **14 A7** 46 14N 79 9W
Bonilla I., *B.C.* **24 B4** 53 28N 130 37W
Bonnechere —►, *Ont.* **15 B9** 45 35N 77 50W
Bonnet, Lac du, *Man.* **21 E15** 50 22N 95 55W
Bonnyville, *Alta.* **22 D10** 54 20N 110 45W
Boothia, Gulf of, *N.W.T.* **27 B7** 71 0N 90 0W
Boothia Pen., *N.W.T.* **27 B6** 71 0N 94 0W
Borden, *P.E.I.* **9 G6** 46 18N 63 47W
Borden, *Sask.* **20 C3** 52 27N 107 14W
Borden I., *N.W.T.* **26 B4** 78 30N 111 30W
Borden L., *Ont.* **17 E13** 47 50N 83 17W
Borden Pen., *N.W.T.* **27 B7** 73 0N 83 0W
Boston, *Ont.* **13 C2** 42 59N 80 16W
Boston Bar, *B.C.* **25 F13** 49 52N 121 30W
Boston Cr. —►, *Ont.* **13 B3** 43 2N 79 56W
Boswell, *B.C.* **25 F18** 49 28N 116 45W
Bothwell, *Ont.* **14 E5** 42 38N 81 52W
Botwood, *Nfld.* **7 D5** 49 6N 55 23W
Bouchard, Île, *Qué.* **12 A4** 45 49N 73 21W
Boucher —►, *Qué.* **11 B13** 49 10N 69 6W
Boucherville, *Qué.* **29 B5** 45 36N 73 27W
Boucherville, Is. de, *Qué.* **29 B5** 45 37N 73 28W
Bouchette, *Qué.* **10 E7** 46 12N 75 57W
Bouchier, L., *Qué.* **10 A5** 50 6N 77 48W
Boundary B., *B.C.* **32 C2** 49 2N 122 57W
Boundary Bay, *B.C.* **32 C3** 49 0N 123 2W
Bourget, *Ont.* **10 F7** 45 26N 75 9W
Bow —►, *Alta.* **23 I9** 49 57N 111 41W
Bow Island, *Alta.* **23 I9** 49 50N 111 23W
Bow Pass, *Alta.* **23 G4** 51 43N 116 30W
Bowden, *Alta.* **23 G6** 51 55N 114 2W
Bowen Island, *B.C.* **25 F11** 49 23N 123 20W
Bowman L., *Ont.* **16 A5** 51 10N 91 25W
Bowmanville, *Ont.* **15 D8** 43 55N 78 41W
Bowron —►, *B.C.* **25 A13** 54 3N 121 50W
Bowron Lake Prov. Park, *B.C.* **25 B13** 53 10N 121 5W
Bowser, *B.C.* **24 F10** 49 27N 124 40W
Bowser L., *B.C.* **18 B3** 56 30N 129 30W
Bowsman, *Man.* **21 C9** 52 14N 101 12W
Bowyer I., *B.C.* **32 A1** 49 26N 123 16W
Boyd L., *Qué.* **6 C2** 52 46N 76 42W
Boyer —►, *Alta.* **18 B5** 58 27N 115 57W
Boyer —►, *Qué.* **30 B5** 46 53N 70 58W
Boyer-Nord —►, *Qué.* **30 B5** 46 44N 70 58W
Boyer-Sud —►, *Qué.* **30 B5** 46 44N 70 58W
Boyle, *Alta.* **22 D8** 54 35N 112 49W
Boylston, *N.S.* **9 H8** 45 26N 61 30W
Boyne, *Ont.* **13 B3** 43 29N 79 50W
Brabant L., *Sask.* **19 B8** 55 58N 103 43W
Bracebridge, *Ont.* **14 B7** 45 2N 79 19W
Bracken, *Sask.* **20 F2** 49 11N 108 6W
Brackendale, *B.C.* **25 F11** 49 48N 123 8W
Bradford, *Ont.* **14 C7** 44 7N 79 34W
Bradore Bay, *Qué.* **7 B3** 51 27N 57 18W
Bradwell, *Sask.* **20 D4** 51 57N 106 14W
Braedale, *Ont.* **13 B4** 43 8N 79 14W
Braeside, *Ont.* **10 F6** 45 28N 76 24W
Bragg Creek, *Alta.* **23 H6** 50 57N 114 35W
Bralorne, *B.C.* **25 E12** 50 50N 122 50W
Bramalea, *Ont.* **28 B1** 43 44N 79 43W
Brampton, *Ont.* **28 B1** 43 45N 79 45W
Branch, *Nfld.* **7 G7** 46 53N 53 57W
Branchton, *Ont.* **13 B2** 43 18N 80 15W
Brandon, *Man.* **21 F11** 49 50N 99 57W
Brant □, *Ont.* **13 B2** 43 10N 80 20W
Brantford, *Ont.* **13 B2** 43 10N 80 15W
Brantville, *N.B.* **9 F5** 47 22N 64 58W
Bras d'Or, L., *N.S.* **9 H9** 45 50N 60 50W
Brazeau —►, *Alta.* **23 F5** 52 55N 115 14W
Brechin, *Ont.* **14 C7** 44 32N 79 10W
Bredenbury, *Sask.* **21 E8** 50 57N 102 3W
Brent, *Ont.* **15 A8** 46 2N 78 29W
Brentwood, *Alta.* **31 F10** 51 7N 114 9W
Breslau, *Ont.* **13 B2** 43 28N 80 25W
Breton, *Alta.* **23 E6** 53 7N 114 28W
Breton, Lac Le, *Qué.* **8 B9** 51 53N 60 9W
Briçonnet, L., *Qué.* **8 B9** 51 27N 60 10W
Bridgenorth, *Ont.* **15 C8** 44 23N 78 23W
Bridgeport, *B.C.* **32 B2** 49 12N 123 8W
Bridgeport, *Ont.* **14 D6** 43 29N 80 29W
Bridgetown, *N.S.* **9 I4** 44 55N 65 18W
Bridgewater, *N.S.* **9 I5** 44 25N 64 31W
Briercrest, *Sask.* **20 E5** 50 10N 105 16W
Brighouse, *B.C.* **32 C2** 49 10N 123 8W
Brighton, *Ont.* **15 C9** 44 2N 77 44W
Brightsand L., *Sask.* **20 B2** 53 36N 108 53W
Brilliant, *B.C.* **25 F17** 49 19N 117 38W
Brimstone, *Ont.* **13 A3** 43 48N 80 0W
Brion, I., *Qué.* **9 F8** 47 46N 61 26W
Brisbane, *Ont.* **13 A2** 43 44N 80 4W
Bristol, *N.B.* **9 G2** 46 28N 67 35W
Bristol, *Qué.* **10 F6** 45 32N 76 28W
Britannia Beach, *B.C.* **25 F11** 49 38N 123 12W
British Columbia □, *B.C.* **18 C3** 55 0N 125 15W
British Mts., *N.W.T.* **26 C2** 68 50N 140 0W
Britt, *Ont.* **14 B6** 45 46N 80 34W
Broach, L., *Qué.* **8 C2** 50 45N 67 59W
Broadback —►, *Qué.* **6 C2** 51 21N 78 52W
Broadview, *Sask.* **20 E8** 50 22N 102 35W
Brochet, *Man.* **19 B8** 57 53N 101 40W
Brochet, L., *Man.* **19 B8** 58 36N 101 35W
Brochet, L. du, *Qué.* **11 B13** 49 40N 69 37W
Brock, *Sask.* **20 D2** 51 26N 108 43W
Brock —►, *Qué.* **10 B7** 50 0N 75 5W
Brock I., *N.W.T.* **26 B4** 77 52N 114 19W
Brock Road, *Ont.* **28 A5** 43 53N 79 5W
Brockville, *Ont.* **15 C11** 44 35N 75 41W
Broderick, *Sask.* **20 D4** 51 30N 106 55W
Brodeur Pen., *N.W.T.* **27 B7** 72 30N 88 10W
Bromont, *Qué.* **11 F10** 45 17N 72 39W
Bromptonville, *Qué.* **11 F11** 45 28N 71 57W
Bronte, *Ont.* **13 B3** 43 24N 79 43W
Bronte Cr. —►, *Ont.* **13 B3** 43 24N 79 43W
Brookdale, *Man.* **21 E11** 50 3N 99 34W
Brookfield, *N.S.* **9 H6** 45 15N 63 17W
Brooklands, *Man.* **31 B2** 49 55N 97 12W
Brooklin, *Ont.* **13 A5** 43 55N 78 55W
Brooklyn, *N.S.* **9 I5** 44 3N 64 42W
Brookmere, *B.C.* **25 F14** 49 52N 120 53W
Brookport, *Qué.* **12 B5** 45 15N 72 50W
Brooks, *Alta.* **23 H9** 50 35N 111 55W
Brooks B., *B.C.* **24 E7** 50 15N 127 55W
Brooks L., *N.W.T.* **19 A7** 61 55N 106 35W
Broquerie, La, *Man.* **21 F14** 49 25N 96 30W
Brossard, *Qué.* **29 C5** 45 26N 73 29W
Brougham, *Ont.* **13 A4** 43 55N 79 6W
Broughton I., *B.C.* **24 E8** 50 48N 126 42W
Broughton Island, *N.W.T.* **27 C9** 67 33N 63 0W
Browning, *Sask.* **20 F8** 49 27N 102 38W
Brownlee, *Sask.* **20 E4** 50 43N 106 1W
Browns Flats, *N.B.* **9 H3** 45 28N 66 8W
Browns Line, *Ont.* **28 C2** 43 36N 79 32W
Brownsburg, *Qué.* **12 A2** 45 41N 74 25W
Bruce, *Alta.* **23 E8** 53 10N 112 2W
Bruce L., *Ont.* **16 B3** 50 49N 93 20W
Bruce Mts., *N.W.T.* **27 B8** 71 12N 72 15W
Bruce Pen., *Ont.* **14 C5** 45 0N 81 30W
Bruderheim, *Alta.* **22 E8** 53 47N 112 56W
Brûlé, *Alta.* **22 E3** 53 15N 117 58W
Brûlé, L., *Nfld.* **8 A6** 52 30N 63 40W
Brunette I., *Nfld.* **7 F5** 47 16N 55 55W
Brunkild, *Man.* **21 F13** 49 36N 97 35W
Bruno, *Sask.* **20 C5** 52 20N 105 30W
Brunswick L., *Ont.* **17 D13** 48 58N 83 23W
Brussels, *Ont.* **14 D5** 43 44N 81 15W
Bryson, *Qué.* **10 F6** 45 41N 76 37W
Buchanan, *Sask.* **20 D8** 51 40N 102 45W
Buchans, *Nfld.* **7 E4** 48 50N 56 52W
Buchans Junction, *Nfld.* **7 E4** 48 51N 56 28W
Buck L., *Alta.* **23 F6** 52 59N 114 46W
Buck Lake, *Alta.* **23 F6** 52 57N 114 47W
Buckhorn L., *Ont.* **15 C8** 44 29N 78 23W
Buckingham, *Qué.* **10 F7** 45 37N 75 24W
Buctouche, *N.B.* **9 G5** 46 30N 64 45W
Buffalo —►, *Alta.* **18 A5** 60 5N 115 5W
Buffalo Creek, *B.C.* **25 D13** 51 44N 121 8W
Buffalo Head Hills, *Alta.* **18 B5** 57 25N 115 55W
Buffalo L., *Alta.* **23 F8** 52 27N 112 54W
Buffalo Narrows, *Sask.* **19 B7** 55 51N 108 29W
Buffalo Pound L., *Sask.* **20 E5** 50 39N 105 30W
Buit, L., *Qué.* **8 C6** 50 59N 63 13W
Bulkley —►, *B.C.* **18 B3** 55 15N 127 40W
Bullocks Corners, *Ont.* **30 D9** 43 17N 79 59W
Bulyea, *Sask.* **20 E6** 50 59N 104 52W
Burdett, *Alta.* **23 I9** 49 50N 111 32W
Burford, *Ont.* **13 B2** 43 7N 80 27W
Burgeo, *Nfld.* **7 F3** 47 37N 57 38W
Burin, *Nfld.* **7 F5** 47 1N 55 14W
Burin Peninsula, *Nfld.* **7 G5** 47 0N 55 40W
Burke Chan., *B.C.* **24 C7** 52 10N 127 30W
Burk's Falls, *Ont.* **14 B7** 45 37N 79 24W
Burleigh Falls, *Ont.* **15 C8** 44 33N 78 12W
Burlington, *Nfld.* **7 D4** 49 45N 56 1W
Burlington, *Ont.* **30 D10** 43 18N 79 45W
Burlington Beach, *Ont.* **30 D10** 43 18N 79 48W
Burnaby, *B.C.* **32 B3** 49 15N 123 0W
Burnaby I., *B.C.* **24 C3** 52 25N 131 19W
Burnaby L., *B.C.* **32 B3** 49 14N 122 56W
Burnhamthorpe, *Ont.* **28 C2** 43 37N 79 36W
Burns Lake, *B.C.* **18 C3** 54 20N 125 45W
Burnside —►, *N.W.T.* **26 C5** 66 51N 108 4W
Burnt Island, *Nfld.* **7 F2** 47 36N 58 53W
Burnt L., *Nfld.* **6 C5** 53 35N 64 4W
Burnt River, *Ont.* **15 C8** 44 41N 78 42W
Burntwood —►, *Man.* **19 B9** 56 8N 96 34W
Burntwood L., *Man.* **19 B8** 55 22N 100 26W
Burquitlam, *B.C.* **32 B3** 49 16N 122 54W
Burrard Inlet, *B.C.* **32 B1** 49 18N 123 15W
Burrows L., *Ont.* **17 C10** 49 57N 86 44W
Burstall, *Sask.* **20 E1** 50 39N 109 54W
Burton, *B.C.* **25 F17** 50 0N 117 53W
Burton L., *Qué.* **6 C2** 54 45N 78 20W
Burtts Corner, *N.B.* **9 G3** 46 3N 66 52W
Burwash, *Ont.* **14 A6** 46 14N 80 51W
Burwash Landing, *Yukon* **26 C2** 61 21N 139 0W
Burwell, Mt., *B.C.* **32 A2** 49 27N 123 1W
Bury, *Qué.* **11 F11** 45 28N 71 30W
Bushell, *Sask.* **19 B7** 59 31N 108 45W
Bute Inlet, *B.C.* **24 E10** 50 40N 124 53W
Butedale, *B.C.* **24 B6** 53 8N 128 42W
Buttle L., *B.C.* **24 F9** 49 42N 125 33W
Button B., *Man.* **19 B10** 58 45N 94 23W
Button Is., *Nfld.* **6 A5** 60 38N 64 40W
Buttonville, *Ont.* **28 A3** 43 51N 79 21W
Byam Martin I., *N.W.T.* **26 B5** 75 15N 104 15W
Bylot I., *N.W.T.* **27 B8** 73 13N 78 34W
Byng Inlet, *Ont.* **14 B6** 45 46N 80 33W

C

Caamano Sd., *B.C.* **24 C5** 52 55N 129 25W
Cabane-Ronde, *Qué.* **29 A4** 45 47N 73 33W
Cabano, *Qué.* **11 D14** 47 40N 68 56W
Cabonga, Réservoir, *Qué.* **10 D6** 47 20N 76 40W
Cabot Strait, *Nfld.* **5 C8** 47 15N 59 40W
Cabri, *Sask.* **20 E2** 50 35N 108 25W
Cache Bay, *Ont.* **14 A7** 46 22N 80 0W
Cache Creek, *B.C.* **25 E13** 50 48N 121 19W
Cadboro Bay, *B.C.* **25 H20** 48 28N 123 17W
Cadillac, *Qué.* **10 C4** 48 14N 78 23W
Cadillac, *Sask.* **20 F3** 49 44N 107 44W
Cadomin, *Alta.* **23 E3** 53 2N 117 20W
Cadotte —►, *Alta.* **22 B3** 56 43N 117 10W
Cains —►, *N.B.* **9 G4** 46 40N 65 47W
Cainsville, *Ont.* **13 B2** 43 9N 80 15W
Cairnside, *Qué.* **12 B3** 45 7N 73 54W
Caistorville, *Ont.* **13 B3** 43 3N 79 44W
Calabogie, *Ont.* **15 B10** 45 18N 76 43W
Caledon, *Ont.* **13 A3** 43 52N 80 0W
Caledon East, *Ont.* **13 A3** 43 52N 79 52W
Caledonia, *N.S.* **9 H7** 45 17N 62 33W
Caledonia, *N.S.* **9 I4** 44 22N 65 2W
Caledonia, *Ont.* **13 B3** 43 7N 79 58W
Calgary, *Alta.* **31 G10** 51 0N 114 10W
Calgary International Airport, *Alta.* **31 F10** 51 4N 114 1W
Callander, *Ont.* **14 A7** 46 13N 79 22W
Calling L., *Alta.* **22 C7** 55 15N 113 20W
Calling Lake, *Alta.* **22 C7** 55 15N 113 12W
Calmar, *Alta.* **22 E7** 53 16N 113 49W
Calstock, *Ont.* **17 C12** 49 47N 84 9W
Calvert C., *B.C.* **24 D7** 51 25N 127 53W

Calvert I., *B.C.* 24 D7 51 30N 128 0W
Camachigama, L., *Qué.* 10 D6 47 50N 76 19W
Cambridge, *N.B.* 9 H4 45 50N 65 58W
Cambridge, *Ont.* 13 B2 43 23N 80 15W
Cambridge Bay, *N.W.T.* 26 C5 69 10N 105 0W
Cameron Falls, *Ont.* 16 C8 49 8N 88 19W
Cameron Hills, *Alta.* 18 B5 59 48N 118 0W
Cameron L., *Ont.* 17 C12 49 1N 84 17W
Camp Borden, *Ont.* 14 C7 44 18N 79 56W
Campania I., *B.C.* 24 B5 53 5N 129 25W
Campbell →, *B.C.* 32 C4 49 1N 122 47W
Campbell Island, *B.C.* 24 C6 52 8N 128 12W
Campbell L., *N.W.T.* 19 A7 63 14N 106 55W
Campbell River, *B.C.* 24 E9 50 5N 125 20W
Campbellford, *Ont.* 15 C9 44 18N 77 48W
Campbell's Bay, *Qué.* 10 F6 45 44N 76 36W
Campbellton, *N.B.* 9 F3 47 57N 66 43W
Campbellton, *Nfld.* 7 D6 49 17N 54 56W
Campbellville, *Ont.* 13 B3 43 29N 79 59W
Camperville, *Man.* 21 D10 51 59N 100 9W
Camrose, *Alta.* 23 F8 53 0N 112 50W
Camsell Portage, *Sask.* 19 B7 59 37N 109 15W
Canaan →, *N.B.* 9 H4 45 55N 65 47W
Canaan Station, *N.B.* 9 G4 46 15N 65 4W
Canada B., *Nfld.* 7 C4 50 43N 56 8W
Canadian Pacific Irrigation Canal, *Alta.* 31 G11 51 0N 114 0W
Canal Flats, *B.C.* 23 H5 50 10N 115 48W
Canboro, *Ont.* 13 C3 42 59N 79 41W
Candiac, *Qué.* 29 C4 45 23N 73 31W
Candle L., *Sask.* 20 B5 53 50N 105 18W
Cando, *Sask.* 20 C2 52 23N 108 14W
Canfield, *Ont.* 13 C3 42 58N 79 45W
Canim, L., *B.C.* 25 D14 51 45N 120 50W
Canim Lake, *B.C.* 25 D14 51 47N 120 54W
Canmore, *Alta.* 23 G5 51 7N 115 18W
Canning, *N.S.* 9 H5 45 9N 64 25W
Cannington, *Ont.* 15 C7 44 20N 79 2W
Canoe, *B.C.* 25 E15 50 45N 119 13W
Canoe L., *Sask.* 19 B7 55 10N 108 15W
Canora, *Sask.* 21 D8 51 40N 102 30W
Canso, *N.S.* 9 H9 45 20N 61 0W
Canterbury, *N.B.* 9 H2 45 53N 67 29W
Cantic, *Qué.* 12 B4 45 4N 73 21W
Canuck, *Sask.* 20 F2 49 12N 108 13W
Canuta, *Qué.* 12 A2 45 42N 74 9W
Canwood, *Sask.* 20 B4 53 22N 106 36W
Canyon Creek, *Alta.* 22 C5 55 22N 115 5W
Caopacho →, *Qué.* 8 B3 51 18N 66 18W
Caopacho, L., *Qué.* 8 B3 52 0N 66 9W
Caotibi, L., *Qué.* 8 C2 50 45N 67 34W
Cap-aux-Meules, *Qué.* 9 F8 47 23N 61 52W
Cap-aux Meules, Î. du, *Qué.* 9 F8 47 23N 61 54W
Cap-Chat, *Qué.* 8 D3 49 6N 66 40W
Cap-de-la-Madeleine, *Qué.* 11 E10 46 22N 72 31W
Cap-des-Rosiers, *Qué.* 8 E5 48 52N 64 13W
Cap d'Espoir, *Qué.* 8 E5 48 26N 64 20W
Cap-Pelé, *N.B.* 9 G5 46 13N 64 18W
Cap-St-Ignace, *Qué.* 11 D12 47 2N 70 28W
Cape Breton Highlands Nat. Park, *N.S.* 9 G9 46 50N 60 40W
Cape Breton I., *N.S.* 9 H9 46 0N 60 30W
Cape Broyle, *Nfld.* 7 F8 47 6N 52 57W
Cape Dorset, *N.W.T.* 27 C8 64 14N 76 32W
Cape Dyer, *N.W.T.* 27 C9 66 30N 61 22W
Cape Ray, *Nfld.* 7 F1 47 38N 59 17W
Cape Scott Prov. Park, *B.C.* 24 E6 50 45N 128 20W
Cape Tormentine, *N.B.* 9 G6 46 8N 63 47W
Capilano →, *B.C.* 32 B2 49 19N 123 7W
Capilano L., *B.C.* 32 A2 49 23N 123 7W
Capitachouane →, *Qué.* 10 D6 47 40N 76 47W
Caplan, *N.B.* 9 E4 48 6N 65 40W
Capreol, *Ont.* 14 A6 46 43N 80 56W
Caramat, *Ont.* 17 C10 49 37N 86 9W
Caraquet, *N.B.* 9 F5 47 48N 64 57W
Carberry, *Man.* 21 F11 49 50N 99 25W
Carbon, *Alta.* 23 G7 51 30N 113 9W
Carbondale, *Alta.* 22 E7 53 45N 113 32W
Carbonear, *Nfld.* 7 F7 47 42N 53 13W
Carcajou, *Alta.* 18 B5 57 47N 117 6W
Cardinal, *Ont.* 15 C11 44 47N 75 23W
Cardinal L., *Alta.* 22 B3 56 14N 117 44W
Cardross, *Sask.* 20 F5 49 50N 105 40W
Cardston, *Alta.* 23 I7 49 15N 113 20W
Careen L., *Sask.* 19 B7 57 0N 108 11W
Carey L., *N.W.T.* 19 A8 62 12N 102 55W
Carheil, L., *Qué.* 8 A2 52 40N 67 5W
Cariboo →, *B.C.* 25 B13 53 3N 121 20W
Cariboo Mts., *B.C.* 25 C14 53 0N 121 0W
Caribou →, *Man.* 19 B10 59 20N 94 44W
Caribou →, *N.W.T.* 18 A3 61 27N 125 45W
Caribou I., *Ont.* 17 E11 47 22N 85 49W
Caribou Is., *N.W.T.* 18 A6 61 55N 113 15W
Caribou L., *Man.* 19 B9 59 21N 96 10W
Caribou L., *Ont.* 16 B7 50 25N 89 5W
Caribou Mts., *Alta.* 18 B5 59 12N 115 40W
Carignan, *Qué.* 12 B4 45 27N 73 19W
Carleton, *N.B.* 9 E3 48 5N 66 4W
Carleton, *N.S.* 9 J4 44 0N 65 56W
Carleton Place, *Ont.* 15 B10 45 8N 76 9W
Carlisle, *Ont.* 13 B3 43 23N 79 59W
Carlyle, *Sask.* 21 F8 49 40N 102 20W
Carmacks, *Yukon* 26 C2 62 5N 136 16W
Carman, *Man.* 21 F13 49 30N 98 0W
Carmangay, *Alta.* 23 H7 50 10N 113 10W
Carmanville, *Nfld.* 7 D6 49 23N 54 19W
Carmi, *B.C.* 25 F15 49 36N 119 8W
Carnduff, *Sask.* 21 F9 49 10N 101 50W
Carnwood, *Alta.* 23 E6 53 11N 114 38W
Caroline, *Alta.* 23 F6 52 5N 114 45W
Caron, *Sask.* 20 E5 50 30N 105 50W
Caron, L., *Qué.* 8 C2 50 57N 67 44W
Carpenter L., *B.C.* 25 E12 50 53N 122 37W
Carragana, *Sask.* 20 C7 52 35N 103 6W
Carrot →, *Sask.* 21 B9 53 50N 101 17W
Carrot River, *Sask.* 20 B7 53 17N 103 35W
Carruthers, *Sask.* 20 C1 52 52N 109 16W
Carstairs, *Alta.* 23 G6 51 34N 114 6W
Cartier, *Ont.* 14 A5 46 42N 81 33W
Cartwright, *Man.* 21 F11 49 6N 99 20W
Cartwright, *Nfld.* 6 C6 53 41N 56 58W
Cartwright Sd., *B.C.* 24 B2 53 13N 132 38W
Casey, *Qué.* 11 D8 47 53N 74 11W
Cashel, *Ont.* 13 A4 43 55N 79 19W
Caslan, *Alta.* 22 D8 54 38N 112 31W
Casselman, *Ont.* 10 F7 45 19N 75 5W
Cassiar, *B.C.* 18 B3 59 16N 129 40W
Cassiar Mts., *B.C.* 18 B2 59 30N 130 30W
Castle Mountain, *Alta.* 23 G5 51 16N 115 55W
Castle Rock, *B.C.* 25 C12 52 32N 122 29W
Castlegar, *B.C.* 25 F17 49 20N 117 40W
Castor, *Alta.* 23 F9 52 15N 111 50W
Castor →, *Qué.* 6 C2 53 24N 78 58W
Casummit Lake, *Ont.* 16 A4 51 29N 92 22W
Cat L., *Ont.* 16 A5 51 40N 91 50W
Catalina, *Nfld.* 7 E7 48 31N 53 4W
Cathcart, *Ont.* 13 B1 43 6N 80 31W
Cathedral Mt., *B.C.* 32 A2 49 28N 123 1W
Cathedral Prov. Park, *B.C.* 25 F15 49 5N 120 0W
Cauchy, L., *Qué.* 8 C9 50 36N 60 46W
Caughnawaga, *Qué.* 29 C3 45 25N 73 41W
Caulfield, *B.C.* 32 A1 49 21N 123 15W
Causapscal, *Qué.* 8 E2 48 19N 67 12W
Causapscal, Parc Prov. de, *Qué.* 8 E3 48 15N 67 0W
Caution C., *B.C.* 24 D7 51 10N 127 47W
Cawasachouane, L., *Qué.* 10 D5 47 27N 77 45W
Caycuse, *B.C.* 24 G10 48 53N 124 22W
Cayley, *Alta.* 23 H7 50 27N 113 51W
Cayuga, *Ont.* 13 C3 42 59N 79 50W
Cazaville, *Qué.* 12 B2 45 5N 74 22W
Cedar L., *Man.* 21 B11 53 10N 100 0W
Cedar L., *Ont.* 15 A8 46 2N 78 30W
Cedar Mills, *Ont.* 13 A3 43 55N 79 48W
Cedar Valley, *Ont.* 13 A2 43 46N 80 10W
Cedarvale, *B.C.* 18 B3 55 1N 128 22W
Cèdres, Les, *Qué.* 29 D1 45 18N 74 3W
Centennial, *Man.* 31 B3 49 54N 97 9W
Central Butte, *Sask.* 20 E4 50 48N 106 31W
Central Patricia, *Ont.* 16 A6 51 30N 90 9W
Centreville, *N.B.* 9 G2 46 26N 67 43W
Centreville, *N.S.* 9 I3 44 33N 66 1W
Cereal, *Alta.* 23 G10 51 25N 110 48W
Cerf, L. de, *Qué.* 10 E7 46 16N 75 30W
Ceylon, *Sask.* 20 F6 49 27N 104 36W
Chaati I., *B.C.* 24 B2 53 7N 132 30W
Chakonipau, L., *Qué.* 6 B4 56 18N 68 30W
Chaleur B., *N.B.* 9 F4 47 55N 65 30W
Chalk River, *Ont.* 15 A9 46 1N 77 27W
Chambly, *Qué.* 12 B4 45 27N 73 17W
Chambly □, *Qué.* 29 C5 45 30N 73 30W
Chambord, *Qué.* 11 C10 48 25N 72 6W
Chamouchouane →, *Qué.* 11 C10 48 37N 72 20W
Champagne, *Yukon* 18 A1 60 49N 136 30W
Champdoré, L., *Qué.* 6 B4 55 55N 65 49W
Champion, *Alta.* 23 H7 50 14N 113 9W
Champlain, *Qué.* 4 C5 46 27N 72 24W
Champneuf, *Qué.* 10 C5 48 35N 77 30W
Chance Harbour, *N.B.* 9 H3 45 7N 66 21W
Chandler, *Qué.* 8 E5 48 18N 64 46W
Change Islands, *Nfld.* 7 D6 49 40N 54 25W
Channel-Port aux Basques, *Nfld.* 7 F1 47 30N 59 9W
Chantrey Inlet, *N.W.T.* 27 C6 67 48N 96 20W
Chapais, *Qué.* 10 B8 49 47N 74 51W
Chapeau, *Qué.* 10 F6 45 54N 77 4W
Chapleau, *Ont.* 17 E13 47 50N 83 24W
Chaplin, *Sask.* 20 E4 50 28N 106 40W
Chaplin L., *Sask.* 20 E4 50 22N 106 36W
Chapman, Mt., *B.C.* 25 D16 51 56N 118 20W
Charcoal L., *Sask.* 19 B8 58 49N 102 22W
Charette, *Qué.* 11 E10 46 27N 72 56W
Charlemagne, *Qué.* 29 A5 45 43N 73 29W
Charles L., *Alta.* 19 B6 59 50N 110 33W
Charlesbourg, *Qué.* 30 A3 46 51N 71 16W
Charleston L., *Ont.* 15 C11 44 32N 76 0W
Charleswood, *Man.* 31 B2 49 51N 97 17W
Charlo, *N.B.* 9 F3 47 59N 66 17W
Charlotte L., *B.C.* 24 C9 52 12N 125 19W
Charlottetown, *P.E.I.* 9 G6 46 14N 63 8W
Charlton I., *N.W.T.* 6 C2 52 0N 79 20W
Charny, *Qué.* 30 B3 46 43N 71 15W
Charron L., *Man.* 21 C15 52 44N 95 15W
Chase, *B.C.* 25 E15 50 50N 119 41W
Chasm, *B.C.* 25 D13 51 13N 121 30W
Châteauguay, *Qué.* 29 C3 45 23N 73 45W
Châteauguay □, *Qué.* 29 D3 45 11N 73 45W
Châteauguay →, *Qué.* 29 C3 45 23N 73 45W
Châteauguay, L., *Qué.* 6 B3 56 26N 70 3W
Châteauguay-Centre, *Qué.* 29 C3 45 21N 73 45W
Châteauvert, L., *Qué.* 11 D9 47 39N 73 56W
Chatham, *N.B.* 9 F4 47 2N 65 28W
Chatham, *Ont.* 14 E4 42 24N 82 11W
Chatham Head, *N.B.* 9 G4 47 0N 65 33W
Chatham Reach, *B.C.* 32 B4 49 15N 122 44W
Chats, L. des, *Qué.* 10 F6 45 30N 76 20W
Chatsworth, *Ont.* 14 C6 44 27N 80 54W
Chaudière →, *Qué.* 11 E11 46 45N 71 17W
Chauvin, *Alta.* 23 F10 52 45N 110 10W
Chavigny, L., *Qué.* 6 B2 58 12N 75 8W
Cheam View, *B.C.* 25 F13 49 15N 121 40W
Checleset B., *B.C.* 24 E7 50 5N 127 35W
Chedabucto B., *N.S.* 9 H8 45 25N 61 8W
Chedoke, *Ont.* 30 D9 43 14N 79 53W
Cheepash →, *Ont.* 17 A16 51 3N 80 59W
Cheepay →, *Ont.* 17 A13 51 25N 83 26W
Cheeseman L., *Ont.* 16 C7 49 27N 89 20W
Chef, R. du →, *Qué.* 11 B9 49 21N 73 25W
Chelsea, *Ont.* 30 D7 45 30N 75 47W
Cheltenham, *Ont.* 13 A3 43 45N 79 55W
Chemainus, *B.C.* 25 G11 48 55N 123 42W
Chénéville, *Qué.* 10 F7 45 53N 75 3W
Chenil, L., *Qué.* 8 B10 51 51N 59 41W
Cherhill, *Alta.* 22 E6 53 49N 114 41W
Cherry Creek, *B.C.* 25 E14 50 43N 120 40W
Cherryville, *B.C.* 25 E16 50 15N 118 37W
Cherrywood, *Ont.* 28 A5 43 52N 79 8W
Cheslatta, *B.C.* 24 B9 53 48N 125 48W
Cheslatta L., *B.C.* 24 B9 53 49N 125 20W
Chesley, *Ont.* 14 C5 44 17N 81 5W
Chester, *N.S.* 9 I5 44 33N 64 15W
Chesterfield Inlet, *N.W.T.* 27 C6 63 30N 90 45W
Chesterville, *Ont.* 10 F7 45 6N 75 14W
Chéticamp, *N.S.* 9 G9 46 37N 60 59W
Chetwynd, *B.C.* 18 B4 55 45N 121 36W
Chezacut, *B.C.* 24 C10 52 24N 124 1W
Chibougamau, *Qué.* 11 B8 49 56N 74 24W
Chibougamau →, *Qué.* 10 B7 49 42N 75 57W
Chibougamau, Parc Prov. de, *Qué.* 11 B9 49 15N 73 45W
Chibougamau L., *Qué.* 11 B8 49 50N 74 20W
Chic-Chocs, Mts., *Qué.* 8 E4 48 55N 66 0W
Chic-Chocs, Parc Prov. des, *Qué.* 8 E3 48 55N 66 20W
Chicobi, L., *Qué.* 10 C4 48 53N 78 30W
Chicoutimi, *Qué.* 5 C5 48 28N 71 5W
Chicoutimi, Parc Prov. de, *Qué.* 11 C12 48 30N 70 20W
Chidley, C., *Nfld.* 6 A5 60 23N 64 26W
Chiefs Pt., *Ont.* 14 C5 44 41N 81 18W
Chignecto, Cape, *N.S.* 9 H5 45 20N 64 57W
Chignecto B., *N.B.* 9 H5 45 30N 64 40W
Chigoubiche, L., *Qué.* 11 B9 49 7N 73 30W
Chilanko →, *B.C.* 24 C11 52 7N 123 41W
Chilanko Forks, *B.C.* 24 C10 52 7N 124 5W
Chilco, *B.C.* 24 A11 54 3N 123 49W
Chilcotin →, *B.C.* 25 D12 51 44N 122 23W
Chilko →, *B.C.* 24 D11 52 0N 123 40W
Chilko, L., *B.C.* 24 D10 51 20N 124 10W
Chilliwack, *B.C.* 25 F13 49 10N 121 54W
Chinchaga →, *Alta.* 22 A2 58 53N 118 20W
Chinook, *Alta.* 23 G10 51 28N 110 59W
Chinook Valley, *Alta.* 22 B3 56 29N 117 39W
Chip L., *Alta.* 22 E5 53 40N 115 23W
Chipewyan L., *Man.* 19 B9 58 0N 98 27W
Chipman, *Alta.* 22 E8 53 42N 112 38W
Chipman, *N.B.* 9 G4 46 6N 65 53W
Chipman L., *Ont.* 17 C10 49 58N 86 15W
Chippawa, *Ont.* 13 B4 43 5N 79 2W
Chiputneticook Lakes, *N.B.* 9 H2 45 37N 67 40W
Chisholm, *Alta.* 22 D6 54 55N 114 10W
Chitek, *Sask.* 20 B3 53 48N 107 45W
Chitek L., *Man.* 21 C11 52 25N 99 25W
Chitek L., *Sask.* 20 B3 53 45N 107 47W
Choelquoit L., *B.C.* 24 D10 51 42N 124 12W
Choiceland, *Sask.* 20 B6 53 29N 104 29W
Choisy, *Qué.* 12 B2 45 29N 74 13W
Chomedey, *Qué.* 29 B3 45 32N 73 45W
Christian I., *Ont.* 10 G2 44 50N 80 12W
Christie B., *N.W.T.* 19 A6 62 32N 111 10W
Christies Corners, *Ont.* 13 B2 43 16N 80 2W
Christina →, *Alta.* 22 B9 56 40N 111 3W
Christina, L., *B.C.* 25 F16 49 3N 118 12W
Christopher Lake, *Sask.* 20 B5 53 32N 105 48W
Chu Chua, *B.C.* 25 D14 51 22N 120 10W
Chuchi L., *B.C.* 18 B4 55 12N 124 30W
Churchbridge, *Sask.* 21 E9 50 54N 101 54W
Churchill, *Man.* 19 B10 58 47N 94 11W
Churchill →, *Man.* 19 B10 58 47N 94 12W
Churchill →, *Nfld.* 6 C5 53 19N 60 10W
Churchill, C., *Man.* 19 B10 58 46N 93 12W
Churchill Falls, *Nfld.* 6 C5 53 36N 64 19W
Churchill L., *Ont.* 16 B5 50 50N 91 50W
Churchill L., *Sask.* 19 B7 55 55N 108 20W
Churchill Pk., *B.C.* 18 B3 58 10N 125 10W
Chute-à-Blondeau, *Qué.* 12 A2 45 35N 74 28W
Chute-aux-Outardes, *Qué.* 11 B14 49 7N 68 24W
Chute-des-Passes, *Qué.* 11 B11 49 52N 71 16W
City View, *Ont.* 30 D7 45 21N 75 45W
Clairambault, L., *Qué.* 6 C4 54 29N 69 0W
Claire, *N.B.* 11 D14 47 15N 68 40W
Claire, L., *Alta.* 18 B6 58 35N 112 5W
Clairmont, *Alta.* 22 C2 55 16N 118 47W
Clandonald, *Alta.* 22 E10 53 34N 110 44W
Clanwilliam, *Man.* 21 E11 50 22N 99 49W
Clapperton I., *Ont.* 14 B4 46 0N 82 14W
Clappisons Corners, *Ont.* 30 D6 43 18N 79 55W
Claremont, *Ont.* 13 A4 43 58N 79 7W
Clarenceville, *Qué.* 12 B4 45 4N 73 15W
Clarendon, *N.B.* 9 H3 45 29N 66 26W
Clarenville, *Nfld.* 7 E6 48 10N 54 1W
Claresholm, *Alta.* 23 I7 50 0N 113 33W
Clark, Pt., *Ont.* 14 C5 44 4N 81 45W
Clarke City, *Qué.* 8 C3 50 12N 66 38W
Clarke L., *Sask.* 20 A4 54 24N 106 54W
Clark's Harbour, *N.S.* 9 J4 43 25N 65 38W
Clarkson, *Ont.* 28 C2 43 31N 79 37W
Claude, *Ont.* 13 A3 43 47N 79 54W
Clay L., *Ont.* 16 B3 50 3N 93 30W
Clear →, *Alta.* 22 B1 56 11N 119 42W
Clear, L., *Ont.* 15 B9 45 26N 77 12W
Clearwater, *B.C.* 25 D14 51 38N 120 2W
Clearwater →, *Alta.* 22 B9 56 44N 111 23W
Clearwater →, *Alta.* 23 F6 52 22N 114 57W
Clearwater →, *B.C.* 25 D14 51 38N 120 3W
Clearwater Cr. →, *N.W.T.* 18 A3 61 36N 125 30W
Clearwater L., *B.C.* 25 C14 52 15N 120 13W
Clearwater Prov. Park, *Man.* 21 B10 54 0N 101 0W
Clementsport, *N.S.* 9 I4 44 40N 65 37W
Clermont, *Qué.* 11 D12 47 41N 70 14W
Climax, *Sask.* 20 F2 49 10N 108 20W
Clinton, *B.C.* 25 D13 51 6N 121 35W
Clinton, *Ont.* 14 D5 43 37N 81 32W
Clinton Colden L., *N.W.T.* 26 C5 63 58N 107 27W
Clinton Creek, *N.W.T.* 26 C1 64 25N 140 37W
Clive, *Alta.* 23 F7 52 28N 113 27W
Clive L., *N.W.T.* 18 A5 63 13N 118 54W
Clova, *Qué.* 10 C7 48 7N 75 22W
Clover Pt., *B.C.* 25 H19 48 24N 123 21W
Cloverdale, *B.C.* 32 C4 49 7N 122 44W
Cloverdale, *N.B.* 9 G2 46 20N 67 22W
Cloyne, *Ont.* 15 C9 44 49N 77 11W
Cluculz L., *B.C.* 24 B11 53 53N 123 33W
Clyde, *Alta.* 22 D7 54 9N 113 39W
Clyde, *Ont.* 13 B2 43 22N 80 14W
Clyde →, *N.S.* 9 J4 43 35N 65 27W
Clyde River, *N.S.* 9 J4 43 38N 65 29W
Clyde River, *N.W.T.* 27 B9 70 30N 68 30W
Coacoachou, L., *Qué.* 8 C9 50 25N 60 14W
Coal →, *B.C.* 18 B3 59 39N 126 57W
Coal Creek, *B.C.* 23 I6 49 30N 114 59W
Coal Harbour, *B.C.* 24 E7 50 36N 127 35W
Coaldale, *Alta.* 23 I8 49 45N 112 35W
Coalhurst, *Alta.* 23 I8 49 45N 112 56W
Coalmont, *B.C.* 25 F14 49 32N 120 42W
Coast Mts., *B.C.* 24 A5 55 0N 129 20W
Coaticook, *Qué.* 11 F11 45 10N 71 46W
Coats I., *N.W.T.* 27 C7 62 30N 83 0W
Cobalt, *Ont.* 10 D3 47 25N 79 42W
Cobaz, L., *Qué.* 8 B9 51 15N 60 21W
Cobden, *Ont.* 15 B10 45 38N 76 53W
Coboconk, *Ont.* 15 C8 44 39N 78 48W
Cobourg, *Ont.* 15 D8 43 58N 78 10W
Coburg I., *N.W.T.* 27 B8 75 57N 79 26W
Cocagne, *N.B.* 9 G5 46 20N 64 37W
Cochenour, *Ont.* 16 A3 51 5N 93 48W
Cochrane, *Alta.* 23 G6 51 11N 114 30W
Cochrane, *Ont.* 4 C3 49 0N 81 0W
Cochrane →, *Sask.* 19 B8 59 0N 103 40W
Cockburn, C., *N.W.T.* 27 B8 74 52N 79 24W
Cockburn I., *Ont.* 14 B3 45 55N 83 22W
Cod I., *Nfld.* 6 B5 57 47N 61 47W
Coderre, *Sask.* 20 E4 50 11N 106 31W
Codette, *Sask.* 20 B7 53 16N 104 0W
Codroy, *Nfld.* 7 F1 47 53N 59 24W
Codroy Pond, *Nfld.* 7 E2 48 4N 58 52W
Coe Hill, *Ont.* 15 C9 44 52N 77 50W
Colborne, *Ont.* 15 D9 44 0N 77 53W
Cold L., *Alta.* 22 D10 54 33N 110 5W
Cold Lake, *Alta.* 22 D10 54 27N 110 10W
Coldwater, *Ont.* 14 C7 44 42N 79 40W
Colebrook, *B.C.* 32 C4 49 6N 122 52W
Coleman, *Alta.* 23 I6 49 40N 114 30W
Coleraine, *Ont.* 28 B1 43 49N 79 41W
Coleville, *Sask.* 20 D1 51 43N 109 15W
Colinet, *Nfld.* 7 F7 47 13N 53 33W
Colinton, *Alta.* 22 D7 54 37N 113 15W
College Bridge, *N.B.* 9 H5 45 57N 64 33W
College Heights, *Alta.* 23 F7 52 28N 113 45W
Collette, *N.B.* 9 G4 46 40N 65 30W
Colleymount, *B.C.* 24 A8 54 2N 126 19W
Collingwood, *Ont.* 14 C6 44 29N 80 13W
Collingwood Corner, *N.S.* 9 H6 45 37N 63 56W
Collins, *Ont.* 16 B7 50 17N 89 27W
Collinson Pen., *N.W.T.* 27 C5 69 58N 101 24W
Colombier, *Qué.* 11 C14 48 52N 68 51W
Colonsay, *Sask.* 20 D5 51 59N 105 52W
Colquitz, *B.C.* 25 H19 48 29N 123 24W
Columbia, Mt., *B.C.* 25 C17 52 8N 117 20W
Columbia L., *B.C.* 23 H5 50 15N 115 52W
Columbus, *Ont.* 13 A5 43 59N 78 55W
Colville Lake, *N.W.T.* 26 C3 67 2N 126 7W
Colwood, *B.C.* 25 H19 48 26N 123 29W
Comber, *Ont.* 14 E4 42 14N 82 33W
Combermere, *Ont.* 15 B9 45 22N 77 37W
Come by Chance, *Nfld.* 7 F7 47 51N 54 0W
Commanda, *Ont.* 14 B7 45 57N 79 36W
Commissaires, L. des, *Qué.* 11 C10 48 10N 72 16W
Commissioner I., *Man.* 21 C13 52 10N 97 16W
Committee B., *N.W.T.* 27 C7 68 30N 86 30W
Como-Est, *Qué.* 12 B2 45 27N 74 7W
Comox, *B.C.* 24 F10 49 42N 124 55W
Compeer, *Alta.* 23 G10 51 52N 110 0W
Compton, *Qué.* 11 F11 45 14N 71 49W
Conception, La, *Qué.* 10 E8 46 9N 74 42W
Conception B., *Nfld.* 7 F8 47 45N 53 0W
Conche, *Nfld.* 7 C5 50 55N 55 58W
Concord, *Ont.* 28 B3 43 48N 79 29W
Conestogo, *Ont.* 13 A2 43 32N 80 30W
Congnarauya, *Qué.* 6 B4 58 35N 68 1W
Coniston, *Ont.* 14 A6 46 29N 80 51W
Conklin, *Alta.* 22 C9 55 38N 111 5W
Connors, *N.B.* 11 D14 47 10N 68 52W
Conquest, *Sask.* 20 D3 51 32N 107 14W
Consecon, *Ont.* 15 D9 44 0N 77 31W
Consort, *Alta.* 23 F10 52 1N 110 46W
Consul, *Sask.* 20 F1 49 20N 109 30W
Contin L., *Man.* 21 B15 53 25N 95 10W
Contrecoeur, *Qué.* 12 A4 45 51N 73 14W
Contwoyto L., *N.W.T.* 26 C4 65 42N 110 50W
Cooking L., *Alta.* 22 E7 53 26N 113 2W
Cook's Harbour, *Nfld.* 7 B5 51 36N 55 52W
Cookshire, *Qué.* 11 F11 45 25N 71 38W
Cooksville, *Ont.* 28 C2 43 36N 79 35W
Coombs, *B.C.* 24 F10 49 18N 124 25W
Copetown, *Ont.* 13 B2 43 14N 80 4W
Copp L., *N.W.T.* 18 A6 60 14N 114 40W
Copper Cliff, *Ont.* 14 A5 46 28N 81 4W
Coppermine, *N.W.T.* 26 C4 67 50N 115 5W
Coppermine →, *N.W.T.* 26 C4 67 49N 116 4W
Coquitlam L., *B.C.* 32 A4 49 23N 122 48W
Coral Harbour, *N.W.T.* 27 C7 64 8N 83 10W
Corbin, *Qué.* 12 B3 45 3N 73 41W
Cormack, *Nfld.* 7 D3 49 18N 57 23W
Cormack L., *N.W.T.* 18 A4 60 56N 121 37W
Cormorant, *Man.* 21 A10 54 14N 100 35W
Cormorant L., *Man.* 21 A10 54 15N 100 50W
Corner Brook, *Nfld.* 7 E3 48 57N 57 58W
Corning, *Sask.* 20 F8 49 58N 102 58W
Cornwall, *Ont.* 15 B12 45 2N 74 44W
Cornwall, *P.E.I.* 9 G6 46 14N 63 13W
Cornwall I., *N.W.T.* 27 B6 77 37N 94 38W
Cornwallis I., *N.W.T.* 27 B6 75 8N 95 0W
Coronach, *Sask.* 20 F5 49 7N 105 31W
Coronation, *Alta.* 23 F9 52 5N 111 27W
Coronation G., *N.W.T.* 26 C5 68 25N 110 0W
Corunna, *Ont.* 14 E4 42 53N 82 26W
Corvette, L. de la, *Qué.* 6 C3 53 25N 74 3W
Corwhin, *Ont.* 13 A2 43 31N 80 4W
Costebelle, L., *Qué.* 8 C7 50 19N 62 23W
Côte-St-Luc, *Qué.* 29 C4 45 28N 73 40W
Coteau Landing, *Qué.* 12 B2 45 15N 74 13W
Cottam, *Ont.* 14 E4 42 8N 82 45W
Coudres, Île aux, *Qué.* 11 D12 47 24N 70 23W
Coulonge →, *Qué.* 10 F6 45 52N 76 46W
Coupeaux, L., *Qué.* 8 B6 51 27N 63 58W
Courtenay, *B.C.* 24 F10 49 45N 125 0W
Courtice, *Ont.* 13 A5 43 55N 78 46W
Courtland, *Ont.* 14 E6 42 51N 80 38W
Courtright, *Ont.* 14 E4 42 49N 82 28W
Courville, *Qué.* 30 A3 46 53N 71 10W
Coutts, *Alta.* 23 J9 49 0N 111 57W
Couture, L., *Qué.* 6 A2 60 7N 75 20W
Cove I., *Ont.* 14 B5 45 17N 81 44W
Coventry L., *N.W.T.* 19 A7 61 15N 106 15W
Covey Hill, *Qué.* 12 B3 45 1N 73 46W
Cow Head, *Nfld.* 7 D3 49 55N 57 48W
Cowan, *Man.* 21 C10 52 5N 100 45W
Cowan L., *Sask.* 20 B3 54 0N 107 15W
Cowansville, *Qué.* 12 B5 45 14N 72 46W
Cowichan L., *B.C.* 24 G10 48 53N 124 17W
Cowley, *Alta.* 23 I6 49 34N 114 5W
Cox I., *B.C.* 24 E6 50 48N 128 36W
Cox's Cove, *Nfld.* 7 D2 49 7N 58 5W
Crabtree, *Qué.* 12 A4 45 58N 73 28W
Cracroft Is., *B.C.* 24 E8 50 32N 126 25W
Craigflower, *B.C.* 25 H19 48 27N 123 26W
Craigmyle, *Alta.* 23 G8 51 40N 112 15W
Craik, *Sask.* 20 D5 51 3N 105 49W
Cranberry Portage, *Man.* 19 C8 54 35N 101 23W
Cranbrook, *B.C.* 23 I5 49 30N 115 46W
Crane I., *Qué.* 11 D12 47 4N 70 33W

Crane L., *Sask.* **20 E1** 50 5N 109 5W
Crane River, *Man.* **21 D11** 51 30N 99 14W
Crapaud, *P.E.I.* **9 G6** 46 14N 63 30W
Crauford, C., *N.W.T.* **27 B7** 73 44N 84 51W
Craven, *Sask.* **20 E6** 50 42N 104 49W
Craven, L., *Qué.* **6 C2** 54 20N 76 56W
Crean L., *Sask.* **20 A4** 54 5N 106 9W
Credit →, *Ont.* **28 C2** 43 33N 79 35W
Crediton, *Ont.* **14 D5** 43 17N 81 33W
Cree →, *Sask.* **19 B7** 58 57N 105 47W
Cree L., *Sask.* **19 B7** 57 30N 106 30W
Creelman, *Sask.* **20 F7** 49 49N 103 18W
Creemore, *Ont.* **14 C6** 44 19N 80 6W
Cremona, *Alta.* **23 G6** 51 33N 114 29W
Crescent Beach, *B.C.* **32 C3** 49 3N 122 53W
Crescent Spur, *B.C.* **25 B14** 53 34N 120 42W
Creston, *B.C.* **23 I4** 49 10N 116 31W
Crete, La, *Alta.* **18 B5** 58 11N 116 24W
Crimson Lake, *Alta.* **23 F5** 52 27N 115 2W
Crimson Lake Prov. Park, *Alta.* **23 F6** 52 28N 114 54W
Crofton, *B.C.* **25 G11** 48 52N 123 38W
Croix, La, L., *Ont.* **16 D4** 48 20N 92 15W
Croker, C., *Ont.* **14 C6** 44 58N 80 59W
Cromarty, *Man.* **19 B10** 58 3N 94 9W
Cromer, *Man.* **21 F9** 49 44N 101 14W
Crooked →, *B.C.* **18 C4** 54 50N 122 54W
Crooked L., *Nfld.* **7 E4** 48 24N 56 17W
Crooked River, *Sask.* **20 C7** 52 51N 103 44W
Cross Creek, *N.B.* **9 G3** 46 19N 66 43W
Cross L., *Man.* **19 C9** 54 45N 97 30W
Crossfield, *Alta.* **23 G7** 51 25N 114 0W
Crow →, *B.C.* **18 B4** 59 41N 124 20W
Crowsnest Pass, *Alta.-B.C.* **23 I6** 49 40N 114 40W
Cry L., *B.C.* **18 B3** 58 45N 129 0W
Crystal Bay, *Ont.* **30 D6** 45 22N 75 51W
Crystal City, *Man.* **21 F12** 49 9N 98 57W
Cudworth, *Sask.* **20 C5** 52 30N 105 44W
Cumberland, *B.C.* **24 F10** 49 40N 125 0W
Cumberland, *Ont.* **15 B11** 45 29N 75 24W
Cumberland House, *Sask.* **21 B8** 53 58N 102 16W
Cumberland L., *Sask.* **21 A8** 54 3N 102 18W
Cumberland Pen., *N.W.T.* **27 C9** 67 0N 64 0W
Cumberland Sd., *N.W.T.* **27 C9** 65 30N 66 0W
Cumnock, *Ont.* **13 A2** 43 46N 80 27W
Cumshewa Inlet, *B.C.* **24 B3** 53 3N 131 50W
Cupar, *Sask.* **20 E6** 50 57N 104 10W
Cushing, *Qué.* **12 A2** 45 36N 74 28W
Cushing, Mt., *B.C.* **18 B3** 57 35N 126 57W
Cusson, Pte., *Qué.* **6 A2** 60 23N 77 46W
Cut Knife, *Sask.* **20 C1** 52 45N 109 1W
Cutbank, *Sask.* **20 D4** 51 18N 106 51W
Cutbank →, *Alta.* **22 D2** 54 43N 118 32W
Cynthia, *Alta.* **22 E5** 53 17N 115 25W
Cypress Hills, *Sask.* **19 D7** 49 40N 109 30W
Cypress Hills Prov. Park, *Sask.* **20 F1** 49 40N 109 30W
Cypress River, *Man.* **21 F11** 49 34N 99 5W
Cyrville, *Ont.* **30 D8** 45 25N 75 38W
Czar, *Alta.* **23 F10** 52 27N 110 50W

D

Dalesville, *Qué.* **12 A2** 45 42N 74 24W
Dalhousie, *N.B.* **9 E3** 48 5N 66 26W
Dalhousie East, *N.S.* **9 I5** 44 43N 64 48W
Dalhousie Station, *Qué.* **12 B2** 45 18N 74 27W
Dalhousie West, *N.S.* **9 I4** 44 43N 65 13W
Dalkeith, *Qué.* **12 B1** 45 27N 74 32W
Dalles, Les, *Qué.* **12 A3** 45 59N 73 31W
Dalmeny, *Sask.* **20 C4** 52 20N 106 46W
Dalton, *Ont.* **17 D12** 48 11N 84 1W
Daly L., *Sask.* **19 B7** 56 32N 105 39W
Damascus, *Ont.* **13 A2** 43 55N 80 29W
Dana, L., *Qué.* **6 C2** 50 53N 77 20W
Danforth, *Ont.* **28 B4** 43 43N 79 15W
Daniel's Harbour, *Nfld.* **7 C3** 50 13N 57 35W
Danielson Prov. Park, *Sask.* **20 D4** 51 16N 106 50W
Danskin, *B.C.* **24 B9** 53 59N 125 47W
Dark Cove, *Nfld.* **7 E6** 48 47N 54 13W
Darnley B., *N.W.T.* **26 C3** 69 30N 123 30W
Dartmouth, *N.S.* **9 I6** 44 40N 63 30W
Dartmouth →, *Qué.* **8 E5** 48 53N 64 34W
Dasserat, L., *Qué.* **10 C3** 48 16N 79 25W
Daulnay, *N.B.* **9 F4** 47 25N 65 28W
Dauphin, *Man.* **21 D10** 51 9N 100 5W
Dauphin L., *Man.* **21 D11** 51 20N 99 45W
David →, *Qué.* **12 A5** 45 58N 72 54W
Davidson, *Sask.* **20 D5** 51 16N 105 59W
Davis Inlet, *Nfld.* **6 B5** 55 50N 60 59W
Davy L., *Sask.* **19 B7** 58 53N 108 18W
Dawson, *Yukon* **26 C2** 64 10N 139 30W
Dawson B., *Man.* **21 C10** 52 53N 100 49W
Dawson Creek, *B.C.* **18 B4** 55 45N 120 15W
Dawson Inlet, *N.W.T.* **19 A10** 61 50N 93 25W
Daysland, *Alta.* **23 F8** 52 50N 112 20W
De Beaujeu, *Qué.* **12 B2** 45 19N 74 20W
De Grau, *Nfld.* **7 E1** 48 29N 59 9W
De Léry, *Qué.* **29 D5** 45 15N 73 26W
De Morhiban, L., *Qué.* **8 B7** 51 50N 62 54W
Deacon, *Man.* **31 B4** 49 51N 96 56W
Deadwood L., *B.C.* **18 B3** 59 10N 128 30W
Dean →, *B.C.* **24 C8** 52 49N 126 58W
Dean Chan., *B.C.* **24 C7** 52 30N 127 15W
Dease →, *B.C.* **18 B3** 59 56N 128 32W
Dease Arm, *N.W.T.* **26 C4** 66 52N 119 37W
Dease L., *B.C.* **18 B2** 58 40N 130 5W
Dease Lake, *B.C.* **18 B2** 58 25N 130 6W
Debden, *Sask.* **20 B4** 53 30N 106 50W
Debec, *N.B.* **9 G2** 46 4N 67 41W
Debert, *N.S.* **9 H6** 45 26N 63 28W
Debolt, *Alta.* **22 C2** 55 12N 118 1W
Decelles, Rés., *Qué.* **10 D4** 47 42N 78 8W
Déception, Fjord, *Qué.* **6 A3** 62 8N 74 41W
Deception L., *Sask.* **19 B8** 56 33N 104 13W
Deep B., *N.W.T.* **18 A5** 61 15N 116 35W
Deep Cove, *B.C.* **32 A3** 49 20N 122 56W
Deer →, *Man.* **19 B10** 58 23N 94 13W
Deer, L., *Nfld.* **7 D3** 49 6N 57 35W
Deer Lake, *Nfld.* **7 D3** 49 11N 57 27W
Deer Lake, *Ont.* **19 C10** 52 36N 94 20W
Deer Pond, *Nfld.* **7 E6** 48 30N 54 45W
Dégelis, *Qué.* **11 D14** 47 30N 68 35W
Delaronde L., *Sask.* **20 A3** 54 3N 107 3W
Delburne, *Alta.* **23 F7** 52 12N 113 14W
Delhi, *Ont.* **14 E6** 42 51N 80 30W
Delia, *Alta.* **23 G8** 51 38N 112 23W
Delisle, *Sask.* **20 D3** 51 55N 107 8W
Deloraine, *Man.* **21 F10** 49 15N 100 29W
Delson, *Qué.* **29 C4** 45 22N 73 33W
Delta □, *B.C.* **32 C2** 49 7N 123 0W
Delta Beach, *Man.* **21 E12** 50 11N 98 19W
Denbigh, *Ont.* **15 B9** 45 8N 77 15W
Denman Island, *B.C.* **24 F10** 49 33N 124 48W
Denzil, *Sask.* **20 C1** 52 14N 109 39W
Departure Bay, *B.C.* **24 F11** 49 13N 123 57W
Deroche, *B.C.* **25 F12** 49 12N 122 4W
Derrynane, *Ont.* **13 A1** 43 56N 80 35W
Derwent, *Alta.* **22 E10** 53 41N 110 58W
Desbarats, *Ont.* **14 A3** 46 20N 83 56W
Desbiens, *Qué.* **11 C11** 48 25N 71 57W
Deschaillons, *Qué.* **11 E10** 46 32N 72 7W
Deschambault, *Qué.* **11 E11** 46 39N 71 56W
Descharme →, *Sask.* **19 B7** 56 51N 109 13W
Deschênes, *Qué.* **10 F7** 45 23N 75 48W
Deschênes, L., *Ont.* **30 D6** 45 22N 75 51W
Deseronto, *Ont.* **15 C9** 44 12N 77 3W
Deskenatlata L., *N.W.T.* **18 A6** 60 55N 112 3W
Desmarais, *Alta.* **22 C7** 55 56N 113 49W
Desmaraisville, *Qué.* **10 B6** 49 32N 76 9W
Desméloizes, *Qué.* **10 C3** 48 57N 79 29W
Desolation Sound Prov. Marine Park, *B.C.* **24 E10** 50 5N 124 25W
Destruction Bay, *N.W.T.* **26 C2** 61 15N 138 48W
Deux-Loutres, L. aux, *Qué.* **8 B7** 51 31N 62 28W
Deux Montagnes, *Qué.* **29 B2** 45 32N 73 53W
Deux Montagnes □, *Qué.* **29 B2** 45 40N 74 0W
Deux Montagnes, Lac des, *Qué.* **29 C2** 45 28N 73 59W
Devastation Chan., *B.C.* **24 B6** 53 40N 128 50W
Devenyns, L., *Qué.* **11 D9** 47 5N 73 50W
Devils Paw, *B.C.* **18 B2** 58 47N 134 0W
Devon, *Alta.* **22 E7** 53 24N 113 44W
Devon I., *N.W.T.* **27 B7** 75 10N 85 0W
Dewberry, *Alta.* **22 E10** 53 35N 110 32W
Dewittville, *Qué.* **12 B2** 45 7N 74 5W
Dezadeash L., *Yukon* **18 A1** 60 28N 136 58W
Diamond City, *Alta.* **23 I8** 49 48N 112 51W
Diana B., *Qué.* **6 A4** 61 20N 70 0W
Didsbury, *Alta.* **23 G6** 51 35N 114 10W
Diefenbaker L., *Sask.* **19 C7** 51 0N 106 55W
Dieppe, *N.B.* **9 G5** 46 6N 64 45W
Digby, *N.S.* **9 I4** 44 38N 65 50W
Digby Neck, *N.S.* **9 I3** 44 30N 66 5W
Digges, *Man.* **19 B10** 58 40N 94 0W
Digges Is., *N.W.T.* **6 A2** 62 40N 77 50W
Dildo, *Nfld.* **7 F7** 47 34N 53 33W
Dilke, *Sask.* **20 E5** 50 52N 105 15W
Dillon, *Sask.* **19 B7** 55 56N 108 35W
Dillon →, *Sask.* **19 B7** 55 56N 108 56W
Dingwall, *N.S.* **9 G9** 46 54N 60 28W
Dinorwic, *Ont.* **16 C4** 49 41N 92 30W
Dinorwic L., *Ont.* **16 C4** 49 37N 92 33W
Dinosaur Prov. Park, *Alta.* **23 H9** 50 47N 111 30W
Dinsmore, *Sask.* **20 D3** 51 20N 107 26W
Dionne, L., *Qué.* **8 D2** 49 26N 67 55W
Disraëli, *Qué.* **11 F11** 45 54N 71 21W
Dixonville, *Alta.* **22 B3** 56 32N 117 40W
Dixville, *Qué.* **11 F11** 45 4N 71 46W
Doaktown, *N.B.* **9 G3** 46 33N 66 8W
Dobie →, *Ont.* **16 A6** 51 41N 90 29W
Dodge L., *Sask.* **19 B7** 59 50N 105 36W
Dodsland, *Sask.* **20 D2** 51 50N 108 45W
Dog →, *Ont.* **16 D7** 48 32N 89 39W
Dog Creek, *B.C.* **25 D12** 51 35N 122 14W
Dog L., *Man.* **21 D12** 51 2N 98 31W
Dog L., *Ont.* **16 D7** 48 48N 89 30W
Dog L., *Ont.* **17 D12** 48 17N 84 8W
Doig →, *B.C.* **18 B4** 56 25N 120 40W
Dolbeau, *Qué.* **11 C10** 48 53N 72 18W
Dollard, *Sask.* **20 F2** 49 37N 108 35W
Dollard-des-Ormeaux, *Qué.* **29 C3** 45 29N 73 49W
Dollarton, *B.C.* **32 B3** 49 18N 122 57W
Dolphin and Union Str., *N.W.T.* **26 C4** 69 5N 114 45W
Dome Creek, *B.C.* **25 B13** 53 44N 121 1W
Dominion, *N.S.* **9 G9** 46 13N 60 1W
Dominion, C., *N.W.T.* **27 C8** 65 30N 74 28W
Dominion City, *Man.* **21 F13** 49 9N 97 9W
Dominion L., *Nfld.* **8 A8** 52 40N 61 45W
Don →, *Ont.* **28 C3** 43 39N 79 21W
Don Mills, *Ont.* **28 B3** 43 42N 79 21W
Don Pen., *B.C.* **24 C6** 52 25N 128 12W
Donald, *B.C.* **25 D17** 51 29N 117 10W
Donalda, *Alta.* **23 F8** 52 35N 112 34W
Donan, *Man.* **31 B3** 49 57N 97 6W
Donkin, *N.S.* **9 G10** 46 11N 59 52W
Donnaconna, *Qué.* **11 E11** 46 41N 71 41W
Donnelly, *Alta.* **22 C3** 55 44N 117 6W
Donovans, *Nfld.* **7 H7** 47 32N 52 50W
Doran L., *N.W.T.* **19 A7** 61 13N 108 6W
Dorchester, *N.B.* **9 H5** 45 54N 64 31W
Dorchester, C., *N.W.T.* **27 C8** 65 27N 77 27W
Dorchester Crossing, *N.B.* **9 G5** 46 10N 64 34W
Doré, L. Le = Lillian L., *Qué.* **8 B8** 51 17N 61 23W
Doré L., *Sask.* **19 C7** 54 46N 107 17W
Doré Lake, *Sask.* **19 C7** 54 38N 107 36W
Dorion, *Ont.* **16 D8** 48 47N 88 39W
Dorion, *Qué.* **11 F8** 45 23N 74 3W
Dorset, *Ont.* **10 F4** 45 14N 78 54W
Dorval, *Qué.* **29 C3** 45 27N 73 44W
Dorval Airport, *Qué.* **29 C3** 45 28N 73 44W
Dosquet, *Qué.* **11 E11** 46 28N 71 32W
Doting Cove, *Nfld.* **7 D7** 49 27N 53 57W
Douglas, *Ont.* **15 B10** 45 31N 76 56W
Douglas Chan., *B.C.* **24 B5** 53 40N 129 20W
Douglas I., *B.C.* **32 B4** 49 13N 122 47W
Douglas Pt., *Ont.* **14 C5** 44 19N 81 37W
Douglas Prov. Park, *Sask.* **20 D4** 51 3N 106 28W
Douglastown, *N.B.* **8 E5** 48 46N 64 24W
Douglastown, *N.B.* **9 F4** 47 1N 65 30W
Dowager I., *B.C.* **24 C6** 52 25N 128 22W
Downeys, *Ont.* **13 B2** 43 29N 80 14W
Downsview, *Ont.* **28 B3** 43 43N 79 29W
Downton, Mt., *B.C.* **24 C10** 52 42N 124 52W
Doyles, *Nfld.* **7 F1** 47 50N 59 12W
Dozois, Rés., *Qué.* **10 D5** 47 30N 77 5W
Dragon, *Qué.* **12 B2** 45 29N 74 16W
Drake, *Sask.* **20 D5** 51 45N 105 1W
Drayton, *Ont.* **14 D6** 43 46N 80 40W
Drayton Valley, *Alta.* **22 E6** 53 12N 114 58W
Dresden, *Ont.* **14 E4** 42 35N 82 11W
Drinkwater, *Sask.* **20 E5** 50 18N 105 8W
Drocourt, *Ont.* **14 B6** 45 46N 80 21W
Drowning →, *Ont.* **17 B12** 50 54N 84 34W
Drumbo, *Ont.* **13 B1** 43 16N 80 35W
Drumheller, *Alta.* **23 G8** 51 25N 112 40W
Drummond, *N.B.* **9 F2** 47 2N 67 41W
Drummondville, *Qué.* **11 F10** 45 55N 72 25W
Drumquin, *Ont.* **13 A3** 43 32N 79 47W
Dryberry L., *Ont.* **16 C3** 49 33N 93 53W
Dryden, *Ont.* **16 C4** 49 47N 92 50W
Du Gué →, *Qué.* **6 B3** 57 21N 70 45W
Dubawnt →, *N.W.T.* **19 A8** 64 33N 100 6W
Dubawnt, L., *N.W.T.* **19 A8** 63 4N 101 42W
Duberger, *Qué.* **30 B3** 46 49N 71 18W
Dubreuilville, *Ont.* **17 D12** 48 21N 84 32W
Dubuc, *Sask.* **21 E8** 50 41N 102 28W
Duchess, *Alta.* **23 H9** 50 43N 111 55W
Duck Bay, *Man.* **21 C10** 52 10N 100 9W
Duck Lake, *Sask.* **20 C4** 52 50N 106 16W
Duck Mountain Prov. Parks, *Man.* **21 D10** 51 45N 101 0W
Dufferin □, *Ont.* **13 A2** 43 55N 80 15W
Duffin →, *Ont.* **28 B5** 43 49N 79 2W
Dufrost, Pte., *Qué.* **6 A2** 60 4N 77 39W
Dugald, *Man.* **31 B4** 49 53N 96 51W
Dumbell L., *Nfld.* **8 A4** 52 28N 65 45W
Dumoine →, *Qué.* **10 E5** 46 13N 77 51W
Dumoine L., *Qué.* **10 E5** 46 55N 77 55W
Dunbarton, *Ont.* **28 B5** 43 50N 79 7W
Duncan, *B.C.* **25 G11** 48 45N 123 40W
Duncan, L., *Qué.* **6 C2** 53 29N 77 58W
Duncan Dam, *B.C.* **25 E18** 50 15N 116 56W
Duncan L., *B.C.* **18 A6** 62 51N 113 58W
Dunchurch, *Ont.* **14 B7** 45 39N 79 51W
Dundalk, *Ont.* **14 C6** 44 10N 80 24W
Dundarave, *B.C.* **32 B1** 49 20N 123 10W
Dundas, *Ont.* **14 D7** 43 17N 79 59W
Dundas I., *B.C.* **18 C2** 54 30N 130 50W
Dundas Pen., *N.W.T.* **26 B4** 74 50N 111 36W
Dundee, *Qué.* **12 C2** 45 0N 74 30W
Dundurn, *Sask.* **20 D4** 51 49N 106 30W
Dundurn Camp, *Sask.* **20 D4** 51 51N 106 34W
Dunedin →, *B.C.* **18 B4** 59 30N 124 5W
Dungannon, *Ont.* **14 D5** 43 51N 81 36W
Dungarvon →, *N.B.* **9 G4** 46 49N 65 54W
Dunham, *Qué.* **12 B5** 45 8N 72 48W
Dunière, Parc Prov. de, *Qué.* **8 E3** 48 45N 66 41W
Dunkley, *B.C.* **25 B12** 53 17N 122 28W
Dunmore, *Alta.* **23 I10** 49 58N 110 36W
Dunnville, *Ont.* **14 E7** 42 54N 79 36W
Dunrankin →, *Ont.* **17 D14** 48 47N 82 51W
Dunster, *B.C.* **25 B15** 53 8N 119 50W
Dunvegan, *Alta.* **22 C2** 55 55N 118 36W
Dunvegan L., *N.W.T.* **19 A7** 60 8N 107 10W
Dunville, *Nfld.* **7 F7** 47 16N 53 54W
Duparquet, *Qué.* **10 C3** 48 30N 79 14W
Duparquet, L., *Qué.* **10 C3** 48 28N 79 16W
Dupuy, *Qué.* **10 C3** 48 50N 79 21W
Durham, *Ont.* **14 C6** 44 10N 80 49W
Durham □, *Ont.* **13 A4** 43 57N 79 5W
Durham Bridge, *N.B.* **9 G3** 46 7N 66 36W
Durocher, L., *Qué.* **8 C8** 50 52N 61 12W
Dusey →, *Ont.* **17 A10** 51 11N 86 21W
Dutton, *Ont.* **14 E5** 42 39N 81 30W
Duval, *Sask.* **20 D6** 51 9N 104 59W
Duvernay, *Qué.* **29 B4** 45 35N 73 40W
Dwight, *Ont.* **10 F3** 45 20N 79 1W
Dyment, *Ont.* **16 C4** 49 37N 92 18W
Dysart, *Sask.* **20 E6** 50 57N 104 2W

E

Eabamet, L., *Ont.* **17 A9** 51 30N 87 46W
Eagle →, *Nfld.* **6 C6** 53 36N 57 26W
Eagle Cr. →, *Sask.* **20 C3** 52 20N 107 30W
Eagle Harbour, *B.C.* **32 A1** 49 22N 123 16W
Eagle I., *Man.* **21 B12** 53 40N 98 55W
Eagle L., *B.C.* **24 D10** 51 55N 124 23W
Eagle L., *Ont.* **16 C3** 49 42N 93 13W
Eagle Lake, *Ont.* **15 B8** 45 8N 78 29W
Eagle River, *Ont.* **16 C3** 49 47N 93 12W
Eaglehead L., *Ont.* **16 C7** 49 2N 89 12W
Eaglesham, *Alta.* **22 C3** 55 47N 117 53W
Ear Falls, *Ont.* **16 B3** 50 38N 93 13W
Earl Grey, *Sask.* **20 E6** 50 57N 104 43W
Earls Cove, *B.C.* **24 F11** 49 45N 124 0W
Earltown, *N.S.* **9 H6** 45 35N 63 8W
East Angus, *Qué.* **11 F11** 45 30N 71 40W
East Bay, *N.S.* **9 G9** 46 1N 60 25W
East Broughton Station, *Qué.* **11 E11** 46 14N 71 5W
East Chezzetcook, *N.S.* **9 I6** 44 43N 63 14W
East Coulee, *Alta.* **23 G8** 51 23N 112 27W
East Don →, *Ont.* **28 C3** 43 39N 79 21W
East Farnham, *Qué.* **12 B5** 45 14N 72 46W
East Humber →, *Ont.* **28 B2** 43 48N 79 35W
East Kildonan, *Man.* **31 B3** 49 55N 97 5W
East Main = Eastmain, *Qué.* **6 C2** 52 10N 78 30W
East Pine, *B.C.* **18 B4** 55 48N 120 12W
East Pt., *P.E.I.* **9 G8** 46 27N 61 58W
East Thurlow I., *B.C.* **24 E9** 50 24N 125 25W
East Trout L., *Sask.* **20 A5** 54 22N 105 5W
East York, *Ont.* **28 B4** 43 42N 79 20W
Eastcap Cr. →, *B.C.* **32 A2** 49 27N 123 6W
Eastend, *Sask.* **20 F2** 49 32N 108 50W
Eastern Passage, *N.S.* **9 L12** 44 37N 63 30W
Easterville, *Man.* **21 B11** 53 8N 99 49W
Eastmain, *Qué.* **6 C2** 52 10N 78 30W
Eastmain →, *Qué.* **6 C2** 52 27N 78 26W
Eastman, *Qué.* **11 F10** 45 18N 72 19W
Eatonia, *Sask.* **20 D1** 51 13N 109 25W
Eatonville, *Qué.* **11 D13** 47 20N 69 41W
Eau-Claire, L. à l', *Nfld.* **8 A4** 52 36N 65 50W
Eau Claire, L. à l', *Qué.* **6 B3** 56 10N 74 25W
Eboulements, Les, *Qué.* **11 D12** 47 28N 70 21W
Echo Bay, *N.W.T.* **26 C4** 66 5N 117 55W
Echo Bay, *Ont.* **14 A2** 46 29N 84 4W
Echoing →, *Man.* **19 B10** 55 51N 92 5W
Échouani, L., *Qué.* **10 D7** 47 46N 75 42W
Eckville, *Alta.* **23 F6** 52 21N 114 22W
Eclipse Sd., *N.W.T.* **27 B8** 72 38N 79 0W
Écorce, L. de l', *Qué.* **10 D6** 47 5N 76 24W
Ecorces, L. des, *Qué.* **12 A1** 46 0N 74 32W
Ecueils, Pte. aux, *Qué.* **6 B2** 59 47N 77 50W
Ecum Secum, *N.S.* **9 I7** 44 58N 62 8W
Edam, *Sask.* **20 B2** 53 11N 108 46W
Edberg, *Alta.* **23 F8** 52 47N 112 47W
Edehon L., *N.W.T.* **19 A9** 60 25N 97 15W
Eden, *Man.* **21 E11** 50 23N 99 28W
Eden L., *Man.* **19 B8** 56 38N 100 15W
Eden Mills, *Ont.* **13 A2** 43 35N 80 9W
Edgeley, *Ont.* **28 B2** 43 48N 79 31W
Edgerton, *Alta.* **23 F10** 52 45N 110 27W
Edgewater, *B.C.* **23 H4** 50 42N 116 5W
Edgewood, *B.C.* **25 F16** 49 47N 118 8W
Edmonds, *B.C.* **32 B3** 49 13N 122 57W
Edmonton, *Alta.* **31 D6** 53 30N 113 30W
Edmund L., *Man.* **19 C10** 54 45N 93 17W
Edmundston, *N.B.* **9 F1** 47 23N 68 20W
Edson, *Alta.* **22 E4** 53 35N 116 28W
Edward I., *Ont.* **16 D8** 48 22N 88 37W
Edzo, *N.W.T.* **18 A5** 62 49N 116 4W
Eel River Crossing, *N.B.* **9 E3** 48 1N 66 25W
Eganville, *Ont.* **15 B9** 45 32N 77 5W
Egenolf L., *Man.* **19 B9** 59 3N 100 0W
Egg L., *Sask.* **19 B7** 55 5N 105 30W
Eglington I., *N.W.T.* **26 B4** 75 48N 118 30W
Egmont, *B.C.* **24 F11** 49 45N 123 56W
Egmont B., *P.E.I.* **9 G5** 46 29N 64 6W
Eholt, *B.C.* **25 F16** 49 10N 118 34W
Eileen L., *N.W.T.* **19 A7** 62 16N 107 37W
Ekwan →, *Ont.* **4 B3** 53 12N 82 15W
Ekwan Pt., *Ont.* **4 B3** 53 16N 82 7W
Elaho →, *B.C.* **24 E11** 50 7N 123 23W
Elbow, *Sask.* **20 D4** 51 7N 106 35W
Elbow →, *Alta.* **31 F10** 51 3N 114 2W
Eldorado, *Ont.* **15 C9** 44 35N 77 31W
Eldorado, *Sask.* **19 B7** 59 35N 108 30W
Eldorado Park, *Ont.* **28 C1** 43 39N 79 46W
Elfrida, *Ont.* **30 D10** 43 10N 79 47W
Elgin, *B.C.* **32 C4** 49 4N 122 49W
Elgin, *Man.* **21 F10** 49 27N 100 16W
Elgin, *N.B.* **5 C6** 45 48N 65 10W
Elgin, *Ont.* **15 C10** 44 36N 76 13W
Elk →, *B.C.* **23 I5** 49 11N 115 14W
Elk Island Nat. Park, *Alta.* **22 E8** 53 35N 112 59W
Elk Lake, *Ont.* **10 D2** 47 40N 80 25W
Elk Lakes Prov. Park, *B.C.* **23 H5** 50 30N 115 10W
Elk Point, *Alta.* **22 E10** 53 54N 110 55W
Elkford, *B.C.* **23 I6** 49 52N 114 53W
Elkhorn, *Man.* **21 F9** 49 59N 101 14W
Elko, *B.C.* **23 I5** 49 20N 115 10W
Ellef Ringnes I., *N.W.T.* **27 B5** 78 30N 102 2W
Ellerslie, *Alta.* **31 E7** 53 26N 113 30W
Ellesmere I., *N.W.T.* **27 B8** 79 30N 80 0W
Elliot L., *Man.* **21 C15** 52 54N 95 18W
Elliot Lake, *Ont.* **14 A4** 46 25N 82 35W
Elliston, *Nfld.* **7 E7** 48 38N 53 3W
Ells →, *Alta.* **22 A9** 57 18N 111 40W
Elm Grove, *Man.* **31 C5** 49 47N 96 49W
Elma, *Man.* **21 F15** 49 52N 95 55W
Elmira, *Ont.* **13 A1** 43 36N 80 33W
Elmsdale, *N.S.* **9 I6** 44 58N 63 30W
Elmvale, *Ont.* **14 C7** 44 35N 79 52W
Elmworth, *Alta.* **22 C1** 55 3N 119 37W
Elnora, *Alta.* **23 G7** 51 59N 113 12W
Elora, *Ont.* **13 A2** 43 41N 80 26W
Elphin, *Ont.* **15 C10** 44 55N 76 37W
Elphinstone, *Man.* **21 E10** 50 32N 100 30W
Elrose, *Sask.* **20 D3** 51 12N 108 0W
Elsa, *N.W.T.* **26 C2** 63 55N 135 29W
Elsas, *Ont.* **17 D14** 48 32N 82 55W
Elsona, *B.C.* **32 B3** 49 12N 122 57W
Embarras Portage, *Alta.* **19 B6** 58 27N 111 28W
Embro, *Ont.* **14 D6** 43 9N 80 54W
Emeril, *Qué.* **6 D2** 47 26N 75 47W
Emerson, *Man.* **21 F13** 49 0N 97 10W
Emo, *Ont.* **16 D3** 48 38N 93 50W
Empress, *Alta.* **23 H10** 50 57N 110 0W
Emsdale, *Ont.* **10 F3** 45 32N 79 19W
Endako, *B.C.* **24 A9** 54 6N 125 2W
Endeavour, *Sask.* **20 C8** 52 10N 102 39W
Enderby, *B.C.* **25 E15** 50 35N 119 10W
Enfield, *N.S.* **9 I6** 44 56N 63 32W
Engemann L., *Sask.* **19 B7** 58 0N 106 55W
Englee, *Nfld.* **7 C4** 50 45N 56 5W
Englefeld, *Sask.* **20 C6** 52 10N 104 39W
Englefield, C., *N.W.T.* **27 C7** 69 49N 85 34W
Englehart, *Ont.* **10 D3** 47 49N 79 52W
Engler L., *Sask.* **19 B7** 59 8N 106 52W
English →, *Ont.* **16 C5** 49 12N 91 5W
English →, *Ont.* **19 C10** 50 35N 93 30W
English B., *B.C.* **32 B1** 49 17N 123 11W
English Harbour East, *Nfld.* **7 F6** 47 38N 54 54W
English River, *Ont.* **16 C6** 49 14N 91 0W
Enilda, *Alta.* **22 C4** 55 25N 116 18W
Ennadai, *N.W.T.* **19 A8** 61 8N 100 53W
Ennadai L., *N.W.T.* **19 A8** 61 0N 101 0W
Ennotville, *Ont.* **13 A2** 43 39N 80 20W
Enterprise, *N.W.T.* **18 A5** 60 47N 115 45W
Entiako L., *B.C.* **24 B9** 53 13N 125 31W
Epiphanie, L', *Qué.* **12 A4** 45 51N 73 29W
Eramosa, *Ont.* **13 A2** 43 37N 80 13W
Eric, *Qué.* **6 C4** 51 56N 65 45W
Eric L., *Qué.* **8 B4** 51 55N 65 36W
Erie, L., *Ont.* **14 E6** 42 15N 81 0W
Erieau, *Ont.* **14 E5** 42 16N 81 57W
Eriksdale, *Man.* **21 E12** 50 52N 98 7W
Erin, *Ont.* **13 A2** 43 45N 80 7W
Erindale, *Ont.* **28 C2** 43 32N 79 39W
Erlandson, L., *Qué.* **6 B4** 57 3N 68 28W
Erskine, *Alta.* **23 F8** 52 20N 112 53W
Escoumins, Les, *Qué.* **11 C13** 48 21N 69 24W
Esker, *Nfld.* **6 C4** 53 53N 66 25W
Eskimo Lakes, *N.W.T.* **26 C2** 69 15N 132 17W
Eskimo Pt., *N.W.T.* **19 A10** 61 10N 94 15W
Esnagami L., *Ont.* **17 B10** 50 19N 86 51W
Esnagi L., *Ont.* **17 D12** 48 36N 84 33W
Espanola, *Ont.* **14 A5** 46 15N 81 46W
Esperanza, *B.C.* **24 F8** 49 52N 126 43W
Esperanza Inlet, *B.C.* **24 F8** 49 51N 126 55W

Esquimalt, B.C. **25 H19** 48 26N 123 25W
Essex, Ont. **14 E4** 42 10N 82 49W
Essondale, B.C. **32 B4** 49 14N 122 48W
Est, Î. de l', Qué. **9 F8** 47 37N 61 23W
Estcourt, Qué. **11 D13** 47 28N 69 14W
Esterhazy, Sask. **21 E8** 50 37N 102 5W
Estevan, Sask. **20 F8** 49 10N 102 59W
Estevan Group, B.C. **24 B5** 53 3N 129 38W
Estevan Sd., B.C. **24 B5** 53 5N 129 34W
Eston, Sask. **20 D2** 51 8N 108 40W
Étamamu, Qué. **8 C10** 50 18N 59 59W
Étang-du-Nord, Qué. **9 F8** 47 22N 61 57W
Etawney L., Man. **19 B9** 57 50N 96 50W
Etchemin →, Qué. **30 B3** 46 46N 71 14W
Ethelbert, Man. **21 D10** 51 32N 100 25W
Etobicoke, Ont. **28 B2** 43 42N 79 34W
Etobicoke Cr. →, Ont. **28 C2** 43 35N 79 32W
Étroits, Les, Qué. **11 D14** 47 24N 68 54W
Etzikom, Alta. **23 I9** 49 29N 111 6W
Eudistes, L. des, Qué. **8 C4** 50 30N 65 13W
Eureka, N.W.T. **27 B7** 80 0N 85 56W
Eureka River, Alta. **22 B2** 56 27N 118 44W
Eutsuk L., B.C. **24 B8** 53 20N 126 45W
Évain, Qué. **10 C3** 48 14N 79 8W
Evans L., Qué. **6 C2** 50 50N 77 0W
Evansburg, Alta. **22 E6** 53 36N 114 59W
Everett Mts., N.W.T. **27 C9** 62 45N 67 12W
Everton, Ont. **13 A2** 43 40N 80 9W
Exeter, Ont. **14 D5** 43 21N 81 29W
Exploits, B. of, Nfld. **7 D6** 49 20N 55 0W
Exshaw, Alta. **23 G5** 51 3N 115 9W
Eyeberry L., N.W.T. **19 A8** 63 8N 104 43W
Eyebrow, Sask. **20 E4** 50 48N 106 9W
Eyehill Cr. →, Alta. **23 F10** 52 14N 110 0W

F

Fabre, Qué. **10 D3** 47 12N 79 22W
Fabreville, Qué. **29 B2** 45 34N 73 51W
Faillon, L., Qué. **10 C6** 48 21N 76 39W
Fair Harbour, B.C. **24 E7** 50 4N 127 10W
Fairfield Plain, Ont. **13 B2** 43 3N 80 24W
Fairford, Man. **21 D12** 51 37N 98 38W
Fairport, Ont. **28 B5** 43 49N 79 5W
Fairvale, N.B. **9 H4** 45 25N 66 0W
Fairview, Alta. **22 B2** 56 5N 118 25W
Fairview, N.S. **9 L11** 44 40N 63 38W
Falcon I., Ont. **16 C2** 49 23N 94 45W
Falconbridge, Ont. **14 A6** 46 35N 80 45W
Falher, Alta. **22 C3** 55 44N 117 15W
Falkland, Ont. **13 B2** 43 10N 80 26W
False Creek, B.C. **32 B2** 49 15N 123 8W
Family L., Man. **21 D15** 51 54N 95 27W
Fanny Bay, B.C. **24 F10** 49 37N 124 48W
Far Mt., B.C. **24 C9** 52 47N 125 20W
Faride, L., Qué. **8 C10** 50 58N 59 55W
Farmers Rapids, Ont. **30 D7** 45 30N 75 45W
Farnham, Qué. **12 B5** 45 17N 72 59W
Farnham Centre, Qué. **12 B5** 45 15N 72 50W
Faro, Yukon **26 C2** 62 11N 133 22W
Farrand, C., N.W.T. **27 B7** 71 45N 90 0W
Fatima, Qué. **9 F8** 47 24N 61 53W
Fauquier, B.C. **25 F16** 49 52N 118 5W
Fauquier, Ont. **17 C14** 49 18N 82 3W
Faust, Alta. **22 C5** 55 19N 115 38W
Favourable Lake, Ont. **4 B1** 52 50N 93 39W
Fawcett, Alta. **22 D6** 54 32N 114 5W
Fawn →, Ont. **4 A2** 55 20N 87 35W
Fenelon Falls, Ont. **15 C8** 44 32N 78 45W
Fenwick, Ont. **13 B4** 43 1N 79 22W
Fergus, Ont. **13 A2** 43 43N 80 24W
Ferintosh, Alta. **23 F8** 52 46N 112 58W
Ferland, Ont. **16 B8** 50 19N 88 27W
Ferland, Sask. **20 F4** 49 27N 106 57W
Ferme-Neuve, Qué. **10 E7** 46 42N 75 27W
Fernie, B.C. **23 I5** 49 30N 115 5W
Feronia, Ont. **14 A7** 46 22N 79 19W
Ferryland, Nfld. **7 F8** 47 2N 52 53W
Feuilles →, Qué. **6 B3** 58 47N 70 4W
Feuilles, B. aux, Qué. **6 B4** 58 55N 69 20W
Field, Ont. **14 A6** 46 31N 80 1W
Fife L., Sask. **20 F5** 49 14N 105 53W
File Axe, L., Qué. **11 A9** 50 18N 73 34W
Fillmore, Sask. **20 F7** 49 50N 103 25W
Fils, L. du, Qué. **10 E4** 46 37N 78 7W
Finch, Ont. **10 F7** 45 11N 75 7W
Findlater, Sask. **20 E5** 50 47N 105 24W
Finger L., Ont. **19 C10** 53 33N 93 30W
Finland, Ont. **16 D3** 48 51N 93 55W
Finlay →, B.C. **18 B3** 57 0N 125 10W
Finmark, Ont. **16 D7** 48 35N 89 45W
Fire River, Ont. **17 D13** 48 47N 83 21W
Firebag →, Alta. **22 A9** 57 45N 111 21W
Firedrake L., N.W.T. **19 A8** 61 25N 104 30W
First Narrows, B.C. **32 B2** 49 19N 123 8W
Firvale, B.C. **24 C8** 52 27N 126 13W
Fish Cr. →, Alta. **31 G10** 50 54N 114 1W
Fisher B., Man. **21 D13** 51 35N 97 13W
Fisher Bay, Man. **21 D13** 51 29N 97 18W
Fisher Branch, Man. **21 D13** 51 5N 97 13W
Fisher Str., N.W.T. **27 C7** 63 15N 83 30W
Fishing L., Man. **21 C15** 52 10N 95 24W
Fitz Hugh Sd., B.C. **24 D7** 51 40N 127 55W
Fitzgerald, Alta. **18 B6** 59 51N 111 36W
Fitzwilliam I., Ont. **14 B5** 45 30N 81 45W
Five Islands, N.S. **9 H5** 45 23N 64 6W
Flaherty I., N.W.T. **6 B2** 56 15N 79 15W
Flamboro Centre, Ont. **30 C9** 43 22N 79 56W
Flanders, Ont. **16 D4** 48 44N 92 5W
Flat →, N.W.T. **18 A3** 61 33N 125 18W
Flat Bay, Nfld. **7 E2** 48 24N 58 36W
Flat L., Alta. **22 D8** 54 38N 112 54W
Flatbush, Alta. **22 D6** 54 42N 114 9W
Flaxcombe, Sask. **20 D1** 51 29N 109 36W
Fleming, Sask. **21 E9** 50 4N 101 31W
Flesherton, Ont. **14 C6** 44 16N 80 33W
Fleur de Lys, Nfld. **7 C4** 50 7N 56 8W
Fleur-de-May, L., Nfld. **8 B4** 52 0N 65 5W
Flin Flon, Man. **19 C8** 54 46N 101 53W
Flint L., Ont. **17 C11** 49 52N 85 53W
Floradale, Ont. **13 A1** 43 37N 80 35W
Florence, N.S. **9 G9** 46 16N 60 16W
Flores I., B.C. **24 F8** 49 20N 126 10W
Flower Sta., Ont. **10 F6** 45 10N 76 41W
Flower's Cove, Nfld. **7 B4** 51 14N 56 46W
Foam Lake, Sask. **20 D7** 51 40N 103 32W
Fogo, Nfld. **7 D6** 49 43N 54 17W
Fogo, C., Nfld. **7 D7** 49 40N 54 0W
Fogo I., Nfld. **7 D6** 49 40N 54 5W
Foins, L. aux, Qué. **10 D4** 47 5N 78 11W
Foley I., N.W.T. **27 C8** 68 32N 75 5W
Foleyet, Ont. **17 D14** 48 15N 82 25W
Fond-du-Lac, Sask. **19 B7** 59 19N 107 12W
Fond-du-Lac →, Sask. **19 B7** 59 17N 106 0W
Fontaine, N.B. **9 G5** 46 51N 64 58W
Fontas →, B.C. **18 B4** 58 14N 121 48W
Fonteneau, L., Qué. **8 B8** 51 55N 61 30W
Foothills, Alta. **23 E4** 53 4N 116 47W
Fording, B.C. **23 H6** 50 12N 114 52W
Foremost, Alta. **23 I8** 49 26N 111 34W
Forest, Ont. **14 D5** 43 6N 82 0W
Forest Grove, B.C. **25 D13** 51 46N 121 5W
Forest Hill, Ont. **28 B3** 43 42N 79 25W
Forestburg, Alta. **23 F8** 52 35N 112 1W
Forestville, Qué. **11 C13** 48 48N 69 2W
Forget, Sask. **20 F8** 49 39N 102 52W
Forillon, Parc National, Qué. **8 E5** 48 46N 64 12W
Fork River, Man. **21 D10** 51 31N 100 1W
Forsythe, Qué. **10 C6** 48 14N 76 26W
Fort Albany, Ont. **4 B3** 52 15N 81 35W
Fort Assiniboine, Alta. **22 D6** 54 20N 114 45W
Fort Chipewyan, Alta. **19 B6** 58 42N 111 8W
Fort-Coulonge, Qué. **10 F6** 45 50N 76 45W
Fort Frances, Ont. **16 D3** 48 36N 93 24W
Fort Fraser, B.C. **24 A10** 54 4N 124 33W
Fort Garry, Man. **31 C3** 49 50N 97 9W
Fort George, Qué. **6 C2** 53 50N 79 0W
Fort Good-Hope, N.W.T. **26 C3** 66 14N 128 40W
Fort Hope, Ont. **17 A9** 51 30N 88 0W
Fort Langley, B.C. **25 F12** 49 10N 122 35W
Fort Liard, N.W.T. **18 A4** 60 14N 123 30W
Fort Mackay, Alta. **22 A9** 57 12N 111 41W
Fort McKenzie, Qué. **6 B4** 57 20N 69 0W
Fort Macleod, Alta. **23 I7** 49 45N 113 30W
Fort McMurray, Alta. **22 B9** 56 44N 111 7W
Fort McPherson, N.W.T. **26 C2** 67 30N 134 55W
Fort Nelson, B.C. **18 B4** 58 50N 122 44W
Fort Nelson →, B.C. **18 B4** 59 32N 124 0W
Fort Norman, N.W.T. **26 C3** 64 57N 125 30W
Fort Providence, N.W.T. **18 A5** 61 3N 117 40W
Fort Qu'Appelle, Sask. **20 E7** 50 45N 103 50W
Fort Resolution, N.W.T. **18 A6** 61 10N 113 40W
Fort Ross, N.W.T. **27 B6** 72 0N 94 14W
Fort Rouge, Man. **31 B3** 49 52N 97 9W
Fort Rupert, B.C. **24 E7** 50 42N 127 23W
Fort Rupert, Qué. **6 C2** 51 30N 78 40W
Fort St. James, B.C. **18 C4** 54 30N 124 10W
Fort St. John, B.C. **18 B4** 56 15N 120 50W
Fort Saskatchewan, Alta. **22 E7** 53 40N 113 15W
Fort Severn, Ont. **4 A2** 56 0N 87 40W
Fort Simpson, N.W.T. **18 A4** 61 45N 121 15W
Fort Smith, Alta. **18 B6** 60 0N 111 51W
Fort Smith Region □, N.W.T. **26 C4** 63 0N 120 0W
Fort Vermilion, Alta. **18 B5** 58 24N 116 0W
Fort Whyte, Man. **31 C2** 49 49N 97 13W
Forteau, Nfld. **7 B4** 51 28N 56 58W
Fortin, L., Qué. **8 C2** 50 50N 67 46W
Fortune, Nfld. **7 F5** 47 4N 55 50W
Fortune B., Nfld. **7 F5** 47 30N 55 22W
Fosheim Pen., N.W.T. **27 B7** 80 0N 85 0W
Fosston, Sask. **20 C7** 52 12N 103 49W
Foster, Qué. **11 F10** 45 17N 72 30W
Foster →, Sask. **19 B7** 55 47N 105 49W
Fourchu, N.S. **9 H9** 45 43N 60 17W
Fourmont, L., Nfld. **8 A9** 52 5N 60 27W
Fournier, L., Qué. **8 B4** 51 33N 65 25W
Fourteen Island Lake, Qué. **12 A2** 45 54N 74 2W
Fox →, Man. **19 B10** 56 3N 93 18W
Fox Creek, Alta. **22 D4** 54 24N 116 48W
Fox Valley, Sask. **20 E1** 50 30N 109 25W
Foxe Basin, N.W.T. **27 C8** 66 0N 77 0W
Foxe Chan., N.W.T. **27 C8** 65 0N 80 0W
Foxe Pen., N.W.T. **27 C8** 65 0N 76 0W
Foxville, Ont. **17 B15** 50 4N 81 38W
Frances →, Yukon **18 A3** 60 16N 129 10W
Frances L., Yukon **18 A3** 61 23N 129 30W
Francis, Sask. **20 E7** 50 6N 103 52W
François, Nfld. **7 F4** 47 35N 56 45W
François L., B.C. **24 B9** 54 0N 125 30W
Frankford, Ont. **15 C9** 44 12N 77 36W
Franklin B., N.W.T. **26 C3** 69 45N 126 0W
Franklin Centre, Qué. **12 B3** 45 2N 73 55W
Franklin Mts., N.W.T. **26 C3** 65 0N 125 0W
Franklin River, B.C. **24 F10** 49 7N 124 48W
Franklin Str., N.W.T. **27 B6** 72 0N 96 0W
Franquelin, Qué. **8 D2** 49 18N 67 54W
Franz, Ont. **17 D12** 48 25N 84 30W
Fraser →, B.C. **25 F11** 49 7N 123 11W
Fraser →, Nfld. **6 B5** 56 39N 62 10W
Fraser Lake, B.C. **24 B10** 54 0N 124 50W
Fraserdale, Ont. **17 C15** 49 55N 81 37W
Fraserwood, Man. **21 E13** 50 38N 97 13W
Frazer L., Ont. **16 C8** 49 15N 88 40W
Fredericton, N.B. **9 H3** 45 57N 66 40W
Fredericton Junc., N.B. **9 H3** 45 41N 66 40W
Freels, C., Nfld. **7 D7** 49 15N 53 30W
Freelton, Ont. **13 B2** 43 24N 80 2W
Freeman →, Alta. **22 D6** 54 19N 114 47W
Freeport, N.S. **9 I3** 44 15N 66 20W
Freeport, Ont. **13 B2** 43 25N 80 25W
Frégate, L., Qué. **4 B5** 53 15N 74 45W
Frelighsburg, Qué. **12 B5** 45 3N 72 50W
French →, Ont. **14 A6** 46 2N 80 34W
French →, Ont. **17 B16** 50 40N 80 59W
French River, Ont. **14 A6** 46 2N 80 34W
Frenchman Butte, Sask. **20 B1** 53 35N 109 38W
Frikson, Man. **21 E11** 50 30N 99 55W
Frobisher, Sask. **21 F8** 49 12N 102 26W
Frobisher B., N.W.T. **27 C9** 62 30N 66 0W
Frobisher Bay, N.W.T. **27 C9** 63 44N 68 31W
Frobisher L., Sask. **19 B7** 56 20N 108 15W
Frog L., Alta. **22 E10** 53 55N 110 20W
Frontier, Sask. **20 F2** 49 12N 108 34W
Fruitland, Ont. **13 B3** 43 13N 79 43W
Fruitvale, B.C. **25 F17** 49 7N 117 33W
Fry L., Ont. **16 A5** 51 14N 91 19W
Fulford Harbour, B.C. **25 G11** 48 47N 123 27W
Fulton, Ont. **13 B3** 43 8N 79 40W
Fundy, B. of, N.B. **9 I4** 45 0N 66 0W
Fundy Nat. Park, N.B. **9 H4** 45 35N 65 10W
Fury and Hecla Str., N.W.T. **27 C7** 69 56N 84 0W

G

Gabarouse, N.S. **9 H9** 45 50N 60 9W
Gabriola I., B.C. **25 F11** 49 9N 123 47W
Gagetown, N.B. **9 H3** 45 46N 66 10W
Gagnon, Qué. **8 B1** 51 50N 68 5W
Gagnon, L., N.W.T. **19 A6** 62 3N 110 27W
Gagnon, L., Qué. **10 E7** 46 7N 75 7W
Gaillarbois, L., Qué. **8 B2** 52 0N 67 27W
Galahad, Alta. **23 F9** 52 31N 111 56W
Galeton, Ont. **17 A16** 51 8N 80 55W
Galissonnière, La, L., Qué. **8 B8** 51 25N 62 0W
Gambier I., B.C. **25 F11** 49 30N 123 23W
Gammon →, Man. **21 D15** 51 24N 95 44W
Gananoque, Ont. **15 C10** 44 20N 76 10W
Gander, Nfld. **7 E6** 48 58N 54 35W
Gander →, Nfld. **7 D6** 49 16N 54 30W
Gander L., Nfld. **7 E6** 48 58N 54 35W
Gang Ranch, B.C. **25 D12** 51 33N 122 20W
Garde L., N.W.T. **19 A7** 62 50N 106 13W
Gardiner L., Alta. **22 A8** 57 32N 112 30W
Gardner Canal, B.C. **24 B6** 53 27N 128 8W
Garibaldi, Mt., B.C. **25 F12** 49 51N 123 0W
Garibaldi Prov. Park, B.C. **25 F12** 49 50N 122 40W
Garneau, L., Qué. **8 B6** 51 43N 63 22W
Garnish, Nfld. **7 F5** 47 14N 55 22W
Garry L., N.W.T. **27 C5** 65 58N 100 18W
Garson L., Alta. **22 B10** 56 19N 110 2W
Gascons, Qué. **8 E5** 48 11N 64 51W
Gaspé, Qué. **8 E5** 48 52N 64 30W
Gaspé, B. de, Qué. **8 E5** 48 46N 64 17W
Gaspé, C. de, Qué. **8 E5** 48 48N 64 7W
Gaspé, Pén. de, Qué. **8 E4** 48 45N 65 40W
Gaspésie, Parc Prov. de la, Qué. **8 E4** 48 55N 65 50W
Gataga →, B.C. **18 B3** 58 35N 126 59W
Gateshead I., N.W.T. **27 B5** 70 36N 100 26W
Gatineau, Qué. **10 F7** 45 29N 75 38W
Gatineau →, Qué. **30 D7** 45 27N 75 42W
Gatineau, Parc de la, Qué. **10 F7** 45 40N 76 0W
Gauer L., Man. **19 B9** 57 0N 97 50W
Gaultois, Nfld. **7 F5** 47 36N 55 54W
Gayot, L., Qué. **6 B3** 55 43N 70 50W
Geary, N.B. **9 H3** 45 46N 66 29W
Geikie →, Sask. **19 B8** 57 45N 103 52W
Geikie I., Ont. **16 C8** 50 0N 88 35W
Gem, Alta. **23 H8** 50 57N 112 11W
Genesee, Alta. **22 E6** 53 21N 114 20W
Geneva, Qué. **12 A2** 45 36N 74 20W
George →, Qué. **5 A6** 58 49N 66 10W
George →, Qué. **6 D4** 49 21N 67 59W
George B., N.S. **9 H8** 45 45N 61 45W
George River = Port Nouveau-Québec, Qué. **6 B4** 58 30N 65 59W
Georgetown, Ont. **13 A3** 43 40N 79 56W
Georgetown, P.E.I. **9 G7** 46 13N 62 24W
Georgia, Str. of, B.C. **24 F11** 49 25N 124 0W
Georgian B., Ont. **14 B6** 45 15N 81 0W
Georgina I., Ont. **14 C7** 44 22N 79 17W
Geraldton, Ont. **17 C10** 49 44N 86 59W
Germain, Grand L., Qué. **8 B3** 51 12N 66 41W
Germansen Landing, B.C. **18 B4** 55 43N 124 40W
Gerrard, B.C. **25 E17** 50 30N 117 17W
Gethsémani, Qué. **8 C9** 50 13N 60 40W
Ghost River, Ont. **16 B5** 50 12N 91 30W
Gibbons, Alta. **22 E7** 53 50N 113 20W
Gibsons, B.C. **25 F11** 49 24N 123 32W
Giffard, Qué. **30 A3** 46 51N 71 12W
Gift Lake, Alta. **22 C5** 55 53N 115 49W
Gil I., B.C. **24 B5** 53 12N 129 15W
Gilbert, Mt., B.C. **24 E10** 50 52N 124 16W
Gilbert Plains, Man. **21 D10** 51 9N 100 28W
Gilford I., B.C. **24 E8** 50 40N 126 30W
Gillam, Man. **19 B10** 56 20N 94 40W
Gillies Bay, B.C. **24 F10** 49 42N 124 29W
Gilmour, Ont. **15 C9** 44 48N 77 37W
Gimli, Man. **19 C9** 50 40N 97 0W
Girardville, Qué. **11 C10** 49 0N 72 32W
Girouxville, Alta. **22 C3** 55 45N 117 20W
Gisborne L., Nfld. **7 F6** 47 48N 54 49W
Gjoa Haven, N.W.T. **27 C6** 68 38N 95 53W
Glace Bay, N.S. **9 G10** 46 11N 59 58W
Glacier Nat. Park, B.C. **25 D17** 51 15N 117 30W
Glacier Str., N.W.T. **27 B8** 76 12N 79 15W
Gladmar, Sask. **20 F6** 49 10N 104 27W
Gladstone, Man. **21 E12** 50 13N 98 57W
Gladys L., B.C. **18 B2** 59 50N 133 0W
Glaslyn, Sask. **20 B2** 53 22N 108 21W
Glen Almond, Qué. **10 F7** 45 42N 75 29W
Glen Cross, Ont. **13 A2** 43 59N 80 3W
Glen Ewen, Sask. **21 F8** 49 12N 102 1W
Glen Gordon, Qué. **12 B1** 45 10N 74 32W
Glen Morris, Ont. **13 B2** 43 16N 80 21W
Glen Robertson, Qué. **12 B2** 45 22N 74 30W
Glen Williams, Ont. **13 A3** 43 40N 79 55W
Glenavon, Sask. **20 E7** 50 12N 103 8W
Glenboro, Man. **21 F11** 49 33N 99 17W
Glenchristie, Ont. **13 B2** 43 28N 80 17W
Glencoe, Ont. **14 E5** 42 45N 81 43W
Glendale, Alta. **31 F10** 51 2N 114 9W
Glendale, N.S. **9 H8** 45 49N 61 18W
Glendon, Alta. **22 D9** 54 15N 111 10W
Gleneagle, Ont. **30 C7** 45 32N 75 48W
Glenella, Man. **21 E11** 50 33N 99 11W
Glengarry □, Qué. **12 B2** 45 15N 74 30W
Glenmoor Res., Alta. **31 G10** 50 59N 114 8W
Glenwood, Alta. **23 I7** 49 21N 113 31W
Glenwood, Nfld. **7 E6** 49 0N 54 58W
Glovertown, Nfld. **5 C9** 48 40N 54 3W
Gobles, Ont. **13 B1** 43 9N 80 34W
Godbout, Qué. **8 D2** 49 20N 67 38W
Godbout →, Qué. **8 D2** 49 19N 67 36W
Goderich, Ont. **14 D5** 43 45N 81 41W
Godham, N.W.T. **27 C9** 60 55N 60 40W
Gods →, Man. **19 B10** 56 22N 92 51W
Gods L., Man. **19 C10** 54 40N 94 15W
Goéland, L. au, Qué. **10 B6** 49 50N 76 48W
Gogama, Ont. **17 E15** 47 35N 81 43W
Gold River, B.C. **24 F8** 49 46N 126 3W
Golden, B.C. **25 D18** 51 20N 116 59W
Golden Ears Prov. Park, B.C. **25 F12** 49 30N 122 25W
Golden Hinde, B.C. **24 F9** 49 40N 125 44W
Golden Lake, Ont. **10 F5** 45 34N 77 21W
Golden Prairie, Sask. **20 E1** 50 13N 109 37W
Goldfields, Sask. **19 B7** 59 28N 108 29W
Goldsand L., Man. **19 B8** 57 2N 101 8W
Good Hope Mt., B.C. **24 D10** 51 9N 124 10W
Good Spirit L., Sask. **20 D8** 51 34N 102 40W
Gooderham, Ont. **15 C8** 44 54N 78 21W
Goodeve, Sask. **20 D7** 51 4N 103 10W
Goodsoil, Sask. **19 C7** 54 24N 109 13W
Goodwater, Sask. **20 F7** 49 24N 103 42W
Goodwood, N.S. **9 L11** 44 37N 63 40W
Goose →, Nfld. **6 C5** 53 20N 60 35W
Goose Cove, Nfld. **7 B5** 51 18N 55 38W
Goose I., B.C. **24 D6** 51 57N 128 26W
Goose L., Man. **21 A9** 54 28N 101 30W
Gordon, Man. **31 B1** 50 0N 97 21W
Gordon Hd., B.C. **25 H20** 48 29N 123 18W
Gordon L., Alta. **22 B10** 56 30N 110 25W
Gordon L., N.W.T. **18 A6** 63 5N 113 11W
Gordonville, Ont. **13 A1** 43 54N 80 33W
Gore Bay, Ont. **14 B4** 45 57N 82 28W
Gormley, Ont. **13 A4** 43 56N 79 23W
Goschen I., B.C. **24 B4** 53 48N 130 33W
Goshen, N.S. **9 H8** 45 23N 61 59W
Gough L., Alta. **23 F8** 52 2N 112 28W
Gouin, Rés., Qué. **10 C8** 48 35N 74 40W
Goulais →, Ont. **17 F12** 46 43N 84 27W
Goulds, Nfld. **7 I7** 47 29N 52 46W
Govan, Sask. **20 D6** 51 20N 105 0W
Goyelle, L., Qué. **8 C9** 50 47N 60 45W
Gracefield, Qué. **10 E6** 46 6N 76 3W
Graham, Ont. **16 C6** 49 20N 90 30W
Graham →, B.C. **18 B4** 56 31N 122 17W
Graham I., B.C. **24 B2** 53 40N 132 30W
Graham I., N.W.T. **27 B6** 77 25N 90 30W
Graham L., Alta. **22 B6** 56 35N 114 33W
Grahamdale, Man. **21 D12** 51 23N 98 30W
Grainland, Sask. **20 E4** 50 59N 106 33W
Granby, Qué. **11 F10** 45 25N 72 45W
Granby →, B.C. **25 F16** 49 2N 118 27W
Grand →, Ont. **13 C3** 42 51N 79 34W
Grand Bank, Nfld. **7 F5** 47 6N 55 48W
Grand Bay, N.B. **9 H3** 45 18N 66 12W
Grand Bend, Ont. **14 D5** 43 19N 81 45W
Grand Bruit, Nfld. **7 F2** 47 40N 58 14W
Grand Calumet, Île du, Qué. **10 F6** 45 44N 76 41W
Grand Centre, Alta. **22 D10** 54 25N 110 13W
Grand Coulee, Sask. **20 E6** 50 26N 104 49W
Grand Falls, N.B.-Nfld. **7 E5** 48 56N 55 40W
Grand Forks, B.C. **25 G16** 49 0N 118 30W
Grand Harbour, N.B. **9 I3** 44 41N 66 46W
Grand I., Man. **21 C11** 52 51N 100 0W
Grand Lac Victoria, Qué. **10 D5** 47 35N 77 35W
Grand L., N.B. **9 H3** 45 57N 66 7W
Grand L., Nfld. **6 C5** 53 40N 60 30W
Grand L., Nfld. **7 E3** 49 0N 57 30W
Grand Le Pierre, Nfld. **7 F6** 47 41N 54 47W
Grand Manan I., N.B. **9 I3** 44 45N 66 52W
Grand-Mère, Qué. **11 E10** 46 36N 72 40W
Grand Piles, Qué. **11 E10** 46 40N 72 40W
Grand Rapids, Man. **21 B11** 53 12N 99 19W
Grand Valley, Ont. **13 A2** 43 54N 80 19W
Grand View, Man. **21 D10** 51 10N 100 42W
Grande, Île, Qué. **12 A4** 45 52N 73 14W
Grande, La →, Qué. **6 C2** 53 50N 79 0W
Grande-Anse, N.B. **9 F4** 47 48N 65 11W
Grande Baie, Qué. **11 C12** 48 19N 70 52W
Grande Baleine, R. de la →, Qué. **6 B2** 55 16N 77 47W
Grande Cache, Alta. **22 E1** 53 53N 119 8W
Grande-Cascapédia, Qué. **8 E4** 48 15N 65 54W
Grande-Entrée, Qué. **9 F8** 47 30N 61 40W
Grande-Ligne, Qué. **12 B4** 45 14N 73 22W
Grande Pointe, Man. **31 C3** 49 46N 97 3W
Grande Prairie, Alta. **22 C2** 55 10N 118 50W
Grande-Rivière, Qué. **8 E5** 48 26N 64 30W
Grande-Vallée, Qué. **8 D4** 49 14N 65 8W
Grandes-Bergeronnes, Qué. **11 C13** 48 16N 69 35W
Grandmesnil, L., Qué. **8 B2** 51 19N 67 33W
Grandoe Mines, B.C. **18 B3** 56 29N 129 54W
Granet, L., Qué. **10 D5** 47 47N 77 31W
Granite Pt., Nfld. **7 C4** 50 31N 56 17W
Granville L., Man. **19 B8** 56 18N 100 30W
Gras, L. de, N.W.T. **26 C4** 64 30N 110 30W
Grass →, Man. **19 B9** 56 3N 96 33W
Grass River Prov. Park, Man. **19 C8** 54 40N 100 50W
Grasset, L., Qué. **10 B4** 49 55N 78 10W
Grassie, Ont. **13 B3** 43 9N 79 37W
Grassy Lake, Alta. **23 I9** 49 49N 111 43W
Gravelbourg, Sask. **20 F4** 49 50N 106 35W
Gravenhurst, Ont. **10 G3** 44 52N 79 20W
Grayling →, B.C. **18 B4** 59 21N 125 0W
Grayson, Sask. **20 E8** 50 45N 102 40W
Greasy L., N.W.T. **18 A4** 62 55N 122 12W
Great Bear →, N.W.T. **26 C3** 65 0N 124 0W
Great Bear L., N.W.T. **26 C4** 65 30N 120 0W
Great Burnt L., Nfld. **7 E4** 48 20N 56 20W
Great Central, B.C. **24 F9** 49 20N 125 10W
Great Central L., B.C. **24 F9** 49 22N 125 10W
Great Duck I., Ont. **14 B4** 45 40N 82 57W
Great Falls, Man. **21 E14** 50 27N 96 1W
Great Harbour Deep, Nfld. **7 C4** 50 25N 56 32W
Great I., Man. **19 B9** 58 53N 96 35W
Great Slave L., N.W.T. **18 A5** 61 23N 115 38W
Greece's Point, Qué. **12 A2** 45 36N 74 30W
Greely Fd., N.W.T. **27 A7** 80 30N 85 0W
Green →, N.B. **9 F1** 47 18N 68 9W
Green B., Nfld. **7 D5** 49 45N 55 55W
Green Cr. →, Ont. **30 D8** 45 28N 75 34W
Green Lake, Sask. **20 A3** 54 17N 107 47W
Green Park, Ont. **13 A2** 43 52N 80 27W
Green River, Ont. **13 A4** 43 53N 79 11W
Greenfield Park, Qué. **29 C5** 45 29N 73 29W
Greenfields, Ont. **13 B2** 43 18N 80 29W
Greenough Pt., Ont. **14 C5** 44 58N 81 26W
Greenwater L., Ont. **16 D6** 48 34N 90 26W

Greenwater Lake, *Sask.* ... **20 C7** 52 30N 103 31W
Greenwater Lake Prov. Park, *Sask.* ... **20 C7** 52 32N 103 30W
Greenwood, *B.C.* ... **25 F16** 49 10N 118 40W
Greenwood, *Ont.* ... **13 A4** 43 56N 79 3W
Grenfell, *Sask.* ... **20 E8** 50 30N 102 56W
Grenville, *Qué.* ... **12 A1** 45 37N 74 36W
Grenville Chan., *B.C.* ... **24 B5** 53 40N 129 46W
Gretna, *Man.* ... **21 F13** 49 1N 97 34W
Greves, Les, *Qué.* ... **12 A4** 45 59N 73 11W
Grey →, *Nfld.* ... **7 F3** 47 34N 57 6W
Grey, Pt., *B.C.* ... **32 B1** 49 16N 123 16W
Grey Is., *Nfld.* ... **7 C5** 50 50N 55 35W
Grey Res., *Nfld.* ... **7 E4** 48 20N 56 30W
Grey River, *Nfld.* ... **7 F3** 47 35N 57 6W
Gribbell I., *B.C.* ... **24 B6** 53 23N 129 0W
Griffith, *Ont.* ... **15 B9** 45 15N 77 10W
Griffith I., *Ont.* ... **14 C6** 44 50N 80 55W
Grimsby, *Ont.* ... **13 B3** 43 12N 79 34W
Grimsby Beach, *Ont.* ... **13 B3** 43 12N 79 32W
Grimshaw, *Alta.* ... **22 B3** 56 10N 117 40W
Grindstone I., *Ont.* ... **15 C10** 44 43N 76 14W
Grise Fiord, *N.W.T.* ... **27 B7** 76 25N 82 57W
Groais I., *Nfld.* ... **7 C5** 50 55N 55 35W
Gronlid, *Sask.* ... **20 B6** 53 6N 104 28W
Gros C., *N.W.T.* ... **18 A6** 61 59N 113 32W
Gros-Morne, *Qué.* ... **8 D4** 49 15N 65 34W
Gros Morne Nat. Park, *Nfld.* ... **7 D3** 49 40N 57 50W
Grosse Isle, *Man.* ... **21 E13** 50 4N 97 27W
Grosses-Roches, *Qué.* ... **8 E2** 48 57N 67 5W
Groswater B., *Nfld.* ... **6 C6** 54 20N 57 40W
Grouard Mission, *Alta.* ... **22 C4** 55 33N 116 9W
Groundhog →, *Ont.* ... **17 D14** 48 45N 82 58W
Grovedale, *Alta.* ... **22 C2** 55 3N 118 52W
Grundy Prov. Park, *Ont.* ... **14 B6** 45 58N 80 30W
Grunthal, *Man.* ... **21 F14** 49 24N 96 51W
Guadeloupe, La, *Qué.* ... **11 F12** 45 57N 70 56W
Guéguen, L., *Qué.* ... **10 C5** 48 6N 77 13W
Guelph, *Ont.* ... **13 A2** 43 35N 80 20W
Guernsey, *Sask.* ... **20 D5** 51 53N 105 11W
Guigues, *Qué.* ... **10 D3** 47 28N 79 26W
Guillaume-Delisle, L., *Qué.* ... **6 B2** 56 15N 76 17W
Guines, L., *Nfld.* ... **8 A8** 52 8N 61 25W
Gull →, *Ont.* ... **16 C8** 49 45N 89 0W
Gull L., *Alta.* ... **23 F7** 52 34N 114 0W
Gull Lake, *Sask.* ... **20 E2** 50 10N 108 29W
Gunisao →, *Man.* ... **21 B13** 53 56N 97 53W
Gunisao L., *Man.* ... **21 B14** 53 33N 96 15W
Guysborough, *N.S.* ... **9 H8** 45 23N 61 30W
Gypsum Pt., *N.W.T.* ... **18 A6** 61 53N 114 35W
Gypsumville, *Man.* ... **21 D12** 51 45N 98 40W

H

Habay, *Alta.* ... **18 B5** 58 50N 118 44W
Hafford, *Sask.* ... **20 C3** 52 43N 107 21W
Hagensborg, *B.C.* ... **24 C8** 52 23N 126 32W
Hagersville, *Ont.* ... **13 C2** 42 58N 80 3W
Haileybury, *Ont.* ... **10 D3** 47 30N 79 38W
Haines Junction, *Yukon* ... **18 A1** 60 45N 137 30W
Halbrite, *Sask.* ... **20 F7** 49 30N 103 33W
Haldimand-Norfolk □, *Ont.* ... **13 C3** 42 57N 79 50W
Half Island Cove, *N.S.* ... **9 H8** 45 21N 61 12W
Halfway →, *B.C.* ... **18 B4** 56 12N 121 32W
Haliburton, *Ont.* ... **15 B8** 45 3N 78 30W
Halifax, *N.S.* ... **9 I6** 44 38N 63 35W
Halkirk, *Alta.* ... **23 F8** 52 17N 112 9W
Hall Beach, *N.W.T.* ... **27 C7** 68 46N 81 12W
Hall Pen., *N.W.T.* ... **27 C9** 63 30N 66 0W
Hallebourg, *Ont.* ... **17 C13** 49 40N 83 31W
Halliday L., *N.W.T.* ... **19 A7** 61 21N 108 56W
Halton □, *Ont.* ... **30 C10** 43 30N 79 53W
Hamber Prov. Park, *B.C.* ... **25 C17** 52 20N 118 0W
Hamilton, *Ont.* ... **30 D9** 43 15N 79 50W
Hamilton Beach, *Ont.* ... **30 D10** 43 17N 79 47W
Hamilton Harbour, *Ont.* ... **30 D10** 43 18N 79 50W
Hamilton Inlet, *Nfld.* ... **5 B8** 54 0N 57 30W
Hamilton Sound, *Nfld.* ... **7 D6** 49 35N 54 15W
Hamilton-Wentworth □, *Ont.* ... **30 D9** 43 15N 79 49W
Hamiota, *Man.* ... **21 E10** 50 11N 100 38W
Hampden, *Nfld.* ... **7 D4** 49 33N 56 51W
Hampstead, *N.B.* ... **9 H3** 45 37N 66 5W
Hampton, *N.B.* ... **9 H4** 45 32N 65 51W
Hampton, *Ont.* ... **15 D8** 43 58N 78 45W
Hanceville, *B.C.* ... **25 D11** 51 55N 123 2W
Handel, *Sask.* ... **20 C2** 52 4N 108 42W
Haney, *B.C.* ... **25 F12** 49 12N 122 40W
Hanlan, *Ont.* ... **28 C2** 43 39N 79 39W
Hanley, *Sask.* ... **20 D4** 51 38N 106 26W
Hanmer, *Ont.* ... **14 A6** 46 39N 80 56W
Hanna, *Alta.* ... **23 G9** 51 40N 111 54W
Hannah B., *Ont.* ... **4 B4** 51 40N 80 0W
Hannon, *Ont.* ... **30 D10** 43 11N 79 50W
Hanover, *Ont.* ... **14 C5** 44 9N 81 2W
Hant's Harbour, *Nfld.* ... **7 E7** 48 1N 53 16W
Hantsport, *N.S.* ... **9 H5** 45 4N 64 11W
Happy Valley-Goose Bay, *Nfld.* ... **6 C5** 53 15N 60 20W
Harbour Breton, *Nfld.* ... **7 F5** 47 29N 55 50W
Harbour Grace, *Nfld.* ... **7 F7** 47 40N 53 22W
Harcourt, *N.B.* ... **9 G4** 46 27N 65 15W
Hardisty, *Alta.* ... **23 F9** 52 40N 111 18W
Hardwicke I., *B.C.* ... **24 E9** 50 27N 125 50W
Hardwicke Island, *B.C.* ... **24 E9** 50 26N 125 55W
Hardwood Ridge, *N.B.* ... **9 G3** 46 10N 66 1W
Hare B., *Nfld.* ... **7 B5** 51 15N 55 45W
Hare Bay, *Nfld.* ... **7 E6** 48 51N 54 1W
Harley, *Ont.* ... **13 B2** 43 4N 80 29W
Harmon L., *Ont.* ... **16 C6** 49 56N 90 13W
Harmony, *Ont.* ... **13 A5** 43 54N 78 50W
Haro Str., *B.C.* ... **25 G11** 48 30N 123 15W
Harp L., *Nfld.* ... **6 B5** 55 5N 61 50W
Harricana →, *Qué.* ... **10 A3** 50 56N 79 32W
Harrington Harbour, *Qué.* ... **8 C10** 50 31N 59 30W
Harris, *Sask.* ... **20 D3** 51 44N 107 35W
Harris Pt., *Ont.* ... **14 D4** 43 6N 82 9W
Harrisburg, *Ont.* ... **13 B2** 43 14N 80 23W
Harrison, C., *Nfld.* ... **6 C6** 54 55N 57 55W
Harrison Hot Springs, *B.C.* ... **25 F13** 49 18N 121 47W
Harrison L., *B.C.* ... **25 F13** 49 33N 121 50W
Harriston, *Ont.* ... **14 D6** 43 57N 80 53W
Harrow, *Ont.* ... **14 E4** 42 2N 82 55W
Harrowsmith, *Ont.* ... **15 C10** 44 24N 76 40W
Hartell, *Alta.* ... **23 H6** 50 36N 114 14W
Hartland, *N.B.* ... **9 G2** 46 20N 67 32W
Hartley Bay, *B.C.* ... **24 B5** 53 25N 129 15W
Hartney, *Man.* ... **21 F10** 49 30N 100 35W
Harty, *Ont.* ... **17 C14** 49 29N 82 41W
Harvey, *N.B.* ... **9 H2** 45 43N 67 1W
Hastings, *Ont.* ... **15 C9** 44 18N 77 57W
Hastings Road, *B.C.* ... **32 B3** 49 16N 122 56W
Hatchet L., *Sask.* ... **19 B8** 58 36N 103 40W
Hattonford, *Alta.* ... **22 E5** 53 46N 115 42W
Haultain →, *Sask.* ... **19 B7** 55 51N 106 46W
Hauterive, *Qué.* ... **11 B14** 49 10N 68 16W
Have, La →, *N.S.* ... **9 I5** 44 14N 64 20W
Havelock, *N.B.* ... **9 G4** 46 2N 65 24W
Havelock, *Ont.* ... **15 C9** 44 26N 77 53W
Havelock, *Qué.* ... **12 B3** 45 3N 73 45W
Havre-Aubert, *Qué.* ... **9 F8** 47 12N 61 56W
Havre Aubert, I., *Qué.* ... **9 F8** 47 13N 61 57W
Havre-aux-Maisons, I., *Qué.* ... **9 F8** 47 25N 61 47W
Havre-St.-Pierre, *Qué.* ... **8 C6** 50 18N 63 33W
Hawarden, *Sask.* ... **20 D4** 51 25N 106 36W
Hawk Junction, *Ont.* ... **17 D12** 48 5N 84 38W
Hawk Lake, *Ont.* ... **16 C3** 49 48N 93 59W
Hawkes Bay, *Nfld.* ... **7 C3** 50 36N 57 10W
Hawkesbury, *Qué.* ... **4 C5** 45 37N 74 37W
Hawkesbury I., *B.C.* ... **24 B5** 53 37N 129 3W
Hay →, *Alta.* ... **18 A5** 60 50N 116 26W
Hay, C., *N.W.T.* ... **26 B4** 74 25N 113 0W
Hay Cove, *N.S.* ... **9 H9** 45 45N 60 44W
Hay I., *Ont.* ... **14 C6** 44 53N 80 58W
Hay L., *Alta.* ... **18 B5** 58 50N 118 50W
Hay Lakes, *Alta.* ... **23 E7** 53 12N 113 2W
Hay River, *N.W.T.* ... **18 A5** 60 51N 115 44W
Hayes →, *Man.* ... **19 B10** 57 3N 92 12W
Hays, *Alta.* ... **23 H9** 50 6N 111 48W
Haysboro, *Alta.* ... **31 G10** 50 59N 114 5W
Hazelmere, *B.C.* ... **32 C4** 49 2N 122 43W
Hazelton, *B.C.* ... **18 B3** 55 20N 127 42W
Hazenmore, *Sask.* ... **20 F3** 49 42N 107 8W
Hazlet, *Sask.* ... **20 E2** 50 24N 108 36W
Head of Bay d'Espoir, *Nfld.* ... **7 F5** 47 56N 55 45W
Head of St. Margarets Bay, *N.S.* ... **9 I6** 44 41N 63 55W
Headingley, *Man.* ... **31 B1** 49 53N 97 24W
Hearne B., *N.W.T.* ... **19 A9** 60 10N 99 10W
Hearne L., *N.W.T.* ... **18 A6** 62 20N 113 10W
Hearst, *Ont.* ... **17 C13** 49 40N 83 41W
Heart's Content, *Nfld.* ... **7 F7** 47 54N 53 27W
Heath Pt., *Qué.* ... **8 D8** 49 8N 61 40W
Heath Steele, *N.B.* ... **9 F3** 47 17N 66 5W
Heatherton, *N.S.* ... **9 H8** 45 35N 61 47W
Heatherton, *Nfld.* ... **7 E2** 48 17N 58 45W
Hebert, *Sask.* ... **20 E3** 50 30N 107 10W
Hebron, *N.S.* ... **9 J3** 43 53N 66 5W
Hebron, *Nfld.* ... **6 B5** 58 5N 62 30W
Hebron Fd., *Nfld.* ... **6 B5** 58 9N 62 45W
Hecate I., *B.C.* ... **24 D7** 51 42N 128 0W
Hecate Str., *B.C.* ... **24 B4** 53 10N 130 30W
Hecks Corner, *Qué.* ... **12 B4** 45 4N 73 12W
Hecla I., *Man.* ... **21 D14** 51 10N 96 43W
Hedley, *B.C.* ... **25 F14** 49 22N 120 4W
Hedley B., *N.W.T.* ... **26 B5** 73 0N 108 0W
Heisler, *Alta.* ... **23 F8** 52 41N 112 13W
Helene L., *Sask.* ... **20 B2** 53 33N 108 12W
Hemford, *N.S.* ... **9 I5** 44 30N 64 47W
Hemmingford, *Qué.* ... **12 B3** 45 3N 73 35W
Henderson, Mt., *B.C.* ... **24 A6** 54 16N 128 4W
Hendrix Lake, *B.C.* ... **25 C14** 52 5N 120 48W
Henley Harbour, *Nfld.* ... **7 A5** 52 2N 55 51W
Henrietta Maria, C., *Ont.* ... **4 A3** 55 9N 82 20W
Henry Kater, C., *N.W.T.* ... **27 C9** 69 8N 66 30W
Henrysburg, *Qué.* ... **12 B4** 45 5N 73 25W
Henryville, *Qué.* ... **12 B4** 45 8N 73 11W
Hensall, *Ont.* ... **14 D5** 43 26N 81 30W
Hepworth, *Ont.* ... **14 C5** 44 37N 81 9W
Herbert Inlet, *B.C.* ... **24 F9** 49 20N 125 58W
Herdman, *Qué.* ... **12 B2** 45 2N 74 6W
Hereford, Mt., *Qué.* ... **11 F11** 45 5N 71 36W
Hereward, *Ont.* ... **13 A2** 43 50N 80 19W
Heriot Bay, *B.C.* ... **24 E9** 50 7N 125 13W
Hermitage, *Nfld.* ... **7 F5** 47 33N 55 56W
Heron Bay, *Ont.* ... **17 D10** 48 40N 86 25W
Hérons, Île aux, *Qué.* ... **29 C4** 45 25N 73 35W
Herring Cove, *N.S.* ... **9 I6** 44 34N 63 34W
Herschel, *Sask.* ... **20 D2** 51 38N 108 21W
Herschel I., *N.W.T.* ... **26 C2** 69 35N 139 5W
Hespeler, *Ont.* ... **13 B2** 43 26N 80 19W
Hewett, C., *N.W.T.* ... **27 B9** 70 16N 67 45W
Hibben I., *B.C.* ... **24 C2** 53 0N 132 18W
Hickmans Harbour, *Nfld.* ... **7 E7** 48 6N 53 44W
High I., *Nfld.* ... **5 A7** 56 40N 61 10W
High I., *Nfld.* ... **6 C6** 52 28N 55 40W
High Level, *Alta.* ... **18 B5** 58 31N 117 8W
High Prairie, *Alta.* ... **22 C4** 55 30N 116 30W
High River, *Alta.* ... **23 H7** 50 30N 113 50W
Highland Creek, *Ont.* ... **28 B5** 43 47N 79 10W
Highland Park, *Alta.* ... **31 F10** 51 6N 114 4W
Highridge, *Alta.* ... **22 D6** 54 3N 114 8W
Highrock L., *Sask.* ... **19 B7** 57 5N 105 32W
Hilda, *Alta.* ... **23 H10** 50 28N 110 3W
Hilden, *N.S.* ... **9 H6** 45 18N 63 18W
Hill Island L., *N.W.T.* ... **19 A7** 60 30N 109 50W
Hill Spring, *Alta.* ... **23 I7** 49 17N 113 38W
Hillhurst, *Alta.* ... **31 F10** 51 3N 114 7W
Hillmond, *Sask.* ... **20 B1** 53 26N 109 41W
Hillsborough B., *P.E.I.* ... **9 G6** 46 8N 63 5W
Hillsburgh, *Ont.* ... **13 A2** 43 47N 80 9W
Hillsport, *Ont.* ... **17 C11** 49 27N 85 34W
Hilton Beach, *Ont.* ... **14 A3** 46 15N 83 53W
Hinds L., *Nfld.* ... **7 E4** 48 58N 57 0W
Hines Creek, *Alta.* ... **22 B2** 56 20N 118 40W
Hinton, *Alta.* ... **22 E3** 53 26N 117 34W
Hitchcock, *Sask.* ... **20 F7** 49 14N 103 7W
Hixon, *B.C.* ... **25 B12** 53 25N 122 35W
Hjalmar L., *N.W.T.* ... **19 A7** 61 33N 109 25W
Hoare B., *N.W.T.* ... **27 C9** 65 17N 62 30W
Hobson L., *B.C.* ... **25 C14** 52 35N 120 15W
Hodges Hill, *Nfld.* ... **7 D5** 49 4N 55 53W
Hodgeville, *Sask.* ... **20 E4** 50 7N 106 58W
Hodgson, *Man.* ... **21 D13** 51 13N 97 36W
Holberg, *B.C.* ... **24 E7** 50 40N 128 0W
Holden, *Alta.* ... **22 E8** 53 13N 112 11W
Holdfast, *Sask.* ... **20 E5** 50 58N 105 25W
Holinshead L., *Ont.* ... **16 C7** 49 39N 89 40W
Holman, *N.W.T.* ... **26 B4** 70 44N 117 44W
Holton, *Nfld.* ... **6 C6** 54 31N 57 12W
Holyrood, *Nfld.* ... **7 F7** 47 27N 53 8W
Homathko →, *B.C.* ... **24 E10** 51 0N 124 56W
Home B., *N.W.T.* ... **27 C9** 68 40N 67 10W
Homer, *Ont.* ... **13 B4** 43 10N 79 11W
Homestead, *Alta.* ... **22 C1** 55 31N 119 22W
Hondo, *Alta.* ... **22 C6** 55 4N 114 2W
Honey Harbour, *Ont.* ... **14 C7** 44 52N 79 49W
Honguedo, Détroit d', *Qué.* ... **8 D6** 49 15N 64 0W
Hooker L., *Ont.* ... **16 B5** 50 35N 91 1W
Hope, *B.C.* ... **25 F13** 49 25N 121 25W
Hope, *Ont.* ... **28 A2** 43 53N 79 31W
Hope I., *B.C.* ... **24 E7** 50 55N 127 53W
Hope I., *Ont.* ... **14 C6** 44 55N 80 11W
Hopedale, *Nfld.* ... **6 B5** 55 28N 60 13W
Hopes Advance, C., *Qué.* ... **6 A4** 61 4N 69 34W
Hopewell, *N.S.* ... **9 H7** 45 29N 62 42W
Hopewell Cape, *N.B.* ... **9 H5** 45 51N 64 35W
Horn →, *N.W.T.* ... **18 A5** 61 30N 118 1W
Horn Mts., *N.W.T.* ... **18 A5** 62 15N 119 15W
Hornaday →, *N.W.T.* ... **26 C3** 69 19N 123 48W
Hornby, *Ont.* ... **13 A3** 43 34N 79 50W
Hornell L., *N.W.T.* ... **18 A5** 62 20N 119 25W
Hornepayne, *Ont.* ... **17 C12** 49 14N 84 48W
Hornings Mills, *Ont.* ... **14 C6** 44 9N 80 12W
Horse Is., *Nfld.* ... **7 C5** 50 15N 55 50W
Horsefly, *B.C.* ... **25 C13** 52 20N 121 25W
Horsefly L., *B.C.* ... **25 C14** 52 25N 121 0W
Horseshoe Bay, *B.C.* ... **32 A1** 49 22N 123 17W
Horton →, *N.W.T.* ... **26 C3** 69 56N 126 52W
Horwood, *Nfld.* ... **7 D6** 49 27N 54 32W
Horwood, L., *Ont.* ... **17 D14** 48 5N 82 20W
Hotchkiss →, *Alta.* ... **22 A3** 57 2N 117 28W
Hottah L., *N.W.T.* ... **26 C4** 65 4N 118 30W
Houston, *B.C.* ... **18 C3** 54 25N 126 39W
Howard L., *N.W.T.* ... **19 A7** 62 15N 105 57W
Howe I., *Ont.* ... **15 C10** 44 16N 76 17W
Howe Sd., *B.C.* ... **25 F11** 49 35N 123 15W
Howick, *Qué.* ... **12 B3** 45 11N 73 51W
Howley, *Nfld.* ... **7 D3** 49 12N 57 2W
Hubbard, *Sask.* ... **20 D7** 51 8N 103 22W
Hubbards, *N.S.* ... **9 I5** 44 38N 64 4W
Hubbart Pt., *Man.* ... **19 B10** 59 21N 94 41W
Hudson, *Ont.* ... **19 C10** 50 6N 92 9W
Hudson, *Qué.* ... **12 B2** 45 27N 74 9W
Hudson Bay, *Sask.* ... **21 C8** 52 51N 102 23W
Hudson Bay, *N.W.T.* ... **27 D7** 60 0N 86 0W
Hudson Heights, *Qué.* ... **12 B2** 45 28N 74 10W
Hudson Str., *N.W.T.* ... **27 C9** 62 0N 70 0W
Hudson's Hope, *B.C.* ... **18 B4** 56 0N 121 54W
Hudwin L., *Man.* ... **21 B15** 53 12N 95 41W
Hull, *Qué.* ... **30 D7** 45 25N 75 44W
Humber, *Ont.* ... **13 A3** 43 54N 79 49W
Humber →, *Ont.* ... **28 C3** 43 38N 79 28W
Humber B., *Ont.* ... **28 C3** 43 38N 79 28W
Humber Bay, *Ont.* ... **28 C3** 43 38N 79 27W
Humboldt, *Sask.* ... **20 C5** 52 15N 105 9W
Hundred and Fifty Mile House, *B.C.* ... **25 C13** 52 7N 121 57W
Hundred Mile House, *B.C.* ... **25 D13** 51 38N 121 18W
Hunter, C., *N.W.T.* ... **27 B8** 71 42N 72 30W
Hunter I., *B.C.* ... **24 D7** 51 55N 128 0W
Huntingdon, *Qué.* ... **12 B2** 45 6N 74 10W
Huntingdon □, *Qué.* ... **12 B2** 45 5N 74 15W
Huntsville, *Ont.* ... **14 B7** 45 20N 79 14W
Hupel, *B.C.* ... **25 E16** 50 37N 118 44W
Huron, L., *Ont.* ... **14 C4** 45 0N 83 0W
Hussar, *Alta.* ... **23 G8** 51 3N 112 41W
Hutte Sauvage, L. de la, *Qué.* ... **6 B5** 56 15N 64 45W
Huttonsville, *Ont.* ... **13 A3** 43 38N 79 48W
Hyas, *Sask.* ... **21 D8** 51 54N 102 16W
Hyde In., *N.W.T.* ... **27 B8** 75 2N 80 0W
Hyland →, *B.C.* ... **18 B3** 59 52N 128 12W
Hymers, *Ont.* ... **16 D7** 48 18N 89 43W
Hythe, *Alta.* ... **22 C1** 55 20N 119 33W

I

Ian L., *B.C.* ... **24 B2** 53 50N 132 45W
Iberville, *Qué.* ... **29 B4** 45 19N 73 17W
Iberville □, *Qué.* ... **29 B4** 45 15N 73 10W
Iberville, Lac D', *Qué.* ... **6 B3** 55 55N 73 15W
Iberville, Mt. d', *Nfld.* ... **6 B5** 58 50N 63 50W
Igloolik, *N.W.T.* ... **27 C7** 69 20N 81 49W
Ignace, *Ont.* ... **16 C5** 49 30N 91 40W
Igornachoix Bay, *Nfld.* ... **7 C3** 50 40N 57 25W
Île-à-la Crosse, *Sask.* ... **19 B7** 55 27N 107 53W
Île-à-la-Crosse, Lac, *Sask.* ... **19 B7** 55 40N 107 45W
Île-aux-Noix, *Qué.* ... **12 B4** 45 8N 73 17W
Île-Bizard, *Qué.* ... **29 C2** 45 29N 73 53W
Île-Cadieux, *Qué.* ... **29 C1** 45 25N 74 1W
Île d'Orleans, Chenal de l', *Qué.* ... **30 A4** 46 58N 71 0W
Île-Perrot, *Qué.* ... **29 C2** 45 23N 73 57W
Île-Perrot-Sud, *Qué.* ... **29 C2** 45 21N 73 54W
Île-Sainte-Thérèse, *Qué.* ... **12 B4** 45 22N 73 15W
Îles, L. des, *Qué.* ... **10 E7** 46 20N 75 18W
Ilford, *Man.* ... **19 B9** 56 4N 95 35W
Illukotat →, *Qué.* ... **6 A2** 60 48N 78 11W
Imperial, *Sask.* ... **20 D5** 51 21N 105 28W
Indian Arm, *B.C.* ... **32 A3** 49 23N 122 53W
Indian Cabins, *Alta.* ... **18 B5** 59 52N 117 40W
Indian Harbour, *Nfld.* ... **6 C6** 54 27N 57 13W
Indian Head, *Sask.* ... **20 E7** 50 30N 103 41W
Indian L., *Ont.* ... **16 B2** 50 14N 94 5W
Ingersoll, *Ont.* ... **14 D6** 43 4N 80 55W
Inglewood, *Ont.* ... **13 A3** 43 47N 79 56W
Ingomar, *N.S.* ... **9 J4** 43 34N 65 22W
Ingonish, *N.S.* ... **9 G9** 46 42N 60 18W
Ingonish Beach, *N.S.* ... **9 G9** 46 38N 60 25W
Inkerman, *N.B.* ... **9 F5** 47 40N 64 49W
Inklin, *B.C.* ... **18 B2** 58 56N 133 5W
Inklin →, *B.C.* ... **18 B2** 58 50N 133 10W
Innerkip, *Ont.* ... **14 D6** 43 13N 80 42W
Innetalling I., *N.W.T.* ... **6 B2** 56 0N 79 0W
Innisfail, *Alta.* ... **23 G7** 52 0N 113 57W
Innisfree, *Alta.* ... **23 E9** 53 22N 111 32W
Inoucdjouac, *Qué.* ... **6 B2** 58 25N 78 15W
Intata Reach, *B.C.* ... **24 B9** 53 38N 125 30W
Inuvik, *N.W.T.* ... **26 C2** 68 16N 133 40W
Inuvik □, *N.W.T.* ... **26 C3** 70 0N 130 0W
Invermay, *Sask.* ... **20 D7** 51 48N 103 9W
Invermere, *B.C.* ... **23 H4** 50 30N 116 2W
Inverness, *N.S.* ... **9 G8** 46 15N 61 19W
Inwood, *Man.* ... **21 E13** 50 30N 97 30W
Ioco, *B.C.* ... **32 B3** 49 18N 122 53W
Iona, *N.S.* ... **9 H9** 45 58N 60 48W
Irma, *Alta.* ... **23 F9** 52 55N 111 14W
Iron Bridge, *Ont.* ... **14 A3** 46 17N 83 14W
Iron Springs, *Alta.* ... **23 I8** 49 56N 112 41W
Ironside, *Ont.* ... **30 D7** 45 27N 75 45W
Iroquois, *Ont.* ... **15 C11** 44 51N 75 19W
Iroquois Falls, *Ont.* ... **10 C2** 48 46N 80 41W
Irvine, *Alta.* ... **23 I10** 49 57N 110 16W
Isachsen, *N.W.T.* ... **27 B5** 78 47N 103 30W
Iskut →, *B.C.* ... **18 B2** 56 45N 131 49W
Island →, *N.W.T.* ... **18 A4** 60 25N 121 12W
Island Falls, *Ont.* ... **17 C15** 49 35N 81 20W
Island L., *Man.* ... **19 C10** 53 47N 94 25W
Island Pond, *Nfld.* ... **7 E4** 48 25N 56 23W
Islands, B. of, *Nfld.* ... **7 D2** 49 11N 58 15W
Islay, *Alta.* ... **22 E10** 53 24N 110 33W
Isle aux Morts, *Nfld.* ... **7 F2** 47 35N 59 0W
Isle L., *Alta.* ... **22 E6** 53 38N 114 44W
Isle Pierre, *B.C.* ... **24 B11** 53 57N 123 16W
Isle Verte, L', *Qué.* ... **11 C13** 48 1N 69 20W
Isles, L. des, *Ont.* ... **16 C7** 49 10N 89 40W
Islington, *Ont.* ... **28 C2** 43 38N 79 32W
Issoudun, *Qué.* ... **11 E11** 46 35N 71 38W
Itomamo, L., *Qué.* ... **11 B12** 49 11N 70 28W
Ituna, *Sask.* ... **20 D7** 51 10N 103 24W
Ivanhoe L., *N.W.T.* ... **19 A7** 60 25N 106 30W
Ivugivik, *Qué.* ... **6 A2** 62 24N 77 55W

J

Jaab L., *Ont.* ... **17 A14** 51 10N 82 58W
Jackfish L., *Sask.* ... **20 B2** 53 9N 108 29W
Jackson's Arm, *Nfld.* ... **7 D4** 49 52N 56 47W
Jacobs, *Ont.* ... **16 B7** 50 15N 89 50W
Jacques-Cartier →, *Qué.* ... **11 E11** 46 40N 71 45W
Jacques Cartier, Dét. de, *Qué.* ... **6 D5** 50 0N 63 30W
Jacques-Cartier, L., *Qué.* ... **11 D11** 47 35N 71 13W
Jacques-Cartier, Mt., *Qué.* ... **8 E4** 48 57N 66 0W
Jacquet River, *N.B.* ... **9 F4** 47 55N 66 0W
James B., *Ont.* ... **4 B4** 51 30N 80 0W
James River, *N.S.* ... **9 H7** 45 35N 62 7W
Jameson, C., *N.W.T.* ... **27 B8** 72 5N 74 14W
Jan L., *Sask.* ... **19 C8** 54 56N 102 55W
Jansen, *Sask.* ... **20 D6** 51 54N 104 45W
Jarvis, *Ont.* ... **14 E6** 42 53N 80 6W
Jarvis River, *Ont.* ... **16 D7** 48 7N 89 21W
Jasper, *Alta.* ... **23 F2** 52 55N 118 5W
Jasper, *Ont.* ... **15 C11** 44 50N 75 56W
Jasper Nat. Park, *Alta.* ... **23 F2** 52 50N 118 8W
Jean Marie River, *N.W.T.* ... **18 A4** 61 32N 120 38W
Jeanette L., *Ont.* ... **16 A4** 51 5N 92 5W
Jeanne-d'Arc, *Ont.* ... **30 C8** 45 28N 75 32W
Jedway, *B.C.* ... **24 C3** 52 17N 131 14W
Jellicoe, *Ont.* ... **17 C9** 49 40N 87 30W
Jemseg, *N.B.* ... **9 H3** 45 50N 66 7W
Jennings →, *B.C.* ... **18 B2** 59 38N 132 5W
Jerome, *Ont.* ... **17 E14** 47 37N 82 14W
Jerseyside, *Nfld.* ... **7 F7** 47 16N 53 58W
Jerseyville, *Ont.* ... **13 B2** 43 12N 80 7W
Jervis Inlet, *B.C.* ... **24 F11** 50 0N 123 57W
Jesus, Île, *Qué.* ... **29 B3** 45 35N 73 45W
Joe Batt's Arm, *Nfld.* ... **7 D6** 49 44N 54 10W
Joffre, Mt., *B.C.* ... **23 H5** 50 32N 115 13W
Joggins, *N.S.* ... **9 H5** 45 42N 64 27W
Jogues, *Ont.* ... **17 C13** 49 36N 83 45W
Jogues, *Qué.* ... **12 B5** 45 29N 72 49W
Johnson's Crossing, *Yukon* ... **18 A2** 60 29N 133 18W
Johnstone Str., *B.C.* ... **24 E9** 50 28N 126 0W
Joir →, *Qué.* ... **8 B9** 51 59N 60 12W
Joliette, *Qué.* ... **11 E9** 46 3N 73 24W
Joliette, Parc. Prov. de, *Qué.* ... **11 E9** 46 30N 74 0W
Jones Sound, *N.W.T.* ... **27 B7** 76 0N 85 0W
Jonquière, *Qué.* ... **11 C11** 48 27N 71 14W
Jordan, L., *N.S.* ... **9 I4** 44 5N 65 14W
Jordan Falls, *N.S.* ... **9 J4** 43 49N 65 14W
Jordan Harbour, *Ont.* ... **13 B4** 43 11N 79 23W
Joseph, L., *Nfld.* ... **8 A4** 52 45N 65 18W
Joseph, L., *Ont.* ... **10 F3** 45 10N 79 44W
Joseph, Petit lac, *Nfld.* ... **8 A4** 52 36N 65 5W
Joussard, *Alta.* ... **22 C5** 55 22N 115 50W
Joy B., *Qué.* ... **6 A3** 61 30N 72 0W
Juan de Fuca Str., *B.C.* ... **24 G10** 48 15N 124 0W
Juan Perez Sd., *B.C.* ... **24 C3** 52 32N 131 24W
Jubilee L., *Nfld.* ... **7 E5** 48 3N 55 11W
Jude I., *Nfld.* ... **7 F6** 47 15N 54 49W
Judique, *N.S.* ... **9 H8** 45 52N 61 30W
Julian L., *Qué.* ... **6 C2** 54 25N 77 57W
Juniper, *N.B.* ... **9 G2** 46 33N 67 13W
Jupiter →, *Qué.* ... **8 D6** 49 29N 63 37W
Juskatla, *B.C.* ... **24 B2** 53 37N 132 18W

K

Kabinakagami →, *Ont.* ... **17 B12** 50 25N 84 20W
Kabinakagami L., *Ont.* ... **17 D12** 48 54N 84 25W
Kaegudeck L., *Nfld.* ... **7 E5** 48 7N 55 12W
Kagaki L., *Ont.* ... **16 C3** 49 13N 93 52W
Kagawong L., *Ont.* ... **14 B4** 45 54N 82 15W
Kagianagami L., *Ont.* ... **17 B9** 50 57N 87 50W
Kagiano L., *Ont.* ... **17 C10** 49 16N 86 26W
Kahniah →, *B.C.* ... **18 B4** 58 15N 120 55W
Kaipokok B., *Nfld.* ... **6 C6** 54 54N 59 47W
Kakabeka Falls, *Ont.* ... **16 D7** 48 24N 89 37W
Kakisa →, *N.W.T.* ... **18 A5** 61 3N 118 10W
Kakisa L., *N.W.T.* ... **18 A5** 60 56N 117 43W
Kakwa →, *Alta.* ... **22 D2** 54 37N 118 28W
Kaladar, *Ont.* ... **15 C9** 44 37N 77 5W
Kamilukuak, L., *N.W.T.* ... **19 A8** 62 22N 101 40W
Kaminak L., *N.W.T.* ... **19 A10** 62 10N 95 0W
Kaministikwia, *Ont.* ... **16 D7** 48 32N 89 35W
Kamloops, *B.C.* ... **25 E14** 50 40N 120 20W
Kamloops L., *B.C.* ... **25 E14** 50 45N 120 40W
Kamouraska, *Qué.* ... **11 D13** 47 34N 69 52W

Kamsack, Sask. 21 D9 51 34N 101 54W
Kamuchawie L., Sask. 19 B8 56 18N 101 59W
Kanaaupscow, Qué. 6 C2 54 2N 76 30W
Kanaaupscow →, Qué. 6 C2 53 39N 77 9W
Kanairiktok →, Nfld. 6 B5 55 2N 60 18W
Kanata, Ont. 15 B11 45 20N 75 59W
Kane Basin, N.W.T. 27 B8 79 1N 73 0W
Kaniapiskau →, Qué. 6 B4 56 40N 69 30W
Kaniapiskau L., Qué. 6 C4 54 10N 69 55W
Kapikotongwa →, Ont. 17 B10 50 39N 86 43W
Kapiskau →, Ont. 4 B3 52 47N 81 55W
Kaposvar Cr. →, Sask. 20 E8 50 31N 101 55W
Kapuskasing, Ont. 17 C14 49 25N 82 30W
Kapuskasing →, Ont. 17 C15 49 49N 82 0W
Kasba L., N.W.T. 19 A8 60 20N 102 10W
Kashabowie, Ont. 16 D6 48 40N 90 26W
Kaskattama →, Man. 19 B10 57 3N 90 4W
Kaslo, B.C. 25 F18 49 55N 116 55W
Kasmere L., Man. 19 B8 59 34N 101 10W
Katimik L., Man. 21 C11 52 53N 99 21W
Kawagama L., Ont. 10 F4 45 18N 78 45W
Kawene, Ont. 16 D5 48 45N 91 15W
Kawinawl, Man. 21 C11 52 50N 99 30W
Kearney, Ont. 14 B7 45 33N 79 13W
Kechika →, B.C. 18 B3 59 41N 127 12W
Kedgwick, N.B. 9 F2 47 40N 67 20W
Keeley L., Sask. 19 C7 54 54N 108 8W
Keene, Ont. 15 C8 44 15N 78 10W
Keewatin, Ont. 16 C2 49 46N 94 34W
Keewatin □, N.W.T. 19 A10 63 20N 95 0W
Keewatin →, Man. 19 B8 56 29N 100 46W
Keezhik L., Ont. 16 A8 51 45N 88 30W
Keg River, Alta. 18 B5 57 54N 117 55W
Kégashka, L., Qué. 8 C8 50 20N 61 25W
Kegaska, Qué. 8 C8 50 9N 61 18W
Keglo, B., Qué. 6 B4 58 40N 66 0W
Keith Arm, N.W.T. 26 C3 64 20N 122 15W
Kejimkujik Nat. Park, N.S. 9 I4 44 25N 65 25W
Kellett C., N.W.T. 26 B3 72 0N 126 0W
Kellett Str., N.W.T. 26 B4 75 45N 117 30W
Kelligrews, Nfld. 7 F7 47 30N 53 1W
Kelliher, Sask. 20 D7 51 16N 103 44W
Kelowna, B.C. 25 F15 49 50N 119 25W
Kelsey Bay, B.C. 24 E9 50 25N 126 0W
Kelvin I., Ont. 16 C8 49 51N 88 40W
Kelvington, Sask. 20 C7 52 10N 103 30W
Kelwood, Man. 21 E11 50 37N 99 28W
Kemano, B.C. 24 B7 53 35N 128 0W
Kempt, L., Qué. 11 D8 47 25N 74 22W
Kemptown, N.S. 9 H6 45 28N 63 5W
Kemptville, Ont. 15 C11 45 0N 75 38W
Kenaston, Sask. 20 D4 51 30N 106 17W
Kennebecasis →, N.B. 9 H3 45 19N 66 4W
Kennedy, B.C. 32 B3 49 10N 122 53W
Kennedy, Sask. 21 E8 50 1N 102 21W
Kennedy I., B.C. 24 A4 54 3N 130 11W
Kennedy L., B.C. 24 F9 49 3N 125 32W
Kennetcook, N.S. 9 H6 45 11N 63 44W
Keno Hill, Yukon 26 C2 63 57N 135 18W
Kénogami, Qué. 11 C11 48 25N 71 15W
Kenogami →, Ont. 17 A12 51 6N 84 28W
Kénogami, L., Qué. 11 C11 48 20N 71 23W
Kenora, Ont. 16 C2 49 47N 94 29W
Kensington, P.E.I. 9 G6 46 28N 63 34W
Kensington, Qué. 12 B2 45 1N 74 18W
Kent Junction, N.B. 9 G4 46 35N 65 20W
Kent Pen., N.W.T. 26 C5 68 30N 107 0W
Kentville, N.S. 9 H5 45 6N 64 29W
Kenville, Man. 21 D9 52 0N 101 20W
Keremeos, B.C. 25 F15 49 13N 119 50W
Kerrobert, Sask. 20 D1 51 56N 109 8W
Kersley, B.C. 25 C12 52 49N 122 25W
Kesagami →, Ont. 4 B4 51 40N 79 45W
Kesagami L., Ont. 4 B3 50 23N 80 15W
Keswick, Ont. 14 C7 44 15N 79 28W
Kettle →, Man. 19 B11 56 40N 89 34W
Kettle →, B.C. 25 G16 48 41N 118 7W
Kettle Pt., Ont. 14 D4 43 13N 82 1W
Key Harbour, Ont. 14 B6 45 50N 80 45W
Khedive, Sask. 20 F6 49 37N 104 31W
Kicking Horse Pass, B.C. 25 D18 51 28N 116 16W
Kiglapait Mts., Nfld. 6 B5 57 6N 61 22W
Kikino, Alta. 22 D8 54 27N 112 8W
Kikkatla, B.C. 24 B4 53 47N 130 25W
Kilbride, Nfld. 7 H7 47 32N 52 45W
Kilbride, Ont. 13 B3 43 25N 79 56W
Kildala Arm, B.C. 24 B6 53 50N 128 29W
Killala L., Ont. 17 C10 49 5N 86 32W
Killaloe Sta., Ont. 10 F5 45 33N 77 25W
Killaly, Sask. 20 E8 50 45N 102 50W
Killam, Alta. 23 F9 52 47N 111 51W
Killarney, Man. 21 F11 49 10N 99 40W
Killarney, Ont. 14 B5 45 55N 81 30W
Killarney Prov. Park, Ont. 14 A5 46 2N 81 35W
Killdeer, Sask. 20 F4 49 6N 106 22W
Killinek I., Nfld. 6 A5 60 24N 64 37W
Killowen, Qué. 12 A2 45 36N 74 15W
Kilmar, Qué. 12 A1 45 46N 74 37W
Kimberley, B.C. 23 I5 49 40N 115 59W
Kimbo, Ont. 13 B3 43 7N 79 36W
Kimiwan L., Alta. 22 C4 55 45N 116 55W
Kimsquit, B.C. 24 C8 52 45N 126 57W
Kinaskan L., B.C. 18 B2 57 38N 130 8W
Kinbasket L., B.C. 25 D16 52 0N 118 10W
Kincaid, Sask. 20 F4 49 40N 107 0W
Kincardine, Ont. 14 C5 44 10N 81 40W
Kindersley, Sask. 20 D1 51 30N 109 10W
King City, Ont. 13 A3 43 56N 79 32W
King George Is., N.W.T. 6 B2 57 20N 78 25W
King I., B.C. 24 C7 52 10N 127 40W
King William I., N.W.T. 27 C6 69 10N 97 25W
Kingcome Inlet, B.C. 24 E8 50 56N 126 29W
Kinghorn, Ont. 28 A2 43 55N 79 34W
King's Point, Nfld. 7 D4 49 35N 56 11W
Kingsey Falls, Qué. 11 F10 45 51N 72 4W
Kingsgate, B.C. 23 I4 49 1N 116 11W
Kingsmere L., Sask. 20 A4 54 6N 106 27W
Kingston, N.S. 9 I5 44 59N 64 57W
Kingston, Ont. 15 C10 44 14N 76 30W
Kingsville, Ont. 14 E4 42 2N 82 45W
Kinistino, Sask. 20 C5 52 57N 105 2W
Kinkora, P.E.I. 9 G6 46 19N 63 36W
Kinmount, Ont. 15 C8 44 48N 78 45W
Kinnaird, B.C. 25 F17 49 17N 117 39W
Kinoje →, Ont. 4 B3 52 8N 81 25W
Kinoje Lakes, Ont. 17 A15 51 35N 81 48W
Kinsale, Ont. 13 A4 43 56N 79 2W
Kinushseo →, Ont. 4 A3 55 15N 83 45W
Kinuso, Alta. 22 C5 55 20N 115 25W
Kiosk, Ont. 15 A8 46 6N 78 53W
Kipahigan L., Man. 19 B8 55 20N 101 55W
Kipawa, Qué. 10 E4 46 47N 78 59W
Kipawa, Parc de, Qué. 10 E4 47 0N 78 50W
Kipawa L., Qué. 10 E4 46 50N 79 0W
Kipling, Sask. 20 E8 50 6N 102 38W
Kippens, Nfld. 7 E2 48 33N 58 38W
Kirkfield, Ont. 15 C8 44 34N 78 59W
Kirkfield Park, Man. 31 B2 49 53N 97 17W
Kirkland, Qué. 29 C2 45 27N 73 52W
Kirkland Lake, Ont. 4 C3 48 9N 80 2W
Kirkwall, Ont. 13 B2 43 21N 80 10W
Kisbey, Sask. 20 F8 49 39N 102 40W
Kiskatinaw →, B.C. 18 B4 56 8N 120 10W
Kiskitto L., Man. 21 A12 54 16N 98 30W
Kiskittogisu L., Man. 21 A12 54 13N 98 20W
Kississing L., Man. 19 B8 55 10N 101 20W
Kitchener, Ont. 13 B2 43 27N 80 29W
Kitikmeot □, N.W.T. 26 C5 70 0N 110 0W
Kitimat, B.C. 24 A6 54 3N 128 38W
Kitimat Arm, B.C. 24 B6 53 55N 128 42W
Kitimat Ranges, B.C. 24 B5 54 0N 129 15W
Kitscoty, Alta. 22 E10 53 20N 110 20W
Kittertoksoak, I., N.W.T. 6 B4 58 50N 65 50W
Kitvitoo, N.W.T. 27 C9 67 56N 64 52W
Klappan →, B.C. 18 B3 58 0N 129 43W
Kleczkowski, L., Qué. 8 C6 50 48N 63 27W
Kleena Kleene, B.C. 24 D10 52 0N 124 59W
Kleinburg, Ont. 28 B2 43 50N 79 38W
Kleindale, B.C. 24 F11 49 38N 123 58W
Klinaklini →, B.C. 24 D9 51 21N 125 40W
Klondike, Yukon 26 C2 64 0N 139 26W
Klotz, L., Qué. 6 A3 60 32N 73 40W
Kluane L., Yukon 26 C2 61 15N 138 40W
Knee L., Man. 19 B10 55 3N 94 45W
Knee L., Sask. 19 B7 55 51N 107 0W
Knewstubb L., B.C. 24 B10 53 33N 124 55W
Knight Inlet, B.C. 24 E9 50 45N 125 40W
Knowlton, Qué. 11 F10 45 13N 72 31W
Knox, C., B.C. 24 A1 54 11N 133 5W
Koartac, Qué. 6 A4 60 55N 69 40W
Kogaluk →, Nfld. 6 B5 56 12N 61 44W
Kokanee Glacier Prov. Park, B.C. 25 F17 49 47N 117 10W
Koocanusa, L., B.C. 23 I5 49 20N 115 15W
Kootenay L., B.C. 25 F18 49 45N 116 50W
Kootenay Nat. Park, B.C. 23 H5 51 0N 116 0W
Kopka →, Ont. 16 B7 50 4N 89 1W
Kormack, Ont. 17 E14 47 38N 82 59W
Koroc →, Qué. 6 B4 58 50N 65 50W
Kotaneelee →, N.W.T. 18 A4 60 11N 123 42W
Kotcho L., B.C. 18 B4 59 7N 121 12W
Kouchibouguac Nat. Park, N.B. 9 G4 46 50N 65 20W
Kovic, B., Qué. 6 A2 61 35N 77 36W
Kowkash, Ont. 17 B9 50 20N 87 12W
Krydor, Sask. 20 C3 52 47N 107 4W
Kugaluk, B., Qué. 6 B2 59 10N 78 40W
Kugong I., N.W.T. 6 B2 56 18N 79 50W
Kukukus L., Ont. 16 C5 49 47N 91 41W
Kunghit I., B.C. 24 C3 52 6N 131 3W
Kuroki, Sask. 20 D7 51 52N 103 29W
Kusawa L., Yukon 18 A1 60 20N 136 13W
Kuujjuaq, Qué. 6 B4 58 6N 68 15W
Kwadacha →, B.C. 18 B3 57 28N 125 38W
Kwataboahegan →, Ont. 17 A16 51 9N 80 50W
Kwinitsa, B.C. 24 A5 54 19N 129 22W
Kyle, Sask. 20 E2 50 50N 108 2W
Kynoch Inlet, B.C. 24 C7 52 45N 128 0W
Kyuquot, B.C. 24 E7 50 3N 127 25W

L

Laberge, L., Yukon 18 A1 61 11N 135 12W
Labrador, Coast of □, Nfld. 5 B7 53 20N 61 0W
Labrador City, Nfld. 8 A3 52 57N 66 55W
Labrieville, Qué. 11 B13 49 18N 69 34W
Lac Allard, Qué. 8 C6 50 33N 63 24W
Lac-Alouette, Qué. 12 A3 45 49N 73 58W
Lac-au-Saumon, Qué. 8 E2 48 25N 67 22W
Lac-aux-Sables, Qué. 11 E10 46 51N 72 24W
Lac Bouchette, Qué. 11 C10 48 16N 72 11W
Lac-Brière, Qué. 12 A3 45 50N 73 58W
Lac Carré, Qué. 11 E8 46 7N 74 29W
Lac-des-Écorces, Qué. 10 E7 46 34N 75 22W
Lac du Bonnet, Man. 21 E14 50 15N 96 4W
Lac Édouard, Qué. 11 D10 47 40N 72 16W
Lac-Etchemin, Qué. 11 E12 46 24N 70 30W
Lac La Biche, Alta. 22 D9 54 45N 111 58W
Lac la Hache, B.C. 25 D13 51 49N 121 27W
Lac la Martre, N.W.T. 26 C4 63 8N 117 16W
Lac-l'Achigan, Qué. 12 A3 45 57N 73 59W
Lac-Lapierre, Qué. 12 A3 45 56N 73 47W
Lac-Marois, Qué. 12 A2 45 51N 74 8W
Lac-Meach, Ont. 30 C6 45 32N 75 51W
Lac-Mégantic, Qué. 11 F12 45 35N 70 53W
Lac-Millette, Qué. 12 A2 45 58N 74 12W
Lac-Rémi, Qué. 10 E8 46 1N 74 46W
Lac-St-Charles, Qué. 30 A2 46 54N 71 23W
Lac-Ste-Marie, Qué. 10 F7 45 57N 75 57W
Lac Seul Res., Ont. 16 B4 50 25N 92 30W
Lacadie, Qué. 29 D5 45 19N 73 21W
Lachenaie, Qué. 29 A4 45 42N 73 30W
Lachine, Qué. 29 C4 45 30N 73 40W
Lachute, Qué. 12 A2 45 39N 74 21W
Laclu, Ont. 16 C2 49 46N 94 41W
Lacolle, Qué. 12 B4 45 5N 73 22W
Lacombe, Alta. 23 F7 52 30N 113 44W
Ladner, B.C. 32 C2 49 5N 123 4W
Lady Ann Str., N.W.T. 27 B8 75 40N 79 50W
Ladysmith, B.C. 24 G10 49 0N 123 49W
Laferte →, N.W.T. 18 A5 61 53N 117 44W
Laflamme →, Qué. 10 B5 49 17N 77 9W
Laflèche, Qué. 12 B4 45 30N 73 28W
Lafleche, Sask. 20 F4 49 45N 106 40W
Lafontaine, Qué. 12 A2 45 48N 74 1W
Laforce, Qué. 10 D4 47 32N 78 44W
Laidlaw, B.C. 25 F13 49 20N 121 36W
Laird, Sask. 20 C4 52 43N 106 35W
Lake Alma, Sask. 20 F6 49 9N 104 12W
Lake Cowichan, B.C. 24 G10 48 49N 124 3W
Lake Harbour, N.W.T. 27 C9 62 50N 69 50W
Lake Hill, B.C. 25 H19 48 28N 123 22W
Lake Lenore, Sask. 20 C6 52 24N 104 59W
Lake Louise, Alta. 23 G4 51 30N 116 10W
Lake River, Ont. 4 B3 54 30N 82 31W
Lake St. Peter, Ont. 15 B8 45 18N 78 2W
Lake Superior Prov. Park, Ont. 17 E12 47 45N 84 45W
Lake View, Ont. 28 C2 43 34N 79 33W
Lakefield, Ont. 15 C8 44 25N 78 16W
Lakefield, Qué. 12 A2 45 45N 74 15W
Lakeview, Ont. 30 D7 45 21N 75 50W
Lakeview, Qué. 12 A1 45 53N 74 34W
Lakitusaki →, Ont. 4 B3 54 21N 82 25W
Lamaline, Nfld. 7 G5 46 52N 55 49W
Lambeth, Ont. 14 E5 42 54N 81 18W
Lambton, Qué. 11 F11 45 50N 71 5W
Lambton, C., N.W.T. 26 B3 71 5N 123 9W
Lambton Mills, Ont. 28 C2 43 39N 79 31W
Lamèque, N.B. 9 F5 47 45N 64 38W
Lamming Mills, B.C. 25 B14 53 20N 120 15W
Lamont, Alta. 22 E8 53 46N 112 50W
Lampman, Sask. 20 F8 49 25N 102 50W
Lamprey, Man. 19 B10 58 33N 94 8W
Lanark, Ont. 10 F6 45 1N 76 22W
Lancaster, Ont. 10 F8 45 10N 74 30W
Lancaster, Qué. 12 B2 45 8N 74 30W
Lancaster Sd., N.W.T. 27 B7 74 13N 84 0W
Lancer, Sask. 20 E2 50 48N 108 53W
Landis, Sask. 20 C2 52 12N 108 27W
Landrienne, Qué. 10 C5 48 30N 77 50W
Lang Bay, B.C. 24 F10 49 45N 124 21W
Langara I., B.C. 24 A1 54 14N 133 1W
Langenburg, Sask. 21 E9 50 51N 101 43W
Langford, B.C. 25 H19 48 27N 123 29W
Langham, Sask. 20 C4 52 22N 106 58W
Langlade, St- P. & M. 7 G4 46 50N 56 20W
Langley, B.C. 25 F12 49 7N 122 39W
Langruth, Man. 21 E12 50 23N 98 40W
Langstaff, Ont. 28 B3 43 50N 79 25W
Lanigan, Sask. 20 D5 51 51N 105 2W
Lanoraie, Qué. 12 A4 45 58N 73 13W
Lansdowne, Ont. 15 C10 44 24N 76 1W
Lansdowne House, Ont. 4 B2 52 14N 87 53W
Lansing, Ont. 28 B3 43 45N 79 25W
Lanz I., B.C. 24 E6 50 49N 128 41W
Lanzville, B.C. 24 F10 49 15N 124 5W
Laprairie □, Qué. 12 B4 45 20N 73 30W
Larder Lake, Ont. 10 C3 48 5N 79 40W
Laredo Sd., B.C. 24 C6 52 30N 128 53W
Lark Harbour, Nfld. 7 D2 49 6N 58 23W
Larrys River, N.S. 9 H8 45 13N 61 23W
Larus L., Ont. 16 A2 51 17N 94 40W
Lasalle, Qué. 29 C4 45 26N 73 38W
Lashburn, Sask. 20 B1 53 10N 109 40W
Lasqueti, B.C. 24 F10 49 30N 124 21W
Lasqueti I., B.C. 24 F10 49 29N 124 16W
Last Mountain L., Sask. 20 D5 51 5N 105 14W
Latchford, Ont. 10 D3 47 20N 79 50W
Latulipe, Qué. 10 D3 47 26N 79 2W
Laurel, Ont. 13 A2 43 57N 80 13W
Laurel, Qué. 12 A2 45 51N 74 28W
Laurentian Plateau, Qué. 6 C4 52 0N 70 0W
Laurentides, Qué. 12 A3 45 51N 73 46W
Laurentides, Parc Prov. des, Qué. 11 D11 47 45N 71 15W
Laurie L., Man. 19 B8 56 35N 101 57W
Laurier, Man. 21 E11 50 53N 99 33W
Laurier-Station, Qué. 11 E11 46 32N 71 38W
Laurierville, Qué. 11 E11 46 18N 71 39W
Lauzon, Qué. 30 B4 46 48N 71 10W
Laval, Qué. 29 B3 45 35N 73 45W
Laval-des-Rapides, Qué. 29 B3 45 33N 73 42W
Laval-Ouest, Qué. 29 B2 45 33N 73 52W
Laval-sur-le-Lac, Qué. 29 B2 45 32N 73 52W
Lavaltrie, Qué. 12 A4 45 53N 73 17W
Lavant Sta., Ont. 15 B10 45 3N 76 42W
Laverlochère, Qué. 10 D3 47 26N 79 18W
Lavieille, L., Ont. 15 B8 45 51N 78 14W
Lavillètte, N.B. 9 F4 47 16N 65 18W
Lavoy, Alta. 22 E9 53 27N 111 52W
Lawn, Nfld. 7 G5 46 57N 55 35W
Lawrence Station, N.B. 9 H2 45 26N 67 11W
Lawrencetown, N.S. 9 I4 44 53N 65 10W
Leach I., Ont. 17 E12 47 28N 84 57W
Leader, Sask. 20 E1 50 50N 109 30W
Leaf L., Sask. 21 B8 53 1N 102 8W
Leamington, Ont. 14 E4 42 3N 82 36W
Leaside, Ont. 28 B3 43 42N 79 22W
Leask, Sask. 20 B4 53 5N 106 45W
Lebel-sur-Quévillon, Qué. 10 B6 49 3N 76 59W
Leduc, Alta. 22 E7 53 15N 113 30W
Leech L., Sask. 20 D8 51 5N 102 28W
Lefebvre, Qué. 11 D13 47 12N 69 49W
Lefroy, Ont. 14 C7 44 16N 79 34W
Legal, Alta. 22 E7 53 55N 113 35W
Légère, N.B. 9 F5 47 25N 64 56W
Leitrim, Ont. 30 E8 45 20N 75 36W
Lejeune, Qué. 11 D14 47 46N 68 34W
Leland Lakes, N.W.T. 19 A6 60 0N 110 59W
Lemberg, Sask. 20 E7 50 44N 103 12W
Lemieux, Qué. 11 E10 46 18N 72 7W
Lemieux, L., Qué. 10 A8 50 19N 74 38W
Lemieux Is., N.W.T. 27 C9 63 40N 64 20W
Lemoine, L., Qué. 10 D5 48 0N 78 0W
Lemoyne, Qué. 29 C5 45 30N 73 30W
Lennoxville, Qué. 11 F11 45 22N 71 51W
Lenore L., Sask. 20 C6 52 30N 104 59W
Leoville, Sask. 20 B3 53 39N 107 33W
Lepellé →, Qué. 6 B3 59 58N 72 24W
Lepreau, N.B. 9 H3 45 10N 66 28W
Leroy, Sask. 20 D6 52 0N 104 44W
Leroy, L., Qué. 6 B4 55 10N 67 15W
Léry, Qué. 29 C3 45 21N 73 48W
Leslieville, Alta. 23 F6 52 23N 114 36W
Lesser Slave L., Alta. 22 C5 55 30N 115 25W
Lesser Slave Lake Prov. Park, Alta. 22 C6 55 26N 114 49W
Lester B. Pearson International Airport, Ont. 28 B2 43 42N 79 38W
Lestock, Sask. 20 D7 51 19N 103 59W
Lethbridge, Alta. 23 I8 49 45N 112 45W
Lethbridge, Nfld. 7 E7 48 22N 53 52W
Levack, Ont. 14 A5 46 38N 81 23W
Lévis, Qué. 30 B4 46 48N 71 9W
Levis, L., N.W.T. 18 A5 62 37N 117 58W
Lewis Hills, Nfld. 7 E2 48 48N 58 30W
Lewisporte, Nfld. 7 D5 49 15N 55 3W
Lewisville, N.B. 9 G5 46 6N 64 46W
Liard →, N.W.T. 18 A4 61 51N 121 18W
Liberty, Sask. 20 D5 51 8N 105 26W
Liddon Gulf, N.W.T. 26 B4 75 3N 113 0W
Lièvre →, Qué. 10 F7 45 31N 75 26W
Likely, B.C. 25 C13 52 37N 121 35W
Lillian L., Qué. 8 B8 51 17N 61 23W
Lillooet, B.C. 25 E13 50 44N 121 57W
Lillooet →, B.C. 25 F13 49 15N 121 57W
Lillooet L., B.C. 25 E12 50 18N 122 35W
Limbour, Ont. 30 D7 45 29N 75 45W
Limehouse, Ont. 13 A3 43 38N 79 58W
Limerick, Sask. 20 F4 49 39N 106 16W
Limestone →, Man. 19 B10 56 31N 94 7W
Limestone B., Man. 21 B12 53 50N 98 53W
Limoges, Ont. 15 B11 45 20N 75 15W
Linaria, Alta. 22 D6 54 19N 114 8W
Lincoln, Ont. 13 B4 43 10N 79 29W
Lincolnville, N.S. 9 H8 45 30N 61 33W
Lindell Beach, B.C. 25 F12 49 2N 122 1W
Linden, Alta. 23 G7 51 36N 113 28W
Lindsay, Ont. 15 C8 44 22N 78 43W
Linière, Qué. 11 E12 46 4N 70 32W
Link L., B.C. 24 C7 52 25N 127 40W
Lintlaw, Sask. 20 C7 52 4N 103 14W
Linton, Ont. 13 A3 43 56N 79 40W
Linton, Qué. 11 D10 47 15N 72 16W
Linwood, Ont. 14 D6 43 35N 80 43W
Lion's Head, Ont. 14 C5 44 58N 81 15W
Lipton, Sask. 20 E7 50 54N 103 51W
Listowel, Ont. 14 D6 43 44N 80 58W
Little Abitibi →, Ont. 17 B15 50 29N 81 32W
Little Bay, Nfld. 7 D5 49 36N 55 57W
Little Bow →, Alta. 23 I8 49 53N 112 29W
Little Burnt Bay, Nfld. 7 D5 49 25N 55 5W
Little Cadotte →, Alta. 22 B3 56 41N 117 6W
Little Churchill →, Man. 19 B9 57 30N 95 22W
Little Corners, Ont. 13 B2 43 20N 80 17W
Little Current, Ont. 14 B5 45 55N 82 0W
Little Current →, Ont. 17 B12 50 57N 84 36W
Little Dover, N.S. 9 H8 45 15N 61 3W
Little Fort, B.C. 25 D14 51 26N 120 13W
Little Grand Rapids, Man. 21 D15 52 0N 95 29W
Little Narrows, N.S. 9 H9 45 59N 60 59W
Little Pic →, Ont. 17 D10 48 48N 86 37W
Little Quill L., Sask. 20 D6 51 55N 104 5W
Little Rouge →, Ont. 28 B5 43 48N 79 8W
Little Smoky →, Alta. 22 D3 54 44N 117 11W
Little White →, Ont. 14 A3 46 23N 83 20W
Lively, Ont. 14 A5 46 26N 81 9W
Liverpool, N.S. 9 I5 44 5N 64 41W
Liverpool, C., N.W.T. 27 B8 73 38N 78 6W
Liverpool Bay, N.W.T. 26 C3 70 0N 128 0W
Lloyd L., Sask. 19 B7 57 22N 108 57W
Lloydminster, Sask. 20 B1 53 17N 110 0W
Lloyds →, Nfld. 7 E3 48 35N 57 15W
Lloydtown, Ont. 13 A3 43 59N 79 42W
Lochdale, B.C. 32 B3 49 17N 122 58W
Loche, La, Sask. 19 B7 56 29N 109 26W
Lockeport, N.S. 9 J4 43 47N 65 4W
Lodgepole, Alta. 23 E5 53 6N 115 19W
Logan, Mount, Qué. 8 E3 48 53N 66 38W
Logan I., Ont. 16 B8 50 7N 88 27W
Loggieville, N.B. 9 F4 47 4N 65 23W
Logy Bay, Nfld. 7 H8 47 38N 52 40W
Lomond, Alta. 23 H8 50 24N 112 36W
London, Ont. 14 E5 42 59N 81 15W
Londonderry, N.S. 9 H6 45 29N 63 36W
Lone Butte, B.C. 25 D13 51 33N 121 12W
Lone Pine, Alta. 22 D5 54 18N 115 7W
Lone Rock, Sask. 20 B1 53 3N 109 53W
Lonely I., Ont. 14 B5 45 34N 81 28W
Long Beach, B.C. 24 F9 49 1N 125 40W
Long Branch, Ont. 28 C2 43 35N 79 32W
Long Cr. →, Sask. 20 F8 49 7N 102 59W
Long I., N.W.T. 6 C2 54 50N 79 20W
Long I., Nfld. 7 F5 47 34N 55 59W
Long L., Alta. 22 D8 54 22N 112 46W
Long L., Ont. 17 C10 49 30N 86 50W
Long Lake, N.S. 9 L11 44 36N 63 38W
Long Pt., Man. 21 B12 53 2N 98 25W
Long Pt., Nfld. 7 E2 48 47N 58 46W
Long Pt., Ont. 14 E6 42 35N 80 2W
Long Point B., Ont. 14 E6 42 40N 80 10W
Long Range Mts., Nfld. 7 D3 49 30N 57 30W
Long Reach, N.B. 9 H3 45 28N 66 5W
Longlac, Ont. 17 C10 49 45N 86 25W
Longlegged L., Ont. 16 B2 50 46N 94 8W
Longue-Pointe-de-Mingan, Qué. 8 C5 50 16N 64 9W
Longueuil, Qué. 11 F9 45 32N 73 30W
Longueuil-St-Hubert, Qué. 12 B4 45 29N 73 26W
Longview, Alta. 23 H6 50 32N 114 10W
Lookout, C., Ont. 4 A3 55 18N 83 56W
Loon →, Alta. 22 A5 57 8N 115 3W
Loon →, Man. 19 B8 55 53N 101 59W
Loon Lake, Sask. 20 A1 54 2N 109 10W
Lord Selkirk, Man. 31 B2 49 56N 97 11W
Lord's Cove, Nfld. 7 G5 46 53N 55 40W
Loreburn, Sask. 20 D4 51 13N 106 36W
Lorette, Man. 21 F14 49 44N 96 52W
Loretteville, Qué. 30 A2 46 51N 71 21W
Lorne, N.B. 9 F3 47 53N 66 8W
Lorne Park, Ont. 28 C2 43 32N 79 36W
Lorraine, Qué. 29 A3 45 41N 73 47W
Lorrainville, Qué. 10 D3 47 21N 79 23W
Lost River, Qué. 12 A1 45 50N 74 33W
Lott Cr. →, Alta. 31 G9 51 0N 114 13W
Lougheed, Alta. 23 F9 52 44N 111 33W
Lougheed I., N.W.T. 26 B5 77 26N 105 6W
Louis Creek, B.C. 25 D14 51 8N 120 7W
Louis XIV, Pte., Qué. 6 C2 54 37N 79 45W
Louisa, L., Qué. 12 A2 45 46N 74 25W
Louisbourg, N.S. 9 H10 45 55N 60 0W
Louisbourg Nat. Historic Park, N.S. 9 H9 45 58N 60 20W
Louisdale, N.S. 9 H8 45 36N 61 4W
Louise I., B.C. 24 C3 52 55N 131 50W
Louiseville, Qué. 11 E10 46 20N 72 56W
Loups Marins, Lacs des, Qué. 6 B3 56 30N 73 45W
Lourdes, Nfld. 7 E2 48 39N 59 0W

Lourdes-du-Blanc-Sablon, Qué. 7 B3 51 24N 57 12W
Love, Sask. 20 B6 53 29N 104 10W
Loverna, Sask. 20 D1 51 40N 110 0W
Low, Qué. 10 F7 45 50N 76 0W
Low, C., N.W.T. 27 C7 63 7N 85 18W
Low L., Qué. 6 B4 55 54N 67 5W
Lowe Farm, Man. 21 F13 49 21N 97 35W
Lower Arrow L., B.C. 25 F16 49 40N 118 5W
Lower Capilano, B.C. 32 B2 49 19N 123 7W
Lower Manitou L., Ont. 16 C4 49 15N 93 0W
Lower Nicola, B.C. 25 E14 50 12N 120 54W
Lower Post, B.C. 18 B3 59 58N 128 30W
Lower West Pubnico, N.S. 9 J4 43 38N 65 48W
Lower Wood Harbour, N.S. 9 J4 43 31N 65 44W
Lowther, Ont. 17 C13 49 32N 83 2W
Lubicon L., Alta. 22 B5 56 23N 115 56W
Lubicon Lake, Alta. 22 B5 56 22N 115 52W
Lucan, Ont. 14 D5 43 11N 81 24W
Lucerne, B.C. 25 C16 52 52N 118 33W
Luceville, Qué. 11 C14 48 32N 68 22W
Luck L., Sask. 20 D3 51 5N 107 5W
Lucknow, Ont. 14 D5 43 57N 81 31W
Lucky Lake, Sask. 20 E3 50 59N 107 8W
Ludlow, N.B. 9 G3 46 29N 66 21W
Lulu I., B.C. 32 C2 49 10N 123 5W
Lumsden, Nfld. 7 D7 49 19N 53 37W
Lumsden, Sask. 20 E6 50 39N 104 52W
Lund, B.C. 24 F10 49 59N 124 45W
Lundar, Man. 21 E12 50 42N 98 2W
Lundbreck, Alta. 23 I6 49 35N 114 10W
Lunenburg, N.S. 9 I5 44 22N 64 18W
Luscar, Alta. 23 E3 53 4N 117 24W
Luseland, Sask. 20 C1 52 5N 109 24W
Luther, L., Ont. 13 A2 43 56N 80 26W
Lyal I., Ont. 14 C5 44 57N 81 24W
Lyell I., B.C. 24 C3 52 40N 131 35W
Lymburn, Alta. 22 C1 55 21N 119 47W
Lynden, Ont. 13 B2 43 14N 80 9W
Lynn Cr. →, B.C. 32 B2 49 18N 123 2W
Lynn Creek, B.C. 32 A2 49 20N 123 2W
Lynn Lake, Man. 19 B8 56 51N 101 3W
Lynnmour, B.C. 32 B2 49 19N 123 3W
Lynx L., N.W.T. 19 A7 62 25N 106 15W
Lyster, Qué. 11 E11 46 22N 71 37W
Lytton, B.C. 25 E13 50 13N 121 31W

M

Ma-Me-O Beach, Alta. 23 F7 52 58N 113 59W
Mabel L., B.C. 25 E16 50 35N 118 43W
Maberly, Ont. 15 C10 44 50N 76 32W
Mabou, N.S. 9 G8 46 4N 61 29W
McAdam, N.B. 9 H2 45 36N 67 20W
Macalister, B.C. 25 C12 52 27N 122 24W
Macamic, Qué. 10 C4 48 45N 79 0W
Macaulay Pt., B.C. 25 H19 48 25N 123 24W
McAuley, Man. 21 E9 50 16N 101 23W
McBride, B.C. 25 B14 53 20N 120 19W
McCallum, Nfld. 7 F4 47 38N 56 14W
Maccan, N.S. 9 H5 45 43N 64 15W
McCauley I., B.C. 24 B4 53 40N 130 15W
McClelland L., Alta. 22 A9 57 29N 111 20W
McClintock, Man. 19 B10 57 50N 94 10W
McClure Str., N.W.T. 26 B4 75 0N 119 0W
McCormick, Qué. 12 B1 45 21N 74 33W
McCreary, Man. 21 E11 50 46N 99 29W
McCusker →, Sask. 19 B7 55 32N 108 39W
McDame, B.C. 18 B3 59 44N 128 59W
Macdiarmid, Ont. 16 C8 49 26N 88 8W
McDonald, L., Qué. 12 A1 45 52N 74 35W
Macdougall L., N.W.T. 27 C6 66 0N 98 27W
MacDowell L., Ont. 4 B1 52 15N 92 45W
Macdun, Sask. 20 F7 49 19N 103 16W
Maces Bay, N.B. 9 H3 45 6N 66 29W
McFarlane →, Sask. 19 B7 59 12N 107 58W
MacGregor, Man. 21 F12 49 57N 98 48W
McGregor →, B.C. 18 B4 55 10N 122 0W
McGregor L., Alta. 23 H8 50 25N 112 52W
Machichi →, Man. 19 B10 57 3N 92 6W
McIntosh, Ont. 16 C3 49 57N 93 36W
McIntosh L., Sask. 19 B8 55 45N 105 0W
McIntyre B., B.C. 24 A3 54 5N 132 0W
Mackay, Alta. 22 E5 53 39N 115 35W
MacKay →, Alta. 22 A9 57 10N 111 38W
McKay L., Ont. 17 C10 49 37N 86 25W
McKellar, Ont. 14 B7 45 30N 79 55W
Mackenzie, B.C. 18 B4 55 20N 123 5W
Mackenzie →, N.W.T. 26 C2 69 10N 134 20W
Mackenzie Bay, N.W.T. 26 C2 69 0N 137 30W
Mackenzie Highway, Alta. 18 B5 58 0N 117 15W
Mackenzie King I., N.W.T. 26 B4 77 45N 111 0W
McKenzie L., Sask. 20 A8 54 12N 102 30W
Mackenzie Mts., Yukon 26 C3 64 0N 130 0W
Macklin, Sask. 20 C1 52 20N 109 56W
McLean, Sask. 20 E6 50 31N 104 4W
Maclean Str., N.W.T. 27 B5 77 30N 103 30W
McLennan, Alta. 22 C4 55 42N 116 50W
McLeod →, Alta. 22 D5 54 9N 115 42W
MacLeod, B., N.W.T. 19 A7 62 53N 110 0W
MacLeod Lake, B.C. 18 C4 54 58N 123 0W
M'Clintock Chan., N.W.T. 26 B5 72 0N 102 0W
McLure, B.C. 25 D14 51 2N 120 13W
McMasterville, Qué. 12 A4 45 33N 73 15W
McMorran, Sask. 20 D2 51 19N 108 42W
McMurray = Fort McMurray, Alta. 22 B9 56 44N 111 7W
McNabs I, N.S. 9 L11 44 37N 63 32W
MacNutt, Sask. 21 D9 51 5N 101 36W
Macoun L., Sask. 19 B8 56 32N 103 40W
MacTier, Ont. 14 B7 45 8N 79 47W
Madame I., N.S. 9 H9 45 30N 60 58W
Madawaska, Ont. 10 F5 45 30N 78 0W
Madawaska →, Ont. 15 B10 45 27N 76 21W
Maddox Cove, Nfld. 7 I7 47 28N 52 42W
Madeira Park, B.C. 24 F11 49 37N 124 0W
Madeleine →, Qué. 8 D4 49 15N 65 19W
Madeleine, Is. de la, Qué. 9 F8 47 30N 61 40W
Madeleine-Centre, Qué. 8 D4 49 15N 65 22W
Madoc, Ont. 15 C9 44 30N 77 28W
Madsen, Ont. 16 B3 50 58N 93 55W
Mafeking, Man. 21 C9 52 40N 101 10W
Magaguadavic, N.B. 9 H2 45 42N 67 12W
Magaguadavic →, N.B. 9 H3 45 7N 66 54W
Magaguadavic L., N.B. 9 H2 45 43N 67 12W
Magnetawan, Ont. 14 B7 45 40N 79 39W
Magog, Qué. 11 F10 45 18N 72 9W
Magpie, Qué. 8 C5 50 19N 64 30W
Magpie →, Ont. 17 E12 47 56N 84 50W
Magpie →, Qué. 8 C5 50 19N 64 27W
Magpie L., Qué. 8 C5 51 0N 64 41W
Magrath, Alta. 23 I8 49 25N 112 50W
Maguse L., N.W.T. 19 A9 61 40N 95 10W
Maguse Pt., N.W.T. 19 A10 61 20N 93 50W
Mahatta River, B.C. 24 E7 50 22N 127 47W
Mahone Bay, N.S. 5 D7 44 30N 64 20W
Mahood Falls, B.C. 25 D14 51 50N 120 38W
Mahood L., B.C. 25 D14 51 50N 120 23W
Maicasagi →, Qué. 10 B6 49 58N 76 33W
Maidstone, Sask. 20 B1 53 5N 109 20W
Maillardville, B.C. 32 B3 49 15N 122 52W
Main-à-Dieu, N.S. 9 H10 46 0N 59 51W
Main Brook, Nfld. 7 B4 51 11N 56 1W
Main Centre, Sask. 20 E3 50 35N 107 21W
Maisonnette, N.B. 9 F5 47 49N 65 0W
Maitland, N.S. 9 H6 45 19N 63 30W
Maitland Bridge, N.S. 9 I4 44 27N 65 12W
Major, Sask. 20 D1 51 52N 109 37W
Makkovik, Nfld. 6 B6 55 10N 59 10W
Makokibatan L., Ont. 17 A9 51 17N 87 20W
Malachi, Ont. 16 C2 49 56N 94 59W
Malartic, Qué. 10 C4 48 9N 78 9W
Malartic, L., Qué. 10 C4 48 15N 78 5W
Malbaie, La, Qué. 11 D12 47 40N 70 10W
Malcolm I., B.C. 24 E8 50 38N 127 0W
Maligne L., Alta. 23 F3 52 40N 117 31W
Mallaig, Alta. 22 D9 54 13N 111 22W
Mallorytown, Ont. 15 C11 44 29N 75 53W
Malton, Ont. 28 B2 43 42N 79 38W
Malvern, Ont. 28 B4 43 48N 79 14W
Mameigwess L., Ont. 16 C5 49 34N 91 49W
Mameigwess L., Ont. 4 B2 52 35N 87 50W
Manawan L., Sask. 19 B8 55 24N 103 14W
Manchester L., N.W.T. 19 A7 61 28N 107 29W
Manicouagan →, Qué. 11 B14 49 30N 68 30W
Manicouagan, Rés., Qué. 6 C4 51 5N 68 40W
Manigotagan, Man. 21 D14 51 6N 96 18W
Manigotagan L., Man. 21 E15 50 52N 95 37W
Manito L., Sask. 20 C1 52 43N 109 43W
Manitoba □, Man. 21 A14 55 30N 97 0W
Manitoba, L., Man. 21 E12 51 0N 98 45W
Manitou, Man. 21 F12 49 15N 98 32W
Manitou, Qué. 8 C4 50 18N 65 15W
Manitou →, Qué. 8 C4 50 18N 65 15W
Manitou L., Ont. 14 B5 45 51N 82 0W
Manitou L., Qué. 8 C4 50 55N 65 17W
Manitoulin I., Ont. 14 B4 45 40N 82 30W
Manitouwadge, Ont. 17 C11 49 8N 85 48W
Manitowaning, Ont. 14 B5 45 46N 81 49W
Maniwaki, Qué. 10 E7 46 23N 75 58W
Mankota, Sask. 20 F3 49 25N 107 5W
Manlius, Man. 31 B3 50 0N 97 2W
Mannheim, Ont. 13 B1 43 24N 80 33W
Manning, Alta. 22 B3 56 53N 117 39W
Manning Park, B.C. 25 F14 49 4N 120 47W
Manning Prov. Park, B.C. 25 F14 49 5N 120 45W
Mannville, Alta. 22 E9 53 20N 111 10W
Manor, Sask. 21 F8 49 36N 102 5W
Manotick, Ont. 15 B11 45 13N 75 41W
Manouane, L., Qué. 11 D8 47 33N 74 6W
Manouane, L., Qué. 6 C3 50 45N 70 45W
Manseau, Qué. 11 E11 46 22N 72 0W
Mansel I., N.W.T. 27 C8 62 0N 80 0W
Manson Creek, B.C. 18 B4 55 37N 124 32W
Manuels, N.B. 9 F5 47 3N 64 59W
Many Island L., Alta. 23 H10 50 8N 110 3W
Manyberries, Alta. 23 I10 49 24N 110 42W
Maple, Ont. 28 A2 43 51N 79 31W
Maple Bay, B.C. 25 G11 48 48N 123 37W
Maple Creek, Sask. 20 F1 49 55N 109 29W
Maple Grove, Qué. 29 D3 45 19N 73 50W
Maples, The, Ont. 13 A2 43 52N 80 10W
Marathon, Ont. 17 D10 48 44N 86 23W
Marblehead, B.C. 25 E18 50 15N 116 58W
Marbleton, Qué. 11 F11 45 37N 71 35W
Marceau, L., Qué. 8 B3 51 25N 66 41W
Marcelin, Sask. 20 C4 52 55N 106 47W
Marconi, Man. 31 B3 49 55N 97 6W
Marden, Ont. 13 A2 43 36N 80 18W
Marelan, Qué. 12 A1 45 38N 74 33W
Marengo, Sask. 20 D1 51 29N 109 47W
Margaree Forks, N.S. 9 G8 46 20N 61 5W
Margaret Bay, B.C. 24 D7 51 20N 127 35W
Margaret L., Alta. 18 B5 58 56N 115 25W
Margo, Sask. 20 D7 51 49N 103 20W
Marguerite, B.C. 25 C12 52 30N 122 25W
Maria, Qué. 8 E4 48 10N 65 59W
Marian L., N.W.T. 18 A5 63 0N 116 15W
Maricourt, Qué. 6 B3 56 34N 70 49W
Marie L., Alta. 22 D10 54 38N 110 18W
Marieville, Qué. 12 B4 45 26N 73 10W
Markdale, Ont. 14 C6 44 19N 80 39W
Markerville, Alta. 23 F6 52 7N 114 10W
Markham, Ont. 28 A4 43 52N 79 16W
Markham L., N.W.T. 19 A8 62 30N 102 35W
Markstay, Ont. 14 A6 46 29N 80 32W
Marlbank, Ont. 15 C9 44 26N 77 6W
Marmion L., Ont. 16 D5 48 55N 91 20W
Marmora, Ont. 15 C9 44 28N 77 41W
Marquette, Man. 21 E13 50 4N 97 44W
Marquette, L., Qué. 11 C9 48 54N 73 54W
Marsden, Sask. 20 C1 52 51N 109 49W
Marshall, Sask. 20 B1 53 11N 109 47W
Marsoui, Qué. 8 D3 49 13N 66 4W
Marsville, Ont. 13 A2 43 50N 80 13W
Marten River, Ont. 14 A7 46 44N 79 49W
Martensville, Sask. 20 C4 52 17N 106 40W
Martre, L., La, N.W.T. 26 C4 63 0N 118 0W
Marwayne, Alta. 22 E10 53 32N 110 20W
Mary Frances L., N.W.T. 19 A7 63 19N 106 13W
Maryen, L., Qué. 8 B9 51 20N 60 28W
Maryfield, Sask. 21 F9 49 50N 101 35W
Maryhill, Ont. 13 A2 43 32N 80 23W
Mary's Harbour, Nfld. 6 C6 52 18N 55 51W
Marystown, Nfld. 7 F5 47 10N 55 10W
Marysville, B.C. 23 I5 49 35N 116 0W
Marysville, N.B. 9 H3 45 59N 66 35W
Mascouche, Qué. 29 A4 45 45N 73 36W
Mascouche →, Qué. 29 A4 45 41N 73 37W
Maskinongé, Qué. 11 E9 46 14N 73 1W
Masset, B.C. 24 A2 54 2N 132 10W
Masset Inlet, B.C. 24 B2 53 43N 132 20W
Massey, Ont. 14 A4 46 12N 82 5W
Masson, Qué. 10 F7 45 32N 75 25W
Massueville, Qué. 12 A5 45 55N 72 56W
Mastigouche, Parc, Qué. 11 E9 46 33N 73 41W
Matachewan, Ont. 4 C3 47 56N 80 39W
Matagami, Qué. 10 B5 49 45N 77 34W
Matagami, L., Qué. 10 B5 49 50N 77 40W
Matamec, L., Qué. 8 C4 50 21N 65 58W
Matane, Qué. 8 E2 48 50N 67 33W
Matane →, Qué. 8 E2 48 50N 67 35W
Matane, Parc Prov. de, Qué. 8 E3 48 40N 67 0W
Matapédia, N.B. 9 F3 48 0N 66 59W
Matapédia, L., Qué. 8 E2 48 35N 67 35W
Matawin →, Qué. 11 E10 46 54N 72 56W
Matawin, Rés., Qué. 11 E9 46 46N 73 50W
Matchi-Manitou, L., Qué. 10 C5 48 0N 77 4W
Matheson Island, Man. 21 D14 51 45N 96 56W
Matinenda L., Ont. 14 A4 46 22N 82 57W
Mattagami →, Ont. 17 B15 50 43N 81 29W
Mattagami L., Ont. 17 E15 47 54N 81 35W
Mattawa, Qué. 4 C4 46 20N 78 45W
Mattawitchewan →, Ont. 17 C13 49 52N 83 12W
Mattice, Ont. 17 C13 49 40N 83 20W
Maugerville, N.B. 9 H3 45 52N 66 27W
Maunoir, L., N.W.T. 26 C3 67 30N 124 55W
Mauricie, Parc Nat. de la, Qué. 11 E10 46 45N 73 0W
Mavillette, N.S. 9 I3 44 6N 66 11W
Mawcook, Qué. 12 B5 45 27N 72 47W
Maxhamish L., B.C. 18 B4 59 50N 123 17W
Maxville, Ont. 10 F8 45 17N 74 51W
Mayerthorpe, Alta. 22 E5 53 57N 115 8W
Mayfair, Sask. 20 C3 52 58N 107 36W
Mayland, Alta. 31 F11 51 3N 114 0W
Maymont, Sask. 20 C3 52 34N 107 42W
Mayne, B.C. 25 G11 48 52N 123 17W
Mayo, Yukon 26 C2 63 38N 135 57W
Mayson L., Sask. 19 B7 57 55N 107 10W
Mazenod, Sask. 20 F4 49 52N 106 13W
Mazhabong L., Ont. 17 F14 46 58N 82 30W
Meacham, Sask. 20 C5 52 6N 105 45W
Meachen, B.C. 23 I4 49 38N 116 17W
Meadow L., Sask. 20 A2 54 7N 108 20W
Meadow Lake, Sask. 20 A2 54 10N 108 26W
Meadow Lake Prov. Park, Sask. 19 C7 54 27N 109 0W
Meaford, Ont. 14 C6 44 36N 80 35W
Meaghers Grant, N.S. 9 I6 44 55N 63 15W
Mealy Mts., Nfld. 5 B8 53 10N 58 0W
Meander River, Alta. 18 B5 59 2N 117 42W
Meares I., B.C. 24 F9 49 12N 125 50W
Meath Park, Sask. 20 B5 53 27N 105 22W
Mecatina, Little →, Nfld. 8 B9 52 0N 60 15W
Méchins, Les, Qué. 8 E3 48 59N 66 59W
Medicine Hat, Alta. 23 I10 50 0N 110 45W
Medley, Alta. 22 D10 54 25N 110 16W
Medstead, Sask. 20 B2 53 19N 108 5W
Meductic, N.B. 9 H2 46 0N 67 29W
Medway →, N.S. 9 I5 44 8N 64 36W
Mégantic, L., Qué. 11 F12 45 32N 70 53W
Mégantic, Mt., Qué. 11 F11 45 28N 71 9W
Mégiscane →, Qué. 10 C7 48 29N 75 38W
Mégiscane, L., Qué. 10 C7 48 35N 75 55W
Meighen I., N.W.T. 27 B6 80 0N 99 30W
Mékinac, L., Qué. 11 D10 47 3N 72 41W
Meldrum Bay, Ont. 14 B3 45 56N 83 6W
Meldrum Creek, B.C. 25 C12 52 6N 122 21W
Mélèzes →, Qué. 6 B4 57 40N 69 29W
Melfort, Sask. 20 C6 52 50N 104 37W
Melita, Man. 21 F10 49 15N 101 0W
Melochville, Qué. 29 D2 45 19N 73 56W
Melville, Sask. 20 E8 50 55N 102 50W
Melville, L., Nfld. 6 C6 53 30N 60 0W
Melville I., N.W.T. 26 B4 75 30N 112 0W
Melville Pen., N.W.T. 27 C7 68 0N 84 0W
Melvin →, Alta. 18 B5 59 11N 117 31W
Memphrémagog, L., Qué. 11 F10 45 8N 72 17W
Ménardville, Qué. 12 B4 45 17N 73 4W
Ménascouagama, L., Qué. 8 B8 51 13N 61 52W
Mendham, Sask. 20 E1 50 46N 109 40W
Menihek, Nfld. 6 C6 54 28N 56 36W
Menihek L., Nfld. 6 C4 54 0N 67 0W
Ménistouc, L., Qué. 8 A3 52 52N 66 29W
Meota, Sask. 20 B2 53 2N 108 27W
Merasheen I., Nfld. 7 F6 47 25N 54 15W
Mercier, Qué. 29 D3 45 19N 73 45W
Mercoal, Alta. 22 E3 53 10N 117 5W
Mercy C., N.W.T. 27 C9 65 0N 63 30W
Merigomish, N.S. 9 H7 45 38N 62 26W
Merivale, Ont. 30 E7 45 19N 75 43W
Merrickville, Ont. 15 C11 44 55N 75 50W
Merritt, B.C. 25 E14 50 10N 120 45W
Merry I., N.W.T. 6 B2 55 29N 77 31W
Mersey →, N.S. 9 I5 44 2N 64 43W
Merton, Ont. 13 B3 43 25N 79 44W
Merville, B.C. 24 F9 49 48N 125 3W
Mervin, Sask. 20 B2 53 20N 108 53W
Mesgouez, L., Qué. 6 C3 51 20N 75 0W
Mesilinka →, B.C. 18 B4 56 6N 124 30W
Mess Cr. →, B.C. 18 B2 57 55N 131 14W
Messine, Qué. 10 E6 46 14N 76 2W
Meteghan, N.S. 9 I3 44 11N 66 10W
Methy L., Sask. 19 B7 56 28N 109 30W
Métis-sur-Mer, Qué. 8 E2 48 40N 67 59W
Meyronne, Sask. 20 F4 49 39N 106 50W
Mica Creek, B.C. 25 C16 52 2N 118 35W
Michaudville, Qué. 12 A4 45 50N 73 4W
Michikamau L., Nfld. 5 B7 54 20N 63 10W
Michipicoten, Ont. 17 E12 47 55N 84 55W
Michipicoten B., Ont. 17 E12 47 53N 84 53W
Michipicoten I., Ont. 17 E11 47 40N 85 40W
Micmac Lake, N.S. 9 K11 44 41N 63 33W
Midale, Sask. 20 F7 49 25N 103 20W
Middle Church, Man. 31 B3 49 59N 97 4W
Middle Lake, Sask. 20 C5 52 29N 105 18W
Middle Musquodoboit, N.S. 9 H6 45 3N 63 9W
Middleton, N.S. 9 I4 44 57N 65 4W
Middlewood, N.S. 9 I5 44 14N 64 34W
Midland, Man. 31 B2 49 54N 97 11W
Midland, Ont. 14 C7 44 45N 79 50W
Midnapore, Alta. 31 G10 50 55N 114 5W
Midway, B.C. 25 F16 49 1N 118 48W
Miette Hotsprings, Alta. 22 E3 53 8N 117 46W
Mikkwa →, Alta. 22 A6 58 25N 114 46W
Milden, Sask. 20 D3 51 29N 107 32W
Mildmay, Ont. 14 C5 44 3N 81 7W
Milestone, Sask. 20 F6 49 59N 104 31W
Milford Station, N.S. 9 H6 45 3N 63 26W
Milk →, N. Amer. 23 I10 48 5N 106 15W
Milk River, Alta. 23 I8 49 10N 112 5W
Mill Cove, N.S. 9 K11 44 43N 63 40W
Mill Cr. →, Alta. 31 D7 53 33N 113 29W
Mill Village, N.S. 9 I5 44 9N 64 39W
Millbridge, Ont. 15 C9 44 41N 77 36W
Millbrook, Ont. 15 C8 44 10N 78 29W
Mille Îles, R. des →, Qué. 29 A4 45 42N 73 32W
Mille Isles, Qué. 12 A2 45 49N 74 14W
Mille Lacs, L. des, Ont. 16 D6 48 45N 90 35W
Millerand, Qué. 9 F8 47 13N 61 59W
Millertown, Nfld. 7 E4 48 49N 56 33W
Millet, Alta. 23 E7 53 6N 113 28W
Millgrove, Ont. 30 C9 43 20N 79 58W
Milliken, Ont. 28 B4 43 49N 79 18W
Mills L., N.W.T. 18 A5 61 30N 118 20W
Millstream, N.B. 9 E2 48 2N 67 2W
Milltown, N.B. 9 H2 45 10N 67 18W
Milltown, Nfld. 7 F5 47 54N 55 46W
Millville, N.B. 9 G2 46 8N 67 12W
Milnesville, Ont. 13 A4 43 55N 79 16W
Milo, Alta. 23 H8 50 34N 112 53W
Milot, Qué. 11 C11 48 54N 71 49W
Milton, N.S. 9 I5 44 4N 64 45W
Milton, Ont. 13 A3 43 31N 79 53W
Milton Heights, Ont. 13 A3 43 31N 79 56W
Milverton, Ont. 14 D6 43 34N 80 55W
Mimico Cr. →, Ont. 28 C3 43 37N 79 30W
Miminegash, P.E.I. 9 G5 46 53N 64 14W
Miminiska L., Ont. 16 A8 51 35N 88 37W
Mimosa, Ont. 13 A2 43 44N 80 13W
Minago →, Man. 21 A12 54 33N 98 59W
Minaki, Ont. 19 D10 49 59N 94 40W
Minas Basin, N.S. 9 H5 45 20N 64 12W
Minas Channel, N.S. 9 H5 45 15N 64 45W
Mindemoya, Ont. 14 B4 45 44N 82 10W
Minden, Ont. 15 C8 44 55N 78 43W
Mine, L., Qué. 8 C5 50 51N 64 43W
Mine Centre, Ont. 16 D4 48 45N 92 37W
Minegan, Îles de, Qué. 8 C6 50 12N 63 35W
Mingan, Qué. 8 C6 50 20N 64 0W
Mingan →, Qué. 8 C6 50 18N 63 59W
Minipi, L., Nfld. 8 A9 52 25N 60 45W
Miniss L., Ont. 16 B6 50 48N 90 50W
Minitonas, Man. 21 C9 52 5N 101 2W
Mink L., N.W.T. 18 A5 61 54N 117 40W
Minnedosa, Man. 21 E11 50 14N 99 50W
Minnitaki L., Ont. 16 C4 49 57N 92 10W
Minstrel Island, B.C. 24 E8 50 37N 126 18W
Minto, N.B. 9 G3 46 5N 66 5W
Minto, L., Qué. 6 B3 57 13N 75 0W
Minton, Sask. 20 F6 49 10N 104 35W
Miquelon, Qué. 10 B6 49 25N 76 27W
Miquelon, St- P. & M. 7 F4 47 1N 56 20W
Mira, N.S. 9 G10 46 2N 59 58W
Mira →, N.S. 9 G10 46 2N 59 58W
Mirabel Airport, Qué. 29 A1 45 41N 74 2W
Miramichi, Little S.W. →, N.B. 9 G4 46 58N 65 40W
Miramichi, N.W. →, N.B. 9 G4 46 57N 65 50W
Miramichi, S.W. →, N.B. 9 G4 46 58N 65 38W
Miramichi B., N.B. 9 F5 47 15N 65 0W
Mirond L., Sask. 19 B8 55 6N 102 47W
Mirror, Alta. 23 F7 52 30N 113 7W
Miscou Centre, N.B. 9 F5 47 57N 64 34W
Miscou I., N.B. 9 F5 47 57N 64 31W
Miscouche, P.E.I. 9 G6 46 26N 63 52W
Misehkow →, Ont. 16 A7 51 26N 89 11W
Missanabie, Ont. 17 D12 48 20N 84 6W
Missinaibi →, Ont. 17 B15 50 43N 81 29W
Missinaibi L., Ont. 17 D13 48 23N 83 40W
Missinaibi Lake Prov. Park, Ont. 17 D13 48 25N 83 30W
Mission City, B.C. 25 F12 49 10N 122 15W
Missipuskiow →, Sask. 20 B7 53 53N 103 18W
Missisa L., Ont. 4 B2 52 20N 85 7W
Missisicabi →, Qué. 6 C2 51 14N 79 31W
Missisquoi □, Qué. 12 B5 45 5N 73 0W
Missisquoi, B., Qué. 12 B4 45 2N 73 9W
Mississagi →, Ont. 14 A3 46 15N 83 9W
Mississagi Prov. Park, Ont. 14 A4 46 30N 82 40W
Mississauga, Ont. 28 C2 43 32N 79 35W
Mississippi L., Ont. 10 F6 45 5N 76 10W
Mistake B., N.W.T. 19 A10 62 8N 93 0W
Mistanipisipou →, Qué. 8 B8 51 32N 61 50W
Mistaouac, L., Qué. 10 B4 49 25N 78 41W
Mistassibi →, Qué. 11 C10 48 53N 72 13W
Mistassibi Nord-Est. →, Qué. 11 B11 49 31N 71 56W
Mistassini, Qué. 11 C10 48 53N 72 12W
Mistassini →, Qué. 11 C10 48 42N 72 20W
Mistassini, Parc. Prov. de, Qué. 11 A9 50 20N 74 0W
Mistassini L., Qué. 6 C3 51 0N 73 30W
Mistastin L., Nfld. 5 A7 55 57N 63 20W
Mistatim, Sask. 20 C7 52 52N 103 22W
Misty L., Man. 19 B8 58 53N 101 40W
Mitchell, Ont. 14 D5 43 28N 81 12W
Mitchell Corners, Ont. 13 A5 43 55N 78 53W
Mitchell Corners, Qué. 12 B4 45 2N 73 1W
Mitchell I., B.C. 32 B2 49 12N 123 5W
Mitchell L., B.C. 25 C14 52 52N 120 37W
Mitchinamécus, Rés., Qué. 10 D7 47 19N 75 9W
Moberly →, B.C. 18 B4 56 12N 120 55W
Moffat, Ont. 13 A2 43 31N 80 3W
Moira →, Ont. 15 C9 44 21N 77 24W
Moisie, Qué. 8 C3 50 12N 66 1W
Moisie →, Qué. 8 C3 50 14N 66 5W
Mojikit L., Ont. 16 B8 50 40N 88 15W
Molson L., Man. 21 A14 54 22N 96 40W
Monarch, Alta. 23 I7 49 48N 113 7W
Monarch Mt., B.C. 18 C3 51 55N 125 57W
Monashee Prov. Park, B.C. 25 E16 50 30N 118 15W
Monck, Ont. 13 A2 43 58N 80 29W
Moncouche, L., Qué. 11 C12 48 45N 70 42W
Moncton, N.B. 9 G5 46 7N 64 51W
Mondonac, L., Qué. 11 D9 47 24N 73 58W
Mongolia, Ont. 13 A4 43 56N 79 13W

Monitor, Alta. 23 G10 51 58N 110 34W
Monkstown, Nfld. 7 F6 47 35N 54 26W
Monkton, Ont. 14 D5 43 35N 81 5W
Monmouth Mt., B.C. 24 E11 51 0N 123 47W
Mono Mills, Ont. 13 A3 43 57N 79 58W
Mono Road Station, Ont. 13 A3 43 51N 79 51W
Mont-Carmel, Qué. 11 D13 47 26N 69 52W
Mont-Gabriel, Qué. 12 A2 45 55N 74 10W
Mont-Joli, Qué. 11 C14 48 37N 68 10W
Mont-Laurier, Qué. 10 E7 46 35N 75 30W
Mont-Louis, Qué. 8 D4 49 15N 65 44W
Mont-Rolland, Qué. 12 A2 45 57N 74 7W
Mont-Royal, Qué. 29 B4 45 31N 73 39W
Mont-St-Grégoire, Qué. 12 B4 45 20N 73 10W
Mont-St-Hilaire, Qué. 12 A4 45 34N 73 12W
Mont St-Pierre, Qué. 8 D4 49 13N 65 49W
Mont-Tremblant, Qué. 10 E8 46 13N 74 36W
Mont Tremblant Prov. Park, Qué. 11 E8 46 30N 74 30W
Montague, P.E.I. 9 G7 46 10N 62 39W
Montcalm □, Qué. 12 A3 45 59N 73 45W
Montcerf, Qué. 10 E6 46 32N 76 3W
Montcevelles, L., Qué. 8 B9 51 7N 60 38W
Montebello, Qué. 10 F8 45 40N 74 55W
Montfort, Qué. 12 A2 45 53N 74 20W
Montgomery, Alta. 31 F10 51 4N 114 10W
Monticello, Ont. 13 A2 43 59N 80 24W
Montmagny, Qué. 11 E12 46 58N 70 34W
Montmartre, Sask. 20 E7 50 14N 103 27W
Montmorency, Qué. 5 C5 46 53N 71 11W
Montmorency →, Qué. 30 A4 46 53N 71 7W
Montréal, Qué. 29 B4 45 31N 73 34W
Montreal →, Ont. 17 E12 47 14N 84 39W
Montréal, Île de, Qué. 29 C4 45 30N 73 40W
Montreal I., Ont. 17 E12 47 19N 84 44W
Montreal L., Sask. 20 A5 54 20N 105 45W
Montreal Lake, Sask. 20 A5 54 3N 105 46W
Montréal-Nord, Qué. 29 B4 45 36N 73 38W
Montreuil, L., Qué. 10 A5 50 12N 77 40W
Montrose, B.C. 25 F17 49 5N 117 35W
Montrose, Ont. 13 B4 43 3N 79 8W
Monts, Pte. des, Qué. 8 D2 49 20N 67 12W
Moonbeam, Ont. 17 C14 49 20N 82 10W
Moore Pt., Ont. 28 B5 43 48N 79 3W
Moores Mill, N.B. 9 H2 45 18N 67 17W
Moose →, Ont. 17 A16 51 20N 80 25W
Moose Creek, Ont. 15 B12 45 15N 74 58W
Moose Factory, Ont. 17 A16 51 16N 80 32W
Moose Heights, B.C. 25 B12 53 4N 122 31W
Moose Hill, Ont. 16 D7 48 15N 89 29W
Moose I., Man. 21 D13 51 42N 97 10W
Moose Jaw, Sask. 20 E5 50 24N 105 30W
Moose Jaw →, Sask. 20 E5 50 34N 105 18W
Moose L., Man. 21 B10 53 46N 100 8W
Moose Lake, Man. 21 B10 53 43N 100 20W
Moose Mountain Cr. →, Sask. 20 F8 49 13N 102 12W
Moose Mountain Prov. Park, Sask. 21 F8 49 48N 102 25W
Moose River, Ont. 17 B15 50 48N 81 17W
Moosomin, Sask. 21 E9 50 9N 101 40W
Moosonee, Ont. 17 A16 51 17N 80 39W
Morden, Man. 21 F12 49 15N 98 10W
Morell, P.E.I. 9 G7 46 25N 62 42W
Moresby I., B.C. 24 C3 52 30N 131 40W
Morice →, B.C. 24 A7 54 12N 127 5W
Morice L., B.C. 24 B7 53 50N 127 40W
Morin-Heights, Qué. 12 A2 45 54N 74 15W
Morinville, Alta. 22 E7 53 49N 113 41W
Morrin, Alta. 23 G8 51 40N 112 47W
Morris, Man. 21 F13 49 25N 97 22W
Morris →, Man. 21 F13 49 21N 97 21W
Morris L., N.S. 9 L12 44 39N 63 30W
Morrisburg, Ont. 15 C11 44 55N 75 7W
Morriston, Ont. 13 B2 43 27N 80 7W
Morse, Sask. 20 E3 50 25N 107 3W
Morson, Ont. 16 C2 49 6N 94 19W
Mortlach, Sask. 20 E4 50 27N 106 4W
Moses Inlet, B.C. 24 D7 51 47N 127 23W
Mosher, Ont. 17 D12 48 42N 84 12W
Mosley Cr. →, B.C. 24 D10 51 18N 124 50W
Mosquito B., Qué. 6 A2 61 10N 78 0W
Mossbank, Sask. 20 F5 49 56N 105 56W
Mossy →, Sask. 20 A8 54 5N 102 58W
Mothe, Rés. La, Qué. 11 C11 48 46N 71 9W
Motte, L. la, Qué. 10 C4 48 20N 78 2W
Mouchalagane →, Qué. 6 C4 50 56N 68 41W
Mould Bay, N.W.T. 26 B4 76 12N 119 25W
Mount Albert, Ont. 14 C7 44 8N 79 19W
Mount Assiniboine Prov. Park, B.C. 23 H5 50 53N 115 39W
Mount Brydges, Ont. 14 E5 42 54N 81 29W
Mount Carleton Prov. Park, N.B. 9 F3 47 25N 66 55W
Mount Carmel, Nfld. 7 F7 47 9N 53 29W
Mount Dennis, Ont. 28 B3 43 41N 79 29W
Mount Forest, Ont. 14 D6 43 59N 80 43W
Mount Hamilton, Ont. 30 D9 43 14N 79 51W
Mount Hope, Ont. 30 E9 43 9N 79 55W
Mount Moriah, Nfld. 7 E2 48 58N 58 2W
Mount Pearl, Nfld. 7 F8 47 31N 52 47W
Mount Pleasant, Alta. 31 F10 51 4N 114 5W
Mount Pleasant, Ont. 13 B2 43 5N 80 19W
Mount Revelstoke Nat. Park, B.C. 25 D16 51 5N 118 30W
Mount Robson Prov. Park, B.C. 25 C16 53 0N 119 0W
Mount Seymour Prov. Park, B.C. 32 A3 49 24N 122 55W
Mount Stewart, P.E.I. 9 G7 46 22N 62 52W
Mount Tolmie, B.C. 25 G20 48 28N 123 20W
Mount Uniacke, N.S. 9 I6 44 54N 63 50W
Mount Vernon, Ont. 13 B2 43 6N 80 24W
Mountain Park, Alta. 23 F3 52 50N 117 15W
Mountain View, Alta. 23 I7 49 8N 113 36W
Muchalat Inlet, B.C. 24 F8 49 38N 126 15W
Mud B., B.C. 32 C3 49 5N 122 53W
Muddy L., Sask. 20 C1 52 19N 109 6W
Mudjatik →, Sask. 19 B7 56 1N 107 36W
Muenster, Sask. 20 C6 52 12N 105 0W
Mukutawa →, Man. 21 B13 53 10N 97 24W
Mulgrave, N.S. 9 H8 45 38N 61 31W
Muncho Lake, B.C. 18 B3 59 0N 125 50W
Mundare, Alta. 22 E8 53 35N 112 20W
Munroe L., Man. 19 B9 59 13N 98 35W
Munson, Alta. 23 G8 51 34N 112 45W
Murchison I., Ont. 16 C8 50 0N 88 21W
Murdochville, Qué. 8 E4 48 58N 65 30W
Murdock, Man. 31 B3 49 56N 97 4W
Muriel L., Alta. 22 D10 54 9N 110 40W
Murphy L., B.C. 25 C13 52 3N 121 15W
Murray →, B.C. 18 B4 56 11N 120 45W
Murray Harbour, P.E.I. 9 H7 46 0N 62 28W
Murray River, P.E.I. 9 G7 46 1N 62 37W
Murtle L., B.C. 25 C15 52 8N 119 38W
Musgrave Harbour, Nfld. 7 D7 49 27N 53 58W
Mushaboom, N.S. 9 I7 44 51N 62 32W
Muskeg →, N.W.T. 18 A4 60 20N 123 20W
Muskeg L., Ont. 16 D6 49 0N 90 2W
Muskeg River, Alta. 22 E2 53 55N 118 39W
Muskoka, L., Ont. 14 C7 45 0N 79 25W
Muskwa →, Alta. 22 B7 56 15N 113 48W
Muskwa →, B.C. 18 B4 58 47N 122 48W
Muskwa L., Alta. 22 B6 56 9N 114 38W
Musquanousse, L., Qué. 8 C8 50 22N 61 5W
Musquaro, Qué. 8 C8 50 10N 61 3W
Musquaro, L., Qué. 8 C8 50 38N 61 5W
Musquash, N.B. 9 H3 45 11N 66 19W
Musquodoboit Harbour, N.S. 9 I6 44 50N 63 9W
Mussel Inlet, B.C. 24 C6 52 53N 128 7W
Myrnam, Alta. 22 E9 53 40N 111 14W
Mystery Lake, Alta. 22 D6 54 10N 114 55W

N

Nabisipi →, Qué. 9 C5 50 14N 62 13W
Nachicapau, L., Qué. 6 B4 56 40N 68 5W
Nachvak Fd., Nfld. 6 B5 59 3N 63 45W
Nackawic, N.B. 9 H2 45 59N 67 17W
Nacmine, Alta. 23 G8 51 28N 112 47W
Nadern Harb., B.C. 24 B2 54 0N 132 36W
Nadina →, B.C. 24 B8 53 58N 126 30W
Nadina L., B.C. 24 B7 53 53N 127 2W
Nagagami →, Ont. 17 C12 49 40N 84 40W
Nagagami L., Ont. 17 C11 49 25N 85 1W
Nagagamisis L., Ont. 17 C12 49 28N 84 40W
Nagas Pt., B.C. 24 C3 52 12N 131 22W
Nagasin L., Ont. 17 E13 47 48N 83 37W
Nahanni Butte, N.W.T. 18 A4 61 2N 123 31W
Nahanni Nat. Park, N.W.T. 18 A4 61 15N 125 0W
Nahlin, B.C. 18 B2 58 55N 131 38W
Naicam, Sask. 20 C6 52 30N 104 30W
Naikoon Prov. Park, B.C. 24 B3 53 55N 131 55W
Nain, Nfld. 6 B5 56 34N 61 40W
Nairn, Ont. 14 A5 46 20N 81 35W
Nakina, B.C. 18 B2 59 12N 132 52W
Nakina, Ont. 17 B10 50 10N 86 40W
Nakusp, B.C. 25 E17 50 20N 117 45W
Namakan L., Ont. 16 D4 48 27N 92 35W
Namew L., Sask. 21 A9 54 14N 101 56W
Namu, B.C. 24 D7 51 52N 127 50W
Namur, Qué. 10 F8 45 54N 74 56W
Nanaimo, B.C. 24 F11 49 10N 124 0W
Nanika L., B.C. 24 B7 53 47N 127 38W
Nanisivik, N.W.T. 27 B7 73 2N 84 33W
Nansen Sd., N.W.T. 27 A6 81 0N 91 0W
Nanton, Alta. 23 H7 50 21N 113 46W
Naococane L., Qué. 6 C3 52 50N 70 45W
Napanee, Ont. 15 C10 44 15N 77 0W
Napartokh B., Nfld. 6 B5 58 1N 62 19W
Napierville, Qué. 11 F9 45 11N 73 25W
Napierville □, Qué. 12 B3 45 10N 73 30W
Napinka, Man. 21 F10 49 19N 100 50W
Narraway →, Alta. 22 C1 55 44N 119 55W
Nash Creek, N.B. 9 F3 47 56N 66 6W
Nashwaak Bridge, N.B. 9 G3 46 14N 66 37W
Nashwaaksis, N.B. 9 H3 45 59N 66 38W
Naskaupi →, Nfld. 6 C5 53 47N 60 51W
Nass →, B.C. 18 C3 55 0N 129 40W
Nastapoka →, Qué. 6 B2 56 55N 76 33W
Nastapoka, Is., N.W.T. 6 B2 56 55N 76 50W
Natal, B.C. 23 I6 49 43N 114 51W
Natalkuz L., B.C. 24 B9 53 36N 125 20W
Natashquan, Qué. 8 C8 50 14N 61 46W
Natashquan →, Qué. 8 C8 50 7N 61 50W
Natashquan-Est →, Qué. 8 B8 51 20N 61 40W
Natashquan Pt., Qué. 8 C8 50 8N 61 40W
Nation →, B.C. 18 B4 55 30N 123 32W
Naughton, Ont. 14 A5 46 24N 81 12W
Navin, Man. 31 B4 49 51N 97 0W
Nazko, B.C. 24 B11 53 1N 123 37W
Nazko →, B.C. 24 B11 53 7N 123 34W
Nechako →, B.C. 25 B12 53 30N 122 44W
Nechako Res., B.C. 24 B7 53 42N 127 30W
Neepawa, Man. 21 E11 50 15N 99 30W
Neguac, N.B. 9 F4 47 15N 65 5W
Neidpath, Sask. 20 E3 50 12N 107 20W
Neilburg, Sask. 20 C1 52 50N 109 38W
Neil's Harbour, N.S. 9 G9 46 48N 60 20W
Nejanilini L., Man. 19 B9 59 33N 97 48W
Nelson, B.C. 25 F17 49 30N 117 20W
Nelson, Ont. 30 C9 43 23N 79 50W
Nelson →, Man. 19 C9 54 33N 98 2W
Nelson Forks, B.C. 18 B4 59 30N 124 0W
Nelson House, Man. 19 B9 55 47N 98 51W
Nelson L., Man. 19 B8 55 48N 100 7W
Nelson-Miramichi, N.B. 9 G4 46 59N 65 34W
Nemegosenda L., Ont. 17 E13 48 0N 83 7W
Nemeiben L., Sask. 19 B7 55 20N 105 20W
Némiscachingue, L., Qué. 10 D8 47 25N 74 30W
Némiscau, Qué. 6 C2 51 18N 76 54W
Némiscau, L., Qué. 6 C2 51 25N 76 40W
Neoskweskau, Qué. 6 C3 51 52N 74 17W
Nepisiguit →, N.B. 9 F4 47 37N 65 38W
Neptune, Sask. 20 F6 49 22N 104 4W
Néret L., Qué. 6 C3 54 45N 70 44W
Nestaocano →, Qué. 11 B9 49 38N 73 28W
Nestor Falls, Ont. 16 C3 49 7N 93 56W
Netherby, Ont. 13 C4 42 57N 79 8W
Nettilling L., N.W.T. 27 C8 66 30N 71 0W
Neudorf, Sask. 20 E7 50 43N 103 1W
Neufchâtel, Qué. 30 A2 46 51N 71 23W
Neustadt, Ont. 14 C6 44 4N 81 0W
Neville, Sask. 20 F3 49 58N 107 39W
New Brigden, Alta. 23 G10 51 42N 110 29W
New Brunswick □, Canada 9 G3 46 50N 66 30W
New Carlisle, N.B. 9 E4 48 1N 65 20W
New Denmark, N.B. 9 F2 47 2N 67 38W
New Denver, B.C. 25 F17 50 0N 117 25W
New Dundee, Ont. 13 B1 43 21N 80 31W
New Durham, Ont. 13 B1 43 3N 80 34W
New Germany, N.S. 9 I5 44 33N 64 43W
New Glasgow, N.S. 9 H7 45 35N 62 36W
New Glasgow, Qué. 12 A3 45 50N 73 53W
New Hamburg, Ont. 14 D6 43 23N 80 42W
New Harbour, N.S. 9 H8 45 13N 61 29W
New Hazelton, B.C. 18 B3 55 20N 127 30W
New Liskeard, Ont. 10 D3 47 31N 79 41W
New Norway, Alta. 23 F8 52 52N 112 57W
New Richmond, Qué. 8 E4 48 15N 65 45W
New Ross, N.S. 9 I5 44 44N 64 27W
New Sarepta, Alta. 22 E7 53 16N 113 8W
New Toronto, Ont. 28 C3 43 36N 79 30W
New Waterford, N.S. 9 G9 46 13N 60 4W
New Westminster, B.C. 25 F12 49 13N 122 55W
New World I., Nfld. 7 D6 49 35N 54 40W
Newboro L., Ont. 15 C10 44 38N 76 20W
Newbrook, Alta. 22 D8 54 24N 112 57W
Newburgh, Ont. 15 C10 44 19N 76 52W
Newcastle, N.B. 9 F4 47 1N 65 38W
Newcastle Bridge, N.B. 9 G3 46 4N 66 3W
Newell, L., Alta. 23 H9 50 26N 111 55W
Newfoundland □, Canada 5 B8 53 0N 58 0W
Newgate, B.C. 23 I5 49 2N 115 12W
Newmarket, Ont. 14 C7 44 3N 79 28W
Newport, Ont. 13 B2 43 6N 80 14W
Newport, Qué. 8 E5 48 16N 64 45W
Newton, B.C. 32 C3 49 8N 122 51W
Newton Brook, Ont. 28 B3 43 48N 79 24W
Newtown, Nfld. 7 D7 49 12N 53 31W
Niagara □, Ont. 13 B4 43 15N 79 4W
Niagara →, Ont. 13 B4 43 16N 79 3W
Niagara Falls, Ont. 13 B4 43 7N 79 5W
Niagara-on-the-Lake, Ont. 13 B4 43 15N 79 4W
Nicola, B.C. 25 E14 50 12N 120 40W
Nicola L., B.C. 25 E14 50 10N 120 32W
Nicolet, Qué. 11 E10 46 17N 72 35W
Nicomekl →, B.C. 32 C3 49 3N 122 52W
Nigel I., B.C. 24 E7 50 53N 127 43W
Nimpkish →, B.C. 24 E8 50 34N 126 58W
Nimpkish L., B.C. 24 E8 50 25N 126 59W
Nimpo L., B.C. 24 C9 52 20N 125 10W
Ninette, Man. 21 F11 49 24N 99 38W
Nioman, Qué. 6 C4 50 25N 66 5W
Nipawin, Sask. 20 B7 53 20N 104 0W
Nipawin Prov. Park, Sask. 20 B6 54 0N 104 37W
Nipekamew →, Sask. 20 A6 54 59N 104 52W
Nipigon, Ont. 16 D8 49 0N 88 17W
Nipigon, L., Ont. 16 C8 49 50N 88 30W
Nipigon B., Ont. 17 D9 48 53N 87 50W
Nipin →, Sask. 19 B7 55 46N 108 35W
Nipishish L., Nfld. 6 C5 54 12N 60 45W
Nipisi L., Alta. 22 C6 55 47N 114 57W
Nipissing L., Ont. 14 A7 46 20N 80 0W
Nipissis →, Qué. 6 C4 50 30N 66 5W
Nipissis, L., Qué. 8 B3 51 2N 66 10W
Nipisso, L., Qué. 8 C4 50 52N 65 50W
Nipper's Harbour, Nfld. 7 D5 49 48N 55 52W
Niskibi →, Ont. 4 A2 56 29N 88 9W
Nisutlin →, Yukon 18 A2 60 14N 132 34W
Nitchequon, Qué. 6 C3 53 10N 70 58W
Nith →, Ont. 14 D6 43 12N 80 23W
Nitinat, B.C. 24 G10 48 56N 124 29W
Nitinat L., B.C. 24 G10 48 45N 124 45W
Niverville, Man. 21 F13 49 36N 97 3W
Nobel, Ont. 14 B6 45 25N 80 6W
Nobleford, Alta. 23 I7 49 53N 113 3W
Nobleton, Ont. 13 A3 43 54N 79 40W
Noel, N.S. 9 H6 45 18N 63 45W
Noelville, Ont. 14 A6 46 8N 80 26W
Noirclair, L., Qué. 8 C9 50 38N 60 23W
Noire →, Qué. 10 F6 45 54N 76 57W
Nokomis, Sask. 20 D6 51 35N 105 0W
Nokomis L., Sask. 19 B8 57 0N 103 0W
Noman L., N.W.T. 19 A7 62 15N 108 55W
Nominingue, Qué. 10 E7 46 24N 75 2W
Nominingue, L., Qué. 10 E8 46 26N 74 59W
Nonacho L., N.W.T. 19 A7 61 42N 109 40W
Nootka, B.C. 24 F8 49 38N 126 38W
Nootka I., B.C. 24 F8 49 32N 126 42W
Noranda, Qué. 10 C4 48 20N 79 0W
Nord →, Qué. 12 A2 45 31N 74 20W
Nord, Grand L. du, Qué. 8 C2 50 54N 67 6W
Nord, Petit L. du, Qué. 8 C2 50 50N 67 10W
Nordegg, Alta. 23 F4 52 29N 116 5W
Norembega, Ont. 10 C2 48 59N 80 43W
Norman Wells, N.W.T. 26 C3 65 17N 126 51W
Normandin, Qué. 11 C10 48 49N 72 31W
Norman's Cove, Nfld. 7 F7 47 33N 53 40W
Normétal, Qué. 10 C3 49 0N 79 22W
Norquay, Sask. 21 D8 51 53N 102 5W
Norris Arm, Nfld. 7 D5 49 5N 55 15W
Norris Point, Nfld. 7 D3 49 31N 57 53W
North →, Nfld. 6 B5 57 30N 61 50W
North, C., N.S. 9 F9 47 2N 60 20W
North Aulatsivik I., Nfld. 6 B5 59 46N 64 5W
North Battleford, Sask. 20 C2 52 50N 108 17W
North Bay, Ont. 14 A7 46 20N 79 30W
North Belcher Is., N.W.T. 6 B2 56 50N 79 50W
North Bend, B.C. 25 F13 49 50N 121 27W
North Buck L., Alta. 22 D8 54 41N 112 32W
North Burnaby, B.C. 32 B3 49 17N 123 0W
North Caribou L., Ont. 4 B1 52 50N 90 40W
North Channel, Ont. 14 B4 46 0N 83 0W
North French →, Ont. 17 A16 51 10N 80 50W
North Gower, Ont. 15 B11 45 8N 75 43W
North Grant, N.S. 9 H7 45 40N 62 2W
North Hatley, Qué. 11 F11 45 17N 71 58W
North Head, N.B. 9 I3 44 46N 66 45W
North Head, Nfld. 7 I8 47 29N 52 38W
North Henik L., N.W.T. 19 A9 61 45N 97 40W
North Knife →, Man. 19 B10 58 53N 94 45W
North Lancaster, Qué. 12 B2 45 13N 74 30W
North Lonsdale, B.C. 32 A2 49 20N 123 4W
North Magnetic Pole, N.W.T. 27 B5 77 5N 102 6W
North Nahanni →, N.W.T. 18 A4 62 15N 123 20W
North Pt., N.B. 9 F6 47 5N 64 0W
North Portal, Sask. 21 F8 49 0N 102 33W
North Ram →, Alta. 23 F6 52 16N 114 38W
North Rustico, P.E.I. 9 G6 46 27N 63 19W
North Saskatchewan →, Sask. 20 B5 53 15N 105 5W
North Seneca, Ont. 13 B3 43 7N 79 56W
North Star, Alta. 22 B3 56 51N 117 38W
North Sydney, N.S. 9 G9 46 12N 60 15W
North Thompson →, B.C. 25 E14 50 40N 120 20W
North Twin I., N.W.T. 6 C2 53 20N 80 0W
North Twin L., Nfld. 7 D5 49 16N 55 56W
North Vancouver, B.C. 25 F11 49 25N 123 3W
North Wabasca L., Alta. 22 C7 56 0N 113 55W
North West River, Nfld. 6 C5 53 30N 60 10W
North West Territories □, N.W.T. 26 C5 67 0N 110 0W
North York, Ont. 28 B3 43 46N 79 30W
Northern Indian L., Man. 19 B9 57 20N 97 20W
Northern Light, L., Ont. 16 D6 48 15N 90 39W
Northmount, Ont. 28 B3 43 46N 79 24W
Northport, N.S. 9 H6 45 46N 63 52W
Northumberland Str., P.E.I. 9 G6 46 20N 64 0W
Northwest Gander →, Nfld. 7 E5 48 55N 55 2W
Norton, N.B. 9 H4 45 38N 65 42W
Norway House, Man. 21 B13 53 59N 97 50W
Norwegian B., N.W.T. 27 B7 77 30N 90 0W
Norwich, Ont. 14 E6 42 59N 80 36W
Norwood, Ont. 15 C9 44 23N 77 59W
Nose Cr. →, Alta. 31 F10 51 3N 114 1W
Notigi Dam, Man. 19 B9 56 40N 99 10W
Notikewin →, Alta. 22 A3 57 2N 117 38W
Notre-Dame, N.B. 9 G5 46 18N 64 46W
Notre-Dame, Qué. 29 C5 45 28N 73 28W
Notre-Dame, Les, Qué. 8 E2 48 10N 68 0W
Notre Dame B., Nfld. 7 D5 49 45N 55 30W
Notre Dame de Koartac = Koartac, Qué. 6 A4 60 55N 69 40W
Notre-Dame-de-la-Doré, Qué. 11 C10 48 43N 72 39W
Notre-Dame-de-l'Île-Perrot, Qué. 29 C2 45 23N 73 56W
Notre Dame de Lourdes, Man. 21 F12 49 32N 98 33W
Notre-Dame-de-Stanbridge, Qué. 12 B4 45 8N 73 2W
Notre-Dame-des-Bois, Qué. 11 F11 45 24N 71 4W
Notre-Dame-des-Laurentides, Qué. 30 A3 46 55N 71 18W
Notre Dame d'Ivugivic = Ivugivik, Qué. 6 A2 62 24N 77 55W
Notre-Dame-du-Bon-Conseil, Qué. 11 F10 46 0N 72 21W
Notre Dame du Lac, Ont. 14 A6 46 18N 80 11W
Notre-Dame-du-Lac, Qué. 11 D14 47 36N 68 48W
Notre-Dame-du-Laus, Qué. 10 E7 46 5N 75 37W
Notre-Dame-du-Nord, Qué. 10 D3 47 36N 79 30W
Notre-Dame-du-Portage, Qué. 11 D13 47 46N 69 37W
Nottawasaga B., Ont. 14 C6 44 35N 80 15W
Nottaway →, Qué. 6 C2 51 22N 78 55W
Nottingham I., N.W.T. 27 C8 63 20N 77 55W
Nottingham Island, N.W.T. 27 C8 63 6N 77 50W
Notukeu Cr. →, Sask. 20 F4 49 56N 106 29W
Nouveau Comptoir, Qué. 6 C2 53 0N 78 49W
Nouveau-Québec, Qué. 6 B3 56 0N 71 0W
Nouvelle, N.B. 9 E3 48 8N 66 19W
Nouvelle →, N.B. 9 E3 48 7N 66 19W
Nouvelle France, C. de, Qué. 6 A3 62 27N 73 42W
Nova Scotia □, Canada 9 H6 45 10N 63 0W
Nova Zembla I., N.W.T. 27 B8 72 11N 74 50W
Novar, Ont. 14 B7 45 27N 79 15W
Nueltin L., N.W.T. 19 A9 60 30N 99 30W
Nulki L., B.C. 24 B10 53 55N 124 7W
Nunaksaluk I., Nfld. 6 B5 55 49N 60 20W
Nungesser L., Ont. 16 A3 51 28N 93 30W
Nut L., Sask. 20 C7 52 22N 103 42W
Nutak, Nfld. 6 B5 57 28N 61 59W
Nuvuk Is., Nfld. 6 A2 62 24N 78 3W
Nyarling →, N.W.T. 18 A6 60 41N 113 23W

O

Oak Bay, B.C. 25 G20 48 26N 123 18W
Oak Bay, N.B. 9 H2 45 14N 67 12W
Oak Bluff, Man. 31 C2 49 46N 97 19W
Oak Hill, N.B. 9 H2 45 20N 67 20W
Oak Lake, Man. 21 F10 49 46N 100 38W
Oak Point, Man. 21 E12 50 30N 98 1W
Oak Ridges, Ont. 13 A4 43 57N 79 28W
Oak River, Man. 21 E10 50 8N 100 26W
Oakbank, Man. 31 B4 49 57N 96 51W
Oakland, Ont. 13 B2 43 2N 80 20W
Oakville, Ont. 13 B3 43 27N 79 41W
Oakville →, Ont. 13 B3 43 27N 79 41W
Oba, Ont. 17 C12 49 4N 84 7W
Oba L., Ont. 17 D12 48 40N 84 16W
Obakamiga L., Ont. 17 C11 49 9N 85 9W
Obalski, L., Qué. 10 C5 48 43N 77 58W
Obamsca, L., Qué. 10 A4 50 24N 78 16W
Obatanga Prov. Park, Ont. 17 D11 48 20N 85 10W
Obed, Alta. 22 E3 53 30N 117 10W
Obedjwan, Qué. 10 C8 48 40N 74 56W
Obonga L., Ont. 16 C7 49 57N 89 22W
Observatory Inlet, B.C. 18 B3 55 10N 129 54W
Ocean Falls, B.C. 24 C7 52 18N 127 48W
Ocean Park, B.C. 32 C3 49 2N 122 52W
Ochre River, Man. 21 D11 51 4N 99 47W
Odei →, Man. 19 B9 56 6N 96 54W
Odessa, Ont. 15 C10 44 17N 76 43W
Odessa, Sask. 20 E7 50 17N 103 47W
Ogahalla, Ont. 17 B11 50 6N 85 51W
Ogascanane, L., Qué. 10 D4 47 5N 78 25W
Ogden, Alta. 31 G11 51 0N 114 0W
Ogema, Sask. 20 F6 49 35N 104 55W
Ogilvie Mts., N.W.T. 26 C2 65 0N 140 0W
Ogoki, Ont. 17 A11 51 38N 85 58W
Ogoki →, Ont. 17 A11 51 38N 85 57W
Ogoki L., Ont. 17 B9 50 50N 87 10W
Ogoki Res., Ont. 16 B8 50 45N 88 15W
Ohsweken, Ont. 13 B2 43 4N 80 7W
Oil Springs, Ont. 14 E4 42 47N 82 7W
Oka, Qué. 12 B2 45 28N 74 5W
Okak, Nfld. 6 B5 57 33N 61 58W

Okak Is., *Nfld.* 6 **B5** 57 30N 61 30W
Okanagan L., *B.C.* 25 **F15** 50 0N 119 30W
Okanagan Mission, *B.C.* 25 **F15** 49 45N 119 30W
Okanagan Mountain Prov. Park, *B.C.* 25 **F15** 49 45N 119 30W
Old Chelsea, *Ont.* 30 **D7** 45 30N 75 49W
Old Crow, *Yukon* 26 **C2** 67 30N 139 55W
Old Fort →, *Alta.* 19 **B6** 58 36N 110 24W
Old Perlican, *Nfld.* 7 **E7** 48 5N 53 1W
Old Wives L., *Sask.* 20 **E5** 50 5N 106 0W
Oldman →, *Alta.* 23 **I9** 49 57N 111 42W
Olds, *Alta.* 23 **G6** 51 50N 114 10W
O'Leary, *P.E.I.* 9 **G5** 46 42N 64 13W
Olga, L., *Qué.* 10 **B5** 49 47N 77 15W
Oliver, *B.C.* 25 **F15** 49 13N 119 37W
Oliver L., *Sask.* 19 **B8** 56 56N 103 22W
Olomane →, *Qué.* 8 **C9** 50 14N 60 37W
Omemee, *Ont.* 15 **C8** 44 18N 78 33W
Omineca →, *B.C.* 18 **B4** 56 3N 124 16W
Ommanney B., *N.W.T.* 27 **B5** 73 0N 101 0W
Onakawana, *Ont.* 17 **B15** 50 36N 81 27W
Onaman →, *Ont.* 17 **C9** 49 59N 88 0W
Onaman L., *Ont.* 17 **C9** 50 0N 87 26W
Onanole, *Man.* 21 **E11** 50 37N 99 58W
Onaping, *Ont.* 14 **A5** 46 37N 81 25W
Onaping →, *Ont.* 14 **A5** 46 37N 81 18W
Onaping L., *Ont.* 17 **E15** 47 3N 81 30W
Onatchiway, L., *Qué.* 11 **B11** 49 3N 71 5W
Onion Lake, *Sask.* 20 **B1** 53 43N 110 0W
Onondaga, *Ont.* 13 **B2** 43 7N 80 7W
Onoway, *Alta.* 22 **E6** 53 42N 114 12W
Ontario □, *Ont.* 4 **B2** 52 0N 88 10W
Ontario, L., *Ont.* 15 **D9** 43 40N 78 0W
Oona River, *B.C.* 24 **B4** 53 57N 130 16W
Ootsa L., *B.C.* 24 **B8** 53 50N 126 2W
Ootsa Lake, *B.C.* 24 **B8** 53 50N 126 5W
Opasatica, L., *Qué.* 10 **C3** 48 5N 79 18W
Opasatika, *Ont.* 17 **C14** 49 30N 82 50W
Opasatika →, *Ont.* 17 **B14** 50 25N 82 25W
Opasatika L., *Ont.* 17 **C13** 49 4N 83 6W
Opasquia, *Ont.* 19 **C10** 53 16N 93 34W
Opataca, L., *Qué.* 10 **A8** 50 22N 74 55W
Opawica, L., *Qué.* 10 **B7** 49 35N 75 55W
Opémisca, L., *Qué.* 10 **B8** 49 56N 74 52W
Opeongo L., *Ont.* 15 **B8** 45 42N 78 23W
Opinaca →, *Qué.* 6 **C2** 52 15N 78 2W
Opinaca L., *Qué.* 6 **C2** 52 39N 76 20W
Opiscoteo, L., *Qué.* 6 **C4** 53 10N 68 10W
Opiskotish, L., *Qué.* 6 **C4** 53 10N 67 50W
Opocopa, L., *Qué.* 8 **A3** 52 38N 66 35W
Orangeville, *Ont.* 13 **A2** 43 55N 80 5W
Orillia, *Ont.* 14 **C7** 44 40N 79 24W
Orléans, I. d', *Qué.* 30 **A5** 46 54N 70 58W
Ormiston, *Sask.* 20 **F5** 49 44N 105 24W
Ormstown, *Qué.* 12 **B3** 45 8N 74 0W
Oromocto, *N.B.* 9 **H3** 45 54N 66 29W
Oromocto, L., *N.B.* 9 **H3** 45 36N 67 0W
Orono, *Ont.* 15 **D8** 43 59N 78 37W
Orsainville, *Qué.* 30 **A3** 46 51N 71 14W
Osawin →, *Ont.* 17 **C11** 49 45N 85 19W
Osborne Corners, *Ont.* 13 **B2** 43 13N 80 16W
Osgoode, *Ont.* 15 **B11** 45 8N 75 36W
Oshawa, *Ont.* 15 **D8** 43 50N 78 50W
Oskélanéo, *Qué.* 10 **C7** 48 5N 75 15W
Osler, *Sask.* 20 **C4** 52 22N 106 33W
Osnaburgh L., *Ont.* 16 **A6** 51 12N 90 9W
Osoyoos, *B.C.* 25 **F15** 49 0N 119 30W
Osoyoos L., *B.C.* 25 **F15** 49 0N 119 27W
Ospika →, *B.C.* 18 **B4** 56 20N 124 0W
Ospringe, *Ont.* 13 **A2** 43 42N 80 7W
Ossokmanuan L., *Nfld.* 6 **C5** 53 25N 65 0W
Ostaboningue, L., *Qué.* 10 **D4** 47 9N 78 53W
O'Sullivan L., *Ont.* 17 **B9** 50 25N 87 2W
Otelnuk L., *Qué.* 6 **B4** 56 9N 68 12W
Otish, Mts., *Qué.* 6 **C3** 52 22N 70 30W
Otoskwin →, *Ont.* 4 **B2** 52 13N 88 6W
Otosquen, *Sask.* 21 **B8** 53 17N 102 1W
Ottawa, *Ont.* 30 **D7** 45 27N 75 42W
Ottawa → = Outaouais →, *Ont.* 12 **B2** 45 27N 74 8W
Ottawa-Carleton □, *Ont.* 30 **D8** 45 23N 75 40W
Ottawa International Airport, *Ont.* 30 **E8** 45 19N 75 40W
Ottawa Is., *N.W.T.* 27 **D7** 59 35N 80 10W
Otter L., *Sask.* 19 **B8** 55 35N 104 39W
Otter Rapids, *Ont.* 17 **B15** 50 11N 81 39W
Otter Rapids, *Sask.* 19 **B8** 55 38N 104 44W
Otterburn Park, *Qué.* 12 **A4** 45 32N 73 13W
Otterville, *Ont.* 14 **E6** 42 55N 80 36W
Ouareau, L., Rés., *Qué.* 11 **E8** 46 17N 74 9W
Ouasiemsca →, *Qué.* 11 **C10** 49 0N 72 30W
Ouest, Pte., *Qué.* 8 **D5** 49 52N 64 40W
Oustic, *Ont.* 13 **A2** 43 42N 80 15W
Outaouais →, *Ont.* 12 **B2** 45 27N 74 8W
Outardes, *Qué.* 11 **A13** 50 20N 69 10W
Outardes →, *Qué.* 11 **B13** 49 24N 69 30W
Outer I., *Qué.* 6 **C6** 51 10N 58 35W
Outlook, *Sask.* 20 **D4** 51 30N 107 0W
Outremount, *Qué.* 29 **B4** 45 31N 73 37W
Overflowing →, *Man.* 21 **B9** 53 8N 101 5W
Owen Sound, *Ont.* 14 **C6** 44 35N 80 55W
Owikeno L., *B.C.* 24 **D8** 51 40N 126 50W
Owl →, *Man.* 19 **B10** 57 51N 92 44W
Oxbow, *Sask.* 21 **F8** 49 14N 102 10W
Oxford, *N.S.* 9 **H6** 45 44N 63 52W
Oxford L., *Man.* 19 **C9** 54 51N 95 37W
Oyama, *B.C.* 25 **E15** 50 7N 119 22W
Oyen, *Alta.* 23 **G10** 51 22N 110 28W
Oyster River, *B.C.* 24 **F9** 49 53N 125 7W

P

Pabos Mills, *Qué.* 8 **E5** 48 19N 64 42W
Pacific, *B.C.* 18 **C3** 54 48N 128 28W
Pacific Rim Nat. Park, *B.C.* 24 **G10** 48 40N 124 45W
Packenham, *Ont.* 15 **B10** 45 22N 76 25W
Pacquet, *Nfld.* 7 **D5** 50 0N 55 53W
Paddockwood, *Sask.* 20 **B5** 53 30N 105 30W
Padle, *N.W.T.* 27 **C6** 62 10N 97 5W
Padloping Island, *N.W.T.* 27 **C9** 67 0N 62 50W
Pagwa River, *Ont.* 17 **B11** 50 2N 85 14W
Pagwachuan →, *Ont.* 17 **B12** 50 12N 84 43W
Paimpont, L., *Qué.* 8 **C8** 50 28N 61 34W
Paint Hills = Nouveau Comptoir, *Qué.* 6 **C2** 53 0N 78 49W
Paint L., *Man.* 19 **B9** 55 28N 97 57W
Paisley, *Ont.* 14 **C5** 44 18N 81 16W
Paix, Îles de la, *Qué.* 29 **D2** 45 20N 73 51W
Pakashkan L., *Ont.* 16 **C6** 49 21N 90 15W
Pakenham, *Ont.* 10 **F6** 45 18N 76 18W
Pakowi L., *Alta.* 23 **I10** 49 20N 111 0W
Pakwash L., *Ont.* 16 **B3** 50 45N 93 30W
Palermo, *Ont.* 13 **B3** 43 26N 79 47W
Palgrave, *Ont.* 13 **A3** 43 57N 79 50W
Palmarolle, *Qué.* 10 **C3** 48 40N 79 12W
Palmerston, *Ont.* 14 **D6** 43 50N 80 51W
Palomar, *Ont.* 17 **D14** 48 10N 82 16W
Panache, L., *Ont.* 14 **A5** 46 15N 81 20W
Pangmar, *Sask.* 20 **F6** 49 39N 104 40W
Panny →, *Alta.* 22 **A6** 57 8N 114 51W
Papineau-Labelle, Parc Prov., *Qué.* 10 **E7** 46 10N 75 15W
Papineauville, *Qué.* 10 **F7** 45 37N 75 1W
Paradis, *Qué.* 10 **C6** 48 15N 76 35W
Paradise →, *Nfld.* 6 **C6** 53 27N 57 19W
Paradise Hill, *Sask.* 20 **B1** 53 32N 109 28W
Paradise Valley, *Alta.* 23 **E10** 53 2N 110 17W
Parent, *Qué.* 10 **D8** 47 55N 74 35W
Parent, L., *Qué.* 10 **C5** 48 31N 77 1W
Parham, *Ont.* 15 **C10** 44 39N 76 43W
Paris, *Ont.* 13 **B2** 43 12N 80 25W
Park Royal, *B.C.* 32 **B2** 49 20N 123 8W
Parker, *Ont.* 13 **A1** 43 46N 80 35W
Parkerview, *Sask.* 20 **D7** 51 21N 103 18W
Parkhill, *Ont.* 14 **D5** 43 15N 81 38W
Parks L., *Ont.* 17 **C9** 49 27N 87 38W
Parkside, *Sask.* 20 **B4** 53 10N 106 33W
Parksville, *B.C.* 24 **F10** 49 20N 124 21W
Parrsboro, *N.S.* 9 **H5** 45 30N 64 25W
Parry Is., *N.W.T.* 26 **B5** 77 0N 110 0W
Parry Sound, *Ont.* 14 **B7** 45 20N 80 0W
Parsnip →, *B.C.* 18 **B4** 55 10N 123 2W
Parson, *B.C.* 25 **D18** 51 5N 116 37W
Parsons Pond, *Nfld.* 7 **D3** 49 59N 57 37W
Parson's Pond, *Nfld.* 7 **C3** 50 2N 57 43W
Partridge →, *Ont.* 17 **A16** 51 19N 80 18W
Partridge Pt., *Nfld.* 7 **C4** 50 10N 56 10W
Pasadena, *Nfld.* 7 **D3** 49 1N 57 36W
Pasfield L., *Sask.* 19 **B7** 58 24N 105 20W
Paspébiac, *N.B.* 9 **E4** 48 3N 65 17W
Pass Island, *Nfld.* 7 **F4** 47 30N 56 12W
Passage Pt., *N.W.T.* 26 **B4** 73 29N 115 16W
Pasteur, L., *Qué.* 8 **C3** 50 13N 66 58W
Patrick's Cove, *Nfld.* 7 **F6** 47 3N 54 7W
Patrie, La, *Qué.* 11 **F11** 45 24N 71 15W
Patterson, *Ont.* 28 **A3** 43 54N 79 28W
Paul I., *Nfld.* 6 **B5** 56 30N 61 20W
Paul-Sauvé, L., *Qué.* 10 **A4** 50 15N 78 20W
Paulatuk, *N.W.T.* 26 **C3** 69 25N 124 0W
Payne Bay = Bellin, *Qué.* 6 **B4** 60 0N 70 0W
Peace →, *Alta.* 18 **B6** 59 0N 111 25W
Peace Point, *Alta.* 18 **B6** 59 7N 112 27W
Peace River, *Alta.* 22 **B3** 56 15N 117 18W
Peachland, *B.C.* 25 **F15** 49 47N 119 45W
Pearl, *Ont.* 16 **D8** 48 40N 88 40W
Pearse I., *B.C.* 18 **C2** 54 52N 130 14W
Peel □, *Ont.* 28 **B1** 43 45N 79 47W
Peel →, *Yukon* 26 **C2** 67 0N 135 0W
Peerless L., *Alta.* 22 **B6** 56 37N 114 40W
Peerless Lake, *Alta.* 22 **B6** 56 40N 114 35W
Peers, *Alta.* 22 **E5** 53 40N 116 0W
Peggy's Cove, *N.S.* 9 **I6** 44 30N 63 55W
Pékans →, *Qué.* 8 **A3** 52 12N 66 49W
Pelee, Pt., *Ont.* 14 **F4** 41 54N 82 31W
Pelee I., *Ont.* 14 **F4** 41 47N 82 40W
Pelham, *Ont.* 13 **B4** 43 3N 79 21W
Pelham Union, *Ont.* 13 **B4** 43 5N 79 23W
Pélican, L., *Qué.* 6 **B3** 59 47N 73 35W
Pelican L., *Man.* 21 **C10** 52 28N 100 20W
Pelican Narrows, *Sask.* 19 **B8** 55 10N 102 56W
Pelican Rapids, *Man.* 21 **C10** 52 45N 100 42W
Pelletier Sta., *Qué.* 11 **D13** 47 33N 69 26W
Pelly, *Sask.* 21 **D9** 51 52N 101 56W
Pelly →, *Yukon* 26 **C2** 62 47N 137 19W
Pelly Bay, *N.W.T.* 27 **C7** 68 38N 89 50W
Pelly Crossing, *N.W.T.* 26 **C2** 62 49N 136 34W
Pelly L., *N.W.T.* 26 **C5** 66 0N 102 0W
Pelly Pt., *B.C.* 32 **C1** 49 7N 123 12W
Pemberton, *B.C.* 25 **E12** 50 25N 122 50W
Pembina →, *Alta.* 22 **D6** 54 45N 114 17W
Pembroke, *Ont.* 15 **B9** 45 50N 77 7W
Penetanguishene, *Nfld.* 7 **H7** 47 36N 52 45W
Penetanguishene, *Ont.* 14 **C7** 44 50N 79 55W
Penhold, *Alta.* 23 **F7** 52 8N 113 52W
Pennant, *Sask.* 20 **E2** 50 32N 108 14W
Penniac, *N.B.* 9 **G3** 46 2N 66 34W
Penny, *B.C.* 25 **B13** 53 51N 121 20W
Penny Highland, *N.W.T.* 27 **C9** 67 19N 66 20W
Penny Str., *N.W.T.* 27 **B6** 76 30N 97 0W
Pense, *Sask.* 20 **E6** 50 25N 104 59W
Pentecôte →, *Qué.* 8 **D2** 49 46N 67 10W
Pentecôte, L., *Qué.* 8 **D2** 49 53N 67 20W
Penticton, *B.C.* 25 **F15** 49 30N 119 38W
Pentland Corners, *Ont.* 13 **A2** 43 40N 80 30W
Penylan L., *N.W.T.* 19 **A7** 61 50N 106 20W
Percé, *Qué.* 8 **E5** 48 31N 64 13W
Perdue, *Sask.* 20 **C3** 52 4N 107 33W
Péribonca →, *Qué.* 11 **C10** 48 45N 72 5W
Péribonca, L., *Qué.* 11 **A11** 50 1N 71 10W
Péribonka, *Qué.* 11 **C10** 48 46N 72 3W
Perow, *B.C.* 18 **C3** 54 35N 126 10W
Perrot, Île, *Qué.* 29 **C2** 45 22N 73 57W
Perry River, *N.W.T.* 27 **C5** 67 43N 102 14W
Perth, *N.B.* 9 **G2** 46 44N 67 42W
Perth, *Ont.* 15 **C10** 44 55N 76 15W
Petawawa, *Ont.* 15 **B9** 45 54N 77 17W
Peter Pond L., *Sask.* 19 **B7** 55 55N 108 44W
Peterbell, *Ont.* 17 **D13** 48 36N 83 21W
Peterborough, *Ont.* 15 **C8** 44 20N 78 20W
Peters, L., *Qué.* 6 **B3** 59 41N 70 53W
Petersfield, *Man.* 21 **E14** 50 18N 96 58W
Petit-Cap, *Qué.* 8 **D5** 49 3N 64 30W
Petit-de-Grat, *N.S.* 9 **H9** 45 30N 60 58W
Petit Étang, *N.S.* 9 **G9** 46 39N 60 58W
Petit Lac Manicouagan, *Qué.* 8 **B2** 51 25N 67 40W
Petit-Mécatina →, *Qué.* 8 **C10** 50 40N 59 30W
Petit-Mécatina, I. du, *Qué.* 6 **C6** 50 30N 59 25W
Petit-Rocher, *N.B.* 9 **F4** 47 46N 65 43W
Petitcodiac, *N.B.* 9 **H4** 45 57N 65 11W
Petite Baleine →, *Qué.* 6 **B2** 56 0N 76 45W
Petite-Cascapédia, Parc Prov. de la, *Qué.* 8 **E4** 48 30N 65 45W
Petite-Rivière, *Qué.* 11 **D12** 47 20N 70 33W
Petite Rivière Bridge, *N.S.* 9 **I5** 44 14N 64 27W
Petite Saguenay, *Qué.* 11 **C12** 48 15N 70 4W
Petitsikapau, L., *Nfld.* 6 **C4** 54 37N 66 25W
Petrolia, *Ont.* 14 **E4** 42 54N 82 9W
Petty Harbour Long Pond, *Nfld.* 7 **F8** 47 31N 52 58W
Phelps L., *Sask.* 19 **B8** 59 15N 103 15W
Philipsburg, *Qué.* 12 **B4** 45 2N 73 5W
Piapot, *Sask.* 20 **F1** 49 59N 109 8W
Piashti, L., *Qué.* 8 **C7** 50 29N 62 52W
Pic →, *Ont.* 17 **D10** 48 36N 86 18W
Pic I., *Ont.* 17 **D10** 48 43N 86 37W
Piccadilly, *Nfld.* 7 **E2** 48 34N 58 55W
Pickerel L., *Ont.* 16 **D5** 48 40N 91 25W
Pickering, *Ont.* 28 **A5** 43 52N 79 2W
Pickering Beach, *Ont.* 13 **A5** 43 50N 78 59W
Pickle Lake, *Ont.* 16 **A6** 51 30N 90 12W
Picton, *Ont.* 15 **C9** 44 1N 77 9W
Pictou, *N.S.* 9 **H7** 45 41N 62 42W
Pictou I., *N.S.* 9 **H7** 45 49N 62 33W
Picture Butte, *Alta.* 23 **I8** 49 55N 112 45W
Pie I., *Ont.* 16 **D7** 48 15N 89 6W
Piedmont, *Qué.* 12 **A2** 45 54N 74 8W
Pierceland, *Sask.* 20 **A1** 54 20N 109 46W
Pierrefonds, *Qué.* 29 **C2** 45 29N 73 52W
Pierreville, *Qué.* 11 **E10** 46 4N 72 49W
Pierson, *Man.* 21 **F9** 49 11N 101 15W
Pigeon Hill, *Qué.* 12 **B5** 45 3N 72 56W
Pigeon L., *Alta.* 23 **E6** 53 1N 114 2W
Pigeon L., *Ont.* 15 **C8** 44 27N 78 30W
Pike River, *Qué.* 12 **B4** 45 4N 73 6W
Pikwitonei, *Man.* 19 **B9** 55 35N 97 9W
Pilot Butte, *Sask.* 20 **E6** 50 28N 104 25W
Pilot Mound, *Man.* 21 **F12** 49 15N 98 54W
Pin-Blanc, L., *Qué.* 10 **E4** 46 45N 78 8W
Pinacle, Le, mt., *Qué.* 12 **B5** 45 2N 72 45W
Pinawa, *Man.* 21 **E15** 50 9N 95 50W
Pincher Creek, *Alta.* 23 **I7** 49 30N 113 57W
Pinchi L., *B.C.* 18 **C4** 54 38N 124 30W
Pincourt, *Qué.* 29 **C2** 45 23N 74 0W
Pine →, *Sask.* 19 **B7** 58 50N 105 38W
Pine, C., *Nfld.* 7 **G7** 46 37N 53 32W
Pine Dock, *Man.* 21 **D14** 51 38N 96 48W
Pine Falls, *Man.* 21 **E14** 50 34N 96 11W
Pine Grove, *Ont.* 28 **B2** 43 48N 79 35W
Pine Hill, *Qué.* 12 **A2** 45 44N 74 29W
Pine Pass, *B.C.* 18 **B4** 55 25N 122 42W
Pine Point, *N.W.T.* 18 **A6** 60 50N 114 28W
Pine Portage, *Ont.* 16 **C8** 49 20N 88 26W
Pine Ridge, *Man.* 31 **B5** 50 0N 96 50W
Pine River, *Man.* 21 **D10** 51 45N 100 30W
Pineview, *B.C.* 25 **B12** 53 50N 122 38W
Pink →, *Sask.* 19 **B8** 56 50N 103 50W
Pins, Pte. aux, *Ont.* 14 **E5** 42 15N 81 51W
Pinware, *Nfld.* 7 **B4** 51 37N 56 42W
Pinware →, *Nfld.* 7 **B4** 51 39N 56 42W
Pipestone →, *Ont.* 4 **B2** 52 53N 89 23W
Pipestone Cr. →, *Man.* 21 **F10** 49 38N 100 15W
Pipmuacan, Rés., *Qué.* 11 **B12** 49 45N 70 30W
Pistol B., *N.W.T.* 19 **A10** 62 25N 92 37W
Pistolet B., *Nfld.* 7 **B5** 51 35N 55 45W
Pitt →, *B.C.* 32 **B4** 49 13N 122 46W
Pitt I., *B.C.* 24 **B5** 53 30N 129 50W
Pitt L., *B.C.* 25 **F12** 49 25N 122 32W
Pitt Meadows, *B.C.* 32 **B4** 49 13N 122 42W
Pivabiska →, *Ont.* 17 **B14** 50 13N 82 52W
Placentia, *Nfld.* 7 **F7** 47 20N 54 0W
Placentia B., *Nfld.* 7 **G6** 47 0N 54 40W
Plage-St-Blaise, *Qué.* 12 **B4** 45 12N 73 16W
Plaine, La, *Qué.* 29 **A3** 45 47N 73 46W
Plamondon, *Alta.* 22 **D8** 54 51N 112 32W
Plaster Rock, *N.B.* 9 **G2** 46 53N 67 22W
Playgreen L., *Man.* 21 **B12** 54 0N 98 15W
Pleasant Bay, *N.S.* 9 **C7** 46 51N 60 48W
Pleasantdale, *Sask.* 20 **C6** 52 35N 104 30W
Pledger L., *Ont.* 17 **B13** 50 53N 83 42W
Plenty, *Sask.* 20 **D2** 51 47N 108 38W
Plessisville, *Qué.* 11 **E11** 46 14N 71 47W
Pletipi L., *Qué.* 6 **C3** 51 44N 70 6W
Plevna, *Ont.* 15 **C10** 44 58N 76 59W
Plonge, Lac la, *Sask.* 19 **B7** 55 8N 107 20W
Plum Coulee, *Man.* 21 **F13** 49 11N 97 45W
Plumas, *Man.* 21 **E11** 50 23N 99 5W
Plunkett, *Sask.* 20 **D5** 51 55N 105 27W
Plympton, *N.S.* 9 **I4** 44 30N 65 55W
Pocatière, La, *Qué.* 11 **D12** 47 22N 70 2W
Pogamasing, *Ont.* 17 **F15** 46 55N 81 50W
Poile, La, *Nfld.* 7 **F2** 47 41N 58 24W
Point Edward, *Ont.* 14 **E4** 43 0N 82 30W
Point L., *N.W.T.* 26 **C4** 65 15N 113 4W
Point Leamington, *Nfld.* 7 **D5** 49 20N 55 24W
Point Pelee Nat. Park, *Ont.* 14 **F4** 41 57N 82 31W
Point Pleasant, *N.S.* 9 **L11** 44 37N 63 34W
Point Sapin, *N.B.* 9 **G5** 46 58N 64 50W
Pointe-à-la-Frégate, *Qué.* 8 **D5** 49 12N 64 55W
Pointe-à-Maurier, *Qué.* 8 **C10** 50 20N 59 48W
Pointe au Baril Sta., *Ont.* 14 **B6** 45 35N 80 23W
Pointe-au-Pic, *Qué.* 11 **D12** 47 38N 70 9W
Pointe-aux-Anglais, *Qué.* 8 **D2** 49 41N 67 10W
Pointe-aux-Outardes, *Qué.* 11 **B14** 49 3N 68 26W
Pointe-aux-Trembles, *Qué.* 29 **B5** 45 40N 73 30W
Pointe-Calumet, *Qué.* 29 **C2** 45 30N 73 58W
Pointe-Claire, *Qué.* 29 **C3** 45 26N 73 50W
Pointe-des-Cascades, *Qué.* 29 **D2** 45 20N 73 58W
Pointe du Bois, *Man.* 21 **E15** 50 18N 95 33W
Pointe-Fortune, *Qué.* 12 **A2** 45 34N 74 23W
Pointe-Gatineau, *Ont.* 30 **D7** 45 28N 75 42W
Pointe-Lebel, *Qué.* 11 **B14** 49 10N 68 12W
Pointe-Parent, *Qué.* 8 **C8** 50 8N 61 47W
Pointe Verte, *N.B.* 9 **F4** 47 51N 65 46W
Poisson-Blanc, L. du, *Qué.* 10 **F7** 46 0N 75 45W
Poltimore, *Qué.* 10 **F7** 45 47N 75 43W
Ponask L., *Ont.* 4 **B1** 54 0N 92 41W
Ponass L., *Sask.* 20 **C7** 52 16N 103 58W
Poncheville, L., *Qué.* 10 **A6** 50 10N 76 55W
Pond Inlet, *N.W.T.* 27 **B8** 72 40N 77 0W
Ponds, I. of, *Nfld.* 6 **C6** 53 27N 55 52W
Ponoka, *Alta.* 23 **F7** 52 42N 113 40W
Ponsonby, *Ont.* 13 **A2** 43 38N 80 22W
Pont-Mousseau, *Qué.* 12 **A3** 45 52N 73 39W
Pont-Rouge, *Qué.* 11 **E11** 46 45N 71 42W
Pont-Viau, *Qué.* 29 **B3** 45 34N 73 41W
Ponteix, *Sask.* 20 **F3** 49 46N 107 29W
Pontiac, Parc, *Qué.* 10 **E6** 46 30N 76 30W
Ponton →, *Alta.* 18 **B5** 58 27N 116 11W
Pontypool, *Ont.* 15 **C8** 44 6N 78 38W
Pooley I., *B.C.* 24 **C6** 52 45N 128 15W
Poplar →, *Man.* 21 **C13** 53 0N 97 19W
Poplar →, *N.W.T.* 18 **A4** 61 22N 121 52W
Poplar Point, *Man.* 21 **E13** 50 4N 97 59W
Poplarfield, *Man.* 21 **E13** 50 53N 97 36W
Porcher I., *B.C.* 24 **B4** 53 50N 130 30W
Porcupine, *Ont.* 17 **D15** 48 30N 81 11W
Porcupine →, *Sask.* 19 **B8** 59 11N 104 46W
Porcupine Plain, *Sask.* 20 **C7** 52 36N 103 15W
Port Alberni, *B.C.* 24 **F10** 49 14N 124 50W
Port Alfred, *Qué.* 11 **C12** 48 18N 70 53W
Port Alice, *B.C.* 24 **E7** 50 20N 127 25W
Port au Choix, *Nfld.* 7 **C3** 50 43N 57 22W
Port au Port, *Nfld.* 7 **E2** 48 33N 58 43W
Port au Port B., *Nfld.* 7 **E2** 48 40N 58 50W
Port Blandford, *Nfld.* 7 **E6** 48 20N 54 10W
Port Burwell, *Ont.* 14 **E6** 42 40N 80 48W
Port Carling, *Ont.* 14 **B7** 45 7N 79 35W
Port-Cartier, *Qué.* 8 **C3** 50 2N 66 50W
Port-Cartier-Ouest, *Qué.* 8 **C3** 50 1N 66 52W
Port Clements, *B.C.* 24 **B2** 53 40N 132 10W
Port Colborne, *Ont.* 14 **E7** 42 50N 79 10W
Port Coquitlam, *B.C.* 25 **F12** 49 15N 122 45W
Port Credit, *Ont.* 28 **C2** 43 33N 79 35W
Port Dalhousie, *Ont.* 13 **B4** 43 13N 79 16W
Port-Daniel, Parc Prov. de, *Qué.* 8 **E5** 48 11N 64 58W
Port Dover, *Ont.* 14 **E6** 42 47N 80 12W
Port Dufferin, *N.S.* 9 **I7** 44 55N 62 23W
Port Edward, *B.C.* 24 **A4** 54 12N 130 10W
Port Elgin, *N.B.* 9 **G5** 46 3N 64 5W
Port Elgin, *Ont.* 14 **C5** 44 25N 81 25W
Port Greville, *N.S.* 9 **H5** 45 24N 64 33W
Port Guichon, *B.C.* 32 **C2** 49 5N 123 7W
Port Hammond, *B.C.* 32 **B5** 49 12N 122 39W
Port Hardy, *B.C.* 24 **E7** 50 41N 127 30W
Port Harrison = Inoucdjouac, *Qué.* 6 **B2** 58 25N 78 15W
Port Hastings, *N.S.* 9 **H8** 45 39N 61 24W
Port Hawkesbury, *N.S.* 9 **H8** 45 36N 61 22W
Port Hood, *N.S.* 9 **H8** 46 0N 61 32W
Port Hope, *Ont.* 15 **D8** 43 56N 78 20W
Port Howe, *N.S.* 9 **H6** 45 51N 63 45W
Port Kells, *B.C.* 32 **C4** 49 10N 122 42W
Port Lewis, *Qué.* 12 **B2** 45 10N 74 17W
Port Loring, *Ont.* 14 **B7** 45 55N 80 0W
Port Lorne, *N.S.* 9 **I4** 44 57N 65 16W
Port McNeill, *B.C.* 24 **E7** 50 35N 127 5W
Port Mann, *B.C.* 32 **B4** 49 12N 122 49W
Port Medway, *N.S.* 9 **I5** 44 8N 64 35W
Port Mellon, *B.C.* 25 **F11** 49 32N 123 31W
Port-Menier, *Qué.* 8 **D5** 49 51N 64 15W
Port Moody, *B.C.* 25 **F12** 49 17N 122 51W
Port Mouton, *N.S.* 9 **J5** 43 58N 64 50W
Port Nelson, *Man.* 19 **B10** 57 3N 92 36W
Port Nelson, *Ont.* 30 **D10** 43 20N 79 46W
Port Nouveau-Québec, *Qué.* 6 **B4** 58 30N 65 59W
Port Perry, *Ont.* 15 **C8** 44 6N 78 56W
Port Radium = Echo Bay, *N.W.T.* 26 **C4** 66 5N 117 55W
Port Renfrew, *B.C.* 24 **G10** 48 30N 124 20W
Port Robinson, *Ont.* 13 **B4** 43 2N 79 13W
Port Rowan, *Ont.* 14 **E6** 42 40N 80 30W
Port Royal, *N.S.* 9 **I4** 44 43N 65 36W
Port Saunders, *Nfld.* 7 **C3** 50 40N 57 18W
Port Severn, *Ont.* 14 **C7** 44 48N 79 43W
Port Simpson, *B.C.* 18 **C2** 54 30N 130 20W
Port Stanley, *Ont.* 14 **E5** 42 40N 81 10W
Port Wallace, *N.S.* 9 **K11** 44 42N 63 33W
Port Weller East, *Ont.* 13 **B4** 43 14N 79 13W
Port Whitby, *Ont.* 13 **A5** 43 51N 78 56W
Portage B., *Man.* 21 **D12** 51 33N 98 50W
Portage La Prairie, *Man.* 21 **F12** 49 58N 98 18W
Porter L., *N.W.T.* 19 **A7** 61 41N 108 5W
Porter L., *Sask.* 19 **B7** 56 20N 107 20W
Portland, *Ont.* 15 **C10** 44 42N 76 12W
Portland Creek Pond, *Nfld.* 7 **C3** 50 11N 57 32W
Portland Prom., *Qué.* 6 **B2** 58 40N 78 33W
Portneuf →, *Qué.* 11 **C13** 48 38N 69 5W
Portneuf, Parc Prov. de, *Qué.* 11 **D10** 47 10N 72 25W
Poste-de-la-Baleine, *Qué.* 6 **B2** 55 17N 77 45W
Pottageville, *Ont.* 13 **A3** 43 59N 79 37W
Pouce Coupé, *B.C.* 18 **B4** 55 40N 120 10W
Pouch Cove, *Nfld.* 7 **F8** 47 46N 52 46W
Poulin-de-Courval, L., *Qué.* 11 **C12** 48 52N 70 27W
Poutrincourt, L., *Qué.* 11 **B8** 49 11N 74 7W
Povungnituk, *Qué.* 6 **A2** 60 2N 77 10W
Povungnituk →, *Qué.* 6 **A2** 60 3N 77 15W
Povungnituk, B., *Qué.* 6 **B2** 60 0N 77 30W
Povungnituk, Mts. de, *Qué.* 6 **A2** 61 30N 75 5W
Powassan, *Ont.* 14 **A7** 46 5N 79 25W
Powell L., *B.C.* 24 **E10** 50 2N 124 25W
Powell River, *B.C.* 24 **F10** 49 50N 124 35W
Prairie, La, *Qué.* 29 **C5** 45 25N 73 30W
Prairies, R. des →, *Qué.* 29 **A5** 45 42N 73 29W
Preeceville, *Sask.* 20 **D8** 51 57N 102 40W
Preissac, L., *Qué.* 10 **C4** 48 20N 78 20W
Prelate, *Sask.* 20 **E1** 50 51N 109 24W
Premier, *B.C.* 18 **B3** 56 4N 129 56W
Prescott, *Ont.* 15 **C11** 44 45N 75 30W
Prescott □, *Qué.* 12 **A2** 45 35N 74 50W
Prescott I., *B.C.* 24 **A4** 54 6N 130 37W
Présentation, La, *Qué.* 12 **A4** 45 39N 73 3W
Preston, *Ont.* 13 **B2** 43 23N 80 21W
Préville, *Qué.* 29 **C5** 45 29N 73 30W
Prevost, *Qué.* 12 **A2** 45 52N 74 5W
Price, *Qué.* 8 **E1** 48 36N 68 7W
Price I., *B.C.* 24 **C6** 52 23N 128 41W
Priestly, *B.C.* 18 **C3** 54 8N 125 20W
Primrose L., *Sask.* 19 **C7** 54 55N 109 45W
Prince, *Sask.* 20 **C2** 52 58N 108 23W
Prince Albert, *Sask.* 20 **B5** 53 15N 105 50W
Prince Albert Nat. Park, *Sask.* 20 **B4** 54 0N 106 25W
Prince Albert Pen., *N.W.T.* 26 **B4** 72 30N 116 0W
Prince Albert Sd., *N.W.T.* 26 **B4** 70 25N 115 0W

Prince Alfred C., *N.W.T.* 26 **B3** 74 20N 124 40W
Prince Charles I., *N.W.T.* 27 **C8** 67 47N 76 12W
Prince Edward I. □, *Canada* 9 **G6** 46 20N 63 20W
Prince Edward Island Nat. Park, *P.E.I.* 9 **G6** 46 26N 63 12W
Prince Edward Pt., *Ont.* 15 **D10** 43 56N 76 52W
Prince George, *B.C.* 25 **B12** 53 55N 122 50W
Prince Gustav Adolf Sea, *N.W.T.* 26 **B5** 78 30N 107 0W
Prince of Wales I., *N.W.T.* 27 **B6** 73 0N 99 0W
Prince of Wales Str., *N.W.T.* 26 **B4** 73 0N 117 0W
Prince Patrick I., *N.W.T.* 26 **B4** 77 0N 120 0W
Prince Regent Inlet, *N.W.T.* 27 **B7** 73 0N 90 0W
Prince Rupert, *B.C.* 24 **A4** 54 20N 130 20W
Princess Margaret Range, *N.W.T.* 27 **A6** 80 30N 92 0W
Princess Royal Chan., *B.C.* 24 **C6** 53 0N 128 31W
Princess Royal I., *B.C.* 24 **C6** 53 0N 128 40W
Princeton, *B.C.* 25 **F14** 49 27N 120 30W
Princeton, *Ont.* 13 **B1** 43 10N 80 32W
Princeville, *Qué.* 11 **E11** 46 10N 71 53W
Principe Chan., *B.C.* 24 **B5** 53 28N 130 0W
Procter, *B.C.* 25 **F18** 49 37N 116 57W
Prophet →, *B.C.* 18 **B4** 58 48N 122 40W
Providence, La, *Qué.* 12 **A5** 45 37N 72 57W
Providence Bay, *Ont.* 14 **B4** 45 41N 82 15W
Provost, *Alta.* 23 **F10** 52 25N 110 20W
Prud'homme, *Sask.* 20 **C5** 52 20N 105 54W
Pugwash, *N.S.* 9 **H6** 45 51N 63 40W
Pukaskwa →, *Ont.* 17 **E11** 48 0N 85 53W
Pukaskwa Nat. Park, *Ont.* 17 **D11** 48 20N 86 0W
Pukatawagan, *Man.* 19 **B8** 55 45N 101 20W
Punnichy, *Sask.* 20 **D6** 51 23N 104 18W
Puntzi L., *B.C.* 24 **C10** 52 12N 124 2W
Puslinch, *Ont.* 13 **B2** 43 26N 80 5W
Puslinch, L., *Ont.* 13 **B2** 43 25N 80 16W
Putahow L., *Man.* 19 **B8** 59 54N 100 40W
Puyjalon, L., *Qué.* 8 **C6** 50 30N 63 25W

Q

Quadra I., *B.C.* 24 **E9** 50 10N 125 15W
Qualicum Beach, *B.C.* 24 **F10** 49 22N 124 26W
Qu'Appelle, *Sask.* 20 **E7** 50 33N 103 53W
Qu'Appelle →, *Sask.* 20 **E8** 50 26N 101 19W
Quarryville, *N.B.* 9 **G4** 46 50N 65 47W
Quathiaski Cove, *B.C.* 24 **E9** 50 3N 125 12W
Quatsino, *B.C.* 24 **E7** 50 30N 127 40W
Quatsino Sd., *B.C.* 24 **E7** 50 25N 127 58W
Québec, *Qué.* 30 **A3** 46 52N 71 13W
Québec □, *Qué.* 5 **C6** 50 0N 70 0W
Queen Charlotte, *B.C.* 24 **B2** 53 15N 132 2W
Queen Charlotte Is., *B.C.* 24 **B2** 53 20N 132 10W
Queen Charlotte Mts., *B.C.* 24 **B2** 53 5N 132 15W
Queen Charlotte Str., *B.C.* 24 **E7** 51 0N 128 0W
Queen Elizabeth Is., *N.W.T.* 27 **B6** 76 0N 95 0W
Queen Maud G., *N.W.T.* 26 **C5** 68 15N 102 30W
Queens Sd., *B.C.* 24 **D6** 51 57N 128 20W
Queensborough, *B.C.* 32 **B3** 49 12N 122 56W
Queenston, *Ont.* 13 **B4** 43 10N 79 3W
Queenstown, *N.B.* 9 **H3** 45 41N 66 7W
Quesnel, *B.C.* 25 **C12** 53 0N 122 30W
Quesnel →, *B.C.* 25 **C12** 52 58N 122 29W
Quesnel L., *B.C.* 25 **C13** 52 30N 121 20W
Quetico Prov. Park, *Ont.* 16 **D5** 48 30N 91 45W
Quévillon, L., *Qué.* 10 **B6** 49 4N 76 57W
Quick, *B.C.* 18 **C3** 54 36N 126 54W
Quidi Vidi, *Nfld.* 7 **H7** 47 35N 52 41W
Quiet L., *Yukon* 18 **A2** 61 5N 133 5W
Quilchena, *B.C.* 25 **E14** 50 10N 120 30W
Quill Lake, *Sask.* 20 **C6** 52 4N 104 15W
Quinton, *Sask.* 20 **D6** 51 23N 104 24W
Quinze, L. des, *Qué.* 10 **D3** 47 35N 79 5W
Quyon, *Qué.* 10 **F6** 45 31N 76 14W

R

Raanes Pen., *N.W.T.* 27 **B7** 78 30N 85 45W
Rabbit →, *B.C.* 18 **B3** 59 41N 127 12W
Rabbit Lake, *Sask.* 20 **B3** 53 8N 107 46W
Rabbitskin →, *N.W.T.* 18 **A4** 61 47N 120 42W
Race, C., *Nfld.* 7 **G7** 46 40N 53 5W
Racine L., *Ont.* 17 **D13** 48 2N 83 20W
Radisson, *Sask.* 20 **C3** 52 30N 107 20W
Radium Hot Springs, *B.C.* 23 **H4** 50 35N 116 2W
Radville, *Sask.* 20 **F6** 49 30N 104 15W
Radway, *Alta.* 22 **D8** 54 4N 112 57W
Rae, *N.W.T.* 18 **A5** 62 50N 116 3W
Rae Isthmus, *N.W.T.* 27 **C7** 66 40N 87 30W
Rainbow Lake, *Alta.* 18 **B5** 58 30N 119 23W
Rainy →, *Ont.* 16 **D2** 48 43N 94 29W
Rainy L., *Ont.* 19 **D10** 48 42N 93 10W
Rainy River, *Ont.* 19 **D10** 48 43N 94 29W
Raleigh, *Nfld.* 7 **B5** 51 34N 55 44W
Ralston, *Alta.* 23 **H9** 50 15N 111 10W
Ram →, *Alta.* 23 **F5** 52 23N 115 25W
Ram →, *N.W.T.* 18 **A4** 62 1N 123 41W
Rama, *Sask.* 20 **D8** 51 46N 103 0W
Ramah, *Nfld.* 6 **B5** 58 52N 63 15W
Ramah B., *Nfld.* 6 **B5** 58 52N 63 13W
Ramea, *Nfld.* 7 **F3** 47 31N 57 23W
Ramea Is., *Nfld.* 7 **F3** 47 31N 57 22W
Ramore, *Ont.* 10 **C2** 48 30N 80 25W
Ramsay I., *B.C.* 24 **C3** 52 33N 131 23W
Ramsayville, *Ont.* 30 **D8** 45 23N 75 34W
Ramsey, *Ont.* 17 **E14** 47 25N 82 20W
Ramsey L., *Ont.* 17 **E14** 47 13N 82 15W
Rancheria →, *Yukon* 18 **A3** 60 13N 129 7W
Random I., *Nfld.* 7 **E7** 48 8N 53 44W
Ranfurly, *Alta.* 22 **E9** 53 25N 111 41W
Rang-des-Dusseau, *Qué.* 12 **B4** 45 11N 73 9W
Ranger L., *Ont.* 17 **F13** 46 52N 83 35W
Rankin Inlet, *N.W.T.* 27 **C6** 62 30N 93 0W
Ranoke, *Ont.* 17 **B15** 50 26N 81 35W
Raper, C., *N.W.T.* 27 **C9** 69 44N 67 6W
Rapid →, *B.C.* 18 **B3** 59 15N 129 5W
Rapid City, *Man.* 21 **E10** 50 7N 100 2W
Rapide-Blanc, *Qué.* 11 **D9** 47 48N 73 2W
Rapide-Mascouche, *Qué.* 29 **A4** 45 46N 73 40W
Rapide-Sept, *Qué.* 10 **D4** 47 46N 78 19W
Rapides des Joachims, *Qué.* 10 **E5** 46 13N 77 43W
Rat →, *Man.* 21 **F13** 49 35N 97 10W
Rat River, *N.W.T.* 18 **A6** 61 7N 112 36W
Rats, R. aux →, *Qué.* 11 **C10** 48 53N 72 14W
Ratz, Mt., *B.C.* 18 **B2** 57 23N 132 12W
Rawdon, *Qué.* 11 **E9** 46 3N 73 40W
Ray, C., *Nfld.* 7 **F1** 47 33N 59 15W
Rayleigh, *B.C.* 25 **E14** 50 49N 120 17W
Raymond, *Alta.* 23 **I8** 49 30N 112 35W
Raymore, *Sask.* 20 **D6** 51 25N 104 31W
Read Island, *N.W.T.* 26 **C4** 69 12N 114 31W
Reading, *Ont.* 13 **A2** 43 50N 80 13W
Red →, *N. Amer.* 31 **C3** 49 45N 97 9W
Red Bay, *Nfld.* 7 **B4** 51 44N 56 25W
Red Deer, *Alta.* 23 **F7** 52 20N 113 50W
Red Deer →, *Alta.* 23 **H10** 50 58N 110 0W
Red Deer →, *Man.* 21 **C9** 52 53N 101 1W
Red Deer L., *Alta.* 23 **F7** 52 43N 113 2W
Red Deer L., *Man.* 21 **C9** 52 55N 101 20W
Red I., *Nfld.* 7 **F6** 47 23N 54 10W
Red Indian L., *Nfld.* 7 **E4** 48 35N 57 0W
Red L., *Ont.* 16 **A3** 51 3N 93 49W
Red Lake, *Ont.* 19 **C10** 51 3N 93 49W
Red Lake Road, *Ont.* 16 **C3** 49 59N 93 25W
Red Pass, *B.C.* 25 **C16** 53 0N 119 0W
Red River Floodway, *Man.* 31 **C4** 49 50N 96 57W
Red Rock, *B.C.* 25 **B12** 53 42N 122 40W
Red Rock, *Ont.* 16 **D8** 48 55N 88 15W
Red Sucker L., *Man.* 19 **C10** 54 9N 93 40W
Redberry L., *Sask.* 20 **C3** 52 45N 107 14W
Redcliff, *Alta.* 23 **H10** 50 10N 110 50W
Redditt, *Ont.* 16 **C2** 49 59N 94 24W
Redknife →, *N.W.T.* 18 **A5** 61 14N 119 22W
Redonda Bay, *B.C.* 24 **E10** 50 17N 124 57W
Redonda Is., *B.C.* 24 **E10** 50 15N 124 50W
Redrock Pt., *N.W.T.* 18 **A5** 62 11N 115 2W
Redvers, *Sask.* 21 **F9** 49 35N 101 40W
Redwater, *Alta.* 22 **E7** 53 55N 113 6W
Redwillow →, *Alta.* 22 **C1** 55 2N 119 18W
Reed, L., *Man.* 19 **C8** 54 38N 100 30W
Regina, *Sask.* 20 **E6** 50 27N 104 35W
Regina Beach, *Sask.* 20 **E6** 50 47N 105 0W
Reid L., *Sask.* 20 **F2** 50 0N 108 9W
Reid Lake, *B.C.* 24 **B11** 53 58N 123 6W
Reindeer →, *Sask.* 19 **B8** 55 36N 103 11W
Reindeer I., *Man.* 21 **C13** 52 30N 98 0W
Reindeer L., *Sask.* 19 **B8** 57 15N 102 15W
Reine, La, *Qué.* 10 **C3** 48 50N 79 30W
Reinland, *Man.* 21 **F13** 49 2N 97 52W
Reliance, *N.W.T.* 19 **A7** 63 0N 109 20W
Remi Lake Prov. Park, *Ont.* 17 **C14** 49 30N 82 15W
Rémigny, *Qué.* 10 **D3** 47 46N 79 12W
Renata, *B.C.* 25 **F16** 49 27N 118 7W
Rencontre East, *Nfld.* 7 **F5** 47 38N 55 12W
Renews, *Nfld.* 7 **G8** 46 56N 52 56W
Renfrew, *Ont.* 15 **B10** 45 30N 76 40W
Renison, *Ont.* 17 **B15** 50 58N 81 7W
Rennell Sd., *B.C.* 24 **B2** 53 23N 132 35W
Rennie, *Man.* 21 **F15** 49 51N 95 33W
Rennison I., *B.C.* 24 **C5** 52 50N 129 20W
Repentigny, *Qué.* 29 **A5** 45 44N 73 28W
Repulse Bay, *N.W.T.* 27 **C7** 66 30N 86 30W
Reserve, *Sask.* 20 **C8** 52 28N 102 39W
Resolute, *N.W.T.* 27 **B6** 74 42N 94 54W
Restigouche →, *N.B.* 9 **F3** 47 50N 67 0W
Reston, *Man.* 21 **F9** 49 33N 101 6W
Revelstoke, *B.C.* 25 **E16** 51 0N 118 10W
Rexdale, *Ont.* 28 **B2** 43 43N 79 33W
Rexton, *N.B.* 9 **G5** 46 39N 64 52W
Reynolds, *Man.* 21 **F15** 49 40N 95 55W
Rhein, *Sask.* 21 **D8** 51 25N 102 15W
Ribstone Cr. →, *Alta.* 23 **F10** 52 52N 110 5W
Rice L., *Ont.* 15 **C8** 44 12N 78 10W
Riceburg, *Qué.* 12 **B5** 45 8N 72 56W
Riceton, *Sask.* 20 **E6** 50 7N 104 19W
Rich, C., *Ont.* 14 **C6** 44 43N 80 38W
Rich Valley, *Alta.* 22 **E6** 53 51N 114 21W
Richan, *Ont.* 16 **C4** 49 59N 92 49W
Richards I., *N.W.T.* 26 **C2** 68 0N 135 0W
Richards L., *Sask.* 19 **B7** 59 10N 107 10W
Richardson →, *Alta.* 19 **B6** 58 25N 111 14W
Richardson Mts., *N.W.T.* 26 **C2** 68 20N 135 45W
Riche, Pte., *Nfld.* 7 **C3** 50 42N 57 25W
Richelieu, *Qué.* 12 **B4** 45 27N 73 15W
Richelieu □, *Qué.* 12 **A5** 45 55N 73 0W
Richelieu →, *Qué.* 12 **A4** 45 0N 73 18W
Richibucto, *N.B.* 9 **G5** 46 42N 64 54W
Richmond, *Ont.* 15 **B11** 45 11N 75 50W
Richmond, *Qué.* 11 **F10** 45 40N 72 9W
Richmond □, *B.C.* 32 **C2** 49 9N 123 7W
Richmond Hill, *Ont.* 28 **A3** 43 52N 79 27W
Richmound, *Sask.* 20 **E1** 50 27N 109 45W
Richvale, *Ont.* 28 **A3** 43 51N 79 26W
Rideau →, *Ont.* 30 **D7** 45 27N 75 42W
Rideau Canal, *Ont.* 30 **D7** 44 53N 76 0W
Ridge →, *Ont.* 17 **B12** 50 25N 84 20W
Ridgedale, *Sask.* 20 **C6** 53 0N 104 10W
Ridgetown, *Ont.* 14 **E5** 42 26N 81 52W
Riding Mt. Nat. Park, *Man.* 21 **E11** 50 50N 100 0W
Rigaud, *Qué.* 12 **B2** 45 29N 74 18W
Rigolet, *Nfld.* 6 **C6** 54 10N 58 23W
Rimbey, *Alta.* 23 **F6** 52 35N 114 15W
Rimouski, *Qué.* 11 **C14** 48 27N 68 30W
Rimouski →, *Qué.* 11 **C14** 48 27N 68 32W
Rimouski, Parc Prov. de, *Qué.* 11 **D14** 48 0N 68 15W
Rimouski-Est, *Qué.* 11 **C14** 48 28N 68 31W
Ringwood, *Ont.* 13 **A4** 43 58N 79 17W
Riondel, *B.C.* 25 **F18** 49 46N 116 51W
Riou L., *Sask.* 19 **B7** 59 7N 106 25W
Ripley, *Ont.* 14 **C5** 44 4N 81 35W
Ripon, *Qué.* 10 **F7** 45 45N 75 10W
Ritchie L., *Nfld.* 8 **A3** 52 58N 66 1W
River Hébert, *N.S.* 9 **H5** 45 42N 64 23W
River John, *N.S.* 9 **H6** 45 45N 63 3W
River Jordan, *B.C.* 24 **G10** 48 26N 124 3W
River of Ponds, *Nfld.* 7 **C3** 50 32N 57 24W
River of Ponds L., *Nfld.* 7 **C3** 50 30N 57 20W
River Valley, *Ont.* 14 **A6** 46 35N 80 11W
Rivercrest, *Man.* 31 **B3** 50 0N 97 3W
Riverfield, *Qué.* 12 **B3** 45 9N 73 49W
Riverhead, *Nfld.* 7 **G7** 46 58N 53 31W
Riverhurst, *Sask.* 20 **E4** 50 55N 106 50W
Riverport, *N.S.* 9 **I5** 44 18N 64 20W
Rivers, *Man.* 21 **E10** 50 2N 100 14W
Rivers, L. of the, *Sask.* 20 **F5** 49 49N 105 44W
Rivers Inlet, *B.C.* 24 **D7** 51 42N 127 15W
Riverside-Albert, *N.B.* 9 **H5** 45 42N 64 45W
Riverton, *Man.* 21 **D14** 51 1N 97 0W
Riverview Heights, *N.B.* 9 **G5** 46 4N 64 48W
Rivière-à-la-Chaloupe, *Qué.* 8 **C4** 50 17N 65 6W
Rivière-à-Pierre, *Qué.* 11 **E10** 46 59N 72 11W
Rivière-au-Renard, *Qué.* 8 **E5** 48 59N 64 23W
Rivière-aux-Rats, *Qué.* 11 **D10** 47 13N 72 53W
Rivière-Beaudette, *Qué.* 12 **B2** 45 14N 74 20W
Rivière-Bersimis, *Qué.* 11 **C14** 48 56N 68 42W
Rivière-de-la-Chaloupe, *Qué.* 8 **D7** 49 8N 62 32W
Rivière-des-Prairies, *Qué.* 29 **B4** 45 39N 73 33W
Rivière-du-Loup, *Qué.* 11 **D13** 47 50N 69 30W
Rivière-Ouelle, *Qué.* 11 **D12** 47 26N 70 1W
Rivière-Pentecôte, *Qué.* 8 **D2** 49 57N 67 1W
Rivière-Pigou, *Qué.* 8 **C4** 50 16N 65 35W
Rivière-Portneuf, *Qué.* 11 **C13** 48 38N 69 6W
Rivière-St-Jean, *Qué.* 8 **C5** 50 17N 64 19W
Rivière-Ste-Marguerite, *Qué.* 8 **C3** 50 8N 66 37W
Rivière Verte, *N.B.* 9 **F1** 47 19N 68 9W
Rivierre-au-Tonnère, *Qué.* 8 **C5** 50 16N 64 47W
Robb, *Alta.* 22 **E4** 53 13N 116 58W
Robe-Noire, L. de la, *Qué.* 8 **C7** 50 42N 62 42W
Robert's Arm, *Nfld.* 7 **D5** 49 29N 55 49W
Roberts Bank Superport, *B.C.* 32 **C1** 49 1N 123 9W
Roberts Creek, *B.C.* 25 **F11** 49 26N 123 38W
Robertsonville, *Qué.* 11 **E11** 46 9N 71 13W
Robertville, *N.B.* 9 **F4** 47 42N 65 46W
Roberval, *Qué.* 11 **C10** 48 32N 72 15W
Roblin, *Man.* 21 **D9** 51 14N 101 21W
Roblin Park, *Man.* 31 **B2** 49 52N 97 17W
Robsart, *Sask.* 20 **F1** 49 23N 109 17W
Robson, Mt., *B.C.* 25 **B15** 53 10N 119 10W
Rocanville, *Sask.* 21 **E9** 50 23N 101 42W
Roche Percée, *Sask.* 20 **F8** 49 4N 102 48W
Rochebaucourt, *Qué.* 10 **C5** 48 41N 77 30W
Rocher River, *N.W.T.* 18 **A6** 61 23N 112 44W
Roches →, *Qué.* 8 **C3** 50 2N 66 55W
Rochester, *Alta.* 22 **D7** 54 22N 113 27W
Rock →, *Yukon* 18 **A3** 60 7N 127 7W
Rock Creek, *B.C.* 25 **F16** 49 4N 119 0W
Rock Island, *Qué.* 11 **F9** 45 26N 73 34W
Rockburn, *Qué.* 12 **B3** 45 1N 74 1W
Rockcliffe Park, *Ont.* 30 **D7** 45 27N 75 41W
Rockglen, *Sask.* 20 **F5** 49 11N 105 57W
Rockingham, *N.S.* 9 **K11** 44 41N 63 39W
Rockland, *Ont.* 10 **F7** 45 33N 75 17W
Rockton, *Ont.* 13 **B2** 43 17N 80 7W
Rockway, *Ont.* 13 **B4** 43 6N 79 20W
Rockwood, *Ont.* 13 **A2** 43 37N 80 8W
Rocky →, *Alta.* 23 **E3** 53 8N 117 59W
Rocky Harbour, *Nfld.* 7 **D3** 49 36N 57 55W
Rocky Island L., *Ont.* 17 **F14** 46 55N 83 0W
Rocky Lane, *Alta.* 18 **B5** 58 31N 116 22W
Rocky Mountain House, *Alta.* 23 **F6** 52 22N 114 55W
Rocky Mts., *Br. Ant. Terr.* 18 **C4** 55 0N 121 0W
Rockyford, *Alta.* 23 **G7** 51 14N 113 10W
Roddickton, *Nfld.* 7 **C4** 50 51N 56 8W
Roderick I., *B.C.* 24 **C6** 52 38N 128 22W
Rodney, *Ont.* 14 **E5** 42 34N 81 41W
Roes Welcome Sd., *N.W.T.* 27 **C7** 65 0N 87 0W
Roger, L., *Qué.* 10 **D4** 47 50N 78 59W
Rogersville, *N.B.* 9 **G4** 46 44N 65 26W
Roggan L., *Qué.* 6 **C2** 54 8N 77 50W
Roggan River, *Qué.* 6 **C2** 54 25N 79 32W
Rohault, L., *Qué.* 11 **B8** 49 23N 74 20W
Roland, *Man.* 21 **F13** 49 22N 97 56W
Rollet, *Qué.* 10 **D3** 47 55N 79 15W
Rolling Hills, *Alta.* 23 **H9** 50 13N 111 46W
Romaine →, *Qué.* 8 **C6** 50 18N 63 47W
Rondeau Prov. Park, *Ont.* 14 **E5** 42 19N 81 51W
Ronge, L. la, *Sask.* 19 **B7** 55 6N 105 17W
Ronge, La, *Sask.* 19 **B7** 55 5N 105 20W
Roosevelt, Mt., *B.C.* 18 **B3** 58 26N 125 20W
Roosville, *B.C.* 23 **J5** 49 0N 115 3W
Rorketon, *Man.* 21 **D11** 51 24N 99 35W
Rosalind, *Alta.* 23 **F8** 52 47N 112 27W
Rose Blanche, *Nfld.* 7 **F2** 47 38N 58 45W
Rose Harbour, *B.C.* 24 **C3** 52 15N 131 10W
Rose Pt., *B.C.* 24 **A3** 54 11N 131 39W
Rose Valley, *Sask.* 20 **C7** 52 19N 103 49W
Rosebud →, *Alta.* 23 **G8** 51 25N 112 38W
Rosedale, *B.C.* 25 **F13** 49 10N 121 48W
Roseisle, *Man.* 21 **F12** 49 30N 98 20W
Rosemary, *Alta.* 23 **H8** 50 46N 112 5W
Rosemère, *Qué.* 11 **F9** 45 38N 73 48W
Rosetown, *Sask.* 20 **D3** 51 35N 107 59W
Ross River, *Yukon* 26 **C2** 62 30N 131 30W
Rossburn, *Man.* 21 **E10** 50 40N 100 49W
Rosseau, *Ont.* 14 **B7** 45 16N 79 39W
Rosseau L., *Ont.* 14 **B7** 45 10N 79 35W
Rosser, *Man.* 31 **B1** 49 59N 97 27W
Rossignol, L., *Qué.* 6 **C3** 52 43N 73 40W
Rossignol Res., *N.S.* 9 **I4** 44 12N 65 10W
Rossland, *B.C.* 25 **F17** 49 6N 117 50W
Rossmore, *Ont.* 15 **C9** 44 8N 77 23W
Rossport, *Ont.* 17 **D9** 48 50N 87 30W
Rosthern, *Sask.* 20 **C4** 52 40N 106 20W
Rothesay, *N.B.* 9 **H4** 45 23N 66 0W
Rouge →, *Ont.* 28 **B5** 43 48N 79 7W
Rouge →, *Qué.* 10 **F8** 45 17N 74 10W
Rouge Hill, *Ont.* 28 **B5** 43 48N 79 8W
Rougemont, *Qué.* 12 **B4** 45 26N 73 3W
Rouleau, *Sask.* 20 **E6** 50 10N 104 56W
Round Hill, *Alta.* 23 **E8** 53 10N 112 38W
Round Hill, *N.S.* 9 **I4** 44 46N 65 24W
Round L., *Nfld.* 7 **B4** 51 15N 56 32W
Round L., *Ont.* 15 **B9** 45 38N 77 30W
Round Pond, *Nfld.* 7 **E5** 48 11N 56 0W
Round Valley, *Alta.* 22 **E6** 53 21N 114 57W
Roussillon, *Qué.* 12 **A2** 45 41N 74 26W
Routhierville, *Qué.* 8 **E2** 48 11N 67 9W
Rouville □, *Qué.* 12 **B4** 45 33N 73 10W
Rouvray, L., *Qué.* 11 **B12** 49 18N 70 49W
Rouyn, *Qué.* 10 **C4** 48 20N 79 0W
Rowan L., *Ont.* 16 **C3** 49 18N 93 32W
Rowley I., *N.W.T.* 27 **C8** 69 6N 77 52W
Roxboro, *Qué.* 29 **B3** 45 31N 73 48W
Roxton Falls, *Qué.* 11 **F10** 45 34N 72 31W
Royal Oak, *B.C.* 25 **H19** 48 29N 123 23W
Ruel, *Ont.* 17 **E15** 47 15N 81 28W
Ruisseau-des-Anges, *Qué.* 12 **A3** 45 48N 73 40W
Ruisseau-Vert, *Qué.* 11 **B14** 49 4N 68 28W
Rummelhardt, *Ont.* 13 **B1** 43 27N 80 34W
Rumsey, *Alta.* 23 **G8** 51 51N 112 48W
Rupert →, *Qué.* 6 **C2** 51 29N 78 45W
Rupert B., *Qué.* 6 **C2** 51 35N 79 0W
Rupert House = Fort Rupert, *Qué.* 6 **C2** 51 30N 78 40W
Rusagonis, *N.B.* 9 **H3** 45 48N 66 37W
Rush L., *Ont.* 17 **E14** 47 45N 82 11W
Rush Lake, *Sask.* 20 **E3** 50 24N 107 24W
Rushoon, *Nfld.* 7 **F6** 47 21N 54 55W
Russell, *Man.* 19 **C8** 50 50N 101 20W
Russell I., *N.W.T.* 27 **B6** 74 0N 98 25W
Russell L., *Man.* 19 **B8** 56 15N 101 30W
Russell L., *N.W.T.* 18 **A5** 63 5N 115 44W
Russelltown, *Qué.* 12 **B3** 45 4N 73 45W
Rutledge →, *N.W.T.* 19 **A6** 61 4N 112 0W
Rutledge L., *N.W.T.* 19 **A6** 61 33N 110 47W
Rutter, *Ont.* 14 **A6** 46 6N 80 40W
Ryans B., *Nfld.* 6 **B5** 59 35N 64 3W
Rycroft, *Alta.* 22 **C2** 55 45N 118 40W
Ryley, *Alta.* 22 **E8** 53 17N 112 26W

S

Saanich, *B.C.* 25 **H19** 48 28N 123 22W
Sable, C., *N.S.* 9 **J4** 43 29N 65 38W
Sable I., *N.S.* 5 **D8** 44 0N 60 0W
Sable River, *N.S.* 9 **J4** 43 51N 65 3W
Sables, R. aux →, *Ont.* 14 **A4** 46 13N 82 3W
Sabourin, L., *Qué.* 10 **D5** 47 58N 77 41W
Sabrevois, *Qué.* 12 **B4** 45 12N 73 14W
Sachigo →, *Ont.* 4 **A2** 55 6N 88 58W
Sachigo L., *Ont.* 4 **B1** 53 50N 92 12W
Sachs Harbour, *N.W.T.* 26 **B3** 71 59N 125 15W
Sackville, *N.B.* 9 **H5** 45 54N 64 22W
Sacré-Coeur-de-Jésus, *Qué.* 11 **C13** 48 14N 69 48W
Saganaga L., *Ont.* 16 **D6** 48 14N 90 52W
Saganash L., *Ont.* 17 **C14** 49 4N 82 35W
Saglek B., *Nfld.* 6 **B5** 58 30N 63 0W
Saglek Fd., *Nfld.* 6 **B5** 58 29N 63 15W
Saglouc, *Qué.* 6 **A2** 62 14N 75 38W
Saguenay →, *Qué.* 11 **C12** 48 22N 71 0W
Sahtaneh →, *B.C.* 18 **B4** 59 2N 122 28W
St-Adalbert, *Qué.* 11 **E13** 46 51N 69 53W
St-Adolphe-d'Howard, *Qué.* 12 **A2** 45 58N 74 20W
St-Agapitville, *Qué.* 11 **E11** 46 34N 71 26W
St. Alban's, *Nfld.* 7 **F5** 47 51N 55 50W
St. Albert, *Alta.* 22 **E7** 53 37N 113 32W
St-Alexandre, *Qué.* 11 **D13** 47 41N 69 38W
St-Alexandre, *Qué.* 12 **B4** 45 14N 73 7W
St-Alexis, *Qué.* 12 **A3** 45 56N 73 37W
St-Alexis-des-Monts, *Qué.* 11 **E9** 46 28N 73 8W
St-Amable, *Qué.* 12 **A4** 45 39N 73 18W
St-Ambroise, *Qué.* 11 **C11** 48 33N 71 20W
St-Anaclet, *Qué.* 11 **C14** 48 29N 68 26W
St-André, *N.B.* 9 **F2** 47 8N 67 45W
St-André-Avellin, *Qué.* 10 **F7** 45 43N 75 3W
St-André-Est, *Qué.* 12 **A2** 45 34N 74 20W
St. Andrews, *N.B.* 9 **H2** 45 7N 67 5W
St. Andrew's, *Nfld.* 7 **F1** 47 45N 59 15W
St-Angèle-de-Monnoir, *Qué.* 12 **B4** 45 23N 73 6W
St-Anicet, *Qué.* 12 **B2** 45 8N 74 22W
St. Annes, *Man.* 21 **F14** 49 40N 96 39W
St. Anns, *Ont.* 13 **B4** 43 5N 79 30W
St. Anns B., *N.S.* 9 **G9** 46 22N 60 25W
St-Anselme, *N.B.* 9 **G5** 46 4N 64 43W
St-Anselme, *Qué.* 11 **E12** 46 37N 70 58W
St. Anthony, *N.B.* 9 **G5** 46 22N 64 45W
St. Anthony, *Nfld.* 7 **B5** 51 22N 55 35W
St-Antoine, *Qué.* 29 **A2** 45 46N 73 59W
St-Antoine-sur-Richelieu, *Qué.* 12 **A4** 45 46N 73 11W
St-Antonin, *Qué.* 11 **D13** 47 46N 69 29W
St-Apolline, *Qué.* 11 **E12** 46 48N 70 12W
St. Arthur, *N.B.* 9 **F2** 47 33N 67 46W
St-Aubert, *Qué.* 11 **D12** 47 11N 70 13W
St-Augustin, *Qué.* 29 **B2** 45 38N 73 59W
St-Augustin →, *Qué.* 6 **C6** 51 16N 58 40W
St-Augustin, L., *Qué.* 30 **B2** 46 45N 71 23W
St-Augustin-de-Desmaures, *Qué.* 30 **B2** 46 45N 71 30W
St-Augustin-Saguenay, *Qué.* 7 **B2** 51 13N 58 38W
St-Barnabé-Sud, *Qué.* 12 **A5** 45 44N 72 55W
St-Barthélémy, *Qué.* 11 **E9** 46 11N 73 8W
St-Basile, *N.B.* 9 **F1** 47 21N 68 14W
St-Basile-le-Grand, *Qué.* 12 **A4** 45 31N 73 17W
St-Basile-Sud, *Qué.* 11 **E11** 46 45N 71 49W
St. Benedict, *Sask.* 20 **C5** 52 34N 105 23W
St-Benoît, *Qué.* 12 **A2** 45 34N 74 6W
St-Bernard-de-Lacolle, *Qué.* 12 **B4** 45 5N 73 25W
St-Blaise, *Qué.* 12 **B4** 45 13N 73 17W
St. Boniface, *Man.* 31 **B3** 49 53N 97 5W
St. Brendan's, *Nfld.* 7 **E7** 48 52N 53 40W
St. Bride's, *Nfld.* 7 **G6** 46 56N 54 10W
St. Brieux, *Sask.* 20 **C6** 52 38N 104 54W
St-Bruno, *Qué.* 11 **C11** 48 28N 71 39W
St-Bruno-de-Montarville, *Qué.* 29 **B5** 45 32N 73 21W
St-Calixte-de-Kilkenny, *Qué.* 12 **A3** 45 57N 73 51W
St-Calixte-Nord, *Qué.* 12 **A3** 45 59N 73 55W
St-Canut, *Qué.* 12 **A2** 45 43N 74 5W
St-Casimir, *Qué.* 11 **E10** 46 40N 72 8W
St. Catharines, *Ont.* 13 **B4** 43 10N 79 15W
St-Césaire, *Qué.* 29 **B4** 45 25N 73 0W
St. Charles, *Man.* 31 **B2** 49 53N 97 19W
St-Charles, *Qué.* 30 **B5** 46 46N 70 57W
St-Charles →, *Qué.* 30 **B3** 46 49N 71 13W
St-Charles, L., *Qué.* 30 **A2** 46 55N 71 23W
St-Charles-sur-Richelieu, *Qué.* 12 **B4** 45 41N 73 11W
St-Chrysostôme, *Qué.* 12 **B3** 45 6N 73 46W
St. Clair, L., *Ont.* 14 **E4** 42 30N 82 45W
St. Claude, *Man.* 21 **F12** 49 40N 98 20W
St-Clet, *Qué.* 12 **B2** 45 21N 74 13W
St-Coeur de Marie, *Qué.* 11 **C11** 48 39N 71 43W

St-Colomban, Qué.	12 A2	45 44N	74 8W
St-Côme, Qué.	11 E9	46 16N	73 47W
St-Constant, Qué.	29 C4	45 22N	73 37W
St-Croix, N.B.	9 H2	45 34N	67 26W
St. Croix →, N. Amer.	9 H2	45 5N	67 6W
St-Cyrille-de-L'Islet, Qué.	11 D12	47 2N	70 17W
St-Damase, Qué.	12 A4	45 31N	73 1W
St-David-de-l'Auberivière, Qué.	30 B3	46 47N	71 12W
St-David-d'Yamaska, Qué.	12 A5	45 57N	72 51W
St. David's, Nfld.	7 E2	48 12N	58 52W
St. Davids, Ont.	13 B4	43 10N	79 6W
St-Denis, Qué.	12 A4	45 47N	73 9W
St-Dominique, Qué.	12 B2	45 20N	74 8W
St-Donat-de-Montcalm, Qué.	11 E8	46 19N	74 13W
St-Édouard-de-Napierville, Qué.	12 B3	45 14N	73 31W
St-Eleanors, P.E.I.	9 G6	46 25N	63 49W
St. Elias Mts., N.W.T.	18 A1	60 33N	139 28W
St-Éloi, Qué.	11 C13	48 2N	69 14W
St-Élouthère, Qué.	11 D13	47 30N	69 15W
St-Émile, Qué.	30 A2	46 52N	71 20W
St-Éphrem-de-Tring, Qué.	11 E12	46 2N	70 59W
St-Esprit, Qué.	12 A3	45 54N	73 40W
St-Étienne-de-Beauharnois, Qué.	29 D2	45 15N	73 55W
St-Étienne-de-Beaumont, Qué.	30 B4	46 50N	71 1W
St. Eugène, Ont.	10 F8	45 30N	74 28W
St-Eugène, Qué.	12 B2	45 30N	74 29W
St-Eusèbe, Qué.	11 D14	47 33N	68 55W
St. Eustache, Man.	21 F13	49 59N	97 47W
St-Eustache, Qué.	29 B2	45 33N	73 54W
St-Fabien, Qué.	11 C14	48 18N	68 52W
St-Félicien, Qué.	11 C10	48 40N	72 25W
St-Félix-de-Valois, Qué.	11 E9	46 10N	73 26W
St-Félix-du-Cap-Rouge, Qué.	30 B2	46 45N	71 22W
St-François, Qué.	11 E12	46 48N	70 49W
St-François, Qué.	29 B4	45 40N	73 35W
St-François →, Qué.	11 E10	46 7N	72 55W
St-François, L., Qué.	11 F8	45 10N	74 22W
St-François, L., Qué.	12 B2	45 10N	74 22W
St-François-du-Lac, Qué.	11 E10	46 5N	72 50W
St. François Xavier, Man.	21 F13	49 55N	97 32W
St-Fulgence, Qué.	11 C12	48 27N	70 54W
St-Gabriel-de-Brandon, Qué.	11 E9	46 17N	73 24W
St-Gabriel-de-Gaspé, Qué.	8 E5	48 31N	64 32W
St-Gabriel-de-Rimouski, Qué.	11 C14	48 25N	68 10W
St-Gabriel-Ouest, Qué.	30 A1	47 2N	71 35W
St-Gédéon, Qué.	11 C11	48 30N	71 46W
St-Gédéon-de-Beauce, Qué.	11 F12	45 45N	70 40W
St. George, N.B.	9 H3	45 11N	66 50W
St. George, Ont.	13 B2	43 15N	80 15W
St. George, C., Nfld.	7 E1	48 30N	59 16W
St. George's, Nfld.	7 E2	48 26N	58 31W
St-Georges, Qué.	11 E12	46 8N	70 40W
St. George's B., Nfld.	7 E2	48 24N	58 53W
St-Georges-de-Bagot, Qué.	12 A5	45 40N	72 50W
St-Georges-de-Cacouna, Qué.	11 D13	47 55N	69 30W
St-Georges-Ouest, Qué.	11 E12	46 7N	70 40W
St-Gérard, Qué.	11 F11	45 46N	71 25W
St-Germain-de-Grantham, Qué.	11 F10	45 50N	72 34W
St-Godefroi, N.B.	9 E4	48 5N	65 6W
St-Guillaume-d'Upton, Qué.	12 A5	45 53N	72 46W
St-Hector-de-Bagot, Qué.	12 A5	45 35N	72 48W
St-Henri, Qué.	30 B4	46 42N	71 4W
St-Hermas, Qué.	12 A2	45 36N	74 11W
St-Hilarion, Qué.	11 D12	47 34N	70 24W
St-Hippolyte-de-Kilkenny, Qué.	12 A2	45 56N	74 1W
St-Honoré, Qué.	11 C11	48 32N	71 5W
St-Hubert, Qué.	29 C5	45 30N	73 25W
St-Hubert-de-Témiscouata, Qué.	11 D13	47 49N	69 9W
St-Hugues, Qué.	12 A5	45 48N	72 52W
St-Hyacinthe, Qué.	11 F10	45 40N	72 58W
St-Hyacinthe □, Qué.	12 A4	45 40N	73 0W
St-Ignace, N.B.	9 G4	46 42N	65 5W
St. Ignace I., Ont.	17 D9	48 45N	88 0W
St-Ignas-de-Stanbridge, Qué.	12 B5	45 10N	72 57W
St-Isidore, Qué.	29 D3	45 20N	73 42W
St-Isidore-Jonction, Qué.	29 C4	45 21N	73 38W
St. Jacobs, Ont.	13 A1	43 32N	80 33W
St-Jacques, N.B.	9 F1	47 26N	68 23W
St-Jacques, Qué.	12 A3	45 57N	73 34W
St-Jacques-le-Mineur, Qué.	29 D5	45 17N	73 25W
St. James-Assiniboia, Man.	31 B2	49 54N	97 15W
St-Janvier, Qué.	29 A2	45 42N	73 56W
St-Jean, Qué.	12 B4	45 20N	73 20W
St-Jean □, Qué.	12 B4	45 15N	73 15W
St-Jean →, Qué.	6 C5	50 17N	64 20W
St-Jean →, Qué.	8 E5	48 46N	64 26W
St-Jean, L., Qué.	11 C11	48 40N	72 0W
St. Jean Baptiste, Man.	21 F13	49 15N	97 20W
St-Jean-Baptiste-de-Restigouche, N.B.	9 F2	47 46N	67 13W
St-Jean-Baptiste-de-Rouville, Qué.	12 A4	45 31N	73 7W
St-Jean-Chrysostôme, Qué.	30 B3	46 43N	71 12W
St-Jean-de-Boischatel, Qué.	30 A4	46 54N	71 9W
St-Jean-de-Dieu, Qué.	11 D13	48 0N	69 3W
St-Jean-Port-Joli, Qué.	11 D12	47 15N	70 13W
St-Jérôme, Qué.	11 C11	48 26N	71 53W
St-Jérôme, Qué.	11 F9	45 47N	74 0W
St-Joachim, Qué.	11 D12	47 4N	70 50W
St-Joachim-de-Tourelle, Qué.	8 D3	49 9N	66 25W
St. John, N.B.	9 H3	45 20N	66 8W
St. John →, N. Amer.	9 H3	45 15N	66 4W
St. John, C., Nfld.	7 D5	50 0N	55 32W
St. John, L., Nfld.	7 E6	48 23N	54 41W
St. John B., Nfld.	7 C3	50 55N	57 9W
Saint John Harbour, N.B.	9 H3	45 15N	66 2W
St. John I., Nfld.	7 C3	50 49N	57 14W
St. Johns, Man.	31 B3	49 55N	97 7W
St. John's, Nfld.	7 F8	47 35N	52 40W
St. John's Airport, Nfld.	7 H7	47 6N	52 45W
St. John's B., Nfld.	7 H8	47 34N	52 38W
St. John's East, Nfld.	7 H7	47 38N	52 42W
St. John's North, Nfld.	7 H7	47 33N	52 49W
St. John's South, Nfld.	7 I7	47 30N	52 43W
St-Joseph, Qué.	12 A5	45 38N	72 56W
St. Joseph, I., Ont.	14 A3	46 12N	83 58W
St. Joseph, L., Ont.	16 A6	51 10N	90 35W
St-Joseph-de-Beauce, Qué.	11 E12	46 18N	70 53W
St-Joseph-de-la-Rivière-Bleue, Qué.	11 D13	47 26N	69 3W
St-Joseph-de-Sorel, Qué.	11 E9	46 2N	73 7W
St-Joseph-du-Lac, Qué.	29 B2	45 32N	74 0W
St-Jovite, Qué.	10 E8	46 8N	74 38W
St-Jude, Qué.	12 A5	45 46N	72 59W
St-Justine, Qué.	11 E12	46 24N	70 21W
St-Lambert, Qué.	29 C5	45 30N	73 30W
St. Laurent, Man.	21 E13	50 25N	97 58W
St-Laurent, Qué.	29 C4	45 30N	73 40W
Saint-Laurent →, Qué.	29 C4	45 25N	73 32W
St-Laurent d'Orléans, Qué.	30 A4	46 51N	71 1W
St. Lawrence, Nfld.	7 G5	46 54N	55 23W
St. Lawrence →, Qué.	5 C6	49 30N	66 0W
St. Lawrence, Gulf of, Qué.	5 C7	48 25N	62 0W
St. Lazare, Man.	21 E9	50 27N	101 18W
St-Lazare-Station, Qué.	12 B2	45 23N	74 6W
St-Léolin, N.B.	9 F4	47 46N	65 10W
St-Léon-le-Grand, Qué.	8 E2	48 23N	67 30W
St. Leonard, N.B.	9 F2	47 12N	67 58W
St-Léonard, Qué.	29 B4	45 35N	73 35W
St-Léonard-de-Portneuf, Qué.	11 E11	46 53N	71 55W
St. Lewis →, Nfld.	6 C6	52 26N	56 11W
St-Liboire, Qué.	12 A5	45 39N	72 46W
St Louis, P.E.I.	9 G5	46 53N	64 8W
St. Louis, Sask.	20 C5	52 55N	105 49W
St-Louis →, Qué.	29 D2	45 19N	73 53W
St-Louis, L., Qué.	29 C3	45 24N	73 48W
St-Louis, Mts, Qué.	6 D3	46 13N	73 36W
St-Louis-de-Gonzague, Qué.	12 B3	45 13N	74 0W
St-Louis-de-Kent, N.B.	9 G5	46 44N	64 58W
St-Louis-de-Pintendre, Qué.	30 B4	46 45N	71 8W
St-Louis-de-Richelieu, Qué.	12 A5	45 51N	72 59W
St-Louis-de-Terrebonne, Qué.	29 A3	45 42N	73 47W
St-Luc, Qué.	12 B4	45 22N	73 18W
St-Luc-de-Matane, Qué.	8 E2	48 48N	67 28W
St-Ludger, Qué.	11 F12	45 45N	70 42W
St. Lunaire-Griquet, Nfld.	7 B5	51 31N	55 28W
St-Magloire, Qué.	11 E12	46 35N	70 17W
St. Malo, Man.	21 F14	49 19N	96 57W
St-Marc, Qué.	12 A4	45 41N	73 12W
St-Marcel-de-Richelieu, Qué.	12 A5	45 52N	72 54W
St. Margarets, N.B.	9 G4	46 54N	65 11W
St-Martin, Qué.	29 B3	45 35N	73 44W
St. Martin L., Man.	21 D12	51 40N	98 30W
St. Martins, N.B.	9 H4	45 22N	65 34W
St. Mary →, B.C.	23 I5	49 37N	115 38W
St. Mary Res., Alta.	23 I7	49 20N	113 11W
St. Marys, Ont.	14 D5	43 20N	81 10W
St. Mary's, C., Nfld.	7 G6	46 50N	54 12W
St. Mary's Alpine Prov. Park, B.C.	23 I4	49 50N	116 25W
St. Mary's B., Nfld.	5 C9	46 50N	53 50W
St. Marys Bay, N.S.	9 I3	44 25N	66 10W
St-Mathias, Qué.	12 B4	45 28N	73 16W
St-Mathieu, Qué.	29 D4	45 19N	73 31W
St-Maurice →, Qué.	11 E10	46 21N	72 31W
St-Maurice, Parc Prov. du, Qué.	11 D9	47 5N	73 15W
St-Michel, Qué.	29 B4	45 34N	73 37W
St-Michel, Qué.	30 A5	46 52N	70 55W
St-Michel-de-Napierville, Qué.	12 B3	45 14N	73 34W
St-Michel-de-Wentworth, Qué.	12 A2	45 46N	74 29W
St-Michel-des-Saints, Qué.	11 E9	46 41N	73 55W
St-Nazaire, Qué.	11 F10	45 44N	72 37W
St-Nicolas, Qué.	30 B2	46 42N	71 24W
St-Noël, Qué.	8 E2	48 35N	67 50W
St. Norbert, Man.	31 C3	49 46N	97 9W
St-Octave-de-l'Aveniro, Qué.	8 E3	49 0N	66 33W
St-Omer, Qué.	11 D13	47 3N	69 43W
St-Ours, Qué.	12 A4	45 53N	73 9W
St-Pacome, Qué.	11 D13	47 24N	69 58W
St-Pamphile, Qué.	11 E13	46 58N	69 48W
St. Pascal, Qué.	11 D13	47 32N	69 48W
St-Patrice, L., Qué.	10 E5	46 22N	77 20W
St. Paul, Alta.	22 E9	54 0N	111 17W
St-Paul, Qué.	12 B5	45 26N	72 53W
St-Paul →, Qué.	6 C6	51 27N	57 42W
St. Paul, I., N.S.	9 F9	47 12N	60 9W
St-Paul-de-Montmigny, Qué.	11 E12	46 44N	70 22W
St-Paul-d'Industrie, Qué.	12 A4	45 59N	73 27W
St-Paul-du-Nord, Qué.	11 C13	48 34N	69 14W
St-Paul-l'Ermite, Qué.	29 A5	45 45N	73 28W
St-Paulin, Qué.	11 E9	46 25N	73 1W
St. Pauls, Nfld.	7 D3	49 52N	57 49W
St. Peters, N.S.	9 H9	45 40N	60 53W
St. Peters, P.E.I.	9 G7	46 25N	62 35W
St-Philemon, Qué.	11 E12	46 41N	70 27W
St-Philippe-d'Argenteuil, Qué.	12 A2	45 37N	74 25W
St-Philippe-de-Lapraire, Qué.	29 C5	45 21N	73 28W
St-Pie, Qué.	12 B5	45 30N	72 54W
St. Pierre, Man.	21 F14	49 26N	96 59W
St.-Pierre, St- P. & M.	7 G4	46 46N	56 12W
St.-Pierre, I., St- P. & M.	7 G4	46 47N	56 11W
St-Pierre, L., Qué.	11 A14	50 8N	68 26W
St-Pierre, L., Qué.	11 E10	46 12N	72 52W
St.-Pierre et Miquelon □, St- P. & M.	7 G4	46 55N	56 10W
St-Placide, Qué.	12 A2	45 31N	74 13W
St-Polycarpe, Qué.	12 B2	45 18N	74 18W
St-Prime, Qué.	11 C10	48 35N	72 20W
St. Quentin, N.B.	9 F2	47 30N	67 23W
St-Raphaël, Qué.	11 E12	46 48N	70 45W
St-Raymond, Qué.	11 E11	46 54N	71 50W
St-Rédemptueur, Qué.	30 B3	46 42N	71 17W
St-Rémi, Qué.	29 D4	45 16N	73 37W
St-Robert, Qué.	12 A5	45 58N	73 0W
St-Roch, Qué.	11 D12	47 18N	70 12W
St-Roch-de-l'Achigan, Qué.	12 A3	45 51N	73 36W
St-Roch-de-Richelieu, Qué.	12 A4	45 53N	73 10W
St-Romuald, Qué.	30 B3	46 46N	71 20W
St-Rose, Qué.	29 B3	45 37N	73 47W
St-Sauveur, N.B.	9 F4	47 32N	65 20W
St-Sauveur-des-Montes, Qué.	12 A2	45 54N	74 10W
St-Sébastien, Qué.	11 F12	45 47N	70 58W
St-Siméon, Qué.	11 D13	47 51N	69 54W
St-Siméon-de-Bonaventure, N.B.	9 E4	48 5N	65 36W
St-Simon-de-Bagot, Qué.	12 A5	45 44N	72 52W
St-Simon-de-Rimouski, Qué.	11 C13	48 12N	69 3W
St-Stanislas-de-Kostka, Qué.	12 B2	45 11N	74 8W
St. Stephen, N.B.	9 H2	45 16N	67 17W
St-Sulpice, Qué.	12 A4	45 50N	73 21W
St-Télesphore, Qué.	12 B2	45 17N	74 23W
St. Thomas, Ont.	14 E5	42 45N	81 10W
St-Timothée, Qué.	29 D1	45 18N	74 2W
St-Tite, Qué.	11 E10	46 45N	72 34W
St-Tite-des-Caps, Qué.	11 D12	47 8N	70 47W
St-Ulric, Qué.	8 E2	48 47N	67 42W
St-Urbain, Qué.	11 D12	47 33N	70 32W
St-Urbain-de-Châteauguay, Qué.	12 B3	45 13N	73 44W
St-Valérien, Qué.	12 A5	45 34N	72 43W
St-Vianney, Qué.	8 E2	48 37N	67 25W
St. Victor, Sask.	20 F5	49 26N	105 52W
St-Vincent-de-Paul, Qué.	29 B4	45 37N	73 39W
St. Vincent's, Nfld.	7 G7	46 48N	53 38W
St. Vital, Man.	31 B3	49 51N	97 7W
St. Walburg, Sask.	20 B1	53 39N	109 12W
St-Yvon, Qué.	8 D5	49 10N	64 48W
St-Zotique, Qué.	12 B2	45 15N	74 15W
St. Marys →, N.S.	9 H8	45 2N	61 53W
Ste-Adèle, Qué.	12 A2	45 57N	74 7W
Ste. Agathe, Man.	21 F13	49 34N	97 11W
Ste-Agathe, Qué.	11 E11	46 23N	71 25W
Ste-Agathe-des-Monts, Qué.	11 E8	46 3N	74 17W
Ste-Agnès-de-Dundee, Qué.	12 B2	45 1N	74 25W
Ste-Angèle-de-Mérici, Qué.	8 E1	48 32N	68 5W
Ste-Angèle-de-Monnoir, Qué.	12 B4	45 23N	73 6W
Ste. Anne, L., Alta.	22 E6	53 42N	114 25W
Ste-Anne, L., Qué.	8 D2	50 0N	67 42W
Ste Anne de Beaupré, Qué.	11 D12	47 2N	70 58W
Ste-Anne-de-Bellevue, Qué.	29 C2	45 24N	73 57W
Ste-Anne-de-Madawaska, N.B.	9 F1	47 15N	68 2W
Ste-Anne-de-Prescott, Qué.	12 B2	45 26N	74 29W
Ste-Anne-des-Monts, Qué.	8 D3	49 8N	66 30W
Ste-Anne-des-Plaines, Qué.	29 A3	45 47N	73 49W
Ste-Anne-du-Lac, Qué.	10 E7	46 48N	75 25W
Ste-Blandine, Qué.	11 C14	48 22N	68 28W
Ste-Brigide-d'Iberville, Qué.	12 B4	45 19N	73 4W
Ste-Cécile-de-Milton, Qué.	12 B5	45 29N	72 44W
Ste-Claire, Qué.	11 E12	46 36N	70 51W
Ste-Clothilde-de-Châteauguay, Qué.	12 B3	45 10N	73 41W
Ste-Croix, Qué.	11 E11	46 38N	71 44W
Ste-Dorothée, Qué.	29 B3	45 32N	73 49W
Ste-Famille, Qué.	11 E12	46 58N	70 58W
Ste-Félicité, Qué.	8 E2	48 54N	67 20W
Ste-Florence, Qué.	8 E2	48 16N	67 14W
Ste-Foy, Qué.	30 B3	46 47N	71 17W
Ste-Françoise, Qué.	11 C13	48 6N	69 4W
Ste-Geneviève, Qué.	29 C2	45 29N	73 52W
Ste-Hélène-de-Bagot, Qué.	12 A5	45 44N	72 44W
Ste-Julie, Qué.	12 A4	45 35N	73 19W
Ste-Julienne, Qué.	12 A3	45 58N	73 43W
Ste-Justine-de-Newton, Qué.	12 B2	45 22N	74 25W
Ste-Madeleine, Qué.	12 A4	45 36N	73 6W
Ste-Marguerite →, Qué.	8 C3	50 9N	66 36W
Ste-Marie de la Madeleine, Qué.	11 E12	46 26N	71 0W
Ste-Marie-Salomé, Qué.	12 A4	45 56N	73 30W
Ste-Marthe, Qué.	12 B2	45 24N	74 18W
Ste-Marthe-de-Gaspé, Qué.	8 D3	49 12N	66 10W
Ste-Marthe-sur-le-Lac, Qué.	29 B2	45 32N	73 57W
Ste-Martine, Qué.	29 D3	45 15N	73 48W
Ste-Monique, Qué.	11 C11	48 44N	71 51W
Ste-Pudentienne, Qué.	11 F10	45 28N	72 40W
Ste-Rosalie, Qué.	12 A5	45 38N	72 54W
Ste-Rose, Qué.	12 A3	45 37N	73 48W
Ste. Rose du lac, Man.	21 D11	51 4N	99 30W
Ste-Sabine, Qué.	12 B4	45 15N	73 2W
Ste-Scholastique, Qué.	12 A2	45 39N	74 5W
Ste-Thècle, Qué.	11 E10	46 49N	72 31W
Ste-Thérèse, Qué.	29 B2	45 38N	73 50W
Ste-Thérèse, Île, Qué.	29 B5	45 40N	73 29W
Ste-Thérèse-de-Lisieux, Qué.	30 A3	46 56N	71 12W
Ste-Thérèse-Ouest, Qué.	29 B3	45 37N	73 50W
Ste-Victoire, Qué.	12 A4	45 57N	73 5W
Sairs, L., Qué.	10 E4	46 49N	78 26W
Sakami, L., Qué.	6 C2	53 15N	77 0W
Salaberry, Île de, Qué.	12 B2	45 17N	74 7W
Salaberry-de-Valleyfield, Qué.	12 B2	45 15N	74 8W
Salem, Ont.	13 A2	43 42N	80 27W
Salisbury, N.B.	9 G4	46 2N	65 3W
Salisbury I., N.W.T.	27 C8	63 30N	77 0W
Sally's Cove, Nfld.	7 D3	49 44N	57 56W
Salmo, B.C.	25 F17	49 10N	117 20W
Salmon →, B.C.	18 C4	54 3N	122 40W
Salmon →, N.B.	9 G4	46 6N	65 56W
Salmon →, Qué.	8 D7	49 25N	62 15W
Salmon Arm, B.C.	25 E15	50 40N	119 15W
Salmon Res., Nfld.	7 E5	48 5N	56 0W
Salmon River, N.S.	9 I3	44 3N	66 10W
Salt →, Alta.	18 B6	60 0N	112 25W
Saltair, B.C.	24 G11	48 57N	123 46W
Saltcoats, Sask.	21 D8	51 5N	102 15W
Saltery Bay, B.C.	24 F10	49 47N	124 10W
Salvador, Sask.	20 C1	52 10N	109 32W
Salvail, Qué.	12 A4	45 40N	73 4W
Salvail →, Qué.	29 A2	45 49N	73 58W
Sambro, N.S.	9 I6	44 28N	63 36W
San Clara, Man.	21 D9	51 29N	101 26W
Sand →, Alta.	22 D9	54 23N	111 2W
Sand L., Ont.	16 B2	50 10N	94 35W
Sandbank L., Ont.	17 A14	51 8N	82 41W
Sandfly L., Sask.	19 B7	55 43N	106 6W
Sandhill, Ont.	13 A3	43 50N	79 52W
Sandspit, B.C.	24 B3	53 14N	131 49W
Sandwich B., Nfld.	6 C6	53 40N	57 15W
Sandy →, Qué.	6 B4	55 30N	68 21W
Sandy Cove, Nfld.	7 B4	51 21N	56 40W
Sandy L., Alta.	22 E6	53 47N	114 2W
Sandy L., Nfld.	7 D4	49 15N	57 0W
Sandy L., Ont.	4 B1	53 2N	93 0W
Sandy Lake, Ont.	4 B1	53 0N	93 15W
Sandy Narrows, Sask.	19 B8	55 5N	103 4W
Sandy Point, N.S.	9 J4	43 42N	65 19W
Sandybeach L., Ont.	16 C4	49 49N	92 21W
Sangudo, Alta.	22 E6	53 50N	114 54W
Sanmaur, Qué.	11 D9	47 54N	73 47W
Sardis, B.C.	25 F13	49 8N	121 58W
Sarnia, Ont.	14 E4	42 58N	82 23W
Sarre, La, Qué.	10 C3	48 45N	79 15W
Sasaginnigak L., Man.	21 D15	51 36N	95 39W
Saseginaga, L., Qué.	10 D4	47 6N	78 35W
Saskatchewan □, Sask.	19 C7	54 40N	106 0W
Saskatchewan →, Sask.	21 B10	53 37N	100 40W
Saskatchewan Landing Prov. Park, Sask.	20 E3	50 38N	107 59W
Saskatoon, Sask.	20 C4	52 10N	106 38W
Saturna, B.C.	25 G11	48 47N	123 11W
Saubosq, L., Qué.	8 B5	51 30N	64 53W
Saugeen →, Ont.	14 C5	44 30N	81 22W
Saulnierville, N.S.	9 I3	44 16N	66 8W
Sault-au-Moulton, Qué.	11 C13	48 33N	69 15W
Sault aux Cochons →, Qué.	11 C13	48 44N	69 4W
Sault Ste. Marie, Ont.	14 A2	46 30N	84 20W
Saumur, L., Qué.	8 B7	51 16N	62 49W
Sauvage, L., Qué.	10 A8	50 6N	74 30W
Savant L., Ont.	16 B6	50 16N	90 44W
Savant Lake, Ont.	16 B6	50 14N	90 40W
Savona, B.C.	25 E14	50 45N	120 50W
Sawyerville, Qué.	11 F11	45 20N	71 34W
Sayabec, Qué.	8 E2	48 35N	67 41W
Scandia, Alta.	23 H9	50 20N	112 0W
Scarborough, Ont.	28 B4	43 45N	79 12W
Scatarie I., N.S.	9 H10	46 0N	59 44W
Sceptre, Sask.	20 E1	50 51N	109 15W
Schefferville, Qué.	6 C4	54 48N	66 50W
Schreiber, Ont.	17 D9	48 45N	87 20W
Schuler, Alta.	23 H10	50 20N	110 6W
Schumacher, Ont.	17 D15	48 30N	81 16W
Scie, La, Nfld.	7 D5	49 57N	55 36W
Scotland, Ont.	13 B2	43 1N	80 22W
Scotstown, Qué.	11 F11	45 32N	71 17W
Scott, Sask.	20 C2	52 22N	108 50W
Scott Chan., B.C.	24 E6	50 45N	128 30W
Scott Inlet, N.W.T.	27 B8	71 0N	71 0W
Scott Is., B.C.	24 E6	50 48N	128 40W
Scott-Jonction, Qué.	11 E11	46 30N	71 4W
Scott L., Sask.	19 B7	59 55N	106 18W
Scugog, L., Ont.	15 C8	44 10N	78 55W
Sea I., B.C.	32 B1	49 12N	123 10W
Seaforth, Ont.	14 D5	43 35N	81 25W
Seager Wheeler L., Sask.	20 A7	54 17N	103 31W
Seahorse L., Nfld.	8 A4	52 12N	65 48W
Seal →, Man.	19 B10	59 4N	94 48W
Seal Cove, N.B.	9 I3	44 39N	66 51W
Seal Cove, Nfld.	7 F4	47 29N	56 4W
Seal Cove, Nfld.	7 D4	49 57N	56 22W
Seal L., Nfld.	6 C5	54 20N	61 30W
Searchmont, Ont.	17 F12	46 47N	84 3W
Searle, Man.	31 B2	49 51N	97 15W
Seba Beach, Alta.	22 E6	53 35N	114 47W
Sebringville, Ont.	14 D5	43 24N	81 4W
Sechelt, B.C.	24 F11	49 25N	123 42W
Second Narrows, B.C.	32 B2	49 18N	123 2W
Sedgewick, Alta.	23 F9	52 48N	111 41W
Sedley, Sask.	20 E7	50 10N	104 0W
Seeley's Bay, Ont.	15 C10	44 29N	76 14W
Sein →, Man.	31 B3	49 54N	97 7W
Selby Lake, Qué.	12 B5	45 6N	72 48W
Selkirk, Man.	21 E14	50 10N	96 55W
Selkirk, Ont.	14 E7	42 49N	79 56W
Selkirk I., Man.	21 B11	53 20N	99 6W
Selkirk Mts., B.C.	18 C5	51 15N	117 40W
Selwyn L., Sask.	19 B8	60 0N	104 30W
Semans, Sask.	20 D6	51 25N	104 44W
Semiahmoo B., B.C.	32 C3	49 1N	122 50W
Sénécal, L., Nfld.	8 A6	52 5N	63 20W
Senneterre, Qué.	10 C5	48 25N	77 15W
Senneville, Qué.	29 C2	45 27N	73 57W
Separation Point, Nfld.	6 C6	53 37N	57 25W
Sept-Îles, Qué.	8 C3	50 13N	66 22W
Sequart L., Nfld.	8 A6	52 26N	63 47W
Sérigny →, Qué.	6 B4	56 47N	66 0W
Serpentine →, B.C.	32 C3	49 5N	122 51W
Seton L., B.C.	25 E12	50 42N	122 8W
Seton Portage, B.C.	25 E12	50 42N	122 17W
Setting L., Man.	19 C9	55 0N	98 38W
Seven Islands B., Nfld.	6 B5	59 25N	63 45W
Seven Sisters, B.C.	18 C3	54 56N	128 10W
Seven Sisters Falls, Man.	21 E14	50 7N	96 2W
Seventy Mile House, B.C.	25 D13	51 18N	121 23W
Severn →, Ont.	4 A2	56 2N	87 36W
Severn L., Ont.	4 B1	53 54N	90 48W
Sewell, B.C.	24 B2	53 47N	132 16W
Sexsmith, Alta.	22 C2	55 21N	118 47W
Seymour →, B.C.	32 B2	49 18N	123 1W
Seymour, Mt., B.C.	32 A3	49 24N	122 57W
Seymour Arm, B.C.	25 D16	51 15N	118 57W
Seymour Heights, B.C.	32 B3	49 19N	123 0W
Seymour Inlet, B.C.	24 D8	51 3N	127 0W
Seymour L., B.C.	32 A3	49 27N	122 57W
Shabogamo L., Nfld.	6 C4	53 15N	66 30W
Shabuskwia L., Ont.	16 A8	51 15N	89 0W
Shakespeare I., Ont.	16 C8	49 38N	88 25W
Shalalth, B.C.	25 E12	50 43N	122 13W
Shallow Lake, Ont.	14 C5	44 36N	81 5W
Shamattawa, Man.	19 B10	55 51N	92 5W
Shamattawa →, Ont.	4 A2	55 1N	85 23W
Shamrock, Sask.	20 E4	50 10N	106 37W
Shannon L., Ont.	17 C13	49 48N	83 24W
Sharbot Lake, Ont.	15 C10	44 46N	76 41W
Sharpe L., Man.	19 C10	54 24N	93 40W
Shaunavon, Sask.	20 F2	49 35N	108 25W
Shawanaga, Ont.	14 B6	45 31N	80 17W
Shawbridge, Qué.	12 A2	45 52N	74 5W
Shawinigan, Qué.	11 E10	46 35N	72 50W
Shawinigan Sud, Qué.	11 E10	46 31N	72 45W
Shawville, Qué.	10 F6	45 36N	76 30W
Shebandowan, Ont.	16 D6	48 38N	90 4W
Shediac, N.B.	9 G5	46 14N	64 32W
Sheet Harbour, N.S.	9 I7	44 56N	62 31W

Sheffield, *Ont.* **13 B2** 43 19N 80 12W
Sheffield L., *Nfld.* **7 D4** 49 20N 56 34W
Sheguiandah, *Ont.* **14 B5** 45 54N 81 55W
Sheho, *Sask.* **20 D7** 51 35N 103 13W
Sheila, *N.B.* **9 F5** 47 29N 64 55W
Shelburne, *N.S.* **9 J4** 43 47N 65 20W
Shelburne, *Ont.* **14 C6** 44 4N 80 15W
Sheldrake, *Qué.* **8 C5** 50 20N 64 51W
Shell Lake, *Sask.* **20 B3** 53 19N 107 2W
Shellbrook, *Sask.* **20 B4** 53 13N 106 24W
Shelley, *B.C.* **25 B12** 54 0N 122 37W
Shellmouth, *Man.* **21 E9** 50 56N 101 29W
Shepard, *Alta.* **31 G11** 50 57N 113 55W
Sherbrooke, *Qué.* **11 F11** 45 28N 71 57W
Sheridan, *Ont.* **28 C2** 43 31N 79 40W
Sheridan L., *B.C.* **25 D14** 51 31N 120 54W
Sherman, *B.C.* **32 A1** 49 21N 123 14W
Sherridon, *Man.* **19 B8** 55 8N 101 5W
Sherrington, *Qué.* **12 B3** 45 10N 73 31W
Sherwood Park, *Alta.* **31 D8** 53 31N 113 19W
Shesley, *B.C.* **18 B2** 58 17N 131 52W
Shesley →, *B.C.* **18 B2** 58 48N 132 5W
Shethanei L., *Man.* **19 B9** 58 48N 97 50W
Shibogama L., *Ont.* **4 B2** 53 35N 88 15W
Shilo, *Man.* **21 F11** 49 49N 99 38W
Shippegan, *N.B.* **9 F5** 47 45N 64 45W
Shippegan I., *N.B.* **9 F5** 47 50N 64 38W
Shoal L., *Ont.* **16 C1** 49 33N 95 1W
Shoal Lake, *Man.* **21 E10** 50 30N 100 35W
Shoals Prov. Park, *Ont.* **17 E13** 47 50N 83 50W
Shubenacadie, *N.S.* **9 H6** 45 5N 63 24W
Shuswap L., *B.C.* **25 E15** 50 55N 119 3W
Sibley Prov. Park, *Ont.* **16 D8** 48 30N 88 45W
Sicamous, *B.C.* **25 E16** 50 49N 119 0W
Sideburned L., *Ont.* **17 E13** 47 45N 83 15W
Sidney, *B.C.* **25 G11** 48 39N 123 24W
Sidney, *Man.* **21 F11** 49 54N 99 4W
Sifton, *Man.* **21 D10** 51 21N 100 8W
Sifton Pass, *B.C.* **18 B3** 57 52N 126 15W
Signal Hill, *Nfld.* **7 H7** 47 35N 52 41W
Sigutlat L., *B.C.* **24 C8** 52 57N 126 12W
Sikkani Chief →, *B.C.* **18 B4** 57 47N 122 15W
Silcox, *Man.* **19 B10** 57 12N 94 10W
Sillery, *Qué.* **30 B3** 46 46N 71 15W
Silver Islet, *Ont.* **16 D8** 48 20N 88 45W
Silver Ridge, *Man.* **21 E12** 50 48N 98 52W
Silver Star Prov. Park, *B.C.* **25 E15** 50 23N 119 5W
Silver Water, *Ont.* **14 B4** 45 52N 82 52W
Silvertip Mt., *B.C.* **25 F13** 49 10N 121 13W
Silverton, *B.C.* **25 F17** 49 57N 117 21W
Simard, L., *Qué.* **10 D4** 47 40N 78 40W
Simcoe, *Ont.* **14 E6** 42 50N 80 20W
Simcoe, L., *Ont.* **14 C7** 44 25N 79 20W
Simmie, *Sask.* **20 F2** 49 56N 108 6W
Simmons, *Ont.* **30 D7** 45 26N 75 49W
Simmons Pen., *N.W.T.* **27 B7** 76 40N 89 7W
Simonette →, *Alta.* **22 C2** 55 9N 118 15W
Simonhouse, *Man.* **21 A9** 54 26N 101 23W
Simpson, *Sask.* **20 D5** 51 27N 105 27W
Simpson I., *Ont.* **17 D9** 48 46N 87 41W
Simpson Pen., *N.W.T.* **27 C7** 68 34N 88 45W
Simpsons Corners, *Ont.* **13 A2** 43 46N 80 18W
Sinclair Mills, *B.C.* **18 C4** 54 5N 121 40W
Sinclair Pass, *B.C.* **23 H5** 50 40N 115 58W
Sintaluta, *Sask.* **20 E7** 50 29N 103 27W
Sioux Lookout, *Ont.* **16 B5** 50 10N 91 50W
Sioux Narrows, *Ont.* **16 C2** 49 25N 94 10W
Sipiwesk L., *Man.* **19 B9** 55 5N 97 35W
Sir Francis Drake, Mt., *B.C.* **24 E10** 50 49N 124 48W
Sir Sandford, Mt., *B.C.* **25 D17** 51 40N 117 52W
Sisipuk L., *Man.* **19 B8** 55 45N 101 50W
Sixteen Island Lake, *Qué.* **12 A2** 45 56N 74 28W
Skeena →, *B.C.* **24 A4** 54 9N 130 5W
Skeena Mts., *B.C.* **18 B3** 56 40N 128 30W
Skidegate, *B.C.* **24 B2** 53 15N 132 1W
Skihist, Mt., *B.C.* **25 E13** 50 12N 121 54W
Skownan, *Man.* **21 D11** 51 58N 99 35W
Slate Is., *Ont.* **17 D10** 48 40N 87 0W
Slave →, *N.W.T.* **18 A6** 61 18N 113 39W
Slave Lake, *Alta.* **22 C6** 55 17N 114 43W
Slave Pt., *N.W.T.* **18 A5** 61 11N 115 56W
Slemon L., *N.W.T.* **18 A5** 63 13N 116 4W
Slocan, *B.C.* **25 F17** 49 48N 117 28W
Slocan L., *B.C.* **25 F17** 49 50N 117 23W
Smalltree L., *N.W.T.* **19 A8** 61 0N 105 0W
Smeaton, *Sask.* **20 B6** 53 30N 104 49W
Smiley, *Sask.* **20 D1** 51 38N 109 29W
Smith, *Alta.* **22 C7** 55 10N 114 0W
Smith →, *B.C.* **18 B3** 59 34N 126 30W
Smith Arm, *N.W.T.* **26 C3** 66 15N 123 0W
Smith I., *N.W.T.* **6 C6** 54 13N 58 18W
Smith Pen., *N.W.T.* **27 B8** 77 12N 78 50W
Smithers, *B.C.* **18 C3** 54 45N 127 10W
Smiths Cove, *N.S.* **9 I4** 44 37N 65 42W
Smiths Falls, *Ont.* **15 C11** 44 55N 76 0W
Smithville, *Ont.* **13 B3** 43 6N 79 33W
Smoky →, *Alta.* **22 B3** 56 10N 117 21W
Smoky Falls, *Ont.* **17 B14** 50 4N 82 10W
Smoky Lake, *Alta.* **22 D8** 54 10N 112 30W
Smooth Rock Falls, *Ont.* **17 C15** 49 17N 81 37W
Smoothrock L., *Ont.* **16 B7** 50 30N 89 30W
Smoothstone L., *Sask.* **19 C7** 54 40N 106 50W
Snake L., *Sask.* **19 B7** 55 32N 106 35W
Snaring, *Alta.* **23 E2** 53 5N 118 4W
Snelgrove, *Ont.* **13 A3** 43 44N 79 49W
Snipe L., *Alta.* **22 C4** 55 7N 116 47W
Snow Lake, *Man.* **19 C8** 54 52N 100 3W
Snowbird L., *N.W.T.* **19 A8** 60 45N 103 0W
Snowdrift, *N.W.T.* **19 A6** 62 24N 110 44W
Snowdrift →, *N.W.T.* **19 A6** 62 24N 110 44W
Snowflake, *Man.* **21 F12** 49 3N 98 39W
Snyder, *Ont.* **13 C4** 42 57N 79 3W
Soeurs, Île des, *Qué.* **29 C4** 45 28N 73 33W
Sointula, *B.C.* **24 E8** 50 38N 127 0W
Solina, *Ont.* **13 A5** 43 58N 78 47W
Sombra, *Ont.* **14 E4** 42 43N 82 29W
Somerset, *Man.* **21 F12** 49 25N 98 39W
Somerset I., *N.W.T.* **27 B6** 73 30N 93 0W
Sonningdale, *Sask.* **20 C3** 52 23N 107 44W
Sonora, *N.S.* **9 H8** 45 4N 61 54W
Sonora I., *B.C.* **24 E9** 50 22N 125 15W
Sooke, *B.C.* **25 G11** 48 13N 123 43W
Sop's Arm, *Nfld.* **7 D4** 49 46N 56 56W
Sorel, *Qué.* **11 F9** 46 0N 73 10W
Soscumica, L., *Qué.* **10 A5** 50 15N 77 27W
Soucy, *Qué.* **10 C7** 48 10N 75 30W
Soulanges □, *Qué.* **12 B2** 45 18N 74 3W
Soulanges, Canal de, *Qué.* **29 D2** 45 20N 73 58W
Sounding Cr. →, *Alta.* **23 F10** 52 6N 110 28W
Sounding L., *Alta.* **23 F10** 52 8N 110 29W
Souris, *Man.* **19 D8** 49 40N 100 20W
Souris, *P.E.I.* **9 G7** 46 21N 62 15W
Souris →, *Man.* **21 F11** 49 40N 99 34W
South Aulatsivik I., *Nfld.* **6 B5** 56 45N 61 30W
South Baymouth, *Ont.* **14 B4** 45 33N 82 1W
South Bentinck Arm, *B.C.* **24 C8** 52 7N 126 47W
South Branch, *Nfld.* **7 F1** 47 55N 59 2W
South Brook, *Nfld.* **7 D4** 49 26N 56 5W
South Burnaby, *B.C.* **32 B3** 49 13N 123 0W
South East Passage, *N.S.* **9 L12** 44 36N 63 28W
South Gillies, *Ont.* **16 D7** 48 14N 89 42W
South Granby, *Qué.* **12 B5** 45 19N 72 43W
South Hd., *Nfld.* **7 D2** 49 9N 58 22W
South Heart →, *Alta.* **22 C4** 55 34N 116 11W
South Henik, L., *N.W.T.* **19 A9** 61 30N 97 30W
South Knife →, *Man.* **19 B10** 58 55N 94 37W
South Lancaster, *Qué.* **12 B2** 45 8N 74 30W
South Nahanni →, *N.W.T.* **18 A4** 61 3N 123 21W
South Nation →, *Ont.* **15 B11** 45 34N 75 6W
South Porcupine, *Ont.* **17 D15** 48 30N 81 12W
South River, *Ont.* **14 B7** 45 52N 79 23W
South Saskatchewan →, *Sask.* **20 B5** 53 15N 105 5W
South Seal →, *Man.* **19 B9** 58 48N 98 8W
South Thompson →, *B.C.* **25 E14** 50 40N 120 20W
South Twin I., *N.W.T.* **6 C2** 53 7N 79 52W
South Twin L., *Nfld.* **7 D5** 49 16N 55 47W
South Wabasca L., *Alta.* **22 C7** 55 55N 113 45W
South West Port Moulton, *N.S.* **9 J5** 43 54N 64 49W
South Westminster, *B.C.* **32 B3** 49 12N 122 53W
Southampton, *N.S.* **9 H5** 45 35N 64 15W
Southampton, *Ont.* **14 C5** 44 30N 81 25W
Southampton I., *N.W.T.* **27 C7** 64 30N 84 0W
Southbank, *B.C.* **24 A9** 54 2N 125 46W
Southdate, *N.S.* **9 L11** 44 40N 63 34W
Southend, *Sask.* **19 B8** 56 19N 103 22W
Southern Indian L., *Man.* **19 B9** 57 10N 98 30W
Southey, *Sask.* **20 E6** 50 56N 104 30W
Sovereign, *Sask.* **20 D3** 51 31N 107 43W
Sowden L., *Ont.* **16 C5** 49 32N 91 12W
Spalding, *Sask.* **20 C6** 52 20N 104 30W
Spaniard's Bay, *Nfld.* **7 F7** 47 38N 53 20W
Spanish, *Ont.* **14 A4** 46 12N 82 20W
Spanish →, *Ont.* **14 A4** 46 11N 82 19W
Sparwood, *B.C.* **23 I6** 49 44N 114 53W
Spatsizi →, *B.C.* **18 B3** 57 42N 128 7W
Spear, C., *Nfld.* **7 H8** 47 31N 52 37W
Speed →, *Ont.* **13 B2** 43 23N 80 22W
Speers, *Sask.* **20 C3** 52 43N 107 34W
Spence Bay, *N.W.T.* **27 C6** 69 32N 93 32W
Spencerville, *Ont.* **15 C11** 44 51N 75 33W
Spences Bridge, *B.C.* **25 E13** 50 25N 121 20W
Sperling, *Man.* **21 F13** 49 30N 97 42W
Spirit River, *Alta.* **22 C2** 55 45N 118 50W
Spiritwood, *Sask.* **20 B3** 53 24N 107 33W
Split L., *Man.* **19 B9** 56 8N 96 15W
Spragge, *Ont.* **14 A4** 46 15N 82 40W
Sprague, *Man.* **21 F15** 49 2N 95 38W
Sprigg's Pt., *Nfld.* **7 H8** 47 33N 52 40W
Spring Coulee, *Alta.* **23 I7** 49 20N 113 3W
Spring Valley, *Sask.* **20 F5** 49 56N 105 24W
Springbrook, *Ont.* **13 A3** 43 39N 79 47W
Springdale, *Nfld.* **7 D4** 49 30N 56 6W
Springfield, *Man.* **31 B4** 49 56N 96 56W
Springfield, *N.S.* **9 I5** 44 38N 64 52W
Springfield, *Ont.* **14 E6** 42 50N 80 56W
Springhill, *N.S.* **9 C7** 45 40N 64 4W
Springhouse, *B.C.* **25 D12** 51 56N 122 7W
Springside, *Sask.* **20 D8** 51 21N 102 44W
Springvale, *Ont.* **30 D9** 43 13N 79 59W
Springwater, *Sask.* **20 D2** 51 58N 108 23W
Sproat L., *B.C.* **24 F9** 49 17N 125 2W
Spruce Grove, *Alta.* **22 E7** 53 32N 114 0W
Spruce I., *Man.* **21 B10** 53 5N 100 40W
Spruce Woods Prov. Park, *Man.* **21 F11** 49 43N 99 5W
Sprucedale, *Ont.* **14 B7** 45 29N 79 28W
Spryfield, *N.S.* **9 L11** 44 37N 63 37W
Spuzzum, *B.C.* **25 F13** 49 37N 121 23W
Squamish, *B.C.* **25 F11** 49 45N 123 10W
Squamish →, *B.C.* **25 F11** 49 45N 123 8W
Square Islands, *Nfld.* **6 C6** 52 47N 55 47W
Squatec, *Qué.* **11 D14** 47 53N 68 43W
Squaw Rapids, *Sask.* **20 B7** 53 41N 103 21W
Stamford, *Ont.* **13 B4** 43 8N 79 6W
Stanbridge East, *Qué.* **12 B5** 45 7N 72 55W
Standard, *Alta.* **23 G8** 51 7N 112 59W
Stanley, *N.B.* **9 G3** 46 20N 66 44W
Stanley, *Sask.* **19 B8** 55 24N 104 22W
Star City, *Sask.* **20 C6** 52 50N 104 20W
Starbuck, *Man.* **21 F13** 49 46N 97 37W
Station-du-Côteau, La, *Qué.* **12 B2** 45 17N 74 14W
Stave Falls, *B.C.* **25 F12** 49 13N 122 22W
Stave L., *B.C.* **25 F12** 49 22N 122 17W
Stavely, *Alta.* **23 H7** 50 10N 113 38W
Stayner, *Ont.* **14 C6** 44 25N 80 5W
Steele, Mt., *N.W.T.* **26 C1** 61 6N 140 23W
Steen River, *Alta.* **18 B5** 59 40N 117 12W
Steensby Inlet, *N.W.T.* **27 B8** 70 15N 78 35W
Steep Rock, *Man.* **21 D12** 51 30N 98 48W
Stefansson I., *N.W.T.* **26 B5** 73 20N 105 45W
Steinbach, *Man.* **21 F14** 49 32N 96 40W
Stellarton, *N.S.* **9 H7** 45 32N 62 30W
Stephens I., *B.C.* **24 A4** 54 10N 130 45W
Stephenville, *Nfld.* **7 E2** 48 31N 58 35W
Stephenville Crossing, *Nfld.* **7 E2** 48 30N 58 26W
Stettler, *Alta.* **23 F8** 52 19N 112 40W
Stevens, *Ont.* **17 C11** 49 33N 85 49W
Stevenson L., *Man.* **21 B15** 53 55N 96 0W
Steveston, *B.C.* **32 C1** 49 8N 123 11W
Stewart, *B.C.* **18 B3** 55 56N 129 57W
Stewart, *N.W.T.* **26 C2** 63 19N 139 26W
Stewart Valley, *Sask.* **20 E3** 50 36N 107 48W
Stewiacke, *N.S.* **9 H6** 45 9N 63 22W
Stickney, *N.B.* **9 G2** 46 23N 67 34W
Stikine →, *B.C.* **18 B2** 56 40N 132 30W
Stirling, *Alta.* **23 I8** 49 30N 112 30W
Stirling, *Ont.* **15 C9** 44 18N 77 33W
Stittsville, *Ont.* **10 F7** 45 15N 75 55W
Stockholm, *Sask.* **21 E8** 50 39N 102 18W
Stokes Bay, *Ont.* **14 C5** 45 0N 81 28W
Stoneham, *Qué.* **11 E11** 47 0N 71 22W
Stoner, *B.C.* **25 B12** 53 38N 122 40W
Stonewall, *Man.* **21 E13** 50 10N 97 19W
Stoney Creek, *Ont.* **14 D7** 43 14N 79 45W
Stony L., *Man.* **19 B9** 58 51N 98 40W
Stony L., *Ont.* **15 C9** 44 30N 78 0W
Stony Mountain, *Man.* **21 E13** 50 5N 97 13W
Stony Plain, *Alta.* **22 E7** 53 32N 114 0W
Stony Rapids, *Sask.* **19 B7** 59 16N 105 50W
Storkerson B., *N.W.T.* **26 B3** 72 56N 124 50W
Stormy L., *Ont.* **16 C4** 49 23N 92 18W
Stouffville, *Ont.* **13 A4** 43 58N 79 15W
Stoughton, *Sask.* **20 F8** 49 40N 103 0W
Stout, L., *Ont.* **19 C10** 52 0N 94 40W
Strachan, Mt., *B.C.* **32 A1** 49 25N 123 12W
Stranraer, *Sask.* **20 D2** 51 43N 108 29W
Strasbourg, *Sask.* **20 D6** 51 4N 104 55W
Stratford, *Ont.* **14 D6** 43 23N 81 0W
Strathcona Prov. Park, *B.C.* **24 F9** 49 38N 125 40W
Strathmore, *Alta.* **23 G7** 51 5N 113 18W
Strathnaver, *B.C.* **25 B12** 53 20N 122 33W
Strathroy, *Ont.* **14 E5** 42 58N 81 38W
Stratton, *Ont.* **16 D2** 48 41N 94 10W
Strawberry Hill, *B.C.* **32 C3** 49 8N 122 53W
Streetsville, *Ont.* **28 C1** 43 35N 79 42W
Strome, *Alta.* **23 F8** 52 48N 112 4W
Strongfield, *Sask.* **20 D4** 51 20N 106 35W
Stroud, *Ont.* **14 C7** 44 19N 79 37W
Struthers, *Ont.* **17 D11** 48 41N 85 51W
Stuart →, *B.C.* **18 C4** 54 0N 123 35W
Stuart L., *B.C.* **18 C4** 54 30N 124 30W
Stull, L., *Ont.* **4 B1** 54 24N 92 34W
Stupart →, *Man.* **19 B10** 56 0N 93 25W
Sturgeon →, *Alta.* **31 D6** 53 46N 113 10W
Sturgeon →, *Ont.* **14 A6** 46 35N 80 11W
Sturgeon →, *Sask.* **20 B5** 53 12N 105 52W
Sturgeon B., *Man.* **21 D13** 52 0N 97 50W
Sturgeon Cr. →, *Man.* **31 B2** 49 52N 97 16W
Sturgeon Falls, *Ont.* **14 A7** 46 25N 79 57W
Sturgeon L., *Alta.* **22 C3** 55 6N 117 32W
Sturgeon L., *Ont.* **15 C8** 44 28N 78 43W
Sturgeon L., *Ont.* **16 C6** 50 0N 90 45W
Sturgeon L., *Ont.* **16 D5** 48 29N 91 38W
Sturgis, *Sask.* **20 D8** 51 56N 102 36W
Success, *Sask.* **20 E2** 50 28N 108 6W
Sud, Pte., *Qué.* **8 D7** 49 3N 62 14W
Sud-Ouest, Pte. du, *Qué.* **8 D6** 49 23N 63 36W
Sudbury, *Ont.* **14 A6** 46 30N 81 0W
Suffield, *Alta.* **23 H9** 50 12N 111 10W
Sugar L., *B.C.* **25 E16** 50 24N 118 30W
Sugarloaf Head, *Nfld.* **7 H8** 47 37N 52 39W
Suggi L., *Sask.* **20 A8** 54 22N 102 47W
Sugluk = Saglouc, *Qué.* **6 A2** 62 14N 75 38W
Sukunka →, *B.C.* **18 B4** 55 45N 121 15W
Sullivan, *B.C.* **32 C4** 49 7N 122 48W
Sullivan, *Qué.* **10 C5** 48 7N 77 50W
Sullivan Bay, *B.C.* **24 E8** 50 55N 126 50W
Sullivan L., *Alta.* **23 G9** 52 0N 112 0W
Sulphur Pt., *N.W.T.* **18 A6** 60 56N 114 48W
Sultan, *Ont.* **17 E14** 47 36N 82 47W
Summerford, *Nfld.* **7 D6** 49 29N 54 47W
Summerland, *B.C.* **25 F15** 49 32N 119 41W
Summerside, *Nfld.* **7 E3** 48 59N 57 59W
Summerside, *P.E.I.* **9 G6** 46 24N 63 47W
Summerstown, *Qué.* **12 B1** 45 4N 74 32W
Summerville, *Nfld.* **7 E7** 48 27N 53 33W
Summerville, *Ont.* **28 C2** 43 37N 79 34W
Summit Lake, *B.C.* **18 C4** 54 20N 122 40W
Sunbury, *B.C.* **32 C3** 49 9N 122 59W
Sunderland, *Ont.* **15 C7** 44 16N 79 4W
Sundown, *Man.* **21 F14** 49 6N 96 16W
Sundre, *Alta.* **23 G6** 51 49N 114 38W
Sundridge, *Ont.* **14 B7** 45 45N 79 25W
Sunny Corner, *N.B.* **9 G4** 46 57N 65 49W
Sunnybrae, *N.S.* **9 H7** 45 24N 62 30W
Sunnyside, *Nfld.* **7 F7** 47 51N 53 55W
Sunwapta Pass, *Alta.* **23 F3** 52 13N 117 10W
Superior, L., *Ont.* **17 E10** 47 40N 87 0W
Surprise, L., *Qué.* **10 B8** 49 20N 74 55W
Surprise L., *B.C.* **18 B2** 59 40N 133 15W
Surrey, *B.C.* **32 B3** 49 12N 122 51W
Surrey □, *B.C.* **32 C4** 49 9N 122 46W
Surrey Centre, *B.C.* **32 C4** 49 7N 122 45W
Sussex, *N.B.* **9 H4** 45 45N 65 37W
Sustut →, *B.C.* **18 B3** 56 20N 127 30W
Sutton, *Ont.* **14 C7** 44 18N 79 22W
Sutton, *Qué.* **11 F10** 45 6N 72 37W
Sutton →, *Ont.* **4 A3** 55 15N 83 45W
Sverdrup Chan., *N.W.T.* **27 B6** 79 56N 96 25W
Sverdrup Is., *N.W.T.* **27 B6** 79 0N 97 0W
Swan →, *Alta.* **22 C5** 55 30N 115 18W
Swan →, *Man.* **21 C10** 52 30N 100 45W
Swan Hills, *Alta.* **22 D5** 54 42N 115 24W
Swan L., *Man.* **21 C10** 52 30N 100 40W
Swan River, *Man.* **21 C9** 52 10N 101 16W
Swansea, *Ont.* **28 C3** 43 38N 79 28W
Swastika, *Ont.* **10 C2** 48 7N 80 6W
Swift Current, *Nfld.* **7 F6** 47 53N 54 12W
Swift Current, *Sask.* **20 E3** 50 20N 107 45W
Swiftcurrent →, *Sask.* **20 E3** 50 38N 107 44W
Swindle, I., *B.C.* **24 C6** 52 30N 128 35W
Sydenham →, *Ont.* **14 E4** 42 33N 82 25W
Sydney, *N.S.* **9 G9** 46 7N 60 7W
Sydney L., *Ont.* **16 B2** 50 41N 94 25W
Sydney Mines, *N.S.* **9 G9** 46 18N 60 15W
Sydney River, *N.S.* **9 G9** 46 6N 60 13W
Sylvan L., *Alta.* **23 F6** 52 21N 114 10W
Sylvan Lake, *Alta.* **23 F6** 52 20N 114 3W
Sylvania, *Sask.* **20 C7** 52 42N 104 0W
Sylvester, *Alta.* **22 D1** 55 0N 119 41W

T

Tabatière, La, *Qué.* **7 C2** 50 50N 58 58W
Taber, *Alta.* **23 I8** 49 47N 112 8W
Table B., *Nfld.* **6 C6** 53 40N 56 25W
Tachick L., *B.C.* **24 B10** 53 57N 124 12W
Tadoule, L., *Man.* **19 B9** 58 36N 98 20W
Tadoussac, *Qué.* **11 C13** 48 11N 69 42W
Tagish, *Yukon* **18 A2** 60 19N 134 16W
Tagish L., *Yukon* **18 A2** 60 10N 134 20W
Tahsis, *B.C.* **24 F8** 49 55N 126 40W
Takiyuak L., *N.W.T.* **26 C4** 65 30N 113 5W
Takla L., *B.C.* **18 B3** 55 15N 125 45W
Takla Landing, *B.C.* **18 B3** 55 30N 125 50W
Taku →, *B.C.* **18 B2** 58 30N 133 50W
Takysie Lake, *B.C.* **24 B9** 53 53N 125 53W
Talbot L., *Man.* **21 B11** 54 0N 99 55W
Taltson →, *N.W.T.* **18 A6** 61 24N 112 46W
Talunkwan I., *B.C.* **24 C3** 52 50N 131 45W
Tamworth, *Ont.* **15 C10** 44 29N 77 0W
Tangier, *N.S.* **9 I7** 44 48N 62 42W
Tansley, *Ont.* **13 B3** 43 25N 79 48W
Tantallon, *Sask.* **21 E9** 50 32N 101 50W
Tanu I., *B.C.* **24 C3** 52 46N 131 40W
Tanzilla →, *B.C.* **18 B2** 58 8N 130 43W
Tapleytown, *Ont.* **30 D10** 43 11N 79 44W
Tara, *Ont.* **14 C5** 44 28N 81 9W
Tarbert, *Ont.* **13 A2** 43 56N 80 20W
Taschereau, *Qué.* **10 C4** 48 40N 78 40W
Taseko →, *B.C.* **24 C11** 52 8N 123 45W
Taseko L., *B.C.* **24 D11** 51 15N 123 35W
Tassialuk, L., *Qué.* **6 B3** 59 3N 74 0W
Tasu, *B.C.* **24 C2** 52 45N 132 5W
Tasu Sd., *B.C.* **24 C2** 52 47N 132 2W
Tatamagouche, *N.S.* **9 H6** 45 43N 63 18W
Tathlina L., *N.W.T.* **18 A5** 60 33N 117 39W
Tatinnai L., *N.W.T.* **19 A9** 60 55N 97 40W
Tatla L., *B.C.* **24 D10** 52 0N 124 20W
Tatlayoko L., *B.C.* **24 D10** 51 35N 124 24W
Tatnam, C., *Man.* **19 B10** 57 16N 91 0W
Tatton, *B.C.* **25 D13** 51 43N 121 22W
Tatuk, L., *B.C.* **24 B10** 53 32N 124 14W
Taunton, *Ont.* **13 A5** 43 56N 78 49W
Tavistock, *Ont.* **14 D6** 43 19N 80 50W
Taylor, *B.C.* **18 B4** 56 13N 120 40W
Tazin L., *Sask.* **19 B7** 59 44N 108 42W
Tchentlo L., *B.C.* **18 B4** 55 15N 125 0W
Tecumseh, *Ont.* **14 E4** 42 19N 82 54W
Tee Lake, *Qué.* **10 E4** 46 40N 79 0W
Teepee Creek, *Alta.* **22 C2** 55 22N 118 24W
Teeswater, *Ont.* **14 D5** 43 59N 81 17W
Telegraph Cove, *B.C.* **24 E8** 50 32N 126 50W
Telegraph Cr. →, *B.C.* **18 B2** 58 0N 131 10W
Telkwa, *B.C.* **18 C3** 54 41N 127 5W
Temiscamie →, *Qué.* **6 C3** 50 59N 73 5W
Témiscaming, *Qué.* **10 E3** 46 44N 79 5W
Témiscamingue, L., *Qué.* **10 D3** 47 10N 79 25W
Temperance Vale, *N.B.* **9 G2** 46 4N 67 15W
Temperanceville, *Ont.* **28 A3** 43 56N 79 28W
Templeman, Mt., *B.C.* **25 E17** 50 42N 117 12W
Templeton, *Ont.* **30 D8** 45 29N 75 35W
Ten Mile L., *Nfld.* **7 B4** 51 6N 56 42W
Tent L., *N.W.T.* **19 A7** 62 25N 107 54W
Terence Bay, *N.S.* **9 I6** 44 28N 63 43W
Terra Cotta, *Ont.* **13 A3** 43 43N 79 56W
Terra Nova, *Nfld.* **7 E6** 48 30N 54 13W
Terra Nova →, *Nfld.* **7 E7** 48 40N 54 0W
Terra Nova Nat. Park, *Nfld.* **7 E7** 48 33N 53 58W
Terrace, *B.C.* **18 C3** 54 30N 128 35W
Terrace Bay, *Ont.* **17 D9** 48 47N 87 5W
Terrasse-Vaudreuil, *Qué.* **29 C2** 45 24N 73 59W
Terrebonne, *Qué.* **29 A4** 45 42N 73 38W
Terrebonne □, *Qué.* **29 A2** 45 50N 74 0W
Terrebonne Heights, *Qué.* **29 A4** 45 44N 73 38W
Terrenceville, *Nfld.* **7 F6** 47 40N 54 44W
Teslin, *Yukon* **18 A2** 60 10N 132 43W
Teslin →, *Yukon* **18 A2** 61 34N 134 35W
Teslin L., *Yukon* **18 A2** 60 15N 132 57W
Tetachuck L., *B.C.* **24 B9** 53 18N 125 55W
Tête-à-la-Baleine, *Qué.* **7 C1** 50 41N 59 20W
Tethul →, *N.W.T.* **18 A6** 60 35N 112 12W
Tetu L., *Ont.* **16 B1** 50 11N 95 2W
Teulon, *Man.* **21 E13** 50 23N 97 16W
Texada I., *B.C.* **24 F10** 49 40N 124 25W
Tezzeron L., *B.C.* **18 C4** 54 43N 124 30W
Tha-anne →, *N.W.T.* **19 A10** 60 31N 94 37W
Thames →, *Ont.* **14 E4** 42 20N 82 25W
Thamesford, *Ont.* **14 D6** 43 4N 81 0W
Thamesville, *Ont.* **14 E5** 42 33N 81 59W
The Pas, *Man.* **21 B9** 53 45N 101 15W
Thedford, *Ont.* **14 D5** 43 9N 81 51W
Thekulthili L., *N.W.T.* **19 A7** 61 3N 110 0W
Thelon →, *N.W.T.* **19 A8** 62 35N 104 3W
Theodore, *Sask.* **20 D8** 51 26N 102 55W
Thesiger B., *N.W.T.* **26 B3** 71 30N 124 5W
Thessalon, *Ont.* **14 A3** 46 20N 83 30W
Thetford Mines, *Qué.* **11 E11** 46 8N 71 18W
Thévet, L., *Qué.* **8 B5** 51 50N 64 12W
Thicket Portage, *Man.* **19 B9** 55 19N 97 42W
Thistletown, *Ont.* **28 B2** 43 44N 79 33W
Thlewiaza →, *Man.* **19 B8** 59 43N 100 5W
Thlewiaza →, *N.W.T.* **19 A10** 60 29N 94 40W
Thoa →, *N.W.T.* **19 A7** 60 31N 109 47W
Thom Bay, *N.W.T.* **27 B6** 70 9N 92 25W
Thomas Hubbard, C., *N.W.T.* **27 A6** 82 0N 94 25W
Thompson, *B.C.* **25 E13** 50 15N 121 24W
Thompson, *Man.* **19 B9** 55 45N 97 52W
Thompson →, *B.C.* **25 E13** 50 15N 121 24W
Thompson Landing, *N.W.T.* **19 A6** 62 56N 110 40W
Thorburn, *N.S.* **9 H7** 45 34N 62 33W
Thorhild, *Alta.* **22 D7** 54 10N 113 7W
Thornburn Road, *Nfld.* **7 H6** 47 35N 52 51W
Thornbury, *Ont.* **14 C6** 44 34N 80 26W
Thornhill, *Man.* **21 F12** 49 12N 98 14W
Thornhill, *Ont.* **28 B3** 43 48N 79 25W
Thorold, *Ont.* **13 B4** 43 7N 79 12W
Thorold South, *Ont.* **13 B4** 43 6N 79 12W
Thorsby, *Alta.* **22 E6** 53 14N 114 3W
Three Hills, *Alta.* **23 G7** 51 43N 113 15W
Three Mile Plains, *N.S.* **9 I5** 44 58N 64 7W
Thubun Lakes, *N.W.T.* **19 A6** 61 30N 112 0W
Thunder Bay, *Ont.* **16 D7** 48 20N 89 15W
Thunder Cr. →, *Sask.* **20 E5** 50 23N 105 32W
Thurso, *Qué.* **10 F7** 45 36N 75 15W
Thutade L., *B.C.* **18 B3** 57 0N 126 55W
Tide Head, *N.B.* **9 F3** 47 59N 66 47W
Tignish, *P.E.I.* **9 G5** 46 58N 64 2W
Tilbury, *Ont.* **14 E4** 42 17N 82 23W
Tillsonburg, *Ont.* **14 E6** 42 53N 80 44W
Tilston, *Man.* **21 F9** 49 23N 101 19W
Timagami L., *Ont.* **10 E2** 47 0N 80 10W
Timberlea, *N.S.* **9 I6** 44 40N 63 45W

Timmins, *Ont.* **17 D15** 48 28N 81 25W
Tintagel, *B.C.* **24 A9** 54 12N 125 35W
Tisdale, *Sask.* **20 C7** 52 50N 104 0W
Tiverton, *N.S.* **9 I3** 44 23N 66 13W
Tiverton, *Ont.* **14 C5** 44 16N 81 32W
Tlell, *B.C.* **24 B3** 53 34N 131 56W
Toad →, *B.C.* **18 B4** 59 25N 124 57W
Toba Inlet, *B.C.* **24 E10** 50 25N 124 35W
Tobermory, *Ont.* **14 B5** 45 12N 81 40W
Tobin L., *Sask.* **20 B7** 53 35N 103 30W
Tobique →, *N.B.* **9 G2** 46 46N 67 42W
Toby Creek, *B.C.* **25 E18** 50 20N 116 25W
Tofield, *Alta.* **22 E8** 53 25N 112 40W
Tofino, *B.C.* **24 F9** 49 11N 125 55W
Togo, *Sask.* **21 D9** 51 24N 101 35W
Tolstoi, *Man.* **21 F14** 49 5N 96 49W
Tomiko L., *Ont.* **14 A7** 46 32N 79 49W
Tompkins, *Sask.* **20 E2** 50 4N 108 47W
Top of the World Prov. Park, *B.C.* **23 I5** 50 0N 115 35W
Topley, *B.C.* **18 C3** 54 49N 126 18W
Torbay, *Nfld.* **7 F8** 47 40N 52 42W
Torch →, *Sask.* **20 B7** 53 50N 103 5W
Tormore, *Ont.* **28 A1** 43 51N 79 42W
Tornado Mt., *B.C.* **18 D6** 49 55N 114 40W
Torngat Mts., *Nfld.* **6 B5** 59 0N 63 40W
Toronto, *Ont.* **28 C4** 43 39N 79 20W
Toronto □, *Ont.* **28 C3** 43 39N 79 23W
Toronto Harbour, *Ont.* **28 C3** 43 38N 79 22W
Toronto I., *Ont.* **28 C3** 43 37N 79 23W
Torquay, *Sask.* **20 F7** 49 9N 103 30W
Torrington, *Alta.* **23 G7** 51 48N 113 35W
Torsill Mts., *N.W.T.* **27 C7** 65 0N 84 30W
Tortue, R. de la →, *Qué.* **29 C2** 45 27N 73 56W
Tottenham, *Ont.* **14 C7** 44 1N 79 49W
Touchwood, *Sask.* **20 D6** 51 21N 104 9W
Toulnustouc →, *Qué.* **8 D1** 49 35N 68 24W
Toulnustouc Nord-Est. →, *Qué.* **8 C2** 50 56N 67 44W
Tracadie, *N.B.* **9 F5** 47 30N 64 55W
Tracy, *N.B.* **9 H3** 45 41N 66 41W
Tracy, *Qué.* **11 E9** 46 1N 73 9W
Trafalgar, *Ont.* **28 D1** 43 29N 79 43W
Trail, *B.C.* **25 F17** 49 5N 117 40W
Trainor L., *N.W.T.* **18 A4** 60 24N 120 17W
Tramping Lake, *Sask.* **20 C2** 52 8N 108 57W
Transcona, *Man.* **31 B4** 49 55N 97 0W
Trappe, La, *Qué.* **29 C1** 45 29N 74 2W
Travers Res., *Alta.* **23 H8** 50 12N 112 51W
Treherne, *Man.* **21 F12** 49 38N 98 42W
Tremblant, Mt., *Qué.* **10 E8** 46 16N 74 35W
Trenche →, *Qué.* **11 D10** 47 46N 72 53W
Trend Village, *Ont.* **30 E7** 45 19N 75 48W
Trent →, *Ont.* **15 C9** 44 6N 77 34W
Trente et un Milles, L. des, *Qué.* **10 E7** 46 12N 75 49W
Trenton, *N.S.* **9 H7** 45 37N 62 38W
Trenton, *Ont.* **15 C9** 44 10N 77 34W
Trepassey, *Nfld.* **7 G7** 46 43N 53 25W
Trepassey B., *Nfld.* **7 G7** 46 37N 53 30W
Tres-St-Redempteur, *Qué.* **12 B2** 45 26N 74 23W
Treuter Mts., *N.W.T.* **27 B7** 75 42N 82 30W
Trêve, L. la, *Qué.* **10 B7** 49 56N 75 30W
Tribune, *Sask.* **20 F7** 49 15N 103 49W
Tring-Jonction, *Qué.* **11 E12** 46 16N 70 59W
Trinity, *Nfld.* **7 E7** 48 59N 53 55W
Trinity B., *Nfld.* **7 E7** 48 20N 53 10W
Triquet, L., *Qué.* **8 C10** 50 42N 59 47W
Trochu, *Alta.* **23 G7** 51 50N 113 13W
Trodely I., *N.W.T.* **6 C2** 52 15N 79 26W
Troilus, L., *Qué.* **6 C3** 50 50N 74 35W
Trois-Pistoles, *Qué.* **11 C13** 48 5N 69 10W
Trois-Rivières, *Qué.* **11 E10** 46 25N 72 34W
Trout →, *N.W.T.* **18 A5** 61 19N 119 51W
Trout Creek, *Ont.* **14 B7** 45 59N 79 22W
Trout L., *N.W.T.* **18 A4** 60 40N 121 14W
Trout L., *Ont.* **19 C10** 51 20N 93 15W
Trout Lake, *B.C.* **25 E17** 50 35N 117 25W
Trout River, *Nfld.* **7 D2** 49 29N 58 8W
Trout River, *Qué.* **12 B2** 45 3N 74 17W
Troy, *N.S.* **9 H8** 45 42N 61 26W
Troy, *Ont.* **13 B2** 43 16N 80 11W
Truite, L. à la, *Qué.* **10 D4** 47 20N 78 20W
Truro, *N.S.* **9 H6** 45 21N 63 14W
Tsacha L., *B.C.* **24 B10** 53 3N 124 50W
Tsawassen, *B.C.* **32 C2** 49 1N 123 6W
Tsitsutl Pk., *B.C.* **24 C9** 52 43N 125 47W
Tsu L., *N.W.T.* **18 A6** 60 40N 111 52W
Tsuniah L., *B.C.* **24 D10** 51 33N 124 4W
Tuchodi →, *B.C.* **18 B4** 58 17N 123 42W
Tudor, L., *Qué.* **6 B4** 55 50N 65 25W
Tugaske, *Sask.* **20 E4** 50 52N 106 17W
Tukarak I., *N.W.T.* **6 B2** 56 15N 78 45W
Tuktoyaktuk, *N.W.T.* **26 C2** 69 27N 133 2W
Tulemalu L., *N.W.T.* **19 A9** 62 58N 99 25W
Tullamore, *Ont.* **28 B1** 43 47N 79 46W
Tulsequah, *B.C.* **18 B2** 58 39N 133 35W
Tungsten, *N.W.T.* **18 A3** 61 57N 128 16W
Tunulic →, *Qué.* **6 B4** 58 57N 66 50W
Tunungayualok I., *Nfld.* **6 B5** 56 0N 61 0W
Tupper, *B.C.* **18 B4** 55 32N 120 1W
Tuque, La, *Qué.* **11 D10** 47 30N 72 50W
Turgeon →, *Qué.* **10 B4** 50 0N 78 56W
Turgeon, L., *Qué.* **10 B3** 49 2N 79 4W
Turin, *Alta.* **23 I8** 49 58N 112 31W
Turnagain →, *B.C.* **18 B3** 59 12N 127 35W
Turner Valley, *Alta.* **23 H6** 50 40N 114 17W
Turnor L., *Sask.* **19 B7** 56 35N 108 35W
Turnour I., *B.C.* **24 E8** 50 36N 126 27W
Turtle →, *Ont.* **16 D4** 48 51N 92 45W
Turtle L., *Sask.* **20 B2** 53 36N 108 38W
Turtle Mt. Prov. Park, *Man.* **21 F10** 49 3N 100 15W
Turtleford, *Sask.* **20 B2** 53 23N 108 57W
Tusket, *N.S.* **9 J4** 43 52N 65 58W
Tusket →, *N.S.* **9 J4** 43 41N 65 57W
Tutshi L., *B.C.* **18 B2** 59 56N 134 30W
Tuxedo, *Man.* **31 B2** 49 52N 97 13W
Tuxford, *Sask.* **20 E5** 50 34N 105 35W
Tuya L., *B.C.* **18 B2** 59 7N 130 35W
Tweed, *Ont.* **15 C9** 44 29N 77 19W
Tweedmuir, *Sask.* **20 B5** 53 34N 105 57W
Tweedside, *N.B.* **9 H2** 45 38N 67 1W
Tweedside, *Ont.* **13 B3** 43 10N 79 41W
Tweedsmuir Prov. Park, *B.C.* **24 C8** 53 0N 126 20W
Twelve Mile L., *Sask.* **20 F4** 49 29N 106 14W
Twenty Mile Creek →, *Ont.* **13 B4** 43 10N 79 22W
Twillingate, *Nfld.* **7 D6** 49 42N 54 45W
Twin City, *Ont.* **16 D7** 48 22N 89 25W
Two Creeks, *Alta.* **22 D4** 54 18N 116 21W
Two Hills, *Alta.* **22 E9** 53 43N 111 52W
Tyndall, *Man.* **21 E14** 50 5N 96 40W
Tyne Valley, *P.E.I.* **9 G6** 46 35N 63 56W
Tyrrell Arm, *N.W.T.* **19 A9** 62 27N 97 30W
Tyrrell L., *N.W.T.* **19 A7** 63 7N 105 27W

U

Uchi Lake, *Ont.* **19 C10** 51 5N 92 35W
Ucluelet, *B.C.* **24 G9** 48 57N 125 32W
Uivuk, C., *Nfld.* **6 B5** 58 29N 62 34W
Umfreville L., *Ont.* **16 B2** 50 18N 94 45W
Ungava B., *Nfld.* **27 D9** 59 30N 67 30W
Ungava Pen., *Qué.* **6 B3** 60 0N 74 0W
Union Bay, *B.C.* **24 F10** 49 35N 124 53W
Union I., *B.C.* **24 F7** 50 0N 127 16W
Unionville, *Ont.* **28 A4** 43 52N 79 18W
United States Range, *N.W.T.* **27 A9** 82 25N 68 0W
Unity, *Sask.* **20 C1** 52 30N 109 5W
University →, *Ont.* **17 E11** 47 55N 85 12W
Unuk →, *B.C.* **18 B2** 56 5N 131 3W
Upper Arrow L., *B.C.* **25 E17** 50 30N 117 50W
Upper Blackville, *N.B.* **9 G4** 46 39N 65 52W
Upper Campbell L., *B.C.* **24 F9** 49 55N 125 39W
Upper Foster L., *Sask.* **19 B7** 56 47N 105 20W
Upper Goose L., *Ont.* **16 A4** 51 43N 92 43W
Upper Humber →, *Nfld.* **7 D3** 49 11N 57 28W
Upper Lachute, *Qué.* **12 A2** 45 40N 74 14W
Upper Manitou L., *Ont.* **16 C4** 49 24N 92 48W
Upper Musquodoboit, *N.S.* **9 H7** 45 10N 62 58W
Upper Stewiacke, *N.S.* **9 H7** 45 13N 63 0W
Upsala, *Ont.* **16 C6** 49 3N 90 28W
Upton, *Qué.* **11 F10** 45 39N 72 41W
Uranium City, *Sask.* **19 B7** 59 34N 108 37W
Ursula Chan., *B.C.* **24 B6** 53 25N 128 55W
Utik L., *Man.* **19 B9** 55 15N 96 0W
Utikuma L., *Alta.* **22 C5** 55 50N 115 30W
Uxbridge, *Ont.* **14 C7** 44 6N 79 7W

V

Val-Alain, *Qué.* **11 E11** 46 24N 71 45W
Val-Barrette, *Qué.* **10 E7** 46 30N 75 21W
Val-Bélair, *Qué.* **30 A2** 46 51N 71 26W
Val Brillant, *Qué.* **8 E2** 48 32N 67 33W
Val Caron, *Ont.* **14 A5** 46 37N 81 1W
Val-des-Bois, *Qué.* **10 F7** 45 54N 75 35W
Val-d'Espoir, *Qué.* **8 E5** 48 31N 64 24W
Val d'Or, *Qué.* **10 C5** 48 7N 77 47W
Val Marie, *Sask.* **20 F3** 49 15N 107 45W
Valcourt, *Qué.* **11 F10** 45 29N 72 18W
Valdes I., *B.C.* **25 F11** 49 4N 123 39W
Valemount, *B.C.* **25 C15** 52 50N 119 15W
Vallée-Jonction, *Qué.* **11 E12** 46 22N 70 55W
Valleyview, *Alta.* **22 C3** 55 5N 117 17W
Valleyview, *B.C.* **25 E14** 50 10N 120 13W
Valora, *Ont.* **16 C5** 49 46N 91 13W
Valrita, *Ont.* **17 C14** 49 27N 82 33W
Van Bruyssel, *Qué.* **11 D10** 47 56N 72 9W
Van Buren, *N.B.* **9 F2** 47 10N 67 55W
Vananda, *B.C.* **24 F10** 49 46N 124 33W
Vancouver, *B.C.* **25 F11** 49 15N 123 10W
Vancouver Harb., *B.C.* **32 B2** 49 18N 123 5W
Vancouver I., *B.C.* **24 F9** 49 50N 126 0W
Vancouver I. Ranges, *B.C.* **24 F9** 49 30N 125 40W
Vancouver International Airport, *B.C.* **32 B1** 48 12N 123 11W
Vanderhoof, *B.C.* **24 B11** 54 0N 124 0W
Vandry, *Qué.* **11 D9** 47 52N 73 34W
Vanessa, *Ont.* **13 C2** 42 58N 80 24W
Vanguard, *Sask.* **20 F3** 49 55N 107 20W
Vanier, *Ont.* **30 D8** 45 27N 75 40W
Vanier, *Qué.* **30 B3** 46 49N 71 15W
Vankleek Hill, *Ont.* **15 B12** 45 32N 74 40W
Vanscoy, *Sask.* **20 D4** 52 0N 106 59W
Vansittart I., *N.W.T.* **27 C7** 65 50N 84 0W
Varennes, *Qué.* **12 A4** 45 39N 73 28W
Vars, *Ont.* **10 F7** 45 21N 75 21W
Vassar, *Man.* **21 F15** 49 10N 95 55W
Vaucluse, *Qué.* **12 A4** 45 54N 73 26W
Vaudreuil, *Qué.* **29 C1** 45 24N 74 1W
Vaudreuil □, *Qué.* **12 B2** 45 25N 74 15W
Vaudreuil-sur-le-Lac, *Qué.* **12 B2** 45 25N 74 3W
Vauxhall, *Alta.* **23 H8** 50 5N 112 9W
Vavenby, *B.C.* **25 D15** 51 36N 119 43W
Vegreville, *Alta.* **22 E8** 53 30N 112 5W
Venise, *Qué.* **12 B4** 45 5N 73 8W
Venosta, *Qué.* **10 F6** 45 52N 76 1W
Verchères, *Qué.* **29 A5** 45 47N 73 21W
Verchères □, *Qué.* **12 A4** 45 45N 73 15W
Verdun, *Qué.* **29 C4** 45 27N 73 34W
Veregin, *Sask.* **21 D8** 51 35N 102 5W
Vérendrye, Parc Prov. de la, *Qué.* **10 D6** 47 20N 76 40W
Verlo, *Sask.* **20 E2** 50 19N 108 35W
Vermeulle, L., *Qué.* **6 C4** 54 43N 69 24W
Vermilion, *Alta.* **22 E10** 53 20N 110 50W
Vermilion →, *Alta.* **22 E10** 53 22N 110 51W
Vermilion →, *Qué.* **11 D10** 47 38N 72 56W
Vermilion Bay, *Ont.* **19 D10** 49 51N 93 34W
Vermilion Chutes, *Alta.* **18 B6** 58 22N 114 51W
Vermilion L., *Ont.* **16 B4** 50 3N 92 13W
Vermilion Pass, *B.C.* **25 D18** 51 15N 116 2W
Verner, *Ont.* **14 A6** 46 25N 80 8W
Vernon, *B.C.* **25 E15** 50 20N 119 15W
Véron, L., *Nfld.* **8 B4** 51 48N 65 7W
Verona, *Ont.* **15 C10** 44 29N 76 42W
Vert I., *Ont.* **16 D8** 48 55N 88 3W
Verte, I., *Qué.* **11 C13** 48 2N 69 26W
Veteran, *Alta.* **23 G9** 52 0N 111 7W
Vibank, *Sask.* **20 E7** 50 20N 103 56W
Viceroy, *Sask.* **20 F5** 49 28N 105 22W
Victor, L., *Qué.* **8 C8** 50 35N 61 50W
Victoria, *B.C.* **25 G19** 48 30N 123 25W
Victoria, *Nfld.* **7 F7** 47 46N 53 14W
Victoria, *Ont.* **13 A3** 43 46N 79 53W
Victoria, Grand L., *Qué.* **10 D5** 47 31N 77 30W
Victoria & Albert Mts., *N.W.T.* **27 A8** 80 45N 72 0W
Victoria Beach, *Man.* **21 E14** 50 40N 96 35W
Victoria Harbour, *Ont.* **14 C7** 44 45N 79 45W
Victoria I., *N.W.T.* **26 B4** 71 0N 111 0W
Victoria Pk., *Alta.* **23 I6** 49 18N 114 8W
Victoria Pk., *B.C.* **24 E8** 50 3N 126 5W
Victoria Res., *Nfld.* **7 E3** 48 20N 57 27W
Victoria Square, *Ont.* **13 A4** 43 54N 79 22W
Victoriaville, *Qué.* **11 E11** 46 4N 71 56W
Vienna, *Ont.* **14 E6** 42 41N 80 48W
Viking, *Alta.* **23 E9** 53 7N 111 50W
Ville-Marie, *Qué.* **10 D3** 47 20N 79 30W
Villebon, L., *Qué.* **10 D5** 47 58N 77 17W
Villemontel, *Qué.* **10 C4** 48 38N 78 22W
Vilna, *Alta.* **22 D9** 54 7N 111 55W
Vimont, *Qué.* **29 B3** 45 36N 73 43W
Vineland, *Ont.* **13 B4** 43 9N 79 24W
Virago Sd., *B.C.* **24 B2** 54 0N 132 30W
Virden, *Man.* **21 F10** 49 50N 100 56W
Virgil, *Ont.* **13 B4** 43 13N 79 8W
Virgin →, *Sask.* **19 B7** 57 2N 108 17W
Virginia Falls, *N.W.T.* **18 A3** 61 38N 125 42W
Virginiatown, *Ont.* **10 C3** 48 9N 79 36W
Viscount, *Sask.* **20 D5** 51 57N 105 39W
Viscount Melville Sd., *N.W.T.* **26 B5** 74 10N 108 0W
Vogar, *Man.* **21 E12** 50 57N 98 39W
Voisey B., *Nfld.* **6 B5** 56 15N 61 50W
Vonda, *Sask.* **20 C4** 52 19N 106 6W
Vulcan, *Alta.* **23 H7** 50 25N 113 15W

W

W.A.C. Bennett Dam, *B.C.* **18 B4** 56 2N 122 6W
Wabakimi L., *Ont.* **16 B7** 50 38N 89 45W
Wabamun, *Alta.* **22 E6** 53 33N 114 28W
Wabana, *Nfld.* **7 F8** 47 40N 53 0W
Wabano →, *Qué.* **11 C8** 48 20N 74 3W
Wabasca, *Alta.* **22 C7** 55 57N 113 56W
Wabasca →, *Alta.* **22 A5** 58 22N 115 20W
Wabaskang L., *Ont.* **16 B3** 50 26N 93 13W
Wabassi →, *Ont.* **17 A10** 51 45N 86 20W
Wabatongushi L., *Ont.* **17 D12** 48 26N 84 13W
Wabigoon, *Ont.* **16 C4** 49 43N 92 35W
Wabigoon L., *Ont.* **19 D10** 49 44N 92 44W
Wabimeig L., *Ont.* **17 A11** 51 28N 85 36W
Wabinosh L., *Ont.* **16 B8** 50 5N 89 0W
Wabowden, *Man.* **19 C9** 54 55N 98 38W
Wabuk Pt., *Ont.* **4 A2** 55 20N 85 5W
Wabush, *Nfld.* **8 A3** 52 55N 66 52W
Waco, *Qué.* **8 B4** 51 27N 65 37W
Waconichi, L., *Qué.* **11 A9** 50 8N 74 0W
Wacouno →, *Qué.* **8 C4** 50 54N 65 57W
Waddington, Mt., *B.C.* **24 D9** 51 23N 125 15W
Wadena, *Sask.* **20 D7** 51 57N 103 47W
Wadhams, *B.C.* **24 D7** 51 30N 127 30W
Wadlin L., *Alta.* **22 A5** 57 44N 115 35W
Wadsley, *B.C.* **32 A1** 49 21N 123 13W
Wager B., *N.W.T.* **27 C7** 65 26N 88 40W
Wager Bay, *N.W.T.* **27 C6** 65 56N 90 49W
Wainwright, *Alta.* **23 F10** 52 50N 110 50W
Wakaw, *Sask.* **20 C5** 52 39N 105 44W
Wakefield, *Qué.* **10 F7** 45 38N 75 56W
Wakeham, *Qué.* **8 E5** 48 50N 64 34W
Wakeham Bay = Maricourt, *Qué.* **6 B3** 56 34N 70 49W
Wakomata L., *Ont.* **14 A3** 46 34N 83 22W
Wakuach L., *Qué.* **6 B4** 55 34N 67 32W
Waldeck, *Sask.* **20 E3** 50 22N 107 36W
Waldheim, *Sask.* **20 C4** 52 39N 106 37W
Wales I., *N.W.T.* **6 A3** 62 0N 72 30W
Walhachin, *B.C.* **25 E14** 50 45N 120 59W
Walker L., *Man.* **19 C9** 54 42N 95 57W
Walker L., *Qué.* **8 C2** 50 20N 67 11W
Walkerton, *Ont.* **14 C5** 44 10N 81 10W
Wallace, *N.S.* **9 H6** 45 48N 63 29W
Wallaceburg, *Ont.* **14 E4** 42 34N 82 23W
Walmsley, L., *N.W.T.* **19 A7** 63 25N 108 36W
Walsh, *Alta.* **23 I10** 49 57N 110 3W
Waltham Sta., *Qué.* **10 F6** 45 57N 76 57W
Walton, *N.S.* **9 H6** 45 14N 64 0W
Wanapitei →, *Ont.* **14 A6** 46 2N 80 51W
Wanapitei L., *Ont.* **14 A6** 46 45N 80 40W
Wanham, *Alta.* **22 C2** 55 44N 118 24W
Wanless, *Man.* **21 A9** 54 11N 101 21W
Wapawekka L., *Sask.* **19 C8** 54 55N 104 40W
Wapella, *Sask.* **21 E9** 50 16N 101 58W
Wapikopa L., *Ont.* **4 B2** 52 56N 87 53W
Wapiti →, *Alta.* **22 C2** 55 5N 118 18W
Warburg, *Alta.* **23 E6** 53 11N 114 19W
Wardlow, *Alta.* **23 H9** 50 56N 111 31W
Wardner, *B.C.* **23 I5** 49 25N 115 26W
Ware, *B.C.* **18 B3** 57 26N 125 41W
Warfield, *B.C.* **25 F17** 49 6N 117 46W
Warman, *Sask.* **20 C4** 52 19N 106 30W
Warner, *Alta.* **23 I8** 49 17N 112 12W
Warren, *Ont.* **14 A6** 46 27N 80 18W
Warrender, C., *N.W.T.* **27 B7** 74 28N 81 46W
Wasaga Beach, *Ont.* **14 C6** 44 31N 80 1W
Waseca, *Sask.* **20 B1** 53 6N 109 28W
Wasekamio L., *Sask.* **19 B7** 56 45N 108 45W
Washago, *Ont.* **14 C7** 44 45N 79 20W
Washi L., *Ont.* **17 A9** 51 24N 87 2W
Washington, *Ont.* **13 B1** 43 18N 80 35W
Waskada, *Man.* **21 F10** 49 6N 100 48W
Waskaiowaka, L., *Man.* **19 B9** 56 33N 96 23W
Waskateena Beach, *Sask.* **20 B5** 53 45N 105 15W
Waskatenau, *Alta.* **22 D8** 54 7N 112 47W
Waskesiu L., *Sask.* **20 B4** 53 58N 106 12W
Waskesiu Lake, *Sask.* **20 B4** 53 55N 106 5W
Waswanipi, *Qué.* **10 B6** 49 40N 76 29W
Waswanipi →, *Qué.* **10 B6** 49 40N 76 25W
Waswanipi, L., *Qué.* **10 B6** 49 35N 76 40W
Waterbury L., *Sask.* **19 B8** 58 10N 104 22W
Waterdown, *Ont.* **14 D7** 43 20N 79 53W
Waterford, *Ont.* **14 E6** 42 56N 80 17W
Waterford →, *Nfld.* **7 H7** 47 33N 52 43W
Waterhen L., *Man.* **21 C11** 52 10N 99 40W
Waterhen L., *Sask.* **19 C7** 54 28N 108 25W
Waterloo, *Ont.* **13 B1** 43 30N 80 32W
Waterloo, *Qué.* **11 F10** 45 22N 72 32W
Waterton Glacier Int. Peace Park, *Alta.* **18 D6** 48 35N 113 40W
Waterton Park, *Alta.* **23 I7** 49 3N 113 55W
Waterville, *N.S.* **9 H5** 45 3N 64 41W
Waterville, *Qué.* **11 F11** 45 16N 71 54W
Watford, *Ont.* **14 E5** 42 57N 81 53W
Wathaman →, *Sask.* **19 B8** 57 16N 102 59W
Watrous, *Sask.* **20 D5** 51 40N 105 25W
Watshishou, L., *Qué.* **8 C9** 50 20N 60 50W
Watson, *Sask.* **20 C6** 52 10N 104 30W
Watson Lake, *Yukon* **18 A3** 60 6N 128 49W
Waubamik, *Ont.* **14 B6** 45 27N 80 1W
Waubaushene, *Ont.* **14 C7** 44 45N 79 42W
Waugh, *Man.* **21 F15** 49 40N 95 11W
Waverley, *N.S.* **9 I6** 44 47N 63 36W
Wawa, *Ont.* **17 E12** 47 59N 84 47W
Wawagosic →, *Qué.* **10 B3** 49 58N 79 6W
Wawanesa, *Man.* **21 F11** 49 36N 99 40W
Wawang L., *Ont.* **16 C6** 49 25N 90 34W
Wayagamac, L., *Qué.* **11 D10** 47 21N 72 39W
Webb, *Sask.* **20 E2** 50 11N 108 12W
Webbwood, *Ont.* **14 A5** 46 16N 81 52W
Wedgeport, *N.S.* **9 J4** 43 44N 65 59W
Weedon-Centre, *Qué.* **11 F11** 45 42N 71 27W
Weekes, *Sask.* **20 C8** 52 34N 102 52W
Weir →, *Man.* **19 B10** 56 54N 93 21W
Weir River, *Man.* **19 B10** 56 49N 94 6W
Weirdale, *Sask.* **20 B5** 53 27N 105 15W
Wekusko L., *Man.* **19 C9** 54 40N 99 50W
Weldon, *Sask.* **20 B5** 53 1N 105 8W
Welland, *Ont.* **13 C4** 43 0N 79 15W
Welland →, *Ont.* **13 B4** 43 4N 79 3W
Welland Canal, *Ont.* **13 B4** 43 3N 79 13W
Wellandport, *Ont.* **13 C4** 43 0N 79 29W
Weller Park, *Ont.* **13 B4** 43 14N 79 13W
Wellington, *B.C.* **24 F11** 49 13N 123 58W
Wellington, *Nfld.* **7 E7** 48 53N 53 58W
Wellington, *Ont.* **15 D9** 43 57N 77 20W
Wellington, *P.E.I.* **9 G6** 46 27N 64 0W
Wellington □, *Ont.* **13 A2** 43 50N 80 30W
Wellington Chan., *N.W.T.* **27 B6** 75 0N 93 0W
Wells, *B.C.* **25 B13** 53 6N 121 36W
Wells Gray Prov. Park, *B.C.* **25 C14** 52 30N 120 15W
Welsford, *N.B.* **9 H3** 45 27N 66 20W
Wembley, *Alta.* **22 C1** 55 9N 119 8W
Wenasaga →, *Ont.* **16 B3** 50 38N 93 10W
Wenebegon →, *Ont.* **17 F13** 46 53N 83 12W
Wenebegon L., *Ont.* **17 E13** 47 23N 83 6W
Wentworth, *N.S.* **9 H6** 45 38N 63 33W
Weslemkoon L., *Ont.* **15 B9** 45 2N 77 25W
Wesleyville, *Nfld.* **7 D7** 49 8N 53 36W
West Don →, *Ont.* **28 B4** 43 42N 79 20W
West Duffin →, *Ont.* **28 A5** 43 51N 79 4W
West Hill, *Ont.* **28 B4** 43 47N 79 12W
West Humber →, *Ont.* **28 B2** 43 44N 79 33W
West Kildonan, *Man.* **31 B3** 49 56N 97 8W
West Lorne, *Ont.* **14 E5** 42 36N 81 36W
West Magpie →, *Qué.* **6 C5** 52 0N 65 0W
West Montrose, *Ont.* **13 A2** 43 35N 80 29W
West Poplar, *Sask.* **20 F4** 49 0N 106 22W
West Road →, *B.C.* **25 B12** 53 18N 122 53W
West Thurlow I., *B.C.* **24 E9** 50 25N 125 35W
West Vancouver, *B.C.* **32 A2** 49 21N 123 8W
Westbourne, *Man.* **21 E12** 50 8N 98 35W
Westdale, *Ont.* **30 D9** 43 17N 79 53W
Western Duck I., *Ont.* **14 B4** 45 45N 83 0W
Western Pen., *Ont.* **16 C2** 49 30N 94 50W
Western Shore, *N.S.* **9 I5** 44 32N 64 19W
Westfield, *N.B.* **9 H3** 45 22N 66 14W
Westham I., *B.C.* **32 C1** 49 5N 123 10W
Westlock, *Alta.* **22 D7** 54 9N 113 55W
Westmount, *Qué.* **29 C4** 45 29N 73 36W
Weston, *Ont.* **28 B2** 43 43N 79 31W
Weston I., *N.W.T.* **6 C2** 52 33N 79 36W
Westover, *Ont.* **13 B2** 43 19N 80 5W
Westport, *N.S.* **9 I3** 44 15N 66 22W
Westport, *Nfld.* **7 D4** 49 47N 56 38W
Westport, *Ont.* **15 C10** 44 40N 76 25W
Westray, *Man.* **21 B9** 53 36N 101 24W
Westree, *Ont.* **17 E15** 47 26N 81 34W
Westsyde, *B.C.* **25 E14** 50 47N 120 21W
Westville, *N.S.* **9 H7** 45 34N 62 43W
Wetaskiwin, *Alta.* **23 F7** 52 55N 113 24W
Wexford, *Ont.* **28 B4** 43 45N 79 18W
Weyburn, *Sask.* **20 F7** 49 40N 103 50W
Weyburn L., *N.W.T.* **18 A5** 63 0N 117 59W
Weymouth, *N.S.* **9 I3** 44 30N 66 1W
Whale →, *Qué.* **6 B4** 58 15N 67 40W
Whale Cove, *N.W.T.* **19 A10** 62 11N 92 36W
Whaletown, *B.C.* **24 E9** 50 7N 125 2W
Wheatley, *Ont.* **14 E4** 42 6N 82 27W
Wheeler →, *Qué.* **6 B4** 57 2N 67 13W
Wheeler →, *Sask.* **19 B7** 57 25N 105 30W
Whiskey Gap, *Alta.* **23 J7** 49 0N 113 3W
Whiskey Jack L., *Man.* **19 B8** 58 23N 101 55W
Whitbourne, *Nfld.* **7 F7** 47 25N 53 32W
Whitby, *Ont.* **15 D8** 43 52N 78 56W
White →, *Ont.* **17 D10** 48 33N 86 16W
White B., *Nfld.* **7 D4** 50 0N 56 35W
White Bear, *Sask.* **20 E2** 50 53N 108 13W
White Bear Res., *Nfld.* **7 E3** 48 10N 57 5W
White Fox, *Sask.* **20 B6** 53 27N 104 5W
White L., *Ont.* **10 F6** 45 18N 76 31W
White L., *Ont.* **17 D11** 48 47N 85 37W
White Otter L., *Ont.* **16 C5** 49 5N 91 55W
White Owl L., *Ont.* **17 E14** 47 10N 82 35W
White Pass, *B.C.* **18 B1** 59 40N 135 3W
White River, *Ont.* **17 D11** 48 35N 85 20W
White Rock, *B.C.* **25 F12** 49 2N 122 48W
Whiteclay L., *Ont.* **16 B8** 50 53N 88 45W
Whitecourt, *Alta.* **22 D5** 54 10N 115 45W
Whitefish, *Ont.* **14 A5** 46 23N 81 19W
Whitefish Falls, *Ont.* **14 A5** 46 7N 81 44W
Whitefish L., *N.W.T.* **19 A7** 62 41N 106 48W
Whitegull, L., *Qué.* **6 B5** 55 27N 64 17W
Whitehorse, *Yukon* **18 A1** 60 43N 135 3W
Whitemouth, *Man.* **21 F15** 49 57N 95 58W
Whitemouth →, *Man.* **21 E14** 50 7N 96 2W
Whitemouth L., *Man.* **21 F15** 49 15N 95 40W

Whitemud Cr. →, *Alta.* **31 E6** 53 31N 113 34W
Whitesand →, *Sask.* **20 D8** 51 34N 102 56W
Whiteshell Prov. Park, *Man.* **21 F15** 50 0N 95 40W
Whiteswan L., *Sask.* **20 A5** 54 5N 105 10W
Whitevale, *Ont.* **28 A5** 43 53N 79 9W
Whitewater →, *Sask.* **20 F3** 49 0N 108 0W
Whitewater L., *Ont.* **16 B7** 50 50N 89 10W
Whitewood, *Sask.* **21 E8** 50 20N 102 20W
Whitney, *Ont.* **10 F4** 45 31N 78 14W
Whittington, *Ont.* **13 A2** 43 59N 80 10W
Wholdaia L., *N.W.T.* **19 A8** 60 43N 104 20W
Whycocomagh, *N.S.* **9 H8** 45 59N 61 7W
Wiarton, *Ont.* **14 C5** 44 40N 81 10W
Wicked Pt., *Ont.* **15 D9** 43 52N 77 15W
Wickham, *Qué.* **11 F10** 45 45N 72 30W
Wikwemikong, *Ont.* **14 B5** 45 48N 81 43W
Wilberforce, *Ont.* **10 F4** 45 2N 78 13W
Wilcox, *Sask.* **20 E6** 50 6N 104 44W
Wilcox Lake, *Ont.* **13 A4** 43 56N 79 25W
Wildfield, *Ont.* **28 B1** 43 49N 79 44W
Wildgoose L., *Ont.* **17 C9** 49 44N 87 11W
Wildhay →, *Alta.* **22 E3** 53 59N 117 20W
Wildwood, *Alta.* **22 E5** 53 37N 115 14W
Wilkie, *Sask.* **20 C2** 52 27N 108 42W
William →, *Sask.* **19 B7** 59 8N 109 19W
William A. Switzer Prov. Park, *Alta.* **22 E3** 53 30N 117 48W
William L., *Man.* **21 B11** 53 54N 99 21W
Williams L., *Ont.* **16 A6** 51 48N 90 45W
Williams Lake, *B.C.* **25 C12** 52 10N 122 10W
Williamsburg, *Ont.* **13 B2** 43 24N 80 30W
Williamstown, *Qué.* **12 B1** 45 9N 74 34W
Willingdon, *Alta.* **22 E8** 53 50N 112 8W
Williston L., *B.C.* **18 B4** 56 0N 124 0W
Willmore Wilderness Park, *Alta.* **22 E1** 53 45N 119 30W
Willow Bunch, *Sask.* **20 F5** 49 20N 105 35W
Willow Bunch L., *Sask.* **20 F5** 49 27N 105 27W
Willow L., *N.W.T.* **18 A5** 62 10N 119 8W
Willowbrook, *Sask.* **20 D8** 51 12N 102 48W
Willowdale, *Ont.* **28 B3** 43 47N 79 26W
Willowlake →, *N.W.T.* **18 A4** 62 42N 123 8W
Wilmot, *N.S.* **9 G7** 46 2N 62 30W
Wilson Creek, *B.C.* **24 F11** 49 27N 123 43W
Wilson Landing, *B.C.* **25 F15** 50 0N 119 30W
Wilsons Beach, *N.B.* **9 I3** 44 56N 66 56W
Wilsonville, *Ont.* **13 C2** 42 58N 80 19W
Winagami L., *Alta.* **22 C4** 55 37N 116 44W
Winagami Lake Prov. Park, *Alta.* **22 C4** 55 37N 116 39W
Winchester, *Ont.* **15 B11** 45 6N 75 21W
Windemere L., *Ont.* **17 E13** 47 58N 83 47W
Windermere, *B.C.* **23 H5** 50 28N 115 59W
Windfall, *Alta.* **22 D4** 54 12N 116 13W
Windflower L., *N.W.T.* **18 A5** 62 52N 118 30W
Windigo →, *Qué.* **11 D9** 47 46N 73 19W
Windsor, *N.S.* **9 I5** 44 59N 64 5W
Windsor, *Nfld.* **7 E5** 48 57N 55 40W
Windsor, *Ont.* **14 E4** 42 18N 83 0W
Windsor, *Qué.* **11 F11** 45 34N 72 0W
Windsor Heights, *Nfld.* **7 H7** 47 36N 52 49W
Windsor L., *Nfld.* **7 H7** 47 36N 52 48W
Windthorst, *Sask.* **20 E8** 50 6N 102 50W
Windy L., *N.W.T.* **19 A8** 60 20N 100 2W
Windy L., *Sask.* **20 A8** 54 22N 102 35W
Winefred L., *Alta.* **22 C10** 55 30N 110 30W
Winfield, *Alta.* **23 F6** 52 58N 114 26W
Wingham, *Ont.* **14 D5** 43 55N 81 20W
Winisk, *Ont.* **4 A2** 55 20N 85 15W
Winisk →, *Ont.* **4 A2** 55 17N 85 5W
Winisk L., *Ont.* **4 B2** 52 55N 87 22W
Winkler, *Man.* **21 F13** 49 10N 97 56W
Winnipeg, *Man.* **31 B3** 49 54N 97 9W
Winnipeg →, *Man.* **21 E14** 50 38N 96 19W
Winnipeg, L., *Man.* **21 D14** 52 0N 97 0W
Winnipeg Beach, *Man.* **21 E14** 50 30N 96 58W
Winnipeg International Airport, *Man.* **31 B2** 49 55N 97 15W
Winnipegosis, *Man.* **21 D11** 51 39N 99 55W
Winnipegosis L., *Man.* **21 C11** 52 30N 100 0W
Winokapau, L., *Nfld.* **6 C5** 53 15N 62 50W
Winona, *Ont.* **13 B3** 43 12N 79 39W
Winter Harbour, *B.C.* **24 E6** 50 31N 128 2W
Winterbourne, *Ont.* **13 A2** 43 33N 80 28W
Wintering L., *Ont.* **17 C9** 49 26N 87 16W
Winterton, *Nfld.* **7 F7** 47 58N 53 20W
Wiseton, *Sask.* **20 D3** 51 19N 107 39W
Wishart, *Sask.* **20 D7** 51 33N 103 59W
Wistaria, *B.C.* **24 B8** 53 52N 126 22W
Withrow, *Alta.* **23 F6** 52 23N 114 30W
Woburn, *Ont.* **28 B4** 43 46N 79 13W
Wolf →, *Yukon* **18 A2** 60 17N 132 33W
Wolf Bay, *Qué.* **8 C9** 50 16N 60 8W
Wolf L., *Yukon* **18 A2** 60 24N 131 40W
Wolfe I., *Ont.* **15 C10** 44 7N 76 20W
Wolfville, *N.S.* **9 H5** 45 5N 64 22W
Wollaston L., *Sask.* **19 B8** 58 7N 103 10W
Wollaston Pen., *N.W.T.* **26 C4** 69 30N 115 0W
Wolseley, *Sask.* **20 E7** 50 25N 103 15W
Wolstenholme, C., *Qué.* **6 A2** 62 35N 77 30W
Wolstenholme Fjord, *N.W.T.* **27 B9** 76 0N 70 0W
Wood →, *Sask.* **20 E4** 50 8N 106 13W
Wood Buffalo Nat. Park, *Alta.* **18 B6** 59 0N 113 41W
Wood L., *Sask.* **19 B8** 55 17N 103 17W
Woodbridge, *Ont.* **28 B2** 43 47N 79 36W
Woodburn, *Ont.* **13 B3** 43 8N 79 45W
Woodfibre, *B.C.* **25 F11** 49 41N 123 15W
Woodhill, *Ont.* **28 B1** 43 45N 79 41W
Woodlands, *Man.* **21 E13** 50 12N 97 40W
Woodpecker, *B.C.* **25 B12** 53 30N 122 40W
Woodridge, *Man.* **21 F14** 49 20N 96 9W
Woods, L., *Nfld.* **6 C4** 54 30N 65 13W
Woods, L. of the, *Ont.* **19 D10** 49 15N 94 45W
Woodside, *N.S.* **9 L11** 44 39N 63 33W
Woodstock, *N.B.* **9 G2** 46 11N 67 37W
Woodstock, *Ont.* **14 D6** 43 10N 80 45W
Woody Point, *Nfld.* **7 D3** 49 30N 57 55W
Worsley, *Alta.* **22 B1** 56 31N 119 8W
Woss Camp, *B.C.* **24 E8** 50 13N 126 35W
Woss L., *B.C.* **24 E8** 50 7N 126 36W
Wottonville, *Qué.* **11 F11** 45 44N 71 48W
Wright, *B.C.* **25 D13** 51 52N 121 40W
Wrigley, *N.W.T.* **26 C3** 63 16N 123 37W
Wrigley Corners, *Ont.* **13 B2** 43 17N 80 22W
Wrottesley, C., *N.W.T.* **26 B3** 74 32N 121 33W
Wroxton, *Sask.* **21 D9** 51 14N 101 53W
Wunnummin L., *Ont.* **4 B2** 52 55N 89 10W
Wymark, *Sask.* **20 E3** 50 7N 107 44W
Wyndham Hills, *Ont.* **13 B2** 43 10N 80 17W
Wyniatt B., *N.W.T.* **26 B4** 72 45N 110 30W
Wynndel, *B.C.* **23 I4** 49 11N 116 33W
Wynyard, *Sask.* **20 D6** 51 45N 104 10W
Wyoming, *Ont.* **14 E4** 42 57N 82 7W

Y

Yahk, *B.C.* **23 I4** 49 6N 116 10W
Yale, *B.C.* **25 F13** 49 34N 121 25W
Yamaska, *Qué.* **11 F10** 46 0N 72 55W
Yamaska □, *Qué.* **12 A5** 46 50N 72 50W
Yamaska →, *Qué.* **12 B5** 45 17N 72 55W
Yamaska, Mt., *Qué.* **12 B5** 45 27N 72 52W
Yarker, *Ont.* **15 C10** 44 23N 76 46W
Yarmouth, *N.S.* **9 J3** 43 50N 66 7W
Yarrow, *B.C.* **25 F12** 49 5N 122 2W
Yasinski, L., *Qué.* **6 C2** 53 16N 77 35W
Yathkyed L., *N.W.T.* **19 A9** 62 40N 98 0W
Yellow Creek, *Sask.* **20 C5** 52 45N 105 15W
Yellow Grass, *Sask.* **20 F6** 49 48N 104 10W
Yellowhead P., *B.C.* **25 C16** 52 53N 118 25W
Yellowknife, *N.W.T.* **18 A6** 62 27N 114 29W
Yellowknife →, *N.W.T.* **18 A6** 62 31N 114 19W
Yoho Nat. Park, *B.C.* **25 D18** 51 25N 116 30W
York, *Ont.* **13 B3** 43 1N 79 53W
York, *Ont.* **28 B3** 43 42N 79 27W
York □, *Ont.* **13 A4** 43 55N 79 30W
York →, *Qué.* **8 E5** 48 49N 64 34W
York, C., *N.W.T.* **27 B9** 76 30N 68 0W
York Mills, *Ont.* **28 B3** 43 45N 79 25W
Yorkton, *Sask.* **21 D8** 51 11N 102 28W
Youbou, *B.C.* **24 G10** 48 53N 124 13W
Young, *Sask.* **20 D5** 51 47N 105 45W
Youngstown, *Alta.* **23 G9** 51 35N 111 10W
Yukon Territory □, *Canada* **26 C2** 63 0N 135 0W

Z

Zealand Station, *N.B.* **9 G3** 46 3N 66 56W
Zealandia, *Sask.* **20 D3** 51 37N 107 45W
Zeballos, *B.C.* **24 F8** 49 59N 126 50W
Zenon Park, *Sask.* **20 B7** 53 4N 103 45W
Zionz L., *Ont.* **16 A5** 51 25N 91 52W
Zurich, *Ont.* **14 D5** 43 26N 81 37W
Zymoetz →, *B.C.* **18 C3** 54 33N 128 31W

ATLAS OF THE WORLD

SETTLEMENTS AND BOUNDARIES

Settlements in order of size :-

LONDON · Stuttgart · Sevilla · Bergen · Bath · *Biarritz* · *Srikolayatji*

International Boundaries · International Boundaries (Undemarcated or Undefined) · Internal Boundaries

These show the de facto situation where there are rival claims to territory.

National and Provincial Parks · ∴ Sites of Archæological or Historical importance

COMMUNICATIONS

Freeways/Motorways

Under construction

Trans-Canada Highway

Principal Roads

Other Roads

Trails and Seasonal Roads

Principal Railroads

Other Railroads

Under construction

Railroad Tunnels

Road Tunnels

Principal Canals

Principal Oil Pipelines

3386 Principal Shipping Routes (Distances in Nautical Miles)

Passes

Airports

PHYSICAL FEATURES

Perennial Streams

Seasonal Streams

▲ 8848 Spot Height in meters/metres

Seasonal Lakes, Salt Flats

Swamps, Marshes

▼ 8050 Sea Depths in meters/metres

Permanent Ice

Wells in Desert

1134 Height of Lake Surface Above Sea Level, in meters/metres

ARCTIC OCEAN
BEAUFORT SEA
ELLESMERE I.
QUEEN ELIZABETH IS.
PARRY IS.
DEVON I.
BANKS I.
VICTORIA I.
Greenland
BAFFIN BAY
DAVIS STR.
SVALBARD
Arctic Circle
ICELAND
C. Farewell
Great Bear L.
Great Slave L.
HUDSON BAY
Alaska
ALEXANDER ARCH.
VANCOUVER I.
NORTH AMERICA
L. Winnipeg
L. Superior
L. Michigan
L. Huron
L. Ontario
L. Erie
Labrador
NEWFOUNDLAND
C. Race
British Isles
GREAT BRITAIN
IRELAND
NORTH SEA
AZORES
MADEIRA
CANARY IS.
BERMUDA
GULF OF MEXICO
BAHAMAS
ATLANTIC OCEAN
Tropic of Cancer
HAWAIIAN IS.
CUBA
HISPANIOLA
JAMAICA
West Indies
9200
LEEWARD IS.
C. VERDE IS.
CARIBBEAN SEA
WINDWARD IS.
PACIFIC OCEAN
CHRISTMAS I.
Equator
GALAPAGOS IS.
GULF OF GUINEA
ASCENSION
MARQUESAS IS.
SOUTH AMERICA
Mato Grosso
Selvas
L. Titicaca
SOCIETY IS.
TUAMOTU ARCH.
COOK IS.
ST. HELENA
Tropic of Capricorn
8050
TUBUAI IS.
Gran Chaco
Pampas
Rio de la Plata
TRISTAN DA CUNHA
FALKLAND IS.
TIERRA DEL FUEGO
C. Horn
S. GEORGIA
SOUTHE
165
150
135
120
105
90
75
60
45
30
15
0
West from Greenwich
East from Gr
Projection: Gall's Stereographic

ARCTIC OCEAN
FRANZ JOSEPH LAND
SEVERNAYA ZEMLYA
BARENTS SEA
NOVAYA ZEMLYA
KARA SEA
LAPTEV SEA
NEW SIBERIAN IS.
WRANGEL I.
BERING STR.
Taimyr Pen.
Siberia
Russia
EUROPE
L. Ladoga
BALTIC SEA
WHITE SEA
Steppe
L. Balkhash
ARAL SEA
CASPIAN SEA
BLACK SEA
MEDITERRANEAN SEA
ASIA
Gobi
Tibet
China
SEA OF OKHOTSK
BERING SEA
ALEUTIAN IS.
SAKHALIN
KURIL IS.
HOKKAIDŌ
SEA OF JAPAN
HONSHŪ
KYŪSHŪ
YELLOW SEA
RYUKYU IS.
MIDWAY IS.
Tropic of Cancer
TAIWAN
LUZON
MARIANA IS.
PACIFIC
GUAM
Philippines
MINDANAO
CAROLINE IS.
MARSHALL IS.
GILBERT IS.
Equator
MOLUCCAS
BORNEO
CELEBES
SOUTH CHINA SEA
THE GULF
Arabia
RED SEA
ARABIAN SEA
BAY OF BENGAL
India
ANDAMAN IS.
LACCADIVE IS.
CEYLON
Malay Pen.
MALDIVES
INDIAN
SUMATRA
East Indies
JAVA
SUNDA IS.
TIMOR
NEW GUINEA
BISMARK ARCH.
OCEAN
SOLOMON IS.
SAMOA
FIJI
TONGA
NEW CALEDONIA
Tropic of Capricorn
CORAL SEA
TIMOR SEA
AUSTRALIA
L. Eyre
TASMAN SEA
TASMANIA
NORTH I.
New Zealand
SOUTH I.
MACQUARIE IS.
SEYCHELLES
CHAGOS ARCH.
COCOS OR KEELING IS.
OCEAN
ZANZIBAR
MOZAMBIQUE CHANNEL
MADAGASCAR
MAURITIUS
RÉUNION
CROZET IS.
KERGUELEN
AFRICA
L. Chad
Congo Basin
L. Tanganyika
L. Malawi
Kalahari
C. of Good Hope
Ras Asir
SOUTHERN OCEAN
15 30 45 60 75 90 105 120 135 150 165 180

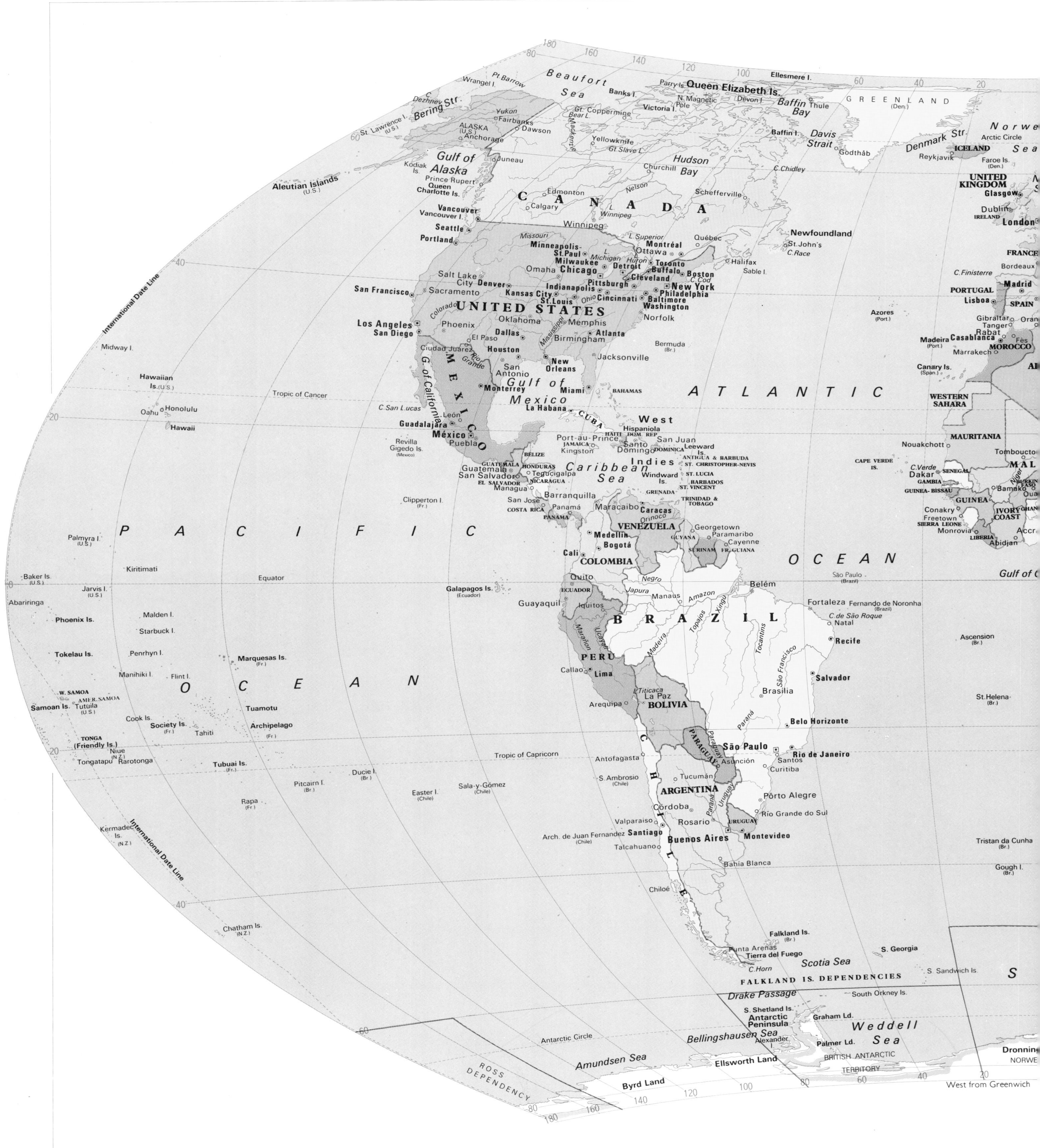
Beaufort Sea
Wrangel I.
Pt. Barrow
Bering Str.
St. Lawrence I. (U.S.)
ALASKA (U.S.)
Yukon
Fairbanks
Dawson
Anchorage
Gulf of Alaska
Juneau
Kodiak Is.
Aleutian Islands (U.S.)
Prince Rupert
Queen Charlotte Is.
Banks I.
Parry Is.
Queen Elizabeth Is.
Ellesmere I.
Victoria I.
N. Magnetic Pole
Bear L.
Gt. Coppermine
Mackenzie
Devon I.
Baffin Bay
Thule
GREENLAND (Den.)
Yellowknife
Gt. Slave L.
Baffin I.
Davis Strait
Godthåb
Denmark Str.
Norwegian Sea
Arctic Circle
ICELAND
Reykjavik
Faroe Is. (Den.)
Hudson Bay
Churchill
Nelson
C. Chidley
Schefferville
CANADA
Edmonton
Calgary
L. Winnipeg
Winnipeg
Vancouver
Vancouver I.
Seattle
Portland
Missouri
Minneapolis-St. Paul
L. Michigan
L. Huron
L. Superior
Montréal
Ottawa
Québec
Newfoundland
St. John's
C. Race
Halifax
Sable I.
Milwaukee
Detroit
Toronto
Buffalo
Boston
C. Cod
Cleveland
New York
Philadelphia
Baltimore
Washington
Omaha
Chicago
Pittsburgh
Salt Lake City
Denver
Indianapolis
San Francisco
Sacramento
Kansas City
Ohio
Cincinnati
St. Louis
Colorado
UNITED STATES
Norfolk
Los Angeles
San Diego
Phoenix
Oklahoma
Memphis
Mississippi
Dallas
Atlanta
El Paso
Birmingham
Ciudad Juárez
Rio Grande
Houston
New Orleans
Jacksonville
Bermuda (Br.)
San Antonio
MEXICO
G. of California
Monterrey
Gulf of Mexico
Miami
BAHAMAS
C. San Lucas
La Habana
CUBA
León
Guadalajara
México
Puebla
Revilla Gigedo Is. (Mexico)
West Indies
Hispaniola
HAITI
DOM. REP.
Port-au-Prince
JAMAICA
Kingston
Santo Domingo
San Juan
DOMINICA
Leeward Is.
ANTIGUA & BARBUDA
ST. CHRISTOPHER-NEVIS
BELIZE
GUATEMALA
HONDURAS
Guatemala
Tegucigalpa
San Salvador
EL SALVADOR
NICARAGUA
Managua
Caribbean Sea
Windward Is.
ST. LUCIA
BARBADOS
ST. VINCENT
GRENADA
TRINIDAD & TOBAGO
Barranquilla
San José
COSTA RICA
Panamá
PANAMA
Maracaibo
Caracas
Orinoco
VENEZUELA
Georgetown
Paramaribo
Cayenne
GUYANA
SURINAM
FR. GUIANA
Clipperton I. (Fr.)
Medellín
Bogotá
Cali
COLOMBIA
Quito
ECUADOR
Guayaquil
Galapagos Is. (Ecuador)
Negro
Japura
Manaus
Amazon
Belém
Iquitos
Tapajós
Xingu
BRAZIL
Fortaleza
Fernando de Noronha (Brazil)
C. de São Roque
Natal
Recife
Marañón
Ucayali
Madeira
Tocantins
São Francisco
PERU
Callao
Lima
Titicaca
La Paz
BOLIVIA
Arequipa
Brasília
Salvador
Paraná
Belo Horizonte
PARAGUAY
Paraguay
São Paulo
Rio de Janeiro
Santos
Curitiba
Asunción
Antofagasta
S. Ambrosio (Chile)
Tucumán
ARGENTINA
Uruguay
Pôrto Alegre
Córdoba
Rio Grande do Sul
URUGUAY
Valparaíso
Rosario
Santiago
Buenos Aires
Montevideo
CHILE
Arch. de Juan Fernandez (Chile)
Talcahuano
Bahia Blanca
Chiloé
Falkland Is. (Br.)
Punta Arenas
Tierra del Fuego
C. Horn
Scotia Sea
S. Georgia
S. Sandwich Is.
FALKLAND IS. DEPENDENCIES
Drake Passage
South Orkney Is.
S. Shetland Is.
Antarctic Peninsula
Graham Ld.
Weddell Sea
Bellingshausen Sea
Alexander I.
Palmer Ld.
BRITISH ANTARCTIC TERRITORY
Ellsworth Land
Amundsen Sea
Byrd Land
ROSS DEPENDENCY
Antarctic Circle
Dronning
NORWE
West from Greenwich
ATLANTIC OCEAN
PACIFIC OCEAN
International Date Line
Midway I.
Hawaiian Is. (U.S.)
Oahu
Honolulu
Hawaii
Tropic of Cancer
Equator
Tropic of Capricorn
Palmyra I. (U.S.)
Kiritimati
Baker Is. (U.S.)
Jarvis I. (U.S.)
Abariringa
Phoenix Is.
Malden I.
Starbuck I.
Tokelau Is.
Penrhyn I.
Marquesas Is. (Fr.)
Manihiki I.
Flint I.
W. SAMOA
AMER. SAMOA
Samoan Is.
Tutuila (U.S.)
Tuamotu Archipelago (Fr.)
Cook Is.
Society Is. (Fr.)
Tahiti
TONGA (Friendly Is.)
Niue (N.Z.)
Tongatapu
Rarotonga
Tubuai Is. (Fr.)
Ducie I. (Br.)
Pitcairn I. (Br.)
Easter I. (Chile)
Sala-y-Gómez (Chile)
Rapa (Fr.)
Kermadec Is. (N.Z.)
Chatham Is. (N.Z.)
UNITED KINGDOM
Glasgow
Dublin
IRELAND
London
FRANCE
Bordeaux
C. Finisterre
PORTUGAL
Madrid
Lisboa
SPAIN
Azores (Port.)
Gibraltar
Oran
Tanger
Rabat
Fès
Madeira (Port.)
Casablanca
Marrakech
MOROCCO
Canary Is. (Span.)
WESTERN SAHARA
MAURITANIA
Nouakchott
Tombouctou
CAPE VERDE IS.
C. Verde
Dakar
SENEGAL
GAMBIA
GUINEA-BISSAU
Bamako
Niger
GUINEA
Conakry
Freetown
SIERRA LEONE
Monrovia
LIBERIA
IVORY COAST
Abidjan
Accra
Gulf of Guinea
São Paulo (Brazil)
Ascension (Br.)
St. Helena (Br.)
Tristan da Cunha (Br.)
Gough I. (Br.)

Projection: *Hammer Equal Area*

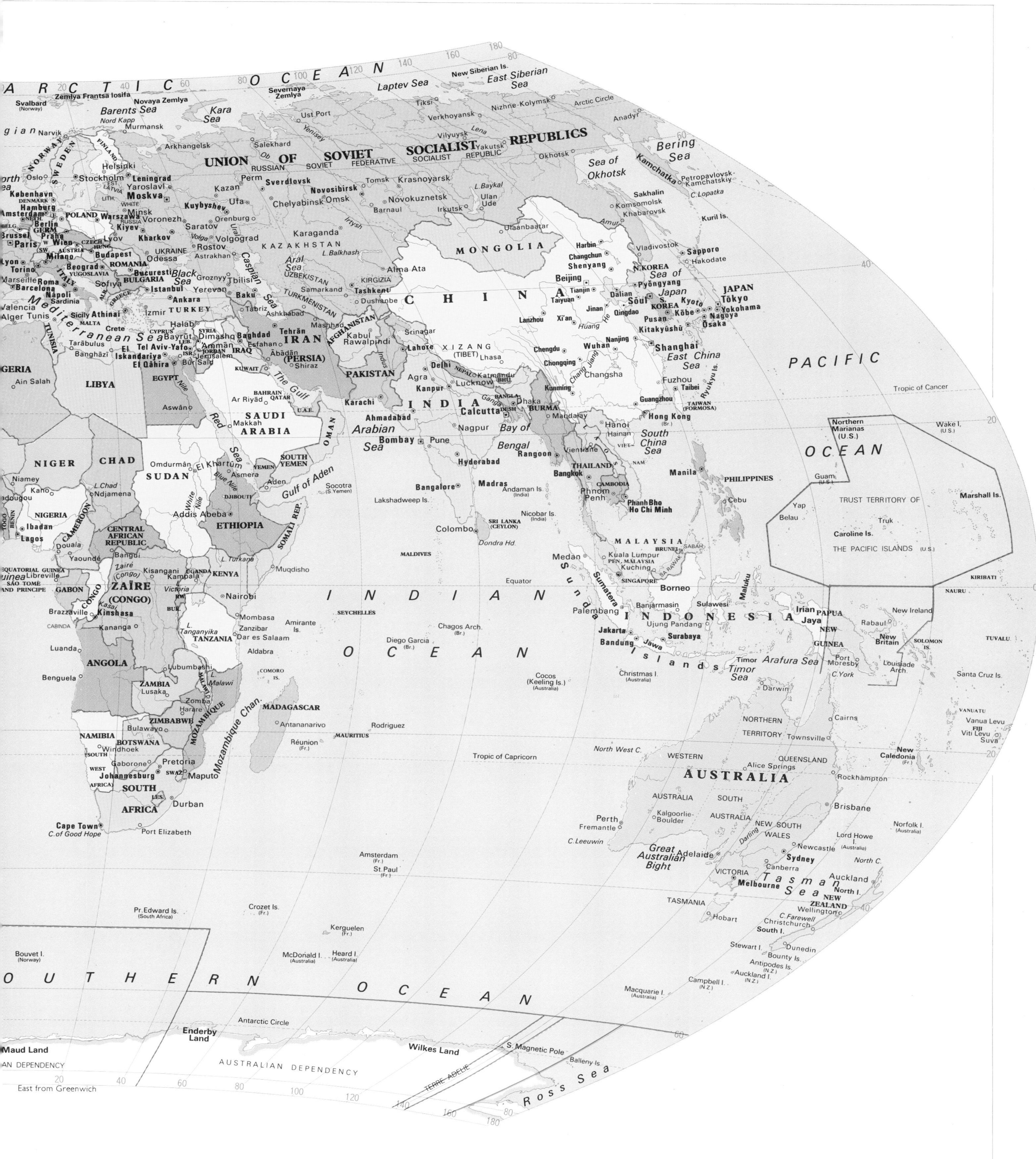
ARCTIC OCEAN
Laptev Sea
East Siberian Sea
Barents Sea
Kara Sea
Bering Sea
Sea of Okhotsk
UNION OF SOVIET SOCIALIST REPUBLICS
MONGOLIA
CHINA
JAPAN
PACIFIC OCEAN
INDIAN OCEAN
SOUTHERN OCEAN
INDIA
PAKISTAN
IRAN (PERSIA)
SAUDI ARABIA
LIBYA
EGYPT
SUDAN
CHAD
NIGER
NIGERIA
ETHIOPIA
ZAÏRE (CONGO)
ANGOLA
ZAMBIA
MADAGASCAR
SOUTH AFRICA
AUSTRALIA
INDONESIA
PHILIPPINES
MALAYSIA
BURMA
THAILAND
TRUST TERRITORY OF THE PACIFIC ISLANDS (U.S.)
NEW ZEALAND
Tasman Sea
Arafura Sea
Timor Sea
South China Sea
East China Sea
Bay of Bengal
Arabian Sea
Mediterranean Sea
Tropic of Cancer
Equator
Tropic of Capricorn
Antarctic Circle
Arctic Circle
AUSTRALIAN DEPENDENCY
Wilkes Land
Enderby Land
Ross Sea
East from Greenwich

1 : 16 000 000

100 0 100 200 300 400 500 miles

100 0 200 400 600 800 km

Projection: Bonne West from Greenwich 0 East from Greenwich

1 : 16 000 000

100 0 100 200 300 400 500 miles

100 0 200 400 600 800 km

Projection: Bonne West from Greenwich 0 East from Greenwich

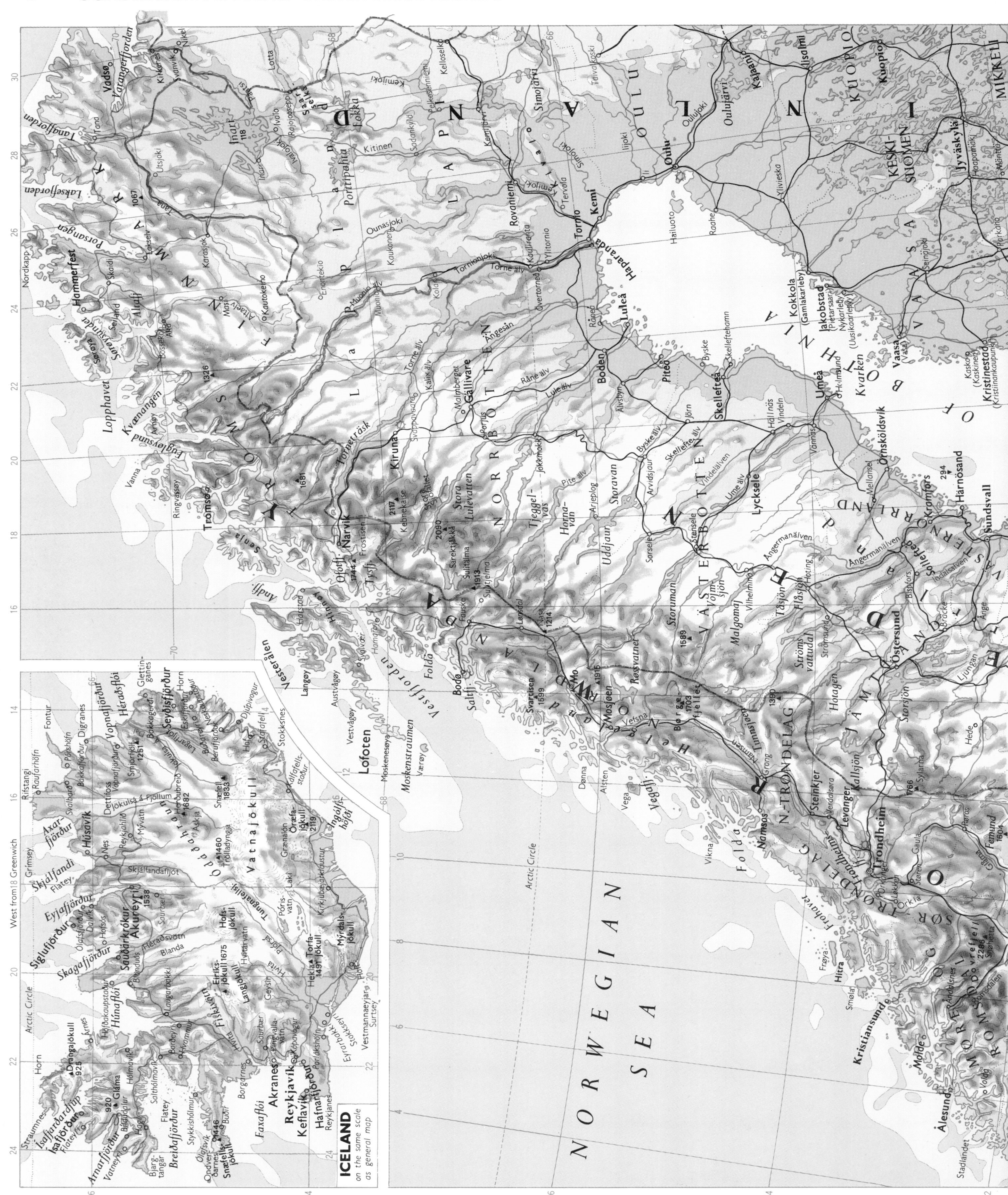

NORWEGIAN SEA
ICELAND
on the same scale as general map
West from Greenwich
Arctic Circle
Vatnajökull
Reykjavík
Akureyri
Lofoten
Vesterålen
Tromsø
Narvik
Kiruna
Bodø
Trondheim
Kristiansund
Ålesund
Molde
Namsos
Östersund
Sundsvall
Härnösand
Umeå
Skellefteå
Piteå
Luleå
Boden
Haparanda
Tornio
Kemi
Oulu
Vaasa
Kokkola
Jakobstad
Jyväskylä
Kuopio
Kajaani
Hammerfest
Vadsø
Kirkenes
Nordkapp
Inari
Gällivare
Lycksele
Vefsna
Saltfjellet
Kebnekaise
Sulitjelma
Svartisen
Mosjøen
Mo
Steinkjer
Levanger
Hitra
Frøya
Smøla
Stadlandet

1 : 4 000 000

20 10 0 20 40 60 80 100 miles

40 20 0 40 80 120 160 km

Projection: Conical with two standard parallels

East from Greenwich

ft	m
6000	2000
4500	1500
3000	1000
1200	400
600	200
0	0
600	200

Gulf of Bothnia
Örnsköldsvik
Härnösand
Sundsvall
Hudiksvall
Söderhamn
Gävle
Uppsala
Norrtälje
STOCKHOLM
Södertälje
Västerås
Eskilstuna
Örebro
Karlstad
Falun
Borlänge
Mora
Östersund
Trondheim
Lillehammer
Hamar
Oslo
Drammen
Skien
Porsmtägrunn
Fredrikstad
Halden
Sarpsborg
Moss
Kongsberg
Arvika
Säffle
Åmål
VÄSTERNORRLANDS LÄN
GÄVLEBORGS LÄN
JÄMTLANDS LÄN
KOPPARBERGS LÄN
VÄRMLANDS LÄN
VÄSTMANLANDS LÄN
SÖDERMANLANDS LÄN
UPPSALA LÄN
STOCKHOLMS LÄN
ÖREBRO LÄN
SØR TRØNDELAG FYLKE
MØRE OG ROMSDAL FYLKE
HEDMARK FYLKE
OPPLAND FYLKE
BUSKERUD
TELEMARK FYLKE
VESTFOLD
ØSTFOLD
AKERSHUS FYLKE
Jotunheimen
Dovrefjell
Transtrandsfjällen
Siljan
Mälaren
Hjälmaren
Glittertind 2470
Galdhøpiggen 2469
Snøhetta 2286

1 : 2 000 000

10 0 10 20 30 40 50 miles

10 0 10 20 30 40 50 60 70 80 km

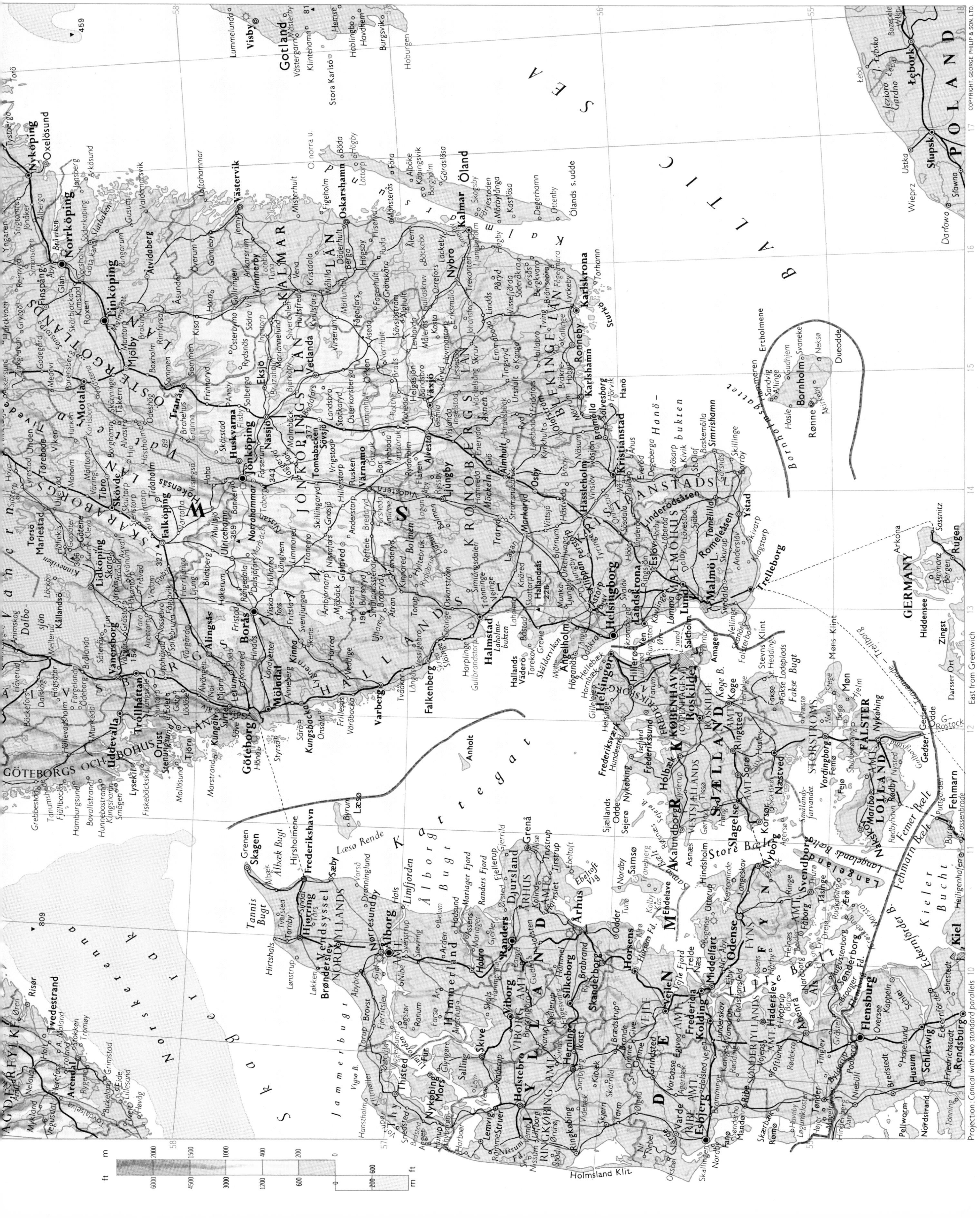

BALTIC SEA

Skagerrak

Kattegat

SWEDEN

DENMARK

NORWAY

GERMANY

POLAND

GÖTEBORGS OCH BOHUS LÄN

ÄLVSBORGS LÄN

SKARABORGS LÄN

ÖSTERGÖTLANDS LÄN

JÖNKÖPINGS LÄN

KALMAR LÄN

KRONOBERGS LÄN

BLEKINGE LÄN

HALLANDS LÄN

KRISTIANSTADS LÄN

MALMÖHUS LÄN

JYLLAND

SJÆLLAND

FYN

LOLLAND

FALSTER

Gotland

Öland

Bornholm

Anholt

Læsø

Samsø

Femer Bælt

Kieler Bucht

Store Bælt

Jammer bugt

ft	m
6000	2000
4500	1500
3000	1000
1200	400
600	200
0	0
200	600

Projection: Conical with two standard parallels

East from Greenwich

NORTH SEA
IRISH SEA
North Channel
SCOTLAND
Southern Uplands
Pennines
Cumbrian Mts.
N. York Moors
York Wolds
Lincoln Wolds
Cheviot Hills
Ochil Hills
Pentland Hills
Lammermuir Hills
Moorfoot Hills
Galloway
Kintyre
Firth of Forth
Firth of Clyde
Solway Firth
HADRIAN'S WALL
NORTHUMBERLAND
TYNE & WEAR
DURHAM
CLEVELAND
CUMBRIA
NORTH YORKSHIRE
W. YORKSHIRE
SOUTH YORKSHIRE
HUMBERSIDE
LANCASHIRE
MERSEYSIDE
GREATER MANCHESTER
CHESHIRE
DERBY
NOTTS
LINCOLN
STAFFORD
NORFOLK
CLWYD
GWYNEDD
ISLE OF MAN
Anglesey
The Wash
The Fens
Holderness
Edinburgh
Glasgow
Stirling
Dundee
Kirkcaldy
Dunfermline
Falkirk
Leith
Paisley
Greenock
Dumbarton
Clydebank
Motherwell
Airdrie
Coatbridge
Hamilton
Kilmarnock
Ayr
Dumfries
Berwick-upon-Tweed
Newcastle
Gateshead
Sunderland
Tynemouth
South Shields
Hartlepool
Middlesbrough
Stockton
Darlington
Carlisle
Penrith
Kendal
Lancaster
Morecambe
Barrow-in-Furness
Blackpool
Preston
Southport
Liverpool
Birkenhead
Manchester
Bolton
Oldham
Stockport
Bradford
Leeds
Harrogate
York
Scarborough
Bridlington
Hull
Grimsby
Scunthorpe
Doncaster
Sheffield
Rotherham
Chesterfield
Lincoln
Nottingham
Derby
Stoke-on-Trent
Chester
Wrexham
Shrewsbury
Boston
Kings Lynn
Norwich
Great Yarmouth
Cromer
Douglas
Belfast
Bangor
Larne
Stranraer
Campbeltown
Holyhead
Caernarfon
Flamborough Hd.
Spurn Hd.
Skegness
Cross Fell 893
The Cheviot 816
Snowdon 1085
Broad Law 840
Merrick 843
Goat Fell 874
Snaefell 620
Sca Fell 978
Skiddaw 931
Helvellyn 950

1 : 1 600 000

10 0 10 20 30 40 50 miles

10 0 10 20 30 40 50 60 70 80 km

ENGLISH CHANNEL

Bristol Channel

Cardigan Bay

Channel Islands

SCILLY ISLES
On same Scale

Isles of Scilly

ft	m
3000	1000
1200	400
600	200
300	100
0	0
150	50
300	100
ft	m

West from Greenwich

East from Greenwich

Projection: Conical with two standard parallels.

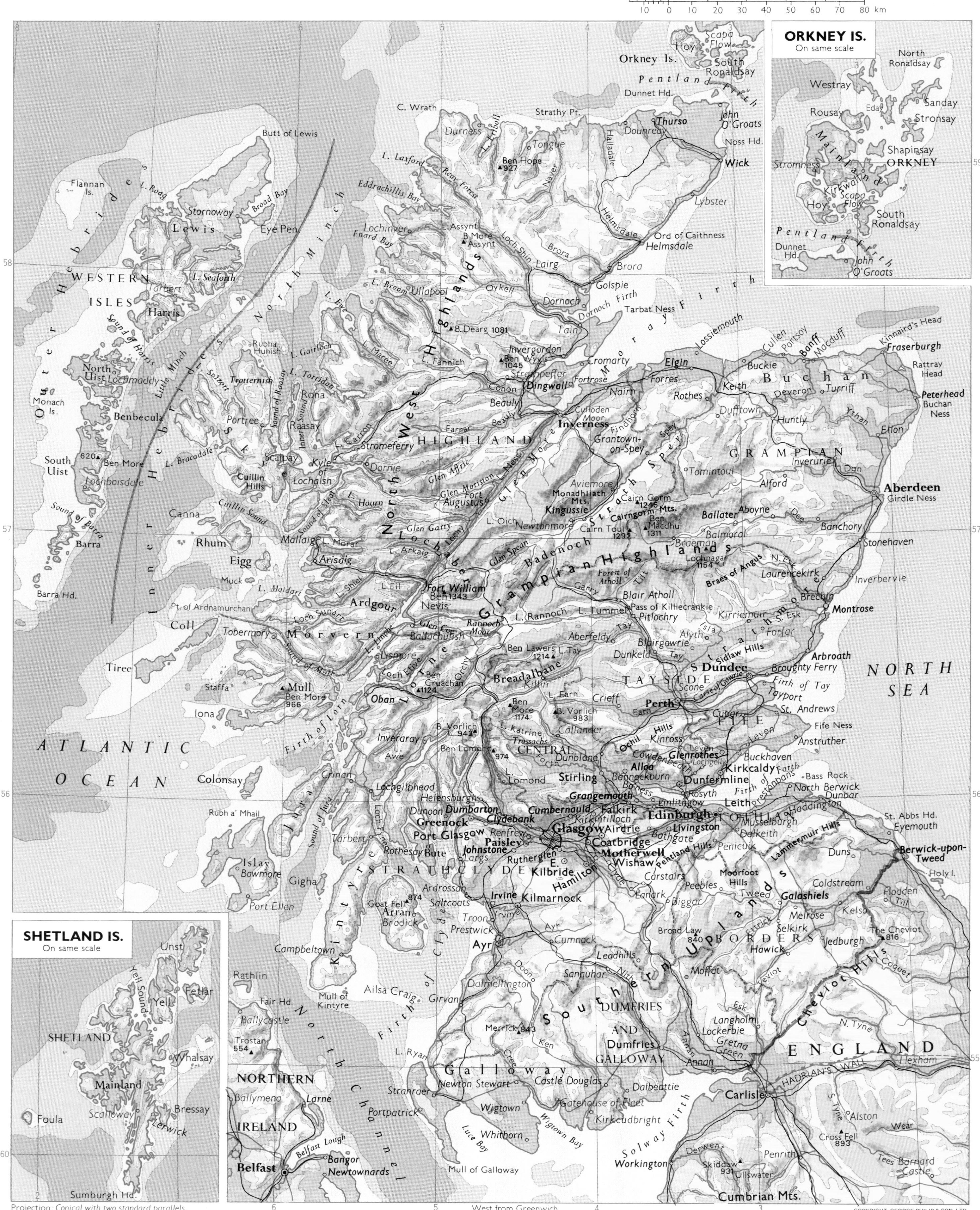
1 : 1 600 000
ORKNEY IS.
On same scale
SHETLAND IS.
On same scale
ATLANTIC OCEAN
NORTH SEA
ENGLAND
NORTHERN IRELAND
Orkney Is.
Pentland Firth
Moray Firth
Outer Hebrides
Inner Hebrides
North West Highlands
Grampian Highlands
Southern Uplands
Cheviot Hills
North Channel
Firth of Clyde
Solway Firth
Edinburgh
Glasgow
Aberdeen
Dundee
Inverness
Perth
Stirling
Carlisle
Belfast
Projection: Conical with two standard parallels.
West from Greenwich
COPYRIGHT, GEORGE PHILIP & SON, LTD.

1 : 1 600 000

10 0 10 20 30 40 50 miles

10 0 10 20 30 40 50 60 70 80 km

ATLANTIC OCEAN
IRISH SEA
North Channel
St. George's Channel
NORTHERN IRELAND
IRELAND
ULSTER
CONNACHT
LEINSTER
MUNSTER
Kintyre
Campbeltown
Arran
Ailsa Craig
Mull of Kintyre
Rathlin I.
Fair Hd.
Giant's Causeway
Portrush
Malin Hd.
Lough Swilly
Carndonagh
Inishowen Pen.
Moville
Buncrana
Lough Foyle
Limavady
Coleraine
Ballymoney
Ballycastle
Trostan 554
Londonderry
Ballymena
Larne
Stranraer
Portpatrick
I. Magee
Sperrin Mts.
Strabane
Sawel 683
Magherafelt
Carrickfergus
Antrim
Belfast L.
Donaghadee
Bangor
Newtownards
Belfast
Lisburn
Cookstown
Omagh
Lough Neagh 16
Dungannon
Irvinestown
Lurgan (Craigavon)
Portadown
Armagh
Banbridge
Downpatrick
Ards Pen.
Strangford L.
Dundrum
Dundrum Bay
Slieve Donard 852
Newcastle
Mourne Mts.
Warrenpoint
Newry
St. Gullion 577
Castleblayney
Carlingford L.
Greenore
Tory I.
Horn Hd.
Sheep Haven
Bloody Foreland
Gweedore
Errigal 752
Derryveagh Mts.
Aran I.
Letterkenny
DONEGAL
Gweebarra B.
Glenties
Finn
Lifford
Loughros More B.
Bluestack 676
Rossan Pt.
Rathlin O Birne I.
Killybegs
Donegal
Donegal Bay
Bundoran
Ballyshannon
L. Erne
Erne
Enniskillen
MONAGHAN
Monaghan
Upper L. Erne
Clones
Downpatrick Hd.
Broad Haven
Killala B.
Erris Hd.
Belmullet
Mullet Peninsula
Blacksod Bay
Killala
Ballina
Sligo B.
Sligo
Collooney
Ox Mts.
SLIGO
LEITRIM
L. Allen
L. Arrow
Leitrim
Boyle
Carrick-on-Shannon
Belturbet
CAVAN
Cavan
Annalee
Cootehill
Carrickmacross
Kingscourt
Louth
LOUTH
Dundalk
Dundalk Bay
Ardee
Achill Hd.
Achill I.
Achill
L. Conn
Nephin 806
MAYO
Castlebar
Clew Bay
Clare I.
Westport
Croagh Patrick 765
Claremorris
ROSCOMMON
Castlereagh
L. Gowna
Granard
Longford
L. Sheelin
Oldcastle
Ceanannas Mor (Kells)
Drogheda
Balbriggan
Killary Harbour
Inishbofin
Mweelrea 819
L. Mask
Robe
LONGFORD
An Uaimh (Navan)
Athboy
MEATH
Trim
Boyne
Ballinrobe
Roscommon
L. Ree
Inny
Mullingar
WESTMEATH
Lambay I.
Swords
Clifden
Twelve Pins
Connemara
Tuam
Suck
Athlone
DUBLIN
Ireland's Eye
Howth Head
Slyne Hd.
L. Corrib
GALWAY
Maynooth
Dublin (Baile Atha Cliath)
Dublin Bay
Ballinasloe
Clara
Edenderry
Clare
Tullamore
Celbridge
Galway
Athenry
Brosna
OFFALY
Daingean
Droichead Nua
Naas
Dun Laoghaire
Bray
Kippure 754
Kilkieran B.
Galway Bay
Loughrea
Shannon
Portarlington
KILDARE
Kildare
Inishmore
Aran Is.
Slieve Aughty
Portumna
Gort
Birr
Sl. Bloom
Mountmellick
Port Laoise
Poulaphouca Res.
Hags Hd.
Liscannor Bay
Ennistymon
L. Derg
Roscrea
LAOIS
Athy
Wicklow
Wicklow Hd.
Lugnaquilla 923
WICKLOW
Wicklow Mts.
Rathdrum
Mal Bay
Miltown Malbay
Ennis
CLARE
Nenagh
Ballina
Killaloe
Keeper 694
Templemore
Nore
Barrow
Carlow
Mizen Hd.
Arklow
Avoca
Tullow
Shillelagh
CARLOW
Kilkee
Rineanna
Ardnacrusha
Kilrush
Limerick
Thurles
TIPPERARY
Kilkenny
KILKENNY
Muine Bheag
Mt. Leinster 796
Slaney
Gorey
Loop Hd.
R. Shannon
Foynes
Rathkeale
Cashel
Callan
Enniscorthy
Cahore Pt.
Listowel
LIMERICK
Newcastle
Golden Vale
Tipperary
Slievenamon 722
WEXFORD
Kerry Hd.
Feale
Fenit
Tralee Bay
Brandon Bay
Rath Luirc (Charleville)
Galtymore 920
Caher
Carrick-on-Suir
New Ross
Wexford
Wexford Harbour
Galty Mts.
Clonmel
Rosslare
Tralee
KERRY
Brandon Mt. 953
Dingle
Sl. Mish
Maine
Newmarket
Mitchelstown
Knockmealdown Mts.
Comeragh Mts.
Suir
Waterford
Tramore
Greenore Pt.
Tuscar Rock
Carnsore Pt
Gt. Blasket I.
Dunmore Hd.
Dingle Bay
Kanturk
Blackwater
Mallow
WATERFORD
Killarney
Laune
Fermoy
Lismore
Dungarvan
Hook Hd.
Waterford Harbour
Saltee Is.
Macgillycuddy's Reeks
Carrauntuohill 1040
Lakes of Killarney
Boggeragh Mts.
CORK
Dungarvan Bay
Valentia Harbour
Valentia I.
Cahirciveen
Blarney
Cork
Youghal
St. David's Hd.
Kenmare
Macroom
Lee
Midleton
Youghal Harbour
Skellig Rocks
Passage West
Cobh
Ballinskelligs B.
Kenmare River
Caha Mts.
Glengariff
Bandon
Crosshaven
Kinsale
Cork Harbour
Castletown Bearhaven
Bantry
Clonakilty
Skibbereen
Bear I.
Crow Hd.
Bantry Bay
Skull
Clonakilty Bay
Old Head of Kinsale
Dunmanus Bay
Baltimore
Galley Hd
Mizen Hd.
Fastnet Rock
Clear I.
C. Clear
West from Greenwich
ft m
3000 1000
1200 400
600 200
300 100
0 0
100 300
200 600
m ft

Towns underlined in Northern Ireland give their names to the Districts in which they stand

The remaining Districts are:—

1	Fermanagh	5	Castlereagh
2	Moyle	6	Ards
3	Newtownabbey	7	Down
4	North Down	8	Newry & Mourne

Projection: *Conical with two standard parallels.*

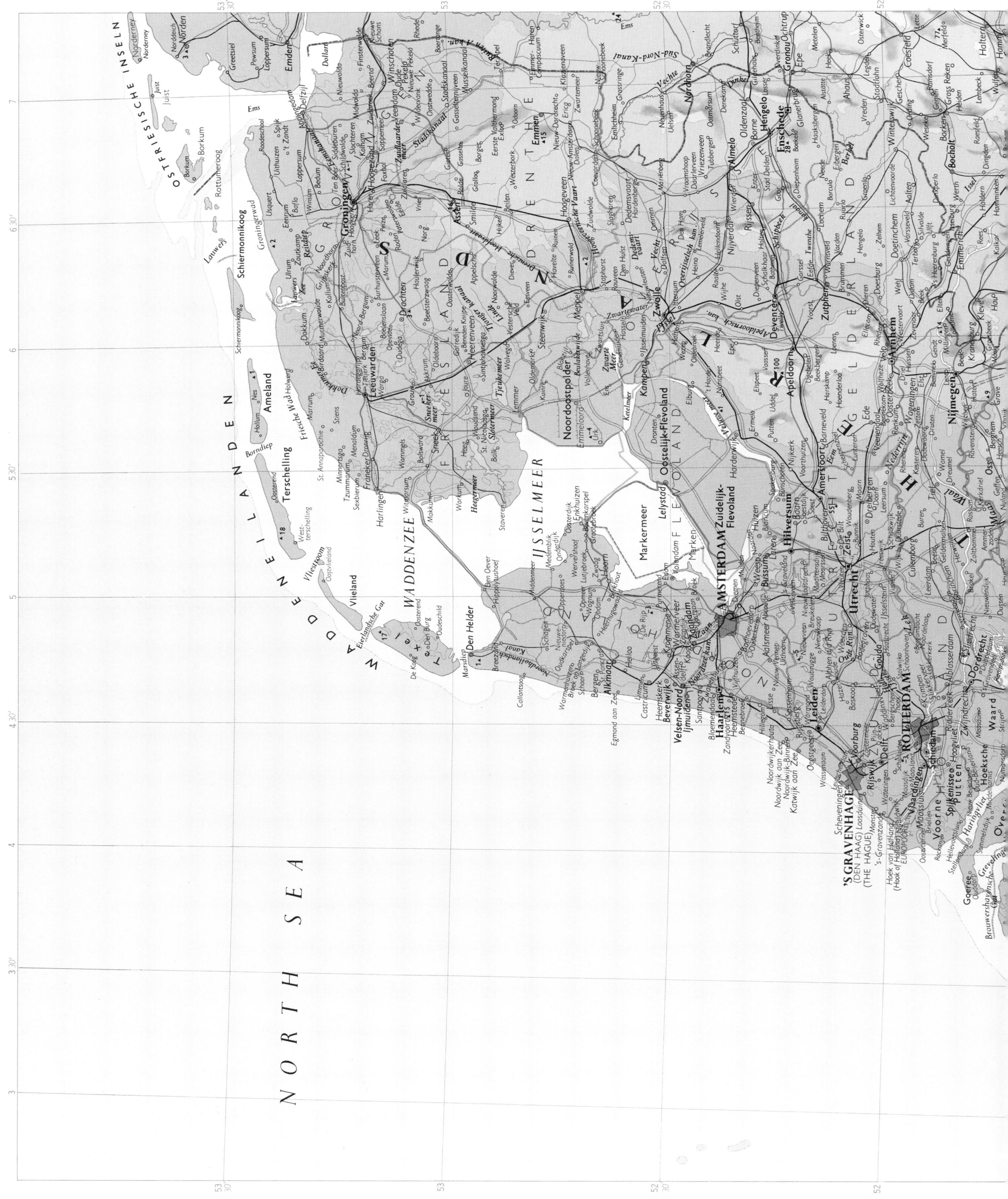
NORTH SEA
WADDENEILANDEN
OSTFRIESISCHE INSELN
WADDENZEE
IJSSELMEER
Markermeer
Texel
Vlieland
Terschelling
Ameland
Schiermonnikoog
Borkum
Den Helder
Alkmaar
Haarlem
AMSTERDAM
Leiden
'S GRAVENHAGE
(DEN HAAG)
(THE HAGUE)
Delft
ROTTERDAM
Schiedam
Dordrecht
Utrecht
Hilversum
Amersfoort
Apeldoorn
Deventer
Zutphen
Arnhem
Nijmegen
Zwolle
Kampen
Lelystad
Oostelijk-Flevoland
Zuidelijk-Flevoland
Noordoostpolder
Leeuwarden
Harlingen
Groningen
Assen
Emmen
Hoogeveen
Meppel
Heerenveen
Almelo
Hengelo
Enschede
Emden
Norden
Ems
Dollard
Lauwers
Ede
Gouda
Zaandam
Velsen-Noord
IJmuiden
Waal
Nederrijn
Lek
Vecht
IJssel
53° 30'
53°
52° 30'
52°
7
6° 30'
6
5° 30'
5
4° 30'
4
3° 30'
3

1 : 1 000 000
5 0 5 10 15 20 25 miles
5 0 10 20 30 40 km
Projection: Conical with two standard parallels
East from Greenwich
COPYRIGHT GEORGE PHILIP & SON, LTD
ft m
1800 600
1200 400
600 200
300 100
150 50
30 10
0 0
G E R M A N Y
B E L G I U M
F R A N C E
LUXEMBOURG
A r d e n n e
BRUSSEL (BRUXELLES)
Antwerpen
(Gand) Gent
Brugge
Oostende
Liège
Namur
Charleroi
Mons
Tournai
Lille
Roubaix
Tourcoing
Valenciennes
Cambrai
St-Quentin
Laon
Charleville-Mézières
Sedan
Luxembourg
Trier
Aachen
Maastricht
Eindhoven
Tilburg
Breda
KÖLN (COLOGNE)
DÜSSELDORF
Bonn
ESSEN
DORTMUND
Duisburg
Wuppertal
Krefeld
Mönchengladbach
Venlo
Hasselt
Leuven
Mechelen
Kortrijk
Roeselare
Vlissingen (Flushing)
Middelburg
Zuid-Beveland
Noordbeveland
Walcheren
Tholen
Bergen op Zoom
Roosendaal
Meuse
Sambre
Escaut
Oise
Moselle
Sauer
Our
Rur
Rhein
Maas
Schwarzwalder Hochwald
Hautes Fagnes

ENGLAND
English Channel
CHANNEL ISLANDS
Alderney
Guernsey
Jersey
St. Peter Port
St. Helier
Baie de la Seine
Golfe de St - Malo
Mer d'Iroise
Baie de Bourgneuf
Pertuis Breton
Pertuis d'Antioche
Lyme Bay
Dartmoor
Exeter
Plymouth
Southampton
Portsmouth
Brighton
Bournemouth
Weymouth
Eastbourne
Hastings
Folkestone
Cherbourg
Le Havre
Rouen
Dieppe
Caen
Bayeux
Lisieux
Brest
Quimper
Lorient
Vannes
St. Brieuc
St. Malo
Rennes
Laval
Le Mans
Alençon
Angers
Nantes
St. Nazaire
Cholet
Tours
Blois
Poitiers
Châtellerault
Niort
La Rochelle
Rochefort
Saintes
Cognac
Angoulême
Limoges
La Roche-sur-Yon
Les Sables-d'Olonne
Ile d'Ouessant
Belle-Ile
Ile de Noirmoutier
Ile d'Yeu
Ile de Ré
Ile d'Oléron
BRETAGNE
NORMANDIE
MAINE
ANJOU
TOURAINE
POITOU
AUNIS
ANGOUMOIS
PERCHE
Loire
Vienne
ft
m
12 000
9000
6000
4500
3000
1200
600
0
200
2000
4000
3000
2000
1500
1000
400
200
0
600
6000
m
ft
DÉPARTEMENTS IN THE PARIS AREA
1 Ville de Paris
2 Seine-St-Denis
3 Val-de-Marne
4 Hauts-de-Seine
Projection: Conical with two standard parallels
West from Greenwich
East from Greenwich

1 : 2 000 000

10 0 10 20 30 40 50 miles

10 0 10 20 30 40 50 60 70 80 km

BELGIUM

LUXEMBOURG

GERMANY

FRANCE

SWITZERLAND

ITALY

SAARLAND

ARDENNES

Champagne

BOURBONNAIS

PARIS

BRUSSEL (Bruxelles)

KÖLN (Cologne)

FRANKFURT

LYON (Lyons)

2 3 4 5 6 7

ATLANTIC
OCEAN
Golfe de
Gascogne
Ile de Noirmoutier
Ile d'Yeu
Ile de Ré
Ile d'Oléron
Pertuis Breton
Pertuis d'Antioche
Cholet
Bourges
Nevers
Châteauroux
Poitiers
Châtellerault
Niort
La Rochelle
Rochefort
AUNIS
ANGOUMOIS
SAINTONGE
Saintes
Cognac
Angoulême
Limoges
Plateau de Millevaches
Clermont-Ferrand
Vichy
Moulins
Montluçon
BOURBONNAIS
Périgueux
DORDOGNE
Bordeaux
Libourne
Bergerac
Arcachon
GIRONDE
LANDES
LOT-ET-GARONNE
Agen
Cahors
Montauban
Toulouse
Albi
Rodez
AVEYRON
Millau
Causse Méjean
Aurillac
CANTAL
Brive-la-Gaillarde
Tulle
CORRÈZE
Castres
Carcassonne
Narbonne
Béziers
Sète
Montpellier
Perpignan
ROUSSILLON
PYRÉNÉES-ORIENTALES
ANDORRA
Pau
Tarbes
Lourdes
HAUTES-PYRÉNÉES
Bayonne
Biarritz
San Sebastián
Pamplona
NAVARRA
Huesca
Zaragoza
Lérida
Gerona
Manresa
Sierra de la Peña
Sierra de Guara
Golfe
ft m
12 000 4000
9000 3000
6000 2000
4500 1500
3000 1000
1200 400
600 200
0 0
200 600
2000 6000
m ft
47
46
45
44
42
Projection: Conical with two standard parallels
West from Greenwich
East from Greenwich
1 0 1 2 3

1 : 2 000 000

10 0 10 20 30 40 50 miles

10 0 10 20 30 40 50 60 70 80 km

SWITZERLAND
ITALY
CORSICA
LIGURIAN SEA
MEDITERRANEAN SEA
Golfo di Génova
du Lion
ALPES-DE-HAUTE-PROVENCE
ALPES-MARITIMES
VAUCLUSE
HAUTE-SAVOIE
SAVOIE
HAUTE-CORSE
CORSE-DU-SUD
ILES D'HYÈRES
LYON
MILANO
TORINO
GENOVA
MARSEILLE
Genève
Lausanne
Bern
Luzern
Grenoble
Chambéry
Avignon
Nîmes
Arles
Aix-en-Provence
Toulon
Nice
Cannes
Monaco
San Remo
Savona
La Spezia
Livorno
Bastia
Ajaccio
Brescia
Bergamo
Parma
Cremona
Piacenza
Novara
Pavia
Alessandria
Asti
Cuneo
Valence
St-Étienne
Mont Blanc 4807
Matterhorn 4478
Gran Paradiso 4061
Monte Cinto 2710
Lac Léman
L. Maggiore
L. di Como
L. di Garda
Rhône
Isère
Durance
Po
Elba
Capraia
Gorgona

BAY OF BISCAY
ATLANTIC OCEAN
San Sebastián
Bilbao
Baracaldo
Santander
Gijón
Oviedo
Mieres
León
Burgos
Vitoria
Logroño
Valladolid
Palencia
Salamanca
Zamora
Segovia
Ávila
MADRID
Toledo
Guadalajara
Alcalá de Henares
Aranjuez
Lugo
Orense
Vigo
Pontevedra
La Coruña (Corunna)
El Ferrol
Santiago de Compostela
Porto (Oporto)
Vila Nova de Gaia
Braga
Bragança
Coimbra
Aveiro
Viseu
Guarda
Plasencia
Sierra de Gredos
Sierra de Gata
Sierra de Guadarrama
Sierra de la Culebra
Sierra de la Demanda
Picos de Europa
Cabo Finisterre
Cabo Ortegal
ASTURIAS
CANTABRIA
GALICIA
VASCONGADAS
LA RIOJA
Duero
Douro
Miño
Ebro
Tajo

1 : 2 000 000

MEDITERRANEAN SEA
Golfo de Cádiz
Strait of Gibraltar
MOROCCO
Costa del Sol
Algarve
Sierra Nevada
Sierra Morena
Montes de Toledo
Sevilla (Seville)
Córdoba
Granada
Málaga
Cádiz
Huelva
Jaén
Almería
Badajoz
Mérida
Évora
Faro
Setúbal
LISBOA (LISBON)
Gibraltar (Br.)
Algeciras
Ceuta (Sp.)
Tanger (Tangier)
Tétouan
Melilla (Sp.)
Alborán (Sp.)
Projection: Conical with two standard parallels
West from Greenwich
COPYRIGHT. GEORGE PHILIP & SON. LTD.

BAY OF BISCAY
Golfe de Gascogne
FRANCE
SPAIN
Menorca
(Minorca)
Mallorca
(Majorca)
BALEARIC ISLANDS
ANDORRA
ROUSSILLON
PYRÉNÉES-ORIENTALES
HAUTES PYRÉNÉES
PYRÉNÉES-ATLANTIQUES
BÉARN
NAVARRE
NAVARRA
VASCONGADAS
CANTABRIA
BARCELONA
Hospitalet de Llobregat
Zaragoza
(Saragossa)
MADRID
Pamplona
San Sebastián
Bilbao
Santander
Logroño
Burgos
Vitoria
Lérida
Tarragona
Castellón de la Plana
Guadalajara
Teruel
Huesca
Tortosa
Toulouse
Perpignan
Narbonne
Béziers
Carcassonne
Bayonne
Biarritz
Tarbes
Pau
Sierra de la Peña
Sierra de Guara
Sa. de Cebollera
Sa. del Moncayo
Montes Universales
Sa. de Albarracín
Mts. del Maestrazgo
Sierra de la Demanda
Ebro
Segre
Cinca
Golfo de San Jorge
Islas Columbretes
Costa Brava
Costa Dorada
LA MANCHA

1 : 2 000 000

10 0 10 20 30 40 50 miles
10 0 10 20 30 40 50 60 70 80 km
MEDITERRANEAN SEA
NORTH ATLANTIC OCEAN
CANARY ISLANDS
1 : 1 600 000
LANZAROTE
FUERTEVENTURA
GRAN CANARIA
TENERIFE
GOMERA
LA PALMA
HIERRO
LAS PALMAS
SANTA CRUZ DE TENERIFE
Arrecife
Puerto del Rosario
Teide 3718
Isla de Lobos
Alegranza
Graciosa
Montaña Clara
Valverde
San Sebastián de la Gomera
Los Llanos de Aridane
Sta. Cruz de la Palma
Puerto de la Cruz
La Laguna
Guía
Telde
Maspalomas
Ibiza (Iviza)
Formentera
Cabrera
VALENCIA
Alicante
Murcia
Cartagena
Albacete
Granada
Almería
Elche
Lorca
Alcoy
Gandía
Játiva
Alcira
Sueca
Orihuela
Torrevieja
Linares
Úbeda
Baeza
Guadix
Motril
Valdepeñas
Manzanares
Daimiel
Tomelloso
Villarrobledo
Hellín
Yecla
Almansa
Villena
Caravaca
Cieza
Jumilla
Águilas
Mazarrón
Golfo de Mazarrón
Golfo de Almería
Cabo de Gata
Cabo de Palos
Cabo de la Nao
Cabo de San Antonio
Mar Menor
Albufera de Valencia
Sierra Nevada
Mulhacén 3478
Sa. de los Filabres
Sierra de Segura
Sa. de Cazorla
Sierra de Alcaraz
Sierra Morena
Sa. Espuña 1584
Sierra de Gádor
Las Alpujarras
Projection: Lambert's Conformal Conic
Projection: Conical with two standard parallels
West from Greenwich
East from Greenwich
COPYRIGHT, GEORGE PHILIP & SON, LTD.
m ft

SWITZERLAND
FRANCE
LIGURIAN SEA
Golfo di Génova
CORSE
(CORSICA)
Côte d'Azur
RIVIERA
ILES D'HYERES
Arcipelago Toscano
VORARLBERG
LIECHTENSTEIN
ST. GALLEN
GRAUBÜNDEN
TICINO
VALAIS
VAUD
FRIBOURG
BERN
LUZERN
UNTER-WALDEN
HAUTE-SAVOIE
SAVOIE
ISÈRE
DRÔME
HAUTES-ALPES
VAUCLUSE
ALPES-DE-HAUTE-PROVENCE
ALPES-MARITIMES
BOUCHES-DU-RHÔNE
PROVENCE
DAUPHINÉ
FRANCHE-COMTÉ
BOURGOGNE
SAÔNE-ET-LOIRE
PIEMONTE
LOMBARDIA
LIGURIA
EMILIA-ROMAGNA
VALLE D'AOSTA
HAUTE-CORSE
CORSE-DU-SUD
Alpi Pennine
Alpi Graie
Alpi Lepontine
Alpi Orobie
Berner Alpen
Lechtaler Alpen
Alpes Maritimes
Appennino Ligure
MILANO
(Milan)
TORINO
(Turin)
GENOVA
(Genoa)
MARSEILLE
(Marseilles)
Lyon
(Lyons)
Genève
Lausanne
Bern
Luzern
Zürich
Grenoble
Chambéry
Annecy
Nice
MONACO
Cannes
Toulon
Avignon
Aix-en-Provence
Arles
Bastia
Ajaccio
Livorno
(Leghorn)
Pisa
Lucca
La Spezia
Parma
Cremona
Piacenza
Bergamo
Bréscia
Novara
Vercelli
Asti
Alessàndria
Cúneo
Savona
Sanremo
Impéria
Lago Maggiore
L. di Como
Lago di Garda
Lac Léman
Rhône
Po
Durance
Isère
Elba
Capraia
Montecristo
Giglio
Gorgona
Pianosa
Mt. Blanc 4807
Matterhorn 4478
Monte Rosa 4634
Gran Paradiso 4061
Monte Viso 3841
Projection: Conical with two standard parallels
East from Greenwich
ft
m
12 000
9000
6000
4500
3000
1200
600
0
200
2000
4000
3000
2000
1500
1000
400
200
0
600
6000
m ft

1 : 2 000 000

10 0 10 20 30 40 50 miles

10 0 10 20 30 40 50 60 70 80 km

Innsbruck
Hohe Tauern
Niedere Tauern
Zillertaler Alpen
Karnische Alpen
Karawanken
Julijske Alpe
Graz
Klagenfurt
Villach
Lienz
Judenburg
Maribor
Ljubljana
Zagreb
Karlovac
Rijeka (Fiume)
Trieste
G. di Trieste
Golfo di Venézia
Venézia (Venice)
Pádova (Padua)
Vicenza
Treviso
Udine
Gorízia
Bolzano
Merano
Belluno
Ferrara
Bologna
Ravenna
Rímini
SAN MARINO
Pésaro
Ancona
Firenze (Florence)
Arezzo
Perúgia
Assisi
Foligno
Terni
Rieti
L'Aquila
Pescara
Chieti
Téramo
Áscoli Piceno
Viterbo
Civitavécchia
ROMA (ROME)
Vatican City
Tívoli
Sulmona
Avezzano
Vasto
Térmoli
Vieste
Monte Sant'Ángelo
Gran Sasso d'Italia
ABRUZZI
UMBRIA
MARCHE
LAZIO
MOLISE
VENEZIA GIULIA
FRIULI
HUNGARY
Balaton
Bakony Hegység
Nagykanizsa
Zalaegerszeg
Keszthely
Bjelovar
Virovitica
Sisak
Banja Luka
Bihać
Gospić
Zadar
Šibenik
Split
Brač
Hvar
Vis
Korčula
Lastovo
Mljet
Pelješac
Dugi Otok
Pag
Krk
Cres
Lošinj
Pula
Poreč
Istra
Kvarner
Kvarnerić
Velebit Planina
Velika Kapela
Mala Kapela
Dinara Planina
DALMACIJA
BOSNA
HERCEGOVINA
ADRIATIC SEA
Palagruža
Tremiti
Pianosa
Golfo di Venézia
Foci del Po
Valli di Comácchio
L. Trasimeno
L. di Bolsena
L. di Bracciano
L. di Lésina
L. di Varano
Monte Argentario
Testa del Gargano
12
13
14
15
16
17
42
43
44
45
46
47

CORSE
CORSICA
CORSE-DU-SUD
G. d'Ajaccio
Porto-Vecchio
Bonifacio
Bouches de Bonifacio
Golfo dell' Asinara
Costa Smeralda
G. di Olbia
Sássari
Alghero
SARDEGNA
SARDINIA
Golfo di Orosei
Monti del Gennargentu
Golfo di Oristano
Oristano
Iglésias
Cagliari
Golfo di Cágliari
San Pietro
Sant' Antíoco
C. Spartivento
ROMA (Rome)
Vatican City
Golfo di Gaeta
Ísole Ponziane
TYRRHENIAN SEA
Ustica
PALERMO
Trápani
Ísole Égadi
Marsala
Sicilian Channel
Iles de la Galite
Bizerte (Binzert)
Golfe de Tunis
TUNIS
C. Bon
TUNISIA
Pantelleria
MEDITE
Projection: Conical with two standard parallels
East from Greenwich

1 : 2 000 000

ADRIATIC SEA
IONIAN SEA
Golfo di Táranto
Strait of Otranto
G. di Manfredónia
Golfo di Squillace
Golfo di Sant'Eufémia
G. di Salerno
G. di Policastro
BASILICATA
CALABRIA
ABRUZZI
MOLISE
Bari
Táranto
Bríndisi
Lecce
Fóggia
Cosenza
Catanzaro
Crotone
Messina
Réggio di Calábria
Catánia
Siracusa
Augusta
Ragusa
Napoli
Salerno
Potenza
Matera
Durrësi (Durazzo)
Tirana (Tiranë)
Vlora (Valona)
Kérkira (Corfu)
Isole Eólie o Lípari (Æolian Is.)
Strómboli
Salina
Lípari
Vulcano
Filicudi
Alicudi
Etna 3340
Monte Pollino 2271
La Sila 1929
Aspromonte 1956
C. Santa Maria di Leuca
C. Spartivento
C. delle Colonne
C. Passero
Str. di Messina
Monti Nébrodi
Monti Iblei
Capri
Golfo di Gela
RRANEAN SEA
Channel

NORTH SEA
BALTIC SEA
DENMARK
POLAND
NETHERLANDS
WEST GERMANY
EAST GERMANY
NORD-FRIESISCHE INSELN
OSTFRIESISCHE INSELN
WADDENEILANDEN
Deutsche Bucht
Mecklenburger Bucht
Fehmarn Belt
SCHLESWIG-HOLSTEIN
NIEDERSACHSEN
NORDRHEIN-WESTFALEN
HESSEN
NEUBRANDENBURG
SCHWERIN
ROSTOCK
POTSDAM
FRANKFURT
MAGDEBURG
HALLE
COTTBUS
LEIPZIG
DRESDEN
ERFURT
GERA
SUHL
KARL-MARX-STADT
HAMBURG
BERLIN
Bremen
Bremerhaven
Hannover
Kiel
Lübeck
Rostock
Schwerin
Stralsund
Greifswald
Szczecin
Flensburg
Oldenburg
Wilhelmshaven
Emden
Groningen
Osnabrück
Münster
Bielefeld
Braunschweig
Wolfsburg
Magdeburg
Potsdam
Frankfurt
Cottbus
Halle
LEIPZIG
DRESDEN
Karl-Marx-Stadt
Zwickau
Erfurt
Weimar
Jena
Gera
Kassel
Göttingen
DORTMUND
ESSEN
DUISBURG
DÜSSELDORF
Wuppertal
KÖLN
Bonn
Aachen
Siegen
Marburg
Giessen
Fulda
Elbe
Weser
Ems
Oder
Spree
Saale
Rügen
Fehmarn
LOLLAND
Falster
Møn

1 : 2 000 000

10 0 10 20 30 40 50 miles
10 0 10 20 30 40 50 60 70 80 km

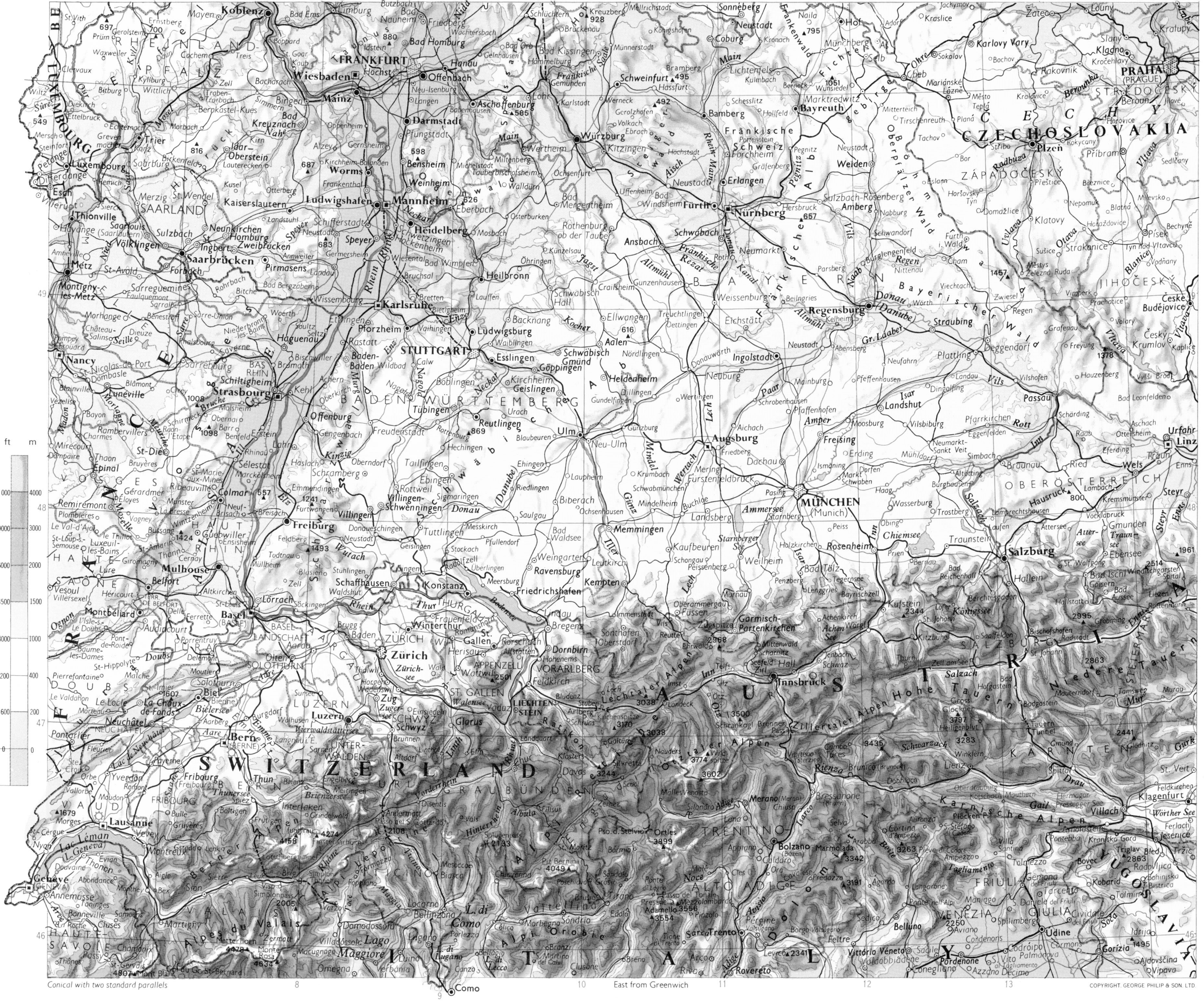

CZECHOSLOVAKIA
SWITZERLAND
AUSTRIA
ITALY
FRANCE
YUGOSLAVIA
LUXEMBOURG
PRAHA (PRAGUE)
Plzeň
České Budějovice
Karlovy Vary
Koblenz
FRANKFURT
Wiesbaden
Mainz
Offenbach
Darmstadt
Würzburg
Bamberg
Bayreuth
Nürnberg
Fürth
Erlangen
Regensburg
Mannheim
Ludwigshafen
Heidelberg
Karlsruhe
Saarbrücken
Metz
Nancy
Strasbourg
STUTTGART
Ulm
Augsburg
Ingolstadt
MÜNCHEN (Munich)
Landshut
Passau
Linz
Salzburg
Innsbruck
Freiburg
Mulhouse
Basel
Zürich
Konstanz
Bodensee
Bern
Luzern
Lausanne
Genève
Lac Léman (L. Geneva)
Bolzano
Trento
Udine
Klagenfurt
Villach
Como
Alpes du Valais
Hohe Tauern
Niedere Tauern
Karnische Alpen
Ötztaler Alpen
Zillertaler Alpen
Lechtaler Alpen
Bayerischer Wald
Oberpfälzer Wald
Conical with two standard parallels
East from Greenwich
COPYRIGHT GEORGE PHILIP & SON LTD
ft
12 000
9000
6000
4500
3000
1200
600
0
m
4000
3000
2000
1500
1000
400
200
0

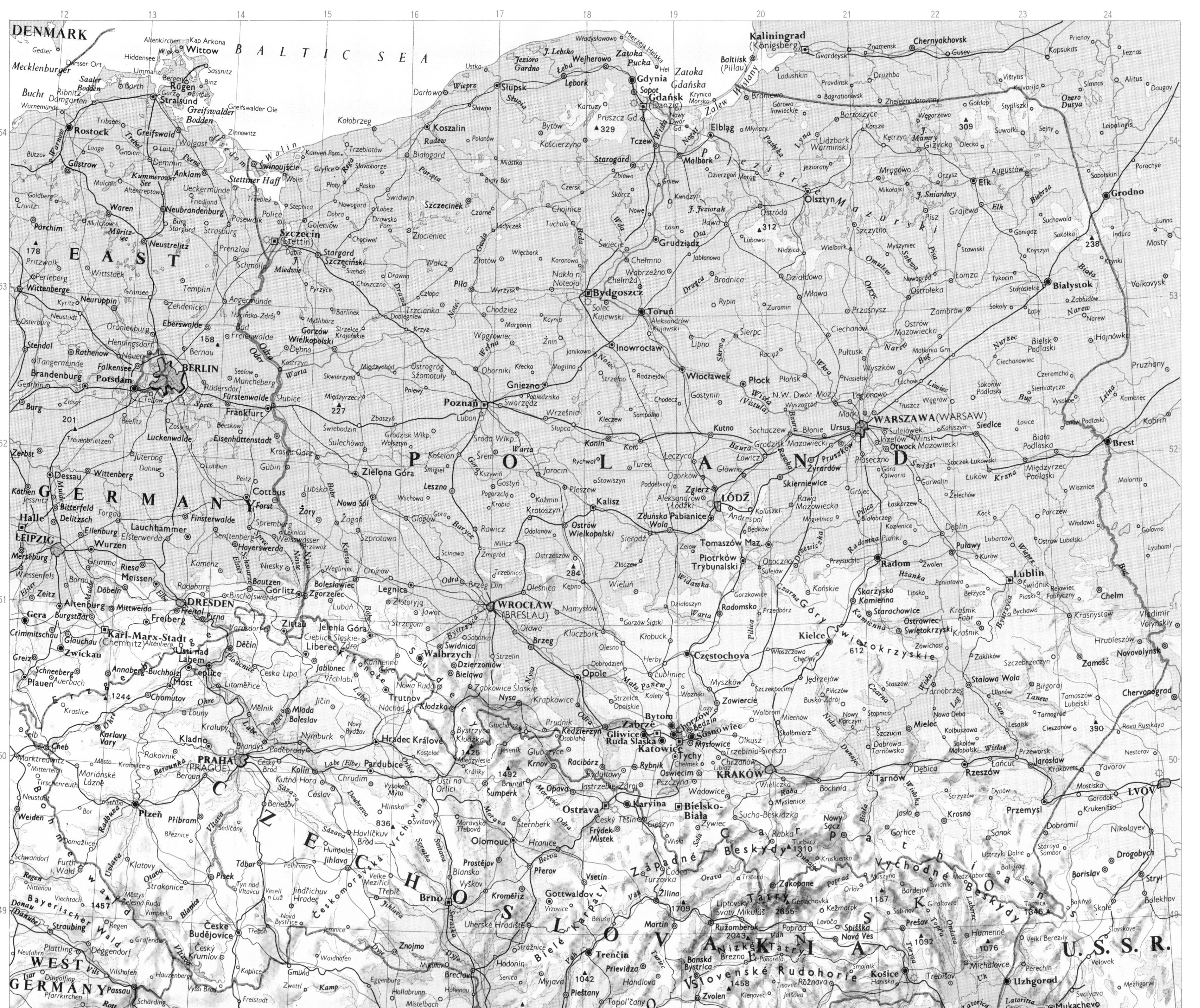
DENMARK
BALTIC SEA
EAST GERMANY
WEST GERMANY
POLAND
CZECHOSLOVAKIA
U.S.S.R.
BERLIN
DRESDEN
LEIPZIG
PRAHA (PRAGUE)
WARSZAWA (WARSAW)
KRAKÓW
WROCŁAW (BRESLAU)
ŁÓDŹ
Poznań
Gdańsk (Danzig)
Szczecin (Stettin)
Kaliningrad (Königsberg)
Grodno
Brest
LVOV
Brno
Ostrava
Katowice
Lublin
Białystok
Rostock
Karl-Marx-Stadt (Chemnitz)
Plzeň
Košice
Uzhgorod

HUNGARY
ROMANIA
YUGOSLAVIA
AUSTRIA
ITALY
ADRIATIC SEA
BUDAPEST
BEOGRAD (BELGRADE)
WIEN (VIENNA)
SOFIYA (SOFIA)
Zagreb
Ljubljana
Sarajevo
Bratislava
Graz
Linz
Salzburg
Trieste
Rijeka (Fiume)
Split
Dubrovnik
Ancona
Pescara
Timişoara
Arad
Oradea
Cluj-Napoca
Debrecen
Miskolc
Szeged
Pécs
Győr
Novi Sad
Osijek
Niš
Titograd
Mostar
Zenica
Tuzla
Banja Luka
Kragujevac
Priština
Duna (Danube)
Dunav (Danube)
Sava
Drava
Tisa
Balaton
Dinara Planina
Velebit Planina
Velika Kapela
Munții Apuseni
BOSNA
HERCEGOVINA
CRNA GORA (MONTENEGRO)
Golfo di Venézia
Projection: Conical with two standard parallels
East from Greenwich

ft m

12 000 4000

9000 3000

6000 2000

4500 1500

3000 1000

1200 400

600 200

0 0

200 600

m ft

1 : 2 800 000

10 0 10 20 30 40 50 100 miles

10 0 10 20 30 40 50 100 150 km

UKRAINIAN S.S.R.
U.S.S.R.
MOLDAVIAN S.S.R.
B E S S A R A B I Y A
M O L D O V A
T R A N S I L V A N I A
R O M A N I A
C a r p a ţ i i M e r i d i o n a l i
V A L A H I A
D O B R U D J A
B U L G A R I A
Y U G O S L A V I A
HUNGARY
CRNA GORA (MONTENEGRO)
B L A C K S E A
BUCUREŞTI (BUCHAREST)
BEOGRAD (BELGRADE)
SOFIYA (SOFIA)
BUDAPEST
Kishinev
Constanţa
Varna
Burgas
Cluj-Napoca
Timişoara
Braşov
Iaşi
Galaţi
Brăila
Ploieşti
Craiova
Ruse
Plovdiv
Debrecen
Szeged
Novi Sad
Niš
Dunărea (Danube)
Duna (Danube)

1 : 2 800 000

10 0 10 20 30 40 50 100 miles

10 0 10 20 30 40 50 100 150 km

East from Greenwich

Projection: Conical with two standard parallels

m	ft
3000	9000
2000	6000
1500	4500
1000	3000
400	1200
200	600
0	0
200	600
2000	6000

G. of Finland
BALTIC SEA
Gotland
Hiiumaa (Khiuma)
Saaremaa (Sarema)
Rizhskiy Zaliv (Gulf of Riga)
LENINGRAD
Tallinn
Riga
Vilnius
Minsk
Kaunas
Kaliningrad
WARSZAWA (Warsaw)
KIYEV (Kiev)
Smolensk
Novgorod
Pskov
Vitebsk
Mogilev
Gomel
Brest
Lvov
Lublin
Grodno
Białystok
Daugavpils
Tartu
ESTONIAN S.S.R.
LATVIAN S.S.R.
LITHUANIAN S.S.R.
BYELORUSSIAN S.S.R. (WHITE RUSSIA)
RUSSIAN SOCIA
POLAND
UKRAINIAN S.
Valdayskaya Vozvyshennost
Carpathians
Projection: Conical with two standard parallels
East from Greenwich

1 : 4 000 000

50 0 50 100 miles
50 0 50 100 150 km

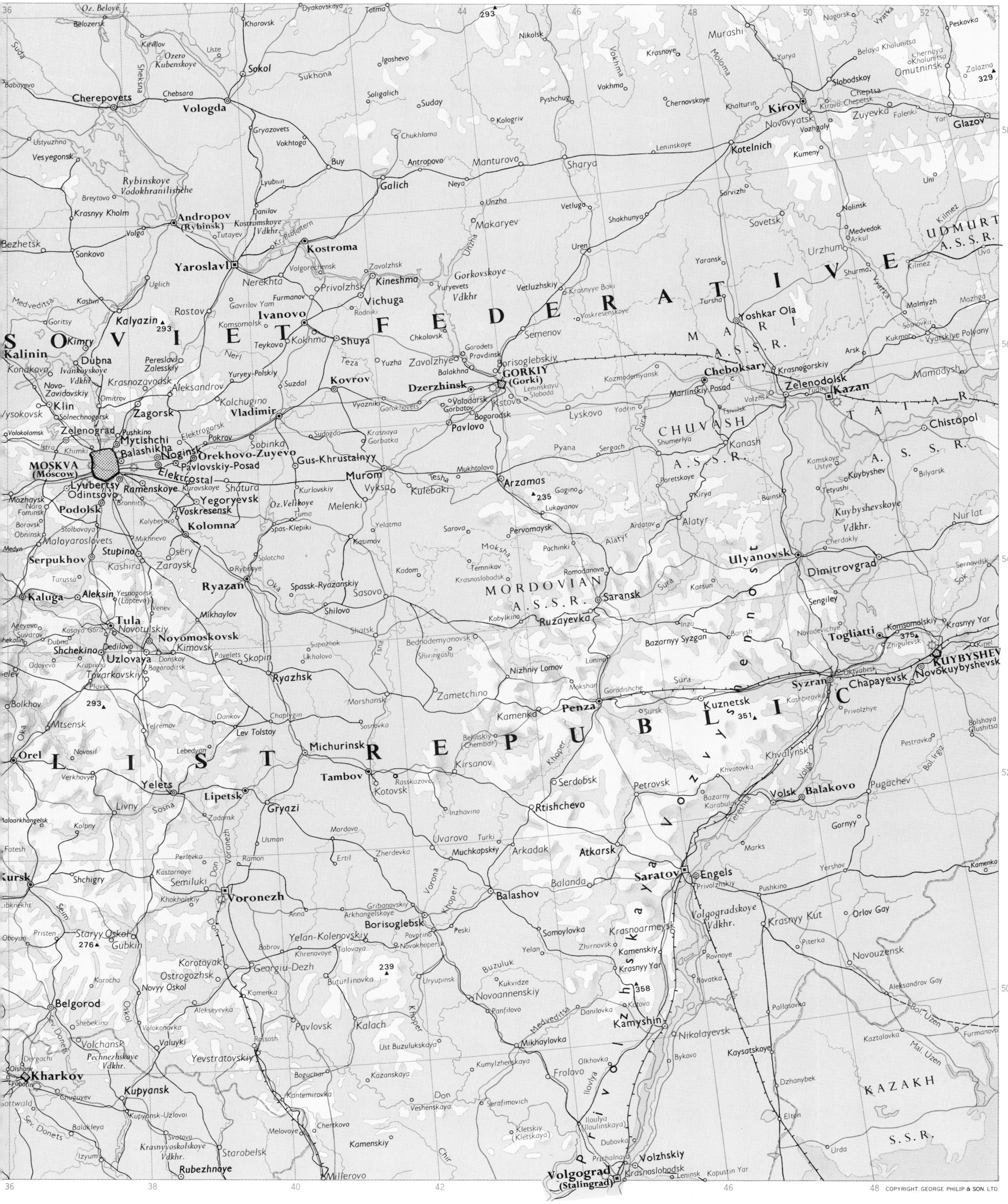

36 40 42 44 46 48 50 52

Oz. Beloye
Belozersk
Dyakovskaya
Totma
293
Kharovsk
Nikolsk
Murashi
Nagorsk
Vyatka
Peskovka
Kama
Suda
Kirillov
Ozero Kubenskoye
Uste
Igoshevo
Vokhma
Krasnoye
Moloma
Yurya
Belaya Kholunitsa
Chernaya Kholunitsa
Omutninsk
Zalazna
329
Sheksna
Sokol
Sukhona
Vokhma
Slobodskoy
Babayevo
Cherepovets
Chebsara
Vologda
Soligalich
Suday
Pyshchug
Chernovskoye
Khalturin
Kirov
Cheptsa
Kirovo-Chepetsk
Zuyevka
Falenki
Yar
Glazov
Novovyatsk
Kologriv
Vozhgaly
58
Ustyuzhna
Gryazovets
Chukhloma
Leninskoye
Kotelnich
Vokhtoga
Vesyegonsk
Buy
Antropovo
Manturovo
Sharya
Kumeny
Rybinskoye Vodokhranilishche
Lyubim
Galich
Neya
Uni
Breytovo
Sorvizhi
Unzha
Nolinsk
Krasnyy Kholm
Danilov
Vetluga
Andropov (Rybinsk)
Kostromskoye Vdkhr.
Makaryev
Shakhunya
Sovetsk
Kilmez
Volga
Tutayev
Kr. Profintern
Medvedok
Arkul
Bezhetsk
UDMURT A.S.S.R.
Kostroma
Uren
Sonkovo
Urzhum
Uva
Yaroslavl
Volgorechensk
Zavolzhsk
Unzha
Yaransk
Kilmez
Uglich
Nerekhta
Kineshma
Gorkovskoye Vdkhr.
Shurma
Privolzhsk
Yuryevets
Vetluzhskiy
Krasnyye Baki
Vyatka
Medveditsa
Kashin
Furmanov
Vichuga
Tursha
Mozhga
Goritsy
Rostov
Gavrilov Yam
Rodniki
Yoshkar Ola
Malmyzh
Kalyazin
293
Ivanovo
Yoshkar Ola
Komsomolsk
Semenov
Sosnovka
Kimry
Teykovo
Kokhma
Shuya
Chkalovsk
MARI A.S.S.R.
Kukmor
Vyatskiye Polyany
Kalinin
Gorodets
Balakhna
Pravdinsk
56
Dubna
Pereslavl Zalesskiy
Nerl
Teza
Yuzha
Zavolzhye
Borisoglebskiy
Arsk
Konakovo
Ivankovskoye Vdkhr.
Yuryev-Polskiy
GORKIY (Gorki)
Cheboksary
Krasnogorskiy
Mamadysh
Novo-Zavidovskiy
Krasnozavodsk
Suzdal
Kovrov
Dzerzhinsk
Leninskaya Sloboda
Kozmodemyansk
Zelenodolsk
Kazan
Klin
Dmitrov
Aleksandrov
Vyazniki
Volodarsk
Kstovo
Marlinskiy Posad
Volzhsk
Yudino
Vysokovsk
Solnechnogorsk
Kolchugino
Gorokhovets
Gorbatov
Bogorodsk
Zagorsk
Vladimir
Lyskovo
Yadrin
Sura
Tsivilsk
TATAR A.S.S.R.
Chistopol
Volokolamsk
Zelenograd
Pushkino
Elektrogorsk
Sudogda
Krasnaya Gorbatka
Pavlovo
CHUVASH A.S.S.R.
Istra
Mytishchi
Pokrov
Sobinka
Shumerlya
Kanash
Khimki
Balashikha
Noginsk
Orekhovo-Zuyevo
Pyana
Sergach
Kamskoye Ustye
MOSKVA (Moscow)
Pavlovskiy-Posad
Gus-Khrustalnyy
Mukhtolovo
Kuybyshev
Bilyarsk
Elektrostal
Murom
Tesha
Arzamas
Poretskoye
Lyubertsy
Ramenskoye
Kurovskoye
Shatura
Kurlovskiy
Vyksa
Kulebaki
235
Gagino
Tetyushi
Mozhaysk
Odintsovo
Bronnitsy
Yegoryevsk
Oz. Velikoye
Melenki
Lukoyanov
Kirya
Buinsk
Naro Fominsk
Podolsk
Voskresensk
Tuma
Kuybyshevskoye Vdkhr.
Borovsk
Kolyberovo
Spas-Klepiki
Yelatma
Sarova
Pervomaysk
Ardatov
Alatyr
Nurlat
Obninsk
Stolbovaya
Kolomna
Alatyr
Maloyaroslavets
Mikhnevo
Kasimov
Moksha
Pochinki
Cherdakly
Medyn
Serpukhov
Stupino
Ozery
Solotcha
Temnikov
Ulyanovsk
Dimitrovgrad
54
Kashira
Zaraysk
Rybnoye
Kadom
Krasnoslobodsk
Romodanovo
Sernovodsk
Tarussa
Ryazan
Spassk-Ryazanskiy
MORDOVIAN A.S.S.R.
Saransk
Sura
Karsun
Sok
Kaluga
Aleksin
Yesnogorsk (Lupeta)
Oka
Sasovo
Venev
Shilovo
Sengiley
Mikhaylov
Kobylkino
Ruzayevka
Inza
Novodevichye
Komsomolskiy
Krasnyy Yar
Ageyevo
Suvorov
Tula
Novotulskiy
Shatsk
Bednodemyanovsk
Bazarnyy Syzgan
Barysh
Togliatti
375
Zhigulevsk
Kinel
Chekalin
Kosaya Gora
Dubna
Noyomoskovsk
Kimovsk
Supozhok
Shchekino
Dedilovo
Ukholovo
Spirinngushi
Lunino
KUYBYSHEV
Odoyevo
Uzlovaya
Donskoy
Pavelets
Skopin
Tsna
Nizhniy Lomov
Oktyabrsk
Novokuybyshevsk
Belev
Krapivna
Bogoroditsk
Sura
Syzran
Chapayevsk
Tovarkovskiy
Ryazhsk
Zametchino
Mokshan
Gorodishche
Plavsk
Bolkhov
293
Dankov
Chaplygin
Morshansk
Kamenka
Penza
Kuznetsk
Kashpirovka
Privolzhye
Mtsensk
Yefremov
Sosnovka
Sursk
351
Bolshaya Glushitsa
Oka
Lev Tolstoy
Belinskiy (Chembar)
Khoper
Orel
Novosil
Lebedyan
Michurinsk
Khvalynsk
Pestravka
Verkhovye
Kirsanov
Serdobsk
Khvatovka
Volga
Bol. Irgiz
52
Yelets
Tambov
Rasskazovo
Petrovsk
Bazarny Karabulak
Tereshka
Volsk
Balakovo
Pugachev
Livny
Lipetsk
Gryazi
Kotovsk
Rtishchevo
Maloarkhangelsk
Sosna
Zadonsk
Inzhavino
Kolpny
Usman
Mordovo
Uvarovo
Turki
Gornyy
Voronezh
Muchkapskiy
Arkadak
Atkarsk
Fatesh
Perlevka
Ramon
Ertil
Zherdevka
Marks
Kastornoye
Don
Vorona
Saratov
Engels
Yershov
Kamenka
Kursk
Shchigry
Semiluki
Khoper
Balanda
Privolzhskiy
Pushkino
Lgov
Khokholskiy
Voronezh
Balashov
Volgogradskoye Vdkhr.
Oboyan
Seim
Anna
Gribanovskiy
Arkhangelskoye
Samoylovka
Krasnoarmeysk
Krasnyy Kut
Orlov Gay
Pristen
Staryy Oskol
Borisoglebsk
Peski
276
Gubkin
Yelan-Kolenovskiy
Povorino
Novokhopersk
Yelan
Zhirnovsk
Kamenskiy
Piterka
Bobrov
Khrenovoye
Talovaya
Krasnyy Yar
Rovnoye
Novouzensk
Korotoyak
239
Buzuluk
Ostrogozhsk
Georgiu-Dezh
Buturlinovka
Uryupinsk
Kukvidze
358
Novatka
Korocha
Novyy Oskol
Kamenka
Novoannenskiy
Kotovo
Aleksandrov Gay
50
Belgorod
Oskol
Alekseyevka
Panfilovo
Medveditsa
Danilovka
Pallasovka
Shebekino
Volokonovka
Pavlovsk
Kalach
Khoper
Kamyshin
Nikolayevsk
Bol. Uzen
Sev. Donets
Valuyki
Mikhaylovka
Kaztalovka
Furmanovo
Volchansk
Pechenezhskoye Vdkhr.
Rossosh
Ust Buzulukskaya
Kaysatskoye
Mal. Uzen
Dergachi
Yevstratovskiy
Bykovo
Olshany
Kharkov
Boguchar
Kumylzhenskaya
Olkhovka
Frolovo
Lyubotin
Kupyansk
Kazanskaya
Dzhanybek
KAZAKH S.S.R.
Chuguyev
Kantemirovka
Don
Serafimovich
Ilovlya
Gottwald
Kupyansk-Uzlovoi
Veshenskaya
Elton
Sev. Donets
Balakleya
Svatovo
Chertkovo
Kletskiy (Kletskaya)
Ilovlya (Ilovlinskaya)
Melovoye
Dubovka
Izyum
Krasnyy Oskolskoye Vdkhr.
Kamenskiy
Chir
Starobelsk
Prishalnaya
Volzhskiy
Urda
Rubezhnoye
Millerovo
Volgograd (Stalingrad)
Krasnoslobodsk
Leninsk
Kapustin Yar
Privolzhskaya Vozvyshennost

SOVIET FEDERATIVE SOCIALIST REPUBLIC

36 38 40 42 46 48

Rovno
Korosten
Kiyevskoye Vdkhr.
Nezhin
Bakhmach
Sumy
Starry Oskol
Lvov
Zhitomir
KIYEV (Kiev)
Priluki
Belgorod
Ternopol
Berdichev
Belaya Tserkov
Kharkov
Khmelnitskiy
Vinnitsa
Kremenchugskoye Vdkhr.
Cherkassy
Poltava
Kupyansk
Ivano-Frankovsk (Stanislav)
Kemenets-Podolskiy
Uman
Kremenchug
Chernovtsy
Kirovograd
Dneprodzerzhinsk
Dnepropetrovsk
Pavlograd
Slavyansk
Kramatorsk
Artemovsk
Konstantinovka
Gorlovka
Yenakiyevo
Makeyevka
Donetsk (Stalino)
Beltsy
Pervomaysk
Krivoy Rog
Zaporozhye
Nikopol
Kishinev
Tiraspol
Bendery
Nikolayev
Kakhovskoye Vdkhr.
Melitopol
Zhdanov
Odessa
Kherson
Berdyansk
ROMANIA
Galati
Braila
Ismail
Karkinitskiy Zaliv
AZOVSKOYE MORE (Sea of Azov)
Dzhankoi
Krymskiy P.-ov. (Crimea)
Yevpatoriya
Kerch
Ploiești
BUCUREȘTI (Bucharest)
Simferopol
Feodosiya
Sevastopol
Yalta
Novorossiysk
Constanța
Ruse (Ruščuk)
BULGARIA
Varna
Burgas
B L A C K S E A
Kirklareli
Edirne
Karadeniz Boğazi (Bosporus)
Zonguldak
Samsun
İstanbul
Üsküdar
MARMARA DENIZI (Sea of Marmara)
İzmit
Adapazari
Bursa
Ankara
T U R K

Projection: Conical with two standard parallels

1 : 4 000 000

50 0 50 100 miles

50 0 50 100 150 km

Volgograd
(Stalingrad)
Rostov
Astrakhan
Krasnodar
Stavropol
Elista
(Stepnoi)
Tbilisi
Yerevan
BAKU
Makhachkala
Groznyy
Ordzhonikidze
Nalchik
Sukhumi
Batumi
Kutaisi
Kirovakan
Leninakan
Kirovabad
Sumgait
Derbent
Guryev
Kamyshin
Nikolayevsk
Volzhskiy
Krasnoslobodsk
Krasnoarmeysk
Voroshilovgrad
(Lugansk)
Kommunarsk
Kirovsk
Stakhanov
Bryanka
Krasnodon
Krasnyy Luch
Thorez
Rovenki
Snezhnoye
Gukovo
Novoshakhtinsk
Shakhty
Novocherkassk
Taganrog
Azov
Bataysk
Zernograd
Salsk
Proletarskaya
Tikhoretsk
Kropotkin
Armavir
Maykop
Nevinnomyssk
Cherkessk
Mineralnyye Vody
Pyatigorsk
Yessentuki
Kislovodsk
Mozdok
Prokhladnyy
Gudermes
Buynaksk
Kaspiysk
Kizlyar
Budennovsk
Zelenokumsk
(Vorontsovo-Aleksandrovskoye)
Svetlograd
(Petrovskoye)
Blagodarnoye
Tuapse
Sochi
Adler
Gagra
Ochamchire
Poti
Kobuleti
Rustavi
Gori
Tskhinvali
(Staliniri)
Zestafoni
Samtredia
Telavi
Mingechaur
Kars
Trabzon
Rize
Bayburt
Millerovo
Kamensk-Shakhtinskiy
Severodonetsk
Starobelsk
Rossosh
Pavlovsk
Kalach
Frolovo
Mikhaylovka
Novoannenskiy
Uryupinsk
Buturlinovka
Georgiu-Dezh
Ostrogozhsk
Korotoyak
Yevstratovskiy
Volgodonsk
Tsimlyansk
Kotelnikovo
Novouzensk
Krasnyy Kut
Volgogradskoye
Vdkhr.
Tsimlyanskoye
Vdkhr.
Veselovskoye
Vdkhr.
Mingechaurskoye
Vdkhr.
Oz. Manych-
Gudilo
Ergeni Vozyshennost
Privolzhskaya Vozyshennost
Prikaspiyskaya Nizmennost
K A L M Y K
A. S. S. R.
K A Z A K H
S. S. R.
CHECHENO-
INGUSH
A.S.S.R.
DAGESTAN
A.S.S.R.
KABARDINO-
BALKAR
A.S.S.R.
N. OSETIAN
A.S.S.R.
ABKHAZ
A.S.S.R.
ADZHAR
A.S.S.R.
G E O R G I A N
S. S. R.
A R M E N I A N
S. S. R.
A Z E R B A I J A N
S. S. R.
Bol'shoy Kavkaz
Malyy Kavkaz
C A S P I A N   S E A
P-ov. Mangyshlak
Mangyshlakskiy Zaliv
Fort Shevchenko
Shevchenko
Elbrus 5633
Kazbek 5047
Tebulos 4492
Bazar Dyuzi 4466
Aragats 4090
Volga
Don
Kuban
Terek
Kura
Ural
East from Greenwich
COPYRIGHT. GEORGE PHILIP & SON. LTD.

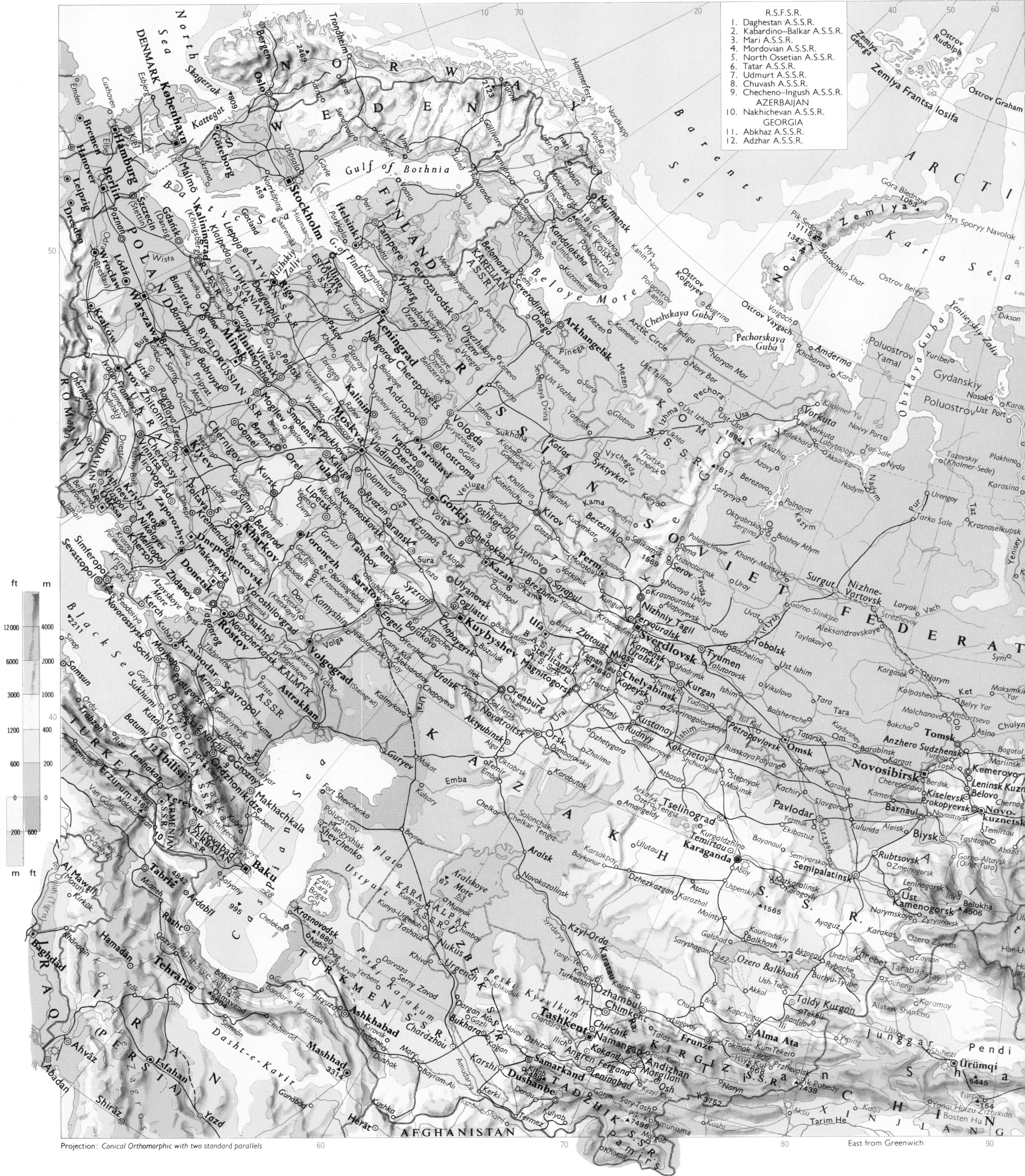
R.S.F.S.R.
1. Daghestan A.S.S.R.
2. Kabardino-Balkar A.S.S.R.
3. Mari A.S.S.R.
4. Mordovian A.S.S.R.
5. North Ossetian A.S.S.R.
6. Tatar A.S.S.R.
7. Udmurt A.S.S.R.
8. Chuvash A.S.S.R.
9. Checheno-Ingush A.S.S.R.
AZERBAIJAN
10. Nakhichevan A.S.S.R.
GEORGIA
11. Abkhaz A.S.S.R.
12. Adzhar A.S.S.R.
ft m
12000 4000
6000 2000
3000 1000
1200 400
600 200
0 0
200 600
m ft
Projection: Conical Orthomorphic with two standard parallels
East from Greenwich

1 : 16 000 000
100 0 100 200 300 400 500 miles
100 0 200 400 600 800 km
Mys Dezhneva (East C.)
St. Lawrence I. (U.S.A.)
Chukotskoye More
Chukotskiy Khrebet
Anadyrskiy Zaliv
Ostrov Vrangelya
East Siberian Sea
Ostrova Medvezhi
Ostrov Henrietta
Ostrov Jeannette
Ostrova Delong
Ostrov Bennett
Ostrov Zhokhova
Novosibirskiye Ostrova
Ostrov Faddeyevskiy
Ostrov Novaya Sibir
Ostrov Belkovskiy
Ostrov Kotelnyy
Ostrov Stolbovoy
Ostrov Malyy Lyakhovskiy
Ostrov Bolshoy Lyakhovskiy
Lyakhovskiye Ostrova
Proliv Dmitriya Lapteva
OCEAN
Laptev Sea
Ostrov Shmidt
Mys Arkticheskiy
Ostrov Komsomolets
Ostrov Pioner
Ostrov Oktyabrskoy Revolyutsii
Ostrov Bolshevik
Severnaya Zemlya
Proliv Vilskutskogo
Poluostrov Taymyr
Gory Byrranga
Oz. Taymyr
Ostrov Bolshoy Begichev
Nordvik
Tiksi
Verkhoyansk
Verkhoyanskiy Khrebet
Khrebet Cherskogo
Pobeda 3147
Srednekolymsk
Kolyma
Okhotsko Kolymskoye
Magadan
Gizhiga
Penzhinskaya Guba
Gizhiginskaya Guba
Zaliv Shelikhova
Koryakskiy Khrebet
Sredinnyy Khrebet
Poluostrov Kamchatka
Petropavlovsk-Kamchatskiy
Komandorskiye Ostrova
Bering Sea
Sea of Okhotsk
Okhotsk
Ayan
Khrebet Dzhugdzur
Sakhalin
Sakhalinskiy Zaliv
Ostrov Bolshoy Shantar
Nikolayevsk-na-Amure
Kurilskiye Ostrova
Yuzhno-Sakhalinsk
Sovetskaya Gavan
Komsomolsk
Khabarovsk
Sikhote Alin
Vladivostok
Nakhodka
Ussuriysk
Sea of JAPAN
Japan Sea
Hokkaido
Sapporo
Hakodate
Honshu
Niigata
Toyama
Kanazawa
YAKUTSK A.S.S.R.
SOCIALIST REPUBLIC
Yakutsk
Vilyuysk
Olekminsk
Aldan
Stanovoy Khrebet
Yablonovyy Khrebet
Chita
Ulan Ude
BURYAT A.S.S.R.
Irkutsk
Angarsk
Bratsk
Kirensk
Krasnoyarsk
Achinsk
Kansk
Norilsk
Igarka
Dudinka
Arctic Circle
Vostochnyy Sayan
Zapadnyy Sayan
TUVA A.S.S.R.
Kyzyl
Abakan
Minusinsk
Blagoveshchensk
Birobidzhan
Qiqihar
Harbin
Jilin
Changchun
Shenyang
Fushun
Anshan
Dalian
Yingkou
Dandong
Beijing
Hohhot
Baotou
Zhangjiakou
Hulun Nur
Da Hinggan Ling
Dongbei
GOBI
MONGOLIA
Ulaanbaatar (Ulan Bator)
Hentiyn Nuruu
Hangayn Nuruu
Hovsgol Nuur
Uvs Nuur
Edrengiyn Nuruu
NORTH KOREA
P'yongyang
SOUTH KOREA
Soul (Seoul)
Inch'on
Taegu
Pusan
Chongjin
Boundaries of U.S.S.R.
Boundaries of S.S.R.
Boundaries of A.S.S.R.

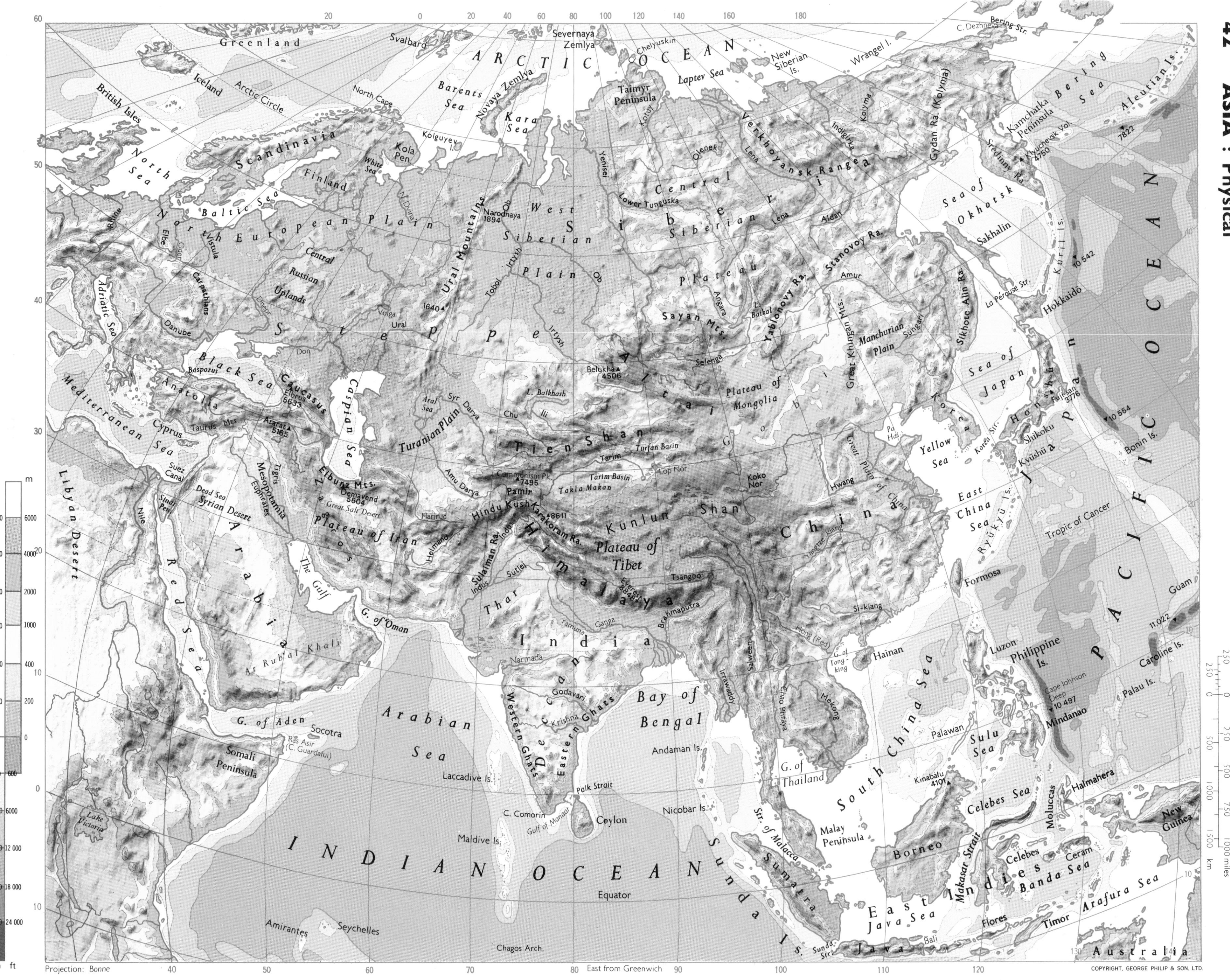
1 : 40 000 000
miles
km
Projection: Bonne
East from Greenwich
COPYRIGHT, GEORGE PHILIP & SON, LTD.
ARCTIC OCEAN
PACIFIC OCEAN
INDIAN OCEAN
Greenland
Svalbard
Severnaya Zemlya
Chelyuskin
Iceland
Arctic Circle
British Isles
North Cape
Barents Sea
Novaya Zemlya
Kara Sea
Taimyr Peninsula
Laptev Sea
New Siberian Is.
Wrangel I.
C. Dezhnev
Bering Str.
Bering Sea
Aleutian Is.
Kamchatka Peninsula
Sredinny Ra.
Klyuchevsk Vol. 4750
Gydan Ra. (Kolyma)
Kolyma
Indigirka
Verkhoyansk Range
Kolguyev I.
Kola Pen.
White Sea
Scandinavia
North Sea
Finland
Baltic Sea
North European Plain
Central Russian Uplands
Ural Mountains
Narodnaya 1894
West Siberian Plain
Central Siberian Plateau
Siberia
Lower Tunguska
Olenek
Yenisei
Lena
Aldan
Sea of Okhotsk
Sakhalin
Kuril Is.
Stanovoy Ra.
Yablonovy Ra.
Amur
Baikal
Angara
Sayan Mts.
Hokkaido
La Pérouse Str.
Sikhote Alin Ra.
Great Khingan Mts.
Manchurian Plain
Sungari
Rhine
Elbe
Oder
Vistula
Carpathians
Danube
Adriatic Sea
Dnepr
Volga
Ural
1640
Tobol
Irtysh
Ob
Steppe
Don
Black Sea
Bosporus
Caucasus
Elbrus 5633
Anatolia
Taurus Mts.
Ararat 5165
Cyprus
Mediterranean Sea
Caspian Sea
Aral Sea
Syr Darya
Turanian Plain
L. Balkhash
Chu
Ili
Belukha 4506
Altai
Selenga
Plateau of Mongolia
Gobi
Sea of Japan
Korea
Honshu
Fujiyama 3776
Japan
10 554
Bonin Is.
Shikoku
Kyushu
Korea Str.
Yellow Sea
Po Hai
Tien Shan
Tarim
Turfan Basin
Tarim Basin
Takla Makan
Lop Nor
Koko Nor
Hwang
Great Plain of China
Suez Canal
Dead Sea
Syrian Desert
Sinai Pen.
Libyan Desert
Nile
Mesopotamia
Tigris
Euphrates
Elburz Mts.
Demavend 5604
Great Salt Desert
Plateau of Iran
Zagros
Harirud
Helmand
Amu Darya
Communism Pk. 7495
Pamir
Hindu Kush
Karakoram Ra.
8611
Kunlun Shan
Plateau of Tibet
China
Yangtze Kiang
East China Sea
Ryukyu Is.
Tropic of Cancer
Formosa
Sulaiman Ra.
Indus
Sutlej
Himalaya
Everest 8848
Tsangpo
Brahmaputra
Si-kiang
Guam
11 022
Caroline Is.
The Gulf
Arabia
Red Sea
G. of Oman
Thar
Yamuna
Ganga
India
Hong (Red)
G. of Tong-king
Hainan
Luzon
Philippine Is.
Ar Rub' al Khali
Narmada
Godavari
Krishna
Deccan
Western Ghats
Eastern Ghats
Bay of Bengal
Irrawaddy
Salween
Chao Phraya
Mekong
South China Sea
Cape Johnson Deep 10 497
Mindanao
Palau Is.
G. of Aden
Socotra
Ras Asir (C. Guardafui)
Somali Peninsula
Arabian Sea
Andaman Is.
G. of Thailand
Palawan
Sulu Sea
Laccadive Is.
Polk Strait
Kinabalu 4101
Celebes Sea
Moluccas
Halmahera
C. Comorin
Gulf of Manaar
Ceylon
Nicobar Is.
Lake Victoria
Maldive Is.
Str. of Malacca
Malay Peninsula
Borneo
Makasar Strait
Celebes
Ceram
Banda Sea
New Guinea
East Indies
Sumatra
Sunda Is.
Equator
Java Sea
Flores
Timor
Arafura Sea
Amirantes
Seychelles
Chagos Arch.
Sunda Str.
Java
Bali
Australia

1 : 40 000 000

250 0 250 500 750 1000 miles

250 0 500 1000 1500 km

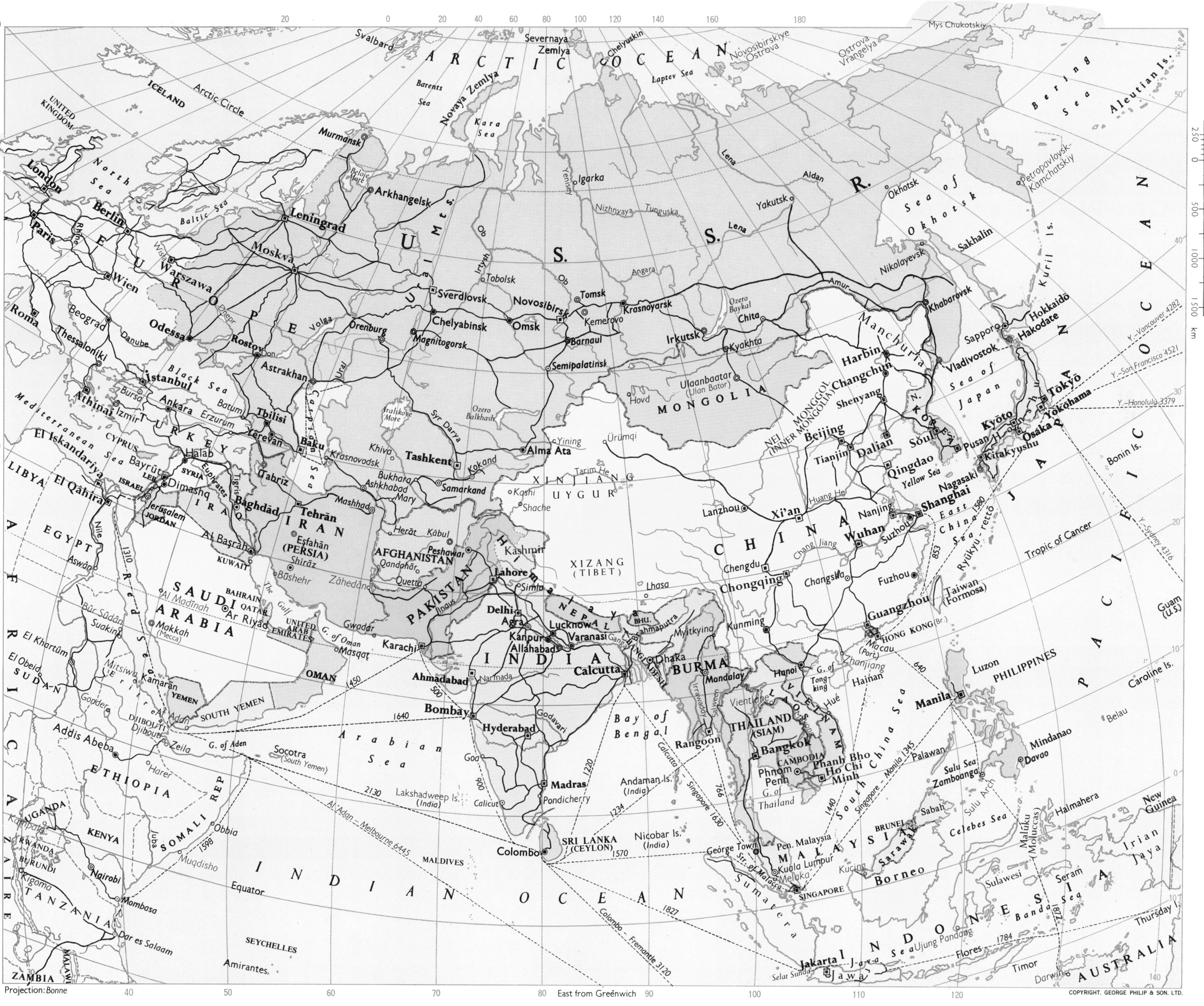
ARCTIC OCEAN
PACIFIC OCEAN
INDIAN OCEAN
U. S. S. R.
EUROPE
AFRICA
AUSTRALIA
CHINA
MONGOLIA
INDIA
IRAN (PERSIA)
AFGHANISTAN
PAKISTAN
SAUDI ARABIA
TURKEY
IRAQ
BURMA
THAILAND (SIAM)
INDONESIA
MALAYSIA
PHILIPPINES
JAPAN
KOREA
NEPAL
SRI LANKA (CEYLON)
OMAN
SOUTH YEMEN
YEMEN
ETHIOPIA
KENYA
TANZANIA
SOMALI REP
EGYPT
SUDAN
XIZANG (TIBET)
XINJIANG UYGUR
Manchuria
Arabian Sea
Bay of Bengal
Sea of Okhotsk
Sea of Japan
South China Sea
East China Sea
Bering Sea
Caspian Sea
Red Sea
Black Sea
Mediterranean Sea
Tropic of Cancer
Equator
Arctic Circle
Beijing
Shanghai
Tokyo
Moskva
Leningrad
Delhi
Calcutta
Bombay
Karachi
Tehrān
Baghdād
Manila
Bangkok
Rangoon
Jakarta
Singapore
Colombo
Madras
Hong Kong (Br.)
Istanbul
London
Paris
Berlin
Roma
Projection: Bonne
East from Greenwich
COPYRIGHT. GEORGE PHILIP & SON, LTD.

44 ISRAEL AND WEST JORDAN

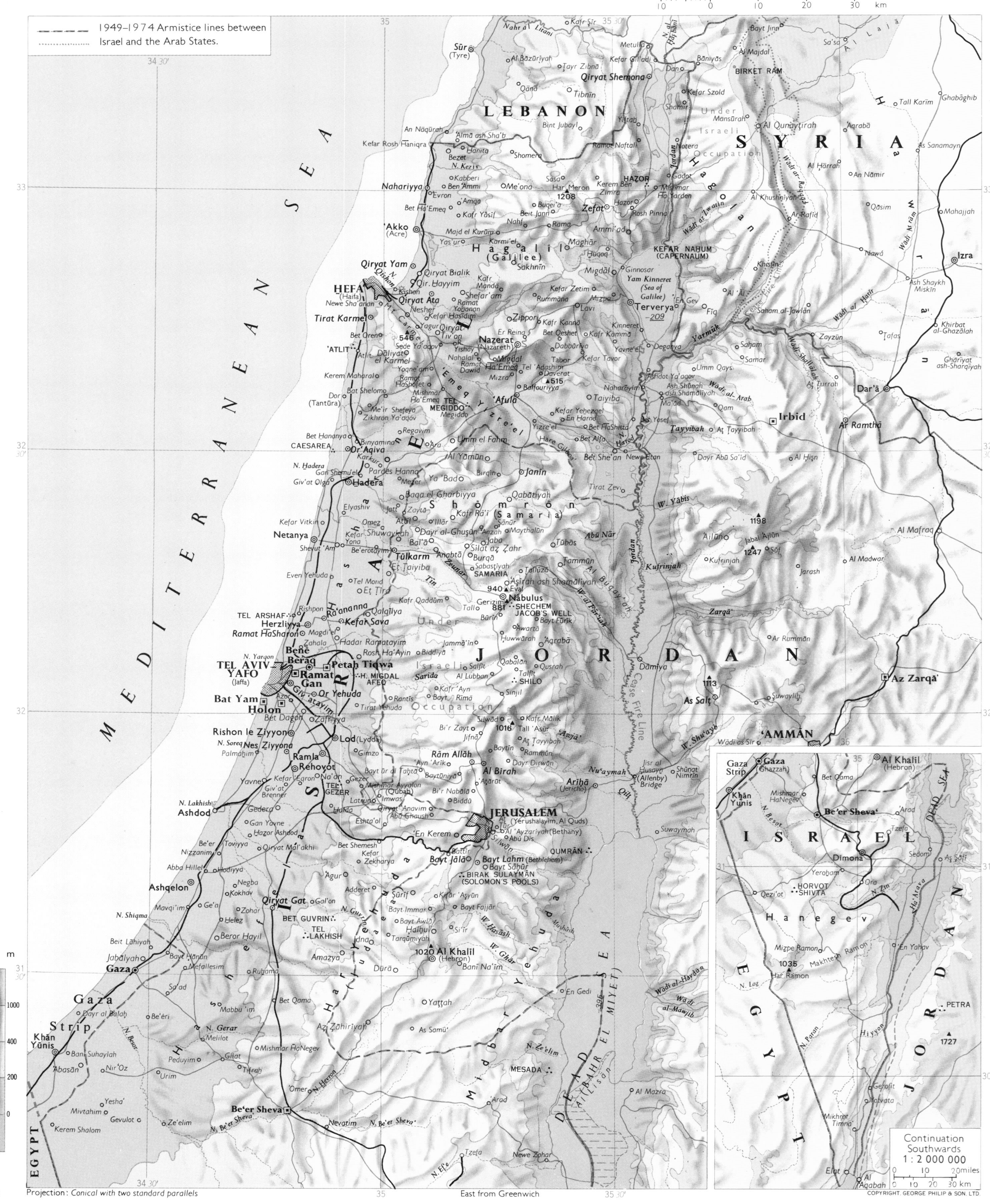

1 : 800 000
10 5 0 10 20 miles
10 0 10 20 30 km
1949–1974 Armistice lines between
Israel and the Arab States.
MEDITERRANEAN SEA
LEBANON
SYRIA
ISRAEL
JORDAN
EGYPT
Gaza Strip
Şūr (Tyre)
Qiryat Shemona
Metulla
Nahariyya
'Akko (Acre)
HEFA (Haifa)
Tirat Karmel
Ha galil (Galilee)
Zefat
Yam Kinneret (Sea of Galilee)
Teverya
Nazerat (Nazareth)
'Afula
Hadera
Netanya
Janin
Shomron (Samaria)
Tūlkarm
Nābulus
Herzliyya
TEL AVIV-YAFO (Jaffa)
Ramat Gan
Petah Tiqwa
Bat Yam
Holon
Rishon le Ziyyon
Lod (Lydda)
Ramla
Rehovot
Rām Allāh
Arīhā (Jericho)
Ashdod
JERUSALEM (Yerushalayim, Al Quds)
Bayt Lahm (Bethlehem)
Ashqelon
Qiryat Gat
Gaza
Khān Yūnis
Al Khalīl (Hebron)
Be'er Sheva'
MESADA
DEAD SEA
Irbid
Dar'ā
Az Zarqā'
As Salț
'AMMĀN
Under Israeli Occupation
Projection: Conical with two standard parallels
East from Greenwich
ft m
3000 1000
1200 400
600 200
0 0
200 600
m ft
Continuation Southwards
1 : 2 000 000
0 10 20 miles
0 10 20 30 km
Dimona
Hanegev
PETRA
Elat
Al 'Aqabah
COPYRIGHT, GEORGE PHILIP & SON, LTD.

1 : 12 000 000

100 0 100 200 300 400 miles

100 0 100 200 300 400 500 600 km

LEBANON
Bayrūt
SYRIA
Dimashq (Damascus)
IRAQ
Baghdād
ISRAEL
Tel Aviv-Yafo
Jerusalem
JORDAN
Amman
Dead Sea
Bādiyat ash Shām
Al Jazīrah (Mesopotamia)
Karbalā
Al Ḥillah
Ar Ruṭbah
Ṭurayf
Badanah
Būr Sa'īd
Ismā'īlīya
El Suweis (Suez)
Borujerd
Kāshān
Khvor
Dezfūl
Eṣfahān
Yazd
Dasht-e Lūt
AFGHANISTAN
IRAN (PERSIA)
Masjed Soleyman
Qomsheh
Ahvāz
Khorramshahr
Al Baṣrah
Ābādān
Kermān
Shīrāz
Kāzerūn
Neyrīz
Bam
Zābol
Zāhedān
Būshehr
Jahrom
KUWAIT
Al Kuwayt (Kuwait)
Faylakah
Būbiyān
Rafḥā
Al Jawf
An Nafūd
Ḥafar al Bāṭin
Tabūk
Qal'at al Akhḍar
Taymā'
Ḥā'il
Al Wajh
Madā'in Ṣāliḥ
Buraydah
'Unayzah
Az Zilfī
Al Majma'ah
Shaqrā'
Al Madīnah
Yanbu' al Baḥr
Ar Riyāḍ (Riyadh)
Duwādimī
SAUDI ARABIA
HIJAZ
NAJD
Ad Dammām
BAHRAIN
Al Manāmah
Al Hufūf
QATAR
Ad Dawḥah
Abū Ẓaby (Abu Dhabi)
Dubayy (Dubai)
Ash Shāriqah
UNITED ARAB EMIRATES
Abū Ẓaby (TRUCIAL STATES)
THE GULF
Bandar 'Abbās
Mīnāb
Jāsk
Gulf of Oman
Ṣuḥār
Masqaṭ (Muscat)
Ṣūr
Maṣīrah
Khalūf
OMAN
Rub 'al Khālī
Ẓufār
Mirbāṭ
Ṣalālah
Jazā'ir Khurīyā Muriyā
Tropic of Cancer
Mastūrah
Rābigh
Jiddah
Makkah (Mecca)
Aṭ Ṭā'if
Turabah
Al Līth
Al Qunfudhah
'ASĪR
Abhā
Jīzān
Jazā'ir Farasān
Ṣa'dah
Nakfa
Jabal Ṭuwayq
Tamrah
Al 'Ubaylah
YEMEN
Ṣanā'
Ma'rib
Al Ḥudaydah
Kamarān
Dhamār
Ibb
Ta'izz
Al Mukhā
Al 'Adan (Aden)
SOUTH YEMEN
Ḥaḍramawt
Shibām
Al Mukallā
Sayḥūt
Ghubbat al Qamar
Gulf of Aden
'Abd al Kūrī
Socotra (South Yemen)
Hadibu
RED SEA
EGYPT
Qena
Luxor
Isna
Idfu
Kôm Ombo
Aswân
Buheiret en Naser (Lake Nasser)
Es Sahrâ en Nûbîya
Wadi Halfa
Abri
Delgo
BAHR EL AHMAR
Bûr Sûdân (Port Sudan)
Suakin
Tokar
Kareima
Merowe
Atbara
Ed Dâmer
Shendî
Omdurmân
El Khartûm (Khartoum)
KASSALA
Kassala
SUDAN
Wad Medanî
GEZIRA
Sennâr
Kôstî
Er Roseires
BLUE NILE (AN NÎL EL AZRAQ)
Kodok
Malakâl
Nasir
JONGLEI
SHARQ EL ISTIWA'IYA
Jûba
Torit
Kapoeta
ERITREA
Asmera (Asmara)
Mitsiwa
Keren
Akordat
Aseb
Dahlak Kebir
Bab el Mandeb
DJIBOUTI
Djibouti
Tadjoura
ETHIOPIA
Addis Abeba (Addis Ababa)
Gonder
L. Tana
Dese (Dessye)
Debre Markos
Gimbi
Gore
Jima
Dire Dawa
Harer
Jijiga
Awash
L. Ziway
L. Shala
L. Abaya
L. Shamo
Chew Bahir (L. Stefanie)
Ogaden
Moyale
SOMALI REP.
Hargeisa
Berbera
Burao
Erigavo
Bosaso
Las Anod
Garoe
Eil
Obbia
Belet Uen
Bulo Burti
Muqdisho (Mogadishu)
Merca
Baidoa
Bardera
Kismayu
INDIAN OCEAN
Ras Asir (C. Guardafui)
UGANDA
L. Kyoga
KENYA
L. Turkana
Lodwar
Marsabit
Wajir
ZAIRE

ft m
12 000 4000
9000 3000
6000 2000
4500 1500
3000 1000
1200 400
600 200
0 0
200 600
2000 6000
4000 12 000
m ft

Projection: Sanson-Flamsteed's Sinusoidal

35 40 East from Greenwich 45 50

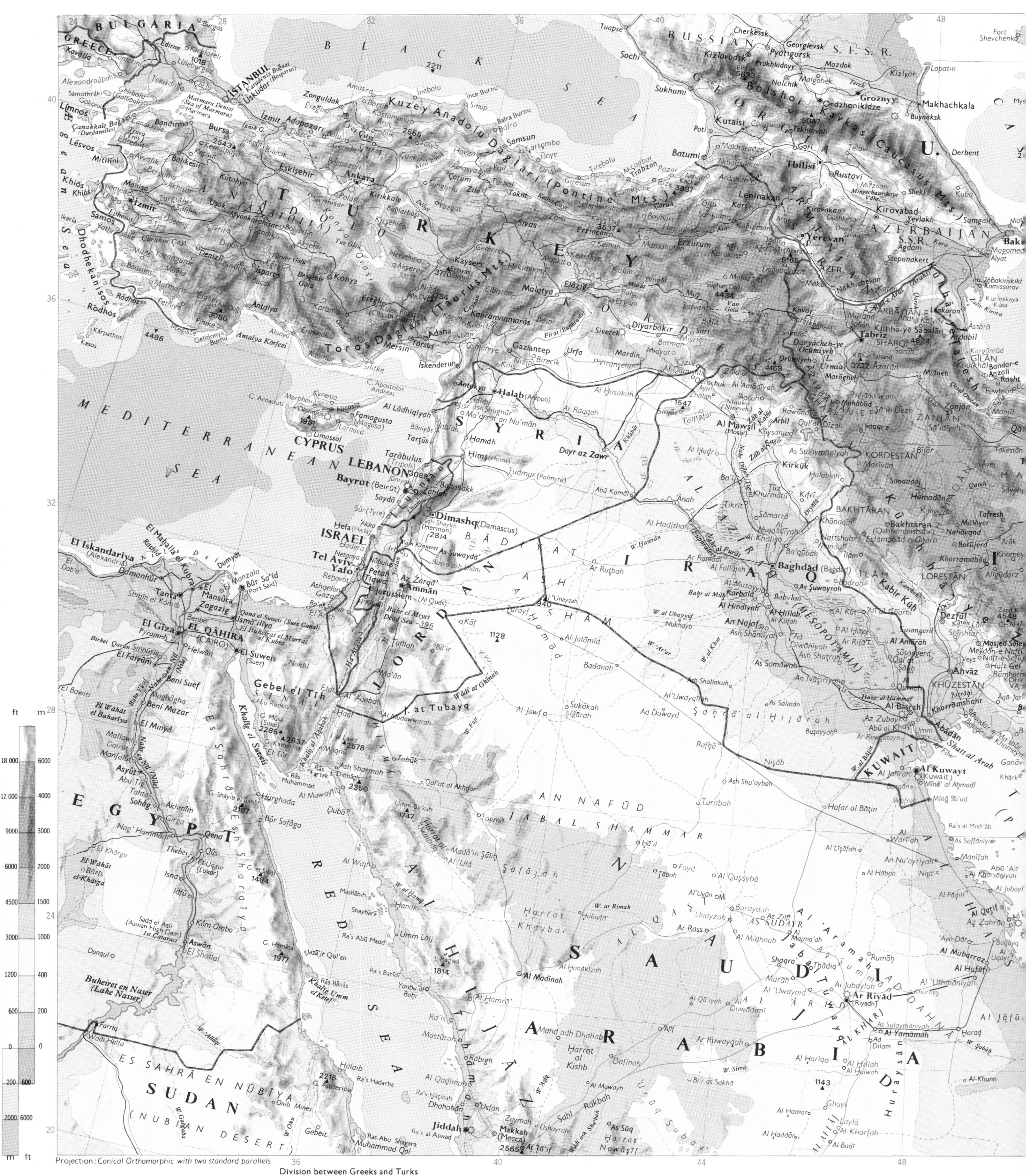
BULGARIA
GREECE
BLACK SEA
RUSSIAN S.F.S.R.
GEORGIA
ARMENIA
AZERBAIJAN S.S.R.
U.
TURKEY
Kuzey Anadolu Dağlari (Pontine Mts.)
Toros Dağlari (Taurus Mts.)
Bolshoi Kavkas (Caucasus Mts.)
ANADOLU (ANATOLIA)
MEDITERRANEAN SEA
CYPRUS
LEBANON
SYRIA
ISRAEL
JORDAN
IRAQ
KUWAIT
EGYPT
SUDAN
SAUDI ARABIA
RED SEA
AL HIJAZ
AN NAFŪD
JABAL SHAMMAR
BĀDIYAT ASH SHAM
ES SAHRÂ EN NÛBÎYA
(NUBIAN DESERT)
Es Sahrâ esh Sharqîya
SINAI
MESOPOTAMIA
AD DAHNA
İstanbul
Ankara
İzmir
Bursa
Konya
Adana
Kayseri
Samsun
Trabzon
Erzurum
Tbilisi
Yerevan
Batumi
Groznyy
Makhachkala
Baku
Tabrīz
Halab (Aleppo)
Hims (Homs)
Dimashq (Damascus)
Bayrūt (Beirūt)
Tarābulus (Tripoli)
Nicosia
Famagusta (Magosa)
Limassol
Tel Aviv-Yafo
Jerusalem (Al Quds)
'Ammān
Dead Sea -395
El Iskandarîya (Alexandria)
Bûr Sa'îd (Port Said)
El Qâhira (Cairo)
El Gîza
El Suweis (Suez)
Aswân
Qena
El Uqsur (Luxor)
Wadi Halfa
Baghdād
Al Mawsil (Mosul)
Kirkūk
Al Basrah
Al Kuwayt (Kuwait)
Ar Riyād (Riyadh)
Al Madīnah
Makkah (Mecca)
Jiddah
Al Hufūf
Dayr az Zawr
Tudmur (Palmyra)
Buheiret en Naser (Lake Nasser)
Gebel el Tîh
Bahr el Miyet
Shatt al Arab
ft m
18 000 6000
12 000 4000
9000 3000
6000 2000
4500 1500
3000 1000
1200 400
600 200
0 0
200 600
2000 6000
m ft

Projection: *Conical Orthomorphic with two standard parallels*

Division between Greeks and Turks in Cyprus; Turks to the North.

1 : 8 000 000

100 0 100 200 300 miles

100 0 100 200 300 400 500 km

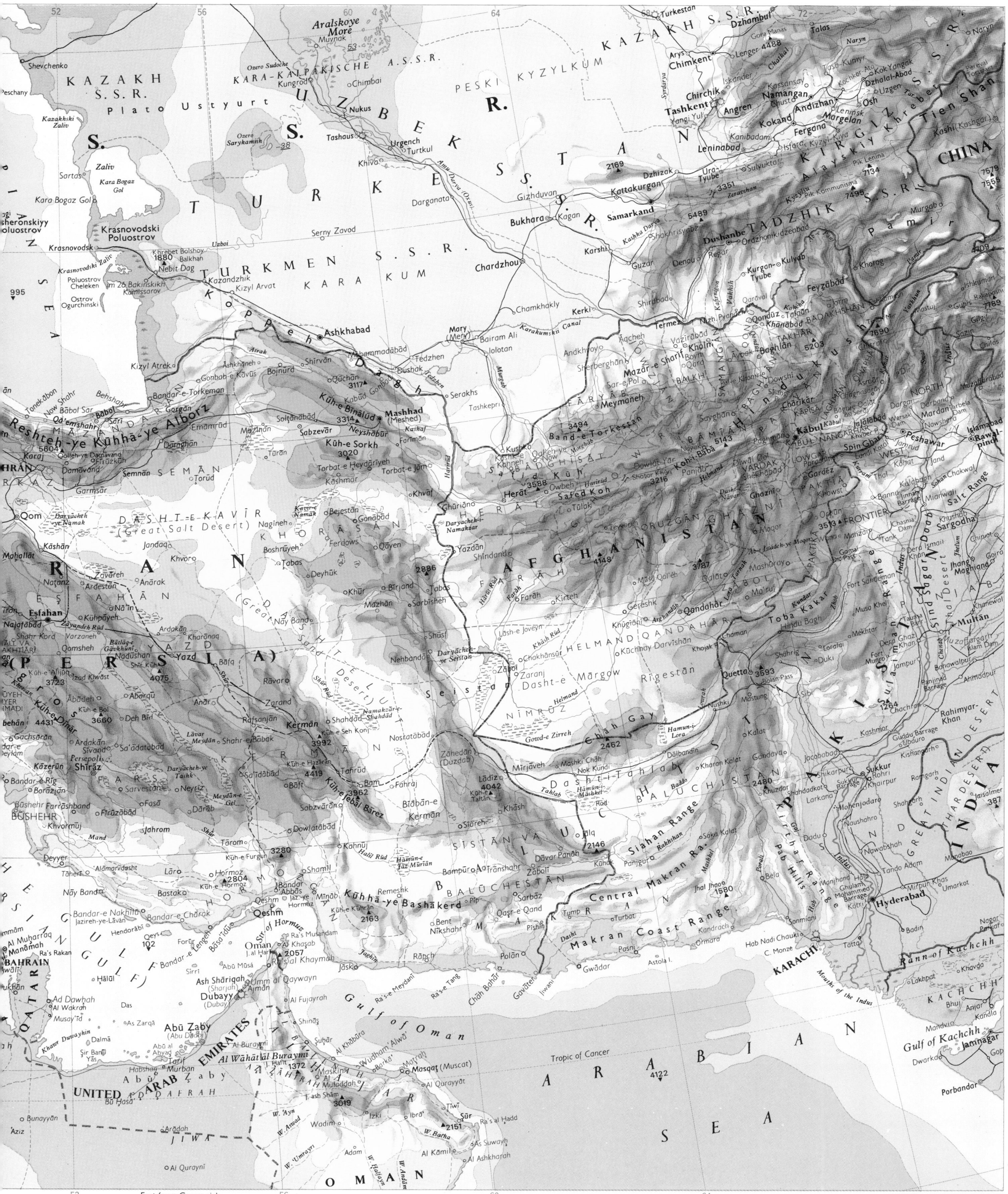

KAZAKH S.S.R.
Plato Ustyurt
Aralskoye More
KARA-KALPAKISCHE A.S.S.R.
PESKI KYZYLKUM
UZBEK S.S.R.
TURKMEN S.S.R.
KARA KUM
Kopet Dagh
Krasnovodski Poluostrov
Kara Bogaz Gol
CASPIAN SEA
Reshteh-ye Kuhha-ye Alborz
DASHT-E KAVIR (Great Salt Desert)
KHORASAN
IRAN (PERSIA)
DASHT-E LUT (Great Sand Desert)
Zagros
FARS
KERMAN
Kuh-e Binalud
Kuh-e Sorkh
Kuh-e Jebal Barez
Kuhha-ye Bashakerd
BALUCHESTAN
SISTAN VA BALUCHESTAN
Seistan
Dasht-e Margow
Rigestan
HELMAND
AFGHANISTAN
Hindu Kush
Band-e Torkestan
Safed Koh
Koh-i-Baba
TADZHIK S.S.R.
KIRGIZ S.S.R.
Pamir
Tien Shan
CHINA
PAKISTAN
BALUCHISTAN
Dasht-i-Tahlab
Chagai
Siahan Range
Central Makran Ra.
Makran Coast Range
Kirthar Range
Sulaiman Range
Pab Hills
Toba Kakar
Salt Range
Sind Sagar Doab
Thal Desert
SIND
THAR DESERT / GREAT INDIAN DESERT
INDIA
Rann of Kachchh
Gulf of Kachchh
KACHCHH
Mouths of the Indus
Gulf of Oman
ARABIAN SEA
Tropic of Cancer
Str. of Hormuz
THE GULF
BAHRAIN
QATAR
UNITED ARAB EMIRATES
OMAN
Al Hajar
Dhafrah
Jiwa
Tashkent
Samarkand
Bukhara
Dushanbe
Ashkhabad
Mashhad (Meshed)
Kabul
Peshawar
Islamabad
Rawalpindi
Quetta
Karachi
Hyderabad
Multan
Herat
Qandahar
Tehran
Esfahan
Shiraz
Kerman
Yazd
Zahedan (Duzdab)
Bandar Abbas
Masqat (Muscat)
Dubayy (Dubai)
Abu Zaby (Abu Dhabi)

52 56 60 64 East from Greenwich

40 36 32 28 24 20

AFGHANISTAN
PAKISTAN
BALUCHISTAN
N.W. FRONTIER PROVINCE
PUNJAB
SIND
RAJASTHAN
HARYANA
HIMACHAL PRADESH
JAMMU AND KASHMIR
GUJARAT
MADHYA PRADESH
THAR DESERT
(Great Indian Desert)
THAL DESERT
ARABIAN SEA
Gulf of Kachchh
Rann of Kachchh
Little Rann
Mouths of the Indus
Kabul
Qandahar
Ghazni
Quetta
Peshawar
Islamabad
Rawalpindi
Srinagar
Jammu
Lahore
Amritsar
Faisalabad
Multan
Bahawalpur
Sukkur
Hyderabad
KARACHI
Simla
Chandigarh
Ludhiana
DELHI
Meerut
Agra
Jaipur
Jodhpur
Bikaner
Ajmer
Udaipur
AHMADABAD
Vadodara
Rajkot
Jamnagar
Bhavnagar
Indore
Bhopal
Ujjain
Gwalior
Kota
Tropic of Cancer
Sulaiman Range
Salt Range
Kirthar Range
Pab Hills
Gir Hills
Toba Kakar
Indus
Sutlej
Chenab
Jhelum
Ravi
Beas
Luni
Narmada
Tapti
Mahi
ft
m
18 000
6000
12 000
4000
9000
3000
6000
2000
4500
1500
3000
1000
1200
400
600
200
0
0
200
600
2000
6000
m
ft
Projection: Conical with two standard parallels

1 : 4 800 000

50 0 50 100 150 miles

50 0 50 100 150 200 250 km

JAMMU AND KASHMIR
On same scale as Main Map
CHINESE REPUBLIC
Nganglong Kangri
Gangdisê Shan
Karakoram Range
Kunlun Shan
Deosai Mountains
Zaskar Mountains
JAMMU AND KASHMIR
N.W. FRONTIER PROVINCE
PUNJAB
HIMACHAL PRADESH
SODA PLAINS
XIZANG
NEPAL
SIKKIM
BHUTAN
ASSAM
BANGLADESH
UTTAR PRADESH
BIHAR
BENGAL
MADHYA PRADESH
Mahabharat Range
Siwalik Range
Kaimur Hills
Maikala Range
Garo Hills
Rajmahal Hills
Mouths of the Ganga
The Sandheads
Sundarbans
KANPUR
Lucknow
Allahabad
Varanasi
Patna
CALCUTTA
Katmandu
Srinagar
Rawalpindi
Islamabad
Jammu
Dhaka
Jabalpur
Ranchi
East from Greenwich

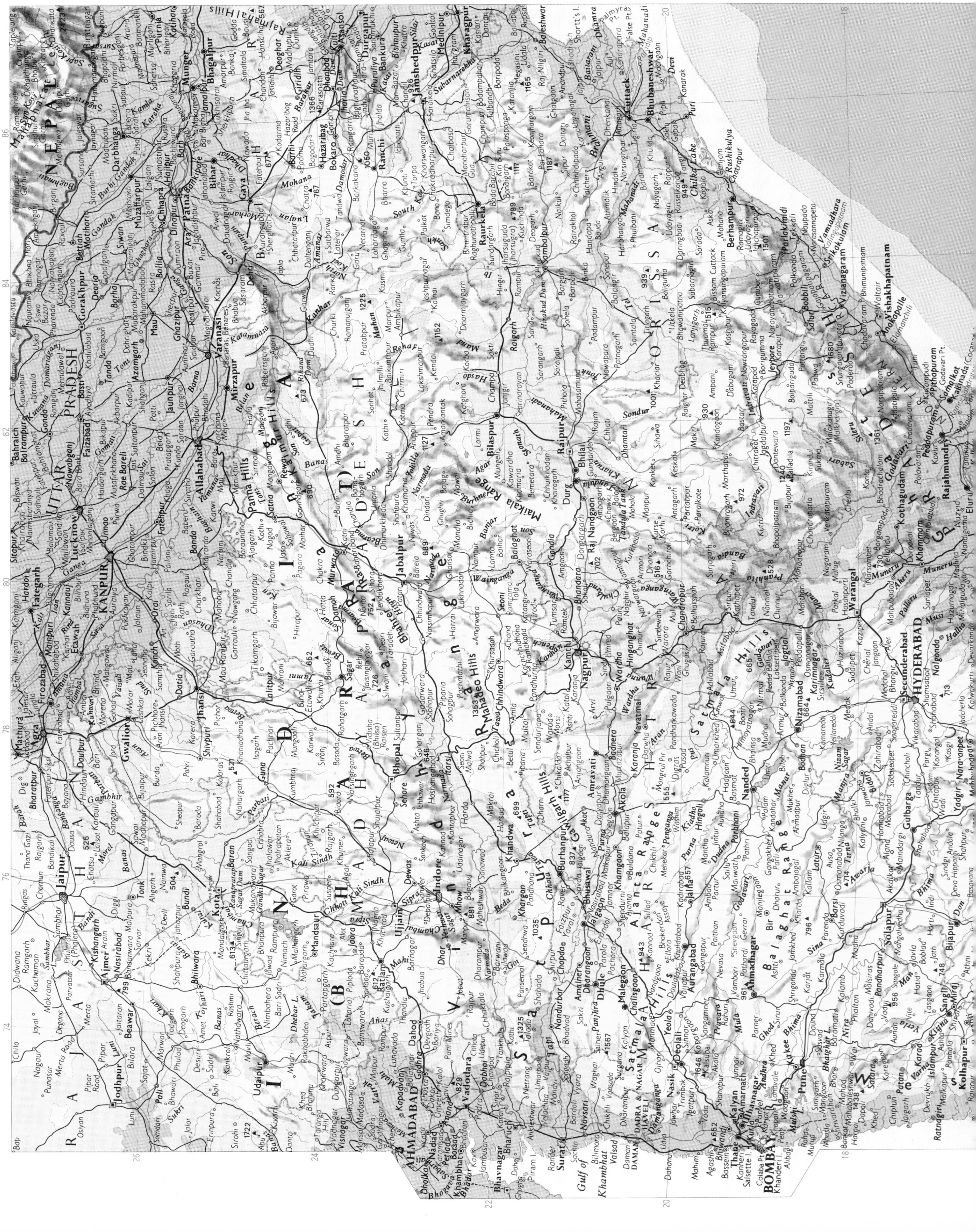
NEPAL
UTTAR PRADESH
MADHYA PRADESH
RAJASTHAN
ORISSA
Lucknow
Kanpur
Allahabad
Varanasi
Patna
Jabalpur
Nagpur
Raipur
Bhopal
Indore
Ujjain
Jaipur
Ajmer
Jodhpur
Udaipur
Ahmadabad
Vadodara
Surat
Bombay
Pune
Nasik
Aurangabad
Hyderabad
Secunderabad
Warangal
Cuttack
Bhubaneshwar
Puri
Vishakhapatnam
Rajahmundry
Agra
Gwalior
Jhansi
Ranchi
Jamshedpur
Gulf of Khambhat
Satpura Range
Vindhya Range
Ajanta Range
Mahadeo Hills
Maikala Range
Chilka Lake

1 : 4 800 000

50 0 50 100 150 miles

50 0 50 100 150 200 250 km

BAY OF BENGAL

Coromandel Coast

ARABIAN SEA

Malabar Coast

Gulf of Mannar (Manaar)

Palk Strait

Palk Bay

SRI LANKA (CEYLON)

TAMIL NADU

KARNATAKA

ANDHRA PRADESH

GOA

MADRAS

BANGALORE

Mysore

Mangalore

Calicut (Kozhikode)

Cochin

Trivandrum

C. Comorin

Pondicherry (Puduchcheri)

Colombo

Kandy

Jaffna

Trincomalee

Galle

Dondra Head

Adam's Bridge

Pearl Banks

Elikalpeni Bank

Androth I.

Kalpeni I.

East from 80 Greenwich

Projection: Conical with two standard parallels

m 3000 2000 1500 1000 400 200 0

ft 9000 6000 4500 3000 1200 600 0

0 200 600 2000 6000 4000 12 000 m ft

BANGLADESH, NORTH EASTERN INDIA AND BURMA

1 : 4 800 000

50 0 50 100 150 miles

50 0 50 100 150 200 250 km

ft m

18 000 6000

12 000 4000

9000 3000

6000 2000

4500 1500

3000 1000

1200 400

600 200

0 0

200 600

2000 6000

m ft

Projection: Conical with two standard parallels

East from Greenwich

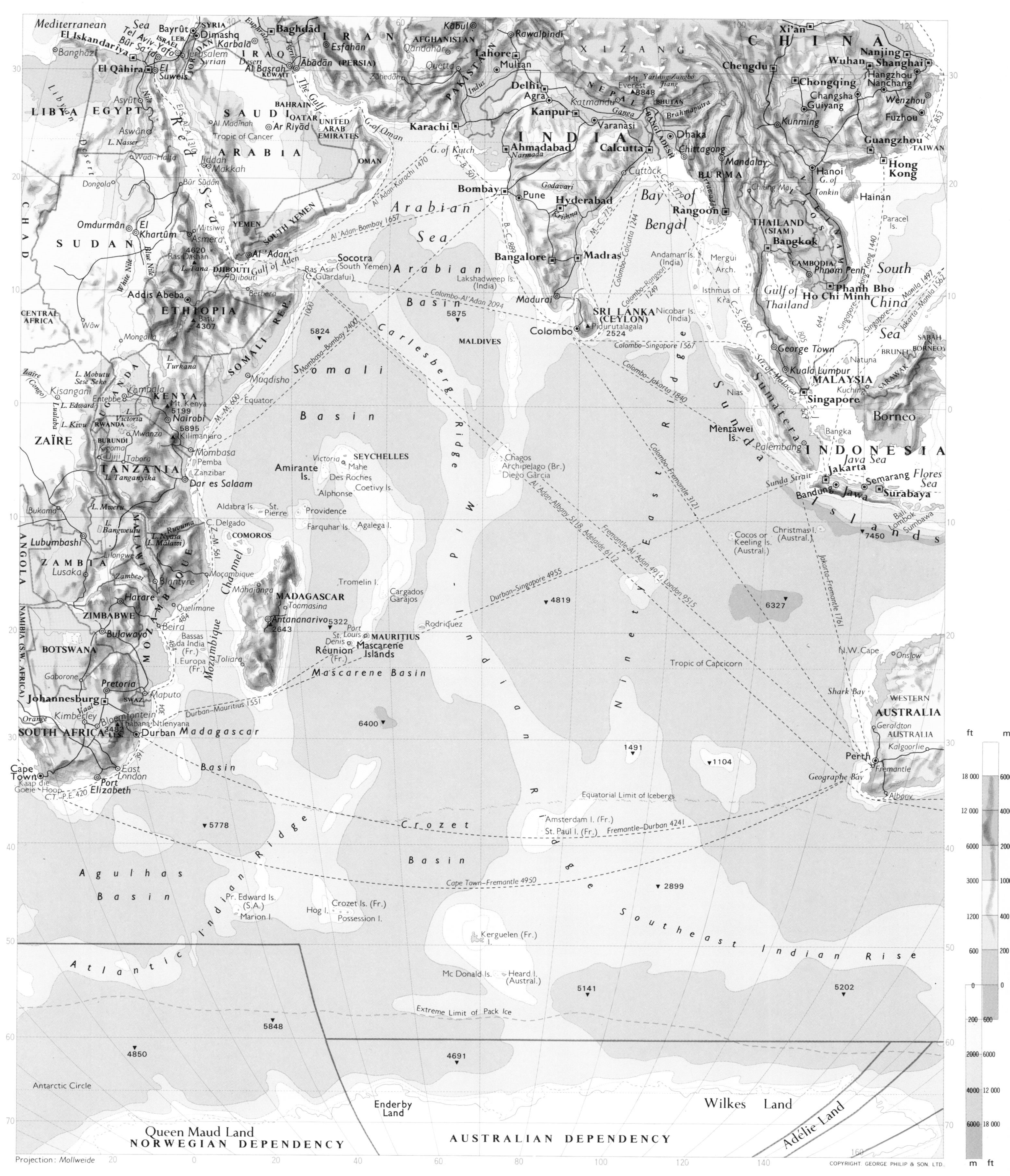
Mediterranean Sea
El Iskandarîya
Bûr Sa'îd
Tel Aviv-Yafo
Bayrût
SYRIA
LEB.
ISRAEL
Dimashq
Jerusalem
JORDAN
Karbalā
Baghdād
IRAN
Esfahān
AFGHANISTAN
Kābul
Rawalpindi
Qandahār
Lahore
Multan
Quetta
Zāhedān
IRAQ
Al Başrah
KUWAIT
Ābādān (PERSIA)
Desert
Syrian
Banghāzī
El Qâhira
El Suweis
Libyan Desert
LIBYA
EGYPT
Asyût
Nile
Aswân
L. Nasser
Wadi Halfa
SAUDI ARABIA
Al Madīnah
Ar Riyāḍ
Tropic of Cancer
Jiddah
Makkah
BAHRAIN
QATAR
UNITED ARAB EMIRATES
The Gulf
G. of Oman
OMAN
Karachi
PAKISTAN
Indus
XIZANG
Delhi
Agra
NEPAL
Mt. Everest 8848
Yarlung Zangbo Jiang
BHUTAN
Katmandu
Ganga
Brahmaputra
Kanpur
Varanasi
BANGLADESH
Dhaka
Chittagong
INDIA
Ahmadabad
Narmada
Calcutta
G. of Kutch
Cuttack
Bombay
Pune
Godavari
Hyderabad
Krishna
Bay of Bengal
Rangoon
Irrawaddy
BURMA
Mandalay
Bangalore
Madras
Madurai
SRI LANKA (CEYLON)
Colombo
Pidurutalagala 2524
CHINA
Xi'an
Chengdu
Chongqing
Wuhan
Nanjing
Shanghai
Hangzhou
Nanchang
Changsha
Guiyang
Wenzhou
Fuzhou
Kunming
Guangzhou
TAIWAN
Hong Kong
Hanoi
G. of Tonkin
Hainan
Paracel Is.
VIETNAM
LAOS
Chiang Mai
THAILAND (SIAM)
Bangkok
CAMBODIA
Phnom Penh
Phanh Bho Ho Chi Minh
Gulf of Thailand
South China Sea
Isthmus of Kra
Mergui Arch.
Andaman Is. (India)
Nicobar Is. (India)
George Town
Kuala Lumpur
MALAYSIA
Singapore
Natuna
BRUNEI
SABAH (N. BORNEO)
SARAWAK
Kuching
Borneo
Str. of Malacca
Sumatera
Nias
Mentawei Is.
Bangka
Palembang
INDONESIA
Java Sea
Jakarta
Semarang
Flores Sea
Surabaya
Bandung
Jawa
Sunda Strait
Sunda Islands
Bali
Lombok
Sumbawa
7450
Christmas I. (Austral.)
Cocos or Keeling Is. (Austral.)
CHAD
SUDAN
Dongola
Omdurmân
El Khartûm
Blue Nile
White Nile
Bûr Sûdân
Red Sea
Mitsiwa
Asmera
4620 Ras Dashan
L. Tana
YEMEN
SOUTH YEMEN
Al 'Adan
Gulf of Aden
DJIBOUTI
Djibouti
Berbera
Socotra (South Yemen)
Ras Asir (Guardafui)
Addis Abeba
ETHIOPIA
Batu 4307
SOMALI REP.
CENTRAL AFRICA
Wāw
Mongalla
L. Turkana
UGANDA
L. Mobutu Sese Seko
Zaïre (Congo)
Kisangani
L. Edward
Entebbe
Kampala
KENYA
Mt. Kenya 5199
Nairobi
Muqdisho
Equator
L. Kivu
RWANDA
L. Victoria
Mwanza
BURUNDI
Kigoma
Ujiji
Tabora
Kilimanjaro 5895
ZAÏRE
Lualaba
Mombasa
Pemba
Zanzibar
TANZANIA
L. Tanganyika
Dar es Salaam
Bukama
L. Mweru
L. Bangweulu
MALAWI
Rovuma
L. Nyasa (L. Malawi)
C. Delgado
Lubumbashi
ZAMBIA
Lilongwe
Lusaka
ANGOLA
Zambezi
MOZAMBIQUE
Moçambique
Blantyre
Harare
Quelimane
ZIMBABWE
Beira
Bulawayo
BOTSWANA
NAMIBIA (S.W. AFRICA)
Gaborone
Pretoria
Johannesburg
SWAZI.
Maputo
Orange
Vaal
Kimberley
Bloemfontein
Thabana Ntlenyana 3482
LES.
SOUTH AFRICA
Durban
Cape Town
Kaap die Goeie Hoop
East London
Port Elizabeth
COMOROS
Mozambique Channel
Mahajanga
MADAGASCAR
Toamasina
Antananarivo
2643
Toliara
Bassas da India (Fr.)
I. Europa (Fr.)
Aldabra Is.
St. Pierre
Providence
Farquhar Is.
Agalega I.
Amirante Is.
Alphonse
Victoria
SEYCHELLES
Mahe
Des Roches
Coetivy Is.
Tromelin I.
Cargados Garajos
Rodriquez
5322
Port St. Louis
Denis
MAURITIUS
Réunion (Fr.)
Mascarene Islands
Mascarene Basin
Arabian Sea
Arabian Basin
Lakshadweep Is. (India)
5875
5824
MALDIVES
Somali Basin
Carlesberg Ridge
Chagos Archipelago (Br.)
Diego Garcia
Mid-Indian Ridge
Ninety East Ridge
4819
6327
Tropic of Capricorn
N.W. Cape
Onslow
Shark Bay
WESTERN AUSTRALIA
Geraldton
Kalgoorlie
Perth
Fremantle
Geographe Bay
Albany
6400
Madagascar Basin
1491
1104
Equatorial Limit of Icebergs
Amsterdam I. (Fr.)
St. Paul I. (Fr.)
Crozet Basin
5778
Agulhas Basin
Atlantic Indian Ridge
Pr. Edward Is. (S.A.)
Marion I.
Hog I.
Crozet Is. (Fr.)
Possession I.
2899
Kerguelen (Fr.)
Southeast Indian Rise
Mc Donald Is.
Heard I. (Austral.)
5141
5202
Extreme Limit of Pack Ice
5848
4850
4691
Antarctic Circle
Enderby Land
Wilkes Land
Adélie Land
Queen Maud Land
NORWEGIAN DEPENDENCY
AUSTRALIAN DEPENDENCY
Al 'Adan-Karachi 1470
Al 'Adan-Bombay 1657
K.-B. 501
B.-C. 889
M.-C. 775
C.-R. 775
Colombo-Calcutta 1244
Colombo-Rangoon 1249
Colombo-Al 'Adan 2094
Colombo-Singapore 1567
Colombo-Jakarta 1840
Colombo-Fremantle 3121
C.-S. 1650
Hong Kong 1440
Manila 1497
Jakarta-Manila 1562
H.-S. 853
Mombasa-Bombay 2400
M.-M. 600
Z.-M. 561
Durban-Singapore 4955
Durban-Mauritius 1551
Al 'Adan-Albany 5118, Adelaide 6112
Fremantle-Al 'Adan 4914, London 9515
Jakarta-Fremantle 1761
Fremantle-Durban 4241
Cape Town-Fremantle 4950
C.T.-P.E. 420
ft m
18 000 6000
12 000 4000
6000 2000
3000 1000
1200 400
600 200
0 0
200 600
2000 6000
4000 12 000
6000 18 000
m ft

Projection: Mollweide

CHINA
YUNNAN
GUANGXI ZHANGZU ZIZHIQU AUTONOMOUS REGION
GUANGDONG
BURMA
SHAN STATE
KAYAH
BAC PHAN (TONKIN)
LAOS
VIETNAM
ANNAM
THAILAND (SIAM)
CAMBODIA
Gulf of Tonkin
Hainan
Gulf of Martaban
Leizhou Bandao
Tanen Tong Dan
Dawna Range
Khorat
Cao Nguyen Khorat
Phnom Dangrek
Chao Phraya Lowlands
Central Highlands
Thiu Khao Phetchabun
Tonle Sap (Great Lake)
Mandalay
Rangoon
Moulmein
Chiang Mai
Vientiane
Luang Prabang
HANOI
Haiphong
Hue
Da Nang (Tourane)
BANGKOK (Krung Thep)
Thon Buri
Nakhon Ratchasima (Khorat)
Ubon Ratchathani
Battambang
Mekong
Red River Delta

1 : 4 800 000

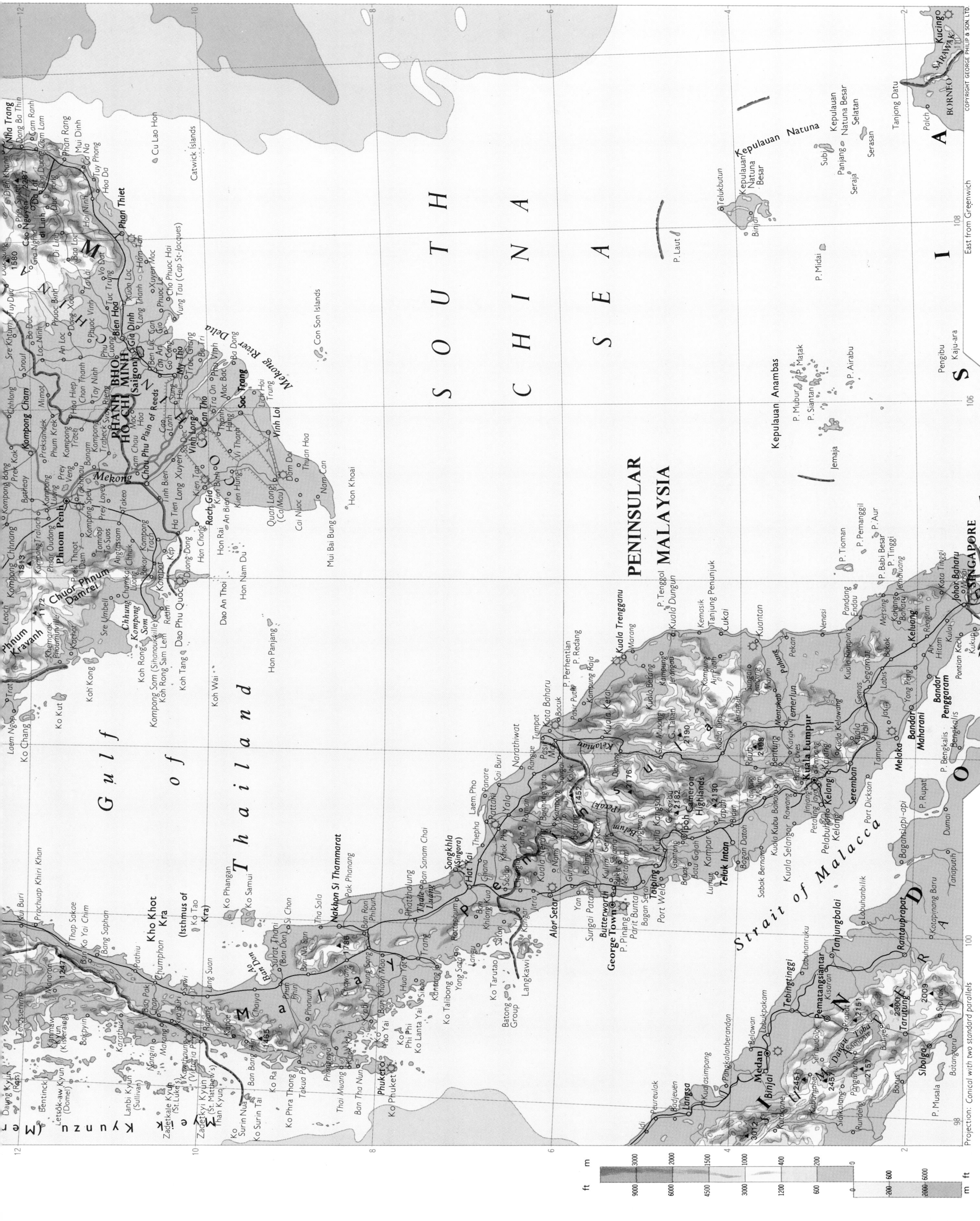

50 0 50 100 150 miles

50 0 50 100 150 200 250 km

SOUTH CHINA SEA

Gulf of Thailand

Strait of Malacca

PENINSULAR MALAYSIA

INDONESIA

Kepulauan Natuna

Kepulauan Anambas

Mekong River Delta

Mekong

Plain of Reeds

Chuor Phnum Damrei

Phnum Kravanh

Kho Khot Kra (Isthmus of Kra)

Cameron Highlands

PHANH BHO HO CHI MINH (Saigon)

Phnom Penh

Kompong Cham

Kompong Som (Sihanoukville)

Kampot

Phu Quoc

Rach Gia

Can Tho

My Tho

Vinh Long

Soc Trang

Vinh Loi

Quan Long (Ca Mau)

Phan Thiet

Phan Rang

Nha Trang

Bien Hoa

Vung Tau (Cap St-Jacques)

Con Son Islands

Catwick Islands

Cu Lao Hon

Hon Khoai

Ko Chang

Ko Kut

Koh Kong

Ko Samui

Ko Phangan

Ko Tao

Surat Thani (Ban Don)

Nakhon Si Thammarat

Songkhla (Singora)

Hat Yai

Pattani

Yala

Narathiwat

Phuket

Ko Phuket

Krabi

Trang

Satun

Langkawi

Alor Setar

George Town

P. Pinang

Butterworth

Taiping

Ipoh

Teluk Intan

Kuala Lumpur

Kelang

Seremban

Port Dickson

Melaka

Kota Baharu

Kuala Trengganu

Kuantan

Mersing

Kluang

Johor Baharu

SINGAPORE

Tanjungpinang

P. Bintan

P. Tioman

Medan

Binjai

Tebingtinggi

Pematangsiantar

Tanjungbalai

Rantauprapat

Sibolga

Tarutung

Langsa

Dumai

P. Rupat

P. Bengkalis

Kucing

SARAWAK

BORNEO

P. Laut

P. Midai

Kyunzu (Mergui Archipelago)

Ko Surin Nua

Ko Surin Tai

Ko Phra Thong

Chumphon

Prachuap Khiri Khan

Projection: Conical with two standard parallels

East from Greenwich

ft m

9000 3000

6000 2000

4500 1500

3000 1000

1200 400

600 200

0 0

200 600

2000 6000

m ft

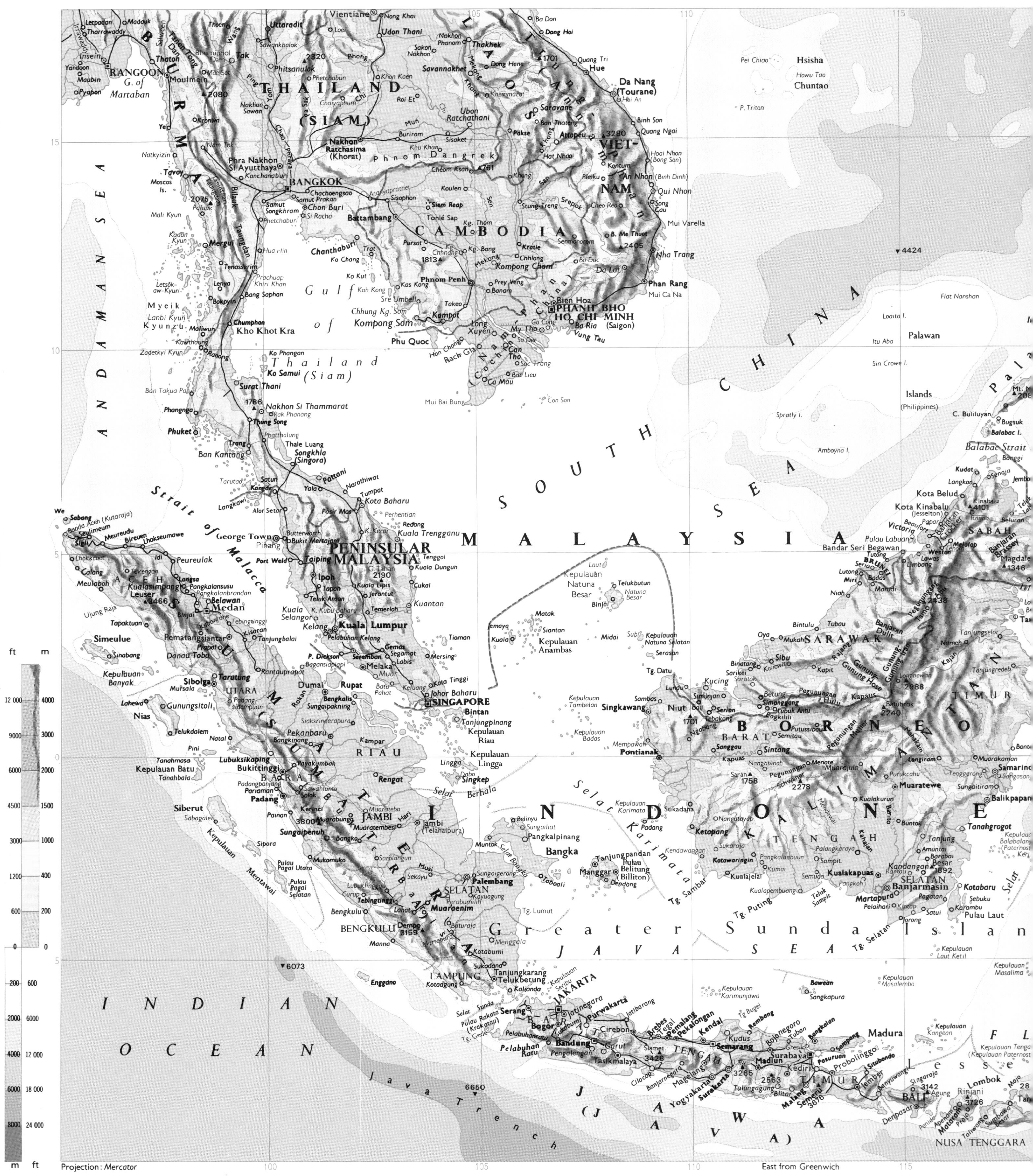

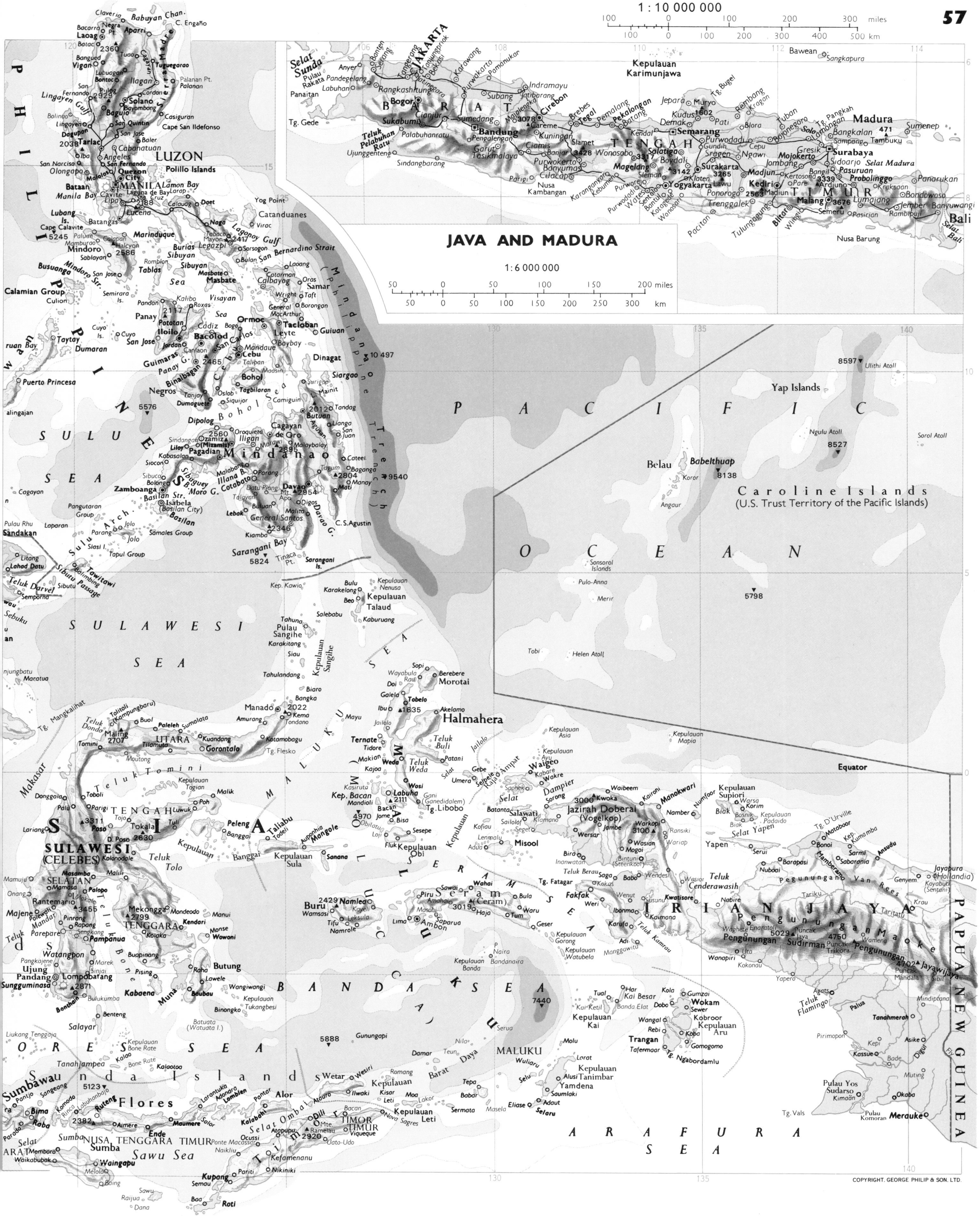

1 : 10 000 000

100 0 100 200 300 miles

100 0 100 200 300 400 500 km

JAVA AND MADURA

1 : 6 000 000

50 0 50 100 150 200 miles

50 0 50 100 150 200 250 300 km

Selat Sunda
JAKARTA
Kepulauan Karimunjawa
Bawean
BARAT
TENGAH
TIMUR
Madura
Selat Madura
Bali
Bandung
Semarang
Surabaya
Yogyakarta
Surakarta
Malang
Cirebon
Bogor
Nusa Kambangan
Nusa Barung

PHILIPPINES
LUZON
MANILA
Mindoro
Panay
Negros
Cebu
Bohol
Leyte
Samar
Mindanao
Sibuyan Sea
Visayan Sea
Bohol Sea
Mindanao Trench (Philippine Trench)
San Bernardino Strait
Sulu Arch.
SULU SEA
SULAWESI SEA
Kepulauan Talaud
Kepulauan Sangihe
MALUKU SEA
Morotai
Halmahera
Yap Islands
Belau
Babelthuap
Caroline Islands
(U.S. Trust Territory of the Pacific Islands)
PACIFIC OCEAN
Equator
SULAWESI (CELEBES)
UTARA
TENGAH
SELATAN
TENGGARA
Teluk Tomini
Teluk Tolo
Teluk Bone
Kepulauan Banggai
Kepulauan Sula
Buru
Seram (Ceram)
Ambon
Seram Sea
BANDA SEA
MALUKU
Kepulauan Kai
Kepulauan Aru
Kepulauan Tanimbar
Yamdena
IRIAN JAYA
Jazirah Doberai (Vogelkop)
Teluk Cenderawasih
Pegunungan Maoke
Puncak Jaya
PAPUA NEW GUINEA
Jayapura (Hollandia)
Merauke
Pulau Yos Sudarso
ARAFURA SEA
FLORES SEA
Sumbawa
Flores
Nusa Tenggara
Sumba
NUSA TENGGARA TIMUR
Sawu Sea
Timor
TIMOR TIMUR
Dili
Kupang
Roti
Wetar
Alor
Timor Sea

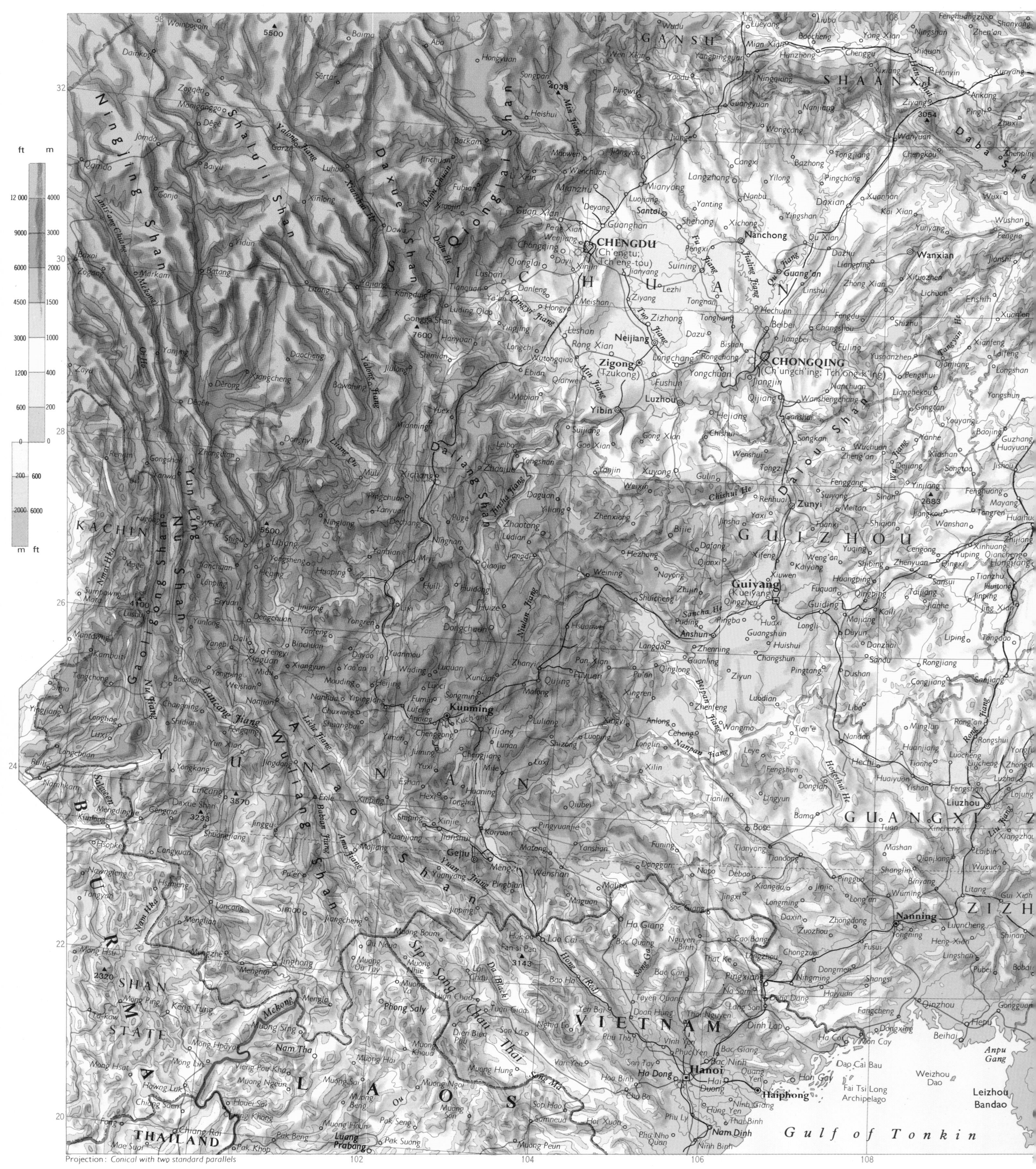
CHENGDU
CHONGQING
Kunming
Guiyang
Nanning
Hanoi
Haiphong
SICHUAN
YUNNAN
GUIZHOU
GUANGXI
VIETNAM
LAOS
THAILAND
BURMA
Gulf of Tonkin
Projection: Conical with two standard parallels

1 : 4 800 000

50 0 50 100 150 miles
50 0 50 100 150 200 250 km

HENAN
ANHUI
JIANGSU
HUBEI
HUNAN
JIANGXI
ZHEJIANG
FUJIAN
GUANGDONG
TAIWAN (FORMOSA)
SOUTH CHINA SEA
Formosa Strait
Luzon Strait
Tropic of Cancer
SHANGHAI (Changhai)
NANJING (Nanking; Nanching)
WUHAN (Wou-han)
Hankou
Changsha
Nanchang
Hangzhou (Hangchou; Hangchow)
Fuzhou (Foochow; Fuchou)
Xiamen (Hsiamen; Amoy)
Shantou (Swatow)
GUANGZHOU (Kuangchou; Canton)
HONG KONG (U.K.)
Kowloon
Macau (Macao) (Port.)
TAIBEI (T'aipei)
Jilong
Gaoxiong (Kaohsiung)
Taizhong (T'aichung)
Tainan
Ningbo (Ningpo)
Wenzhou (Wenchow)
Quanzhou (Ch'uanchou)
Zhangzhou
Suzhou (Suchou)
Wuxi (Wuhsi)
Changzhou (Ch'angchou)
Zhenjiang (Chenchiang)
Hefei
Huainan
Bengbu
Nanyang
Xinyang
Xiangfan
Yichang (Ich'ang)
Changde
Zhuzhou
Xiangtan
Hengyang
Shaoyang
Guilin
Wuzhou
Zhanjiang
Shaoguan
Ganzhou
Jingdezhen
Jiujiang
Anqing
Wuhu
Nantong
Dabie Shan
Wuyi Shan
Jiuling Shan
Mufu Shan
Chang Jiang (Yangtze)
Poyang Hu
Dongting Hu
Chongming Dao
Zhoushan Dao
Hainan
Leizhou Wan
Tungsha Tao
Dangan Liedao
Honghai Wan
Hangzhou Wan
Xinghua Wan
Lan Yu
Huoshao Dao
3997
3931
2393
2164
2120
1810
1725
1703
1629
1834
112
114
116
118
120
122
32
30
28
26
24
22
20

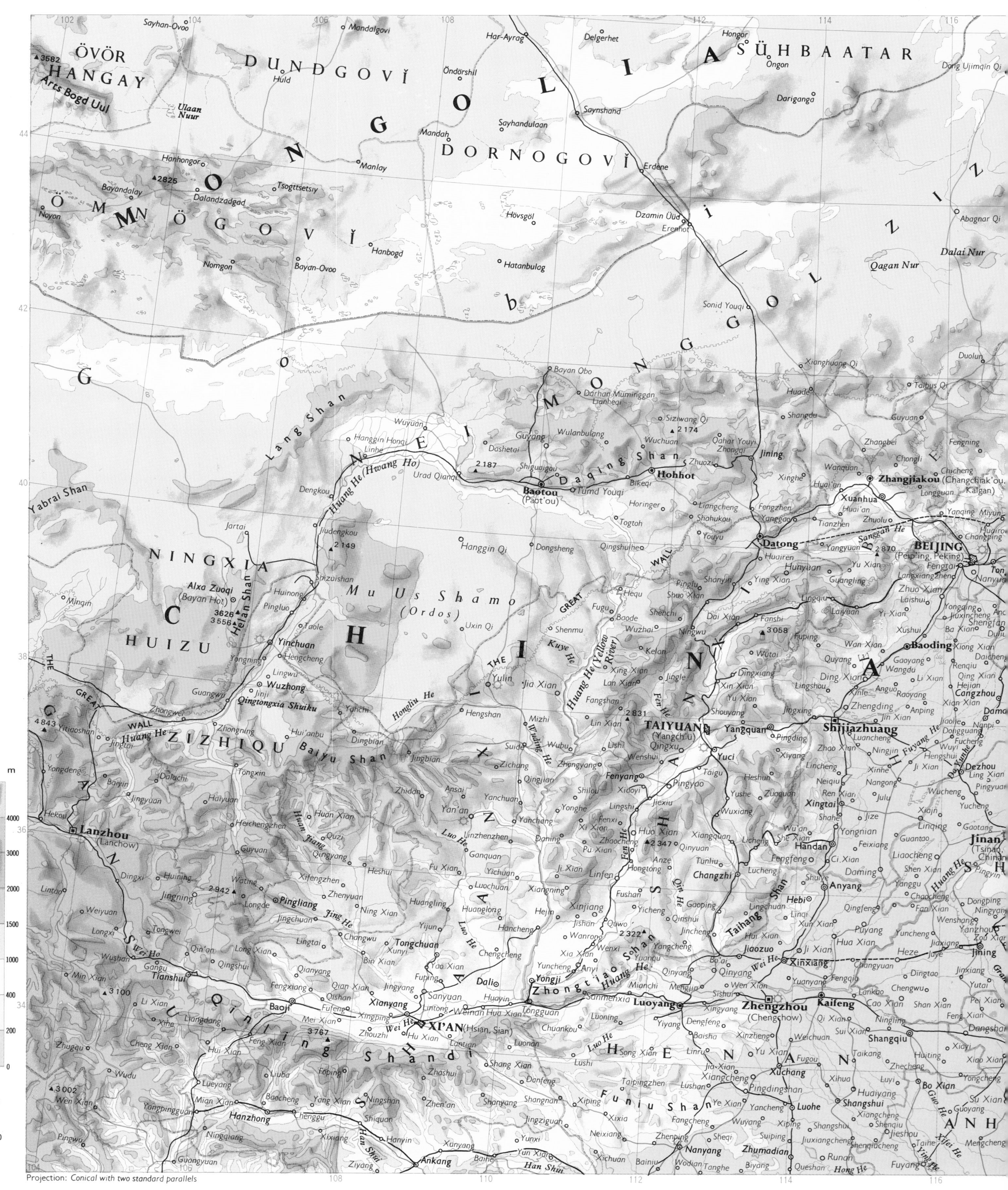
MONGOLIA
ÖVÖR HANGAY
DUNDGOVĬ
DORNOGOVĬ
ÖMNÖGOVĬ
SÜHBAATAR
Arts Bogd Uul
Ulaan Nuur
Sayhan-Ovoo
Mandalgovi
Har-Ayrag
Delgerhet
Hongor
Ongon
Huld
Öndörshil
Dariganga
Dong Ujimqin Qi
Saynshand
Sayhandulaan
Mandah
Manlay
Hanhongor
Erdene
Bayandalay
Tsogttsetsiy
Dalandzadgad
Noyon
Hövsgöl
Dzamin Üüd
Erenhot
Abagnar Qi
Hanbogd
Nomgon
Bayan-Ovoo
Hatanbulag
Dalai Nur
Qagan Nur
Gobi
NEI MONGGOL ZIZHIQU
Sonid Youqi
Xianghuang Qi
Duolun
Huade
Taibus Qi
Bayan Obo
Darhan Muminggan Lianheqi
Siziwang Qi
Shangdu
Guyuan
Lang Shan
Wuyuan
Hanggin Houqi
Linhe
Dashetai
Guyang
Wulanbulang
Wuchuan
Qahar Youyi Zhongqi
Zhangbei
Fengning
Chongli
Daqing Shan
Hohhot
Zhuozi
Jining
Xinghe
Wanquan
Zhangjiakou (Changchiak'ou, Kalgan)
Chicheng
Urad Qianqi
Shiguaigou
Baotou (Paot'ou)
Tumd Youqi
Bikeqi
Huang He (Hwang Ho)
Dengkou
Yabrai Shan
Horinger
Liangcheng
Fengzhen
Xuanhua
Huai'an
Longguan
Yanqing
Miyun
Togtoh
Shahukou
Yanggao
Tianzhen
Zhuolu
Sanggan He
Jartai
Jiudengkou
Hanggin Qi
Dongsheng
Qingshuihe
Youyu
Datong
Yangyuan
BEIJING (Pei-ching, Peking)
Fengtai
NINGXIA HUIZU ZIZHIQU
Mu Us Shamo (Ordos)
Huairen
Hunyuan
Yu Xian
Guangling
Shizuishan
Huinong
Pingluo
Alxa Zuoqi (Bayan Hot)
Helan Shan
Mingin
Hequ
Pinglu
Shuo Xian
Shanyin
Ying Xian
Lingqiu
Laiyuan
Zhuo Xian
Yongqing
Fugu
Baode
Shenchi
Wuzhai
Dai Xian
Fanshi
Xushui
Ba Xian
Uxin Qi
Taole
Yinchuan
Shenmu
Ningwu
Fuping
Wan Xian
Baoding
Yongning
Hengcheng
Kelan
Wutai
Kuye He
Huang He (Yellow River)
Quyang
Gaoyang
Wangdu
Lingwu
Wuzhong
Yulin
Jia Xian
Xing Xian
Dingxiang
Ding Xian
Guangwu
Jinji
Qingtongxia Shuiku
Lan Xian
Jingle
Xin Xian
Hejian
Cangzhou
Zhongwei
Yanchi
Hongliu He
Hengshan
Fangshan
Yu Xian
Lingshou
Anguo
Raoyang
Mizhi
Shouyang
Zhengding
Jin Xian
Anping
GREAT WALL
Yitiaoshan
Huang He
Zhongning
Hui'anbu
Lin Xian
TAIYUAN (Yangch'ü)
Yangquan
Shijiazhuang
Jingtai
Dingbian
Wuding He
Wubu
Lishi
Qingxu
Pingding
Luancheng
Baiyu Shan
Suide
Yuci
Zhao Xian
Ningjin
Fuyang He
Yongdeng
Jingbian
Zichang
Zhongyang
Wenshui
Xiyang
Lincheng
Xinhe
Ji Xian
Dezhou
Tongxin
Baiyin
Jingyuan
Haiyuan
Dalachi
Ansai
Qingjian
Fenyang
Pingyao
Taigu
Heshun
Neiqiu
Nangong
Zhidan
Yanchuan
Shilou
Xiaoyi
Jiexiu
Yushe
Zuoquan
Ren Xian
Xingtai
Wucheng
Hekou
Lanzhou (Lanchow)
Huan Xian
Yan'an
Yanchang
Yonghe
Lingshi
Wuxiang
Shahe
Jize
Yongnian
Feixiang
Guantao
Linqing
Jinan (Tsinan)
Herchengzhen
Huan Jiang
Quzi
Linzhenzhen
Luo He
Daning
Fenxi
Xi Xian
Huo Xian
Zhaocheng
Fen He
Xiangyuan
Qinyuan
Wu'an
She Xian
Handan
Ci Xian
Liaocheng
Qingyang
Guyuan
Ganquan
Pu Xian
Tunliu
Lucheng
Changzhi
Fengfeng
Daming
Shen Xian
Anyang
Dingxi
Huining
Heshui
Fu Xian
Yichuan
Ji Xian
Anze
Hongtong
Linfen
Zhongtiao Shan
Taihang Shan
Lintao
Jingning
Wating
Xifengzhen
Zhenyuan
Luochuan
Xiangning
Fushan
Linzhou
Shulin
Hebi
Yanggu
Chaocheng
Weiyuan
Longde
Pingliang
Ning Xian
Huangling
Huanglong
Xinjiang
Jishan
Yicheng
Qin He
Gaoping
Lingchuan
Linqi
Qingfeng
Fan Xian
Dongping
Ningyang
Jingchuan
Jing He
Yijun
Hancheng
Hejin
Qinshui
Jincheng
Xun Xian
Puyang
Wenshang
Longxi
Tongwei
Changwu
Lingtai
Tongchuan
Xunyi
Chengcheng
Wanrong
Wenxi
Huixian
Hua Xian
Yuncheng
Juancheng
Yanzhou
Zou Xian
Wushan
Wei He
Qin'an
Long Xian
Qingshui
Bin Xian
Yao Xian
Pucheng
Xia Xian
Yuncheng
Anyi
Jiaozuo
Ji Xian
Xinxiang
Heze
Juye
Jining
Gangu
Tianshui
Qianyang
Fengxiang
Qian Xian
Qishan
Jingyang
Fuping
Sanyuan
Dali
Yongji
Huang He
Qinyang
Wen Xian
Changyuan
Dingtao
Jinxiang
Min Xian
Li Xian
Xihe
Liangdang
Baoji
Fufeng
Mei Xian
Xianyang
Xingping
Lintong
Weinan
Hua Xian
Huayin
Tongguan
Sanmenxia
Mianchi
Mengjin
Luoyang
Zhengzhou (Chengchow)
Kaifeng
Lankao
Chengwu
Cao Xian
Shan Xian
Yutai
Pei Xian
XI'AN (Hsian, Sian)
Zhouzhi
Hu Xian
Lantian
Luonan
Chuankou
Luoning
Yiyang
Xingyang
Dengfeng
Qi Xian
Ningling
Feng Xian
Dangshan
Zhugqu
Cheng Xian
Feng Xian
Qinling Shandi
Shang Xian
Baisha
Xinzheng
Weichuan
Sui Xian
Shangqiu
Hui Xian
Luo He
Song Xian
Ruzhou
Yu Xian
Fugou
Taikang
Huiting
Xiayi
Wudu
Liuba
Foping
Zhashui
Lushi
Jia Xian
Xuchang
Xihua
Zhecheng
Luyi
Lueyang
Danfeng
Taipingzhen
Xiangcheng
Lushan
Pingdingshan
Huaiyang
Bo Xian
Yongcheng
Wen Xian
Mian Xian
Baocheng
Yang Xian
Ningshan
Zhen'an
Shanyang
Shangnan
Xiping
Funiu Shan
Ye Xian
Yancheng
Luohe
Shangshui
Guoyang
Yangpingguan
Hanzhong
Chenggu
Shiquan
Jingziguan
Xixia
Fangcheng
Wuyang
Xiping
Xiangcheng
Shenqiu
Jieshou
Pingwu
Ningqiang
Xixiang
Han Shui
Hanyin
Xunyang
Yunxi
Neixiang
Zhenping
Nanyang
Sheqi
Suiping
Zhumadian
Jiuxiangcheng
Shenqiucheng
Taihe
Mengcheng
Guangyuan
Ankang
Baihe
Yun Xian
Han Shui
Xichuan
Bainiu
Wodian
Tanghe
Biyang
Queshan
Runan
Hong He
Fuyang
Ziyang
HENAN
SHANXI
SHAANXI
HEBEI
GANSU
CHINA
ANHUI
3582
2825
2174
2187
2149
3626
3556
3058
2870
2831
4843
2942
2347
2322
3100
3767
3002
102
104
106
108
110
112
114
116
44
42
40
38
36
34
ft
m
12 000
9000
6000
4500
3000
1200
600
0
200
2000
4000
3000
2000
1500
1000
400
200
0
600
6000
m
ft

Projection: *Conical with two standard parallels*

1 : 4 800 000

50 0 50 100 150 miles

50 0 50 100 150 200 km

HARBIN (Haerhpin)
HEILONGJIANG
JILIN
LIAONING
Changchun
Jilin (Kirin, Chilin)
Shenyang (Mukden)
Fushun
Anshan
Benxi
Liaoyang
Jinzhou
Dandong
Dalian (Lüda)
Lüshun
Tianjin (Tientsin, T'ienching)
Tangshan
Qinhuangdao
Zibo
Weifang
Qingdao (Ch'ingtao)
Yantai
Weihai
Lianyungang (Hsinhaihlen)
Xuzhou (Hsuchow, Suchow)
Bengbu
Huai'an
Qingjiang
Chifeng
Fuxin
Shuangliao
Siping
Tongliao
Tao'an
Baicheng
Mudanjiang
Jixi
Vladivostok
Ussuriysk (Voroshilov)
U.S.S.R.
Yanji
Tumen
Dunhua
Tonghua
Changbai Shan
Paektu-san
Zhangguangcai Ling
Manchuria
Liaodong Bandao
Liaodong Wan
Bo Hai (Gulf of Chihli)
Laizhou Wan
Shandong Bandao
Haizhou Wan
Jiaozhou Wan
Korea Bay
HUANG HAI (Yellow Sea)
SEA OF JAPAN
Tongjosŏn Man
Korea Strait
Tsushima-kaikyō
Tsushima
Iki
JAPAN
Sasebo
Nagasaki
Karatsu
Imari
Ōmura
Isahaya
Kuchinotsu
Nakadōri-jima
Fukue-jima
Izuhara
NORTH KOREA
SOUTH KOREA
P'yŏngyang
Sinŭiju
Ch'ŏngjin
Hamhŭng
Hŭngnam
Wŏnsan
Kimch'aek
Kaesŏng
Haeju
Nampo
SŎUL (Seoul)
Inch'ŏn
Yŏngdŭngpo
Suwŏn
Ch'unch'ŏn
Kangnŭng
Wŏnju
Ch'ŏngju
Taejŏn
Chŏnju
Kunsan
Kwangju
Mokp'o
Yŏsu
Chinju
Masan
Chinhae
PUSAN
Taegu
P'ohang
Ulsan
Kyŏngju
Andong
Ullŭng-do
Cheju-do
Cheju
Sŏgwi-po
Cease Fire Line
Paengnyong-do
Yalu Jiang
Tumen
Songhua Jiang
Liao He
Xiliao He
Huang He
Willow Wall

1 : 16 000 000

100 0 100 200 300 400 miles

100 0 100 200 300 400 500 600 km

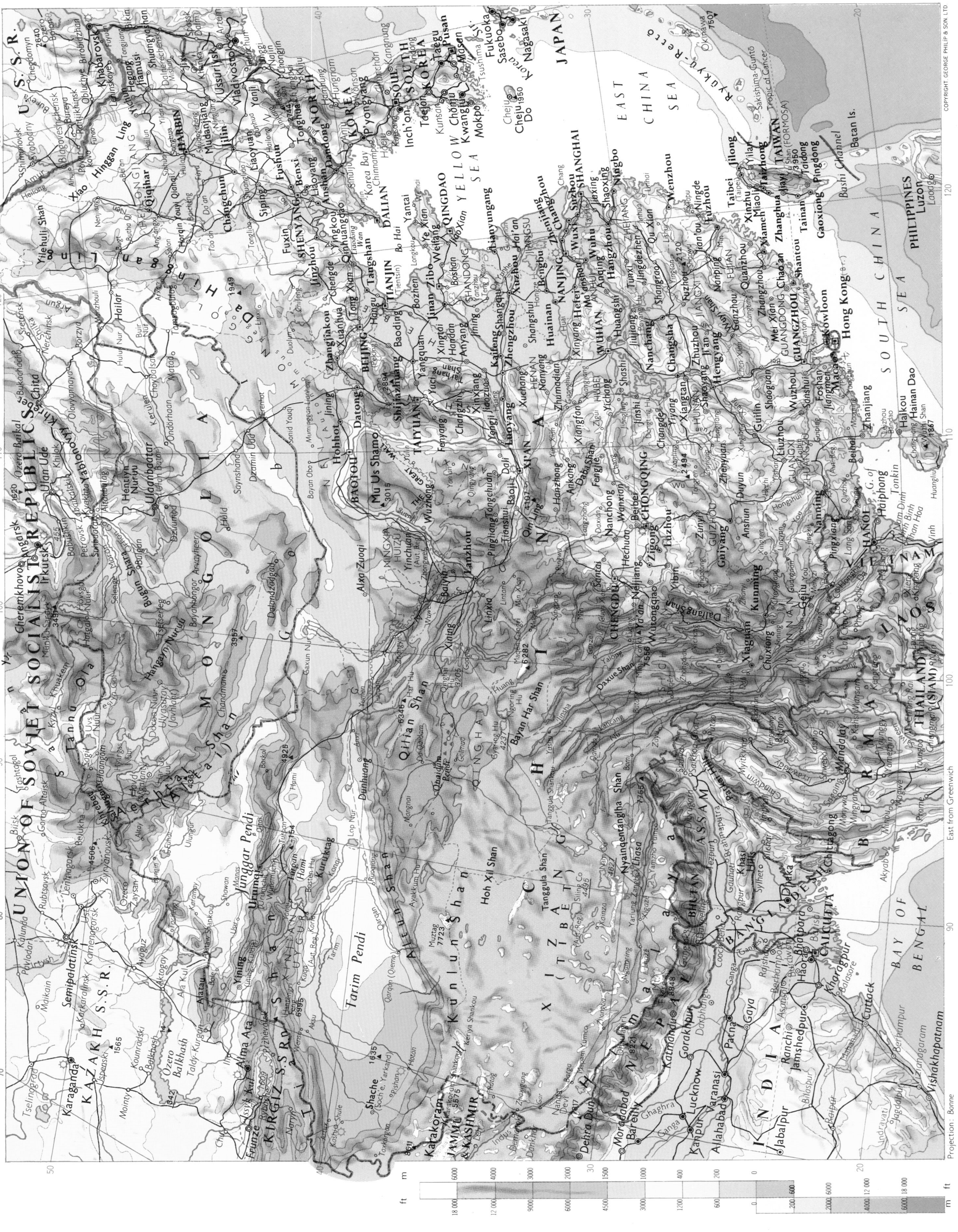

East from Greenwich

Projection: Bonne

U.S.S.R.

UNION OF SOVIET SOCIALIST REPUBLICS

MONGOLIA

KAZAKH S.S.R.

KIRGIZ S.S.R.

NORTH KOREA

SOUTH KOREA

JAPAN

EAST CHINA SEA

YELLOW SEA

SOUTH CHINA SEA

BAY OF BENGAL

PHILIPPINES

VIETNAM

LAOS

THAILAND (SIAM)

BURMA

INDIA

NEPAL

BHUTAN

ASSAM

JAMMU & KASHMIR

TAIWAN (FORMOSA)

Ryūkyū-Rettō

Hong Kong

Macau

Hainan Dao

Tarim Pendi

Junggar Pendi

Dzungaria

XINJIANG UYGUR (Aut. Reg.)

XIZANG (TIBET)

QINGHAI

GANSU

NINGXIA HUIZU

MONGOLIA

Kunlun Shan

Qilian Shan

Altun Shan

Tian Shan

Altai

Himalaya

Bayan Har Shan

Daxue Shan

Nyainqentanglha Shan

Lop Nur

BEIJING

SHANGHAI

TIANJIN

SHENYANG

HARBIN

TAIYUAN

XI'AN

WUHAN

CHONGQING

CHENGDU

GUANGZHOU

KUNMING

GUIZHOU

HENAN

HEBEI

SHANDONG

JIANGSU

FUJIAN

QINGDAO

DALIAN

NANJING

Hangzhou

Ningbo

Wenzhou

Fuzhou

Xiamen

Shantou

Lhasa

Lanzhou

Yinchuan

Hohhot

Baotou

Datong

Pyongyang

Seoul

Pusan

Taegu

Taibei

Vladivostok

Hanoi

Haiphong

Dhaka

Calcutta

Katmandu

Lucknow

Varanasi

Patna

Alma Ata

Frunze

Karaganda

Ozero Balkhash

Ozero Baikal

1 : 6 000 000

50 0 50 100 150 200 miles
50 0 50 100 150 200 250 300 km
SEA OF JAPAN
PACIFIC OCEAN
Sea of Okhotsk
CHINA
U. S. S. R.
NORTH KOREA
SOUTH KOREA
Sikhote Alin
Mudanjiang
Ningan
Turii Rog
Ozero Khanka
Spassk-Dalni
Varfolomeyevka
Verkhove
Tetyukhe
Ussurysk (Voroshilov)
Uglovaya
Vladivostok
Suchan
Nakhodka
Tumen
Hunchun
Najin
Zaliv Petra Velikogo
Chongjin
Songjin
Tanchon
Kosŏng
Samchok
Ullung Do
Pusan
KOREA STRAIT
Tsushima
Tsushima-Kaikyō
Iki
Rebun-Tō
Rishiri-Tō
Wakkanai
Teshio
Otoineppu
Enbetsu
HOKKAIDŌ
Monbetsu
Yūbetsu
Abashiri-Wan
Nemuro-Kaikyō
Rumoi
Shibetsu
Kitami
Abashiri
Daisetsu-Zan 2290
Asahigawa
Atsuta
Ishikari-Wan (Otaru-Wan)
HOKKAIDŌ
Nemuro
Kamui-Misaki
Bibai
Iwamisawa
Obihiro
Honbetsu
Otaru
Yūbari
Kushiro
Iwanai
Sapporo
Tomakomai
Tokachi
2052
Poroshiri Dake
Shiraoi
Mombetsu
Setana
Uchiura-Wan
Muroran
Urakawa
Samani
Okushiri-Tō
Erimo-Misaki
Esashi
Hakodate
Esan-Misaki
Tsugaru-Kaikyō
Shiriya-Zaki
Matsumae
Mutsu
Mutsu-Wan
Aomori
Hirosaki
Hachinohe
Towada-Ko
Odate
Kuji
Noshiro
Yoneshiro
Oga-Hantō
Iwate-San 2041
Akita
Morioka
Miyako
Omono
Honjō
Hanamaki
Kamaishi
Yokote
Kitakami
Ichinoseki
Sakata
Tsuruoka
Mogami
Shinjō
TŌHOKU
Kogota
Ishinomaki
Shiogama
Yamagata
Sendai
Iwanuma
Sado
Niigata
Shibata
Yonezawa
Agano
Fukushima
Bandai San 1819
Suzu-Misaki
Nagaoka
Wajima
Kashiwazaki
Aizuwakamatsu
Naoetsu
Koriyama
Tajima
Toyama-Wan
Nanao
Takada
Iwaki
Himi
Takaoka
Nikkō
Kanazawa
Toyama
Nagano
Hitachi
Shinano
CHŪBU
Matsumoto
Maebashi
Kiryū
Utsunomiya
Ueda
Tochigi
Nakaminato
Fukui
Takasaki
Mito
Chichibu
Gyoda
Takayama
Omiya
Tsuchiura
KANTŌ
Kawagoe
Suwa
Suwa-Ko
Urawa
Shin-Tone
Sawara
Takefu
Ontake 3063
Ina
Kawaguchi
Ichikawa
Chōshi
Kyō-ga-Saki
Wakasa-Wan
Tenryū
Kōfu
TŌKYŌ
Tsuruga
Fuji-San
Kawasaki
Chiba
Hi-no-Misaki
Matsue
Tottori
Toyooka
Maizuru
Ayabe
Gifu
Yokohama
Yokosuka
Izumo
Yonago
Biwa-Ko
Ichinomiya
Fuji-no-miya
3776
Fujisawa
CHŪGOKU
Tsuyama
Okyoto
Hikone
Kuwana
Nagoya
Numazu
Atami
Hamada
Himeji
Otsu
Yokkaichi
Okazaki
Shimizu
Shizuoka
Katsuura
Masuda
Kurashiki
Amagasaki
Kōbe
Ōsaka
Suruga-Wan
Itō
Tateyama
Fukuyama
Okayama
Akashi
Onomichi
Nara
Tsu
Hamamatsu
Shimada
Ō-Shima
Hagi
Hiroshima
Mihara
Sakai
Matsusaka
Toyohashi
Yamaguchi
Kure
Takamatsu
Kishiwada
Toba
Ise-Wan
Nii-Jima
Shimonoseki
Ube
Tokuyama
Marugame
Wakayama
Tokushima
Owase
Daiō-Misaki
Miyake-Jima
Suō-Nada
Seto Naikai
Niihama
KINKI
Fukuoka
Kitakyūshū
Matsuyama
SHIKOKU
Kii-Suidō
Mikura-Jima
Karatsu
Nakatsu
Shingū
Sasebo
Saga
Kurume
Beppu
Ōita
Yawatahama
Kōchi
Shio-no-Misaki
Ōmuta
Usuki
Uwajima
Tosa-Wan
Muroto-Misaki
Nakadori-Jima
Kashima
Aso-zan 1592
Saiki
Bungo-Suidō
SHIKOKU
Isahaya
Nagasaki
Kumamoto
Nakamura
Hachijō-Jima
Fukue-Jima
Shimabara
Yatsushiro
Nobeoka
Ashizuri-zaki
Shimo-Jima
KYŪSHŪ
Minamata
Aoga-Shima
Sendai
Miyazaki
Kobayashi
Kagoshima
Miyakonojō
KYŪSHŪ
Kanoya
Makurazaki
Kagoshima-Wan
Shibushi-Wan
Ōsumi-Kaikyō
Nishinoomote
Ōsumi-Shotō
Tane-ga-Shima
Kuchinoerabu-Jima
Yaku-Jima
Tokara-Kaikyō
Naka-no-Shima
Suwanose-Jima
Ōsumi-Shotō
Kuchinoerabu-Jima
Tokara-Kaikyō
Yaku-Jima
Naka-no-Shima
Suwanose-Shima
Satsuna-Shotō
Nansei Shotō (Ryūkyū-Shotō)
Okinawa-Shotō
Kikai-Jima
Naze
Amami Ō Shima
Setouchi
Tokunoshima
Okinoerabu-Jima
Okinawa-Jima
Ishikawa
Ginowan
Koza
Kerama-Shotō
Naha
Nansei-Shoto Trench
7507
PACIFIC
OCEAN
Miyako-Jima
Hirara
Yaeyama-Shotō
Yonaguni-Jima
Ishigaki-Jima
Ishigaki
Iriomote-Jima
RYŪKYŪ ISLANDS
Continuation southwards in same scale
ft m
4500 1500
3000 1000
1200 400
600 200
0 0
200 600
m ft
Projection: Bonne
East from Greenwich
COPYRIGHT. GEORGE PHILIP & SON LTD

SEA OF JAPAN
SOUTH KOREA
HONSHU
Oki-Shotō
Dōgo
Saigō
CHŪGOKU - DISTRICT
Shimane-Hantō
Matsue
Sakaiminato
Yonago
Tottori
Izumo
Hiroshima
HIROSHIMA
SHIMANE
OKAYAMA
TOTTORI
YAMAGUCHI
HYOGO
Himeji
Okayama
Kurashiki
Fukuyama
Onomichi
Kure
Iwakuni
Yamaguchi
Hagi
Shimonoseki
KITAKYŪSHŪ
Ube
Tokuyama
Takamatsu
Tokushima
Matsuyama
Imabari
Niihama
Kōchi
SHIKOKU
SHIKOKU - DISTRICT
KAGAWA
TOKUSHIMA
EHIME
KOCHI
Tosa-Wan
Muroto
Muroto-Misaki
Ashizuri-Zaki
Iyo-Nada
Suō-Nada
Hibiki-Nada
Genkai-Nada
Tsushima
Izuhara
Iki
FUKUOKA
Saga
Kurume
Ōmuta
Sasebo
Nagasaki
Kumamoto
Ōita
Beppu
Beppu-Wan
Nobeoka
Miyazaki
Miyakonojō
Kagoshima
Kagoshima-Wan
Yatsushiro
Amakusa-Nada
Amakusa-Shotō
Koshiki-Rettō
KYŪSHŪ
KYŪSHŪ - DISTRICT
KUMAMOTO
MIYAZAKI
KAGOSHIMA
NAGASAKI
ŌITA
Bungo-Suidō
Hōyo-Kaikyō
Kii-Suidō
Awaji-Shima
Sata-Misaki
Projection: Lambert's Conformal Conic

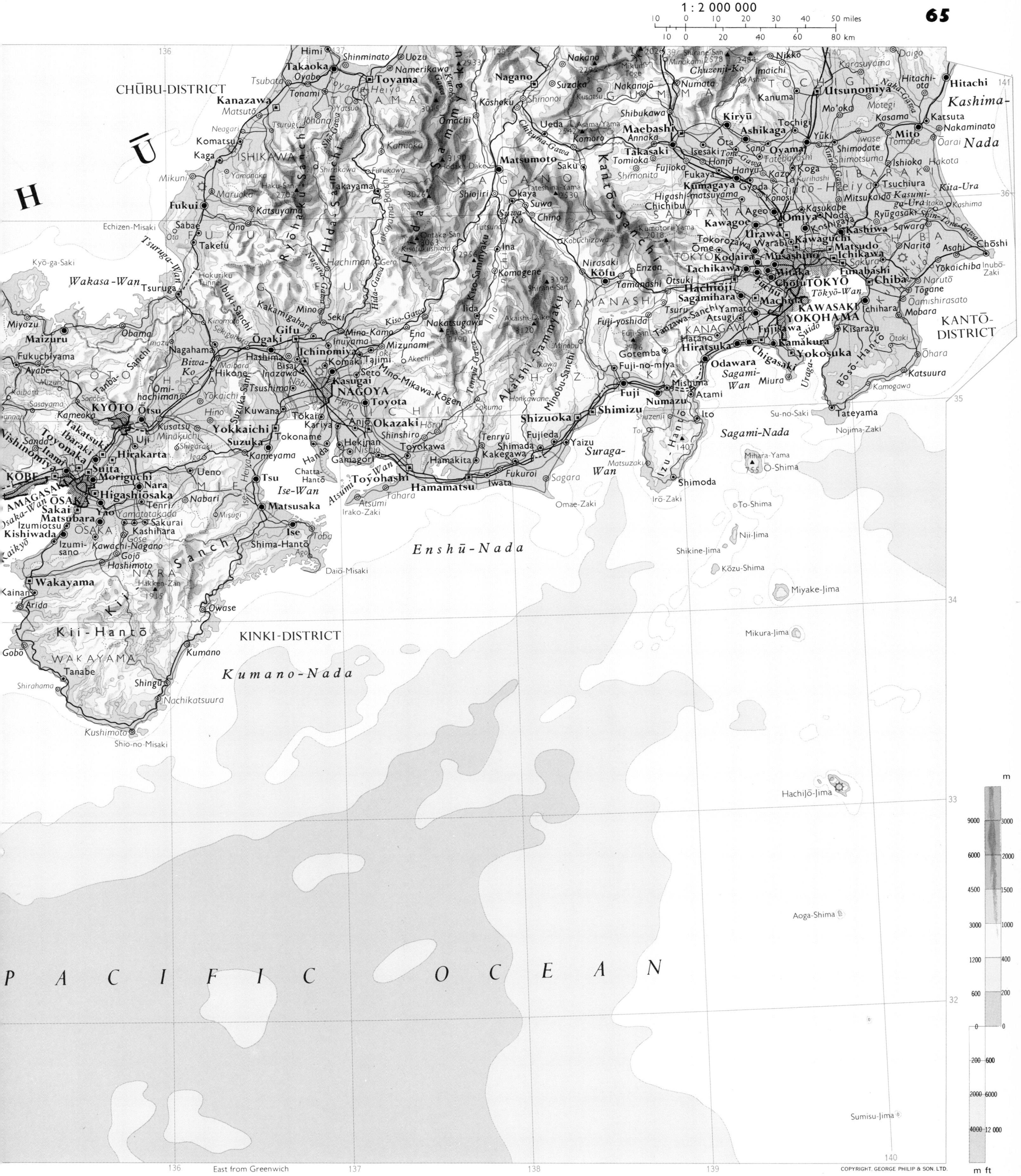

1 : 2 000 000

10 0 10 20 30 40 50 miles

10 0 20 40 60 80 km

CHŪBU-DISTRICT

H O N S H Ū

Himi Takaoka Oyabe Toyama Shinminato Uozu Namerikawa Tonami Tsubata Kanazawa Matsutō Neagari Komatsu Kaga Mikuni ISHIKAWA Tsurugi Jōhana Fukui Maruoka Katsuyama Sabae Ōno Takefu Ōta FUKUI Echizen-Misaki Tsuruga-Wan Tsuruga Kyō-ga-Saki Wakasa-Wan Hokuriku Tunnel

TOYAMA Ōmachi Shirakawa Furukawa Takayama Hida-Sanchi Ryōhaku-Sanchi Hachiman Gero Nagara-Gawa Hida-Gawa GIFU Ibuki-Sanchi Kakamigahara Mino Seki Gifu Ōgaki Ichinomiya Kasugai Komaki Inuyama Tajimi Mizunami Mino-Kamo Kiso-Gawa Ena Akechi Toki Seto Nagoya

Nagano Suzaka Kōshoku Shinonoi Nakanojō Ueda Komoro Asama-Yama Saku Matsumoto Shiojiri Okaya Suwa Suwa-Ko Chino Tateshina-Yama Ina Komagene Iida Nakatsugawa Ena-San Hotaka-Dake Ontake-San Kiso-Sammyaku Kiso-Komagatake NAGANO Akaishi-Dake Akaishi-Sammyaku Shirane-San Hida-Sammyaku Tenryū-Gawa Tenryū

Maizuru Miyazu Obama Fukuchiyama Ayabe Kameoka Kyōto KYOTO Ōtsu Biwa-Ko Nagahama Hikone Ōmi-hachiman Yōkaichi SHIGA Kusatsu Minakuchi Uji Takatsuki Ibaraki Toyonaka Itami Nishinomiya Kōbe Amagasaki Suita Moriguchi Hirakata Ōsaka Higashiōsaka Sakai Matsubara Yao Izumiotsu Kishiwada Izumi-sano Ōsaka-Wan Nara Tenri Sakurai Kashihara Gojō Hashimoto Kawachi-Nagano NARA Hakken-Zan Wakayama Kainan Arida Gobo Kii-Hantō Kii-Sanchi WAKAYAMA Tanabe Shirahama Shingū Nachikatsuura Kushimoto Shio-no-Misaki Kumano Owase Kumano-Nada KINKI-DISTRICT

Ueno Nabari MIE Suzuka Yokkaichi Kuwana Kameyama Tsu Ise-Wan Matsusaka Ise Toba Shima-Hantō Ago Daiō-Misaki Tsushima Inazawa Tōkai Kariya Anjō Okazaki Toyota Hekinan Nishio Gamagōri Handa Chatta-Hantō Tokoname Toyohashi Atsumi Atsumi-Wan Tahara Irako-Zaki AICHI Shinshiro Toyokawa Hamakita Hamamatsu Iwata Mino-Mikawa-Kōgen Enshū-Nada

Shizuoka Shimizu Fujieda Shimada Kakegawa Yaizu Fukuroi Sagara Omae-Zaki Suruga-Wan Fuji Fuji-no-miya Gotemba Numazu Mishima Atami Itō Shuzenji Izu-Hantō Shimoda Irō-Zaki Matsuzaki Minobu-Sanchi SHIZUOKA Fuji-San Fuji-yoshida YAMANASHI Kōfu Nirasaki Enzan Yamanashi

Nikkō Shirane-San Chūzenji-Ko Imaichi Numata Ashio Utsunomiya TOCHIGI Kanuma Kiryū Ashikaga Tochigi Ōta GUMMA Shibukawa Maebashi Takasaki Annaka Tomioka Shimonita Fujioka Isesaki Honjō Kantō-Sanchi Chichibu Higashi-matsuyama Kumagaya Gyōda Konosu Fukaya Hanyū Kazo Koga Kumotori-Yama SAITAMA Kawagoe Ageo Ōmiya Urawa Kawaguchi Tokorozawa Ōme Kodaira Musashino Tachikawa Hachiōji Mitaka Chōfu Fuchū TŌKYŌ Machida Sagamihara Kawasaki Yokohama Yamato Atsugi Hadano Hiratsuka Chigasaki Fujisawa Kamakura Yokosuka Odawara Sagami-Wan Miura Uraga-Suidō Tanzawa-Sanchi KANAGAWA Tōkyō-Wan

Daigo Karasuyama Hitachi-ōta Hitachi Kashima-Nada Katsuta Nakaminato Mito Ōarai Kasama Moʼoka Shimodate Shimotsuma Yūki Oyama Ishioka Hokota IBARAKI Tsuchiura Kasumi-ga-Ura Kita-Ura Itako Kashima Mitsukaidō Ryūgasaki Noda Kasukabe Kashiwa Matsudo Ichikawa Funabashi Chiba Narita Sawara Chōshi Asahi Inubō-Zaki Yōkaichiba Narutō Tōgane Ōamishirasato Mobara Ichihara Kisarazu KANTŌ-DISTRICT CHIBA Ōtaki Ōhara Bōsō-Hantō Katsuura Kamogawa Tateyama Nojima-Zaki Su-no-Saki

Sagami-Nada Mihara-Yama Ō-Shima To-Shima Nii-Jima Shikine-Jima Kōzu-Shima Miyake-Jima Mikura-Jima Hachijō-Jima Aoga-Shima Sumisu-Jima

P A C I F I C O C E A N

136 137 138 139 140 141 36 35 34 33 32

East from Greenwich

m	ft
9000	3000
6000	2000
4500	1500
3000	1000
1200	400
600	200
0	0
200	600
2000	6000
4000	12 000

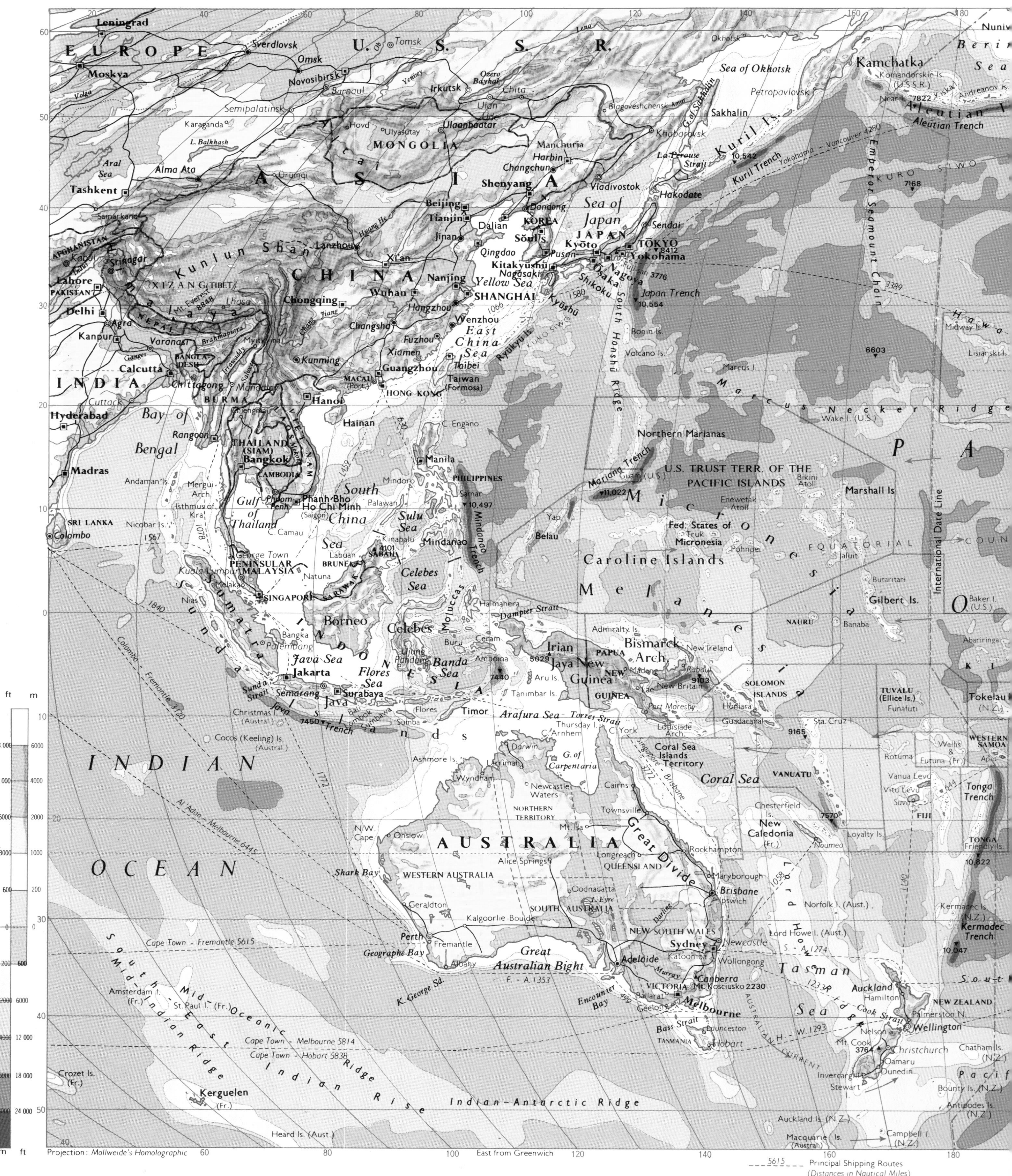

EUROPE
U. S. S. R.
ASIA
CHINA
MONGOLIA
INDIA
AUSTRALIA
INDIAN OCEAN
Sea of Okhotsk
Sea of Japan
Yellow Sea
East China Sea
South China Sea
Bay of Bengal
Gulf of Thailand
Java Sea
Flores Sea
Banda Sea
Celebes Sea
Sulu Sea
Arafura Sea
Coral Sea
Tasman Sea
Great Australian Bight
Micronesia
Melanesia
Caroline Islands
Marshall Is.
Gilbert Is.
U.S. TRUST TERR. OF THE PACIFIC ISLANDS
Fed. States of Micronesia
International Date Line
Kuril Trench
Japan Trench
Mariana Trench
Mindanao Trench
Java Trench
Tonga Trench
Kermadec Trench
Aleutian Trench
Emperor Seamount Chain
Marcus Necker Ridge
Great Dividing Range
Mid-Oceanic Ridge
South-East Indian Rise
Mid-Indian Ridge
Indian-Antarctic Ridge
Lord Howe Rise
NEW ZEALAND
Kerguelen
Projection: Mollweide's Homolographic
East from Greenwich
5615 Principal Shipping Routes (Distances in Nautical Miles)

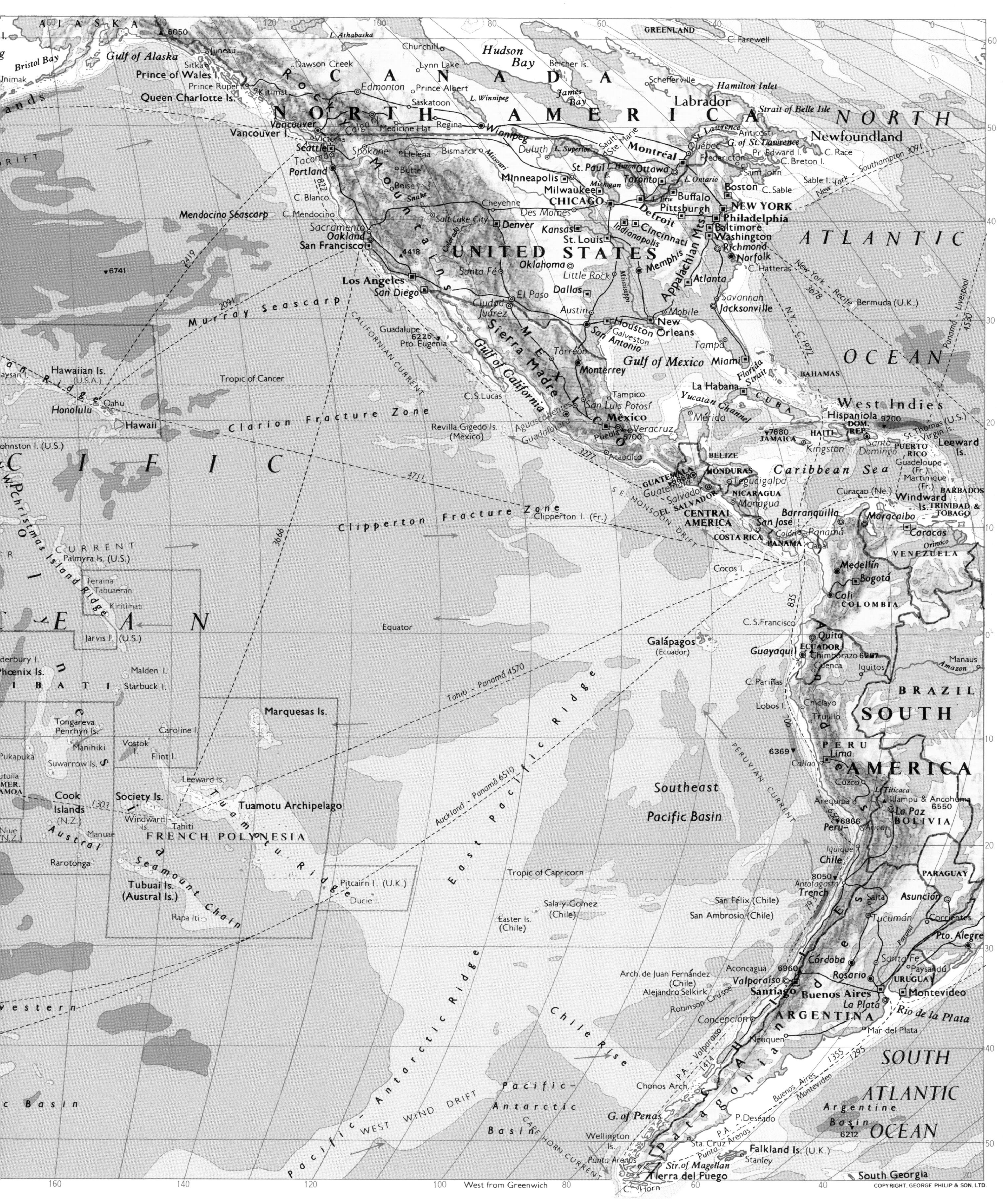
NORTH AMERICA
CANADA
UNITED STATES
ATLANTIC OCEAN
PACIFIC OCEAN
SOUTH AMERICA
SOUTH ATLANTIC OCEAN
Gulf of Mexico
Caribbean Sea
Hudson Bay
Southeast Pacific Basin
East Pacific Ridge
Clipperton Fracture Zone
Clarion Fracture Zone
Murray Seascarp
Mendocino Seascarp
Galápagos (Ecuador)
FRENCH POLYNESIA
Tuamotu Archipelago
Marquesas Is.
Hawaiian Is. (U.S.A.)
Tropic of Cancer
Equator
Tropic of Capricorn
West from Greenwich

1 : 4 000 000

50 0 50 100 miles

50 0 50 100 150 km

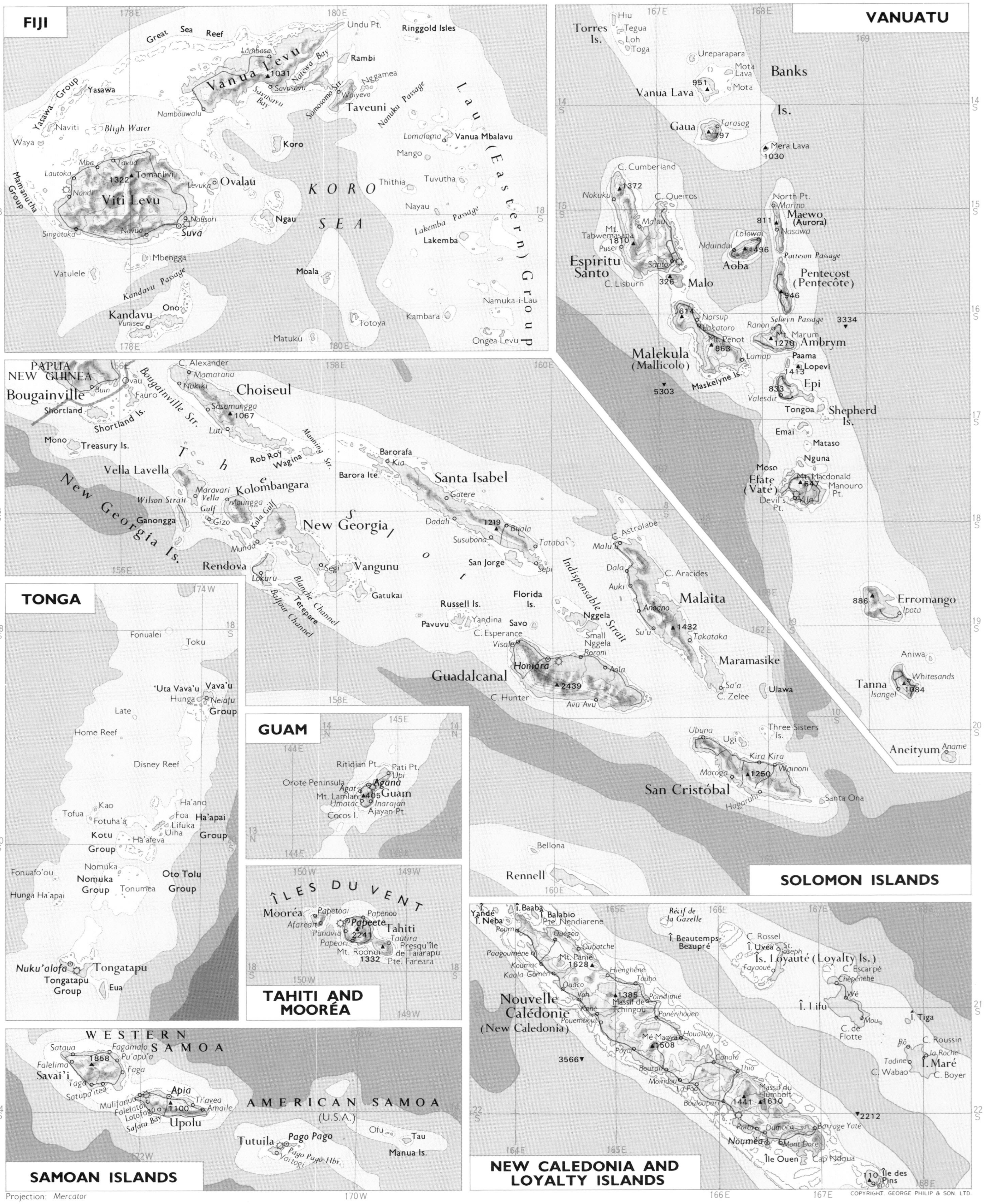

FIJI

Great Sea Reef, Undu Pt., Ringgold Isles, Lambasa, Vanua Levu, 1031, Natewa Bay, Rambi, Savusavu, Savusavu Bay, Nggamea, Somosomo Str., Naiyevo, Taveuni, Nanuku Passage, Yasawa Group, Yasawa, Nambouwalu, Naviti, Bligh Water, Waya, Koro, Lau (Eastern) Group, Lomaloma, Vanua Mbalavu, Mango, Mamanutha Group, Lautoka, Mba, Tavua, 1322, Tomanivi, Levuka, Ovalau, Nandi, Viti Levu, Thithia, Tuvutha, Koro Sea, Nayau, Navua, Nausori, Suva, Singatoka, Ngau, Lakemba Passage, Lakemba, Mbengga, Vatulele, Moala, Kandavu Passage, Namuka-i-Lau, Kandavu, Ono, Vunisea, Totoya, Kambara, Matuku, Ongea Levu

VANUATU

Hiu, Torres Is., Tegua, Loh, Toga, Ureparapara, Mota Lava, Mota, Banks Is., 951, Vanua Lava, Gaua, Tarasag, 797, Mera Lava, 1030, C. Cumberland, 1372, Nokuku, C. Queiros, North Pt., Marino, Maewo (Aurora), 811, Nasawa, Mt. Tabwemasana, 1810, Pusei, Malau, Lolowai, 1496, Nduindui, Aoba, Patteson Passage, Espiritu Santo, Santo, C. Lisburn, 326, Malo, Pentecost (Pentecôte), 946, 614, Norsup, Lakatoro, Selwyn Passage, 3334, Ranon, Mt. Marum, 1270, Ambrym, Mt. Penot, 863, Lamap, Malekula (Mallicolo), Maskelyne Is., Paama, Lopevi, 1413, 5303, 833, Epi, Valesdir, Tongoa, Shepherd Is., Emai, Mataso, Nguna, Moso, Efate (Vaté), Mt. Macdonald, 647, Manouro Pt., Devil's Pt., Vila, 886, Erromango, Ipota, Aniwa, Whitesands, Tanna, Isangel, 1084, Aneityum, Aname

SOLOMON ISLANDS

Papua New Guinea, Bougainville, Buin, Ovau, Fauro, Shortland, Shortland Is., Bougainville Str., C. Alexander, Mamarana, Nukiki, Choiseul, Sasamungga, 1067, Luti, Mono, Treasury Is., Manning Str., Rob Roy, Wagina, Barorafa, Kia, Vella Lavella, The Slot, Barora Ite, Santa Isabel, Maravari, Vella Gulf, Kolombangara, Gatere, New Georgia Is., Wilson Strait, Ganongga, Gizo, Kula Gulf, Noungga, New Georgia, Dadali, 1219, Buala, Susubona, Tataba, Astrolabe, Munda, Rendova, Segi, Vangunu, San Jorge, Sepi, Malu'u, Lokuru, Blanche Channel, Tetepare, Balfour Channel, Gatukai, Dala, C. Aracides, Auki, Indispensable Strait, Malaita, Florida Is., Russell Is., Yandina, Nggela, Anoano, Pavuvu, Savo, C. Esperance, Small Nggela, 1432, Su'u, Takataka, Visale, Honiara, Roroni, Aola, Maramasike, Guadalcanal, 2439, C. Hunter, Avu Avu, Sa'a, C. Zelee, Ulawa, Ubuna, Ugi, Three Sisters Is., Kira Kira, Wainoni, Marogu, 1250, San Cristóbal, Hagaruhi, Santa Ona, Bellona, Rennell

TONGA

Fonualei, Toku, 'Uta Vava'u, Vava'u, Hunga, Neiafu, Group, Late, Home Reef, Disney Reef, Kao, Tofua, Ha'ano, Fotuha'a, Foa, Lifuka, Ha'apai Group, Uiha, Kotu Group, Ha'afeva, Nomuka, Nomuka Group, Fonuafo'ou, Tonumea, Oto Tolu Group, Hunga Ha'apai, Nuku'alofa, Tongatapu, Tongatapu Group, Eua

GUAM

Ritidian Pt., Pati Pt., Upi, Orote Peninsula, Agat, Agana, Mt. Lamlam, 405, Guam, Umatac, Inarajan, Cocos I., Ajayan Pt.

TAHITI AND MOORÉA

Îles du Vent, Mooréa, Papetoai, Afareaitu, Papenoo, Papeete, Tahiti, Punavia, 2241, Tautira, Papeari, Presqu'île de Taiarapu, Mt. Roonui, 1332, Pte. Fareara

SAMOAN ISLANDS

Western Samoa, Sataua, Fagamalo, Pu'apu'a, Falelima, 1858, Faga, Savai'i, Taga, Satupa'itea, Apia, Ti'avea, Mulifanua, Falelatai, Lotofaga, 1100, Amaile, Safata Bay, Upolu, American Samoa (U.S.A.), Ofu, Tau, Tutuila, Pago Pago, Pago Pago Hbr., Vaitogi, Manua Is.

NEW CALEDONIA AND LOYALTY ISLANDS

Yandé, Î. Neba, Î. Baaba, Î. Balabio, Pte. Nendiarene, Récif de la Gazelle, Poum, Ouegoa, Î. Beautemps-Beaupré, C. Rossel, Î. Uvéa, St. Joseph, Îs. Loyauté (Loyalty Is.), Fayaoué, C. Escarpé, Chépénéhé, Pam, Ouébatche, Paagoumène, Mt. Panié, 1628, Koumac, Kaala-Gomen, Hienghène, Touho, Ouaco, Voh, 1385, Massif de Tchingou, Poindimié, Nouvelle-Calédonie (New Caledonia), Koné, Pouembout, Ponérihouen, Wé, Î. Lifou, C. de Flotte, Mou, Î. Tiga, Mé Maoya, 1508, Houaïlou, Poya, Canala, Thio, 3566, Bourail, Moindou, La Foa, Bô, C. Roussin, La Roche, Tadine, Î. Maré, C. Wabao, C. Boyer, Massif du Humboldt, 1441, 1610, Boulouparis, 2212, Païta, Dumbéa, Barrage Yaté, Nouméa, Mont Dore, Île Ouen, Cap Ndoua, 110, Île des Pins, Vao

Projection: Mercator

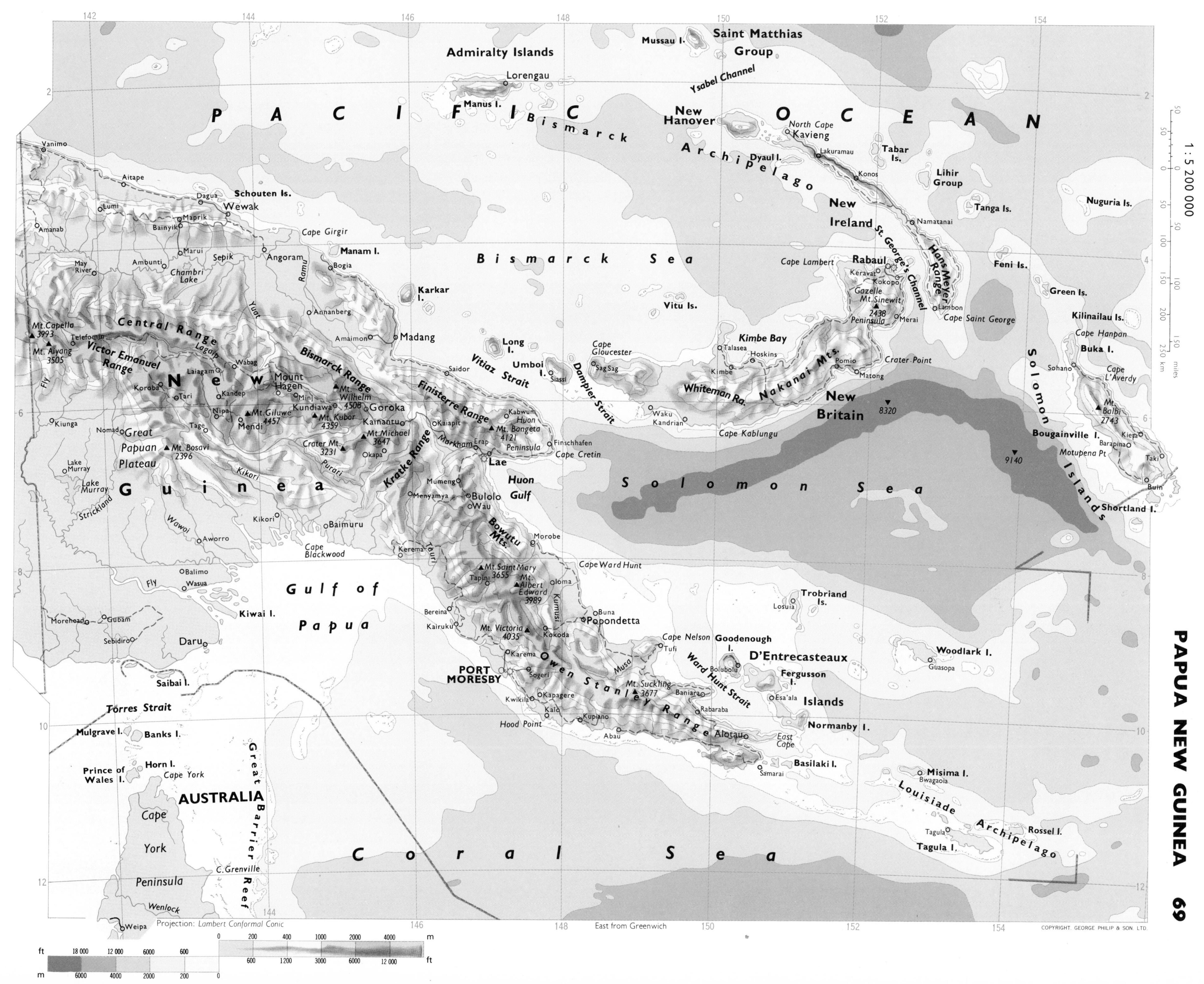
1 : 5 200 000
miles
km
PACIFIC OCEAN
Bismarck Sea
Solomon Sea
Coral Sea
Gulf of Papua
Huon Gulf
New Guinea
New Britain
New Ireland
New Hanover
Bismarck Archipelago
Admiralty Islands
Manus I.
Lorengau
Saint Matthias Group
Mussau I.
Ysabel Channel
Solomon Islands
Bougainville I.
Buka I.
Shortland I.
Mt. Balbi 2743
Kieta
Buin
Nuguria Is.
Kilinailau Is.
Green Is.
Feni Is.
Tanga Is.
Lihir Group
Tabar Is.
Hans Meyer Range
St. George's Channel
Rabaul
Kokopo
Gazelle Peninsula
Mt. Sinewit 2438
Nakanai Mts.
Whiteman Ra.
Kimbe Bay
Cape Gloucester
Dampier Strait
Vitiaz Strait
Umboi I.
Long I.
Karkar I.
Manam I.
Schouten Is.
Wewak
Madang
Finisterre Range
Mt. Bangeta 4121
Huon Peninsula
Finschhafen
Lae
Bulolo
Wau
Bowutu Mts.
Kratke Range
Bismarck Range
Mt. Wilhelm 4508
Goroka
Mt. Michael 3647
Mt. Kubor 4359
Kundiawa
Mount Hagen
Mt. Giluwe 4457
Mendi
Crater Mt. 3231
Sepik
Ramu
Central Range
Victor Emanuel Range
Mt. Capella 3993
Mt. Aiyang 3505
Great Papuan Plateau
Mt. Bosavi 2396
Lake Murray
Strickland
Fly
Kikori
Purari
Owen Stanley Range
Mt. Victoria 4035
Mt. Albert Edward 3989
Mt. Saint Mary 3655
Mt. Suckling 3677
Kokoda
Popondetta
PORT MORESBY
Hood Point
Kiwai I.
Daru
Torres Strait
Saibai I.
Mulgrave I.
Prince of Wales I.
Horn I.
Banks I.
Cape York
AUSTRALIA
Cape York Peninsula
Weipa
Great Barrier Reef
Trobriand Is.
Woodlark I.
D'Entrecasteaux Islands
Goodenough I.
Fergusson I.
Normanby I.
Ward Hunt Strait
Alotau
Misima I.
Louisiade Archipelago
Tagula I.
Rossel I.
Basilaki I.
East Cape
9140
8320
East from Greenwich
Projection: Lambert Conformal Conic
COPYRIGHT GEORGE PHILIP & SON. LTD.

Java Trench
TIMOR SEA
INDIAN OCEAN
WESTERN AUSTRALIA
NORTHERN TERRIT
SOUTH AU
Ashmore Reef
Cartier I.
Scott Reef
Rowley Shoals
Bonaparte Archipelago
C. Londonderry
C. Talbot
C. Bougainville
Vansittart B.
Admiralty G.
Montague Sd.
York Sd.
Brunswick B.
Cambridge G.
Jos. Bonaparte Gulf
Queens Chan.
Drysdale
Collier B.
King Sd.
C. Levêque
Lacepede Is.
Mt. Hann
776
Kimberley
King Leopold Ras.
Mt. Ord
1007
Durack Range
Ord
Wyndham
Kununurra
Victoria
Victoria River Downs
Derby
Carnot B.
C. Boileau
Broome
Fitzroy
Fitzroy Crossing
Hall's Creek
GREAT NORTHERN
Sturt Cr.
Gordon Downs
Roebuck B.
C. Latouche Treville
Lagrange
Eighty Mile Beach
Gregory Lake
Horden Hills
Great Sandy Desert
Dampier Archipelago
P. Hedland
Goldsworthy
De Grey
Monte Bello Is.
Barrow I.
C. Preston
Dampier
Karratha
Roebourne
Yule
Shaw
Marble Bar
Pilbara
Fortescue
Hamersley
Wittenoom
Mt. Bruce
1235
Nullagine
Throssell Ra.
L. Dora
L. Blanche
L. Mackay
Pannawonica
Onslow
N.W. Cape
Exmouth
Exmouth G.
Learmonth
Pt. Cloates
N.W. COASTAL
Tom Price
Ophthalmia Ra.
1053
Newman
Paraburdoo
Ashburton
Robertson Ra.
L. Disappointment
Gibson Desert
Rawlinson Ra.
C. Farquhar
L. McLeod
Lyons
Mt. Augustus
1105
C. Cuvier
Geographe Chan.
Bernier I.
Carnarvon
Gascoyne
Dorre I.
Naturaliste Chan.
Dirk Hartog I.
Shark B.
Denham
S. Passage
Steep Pt.
Wooramel
Robinson Ras.
Peak Hill
L. Buchanan
L. Carnegie
L. Wells
712
Wiluna
Meekatharra
Murchison
Sanford
Cue
L. Austin
Sandstone
L. Yeo
Great Victoria Desert
Laverton
L. Rason
Gantheaume B.
Tallering Peak
439
Mt. Magnet
Yalgoo
Leonora
Malcolm
L. Carey
L. Minigwal
Houtman Abrolhos
Northampton
Pindar
Mullewa
Geraldton
Mongers Lake
L. Barlee
L. Raeside
L. Ballard
Menzies
Dongara
L. Moore
Darling Range
GERALDTON
Bonnie Rock
Bencubbin
Kanowna
Kalgoorlie-Boulder
Zanthus
Rawlinna
Forrest
Deakin
Coolgardie
Southern Cross
EASTERN
GREAT
L. Lefroy
L. Cowan
Norseman
L. Dundas
L. Johnston
Northam
Merredin
Kellerberrin
Swan
Perth
Fremantle
York
Beverley
Brookton
Narrogin
Kwinana
New Town
Pinjarra
ALBANY
Newdegate
Ravensthorpe
Hopetoun
Esperance
Esperance B.
Bunbury
Geographe B.
Collie
Wagin
Nyabing
Katanning
Gnowangerup
C. Naturaliste
Busselton
Bridgetown
Manjimup
Pemberton
Stirling Ra.
Mt. Barker
Albany
Augusta
C. Leeuwin
Flinders B.
Pt. d'Entrecasteaux
Pt. Nuyts
Denmark
C. Knob
Hood Pt.
C. Pasley
C. Arid
Archipelago of the Recherche
Nullarbor Plain
Hampton Tableland
EYRE
Eyre
Eucla Motel
Pt. Dover
Pt. Culver
Great Australian Bight
Head of Bight
Croker I.
Melville I.
Bathurst I.
Dundas Str.
Coburg Pen.
Van Diemen Gulf
Clarence Str.
P. Darwin
Darwin
Goulburn Is.
Junction
Crocodile
Castlereagh
Jabiru
Arnhem Land
Rum Jungle
Pt. Blaze
Anson B.
C. Scott
Batchelor
Pine Creek
Daly
Katherine
Roper
Mataranka
Larrimah
Birdum
Daly Waters
Wave Hill
Newcastle Waters
L. Woods
STUART
Renner Springs T.O.
Tanami Desert
Tennant Creek
Barrow Creek
Reynolds Ra.
Mt. Zeil
1510
L. Macdonald
Macdonnell Ras.
Alice Springs
James Ra.
Palmer
Finke
Hugh
L. Amadeus
Mt. Olga
1069
Ayers Rock
868
Blackstone Ra.
Musgrave Ranges
1549
Mt. Woodroffe
The Hamilton
The Alberga
Everard Ras.
Coober Pedy
L. Maurice
Maralinga
Ooldea
Tarcoola
L. Everard
Penong
Ceduna
C. Adieu
Fowlers B.
Nuyts Archipelago
Streaky B.
C. Radstock
Anxious B.
Investigator Group
Coffin B. Penin
ft
m
6000
2000
4500
1500
3000
1000
1200
400
600
200
0
0
200
600
2000
6000
4000
12 000
6000
18 000
m
ft
10
15
20
25
30
35
110
115
120
125
105
130
Projection: Bonne
East from Greenwich

1 : 11 200 000

100 50 0 100 200 300 400 miles

100 0 100 200 300 400 500 600 km

CORAL SEA

CORAL SEA ISLANDS TERRITORY

PACIFIC OCEAN

TASMAN SEA

Gulf of Carpentaria

QUEENSLAND

NEW SOUTH WALES

VICTORIA

TASMANIA

Great Barrier Reef

Great Dividing Range

Cape York Peninsula

Simpson Desert

Barkly Tableland

Great Dividing Range

Grey Range

Australian Alps

Bass Strait

Louisiade Archipelago

Chesterfield Is.

Lord Howe I.

Tropic of Capricorn

Thursday I. Banks I. Prince of Wales I. C. York

Groote Eylandt

Mount Isa Cloncurry Townsville Cairns Mackay Rockhampton Gladstone Bundaberg Maryborough Brisbane Gold Coast Toowoomba Ipswich

Longreach Charleville Roma Cunnamulla Winton Hughenden

Coffs Harbour Lismore Tamworth Armidale Maitland Newcastle Cessnock SYDNEY Wollongong Shellharbour Goulburn Canberra Wagga Wagga Orange Dubbo Broken Hill

Adelaide Elizabeth Whyalla Mildura Bendigo Ballarat Geelong MELBOURNE Shepparton

Devonport Burnie Launceston Hobart Glenorchy

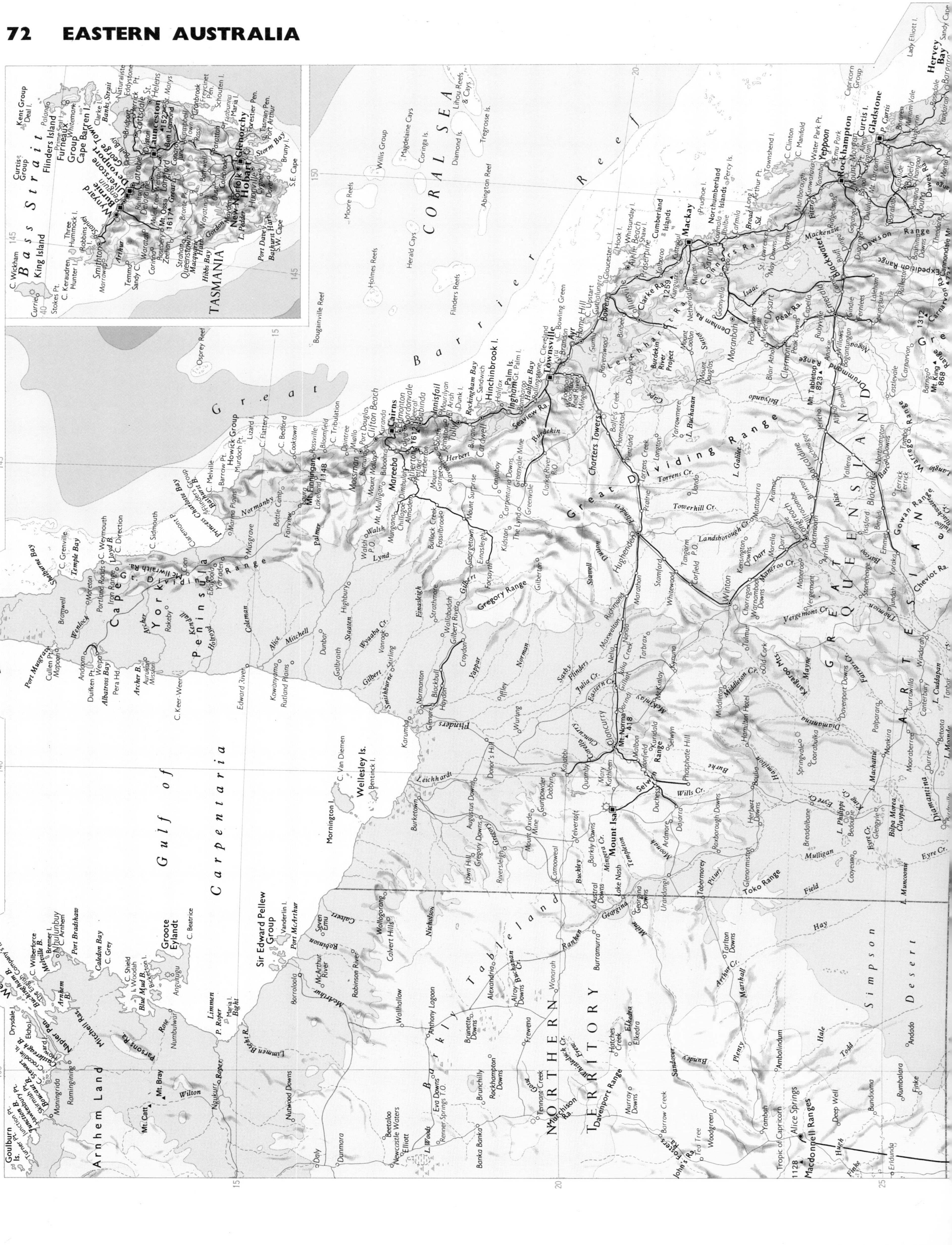

TASMANIA
Bass Strait
CORAL SEA
Great Barrier Reef
Gulf of Carpentaria
Cape York Peninsula
Great Dividing Range
QUEENSLAND
GREAT ARTESIAN BASIN
NORTHERN TERRITORY
Barkly Tableland
Arnhem Land
Simpson Desert

SOUTH AUSTRALIA
NEW SOUTH WALES
TASMAN SEA
Bass Strait
SYDNEY
CANBERRA
MELBOURNE
ADELAIDE
BRISBANE
Newcastle
Wollongong
Geelong
Ballarat
Bendigo
Broken Hill
Mildura
Port Augusta
Port Pirie
Whyalla
Port Lincoln
Kangaroo I.
King Island
Flinders Island
Furneaux Group
Lake Eyre (North)
Lake Torrens
Lake Gairdner
Lake Frome
Spencer Gulf
Grey Range
Barrier Range
Flinders Ranges
Stuart Range
Toowoomba
Ipswich
Gold Coast
Coffs Harbour
Tamworth
Armidale
Dubbo
Orange
Bathurst
Wagga Wagga
Albury
Mount Gambier
Warrnambool
1 : 6 400 000
50 0 50 100 150 200 miles
50 0 50 100 150 200 250 300 km
Projection: Bonne
East from Greenwich
COPYRIGHT. GEORGE PHILIP & SON. LTD.
ft m
4500 1500
3000 1000
1200 400
600 200
0 0
200 600
2000 6000
4000 12 000
m ft

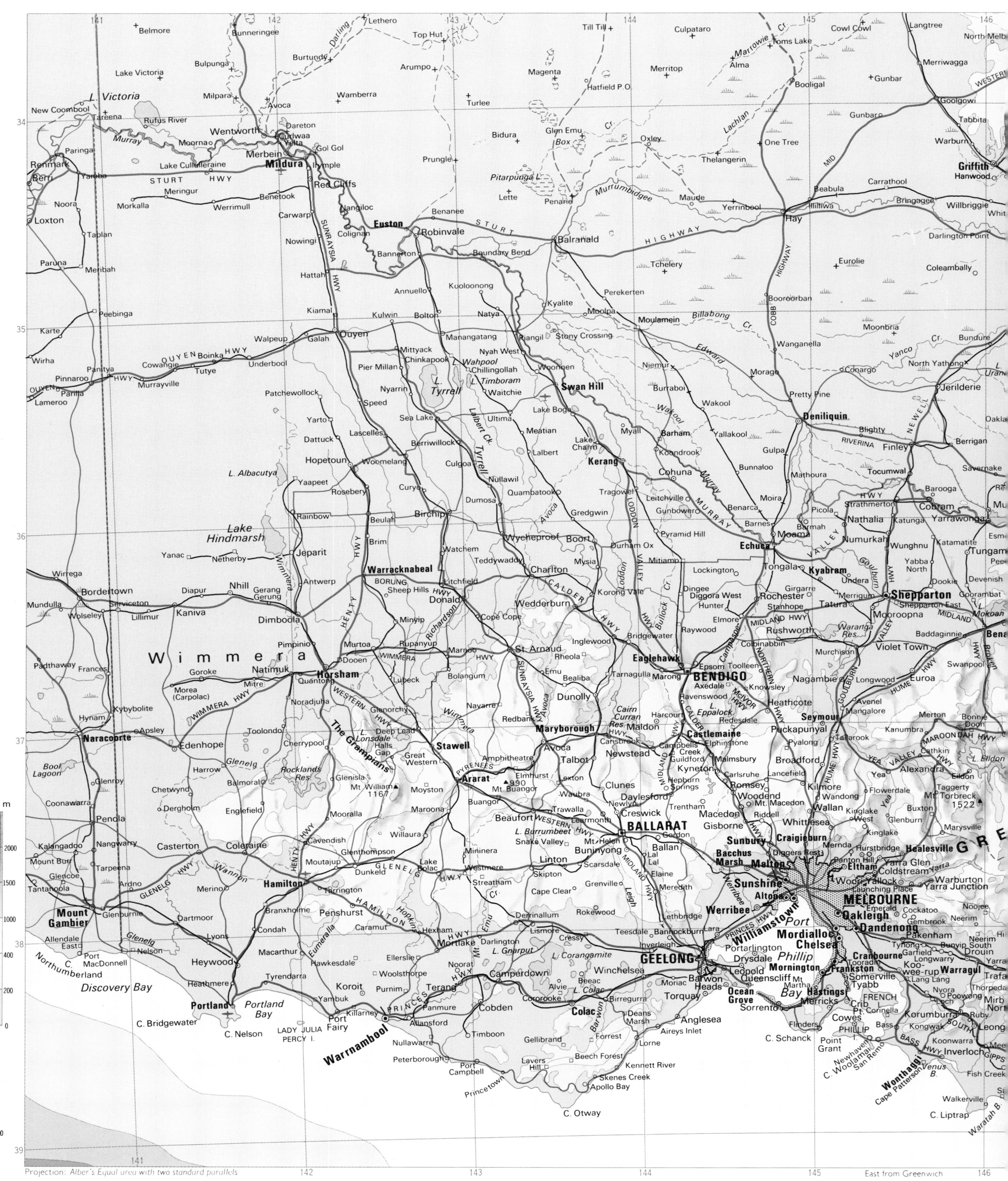
MELBOURNE
GEELONG
BALLARAT
BENDIGO
Mildura
Swan Hill
Horsham
Hamilton
Warrnambool
Portland
Wimmera
The Grampians
Discovery Bay
Port Phillip Bay
C. Otway
Projection: Alber's Equal area with two standard parallels
East from Greenwich

Woy Woy
Broken Bay
Berowra
Hornsby
Manly
Port Jackson
SYDNEY
Botany Bay
Cronulla
Sutherland
Richmond
Springwood
Penrith
Blacktown
Windsor
Kurrajong
Cowra
Mt. Victoria
Blackheath
Katoomba
Glenbrook
St. Marys
Parramatta
Fairfield
Liverpool
Wallacia
Werombi
Camden
The Oaks
Menangle
Campbelltown
Woronora Res.
Appin
Helensburgh
Stanwell Park
Picton
Thirlmere
Cataract Res.
Bulli
Woonona
WOLLONGONG
Port Kembla
Lake Illawarra
Shellharbour
Bass Pt.
Kiama
Dapto
Albion Park
Cordeaux Res.
Unanderra
Avon Res.
Bargo
Buxton
Nepean Res.
Mittagong
Berrima
Bowral
Moss Vale
Robertson
Bundanoon
Berry
Gerringong
Kangaroo Valley
Nowra
Bomaderry
Falls Creek
Beecroft Hd.
Huskisson
Jervis Bay (Commonwealth Territory)
Jervis Bay
St. Georges Hd.
Wandandian
Nerriga
Milton
Mollymook
Ulladulla
Warden Hd.
Termeil
BRUSH ISLAND
East Lynne
Brooman
Batemans Bay
Bateman's Bay
Mogo
Burrewarra Pt.
Moruya
Moruya Heads
Tuross Head
Bodalla
Eurobodalla
Narooma
MONTAGUE I.
C. Dromedary
Central Tilba
Cobargo
Quaama
Goalen Hd.
Bega
Tathra
Candelo
Merimbula
Pambula
Eden
Twofold Bay
Towamba
Wonboyn
Green C.
Disaster B.
C. Howe
GABO I.
Mallacoota
Mallacoota Inlet
Genoa
Noorinbee
Cann River
Point Hicks
Ram Head
Bemm River
C. Conran
Marlo
Orbost
Newmerella
Lakes Entrance
Lake Tyers
Paynesville
Metung
Swan Reach
Nowa Nowa
Tostaree
Bairnsdale
Bruthen
Lindenow
Bengworden
L. King
Stratford
Maffra
Sale
Meerlieu
Victoria
Beach
Loch Sport
L. Wellington
L. Reeve
Ninety Mile Beach
Seaspray
Heyfield
Newry
Munro
Briagolong
Glenmaggie
Walhalla
Erica
Thompson
Moondarra
Cowwarr
Glengarry
Latrobe
Kilmany
Rosedale
Traralgon
Moe
PRINCES HWY
Morwell
Yinnar
Churchill
Gormandale
Boolarra
Carrajung
Darriman
Mirboo
Wonwron
Yarram
MIDLAND HWY
Woodside
Welshpool
Toora
Port Welshpool
Port Albert
The Ninety Mile Beach
ST. MARGARET I.
SUNDAY I.
SNAKE I.
Corner Inlet
Wilsons Promontory
NATIONAL PARK
C. Wellington
Mt. Baw Baw 1563
Aberfeldy
Licola
Mt. Tamboritha 1640
Macalister
Wonnangatta
Dargo
Mitchell
Gippsland
Ensay
Swifts Creek
Tambo
Buchan
Omeo
Bowen Mts.
Benambra
Hotham Heights
Mt. Hotham
Mt. Buller 1806
Mt. Buller
Howqua
Jamieson
Mansfield
Tolmie
Whitfield
Mt. Feathertop 1922
Falls Creek
Glen Valley
Morass
Mt. Bogong 1986
Tawonga
Mount Beauty
Bright
Porepunkah
Buffalo
Ovens
Myrtleford
Moyhu
King
Whorouly
Glenrowan
Oxley
Everton
Wangaratta
Beechworth
Yackandandah
Dederang
Eskdale
Kiewa
Mitta Mitta
Mt. Benambra 1476
L. Dartmouth
OMEO HWY
KIEWA VALLEY HWY
Tallangatta
Corryong
Cudgewa
Koetong
Granya
Bandiana
Wodonga
Ebden
Bonegilla
L. Hume (Res.)
Albury
Chiltern
Barnawartha
Rutherglen
Corowa
Wahgunyah
Springhurst
Woorragee
Bowser
Table Top
Gerogery
Brocklesby
Balldale
Talmalmo
Jingellic
Walwa
Tintaldra
Towong
MURRAY VALLEY HWY
Woomargama
Walla Walla
Culcairn
Walbundrie
Goombargana Hill 403
Daysdale
Holbrook
Henty
HUME
OLYMPIC WAY
Little Billabong
Carabost
Rosewood
Mannus
Tumbarumba
Laurel Hill
Bogandyera Mt 1059
Tumut 2 Dam
Cabramurra
Tumut Pond Dam
Tooma Res.
Tooma
Mt. Jagungal 2060
Khancoban
Murray
Geehi
Mt. Townsend 2209
2230
Mt. Kosciusko
Thredbo Village
Guthega Dam
Island Bend
Snowy Mts.
Snowy
Australian Alps
Happy Jacks Dam
Adaminaby
L. Eucumbene
Eucumbene
Kiandra
Talbingo Dam
Blowering Dam
Batlow
Kunama
Wondalga
Gilmore
Tumut
Adelong
Tumblong
Humula
Kyeamba
Tarcutta
Mangoplah
Yerong Creek
Pleasant Hills
The Rock
555 Hanging Rock
Urangeline East
Rand
Billabong
Urana
Osborne
Milbrulong
Lockhart
Cullivel
L. Cullivel
Bullenbung
Uranquinty
Alfred Town
Wagga Wagga
Wantabadgery
Galore
Yuluma
Borea Creek
Kywong
Morundah
Narrandera
Murrumbidgee
Grong Grong
Matong
Ganmain
Coolamon
Marrar
Old Junee
Junee
Bethungra
Cootamundra
Mimosa
Methul
Leeton
Yanco
Murrami
Ardlethan
Beckom
Barellan
Binya
Yenda
Mt. Ringa 455
South Yalgogrin
Tallimba
Narriah
Weethalle
Yalgorin
Rankins Springs
Kikoira
Gubbata
Ungarie
Girral
Calleen
Lake Cowal
L. Cowal
Wirrinya
Marsden
West Wyalong
Wyalong
Alleena
Bellarwi
Barmedman
Mirrool
Reefton
Quandialla
Caragabal
Morangarell
Ariah Park
Temora
Grogan
Stockinbingal
Milvale
Young
Wombat
Murringo
Bribbaree
Thuddungra
Tyagong
Piney Range
Bogalong Creek
Grenfell
Greenethorpe
Pullabooka
Gooloogong
Garema
MID WESTERN HWY
Koorawatha
Bendick Murrell
OLYMPIC WAY
Cowra
Canowindra
Billimari
Broula
Darby Falls
Woodstock
Wyangala Res.
Lyndhurst
Carcoar
Mandurama
Mt. Macquarie 1204
Barry
Neville
Newbridge
Ben Chifley Res.
Rockley
Oberon
Fish River Res.
Hampton
Jenolan Caves
Abercrombie
Burraga
Porters Retreat
Lake Burragorang
Nattai River
Wollondilly
Range
GREAT DIVIDING RANGE
Cullarin Range
Wombeyan Caves
Golspie
Taralga
Laggan
Binda
Peelwood
Tuena
Bigga
Reids Flat
Graham
Godfreys Creek
Frogmore
Lachlan
Rugby
Crookwell
Roslyn
Rye Park
Boorowa
Murrumburrah
Harden
Wallendbeen
Galong
Binalong
McMahon's Reef
Muttama
Bowning
HIGHWAY
Bookham
Jugiong
Yass
Gunning
Dalton
HUME
Kenmore
Goulburn
Marulan
Wingello
Bungonia
Marulan South
Breadalbane
Collector
Inveralochy
L. Bathurst
Tarago
L. George
Shoalhaven
Marlow
Doughboy
Braidwood
1131
Currockbilly
Majors Creek
Araluen
Nelligen
Hoskinstown
Captains Flat
Michelago
Royalla
Queanbeyan
Bungendore
Sutton
Gundaroo
Hall
CANBERRA
AUSTRALIAN CAPITAL TERRITORY
Tharwa
Brindabella
Argalong
Wee Jasper
Burrinjuck Res.
Burrinjuck Dam
Brungle
Gundagai
Nangus
Pettitts
Murrumbateman
BARTON HWY
FEDERAL HWY
Bimberi Pk. 1910
Tantangara Res.
Collinton
Shannons Flat
Jerangle
Bredbo
Bunyan
Cooma
Rock Flat
Nimmitabel
Berridale
Jindabyne
L. Jindabyne
Dalgety
Ingebyra
Jimenbuen
Cambalong
Bombala
Tombong
Corrowidgie
Bibbenluke
Cathcart
Bemboka
MONARO HWY
Wyndham
Wolumla
Yowrie
Burragate
Rowes
Delegate
Rockton
Nungatta
Bonang
BONANG HWY
Mt. Ellery 1297
Brodribb
CANN VALLEY HWY
Cann
Genoa
Club Terrace
PRINCES HWY
Mt. Bowen 1372
Gelantipy
Buchan
1836
Mt. Cobberas
Mt. Gibbo 1757
SOUTH PACIFIC OCEAN
TASMAN SEA
34
35
36
37
38
39
147
148
149
150
151

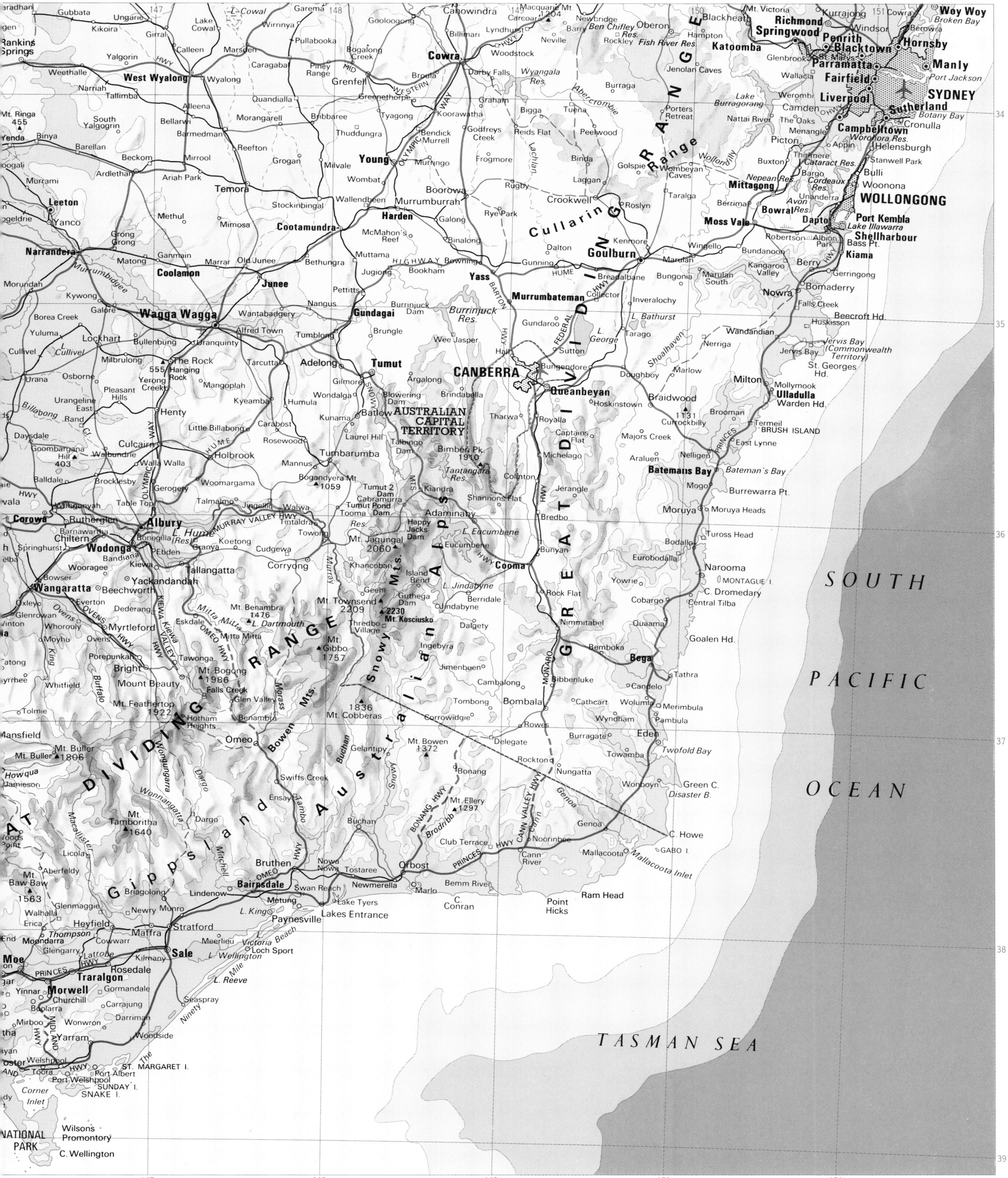

1 : 2 000 000

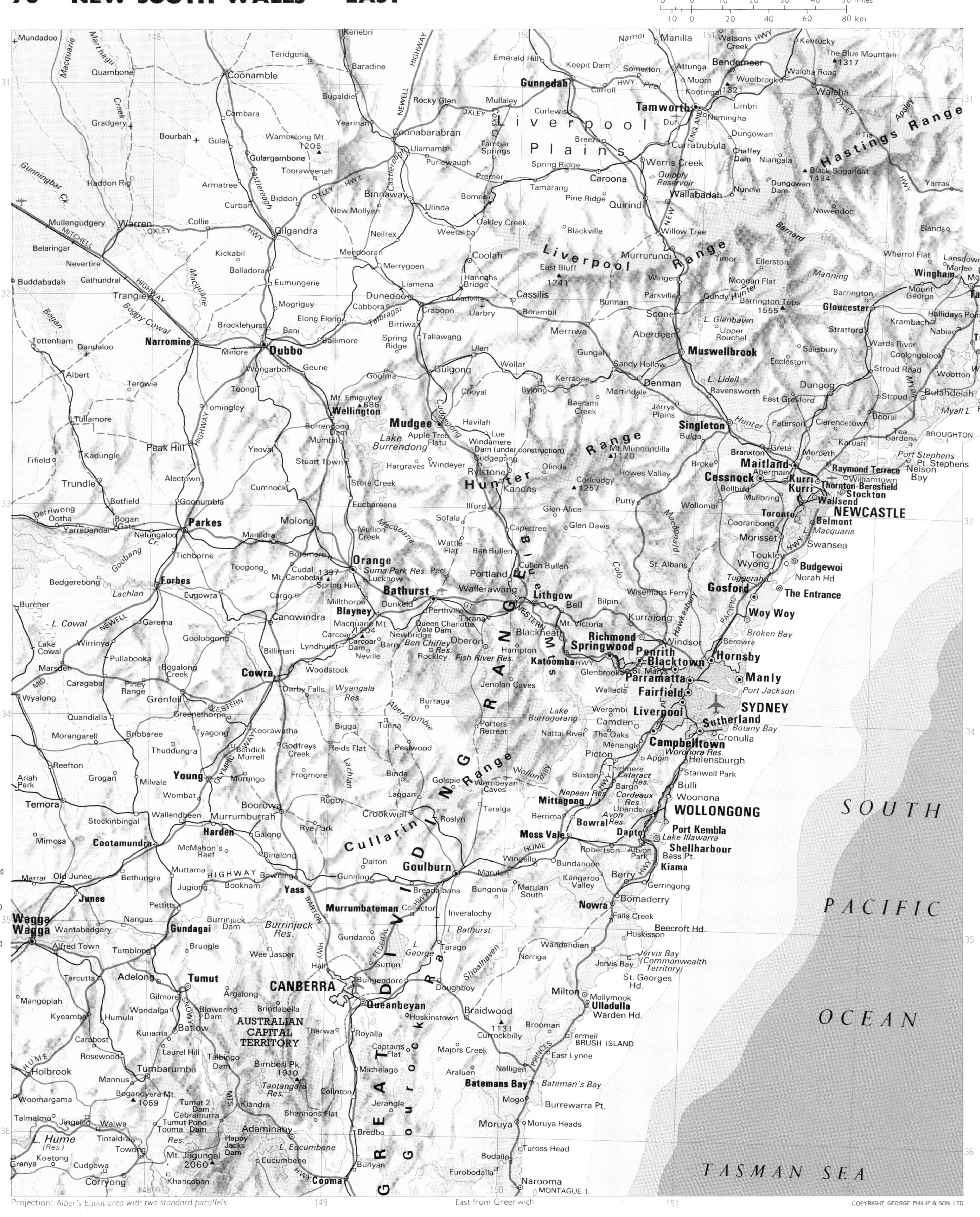

10 0 10 20 30 40 50 miles
10 0 20 40 60 80 km
Coonamble
Gunnedah
Tamworth
Manilla
Bendemeer
Walcha
Liverpool Plains
Coonabarabran
Hastings Range
Gilgandra
Warren
Liverpool Range
Wingham
Taree
Gloucester
Narromine
Dubbo
Muswellbrook
Mudgee
Wellington
Singleton
Maitland
Cessnock
NEWCASTLE
Parkes
Orange
Bathurst
Forbes
Lithgow
Gosford
Cowra
Katoomba
Penrith
Parramatta
SYDNEY
Manly
Liverpool
Campbelltown
Young
WOLLONGONG
Goulburn
Cootamundra
Yass
Gundagai
Wagga Wagga
Tumut
CANBERRA
AUSTRALIAN CAPITAL TERRITORY
Queanbeyan
Batemans Bay
Cooma
GREAT DIVIDING RANGE
Blue Mts
Cullarin Range
Gourock Ra.
SOUTH PACIFIC OCEAN
TASMAN SEA
ft m
Projection: Alber's Equal area with two standard parallels
East from Greenwich

1 : 2 000 000

10 0 10 20 30 40 50 miles

10 0 20 40 60 80 km

Surat, Glenmorgan, Meandarra, Cabawin, Tara, Kogan, Kumbarilla, Ducklo, Dalby, Blaxland, Kaimkillenbun, 748, Wutul, Djuan, Maclagan, Quinalow, Toogoolawah, Brisbane, Wamuran, Caboolture, C. Moreton, Bongaree, Mt. Tempest, MORETON I., 282, Moreton Bay, Deception Bay, Somerset Dam, Beachmere, Dayboro, Murrumba, Redcliffe, Bald Hills, 745, Sandgate, Esk, L. Wivenhoe (under construction), Chermside, Hagen, 763, Crows Nest, Ravensbourne, Goombungee, Acland, Bowenville, Jondaryan, Tipton, Broadwater Lagoon, 418, Currajong, Darling, Darling, Oakey, 808, Coominya, Mt. Perseverance, Newmarket, Mount Nebo, BRISBANE, Wynnum, Pt. Lookout, Dunwich, Cleveland, N. STRADBROKE I., Meringandan, L. Clarendon, Lowood, Fernvale, Gowrie Junc., Helidon, Gatton, Marburg, Cecil Plains, Mount Tyson, Coomrith, Bongeen, 678, TOOWOOMBA, Grantham, Forest Hill, Laidley, Ipswich, Goodna, Holland Park, Redland Bay, Russell Island, Dunmore, Wyreema, Blenheim, Rosewood, Bennleigh, Southbrook, Grandchester, Greenbank, Waterford, Cooroorah, Moonie, Weir, Brookstead, Pittsworth, Mt. Sylvia, Mulgowie, Ripley, Jimboomba, Pimpama, S. STRADBROKE I., MOONIE HIGHWAY, Moonie, Felton East, Greenmount, Mount Walker, Harrisville, 679, Millmerran, Rosevale, Thomby, Downs, Flinton, Boondandilla, Nobby, Townson, Kagaru, Tamborine North, Southport, Westmar, Downs, Clifton, Upper Pilton, 1013, Aratula, Kalbar, Nerang, Surfers Paradise, Alton, Mt. Domville 645, Leyburn, Hendon, Allora, Boonah, Beaudesert, Mudgeeraba, GOLD, Maryvale, Mt. Alford, Advancetown Lake, Burleigh Heads, Pratten, Laravale, Coolangatta, Yarrill Cr., Karara, Greymare, Emu Vale, Innisplain, Point Danger, COAST, Warwick, 1381, Rathdowney, 1204, McPherson Ra., Tweed Heads, Gore, Mt. Barney 1359, Palen Creek, Tumbulgum, Kingscliff-Fingal, Chillingham, Graysholm, Yuraraba, Killarney, Murwillumbah, BARWON, Weir, Commoron Cr., Bungunya, Toobeah, Gooray, Inglewood, Cobba-da-mana, Mt. Magnus 990, Cherry Gully, Woodenbong, Tyalgum, Mt. Warning 1156, Burringbar, Uki, HWY, Talwood, Legume, Unumgar, Grevillia, Gradule, Goondiwindi, Yelarbon, Whetstone, CUNNINGHAM, Cottonvale, MT. LINDESAY, Urbenville, Wiangaree, Mullumbimby, Brunswick Heads, Daymar, Macintyre, Boggabilla, Amiens, Stanthorpe, Tooloom, Toonumbar Dam, Cawongla, Nimbin, C. Byron, Liston, Toonumbar, Rock Creek Res., Byron Bay, Kurumbul, Beebo, Limevale, Pikedale, Kyogle, Boomi, Bonalbo, Dunoon, Whalan Cr., Caloona, Texas, Ballandean, Silverspur, Dumaresq, Macintyre, Tabulam, Mummulgum, Alstonville, Lismore, Ballina, Wallangarra, Mallanganee, Casino, Mungindi, Yetman, Drake, Wardell, Weemelah, Gil Gil Cr., 1328, Tatham, Coraki, Neeworra, Garah, Bonshaw, Tenterfield, BRUXNER, Wyan, Cropp Cr., Ottleys Cr., Rappville, Woodburn, Evans Head, Snapper Point, Croppa Creek, Mole, Timbarra, Baryulgil, Richmond, PACIFIC, Coolatai, Wallangra, Bolivia, Mt. Bajimba 1446, Camira Cr., CORAL, Medgun, Ashley, Crooble, Ashford, Torrington, Beardy, Whiporie, Banyabba, Pindari Res., Clarence, Woody Head, GWYDIR, Pallamallawa, Emmaville, Fine Flower Cr., Maclean, Yamba, Moree, Gwydir, HWY, Warialda, Graman, Macintyre, Bukkulla, Severn, Deepwater, Cangai, Dilkoon, Lawrence, Biniguy, Gravesend, Delungra, Oakwood, Dundee, GWYDIR, Jackadgery, Copmanhurst, SEA, Koloona, Byron, Glen Innes, Mann, Ulmarra, Grafton, Moomin Cr., Gurley, NEWELL, Terry Hie Hie, Little Plain, Inverell, Newton Boyd, Sandon Bluffs, Red Range, Nymboida, Coutts Crossing, Pillar Valley, Stannifer, Mt. Rumbee 1503, Dalmorton, Halfway Creek, Wooli, N. SOLITARY I., Bellata, Bingara, Gilgai, Copeton Dam, Howell, Tingha, Boyd, Nymboida, Orara, Kungala, Red Rock, N.W. SOLITARY I., Haystack Mountain 516, Caroda, Gwydir, 1520, Ben Lomond, Ben Lomond, Glenreagh, Corindi, Clouds Creek, Burren Junction, Edgeroi, Upper Horton, Llangothlin, Blackwater, Mt. Hyland 1439, Woolgoolga, Merah North, Namoi, Bundarra, Nana Glen, Cubbaroo, Kaputar 1508, Cobbadah, Guyra, Chandlers Pk. 1470, Aberfoyle, Ulong, Coramba, S. SOLITARY I., Wee Waa, Nandewar Range, Black Mountain, Tyringham, Cascade, Coffs Harbour, MUTTON BIRD I., Narrabri, Gwydir, Ebor, Dorrigo, HIGHWAY, Sawtell, Barraba, Woods Reef, Yarrowyck, Rockvale, Bellingen, Raleigh, Narrabri W., Bohena Cr., Turrawan, Kingstown, England, 1608 Round Mt., 1566 Point Lookout, Wollomombi, Gwabegar, Armidale, Wollomombi Falls, Urunga, Baan Baa, Upper Manilla, Mac Donald, Rocky River, New, Bowraville, Boggabri, Watsons Creek, Uralla, Macksville, Nambucca Heads, Kenebri, HWY, Namoi, Manilla, Kentucky, Bellbrook, Taylors Arm, Trial Bay, ENGLAND, The Blue Mountain 1317, South West Rocks, Baradine, NEWELL, Emerald Hill, Keepit Dam, Attunga, Bendemeer, Macleay, Smoky Cape, Somerton, Moore, Woolbrook, Walcha Road, Willawarrin, Jerseyville, Smithtown, Gunnedah, Carroll, HWY, Peel, Kootingal, 1321, Walcha, Frederickton, Bugaldie, Rocky Glen, Mullaley, Tamworth, Limbri, Apsley, Range, Kempsey, Korogoro Pt., OXLEY, Curlewis, Liverpool, Nemingha, Duri, Mt. Banda Banda 1258, Yearinan, Coxs Cr., Duri Mountain 947, Dungowan, Crescent Head, Coonabarabran, GREAT DIVIDING RANGE, Tambar Springs, Plains, Breeza, Currabubula, Hastings, Ulamambri, Werris Creek, Niangala, Rollands Plains, Telegraph Point, Purlewaugh, Spring Ridge, Quipolly Res., Chaffey Dam, Black Sugarloaf 1494, Castlereagh, Premer, Caroona, Dungowan Dam, Yarras, Wauchope, Port Macquarie, Tamarang, Nundle, Ellenborough, Hastings, Binnaway, Bomera, Pine Ridge, Quirindi, Wallabadah, Nowendoc, Comboyne, Kendall, New Mollyan, Ulinda, Oakley Creek, Blackville, Willow Tree, Barnard, Elands, Lorne, Perpendicular Pt., Weetaliba, Laurieton, Neilrex, Murrurundi, Range, Wherrol Flat, Marlee, Moorland, TASMAN, Mendooran, Coolah, Liverpool, Timor, Ellerston, Manning, Wingham, Lansdowne, Merrygoen, East Bluff 1241, Moonan Flat, Crowdy Hd., Hannahs Bridge, Wingen, Mount George, Taree, Liamena, Parkville, Hunter, Barrington, Dunedoo, Leadville, Cassilis, Gundy, Barrington Tops 1555, Cabbora, Bunnan, Gloucester, Halliday's Point, Talbragar, Craboon, Uarbry, Borambil, Scone, L. Glenbawn, Krambach, SEA, Elong Elong, Birriwa, Merriwa, Aberdeen, Upper Rouchel, Stratford, Nabiac, Tuncurry, Ballimore, Spring Ridge, Tallawang, Salisbury, Wards River, Forster, C. Hawke, Ulan, Gungal, Muswellbrook, Chichester Res., Coolongolook, Wallis L., Wollar, Sandy Hollow, Eccleston, Stroud Road, Wootton, Gulgong, Denman, Lostock Dam, Dungog, Myall, Bulahdelah, Goolma, Kerrabee, Jerrys Plains, Ravensworth, East Gresford, Stroud, Seal Rocks, Cooyal, Bylong, Baerami Creek, Martindale, Booral, Myall L.

27, 28, 29, 30, 31, 32

150, 151, 152, 153, 154

Projection: Alber's Equal area with two standard parallels

East from Greenwich

ft m

4500 1500

3000 1000

1200 400

600 200

0 0

200 600

2000 6000

4000 12 000

m ft

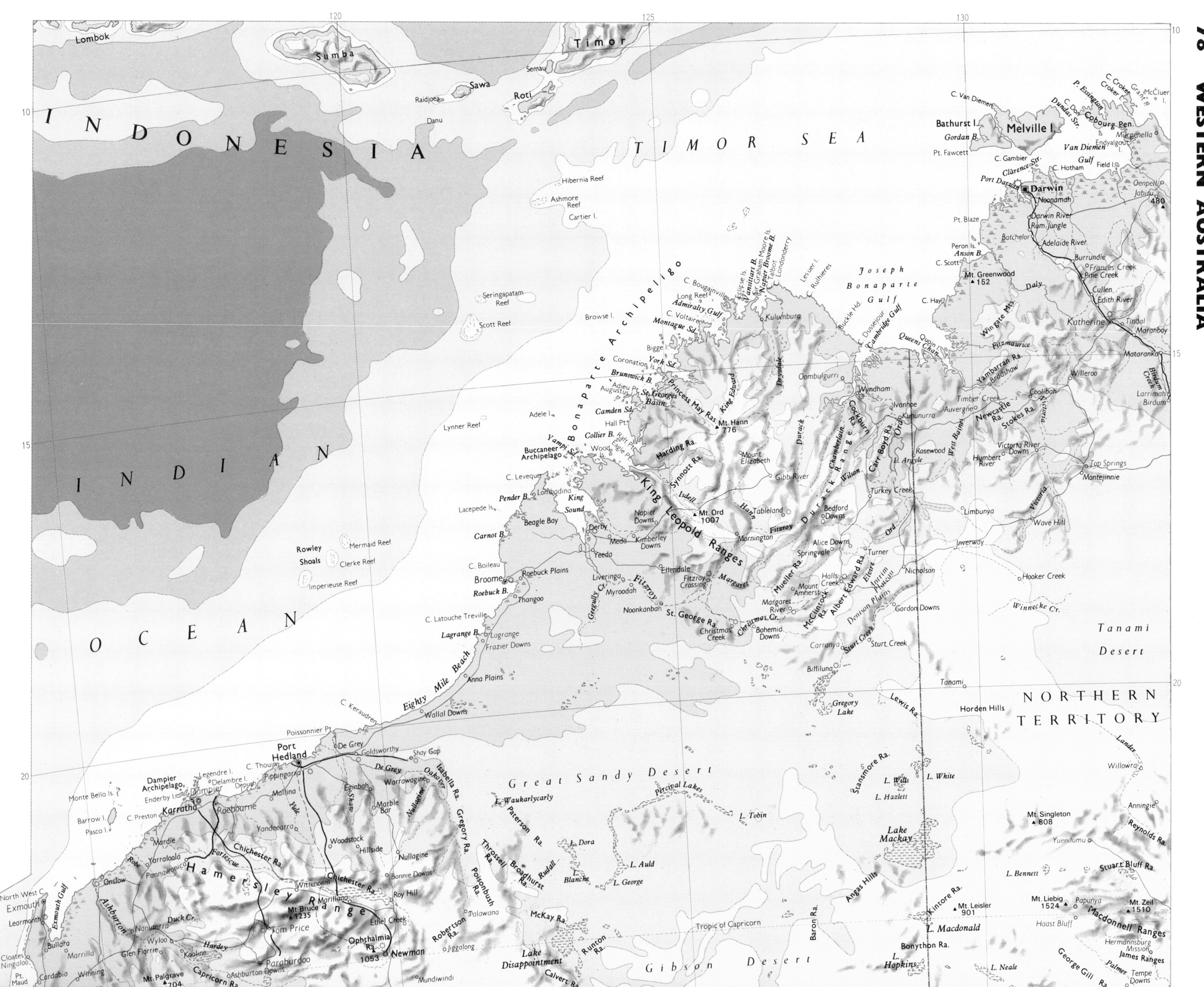

T I M O R S E A
I N D O N E S I A
I N D I A N
O C E A N
N O R T H E R N
T E R R I T O R Y
Lombok
Sumba
Timor
Sawa
Roti
Semau
Raijoea
Danu
Melville I.
Bathurst I.
Darwin
Katherine
Joseph Bonaparte Gulf
Bonaparte Archipelago
Cambridge Gulf
King Sound
Exmouth Gulf
Eighty Mile Beach
King Leopold Ranges
Durack Range
Hamersley Range
Macdonnell Ranges
Tanami Desert
Great Sandy Desert
Gibson Desert
Lake Mackay
Lake Disappointment
L. Macdonald
L. Argyle
Gregory Lake
Tropic of Capricorn
Wyndham
Kununurra
Halls Creek
Fitzroy Crossing
Derby
Broome
Port Hedland
Karratha
Dampier
Roebourne
Newman
Tom Price
Paraburdoo
Onslow
Exmouth
Ord
Fitzroy
Victoria River Downs
Kimberley Downs
Rowley Shoals
Scott Reef
Browse I.
Cartier I.
Ashmore Reef
Hibernia Reef
Adele I.
Lacepede Is.
Mt. Ord 1007
Mt. Hann 776
Mt. Bruce 1235
Mt. Greenwood 152
Mt. Singleton 808
Mt. Leisler 901
Mt. Liebig 1524
Mt. Zeil 1510
Mt. Palgrave 704
10
15
20
120
125
130

1 : 6 400 000

50 0 50 100 150 200 miles

50 0 50 100 150 200 250 300 km

SOUTHERN OCEAN

Great Australian Bight

WESTERN AUSTRALIA

SOUTH AUSTRALIA

Great Victoria Desert

Nullarbor Plain

Hampton Tableland

Archipelago of the Recherche

PERTH
Fremantle
Rockingham
Kwinana
Mandurah
Bunbury
Busselton
Albany
Esperance
Geraldton
Carnarvon
Kalgoorlie-Boulder
Norseman
Northam
Merredin
Narrogin
Katanning
Collie
Bridgetown
Manjimup
Denham
Wiluna
Meekatharra
Cue
Mount Magnet
Laverton
Leonora
Menzies
Coolgardie
Southern Cross
Kellerberrin
Moora
Dongara
Eucla Motel
Madura Motel
Cocklebiddy Motel
Nullarbor
Cook
Ooldea
Forrest
Rawlinna
Kitchener
Zanthus

Shark Bay
Hamelin Pool
Dirk Hartog I.
Houtman Abrolhos
Rottnest I.
C. Leeuwin
C. Naturaliste
Pt. D'Entrecasteaux
Head of Bight

L. Amadeus
L. Carnegie
L. Wells
L. Carey
L. Barlee
L. Moore
L. Austin
L. Cowan
L. Dundas
L. Lefroy
L. Minigwal
L. Yindarlgooda
L. Hope
L. Magenta
L. Grace

Ayers Rock 868
Mt. Olga 1069
Musgrave Ranges
Mt. Woodroffe 1549
Mt. Morris 1387
Mann Ras. 1174
Everard Ranges
Warburton Ra.
Rawlinson Ra. 1126
Mt. Augustus 1105
Mt. Essendon 906
Mt. Eureka 499
Mt. Singleton 677
Mt. Ragged 585
Peak Eleanora 503
Stirling Ra. 1073
Mt. Barker
Mt. Ridley
Ernest Giles Ra. 712
Kennedy Ra.
Collier Ra.
Robinson Ra.
Barr Smith Ra.
Montague Ra.
Dividing Ra.
Tallering Peak 439

East from Greenwich

Projection: Bonne

m ft

0 0
200 600
400 1200
1000 3000

0 0
200 600
2000 6000
4000 12 000

1 : 2 800 000

20 0 20 40 60 80 miles

20 0 20 40 60 80 100 120km

PACIFIC

OCEAN

TASMAN

SEA

NORTHLAND

CENTRAL AUCKLAND

SOUTH AUCKLAND BAY OF PLENTY

TARANAKI

WELLINGTON

HAWKE'S BAY

EAST COAST

C. Reinga
C. Maria van Diemen
North C.
Parengarenga Harb.
Ninety Mile Beach
Rangaunu B.
C. Karikari
Houhora
Doubtless B.
Mangonui
Whangaroa Harb.
Awanui
Kaitaia
Ahipara B.
Cavalli I.
Bay of Islands
C. Brett
Kerikeri
Russell
Okaihau
Herekino
Kohukohu
Kaikohe
Kawakawa
Whangaruru Harb.
Poor Knights Island
Hokianga Harb.
Rawene
776
Omapere
Hikurangi
Wairoa
Kamo
Whangarei
Donnelly's Crossing
Aranga
Onerahi
Whangarei Harb.
Bream Head
Kirikopuni
Bream Bay
Hen & Chickens Islands
Dargaville
Waikiekie
Waipu
Bream Tail
Te Kopuru
Ruawai
Paparoa
Maungaturoto
Needles Point
Port Fitzroy
Great Barrier I.
Lit. Barrier I.
Wellsford
C. Rodney
C. Barrier
Kaipara Harb.
Matakana
Kawau I.
Cuvier I.
Warkworth
C. Colville
Hauraki Gulf
Port Charles
Mercury Is.
Helensville
Coromandel
Takapuna
Devonport
Birkenhead
Mercury B.
Whitianga
AUCKLAND
Waiheke I.
Firth of Thames
Mt. Roskill
Howick
Coromandel Ra.
Onehunga
Mt. Wellington
836
Coromandel Peninsula
Papatoetoe
Otahuhu
Manukau
Manukau Harb.
Papakura
Thames
Pukekohe
Tuakau
Whangamata
Mayor I.
Waiuku
Mercer
Waikato
Te Kauwhata
Waikare L.
Paeroa
Waihi
White I.
Te Aroha
Katikati
Tauranga Harb.
Huntly
Waitoa
Matakana I.
Motiti I.
Glen Afton
Glen Massey
Morrinsville
Mt. Maunganui
Ngaruawahia
Bay of Plenty
C. Runaway
Hicks Bay
Te Araroa
East C.
Raglan Harb.
Frankton
Hamilton
Tauranga
Te Puke
Te Kaha
Raglan
Waharoa
Cambridge
Matamata
Paengaroa
Motata
Whakatane
Edgecumbe
Ohiwa Harbour
Hikurangi
1753
Waiapu
Raukumara Ra.
Ruatoria
Aotea Harb.
Ohaupo
Te Awamutu
Karapiro
Tirau
Putaruru
Rotorua
Rotoiti
Rotoehu
Rotoma
Kawerau
Teko
Opotiki
Waipiro
Kawhia Harb.
Albatross Pt.
Arapuni
Kihikihi
Mamaku
Ngongotaha
L. Tarawera
Mt. Tarawera
1111
Motu
Tokomaru Bay
Otorohanga
Tokoroa
Rotorua
Te Kuiti
Waipa
Rangitoto Ra.
Mangakino
Kinleith
Atiamuri
Waiotapu
Whakatane
Motuhora
Galatea
Tirua Pt.
KAINGAROA STATE FOREST
Murupara
Tolaga Bay
Te Karaka
Ormond
1165
Whakamaru
Hauhungaroa Ra.
Mokau
Aria
Mokai
Wairakei
Waikato
Taupo
Rangitaiki
1403
Waikare Iti
Ngatapa
Patutahi
Gisborne
Ongarue
Ohakuri
North Taranaki Bight
Taumarunui
369
Lake Taupo
Waikaremoana
Tuai
L. Waikaremoana
Poverty Bay
Ohura
Rangitaiki
Huiarau Ra.
Pukearuhe
Waitara
Manunui
Tokaanu
1383
Frasertown
New Plymouth
Tahora
Owhango
Rotoaira
Ahimanawa Ra.
Tarawera
Mohaka
Waikokopu
Inglewood
Okato
Whangamomona
Ngauruhoe
2291
Kaimanawa Mts.
Putorino
Wairoa
Nuhaka
Mahia Peninsula
C. Egmont
Mt. Egmont
2518
Rahotu
Midhurst
Huiroa
NAT. PARK
Ruapehu
2796
Rangataua
Kaweka Ra.
Ngaruroro
Portland I.
Stratford
Kopongo
Eltham
Ohakune
Pipiriki
Raetihi
Hawke Bay
Bay View
Napier
Opunake
Kapuni
Normanby
Hawera
Manaia
Waitotara
Wanganui
Whangaehu
Turakina
Waiouru
Rangitikei
Taradale
Clive
Hastings
C. Kidnappers
Havelock North
South Taranaki Bight
Patea
Waverley
Maxwell
Taihape
Mangaweka
Opapa
Tukituki
Otane
1733
Castlecliff
Wanganui
Hunterville
Apiti
Ruahine Ra.
Waipawa
Waipukurau
Turakina
Marton
Halcombe
Norsewood
Takapau
Wanstead
Ormondville
Bulls
Feilding
Rangitikei
Bunnythorpe
Ashhurst
Dannevirke
Rongotea
Palmerston North
Woodville
Porangahau
Longburn
Manawatu
Foxton
Shannon
Pahiatua
Puketoi Ra.
Weber
C. Turnagain
Herbertville
Levin
Eketahuna
Alfredton
Otaki
Tararua Ra.
Mauriceville
Mitre
1571
Tinui
Castlepoint
Kapiti I.
Paraparaumu
Paekakariki
Masterton
Carterton
Titahi Bay
Upper Hutt
Lr. Hutt
Greytown
Featherston
Johnsonville
Petone
Martinborough
Flat Pt.
Wainuiomata
Wairarapa
L. Onoke
Aorangi Mts.
983
Port Nicholson
WELLINGTON
Eastbourne
Turakirae Head
Ruamahanga
Palliser Bay
C. Palliser
C. Farewell
Golden Bay
Collingwood
C. Stephens
Stephens I.
Separation Pt.
D'Urville Island
Kahurangi Pt.
Takaka
French Pass
Tasman Bay
Pelorus Sd.
Forsyth I.
Cook Strait
Devil River Pk.
1775
Riwaka
Motueka
Tasman Mts.
Queen Charlotte Sd.
Arapawa I.
Karamea
Nelson
Pelorus
Havelock
Terawhiti
Stoke
Picton
Brightwater
Wakefield
Richmond
Tadmor
Mt. Richmond
1760
Tuamarina
Cloudy B.
Mt. Owen
1875
Belgrove
Richmond Ra.
Wairau
Blenheim
Renwicktown
Mokihinui
Lyell Ra.
Buller
Glenhope
Seddon
Lyell
Murchison
L. Rotoiti
Awatere
C. Campbell
Ward
2297

ft m
9000 3000
6000 2000
3000 1000
1200 400
600 200
0 0
200 600
2000 6000
m ft

173 174 175 176 177 178 179

35 36 37 38 39 40 41

Projection: Conical with two standard parallels

East from Greenwich

1 : 2 800 000

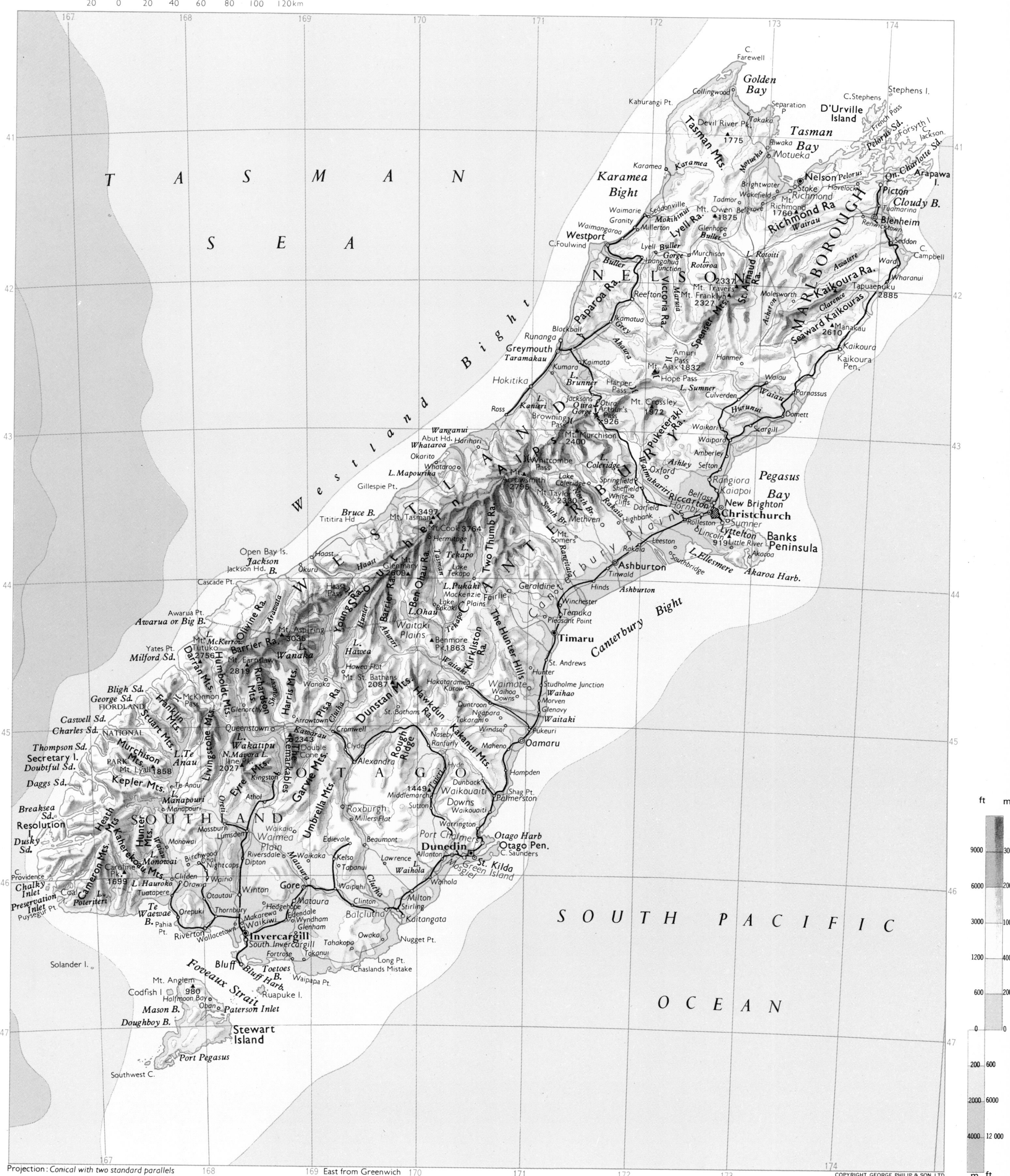
TASMAN SEA
SOUTH PACIFIC OCEAN
Westland Bight
Karamea Bight
Golden Bay
Tasman Bay
Pegasus Bay
Canterbury Bight
Foveaux Strait
NELSON
MARLBOROUGH
WESTLAND
CANTERBURY
OTAGO
SOUTHLAND
Southern Alps
Canterbury Plains
C. Farewell
Collingwood
Kahurangi Pt.
Separation Pt.
D'Urville Island
C. Stephens
Stephens I.
French Pass
Pelorus Sd.
Forsyth I.
C. Jackson
Qn. Charlotte Sd.
Arapawa I.
Tasman Mts.
1775
Devil River Pk.
Takaka
Riwaka
Motueka
Karamea
Nelson
Stoke
Richmond
Brightwater
Wakefield
Tadmor
Mt. Owen 1875
Mt. Richmond 1760
Richmond Ra.
Wairau
Picton
Havelock
Cloudy B.
Blenheim
Renwick
Seddon
C. Campbell
Ward
Waimarie
Seddonville
Granity
Mokihinui
Millerton
Lyell Ra.
Westport
C. Foulwind
Buller
Lyell
Murchison
L. Rotoroa
L. Rotoiti
St. Arnaud Ra.
Mt. Travers 2337
Mt. Franklyn 2327
Spenser Mts.
Victoria Ra.
Reefton
Paparoa Ra.
Molesworth
Kaikoura Ra.
Tapuaenuku 2885
Seaward Kaikouras
Manakau 2610
Kaikoura
Kaikoura Pen.
Blackball
Runanga
Greymouth
Taramakau
Kumara
L. Brunner
Hokitika
Amuri Pass
Mt. Ajax 1832
Hope Pass
Hanmer
L. Sumner
Culverden
Waiau
Hurunui
Parnassus
Domett
Ross
L. Kanieri
Harper Pass
Jacksons
Otira
Arthur's Pass 926
Mt. Crossley 1972
Browning Pass
Mt. Murchison 2400
Waikari
Waipara
Scargill
Amberley
Sefton
Wanganui
Abut Hd.
Harihari
Whataroa
Okarito
L. Mapourika
Whitcombe Pass
L. Coleridge
Oxford
Ashley
Rangiora
Kaiapoi
Mt. Arrowsmith 2795
Mt. Taylor 2330
Springfield
Sheffield
Darfield
Gillespie Pt.
Bruce B.
Tititira Hd
Mt. Tasman 3497
Mt. Cook 3764
Hermitage
Methven
Belfast
Hornby
Riccarton
New Brighton
Christchurch
Sumner
Rolleston
Lincoln
Lyttelton
919
Little River
Banks Peninsula
Akaroa
Akaroa Harb.
L. Ellesmere
Southbridge
Leeston
Rakaia
Ashburton
Tinwald
Hinds
Mt. Somers
Open Bay Is.
Jackson B.
Jackson Hd.
Haast
Okuru
Haast Pass
Two Thumb Ra.
L. Tekapo
Mt. Glenmary 2609
Ben Ohau Ra.
L. Pukaki
Mackenzie Plains
L. Ohau
Fairlie
Geraldine
Winchester
Temuka
Pleasant Point
Timaru
Cascade Pt.
Awarua Pt.
Awarua or Big B.
Olivine Ra.
Mt. Aspiring 3036
Barrier Ra.
L. Wanaka
L. Hawea
Young Ra.
Waitaki Plains
Benmore Pk. 1863
Kirkliston Ra.
The Hunter Hills
St. Andrews
Hunter
Studholme Junction
Waimate
Yates Pt.
Milford Sd.
Mt. Tutuko 2756
Darran Mts.
Humboldt Mts.
Mt. Earnslaw 2815
Richardson Mts.
Harris Mts.
Pisa Ra.
Mt. St. Bathans 2087
Dunstan Mts.
Hawkdun Ra.
Hakataramea
Kurow
Waihao Downs
Waihao
Morven
Glenavy
Waitaki
Bligh Sd.
George Sd.
FIORDLAND NATIONAL PARK
McKinnon Pass
Franklin Mts.
Stuart Mts.
Caswell Sd.
Charles Sd.
Glenorchy
Queenstown
Arrowtown
Cromwell
Clyde
Alexandra
Rough Ridge
St. Bathans Ra.
Duntroon
Ngapara
Tokarahi
Windsor
Pukeuri
Oamaru
Kakanui Mts.
Maheno
Naseby
Ranfurly
Thompson Sd.
Secretary I.
Doubtful Sd.
Murchison Mts.
L. Te Anau
L. Wakatipu
Kawarau 2343
Double Cone
Livingstone Mts.
Mt. Lyall 1858
Jane Pk. 2027
Eyre Mts.
The Remarkables
Kingston
Garvie Mts.
Hampden
Daggs Sd.
Kepler Mts.
Te Anau
L. Manapouri
Manapouri
Athol
Umbrella Mts.
Roxburgh
Millers Flat
1449
Middlemarch
Sutton
Hyde
Dunback
Waikouaiti Downs
Waikouaiti
Shag Pt.
Palmerston
Breaksea Sd.
Resolution I.
Dusky Sd.
Heath Mts.
Kaherekoau Mts.
Hunter Mts.
Mossburn
Lumsden
Waikaia
Waimea Plain
Warrington
Port Chalmers
Otago Harb
Otago Pen.
Dunedin
C. Saunders
St. Kilda
Mosgiel
Green Island
Allanton
Lawrence
L. Waihola
Waihola
Monowai
L. Monowai
Riversdale
Dipton
Waikaka
Edievale
Beaumont
Kelso
Tapanui
C. Providence
Chalky Inlet
Caroline Pk. 1699
Cameron Mts.
L. Poteriteri
L. Hauroko
Clifden
Orawia
Wairio
Nightcaps
Ohai
Birchwood
Tuatapere
Otautau
Winton
Gore
Waipahi
Clinton
Milton
Preservation Inlet
Puysegur Pt.
Te Waewae B.
Orepuki
Thornbury
Makarewa
Waikiwi
Hedgehope
Mataura
Edendale
Wyndham
Glenham
Balclutha
Stirling
Kaitangata
Pahia Pt.
Riverton
Wallacetown
Invercargill
South Invercargill
Owaka
Nugget Pt.
Tahakopa
Fortrose
Tokanui
Long Pt.
Chaslands Mistake
Bluff
Toetoes B.
Bluff Harb.
Waipapa Pt.
Solander I.
Ruapuke I.
Mt. Anglem 980
Codfish I.
Halfmoon Bay
Oban
Paterson Inlet
Mason B.
Doughboy B.
Stewart Island
Port Pegasus
Southwest C.
Projection: Conical with two standard parallels
East from Greenwich
COPYRIGHT, GEORGE PHILIP & SON, LTD.

1 : 32 000 000

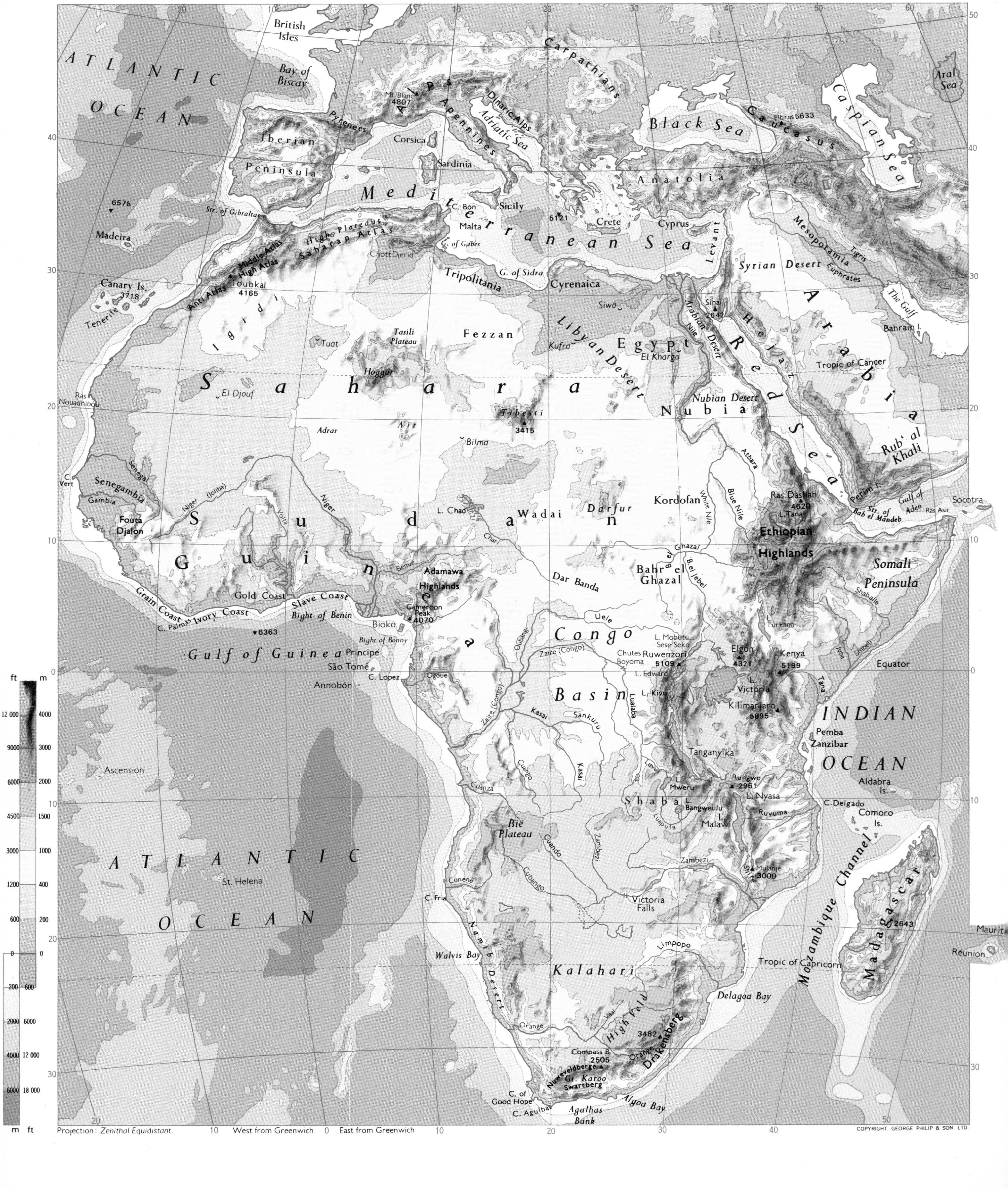

200 0 200 400 600 800 1000 miles

200 0 200 400 600 800 1000 1200 1400 1600 km

ATLANTIC OCEAN
British Isles
Bay of Biscay
Carpathians
Aral Sea
Caspian Sea
Mt. Blanc 4807
Alps
Dinaric Alps
Apennines
Adriatic Sea
Pyrenees
Black Sea
Caucasus
Elbrus 5633
Iberian Peninsula
Corsica
Sardinia
Anatolia
Mediterranean Sea
6576
Str. of Gibraltar
High Plateaus
Saharan Atlas
C. Bon
Sicily
Malta
5121
Crete
Cyprus
Levant
Mesopotamia
Tigris
Madeira
Middle Atlas
High Atlas
G. of Gabes
Chott Djerid
Syrian Desert
Euphrates
Canary Is. 3718
Anti Atlas
Toubkal 4165
Tripolitania
G. of Sidra
Cyrenaica
The Gulf
Tenerife
Igidi
Siwa
Sinai 2642
Arabian Desert
Nile
Hejaz
Arabia
Bahrain
Tuat
Tasili Plateau
Fezzan
Libyan Desert
Kufra
Egypt
El Kharga
Red Sea
Tropic of Cancer
Hoggar
Sahara
El Djouf
Ras Nouadhibou
Tibesti 3415
Nubian Desert
Nubia
Adrar
Aïr
Bilma
Rub' al Khali
Atbara
C. Vert
Senegal
Senegambia
Gambia
Niger (Joliba)
Niger
Volta
Fouta Djalon
Sudan
L. Chad
Wadai
Darfur
Kordofan
White Nile
Blue Nile
Ras Dashan 4620
L. Tana
Perim I.
Str. of Bab el Mandeb
Gulf of Aden
Ras Asir
Socotra
Chari
Ethiopian Highlands
Somali Peninsula
Guinea
Benue
Adamawa Highlands
Dar Banda
Bahr el Ghazal
Bel Ghazal
Bel Jebel
Shabelle
Grain Coast
Gold Coast
Slave Coast
Bight of Benin
Cameroon Peak 4070
C. Palmas
Ivory Coast
6363
Bioko
Uele
Turkana
Bight of Bonny
Congo Basin
Oubangi
L. Mobutu Sese Seko
Elgon 4321
Kenya 5199
Juba
Shibeli
Gulf of Guinea
Principe
São Tomé
Zaire (Congo)
Chutes Boyoma
Ruwenzori 5109
Equator
C. Lopez
Ogoue
L. Edward
Annobón
L. Kivu
L. Victoria
Tana
Lualaba
Kilimanjaro 5895
INDIAN OCEAN
Zaire (Congo)
Kasai
Sankuru
Pemba
Zanzibar
Kasai
Cuango
L. Tanganyika
Ascension
Luvua
L. Mweru
Rungwe 2961
Aldabra Is.
Cuanza
Shaba
L. Nyasa
L. Bangweulu
C. Delgado
Luapula
Ruvuma
Comoro Is.
Bié Plateau
L. Malawi
Cuando
Zambezi
Mozambique Channel
Zambezi
ATLANTIC OCEAN
St. Helena
Cunene
Cubango
Mulanje 3000
Shire
C. Fria
Victoria Falls
Madagascar
2643
Namib Desert
Mauritius
Limpopo
Walvis Bay
Tropic of Capricorn
Réunion
Kalahari
Delagoa Bay
Vaal
High Veld
3482
Drakensberg
Orange
Compass B. 2505
Orange
Nuweveldberge
Gt. Karoo
Swartberg
C. of Good Hope
C. Agulhas
Agulhas Bank
Algoa Bay

ft m
12 000 4000
9000 3000
6000 2000
4500 1500
3000 1000
1200 400
600 200
0 0
200 600
2000 6000
4000 12 000
6000 18 000
m ft

Projection: *Zenithal Equidistant.* 10 West from Greenwich 0 East from Greenwich 10 20 30 40

1 : 32 000 000

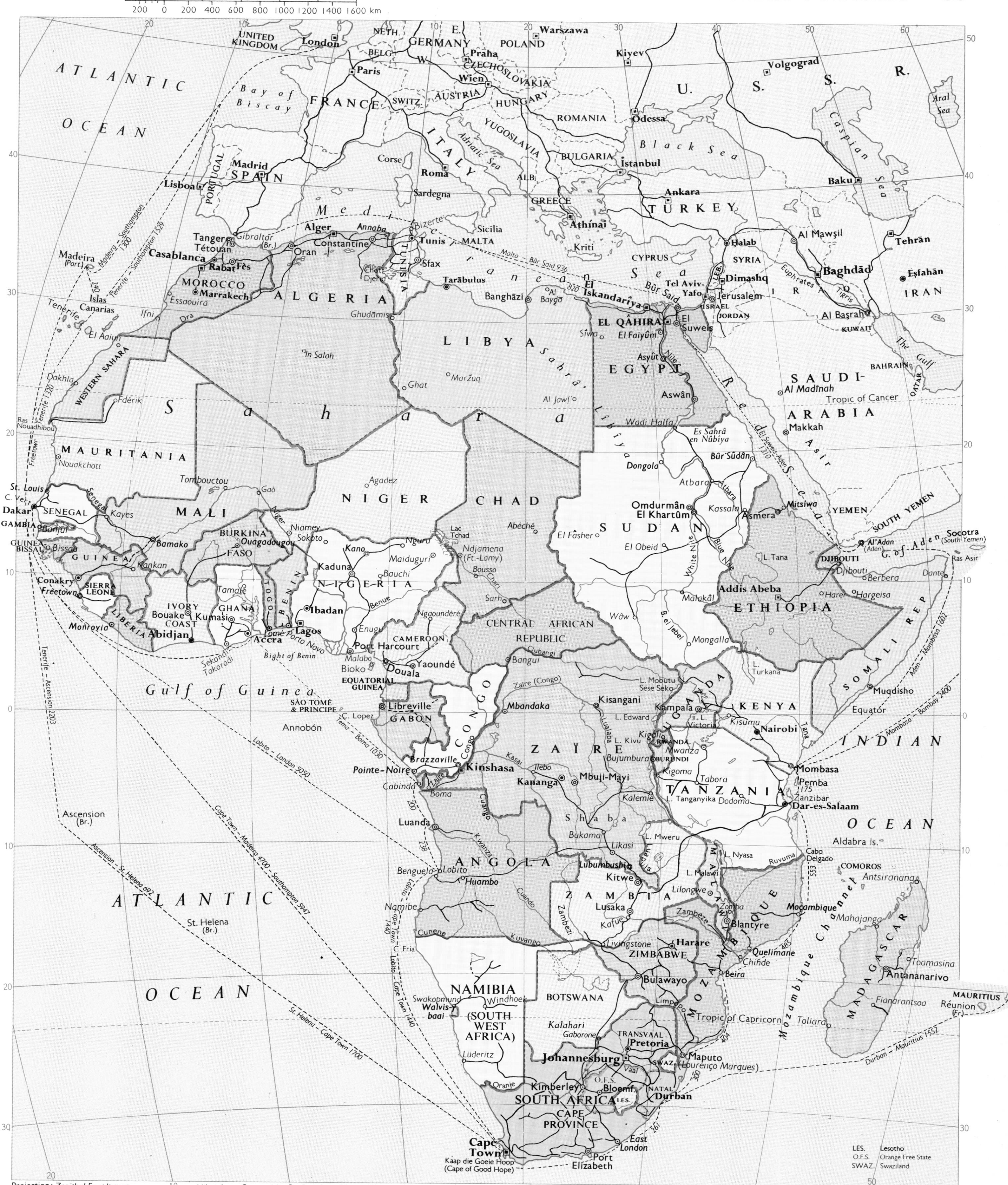
ATLANTIC OCEAN
INDIAN OCEAN
ALGERIA
LIBYA
EGYPT
SUDAN
ETHIOPIA
NIGER
CHAD
MALI
MAURITANIA
NIGERIA
ZAÏRE
ANGOLA
ZAMBIA
TANZANIA
KENYA
SOUTH AFRICA
NAMIBIA (SOUTH WEST AFRICA)
BOTSWANA
ZIMBABWE
MOZAMBIQUE
MADAGASCAR
MOROCCO
WESTERN SAHARA
SENEGAL
GAMBIA
GUINEA
SIERRA LEONE
LIBERIA
IVORY COAST
GHANA
TOGO
BENIN
BURKINA FASO
CAMEROON
CENTRAL AFRICAN REPUBLIC
GABON
CONGO
UGANDA
SOMALI REP.
DJIBOUTI
Gulf of Guinea
Mozambique Channel
Mediterranean Sea
Sahara
LES. Lesotho
O.F.S. Orange Free State
SWAZ. Swaziland
Projection: Zenithal Equidistant.
West from Greenwich 0 East from Greenwich

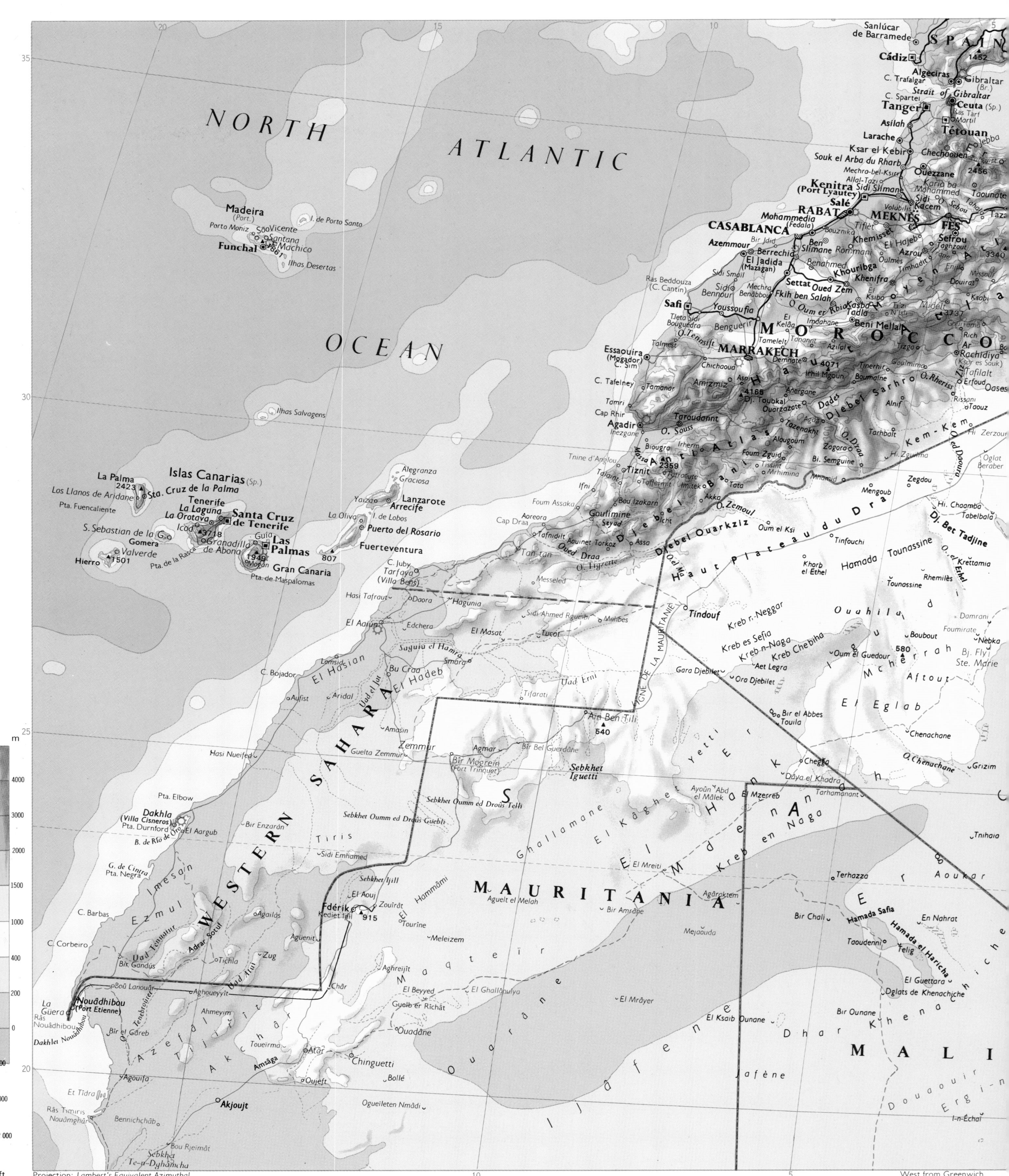
NORTH ATLANTIC OCEAN
Madeira (Port.)
Porto Moniz
São Vicente
Santana
Machico
Funchal
I. de Porto Santo
Ilhas Desertas
Ilhas Salvagens
Islas Canarias (Sp.)
La Palma
Los Llanos de Aridane
Sta. Cruz de la Palma
Pta. Fuencaliente
Tenerife
La Laguna
La Orotava
Santa Cruz de Tenerife
Icod
3718
Guía
Granadilla de Abona
Pta. de la Rasca
S. Sebastian de la Gomera
Gomera
Valverde
Hierro
1501
Las Palmas
1949
Mogán
Gran Canaria
Pta. de Maspalomas
Alegranza
Graciosa
Lanzarote
Arrecife
Yaiza
La Oliva
I. de Lobos
Puerto del Rosario
Fuerteventura
807
Sanlúcar de Barrameda
Cádiz
SPAIN
Algeciras
Gibraltar (Br.)
C. Trafalgar
Strait of Gibraltar
C. Spartel
Ceuta (Sp.)
Tanger
Ras Tarf
Martil
Asilah
Tétouan
Larache
Ksar el Kebir
Chechaouen
Souk el Arba du Rharb
Mechra-bel-Ksiri
Ouezzane
Kenitra (Port Lyautey)
Sidi Slimane
Sidi Kacem
Taounate
Salé
RABAT
MEKNÈS
FES
Mohammedia (Fedala)
CASABLANCA
Sefrou
Azemmour
El Jadida (Mazagan)
Berrechid
Ben Slimane
Khouribga
Azrou
Settat
Oued Zem
Khenifra
Ras Beddouza (C. Cantin)
Safi
Youssoufia
Fkih ben Salah
Kasba Tadla
Beni Mellal
Benguerir
MOROCCO
Essaouira (Mogador)
C. Sim
MARRAKECH
Amizmiz
Demnate
Tamanar
C. Tafelney
4165
Dj. Toubkal
Ouarzazate
Tamri
Cap Rhir
Agadir
Inezgane
Taroudannt
O. Souss
Djebel Sarhro
Rachidiya (Ksar es Souk)
Tafilalt
Erfoud
Rissani
Taouz
Alnif
Tazenakht
Zagora
Tarhbalt
Kem-Kem
Hi. Zerzour
Hi. Zguilma
O. Draa
Foum Zguid
Tiznit
Tafraoute
Bi. Semguine
Ifni
Foum Assaka
Bou Izakarn
Akka
Goulimine
Cap Draa
Tan-tan
Djebel Ouarkziz
Oued Draa
Haut Plateau du Dra
Hamada Tounassine
Dj. Bet Tadjine
Tindouf
C. Juby
Tarfaya (Villa Bens)
Hasi Tafrout
Daora
Haguinia
El Aaiún
Edchera
El Masat
Saguia el Hamra
Smara
C. Bojador
El Hasian
Bu Craa
El Hadeb
Aufist
Aridal
Amasin
Ain Ben Tili
540
Zemmur
Guelta Zemmur
Hasi Nueifed
Bir Mogrein (Fort Trinquet)
Sebkhet Iguetti
Pta. Elbow
Dakhla (Villa Cisneros)
Pta. Durnford
B. de Río de Oro
El Aargub
Bir Enzaran
Tiris
Sidi Emhamed
G. de Cintra
Pta. Negra
Imesan
WESTERN SAHARA
C. Barbas
Ezmul
Agaildis
Sebkhet Ijill
Fdérik
Kediet Ijill
915
Zouîrât
C. Corbeiro
Adrar Sotuf
Tichla
Zug
Bir Gandus
Boû Lanouâr
Aghoueyît
Nouâdhibou (Port Etienne)
La Güera
Râs Nouâdhibou
Dakhlet Nouâdhibou
Bir el Gareb
Ahmeyim
Tijirit
Akchâr
Inchiri
Atâr
Chinguetti
Ouadâne
Amsâga
Ouajeft
Akjoujt
Agouifa
Et Tidra
Râs Timirist
Nouâmghâr
Bennichchâb
Bou Rjeimât
Sebkha Te-n-Dghâmcha
Char
Aghreijît
Maqteïr
Ouarâne
El Beyyed
Guelb er Richât
MAURITANIA
El Hank
Tarhamanant
Chegga
Dâya el Khadra
Ayoûn Abd el Mâlek
El Mzereb
Kreb en Naga
El Mreiti
Erg Chech
El Eglab
Aftout
Mcherrah
Oum el Guedour
Bir el Abbes
Touila
Chenachane
O. Chenachane
Grizim
Terhazza
Aoukar
Bir Chali
Hamada Safia
Taoudenni
Hamada el Haricha
El Guettara
Dglats de Khenachiche
Bir Ounane
Khenachich
El Ksaib Ounane
Dhar
Ijâfene
Jafène
Oueileten Nmâdi
MALI
Douaouir
Erg in-Echaï
In-Echaï
Projection: Lambert's Equivalent Azimuthal
West from Greenwich

1 : 6 400 000

50 0 50 100 150 200 miles

50 0 50 100 150 200 250 300 km

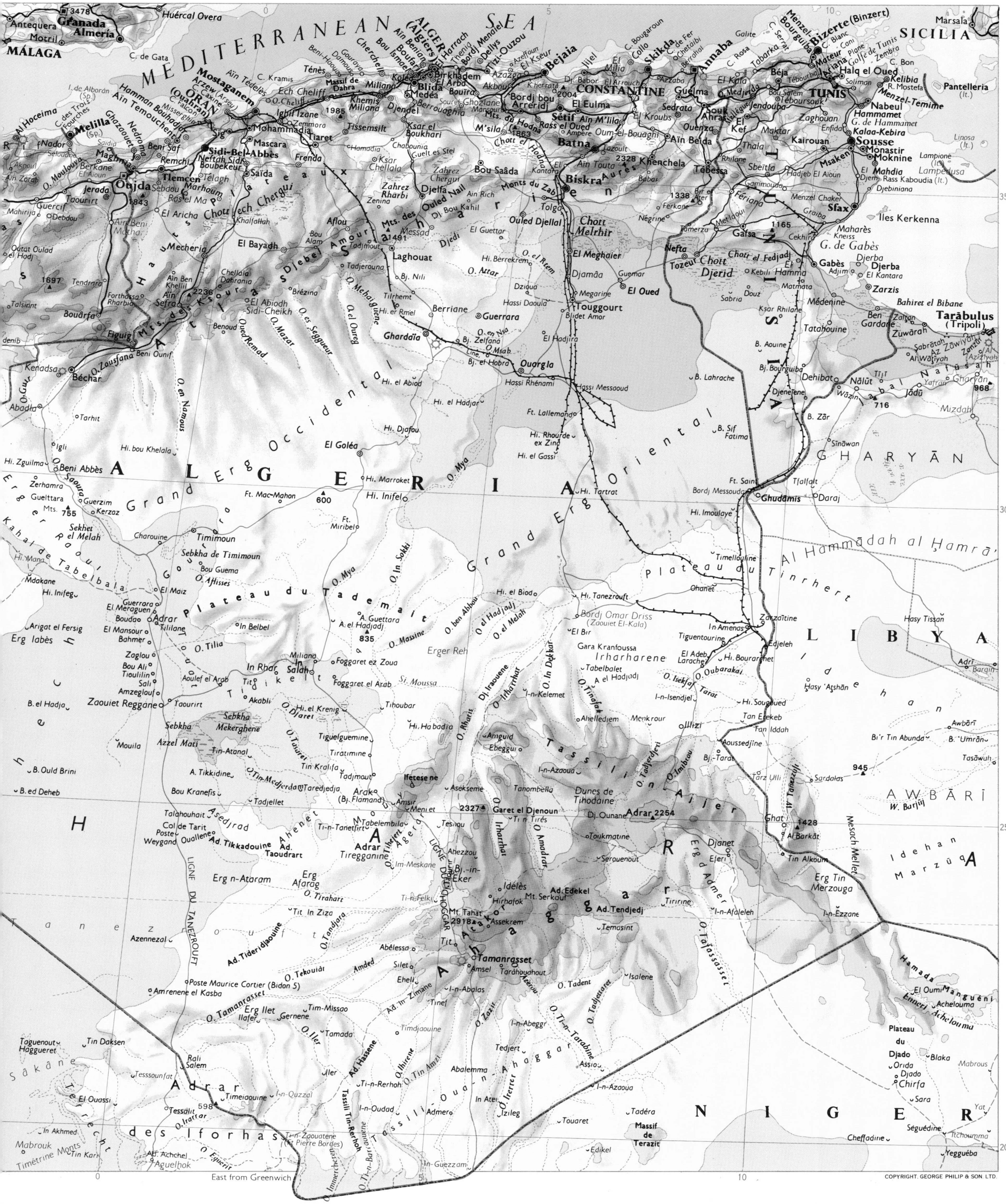

MEDITERRANEAN SEA

SICILIA

ALGERIA

TUNISIA

LIBYA

NIGER

Málaga
Antequera
Granada
Almería
Motril
Huércal Overa
C. de Gata
Melilla (Sp.)
Al Hoceima
Nador
Oujda
Taourirt
Jerada
Berkane
Figuig
Béchar
Kenadsa
Abadla
Beni Abbès
Igli
Tarhit
Oran (Ouahran)
Arzew
Mostaganem
Sidi-Bel-Abbès
Tlemcen
Maghnia
Ghazaouet
Nedroma
Beni Saf
Aïn Temouchent
Hamman Bouhadjar
Mascara
Saïda
Frenda
Tiaret
Relizane
Mohammadia
Ech Cheliff
Ténès
Miliana
Khemis Miliana
Tissemsilt
Médéa
Blida
Alger (Algiers)
Birkhadem
Boufarik
Cherchell
Tipaza
Boumerdès
Dellys
Tizi-Ouzou
Bouïra
Bordj Menaïel
Azazga
Akbou
Bejaïa
Jijel
El Milia
Collo
C. Bougaroun
Skikda
Annaba
El Kala
Guelma
Souk Ahras
Sedrata
Constantine
El Eulma
Sétif
Bordj bou Arreridj
M'sila
Aïn M'lila
Oum-el-Bouaghi
Aïn Beïda
Khenchela
Tebessa
Batna
Biskra
Tolga
Bou Saâda
Djelfa
Ksar el Boukhari
Laghouat
Aflou
El Bayadh
Mecheria
El Aricha
Aïn Sefra
El Abiodh Sidi-Cheikh
Chott ech Chergui
Chott el Hodna
Chott Melrhir
Hauts Plateaux
Atlas Saharien
Djebel Amour
Monts des Ouled Naïl
Monts du Zab
Monts du Hodna
Aurès
Monts des Ksour
El Meghaier
Djamâa
Touggourt
El Oued
Guemar
Ghardaïa
Berriane
Guerrara
Metlili
Ouargla
Hassi Messaoud
El Goléa
Timimoun
Adrar
Reggane
In Salah
Grand Erg Occidental
Grand Erg Oriental
Plateau du Tademaït
Plateau du Tinrhert
Erg Iguidi
Tanezrouft
Tidikelt
Gourara
Touat
Hoggar
Ahaggar
Tamanrasset
Mt. Tahat 2918
Assekrem
Tassili n Ajjer
Tassili-Oua-n-Ahaggar
Adrar des Iforhas
Djanet
Illizi
In Amenas
Bordj Omar Driss
Tin Zaouatene
In Guezzam
Bordj Mokhtar
Tunis
Bizerte (Binzert)
Menzel Bourguiba
Béja
Jendouba
Le Kef
Kairouan
Sousse
Monastir
Mahdia
Sfax
Gafsa
Tozeur
Nefta
Chott el Djerid
Chott el Fedjadj
Kebili
Gabès
G. de Gabès
Djerba
Zarzis
Médenine
Tataouine
Ben Gardane
Nabeul
Hammamet
G. de Hammamet
Kelibia
Pantelleria (It.)
Lampedusa (It.)
Linosa (It.)
Iles Kerkenna
Tarābulus (Tripoli)
Zuwārah
Az Zāwiyah
Sabrātah
Gharyān
Nālūt
Ghudāmis
Al Ḩammādah al Ḩamrā'
Awbārī
Ghāt
Idehan Marzūq
Hamada Manguéni
Plateau du Djado
Djado
Chirfa
Séguédine
Yeggueba
Massif de Terazit

East from Greenwich

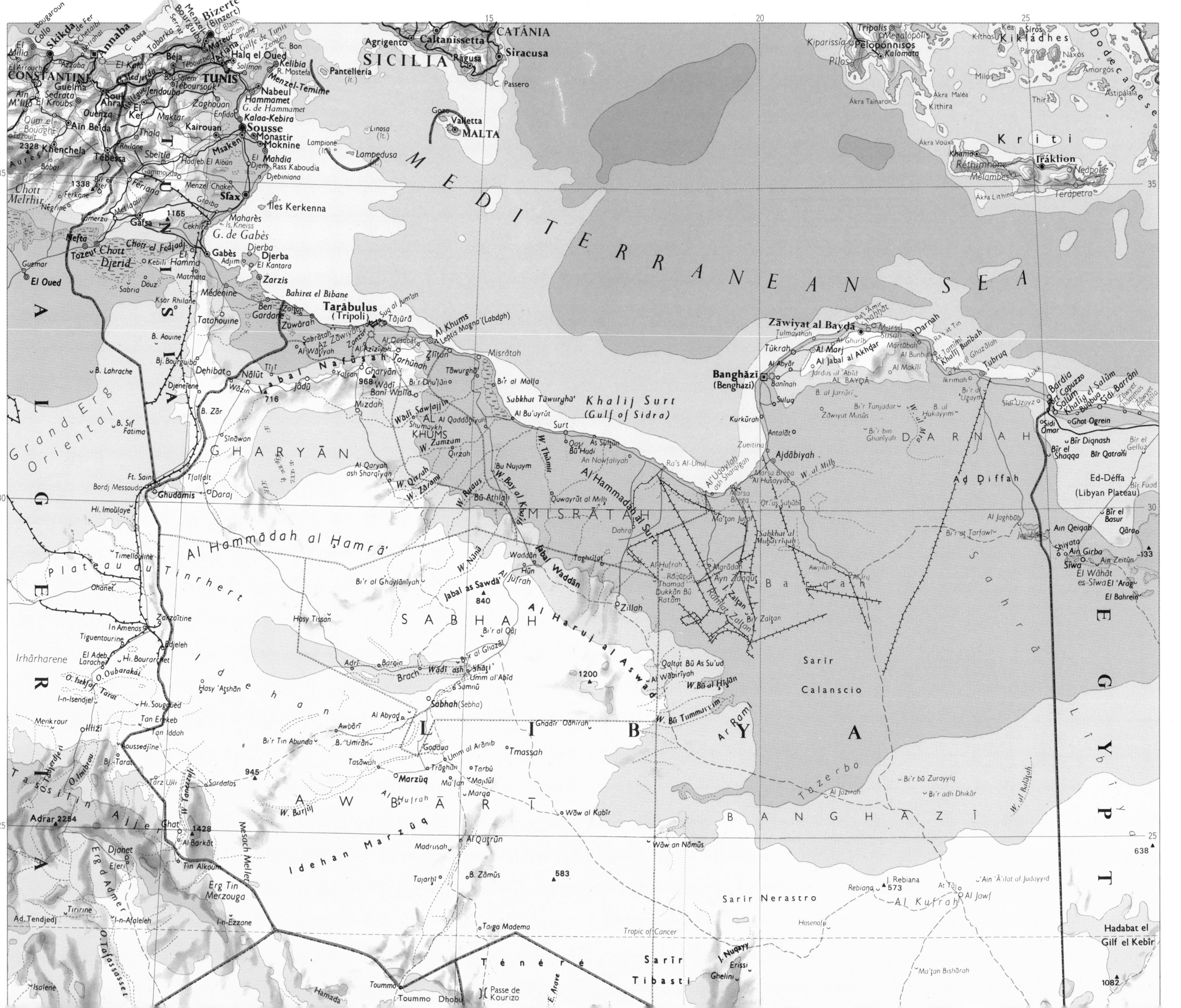
MEDITERRANEAN SEA
SICILIA
CATÁNIA
Siracusa
Caltanissetta
Agrigento
Ragusa
Valletta
MALTA
Pantelleria (It.)
Linosa (It.)
Lampedusa (It.)
Peloponnisos
Kiklådhes
Dodecanese
Kriti
Iráklion
TUNISIA
TUNIS
Bizerte (Binzert)
Sousse
Sfax
Kairouan
Gabès
G. de Gabès
Djerba
Zarzis
Îles Kerkenna
G. de Hammamet
Chott Djerid
Chott el Fedjadj
Chott Melrhir
ALGERIA
Annaba
Skikda
CONSTANTINE
El Oued
Grand Erg Oriental
Plateau du Tinrhert
Tassili n'Ajjer
Erg d'Admer
Adrar 2254
LIBYA
Tarābulus (Tripoli)
Al Khums
Misrātah
Gharyān
Jabal Nafūsah
Ghudāmis
Khalij Surt (Gulf of Sidra)
Surt
Banghāzī (Benghazi)
Zāwiyat al Bayḍā
Darnah
Tubruq
Al Jabal al Akhḍar
Ajdābiyah
Al Hammādah al Hamrā'
Al Hammadah al Surt
Jabal Waddān
Jabal as Sawdā'
Al Haruj al Aswad
SABHAH
Sabhah (Sebha)
Marzūq
Idehan Marzūq
Idehan Awbārī
AWBĀRĪ
GHARYĀN
KHUMS
MISRĀTAH
DARNAH
BANGHĀZĪ
Barqah
Ramlat Zaltan
Sarir Calanscio
Sarir Nerastro
Sarir Tibasti
Ad Diffah
Al Kufrah
Rebiana
Tazerbo
Ténéré
Tropic of Cancer
EGYPT
Sahra Lībīya
Siwa
Ed-Déffa (Libyan Plateau)
Hadabat el Gilf el Kebir
15
20
25
30
35

1 : 6 400 000

50 0 50 100 150 200 miles

50 0 50 100 150 200 250 300 km

CHAD

SUDAN

NIGER

NIGERIA

CAMEROON

CENTRAL AFRICAN REPUBLIC

SHAMÂL DÂRFÛR

JANUB DÂRFÛR

Tibesti

Ennedi

L. Tchad

Ndjamena

m ft

3000 9000

2000 6000

1500 4500

1000 3000

400 1200

200 600

0 0

200 600

2000 6000

4000 12 000

Projection: Lambert's Equivalent Azimuthal

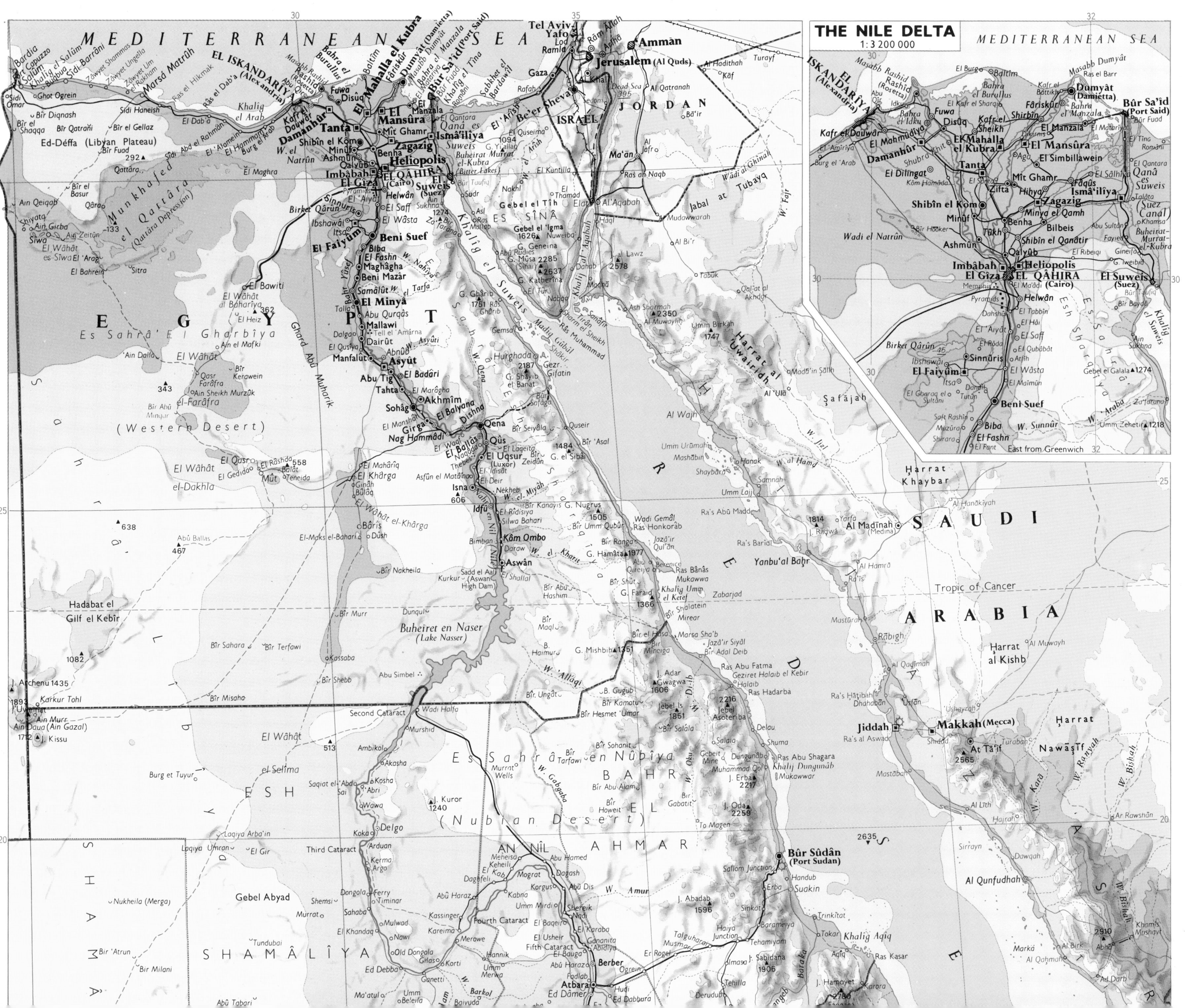
THE NILE DELTA
1:3 200 000
MEDITERRANEAN SEA
East from Greenwich
EL ISKANDARÎYA (Alexandria)
EL QÂHIRA (Cairo)
Bûr Sa'îd (Port Said)
Dumyât (Damietta)
El Suweis (Suez)
Khalîg el Suweis
Es Sahrâ' El Gharbîya
(Western Desert)
Qattara Depression
Libyan Plateau
Tropic of Cancer
SAUDI
ARABIA
JORDAN
ISRAEL
EGYPT
Jerusalem (Al Quds)
Ammân
Tel Aviv-Yafo
Gaza
Makkah (Mecca)
Al Madînah (Medina)
Jiddah
Bûr Sûdân (Port Sudan)
Aswân
El Uqsur (Luxor)
Asyût
Buheiret en Naser (Lake Nasser)
Es Sahrâ en Nûbîya
(Nubian Desert)
Second Cataract
Third Cataract
Fourth Cataract
Fifth Cataract
Wadi Halfa
Atbara
Berber
Hadabat el Gilf el Kebir

1 : 6 400 000

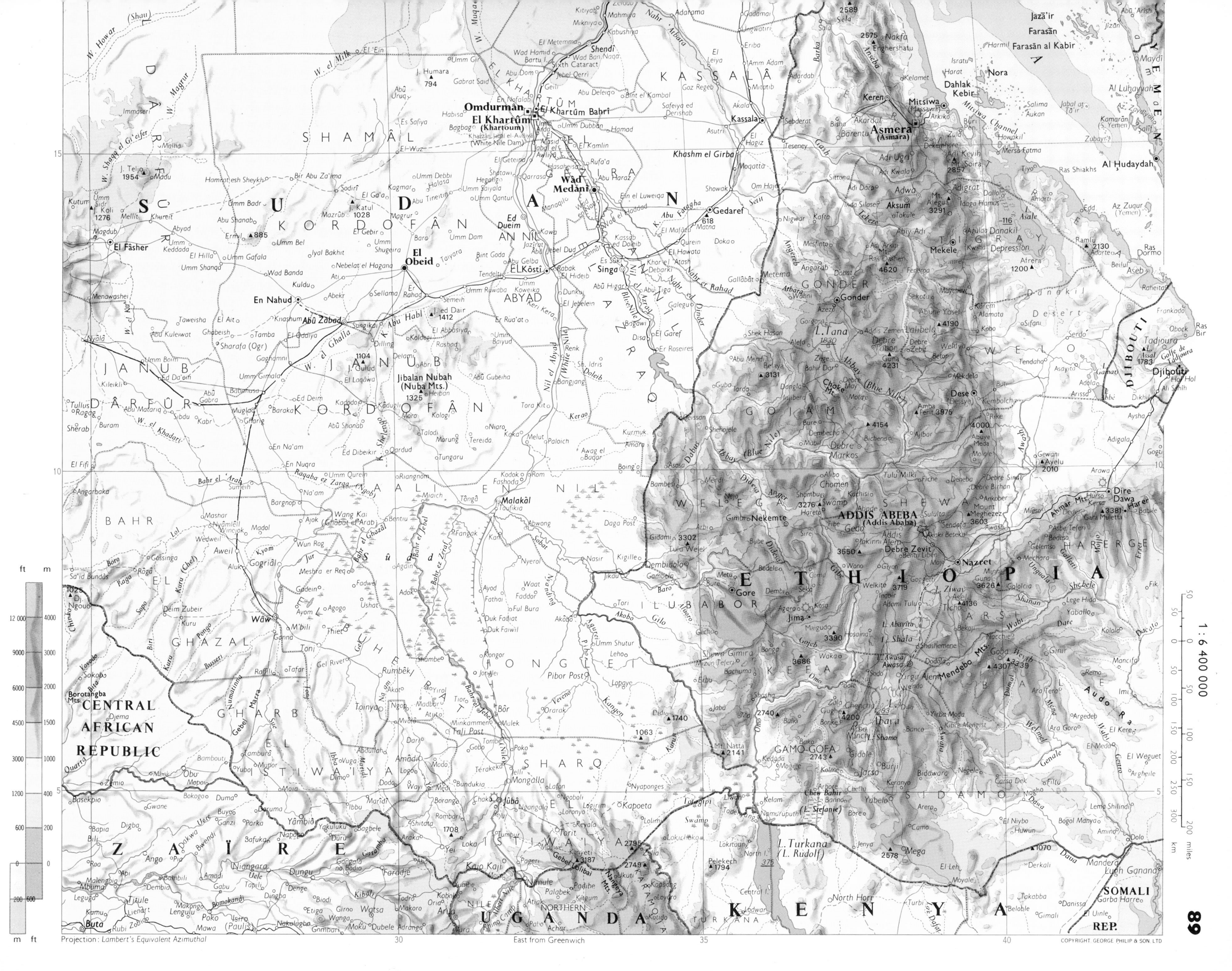

50 0 50 100 150 200 miles
50 0 50 100 150 200 250 300 km
YEMEN
DJIBOUTI
ETHIOPIA
SUDAN
KENYA
UGANDA
SOMALI REP.
CENTRAL AFRICAN REPUBLIC
ZAÏRE
ADDIS ABEBA (Addis Ababa)
El Khartûm (Khartoum)
Omdurmân
Asmera (Asmara)
L. Turkana (L. Rudolf)
East from Greenwich
Projection: Lambert's Equivalent Azimuthal

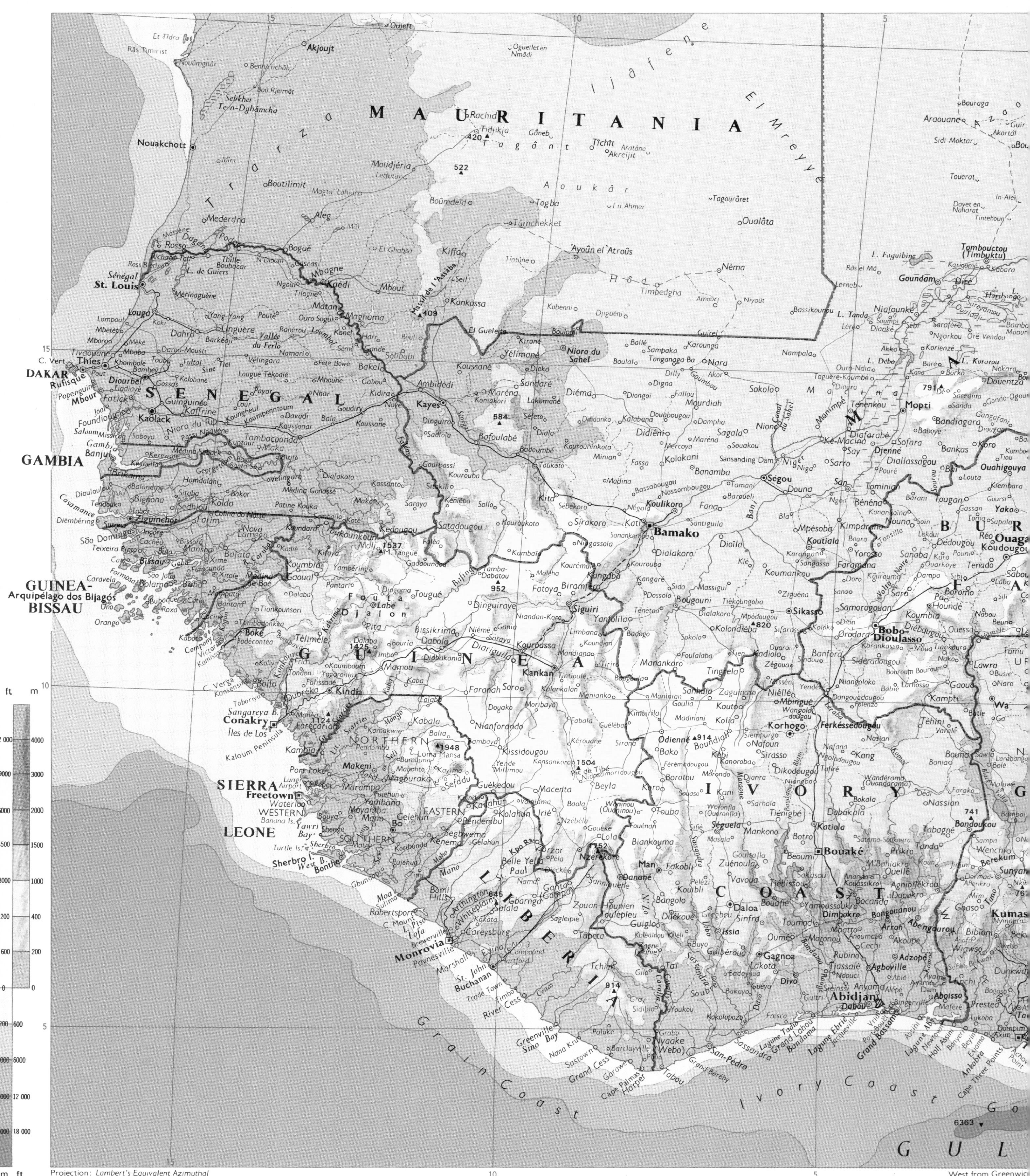
MAURITANIA
SENEGAL
GAMBIA
GUINEA-BISSAU
GUINEA
SIERRA LEONE
LIBERIA
IVORY COAST
Nouakchott
Akjoujt
Tidjikja
Tîchît
Oualâta
Néma
Kiffa
Aleg
Boutilimit
Rosso
St. Louis
Kaédi
Sélibabi
Nioro du Sahel
Kayes
DAKAR
Thiès
Rufisque
Diourbel
Mbour
Kaolack
Ziguinchor
Banjul
Bissau
Arquipélago dos Bijagós
Tambacounda
Bamako
Koulikoro
Ségou
Mopti
San
Sikasso
Tombouctou (Timbuktu)
Goundam
Bobo-Dioulasso
Boké
Kindia
Conakry
Îles de Los
Labé
Fouta Djalon
Kankan
Siguiri
Faranah
Kissidougou
Guékédou
Macenta
Nzérékoré
Freetown
Makeni
Bo
Kenema
Sherbro I.
Monrovia
Buchanan
Robertsport
Harper
Cape Palmas
Greenville
River Cess
Grain Coast
Ivory Coast
Odienné
Korhogo
Man
Daloa
Bouaké
Gagnoa
Abidjan
Grand Bassam
Sassandra
San-Pédro
Tabou
Dimbokro
Agboville
Katiola
Bondoukou
Kumasi
GULF
Projection: Lambert's Equivalent Azimuthal
West from Greenwich
ft
m
12 000
9000
6000
4500
3000
1200
600
0
4000
3000
2000
1500
1000
400
200
200
2000
4000
6000
600
6000
12 000
18 000

1 : 6 400 000

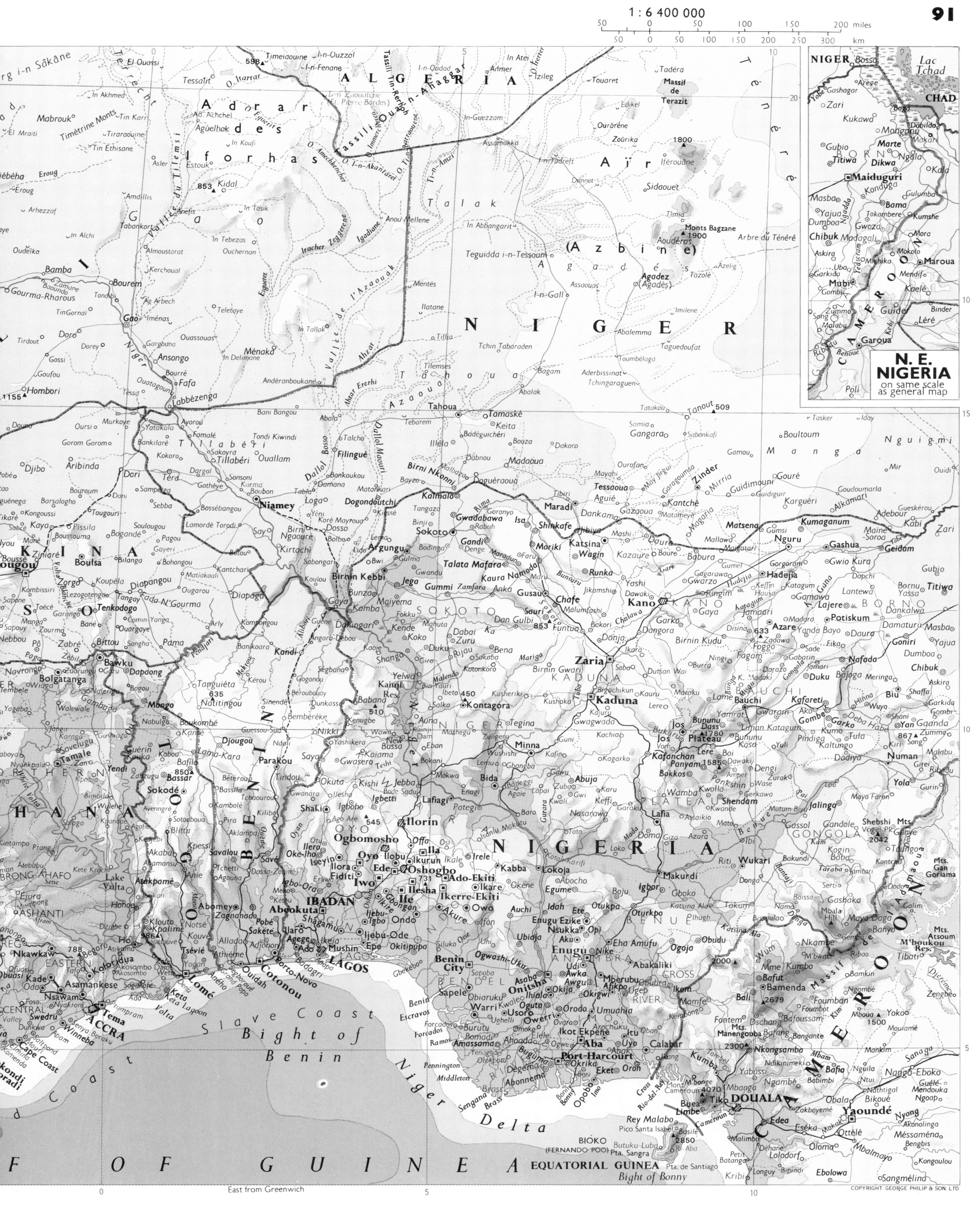
ALGERIA
NIGER
NIGERIA
BENIN
GHANA
N.E. NIGERIA
on same scale as general map
Bight of Benin
Slave Coast
Niger Delta
GULF OF GUINEA
EQUATORIAL GUINEA
Bight of Bonny
Niamey
Kano
Kaduna
Zaria
Sokoto
Ibadan
Lagos
Porto-Novo
Cotonou
Lomé
Accra
Douala
Yaoundé
Maiduguri
Zinder
Agadez
Maradi
Tahoua
Enugu
Port-Harcourt
Jos
Ilorin
Ogbomosho
Oshogbo
Abeokuta
Benin City
Onitsha
Aba
Makurdi
Lokoja
Minna
Bida
Parakou
Kandi
Djougou
Tamale
Bolgatanga
Ouagadougou
Dori
Gao
Tillabéri
East from Greenwich

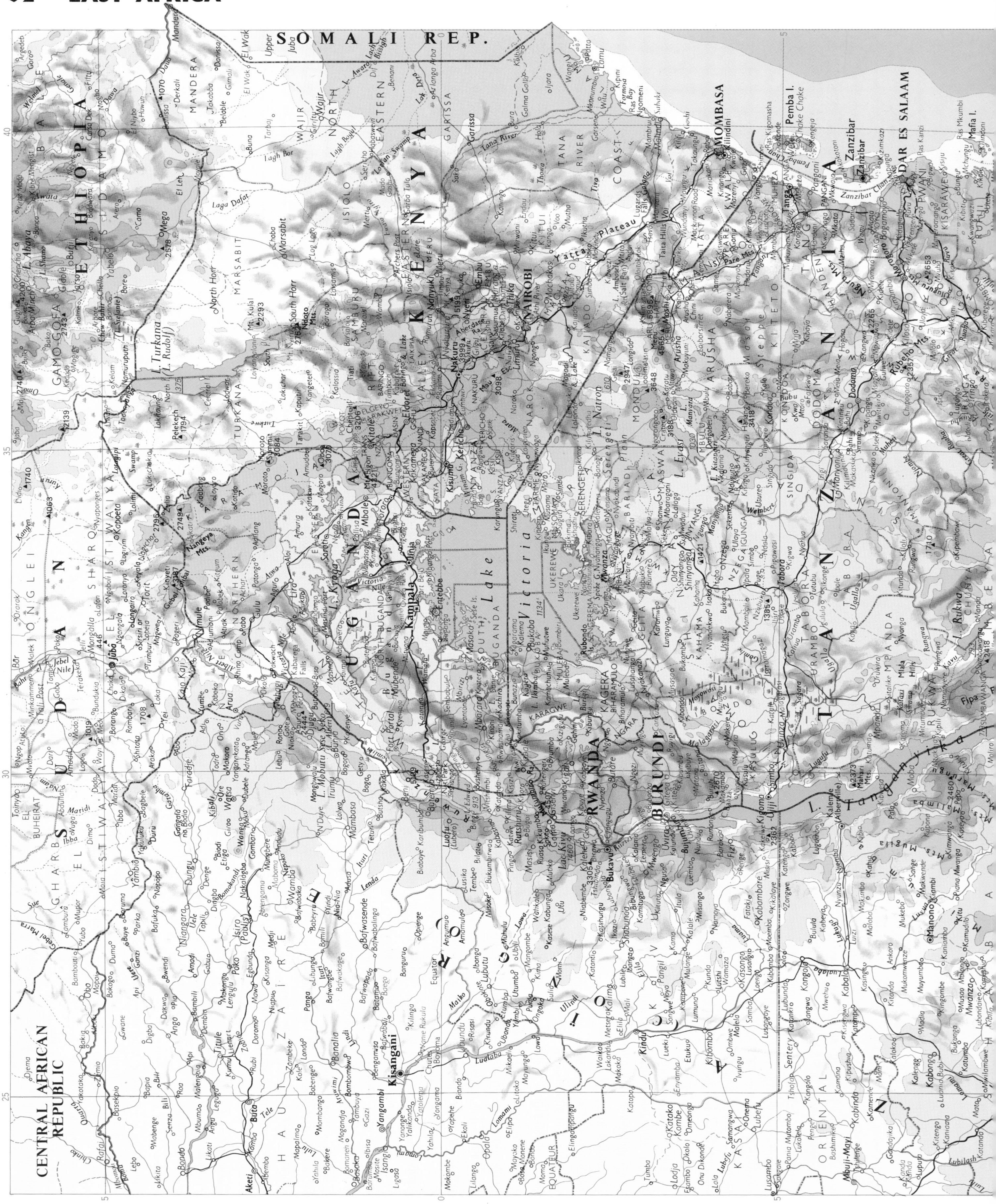

SOMALI REP.
ETHIOPIA
KENYA
UGANDA
TANZANIA
RWANDA
BURUNDI
SUDAN
ZAIRE
CENTRAL AFRICAN REPUBLIC
NAIROBI
MOMBASA
DAR ES SALAAM
Kampala
Kisangani
Zanzibar
Pemba I.
Mafia I.
L. Turkana (L. Rudolf)
Lake Victoria
L. Tanganyika

1 : 6 400 000

50 0 50 100 150 200 miles

50 0 100 200 300 km

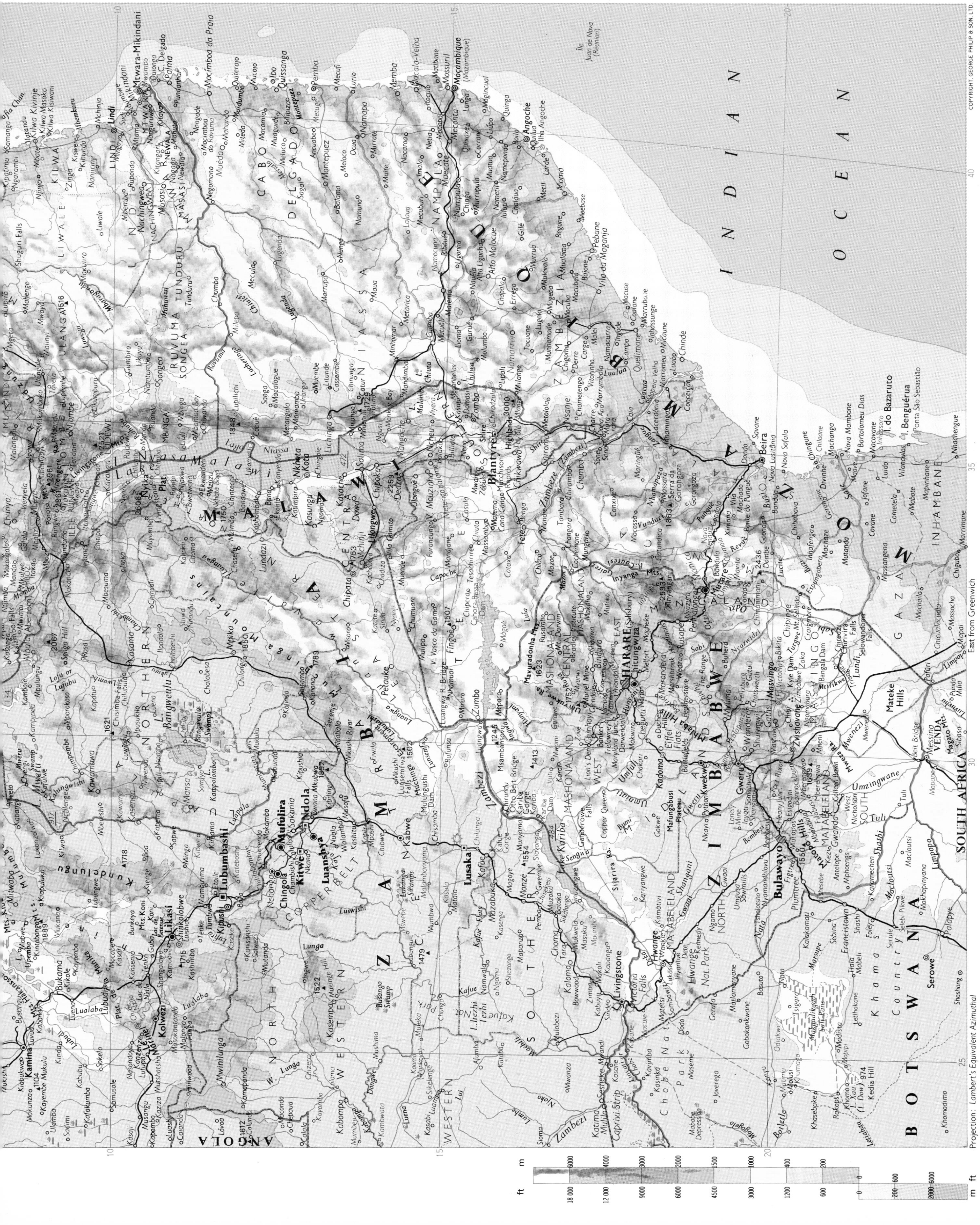

Projection: Lambert's Equivalent Azimuthal

East from Greenwich

INDIAN OCEAN

MOÇAMBIQUE

MALAWI

ZAMBIA

ZIMBABWE

BOTSWANA

ANGOLA

SOUTH AFRICA

m	6000	4000	3000	2000	1500	1000	400	200	0
ft	18 000	12 000	9000	6000	4500	3000	1200	600	0

m	0	200-600	2000-6000
ft	0	600	6000

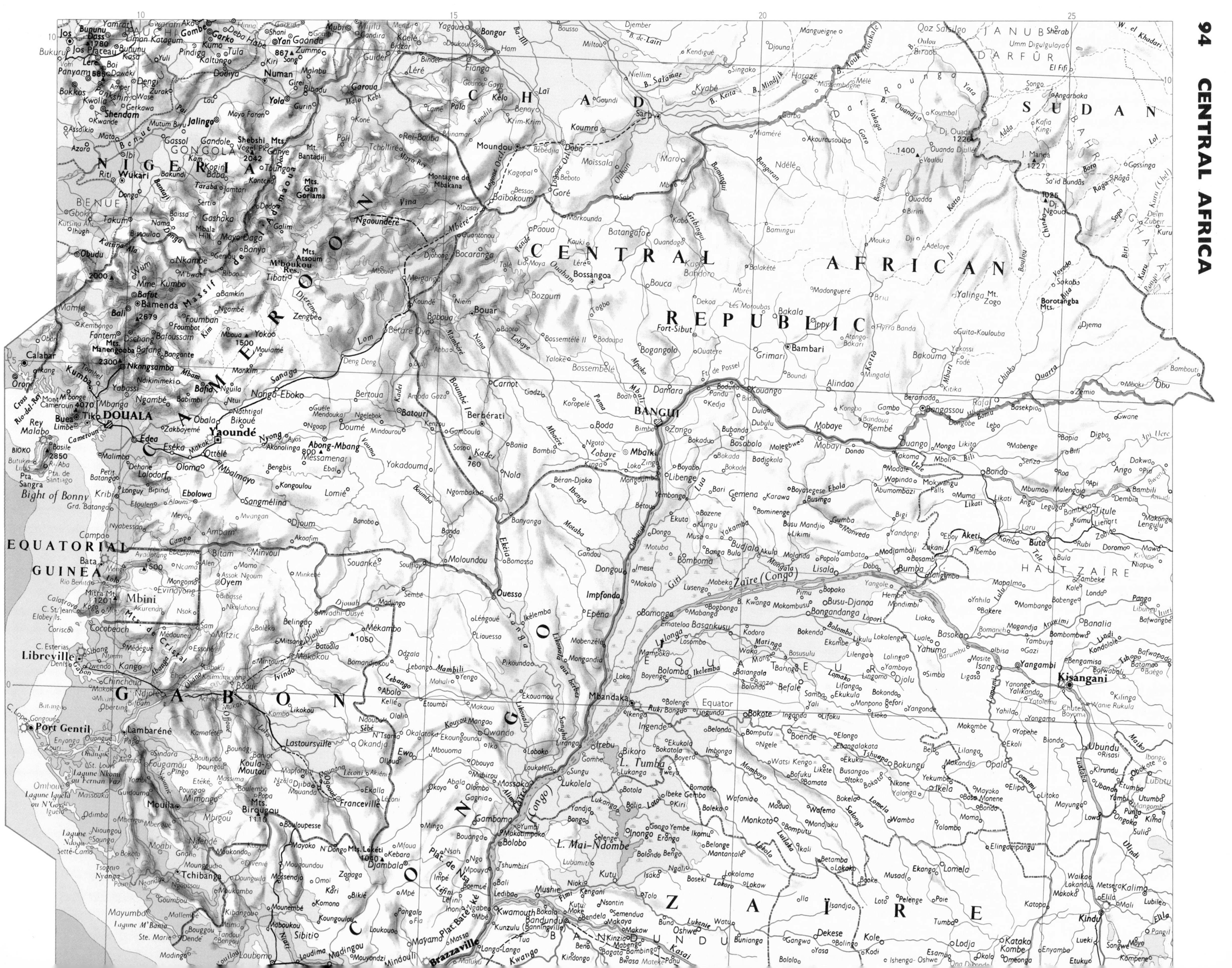

SUDAN
CHAD
CENTRAL AFRICAN REPUBLIC
NIGERIA
CAMEROON
EQUATORIAL GUINEA
GABON
CONGO
ZAÏRE
Bangui
Yaoundé
Douala
Libreville
Port Gentil
Kisangani
Mbandaka
Brazzaville
Bambari
Berbérati
Bangassou
Bouar
Bossangoa
Moundou
Sarh
Garoua
Ngaoundéré
Lambaréné
Franceville
Ouesso
Impfondo
Malabo
BIOKO
Bight of Bonny
Equator
Zaïre (Congo)
Lualaba
Mbini
L. Tumba
L. Mai-Ndombe

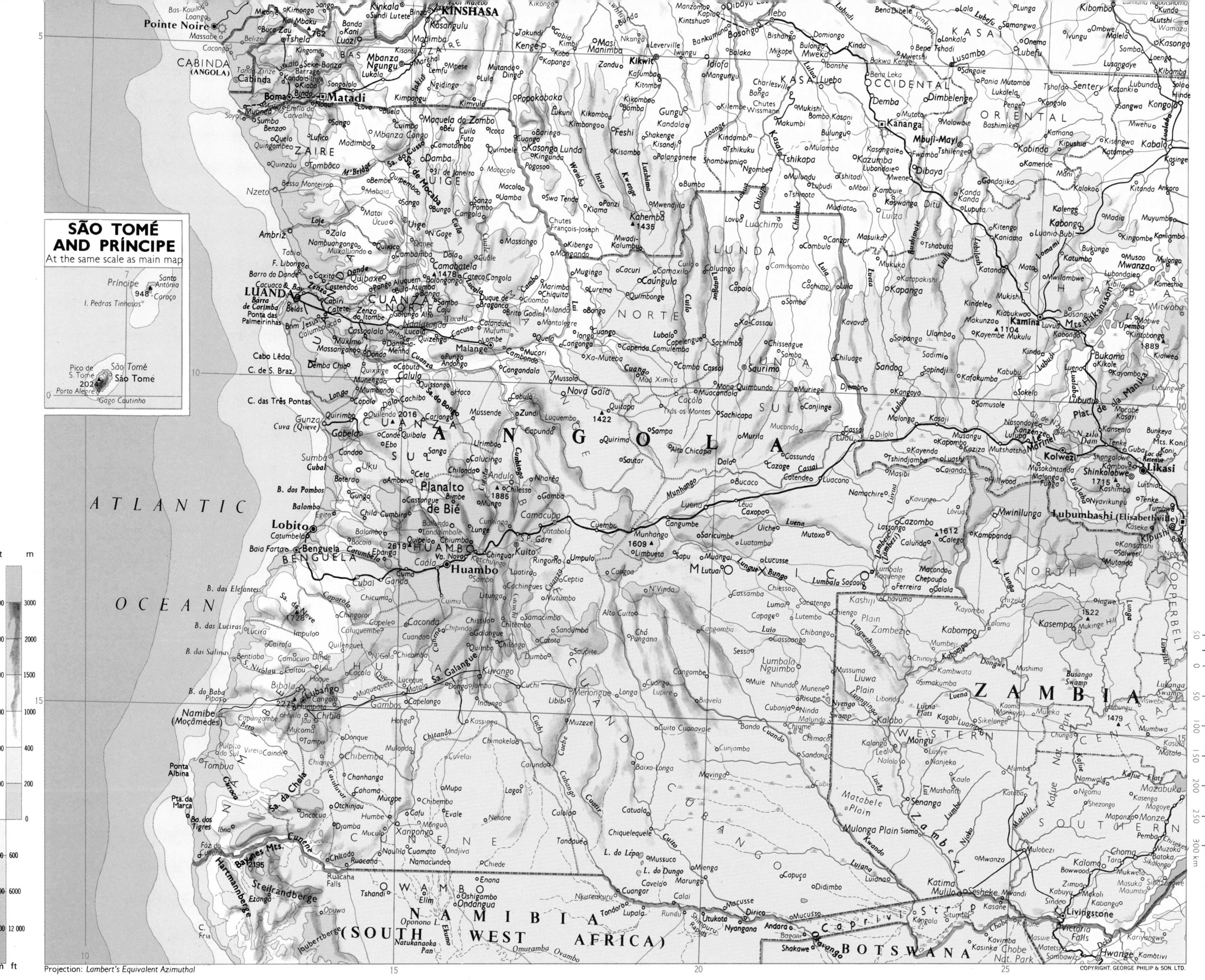

SÃO TOMÉ AND PRÍNCIPE
At the same scale as main map
Príncipe
Santo António
948
Coroço
I. Pedras Tinhosas
Pico de S. Tomé
2024
São Tomé
São Tome
Porto Alegre
Gago Coutinho
ATLANTIC
OCEAN
ANGOLA
ZAMBIA
ZAIRE
NAMIBIA (SOUTH WEST AFRICA)
BOTSWANA
CABINDA (ANGOLA)
KINSHASA
Pointe Noire
Matadi
Boma
LUANDA
Malange
Lobito
Benguela
Huambo
Planalto de Bié
Namibe (Moçâmedes)
Lubango
Kananga
Mbuji-Mayi
Tshikapa
Kolwezi
Likasi
Lubumbashi (Elisabethville)
Livingstone
Victoria Falls
Hwange
Mongu
Katima Mulilo
COPPERBELT

1 : 6 400 000

50 0 50 100 150 200 miles

50 0 50 100 150 200 250 300 km

m 3000 2000 1500 1000 400 200 0

ft 9000 6000 4500 3000 1200 600 0

0 200 600 2000 6000 4000 12 000 m ft

Projection: Lambert's Equivalent Azimuthal

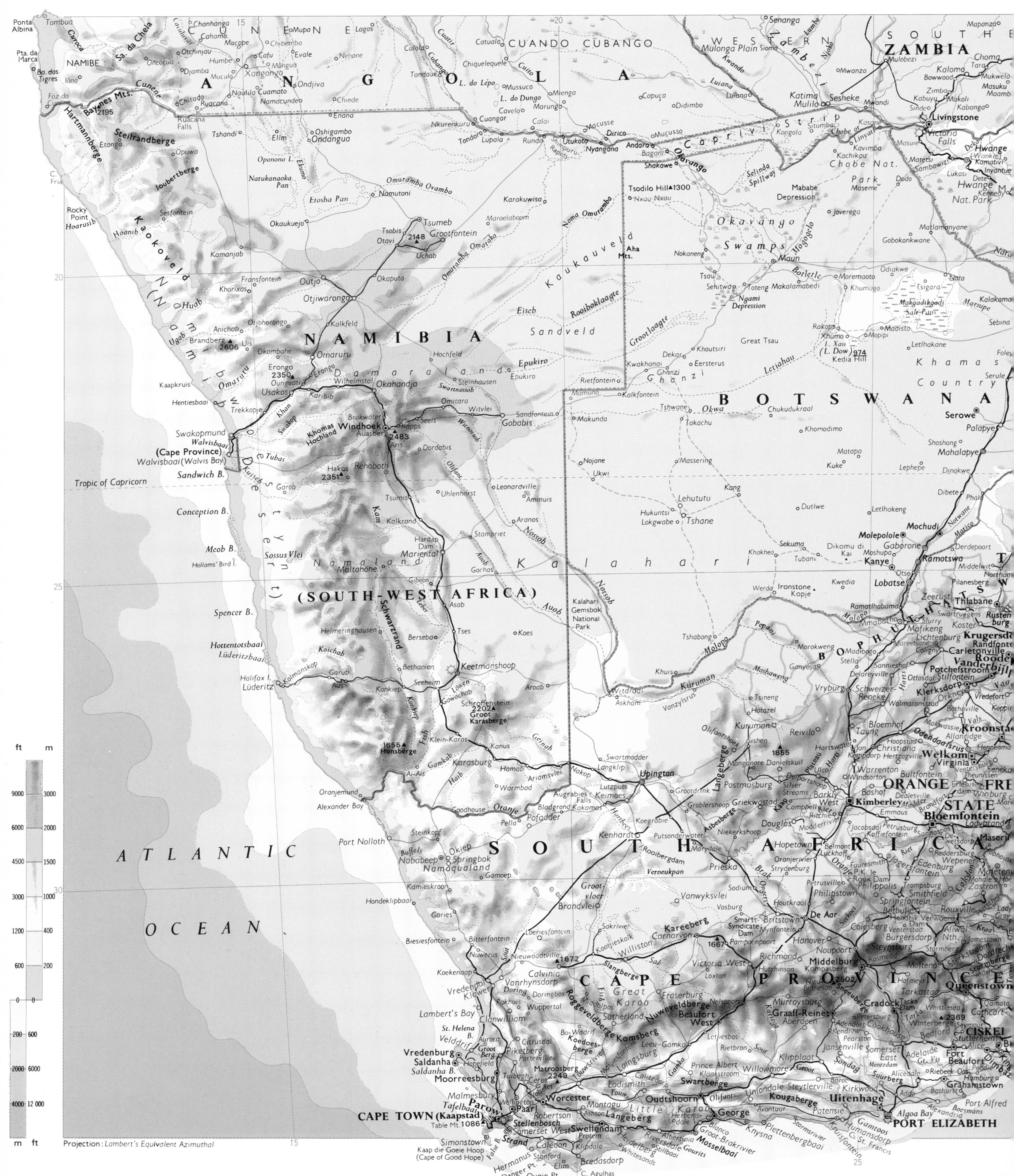
ANGOLA
CUNENE
CUANDO CUBANGO
ZAMBIA
WESTERN
Caprivi Strip
NAMIBIA
(SOUTH-WEST AFRICA)
BOTSWANA
SOUTH AFRICA
CAPE PROVINCE
ORANGE FREE STATE
BOPHUTHATSWANA
CISKEI
ATLANTIC
OCEAN
Tropic of Capricorn
Kaokoveld
Namib Desert
Damaraland
Namaland
Kalahari
Sandveld
Okavango Swamps
Makgadikgadi Salt Pan
Khama's Country
Ghanzi
Namaqualand
Great Karoo
Little Karoo
Etosha Pan
Ngami Depression
Chobe Nat. Park
Hwange Nat. Park
Kalahari Gemsbok National Park
Windhoek
Walvisbaai (Walvis Bay)
(Cape Province)
Swakopmund
Lüderitz
Keetmanshoop
Tsumeb
Gaborone
Kimberley
Bloemfontein
Upington
Livingstone
CAPE TOWN (Kaapstad)
PORT ELIZABETH
Kaap die Goeie Hoop (Cape of Good Hope)
C. Agulhas
Projection: Lambert's Equivalent Azimuthal
ft
m
9000
3000
6000
2000
4500
1500
3000
1000
1200
400
600
200
0
0
200
600
2000
6000
4000
12 000
m
ft

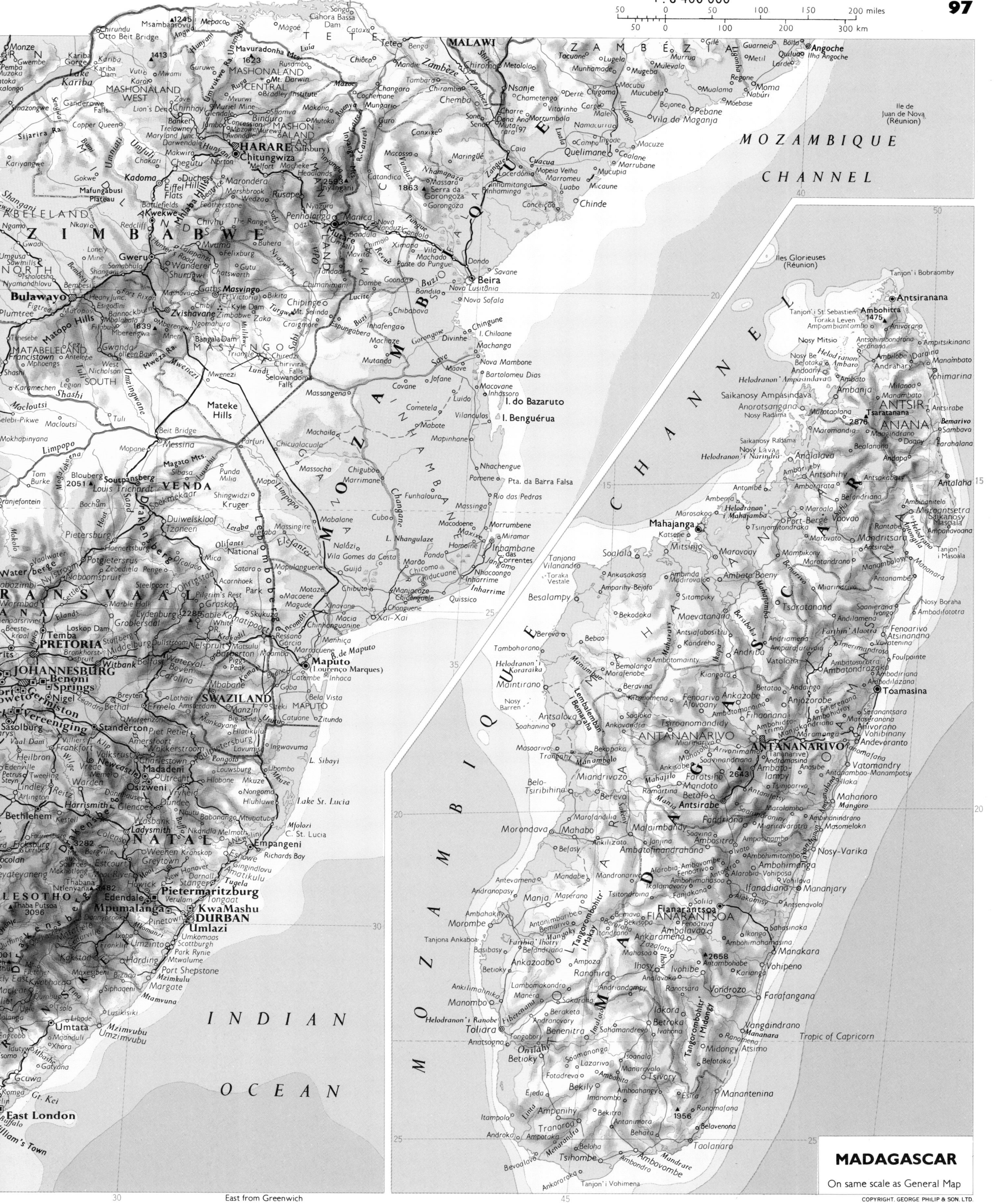
1 : 6 400 000
50 0 50 100 150 200 miles
50 0 100 200 300 km
MALAWI
ZAMBÉZIA
TETE
ZIMBABWE
MASHONALAND WEST
MASHONALAND CENTRAL
MASHONALAND EAST
MATABELELAND SOUTH
MASVINGO
MANICALAND
MOZAMBIQUE
SOFALA
INHAMBANE
GAZA
MAPUTO
TRANSVAAL
VENDA
SWAZILAND
NATAL
LESOTHO
HARARE (Salisbury)
Chitungwiza
Bulawayo
Gweru
Kwekwe
Masvingo
Mutare
Beira
Quelimane
Chinde
Angoche
Maputo (Lourenço Marques)
Inhambane
Xai-Xai
PRETORIA
JOHANNESBURG
Soweto
Benoni
Springs
Germiston
Vereeniging
Pietermaritzburg
DURBAN
Umlazi
KwaMashu
East London
Umtata
Lake Kariba
Limpopo
Zambeze
I. do Bazaruto
I. Benguérua
Pta. da Barra Falsa
C. das Correntes
MOZAMBIQUE CHANNEL
INDIAN OCEAN
Ile de Juan de Nova (Réunion)
Iles Glorieuses (Réunion)
MADAGASCAR
ANTSIRANANA
MAHAJANGA
ANTANANARIVO
TOAMASINA
FIANARANTSOA
TOLIARA
Antsiranana
Mahajanga
Antananarivo
Toamasina
Antsirabe
Fianarantsoa
Toliara
Taolanaro
Morondava
Maintirano
Tropic of Capricorn
East from Greenwich
MADAGASCAR
On same scale as General Map

1 : 6 400 000

50 0 50 100 150 200 miles
50 0 50 100 150 200 250 300 km

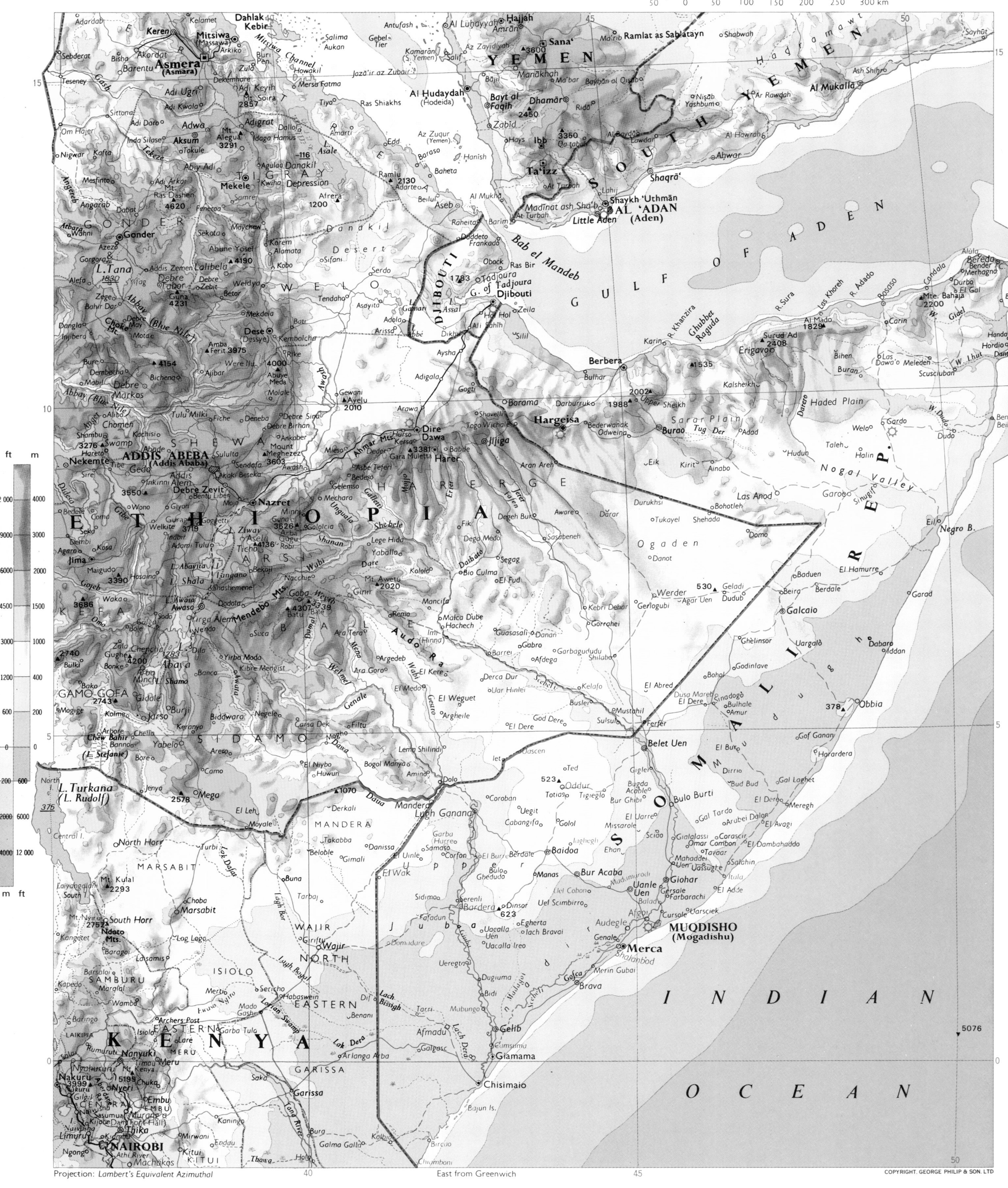
ETHIOPIA
SOMALI REP.
KENYA
YEMEN
SOUTH YEMEN
DJIBOUTI
GULF OF ADEN
INDIAN OCEAN
ADDIS ABEBA
(Addis Ababa)
MUQDISHO
(Mogadishu)
Djibouti
AL 'ADAN
(Aden)
NAIROBI
Sana'
Asmera
(Asmara)
Mitsiwa
(Massawa)
Keren
Dahlak Kebir
Gonder
Mekele
Aksum
Adigrat
Dese
(Dessye)
Debre Markos
Nazret
Dire Dawa
Harer
Jijiga
Hargeisa
Berbera
Burao
Erigavo
Las Anod
Galcaio
Obbia
Belet Uen
Bulo Burti
Giohar
Merca
Brava
Chisimaio
Giamama
Gelib
Baidoa
Bur Acaba
Lugh Ganana
Dolo
Mandera
Moyale
Marsabit
Wajir
Garissa
Nanyuki
Nyeri
Nakuru
Thika
Embu
Meru
Jima
Awasa
Al Hudaydah
(Hodeida)
Ta'izz
Al Mukalla
Shaqrā'
Assab
Bab el Mandeb
G. of Tadjoura
Tadjoura
Obock
Zeila
L. Tana
L. Turkana
(L. Rudolf)
Chew Bahir
(L. Stefanie)
L. Ziway
L. Abaya
L. Shala
Danakil Depression
Danakil Desert
Ogaden
Haded Plain
Sarar Plain
Nogal Valley
Abbay (Blue Nile)
Awash
Shebele
Genale
Dawa
Juba
Webi Shabeelle
Mendebo Mts.
Ahmar Mts.
Ras Dashen
4620
GONDER
WELO
SHEWA
HARERGE
ARSI
BALE
SIDAMO
GAMO GOFA
KEFA
TIGRAY
MANDERA
MARSABIT
WAJIR
ISIOLO
SAMBURU
EASTERN
NORTH EASTERN
GARISSA
Hadramawt
Ramlat as Sab'atayn
Negro B.
Ras Binna
Mudug
Nugaal
5076

Projection: Lambert's Equivalent Azimuthal

East from Greenwich

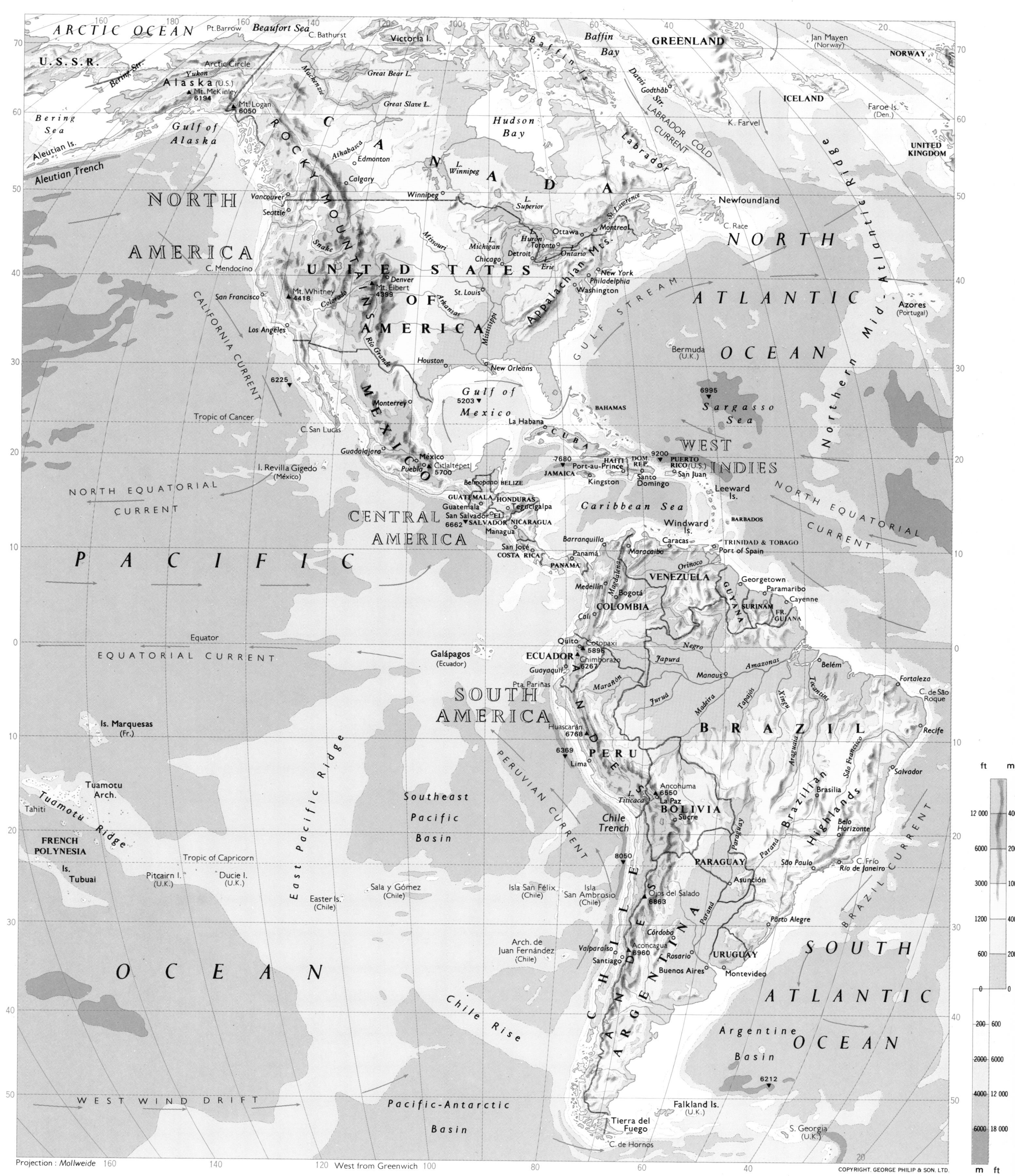
ARCTIC OCEAN
Beaufort Sea
Pt. Barrow
C. Bathurst
Victoria I.
Baffin Bay
GREENLAND
Jan Mayen (Norway)
NORWAY
U.S.S.R.
Bering Str.
Arctic Circle
Yukon
Alaska (U.S.)
Mt. McKinley 6194
Mt. Logan 6050
Mackenzie
Great Bear L.
Great Slave L.
Davis Str.
Godthåb
LABRADOR COLD CURRENT
ICELAND
Faroe Is. (Den.)
Bering Sea
Gulf of Alaska
Aleutian Is.
Aleutian Trench
ROCKY MOUNTAINS
CANADA
Athabasca
Edmonton
Calgary
Hudson Bay
L. Winnipeg
Winnipeg
Labrador
K. Farvel
UNITED KINGDOM
Northern Mid-Atlantic Ridge
NORTH AMERICA
Vancouver
Seattle
L. Superior
St. Lawrence
Newfoundland
C. Race
Ottawa
Montreal
Huron
Toronto
Ontario
L. Michigan
Detroit
Erie
Chicago
Snake
Missouri
C. Mendocino
UNITED STATES OF AMERICA
Denver
Mt. Elbert 4399
Mt. Whitney 4418
San Francisco
Colorado
Arkansas
St. Louis
Appalachian Mts.
New York
Philadelphia
Washington
GULF STREAM
NORTH ATLANTIC OCEAN
Azores (Portugal)
CALIFORNIA CURRENT
Los Angeles
Mississippi
Rio Grande
Houston
New Orleans
Bermuda (U.K.)
6225
MEXICO
Monterrey
Gulf of Mexico
5203
BAHAMAS
6995
Sargasso Sea
Tropic of Cancer
C. San Lucas
La Habana
CUBA
WEST INDIES
Guadalajara
México
Citlaltépetl 5700
Puebla
7680
HAITI
DOM. REP.
9200
PUERTO RICO (U.S.)
San Juan
JAMAICA
Port-au-Prince
Kingston
Santo Domingo
I. Revilla Gigedo (México)
Belmopan
BELIZE
Leeward Is.
NORTH EQUATORIAL CURRENT
GUATEMALA
HONDURAS
Guatemala
Tegucigalpa
Caribbean Sea
San Salvador
EL SALVADOR
6662
NICARAGUA
Managua
CENTRAL AMERICA
Windward Is.
BARBADOS
Barranquilla
Caracas
TRINIDAD & TOBAGO
Port of Spain
San José
COSTA RICA
Panamá
PANAMA
Maracaibo
Orinoco
PACIFIC OCEAN
VENEZUELA
Georgetown
Paramaribo
Cayenne
GUYANA
SURINAM
FR. GUIANA
Medellín
Magdalena
Bogotá
COLOMBIA
Cali
Equator
EQUATORIAL CURRENT
Quito
Cotopaxi 5896
Negro
Galápagos (Ecuador)
ECUADOR
Chimborazo 6267
Japurá
Amazonas
Belém
Guayaquil
Manaus
Fortaleza
Pta. Pariñas
Marañón
C. de São Roque
SOUTH AMERICA
Juruá
Madeira
Tapajós
Xingu
Tocantins
Is. Marquesas (Fr.)
Huascarán 6768
BRAZIL
Recife
East Pacific Ridge
PERUVIAN CURRENT
6369
PERU
Lima
ANDES
Araguaia
São Francisco
Salvador
Tuamotu Arch.
Tuamotu Ridge
Tahiti
Southeast Pacific Basin
L. Titicaca
Ancohuma 6550
La Paz
BOLIVIA
Sucre
Brazilian Highlands
Brasilia
Chile Trench
Belo Horizonte
FRENCH POLYNESIA
Is. Tubuai
Tropic of Capricorn
Pitcairn I. (U.K.)
Ducie I. (U.K.)
8050
Paraguay
PARAGUAY
Paraná
São Paulo
C. Frio
Rio de Janeiro
BRAZIL CURRENT
Easter Is. (Chile)
Sala y Gómez (Chile)
Isla San Félix (Chile)
Isla San Ambrosio (Chile)
Ojos del Salado 6863
Asunción
Pôrto Alegre
Arch. de Juan Fernández (Chile)
Córdoba
Valparaíso
Aconcagua 6960
Santiago
Rosario
URUGUAY
Buenos Aires
Montevideo
CHILE
ARGENTINA
SOUTH ATLANTIC OCEAN
Chile Rise
Argentine Basin
6212
WEST WIND DRIFT
Pacific-Antarctic Basin
Falkland Is. (U.K.)
Tierra del Fuego
C. de Hornos
S. Georgia (U.K.)
Projection : Mollweide
West from Greenwich
ft m
12 000 4000
6000 2000
3000 1000
1200 400
600 200
0 0
200 600
2000 6000
4000 12 000
6000 18 000
m ft

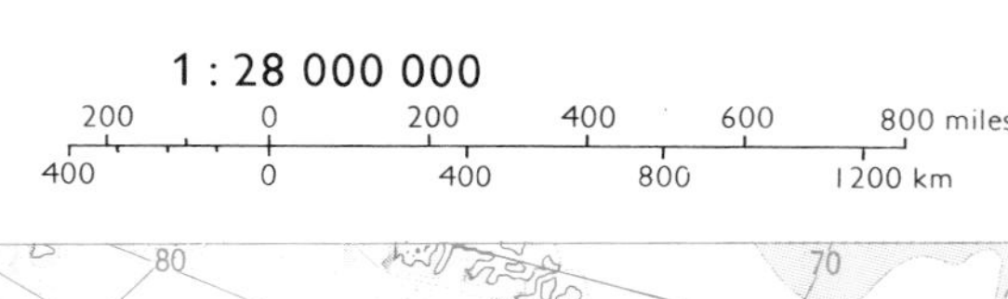
1 : 28 000 000
200 0 200 400 600 800 miles
400 0 400 800 1200 km

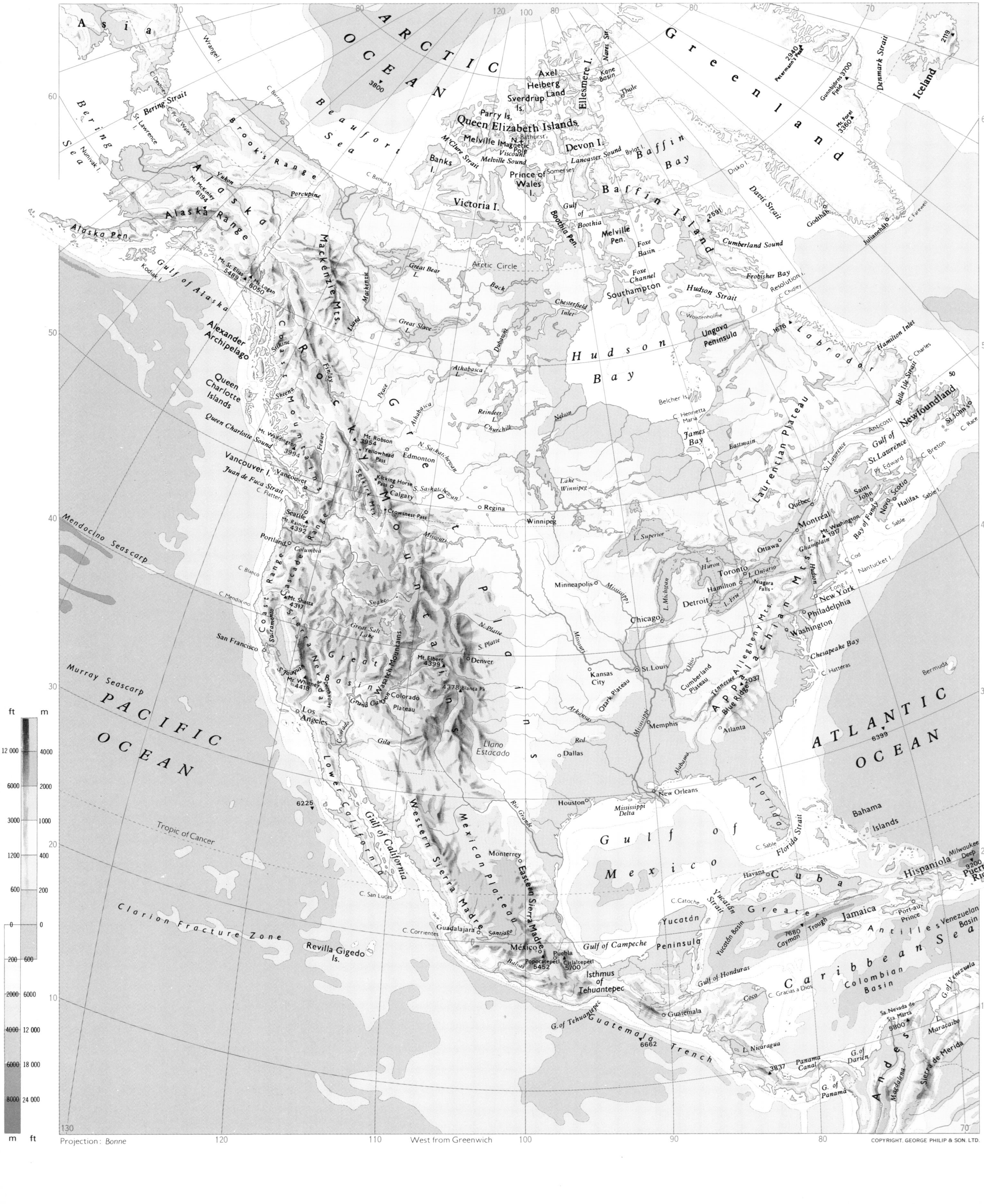

Projection: *Bonne*

West from Greenwich

1 : 28 000 000

200 0 200 400 600 800 miles
400 0 400 800 1200 km

ARCTIC OCEAN
U.S.S.R.
Bering Sea
Bering Strait
Beaufort Sea
Queen Elizabeth Is.
Ellesmere I.
GREENLAND (Denmark)
Denmark Strait
ICELAND
Reykjavik
Baffin Bay
Davis Strait
Godthåb
C. Farvel
Victoria I.
Baffin I.
ALASKA
Arctic Circle
Yukon
Porcupine
Fairbanks
Anchorage
Gulf of Alaska
INUVIK
KITIKMEOT
BAFFIN
YUKON TERRITORY
NORTHWEST TERRITORIES
Mackenzie
Great Bear L.
Back
Whitehorse
FORT SMITH
Yellowknife
Liard
Great Slave L.
Dubawnt
KEEWATIN
Hudson Strait
Hudson Bay
NEWFOUNDLAND
Labrador
Juneau
CANADA
BRITISH COLUMBIA
Finlay
Skeena
Peace
L. Athabasca
Athabasca
ALBERTA
Edmonton
N. Saskatchewan
SASKATCHEWAN
Churchill
Nelson
MANITOBA
Eastmain
QUÉBEC
St. Lawrence
St. John's
SPM
PR. EDWARD I.
Charlottetown
NEW BRUNSWICK
NOVA SCOTIA
Halifax
Fraser
Calgary
L. Winnipeg
Victoria
Vancouver
S. Saskatchewan
Regina
ONTARIO
Québec
Fredericton
MAINE
Augusta
Montpelier
Winnipeg
L. Superior
Montréal
Ottawa
WASHINGTON
Olympia
Seattle
Portland
Columbia
Salem
OREGON
Missouri
MONTANA
Helena
NORTH DAKOTA
Bismarck
MINNESOTA
IDAHO
Boise
Snake
SOUTH DAKOTA
Pierre
Minneapolis
St. Paul
WISCONSIN
L. Michigan
MICHIGAN
Lansing
Huron
Toronto
L. Ontario
Buffalo
NEW YORK
Albany
VER.
N.H.
Concord
MASS.
Boston
Hartford
C.
R.I.
Providence
NEW YORK
Trenton
Philadelphia
WYOMING
Cheyenne
Madison
Milwaukee
Detroit
Erie
Cleveland
PENNSYLVANIA
Harrisburg
Annapolis
Dover
Sacramento
Carson City
Salt Lake City
N. Platte
NEBRASKA
Des Moines
IOWA
Chicago
Toledo
Pittsburgh
Columbus
OHIO
Baltimore
D.C.
M.
D.
San Francisco
San Jose
NEVADA
UTAH
UNITED STATES
Lincoln
ILLINOIS
INDIANA
Indianapolis
WEST VIRGINIA
Washington
Richmond
Kansas City
Springfield
Jefferson City
Cincinnati
Frankfort
Charleston
VIRGINIA
CALIFORNIA
COLORADO
Denver
Topeka
KANSAS
MISSOURI
St. Louis
KENTUCKY
Arkansas
Raleigh
NORTH CAROLINA
Nashville
TENNESSEE
Tennessee
Columbia
SOUTH CAROLINA
Bermuda
PACIFIC OCEAN
ATLANTIC OCEAN
Las Vegas
Colorado
LOS ANGELES
Santa Fe
Albuquerque
ARIZONA
Phoenix
Gila
NEW MEXICO
OKLAHOMA
Oklahoma City
ARKANSAS
Little Rock
Memphis
Mississippi
Alabama
Atlanta
GEORGIA
San Diego
Red River
Dallas
Birmingham
MISSISSIPPI
Jackson
Montgomery
ALABAMA
Jacksonville
Tucson
El Paso
TEXAS
LOUISIANA
Baton Rouge
Tallahassee
FLORIDA
Austin
New Orleans
Houston
Tampa
Rio Grande
Tropic of Cancer
Miami
Str. of Florida
C. Sable
Nassau
BAHAMAS
Gulf of Mexico
MEXICO
Monterrey
Havana
CUBA
DOMINICAN REP.
San Juan
PUERTO RICO
HAITI
Port-au-Prince
Santo Domingo
JAMAICA
Kingston
Guadalajara
MEXICO
Caribbean Sea
Belmopan
BELIZE
GUATEMALA
HONDURAS
Guatemala
Tegucigalpa
Maracaibo
San Salvador
EL SALVADOR
NICARAGUA
L. Nicaragua
Managua
Barranquilla
VENEZUELA
Panamá
San José
COSTA RICA
PANAMA
SOUTH AMERICA
Medellín
COLOMBIA
Bogotá
State capital
C. CONNECTICUT
D. DELAWARE
D.C. DISTRICT OF COLUMBIA
M. MARYLAND
MASS. MASSACHUSETTS
N.H. NEW HAMPSHIRE
N.J. NEW JERSEY
R.I. RHODE ISLAND
VER. VERMONT
SPM ST. PIERRE ET MIQUELON
Projection: Bonne
West from Greenwich
COPYRIGHT. GEORGE PHILIP & SON. LTD.

ALASKA
1 : 24 000 000
Projection: Bonne
PACIFIC OCEAN
BRITISH COLUMBIA
ALBERTA
SASKATCHEWAN
MANITOBA
YUKON TERRITORY
NORTHWEST TERRITORIES
Vancouver
Calgary
Edmonton
Regina
Winnipeg
Saskatoon
Whitehorse
Yellowknife
Anchorage
Fairbanks
Seattle
Minneapolis
West from Greenwich

1 : 12 000 000

100 50 0 100 200 300 400 miles

100 0 100 200 300 400 500 600 km

Devon Island
Lancaster Sound
Baffin Bay
Bylot I.
Pond Inlet
Arctic Bay
Brodeur Peninsula
Milne Inlet
Gulf of Boothia
Scott I.
Clyde
C. Hewett
Disko
Disko B.
Svartenhuk Halvø
Christianshåb
GREENLAND
Søndre Strømfjord
Kong Frederik VI Kyst
Angmagssalik
Holsteinsborg
Sukkertoppen
Godthåb
Fiskenæsset
Frederikshåb
Ivigtut
Julianehåb
Nanortalik
Kap Farvel
Davis Strait
Home B.
Broughton Island
Padloping Island
C. Dyer
Cape Dyer
Cumberland Peninsula
Pangnirtung
Hoare B.
C. Mercy
Cumberland Sd.
Fury & Hecla Str.
Igloolik Island
Hall Lake
Pelly Bay
Committee B.
Melville Peninsula
Prince Charles I.
Foxe Basin
Nettilling L.
Rae Isthmus
Repulse Bay
Circle
Wager Bay
Wager B.
Roes Welcome Sd.
Foxe Channel
C. Dorchester
Foxe Penin.
Amadjuak L.
Amadjuak
Cape Dorset
Frobisher Bay
Lake Harbour
Southampton I.
Coral Harbour
Bell Pen.
Resolution I.
Hudson Strait
C. Chidley
Digges Is.
Coats I.
Mansel I.
Ivujivik
Saglouc (Sugluk)
Maricourt (Wakeham)
Koartac (Notre Dame de Koartac)
Akpatok I.
Arnaud
Bellin (Payne Bay)
Ungava Bay
Ungava Peninsula
Port Nouveau-Quebec (George R.)
Hebron
Payne L.
Ottawa Isv.
Portland Promontory
Inoucdjouac (Port Harrison)
Feuilles
Koksoak
Kuujjuaq
George
Whale
Kaniapiskau
Nain
Hopedale
C. Harrison
Indian Harbour
Rigolet
L. Melville
Cartwright
Hudson Bay
257
L. Minto
Mélèzes
Sleeper Is.
King George Is.
Baker's Dozen Is.
C. Tatnam
Belcher Is.
COAST OF LABRADOR
Schefferville
Petitsikapau L.
Churchill Falls
Churchill
North West R.
Goose Bay
Bottle Harb.
Belle Isle
L. Eau Claire
Lac Bienville
Ft. Severn
Severn
Winisk
Grand Baleine
Poste-de-la-Baleine (Great Whale River)
C. Henrietta Maria
Pte. Louis-XIV
Kanaaupscow
La Grande
Kaniapiskau
Ft. George
Ashuanipi L.
Natashquan
St-Augustin Saguenay
Str. of Belle Isle
Notre Dame B.
Twillingate
Lewisporte
Gander
Bonavista
Trinity B.
Carbonear
St. John's
Grand Falls
NEWFOUNDLAND
Harbour Grace
Placentia B.
Placentia
Trepassey
C. Race
Corner Brook
Port aux Basques
C. Ray
Big Trout L.
Attawapiskat
James Bay
Akimiski I.
Nouveau Comptoir (Paint Hills)
Eastmain
Charlton I.
Ft. Albany
Albany
Moosonee
Fort Rupert (Rupert House)
Rupert
Nottaway
Mistassini L.
L. Albanel
QUEBEC
Moisie
Sept Îles
Port-Cartier
Mingan
Romaine
I. d'Anticosti
Manicouagan
Gagnon
Gulf of St. Lawrence
C. de Gaspé
Gaspé
Pén. de Gaspé
Matane
Campbellton
Dalhousie
Îs. de la Madeleine
Cabot Str.
ST.-PIERRE et MIQUELON (Fr.)
L. St. Joseph
Armstrong
Nakina
Kenogami
Missinaibi
Harricana
Chibougamau
Péribonca
Baie-Comeau
Betsiamites
R. St. Lawrence
Rimouski
Rivière-du-Loup
Bathurst
Chatham
Tignish
PR. EDWARD I.
Summerside
Charlottetown
C. North
Cape Breton I.
Glace Bay
Sydney
Port Hawkesbury
Mulgrave
Northumberland Str.
Pictou
New Glasgow
Truro
Sable I. (Nova Scotia)
Windsor
Dartmouth
Halifax
Bridgewater
Liverpool
Shelburne
C. Sable
Yarmouth
Digby
NOVA SCOTIA
Kentville
Amherst
Springhill
Moncton
NEW BRUNSWICK
Newcastle
Saint John
Fredericton
Woodstock
Edmundston
St. Leonard
B. of Fundy
MAINE
Bangor
Augusta
Lewiston
Portland
NEW HAMPSHIRE
Manchester
Concord
Lowell
Boston
MASS.
C. Cod
Providence
RHODE I.
New Haven
CONN.
NEW YORK
Worcester
Springfield
Waterbury
Bridgeport
Jersey City
Newark
NEW JERSEY
Trenton
Reading
Allentown
Scranton
Binghamton
Elmira
Jamestown
Williamsport
PENNSYLVANIA
Youngstown
Cleveland
Akron
Erie
L. Erie
Buffalo
Niagara Falls
St. Catharines
Hamilton
Brantford
Rochester
Syracuse
Utica
Albany
Glens Falls
Watertown
L. Ontario
Oshawa
Cobourg
TORONTO
Guelph
Kitchener
Stratford
London
Sarnia
Chatham
Windsor
DETROIT
Toledo
OHIO
INDIANA
South Bend
Gary
CHICAGO
ILLINOIS
Evanston
Kenosha
Racine
Milwaukee
Sheboygan
Manitowoc
Madison
Rockford
Kalamazoo
Grand Rapids
Muskegon
Saginaw
Ludington
Cadillac
Traverse City
Appleton
Green Bay
Wausau
Menominee
Antigo
Iron Mt.
Rhinelander
Petoskey
Cheboygan
Manistique
Sault Ste. Marie
Escanaba
L. Michigan
Lake Huron
Georgian Bay
Owen Sound
Orillia
Peterborough
Belleville
Kingston
Burlington
Cornwall
Ottawa
Arnprior
Pembroke
Parry Sound
North Bay
Sudbury
Copper Cliff
North Chan.
Ironwood
Bessemer
Marquette
Laurium
Calumet
Keweenaw Bay
Lake Superior
Michipicoten
Thunder Bay
Nipigon
L. Nipigon
Longlac
Hearst
Heron Bay
Oba
Franz
Mattagami
Cochrane
L. Abitibi
Timmins
Noranda
Rouyn
Kirkland Lake
Haileybury
Cobalt
L. Témiscamingue
Rés. de Cabonga
Taschereau
Senneterre
Val d'Or
Matagami
Rés. de Gouin
Roberval
Dolbeau
St-Jean
Saguenay
Jonquière
Chicoutimi
Tadoussac
La Tuque
Shawinigan
Trois-Rivières
Joliette
Sorel
St. Hyacinthe
Québec
Lévis
Thetford Mines
Sherbrooke
MONTRÉAL
Hull
Lachine
Granby
L. Champlain
VERMONT
1917
1190
1128
1676
2591
1890
2136
2850
3809
6309
West from Greenwich

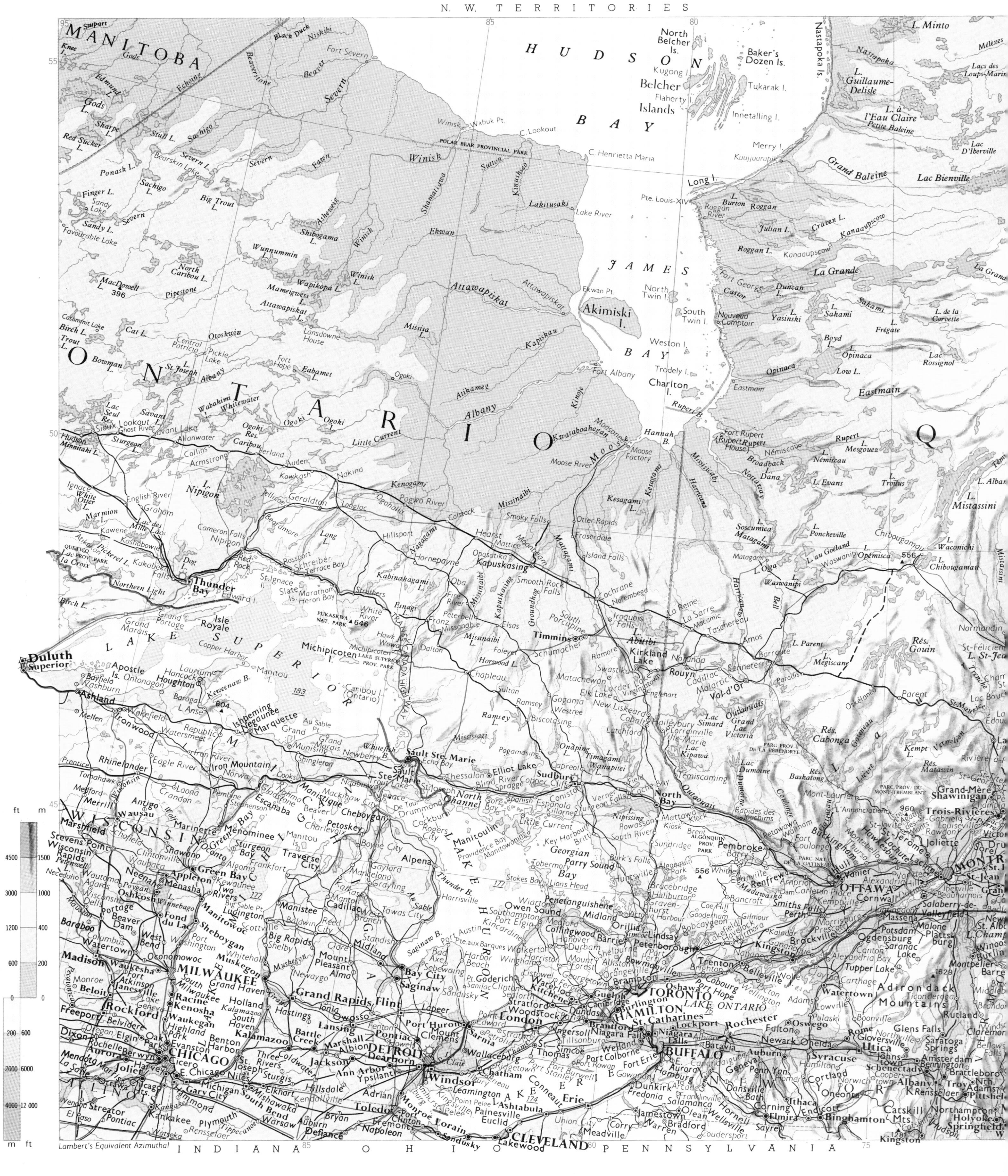

N. W. TERRITORIES

MANITOBA

HUDSON BAY

JAMES BAY

ONTARIO

Q

LAKE SUPERIOR

LAKE MICHIGAN

LAKE HURON

LAKE ERIE

LAKE ONTARIO

WISCONSIN

ILLINOIS

NEW YORK

ft	m
4500	1500
3000	1000
1200	400
600	200
0	0
200	600
2000	6000
4000	12 000
m	ft

Lambert's Equivalent Azimuthal

INDIANA OHIO PENNSYLVANIA

1 : 5 600 000

50 0 50 100 150 200 miles
50 0 50 100 150 200 250 300 km

South Aulatsivik I.
High I.
Nain
Paul I.
Erlandson
Whale L.
George L.
Fraser
Du Gué
Fort McKenzie
L. Nachicapau
Chakonipau L.
Otelnuk L.
Wheeler
L. de la Hutte Sauvage
Voisey's Bay
Kogaluk
Davis Inlet
Nunaksaluk I.
Sérigny
Sandy
610
L. Tudor
Whitegull L.
Woods L.
Big Bay
Hopedale
Kaipokok B.
Aillik
Makkovik
Adlavik Is.
C. Harrison
COAST
OF
Harp L.
Kanairiktok
Nascaupi
Seal L.
Nipishish
Rigolet
Holton
Indian Harbour
Groswater B.
Néret
Petitsikapau L.
Schefferville
Attikamagen L.
Michikamau Lake
L. Melville
1128
Mealy Mts.
Cartwright
Sandwich B.
Island of Ponds
Kaniapiskau L.
North-West River
Goose
Happy Valley-Goose Bay
Separation Point
Eagle
Square Islands
Nitchequon
L. Bermen
Churchill Falls
Ossokmanuan L.
LABRADOR
Paradise
Alexis
St. Lewis
Battle Harbour
L. Plétipi
Shabogamo L.
Opiskotish L.
Winokapau L.
Churchill
Minipi L.
u Z
St. Lewis
Red Bay
Mary's Harbour
Naococane
Opiscoteo L.
Lac Joseph
Atikonak L.
Burnt L.
Little Mecatina
Forteau
Anse au Loup
St. Lunaire-Griquet
St. Anthony
Hare B.
1128
Labrador City
Wabush
Ashuanipi L.
Ménihek Lakes
West Meganie
Romaine
Natashquan
St-Augustin Saguenay
a
St-Augustin
St-Paul
Bradore Bay
Lourdes-de-Blanc-Sablon
Flower's Cove
Groais I.
Conche
Bell I.
U E
B
Gagnon
Rés.
Manicouagan
1048
Nipissis L.
L. Manitou
St-Jean
Magpie L.
Sheldrake
P
Aguanus
Nabisipi
E
Olomane L.
C
Harrington Harbour
I. du Petit-Mécatina
Daniel's Harbour
Port Saunders
I. Quirpon
Roddickton
Englee
Long-Range Mts.
Seal Cove
White B.
Horse Is.
C. St. John
Monchalagan L.
Moisie
St-Marguerite
Ste-Marguerite
Réservoir
Clarke City
L. Pléti
Manouane
Ouiatchouan
Péribonca
Rés. Pipmuacan
Walker
Moisie
Sept-Îles
Port-Cartier
Rivière-Pentecôte
Godbout
Baie-Trinité
Ste-Anne
Mont-Louis
Dét. de Jacques-Cartier
Mingan
Havre-St-Pierre
Aguanish
Natashquan
Kegaska
Gethsémoni
Etamamu
Natashquan
L. Musquaro
Musquaro
Î. d'Anticosti
Jupiter
Heath Pt.
GROS MORNE NAT. PARK
Trout River
Deer Lake
Great Harbour Deep
Sop's Arm
La Scie
Notre Dame B.
Twillingate
Fogo I.
Change Is.
C. Freels
Mistassini
Péribonca L.
Betsiamites
St. Lawrence
Baie-Comeau
Cap-Chat
Ste-Anne
Matane
Mont-Joli
1268
Mt. Jacques-Cartier
Grande-Vallée
Sud Ouest
C. de Gaspé
Douglastown
Percé
572
GULF OF
Î. Brion
Grande-Entrée
Springdale
Howley
Badger
South Brook
Windsor
Grand Falls
Botwood
Bishop's Falls
Gander
Lewisporte
Gander
Glenwood
Dark Cove
Carmanville
Wesleyville
Bonavista
Benton
C. Bonavista
Catalina
Dolbeau
Alma
Mistassini L.
Saguenay
Chicoutimi
Jonquière
Tadoussac
Les Escoumins
Betsiamites
Forestville
Houteville
Baie-Comeau
St. Lawrence
Rimouski
Trois-Pistoles
Sayabec
Amqui
Causapscal
Matapédia
Bonaventure
Paspébiac
Chandler
Grande-Rivière
ST. LAWRENCE
Îs. de la Madeleine (Quebec)
Cap-aux-Meules
Havre-Aubert
St. Paul
C. North
Cabot Strait
Corner Brook
814
Long Pt.
Port au Port B.
Bay of Islands
Stephenville
South Brook
Buchans
Grand Indian
Red Indian L.
Victoria Res.
Grey Res.
Terra Nova
Port Blandford
Clarenville
Trinity
Bay de Verde
Old Perlican
Carbonear
Harbour Grace
Spaniard's Bay
Conception B.
NEWFOUNDLAND
Trinity B.
Lac-St-Jean
Roberval
Chambord
St-Félicien
Kénogami
Dolbeau
La Malbaie
St-Siméon
Baie-St-Paul
PARC PROV. DES LAURENTIDES
1190
Rivière-du-Loup
Cabano
St-Pascal
Édmundston
Grand Falls
Plaster Rock
Bathurst
Dalhousie
Campbellton
Atholville
Belledune
Chaleur Bay
Caraquet
Lamèque
Shippegan
Tracadie
Miscou I.
Miramichi B.
St-Pierre
Miquelon
Langlade
SAINT-PIERRE ET MIQUELON (Fr.)
C. St. George
St. George's B.
George's L.
St. David's
South Branch
St. Andrew's
C. Ray
Channel-Port aux Basques
Burgeo
Ramea
François
Harbour Breton
Marystown
Grand Banks
Fortune
Placentia
St. Lawrence
Argentia
Placentia B.
Grand Bank
St. Mary's B.
C. Pine
C. St. Mary's
C. Race
Trepassey
AVALON PENINSULA
Holyrood
St. John's
C. Spear
Mt. Pearl
QUÉBEC
Montmorency
Lévis
Lauzon
Île d'Orléans
Deschaillons
St-Jean-Port-Joli
Montmagny
St-Pamphile
Van Buren
Caribou
St. Leonard
819
Grand Falls
Plaster Rock
NEW BRUNSWICK
Newcastle
Chatham
Blackville
Chipman Dam
Notre Dame
Rexton
Richibucto
Buctouche
NOVA SCOTIA
Prince Edward Island
Summerside
Kensington
Charlottetown
Montague
Souris
E
a
s
t
Pt.
Tignish
Alberton
North Pt.
Cape Breton Nat. Park
532
Ingonish
Chéticamp
Pleasant Bay
C. North
St. Ann's B.
Cape Breton Island
Sydney Mines
New Waterford
N. Sydney
Sydney
Glace Bay
Louisbourg
Bras d'Or L.
Fourchu
Asbestos
East Angus
Lac-Mégantic
Megantic
Eagle L.
Island Falls
Houlton
Woodstock
Hartland
Stanley
Minto
Grand L.
Havelock
Petitcodiac
Sussex
Moncton
Shediac
Amherst
Sackville
Springhill
Parrsboro
Pictou
New Glasgow
Stellarton
Antigonish
Mulgrave
Canso
Chedabucto B.
I. Madame
Sherbrooke
Thetford Mines
Magog
Sherbrooke
Coaticook
St-Georges
Plessisville
Victoriaville
Drummondville
Richmond
MAINE
Jackman
Bingham
Greenville
Moosehead L.
Mattawamkeag
Lincoln
Milo
Dover-Foxcroft
Guilford
Mooselookmeguntic L.
Rumford
Skowhegan
Waterville
Bangor
Old Town
Brewer
Ellsworth
Bar Harbor
Mt. Desert I.
Machias
Jonesport
Calais
Eastport
Blacks Hr.
Grand Manan I.
St. Stephen
St. George
Fredericton
Gagetown
Oromocto
Rothesay
Saint John
St. Martins
Chignecto B.
Joggins
Minas Basin
Truro
Upper Musquodoboit
Stewiacke
Shubenacadie
Windsor
Kentville
Middleton
Annapolis Royal
Bridgetown
Digby
Weymouth
Bridgewater
Mahone Bay
Lunenburg
Liverpool
L. Rossignol
Port Mouton
Shelburne
Yarmouth
Wedgeport
Clark's Harbour
C. Sable
BAY OF FUNDY
Dartmouth
Halifax
Musquodoboit Hr.
Sheet Hr.
Sable I. (Nova Scotia)
A T L A N T I C
O C E A N
St. Johnsbury
1917
Washington
Berlin
Bethel
Augusta
Belfast
Camden
Rockland
Auburn
Lewiston
Bath
Brunswick
Portland
Saco
Biddeford
Sanford
Sebago L.
Conway
Laconia
Rochester
Concord
Dover
Portsmouth
Manchester
Haverhill
Lawrence
Nashua
Keene
Fitchburg
Lowell
Gloucester
C. Ann
Lynn
Waltham
BOSTON
Brockton
Worcester
Woonsocket

West from Greenwich

Timmins
Cochrane
Iroquois Falls
Lake Abitibi
La Sarre
Amos
Matagami
Chapais
Lebel-sur-Quévillon
Senneterre
Val-d'Or
Malartic
Rouyn
Noranda
Kirkland Lake
New Liskeard
Haileybury
Cobalt
Lake Timiskaming
Témiscaming
Sudbury
North Bay
Lake Nipissing
Sturgeon Falls
Mattawa
Deep River
Petawawa
Pembroke
Renfrew
Arnprior
Hull
OTTAWA
Gatineau
Pointe-Gatineau
Aylmer
Buckingham
Hawkesbury
Cornwall
Massena
Maniwaki
Mont-Laurier
Parry Sound
Huntsville
Bracebridge
Gravenhurst
Georgian Bay
ALGONQUIN PROV. PARK
PARC PROV. DE LA VÉRENDRYE
Réservoir Gouin
Réservoir Cabonga
Réservoir Dozois
Réservoir Decelles
O N T A R I O
Q U É
Projection: Bonne

1 : 2 000 000

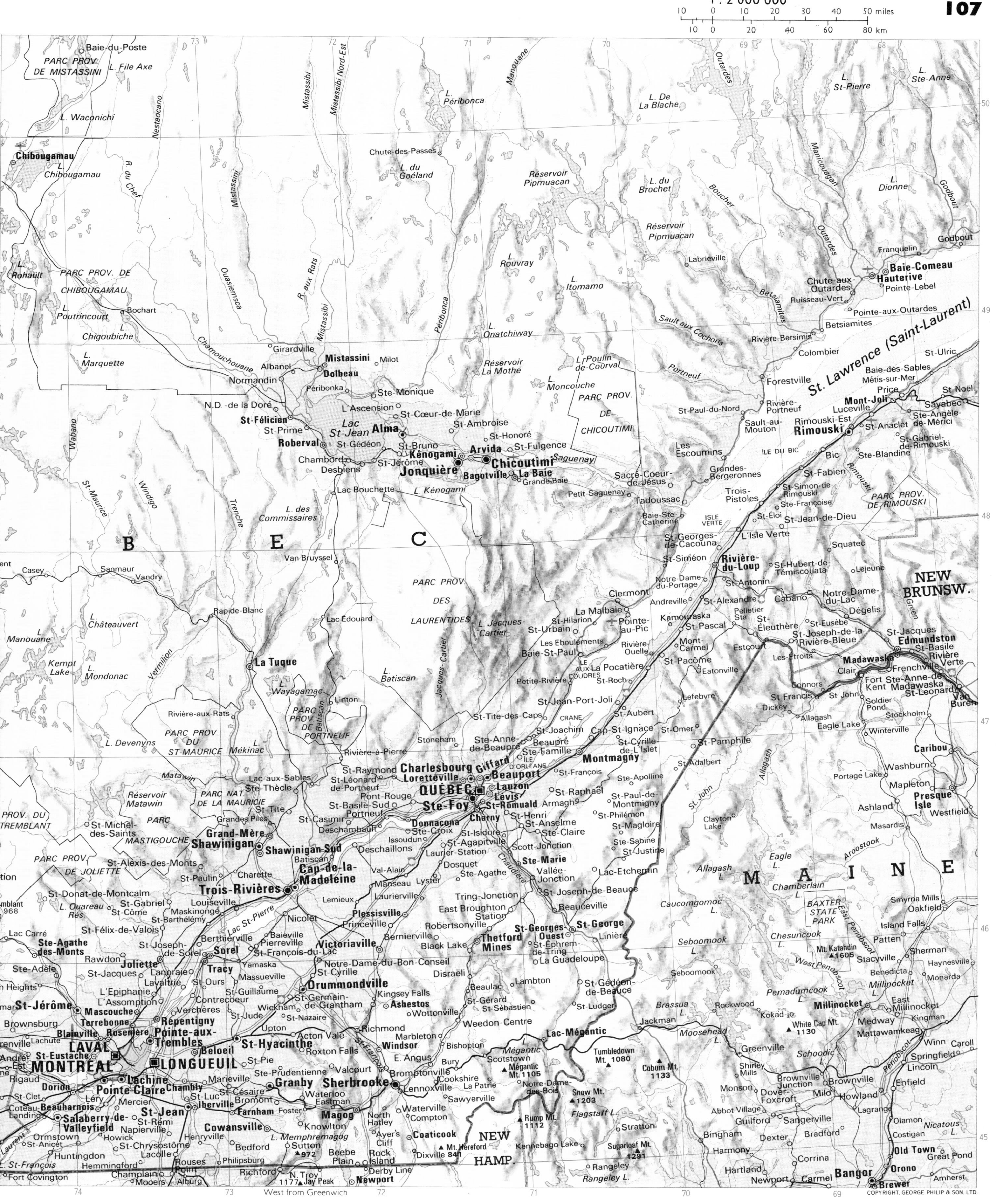
10 0 10 20 30 40 50 miles
10 0 20 40 60 80 km
74
73
72
71
70
69
68
50
49
48
47
46
45
West from Greenwich
Baie-du-Poste
PARC PROV. DE MISTASSINI
L. File Axe
L. Waconichi
Nestaocano
Mistassibi
Mistassibi Nord-Est
Manouane
L. Péribonca
Outardes
L. De La Blache
L. St-Pierre
L. Ste-Anne
Chibougamau
L. Chibougamau
R. du Chef
Mistassini
Chute-des-Passes
L. du Goéland
Réservoir Pipmuacan
L. du Brochet
Boucher
Manicouagan
L. Dionne
Godbout
Réservoir Pipmuacan
Franquelin
L. Rohault
PARC PROV. DE CHIBOUGAMAU
Ouasiemsca
R. aux Rats
Mistassibi
Péribonca
L. Rouvray
L. Itomamo
Labrieville
Baie-Comeau
Hauterive
Pointe-Lebel
Chute-aux-Outardes
Ruisseau-Vert
Betsiamites
L. Poutrincourt
Bochart
L. Chigoubiche
Chamouchouane
L. Onatchiway
Sault aux Cochons
Pointe-aux-Outardes
Betsiamites
Rivière-Bersimis
St. Lawrence (Saint-Laurent)
Girardville
Mistassini
Milot
L. Marquette
Albanel
Dolbeau
Normandin
Réservoir La Mothe
L. Poulin-de-Courval
Portneuf
Colombier
St-Ulric
Baie-des-Sables
Métis-sur-Mer
Forestville
Péribonka
Ste-Monique
L. Moncouche
PARC PROV. DE CHICOUTIMI
Price
St-Noël
Mont-Joli
Sayabec
N.D.-de la Doré
L'Ascension
St-Cœur-de-Marie
Rivière-Portneuf
St-Paul-du-Nord
Luceville
Ste-Angèle-de-Mérici
St-Félicien
St-Prime
Lac St-Jean
Alma
St-Ambroise
Sault-au-Mouton
Rimouski-Est
Rimouski
St-Anaclet
Roberval
St-Gédéon
St-Bruno
St-Honoré
St-Fulgence
Les Escoumins
ÎLE DU BIC
Bic
St-Gabriel-de-Rimouski
Ste-Blandine
Wabano
Chambord
Kénogami
Arvida
Chicoutimi
Saguenay
Desbiens
St-Jérôme
Jonquière
Bagotville
La Baie
Grande-Baie
Sacré-Coeur-de-Jésus
Grandes-Bergeronnes
St-Fabien
Rimouski
St-Maurice
Windigo
Lac Bouchette
L. Kénogami
Petit-Saguenay
Tadoussac
Trois-Pistoles
St-Simon-de-Rimouski
Ste-Françoise
PARC PROV. DE RIMOUSKI
Trenche
L. des Commissaires
Baie-Ste-Catherine
ISLE VERTE
St-Éloi
St-Jean-de-Dieu
B
E
C
St-Georges-de-Cacouna
L'Isle Verte
Squatec
Van Bruyssel
St-Siméon
Rivière-du-Loup
St-Hubert-de-Témiscouata
Lejeune
Casey
Sanmaur
Vandry
PARC PROV. DES LAURENTIDES
Notre-Dame-du-Portage
St-Antonin
NEW BRUNSW.
Clermont
Andreville
St-Alexandre
Cabano
Notre-Dame-du-Lac
Green
Rapide-Blanc
La Malbaie
Kamouraska
Dégelis
L. Châteauvert
Lac Édouard
L. Jacques-Cartier
St-Hilarion
Pointe-au-Pic
St-Pascal
Pelletier Sta.
St-Éleuthère
St-Eusèbe
St-Joseph-de-la-Rivière-Bleue
St-Jacques
Edmundston
L. Manouane
St-Urbain
Mont-Carmel
St-Basile
Les Eboulements
Rivière-Ouelle
Estcourt
Rivière Verte
Kempt Lake
L. Mondonac
Vermillion
La Tuque
Jacques-Cartier
Baie-St-Paul
ÎLE AUX COUDRES
La Pocatière
St-Pacôme
Les Étroits
Madawaska
Frenchville
Eatonville
Clair
Fort Kent
Ste-Anne-de-Madawaska
L. Batiscan
Petite-Rivière
St-Roch
St-Leonard
L. Wayagamac
Linton
Connors
Van Buren
St-Jean-Port-Joli
Lefebvre
St Francis
St John
Soldier Pond
Rivière-aux-Rats
PARC PROV. DE PORTNEUF
Batiscan
St-Tite-des-Caps
CRANE
St-Aubert
Dickey
Allagash
Stockholm
Eagle Lake
PARC PROV. DU ST-MAURICE
St-Joachim
Cap-St-Ignace
St-Omer
Winterville
L. Devenyns
Mékinac
Stoneham
Ste-Anne-de-Beaupré
Beaupré
Ste-Famille
St-Cyrille-de-L'Islet
St-Pamphile
Rivière-à-Pierre
Giffard
ÎLE D'ORLÉANS
Montmagny
St-Adalbert
Caribou
Matawin
St-Raymond
Charlesbourg
Beauport
St-François
Ste-Apolline
Washburn
Lac-aux-Sables
St-Léonard-de-Portneuf
Loretteville
Lauzon
Allagash
Portage Lake
Mapleton
Réservoir Matawin
PARC NAT. DE LA MAURICIE
Ste-Thècle
QUÉBEC
Lévis
St-Raphaël
St-Paul-de-Montmigny
St. John
Ashland
Presque Isle
PROV. DU TREMBLANT
PARC
Grandes Piles
St-Tite
Pont-Rouge
St-Basile-Sud
Portneuf
Ste-Foy
St-Romuald
Armagh
St-Philémon
Clayton Lake
Westfield
St-Michel-des-Saints
MASTIGOUCHE
Grand-Mère
St-Casimir
Deschambault
Charny
St-Henri
St-Anselme
Ste-Claire
St-Magloire
Masardis
Shawinigan
Shawinigan-Sud
Donnacona
Ste-Croix
Issoudun
St-Isidore
St-Agapitville
Scott-Jonction
Ste-Sabine
St-Justine
Aroostook
PARC PROV. DE JOLIETTE
St-Alexis-des-Monts
Deschaillons
Laurier-Station
Ste-Marie
Eagle L.
Batiscan
Cap-de-la-Madeleine
Val-Alain
Dosquet
Chaudière
Allagash L.
M A I N E
St-Paulin
Charette
Ste-Agathe
Vallée-Jonction
Lac-Etchemin
Trois-Rivières
Manseau
Lyster
St-Joseph-de-Beauce
Chamberlain L.
Tremblant 968
St-Donat-de-Montcalm
Madeleine
Laurierville
St-Gabriel
Louiseville
Lemieux
Tring-Jonction
Beauceville
Caucomgomoc L.
Smyrna Mills
Oakfield
L. Ouareau Rés.
St-Côme
Maskinongé
Lac St-Pierre
Plessisville
East Broughton Station
BAXTER STATE PARK
Island Falls
St-Barthélémy
Nicolet
Princeville
Robertsonville
St-Georges-Ouest
St-George
East Penobscot
Lac Carré
St-Félix-de-Valois
Berthierville
Baieville
Victoriaville
Bernierville
Thetford Mines
Linière
Seboomook L.
Chesuncook L.
Patten
Ste-Agathe-des-Monts
St-Joseph-de-Sorel
Pierreville
Black Lake
St-Éphrem-de-Tring
Mt. Katahdin 1605
Sherman
Rawdon
Joliette
Sorel
St-François-du-Lac
Notre-Dame-du-Bon-Conseil
La Guadeloupe
Stacyville
Ste-Adèle
St-Jacques
Lanoraie
Tracy
Yamaska
St-Cyrille
Disraëli
Seboomook
West Penobscot
Benedicta
Haynesville
Lavaltrie
St-Ours
Massueville
Lambton
St-Gédéon-de-Beauce
Pemadumcook L.
Millinocket L.
Monarda
L'Epiphanie
St-Guillaume
Drummondville
Kingsey Falls
Beaulac
St-Jérôme
Mascouche
L'Assomption
Contrecœur
St-Germain-de-Grantham
Asbestos
St-Gérard
St-Sébastien
St-Ludger
Brassua L.
Rockwood
Millinocket
East Millinocket
Brownsburg
Terrebonne
Repentigny
Verchères
Wickham
Wottonville
Jackman
Kokad-jo
Medway
Kingman
Lachute
Blainville
Rosemère
Pointe-aux-Trembles
St-Jude
St-Nazaire
Weedon-Centre
White Cap Mt. 1130
Mattawamkeag
Upton
Richmond
Lac-Mégantic
Moosehead L.
LAVAL
St-Eustache
Beloeil
St-Hyacinthe
Acton Vale
Marbleton
Bishopton
L. Mégantic
Tumbledown Mt. 1080
Greenville
Winn
Caroll
Roxton Falls
Windsor
Scotstown
Coburn Mt. 1133
Schoodic L.
Springfield
MONTREAL
LONGUEUIL
St-Pie
E. Angus
Bury
Mégantic Mt. 1105
Shirley Mills
Lincoln
Rigaud
Lachine
Marieville
Ste-Prudentienne
Valcourt
Bromptonville
Cookshire
Notre-Dame-des-Bois
Brownville Junction
Brownville
Dorion
Pointe-Claire
Chambly
St-Césaire
Granby
Sherbrooke
Lennoxville
La Patrie
Snow Mt. 1203
Monson
Dover-Foxcroft
Milo
Enfield
St-Clet
Léry
St-Luc
Waterloo
Sawyerville
Howland
Coteau Landing
Beauharnois
Mercier
Iberville
Bromont
Eastman
Lagrange
St-Jean
Farnham
Foster
Waterville
Flagstaff L.
Abbot Village
Salaberry-de-Valleyfield
St-Rémi
Napierville
Magog
North Hatley
Compton
Rump Mt. 1112
Guilford
Sangerville
Olamon
Nicatous L.
Ormstown
Cowansville
Knowlton
Stratton
St-Anicet
Howick
Henryville
Ste-Chrysostôme
L. Memphremagog
Ayer's Cliff
Coaticook
NEW HAMP.
Kennebago Lake
Bingham
Dexter
Bradford
Costigan
St-Laurent
Huntingdon
Lacolle
Bedford
Sutton ▲972
Mt. Hereford
Dixville 841
Sugarloaf Mt. 1291
Harmony
Corrina
Old Town
Great Pond
L. St-François
Hemmingford
Rouses Point
Philipsburg
Beebe Plain
Rock Island
Rangeley
Orono
Fort Covington
Champlain
Richford
N. Troy
Derby Line
Rangeley L.
Hartland
Bangor
Amherst
Mooers
Alburg
1177 Jay Peak
Newport
Newport
Carmel
Brewer
COPYRIGHT, GEORGE PHILIP & SON, LTD.

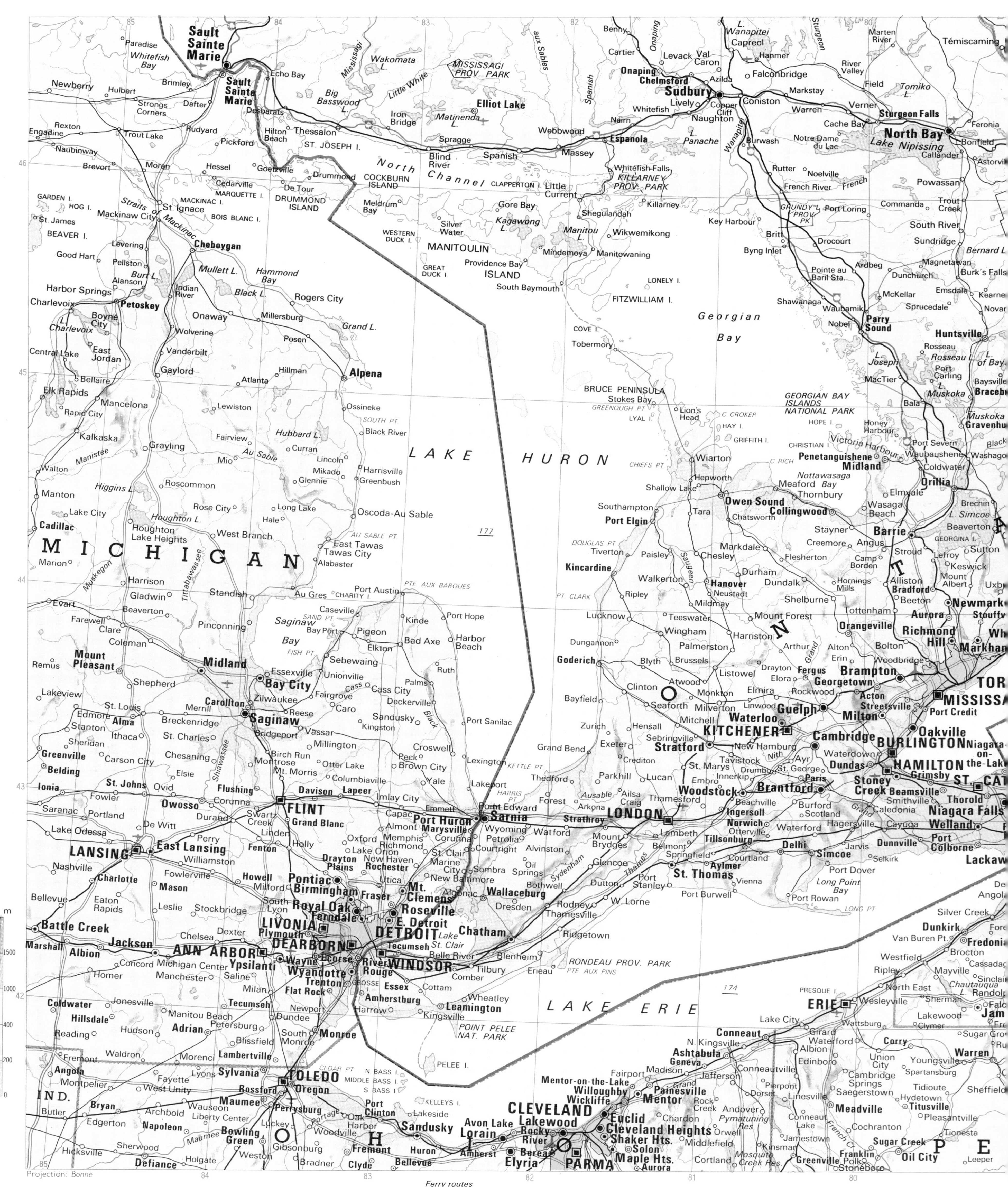
Sault Sainte Marie
Sault Sainte Marie
Paradise
Whitefish Bay
Newberry
Hulbert
Strongs Corners
Dafter
Brimley
Echo Bay
Rexton
Engadine
Naubinway
Trout Lake
Rudyard
Pickford
Desbarats
Thessalon
Hilton Beach
ST. JOSEPH I.
Brevort
Moran
Hessel
Cedarville
MARQUETTE I.
Goetzville
Drummond
De Tour
DRUMMOND ISLAND
COCKBURN ISLAND
GARDEN I.
HOG I.
St. James
BEAVER I.
Mackinaw City
St. Ignace
MACKINAC I.
BOIS BLANC I.
Straits of Mackinac
Cheboygan
Levering
Good Hart
Pellston
Alanson
Burt L.
Mullett L.
Hammond Bay
Indian River
Harbor Springs
Petoskey
Charlevoix
Boyne City
L. Charlevoix
Black L.
Rogers City
Onaway
Millersburg
Wolverine
Grand L.
Posen
Central Lake
East Jordan
Vanderbilt
Gaylord
Hillman
Alpena
Atlanta
Bellaire
Elk Rapids
Mancelona
Lewiston
Ossineke
SOUTH PT
Black River
Rapid City
Kalkaska
Fairview
Hubbard L.
Curran
Grayling
Manistee
Au Sable
Mio
Lincoln
Mikado
Harrisville
Glennie
Greenbush
Walton
Manton
Higgins L.
Roscommon
Rose City
Long Lake
Hale
Oscoda-Au Sable
Lake City
Cadillac
Houghton L.
Houghton Lake Heights
West Branch
AU SABLE PT
East Tawas
Tawas City
Alabaster
MICHIGAN
Marion
Muskegon
Tittabawassee
Harrison
Gladwin
Standish
Au Gres
CHARITY I.
Port Austin
PTE AUX BARQUES
Evart
Beaverton
Farwell
Clare
Pinconning
Saginaw Bay
SAND PT
Caseville
Bay Port
Pigeon
Kinde
Port Hope
Harbor Beach
Elkton
Bad Axe
FISH PT
Coleman
Remus
Mount Pleasant
Midland
Sebewaing
Essexville
Bay City
Unionville
Ruth
Shepherd
Zilwaukee
Fairgrove
Cass
Cass City
Palms
Lakeview
Carollton
Merrill
Saginaw
Reese
Caro
Deckerville
St. Louis
Edmore
Alma
Breckenridge
Sandusky
Kingston
Black
Port Sanilac
Stanton
Ithaca
St. Charles
Bridgeport
Vassar
Sheridan
Millington
Croswell
Greenville
Carson City
Chesaning
Birch Run
Peck
Lexington
KETTLE PT
Belding
Montrose
Otter Lake
Brown City
Elsie
Shiawassee
Mt. Morris
Columbiaville
Yale
Ionia
St. Johns
Ovid
Flushing
Lakeport
Fowler
Corunna
Davison
Lapeer
HARRIS PT
Saranac
Owosso
FLINT
Imlay City
Emmett
Point Edward
Portland
Durand
Swartz Creek
Grand Blanc
Capac
Port Huron
Sarnia
Lake Odessa
De Witt
Linden
Almont
Marysville
Wyoming
Perry
Memphis
Corunna
Petrolia
LANSING
East Lansing
Fenton
Holly
Oxford
Richmond
Courtright
Williamston
Lake Orion
Nashville
Fowlerville
Drayton Plains
New Haven
St. Clair
Marine City
Sombra
Charlotte
Mason
Howell
Milford
Pontiac
Rochester
Utica
Birmingham
Mt. Clemens
Fraser
New Baltimore
Bellevue
Eaton Rapids
Leslie
Stockbridge
South Lyon
Royal Oak
Algonac
Roseville
Ferndale
E. Detroit
Battle Creek
LIVONIA
Chelsea
Dexter
Plymouth
DETROIT
Lake St. Clair
DEARBORN
Jackson
ANN ARBOR
Marshall
Albion
Concord
Michigan Center
Ypsilanti
Wayne
Ecorse
River Rouge
Wyandotte
Tecumseh
WINDSOR
Homer
Manchester
Saline
Trenton
Milan
Flat Rock
GROSSE ILE
Essex
Coldwater
Jonesville
Tecumseh
Amherstburg
Hillsdale
Manitou Beach
Newport
Harrow
Adrian
Petersburg
Dundee
Reading
Hudson
Blissfield
South Monroe
Monroe
Fremont
Waldron
Morenci
Lambertville
Angola
Fayette
Lyons
Sylvania
TOLEDO
CEDAR PT
N. BASS I.
MIDDLE BASS I.
S. BASS I.
Montpelier
West Unity
Rossford
Oregon
IND.
Butler
Bryan
Wauseon
Archbold
Maumee
Perrysburg
Port Clinton
KELLEYS I.
Lakeside
Edgerton
Liberty Center
Napoleon
Bowling Green
Luckey
Portage
Oak Harbor
Sandusky
Sherwood
Maumee
Woodville
Hicksville
Gibsonburg
Weston
Fremont
Defiance
Holgate
Bradner
Clyde
Bellevue
Huron
Avon Lake
Lorain
Amherst
Elyria
Berea
Rocky River
Lakewood
CLEVELAND
PARMA
OHIO
Euclid
Cleveland Heights
Shaker Hts.
Solon
Maple Hts.
Aurora
Mentor-on-the-Lake
Willoughby
Wickliffe
Mentor
Painesville
Fairport
Madison
Geneva
Ashtabula
Jefferson
Grand
N. Kingsville
Conneaut
Conneautville
Rock Creek
Chardon
Andover
Pymatuning Res.
Orwell
Middlefield
Mosquito Creek Res.
Cortland
Kinsman
Greenville
Dorset
Pierpont
Linesville
Conneaut Lake
Jamestown
French Cr.
Meadville
Cochranton
Sugar Creek
Franklin
Polk
Stoneboro
Oil City
Leeper
Tionesta
Pleasantville
Titusville
Hydetown
Tidioute
Sheffield
Spartansburg
Saegerstown
Cambridge Springs
Union City
Youngsville
Warren
Edinboro
Albion
Waterford
Corry
Girard
Wattsburg
Lake City
ERIE
PRESQUE I.
Wesleyville
North East
Lakewood
Clymer
Sugar Grove
Sherman
Chautauqua L.
Randolph
Jamestown
Sinclairville
Mayville
Cassadaga
Brocton
Ripley
Westfield
Fredonia
Dunkirk
Van Buren Pt.
Silver Creek
LONG PT
Angola
Port Rowan
Long Point Bay
Port Dover
Simcoe
Jarvis
Selkirk
Dunnville
Port Colborne
Welland
Niagara Falls
Thorold
ST. CATHARINES
Grimsby
Beamsville
Smithville
Caledonia
Cayuga
Hagersville
Waterford
Delhi
Tillsonburg
Norwich
Otterville
Burford
Scotland
Brantford
Paris
St. George
Ayr
Drumbo
Innerkip
Embro
Woodstock
Beachville
Ingersoll
Thamesford
Tavistock
New Hamburg
St. Marys
Stratford
Sebringville
Mitchell
KITCHENER
Waterloo
Cambridge
Guelph
Waterdown
Dundas
HAMILTON
BURLINGTON
Stoney Creek
Niagara-on-the-Lake
Oakville
Milton
Acton
Streetsville
Port Credit
MISSISSAUGA
TORONTO
Georgetown
Brampton
Rockwood
Fergus
Elora
Drayton
Erin
Alton
Woodbridge
Markham
Richmond Hill
Bolton
Orangeville
Aurora
Stouffville
Newmarket
Tottenham
Beeton
Bradford
Alliston
Uxbridge
Mount Albert
Keswick
Lefroy
Sutton
Stroud
Camp Borden
Angus
Barrie
GEORGIA I.
Beaverton
L. Simcoe
Brechin
Orillia
Elmvale
Wasaga Beach
Stayner
Creemore
Collingwood
Thornbury
Meaford
Nottawasaga Bay
Midland
Penetanguishene
Coldwater
Waubaushene
Port Severn
Victoria Harbour
Washago
Gravenhurst
Muskoka
Bracebridge
L. Muskoka
Port Carling
Rosseau
L. Rosseau
L. of Bays
Baysville
Huntsville
Bala
MacTier
L. Joseph
Honey Harbour
GEORGIAN BAY ISLANDS NATIONAL PARK
HOPE I.
CHRISTIAN I.
GRIFFITH I.
HAY I.
C. CROKER
C. RICH
CHIEFS PT
Lion's Head
LYAL I.
GREENOUGH PT
Stokes Bay
BRUCE PENINSULA
Tobermory
COVE I.
Wiarton
Hepworth
Shallow Lake
Owen Sound
Chatsworth
Tara
Southampton
Port Elgin
Paisley
Chesley
Markdale
Flesherton
Durham
Dundalk
Shelburne
Hornings Mills
Hanover
Neustadt
Walkerton
Saugeen
Kincardine
Tiverton
DOUGLAS PT
Ripley
PT. CLARK
Mildmay
Mount Forest
Teeswater
Lucknow
Wingham
Harriston
Palmerston
Arthur
Grand
Dungannon
Goderich
Blyth
Brussels
Listowel
Clinton
Atwood
Monkton
Elmira
Linwood
Bayfield
Seaforth
Milverton
Zurich
Hensall
Grand Bend
Exeter
Crediton
Parkhill
Lucan
Thedford
Ausable
Ailsa Craig
Arkona
Forest
LONDON
Strathroy
Watford
Alvinston
Mount Brydges
Lambeth
Belmont
Springfield
Aylmer
Courtland
St. Thomas
Port Stanley
Vienna
Port Burwell
Glencoe
Thames
Sydenham
Oil Springs
Bothwell
Dutton
Rodney
W. Lorne
Wallaceburg
Dresden
Thamesville
Chatham
Ridgetown
Blenheim
RONDEAU PROV. PARK
PTE AUX PINS
Erieau
Tilbury
Belle River
Comber
Cottam
Wheatley
Leamington
Kingsville
POINT PELEE NAT. PARK
PELEE I.
LAKE ERIE
LAKE HURON
Georgian Bay
North Channel
MANITOULIN ISLAND
Gore Bay
Kagawong L.
Manitou L.
Silver Water
Meldrum Bay
WESTERN DUCK I.
GREAT DUCK I.
Providence Bay
South Baymouth
Mindemoya
Manitowaning
Wikwemikong
Sheguiandah
Little Current
CLAPPERTON I.
Killarney
KILLARNEY PROV. PARK
Whitefish Falls
LONELY I.
FITZWILLIAM I.
Espanola
Massey
Webbwood
Spanish
Spragge
Blind River
Iron Bridge
Matinenda L.
Elliot Lake
Little White
Big Basswood L.
Mississagi
Wakomata L.
MISSISSAGI PROV. PARK
aux Sables
Spanish
Onaping
Benny
Cartier
Levack
Val Caron
Onaping
Chelmsford
Azilda
Sudbury
Lively
Copper Cliff
Naughton
Whitefish
Nairn
Coniston
Falconbridge
Hanmer
Capreol
L. Wanapitei
Wanapitei
Sturgeon
L. Panache
Burwash
Markstay
Warren
Verner
Sturgeon Falls
Cache Bay
North Bay
Lake Nipissing
Notre Dame du Lac
Callander
Bonfield
Feronia
Astorville
Field
River Valley
Tomiko L.
Marten River
Témiscaming
Rutter
Noelville
French River
French
Powassan
Commanda
Trout Creek
Port Loring
GRUNDY L. PROV. PK
Key Harbour
Britt
South River
Sundridge
Drocourt
Byng Inlet
Ardbeg
Magnetawan
Burk's Falls
Bernard L.
Dunchurch
Pointe au Baril Sta.
Emsdale
Kearney
Shawanaga
McKellar
Waubamik
Sprucedale
Novar
Nobel
Parry Sound
177
174
Projection: Bonne
Ferry routes
85
84
83
82
81
80
46
45
44
43
42
ft
m
4500
1500
3000
1000
1200
400
600
200
0
0
200
600
m
ft

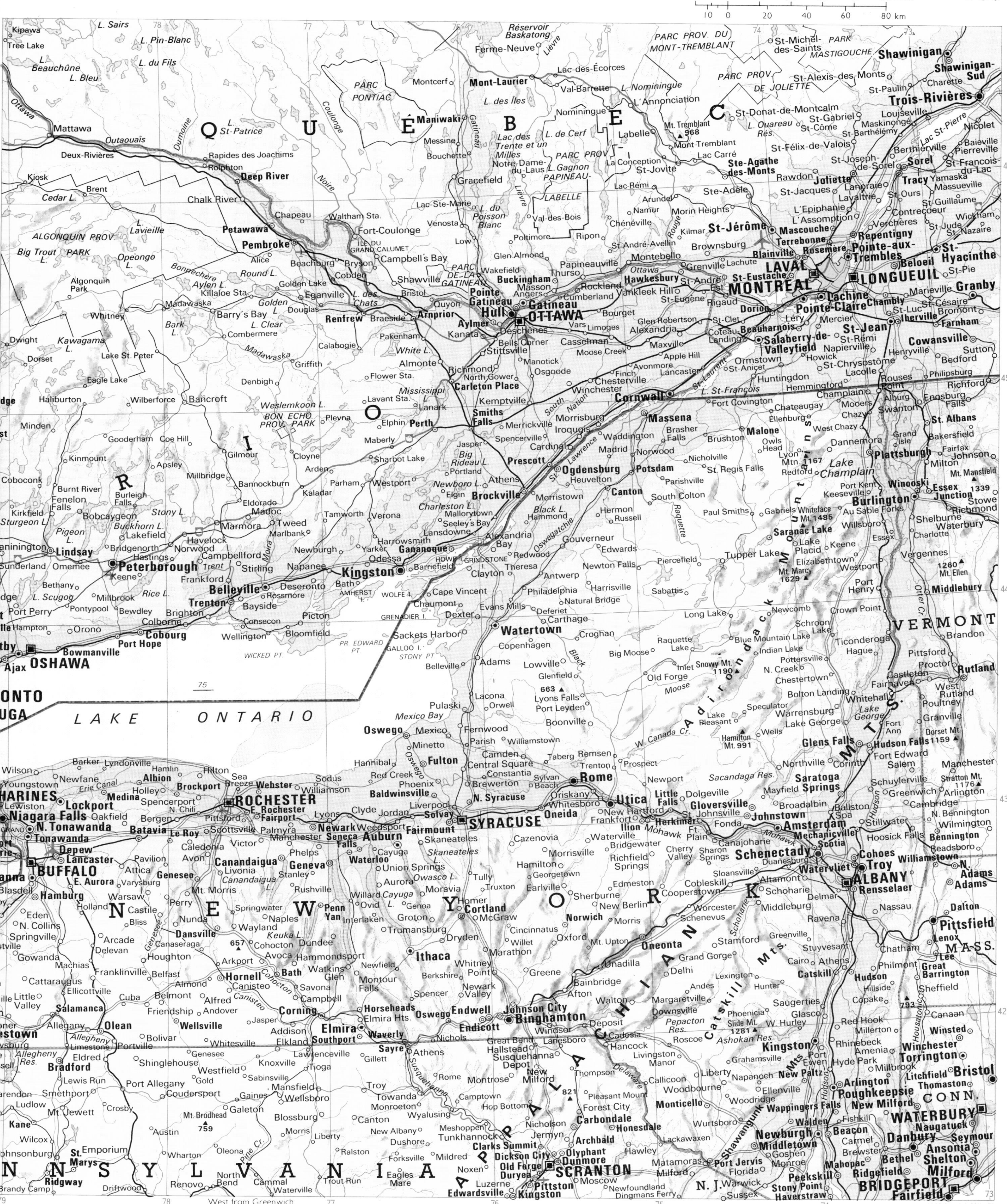
1 : 2 000 000
50 miles
80 km
QUÉBEC
ONTARIO
NEW YORK
VERMONT
MASS.
CONN.
PENNSYLVANIA
N. J.
LAKE ONTARIO
ADIRONDACK MOUNTAINS
APPALACHIAN
Catskill Mts.
Green Mts.
PARC PROV. DU MONT-TREMBLANT
PARC PROV. DE JOLIETTE
PARC PONTIAC
ALGONQUIN PROV. PARK
Lake Champlain
MONTREAL
LAVAL
LONGUEUIL
OTTAWA
Hull
Trois-Rivières
Kingston
Peterborough
OSHAWA
ROCHESTER
BUFFALO
Niagara Falls
SYRACUSE
Utica
Rome
Schenectady
ALBANY
Troy
Binghamton
Elmira
Ithaca
SCRANTON
Watertown
Plattsburgh
Burlington
Rutland
Pittsfield
WATERBURY
BRIDGEPORT
Newburgh
Poughkeepsie
Kingston
Cornwall
Brockville
Belleville
St-Jérôme
St-Jean
Granby
Sorel
West from Greenwich

YUKON TERRITORY
NORTHWEST TERRITORIES
FORT SMITH
FORT NELSON
BRITISH COLUMBIA
ALBERTA
WASHINGTON
IDAHO
ALASKA
PACIFIC OCEAN
QUEEN CHARLOTTE ISLANDS
VANCOUVER ISLAND
ALEXANDER ARCH.
GREAT SLAVE LAKE
WOOD BUFFALO NATIONAL PARK
ROCKY MOUNTAINS
Coast Mountains
Cariboo Mountains
Selkirk Mountains
Skeena Mountains
Cassiar Mountains
Birch Mountains
Caribou Mts.
Horn Mts.
Whitehorse
Yellowknife
Prince Rupert
Prince George
Dawson Creek
Grande Prairie
EDMONTON
Calgary
Red Deer
Lethbridge
Kamloops
Kelowna
VANCOUVER
Victoria
SEATTLE
Bellingham
Nanaimo
Penticton
Nelson
Cranbrook
Kimberley
JASPER NATIONAL PARK
Fort McMurray
Peace River
Dixon Entrance
Hecate Strait
Queen Charlotte Str.
Juan de Fuca Str.
Projection: Lambert's Equivalent Azimuthal
West from Greenwich
ft
m
12 000
9000
6000
4500
3000
1200
600
0
200
2000
4000
3000
2000
1500
1000
400
200
0
600
6000
m
ft

1 : 5 600 000

50 0 50 100 150 200 miles

50 0 50 100 150 200 250 300 km

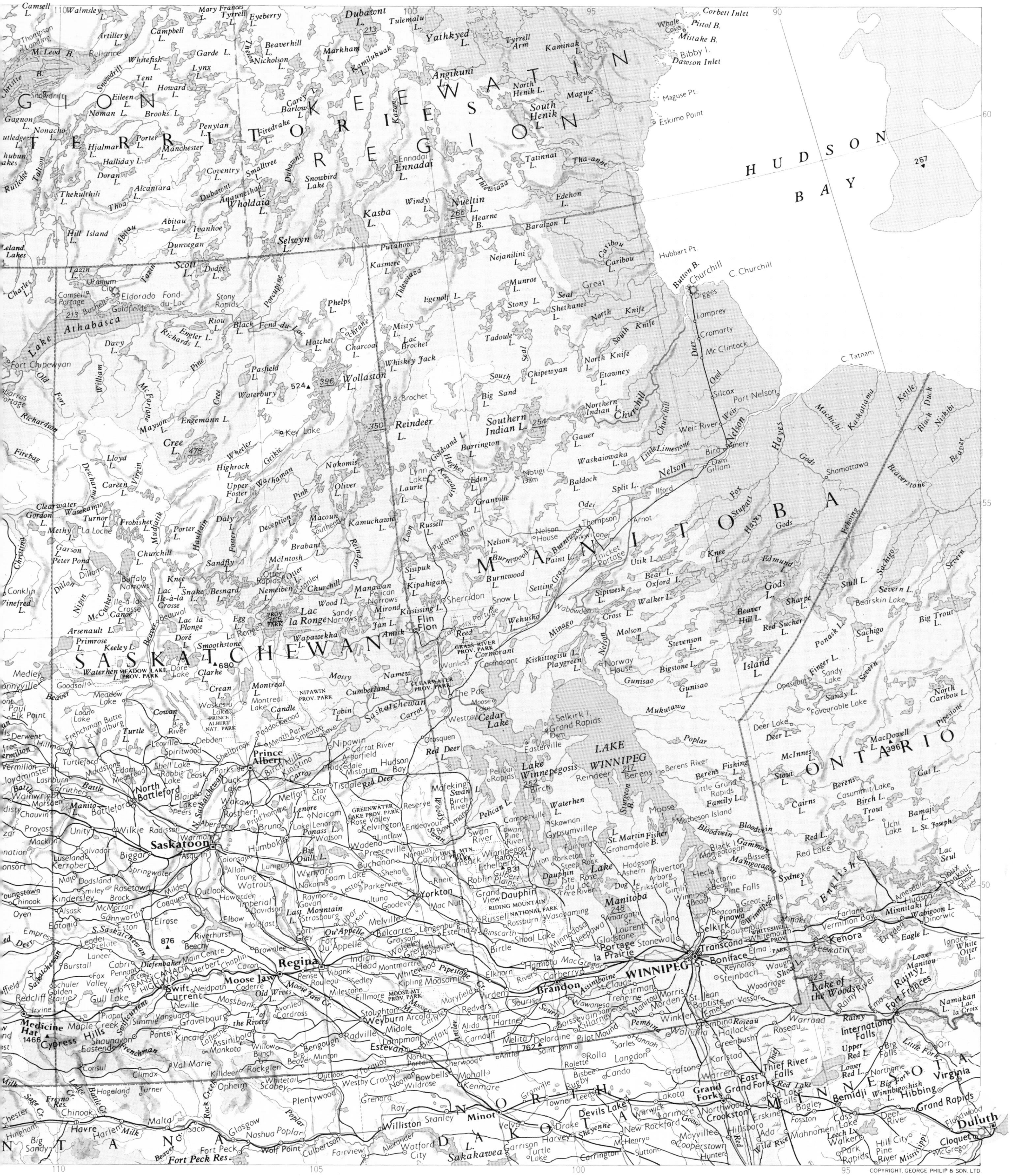

KEEWATIN

REGION

HUDSON BAY

SASKATCHEWAN

MANITOBA

ONTARIO

LAKE WINNIPEG

NORTH DAKOTA

MINNESOTA

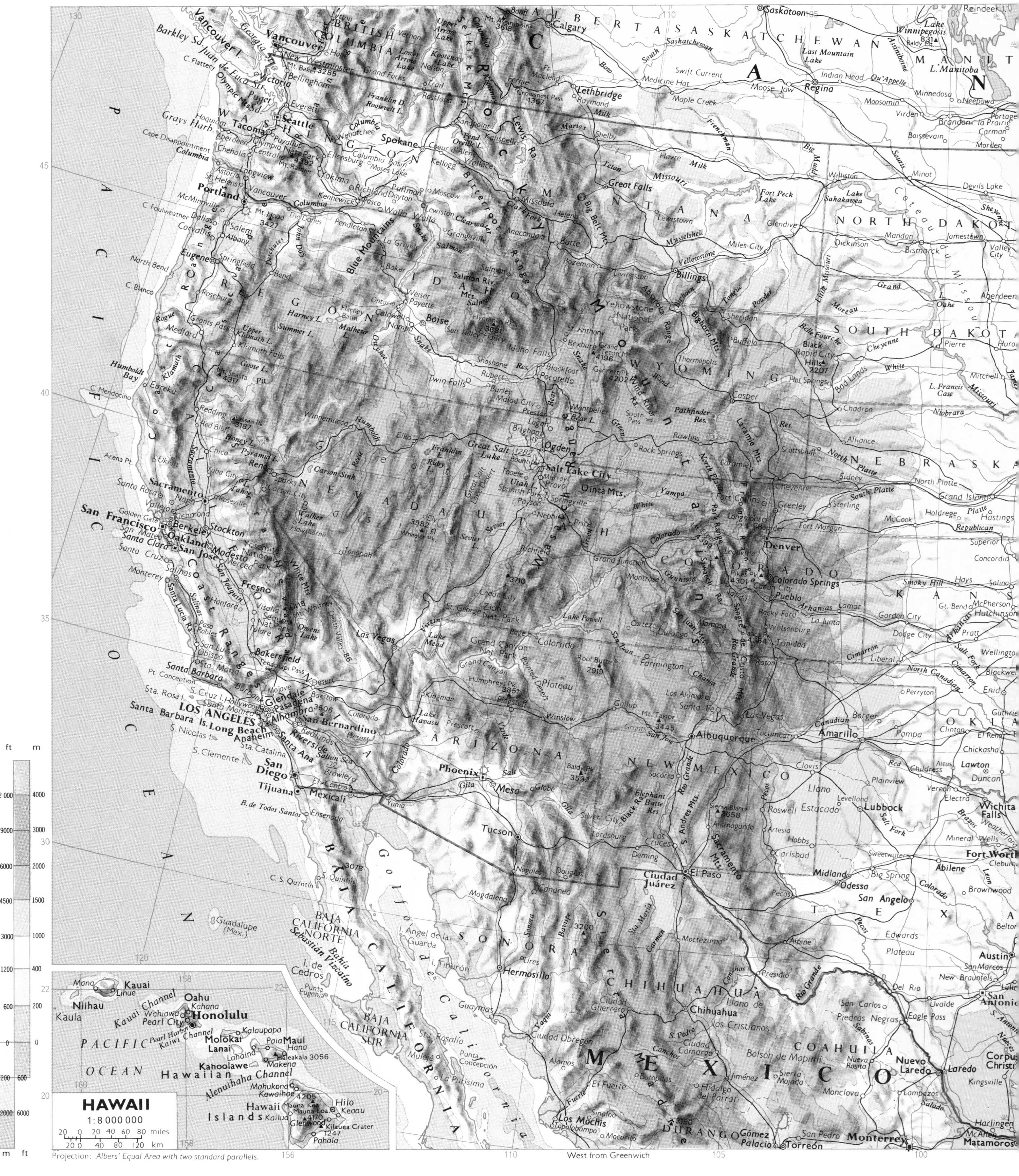

PACIFIC OCEAN
CANADA
BRITISH COLUMBIA
ALBERTA
SASKATCHEWAN
MANITOBA
WASHINGTON
OREGON
IDAHO
MONTANA
WYOMING
NORTH DAKOTA
SOUTH DAKOTA
NEBRASKA
CALIFORNIA
NEVADA
UTAH
COLORADO
KANSAS
ARIZONA
NEW MEXICO
OKLAHOMA
TEXAS
MEXICO
BAJA CALIFORNIA NORTE
BAJA CALIFORNIA SUR
SONORA
CHIHUAHUA
COAHUILA
DURANGO
Golfo de California
Vancouver
Victoria
Seattle
Tacoma
Spokane
Portland
Eugene
Calgary
Lethbridge
Saskatoon
Regina
Great Falls
Billings
Boise
Salt Lake City
Ogden
Denver
Colorado Springs
Pueblo
Cheyenne
Sacramento
San Francisco
Oakland
Berkeley
San Jose
Stockton
Fresno
Bakersfield
LOS ANGELES
Long Beach
Pasadena
Glendale
San Bernardino
Santa Barbara
San Diego
Tijuana
Mexicali
Las Vegas
Reno
Phoenix
Mesa
Tucson
Albuquerque
Santa Fe
El Paso
Ciudad Juárez
Amarillo
Lubbock
Midland
Odessa
San Angelo
Abilene
Austin
San Antonio
Laredo
Nuevo Laredo
Monterrey
Torreón
Chihuahua
Hermosillo
Los Mochis
Rocky Mts.
Sierra Nevada
Cascade Range
Coast Ranges
Great Salt Lake
Great Basin
Mojave Desert
Grand Canyon
Yellowstone National Park
Snake
Columbia
Missouri
Colorado
Rio Grande
Llano Estacado
Sierra Madre
HAWAII
1:8 000 000
Kauai
Niihau
Oahu
Honolulu
Molokai
Lanai
Maui
Kahoolawe
Hawaii
Hilo
PACIFIC OCEAN
Hawaiian Islands
miles
km
ft
m
West from Greenwich

Projection: *Albers' Equal Area with two standard parallels.*

1 : 9 600 000

50 0 50 100 150 200 250 300 miles

50 0 50 100 150 200 250 300 350 400 450 km

CANADA
ONTARIO
QUEBEC
Lake Winnipeg
Winnipeg
Lake of the Woods
Thunder Bay
Lake Superior
Lake Nipigon
Sault Ste. Marie
Sudbury
L. Nipissing
Georgian Bay
Lake Huron
Lake Michigan
Lake Erie
Lake Ontario
L. Champlain
MONTREAL
Ottawa
Québec
TORONTO
Hamilton
Kingston
Kitchener
London
Windsor
DETROIT
Toledo
Cleveland
Akron
Youngstown
Erie
Buffalo
Niagara Falls
Rochester
Syracuse
Utica
Albany
Schenectady
Binghamton
Scranton
Wilkes Barre
Allentown
Reading
Harrisburg
Lancaster
York
PHILADELPHIA
Camden
Trenton
Newark
Paterson
Jersey City
NEW YORK
Bridgeport
New Haven
Waterbury
Hartford
Springfield
Worcester
Providence
Fall River
New Bedford
Brockton
Boston
Lowell
Lawrence
Manchester
Portland
Bangor
Penobscot Bay
Moosehead L.
Sherbrooke
MAINE
NEW BRUNSWICK
VERMONT
NEW HAMPSHIRE
White Mts.
Adirondack Mts.
Catskill Mts.
Martha's Vineyard
C. Cod
Wilmington
Baltimore
Washington D.C.
Annapolis
Delaware Bay
Atlantic City
C. May
Chesapeake Bay
Richmond
Newport News
Norfolk
Portsmouth
Virginia Beach
Lynchburg
Roanoke
Charleston
Huntington
Pittsburgh
Wheeling
Columbus
Dayton
Cincinnati
Lexington
Louisville
Evansville
Indianapolis
Terre Haute
Fort Wayne
South Bend
Gary
Hammond
CHICAGO
Joliet
Aurora
Rockford
Milwaukee
Racine
Kenosha
Madison
Green Bay
Grand Rapids
Lansing
Flint
Saginaw
Bay City
Duluth
Superior
Minneapolis
St. Paul
Rochester
Des Moines
Cedar Rapids
Davenport
Rock Island
Peoria
Springfield
Decatur
Omaha
Council Bluffs
Lincoln
Sioux City
Sioux Falls
St. Joseph
Kansas City
Topeka
Wichita
Tulsa
Oklahoma City
Fort Smith
Little Rock
St. Louis
Springfield
Memphis
Nashville
Knoxville
Chattanooga
Birmingham
Huntsville
Atlanta
Macon
Augusta
Columbia
Charlotte
Winston Salem
Greensboro
Durham
Raleigh
Asheville
Greenville
Savannah
Charleston
Columbus
Montgomery
Mobile
Jackson
Shreveport
Dallas
Waco
Houston
Pasadena
Galveston
Beaumont
Port Arthur
Lake Charles
Baton Rouge
New Orleans
Delta of the Mississippi
Pensacola
Tallahassee
Jacksonville
St. Augustine
Daytona Beach
C. Canaveral
Orlando
Tampa
St. Petersburg
Lakeland
Ft. Pierce
West Palm Beach
Fort Lauderdale
Miami
Key West
Florida Bay
Florida Keys
Everglades
L. Okeechobee
Charlotte Harb.
Apalachee B.
GULF OF MEXICO
ATLANTIC OCEAN
BAHAMAS
Grand Bahama I.
Gt. Abaco
Eleuthera I.
Andros I.
Nassau
New Providence
Cat I.
Long I.
N.W. Providence Chan.
N.E. Providence Channel
Exuma Sound
MINNESOTA
WISCONSIN
MICHIGAN
IOWA
ILLINOIS
INDIANA
OHIO
PENNSYLVANIA
NEW YORK
WEST VIRGINIA
VIRGINIA
MARYLAND
KENTUCKY
TENNESSEE
NORTH CAROLINA
SOUTH CAROLINA
GEORGIA
ALABAMA
MISSISSIPPI
LOUISIANA
ARKANSAS
MISSOURI
FLORIDA
Ozark Plateau
Ouachita Mts.
Boston Mts.
Cumberland Plateau
Allegheny Mts.
Blue Ridge
Albemarle Sd.
Pamlico Sd.
C. Hatteras
Onslow Bay
Raleigh Bay
Long Bay
C. Fear
Mississippi
Ohio
Missouri
Tennessee
Cumberland
Red River
Arkansas
Padre I.
Laguna Madre
Brownsville
Rio Grande
Matagorda I.
Aransas Pass

LAKE SUPERIOR
LAKE HURON
LAKE MICHIGAN
LAKE ERIE
LAKE ONTARIO
Georgian Bay
ONTARIO
QUEBEC
MICHIGAN
WISCONSIN
ILLINOIS
INDIANA
OHIO
KENTUCKY
WEST VIRGINIA
VIRGINIA
PENNSYLVANIA
NEW YORK
NEW JERSEY
MARYLAND
DELAWARE
VERMONT
NEW HAMPSHIRE
MASSACHUSETTS
CHICAGO
MILWAUKEE
DETROIT
TORONTO
MONTREAL
Ottawa
Quebec
CLEVELAND
PITTSBURGH
COLUMBUS
INDIANAPOLIS
Cincinnati
PHILADELPHIA
BALTIMORE
WASHINGTON D.C.
NEW YORK
BOSTON
Buffalo
Rochester
Hamilton

1 : 4 800 000
miles
km
TENNESSEE
NORTH CAROLINA
SOUTH CAROLINA
GEORGIA
ALABAMA
FLORIDA
MISSISSIPPI
MAINE
NEW HAMPSHIRE
CANADA
BAHAMAS
ATLANTIC OCEAN
GULF OF MEXICO
NASHVILLE
ATLANTA
JACKSONVILLE
Charlotte
Columbia
Charleston
Savannah
Birmingham
Montgomery
Mobile
Tallahassee
Tampa
St. Petersburg
Orlando
Miami
Continuation Eastwards On same scale
West from Greenwich
Projection: Alber's Equal Area with two standard parallels
COPYRIGHT GEORGE PHILIP & SON LTD.

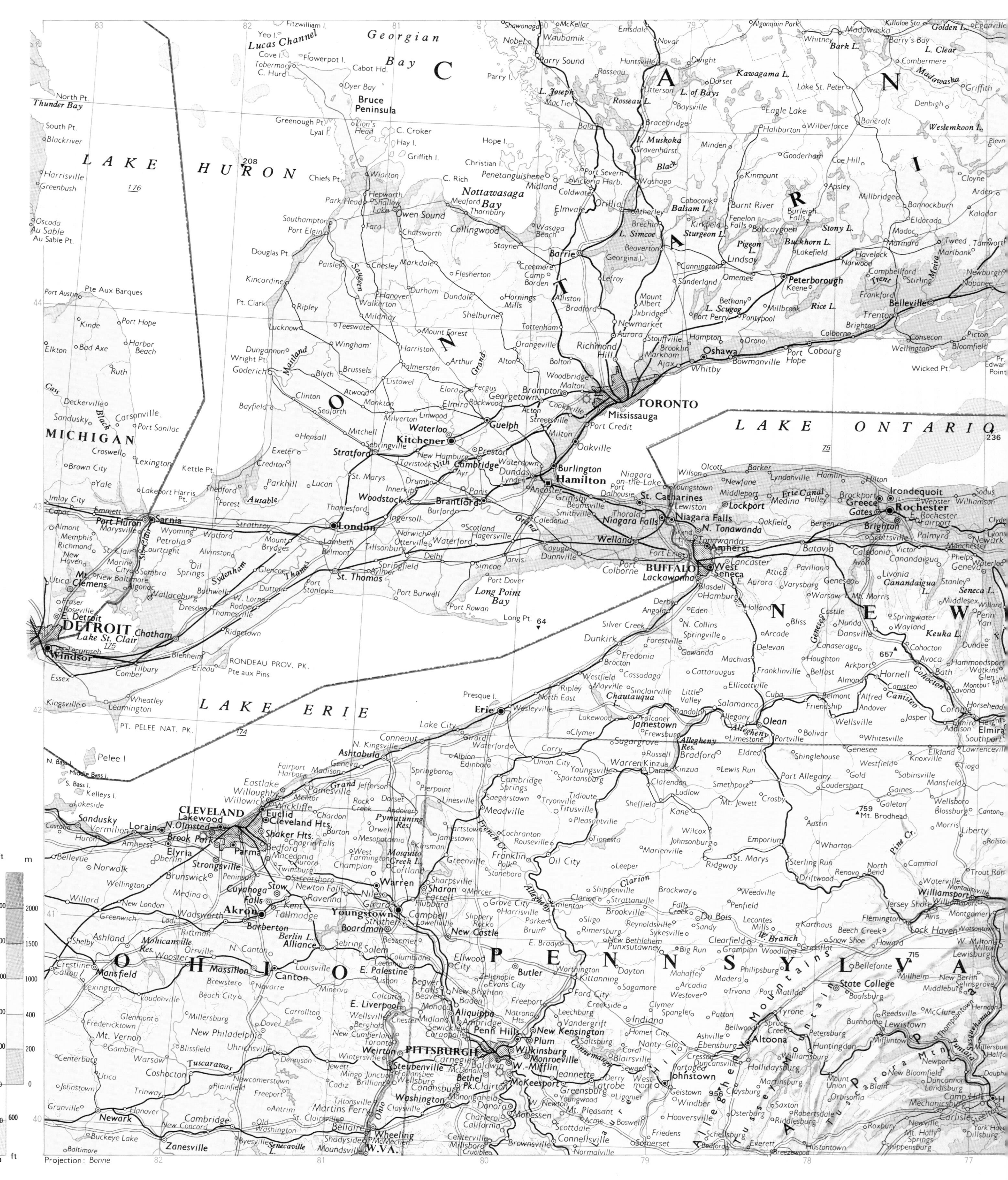
Georgian Bay
Lucas Channel
Bruce Peninsula
LAKE HURON
Thunder Bay
Nottawasaga Bay
C A N A D A
O N T A R I O
L. Simcoe
L. Muskoka
L. Joseph
Rosseau L.
Parry Sound
Huntsville
Owen Sound
Collingwood
Barrie
Orillia
Peterborough
Belleville
Oshawa
Whitby
TORONTO
Mississauga
Oakville
Burlington
Hamilton
St. Catharines
Niagara Falls
Welland
Kitchener
Waterloo
Guelph
Cambridge
Brantford
Stratford
Woodstock
London
St. Thomas
Sarnia
Chatham
Windsor
DETROIT
Lake St. Clair
MICHIGAN
Port Huron
Mt. Clemens
LAKE ONTARIO
LAKE ERIE
Long Point Bay
RONDEAU PROV. PK.
PT. PELEE NAT. PK.
Pelee I.
BUFFALO
Lackawanna
Amherst
N. Tonawanda
Lockport
Rochester
Irondequoit
Greece
Gates
Brighton
Batavia
Jamestown
Olean
Salamanca
Dunkirk
Erie
N E W
Chautauqua L.
Allegheny Res.
Elmira
Corning
Hornell
Canandaigua L.
Keuka L.
Seneca L.
Erie Canal
CLEVELAND
Lakewood
Euclid
Cleveland Hts.
Shaker Hts.
Parma
Elyria
Lorain
Sandusky
Akron
Canton
Youngstown
Warren
Ashtabula
Massillon
Mansfield
O H I O
P E N N S Y L V A N I A
PITTSBURGH
Penn Hills
Monroeville
McKeesport
Butler
New Castle
Meadville
Oil City
Franklin
Bradford
Warren
Williamsport
State College
Altoona
Johnstown
Wheeling
W.VA.
Steubenville
Weirton
Washington
Zanesville
Newark
Allegheny Mountains
Tussey Mountain
Tuscarawas
Susquehanna
Juniata
Ohio
Projection: Bonne
ft
m
6000
4500
3000
1200
600
0
200
2000
1500
1000
400
83
82
81
80
79
78
77
44
43
42
41
40

1 : 2 000 000

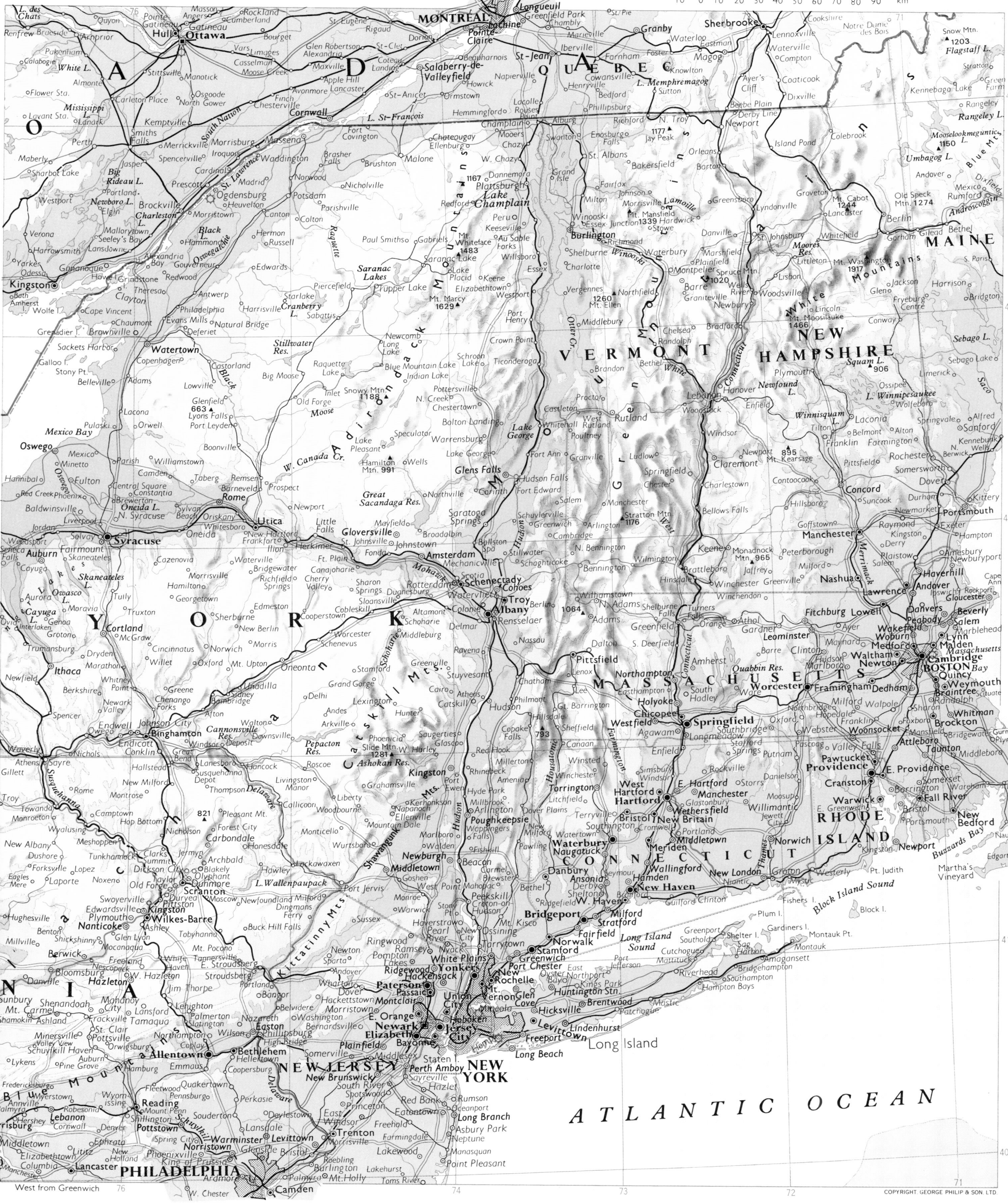

10 0 10 20 30 40 50 60 miles

10 0 10 20 30 40 50 60 70 80 90 km

CANADA

QUEBEC

ONTARIO

NEW YORK

VERMONT

NEW HAMPSHIRE

MAINE

MASSACHUSETTS

CONNECTICUT

RHODE ISLAND

NEW JERSEY

PENNSYLVANIA

ATLANTIC OCEAN

Long Island

MONTREAL

Ottawa

Sherbrooke

Kingston

Syracuse

Utica

Albany

Schenectady

Troy

Binghamton

Scranton

Wilkes-Barre

Allentown

Reading

PHILADELPHIA

Trenton

Newark

NEW YORK

Bridgeport

New Haven

Hartford

Springfield

Worcester

BOSTON

Providence

Manchester

Concord

Portsmouth

Burlington

Lake Champlain

Adirondack Mountains

Green Mountains

White Mountains

Catskill Mts.

West from Greenwich

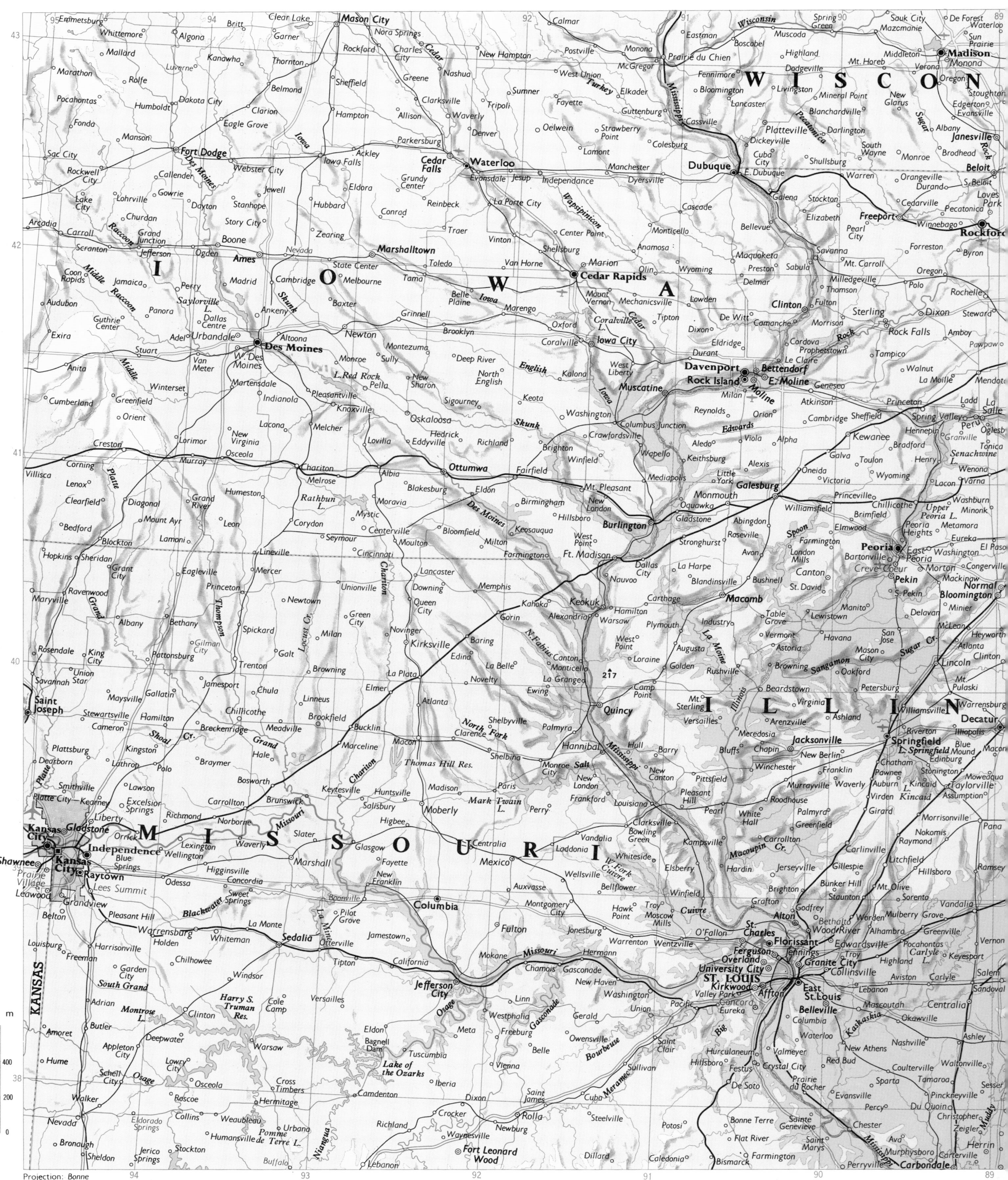
IOWA
WISCON
ILLIN
MISSOURI
KANSAS
Emmetsburg
Whittemore
Algona
Britt
Clear Lake
Mason City
Nora Springs
Calmar
Wisconsin
Spring Green
Sauk City
Mazomanie
De Forest
Waterloo
Sun Prairie
Madison
Monona
Mallard
Kanawha
Garner
Thornton
Rockford
Charles City
Cedar
New Hampton
Postville
Monona
Eastman
Prairie du Chien
Boscobel
Muscoda
Highland
Mt. Horeb
Middleton
Verona
Oregon
Stoughton
Marathon
Rolfe
Belmont
Sheffield
Greene
Nashua
West Union
McGregor
Fennimore
Bloomington
Dodgeville
Livingston
Mineral Point
New Glarus
Edgerton
Evansville
Pocahontas
Humboldt
Dakota City
Clarion
Clarksville
Sumner
Tripoli
Fayette
Turkey
Elkader
Guttenburg
Mississippi
Lancaster
Cassville
Platteville
Blanchardville
Darlington
Pecatonica
Sugar
Albany
Fonda
Eagle Grove
Hampton
Allison
Waverly
Oelwein
Strawberry Point
Colesburg
Dickeyville
Janesville
Manson
Fort Dodge
Parkersburg
Denver
Lamont
Cuba City
South Wayne
Monroe
Brodhead
Rock
Sac City
Des Moines
Webster City
Iowa
Iowa Falls
Ackley
Cedar Falls
Waterloo
Manchester
Dubuque
E. Dubuque
Shullsburg
Warren
Orangeville
Durand
Beloit
S. Beloit
Rockwell City
Callender
Gowrie
Jewell
Grundy Center
Eldora
Evansdale
Jesup
Independance
Dyersville
Galena
Stockton
Loves Park
Lake City
Lohrville
Dayton
Stanhope
Hubbard
Conrad
Reinbeck
La Porte City
Wapsipinicon
Cascade
Elizabeth
Freeport
Cedarville
Pecatonica
Winnebago
Rockford
Arcadia
Carroll
Churdan
Raccoon
Grand Junction
Story City
Zearing
Traer
Center Point
Monticello
Bellevue
Pearl City
Scranton
Jefferson
Boone
Ogden
Ames
Nevada
Marshalltown
Vinton
Shellsburg
Anamosa
Maquoketa
Savanna
Forreston
Byron
Coon Rapids
Middle
Jamaica
Perry
Madrid
Cambridge
State Center
Melbourne
Toledo
Tama
Van Horne
Marion
Cedar Rapids
Olin
Wyoming
Preston
Sabula
Mt. Carroll
Oregon
Raccoon
Saylorville L.
Dallas Centre
Panora
Ankeny
Skunk
Baxter
Delmar
Milledgeville
Thomson
Polo
Rochelle
Audubon
Guthrie Center
Belle Plaine
Marengo
Mount Vernon
Mechanicsville
Lowden
Clinton
Fulton
Sterling
Dixon
Steward
Exira
Adel
Urbandale
Altoona
Des Moines
Grinnell
Newton
Brooklyn
Oxford
Coralville L.
Tipton
De Witt
Camanche
Morrison
Rock
Rock Falls
Amboy
Stuart
W. Des Moines
Montezuma
Coralville
Iowa City
Eldridge
Cordova
Prophetstown
Tampico
Pawpaw
Anita
Van Meter
Monroe
Sully
Deep River
North English
English
Kalona
West Liberty
Durant
Le Claire
Davenport
Bettendorf
Walnut
Rock Island
E. Moline
Moline
Geneseo
La Moille
Mendota
Winterset
Martensdale
L. Red Rock
Pella
New Sharon
Muscatine
Milan
Cumberland
Greenfield
Indianola
Pleasantville
Knoxville
Sigourney
Keota
Reynolds
Atkinson
Orion
Princeton
Ladd
La Salle
Orient
Lacona
Melcher
Oskaloosa
Hedrick
Washington
Columbus Junction
Edwards
Cambridge
Sheffield
Spring Valley
Peru
Oglesby
Creston
Lorimor
New Virginia
Osceola
Lovilia
Eddyville
Richland
Skunk
Crawfordsville
Aledo
Viola
Alpha
Kewanee
Hennepin
Granville
Tonica
Corning
Murray
Chariton
Albia
Ottumwa
Fairfield
Brighton
Winfield
Wapello
Keithsburg
Alexis
Galva
Bradford
Senachwine L.
Villisca
Lenox
Platte
Humeston
Melrose
Blakesburg
Eldon
Mt. Pleasant
Mediapolis
Little York
Galesburg
Oneida
Victoria
Toulon
Wyoming
Henry
Wenona
Lacon
Varna
Clearfield
Diagonal
Grand River
Rathbun L.
Moravia
Birmingham
New London
Monmouth
Oquawka
Williamsfield
Princeville
Chillicothe
Washburn
Minonk
Bedford
Mount Ayr
Leon
Corydon
Mystic
Des Moines
Hillsboro
Burlington
Gladstone
Abingdon
Brimfield
Upper Peoria L.
Blockton
Lamoni
Seymour
Centerville
Moulton
Bloomfield
Keosauqua
West Point
Stronghurst
Roseville
Elmwood
Peoria Heights
Metamora
Hopkins
Sheridan
Lineville
Cincinnati
Milton
Farmington
Ft. Madison
Spoon
Farmington
Peoria
Eureka
El Paso
Grant City
Eagleville
Mercer
Chariton
Lancaster
Dallas City
La Harpe
London Mills
Bartonville
East Peoria
Washington
Congerville
Ravenwood
Princeton
Unionville
Downing
Memphis
Nauvoo
Blandinsville
Canton
Creve Coeur
Morton
Maryville
Grand
Thompson
Newtown
Queen City
Kahoka
Keokuk
Hamilton
Carthage
Bushnell
St. David
Pekin
Mackinaw
Normal
Bloomington
S. Pekin
Albany
Bethany
Spickard
Green City
Novinger
Gorin
Alexandria
Warsaw
Macomb
Table Grove
Manito
Minier
Locust Cr.
Milan
Kirksville
Baring
N. Fabius
Plymouth
Industry
Lewistown
Delavan
McLean
Rosendale
King City
Gilman City
Pattonsburg
Trenton
Galt
Edina
West Point
La Moine
Vermont
Havana
San Jose
Heyworth
Union Star
Savannah
Jamesport
Browning
La Plata
Novelty
La Belle
Canton
Monticello
La Grange
Loraine
Augusta
Astoria
Mason City
Sugar Cr.
Atlanta
Clinton
Saint Joseph
Maysville
Gallatin
Chula
Linneus
Elmer
Ewing
Camp Point
Golden
Rushville
Browning
Sangamon
Oakford
Lincoln
Mt. Pulaski
Stewartsville
Hamilton
Chillicothe
Brookfield
Atlanta
Shelbyville
Palmyra
Quincy
Mt. Sterling
Illinois
Beardstown
Virginia
Petersburg
Williamsville
Warrensburg
Decatur
Cameron
Breckenridge
Meadville
Bucklin
North Fork
Clarence
Versailles
Arenzville
Ashland
Riverton
Illiopolis
Plattsburg
Kingston
Shoal Cr.
Grand
Hale
Marceline
Macon
Shelbina
Hannibal
Hull
Barry
Meredosia
Jacksonville
Springfield
Blue Mound
Macon
Dearborn
Lathrop
Polo
Braymer
Chariton
Thomas Hill Res.
Monroe City
Salt
Mississippi
New Canton
Bluffs
Chapin
New Berlin
L. Springfield
Chatham
Edinburg
Platte
Smithville
Lawson
Bosworth
Keytesville
Huntsville
Madison
Paris
New London
Pittsfield
Winchester
Franklin
Pawnee
Stonington
Moweaqua
Platte City
Kearney
Excelsior Springs
Carrollton
Brunswick
Salisbury
Moberly
Mark Twain L.
Perry
Frankford
Louisiana
Pleasant Hill
Murrayville
Waverly
Auburn
Kincaid
Taylorville
Liberty
Richmond
Norborne
Missouri
Higbee
Clarksville
Pearl
Roodhouse
Virden
Kincaid
Assumption
Kansas City
Gladstone
Orrick
Lexington
Waverly
Slater
Glasgow
Centralia
Vandalia
Bowling Green
White Hall
Palmyra
Girard
Morrisonville
Pana
Independence
Wellington
Marshall
Fayette
Mexico
Laddonia
Whiteside
Kampsville
Greenfield
Carrollton
Nokomis
Raymond
Shawnee
Kansas City
Blue Springs
Higginsville
Concordia
New Franklin
W. Fork Cuivre
Wellsville
Elsberry
Macoupin Cr.
Hardin
Jerseyville
Carlinville
Litchfield
Ramsey
Prairie Village
Raytown
Odessa
Sweet Springs
Auxvasse
Bellflower
Winfield
Gillespie
Hillsboro
Leawood
Lees Summit
Grandview
Blackwater
Boonville
Columbia
Montgomery City
Troy
Hawk Point
Moscow Mills
Cuivre
Bunker Hill
Brighton
Staunton
Mt. Olive
Sorento
Vandalia
Belton
Pleasant Hill
La Monte
Pilot Grove
La Mine
Fulton
Grafton
Alton
Godfrey
Bethalto
Worden
Mulberry Grove
Warrensburg
Whiteman
Sedalia
Otterville
Jamestown
Jonesburg
Warrenton
Wentzville
O'Fallon
St. Charles
Florissant
Wood River
Alhambra
Greenville
Louisburg
Harrisonville
Holden
Tipton
California
Mokane
Missouri
Hermann
Ferguson
Overland
Jennings
Edwardsville
Pocahontas
Vernon
Freeman
Chilhowee
Garden City
Windsor
Jefferson City
Chamois
Gasconade
University City
St. Louis
Granite City
Troy
Highland
Carlyle L.
Keyesport
South Grand
New Haven
Kirkwood
Collinsville
Aviston
Carlyle
Salem
Adrian
Harry S. Truman Res.
Cole Camp
Versailles
Osage
Linn
Washington
Valley Park
Affton
East St. Louis
Lebanon
Sandoval
Montrose L.
Clinton
Westphalia
Gasconade
Gerald
Union
Pacific
Concord
Eureka
Belleville
Mascoutah
Centralia
Butler
Deepwater
Eldon
Meta
Freeburg
Owensville
Columbia
Kaskaskia
Okawville
Amoret
Appleton City
Warsaw
Bagnell Dam
Tuscumbia
Belle
Bourbeuse
Saint Clair
Waterloo
Big
Ashley
Hume
Lowry City
Lake of the Ozarks
Vienna
Sullivan
Hurculaneum
Valmeyer
New Athens
Nashville
Schell City
Osage
Osceola
Cross Timbers
Iberia
Meramec
Hillsboro
Festus
Crystal City
Red Bud
Coulterville
Waltonville
Roscoe
Hermitage
Camdenton
Dixon
Saint James
Cuba
De Soto
Prairie du Rocher
Sparta
Tamaroa
Sesser
Walker
Collins
Weaubleau
Urbana
Richland
Crocker
Rolla
Steelville
Potosi
Bonne Terre
Sainte Genevieve
Evansville
Percy
Pinckneyville
Du Quoin
Nevada
Eldorado Springs
Humansville
Pomme de Terre L.
Niangua
Waynesville
Newburg
Flat River
Saint Marys
Chester
Christopher
Zeigler
Muddy
Bronaugh
Sheldon
Jerico Springs
Stockton
Buffalo
Lebanon
Fort Leonard Wood
Dillard
Caledonia
Farmington
Bismarck
Ava
Murphysboro
Carterville
Herrin
Perryville
Carbondale
Mississippi
ft
m
1200
400
600
200
0
0
Projection: Bonne
95
94
93
92
91
90
89
43
42
41
40
38
217

1 : 2 000 000

10 0 10 20 30 40 50 miles

10 0 20 40 60 80 km

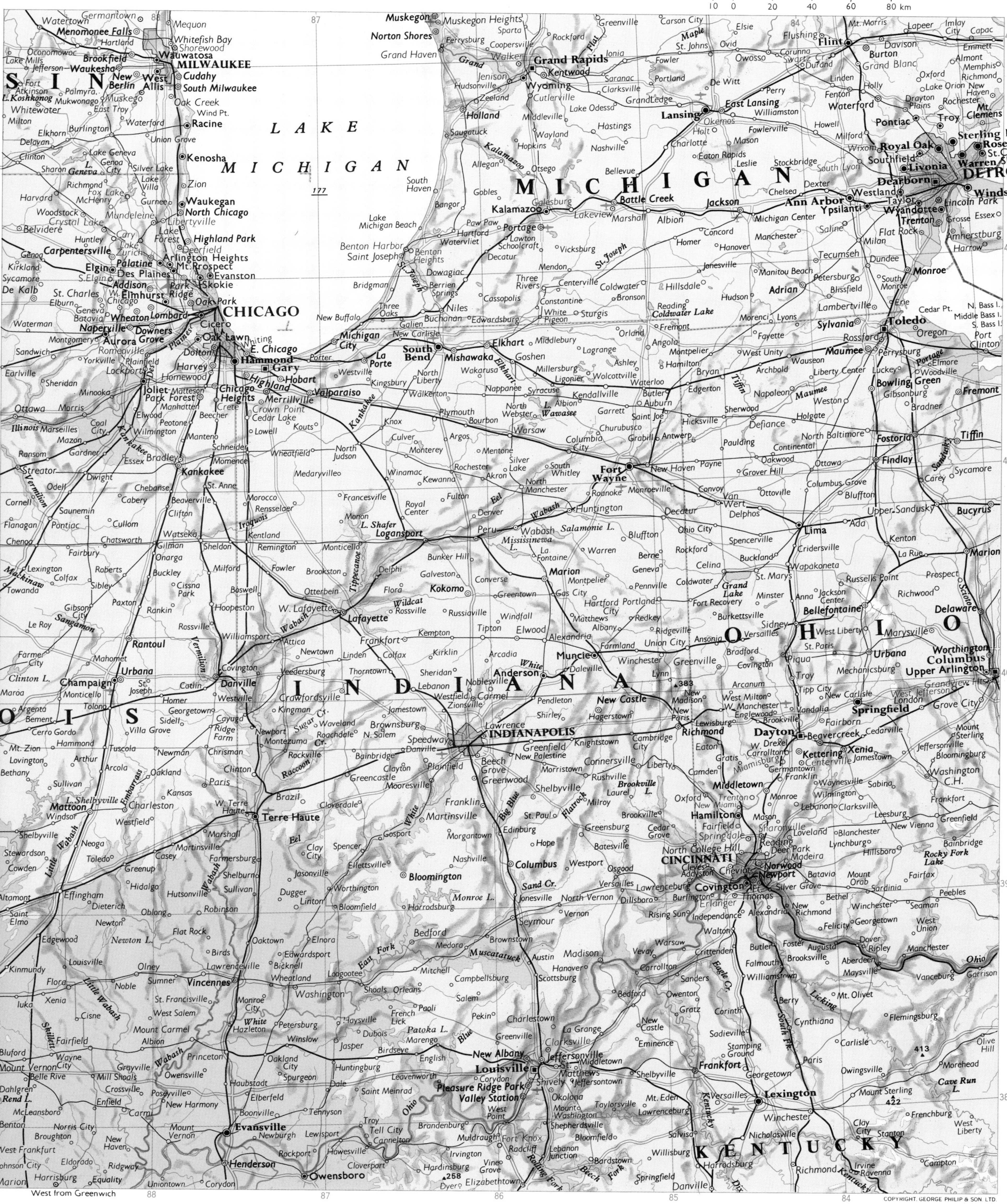

LAKE MICHIGAN

MICHIGAN

INDIANA

OHIO

KENTUCKY

West from Greenwich

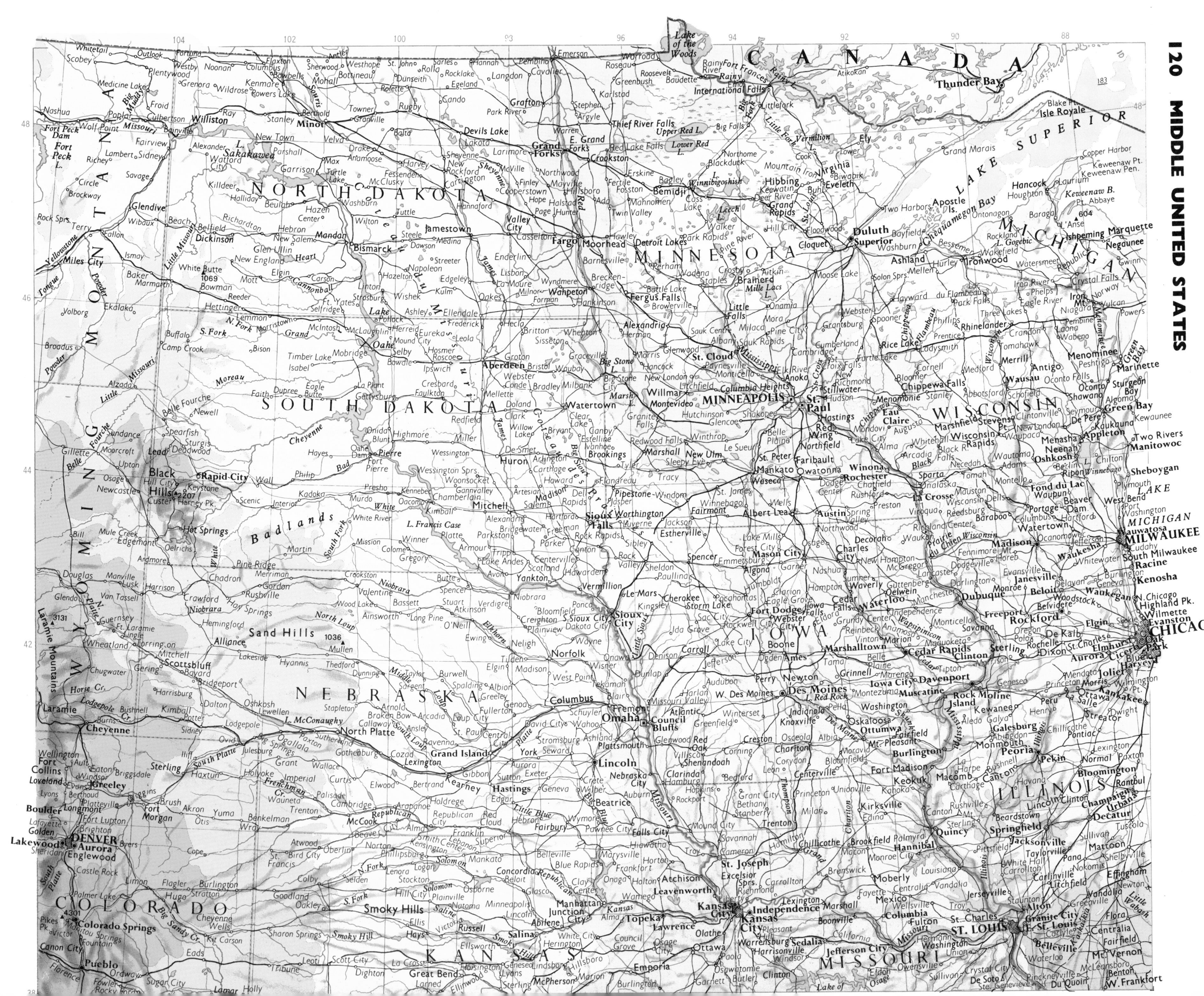
CANADA
LAKE SUPERIOR
LAKE MICHIGAN
NORTH DAKOTA
SOUTH DAKOTA
MINNESOTA
WISCONSIN
MICHIGAN
IOWA
ILLINOIS
NEBRASKA
KANSAS
MISSOURI
MONTANA
WYOMING
COLORADO
CHICAGO
MILWAUKEE
MINNEAPOLIS
St. Paul
ST. LOUIS
DENVER
Kansas City
Omaha
Des Moines
Duluth
Bismarck
Pierre
Cheyenne
Topeka
Madison
Lincoln
Springfield
Fargo
Sioux Falls
Rapid City
Black Hills
Badlands
Sand Hills
Smoky Hills
Laramie Mountains
Lake of the Woods
Thunder Bay
Isle Royale
104
102
100
98
96
94
92
90
88
48
46
44
42

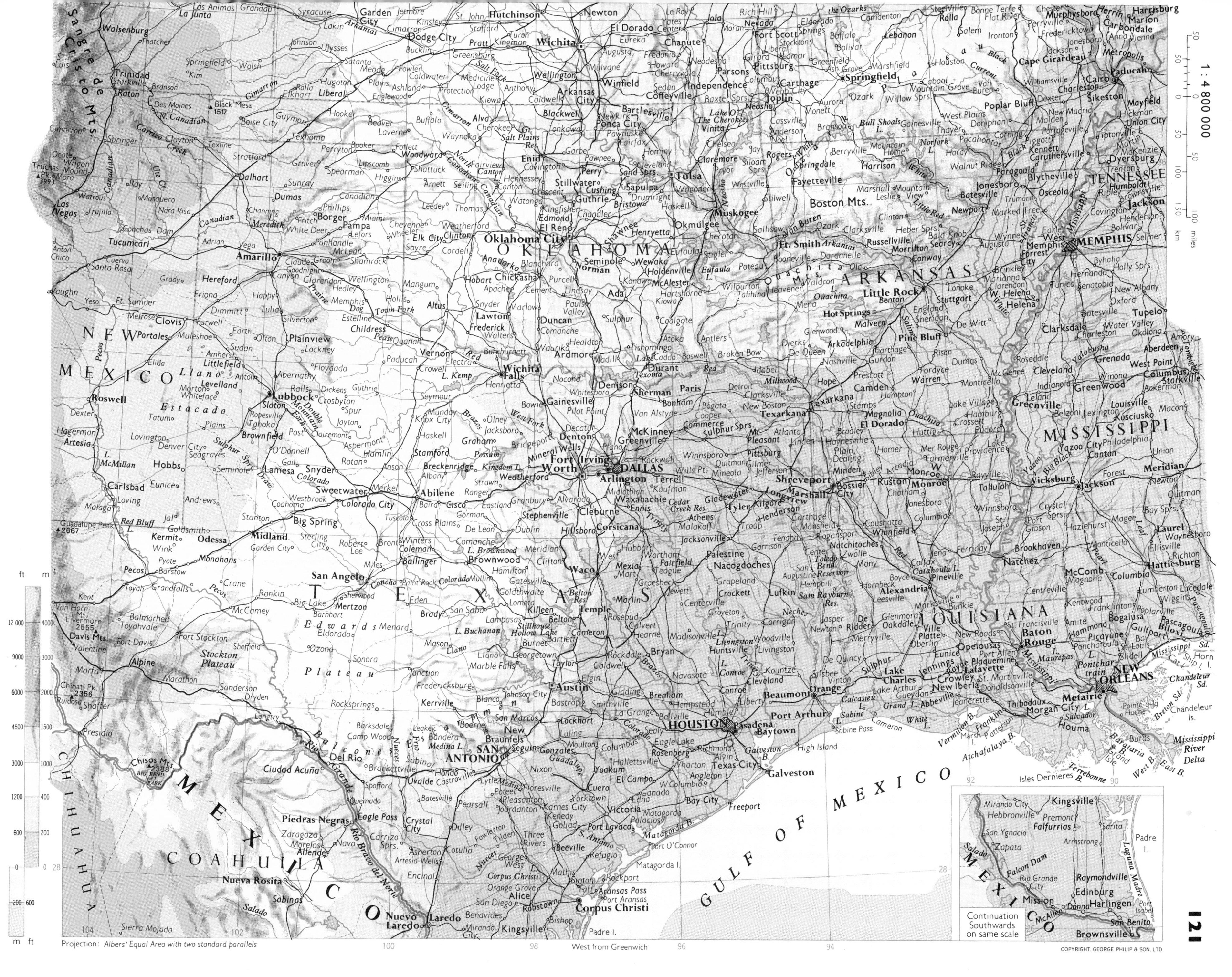
1 : 4 800 000
50 0 50 100 miles
50 0 50 100 150 km
NEW MEXICO
TEXAS
OKLAHOMA
ARKANSAS
LOUISIANA
MISSISSIPPI
TENNESSEE
MEXICO
COAHUILA
CHIHUAHUA
GULF OF MEXICO
Sangre de Cristo Mts.
Llano Estacado
Edwards Plateau
Balcones Escarpment
Ouachita Mts.
Boston Mts.
the Ozarks
Stockton Plateau
Chisos Mts.
Mississippi River Delta
Laguna Madre
Padre I.
Rio Grande
Rio Bravo del Norte
DALLAS
HOUSTON
SAN ANTONIO
MEMPHIS
NEW ORLEANS
Oklahoma City
Tulsa
Little Rock
Fort Worth
Austin
Amarillo
Lubbock
Abilene
Wichita
Wichita Falls
Shreveport
Jackson
Baton Rouge
Corpus Christi
Laredo
Nuevo Laredo
Brownsville
Galveston
Beaumont
Port Arthur
Lake Charles
Waco
San Angelo
Midland
Odessa
Roswell
Clovis
Tucumcari
Trinidad
Raton
Springfield
Ft. Smith
Texarkana
Monroe
Alexandria
Vicksburg
Hattiesburg
Meridian
Tupelo
Pine Bluff
Hot Springs
Continuation Southwards on same scale
Isles Dernieres
ft m
12 000 4000
9000 3000
6000 2000
4500 1500
3000 1000
1200 400
600 200
0 0
200 600
m ft

Projection: Albers' Equal Area with two standard parallels

West from Greenwich

1 : 4 800 000

50 0 50 100 miles

50 0 50 100 150 km

SASKATCHEWAN
ALBERTA
CANADA
BRITISH COLUMBIA
MONTANA
WYOMING
IDAHO
WASHINGTON
OREGON
NEVADA
UTAH
Bighorn Mountains
Medicine Bow Mts.
Park Range
Wind River Range
Uinta Mountains
Little Belt Mts.
Big Belt Mts.
Crazy Mts.
Lewis Range
Bitterroot Range
Lemhi Range
Salmon River Mountains
Sawtooth Ra.
Clearwater Mountains
Cabinet Mountains
Blue Mountains
Wallowa Mts.
Olympic Mts.
Harney Basin
Great Sandy Desert
Great Salt Lake Desert
GREAT SALT LAKE
Snake River Plain
Columbia Basin
Warner Mts.
Cascade Range
Coast Ranges
Klamath Mts.
Shoshone Mountains
Toiyabe Ra.
Ruby Mts.
Independence Mts.
Santa Rosa Ra.
Stillwater Ra.
Trinity Mts.
Diamond Mts.
Schell Creek Ra.
VANCOUVER
Victoria
SEATTLE
Tacoma
Olympia
Spokane
PORTLAND
Salem
Eugene
Bend
Medford
Boise
Nampa
Idaho Falls
Pocatello
Twin Falls
Salt Lake City
Ogden
Provo
Elko
Reno
Sacramento
Berkeley
Richmond
Helena
Great Falls
Butte
Missoula
Kalispell
Billings
Bozeman
Casper
Sheridan
Rock Springs
Lethbridge
Medicine Hat
Juan de Fuca Strait
Pacific Ocean
Yellowstone
Snake
Columbia
Missouri

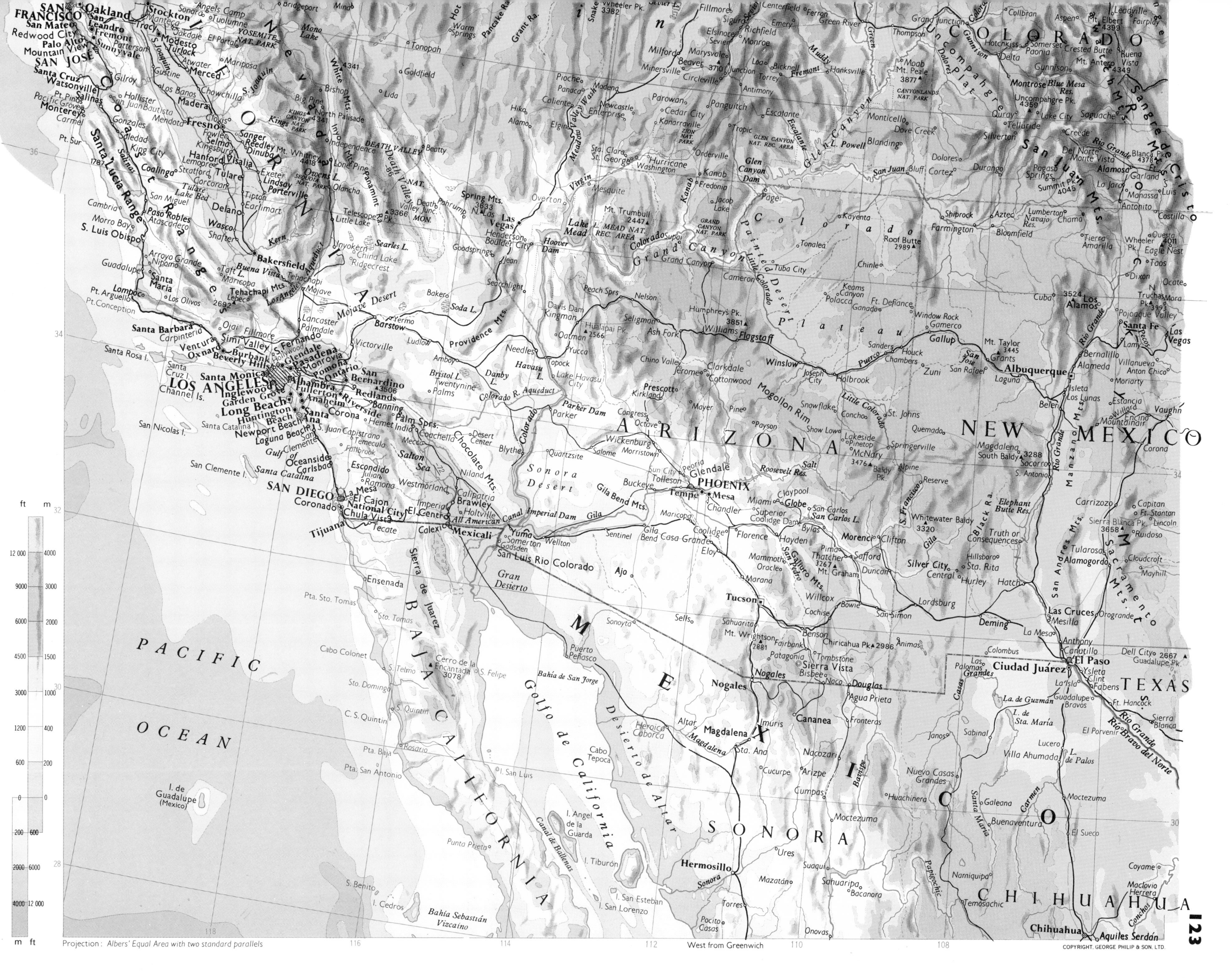
COLORADO
NEW MEXICO
ARIZONA
TEXAS
CHIHUAHUA
SONORA
MEXICO
BAJA CALIFORNIA
PACIFIC OCEAN
Golfo de California
Desierto de Altar
Sonora Desert
Gran Desierto
Colorado Plateau
Painted Desert
Grand Canyon
Death Valley
Mojave Desert
Sierra de Juarez
San Juan Mts.
Sangre de Cristo
Sacramento Mts.
Santa Lucia Range
Rio Grande
Colorado
Gila
Salton Sea
LOS ANGELES
SAN DIEGO
SAN FRANCISCO
SAN JOSE
Oakland
PHOENIX
Tucson
Albuquerque
Santa Fe
El Paso
Ciudad Juárez
Chihuahua
Hermosillo
Nogales
Mexicali
Tijuana
Las Vegas
Bakersfield
Fresno
Santa Barbara
Flagstaff
Yuma
ft m
12 000 4000
9000 3000
6000 2000
4500 1500
3000 1000
1200 400
600 200
0 0
200 600
2000 6000
4000 12 000
m ft
Projection: Albers' Equal Area with two standard parallels
West from Greenwich
COPYRIGHT. GEORGE PHILIP & SON. LTD.

SEATTLE-PORTLAND REGION
On same scale
PACIFIC OCEAN
WASHINGTON
OREGON
VANCOUVER
Vancouver Island
Strait of Georgia
Juan de Fuca Strait
Olympic Mountains
SEATTLE
Tacoma
PORTLAND
Victoria
SAN FRANCISCO
SAN JOSE
Oakland
Sacramento
Stockton
Fresno
Sierra Nevada
Santa Lucia Range
Diablo Range
San Joaquin
Sacramento
Pahute Mesa
White Mts.
Inyo Mts.

1 : 2 000 000
10 0 10 20 30 40 50 miles
10 0 20 40 60 80 km
N E V A D A
A R I Z O N A
C A L I F O R N I A
M E X I C O
P A C I F I C O C E A N
Lake Mead
LAKE MEAD NATIONAL RECREATION AREA
Meadow Valley Wash
Hoover Dam
Boulder City
Henderson
Sunrise Manor
North Las Vegas
Las Vegas
Paradise
Kingman
Needles
L. Mohave
L. Havasu
Lake Havasu City
Parker Dam
Parker
Blythe
Sonora Desert
Colorado R. Aqueduct
Providence Mts.
Mojave Desert
Amargosa Range
Death Valley
Avawatz Mts.
Chocolate Mts.
Coachella Canal
Imperial Valley
Imperial Res.
Imperial Dam
Yuma
Salton Sea
Mexicali
El Centro
Calexico
Brawley
Indio
Palm Springs
Palm Desert
Twentynine Palms
JOSHUA TREE NAT. MON.
ANZA BORREGO DESERT STATE PARK
San Bernardino Mts.
SAN BERNARDINO
Riverside
Redlands
Barstow
Victorville
Lancaster
Palmdale
Bakersfield
Oildale
Tehachapi Mts.
Los Angeles Aqueduct
Mojave
Edwards
Pasadena
Glendale
Burbank
Beverly Hills
Santa Monica
LOS ANGELES
Inglewood
Torrance
Long Beach
Garden Grove
Anaheim
Santa Ana
Huntington Beach
Newport Beach
Orange
Fullerton
Pomona
Ontario
Whittier
Mission Viejo
Oceanside
Escondido
Vista
SAN DIEGO
National City
Chula Vista
El Cajon
Tijuana
San Pedro Channel
Gulf of Santa Catalina
Santa Catalina I.
San Clemente I.
Channel Islands
Santa Barbara Channel
Santa Barbara
Ventura
Oxnard
San Luis Obispo
Santa Maria
Lompoc
San Nicolas I.
Santa Cruz I.
Santa Rosa I.
San Miguel I.
Pt. Conception
Pt. Arguello
West from Greenwich
Projection: Bonne
COPYRIGHT, GEORGE PHILIP & SON, LTD.
m ft
4000 12 000
3000 9000
2000 6000
1500 4500
1000 3000
400 1200
200 600
0 0
200 600
2000 6000

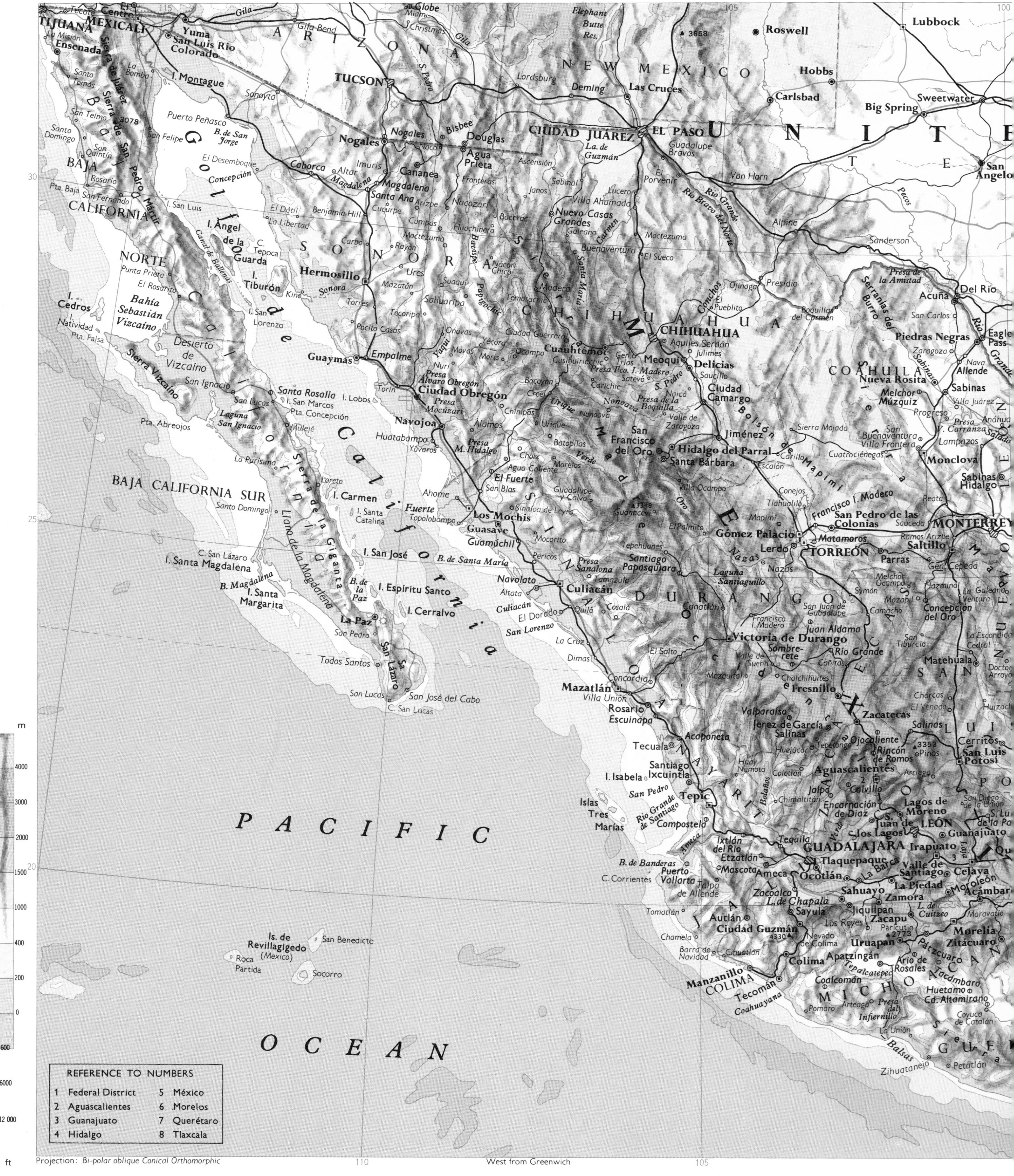
REFERENCE TO NUMBERS
1 Federal District
2 Aguascalientes
3 Guanajuato
4 Hidalgo
5 México
6 Morelos
7 Querétaro
8 Tlaxcala
Projection: Bi-polar oblique Conical Orthomorphic
West from Greenwich
110
105
ft
m
12 000
9000
6000
4500
3000
1200
600
0
200
2000
4000
4000
3000
2000
1500
1000
400
200
0
600
6000
12 000
PACIFIC
OCEAN
Golfo de California
BAJA CALIFORNIA
BAJA CALIFORNIA SUR
NORTE
SONORA
CHIHUAHUA
COAHUILA
DURANGO
SINALOA
NAYARIT
ZACATECAS
JALISCO
COLIMA
MICHOACAN
ARIZONA
NEW MEXICO
TIJUANA
MEXICALI
Ensenada
Yuma
San Luis Rio Colorado
TUCSON
Globe
Lubbock
Roswell
Hobbs
Carlsbad
Las Cruces
Deming
Lordsburg
Big Spring
Sweetwater
San Angelo
CIUDAD JUÁREZ
EL PASO
Nogales
Douglas
Agua Prieta
Bisbee
Cananea
Caborca
Magdalena
Santa Ana
Puerto Peñasco
Hermosillo
Guaymas
Empalme
Ciudad Obregón
Navojoa
Huatabampo
Los Mochis
Guasave
Guamúchil
Culiacán
Navolato
Mazatlán
Villa Unión
Rosario
Escuinapa
Acaponeta
Tecuala
Santiago Ixcuintla
Tepic
Compostela
Puerto Vallarta
Manzanillo
Tecomán
Colima
Ciudad Guzmán
Autlán
GUADALAJARA
Tlaquepaque
Ocotlán
Zacatecas
Fresnillo
Aguascalientes
LEÓN
Irapuato
Celaya
Morelia
Uruapan
Zamora
La Piedad
Zitácuaro
Apatzingán
CHIHUAHUA
Cuauhtémoc
Delicias
Meoqui
Ciudad Camargo
Jiménez
Hidalgo del Parral
Santa Bárbara
Gómez Palacio
TORREÓN
Lerdo
Victoria de Durango
Saltillo
MONTERREY
Monclova
Piedras Negras
Acuña
Del Rio
Eagle Pass
Nueva Rosita
Sabinas
San Luis Potosí
Matehuala
La Paz
Santa Rosalía
San José del Cabo
San Lucas
Todos Santos
I. Cedros
I. Ángel de la Guarda
I. Tiburón
I. Carmen
I. San José
I. Espíritu Santo
I. Cerralvo
I. Santa Magdalena
I. Santa Margarita
Bahía Sebastián Vizcaíno
Desierto de Vizcaíno
Islas Tres Marías
Is. de Revillagigedo (Mexico)
San Benedicto
Socorro
Roca Partida
B. de Banderas
C. Corrientes
L. de Chapala

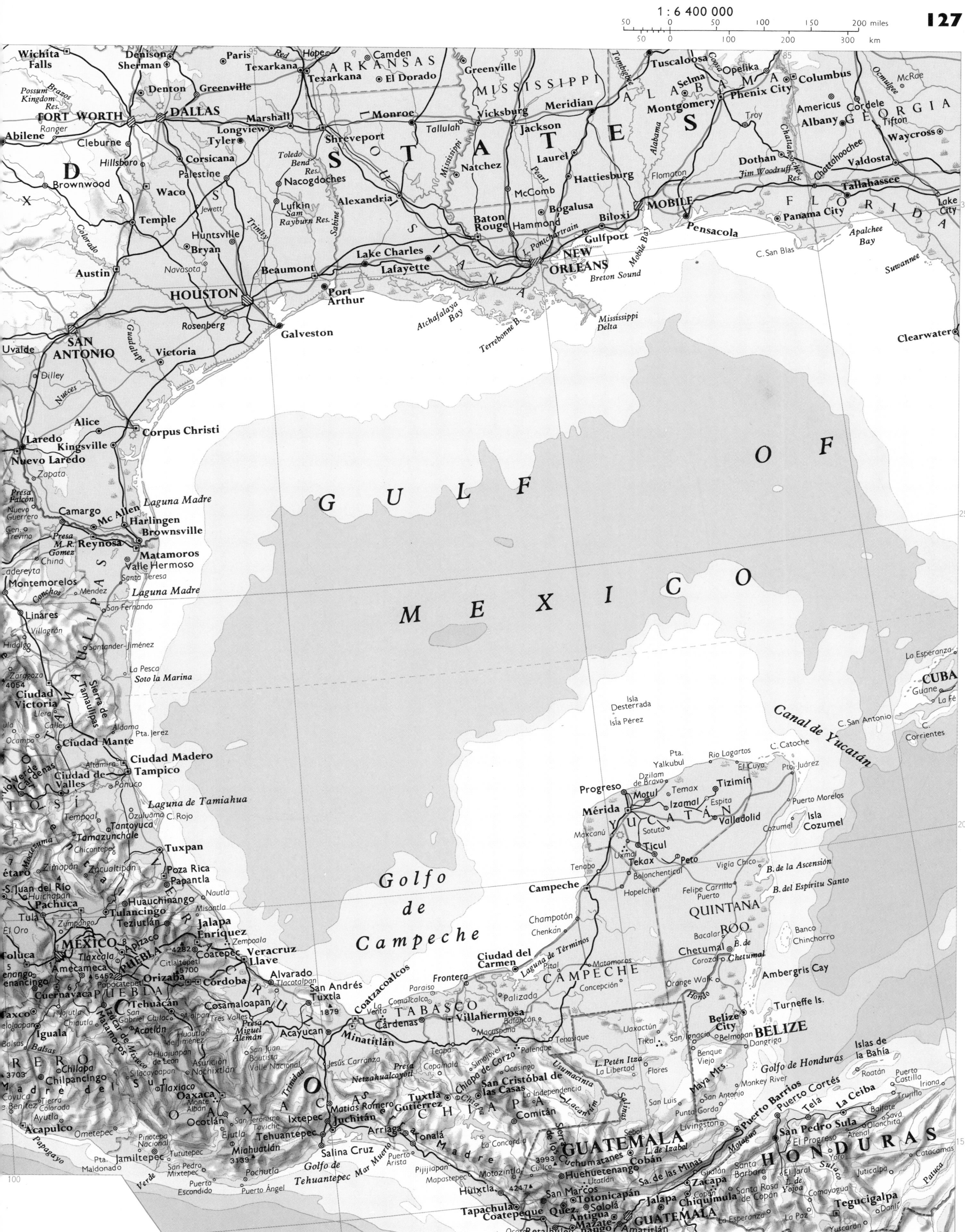
1 : 6 400 000
50 0 50 100 150 200 miles
50 0 100 200 300 km
GULF OF MEXICO
Golfo de Campeche
Canal de Yucatán
Golfo de Honduras
Golfo de Tehuantepec
UNITED STATES
ARKANSAS
MISSISSIPPI
ALABAMA
GEORGIA
FLORIDA
LOUISIANA
TEXAS
TAMAULIPAS
VERACRUZ
OAXACA
CHIAPAS
TABASCO
CAMPECHE
YUCATÁN
QUINTANA ROO
GUATEMALA
BELIZE
HONDURAS
CUBA
Wichita Falls
Denison
Sherman
Paris
Texarkana
Camden
El Dorado
Greenville
Tuscaloosa
Opelika
Columbus
Selma
Phenix City
McRae
Denton
Dallas
Fort Worth
Marshall
Monroe
Vicksburg
Meridian
Montgomery
Americus
Cordele
Albany
Tifton
Waycross
Abilene
Ranger
Cleburne
Longview
Tyler
Shreveport
Tallulah
Jackson
Troy
Hillsboro
Corsicana
Natchez
Laurel
Dothan
Valdosta
Brownwood
Palestine
Nacogdoches
Hattiesburg
Flomaton
Tallahassee
Waco
Temple
Lufkin
Alexandria
McComb
Bogalusa
Mobile
Panama City
Lake City
Huntsville
Bryan
Baton Rouge
Hammond
Biloxi
Pensacola
Gulfport
Apalachee Bay
Austin
Navasota
Beaumont
Lake Charles
Lafayette
New Orleans
Breton Sound
C. San Blas
Suwannee
Houston
Port Arthur
Rosenberg
Galveston
Atchafalaya Bay
Terrebonne B.
Mississippi Delta
Clearwater
Uvalde
San Antonio
Victoria
Dilley
Alice
Corpus Christi
Laredo
Kingsville
Nuevo Laredo
Zapata
Camargo
Mc Allen
Harlingen
Brownsville
Laguna Madre
Reynosa
Matamoros
Valle Hermoso
Montemorelos
Linares
San Fernando
Hidalgo
Santander-Jiménez
La Pesca
Soto la Marina
Ciudad Victoria
Sierra de Tamaulipas
Aldama
Pta. Jerez
Ciudad Mante
Ciudad Madero
Tampico
Ciudad de Valles
Pánuco
Laguna de Tamiahua
Ozuluama
C. Rojo
Tantoyuca
Tamazunchale
Tuxpan
Poza Rica
Papantla
Nautla
Misantla
Pachuca
Huauchinango
Tulancingo
Teziutlán
Jalapa Enriquez
Zempoala
Veracruz Llave
Tula
México
Toluca
Tlaxcala
Apizaco
Puebla
Coatepec
Orizaba
Córdoba
Alvarado
Tlacotalpan
Amecameca
Popocatépetl
Cuernavaca
Tehuacán
Cosamaloapan
San Andrés Tuxtla
Coatzacoalcos
Frontera
Ciudad del Carmen
Laguna de Términos
Champotón
Chenkán
Campeche
Taxco
Iguala
Acatlán
Acayucan
Minatitlán
Cárdenas
Villahermosa
Palizada
Macuspana
Chilapa
Chilpancingo
Oaxaca
Miahuatlán
Pochutla
Puerto Ángel
Puerto Escondido
Acapulco
Ometepec
Jamiltepec
Pinotepa Nacional
Ocotlán
Tehuantepec
Salina Cruz
Juchitán
Ixtepec
Matías Romero
Arriaga
Tonalá
Pijijiapan
Mapastepec
Huixtla
Tapachula
Tuxtla Gutiérrez
San Cristóbal de las Casas
Comitán
Ocosingo
Palenque
Tenosique
Usumacinta
Progreso
Mérida
Motul
Izamal
Temax
Tizimín
Espita
Valladolid
Maxcanú
Ticul
Tekax
Peto
Sotuta
Uxmal
Tenabo
Hopelchén
Bolonchenticul
Felipe Carrillo Puerto
Vigía Chico
Río Lagartos
El Cuyo
C. Catoche
Pto. Juárez
Puerto Morelos
Isla Cozumel
Cozumel
B. de la Ascensión
B. del Espíritu Santo
Bacalar
Chetumal
B. de Chetumal
Corozal
Orange Walk
Banco Chinchorro
Ambergris Cay
Turneffe Is.
Belize City
Belmopan
Dangriga
Uaxactún
Tikal
L. Petén Itzá
Flores
La Libertad
San Luis
Benque Viejo
Maya Mts.
Punta Gorda
San Antonio
Monkey River
Livingston
Puerto Barrios
Puerto Cortés
Tela
La Ceiba
San Pedro Sula
El Progreso
Trujillo
Islas de la Bahía
Roatán
Puerto Castilla
Cobán
Huehuetenango
Quezaltenango
Totonicapán
Sololá
Antigua
Guatemala
Jalapa
Chiquimula
Zacapa
Santa Rosa de Copán
Comayagua
Tegucigalpa
Yoro
Juticalpa
Catacamas
Isla Desterrada
Isla Pérez
Pta. Yalkubul
C. San Antonio
C. Corrientes
La Esperanza
Guane
La Fé
Coatepeque
Retalhuleu
Mazatenango
Amatitlán
Escuintla
Dzilam de Bravo
Sierra de los Cuchumatanes
COPYRIGHT, GEORGE PHILIP & SON, LTD.

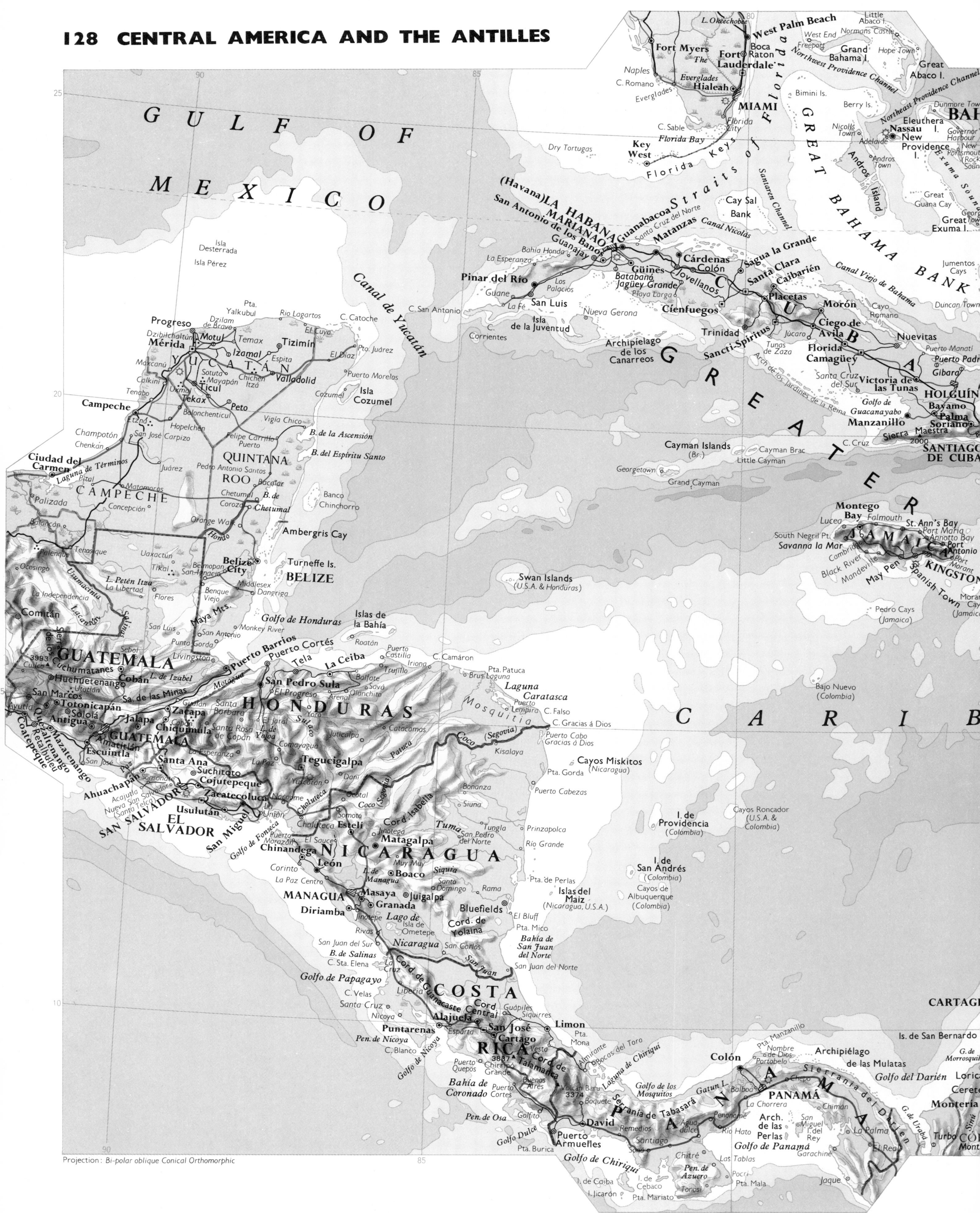
GULF OF MEXICO
GREATER
CARIB
Canal de Yucatán
Straits of Florida
GREAT BAHAMA BANK
Northwest Providence Channel
Northeast Providence Channel
Santaren Channel
Canal Nicolás
Canal Viejo de Bahama
Exuma Sound
L. Okeechobee
West Palm Beach
Boca Raton
Fort Myers
The Everglades
Fort Lauderdale
Naples
C. Romano
Hialeah
MIAMI
C. Sable
Florida Bay
Florida City
Key West
Florida Keys
Dry Tortugas
West End
Freeport
Grand Bahama I.
Little Abaco I.
Normans Castle
Hope Town
Great Abaco I.
Bimini Is.
Berry Is.
Dunmore Town
Eleuthera I.
Nassau
New Providence I.
Governor Harbour
Nicolls Town
Adelaide
Andros Town
Andros Island
Great Guana Cay
Great Exuma I.
Jumentos Cays
Duncan Town
Cay Sal Bank
(Havana) LA HABANA
MARIANAO
Guanabacoa
Santa Cruz del Norte
San Antonio de los Baños
Guanajay
Matanzas
Bahía Honda
La Esperanza
Cárdenas
Colón
Sagua la Grande
Güines
Batabanó
Jagüey Grande
Jovellanos
Playa Larga
Santa Clara
Caibarién
Pinar del Río
Los Palacios
Guane
La Fé
San Luis
C. San Antonio
C. Corrientes
Isla de la Juventud
Nueva Gerona
Cienfuegos
Placetas
Morón
Cayo Romano
Trinidad
Sancti-Spíritus
Júcaro
Ciego de Avila
Tunas de Zaza
Nuevitas
Archipiélago de los Canarreos
Florida
Camagüey
Puerto Manatí
Puerto Padre
Gibara
Arch. de los Jardines de la Reina
Santa Cruz del Sur
Victoria de las Tunas
HOLGUÍN
Golfo de Guacanayabo
Bayamo
Palma Soriano
Manzanillo
Sierra Maestra
2000
C. Cruz
SANTIAGO DE CUBA
CUBA
Cayman Islands (Br.)
Cayman Brac
Little Cayman
Georgetown
Grand Cayman
Montego Bay
Lucea
Falmouth
St. Ann's Bay
Port Maria
Annotto Bay
Port Antonio
South Negril Pt.
Savanna la Mar
Cambridge
Black River
Mandeville
May Pen
Spanish Town
KINGSTON
Morant Pt.
JAMAICA
Pedro Cays (Jamaica)
Swan Islands (U.S.A. & Honduras)
Bajo Nuevo (Colombia)
Isla Desterrada
Isla Pérez
Pta. Yalkubul
Progreso
Dzilam de Bravo
Río Lagartos
C. Catoche
El Cuyo
Dzibilchaltún
Mérida
Motul
Temax
Tizimín
Izamal
Espita
El Díaz
Pto. Juárez
Maxcanú
YUCATAN
Sotuta
Mayapán
Chichén Itzá
Valladolid
Puerto Morelos
Calkiní
Uxmal
Ticul
Cozumel
Isla Cozumel
Tenabo
Tekax
Peto
Campeche
Bolonchenticul
Vigía Chico
Edzná
Hopelchén
Felipe Carrillo Puerto
B. de la Ascensión
Champotón
Chenkán
San José Carpizo
B. del Espíritu Santo
Ciudad del Carmen
Laguna de Términos
QUINTANA ROO
Pedro Antonio Santos
Juárez
Bacalar
Pital
Matamoros
CAMPECHE
Chetumal
B. de Chetumal
Banco Chinchorro
Palizada
Concepción
Corozal
Orange Walk
Hondo
Ambergris Cay
Balancán
Tenosique
Palenque
Uaxactún
Tikal
San Ignacio
Belmopan
Belize City
Turneffe Is.
BELIZE
Ocosingo
Usumacinta
L. Petén Itzá
La Libertad
Flores
Benque Viejo
Middlesex
Dangriga
La Independencia
Lacantún
Comitán
Salinas
Maya Mts.
San Luis
Monkey River
San Antonio
Punta Gorda
Golfo de Honduras
Islas de la Bahía
Roatán
Sierra de los Cuchumatanes
3993
Culico
GUATEMALA
Sebol
Livingston
Puerto Barrios
Puerto Cortés
Tela
La Ceiba
Puerto Castilla
Trujillo
Iriona
C. Camarón
Huehuetenango
Cobán
L. de Izabel
Motagua
San Pedro Sula
El Progreso
Balfate
Sová
Olanchito
Arenal
Pta. Patuca
Brus Laguna
Laguna Caratasca
San Marcos
Utatlán
Sa. de las Minas
Totonicapán
Sololá
Zacapa
Gualán
Santa Bárbara
HONDURAS
Puerto Lempira
C. Falso
Mosquitia
C. Gracias á Dios
Ayutla
Quezaltenango
Retalhuleu
Coatepeque
Mazatenango
Antigua
Jalapa
Chiquimula
Copán
Santa Rosa de Copán
El Jaral
Yoro
Sulaco
L. de Yojoa
Catacamas
Juticalpa
Coco (Segovia)
Puerto Cabo Gracias á Dios
Kisalaya
GUATEMALA
Amatitlán
Escuintla
San José
La Esperanza
Comayagua
Patuca
Tegucigalpa
Santa Ana
Suchitoto
Lempa
La Paz
Danlí
Cayos Miskitos (Nicaragua)
Pta. Gorda
Puerto Cabezas
Ahuachapán
Sonsonate
Cojutepeque
Acajutla
Nueva San Salvador (Santa Tecla)
SAN SALVADOR
Zacatecoluca
Yuscarán
Nacaome
Choluteca
Ocotal
Coco (Segovia)
Cord. Isabella
Bonanza
Siuna
Usulután
EL SALVADOR
San Miguel
La Unión
Golfo de Fonseca
Puerto Morazán
Somoto
Estelí
Tuma
Tungla
San Pedro del Norte
Prinzapolca
Río Grande
El Sauce
Jinotega
Matagalpa
Chinandega
NICARAGUA
Corinto
León
Muy Muy
L. de Managua
Boaco
Siquia
Santo Domingo
Rama
La Paz Centro
MANAGUA
Masaya
Granada
Juigalpa
Diriamba
Jinotepe
Lago de Nicaragua
Isla de Ometepe
Rivas
Bluefields
El Bluff
Cord. de Yolaina
Pta. Mico
Bahía de San Juan del Norte
San Juan del Norte
San Juan del Sur
B. de Salinas
C. Sta. Elena
San Carlos
San Juan
Golfo de Papagayo
La Cruz
Cord. de Guanacaste
Liberia
C. Velas
Santa Cruz
Nicoya
COSTA RICA
Cord. Central
Guápiles
Siquirres
Alajuela
San José
Cartago
Limón
Puntarenas
Esparta
Pta. Mona
Pen. de Nicoya
C. Blanco
Golfo de Nicoya
Puerto Quepos
Chirripó Grande
3837
Cord. de Talamanca
Almirante
Bocas del Toro
Laguna de Chiriquí
Bahía de Coronado
Puerto Cortés
Buenos Aires
Volcán Barú
3374
Boquete
Golfo de los Mosquitos
Serranía de Tabasará
Pen. de Osa
Golfito
Golfo Dulce
Puerto Armuelles
David
Remedios
Pta. Burica
Golfo de Chiriquí
Santiago
Soná
Agua dulce
I. de Coiba
I. de Cebaco
I. Jicarón
Pta. Mariato
Chitré
Pen. de Azuero
Tonosí
Las Tablas
Pocrí
Pta. Mala
Colón
Pta. Manzanillo
Nombre de Dios
Portobelo
Gatun L.
Balboa
PANAMÁ
PANAMA
La Chorrera
Penonomé
Río Hato
Chepo
Chimán
Arch. de las Perlas
San Miguel
I. del Rey
Golfo de Panamá
Garachiné
Jaque
Archipiélago de las Mulatas
Serranía del Darién
Golfo del Darién
La Palma
El Real
G. de Urabá
Turbo
Is. de San Bernardo
G. de Morrosquillo
Lorica
Cereté
Montería
CARTAGENA
I. de Providencia (Colombia)
Cayos Roncador (U.S.A. & Colombia)
I. de San Andrés (Colombia)
Cayos de Albuquerque (Colombia)
Pta. de Perlas
Islas del Maíz (Nicaragua, U.S.A.)
25
20
15
10
90
85
80

Projection: Bi-polar oblique Conical Orthomorphic

1 : 6 400 000
ATLANTIC OCEAN
CARIBBEAN SEA
Tropic of Cancer
HAITI
DOMINICAN REP.
HISPANIOLA
ANTILLES
PUERTO RICO (U.S.A.)
LESSER ANTILLES
LEEWARD ISLANDS
WINDWARD ISLANDS
SAN JUAN
SANTO DOMINGO
PORT-AU-PRINCE
CARACAS
MARACAIBO
BARQUISIMETO
VENEZUELA
GUADELOUPE
DOMINICA
MARTINIQUE
ST. LUCIA
ST. VINCENT
BARBADOS
GRENADA
TRINIDAD & TOBAGO
ANTIGUA & BARBUDA
NETH. ANTILLES
West from Greenwich
COPYRIGHT. GEORGE PHILIP & SON. LTD.

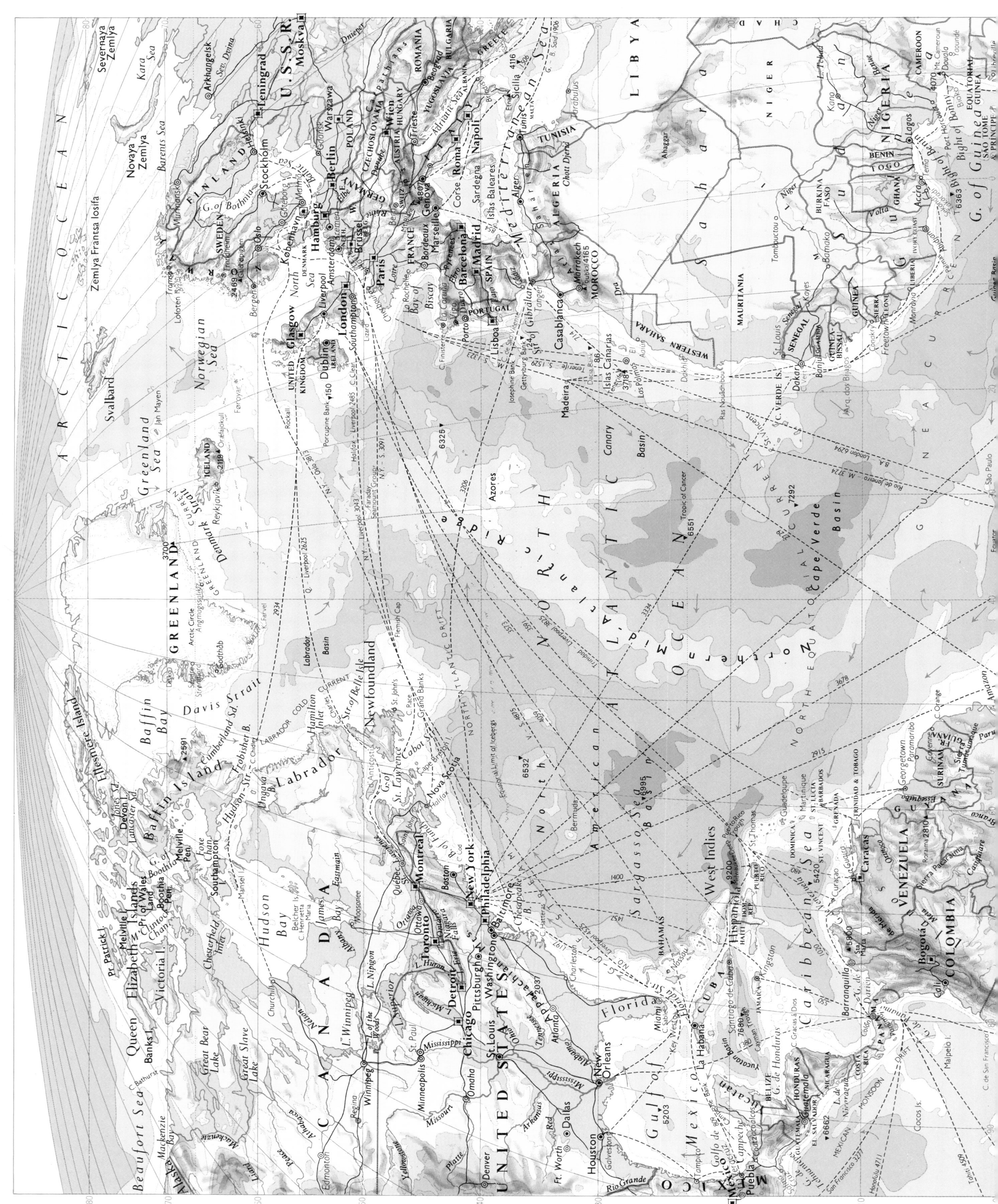
ARCTIC OCEAN
NORTH ATLANTIC OCEAN
Norwegian Sea
Greenland Sea
Labrador Basin
Canary Basin
Cape Verde Basin
Sargasso Sea
Caribbean Sea
Gulf of Mexico
G. of Guinea
Hudson Bay
Baffin Bay
Davis Strait
Denmark Strait
Barents Sea
Kara Sea
Beaufort Sea
Mediterranean Sea
Northern Mid-Atlantic Ridge
GREENLAND
ICELAND
Svalbard
CANADA
UNITED STATES
MEXICO
CUBA
West Indies
VENEZUELA
COLOMBIA
U.S.S.R.
FINLAND
SWEDEN
UNITED KINGDOM
IRELAND
FRANCE
SPAIN
PORTUGAL
MOROCCO
ALGERIA
TUNISIA
LIBYA
MAURITANIA
WESTERN SAHARA
SENEGAL
NIGERIA
Azores
Madeira
Islas Canarias
Bermuda
Newfoundland
Labrador
New York
London
Paris
Madrid
Lisboa
Montreal
Toronto
Chicago
Philadelphia
Washington
Tropic of Cancer
Equator

SOUTH ATLANTIC OCEAN
PACIFIC OCEAN
SOUTHERN OCEAN
BRAZIL
BOLIVIA
PERU
ECUADOR
ARGENTINA
CHILE
PARAGUAY
URUGUAY
FALKLAND IS. (Islas Malvinas)
FALKLAND IS. DEPENDENCIES
BRITISH ANTARCTIC TERRITORY
Weddell Sea
Scotia Sea
Ross Sea
Drake Passage
Brazil Basin
Angola Basin
Cape Basin
Argentine Basin
Agulhas Basin
South East Pacific Basin
Southern Mid-Atlantic Ridge
Walvis Ridge
Atlantic Indian Ridge
Chile Rise
Antarctic Basin
Antarctic (Southern Pacific) Basin
BENGUELA COLD CURRENT
PERUVIAN COLD CURRENT
SOUTH EQUATORIAL CURRENT
BRAZIL CURRENT
CAPE HORN COLD CURRENT
WEST WIND DRIFT
Dronning Maud Land
Coats Land
Enderby Land
Ellsworth Land
Byrd Land
Graham Land
Palmer Land
Antarctic Peninsula
Tierra del Fuego
Galápagos
Lima
Quito
La Paz
Santiago
Buenos Aires
Montevideo
São Paulo
Rio de Janeiro
Belo Horizonte
Salvador
Recife
Fortaleza
Brasília
Belém
Manaus
Asunción
Córdoba
Rosario
Valparaíso
Pôrto Alegre
Cape Town
St. Helena
Ascension
Tristan da Cunha
Gough I.
South Georgia
South Sandwich Is.
South Orkney Is.
South Shetland Is.
Tropic of Capricorn
Antarctic Circle
Equatorial Limit of Icebergs
Principal Shipping Routes (Distances in Nautical Miles)
Principal Air Routes
Direction of Currents
Projection: Mollweide
COPYRIGHT GEORGE PHILIP & SON, LTD.

1 : 24 000 000

100 0 100 200 300 400 500 miles
100 0 200 400 600 800 km
ATLANTIC OCEAN
PACIFIC OCEAN
SOUTH ATLANTIC OCEAN
Equator
Tropic of Capricorn
Andes
Llanos
Guiana Highlands
Selvas
Brazilian Highlands
Plateau of Mato Grosso
Plateau of Borborema
Bolivian Plateau
Gran Chaco
Pampas
Patagonia
Atacama Desert
Peru Chile Trench
Chile Rise
Argentine Basin
Caracas
Georgetown
Bogotá
Medellín
Cali
Quito
Guayaquil
Lima
La Paz
Manaus
Belém
Fortaleza
Recife
Salvador
Brasília
Belo Horizonte
São Paulo
Rio de Janeiro
Asunción
Pôrto Alegre
Montevideo
Buenos Aires
La Plata
Rosario
Córdoba
Tucumán
Santiago
Valparaíso
Falkland Islands
West Falkland
East Falkland
Tierra del Fuego
Magellan's Strait
C. Horn
Staten I.
Trinidad
Amazon
Orinoco
Paraná
Paraguay
Uruguay
São Francisco
Madeira
Negro
Xingu
Tapajós
Tocantins
Aconcagua 6960
Ojos del Salado 6863
Ancohuma & Illampu 6550
Huascarán 6768
Chimborazo 6267
Cotopaxi 5897
Roraima 2810
Pico da Bandeira 2890
S. Valentin 4058
L. Titicaca
L. Poopó
Projection: Lambert's Equivalent Azimuthal
West from Greenwich

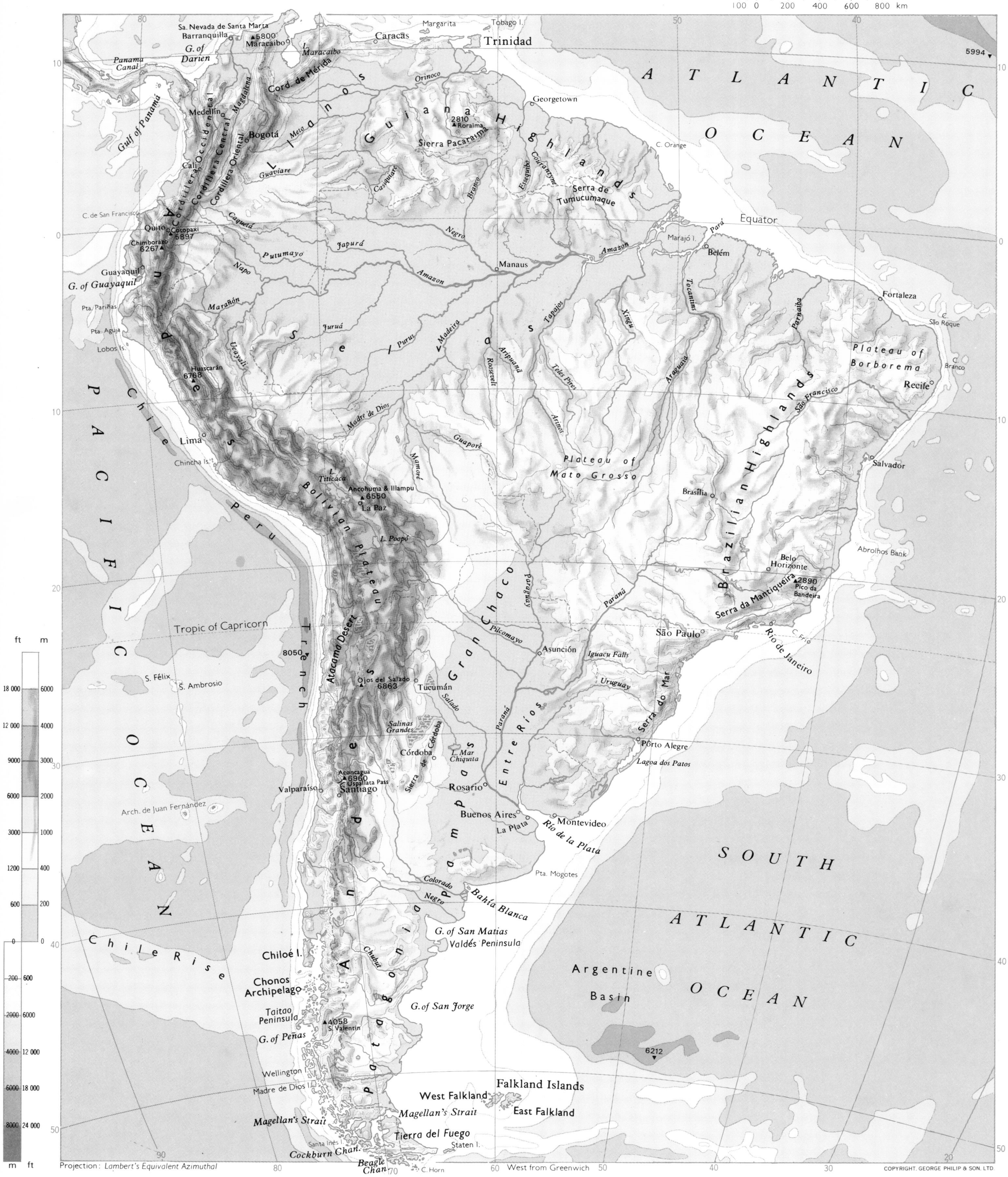

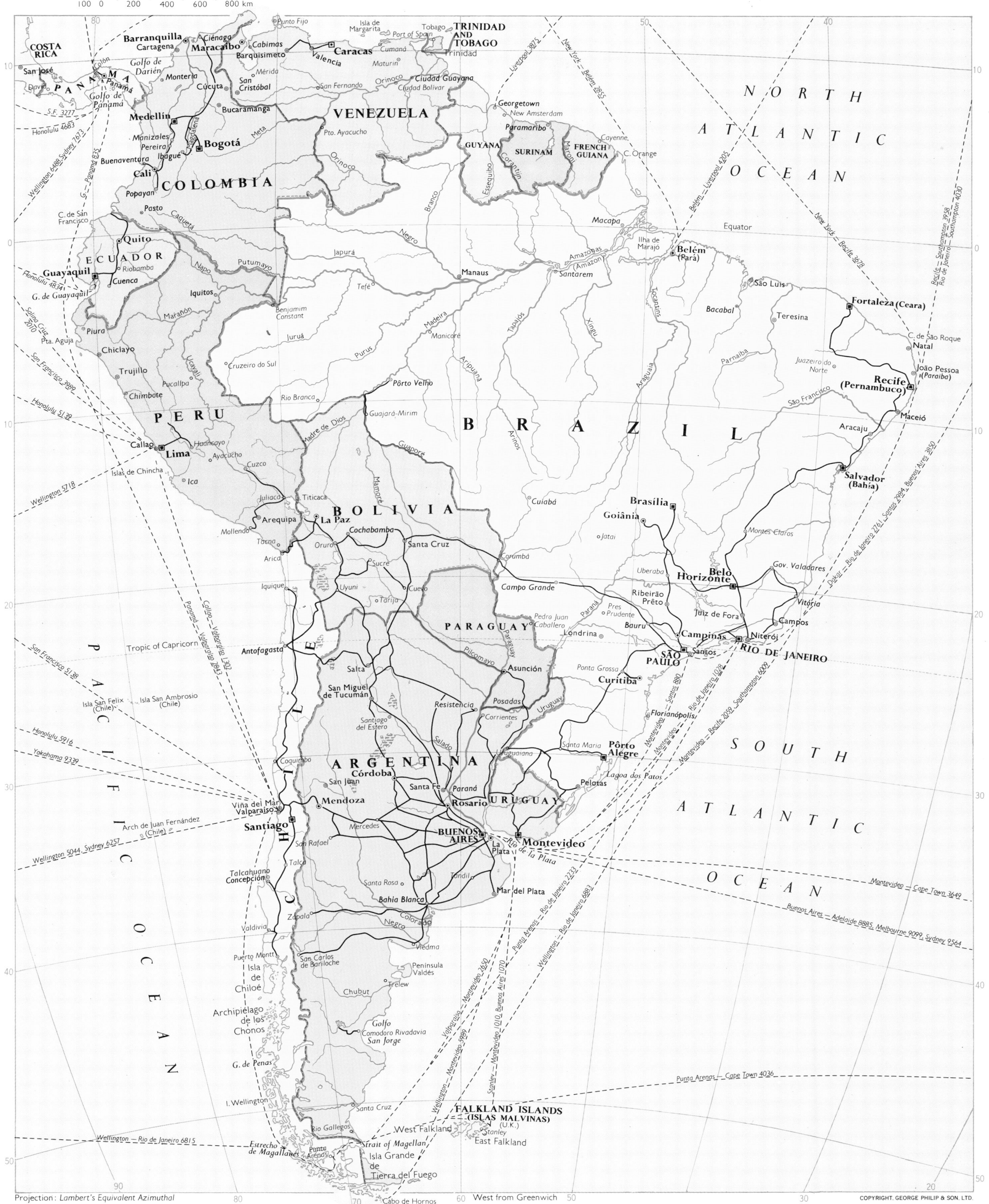
1 : 24 000 000
NORTH ATLANTIC OCEAN
SOUTH ATLANTIC OCEAN
PACIFIC OCEAN
BRAZIL
ARGENTINA
BOLIVIA
PERU
COLOMBIA
VENEZUELA
ECUADOR
CHILE
PARAGUAY
URUGUAY
GUYANA
SURINAM
FRENCH GUIANA
PANAMA
COSTA RICA
TRINIDAD AND TOBAGO
FALKLAND ISLANDS (ISLAS MALVINAS) (U.K.)
Projection: Lambert's Equivalent Azimuthal
West from Greenwich

CARIBBEAN SEA
PACIFIC OCEAN
NETH. ANTILLES
Aruba (Neth.)
Curaçao (Neth.)
Bonaire (Neth.)
Willemstad
Península de la Guajira
Golfo de Venezuela
Punto Fijo
Coro
FALCÓN
DISTRITO FEDERAL
Maiquetía
La Guaira
CARACAS
Los Teques
Valencia
Maracay
Pto. Cabello
Barquisimeto
LARA
ZULIA
MARACAIBO
Lago de Maracaibo
Cabimas
Mérida
Barinas
BARINAS
APURE
San Fernando de Apure
GUÁRICO
PORTUGUESA
COJEDES
San Cristóbal
TÁCHIRA
Cúcuta
VENEZUELA
Santa Marta
BARRANQUILLA
CARTAGENA
ATLÁNTICO
MAGDALENA
CÉSAR
GUAJIRA
Ríohacha
Valledupar
BOLÍVAR
SUCRE
CÓRDOBA
Montería
Sincelejo
Colón
PANAMÁ
PANAMA
Golfo de Panamá
Golfo del Darién
DARIÉN
NORTE SANTANDER
SANTANDER
BUCARAMANGA
Barrancabermeja
ANTIOQUIA
MEDELLÍN
CHOCÓ
Quibdó
Golfo de Tribugá
BOYACÁ
Tunja
Sogamoso
ARAUCA
Arauca
CASANARE
MANIZALES
Pereira
Armenia
Ibagué
TOLIMA
BOGOTÁ
Villavicencio
META
VICHADA
COLOMBIA
GUAINÍA
VAUPÉS
CAQUETÁ
Florencia
HUILA
Neiva
VALLE
CALI
Buenaventura
CAUCA
Popayán
NARIÑO
Pasto
Tumaco
Ipiales
PUTUMAYO
Tulcán
CARCHI
Esmeraldas
ESMERALDAS
IMBABURA
Ibarra
QUITO
PICHINCHA
NAPO
ECUADOR
MANABÍ
Manta
Portoviejo
Latacunga
Ambato
Riobamba
Chimborazo 6267
GUAYAQUIL
GUAYAS
Golfo de Guayaquil
Isla de Puná
PASTAZA
MORONA-SANTIAGO
Cuenca
AZUAY
Machala
EL ORO
Loja
LOJA
ZAMORA-CHINCHIPE
AMAZONAS
PERU
LORETO
Iquitos
Amazonas
Marañón
Napo
Putumayo
Caquetá
Leticia
Benjamin Constant
Tumbes
Sullana
PIURA
Orinoco
Puerto Ayacucho
Meta
Guaviare
Apaporis
Japurá
Solimões
ft m
18 000 6000
12 000 4000
9000 3000
6000 2000
4500 1500
3000 1000
1200 400
600 200
0 0
200 600
2000 6000
4000 12 000
m ft
75
70
80
10
5
0

Projection: *Lambert's Equivalent Azimuthal*

1 : 6 400 000

50 0 50 100 150 200 miles

50 0 100 200 300 km

ATLANTIC OCEAN

VENEZUELA

GUYANA

SURINAM

FRENCH GUIANA

BRAZIL

West from Greenwich

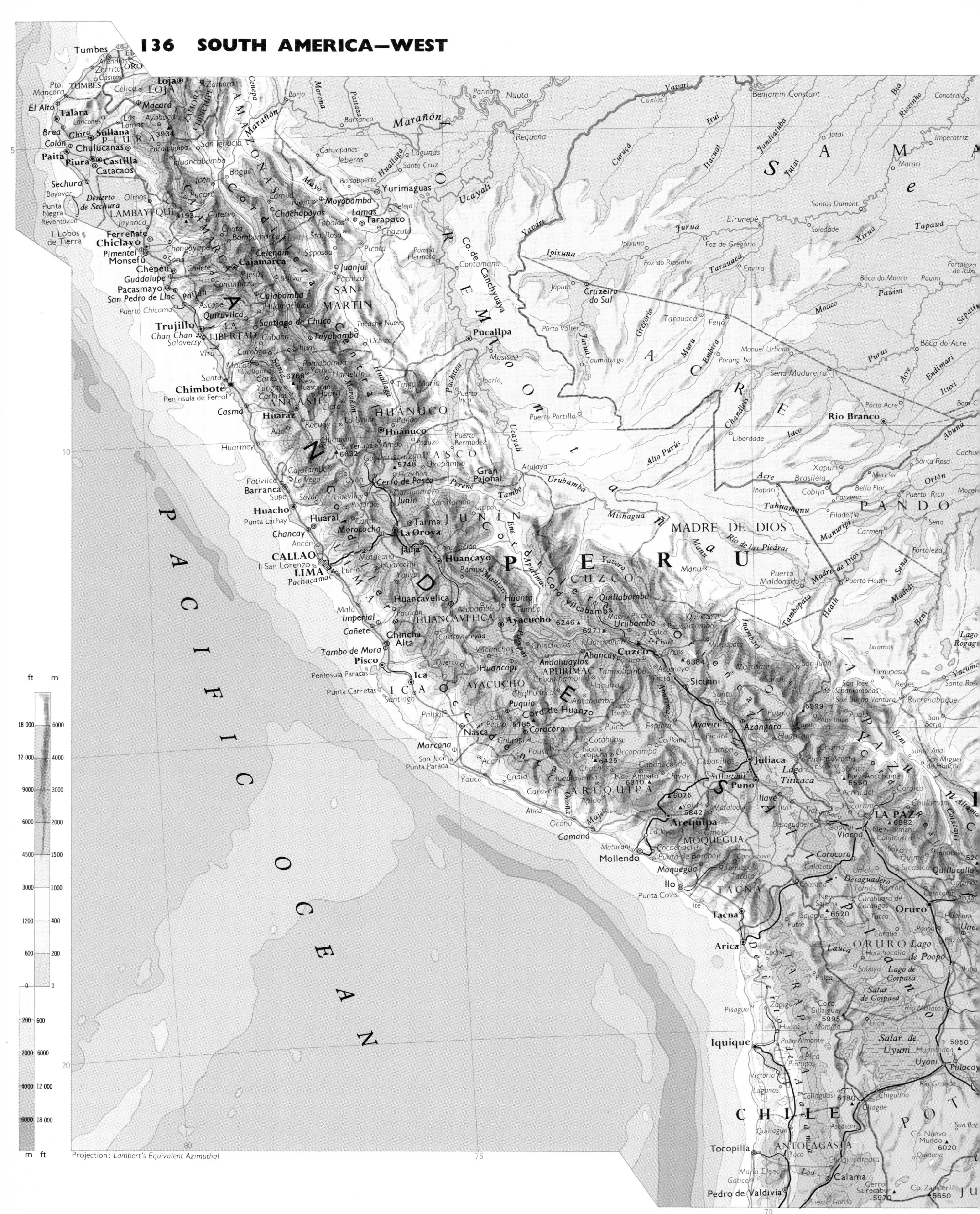
PACIFIC OCEAN
PERU
CHILE
ANDES
Cordillera Central
Cordillera Occidental
Cordillera Oriental
Montaña
Desierto de Atacama
Desierto de Sechura
Tumbes
Talara
Sullana
Piura
Paita
Castilla
Catacaos
Sechura
Loja
Chiclayo
Lambayeque
Cajamarca
Chachapoyas
Moyobamba
Tarapoto
Yurimaguas
Trujillo
Chan Chan
Chimbote
Casma
Huaraz
Huarmey
Huánuco
Tingo María
Pucallpa
Cerro de Pasco
Huacho
Huaral
Tarma
La Oroya
Jauja
Huancayo
CALLAO
LIMA
Pachacamac
Huancavelica
Ayacucho
Cañete
Chincha Alta
Pisco
Ica
Nasca
Marcona
Abancay
Cuzco
Urubamba
Quillabamba
Sicuani
Juliaca
Puno
Lago Titicaca
Arequipa
Mollendo
Camaná
Moquegua
Ilo
Tacna
Arica
Iquique
Tocopilla
Calama
Pedro de Valdivia
LA PAZ
Oruro
Lago de Poopó
Salar de Uyuni
Salar de Coipasa
Rio Branco
Cruzeiro do Sul
Benjamin Constant
Requena
Nauta
Iquitos
Marañón
Ucayali
Huallaga
Urubamba
Madre de Dios
Purus
Juruá
AMAZONAS
SAN MARTIN
LA LIBERTAD
ANCASH
HUANUCO
PASCO
JUNIN
HUANCAVELICA
AYACUCHO
APURIMAC
CUZCO
MADRE DE DIOS
AREQUIPA
MOQUEGUA
TACNA
ICA
PIURA
ACRE
PANDO
ORURO
TARAPACA
ANTOFAGASTA
Projection: Lambert's Equivalent Azimuthal

1 : 6 400 000

50 0 50 100 150 200 miles
50 0 100 200 300 km

AMAZONAS
BRAZIL
PARÁ
RONDÔNIA
MATO GROSSO
MATO GROSSO DO SUL
BOLIVIA
BENI
SANTA CRUZ
CHUQUISACA
TARIJA
PARAGUAY
OLIMPO
BOQUERÓN
Chaco Boreal
JUJUY
SALTA

L. de Coari
Coari
Paricatuba
Axinim
Canumã
Itanhauã
Tefé
Purus
Arumã
Borba
Itaboca
Prêto do Igapó-Açu
Maués
Abacaxis
Mundurucus
Itaituba
Tapajós
Iriri
Pôrto Alegre
Bacajá
Abufari
Madeira
Novo Aripuanã
Jaburu
Itapinima
Capoeira
Tucunaré
Coari
Tapauá
Itatuba
Tapauá
Manicoré
Entre Rios
Santa Maria dos Marmeles
Aripuanã
Canutama
Manicoré
Canumã
Miriti
Sai-Cinza
Jamanxim
Crepori
Curuá
Iriri
Nazaré
Pinhuã
Axioma
Carandpatuba
Canumã
Três Casas
Ipixuna
Purus
Lábrea
Prainha
São Félix
Majuriã
Mucuim
Humaitá
Maici
Marmelos
Canudos
Ituxi
Calama
Samaúma
Cururu
Teles Pires
Xingu
Riosinho
Serra do Cachimbo
Juruena
Estremo
Madeira
Jamari
Aripuanã
Recreio
Curuá
Curuaés
Jiparaná
Pôrto Velho
Tabajara
Barracão do Barreto
Aripuanã
Cachimbo
404
Jaciparaná
Caritianas
S. Benedito
Alto Iriri
Bom Comércio
Abunã
Manoa
Candeias
Jamari
Ariquemes
Roosevelt
Serra dos Apiacás
Iriri Novo
Villa Bella
Esperanza
Nova Vida
Serra do Norte
Moreru
Beni
Guajará-Mirim
Sa. dos Pacaás Novos
Jaru
Jaru
Peixoto de Azevedo
Riberalta
Guayaramerín
Rondônia
Jiparaná
Aripuanã
Serra do Tombador
Serra dos Caiabis
Serra Formosa
Liberdade
Mamoré
Presidente Hermes
Pôrto Cajueiro
Manitsauá-Missu
Campo de Diauarum
Pimenta Bueno
Barão de Melgaço
Tenente Marques
Arinos
Sangue
Pouso Alegre
Yata
Serra Apidiá
Arraias
Suiá Missu
Serra do Roncador
Principe da Beira
Camararé
Saturnina
Xingu
663
Vilhena
Nhambiquara
Juruena
Pedras Negras
Puerto Siles
Lago Rogoaguado
San Joaquin
Versalles
Mategua
Exaltación
Itonamas
Magdalena
Guaporé
Teles Pires
Ronuro
Pôrto dos Meinacos
San Ramón
Baures
Puerto Villazón
Utiariti
Verde
Culiseu
Santa Ana
Mamoré
Lago de San Luis
Juruena
Sangue
El Carmen
San Joaquín
San Martín
Serranía de Huanchaca
Serra dos Parecis
Planalto do Mato Grosso
Apere
Paraguá
669
Nortelândia
Arinos
Diamantino
Cuiabá
San Javier
Arenápolis
Alto Paraguai
Culuene
San Ignacio
Trinidad
Blanco
Perseverancia
Tapirapuã
Serra Azul
Chavantina
Llanos de Mojos
Loreto
San Miguel
Mato Grosso
Guaporé
Rosário Oeste
Barra do Bugres
915
Mato Grosso
Aruanã
San Francisco
1995
Acorizal
Chapada dos Guimarães
Mortes
San Lorenzo
Negro
Paraguai
Jauru
Araguaia
Sécure
Añez
Várzea Grande
Cuiabá
Coronel Ponce
Santa Rosa de la Roca
Pôrto Esperidião
Nossa Senhora do Livramento
Santo Antônio do Leverger
Poxoreu
Barra do Garças
Grande
Yapacani
Concepción
San Ignacio
Aguapeí
Cáceres
Jaciara
Tesouro
Rio das Garças
Araguaiana
Chaparé
San Javier
Santa Ana
San Matías
Barão de Melgaço
Guiratinga
Baliza
Aragarças
Ichilo
Piray
Santa Rosa del Palmar
Poconé
Rondonópolis
Ponte Branca
Iporá
Ivolândia
Cochabamba
Portachuelo
San Miguel
Cuiabá
São Lourenço
Caiapônia
Punata
San Carlos
Montero
Warnes
Lagoa Uberaba
Alto Garças
Araguaia
Sa. das Divisões
Cliza
Totora
Buena Vista
Laguna Concepción
Itiquira
Santa Rita do Araguaia
Santa Cruz
El Cerro
San José
Pôrto Jofre
Itiquira
Alto Araguaia
Caiapó
Caine
Comarapa
Cotoca
Correntes
Rio Verde
Toroto
Aiquile
Pampa Grande
Llanos de Chiquitos
Santo Corazón
Pantanal do São Lourenço
Mineiros
El Palmar
Samaipata
Serra do Caiapó
Pasorapa
Vallegrande
1425
Serr. de Santiago
Santiago
La Cal
Taquari
Jataí
Lagoa Mandioré
Presto
Grande
Bañados de Izozog
Roboré
Colquechaca
Taquari
Verde
Claro
Ocurí
Tarabuco
Serr. de Santiago
Sucre
Zudáñez
Abapó
Puerto Suárez
Coxim
Baús
Santa Ana
Paraguai
Padilla
Corumbá
Pantanal do Rio Negro
Rio Verde de Mato Grosso
Cordillera Oriental
Cordillera Central
Caçu
Potosí
Betanzos
Sopachuy
Gutiérrez
Parapetí
Ladário
Nhecolândia
Itarumã
Fortín General Pando
Aporé
Cachoeira Alta
Lagunillas
Albuquerque
Paraíso
Cassilândia
Puna
Monteagudo
Charagua
Porto Esperança
Negro
Aporé
Fortín Ingavi
Alto Sucuriú
Sucuriú
Paranaíba
Porco
Azurduy
Camiri
Coimbra
Coxim
Paranaíba
Corguinho
Miranda
Rochedo
Inocência
Sucre
Lucas
Fortín Coronel Eugenio Garay
Bahía Negra
Paraguai
Miranda
Miranda
Verde
Jaraguari
Aparecida do Taboado
Cuevo
Carandaiti
Terenos
Aquidauana
Ribas do Rio Pardo
Camargo
Pilcomayo
Sa. da Bodoquena
Aquidauana
Jango
Campo Grande
Água Clara
Bodoquena
Cotagaita
Huacaya
Fortín Madrejón
Pardo
Garcias
Pereira Barreto
Chorolque
Pilaya
Villa Montes
Fuerte Olimpo
5614
San Juan
Villa Abecia
Bonito
Nioaque
Sidrolândia
Três Lagoas
Lussanvira
Tupiza
San Lorenzo
Entre Ríos
Fortín Garrapatal
Puerto Guaraní
Serra de Maracaju
Xavantina
Andradina
Iscayachi
Tarija
Jardim
Anhanduí
Mirandópolis
Uriondo
Sanandita
Guia Lopes da Laguna
Panorama
Villazón
Cuevas
Padcaya
Pôrto Murtinho
Maracaju
Aguapeí
Quiaca
5603
Yacuiba
Rinconada
La Esmeralda
Abra Pampa
Tartagal

60
55
West from Greenwich
65
5
10
15
20

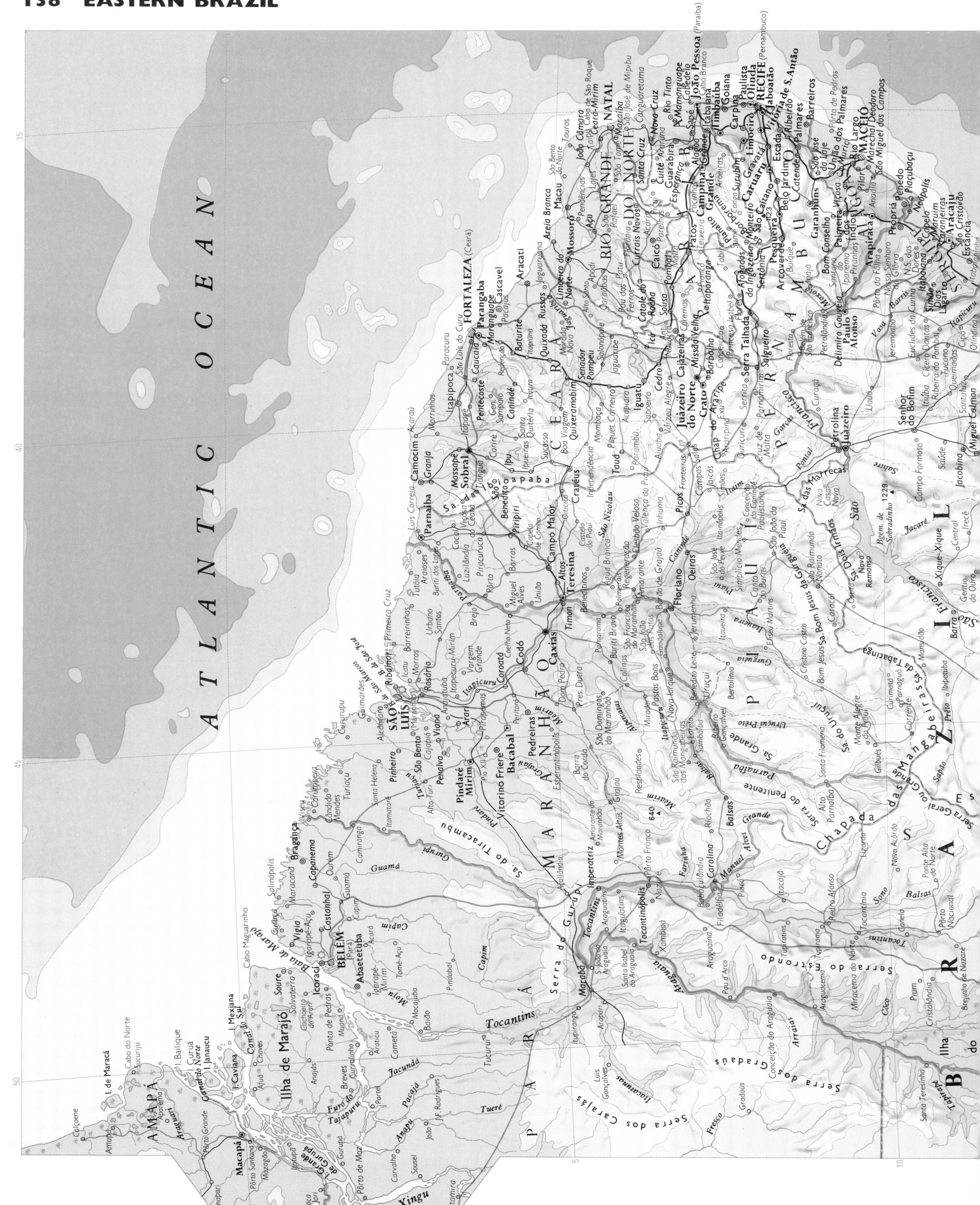
ATLANTIC OCEAN
AMAPÁ
PARÁ
MARANHÃO
CEARÁ
PIAUÍ
RIO GRANDE DO NORTE
PERNAMBUCO
ALAGOAS
BRAZIL
FORTALEZA (Ceará)
NATAL
RECIFE (Pernambuco)
João Pessoa (Paraíba)
MACEIÓ
Aracaju
SÃO LUÍS
Teresina
BELÉM (Pará)
Macapá
Ilha de Marajó
Tocantins
Xingu
Serra dos Carajás
Serra do Gurupi
Serra Geral ou Grande das Mangabeiras
Chapada das Mangabeiras
Serra do Estrondo
Serra dos Gradaús
Serra do Penitente
Sa. do Tiracambu
Sa. da Ibiapaba
Parnaíba
Caxias
Imperatriz
Marabá
Juàzeiro do Norte
Crato
Mossoró
Campina Grande
Caruaru
Petrolina
Juàzeiro
Floriano
Oeiras
Picos
Sobral
Camocim
Bacabal
Codó
Bragança
Castanhal
Abaetetuba
Carolina
Balsas

1 : 6 400 000

50 0 50 100 150 200 miles

50 0 100 200 300 km

ATLANTIC OCEAN
ESPÍRITO SANTO
Tropic of Capricorn
West from Greenwich
SALVADOR (Bahia)
Baía de Todos os Santos
Feira de Santana
Alagoinhas
Ilhéus
Itabuna
Jequié
Vitória da Conquista
Canavieiras
Belmonte
Pôrto Seguro
Caravelas
Banka Abrolhos
São Mateus
Linhares
Colatina
Vitória
Vila Velha
Cachoeiro de Itapemirim
CAMPOS
Cabo de São Tomé
RIO DE JANEIRO
NITERÓI
SÃO GONÇALO
DUQUE DE CAXIAS
Petrópolis
Nova Friburgo
Macaé
Cabo Frio
Volta Redonda
Barra Mansa
Angra dos Reis
Ilha Grande
Teófilo Otoni
Gov. Valadares
Caratinga
Ipatinga
Itabira
Diamantina
Montes Claros
Pirapora
Curvelo
Sete Lagoas
BELO HORIZONTE
Ouro Prêto
Barbacena
Juiz de Fora
São João del Rei
Divinópolis
Uberaba
Uberlândia
Araguari
Patos de Minas
Paracatu
Franca
Ribeirão Prêto
SÃO PAULO
CAMPINAS
SANTOS
SANTO ANDRÉ
Jundiaí
Sorocaba
Piracicaba
Bauru
Marília
Presidente Prudente
Londrina
Maringá
Ponta Grossa
CURITIBA
Paranaguá
Guarapuava
BRASÍLIA
DISTRITO FEDERAL
Anápolis
GOIÂNIA
Serra Geral de Goiás
Serra do Espinhaço
Sa. da Canastra
Mantiqueira
São Francisco
Paranaíba
Grande
Tietê
Paranapanema
Araguaia
Serra do Roncador
BAHIA
MINAS GERAIS
GOIÁS
SÃO PAULO
PARANÁ
RIO DE JANEIRO

Projection: Lambert's Equivalent Azimuthal

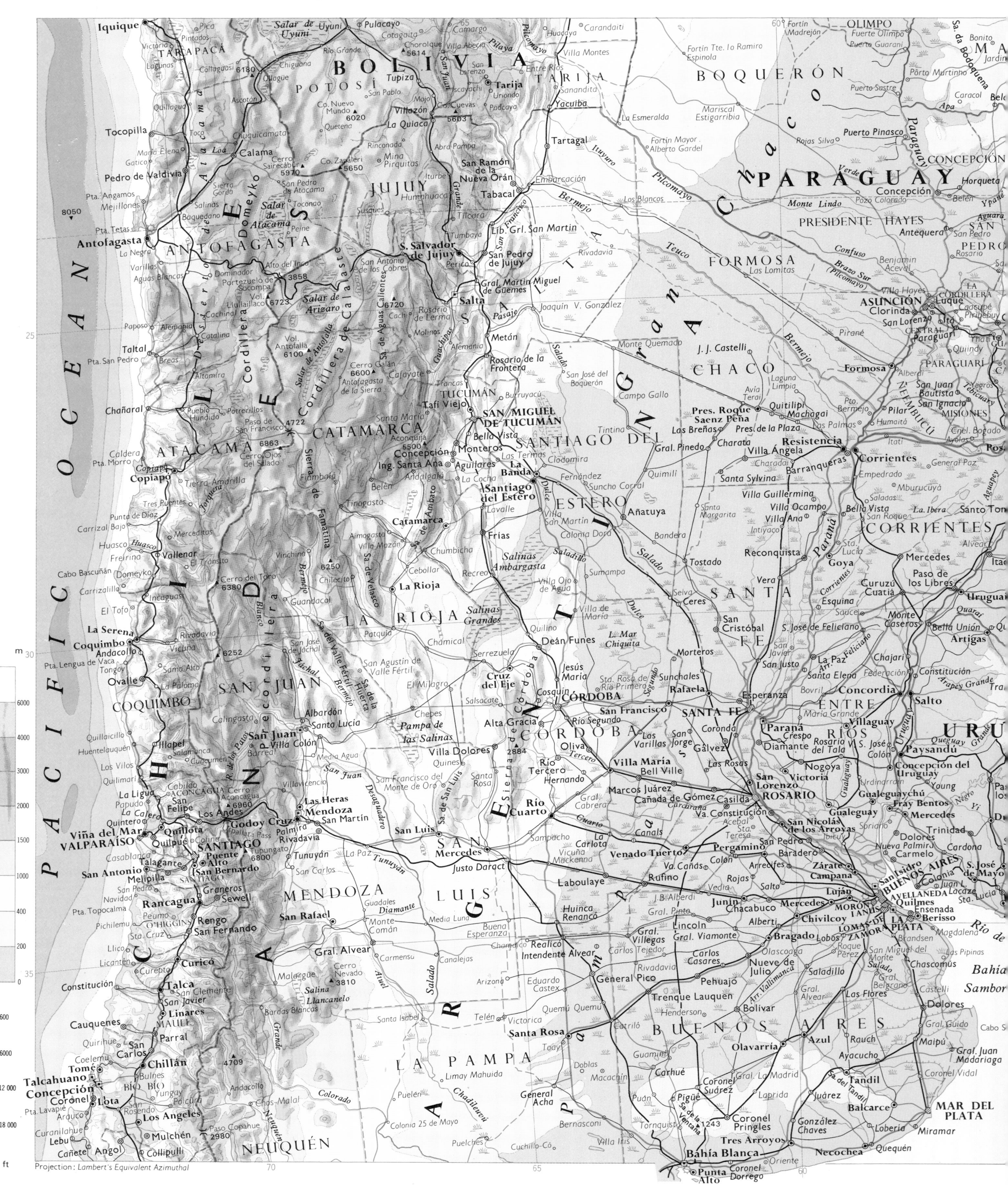
PACIFIC OCEAN
BOLIVIA
PARAGUAY
CHILE
ARGENTINA
URU
Gran Chaco
Desierto de Atacama
Cordillera Domeyko
Cordillera de Claudio
Cordillera de la Sierra
LOS ANDES
Cordillera
Cordillera de San Buenaventura
Salar de Uyuni
Salar de Atacama
Salar de Arizaro
Salar de Antofalla
Salinas Grandes
Salinas Ambargasta
Pampa de las Salinas
Salina Llancanelo
Sierra de Famatina
Sierra de Córdoba
Sierra de San Luis
POTOSÍ
TARIJA
BOQUERÓN
TARAPACÁ
ANTOFAGASTA
ATACAMA
COQUIMBO
ACONCAGUA
SANTIAGO
O'HIGGINS
MAULE
BÍO BÍO
JUJUY
SALTA
FORMOSA
CHACO
TUCUMÁN
CATAMARCA
SANTIAGO DEL ESTERO
LA RIOJA
SAN JUAN
CÓRDOBA
SANTA FE
CORRIENTES
ENTRE RÍOS
MISIONES
MENDOZA
SAN LUIS
LA PAMPA
BUENOS AIRES
NEUQUÉN
PRESIDENTE HAYES
CONCEPCIÓN
OLIMPO
CENTRAL
PARAGUARÍ
CORDILLERA
Iquique
Tocopilla
Calama
Antofagasta
Taltal
Chañaral
Copiapó
Vallenar
La Serena
Coquimbo
Ovalle
Illapel
Viña del Mar
VALPARAÍSO
SANTIAGO
San Antonio
Rancagua
Curicó
Talca
Linares
Chillán
Talcahuano
Concepción
Los Angeles
Tarija
Tupiza
Villazón
Yacuiba
San Salvador de Jujuy
Salta
San Miguel de Tucumán
Santiago del Estero
Catamarca
La Rioja
San Juan
Mendoza
San Luis
CÓRDOBA
Río Cuarto
SANTA FE
Paraná
ROSARIO
BUENOS AIRES
LA PLATA
MAR DEL PLATA
Bahía Blanca
Santa Rosa
Resistencia
Corrientes
Formosa
ASUNCIÓN
Concepción
Paysandú
Salto
Concordia
Tandil
Necochea
Olavarría
Azul
Aconcagua
6960
6863
6723
6880
6720
6600
6380
6250
6252
5970
5650
6020
6180
5614
5603
4722
3858
3810
2884
2980
4709
1243
8050
Salado
Bermejo
Pilcomayo
Dulce
Colorado
Tercero
Cuarto
Paraná
Uruguay
Paraguay
Río de la Plata
ft
m
18 000
12 000
9000
6000
4500
3000
1200
600
0
6000
4000
3000
2000
1500
1000
400
200
0
200
600
2000
6000
4000
12 000
6000
18 000
m
ft
25
30
35
70
65
60
Projection: Lambert's Equivalent Azimuthal

1 : 6 400 000
50 0 50 100 150 miles
50 0 50 100 150 200 km
BELO HORIZONTE
N. Lima
Itabirito
Congonhas
Cons. Lafaiete
Ouro Prêto
Ponte Nova
Vitória
Vila Velha
Itaquari
Guarapari
Pico da Bandeira 2890
Castelo
Cachoeiro de Itapemirim
Carangola
Muriaé
Alegre
Ubá
Itaperuna
Cataguases
Leopoldina
Cambuci
Guarus
CAMPOS
Cabo de São Tomé
RIO DE JANEIRO
Além Paraíba
Três Rios
Petrópolis
Nova Friburgo
Macaé
DUQUE DE CAXIAS
SÃO GONÇALO
NITERÓI
RIO DE JANEIRO
Cabo Frio
La. de Araruama
Tropic of Capricorn
Barra do Piraí
Volta Redonda
Barra Mansa
Nova Iguaçu
Juiz de Fora
Santos Dumont
Barbacena
São João del Rei
Oliveira
Campo Belo
Lavras
Três Corações
São Lourenço
Mantiqueira
Itajubá
Cruzeiro
Guaratinguetá
Taubaté
S. J. dos Campos
Jacareí
Mogi das Cruzes
Angra dos Reis
Ilha Grande
Baía da Ilha Grande
Pta. de Juatinga
Ilha de São Sebastião
Pta. do Boi
SANTOS
Guarujá
São Vicente
SANTO ANDRÉ
São Bernardo do Campo
SÃO PAULO
Itanhaém
Jundiaí
Bragança Paulista
Itu
Sorocaba
CAMPINAS
Americana
Mogi-Mirim
Limeira
Piracicaba
Rio Claro
São Carlos
Araraquara
Ribeirão Prêto
Franca
Passos
Batatais
São Seb. do Paraíso
Guaxupé
Alfenas
Varginha
Três Pontas
Represa de Furnas
Poços de Caldas
Pouso Alegre
Ouro Fino
Pinhal
São João da Boa Vista
Araras
Mococa
Casa Branca
Jaboticabal
Bebedouro
Olímpia
S. José do Rio Prêto
Mirassol
Catanduva
Taquaritinga
Novo Horizonte
Lins
Penápolis
Birigui
Araçatuba
Andradina
Três Lagoas
Mirandópolis
Adamantina
Tupã
Marília
Garça
Bauru
Jaú
Bariri
Pirajuí
Paraguaçu Paulista
Martinópolis
Presidente Prudente
Rancharia
Santo Anastácio
Pres. Epitácio
Assis
Ourinhos
Santa Cruz do Rio Pardo
Botucatu
Avaré
Tatuí
Itapetininga
Itaporanga
Itararé
Itapeva
Jaguariaíva
Paranapiacaba
Juquiá
Registro
Iguape
Ilha Comprida
Ilha do Cardoso
SÃO PAULO
Paranapanema
Porecatu
Londrina
Rolândia
Cornélio Procópio
Jacarèzinho
Cambará
Arapongas
Apucarana
Maringá
Mandaguari
Nova Esperança
Paranavaí
Cianorte
Umuarama
Cruzeiro do Oeste
Campo Mourão
Guaíra
Pto. Mendes
Cascavel
Foz do Iguaçu
Itaipu Dam
Iguazú Falls
Guarapuava
Ponta Grossa
Castro
Pitanga
Prudentópolis
Palmeira
CURITIBA
Antonina
Paranaguá
Guaratuba
Irati
Lapa
União da Vitória
Rio Negro
Mafra
São Francisco do Sul
Joinvile
Pto. União
Caçador
Blumenau
Itajaí
Brusque
Joaçaba
Chapecó
SANTA CATARINA
Campos Novos
Rio do Sul
Ilha de Santa Catarina
Florianópolis
Lajes
Tubarão
Laguna
Cabo Santa Marta Grande
Criciúma
Araranguá
Vacaria
Caxias do Sul
Bento Gonçalves
Erechim
Passo Fundo
Carazinho
Cruz Alta
Santo Ângelo
São Luís Gonzaga
São Borja
Santiago
Santa Maria
Santa Cruz do Sul
Montenegro
Nôvo Hamburgo
Taquara
São Leopoldo
Canoas
Osorio
PÔRTO ALEGRE
Viamão
Rio Pardo
Cachoeira do Sul
Alegrete
Rosário do Sul
São Gabriel
Santana do Livramento
Rivera
Dom Pedrito
Bagé
Caçapava do Sul
Camaquã
Canguçu
Mostardas
Lagoa dos Patos
Pelotas
Rio Grande
Jaguarão
Lagoa Mirim
Lagoa Mangueira
Santa Vitória do Palmar
RIO GRANDE DO SUL
BRAZIL
PARANÁ
MATO GROSSO DO SUL
Pedro Juan Caballero
Ponta Porã
Dourados
Nioaque
Maracaju
Amambai
ALTO PARANÁ
CAAGUAZÚ
ITAPÚA
MISIONES
Encarnación
Posadas
Oberá
Eldorado
Santa Rosa
San Javier
URUGUAY
Tacuarembó
Melo
Rio Branco
San Gregorio
Treinta y Tres
José Batlle y Ordóñez
Minas
Rocha
Aigua
Castillos
Lascano
Canelones
Las Piedras
Pando
San Carlos
Maldonado
MONTEVIDEO
Florida
ATLANTIC
OCEAN
5304
West from Greenwich
55
50
45
40
25
30
35
COPYRIGHT, GEORGE PHILIP & SON, LTD

1 : 6 400 000
miles
km
SOUTH ATLANTIC OCEAN
PACIFIC OCEAN
ARGENTINA
CHILE
Patagonia
NEUQUÉN
RÍO NEGRO
CHUBUT
SANTA CRUZ
LA PAMPA
BUENOS AIRES
ARAUCANIA
LOS LAGOS
Golfo San Matías
Golfo San Jorge
Bahía Grande
Golfo de Penas
Archipiélago de los Chonos
Isla de Chiloé
Isla Grande de Tierra del Fuego
TIERRA DEL FUEGO
Strait of Magellan
Estrecho de Magallanes
FALKLAND ISLANDS
(ISLAS MALVINAS)
West Falkland
East Falkland
Stanley
Comodoro Rivadavia
Bahía Blanca
Río Gallegos
Punta Arenas
Ushuaia
Puerto Montt
Valdivia
Temuco
Neuquén
Trelew
Viedma
Cabo de Hornos
(Cape Horn)
Projection: Lambert's Equivalent Azimuthal
West from Greenwich
COPYRIGHT, GEORGE PHILIP & SON, LTD.

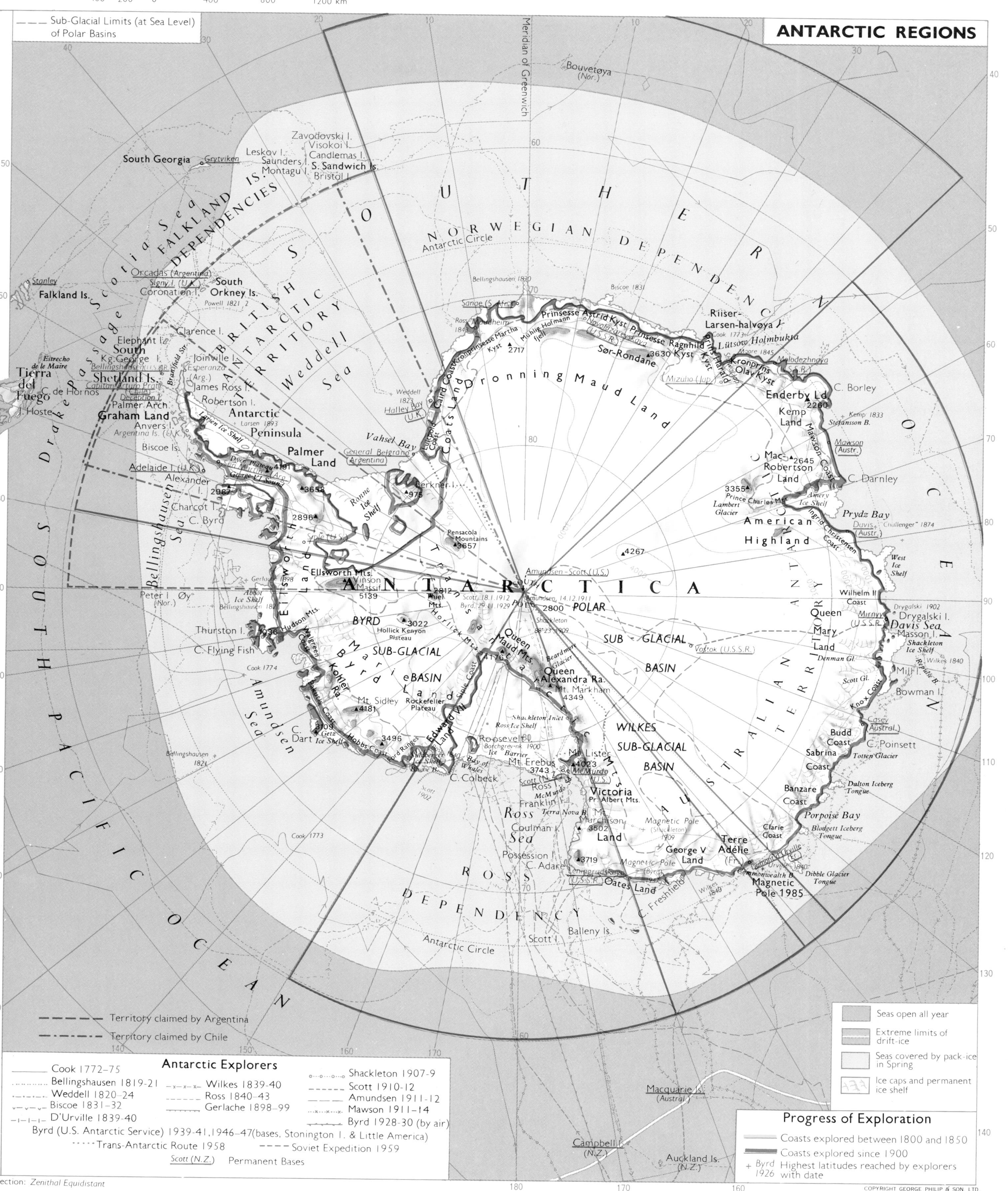
1 : 28 000 000
ANTARCTIC REGIONS
Sub-Glacial Limits (at Sea Level) of Polar Basins
Territory claimed by Argentina
Territory claimed by Chile
Antarctic Explorers
Cook 1772–75
Bellingshausen 1819–21
Weddell 1820–24
Biscoe 1831–32
D'Urville 1839–40
Wilkes 1839–40
Ross 1840–43
Gerlache 1898–99
Shackleton 1907–9
Scott 1910–12
Amundsen 1911–12
Mawson 1911–14
Byrd 1928–30 (by air)
Byrd (U.S. Antarctic Service) 1939–41, 1946–47 (bases, Stonington I. & Little America)
Trans-Antarctic Route 1958
Soviet Expedition 1959
Scott (N.Z.) Permanent Bases
Seas open all year
Extreme limits of drift-ice
Seas covered by pack-ice in Spring
Ice caps and permanent ice shelf
Progress of Exploration
Coasts explored between 1800 and 1850
Coasts explored since 1900
Byrd 1926 Highest latitudes reached by explorers with date
Projection: Zenithal Equidistant
COPYRIGHT GEORGE PHILIP & SON. LTD.

1 : 28 000 000

200 100 0 200 400 600 miles

400 200 0 400 800 1200 km

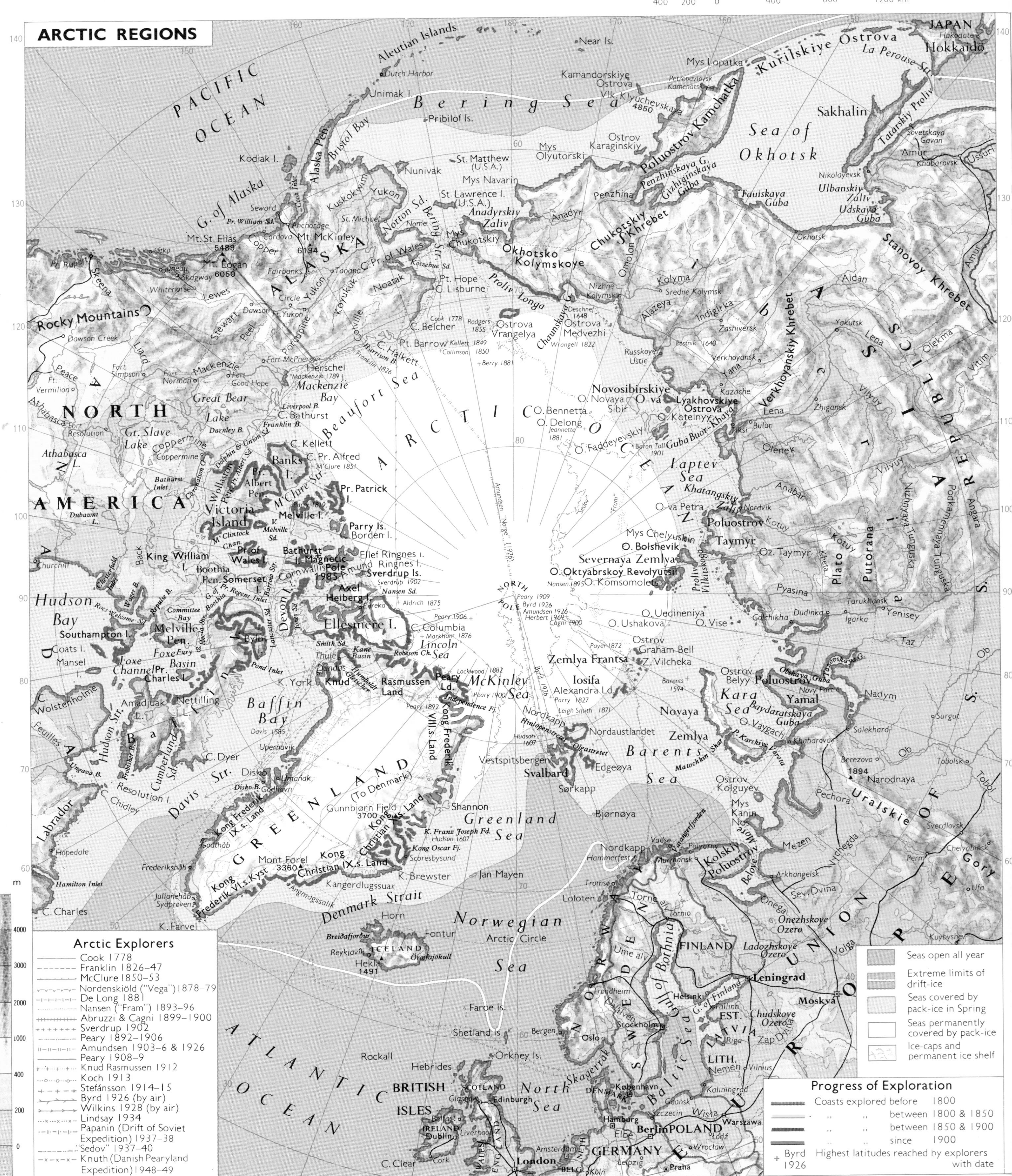
ARCTIC REGIONS
PACIFIC OCEAN
ATLANTIC OCEAN
ARCTIC OCEAN
NORTH AMERICA
ALASKA
GREENLAND (To Denmark)
Bering Sea
Sea of Okhotsk
Beaufort Sea
Laptev Sea
Kara Sea
Barents Sea
Greenland Sea
Norwegian Sea
North Sea
Baffin Bay
Hudson Bay
Davis Str.
Denmark Strait
Arctic Circle
Lincoln Sea
McKinley Sea
ICELAND
BRITISH ISLES
FINLAND
GERMANY
POLAND
JAPAN
Svalbard
Novaya Zemlya
Severnaya Zemlya
Zemlya Frantsa Iosifa
Ellesmere I.
Victoria Island
Baffin I.
Arctic Explorers
Cook 1778
Franklin 1826–47
McClure 1850–53
Nordenskiöld ("Vega") 1878–79
De Long 1881
Nansen ("Fram") 1893–96
Abruzzi & Cagni 1899–1900
Sverdrup 1902
Peary 1892–1906
Amundsen 1903–6 & 1926
Peary 1908–9
Knud Rasmussen 1912
Koch 1913
Stefánsson 1914–15
Byrd 1926 (by air)
Wilkins 1928 (by air)
Lindsay 1934
Papanin (Drift of Soviet Expedition) 1937–38
"Sedov" 1937–40
Knuth (Danish Pearyland Expedition) 1948–49
Seas open all year
Extreme limits of drift-ice
Seas covered by pack-ice in Spring
Seas permanently covered by pack-ice
Ice-caps and permanent ice shelf
Progress of Exploration
Coasts explored before 1800
,, ,, between 1800 & 1850
,, ,, between 1850 & 1900
,, ,, since 1900
+ Byrd 1926 Highest latitudes reached by explorers with date
ft m
12 000 4000
9000 3000
6000 2000
3000 1000
1200 400
600 200
0 0
Projection: Zenithal Equidistant

INDEX

The number printed in bold type against each index entry indicates the map page where the feature will be found. The geographical coordinates which follow the name are sometimes only approximate but are close enough for the place name to be located. Rivers have been indexed to their mouth or confluence.

An open square □ signifies that the name refers to an administrative subdivision of a country while a solid square ■ follows the name of a country. An arrow → follows the name of a river.

The alphabetic order of names composed of two or more words is governed primarily by the first word and then by the second. This rule applies even if the second word is a description or its abbreviation, R., L., I. for example. Names composed of a proper name (Gibraltar) and a description (Strait of) are positioned alphabetically by the proper name. If the same place name occurs twice or more times in the index and all are in the same country, each is followed by the name of the administrative subdivision in which it is located. The names are placed in the alphabetical order of the subdivisions. If the same place name occurs twice or more in the index and the places are in different countries, the latter governs the alphabetical order. In a mixture of these situations the primary order is fixed by the alphabetical sequence of the countries and the secondary order by that of the country subdivisions.

Abbreviations used in the index

A.C.T. — Australian Capital Territory
A.R. — Autonomous Region
A.S.S.R. — Autonomous Soviet Socialist Republic
Afghan. — Afghanistan
Ala. — Alabama
Alta. — Alberta
Amer. — America(n)
And. P. — Andhra Pradesh
Arch. — Archipelago
Ariz. — Arizona
Ark. — Arkansas
Atl. Oc. — Atlantic Ocean
B. — Baie, Bahía, Bay, Bucht, Bugt
B.A. — Buenos Aires
B.C. — British Columbia
Baden-W. — Baden-Württemburg
Bangla. — Bangladesh
Barr. — Barrage
Bay. — Bayern
Beds. — Bedfordshire
Berks. — Berkshire
Br. — British
Bri. — Bridge
Bucks. — Buckinghamshire
C. — Cabo, Cap, Cape, Coast
C.A.R. — Central African Republic
C. Prov. — Cape Province
Calif. — California
Cambs. — Cambridgeshire
Cent. — Central
Chan. — Channel
Colo. — Colorado
Conn. — Connecticut
Cord. — Cordillera
Cr. — Creek
Cumb. — Cumbria
Czech. — Czechoslovakia
D.C. — District of Columbia
Del. — Delaware
Dep. — Dependency
Derby. — Derbyshire
Des. — Desert
Dist. — District
Dj. — Djebel
Domin. — Dominica
Dom. Rep. — Dominican Republic
Dumf. & Gall. — Dumfries & Galloway
E. — East
El Salv. — El Salvador
Eng. — England
Eq. Guin. — Equatorial Guinea
Fla. — Florida
Ft. — Fort
Falk. Is. — Falkland Is.
G. — Golfe, Golfo, Gulf, Guba
Ga. — Georgia
Gib. — Gibraltar
Gloucs. — Gloucester
Gt. — Great, Greater
Guinea-Biss. — Guinea-Bissau
H.K. — Hong Kong
H.P. — Himachal Pradesh
Hants. — Hampshire
Harb. — Harbor, Harbour
Hd. — Head
Hereford & Worcs. — Hereford & Worcester
Herts. — Hertfordshire
Hts. — Heights
I. of M. — Isle of Man
I.(s). — Île, Ilha, Insel, Isla, Island, Isle
Ill. — Illinois
Ind. — Indiana
Ind. Oc. — Indian Ocean
Ivory C. — Ivory Coast
J. — Jabal, Jebel, Jazira
Junc. — Junction
K. — Kap, Kapp
Kans. — Kansas
Kep. — Kepulauan
Ky. — Kentucky
L. — Lac, Lacul, Lago, Lagoa, Lake, Limni, Loch, Lough
La. — Louisiana
Lancs. — Lancashire
Leics. — Leicestershire
Liech. — Liechtenstein
Lim. — Limerick
Lincs. — Lincolnshire
Lit. — Little
Lr. — Lower
Lux. — Luxembourg
Mad. P. — Madhya Pradesh
Madag. — Madagascar
Man. — Manitoba
Mass. — Massachusetts
Md. — Maryland
Me. — Maine
Medit. S. — Mediterranean Sea
Mich. — Michigan
Minn. — Minnesota
Miss. — Mississippi
Mo. — Missouri
Mont. — Montana
Mozam. — Mozambique
Mt.(e). — Mont, Monte, Monti, Montaña, Mountain
N. — Nord, Norte, North, Northern, Nouveau
N.B. — New Brunswick
N.C. — North Carolina
N. Cal. — New Caledonia
N. Dak. — North Dakota
N.H. — New Hampshire
N.I. — North Island
N.J. — New Jersey
N. Mex. — New Mexico
N.S. — Nova Scotia
N.S.W. — New South Wales
N. Terr. — Northern Territory
N.W.T. — North West Territory
N.Y. — New York
N.Z. — New Zealand
Nat. — National
Nebr. — Nebraska
Neths. — Netherlands
Neth. Ant. — Netherlands Antilles
Nev. — Nevada
Nfld. — Newfoundland
Nic. — Nicaragua
Northants. — Northamptonshire
Northumb. — Northumberland
Notts. — Nottinghamshire
O. — Oued, Ouadi
Occ. — Occidentale
O.F.S. — Orange Free State
Okla. — Oklahoma
Ont. — Ontario
Or. — Orientale
Oreg. — Oregon
Os. — Ostrov
Oxon. — Oxfordshire
Oz. — Ozero
P. — Pass, Passo, Pasul, Pulau
P.E.I. — Prince Edward Island
P.O. — Post Office
Pa. — Pennsylvania
Pac. Oc. — Pacific Ocean
Papua N.G. — Papua New Guinea
Pass. — Passage
Pen. — Peninsula, Péninsule
Phil. — Philippines
Pk. — Park, Peak
Plat. — Plateau
P-ov. — Poluostrov
Prom. — Promontory
Prov. — Province, Provincial
Pt. — Point
Pta. — Ponta, Punta
Pte. — Pointe
Qué. — Québec
Queens. — Queensland
R. — Rio, River
R.I. — Rhode Island
R.S.F.S.R. — Russian Soviet Federative Socialist Republic
Ra.(s). — Range(s)
Raj. — Rajasthan
Reg. — Region
Rep. — Republic
Res. — Reserve, Reservoir
Rhld.-Pfz. — Rheinland-Pfalz
S. — San, South, Sea
Si. Arabia — Saudi Arabia
S. Austral. — South Australia
S.C. — South Carolina
S. Dak. — South Dakota
S.-Holst. — Schleswig-Holstein
S.I. — South Island
S. Leone — Sierra Leone
S.S.R. — Soviet Socialist Republic
Sa. — Serra, Sierra
Sard. — Sardinia
Sask. — Saskatchewan
Scot. — Scotland
Sd. — Sound
Sept. — Septentrionale
Sev. — Severnaya
Sib. — Siberia
Som. — Somerset
Sprs. — Springs
St. — Saint, Sankt, Sint
St.P. & M. — St. Pierre & Miquelon
Sta. — Santa, Station
Staffs. — Staffordshire
Ste. — Sainte
Sto. — Santo
Str. — Strait, Stretto
Switz. — Switzerland
T.O. — Telegraph Office
Tas. — Tasmania
Tenn. — Tennessee
Terr. — Territory
Tex. — Texas
Tg. — Tanjung
Tipp. — Tipperary
Trans. — Transvaal
Trin. & Tob. — Trinidad & Tobago
U.A.E. — United Arab Emirates
U.K. — United Kingdom
U.S.A. — United States of America
U.S.S.R. — Union of Soviet Socialist Republics
Ukr. — Ukraine
Ut. P. — Uttar Pradesh
Va. — Virginia
Vdkhr. — Vodokhranilishche
Vic. — Victoria
Vol. — Volcano
Vt. — Vermont
W. — Wadi, West
W. Austral. — Western Australia
W. Isles — Western Isles
W. Va. — West Virginia
Wall. & F. Is. — Wallis & Futuna Is.
Wash. — Washington
Wilts. — Wiltshire
Wis. — Wisconsin
Wlkp. — Wielkopolski
Wyo. — Wyoming
Yorks. — Yorkshire

A

Aachen, W. Germany 30 50 47N 6 4 E
Aalborg = Ålborg, Denmark 11 57 2N 9 54 E
Aalen, W. Germany 31 48 49N 10 6 E
A'âli en Nîl □, Sudan 89 9 30N 31 30 E
Aalsmeer, Neths. 16 52 17N 4 43 E
Aalst, Belgium 17 50 56N 4 2 E
Aalst, Neths. 17 51 23N 5 29 E
Aalten, Neths. 16 51 56N 6 35 E
Aalter, Belgium 17 51 5N 3 28 E
Aarau, Switz. 31 47 23N 8 4 E
Aarberg, Switz. 31 47 2N 7 16 E
Aardenburg, Belgium 17 51 16N 3 28 E
Aare →, Switz. 31 47 33N 8 14 E
Aargau □, Switz. 31 47 26N 8 10 E
Aarhus = Århus, Denmark 11 56 8N 10 11 E
Aarle, Neths. 17 51 30N 5 38 E
Aarschot, Belgium 17 50 59N 4 49 E
Aarsele, Belgium 17 51 0N 3 26 E
Aartrijke, Belgium 17 51 7N 3 6 E
Aba, China 58 32 59N 101 42 E
Aba, Nigeria 91 5 10N 7 19 E
Aba, Zaïre 92 3 58N 30 17 E
Âbâ, Jazîrat, Sudan 89 13 30N 32 31 E
Abacaxis →, Brazil 135 3 54 S 58 47W
Ābādān, Iran 46 30 22N 48 20 E
Abade, Ethiopia 89 9 22N 38 3 E
Ābādeh, Iran 47 31 8N 52 40 E
Abadin, Spain 22 43 21N 7 29W
Abadla, Algeria 85 31 2N 2 45W
Abaeté, Brazil 139 19 9 S 45 27W
Abaeté →, Brazil 139 18 2 S 45 12W
Abaetetuba, Brazil 138 1 40 S 48 50W
Abagnar Qi, China 60 43 52N 116 2 E
Abai, Paraguay 141 25 58 S 55 54W
Abak, Nigeria 91 4 58N 7 50 E
Abakaliki, Nigeria 91 6 22N 8 2 E
Abakan, U.S.S.R. 41 53 40N 91 10 E
Abalemma, Niger 91 16 12N 7 50 E
Abancay, Peru 136 13 35 S 72 55W
Abanilla, Spain 25 38 12N 1 3W
Abano Terme, Italy 27 45 22N 11 46 E
Abapó, Bolivia 137 18 48 S 63 25W
Abarán, Spain 25 38 12N 1 23W
Abariringa, Kiribati 66 2 50 S 171 40W
Abarqū, Iran 47 31 10N 53 20 E
'Abasān, Egypt 44 31 19N 34 21 E
Abashiri, Japan 63 44 0N 144 15 E
Abashiri-Wan, Japan 63 44 0N 144 30 E
Abau, Papua N. G. 69 10 11 S 148 46 E
Abaújszántó, Hungary 33 48 16N 21 12 E
Abay, U.S.S.R. 40 49 38N 72 53 E
Abaya, L., Ethiopia 89 6 30N 37 50 E
Abaza, U.S.S.R. 40 52 39N 90 6 E
Abbadia San Salvatore, Italy 27 42 53N 11 40 E
Abbay = Nîl el Azraq →, Sudan 89 15 38N 32 31 E
Abbaye, Pt., U.S.A. 114 46 58N 88 4W
Abbé, L., Ethiopia 89 11 8N 41 47 E
Abbeville, France 19 50 6N 1 49 E
Abbeville, La., U.S.A. 121 30 0N 92 7W
Abbeville, S.C., U.S.A. 115 34 12N 82 21W
Abbiategrasso, Italy 26 45 23N 8 55 E
Abbieglassie, Australia 73 27 15 S 147 28 E
Abbot Ice Shelf, Antarctica 143 73 0 S 92 0W
Abbotsford, Canada 110 49 5N 122 20W
Abbotsford, U.S.A. 120 44 55N 90 20W
Abbottabad, Pakistan 48 34 10N 73 15 E
Abcoude, Neths. 16 52 17N 4 59 E
Abd al Kūrī, Ind. Oc. 45 12 5N 52 20 E
Abéché, Chad 87 13 50N 20 35 E
Abejar, Spain 24 41 48N 2 47W
Abekr, Sudan 89 12 45N 28 50 E
Abêlessa, Algeria 85 22 58N 4 47 E
Abengourou, Ivory C. 90 6 42N 3 27W
Åbenrå, Denmark 11 55 3N 9 25 E
Abensberg, W. Germany 31 48 49N 11 51 E
Abeokuta, Nigeria 91 7 3N 3 19 E
Aber, Uganda 92 2 12N 32 25 E
Aberaeron, U.K. 13 52 15N 4 16W
Aberayron = Aberaeron, U.K. 13 52 15N 4 16W
Abercorn = Mbala, Zambia 93 8 46 S 31 24 E
Abercorn, Australia 73 25 12 S 151 5 E
Abercrombie →, Australia 76 33 54 S 149 8 E
Aberdare, U.K. 13 51 43N 3 27W
Aberdare Ra., Kenya 92 0 15 S 36 50 E
Aberdeen, Australia 77 32 9 S 150 56 E
Aberdeen, Canada 111 52 20N 106 8W
Aberdeen, S. Africa 96 32 28 S 24 2 E
Aberdeen, U.K. 14 57 9N 2 6W
Aberdeen, Ala., U.S.A. 115 33 49N 88 33W
Aberdeen, Idaho, U.S.A. 122 42 57N 112 50W
Aberdeen, Ohio, U.S.A. 119 38 39N 83 46W
Aberdeen, S. Dak., U.S.A. 120 45 30N 98 30W
Aberdeen, Wash., U.S.A. 124 47 0N 123 50W
Aberdovey, U.K. 13 52 33N 4 3W
Aberfeldy, Australia 75 37 42 S 146 22 E
Aberfeldy, U.K. 14 56 37N 3 50W
Abergaria-a-Velha, Portugal 22 40 41N 8 32W
Abergavenny, U.K. 13 51 49N 3 1W
Abermain, Australia 76 32 49 S 151 26 E
Abernathy, U.S.A. 121 33 49N 101 49W
Abert, L., U.S.A. 122 42 40N 120 8W
Aberystwyth, U.K. 13 52 25N 4 6W
Abha, Si. Arabia 88 18 0N 42 34 E
Abhayapuri, India 52 26 24N 90 38 E
Abidiya, Sudan 88 18 18N 34 3 E
Abidjan, Ivory C. 90 5 26N 3 58W
Abilene, Kans., U.S.A. 120 39 0N 97 16W
Abilene, Tex., U.S.A. 121 32 22N 99 40W
Abingdon, U.K. 13 51 40N 1 17W
Abingdon, Ill., U.S.A. 118 40 53N 90 23W
Abingdon, Va., U.S.A. 115 36 46N 81 56W
Abington Reef, Australia 72 18 0 S 149 35 E
Abitau →, Canada 111 59 53N 109 3W
Abitau L., Canada 111 60 27N 107 15W
Abitibi L., Canada 104 48 40N 79 40W
Abiy Adi, Ethiopia 89 13 39N 39 3 E
Abkhaz A.S.S.R. □, U.S.S.R. 39 43 0N 41 0 E
Abkit, U.S.S.R. 41 64 10N 157 10 E
Abminga, Australia 73 26 8 S 134 51 E
Abnûb, Egypt 88 27 18N 31 4 E
Abo, Massif d', Chad 87 21 41N 16 8 E
Abocho, Nigeria 91 7 35N 6 56 E
Abohar, India 48 30 10N 74 10 E
Aboisso, Ivory C. 90 5 30N 3 5W
Abolo, Congo 94 0 8N 14 16 E
Aboméy, Benin 91 7 10N 2 5 E
Abondance, France 21 46 18N 6 43 E
Abong-Mbang, Cameroon 94 4 0N 13 8 E
Abonnema, Nigeria 91 4 41N 6 49 E
Abony, Hungary 33 47 12N 20 3 E
Aboso, Ghana 90 5 23N 1 57W
Abou-Deïa, Chad 87 11 20N 19 20 E
Abou Goulem, Chad 87 13 37N 21 38 E
Aboyne, U.K. 14 57 4N 2 48W
Abra Pampa, Argentina 140 22 43 S 65 42W
Abrantes, Portugal 23 39 24N 8 7W
Abraveses, Portugal 22 40 41N 7 55W
Abreojos, Pta., Mexico 126 26 50N 113 40W
Abreschviller, France 19 48 39N 7 6 E
Abrets, Les, France 21 45 32N 5 35 E
Abri, Esh Shamâliya, Sudan 88 20 50N 30 27 E
Abri, Janub Kordofân, Sudan 89 11 40N 30 21 E
Abrolhos, Banka, Brazil 139 18 0 S 38 0W
Abruzzi □, Italy 27 42 15N 14 0 E
Absaroka Ra., U.S.A. 122 44 40N 110 0W
Abū al Khaṣīb, Iraq 46 30 25N 48 0 E
Abū 'Alī, Si. Arabia 46 27 20N 49 27 E
Abu 'Arīsh, Si. Arabia 45 16 53N 42 48 E
Abû Ballas, Egypt 88 24 26N 27 36 E
Abu Deleiq, Sudan 89 15 57N 33 48 E
Abu Dhabi = Abū Ẓāby, Oman 47 24 28N 54 22 E
Abū Dīs, Jordan 44 31 47N 35 16 E
Abû Dis, Sudan 88 19 12N 33 38 E
Abû Dom, Sudan 89 16 18N 32 25 E
Abû Gabra, Sudan 89 11 2N 26 50 E
Abū Ghaush, Israel 44 31 48N 35 6 E
Abû Gubeiha, Sudan 89 11 30N 31 15 E
Abu Habl, Khawr →, Sudan 89 12 37N 31 0 E
Abu Hamed, Sudan 88 19 32N 33 13 E
Abu Haraz, An Nîl el Azraq, Sudan 89 14 35N 33 30 E
Abû Haraz, Esh Shamâliya, Sudan 88 19 8N 32 18 E
Abû Higar, Sudan 89 12 50N 33 59 E
Abū Kamāl, Syria 46 34 30N 41 0 E
Abū Madd, Ra's, Si. Arabia 46 24 50N 37 7 E
Abu Matariq, Sudan 89 10 59N 26 9 E
Abu Qir, Egypt 88 31 18N 30 0 E
Abu Qireiya, Egypt 88 24 5N 35 28 E
Abu Qurqâs, Egypt 88 28 1N 30 44 E
Abu Rudeis, Egypt 46 28 54N 33 11 E
Abû Simbel, Egypt 88 22 18N 31 40 E
Abu Tig, Egypt 88 27 4N 31 15 E
Abu Tiga, Sudan 89 12 47N 34 12 E
Abû Zabad, Sudan 89 12 25N 29 10 E
Abū Ẓāby, Oman 47 24 28N 54 22 E
Abufari, Brazil 137 5 25 S 62 59W
Abuja, Nigeria 91 9 16N 7 2 E
Abumombazi, Zaïre 94 3 42N 22 10 E
Abunã, Brazil 137 9 40 S 65 20W
Abunã →, Brazil 137 9 41 S 65 20W
Aburatsu, Japan 64 31 34N 131 24 E
Aburo, Zaïre 92 2 4N 30 53 E
Abut Hd., N.Z. 81 43 7 S 170 15 E
Abwong, Sudan 89 9 2N 32 14 E
Åby, Sweden 11 58 40N 16 10 E
Aby, Lagune, Ivory C. 90 5 15N 3 14W
Acacías, Colombia 134 3 59N 73 46W
Acajutla, El Salv. 128 13 36N 89 50W
Açailândia, Brazil 138 5 0 S 47 50W
Acámbaro, Mexico 126 20 0N 100 40W
Acaponeta, Mexico 126 22 30N 105 20W
Acapulco, Mexico 127 16 51N 99 56W
Acarai, Serra, Brazil 135 1 50N 57 50W
Acaraú, Brazil 138 2 53 S 40 7W
Acari, Brazil 138 6 31 S 36 38W
Acarí, Peru 136 15 25 S 74 36W
Acarigua, Venezuela 134 9 33N 69 12W
Acatlán, Mexico 127 18 10N 98 3W
Acayucan, Mexico 127 17 59N 94 58W
Accéglio, Italy 26 44 28N 6 59 E
Accomac, U.S.A. 114 37 43N 75 40W
Accous, France 20 43 0N 0 36W
Accra, Ghana 91 5 35N 0 6W
Accrington, U.K. 12 53 46N 2 22W
Acebal, Argentina 140 33 20 S 60 50W
Aceh □, Indonesia 56 4 15N 97 30 E
Acerenza, Italy 29 40 50N 15 58 E
Acerra, Italy 29 40 57N 14 22 E
Aceuchal, Spain 23 38 39N 6 30W
Achacachi, Bolivia 136 16 3 S 68 43W
Achaguas, Venezuela 134 7 46N 68 14W
Achalpur, India 50 21 22N 77 32 E
Achao, Chile 142 42 28 S 73 30W
Achel, Belgium 17 51 15N 5 29 E
Acheng, China 61 45 30N 126 58 E
Achenkirch, Austria 31 47 32N 11 45 E
Achensee, Austria 31 47 26N 11 45 E
Acher, India 48 23 10N 72 32 E
Achern, W. Germany 31 48 37N 8 5 E
Acheron →, N.Z. 81 42 16 S 173 4 E
Achill, Ireland 15 53 56N 9 55W
Achill Hd., Ireland 15 53 59N 10 15W
Achill I., Ireland 15 53 58N 10 5W
Achill Sound, Ireland 15 53 53N 9 55W
Achim, W. Germany 30 53 1N 9 2 E
Achinsk, U.S.S.R. 41 56 20N 90 20 E
Achol, Sudan 89 6 35N 31 32 E
Acireale, Italy 29 37 37N 15 9 E
Ackerman, U.S.A. 121 33 20N 89 8W
Ackley, U.S.A. 118 42 33N 93 3W
Acklins I., Bahamas 129 22 30N 74 0W
Acme, Canada 110 51 33N 113 30W
Acobamba, Peru 136 12 52 S 74 35W
Acomayo, Peru 136 13 55 S 71 38W
Aconcagua □, Chile 140 32 15 S 70 30W
Aconcagua, Cerro, Argentina 140 32 39 S 70 0W
Aconquija, Mt., Argentina 140 27 0 S 66 0W
Acopiara, Brazil 138 6 6 S 39 27W
Açores, Is. dos = Azores, Atl. Oc. 4 38 44N 29 0W
Acorizal, Brazil 137 15 12 S 56 22W
Acquapendente, Italy 27 42 45N 11 50 E
Acquasanta, Italy 27 42 46N 13 24 E
Acquaviva delle Fonti, Italy 29 40 53N 16 50 E
Acqui, Italy 26 44 40N 8 28 E
Acre = 'Akko, Israel 44 32 55N 35 4 E
Acre □, Brazil 136 9 1 S 71 0W
Acre →, Brazil 136 8 45 S 67 22W
Acri, Italy 29 39 29N 16 23 E
Acs, Hungary 33 47 42N 18 0 E
Acton, Canada 108 43 38N 80 3W
Acton Vale, Canada 107 45 39N 72 34W
Açu, Brazil 138 5 34 S 36 54W
Ad Dahnā, Si. Arabia 46 24 30N 48 10 E
Ad Dammām, Si. Arabia 46 26 20N 50 5 E
Ad Dawhah, Qatar 47 25 15N 51 35 E
Aḍ Ḍiffah, Libya 86 30 30N 24 30 E
Ad Dilam, Si. Arabia 46 23 55N 47 10 E
Ad Dīwānīyah, Iraq 46 32 0N 45 0 E
Ada, Ghana 91 5 44N 0 40 E
Ada, Minn., U.S.A. 120 47 20N 96 30W
Ada, Ohio, U.S.A. 119 40 46N 83 49W
Ada, Okla., U.S.A. 121 34 50N 96 45W
Ada, Yugoslavia 33 45 49N 20 9 E
Adad, Somali Rep. 98 9 27N 46 49 E
Adaja →, Spain 22 41 32N 4 52W
Ådalslinden, Sweden 10 63 27N 16 55 E
Adam, Oman 47 22 15N 57 28 E
Adam, Mt., Falk. Is. 142 51 34 S 60 4W
Adamantina, Brazil 139 21 42 S 51 4W
Adamaoua, Massif de l', Cameroon 91 7 20N 12 20 E
Adamawa Highlands = Adamaoua, Massif de l', Cameroon 91 7 20N 12 20 E
Adamello, Mt., Italy 26 46 10N 10 34 E
Adami Tulu, Ethiopia 89 7 53N 38 41 E
Adaminaby, Australia 75 36 0 S 148 45 E
Adams, Mass., U.S.A. 117 42 38N 73 8W
Adams, N.Y., U.S.A. 117 43 50N 76 3W
Adams, Wis., U.S.A. 120 43 59N 89 50W
Adams, Mt., U.S.A. 124 46 10N 121 28W
Adam's Bridge, Sri Lanka 51 9 15N 79 40 E
Adams L., Canada 110 51 10N 119 40W
Adam's Peak, Sri Lanka 51 6 48N 80 30 E
Adamuz, Spain 23 38 2N 4 32W
Adana, Turkey 46 37 0N 35 16 E
Adanero, Spain 22 40 56N 4 36W
Adapazarı, Turkey 46 40 48N 30 25 E
Adarama, Sudan 89 17 10N 34 52 E
Adare, C., Antarctica 143 71 0 S 171 0 E
Adaut, Indonesia 57 8 8 S 131 7 E
Adavale, Australia 73 25 52 S 144 32 E
Adda →, Italy 26 45 8N 9 53 E
Addis Ababa = Addis Abeba, Ethiopia 89 9 2N 38 42 E
Addis Abeba, Ethiopia 89 9 2N 38 42 E
Addis Alem, Ethiopia 89 9 0N 38 17 E
Addison, Ill., U.S.A. 119 41 56N 88 2W
Addison, N.Y., U.S.A. 116 42 9N 77 15W
Addo, S. Africa 96 33 32 S 25 45 E
Addyston, U.S.A. 119 39 8N 84 43W
Adebour, Niger 91 13 17N 11 50 E
Adel, Ga., U.S.A. 115 31 10N 83 28W
Adel, Iowa, U.S.A. 118 41 37N 94 1W
Adelaide, Australia 73 34 52 S 138 30 E
Adelaide, Bahamas 128 25 0N 77 31W
Adelaide, S. Africa 97 32 42 S 26 20 E
Adelaide I., Antarctica 143 67 15 S 68 30W
Adelaide Pen., Canada 102 68 15N 97 30W
Adelaide River, Australia 78 13 15 S 131 7 E
Adelanto, U.S.A. 125 34 35N 117 22W
Adele, I., Australia 78 15 32 S 123 9 E
Adélie, Terre, Antarctica 143 68 0 S 140 0 E
Adelong, Australia 76 35 16 S 148 4 E
Ademuz, Spain 24 40 5N 1 13W
Aden = Al 'Adan, S. Yemen 45 12 45N 45 0 E
Aden, G. of, Asia 45 12 30N 47 30 E
Adendorp, S. Africa 96 32 15 S 24 30 E
Adhoi, India 48 23 26N 70 32 E
Adi, Indonesia 57 4 15 S 133 30 E
Adi Daro, Ethiopia 89 14 20N 38 14 E
Adi Keyih, Ethiopia 89 14 51N 39 22 E
Adi Kwala, Ethiopia 89 14 38N 38 48 E
Adi Ugri, Ethiopia 89 14 58N 38 48 E
Adieu, C., Australia 79 32 0 S 132 10 E
Adieu Pt., Australia 78 15 14 S 124 35 E
Adigala, Ethiopia 89 10 24N 42 15 E
Adige →, Italy 27 45 9N 12 20 E
Adigrat, Ethiopia 89 14 20N 39 26 E
Adilabad, India 50 19 33N 78 20 E
Adin, U.S.A. 122 41 10N 121 0W
Adin Khel, Afghan. 47 32 45N 68 5 E
Adinkerke, Belgium 17 51 5N 2 36 E
Adirondack Mts., U.S.A. 117 44 0N 74 15W
Adjim, Tunisia 86 33 47N 10 50 E
Adjohon, Benin 91 6 41N 2 32 E
Adjud, Romania 34 46 7N 27 10 E
Adjumani, Uganda 92 3 20N 31 50 E
Adlavik Is., Canada 105 55 2N 57 45W
Adler, U.S.S.R. 39 43 28N 39 52 E
Admer, Algeria 85 20 21N 5 27 E
Admer, Erg d', Algeria 85 24 0N 9 5 E
Admiralty G., Australia 78 14 20 S 125 55 E
Admiralty I., U.S.A. 102 57 40N 134 35W
Admiralty Inlet, U.S.A. 122 48 0N 122 40W
Admiralty Is., Papua N. G. 69 2 0 S 147 0 E
Ado, Nigeria 91 6 36N 2 56 E
Ado Ekiti, Nigeria 91 7 38N 5 12 E
Adok, Sudan 89 8 10N 30 20 E
Adola, Ethiopia 89 11 14N 41 44 E
Adonara, Indonesia 57 8 15 S 123 5 E
Adoni, India 51 15 33N 77 18 E
Adony, Hungary 33 47 6N 18 52 E
Adour →, France 20 43 32N 1 32W
Adra, India 49 23 30N 86 42 E
Adra, Spain 25 36 43N 3 3W
Adrano, Italy 29 37 40N 14 49 E
Adrar, Algeria 85 27 51N 0 11W
Adré, Chad 87 13 40N 22 20 E
Adrī, Libya 86 27 32N 13 2 E
Ádria, Italy 27 45 4N 12 3 E
Adrian, Mich., U.S.A. 119 41 55N 84 0W
Adrian, Mo., U.S.A. 118 38 24N 94 21W
Adrian, Tex., U.S.A. 121 35 19N 102 37W
Adriatic Sea, Europe 6 43 0N 16 0 E
Adua, Indonesia 57 1 45 S 129 50 E
Adung Long, Burma 52 28 7N 97 42 E
Adur, India 51 9 8N 76 40 E
Adwa, Ethiopia 89 14 15N 38 52 E
Adzhar A.S.S.R. □, U.S.S.R. 39 42 0N 42 0 E
Adzopé, Ivory C. 90 6 7N 3 49W
Ægean Sea, Europe 35 37 0N 25 0 E
Æolian Is. = Eólie, Is., Italy 29 38 30N 14 50 E
Aerht'ai Shan, Mongolia 62 46 40N 92 45 E
Ærø, Denmark 11 54 52N 10 25 E
Ærøskøbing, Denmark 11 54 53N 10 24 E
Afafi, Massif d', Niger 87 22 11N 15 10 E
Afándou, Greece 35 36 18N 28 12 E
Afarag, Erg, Algeria 85 23 50N 2 47 E
Afareaitu, Tahiti 68 17 33 S 149 47W
Afars & Issas, Terr. of = Djibouti ■, Africa 89 12 0N 43 0 E
Afdega, Ethiopia 98 6 4N 43 30 E
Affreville = Khemis Miliana, Algeria 85 36 11N 2 14 E
Affton, U.S.A. 118 38 33N 90 20W
Afghanistan ■, Asia 47 33 0N 65 0 E
Afgoi, Somali Rep. 98 2 7N 44 59 E
'Afif, Si. Arabia 46 23 53N 42 56 E
Afikpo, Nigeria 91 5 53N 7 54 E
Aflou, Algeria 85 34 7N 2 3 E
Afmadu, Somali Rep. 98 0 31N 42 4 E
Afogados da Ingàzeira, Brazil 138 7 45 S 37 39W
Afognak I., U.S.A. 102 58 10N 152 50W
Afragola, Italy 29 40 54N 14 15 E
Afrera, Ethiopia 89 13 16N 41 5 E
Africa 82 10 0N 20 0 E
Afton, U.S.A. 117 42 14N 75 31W
Aftout, Algeria 84 26 50N 3 45W
Afuá, Brazil 138 0 15 S 50 20W
Afula, Israel 44 32 37N 35 17 E
Afyonkarahisar, Turkey 46 38 45N 30 33 E
Aga, Egypt 88 30 55N 31 10 E
Agadès = Agadez, Niger 91 16 58N 7 59 E
Agadez, Niger 91 16 58N 7 59 E
Agadir, Morocco 84 30 28N 9 55W
Agaete, Canary Is. 25 28 6N 15 43W

Agailás, *Mauritania* **84** 22 37N 14 22W
Agana, *Guam* **68** 13 28N 144 45 E
Agano →, *Japan* **63** 37 57N 139 8 E
Agapa, *U.S.S.R.* **41** 71 27N 89 15 E
Agar, *India* **48** 23 40N 76 2 E
Agaro, *Ethiopia* **89** 7 50N 36 38 E
Agartala, *India* **52** 23 50N 91 23 E
Agassiz, *Canada* **110** 49 14N 121 46W
Agats, *Indonesia* **57** 5 33 S 138 0 E
Agbélouvé, *Togo* **91** 6 35N 1 14 E
Agboville, *Ivory C.* **90** 5 55N 4 15W
Agdam, *U.S.S.R.* **39** 40 0N 46 58 E
Agdash, *U.S.S.R.* **39** 40 44N 47 22 E
Agde, *France* **20** 43 19N 3 28 E
Agde, C. d', *France* **20** 43 16N 3 28 E
Agdz, *Morocco* **84** 30 47N 6 30W
Agdzhabedi, *U.S.S.R.* **39** 40 5N 47 27 E
Agen, *France* **20** 44 12N 0 38 E
Ageo, *Japan* **65** 35 58N 139 36 E
Ager Tay, *Chad* **87** 20 0N 17 41 E
Agersø, *Denmark* **11** 55 13N 11 12 E
Ageyevo, *U.S.S.R.* **37** 54 10N 36 27 E
Agger, *Denmark* **11** 56 47N 8 13 E
Aggius, *Italy* **28** 40 56N 9 4 E
Aghil Mts., *China* **49** 36 0N 77 0 E
Aghoueyyît, *Mauritania* **84** 21 10N 15 6W
Aginskoye, *U.S.S.R.* **41** 51 6N 114 32 E
Agira, *Italy* **29** 37 40N 14 30 E
Agly →, *France* **20** 42 46N 3 3 E
Agnibilékrou, *Ivory C.* **90** 7 10N 3 11W
Agnita, *Romania* **34** 45 59N 24 40 E
Agnone, *Italy* **29** 41 49N 14 20 E
Ago, *Japan* **65** 34 20N 136 51 E
Agofie, *Ghana* **91** 8 27N 0 15 E
Agogna →, *Italy* **26** 45 4N 8 52 E
Agogo, *Sudan* **89** 7 50N 28 45 E
Agon, *France* **18** 49 2N 1 34W
Agön, *Sweden* **10** 61 34N 17 23 E
Agordo, *Italy* **27** 46 18N 12 2 E
Agout →, *France* **20** 43 47N 1 41 E
Agra, *India* **48** 27 17N 77 58 E
Agramunt, *Spain* **24** 41 48N 1 6 E
Agreda, *Spain* **24** 41 51N 1 55W
Agri →, *Italy* **29** 40 13N 16 44 E
Ağri Daği, *Turkey* **46** 39 50N 44 15 E
Ağri Karakose, *Turkey* **46** 39 44N 43 3 E
Agrigento, *Italy* **28** 37 19N 13 33 E
Agrinion, *Greece* **35** 38 37N 21 27 E
Agrópoli, *Italy* **29** 40 23N 14 59 E
Água Branca, *Brazil* **138** 5 50 S 42 40W
Agua Caliente, *Baja Calif. N., Mexico* **125** 32 29N 116 59W
Agua Caliente, *Sinaloa, Mexico* **126** 26 30N 108 20W
Agua Caliente Springs, *U.S.A.* **125** 32 56N 116 19W
Água Clara, *Brazil* **137** 20 25 S 52 45W
Agua Hechicero, *Mexico* **125** 32 26N 116 14W
Agua Preta →, *Brazil* **135** 1 41 S 63 48W
Agua Prieta, *Mexico* **126** 31 20N 109 32W
Aguachica, *Colombia* **134** 8 19N 73 38W
Aguada Cecilio, *Argentina* **142** 40 51 S 65 51W
Aguadas, *Colombia* **134** 5 40N 75 38W
Aguadilla, *Puerto Rico* **129** 18 27N 67 10W
Aguadulce, *Panama* **128** 8 15N 80 32W
Aguanga, *U.S.A.* **125** 33 27N 116 51W
Aguanish, *Canada* **105** 50 14N 62 2W
Aguanus →, *Canada* **105** 50 13N 62 5W
Aguapeí, *Brazil* **137** 16 12 S 59 43W
Aguapeí →, *Brazil* **139** 21 0 S 51 0W
Aguapey →, *Argentina* **140** 29 7 S 56 36W
Aguaray Guazú →, *Paraguay* **140** 24 47 S 57 19W
Aguarico →, *Ecuador* **134** 0 59 S 75 11W
Aguas →, *Spain* **24** 41 20N 0 30W
Aguas Blancas, *Chile* **140** 24 15 S 69 55W
Aguas Calientes, Sierra de, *Argentina* **140** 25 26 S 66 40W
Águas Formosas, *Brazil* **139** 17 5 S 40 57W
Aguascalientes, *Mexico* **126** 21 53N 102 12W
Aguascalientes □, *Mexico* **126** 22 0N 102 20W
Agudo, *Spain* **23** 38 59N 4 52W
Águeda, *Portugal* **22** 40 34N 8 27W
Agueda →, *Spain* **22** 41 2N 6 56W
Aguié, *Niger* **91** 13 31N 7 46 E
Aguilafuente, *Spain* **22** 41 13N 4 7W
Aguilar, *Spain* **23** 37 31N 4 40W
Aguilar de Campóo, *Spain* **22** 42 47N 4 15W
Aguilares, *Argentina* **140** 27 26 S 65 35W
Aguilas, *Spain* **25** 37 23N 1 35W
Agüimes, *Canary Is.* **25** 27 58N 15 27W
Aguja, C. de la, *Colombia* **134** 11 18N 74 12W
Agulaa, *Ethiopia* **89** 13 40N 39 40 E
Agulhas, C., *S. Africa* **96** 34 52 S 20 0 E
Agulo, *Canary Is.* **25** 28 11N 17 12W
Agung, *Indonesia* **56** 8 20 S 115 28 E
'Agur, *Israel* **44** 31 42N 34 55 E
Agur, *Uganda* **92** 2 28N 32 55 E
Agusan →, *Phil.* **57** 9 0N 125 30 E
Agustín Codazzi, *Colombia* **134** 10 2N 73 14W
Agvali, *U.S.S.R.* **39** 42 36N 46 8 E
Aha Mts., *Botswana* **96** 19 45 S 21 0 E
Ahaggar, *Algeria* **85** 23 0N 6 30 E
Ahamansu, *Ghana* **91** 7 38N 0 35 E
Ahar, *Iran* **46** 38 35N 47 0 E
Ahaura →, *N.Z.* **81** 42 21 S 171 34 E
Ahaus, *W. Germany* **30** 52 4N 7 1 E
Ahelledjem, *Algeria* **85** 26 37N 6 58 E
Ahipara B., *N.Z.* **80** 35 5 S 173 5 E
Ahiri, *India* **50** 19 30N 80 0 E
Ahlen, *W. Germany* **30** 51 45N 7 52 E
Ahmad Wal, *Pakistan* **48** 29 18N 65 58 E
Ahmadabad, *India* **48** 23 0N 72 40 E
Ahmadnagar, *India* **50** 19 7N 74 46 E
Ahmadpur, *Pakistan* **48** 29 12N 71 10 E
Ahmar Mts., *Ethiopia* **89** 9 20N 41 15 E
Ahmedabad = Ahmadabad, *India* **48** 23 0N 72 40 E
Ahmednagar = Ahmadnagar, *India* **50** 19 7N 74 46 E
Ahoada, *Nigeria* **91** 5 8N 6 36 E
Ahome, *Mexico* **126** 25 55N 109 11W
Ahr →, *W. Germany* **30** 50 33N 7 17 E
Ahrensbök, *W. Germany* **30** 54 0N 10 34 E
Ahrweiler, *W. Germany* **30** 50 31N 7 3 E
Ahuachapán, *El Salv.* **128** 13 54N 89 52W
Ahuriri →, *N.Z.* **81** 44 31 S 170 12 E
Åhus, *Sweden* **11** 55 56N 14 18 E
Ahvāz, *Iran* **46** 31 20N 48 40 E
Ahvenanmaa = Åland, *Finland* **9** 60 15N 20 0 E
Aḥwar, *S. Yemen* **45** 13 30N 46 40 E
Ahzar, *Mali* **91** 15 30N 3 20 E
Aiari →, *Brazil* **134** 1 22N 68 36W
Aichach, *W. Germany* **31** 48 28N 11 9 E
Aichi □, *Japan* **65** 35 0N 137 15 E
Aidone, *Italy* **29** 37 26N 14 26 E
Aiello Cálabro, *Italy* **29** 39 6N 16 12 E
Aigle, *Switz.* **31** 46 18N 6 58 E
Aigle, L', *France* **18** 48 46N 0 38 E
Aignay-le-Duc, *France* **19** 47 40N 4 43 E
Aigoual, Mt., *France* **20** 44 8N 3 35 E
Aigre, *France* **20** 45 54N 0 1 E
Aigua, *Uruguay* **141** 34 13 S 54 46W
Aiguebelle, Parc, *Canada* **106** 48 30N 78 45W
Aigueperse, *France* **20** 46 3N 3 13 E
Aigues →, *France* **21** 44 7N 4 43 E
Aigues-Mortes, *France* **21** 43 35N 4 12 E
Aigues-Mortes, G. d', *France* **21** 43 31N 4 3 E
Aiguilles, *France* **21** 44 47N 6 51 E
Aiguillon, *France* **20** 44 18N 0 21 E
Aiguillon-sur-Mer, L', *France* **20** 46 20N 1 18W
Aigurande, *France* **20** 46 27N 1 49 E
Aihui, *China* **62** 50 10N 127 30 E
Aija, *Peru* **136** 9 50 S 77 45W
Aiken, *U.S.A.* **115** 33 34N 81 50W
Ailao Shan, *China* **58** 24 0N 101 20 E
Aillant-sur-Tholon, *France* **19** 47 52N 3 20 E
Aillik, *Canada* **105** 55 11N 59 18W
Ailly-sur-Noye, *France* **19** 49 45N 2 20 E
Ailsa Craig, *Canada* **108** 43 8N 81 33W
Ailsa Craig, *U.K.* **14** 55 15N 5 7W
'Ailūn, *Jordan* **44** 32 18N 35 47 E
Aim, *U.S.S.R.* **41** 59 0N 133 55 E
Aimere, *Indonesia* **57** 8 45 S 121 3 E
Aimogasta, *Argentina* **140** 28 33 S 66 50W
Aimorés, *Brazil* **139** 19 30 S 41 4W
Ain □, *France* **21** 46 5N 5 20 E
Ain →, *France* **21** 45 45N 5 11 E
Ain Banaiyan, *Si. Arabia* **47** 23 0N 51 0 E
Aïn Beïda, *Algeria* **85** 35 50N 7 29 E
Aïn Ben Khellil, *Algeria* **85** 33 15N 0 49W
Aïn Ben Tili, *Mauritania* **84** 25 59N 9 27W
Aïn Beni Mathar, *Morocco* **85** 34 1N 2 0W
Aïn Benian, *Algeria* **85** 36 48N 2 55 E
Ain Dalla, *Egypt* **88** 27 20N 27 23 E
Ain el Mafki, *Egypt* **88** 27 30N 28 15 E
Ain Girba, *Egypt* **88** 29 20N 25 14 E
Aïn M'lila, *Algeria* **85** 36 2N 6 35 E
Ain Qeiqab, *Egypt* **88** 29 42N 24 55 E
Aïn-Sefra, *Algeria* **85** 32 47N 0 37W
Ain Sheikh Murzûk, *Egypt* **88** 26 47N 27 45 E
Ain Sukhna, *Egypt* **88** 29 32N 32 20 E
Aïn Tédelès, *Algeria* **85** 36 0N 0 21 E
Aïn-Témouchent, *Algeria* **85** 35 16N 1 8W
Aïn Touta, *Algeria* **85** 35 26N 5 54 E
Ain Zeitûn, *Egypt* **88** 29 10N 25 48 E
Aïn Zorah, *Morocco* **85** 34 37N 3 32W
Ainabo, *Somali Rep.* **98** 9 0N 46 25 E
Ainaži, *U.S.S.R.* **36** 57 50N 24 24 E
Aínos Óros, *Greece* **35** 38 10N 20 35 E
Ainsworth, *U.S.A.* **120** 42 33N 99 52W
Aioi, *Japan* **64** 34 48N 134 28 E
Aipe, *Colombia* **134** 3 13N 75 15W
Aiquile, *Bolivia* **137** 18 10 S 65 10W
Aïr, *Niger* **91** 18 30N 8 0 E
Air Hitam, *Malaysia* **55** 1 55N 103 11 E
Airaines, *France* **19** 49 58N 1 55 E
Airão, *Brazil* **135** 1 56 S 61 22W
Airdrie, *U.K.* **14** 55 53N 3 57W
Aire →, *France* **19** 49 18N 4 49 E
Aire →, *U.K.* **12** 53 42N 0 55W
Aire, I. del, *Spain* **24** 39 48N 4 16 E
Aire-sur-la-Lys, *France* **19** 50 37N 2 22 E
Aire-sur-l'Adour, *France* **20** 43 42N 0 15W
Aireys Inlet, *Australia* **74** 38 29 S 144 5 E
Airlie Beach, *Australia* **72** 20 16 S 148 43 E
Airvault, *France* **18** 46 50N 0 8W
Aisch →, *W. Germany* **31** 49 46N 11 1 E
Aisen □, *Chile* **142** 46 30 S 73 0W
Aisne □, *France* **19** 49 42N 3 40 E
Aisne →, *France* **19** 49 26N 2 50 E
Aitana, Sierra de, *Spain* **25** 38 35N 0 24W
Aitape, *Papua N. G.* **69** 3 11 S 142 22 E
Aitkin, *U.S.A.* **120** 46 32N 93 43W
Aitolikón, *Greece* **35** 38 26N 21 21 E
Aiuaba, *Brazil* **138** 6 38 S 40 7W
Aiud, *Romania* **34** 46 19N 23 44 E
Aix-en-Provence, *France* **21** 43 32N 5 27 E
Aix-la-Chapelle = Aachen, *W. Germany* **30** 50 47N 6 4 E
Aix-les-Bains, *France* **21** 45 41N 5 53 E
Aixe-sur-Vienne, *France* **20** 45 47N 1 9 E
Aiyang, Mt., *Papua N. G.* **69** 5 10 S 141 20 E
Aiyansh, *Canada* **110** 55 17N 129 2W
Áíyina, *Greece* **35** 37 45N 23 26 E
Aiyínion, *Greece* **35** 40 28N 22 28 E
Aiyion, *Greece* **35** 38 15N 22 5 E
Aizawl, *India* **52** 23 40N 92 44 E
Aizenay, *France* **18** 46 44N 1 38W
Aizpute, *U.S.S.R.* **36** 56 43N 21 40 E
Aizuwakamatsu, *Japan* **63** 37 30N 139 56 E
Ajaccio, *France* **21** 41 55N 8 40 E
Ajaccio, G. d', *France* **21** 41 52N 8 40 E
Ajaju →, *Colombia* **134** 0 59N 72 20W
Ajalpan, *Mexico* **127** 18 22N 97 15W
Ajanta Ra., *India* **50** 20 28N 75 50 E
Ajax, *Canada* **109** 43 50N 79 1W
Ajax, Mt., *N.Z.* **81** 42 35 S 172 5 E
Ajayan Pt., *Guam* **68** 13 15N 144 43 E
Ajdâbiyah, *Libya* **86** 30 54N 20 4 E
Ajdovščina, *Yugoslavia* **27** 45 54N 13 54 E
Ajibar, *Ethiopia* **89** 10 35N 38 36 E
Ajka, *Hungary* **33** 47 4N 17 31 E
'Ajmān, *Asia* **47** 25 25N 55 30 E
Ajmer, *India* **48** 26 28N 74 37 E
Ajo, *U.S.A.* **123** 32 18N 112 54W
Ajok, *Sudan* **89** 9 15N 28 28 E
Ak Dağ, *Turkey* **46** 36 30N 30 0 E
Akaba, *Togo* **91** 8 10N 1 2 E
Akabli, *Algeria* **85** 26 49N 1 31 E
Akaishi-Dake, *Japan* **65** 35 27N 138 9 E
Akaishi-Sammyaku, *Japan* **65** 35 25N 138 10 E
Akaki Beseka, *Ethiopia* **89** 8 55N 38 45 E
Akala, *Sudan* **89** 15 39N 36 13 E
Akaroa, *N.Z.* **81** 43 49 S 172 59 E
Akasha, *Sudan* **88** 21 10N 30 32 E
Akashi, *Japan* **64** 34 45N 135 0 E
Akbou, *Algeria* **85** 36 31N 4 31 E
Akchâr, *Mauritania* **84** 20 20N 14 28W
Akechi, *Japan* **65** 35 18N 137 23 E
Akelamo, *Indonesia* **57** 1 35N 129 40 E
Akershus fylke □, *Norway* **10** 60 0N 11 10 E
Akeru →, *India* **50** 17 25N 80 0 E
Aketi, *Zaïre* **94** 2 38N 23 47 E
Akhalkalaki, *U.S.S.R.* **39** 41 27N 43 25 E
Akhaltsikhe, *U.S.S.R.* **39** 41 40N 43 0 E
Akharnaí, *Greece* **35** 38 5N 23 44 E
Akhelóös →, *Greece* **35** 38 36N 21 14 E
Akhendria, *Greece* **35** 34 58N 25 16 E
Akhéron →, *Greece* **35** 39 20N 20 29 E
Akhisar, *Turkey* **46** 38 56N 27 48 E
Akhladhókambos, *Greece* **35** 37 31N 22 35 E
Akhmîm, *Egypt* **88** 26 31N 31 47 E
Akhnur, *India* **49** 32 52N 74 45 E
Akhtubinsk, *U.S.S.R.* **39** 48 13N 46 7 E
Akhty, *U.S.S.R.* **39** 41 30N 47 45 E
Akhtyrka, *U.S.S.R.* **36** 50 25N 35 0 E
Aki, *Japan* **64** 33 30N 133 54 E
Aki-Nada, *Japan* **64** 34 5N 132 40 E
Akiéni, *Gabon* **94** 1 11 S 13 53 E
Akimiski I., *Canada* **104** 52 50N 81 30W
Akimovka, *U.S.S.R.* **38** 46 44N 35 0 E
Åkirkeby, *Denmark* **11** 55 4N 14 55 E
Akita, *Japan* **63** 39 45N 140 7 E
Akjoujt, *Mauritania* **90** 19 45N 14 15W
Akka, *Morocco* **84** 29 22N 8 9W
'Akko, *Israel* **44** 32 55N 35 4 E
Akkol, *U.S.S.R.* **40** 45 0N 75 39 E
Akkrum, *Neths.* **16** 53 3N 5 50 E
Aklampa, *Benin* **91** 8 15N 2 10 E
Aklavik, *Canada* **102** 68 12N 135 0W
Akmonte, *Spain* **23** 37 13N 6 38W
Aknoul, *Morocco* **85** 34 40N 3 55W
Akō, *Japan* **64** 34 45N 134 24 E
Ako, *Nigeria* **91** 10 19N 10 48 E
Akobo →, *Ethiopia* **89** 7 48N 33 3 E
Akola, *India* **50** 20 42N 77 2 E
Akonolinga, *Cameroon* **91** 3 50N 12 18 E
Akordat, *Ethiopia* **89** 15 30N 37 40 E
Akosombo Dam, *Ghana* **91** 6 20N 0 5 E
Akot, *India* **50** 21 10N 77 10 E
Akot, *Sudan* **89** 6 31N 30 9 E
Akpatok I., *Canada* **103** 60 25N 68 8W
Akranes, *Iceland* **8** 64 19N 21 58W
Akreïjit, *Mauritania* **90** 18 19N 9 11W
Akrítas Venétiko, Ákra, *Greece* **35** 36 43N 21 54 E
Akron, *Colo., U.S.A.* **120** 40 13N 103 15W
Akron, *Ind., U.S.A.* **119** 41 2N 86 1W
Akron, *Ohio, U.S.A.* **116** 41 7N 81 31W
Akrotíri, Ákra, *Greece* **35** 40 26N 25 27 E
Aksai Chih, *India* **49** 35 15N 79 55 E
Aksaray, *Turkey* **46** 38 25N 34 2 E
Aksarka, *U.S.S.R.* **40** 66 31N 67 50 E
Aksay, *U.S.S.R.* **40** 51 11N 53 0 E
Akşehir, *Turkey* **46** 38 18N 31 30 E
Aksenovo Zilovskoye, *U.S.S.R.* **41** 53 20N 117 40 E
Akstafa, *U.S.S.R.* **39** 41 7N 45 27 E
Aksu, *China* **62** 41 5N 80 10 E
Aksum, *Ethiopia* **89** 14 5N 38 40 E
Aktogay, *U.S.S.R.* **40** 46 57N 79 40 E
Aktyubinsk, *U.S.S.R.* **40** 50 17N 57 10 E
Aku, *Nigeria* **91** 6 40N 7 18 E
Akula, *Zaïre* **94** 2 22N 20 12 E
Akune, *Japan* **64** 32 1N 130 12 E
Akure, *Nigeria* **91** 7 15N 5 5 E
Akureyri, *Iceland* **8** 65 40N 18 6W
Akusha, *U.S.S.R.* **39** 42 18N 47 30 E
Akyab = Sittwe, *Burma* **52** 20 18N 92 45 E
Al Abyār, *Libya* **86** 32 9N 20 29 E
Al 'Adan, *S. Yemen* **45** 12 45N 45 0 E
Al Aḥsā, *Si. Arabia* **46** 25 50N 49 0 E
Al Amādīyah, *Iraq* **46** 37 5N 43 30 E
Al Amārah, *Iraq* **46** 31 55N 47 15 E
Al 'Aqabah, *Jordan* **44** 29 31N 35 0 E
Al 'Aramah, *Si. Arabia* **46** 25 30N 46 0 E
Al Ashkhara, *Oman* **47** 21 50N 59 30 E
Al 'Ayzarīyah, *Jordan* **44** 31 47N 35 15 E
Al 'Azīzīyah, *Libya* **86** 32 30N 13 1 E
Al Badī', *Si. Arabia* **46** 22 0N 46 35 E
Al Barkāt, *Libya* **86** 24 56N 10 14 E
Al Başrah, *Iraq* **46** 30 30N 47 50 E
Al Baydā □, *Libya* **86** 32 0N 21 30 E
Al Bāzūrīyah, *Lebanon* **44** 33 15N 35 16 E
Al Bīrah, *Jordan* **44** 31 55N 35 12 E
Al Bu'ayrāt, *Libya* **86** 31 24N 15 44 E
Al Buqay'ah, *Jordan* **44** 32 15N 35 30 E
Al Fallūjah, *Iraq* **46** 33 20N 43 55 E
Al Fāw, *Iraq* **46** 30 0N 48 30 E
Al Fujayrah, *Asia* **47** 25 7N 56 18 E
Al Gharīb, *Libya* **86** 32 35N 21 11 E
Al Hābah, *Si. Arabia* **46** 27 10N 47 0 E
Al Haddār, *Si. Arabia* **46** 21 58N 45 57 E
Al Ḥadīthah, *Iraq* **46** 34 0N 41 13 E
Al Hāmad, *Si. Arabia* **46** 31 30N 39 30 E
Al Ḥamar, *Si. Arabia* **46** 22 23N 46 6 E
Al Hammādah al Ḥamrā', *Libya* **86** 29 30N 12 0 E
Al Ḥamrā', *Si. Arabia* **46** 24 2N 38 55 E
Al Ḥarīq, *Si. Arabia* **46** 23 29N 46 27 E
Al Harīr, W. →, *Syria* **44** 32 44N 35 59 E
Al Harūj al Aswad, *Libya* **86** 27 0N 17 10 E
Al Ḥasakah, *Syria* **46** 36 35N 40 45 E
Al Ḥawrah, *S. Yemen* **45** 13 50N 47 35 E
Al Ḥayy, *Iraq* **46** 32 5N 46 5 E
Al Ḥijāz, *Si. Arabia* **46** 26 0N 37 30 E
Al Ḥillah, *Iraq* **46** 32 30N 44 25 E
Al Ḥillah, *Si. Arabia* **46** 23 35N 46 50 E
Al Hindīyah, *Iraq* **46** 32 30N 44 10 E
Al Ḥişn, *Jordan* **44** 32 29N 35 52 E
Al Hoceïma, *Morocco* **84** 35 8N 3 58W
Al Ḥudaydah, *Yemen* **45** 14 50N 43 0 E
Al Ḥufrah, *Awbārī, Libya* **86** 25 32N 14 1 E
Al Ḥufrah, *Misrātah, Libya* **86** 29 5N 18 3 E
Al Hufūf, *Si. Arabia* **46** 25 25N 49 45 E
Al Ḥulwah, *Si. Arabia* **46** 23 24N 46 48 E
Al Husayyāt, *Libya* **86** 30 24N 20 37 E
Al Irq, *Libya* **86** 29 5N 21 35 E
Al Ittihad = Madīnat ash Sha'b, *S. Yemen* **45** 12 50N 45 0 E
Al Jabal al Akhḍar, *Libya* **86** 32 0N 21 30 E
Al Jāfūrah, *Si. Arabia* **46** 25 0N 50 15 E
Al Jaghbūb, *Libya* **86** 29 42N 24 38 E
Al Jahrah, *Kuwait* **46** 29 25N 47 40 E
Al Jalāmīd, *Si. Arabia* **46** 31 20N 39 45 E
Al Jawf, *Libya* **86** 24 10N 23 24 E
Al Jawf, *Si. Arabia* **46** 29 55N 39 40 E
Al Jazirah, *Iraq* **46** 33 30N 44 0 E
Al Jazirah, *Libya* **86** 26 10N 21 20 E
Al Jubayl, *Si. Arabia* **46** 27 0N 49 50 E
Al Jubaylah, *Si. Arabia* **46** 24 55N 46 25 E
Al Junaynah, *Sudan* **87** 13 27N 22 45 E
Al Khābūra, *Oman* **47** 23 57N 57 5 E
Al Khalīl, *Jordan* **44** 31 32N 35 6 E
Al Khalūf, *Oman* **45** 20 30N 58 13 E
Al Kharfah, *Si. Arabia* **46** 22 0N 46 35 E
Al Kharj, *Si. Arabia* **46** 24 0N 47 0 E
Al Khasab, *Oman* **47** 26 14N 56 15 E
Al Khums, *Libya* **86** 32 40N 14 17 E
Al Khums □, *Libya* **86** 31 20N 14 10 E
Al Kufrah, *Libya* **86** 24 17N 23 15 E
Al Kūt, *Iraq* **46** 32 30N 46 0 E
Al Kuwayt, *Kuwait* **46** 29 30N 48 0 E
Al Lādhiqīyah, *Syria* **46** 35 30N 35 45 E
Al Līth, *Si. Arabia* **88** 20 9N 40 15 E
Al Lubban, *Jordan* **44** 32 9N 35 14 E
Al Luḥayyah, *Yemen* **45** 15 45N 42 40 E
Al Madīnah, *Si. Arabia* **46** 24 35N 39 52 E
Al-Mafraq, *Jordan* **44** 32 17N 36 14 E
Al Majma'ah, *Si. Arabia* **46** 25 57N 45 22 E
Al Makīlī, *Libya* **86** 32 10N 22 17 E
Al Manāmah, *Bahrain* **47** 26 10N 50 30 E
Al Marj, *Libya* **86** 32 25N 20 30 E
Al Mawşil, *Iraq* **46** 36 15N 43 5 E
Al Mazra, *Jordan* **44** 31 16N 35 31 E
Al Midhnab, *Si. Arabia* **46** 25 50N 44 18 E
Al Miqdādīyah, *Iraq* **46** 34 0N 45 0 E
Al Mish'āb, *Si. Arabia* **46** 28 12N 48 36 E

Al Mubarraz, *Si. Arabia* **46** 25 30N 49 40 E
Al Muḩarraq, *Bahrain* **47** 26 15N 50 40 E
Al Mukallā, *S. Yemen* **45** 14 33N 49 2 E
Al Mukhā, *Yemen* **45** 13 18N 43 15 E
Al Musayyib, *Iraq* **46** 32 40N 44 25 E
Al Muwayliḩ, *Si. Arabia* **46** 27 40N 35 30 E
Al Owuho = Otukpa, *Nigeria* **91** 7 9N 7 41 E
Al Qaddāhīyah, *Libya* **86** 31 15N 15 9 E
Al Qaḑīmah, *Si. Arabia* **46** 22 20N 39 13 E
Al Qā'iyah, *Si. Arabia* **46** 24 33N 43 15 E
Al Qāmishli, *Turkey* **46** 37 10N 41 10 E
Al Qaryah ash Sharqīyah, *Libya* **86** 30 28N 13 40 E
Al Qaşabát, *Libya* **86** 32 39N 14 1 E
Al Qaşīm, *Si. Arabia* **46** 26 0N 43 0 E
Al Qaţīf, *Si. Arabia* **46** 26 35N 50 0 E
Al Qaţrūn, *Libya* **86** 24 56N 15 3 E
Al Quaisūmah, *Si. Arabia* **46** 28 10N 46 20 E
Al Quds = Jerusalem, *Israel* **44** 31 47N 35 10 E
Al Qunfudhah, *Si. Arabia* **88** 19 3N 41 4 E
Al Qurayyāt, *Oman* **47** 23 17N 58 53 E
Al Qurnah, *Iraq* **46** 31 1N 47 25 E
Al 'Ulā, *Si. Arabia* **46** 26 35N 38 0 E
Al Uqaylah ash Sharqīgah, *Libya* **86** 30 12N 19 10 E
Al Uqayr, *Si. Arabia* **46** 25 40N 50 15 E
Al 'Uthmānīyah, *Si. Arabia* **46** 25 5N 49 22 E
Al 'Uwaynid, *Si. Arabia* **46** 24 50N 46 0 E
Al' 'Uwayqīlah, *Si. Arabia* **46** 30 30N 42 10 E
Al 'Uyūn, *Si. Arabia* **46** 26 30N 43 50 E
Al Wajh, *Si. Arabia* **88** 26 10N 36 30 E
Al Wakrah, *Qatar* **47** 25 10N 51 40 E
Al Wari'āh, *Si. Arabia* **46** 27 51N 47 25 E
Al Wātīyah, *Libya* **86** 32 28N 11 57 E
Al Yamāmah, *Si. Arabia* **46** 24 5N 47 30 E
Al Yāmūn, *Jordan* **44** 32 29N 35 14 E
Ala, *Italy* **26** 45 46N 11 0 E
Alabama □, *U.S.A.* **115** 33 0N 87 0W
Alabama →, *U.S.A.* **115** 31 8N 87 57W
Alaejos, *Spain* **22** 41 18N 5 13W
Alagna Valsésia, *Italy* **26** 45 51N 7 56 E
Alagoa Grande, *Brazil* **138** 7 3 S 35 35W
Alagoas □, *Brazil* **138** 9 0 S 36 0W
Alagoinhas, *Brazil* **139** 12 7 S 38 20W
Alagón, *Spain* **24** 41 46N 1 12W
Alagón →, *Spain* **23** 39 44N 6 53W
Alajero, *Canary Is.* **25** 28 3N 17 13W
Alajuela, *Costa Rica* **128** 10 2N 84 8W
Alakamisy, *Madag.* **97** 21 19 S 47 14 E
Alalapura, *Surinam* **135** 2 20N 56 25W
Alalaú →, *Brazil* **135** 0 30 S 61 9W
Alameda, *Spain* **23** 37 12N 4 39W
Alameda, *Calif., U.S.A.* **124** 37 46N 122 15W
Alameda, *N. Mex., U.S.A.* **123** 35 10N 106 43W
Alamo, *U.S.A.* **125** 36 21N 115 10W
Alamo Crossing, *U.S.A.* **125** 34 16N 113 33W
Alamogordo, *U.S.A.* **123** 32 59N 106 0W
Alamos, *Mexico* **126** 27 0N 109 0W
Alamosa, *U.S.A.* **123** 37 30N 106 0W
Åland, *Finland* **9** 60 15N 20 0 E
Aland, *India* **50** 17 36N 76 35 E
Alandroal, *Portugal* **23** 38 41N 7 24W
Ålands hav, *Sweden* **9** 60 0N 19 30 E
Alandur, *India* **51** 13 0N 80 15 E
Alange, Presa de, *Spain* **23** 38 45N 6 18W
Alanis, *Spain* **23** 38 3N 5 43W
Alanya, *Turkey* **46** 36 38N 32 0 E
Alaotra, Farihin', *Madag.* **97** 17 30 S 48 30 E
Alapayevsk, *U.S.S.R.* **40** 57 52N 61 42 E
Alar del Rey, *Spain* **22** 42 38N 4 20W
Alaraz, *Spain* **22** 40 45N 5 17W
Alaska □, *U.S.A.* **102** 65 0N 150 0W
Alaska, G. of, *Pac. Oc.* **102** 58 0N 145 0W
Alaska Highway, *Canada* **110** 60 0N 130 0W
Alaska Pen., *U.S.A.* **102** 56 0N 160 0W
Alaska Range, *U.S.A.* **102** 62 50N 151 0W
Alássio, *Italy* **26** 44 1N 8 10 E
Alataw Shankou, *China* **62** 45 5N 81 57 E
Alatri, *Italy* **28** 41 44N 13 21 E
Alatyr, *U.S.S.R.* **37** 54 45N 46 35 E
Alatyr →, *U.S.S.R.* **37** 54 52N 46 36 E
Alausi, *Ecuador* **134** 2 0 S 78 50W
Álava □, *Spain* **24** 42 48N 2 28W
Alava, C., *U.S.A.* **122** 48 10N 124 40W
Alaverdi, *U.S.S.R.* **39** 41 15N 44 37 E
Alawoona, *Australia* **73** 34 45 S 140 30 E
Alayor, *Spain* **24** 39 57N 4 8 E
Alazan →, *U.S.S.R.* **39** 41 5N 46 40 E
Alba, *Italy* **26** 44 41N 8 1 E
Alba de Tormes, *Spain* **22** 40 50N 5 30W
Alba Iulia, *Romania* **34** 46 8N 23 39 E
Albac, *Romania* **34** 46 28N 23 1 E
Albacete, *Spain* **25** 39 0N 1 50W
Albacete □, *Spain* **25** 38 50N 2 0W
Albacutya, L., *Australia* **74** 35 45 S 141 58 E
Ålbæk, *Denmark* **11** 57 36N 10 25 E
Ålbæk Bugt, *Denmark* **11** 57 35N 10 40 E
Albaida, *Spain* **25** 38 51N 0 31W
Albalate de las Nogueras, *Spain* **24** 40 22N 2 18W
Albalate del Arzobispo, *Spain* **24** 41 6N 0 31W
Albanel, *Canada* **107** 48 53N 72 27W
Albania ■, *Europe* **35** 41 0N 20 0 E
Albano Laziale, *Italy* **28** 41 44N 12 40 E
Albany, *Australia* **79** 35 1 S 117 58 E
Albany, *Ga., U.S.A.* **115** 31 40N 84 10W
Albany, *Ind., U.S.A.* **119** 40 18N 85 13W
Albany, *Minn., U.S.A.* **120** 45 37N 94 38W
Albany, *Mo., U.S.A.* **118** 40 15N 94 20W
Albany, *N.Y., U.S.A.* **117** 42 35N 73 47W
Albany, *Oreg., U.S.A.* **122** 44 41N 123 0W
Albany, *Tex., U.S.A.* **121** 32 45N 99 20W
Albany, *Wis., U.S.A.* **118** 42 43N 89 26W
Albany →, *Canada* **104** 52 17N 81 31W
Albardón, *Argentina* **140** 31 20 S 68 30W
Albarracín, *Spain* **24** 40 25N 1 26W
Albarracín, Sierra de, *Spain* **24** 40 30N 1 30W
Albatross B., *Australia* **72** 12 45 S 141 30 E
Albatross Pt., *N.Z.* **80** 38 7 S 174 44 E
Albegna →, *Italy* **27** 42 30N 11 11 E
Albemarle, *U.S.A.* **115** 35 27N 80 15W
Albemarle Sd., *U.S.A.* **115** 36 0N 76 30W
Albenga, *Italy* **26** 44 3N 8 12 E
Alberche →, *Spain* **22** 39 58N 4 46W
Alberdi, *Paraguay* **140** 26 14 S 58 20W
Alberes, Mts., *Spain* **24** 42 28N 2 56 E
Alberique, *Spain* **25** 39 7N 0 31W
Albersdorf, *W. Germany* **30** 54 8N 9 19 E
Albert, *Australia* **76** 32 22 S 147 30 E
Albert, *France* **19** 50 0N 2 38 E
Albert, L. = Mobutu Sese Seko, L., *Africa* **92** 1 30N 31 0 E
Albert, L., *Australia* **73** 35 30 S 139 10 E
Albert Canyon, *Canada* **110** 51 8N 117 41W
Albert Edward, Mt., *Papua N. G.* **69** 8 20 S 147 24 E
Albert Edward Ra., *Australia* **78** 18 17 S 127 57 E
Albert Lea, *U.S.A.* **120** 43 32N 93 20W
Albert Nile →, *Uganda* **92** 3 36N 32 2 E
Albert Town, *Bahamas* **129** 22 37N 74 33 E
Alberta □, *Canada* **110** 54 40N 115 0W
Alberti, *Argentina* **140** 35 1 S 60 16W
Albertinia, *S. Africa* **96** 34 11 S 21 34 E
Albertkanaal →, *Belgium* **17** 51 14N 4 26 E
Alberton, *Canada* **105** 46 50N 64 0W
Albertville = Kalemie, *Zaïre* **92** 5 55 S 29 9 E
Albertville, *France* **21** 45 40N 6 22 E
Albi, *France* **20** 43 56N 2 9 E
Albia, *U.S.A.* **118** 41 0N 92 50W
Albina, *Surinam* **135** 5 37N 54 15W
Albina, Ponta, *Angola* **95** 15 52 S 11 44 E
Albino, *Italy* **26** 45 47N 9 48 E
Albion, *Idaho, U.S.A.* **122** 42 21N 113 37W
Albion, *Ill., U.S.A.* **119** 38 23N 88 4W
Albion, *Ind., U.S.A.* **119** 41 24N 85 25W
Albion, *Mich., U.S.A.* **119** 42 15N 84 45W
Albion, *Nebr., U.S.A.* **120** 41 47N 98 0W
Albion, *Pa., U.S.A.* **116** 41 53N 80 21W
Albion Park, *Australia* **76** 34 36 S 150 45 E
Alblasserdam, *Neths.* **16** 51 52N 4 40 E
Albocácer, *Spain* **24** 40 21N 0 1 E
Alböke, *Sweden* **11** 56 57N 16 47 E
Alborán, *Medit. S.* **23** 35 57N 3 0W
Alborea, *Spain* **25** 39 17N 1 24W
Ålborg, *Denmark* **11** 57 2N 9 54 E
Ålborg Bugt, *Denmark* **11** 56 50N 10 35 E
Alborz, Reshteh-ye Kūhhā-ye, *Iran* **47** 36 0N 52 0 E
Albox, *Spain* **25** 37 23N 2 8W
Albreda, *Canada* **110** 52 35N 119 10W
Albuera, La, *Spain* **23** 38 45N 6 49W
Albufeira, *Portugal* **23** 37 5N 8 15W
Albula →, *Switz.* **31** 46 38N 9 30 E
Albuñol, *Spain* **25** 36 48N 3 11W
Albuquerque, *Brazil* **137** 19 23 S 57 26W
Albuquerque, *U.S.A.* **123** 35 5N 106 47W
Albuquerque, Cayos de, *Caribbean* **128** 12 10N 81 50W
Alburg, *U.S.A.* **117** 44 58N 73 19W
Alburno, Mte., *Italy* **29** 40 32N 15 15 E
Alburquerque, *Spain* **23** 39 15N 6 59W
Albury, *Australia* **75** 36 3 S 146 56 E
Alby, *Sweden* **10** 62 30N 15 28 E
Alcácer do Sal, *Portugal* **23** 38 22N 8 33W
Alcaçovas, *Portugal* **23** 38 23N 8 9W
Alcalá de Chisvert, *Spain* **24** 40 19N 0 13 E
Alcalá de Guadaira, *Spain* **23** 37 20N 5 50W
Alcalá de Henares, *Spain* **24** 40 28N 3 22W
Alcalá de los Gazules, *Spain* **23** 36 29N 5 43W
Alcalá la Real, *Spain* **23** 37 27N 3 57W
Alcamo, *Italy* **28** 37 59N 12 55 E
Alcanadre, *Spain* **24** 42 24N 2 7W
Alcanadre →, *Spain* **24** 41 43N 0 12W
Alcanar, *Spain* **24** 40 33N 0 28 E
Alcanede, *Portugal* **23** 39 25N 8 49W
Alcanena, *Portugal* **23** 39 27N 8 40W
Alcañices, *Spain* **22** 41 41N 6 21W
Alcañiz, *Spain* **24** 41 2N 0 8W
Alcântara, *Brazil* **138** 2 20 S 44 30W
Alcántara, *Spain* **23** 39 41N 6 57W
Alcantara L., *Canada* **111** 60 57N 108 9W
Alcantarilla, *Spain* **25** 37 59N 1 12W
Alcaracejos, *Spain* **23** 38 24N 4 58W
Alcaraz, *Spain* **25** 38 40N 2 29W
Alcaraz, Sierra de, *Spain* **25** 38 40N 2 20W
Alcarria, La, *Spain* **24** 40 31N 2 45W
Alcaudete, *Spain* **23** 37 35N 4 5W
Alcázar de San Juan, *Spain* **25** 39 24N 3 12W
Alcira, *Spain* **25** 39 9N 0 30W
Alcoa, *U.S.A.* **115** 35 50N 84 0W
Alcobaça, *Portugal* **23** 39 32N 9 0W
Alcobendas, *Spain* **24** 40 32N 3 38W
Alcolea del Pinar, *Spain* **24** 41 2N 2 28W
Alcora, *Spain* **24** 40 5N 0 14W
Alcoutim, *Portugal* **23** 37 25N 7 28W
Alcova, *U.S.A.* **122** 42 37N 106 52W
Alcoy, *Spain* **25** 38 43N 0 30W
Alcubierre, Sierra de, *Spain* **24** 41 45N 0 22W
Alcublas, *Spain* **24** 39 48N 0 43W
Alcudia, *Spain* **24** 39 51N 3 7 E
Alcudia, B. de, *Spain* **24** 39 47N 3 15 E
Alcudia, Sierra de la, *Spain* **23** 38 34N 4 30W
Aldabra Is., *Seychelles* **53** 9 22 S 46 28 E
Aldama, *Mexico* **127** 23 0N 98 4W
Aldan, *U.S.S.R.* **41** 58 40N 125 30 E
Aldan →, *U.S.S.R.* **41** 63 28N 129 35 E
Aldea, Pta. de la, *Canary Is.* **25** 28 0N 15 50W
Aldeburgh, *U.K.* **13** 52 9N 1 35 E
Aldeia Nova, *Portugal* **23** 37 55N 7 24W
Alder, *U.S.A.* **122** 45 27N 112 3W
Alder Pk., *U.S.A.* **124** 35 53N 121 22W
Alderney, *Chan. Is.* **18** 49 42N 2 12W
Aldershot, *U.K.* **13** 51 15N 0 43W
Alectown, *Australia* **76** 32 53 S 148 17 E
Aledo, *U.S.A.* **118** 41 10N 90 50W
Alefa, *Ethiopia* **89** 11 55N 36 55 E
Aleg, *Mauritania* **90** 17 3N 13 55W
Alegranza, *Canary Is.* **25** 29 23N 13 32W
Alegranza, I., *Canary Is.* **25** 29 23N 13 32W
Alegre, *Brazil* **139** 20 50 S 41 30W
Alegrete, *Brazil* **141** 29 40 S 56 0W
Aleisk, *U.S.S.R.* **40** 52 40N 83 0 E
Alejandro Selkirk, I., *Pac. Oc.* **67** 33 50 S 80 15W
Aleksandriya, *Ukraine S.S.R., U.S.S.R.* **36** 50 37N 26 19 E
Aleksandriya, *Ukraine S.S.R., U.S.S.R.* **38** 48 42N 33 3 E
Aleksandriyskaya, *U.S.S.R.* **39** 43 59N 47 0 E
Aleksandrov, *U.S.S.R.* **37** 56 23N 38 44 E
Aleksandrovac, *Yugoslavia* **33** 44 28N 21 13 E
Aleksandrovka, *U.S.S.R.* **38** 48 55N 32 20 E
Aleksandrovo, *Bulgaria* **34** 43 14N 24 51 E
Aleksandrovsk-Sakhalinskiy, *U.S.S.R.* **41** 50 50N 142 20 E
Aleksandrovskiy Zavod, *U.S.S.R.* **41** 50 40N 117 50 E
Aleksandrovskoye, *U.S.S.R.* **40** 60 35N 77 50 E
Aleksandrów Kujawski, *Poland* **32** 52 53N 18 43 E
Aleksandrów Łódźki, *Poland* **32** 51 49N 19 17 E
Alekseyevka, *U.S.S.R.* **37** 50 43N 38 40 E
Aleksin, *U.S.S.R.* **37** 54 31N 37 9 E
Aleksinac, *Yugoslavia* **33** 43 31N 21 42 E
Além Paraíba, *Brazil* **139** 21 52 S 42 41W
Alemania, *Argentina* **140** 25 40 S 65 30W
Alemania, *Chile* **140** 25 10 S 69 55W
Ålen, *Norway* **10** 62 51N 11 17 E
Alençon, *France* **18** 48 27N 0 4 E
Alenuihaha Chan., *U.S.A.* **112** 20 25N 156 0W
Aleppo = Ḩalab, *Syria* **46** 36 10N 37 15 E
Aléria, *France* **21** 42 5N 9 26 E
Alert Bay, *Canada* **110** 50 30N 126 55W
Alès, *France* **21** 44 9N 4 5 E
Aleşd, *Romania* **34** 47 3N 22 22 E
Alessándria, *Italy* **26** 44 54N 8 37 E
Ålestrup, *Denmark* **11** 56 42N 9 29 E
Ålesund, *Norway* **8** 62 28N 6 12 E
Alet-les-Bains, *France* **20** 42 59N 2 14 E
Aleutian Is., *Pac. Oc.* **102** 52 0N 175 0W
Aleutian Trench, *Pac. Oc.* **66** 48 0N 180 0 E
Alexander, *U.S.A.* **120** 47 51N 103 40W
Alexander, C., *Solomon Is.* **68** 6 35 S 156 30 E
Alexander, Mt., *Australia* **79** 28 58 S 120 16 E
Alexander Arch., *U.S.A.* **102** 57 0N 135 0W
Alexander B., *S. Africa* **96** 28 36 S 16 33 E
Alexander Bay, *S. Africa* **96** 28 40 S 16 30 E
Alexander City, *U.S.A.* **115** 32 58N 85 57W
Alexander I., *Antarctica* **143** 69 0 S 70 0W
Alexandra, *Australia* **74** 37 8 S 145 40 E
Alexandra, *N.Z.* **81** 45 14 S 169 25 E
Alexandra Falls, *Canada* **110** 60 29N 116 18W
Alexandretta = İskenderun, *Turkey* **46** 36 32N 36 10 E
Alexandria = El Iskandarîya, *Egypt* **88** 31 0N 30 0 E
Alexandria, *Australia* **72** 19 5 S 136 40 E
Alexandria, *B.C., Canada* **110** 52 35N 122 27W
Alexandria, *Ont., Canada* **109** 45 19N 74 38W
Alexandria, *Romania* **34** 43 57N 25 24 E
Alexandria, *S. Africa* **96** 33 38 S 26 28 E
Alexandria, *Ind., U.S.A.* **119** 40 18N 85 40W
Alexandria, *Ky., U.S.A.* **119** 38 58N 84 23W
Alexandria, *La., U.S.A.* **121** 31 20N 92 30W
Alexandria, *Minn., U.S.A.* **120** 45 50N 95 20W
Alexandria, *Mo., U.S.A.* **118** 40 27N 91 28W
Alexandria, *S. Dak., U.S.A.* **120** 43 40N 97 45W
Alexandria, *Va., U.S.A.* **114** 38 47N 77 1W
Alexandria Bay, *U.S.A.* **117** 44 20N 75 52W
Alexandrina, L., *Australia* **73** 35 25 S 139 10 E
Alexandroúpolis, *Greece* **35** 40 50N 25 54 E
Alexis, *U.S.A.* **118** 41 4N 90 33W
Alexis →, *Canada* **105** 52 33N 56 8W
Alexis Creek, *Canada* **110** 52 10N 123 20W
Alfambra, *Spain* **24** 40 33N 1 5W
Alfândega da Fé, *Portugal* **22** 41 20N 6 59W
Alfaro, *Spain* **24** 42 10N 1 50W
Alfeld, *W. Germany* **30** 52 0N 9 49 E
Alfenas, *Brazil* **141** 21 20 S 46 10W
Alfiós →, *Greece* **35** 37 40N 21 33 E
Alfonsine, *Italy* **27** 44 30N 12 1 E
Alford, *U.K.* **14** 57 13N 2 42W
Alfred, *Maine, U.S.A.* **117** 43 28N 70 40W
Alfred, *N.Y., U.S.A.* **116** 42 15N 77 45W
Alfred Town, *Australia* **76** 35 8 S 147 30 E
Alfredton, *N.Z.* **80** 40 41 S 175 54 E
Alfreton, *U.K.* **12** 53 6N 1 22W
Alfta, *Sweden* **10** 61 21N 16 4 E
Alga, *U.S.S.R.* **40** 49 53N 57 20 E
Algaba, La, *Spain* **23** 37 27N 6 1W
Algar, *Spain* **23** 36 40N 5 39W
Algarinejo, *Spain* **23** 37 19N 4 9W
Algarve, *Portugal* **23** 36 58N 8 20W
Algeciras, *Spain* **23** 36 9N 5 28W
Algemesí, *Spain* **25** 39 11N 0 27W
Alger, *Algeria* **85** 36 42N 3 8 E
Algeria ■, *Africa* **85** 28 30N 2 0 E
Alghero, *Italy* **28** 40 34N 8 20 E
Algiers = Alger, *Algeria* **85** 36 42N 3 8 E
Algoa B., *S. Africa* **96** 33 50 S 25 45 E
Algodonales, *Spain* **23** 36 54N 5 24W
Algodor →, *Spain* **22** 39 55N 3 53W
Algoma, *U.S.A.* **114** 44 35N 87 27W
Algona, *U.S.A.* **118** 43 4N 94 14W
Algonac, *U.S.A.* **116** 42 37N 82 32W
Algonquin Prov. Park, *Canada* **109** 45 50N 78 30W
Alhama de Almería, *Spain* **25** 36 57N 2 34W
Alhama de Aragón, *Spain* **24** 41 18N 1 54W
Alhama de Granada, *Spain* **23** 37 0N 3 59W
Alhama de Murcia, *Spain* **25** 37 51N 1 25W
Alhambra, *Spain* **25** 38 54N 3 4W
Alhambra, *Calif., U.S.A.* **125** 34 2N 118 10W
Alhambra, *Ill., U.S.A.* **118** 38 52N 89 45W
Alhaurín el Grande, *Spain* **23** 36 39N 4 41W
Alhucemas = Al Hoceïma, *Morocco* **84** 35 8N 3 58W
'Alī al Gharbī, *Iraq* **46** 32 30N 46 45 E
Ali Bayramly, *U.S.S.R.* **39** 39 59N 48 52 E
'Alī Khēl, *Afghan.* **48** 33 57N 69 43 E
Ali Sahīh, *Djibouti* **89** 11 10N 42 44 E
Ália, *Italy* **28** 37 47N 13 42 E
Aliaga, *Spain* **24** 40 40N 0 42W
Aliákmon →, *Greece* **35** 40 30N 22 36 E
Alibag, *India* **50** 18 38N 72 56 E
Alibo, *Ethiopia* **89** 9 52N 37 5 E
Alibunar, *Yugoslavia* **33** 45 5N 20 57 E
Alicante, *Spain* **25** 38 23N 0 30W
Alicante □, *Spain* **25** 38 30N 0 37W
Alice, *Canada* **109** 45 47N 77 14W
Alice, *S. Africa* **96** 32 48 S 26 55 E
Alice, *U.S.A.* **121** 27 47N 98 1W
Alice →, *Queens., Australia* **72** 24 2 S 144 50 E
Alice →, *Queens., Australia* **72** 15 35 S 142 20 E
Alice, Punta dell', *Italy* **29** 39 23N 17 10 E
Alice Arm, *Canada* **110** 55 29N 129 31W
Alice Downs, *Australia* **78** 17 45 S 127 56 E
Alice Springs, *Australia* **72** 23 40 S 133 50 E
Alicedale, *S. Africa* **96** 33 15 S 26 4 E
Aliceville, *U.S.A.* **115** 33 9N 88 10W
Alick Cr. →, *Australia* **72** 20 55 S 142 20 E
Alicudi, I., *Italy* **29** 38 33N 14 20 E

Alida, Canada 111 49 25N 101 55W
Aligarh, Raj., India 48 25 55N 76 15 E
Aligarh, Ut. P., India 48 27 55N 78 10 E
Aligūdarz, Iran 46 33 25N 49 45 E
Alijó, Portugal 22 41 16N 7 27W
Alimena, Italy 29 37 42N 14 4 E
Alindao, C.A.R. 94 5 2N 21 13 E
Alingsås, Sweden 11 57 56N 12 31 E
Alipur, Pakistan 48 29 25N 70 55 E
Alipur Duar, India 52 26 30N 89 35 E
Aliquippa, U.S.A. 116 40 38N 80 18W
Aliste →, Spain 22 41 34N 5 58W
Alitus, U.S.S.R. 36 54 24N 24 3 E
Alivérion, Greece 35 38 24N 24 2 E
Aliwal North, S. Africa 96 30 45 S 26 45 E
Alix, Canada 110 52 24N 113 11W
Aljezur, Portugal 23 37 18N 8 49W
Aljustrel, Portugal 23 37 55N 8 10W
Alkamari, Niger 91 13 27N 11 10 E
Alken, Belgium 17 50 53N 5 18 E
Alkmaar, Neths. 16 52 37N 4 45 E
All American Canal, U.S.A. 123 32 45N 115 0W
Allada, Benin 91 6 41N 2 9 E
Allah Dad, Pakistan 48 25 38N 67 34 E
Allahabad, India 49 25 25N 81 58 E
Allakh-Yun, U.S.S.R. 41 60 50N 137 5 E
Allal Tazi, Morocco 84 34 30N 6 20W
Allan, Canada 111 51 53N 106 4W
Allanche, France 20 45 14N 2 57 E
Allanmyo, Burma 52 19 30N 95 17 E
Allanridge, S. Africa 96 27 45 S 26 40 E
Allansford, Australia 74 38 26 S 142 39 E
Allanton, N.Z. 81 45 55 S 170 15 E
Allanwater, Canada 104 50 14N 90 10W
Allaqi, Wadi →, Egypt 88 23 7N 32 47 E
Allariz, Spain 22 42 11N 7 50W
Allassac, France 20 45 15N 1 29 E
Alle, Belgium 17 49 51N 4 58 E
Allegan, U.S.A. 119 42 32N 85 52W
Allegany, U.S.A. 116 42 6N 78 30W
Allegheny →, U.S.A. 116 40 27N 80 0W
Allegheny Mts., U.S.A. 114 38 0N 80 0W
Allegheny Res., U.S.A. 116 42 0N 78 55W
Allègre, France 20 45 12N 3 41 E
Allen, Argentina 142 38 58 S 67 50W
Allen, Bog of, Ireland 15 53 15N 7 0W
Allen, L., Ireland 15 54 12N 8 5W
Allenby Br. = Jisr al Ḩusayn, Jordan 44 31 53N 35 33 E
Allende, Mexico 126 28 20N 100 50W
Allentown, U.S.A. 117 40 36N 75 30W
Alleppey, India 51 9 30N 76 28 E
Aller →, W. Germany 30 52 57N 9 10 E
Alleur, Belgium 17 50 39N 5 31 E
Allevard, France 21 45 24N 6 5 E
Alliance, Surinam 135 5 50N 54 50W
Alliance, Nebr., U.S.A. 120 42 10N 102 50W
Alliance, Ohio, U.S.A. 116 40 53N 81 7W
Allier □, France 20 46 25N 3 0 E
Allier →, France 19 46 57N 3 4 E
Allingåbro, Denmark 11 56 28N 10 20 E
Allinge, Denmark 11 55 17N 14 50 E
Allison, U.S.A. 118 42 45N 92 48W
Alliston, Canada 108 44 9N 79 52W
Alloa, U.K. 14 56 7N 3 49W
Allora, Australia 77 28 2 S 152 0 E
Allos, France 21 44 15N 6 38 E
Alma, Canada 107 48 35N 71 40W
Alma, Ga., U.S.A. 115 31 33N 82 28W
Alma, Kans., U.S.A. 120 39 1N 96 22W
Alma, Mich., U.S.A. 104 43 25N 84 40W
Alma, Nebr., U.S.A. 120 40 10N 99 25W
Alma, Wis., U.S.A. 120 44 19N 91 54W
'Almā ash Sha'b, Lebanon 44 33 7N 35 9 E
Alma Ata, U.S.S.R. 40 43 15N 76 57 E
Almada, Portugal 23 38 40N 9 9W
Almaden, Australia 72 17 22 S 144 40 E
Almadén, Spain 23 38 49N 4 52W
Almagro, Spain 23 38 50N 3 45W
Almanor, L., U.S.A. 122 40 15N 121 11W
Almansa, Spain 25 38 51N 1 5W
Almanza, Spain 22 42 39N 5 3W
Almanzor, Pico de, Spain 22 40 15N 5 18W
Almanzora →, Spain 25 37 14N 1 46W
Almarcha, La, Spain 24 39 41N 2 24W
Almas, Brazil 139 11 33 S 47 9W
Almazán, Spain 24 41 30N 2 30W
Almazora, Spain 24 39 57N 0 3W
Almeirim, Brazil 135 1 30 S 52 34W
Almeirim, Portugal 23 39 12N 8 37W
Almelo, Neths. 16 52 22N 6 42 E
Almenar, Spain 24 41 43N 2 12W
Almenara, Brazil 139 16 11 S 40 42W
Almenara, Spain 24 39 46N 0 14W
Almenara, Sierra de, Spain 25 37 34N 1 32W
Almendralejo, Spain 23 38 41N 6 26W
Almería, Spain 25 36 52N 2 27W
Almería □, Spain 25 37 20N 2 20W
Almería, G. de, Spain 25 36 41N 2 28W
Älmhult, Sweden 11 56 33N 14 8 E
Almirante, Panama 128 9 10N 82 30W
Almirante Montt, G., Chile 142 51 52 S 72 50W
Almirós, Greece 35 39 11N 22 45 E
Almodôvar, Portugal 23 37 31N 8 2W
Almodóvar del Campo, Spain 23 38 43N 4 10W
Almogia, Spain 23 36 50N 4 32W
Almonaster la Real, Spain 23 37 52N 6 48W
Almont, U.S.A. 116 42 53N 83 2W
Almonte, Canada 106 45 14N 76 12W
Almonte →, Spain 23 39 41N 6 28W
Almora, India 49 29 38N 79 40 E
Almoradi, Spain 25 38 7N 0 46W
Almorox, Spain 22 40 14N 4 24W
Almoustarat, Mali 91 17 35N 0 8 E
Almuñécar, Spain 23 36 43N 3 41W
Almunia de Doña Godina, La, Spain 24 41 29N 1 23W
Alnif, Morocco 84 31 10N 5 8W
Alnwick, U.K. 12 55 25N 1 42W
Aloi, Uganda 92 2 16N 33 10 E
Alon, Burma 52 22 12N 95 5 E
Alor, Indonesia 57 8 15 S 124 30 E
Alor Setar, Malaysia 55 6 7N 100 22 E
Alora, Spain 23 36 49N 4 46W
Alosno, Spain 23 37 33N 7 7W
Alotau, Papua N. G. 69 10 16 S 150 30 E
Alougoum, Morocco 84 30 17N 6 56W
Aloysius Mt., Australia 79 26 0 S 128 38 E
Alpaugh, U.S.A. 124 35 53N 119 29W
Alpedrinha, Portugal 22 40 6N 7 27W
Alpena, U.S.A. 104 45 6N 83 24W
Alpercatas →, Brazil 138 6 2 S 44 19W
Alpes-de-Haute-Provence □, France 21 44 8N 6 10 E
Alpes-Maritimes □, France 21 43 55N 7 10 E
Alpha, Australia 72 23 39 S 146 37 E
Alpha, U.S.A. 118 41 11N 90 23W
Alphen, Neths. 17 51 29N 4 58 E
Alphen aan den Rijn, Neths. 16 52 7N 4 40 E
Alphonse, Seychelles 53 7 0 S 52 45 E
Alpiarça, Portugal 23 39 15N 8 35W
Alpine, Ariz., U.S.A. 123 33 57N 109 4W
Alpine, Calif., U.S.A. 125 32 50N 116 46W
Alpine, Tex., U.S.A. 121 30 25N 103 35W
Alps, Europe 6 47 0N 8 0 E
Alpujarras, Las, Spain 25 36 55N 3 20W
Alrø, Denmark 11 55 52N 10 5 E
Alroy Downs, Australia 72 19 20 S 136 5 E
Alsace, France 19 48 15N 7 25 E
Alsask, Canada 111 51 21N 109 59W
Alsásua, Spain 24 42 54N 2 10W
Alsen, Sweden 10 63 23N 13 56 E
Alsfeld, W. Germany 30 50 44N 9 19 E
Alsten, Norway 8 65 58N 12 40 E
Alstonville, Australia 77 28 51 S 153 27 E
Alta, Norway 8 69 57N 23 10 E
Alta, Sierra, Spain 24 40 31N 1 30W
Alta Gracia, Argentina 140 31 40 S 64 30W
Alta Lake, Canada 110 50 10N 123 0W
Alta Sierra, U.S.A. 125 35 42N 118 33W
Altaelva →, Norway 8 69 46N 23 45 E
Altafjorden, Norway 8 70 5N 23 5 E
Altagracia, Venezuela 134 10 45N 71 30W
Altagracia de Orituco, Venezuela 134 9 52N 66 23W
Altai = Aerht'ai Shan, Mongolia 62 46 40N 92 45 E
Altamachi →, Bolivia 136 16 8 S 66 50W
Altamaha →, U.S.A. 115 31 19N 81 17W
Altamira, Brazil 135 3 12 S 52 10W
Altamira, Chile 140 25 47 S 69 51W
Altamira, Colombia 134 2 3N 75 47W
Altamira, Mexico 127 22 24N 97 55W
Altamira, Cuevas de, Spain 22 43 20N 4 5W
Altamont, Ill., U.S.A. 119 39 4N 88 45W
Altamont, N.Y., U.S.A. 117 42 43N 74 3W
Altamura, Italy 29 40 50N 16 33 E
Altanbulag, Mongolia 62 50 16N 106 30 E
Altar, Mexico 126 30 40N 111 50W
Altata, Mexico 126 24 30N 108 0W
Altavista, U.S.A. 114 37 9N 79 22W
Altay, China 62 47 48N 88 10 E
Altdorf, Switz. 31 46 52N 8 36 E
Alte Mellum, W. Germany 30 53 45N 8 6 E
Altea, Spain 25 38 38N 0 2W
Altenberg, E. Germany 30 50 46N 13 47 E
Altenbruch, W. Germany 30 53 48N 8 44 E
Altenburg, E. Germany 30 50 59N 12 28 E
Altenkirchen, E. Germany 30 54 38N 13 20 E
Altenkirchen, W. Germany 30 50 41N 7 38 E
Altenteptow, E. Germany 30 53 42N 13 15 E
Alter do Chão, Portugal 23 39 12N 7 40W
Altiplano, Bolivia 136 17 0 S 68 0W
Altkirch, France 19 47 37N 7 15 E
Altmühl →, W. Germany 31 48 54N 11 54 E
Alto Adige = Trentino-Alto Adige □, Italy 26 46 30N 11 0 E
Alto Araguaia, Brazil 137 17 15 S 53 20W
Alto Chindio, Mozam. 93 16 19 S 35 25 E
Alto Cuchumatanes = Cuchumatanes, Sierra de los, Guatemala 128 15 35N 91 25W
Alto Cuito, Angola 95 13 27 S 18 49 E
Alto del Inca, Chile 140 24 10 S 68 10W
Alto Garças, Brazil 137 16 56 S 53 32W
Alto Iriri →, Brazil 137 8 50 S 53 25W
Alto Ligonha, Mozam. 93 15 30 S 38 11 E
Alto Molocue, Mozam. 93 15 50 S 37 35 E
Alto Paraguai, Brazil 137 14 30 S 56 31W
Alto Paraná □, Paraguay 141 25 0 S 54 50W
Alto Parnaíba, Brazil 138 9 6 S 45 57W
Alto Purús →, Peru 136 9 12 S 70 28W
Alto Río Senguerr, Argentina 142 45 2 S 70 50W
Alto Santo, Brazil 138 5 31 S 38 15W
Alto Sucuriú, Brazil 137 19 19 S 52 47W
Alto Turi, Brazil 138 2 54 S 45 38W
Alton, Australia 77 28 0 S 149 16 E
Alton, Canada 108 43 54N 80 5W
Alton, U.S.A. 118 38 55N 90 5W
Alton Downs, Australia 73 26 7 S 138 57 E
Altona, Australia 74 37 51 S 144 50 E
Altona, W. Germany 30 53 32N 9 56 E
Altoona, Iowa, U.S.A. 118 41 39N 93 28W
Altoona, Pa., U.S.A. 116 40 32N 78 24W
Altopáscio, Italy 26 43 50N 10 40 E
Altos, Brazil 138 5 3 S 42 28W
Altötting, W. Germany 31 48 14N 12 41 E
Altstätten, Switz. 31 47 22N 9 33 E
Altun Shan, China 62 38 30N 88 0 E
Alturas, U.S.A. 122 41 36N 120 37W
Altus, U.S.A. 121 34 30N 99 25W
Alucra, Turkey 39 40 22N 38 47 E
Aluksne, U.S.S.R. 36 57 24N 27 3 E
Alùla, Somali Rep. 98 11 50N 50 45 E
Alunite, U.S.A. 125 35 59N 114 55W
Alupka, U.S.S.R. 38 44 23N 34 2 E
Alushta, U.S.S.R. 38 44 40N 34 25 E
Alusi, Indonesia 57 7 35 S 131 40 E
Alustante, Spain 24 40 36N 1 40W
Alva, U.S.A. 121 36 50N 98 50W
Alvaiázere, Portugal 22 39 49N 8 23W
Älvängen, Sweden 11 57 58N 12 8 E
Alvarado, Mexico 127 18 40N 95 50W
Alvarado, U.S.A. 121 32 25N 97 15W
Alvarães, Brazil 135 3 12 S 64 50W
Alvaro Obregón, Presa, Mexico 126 27 55N 109 52W
Alvdal, Norway 10 62 6N 10 37 E
Alvear, Argentina 140 29 5 S 56 30W
Alverca, Portugal 23 38 56N 9 1W
Alveringen, Belgium 17 51 1N 2 43 E
Alvesta, Sweden 11 56 54N 14 35 E
Alvie, Australia 74 38 14 S 143 30 E
Alvin, U.S.A. 121 29 23N 95 12W
Alvinston, Canada 108 42 49N 81 52W
Alvito, Portugal 23 38 15N 8 0W
Älvkarleby, Sweden 9 60 34N 17 26 E
Älvros, Sweden 10 62 3N 14 38 E
Älvsborgs län □, Sweden 11 58 30N 12 30 E
Älvsbyn, Sweden 8 65 40N 21 0 E
Älvsered, Sweden 11 57 14N 12 51 E
Alwar, India 48 27 38N 76 34 E
Alwaye, India 51 10 8N 76 24 E
Alxa Zuoqi, China 60 38 50N 105 40 E
Alyaskitovyy, U.S.S.R. 41 64 45N 141 30 E
Alyata, U.S.S.R. 39 39 58N 49 25 E
Alyth, U.K. 14 56 38N 3 15W
Alzada, U.S.A. 120 45 3N 104 22W
Alzano Lombardo, Italy 26 45 44N 9 43 E
Alzette →, Lux. 17 49 45N 6 6 E
Alzey, W. Germany 31 49 48N 8 4 E
Am Dam, Chad 87 12 40N 20 35 E
Am Géréda, Chad 87 12 53N 21 14 E
Am-Timan, Chad 87 11 0N 20 10 E
Amacuro □, Venezuela 135 8 50N 61 5W
Amadeus, L., Australia 79 24 54 S 131 0 E
Amâdi, Sudan 89 5 29N 30 25 E
Amadi, Zaïre 92 3 40N 26 40 E
Amadjuak, Canada 103 64 0N 72 39W
Amadjuak L., Canada 103 65 0N 71 8W
Amadora, Portugal 23 38 45N 9 13W
Amagasaki, Japan 65 34 42N 135 20 E
Amager, Denmark 11 55 37N 12 35 E
Amagi, Japan 64 33 25N 130 39 E
Amaimon, Papua N. G. 69 5 12 S 145 30 E
Amakusa-Nada, Japan 64 32 35N 130 5 E
Amakusa-Shotō, Japan 64 32 15N 130 10 E
Åmål, Sweden 10 59 3N 12 42 E
Amalapuram, India 51 16 35N 81 55 E
Amalfi, Colombia 134 6 55N 75 4W
Amalfi, Italy 29 40 39N 14 34 E
Amaliás, Greece 35 37 47N 21 22 E
Amalner, India 50 21 5N 75 5 E
Amambaí, Brazil 141 23 5 S 55 13W
Amambaí →, Brazil 141 23 22 S 53 56W
Amambay □, Paraguay 141 23 0 S 56 0W
Amambay, Cordillera de, S. Amer. 141 23 0 S 55 45W
Amana →, Venezuela 135 9 45N 62 39W
Amaná, L., Brazil 135 2 35 S 64 40W
Amanab, Papua N. G. 69 3 40 S 141 14 E
Amanda Park, U.S.A. 124 47 28N 123 55W
Amándola, Italy 27 42 59N 13 21 E
Amangeldy, U.S.S.R. 40 50 10N 65 10 E
Amantea, Italy 29 39 8N 16 3 E
Amapá, Brazil 138 2 5N 50 50W
Amapá □, Brazil 138 1 40N 52 0W
Amapari, Brazil 135 0 37N 51 39W
Amara, Sudan 89 10 25N 34 10 E
Amarante, Brazil 138 6 14 S 42 50W
Amarante, Portugal 22 41 16N 8 5W
Amarante do Maranhão, Brazil 138 5 36 S 46 45W
Amaranth, Canada 111 50 36N 98 43W
Amarapura, Burma 52 21 54N 96 3 E
Amaravati →, India 51 11 0N 78 15 E
Amareleja, Portugal 23 38 12N 7 13W
Amargosa, Brazil 139 13 2 S 39 36W
Amargosa →, U.S.A. 125 36 14N 116 51W
Amargosa Ra., U.S.A. 125 36 25N 116 40W
Amarillo, U.S.A. 121 35 14N 101 46W
Amarnath, India 50 19 12N 73 22 E
Amaro, Mt., Italy 27 42 5N 14 6 E
Amaro Leite, Brazil 139 13 58 S 49 9W
Amarpur, India 49 25 5N 87 0 E
Amasra, Turkey 46 41 45N 32 30 E
Amassama, Nigeria 91 5 1N 6 2 E
Amasya, Turkey 46 40 40N 35 50 E
Amataurá, Brazil 134 3 29 S 68 6W
Amatikulu, S. Africa 97 29 3 S 31 33 E
Amatitlán, Guatemala 128 14 29N 90 38W
Amatrice, Italy 27 42 38N 13 16 E
Amay, Belgium 17 50 33N 5 19 E
Amazon = Amazonas →, S. Amer. 135 0 5 S 50 0W
Amazonas □, Brazil 136 4 0 S 62 0W
Amazonas □, Peru 136 5 0 S 78 0W
Amazonas □, Venezuela 134 3 30N 66 0W
Amazonas →, S. Amer. 135 0 5 S 50 0W
Ambad, India 50 19 38N 75 50 E
Ambahakily, Madag. 97 21 36 S 43 41 E
Ambala, India 48 30 23N 76 56 E
Ambalangoda, Sri Lanka 51 6 15N 80 5 E
Ambalapulai, India 51 9 25N 76 25 E
Ambalavao, Madag. 97 21 50 S 46 56 E
Ambalindum, Australia 72 23 23 S 135 0 E
Ambam, Cameroon 94 2 20N 11 15 E
Ambanja, Madag. 97 13 40 S 48 27 E
Ambarchik, U.S.S.R. 41 69 40N 162 20 E
Ambarijeby, Madag. 97 14 56 S 47 41 E
Ambaro, Helodranon', Madag. 97 13 23 S 48 38 E
Ambartsevo, U.S.S.R. 40 57 30N 83 52 E
Ambasamudram, India 51 8 43N 77 25 E
Ambato, Ecuador 134 1 5 S 78 42W
Ambato, Sierra de, Argentina 140 28 25 S 66 10W
Ambato Boeny, Madag. 97 16 28 S 46 43 E
Ambatofinandrahana, Madag. 97 20 33 S 46 48 E
Ambatolampy, Madag. 97 19 20 S 47 35 E
Ambatondrazaka, Madag. 97 17 55 S 48 28 E
Ambatosoratra, Madag. 97 17 37 S 48 31 E
Ambenja, Madag. 97 15 17 S 46 58 E
Amberg, W. Germany 31 49 25N 11 52 E
Ambergris Cay, Belize 127 18 0N 88 0W
Ambérieu-en-Bugey, France 21 45 57N 5 20 E
Amberley, N.Z. 81 43 9 S 172 44 E
Ambert, France 20 45 33N 3 44 E
Ambidédi, Mali 90 14 35N 11 47W
Ambikapur, India 49 23 15N 83 15 E
Ambikol, Sudan 88 21 20N 30 50 E
Ambilobé, Madag. 97 13 10 S 49 3 E
Ambinanindrano, Madag. 97 20 5 S 48 23 E
Ambjörnarp, Sweden 11 57 25N 13 17 E
Ambleside, U.K. 12 54 26N 2 58W
Amblève, Belgium 17 50 21N 6 10 E
Amblève →, Belgium 17 50 25N 5 45 E
Ambo, Ethiopia 89 12 20N 37 30 E
Ambo, Peru 136 10 5 S 76 10W
Ambodifototra, Madag. 97 16 59 S 49 52 E
Ambodilazana, Madag. 97 18 6 S 49 10 E
Ambohimahasoa, Madag. 97 21 7 S 47 13 E
Ambohimanga, Madag. 97 20 52 S 47 36 E
Ambohitra, Madag. 97 12 30 S 49 10 E
Ambon, Indonesia 57 3 35 S 128 20 E
Amboseli L., Kenya 92 2 40 S 37 10 E
Ambositra, Madag. 97 20 31 S 47 25 E
Ambovombé, Madag. 97 25 11 S 46 5 E
Amboy, Calif., U.S.A. 125 34 33N 115 51W
Amboy, Ill., U.S.A. 118 41 44N 89 20W
Amboyna I., S. China Sea 56 7 50N 112 50 E
Ambridge, U.S.A. 116 40 36N 80 15W
Ambriz, Angola 95 7 48 S 13 8 E
Ambrym, Vanuatu 68 16 15 S 168 10 E
Ambunti, Papua N. G. 69 4 13 S 142 52 E
Ambur, India 51 12 48N 78 43 E
Amby, Australia 73 26 30 S 148 11 E
Amchitka I., U.S.A. 102 51 30N 179 0W
Amderma, U.S.S.R. 40 69 45N 61 30 E
Ameca, Mexico 126 20 30N 104 0W
Ameca →, Mexico 126 20 40N 105 15W
Amecameca, Mexico 127 19 7N 98 46W
Ameland, Neths. 16 53 27N 5 45 E
Amélia, Italy 27 42 34N 12 25 E
Amélie-les-Bains-Palalda, France 20 42 29N 2 41 E
Amen, U.S.S.R. 41 68 45N 180 0 E
Amendolaro, Italy 29 39 58N 16 34 E
America, Neths. 17 51 27N 5 59 E
American Falls, U.S.A. 122 42 46N 112 56W
American Falls Res., U.S.A. 122 43 0N 112 50W
American Highland, Antarctica 143 73 0 S 75 0 E
American Samoa ■, Pac. Oc. 68 14 20 S 170 40W
Americana, Brazil 141 22 45 S 47 20W
Americus, U.S.A. 115 32 0N 84 10W
Amersfoort, Neths. 16 52 9N 5 23 E
Amersfoort, S. Africa 97 26 59 S 29 53 E

Amery, *Australia* **79** 31 9 S 117 5 E
Amery, *Canada* **111** 56 34N 94 3W
Amery Ice Shelf, *Antarctica* **143** 69 30 S 72 0 E
Ames, *U.S.A.* **118** 42 0N 93 40W
Amesbury, *U.S.A.* **117** 42 50N 70 52W
Amfíklia, *Greece* **35** 38 38N 22 35 E
Amfilokhía, *Greece* **35** 38 52N 21 9 E
Amga, *U.S.S.R.* **41** 60 50N 132 0 E
Amga →, *U.S.S.R.* **41** 62 38N 134 32 E
Amgu, *U.S.S.R.* **41** 45 45N 137 15 E
Amgun →, *U.S.S.R.* **41** 52 56N 139 38 E
Amherst, *Canada* **105** 45 48N 64 8W
Amherst, *Mass., U.S.A.* **117** 42 21N 72 30W
Amherst, *N.Y., U.S.A.* **116** 42 59N 78 48W
Amherst, *Ohio, U.S.A.* **116** 41 23N 82 15W
Amherst, *Tex., U.S.A.* **121** 34 0N 102 24W
Amherst I., *Canada* **109** 44 8N 76 43W
Amherstburg, *Canada* **108** 42 6N 83 6W
Amiata, Mte., *Italy* **27** 42 54N 11 40 E
Amiens, *Australia* **77** 28 35 S 151 48 E
Amiens, *France* **19** 49 54N 2 16 E
Amili, *India* **52** 28 25N 95 52 E
Amindaion, *Greece* **35** 40 42N 21 42 E
Amirante Is., *Seychelles* **53** 6 0 S 53 0 E
Amisk L., *Canada* **111** 54 35N 102 15W
Amistad, Presa de la, *Mexico* **126** 29 24N 101 0W
Amite, *U.S.A.* **121** 30 47N 90 31W
Amizmiz, *Morocco* **84** 31 12N 8 15W
Åmli, *Norway* **11** 58 45N 8 32 E
Amlwch, *U.K.* **12** 53 24N 4 21W
Amm Adam, *Sudan* **89** 16 20N 36 1 E
'Ammān, *Jordan* **44** 31 57N 35 52 E
Ammanford, *U.K.* **13** 51 48N 4 0W
Ammerån, *Sweden* **10** 63 9N 16 13 E
Ammerån →, *Sweden* **10** 63 9N 16 13 E
Ammersee, *W. Germany* **31** 48 0N 11 7 E
Ammerzoden, *Neths.* **16** 51 45N 5 13 E
Ammi'ad, *Israel* **44** 32 55N 35 32 E
Amnat Charoen, *Thailand* **54** 15 51N 104 38 E
Amo Jiang →, *China* **58** 23 0N 101 50 E
Amorebieta, *Spain* **24** 43 13N 2 44W
Amoret, *U.S.A.* **118** 38 15N 94 35W
Amorgós, *Greece* **35** 36 50N 25 57 E
Amory, *U.S.A.* **115** 33 59N 88 29W
Amos, *Canada* **106** 48 35N 78 5W
Åmot, *Buskerud, Norway* **10** 59 54N 9 54 E
Åmot, *Telemark, Norway* **10** 59 34N 8 0 E
Åmotsdal, *Norway* **10** 59 37N 8 26 E
Amour, Djebel, *Algeria* **85** 33 42N 1 37 E
Amoy = Xiamen, *China* **59** 24 25N 118 4 E
Ampang, *Malaysia* **55** 3 8N 101 45 E
Ampanihy, *Madag.* **97** 24 40 S 44 45 E
Ampasindava, Helodranon', *Madag.* **97** 13 40 S 48 15 E
Ampasindava, Saikanosy, *Madag.* **97** 13 42 S 47 55 E
Ampato, Nevado, *Peru* **136** 15 40 S 71 56W
Ampenan, *Indonesia* **56** 8 35 S 116 13 E
Amper, *Nigeria* **91** 9 25N 9 40 E
Amper →, *W. Germany* **31** 48 30N 11 57 E
Ampère, *Algeria* **85** 35 44N 5 27 E
Ampezzo, *Italy* **27** 46 25N 12 48 E
Amphitheatre, *Australia* **74** 37 11 S 143 22 E
Amposta, *Spain* **24** 40 43N 0 34 E
Ampotaka, *Madag.* **97** 25 3 S 44 41 E
Ampoza, *Madag.* **97** 22 20 S 44 44 E
Amqa, *Israel* **44** 32 59N 35 10 E
Amqui, *Canada* **105** 48 28N 67 27W
Amravati, *India* **50** 20 55N 77 45 E
Amreli, *India* **48** 21 35N 71 17 E
Amrenene el Kasba, *Algeria* **85** 22 10N 0 30 E
Amritsar, *India* **48** 31 35N 74 57 E
Amroha, *India* **49** 28 53N 78 30 E
Amrum, *W. Germany* **30** 54 37N 8 21 E
Amsel, *Algeria* **85** 22 47N 5 29 E
Amsterdam, *Neths.* **16** 52 23N 4 54 E
Amsterdam, *U.S.A.* **117** 42 58N 74 10W
Amsterdam, I., *Ind. Oc.* **53** 38 30 S 77 30 E
Amstetten, *Austria* **33** 48 7N 14 51 E
Amudarya →, *U.S.S.R.* **40** 43 40N 59 0 E
Amund Ringnes I., *Canada* **144** 78 20N 96 25W
Amundsen Gulf, *Canada* **102** 71 0N 124 0W
Amundsen Sea, *Antarctica* **143** 72 0 S 115 0W
Amungen, *Sweden* **10** 61 10N 15 40 E
Amuntai, *Indonesia* **56** 2 28 S 115 25 E
Amur, *Somali Rep.* **98** 5 16N 46 30 E
Amur →, *U.S.S.R.* **41** 52 56N 141 10 E
Amurang, *Indonesia* **57** 1 5N 124 40 E
Amuri Pass, *N.Z.* **81** 42 31 S 172 11 E
Amurrio, *Spain* **24** 43 3N 3 0W
Amursk, *U.S.S.R.* **41** 50 14N 136 54 E
Amurzet, *U.S.S.R.* **41** 47 50N 131 5 E
Amusco, *Spain* **22** 42 10N 4 28W
Amvrakikós Kólpos, *Greece* **35** 39 0N 20 55 E
Amvrosiyevka, *U.S.S.R.* **39** 47 43N 38 30 E
Amzeglouf, *Algeria* **85** 26 50N 0 1 E
An, *Burma* **52** 19 48N 94 0W
An Bien, *Vietnam* **55** 9 45N 105 0 E
An Hoa, *Vietnam* **54** 15 40N 108 5 E
An Khe, *Vietnam* **54** 13 57N 108 39 E
An Nafūd, *Si. Arabia* **46** 28 15N 41 0 E
An Najaf, *Iraq* **46** 32 3N 44 15 E
An Nāqūrah, *Lebanon* **44** 33 7N 35 8 E
An Nāṣirīyah, *Iraq* **46** 31 0N 46 15 E
An Nawfaliyah, *Libya* **86** 30 54N 17 58 E
An Nhon, *Vietnam* **54** 13 55N 109 7 E
An Nîl □, *Sudan* **88** 19 30N 33 0 E
An Nîl el Abyad □, *Sudan* **89** 14 0N 32 15 E
An Nîl el Azraq □, *Sudan* **89** 12 30N 34 30 E
An Nu'ayrīyah, *Si. Arabia* **46** 27 30N 48 30 E
An Thoi, Dao, *Vietnam* **55** 9 58N 104 0 E
An Uaimh, *Ireland* **15** 53 39N 6 40W
Anabar →, *U.S.S.R.* **41** 73 8N 113 36 E
'Anabtā, *Jordan* **44** 32 19N 35 7 E
Anabuki, *Japan* **64** 34 2N 134 11 E
Anaco, *Venezuela* **135** 9 27N 64 28W
Anaconda, *U.S.A.* **122** 46 7N 113 0W
Anacortes, *U.S.A.* **110** 48 30N 122 40W
Anadarko, *U.S.A.* **121** 35 4N 98 15W
Anadia, *Brazil* **138** 9 42 S 36 18W
Anadia, *Portugal* **22** 40 26N 8 27W
Anadolu, *Turkey* **46** 38 0N 30 0 E
Anadyr, *U.S.S.R.* **41** 64 35N 177 20 E
Anadyr →, *U.S.S.R.* **41** 64 55N 176 5 E
Anadyrskiy Zaliv, *U.S.S.R.* **41** 64 0N 180 0 E
Anáfi, *Greece* **35** 36 22N 25 48 E
Anafópoulo, *Greece* **35** 36 17N 25 50 E
Anaga, Pta. de, *Canary Is.* **25** 28 34N 16 9W
Anagni, *Italy* **28** 41 44N 13 8 E
'Ānah, *Iraq* **46** 34 25N 42 0 E
Anaheim, *U.S.A.* **125** 33 50N 118 0W
Anahim Lake, *Canada* **110** 52 28N 125 18W
Anáhuac, *Mexico* **126** 27 14N 100 9W
Anai Mudi, Mt., *India* **51** 10 12N 77 4 E
Anaimalai Hills, *India* **51** 10 20N 76 40 E
Anajás, *Brazil* **138** 0 59 S 49 57W
Anajatuba, *Brazil* **138** 3 16 S 44 37W
Anakapalle, *India* **50** 17 42N 83 6 E
Anakie, *Australia* **72** 23 32 S 147 45 E
Anaklia, *U.S.S.R.* **39** 42 22N 41 35 E
Analalava, *Madag.* **97** 14 35 S 48 0 E
Anamã, *Brazil* **135** 3 35 S 61 22W
Anambar →, *Pakistan* **48** 30 15N 68 50 E
Anambas, Kepulauan, *Indonesia* **56** 3 20N 106 30 E
Aname, *Vanuatu* **68** 20 8 S 169 47 E
Anamoose, *U.S.A.* **120** 47 55N 100 20W
Anamosa, *U.S.A.* **118** 42 7N 91 30W
Anamur, *Turkey* **46** 36 8N 32 58 E
Anan, *Japan* **64** 33 54N 134 40 E
Anand, *India* **48** 22 32N 72 59 E
Anandpur, *India* **50** 21 16N 86 13 E
Anantapur, *India* **51** 14 39N 77 42 E
Anantnag, *India* **49** 33 45N 75 10 E
Ananyev, *U.S.S.R.* **38** 47 44N 29 47 E
Anapa, *U.S.S.R.* **38** 44 55N 37 25 E
Anápolis, *Brazil* **139** 16 15 S 48 50W
Anapu →, *Brazil* **135** 1 53 S 50 53W
Anār, *Iran* **47** 30 55N 55 13 E
Anārak, *Iran* **47** 33 25N 53 40 E
Anatolia = Anadolu, *Turkey* **46** 38 0N 30 0 E
Anatone, *U.S.A.* **122** 46 9N 117 4W
Anatsogno, *Madag.* **97** 23 33 S 43 46 E
Añatuya, *Argentina* **140** 28 20 S 62 50W
Anauá →, *Brazil* **135** 0 58N 61 21W
Anaunethad L., *Canada* **111** 60 55N 104 25W
Anavilhanas, Arquipélago das, *Brazil* **135** 2 42 S 60 45W
Anaye, *Niger* **87** 19 15N 12 50 E
Ancash □, *Peru* **136** 9 30 S 77 45W
Ancenis, *France* **18** 47 21N 1 10W
Ancho, Canal, *Chile* **142** 50 0 S 74 20W
Anchor Bay, *U.S.A.* **124** 38 48N 123 34W
Anchorage, *U.S.A.* **102** 61 10N 149 50W
Anci, *China* **60** 39 20N 116 40 E
Ancohuma, Nevada, *Bolivia* **136** 16 0 S 68 50W
Ancón, *Peru* **136** 11 50 S 77 10W
Ancona, *Italy* **27** 43 37N 13 30 E
Ancud, *Chile* **142** 42 0 S 73 50W
Ancud, G. de, *Chile* **142** 42 0 S 73 0W
Andacollo, *Argentina* **140** 37 10 S 70 42W
Andacollo, *Chile* **140** 30 5 S 71 10W
Andado, *Australia* **72** 25 25 S 135 15 E
Andahuaylas, *Peru* **136** 13 40 S 73 25W
Andalgalá, *Argentina* **140** 27 40 S 66 30W
Åndalsnes, *Norway* **10** 62 35N 7 43 E
Andalucía □, *Spain* **23** 37 35N 5 0W
Andalusia, *U.S.A.* **115** 31 19N 86 30W
Andalusia □ = Andalucía □, *Spain* **23** 37 35N 5 0W
Andaman Is., *Ind. Oc.* **53** 12 30N 92 30 E
Andaman Sea, *Ind. Oc.* **56** 13 0N 96 0 E
Andara, *Namibia* **96** 18 2 S 21 9 E
Andaraí, *Brazil* **139** 12 48 S 41 20W
Andelot, *France* **19** 48 15N 5 18 E
Andelys, Les, *France* **18** 49 15N 1 25 E
Andenne, *Belgium* **17** 50 30N 5 5 E
Andéranboukane, *Mali* **91** 15 26N 3 2 E
Anderlecht, *Belgium* **17** 50 50N 4 19 E
Anderlues, *Belgium* **17** 50 25N 4 16 E
Andermatt, *Switz.* **31** 46 38N 8 35 E
Andernach, *W. Germany* **30** 50 24N 7 25 E
Andernos-les-Bains, *France* **20** 44 44N 1 6W
Anderslöv, *Sweden* **11** 55 26N 13 19 E
Anderson, *Calif., U.S.A.* **122** 40 30N 122 19W
Anderson, *Ind., U.S.A.* **119** 40 5N 85 40W
Anderson, *Mo., U.S.A.* **121** 36 43N 94 29W
Anderson, *S.C., U.S.A.* **115** 34 32N 82 40W
Anderson →, *Canada* **102** 69 42N 129 0W
Anderson, Mt., *S. Africa* **97** 25 5 S 30 42 E
Anderstorp, *Sweden* **11** 57 19N 13 39 E
Andes, *Colombia* **136** 5 40N 75 53W
Andes, Cord. de los, *S. Amer.* **136** 20 0 S 68 0W
Andfjorden, *Norway* **8** 69 10N 16 20 E
Andhra, L., *India* **50** 18 54N 73 32 E
Andhra Pradesh □, *India* **51** 16 0N 79 0 E
Andikíthira, *Greece* **35** 35 52N 23 15 E
Andímilos, *Greece* **35** 36 47N 24 12 E
Andípaxoi, *Greece* **35** 39 9N 20 13 E
Andizhan, *U.S.S.R.* **40** 41 10N 72 0 E
Andkhvoy, *Afghan.* **47** 36 52N 65 8 E
Andoany, *Madag.* **97** 13 25 S 48 16 E
Andoas, *Peru* **134** 2 55 S 76 25W
Andol, *India* **50** 17 51N 78 4 E
Andong, *S. Korea* **61** 36 40N 128 43 E
Andongwei, *China* **61** 35 6N 119 20 E
Andorra ■, *Europe* **24** 42 30N 1 30 E
Andorra La Vella, *Andorra* **24** 42 31N 1 32 E
Andover, *U.K.* **13** 51 13N 1 29W
Andover, *Mass., U.S.A.* **117** 42 40N 71 8W
Andover, *N.Y., U.S.A.* **116** 42 11N 77 48W
Andover, *Ohio, U.S.A.* **116** 41 35N 80 35W
Andradina, *Brazil* **139** 20 54 S 51 23W
Andrahary, Mt., *Madag.* **97** 13 37 S 49 17 E
Andraitx, *Spain* **24** 39 39N 2 25 E
Andramasina, *Madag.* **97** 19 11 S 47 35 E
Andranopasy, *Madag.* **97** 21 17 S 43 44 E
Andreanof Is., *U.S.A.* **102** 52 0N 178 0W
Andreapol, *U.S.S.R.* **36** 56 40N 32 17 E
Andrespol, *Poland* **32** 51 45N 19 34 E
Andreville, *Canada* **107** 47 41N 69 44W
Andrewilla, *Australia* **73** 26 31 S 139 17 E
Andrews, *S.C., U.S.A.* **115** 33 29N 79 30W
Andrews, *Tex., U.S.A.* **121** 32 18N 102 33W
Ándria, *Italy* **29** 41 13N 16 17 E
Andriba, *Madag.* **97** 17 30 S 46 58 E
Andrijevica, *Yugoslavia* **33** 42 45N 19 48 E
Andrítsaina, *Greece* **35** 37 29N 21 52 E
Androka, *Madag.* **97** 24 58 S 44 2 E
Andropov, *U.S.S.R.* **37** 58 5N 38 50 E
Ándros, *Greece* **35** 37 50N 24 57 E
Andros I., *Bahamas* **128** 24 30N 78 0W
Andros Town, *Bahamas* **128** 24 43N 77 47W
Andújar, *Spain* **23** 38 3N 4 5W
Andulo, *Angola* **95** 11 25 S 16 45 E
Aneby, *Sweden* **11** 57 48N 14 49 E
Anegada, B., *Argentina* **142** 40 20 S 62 20W
Anegada I., *Virgin Is.* **129** 18 45N 64 20W
Anegada Passage, *W. Indies* **129** 18 15N 63 45W
Anécho, *Togo* **91** 6 12N 1 34 E
Aneityum, *Vanuatu* **68** 20 12 S 169 45 E
Añelo, *Argentina* **142** 38 20 S 68 45W
Anergane, *Morocco* **84** 31 4N 7 14W
Aneto, Pico de, *Spain* **24** 42 37N 0 40 E
Añez, *Bolivia* **137** 15 40 S 63 10W
Anfu, *China* **59** 27 21N 114 40 E
Ang Thong, *Thailand* **54** 14 35N 100 31 E
Angamos, Punta, *Chile* **140** 23 1 S 70 32W
Ang'angxi, *China* **62** 47 10N 123 48 E
Angara →, *U.S.S.R.* **41** 58 30N 97 0 E
Angarab, *Ethiopia* **89** 13 11N 37 7 E
Angarsk, *U.S.S.R.* **41** 52 30N 104 0 E
Angas Downs, *Australia* **79** 25 2 S 132 14 E
Angas Hills, *Australia* **78** 23 0 S 127 50 E
Angaston, *Australia* **73** 34 30 S 139 8 E
Ånge, *Sweden* **10** 62 31N 15 35 E
Ángel de la Guarda, I., *Mexico* **126** 29 30N 113 30W
Angel Falls, *Venezuela* **135** 5 57N 62 30W
Angeles, *Phil.* **57** 15 9N 120 33 E
Ängelholm, *Sweden* **11** 56 15N 12 58 E
Angellala, *Australia* **73** 26 24 S 146 54 E
Angels Camp, *U.S.A.* **124** 38 8N 120 30W
Ängelsberg, *Sweden* **10** 59 58N 16 0 E
Anger →, *Ethiopia* **89** 9 37N 36 6 E
Angereb →, *Ethiopia* **89** 13 45N 36 40 E
Ångermanälven →, *Sweden* **10** 62 40N 18 0 E
Angermünde, *E. Germany* **30** 53 1N 14 0 E
Angers, *Canada* **117** 45 31N 75 29W
Angers, *France* **18** 47 30N 0 35W
Angerville, *France* **19** 48 19N 2 0 E
Ängesån →, *Sweden* **8** 66 50N 22 15 E
Anghiari, *Italy* **27** 43 32N 12 3 E
Angical, *Brazil* **139** 12 0 S 44 42W
Angikuni L., *Canada* **111** 62 0N 100 0W
Angkor, *Cambodia* **54** 13 22N 103 50 E
Anglem Mt., *N.Z.* **81** 46 45 S 167 53 E
Anglés, *Spain* **24** 41 57N 2 38 E
Anglesea, *Australia* **74** 38 25 S 144 12 E
Anglesey, *U.K.* **12** 53 17N 4 20W
Anglet, *France* **20** 43 29N 1 31W
Angleton, *U.S.A.* **121** 29 12N 95 23W
Angleur, *Belgium* **17** 50 36N 5 35 E
Angliers, *Canada* **106** 47 33N 79 14W
Anglin →, *France* **20** 46 42N 0 52 E
Anglure, *France* **19** 48 35N 3 50 E
Angmagssalik, *Greenland* **144** 65 40N 37 20W
Ango, *Zaïre* **92** 4 10N 26 5 E
Angoche, *Mozam.* **93** 16 8 S 40 0 E
Angoche, I., *Mozam.* **93** 16 20 S 39 50 E
Angol, *Chile* **140** 37 56 S 72 45W
Angola, *Ind., U.S.A.* **119** 41 40N 85 0W
Angola, *N.Y., U.S.A.* **116** 42 38N 79 2W
Angola ■, *Africa* **95** 12 0 S 18 0 E
Angoon, *U.S.A.* **110** 57 40N 134 40W
Angoram, *Papua N. G.* **69** 4 4 S 144 4 E
Angoulême, *France* **20** 45 39N 0 10 E
Angoumois, *France* **20** 45 50N 0 25 E
Angra dos Reis, *Brazil* **141** 23 0 S 44 10W
Angren, *U.S.S.R.* **40** 41 1N 70 12 E
Angtassom, *Cambodia* **55** 11 1N 104 41 E
Angu, *Zaïre* **92** 3 25N 24 28 E
Anguang, *China* **61** 45 15N 123 45 E
Anguilla, *W. Indies* **129** 18 14N 63 5W
Anguo, *China* **60** 38 28N 115 15 E
Angurugu, *Australia* **72** 14 0 S 136 25 E
Angus, *Canada* **108** 44 19N 79 53W
Angus, Braes of, *U.K.* **14** 56 51N 3 10W
Anhanduí →, *Brazil* **141** 21 46 S 52 9W
Anhée, *Belgium* **17** 50 18N 4 53 E
Anholt, *Denmark* **11** 56 42N 11 33 E
Anhua, *China* **59** 28 23N 111 12 E
Anhui □, *China* **61** 32 0N 117 0 E
Anhwei □ = Anhui □, *China* **61** 32 0N 117 0 E
Anichab, *Namibia* **96** 21 0 S 14 46 E
Anicuns, *Brazil* **139** 16 28 S 49 58W
Ánidhros, *Greece* **35** 36 38N 25 43 E
Anie, *Togo* **91** 7 42N 1 8 E
Animas, *U.S.A.* **123** 31 58N 108 58W
Ånimskog, *Sweden* **11** 58 53N 12 35 E
Anina, *Romania* **34** 45 6N 21 51 E
Anita, *U.S.A.* **118** 41 27N 94 46W
Anivorano, *Madag.* **97** 18 44 S 48 58 E
Aniwa, *Vanuatu* **68** 19 17 S 169 35 E
Anjangaon, *India* **50** 21 10N 77 20 E
Anjar, *India* **48** 23 6N 70 10 E
Anjidiv I., *India* **51** 14 40N 74 10 E
Anjō, *Japan* **65** 34 57N 137 5 E
Anjou, *France* **18** 47 20N 0 15W
Anjozorobe, *Madag.* **97** 18 22 S 47 52 E
Anju, *N. Korea* **61** 39 36N 125 40 E
Anka, *Nigeria* **91** 12 13N 5 58 E
Ankaboa, Tanjona, *Madag.* **97** 21 58 S 43 20 E
Ankang, *China* **60** 32 40N 109 1 E
Ankara, *Turkey* **46** 40 0N 32 54 E
Ankaramena, *Madag.* **97** 21 57 S 46 39 E
Ankazoabo, *Madag.* **97** 22 18 S 44 31 E
Ankazobe, *Madag.* **97** 18 20 S 47 10 E
Ankeny, *U.S.A.* **118** 41 44N 93 36W
Ankisabe, *Madag.* **97** 19 17 S 46 29 E
Anklam, *E. Germany* **30** 53 48N 13 40 E
Ankleshwar, *India* **50** 21 38N 73 3 E
Ankober, *Ethiopia* **89** 9 35N 39 40 E
Ankoro, *Zaïre* **92** 6 45 S 26 55 E
Anlong, *China* **58** 25 2N 105 27 E
Anlu, *China* **59** 31 15N 113 45 E
Ånn, *Sweden* **10** 63 19N 12 34 E
Ann, C., *U.S.A.* **117** 42 39N 70 37W
Ann Arbor, *U.S.A.* **104** 42 17N 83 45W
Anna, *Ill., U.S.A.* **121** 37 28N 89 10W
Anna, *Ohio, U.S.A.* **119** 40 24N 84 11W
Anna, *U.S.S.R.* **37** 51 28N 40 23 E
Anna Plains, *Australia* **78** 19 17 S 121 37 E
Anna Regina, *Guyana* **135** 7 10N 58 30W
Annaba, *Algeria* **85** 36 50N 7 46 E
Annaberg-Buchholz, *E. Germany* **30** 50 34N 12 58 E
Annaka, *Japan* **65** 36 19N 138 54 E
Annalee →, *Ireland* **15** 54 3N 7 15W
Annam = Trung-Phan, *Vietnam* **54** 16 0N 108 0 E
Annamitique, Chaîne, *Asia* **54** 17 0N 106 0 E
Annan, *U.K.* **14** 55 0N 3 17W
Annan →, *U.K.* **14** 54 58N 3 18W
Annanberg, *Papua N. G.* **69** 4 52 S 144 42 E
Annapolis, *U.S.A.* **114** 39 0N 76 30W
Annapolis Royal, *Canada* **105** 44 44N 65 32W
Annapurna, *Nepal* **49** 28 34N 83 50 E
Annean, L., *Australia* **79** 26 54 S 118 14 E
Anneberg, *Sweden* **11** 57 32N 12 6 E
Annecy, *France* **21** 45 55N 6 8 E
Annecy, L. d', *France* **21** 45 52N 6 10 E
Annemasse, *France* **21** 46 12N 6 16 E
Anning, *China* **58** 24 55N 102 26 E
Anningie, *Australia* **78** 21 50 S 133 7 E
Anniston, *U.S.A.* **115** 33 45N 85 50W
Annobón, *Atl. Oc.* **83** 1 25 S 5 36 E
Annonay, *France* **21** 45 15N 4 40 E
Annonciation, L', *Canada* **106** 46 25N 74 55W
Annot, *France* **21** 43 58N 6 38 E
Annotto Bay, *Jamaica* **128** 18 17N 77 3W
Annuello, *Australia* **74** 34 53 S 142 55 E
Annville, *U.S.A.* **117** 40 18N 76 32W
Annweiler, *W. Germany* **31** 49 12N 7 58 E
Áno Viánnos, *Greece* **35** 35 2N 25 21 E
Anoano, *Solomon Is.* **68** 8 59 S 160 46 E
Anoka, *U.S.A.* **120** 45 10N 93 26W

Anorotsangana, *Madag.* **97** 13 56 S 47 55 E
Anping, *Hebei, China* **60** 38 15N 115 30 E
Anping, *Liaoning, China* **61** 41 5N 123 30 E
Anpu Gang, *China* **58** 21 25N 109 50 E
Anqing, *China* **59** 30 30N 117 3 E
Anqiu, *China* **61** 36 25N 119 10 E
Anren, *China* **59** 26 43N 113 18 E
Ans, *Belgium* **17** 50 39N 5 32 E
Ansāb, *Si. Arabia* **46** 29 11N 44 43 E
Ansai, *China* **60** 36 50N 109 20 E
Ansbach, *W. Germany* **31** 49 17N 10 34 E
Anse, L', *U.S.A.* **104** 46 47N 88 28W
Anse au Loup, L', *Canada* **105** 51 32N 56 50W
Anseba →, *Ethiopia* **89** 16 0N 38 30 E
Anserma, *Colombia* **134** 5 13N 75 48W
Anseroeul, *Belgium* **17** 50 43N 3 32 E
Anshan, *China* **61** 41 5N 122 58 E
Anshun, *China* **58** 26 18N 105 57 E
Ansião, *Portugal* **22** 39 56N 8 27W
Ansirabe, *Madag.* **97** 19 55 S 47 2 E
Ansley, *U.S.A.* **120** 41 19N 99 24W
Ansó, *Spain* **24** 42 51N 0 48W
Anson, *U.S.A.* **121** 32 46N 99 54W
Anson B., *Australia* **78** 13 20 S 130 6 E
Ansongo, *Mali* **91** 15 25N 0 35 E
Ansonia, *Conn., U.S.A.* **117** 41 21N 73 6W
Ansonia, *Ohio, U.S.A.* **119** 40 13N 84 38W
Anstruther, *U.K.* **14** 56 14N 2 40W
Ansudu, *Indonesia* **57** 2 11 S 139 22 E
Antabamba, *Peru* **136** 14 40 S 73 0W
Antakya, *Turkey* **46** 36 14N 36 10 E
Antalaha, *Madag.* **97** 14 57 S 50 20 E
Antalya, *Turkey* **46** 36 52N 30 45 E
Antalya Körfezi, *Turkey* **46** 36 15N 31 30 E
Antananarivo, *Madag.* **97** 18 55 S 47 31 E
Antananarivo □, *Madag.* **97** 19 0 S 47 0 E
Antanimbaribe, *Madag.* **97** 21 30 S 44 48 E
Antarctic Pen., *Antarctica* **143** 67 0 S 60 0W
Antarctica **143** 90 0 S 0 0 E
Antelope, *Zimb.* **93** 21 2 S 28 31 E
Antenor Navarro, *Brazil* **138** 6 44 S 38 27W
Antequera, *Paraguay* **140** 24 8 S 57 7W
Antequera, *Spain* **23** 37 5N 4 33W
Antero Mt., *U.S.A.* **123** 38 45N 106 15W
Anthony, *Kans., U.S.A.* **121** 37 8N 98 2W
Anthony, *N. Mex., U.S.A.* **123** 32 1N 106 37W
Anthony Lagoon, *Australia* **72** 18 0 S 135 30 E
Anti Atlas, *Morocco* **84** 30 0N 8 30W
Antibes, *France* **21** 43 34N 7 6 E
Antibes, C. d', *France* **21** 43 31N 7 7 E
Anticosti, I. d', *Canada* **105** 49 30N 63 0W
Antifer, C. d', *France* **18** 49 41N 0 10 E
Antigo, *U.S.A.* **120** 45 8N 89 5W
Antigonish, *Canada* **105** 45 38N 61 58W
Antigua, *Canary Is.* **25** 28 24N 14 1W
Antigua, *Guatemala* **128** 14 34N 90 41W
Antigua, *W. Indies* **129** 17 0N 61 50W
Antigua & Barbuda ■, *W. Indies* **129** 17 20N 61 48W
Antilla, *Cuba* **128** 20 40N 75 50W
Antimony, *U.S.A.* **123** 38 7N 112 0W
Antioch, *U.S.A.* **124** 38 0N 121 45W
Antioche, Pertuis d', *France* **20** 46 6N 1 20W
Antioquia, *Colombia* **134** 6 40N 75 55W
Antioquia □, *Colombia* **134** 7 0N 75 30W
Antipodes Is., *Pac. Oc.* **66** 49 45 S 178 40 E
Antler, *U.S.A.* **120** 48 58N 101 18W
Antler →, *Canada* **111** 49 8N 101 0W
Antlers, *U.S.A.* **121** 34 15N 95 35W
Antofagasta, *Chile* **140** 23 50 S 70 30W
Antofagasta □, *Chile* **140** 24 0 S 69 0W
Antofagasta de la Sierra, *Argentina* **140** 26 5 S 67 20W
Antofalla, *Argentina* **140** 25 30 S 68 5W
Antofalla, Salar de, *Argentina* **140** 25 40 S 67 45W
Antoing, *Belgium* **17** 50 34N 3 27 E
Anton, *U.S.A.* **121** 33 49N 102 5W
Anton Chico, *U.S.A.* **123** 35 12N 105 5W
Antongila, Helodrano, *Madag.* **97** 15 30 S 49 50 E
Antonibé, *Madag.* **97** 15 7 S 47 24 E
Antonibé, Presqu'île d', *Madag.* **97** 14 55 S 47 20 E
Antonina, *Brazil* **141** 25 26 S 48 42W
Antonito, *U.S.A.* **123** 37 4N 106 1W
Antonovo, *U.S.S.R.* **39** 49 25N 51 42 E
Antrain, *France* **18** 48 28N 1 30W
Antrim, *U.K.* **15** 54 43N 6 13W
Antrim □, *U.K.* **15** 54 55N 6 20W
Antrim, Mts. of, *U.K.* **15** 54 57N 6 8W
Antrim Plateau, *Australia* **78** 18 8 S 128 20 E
Antrodoco, *Italy* **27** 42 25N 13 4 E
Antropovo, *U.S.S.R.* **37** 58 26N 42 51 E
Antsalova, *Madag.* **97** 18 40 S 44 37 E
Antsiranana, *Madag.* **97** 12 25 S 49 20 E
Antsohihy, *Madag.* **97** 14 50 S 47 59 E
Antsohimbondrona Seranana, *Madag.* **97** 13 7 S 48 48 E
Antu, *China* **61** 42 30N 128 20 E
Antwerp = Antwerpen, *Belgium* **17** 51 13N 4 25 E
Antwerp, *Australia* **74** 36 17 S 142 4 E
Antwerp, *N.Y., U.S.A.* **117** 44 12N 75 36W
Antwerp, *Ohio, U.S.A.* **119** 41 11N 84 45W
Antwerpen, *Belgium* **17** 51 13N 4 25 E
Antwerpen □, *Belgium* **17** 51 15N 4 40 E
Anupgarh, *India* **48** 29 10N 73 10 E
Anuradhapura, *Sri Lanka* **51** 8 22N 80 28 E
Anvers = Antwerpen, *Belgium* **17** 51 13N 4 25 E
Anvers I., *Antarctica* **143** 64 30 S 63 40W
Anvik, *U.S.A.* **102** 62 37N 160 20W
Anxi, *Fujian, China* **59** 25 2N 118 12 E
Anxi, *Gansu, China* **62** 40 30N 95 43 E
Anxiang, *China* **59** 29 27N 112 11 E
Anxious B., *Australia* **73** 33 24 S 134 45 E
Anyama, *Ivory C.* **90** 5 30N 4 3W
Anyang, *China* **60** 36 5N 114 21 E
Anyi, *Jiangxi, China* **59** 28 49N 115 25 E
Anyi, *Shanxi, China* **60** 35 2N 111 2 E
Anyuan, *China* **59** 25 9N 115 21 E
Anza, *U.S.A.* **125** 33 35N 116 39W
'Anzah, *Jordan* **44** 32 22N 35 12 E
Anze, *China* **60** 36 10N 112 12 E
Anzhero-Sudzhensk, *U.S.S.R.* **40** 56 10N 86 0 E
Ánzio, *Italy* **28** 41 28N 12 37 E
Anzoátegui □, *Venezuela* **135** 9 0N 64 30W
Aoba, *Vanuatu* **68** 15 25 S 167 50 E
Aoga-Shima, *Japan* **65** 32 28N 139 46 E
Aoiz, *Spain* **24** 42 46N 1 22W
Aomori, *Japan* **63** 40 45N 140 45 E
Aonla, *India* **49** 28 16N 79 11 E
Aono-Yama, *Japan* **64** 34 28N 131 48 E
Aorangi Mts., *N.Z.* **80** 41 28 S 175 22 E
Aosta, *Italy* **26** 45 43N 7 20 E
Aoudéras, *Niger* **91** 17 45N 8 20 E
Aouinet Torkoz, *Morocco* **84** 28 31N 9 46W
Aoukar, *Mali* **84** 23 50N 2 45W
Aouker, *Mauritania* **90** 17 40N 10 0W
Aoulef el Arab, *Algeria* **85** 26 55N 1 2 E
Apa →, *S. Amer.* **140** 22 6 S 58 2W
Apache, *U.S.A.* **121** 34 53N 98 22W
Apalachee B., *U.S.A.* **115** 30 0N 84 0W
Apalachicola, *U.S.A.* **115** 29 40N 85 0W
Apalachicola →, *U.S.A.* **115** 29 40N 85 0W
Apapa, *Nigeria* **91** 6 25N 3 25 E
Apaporis →, *Colombia* **134** 1 23 S 69 25W
Aparecida do Taboado, *Brazil* **139** 20 5 S 51 5W
Aparri, *Phil.* **57** 18 22N 121 38 E
Aparurén, *Venezuela* **135** 5 6N 62 8W
Apateu, *Romania* **34** 46 36N 21 47 E
Apatin, *Yugoslavia* **33** 45 40N 19 0 E
Apatzingán, *Mexico* **126** 19 0N 102 20W
Apeldoorn, *Neths.* **16** 52 13N 5 57 E
Apeldoornsch Kanal →, *Neths.* **16** 52 29N 6 5 E
Apen, *W. Germany* **30** 53 12N 7 47 E
Apere →, *Bolivia* **137** 13 44 S 65 18W
Apia, *W. Samoa* **68** 13 50 S 171 50W
Apiacás, Serra dos, *Brazil* **137** 9 50 S 57 0W
Apiaú →, *Brazil* **135** 2 39N 61 12W
Apiaú, Serra do, *Brazil* **135** 2 30N 62 0W
Apidiá →, *Brazil* **137** 11 39 S 61 11W
Apinajé, *Brazil* **139** 11 31 S 48 18W
Apiti, *N.Z.* **80** 39 58 S 175 54 E
Apizaco, *Mexico* **127** 19 26N 98 9W
Aplao, *Peru* **136** 16 0 S 72 40W
Apo, Mt., *Phil.* **57** 6 53N 125 14 E
Apodi, *Brazil* **138** 5 39 S 37 48W
Apolda, *E. Germany* **30** 51 1N 11 30 E
Apollo Bay, *Australia* **74** 38 45 S 143 40 E
Apollonia = Marsá Susah, *Libya* **86** 32 52N 21 59 E
Apollonia, *Greece* **35** 36 58N 24 43 E
Apolo, *Bolivia* **136** 14 30 S 68 30W
Apónguao →, *Venezuela* **135** 4 48N 61 36W
Aporé, *Brazil* **137** 18 58 S 52 1W
Aporé →, *Brazil* **139** 19 27 S 50 57W
Aporema, *Brazil* **138** 1 14N 50 49W
Apostle Is., *U.S.A.* **120** 47 0N 90 30W
Apóstoles, *Argentina* **141** 28 0 S 56 0W
Apostolovo, *U.S.S.R.* **38** 47 39N 33 39 E
Apoteri, *Guyana* **135** 4 2N 58 32W
Appalachian Mts., *U.S.A.* **114** 38 0N 80 0W
Appelscha, *Neths.* **16** 52 57N 6 21 E
Appenines = Appennini, *Italy* **26** 44 0N 11 0 E
Appennini, *Italy* **26** 44 0N 11 0 E
Appennino Ligure, *Italy* **26** 44 30N 9 0 E
Appenzell-Ausser Rhoden □, *Switz.* **31** 47 23N 9 23 E
Appenzell-Inner Rhoden □, *Switz.* **31** 47 20N 9 25 E
Appiano, *Italy* **27** 46 27N 11 17 E
Appin, *Australia* **76** 34 11 S 150 45 E
Appingedam, *Neths.* **16** 53 19N 6 51 E
Apple Hill, *Canada* **109** 45 13N 74 46W
Apple Tree Flat, *Australia* **76** 32 40 S 149 36 E
Apple Valley, *U.S.A.* **125** 34 30N 117 11W
Appleby, *U.K.* **12** 54 35N 2 29W
Appleton, *U.S.A.* **114** 44 17N 88 25W
Appleton City, *U.S.A.* **118** 38 11N 94 2W
Approuague, *Fr. Guiana* **135** 4 20N 52 0W
Approuague →, *Fr. Guiana* **135** 4 30N 51 57W
Apricena, *Italy* **29** 41 47N 15 25 E
Aprigliano, *Italy* **29** 39 17N 16 19 E
Aprília, *Italy* **28** 41 38N 12 38 E
Apsheronsk, *U.S.S.R.* **39** 44 28N 39 42 E
Apsley, *Australia* **74** 36 58 S 141 5 E
Apsley, *Canada* **109** 44 45N 78 6W
Apt, *France* **21** 43 53N 5 24 E
Apuane, Alpi, *Italy* **26** 44 7N 10 14 E
Apuaú, *Brazil* **135** 2 25 S 60 53W
Apucarana, *Brazil* **141** 23 55 S 51 33W
Apulia = Púglia □, *Italy* **29** 41 0N 16 30 E
Apure □, *Venezuela* **134** 7 10N 68 50W
Apure →, *Venezuela* **134** 7 37N 66 25W
Apurímac □, *Peru* **136** 14 0 S 73 0W
Apurimac →, *Peru* **136** 12 17 S 73 56W
Apuseni, Munţii, *Romania* **34** 46 30N 22 45 E
Aqabah = Al 'Aqabah, *Jordan* **44** 29 31N 35 0 E
'Aqabah, Khalīj al, *Red Sea* **46** 28 15N 33 20 E
Āqcheh, *Afghan.* **47** 37 0N 66 5 E
Aqîq, *Sudan* **88** 18 14N 38 12 E
Aqîq, Khalîg, *Sudan* **88** 18 20N 38 10 E
Aqrabā, *Jordan* **44** 32 9N 35 20 E
Aqrah, *Iraq* **46** 36 46N 43 45 E
Aquidauana, *Brazil* **137** 20 30 S 55 50W
Aquidauana →, *Brazil* **137** 19 44 S 56 50W
Áquila, L', *Italy* **27** 42 21N 13 24 E
Aquiles Serdán, *Mexico* **126** 28 37N 105 54W
Aquin, *Haiti* **129** 18 16N 73 24W
Ar Rachidiya, *Morocco* **84** 31 58N 4 20W
Ar Rafīd, *Syria* **44** 32 57N 35 52 E
Ar Ramādī, *Iraq* **46** 33 25N 43 20 E
Ar Raml, *Libya* **86** 26 45N 19 40 E
Ar Ramthā, *Jordan* **44** 32 34N 36 0 E
Ar Raqqah, *Syria* **46** 36 0N 38 55 E
Ar Rass, *Si. Arabia* **46** 25 50N 43 40 E
Ar Rifā'ī, *Iraq* **46** 31 50N 46 10 E
Ar Riyāḍ, *Si. Arabia* **46** 24 41N 46 42 E
Ar Rummān, *Jordan* **44** 32 9N 35 48 E
Ar Ruṭbah, *Iraq* **46** 33 0N 40 15 E
Ar Ruwayḍah, *Si. Arabia* **46** 23 40N 44 40 E
Ara, *India* **49** 25 35N 84 32 E
'Arab, Bahr el →, *Sudan* **89** 9 0N 29 30 E
Arab, Khalîg el, *Egypt* **88** 30 55N 29 0 E
Arab, Shatt al, *Asia* **46** 30 0N 48 31 E
Arabatskaya Strelka, *U.S.S.R.* **38** 45 40N 35 0 E
Arabba, *Italy* **27** 46 30N 11 51 E
Arabelo, *Venezuela* **135** 4 55N 64 13W
Arabia, *Asia* **45** 25 0N 45 0 E
Arabian Desert = Es Sahrâ' Esh Sharqîya, *Egypt* **88** 27 30N 32 30 E
Arabian Gulf = Gulf, The, *Asia* **47** 27 0N 50 0 E
Arabian Sea, *Ind. Oc.* **42** 16 0N 65 0 E
Arac, *Turkey* **46** 41 15N 33 21 E
Aracaju, *Brazil* **138** 10 55 S 37 4W
Aracataca, *Colombia* **134** 10 38N 74 9W
Aracati, *Brazil* **138** 4 30 S 37 44W
Araçatuba, *Brazil* **141** 21 10 S 50 30W
Aracena, *Spain* **23** 37 53N 6 38W
Aracena, Sierra de, *Spain* **23** 37 50N 6 50W
Aracides, C., *Solomon Is.* **68** 8 21 S 161 0 E
Araçuaí, *Brazil* **139** 16 52 S 42 4W
Araçuaí →, *Brazil* **139** 16 46 S 42 2W
'Arad, *Israel* **44** 31 15N 35 12 E
Arad, *Romania* **34** 46 10N 21 20 E
Arada, *Chad* **87** 15 0N 20 20 E
Arafura Sea, *E. Indies* **57** 9 0 S 135 0 E
Aragarças, *Brazil* **137** 15 55 S 52 15W
Aragats, *U.S.S.R.* **39** 40 30N 44 15 E
Aragón □, *Spain* **24** 41 25N 1 0W
Aragón →, *Spain* **24** 42 13N 1 44W
Aragona, *Italy* **28** 37 24N 13 36 E
Aragua □, *Venezuela* **134** 10 0N 67 10W
Aragua de Barcelona, *Venezuela* **135** 9 28N 64 49W
Araguacema, *Brazil* **138** 8 50 S 49 20W
Araguaçu, *Brazil* **139** 12 49 S 49 51W
Araguaia →, *Brazil* **138** 5 21 S 48 41W
Araguaiana, *Brazil* **137** 15 43 S 51 51W
Araguaína, *Brazil* **138** 7 12 S 48 12W
Araguari, *Brazil* **139** 18 38 S 48 11W
Araguari →, *Brazil* **138** 1 15N 49 55W
Araguatins, *Brazil* **138** 5 38 S 48 7W
Araioses, *Brazil* **138** 2 53 S 41 55W
Arak, *Algeria* **85** 25 20N 3 45 E
Arāk, *Iran* **46** 34 0N 49 40 E
Arakan □, *Burma* **52** 19 0N 94 15 E
Arakan Yoma, *Burma* **52** 20 0N 94 40 E
Arakkonam, *India* **51** 13 7N 79 43 E
Araks = Aras, Rūd-e →, *Iran* **46** 39 10N 47 10 E
Aral Sea = Aralskoye More, *U.S.S.R.* **40** 44 30N 60 0 E
Aralsk, *U.S.S.R.* **40** 46 50N 61 20 E
Aralskoye More, *U.S.S.R.* **40** 44 30N 60 0 E
Araluen, *Australia* **76** 35 36 S 149 49 E
Aramac, *Australia* **72** 22 58 S 145 14 E
Arambag, *India* **49** 22 53N 87 48 E
Aran Areh, *Ethiopia* **98** 9 2N 43 54 E
Aran I., *Ireland* **15** 55 0N 8 30W
Aran Is., *Ireland* **15** 53 5N 9 42W
Aranda de Duero, *Spain* **24** 41 39N 3 42W
Aranga, *N.Z.* **80** 35 44 S 173 40 E
Arani, *India* **51** 12 43N 79 19 E
Aranjuez, *Spain* **22** 40 1N 3 40W
Aranos, *Namibia* **96** 24 9 S 19 7 E
Aransas Pass, *U.S.A.* **121** 27 55N 97 9W
Aranzazu, *Colombia* **134** 5 16N 75 30W
Arao, *Japan* **64** 32 59N 130 25 E
Araouane, *Mali* **90** 18 55N 3 30W
Arapahoe, *U.S.A.* **120** 40 22N 99 53W
Arapari, *Brazil* **138** 5 34 S 49 15W
Arapey Grande →, *Uruguay* **140** 30 55 S 57 49W
Arapiraca, *Brazil* **138** 9 45 S 36 39W
Arapkir, *Turkey* **46** 39 5N 38 30 E
Arapongas, *Brazil* **141** 23 29 S 51 28W
Araracuara, *Colombia* **134** 0 24 S 72 17W
Araranguá, *Brazil* **141** 29 0 S 49 30W
Araraquara, *Brazil* **139** 21 50 S 48 0W
Ararás, Serra das, *Brazil* **141** 25 0 S 53 10W
Ararat, *Australia* **74** 37 16 S 143 0 E
Ararat, Mt. = Ağri Daği, *Turkey* **46** 39 50N 44 15 E
Arari, *Brazil* **138** 3 28 S 44 47W
Araria, *India* **49** 26 9N 87 33 E
Araripe, Chapada do, *Brazil* **138** 7 20 S 40 0W
Araripina, *Brazil* **138** 7 33 S 40 34W
Araruama, L. de, *Brazil* **139** 22 53 S 42 12W
Araruna, *Brazil* **138** 6 52 S 35 44W
Aras, Rūd-e →, *Iran* **46** 39 10N 47 10 E
Araticu, *Brazil* **138** 1 58 S 49 51W
Arauca, *Colombia* **134** 7 0N 70 40W
Arauca □, *Colombia* **134** 6 40N 71 0W
Arauca →, *Venezuela* **134** 7 24N 66 35W
Arauco, *Chile* **140** 37 16 S 73 25W
Arauco □, *Chile* **140** 37 40 S 73 25W
Araújos, *Brazil* **139** 19 56 S 45 14W
Arauquita, *Colombia* **134** 7 2N 71 25W
Araure, *Venezuela* **134** 9 34N 69 13W
Arawa, *Ethiopia* **89** 9 57N 41 58 E
Arawata →, *N.Z.* **81** 44 0 S 168 40 E
Araxá, *Brazil* **139** 19 35 S 46 55W
Araya, Pen. de, *Venezuela* **135** 10 40N 64 0W
Arba Minch, *Ethiopia* **89** 6 0N 37 30 E
Arbatax, *Italy* **28** 39 57N 9 42 E
Arbaza, *U.S.S.R.* **41** 52 40N 92 30 E
Arbīl, *Iraq* **46** 36 15N 44 5 E
Arboga, *Sweden* **10** 59 24N 15 52 E
Arbois, *France* **19** 46 55N 5 46 E
Arboletes, *Colombia* **134** 8 51N 76 26W
Arbore, *Ethiopia* **89** 5 3N 36 50 E
Arborea, *Italy* **28** 39 46N 8 34 E
Arborfield, *Canada* **111** 53 6N 103 39W
Arborg, *Canada* **111** 50 54N 97 13W
Arbrå, *Sweden* **10** 61 28N 16 22 E
Arbresle, L', *France* **21** 45 50N 4 36 E
Arbroath, *U.K.* **14** 56 34N 2 35W
Arbuckle, *U.S.A.* **124** 39 3N 122 2W
Arbus, *Italy* **28** 39 30N 8 33 E
Arbuzinka, *U.S.S.R.* **38** 47 0N 31 59 E
Arc, *France* **19** 47 28N 5 34 E
Arc →, *France* **21** 45 34N 6 12 E
Arcachon, *France* **20** 44 40N 1 10W
Arcachon, Bassin d', *France* **20** 44 42N 1 10W
Arcade, *Calif., U.S.A.* **124** 34 2N 118 15W
Arcade, *U.S.A.* **116** 42 34N 78 25W
Arcadia, *Fla., U.S.A.* **115** 27 20N 81 50W
Arcadia, *Ind., U.S.A.* **119** 40 10N 86 1W
Arcadia, *Iowa, U.S.A.* **118** 42 5N 95 3W
Arcadia, *La., U.S.A.* **121** 32 34N 92 53W
Arcadia, *Nebr., U.S.A.* **120** 41 29N 99 4W
Arcadia, *Pa., U.S.A.* **116** 40 46N 78 54W
Arcadia, *Wis., U.S.A.* **120** 44 13N 91 29W
Arcanum, *U.S.A.* **119** 39 59N 84 33W
Arcata, *U.S.A.* **122** 40 55N 124 4W
Arcévia, *Italy* **27** 43 29N 12 58 E
Archangel = Arkhangelsk, *U.S.S.R.* **40** 64 40N 41 0 E
Archar, *Bulgaria* **34** 43 50N 22 54 E
Archbald, *U.S.A.* **117** 41 30N 75 31W
Archbold, *U.S.A.* **119** 41 31N 84 18W
Archena, *Spain* **25** 38 9N 1 16W
Archer →, *Australia* **72** 13 28 S 141 41 E
Archer B., *Australia* **72** 13 20 S 141 30 E
Archers Post, *Kenya* **92** 0 35N 37 35 E
Archidona, *Spain* **23** 37 6N 4 22W
Arci, Monte, *Italy* **28** 39 47N 8 44 E
Arcidosso, *Italy* **27** 42 51N 11 30 E
Arcila = Asilah, *Morocco* **84** 35 29N 6 0W
Arcis-sur-Aube, *France* **19** 48 32N 4 10 E
Arckaringa, *Australia* **73** 27 56 S 134 45 E
Arckaringa Cr. →, *Australia* **73** 28 10 S 135 22 E
Arco, *Italy* **26** 45 55N 10 54 E
Arco, *U.S.A.* **122** 43 45N 113 16W
Arcola, *Canada* **111** 49 40N 102 30W
Arcola, *U.S.A.* **119** 39 41N 88 19W
Arcos, *Spain* **24** 41 12N 2 16W
Arcos de los Frontera, *Spain* **23** 36 45N 5 49W
Arcos de Valdevez, *Portugal* **22** 41 55N 8 22W

Arcot, *India* **51** 12 53N 79 20 E
Arcoverde, *Brazil* **138** 8 25 S 37 4W
Arcs, Les, *France* **21** 43 27N 6 29 E
Arctic Bay, *Canada* **103** 73 1N 85 7W
Arctic Ocean, *Arctic* **144** 78 0N 160 0W
Arctic Red River, *Canada* **102** 67 15N 134 0W
Arda →, *Bulgaria* **35** 41 40N 26 29 E
Arda →, *Italy* **26** 44 53N 9 52 E
Ardabīl, *Iran* **46** 38 15N 48 18 E
Ardahan, *Turkey* **46** 41 7N 42 41 E
Ardakān = Sepīdān, *Iran* **47** 30 20N 52 5 E
Ardales, *Spain* **23** 36 53N 4 51W
Årdalstangen, *Norway* **10** 61 14N 7 43 E
Ardatov, *U.S.S.R.* **37** 54 51N 46 15 E
Ardbeg, *Canada* **108** 45 38N 80 5W
Ardea, *Greece* **35** 40 58N 22 3 E
Ardèche □, *France* **21** 44 42N 4 16 E
Ardèche →, *France* **21** 44 16N 4 39 E
Ardee, *Ireland* **15** 53 51N 6 32W
Arden, *Canada* **109** 44 43N 76 56W
Arden, *Calif., U.S.A.* **124** 38 36N 121 33W
Arden, *U.S.A.* **125** 36 1N 115 14W
Arden Stby., *Denmark* **11** 56 46N 9 52 E
Ardenne, *Belgium* **19** 50 0N 5 10 E
Ardennes □, *France* **19** 49 35N 4 40 E
Ardentes, *France* **19** 46 45N 1 50 E
Ardestān, *Iran* **47** 33 20N 52 25 E
Ardgour, *U.K.* **14** 56 45N 5 25W
Árdhas →, *Greece* **35** 41 36N 26 25 E
Ardila →, *Portugal* **23** 38 12N 7 28W
Ardlethan, *Australia* **75** 34 22 S 146 53 E
Ardmore, *Australia* **72** 21 39 S 139 11 E
Ardmore, *Okla., U.S.A.* **121** 34 10N 97 5W
Ardmore, *Pa., U.S.A.* **117** 39 58N 75 18W
Ardmore, *S. Dak., U.S.A.* **120** 43 0N 103 40W
Ardnacrusha, *Ireland* **15** 52 43N 8 38W
Ardnamurchan, Pt. of, *U.K.* **14** 56 44N 6 14W
Ardno, *Australia* **74** 37 49 S 141 3 E
Ardooie, *Belgium* **17** 50 59N 3 13 E
Ardore Marina, *Italy* **29** 38 11N 16 10 E
Ardres, *France* **19** 50 50N 2 0 E
Ardrossan, *Australia* **73** 34 26 S 137 53 E
Ardrossan, *U.K.* **14** 55 39N 4 50W
Ards □, *U.K.* **15** 54 35N 5 30W
Ards Pen., *U.K.* **15** 54 30N 5 25W
Ardud, *Romania* **34** 47 37N 22 52 E
Ardunac, *Turkey* **39** 41 8N 42 5 E
Åre, *Sweden* **10** 63 22N 13 15 E
Arecibo, *Puerto Rico* **129** 18 29N 66 42W
Areia Branca, *Brazil* **138** 5 0 S 37 0W
Arena, Pt., *U.S.A.* **124** 38 57N 123 44W
Arenales, Cerro, *Chile* **142** 47 5 S 73 40W
Arenápolis, *Brazil* **137** 14 26 S 56 49W
Arenas, *Spain* **22** 43 17N 4 50W
Arenas de San Pedro, *Spain* **22** 40 12N 5 5W
Arendal, *Norway* **11** 58 28N 8 46 E
Arendonk, *Belgium* **17** 51 19N 5 5 E
Arendsee, *E. Germany* **30** 52 52N 11 27 E
Arenillas, *Ecuador* **134** 3 33 S 80 10W
Arenys de Mar, *Spain* **24** 41 35N 2 33 E
Arenzano, *Italy* **26** 44 24N 8 40 E
Arenzville, *U.S.A.* **118** 39 53N 90 22W
Areópolis, *Greece* **35** 36 40N 22 22 E
Arequipa, *Peru* **136** 16 20 S 71 30W
Arequipa □, *Peru* **136** 16 0 S 72 50W
Arere, *Brazil* **135** 0 16 S 53 52W
Arero, *Ethiopia* **89** 4 41N 38 50 E
Arès, *France* **20** 44 47N 1 8W
Arévalo, *Spain* **22** 41 3N 4 43W
Arezzo, *Italy* **27** 43 28N 11 50 E
Arga →, *Spain* **24** 42 18N 1 47W
Argalastí, *Greece* **35** 39 13N 23 13 E
Argalong, *Australia* **76** 35 18 S 148 27 E
Argamakmur, *Indonesia* **56** 3 35 S 102 0 E
Argamasilla de Alba, *Spain* **25** 39 8N 3 5W
Arganda, *Spain* **24** 40 19N 3 26W
Arganil, *Portugal* **22** 40 13N 8 3W
Argelès-Gazost, *France* **20** 43 0N 0 6W
Argelès-sur-Mer, *France* **20** 42 34N 3 1 E
Argens →, *France* **21** 43 24N 6 44 E
Argent-sur-Sauldre, *France* **19** 47 33N 2 25 E
Argenta, *Italy* **27** 44 37N 11 50 E
Argenta, *U.S.A.* **119** 39 59N 88 49W
Argentan, *France* **18** 48 45N 0 1W
Argentário, Mte., *Italy* **27** 42 23N 11 11 E
Argentat, *France* **20** 45 6N 1 56 E
Argentera, *Italy* **26** 44 23N 6 58 E
Argentera, Monte del, *Italy* **26** 44 12N 7 5 E
Argenteuil, *France* **19** 48 57N 2 14 E
Argentia, *Canada* **105** 47 18N 53 58W
Argentiera, C. dell', *Italy* **28** 40 44N 8 8 E
Argentière-la-Bessée, L', *France* **21** 44 47N 6 33 E
Argentina ■, *S. Amer.* **142** 35 0 S 66 0W
Argentina Is., *Antarctica* **143** 66 0 S 64 0W
Argentino, L., *Argentina* **142** 50 10 S 73 0W
Argenton-Château, *France* **18** 46 59N 0 27W
Argenton-sur-Creuse, *France* **20** 46 36N 1 30 E
Argeş →, *Romania* **34** 44 12N 26 14 E
Arghandab →, *Afghan.* **48** 31 30N 64 15 E
Argo, *Sudan* **88** 19 28N 30 30 E
Argolikós Kólpos, *Greece* **35** 37 20N 22 52 E
Argonne, *France* **19** 49 10N 5 0 E
Árgos, *Greece* **35** 37 40N 22 43 E
Argos, *U.S.A.* **119** 41 14N 86 15W
Argostólion, *Greece* **35** 38 12N 20 33 E
Arguedas, *Spain* **24** 42 11N 1 36W
Arguello, Pt., *U.S.A.* **125** 34 34N 120 40W
Arguineguín, *Canary Is.* **25** 27 46N 15 41W
Argun →, *U.S.S.R.* **41** 53 20N 121 28 E
Argungu, *Nigeria* **91** 12 40N 4 31 E
Argus Pk., *U.S.A.* **125** 35 52N 117 26W
Argyle, *U.S.A.* **120** 48 23N 96 49W
Argyle, L., *Australia* **78** 16 20 S 128 40 E
Argyrádhes, *Greece* **35** 39 27N 19 58 E
Århus, *Denmark* **11** 56 8N 10 11 E
Århus Amtskommune □, *Denmark* **11** 56 15N 10 15 E
Aria, *N.Z.* **80** 38 33 S 175 0 E
Ariah Park, *Australia* **76** 34 22 S 147 16 E
Ariamsvlei, *Namibia* **96** 28 9 S 19 51 E
Ariana, *Tunisia* **86** 36 52N 10 12 E
Ariano Irpino, *Italy* **29** 41 10N 15 4 E
Ariano nel Polèsine, *Italy* **27** 44 56N 12 5 E
Ariari →, *Colombia* **134** 2 35N 72 47W
Aribinda, *Burkina Faso* **91** 14 17N 0 52W
Arica, *Chile* **136** 18 32 S 70 20W
Arica, *Colombia* **134** 2 0 S 71 50W
Arico, *Canary Is.* **25** 28 9N 16 29W
Arid, C., *Australia* **79** 34 1 S 123 10 E
Arida, *Japan* **65** 34 5N 135 8 E
Aridh, *Si. Arabia* **46** 25 0N 46 0 E
Ariège □, *France* **20** 42 56N 1 30 E
Ariège →, *France* **20** 43 30N 1 25 E
Arieş →, *Romania* **34** 46 24N 23 20 E
Arima, *Trin. & Tob.* **129** 10 38N 61 17W
Arinos →, *Brazil* **137** 10 25 S 58 20W
Ario de Rosales, *Mexico* **126** 19 12N 102 0W
Aripuanã, *Brazil* **137** 9 25 S 60 30W
Aripuanã →, *Brazil* **137** 5 7 S 60 25W
Ariquemes, *Brazil* **137** 9 55 S 63 6W
Arisaig, *U.K.* **14** 56 55N 5 50W
Arîsh, W. el →, *Egypt* **88** 31 9N 33 49 E
Arismendi, *Venezuela* **134** 8 29N 68 22W
Arissa, *Ethiopia* **89** 11 10N 41 35 E
Aristazabal I., *Canada* **110** 52 40N 129 10W
Arita, *Japan* **64** 33 11N 129 54 E
Arivaca, *U.S.A.* **123** 31 37N 111 25W
Arivonimamo, *Madag.* **97** 19 1 S 47 11 E
Ariyalur, *India* **51** 11 8N 79 8 E
Ariza, *Spain* **24** 41 19N 2 3W
Arizaro, Salar de, *Argentina* **140** 24 40 S 67 50W
Arizona, *Argentina* **140** 35 45 S 65 25W
Arizona □, *U.S.A.* **123** 34 20N 111 30W
Arizpe, *Mexico* **126** 30 20N 110 11W
Årjäng, *Sweden* **10** 59 24N 12 8 E
Arjeplog, *Sweden* **8** 66 3N 18 2 E
Arjona, *Colombia* **134** 10 14N 75 22W
Arjona, *Spain* **23** 37 56N 4 4W
Arjuno, *Indonesia* **57** 7 49 S 112 34 E
Arka, *U.S.S.R.* **41** 60 15N 142 0 E
Arkadak, *U.S.S.R.* **37** 51 58N 43 19 E
Arkadelphia, *U.S.A.* **121** 34 5N 93 0W
Arkaig, L., *U.K.* **14** 56 58N 5 10W
Arkalyk, *U.S.S.R.* **40** 50 13N 66 50 E
Arkansas □, *U.S.A.* **121** 35 0N 92 30W
Arkansas →, *U.S.A.* **121** 33 48N 91 4W
Arkansas City, *U.S.A.* **121** 37 4N 97 3W
Árkathos →, *Greece* **35** 39 20N 21 4 E
Arkhangelsk, *U.S.S.R.* **40** 64 40N 41 0 E
Arkhangelskoye, *U.S.S.R.* **37** 51 32N 40 58 E
Arkiko, *Ethiopia* **89** 15 33N 39 30 E
Arklow, *Ireland* **15** 52 48N 6 10W
Arkona, *Canada* **108** 43 4N 81 50W
Arkona, Kap, *E. Germany* **30** 54 41N 13 26 E
Arkösund, *Sweden* **11** 58 29N 16 56 E
Arkticheskiy, Mys, *U.S.S.R.* **41** 81 10N 95 0 E
Arkul, *U.S.S.R.* **37** 57 17N 50 3 E
Arlanc, *France* **20** 45 25N 3 42 E
Arlanza →, *Spain* **22** 42 6N 4 9W
Arlanzón →, *Spain* **22** 42 3N 4 17W
Arlberg Pass, *Austria* **31** 47 9N 10 12 E
Arlee, *U.S.A.* **122** 47 10N 114 4W
Arles, *France* **21** 43 41N 4 40 E
Arlington, *S. Africa* **97** 28 1 S 27 53 E
Arlington, *Oreg., U.S.A.* **122** 45 48N 120 6W
Arlington, *S. Dak., U.S.A.* **120** 44 25N 97 4W
Arlington, *Va., U.S.A.* **114** 38 52N 77 5W
Arlington, *Wash., U.S.A.* **110** 48 11N 122 4W
Arlington Heights, *U.S.A.* **119** 42 5N 87 59W
Arlon, *Belgium* **17** 49 42N 5 49 E
Arlöv, *Sweden* **11** 55 38N 13 5 E
Arly, *Burkina Faso* **91** 11 35N 1 28 E
Armagh, *Canada* **107** 46 41N 70 32W
Armagh, *U.K.* **15** 54 22N 6 40W
Armagh □, *U.K.* **15** 54 18N 6 37W
Armagnac, *France* **20** 43 50N 0 10 E
Armançon →, *France* **19** 47 59N 3 30 E
Armavir, *U.S.S.R.* **39** 45 2N 41 7 E
Armenia, *Colombia* **134** 4 35N 75 45W
Armenian S.S.R. □, *U.S.S.R.* **39** 40 0N 44 0 E
Armentières, *France* **19** 50 40N 2 50 E
Armidale, *Australia* **77** 30 30 S 151 40 E
Armour, *U.S.A.* **120** 43 20N 98 25W
Armstrong, *B.C., Canada* **110** 50 25N 119 10W
Armstrong, *Ont., Canada* **104** 50 18N 89 4W
Armstrong, *U.S.A.* **121** 26 59N 97 48W
Armstrong Cr. →, *Australia* **78** 16 35 S 131 40 E
Armur, *India* **50** 18 48N 78 16 E
Arnaouti, C., *Cyprus* **46** 35 6N 32 17 E
Arnarfjörður, *Iceland* **8** 65 48N 23 40W
Arnaud →, *Canada* **103** 60 0N 70 0W
Arnay-le-Duc, *France* **19** 47 10N 4 27 E
Arnedillo, *Spain* **24** 42 13N 2 14W
Arnedo, *Spain* **24** 42 12N 2 5W
Arnemuiden, *Neths.* **17** 51 30N 3 40 E
Árnes, *Iceland* **8** 66 1N 21 31W
Årnes, *Norway* **10** 60 7N 11 28 E
Arnett, *U.S.A.* **121** 36 9N 99 44W
Arnhem, *Neths.* **16** 51 58N 5 55 E
Arnhem, C., *Australia* **72** 12 20 S 137 30 E
Arnhem B., *Australia* **72** 12 20 S 136 10 E
Arnhem Land, *Australia* **72** 13 10 S 134 30 E
Arno →, *Italy* **26** 43 41N 10 17 E
Arno Bay, *Australia* **73** 33 54 S 136 34 E
Arnold, *Calif., U.S.A.* **124** 38 15N 120 20W
Arnold, *Nebr., U.S.A.* **120** 41 29N 100 10W
Arnoldstein, *Austria* **33** 46 33N 13 43 E
Arnon →, *France* **19** 47 13N 2 1 E
Arnot, *Canada* **111** 55 56N 96 41W
Arnøy, *Norway* **8** 70 9N 20 40 E
Arnprior, *Canada* **109** 45 26N 76 21W
Arnsberg, *W. Germany* **30** 51 25N 8 2 E
Arnstadt, *E. Germany* **30** 50 50N 10 56 E
Arntfield, *Canada* **106** 48 12N 79 15W
Aro →, *Venezuela* **135** 8 1N 64 11W
Aroab, *Namibia* **96** 26 41 S 19 39 E
Aroche, *Spain* **23** 37 56N 6 57W
Aroeiras, *Brazil* **138** 7 31 S 35 41W
Arolsen, *W. Germany* **30** 51 23N 9 1 E
Aron →, *France* **20** 46 50N 3 28 E
Arona, *Italy* **26** 45 45N 8 32 E
Arosa, Ria de, *Spain* **22** 42 28N 8 57W
Arpajon, *France* **19** 48 36N 2 15 E
Arpajon-sur-Cère, *France* **20** 44 53N 2 28 E
Arpino, *Italy* **28** 41 40N 13 35 E
Arque, *Bolivia* **136** 17 48 S 66 23W
Arrabury, *Australia* **73** 26 45 S 141 0 E
Arraias, *Brazil* **139** 12 56 S 46 57W
Arraias →, *Mato Grosso, Brazil* **137** 11 10 S 53 35W
Arraias →, *Pará, Brazil* **138** 7 30 S 49 20W
Arraiolos, *Portugal* **23** 38 44N 7 59W
Arran, *U.K.* **14** 55 34N 5 12W
Arrandale, *Canada* **110** 54 57N 130 0W
Arras, *France* **19** 50 17N 2 46 E
Arrats →, *France* **20** 44 6N 0 52 E
Arreau, *France* **20** 42 54N 0 22 E
Arrecife, *Canary Is.* **25** 28 57N 13 37W
Arrecifes, *Argentina* **140** 34 6 S 60 9W
Arrée, Mts. d', *France* **18** 48 26N 3 55W
Arriaga, *Chiapas, Mexico* **127** 16 15N 93 52W
Arriaga, *San Luis Potosí, Mexico* **126** 21 55N 101 23W
Arrilalah P.O., *Australia* **72** 23 43 S 143 54 E
Arrino, *Australia* **79** 29 30 S 115 40 E
Arrojado →, *Brazil* **139** 13 24 S 44 20W
Arromanches-les-Bains, *France* **18** 49 20N 0 38W
Arronches, *Portugal* **23** 39 8N 7 16W
Arros →, *France* **20** 43 40N 0 2W
Arrou, *France* **18** 48 6N 1 8 E
Arrow, L., *Ireland* **15** 54 3N 8 20W
Arrow Rock Res., *U.S.A.* **122** 43 45N 115 50W
Arrowhead, *Canada* **110** 50 40N 117 55W
Arrowhead, L., *U.S.A.* **125** 34 16N 117 10W
Arrowsmith, Mt., *N.Z.* **81** 43 20 S 170 55 E
Arrowtown, *N.Z.* **81** 44 57 S 168 50 E
Arroyo de la Luz, *Spain* **23** 39 30N 6 38W
Arroyo Grande, *U.S.A.* **125** 35 9N 120 32W
Års, *Denmark* **11** 56 48N 9 30 E
Ars-en-Ré, *France* **20** 46 12N 1 31W
Ars-sur-Moselle, *France* **19** 49 5N 6 4 E
Arsenault L., *Canada* **111** 55 6N 108 32W
Arsi □, *Ethiopia* **89** 7 45N 39 0 E
Arsiero, *Italy* **27** 45 49N 11 22 E
Arsikere, *India* **51** 13 15N 76 15 E
Arsk, *U.S.S.R.* **37** 56 10N 49 50 E
Árta, *Greece* **35** 39 8N 21 2 E
Artá, *Spain* **24** 39 41N 3 21 E
Arteaga, *Mexico* **126** 18 50N 102 20W
Arteijo, *Spain* **22** 43 19N 8 29W
Artem, Ostrov, *U.S.S.R.* **39** 40 28N 50 20 E
Artemovsk, *R.S.F.S.R., U.S.S.R.* **41** 54 45N 93 35 E
Artemovsk, *Ukraine S.S.R., U.S.S.R.* **38** 48 35N 38 0 E
Artemovski, *U.S.S.R.* **39** 47 45N 40 16 E
Artenay, *France* **19** 48 5N 1 50 E
Artern, *E. Germany* **30** 51 22N 11 18 E
Artesa de Segre, *Spain* **24** 41 54N 1 3 E
Artesia = Mosomane, *Botswana* **96** 24 2 S 26 19 E
Artesia, *U.S.A.* **121** 32 55N 104 25W
Artesia Wells, *U.S.A.* **121** 28 17N 99 18W
Artesian, *U.S.A.* **120** 44 2N 97 54W
Arthez-de-Béarn, *France* **20** 43 29N 0 38W
Arthington, *Liberia* **90** 6 35N 10 45W
Arthur, *Canada* **108** 43 50N 80 32W
Arthur, *U.S.A.* **119** 39 43N 88 28W
Arthur →, *Australia* **72** 41 2 S 144 40 E
Arthur Cr. →, *Australia* **72** 22 30 S 136 25 E
Arthur Pt., *Australia* **72** 22 7 S 150 3 E
Arthur's Pass, *N.Z.* **81** 42 54 S 171 35 E
Arthur's Town, *Bahamas* **129** 24 38N 75 42W
Artigas, *Uruguay* **140** 30 20 S 56 30W
Artik, *U.S.S.R.* **39** 40 38N 43 58 E
Artillery L., *Canada* **111** 63 9N 107 52W
Artois, *France* **19** 50 20N 2 30 E
Artsiz, *U.S.S.R.* **38** 46 4N 29 26 E
Artvin, *Turkey* **46** 41 14N 41 44 E
Aru, Kepulauan, *Indonesia* **57** 6 0 S 134 30 E
Aru Meru □, *Tanzania* **92** 3 20 S 36 50 E
Arua, *Uganda* **92** 3 1N 30 58 E
Aruanã, *Brazil* **139** 14 54 S 51 10W
Aruba, *Neth. Ant.* **129** 12 30N 70 0W
Arucas, *Canary Is.* **25** 28 7N 15 32W
Arudy, *France* **20** 43 7N 0 28W
Arumã, *Brazil* **135** 4 44 S 62 8W
Arumpo, *Australia* **74** 33 48 S 142 55 E
Arun →, *Nepal* **49** 26 55N 87 10 E
Arunachal Pradesh □, *India* **52** 28 0N 95 0 E
Arundel, *Canada* **106** 45 58N 74 37W
Aruppukkottai, *India* **51** 9 31N 78 8 E
Arusha, *Tanzania* **92** 3 20 S 36 40 E
Arusha □, *Tanzania* **92** 4 0 S 36 30 E
Arusha Chini, *Tanzania* **92** 3 32 S 37 20 E
Aruvi →, *Sri Lanka* **51** 8 48N 79 53 E
Aruwimi →, *Zaïre* **92** 1 13N 23 36 E
Arvada, *U.S.A.* **122** 44 43N 106 6W
Arvakalu, *Sri Lanka* **51** 8 20N 79 58 E
Arvayheer, *Mongolia* **62** 46 15N 102 48 E
Arve →, *France* **21** 46 11N 6 8 E
Arvi, *India* **50** 20 59N 78 16 E
Arvida, *Canada* **107** 48 25N 71 14W
Arvidsjaur, *Sweden* **8** 65 35N 19 10 E
Arvika, *Sweden* **10** 59 40N 12 36 E
Arvin, *U.S.A.* **125** 35 12N 118 50W
Arxan, *China* **62** 47 11N 119 57 E
Arys, *U.S.S.R.* **40** 42 26N 68 48 E
Arzachena, *Italy* **28** 41 5N 9 27 E
Arzamas, *U.S.S.R.* **37** 55 27N 43 55 E
Arzew, *Algeria* **85** 35 50N 0 23W
Arzgir, *U.S.S.R.* **39** 45 18N 44 23 E
Arzignano, *Italy* **27** 45 30N 11 20 E
As, *Belgium* **17** 51 1N 5 35 E
'As Saffānīyah, *Si. Arabia* **46** 28 5N 48 50 E
Aş Şāfī, *Jordan* **44** 31 2N 35 28 E
As Salt, *Jordan* **44** 32 2N 35 43 E
As Samāwah, *Iraq* **46** 31 15N 45 15 E
As Samū', *Jordan* **44** 31 24N 35 4 E
As Sanamayn, *Syria* **44** 33 3N 36 10 E
As Sulaymānīyah, *Iraq* **46** 35 35N 45 29 E
As Sulaymānīyah, *Si. Arabia* **46** 24 9N 47 18 E
As Sulţan, *Libya* **86** 31 4N 17 8 E
As Summān, *Si. Arabia* **46** 25 0N 47 0 E
As Sūq, *Si. Arabia* **46** 21 58N 42 3 E
As Suwaydā', *Syria* **46** 32 40N 36 30 E
As Suwayh, *Oman* **47** 22 10N 59 33 E
Aş Şuwayrah, *Iraq* **46** 32 55N 45 0 E
Asab, *Namibia* **96** 25 30 S 18 0 E
Asaba, *Nigeria* **91** 6 12N 6 38 E
Asafo, *Ghana* **90** 6 20N 2 40W
Asahi, *Japan* **65** 35 43N 140 39 E
Asahi-Gawa →, *Japan* **64** 34 36N 133 58 E
Asahigawa, *Japan* **63** 43 46N 142 22 E
Asale, L., *Ethiopia* **89** 14 0N 40 20 E
Asama-Yama, *Japan* **65** 36 24N 138 31 E
Asamankese, *Ghana* **91** 5 50N 0 40W
Asansol, *India* **49** 23 40N 87 1 E
Åsarna, *Sweden* **10** 62 39N 14 22 E
Asbe Teferi, *Ethiopia* **89** 9 4N 40 49 E
Asbesberge, *S. Africa* **96** 29 0 S 23 0 E
Asbestos, *Canada* **105** 45 47N 71 58W
Asbury Park, *U.S.A.* **117** 40 15N 74 1W
Ascensión, *Mexico* **126** 31 6N 107 59W
Ascensión, B. de la, *Mexico* **127** 19 50N 87 20W
Ascension I., *Atl. Oc.* **4** 8 0 S 14 15W
Aschaffenburg, *W. Germany* **31** 49 58N 9 8 E
Aschendorf, *W. Germany* **30** 53 2N 7 22 E
Aschersleben, *E. Germany* **30** 51 45N 11 28 E
Asciano, *Italy* **27** 43 14N 11 32 E
Áscoli Piceno, *Italy* **27** 42 51N 13 34 E
Áscoli Satriano, *Italy* **29** 41 11N 15 32 E
Ascope, *Peru* **136** 7 46 S 79 8W
Ascotán, *Chile* **140** 21 45 S 68 17W
Aseb, *Ethiopia* **89** 13 0N 42 40 E
Åseda, *Sweden* **11** 57 10N 15 20 E
Asedjrad, *Algeria* **85** 24 51N 1 29 E
Asela, *Ethiopia* **89** 8 0N 39 0 E

Asenovgrad, *Bulgaria* . **35** 42 1N 24 51 E
Asfeld, *France* ...... **19** 49 27N 4 5 E
Asfûn el Matâ'na, *Egypt* .... **88** 25 26N 32 30 E
Åsgårdstrand, *Norway* **10** 59 22N 10 27 E
Ash Fork, *U.S.A.* **123** 35 14N 112 32W
Ash Grove, *U.S.A.* ... **121** 37 21N 93 36W
Ash Shām, Bādiyat, *Asia* .... **46** 32 0N 40 0 E
Ash Shāmīyah, *Iraq* .. **46** 31 55N 44 35 E
Ash Shāriqah, *U.A.E.* **47** 25 23N 55 26 E
Ash Shaṭrah, *Iraq* .... **46** 31 30N 46 10 E
Ash Shaykh, J., *Lebanon* .... **46** 33 25N 35 50 E
Ash Shu'aybah, *Si. Arabia* .... **46** 27 53N 44 43 E
Ash Shu'bah, *Si. Arabia* .... **46** 28 54N 44 44 E
Ash Shūnah ash Shamālīyah, *Jordan* . **44** 32 37N 35 34 E
Ashanti □, *Ghana* **91** 7 30N 1 30W
Ashau, *Vietnam* ...... **54** 16 6N 107 22 E
Ashburn, *U.S.A.* **115** 31 42N 83 40W
Ashburton, *N.Z.* ..... **81** 43 53 S 171 48 E
Ashburton →, *Australia* .... **78** 21 40 S 114 56 E
Ashburton, North Branch →, *N.Z.* ... **81** 43 54 S 171 44 E
Ashburton, South Branch →, *N.Z.* ... **81** 43 54 S 171 44 E
Ashburton Downs, *Australia* .... **78** 23 25 S 117 4 E
Ashby-de-la-Zouch, *U.K.* **12** 52 45N 1 29W
Ashcroft, *Canada* **110** 50 40N 121 20W
Ashdod, *Israel* .... **44** 31 49N 34 35 E
Ashdot Yaaqov, *Israel* **44** 32 39N 35 35 E
Asheboro, *U.S.A.* **115** 35 43N 79 46W
Asherton, *U.S.A.* **121** 28 25N 99 43W
Asheville, *U.S.A.* **115** 35 39N 82 30W
Asheweig →, *Canada* **104** 54 17N 87 12W
Ashford, *Australia* .... **77** 29 15 S 151 3 E
Ashford, *U.K.* .... **13** 51 8N 0 53 E
Ashford, *U.S.A.* **122** 46 45N 122 2W
Ashikaga, *Japan* ..... **65** 36 28N 139 29 E
Ashio, *Japan* .... **65** 36 38N 139 27 E
Ashizuri-Zaki, *Japan* . **64** 32 44N 133 0 E
Ashkarkot, *Afghan.* .. **48** 33 3N 67 58 E
Ashkhabad, *U.S.S.R.* . **40** 38 0N 57 50 E
Ashland, *Ill., U.S.A.* . **118** 39 53N 90 0W
Ashland, *Kans., U.S.A.* **121** 37 13N 99 43W
Ashland, *Ky., U.S.A.* . **114** 38 25N 82 40W
Ashland, *Maine, U.S.A.* **105** 46 34N 68 26W
Ashland, *Mont., U.S.A.* **122** 45 41N 106 12W
Ashland, *Nebr., U.S.A.* **120** 41 5N 96 27W
Ashland, *Ohio, U.S.A.* **116** 40 52N 82 20W
Ashland, *Oreg., U.S.A.* **122** 42 10N 122 38W
Ashland, *Pa., U.S.A.* . **117** 40 45N 76 22W
Ashland, *Va., U.S.A.* . **114** 37 46N 77 30W
Ashland, *Wis., U.S.A.* **120** 46 40N 90 52W
Ashley, *Australia* ..... **77** 29 18 S 149 52 E
Ashley, *Ill., U.S.A.* ... **118** 38 20N 89 11W
Ashley, *Ind., U.S.A.* . **119** 41 32N 85 4W
Ashley, *N. Dak., U.S.A.* **120** 46 3N 99 23W
Ashley, *Pa., U.S.A.* .. **117** 41 12N 75 55W
Ashmont, *Canada* **110** 54 7N 111 35W
Ashmore Reef, *Australia* .... **78** 12 14 S 123 5 E
Ashmûn, *Egypt* ...... **88** 30 18N 30 55 E
Ashq'elon, *Israel* .... **44** 31 42N 34 35 E
Ashtabula, *U.S.A.* **116** 41 52N 80 50W
Ashti, *India* .... **50** 18 50N 75 15 E
Ashton, *S. Africa* .... **96** 33 50 S 20 5 E
Ashton, *U.S.A.* **122** 44 6N 111 30W
Ashton-under-Lyne, *U.K.* **12** 53 30N 2 8W
Ashuanipi, L., *Canada* **105** 52 45N 66 15W
Ashurst, *N.Z.* .... **80** 40 16 S 175 45 E
Asia .... **42** 45 0N 75 0 E
Asia, Kepulauan, *Indonesia* .... **57** 1 0N 131 13 E
Asiago, *Italy* .... **27** 45 52N 11 30 E
Asidonhoppo, *Surinam* **135** 3 50N 55 30W
Asifabad, *India* ...... **50** 19 20N 79 24 E
Asike, *Indonesia* ..... **57** 6 39 S 140 24 E
Asilah, *Morocco* **84** 35 29N 6 0W
Asinara, *Italy* .... **28** 41 5N 8 15 E
Asinara, G. dell', *Italy* **28** 41 0N 8 30 E
Asino, *U.S.S.R.* ...... **40** 57 0N 86 0 E
'Asīr □, *Si. Arabia* ... **45** 18 40N 42 30 E
Asir, Ras, *Somali Rep.* **98** 11 55N 51 10 E
Aska, *India* .... **50** 19 2N 84 42 E
Asker, *Norway* .... **10** 59 50N 10 26 E
Askersund, *Sweden* ... **11** 58 53N 14 55 E
Askham, *S. Africa* .... **96** 26 59 S 20 47 E
Askim, *Norway* ...... **10** 59 35N 11 10 E
Askja, *Iceland* **8** 65 3N 16 48W
Asl, *Egypt* .... **88** 29 33N 32 44 E
Āsmār, *Afghan.* ...... **47** 35 10N 71 27 E
Asmara = Asmera, *Ethiopia* .... **89** 15 19N 38 55 E
Asmera, *Ethiopia* ..... **89** 15 19N 38 55 E
Asnæs, *Denmark* ..... **11** 55 40N 11 0 E
Asni, *Morocco* **84** 31 17N 7 58W
Aso, *Japan* .... **64** 33 0N 131 5 E
Aso-Zan, *Japan* ...... **64** 32 53N 131 6 E
Asola, *Italy* .... **26** 45 12N 10 25 E
Asoteriba, Jebel, *Sudan* **88** 21 51N 36 30 E
Asotin, *U.S.A.* **122** 46 20N 117 3W
Aspe, *Spain* **25** 38 20N 0 40W
Aspen, *U.S.A.* **123** 39 12N 106 56W
Aspermont, *U.S.A.* ... **121** 33 11N 100 15W
Aspiring, Mt., *N.Z.* .. **81** 44 23 S 168 46 E
Aspres-sur-Buëch, *France* .... **21** 44 32N 5 44 E
Aspromonte, *Italy* .... **29** 38 10N 16 0 E
Aspur, *India* .... **48** 23 58N 74 7 E
Asquith, *Canada* **111** 52 8N 107 13W
Assa, *Morocco* **84** 28 35N 9 6W
Assâba, *Mauritania* ... **90** 16 10N 11 45W
Assam □, *India* ...... **52** 26 0N 93 0 E
Assamakka, *Niger* .... **91** 19 21N 5 38 E
Asse, *Belgium* .... **17** 50 24N 4 10 E
Assebroek, *Belgium* .. **17** 51 11N 3 17 E
Assekrem, *Algeria* .... **85** 23 16N 5 49 E
Assémini, *Italy* ...... **28** 39 18N 9 0 E
Assen, *Neths.* .... **16** 53 0N 6 35 E
Assendelft, *Neths.* .... **16** 52 29N 4 45 E
Assenede, *Belgium* ... **17** 51 14N 3 46 E
Assens, *Århus, Denmark* .... **11** 56 41N 10 3 E
Assens, *Fyn, Denmark* **11** 55 16N 9 55 E
Assesse, *Belgium* ..... **17** 50 22N 5 2 E
Assini, *Ivory C.* **90** 5 9N 3 17W
Assiniboia, *Canada* ... **111** 49 40N 105 59W
Assiniboine →, *Canada* **111** 49 53N 97 8W
Assis, *Brazil* .... **141** 22 40 S 50 20W
Assisi, *Italy* .... **27** 43 4N 12 36 E
Assumption, *U.S.A.* .. **118** 39 31N 89 3W
Assynt, L., *U.K.* **14** 58 25N 5 15W
Astaffort, *France* ..... **20** 44 4N 0 40 E
Asten, *Neths.* .... **17** 51 24N 5 45 E
Asti, *Italy* .... **26** 44 54N 8 11 E
Astipálaia, *Greece* .... **35** 36 32N 26 22 E
Astorga, *Spain* **22** 42 29N 6 8W
Astoria, *Ill., U.S.A.* .. **118** 40 14N 90 21W
Astoria, *Oreg., U.S.A.* **124** 46 16N 123 50W
Åstorp, *Sweden* ...... **11** 56 6N 12 55 E
Astorville, *Canada* ... **108** 46 11N 79 17W
Astrakhan, *U.S.S.R.* .. **39** 46 25N 48 5 E
Astrolabe, C., *Solomon Is.* .... **68** 8 20 S 160 34 E
Astudillo, *Spain* **22** 42 12N 4 22W
Asturias, *Spain* **22** 43 15N 6 0W
Asunción, *Paraguay* .. **140** 25 10 S 57 30W
Asunción, La, *Venezuela* **135** 11 2N 63 53W
Asunción Nochixtlán, *Mexico* **127** 17 28N 97 14W
Asutri, *Sudan* .... **89** 15 25N 35 45 E
Aswa →, *Uganda* .... **92** 3 43N 31 55 E
Aswad, Ras al, *Si. Arabia* .... **88** 21 20N 39 0 E
Aswân, *Egypt* .... **88** 24 4N 32 57 E
Aswân High Dam = Sadd el Aali, *Egypt* . **88** 23 54N 32 54 E
Asyût, *Egypt* .... **88** 27 11N 31 4 E
Asyûti, Wadi →, *Egypt* **88** 27 11N 31 16 E
Aszód, *Hungary* ...... **33** 47 39N 19 28 E
At Ṭafīlah, *Jordan* .... **46** 30 45N 35 30 E
At Tā'if, *Si. Arabia* .. **45** 21 5N 40 27 E
At Tāj, *Libya* .... **86** 24 13N 23 18 E
At Tamīmī, *Libya* .... **86** 32 20N 23 4 E
Aṭ Ṭur, *Jordan* ...... **44** 31 47N 35 14 E
Aṭ Ṭurrah, *Jordan* .... **44** 32 39N 35 59 E
Atacama □, *Chile* .... **140** 27 30 S 70 0W
Atacama, Desierto de, *Chile* .... **140** 24 0 S 69 20W
Atacama, Salar de, *Chile* .... **140** 23 30 S 68 20W
Ataco, *Colombia* **134** 3 35N 75 23W
Atakor, *Algeria* ...... **85** 23 27N 5 31 E
Atakpamé, *Togo* ..... **91** 7 31N 1 13 E
Atalándi, *Greece* ..... **35** 38 39N 22 58 E
Atalaya, *Peru* .... **136** 10 45 S 73 50W
Atalaya de Femes, *Canary Is.* **25** 28 56N 13 47W
Ataléia, *Brazil* .... **139** 18 3 S 41 6W
Atami, *Japan* .... **65** 35 5N 139 4 E
Atankawng, *Burma* ... **52** 25 50N 97 47 E
Atapupu, *Indonesia* ... **57** 9 0 S 124 51 E
Atâr, *Mauritania* **84** 20 30N 13 5W
Atara, *U.S.S.R.* ...... **41** 63 10N 129 10 E
Ataram, Erg n-, *Algeria* **85** 23 57N 2 0 E
Atarfe, *Spain* **23** 37 13N 3 40W
Atascadero, *Calif., U.S.A.* **124** 35 29N 120 40W
Atascadero, *U.S.A.* ... **123** 35 32N 120 44W
Atasu, *U.S.S.R.* ...... **40** 48 30N 71 0 E
Atauro, *Indonesia* .... **57** 8 10 S 125 30 E
Atbara, *Sudan* .... **88** 17 42N 33 59 E
'Atbara →, *Sudan* ... **88** 17 40N 33 56 E
Atbasar, *U.S.S.R.* .... **40** 51 48N 68 20 E
Atchafalaya B., *U.S.A.* **121** 29 30N 91 20W
Atchison, *U.S.A.* **120** 39 40N 95 10W
Atebubu, *Ghana* **91** 7 47N 1 0W
Ateca, *Spain* **24** 41 20N 1 49W
Aterno →, *Italy* ..... **27** 42 11N 13 51 E
Atesine, Alpi, *Italy* ... **26** 46 55N 11 30 E
Atessa, *Italy* .... **27** 42 5N 14 27 E
Ath, *Belgium* .... **17** 50 38N 3 47 E
Athabasca, *Canada* ... **110** 54 45N 113 20W
Athabasca →, *Canada* **111** 58 40N 110 50W
Athabasca, L., *Canada* **111** 59 15N 109 15W
Athboy, *Ireland* **15** 53 37N 6 55W
Athenry, *Ireland* **15** 53 18N 8 45W
Athens = Athínai, *Greece* .... **35** 37 58N 23 46 E
Athens, *Canada* **109** 44 38N 75 57W
Athens, *Ala., U.S.A.* . **115** 34 49N 86 58W
Athens, *Ga., U.S.A.* . **115** 33 56N 83 24W
Athens, *N.Y., U.S.A.* . **117** 42 15N 73 48W
Athens, *Ohio, U.S.A.* **114** 39 25N 82 6W
Athens, *Pa., U.S.A.* .. **117** 41 57N 76 36W
Athens, *Tenn., U.S.A.* **115** 35 45N 84 38W
Athens, *Tex., U.S.A.* . **121** 32 11N 95 48W
Atherley, *Canada* **108** 44 37N 79 20W
Atherton, *Australia* ... **72** 17 17 S 145 30 E
Athiéme, *Benin* ...... **91** 6 37N 1 40 E
Athínai, *Greece* ...... **35** 37 58N 23 46 E
Athlone, *Ireland* **15** 53 26N 7 57W
Athni, *India* .... **50** 16 44N 75 6 E
Athol, *N.Z.* .... **81** 45 30 S 168 35 E
Atholl, Forest of, *U.K.* **14** 56 51N 3 50W
Atholville, *Canada* ... **105** 47 59N 66 43W
Áthos, *Greece* .... **35** 40 9N 24 22 E
Athus, *Belgium* ...... **17** 49 34N 5 50 E
Athy, *Ireland* **15** 53 0N 7 0W
Ati, *Chad* .... **87** 13 13N 18 20 E
Ati, *Sudan* .... **89** 13 5N 29 2 E
Atiak, *Uganda* ...... **92** 3 12N 32 2 E
Atiamuri, *N.Z.* ...... **80** 38 24 S 176 5 E
Atico, *Peru* .... **136** 16 14 S 73 40W
Atienza, *Spain* **24** 41 12N 2 52W
Atikokan, *Canada* **104** 48 45N 91 37W
Atikonak L., *Canada* . **105** 52 40N 64 32W
Atirampattinam, *India* **51** 10 28N 79 20 E
Atka, *U.S.S.R.* ...... **41** 60 50N 151 48 E
Atkarsk, *U.S.S.R.* .... **37** 51 55N 45 2 E
Atkinson, *Ill., U.S.A.* . **118** 41 25N 90 1W
Atkinson, *Nebr., U.S.A.* **120** 42 35N 98 59W
Atlanta, *Ga., U.S.A.* . **115** 33 50N 84 24W
Atlanta, *Ill., U.S.A.* .. **118** 40 16N 89 14W
Atlanta, *Mo., U.S.A.* . **118** 39 54N 92 29W
Atlanta, *Tex., U.S.A.* . **121** 33 7N 94 8W
Atlantic, *U.S.A.* **120** 41 25N 95 0W
Atlantic City, *U.S.A.* . **114** 39 25N 74 25W
Atlantic Ocean **4** 0 0 20 0W
Atlántico □, *Colombia* **134** 10 45N 75 0W
Atlas Mts. = Haut Atlas, *Morocco* **84** 32 30N 5 0W
Atlin, *Canada* **102** 59 31N 133 41W
Atlin, L., *Canada* **110** 59 26N 133 45W
'Atlit, *Israel* .... **44** 32 42N 34 56 E
Atmakur, *India* ...... **51** 14 37N 79 40 E
Atmore, *U.S.A.* **115** 31 2N 87 30W
Atō, *Japan* .... **64** 34 25N 131 40 E
Atoka, *U.S.A.* **121** 34 22N 96 10W
Átokos, *Greece* ...... **35** 38 28N 20 49 E
Atolia, *U.S.A.* **125** 35 19N 117 37W
Atouguia, *Portugal* ... **23** 39 20N 9 20W
Atoyac →, *Mexico* ... **127** 16 30N 97 31W
Atrak →, *Iran* .... **47** 37 50N 57 0 E
Ätran, *Sweden* ...... **11** 57 7N 12 57 E
Atrato →, *Colombia* . **134** 8 17N 76 58W
Atrauli, *India* .... **48** 28 2N 78 20 E
Atri, *Italy* .... **27** 42 35N 14 0 E
Atsbi, *Ethiopia* .... **89** 13 52N 39 50 E
Atsoum, Mts., *Cameroon* .... **91** 6 41N 12 57 E
Atsugi, *Japan* .... **65** 35 25N 139 21 E
Atsumi, *Japan* .... **65** 34 35N 137 4 E
Atsumi-Wan, *Japan* .. **65** 34 44N 137 13 E
Atsuta, *Japan* .... **63** 43 24N 141 26 E
Attalla, *U.S.A.* **115** 34 2N 86 5W
Attawapiskat, *Canada* **104** 52 56N 82 24W
Attawapiskat →, *Canada* **104** 52 57N 82 18W
Attawapiskat, L., *Canada* **104** 52 18N 87 54W
Attendorn, *W. Germany* .... **30** 51 8N 7 54 E
Attert, *Belgium* ...... **17** 49 45N 5 47 E
Attica, *U.S.A.* **119** 40 20N 87 15W
Attichy, *France* ...... **19** 49 25N 3 3 E
Attigny, *France* ...... **19** 49 28N 4 35 E
Attikamagen L., *Canada* **105** 55 0N 66 30W
'Attīl, *Jordan* .... **44** 32 23N 35 4 E
Attleboro, *U.S.A.* **117** 41 56N 71 18W
Attock, *Pakistan* ..... **48** 33 52N 72 20 E
Attopeu, *Laos* .... **54** 14 48N 106 50 E
Attunga, *Australia* .... **77** 30 55 S 150 50 E
Attur, *India* .... **51** 11 35N 78 30 E
Atuel →, *Argentina* .. **140** 36 17 S 66 50W
Åtvidaberg, *Sweden* .. **11** 58 12N 16 0 E
Atwater, *U.S.A.* **124** 37 21N 120 37W
Atwood, *Canada* **108** 43 40N 81 1W
Atwood, *U.S.A.* **120** 39 52N 101 3W
Au Sable →, *U.S.A.* . **104** 44 25N 83 20W
Au Sable Pt., *U.S.A.* . **104** 46 40N 86 10W
Aubagne, *France* ..... **21** 43 17N 5 37 E
Aubange, *Belgium* .... **17** 49 34N 5 48 E
Aube □, *France* ..... **19** 48 15N 4 10 E
Aube →, *France* ..... **19** 48 34N 3 43 E
Aubel, *Belgium* ...... **17** 50 42N 5 51 E
Aubenas, *France* ..... **21** 44 37N 4 24 E
Aubenton, *France* .... **19** 49 50N 4 12 E
Auberry, *U.S.A.* **124** 37 7N 119 29W
Aubigny-sur-Nère, *France* .... **19** 47 30N 2 24 E
Aubin, *France* .... **20** 44 33N 2 15 E
Aubrac, Mts. d', *France* **20** 44 40N 3 2 E
Auburn, *Ala., U.S.A.* . **115** 32 37N 85 30W
Auburn, *Calif., U.S.A.* **124** 38 53N 121 4W
Auburn, *Ill., U.S.A.* .. **118** 39 36N 89 45W
Auburn, *Ind., U.S.A.* . **119** 41 20N 85 0W
Auburn, *N.Y., U.S.A.* **117** 42 57N 76 39W
Auburn, *Nebr., U.S.A.* **120** 40 25N 95 50W
Auburn, *Wash., U.S.A.* **124** 47 18N 122 13W
Auburn Range, *Australia* .... **73** 25 15 S 150 30 E
Auburndale, *U.S.A.* .. **115** 28 5N 81 45W
Aubusson, *France* .... **20** 45 57N 2 11 E
Auch, *France* .... **20** 43 39N 0 36 E
Auchel, *France* ...... **19** 50 30N 2 29 E
Auchi, *Nigeria* ...... **91** 7 6N 6 13 E
Auckland, *N.Z.* ...... **80** 36 52 S 174 46 E
Auckland □, *N.Z.* .... **80** 38 35 S 177 0 E
Auckland Is., *Pac. Oc.* **66** 50 40 S 166 5 E
Aude □, *France* ...... **20** 43 8N 2 28 E
Aude →, *France* ..... **20** 43 13N 3 14 E
Audegle, *Somali Rep.* . **98** 1 59N 44 50 E
Auden, *Canada* **104** 50 14N 87 53W
Auderghem, *Belgium* . **17** 50 49N 4 26 E
Auderville, *France* **18** 49 43N 1 57W
Audierne, *France* **18** 48 1N 4 34W
Audincourt, *France* ... **19** 47 30N 6 50 E
Audo Ra., *Ethiopia* .. **89** 6 20N 41 50 E
Audubon, *U.S.A.* **118** 41 43N 94 56W
Aue, *E. Germany* .... **30** 50 34N 12 43 E
Auerbach, *E. Germany* **30** 50 30N 12 25 E
Aueti Paraná →, *Brazil* .... **134** 1 51 S 65 37W
Aufist, *W. Sahara* **84** 25 44N 14 39W
Augathella, *Australia* . **73** 25 48 S 146 35 E
Augrabies Falls, *S. Africa* .... **96** 28 35 S 20 20 E
Augsburg, *W. Germany* **31** 48 22N 10 54 E
Augusta, *Italy* .... **29** 37 14N 15 12 E
Augusta, *Ark., U.S.A.* **121** 35 17N 91 25W
Augusta, *Ga., U.S.A.* . **115** 33 29N 81 59W
Augusta, *Ill., U.S.A.* . **118** 40 14N 90 57W
Augusta, *Kans., U.S.A.* **121** 37 40N 97 0W
Augusta, *Ky., U.S.A.* . **119** 38 47N 84 0W
Augusta, *Maine, U.S.A.* **105** 44 20N 69 46W
Augusta, *Mont., U.S.A.* **122** 47 30N 112 29W
Augusta, *Wis., U.S.A.* **120** 44 41N 91 8W
Augustenborg, *Denmark* .... **11** 54 57N 9 53 E
Augustines, L. des, *Canada* **106** 47 37N 75 56W
Augustów, *Poland* .... **32** 53 51N 23 0 E
Augustus, Mt., *Australia* .... **79** 24 20 S 116 50 E
Augustus Downs, *Australia* .... **72** 18 35 S 139 55 E
Augustus I., *Australia* . **78** 15 20 S 124 30 E
Aukan, *Ethiopia* ..... **89** 15 29N 40 50 E
Auki, *Solomon Is.* ... **68** 8 45 S 160 42 E
Aukum, *U.S.A.* **124** 38 34N 120 43W
Aulla, *Italy* .... **26** 44 12N 10 0 E
Aulnay, *France* **20** 46 2N 0 22W
Aulne →, *France* **18** 48 17N 4 16W
Aulnoye-Aymeries, *France* .... **19** 50 12N 3 50 E
Ault, *France* .... **18** 50 8N 1 26 E
Ault, *U.S.A.* **120** 40 40N 104 42W
Aulus-les-Bains, *France* **20** 42 49N 1 19 E
Aumale, *France* ...... **19** 49 46N 1 46 E
Aumont-Aubrac, *France* .... **20** 44 43N 3 17 E
Auna, *Nigeria* .... **91** 10 9N 4 42 E
Aundh, *India* .... **50** 17 33N 74 23 E
Aunis, *France* **20** 46 5N 0 50W
Auponhia, *Indonesia* .. **57** 1 58 S 125 27 E
Aups, *France* .... **21** 43 37N 6 15 E
Aur, P., *Malaysia* .... **55** 2 35N 104 10 E
Aura, *Burma* .... **52** 26 59N 97 57 E
Auraiya, *India* .... **49** 26 28N 79 33 E
Aurangabad, *Bihar, India* .... **49** 24 45N 84 18 E
Aurangabad, *Maharashtra, India* . **50** 19 50N 75 23 E
Auray, *France* **18** 47 40N 2 59W
Aurès, *Algeria* .... **85** 35 8N 6 30 E
Aurich, *W. Germany* . **30** 53 28N 7 30 E
Aurilândia, *Brazil* .... **139** 16 44 S 50 28W
Aurillac, *France* ..... **20** 44 55N 2 26 E
Auronza, *Italy* .... **27** 46 33N 12 27 E
Aurora = Maewo, *Vanuatu* .... **68** 15 10 S 168 10 E
Aurora, *Canada* **116** 44 0N 79 28W
Aurora, *S. Africa* .... **96** 32 40 S 18 29 E
Aurora, *Colo., U.S.A.* **120** 39 44N 104 55W
Aurora, *Ill., U.S.A.* .. **119** 41 42N 88 12W
Aurora, *Mo., U.S.A.* . **121** 36 58N 93 42W
Aurora, *Nebr., U.S.A.* **120** 40 55N 98 0W
Aurora, *Ohio, U.S.A.* **116** 41 21N 81 20W
Aurskog, *Norway* .... **10** 59 55N 11 26 E
Aurukun Mission, *Australia* .... **72** 13 20 S 141 45 E
Aus, *Namibia* .... **96** 26 35 S 16 12 E
Ausable →, *Canada* .. **108** 43 19N 81 46W
Aust-Agder fylke □, *Norway* .... **9** 58 55N 7 40 E
Austin, *Ind., U.S.A.* .. **119** 38 45N 85 49W
Austin, *Minn., U.S.A.* **120** 43 37N 92 59W
Austin, *Nev., U.S.A.* . **122** 39 30N 117 1W
Austin, *Pa., U.S.A.* .. **116** 41 40N 78 7W
Austin, *Tex., U.S.A.* . **121** 30 20N 97 45W
Austin, L., *Australia* .. **79** 27 40 S 118 0 E
Austral Downs, *Australia* .... **72** 20 30 S 137 45 E
Austral Is. = Tubuai Is., *Pac. Oc.* .... **67** 25 0 S 150 0W
Austral Seamount Chain, *Pac. Oc.* .... **67** 24 0 S 150 0W
Australia ■, *Oceania* . **66** 23 0 S 135 0 E
Australian Alps, *Australia* .... **75** 36 30 S 148 30 E
Australian Cap. Terr. □, *Australia* .. **75** 35 30 S 149 0 E
Australian Dependency □, *Antarctica* .... **143** 73 0 S 90 0 E
Austria ■, *Europe* ... **33** 47 0N 14 0 E
Austvågøy, *Norway* ... **8** 68 20N 14 40 E

Autazes, Brazil 135 3 35 S 59 8W
Autelbas, Belgium 17 49 39N 5 52 E
Auterive, France 20 43 21N 1 29 E
Authie →, France 19 50 22N 1 38 E
Authon-du-Perche, France 18 48 12N 0 54 E
Autlán, Mexico 126 19 40N 104 30W
Autun, France 19 46 58N 4 17 E
Auvelais, Belgium 17 50 27N 4 38 E
Auvergne, Australia 78 15 39 S 130 1 E
Auvergne, France 20 45 20N 3 15 E
Auvergne, Mts. d', France 20 45 20N 2 55 E
Auvézére →, France 20 45 12N 0 50 E
Auxerre, France 19 47 48N 3 32 E
Auxi-le-Château, France 19 50 15N 2 8 E
Auxonne, France 19 47 10N 5 20 E
Auxvasse, U.S.A. 118 39 1N 91 54W
Auzances, France 20 46 2N 2 30 E
Auzat-sur-Allier, France 20 45 27N 3 19 E
Ava, U.S.A. 118 37 53N 89 30W
Avallon, France 19 47 30N 3 53 E
Avalon, U.S.A. 125 33 21N 118 20W
Avalon Pen., Canada 105 47 30N 53 20W
Avanigadda, India 51 16 0N 80 56 E
Avaré, Brazil 141 23 4 S 48 58W
Ávas, Greece 35 40 57N 25 56 E
Avawatz Mts., U.S.A. 125 35 30N 116 20W
Aveiro, Brazil 135 3 10 S 55 5W
Aveiro, Portugal 22 40 37N 8 38W
Aveiro □, Portugal 22 40 40N 8 35W
Āvej, Iran 46 35 40N 49 15 E
Avelgem, Belgium 17 50 47N 3 27 E
Avellaneda, Argentina 140 34 50 S 58 10W
Avellino, Italy 29 40 54N 14 46 E
Avenal, U.S.A. 124 36 0N 120 8W
Avenel, Australia 74 36 53 S 145 15 E
Averøya, Norway 10 63 0N 7 35 E
Aversa, Italy 29 40 58N 14 11 E
Avery, U.S.A. 122 47 22N 115 56W
Aves, I. de, W. Indies 129 15 45N 63 55W
Aves, Is. de, Venezuela 129 12 0N 67 30W
Avesnes-sur-Helpe, France 19 50 8N 3 55 E
Avesta, Sweden 10 60 9N 16 10 E
Aveyron □, France 20 44 22N 2 45 E
Aveyron →, France 20 44 5N 1 16 E
Avezzano, Italy 27 42 2N 13 24 E
Aviá Terai, Argentina 140 26 45 S 60 50W
Aviano, Italy 27 46 3N 12 35 E
Avigliana, Italy 26 45 7N 7 13 E
Avigliano, Italy 29 40 44N 15 41 E
Avignon, France 21 43 57N 4 50 E
Ávila, Spain 22 40 39N 4 43W
Ávila □, Spain 22 40 30N 5 0W
Ávila, Sierra de, Spain 22 40 40N 5 0W
Avila Beach, U.S.A. 125 35 11N 120 44W
Avilés, Spain 22 43 35N 5 57W
Avisio →, Italy 27 46 7N 11 5 E
Aviston, U.S.A. 118 38 36N 89 36W
Aviz, Portugal 23 39 4N 7 53W
Avize, France 19 48 59N 4 0 E
Avoca, Australia 74 37 5 S 143 26 E
Avoca, Ireland 15 52 52N 6 13W
Avoca, U.S.A. 116 42 24N 77 25W
Avoca →, Australia 74 35 40 S 143 43 E
Avola, Canada 110 51 45N 119 19W
Avola, Italy 29 36 56N 15 7 E
Avon, Ill., U.S.A. 118 40 40N 90 26W
Avon, N.Y., U.S.A. 116 42 55N 77 42W
Avon, S. Dak., U.S.A. 120 43 0N 98 3W
Avon □, U.K. 13 51 30N 2 40W
Avon →, Australia 79 31 40 S 116 7 E
Avon →, Avon, U.K. 13 51 30N 2 43W
Avon →, Hants., U.K. 13 50 44N 1 45W
Avon →, Warwick, U.K. 13 52 0N 2 9W
Avondale, Zimb. 93 17 43 S 30 58 E
Avonlea, Canada 111 50 0N 105 0W
Avonmore, Canada 106 45 10N 74 58W
Avonmouth, U.K. 13 51 30N 2 42W
Avranches, France 18 48 40N 1 20W
Avre →, France 18 48 47N 1 22 E
Avu Avu, Solomon Is. 68 9 50 S 160 22 E
Awag el Baqar, Sudan 89 10 10N 33 10 E
Awaji, Japan 65 34 32N 135 1 E
Awaji-Shima, Japan 64 34 30N 134 50 E
'Awālī, Bahrain 47 26 0N 50 30 E
Awantipur, India 49 33 55N 75 3 E
Awanui, N.Z. 80 35 4 S 173 17 E
Awarja →, India 50 17 5N 76 15 E
'Awartā, Jordan 44 32 10N 35 17 E
Awarua Pt., N.Z. 81 44 15 S 168 5 E
Awasa, L., Ethiopia 89 7 0N 38 30 E
Awash, Ethiopia 89 9 1N 40 10 E
Awash →, Ethiopia 89 11 45N 41 5 E
Awaso, Ghana 90 6 15N 2 22W
Awatere →, N.Z. 81 41 37 S 174 10 E
Awbārī, Libya 86 26 46N 12 57 E
Awbārī □, Libya 86 26 35N 12 46 E
Awe, L., U.K. 14 56 15N 5 15W
Aweil, Sudan 89 8 42N 27 20 E
Awgu, Nigeria 91 6 4N 7 24 E
Awjilah, Libya 86 29 8N 21 7 E
Aworro, Papua N. G. 69 7 43 S 143 11 E
Ax-les-Thermes, France 20 42 44N 1 50 E
Axarfjörður, Iceland 8 66 15N 16 45W
Axedale, Australia 74 36 47 S 144 30 E
Axel, Neths. 17 51 16N 3 55 E
Axel Heiberg I., Canada 144 80 0N 90 0W
Axim, Ghana 90 4 51N 2 15W
Aximim, Brazil 135 4 2 S 59 22W
Axintele, Romania 34 44 37N 26 47 E
Axioma, Brazil 137 6 45 S 64 31W
Axiós →, Greece 35 40 57N 22 35 E
Axmarsbruk, Sweden 10 61 3N 17 10 E
Axminster, U.K. 13 50 47N 3 1W
Axstedt, W. Germany 30 53 26N 8 43 E
Axvall, Sweden 11 58 23N 13 34 E
Aÿ, France 19 49 3N 4 0 E
Ayaantang, Eq. Guin. 94 1 58N 10 24 E
Ayabaca, Peru 136 4 40 S 79 53W
Ayabe, Japan 65 35 20N 135 20 E
Ayacucho, Argentina 140 37 5 S 58 20W
Ayacucho, Peru 136 13 0 S 74 0W
Ayaguz, U.S.S.R. 40 48 10N 80 0 E
Ayakudi, India 51 10 28N 77 56 E
Ayamonte, Spain 23 37 12N 7 24W
Ayan, U.S.S.R. 41 56 30N 138 16 E
Ayancık, Turkey 38 41 57N 34 18 E
Ayapel, Colombia 134 8 19N 75 9W
Ayas, Turkey 38 40 10N 32 14 E
Ayaviri, Peru 136 14 50 S 70 35W
Āybak, Afghan. 47 36 15N 68 5 E
Aye, Belgium 17 50 14N 5 18 E
Ayenngré, Togo 91 8 40N 1 1 E
Ayer's Cliff, Canada 117 45 10N 72 3W
Ayers Rock, Australia 79 25 23 S 131 5 E
Ayiá, Greece 35 39 43N 22 45 E
Ayía Marína, Greece 35 37 11N 26 48 E
Ayía Paraskeví, Greece 35 39 14N 26 16 E
Ayía Rouméli, Greece 35 35 14N 23 58 E
Áyios Andréas, Greece 35 37 21N 22 45 E
Ayíos Evstrátios, Greece 35 39 34N 24 58 E
Áyios Ioannis, Ákra, Greece 35 35 20N 25 40 E
Áyios Kiríkos, Greece 35 37 34N 26 17 E
Áyios Mírono, Greece 35 35 15N 25 1 E
Áyios Nikólaos, Greece 35 35 11N 25 41 E
Aykathonisi, Greece 35 37 28N 27 0 E
Aylen L., Canada 109 45 37N 77 51W
Aylesbury, U.K. 13 51 48N 0 49W
Aylmer, Ont., Canada 108 42 46N 80 59W
Aylmer, Qué., Canada 106 45 24N 75 51W
Aylmer L., Canada 102 64 0N 110 8W
'Ayn al Ghazālah, Libya 86 32 10N 23 20 E
'Ayn 'Arīk, Jordan 44 31 54N 35 8 E
Ayn Dār, Si. Arabia 46 25 55N 49 10 E
Ayn Zālah, Iraq 46 36 45N 42 35 E
'Ayn Zaqqūt, Libya 86 29 0N 19 30 E
Ayna, Spain 25 38 34N 2 3W
Ayolas, Paraguay 140 27 10 S 56 59W
Ayom, Sudan 89 7 49N 28 23 E
Ayon, Ostrov, U.S.S.R. 41 69 50N 169 0 E
Ayora, Spain 25 39 3N 1 3W
Ayr, Australia 72 19 35 S 147 25 E
Ayr, Canada 108 43 17N 80 27W
Ayr, U.K. 14 55 28N 4 37W
Ayr →, U.K. 14 55 29N 4 40W
Ayre, Pt. of, U.K. 12 54 27N 4 21W
Aysha, Ethiopia 89 10 50N 42 23 E
Aytos, Bulgaria 34 42 42N 27 16 E
Ayu, Kepulauan, Indonesia 57 0 35N 131 5 E
Ayutla, Guatemala 128 14 40N 92 10W
Ayutla, Mexico 127 16 58N 99 17W
Ayvalık, Turkey 46 39 20N 26 46 E
Aywaille, Belgium 17 50 28N 5 40 E
Az Ẓahrān, Si. Arabia 46 26 10N 50 7 E
Az Zarqā, Jordan 44 32 5N 36 4 E
Az Zāwiyah, Libya 86 32 52N 12 56 E
Az-Zilfī, Si. Arabia 46 26 12N 44 52 E
Az Zubayr, Iraq 46 30 20N 47 50 E
Azambuja, Portugal 23 39 4N 8 51W
Azamgarh, India 49 26 5N 83 13 E
Azangaro, Peru 136 14 55 S 70 13W
Azaouak, Vallée de l', Mali 91 15 50N 3 20 E
Āzarbāyjān-e Gharbī □, Iran 46 37 0N 44 30 E
Āzarbāyjān-e Sharqī □, Iran 46 37 20N 47 0 E
Azare, Nigeria 91 11 55N 10 10 E
Azay-le-Rideau, France 18 47 16N 0 30 E
Azazga, Algeria 85 36 48N 4 22 E
Azbine = Aïr, Niger 91 18 30N 8 0 E
Azefal, Mauritania 84 21 0N 14 45W
Azeffoun, Algeria 85 36 51N 4 26 E
Azemmour, Morocco 85 33 20N 9 20W
Azerbaijan S.S.R. □, U.S.S.R. 39 40 20N 48 0 E
Azezo, Ethiopia 89 12 28N 37 15 E
Azilda, Canada 108 46 33N 81 6W
Azimganj, India 49 24 14N 88 16 E
Aznalcóllar, Spain 23 37 32N 6 17W
Azogues, Ecuador 134 2 35 S 78 0W
Azor, Israel 44 32 2N 34 48 E
Azores, Atl. Oc. 4 38 44N 29 0W
Azov, U.S.S.R. 39 47 3N 39 25 E
Azov Sea = Azovskoye More, U.S.S.R. 40 46 0N 36 30 E
Azovskoye More, U.S.S.R. 40 46 0N 36 30 E
Azovy, U.S.S.R. 40 64 55N 64 35 E
Azpeitia, Spain 24 43 12N 2 19W
Azrou, Morocco 84 33 28N 5 19W
Aztec, U.S.A. 123 36 54N 108 0W
Azúa de Compostela, Dom. Rep. 129 18 25N 70 44W
Azuaga, Spain 23 38 16N 5 39W
Azuara, Spain 24 41 15N 0 53W
Azuay □, Ecuador 134 2 55 S 79 0W
Azuer →, Spain 23 39 8N 3 36W
Azuero, Pen. de, Panama 128 7 30N 80 30W
Azul, Argentina 140 36 42 S 59 43W
Azul, Serra, Brazil 137 14 50 S 54 50W
Azurduy, Bolivia 137 19 59 S 64 29W
Azusa, U.S.A. 125 34 8N 117 52W
Azzaba, Algeria 85 36 48N 7 6 E
Azzano Décimo, Italy 27 45 53N 12 46 E

B

Ba Don, Vietnam 54 17 45N 106 26 E
Ba Dong, Vietnam 55 9 40N 106 33 E
Ba Ngoi = Cam Lam, Vietnam 55 11 54N 109 10 E
Ba Ria, Vietnam 55 10 30N 107 10 E
Ba Tri, Vietnam 55 10 2N 106 36 E
Ba Xian, China 60 39 8N 116 22 E
Baa, Indonesia 57 10 50 S 123 0 E
Baaba, I., N. Cal. 68 20 3 S 164 59 E
Baamonde, Spain 22 43 7N 7 44W
Baan Baa, Australia 77 30 36 S 149 56 E
Baarle Nassau, Belgium 17 51 27N 4 56 E
Baarlo, Neths. 17 51 20N 6 6 E
Baarn, Neths. 16 52 12N 5 17 E
Bab el Mandeb, Red Sea 45 12 35N 43 25 E
Baba dag, U.S.S.R. 39 41 0N 48 19 E
Babaçulândia, Brazil 138 7 13 S 47 46W
Babadag, Romania 34 44 53N 28 44 E
Babahoyo, Ecuador 134 1 40 S 79 30W
Babakin, Australia 79 32 7 S 118 1 E
Babana, Nigeria 91 10 31N 3 46 E
Babar, Algeria 85 35 10N 7 6 E
Babar, Indonesia 57 8 0 S 129 30 E
Babar, Pakistan 48 31 7N 69 32 E
Babarkach, Pakistan 48 29 45N 68 0 E
Babayevo, U.S.S.R. 37 59 24N 35 55 E
Babb, U.S.A. 122 48 56N 113 27W
Babenhausen, W. Germany 31 49 57N 8 56 E
Babi Besar, P., Malaysia 55 2 25N 103 59 E
Babian Jiang →, China 58 22 55N 101 47 E
Babile, Ethiopia 89 9 16N 42 11 E
Babinda, Australia 72 17 20 S 145 56 E
Babine, Canada 110 55 22N 126 37W
Babine →, Canada 110 55 45N 127 44W
Babine L., Canada 110 54 48N 126 0W
Babo, Indonesia 57 2 30 S 133 30 E
Bābol, Iran 47 36 40N 52 50 E
Bābol Sar, Iran 47 36 45N 52 45 E
Baboua, C.A.R. 94 5 49N 14 58 E
Babura, Nigeria 91 12 51N 8 59 E
Babusar Pass, Pakistan 49 35 12N 73 59 E
Babušnica, Yugoslavia 33 43 7N 22 27 E
Babuyan Chan., Phil. 57 18 40N 121 30 E
Babylon, Iraq 46 32 40N 44 30 E
Bac Can, Vietnam 54 22 8N 105 49 E
Bac Giang, Vietnam 54 21 16N 106 11 E
Bac Ninh, Vietnam 54 21 13N 106 4 E
Bac Phan, Vietnam 54 22 0N 105 0 E
Bac Quang, Vietnam 54 22 30N 104 48 E
Bacabal, Brazil 138 4 15 S 44 45W
Bacajá →, Brazil 135 3 25 S 51 50W
Bacalar, Mexico 127 18 50N 87 27W
Bacan, Indonesia 57 8 27 S 126 27 E
Bacan, Kepulauan, Indonesia 57 0 35 S 127 30 E
Bacan, Pulau, Indonesia 57 0 50 S 127 30 E
Bacarra, Phil. 57 18 15N 120 37 E
Bacău, Romania 34 46 35N 26 55 E
Baccarat, France 19 48 28N 6 42 E
Bacchus Marsh, Australia 74 37 43 S 144 27 E
Bacerac, Mexico 126 30 18N 108 50W
Băceşti, Romania 34 46 50N 27 11 E
Bach Long Vi, Dao, Vietnam 54 20 10N 107 40 E
Bachaquero, Venezuela 134 9 56N 71 8W
Bacharach, W. Germany 31 50 3N 7 46 E
Bachelina, U.S.S.R. 40 57 45N 67 20 E
Bachuma, Ethiopia 89 6 48N 35 53 E
Bačina, Yugoslavia 33 43 42N 21 23 E
Back →, Canada 102 65 10N 104 0W
Bačka Palanka, Yugoslavia 33 45 17N 19 27 E
Bačka Topola, Yugoslavia 33 45 49N 19 39 E
Bäckefors, Sweden 11 58 48N 12 9 E
Backnang, W. Germany 31 48 57N 9 26 E
Backstairs Passage, Australia 73 35 40 S 138 5 E
Bacolod, Phil. 57 10 40N 122 57 E
Bacqueville-en-Caux, France 18 49 47N 1 0 E
Bácsalmás, Hungary 33 46 8N 19 17 E
Bacuk, Malaysia 55 6 4N 102 25 E
Bad →, U.S.A. 120 44 22N 100 22W
Bad Axe, U.S.A. 116 43 48N 82 59W
Bad Bergzabern, W. Germany 31 49 6N 8 0 E
Bad Bramstedt, W. Germany 30 53 56N 9 53 E
Bad Doberan, E. Germany 30 54 6N 11 55 E
Bad Driburg, W. Germany 30 51 44N 9 0 E
Bad Ems, W. Germany 31 50 22N 7 44 E
Bad Frankenhausen, E. Germany 30 51 21N 11 3 E
Bad Freienwalde, E. Germany 30 52 47N 14 3 E
Bad Godesberg, W. Germany 30 50 41N 7 4 E
Bad Hersfeld, W. Germany 30 50 52N 9 42 E
Bad Hofgastein, Austria 33 47 17N 13 6 E
Bad Homburg, W. Germany 31 50 17N 8 33 E
Bad Honnef, W. Germany 30 50 39N 7 13 E
Bad Ischl, Austria 33 47 44N 13 38 E
Bad Kissingen, W. Germany 31 50 11N 10 5 E
Bad Kreuznach, W. Germany 31 49 47N 7 47 E
Bad Lands, U.S.A. 120 43 40N 102 10W
Bad Langensalza, E. Germany 30 51 6N 10 40 E
Bad Lauterberg, W. Germany 30 51 38N 10 29 E
Bad Lippspringe, W. Germany 30 51 47N 8 46 E
Bad Mergentheim, W. Germany 31 49 29N 9 47 E
Bad Münstereifel, W. Germany 30 50 33N 6 46 E
Bad Muskau, E. Germany 30 51 33N 14 43 E
Bad Nauheim, W. Germany 31 50 24N 8 45 E
Bad Oeynhausen, W. Germany 30 52 16N 8 45 E
Bad Oldesloe, W. Germany 30 53 48N 10 22 E
Bad Orb, W. Germany 31 50 16N 9 21 E
Bad Pyrmont, W. Germany 30 51 59N 9 15 E
Bad Reichenhall, W. Germany 31 47 44N 12 53 E
Bad St.-Peter, W. Germany 30 54 23N 8 32 E
Bad Salzuflen, W. Germany 30 52 8N 8 44 E
Bad Segeberg, W. Germany 30 53 58N 10 16 E
Bad Tölz, W. Germany 31 47 43N 11 34 E
Bad Waldsee, W. Germany 31 47 56N 9 46 E
Bad Wildungen, W. Germany 30 51 7N 9 10 E
Bad Wimpfen, W. Germany 31 49 12N 9 10 E
Bad Windsheim, W. Germany 31 49 29N 10 25 E
Badagara, India 51 11 35N 75 40 E
Badagri, Nigeria 91 6 25N 2 55 E
Badajós, L., Brazil 135 3 15 S 62 50W
Badajoz, Spain 23 38 50N 6 59W
Badajoz □, Spain 23 38 40N 6 30W
Badakhshān □, Afghan. 47 36 30N 71 0 E
Badalona, Spain 24 41 26N 2 15 E
Badalzai, Afghan. 48 29 50N 65 35 E
Badampahar, India 50 22 10N 86 10 E
Badanah, Si. Arabia 46 30 58N 41 30 E
Badarinath, India 49 30 45N 79 30 E
Badas, Brunei 56 4 33N 114 25 E
Badas, Kepulauan, Indonesia 56 0 45N 107 5 E
Baddaginnie, Australia 74 36 34 S 145 52 E
Baddo →, Pakistan 47 28 0N 64 20 E
Bade, Indonesia 57 7 10 S 139 35 E
Baden, Austria 33 48 1N 16 13 E
Baden, Switz. 31 47 28N 8 18 E
Baden-Baden, W. Germany 31 48 45N 8 15 E
Baden-Württemberg □, W. Germany 31 48 40N 9 0 E
Badger, Canada 105 49 0N 56 4W
Badger, U.S.A. 124 36 38N 119 1W
Bādghīsāt □, Afghan. 47 35 0N 63 0 E
Badgom, India 49 34 1N 74 45 E
Badhoevedorp, Neths. 16 52 20N 4 47 E
Badia Polèsine, Italy 27 45 6N 11 30 E
Badin, Pakistan 48 24 38N 68 54 E
Badnera, India 50 20 48N 77 44 E
Badogo, Mali 90 11 2N 8 13W
Badong, China 59 31 1N 110 23 E
Baduen, Somali Rep. 98 7 15N 47 40 E
Badulla, Sri Lanka 51 7 1N 81 7 E
Badupi, Burma 52 21 36N 93 27 E
Baena, Spain 23 37 37N 4 20W
Baerami Creek, Australia 76 32 27 S 150 27 E
Baexem, Neths. 17 51 13N 5 53 E
Baeza, Ecuador 134 0 25 S 77 53W
Baeza, Spain 25 37 57N 3 25W
Bafang, Cameroon 91 5 9N 10 11 E
Bafatá, Guinea-Biss. 90 12 8N 14 40W
Baffin B., Canada 144 72 0N 64 0W
Baffin I., Canada 103 68 0N 75 0W
Bafia, Cameroon 91 4 40N 11 10 E
Bafilo, Togo 91 9 22N 1 22 E
Bafing →, Mali 90 13 49N 10 50W
Baflo, Neths. 16 53 22N 6 31 E
Bafoulabé, Mali 90 13 50N 10 55W
Bafoussam, Cameroon 91 5 28N 10 25 E
Bāfq, Iran 47 31 40N 55 25 E

Bafra, *Turkey* **38** 41 34N 35 54 E
Bafra, C., *Turkey* **38** 41 44N 35 58 E
Bāft, *Iran* **47** 29 15N 56 38 E
Bafut, *Cameroon* **91** 6 6N 10 2 E
Bafwasende, *Zaïre* **92** 1 3N 27 5 E
Bagalkot, *India* **51** 16 10N 75 40 E
Bagamoyo, *Tanzania* **92** 6 28 S 38 55 E
Bagamoyo □, *Tanzania* **92** 6 20 S 38 30 E
Bagan Datoh, *Malaysia* **55** 3 59N 100 47 E
Bagan Serai, *Malaysia* **55** 5 1N 100 32 E
Baganga, *Phil.* **57** 7 34N 126 33 E
Bagani, *Namibia* **96** 18 7 S 21 41 E
Bagansiapiapi, *Indonesia* **56** 2 12N 100 50 E
Bagasra, *India* **48** 21 30N 71 0 E
Bagata, *Zaïre* **94** 3 44 S 17 57 E
Bagawi, *Sudan* **89** 12 20N 34 18 E
Bagdad, *U.S.A.* **125** 34 35N 115 53W
Bagdarin, *U.S.S.R.* **41** 54 26N 113 36 E
Bagé, *Brazil* **141** 31 20 S 54 15W
Bagenalstown = Muine Bheag, *Ireland* **15** 52 42N 6 57W
Baggs, *U.S.A.* **122** 41 8N 107 46W
Bagh, *Pakistan* **49** 33 59N 73 45 E
Baghdād, *Iraq* **46** 33 20N 44 30 E
Bagherhat, *Bangla.* **52** 22 40N 89 47 E
Bagheria, *Italy* **28** 38 5N 13 30 E
Baghlān, *Afghan.* **47** 36 12N 69 0 E
Baghlān □, *Afghan.* **47** 36 0N 68 30 E
Bagley, *U.S.A.* **120** 47 30N 95 22W
Bagnacavallo, *Italy* **27** 44 25N 11 58 E
Bagnara Cálabra, *Italy* **29** 38 16N 15 49 E
Bagnell Dam, *U.S.A.* **118** 38 14N 92 36W
Bagnères-de-Bigorre, *France* **20** 43 5N 0 9 E
Bagnères-de-Luchon, *France* **20** 42 47N 0 38 E
Bagni di Lucca, *Italy* **26** 44 1N 10 37 E
Bagno di Romagna, *Italy* **27** 43 50N 11 59 E
Bagnoles-de-l'Orne, *France* **18** 48 32N 0 25W
Bagnoli di Sopra, *Italy* **27** 45 13N 11 55 E
Bagnolo Mella, *Italy* **26** 45 27N 10 14 E
Bagnols-sur-Cèze, *France* **21** 44 10N 4 36 E
Bagnorégio, *Italy* **27** 42 38N 12 7 E
Bagolino, *Italy* **26** 45 49N 10 28 E
Bagotville, *Canada* **107** 48 22N 70 54W
Bagua, *Peru* **136** 5 35 S 78 22W
Baguio, *Phil.* **57** 16 26N 120 34 E
Bahabón de Esgueva, *Spain* **24** 41 52N 3 43W
Bahadurabad Ghat, *Bangla.* **52** 25 11N 89 44 E
Bahadurgarh, *India* **48** 28 40N 76 57 E
Bahama, Canal Viejo de, *W. Indies* **128** 22 10N 77 30W
Bahamas ■, *N. Amer.* **129** 24 0N 75 0W
Baharampur, *India* **49** 24 2N 88 27 E
Bahariya, El Wâhât al, *Egypt* **88** 28 0N 28 50 E
Bahau, *Malaysia* **55** 2 48N 102 26 E
Bahawalnagar, *Pakistan* **48** 30 0N 73 15 E
Bahawalpur, *Pakistan* **48** 29 24N 71 40 E
Baheri, *India* **49** 28 45N 79 34 E
Bahi, *Tanzania* **92** 5 58 S 35 21 E
Bahi Swamp, *Tanzania* **92** 6 10 S 35 0 E
Bahía = Salvador, *Brazil* **139** 13 0 S 38 30W
Bahía □, *Brazil* **139** 12 0 S 42 0W
Bahía, Is. de la, *Honduras* **128** 16 45N 86 15W
Bahía Blanca, *Argentina* **140** 38 35 S 62 13W
Bahía de Caráquez, *Ecuador* **134** 0 40 S 80 27W
Bahía Honda, *Cuba* **128** 22 54N 83 10W
Bahía Laura, *Argentina* **142** 48 10 S 66 30W
Bahía Negra, *Paraguay* **137** 20 5 S 58 5W
Bahir Dar, *Ethiopia* **89** 11 37N 37 10 E
Bahmer, *Algeria* **85** 27 32N 0 10W
Bahönye, *Hungary* **33** 46 25N 17 28 E
Bahr Aouk →, *C.A.R.* **94** 8 40N 19 0 E
Bahr el Ahmar □, *Sudan* **88** 20 0N 35 0 E
Bahr el Ghazâl □, *Sudan* **89** 7 0N 28 0 E
Bahr Salamat →, *Chad* **87** 9 20N 18 0 E
Bahr Yûsef →, *Egypt* **88** 28 25N 30 35 E
Bahra el Burullus, *Egypt* **88** 31 28N 30 48 E
Bahraich, *India* **49** 27 38N 81 37 E
Bahrain ■, *Asia* **47** 26 0N 50 35 E
Bahror, *India* **48** 27 51N 76 20 E
Bai, *Mali* **90** 13 35N 3 28W
Bai Bung, Mui, *Vietnam* **55** 8 38N 104 44 E
Bai Duc, *Vietnam* **54** 18 3N 105 49 E
Bai Thuong, *Vietnam* **54** 19 54N 105 23 E
Baia Farta, *Angola* **95** 12 40 S 13 11 E
Baia Mare, *Romania* **34** 47 40N 23 35 E
Baia-Sprie, *Romania* **34** 47 41N 23 43 E
Baião, *Brazil* **138** 2 40 S 49 40W
Baïbokoum, *Chad* **87** 7 46N 15 43 E
Baicheng, *China* **61** 45 38N 122 42 E
Baidoa, *Somali Rep.* **98** 3 8N 43 30 E
Baie Comeau, *Canada* **105** 49 12N 68 10W
Baie-du-Poste, *Canada* **107** 50 24N 73 56W
Baie-St-Paul, *Canada* **107** 47 28N 70 32W
Baie-Ste-Catherine, *Canada* **107** 48 6N 69 44W
Baie Trinité, *Canada* **105** 49 25N 67 20W
Baie Verte, *Canada* **105** 49 55N 56 12W
Baieville, *Canada* **107** 46 8N 72 43W
Baignes-Ste.-Radegonde, *France* **20** 45 23N 0 25W
Baigneux-les-Juifs, *France* **19** 47 31N 4 39 E
Baihe, *China* **60** 32 50N 110 5 E
Baihe, *Taiwan* **59** 23 24N 120 24 E
Ba'ījī, *Iraq* **46** 35 0N 43 30 E
Baikal, L. = Baykal, Oz., *U.S.S.R.* **41** 53 0N 108 0 E
Bailadila, Mt., *India* **50** 18 43N 81 15 E
Baile Atha Cliath = Dublin, *Ireland* **15** 53 20N 6 18W
Bailei, *Ethiopia* **89** 6 44N 40 18 E
Bailén, *Spain* **23** 38 8N 3 48W
Băileşti, *Romania* **34** 44 1N 23 20 E
Baileux, *Belgium* **17** 50 2N 4 23 E
Bailhongal, *India* **51** 15 55N 74 53 E
Bailique, Ilha, *Brazil* **138** 1 2N 49 58W
Bailleul, *France* **19** 50 44N 2 41 E
Bailundo, *Angola* **95** 12 10 S 15 50 E
Baima, *China* **58** 33 0N 100 26 E
Baimuru, *Papua N. G.* **69** 7 35 S 144 51 E
Bain-de-Bretagne, *France* **18** 47 50N 1 40W
Bainbridge, *Ga., U.S.A.* **115** 30 53N 84 34W
Bainbridge, *Ind., U.S.A.* **119** 39 46N 86 49W
Bainbridge, *N.Y., U.S.A.* **117** 42 17N 75 29W
Bainbridge, *Ohio, U.S.A.* **119** 39 14N 83 16W
Baing, *Indonesia* **57** 10 14 S 120 34 E
Bainiu, *China* **60** 32 50N 112 15 E
Bainville, *U.S.A.* **120** 48 8N 104 10W
Bainyik, *Papua N. G.* **69** 3 40 S 143 4 E
Bā'ir, *Jordan* **46** 30 45N 36 55 E
Baird, *U.S.A.* **121** 32 25N 99 25W
Baird Mts., *U.S.A.* **102** 67 10N 160 15W
Bairin Youqi, *China* **61** 43 30N 118 35 E
Bairin Zuoqi, *China* **61** 43 58N 119 15 E
Bairnsdale, *Australia* **75** 37 48 S 147 36 E
Baisha, *China* **60** 34 20N 112 32 E
Baïsole →, *France* **20** 43 26N 0 25 E
Baissa, *Nigeria* **91** 7 14N 10 38 E
Baitadi, *Nepal* **49** 29 35N 80 25 E
Baixa Grande, *Brazil* **139** 11 57 S 40 11W
Baiyin, *China* **60** 36 45N 104 14 E
Baiyü, *China* **58** 31 16N 98 50 E
Baiyu Shan, *China* **60** 37 15N 107 30 E
Baiyuda, *Sudan* **88** 17 35N 32 7 E
Baj Baj, *India* **49** 22 30N 88 5 E
Baja, *Hungary* **33** 46 12N 18 59 E
Baja, Pta., *Mexico* **126** 29 50N 116 0W
Baja California, *Mexico* **126** 31 10N 115 12W
Bajana, *India* **48** 23 7N 71 49 E
Bajimba, Mt., *Australia* **77** 29 17 S 152 6 E
Bajo Nuevo, *Caribbean* **128** 15 40N 78 50W
Bajoga, *Nigeria* **91** 10 57N 11 20 E
Bajool, *Australia* **72** 23 40 S 150 35 E
Bakala, *C.A.R.* **94** 6 15N 20 20 E
Bakar, *Yugoslavia* **27** 45 18N 14 32 E
Bakchar, *U.S.S.R.* **40** 57 1N 82 5 E
Bakel, *Neths.* **17** 51 30N 5 45 E
Bakel, *Senegal* **90** 14 56N 12 20W
Baker, *Calif., U.S.A.* **125** 35 16N 116 8W
Baker, *Mont., U.S.A.* **120** 46 22N 104 12W
Baker, *Oreg., U.S.A.* **122** 44 50N 117 55W
Baker, Canal, *Chile* **142** 47 45 S 74 45W
Baker, L., *Australia* **79** 26 54 S 126 5 E
Baker, L., *Canada* **102** 64 0N 96 0W
Baker I., *Pac. Oc.* **66** 0 10N 176 35W
Baker Lake, *Canada* **102** 64 20N 96 3W
Baker Mt., *U.S.A.* **122** 48 50N 121 49W
Bakers Creek, *Australia* **72** 21 13 S 149 7 E
Baker's Dozen Is., *Canada* **104** 56 45N 78 45W
Bakersfield, *Calif., U.S.A.* **125** 35 25N 119 0W
Bakersfield, *Vt., U.S.A.* **117** 44 46N 72 48W
Bakhchisaray, *U.S.S.R.* **38** 44 40N 33 45 E
Bakhmach, *U.S.S.R.* **36** 51 10N 32 45 E
Bākhtarān, *Iran* **46** 34 23N 47 0 E
Bakhtārān □, *Iran* **46** 34 0N 46 30 E
Bakinskikh Komissarov, im. 26, *U.S.S.R.* **46** 39 20N 49 15 E
Bakırköy, *Turkey* **35** 40 59N 28 53 E
Bakkafjörður, *Iceland* **8** 66 2N 14 48W
Bakkagerði, *Iceland* **8** 65 31N 13 49W
Bakony →, *Hungary* **33** 47 35N 17 54 E
Bakony Forest = Bakony Hegyseg, *Hungary* **33** 47 10N 17 30 E
Bakony Hegyseg, *Hungary* **33** 47 10N 17 30 E
Bakori, *Nigeria* **91** 11 34N 7 25 E
Bakouma, *C.A.R.* **94** 5 40N 22 56 E
Baku, *U.S.S.R.* **39** 40 25N 49 45 E
Bakutis Coast, *Antarctica* **143** 74 0 S 120 0W
Bakwa-Kenge, *Zaïre* **95** 4 51 S 22 4 E
Bala, *Canada* **108** 45 1N 79 37W
Bal'ā, *Jordan* **44** 32 20N 35 6 E
Bala, L., *U.K.* **12** 52 53N 3 38W
Balabac, Str., *E. Indies* **56** 7 53N 117 5 E
Balabac I., *Phil.* **56** 8 0N 117 0 E
Balabagh, *Afghan.* **48** 34 25N 70 12 E
Balabakk, *Lebanon* **46** 34 0N 36 10 E
Balabalangan, Kepulauan, *Indonesia* **56** 2 20 S 117 30 E
Balabio, I., *N. Cal.* **68** 20 7 S 164 11 E
Bălăciţa, *Romania* **34** 44 23N 23 8 E
Balaghat, *India* **50** 21 49N 80 12 E
Balaghat Ra., *India* **50** 18 50N 76 30 E
Balaguer, *Spain* **24** 41 50N 0 50 E
Balakété, *C.A.R.* **94** 6 56N 19 54 E
Balakhna, *U.S.S.R.* **37** 56 25N 43 32 E
Balaklava, *Australia* **73** 34 7 S 138 22 E
Balaklava, *U.S.S.R.* **38** 44 30N 33 30 E
Balakleya, *U.S.S.R.* **38** 49 28N 36 55 E
Balakovo, *U.S.S.R.* **37** 52 4N 47 55 E
Balancán, *Mexico* **127** 17 48N 91 32W
Balanda, *U.S.S.R.* **37** 51 30N 44 40 E
Balangir, *India* **50** 20 43N 83 35 E
Balapur, *India* **50** 20 40N 76 45 E
Balashikha, *U.S.S.R.* **37** 55 49N 37 59 E
Balashov, *U.S.S.R.* **37** 51 30N 43 10 E
Balasinor, *India* **48** 22 57N 73 23 E
Balasore = Baleshwar, *India* **50** 21 35N 87 3 E
Balassagyarmat, *Hungary* **33** 48 4N 19 15 E
Balât, *Egypt* **88** 25 36N 29 19 E
Balaton, *Hungary* **33** 46 50N 17 40 E
Balazote, *Spain* **25** 38 54N 2 9W
Balbi, Mt., *Papua N. G.* **69** 5 55 S 154 58 E
Balboa, *Panama* **128** 9 0N 79 30W
Balbriggan, *Ireland* **15** 53 35N 6 10W
Balcarce, *Argentina* **140** 38 0 S 58 10W
Balcarres, *Canada* **111** 50 50N 103 35W
Balchik, *Bulgaria* **34** 43 28N 28 11 E
Balclutha, *N.Z.* **81** 46 15 S 169 45 E
Balcombe, *Australia* **74** 38 16 S 145 2 E
Bald Hd., *Australia* **79** 35 6 S 118 1 E
Bald I., *Australia* **79** 34 57 S 118 27 E
Bald Knob, *U.S.A.* **121** 35 20N 91 35W
Baldock L., *Canada* **111** 56 33N 97 57W
Baldwin, *Fla., U.S.A.* **115** 30 15N 82 10W
Baldwin, *Mich., U.S.A.* **114** 43 54N 85 53W
Baldwinsville, *U.S.A.* **117** 43 10N 76 19W
Bale, *Yugoslavia* **27** 45 4N 13 46 E
Bale □, *Ethiopia* **89** 6 20N 41 30 E
Baleares □, *Spain* **24** 39 30N 3 0 E
Baleares, Is., *Spain* **24** 39 30N 3 0 E
Balearic Is. = Baleares, Is., *Spain* **24** 39 30N 3 0 E
Baleia, Pta. da, *Brazil* **139** 17 40 S 39 7W
Balen, *Belgium* **17** 51 10N 5 10 E
Baler, *Phil.* **57** 15 46N 121 34 E
Baleshwar, *India* **50** 21 35N 87 3 E
Balfate, *Honduras* **128** 15 48N 86 25W
Balfe's Creek, *Australia* **72** 20 12 S 145 55 E
Balfour, *S. Africa* **97** 26 38 S 28 35 E
Balfour Channel, *Solomon Is.* **68** 8 43 S 157 27 E
Balfouriyya, *Israel* **44** 32 38N 35 18 E
Balharshah, *India* **50** 19 50N 79 23 E
Bali, *Cameroon* **91** 5 54N 10 0 E
Bali, *Indonesia* **56** 8 20 S 115 0 E
Bali □, *Indonesia* **56** 8 20 S 115 0 E
Bali, Selat, *Indonesia* **57** 8 18 S 114 25 E
Baligród, *Poland* **32** 49 20N 22 17 E
Balikesir, *Turkey* **46** 39 35N 27 58 E
Balikpapan, *Indonesia* **56** 1 10 S 116 55 E
Balimbing, *Phil.* **57** 5 5N 119 58 E
Balimo, *Papua N. G.* **69** 8 6 S 142 57 E
Baling, *Malaysia* **55** 5 41N 100 55 E
Baliza, *Brazil* **137** 16 0 S 52 20W
Balk, *Neths.* **16** 52 54N 5 35 E
Balkan Mts. = Stara Planina, *Bulgaria* **34** 43 15N 23 0 E
Balkan Pen., *Europe* **6** 42 0N 22 0 E
Balkh, *Afghan.* **47** 36 44N 66 47 E
Balkh □, *Afghan.* **47** 36 30N 67 0 E
Balkhash, *U.S.S.R.* **40** 46 50N 74 50 E
Balkhash, Ozero, *U.S.S.R.* **40** 46 0N 74 50 E
Ballachulish, *U.K.* **14** 56 40N 5 10W
Balladonia, *Australia* **79** 32 27 S 123 51 E
Balladoran, *Australia* **76** 31 52 S 148 39 E
Ballan, *Australia* **74** 37 35 S 144 13 E
Ballandean, *Australia* **77** 28 46 S 151 50 E
Ballarat, *Australia* **74** 37 33 S 143 50 E
Ballard, L., *Australia* **79** 29 20 S 120 10 E
Ballater, *U.K.* **14** 57 2N 3 2W
Ballenas, Canal de, *Mexico* **126** 29 10N 113 45W
Balleny Is., *Antarctica* **143** 66 30 S 163 0 E
Ballia, *India* **49** 25 46N 84 12 E
Ballidu, *Australia* **79** 30 35 S 116 45 E
Ballimore, *Australia* **76** 32 12 S 148 55 E
Ballina, *Australia* **77** 28 50 S 153 31 E
Ballina, *Mayo, Ireland* **15** 54 7N 9 10W
Ballina, *Tipp., Ireland* **15** 52 49N 8 27W
Ballinasloe, *Ireland* **15** 53 20N 8 12W
Ballinger, *U.S.A.* **121** 31 45N 99 58W
Ballinrobe, *Ireland* **15** 53 36N 9 13W
Ballinskelligs B., *Ireland* **15** 51 46N 10 11W
Ballon, *France* **18** 48 10N 0 14 E
Ballycastle, *U.K.* **15** 55 12N 6 15W
Ballymena, *U.K.* **15** 54 53N 6 18W
Ballymena □, *U.K.* **15** 54 53N 6 18W
Ballymoney, *U.K.* **15** 55 5N 6 30W
Ballymoney □, *U.K.* **15** 55 5N 6 23W
Ballyshannon, *Ireland* **15** 54 30N 8 10W
Balmaceda, *Chile* **142** 46 0 S 71 50W
Balmazújváros, *Hungary* **33** 47 37N 21 21 E
Balmoral, *Australia* **74** 37 15 S 141 48 E
Balmoral, *U.K.* **14** 57 3N 3 13W
Balmorhea, *U.S.A.* **121** 31 2N 103 41W
Balombo, *Angola* **95** 12 21 S 14 46 E
Balonne →, *Australia* **73** 28 47 S 147 56 E
Balrampur, *India* **49** 27 30N 82 20 E
Balranald, *Australia* **74** 34 38 S 143 33 E
Balş, *Romania* **34** 44 22N 24 5 E
Balsapuerto, *Peru* **136** 5 48 S 76 33W
Balsas, *Mexico* **127** 18 0N 99 40W
Balsas →, *Goiás, Brazil* **138** 9 58 S 47 52W
Balsas →, *Maranhão, Brazil* **138** 7 15 S 44 35W
Balsas →, *Mexico* **126** 17 55N 102 10W
Bålsta, *Sweden* **10** 59 35N 17 30 E
Balston Spa, *U.S.A.* **117** 43 0N 73 52W
Balta, *Romania* **34** 44 54N 22 38 E
Balta, *U.S.A.* **120** 48 12N 100 7W
Balta, *R.S.F.S.R., U.S.S.R.* **39** 42 58N 44 32 E
Balta, *Ukraine S.S.R., U.S.S.R.* **38** 48 2N 29 45 E
Baltanás, *Spain* **22** 41 56N 4 15W
Baltic Sea, *Europe* **9** 56 0N 20 0 E
Baltîm, *Egypt* **88** 31 35N 31 10 E
Baltimore, *Ireland* **15** 51 29N 9 22W
Baltimore, *U.S.A.* **114** 39 18N 76 37W
Baltit, *Pakistan* **49** 36 15N 74 40 E
Baltrum, *W. Germany* **30** 53 43N 7 25 E
Baluchistan □, *Pakistan* **47** 27 30N 65 0 E
Balurghat, *India* **49** 25 15N 88 44 E
Balygychan, *U.S.S.R.* **41** 63 56N 154 12 E
Balzar, *Ecuador* **134** 2 2 S 79 54W
Bam, *Iran* **47** 29 7N 58 14 E
Bama, *China* **58** 24 8N 107 12 E
Bama, *Nigeria* **91** 11 33N 13 41 E
Bamako, *Mali* **90** 12 34N 7 55W
Bamba, *Mali* **91** 17 5N 1 24W
Bamba, *Zaïre* **95** 5 45 S 18 23 E
Bambamarca, *Peru* **136** 6 36 S 78 32W
Bambari, *C.A.R.* **94** 5 40N 20 35 E
Bambaroo, *Australia* **72** 18 50 S 146 10 E
Bamberg, *U.S.A.* **115** 33 19N 81 1W
Bamberg, *W. Germany* **31** 49 54N 10 53 E
Bambesi, *Ethiopia* **89** 9 45N 34 40 E
Bambey, *Senegal* **90** 14 42N 16 28W
Bambili, *Zaïre* **92** 3 40N 26 0 E
Bambuí, *Brazil* **139** 20 1 S 45 58W
Bamenda, *Cameroon* **91** 5 57N 10 11 E
Bamfield, *Canada* **110** 48 45N 125 10W
Bāmīān □, *Afghan.* **47** 35 0N 67 0 E
Bamiancheng, *China* **61** 43 15N 124 2 E
Bamingui, *C.A.R.* **94** 7 34N 20 11 E
Bamkin, *Cameroon* **91** 6 3N 11 27 E
Bampūr, *Iran* **47** 27 15N 60 21 E
Ban Aranyaprathet, *Thailand* **54** 13 41N 102 30 E
Ban Ban, *Laos* **54** 19 31N 103 30 E
Ban Bang Hin, *Thailand* **55** 9 32N 98 35 E
Ban Chiang Klang, *Thailand* **54** 19 25N 100 55 E
Ban Chik, *Laos* **54** 17 15N 102 22 E
Ban Choho, *Thailand* **54** 15 2N 102 9 E
Ban Dan Lan Hoi, *Thailand* **54** 17 0N 99 35 E
Ban Don = Surat Thani, *Thailand* **55** 9 6N 99 20 E
Ban Don, *Vietnam* **54** 12 53N 107 48 E
Ban Don, Ao, *Thailand* **55** 9 20N 99 25 E
Ban Dong, *Thailand* **54** 19 30N 100 59 E
Ban Hong, *Thailand* **54** 18 18N 98 50 E
Ban Kaeng, *Thailand* **54** 17 29N 100 7 E
Ban Keun, *Laos* **54** 18 22N 102 35 E
Ban Khai, *Thailand* **54** 12 46N 101 18 E
Ban Kheun, *Laos* **54** 20 13N 101 7 E
Ban Khlong Kua, *Thailand* **55** 6 57N 100 8 E
Ban Khuan Mao, *Thailand* **55** 7 50N 99 37 E
Ban Khun Yuam, *Thailand* **54** 18 49N 97 57 E
Ban Ko Yai Chim, *Thailand* **55** 11 17N 99 26 E
Ban Kok, *Thailand* **54** 16 40N 103 40 E
Ban Laem, *Thailand* **54** 13 13N 99 59 E
Ban Lao Ngam, *Laos* **54** 15 28N 106 10 E
Ban Le Kathe, *Thailand* **54** 15 49N 98 53 E
Ban Mae Chedi, *Thailand* **54** 19 11N 99 31 E
Ban Mae Laeng, *Thailand* **54** 20 1N 99 17 E
Ban Mae Sariang, *Thailand* **54** 18 10N 97 56 E
Ban Mi, *Thailand* **54** 15 3N 100 32 E
Ban Muong Mo, *Laos* **54** 19 4N 103 58 E
Ban Na Mo, *Laos* **54** 17 7N 105 40 E
Ban Na San, *Thailand* **55** 8 53N 99 52 E
Ban Na Tong, *Laos* **54** 20 56N 101 47 E
Ban Nam Bac, *Laos* **54** 20 38N 102 20 E
Ban Nam Ma, *Laos* **54** 22 2N 101 37 E
Ban Ngang, *Laos* **54** 15 59N 106 11 E
Ban Nong Bok, *Laos* **54** 17 5N 104 48 E
Ban Nong Boua, *Laos* **54** 15 40N 106 33 E
Ban Nong Pling, *Thailand* **54** 15 40N 100 10 E
Ban Pak Chan, *Thailand* **55** 10 32N 98 51 E
Ban Phai, *Thailand* **54** 16 4N 102 44 E
Ban Pong, *Thailand* **54** 13 50N 99 55 E
Ban Ron Phibun, *Thailand* **55** 8 9N 99 51 E
Ban Sanam Chai, *Thailand* **55** 7 33N 100 25 E
Ban Sangkha, *Thailand* **54** 14 37N 103 52 E

Ban Tak, *Thailand* **54** 17 2N 99 4 E
Ban Tako, *Thailand* **54** 14 5N 102 40 E
Ban Tha Dua, *Thailand* **54** 17 59N 98 39 E
Ban Tha Li, *Thailand* **54** 17 37N 101 25 E
Ban Tha Nun, *Thailand* **55** 8 12N 98 18 E
Ban Thahine, *Laos* **54** 14 12N 105 33 E
Ban Xien Kok, *Laos* **54** 20 54N 100 39 E
Ban Yen Nhan, *Vietnam* **54** 20 57N 106 2 E
Baña, Punta de la, *Spain* **24** 40 33N 0 40 E
Banaba, *Kiribati* **66** 0 45 S 169 50 E
Banalia, *Zaïre* **92** 1 32N 25 5 E
Banam, *Cambodia* **55** 11 20N 105 17 E
Banamba, *Mali* **90** 13 29N 7 22W
Banana, *Australia* **72** 24 28 S 150 8 E
Bananal, I. do, *Brazil* **139** 11 30 S 50 30W
Banaras = Varanasi, *India* **49** 25 22N 83 0 E
Banas →, *Gujarat, India* **48** 23 45N 71 25 E
Banas →, *Mad. P., India* **49** 24 15N 81 30 E
Bânâs, Ras, *Egypt* **88** 23 57N 35 50 E
Banbridge, *U.K.* **15** 54 21N 6 17W
Banbridge □, *U.K.* **15** 54 21N 6 16W
Banbury, *U.K.* **13** 52 4N 1 21W
Banchory, *U.K.* **14** 57 3N 2 30W
Bancroft, *Canada* **109** 45 3N 77 51W
Band-e Torkestān, *Afghan.* **47** 35 30N 64 0 E
Banda, *Cameroon* **94** 3 58N 14 32 E
Banda, *India* **49** 25 30N 80 26 E
Banda, Kepulauan, *Indonesia* **57** 4 37 S 129 50 E
Banda, La, *Argentina* **140** 27 45 S 64 10W
Banda Aceh, *Indonesia* **56** 5 35N 95 20 E
Banda Banda, Mt., *Australia* **77** 31 10 S 152 28 E
Banda Elat, *Indonesia* **57** 5 40 S 133 5 E
Banda Sea, *Indonesia* **57** 6 0 S 130 0 E
Bandai-San, *Japan* **63** 37 36N 140 4 E
Bandama →, *Ivory C.* **90** 6 32N 5 30W
Bandanaira, *Indonesia* **57** 4 32 S 129 54 E
Bandanwara, *India* **48** 26 9N 74 38 E
Bandar = Machilipatnam, *India* **51** 16 12N 81 8 E
Bandār 'Abbās, *Iran* **47** 27 15N 56 15 E
Bandar-e Anzalī, *Iran* **46** 37 30N 49 30 E
Bandar-e Chārak, *Iran* **47** 26 45N 54 20 E
Bandar-e Deylam, *Iran* **46** 30 5N 50 10 E
Bandar-e Khomeyni, *Iran* **46** 30 30N 49 5 E
Bandar-e Lengeh, *Iran* **47** 26 35N 54 58 E
Bandar-e Ma'shur, *Iran* **46** 30 35N 49 10 E
Bandar-e Nakhīlū, *Iran* **47** 26 58N 53 30 E
Bandar-e Rīg, *Iran* **47** 29 29N 50 38 E
Bandar-e Torkeman, *Iran* **47** 37 0N 54 10 E
Bandar Maharani = Muar, *Malaysia* **55** 2 3N 102 34 E
Bandar Penggaram = Batu Pahat, *Malaysia* **55** 1 50N 102 56 E
Bandar Seri Begawan, *Brunei* **56** 4 52N 115 0 E
Bandawe, *Malawi* **93** 11 58 S 34 5 E
Bande, *Belgium* **17** 50 10N 5 25 E
Bande, *Spain* **22** 42 3N 7 58W
Bandeira, Pico da, *Brazil* **139** 20 26 S 41 47W
Bandeirante, *Brazil* **139** 13 41 S 50 48W
Bandera, *Argentina* **140** 28 55 S 62 20W
Bandera, *U.S.A.* **121** 29 45N 99 3W
Banderas, B. de, *Mexico* **126** 20 40N 105 30W
Bandia →, *India* **50** 19 2N 80 28 E
Bandiagara, *Mali* **90** 14 12N 3 29W
Bandiana, *Australia* **75** 36 10 S 146 55 E
Bandırma, *Turkey* **46** 40 20N 28 0 E
Bandon, *Ireland* **15** 51 44N 8 45W
Bandon →, *Ireland* **15** 51 40N 8 41W
Bandoua, *C.A.R.* **94** 4 39N 21 42 E
Bandula, *Mozam.* **93** 19 0 S 33 7 E
Bandundu, *Zaïre* **94** 3 15 S 17 22 E
Bandung, *Indonesia* **57** 6 54 S 107 36 E
Bandya, *Australia* **79** 27 40 S 122 5 E
Bañeres, *Spain* **25** 38 44N 0 38W
Banes, *Cuba* **129** 21 0N 75 42W
Bañeza, La, *Spain* **22** 42 17N 5 54W
Banff, *Canada* **110** 51 10N 115 34W
Banff, *U.K.* **14** 57 40N 2 32W
Banff Nat. Park, *Canada* **110** 51 30N 116 15W
Banfora, *Burkina Faso* **90** 10 40N 4 40W
Bang Fai →, *Laos* **54** 16 57N 104 45 E
Bang Hieng →, *Laos* **54** 16 10N 105 10 E
Bang Krathum, *Thailand* **54** 16 34N 100 18 E
Bang Lamung, *Thailand* **54** 13 3N 100 56 E
Bang Mun Nak, *Thailand* **54** 16 2N 100 23 E
Bang Pa In, *Thailand* **54** 14 14N 100 35 E
Bang Rakam, *Thailand* **54** 16 45N 100 7 E
Bang Saphan, *Thailand* **55** 11 14N 99 28 E
Bangala Dam, *Zimb.* **93** 21 7 S 31 25 E
Bangalore, *India* **51** 12 59N 77 40 E
Bangalow, *Australia* **77** 28 41 S 153 30 E
Bangante, *Cameroon* **91** 5 8N 10 32 E
Bangaon, *India* **49** 23 0N 88 47 E
Bangassou, *C.A.R.* **94** 4 55N 23 7 E
Bangeta, Mt., *Papua N. G.* **69** 6 21 S 147 3 E
Banggai, *Indonesia* **57** 1 40 S 123 30 E
Banggi, P., *Malaysia* **56** 7 17N 117 12 E
Banghāzī, *Libya* **86** 32 11N 20 3 E
Banghāzī □, *Libya* **86** 32 7N 20 4 E
Bangil, *Indonesia* **57** 7 36 S 112 50 E
Bangjang, *Sudan* **89** 11 23N 32 41 E
Bangka, P., *Sulawesi, Indonesia* **57** 1 50N 125 5 E
Bangka, P., *Sumatera, Indonesia* **56** 2 0 S 105 50 E
Bangka, Selat, *Indonesia* **56** 2 30 S 105 30 E
Bangkalan, *Indonesia* **57** 7 2 S 112 46 E
Bangkinang, *Indonesia* **56** 0 18N 101 5 E
Bangko, *Indonesia* **56** 2 5 S 102 9 E
Bangkok, *Thailand* **54** 13 45N 100 35 E
Bangladesh ■, *Asia* **52** 24 0N 90 0 E
Bangolo, *Ivory C.* **90** 7 1N 7 29W
Bangong Co, *India* **49** 35 50N 79 20 E
Bangor, *N. Ireland, U.K.* **15** 54 40N 5 40W
Bangor, *Wales, U.K.* **12** 53 13N 4 9W
Bangor, *Maine, U.S.A.* **105** 44 48N 68 42W
Bangor, *Mich., U.S.A.* **119** 42 18N 86 7W
Bangor, *Pa., U.S.A.* **117** 40 51N 75 13W
Bangu, *Zaïre* **94** 0 3 S 19 12 E
Bangued, *Phil.* **57** 17 40N 120 37 E
Bangui, *C.A.R.* **94** 4 23N 18 35 E
Banguru, *Zaïre* **92** 0 30N 27 10 E
Bangweulu, L., *Zambia* **93** 11 0 S 30 0 E
Bangweulu Swamp, *Zambia* **93** 11 20 S 30 15 E
Bani, *Dom. Rep.* **129** 18 16N 70 22W
Bani →, *Mali* **90** 14 30N 4 12W
Bani, Djebel, *Morocco* **84** 29 16N 8 0W
Bani Bangou, *Niger* **91** 15 3N 2 42 E
Banī Na'īm, *Jordan* **44** 31 31N 35 10 E
Banī Suhaylah, *Egypt* **44** 31 21N 34 19 E
Banī Walīd, *Libya* **86** 31 36N 13 53 E
Bania, *Ivory C.* **90** 9 4N 3 6W
Baniara, *Papua N. G.* **69** 9 44 S 149 54 E
Banihal Pass, *India* **49** 33 30N 75 12 E
Banīnah, *Libya* **86** 32 0N 20 12 E
Bāniyās, *Syria* **46** 35 10N 36 0 E
Banja Luka, *Yugoslavia* **33** 44 49N 17 11 E
Banjar, *Indonesia* **57** 7 24 S 108 30 E
Banjarmasin, *Indonesia* **56** 3 20 S 114 35 E
Banjarnegara, *Indonesia* **57** 7 24 S 109 42 E
Banjul, *Gambia* **90** 13 28N 16 40W
Banka Banka, *Australia* **72** 18 50 S 134 0 E
Bankeryd, *Sweden* **11** 57 53N 14 6 E
Banket, *Zimb.* **93** 17 27 S 30 19 E
Bankilaré, *Niger* **91** 14 35N 0 44 E
Bankipore, *India* **49** 25 35N 85 10 E
Banks, Is., *Vanuatu* **68** 13 50 S 167 30 E
Banks C., *Australia* **77** 34 0 S 151 15 E
Banks I., *B.C., Canada* **110** 53 20N 130 0W
Banks I., *N.W.T., Canada* **102** 73 15N 121 30W
Banks I., *Papua N. G.* **69** 10 10 S 142 15 E
Banks Pen., *N.Z.* **81** 43 45 S 173 15 E
Banks Str., *Australia* **72** 40 40 S 148 10 E
Bankura, *India* **49** 23 11N 87 18 E
Bann →, *Down, U.K.* **15** 54 30N 6 31W
Bann →, *Londonderry, U.K.* **15** 55 10N 6 34W
Bannalec, *France* **18** 47 57N 3 42W
Bannang Sata, *Thailand* **55** 6 16N 101 16 E
Bannerton, *Australia* **74** 34 42 S 142 47 E
Banning, *U.S.A.* **125** 33 58N 116 52W
Banningville = Bandundu, *Zaïre* **94** 3 15 S 17 22 E
Bannockburn, *Australia* **74** 38 3 S 144 10 E
Bannockburn, *Canada* **109** 44 39N 77 33W
Bannockburn, *U.K.* **14** 56 5N 3 55W
Bannockburn, *Zimb.* **93** 20 17 S 29 48 E
Bañolas, *Spain* **24** 42 16N 2 44 E
Banon, *France* **21** 44 2N 5 38 E
Baños de la Encina, *Spain* **23** 38 10N 3 46W
Baños de Molgas, *Spain* **22** 42 15N 7 40W
Banská Bystrica, *Czech.* **32** 48 46N 19 14 E
Banská Štiavnica, *Czech.* **33** 48 25N 18 55 E
Banswara, *India* **48** 23 32N 74 24 E
Banten, *Indonesia* **57** 6 5 S 106 8 E
Bantry, *Ireland* **15** 51 40N 9 28W
Bantry, B., *Ireland* **15** 51 35N 9 50W
Bantul, *Indonesia* **57** 7 55 S 110 19 E
Bantva, *India* **48** 21 29N 70 12 E
Bantval, *India* **51** 12 55N 75 0 E
Banyabba, *Australia* **77** 29 22 S 153 2 E
Banyak, Kepulauan, *Indonesia* **56** 2 10N 97 10 E
Banyo, *Cameroon* **91** 6 52N 11 45 E
Banyuls-sur-Mer, *France* **20** 42 28N 3 8 E
Banyumas, *Indonesia* **57** 7 32 S 109 18 E
Banyuwangi, *Indonesia* **57** 8 13 S 114 21 E
Banzare Coast, *Antarctica* **143** 68 0 S 125 0 E
Banzyville = Mobayi, *Zaïre* **94** 4 15N 21 8 E
Bao Ha, *Vietnam* **54** 22 11N 104 21 E
Bao Lac, *Vietnam* **54** 22 57N 105 40 E
Bao Loc, *Vietnam* **55** 11 32N 107 48 E
Bao'an, *China* **59** 22 27N 114 10 E
Baocheng, *China* **60** 33 12N 106 56 E
Baode, *China* **60** 39 1N 111 5 E
Baodi, *China* **61** 39 38N 117 20 E
Baoding, *China* **60** 38 50N 115 28 E
Baoji, *China* **60** 34 20N 107 5 E
Baojing, *China* **58** 28 45N 109 41 E
Baokang, *China* **59** 31 54N 111 12 E
Baoro, *C.A.R.* **94** 5 40N 15 58 E
Baoshan, *Shanghai, China* **59** 31 27N 121 26 E
Baoshan, *Yunnan, China* **58** 25 10N 99 5 E
Baotou, *China* **60** 40 32N 110 2 E
Baoying, *China* **61** 33 17N 119 20 E
Bap, *India* **48** 27 23N 72 18 E
Bapatla, *India* **51** 15 55N 80 30 E
Bapaume, *France* **19** 50 7N 2 50 E
Bāqa el Gharbīyya, *Israel* **44** 32 25N 35 2 E
Ba'qūbah, *Iraq* **46** 33 45N 44 50 E
Baquedano, *Chile* **140** 23 20 S 69 52W
Bar, *U.S.S.R.* **38** 49 4N 27 40 E
Bar, *Yugoslavia* **33** 42 8N 19 8 E
Bar Bigha, *India* **49** 25 21N 85 47 E
Bar Harbor, *U.S.A.* **105** 44 15N 68 20W
Bar-le-Duc, *France* **19** 48 47N 5 10 E
Bar-sur-Aube, *France* **19** 48 14N 4 40 E
Bar-sur-Seine, *France* **19** 48 7N 4 20 E
Barabai, *Indonesia* **56** 2 32 S 115 34 E
Barabinsk, *U.S.S.R.* **40** 55 20N 78 20 E
Baraboo, *U.S.A.* **120** 43 28N 89 46W
Baracaldo, *Spain* **24** 43 18N 2 59W
Baracoa, *Cuba* **129** 20 20N 74 30W
Baradero, *Argentina* **140** 33 52 S 59 29W
Baradine, *Australia* **77** 30 56 S 149 4 E
Baraga, *U.S.A.* **120** 46 49N 88 29W
Barahona, *Dom. Rep.* **129** 18 13N 71 7W
Barahona, *Spain* **24** 41 17N 2 39W
Baraka →, *Sudan* **88** 18 13N 37 35 E
Barakot, *India* **49** 21 33N 84 59 E
Barakpur, *India* **49** 22 44N 88 30 E
Barakula, *Australia* **73** 26 30 S 150 33 E
Baralaba, *Australia* **72** 24 13 S 149 50 E
Baralzon L., *Canada* **111** 60 0N 98 3W
Baramati, *India* **50** 18 11N 74 33 E
Baramba, *India* **50** 20 25N 85 23 E
Barameiya, *Sudan* **88** 18 32N 36 38 E
Baramula, *India* **49** 34 15N 74 20 E
Baran, *India* **48** 25 9N 76 40 E
Baranoa, *Colombia* **134** 10 48N 74 55W
Baranof I., *U.S.A.* **102** 57 0N 135 10W
Baranovichi, *U.S.S.R.* **36** 53 10N 26 0 E
Barão de Cocais, *Brazil* **139** 19 56 S 43 28W
Barão de Grajaú, *Brazil* **138** 6 45 S 43 1W
Barão de Melgaço, *Mato Grosso, Brazil* **137** 16 14 S 55 52W
Barão de Melgaço, *Rondônia, Brazil* **137** 11 50 S 60 45W
Baraolt, *Romania* **34** 46 5N 25 34 E
Barapasi, *Indonesia* **57** 2 15 S 137 5 E
Barapina, *Papua N. G.* **69** 6 21 S 155 25 E
Barasat, *India* **49** 22 46N 88 31 E
Barat Daya, Kepulauan, *Indonesia* **57** 7 30 S 128 0 E
Barataria B., *U.S.A.* **121** 29 15N 89 45W
Baraut, *India* **48** 29 13N 77 7 E
Baraya, *Colombia* **134** 3 10N 75 4W
Barbacena, *Brazil* **139** 21 15 S 43 56W
Barbacoas, *Colombia* **134** 1 45N 78 0W
Barbacoas, *Venezuela* **134** 9 29N 66 58W
Barbados ■, *W. Indies* **129** 13 0N 59 30W
Barbalha, *Brazil* **138** 7 19 S 39 17W
Barban, *Yugoslavia* **27** 45 5N 14 4 E
Barbastro, *Spain* **24** 42 2N 0 5 E
Barbate, *Spain* **23** 36 13N 5 56W
Barberino di Mugello, *Italy* **27** 44 1N 11 15 E
Barberton, *S. Africa* **97** 25 42 S 31 2 E
Barberton, *U.S.A.* **116** 41 0N 81 40W
Barbezieux, *France* **20** 45 28N 0 9W
Barbosa, *Colombia* **134** 5 57N 73 37W
Barbourville, *U.S.A.* **115** 36 57N 83 52W
Barbuda I., *W. Indies* **129** 17 30N 61 40W
Barca, La, *Mexico* **126** 20 20N 102 40W
Barcaldine, *Australia* **72** 23 43 S 145 6 E
Barcarès, Le, *France* **20** 42 47N 3 2 E
Barcarrota, *Spain* **23** 38 31N 6 51W
Barcellona Pozzo di Gotto, *Italy* **29** 38 8N 15 15 E
Barcelona, *Spain* **24** 41 21N 2 10 E
Barcelona, *Venezuela* **135** 10 10N 64 40W
Barcelona □, *Spain* **24** 41 30N 2 0 E
Barcelonette, *France* **21** 44 23N 6 40 E
Barcelos, *Brazil* **135** 1 0 S 63 0W
Barcoo →, *Australia* **72** 25 30 S 142 50 E
Barcs, *Hungary* **33** 45 58N 17 28 E
Barda, *U.S.S.R.* **39** 40 25N 47 10 E
Barda del Medio, *Argentina* **142** 38 45 S 68 11W
Bardai, *Chad* **87** 21 25N 17 0 E
Bardas Blancas, *Argentina* **140** 35 49 S 69 45W
Barddhaman, *India* **49** 23 14N 87 39 E
Bardejov, *Czech.* **32** 49 18N 21 15 E
Bardera, *Somali Rep.* **98** 2 20N 42 27 E
Bardi, *Italy* **26** 44 38N 9 43 E
Bardi, Ra's, *Si. Arabia* **46** 24 17N 37 31 E
Bardia, *Libya* **86** 31 45N 25 0 E
Bardoli, *India* **50** 21 12N 73 5 E
Bardolino, *Italy* **26** 45 33N 10 43 E
Bardsey I., *U.K.* **12** 52 46N 4 47W
Bardstown, *U.S.A.* **119** 37 50N 85 29W
Bareilly, *India* **49** 28 22N 79 27 E
Barentin, *France* **18** 49 33N 0 58 E
Barenton, *France* **18** 48 38N 0 50W
Barents Sea, *Arctic* **144** 73 0N 39 0 E
Barentu, *Ethiopia* **89** 15 2N 37 35 E
Barfleur, *France* **18** 49 40N 1 17W
Barfleur, Pte. de, *France* **18** 49 42N 1 16W
Barga, *China* **62** 30 40N 81 20 E
Barga, *Italy* **26** 44 5N 10 30 E
Bargal, *Somali Rep.* **98** 11 25N 51 0 E
Bargara, *Australia* **72** 24 50 S 152 25 E
Barge, *Italy* **26** 44 43N 7 19 E
Barge, La, *U.S.A.* **122** 42 12N 110 4W
Bargnop, *Sudan* **89** 9 32N 28 25 E
Bargo, *Australia* **76** 34 18 S 150 35 E
Bargteheide, *W. Germany* **30** 53 42N 10 13 E
Barguzin, *U.S.S.R.* **41** 53 37N 109 37 E
Barh, *India* **49** 25 29N 85 46 E
Barhaj, *India* **49** 26 18N 83 44 E
Barhi, *India* **49** 24 15N 85 25 E
Bari, *India* **48** 26 39N 77 39 E
Bari, *Italy* **29** 41 6N 16 52 E
Bari Doab, *Pakistan* **48** 30 20N 73 0 E
Bariadi □, *Tanzania* **92** 2 45 S 34 40 E
Barīm, *S. Yemen* **45** 12 39N 43 25 E
Barima →, *Guyana* **135** 8 33N 60 25W
Barinas, *Venezuela* **134** 8 36N 70 15W
Barinas □, *Venezuela* **134** 8 10N 69 50W
Baring, *U.S.A.* **118** 40 15N 92 12W
Baring, C., *Canada* **102** 70 0N 117 30W
Baringa, *Zaïre* **94** 0 45N 20 52 E
Baringo, *Kenya* **92** 0 47N 36 16 E
Baringo □, *Kenya* **92** 0 55N 36 0 E
Baringo, L., *Kenya* **92** 0 47N 36 16 E
Barinitas, *Venezuela* **134** 8 45N 70 25W
Baripada, *India* **50** 21 57N 86 45 E
Bariri, *Brazil* **139** 22 4 S 48 44W
Bârîs, *Egypt* **88** 24 42N 30 31 E
Barisal, *Bangla.* **52** 22 45N 90 20 E
Barisan, Bukit, *Indonesia* **56** 3 30 S 102 15 E
Barito →, *Indonesia* **56** 4 0 S 114 50 E
Barjac, *France* **21** 44 20N 4 22 E
Barjols, *France* **21** 43 34N 6 2 E
Barjūj, Wadi →, *Libya* **86** 25 26N 12 12 E
Bark L., *Canada* **106** 45 27N 77 51W
Barka = Baraka →, *Sudan* **88** 18 13N 37 35 E
Barkā', *Oman* **47** 23 40N 58 0 E
Barkam, *China* **58** 31 51N 102 28 E
Barker, *U.S.A.* **116** 43 20N 78 35W
Barkley Sound, *Canada* **110** 48 50N 125 10W
Barkly Downs, *Australia* **72** 20 30 S 138 30 E
Barkly East, *S. Africa* **96** 30 58 S 27 33 E
Barkly Tableland, *Australia* **72** 17 50 S 136 40 E
Barkly West, *S. Africa* **96** 28 5 S 24 31 E
Barkol, Wadi →, *Sudan* **88** 17 40N 32 0 E
Barksdale, *U.S.A.* **121** 29 47N 100 2W
Barlee, L., *Australia* **79** 29 15 S 119 30 E
Barletta, *Italy* **29** 41 20N 16 17 E
Barlinek, *Poland* **32** 53 0N 15 15 E
Barlovento, *Canary Is.* **25** 28 48N 17 48W
Barlow L., *Canada* **111** 62 0N 103 0W
Barmah, *Australia* **74** 36 2 S 144 58 E
Barmedman, *Australia* **76** 34 9 S 147 21 E
Barmer, *India* **48** 25 45N 71 20 E
Barmera, *Australia* **73** 34 15 S 140 28 E
Barmouth, *U.K.* **12** 52 44N 4 3W
Barmstedt, *W. Germany* **30** 53 47N 9 46 E
Barnagar, *India* **48** 23 7N 75 19 E
Barnard Castle, *U.K.* **12** 54 33N 1 55W
Barnato, *Australia* **73** 31 38 S 145 0 E
Barnaul, *U.S.S.R.* **40** 53 20N 83 40 E
Barnawatha, *Australia* **75** 36 6 S 146 44 E
Barnesville, *U.S.A.* **115** 33 6N 84 9W
Barnet, *U.K.* **13** 51 37N 0 15W
Barneveld, *Neths.* **16** 52 7N 5 36 E
Barneveld, *U.S.A.* **117** 43 16N 75 14W
Barneville-Cartevert, *France* **18** 49 23N 1 46W
Barney, Mt., *Australia* **77** 28 17 S 152 44 E
Barngo, *Australia* **72** 25 3 S 147 20 E
Barnhart, *U.S.A.* **121** 31 10N 101 8W
Barnsley, *U.K.* **12** 53 33N 1 29W
Barnstaple, *U.K.* **13** 51 5N 4 3W
Barnsville, *U.S.A.* **120** 46 43N 96 28W
Baro, *Nigeria* **91** 8 35N 6 18 E
Baro →, *Ethiopia* **89** 8 26N 33 13 E
Baroda = Vadodara, *India* **48** 22 20N 73 10 E
Baroda, *India* **48** 25 29N 76 35 E
Baroe, *S. Africa* **96** 33 13 S 24 33 E
Baron Ra., *Australia* **78** 23 30 S 127 45 E
Barora Ite, *Solomon Is.* **68** 7 36 S 158 24 E
Barorafa, *Solomon Is.* **68** 7 30 S 158 20 E
Barpali, *India* **50** 21 11N 83 35 E
Barpathar, *India* **52** 26 17N 93 53 E
Barpeta, *India* **52** 26 20N 91 10 E
Barqin, *Libya* **86** 27 33N 13 34 E
Barques, Pte. aux, *U.S.A.* **114** 44 5N 82 55W
Barquinha, *Portugal* **23** 39 28N 8 25W
Barquísimeto, *Venezuela* **134** 10 4N 69 19W
Barr, *France* **19** 48 25N 7 28 E
Barra, *Brazil* **138** 11 5 S 43 10W
Barra, *U.K.* **14** 57 0N 7 30W
Barra, Sd. of, *U.K.* **14** 57 4N 7 25W
Barra da Estiva, *Brazil* **139** 13 38 S 41 19W
Barra de Navidad, *Mexico* **126** 19 12N 104 41W
Barra do Corda, *Brazil* **138** 5 30 S 45 10W

Barra do Dande, Angola 95 8 28 S 13 22 E
Barra do Mendes, Brazil 139 11 43 S 42 4W
Barra do Piraí, Brazil 139 22 30 S 43 50W
Barra Falsa, Pta. da, Mozam. 97 22 58 S 35 37 E
Barra Hd., U.K. 14 56 47N 7 40W
Barra Mansa, Brazil 141 22 35 S 44 12W
Barraba, Australia 77 30 21 S 150 35 E
Barracão do Barreto, Brazil 137 8 48 S 58 24W
Barrackpur = Barakpur, India 49 22 44N 88 30 E
Barrafranca, Italy 29 37 22N 14 10 E
Barranca, Lima, Peru 136 10 45 S 77 50W
Barranca, Loreto, Peru 134 4 50 S 76 50W
Barrancabermeja, Colombia 134 7 0N 73 50W
Barrancas, Colombia 134 10 57N 72 50W
Barrancas, Venezuela 135 8 55N 62 5W
Barrancos, Portugal 23 38 10N 6 58W
Barranqueras, Argentina 140 27 30 S 59 0W
Barranquilla, Colombia 134 11 0N 74 50W
Barras, Brazil 138 4 15 S 42 18W
Barras, Colombia 134 1 45 S 73 13W
Barraute, Canada 106 48 26N 77 38W
Barre, U.S.A. 117 44 15N 72 30W
Barre do Bugres, Brazil 137 15 0 S 57 11W
Barreal, Argentina 140 31 33 S 69 28W
Barrei, Ethiopia 98 6 10N 42 49 E
Barreiras, Brazil 139 12 8 S 45 0W
Barreirinha, Brazil 135 2 47 S 57 3W
Barreirinhas, Brazil 138 2 30 S 42 50W
Barreiro, Portugal 23 38 40N 9 6W
Barreiros, Brazil 138 8 49 S 35 12W
Barrême, France 21 43 57N 6 23 E
Barren, Nosy, Madag. 97 18 25 S 43 40 E
Barretos, Brazil 139 20 30 S 48 35W
Barrhead, Canada 110 54 10N 114 24W
Barrie, Canada 108 44 24N 79 40W
Barriefield, Canada 109 44 14N 76 28W
Barrier, C., N.Z. 80 36 25 S 175 32 E
Barrier Ra., Australia 73 31 0 S 141 30 E
Barrier Ra., N.Z. 81 44 5 S 169 42 E
Barrière, Canada 110 51 12N 120 7W
Barrington, Australia 77 31 58 S 151 55 E
Barrington, U.S.A. 117 41 43N 71 20W
Barrington L., Canada 111 56 55N 100 15W
Barrington Tops, Australia 77 32 6 S 151 28 E
Barringun, Australia 73 29 1 S 145 41 E
Barro do Garças, Brazil 137 15 54 S 52 16W
Barrow, U.S.A. 102 71 16N 156 50W
Barrow →, Ireland 15 52 10N 6 57W
Barrow Creek, Australia 72 21 30 S 133 55 E
Barrow I., Australia 78 20 45 S 115 20 E
Barrow-in-Furness, U.K. 12 54 8N 3 15W
Barrow Pt., Australia 72 14 20 S 144 40 E
Barrow Ra., Australia 79 26 0 S 127 40 E
Barrow Str., Canada 144 74 20N 95 0W
Barruecopardo, Spain 22 41 4N 6 40W
Barruelo, Spain 22 42 54N 4 17W
Barry, Australia 76 33 38 S 149 16 E
Barry, U.K. 13 51 23N 3 19W
Barry, U.S.A. 118 39 42N 91 2W
Barry's Bay, Canada 109 45 29N 77 41W
Barsalogho, Burkina Faso 91 13 25N 1 3W
Barsat, Pakistan 49 36 10N 72 45 E
Barsi, India 50 18 10N 75 50 E
Barsø, Denmark 11 55 7N 9 33 E
Barstow, Calif., U.S.A. 125 34 58N 117 2W
Barstow, Tex., U.S.A. 121 31 28N 103 24W
Barth, E. Germany 30 54 20N 12 36 E
Barthélemy, Col, Vietnam 54 19 26N 104 6 E
Bartica, Guyana 135 6 25N 58 40W
Bartin, Turkey 46 41 38N 32 21 E
Bartlesville, U.S.A. 121 36 50N 95 58W
Bartlett, Calif., U.S.A. 124 36 29N 118 2W
Bartlett, Tex., U.S.A. 121 30 46N 97 30W
Bartlett, L., Canada 110 63 5N 118 20W
Bartolomeu Dias, Mozam. 93 21 10 S 35 8 E
Barton, Australia 79 30 31 S 132 39 E
Barton-upon-Humber, U.K. 12 53 41N 0 27W
Bartonville, U.S.A. 118 40 39N 89 39W
Bartoszyce, Poland 32 54 15N 20 55 E
Bartow, U.S.A. 115 27 53N 81 49W
Barú, I. de, Colombia 134 10 15N 75 35W
Barú, Volcan, Panama 128 8 55N 82 35W
Barumba, Zaïre 92 1 3N 23 37 E
Baruth, E. Germany 30 52 3N 13 31 E
Barvaux, Belgium 17 50 21N 5 29 E
Barvenkovo, U.S.S.R. 38 48 57N 37 0 E
Barwani, India 48 22 2N 74 57 E
Barwon →, Australia 74 38 8 S 144 3 E
Barwon Heads, Australia 74 38 17 S 144 30 E
Barysh, U.S.S.R. 37 53 39N 47 8 E
Baryulgil, Australia 77 29 12 S 152 38 E
Bas-Rhin □, France 19 48 40N 7 30 E
Bašaid, Yugoslavia 33 45 38N 20 25 E
Bāsa'idū, Iran 47 26 35N 55 20 E
Basal, Pakistan 48 33 33N 72 13 E
Basankusa, Zaïre 94 1 5N 19 50 E
Basawa, Afghan. 48 34 15N 70 50 E
Bascharage, Lux. 17 49 34N 5 55 E
Bascuñán, C., Chile 140 28 52 S 71 35W
Basècles, Belgium 17 50 32N 3 39 E
Basel, Switz. 31 47 35N 7 35 E
Basel-Stadt □, Switz. 31 47 35N 7 35 E
Baselland □, Switz. 31 47 26N 7 45 E
Basento →, Italy 29 40 21N 16 50 E
Bashkir A.S.S.R. □, U.S.S.R. 40 54 0N 57 0 E
Basilaki I., Papua N. G. 69 10 35 S 151 0 E
Basilan, Phil. 57 6 35N 122 0 E
Basilan Str., Phil. 57 6 50N 122 0 E
Basildon, U.K. 13 51 34N 0 29 E
Basilicata □, Italy 29 40 30N 16 0 E
Basim = Washim, India 50 20 3N 77 0 E
Basin, U.S.A. 122 44 22N 108 2W
Basingstoke, U.K. 13 51 15N 1 5W
Basirhat, Bangla. 52 22 40N 88 54 E
Baška, Yugoslavia 27 44 58N 14 45 E
Baskatong, Rés., Canada 106 46 46N 75 50W
Basle = Basel, Switz. 31 47 35N 7 35 E
Basmat, India 50 19 15N 77 12 E
Basoda, India 48 23 52N 77 54 E
Basoka, Zaïre 92 1 16N 23 40 E
Basongo, Zaïre 95 4 15 S 20 20 E
Basque, Pays, France 20 43 15N 1 20W
Basque Provinces = Vascongadas □, Spain 24 42 50N 2 45W
Basra = Al Başrah, Iraq 46 30 30N 47 50 E
Bass, Australia 74 38 29 S 145 28 E
Bass Point, Australia 77 34 36 S 150 54 E
Bass Rock, U.K. 14 56 5N 2 40W
Bass Str., Australia 72 39 15 S 146 30 E
Bassano, Canada 110 50 48N 112 20W
Bassano del Grappa, Italy 27 45 45N 11 45 E
Bassar, Togo 91 9 19N 0 57 E
Basse Santa-Su, Gambia 90 13 13N 14 15W
Basse-Terre, Guadeloupe 129 16 0N 61 40W
Bassée, La, France 19 50 31N 2 49 E
Bassein, Burma 52 16 45N 94 30 E
Bassein, India 50 19 26N 72 48 E
Basseterre, St. Christopher-Nevis 129 17 17N 62 43W
Bassett, Nebr., U.S.A. 120 42 37N 99 30W
Bassett, Va., U.S.A. 115 36 48N 79 59W
Bassevelde, Belgium 17 51 15N 3 41 E
Bassi, India 48 30 44N 76 21 E
Bassigny, France 19 48 0N 5 30 E
Bassikounou, Mauritania 90 15 55N 6 1W
Bassilly, Belgium 17 50 40N 3 56 E
Bassum, W. Germany 30 52 50N 8 42 E
Båstad, Sweden 11 56 25N 12 51 E
Bastak, Iran 47 27 15N 54 25 E
Bastar, India 50 19 15N 81 40 E
Bastelica, France 21 42 1N 9 3 E
Basti, India 49 26 52N 82 55 E
Bastia, France 21 42 40N 9 30 E
Bastia Umbra, Italy 27 43 4N 12 34 E
Bastide-Puylaurent, La, France 20 44 35N 3 55 E
Bastogne, Belgium 17 50 1N 5 43 E
Bastrop, U.S.A. 121 30 5N 97 22W
Bat Yam, Israel 44 32 2N 34 44 E
Bata, Eq. Guin. 94 1 57N 9 50 E
Bata, Romania 34 46 1N 22 4 E
Bataan, Phil. 57 14 40N 120 25 E
Batabanó, Cuba 128 22 40N 82 20W
Batabanó, G. de, Cuba 128 22 30N 82 30W
Batac, Phil. 57 18 3N 120 34 E
Batagoy, U.S.S.R. 41 67 38N 134 38 E
Batak, Bulgaria 35 41 57N 24 12 E
Batalha, Portugal 23 39 40N 8 50W
Batama, Zaïre 92 0 58N 26 33 E
Batamay, U.S.S.R. 41 63 30N 129 15 E
Batang, China 58 30 1N 99 0 E
Batang, Indonesia 57 6 55 S 109 45 E
Batangafo, C.A.R. 94 7 25N 18 20 E
Batangas, Phil. 57 13 35N 121 10 E
Batanta, Indonesia 57 0 55 S 130 40 E
Batatais, Brazil 141 20 54 S 47 37W
Batavia, Ind., U.S.A. 119 41 55N 88 17W
Batavia, N.Y., U.S.A. 116 43 0N 78 10W
Batavia, Ohio, U.S.A. 119 39 5N 84 11W
Bataysk, U.S.S.R. 39 47 3N 39 45 E
Batchelor, Australia 78 13 4 S 131 1 E
Batéké, Plateau, Congo 94 3 30 S 15 45 E
Bateman's B., Australia 76 35 40 S 150 12 E
Batemans Bay, Australia 76 35 44 S 150 11 E
Batesburg, U.S.A. 115 33 54N 81 32W
Batesville, Ark., U.S.A. 121 35 48N 91 40W
Batesville, Ind., U.S.A. 119 39 18N 85 13W
Batesville, Miss., U.S.A. 121 34 17N 89 58W
Batesville, Tex., U.S.A. 121 28 59N 99 38W
Bath, Canada 109 44 11N 76 47W
Bath, U.K. 13 51 22N 2 22W
Bath, Maine, U.S.A. 105 43 50N 69 49W
Bath, N.Y., U.S.A. 116 42 20N 77 17W
Batheay, Cambodia 55 11 59N 104 57 E
Bathgate, U.K. 14 55 54N 3 38W
Bathmen, Neths. 16 52 15N 6 29 E
Bathurst = Banjul, Gambia 90 13 28N 16 40W
Bathurst, Australia 76 33 25 S 149 31 E
Bathurst, Canada 105 47 37N 65 43W
Bathurst, S. Africa 96 33 30 S 26 50 E
Bathurst, C., Canada 102 70 34N 128 0W
Bathurst B., Australia 72 14 16 S 144 25 E
Bathurst Harb., Australia 72 43 15 S 146 10 E
Bathurst I., Australia 78 11 30 S 130 10 E
Bathurst I., Canada 144 76 0N 100 30W
Bathurst Inlet, Canada 102 66 50N 108 1W
Bathurst L., Australia 76 35 3 S 149 44 E
Batie, Burkina Faso 90 9 53N 2 53W
Batinah, Oman 47 24 0N 56 0 E
Batiscan, Canada 107 46 30N 72 15W
Batiscan →, Canada 107 46 16N 72 15W
Batiscan, L., Canada 107 47 22N 71 55W
Batlow, Australia 76 35 31 S 148 9 E
Batman, Turkey 46 37 55N 41 5 E
Batna, Algeria 85 35 34N 6 15 E
Batoala, Gabon 94 0 48N 13 27 E
Batoka, Zambia 93 16 45 S 27 15 E
Baton Rouge, U.S.A. 121 30 30N 91 5W
Batong, Ko, Thailand 55 6 32N 99 12 E
Batopilas, Mexico 126 27 0N 107 45W
Batouri, Cameroon 94 4 30N 14 25 E
Battambang, Cambodia 54 13 7N 103 12 E
Batticaloa, Sri Lanka 51 7 43N 81 45 E
Battice, Belgium 17 50 39N 5 50 E
Battipáglia, Italy 29 40 38N 15 0 E
Battīr, Israel 44 31 44N 35 8 E
Battle, U.K. 13 50 55N 0 30 E
Battle →, Canada 111 52 43N 108 15W
Battle Camp, Australia 72 15 20 S 144 40 E
Battle Creek, U.S.A. 119 42 20N 85 6W
Battle Ground, U.S.A. 124 45 47N 122 32W
Battle Harbour, Canada 105 52 16N 55 35W
Battle Lake, U.S.A. 120 46 20N 95 43W
Battle Mountain, U.S.A. 122 40 45N 117 0W
Battlefields, Zimb. 93 18 37 S 29 47 E
Battleford, Canada 111 52 45N 108 15W
Battonya, Hungary 33 46 16N 21 3 E
Batu, Kepulauan, Indonesia 56 0 30 S 98 25 E
Batu Caves, Malaysia 55 3 15N 101 40 E
Batu Gajah, Malaysia 55 4 28N 101 3 E
Batu Pahat, Malaysia 55 1 50N 102 56 E
Batuata, Indonesia 57 6 12 S 122 42 E
Batumi, U.S.S.R. 39 41 30N 41 30 E
Baturaja, Indonesia 56 4 11 S 104 15 E
Baturité, Brazil 138 4 28 S 38 45W
Bau, Malaysia 56 1 25N 110 9 E
Baubau, Indonesia 57 5 25 S 122 38 E
Bauchi, Nigeria 91 10 22N 9 48 E
Bauchi □, Nigeria 91 10 30N 10 0 E
Baud, France 18 47 52N 3 1W
Baudette, U.S.A. 120 48 46N 94 35W
Baudour, Belgium 17 50 29N 3 50 E
Bauer, C., Australia 73 32 44 S 134 4 E
Baugé, France 18 47 31N 0 8W
Bauhinia Downs, Australia 72 24 35 S 149 18 E
Baule, La, France 18 47 17N 2 24W
Baume-les-Dames, France 19 47 22N 6 22 E
Baunatal, W. Germany 30 51 13N 9 25 E
Baunei, Italy 28 40 2N 9 41 E
Baures, Bolivia 137 13 35 S 63 35W
Bauru, Brazil 141 22 10 S 49 0W
Baús, Brazil 137 18 22 S 52 47W
Bauska, U.S.S.R. 36 56 24N 25 15 E
Bautzen, E. Germany 30 51 11N 14 25 E
Baux-de-Provence, Les, France 21 43 45N 4 51 E
Bavaria = Bayern □, W. Germany 31 49 7N 11 30 E
Båven, Sweden 10 59 0N 16 56 E
Bavi Sadri, India 48 24 28N 74 30 E
Bavispe →, Mexico 126 29 30N 109 11W
Baw Baw, Mt., Australia 75 37 49 S 146 19 E
Bawdwin, Burma 52 23 5N 97 20 E
Bawean, Indonesia 56 5 46 S 112 35 E
Bawku, Ghana 91 11 3N 0 19W
Bawlake, Burma 52 19 11N 97 21 E
Bawolung, China 58 28 50N 101 16 E
Baxley, U.S.A. 115 31 43N 82 23W
Baxoi, China 58 30 1N 96 50 E
Baxter, U.S.A. 118 41 49N 93 9W
Baxter Springs, U.S.A. 121 37 3N 94 45W
Bay, L. de, Phil. 57 14 20N 121 11 E
Bay Bulls, Canada 105 47 19N 52 50W
Bay City, Mich., U.S.A. 104 43 35N 83 51W
Bay City, Oreg., U.S.A. 122 45 45N 123 58W
Bay City, Tex., U.S.A. 121 28 59N 95 55W
Bay de Verde, Canada 105 48 5N 52 54W
Bay Minette, U.S.A. 115 30 54N 87 43W
Bay St. Louis, U.S.A. 121 30 18N 89 22W
Bay Springs, U.S.A. 121 31 58N 89 18W
Bay View, N.Z. 80 39 25 S 176 50 E
Baya, Zaïre 93 11 53 S 27 25 E
Bayamo, Cuba 128 20 20N 76 40W
Bayamón, Puerto Rico 129 18 24N 66 10W
Bayan Har Shan, China 62 34 0N 98 0 E
Bayan Hot = Alxa Zuoqi, China 60 38 50N 105 40 E
Bayan Obo, China 60 41 52N 109 59 E
Bayan-Ovoo, Mongolia 60 42 55N 106 5 E
Bayana, India 48 26 55N 77 18 E
Bayanaul, U.S.S.R. 40 50 45N 75 45 E
Bayandalay, Mongolia 60 43 30N 103 29 E
Bayanhongor, Mongolia 62 46 8N 102 43 E
Bayard, U.S.A. 120 41 48N 103 17W
Bayázeh, Iran 47 33 30N 54 40 E
Baybay, Phil. 57 10 40N 124 55 E
Bayburt, Turkey 46 40 15N 40 20 E
Bayerischer Wald, W. Germany 31 49 0N 13 0 E
Bayern □, W. Germany 31 49 7N 11 30 E
Bayeux, France 18 49 17N 0 42W
Bayfield, Canada 108 43 34N 81 42W
Bayfield, U.S.A. 120 46 50N 90 48W
Baykal, Oz., U.S.S.R. 41 53 0N 108 0 E
Baykit, U.S.S.R. 41 61 50N 95 50 E
Baykonur, U.S.S.R. 40 47 48N 65 50 E
Baynes Mts., Namibia 96 17 15 S 13 0 E
Bayombong, Phil. 57 16 30N 121 10 E
Bayon, France 19 48 30N 6 20 E
Bayona, Spain 22 42 6N 8 52W
Bayonne, France 20 43 30N 1 28W
Bayonne, U.S.A. 117 40 41N 74 7W
Bayovar, Peru 136 5 50 S 81 0W
Bayram-Ali, U.S.S.R. 40 37 37N 62 10 E
Bayreuth, W. Germany 31 49 56N 11 35 E
Bayrischzell, W. Germany 31 47 39N 12 1 E
Bayrūt, Lebanon 46 33 53N 35 31 E
Bays, L. of, Canada 108 45 15N 79 4W
Bayside, Canada 109 44 7N 77 30W
Baysville, Canada 108 45 9N 79 7W
Bayt Awlá, Jordan 44 31 37N 35 2 E
Bayt Fajjār, Jordan 44 31 38N 35 9 E
Bayt Fūrīk, Jordan 44 32 11N 35 20 E
Bayt Ḩānūn, Egypt 44 31 32N 34 32 E
Bayt Jālā, Jordan 44 31 43N 35 11 E
Bayt Lahm, Jordan 44 31 43N 35 12 E
Bayt Rīma, Jordan 44 32 2N 35 6 E
Bayt Sāḩūr, Jordan 44 31 42N 35 13 E
Bayt Ummar, Jordan 44 31 38N 35 7 E
Bayt 'ūr al Taḩtā, Jordan 44 31 54N 35 5 E
Baytīn, Jordan 44 31 56N 35 14 E
Baytown, U.S.A. 121 29 42N 94 57W
Baytūniyā, Jordan 44 31 54N 35 10 E
Bayzo, Niger 91 13 52N 4 35 E
Baza, Spain 25 37 30N 2 47W
Bazar Dyuzi, U.S.S.R. 39 41 12N 47 50 E
Bazarny Karabulak, U.S.S.R. 37 52 15N 46 20 E
Bazarnyy Syzgan, U.S.S.R. 37 53 45N 46 40 E
Bazartobe, U.S.S.R. 39 49 26N 51 45 E
Bazaruto, I. do, Mozam. 97 21 40 S 35 28 E
Bazas, France 20 44 27N 0 13W
Bazhong, China 58 31 52N 106 46 E
Bazin →, Canada 106 47 29N 75 22W
Beach, U.S.A. 120 46 57N 103 58W
Beach City, U.S.A. 116 40 38N 81 35W
Beachburg, Canada 109 45 44N 76 51W
Beachport, Australia 73 37 29 S 140 0 E
Beachville, Canada 108 43 5N 80 49W
Beachy Head, U.K. 13 50 44N 0 16 E
Beacon, Australia 79 30 26 S 117 52 E
Beacon, U.S.A. 117 41 32N 73 58W
Beaconia, Canada 111 50 25N 96 31W
Beagle, Canal, S. Amer. 142 55 0 S 68 30W
Beagle Bay, Australia 78 16 58 S 122 40 E
Bealanana, Madag. 97 14 33 S 48 44 E
Bealiba, Australia 74 36 48 S 143 34 E
Beamsville, Canada 108 43 12N 79 28W
Bear →, U.S.A. 124 38 56N 121 36W
Béar, C., France 20 42 31N 3 8 E
Bear I., Ireland 15 51 38N 9 50W
Bear L., B.C., Canada 110 56 10N 126 52W
Bear L., Man., Canada 111 55 8N 96 0W
Bear L., U.S.A. 122 42 0N 111 20W
Bearcreek, U.S.A. 122 45 11N 109 6W
Beardmore, Canada 104 49 36N 87 57W
Beardmore Glacier, Antarctica 143 84 30 S 170 0 E
Beardstown, U.S.A. 118 40 0N 90 25W
Béarn, Canada 106 47 17N 79 20W
Béarn, France 20 43 20N 0 30W
Bearpaw Mts., U.S.A. 122 48 15N 109 30W
Bearskin Lake, Canada 104 53 58N 91 2W
Beas de Segura, Spain 25 38 15N 2 53W
Beasain, Spain 24 43 3N 2 11W
Beata, C., Dom. Rep. 129 17 40N 71 30W
Beata, I., Dom. Rep. 129 17 34N 71 31W
Beatrice, U.S.A. 120 40 20N 96 40W
Beatrice, Zimb. 93 18 15 S 30 55 E
Beatrice, C., Australia 72 14 20 S 136 55 E
Beatton →, Canada 110 56 15N 120 45W
Beatton River, Canada 110 57 26N 121 20W
Beatty, U.S.A. 124 36 58N 116 46W
Beaucaire, France 21 43 48N 4 39 E
Beauce, Plaine de la, France 19 48 10N 1 45 E
Beauceville, Canada 107 46 13N 70 46W
Beauchêne, I., Falk. Is. 142 52 55 S 59 15W
Beauchûne, L., Canada 106 46 35N 78 55W
Beaudesert, Australia 77 27 59 S 153 0 E
Beaufort, Australia 74 37 25 S 143 25 E
Beaufort, Malaysia 56 5 30N 115 40 E
Beaufort, N.C., U.S.A. 115 34 45N 76 40W
Beaufort, S.C., U.S.A. 115 32 25N 80 40W
Beaufort Sea, Arctic 144 72 0N 140 0W
Beaufort West, S. Africa 96 32 18 S 22 36 E
Beaugency, France 19 47 47N 1 38 E
Beauharnois, Canada 107 45 20N 73 52W
Beaujeu, France 21 46 10N 4 35 E
Beaulac, Canada 107 45 23N 71 23W
Beaulieu →, Canada 110 62 3N 113 11W

Beaulieu-sur-Dordogne, France 20 44 58N 1 50 E
Beaulieu-sur-Mer, France 21 43 42N 7 20 E
Beauly, U.K. 14 57 29N 4 27W
Beauly →, U.K. 14 57 26N 4 28W
Beaumaris, U.K. 12 53 16N 4 7W
Beaumetz-lès-Loges, France 19 50 15N 2 38 E
Beaumont, Belgium 17 50 15N 4 14 E
Beaumont, France 20 44 45N 0 46 E
Beaumont, N.Z. 81 45 50 S 169 33 E
Beaumont, Calif., U.S.A. 125 33 56N 116 58W
Beaumont, Tex., U.S.A. 121 30 5N 94 8W
Beaumont-de-Lomagne, France 20 43 53N 1 0 E
Beaumont-le-Roger, France 18 49 4N 0 47 E
Beaumont-sur-Oise, France 19 49 9N 2 17 E
Beaumont-sur-Sarthe, France 18 48 13N 0 8 E
Beaune, France 19 47 2N 4 50 E
Beaune-la-Rolande, France 19 48 4N 2 25 E
Beauport, Canada 107 46 52N 71 11W
Beaupré, Canada 107 47 3N 70 54W
Beaupréau, France 18 47 12N 0 59W
Beauraing, Belgium 17 50 7N 4 57 E
Beauséjour, Canada 111 50 5N 96 35W
Beausset, Le, France 21 43 12N 5 48 E
Beautemps-Beaupré, I., N. Cal. 68 20 24 S 166 9 E
Beauvais, France 19 49 25N 2 8 E
Beauval, Canada 111 55 9N 107 37W
Beauvoir-sur-Mer, France 18 46 55N 2 2W
Beauvoir-sur-Niort, France 20 46 12N 0 30W
Beaver, Alaska, U.S.A. 102 66 20N 147 30W
Beaver, Okla., U.S.A. 121 36 52N 100 31W
Beaver, Pa., U.S.A. 116 40 40N 80 18W
Beaver, Utah, U.S.A. 123 38 20N 112 45W
Beaver →, B.C., Canada 110 59 52N 124 20W
Beaver →, Ont., Canada 104 55 55N 87 48W
Beaver →, Sask., Canada 111 55 26N 107 45W
Beaver City, U.S.A. 120 40 13N 99 50W
Beaver Dam, U.S.A. 120 43 28N 88 50W
Beaver Falls, U.S.A. 116 40 44N 80 20W
Beaver Hill L., Canada 111 54 5N 94 50W
Beaver I., U.S.A. 104 45 40N 85 31W
Beavercreek, U.S.A. 119 39 43N 84 11W
Beaverhill L., Alta., Canada 110 53 27N 112 32W
Beaverhill L., N.W.T., Canada 111 63 2N 104 22W
Beaverlodge, Canada 110 55 11N 119 29W
Beavermouth, Canada 110 51 32N 117 23W
Beaverstone →, Canada 104 54 59N 89 25W
Beaverton, Canada 108 44 26N 79 9W
Beaverton, U.S.A. 124 45 29N 122 48W
Beaverville, U.S.A. 119 40 57N 87 39W
Beawar, India 48 26 3N 74 18 E
Bebedouro, Brazil 141 21 0 S 48 25W
Beboa, Madag. 97 17 22 S 44 33 E
Bebra, W. Germany 30 50 59N 9 48 E
Beccles, U.K. 13 52 27N 1 33 E
Bečej, Yugoslavia 33 45 36N 20 3 E
Becerreá, Spain 22 42 51N 7 10W
Béchar, Algeria 85 31 38N 2 18W
Beckley, U.S.A. 114 37 50N 81 8W
Beckum, W. Germany 30 51 46N 8 3 E
Bečva →, Czech. 32 49 31N 17 40 E
Bédar, Spain 25 37 11N 1 59W
Bédarieux, France 20 43 37N 3 10 E
Bédarrides, France 21 44 2N 4 54 E
Beddouza, Ras, Morocco 84 32 33N 9 9W
Bedele, Ethiopia 89 8 31N 36 23 E
Bederkesa, W. Germany 30 53 37N 8 50 E
Bederwanak, Somali Rep. 98 9 34N 44 23 E
Bedeso, Ethiopia 89 9 58N 40 52 E
Bedford, Canada 107 45 7N 72 59W
Bedford, S. Africa 96 32 40 S 26 10 E
Bedford, U.K. 13 52 8N 0 29W
Bedford, Ind., U.S.A. 119 38 50N 86 30W
Bedford, Iowa, U.S.A. 118 40 40N 94 41W
Bedford, Ky., U.S.A. 119 38 36N 85 19W
Bedford, Ohio, U.S.A. 116 41 23N 81 32W
Bedford, Pa., U.S.A. 116 40 1N 78 30W
Bedford, Va., U.S.A. 114 37 25N 79 30W
Bedford □, U.K. 13 52 4N 0 28W
Bedford, C., Australia 72 15 14 S 145 21 E
Bedford Downs, Australia 78 17 19 S 127 20 E
Bedgerebong, Australia 76 33 21 S 147 43 E
Bedi, Chad 87 11 6N 18 33 E
Będków, Poland 32 51 36N 19 44 E
Bednja →, Yugoslavia 27 46 12N 16 25 E
Bednodemyanovsk, U.S.S.R. 37 53 55N 43 15 E
Bedónia, Italy 26 44 28N 9 36 E
Bedourie, Australia 72 24 30 S 139 30 E
Bedum, Neths. 16 53 18N 6 36 E
Będzin, Poland 32 50 19N 19 7 E
Beeac, Australia 74 38 13 S 143 37 E
Beebe Plain, Canada 107 45 1N 72 9W
Beebo, Australia 77 28 43 S 150 59 E
Beech Fork →, U.S.A. 119 37 55N 85 50W
Beech Grove, U.S.A. 119 39 40N 86 2W
Beecher, U.S.A. 119 41 21N 87 38W
Beechworth, Australia 75 36 22 S 146 43 E
Beechy, Canada 111 50 53N 107 24W
Beecroft Head, Australia 77 35 0 S 150 51 E
Beek, Gelderland, Neths. 16 51 55N 6 11 E
Beek, Limburg, Neths. 17 50 57N 5 48 E
Beek, Noord-Brabant, Neths. 17 51 32N 5 38 E
Beekbergen, Neths. 16 52 10N 5 58 E
Beelitz, E. Germany 30 52 14N 12 58 E
Beenleigh, Australia 77 27 43 S 153 10 E
Be'er Sheva', Israel 44 31 15N 34 48 E
Be'er Sheva' →, Israel 44 31 12N 34 40 E
Be'er Toviyya, Israel 44 31 44N 34 42 E
Be'eri, Israel 44 31 25N 34 30 E
Be'erotayim, Israel 44 32 19N 34 59 E
Beersheba = Be'er Sheva', Israel 44 31 15N 34 48 E
Beerta, Neths. 16 53 11N 7 6 E
Beerze →, Neths. 16 51 39N 5 20 E
Beesd, Neths. 16 51 53N 5 11 E
Beeskow, E. Germany 30 52 9N 14 14 E
Beeston, U.K. 12 52 55N 1 11W
Beetaloo, Australia 72 17 15 S 133 50 E
Beeton, Canada 108 44 5N 79 47W
Beetsterzwaag, Neths. 16 53 4N 6 5 E
Beetzendorf, E. Germany 30 52 42N 11 6 E
Beeville, U.S.A. 121 28 27N 97 44W
Befale, Zaïre 94 0 25N 20 45 E
Befandriana, Madag. 97 21 55 S 44 0 E
Befotaka, Madag. 97 23 49 S 47 0 E
Bega, Australia 75 36 41 S 149 51 E
Bega, Canalul, Romania 34 45 37N 20 46 E
Bégard, France 18 48 38N 3 18W
Bègles, France 20 44 45N 0 35W
Begna →, Norway 10 60 41N 10 0 E
Begonte, Spain 22 43 10N 7 40W
Begusarai, India 49 25 24N 86 9 E
Behara, Madag. 97 24 55 S 46 20 E
Behbehān, Iran 46 30 30N 50 15 E
Behshahr, Iran 47 36 45N 53 35 E
Bei Jiang →, China 59 23 2N 112 58 E
Bei'an, China 62 48 10N 126 20 E
Beibei, China 62 29 47N 106 22 E
Beigang, Taiwan 59 23 38N 120 16 E
Beihai, China 58 21 28N 109 6 E
Beijing, China 60 39 55N 116 20 E
Beijing □, China 60 39 55N 116 20 E
Beilen, Neths. 16 52 52N 6 27 E
Beiliu, China 59 22 41N 110 21 E
Beilngries, W. Germany 31 49 1N 11 27 E
Beilpajah, Australia 73 32 54 S 143 52 E
Beilul, Ethiopia 89 13 2N 42 20 E
Beipiao, China 61 41 52N 120 32 E
Beira, Mozam. 93 19 50 S 34 52 E
Beira, Somali Rep. 98 6 57N 47 19 E
Beirut = Bayrūt, Lebanon 46 33 53N 35 31 E
Beit Lāhiyah, Egypt 44 31 32N 34 30 E
Beitaolaizhao, China 61 44 58N 125 58 E
Beitbridge, Zimb. 93 22 12 S 30 0 E
Beiuş, Romania 34 46 40N 22 21 E
Beizhen, Liaoning, China 61 41 38N 121 54 E
Beizhen, Shandong, China 61 37 20N 118 2 E
Beizhengzhen, China 61 44 31N 123 30 E
Beja, Portugal 23 38 2N 7 53W
Béja, Tunisia 86 36 43N 9 12 E
Beja □, Portugal 23 37 55N 7 55W
Bejaia, Algeria 85 36 42N 5 2 E
Béjar, Spain 22 40 23N 5 46W
Bejestān, Iran 47 34 30N 58 5 E
Bekasi, Indonesia 57 6 14 S 106 59 E
Békés, Hungary 33 46 47N 21 9 E
Békéscsaba, Hungary 33 46 40N 21 5 E
Bekily, Madag. 97 24 13 S 45 19 E
Bekkevoort, Belgium 17 50 57N 4 58 E
Bekoji, Ethiopia 89 7 40N 39 17 E
Bekok, Malaysia 55 2 20N 103 7 E
Bekwai, Ghana 91 6 30N 1 34W
Bela, India 49 25 50N 82 0 E
Bela, Pakistan 48 26 12N 66 20 E
Bela Crkva, Yugoslavia 33 44 55N 21 27 E
Bela Palanka, Yugoslavia 33 43 13N 22 17 E
Bela Vista, Brazil 140 22 12 S 56 20W
Bela Vista, Mozam. 97 26 10 S 32 44 E
Bélâbre, France 20 46 34N 1 8 E
Belalcázar, Spain 23 38 35N 5 10W
Belaringar, Australia 76 31 45 S 147 34 E
Belas, Angola 95 8 55 S 13 9 E
Belau Is., Pac. Oc. 66 7 30N 134 30 E
Belavenona, Madag. 97 24 50 S 47 4 E
Belawan, Indonesia 56 3 33N 98 32 E
Belaya, Mt., Ethiopia 89 11 25N 36 8 E
Belaya Glina, U.S.S.R. 39 46 5N 40 48 E
Belaya Kalitva, U.S.S.R. 39 48 13N 40 50 E
Belaya Kholunitsa, U.S.S.R. 37 58 41N 50 13 E
Belaya Tserkov, U.S.S.R. 36 49 45N 30 10 E
Belcher Is., Canada 104 56 15N 78 45W
Belchite, Spain 24 41 18N 0 43W
Belcourt, Canada 106 48 24N 77 21W
Belden, U.S.A. 124 40 2N 121 17W
Belém, Brazil 138 1 20 S 48 30W
Belém de São Francisco, Brazil 138 8 46 S 38 58W
Belén, Argentina 140 27 40 S 67 5W
Belén, Colombia 134 1 26N 75 56W
Belén, Paraguay 140 23 30 S 57 6W
Belen, U.S.A. 123 34 40N 106 50W
Bélesta, France 20 42 55N 1 56 E
Belet Uen, Somali Rep. 98 4 30N 45 5 E
Belev, U.S.S.R. 37 53 50N 36 5 E
Belfair, U.S.A. 124 47 27N 122 50W
Belfast, N.Z. 81 43 27 S 172 39 E
Belfast, S. Africa 97 25 42 S 30 2 E
Belfast, U.K. 15 54 35N 5 56W
Belfast, Maine, U.S.A. 105 44 30N 69 0W
Belfast, N.Y., U.S.A. 116 42 21N 78 9W
Belfast □, U.K. 15 54 35N 5 56W
Belfast, L., U.K. 15 54 40N 5 50W
Belfeld, Neths. 17 51 18N 6 6 E
Belfield, U.S.A. 120 46 54N 103 11W
Belfort, France 19 47 38N 6 50 E
Belfry, U.S.A. 122 45 10N 109 2W
Belgaum, India 51 15 55N 74 35 E
Belgioioso, Italy 26 45 9N 9 21 E
Belgium ■, Europe 17 50 30N 5 0 E
Belgorod, U.S.S.R. 38 50 35N 36 35 E
Belgorod-Dnestrovskiy, U.S.S.R. 38 46 11N 30 23 E
Belgrade = Beograd, Yugoslavia 33 44 50N 20 37 E
Belgrade, U.S.A. 122 45 50N 111 10W
Belgrove, N.Z. 81 41 27 S 172 59 E
Belhaven, U.S.A. 115 35 34N 76 35W
Beli Drim →, Europe 33 42 6N 20 25 E
Beli Manastir, Yugoslavia 33 45 45N 18 36 E
Belice →, Italy 28 37 35N 12 55 E
Belin-Béliet, France 20 44 29N 0 47W
Belinga, Gabon 94 1 10N 13 2 E
Belinskiy, U.S.S.R. 37 53 0N 43 25 E
Belinyu, Indonesia 56 1 35 S 105 50 E
Belitung, Indonesia 56 3 10 S 107 50 E
Beliu, Romania 34 46 30N 22 0 E
Belize ■, Cent. Amer. 127 17 0N 88 30W
Belize City, Belize 127 17 25N 88 0W
Beljanica, Yugoslavia 33 44 8N 21 43 E
Belkovskiy, Ostrov, U.S.S.R. 41 75 32N 135 44 E
Bell, Australia 76 33 28 S 150 17 E
Bell →, Canada 106 49 48N 77 38W
Bell Bay, Australia 72 41 6 S 146 53 E
Bell I., Canada 105 50 46N 55 35W
Bell-Irving →, Canada 110 56 12N 129 5W
Bell Peninsula, Canada 103 63 50N 82 0W
Bell Ville, Argentina 140 32 40 S 62 40W
Bella Bella, Canada 110 52 10N 128 10W
Bella Coola, Canada 110 52 25N 126 40W
Bella Flor, Bolivia 136 11 9 S 67 49W
Bella Unión, Uruguay 140 30 15 S 57 40W
Bella Vista, Corrientes, Argentina 140 28 33 S 59 0W
Bella Vista, Tucuman, Argentina 140 27 10 S 65 25W
Bellac, France 20 46 7N 1 3 E
Bellágio, Italy 26 45 59N 9 15 E
Bellaire, U.S.A. 116 40 1N 80 46W
Bellary, India 51 15 10N 76 56 E
Bellata, Australia 77 29 53 S 149 46 E
Bellbird, Australia 76 32 52 S 151 19 E
Bellbrook, Australia 77 30 47 S 152 31 E
Belle, U.S.A. 118 38 17N 91 43W
Belle, La, Fla., U.S.A. 115 26 45N 81 22W
Belle, La, Mo., U.S.A. 118 40 7N 91 55W
Belle Fourche, U.S.A. 120 44 43N 103 52W
Belle Fourche →, U.S.A. 120 44 25N 102 19W
Belle Glade, U.S.A. 115 26 43N 80 38W
Belle-Ile, France 18 47 20N 3 10W
Belle Isle, Canada 105 51 57N 55 25W
Belle Isle, Str. of, Canada 105 51 30N 56 30W
Belle-Isle-en-Terre, France 18 48 33N 3 23W
Belle Plaine, Iowa, U.S.A. 118 41 51N 92 18W
Belle Plaine, Minn., U.S.A. 120 44 35N 93 48W
Belle Rive, U.S.A. 119 38 14N 88 45W
Belle River, Canada 108 42 18N 82 43W
Belle Yella, Liberia 90 7 24N 10 0W
Belledonne, Chaîne de, France 21 45 20N 6 10 E
Belledune, Canada 105 47 55N 65 50W
Bellefontaine, U.S.A. 119 40 20N 83 45W
Bellefonte, U.S.A. 116 40 56N 77 45W
Bellegarde, France 19 47 59N 2 26 E
Bellegarde-en-Marche, France 20 45 59N 2 18 E
Bellegarde-sur-Valserine, France 21 46 4N 5 50 E
Bellême, France 18 48 22N 0 34 E
Belleoram, Canada 105 47 31N 55 25W
Belleterre, Canada 106 47 25N 78 41W
Belleville, Canada 109 44 10N 77 23W
Belleville, France 21 46 7N 4 45 E
Belleville, Ill., U.S.A. 118 38 30N 90 0W
Belleville, Kans., U.S.A. 120 39 51N 97 38W
Belleville, N.Y., U.S.A. 117 43 46N 76 10W
Belleville-sur-Vie, France 18 46 46N 1 25W
Bellevue, Canada 110 49 35N 114 22W
Bellevue, Idaho, U.S.A. 122 43 25N 114 23W
Bellevue, Iowa, U.S.A. 118 42 16N 90 26W
Bellevue, Mich., U.S.A. 119 42 27N 85 1W
Bellevue, Ohio, U.S.A. 116 41 20N 82 48W
Bellevue, Wash., U.S.A. 124 47 37N 122 12W
Belley, France 21 45 46N 5 41 E
Bellflower, U.S.A. 118 39 0N 91 21W
Bellin, Canada 103 60 0N 70 0W
Bellingen, Australia 77 30 25 S 152 50 E
Bellingham, U.S.A. 110 48 45N 122 27W
Bellingshausen, Antarctica 143 62 0 S 59 0W
Bellingshausen Sea, Antarctica 143 66 0 S 80 0W
Bellinzona, Switz. 31 46 11N 9 1 E
Bello, Colombia 134 6 20N 75 33W
Bellona, Solomon Is. 68 11 17 S 159 47 E
Bellows Falls, U.S.A. 117 43 10N 72 30W
Bellpat, Pakistan 48 29 0N 68 5 E
Bellpuig, Spain 24 41 37N 1 1 E
Bells Corners, Canada 109 45 19N 75 50W
Belluno, Italy 27 46 8N 12 13 E
Bellville, U.S.A. 121 29 58N 96 18W
Bellwood, U.S.A. 116 40 36N 78 21W
Bélmez, Spain 23 38 17N 5 17W
Belmond, U.S.A. 118 42 51N 93 37W
Belmont, Australia 76 33 4 S 151 42 E
Belmont, Canada 108 42 53N 81 5W
Belmont, S. Africa 96 29 28 S 24 22 E
Belmont, U.S.A. 116 42 14N 78 3W
Belmonte, Brazil 139 16 0 S 39 0W
Belmonte, Portugal 22 40 21N 7 20W
Belmonte, Spain 24 39 34N 2 43W
Belmopan, Belize 127 17 18N 88 30W
Belmullet, Ireland 15 54 13N 9 58W
Belo Horizonte, Brazil 139 19 55 S 43 56W
Belo Jardim, Brazil 138 8 20 S 36 26W
Belo-sur-Mer, Madag. 97 20 42 S 44 0 E
Belo-Tsiribihina, Madag. 97 19 40 S 44 30 E
Beloeil, Canada 107 45 34N 73 12W
Belogorsk, R.S.F.S.R., U.S.S.R. 41 51 0N 128 20 E
Belogorsk, Ukraine S.S.R., U.S.S.R. 38 45 3N 34 35 E
Belogradchik, Bulgaria 34 43 53N 22 15 E
Beloha, Madag. 97 25 10 S 45 3 E
Beloit, Kans., U.S.A. 120 39 32N 98 9W
Beloit, Wis., U.S.A. 118 42 35N 89 0W
Belokorovichi, U.S.S.R. 36 51 7N 28 2 E
Belomorsk, U.S.S.R. 40 64 35N 34 30 E
Belonia, India 52 23 15N 91 30 E
Belopolye, U.S.S.R. 36 51 14N 34 20 E
Belovo, U.S.S.R. 40 54 30N 86 0 E
Beloye More, U.S.S.R. 40 66 30N 38 0 E
Beloye Ozero, U.S.S.R. 39 45 15N 46 50 E
Belozersk, U.S.S.R. 37 60 0N 37 30 E
Belpasso, Italy 29 37 37N 15 0 E
Belsele, Belgium 17 51 9N 4 6 E
Belsito, Italy 28 37 50N 13 47 E
Beltana, Australia 73 30 48 S 138 25 E
Belterra, Brazil 135 2 45 S 55 0W
Beltinci, Yugoslavia 27 46 37N 16 20 E
Belton, S.C., U.S.A. 115 34 31N 82 39W
Belton, Tex., U.S.A. 121 31 4N 97 30W
Belton Res., U.S.A. 121 31 8N 97 32W
Beltsy, U.S.S.R. 38 47 48N 28 0 E
Belturbet, Ireland 15 54 6N 7 28W
Belukha, U.S.S.R. 40 49 50N 86 50 E
Beluran, Malaysia 56 5 48N 117 35 E
Belvedere Maríttimo, Italy 29 39 37N 15 52 E
Belvès, France 20 44 46N 1 0 E
Belvidere, Ill., U.S.A. 119 42 15N 88 55W
Belvidere, N.J., U.S.A. 117 40 48N 75 5W
Belvis de la Jara, Spain 23 39 45N 4 57W
Belyando →, Australia 72 21 38 S 146 50 E
Belyy, U.S.S.R. 36 55 48N 32 51 E
Belyy, Ostrov, U.S.S.R. 40 73 30N 71 0 E
Belyy Yar, U.S.S.R. 40 58 26N 84 39 E
Belzig, E. Germany 30 52 8N 12 36 E
Belzoni, U.S.A. 121 33 12N 90 30W
Bemaraha, Lembalemban' i, Madag. 97 18 40 S 44 45 E
Bemarivo, Madag. 97 21 45 S 44 45 E
Bemarivo →, Madag. 97 15 27 S 47 40 E
Bemavo, Madag. 97 21 33 S 45 25 E
Bembéréke, Benin 91 10 11N 2 43 E
Bembesi, Zimb. 93 20 0 S 28 58 E
Bembesi →, Zimb. 93 18 57 S 27 47 E
Bembézar →, Spain 23 37 45N 5 13W
Bemboka, Australia 75 36 38 S 149 34 E
Bement, U.S.A. 119 39 55N 88 34W
Bemidji, U.S.A. 120 47 30N 94 50W
Bemm River, Australia 75 37 47 S 148 58 E
Bemmel, Neths. 16 51 54N 5 54 E
Ben 'Ammi, Israel 44 33 0N 35 7 E
Ben Bullen, Australia 76 33 12 S 150 2 E
Ben Cruachan, U.K. 14 56 26N 5 8W
Ben Dearg, U.K. 14 57 47N 4 58W
Ben Gardane, Tunisia 86 33 11N 11 11 E
Ben Hope, U.K. 14 58 24N 4 36W
Ben Lawers, U.K. 14 56 33N 4 13W
Ben Lomond, N.S.W., Australia 77 30 1 S 151 43 E

Ben Lomond, *Tas., Australia* **72** 41 38 S 147 42 E
Ben Lomond, *U.K.* **14** 56 12N 4 39W
Ben Luc, *Vietnam* **55** 10 39N 106 29 E
Ben Macdhui, *U.K.* **14** 57 4N 3 40W
Ben Mhor, *U.K.* **14** 57 16N 7 21W
Ben More, *Central, U.K.* **14** 56 23N 4 31W
Ben More, *Strathclyde, U.K.* **14** 56 26N 6 2W
Ben More Assynt, *U.K.* **14** 58 7N 4 51W
Ben Nevis, *U.K.* **14** 56 48N 5 0W
Ben Ohau Ra., *N.Z.* **81** 44 1 S 170 4 E
Ben Quang, *Vietnam* **54** 17 3N 106 55 E
Ben Slimane, *Morocco* **84** 33 38N 7 7W
Ben Tre, *Vietnam* **55** 10 3N 106 36 E
Ben Vorlich, *U.K.* **14** 56 22N 4 15W
Ben Wyvis, *U.K.* **14** 57 40N 4 35W
Bena, *Nigeria* **91** 11 20N 5 50 E
Bena Dibele, *Zaïre* **95** 4 4 S 22 50 E
Bena-Leka, *Zaïre* **95** 5 8 S 22 10 E
Bena-Tshadi, *Zaïre* **95** 4 40 S 22 49 E
Benadir □, *Somali Rep.* **98** 1 30N 44 30 E
Benagalbón, *Spain* **23** 36 45N 4 15W
Benagerie, *Australia* **73** 31 25 S 140 22 E
Benahmed, *Morocco* **84** 33 4N 7 9W
Benalla, *Australia* **74** 36 30 S 146 0 E
Benamejí, *Spain* **23** 37 16N 4 33W
Benares = Varanasi, *India* **49** 25 22N 83 0 E
Bénat, C., *France* **21** 43 5N 6 22 E
Benavente, *Portugal* **23** 38 59N 8 49W
Benavente, *Spain* **22** 42 2N 5 43W
Benavides, *Spain* **22** 42 30N 5 54W
Benavides, *U.S.A.* **121** 27 35N 98 28W
Benbecula, *U.K.* **14** 57 26N 7 21W
Benbonyathe, Mt., *Australia* **73** 30 25 S 139 11 E
Bencubbin, *Australia* **79** 30 48 S 117 52 E
Bend, *U.S.A.* **122** 44 2N 121 15W
Bendel □, *Nigeria* **91** 6 0N 6 0 E
Bendela, *Zaïre* **94** 3 18 S 17 36 E
Bendemeer, *Australia* **77** 30 53 S 151 8 E
Bender Beila, *Somali Rep.* **98** 9 30N 50 48 E
Bender Merchagno, *Somali Rep.* **98** 11 41N 50 34 E
Bendering, *Australia* **79** 32 23 S 118 18 E
Bendery, *U.S.S.R.* **38** 46 50N 29 30 E
Bendick Murrell, *Australia* **76** 34 8 S 148 28 E
Bendigo, *Australia* **74** 36 40 S 144 15 E
Bendorf, *W. Germany* **30** 50 26N 7 34 E
Benē Beraq, *Israel* **44** 32 6N 34 51 E
Beneden Knijpe, *Neths.* **16** 52 58N 5 59 E
Beneditinos, *Brazil* **138** 5 27 S 42 22W
Benedito Leite, *Brazil* **138** 7 13 S 44 34W
Bénéna, *Mali* **90** 13 9N 4 17W
Benenitra, *Madag.* **97** 23 27 S 45 5 E
Benešŏv, *Czech.* **32** 49 46N 14 41 E
Bénestroff, *France* **19** 48 54N 6 45 E
Benet, *France* **20** 46 22N 0 35W
Benetook, *Australia* **74** 34 22 S 142 0 E
Benevento, *Italy* **29** 41 7N 14 45 E
Benfeld, *France* **19** 48 22N 7 34 E
Benga, *Mozam.* **93** 16 11 S 33 40 E
Bengal, Bay of, *Ind. Oc.* **42** 15 0N 90 0 E
Bengbu, *China* **61** 32 58N 117 20 E
Benghazi = Banghāzī, *Libya* **86** 32 11N 20 3 E
Bengkalis, *Indonesia* **56** 1 30N 102 10 E
Bengkulu, *Indonesia* **56** 3 50 S 102 12 E
Bengkulu □, *Indonesia* **56** 3 48 S 102 16 E
Bengough, *Canada* **111** 49 25N 105 10W
Benguela, *Angola* **95** 12 37 S 13 25 E
Benguela □, *Angola* **95** 13 0 S 13 30 E
Benguerir, *Morocco* **84** 32 16N 7 56W
Benguérua, I., *Mozam.* **97** 21 58 S 35 28 E
Benha, *Egypt* **88** 30 26N 31 8 E
Beni, *Australia* **76** 32 11 S 148 43 E
Beni, *Zaïre* **92** 0 30N 29 27 E
Beni □, *Bolivia* **137** 14 0 S 65 0W
Beni →, *Bolivia* **137** 10 23 S 65 24W
Beni Abbès, *Algeria* **85** 30 5N 2 5W
Beni-Haoua, *Algeria* **85** 36 30N 1 30 E
Beni Mazâr, *Egypt* **88** 28 32N 30 44 E
Beni Mellal, *Morocco* **84** 32 21N 6 21W
Beni Ounif, *Algeria* **85** 32 0N 1 10W
Beni Saf, *Algeria* **85** 35 17N 1 15W
Beni Suef, *Egypt* **88** 29 5N 31 6 E
Beniah L., *Canada* **110** 63 23N 112 17W
Benicarló, *Spain* **24** 40 23N 0 23 E
Benicia, *U.S.A.* **124** 38 3N 122 9W
Benidorm, *Spain* **25** 38 33N 0 9W
Benidorm, Islote de, *Spain* **25** 38 31N 0 9W
Benin ■, *Africa* **91** 10 0N 2 0 E
Benin, Bight of, *W. Afr.* **91** 5 0N 3 0 E
Benin City, *Nigeria* **91** 6 20N 5 31 E
Benisa, *Spain* **25** 38 43N 0 3 E
Benjamin Aceval, *Paraguay* **140** 24 58 S 57 34W
Benjamin Constant, *Brazil* **134** 4 40 S 70 15W
Benjamin Hill, *Mexico* **126** 30 10N 111 10W
Benkelman, *U.S.A.* **120** 40 7N 101 32W
Benkovac, *Yugoslavia* **27** 44 2N 15 37 E
Benlidi, *Australia* **72** 24 35 S 144 50 E
Benmore Pk., *N.Z.* **81** 44 25 S 170 8 E
Bennebroek, *Neths.* **16** 52 19N 4 36 E
Bennekom, *Neths.* **16** 52 0N 5 41 E
Bennett, *Canada* **110** 59 56N 134 53W
Bennett, Ostrov, *U.S.S.R.* **41** 76 21N 148 56 E
Bennettsville, *U.S.A.* **115** 34 38N 79 39W
Bennington, *U.S.A.* **117** 42 52N 73 12W
Benny, *Canada* **108** 46 47N 81 38W
Bénodet, *France* **18** 47 53N 4 7W
Benoni, *S. Africa* **97** 26 11 S 28 18 E
Benoud, *Algeria* **85** 32 20N 0 16 E
Benoy, *Chad* **87** 8 59N 16 19 E
Benque Viejo, *Belize* **127** 17 5N 89 8W
Bensheim, *W. Germany* **31** 49 40N 8 38 E
Benson, *U.S.A.* **123** 31 59N 110 19W
Bent, *Iran* **47** 26 20N 59 31 E
Benteng, *Indonesia* **57** 6 10 S 120 30 E
Bentinck I., *Australia* **72** 17 3 S 139 35 E
Bentiu, *Sudan* **89** 9 10N 29 55 E
Bento Gonçalves, *Brazil* **141** 29 10 S 51 31W
Benton, *Ark., U.S.A.* **121** 34 30N 92 35W
Benton, *Calif., U.S.A.* **124** 37 48N 118 32W
Benton, *Ill., U.S.A.* **118** 38 0N 88 55W
Benton Harbor, *U.S.A.* **119** 42 10N 86 28W
Bentu Liben, *Ethiopia* **89** 8 32N 38 21 E
Bentung, *Malaysia* **55** 3 31N 101 55 E
Benue □, *Nigeria* **91** 7 30N 7 30 E
Benue →, *Nigeria* **91** 7 48N 6 46 E
Benxi, *China* **61** 41 20N 123 48 E
Benzdorp, *Surinam* **135** 3 44N 54 5W
Beo, *Indonesia* **57** 4 25N 126 50 E
Beograd, *Yugoslavia* **33** 44 50N 20 37 E
Beowawe, *U.S.A.* **122** 40 35N 116 30W
Bepan Jiang →, *China* **58** 24 55N 106 5 E
Beppu, *Japan* **64** 33 15N 131 30 E
Beppu-Wan, *Japan* **64** 33 18N 131 34 E
Bera, *Bangla.* **52** 24 5N 89 37 E
Berati, *Albania* **35** 40 43N 19 59 E
Berau, Teluk, *Indonesia* **57** 2 30 S 132 30 E
Berber, *Sudan* **88** 18 0N 34 0 E
Berbera, *Somali Rep.* **98** 10 30N 45 2 E
Berbérati, *C.A.R.* **94** 4 15N 15 40 E
Berberia, C. del, *Spain* **25** 38 39N 1 24 E
Berbice □, *Guyana* **135** 4 0N 58 0W
Berbice →, *Guyana* **135** 6 20N 57 32W
Berceto, *Italy* **26** 44 30N 10 0 E
Berchtesgaden, *W. Germany* **31** 47 37N 12 58 E
Berdale, *Somali Rep.* **98** 7 4N 47 51 E
Berdichev, *U.S.S.R.* **38** 49 57N 28 30 E
Berdsk, *U.S.S.R.* **40** 54 47N 83 2 E
Berdyansk, *U.S.S.R.* **38** 46 45N 36 50 E
Berea, *U.S.A.* **114** 37 35N 84 18W
Berebere, *Indonesia* **57** 2 25N 128 45 E
Bereda, *Somali Rep.* **98** 11 45N 51 0 E
Bereina, *Papua N. G.* **69** 8 39 S 146 30 E
Berekum, *Ghana* **90** 7 29N 2 34W
Berenice, *Egypt* **88** 24 2N 35 25 E
Berens →, *Canada* **111** 52 25N 97 2W
Berens I., *Canada* **111** 52 18N 97 18W
Berens River, *Canada* **111** 52 25N 97 0W
Berestechko, *U.S.S.R.* **36** 50 22N 25 5 E
Bereşti, *Romania* **34** 46 6N 27 50 E
Beretău →, *Romania* **34** 47 10N 21 50 E
Berettyo →, *Hungary* **33** 46 59N 21 7 E
Berettyóújfalu, *Hungary* **33** 47 13N 21 33 E
Berevo, *Mahajanga, Madag.* **97** 17 14 S 44 17 E
Berevo, *Toliara, Madag.* **97** 19 44 S 44 58 E
Bereza, *U.S.S.R.* **36** 52 31N 24 51 E
Berezhany, *U.S.S.R.* **36** 49 26N 24 58 E
Berezina →, *U.S.S.R.* **36** 52 33N 30 14 E
Berezna, *U.S.S.R.* **37** 51 35N 31 46 E
Berezniki, *U.S.S.R.* **40** 59 24N 56 46 E
Berezovka, *U.S.S.R.* **38** 47 14N 30 55 E
Berezovo, *U.S.S.R.* **40** 64 0N 65 0 E
Berga, *Spain* **24** 42 6N 1 48 E
Berga, *Sweden* **11** 57 14N 16 3 E
Bergama, *Turkey* **46** 39 8N 27 15 E
Bergambacht, *Neths.* **16** 51 56N 4 48 E
Bérgamo, *Italy* **26** 45 42N 9 40 E
Bergantiños, *Spain* **22** 43 20N 8 40W
Bergara, *Spain* **24** 43 9N 2 28W
Bergedorf, *W. Germany* **30** 53 28N 10 12 E
Bergeijk, *Neths.* **17** 51 19N 5 21 E
Bergen, *E. Germany* **30** 54 24N 13 26 E
Bergen, *Neths.* **16** 52 40N 4 43 E
Bergen, *Norway* **9** 60 23N 5 20 E
Bergen, *U.S.A.* **116** 43 5N 77 56W
Bergen-op-Zoom, *Neths.* **17** 51 30N 4 18 E
Bergerac, *France* **20** 44 51N 0 30 E
Bergheim, *W. Germany* **30** 50 57N 6 38 E
Berghem, *Neths.* **16** 51 46N 5 33 E
Bergisch-Gladbach, *W. Germany* **30** 50 59N 7 9 E
Bergkvara, *Sweden* **11** 56 23N 16 5 E
Bergschenhoek, *Neths.* **16** 51 59N 4 30 E
Bergsjö, *Sweden* **10** 61 59N 17 3 E
Bergues, *France* **19** 50 58N 2 24 E
Bergum, *Neths.* **16** 53 13N 5 59 E
Bergvik, *Sweden* **10** 61 16N 16 50 E
Bergville, *S. Africa* **97** 28 52 S 29 18 E
Berhala, Selat, *Indonesia* **56** 1 0 S 104 15 E
Berhampore = Baharampur, *India* **49** 24 2N 88 27 E
Berhampur, *India* **50** 19 15N 84 54 E
Berheci →, *Romania* **34** 46 7N 27 19 E
Bering Sea, *Pac. Oc.* **102** 58 0N 167 0 E
Bering Str., *U.S.A.* **102** 66 0N 170 0W
Beringen, *Belgium* **17** 51 3N 5 14 E
Beringovskiy, *U.S.S.R.* **41** 63 3N 179 19 E
Berislav, *U.S.S.R.* **38** 46 50N 33 30 E
Berisso, *Argentina* **140** 34 56 S 57 50W
Berja, *Spain* **25** 36 50N 2 56W
Berkane, *Morocco* **85** 34 52N 2 20W
Berkel →, *Neths.* **16** 52 8N 6 12 E
Berkeley, *U.K.* **13** 51 41N 2 28W
Berkeley, *U.S.A.* **124** 37 52N 122 20W
Berkeley Springs, *U.S.A.* **114** 39 38N 78 12W
Berkhout, *Neths.* **16** 52 38N 4 59 E
Berkner I., *Antarctica* **143** 79 30 S 50 0W
Berkovitsa, *Bulgaria* **34** 43 16N 23 8 E
Berkshire □, *U.K.* **13** 51 30N 1 20W
Berlaar, *Belgium* **17** 51 7N 4 39 E
Berland →, *Canada* **110** 54 0N 116 50W
Berlanga, *Spain* **23** 38 17N 5 50W
Berlare, *Belgium* **17** 51 2N 4 0 E
Berleburg, *W. Germany* **30** 51 3N 8 22 E
Berlenga, I., *Portugal* **23** 39 25N 9 30W
Berlin, *Germany* **30** 52 32N 13 24 E
Berlin, *Md., U.S.A.* **114** 38 19N 75 12W
Berlin, *N.H., U.S.A.* **117** 44 29N 71 10W
Berlin, *Wis., U.S.A.* **114** 43 58N 88 55W
Bermeja, Sierra, *Spain* **23** 36 30N 5 11W
Bermejo →, *Formosa, Argentina* **140** 26 51 S 58 23W
Bermejo →, *San Juan, Argentina* **140** 32 30 S 67 30W
Bermeo, *Spain* **24** 43 25N 2 47W
Bermillo de Sayago, *Spain* **22** 41 22N 6 8W
Bermuda ■, *Atl. Oc.* **4** 32 45N 65 0W
Bern, *Switz.* **31** 46 57N 7 28 E
Bern □, *Switz.* **31** 46 45N 7 40 E
Bernado, *U.S.A.* **123** 34 30N 106 53W
Bernalda, *Italy* **29** 40 24N 16 44 E
Bernalillo, *U.S.A.* **123** 35 17N 106 37W
Bernard L., *Canada* **108** 45 45N 79 23W
Bernardo de Irigoyen, *Argentina* **141** 26 15 S 53 40W
Bernardo O'Higgins □, *Chile* **140** 34 15 S 70 45W
Bernasconi, *Argentina* **140** 37 55 S 63 44W
Bernau, *E. Germany* **30** 52 40N 13 35 E
Bernau, *W. Germany* **31** 47 45N 12 20 E
Bernay, *France* **18** 49 5N 0 35 E
Bernburg, *E. Germany* **30** 51 40N 11 42 E
Berne = Bern, *Switz.* **31** 46 57N 7 28 E
Berne, *U.S.A.* **119** 40 39N 84 57W
Berne □ = Bern □, *Switz.* **31** 46 45N 7 40 E
Berneck, *E. Germany* **31** 51 3N 11 40 E
Berner Alpen, *Switz.* **31** 46 27N 7 35 E
Bernese Oberland = Oberland, *Switz.* **31** 46 30N 7 30 E
Bernier I., *Australia* **79** 24 50 S 113 12 E
Bernierville, *Canada* **107** 46 6N 71 34W
Bernina, Piz, *Switz.* **31** 46 20N 9 54 E
Bernissart, *Belgium* **17** 50 28N 3 39 E
Bernkastel-Kues, *W. Germany* **31** 49 55N 7 4 E
Beror Hayil, *Israel* **44** 31 34N 34 38 E
Beroroha, *Madag.* **97** 21 40 S 45 10 E
Béroubouay, *Benin* **91** 10 34N 2 46 E
Beroun, *Czech.* **32** 49 57N 14 5 E
Berounka →, *Czech.* **32** 50 0N 13 47 E
Berovo, *Yugoslavia* **35** 41 38N 22 51 E
Berrahal, *Algeria* **85** 36 54N 7 33 E
Berre, Étang de, *France* **21** 43 27N 5 5 E
Berrechid, *Morocco* **84** 33 18N 7 36W
Berri, *Australia* **73** 34 14 S 140 35 E
Berriane, *Algeria* **85** 32 50N 3 46 E
Berridale, *Australia* **75** 36 22 S 148 48 E
Berrien Springs, *U.S.A.* **119** 41 57N 86 20W
Berrima, *Australia* **76** 34 28 S 150 20 E
Berriwillock, *Australia* **74** 35 36 S 142 59 E
Berrouaghia, *Algeria* **85** 36 10N 2 53 E
Berry, *Australia* **76** 34 46 S 150 43 E
Berry, *France* **19** 46 50N 2 0 E
Berry, *U.S.A.* **119** 38 31N 84 23W
Berry Is., *Bahamas* **128** 25 40N 77 50W
Berryessa, L., *U.S.A.* **124** 38 31N 122 6W
Berryville, *U.S.A.* **121** 36 23N 93 35W
Bersenbrück, *W. Germany* **30** 52 33N 7 56 E
Berthierville, *Canada* **107** 46 5N 73 10W
Berthold, *U.S.A.* **120** 48 19N 101 45W
Berthoud, *U.S.A.* **120** 40 21N 105 5W
Bertincourt, *France* **19** 50 5N 2 58 E
Bertoua, *Cameroon* **94** 4 30N 13 45 E
Bertrand, *U.S.A.* **120** 40 35N 99 38W
Bertrange, *Lux.* **17** 49 37N 6 3 E
Bertrix, *Belgium* **17** 49 51N 5 15 E
Berufjörður, *Iceland* **8** 64 48N 14 29W
Beruri, *Brazil* **135** 3 54 S 61 22W
Berwick, *Australia* **74** 38 2 S 145 23 E
Berwick, *U.S.A.* **117** 41 4N 76 17W
Berwick-upon-Tweed, *U.K.* **12** 55 47N 2 0W
Berwyn Mts., *U.K.* **12** 52 54N 3 26W
Berzasca, *Romania* **34** 44 39N 21 58 E
Besal, *Pakistan* **49** 35 4N 73 56 E
Besalampy, *Madag.* **97** 16 43 S 44 29 E
Besançon, *France* **19** 47 15N 6 0 E
Besar, *Indonesia* **56** 2 40 S 116 0 E
Beshenkovichi, *U.S.S.R.* **36** 55 2N 29 29 E
Beslan, *U.S.S.R.* **39** 43 15N 44 28 E
Besnard L., *Canada* **111** 55 25N 106 0W
Besni, *Turkey* **46** 37 41N 37 52 E
Besor, N. →, *Egypt* **44** 31 28N 34 22 E
Bessa Monteiro, *Angola* **95** 7 7 S 13 44 E
Bessarabka, *U.S.S.R.* **38** 46 21N 28 58 E
Bessèges, *France* **21** 44 18N 4 8 E
Bessemer, *Ala., U.S.A.* **115** 33 25N 86 57W
Bessemer, *Mich., U.S.A.* **120** 46 27N 90 0W
Bessin, *France* **18** 49 18N 1 0W
Bessines-sur-Gartempe, *France* **20** 46 6N 1 22 E
Best, *Neths.* **17** 51 31N 5 23 E
Bet Alfa, *Israel* **44** 32 31N 35 25 E
Bet Dagan, *Israel* **44** 32 1N 34 49 E
Bet Guvrin, *Israel* **44** 31 37N 34 54 E
Bet Ha'Emeq, *Israel* **44** 32 58N 35 8 E
Bet Hashitta, *Israel* **44** 32 31N 35 27 E
Bet Qeshet, *Israel* **44** 32 41N 35 21 E
Bet She'an, *Israel* **44** 32 30N 35 30 E
Bet Shemesh, *Israel* **44** 31 44N 35 0 E
Bet Tadjine, Djebel, *Algeria* **84** 29 0N 3 30W
Bet Yosef, *Israel* **44** 32 34N 35 33 E
Betafo, *Madag.* **97** 19 50 S 46 51 E
Betancuria, *Canary Is.* **25** 28 25N 14 3W
Betanzos, *Bolivia* **137** 19 34 S 65 27W
Betanzos, *Spain* **22** 43 15N 8 12W
Bétaré Oya, *Cameroon* **94** 5 40N 14 5 E
Bétera, *Spain* **24** 39 35N 0 28W
Bethal, *S. Africa* **97** 26 27 S 29 28 E
Bethanien, *Namibia* **96** 26 31 S 17 8 E
Bethany = Al 'Ayzarīyah, *Jordan* **44** 31 47N 35 15 E
Bethany, *Canada* **109** 44 11N 78 34W
Bethany, *S. Africa* **96** 29 34 S 25 59 E
Bethany, *Ill., U.S.A.* **119** 39 39N 88 45W
Bethany, *Mo., U.S.A.* **118** 40 18N 94 0W
Bethel, *Alaska, U.S.A.* **102** 60 50N 161 50W
Bethel, *Ohio, U.S.A.* **119** 38 58N 84 5W
Bethel, *Vt., U.S.A.* **117** 43 50N 72 37W
Bethel Park, *U.S.A.* **116** 40 20N 80 2W
Bethlehem = Bayt Lahm, *Jordan* **44** 31 43N 35 12 E
Bethlehem, *S. Africa* **97** 28 14 S 28 18 E
Bethlehem, *U.S.A.* **117** 40 39N 75 24W
Bethulie, *S. Africa* **96** 30 30 S 25 59 E
Béthune, *France* **19** 50 30N 2 38 E
Béthune →, *France* **18** 49 53N 1 9 E
Bethungra, *Australia* **76** 34 45 S 147 51 E
Betijoque, *Venezuela* **134** 9 23N 70 44W
Betim, *Brazil* **139** 19 58 S 44 7W
Betioky, *Madag.* **97** 23 48 S 44 20 E
Beton-Bazoches, *France* **19** 48 42N 3 15 E
Betong, *Thailand* **55** 5 45N 101 5 E
Betoota, *Australia* **72** 25 45 S 140 42 E
Betroka, *Madag.* **97** 23 16 S 46 0 E
Betsiamites, *Canada* **107** 48 56N 68 40W
Betsiamites →, *Canada* **107** 48 56N 68 38W
Betsiboka →, *Madag.* **97** 16 3 S 46 36 E
Betsjoeanaland, *S. Africa* **96** 26 30 S 22 30 E
Bettembourg, *Lux.* **17** 49 31N 6 6 E
Bettendorf, *U.S.A.* **118** 41 32N 90 30W
Bettiah, *India* **49** 26 48N 84 33 E
Béttola, *Italy* **26** 44 42N 9 32 E
Betul, *India* **50** 21 58N 77 59 E
Betung, *Malaysia* **56** 1 24N 111 31 E
Betzdorf, *W. Germany* **30** 50 47N 7 53 E
Beuca, *Romania* **34** 44 14N 24 56 E
Beuil, *France* **21** 44 6N 6 59 E
Beulah, *Australia* **74** 35 58 S 142 29 E
Beulah, *U.S.A.* **120** 47 18N 101 47W
Beuvron →, *France* **18** 47 29N 1 15 E
Bevensen, *W. Germany* **30** 53 5N 10 34 E
Beveren, *Belgium* **17** 51 12N 4 16 E
Beverley, *Australia* **79** 32 9 S 116 56 E
Beverley, *U.K.* **12** 53 52N 0 26W
Beverlo, *Belgium* **17** 51 7N 5 13 E
Beverly, *Mass., U.S.A.* **117** 42 32N 70 50W
Beverly, *Wash., U.S.A.* **122** 46 55N 119 59W
Beverly Hills, *U.S.A.* **125** 34 4N 118 29W
Beverwijk, *Neths.* **16** 52 28N 4 38 E
Bewdley, *Canada* **109** 44 5N 78 19W
Bex, *Switz.* **31** 46 15N 7 0 E
Beyin, *Ghana* **90** 5 1N 2 41W
Beykoz, *Turkey* **35** 41 8N 29 7 E
Beyla, *Guinea* **90** 8 30N 8 38W
Beynat, *France* **20** 45 8N 1 44 E
Beyneu, *U.S.S.R.* **40** 45 10N 55 3 E
Beypazarı, *Turkey* **46** 40 10N 31 56 E
Beypore →, *India* **51** 11 10N 75 47 E
Beyşehir Gölü, *Turkey* **46** 37 40N 31 45 E
Bezet, *Israel* **44** 33 4N 35 8 E
Bezhetsk, *U.S.S.R.* **37** 57 47N 36 39 E
Bezhitsa, *U.S.S.R.* **36** 53 19N 34 17 E
Béziers, *France* **20** 43 20N 3 12 E
Bezwada = Vijayawada, *India* **51** 16 31N 80 39 E
Bhadarwah, *India* **49** 32 58N 75 46 E
Bhadra →, *India* **51** 14 0N 75 20 E
Bhadrakh, *India* **50** 21 10N 86 30 E
Bhadravati, *India* **51** 13 49N 75 40 E
Bhagalpur, *India* **49** 25 10N 87 0 E
Bhainsa, *India* **50** 19 10N 77 58 E
Bhairab →, *Bangla.* **52** 22 51N 89 34 E
Bhairab Bazar, *Bangla.* **52** 24 4N 90 58 E
Bhakkar, *Pakistan* **48** 31 40N 71 5 E
Bhakra Dam, *India* **48** 31 30N 76 45 E
Bhamo, *Burma* **52** 24 15N 97 15 E
Bhamragarh, *India* **50** 19 30N 80 40 E
Bhandara, *India* **50** 21 5N 79 42 E
Bhanrer Ra., *India* **48** 23 40N 79 45 E
Bharat = India ■, *Asia* **5** 20 0N 78 0 E
Bharatpur, *India* **48** 27 15N 77 30 E
Bharuch, *India* **50** 21 47N 73 0 E
Bhatghar L., *India* **50** 18 10N 73 48 E

Bhatiapara Ghat, *Bangla.* **52** 23 13N 89 42 E
Bhatinda, *India* **48** 30 15N 74 57 E
Bhatkal, *India* **51** 13 58N 74 35 E
Bhatpara, *India* **49** 22 50N 88 25 E
Bhattiprolu, *India* **51** 16 7N 80 45 E
Bhaun, *Pakistan* **48** 32 55N 72 40 E
Bhaunagar = Bhavnagar, *India* **48** 21 45N 72 10 E
Bhavani, *India* **51** 11 27N 77 43 E
Bhavani →, *India* **51** 11 0N 78 15 E
Bhavnagar, *India* **48** 21 45N 72 10 E
Bhawanipatna, *India* **50** 19 55N 80 10 E
Bhera, *Pakistan* **48** 32 29N 72 57 E
Bhilsa = Vidisha, *India* **48** 23 28N 77 53 E
Bhilwara, *India* **48** 25 25N 74 38 E
Bhima →, *India* **50** 16 25N 77 17 E
Bhimavaram, *India* **51** 16 30N 81 30 E
Bhimbar, *Pakistan* **48** 32 59N 74 3 E
Bhind, *India* **49** 26 30N 78 46 E
Bhiwandi, *India* **50** 19 20N 73 0 E
Bhiwani, *India* **48** 28 50N 76 9 E
Bhola, *Bangla.* **52** 22 45N 90 35 E
Bhongir, *India* **50** 17 30N 78 56 E
Bhopal, *India* **48** 23 20N 77 30 E
Bhor, *India* **50** 18 12N 73 53 E
Bhubaneshwar, *India* **50** 20 15N 85 50 E
Bhuj, *India* **48** 23 15N 69 49 E
Bhumibol Dam, *Thailand* **54** 17 15N 98 58 E
Bhusaval, *India* **50** 21 3N 75 46 E
Bhutan ■, *Asia* **52** 27 25N 90 30 E
Biá →, *Brazil* **134** 3 28 S 67 23W
Biafra, B. of = Bonny, Bight of, *Africa* **91** 3 30N 9 20 E
Biak, *Indonesia* **57** 1 10 S 136 6 E
Biała →, *Poland* **32** 50 3N 20 55 E
Biała Podlaska, *Poland* **32** 52 4N 23 6 E
Białogard, *Poland* **32** 54 2N 15 58 E
Białystok, *Poland* **32** 53 10N 23 10 E
Biancavilla, *Italy* **29** 37 39N 14 50 E
Biaro, *Indonesia* **57** 2 5N 125 26 E
Biarritz, *France* **20** 43 29N 1 33W
Biasca, *Switz.* **31** 46 22N 8 58 E
Biba, *Egypt* **88** 28 55N 31 0 E
Bibai, *Japan* **63** 43 19N 141 52 E
Bibala, *Angola* **95** 14 44 S 13 24 E
Bibane, Bahiret el, *Tunisia* **86** 33 16N 11 13 E
Bibassé, *Gabon* **94** 1 27N 11 37 E
Bibbenluke, *Australia* **75** 36 48 S 149 17 E
Bibbiena, *Italy* **27** 43 43N 11 50 E
Bibby I., *Canada* **111** 61 55N 93 0W
Biberach, *W. Germany* **31** 48 5N 9 49 E
Bibey →, *Spain* **22** 42 24N 7 13W
Bibiani, *Ghana* **90** 6 30N 2 8W
Bibile, *Sri Lanka* **51** 7 10N 81 25 E
Biboohra, *Australia* **72** 16 56 S 145 25 E
Bibungwa, *Zaïre* **92** 2 40 S 28 15 E
Bic, *Canada* **107** 48 20N 68 41W
Bic, Île du, *Canada* **107** 48 24N 68 52W
Bicaz, *Romania* **34** 46 53N 26 5 E
Biccari, *Italy* **29** 41 23N 15 12 E
Biche, La →, *Canada* **110** 59 57N 123 50W
Bichena, *Ethiopia* **89** 10 28N 38 10 E
Bickerton I., *Australia* **72** 13 45 S 136 10 E
Bicknell, *Ind., U.S.A.* **119** 38 50N 87 20W
Bicknell, *Utah, U.S.A.* **123** 38 16N 111 35W
Bida, *Nigeria* **91** 9 3N 5 58 E
Bida, *Zaïre* **94** 4 55N 19 56 E
Bidar, *India* **50** 17 55N 77 35 E
Biddeford, *U.S.A.* **105** 43 30N 70 28W
Biddiyā, *Jordan* **44** 32 7N 35 4 E
Biddon, *Australia* **76** 31 30 S 148 47 E
Biddū, *Jordan* **44** 31 50N 35 8 E
Biddwara, *Ethiopia* **89** 5 11N 38 34 E
Bideford, *U.K.* **13** 51 1N 4 13W
Bidon 5 = Poste Maurice Cortier, *Algeria* **85** 22 14N 1 2 E
Bidor, *Malaysia* **55** 4 6N 101 15 E
Bié □, *Angola* **95** 12 30 S 17 0 E
Bié, Planalto de, *Angola* **95** 12 0 S 16 0 E
Bieber, *U.S.A.* **122** 41 4N 121 6W
Biel, *Switz.* **31** 47 8N 7 14 E
Bielawa, *Poland* **32** 50 43N 16 37 E
Bielé Karpaty, *Czech.* **32** 49 5N 18 0 E
Bielefeld, *W. Germany* **30** 52 2N 8 31 E
Bielersee, *Switz.* **31** 47 6N 7 5 E
Biella, *Italy* **26** 45 33N 8 3 E
Bielsk Podlaski, *Poland* **32** 52 47N 23 12 E
Bielsko-Biała, *Poland* **32** 49 50N 19 2 E
Bien Hoa, *Vietnam* **55** 10 57N 106 49 E
Bienfait, *Canada* **111** 49 10N 102 50W
Bienne = Biel, *Switz.* **31** 47 8N 7 14 E
Bienvenida, *Spain* **23** 38 18N 6 12W
Bienvenue, *Fr. Guiana* **135** 3 0N 52 30W
Bienville, L., *Canada* **104** 55 5N 72 40W
Biescas, *Spain* **24** 42 37N 0 20W
Biese →, *E. Germany* **30** 52 53N 11 46 E
Biesiesfontein, *S. Africa* **96** 30 57 S 17 58 E
Bietigheim, *W. Germany* **31** 48 57N 9 8 E
Bievre, *Belgium* **17** 49 57N 5 1 E
Biferno →, *Italy* **29** 41 59N 15 2 E
Bifoum, *Gabon* **94** 0 20 S 10 23 E
Big →, *Canada* **105** 54 50N 58 55W
Big →, *U.S.A.* **118** 38 27N 90 37W
Big B., *Canada* **105** 55 43N 60 35W
Big Basswood L., *Canada* **108** 46 25N 83 23W
Big Bear City, *U.S.A.* **125** 34 16N 116 51W
Big Bear L., *U.S.A.* **125** 34 15N 116 56W
Big Beaver, *Canada* **111** 49 10N 105 10W
Big Belt Mts., *U.S.A.* **122** 46 50N 111 30W
Big Bend, *Swaziland* **97** 26 50 S 31 58 E
Big Bend Nat. Park, *U.S.A.* **121** 29 15N 103 15W
Big Black →, *U.S.A.* **121** 32 0N 91 5W
Big Blue →, *Ind., U.S.A.* **119** 39 12N 85 56W
Big Blue →, *Kans., U.S.A.* **120** 39 11N 96 40W
Big Cr. →, *Canada* **110** 51 42N 122 41W
Big Creek, *U.S.A.* **124** 37 11N 119 14W
Big Cypress Swamp, *U.S.A.* **115** 26 12N 81 10W
Big Falls, *U.S.A.* **120** 48 11N 93 48W
Big Fork →, *U.S.A.* **120** 48 31N 93 43W
Big Horn Mts. = Bighorn Mts., *U.S.A.* **122** 44 30N 107 30W
Big Lake, *U.S.A.* **121** 31 12N 101 25W
Big Moose, *U.S.A.* **117** 43 49N 74 58W
Big Muddy →, *Ill., U.S.A.* **118** 38 0N 89 0W
Big Muddy →, *Mont., U.S.A.* **120** 48 8N 104 36W
Big Pine, *U.S.A.* **124** 37 12N 118 17W
Big Piney, *U.S.A.* **122** 42 32N 110 3W
Big Quill L., *Canada* **111** 51 55N 104 50W
Big Rapids, *U.S.A.* **114** 43 42N 85 27W
Big Rideau L., *Canada* **109** 44 40N 76 15W
Big River, *Canada* **111** 53 50N 107 0W
Big Run, *U.S.A.* **116** 40 57N 78 55W
Big Sable Pt., *U.S.A.* **114** 44 5N 86 30W
Big Sand L., *Canada* **111** 57 45N 99 45W
Big Sandy, *U.S.A.* **122** 48 12N 110 9W
Big Sandy Cr. →, *U.S.A.* **120** 38 6N 102 29W
Big Sioux →, *U.S.A.* **120** 42 30N 96 25W
Big Spring, *U.S.A.* **121** 32 10N 101 25W
Big Springs, *U.S.A.* **120** 41 4N 102 3W
Big Stone City, *U.S.A.* **120** 45 20N 96 30W
Big Stone Gap, *U.S.A.* **115** 36 52N 82 45W
Big Stone L., *U.S.A.* **120** 45 30N 96 35W
Big Sur, *U.S.A.* **124** 36 15N 121 48W
Big Timber, *U.S.A.* **122** 45 53N 110 0W
Big Trout L., *Ont., Canada* **104** 53 40N 90 0W
Big Trout L., *Ont., Canada* **109** 45 46N 78 37W
Biganos, *France* **20** 44 39N 0 59W
Bigfork, *U.S.A.* **122** 48 3N 114 2W
Bigga, *Australia* **76** 34 4 S 149 9 E
Biggar, *Canada* **111** 52 4N 108 0W
Biggar, *U.K.* **14** 55 38N 3 31W
Bigge I., *Australia* **78** 14 35 S 125 10 E
Biggenden, *Australia* **73** 25 31 S 152 4 E
Biggs, *U.S.A.* **124** 39 24N 121 43W
Bighorn, *U.S.A.* **122** 46 11N 107 25W
Bighorn →, *U.S.A.* **122** 46 9N 107 28W
Bighorn Mts., *U.S.A.* **122** 44 30N 107 30W
Bigniba →, *Canada* **106** 49 18N 77 20W
Bignona, *Senegal* **90** 12 52N 16 14W
Bigorre, *France* **20** 43 10N 0 5 E
Bigstone L., *Canada* **111** 53 42N 95 44W
Bigwa, *Tanzania* **92** 7 10 S 39 10 E
Bihać, *Yugoslavia* **27** 44 49N 15 57 E
Bihar, *India* **49** 25 5N 85 40 E
Bihar □, *India* **49** 25 0N 86 0 E
Biharamulo, *Tanzania* **92** 2 25 S 31 25 E
Biharamulo □, *Tanzania* **92** 2 30 S 31 20 E
Bihor, Munţii, *Romania* **34** 46 29N 22 47 E
Bijagós, Arquipélago dos, *Guinea-Biss.* **90** 11 15N 16 10W
Bijaipur, *India* **48** 26 2N 77 20 E
Bijapur, *Karnataka, India* **50** 16 50N 75 55 E
Bijapur, *Mad. P., India* **50** 18 50N 80 50 E
Bījār, *Iran* **46** 35 52N 47 35 E
Bijeljina, *Yugoslavia* **33** 44 46N 19 17 E
Bijelo Polje, *Yugoslavia* **33** 43 1N 19 45 E
Bijie, *China* **58** 27 20N 105 16 E
Bijni, *India* **52** 26 30N 90 40 E
Bijnor, *India* **48** 29 27N 78 11 E
Bikaner, *India* **48** 28 2N 73 18 E
Bikapur, *India* **49** 26 30N 82 7 E
Bikeqi, *China* **60** 40 43N 111 20 E
Bikin, *U.S.S.R.* **41** 46 50N 134 20 E
Bikini Atoll, *Pac. Oc.* **66** 12 0N 167 30 E
Bikoro, *Zaïre* **94** 0 48 S 18 15 E
Bikoué, *Cameroon* **91** 3 55N 11 50 E
Bilara, *India* **48** 26 14N 73 53 E
Bilaspara, *India* **52** 26 13N 90 14 E
Bilaspur, *Mad. P., India* **49** 22 2N 82 15 E
Bilaspur, *Punjab, India* **48** 31 19N 76 50 E
Bilauk Taungdan, *Thailand* **54** 13 0N 99 0 E
Bilbao, *Spain* **24** 43 16N 2 56W
Bilbeis, *Egypt* **88** 30 25N 31 34 E
Bilbor, *Romania* **34** 47 6N 25 30 E
Bíldudalur, *Iceland* **8** 65 41N 23 36W
Bileća, *Yugoslavia* **33** 42 53N 18 27 E
Bilecik, *Turkey* **46** 40 5N 30 5 E
Biłgoraj, *Poland* **32** 50 33N 22 42 E
Bilibino, *U.S.S.R.* **41** 68 3N 166 20 E
Bilibiza, *Mozam.* **93** 12 30 S 40 20 E
Bilin, *Burma* **52** 17 14N 97 15 E
Bilir, *U.S.S.R.* **41** 65 40N 131 20 E
Bill, *U.S.A.* **120** 43 18N 105 18W
Billabalong, *Australia* **79** 27 25 S 115 49 E
Billiluna, *Australia* **78** 19 37 S 127 41 E
Billingham, *U.K.* **12** 54 36N 1 18W
Billings, *U.S.A.* **122** 45 43N 108 29W
Billingsfors, *Sweden* **10** 58 59N 12 15 E
Billiton Is. = Belitung, *Indonesia* **56** 3 10 S 107 50 E
Billom, *France* **20** 45 43N 3 20 E
Bilma, *Niger* **87** 18 50N 13 30 E
Bilo Gora, *Yugoslavia* **33** 45 53N 17 15 E
Biloela, *Australia* **72** 24 24 S 150 31 E
Biloku, *Guyana* **135** 1 50N 58 25W
Biloxi, *U.S.A.* **121** 30 24N 88 53W
Bilpa Morea Claypan, *Australia* **72** 25 0 S 140 0 E
Bilpin, *Australia* **76** 33 28 S 150 31 E
Bilthoven, *Neths.* **16** 52 8N 5 12 E
Biltine, *Chad* **87** 14 40N 20 50 E
Bilugyun, *Burma* **52** 16 24N 97 32 E
Bilyana, *Australia* **72** 18 5 S 145 50 E
Bilyarsk, *U.S.S.R.* **37** 54 58N 50 22 E
Bilzen, *Belgium* **17** 50 52N 5 31 E
Bima, *Indonesia* **57** 8 22 S 118 49 E
Bimban, *Egypt* **88** 24 24N 32 54 E
Bimberi Peak, *Australia* **76** 35 44 S 148 51 E
Bimbila, *Ghana* **91** 8 54N 0 5 E
Bimbo, *C.A.R.* **94** 4 15N 18 33 E
Bimini Is., *Bahamas* **128** 25 42N 79 25W
Bin Xian, *Heilongjiang, China* **61** 45 42N 127 32 E
Bin Xian, *Shaanxi, China* **60** 35 2N 108 4 E
Bina-Etawah, *India* **48** 24 13N 78 14 E
Binalbagan, *Phil.* **57** 10 12N 122 50 E
Bīnālūd, Kūh-e, *Iran* **47** 36 30N 58 30 E
Binatang, *Malaysia* **56** 2 10N 111 40 E
Binbee, *Australia* **72** 20 19 S 147 56 E
Binche, *Belgium* **17** 50 26N 4 10 E
Binchuan, *China* **58** 25 42N 100 38 E
Binda, *Australia* **73** 27 52 S 147 21 E
Binda, *Zaïre* **95** 5 52 S 13 14 E
Bindi Bindi, *Australia* **79** 30 37 S 116 22 E
Bindle, *Australia* **73** 27 40 S 148 45 E
Bindura, *Zimb.* **93** 17 18 S 31 18 E
Bingara, *N.S.W., Australia* **77** 29 52 S 150 36 E
Bingara, *Queens., Australia* **73** 28 10 S 144 37 E
Bingen, *W. Germany* **31** 49 57N 7 53 E
Bingerville, *Ivory C.* **90** 5 18N 3 49W
Bingham, *U.S.A.* **105** 45 5N 69 50W
Bingham Canyon, *U.S.A.* **122** 40 31N 112 10W
Binghamton, *U.S.A.* **117** 42 9N 75 54W
Bingöl, *Turkey* **46** 38 53N 40 29 E
Binh Dinh = An Nhon, *Vietnam* **54** 13 55N 109 7 E
Binh Khe, *Vietnam* **54** 13 57N 108 51 E
Binh Son, *Vietnam* **54** 15 20N 108 40 E
Binhai, *China* **61** 34 2N 119 49 E
Biniguy, *Australia* **77** 29 34 S 150 14 E
Binjai, *Indonesia* **56** 3 20N 98 30 E
Binnaway, *Australia* **77** 31 28 S 149 24 E
Binongko, *Indonesia* **57** 5 55 S 123 55 E
Binscarth, *Canada* **111** 50 37N 101 17W
Bint Jubayl, *Lebanon* **44** 33 8N 35 25 E
Bintan, *Indonesia* **56** 1 0N 104 0 E
Bintulu, *Malaysia* **56** 3 10N 113 0 E
Bintuni, *Indonesia* **57** 2 7 S 133 32 E
Binyamina, *Israel* **44** 32 32N 34 56 E
Binyang, *China* **58** 23 12N 108 47 E
Binz, *E. Germany* **30** 54 23N 13 37 E
Binza, *Zaïre* **95** 4 21 S 15 14 E
Binzert = Bizerte, *Tunisia* **86** 37 15N 9 50 E
Bío Bío □, *Chile* **140** 37 35 S 72 0W
Biograd, *Yugoslavia* **27** 43 56N 15 29 E
Bioko, *Eq. Guin.* **91** 3 30N 8 40 E
Biougra, *Morocco* **84** 30 15N 9 14W
Biq'at Bet Netofa, *Israel* **44** 32 49N 35 22 E
Bir, *India* **50** 19 4N 75 46 E
Bir, Ras, *Djibouti* **89** 12 0N 43 20 E
Bîr Abu Hashim, *Egypt* **88** 23 42N 34 6 E
Bîr Abu M'nqar, *Egypt* **88** 26 33N 27 33 E
Bîr Adal Deib, *Sudan* **88** 22 35N 36 10 E
Bi'r al Malfa, *Libya* **86** 31 58N 15 18 E
Bir Aouine, *Tunisia* **86** 32 25N 9 18 E
Bîr 'Asal, *Egypt* **88** 25 55N 34 20 E
Bîr Autrun, *Sudan* **88** 18 15N 26 40 E
Bi'r Dhu'fān, *Libya* **86** 31 59N 14 32 E
Bîr Diqnash, *Egypt* **88** 31 3N 25 23 E
Bir el Abbes, *Algeria* **84** 26 7N 6 9W
Bir el Ater, *Algeria* **85** 34 46N 8 3 E
Bîr el Basur, *Egypt* **88** 29 51N 25 49 E
Bîr el Gellaz, *Egypt* **88** 30 50N 26 40 E
Bîr el Shaqqa, *Egypt* **88** 30 54N 25 1 E
Bîr Fuad, *Egypt* **88** 30 35N 26 28 E
Bir Gara, *Chad* **87** 13 11N 15 58 E
Bîr Haimur, *Egypt* **88** 22 45N 33 40 E
Bir Jdid, *Morocco* **84** 33 26N 8 0W
Bîr Kanayis, *Egypt* **88** 24 59N 33 15 E
Bîr Kerawein, *Egypt* **88** 27 10N 28 25 E
Bir Lahrache, *Algeria* **85** 32 1N 8 12 E
Bîr Maql, *Egypt* **88** 23 7N 33 40 E
Bîr Misaha, *Egypt* **88** 22 13N 27 59 E
Bir Mogrein, *Mauritania* **84** 25 10N 11 25W
Bîr Murr, *Egypt* **88** 23 28N 30 10 E
Bi'r Nabālā, *Jordan* **44** 31 52N 35 12 E
Bîr Nakheila, *Egypt* **88** 24 1N 30 50 E
Bîr Qatrani, *Egypt* **88** 30 55N 26 10 E
Bîr Ranga, *Egypt* **88** 24 25N 35 15 E
Bîr Sahara, *Egypt* **88** 22 54N 28 40 E
Bîr Seiyâla, *Egypt* **88** 26 10N 33 50 E
Bir Semguine, *Morocco* **84** 30 1N 5 39W
Bîr Shalatein, *Egypt* **88** 23 5N 35 25 E
Bîr Shebb, *Egypt* **88** 22 25N 29 40 E
Bîr Shût, *Egypt* **88** 23 50N 35 15 E
Bîr Terfawi, *Egypt* **88** 22 57N 28 55 E
Bîr Umm Qubûr, *Egypt* **88** 24 35N 34 2 E
Bîr Ungât, *Egypt* **88** 22 8N 33 48 E
Bîr Za'farâna, *Egypt* **88** 29 10N 32 40 E
Bîr Zāmūs, *Libya* **86** 24 16N 15 6 E
Bi'r Zayt, *Jordan* **44** 31 59N 35 11 E
Bîr Zeidûn, *Egypt* **88** 25 45N 33 40 E
Bira, *Indonesia* **57** 2 3 S 132 2 E
Bîra, *Romania* **34** 47 2N 27 3 E
Birak Sulaymān, *Jordan* **44** 31 42N 35 7 E
Biramféro, *Guinea* **90** 11 40N 9 10W
Birao, *C.A.R.* **94** 10 20N 22 47 E
Birawa, *Zaïre* **92** 2 20 S 28 48 E
Bîrca, *Romania* **34** 43 59N 23 36 E
Birch Hills, *Canada* **111** 52 59N 105 25W
Birch I., *Canada* **111** 52 26N 99 54W
Birch L., *N.W.T., Canada* **110** 62 4N 116 33W
Birch L., *Ont., Canada* **104** 51 23N 92 18W
Birch L., *U.S.A.* **104** 47 48N 91 43W
Birch Mts., *Canada* **110** 57 30N 113 10W
Birch River, *Canada* **111** 52 24N 101 6W
Birchip, *Australia* **74** 35 56 S 142 55 E
Birchwood, *N.Z.* **81** 45 55 S 167 53 E
Bird, *Canada* **111** 56 30N 94 13W
Bird City, *U.S.A.* **120** 39 48N 101 33W
Bird I. = Aves, I. de, *W. Indies* **129** 15 45N 63 55W
Bird I., *S. Africa* **96** 32 3 S 18 17 E
Birdaard, *Neths.* **16** 53 18N 5 53 E
Birdlip, *U.K.* **13** 51 50N 2 7W
Birds, *U.S.A.* **119** 38 50N 87 40W
Birdseye, *U.S.A.* **119** 38 19N 86 42W
Birdsville, *Australia* **72** 25 51 S 139 20 E
Birdum, *Australia* **78** 15 39 S 133 13 E
Birecik, *Turkey* **46** 37 0N 38 0 E
Bireuen, *Indonesia* **56** 5 14N 96 39 E
Birifo, *Gambia* **90** 13 30N 14 0W
Birigui, *Brazil* **141** 21 18 S 50 16W
Birini, *C.A.R.* **94** 7 51N 22 24 E
Birkenfeld, *W. Germany* **31** 49 39N 7 11 E
Birkenhead, *N.Z.* **80** 36 49 S 174 46 E
Birkenhead, *U.K.* **12** 53 24N 3 1W
Birket Qârûn, *Egypt* **88** 29 30N 30 40 E
Birkhadem, *Algeria* **85** 36 43N 3 3 E
Bîrlad, *Romania* **34** 46 15N 27 38 E
Birmingham, *U.K.* **13** 52 30N 1 55W
Birmingham, *Ala., U.S.A.* **115** 33 31N 86 50W
Birmingham, *Iowa, U.S.A.* **118** 40 53N 91 57W
Birmitrapur, *India* **50** 22 24N 84 46 E
Birni Ngaouré, *Niger* **91** 13 5N 2 51 E
Birni Nkonni, *Niger* **91** 13 55N 5 15 E
Birnin Gwari, *Nigeria* **91** 11 0N 6 45 E
Birnin Kebbi, *Nigeria* **91** 12 32N 4 12 E
Birnin Kudu, *Nigeria* **91** 11 30N 9 29 E
Birobidzhan, *U.S.S.R.* **41** 48 50N 132 50 E
Birougou, Mts., *Gabon* **94** 1 51 S 12 20 E
Birqīn, *Jordan* **44** 32 27N 35 15 E
Birr, *Ireland* **15** 53 7N 7 55W
Birregurra, *Australia* **74** 38 20 S 143 46 E
Birrie →, *Australia* **73** 29 43 S 146 37 E
Birriwa, *Australia* **77** 32 7 S 149 28 E
Birsilpur, *India* **48** 28 11N 72 15 E
Birsk, *U.S.S.R.* **40** 55 25N 55 30 E
Birtin, *Romania* **34** 46 59N 22 31 E
Birtle, *Canada* **111** 50 30N 101 5W
Biryuchiy, *U.S.S.R.* **38** 46 10N 35 0 E
Birzai, *U.S.S.R.* **36** 56 11N 24 45 E
Bîrzava, *Romania* **34** 46 7N 21 59 E
Bisa, *Indonesia* **57** 1 15 S 127 28 E
Bisáccia, *Italy* **29** 41 0N 15 20 E
Bisacquino, *Italy* **28** 37 42N 13 13 E
Bisai, *Japan* **65** 35 16N 136 44 E
Bisalpur, *India* **49** 28 14N 79 48 E
Bisbal, La, *Spain* **24** 41 58N 3 2 E
Bisbee, *U.S.A.* **123** 31 30N 110 0W
Biscarrosse et de Parentis, Étang de, *France* **20** 44 21N 1 10W
Biscay, B. of, *Atl. Oc.* **130** 45 0N 2 0W
Biscayne B., *U.S.A.* **115** 25 40N 80 12W
Biscéglie, *Italy* **29** 41 14N 16 30 E
Bischofshofen, *Austria* **33** 47 26N 13 14 E
Bischofswerda, *E. Germany* **30** 51 8N 14 11 E
Bischwiller, *France* **19** 48 46N 7 50 E
Biscoe Bay, *Antarctica* **143** 77 0 S 152 0W
Biscoe Is., *Antarctica* **143** 66 0 S 67 0W
Biscostasing, *Canada* **104** 47 18N 82 9W
Biscucuy, *Venezuela* **134** 9 22N 69 59W
Biševo, *Yugoslavia* **27** 42 57N 16 3 E
Bisha, *Ethiopia* **89** 15 30N 37 31 E
Bishah, W. →, *Si. Arabia* **88** 21 24N 43 26 E
Bishan, *China* **58** 29 33N 106 12 E
Bishnupur, *India* **49** 23 8N 87 20 E
Bisho, *S. Africa* **97** 32 50 S 27 23 E
Bishop, *Calif., U.S.A.* **124** 37 20N 118 26W
Bishop, *Tex., U.S.A.* **121** 27 35N 97 49W
Bishop Auckland, *U.K.* **12** 54 40N 1 40W
Bishop's Falls, *Canada* **105** 49 2N 55 30W
Bishop's Stortford, *U.K.* **13** 51 52N 0 11 E
Bishopton, *Canada* **107** 45 35N 71 35W
Bisignano, *Italy* **29** 39 30N 16 17 E
Bisina, L., *Uganda* **92** 1 38N 33 56 E
Biskra, *Algeria* **85** 34 50N 5 44 E

Bislig, *Phil.* **57** 8 15N 126 27 E
Bismarck, *Mo., U.S.A.* **118** 37 46N 90 38W
Bismarck, *N. Dak., U.S.A.* **120** 46 49N 100 49W
Bismarck Arch., *Papua N. G.* **69** 2 30S 150 0 E
Bismarck Ra., *Papua N. G.* **69** 5 35S 145 0 E
Bismarck Sea, *Papua N. G.* **69** 4 10S 146 50 E
Bismark, *E. Germany* **30** 52 39N 11 31 E
Biso, *Uganda* **92** 1 44N 31 26 E
Bison, *U.S.A.* **120** 45 34N 102 28W
Bispfors, *Sweden* **8** 63 1N 16 37 E
Bispgården, *Sweden* **10** 63 2N 16 40 E
Bissagos = Bijagós, Arquipélago dos, *Guinea-Biss.* **90** 11 15N 16 10W
Bissau, *Guinea-Biss.* **90** 11 45N 15 45W
Bissett, *Canada* **111** 51 2N 95 41W
Bissikrima, *Guinea* **90** 10 50N 10 58W
Bistcho L., *Canada* **110** 59 45N 118 50W
Bistreţu, *Romania* **34** 43 54N 23 23 E
Bistrica = Ilirska-Bistrica, *Yugoslavia* **27** 45 34N 14 14 E
Bistriţa, *Romania* **34** 47 9N 24 35 E
Bistriţa →, *Romania* **34** 46 30N 26 57 E
Bistriţei, Munţii, *Romania* **34** 47 15N 25 40 E
Biswan, *India* **49** 27 29N 81 2 E
Bitam, *Gabon* **94** 2 5N 11 25 E
Bitburg, *W. Germany* **31** 49 58N 6 32 E
Bitche, *France* **19** 49 2N 7 25 E
Bitkine, *Chad* **87** 11 59N 18 13 E
Bitlis, *Turkey* **46** 38 20N 42 3 E
Bitola, *Yugoslavia* **35** 41 5N 21 10 E
Bitolj = Bitola, *Yugoslavia* **35** 41 5N 21 10 E
Bitonto, *Italy* **29** 41 7N 16 40 E
Bitter Creek, *U.S.A.* **122** 41 39N 108 36W
Bitter L. = Buheirat-Murrat-el-Kubra, *Egypt* **88** 30 15N 32 40 E
Bitterfeld, *E. Germany* **30** 51 36N 12 20 E
Bitterfontein, *S. Africa* **96** 31 1S 18 32 E
Bitterroot →, *U.S.A.* **122** 46 52N 114 6W
Bitterroot Range, *U.S.A.* **122** 46 0N 114 20W
Bitterwater, *U.S.A.* **124** 36 23N 121 0W
Bitti, *Italy* **28** 40 29N 9 20 E
Bittou, *Burkina Faso* **91** 11 17N 0 18W
Biu, *Nigeria* **91** 10 40N 12 3 E
Bivolari, *Romania* **34** 47 31N 27 27 E
Biwa-Ko, *Japan* **65** 35 15N 136 10 E
Biwabik, *U.S.A.* **120** 47 33N 92 19W
Bixad, *Romania* **34** 47 56N 23 28 E
Biyang, *China* **60** 32 38N 113 21 E
Biysk, *U.S.S.R.* **40** 52 40N 85 0 E
Bizana, *S. Africa* **97** 30 50S 29 52 E
Bizen, *Japan* **64** 34 43N 134 8 E
Bizerte, *Tunisia* **86** 37 15N 9 50 E
Bjargtangar, *Iceland* **8** 65 30N 24 30W
Bjelasica, *Yugoslavia* **33** 42 50N 19 40 E
Bjelovar, *Yugoslavia* **33** 45 56N 16 49 E
Bjerringbro, *Denmark* **11** 56 23N 9 39 E
Björbo, *Sweden* **10** 60 27N 14 44 E
Björneborg, *Sweden* **10** 59 14N 14 16 E
Bjørnøya, *Arctic* **144** 74 30N 19 0 E
Bjuv, *Sweden* **11** 56 5N 12 55 E
Blace, *Yugoslavia* **33** 43 18N 21 17 E
Blache, L. de la, *Canada* **107** 50 5N 69 29W
Black → = Da →, *Vietnam* **54** 21 15N 105 20 E
Black →, *Canada* **108** 44 42N 79 19W
Black →, *Ark., U.S.A.* **121** 35 38N 91 19W
Black →, *N.Y., U.S.A.* **117** 43 59N 76 4W
Black →, *Wis., U.S.A.* **120** 43 52N 91 22W
Black Diamond, *Canada* **110** 50 45N 114 14W
Black Forest = Schwarzwald, *W. Germany* **31** 48 0N 8 0 E
Black Hills, *U.S.A.* **120** 44 0N 103 50W
Black I., *Canada* **111** 51 12N 96 30W
Black L., *Canada* **111** 59 12N 105 15W
Black L., *U.S.A.* **114** 45 28N 84 15W
Black Lake, *Canada* **107** 46 1N 71 22W
Black Mesa, Mt., *U.S.A.* **121** 36 57N 102 55W
Black Mt. = Mynydd Du, *U.K.* **13** 51 45N 3 45W
Black Mountain, *Australia* **77** 30 18S 151 39 E
Black Mts., *U.K.* **13** 51 52N 3 5W
Black Range, *U.S.A.* **123** 33 30N 107 55W
Black River, *Jamaica* **128** 18 0N 77 50W
Black River Falls, *U.S.A.* **120** 44 23N 90 52W
Black Sea, *Europe* **38** 43 30N 35 0 E
Black Sugarloaf, Mt., *Australia* **77** 31 18S 151 35 E
Black Volta →, *Africa* **90** 8 41N 1 33W
Black Warrior →, *U.S.A.* **115** 32 32N 87 51W
Blackall, *Australia* **72** 24 25S 145 45 E
Blackball, *N.Z.* **81** 42 22S 171 26 E
Blackbull, *Australia* **72** 17 55S 141 45 E
Blackburn, *U.K.* **12** 53 44N 2 30W
Blackduck, *U.S.A.* **120** 47 43N 94 32W
Blackfoot, *U.S.A.* **122** 43 13N 112 12W
Blackfoot →, *U.S.A.* **122** 46 52N 113 53W
Blackfoot Res., *U.S.A.* **122** 43 0N 111 35W
Blackheath, *Australia* **76** 33 39S 150 17 E
Blackie, *Canada* **110** 50 36N 113 37W
Blackpool, *U.K.* **12** 53 48N 3 3W
Blackriver, *U.S.A.* **116** 44 46N 83 17W
Blacks Harbour, *Canada* **105** 45 3N 66 49W
Blacksburg, *U.S.A.* **114** 37 17N 80 23W
Blacksod B., *Ireland* **15** 54 6N 10 0W
Blackstone, *U.S.A.* **114** 37 6N 78 0W
Blackstone →, *Canada* **110** 61 5N 122 55W
Blackstone Ra., *Australia* **79** 26 0S 128 30 E
Blacktown, *Australia* **76** 33 48S 150 55 E
Blackville, *Australia* **77** 31 40S 150 15 E
Blackville, *Canada* **105** 46 44N 65 50W
Blackwater, *N.S.W., Australia* **77** 30 4S 151 53 E
Blackwater, *Queens., Australia* **72** 23 35S 148 53 E
Blackwater →, *Ireland* **15** 51 55N 7 50W
Blackwater →, *U.K.* **15** 54 31N 6 35W
Blackwater →, *U.S.A.* **118** 38 59N 92 59W
Blackwater Cr. →, *Australia* **73** 25 56S 144 30 E
Blackwell, *U.S.A.* **121** 36 55N 97 20W
Blackwells Corner, *U.S.A.* **125** 35 37N 119 47W
Blackwood, C., *Papua N. G.* **69** 7 49S 144 31 E
Bladel, *Neths.* **17** 51 22N 5 13 E
Blaenau Ffestiniog, *U.K.* **12** 53 0N 3 57W
Blagodarnoye, *U.S.S.R.* **39** 45 7N 43 37 E
Blagoevgrad, *Bulgaria* **35** 42 2N 23 5 E
Blagoveshchensk, *U.S.S.R.* **41** 50 20N 127 30 E
Blain, *France* **18** 47 29N 1 45W
Blaine, *U.S.A.* **110** 48 59N 122 43W
Blaine Lake, *Canada* **111** 52 51N 106 52W
Blainville, *Canada* **107** 45 40N 73 52W
Blainville-sur-l'Eau, *France* **19** 48 33N 6 23 E
Blair, *U.S.A.* **120** 41 38N 96 10W
Blair Athol, *Australia* **72** 22 42S 147 31 E
Blair Atholl, *U.K.* **14** 56 46N 3 50W
Blairgowrie, *U.K.* **14** 56 36N 3 20W
Blairmore, *Canada* **110** 49 40N 114 25W
Blairsden, *U.S.A.* **124** 39 47N 120 37W
Blairsville, *U.S.A.* **116** 40 27N 79 15W
Blaj, *Romania* **34** 46 10N 23 57 E
Blake Pt., *U.S.A.* **120** 48 12N 88 27W
Blakely, *U.S.A.* **115** 31 22N 85 0W
Blakesburg, *U.S.A.* **118** 40 58N 92 38W
Blâmont, *France* **19** 48 35N 6 50 E
Blanc, C., *Tunisia* **86** 37 15N 9 56 E
Blanc, Le, *France* **20** 46 37N 1 3 E
Blanc, Mont, *Alps* **21** 45 48N 6 50 E
Blanca, B., *Argentina* **142** 39 10S 61 30W
Blanca Peak, *U.S.A.* **123** 37 35N 105 29W
Blanchard, *U.S.A.* **121** 35 8N 97 40W
Blanchardville, *U.S.A.* **118** 42 48N 89 52W
Blanche, C., *Australia* **73** 33 1S 134 9 E
Blanche Channel, *Solomon Is.* **68** 8 30S 157 30 E
Blanche L., *S. Austral., Australia* **73** 29 15S 139 40 E
Blanche L., *W. Austral., Australia* **78** 22 25S 123 17 E
Blanchester, *U.S.A.* **119** 39 17N 83 59W
Blanco, *S. Africa* **96** 33 55S 22 23 E
Blanco, *U.S.A.* **121** 30 7N 98 30W
Blanco →, *Argentina* **140** 30 20S 68 42W
Blanco, C., *Costa Rica* **128** 9 34N 85 8W
Blanco, C., *Spain* **25** 39 21N 2 51 E
Blanco, C., *U.S.A.* **122** 42 50N 124 40W
Blanda →, *Iceland* **8** 65 20N 19 40W
Blandford Forum, *U.K.* **13** 50 52N 2 10W
Blanding, *U.S.A.* **123** 37 35N 109 30W
Blandinsville, *U.S.A.* **118** 40 33N 90 52W
Blanes, *Spain* **24** 41 40N 2 48 E
Blangy-sur-Bresle, *France* **19** 49 55N 1 37 E
Blanice →, *Czech.* **32** 49 10N 14 5 E
Blankenberge, *Belgium* **17** 51 20N 3 9 E
Blankenburg, *E. Germany* **30** 51 46N 10 56 E
Blanquefort, *France* **20** 44 55N 0 38W
Blanquilla, La, *Venezuela* **135** 11 51N 64 37W
Blanquillo, *Uruguay* **141** 32 53S 55 37W
Blansko, *Czech.* **32** 49 22N 16 40 E
Blantyre, *Malawi* **93** 15 45S 35 0 E
Blaricum, *Neths.* **16** 52 16N 5 14 E
Blarney, *Ireland* **15** 51 57N 8 35W
Blato, *Yugoslavia* **27** 42 56N 16 48 E
Blaubeuren, *W. Germany* **31** 48 24N 9 47 E
Blåvands Huk, *Denmark* **9** 55 33N 8 4 E
Blaydon, *U.K.* **12** 54 56N 1 47W
Blaye, *France* **20** 45 8N 0 40W
Blaye-les-Mines, *France* **20** 44 1N 2 8 E
Blayney, *Australia* **76** 33 32S 149 14 E
Blaze, Pt., *Australia* **78** 12 56S 130 11 E
Bleckede, *W. Germany* **30** 53 18N 10 43 E
Bled, *Yugoslavia* **27** 46 27N 14 7 E
Blednaya, Gora, *U.S.S.R.* **40** 76 20N 65 0 E
Bléharis, *Belgium* **17** 50 31N 3 25 E
Blejeşti, *Romania* **34** 44 19N 25 27 E
Blekinge län □, *Sweden* **11** 56 20N 15 20 E
Blenheim, *Canada* **108** 42 20N 82 0W
Blenheim, *N.Z.* **81** 41 38S 173 57 E
Bléone →, *France* **21** 44 5N 6 0 E
Blerick, *Neths.* **17** 51 22N 6 9 E
Bletchley, *U.K.* **13** 51 59N 0 44W
Bleu, L., *Canada* **106** 46 35N 78 24W
Bleymard, Le, *France* **20** 44 30N 3 42 E
Blida, *Algeria* **85** 36 30N 2 49 E
Blidet Amor, *Algeria* **85** 32 59N 5 58 E
Blidö, *Sweden* **10** 59 37N 18 53 E
Blidsberg, *Sweden* **11** 57 56N 13 30 E
Bligh Sound, *N.Z.* **81** 44 47S 167 32 E
Bligh Water, *Fiji* **68** 17 0S 178 0 E
Blind River, *Canada* **108** 46 10N 82 58W
Blissfield, *U.S.A.* **119** 41 50N 83 52W
Blitar, *Indonesia* **57** 8 5S 112 11 E
Blitta, *Togo* **91** 8 23N 1 6 E
Block I., *U.S.A.* **117** 41 11N 71 35W
Block Island Sd., *U.S.A.* **117** 41 17N 71 35W
Blockton, *U.S.A.* **118** 40 37N 94 29W
Blodgett Iceberg Tongue, *Antarctica* **143** 66 8S 130 35 E
Bloemendaäl, *Neths.* **16** 52 24N 4 39 E
Bloemfontein, *S. Africa* **96** 29 6S 26 7 E
Bloemhof, *S. Africa* **96** 27 38S 25 32 E
Blois, *France* **18** 47 35N 1 20 E
Blokziji, *Neths.* **16** 52 43N 5 58 E
Blomskog, *Sweden* **10** 59 16N 12 2 E
Blönduós, *Iceland* **8** 65 40N 20 12W
Bloodvein →, *Canada* **111** 51 47N 96 43W
Bloody Foreland, *Ireland* **15** 55 10N 8 18W
Bloomer, *U.S.A.* **120** 45 8N 91 30W
Bloomfield, *Australia* **72** 15 56S 145 22 E
Bloomfield, *Canada* **109** 43 59N 77 14W
Bloomfield, *Ind., U.S.A.* **119** 39 1N 86 57W
Bloomfield, *Iowa, U.S.A.* **118** 40 44N 92 26W
Bloomfield, *Ky., U.S.A.* **119** 37 55N 85 19W
Bloomfield, *N. Mex., U.S.A.* **123** 36 46N 107 59W
Bloomfield, *Nebr., U.S.A.* **120** 42 38N 97 40W
Bloomingburg, *U.S.A.* **119** 39 36N 83 24W
Bloomington, *Ill., U.S.A.* **118** 40 27N 89 0W
Bloomington, *Ind., U.S.A.* **119** 39 10N 86 30W
Bloomington, *Wis., U.S.A.* **118** 42 53N 90 55W
Bloomsburg, *U.S.A.* **117** 41 0N 76 30W
Blora, *Indonesia* **57** 6 57S 111 25 E
Blossburg, *U.S.A.* **116** 41 40N 77 4W
Blouberg, *S. Africa* **97** 23 8S 28 59 E
Blountstown, *U.S.A.* **115** 30 28N 85 5W
Blowering Dam, *Australia* **76** 35 26S 148 16 E
Bludenz, *Austria* **31** 47 10N 9 50 E
Blue →, *U.S.A.* **119** 38 11N 86 18W
Blue Island, *U.S.A.* **114** 41 40N 87 40W
Blue Lake, *U.S.A.* **122** 40 53N 124 0W
Blue Mesa Res., *U.S.A.* **123** 38 30N 107 15W
Blue Mound, *U.S.A.* **118** 39 42N 89 7W
Blue Mts., *Australia* **76** 33 40S 150 0 E
Blue Mts., *Oreg., U.S.A.* **122** 45 15N 119 0W
Blue Mts., *Pa., U.S.A.* **117** 40 30N 76 30W
Blue Mud B., *Australia* **72** 13 30S 136 0 E
Blue Nile = An Nîl el Azraq □, *Sudan* **89** 12 30N 34 30 E
Blue Nile = Nîl el Azraq →, *Sudan* **89** 15 38N 32 31 E
Blue Rapids, *U.S.A.* **120** 39 41N 96 39W
Blue Ridge Mts., *U.S.A.* **115** 36 30N 80 15W
Blue Springs, *U.S.A.* **118** 39 1N 94 17W
Blue Stack Mts., *Ireland* **15** 54 46N 8 5W
Blueberry →, *Canada* **110** 56 45N 120 49W
Bluefield, *U.S.A.* **114** 37 18N 81 14W
Bluefields, *Nic.* **128** 12 20N 83 50W
Blueskin B., *N.Z.* **81** 45 44S 170 38 E
Bluff, *Australia* **72** 23 35S 149 4 E
Bluff, *N.Z.* **81** 46 37S 168 20 E
Bluff, *U.S.A.* **123** 37 17N 109 33W
Bluff Harbour, *N.Z.* **81** 46 36S 168 21 E
Bluff Knoll, *Australia* **79** 34 24S 118 15 E
Bluff Pt., *Australia* **79** 27 50S 114 5 E
Bluffs, *U.S.A.* **118** 39 45N 90 32W
Bluffton, *Ind., U.S.A.* **119** 40 43N 85 9W
Bluffton, *Ohio, U.S.A.* **119** 40 54N 83 54W
Bluford, *U.S.A.* **119** 38 20N 88 45W
Blumenau, *Brazil* **141** 27 0S 49 0W
Blumenthal, *W. Germany* **30** 53 5N 8 20 E
Blunt, *U.S.A.* **120** 44 32N 100 0W
Bly, *U.S.A.* **122** 42 23N 121 0W
Blyberg, *Sweden* **10** 61 9N 14 11 E
Blyth, *Canada* **108** 43 44N 81 26W
Blyth, *U.K.* **12** 55 8N 1 32W
Blythe, *U.S.A.* **125** 33 40N 114 33W
Bø, *Norway* **10** 59 25N 9 3 E
Bo, *S. Leone* **90** 7 55N 11 50W
Bo Duc, *Vietnam* **55** 11 58N 106 50 E
Bo Hai, *China* **61** 39 0N 120 0 E
Bō-no-Misaki, *Japan* **64** 31 15N 130 13 E
Bo Xian, *China* **60** 33 50N 115 45 E
Boa Esperança, *Brazil* **135** 3 21N 61 23W
Boa Nova, *Brazil* **139** 14 22S 40 10W
Boa Viagem, *Brazil* **138** 5 7S 39 44W
Boa Vista, *Brazil* **135** 2 48N 60 30W
Boaco, *Nic.* **128** 12 29N 85 35W
Bo'ai, *China* **60** 35 10N 113 3 E
Boal, *Spain* **22** 43 25N 6 49W
Boali, *C.A.R.* **94** 4 48N 18 7 E
Boardman, *U.S.A.* **116** 41 2N 80 40W
Boatman, *Australia* **73** 27 16S 146 55 E
Bobadah, *Australia* **73** 32 19S 146 41 E
Bobai, *China* **58** 22 17N 109 59 E
Bobbili, *India* **50** 18 35N 83 30 E
Bòbbio, *Italy* **26** 44 47N 9 22 E
Bobcaygeon, *Canada* **109** 44 33N 78 33W
Böblingen, *W. Germany* **31** 48 41N 9 1 E
Bobo-Dioulasso, *Burkina Faso* **90** 11 8N 4 13W
Boboc, *Romania* **34** 45 13N 26 59 E
Bobonaza →, *Ecuador* **134** 2 36S 76 38W
Bobov Dol, *Bulgaria* **34** 42 20N 23 0 E
Bóbr →, *Poland* **32** 52 4N 15 4 E
Bobraomby, Tanjon' i, *Madag.* **97** 12 40S 49 10 E
Bobrinets, *U.S.S.R.* **38** 48 4N 32 5 E
Bobrov, *U.S.S.R.* **37** 51 5N 40 2 E
Bobruysk, *U.S.S.R.* **36** 53 10N 29 15 E
Bobures, *Venezuela* **134** 9 15N 71 11W
Boca de Drago, *Venezuela* **135** 11 0N 61 50W
Boca de Uracoa, *Venezuela* **134** 9 8N 62 20W
Bôca do Acre, *Brazil* **136** 8 50S 67 27W
Bôca do Jari, *Brazil* **135** 1 7S 51 58W
Bôca do Moaco, *Brazil* **136** 7 41S 68 17W
Boca Grande, *Venezuela* **135** 8 40N 60 40W
Boca Raton, *U.S.A.* **115** 26 21N 80 5W
Bocaiúva, *Brazil* **139** 17 7S 43 49W
Bocanda, *Ivory C.* **90** 7 5N 4 31W
Bocaranga, *C.A.R.* **94** 7 0N 15 35 E
Bocas del Toro, *Panama* **128** 9 15N 82 20W
Boceguillas, *Spain* **24** 41 20N 3 39W
Bochart, *Canada* **107** 49 10N 73 30W
Bochnia, *Poland* **32** 49 58N 20 27 E
Bocholt, *Belgium* **17** 51 10N 5 35 E
Bocholt, *W. Germany* **30** 51 50N 6 35 E
Bochum, *W. Germany* **30** 51 28N 7 12 E
Bockenem, *W. Germany* **30** 52 1N 10 8 E
Bocognano, *France* **21** 42 5N 9 4 E
Boconó, *Venezuela* **134** 9 15N 70 16W
Boconó →, *Venezuela* **134** 8 43N 69 34W
Bocoyna, *Mexico* **126** 27 52N 107 35W
Bocq →, *Belgium* **17** 50 20N 4 55 E
Boda, *C.A.R.* **94** 4 19N 17 26 E
Böda, *Sweden* **11** 57 15N 17 3 E
Bodafors, *Sweden* **11** 57 48N 14 23 E
Bodalla, *Australia* **76** 36 4S 150 4 E
Bodaybo, *U.S.S.R.* **41** 57 50N 114 0 E
Boddington, *Australia* **79** 32 50S 116 30 E
Bodega Bay, *U.S.A.* **124** 38 20N 123 3W
Bodegraven, *Neths.* **16** 52 5N 4 46 E
Boden, *Sweden* **8** 65 50N 21 42 E
Bodensee, *W. Germany* **31** 47 35N 9 25 E
Bodenteich, *W. Germany* **30** 52 49N 10 41 E
Bodhan, *India* **50** 18 40N 77 44 E
Bodinayakkanur, *India* **51** 10 2N 77 10 E
Bodinga, *Nigeria* **91** 12 58N 5 10 E
Bodmin, *U.K.* **13** 50 28N 4 44W
Bodmin Moor, *U.K.* **13** 50 33N 4 36W
Bodoquena, Serra da, *Brazil* **137** 21 0S 56 50W
Bodoupa, *C.A.R.* **94** 5 43N 17 36 E
Bodrog →, *Hungary* **33** 48 15N 21 35 E
Bodrum, *Turkey* **46** 37 5N 27 30 E
Boechout, *Belgium* **17** 51 10N 4 30 E
Boegoebergdam, *S. Africa* **96** 29 7S 22 9 E
Boekelo, *Neths.* **16** 52 12N 6 49 E
Boelenslaan, *Neths.* **16** 53 10N 6 10 E
Boembé, *Congo* **94** 2 54S 15 39 E
Boën, *France* **21** 45 44N 4 0 E
Boende, *Zaïre* **94** 0 24S 21 12 E
Boerne, *U.S.A.* **121** 29 48N 98 41W
Boertange, *Neths.* **16** 53 1N 7 12 E
Boezinge, *Belgium* **17** 50 54N 2 52 E
Boffa, *Guinea* **90** 10 16N 14 3W
Bogale, *Burma* **52** 16 17N 95 24 E
Bogalong Creek, *Australia* **76** 33 50S 148 6 E
Bogalusa, *U.S.A.* **121** 30 50N 89 55W
Bogan →, *Australia* **76** 29 59S 146 17 E
Bogan Gate, *Australia* **76** 33 7S 147 49 E
Bogangolo, *C.A.R.* **94** 5 34N 18 15 E
Bogantungan, *Australia* **72** 23 41S 147 17 E
Bogata, *U.S.A.* **121** 33 26N 95 10W
Bogatić, *Yugoslavia* **33** 44 51N 19 30 E
Bogense, *Denmark* **11** 55 34N 10 5 E
Boggabilla, *Australia* **77** 28 36S 150 24 E
Boggabri, *Australia* **77** 30 45S 150 0 E
Boggeragh Mts., *Ireland* **15** 52 2N 8 55W
Boggy Cowal →, *Australia* **76** 32 10S 148 0 E
Bogia, *Papua N. G.* **69** 4 9S 145 0 E
Bognor Regis, *U.K.* **13** 50 47N 0 40W
Bogø, *Denmark* **11** 54 55N 12 2 E
Bogo, *Phil.* **57** 11 3N 124 0 E
Bogodukhov, *U.S.S.R.* **36** 50 9N 35 33 E
Bogong, Mt., *Australia* **75** 36 47S 147 17 E
Bogor, *Indonesia* **57** 6 36S 106 48 E
Bogoroditsk, *U.S.S.R.* **37** 53 47N 38 8 E
Bogorodsk, *U.S.S.R.* **37** 56 4N 43 30 E

Bogorodskoye, U.S.S.R. 41 52 22N 140 30 E
Bogoso, Ghana 90 5 38N 2 3W
Bogotá, Colombia 134 4 34N 74 0W
Bogotol, U.S.S.R. 40 56 15N 89 50 E
Bogra, Bangla. 52 24 51N 89 22 E
Boguchany, U.S.S.R. 41 58 40N 97 30 E
Boguchar, U.S.S.R. 39 49 55N 40 32 E
Bogué, Mauritania 90 16 45N 14 10W
Boguslav, U.S.S.R. 38 49 47N 30 53 E
Bohain-en-Vermandois, France 19 49 59N 3 28 E
Bohemia Downs, Australia 78 18 53 S 126 14 E
Bohemian Forest = Böhmerwald, W. Germany 31 49 30N 12 40 E
Bohena Cr. →, Australia 77 30 17 S 149 42 E
Bohinjska Bistrica, Yugoslavia 27 46 17N 14 1 E
Böhmerwald, W. Germany 31 49 30N 12 40 E
Bohmte, W. Germany 30 52 24N 8 20 E
Bohol, Phil. 57 9 50N 124 10 E
Bohol, Somali Rep. 98 5 45N 46 9 E
Bohol Sea, Phil. 57 9 0N 124 0 E
Bohotleh, Somali Rep. 98 8 20N 46 25 E
Boi, Nigeria 91 9 35N 9 27 E
Boi, Pta. de, Brazil 141 23 55 S 45 15W
Boiaçu, Brazil 135 0 27 S 61 46W
Boiano, Italy 29 41 28N 14 29 E
Boileau, C., Australia 78 17 40 S 122 7 E
Boinka, Australia 74 35 11 S 141 36 E
Boipeba, I. de, Brazil 139 13 39 S 38 55W
Bois →, Brazil 139 18 35 S 50 2W
Boischot, Belgium 17 51 3N 4 47 E
Boise, U.S.A. 122 43 43N 116 9W
Boise City, U.S.A. 121 36 45N 102 30W
Boissevain, Canada 111 49 15N 100 5W
Boite →, Italy 27 46 5N 12 5 E
Boitzenburg, E. Germany 30 53 16N 13 36 E
Boizenburg, E. Germany 30 53 22N 10 42 E
Bojador C., W. Sahara 84 26 0N 14 30W
Bojnūrd, Iran 47 37 30N 57 20 E
Bojonegoro, Indonesia 57 7 11 S 111 54 E
Boju, Nigeria 91 7 22N 7 55 E
Boka Kotorska, Yugoslavia 33 42 23N 18 32 E
Bokada, Zaïre 94 4 8N 19 23 E
Bokala, Ivory C. 90 8 31N 4 33W
Bokatola, Zaïre 94 0 38 S 18 46 E
Boké, Guinea 90 10 56N 14 17W
Bokhara →, Australia 73 29 55 S 146 42 E
Bokkos, Nigeria 91 9 17N 9 1 E
Boknafjorden, Norway 9 59 14N 5 40 E
Bokoro, Chad 87 12 25N 17 14 E
Bokote, Zaïre 94 0 12 S 21 8 E
Boksitogorsk, U.S.S.R. 36 59 32N 33 56 E
Bokungu, Zaïre 94 0 35 S 22 50 E
Bol, Chad 87 13 30N 15 0 E
Bol, Yugoslavia 27 43 18N 16 38 E
Bolac, L., Australia 74 37 43 S 142 57 E
Bolama, Guinea-Biss. 90 11 30N 15 30W
Bolan Pass, Pakistan 47 29 50N 67 20 E
Bolangum, Australia 74 36 42 S 142 54 E
Bolaños →, Mexico 126 21 14N 104 8W
Bolbec, France 18 49 30N 0 30 E
Boldeşti, Romania 34 45 3N 26 2 E
Bole, China 62 45 11N 81 37 E
Bole, Ethiopia 89 6 36N 37 20 E
Bolekhov, U.S.S.R. 36 49 0N 24 0 E
Bolesławiec, Poland 32 51 17N 15 37 E
Bolgatanga, Ghana 91 10 44N 0 53W
Bolgrad, U.S.S.R. 38 45 40N 28 32 E
Boli, Sudan 89 6 2N 28 48 E
Bolinao C., Phil. 57 16 23N 119 55 E
Bolívar, Argentina 140 36 15 S 60 53W
Bolívar, Antioquía, Colombia 134 5 50N 76 1W
Bolívar, Cauca, Colombia 134 2 0N 77 0W
Bolívar, Peru 136 7 18 S 77 48W
Bolivar, Mo., U.S.A. 121 37 38N 93 22W
Bolivar, Tenn., U.S.A. 121 35 14N 89 0W
Bolívar □, Colombia 134 9 0N 74 40W
Bolívar □, Ecuador 134 1 15 S 79 5W
Bolívar □, Venezuela 135 6 20N 63 30W
Bolivia, Australia 77 29 17 S 151 59 E
Bolivia ■, S. Amer. 137 17 6 S 64 0W
Bolivian Plateau, S. Amer. 132 20 0 S 67 30W
Bolkhov, U.S.S.R. 37 53 25N 36 0 E
Bollène, France 21 44 18N 4 45 E
Bollnäs, Sweden 10 61 21N 16 24 E
Bollon, Australia 73 28 2 S 147 29 E
Bollstabruk, Sweden 10 63 1N 17 40 E
Bollullos, Spain 23 37 19N 6 32W
Bolmen, Sweden 11 56 55N 13 40 E
Bolobo, Zaïre 94 2 6 S 16 20 E
Bologna, Italy 27 44 30N 11 20 E
Bologne, France 19 48 10N 5 8 E
Bologoye, U.S.S.R. 36 57 55N 34 0 E
Bolomba, Zaïre 94 0 35N 19 0 E
Bolonchenticul, Mexico 127 20 0N 89 49W
Bolong, Phil. 57 7 6N 122 14 E
Boloven, Cao Nguyen, Laos 54 15 10N 106 30 E
Bolpur, India 49 23 40N 87 45 E
Bolsena, Italy 27 42 40N 11 58 E
Bolsena, L. di, Italy 27 42 35N 11 55 E
Bolshaya Glushitsa, U.S.S.R. 37 52 28N 50 30 E
Bolshaya Martynovka, U.S.S.R. 39 47 12N 41 46 E
Bolshaya Vradiyevka, U.S.S.R. 38 47 50N 30 40 E
Bolshereche, U.S.S.R. 40 56 4N 74 45 E
Bolshevik, Ostrov, U.S.S.R. 41 78 30N 102 0 E
Bolshoi Kavkas, U.S.S.R. 39 42 50N 44 0 E
Bolshoy Anyuy →, U.S.S.R. 41 68 30N 160 49 E
Bolshoy Atlym, U.S.S.R. 40 62 25N 66 50 E
Bolshoy Begichev, Ostrov, U.S.S.R. 41 74 20N 112 30 E
Bolshoy Lyakhovskiy, Ostrov, U.S.S.R. 41 73 35N 142 0 E
Bolshoy Tokmak, U.S.S.R. 38 47 16N 35 42 E
Bol'shoy Tyuters, Ostrov, U.S.S.R. 36 59 51N 27 13 E
Bolsward, Neths. 16 53 3N 5 32 E
Boltaña, Spain 24 42 28N 0 4 E
Boltigen, Switz. 31 46 38N 7 24 E
Bolton, Australia 74 34 58 S 142 54 E
Bolton, Canada 108 43 54N 79 45W
Bolton, U.K. 12 53 35N 2 26W
Bolu, Turkey 46 40 45N 31 35 E
Bolubolu, Papua N. G. 69 9 21 S 150 20 E
Boluo, China 59 23 3N 114 21 E
Bolvadin, Turkey 46 38 45N 31 4 E
Bolzano, Italy 27 46 30N 11 20 E
Bom Comércio, Brazil 137 9 45 S 65 54W
Bom Conselho, Brazil 138 9 10 S 36 41W
Bom Despacho, Brazil 139 19 43 S 45 15W
Bom Jesus, Brazil 138 9 4 S 44 22W
Bom Jesus da Gurguéia, Serra, Brazil 138 9 0 S 43 0W
Bom Jesus da Lapa, Brazil 139 13 15 S 43 25W
Boma, Zaïre 95 5 50 S 13 4 E
Bomaderry, Australia 76 34 52 S 150 37 E
Bomandjokou, Congo 94 0 34N 14 23 E
Bomassa, Congo 94 2 12N 16 12 E
Bomba, La, Mexico 126 31 53N 115 2W
Bombala, Australia 75 36 56 S 149 15 E
Bombarral, Portugal 23 39 15N 9 9W
Bombay, India 50 18 55N 72 50 E
Bomboma, Zaïre 94 2 25N 18 55 E
Bombombwa, Zaïre 92 1 40N 25 40 E
Bomera, Australia 77 31 33 S 149 49 E
Bomi Hills, Liberia 90 7 1N 10 38W
Bomili, Zaïre 92 1 45N 27 5 E
Bommel, Neths. 16 51 43N 4 26 E
Bomokandi →, Zaïre 92 3 39N 26 8 E
Bomongo, Zaïre 94 1 27N 18 21 E
Bomu →, C.A.R. 94 4 40N 22 30 E
Bon, C., Tunisia 86 37 1N 11 2 E
Bon Echo Prov. Park, Canada 109 45 0N 77 20W
Bon Sar Pa, Vietnam 54 12 24N 107 35 E
Bonaire, Neth. Ant. 129 12 10N 68 15W
Bonalbo, Australia 77 28 44 S 152 37 E
Bonang, Australia 75 37 11 S 148 41 E
Bonanza, Nic. 128 13 54N 84 35W
Bonaparte Archipelago, Australia 78 14 0 S 124 30 E
Boñar, Spain 22 42 52N 5 19W
Bonaventure, Canada 105 48 5N 65 32W
Bonavista, Canada 105 48 40N 53 5W
Bonavista, C., Canada 105 48 42N 53 5W
Bondeno, Italy 27 44 53N 11 22 E
Bondo, Zaïre 92 3 55N 23 53 E
Bondoukou, Ivory C. 90 8 2N 2 47W
Bondowoso, Indonesia 57 7 55 S 113 49 E
Bone, Teluk, Indonesia 57 4 10 S 120 50 E
Bone Rate, Indonesia 57 7 25 S 121 5 E
Bone Rate, Kepulauan, Indonesia 57 6 30 S 121 10 E
Bonefro, Italy 29 41 42N 14 55 E
Bonegilla, Australia 75 36 8 S 146 58 E
Bo'ness, U.K. 14 56 0N 3 38W
Bonfield, Canada 108 46 14N 79 9W
Bong Son = Hoai Nhon, Vietnam 54 14 28N 109 1 E
Bongandanga, Zaïre 94 1 24N 21 3 E
Bongo, Zaïre 94 1 47 S 17 41 E
Bongor, Chad 87 10 35N 15 20 E
Bongouanou, Ivory C. 90 6 42N 4 15W
Bonham, U.S.A. 121 33 30N 96 10W
Bonheiden, Belgium 17 51 1N 4 32 E
Bonifacio, France 21 41 24N 9 10 E
Bonifacio, Bouches de, Medit. S. 28 41 12N 9 15 E
Bonin Is., Pac. Oc. 66 27 0N 142 0 E
Bonke, Ethiopia 89 6 5N 37 16 E
Bonn, W. Germany 30 50 43N 7 6 E
Bonnat, France 20 46 20N 1 54 E
Bonne Terre, U.S.A. 118 37 57N 90 33W
Bonnechere →, Canada 109 45 35N 77 50W
Bonners Ferry, U.S.A. 122 48 38N 116 21W
Bonnétable, France 18 48 11N 0 25 E
Bonneuil-Matours, France 18 46 41N 0 34 E
Bonneval, France 18 48 11N 1 24 E
Bonneville, France 21 46 4N 6 24 E
Bonney, L., Australia 73 37 50 S 140 20 E
Bonnie Doon, Australia 74 37 2 S 145 53 E
Bonnie Downs, Australia 72 22 7 S 143 50 E
Bonnie Rock, Australia 79 30 29 S 118 22 E
Bonny, Nigeria 91 4 25N 7 13 E
Bonny →, Nigeria 91 4 20N 7 10 E
Bonny, Bight of, Africa 91 3 30N 9 20 E
Bonny-sur-Loire, France 19 47 33N 2 50 E
Bonnyville, Canada 111 54 20N 110 45W
Bonoi, Indonesia 57 1 45 S 137 41 E
Bonorva, Italy 28 40 25N 8 47 E
Bonsall, U.S.A. 125 33 16N 117 14W
Bonshaw, Australia 77 29 2 S 151 16 E
Bontang, Indonesia 56 0 10N 117 30 E
Bonthain, Indonesia 57 5 34 S 119 56 E
Bonthe, S. Leone 90 7 30N 12 33W
Bontoc, Phil. 57 17 7N 120 58 E
Bonyeri, Ghana 90 5 1N 2 46W
Bonython Ra., Australia 78 23 40 S 128 45 E
Boogardie, Australia 79 28 2 S 117 45 E
Bookabie, Australia 79 31 50 S 132 41 E
Booker, U.S.A. 121 36 29N 100 30W
Bookham, Australia 76 34 48 S 148 36 E
Boolaboolka, L., Australia 73 32 38 S 143 10 E
Boolarra, Australia 75 38 20 S 146 20 E
Booligal, Australia 74 33 58 S 144 53 E
Boom, Belgium 17 51 6N 4 20 E
Boomi, Australia 77 28 44 S 149 34 E
Boonah, Australia 77 27 58 S 152 41 E
Boone, Iowa, U.S.A. 118 42 5N 93 53W
Boone, N.C., U.S.A. 115 36 14N 81 43W
Booneville, Ark., U.S.A. 121 35 10N 93 54W
Booneville, Miss., U.S.A. 115 34 39N 88 34W
Boonville, Calif., U.S.A. 124 39 1N 123 22W
Boonville, Ind., U.S.A. 119 38 3N 87 13W
Boonville, Mo., U.S.A. 118 38 57N 92 45W
Boonville, N.Y., U.S.A. 117 43 31N 75 20W
Booral, Australia 76 32 30 S 151 56 E
Boorindal, Australia 73 30 22 S 146 11 E
Boorowa, Australia 76 34 28 S 148 44 E
Boort, Australia 74 36 7 S 143 46 E
Boothia, Gulf of, Canada 103 71 0N 90 0W
Boothia Pen., Canada 102 71 0N 94 0W
Bootle, Cumbria, U.K. 12 54 17N 3 24W
Bootle, Merseyside, U.K. 12 53 28N 3 1W
Booué, Gabon 94 0 5 S 11 55 E
Bophuthatswana □, S. Africa 96 25 49 S 25 30 E
Boppard, W. Germany 31 50 13N 7 36 E
Boquerón □, Paraguay 137 21 30 S 60 0W
Boquete, Panama 128 8 46N 82 27W
Boquilla, Presa de la, Mexico 126 27 40N 105 30W
Boquillas del Carmen, Mexico 126 29 17N 102 53W
Bor, Czech. 32 49 41N 12 45 E
Bôr, Sudan 89 6 10N 31 40 E
Bor, Sweden 11 57 9N 14 10 E
Bor, Yugoslavia 33 44 8N 22 7 E
Borah, Pk., U.S.A. 122 44 19N 113 46W
Borama, Somali Rep. 98 9 55N 43 7 E
Borambil, Australia 77 32 4 S 150 1 E
Borang, Sudan 89 4 50N 30 59 E
Borangapara, India 52 25 14N 90 14 E
Borås, Sweden 11 57 43N 12 56 E
Borāzjān, Iran 47 29 22N 51 10 E
Borba, Brazil 135 4 12 S 59 34W
Borba, Portugal 23 38 50N 7 26W
Borborema, Planalto da, Brazil 138 7 0 S 37 0W
Borçka, Turkey 39 41 25N 41 41 E
Borculo, Neths. 16 52 7N 6 31 E
Borda, C., Australia 73 35 45 S 136 34 E
Bordeaux, France 20 44 50N 0 36W
Borden, Australia 79 34 3 S 118 12 E
Borden, Canada 105 46 18N 63 47W
Borden I., Canada 144 78 30N 111 30W
Borders □, U.K. 14 55 35N 2 50W
Bordertown, Australia 73 36 19 S 140 45 E
Borðeyri, Iceland 8 65 12N 21 6W
Bordighera, Italy 26 43 47N 7 40 E
Bordj bou Arreridj, Algeria 85 36 4N 4 45 E
Bordj Bourguiba, Tunisia 86 32 12N 10 2 E
Bordj el Hobra, Algeria 85 32 9N 4 51 E
Bordj Fly Ste. Marie, Algeria 84 27 19N 2 32W
Bordj-in-Eker, Algeria 85 24 9N 5 3 E
Bordj Menaiel, Algeria 85 36 46N 3 43 E
Bordj Messouda, Algeria 85 30 12N 9 25 E
Bordj Nili, Algeria 85 33 28N 3 2 E
Bordj Omar Driss, Algeria 85 28 10N 6 40 E
Bordj-Tarat, Algeria 85 25 55N 9 3 E
Bordj Zelfana, Algeria 85 32 27N 4 15 E
Boremore, Australia 76 33 15 S 149 0 E
Borensberg, Sweden 11 58 34N 15 17 E
Borgarnes, Iceland 8 64 32N 21 55W
Børgefjellet, Norway 8 65 20N 13 45 E
Borger, Neths. 16 52 54N 6 44 E
Borger, U.S.A. 121 35 40N 101 20W
Borgerhout, Belgium 17 51 12N 4 28 E
Borghamn, Sweden 11 58 23N 14 41 E
Borgholm, Sweden 11 56 52N 16 39 E
Bórgia, Italy 29 38 50N 16 30 E
Borgloon, Belgium 17 50 48N 5 21 E
Borgo San Dalmazzo, Italy 26 44 19N 7 29 E
Borgo San Lorenzo, Italy 27 43 57N 11 21 E
Borgo Valsugano, Italy 27 46 3N 11 27 E
Borgomanero, Italy 26 45 41N 8 28 E
Borgonovo Val Tidone, Italy 26 45 1N 9 28 E
Borgorose, Italy 27 42 12N 13 14 E
Borgosésia, Italy 26 45 43N 8 17 E
Borgvattnet, Sweden 10 63 26N 15 48 E
Borikhane, Laos 54 18 33N 103 43 E
Borislav, U.S.S.R. 36 49 18N 23 28 E
Borisoglebsk, U.S.S.R. 37 51 27N 42 5 E
Borisoglebskiy, U.S.S.R. 37 56 28N 43 59 E
Borisov, U.S.S.R. 36 54 17N 28 28 E
Borispol, U.S.S.R. 36 50 21N 30 59 E
Borja, Peru 134 4 20 S 77 40W
Borja, Spain 24 41 48N 1 34W
Borjas Blancas, Spain 24 41 31N 0 52 E
Borken, W. Germany 30 51 51N 6 52 E
Borkou, Chad 87 18 15N 18 50 E
Borkum, W. Germany 30 53 36N 6 42 E
Borlänge, Sweden 10 60 29N 15 26 E
Borley, C., Antarctica 143 66 15 S 52 30 E
Bormida →, Italy 26 44 23N 8 13 E
Bórmio, Italy 26 46 28N 10 22 E
Born, Neths. 17 51 2N 5 49 E
Borna, E. Germany 30 51 8N 12 31 E
Borndiep, Neths. 16 53 27N 5 35 E
Borne, Neths. 16 52 18N 6 46 E
Bornem, Belgium 17 51 6N 4 14 E
Borneo, E. Indies 56 1 0N 115 0 E
Bornholm, Denmark 11 55 10N 15 0 E
Bornholmsgattet, Europe 11 55 15N 14 20 E
Borno □, Nigeria 91 12 30N 12 30 E
Bornos, Spain 23 36 48N 5 42W
Bornu Yassa, Nigeria 91 12 14N 12 25 E
Borobudur, Indonesia 57 7 36 S 110 13 E
Borodino, U.S.S.R. 36 55 31N 35 40 E
Borogontsy, U.S.S.R. 41 62 42N 131 8 E
Boromo, Burkina Faso 90 11 45N 2 58W
Boron, U.S.A. 125 35 0N 117 39W
Boronga Is., Burma 52 19 58N 93 6 E
Borongan, Phil. 57 11 37N 125 26 E
Bororen, Australia 72 24 13 S 151 33 E
Borotangba Mts., C.A.R. 89 6 30N 25 0 E
Borovan, Bulgaria 34 43 27N 23 45 E
Borovichi, U.S.S.R. 36 58 25N 33 55 E
Borovsk, U.S.S.R. 37 55 12N 36 24 E
Borrby, Sweden 11 55 27N 14 10 E
Borrego Springs, U.S.A. 125 33 15N 116 23W
Borriol, Spain 24 40 4N 0 4W
Borroloola, Australia 72 16 4 S 136 17 E
Borşa, Romania 34 47 41N 24 50 E
Borssele, Neths. 17 51 26N 3 45 E
Bort-les-Orgues, France 20 45 24N 2 29 E
Borth, U.K. 13 52 29N 4 3W
Borujerd, Iran 46 33 55N 48 50 E
Borzhomi, U.S.S.R. 39 41 48N 43 28 E
Borzna, U.S.S.R. 36 51 18N 32 26 E
Borzya, U.S.S.R. 41 50 24N 116 31 E
Bosa, Italy 28 40 17N 8 32 E
Bosanska Dubica, Yugoslavia 27 45 10N 16 50 E
Bosanska Gradiška, Yugoslavia 33 45 10N 17 15 E
Bosanska Kostajnica, Yugoslavia 27 45 11N 16 33 E
Bosanska Krupa, Yugoslavia 27 44 53N 16 10 E
Bosanski Novi, Yugoslavia 27 45 2N 16 22 E
Bosanski Šamac, Yugoslavia 33 45 3N 18 29 E
Bosansko Grahovo, Yugoslavia 27 44 12N 16 26 E
Bosansko Petrovac, Yugoslavia 27 44 35N 16 21 E
Bosaso, Somali Rep. 98 11 12N 49 18 E
Bosavi, Mt., Papua N. G. 69 6 30 S 142 49 E
Boscastle, U.K. 13 50 42N 4 42W
Boscobel, U.S.A. 118 43 8N 90 42W
Boscotrecase, Italy 29 40 46N 14 28 E
Bose, China 58 23 53N 106 35 E
Boshan, China 61 36 28N 117 49 E
Boshoek, S. Africa 96 25 30 S 27 9 E
Boshof, S. Africa 96 28 31 S 25 13 E
Boshrūyeh, Iran 47 33 50N 57 30 E
Bosilegrad, Yugoslavia 33 42 30N 22 27 E
Boskoop, Neths. 16 52 4N 4 40 E
Bosna →, Yugoslavia 33 45 4N 18 29 E
Bosna i Hercegovina □, Yugoslavia 33 44 0N 18 0 E
Bosnia = Bosna i Hercegovina □, Yugoslavia 33 44 0N 18 0 E
Bosnik, Indonesia 57 1 5 S 136 10 E
Bōsō-Hantō, Japan 65 35 20N 140 20 E
Bosobolo, Zaïre 94 4 15N 19 50 E
Bosporus = Karadeniz Boğazı, Turkey 46 41 10N 29 10 E
Bossangoa, C.A.R. 94 6 35N 17 30 E
Bossekop, Norway 8 69 57N 23 15 E
Bossembélé, C.A.R. 94 5 25N 17 40 E

Bossembélé II, *C.A.R.* **94** 5 41N 16 38 E
Bossier City, *U.S.A.* **121** 32 28N 93 48W
Bosso, *Niger* **91** 13 43N 13 19 E
Bosten Hu, *China* **62** 41 55N 87 40 E
Boston, *U.K.* **12** 52 59N 0 2W
Boston, *U.S.A.* **117** 42 20N 71 0W
Boston Bar, *Canada* **110** 49 52N 121 30W
Bosusulu, *Zaïre* **94** 0 50N 20 45 E
Bosut →, *Yugoslavia* **33** 45 20N 19 0 E
Boswell, *Canada* **110** 49 28N 116 45W
Boswell, *Ind., U.S.A.* **119** 40 30N 87 23W
Boswell, *Okla., U.S.A.* **121** 34 1N 95 50W
Boswell, *Pa., U.S.A.* **116** 40 9N 79 2W
Bosworth, *U.S.A.* **118** 39 28N 93 20W
Botad, *India* **48** 22 15N 71 40 E
Botany Bay, *Australia* **76** 34 0 S 151 14 E
Botene, *Laos* **54** 17 35N 101 12 E
Botevgrad, *Bulgaria* **34** 42 55N 23 47 E
Botfield, *Australia* **76** 33 1 S 147 46 E
Bothaville, *S. Africa* **96** 27 23 S 26 34 E
Bothnia, G. of, *Europe* **8** 63 0N 20 0 E
Bothwell, *Australia* **72** 42 20 S 147 1 E
Bothwell, *Canada* **108** 42 38N 81 52W
Boticas, *Portugal* **22** 41 41N 7 40W
Botletle →, *Botswana* **96** 20 10 S 23 15 E
Botoşani, *Romania* **34** 47 42N 26 41 E
Botro, *Ivory C.* **90** 7 51N 5 19W
Botswana ■, *Africa* **96** 22 0 S 24 0 E
Bottineau, *U.S.A.* **120** 48 49N 100 25W
Bottrop, *W. Germany* **17** 51 34N 6 59 E
Botucatu, *Brazil* **141** 22 55 S 48 30W
Botwood, *Canada* **105** 49 6N 55 23W
Bou Alam, *Algeria* **85** 33 50N 1 26 E
Bou Ali, *Algeria* **85** 27 11N 0 4W
Bou Djébéha, *Mali* **90** 18 25N 2 45W
Bou Guema, *Algeria* **85** 28 49N 0 19 E
Bou Ismael, *Algeria* **85** 36 38N 2 42 E
Bou Izakarn, *Morocco* **84** 29 12N 9 46W
Boû Lanouâr, *Mauritania* **84** 21 12N 16 34W
Bou Saâda, *Algeria* **85** 35 11N 4 9 E
Bou Salem, *Tunisia* **86** 36 45N 9 2 E
Bouaké, *Ivory C.* **90** 7 40N 5 2W
Bouanga, *Congo* **94** 2 7 S 16 8 E
Bouar, *C.A.R.* **94** 6 0N 15 40 E
Bouârfa, *Morocco* **85** 32 32N 1 58W
Bouca, *C.A.R.* **94** 6 45N 18 25 E
Boucau, *France* **20** 43 32N 1 29W
Boucaut B., *Australia* **72** 12 0 S 134 25 E
Boucher →, *Canada* **107** 49 10N 69 6W
Bouches-du-Rhône □, *France* **21** 43 37N 5 2 E
Bouchette, *Canada* **106** 46 12N 75 57W
Bouchier, L., *Canada* **106** 50 6N 77 48W
Bouda, *Algeria* **85** 27 50N 0 27W
Boudenib, *Morocco* **84** 31 59N 3 31W
Boufarik, *Algeria* **85** 36 34N 2 58 E
Bougainville C., *Australia* **78** 13 57 S 126 4 E
Bougainville I., *Solomon Is.* **69** 6 0 S 155 0 E
Bougainville Reef, *Australia* **72** 15 30 S 147 5 E
Bougainville Str., *Solomon Is.* **68** 6 40 S 156 10 E
Bougaroun, C., *Algeria* **85** 37 6N 6 30 E
Bougie = Bejaia, *Algeria* **85** 36 42N 5 2 E
Bougouni, *Mali* **90** 11 30N 7 20W
Bouillon, *Belgium* **17** 49 44N 5 3 E
Bouïra, *Algeria* **85** 36 20N 3 59 E
Boulder, *Colo., U.S.A.* **120** 40 3N 105 10W
Boulder, *Mont., U.S.A.* **122** 46 14N 112 4W
Boulder City, *U.S.A.* **125** 35 58N 114 50W
Boulder Creek, *U.S.A.* **124** 37 7N 122 7W
Boulder Dam = Hoover Dam, *U.S.A.* **125** 36 0N 114 45W
Boulembo, *Gabon* **94** 1 26 S 12 0 E
Bouli, *Mauritania* **90** 15 17N 12 18W
Boulia, *Australia* **72** 22 52 S 139 51 E
Bouligny, *France* **19** 49 17N 5 45 E
Boulogne →, *France* **18** 47 12N 1 47W
Boulogne-sur-Gesse, *France* **20** 43 18N 0 38 E
Boulogne-sur-Mer, *France* **19** 50 42N 1 36 E
Bouloire, *France* **18** 47 59N 0 45 E
Bouloupari, *N. Cal.* **68** 21 52 S 166 4 E
Boulsa, *Burkina Faso* **91** 12 39N 0 34W
Boultoum, *Niger* **91** 14 45N 10 25 E
Boumalne, *Morocco* **84** 31 25N 6 0W
Boun Neua, *Laos* **54** 21 38N 101 54 E
Boun Tai, *Laos* **54** 21 23N 101 58 E
Bouna, *Ivory C.* **90** 9 10N 3 0W
Boundary Bend, *Australia* **74** 34 43 S 143 8 E
Boundary Pk., *U.S.A.* **124** 37 51N 118 21W
Boundiali, *Ivory C.* **90** 9 30N 6 20W
Bountiful, *U.S.A.* **122** 40 57N 111 58W
Bounty I., *Pac. Oc.* **66** 48 0 S 178 30 E
Bourail, *N. Cal.* **68** 21 34 S 165 30 E
Bourbah, *Australia* **76** 31 18 S 148 20 E
Bourbeuse →, *U.S.A.* **118** 38 24N 90 54W
Bourbon, *U.S.A.* **119** 41 18N 86 7W
Bourbon-Lancy, *France* **20** 46 37N 3 45 E
Bourbon-l'Archambault, *France* **20** 46 36N 3 4 E
Bourbonnais, *France* **20** 46 28N 3 0 E
Bourbonne-les-Bains, *France* **19** 47 54N 5 45 E
Bourem, *Mali* **91** 17 0N 0 24W
Bourg, *France* **20** 45 3N 0 34W
Bourg-Argental, *France* **21** 45 18N 4 32 E
Bourg-de-Péage, *France* **21** 45 2N 5 3 E
Bourg-en-Bresse, *France* **21** 46 13N 5 12 E
Bourg-St.-Andéol, *France* **21** 44 23N 4 39 E
Bourg-St.-Maurice, *France* **21** 45 35N 6 46 E
Bourganeuf, *France* **20** 45 57N 1 45 E
Bourges, *France* **19** 47 9N 2 25 E
Bourget, *Canada* **106** 45 26N 75 9W
Bourget, L. du, *France* **21** 45 44N 5 52 E
Bourgneuf, B. de, *France* **18** 47 3N 2 10W
Bourgneuf-en-Retz, *France* **18** 47 2N 1 58W
Bourgneuf-la-Fôret, Le, *France* **18** 48 10N 0 59W
Bourgogne, *France* **19** 47 0N 4 50 E
Bourgoin-Jallieu, *France* **21** 45 36N 5 17 E
Bourgueil, *France* **18** 47 17N 0 10 E
Bourke, *Australia* **73** 30 8 S 145 55 E
Bournemouth, *U.K.* **13** 50 43N 1 53W
Bourriot-Bergonce, *France* **20** 44 7N 0 14W
Bouscat, Le, *France* **20** 44 53N 0 37W
Bouse, *U.S.A.* **125** 33 55N 114 0W
Boussac, *France* **20** 46 22N 2 13 E
Boussens, *France* **20** 43 12N 0 58 E
Bousso, *Chad* **87** 10 34N 16 52 E
Boussu, *Belgium* **17** 50 26N 3 48 E
Boutilimit, *Mauritania* **90** 17 45N 14 40W
Bouvet I. = Bouvetøya, *Antarctica* **143** 54 26 S 3 24 E
Bouvetøya, *Antarctica* **143** 54 26 S 3 24 E
Bouznika, *Morocco* **84** 33 46N 7 6W
Bouzonville, *France* **19** 49 17N 6 32 E
Bova Marina, *Italy* **29** 37 59N 15 56 E
Bovalino Marina, *Italy* **29** 38 9N 16 10 E
Bovec, *Yugoslavia* **27** 46 20N 13 33 E
Bovenkarspel, *Neths.* **16** 52 41N 5 14 E
Bovigny, *Belgium* **17** 50 12N 5 55 E
Bovill, *U.S.A.* **122** 46 58N 116 27W
Bovino, *Italy* **29** 41 15N 15 20 E
Bow Island, *Canada* **110** 49 50N 111 23W
Bowbells, *U.S.A.* **120** 48 47N 102 19W
Bowdle, *U.S.A.* **120** 45 30N 99 40W
Bowelling, *Australia* **79** 33 25 S 116 30 E
Bowen, *Australia* **72** 20 0 S 148 16 E
Bowen, Mt., *Australia* **75** 37 9 S 148 35 E
Bowen Mts., *Australia* **75** 37 0 S 148 0 E
Bowie, *Ariz., U.S.A.* **123** 32 15N 109 30W
Bowie, *Tex., U.S.A.* **121** 33 33N 97 50W
Bowland, Forest of, *U.K.* **12** 54 0N 2 30W
Bowling Green, *Ky., U.S.A.* **114** 37 0N 86 25W
Bowling Green, *Mo., U.S.A.* **118** 39 21N 91 12W
Bowling Green, *Ohio, U.S.A.* **119** 41 22N 83 40W
Bowling Green, C., *Australia* **72** 19 19 S 147 25 E
Bowman, *U.S.A.* **120** 46 12N 103 21W
Bowman I., *Antarctica* **143** 65 0 S 104 0 E
Bowmans, *Australia* **73** 34 10 S 138 17 E
Bowmanville, *Canada* **109** 43 55N 78 41W
Bowmore, *U.K.* **14** 55 45N 6 18W
Bowning, *Australia* **76** 34 46 S 148 50 E
Bowral, *Australia* **76** 34 26 S 150 27 E
Bowraville, *Australia* **77** 30 37 S 152 52 E
Bowron →, *Canada* **110** 54 3N 121 50W
Bowser, *Australia* **75** 36 19 S 146 23 E
Bowser L., *Canada* **110** 56 30N 129 30W
Bowsman, *Canada* **111** 52 14N 101 12W
Bowutu Mts., *Papua N. G.* **69** 7 45 S 147 10 E
Bowwood, *Zambia* **93** 17 5 S 26 20 E
Boxholm, *Sweden* **11** 58 12N 15 3 E
Boxmeer, *Neths.* **17** 51 38N 5 56 E
Boxtel, *Neths.* **17** 51 36N 5 20 E
Boyabat, *Turkey* **38** 41 28N 34 42 E
Boyabo, *Zaïre* **94** 3 43N 18 46 E
Boyaca □, *Colombia* **134** 5 30N 72 30W
Boyce, *U.S.A.* **121** 31 25N 92 39W
Boyer →, *Canada* **110** 58 27N 115 57W
Boyer, C., *N. Cal.* **68** 21 37 S 168 6 E
Boyle, *Ireland* **15** 53 58N 8 19W
Boyne →, *Ireland* **15** 53 43N 6 15W
Boyne City, *U.S.A.* **104** 45 13N 85 1W
Boyni Qara, *Afghan.* **47** 36 20N 67 0 E
Boynton Beach, *U.S.A.* **115** 26 31N 80 3W
Boyoma, Chutes, *Zaïre* **92** 0 35N 25 23 E
Boyup Brook, *Australia* **79** 33 50 S 116 23 E
Bozeman, *U.S.A.* **122** 45 40N 111 0W
Bozen = Bolzano, *Italy* **27** 46 30N 11 20 E
Bozene, *Zaïre* **94** 2 56N 19 12 E
Bozouls, *France* **20** 44 28N 2 43 E
Bozoum, *C.A.R.* **94** 6 25N 16 35 E
Bozovici, *Romania* **34** 44 56N 22 1 E
Bra, *Italy* **26** 44 41N 7 50 E
Brabant □, *Belgium* **17** 50 46N 4 30 E
Brabant L., *Canada* **111** 55 58N 103 43W
Brabrand, *Denmark* **11** 56 9N 10 7 E
Brač, *Yugoslavia* **27** 43 20N 16 40 E
Bracadale, L., *U.K.* **14** 57 20N 6 30W
Bracciano, *Italy* **27** 42 6N 12 10 E
Bracciano, L. di, *Italy* **27** 42 8N 12 11 E
Bracebridge, *Canada* **108** 45 2N 79 19W
Brach, *Libya* **86** 27 31N 14 20 E
Bracieux, *France* **19** 47 30N 1 30 E
Bräcke, *Sweden* **10** 62 45N 15 26 E
Brackettville, *U.S.A.* **121** 29 21N 100 20W
Brački Kanal, *Yugoslavia* **27** 43 24N 16 40 E
Brad, *Romania* **34** 46 10N 22 50 E
Brădano →, *Italy* **29** 40 23N 16 51 E
Bradenton, *U.S.A.* **115** 27 25N 82 35W
Bradford, *Canada* **108** 44 7N 79 34W
Bradford, *U.K.* **12** 53 47N 1 45W
Bradford, *Ill., U.S.A.* **118** 41 11N 89 39W
Bradford, *Ohio, U.S.A.* **119** 40 8N 84 27W
Bradford, *Pa., U.S.A.* **116** 41 58N 78 41W
Bradford, *Vt., U.S.A.* **117** 43 59N 72 9W
Brădiceni, *Romania* **34** 45 3N 23 4 E
Bradley, *Ark., U.S.A.* **121** 33 7N 93 39W
Bradley, *Calif., U.S.A.* **124** 35 52N 120 48W
Bradley, *Ill., U.S.A.* **119** 41 9N 87 52W
Bradley, *S. Dak., U.S.A.* **120** 45 10N 97 40W
Bradley Institute, *Zimb.* **93** 17 7 S 31 25 E
Bradore Bay, *Canada* **105** 51 27N 57 18W
Bradshaw, *Australia* **78** 15 21 S 130 16 E
Brady, *U.S.A.* **121** 31 8N 99 25W
Brædstrup, *Denmark* **11** 55 58N 9 37 E
Braemar, *Australia* **73** 33 12 S 139 35 E
Braeside, *Canada* **106** 45 28N 76 24W
Braga, *Portugal* **22** 41 35N 8 25W
Braga □, *Portugal* **22** 41 30N 8 30W
Bragado, *Argentina* **140** 35 2 S 60 27W
Bragança, *Brazil* **138** 1 0 S 47 2W
Bragança, *Portugal* **22** 41 48N 6 50W
Bragança □, *Portugal* **22** 41 30N 6 45W
Bragança Paulista, *Brazil* **141** 22 55 S 46 32W
Brahmanbaria, *Bangla.* **52** 23 58N 91 15 E
Brahmani →, *India* **50** 20 39N 86 46 E
Brahmaputra →, *India* **49** 24 2N 90 59 E
Braich-y-pwll, *U.K.* **12** 52 47N 4 46W
Braidwood, *Australia* **76** 35 27 S 149 49 E
Brăila, *Romania* **34** 45 19N 27 59 E
Braine-l'Alleud, *Belgium* **17** 50 42N 4 23 E
Braine-le-Comte, *Belgium* **17** 50 37N 4 8 E
Brainerd, *U.S.A.* **120** 46 20N 94 10W
Braintree, *U.K.* **13** 51 53N 0 34 E
Braintree, *U.S.A.* **117** 42 11N 71 0W
Brak →, *S. Africa* **96** 29 35 S 22 55 E
Brake, *Niedersachsen, W. Germany* **30** 53 19N 8 30 E
Brake, *Nordrhein-Westfalen, W. Germany* **30** 51 43N 9 12 E
Brakel, *Neths.* **16** 51 49N 5 5 E
Bräkne-Hoby, *Sweden* **11** 56 14N 15 6 E
Brakwater, *Namibia* **96** 22 28 S 17 3 E
Brålanda, *Sweden* **11** 58 34N 12 21 E
Bralorne, *Canada* **110** 50 50N 122 50W
Bramberg, *W. Germany* **31** 50 6N 10 40 E
Bramminge, *Denmark* **11** 55 28N 8 42 E
Brämön, *Sweden* **10** 62 14N 17 40 E
Brampton, *Canada* **108** 43 45N 79 45W
Bramsche, *W. Germany* **30** 52 25N 7 58 E
Bramwell, *Australia* **72** 12 8 S 142 37 E
Branco →, *Brazil* **135** 1 20 S 61 50W
Branco, C., *Brazil* **138** 7 9 S 34 47W
Brande, *Denmark* **11** 55 57N 9 8 E
Brandenburg, *E. Germany* **30** 52 24N 12 33 E
Brandenburg, *U.S.A.* **119** 38 0N 86 10W
Brandfort, *S. Africa* **96** 28 40 S 26 30 E
Brandon, *Canada* **111** 49 50N 99 57W
Brandon, *U.S.A.* **117** 43 48N 73 4W
Brandon, Mt., *Ireland* **15** 52 15N 10 15W
Brandon B., *Ireland* **15** 52 17N 10 8W
Brandsen, *Argentina* **140** 35 10 S 58 15W
Brandval, *Norway* **10** 60 19N 12 1 E
Brandvlei, *S. Africa* **96** 30 25 S 20 30 E
Brandýs, *Czech.* **32** 50 10N 14 40 E
Branford, *U.S.A.* **117** 41 15N 72 48W
Braniewo, *Poland* **32** 54 25N 19 50 E
Bransfield Str., *Antarctica* **143** 63 0 S 59 0W
Branson, *Colo., U.S.A.* **121** 37 4N 103 53W
Branson, *Mo., U.S.A.* **121** 36 40N 93 18W
Brantford, *Canada* **108** 43 10N 80 15W
Brantôme, *France* **20** 45 22N 0 39 E
Branxholme, *Australia* **74** 37 52 S 141 49 E
Branxton, *Australia* **76** 32 38 S 151 21 E
Branzi, *Italy* **26** 46 0N 9 46 E
Bras d'Or, L., *Canada* **105** 45 50N 60 50W
Brasil, Planalto, *Brazil* **132** 18 0 S 46 30W
Brasiléia, *Brazil* **136** 11 0 S 68 45W
Brasília, *Brazil* **139** 15 47 S 47 55W
Brasília Legal, *Brazil* **135** 3 49 S 55 36W
Braslav, *U.S.S.R.* **36** 55 38N 27 0 E
Braslovce, *Yugoslavia* **27** 46 21N 15 3 E
Braşov, *Romania* **34** 45 38N 25 35 E
Brass, *Nigeria* **91** 4 35N 6 14 E
Brass →, *Nigeria* **91** 4 15N 6 13 E
Brassac-les-Mines, *France* **20** 45 24N 3 20 E
Brasschaat, *Belgium* **17** 51 19N 4 27 E
Brassey, Banjaran, *Malaysia* **56** 5 0N 117 15 E
Brassey Ra., *Australia* **79** 25 8 S 122 15 E
Brasstown Bald, Mt., *U.S.A.* **115** 34 54N 83 45W
Bratislava, *Czech.* **33** 48 10N 17 7 E
Bratsk, *U.S.S.R.* **41** 56 10N 101 30 E
Brattleboro, *U.S.A.* **117** 42 53N 72 37W
Braţul Chilia →, *Romania* **34** 45 25N 29 20 E
Braţul Sfîntu Gheorghe →, *Romania* **34** 45 0N 29 20 E
Braţul Sulina →, *Romania* **34** 45 10N 29 20 E
Braunau, *Austria* **33** 48 15N 13 3 E
Braunschweig, *W. Germany* **30** 52 17N 10 28 E
Braunton, *U.K.* **13** 51 6N 4 9W
Brava, *Somali Rep.* **98** 1 20N 44 8 E
Bråviken, *Sweden* **10** 58 38N 16 32 E
Bravo del Norte →, *Mexico* **126** 25 57N 97 9W
Brawley, *U.S.A.* **125** 32 58N 115 30W
Bray, *Ireland* **15** 53 12N 6 6W
Bray, Mt., *Australia* **72** 14 0 S 134 30 E
Bray, Pays de, *France* **19** 49 46N 1 26 E
Bray-sur-Seine, *France* **19** 48 25N 3 14 E
Braymer, *U.S.A.* **118** 39 35N 93 48W
Brazeau →, *Canada* **110** 52 55N 115 14W
Brazil, *U.S.A.* **119** 39 32N 87 8W
Brazil ■, *S. Amer.* **139** 12 0 S 50 0W
Brazilian Highlands = Brasil, Planalto, *Brazil* **132** 18 0 S 46 30W
Brazo Sur →, *S. Amer.* **140** 25 21 S 57 42W
Brazos →, *U.S.A.* **121** 28 53N 95 23W
Brazzaville, *Congo* **95** 4 9 S 15 12 E
Brčko, *Yugoslavia* **33** 44 54N 18 46 E
Brea, *Peru* **136** 4 40 S 81 7W
Breadalbane, *N.S.W., Australia* **76** 34 48 S 149 28 E
Breadalbane, *Queens., Australia* **72** 23 50 S 139 35 E
Breadalbane, *U.K.* **14** 56 30N 4 15W
Breaden, L., *Australia* **79** 25 51 S 125 28 E
Breaksea Sd., *N.Z.* **81** 45 35 S 166 35 E
Bream Bay, *N.Z.* **80** 35 56 S 174 28 E
Bream Head, *N.Z.* **80** 35 51 S 174 36 E
Bream Tail, *N.Z.* **80** 36 3 S 174 36 E
Breas, *Chile* **140** 25 29 S 70 24W
Brebes, *Indonesia* **57** 6 52 S 109 3 E
Brechin, *Canada* **108** 44 32N 79 10W
Brechin, *U.K.* **14** 56 44N 2 40W
Brecht, *Belgium* **17** 51 21N 4 38 E
Breckenridge, *Colo., U.S.A.* **122** 39 30N 106 2W
Breckenridge, *Minn., U.S.A.* **120** 46 20N 96 36W
Breckenridge, *Mo., U.S.A.* **118** 39 46N 93 48W
Breckenridge, *Tex., U.S.A.* **121** 32 48N 98 55W
Brecknock, Pen., *Chile* **142** 54 35 S 71 30W
Břeclav, *Czech.* **32** 48 46N 16 53 E
Brecon, *U.K.* **13** 51 57N 3 23W
Brecon Beacons, *U.K.* **13** 51 53N 3 27W
Breda, *Neths.* **17** 51 35N 4 45 E
Bredaryd, *Sweden* **11** 57 10N 13 45 E
Bredasdorp, *S. Africa* **96** 34 33 S 20 2 E
Bredbo, *Australia* **76** 35 58 S 149 10 E
Bredene, *Belgium* **17** 51 14N 2 59 E
Bredstedt, *W. Germany* **30** 54 37N 8 59 E
Bree, *Belgium* **17** 51 8N 5 35 E
Breeza, *Australia* **77** 31 15 S 150 27 E
Breezand, *Neths.* **16** 52 53N 4 49 E
Bregalnica →, *Yugoslavia* **35** 41 43N 22 9 E
Bregenz, *Austria* **31** 47 30N 9 45 E
Bréhal, *France* **18** 48 53N 1 30W
Bréhat, I. de, *France* **18** 48 51N 3 0W
Breiðafjörður, *Iceland* **8** 65 15N 23 15W
Breil-sur-Roya, *France* **21** 43 56N 7 31 E
Breisach, *W. Germany* **31** 48 2N 7 37 E
Brejinho de Nazaré, *Brazil* **138** 11 1 S 48 34W
Brejo, *Brazil* **138** 3 41 S 42 47W
Bremen, *W. Germany* **30** 53 4N 8 47 E
Bremen □, *W. Germany* **30** 53 6N 8 46 E
Bremer I., *Australia* **72** 12 5 S 136 45 E
Bremerhaven, *W. Germany* **30** 53 34N 8 35 E
Bremerton, *U.S.A.* **124** 47 30N 122 38W
Bremervörde, *W. Germany* **30** 53 28N 9 10 E
Bremsnes, *Norway* **10** 63 6N 7 40 E
Brenes, *Spain* **23** 37 32N 5 54W
Brenham, *U.S.A.* **121** 30 5N 96 27W
Brenner Pass, *Alps* **31** 47 0N 11 30 E
Breno, *Italy* **26** 45 57N 10 20 E
Brent, *Canada* **109** 46 2N 78 29W
Brent, *U.K.* **13** 51 33N 0 18W
Brenta →, *Italy* **27** 45 11N 12 18 E
Brentwood, *U.K.* **13** 51 37N 0 19 E
Brentwood, *U.S.A.* **117** 40 47N 73 15W
Bréscia, *Italy* **26** 45 33N 10 13 E
Breskens, *Neths.* **17** 51 23N 3 33 E
Breslau = Wrocław, *Poland* **32** 51 5N 17 5 E
Bresle →, *France* **18** 50 4N 1 22 E
Bresles, *France* **19** 49 25N 2 13 E
Bressanone, *Italy* **27** 46 43N 11 40 E
Bressay I., *U.K.* **14** 60 10N 1 5W
Bresse, *France* **19** 46 50N 5 10 E
Bresse, La, *France* **19** 48 0N 6 53 E
Bressuire, *France* **18** 46 51N 0 30W
Brest, *France* **18** 48 24N 4 31W
Brest, *U.S.S.R.* **36** 52 10N 23 40 E
Bretagne, *France* **18** 48 0N 3 0W
Bretçu, *Romania* **34** 46 7N 26 18 E
Breteuil, *Eure, France* **18** 48 50N 0 53 E
Breteuil, *Oise, France* **19** 49 38N 2 18 E

Breton, *Canada* **110** 53 7N 114 28W
Breton, Pertuis, *France* **20** 46 17N 1 25W
Breton Sd., *U.S.A.* **121** 29 40N 89 12W
Brett, C., *N.Z.* **80** 35 10 S 174 20 E
Bretten, *W. Germany* **31** 49 2N 8 43 E
Breukelen, *Neths.* **16** 52 10N 5 0 E
Brevard, *U.S.A.* **115** 35 19N 82 42W
Breves, *Brazil* **138** 1 40 S 50 29W
Brevik, *Norway* **10** 59 4N 9 42 E
Brewarrina, *Australia* **73** 30 0 S 146 51 E
Brewer, *U.S.A.* **105** 44 43N 68 50W
Brewer, Mt., *U.S.A.* **124** 36 44N 118 28W
Brewster, *N.Y., U.S.A.* **117** 41 23N 73 37W
Brewster, *Wash., U.S.A.* **122** 48 10N 119 51W
Brewster, Kap, *Greenland* **144** 70 7N 22 0W
Brewton, *U.S.A.* **115** 31 9N 87 2W
Breyten, *S. Africa* **97** 26 16 S 30 0 E
Breytovo, *U.S.S.R.* **37** 58 18N 37 50 E
Brezhnev, *U.S.S.R.* **40** 55 42N 52 19 E
Brežice, *Yugoslavia* **27** 45 54N 15 35 E
Brézina, *Algeria* **85** 33 4N 1 14 E
Březnice, *Czech.* **32** 49 32N 13 57 E
Breznik, *Bulgaria* **34** 42 44N 22 50 E
Brezno, *Czech.* **32** 48 50N 19 40 E
Bria, *C.A.R.* **94** 6 30N 21 58 E
Briagolong, *Australia* **75** 37 51 S 147 5 E
Briançon, *France* **21** 44 54N 6 39 E
Briare, *France* **19** 47 38N 2 45 E
Bribbaree, *Australia* **76** 34 10 S 147 51 E
Bribie I., *Australia* **73** 27 0 S 152 58 E
Bricquebec, *France* **18** 49 28N 1 38W
Bridgehampton, *U.S.A.* **117** 40 56N 72 19W
Bridgend, *U.K.* **13** 51 30N 3 35W
Bridgenorth, *Canada* **109** 44 23N 78 23W
Bridgeport, *Canada* **108** 43 29N 80 29W
Bridgeport, *Calif., U.S.A.* **124** 38 14N 119 15W
Bridgeport, *Conn., U.S.A.* **117** 41 12N 73 12W
Bridgeport, *Nebr., U.S.A.* **120** 41 42N 103 10W
Bridgeport, *Tex., U.S.A.* **121** 33 15N 97 45W
Bridger, *U.S.A.* **122** 45 20N 108 58W
Bridgeton, *U.S.A.* **114** 39 29N 75 10W
Bridgetown, *Australia* **79** 33 58 S 116 7 E
Bridgetown, *Barbados* **129** 13 0N 59 30W
Bridgetown, *Canada* **105** 44 55N 65 18W
Bridgewater, *Australia* **74** 36 36 S 143 59 E
Bridgewater, *Canada* **105** 44 25N 64 31W
Bridgewater, *Mass., U.S.A.* **117** 41 59N 70 56W
Bridgewater, *S. Dak., U.S.A.* **120** 43 34N 97 29W
Bridgewater, C., *Australia* **74** 38 23 S 141 23 E
Bridgman, *U.S.A.* **119** 41 57N 86 33W
Bridgnorth, *U.K.* **13** 52 33N 2 25W
Bridgton, *U.S.A.* **117** 44 5N 70 41W
Bridgwater, *U.K.* **13** 51 7N 3 0W
Bridlington, *U.K.* **12** 54 6N 0 11W
Bridport, *Australia* **72** 40 59 S 147 23 E
Bridport, *U.K.* **13** 50 43N 2 45W
Brie, Plaine de la, *France* **19** 48 35N 3 10 E
Brie-Comte-Robert, *France* **19** 48 40N 2 35 E
Briec, *France* **18** 48 6N 4 0W
Brielle, *Neths.* **16** 51 54N 4 10 E
Brienne-le-Château, *France* **19** 48 24N 4 30 E
Brienon-sur-Armançon, *France* **19** 47 59N 3 38 E
Brienz, *Switz.* **31** 46 46N 8 2 E
Brienzersee, *Switz.* **31** 46 44N 7 53 E
Briey, *France* **19** 49 14N 5 57 E
Brig, *Switz.* **31** 46 18N 7 59 E
Brigg, *U.K.* **12** 53 33N 0 30W
Briggsdale, *U.S.A.* **120** 40 40N 104 20W
Brigham City, *U.S.A.* **122** 41 30N 112 1W
Bright, *Australia* **75** 36 42 S 146 56 E
Brighton, *Australia* **73** 35 5 S 138 30 E
Brighton, *Canada* **109** 44 2N 77 44W
Brighton, *U.K.* **13** 50 50N 0 9W
Brighton, *Colo., U.S.A.* **120** 39 59N 104 50W
Brighton, *Ill., U.S.A.* **118** 39 2N 90 8W
Brighton, *Iowa, U.S.A.* **118** 41 10N 91 49W
Brightwater, *N.Z.* **81** 41 22 S 173 9 E
Brignogan-Plage, *France* **18** 48 40N 4 20W
Brignoles, *France* **21** 43 25N 6 5 E
Brihuega, *Spain* **24** 40 45N 2 52W
Brikama, *Gambia* **90** 13 15N 16 45W
Brilliant, *Canada* **110** 49 19N 117 38W
Brilliant, *U.S.A.* **116** 40 15N 80 39W
Brilon, *W. Germany* **30** 51 23N 8 32 E
Brim, *Australia* **74** 36 3 S 142 27 E
Brimfield, *U.S.A.* **118** 40 50N 89 53W
Brindabella, *Australia* **76** 35 22 S 148 44 E
Bríndisi, *Italy* **29** 40 39N 17 55 E
Brinje, *Yugoslavia* **27** 45 0N 15 9 E
Brinkley, *U.S.A.* **121** 34 55N 91 15W
Brinkworth, *Australia* **73** 33 42 S 138 26 E
Brinnon, *U.S.A.* **124** 47 41N 122 54W
Brion, I., *Canada* **105** 47 46N 61 26W
Brionne, *France* **18** 49 11N 0 43 E
Brionski, *Yugoslavia* **27** 44 55N 13 45 E
Brioude, *France* **20** 45 18N 3 24 E
Briouze, *France* **18** 48 42N 0 23W
Brisbane, *Australia* **77** 27 25 S 153 2 E
Brisbane →, *Australia* **77** 27 24 S 153 9 E
Brisighella, *Italy* **27** 44 14N 11 46 E
Bristol, *Canada* **106** 45 32N 76 28W
Bristol, *U.K.* **13** 51 26N 2 35W
Bristol, *Conn., U.S.A.* **117** 41 44N 72 57W
Bristol, *Pa., U.S.A.* **117** 40 6N 74 52W
Bristol, *R.I., U.S.A.* **117** 41 40N 71 15W
Bristol, *S. Dak., U.S.A.* **120** 45 25N 97 43W
Bristol, *Tenn., U.S.A.* **115** 36 36N 82 11W
Bristol B., *U.S.A.* **102** 58 0N 160 0W
Bristol Channel, *U.K.* **13** 51 18N 4 30W
Bristol I., *Antarctica* **143** 58 45 S 28 0W
Bristol L., *U.S.A.* **123** 34 23N 116 50W
Bristow, *U.S.A.* **121** 35 55N 96 28W
British Antarctic Territory □, *Antarctica* **143** 66 0 S 45 0W
British Columbia □, *Canada* **110** 55 0N 125 15W
British Guiana = Guyana ■, *S. Amer.* **136** 5 0N 59 0W
British Honduras = Belize ■, *Cent. Amer.* **127** 17 0N 88 30W
British Isles, *Europe* **6** 55 0N 4 0W
Brits, *S. Africa* **97** 25 37 S 27 48 E
Britstown, *S. Africa* **96** 30 37 S 23 30 E
Britt, *Canada* **108** 45 46N 80 34W
Britt, *U.S.A.* **118** 43 6N 93 48W
Brittany = Bretagne, *France* **18** 48 0N 3 0W
Britton, *U.S.A.* **120** 45 50N 97 47W
Brive-la-Gaillarde, *France* **20** 45 10N 1 32 E
Briviesca, *Spain* **24** 42 32N 3 19W
Brixton, *Australia* **72** 23 32 S 144 57 E
Brlik, *U.S.S.R.* **40** 43 40N 73 49 E
Brno, *Czech.* **32** 49 10N 16 35 E
Bro, *Sweden* **10** 59 31N 17 38 E
Broach = Bharuch, *India* **50** 21 47N 73 0 E
Broad →, *U.S.A.* **115** 33 59N 82 39W
Broad Arrow, *Australia* **79** 30 23 S 121 15 E
Broad B., *U.K.* **14** 58 14N 6 16W
Broad Haven, *Ireland* **15** 54 20N 9 55W
Broad Law, *U.K.* **14** 55 30N 3 22W
Broad Sd., *Australia* **72** 22 0 S 149 45 E
Broadford, *Australia* **74** 37 14 S 145 4 E
Broadhurst Ra., *Australia* **78** 22 30 S 122 30 E
Broads, The, *U.K.* **12** 52 45N 1 30 E
Broadus, *U.S.A.* **120** 45 28N 105 27W
Broadview, *Canada* **111** 50 22N 102 35W
Broadwater, *Australia* **77** 28 59 S 153 29 E
Broager, *Denmark* **11** 54 53N 9 40 E
Broaryd, *Sweden* **11** 57 7N 13 15 E
Brochet, *Canada* **111** 57 53N 101 40W
Brochet, L., *Canada* **111** 58 36N 101 35W
Brochet, L. du, *Canada* **107** 49 40N 69 37W
Brock, *Canada* **111** 51 26N 108 43W
Brock →, *Canada* **106** 50 0N 75 5W
Brocken, *E. Germany* **30** 51 48N 10 40 E
Brocklehurst, *Australia* **76** 32 9 S 148 38 E
Brockport, *U.S.A.* **116** 43 12N 77 56W
Brockton, *U.S.A.* **117** 42 8N 71 2W
Brockville, *Canada* **109** 44 35N 75 41W
Brockway, *Mont., U.S.A.* **120** 47 18N 105 46W
Brockway, *Pa., U.S.A.* **116** 41 14N 78 48W
Brocton, *U.S.A.* **116** 42 25N 79 26W
Brod, *Yugoslavia* **35** 41 35N 21 17 E
Brodarevo, *Yugoslavia* **33** 43 14N 19 44 E
Brodeur Pen., *Canada* **103** 72 30N 88 10W
Brodhead, *U.S.A.* **118** 42 37N 89 22W
Brodick, *U.K.* **14** 55 34N 5 9W
Brodnica, *Poland* **32** 53 15N 19 25 E
Brodribb →, *Australia* **75** 37 29 S 148 35 E
Brody, *U.S.S.R.* **36** 50 5N 25 10 E
Broechem, *Belgium* **17** 51 11N 4 38 E
Broek, *Neths.* **16** 52 26N 5 0 E
Broek op Langedijk, *Neths.* **16** 52 41N 4 49 E
Brogan, *U.S.A.* **122** 44 14N 117 32W
Broglie, *France* **18** 49 0N 0 30 E
Broke, *Australia* **76** 32 45 S 151 7 E
Broken →, *Australia* **74** 36 24 S 145 24 E
Broken Bay, *Australia* **76** 33 30 S 151 15 E
Broken Bow, *Nebr., U.S.A.* **120** 41 25N 99 35W
Broken Bow, *Okla., U.S.A.* **121** 34 2N 94 43W
Broken Hill = Kabwe, *Zambia* **93** 14 30 S 28 29 E
Broken Hill, *Australia* **73** 31 58 S 141 29 E
Brokind, *Sweden* **11** 58 13N 15 42 E
Brokopondo, *Surinam* **135** 5 3N 54 59W
Brokopondo □, *Surinam* **135** 4 30N 55 30W
Bromfield, *U.K.* **13** 52 25N 2 45W
Bromley, *U.K.* **13** 51 20N 0 5 E
Bromölla, *Sweden* **11** 56 5N 14 28 E
Bromont, *Canada* **107** 45 17N 72 39W
Bromptonville, *Canada* **107** 45 28N 71 57W
Bronaugh, *U.S.A.* **118** 37 41N 94 28W
Brønderslev, *Denmark* **11** 57 16N 9 57 E
Brong-Ahafo □, *Ghana* **90** 7 50N 2 0W
Bronkhorstspruit, *S. Africa* **97** 25 46 S 28 45 E
Bronnitsy, *U.S.S.R.* **37** 55 27N 38 10 E
Bronson, *U.S.A.* **119** 41 52N 85 12W
Bronte, *Italy* **29** 37 48N 14 49 E
Bronte, *U.S.A.* **121** 31 54N 100 18W
Bronte Park, *Australia* **72** 42 8 S 146 30 E
Brook Park, *U.S.A.* **116** 41 24N 80 51W
Brookfield, *U.S.A.* **118** 39 50N 93 4W
Brookhaven, *U.S.A.* **121** 31 40N 90 25W
Brookings, *Oreg., U.S.A.* **122** 42 4N 124 10W
Brookings, *S. Dak., U.S.A.* **120** 44 20N 96 45W
Brooklin, *Canada* **116** 43 55N 78 55W
Brooklyn, *U.S.A.* **118** 41 44N 92 27W
Brookmere, *Canada* **110** 49 52N 120 53W
Brooks, *Canada* **110** 50 35N 111 55W
Brooks B., *Canada* **110** 50 15N 127 55W
Brooks L., *Canada* **111** 61 55N 106 35W
Brooks Ra., *U.S.A.* **102** 68 40N 147 0W
Brookston, *U.S.A.* **119** 40 36N 86 52W
Brooksville, *Fla., U.S.A.* **115** 28 32N 82 21W
Brooksville, *Ky., U.S.A.* **119** 38 41N 84 4W
Brookville, *U.S.A.* **119** 39 25N 85 0W
Brooloo, *Australia* **73** 26 30 S 152 43 E
Broom, L., *U.K.* **14** 57 55N 5 15W
Brooman, *Australia* **76** 35 29 S 150 17 E
Broome, *Australia* **78** 18 0 S 122 15 E
Broomehill, *Australia* **79** 33 51 S 117 39 E
Broons, *France* **18** 48 20N 2 16W
Brora, *U.K.* **14** 58 0N 3 50W
Brora →, *U.K.* **14** 58 4N 3 52W
Brösarp, *Sweden* **11** 55 43N 14 6 E
Brosna →, *Ireland* **15** 53 8N 8 0W
Broşteni, *Romania* **34** 47 14N 25 43 E
Brotas de Macaúbas, *Brazil* **139** 12 0 S 42 38W
Brothers, *U.S.A.* **122** 43 56N 120 39W
Brøttum, *Norway* **10** 61 2N 10 34 E
Brou, *France* **18** 48 13N 1 11 E
Broughton, *U.S.A.* **119** 37 56N 88 27W
Broughton I., *Australia* **76** 32 37 S 152 20 E
Broughton Island, *Canada* **103** 67 33N 63 0W
Broughty Ferry, *U.K.* **14** 56 29N 2 50W
Brouwershaven, *Neths.* **16** 51 45N 3 55 E
Brouwershavensche Gat, *Neths.* **16** 51 46N 3 50 E
Brovary, *U.S.S.R.* **36** 50 34N 30 48 E
Brovst, *Denmark* **11** 57 6N 9 31 E
Browerville, *U.S.A.* **120** 46 3N 94 50W
Brown, Pt., *Australia* **73** 32 32 S 133 50 E
Brown Willy, *U.K.* **13** 50 35N 4 34W
Brownfield, *U.S.A.* **121** 33 10N 102 15W
Browning, *Ill., U.S.A.* **118** 40 7N 90 22W
Browning, *Mo., U.S.A.* **118** 40 3N 93 12W
Browning, *Mont., U.S.A.* **122** 48 35N 113 0W
Brownlee, *Canada* **111** 50 43N 106 1W
Brownsburg, *Canada* **107** 45 41N 74 25W
Brownsburg, *U.S.A.* **119** 39 50N 86 26W
Brownstown, *U.S.A.* **119** 38 53N 86 3W
Brownsville, *Oreg., U.S.A.* **122** 44 29N 123 0W
Brownsville, *Tenn., U.S.A.* **121** 35 35N 89 15W
Brownsville, *Tex., U.S.A.* **121** 25 56N 97 25W
Brownsweg, *Surinam* **135** 5 5N 55 15W
Brownwood, *U.S.A.* **121** 31 45N 99 0W
Brownwood, L., *U.S.A.* **121** 31 51N 98 35W
Browse I., *Australia* **78** 14 7 S 123 33 E
Brozas, *Spain* **23** 39 37N 6 47W
Bruas, *Malaysia* **55** 4 30N 100 47 E
Bruay-en-Artois, *France* **19** 50 29N 2 33 E
Bruce, Mt., *Australia* **78** 22 37 S 118 8 E
Bruce B., *N.Z.* **81** 43 35 S 169 42 E
Bruce Pen., *Canada* **108** 45 0N 81 30W
Bruce Rock, *Australia* **79** 31 52 S 118 8 E
Bruche →, *France* **19** 48 34N 7 43 E
Bruchsal, *W. Germany* **31** 49 9N 8 39 E
Bruck an der Leitha, *Austria* **33** 48 1N 16 47 E
Bruck an der Mur, *Austria* **33** 47 24N 15 16 E
Brückenau, *W. Germany* **31** 50 17N 9 48 E
Brue →, *U.K.* **13** 51 10N 2 59W
Brugelette, *Belgium* **17** 50 35N 3 52 E
Bruges = Brugge, *Belgium* **17** 51 13N 3 13 E
Brugg, *Switz.* **31** 47 29N 8 11 E
Brugge, *Belgium* **17** 51 13N 3 13 E
Brühl, *W. Germany* **30** 50 49N 6 51 E
Bruinisse, *Neths.* **17** 51 40N 4 5 E
Brûlé, *Canada* **110** 53 15N 117 58W
Brûlon, *France* **18** 47 58N 0 15W
Brûly, *Belgium* **17** 49 58N 4 32 E
Brumado, *Brazil* **139** 14 14 S 41 40W
Brumado →, *Brazil* **139** 14 13 S 41 40W
Brumath, *France* **19** 48 43N 7 40 E
Brummen, *Neths.* **16** 52 5N 6 10 E
Brumunddal, *Norway* **10** 60 53N 10 56 E
Brunchilly, *Australia* **72** 18 50 S 134 30 E
Brundidge, *U.S.A.* **115** 31 43N 85 45W
Bruneau, *U.S.A.* **122** 42 57N 115 55W
Bruneau →, *U.S.A.* **122** 42 57N 115 58W
Brunei = Bandar Seri Begawan, *Brunei* **56** 4 52N 115 0 E
Brunei ■, *Asia* **56** 4 50N 115 0 E
Brunette Downs, *Australia* **72** 18 40 S 135 55 E
Brunflo, *Sweden* **10** 63 5N 14 50 E
Brungle, *Australia* **76** 35 8 S 148 13 E
Brunico, *Italy* **27** 46 50N 11 55 E
Brunkeberg, *Norway* **10** 59 26N 8 28 E
Brunna, *Sweden* **10** 59 52N 17 25 E
Brunnen, *Switz.* **31** 46 59N 8 37 E
Brunner, L., *N.Z.* **81** 42 37 S 171 27 E
Brunnsvik, *Sweden* **10** 60 12N 15 8 E
Bruno, *Canada* **111** 52 20N 105 30W
Brunsbüttelkoog, *W. Germany* **30** 53 52N 9 13 E
Brunssum, *Neths.* **17** 50 57N 5 59 E
Brunswick = Braunschweig, *W. Germany* **30** 52 17N 10 28 E
Brunswick, *Ga., U.S.A.* **115** 31 10N 81 30W
Brunswick, *Maine, U.S.A.* **105** 43 53N 69 50W
Brunswick, *Md., U.S.A.* **114** 39 20N 77 38W
Brunswick, *Mo., U.S.A.* **118** 39 26N 93 10W
Brunswick, *Ohio, U.S.A.* **116** 41 15N 81 50W
Brunswick, Pen. de, *Chile* **142** 53 30 S 71 30W
Brunswick B., *Australia* **78** 15 15 S 124 50 E
Brunswick Heads, *Australia* **77** 28 32 S 153 33 E
Brunswick Junction, *Australia* **79** 33 15 S 115 50 E
Bruntál, *Czech.* **32** 50 0N 17 27 E
Bruny I., *Australia* **72** 43 20 S 147 15 E
Brus Laguna, *Honduras* **128** 15 47N 84 35W
Brusartsi, *Bulgaria* **34** 43 40N 23 5 E
Brush, *U.S.A.* **120** 40 17N 103 33W
Brush Island, *Australia* **77** 35 32 S 150 25 E
Brushton, *U.S.A.* **117** 44 50N 74 32W
Brusio, *Switz.* **31** 46 14N 10 8 E
Brusque, *Brazil* **141** 27 5 S 49 0W
Brussel, *Belgium* **17** 50 51N 4 21 E
Brussels = Brussel, *Belgium* **17** 50 51N 4 21 E
Brussels, *Canada* **108** 43 44N 81 15W
Brustem, *Belgium* **17** 50 48N 5 14 E
Bruthen, *Australia* **75** 37 42 S 147 50 E
Bruxelles = Brussel, *Belgium* **17** 50 51N 4 21 E
Bruyères, *France* **19** 48 10N 6 40 E
Bryan, *Ohio, U.S.A.* **119** 41 30N 84 30W
Bryan, *Tex., U.S.A.* **121** 30 40N 96 27W
Bryan, Mt., *Australia* **73** 33 30 S 139 0 E
Bryanka, *U.S.S.R.* **39** 48 32N 38 45 E
Bryansk, *U.S.S.R.* **36** 53 13N 34 25 E
Bryanskoye, *U.S.S.R.* **39** 44 20N 47 10 E
Bryant, *U.S.A.* **120** 44 35N 97 28W
Bryne, *Norway* **9** 58 44N 5 38 E
Bryson, *Canada* **106** 45 41N 76 37W
Bryson City, *U.S.A.* **115** 35 28N 83 25W
Brza Palanka, *Yugoslavia* **33** 44 28N 22 27 E
Brzava →, *Yugoslavia* **33** 45 21N 20 45 E
Brzeg, *Poland* **32** 50 52N 17 30 E
Brzeg Din, *Poland* **32** 51 16N 16 41 E
Bū Athlah, *Libya* **86** 30 9N 15 39 E
Bu Craa, *W. Sahara* **84** 26 45N 12 50W
Bua Yai, *Thailand* **54** 15 33N 102 26 E
Buala, *Solomon Is.* **68** 8 10 S 159 35 E
Buangor, *Australia* **74** 37 20 S 143 10 E
Buangor, Mt., *Australia* **74** 37 16 S 143 13 E
Buapinang, *Indonesia* **57** 4 40 S 121 30 E
Buayan, *Phil.* **57** 6 3N 125 6 E
Buba, *Guinea-Biss.* **90** 11 40N 14 59W
Bubanda, *Zaïre* **94** 4 14N 19 38 E
Bubanza, *Burundi* **92** 3 6 S 29 23 E
Bucak, *Turkey* **46** 37 28N 30 36 E
Bucaramanga, *Colombia* **134** 7 0N 73 0W
Buccaneer Arch., *Australia* **78** 16 7 S 123 20 E
Bucchiánico, *Italy* **27** 42 20N 14 10 E
Bucecea, *Romania* **34** 47 47N 26 28 E
Buchach, *U.S.S.R.* **36** 49 5N 25 25 E
Buchan, *Australia* **75** 37 30 S 148 12 E
Buchan, *U.K.* **14** 57 32N 2 8W
Buchan →, *Australia* **75** 37 22 S 148 9 E
Buchan Ness, *U.K.* **14** 57 29N 1 48W
Buchanan, *Canada* **111** 51 40N 102 45W
Buchanan, *Liberia* **90** 5 57N 10 2W
Buchanan, *U.S.A.* **119** 41 50N 86 22W
Buchanan, L., *Queens., Australia* **72** 21 35 S 145 52 E
Buchanan, L., *W. Austral., Australia* **79** 25 33 S 123 2 E
Buchanan, L., *U.S.A.* **121** 30 50N 98 25W
Buchans, *Canada* **105** 48 50N 56 52W
Bucharest = Bucureşti, *Romania* **34** 44 27N 26 10 E
Buchholz, *W. Germany* **30** 53 19N 9 51 E
Buchloe, *W. Germany* **31** 48 3N 10 45 E
Buchon, Pt., *U.S.A.* **124** 35 15N 120 54W
Bückeburg, *W. Germany* **30** 52 16N 9 2 E
Buckeye, *U.S.A.* **123** 33 28N 112 40W
Buckhannon, *U.S.A.* **114** 39 2N 80 10W
Buckhaven, *U.K.* **14** 56 10N 3 2W
Buckhorn L., *Canada* **109** 44 29N 78 23W
Buckie, *U.K.* **14** 57 40N 2 58W
Buckingham, *Canada* **106** 45 37N 75 24W
Buckingham, *U.K.* **13** 52 0N 0 59W
Buckingham □, *U.K.* **13** 51 50N 0 55W
Buckingham B., *Australia* **72** 12 10 S 135 40 E
Buckingham Can., *India* **51** 14 0N 80 5 E
Buckland, *U.S.A.* **119** 40 37N 84 16W
Buckland Newton, *U.K.* **13** 50 45N 2 25W

Buckle Hd., Australia 78 14 26 S 127 52 E
Buckleboo, Australia 73 32 54 S 136 12 E
Buckley, Ill., U.S.A. 119 40 35N 88 2W
Buckley, Wash., U.S.A. 122 47 10N 122 2W
Bucklin, Kans., U.S.A. 121 37 37N 99 40W
Bucklin, Mo., U.S.A. 118 39 47N 92 53W
Bucks L., U.S.A. 124 39 54N 121 12W
Buco Zau, Angola 95 4 46 S 12 33 E
Bucquoy, France 19 50 9N 2 43 E
Buctouche, Canada 105 46 30N 64 45W
Bucureşti, Romania 34 44 27N 26 10 E
Bucyrus, U.S.A. 119 40 48N 83 0W
Budafok, Hungary 33 47 26N 19 2 E
Budalin, Burma 52 22 20N 95 10 E
Budapest, Hungary 33 47 29N 19 5 E
Budaun, India 49 28 5N 79 10 E
Budd Coast, Antarctica 143 68 0 S 112 0 E
Buddabadah, Australia 76 31 56 S 147 14 E
Buddusò, Italy 28 40 35N 9 18 E
Bude, U.K. 13 50 49N 4 33W
Budel, Neths. 17 51 17N 5 34 E
Budennovsk, U.S.S.R. 39 44 50N 44 10 E
Budeşti, Romania 34 44 13N 26 30 E
Budge Budge = Baj Baj, India 49 22 30N 88 5 E
Budgewoi Lake, Australia 76 33 13 S 151 34 E
Búðareyri, Iceland 8 65 2N 14 13W
Búðir, Iceland 8 64 49N 23 23W
Budia, Spain 24 40 38N 2 46W
Budjala, Zaïre 94 2 50N 19 40 E
Búdrio, Italy 27 44 31N 11 31 E
Buea, Cameroon 91 4 10N 9 9 E
Buellton, U.S.A. 125 34 37N 120 12W
Buena Vista, Bolivia 137 17 27 S 63 40W
Buena Vista, Colo., U.S.A. 123 38 56N 106 6W
Buena Vista, Va., U.S.A. 114 37 47N 79 23W
Buena Vista L., U.S.A. 125 35 15N 119 21W
Buenaventura, Colombia 134 3 53N 77 4W
Buenaventura, Mexico 126 29 50N 107 30W
Buenaventura, B. de, Colombia 134 3 48N 77 17W
Buendía, Pantano de, Spain 24 40 25N 2 43W
Buenópolis, Brazil 139 17 54 S 44 11W
Buenos Aires, Argentina 140 34 30 S 58 20W
Buenos Aires, Colombia 134 1 36N 73 18W
Buenos Aires, Costa Rica 128 9 10N 83 20W
Buenos Aires □, Argentina 140 36 30 S 60 0W
Buenos Aires, L., Chile 142 46 35 S 72 30W
Buesaco, Colombia 134 1 23N 77 9W
Buffalo, Mo., U.S.A. 118 37 40N 93 5W
Buffalo, N.Y., U.S.A. 116 42 55N 78 50W
Buffalo, Okla., U.S.A. 121 36 55N 99 42W
Buffalo, S. Dak., U.S.A. 120 45 39N 103 31W
Buffalo, Wyo., U.S.A. 122 44 25N 106 50W
Buffalo →, Australia 77 36 42 S 146 40 E
Buffalo →, Canada 110 60 5N 115 5W
Buffalo Head Hills, Canada 110 57 25N 115 55W
Buffalo L., Canada 110 52 27N 112 54W
Buffalo Narrows, Canada 111 55 51N 108 29W
Buffels →, S. Africa 96 29 36 S 17 3 E
Buford, U.S.A. 115 34 5N 84 0W
Bug →, Poland 32 52 31N 21 5 E
Bug →, U.S.S.R. 38 46 59N 31 58 E
Buga, Colombia 134 4 0N 76 15W
Bugaldie, Australia 77 31 2 S 149 6 E
Buganda □, Uganda 92 0 0 31 30 E
Buganga, Uganda 92 0 3 S 32 0 E
Bugeat, France 20 45 36N 1 55 E
Bugel, Tanjung, Indonesia 56 6 26 S 111 3 E
Buggenhout, Belgium 17 51 1N 4 12 E
Bugsuk, Phil. 56 8 15N 117 15 E
Bugue, Le, France 20 44 55N 0 56 E
Buguma, Nigeria 91 4 42N 6 55 E
Buguruslan, U.S.S.R. 40 53 39N 52 26 E
Buhăeşti, Romania 34 46 47N 27 32 E
Buheirat-Murrat-el-Kubra, Egypt 88 30 15N 32 40 E
Buhl, Idaho, U.S.A. 122 42 35N 114 54W
Buhl, Minn., U.S.A. 120 47 30N 92 46W
Buick, U.S.A. 121 37 38N 91 2W
Builth Wells, U.K. 13 52 10N 3 26W
Buin, Papua N. G. 68 6 48 S 155 42 E
Buinsk, U.S.S.R. 37 55 0N 48 18 E
Buíque, Brazil 138 8 37 S 37 9W
Buir Nur, Mongolia 62 47 50N 117 42 E
Buis-les-Baronnies, France 21 44 17N 5 16 E
Buitenpost, Neths. 16 53 15N 6 9 E
Buitrago, Spain 22 41 0N 3 38W
Bujalance, Spain 23 37 54N 4 23W
Buján, Spain 22 42 59N 8 36W
Bujaraloz, Spain 24 41 29N 0 10W
Buje, Yugoslavia 27 45 24N 13 39 E
Buji, Papua N. G. 69 9 8 S 142 11 E
Bujumbura, Burundi 92 3 16 S 29 18 E
Buka I., Papua N. G. 69 5 10 S 154 35 E
Bukachacha, U.S.S.R. 41 52 55N 116 50 E
Bukama, Zaïre 93 9 10 S 25 50 E
Bukavu, Zaïre 92 2 20 S 28 52 E
Bukene, Tanzania 92 4 15 S 32 48 E
Bukhara, U.S.S.R. 40 39 48N 64 25 E
Bukima, Tanzania 92 1 50 S 33 25 E
Bukit Mertajam, Malaysia 55 5 22N 100 28 E
Bukittinggi, Indonesia 56 0 20 S 100 20 E
Bukkapatnam, India 51 14 14N 77 46 E
Bukkulla, Australia 77 29 30 S 151 8 E
Bukoba, Tanzania 92 1 20 S 31 49 E
Bukoba □, Tanzania 92 1 30 S 32 0 E
Bukuru, Nigeria 91 9 42N 8 48 E
Bukuya, Uganda 92 0 40N 31 52 E
Bula, Guinea-Biss. 90 12 7N 15 43W
Bula, Indonesia 57 3 6 S 130 30 E
Bulahdelah, Australia 76 32 23 S 152 13 E
Bulan, Phil. 57 12 40N 123 52 E
Bulandshahr, India 48 28 28N 77 51 E
Bûlâq, Egypt 88 25 10N 30 38 E
Bulawayo, Zimb. 93 20 7 S 28 32 E
Buldana, India 50 20 30N 76 18 E
Bulga, Australia 76 32 39 S 151 2 E
Bulgan, Mongolia 62 48 45N 103 34 E
Bulgaria ■, Europe 34 42 35N 25 30 E
Bulgroo, Australia 73 25 47 S 143 58 E
Bulgunnia, Australia 73 30 10 S 134 53 E
Bulhale, Somali Rep. 98 5 20N 46 29 E
Bulhar, Somali Rep. 98 10 25N 44 30 E
Buli, Teluk, Indonesia 57 1 5N 128 25 E
Buliluyan, C., Phil. 56 8 20N 117 15 E
Bulki, Ethiopia 89 6 11N 36 31 E
Bulkley →, Canada 110 55 15N 127 40W
Bull Shoals L., U.S.A. 121 36 40N 93 5W
Bullange, Belgium 17 50 24N 6 15 E
Bullaque →, Spain 23 38 59N 4 17W
Bullara, Australia 78 22 40 S 114 3 E
Bullaring, Australia 79 32 30 S 117 45 E
Bullas, Spain 25 38 2N 1 40W
Bulle, Switz. 31 46 37N 7 3 E
Buller →, N.Z. 81 41 44 S 171 36 E
Buller, Mt., Australia 75 37 10 S 146 28 E
Buller Gorge, N.Z. 81 41 40 S 172 10 E
Bulli, Australia 76 34 15 S 150 57 E
Bullock Cr. →, Australia 74 35 42 S 143 54 E
Bullock Creek, Australia 72 17 43 S 144 31 E
Bulloo →, Australia 73 28 43 S 142 30 E
Bulloo Downs, Queens., Australia 73 28 31 S 142 57 E
Bulloo Downs, W. Austral., Australia 79 24 0 S 119 32 E
Bulloo L., Australia 73 28 43 S 142 25 E
Bulls, N.Z. 80 40 10 S 175 24 E
Bully-les-Mines, France 19 50 27N 2 44 E
Bulnes, Chile 140 36 42 S 72 19W
Bulo Burti, Somali Rep. 98 3 50N 45 33 E
Bulo Ghedudo, Somali Rep. 98 2 52N 43 1 E
Buloke, L., Australia 74 36 15 S 142 58 E
Bulolo, Papua N. G. 69 7 10 S 146 40 E
Bulongo, Zaïre 95 4 45 S 21 30 E
Bulsar = Valsad, India 50 20 40N 72 58 E
Bultfontein, S. Africa 96 28 18 S 26 10 E
Bulu Karakelong, Indonesia 57 4 35N 126 50 E
Bulukumba, Indonesia 57 5 33 S 120 11 E
Bulun, U.S.S.R. 41 70 37N 127 30 E
Bulungu, Zaïre 95 6 4 S 21 54 E
Bumba, Zaïre 94 2 13N 22 30 E
Bumbiri I., Tanzania 92 1 40 S 31 55 E
Bumhkang, Burma 52 26 51N 97 40 E
Bumhpa Bum, Burma 52 26 51N 97 14 E
Bumi →, Zimb. 93 17 0 S 28 20 E
Bumtang →, Bhutan 52 26 56N 90 53 E
Buna, Kenya 92 2 58N 39 30 E
Buna, Papua N. G. 69 8 42 S 148 27 E
Bunazi, Tanzania 92 1 3 S 31 23 E
Bunbah, Khalīj, Libya 86 32 20N 23 15 E
Bunbury, Australia 79 33 20 S 115 35 E
Buncrana, Ireland 15 55 8N 7 28W
Bundaberg, Australia 73 24 54 S 152 22 E
Bundanoon, Australia 76 34 40 S 150 16 E
Bundarra, Australia 77 30 4 S 151 0 E
Bünde, W. Germany 30 52 11N 8 33 E
Bundey →, Australia 72 21 46 S 135 37 E
Bundi, India 48 25 30N 75 35 E
Bundooma, Australia 72 24 54 S 134 16 E
Bundoran, Ireland 15 54 24N 8 17W
Bundukia, Sudan 89 5 14N 30 55 E
Bung Kan, Thailand 54 18 23N 103 37 E
Bungatakada, Japan 64 33 35N 131 25 E
Bungil Cr. →, Australia 72 27 5 S 149 5 E
Bungo-Suidō, Japan 64 33 0N 132 15 E
Bungoma, Kenya 92 0 34N 34 34 E
Bungonia, Australia 76 34 51 S 149 57 E
Bungu, Tanzania 92 7 35 S 39 0 E
Bungun Shara, Mongolia 62 49 0N 104 0 E
Bungunya, Australia 77 28 25 S 149 42 E
Bunia, Zaïre 92 1 35N 30 20 E
Buninyong, Australia 74 37 36 S 143 54 E
Bunji, Pakistan 49 35 45N 74 40 E
Bunker Hill, Ill., U.S.A. 118 39 3N 89 57W
Bunker Hill, Ind., U.S.A. 119 40 40N 86 6W
Bunkie, U.S.A. 121 31 1N 92 12W
Bunnan, Australia 77 32 2 S 150 37 E
Bunnell, U.S.A. 115 29 28N 81 12W
Bunnik, Neths. 16 52 4N 5 12 E
Bunnythorpe, N.Z. 80 40 16 S 175 39 E
Buñol, Spain 25 39 25N 0 47W
Bunsbeek, Belgium 17 50 50N 4 56 E
Bunschoten, Neths. 16 52 14N 5 22 E
Buntok, Indonesia 56 1 40 S 114 58 E
Bununu, Nigeria 91 9 51N 9 32 E
Bununu Dass, Nigeria 91 10 0N 9 31 E
Bunyan, Australia 76 36 10 S 149 11 E
Bunyip, Australia 74 38 6 S 145 43 E
Bunyu, Indonesia 56 3 35N 117 50 E
Bunza, Nigeria 91 12 8N 4 0 E
Buol, Indonesia 57 1 15N 121 32 E
Buon Brieng, Vietnam 54 13 9N 108 12 E
Buon Me Thuot, Vietnam 54 12 40N 108 3 E
Buong Long, Cambodia 54 13 44N 106 59 E
Buorkhaya, Mys, U.S.S.R. 41 71 50N 132 40 E
Buqayq, Si. Arabia 46 26 0N 49 45 E
Buqbua, Egypt 88 31 29N 25 29 E
Buqei'a, Israel 44 32 58N 35 20 E
Bur Acaba, Somali Rep. 98 3 12N 44 20 E
Bûr Fuad, Egypt 88 31 15N 32 20 E
Bur Ghibi, Somali Rep. 98 3 56N 45 7 E
Bûr Safâga, Egypt 88 26 43N 33 57 E
Bûr Sa'îd, Egypt 88 31 16N 32 18 E
Bûr Sûdân, Sudan 88 19 32N 37 9 E
Bûr Taufiq, Egypt 88 29 54N 32 32 E
Bura, Kenya 92 1 4 S 39 58 E
Buran, Somali Rep. 98 10 14N 48 44 E
Burao, Somali Rep. 98 9 32N 45 32 E
Buras, U.S.A. 121 29 20N 89 33W
Buraydah, Si. Arabia 46 26 20N 44 8 E
Buraymī, Al Wāhāt al, Oman 47 24 10N 55 43 E
Burbank, U.S.A. 125 34 9N 118 23W
Burcher, Australia 76 33 30 S 147 16 E
Burdekin →, Australia 72 19 38 S 147 25 E
Burdett, Canada 110 49 50N 111 32W
Burdur, Turkey 46 37 45N 30 22 E
Burdwan = Barddhaman, India 49 23 14N 87 39 E
Bure, Ethiopia 89 10 40N 37 4 E
Bure →, U.K. 12 52 38N 1 45 E
Bureba, La, Spain 24 42 36N 3 24W
Buren, Neths. 16 51 55N 5 20 E
Büren, W. Germany 30 51 33N 8 34 E
Bureya →, U.S.S.R. 41 49 27N 129 30 E
Burford, Canada 108 43 7N 80 27W
Burg, E. Germany 30 52 16N 11 50 E
Burg, W. Germany 30 54 25N 11 10 E
Burg el Arab, Egypt 88 30 54N 29 32 E
Burg et Tuyur, Sudan 88 20 55N 27 56 E
Burg Stargard, E. Germany 30 53 29N 13 19 E
Burgas, Bulgaria 34 42 33N 27 29 E
Burgdorf, Switz. 31 47 3N 7 37 E
Burgdorf, W. Germany 30 52 27N 10 0 E
Burgeo, Canada 105 47 37N 57 38W
Burgersdorp, S. Africa 96 31 0 S 26 20 E
Burges, Mt., Australia 79 30 50 S 121 5 E
Burghausen, W. Germany 31 48 10N 12 50 E
Búrgio, Italy 28 37 35N 13 18 E
Burglengenfeld, W. Germany 31 49 11N 12 2 E
Burgo de Osma, Spain 24 41 35N 3 4W
Burgohondo, Spain 22 40 26N 4 47W
Burgos, Spain 24 42 21N 3 41W
Burgos □, Spain 24 42 21N 3 42W
Burgstädt, E. Germany 30 50 55N 12 49 E
Burgsteinfurt, W. Germany 30 52 9N 7 23 E
Burgsvik, Sweden 11 57 3N 18 19 E
Burguillos del Cerro, Spain 23 38 23N 6 35W
Burgundy = Bourgogne, France 19 47 0N 4 50 E
Burhanpur, India 50 21 18N 76 14 E
Burhou, U.K. 18 49 45N 2 15W
Buri Pen., Ethiopia 89 15 25N 39 55 E
Burias, Phil. 57 12 55N 123 5 E
Burica, Pta., Costa Rica 128 8 3N 82 51W
Burigi, L., Tanzania 92 2 2 S 31 22 E
Burin, Canada 105 47 1N 55 14W
Būrīn, Jordan 44 32 11N 35 15 E
Buriram, Thailand 54 15 0N 103 0 E
Buriti Alegre, Brazil 139 18 9 S 49 3W
Buriti Bravo, Brazil 138 5 50 S 43 50W
Buriti dos Lopes, Brazil 138 3 10 S 41 52W
Burji, Ethiopia 89 5 29N 37 51 E
Burkburnett, U.S.A. 121 34 7N 98 35W
Burke, U.S.A. 122 47 31N 115 56W
Burke →, Australia 72 23 12 S 139 33 E
Burketown, Australia 72 17 45 S 139 33 E
Burkettsville, U.S.A. 119 40 21N 84 39W
Burkina Faso ■, Africa 90 12 0N 1 0W
Burk's Falls, Canada 108 45 37N 79 24W
Burleigh Falls, Canada 109 44 33N 78 12W
Burleigh Heads, Australia 77 28 5 S 153 25 E
Burley, U.S.A. 122 42 37N 113 55W
Burlingame, U.S.A. 124 37 35N 122 21W
Burlington, Canada 108 43 18N 79 45W
Burlington, Colo., U.S.A. 120 39 21N 102 18W
Burlington, Ill., U.S.A. 119 42 43N 88 33W
Burlington, Iowa, U.S.A. 118 40 50N 91 5W
Burlington, Kans., U.S.A. 120 38 15N 95 47W
Burlington, Ky., U.S.A. 119 39 2N 84 43W
Burlington, N.C., U.S.A. 115 36 7N 79 27W
Burlington, N.J., U.S.A. 117 40 5N 74 50W
Burlington, Vt., U.S.A. 117 44 27N 73 14W
Burlington, Wash., U.S.A. 110 48 29N 122 19W
Burlington, Wis., U.S.A. 114 42 41N 88 18W
Burlyu-Tyube, U.S.S.R. 40 46 30N 79 10 E
Burma ■, Asia 52 21 0N 96 30 E
Burnaby I., Canada 110 52 25N 131 19W
Burnet, U.S.A. 121 30 45N 98 11W
Burney, U.S.A. 122 40 56N 121 41W
Burngup, Australia 79 33 2 S 118 42 E
Burnham, U.S.A. 116 40 37N 77 34W
Burnie, Australia 72 41 4 S 145 56 E
Burnley, U.K. 12 53 47N 2 15W
Burns, Oreg., U.S.A. 122 43 40N 119 4W
Burns, Wyo., U.S.A. 120 41 13N 104 18W
Burns Lake, Canada 110 54 20N 125 45W
Burnside →, Canada 102 66 51N 108 4W
Burnside, L., Australia 79 25 22 S 123 0 E
Burnt River, Canada 109 44 41N 78 42W
Burntwood →, Canada 111 56 8N 96 34W
Burntwood L., Canada 111 55 22N 100 26W
Burpengary, Australia 77 27 10 S 152 57 E
Burqā, Jordan 44 32 18N 35 11 E
Burqān, Kuwait 46 29 0N 47 57 E
Burqin, China 62 47 43N 87 0 E
Burra, Australia 73 33 40 S 138 55 E
Burraga, Australia 76 33 57 S 149 32 E
Burragate, Australia 75 37 2 S 149 38 E
Burragorang, L., Australia 76 33 52 S 150 37 E
Burramurra, Australia 72 20 25 S 137 15 E
Burreli, Albania 35 41 36N 20 1 E
Burren Junction, Australia 73 30 7 S 148 59 E
Burrendong, L., Australia 76 32 45 S 149 10 E
Burrendong Dam, Australia 76 32 39 S 149 6 E
Burrewarra Pt., Australia 76 35 50 S 150 15 E
Burriana, Spain 24 39 50N 0 4W
Burringbar, Australia 77 28 25 S 153 29 E
Burrinjuck Dam, Australia 76 35 0 S 148 34 E
Burrinjuck Res., Australia 76 35 0 S 148 36 E
Burro, Serranías del, Mexico 126 29 0N 102 0W
Burrumbeet, L., Australia 74 37 30 S 143 39 E
Burrundie, Australia 78 13 32 S 131 42 E
Burruyacú, Argentina 140 26 30 S 64 40W
Burry Port, U.K. 13 51 41N 4 17W
Bursa, Turkey 46 40 15N 29 5 E
Burseryd, Sweden 11 57 12N 13 17 E
Burstall, Canada 111 50 39N 109 54W
Burton, U.S.A. 119 43 0N 83 40W
Burton L., Canada 104 54 45N 78 20W
Burton-upon-Trent, U.K. 12 52 48N 1 39W
Burtundy, Australia 74 33 45 S 142 15 E
Buru, Indonesia 57 3 30 S 126 30 E
Burullus, Bahra el, Egypt 88 31 25N 31 0 E
Burundi ■, Africa 92 3 15 S 30 0 E
Bururi, Burundi 92 3 57 S 29 37 E
Burutu, Nigeria 91 5 20N 5 29 E
Burwash, Canada 108 46 14N 80 51W
Burwell, U.S.A. 120 41 49N 99 8W
Bury, Canada 107 45 28N 71 30W
Bury, U.K. 12 53 36N 2 19W
Bury St. Edmunds, U.K. 13 52 15N 0 42 E
Buryat A.S.S.R. □, U.S.S.R. 41 53 0N 110 0 E
Buryn, U.S.S.R. 36 51 13N 33 50 E
Busalla, Italy 26 44 34N 8 58 E
Busango Swamp, Zambia 93 14 15 S 25 45 E
Buşayyah, Iraq 46 30 0N 46 10 E
Busca, Italy 26 44 31N 7 29 E
Būshehr, Iran 47 28 55N 50 55 E
Būshehr □, Iran 47 28 20N 51 45 E
Bushell, Canada 111 59 31N 108 45W
Bushenyi, Uganda 92 0 35 S 30 10 E
Bushire = Būshehr, Iran 47 28 55N 50 55 E
Bushnell, Ill., U.S.A. 120 40 32N 90 30W
Bushnell, Nebr., U.S.A. 120 41 18N 103 50W
Busia □, Kenya 92 0 25N 34 6 E
Busie, Ghana 90 10 29N 2 22W
Businga, Zaïre 94 3 16N 20 59 E
Buskerud fylke □, Norway 10 60 13N 9 0 E
Busko Zdrój, Poland 32 50 28N 20 42 E
Buslei, Ethiopia 98 5 28N 44 25 E
Busoga □, Uganda 92 0 5N 33 30 E
Busovača, Yugoslavia 33 44 6N 17 53 E
Busra ash Shām, Syria 46 32 30N 36 25 E
Bussang, France 19 47 50N 6 50 E
Busselton, Australia 79 33 42 S 115 15 E
Busseto, Italy 26 44 59N 10 2 E
Bussum, Neths. 16 52 16N 5 10 E
Bustamante, B., Argentina 142 45 5 S 66 18W
Busto, C., Spain 22 43 34N 6 28W
Busto Arsizio, Italy 26 45 40N 8 50 E
Busu-Djanoa, Zaïre 94 1 43N 21 23 E
Busuanga, Phil. 57 12 10N 120 0 E
Büsum, W. Germany 30 54 7N 8 50 E

Buta, *Zaïre* **92** 2 50N 24 53 E
Butare, *Rwanda* **92** 2 31 S 29 52 E
Butaritari, *Kiribati* **66** 3 30N 174 0 E
Bute, *U.K.* **14** 55 48N 5 2W
Bute Inlet, *Canada* **110** 50 40N 124 53W
Butemba, *Uganda* **92** 1 9N 31 37 E
Butembo, *Zaïre* **92** 0 9N 29 18 E
Butera, *Italy* **29** 37 10N 14 10 E
Bütgenbach, *Belgium* **17** 50 26N 6 12 E
Butha Qi, *China* **62** 48 0N 122 32 E
Buthidaung, *Burma* **52** 20 52N 92 32 E
Butiaba, *Uganda* **92** 1 50N 31 20 E
Butler, *Ind., U.S.A.* **119** 41 26N 84 52W
Butler, *Ky., U.S.A.* **119** 38 47N 84 22W
Butler, *Mo., U.S.A.* **118** 38 17N 94 18W
Butler, *Pa., U.S.A.* **116** 40 52N 79 52W
Butte, *Mont., U.S.A.* **122** 46 0N 112 31W
Butte, *Nebr., U.S.A.* **120** 42 56N 98 54W
Butte Creek →, *U.S.A.* **124** 39 12N 121 56W
Butterworth = Gcuwa, *S. Africa* **97** 32 20 S 28 11 E
Butterworth, *Malaysia* **55** 5 24N 100 23 E
Buttfield, Mt., *Australia* **79** 24 45 S 128 9 E
Button B., *Canada* **111** 58 45N 94 23W
Buttonwillow, *U.S.A.* **125** 35 24N 119 28W
Butty Hd., *Australia* **79** 33 54 S 121 39 E
Butuan, *Phil.* **57** 8 57N 125 33 E
Butuku-Luba, *Eq. Guin.* **91** 3 29N 8 33 E
Butung, *Indonesia* **57** 5 0 S 122 45 E
Buturlinovka, *U.S.S.R.* **37** 50 50N 40 35 E
Butzbach, *W. Germany* **30** 50 24N 8 40 E
Bützow, *E. Germany* **30** 53 51N 11 59 E
Buxar, *India* **49** 25 34N 83 58 E
Buxton, *N.S.W., Australia* **76** 34 15 S 150 32 E
Buxton, *Vic., Australia* **74** 37 26 S 145 42 E
Buxton, *Guyana* **135** 6 48N 58 2W
Buxton, *S. Africa* **96** 27 38 S 24 42 E
Buxton, *U.K.* **12** 53 16N 1 54W
Buxy, *France* **19** 46 44N 4 40 E
Buy, *U.S.S.R.* **37** 58 28N 41 28 E
Buyaga, *U.S.S.R.* **41** 59 50N 127 0 E
Buynaksk, *U.S.S.R.* **39** 42 48N 47 7 E
Büyük Çekmece, *Turkey* **35** 41 2N 28 35 E
Buzançais, *France* **18** 46 54N 1 25 E
Buzău, *Romania* **34** 45 10N 26 50 E
Buzău →, *Romania* **34** 45 26N 27 44 E
Buzău, Pasul, *Romania* **34** 45 35N 26 12 E
Buzen, *Japan* **64** 33 35N 131 5 E
Buzet, *Yugoslavia* **27** 45 24N 13 58 E
Buzi →, *Mozam.* **93** 19 50 S 34 43 E
Buziaş, *Romania* **34** 45 38N 21 36 E
Buzuluk, *U.S.S.R.* **40** 52 48N 52 12 E
Buzuluk →, *U.S.S.R.* **37** 50 15N 42 7 E
Buzzards Bay, *U.S.A.* **117** 41 45N 70 38W
Bwagaoia, *Papua N. G.* **69** 10 40 S 152 52 E
Bwana Mkubwe, *Zaïre* **93** 13 8 S 28 38 E
Byala, *Bulgaria* **34** 43 28N 25 44 E
Byala Slatina, *Bulgaria* **34** 43 26N 23 55 E
Byandovan, Mys, *U.S.S.R.* **39** 39 45N 49 28 E
Bychawa, *Poland* **32** 51 1N 22 36 E
Bydgoszcz, *Poland* **32** 53 10N 18 0 E
Byelorussian S.S.R. □, *U.S.S.R.* **36** 53 30N 27 0 E
Byers, *U.S.A.* **120** 39 46N 104 13W
Byesville, *U.S.A.* **116** 39 56N 81 32W
Byhalia, *U.S.A.* **121** 34 53N 89 41W
Bykhov, *U.S.S.R.* **36** 53 31N 30 14 E
Bykovo, *U.S.S.R.* **39** 49 50N 45 25 E
Bylas, *U.S.A.* **123** 33 11N 110 9W
Bylderup, *Denmark* **11** 54 57N 9 6 E
Bylong, *Australia* **76** 32 24 S 150 8 E
Bylot I., *Canada* **103** 73 13N 78 34W
Byng Inlet, *Canada* **108** 45 46N 80 33W
Byrd, C., *Antarctica* **143** 69 38 S 76 7W
Byrd Land, *Antarctica* **143** 79 30 S 125 0W
Byrd Sub-Glacial Basin, *Antarctica* **143** 82 0 S 120 0W
Byro, *Australia* **79** 26 5 S 116 11 E
Byrock, *Australia* **73** 30 40 S 146 27 E
Byron, *Australia* **77** 29 40 S 151 7 E
Byron, *U.S.A.* **118** 42 8N 89 15W
Byron, C., *Australia* **77** 28 38 S 153 40 E
Byron Bay, *Australia* **77** 28 43 S 153 37 E
Byrranga, Gory, *U.S.S.R.* **41** 75 0N 100 0 E
Byrum, *Denmark* **11** 57 16N 11 0 E
Byske, *Sweden* **8** 64 57N 21 11 E
Byske älv →, *Sweden* **8** 64 57N 21 13 E
Bystrzyca Kłodzka, *Poland* **32** 50 19N 16 39 E
Byten, *U.S.S.R.* **36** 52 50N 25 27 E
Bytom, *Poland* **32** 50 25N 18 54 E
Bytów, *Poland* **32** 54 10N 17 30 E
Byumba, *Rwanda* **92** 1 35 S 30 4 E

C

Ca →, *Vietnam* **54** 18 45N 105 45 E
Ca Mau = Quan Long, *Vietnam* **55** 9 7N 105 8 E
Ca Mau, Mui = Bai Bung, Mui, *Vietnam* **55** 8 38N 104 44 E
Ca Na, *Vietnam* **55** 11 20N 108 54 E
Caacupé, *Paraguay* **140** 25 23 S 57 5W
Caála, *Angola* **95** 12 46 S 15 30 E
Caamano Sd., *Canada* **110** 52 55N 129 25W
Caapiranga, *Brazil* **135** 3 18 S 61 13W
Caazapá, *Paraguay* **140** 26 8 S 56 19W
Caazapá □, *Paraguay* **141** 26 10 S 56 0W
Caballeria, C. de, *Spain* **24** 40 5N 4 5 E
Cabana, *Peru* **136** 8 25 S 78 5W
Cabanaconde, *Peru* **136** 15 38 S 71 58W
Cabañaquinta, *Spain* **22** 43 10N 5 38W
Cabanatuan, *Phil.* **57** 15 30N 120 58 E
Cabanes, *Spain* **24** 40 9N 0 2 E
Cabanillas, *Peru* **136** 15 36 S 70 28W
Cabano, *Canada* **107** 47 40N 68 56W
Čabar, *Yugoslavia* **27** 45 36N 14 39 E
Cabazon, *U.S.A.* **125** 33 55N 116 47W
Cabbora →, *Australia* **77** 32 2 S 149 17 E
Cabedelo, *Brazil* **138** 7 0 S 34 50W
Cabery, *U.S.A.* **119** 40 59N 88 12W
Cabeza del Buey, *Spain* **23** 38 44N 5 13W
Cabildo, *Chile* **140** 32 30 S 71 5W
Cabimas, *Venezuela* **134** 10 23N 71 25W
Cabinda, *Angola* **95** 5 33 S 12 11 E
Cabinda □, *Angola* **95** 5 0 S 12 30 E
Cabinet Mts., *U.S.A.* **122** 48 0N 115 30W
Cabiri, *Angola* **95** 8 52 S 13 39 E
Cabo Blanco, *Argentina* **142** 47 15 S 65 47W
Cabo Frio, *Brazil* **139** 22 51 S 42 3W
Cabo Pantoja, *Peru* **134** 1 0 S 75 10W
Cabo Raso, *Argentina* **142** 44 20 S 65 15W
Cabonga, Réservoir, *Canada* **106** 47 20N 76 40W
Cabool, *U.S.A.* **121** 37 10N 92 8W
Caboolture, *Australia* **73** 27 5 S 152 58 E
Cabora Bassa Dam, *Mozam.* **93** 15 20 S 32 50 E
Caborca, *Mexico* **126** 30 40N 112 10W
Cabot, Mt., *U.S.A.* **117** 44 30N 71 25W
Cabot Strait, *Canada* **105** 47 15N 59 40W
Cabra, *Spain* **23** 37 30N 4 28W
Cabra del Santo Cristo, *Spain* **25** 37 42N 3 16W
Cabramurra, *Australia* **76** 35 56 S 148 26 E
Cábras, *Italy* **28** 39 57N 8 30 E
Cabrera, I., *Spain* **25** 39 8N 2 57 E
Cabrera, Sierra, *Spain* **22** 42 12N 6 40W
Cabri, *Canada* **111** 50 35N 108 25W
Cabriel →, *Spain* **25** 39 14N 1 3W
Cabruta, *Venezuela* **134** 7 50N 66 10W
Cabuyaro, *Colombia* **134** 4 18N 72 49W
Cacabelos, *Spain* **22** 42 36N 6 44W
Čačak, *Yugoslavia* **33** 43 54N 20 20 E
Cacao, *Fr. Guiana* **135** 4 33N 52 26W
Cáceres, *Brazil* **137** 16 5 S 57 40W
Cáceres, *Colombia* **134** 7 35N 75 20W
Cáceres, *Spain* **23** 39 26N 6 23W
Cáceres □, *Spain* **23** 39 45N 6 0W
Cache Bay, *Canada* **108** 46 22N 80 0W
Cache Cr. →, *U.S.A.* **124** 38 45N 121 43W
Cachepo, *Portugal* **23** 37 20N 7 49W
Cachéu, *Guinea-Biss.* **90** 12 14N 16 8W
Cachi, *Argentina* **140** 25 5 S 66 10W
Cachimbo, *Brazil* **137** 8 57 S 54 54W
Cachimbo, Serra do, *Brazil* **137** 9 30 S 55 0W
Cachingues, *Angola* **95** 13 5 S 16 43 E
Cachoeira, *Brazil* **139** 12 30 S 39 0W
Cachoeira Alta, *Brazil* **139** 18 48 S 50 58W
Cachoeira de Itapemirim, *Brazil* **141** 20 51 S 41 7W
Cachoeira do Sul, *Brazil* **141** 30 3 S 52 53W
Cachoeiro do Arari, *Brazil* **138** 1 1 S 48 58W
Cachopo, *Portugal* **23** 37 20N 7 49W
Cachuela Esperanza, *Bolivia* **137** 10 32 S 65 38W
Cacólo, *Angola* **95** 10 9 S 19 21 E
Caconda, *Angola* **95** 13 48 S 15 8 E
Cacongo, *Angola* **95** 5 11 S 12 5 E
Caçu, *Brazil* **139** 18 37 S 51 4W
Cacula, *Angola* **95** 14 29 S 14 10 E
Caculé, *Brazil* **139** 14 30 S 42 13W
Cacuso, *Angola* **95** 9 25 S 15 45 E
Cadarache, *France* **21** 43 41N 5 43 E
Čadca, *Czech.* **32** 49 26N 18 45 E
Caddo, *U.S.A.* **121** 34 8N 96 18W
Cadell Cr. →, *Australia* **72** 22 35 S 141 51 E
Cader Idris, *U.K.* **12** 52 43N 3 56W
Cadí, Sierra del, *Spain* **24** 42 17N 1 42 E
Cadibarrawirracanna, L., *Australia* **73** 28 52 S 135 27 E
Cadillac, *Canada* **106** 48 14N 78 23W
Cadillac, *France* **20** 44 38N 0 20W
Cadillac, *U.S.A.* **104** 44 16N 85 25W
Cadiz, *Phil.* **57** 10 57N 123 15 E
Cádiz, *Spain* **23** 36 30N 6 20W
Cadiz, *U.S.A.* **116** 40 13N 81 0W
Cádiz □, *Spain* **23** 36 36N 5 45W
Cádiz, G. de, *Spain* **23** 36 40N 7 0W
Cadney Park, *Australia* **73** 27 55 S 134 3 E
Cadomin, *Canada* **110** 53 2N 117 20W
Cadotte →, *Canada* **110** 56 43N 117 10W
Cadours, *France* **20** 43 44N 1 2 E
Cadoux, *Australia* **79** 30 46 S 117 7 E
Caen, *France* **18** 49 10N 0 22W
Caernarfon, *U.K.* **12** 53 8N 4 17W
Caernarfon B., *U.K.* **12** 53 4N 4 40W
Caernarvon = Caernarfon, *U.K.* **12** 53 8N 4 17W
Caerphilly, *U.K.* **13** 51 34N 3 13W
Caesarea, *Israel* **44** 32 30N 34 53 E
Caeté, *Brazil* **139** 19 55 S 43 40W
Caetité, *Brazil* **139** 13 50 S 42 32W
Cafayate, *Argentina* **140** 26 2 S 66 0W
Cafifi, *Colombia* **134** 5 13N 71 4W
Cafu, *Angola* **95** 16 30 S 15 8 E
Cagayan →, *Phil.* **57** 18 25N 121 42 E
Cagayan de Oro, *Phil.* **57** 8 30N 124 40 E
Cagli, *Italy* **27** 43 32N 12 38 E
Cágliari, *Italy* **28** 39 15N 9 6 E
Cágliari, G. di, *Italy* **28** 39 8N 9 10 E
Cagnano Varano, *Italy* **29** 41 49N 15 47 E
Cagnes-sur-Mer, *France* **21** 43 40N 7 9 E
Caguán →, *Colombia* **134** 0 8 S 74 18W
Caguas, *Puerto Rico* **129** 18 14N 66 4W
Caha Mts., *Ireland* **15** 51 45N 9 40W
Cahama, *Angola* **95** 16 17 S 14 19 E
Caher, *Ireland* **15** 52 23N 7 56W
Cahersiveen, *Ireland* **15** 51 57N 10 13W
Cahore Pt., *Ireland* **15** 52 34N 6 11W
Cahors, *France* **20** 44 27N 1 27 E
Cahuapanas, *Peru* **136** 5 15 S 77 0W
Cahuinari →, *Colombia* **134** 1 21 S 70 44W
Cai Bau, Dao, *Vietnam* **54** 21 10N 107 27 E
Cai Nuoc, *Vietnam* **55** 8 56N 105 1 E
Caia, *Mozam.* **93** 17 51 S 35 24 E
Caiabis, Serra dos, *Brazil* **137** 11 30 S 56 30W
Caianda, *Angola* **93** 11 2 S 23 31 E
Caiapó, Serra do, *Brazil* **137** 17 0 S 52 0W
Caiapônia, *Brazil* **137** 16 57 S 51 49W
Caibarién, *Cuba* **128** 22 30N 79 30W
Caicara, *Bolívar, Venezuela* **134** 7 38N 66 10W
Caicara, *Monagas, Venezuela* **135** 9 52N 63 38W
Caicó, *Brazil* **138** 6 20 S 37 0W
Caicos Is., *W. Indies* **129** 21 40N 71 40W
Caicos Passage, *W. Indies* **129** 22 45N 72 45W
Cailloma, *Peru* **136** 15 9 S 71 45W
Caine →, *Bolivia* **137** 18 23 S 65 21W
Caird Coast, *Antarctica* **143** 75 0 S 25 0W
Cairn Curran Res., *Australia* **74** 37 5 S 144 2 E
Cairn Gorm, *U.K.* **14** 57 7N 3 40W
Cairn Toul, *U.K.* **14** 57 3N 3 44W
Cairngorm Mts., *U.K.* **14** 57 6N 3 42W
Cairns, *Australia* **72** 16 57 S 145 45 E
Cairo = El Qâhira, *Egypt* **88** 30 1N 31 14 E
Cairo, *Ga., U.S.A.* **115** 30 52N 84 12W
Cairo, *Ill., U.S.A.* **121** 37 0N 89 10W
Cairo Montenotte, *Italy* **26** 44 23N 8 16 E
Caithness, Ord of, *U.K.* **14** 58 9N 3 37W
Caiundo, *Angola* **95** 15 50 S 17 28 E
Caiza, *Bolivia* **137** 20 2 S 65 40W
Cajabamba, *Peru* **136** 7 38 S 78 4W
Cajamarca, *Peru* **136** 7 5 S 78 28W
Cajamarca □, *Peru* **136** 6 15 S 78 50W
Cajapió, *Brazil* **138** 2 58 S 44 48W
Cajarc, *France* **20** 44 29N 1 50 E
Cajatambo, *Peru* **136** 10 30 S 77 2W
Cajàzeiras, *Brazil* **138** 6 52 S 38 30W
Čajetina, *Yugoslavia* **33** 43 47N 19 42 E
Çakirgol, *Turkey* **39** 40 33N 39 40 E
Čakovec, *Yugoslavia* **27** 46 23N 16 26 E
Cal, La →, *Bolivia* **137** 17 27 S 58 15W
Cala, *Spain* **23** 37 59N 6 21W
Cala →, *Spain* **23** 37 38N 6 5W
Cala Cadolar, Punta de, *Spain* **25** 38 38N 1 35 E
Calabar, *Nigeria* **91** 4 57N 8 20 E
Calabogie, *Canada* **109** 45 18N 76 43W
Calabozo, *Venezuela* **134** 9 0N 67 28W
Calábria □, *Italy* **29** 39 24N 16 30 E
Calaburras, Pta. de, *Spain* **23** 36 30N 4 38W
Calaceite, *Spain* **24** 41 1N 0 11 E
Calacota, *Bolivia* **136** 17 16 S 68 38W
Calafate, *Argentina* **142** 50 19 S 72 15W
Calahorra, *Spain* **24** 42 18N 1 59W
Calais, *France* **19** 50 57N 1 56 E
Calais, *U.S.A.* **105** 45 11N 67 20W
Calais, Pas de, *France* **19** 51 0N 1 20 E
Calalaste, Cord. de, *Argentina* **140** 25 0 S 67 0W
Calama, *Brazil* **137** 8 0 S 62 50W
Calama, *Chile* **140** 22 30 S 68 55W
Calamar, *Bolívar, Colombia* **134** 10 15N 74 55W
Calamar, *Vaupés, Colombia* **134** 1 58N 72 32W
Calamarca, *Bolivia* **136** 16 55 S 68 9W
Calamian Group, *Phil.* **57** 11 50N 119 55 E
Calamocha, *Spain* **24** 40 50N 1 17W
Calañas, *Spain* **23** 37 40N 6 53W
Calanda, *Spain* **24** 40 56N 0 15W
Calandula, *Angola* **95** 9 6 S 15 57 E
Calang, *Indonesia* **56** 4 37N 95 37 E
Calangiánus, *Italy* **28** 40 56N 9 12 E
Calanscio, Sarīr, *Libya* **86** 27 0N 21 30 E
Calapan, *Phil.* **57** 13 25N 121 7 E
Călăraşi, *Romania* **34** 44 12N 27 20 E
Călăraşi □, *Romania* **34** 44 10N 27 0 E
Calasparra, *Spain* **25** 38 14N 1 41W
Calatafimi, *Italy* **28** 37 56N 12 50 E
Calatayud, *Spain* **24** 41 20N 1 40W
Calato = Kálathos, *Greece* **35** 36 9N 28 8 E
Calauag, *Phil.* **57** 13 55N 122 15 E
Calavà, C., *Italy* **29** 38 11N 14 55 E
Calavite, Cape, *Phil.* **57** 13 26N 120 20 E
Calbayog, *Phil.* **57** 12 4N 124 38 E
Calbe, *E. Germany* **30** 51 57N 11 47 E
Calca, *Peru* **136** 13 22 S 72 0W
Calcasieu L., *U.S.A.* **121** 30 0N 93 17W
Calci, *Italy* **26** 43 44N 10 31 E
Calcutta, *India* **49** 22 36N 88 24 E
Caldaro, *Italy* **27** 46 23N 11 15 E
Caldas □, *Colombia* **134** 5 15N 75 30W
Caldas da Rainha, *Portugal* **23** 39 24N 9 8W
Caldas de Reyes, *Spain* **22** 42 36N 8 39W
Caldas Novas, *Brazil* **139** 17 45 S 48 38W
Calder →, *U.K.* **12** 53 44N 1 21W
Caldera, *Chile* **140** 27 5 S 70 55W
Caldwell, *Idaho, U.S.A.* **122** 43 45N 116 42W
Caldwell, *Kans., U.S.A.* **121** 37 5N 97 37W
Caldwell, *Tex., U.S.A.* **121** 30 30N 96 42W
Caledon, *S. Africa* **96** 34 14 S 19 26 E
Caledon →, *S. Africa* **96** 30 31 S 26 5 E
Caledon B., *Australia* **72** 12 45 S 137 0 E
Caledonia, *Canada* **108** 43 7N 79 58W
Caledonia, *Mo., U.S.A.* **118** 37 45N 90 46W
Caledonia, *N.Y., U.S.A.* **116** 42 57N 77 54W
Calella, *Spain* **24** 41 37N 2 40 E
Calemba, *Angola* **96** 16 0 S 15 44 E
Calenzana, *France* **21** 42 31N 8 51 E
Calera, La, *Chile* **140** 32 50 S 71 10W
Caleta Olivia, *Argentina* **142** 46 25 S 67 25W
Calexico, *U.S.A.* **125** 32 40N 115 33W
Calf of Man, *I. of Man* **12** 54 4N 4 48W
Calgary, *Canada* **110** 51 0N 114 10W
Calhoun, *U.S.A.* **115** 34 30N 84 55W
Cali, *Colombia* **134** 3 25N 76 35W
Calicut, *India* **51** 11 15N 75 43 E
Caliente, *U.S.A.* **123** 37 36N 114 34W
California, *Mo., U.S.A.* **118** 38 37N 92 30W
California, *Pa., U.S.A.* **116** 40 5N 79 55W
California □, *U.S.A.* **123** 37 25N 120 0W
California, Baja, *Mexico* **126** 32 10N 115 12W
California, Baja, T.N. □, *Mexico* **126** 30 0N 115 0W
California, Baja, T.S. □, *Mexico* **126** 25 50N 111 50W
California, G. de, *Mexico* **126** 27 0N 111 0W
California, Lr. = California, Baja, *Mexico* **126** 32 10N 115 12W
California City, *U.S.A.* **125** 35 7N 117 57W
California Hot Springs, *U.S.A.* **125** 35 51N 118 41W
Călimăneşti, *Romania* **34** 45 14N 24 20 E
Călimani, Munţii, *Romania* **34** 47 12N 25 0 E
Călineşti, *Romania* **34** 45 21N 24 18 E
Calingasta, *Argentina* **140** 31 15 S 69 30W
Calipatria, *U.S.A.* **125** 33 8N 115 30W
Calistoga, *U.S.A.* **124** 38 36N 122 32W
Calitri, *Italy* **29** 40 54N 15 25 E
Calitzdorp, *S. Africa* **96** 33 33 S 21 42 E
Callabonna, L., *Australia* **73** 29 40 S 140 5 E
Callac, *France* **18** 48 25N 3 27W
Callan, *Ireland* **15** 52 33N 7 25W
Callander, *Canada* **108** 46 13N 79 22W
Callander, *U.K.* **14** 56 15N 4 14W
Callantsoog, *Neths.* **16** 52 50N 4 42 E
Callao, *Peru* **136** 12 0 S 77 0W
Callaway, *U.S.A.* **120** 41 20N 99 56W
Callender, *U.S.A.* **118** 42 22N 94 17W
Calles, *Mexico* **127** 23 2N 98 42W
Callide, *Australia* **72** 24 18 S 150 28 E
Calling Lake, *Canada* **110** 55 15N 113 12W
Calliope, *Australia* **72** 24 0 S 151 16 E
Callosa de Ensarriá, *Spain* **25** 38 40N 0 8W
Callosa de Segura, *Spain* **25** 38 7N 0 53W
Calmar, *U.S.A.* **118** 43 11N 91 52W
Calne, *U.K.* **12** 51 26N 2 0W
Calola, *Angola* **95** 16 25 S 17 48 E
Caloona, *Australia* **77** 28 52 S 149 11 E
Calore →, *Italy* **29** 41 11N 14 28 E
Caloundra, *Australia* **73** 26 45 S 153 10 E
Calpe, *Spain* **25** 38 39N 0 3 E
Calpella, *U.S.A.* **124** 39 14N 123 12W
Calpine, *U.S.A.* **124** 39 40N 120 27W
Calstock, *Canada* **104** 49 47N 84 9W
Caltabellotta, *Italy* **28** 37 36N 13 11 E
Caltagirone, *Italy* **29** 37 13N 14 30 E
Caltanissetta, *Italy* **29** 37 30N 14 3 E
Calucinga, *Angola* **95** 11 18 S 16 12 E
Calulo, *Angola* **95** 10 1 S 14 56 E
Calumet, *U.S.A.* **114** 47 14N 88 27W
Calunda, *Angola* **95** 12 7 S 23 36 E
Caluquembe, *Angola* **95** 13 47 S 14 44 E
Caluso, *Italy* **26** 45 18N 7 52 E
Calvados □, *France* **18** 49 5N 0 15W
Calvert, *U.S.A.* **121** 30 59N 96 40W
Calvert →, *Australia* **72** 16 17 S 137 44 E
Calvert Hills, *Australia* **72** 17 15 S 137 20 E
Calvert I., *Canada* **110** 51 30N 128 0W
Calvert Ra., *Australia* **78** 24 0 S 122 30 E
Calvi, *France* **21** 42 34N 8 45 E
Calvillo, *Mexico* **126** 21 51N 102 43W
Calvinia, *S. Africa* **96** 31 28 S 19 45 E
Calw, *W. Germany* **31** 48 43N 8 44 E
Calwa, *U.S.A.* **124** 36 42N 119 46W
Calzada Almuradiel, *Spain* **25** 38 32N 3 28W

Calzada de Calatrava, *Spain* **23** 38 42N 3 46W
Cam →, *U.K.* **13** 52 21N 0 16 E
Cam Lam, *Vietnam* **55** 11 54N 109 10 E
Cam Pha, *Vietnam* **54** 21 7N 107 18 E
Cam Ranh, *Vietnam* **55** 11 54N 109 12 E
Cam Xuyen, *Vietnam* **54** 18 15N 106 0 E
Camabatela, *Angola* **95** 8 20 S 15 26 E
Camacã, *Brazil* **139** 15 24 S 39 30W
Camaçari, *Brazil* **139** 12 41 S 38 18W
Camachigama, L., *Canada* **106** 47 50N 76 19W
Camacho, *Mexico* **126** 24 25N 102 18W
Camacupa, *Angola* **95** 11 58 S 17 22 E
Camaguán, *Venezuela* **134** 8 6N 67 36W
Camagüey, *Cuba* **128** 21 20N 78 0W
Camaiore, *Italy* **26** 43 57N 10 18 E
Camamu, *Brazil* **139** 13 57 S 39 7W
Camaná, *Peru* **136** 16 30 S 72 50W
Camanche, *U.S.A.* **118** 41 47N 90 15W
Camanche Res., *U.S.A.* **124** 38 16N 120 51W
Camanongue, *Angola* **95** 11 24 S 20 17 E
Camaquã →, *Brazil* **141** 31 17 S 51 47W
Camararé →, *Brazil* **137** 12 15 S 58 55W
Camarat, C., *France* **21** 43 12N 6 41 E
Camaret, *France* **18** 48 16N 4 37W
Camargo, *Bolivia* **137** 20 38 S 65 15W
Camargue, *France* **21** 43 34N 4 34 E
Camarillo, *U.S.A.* **125** 34 13N 119 2W
Camariñas, *Spain* **22** 43 8N 9 12W
Camarón, C., *Honduras* **128** 16 0N 85 0W
Camarones, *Argentina* **142** 44 50 S 65 40W
Camarones, B., *Argentina* **142** 44 45 S 65 35W
Camas, *U.S.A.* **124** 45 35N 122 24W
Camas Valley, *U.S.A.* **122** 43 0N 123 46W
Camaxilo, *Angola* **95** 8 21 S 18 56 E
Cambados, *Spain* **22** 42 31N 8 49W
Cambalong, *Australia* **75** 36 49 S 149 7 E
Cambamba, *Angola* **95** 8 53 S 14 44 E
Cambará, *Brazil* **141** 23 2 S 50 5W
Cambay = Khambhat, *India* **48** 22 23N 72 33 E
Cambil, *Spain* **25** 37 40N 3 33W
Cambo-les-Bains, *France* **20** 43 22N 1 23W
Cambodia ■, *Asia* **54** 12 15N 105 0 E
Camborne, *U.K.* **13** 50 13N 5 18W
Cambrai, *France* **19** 50 11N 3 14 E
Cambria, *U.S.A.* **124** 35 39N 121 6W
Cambrian Mts., *U.K.* **13** 52 25N 3 52W
Cambridge, *Canada* **108** 43 23N 80 15W
Cambridge, *Jamaica* **128** 18 18N 77 54W
Cambridge, *N.Z.* **80** 37 54 S 175 29 E
Cambridge, *U.K.* **13** 52 13N 0 8 E
Cambridge, *Idaho, U.S.A.* **122** 44 36N 116 40W
Cambridge, *Ill., U.S.A.* **118** 41 18N 90 12W
Cambridge, *Iowa, U.S.A.* **118** 41 54N 93 32W
Cambridge, *Mass., U.S.A.* **117** 42 20N 71 8W
Cambridge, *Md., U.S.A.* **114** 38 33N 76 2W
Cambridge, *Minn., U.S.A.* **120** 45 34N 93 15W
Cambridge, *N.Y., U.S.A.* **117** 43 2N 73 22W
Cambridge, *Nebr., U.S.A.* **120** 40 20N 100 12W
Cambridge, *Ohio, U.S.A.* **116** 40 1N 81 35W
Cambridge Bay, *Canada* **102** 69 10N 105 0W
Cambridge City, *U.S.A.* **119** 39 49N 85 10W
Cambridge Gulf, *Australia* **78** 14 55 S 128 15 E
Cambridge Springs, *U.S.A.* **116** 41 47N 80 4W
Cambridgeshire □, *U.K.* **13** 52 12N 0 7 E
Cambrils, *Spain* **24** 41 8N 1 3 E
Cambuci, *Brazil* **139** 21 35 S 41 55W
Camden, *Australia* **76** 34 1 S 150 43 E
Camden, *Ala., U.S.A.* **115** 31 59N 87 15W
Camden, *Ark., U.S.A.* **121** 33 40N 92 50W
Camden, *Maine, U.S.A.* **105** 44 14N 69 6W
Camden, *N.J., U.S.A.* **117** 39 57N 75 7W
Camden, *Ohio, U.S.A.* **119** 39 38N 84 39W
Camden, *S.C., U.S.A.* **115** 34 17N 80 34W
Camden Sound, *Australia* **78** 15 27 S 124 25 E
Camdenton, *U.S.A.* **118** 38 1N 92 45W
Camembert, *France* **18** 48 53N 0 10 E
Cámeri, *Italy* **26** 45 30N 8 40 E
Camerino, *Italy* **27** 43 10N 13 4 E
Cameron, *Ariz., U.S.A.* **123** 35 55N 111 31W
Cameron, *La., U.S.A.* **121** 29 50N 93 18W
Cameron, *Mo., U.S.A.* **118** 39 42N 94 14W
Cameron, *Tex., U.S.A.* **121** 30 53N 97 0W
Cameron Falls, *Canada* **104** 49 8N 88 19W
Cameron Highlands, *Malaysia* **55** 4 27N 101 22 E
Cameron Hills, *Canada* **110** 59 48N 118 0W
Cameron Mts., *N.Z.* **81** 46 1 S 167 0 E
Cameroon ■, *Africa* **94** 6 0N 12 30 E
Camerota, *Italy* **29** 40 2N 15 21 E
Cameroun →, *Cameroon* **91** 4 0N 9 35 E
Cameroun, Mt., *Cameroon* **91** 4 13N 9 10 E
Cametá, *Brazil* **138** 2 12 S 49 30W
Caminha, *Portugal* **22** 41 50N 8 50W
Camino, *U.S.A.* **124** 38 47N 120 40W
Camira Creek, *Australia* **77** 29 15 S 152 58 E
Camiranga, *Brazil* **138** 1 48 S 46 17W
Camiri, *Bolivia* **137** 20 3 S 63 31W
Camissombo, *Angola* **95** 8 7 S 20 38 E
Cammal, *U.S.A.* **116** 41 24N 77 28W
Camocim, *Brazil* **138** 2 55 S 40 50W
Camogli, *Italy* **26** 44 21N 9 9 E
Camooweal, *Australia* **72** 19 56 S 138 7 E
Camopi, *Fr. Guiana* **135** 3 12N 52 17W
Camopi →, *Fr. Guiana* **135** 3 10N 52 20W
Camp Borden, *Canada* **108** 44 18N 79 56W
Camp Crook, *U.S.A.* **120** 45 36N 103 59W
Camp Nelson, *U.S.A.* **125** 36 8N 118 39W
Camp Point, *U.S.A.* **118** 40 3N 91 4W
Camp Wood, *U.S.A.* **121** 29 41N 100 0W
Campagna, *Italy* **29** 40 40N 15 5 E
Campana, *Argentina* **140** 34 10 S 58 55W
Campana, I., *Chile* **142** 48 20 S 75 20W
Campanario, *Spain* **23** 38 52N 5 36W
Campania □, *Italy* **29** 40 50N 14 45 E
Campaspe →, *Australia* **74** 36 13 S 144 45 E
Campbell, *S. Africa* **96** 28 48 S 23 44 E
Campbell, *Calif., U.S.A.* **124** 37 17N 121 57W
Campbell, *Ohio, U.S.A.* **116** 41 5N 80 36W
Campbell, C., *N.Z.* **81** 41 47 S 174 18 E
Campbell I., *Pac. Oc.* **66** 52 30 S 169 0 E
Campbell L., *Canada* **111** 63 14N 106 55W
Campbell River, *Canada* **110** 50 5N 125 20W
Campbell Town, *Australia* **72** 41 52 S 147 30 E
Campbellford, *Canada* **109** 44 18N 77 48W
Campbellpur, *Pakistan* **48** 33 46N 72 26 E
Campbell's Bay, *Canada* **106** 45 44N 76 36W
Campbells Creek, *Australia* **74** 37 6 S 144 12 E
Campbellsburg, *U.S.A.* **119** 38 39N 86 16W
Campbellsville, *U.S.A.* **114** 37 23N 85 21W
Campbellton, *Canada* **105** 47 57N 66 43W
Campbelltown, *Australia* **76** 34 4 S 150 49 E
Campbeltown, *U.K.* **14** 55 25N 5 36W
Campeche, *Mexico* **127** 19 50N 90 32W
Campeche □, *Mexico* **127** 19 50N 90 32W
Campeche, B. de, *Mexico* **127** 19 30N 93 0W
Camperdown, *Australia* **74** 38 14 S 143 9 E
Camperville, *Canada* **111** 51 59N 100 9W
Campi Salentina, *Italy* **29** 40 22N 18 2 E
Campidano, *Italy* **28** 39 30N 8 40 E
Campíglia Maríttima, *Italy* **26** 43 4N 10 37 E
Campillo de Altobuey, *Spain* **24** 39 36N 1 49W
Campillo de Llerena, *Spain* **23** 38 30N 5 50W
Campillos, *Spain* **23** 37 4N 4 51W
Campiña, La, *Spain* **23** 37 45N 4 45W
Campina Grande, *Brazil* **138** 7 20 S 35 47W
Campina Verde, *Brazil* **139** 19 31 S 49 28W
Campinas, *Brazil* **141** 22 50 S 47 0W
Campine, *Belgium* **17** 51 8N 5 20 E
Campli, *Italy* **27** 42 44N 13 40 E
Campo, *Cameroon* **94** 2 22N 9 50 E
Campo, *Spain* **24** 42 25N 0 24 E
Campo Belo, *Brazil* **139** 20 52 S 45 16W
Campo de Criptana, *Spain* **25** 39 24N 3 7W
Campo de Diauarum, *Brazil* **137** 11 12 S 53 14W
Campo de Gibraltar, *Spain* **23** 36 15N 5 25W
Campo Flórido, *Brazil* **139** 19 47 S 48 35W
Campo Formoso, *Brazil* **138** 10 30 S 40 20W
Campo Grande, *Brazil* **137** 20 25 S 54 40W
Campo Maíor, *Brazil* **138** 4 50 S 42 12W
Campo Maior, *Portugal* **23** 38 59N 7 7W
Campo Mourão, *Brazil* **141** 24 3 S 52 22W
Campo Túres, *Italy* **27** 46 53N 11 55 E
Campoalegre, *Colombia* **134** 2 41N 75 20W
Campobasso, *Italy* **29** 41 34N 14 40 E
Campobello di Licata, *Italy* **28** 37 16N 13 55 E
Campobello di Mazara, *Italy* **28** 37 38N 12 45 E
Campofelice, *Italy* **28** 37 54N 13 53 E
Camporeale, *Italy* **28** 37 53N 13 3 E
Campos, *Brazil* **139** 21 50 S 41 20W
Campos Altos, *Brazil* **139** 19 47 S 46 10W
Campos Belos, *Brazil* **139** 13 10 S 47 3W
Campos del Puerto, *Spain* **25** 39 26N 3 1 E
Campos Novos, *Brazil* **141** 27 21 S 51 50W
Campos Sales, *Brazil* **138** 7 4 S 40 23W
Camprodón, *Spain* **24** 42 19N 2 23 E
Campton, *U.S.A.* **119** 37 44N 83 33W
Camptonville, *U.S.A.* **124** 39 27N 121 3W
Campuya →, *Peru* **134** 1 40 S 73 30W
Camrose, *Canada* **110** 53 0N 112 50W
Camsell Portage, *Canada* **111** 59 37N 109 15W
Can Gio, *Vietnam* **55** 10 25N 106 58 E
Can Tho, *Vietnam* **55** 10 2N 105 46 E
Canaan, *U.S.A.* **117** 42 1N 73 20W
Canada ■, *N. Amer.* **102** 60 0N 100 0W
Cañada de Gómez, *Argentina* **140** 32 40 S 61 30W
Canadian, *U.S.A.* **121** 35 56N 100 25W
Canadian →, *U.S.A.* **121** 35 27N 95 3W
Çanakkale, *Turkey* **46** 40 8N 26 30 E
Çanakkale Boğazı, *Turkey* **46** 40 3N 26 12 E
Canal Flats, *Canada* **110** 50 10N 115 48W
Canala, *N. Cal.* **68** 21 32 S 165 57 E
Canalejas, *Argentina* **140** 35 15 S 66 34W
Canals, *Argentina* **140** 33 35 S 62 53W
Canals, *Spain* **25** 38 58N 0 35W
Canandaigua, *U.S.A.* **116** 42 55N 77 18W
Cananea, *Mexico* **126** 31 0N 110 20W
Cañar, *Ecuador* **134** 2 33 S 78 56W
Cañar □, *Ecuador* **134** 2 30 S 79 0W
Canarias, Is., *Atl. Oc.* **25** 28 30N 16 0W
Canarreos, Arch. de los, *Cuba* **128** 21 35N 81 40W
Canary Is. = Canarias, Is., *Atl. Oc.* **25** 28 30N 16 0W
Canastra, Serra da, *Brazil* **139** 20 0 S 46 20W
Canatlán, *Mexico* **126** 24 31N 104 47W
Canaveral, C., *U.S.A.* **115** 28 28N 80 31W
Cañaveras, *Spain* **24** 40 27N 2 24W
Canavieiras, *Brazil* **139** 15 39 S 39 0W
Canbelego, *Australia* **73** 31 32 S 146 18 E
Canberra, *Australia* **76** 35 15 S 149 8 E
Canby, *Calif., U.S.A.* **122** 41 26N 120 58W
Canby, *Minn., U.S.A.* **120** 44 44N 96 15W
Canby, *Oreg., U.S.A.* **124** 45 16N 122 42W
Cancale, *France* **18** 48 40N 1 50W
Canche →, *France* **19** 50 31N 1 39 E
Canchyuaya, Cordillera de, *Peru* **136** 7 30 S 74 0W
Cancún, *Mexico* **127** 21 8N 86 44W
Candala, *Somali Rep.* **98** 11 30N 49 58 E
Candarave, *Peru* **136** 17 15 S 70 13W
Candas, *Spain* **22** 43 35N 5 45W
Candé, *France* **18** 47 34N 1 0W
Candeias →, *Brazil* **137** 8 39 S 63 31W
Candela, *Italy* **29** 41 8N 15 31 E
Candelaria, *Argentina* **141** 27 29 S 55 44W
Candelaria, Pta. de la, *Spain* **22** 43 45N 8 0W
Candeleda, *Spain* **22** 40 10N 5 14W
Candelo, *Australia* **75** 36 47 S 149 43 E
Candia = Iráklion, *Greece* **35** 35 20N 25 12 E
Candia, Sea of = Crete, Sea of, *Greece* **35** 36 0N 25 0 E
Cândido de Abreu, *Brazil* **139** 24 35 S 51 20W
Cândido Mendes, *Brazil* **138** 1 27 S 45 43W
Candle L., *Canada* **111** 53 50N 105 18W
Candlemas I., *Antarctica* **143** 57 3 S 26 40W
Cando, *U.S.A.* **120** 48 30N 99 14W
Canea = Khaniá, *Greece* **35** 35 30N 24 4 E
Canela, *Brazil* **138** 10 15 S 48 25W
Canelli, *Italy* **26** 44 44N 8 18 E
Canelones, *Uruguay* **141** 34 32 S 56 17W
Canet-Plage, *France* **20** 42 41N 3 2 E
Cañete, *Chile* **140** 37 50 S 73 30W
Cañete, *Peru* **136** 13 8 S 76 30W
Cañete, *Spain* **24** 40 3N 1 54W
Cañete de las Torres, *Spain* **23** 37 53N 4 19W
Canfranc, *Spain* **24** 42 42N 0 31W
Cangai, *Australia* **77** 29 30 S 152 30 E
Cangamba, *Angola* **95** 13 40 S 19 54 E
Cangandala, *Angola* **95** 9 45 S 16 33 E
Cangas, *Spain* **22** 42 16N 8 47W
Cangas de Narcea, *Spain* **22** 43 10N 6 32W
Cangas de Onís, *Spain* **22** 43 21N 5 8W
Cangoa, *Angola* **95** 13 8 S 18 30 E
Cangombo, *Angola* **95** 14 24 S 19 59 E
Cangongo, *Angola* **95** 9 24 S 17 30 E
Canguaretama, *Brazil* **138** 6 20 S 35 5W
Canguçu, *Brazil* **141** 31 22 S 52 43W
Cangxi, *China* **58** 31 47N 105 59 E
Cangyuan, *China* **58** 23 12N 99 14 E
Cangzhou, *China* **60** 38 19N 116 52 E
Canhoca, *Angola* **95** 9 15 S 14 41 E
Cani, I., *Tunisia* **86** 36 21N 10 5 E
Canicattì, *Italy* **28** 37 21N 13 50 E
Canicattini, *Italy* **29** 37 1N 15 3 E
Canim Lake, *Canada* **110** 51 47N 120 54W
Canindé, *Brazil* **138** 4 22 S 39 19W
Canindé →, *Brazil* **138** 6 15 S 42 52W
Canipaan, *Phil.* **56** 8 33N 117 15 E
Canisteo, *U.S.A.* **116** 42 17N 77 37W
Canisteo →, *U.S.A.* **116** 42 5N 77 8W
Cañitas, *Mexico* **126** 23 36N 102 43W
Cañiza, La, *Spain* **22** 42 13N 8 16W
Cañizal, *Spain* **22** 41 12N 5 22W
Canjáyar, *Spain* **25** 37 1N 2 44W
Canjinge, *Angola* **95** 10 12 S 21 17 E
Çankırı, *Turkey* **46** 40 40N 33 37 E
Cankuzo, *Burundi* **92** 3 10 S 30 31 E
Canmore, *Canada* **110** 51 7N 115 18W
Cann →, *Australia* **75** 37 44 S 149 7 E
Cann River, *Australia* **75** 37 35 S 149 7 E
Canna, *U.K.* **14** 57 3N 6 33W
Cannanore, *India* **51** 11 53N 75 27 E
Cannelton, *U.S.A.* **119** 37 55N 86 45W
Cannes, *France* **21** 43 32N 7 0 E
Canning Town = Port Canning, *India* **49** 22 23N 88 40 E
Cannington, *Canada* **109** 44 20N 79 2W
Cannock, *U.K.* **12** 52 42N 2 2W
Cannon Ball →, *U.S.A.* **120** 46 20N 100 38W
Cannondale, Mt., *Australia* **72** 25 13 S 148 57 E
Caño Colorado, *Colombia* **134** 2 18N 68 22W
Canoas, *Brazil* **141** 29 56 S 51 11W
Canoe L., *Canada* **111** 55 10N 108 15W
Canon City, *U.S.A.* **120** 38 27N 105 14W
Canora, *Canada* **111** 51 40N 102 30W
Canosa di Púglia, *Italy* **29** 41 13N 16 4 E
Canourgue, Le, *France* **20** 44 26N 3 13 E
Canowindra, *Australia* **76** 33 35 S 148 38 E
Canso, *Canada* **105** 45 20N 61 0W
Canta, *Peru* **136** 11 29 S 76 37W
Cantabria □, *Spain* **22** 43 10N 4 0W
Cantabria, Sierra de, *Spain* **24** 42 40N 2 30W
Cantabrian Mts. = Cantábrica, Cordillera, *Spain* **22** 43 0N 5 10W
Cantábrica, Cordillera, *Spain* **22** 43 0N 5 10W
Cantal □, *France* **20** 45 5N 2 45 E
Cantal, Plomb du, *France* **20** 45 3N 2 45 E
Cantanhede, *Portugal* **22** 40 20N 8 36W
Cantaura, *Venezuela* **135** 9 19N 64 21W
Cantavieja, *Spain* **24** 40 31N 0 25W
Canterbury, *Australia* **72** 25 23 S 141 53 E
Canterbury, *U.K.* **13** 51 17N 1 5 E
Canterbury □, *N.Z.* **81** 43 45 S 171 19 E
Canterbury Bight, *N.Z.* **81** 44 16 S 171 55 E
Canterbury Plains, *N.Z.* **81** 43 55 S 171 22 E
Cantil, *U.S.A.* **125** 35 18N 117 58W
Cantillana, *Spain* **23** 37 36N 5 50W
Canto do Buriti, *Brazil* **138** 8 7 S 42 58W
Canton = Guangzhou, *China* **59** 23 5N 113 10 E
Canton, *Ga., U.S.A.* **115** 34 13N 84 29W
Canton, *Ill., U.S.A.* **118** 40 32N 90 0W
Canton, *Miss., U.S.A.* **121** 32 40N 90 1W
Canton, *Mo., U.S.A.* **118** 40 10N 91 33W
Canton, *N.Y., U.S.A.* **117** 44 32N 75 3W
Canton, *Ohio, U.S.A.* **116** 40 47N 81 22W
Canton, *Okla., U.S.A.* **121** 36 5N 98 36W
Canton, *S. Dak., U.S.A.* **120** 43 20N 96 35W
Canton L., *U.S.A.* **121** 36 12N 98 40W
Cantù, *Italy* **26** 45 44N 9 8 E
Canudos, *Brazil* **137** 7 13 S 58 5W
Canumã, *Amazonas, Brazil* **135** 4 2 S 59 4W
Canumã, *Amazonas, Brazil* **137** 6 8 S 60 10W
Canumã →, *Brazil* **137** 3 55 S 59 10W
Canungra, *Australia* **77** 28 1 S 153 10 E
Canutama, *Brazil* **137** 6 30 S 64 20W
Canutillo, *U.S.A.* **123** 31 58N 106 36W
Canyon, *Tex., U.S.A.* **121** 35 0N 101 57W
Canyon, *Wyo., U.S.A.* **122** 44 43N 110 36W
Canyonlands Nat. Park, *U.S.A.* **123** 38 25N 109 30W
Canyonville, *U.S.A.* **122** 42 55N 123 14W
Canzo, *Italy* **26** 45 54N 9 18 E
Cao Bang, *Vietnam* **54** 22 40N 106 15 E
Cao He →, *China* **61** 40 10N 124 32 E
Cao Lanh, *Vietnam* **55** 10 27N 105 38 E
Cao Xian, *China* **60** 34 50N 115 35 E
Cáorle, *Italy* **27** 45 36N 12 51 E
Cap-aux-Meules, *Canada* **105** 47 23N 61 52W
Cap-Chat, *Canada* **105** 49 6N 66 40W
Cap-de-la-Madeleine, *Canada* **107** 46 22N 72 31W
Cap-Haïtien, *Haiti* **129** 19 40N 72 20W
Cap-St-Ignace, *Canada* **107** 47 2N 70 28W
Cap St.-Jacques = Vung Tau, *Vietnam* **55** 10 21N 107 4 E
Capa, *Vietnam* **54** 22 21N 103 50 E
Capa Stilo, *Italy* **29** 38 25N 16 35 E
Capáccio, *Italy* **29** 40 26N 15 4 E
Capaia, *Angola* **95** 8 27 S 20 13 E
Capanaparo →, *Venezuela* **134** 7 1N 67 7W
Capanema, *Brazil* **138** 1 12 S 47 11W
Caparo →, *Barinas, Venezuela* **134** 7 46N 70 23W
Caparo →, *Bolívar, Venezuela* **135** 7 30N 64 0W
Capatárida, *Venezuela* **134** 11 11N 70 37W
Capbreton, *France* **20** 43 39N 1 26W
Capdenac, *France* **20** 44 34N 2 5 E
Cape →, *Australia* **72** 20 49 S 146 51 E
Cape Barren I., *Australia* **72** 40 25 S 148 15 E
Cape Breton Highlands Nat. Park, *Canada* **105** 46 50N 60 40W
Cape Breton I., *Canada* **105** 46 0N 60 30W
Cape Charles, *U.S.A.* **114** 37 15N 75 59W
Cape Clear, *Australia* **74** 37 47 S 143 36 E
Cape Coast, *Ghana* **91** 5 5N 1 15W
Cape Dorset, *Canada* **103** 64 14N 76 32W
Cape Dyer, *Canada* **103** 66 30N 61 22W
Cape Fear →, *U.S.A.* **115** 34 30N 78 25W
Cape Girardeau, *U.S.A.* **121** 37 20N 89 30W
Cape Jervis, *Australia* **73** 35 40 S 138 5 E
Cape May, *U.S.A.* **114** 39 1N 74 53W
Cape Palmas, *Liberia* **90** 4 25N 7 49W

Cape Patterson, Australia 74 38 40 S 145 37 E
Cape Preston, Australia 78 20 51 S 116 12 E
Cape Province □, S. Africa 96 32 0 S 23 0 E
Cape Tormentine, Canada 105 46 8N 63 47W
Cape Town, S. Africa 96 33 55 S 18 22 E
Cape Verde Is. ■, Atl. Oc. 4 17 10N 25 20W
Cape Vincent, U.S.A. 117 44 9N 76 21W
Cape York Peninsula, Australia 72 12 0 S 142 30 E
Capela, Brazil 138 10 30 S 37 0W
Capela de Campo, Brazil 138 4 40 S 41 55W
Capele, Angola 95 13 39 S 14 53 E
Capelinha, Brazil 139 17 42 S 42 31W
Capella, Australia 72 23 2 S 148 1 E
Capella, Mt., Papua N. G. 69 5 4 S 141 8 E
Capelle, La, France 19 49 59N 3 50 E
Capenda Camulemba, Angola 95 9 24 S 18 27 E
Capendu, France 20 43 11N 2 31 E
Capernaum = Kefar Nahum, Israel 44 32 54N 35 34 E
Capertree, Australia 76 33 6 S 149 58 E
Capestang, France 20 43 20N 3 2 E
Capim, Brazil 138 1 41 S 47 47W
Capim →, Brazil 138 1 40 S 47 47W
Capinópolis, Brazil 139 18 41 S 49 35W
Capinota, Bolivia 136 17 43 S 66 14W
Capitachouane →, Canada 106 47 40N 76 47W
Capitan, U.S.A. 123 33 33N 105 41W
Capitán Aracena, I., Chile 142 54 10 S 71 20W
Capitan Arturo Prat, Antarctica 143 63 0 S 60 15W
Capitán Pastene, Chile 142 38 13 S 73 1W
Capitola, U.S.A. 124 36 59N 121 57W
Capivara, Serra da, Brazil 139 14 35 S 45 0W
Capizzi, Italy 29 37 50N 14 26 E
Čapljina, Yugoslavia 33 43 10N 17 43 E
Capoche →, Mozam. 93 15 35 S 33 0 E
Capoeira, Brazil 137 5 37 S 59 33W
Capolo, Angola 95 10 22 S 14 7 E
Capraia, Italy 26 43 2N 9 50 E
Caprarola, Italy 27 42 21N 12 11 E
Capreol, Canada 108 46 43N 80 56W
Caprera, Italy 28 41 12N 9 28 E
Capri, Italy 29 40 34N 14 15 E
Capricorn Group, Australia 72 23 30 S 151 55 E
Capricorn Ra., Australia 78 23 20 S 116 50 E
Caprino Veronese, Italy 26 45 37N 10 47 E
Caprivi Strip, Namibia 96 18 0 S 23 0 E
Captainganj, India 49 26 55N 83 45 E
Captain's Flat, Australia 76 35 35 S 149 27 E
Captieux, France 20 44 18N 0 16W
Cápua, Italy 29 41 7N 14 15 E
Caquetá □, Colombia 134 1 0N 74 0W
Caquetá →, Colombia 134 1 15 S 69 15W
Carabobo, Venezuela 134 10 2N 68 5W
Carabobo □, Venezuela 134 10 10N 68 5W
Carabost, Australia 76 35 35 S 147 43 E
Caracal, Romania 34 44 8N 24 22 E
Caracaraí, Brazil 135 1 50N 61 8W
Caracas, Venezuela 134 10 30N 66 55W
Caracol, Brazil 138 9 15 S 43 22W
Caracollo, Bolivia 136 17 39 S 67 10W
Caradoc, Australia 73 30 35 S 143 5 E
Caragabal, Australia 76 33 49 S 147 45 E
Caráglio, Italy 26 44 25N 7 25 E
Carahue, Chile 142 38 43 S 73 12W
Caraí, Brazil 139 17 12 S 41 42W
Carajás, Serra dos, Brazil 138 6 0 S 51 30W
Caramut, Australia 74 37 56 S 142 31 E
Caranapatuba, Brazil 137 6 38 S 62 34W
Carandaiti, Bolivia 137 20 45 S 63 4W
Carangola, Brazil 139 20 44 S 42 5W
Carani, Australia 79 30 57 S 116 28 E
Caransebeş, Romania 34 45 28N 22 18 E
Carantec, France 18 48 40N 3 55W
Caraparaná →, Colombia 134 1 45 S 73 13W
Carapelle →, Italy 29 41 3N 15 55 E
Caras, Peru 136 9 3 S 77 47W
Caratasca, L., Honduras 128 15 20N 83 40W
Caratinga, Brazil 139 19 50 S 42 10W
Caraúbas, Brazil 138 5 43 S 37 33W
Caravaca, Spain 25 38 8N 1 52W
Caravággio, Italy 26 45 30N 9 39 E
Caravelas, Brazil 139 17 45 S 39 15W
Caraveli, Peru 136 15 45 S 73 25W
Caràzinho, Brazil 141 28 16 S 52 46W
Carballino, Spain 22 42 26N 8 5W
Carballo, Spain 22 43 13N 8 41W
Carberry, Canada 111 49 50N 99 25W
Carbia, Spain 22 42 48N 8 14W
Carbó, Mexico 126 29 42N 110 58W
Carbon, Canada 110 51 30N 113 9W
Carbonara, C., Italy 28 39 8N 9 30 E
Carbondale, Colo., U.S.A. 122 39 30N 107 10W
Carbondale, Ill., U.S.A. 118 37 45N 89 10W
Carbondale, Pa., U.S.A. 117 41 37N 75 30W
Carbonear, Canada 105 47 42N 53 13W
Carboneras, Spain 25 37 0N 1 53W
Carboneras de Guadazaón, Spain 24 39 54N 1 50W
Carbonia, Italy 28 39 10N 8 30 E
Carcabuey, Spain 23 37 27N 4 17W
Carcagente, Spain 25 39 8N 0 28W
Carcajou, Canada 110 57 47N 117 6W
Carcasse, C., Haiti 129 18 30N 74 28W
Carcassonne, France 20 43 13N 2 20 E
Carche, Spain 25 38 26N 1 9W
Carchi □, Ecuador 134 0 45N 78 0W
Carcoar, Australia 76 33 36 S 149 8 E
Carcross, Canada 102 60 13N 134 45W
Cardabia, Australia 78 23 2 S 113 48 E
Cardamon Hills, India 51 9 30N 77 15 E
Cárdenas, Cuba 128 23 0N 81 30W
Cárdenas, San Luis Potosí, Mexico 127 22 0N 99 41W
Cárdenas, Tabasco, Mexico 127 17 59N 93 21W
Cardenete, Spain 24 39 46N 1 41W
Cardiel, L., Argentina 142 48 55 S 71 10W
Cardiff, U.K. 13 51 28N 3 11W
Cardiff-by-the-Sea, U.S.A. 125 33 1N 117 17W
Cardigan, U.K. 13 52 6N 4 41W
Cardigan B., U.K. 13 52 30N 4 30W
Cardinal, Canada 109 44 47N 75 23W
Cardón, Punta, Venezuela 134 11 37N 70 14W
Cardona, Spain 24 41 56N 1 40 E
Cardona, Uruguay 140 33 53 S 57 18W
Cardoner →, Spain 24 41 41N 1 51 E
Cardross, Canada 111 49 50N 105 40W
Cardston, Canada 110 49 15N 113 20W
Cardwell, Australia 72 18 14 S 146 2 E
Careen L., Canada 111 57 0N 108 11W
Carei, Romania 34 47 40N 22 29 E
Careiro, Brazil 135 3 12 S 59 45W
Careme, Indonesia 57 6 55 S 108 27 E
Carentan, France 18 49 19N 1 15W
Carey, Idaho, U.S.A. 122 43 19N 113 58W
Carey, Ohio, U.S.A. 119 40 58N 83 22W
Carey, L., Australia 79 29 0 S 122 15 E
Carey L., Canada 111 62 12N 102 55W
Careysburg, Liberia 90 6 34N 10 30W
Cargados Garajos, Ind. Oc. 53 17 0 S 59 0 E
Cargèse, France 21 42 7N 8 35 E
Cargo, Australia 76 33 25 S 148 48 E
Carhaix-Plouguer, France 18 48 18N 3 36W
Carhuamayo, Peru 136 10 51 S 76 4W
Carhuas, Peru 136 9 15 S 77 39W
Carhué, Argentina 140 37 10 S 62 50W
Cariacica, Brazil 139 20 16 S 40 25W
Cariango, Angola 95 10 37 S 15 20 E
Caribbean Sea, W. Indies 129 15 0N 75 0W
Cariboo Mts., Canada 110 53 0N 121 0W
Caribou, U.S.A. 105 46 55N 68 0W
Caribou →, Man., Canada 111 59 20N 94 44W
Caribou →, N.W.T., Canada 110 61 27N 125 45W
Caribou I., Canada 104 47 22N 85 49W
Caribou Is., Canada 110 61 55N 113 15W
Caribou L., Man., Canada 111 59 21N 96 10W
Caribou L., Ont., Canada 104 50 25N 89 5W
Caribou Mts., Canada 110 59 12N 115 40W
Carichic, Mexico 126 27 56N 107 3W
Carignan, France 19 49 38N 5 10 E
Carignano, Italy 26 44 55N 7 40 E
Carillo, Mexico 126 26 50N 103 55W
Carin, Somali Rep. 98 10 59N 49 13 E
Carinda, Australia 73 30 28 S 147 41 E
Cariñena, Spain 24 41 20N 1 13W
Carinhanha, Brazil 139 14 15 S 44 46W
Carinhanha →, Brazil 139 14 20 S 43 47W
Carini, Italy 28 38 9N 13 10 E
Carinola, Italy 28 41 11N 13 58 E
Caripito, Venezuela 135 10 8N 63 6W
Carisbrook, Australia 74 37 3 S 143 49 E
Caritianas, Brazil 137 9 20 S 63 6W
Carlbrod = Dimitrovgrad, Yugoslavia 33 43 0N 22 48 E
Carlentini, Italy 29 37 15N 15 2 E
Carleton Place, Canada 109 45 8N 76 9W
Carletonville, S. Africa 96 26 23 S 27 22 E
Carlin, U.S.A. 122 40 44N 116 5W
Carlingford, L., Ireland 15 54 0N 6 5W
Carlinville, U.S.A. 118 39 20N 89 55W
Carlisle, U.K. 12 54 54N 2 55W
Carlisle, Ky., U.S.A. 119 38 18N 84 1W
Carlisle, Pa., U.S.A. 116 40 12N 77 10W
Carlit, Pic, France 20 42 35N 1 55 E
Carloforte, Italy 28 39 10N 8 18 E
Carlos Casares, Argentina 140 35 32 S 61 20W
Carlos Chagas, Brazil 139 17 43 S 40 45W
Carlos Tejedor, Argentina 140 35 25 S 62 25W
Carlota, La, Argentina 140 33 30 S 63 20W
Carlow, Ireland 15 52 50N 6 58W
Carlow □, Ireland 15 52 43N 6 50W
Carlsbad, Calif., U.S.A. 125 33 11N 117 25W
Carlsbad, N. Mex., U.S.A. 121 32 20N 104 14W
Carlsruhe, Australia 74 37 16 S 144 30 E
Carlyle, Canada 111 49 40N 102 20W
Carlyle, U.S.A. 120 38 38N 89 23W
Carlyle Resr., U.S.A. 118 38 37N 89 21W
Carmacks, Canada 102 62 5N 136 16W
Carmagnola, Italy 26 44 50N 7 42 E
Carman, Canada 111 49 30N 98 0W
Carmangay, Canada 110 50 10N 113 10W
Carmanville, Canada 105 49 23N 54 19W
Carmarthen, U.K. 13 51 52N 4 20W
Carmarthen B., U.K. 13 51 40N 4 30W
Carmaux, France 20 44 3N 2 10 E
Carmel, Ind., U.S.A. 119 39 59N 86 8W
Carmel, N.Y., U.S.A. 117 41 25N 73 38W
Carmel-by-the-Sea, U.S.A. 124 36 38N 121 55W
Carmel Mt., Israel 44 32 45N 35 3 E
Carmel Valley, U.S.A. 124 36 29N 121 43W
Carmelo, Uruguay 140 34 0 S 58 20W
Carmen, Bolivia 136 11 40 S 67 51W
Carmen, Colombia 134 9 43N 75 8W
Carmen, Paraguay 141 27 13 S 56 12W
Carmen →, Mexico 126 30 42N 106 29W
Carmen, I., Mexico 126 26 0N 111 20W
Carmen de Patagones, Argentina 142 40 50 S 63 0W
Cármenes, Spain 22 42 58N 5 34W
Carmensa, Argentina 140 35 15 S 67 40W
Carmi, U.S.A. 119 38 6N 88 10W
Carmichael, U.S.A. 124 38 38N 121 19W
Carmila, Australia 72 21 55 S 149 24 E
Carmona, Spain 23 37 28N 5 42W
Carnarvon, Queens., Australia 72 24 48 S 147 45 E
Carnarvon, W. Austral., Australia 79 24 51 S 113 42 E
Carnarvon, S. Africa 96 30 56 S 22 8 E
Carnarvon Ra., Queens., Australia 72 25 15 S 148 30 E
Carnarvon Ra., W. Austral., Australia 79 25 20 S 120 45 E
Carnation, U.S.A. 124 47 39N 121 55W
Carnaxide, Portugal 23 38 43N 9 14W
Carndonagh, Ireland 15 55 15N 7 16W
Carnduff, Canada 111 49 10N 101 50W
Carnegie, U.S.A. 116 40 24N 80 4W
Carnegie, L., Australia 79 26 5 S 122 30 E
Carnic Alps = Karnische Alpen, Europe 33 46 36N 13 0 E
Carnot, C.A.R. 94 4 59N 15 56 E
Carnot B., Australia 78 17 20 S 122 15 E
Carnsore Pt., Ireland 15 52 10N 6 20W
Caro, U.S.A. 114 43 29N 83 27W
Caroda, Australia 77 29 59 S 150 22 E
Carol City, U.S.A. 115 25 5N 80 16W
Carolina, Brazil 138 7 10 S 47 30W
Carolina, Puerto Rico 129 18 23N 65 57W
Carolina, S. Africa 97 26 5 S 30 6 E
Carolina, La, Spain 23 38 17N 3 38W
Caroline I., Kiribati 67 9 15 S 150 3W
Caroline Is., Pac. Oc. 66 8 0N 150 0 E
Caroline Pk., N.Z. 81 45 57 S 167 15 E
Caron, Canada 111 50 30N 105 50W
Caroni →, Venezuela 135 8 21N 62 43W
Caroona, Australia 77 31 24 S 150 26 E
Carora, Venezuela 134 10 11N 70 5W
Carovigno, Italy 29 40 42N 17 40 E
Carpathians, Mts., Europe 32 49 30N 21 0 E
Carpaţii Meridionali, Romania 34 45 30N 25 0 E
Carpenédolo, Italy 26 45 22N 10 25 E
Carpentaria, G. of, Australia 72 14 0 S 139 0 E
Carpentaria Downs, Australia 72 18 44 S 144 20 E
Carpentersville, U.S.A. 119 42 6N 88 17W
Carpentras, France 21 44 3N 5 2 E
Carpi, Italy 26 44 47N 10 52 E
Carpina, Brazil 138 7 51 S 35 15W
Carpino, Italy 29 41 50N 15 51 E
Carpinteria, U.S.A. 125 34 25N 119 31W
Carpio, Spain 22 41 13N 5 7W
Carpolac = Morea, Australia 74 36 45 S 141 18 E
Carr Boyd Ra., Australia 78 16 15 S 128 35 E
Carrabelle, U.S.A. 115 29 52N 84 40W
Carrajung, Australia 75 38 22 S 146 44 E
Carranya, Australia 78 19 14 S 127 46 E
Carrara, Italy 26 44 5N 10 7 E
Carrascosa del Campo, Spain 24 40 2N 2 45W
Carrauntoohill, Mt., Ireland 15 52 0N 9 49W
Carretas, Punta, Peru 136 14 12 S 76 17W
Carrick-on-Shannon, Ireland 15 53 57N 8 7W
Carrick-on-Suir, Ireland 15 52 22N 7 30W
Carrickfergus, U.K. 15 54 43N 5 50W
Carrickfergus □, U.K. 15 54 43N 5 49W
Carrickmacross, Ireland 15 54 0N 6 43W
Carrieton, Australia 73 32 25 S 138 31 E
Carrington, U.S.A. 120 47 30N 99 7W
Carrión →, Spain 22 41 53N 4 32W
Carrión de los Condes, Spain 22 42 20N 4 37W
Carrizal Bajo, Chile 140 28 5 S 71 20W
Carrizalillo, Chile 140 29 5 S 71 30W
Carrizo Cr. →, U.S.A. 121 36 30N 103 40W
Carrizo Springs, U.S.A. 121 28 28N 99 50W
Carrizozo, U.S.A. 123 33 40N 105 57W
Carroll, Australia 77 30 58 S 150 27 E
Carroll, U.S.A. 118 42 2N 94 55W
Carrollton, Ga., U.S.A. 115 33 36N 85 5W
Carrollton, Ill., U.S.A. 120 39 20N 90 25W
Carrollton, Ky., U.S.A. 119 38 40N 85 10W
Carrollton, Mo., U.S.A. 118 39 19N 93 24W
Carrollton, Ohio, U.S.A. 116 40 31N 81 9W
Carron →, U.K. 14 57 30N 5 30W
Carron, L., U.K. 14 57 22N 5 35W
Carrot →, Canada 111 53 50N 101 17W
Carrot River, Canada 111 53 17N 103 35W
Carrouges, France 18 48 34N 0 10W
Carruthers, Canada 111 52 52N 109 16W
Çarşamba, Turkey 46 41 15N 36 45 E
Carse of Gowrie, U.K. 14 56 30N 3 10W
Carsoli, Italy 27 42 7N 13 3 E
Carson, Calif., U.S.A. 125 33 48N 118 17W
Carson, U.S.A. 120 46 27N 101 29W
Carson →, U.S.A. 124 39 45N 118 40W
Carson City, Mich., U.S.A. 119 43 11N 84 51W
Carson City, Nev., U.S.A. 124 39 12N 119 46W
Carson Sink, U.S.A. 122 39 50N 118 40W
Carstairs, U.K. 14 55 42N 3 41W
Cartagena, Colombia 134 10 25N 75 33W
Cartagena, Spain 25 37 38N 0 59W
Cartago, Colombia 134 4 45N 75 55W
Cartago, Costa Rica 128 9 50N 85 52W
Cartaxo, Portugal 23 39 10N 8 47W
Cartaya, Spain 23 37 16N 7 9W
Carteret, France 18 49 23N 1 47W
Cartersville, U.S.A. 115 34 11N 84 48W
Carterton, N.Z. 80 41 2 S 175 31 E
Carterville, U.S.A. 118 37 46N 89 5W
Carthage, Ark., U.S.A. 121 34 4N 92 32W
Carthage, Ill., U.S.A. 118 40 25N 91 10W
Carthage, Mo., U.S.A. 121 37 10N 94 20W
Carthage, S. Dak., U.S.A. 120 44 14N 97 38W
Carthage, Tex., U.S.A. 121 32 8N 94 20W
Cartier, Canada 108 46 42N 81 33W
Cartier I., Australia 78 12 31 S 123 29 E
Cartwright, Canada 105 53 41N 56 58W
Caruaru, Brazil 138 8 15 S 35 55W
Carúpano, Venezuela 135 10 39N 63 15W
Carutapera, Brazil 138 1 13 S 46 1W
Caruthersville, U.S.A. 121 36 10N 89 40W
Carvalho, Brazil 135 2 16 S 51 29W
Carvin, France 19 50 30N 2 57 E
Carvoeiro, Brazil 135 1 30 S 61 59W
Carvoeiro, C., Portugal 23 39 21N 9 24W
Carwarp, Australia 74 34 28 S 142 11 E
Casa Branca, Brazil 139 21 46 S 47 4W
Casa Branca, Portugal 23 38 29N 8 12W
Casa Grande, U.S.A. 123 32 53N 111 51W
Casablanca, Chile 140 33 20 S 71 25W
Casablanca, Morocco 84 33 36N 7 36W
Casacalenda, Italy 29 41 45N 14 50 E
Casal di Principe, Italy 29 41 0N 14 8 E
Casalbordino, Italy 27 42 10N 14 34 E
Casale Monferrato, Italy 26 45 8N 8 28 E
Casalmaggiore, Italy 26 44 59N 10 25 E
Casalpusterlengo, Italy 26 45 10N 9 40 E
Casamance →, Senegal 90 12 33N 16 46W
Casamássima, Italy 29 40 58N 16 55 E
Casanare →, Colombia 134 6 2N 69 51W
Casarano, Italy 29 40 0N 18 10 E
Casares, Spain 23 36 27N 5 16W
Casas Grandes, Mexico 126 30 22N 108 0W
Casas Ibañez, Spain 25 39 17N 1 30W
Casasimarro, Spain 25 39 22N 2 3W
Casatejada, Spain 22 39 54N 5 40W
Casavieja, Spain 22 40 17N 4 46W
Cascade, Idaho, U.S.A. 122 44 30N 116 2W
Cascade, Iowa, U.S.A. 118 42 18N 91 0W
Cascade, Mont., U.S.A. 122 47 16N 111 46W
Cascade →, Australia 77 30 15 S 152 48 E
Cascade Locks, U.S.A. 124 45 44N 121 54W
Cascade Pt., N.Z. 81 44 1 S 168 20 E
Cascade Ra., U.S.A. 124 47 0N 121 30W
Cascais, Portugal 23 38 41N 9 25W
Cascavel, Brazil 141 24 57 S 53 28W
Cáscina, Italy 26 43 40N 10 32 E
Caselle Torinese, Italy 26 45 12N 7 39 E
Caserta, Italy 29 41 5N 14 20 E
Casey, Canada 107 47 53N 74 11W
Cashel, Ireland 15 52 31N 7 53W
Cashmere, U.S.A. 122 47 31N 120 30W
Cashmere Downs, Australia 79 28 57 S 119 35 E
Casibare →, Colombia 134 3 48N 72 18W
Casiguran, Phil. 57 16 22N 122 7 E
Casilda, Argentina 140 33 10 S 61 10W
Casino, Australia 77 28 52 S 153 3 E
Casiquiare →, Venezuela 134 2 1N 67 7W
Casitas, Peru 136 3 54 S 80 39W
Caslan, Canada 110 54 38N 112 31W
Čáslav, Czech. 32 49 54N 15 22 E
Casma, Peru 136 9 30 S 78 20W
Casmalia, U.S.A. 125 34 50N 120 32W
Casola Valsenio, Italy 27 44 12N 11 40 E
Cásoli, Italy 27 42 7N 14 18 E
Caspe, Spain 24 41 14N 0 1W
Casper, U.S.A. 122 42 52N 106 20W
Caspian Sea, U.S.S.R. 40 43 0N 50 0 E
Casquets, Chan. Is. 18 49 46N 2 15W

Cass City, *U.S.A.* **114** 43 34N 83 24W
Cass Lake, *U.S.A.* **120** 47 23N 94 38W
Cassá de la Selva, *Spain* **24** 41 53N 2 52 E
Cassai, *Angola* **95** 10 33 S 21 59 E
Cassamba, *Angola* **95** 13 6 S 20 18 E
Cassano Iónio, *Italy* **29** 39 47N 16 20 E
Cassel, *France* **19** 50 48N 2 30 E
Casselman, *Canada* **106** 45 19N 75 5W
Casselton, *U.S.A.* **120** 47 0N 97 15W
Cassiar, *Canada* **110** 59 16N 129 40W
Cassiar Mts., *Canada* **110** 59 30N 130 30W
Cassilândia, *Brazil* **137** 19 9 S 51 45W
Cassilis, *Australia* **77** 32 3 S 149 58 E
Cassinga, *Angola* **95** 15 5 S 16 4 E
Cassino, *Italy* **28** 41 30N 13 50 E
Cassis, *France* **21** 43 14N 5 32 E
Cassoalala, *Angola* **95** 9 30 S 14 22 E
Cassoango, *Angola* **95** 13 42 S 20 56 E
Cassopolis, *U.S.A.* **119** 41 55N 86 1W
Cassunda, *Angola* **95** 10 57 S 21 3 E
Cassville, *Mo., U.S.A.* **121** 36 45N 93 52W
Cassville, *Wis., U.S.A.* **118** 42 43N 90 59W
Cástagneto Carducci, *Italy* **26** 43 9N 10 36 E
Castaic, *U.S.A.* **125** 34 30N 118 38W
Castanhal, *Brazil* **138** 1 18 S 47 55W
Casteau, *Belgium* **17** 50 32N 4 2 E
Castéggio, *Italy* **26** 45 1N 9 8 E
Castejón de Monegros, *Spain* **24** 41 37N 0 15W
Castel di Sangro, *Italy* **27** 41 47N 14 6 E
Castel San Giovanni, *Italy* **26** 45 4N 9 25 E
Castel San Pietro, *Italy* **27** 44 23N 11 30 E
Castelbuono, *Italy* **29** 37 56N 14 4 E
Casteldelfino, *Italy* **26** 44 35N 7 4 E
Castelfiorentino, *Italy* **26** 43 36N 10 58 E
Castelfranco Emília, *Italy* **26** 44 37N 11 2 E
Castelfranco Véneto, *Italy* **27** 45 40N 11 56 E
Casteljaloux, *France* **20** 44 19N 0 6 E
Castellabate, *Italy* **29** 40 18N 14 55 E
Castellammare, G. di, *Italy* **28** 38 5N 12 55 E
Castellammare del Golfo, *Italy* **28** 38 2N 12 53 E
Castellammare di Stábia, *Italy* **29** 40 47N 14 29 E
Castellamonte, *Italy* **26** 45 23N 7 42 E
Castellana Grotte, *Italy* **29** 40 53N 17 10 E
Castellane, *France* **21** 43 50N 6 31 E
Castellaneta, *Italy* **29** 40 40N 16 57 E
Castellar de Santisteban, *Spain* **25** 38 16N 3 8W
Castelleone, *Italy* **26** 45 19N 9 47 E
Castelli, *Argentina* **140** 36 7 S 57 47W
Castelló de Ampurias, *Spain* **24** 42 15N 3 4 E
Castellón □, *Spain* **24** 40 15N 0 5W
Castellón de la Plana, *Spain* **24** 39 58N 0 3W
Castellote, *Spain* **24** 40 48N 0 15W
Castelltersol, *Spain* **24** 41 45N 2 8 E
Castelmáuro, *Italy* **29** 41 50N 14 40 E
Castelnau-de-Médoc, *France* **20** 45 2N 0 48W
Castelnaudary, *France* **20** 43 20N 1 58 E
Castelnovo ne' Monti, *Italy* **26** 44 27N 10 26 E
Castelnuovo di Val di Cécina, *Italy* **26** 43 12N 10 54 E
Castelo, *Brazil* **139** 20 33 S 41 14W
Castelo Branco, *Portugal* **22** 39 50N 7 31W
Castelo Branco □, *Portugal* **22** 39 52N 7 45W
Castelo de Paiva, *Portugal* **22** 41 2N 8 16W
Castelo de Vide, *Portugal* **23** 39 25N 7 27W
Castelo do Piauí, *Brazil* **138** 5 20 S 41 33W
Castelsarrasin, *France* **20** 44 2N 1 7 E
Casteltérmini, *Italy* **28** 37 32N 13 38 E
Castelvetrano, *Italy* **28** 37 40N 12 46 E
Castendo, *Angola* **95** 8 39 S 14 10 E
Casterton, *Australia* **74** 37 30 S 141 30 E
Castets, *France* **20** 43 52N 1 6W
Castiglione del Lago, *Italy* **27** 43 7N 12 3 E
Castiglione della Pescáia, *Italy* **26** 42 46N 10 53 E
Castiglione della Stiviere, *Italy* **26** 45 23N 10 30 E
Castiglione Fiorentino, *Italy* **27** 43 20N 11 55 E
Castilblanco, *Spain* **23** 39 17N 5 5W
Castilla, *Peru* **136** 5 12 S 80 38W
Castilla, Playa de, *Spain* **23** 37 0N 6 33W
Castilla La Mancha □, *Spain* **23** 39 30N 3 30W
Castilla La Nueva, *Spain* **23** 39 45N 3 20W
Castilla La Vieja, *Spain* **22** 41 55N 4 0W
Castilla y Leon □, *Spain* **22** 42 0N 5 0W
Castillon, Barr. de, *France* **21** 43 53N 6 33 E
Castillon-en-Couserans, *France* **20** 42 56N 1 1 E
Castillon-la-Bataille, *France* **20** 44 51N 0 2W
Castillonès, *France* **20** 44 39N 0 37 E
Castillos, *Uruguay* **141** 34 12 S 53 52W
Castle Dale, *U.S.A.* **122** 39 11N 111 1W
Castle Douglas, *U.K.* **14** 54 57N 3 57W
Castle Point, *N.Z.* **80** 40 54 S 176 15 E
Castle Rock, *Colo., U.S.A.* **120** 39 26N 104 50W
Castle Rock, *Wash., U.S.A.* **124** 46 20N 122 58W
Castlebar, *Ireland* **15** 53 52N 9 17W
Castleblaney, *Ireland* **15** 54 7N 6 44W
Castlecliff, *N.Z.* **80** 39 57 S 174 59 E
Castlegar, *Canada* **110** 49 20N 117 40W
Castlemaine, *Australia* **74** 37 2 S 144 12 E
Castlereagh, *Ireland* **15** 53 47N 8 30W
Castlereagh □, *U.K.* **15** 54 33N 5 53W
Castlereagh →, *Australia* **73** 30 12 S 147 32 E
Castlereagh B., *Australia* **72** 12 10 S 135 10 E
Castletown, *I. of Man* **12** 54 4N 4 40W
Castletown Bearhaven, *Ireland* **15** 51 40N 9 54W
Castlevale, *Australia* **72** 24 30 S 146 48 E
Castor, *Canada* **110** 52 15N 111 50W
Castres, *France* **20** 43 37N 2 13 E
Castricum, *Neths.* **16** 52 33N 4 40 E
Castries, *St. Lucia* **129** 14 0N 60 50W
Castril, *Spain* **25** 37 48N 2 46W
Castro, *Brazil* **141** 24 45 S 50 0W
Castro, *Chile* **142** 42 30 S 73 50W
Castro Alves, *Brazil* **139** 12 46 S 39 33W
Castro del Río, *Spain* **23** 37 41N 4 29W
Castro Marim, *Portugal* **23** 37 13N 7 26W
Castro Urdiales, *Spain* **24** 43 23N 3 11W
Castro Verde, *Portugal* **23** 37 41N 8 4W
Castrojeriz, *Spain* **22** 42 17N 4 9W
Castropol, *Spain* **22** 43 32N 7 0W
Castroreale, *Italy* **29** 38 5N 15 15 E
Castrovíllari, *Italy* **29** 39 49N 16 11 E
Castroville, *Calif., U.S.A.* **124** 36 46N 121 45W
Castroville, *Tex., U.S.A.* **121** 29 20N 98 53W
Castrovirreyna, *Peru* **136** 13 20 S 75 18W
Castuera, *Spain* **23** 38 43N 5 37W
Casummit Lake, *Canada* **104** 51 29N 92 22W
Cat Ba, Dao, *Vietnam* **54** 20 50N 107 0 E
Cat I., *Bahamas* **129** 24 30N 75 30W
Cat I., *U.S.A.* **121** 30 15N 89 7W
Cat L., *Canada* **104** 51 40N 91 50W
Catabola, *Angola* **95** 12 9 S 17 16 E
Catacamas, *Honduras* **128** 14 54N 85 56W
Catacáos, *Peru* **136** 5 20 S 80 45W
Cataguases, *Brazil* **139** 21 23 S 42 39W
Catahoula L., *U.S.A.* **121** 31 30N 92 5W
Catalão, *Brazil* **139** 18 10 S 47 57W
Catalina, *Canada* **105** 48 31N 53 4W
Catalonia = Cataluña □, *Spain* **24** 41 40N 1 15 E
Cataluña □, *Spain* **24** 41 40N 1 15 E
Catamarca, *Argentina* **140** 28 30 S 65 50W
Catamarca □, *Argentina* **140** 27 0 S 65 50W
Catanduanes, *Phil.* **57** 13 50N 124 20 E
Catanduva, *Brazil* **141** 21 5 S 48 58W
Catánia, *Italy* **29** 37 31N 15 4 E
Catánia, G. di, *Italy* **29** 37 25N 15 8 E
Catanzaro, *Italy* **29** 38 54N 16 38 E
Catarman, *Phil.* **57** 12 28N 124 35 E
Cateau, Le, *France* **19** 50 7N 3 32 E
Cateel, *Phil.* **57** 7 47N 126 24 E
Catende, *Angola* **95** 11 14 S 21 30 E
Catende, *Brazil* **138** 8 40 S 35 43W
Catete, *Angola* **95** 9 6 S 13 43 E
Cathcart, *Australia* **75** 36 52 S 149 24 E
Cathcart, *S. Africa* **96** 32 18 S 27 10 E
Cathkin, *Australia* **74** 37 10 S 145 38 E
Cathlamet, *U.S.A.* **124** 46 12N 123 23W
Cathundral, *Australia* **76** 31 55 S 147 51 E
Catio, *Guinea-Biss.* **90** 11 17N 15 15W
Catismiña, *Venezuela* **135** 4 5N 63 40W
Catita, *Brazil* **138** 9 31 S 43 1W
Catlettsburg, *U.S.A.* **118** 38 23N 82 38W
Catlin, *U.S.A.* **119** 40 4N 87 42W
Catoche, C., *Mexico* **127** 21 40N 87 8W
Catolé do Rocha, *Brazil* **138** 6 21 S 37 45W
Catral, *Spain* **25** 38 10N 0 47W
Catria, Mt., *Italy* **27** 43 28N 12 42 E
Catrimani, *Brazil* **135** 0 27N 61 41W
Catrimani →, *Brazil* **135** 0 28N 61 44W
Catskill, *U.S.A.* **117** 42 14N 73 52W
Catskill Mts., *U.S.A.* **117** 42 15N 74 15W
Catt, Mt., *Australia* **72** 13 49 S 134 23 E
Cattaraugus, *U.S.A.* **116** 42 22N 78 52W
Cattólica, *Italy* **27** 43 58N 12 43 E
Cattólica Eraclea, *Italy* **28** 37 27N 13 24 E
Catu, *Brazil* **139** 12 21 S 38 23W
Catuala, *Angola* **95** 16 25 S 19 2 E
Catumbela, *Angola* **95** 12 25 S 13 34 E
Catur, *Mozam.* **93** 13 45 S 35 30 E
Catwick Is., *Vietnam* **55** 10 0N 109 0 E
Cauca □, *Colombia* **134** 2 30N 76 50W
Cauca →, *Colombia* **134** 8 54N 74 28W
Caucaia, *Brazil* **138** 3 40 S 38 35W
Caucasia, *Colombia* **134** 8 0N 75 12W
Caucasus Mts. = Bolshoi Kavkas, *U.S.S.R.* **39** 42 50N 44 0 E
Caudebec-en-Caux, *France* **18** 49 30N 0 42 E
Caudete, *Spain* **25** 38 42N 1 2W
Caudry, *France* **19** 50 7N 3 22 E
Caulnes, *France* **18** 48 18N 2 10W
Caulónia, *Italy* **29** 38 23N 16 25 E
Caúngula, *Angola* **95** 8 26 S 18 38 E
Cauquenes, *Chile* **140** 36 0 S 72 22W
Caura →, *Venezuela* **135** 7 38N 64 53W
Caurés →, *Brazil* **135** 1 21 S 62 20W
Cauresi →, *Mozam.* **93** 17 8 S 33 0 E
Causapscal, *Canada* **105** 48 19N 67 12W
Caussade, *France* **20** 44 10N 1 33 E
Causse-Méjean, *France* **20** 44 18N 3 42 E
Cauterets, *France* **20** 42 52N 0 8W
Cautín □, *Chile* **142** 39 0 S 72 30W
Caux, Pays de, *France* **18** 49 38N 0 35 E
Cava dei Tirreni, *Italy* **29** 40 42N 14 42 E
Cávado →, *Portugal* **22** 41 32N 8 48W
Cavaillon, *France* **21** 43 50N 5 2 E
Cavalaire-sur-Mer, *France* **21** 43 10N 6 33 E
Cavalcante, *Brazil* **139** 13 48 S 47 30W
Cavalerie, La, *France* **20** 44 0N 3 10 E
Cavalese, *Italy* **27** 46 17N 11 29 E
Cavalier, *U.S.A.* **120** 48 50N 97 39W
Cavalla = Cavally →, *Africa* **90** 4 22N 7 32W
Cavalli Is., *N.Z.* **80** 35 0 S 173 58 E
Cavallo, I. de, *France* **21** 41 22N 9 16 E
Cavally →, *Africa* **90** 4 22N 7 32W
Cavan, *Ireland* **15** 54 0N 7 22W
Cavan □, *Ireland* **15** 53 58N 7 10W
Cavárzere, *Italy* **27** 45 8N 12 6 E
Cave City, *U.S.A.* **114** 37 13N 85 57W
Cavenagh Range, *Australia* **79** 26 12 S 127 55 E
Cavendish, *Australia* **74** 37 31 S 142 2 E
Caviana, I., *Brazil* **138** 0 10N 50 10W
Cavite, *Phil.* **57** 14 29N 120 55 E
Cavour, *Italy* **26** 44 47N 7 22 E
Cavtat, *Yugoslavia* **33** 42 35N 18 13 E
Cawasachouane, L., *Canada* **106** 47 27N 77 45W
Cawndilla, L., *Australia* **73** 32 30 S 142 15 E
Cawnpore = Kanpur, *India* **49** 26 28N 80 20 E
Caxias, *Brazil* **138** 4 55 S 43 20W
Caxias do Sul, *Brazil* **141** 29 10 S 51 10W
Caxine, C., *Algeria* **85** 35 56N 0 27W
Caxito, *Angola* **95** 8 30 S 13 30 E
Caxopa, *Angola* **95** 11 52 S 20 52 E
Cay Sal Bank, *Bahamas* **128** 23 45N 80 0W
Cayambe, *Ecuador* **134** 0 3N 78 8W
Cayambe, Vol., *Ecuador* **134** 0 2N 77 59W
Cayenne, *Fr. Guiana* **135** 5 0N 52 18W
Cayenne □, *Fr. Guiana* **135** 4 0N 53 0W
Cayes, Les, *Haiti* **129** 18 15N 73 46W
Cayeux-sur-Mer, *France* **19** 50 10N 1 30 E
Caylus, *France* **20** 44 15N 1 47 E
Cayman Brac, *Cayman Is.* **128** 19 43N 79 49W
Cayman Is., *W. Indies* **128** 19 40N 80 30W
Cayo Romano, *Cuba* **129** 22 0N 78 0W
Cayuga, *Canada* **108** 42 59N 79 50W
Cayuga, *Ind., U.S.A.* **119** 39 57N 87 38W
Cayuga, *N.Y., U.S.A.* **117** 42 54N 76 44W
Cayuga L., *U.S.A.* **117** 42 45N 76 45W
Cazaje, *Angola* **95** 11 2 S 20 45 E
Cazalla de la Sierra, *Spain* **23** 37 56N 5 45W
Căzăneşti, *Romania* **34** 44 36N 27 3 E
Cazaux et de Sanguinet, Étang de, *France* **20** 44 29N 1 10W
Cazères, *France* **20** 43 13N 1 5 E
Cazin, *Yugoslavia* **27** 44 57N 15 57 E
Čazma, *Yugoslavia* **27** 45 45N 16 39 E
Čazma →, *Yugoslavia* **27** 45 35N 16 29 E
Cazombo, *Angola* **95** 11 54 S 22 56 E
Cazorla, *Spain* **25** 37 55N 3 2W
Cazorla, *Venezuela* **134** 8 1N 67 0W
Cazorla, Sierra de, *Spain* **25** 38 5N 2 55W
Cea →, *Spain* **22** 42 0N 5 36W
Ceanannus Mor, *Ireland* **15** 53 42N 6 53W
Ceará = Fortaleza, *Brazil* **138** 3 45 S 38 35W
Ceará □, *Brazil* **138** 5 0 S 40 0W
Ceará Mirim, *Brazil* **138** 5 38 S 35 25W
Cebaco, I. de, *Panama* **128** 7 33N 81 9W
Cebollar, *Argentina* **140** 29 10 S 66 35W
Cebollera, Sierra de, *Spain* **24** 42 0N 2 30W
Cebreros, *Spain* **22** 40 27N 4 28W
Cebu, *Phil.* **57** 10 18N 123 54 E
Ceccano, *Italy* **28** 41 34N 13 18 E
Cechi, *Ivory C.* **90** 6 15N 4 25W
Cecil Plains, *Australia* **77** 27 30 S 151 11 E
Cécina, *Italy* **26** 43 19N 10 33 E
Cécina →, *Italy* **26** 43 19N 10 29 E
Ceclavin, *Spain* **22** 39 50N 6 45W
Cedar →, *U.S.A.* **118** 41 17N 91 21W
Cedar City, *U.S.A.* **123** 37 41N 113 3W
Cedar Creek Res., *U.S.A.* **121** 32 4N 96 5W
Cedar Falls, *Iowa, U.S.A.* **118** 42 39N 92 29W
Cedar Falls, *Wash., U.S.A.* **124** 47 25N 121 45W
Cedar Grove, *U.S.A.* **119** 39 22N 84 56W
Cedar Key, *U.S.A.* **115** 29 9N 83 5W
Cedar L., *Man., Canada* **111** 53 10N 100 0W
Cedar L., *Ont., Canada* **109** 46 2N 78 30W
Cedar Lake, *U.S.A.* **119** 41 20N 87 25W
Cedar Point, *U.S.A.* **119** 41 44N 83 21W
Cedar Rapids, *U.S.A.* **118** 42 0N 91 38W
Cedartown, *U.S.A.* **115** 34 1N 85 15W
Cedarvale, *Canada* **110** 55 1N 128 22W
Cedarville, *S. Africa* **97** 30 23 S 29 3 E
Cedarville, *Calif., U.S.A.* **122** 41 37N 120 13W
Cedarville, *Ill., U.S.A.* **118** 42 23N 89 38W
Cedarville, *Ohio, U.S.A.* **119** 39 44N 83 49W
Cedeira, *Spain* **22** 43 39N 8 2W
Cedral, *Mexico* **126** 23 50N 100 42W
Cedrino →, *Italy* **28** 40 23N 9 44 E
Cedro, *Brazil* **138** 6 34 S 39 3W
Cedros, I. de, *Mexico* **126** 28 10N 115 20W
Ceduna, *Australia* **73** 32 7 S 133 46 E
Cefalù, *Italy* **29** 38 3N 14 1 E
Cega →, *Spain* **22** 41 33N 4 46W
Cegléd, *Hungary* **33** 47 11N 19 47 E
Céglie Messápico, *Italy* **29** 40 39N 17 31 E
Cehegín, *Spain* **25** 38 6N 1 48W
Ceheng, *China* **58** 24 58N 105 48 E
Cehu-Silvaniei, *Romania* **34** 47 24N 23 9 E
Ceiba, La, *Honduras* **128** 15 40N 86 50W
Ceira →, *Portugal* **22** 40 13N 8 16W
Cekhira, *Tunisia* **86** 34 20N 10 5 E
Cela, *Angola* **95** 11 25 S 15 7 E
Celano, *Italy* **27** 42 6N 13 30 E
Celanova, *Spain* **22** 42 9N 7 58W
Celaya, *Mexico* **126** 20 31N 100 37W
Celbridge, *Ireland* **15** 53 20N 6 33W
Celebes = Sulawesi □, *Indonesia* **57** 2 0 S 120 0 E
Celebes Sea, *Indonesia* **57** 3 0N 123 0 E
Celendín, *Peru* **136** 6 52 S 78 10W
Čelić, *Yugoslavia* **33** 44 43N 18 47 E
Celica, *Ecuador* **134** 4 7 S 79 59W
Celina, *U.S.A.* **119** 40 32N 84 31W
Celje, *Yugoslavia* **27** 46 16N 15 18 E
Celle, *W. Germany* **30** 52 37N 10 4 E
Celles, *Belgium* **17** 50 42N 3 28 E
Celorico da Beira, *Portugal* **22** 40 38N 7 24W
Cement, *U.S.A.* **121** 34 56N 98 8W
Cenepa →, *Peru* **134** 4 40 S 78 10W
Cengong, *China* **58** 27 13N 108 44 E
Cenis, Col du Mont, *France* **21** 45 15N 6 55 E
Ceno →, *Italy* **26** 44 4N 10 5 E
Centallo, *Italy* **26** 44 30N 7 35 E
Centenário do Sul, *Brazil* **139** 22 48 S 51 36W
Center, *N. Dak., U.S.A.* **120** 47 9N 101 17W
Center, *Tex., U.S.A.* **121** 31 50N 94 10W
Center Point, *U.S.A.* **118** 42 12N 91 46W
Centerfield, *U.S.A.* **123** 39 9N 111 56W
Centerville, *Calif., U.S.A.* **124** 36 44N 119 30W
Centerville, *Iowa, U.S.A.* **118** 40 45N 92 57W
Centerville, *Mich., U.S.A.* **119** 41 55N 85 32W
Centerville, *Pa., U.S.A.* **116** 40 3N 79 59W
Centerville, *S. Dak., U.S.A.* **120** 43 10N 96 58W
Centerville, *Tenn., U.S.A.* **115** 35 46N 87 29W
Centerville, *Tex., U.S.A.* **121** 31 15N 95 56W
Cento, *Italy* **27** 44 43N 11 16 E
Central, *Brazil* **138** 11 8 S 42 8W
Central, *U.S.A.* **123** 32 46N 108 9W
Central □, *Kenya* **92** 0 30 S 37 30 E
Central □, *Malawi* **93** 13 30 S 33 30 E
Central □, *U.K.* **14** 56 10N 4 30W
Central □, *Zambia* **93** 14 25 S 28 50 E
Central, Cordillera, *Bolivia* **137** 18 30 S 64 55W
Central, Cordillera, *Colombia* **134** 5 0N 75 0W
Central, Cordillera, *Costa Rica* **128** 10 10N 84 5W
Central, Cordillera, *Dom. Rep.* **129** 19 15N 71 0W
Central, Cordillera, *Peru* **136** 7 0 S 77 30W
Central African Republic ■, *Africa* **94** 7 0N 20 0 E
Central City, *Ky., U.S.A.* **114** 37 20N 87 7W
Central City, *Nebr., U.S.A.* **120** 41 8N 98 0W
Central I., *Kenya* **92** 3 30N 36 0 E
Central Makran Range, *Pakistan* **47** 26 30N 64 15 E
Central Patricia, *Canada* **104** 51 30N 90 9W
Central Ra., *Papua N. G.* **69** 5 0 S 143 0 E
Central Russian Uplands, *Europe* **6** 54 0N 36 0 E
Central Siberian Plateau, *U.S.S.R.* **42** 65 0N 105 0 E
Central Tilba, *Australia* **75** 36 20 S 150 4 E
Centralia, *Ill., U.S.A.* **118** 38 32N 89 5W
Centralia, *Mo., U.S.A.* **118** 39 12N 92 6W
Centralia, *Wash., U.S.A.* **124** 46 46N 122 59W

Centreville, Ala., U.S.A. 115 32 55N 87 7W
Centreville, Miss., U.S.A. 121 31 10N 91 3W
Centúripe, Italy 29 37 37N 14 41 E
Cephalonia = Kefallinía, Greece 35 38 20N 20 30 E
Ceprano, Italy 28 41 33N 13 30 E
Cepu, Indonesia 57 7 9 S 111 35 E
Ceram = Seram, Indonesia 57 3 10 S 129 0 E
Ceram Sea = Seram Sea, Indonesia 57 2 30 S 128 30 E
Cerbère, France 20 42 26N 3 10 E
Cerbicales, Is., France 21 41 33N 9 22 E
Cercal, Portugal 23 37 48N 8 40W
Cercemaggiore, Italy 29 41 27N 14 43 E
Cerdaña, Spain 24 42 22N 1 35 E
Cerdedo, Spain 22 42 33N 8 23W
Cère →, France 20 44 55N 1 49 E
Cerea, Italy 27 45 12N 11 13 E
Ceres, Argentina 140 29 55 S 61 55W
Ceres, Brazil 139 15 17 S 49 35W
Ceres, Italy 26 45 19N 7 22 E
Ceres, S. Africa 96 33 21 S 19 18 E
Ceres, U.S.A. 124 37 35N 120 57W
Céret, France 20 42 30N 2 42 E
Cereté, Colombia 134 8 53N 75 48W
Cerf, L. de, Canada 106 46 16N 75 30W
Cerfontaine, Belgium 17 50 11N 4 26 E
Cerignola, Italy 29 41 17N 15 53 E
Cerigo = Kíthira, Greece 35 36 9N 23 0 E
Cérilly, France 20 46 37N 2 50 E
Cerisiers, France 19 48 8N 3 30 E
Cerizay, France 18 46 50N 0 40W
Çerkeş, Turkey 46 40 49N 32 52 E
Cerknica, Yugoslavia 27 45 48N 14 21 E
Cerna →, Romania 34 44 45N 24 0 E
Cernavodă, Romania 34 44 22N 28 3 E
Cernay, France 19 47 44N 7 10 E
Cernik, Yugoslavia 33 45 17N 17 22 E
Cerralvo, I., Mexico 126 24 20N 109 45 E
Cerreto Sannita, Italy 29 41 17N 14 34 E
Cerritos, Mexico 126 22 27N 100 20W
Cerro Gordo, U.S.A. 119 39 53N 88 44W
Cerro Sombrero, Chile 142 52 45 S 69 15W
Certaldo, Italy 26 43 32N 11 2 E
Cervaro →, Italy 29 41 30N 15 52 E
Cervera, Spain 24 41 40N 1 16 E
Cervera de Pisuerga, Spain 22 42 51N 4 30W
Cervera del Río Alhama, Spain 24 42 2N 1 58W
Cérvia, Italy 27 44 15N 12 20 E
Cervignano del Friuli, Italy 27 45 49N 13 20 E
Cervinara, Italy 29 41 2N 14 36 E
Cervione, France 21 42 20N 9 29 E
Cervo, Spain 22 43 40N 7 24W
César □, Colombia 134 9 0N 73 30W
Cesaro, Italy 29 37 50N 14 38 E
Cesena, Italy 27 44 9N 12 14 E
Cesenático, Italy 27 44 12N 12 22 E
Cēsis, U.S.S.R. 36 57 17N 25 28 E
Česká Lípa, Czech. 32 50 45N 14 30 E
České Budějovice, Czech. 32 48 55N 14 25 E
Ceskomoravská Vrchovina, Czech. 32 49 30N 15 40 E
Český Brod, Czech. 32 50 4N 14 52 E
Český Krumlov, Czech. 32 48 43N 14 21 E
Český Těšin, Czech. 32 49 45N 18 39 E
Cessnock, Australia 76 32 50 S 151 21 E
Cestos →, Liberia 90 5 40N 9 10W
Cétin Grad, Yugoslavia 27 45 9N 15 45 E
Cetina →, Yugoslavia 27 43 26N 16 42 E
Cetraro, Italy 29 39 30N 15 56 E
Ceuta, Morocco 84 35 52N 5 18W
Ceva, Italy 26 44 23N 8 3 E
Cévennes, France 20 44 10N 3 50 E
Ceyhan, Turkey 46 37 4N 35 47 E
Ceylon = Sri Lanka ■, Asia 51 7 30N 80 50 E
Cèze →, France 21 44 6N 4 43 E
Cha-am, Thailand 54 12 48N 99 58 E
Chá Pungana, Angola 95 13 44 S 18 39 E
Chaam, Neths. 17 51 30N 4 52 E
Chabeuil, France 21 44 54N 5 3 E
Chablais, France 21 46 20N 6 36 E
Chablis, France 19 47 47N 3 48 E
Chabounia, Algeria 85 35 30N 2 38 E
Chacabuco, Argentina 140 34 40 S 60 27W
Chachapoyas, Peru 136 6 15 S 77 50W
Chachasp, Peru 136 15 30 S 72 15W
Chachoengsao, Thailand 54 13 42N 101 5 E
Chachro, Pakistan 48 25 5N 70 15 E
Chaco □, Argentina 140 26 30 S 61 0W
Chad ■, Africa 87 15 0N 17 15 E
Chad, L. = Tchad, L., Chad 87 13 30N 14 30 E
Chadan, U.S.S.R. 41 51 17N 91 35 E
Chadileuvú →, Argentina 140 37 46 S 66 0W
Chadiza, Zambia 93 14 45 S 32 27 E
Chadron, U.S.A. 120 42 50N 103 0W
Chadyr-Lunga, U.S.S.R. 38 46 3N 28 51 E
Chae Hom, Thailand 54 18 43N 99 35 E
Chaem →, Thailand 54 18 11N 98 38 E
Chagda, U.S.S.R. 41 58 45N 130 38 E
Chagny, France 19 46 57N 4 45 E
Chagoda, U.S.S.R. 36 59 10N 35 15 E
Chagos Arch., Ind. Oc. 53 6 0 S 72 0 E
Chāh Bahār, Iran 47 25 20N 60 40 E
Chāh Gay Hills, Afghan. 47 29 30N 64 0 E
Chahār Mahāll va Bakhtīarī □, Iran 46 32 0N 49 0 E
Chahtung, Burma 52 26 41N 98 10 E
Chaillé-les-Marais, France 20 46 25N 1 2W
Chainat, Thailand 54 15 11N 100 8 E
Chaise-Dieu, La, France 20 45 18N 3 42 E
Chaitén, Chile 142 42 55 S 72 43W
Chaiya, Thailand 55 9 23N 99 14 E
Chaize-le-Vicomte, La, France 18 46 40N 1 18W
Chaj Doab, Pakistan 48 32 15N 73 0 E
Chajari, Argentina 140 30 42 S 58 0W
Chakaria, Bangla. 52 21 45N 92 5 E
Chake Chake, Tanzania 92 5 15 S 39 45 E
Chakhānsūr, Afghan. 47 31 10N 62 0 E
Chakonipau, L., Canada 105 56 18N 68 30W
Chakradharpur, India 49 22 45N 85 40 E
Chakwadam, Burma 52 27 29N 98 31 E
Chakwal, Pakistan 48 32 56N 72 53 E
Chala, Peru 136 15 48 S 74 20W
Chalais, France 20 45 16N 0 3 E
Chalakudi, India 51 10 18N 76 20 E
Chalchihuites, Mexico 126 23 29N 103 53W
Chalcis = Khalkís, Greece 35 38 27N 23 42 E
Chaleur B., Canada 105 47 55N 65 30W
Chalfant, U.S.A. 124 37 32N 118 21W
Chalhuanca, Peru 136 14 15 S 73 15W
Chalindrey, France 19 47 43N 5 26 E
Chaling, China 59 26 58N 113 30 E
Chalisgaon, India 50 20 30N 75 10 E
Chalk River, Canada 109 46 1N 77 27W
Chalkar, U.S.S.R. 39 50 40N 51 53 E
Chalkar, Ozero, U.S.S.R. 39 50 50N 51 50 E
Chalky Inlet, N.Z. 81 46 3 S 166 31 E
Challans, France 18 46 50N 1 52W
Challapata, Bolivia 136 18 53 S 66 50W
Challis, U.S.A. 122 44 32N 114 25W
Chalna, India 49 22 36N 89 35 E
Chalon-sur-Saône, France 19 46 48N 4 50 E
Chalonnes-sur-Loire, France 18 47 20N 0 45W
Châlons-sur-Marne, France 19 48 58N 4 20 E
Châlus, France 20 45 39N 0 58 E
Chalyaphum, Thailand 54 15 48N 102 2 E
Cham, W. Germany 31 49 12N 12 40 E
Cham, Cu Lao, Vietnam 54 15 57N 108 30 E
Chama, U.S.A. 123 36 54N 106 35W
Chaman, Pakistan 47 30 58N 66 25 E
Chamartín de la Rosa, Spain 24 40 28N 3 40W
Chamba, India 48 32 35N 76 10 E
Chamba, Tanzania 93 11 37 S 37 0 E
Chambal →, India 49 26 29N 79 15 E
Chamberlain, U.S.A. 120 43 50N 99 21W
Chamberlain →, Australia 78 15 30 S 127 54 E
Chambers, U.S.A. 123 35 13N 109 30W
Chambersburg, U.S.A. 114 39 53N 77 41W
Chambéry, France 21 45 34N 5 55 E
Chambly, Canada 117 45 27N 73 17W
Chambon-Feugerolles, Le, France 21 45 24N 4 19 E
Chambord, Canada 107 48 25N 72 6W
Chambri L., Papua N. G. 69 4 15 S 143 10 E
Chamela, Mexico 126 19 32N 105 5W
Chamical, Argentina 140 30 22 S 66 27W
Chamkar Luong, Cambodia 55 11 0N 103 45 E
Chamois, U.S.A. 118 38 41N 91 46W
Chamonix-Mont-Blanc, France 21 45 55N 6 51 E
Chamouchouane →, Canada 107 48 37N 72 20W
Champa, India 49 22 2N 82 43 E
Champagne, Canada 110 60 49N 136 30W
Champagne, France 19 48 40N 4 20 E
Champagne, Plaine de, France 19 49 0N 4 30 E
Champagnole, France 19 46 45N 5 55 E
Champaign, U.S.A. 119 40 8N 88 14W
Champassak, Laos 54 14 53N 105 52 E
Champaubert, France 19 48 50N 3 45 E
Champdeniers, France 20 46 29N 0 25W
Champeix, France 20 45 37N 3 8 E
Champlain, Canada 104 46 27N 72 24W
Champlain, U.S.A. 117 44 59N 73 27W
Champlain, L., U.S.A. 117 44 30N 73 20W
Champneuf, Canada 106 48 35N 77 30W
Champotón, Mexico 127 19 20N 90 50W
Chamrajnagar, India 51 11 52N 76 52 E
Chamusca, Portugal 23 39 21N 8 29W
Chan Chan, Peru 136 8 7 S 79 0W
Chana, Thailand 55 6 55N 100 44 E
Chañaral, Chile 140 26 23 S 70 40W
Chanasma, India 48 23 44N 72 5 E
Chancay, Peru 136 11 32 S 77 25W
Chandalar, U.S.A. 102 67 30N 148 35W
Chandannagar, India 49 22 52N 88 24 E
Chandausi, India 49 28 27N 78 49 E
Chandeleur Is., U.S.A. 121 29 48N 88 51W
Chandeleur Sd., U.S.A. 121 29 58N 88 40W
Chandigarh, India 48 30 43N 76 47 E
Chandler, Australia 73 27 0 S 133 19 E
Chandler, Canada 105 48 18N 64 46W
Chandler, Ariz., U.S.A. 123 33 20N 111 56W
Chandler, Okla., U.S.A. 121 35 43N 96 53W
Chandlers Peak, Australia 77 30 15 S 151 48 E
Chandless →, Brazil 136 9 8 S 69 51W
Chandmani, Mongolia 62 45 22N 98 2 E
Chandpur, Bangla. 52 23 8N 90 45 E
Chandpur, India 48 29 8N 78 19 E
Chandrapur, India 50 19 57N 79 25 E
Chang, Pakistan 48 26 59N 68 30 E
Chang, Ko, Thailand 55 12 0N 102 23 E
Chang Jiang →, China 59 31 48N 121 10 E
Changa, India 49 33 53N 77 35 E
Changanacheri, India 51 9 25N 76 31 E
Changane →, Mozam. 97 24 30 S 33 30 E
Changbai, China 61 41 25N 128 5 E
Changbai Shan, China 61 42 20N 129 0 E
Changchiak'ou = Zhangjiakou, China 60 40 48N 114 55 E
Ch'angchou = Changzhou, China 59 31 47N 119 58 E
Changchun, China 61 43 57N 125 17 E
Changchunling, China 61 45 18N 125 27 E
Changde, China 59 29 4N 111 35 E
Changfeng, China 59 32 28N 117 10 E
Changhai = Shanghai, China 59 31 15N 121 26 E
Changhua, China 59 30 12N 119 12 E
Changjiang, China 54 19 20N 108 55 E
Changjin-chŏsuji, N. Korea 61 40 30N 127 15 E
Changle, China 59 25 59N 119 27 E
Changli, China 61 39 40N 119 13 E
Changling, China 61 44 20N 123 58 E
Changlun, Malaysia 55 6 25N 100 26 E
Changning, Hunan, China 59 26 28N 112 22 E
Changning, Yunnan, China 58 24 45N 99 30 E
Changping, China 60 40 14N 116 12 E
Changsha, China 59 28 12N 113 0 E
Changshan, China 59 28 55N 118 27 E
Changshou, China 58 29 51N 107 8 E
Changshu, China 59 31 38N 120 43 E
Changshun, China 58 26 3N 106 25 E
Changtai, China 59 24 35N 117 42 E
Changting, China 59 25 50N 116 22 E
Changwu, China 60 35 10N 107 45 E
Changxing, China 59 31 0N 119 55 E
Changyang, China 59 30 30N 111 10 E
Changyi, China 61 36 40N 119 30 E
Changyuan, China 60 35 15N 114 42 E
Changzhi, China 60 36 10N 113 6 E
Changzhou, China 59 31 47N 119 58 E
Chanhanga, Angola 95 16 0 S 14 8 E
Chanlar, U.S.S.R. 39 40 25N 46 10 E
Channapatna, India 51 12 40N 77 15 E
Channel Is., U.K. 18 49 30N 2 40W
Channel Is., U.S.A. 125 33 55N 119 26W
Channel-Port aux Basques, Canada 105 47 30N 59 9W
Channing, Mich., U.S.A. 114 46 9N 88 1W
Channing, Tex., U.S.A. 121 35 45N 102 20W
Chantada, Spain 22 42 36N 7 46W
Chanthaburi, Thailand 54 12 38N 102 12 E
Chantilly, France 19 49 12N 2 29 E
Chantonnay, France 18 46 40N 1 3W
Chantrey Inlet, Canada 102 67 48N 96 20W
Chanute, U.S.A. 121 37 45N 95 25W
Chanza →, Spain 23 37 32N 7 30W
Chao Hu, China 59 31 30N 117 30 E
Chao Phraya →, Thailand 54 13 32N 100 36 E
Chao Phraya Lowlands, Thailand 54 15 30N 100 0 E
Chao Xian, China 59 31 38N 117 50 E
Chao'an, China 59 23 42N 116 32 E
Chaocheng, China 60 36 4N 115 37 E
Chaoyang, Guangdong, China 59 23 17N 116 30 E
Chaoyang, Liaoning, China 61 41 35N 120 22 E
Chapada dos Guimarães, Brazil 137 15 26 S 55 45W
Chapais, Canada 106 49 47N 74 51W
Chapala, Mozam. 93 15 50 S 37 35 E
Chapala, L. de, Mexico 126 20 10N 103 20W
Chaparé →, Bolivia 137 15 58 S 64 42W
Chaparmukh, India 52 26 12N 92 31 E
Chaparral, Colombia 134 3 43N 75 28W
Chapayevo, U.S.S.R. 39 50 25N 51 10 E
Chapayevsk, U.S.S.R. 37 53 0N 49 40 E
Chapeau, Canada 106 45 54N 77 4W
Chapecó, Brazil 141 27 14 S 52 41W
Chapel Hill, U.S.A. 115 35 53N 79 3W
Chapelle d'Angillon, La, France 19 47 21N 2 25 E
Chapelle-Glain, La, France 18 47 38N 1 11W
Chapin, U.S.A. 118 39 46N 90 24W
Chapleau, Canada 104 47 50N 83 24W
Chaplin, Canada 111 50 28N 106 40W
Chaplino, U.S.S.R. 38 48 8N 36 15 E
Chaplygin, U.S.S.R. 37 53 15N 40 0 E
Châr, Mauritania 84 21 32N 12 45W
Chara, U.S.S.R. 41 56 54N 118 20 E
Charadai, Argentina 140 27 35 S 60 0W
Charagua, Bolivia 137 19 45 S 63 10W
Charalá, Colombia 134 6 17N 73 10W
Charambirá, Punta, Colombia 134 4 16N 77 32W
Charaña, Bolivia 136 17 30 S 69 25W
Charapita, Colombia 134 0 37 S 74 21W
Charata, Argentina 140 27 13 S 61 14W
Charcas, Mexico 126 23 10N 101 20W
Charcoal L., Canada 111 58 49N 102 22W
Chard, U.K. 13 50 52N 2 59W
Chardara, U.S.S.R. 40 41 16N 67 59 E
Chardon, U.S.A. 116 41 34N 81 17W
Charduar, India 52 26 51N 92 46 E
Chardzhou, U.S.S.R. 40 39 6N 63 34 E
Charente □, France 20 45 50N 0 16 E
Charente →, France 20 45 57N 1 5W
Charente-Maritime □, France 20 45 45N 0 45W
Charentsavan, U.S.S.R. 39 40 35N 44 41 E
Charette, Canada 107 46 27N 72 56W
Chari →, Chad 87 12 58N 14 31 E
Chārīkār, Afghan. 47 35 0N 69 10 E
Charité-sur-Loire, La, France 19 47 10N 3 1 E
Chariton, U.S.A. 118 41 1N 93 19W
Chariton →, U.S.A. 118 39 19N 92 58W
Charity, Guyana 135 7 24N 58 36W
Charkhari, India 49 25 24N 79 45 E
Charkhi Dadri, India 48 28 37N 76 17 E
Charleroi, Belgium 17 50 24N 4 27 E
Charleroi, U.S.A. 116 40 8N 79 54W
Charles, C., U.S.A. 114 37 10N 75 59W
Charles City, U.S.A. 118 43 2N 92 41W
Charles L., Canada 111 59 50N 110 33W
Charles Town, U.S.A. 114 39 20N 77 50W
Charlesbourg, Canada 107 46 51N 71 16W
Charleston, Ill., U.S.A. 114 39 30N 88 10W
Charleston, Ill., U.S.A. 119 39 30N 88 10W
Charleston, Miss., U.S.A. 121 34 2N 90 3W
Charleston, Mo., U.S.A. 121 36 52N 89 20W
Charleston, S.C., U.S.A. 115 32 47N 79 56W
Charleston, W. Va., U.S.A. 114 38 24N 81 36W
Charleston L., Canada 109 44 32N 76 0W
Charleston Park, U.S.A. 125 36 17N 115 37W
Charleston Pk., U.S.A. 125 36 16N 115 42W
Charlestown, S. Africa 97 27 26 S 29 53 E
Charlestown, U.S.A. 119 38 29N 85 40W
Charlesville, Zaïre 95 5 27 S 20 59 E
Charleville = Rath Luirc, Ireland 15 52 21N 8 40W
Charleville, Australia 73 26 24 S 146 15 E
Charleville-Mézières, France 19 49 44N 4 40 E
Charlevoix, U.S.A. 104 45 19N 85 14W
Charlieu, France 21 46 10N 4 10 E
Charlotte, Mich., U.S.A. 119 42 36N 84 48W
Charlotte, N.C., U.S.A. 115 35 16N 80 46W
Charlotte Amalie, Virgin Is. 129 18 22N 64 56W
Charlotte Harbor, U.S.A. 115 26 58N 82 4W
Charlottenberg, Sweden 10 59 54N 12 17 E
Charlottesville, U.S.A. 114 38 1N 78 30W
Charlottetown, Canada 105 46 14N 63 8W
Charlton, Australia 74 36 16 S 143 24 E
Charlton, U.S.A. 120 40 59N 93 20W
Charlton I., Canada 104 52 0N 79 20W
Charmes, France 19 48 22N 6 17 E
Charny, Canada 107 46 43N 71 15W
Charolles, France 21 46 27N 4 16 E
Chârost, France 19 46 58N 2 7 E
Charouine, Algeria 85 29 0N 0 15W
Charre, Mozam. 93 17 13 S 35 10 E
Charroux, France 20 46 9N 0 25 E
Charsadda, Pakistan 48 34 7N 71 45 E
Charters Towers, Australia 72 20 5 S 146 13 E
Chartre-sur-le-Loir, La, France 18 47 44N 0 34 E
Chartres, France 18 48 29N 1 30 E
Chascomús, Argentina 140 35 30 S 58 0W
Chasefu, Zambia 93 11 55 S 33 8 E
Chaslands Mistake, N.Z. 81 46 38 S 169 22 E
Chasovnya-Uchurskaya, U.S.S.R. 41 57 15N 132 50 E
Chasseneuil-sur-Bonnieure, France 20 45 52N 0 29 E
Châtaigneraie, La, France 20 46 39N 0 44W
Chatal Balkan = Udvoy Balkan, Bulgaria 34 42 50N 26 50 E
Château-Arnoux, France 21 44 6N 6 0 E
Château-Chinon, France 19 47 4N 3 56 E
Château-d'Oléron, Le, France 20 45 54N 1 12W
Château-du-Loir, France 18 47 40N 0 25 E
Château-Gontier, France 18 47 50N 0 48W
Château-la-Vallière, France 18 47 30N 0 20 E
Château-Landon, France 19 48 8N 2 40 E

Château-Porcien, *France* **19** 49 31N 4 13 E
Château-Renault, *France* **18** 47 36N 0 56 E
Château-Salins, *France* **19** 48 50N 6 30 E
Château-Thierry, *France* **19** 49 3N 3 20 E
Châteaubourg, *France* **18** 48 7N 1 25W
Châteaubriant, *France* **18** 47 43N 1 23W
Châteaudun, *France* **18** 48 3N 1 20 E
Châteaugiron, *France* **18** 48 3N 1 30W
Châteaulin, *France* **18** 48 11N 4 8W
Châteaumeillant, *France* **20** 46 35N 2 12 E
Châteauneuf-du-Faou, *France* **18** 48 11N 3 50W
Châteauneuf-en-Thymerais, *France* **18** 48 35N 1 13 E
Châteauneuf-sur-Charente, *France* **20** 45 36N 0 3W
Châteauneuf-sur-Cher, *France* **19** 46 52N 2 18 E
Châteauneuf-sur-Loire, *France* **19** 47 52N 2 13 E
Châteaurenard, *Bouches-du-Rhône, France* **21** 43 53N 4 51 E
Châteaurenard, *Loiret, France* **19** 47 56N 2 55 E
Châteauroux, *France* **19** 46 50N 1 40 E
Châteauvert, L., *Canada* **107** 47 39N 73 56W
Châtelaillon-Plage, *France* **20** 46 5N 1 5W
Châtelaudren, *France* **18** 48 33N 2 59W
Chatelet, *Belgium* **17** 50 24N 4 32 E
Châtelet, Le, *France* **20** 46 38N 2 16 E
Châtelet-en-Brie, Le, *France* **19** 48 31N 2 48 E
Châtelguyon, *France* **20** 45 55N 3 4 E
Châtellerault, *France* **18** 46 50N 0 30 E
Châtelus-Malvaleix, *France* **20** 46 18N 2 1 E
Chatfield, *U.S.A.* **120** 43 15N 91 58W
Chatham, *N.B., Canada* **105** 47 2N 65 28W
Chatham, *Ont., Canada* **108** 42 24N 82 11W
Chatham, *U.K.* **13** 51 22N 0 32 E
Chatham, *Ill., U.S.A.* **118** 39 40N 89 42W
Chatham, *La., U.S.A.* **121** 32 22N 92 26W
Chatham, *N.Y., U.S.A.* **117** 42 21N 73 32W
Chatham, I., *Chile* **142** 50 40 S 74 25W
Chatham Is., *Pac. Oc.* **66** 44 0 S 176 40W
Chatham Str., *U.S.A.* **110** 57 0N 134 40W
Chatillon, *Italy* **26** 45 45N 7 40 E
Châtillon-Coligny, *France* **19** 47 50N 2 51 E
Châtillon-en-Bazois, *France* **19** 47 3N 3 39 E
Châtillon-en-Diois, *France* **21** 44 41N 5 29 E
Châtillon-sur-Indre, *France* **18** 46 59N 1 10 E
Châtillon-sur-Loire, *France* **19** 47 35N 2 44 E
Châtillon-sur-Marne, *France* **19** 49 6N 3 44 E
Châtillon-sur-Seine, *France* **19** 47 50N 4 33 E
Chatmohar, *Bangla.* **49** 24 15N 89 15 E
Chatra, *India* **49** 24 12N 84 56 E
Chatrapur, *India* **50** 19 22N 85 2 E
Châtre, La, *France* **20** 46 35N 2 0 E
Chats, L. des, *Canada* **106** 45 30N 76 20W
Chatsworth, *Canada* **108** 44 27N 80 54W
Chatsworth, *U.S.A.* **119** 40 45N 88 18W
Chatsworth, *Zimb.* **93** 19 38 S 31 13 E
Chatta-Hantō, *Japan* **65** 34 45N 136 55 E
Chattahoochee →, *U.S.A.* **115** 30 43N 84 51W
Chattanooga, *U.S.A.* **115** 35 2N 85 17W
Chaturat, *Thailand* **54** 15 40N 101 51 E
Chau Doc, *Vietnam* **55** 10 42N 105 7 E
Chaudanne, Barr. de, *France* **21** 43 51N 6 32 E
Chaudes-Aigues, *France* **20** 44 51N 3 1 E
Chaudière →, *Canada* **107** 46 45N 71 17W
Chauffailles, *France* **21** 46 13N 4 20 E
Chauk, *Burma* **52** 20 53N 94 49 E
Chaukan Pass, *Burma* **52** 27 8N 97 10 E
Chaulnes, *France* **19** 49 48N 2 47 E
Chaumont, *France* **19** 48 7N 5 8 E
Chaumont, *U.S.A.* **117** 44 4N 76 9W
Chaumont-en-Vexin, *France* **19** 49 16N 1 53 E
Chaumont-sur-Loire, *France* **18** 47 29N 1 11 E
Chaunay, *France* **20** 46 13N 0 9 E
Chauny, *France* **19** 49 37N 3 12 E
Chausey, Is., *France* **18** 48 52N 1 49W
Chaussin, *France* **19** 46 59N 5 22 E
Chautauqua L., *U.S.A.* **116** 42 7N 79 30W
Chauvigny, *France* **18** 46 34N 0 39 E
Chauvin, *Canada* **111** 52 45N 110 10W
Chaux-de-Fonds, La, *Switz.* **31** 47 7N 6 50 E
Chavantina, *Brazil* **137** 14 40 S 52 21W
Chaves, *Brazil* **138** 0 15 S 49 55W
Chaves, *Portugal* **22** 41 45N 7 32W
Chavuma, *Zambia* **95** 13 4 S 22 40 E
Chawang, *Thailand* **55** 8 25N 99 30 E
Chazelles-sur-Lyon, *France* **21** 45 39N 4 22 E
Chazuta, *Peru* **136** 6 30 S 76 0W
Chazy, *U.S.A.* **117** 44 52N 73 28W
Cheb, *Czech.* **32** 50 9N 12 28 E
Chebanse, *U.S.A.* **119** 41 0N 87 54W
Cheboksary, *U.S.S.R.* **37** 56 8N 47 12 E
Cheboygan, *U.S.A.* **104** 45 38N 84 29W
Chebsara, *U.S.S.R.* **37** 59 10N 38 59 E
Chech, Erg, *Africa* **84** 25 0N 2 15W
Chechaouen, *Morocco* **84** 35 9N 5 15W
Chechen, Os., *U.S.S.R.* **39** 43 59N 47 40 E
Checheno-Ingush A.S.S.R. □, *U.S.S.R.* **39** 43 30N 45 29 E
Chęciny, *Poland* **32** 50 46N 20 28 E
Checleset B., *Canada* **110** 50 5N 127 35W
Checotah, *U.S.A.* **121** 35 31N 95 30W
Chedabucto B., *Canada* **105** 45 25N 61 8W
Cheduba I., *Burma* **52** 18 45N 93 40 E
Cheepie, *Australia* **73** 26 33 S 145 1 E
Chef, R. du →, *Canada* **107** 49 21N 73 25W
Chef-Boutonne, *France* **20** 46 7N 0 4W
Chegdomyn, *U.S.S.R.* **41** 51 7N 133 1 E
Chegga, *Mauritania* **84** 25 27N 5 40W
Chegutu, *Zimb.* **93** 18 10 S 30 14 E
Chehalis, *U.S.A.* **124** 46 44N 122 59W
Cheiron, Mt., *France* **21** 43 49N 6 58 E
Cheju Do, *S. Korea* **61** 33 29N 126 34 E
Chekalin, *U.S.S.R.* **37** 54 10N 36 10 E
Chekiang = Zhejiang □, *China* **59** 29 0N 120 0 E
Chel = Kuru, Bahr el →, *Sudan* **89** 8 10N 26 50 E
Chela, Sa. da, *Angola* **95** 16 20 S 13 20 E
Chelan, *U.S.A.* **122** 47 49N 120 0W
Chelan, L., *U.S.A.* **122** 48 5N 120 30W
Cheleken, *U.S.S.R.* **40** 39 26N 53 7 E
Chelforó, *Argentina* **142** 39 0 S 66 33W
Chéliff, O. →, *Algeria* **85** 36 0N 0 8 E
Chelkar, *U.S.S.R.* **40** 47 48N 59 39 E
Chelkar Tengiz, Solonchak, *U.S.S.R.* **40** 48 0N 62 30 E
Chellala Dahrania, *Algeria* **85** 33 2N 0 1 E
Chelles, *France* **19** 48 52N 2 33 E
Chełm, *Poland* **32** 51 8N 23 30 E
Chełmek, *Poland* **32** 50 6N 19 16 E
Chełmno, *Poland* **32** 53 20N 18 30 E
Chelmsford, *U.K.* **13** 51 44N 0 29 E
Chelmsford Dam, *S. Africa* **97** 27 55 S 29 59 E
Chelmża, *Poland* **32** 53 10N 18 39 E
Chelsea, *Australia* **74** 38 5 S 145 8 E
Chelsea, *Mich., U.S.A.* **119** 42 19N 84 1W
Chelsea, *Okla., U.S.A.* **121** 36 35N 95 35W
Chelsea, *Vt., U.S.A.* **117** 43 59N 72 27W
Cheltenham, *U.K.* **13** 51 55N 2 5W
Chelva, *Spain* **24** 39 45N 1 0W
Chelyabinsk, *U.S.S.R.* **40** 55 10N 61 24 E
Chelyuskin, C., *U.S.S.R.* **42** 77 30N 103 0 E
Chemainus, *Canada* **110** 48 55N 123 42W
Chembar = Belinskiy, *U.S.S.R.* **37** 53 0N 43 25 E
Chemillé, *France* **18** 47 14N 0 45W
Chemnitz = Karl-Marx-Stadt, *E. Germany* **30** 50 50N 12 55 E
Chemult, *U.S.A.* **122** 43 14N 121 47W
Chen, Gora, *U.S.S.R.* **41** 65 16N 141 50 E
Chen Xian, *China* **59** 25 47N 113 1 E
Chenab →, *Pakistan* **48** 30 23N 71 2 E
Chenachane, O. →, *Algeria* **84** 25 20N 3 20W
Chenango Forks, *U.S.A.* **117** 42 15N 75 51W
Chencha, *Ethiopia* **89** 6 15N 37 32 E
Chenchiang = Zhenjiang, *China* **59** 32 11N 119 26 E
Chênée, *Belgium* **17** 50 37N 5 37 E
Chénéville, *Canada* **106** 45 53N 75 3W
Cheney, *U.S.A.* **122** 47 29N 117 34W
Cheng Xian, *China* **60** 33 43N 105 42 E
Chengalpattu, *India* **51** 12 42N 79 58 E
Chengbu, *China* **59** 26 18N 110 16 E
Chengcheng, *China* **60** 35 8N 109 56 E
Chengchou = Zhengzhou, *China* **60** 34 45N 113 34 E
Chengde, *China* **61** 40 59N 117 58 E
Chengdong Hu, *China* **59** 32 15N 116 20 E
Chengdu, *China* **58** 30 38N 104 2 E
Chengele, *India* **52** 28 47N 96 16 E
Chenggong, *China* **58** 24 52N 102 56 E
Chenggu, *China* **60** 33 10N 107 21 E
Chengjiang, *China* **58** 24 39N 103 0 E
Chengkou, *China* **58** 31 54N 108 31 E
Ch'engtu = Chengdu, *China* **58** 30 38N 104 2 E
Chengwu, *China* **60** 34 58N 115 50 E
Chengxi Hu, *China* **59** 32 15N 116 10 E
Chengyang, *China* **61** 36 18N 120 21 E
Chenjiagang, *China* **61** 34 23N 119 47 E
Chenkán, *Mexico* **127** 19 8N 90 58W
Chenoa, *U.S.A.* **119** 40 45N 88 42W
Chenxi, *China* **59** 28 2N 110 12 E
Cheo Reo, *Vietnam* **54** 13 25N 108 28 E
Cheom Ksan, *Cambodia* **54** 14 13N 104 56 E
Chepelare, *Bulgaria* **35** 41 44N 24 40 E
Chepén, *Peru* **136** 7 15 S 79 23W
Chépénéhé, *Vanuatu* **68** 20 47 S 167 9 E
Chepes, *Argentina* **140** 31 20 S 66 35W
Chepo, *Panama* **128** 9 10N 79 6W
Cheptsa →, *U.S.S.R.* **37** 58 36N 50 4 E
Cheptulil, Mt., *Kenya* **92** 1 25N 35 35 E
Chequamegon B., *U.S.A.* **120** 46 40N 90 30W
Cher □, *France* **19** 47 10N 2 30 E
Cher →, *France* **18** 47 21N 0 29 E
Cheran, *India* **52** 25 45N 90 44 E
Cherasco, *Italy* **26** 44 39N 7 50 E
Cheratte, *Belgium* **17** 50 40N 5 41 E
Cheraw, *U.S.A.* **115** 34 42N 79 54W
Cherbourg, *France* **18** 49 39N 1 40W
Cherchell, *Algeria* **85** 36 35N 2 12 E
Cherdakly, *U.S.S.R.* **37** 54 25N 48 50 E
Cherdyn, *U.S.S.R.* **40** 60 24N 56 29 E
Cheremkhovo, *U.S.S.R.* **41** 53 8N 103 1 E
Cherepanovo, *U.S.S.R.* **40** 54 15N 83 30 E
Cherepovets, *U.S.S.R.* **37** 59 5N 37 55 E
Chergui, Chott ech, *Algeria* **85** 34 21N 0 25 E
Cherikov, *U.S.S.R.* **36** 53 32N 31 20 E
Cherkassy, *U.S.S.R.* **38** 49 27N 32 4 E
Cherkessk, *U.S.S.R.* **39** 44 15N 42 5 E
Cherlak, *U.S.S.R.* **40** 54 15N 74 55 E
Chernaya Kholunitsa, *U.S.S.R.* **37** 58 51N 51 52 E
Cherni, *Bulgaria* **34** 42 35N 23 18 E
Chernigov, *U.S.S.R.* **36** 51 28N 31 20 E
Chernobyl, *U.S.S.R.* **36** 51 13N 30 15 E
Chernogorsk, *U.S.S.R.* **41** 53 49N 91 18 E
Chernomorskoye, *U.S.S.R.* **38** 45 31N 32 40 E
Chernovskoye, *U.S.S.R.* **37** 58 48N 47 20 E
Chernovtsy, *U.S.S.R.* **38** 48 15N 25 52 E
Chernoye, *U.S.S.R.* **41** 70 30N 89 10 E
Chernyakhovsk, *U.S.S.R.* **36** 54 36N 21 48 E
Chernyshkovskiy, *U.S.S.R.* **39** 48 30N 42 13 E
Chernyshovskiy, *U.S.S.R.* **41** 63 0N 112 30 E
Cherokee, *Iowa, U.S.A.* **120** 42 40N 95 30W
Cherokee, *Okla., U.S.A.* **121** 36 45N 98 25W
Cherokees, L. O'The, *U.S.A.* **121** 36 50N 95 12W
Cherquenco, *Chile* **142** 38 35 S 72 0W
Cherry Creek, *U.S.A.* **122** 39 50N 114 58W
Cherry Gully, *Australia* **77** 28 25 S 152 1 E
Cherry Valley, *U.S.A.* **125** 33 59N 116 57W
Cherrypool, *Australia* **74** 37 7 S 142 13 E
Cherryvale, *U.S.A.* **121** 37 20N 95 33W
Cherskiy, *U.S.S.R.* **41** 68 45N 161 18 E
Cherskogo Khrebet, *U.S.S.R.* **41** 65 0N 143 0 E
Chertkovo, *U.S.S.R.* **39** 49 25N 40 19 E
Cherven, *U.S.S.R.* **36** 53 45N 28 28 E
Cherven-Bryag, *Bulgaria* **34** 43 17N 24 7 E
Chervonograd, *U.S.S.R.* **36** 50 25N 24 10 E
Cherwell →, *U.K.* **13** 51 46N 1 18W
Chesapeake, *U.S.A.* **114** 36 43N 76 15W
Chesapeake Bay, *U.S.A.* **114** 38 0N 76 12W
Cheshire □, *U.K.* **12** 53 14N 2 30W
Cheshskaya Guba, *U.S.S.R.* **40** 67 20N 47 0 E
Cheslatta L., *Canada* **110** 53 49N 125 20W
Chesley, *Canada* **108** 44 17N 81 5W
Chesne, Le, *France* **19** 49 30N 4 45 E
Cheste, *Spain* **25** 39 30N 0 41W
Chester, *U.K.* **12** 53 12N 2 53W
Chester, *Calif., U.S.A.* **122** 40 22N 121 14W
Chester, *Ill., U.S.A.* **118** 37 58N 89 50W
Chester, *Mont., U.S.A.* **122** 48 31N 111 0W
Chester, *Pa., U.S.A.* **114** 39 54N 75 20W
Chester, *S.C., U.S.A.* **115** 34 44N 81 13W
Chesterfield, *U.K.* **12** 53 14N 1 26W
Chesterfield, Is., *N. Cal.* **66** 19 52 S 158 15 E
Chesterfield Inlet, *Canada* **102** 63 30N 90 45W
Chesterton Range, *Australia* **73** 25 30 S 147 27 E
Chesterville, *Canada* **106** 45 6N 75 14W
Chesuncook L., *U.S.A.* **105** 46 0N 69 10W
Chetaibi, *Algeria* **85** 37 1N 7 20 E
Chéticamp, *Canada* **105** 46 37N 60 59W
Chetumal, *Mexico* **127** 18 30N 88 20W
Chetumal, B. de, *Mexico* **127** 18 40N 88 10W
Chetwynd, *Australia* **74** 37 17 S 141 23 E
Chetwynd, *Canada* **110** 55 45N 121 36W
Chevanceaux, *France* **20** 45 18N 0 14W
Cheviot, *U.S.A.* **119** 39 10N 84 37W
Cheviot, The, *U.K.* **12** 55 29N 2 8W
Cheviot Hills, *U.K.* **12** 55 20N 2 30W
Cheviot Ra., *Australia* **72** 25 20 S 143 45 E
Chew Bahir, *Ethiopia* **89** 4 40N 36 50 E
Chewelah, *U.S.A.* **122** 48 17N 117 43W
Cheyenne, *Okla., U.S.A.* **121** 35 35N 99 40W
Cheyenne, *Wyo., U.S.A.* **120** 41 9N 104 49W
Cheyenne →, *U.S.A.* **120** 44 40N 101 15W
Cheyenne Wells, *U.S.A.* **120** 38 51N 102 10W
Cheylard, Le, *France* **21** 44 55N 4 25 E
Cheyne B., *Australia* **79** 34 35 S 118 50 E
Chhabra, *India* **48** 24 40N 76 54 E
Chhapra, *India* **49** 25 48N 84 44 E
Chhata, *India* **48** 27 42N 77 30 E
Chhatak, *Bangla.* **52** 25 5N 91 37 E
Chhatarpur, *India* **49** 24 55N 79 35 E
Chhep, *Cambodia* **54** 13 45N 105 24 E
Chhindwara, *India* **49** 22 2N 78 59 E
Chhlong, *Cambodia* **55** 12 15N 105 58 E
Chhuk, *Cambodia* **55** 10 46N 104 28 E
Chi →, *Thailand* **54** 15 11N 104 43 E
Chiamis, *Indonesia* **57** 7 20 S 108 21 E
Chiamussu = Jiamusi, *China* **62** 46 40N 130 26 E
Chiang Dao, *Thailand* **54** 19 22N 98 58 E
Chiang Kham, *Thailand* **54** 19 32N 100 18 E
Chiang Khan, *Thailand* **54** 17 52N 101 36 E
Chiang Khong, *Thailand* **54** 20 17N 100 24 E
Chiang Mai, *Thailand* **54** 18 47N 98 59 E
Chiang Saen, *Thailand* **54** 20 16N 100 5 E
Chiange, *Angola* **95** 15 35 S 13 40 E
Chiapa →, *Mexico* **127** 16 42N 93 0W
Chiapa de Corzo, *Mexico* **127** 16 42N 93 0W
Chiapas □, *Mexico* **127** 17 0N 92 45W
Chiaramonte Gulfi, *Italy* **29** 37 1N 14 41 E
Chiaravalle, *Italy* **27** 43 38N 13 17 E
Chiaravalle Centrale, *Italy* **29** 38 41N 16 25 E
Chiari, *Italy* **26** 45 31N 9 55 E
Chiatura, *U.S.S.R.* **39** 42 15N 43 17 E
Chiautla, *Mexico* **127** 18 18N 98 34W
Chiávari, *Italy* **26** 44 20N 9 20 E
Chiavenna, *Italy* **26** 46 18N 9 23 E
Chiba, *Japan* **65** 35 30N 140 7 E
Chiba □, *Japan* **65** 35 30N 140 20 E
Chibabava, *Mozam.* **97** 20 17 S 33 35 E
Chibatu, *Indonesia* **57** 7 6 S 107 59 E
Chibemba, *Cunene, Angola* **95** 15 48 S 14 8 E
Chibemba, *Huila, Angola* **95** 16 20 S 15 20 E
Chibia, *Angola* **95** 15 10 S 13 42 E
Chibougamau, *Canada* **107** 49 56N 74 24W
Chibougamau →, *Canada* **106** 49 42N 75 57W
Chibougamau, Parc Prov. de, *Canada* **107** 49 15N 73 45W
Chibougamau L., *Canada* **107** 49 50N 74 20W
Chibuk, *Nigeria* **91** 10 52N 12 50 E
Chic-Chocs, Mts., *Canada* **105** 48 55N 66 0W
Chicacole = Srikakulam, *India* **50** 18 14N 83 58 E
Chicago, *U.S.A.* **119** 41 53N 87 40W
Chicago Heights, *U.S.A.* **119** 41 29N 87 37W
Chichagof I., *U.S.A.* **110** 58 0N 136 0W
Chichaoua, *Morocco* **84** 31 32N 8 44W
Chicheng, *China* **60** 40 55N 115 55 E
Chichester, *U.K.* **13** 50 50N 0 47W
Chichibu, *Japan* **65** 36 5N 139 10 E
Ch'ich'ihaerh = Qiqihar, *China* **62** 47 26N 124 0 E
Chickasha, *U.S.A.* **121** 35 0N 98 0W
Chiclana de la Frontera, *Spain* **23** 36 26N 6 9W
Chiclayo, *Peru* **136** 6 42 S 79 50W
Chico, *U.S.A.* **124** 39 45N 121 54W
Chico →, *Chubut, Argentina* **142** 44 0 S 67 0W
Chico →, *Santa Cruz, Argentina* **142** 50 0 S 68 30W
Chicobi, L., *Canada* **106** 48 53N 78 30W
Chicomo, *Mozam.* **97** 24 31 S 34 6 E
Chicontepec, *Mexico* **127** 20 58N 98 10W
Chicopee, *U.S.A.* **117** 42 6N 72 37W
Chicoutimi, *Canada* **105** 48 28N 71 5W
Chicoutimi, Parc Prov. de, *Canada* **107** 48 30N 70 20W
Chicualacuala, *Mozam.* **97** 22 6 S 31 42 E
Chidambaram, *India* **51** 11 20N 79 45 E
Chidenguele, *Mozam.* **97** 24 55 S 34 11 E
Chidley, C., *Canada* **103** 60 23N 64 26W
Chiede, *Angola* **95** 17 15 S 16 22 E
Chiefs Pt., *Canada* **108** 44 41N 81 18W
Chiem Hoa, *Vietnam* **54** 22 12N 105 17 E
Chiemsee, *W. Germany* **31** 47 53N 12 27 E
Chiengi, *Zambia* **93** 8 45 S 29 10 E
Chiengmai = Chiang Mai, *Thailand* **54** 18 47N 98 59 E
Chiengo, *Angola* **95** 13 20 S 21 55 E
Chienti →, *Italy* **27** 43 18N 13 45 E
Chieri, *Italy* **26** 45 0N 7 50 E
Chiers →, *France* **19** 49 39N 5 0 E
Chiese →, *Italy* **26** 45 8N 10 25 E
Chieti, *Italy* **27** 42 22N 14 10 E
Chièvres, *Belgium* **17** 50 35N 3 48 E
Chifeng, *China* **61** 42 18N 118 58 E
Chigasaki, *Japan* **65** 35 19N 139 24 E
Chigirin, *U.S.S.R.* **38** 49 4N 32 38 E
Chignecto B., *Canada* **105** 45 30N 64 40W
Chigorodó, *Colombia* **134** 7 41N 76 42W
Chigoubiche, L., *Canada* **107** 49 7N 73 30W
Chiguana, *Bolivia* **140** 21 0 S 67 58W
Chihli, G. of = Bo Hai, *China* **61** 39 0N 120 0 E
Chihuahua, *Mexico* **126** 28 40N 106 3W
Chihuahua □, *Mexico* **126** 28 40N 106 3W
Chiili, *U.S.S.R.* **40** 44 20N 66 15 E
Chik Bollapur, *India* **51** 13 25N 77 45 E
Chikhli, *India* **50** 20 20N 76 18 E

Chikmagalur, *India* **51** 13 15N 75 45 E
Chikodi, *India* **51** 16 26N 74 38 E
Chikugo, *Japan* **64** 33 14N 130 28 E
Chikuma-Gawa →, *Japan* **65** 36 59N 138 35 E
Chikwawa, *Malawi* **93** 16 2 S 34 50 E
Chilac, *Mexico* **127** 18 20N 97 24W
Chilako →, *Canada* **110** 53 53N 122 57W
Chilam Chavki, *Pakistan* **49** 35 5N 75 5 E
Chilanga, *Zambia* **93** 15 33 S 28 16 E
Chilapa, *Mexico* **127** 17 40N 99 11W
Chilas, *Pakistan* **49** 35 25N 74 5 E
Chilcotin →, *Canada* **110** 51 44N 122 23W
Childers, *Australia* **73** 25 15 S 152 17 E
Childress, *U.S.A.* **121** 34 30N 100 15W
Chile ■, *S. Amer.* **142** 35 0 S 72 0W
Chile Chico, *Chile* **142** 46 33 S 71 44W
Chile Rise, *Pac. Oc.* **67** 38 0 S 92 0W
Chilecito, *Argentina* **140** 29 10 S 67 30W
Chilete, *Peru* **136** 7 10 S 78 50W
Chilhowee, *U.S.A.* **118** 38 36N 93 51W
Chililabombwe, *Zambia* **93** 12 18 S 27 43 E
Chilin = Jilin, *China* **61** 43 44N 126 30 E
Chilka L., *India* **50** 19 40N 85 25 E
Chilko →, *Canada* **110** 52 0N 123 40W
Chilko, L., *Canada* **110** 51 20N 124 10W
Chillagoe, *Australia* **72** 17 7 S 144 33 E
Chillán, *Chile* **140** 36 40 S 72 10W
Chillicothe, *Ill., U.S.A.* **118** 40 55N 89 32W
Chillicothe, *Mo., U.S.A.* **118** 39 45N 93 30W
Chillicothe, *Ohio, U.S.A.* **114** 39 20N 82 58W
Chillingham, *Australia* **77** 28 20 S 153 17 E
Chillingollah, *Australia* **74** 35 16 S 143 3 E
Chilliwack, *Canada* **110** 49 10N 121 54W
Chilo, *India* **48** 27 25N 73 32 E
Chiloane, I., *Mozam.* **97** 20 40 S 34 55 E
Chiloé □, *Chile* **142** 43 0 S 73 0W
Chiloé, I. de, *Chile* **142** 42 30 S 73 50W
Chilonda, *Angola* **95** 11 19 S 16 12 E
Chilpancingo, *Mexico* **127** 17 30N 99 30W
Chiltern, *Australia* **75** 36 10 S 146 36 E
Chiltern Hills, *U.K.* **13** 51 44N 0 42W
Chilton, *U.S.A.* **114** 44 1N 88 12W
Chiluage, *Angola* **95** 9 30 S 21 50 E
Chilubula, *Zambia* **93** 10 14 S 30 51 E
Chilumba, *Malawi* **93** 10 28 S 34 12 E
Chilwa, L., *Malawi* **93** 15 15 S 35 40 E
Chimaltitán, *Mexico* **126** 21 46N 103 50W
Chimán, *Panama* **128** 8 45N 78 40W
Chimay, *Belgium* **17** 50 3N 4 20 E
Chimbay, *U.S.S.R.* **40** 42 57N 59 47 E
Chimborazo, *Ecuador* **134** 1 29 S 78 55W
Chimborazo □, *Ecuador* **134** 1 0 S 78 40W
Chimbote, *Peru* **136** 9 0 S 78 35W
Chimkent, *U.S.S.R.* **40** 42 18N 69 36 E
Chimoio, *Mozam.* **93** 19 4 S 33 30 E
Chimpembe, *Zambia* **93** 9 31 S 29 33 E
Chin □, *Burma* **52** 22 0N 93 0 E
Chin Hills, *Burma* **52** 22 30N 93 30 E
Chin Ling Shan = Qinling Shandi, *China* **60** 33 50N 108 10 E
China, *Mexico* **127** 25 40N 99 20W
China ■, *Asia* **62** 30 0N 110 0 E
China Lake, *U.S.A.* **125** 35 44N 117 37W
Chinacota, *Colombia* **134** 7 37N 72 36W
Chinan = Jinan, *China* **60** 36 38N 117 1 E
Chinandega, *Nic.* **128** 12 35N 87 12W
Chinati Pk., *U.S.A.* **121** 30 0N 104 25W
Chincha Alta, *Peru* **136** 13 25 S 76 7W
Chinchilla, *Australia* **73** 26 45 S 150 38 E
Chinchilla de Monte Aragón, *Spain* **25** 38 53N 1 40W
Chinchón, *Spain* **24** 40 9N 3 26W
Chinchorro, Banco, *Mexico* **127** 18 35N 87 20W
Chinchou = Jinzhou, *China* **61** 41 5N 121 3 E
Chinchoua, *Gabon* **94** 0 1N 9 48 E
Chincoteague, *U.S.A.* **114** 37 58N 75 21W
Chinde, *Mozam.* **93** 18 35 S 36 30 E
Chindwin →, *Burma* **52** 21 26N 95 15 E
Chineni, *India* **49** 33 2N 75 15 E
Chinga, *Mozam.* **93** 15 13 S 38 35 E
Chingola, *Zambia* **93** 12 31 S 27 53 E
Chingole, *Malawi* **93** 13 4 S 34 17 E
Chingoroi, *Angola* **95** 13 37 S 14 1 E
Ch'ingtao = Qingdao, *China* **61** 36 5N 120 20 E
Chinguar, *Angola* **95** 12 25 S 16 45 E
Chinguetti, *Mauritania* **84** 20 25N 12 24W
Chingune, *Mozam.* **97** 20 33 S 35 0 E
Chinhae, *S. Korea* **61** 35 9N 128 47 E
Chinhanguanine, *Mozam.* **97** 25 21 S 32 30 E
Chinhoyi, *Zimb.* **93** 17 20 S 30 8 E
Chiniot, *Pakistan* **48** 31 45N 73 0 E
Chínipas, *Mexico* **126** 27 22N 108 32W
Chinju, *S. Korea* **61** 35 12N 128 2 E
Chinkapook, *Australia* **74** 35 11 S 142 57 E
Chinle, *U.S.A.* **123** 36 14N 109 38W
Chinnamanur, *India* **51** 9 50N 77 24 E
Chinnampo, *N. Korea* **61** 38 52N 125 10 E
Chinnur, *India* **50** 18 57N 79 49 E
Chino, *Japan* **65** 35 59N 138 9 E
Chino, *U.S.A.* **125** 34 1N 117 41W
Chino Valley, *U.S.A.* **123** 34 54N 112 28W
Chinon, *France* **18** 47 10N 0 15 E
Chinook, *Canada* **111** 51 28N 110 59W
Chinook, *U.S.A.* **122** 48 35N 109 19W
Chinsali, *Zambia* **93** 10 30 S 32 2 E
Chintamani, *India* **51** 13 26N 78 3 E
Chióggia, *Italy* **27** 45 13N 12 15 E
Chíos = Khíos, *Greece* **35** 38 27N 26 9 E
Chipata, *Zambia* **93** 13 38 S 32 28 E
Chipatujah, *Indonesia* **57** 7 45 S 108 0 E
Chipewyan L., *Canada* **111** 58 0N 98 27W
Chipinge, *Zimb.* **93** 20 13 S 32 28 E
Chipiona, *Spain* **23** 36 44N 6 26W
Chipley, *U.S.A.* **115** 30 45N 85 32W
Chiplun, *India* **50** 17 31N 73 34 E
Chipman, *Canada* **105** 46 6N 65 53W
Chipoka, *Malawi* **93** 13 57 S 34 28 E
Chippenham, *U.K.* **13** 51 27N 2 7W
Chippewa →, *U.S.A.* **120** 44 25N 92 10W
Chippewa Falls, *U.S.A.* **120** 44 55N 91 22W
Chiquián, *Peru* **136** 10 10 S 77 0W
Chiquimula, *Guatemala* **128** 14 51N 89 37W
Chiquinquira, *Colombia* **134** 5 37N 73 50W
Chiquitos, Llanos de, *Bolivia* **137** 18 0 S 61 30W
Chir →, *U.S.S.R.* **39** 48 30N 43 0 E
Chirala, *India* **51** 15 50N 80 26 E
Chiramba, *Mozam.* **93** 16 55 S 34 39 E
Chiran, *Japan* **64** 31 22N 130 27 E
Chirawa, *India* **48** 28 14N 75 42 E
Chirayinkil, *India* **51** 8 41N 76 49 E
Chirchik, *U.S.S.R.* **40** 41 29N 69 35 E
Chirfa, *Niger* **87** 20 55N 12 22 E
Chirgua →, *Venezuela* **134** 8 54N 67 58W
Chiricahua Pk., *U.S.A.* **123** 31 53N 109 14W
Chirikof I., *U.S.A.* **102** 55 50N 155 40W
Chiriquí, G. de, *Panama* **128** 8 0N 82 10W
Chiriquí, L. de, *Panama* **128** 9 10N 82 0W
Chirivira Falls, *Zimb.* **93** 21 10 S 32 12 E
Chirpan, *Bulgaria* **34** 42 10N 25 19 E
Chirripó Grande, Cerro, *Costa Rica* **128** 9 29N 83 29W
Chisamba, *Zambia* **93** 14 55 S 28 20 E
Chisholm, *Canada* **110** 54 55N 114 10W
Chishtian Mandi, *Pakistan* **48** 29 50N 72 55 E
Chishui, *China* **58** 28 30N 105 42 E
Chishui He →, *China* **58** 28 49N 105 50 E
Chisimaio, *Somali Rep.* **98** 0 22 S 42 32 E
Chisimba Falls, *Zambia* **93** 10 12 S 30 56 E
Chisone →, *Italy* **26** 44 49N 7 25 E
Chisos Mts., *U.S.A.* **121** 29 20N 103 15W
Chistopol, *U.S.S.R.* **37** 55 25N 50 38 E
Chita, *Colombia* **134** 6 11N 72 28W
Chita, *U.S.S.R.* **41** 52 0N 113 35 E
Chitado, *Angola* **95** 17 10 S 14 8 E
Chitapur, *India* **50** 17 10N 77 5 E
Chitembo, *Angola* **95** 13 30 S 16 50 E
Chitipa, *Malawi* **93** 9 41 S 33 19 E
Chitrakot, *India* **50** 19 10N 81 40 E
Chitral, *Pakistan* **47** 35 50N 71 56 E
Chitravati →, *India* **51** 14 45N 78 15 E
Chitré, *Panama* **128** 7 59N 80 27W
Chittagong, *Bangla.* **52** 22 19N 91 48 E
Chittagong □, *Bangla.* **52** 24 5N 91 0 E
Chittaurgarh, *India* **48** 24 52N 74 38 E
Chittoor, *India* **51** 13 15N 79 5 E
Chittur, *India* **51** 10 40N 76 45 E
Chiumba, *Angola* **95** 12 29 S 16 8 E
Chiume, *Angola* **95** 15 3 S 21 14 E
Chiusa, *Italy* **27** 46 38N 11 34 E
Chiusi, *Italy* **27** 43 1N 11 58 E
Chiva, *Spain* **25** 39 27N 0 41W
Chivacoa, *Venezuela* **134** 10 10N 68 54W
Chivasso, *Italy* **26** 45 10N 7 52 E
Chivay, *Peru* **136** 15 40 S 71 35W
Chivhu, *Zimb.* **93** 19 2 S 30 52 E
Chivilcoy, *Argentina* **140** 34 55 S 60 0W
Chiwanda, *Tanzania* **93** 11 23 S 34 55 E
Chixi, *China* **59** 22 0N 112 58 E
Chizela, *Zambia* **93** 13 10 S 25 0 E
Chkalov = Orenburg, *U.S.S.R.* **40** 51 45N 55 6 E
Chkolovsk, *U.S.S.R.* **37** 56 50N 43 10 E
Chloride, *U.S.A.* **125** 35 25N 114 12W
Cho Bo, *Vietnam* **54** 20 46N 105 10 E
Cho Phuoc Hai, *Vietnam* **55** 10 26N 107 18 E
Choba, *Kenya* **92** 2 30N 38 5 E
Chobe National Park, *Botswana* **96** 18 0 S 25 0 E
Chociwel, *Poland* **32** 53 29N 15 21 E
Chocó □, *Colombia* **134** 6 0N 77 0W
Chocontá, *Colombia* **134** 5 9N 73 41W
Chodavaram, *India* **50** 17 50N 82 57 E
Chodecz, *Poland* **32** 52 24N 19 2 E
Chodziez, *Poland* **32** 52 58N 16 58 E
Choele Choel, *Argentina* **142** 39 11 S 65 40W
Chōfu, *Japan* **65** 35 39N 139 33 E
Choiseul, *Solomon Is.* **68** 7 0 S 156 40 E
Choisy-le-Roi, *France* **19** 48 45N 2 24 E
Choix, *Mexico* **126** 26 40N 108 23W
Chojnice, *Poland* **32** 53 42N 17 32 E
Chojnów, *Poland* **32** 51 18N 15 58 E
Choke Mts., *Ethiopia* **89** 11 18N 37 15 E
Chokurdakh, *U.S.S.R.* **41** 70 38N 147 55 E
Cholame, *U.S.A.* **124** 35 44N 120 18W
Cholet, *France* **18** 47 4N 0 52W
Choluteca, *Honduras* **128** 13 20N 87 14W
Choluteca →, *Honduras* **128** 13 0N 87 20W
Chom Bung, *Thailand* **54** 13 37N 99 36 E
Chom Thong, *Thailand* **54** 18 25N 98 41 E
Choma, *Zambia* **93** 16 48 S 26 59 E
Chomen Swamp, *Ethiopia* **89** 9 20N 37 10 E
Chomun, *India* **48** 27 15N 75 40 E
Chomutov, *Czech.* **32** 50 28N 13 23 E
Chon Buri, *Thailand* **54** 13 21N 101 1 E
Chon Thanh, *Vietnam* **55** 11 24N 106 36 E
Chonan, *S. Korea* **61** 36 48N 127 9 E
Chone, *Ecuador* **134** 0 40 S 80 0W
Chong Kai, *Cambodia* **54** 13 57N 103 35 E
Chong Mek, *Thailand* **54** 15 10N 105 27 E
Chong'an, *China* **59** 27 45N 118 0 E
Chongde, *China* **59** 30 32N 120 26 E
Chongjin, *N. Korea* **61** 41 47N 129 50 E
Chŏngju, *N. Korea* **61** 39 40N 125 5 E
Chŏngju, *S. Korea* **61** 36 39N 127 27 E
Chongli, *China* **60** 40 58N 115 15 E
Chongming, *China* **59** 31 38N 121 23 E
Chongming Dao, *China* **59** 31 40N 121 30 E
Chongoyape, *Peru* **136** 6 35 S 79 25W
Chongqing, *Sichuan, China* **58** 29 35N 106 25 E
Chongqing, *Sichuan, China* **58** 30 38N 103 40 E
Chongren, *China* **59** 27 46N 116 3 E
Chongzuo, *China* **58** 22 23N 107 20 E
Chŏnju, *S. Korea* **61** 35 50N 127 4 E
Chonos, Arch. de los, *Chile* **142** 45 0 S 75 0W
Chopda, *India* **50** 21 20N 75 15 E
Chopim →, *Brazil* **141** 25 35 S 53 5W
Chorbat La, *India* **49** 34 42N 76 37 E
Chorley, *U.K.* **12** 53 39N 2 39W
Chorolque, Cerro, *Bolivia* **140** 20 59 S 66 5W
Chorregon, *Australia* **72** 22 40 S 143 32 E
Chorrera, La, *Colombia* **134** 0 44 S 73 1W
Chortkov, *U.S.S.R.* **36** 49 2N 25 46 E
Chŏrwŏn, *S. Korea* **61** 38 15N 127 10 E
Chorzów, *Poland* **32** 50 18N 18 57 E
Chos-Malal, *Argentina* **140** 37 20 S 70 15W
Chosan, *N. Korea* **61** 40 50N 125 47 E
Chōshi, *Japan* **65** 35 45N 140 51 E
Choszczno, *Poland* **32** 53 7N 15 25 E
Chota, *Peru* **136** 6 33 S 78 39W
Choteau, *U.S.A.* **122** 47 50N 112 10W
Chotila, *India* **48** 22 23N 71 15 E
Chowchilla, *U.S.A.* **124** 37 11N 120 12W
Chowkham, *Burma* **52** 20 52N 97 28 E
Choybalsan, *Mongolia* **62** 48 4N 114 30 E
Chrisman, *U.S.A.* **119** 39 48N 87 41W
Christchurch, *N.Z.* **81** 43 33 S 172 47 E
Christchurch, *U.K.* **13** 50 44N 1 33W
Christian I., *Canada* **106** 44 50N 80 12W
Christiana, *S. Africa* **96** 27 52 S 25 8 E
Christiansfeld, *Denmark* **11** 55 21N 9 29 E
Christiansted, *Virgin Is.* **129** 17 45N 64 42W
Christie B., *Canada* **111** 62 32N 111 10W
Christina →, *Canada* **111** 56 40N 111 3W
Christmas Cr. →, *Australia* **78** 18 29 S 125 23 E
Christmas Creek, *Australia* **78** 18 29 S 125 23 E
Christmas I. = Kiritimati, *Kiribati* **67** 1 58N 157 27W
Christmas I., *Ind. Oc.* **53** 10 30 S 105 40 E
Christopher L., *Australia* **79** 24 49 S 127 42 E
Chrudim, *Czech.* **32** 49 58N 15 43 E
Chrzanów, *Poland* **32** 50 10N 19 21 E
Chtimba, *Malawi* **93** 10 35 S 34 13 E
Chu, *U.S.S.R.* **40** 43 36N 73 42 E
Chu →, *Vietnam* **54** 19 53N 105 45 E
Chu Chua, *Canada* **110** 51 22N 120 10W
Chu Lai, *Vietnam* **54** 15 28N 108 45 E
Chu Xian, *China* **59** 32 19N 118 20 E
Chuadanga, *Bangla.* **52** 23 38N 88 51 E
Ch'uanchou = Quanzhou, *China* **59** 24 55N 118 34 E
Chuankou, *China* **60** 34 20N 110 59 E
Chūbu □, *Japan* **65** 36 45N 137 30 E
Chubut □, *Argentina* **142** 43 30 S 69 0W
Chubut →, *Argentina* **142** 43 20 S 65 5W
Chuchi L., *Canada* **110** 55 12N 124 30W
Chudovo, *U.S.S.R.* **36** 59 10N 31 41 E
Chudskoye, Oz., *U.S.S.R.* **36** 58 13N 27 30 E
Chūgoku □, *Japan* **64** 35 0N 133 0 E
Chūgoku-Sanchi, *Japan* **64** 35 0N 133 0 E
Chuguyev, *U.S.S.R.* **38** 49 55N 36 45 E
Chugwater, *U.S.A.* **120** 41 48N 104 47W
Chukhloma, *U.S.S.R.* **37** 58 45N 42 40 E
Chukotskiy Khrebet, *U.S.S.R.* **41** 68 0N 175 0 E
Chukotskoye More, *U.S.S.R.* **41** 68 0N 175 0W
Chula, *U.S.A.* **118** 39 55N 93 29W
Chula Vista, *U.S.A.* **125** 32 39N 117 8W
Chulman, *U.S.S.R.* **41** 56 52N 124 52 E
Chulucanas, *Peru* **136** 5 8 S 80 10W
Chulumani, *Bolivia* **136** 16 24 S 67 31W
Chulym →, *U.S.S.R.* **40** 57 43N 83 51 E
Chum Phae, *Thailand* **54** 16 40N 102 6 E
Chum Saeng, *Thailand* **54** 15 55N 100 15 E
Chuma, *Bolivia* **136** 15 24 S 68 56W
Chumar, *India* **49** 32 40N 78 35 E
Chumbicha, *Argentina* **140** 29 0 S 66 10W
Chumerna, *Bulgaria* **34** 42 45N 25 55 E
Chumikan, *U.S.S.R.* **41** 54 40N 135 10 E
Chumphon, *Thailand* **55** 10 35N 99 14 E
Chumpi, *Peru* **136** 15 4 S 73 46W
Chumuare, *Mozam.* **93** 14 31 S 31 50 E
Chuna →, *U.S.S.R.* **41** 57 47N 94 37 E
Chun'an, *China* **59** 29 35N 119 3 E
Chunchŏn, *S. Korea* **61** 37 58N 127 44 E
Chunchura, *India* **49** 22 53N 88 27 E
Chunga, *Zambia* **93** 15 0 S 26 2 E
Chungking = Chongqing, *China* **58** 29 35N 106 25 E
Chungt'iaoshan = Zhongtiao Shan, *China* **60** 35 0N 111 10 E
Chunian, *Pakistan* **48** 30 57N 74 0 E
Chunya, *Tanzania* **93** 8 30 S 33 27 E
Chunya □, *Tanzania* **92** 7 48 S 33 0 E
Chunyang, *China* **61** 43 38N 129 23 E
Chuquibamba, *Peru* **136** 15 47 S 72 44W
Chuquibambilla, *Peru* **136** 14 7 S 72 41W
Chuquicamata, *Chile* **140** 22 15 S 69 0W
Chuquisaca □, *Bolivia* **137** 20 30 S 63 30W
Chur, *Switz.* **31** 46 52N 9 32 E
Churachandpur, *India* **52** 24 20N 93 40 E
Churchill, *Australia* **75** 38 19 S 146 25 E
Churchill, *Canada* **111** 58 47N 94 11W
Churchill →, *Man., Canada* **111** 58 47N 94 12W
Churchill →, *Nfld., Canada* **105** 53 19N 60 10W
Churchill, C., *Canada* **111** 58 46N 93 12W
Churchill Falls, *Canada* **105** 53 36N 64 19W
Churchill L., *Canada* **111** 55 55N 108 20W
Churchill Pk., *Canada* **110** 58 10N 125 10W
Churdan, *U.S.A.* **118** 42 9N 94 29W
Churu, *India* **48** 28 20N 74 50 E
Churubusco, *U.S.A.* **119** 41 14N 85 19W
Chushal, *India* **49** 33 40N 78 40 E
Chusovoy, *U.S.S.R.* **40** 58 15N 57 40 E
Chute-aux-Outardes, *Canada* **107** 49 7N 68 24W
Chute-des-Passes, *Canada* **107** 49 52N 71 16W
Chuvash A.S.S.R.□, *U.S.S.R.* **37** 55 30N 47 0 E
Chuxiong, *China* **58** 25 2N 101 28 E
Ci Xian, *China* **60** 36 20N 114 25 E
Ciacova, *Romania* **34** 45 35N 21 10 E
Cianjur, *Indonesia* **57** 6 49 S 107 8 E
Cibadok, *Indonesia* **57** 6 53 S 106 47 E
Cibatu, *Indonesia* **57** 7 8 S 107 59 E
Cibola, *U.S.A.* **125** 33 17N 114 42W
Cicero, *Ill., U.S.A.* **119** 41 51N 87 45W
Cicero, *U.S.A.* **114** 41 48N 87 48W
Cícero Dantas, *Brazil* **138** 10 36 S 38 23W
Cidacos →, *Spain* **24** 42 21N 1 38W
Cide, *Turkey* **38** 41 53N 33 1 E
Ciechanów, *Poland* **32** 52 52N 20 38 E
Ciego de Avila, *Cuba* **128** 21 50N 78 50W
Ciénaga, *Colombia* **134** 11 1N 74 15W
Ciénaga de Oro, *Colombia* **134** 8 53N 75 37W
Cienfuegos, *Cuba* **128** 22 10N 80 30W
Cieplice Śląskie Zdrój, *Poland* **32** 50 50N 15 40 E
Cierp, *France* **20** 42 55N 0 40 E
Cíes, Is., *Spain* **22** 42 12N 8 55W
Cieszyn, *Poland* **32** 49 45N 18 35 E
Cieza, *Spain* **25** 38 17N 1 23W
Cifuentes, *Spain* **24** 40 47N 2 37W
Cihuatlán, *Mexico* **126** 19 14N 104 35W
Cijara, Pantano de, *Spain* **23** 39 18N 4 52W
Cijulang, *Indonesia* **57** 7 42 S 108 27 E
Cikajang, *Indonesia* **57** 7 25 S 107 48 E
Cikampek, *Indonesia* **57** 6 23 S 107 28 E
Cilacap, *Indonesia* **57** 7 43 S 109 0 E
Çıldır, *Turkey* **39** 41 10N 43 20 E
Cili, *China* **59** 29 30N 111 8 E
Cilician Gates P., *Turkey* **46** 37 20N 34 52 E
Cima, *U.S.A.* **125** 35 14N 115 30W
Cimahi, *Indonesia* **57** 6 53 S 107 33 E
Cimarron, *Kans., U.S.A.* **121** 37 50N 100 20W
Cimarron, *N. Mex., U.S.A.* **121** 36 30N 104 52W
Cimarron →, *U.S.A.* **121** 36 10N 96 17W
Cimone, Mte., *Italy* **26** 44 10N 10 40 E
Cîmpina, *Romania* **34** 45 10N 25 45 E
Cîmpulung, *Argeş, Romania* **34** 45 17N 25 3 E
Cîmpulung, *Suceava, Romania* **34** 47 32N 25 30 E
Cinca →, *Spain* **24** 41 26N 0 21 E
Cincinnati, *Iowa, U.S.A.* **118** 40 38N 92 56W
Cincinnati, *Ohio, U.S.A.* **119** 39 10N 84 26W
Cîndeşti, *Romania* **34** 45 15N 26 42 E
Ciney, *Belgium* **17** 50 18N 5 5 E
Cíngoli, *Italy* **27** 43 23N 13 10 E
Cinigiano, *Italy* **27** 42 53N 11 23 E
Cinto, Mte., *France* **21** 42 24N 8 54 E
Ciorani, *Romania* **34** 44 45N 26 25 E
Ciotat, La, *France* **21** 43 10N 5 37 E
Čiovo, *Yugoslavia* **27** 43 30N 16 17 E
Cipó, *Brazil* **138** 11 6 S 38 31W
Circeo, Monte, *Italy* **28** 41 14N 13 3 E
Circle, *Alaska, U.S.A.* **102** 65 50N 144 10W
Circle, *Mont., U.S.A.* **120** 47 26N 105 35W
Circleville, *Ohio, U.S.A.* **114** 39 35N 82 57W
Circleville, *Utah, U.S.A.* **123** 38 12N 112 24W
Cirebon, *Indonesia* **57** 6 45 S 108 32 E
Cirencester, *U.K.* **13** 51 43N 1 59W

Cirey-sur-Vezouze, France **19** 48 35N 6 57 E
Ciriè, Italy **26** 45 14N 7 35 E
Cirò, Italy **29** 39 23N 17 3 E
Ciron →, France **20** 44 36N 0 18W
Cisco, U.S.A. **121** 32 25N 99 0W
Ciskei □, S. Africa **97** 33 0 S 27 0 E
Cislău, Romania **34** 45 14N 26 20 E
Cisne, U.S.A. **119** 38 31N 88 26W
Cisneros, Colombia **134** 6 33N 75 4W
Cissna Park, U.S.A. **119** 40 34N 87 54W
Cisterna di Latina, Italy **28** 41 35N 12 50 E
Cisternino, Italy **29** 40 45N 17 26 E
Citaré →, Brazil **135** 1 11N 54 41W
Citeli-Ckaro, U.S.S.R. **39** 41 33N 46 0 E
Citlaltépetl, Mexico **127** 19 0N 97 20W
Citrus Heights, U.S.A. **124** 38 42N 121 17W
Citrusdal, S. Africa **96** 32 35 S 19 0 E
Città della Pieve, Italy **27** 42 57N 12 0 E
Città di Castello, Italy **27** 43 27N 12 14 E
Città Sant' Angelo, Italy **27** 42 32N 14 5 E
Cittadella, Italy **27** 45 39N 11 48 E
Cittaducale, Italy **27** 42 24N 12 58 E
Cittanova, Italy **29** 38 22N 16 5 E
Ciucaş, Romania **34** 45 31N 25 56 E
Ciudad Altamirano, Mexico **126** 18 20N 100 40W
Ciudad Bolívar, Venezuela **135** 8 5N 63 36W
Ciudad Camargo, Mexico **126** 27 41N 105 10W
Ciudad de Valles, Mexico **127** 22 0N 99 0W
Ciudad del Carmen, Mexico **127** 18 38N 91 50W
Ciudad Delicias = Delicias, Mexico **126** 28 10N 105 30W
Ciudad Guayana, Venezuela **135** 8 0N 62 30W
Ciudad Guerrero, Mexico **126** 28 33N 107 28W
Ciudad Guzmán, Mexico **126** 19 40N 103 30W
Ciudad Juárez, Mexico **126** 31 40N 106 28W
Ciudad Madero, Mexico **127** 22 19N 97 50W
Ciudad Mante, Mexico **127** 22 50N 99 0W
Ciudad Obregón, Mexico **126** 27 28N 109 59W
Ciudad Ojeda, Venezuela **134** 10 12N 71 19W
Ciudad Real, Spain **23** 38 59N 3 55W
Ciudad Real □, Spain **23** 38 50N 4 0W
Ciudad Rodrigo, Spain **22** 40 35N 6 32W
Ciudad Trujillo = Santo Domingo, Dom. Rep. **129** 18 30N 69 59W
Ciudad Victoria, Mexico **127** 23 41N 99 9W
Ciudadela, Spain **24** 40 0N 3 50 E
Ciulniţa, Romania **34** 44 26N 27 22 E
Cividale del Friuli, Italy **27** 46 6N 13 25 E
Cívita Castellana, Italy **27** 42 18N 12 24 E
Civitanova Marche, Italy **27** 43 18N 13 41 E
Civitavécchia, Italy **27** 42 6N 11 46 E
Civitella del Tronto, Italy **27** 42 48N 13 40 E
Civray, France **20** 46 10N 0 17 E
Çivril, Turkey **46** 38 20N 29 43 E
Cixerri →, Italy **28** 39 20N 8 40 E
Cizre, Turkey **46** 37 19N 42 10 E
Clackline, Australia **79** 31 40 S 116 32 E
Clacton-on-Sea, U.K. **13** 51 47N 1 10 E
Clain →, France **18** 46 47N 0 33 E
Claire, Canada **107** 47 15N 68 40W
Claire, L., Canada **110** 58 35N 112 5W
Claire, Le, U.S.A. **118** 41 36N 90 21W
Clairemont, U.S.A. **121** 33 9N 100 44W
Clairton, U.S.A. **116** 40 18N 79 54W
Clairvaux-les-Lacs, France **21** 46 35N 5 45 E
Clallam Bay, U.S.A. **124** 48 15N 124 16W
Clamecy, France **19** 47 28N 3 30 E
Clanton, U.S.A. **115** 32 48N 86 36W
Clanwilliam, S. Africa **96** 32 11 S 18 52 E
Clapperton I., Canada **108** 46 0N 82 14W
Clara, Ireland **15** 53 20N 7 38W
Clara →, Australia **72** 19 8 S 142 30 E
Claraville, U.S.A. **125** 35 24N 118 20W
Clare, Australia **73** 33 50 S 138 37 E
Clare, U.S.A. **104** 43 47N 84 45W
Clare □, Ireland **15** 52 20N 9 0W
Clare →, Ireland **15** 53 22N 9 5W
Clare I., Ireland **15** 53 48N 10 0W
Claremont, Calif., U.S.A. **125** 34 6N 117 43W
Claremont, U.S.A. **117** 43 23N 72 20W
Claremont Pt., Australia **72** 14 1 S 143 41 E
Claremore, U.S.A. **121** 36 40N 95 37W
Claremorris, Ireland **15** 53 45N 9 0W
Clarence, U.S.A. **118** 39 45N 92 16W
Clarence →, Australia **77** 29 25 S 153 22 E
Clarence →, N.Z. **81** 42 10 S 173 56 E
Clarence, I., Chile **142** 54 0 S 72 0W
Clarence I., Antarctica **143** 61 10 S 54 0W
Clarence Str., Australia **78** 12 0 S 131 0 E
Clarence Str., U.S.A. **110** 55 40N 132 10W
Clarence Town, Bahamas **129** 23 6N 74 59W
Clarencetown, Australia **76** 32 34 S 151 46 E
Clarendon, Ark., U.S.A. **121** 34 41N 91 20W
Clarendon, Tex., U.S.A. **121** 34 58N 100 54W
Clarenville, Canada **105** 48 10N 54 1W
Claresholm, Canada **110** 50 0N 113 33W
Clarie Coast, Antarctica **143** 68 0 S 135 0 E
Clarinda, U.S.A. **120** 40 45N 95 0W
Clarion, Iowa, U.S.A. **118** 42 41N 93 46W
Clarion, Pa., U.S.A. **116** 41 12N 79 22W
Clarion →, U.S.A. **116** 41 9N 79 41W
Clarion Fracture Zone, Pac. Oc. **67** 20 0N 120 0W
Clark, U.S.A. **120** 44 55N 97 45W
Clark, Pt., Canada **108** 44 4N 81 45W
Clark Fork, U.S.A. **122** 48 9N 116 9W
Clark Fork →, U.S.A. **122** 48 9N 116 15W
Clark Hill Res., U.S.A. **115** 33 45N 82 20W
Clarkdale, U.S.A. **123** 34 53N 112 3W
Clarke City, Canada **105** 50 12N 66 38W
Clarke I., Australia **72** 40 32 S 148 10 E
Clarke L., Canada **111** 54 24N 106 54W
Clarke Ra., Australia **72** 20 45 S 148 20 E
Clark's Fork →, U.S.A. **122** 45 39N 108 43W
Clark's Harbour, Canada **105** 43 25N 65 38W
Clarks Summit, U.S.A. **117** 41 31N 75 44W
Clarksburg, U.S.A. **114** 39 18N 80 21W
Clarksdale, U.S.A. **121** 34 12N 90 33W
Clarkston, U.S.A. **122** 46 28N 117 2W
Clarksville, Ark., U.S.A. **121** 35 29N 93 27W
Clarksville, Iowa, U.S.A. **118** 42 47N 92 40W
Clarksville, Mich., U.S.A. **119** 42 50N 85 15W
Clarksville, Ohio, U.S.A. **119** 39 24N 83 59W
Clarksville, Tenn., U.S.A. **115** 36 32N 87 20W
Clarksville, Tex., U.S.A. **121** 33 37N 94 59W
Claro →, Brazil **139** 19 8 S 50 40W
Clatskanie, U.S.A. **124** 46 9N 123 12W
Claude, U.S.A. **121** 35 8N 101 22W
Claveria, Phil. **57** 18 37N 121 4 E
Clay, U.S.A. **124** 38 17N 121 10W
Clay Center, U.S.A. **120** 39 27N 97 9W
Clay City, Ind., U.S.A. **119** 39 17N 87 7W
Clay City, Ky., U.S.A. **119** 37 52N 83 55W
Clayette, La, France **21** 46 17N 4 19 E
Claypool, U.S.A. **123** 33 27N 110 55W
Claysville, U.S.A. **116** 40 5N 80 25W
Clayton, Idaho, U.S.A. **122** 44 12N 114 31W
Clayton, Ind., U.S.A. **119** 39 41N 86 31W
Clayton, N. Mex., U.S.A. **121** 36 30N 103 10W
Cle Elum, U.S.A. **122** 47 15N 120 57W
Clear, C., Ireland **15** 51 26N 9 30W
Clear, L., Canada **109** 45 26N 77 12W
Clear I., Ireland **15** 51 26N 9 30W
Clear L., U.S.A. **124** 39 5N 122 47W
Clear Lake, Iowa, U.S.A. **118** 43 8N 93 23W
Clear Lake, S. Dak., U.S.A. **120** 44 48N 96 41W
Clear Lake, Wash., U.S.A. **122** 48 27N 122 15W
Clear Lake Res., U.S.A. **122** 41 55N 121 10W
Clearfield, Iowa, U.S.A. **118** 40 48N 94 29W
Clearfield, Pa., U.S.A. **114** 41 0N 78 27W
Clearfield, Utah, U.S.A. **122** 41 10N 112 0W
Clearlake Highlands, U.S.A. **124** 38 57N 122 38W
Clearmont, U.S.A. **122** 44 43N 106 29W
Clearwater, Canada **110** 51 38N 120 2W
Clearwater, U.S.A. **115** 27 58N 82 45W
Clearwater →, Alta., Canada **110** 52 22N 114 57W
Clearwater →, Alta., Canada **111** 56 44N 111 23W
Clearwater Cr. →, Canada **110** 61 36N 125 30W
Clearwater Mts., U.S.A. **122** 46 20N 115 30W
Clearwater Prov. Park, Canada **111** 54 0N 101 0W
Cleburne, U.S.A. **121** 32 18N 97 25W
Cleethorpes, U.K. **12** 53 33N 0 2W
Cleeve Cloud, U.K. **13** 51 56N 2 0W
Clelles, France **21** 44 50N 5 38 E
Clemency, Lux. **17** 49 35N 5 53 E
Clerke Reef, Australia **78** 17 22 S 119 20 E
Clermont, Australia **72** 22 49 S 147 39 E
Clermont, Canada **107** 47 41N 70 14W
Clermont, France **19** 49 23N 2 24 E
Clermont-en-Argonne, France **19** 49 5N 5 4 E
Clermont-Ferrand, France **20** 45 46N 3 4 E
Clermont-l'Hérault, France **20** 43 38N 3 26 E
Clerval, France **19** 47 25N 6 30 E
Clervaux, Lux. **17** 50 4N 6 2 E
Cléry-St.-André, France **19** 47 50N 1 46 E
Cles, Italy **26** 46 21N 11 4 E
Cleveland, Australia **77** 27 30 S 153 15 E
Cleveland, Miss., U.S.A. **121** 33 43N 90 43W
Cleveland, Ohio, U.S.A. **116** 41 28N 81 43W
Cleveland, Okla., U.S.A. **121** 36 21N 96 33W
Cleveland, Tenn., U.S.A. **115** 35 9N 84 52W
Cleveland, Tex., U.S.A. **121** 30 18N 95 0W
Cleveland □, U.K. **12** 54 35N 1 8 E
Cleveland, C., Australia **72** 19 11 S 147 1 E
Cleveland Heights, U.S.A. **116** 41 32N 81 30W
Clevelândia, Brazil **141** 26 24 S 52 23W
Clevelândia do Norte, Brazil **135** 3 49N 51 52W
Cleves, U.S.A. **119** 39 10N 84 45W
Clew B., Ireland **15** 53 54N 9 50W
Clewiston, U.S.A. **115** 26 44N 80 50W
Clifden, Ireland **15** 53 30N 10 2W
Clifden, N.Z. **81** 46 1 S 167 42 E
Cliffdell, U.S.A. **124** 46 56N 121 5W
Clifton, Australia **77** 27 59 S 151 53 E
Clifton, Ariz., U.S.A. **123** 33 8N 109 23W
Clifton, Ill., U.S.A. **119** 40 56N 87 56W
Clifton, Tex., U.S.A. **121** 31 46N 97 35W
Clifton Beach, Australia **72** 16 46 S 145 39 E
Clifton Forge, U.S.A. **114** 37 49N 79 51W
Clifton Hills, Australia **73** 27 1 S 138 54 E
Climax, Canada **111** 49 10N 108 20W
Clinch →, U.S.A. **115** 36 0N 84 29W
Clingmans Dome, U.S.A. **115** 35 35N 83 30W
Clint, U.S.A. **123** 31 37N 106 11W
Clinton, B.C., Canada **110** 51 6N 121 35W
Clinton, Ont., Canada **108** 43 37N 81 32W
Clinton, N.Z. **81** 46 12 S 169 23 E
Clinton, Ark., U.S.A. **121** 35 37N 92 30W
Clinton, Ill., U.S.A. **120** 40 8N 89 0W
Clinton, Ind., U.S.A. **119** 39 40N 87 22W
Clinton, Iowa, U.S.A. **118** 41 50N 90 12W
Clinton, Mass., U.S.A. **117** 42 26N 71 40W
Clinton, Mo., U.S.A. **118** 38 20N 93 46W
Clinton, N.C., U.S.A. **115** 35 5N 78 15W
Clinton, Okla., U.S.A. **121** 35 30N 99 0W
Clinton, S.C., U.S.A. **115** 34 30N 81 54W
Clinton, Tenn., U.S.A. **115** 36 6N 84 10W
Clinton, Wash., U.S.A. **124** 47 59N 122 22W
Clinton, Wis., U.S.A. **119** 42 34N 88 52W
Clinton C., Australia **72** 22 30 S 150 45 E
Clinton Colden L., Canada **102** 63 58N 107 27W
Clintonville, U.S.A. **120** 44 35N 88 46W
Clipperton, I., Pac. Oc. **67** 10 18N 109 13W
Clipperton Fracture Zone, Pac. Oc. **67** 19 0N 122 0W
Clisson, France **18** 47 5N 1 16W
Clive, N.Z. **80** 39 36 S 176 58 E
Clive L., Canada **110** 63 13N 118 54W
Cliza, Bolivia **137** 17 36 S 65 56W
Cloates, Pt., Australia **78** 22 43 S 113 40 E
Clocolan, S. Africa **97** 28 55 S 27 34 E
Clodomira, Argentina **140** 27 35 S 64 14W
Clonakilty, Ireland **15** 51 37N 8 53W
Clonakilty B., Ireland **15** 51 33N 8 50W
Cloncurry, Australia **72** 20 40 S 140 28 E
Cloncurry →, Australia **72** 18 37 S 140 40 E
Clones, Ireland **15** 54 10N 7 13W
Clonmel, Ireland **15** 52 22N 7 42W
Cloppenburg, W. Germany **30** 52 50N 8 3 E
Cloquet, U.S.A. **120** 46 40N 92 30W
Clorinda, Argentina **140** 25 16 S 57 45W
Cloud Peak, U.S.A. **122** 44 23N 107 10W
Cloudcroft, U.S.A. **123** 33 0N 105 48W
Clouds Creek, Australia **77** 30 4 S 152 42 E
Cloudy B., N.Z. **81** 41 25 S 174 10 E
Clova, Canada **106** 48 7N 75 22W
Cloverdale, Calif., U.S.A. **124** 38 49N 123 0W
Cloverdale, Ind., U.S.A. **119** 39 31N 86 47W
Cloverport, U.S.A. **119** 37 50N 86 38W
Clovis, Calif., U.S.A. **124** 36 47N 119 45W
Clovis, N. Mex., U.S.A. **121** 34 20N 103 10W
Cloyes-sur-le-Loir, France **18** 48 0N 1 14 E
Cloyne, Canada **109** 44 49N 77 11W
Club Terrace, Australia **75** 37 35 S 148 58 E
Cluj-Napoca, Romania **34** 46 47N 23 38 E
Clunes, Australia **74** 37 20 S 143 45 E
Cluny, France **21** 46 26N 4 38 E
Cluses, France **21** 46 5N 6 35 E
Clusone, Italy **26** 45 54N 9 58 E
Clutha →, N.Z. **81** 46 20 S 169 49 E
Clwyd □, U.K. **12** 53 5N 3 20W
Clwyd →, U.K. **12** 53 20N 3 30W
Clyde, N.Z. **81** 45 12 S 169 20 E
Clyde, U.S.A. **116** 43 8N 76 52W
Clyde →, U.K. **14** 55 56N 4 29W
Clyde, Firth of, U.K. **14** 55 20N 5 0W
Clyde River, Canada **103** 70 30N 68 30W
Clydebank, U.K. **14** 55 54N 4 25W
Clymer, U.S.A. **116** 42 3N 79 39W
Côa →, Portugal **22** 41 5N 7 6W
Coachella, U.S.A. **125** 33 44N 116 13W
Coachella Canal, U.S.A. **125** 32 43N 114 57W
Coahoma, U.S.A. **121** 32 17N 101 20W
Coahuayana →, Mexico **126** 18 41N 103 45W
Coahuayutla, Mexico **126** 18 19N 101 42W
Coahuila □, Mexico **126** 27 0N 103 0W
Coal →, Canada **110** 59 39N 126 57W
Coal City, U.S.A. **119** 41 17N 88 17W
Coal I., N.Z. **81** 46 8 S 166 40 E
Coalane, Mozam. **93** 17 48 S 37 2 E
Coalcomán, Mexico **126** 18 40N 103 10W
Coaldale, Canada **110** 49 45N 112 35W
Coalgate, U.S.A. **121** 34 35N 96 13W
Coalinga, U.S.A. **124** 36 10N 120 21W
Coalville, U.K. **12** 52 43N 1 21W
Coalville, U.S.A. **122** 40 58N 111 24W
Coaraci, Brazil **139** 14 38 S 39 32W
Coari, Brazil **135** 4 8 S 63 7W
Coari →, Brazil **135** 4 30 S 63 33W
Coari, L. de, Brazil **135** 4 15 S 63 22W
Coast □, Kenya **92** 2 40 S 39 45 E
Coast Mts., Canada **110** 55 0N 129 20W
Coast Ranges, U.S.A. **124** 41 0N 123 0W
Coastal Plains Basin, Australia **79** 30 10 S 115 30 E
Coatbridge, U.K. **14** 55 52N 4 2W
Coatepec, Mexico **127** 19 27N 96 58W
Coatepeque, Guatemala **128** 14 46N 91 55W
Coatesville, U.S.A. **114** 39 59N 75 55W
Coaticook, Canada **107** 45 10N 71 46W
Coats I., Canada **103** 62 30N 83 0W
Coats Land, Antarctica **143** 77 0 S 25 0W
Coatzacoalcos, Mexico **127** 18 7N 94 25W
Cobalt, Canada **106** 47 25N 79 42W
Cobán, Guatemala **128** 15 30N 90 21W
Cobar, Australia **73** 31 27 S 145 48 E
Cobargo, Australia **75** 36 20 S 149 55 E
Cobba-da-mana, Australia **77** 28 24 S 151 14 E
Cobberas, Mt., Australia **75** 36 53 S 148 12 E
Cobden, Australia **74** 38 20 S 143 3 E
Cobden, Canada **109** 45 38N 76 53W
Cóbh, Ireland **15** 51 50N 8 18W
Cobham, Australia **73** 30 18 S 142 7 E
Cobija, Bolivia **136** 11 0 S 68 50W
Cobleskill, U.S.A. **117** 42 40N 74 30W
Coboconk, Canada **109** 44 39N 78 48W
Cobourg, Canada **109** 43 58N 78 10W
Cobourg Pen., Australia **78** 11 20 S 132 15 E
Cobram, Australia **74** 35 54 S 145 40 E
Cobre, U.S.A. **122** 41 6N 114 25W
Cóbué, Mozam. **93** 12 0 S 34 58 E
Coburg, W. Germany **31** 50 15N 10 58 E
Coca, Spain **22** 41 13N 4 32W
Coca →, Ecuador **134** 0 29 S 76 58W
Cocachacra, Peru **136** 17 5 S 71 45W
Cocal, Brazil **138** 3 28 S 41 34W
Cocanada = Kakinada, India **50** 16 57N 82 11 E
Cocentaina, Spain **25** 38 45N 0 27W
Cocha, La, Argentina **140** 27 50 S 65 40W
Cochabamba, Bolivia **137** 17 26 S 66 10W
Coche, I., Venezuela **135** 10 47N 63 56W
Cochem, W. Germany **31** 50 8N 7 7 E
Cochemane, Mozam. **93** 17 0 S 32 54 E
Cochin, India **51** 9 59N 76 22 E
Cochin China = Nam-Phan, Vietnam **55** 10 30N 106 0 E
Cochise, U.S.A. **123** 32 6N 109 58W
Cochran, U.S.A. **115** 32 25N 83 23W
Cochrane, Alta., Canada **110** 51 11N 114 30W
Cochrane, Ont., Canada **104** 49 0N 81 0W
Cochrane →, Canada **111** 59 0N 103 40W
Cochrane, L., Chile **142** 47 10 S 72 0W
Cockatoo, Australia **74** 37 57 S 145 32 E
Cockburn, Australia **73** 32 5 S 141 0 E
Cockburn, Canal, Chile **142** 54 30 S 72 0W
Cockburn I., Canada **108** 45 55N 83 22W
Cockburn Ra., Australia **78** 15 46 S 128 0 E
Cocklebiddy Motel, Australia **79** 32 0 S 126 3 E
Coco →, Cent. Amer. **128** 15 0N 83 8W
Coco, Pta., Colombia **134** 2 58N 77 43W
Cocoa, U.S.A. **115** 28 22N 80 40W
Cocobeach, Gabon **94** 0 59N 9 34 E
Côcos, Brazil **139** 14 10 S 44 33W
Côcos →, Brazil **139** 12 44 S 44 48W
Cocos I., Guam **68** 13 14N 144 39 E
Cocos I., Pac. Oc. **67** 5 25N 87 55W
Cocos Is., Ind. Oc. **53** 12 10 S 96 55 E
Cod, C., U.S.A. **113** 42 8N 70 10W
Codajás, Brazil **135** 3 55 S 62 0W
Codera, C., Venezuela **134** 10 35N 66 4W
Coderre, Canada **111** 50 11N 106 31W
Codigoro, Italy **27** 44 50N 12 5 E
Codó, Brazil **138** 4 30 S 43 55W
Codogno, Italy **26** 45 10N 9 42 E
Codpa, Chile **136** 18 50 S 69 44W
Codróipo, Italy **27** 45 57N 13 0 E
Cody, U.S.A. **122** 44 35N 109 0W
Coe Hill, Canada **109** 44 52N 77 50W
Coelemu, Chile **140** 36 30 S 72 48W
Coelho Neto, Brazil **138** 4 15 S 43 0W
Coen, Australia **72** 13 52 S 143 12 E
Coeroeni →, Surinam **135** 3 21N 57 31W
Coesfeld, W. Germany **30** 51 56N 7 10 E
Coetivy Is., Seychelles **53** 7 8 S 56 16 E
Cœur d'Alene, U.S.A. **122** 47 45N 116 51W
Cœur d'Alene L., U.S.A. **122** 47 32N 116 48W
Coevorden, Neths. **16** 52 40N 6 44 E
Cofete, Canary Is. **25** 28 6N 14 23W
Coffeyville, U.S.A. **121** 37 0N 95 40W
Coffs Harbour, Australia **77** 30 16 S 153 5 E
Cofrentes, Spain **25** 39 13N 1 5W

Cogealac, Romania 34 44 36N 28 36 E
Coghinas →, Italy 28 40 55N 8 48 E
Coghinas, L. di, Italy 28 40 46N 9 3 E
Cognac, France 20 45 41N 0 20W
Cogne, Italy 26 45 37N 7 21 E
Cogolludo, Spain 24 40 59N 3 10W
Cohagen, U.S.A. 122 47 2N 106 36W
Cohoes, U.S.A. 117 42 47N 73 42W
Cohuna, Australia 74 35 45 S 144 15 E
Coiba, I., Panama 128 7 30N 81 40W
Coig →, Argentina 142 51 0 S 69 10W
Coihaique, Chile 142 45 30 S 71 45W
Coimbatore, India 51 11 2N 76 59 E
Coimbra, Brazil 136 19 55 S 57 48W
Coimbra, Portugal 22 40 15N 8 27W
Coimbra □, Portugal 22 40 12N 8 25W
Coín, Spain 23 36 40N 4 48W
Coipasa, L. de, Bolivia 136 19 12 S 68 7W
Coipasa, Salar de, Bolivia 136 19 26 S 68 9W
Cojata, Peru 136 15 2 S 69 25W
Cojedes □, Venezuela 134 9 20N 68 20W
Cojedes →, Venezuela 134 8 34N 68 5W
Cojimies, Ecuador 136 0 20N 80 0W
Cojocna, Romania 34 46 45N 23 50 E
Cojutepequé, El Salv. 128 13 41N 88 54W
Cokeville, U.S.A. 122 42 4N 111 0W
Colaba Pt., India 50 18 54N 72 47 E
Colac, Australia 74 38 21 S 143 35 E
Colac, L., Australia 74 38 18 S 143 36 E
Colachel = Kolachel, India 51 8 10N 77 15 E
Colares, Portugal 23 38 48N 9 30W
Colatina, Brazil 139 19 32 S 40 37W
Colbeck, C., Antarctica 143 77 6 S 157 48W
Colbinabbin, Australia 74 36 38 S 144 48 E
Colborne, Canada 109 44 0N 77 53W
Colby, U.S.A. 120 39 27N 101 2W
Colchagua □, Chile 140 34 30 S 71 0W
Colchester, U.K. 13 51 54N 0 55 E
Coldstream, Australia 74 37 43 S 145 22 E
Coldstream, U.K. 14 55 39N 2 14W
Coldwater, Canada 108 44 42N 79 40W
Coldwater, Kans., U.S.A. 121 37 18N 99 24W
Coldwater, Mich., U.S.A. 119 41 57N 85 0W
Coldwater, Ohio, U.S.A. 119 40 29N 84 38W
Coldwater, L., U.S.A. 119 41 48N 84 59W
Cole Camp, U.S.A. 118 38 28N 93 12W
Colebrook, Australia 72 42 31 S 147 21 E
Colebrook, U.S.A. 117 44 54N 71 29W
Coleman, Canada 110 49 40N 114 30W
Coleman, U.S.A. 121 31 52N 99 30W
Coleman →, Australia 72 15 6 S 141 38 E
Colenso, S. Africa 97 28 44 S 29 50 E
Coleraine, Australia 74 37 36 S 141 40 E
Coleraine, U.K. 15 55 8N 6 40W
Coleraine □, U.K. 15 55 8N 6 40W
Coleridge, L., N.Z. 81 43 17 S 171 30 E
Coleroon →, India 51 11 25N 79 50 E
Colesberg, S. Africa 96 30 45 S 25 5 E
Colesburg, U.S.A. 118 42 38N 91 12W
Coleville, U.S.A. 124 38 34N 119 30W
Colfax, Calif., U.S.A. 124 39 6N 120 57W
Colfax, Ill., U.S.A. 119 40 34N 88 37W
Colfax, Ind., U.S.A. 119 40 12N 86 40W
Colfax, La., U.S.A. 121 31 35N 92 39W
Colfax, Wash., U.S.A. 122 46 57N 117 28W
Colhué Huapi, L., Argentina 142 45 30 S 69 0W
Cólico, Italy 26 46 8N 9 22 E
Coligny, France 21 46 23N 5 21 E
Coligny, S. Africa 97 26 17 S 26 15 E
Colima, Mexico 126 19 10N 103 40W
Colima □, Mexico 126 19 10N 103 40W
Colima, Nevado de, Mexico 126 19 35N 103 45W
Colina, Chile 140 33 13 S 70 45W
Colina do Norte, Guinea-Biss. 90 12 28N 15 0W
Colinas, Goiás, Brazil 139 14 15 S 48 2W
Colinas, Maranhão, Brazil 138 6 0 S 44 10W
Colinton, Australia 76 35 50 S 149 10 E
Coll, U.K. 14 56 40N 6 35W
Collaguasi, Chile 140 21 5 S 68 45W
Collarada, Peña, Spain 24 42 43N 0 29W
Collarenebri, Australia 73 29 33 S 148 34 E
Collbran, U.S.A. 123 39 16N 107 58W
Colle di Val d'Elsa, Italy 27 43 25N 11 7 E
Colle Salvetti, Italy 26 43 34N 10 27 E
Colle Sannita, Italy 29 41 22N 14 48 E
Collécchio, Italy 26 44 45N 10 10 E
Collector, Australia 76 34 56 S 149 29 E
Colleen Bawn, Zimb. 93 21 0 S 29 12 E
College Park, U.S.A. 115 33 42N 84 27W
Collette, Canada 105 46 40N 65 30W
Collie, N.S.W., Australia 76 31 41 S 148 18 E
Collie, W. Austral., Australia 79 33 22 S 116 8 E
Collier B., Australia 78 16 10 S 124 15 E
Collier Ra., Australia 79 24 45 S 119 10 E
Colline Metallifere, Italy 26 43 10N 11 0 E
Collingwood, Canada 108 44 29N 80 13W
Collingwood, N.Z. 81 40 41 S 172 40 E
Collins, Canada 104 50 17N 89 27W
Collins, U.S.A. 118 37 54N 93 37W
Collinsville, Australia 72 20 30 S 147 56 E
Collinsville, U.S.A. 118 38 40N 89 59W
Collipulli, Chile 140 37 55 S 72 30W
Collo, Algeria 85 36 58N 6 37 E
Collonges, France 21 46 9N 5 52 E
Collooney, Ireland 15 54 11N 8 28W
Colmar, France 19 48 5N 7 20 E
Colmars, France 21 44 11N 6 39 E
Colmenar, Spain 23 36 54N 4 20W
Colmenar de Oreja, Spain 24 40 6N 3 25W
Colmenar Viejo, Spain 22 40 39N 3 47W
Colne, U.K. 12 53 51N 2 11W
Colo →, Australia 76 33 25 S 150 52 E
Cologna Véneta, Italy 27 45 19N 11 21 E
Cologne = Köln, W. Germany 30 50 56N 6 58 E
Coloma, U.S.A. 124 38 49N 120 53W
Colomb-Béchar = Béchar, Algeria 85 31 38N 2 18W
Colombey-les-Belles, France 19 48 32N 5 54 E
Colombey-les-Deux-Églises, France 19 48 13N 4 50 E
Colômbia, Brazil 139 20 10 S 48 40W
Colombia ■, S. Amer. 134 3 45N 73 0W
Colombier, Canada 107 48 52N 68 51W
Colombo, Sri Lanka 51 6 56N 79 58 E
Colombus, U.S.A. 123 31 54N 107 43W
Colome, U.S.A. 120 43 20N 99 44W
Colón, Argentina 140 32 12 S 58 10W
Colón, Cuba 128 22 42N 80 54W
Colón, Panama 128 9 20N 79 54W
Colón, Peru 136 5 0 S 81 0W
Colonella, Italy 27 42 52N 13 50 E
Colonia, Uruguay 140 34 25 S 57 50W
Colonia Dora, Argentina 140 28 34 S 62 59W
Colonial Hts., U.S.A. 114 37 19N 77 25W
Colonne, C. delle, Italy 29 39 2N 17 11 E
Colonsay, Canada 111 51 59N 105 52W
Colonsay, U.K. 14 56 4N 6 12W
Colorado □, U.S.A. 112 37 40N 106 0W
Colorado →, Argentina 142 39 50 S 62 8W
Colorado →, N. Amer. 123 31 45N 114 40W
Colorado →, U.S.A. 121 28 36N 95 58W
Colorado City, U.S.A. 121 32 25N 100 50W
Colorado Desert, U.S.A. 112 34 20N 116 0W
Colorado Plateau, U.S.A. 123 36 40N 110 30W
Colorado R. Aqueduct, U.S.A. 125 34 17N 114 10W
Colorado Springs, U.S.A. 120 38 55N 104 50W
Colorno, Italy 26 44 55N 10 21 E
Colotlán, Mexico 126 22 6N 103 16W
Colquechaca, Bolivia 137 18 40 S 66 1W
Colton, Calif., U.S.A. 125 34 4N 117 20W
Colton, N.Y., U.S.A. 117 44 34N 74 58W
Colton, Wash., U.S.A. 122 46 41N 117 6W
Columbia, Ill., U.S.A. 118 38 26N 90 12W
Columbia, La., U.S.A. 121 32 7N 92 5W
Columbia, Miss., U.S.A. 121 31 16N 89 50W
Columbia, Mo., U.S.A. 118 38 58N 92 20W
Columbia, Pa., U.S.A. 117 40 2N 76 30W
Columbia, S.C., U.S.A. 115 34 0N 81 0W
Columbia, Tenn., U.S.A. 115 35 40N 87 0W
Columbia →, N. Amer. 122 46 15N 124 5W
Columbia, C., Canada 144 83 0N 70 0W
Columbia, District of □, U.S.A. 114 38 55N 77 0W
Columbia, Mt., Canada 110 52 8N 117 20W
Columbia Basin, U.S.A. 122 47 30N 118 30W
Columbia Falls, U.S.A. 122 48 25N 114 16W
Columbia Heights, U.S.A. 120 45 5N 93 10W
Columbiana, U.S.A. 116 40 53N 80 40W
Columbretes, Is., Spain 24 39 50N 0 50 E
Columbus, Ga., U.S.A. 115 32 30N 84 58W
Columbus, Ind., U.S.A. 119 39 14N 85 55W
Columbus, Kans., U.S.A. 121 37 15N 94 30W
Columbus, Miss., U.S.A. 115 33 30N 88 26W
Columbus, Mont., U.S.A. 122 45 38N 109 14W
Columbus, N. Dak., U.S.A. 120 48 52N 102 48W
Columbus, Nebr., U.S.A. 120 41 30N 97 25W
Columbus, Ohio, U.S.A. 119 39 57N 83 1W
Columbus, Tex., U.S.A. 121 29 42N 96 33W
Columbus, Wis., U.S.A. 120 43 20N 89 2W
Columbus Grove, U.S.A. 119 40 55N 84 4W
Columbus Junction, U.S.A. 118 41 17N 91 22W
Colunga, Spain 22 43 29N 5 16W
Colusa, U.S.A. 124 39 15N 122 1W
Colville, U.S.A. 122 48 33N 117 54W
Colville →, U.S.A. 102 70 25N 151 0W
Colville, C., N.Z. 80 36 29 S 175 21 E
Colwyn Bay, U.K. 12 53 17N 3 44W
Coma, Ethiopia 89 8 29N 36 53 E
Comácchio, Italy 27 44 41N 12 10 E
Comalcalco, Mexico 127 18 16N 93 13W
Comallo, Argentina 142 41 0 S 70 5W
Comanche, Okla., U.S.A. 121 34 27N 97 58W
Comanche, Tex., U.S.A. 121 31 55N 98 35W
Comandante Luis Piedrabuena, Argentina 142 49 59 S 68 54W
Comănești, Romania 34 46 25N 26 26 E
Comarapa, Bolivia 137 17 54 S 64 29W
Comayagua, Honduras 128 14 25N 87 37W
Combahee →, U.S.A. 115 32 30N 80 31W
Combara, Australia 76 31 10 S 148 22 E
Combeaufontaine, France 19 47 38N 5 54 E
Comber, Canada 108 42 14N 82 33W
Combermere, Canada 109 45 22N 77 37W
Combermere Bay, Burma 52 19 37N 93 34 E
Comblain-au-Pont, Belgium 17 50 29N 5 35 E
Combles, France 19 50 0N 2 50 E
Combourg, France 18 48 25N 1 46W
Comboyne, Australia 77 31 34 S 152 27 E
Combronde, France 20 45 58N 3 5 E
Comeragh Mts., Ireland 15 52 17N 7 35W
Comet, Australia 72 23 36 S 148 38 E
Comet Vale, Australia 79 29 55 S 121 4 E
Comilla, Bangla. 52 23 28N 91 10 E
Comines, Belgium 17 50 46N 3 0 E
Comino, C., Italy 28 40 28N 9 47 E
Cómiso, Italy 29 36 57N 14 35 E
Comitán, Mexico 127 16 18N 92 9W
Commanda, Canada 108 45 57N 79 36W
Commentry, France 20 46 20N 2 46 E
Commerce, Ga., U.S.A. 115 34 10N 83 25W
Commerce, Tex., U.S.A. 121 33 15N 95 50W
Commercy, France 19 48 43N 5 34 E
Commewijne □, Surinam 135 5 25N 54 45W
Commissaires, L. des, Canada 107 48 10N 72 16W
Committee B., Canada 103 68 30N 86 30W
Commonwealth B., Antarctica 143 67 0 S 144 0 E
Commoron Cr. →, Australia 77 28 22 S 150 8 E
Communism Pk. = Kommunizma, Pik, U.S.S.R. 47 39 0N 72 2 E
Como, Italy 26 45 48N 9 5 E
Como, L. di, Italy 26 46 5N 9 17 E
Comodoro Rivadavia, Argentina 142 45 50 S 67 40W
Comorin, C., India 51 8 3N 77 40 E
Comoro Is. ■, Ind. Oc. 53 12 10 S 44 15 E
Comox, Canada 110 49 42N 124 55W
Compiègne, France 19 49 24N 2 50 E
Comporta, Portugal 23 38 22N 8 46W
Compostela, Mexico 126 21 15N 104 53W
Comprida, I., Brazil 141 24 50 S 47 42W
Compton, Canada 107 45 14N 71 49W
Compton, U.S.A. 125 33 54N 118 13W
Compton Downs, Australia 73 30 28 S 146 30 E
Con Cuong, Vietnam 54 19 2N 104 54 E
Con Son, Is., Vietnam 55 8 41N 106 37 E
Cona Niyeu, Argentina 142 41 58 S 67 0W
Conakry, Guinea 90 9 29N 13 49W
Conara Junction, Australia 72 41 50 S 147 26 E
Concarneau, France 18 47 52N 3 56W
Conceição, Brazil 138 7 33 S 38 31W
Conceição, Mozam. 93 18 47 S 36 7 E
Conceição da Barra, Brazil 139 18 35 S 39 45W
Conceição do Araguaia, Brazil 138 8 0 S 49 2W
Conceição do Canindé, Brazil 138 7 54 S 41 34W
Concepción, Argentina 140 27 20 S 65 35W
Concepción, Bolivia 137 16 15 S 62 8W
Concepción, Chile 140 36 50 S 73 0W
Concepción, Mexico 127 18 15N 90 5W
Concepción, Paraguay 140 23 22 S 57 26W
Concepción, Peru 136 11 54 S 75 19W
Concepción □, Chile 140 37 0 S 72 30W
Concepción →, Mexico 126 30 32N 113 2W
Concepción, Est. de, Chile 142 50 30 S 74 55W
Concepción, L., Bolivia 137 17 20 S 61 20W
Concepción, La = Ri-Aba, Eq. Guin. 91 3 28N 8 40 E
Concepción, La, Venezuela 134 10 30N 71 50W
Concepción, Punta, Mexico 126 26 55N 111 59W
Concepción del Oro, Mexico 126 24 40N 101 30W
Concepción del Uruguay, Argentina 140 32 35 S 58 20W
Conception, La, Canada 106 46 9N 74 42W
Conception, Pt., U.S.A. 125 34 30N 120 34W
Conception B., Namibia 96 23 55 S 14 22 E
Conception I., Bahamas 129 23 52N 75 9W
Concession, Zimb. 93 17 27 S 30 56 E
Conchas Dam, U.S.A. 121 35 25N 104 10W
Conche, Canada 105 50 55N 55 58W
Concho, U.S.A. 123 34 32N 109 43W
Concho →, U.S.A. 121 31 30N 99 45W
Conchos →, Chihuahua, Mexico 126 29 32N 104 25W
Conchos →, Tamaulipas, Mexico 127 25 9N 98 35W
Concord, Calif., U.S.A. 124 37 59N 122 2W
Concord, Mich., U.S.A. 119 42 11N 84 38W
Concord, N.C., U.S.A. 115 35 28N 80 35W
Concord, N.H., U.S.A. 117 43 12N 71 30W
Concordia, Argentina 140 31 20 S 58 2W
Concórdia, Brazil 134 4 36 S 66 36W
Concordia, Mexico 126 23 18N 106 2W
Concordia, Kans., U.S.A. 120 39 35N 97 40W
Concordia, Mo., U.S.A. 118 38 59N 93 34W
Concordia, La, Mexico 127 16 8N 92 38W
Concots, France 20 44 26N 1 40 E
Concrete, U.S.A. 122 48 35N 121 49W
Condah, Australia 74 37 57 S 141 44 E
Condamine, Australia 73 26 56 S 150 9 E
Condat, France 20 45 21N 2 46 E
Condé, Angola 95 10 50 S 14 37 E
Conde, Brazil 139 11 49 S 37 37W
Conde, U.S.A. 120 45 13N 98 5W
Condé-sur-l'Escaut, France 19 50 26N 3 34 E
Condé-sur-Noireau, France 18 48 51N 0 33W
Condeúba, Brazil 139 14 52 S 42 0W
Condobolin, Australia 76 33 4 S 147 6 E
Condom, France 20 43 57N 0 22 E
Condon, U.S.A. 122 45 15N 120 8W
Condove, Italy 26 45 8N 7 19 E
Conegliano, Italy 27 45 53N 12 18 E
Conejera, I., Spain 25 39 11N 2 58 E
Conejos, Mexico 126 26 14N 103 53W
Conflans-en-Jarnisy, France 19 49 10N 5 52 E
Confolens, France 20 46 2N 0 40 E
Confuso →, Paraguay 140 25 9 S 57 34W
Congjiang, China 58 25 43N 108 52 E
Congleton, U.K. 12 53 10N 2 12W
Congo = Zaïre →, Africa 94 6 4 S 12 24 E
Congo, Brazil 138 7 48 S 36 40W
Congo (Kinshasa) = Zaïre ■, Africa 95 3 0 S 23 0 E
Congo ■, Africa 94 1 0 S 16 0 E
Congo Basin, Africa 82 0 10 S 24 30 E
Congonhas, Brazil 139 20 30 S 43 52W
Congress, U.S.A. 123 34 11N 112 56W
Conil, Spain 23 36 17N 6 10W
Coniston, Canada 108 46 29N 80 51W
Conjeeveram = Kanchipuram, India 51 12 52N 79 45 E
Conjuboy, Australia 72 18 35 S 144 35 E
Conklin, Canada 111 55 38N 111 5W
Conlea, Australia 73 30 7 S 144 35 E
Conn, L., Ireland 15 54 3N 9 15W
Connacht, Ireland 15 53 23N 8 40W
Conneaut, U.S.A. 116 41 55N 80 32W
Connecticut □, U.S.A. 117 41 40N 72 40W
Connecticut →, U.S.A. 117 41 17N 72 21W
Connell, U.S.A. 122 46 36N 118 51W
Connellsville, U.S.A. 116 40 3N 79 32W
Connemara, Ireland 15 53 29N 9 45W
Connemaugh →, U.S.A. 116 40 38N 79 42W
Conner, La, U.S.A. 122 48 22N 122 27W
Connerré, France 18 48 3N 0 30 E
Connersville, U.S.A. 119 39 40N 85 10W
Connors, Canada 107 47 10N 68 52W
Connors Ra., Australia 72 21 40 S 149 10 E
Conoble, Australia 73 32 55 S 144 33 E
Conon →, U.K. 14 57 33N 4 28W
Cononaco →, Ecuador 134 1 32 S 75 35W
Cononbridge, U.K. 14 57 32N 4 30W
Conquest, Canada 111 51 32N 107 14W
Conquet, Le, France 18 48 21N 4 46W
Conrad, Iowa, U.S.A. 118 42 14N 92 52W
Conrad, Mont., U.S.A. 122 48 11N 112 0W
Conran, C., Australia 75 37 49 S 148 44 E
Conroe, U.S.A. 121 30 15N 95 28W
Consecon, Canada 109 44 0N 77 31W
Conselheiro Lafaiete, Brazil 141 20 40 S 43 48W
Conselheiro Pena, Brazil 139 19 10 S 41 30W
Consort, Canada 111 52 1N 110 46W
Constance = Konstanz, W. Germany 31 47 39N 9 10 E
Constance, L. = Bodensee, W. Germany 31 47 35N 9 25 E
Constanța, Romania 34 44 14N 28 38 E
Constantina, Spain 23 37 51N 5 40W
Constantine, Algeria 85 36 25N 6 42 E
Constantine, U.S.A. 119 41 50N 85 40W
Constitución, Chile 140 35 20 S 72 30W
Constitución, Uruguay 140 31 0 S 57 50W
Consuegra, Spain 23 39 28N 3 36W
Consul, Canada 111 49 20N 109 30W
Contact, U.S.A. 122 41 50N 114 56W
Contai, India 49 21 54N 87 46 E
Contamana, Peru 136 7 19 S 74 55W
Contarina, Italy 27 45 2N 12 13 E
Contas →, Brazil 139 14 17 S 39 1W
Contes, France 21 43 49N 7 19 E
Continental, U.S.A. 119 41 6N 84 16W
Contoocook, U.S.A. 117 43 13N 71 45W
Contra Costa, Mozam. 97 25 9 S 33 30 E
Contrecoeur, Canada 107 45 51N 73 14W
Contres, France 18 47 24N 1 26 E

Contrexéville, *France* **19** 48 10N 5 53 E
Contumaza, *Peru* **136** 7 23 S 78 57W
Convención, *Colombia* **134** 8 28N 73 21W
Conversano, *Italy* **29** 40 57N 17 8 E
Converse, *U.S.A.* **119** 40 34N 85 52W
Convoy, *U.S.A.* **119** 40 55N 84 43W
Conway = Conwy, *U.K.* **12** 53 17N 3 50W
Conway = Conwy →, *U.K.* **12** 53 18N 3 50W
Conway, *Ark., U.S.A.* **121** 35 5N 92 30W
Conway, *N.H., U.S.A.* **117** 43 58N 71 8W
Conway, *S.C., U.S.A.* **115** 33 49N 79 2W
Conway, L., *Australia* **73** 28 17 S 135 35 E
Conwy, *U.K.* **12** 53 17N 3 50W
Conwy →, *U.K.* **12** 53 18N 3 50W
Cooch Behar = Koch Bihar, *India* **52** 26 22N 89 29 E
Coodardy, *Australia* **79** 27 15 S 117 39 E
Cook, *Australia* **79** 30 37 S 130 25 E
Cook, *U.S.A.* **120** 47 49N 92 39W
Cook, B., *Chile* **142** 55 10 S 70 0W
Cook, Mt., *N.Z.* **81** 43 36 S 170 9 E
Cook Inlet, *U.S.A.* **102** 59 0N 151 0W
Cook Is., *Pac. Oc.* **67** 17 0 S 160 0W
Cook Strait, *N.Z.* **81** 41 15 S 174 29 E
Cookeville, *U.S.A.* **115** 36 12N 85 30W
Cookhouse, *S. Africa* **96** 32 44 S 25 47 E
Cookshire, *Canada* **117** 45 25N 71 38W
Cookstown, *U.K.* **15** 54 40N 6 43W
Cookstown □, *U.K.* **15** 54 40N 6 43W
Cooksville, *Canada* **116** 43 36N 79 35W
Cooktown, *Australia* **72** 15 30 S 145 16 E
Coolabah, *Australia* **73** 31 1 S 146 43 E
Cooladdi, *Australia* **73** 26 37 S 145 23 E
Coolah, *Australia* **77** 31 48 S 149 41 E
Coolamon, *Australia* **76** 34 46 S 147 8 E
Coolangatta, *Australia* **77** 28 11 S 153 29 E
Coolatai, *Australia* **77** 29 15 S 150 45 E
Coolgardie, *Australia* **79** 30 55 S 121 8 E
Coolibah, *Australia* **78** 15 33 S 130 56 E
Coolidge, *U.S.A.* **123** 33 1N 111 35W
Coolidge Dam, *U.S.A.* **123** 33 10N 110 30W
Coolongoolook, *Australia* **77** 32 12 S 152 20 E
Cooma, *Australia* **75** 36 12 S 149 8 E
Coon Rapids, *U.S.A.* **118** 41 53N 94 41W
Coonabarabran, *Australia* **76** 31 14 S 149 18 E
Coonamble, *Australia* **76** 30 56 S 148 27 E
Coonana, *Australia* **79** 31 0 S 123 0 E
Coondapoor, *India* **51** 13 42N 74 40 E
Coongie, *Australia* **73** 27 9 S 140 8 E
Coongoola, *Australia* **73** 27 43 S 145 51 E
Cooninie, L., *Australia* **73** 26 4 S 139 59 E
Coonoor, *India* **51** 11 21N 76 45 E
Cooper, *U.S.A.* **121** 33 20N 95 40W
Cooper →, *U.S.A.* **115** 33 0N 79 55W
Coopers Cr. →, *Australia* **73** 28 29 S 137 46 E
Cooperstown, *N. Dak., U.S.A.* **120** 47 30N 98 6W
Cooperstown, *N.Y., U.S.A.* **117** 42 42N 74 57W
Coopersville, *U.S.A.* **119** 43 4N 85 57W
Coorabie, *Australia* **79** 31 54 S 132 18 E
Coorabulka, *Australia* **72** 23 41 S 140 20 E
Cooranbong, *Australia* **76** 33 4 S 151 28 E
Coorong, The, *Australia* **73** 35 50 S 139 20 E
Coorow, *Australia* **79** 29 53 S 116 2 E
Cooroy, *Australia* **73** 26 22 S 152 54 E
Coos Bay, *U.S.A.* **122** 43 26N 124 7W
Cootamundra, *Australia* **76** 34 36 S 148 1 E
Cootehill, *Ireland* **15** 54 5N 7 5W
Cooyal, *Australia* **76** 32 25 S 149 45 E
Cooyar, *Australia* **73** 26 59 S 151 51 E
Cooyeana, *Australia* **72** 24 29 S 138 45 E
Copahue Paso, *Argentina* **140** 37 49 S 71 8W
Copainalá, *Mexico* **127** 17 8N 93 11W
Copán, *Honduras* **128** 14 50N 89 9W
Copatana, *Brazil* **134** 2 48 S 67 4W
Cope, *U.S.A.* **120** 39 44N 102 50W
Cope, C., *Spain* **25** 37 26N 1 28W
Cope Cope, *Australia* **74** 36 27 S 143 5 E
Copenhagen = København, *Denmark* **11** 55 41N 12 34 E
Copertino, *Italy* **29** 40 17N 18 2 E
Copiapó, *Chile* **140** 27 30 S 70 20W
Copiapó →, *Chile* **140** 27 19 S 70 56W
Copley, *Australia* **73** 30 36 S 138 26 E
Copmanhurst, *Australia* **77** 29 33 S 152 49 E
Copp L., *Canada* **110** 60 14N 114 40W
Coppadah, *Australia* **77** 30 12 S 150 34 E
Copparo, *Italy* **27** 44 52N 11 49 E
Coppename →, *Surinam* **135** 5 48N 55 55W
Copper Center, *U.S.A.* **102** 62 10N 145 25W
Copper Cliff, *Canada* **108** 46 28N 81 4W
Copper Harbor, *U.S.A.* **104** 47 31N 87 55W
Copper Queen, *Zimb.* **93** 17 29 S 29 18 E
Copperbelt □, *Zambia* **93** 13 15 S 27 30 E
Coppermine, *Canada* **102** 67 50N 115 5W
Coppermine →, *Canada* **102** 67 49N 116 4W
Copperopolis, *U.S.A.* **124** 37 58N 120 38W
Coquet →, *U.K.* **12** 55 18N 1 45W
Coquilhatville = Mbandaka, *Zaïre* **94** 0 1N 18 18 E
Coquille, *U.S.A.* **122** 43 15N 124 12W
Coquimbo, *Chile* **140** 30 0 S 71 20W
Coquimbo □, *Chile* **140** 31 0 S 71 0W
Corabia, *Romania* **34** 43 48N 24 30 E
Coração de Jesus, *Brazil* **139** 16 43 S 44 22W
Coracora, *Peru* **136** 15 5 S 73 45W
Coradi, Is., *Italy* **29** 40 27N 17 10 E
Coraki, *Australia* **77** 28 59 S 153 17 E
Coral Gables, *U.S.A.* **115** 25 45N 80 16W
Coral Harbour, *Canada* **103** 64 8N 83 10W
Coral Sea, *Pac. Oc.* **66** 15 0 S 150 0 E
Coralville, *U.S.A.* **118** 41 42N 91 34W
Coralville Res., *U.S.A.* **118** 41 50N 91 40W
Coramba, *Australia* **77** 30 12 S 153 3 E
Corangamite, L., *Australia* **74** 38 0 S 143 30 E
Corantijn →, *Surinam* **135** 5 50N 57 8W
Coraopolis, *U.S.A.* **116** 40 30N 80 10W
Corato, *Italy* **29** 41 12N 16 22 E
Corbeil-Essonnes, *France* **19** 48 36N 2 26 E
Corbie, *France* **19** 49 54N 2 30 E
Corbières, *France* **20** 42 55N 2 35 E
Corbigny, *France* **19** 47 16N 3 40 E
Corbin, *U.S.A.* **114** 37 0N 84 3W
Corbion, *Belgium* **17** 49 48N 5 0 E
Corbones →, *Spain* **23** 37 36N 5 39W
Corby, *U.K.* **13** 52 49N 0 31W
Corcoles →, *Spain* **25** 39 40N 3 18W
Corcoran, *U.S.A.* **124** 36 6N 119 35W
Corcubión, *Spain* **22** 42 56N 9 12W
Cordele, *U.S.A.* **115** 31 55N 83 49W
Cordell, *U.S.A.* **121** 35 18N 99 0W
Cordenons, *Italy* **27** 45 59N 12 42 E
Cordes, *France* **20** 44 5N 1 57 E
Cordisburgo, *Brazil* **139** 19 7 S 44 21W
Córdoba, *Argentina* **140** 31 20 S 64 10W
Córdoba, *Mexico* **127** 18 50N 97 0W
Córdoba, *Spain* **23** 37 50N 4 50W
Córdoba □, *Argentina* **140** 31 22 S 64 15W
Córdoba □, *Colombia* **134** 8 20N 75 40W
Córdoba □, *Spain* **23** 38 5N 5 0W
Córdoba, Sierra de, *Argentina* **140** 31 10 S 64 25W
Cordon, *Phil.* **57** 16 42N 121 32 E
Cordova, *Ala., U.S.A.* **115** 33 45N 87 12W
Cordova, *Alaska, U.S.A.* **102** 60 36N 145 45W
Cordova, *Ill., U.S.A.* **118** 41 41N 90 19W
Corella, *Spain* **24** 42 7N 1 48W
Corella →, *Australia* **72** 19 34 S 140 47 E
Coremas, *Brazil* **138** 7 1 S 37 58W
Corentyne →, *Guyana* **135** 5 50N 57 8W
Corfield, *Australia* **72** 21 40 S 143 21 E
Corfu = Kérkira, *Greece* **35** 39 38N 19 50 E
Corgo, *Spain* **22** 42 56N 7 25W
Corguinho, *Brazil* **137** 19 53 S 54 52W
Cori, *Italy* **28** 41 39N 12 53 E
Coria, *Spain* **22** 40 0N 6 33W
Coricudgy, Mt., *Australia* **76** 32 51 S 150 24 E
Corigliano Cálabro, *Italy* **29** 39 36N 16 31 E
Corindi, *Australia* **77** 30 1 S 153 12 E
Corinella, *Australia* **74** 38 25 S 145 25 E
Coringa Is., *Australia* **72** 16 58 S 149 58 E
Corinna, *Australia* **72** 41 35 S 145 10 E
Corinth = Kórinthos, *Greece* **35** 37 56N 22 55 E
Corinth, *Ky., U.S.A.* **119** 38 30N 84 34W
Corinth, *Miss., U.S.A.* **115** 34 54N 88 30W
Corinth, *N.Y., U.S.A.* **117** 43 15N 73 50W
Corinth, G. of = Korinthiakós Kólpos, *Greece* **35** 38 16N 22 30 E
Corinth Canal, *Greece* **35** 37 58N 23 0 E
Corinto, *Brazil* **139** 18 20 S 44 30W
Corinto, *Nic.* **128** 12 30N 87 10W
Cork, *Ireland* **15** 51 54N 8 30W
Cork □, *Ireland* **15** 51 50N 8 50W
Cork Harbour, *Ireland* **15** 51 46N 8 16W
Corlay, *France* **18** 48 20N 3 5W
Corleone, *Italy* **28** 37 48N 13 16 E
Corleto Perticara, *Italy* **29** 40 23N 16 2 E
Çorlu, *Turkey* **46** 41 11N 27 49 E
Cormack L., *Canada* **110** 60 56N 121 37W
Cormóns, *Italy* **27** 45 58N 13 29 E
Cormorant, *Canada* **111** 54 14N 100 35W
Cormorant L., *Canada* **111** 54 15N 100 50W
Corn Is. = Maiz, Is. del, *Nic.* **128** 12 15N 83 4W
Cornélio Procópio, *Brazil* **141** 23 7 S 50 40W
Cornell, *Ill., U.S.A.* **119** 40 58N 88 43W
Cornell, *Wis., U.S.A.* **120** 45 10N 91 8W
Corner Brook, *Canada* **105** 48 57N 57 58W
Corner Inlet, *Australia* **75** 38 45 S 146 20 E
Corníglio, *Italy* **26** 44 29N 10 5 E
Corning, *Ark., U.S.A.* **121** 36 27N 90 34W
Corning, *Calif., U.S.A.* **122** 39 56N 122 9W
Corning, *Iowa, U.S.A.* **118** 40 57N 94 40W
Corning, *N.Y., U.S.A.* **116** 42 10N 77 3W
Corno, Monte, *Italy* **27** 42 28N 13 34 E
Cornwall, *Canada* **109** 45 2N 74 44W
Cornwall □, *U.K.* **13** 50 26N 4 40W
Cornwallis I., *Canada* **144** 75 8N 95 0W
Corny Pt., *Australia* **73** 34 55 S 137 0 E
Coro, *Venezuela* **134** 11 25N 69 41W
Coroaci, *Brazil* **139** 18 35 S 42 17W
Coroatá, *Brazil* **138** 4 8 S 44 0W
Coroban, *Somali Rep.* **98** 3 58N 42 44 E
Corocoro, *Bolivia* **136** 17 15 S 68 28W
Corocoro, I., *Venezuela* **135** 8 30N 60 10W
Coroico, *Bolivia* **136** 16 0 S 67 50W
Coromandel, *Brazil* **139** 18 28 S 47 13W
Coromandel, *N.Z.* **80** 36 45 S 175 31 E
Coromandel Coast, *India* **51** 12 30N 81 0 E
Coromandel Pen., *N.Z.* **80** 37 0 S 175 45 E
Coromandel Ra., *N.Z.* **80** 37 0 S 175 40 E
Corona, *Australia* **73** 31 16 S 141 24 E
Corona, *Calif., U.S.A.* **125** 33 49N 117 36W
Corona, *N. Mex., U.S.A.* **123** 34 15N 105 32W
Coronada, *U.S.A.* **125** 32 45N 117 9W
Coronado, B. de, *Costa Rica* **128** 9 0N 83 40W
Coronados, G. de los, *Chile* **142** 41 40 S 74 0W
Coronados, Is. los, *U.S.A.* **125** 32 25N 117 15W
Coronation, *Canada* **110** 52 5N 111 27W
Coronation Gulf, *Canada* **102** 68 25N 110 0W
Coronation I., *Antarctica* **143** 60 45 S 46 0W
Coronation I., *U.S.A.* **110** 55 52N 134 20W
Coronation Is., *Australia* **78** 14 57 S 124 55 E
Coronda, *Argentina* **140** 31 58 S 60 56W
Coronel, *Chile* **140** 37 0 S 73 10W
Coronel Bogado, *Paraguay* **140** 27 11 S 56 18W
Coronel Dorrego, *Argentina* **140** 38 40 S 61 10W
Coronel Fabriciano, *Brazil* **139** 19 31 S 42 38W
Coronel Murta, *Brazil* **139** 16 37 S 42 11W
Coronel Oviedo, *Paraguay* **140** 25 24 S 56 30W
Coronel Ponce, *Brazil* **137** 15 34 S 55 1W
Coronel Pringles, *Argentina* **140** 38 0 S 61 30W
Coronel Suárez, *Argentina* **140** 37 30 S 61 52W
Coronel Vidal, *Argentina* **140** 37 28 S 57 45W
Corongo, *Peru* **136** 8 30 S 77 53W
Coronie □, *Surinam* **135** 5 55N 56 20W
Coropuna, Nevado, *Peru* **136** 15 30 S 72 41W
Cororooke, *Australia* **74** 38 17 S 143 31 E
Çorovoda, *Albania* **35** 40 31N 20 14 E
Corowa, *Australia* **75** 35 58 S 146 21 E
Corozal, *Belize* **127** 18 23N 88 23W
Corozal, *Colombia* **134** 9 19N 75 18W
Corps, *France* **21** 44 50N 5 56 E
Corpus, *Argentina* **141** 27 10 S 55 30W
Corpus Christi, *U.S.A.* **121** 27 50N 97 28W
Corpus Christi, L., *U.S.A.* **121** 28 5N 97 54W
Corque, *Bolivia* **136** 18 20 S 67 41W
Corral, *Chile* **142** 39 52 S 73 26W
Corral de Almaguer, *Spain* **24** 39 45N 3 10W
Corralejo, *Canary Is.* **25** 28 43N 13 53W
Corréggio, *Italy* **26** 44 46N 10 47 E
Corrente, *Brazil* **138** 10 27 S 45 10W
Corrente →, *Brazil* **139** 13 8 S 43 28W
Correntes →, *Brazil* **137** 17 38 S 55 8W
Correntes, C. das, *Mozam.* **97** 24 6 S 35 34 E
Correntina, *Brazil* **139** 13 20 S 44 39W
Corrèze □, *France* **20** 45 20N 1 45 E
Corrèze →, *France* **20** 45 10N 1 28 E
Corrib, L., *Ireland* **15** 53 5N 9 10W
Corrientes, *Argentina* **140** 27 30 S 58 45W
Corrientes □, *Argentina* **140** 28 0 S 57 0W
Corrientes →, *Argentina* **140** 30 42 S 59 38W
Corrientes →, *Peru* **136** 3 43 S 74 35W
Corrientes, C., *Colombia* **134** 5 30N 77 34W
Corrientes, C., *Cuba* **128** 21 43N 84 30W
Corrientes, C., *Mexico* **126** 20 25N 105 42W
Corrigan, *U.S.A.* **121** 31 0N 94 48W
Corrigin, *Australia* **79** 32 20 S 117 53 E
Corrowidgie, *Australia* **75** 36 56 S 148 50 E
Corry, *U.S.A.* **116** 41 55N 79 39W
Corryong, *Australia* **75** 36 12 S 147 53 E
Corse, *France* **21** 42 0N 9 0 E
Corse, C., *France* **21** 43 1N 9 25 E
Corse-du-Sud □, *France* **21** 41 45N 9 0 E
Corsica = Corse, *France* **21** 42 0N 9 0 E
Corsicana, *U.S.A.* **121** 32 5N 96 30W
Corte, *France* **21** 42 19N 9 11 E
Corte do Pinto, *Portugal* **23** 37 42N 7 29W
Cortegana, *Spain* **23** 37 52N 6 49W
Cortez, *U.S.A.* **123** 37 24N 108 35W
Cortina d'Ampezzo, *Italy* **27** 46 32N 12 9 E
Cortland, *U.S.A.* **117** 42 35N 76 11W
Cortona, *Italy* **27** 43 16N 12 0 E
Coruche, *Portugal* **23** 38 57N 8 30W
Çorum, *Turkey* **46** 40 30N 34 57 E
Corumbá, *Brazil* **137** 19 0 S 57 30W
Corumbá →, *Brazil* **139** 18 19 S 48 55W
Corumbá de Goiás, *Brazil* **139** 16 0 S 48 50W
Corumbaíba, *Brazil* **139** 18 9 S 48 34W
Coruña, La, *Spain* **22** 43 20N 8 25W
Coruña, La □, *Spain* **22** 43 10N 8 30W
Corunna = Coruña, La, *Spain* **22** 43 20N 8 25W
Corunna, *Canada* **108** 42 53N 82 26W
Corunna, *U.S.A.* **119** 42 59N 84 7W
Corvallis, *U.S.A.* **122** 44 36N 123 15W
Corvette, L. de la, *Canada* **104** 53 25N 74 3W
Corydon, *Ind., U.S.A.* **119** 38 13N 86 7W
Corydon, *Iowa, U.S.A.* **118** 40 42N 93 22W
Corydon, *Ky., U.S.A.* **119** 37 44N 87 43W
Cosalá, *Mexico* **126** 24 28N 106 40W
Cosamaloapan, *Mexico* **127** 18 23N 95 50W
Cosenza, *Italy* **29** 39 17N 16 14 E
Coshocton, *U.S.A.* **116** 40 17N 81 51W
Cosmo Newberry, *Australia* **79** 28 0 S 122 54 E
Cosne-sur-Loire, *France* **19** 47 24N 2 54 E
Coso Junction, *U.S.A.* **125** 36 3N 117 57W
Coso Pk., *U.S.A.* **125** 36 13N 117 44W
Cospeito, *Spain* **22** 43 12N 7 34W
Cosquín, *Argentina* **140** 31 15 S 64 30W
Cossato, *Italy* **26** 45 34N 8 10 E
Cossé-le-Vivien, *France* **18** 47 57N 0 54W
Cosson →, *France* **18** 47 30N 1 15 E
Costa Blanca, *Spain* **25** 38 25N 0 10W
Costa Brava, *Spain* **24** 41 30N 3 0 E
Costa del Sol, *Spain* **23** 36 30N 4 30W
Costa Dorada, *Spain* **24** 40 45N 1 15 E
Costa Mesa, *U.S.A.* **125** 33 39N 117 55W
Costa Rica ■, *Cent. Amer.* **128** 10 0N 84 0W
Costa Smeralda, *Italy* **28** 41 5N 9 35 E
Costigliole d'Asti, *Italy* **26** 44 48N 8 11 E
Costilla, *U.S.A.* **123** 37 0N 105 30W
Cosumnes →, *U.S.A.* **124** 38 14N 121 25W
Coswig, *E. Germany* **30** 51 52N 12 31 E
Cotabato, *Phil.* **57** 7 14N 124 15 E
Cotacajes →, *Bolivia* **136** 16 0 S 67 1W
Cotagaita, *Bolivia* **140** 20 45 S 65 40W
Cotahuasi, *Peru* **136** 15 12 S 72 50W
Côte d'Azur, *France* **21** 43 25N 7 10 E
Côte d'Or, *France* **19** 47 10N 4 50 E
Côte-d'Or □, *France* **19** 47 30N 4 50 E
Côte-St.-André, La, *France* **21** 45 24N 5 15 E
Coteau des Prairies, *U.S.A.* **120** 44 30N 97 0W
Coteau du Missouri, *U.S.A.* **120** 47 0N 101 0W
Coteau Landing, *Canada* **117** 45 15N 74 13W
Cotegipe, *Brazil* **139** 12 2 S 44 15W
Cotentin, *France* **18** 49 15N 1 30W
Côtes de Meuse, *France* **19** 49 15N 5 22 E
Côtes-du-Nord □, *France* **18** 48 25N 2 40W
Cotiella, *Spain* **24** 42 31N 0 19 E
Cotina →, *Yugoslavia* **33** 43 36N 18 50 E
Cotoca, *Bolivia* **137** 17 49 S 63 3W
Cotonou, *Benin* **91** 6 20N 2 25 E
Cotopaxi □, *Ecuador* **134** 0 5 S 78 55W
Cotopaxi, Vol., *Ecuador* **134** 0 40 S 78 30W
Cotronei, *Italy* **29** 39 9N 16 45 E
Cotswold Hills, *U.K.* **13** 51 42N 2 10W
Cottage Grove, *U.S.A.* **122** 43 48N 123 2W
Cottam, *Canada* **108** 42 8N 82 45W
Cottbus, *E. Germany* **30** 51 44N 14 20 E
Cottbus □, *E. Germany* **30** 51 43N 13 30 E
Cottonvale, *Australia* **77** 28 31 S 151 57 E
Cottonwood, *U.S.A.* **123** 34 48N 112 1W
Cotulla, *U.S.A.* **121** 28 26N 99 14W
Coubre, Pte. de la, *France* **20** 45 42N 1 15W
Couches, *France* **19** 46 53N 4 30 E
Couço, *Portugal* **23** 38 59N 8 17W
Coudersport, *U.S.A.* **116** 41 45N 78 1W
Coudres, Île aux, *Canada* **107** 47 24N 70 23W
Couedic, C. du, *Australia* **73** 36 5 S 136 40 E
Couëron, *France* **18** 47 13N 1 44W
Couesnon →, *France* **18** 48 38N 1 32W
Couhé, *France* **20** 46 17N 0 11 E
Coulanges-sur-Yonne, *France* **19** 47 31N 3 33 E
Coulee City, *U.S.A.* **122** 47 36N 119 18W
Coulman I., *Antarctica* **143** 73 35 S 170 0 E
Coulommiers, *France* **19** 48 50N 3 3 E
Coulonge →, *Canada* **106** 45 52N 76 46W
Coulonges-sur-l'Autize, *France* **20** 46 29N 0 36W
Coulterville, *Calif., U.S.A.* **124** 37 42N 120 12W
Coulterville, *Ill., U.S.A.* **118** 38 11N 89 36W
Council, *Alaska, U.S.A.* **102** 64 55N 163 45W
Council, *Idaho, U.S.A.* **122** 44 44N 116 26W
Council Bluffs, *U.S.A.* **120** 41 20N 95 50W
Council Grove, *U.S.A.* **120** 38 41N 96 30W
Coupeville, *U.S.A.* **124** 48 13N 122 41W
Courantyne →, *S. Amer.* **136** 5 55N 57 5W
Courcelles, *Belgium* **17** 50 28N 4 22 E
Courçon, *France* **20** 46 15N 0 50W
Couronne, C., *France* **21** 43 19N 5 3 E
Cours-la-Ville, *France* **21** 46 7N 4 19 E
Coursan, *France* **20** 43 14N 3 4 E
Courseulles-sur-Mer, *France* **18** 49 20N 0 29W
Court-St.-Etienne, *Belgium* **17** 50 38N 4 34 E
Courtenay, *Canada* **110** 49 45N 125 0W

Courtine-le-Trucq, La, *France* 20 45 41N 2 15 E
Courtland, *Canada* 108 42 51N 80 38W
Courtland, *U.S.A.* 124 38 20N 121 34W
Courtrai = Kortrijk, *Belgium* 17 50 50N 3 17 E
Courtright, *Canada* 108 42 49N 82 28W
Courville-sur-Eure, *France* 18 48 28N 1 15 E
Coushatta, *U.S.A.* 121 32 0N 93 21W
Coutances, *France* 18 49 3N 1 28W
Couterne, *France* 18 48 30N 0 25W
Coutras, *France* 20 45 3N 0 8W
Coutts, *Canada* 110 49 0N 111 57W
Coutts Crossing, *Australia* 77 29 49 S 152 55 E
Couvin, *Belgium* 17 50 3N 4 29 E
Covarrubias, *Spain* 24 42 4N 3 31W
Cove I., *Canada* 108 45 17N 81 44W
Coveñas, *Colombia* 134 9 24N 75 44W
Coventry, *U.K.* 13 52 25N 1 31W
Coventry L., *Canada* 111 61 15N 106 15W
Covilhã, *Portugal* 22 40 17N 7 31W
Covington, *Ga., U.S.A.* 115 33 36N 83 50W
Covington, *Ind., U.S.A.* 119 40 9N 87 24W
Covington, *Ky., U.S.A.* 119 39 5N 84 30W
Covington, *Ohio, U.S.A.* 119 40 8N 84 20W
Covington, *Okla., U.S.A.* 121 36 21N 97 36W
Covington, *Tenn., U.S.A.* 121 35 34N 89 39W
Cowal, L., *Australia* 76 33 40 S 147 25 E
Cowan, *Canada* 111 52 5N 100 45W
Cowan, L., *Australia* 79 31 45 S 121 45 E
Cowan L., *Canada* 111 54 0N 107 15W
Cowangie, *Australia* 74 35 12 S 141 26 E
Cowansville, *Canada* 117 45 14N 72 46W
Cowarie, *Australia* 73 27 45 S 138 15 E
Cowcowing Lakes, *Australia* 79 30 55 S 117 20 E
Cowden, *U.S.A.* 119 39 15N 88 52W
Cowdenbeath, *U.K.* 14 56 7N 3 20W
Cowell, *Australia* 73 33 39 S 136 56 E
Cowes, *Australia* 74 38 28 S 145 14 E
Cowes, *U.K.* 13 50 45N 1 18W
Cowlitz →, *U.S.A.* 124 46 5N 122 53W
Cowra, *Australia* 76 33 49 S 148 42 E
Cowwarr, *Australia* 75 38 2 S 146 42 E
Coxilha Grande, *Brazil* 141 28 18 S 51 30W
Coxim, *Brazil* 137 18 30 S 54 55W
Coxim →, *Brazil* 137 18 34 S 54 46W
Cox's Bazar, *Bangla.* 52 21 26N 91 59 E
Cox's Cove, *Canada* 105 49 7N 58 5W
Coyame, *Mexico* 126 29 28N 105 6W
Coyote Wells, *U.S.A.* 125 32 44N 115 58W
Coyuca de Benítez, *Mexico* 127 17 1N 100 8W
Coyuca de Catalan, *Mexico* 126 18 18N 100 41W
Cozad, *U.S.A.* 120 40 55N 99 57W
Cozumel, *Mexico* 127 20 31N 86 55W
Cozumel, I. de, *Mexico* 127 20 30N 86 40W
Craboon, *Australia* 77 32 3 S 149 30 E
Cracow = Kraków, *Poland* 32 50 4N 19 57 E
Cracow, *Australia* 73 25 17 S 150 17 E
Cradock, *S. Africa* 96 32 8 S 25 36 E
Craig, *Alaska, U.S.A.* 110 55 30N 133 5W
Craig, *Colo., U.S.A.* 122 40 32N 107 33W
Craigieburn, *Australia* 74 37 36 S 144 56 E
Craigmore, *Zimb.* 93 20 28 S 32 50 E
Crailsheim, *W. Germany* 31 49 7N 10 5 E
Craiova, *Romania* 34 44 21N 23 48 E
Cramsie, *Australia* 72 23 20 S 144 15 E
Cranberry Portage, *Canada* 111 54 35N 101 23W
Cranbourne, *Australia* 74 38 7 S 145 20 E
Cranbrook, *Tas., Australia* 72 42 0 S 148 5 E
Cranbrook, *W. Austral., Australia* 79 34 18 S 117 33 E
Cranbrook, *Canada* 110 49 30N 115 46W
Crandon, *U.S.A.* 120 45 32N 88 52W
Crane, *Oreg., U.S.A.* 122 43 21N 118 39W
Crane, *Tex., U.S.A.* 121 31 26N 102 27W
Crane I., *Canada* 107 47 4N 70 33W
Cranston, *U.S.A.* 117 41 47N 71 27W
Craon, *France* 18 47 50N 0 58W
Craonne, *France* 19 49 27N 3 46 E
Craponne-sur-Arzon, *France* 20 45 19N 3 51 E
Crasna, *Romania* 34 46 32N 27 51 E
Crater, L., *U.S.A.* 122 42 55N 122 3W
Crater Mt., *Papua N. G.* 69 6 37 S 145 7 E
Crater Pt., *Papua N. G.* 69 5 25 S 152 9 E
Crateús, *Brazil* 138 5 10 S 40 39W
Crati →, *Italy* 29 39 41N 16 30 E
Crato, *Brazil* 138 7 10 S 39 25W
Crato, *Portugal* 23 39 16N 7 39W
Crau, La, *France* 21 43 32N 4 40 E
Cravo Norte, *Colombia* 134 6 18N 70 12W
Cravo Norte →, *Colombia* 134 6 18N 70 12W
Crawford, *U.S.A.* 120 42 40N 103 25W
Crawfordsville, *U.S.A.* 119 40 2N 86 51W
Crawley, *U.K.* 13 51 7N 0 10W
Crazy Mts., *U.S.A.* 122 46 14N 110 30W
Crean L., *Canada* 111 54 5N 106 9W
Crécy-en-Brie, *France* 19 48 50N 2 53 E
Crécy-en-Ponthieu, *France* 19 50 15N 1 53 E
Crediton, *Canada* 108 43 17N 81 33W
Credo, *Australia* 79 30 28 S 120 45 E
Cree →, *Canada* 111 58 57N 105 47W
Cree →, *U.K.* 14 54 51N 4 24W
Cree L., *Canada* 111 57 30N 106 30W
Creede, *U.S.A.* 123 37 56N 106 59W
Creel, *Mexico* 126 27 45N 107 38W
Creemore, *Canada* 108 44 19N 80 6W
Creighton, *U.S.A.* 120 42 30N 97 52W
Creil, *France* 19 49 15N 2 29 E
Crema, *Italy* 26 45 21N 9 40 E
Cremona, *Italy* 26 45 8N 10 2 E
Crepori →, *Brazil* 137 5 42 S 57 8W
Crépy, *France* 19 49 35N 3 32 E
Crépy-en-Valois, *France* 19 49 14N 2 54 E
Cres, *Yugoslavia* 27 44 58N 14 25 E
Cresbard, *U.S.A.* 120 45 13N 98 57W
Crescent, *Okla., U.S.A.* 121 35 58N 97 36W
Crescent, *Oreg., U.S.A.* 122 43 30N 121 37W
Crescent City, *U.S.A.* 122 41 45N 124 12W
Crescent Head, *Australia* 77 31 11 S 152 59 E
Crescentino, *Italy* 26 45 11N 8 7 E
Crespino, *Italy* 27 44 59N 11 51 E
Crespo, *Argentina* 140 32 2 S 60 19W
Cressy, *Australia* 74 38 2 S 143 40 E
Crest, *France* 21 44 44N 5 2 E
Crested Butte, *U.S.A.* 123 38 57N 107 0W
Crestline, *Calif., U.S.A.* 125 34 14N 117 18W
Crestline, *Ohio, U.S.A.* 116 40 46N 82 45W
Creston, *Canada* 110 49 10N 116 31W
Creston, *Calif., U.S.A.* 124 35 32N 120 33W
Creston, *Iowa, U.S.A.* 118 41 0N 94 20W
Creston, *Wash., U.S.A.* 122 47 47N 118 36W
Crestview, *Calif., U.S.A.* 124 37 46N 118 58W
Crestview, *Fla., U.S.A.* 115 30 45N 86 35W
Creswick, *Australia* 74 37 25 S 143 58 E
Crete = Kríti, *Greece* 35 35 15N 25 0 E
Crete, *U.S.A.* 120 40 38N 96 58W
Crete, La, *Canada* 110 58 11N 116 24W
Crete, Sea of, *Greece* 35 36 0N 25 0 E
Cretin, C., *Papua N. G.* 69 6 40 S 147 53 E
Creus, C., *Spain* 24 42 20N 3 19 E
Creuse □, *France* 20 46 10N 2 0 E
Creuse →, *France* 20 47 0N 0 34 E
Creusot, Le, *France* 19 46 48N 4 24 E
Creuzburg, *E. Germany* 30 51 3N 10 15 E
Crevalcore, *Italy* 27 44 41N 11 10 E
Crèvecœur-le-Grand, *France* 19 49 37N 2 5 E
Crevillente, *Spain* 25 38 12N 0 48W
Crewe, *U.K.* 12 53 6N 2 28W
Crib Point, *Australia* 74 38 22 S 145 13 E
Criciúma, *Brazil* 141 28 40 S 49 23W
Cridersville, *U.S.A.* 119 40 39N 84 9W
Crieff, *U.K.* 14 56 22N 3 50W
Crikvenica, *Yugoslavia* 27 45 11N 14 40 E
Crimea = Krymskiy Poluostrov, *U.S.S.R.* 38 45 0N 34 0 E
Crimmitschau, *E. Germany* 30 50 48N 12 23 E
Crinan, *U.K.* 14 56 6N 5 34W
Cristal, Mts. de, *Gabon* 94 0 30N 10 30 E
Cristalândia, *Brazil* 138 10 36 S 49 11W
Cristino Castro, *Brazil* 138 8 49 S 44 13W
Crişu Alb →, *Romania* 34 46 42N 21 17 E
Crişu Negru →, *Romania* 34 46 42N 21 16 E
Crişul Repede →, *Romania* 34 46 55N 20 59 E
Crittenden, *U.S.A.* 119 38 47N 84 36W
Crivitz, *E. Germany* 30 53 35N 11 39 E
Crixás, *Brazil* 139 14 27 S 49 58W
Crna Gora □, *Yugoslavia* 33 42 40N 19 20 E
Crni Drim →, *Yugoslavia* 35 41 17N 20 40 E
Črnomelj, *Yugoslavia* 27 45 33N 15 10 E
Croaghpatrick, *Ireland* 15 53 46N 9 40W
Croatia = Hrvatska □, *Yugoslavia* 27 45 20N 18 0 E
Crocker, *U.S.A.* 118 37 57N 92 16W
Crocker, Banjaran, *Malaysia* 56 5 40N 116 30 E
Crocker I., *Australia* 79 11 12 S 132 32 E
Crockett, *U.S.A.* 121 31 20N 95 30W
Crocodile = Krokodil →, *Mozam.* 97 25 14 S 32 18 E
Crocodile Is., *Australia* 72 12 3 S 134 58 E
Crocq, *France* 20 45 52N 2 21 E
Croisette, C., *France* 21 43 14N 5 22 E
Croisic, Le, *France* 18 47 18N 2 30W
Croisic, Pte. du, *France* 18 47 19N 2 31W
Croix, La, L., *Canada* 104 48 20N 92 15W
Croker, C., *Australia* 78 10 58 S 132 35 E
Croker, C., *Canada* 108 44 58N 80 59W
Cromarty, *Canada* 111 58 3N 94 9W
Cromarty, *U.K.* 14 57 40N 4 2W
Cromer, *U.K.* 12 52 56N 1 18 E
Cromwell, *N.Z.* 81 45 3 S 169 14 E
Cronat, *France* 19 46 43N 3 40 E
Cronulla, *Australia* 76 34 3 S 151 8 E
Crooble, *Australia* 77 29 16 S 150 16 E
Crooked →, *Canada* 110 54 50N 122 54W
Crooked →, *U.S.A.* 122 44 30N 121 16W
Crooked I., *Bahamas* 129 22 50N 74 10W
Crooked Island Passage, *Bahamas* 129 23 0N 74 30W
Crookston, *Minn., U.S.A.* 120 47 50N 96 40W
Crookston, *Nebr., U.S.A.* 120 42 56N 100 45W
Crooksville, *U.S.A.* 114 39 45N 82 8W
Crookwell, *Australia* 76 34 28 S 149 24 E
Croppa Cr. →, *Australia* 77 28 48 S 150 4 E
Croppa Creek, *Australia* 77 28 9 S 150 20 E
Crosby, *Minn., U.S.A.* 120 46 28N 93 57W
Crosby, *N. Dak., U.S.A.* 111 48 55N 103 18W
Crosby, *Pa., U.S.A.* 116 41 45N 78 23W
Crosbyton, *U.S.A.* 121 33 37N 101 12W
Cross →, *Nigeria* 91 4 42N 8 21 E
Cross City, *U.S.A.* 115 29 35N 83 5W
Cross Fell, *U.K.* 12 54 44N 2 29W
Cross L., *Canada* 111 54 45N 97 30W
Cross Plains, *U.S.A.* 121 32 8N 99 7W
Cross River □, *Nigeria* 91 6 0N 8 0 E
Cross Sound, *U.S.A.* 102 58 20N 136 30W
Cross Timbers, *U.S.A.* 118 38 1N 93 14W
Crosse, La, *Kans., U.S.A.* 120 38 33N 99 20W
Crosse, La, *Wis., U.S.A.* 120 43 48N 91 13W
Crossett, *U.S.A.* 121 33 10N 91 57W
Crossfield, *Canada* 110 51 25N 114 0W
Crosshaven, *Ireland* 15 51 48N 8 19W
Crossley, Mt., *N.Z.* 81 42 50 S 172 5 E
Crossville, *U.S.A.* 119 38 10N 88 4W
Croton-on-Hudson, *U.S.A.* 117 41 12N 73 55W
Crotone, *Italy* 29 39 5N 17 6 E
Crow →, *Canada* 110 59 41N 124 20W
Crow Agency, *U.S.A.* 122 45 40N 107 30W
Crow Hd., *Ireland* 15 51 34N 10 9W
Crowdy Hd., *Australia* 77 31 48 S 152 44 E
Crowell, *U.S.A.* 121 33 59N 99 45W
Crowley, *U.S.A.* 121 30 15N 92 20W
Crowley, L., *U.S.A.* 124 37 33N 118 42W
Crown Point, *U.S.A.* 119 41 24N 87 23W
Crows Landing, *U.S.A.* 124 37 23N 121 6W
Crows Nest, *Australia* 73 27 16 S 152 4 E
Crowsnest Pass, *Canada* 110 49 40N 114 40W
Croydon, *Australia* 72 18 13 S 142 14 E
Croydon, *U.K.* 13 51 18N 0 5W
Crozet Is., *Ind. Oc.* 53 46 27 S 52 0 E
Crozon, *France* 18 48 15N 4 30W
Cruz, C., *Cuba* 128 19 50N 77 50W
Cruz, La, *Costa Rica* 128 11 4N 85 39W
Cruz, La, *Mexico* 126 23 55N 106 54W
Cruz Alta, *Brazil* 141 28 45 S 53 40W
Cruz das Almas, *Brazil* 139 12 0 S 39 6W
Cruz de Malta, *Brazil* 138 8 15 S 40 20W
Cruz del Eje, *Argentina* 140 30 45 S 64 50W
Cruzeiro, *Brazil* 139 22 33 S 45 0W
Cruzeiro do Oeste, *Brazil* 141 23 46 S 53 4W
Cruzeiro do Sul, *Brazil* 136 7 35 S 72 35W
Cry L., *Canada* 110 58 45N 129 0W
Crystal Bay, *U.S.A.* 124 39 15N 119 58W
Crystal Brook, *Australia* 73 33 21 S 138 12 E
Crystal City, *Mo., U.S.A.* 118 38 15N 90 23W
Crystal City, *Tex., U.S.A.* 121 28 40N 99 50W
Crystal Falls, *U.S.A.* 114 46 9N 88 11W
Crystal Lake, *U.S.A.* 119 42 14N 88 19W
Crystal River, *U.S.A.* 115 28 54N 82 35W
Crystal Springs, *U.S.A.* 121 31 59N 90 25W
Csongrád, *Hungary* 33 46 43N 20 12 E
Csorna, *Hungary* 33 47 38N 17 18 E
Csurgo, *Hungary* 33 46 16N 17 9 E
Cu Lao Hon, *Vietnam* 55 10 54N 108 18 E
Cua Rao, *Vietnam* 54 19 16N 104 27 E
Cuácua →, *Mozam.* 93 17 54 S 37 0 E
Cuamato, *Angola* 95 17 2 S 15 7 E
Cuamba, *Mozam.* 93 14 45 S 36 22 E
Cuando →, *Angola* 95 17 30 S 23 15 E
Cuando Cubango □, *Angola* 95 16 25 S 20 0 E
Cuangar, *Angola* 95 17 36 S 18 39 E
Cuango, *Angola* 95 6 15 S 16 42 E
Cuanza →, *Angola* 82 9 2 S 13 30 E
Cuanza Norte □, *Angola* 95 8 50 S 14 30 E
Cuanza Sul □, *Angola* 95 10 50 S 14 50 E
Cuarto →, *Argentina* 140 33 25 S 63 2W
Cuatrociénegas, *Mexico* 126 26 59N 102 5W
Cuauhtémoc, *Mexico* 126 28 25N 106 52W
Cuba, *Portugal* 23 38 10N 7 54W
Cuba, *Mo., U.S.A.* 118 38 4N 91 24W
Cuba, *N. Mex., U.S.A.* 123 36 0N 107 0W
Cuba, *N.Y., U.S.A.* 116 42 12N 78 18W
Cuba ■, *W. Indies* 128 22 0N 79 0W
Cuba City, *U.S.A.* 118 42 36N 90 26W
Cubal, *Angola* 95 12 26 S 14 3 E
Cuballing, *Australia* 79 32 50 S 117 10 E
Cubango →, *Africa* 95 18 50 S 22 25 E
Cubanja, *Angola* 95 14 49 S 21 20 E
Cubbaroo, *Australia* 77 30 10 S 149 7 E
Cubia, *Angola* 95 15 58 S 21 42 E
Cucamonga, *U.S.A.* 125 34 10N 117 30W
Cuchi, *Angola* 95 14 37 S 16 58 E
Cuchillo-Có, *Argentina* 142 38 20 S 64 37W
Cuchivero →, *Venezuela* 134 7 40N 65 57W
Cuchumatanes, Sierra de los, *Guatemala* 128 15 35N 91 25W
Cucuí, *Brazil* 134 1 12N 66 50W
Cucurpe, *Mexico* 126 30 20N 110 43W
Cucurrupí, *Colombia* 134 4 23N 76 56W
Cúcuta, *Colombia* 134 7 54N 72 31W
Cudahy, *U.S.A.* 119 42 54N 87 50W
Cudal, *Australia* 76 33 16 S 148 46 E
Cudalbi, *Romania* 34 45 46N 27 41 E
Cuddalore, *India* 51 11 46N 79 45 E
Cuddapah, *India* 51 14 30N 78 47 E
Cuddapan, L., *Australia* 72 25 45 S 141 26 E
Cudgegong, *Australia* 76 32 47 S 149 48 E
Cudgegong →, *Australia* 76 32 37 S 149 43 E
Cudgewa, *Australia* 75 36 10 S 147 42 E
Cudillero, *Spain* 22 43 33N 6 9W
Cue, *Australia* 79 27 25 S 117 54 E
Cuéllar, *Spain* 22 41 23N 4 21W
Cuemba, *Angola* 95 11 50 S 17 42 E
Cuenca, *Ecuador* 134 2 50 S 79 9W
Cuenca, *Spain* 24 40 5N 2 10W
Cuenca □, *Spain* 24 40 0N 2 0W
Cuenca, Serranía de, *Spain* 24 39 55N 1 50W
Cuerdo del Pozo, Pantano de la, *Spain* 24 41 51N 2 44W
Cuernavaca, *Mexico* 127 18 50N 99 20W
Cuero, *U.S.A.* 121 29 5N 97 17W
Cuers, *France* 21 43 14N 6 5 E
Cuervo, *U.S.A.* 121 35 5N 104 25W
Cuesmes, *Belgium* 17 50 26N 3 56 E
Cuevas, Cerro, *Bolivia* 137 22 0 S 65 12W
Cuevas del Almanzora, *Spain* 25 37 18N 1 58W
Cuevo, *Bolivia* 136 20 15 S 63 30W
Cuiabá, *Brazil* 137 15 30 S 56 0W
Cuiabá →, *Brazil* 137 17 5 S 56 36W
Cuilco, *Guatemala* 128 15 24N 91 58W
Cuillin Hills, *U.K.* 14 57 14N 6 15W
Cuillin Sd., *U.K.* 14 57 4N 6 20W
Cuima, *Angola* 95 13 25 S 15 45 E
Cuiseaux, *France* 21 46 30N 5 22 E
Cuité, *Brazil* 138 6 29 S 36 9W
Cuito →, *Angola* 95 18 1 S 20 48 E
Cuito Cuanavale, *Angola* 95 15 10 S 19 10 E
Cuitzeo, L. de, *Mexico* 126 19 55N 101 5W
Cuiuni →, *Brazil* 135 0 45 S 63 7W
Cuivre →, *U.S.A.* 118 38 55N 90 44W
Cuivre, West Fork →, *U.S.A.* 118 39 2N 90 58W
Cukai, *Malaysia* 55 4 13N 103 25 E
Culan, *France* 20 46 34N 2 20 E
Culbertson, *U.S.A.* 120 48 9N 104 30W
Culcairn, *Australia* 76 35 41 S 147 3 E
Culebra, Sierra de la, *Spain* 22 41 55N 6 20W
Culemborg, *Neths.* 16 51 58N 5 14 E
Culgoa, *Australia* 74 35 44 S 143 6 E
Culgoa →, *Australia* 73 29 56 S 146 20 E
Culiacán, *Mexico* 126 24 50N 107 23W
Culiacán →, *Mexico* 126 24 30N 107 42W
Culion, *Phil.* 57 11 54N 120 1 E
Culiseu →, *Brazil* 137 12 14 S 53 17W
Cúllar de Baza, *Spain* 25 37 35N 2 34W
Cullarin Range, *Australia* 76 34 30 S 149 30 E
Cullen, *Australia* 78 13 58 S 131 54 E
Cullen, *U.K.* 14 57 45N 2 50W
Cullen Bullen, *Australia* 76 33 18 S 150 2 E
Cullen Pt., *Australia* 72 11 57 S 141 54 E
Cullera, *Spain* 25 39 9N 0 17W
Cullman, *U.S.A.* 115 34 13N 86 50W
Culloden Moor, *U.K.* 14 57 29N 4 7W
Cullom, *U.S.A.* 119 40 53N 88 16W
Culoz, *France* 21 45 47N 5 46 E
Culpeper, *U.S.A.* 114 38 29N 77 59W
Culuene →, *Brazil* 137 12 56 S 52 51W
Culver, *U.S.A.* 119 41 13N 86 25W
Culver, Pt., *Australia* 79 32 54 S 124 43 E
Culverden, *N.Z.* 81 42 47 S 172 49 E
Cuma, *Angola* 95 12 52 S 15 5 E
Cumaná, *Venezuela* 135 10 30N 64 5W
Cumare, *Colombia* 134 0 49N 72 32W
Cumari, *Brazil* 139 18 16 S 48 11W
Cumberland, *B.C., Canada* 110 49 40N 125 0W
Cumberland, *Ont., Canada* 109 45 29N 75 24W
Cumberland, *Iowa, U.S.A.* 118 41 16N 94 52W
Cumberland, *Md., U.S.A.* 114 39 40N 78 43W
Cumberland, *Wis., U.S.A.* 120 45 32N 92 3W
Cumberland →, *U.S.A.* 115 36 15N 87 0W
Cumberland, C., *Vanuatu* 68 14 39 S 166 37 E
Cumberland I., *U.S.A.* 115 30 52N 81 30W
Cumberland Is., *Australia* 72 20 35 S 149 10 E
Cumberland L., *Canada* 111 54 3N 102 18W
Cumberland Pen., *Canada* 103 67 0N 64 0W
Cumberland Plateau, *U.S.A.* 115 36 0N 84 30W
Cumberland Sd., *Canada* 103 65 30N 66 0W
Cumborah, *Australia* 73 29 40 S 147 45 E
Cumbres Mayores, *Spain* 23 38 4N 6 39W

Cumbria □, U.K. 12 54 35N 2 55W
Cumbrian Mts., U.K. 12 54 30N 3 0W
Cumbum, India 51 15 40N 79 10 E
Cuminá →, Brazil 135 1 30 S 56 0W
Cuminapanema →, Brazil 135 1 9 S 54 54W
Cummings Mt., U.S.A. 125 35 2N 118 34W
Cummins, Australia 73 34 16 S 135 43 E
Cumnock, Australia 76 32 59 S 148 46 E
Cumnock, U.K. 14 55 27N 4 18W
Cumpas, Mexico 126 30 0N 109 48W
Cumplida, Pta., Canary Is. 25 28 50N 17 48W
Cuncumén, Chile 140 31 53 S 70 38W
Cundeelee, Australia 79 30 43 S 123 26 E
Cunderdin, Australia 79 31 37 S 117 12 E
Cundinamarca □, Colombia 134 5 0N 74 0W
Cunene □, Angola 95 16 30 S 15 0 E
Cunene →, Angola 95 17 20 S 11 50 E
Cúneo, Italy 26 44 23N 7 31 E
Cunhinga, Angola 95 12 11 S 16 47 E
Cunillera, I., Spain 25 38 59N 1 13 E
Cunjamba, Angola 95 15 27 S 20 10 E
Cunlhat, France 20 45 38N 3 32 E
Cunnamulla, Australia 73 28 2 S 145 38 E
Cuorgnè, Italy 26 45 23N 7 39 E
Cupar, Canada 111 50 57N 104 10W
Cupar, U.K. 14 56 20N 3 0W
Cupica, G. de, Colombia 134 6 25N 77 30W
Ćuprija, Yugoslavia 33 43 57N 21 26 E
Curaçá, Brazil 138 8 59 S 39 54W
Curaçao, Neth. Ant. 129 12 10N 69 0W
Curacautín, Chile 142 38 26 S 71 53W
Curahuara de Carangas, Bolivia 136 17 52 S 68 26W
Curanilahue, Chile 140 37 29 S 73 28W
Curaray →, Peru 134 2 20 S 74 5W
Curatabaca, Venezuela 135 6 19N 62 51W
Curban, Australia 76 31 33 S 148 32 E
Cure →, France 19 47 40N 3 41 E
Curepto, Chile 140 35 8 S 72 1W
Curiapo, Venezuela 136 8 33N 61 5W
Curicó, Chile 140 34 55 S 71 20W
Curicó □, Chile 140 34 50 S 71 15W
Curicuriari →, Brazil 134 0 14 S 66 48W
Curimatá, Brazil 138 10 2 S 44 17W
Curiplaya, Colombia 134 0 16N 74 52W
Curitiba, Brazil 141 25 20 S 49 10W
Curlewis, Australia 77 31 7 S 150 16 E
Currabubula, Australia 77 31 16 S 150 44 E
Currais Novos, Brazil 138 6 13 S 36 30W
Curralinho, Brazil 138 1 45 S 49 46W
Currant, U.S.A. 122 38 51N 115 32W
Curraweena, Australia 73 30 47 S 145 54 E
Currawilla, Australia 72 25 10 S 141 20 E
Current →, U.S.A. 121 37 15N 91 10W
Currie, Australia 72 39 56 S 143 53 E
Currie, U.S.A. 122 40 16N 114 45W
Currie, Mt., S. Africa 97 30 29 S 29 21 E
Currituck Sd., U.S.A. 115 36 20N 75 50W
Currockbilly Mt., Australia 76 35 25 S 150 0 E
Cursole, Somali Rep. 98 2 14N 45 25 E
Curtea de Argeş, Romania 34 45 12N 24 42 E
Curtis, Spain 22 43 7N 8 4W
Curtis, U.S.A. 120 40 41N 100 32W
Curtis Group, Australia 72 39 30 S 146 37 E
Curtis I., Australia 72 23 35 S 151 10 E
Curuá →, Pará, Brazil 135 2 24 S 54 5W
Curuá →, Pará, Brazil 137 5 23 S 54 22W
Curuá, I., Brazil 138 0 48N 50 10W
Curuaés →, Brazil 137 7 30 S 54 45W
Curuápanema →, Brazil 135 2 25 S 55 2W
Curuçá, Brazil 138 0 43 S 47 50W
Curuguaty, Paraguay 141 24 31 S 55 42W
Çürüksu Çayi →, Turkey 46 37 27N 27 11 E
Curup, Indonesia 56 4 26 S 102 13 E
Curupira, Serra, S. Amer. 135 1 25N 64 30W
Cururu →, Brazil 137 7 12 S 58 3W
Cururupu, Brazil 138 1 50 S 44 50W
Curuzú Cuatiá, Argentina 140 29 50 S 58 5W
Curvelo, Brazil 139 18 45 S 44 27W
Curyo, Australia 74 35 50 S 142 47 E
Cushing, U.S.A. 121 35 59N 96 46W
Cushing, Mt., Canada 110 57 35N 126 57W
Cusihuiriáchic, Mexico 126 28 10N 106 50W
Cusna, Monte, Italy 26 44 13N 10 25 E
Cusset, France 20 46 8N 3 28 E
Custer, U.S.A. 120 43 45N 103 38W
Cut Bank, U.S.A. 122 48 40N 112 15W
Cutervo, Peru 136 6 25 S 78 55W
Cuthbert, U.S.A. 115 31 47N 84 47W
Cutler, U.S.A. 124 36 31N 119 17W
Cutral-Có, Argentina 142 38 58 S 69 15W
Cutro, Italy 29 39 1N 16 58 E
Cuttaburra →, Australia 73 29 43 S 144 22 E
Cuttack, India 50 20 25N 85 57 E
Cuvelai, Angola 95 15 44 S 15 50 E
Cuvier, C., Australia 79 23 14 S 113 22 E
Cuvier I., N.Z. 80 36 27 S 175 50 E
Cuxhaven, W. Germany 30 53 51N 8 41 E
Cuyabeno, Ecuador 134 0 16 S 75 53W
Cuyahoga Falls, U.S.A. 116 41 8N 81 30W
Cuyo, Phil. 57 10 50N 121 5 E
Cuyuni →, Guyana 135 6 23N 58 41W
Cuzco, Bolivia 136 20 0 S 66 50W
Cuzco, Peru 136 13 32 S 72 0W
Cuzco □, Peru 136 13 31 S 71 59W
Cwmbran, U.K. 13 51 39N 3 0W
Cyangugu, Rwanda 92 2 29 S 28 54 E
Cyclades = Kikládhes, Greece 35 37 20N 24 30 E
Cygnet, Australia 72 43 8 S 147 1 E
Cynthiana, U.S.A. 119 38 23N 84 10W
Cypress Hills, Canada 111 49 40N 109 30W
Cyprus ■, Medit. S. 46 35 0N 33 0 E
Cyrenaica, Libya 82 27 0N 23 0 E
Cyrene = Shaḩḩāt, Libya 86 32 48N 21 54 E
Czar, Canada 111 52 27N 110 50W
Czarne, Poland 32 53 42N 16 58 E
Czechoslovakia ■, Europe 32 49 0N 17 0 E
Czersk, Poland 32 53 46N 17 58 E
Częstochowa, Poland 32 50 49N 19 7 E

D

Da →, Vietnam 54 21 15N 105 20 E
Da Hinggan Ling, China 62 48 0N 121 0 E
Da Lat, Vietnam 55 11 56N 108 25 E
Da Nang, Vietnam 54 16 4N 108 13 E
Da Qaidam, China 62 37 50N 95 15 E
Da Yunhe →, China 61 34 25N 120 5 E
Da'an, China 61 45 30N 124 7 E
Daarlerveen, Neths. 16 52 26N 6 34 E
Dab'a, Râs el, Egypt 88 31 3N 28 31 E
Daba Shan, China 58 32 0N 109 0 E
Dabai, Nigeria 91 11 25N 5 15 E
Dabajuro, Venezuela 134 11 2N 70 40W
Dabakala, Ivory C. 90 8 15N 4 20W
Dabaro, Somali Rep. 98 6 21N 48 43 E
Dabbūrīya, Israel 44 32 42N 35 22 E
Dabeiba, Colombia 134 7 1N 76 16W
Dabhoi, India 48 22 10N 73 20 E
Dąbie, Poland 32 53 27N 14 45 E
Dabie Shan, China 59 31 20N 115 20 E
Dabo, Indonesia 56 0 30 S 104 33 E
Dabola, Guinea 90 10 50N 11 5W
Dabou, Ivory C. 90 5 20N 4 23W
Daboya, Ghana 91 9 30N 1 20W
Dabrowa Tarnówska, Poland 32 50 10N 20 59 E
Dabu, China 59 24 22N 116 41 E
Dabung, Malaysia 55 5 23N 102 1 E
Dabus →, Ethiopia 89 10 48N 35 10 E
Dacato →, Ethiopia 89 7 25N 42 40 E
Dacca = Dhaka, Bangla. 52 23 43N 90 26 E
Dacca □ = Dhaka □, Bangla. 52 24 25N 90 25 E
Dachau, W. Germany 31 48 16N 11 27 E
Dadale, Solomon Is. 68 8 7 S 159 6 E
Dadanawa, Guyana 135 2 50N 59 30W
Daday, Turkey 38 41 28N 33 27 E
Dade City, U.S.A. 115 28 20N 82 12W
Dades, Oued →, Morocco 84 30 58N 6 44W
Dadiya, Nigeria 91 9 35N 11 24 E
Dadra and Nagar Haveli □, India 50 20 5N 73 0 E
Dadri = Charkhi Dadri, India 48 28 37N 76 17 E
Dadu, Pakistan 48 26 45N 67 45 E
Dadu He →, China 58 29 31N 103 46 E
Dăeni, Romania 34 44 51N 28 10 E
Daet, Phil. 57 14 2N 122 55 E
Dafang, China 58 27 9N 105 39 E
Dagana, Senegal 90 16 30N 15 35W
Dagash, Sudan 88 19 19N 33 25 E
Dagestanskiye Ogni, U.S.S.R. 39 42 6N 48 12 E
Dagg Sd., N.Z. 81 45 23 S 166 45 E
Daggett, U.S.A. 125 34 52N 116 52W
Daghestan A.S.S.R. □, U.S.S.R. 39 42 30N 47 0 E
Daghfeli, Sudan 88 19 18N 32 40 E
Dagö = Hiiumaa, U.S.S.R. 36 58 50N 22 45 E
Dagu, China 61 38 59N 117 40 E
Dagua, Papua N. G. 69 3 27 S 143 20 E
Daguan, China 58 27 43N 103 56 E
Dagupan, Phil. 57 16 3N 120 20 E
Dahab, Egypt 88 28 31N 34 31 E
Dahlak Kebir, Ethiopia 89 15 50N 40 10 E
Dahlenburg, W. Germany 30 53 11N 10 43 E
Dahlgren, U.S.A. 119 38 12N 88 41W
Dahlonega, U.S.A. 115 34 35N 83 59W
Dahme, E. Germany 30 51 51N 13 25 E
Dahme, W. Germany 30 54 13N 11 5 E
Dahod, India 48 22 50N 74 15 E
Dahomey = Benin ■, Africa 91 10 0N 2 0 E
Dahong Shan, China 59 31 25N 113 0 E
Dahra, Senegal 90 15 22N 15 30W
Dahra, Massif de, Algeria 85 36 7N 1 21 E
Dai Hao, Vietnam 54 18 1N 106 25 E
Dai-Sen, Japan 64 35 22N 133 32 E
Dai Shan, China 59 30 25N 122 10 E
Dai Xian, China 60 39 4N 112 58 E
Daicheng, China 60 38 42N 116 38 E
Daigo, Japan 65 36 46N 140 21 E
Daimanji-San, Japan 64 36 14N 133 20 E
Daimiel, Spain 25 39 5N 3 35W
Daingean, Ireland 15 53 18N 7 15W
Dainkog, China 58 32 30N 97 58 E
Daintree, Australia 72 16 20 S 145 20 E
Daiō-Misaki, Japan 65 34 15N 136 45 E
Dairût, Egypt 88 27 34N 30 43 E
Daisetsu-Zan, Japan 63 43 30N 142 57 E
Daitari, India 50 21 10N 85 46 E
Daito, Japan 64 35 19N 132 58 E
Dajarra, Australia 72 21 42 S 139 30 E
Dajia, Taiwan 59 24 22N 120 37 E
Dajin Chuan →, China 58 31 16N 101 59 E
Dak Dam, Cambodia 54 12 20N 107 21 E
Dak Nhe, Vietnam 54 15 28N 107 48 E
Dak Pek, Vietnam 54 15 4N 107 44 E
Dak Song, Vietnam 55 12 19N 107 35 E
Dak Sui, Vietnam 54 14 55N 107 43 E
Dakar, Senegal 90 14 34N 17 29W
Dakhla, Mauritania 84 23 50N 15 53W
Dakhla, El Wâhât el-, Egypt 88 25 30N 28 50 E
Dakhovskaya, U.S.S.R. 39 44 13N 40 13 E
Dakingari, Nigeria 91 11 37N 4 1 E
Dakor, India 48 22 45N 73 11 E
Dakoro, Niger 91 14 31N 6 46 E
Dakota City, Iowa, U.S.A. 118 42 43N 94 12W
Dakota City, Nebr., U.S.A. 120 42 27N 96 28W
Đakovica, Yugoslavia 33 42 22N 20 26 E
Đakovo, Yugoslavia 33 45 19N 18 24 E
Dala, Angola 95 11 3 S 20 17 E
Dala, Solomon Is. 68 8 30 S 160 41 E
Dalaba, Guinea 90 10 42N 12 15W
Dalachi, China 60 36 48N 105 0 E
Dalai Nur, China 60 43 20N 116 45 E
Dalälven, Sweden 9 60 12N 16 43 E
Dalandzadgad, Mongolia 60 43 27N 104 30 E
Dalarö, Sweden 9 59 8N 18 24 E
Dālbandīn, Pakistan 47 29 0N 64 23 E
Dalbeattie, U.K. 14 54 55N 3 50W
Dalbosjön, Sweden 11 58 40N 12 45 E
Dalby, Australia 77 27 10 S 151 17 E
Dalby, Sweden 11 55 40N 13 22 E
Dale, U.S.A. 119 38 10N 86 59W
Dalen, Neths. 16 52 42N 6 46 E
Dalen, Norway 10 59 26N 8 0 E
Dalet, Burma 52 19 59N 93 51 E
Daletme, Burma 52 21 36N 92 46 E
Daleville, U.S.A. 119 40 7N 85 33W
Dalfsen, Neths. 16 52 31N 6 16 E
Dalga, Egypt 88 27 39N 30 41 E
Dalgaranger, Mt., Australia 79 27 50 S 117 5 E
Dalgety, Australia 75 36 29 S 148 50 E
Dalhart, U.S.A. 121 36 10N 102 30W
Dalhousie, Canada 105 48 5N 66 26W
Dalhousie, India 48 32 38N 76 0 E
Dali, Shaanxi, China 60 34 48N 109 58 E
Dali, Yunnan, China 58 25 40N 100 10 E
Dalian, China 61 38 50N 121 40 E
Daliang Shan, China 58 28 0N 102 45 E
Dalias, Spain 25 36 49N 2 52W
Daling He →, China 61 40 55N 121 40 E
Dāliyat el Karmel, Israel 44 32 43N 35 2 E
Dalkeith, U.K. 14 55 54N 3 5W
Dall I., U.S.A. 110 54 59N 133 25W
Dallarnil, Australia 73 25 19 S 152 2 E
Dallas, Oreg., U.S.A. 122 45 0N 123 15W
Dallas, Tex., U.S.A. 121 32 50N 96 50W
Dallas Center, U.S.A. 118 41 41N 93 58W
Dallas City, U.S.A. 118 40 38N 91 10W
Dallol, Ethiopia 89 14 14N 40 17 E
Dalmacija □, Yugoslavia 33 43 20N 17 0 E
Dalmatia = Dalmacija □, Yugoslavia 33 43 20N 17 0 E
Dalmellington, U.K. 14 55 20N 4 25W
Dalmorton, Australia 77 29 50 S 152 28 E
Dalnegorsk, U.S.S.R. 41 44 32N 135 33 E
Dalneretchensk, U.S.S.R. 41 45 50N 133 40 E
Daloa, Ivory C. 90 7 0N 6 30W
Dalou Shan, China 58 28 15N 107 0 E
Dalsjöfors, Sweden 11 57 46N 13 5 E
Dalskog, Sweden 11 58 44N 12 18 E
Daltenganj, India 49 24 0N 84 4 E
Dalton, Australia 76 34 43 S 149 12 E
Dalton, Canada 104 48 11N 84 1W
Dalton, Ga., U.S.A. 115 34 47N 84 58W
Dalton, Mass., U.S.A. 117 42 28N 73 11W
Dalton, Nebr., U.S.A. 120 41 27N 103 0W
Dalton Iceberg Tongue, Antarctica 143 66 15 S 121 30 E
Dalvík, Iceland 8 65 58N 18 32W
Daly →, Australia 78 13 35 S 130 19 E
Daly City, U.S.A. 124 37 42N 122 28W
Daly L., Canada 111 56 32N 105 39W
Daly Waters, Australia 72 16 15 S 133 24 E
Dam Doi, Vietnam 55 8 50N 105 12 E
Dam Ha, Vietnam 54 21 21N 107 36 E
Daman, India 50 20 25N 72 57 E
Daman □, India 50 20 25N 72 58 E
Damanhûr, Egypt 88 31 0N 30 30 E
Damanzhuang, China 60 38 5N 116 35 E
Damar, Indonesia 57 7 7 S 128 40 E
Damara, C.A.R. 94 4 58N 18 42 E
Damaraland, Namibia 96 21 0 S 17 0 E
Damascus = Dimashq, Syria 46 33 30N 36 18 E
Damaturu, Nigeria 91 11 45N 11 55 E
Damāvand, Iran 47 35 47N 52 0 E
Damāvand, Qolleh-ye, Iran 47 35 56N 52 10 E
Damba, Angola 95 6 44 S 15 20 E
Dame Marie, Haiti 129 18 36N 74 26W
Dāmghān, Iran 47 36 10N 54 17 E
Dămienesti, Romania 34 46 44N 27 1 E
Damietta = Dumyât, Egypt 88 31 24N 31 48 E
Daming, China 60 36 15N 115 6 E
Dāmīya, Jordan 44 32 6N 35 34 E
Dammarie, France 18 48 20N 1 30 E
Dammartin-en-Goële, France 19 49 3N 2 41 E
Damme, W. Germany 30 52 32N 8 12 E
Damodar →, India 49 23 17N 87 35 E
Damoh, India 49 23 50N 79 28 E
Damous, Algeria 85 36 31N 1 42 E
Dampier, Australia 78 20 41 S 116 42 E
Dampier, Selat, Indonesia 57 0 40 S 131 0 E
Dampier Arch., Australia 78 20 38 S 116 32 E
Dampier Str., Papua N. G. 69 5 50 S 148 0 E
Damrei, Chuor Phnum, Cambodia 55 11 30N 103 0 E
Damville, France 18 48 51N 1 5 E
Damvillers, France 19 49 20N 5 21 E
Dan-Gulbi, Nigeria 91 11 40N 6 15 E
Dana, Indonesia 57 11 0 S 122 52 E
Dana, L., Canada 104 50 53N 77 20W
Dana, Mt., U.S.A. 124 37 54N 119 12W
Danakil Depression, Ethiopia 89 12 45N 41 0 E
Danbury, U.S.A. 117 41 23N 73 29W
Danby L., U.S.A. 123 34 17N 115 0W
Dand, Afghan. 48 31 28N 65 32 E
Dandaloo, Australia 76 32 16 S 147 38 E
Dandaragan, Australia 79 30 40 S 115 40 E
Dandeldhura, Nepal 49 29 20N 80 35 E
Dandenong, Australia 74 38 0 S 145 15 E
Dandong, China 61 40 10N 124 20 E
Danfeng, China 60 33 45N 110 25 E
Danforth, U.S.A. 105 45 39N 67 57W
Dangan Liedao, China 59 22 2N 114 8 E
Danger Is. = Pukapuka, Cook Is. 67 10 53 S 165 49W
Danger Pt., S. Africa 96 34 40 S 19 17 E
Dangla, Ethiopia 89 11 18N 36 56 E
Dangora, Nigeria 91 11 30N 8 7 E
Dangrek, Phnom, Thailand 54 14 15N 105 0 E
Dangriga, Belize 127 17 0N 88 13W
Dangshan, China 60 34 27N 116 22 E
Dangtu, China 59 31 32N 118 25 E
Dangyang, China 59 30 52N 111 44 E
Daniel, U.S.A. 122 42 56N 110 2W
Daniel's Harbour, Canada 105 50 13N 57 35W
Danielskuil, S. Africa 96 28 11 S 23 33 E
Danielson, U.S.A. 117 41 50N 71 52W
Danilov, U.S.S.R. 37 58 16N 40 13 E
Danilovka, U.S.S.R. 37 50 25N 44 12 E
Daning, China 60 36 28N 110 45 E
Danissa, Kenya 92 3 15N 40 58 E
Danja, Nigeria 91 11 21N 7 30 E
Danje-ia-Menha, Angola 95 9 32 S 14 39 E
Dankalwa, Nigeria 91 11 52N 12 12 E
Dankama, Nigeria 91 13 20N 7 44 E
Dankov, U.S.S.R. 37 53 20N 39 5 E
Danleng, China 58 30 1N 103 31 E
Danlí, Honduras 128 14 4N 86 35W
Dannemora, Sweden 10 60 12N 17 51 E
Dannemora, U.S.A. 117 44 41N 73 44W
Dannenberg, W. Germany 30 53 7N 11 4 E
Dannevirke, N.Z. 80 40 12 S 176 8 E
Dannhauser, S. Africa 97 28 0 S 30 3 E
Danot, Ethiopia 98 7 33N 45 17 E
Danshui, Taiwan 59 25 12N 121 25 E
Dansville, U.S.A. 116 42 32N 77 41W
Dantan, India 49 21 57N 87 20 E
Dante, Somali Rep. 45 10 25N 51 16 E
Danubyu, Burma 52 17 15N 95 35 E
Danukandi, Bangla. 52 23 32N 90 43 E
Danvers, U.S.A. 117 42 34N 70 55W
Danville, Ill., U.S.A. 119 40 10N 87 40W
Danville, Ind., U.S.A. 119 39 46N 86 32W
Danville, Ky., U.S.A. 119 37 40N 84 45W
Danville, Va., U.S.A. 115 36 40N 79 20W
Danyang, China 59 32 0N 119 31 E
Danzhai, China 58 26 11N 107 48 E
Danzig = Gdańsk, Poland 32 54 22N 18 40 E
Dao, Phil. 57 10 30N 121 57 E
Dão →, Portugal 22 40 20N 8 11W
Dao Xian, China 59 25 36N 111 31 E
Daocheng, China 58 29 0N 100 10 E
Daora, W. Sahara 84 27 5N 12 59W
Daoud = Aïn Beïda, Algeria 85 35 50N 7 29 E
Daoulas, France 18 48 22N 4 17W
Dapong, Togo 91 10 55N 0 16 E
Dapto, Australia 76 34 30 S 150 47 E
Daqing Shan, China 60 40 40N 111 0 E
Daqu Shan, China 59 30 25N 122 20 E
Dar es Salaam, Tanzania 92 6 50 S 39 12 E

Dar'ā, *Syria* **44** 32 36N 36 7 E
Dārāb, *Iran* **47** 28 50N 54 30 E
Daraj, *Libya* **86** 30 10N 10 28 E
Daravica, *Yugoslavia* **33** 42 32N 20 8 E
Daraw, *Egypt* **88** 24 22N 32 51 E
Darazo, *Nigeria* **91** 11 1N 10 24 E
Darband, *Pakistan* **48** 34 20N 72 50 E
Darbhanga, *India* **49** 26 15N 85 55 E
Darburruk, *Somali Rep.* **98** 9 44N 44 31 E
Darby, *U.S.A.* **122** 46 2N 114 7W
Darby Falls, *Australia* **76** 33 53 S 148 52 E
Dardanelle, *Ark., U.S.A.* **121** 35 12N 93 9W
Dardanelle, *Calif., U.S.A.* **124** 38 15N 119 50W
Dardanelles = Çanakkale Boğazı, *Turkey* **46** 40 3N 26 12 E
Darfield, *N.Z.* **81** 43 29 S 172 7 E
Darfo, *Italy* **26** 45 52N 10 11 E
Dargai, *Pakistan* **48** 34 25N 71 55 E
Dargan Ata, *U.S.S.R.* **40** 40 29N 62 10 E
Dargaville, *N.Z.* **80** 35 57 S 173 52 E
Dargo, *Australia* **75** 37 27 S 147 15 E
Dargo →, *Australia* **75** 37 32 S 147 15 E
Darhan Muminggan Lianheqi, *China* **60** 41 40N 110 28 E
Dari, *Sudan* **89** 5 48N 30 26 E
Darién, G. del, *Colombia* **134** 9 0N 77 0W
Darién, Serranía del, *Colombia* **134** 8 30N 77 30W
Dariganga, *Mongolia* **60** 45 21N 113 45 E
Darjeeling = Darjiling, *India* **49** 27 3N 88 18 E
Darjiling, *India* **49** 27 3N 88 18 E
Dark Cove, *Canada* **105** 48 47N 54 13W
Darkan, *Australia* **79** 33 20 S 116 43 E
Darkot Pass, *Pakistan* **49** 36 45N 73 26 E
Darling →, *Australia* **73** 34 4 S 141 54 E
Darling Downs, *Australia* **77** 27 30 S 150 30 E
Darling Ra., *Australia* **79** 32 30 S 116 0 E
Darlington, *U.K.* **12** 54 33N 1 33W
Darlington, *S.C., U.S.A.* **115** 34 18N 79 50W
Darlington, *Wis., U.S.A.* **118** 42 43N 90 7W
Darlot, L., *Australia* **79** 27 48 S 121 35 E
Darłowo, *Poland* **32** 54 25N 16 25 E
Darmstadt, *W. Germany* **31** 49 51N 8 40 E
Darnah, *Libya* **86** 32 40N 22 35 E
Darnah □, *Libya* **86** 31 0N 23 40 E
Darnall, *S. Africa* **97** 29 23 S 31 18 E
Darnétal, *France* **18** 49 25N 1 10 E
Darney, *France* **19** 48 5N 6 2 E
Darnley, C., *Antarctica* **143** 68 0 S 69 0 E
Darnley B., *Canada* **102** 69 30N 123 30W
Daroca, *Spain* **24** 41 9N 1 25W
Darr, *Australia* **72** 23 13 S 144 7 E
Darr →, *Australia* **72** 23 39 S 143 50 E
Darran Mts., *N.Z.* **81** 44 37 S 167 59 E
Darriman, *Australia* **75** 38 26 S 146 59 E
Darrington, *U.S.A.* **122** 48 14N 121 37W
Darror →, *Somali Rep.* **45** 10 30N 50 0 E
Darsana, *Bangla.* **52** 23 35N 88 48 E
Darsi, *India* **51** 15 46N 79 44 E
Darsser Ort, *E. Germany* **30** 54 29N 12 31 E
Dart →, *U.K.* **13** 50 24N 3 36W
Dart, C., *Antarctica* **143** 73 6 S 126 20W
Dartmoor, *Australia* **74** 37 56 S 141 19 E
Dartmoor, *U.K.* **13** 50 36N 4 0W
Dartmouth, *Australia* **72** 23 31 S 144 44 E
Dartmouth, *Canada* **105** 44 40N 63 30W
Dartmouth, *U.K.* **13** 50 21N 3 35W
Dartmouth, L., *Queens., Australia* **73** 26 4 S 145 18 E
Dartmouth, L., *Vic., Australia* **75** 36 34 S 147 32 E
Dartuch, C., *Spain* **24** 39 55N 3 49 E
Daru, *Papua N. G.* **69** 9 3 S 143 13 E
Darvaza, *U.S.S.R.* **40** 40 11N 58 24 E
Darvel, Teluk, *Malaysia* **57** 4 50N 118 20 E
Darwha, *India* **50** 20 15N 77 45 E
Darwin, *Australia* **78** 12 25 S 130 51 E
Darwin, *U.S.A.* **125** 36 15N 117 35W
Darwin, Mt., *Chile* **142** 54 47 S 69 55W
Darwin River, *Australia* **78** 12 50 S 130 58 E
Daryapur, *India* **50** 20 55N 77 20 E
Dās, *U.A.E.* **47** 25 20N 53 30 E
Dashetai, *China* **60** 41 0N 109 5 E
Dashkesan, *U.S.S.R.* **39** 40 40N 46 0 E
Dasht →, *Pakistan* **47** 25 10N 61 40 E
Dasht-e Kavīr, *Iran* **47** 34 30N 55 0 E
Dasht-e Lūt, *Iran* **47** 31 30N 58 0 E
Dasht-e Mārgow, *Afghan.* **47** 30 40N 62 30 E
Dasht-i-Nawar, *Afghan.* **48** 33 52N 68 0 E
Daska, *Pakistan* **48** 32 20N 74 20 E
Dassa-Zoume, *Benin* **91** 7 46N 2 14 E
Dasseneiland, *S. Africa* **96** 33 25 S 18 3 E
Dasserat, L., *Canada* **106** 48 16N 79 25W
Datia, *India* **49** 25 39N 78 27 E
Datian, *China* **59** 25 40N 117 50 E
Datong, *Anhui, China* **59** 30 48N 117 44 E
Datong, *Shanxi, China* **60** 40 6N 113 18 E
Dattapur = Dhamangaon, *India* **50** 20 45N 78 15 E
Dattuck, *Australia* **74** 35 34 S 142 17 E
Datu, Tanjung, *Indonesia* **56** 2 5N 109 39 E
Datu Piang, *Phil.* **57** 7 2N 124 30 E
Daugava →, *U.S.S.R.* **36** 57 4N 24 3 E
Daugavpils, *U.S.S.R.* **36** 55 53N 26 32 E
Daulatabad, *India* **50** 19 57N 75 15 E
Daule, *Ecuador* **134** 1 56 S 79 56W
Daule →, *Ecuador* **134** 2 10 S 79 52W
Daulpur, *India* **48** 26 45N 77 59 E
Daun, *W. Germany* **31** 50 10N 6 53 E
Daund, *India* **50** 18 26N 74 40 E
Dauphin, *Canada* **111** 51 9N 100 5W
Dauphin I., *U.S.A.* **115** 30 16N 88 10W
Dauphin L., *Canada* **111** 51 20N 99 45W
Dauphiné, *France* **21** 45 15N 5 25 E
Daura, *Borno, Nigeria* **91** 11 31N 11 24 E
Daura, *Kaduna, Nigeria* **91** 13 2N 8 21 E
Dausa, *India* **48** 26 52N 76 20 E
Davangere, *India* **51** 14 25N 75 55 E
Davao, *Phil.* **57** 7 0N 125 40 E
Davao, G. of, *Phil.* **57** 6 30N 125 48 E
Dāvar Panāh, *Iran* **47** 27 25N 62 15 E
Davenport, *Calif., U.S.A.* **124** 37 1N 122 12W
Davenport, *Iowa, U.S.A.* **118** 41 30N 90 40W
Davenport, *Wash., U.S.A.* **122** 47 40N 118 5W
Davenport Downs, *Australia* **72** 24 8 S 141 7 E
Davenport Ra., *Australia* **72** 20 28 S 134 0 E
David, *Panama* **128** 8 30N 82 30W
David City, *U.S.A.* **120** 41 18N 97 10W
David Gorodok, *U.S.S.R.* **36** 52 4N 27 8 E
Davidson, *Canada* **111** 51 16N 105 59W
Davis, *Antarctica* **143** 68 34 S 17 55 E
Davis, *U.S.A.* **124** 38 33N 121 44W
Davis Dam, *U.S.A.* **125** 35 11N 114 35W
Davis Inlet, *Canada* **105** 55 50N 60 59W
Davis Mts., *U.S.A.* **121** 30 42N 104 15W
Davis Sea, *Antarctica* **143** 66 0 S 92 0 E
Davis Str., *N. Amer.* **103** 65 0N 58 0W
Davos, *Switz.* **31** 46 48N 9 49 E
Davy L., *Canada* **111** 58 53N 108 18W
Dawa →, *Ethiopia* **89** 4 11N 42 6 E
Dawaki, *Bauchi, Nigeria* **91** 9 25N 9 33 E
Dawaki, *Kano, Nigeria* **91** 12 5N 8 23 E
Dawes Ra., *Australia* **72** 24 40 S 150 40 E
Dawna Range, *Burma* **52** 16 30N 98 30 E
Dawnyein, *Burma* **52** 15 54N 95 36 E
Dawson, *Canada* **102** 64 10N 139 30W
Dawson, *Ga., U.S.A.* **115** 31 45N 84 28W
Dawson, *N. Dak., U.S.A.* **120** 46 56N 99 45W
Dawson, I., *Chile* **142** 53 50 S 70 50W
Dawson Creek, *Canada* **110** 55 45N 120 15W
Dawson Inlet, *Canada* **111** 61 50N 93 25W
Dawson Range, *Australia* **72** 24 30 S 149 48 E
Dawu, *China* **58** 30 55N 101 10 E
Dax, *France* **20** 43 44N 1 3W
Daxi, *Taiwan* **59** 24 52N 121 20 E
Daxian, *China* **58** 31 15N 107 23 E
Daxin, *China* **58** 22 50N 107 11 E
Daxindian, *China* **61** 37 30N 120 50 E
Daxinggou, *China* **61** 43 25N 129 40 E
Daxue Shan, *Sichuan, China* **58** 30 30N 101 30 E
Daxue Shan, *Yunnan, China* **58** 23 42N 99 48 E
Dayao, *China* **58** 25 43N 101 20 E
Daye, *China* **59** 30 6N 114 58 E
Dayi, *China* **58** 30 41N 103 29 E
Daymar, *Australia* **77** 28 37 S 148 59 E
Dayong, *China* **59** 29 11N 110 30 E
Dayr Abū Sa'īd, *Jordan* **44** 32 30N 35 42 E
Dayr al-Ghuṣūn, *Jordan* **44** 32 21N 35 4 E
Dayr az Zawr, *Syria* **46** 35 20N 40 5 E
Dayr Dirwān, *Jordan* **44** 31 55N 35 15 E
Daysland, *Canada* **110** 52 50N 112 20W
Dayton, *Iowa, U.S.A.* **118** 42 14N 94 6W
Dayton, *Ky., U.S.A.* **119** 39 47N 84 28W
Dayton, *Nev., U.S.A.* **124** 39 15N 119 34W
Dayton, *Ohio, U.S.A.* **114** 39 45N 84 10W
Dayton, *Pa., U.S.A.* **116** 40 54N 79 18W
Dayton, *Tenn., U.S.A.* **115** 35 30N 85 1W
Dayton, *Wash., U.S.A.* **122** 46 20N 118 10W
Daytona Beach, *U.S.A.* **115** 29 14N 81 0W
Dayu, *China* **59** 25 24N 114 22 E
Dayville, *U.S.A.* **122** 44 33N 119 37W
Dazhu, *China* **58** 30 41N 107 15 E
Dazu, *China* **58** 29 40N 105 42 E
De Aar, *S. Africa* **96** 30 39 S 24 0 E
De Bilt, *Neths.* **16** 52 6N 5 11 E
De Forest, *U.S.A.* **118** 43 15N 89 20W
De Funiak Springs, *U.S.A.* **115** 30 42N 86 10W
De Grey, *Australia* **78** 20 12 S 119 12 E
De Grey →, *Australia* **78** 20 12 S 119 13 E
De Kalb, *U.S.A.* **119** 41 55N 88 45W
De Koog, *Neths.* **16** 53 6N 4 46 E
De Land, *U.S.A.* **115** 29 1N 81 19W
De Leon, *U.S.A.* **121** 32 9N 98 35W
De Panne, *Belgium* **17** 51 6N 2 34 E
De Pere, *U.S.A.* **114** 44 28N 88 1W
De Queen, *U.S.A.* **121** 34 3N 94 24W
De Quincy, *U.S.A.* **121** 30 30N 93 27W
De Ridder, *U.S.A.* **121** 30 48N 93 15W
De Rijp, *Neths.* **16** 52 33N 4 51 E
De Smet, *U.S.A.* **120** 44 25N 97 35W
De Soto, *U.S.A.* **118** 38 7N 90 33W
De Tour, *U.S.A.* **114** 45 59N 83 56W
De Witt, *Ark., U.S.A.* **121** 34 19N 91 20W
De Witt, *Iowa, U.S.A.* **118** 41 49N 90 33W
De Witt, *Mich., U.S.A.* **119** 42 50N 84 33W
Dead Sea, *Asia* **44** 31 30N 35 30 E
Deadwood, *U.S.A.* **120** 44 23N 103 44W
Deadwood L., *Canada* **110** 59 10N 128 30W
Deakin, *Australia* **79** 30 46 S 128 58 E
Deal, *U.K.* **13** 51 13N 1 25 E
Deal I., *Australia* **72** 39 30 S 147 20 E
Dealesville, *S. Africa* **96** 28 41 S 25 44 E
De'an, *China* **59** 29 21N 115 46 E
Dean, Forest of, *U.K.* **13** 51 50N 2 35W
Deán Funes, *Argentina* **140** 30 20 S 64 20W
Deans Marsh, *Australia* **74** 38 25 S 143 52 E
Dearborn, *Mich., U.S.A.* **104** 42 18N 83 15W
Dearborn, *Mo., U.S.A.* **118** 39 32N 94 46W
Dease →, *Canada* **110** 59 56N 128 32W
Dease L., *Canada* **110** 58 40N 130 5W
Dease Lake, *Canada* **110** 58 25N 130 6W
Death Valley, *U.S.A.* **125** 36 19N 116 52W
Death Valley Junc., *U.S.A.* **125** 36 21N 116 30W
Death Valley Nat. Monument, *U.S.A.* **125** 36 30N 117 0W
Deauville, *France* **18** 49 23N 0 2 E
Deba Habe, *Nigeria* **91** 10 14N 11 20 E
Debaltsevo, *U.S.S.R.* **38** 48 22N 38 26 E
Debao, *China* **58** 23 21N 106 46 E
Debar, *Yugoslavia* **35** 41 31N 20 30 E
Debden, *Canada* **111** 53 30N 106 50W
Debdou, *Morocco* **85** 33 59N 3 0W
Dębica, *Poland* **32** 50 2N 21 25 E
Dęblin, *Poland* **32** 51 34N 21 50 E
Débo, L., *Mali* **90** 15 14N 4 15W
Debolt, *Canada* **110** 55 12N 118 1W
Deborah East, L., *Australia* **79** 30 45 S 119 0 E
Deborah West, L., *Australia* **79** 30 45 S 118 50 E
Debre Birhan, *Ethiopia* **89** 9 41N 39 31 E
Debre Markos, *Ethiopia* **89** 10 20N 37 40 E
Debre May, *Ethiopia* **89** 11 20N 37 25 E
Debre Sina, *Ethiopia* **89** 9 51N 39 50 E
Debre Tabor, *Ethiopia* **89** 11 50N 38 26 E
Debre Zebit, *Ethiopia* **89** 11 48N 38 30 E
Debrecen, *Hungary* **33** 47 33N 21 42 E
Dečani, *Yugoslavia* **33** 42 30N 20 10 E
Decatur, *Ala., U.S.A.* **115** 34 35N 87 0W
Decatur, *Ga., U.S.A.* **115** 33 47N 84 17W
Decatur, *Ill., U.S.A.* **118** 39 50N 89 0W
Decatur, *Ind., U.S.A.* **119** 40 50N 84 56W
Decatur, *Mich., U.S.A.* **119** 42 7N 85 58W
Decatur, *Tex., U.S.A.* **121** 33 15N 97 35W
Decazeville, *France* **20** 44 34N 2 15 E
Deccan, *India* **50** 18 0N 79 0 E
Decelles, Rés., *Canada* **106** 47 42N 78 8W
Deception I., *Antarctica* **143** 63 0 S 60 15W
Deception L., *Canada* **111** 56 33N 104 13W
Dechang, *China* **58** 27 25N 102 11 E
Děčín, *Czech.* **32** 50 47N 14 12 E
Decize, *France* **19** 46 50N 3 28 E
Deckerville, *U.S.A.* **116** 43 33N 82 46W
Decollatura, *Italy* **29** 39 2N 16 21 E
Decorah, *U.S.A.* **120** 43 20N 91 50W
Dedaye, *Burma* **52** 16 24N 95 53 E
Dedéagach = Alexandroúpolis, *Greece* **35** 40 50N 25 54 E
Dedemsvaart, *Neths.* **16** 52 36N 6 28 E
Dederang, *Australia* **75** 36 28 S 147 1 E
Dedham, *U.S.A.* **117** 42 14N 71 10W
Dedilovo, *U.S.S.R.* **37** 53 59N 37 50 E
Dédougou, *Burkina Faso* **90** 12 30N 3 25W
Deduru Oya, *Sri Lanka* **51** 7 32N 79 50 E
Dedza, *Malawi* **93** 14 20 S 34 20 E
Dee →, *Scotland, U.K.* **14** 57 4N 2 7W
Dee →, *Wales, U.K.* **12** 53 15N 3 7W
Deep B., *Canada* **110** 61 15N 116 35W
Deep Lead, *Australia* **74** 37 0 S 142 43 E
Deep River, *U.S.A.* **118** 41 35N 92 22W
Deep Well, *Australia* **72** 24 20 S 134 0 E
Deepwater, *Australia* **77** 29 25 S 151 51 E
Deepwater, *U.S.A.* **118** 38 18N 93 46W
Deer →, *Canada* **111** 58 23N 94 13W
Deer Lake, *Nfld., Canada* **105** 49 11N 57 27W
Deer Lake, *Ont., Canada* **111** 52 36N 94 20W
Deer Lodge, *U.S.A.* **122** 46 25N 112 40W
Deer Park, *Ohio, U.S.A.* **119** 39 13N 84 23W
Deer Park, *Wash., U.S.A.* **122** 47 55N 117 21W
Deer River, *U.S.A.* **120** 47 21N 93 44W
Deeral, *Australia* **72** 17 14 S 145 55 E
Deerdepoort, *S. Africa* **96** 24 37 S 26 27 E
Deerlijk, *Belgium* **17** 50 51N 3 22 E
Deferiet, *U.S.A.* **117** 44 2N 75 41W
Defiance, *U.S.A.* **119** 41 20N 84 20W
Deganya, *Israel* **44** 32 43N 35 34 E
Dêgê, *China* **58** 31 44N 98 39 E
Degebe →, *Portugal* **23** 38 13N 7 29W
Degeh Bur, *Ethiopia* **98** 8 11N 43 31 E
Dégelis, *Canada* **107** 47 30N 68 35W
Degema, *Nigeria* **91** 4 50N 6 48 E
Deggendorf, *W. Germany* **31** 48 49N 12 59 E
Deh Bīd, *Iran* **47** 30 39N 53 11 E
Dehibat, *Tunisia* **86** 32 0N 10 47 E
Dehiwala, *Sri Lanka* **51** 6 50N 79 51 E
Dehkareqan, *Iran* **46** 37 43N 45 55 E
Dehra Dun, *India* **48** 30 20N 78 4 E
Dehri, *India* **49** 24 50N 84 15 E
Dehua, *China* **59** 25 26N 118 14 E
Dehui, *China* **61** 44 30N 125 40 E
Deinze, *Belgium* **17** 50 59N 3 32 E
Dej, *Romania* **34** 47 10N 23 52 E
Deje, *Sweden* **10** 59 35N 13 29 E
Dejiang, *China* **58** 28 18N 108 7 E
Dekemhare, *Ethiopia* **89** 15 6N 39 0 E
Dekese, *Zaïre* **94** 3 24 S 21 24 E
Dekoa, *C.A.R.* **94** 6 19N 19 4 E
Del Mar, *U.S.A.* **125** 32 58N 117 16W
Del Norte, *U.S.A.* **123** 37 40N 106 27W
Del Rio, *U.S.A.* **121** 29 23N 100 50W
Delai, *Sudan* **88** 17 21N 36 6 E
Delano, *U.S.A.* **125** 35 48N 119 13W
Delareyville, *S. Africa* **96** 26 41 S 25 26 E
Delavan, *Ill., U.S.A.* **118** 40 22N 89 33W
Delavan, *Wis., U.S.A.* **119** 42 40N 88 39W
Delaware, *U.S.A.* **119** 40 20N 83 0W
Delaware □, *U.S.A.* **114** 39 0N 75 40W
Delaware →, *U.S.A.* **114** 39 20N 75 25W
Delegate, *Australia* **75** 37 4 S 148 56 E
Delémont, *Switz.* **31** 47 22N 7 20 E
Delft, *Neths.* **16** 52 1N 4 22 E
Delft I., *Sri Lanka* **51** 9 30N 79 40 E
Delfzijl, *Neths.* **16** 53 20N 6 55 E
Delgado, C., *Mozam.* **93** 10 45 S 40 40 E
Delgerhet, *Mongolia* **60** 45 50N 110 30 E
Delgo, *Sudan* **88** 20 6N 30 40 E
Delhi, *Canada* **108** 42 51N 80 30W
Delhi, *India* **48** 28 38N 77 17 E
Delhi, *U.S.A.* **117** 42 17N 74 56W
Delia, *Canada* **110** 51 38N 112 23W
Delice →, *Turkey* **46** 39 45N 34 15 E
Delicias, *Mexico* **126** 28 10N 105 30W
Delitzsch, *E. Germany* **30** 51 32N 12 22 E
Dell City, *U.S.A.* **123** 31 58N 105 19W
Dell Rapids, *U.S.A.* **120** 43 53N 96 44W
Delle, *France* **19** 47 30N 7 2 E
Dellys, *Algeria* **85** 36 57N 3 57 E
Delmar, *Iowa, U.S.A.* **118** 42 0N 90 37W
Delmar, *N.Y., U.S.A.* **117** 42 37N 73 47W
Delmenhorst, *W. Germany* **30** 53 3N 8 37 E
Delmiro Gouveia, *Brazil* **138** 9 24 S 38 6W
Delnice, *Yugoslavia* **27** 45 23N 14 50 E
Delong, Ostrova, *U.S.S.R.* **41** 76 40N 149 20 E
Deloraine, *Australia* **72** 41 30 S 146 40 E
Deloraine, *Canada* **111** 49 15N 100 29W
Delphi, *U.S.A.* **119** 40 37N 86 40W
Delphos, *U.S.A.* **119** 40 51N 84 17W
Delportshoop, *S. Africa* **96** 28 22 S 24 20 E
Delray Beach, *U.S.A.* **115** 26 27N 80 4W
Delsbo, *Sweden* **10** 61 48N 16 32 E
Delta, *Colo., U.S.A.* **123** 38 44N 108 5W
Delta, *Utah, U.S.A.* **122** 39 21N 112 29W
Delta Amacuro □, *Venezuela* **135** 8 30N 61 30W
Delungra, *Australia* **77** 29 39 S 150 51 E
Delvina, *Albania* **35** 39 59N 20 4 E
Delvinákion, *Greece* **35** 39 57N 20 32 E
Demanda, Sierra de la, *Spain* **24** 42 15N 3 0W
Demba, *Zaïre* **95** 5 28 S 22 15 E
Demba Chio, *Angola* **95** 9 41 S 13 41 E
Dembecha, *Ethiopia* **89** 10 32N 37 30 E
Dembi, *Ethiopia* **89** 8 5N 36 25 E
Dembia, *Zaïre* **92** 3 33N 25 48 E
Dembidolo, *Ethiopia* **89** 8 34N 34 50 E
Demer →, *Belgium* **17** 50 57N 4 42 E
Demerara □, *Guyana* **135** 6 0N 58 30W
Demidov, *U.S.S.R.* **36** 55 16N 31 30 E
Deming, *N. Mex., U.S.A.* **123** 32 10N 107 50W
Deming, *Wash., U.S.A.* **124** 48 49N 122 13W
Demini →, *Brazil* **135** 0 46 S 62 56W
Demmin, *E. Germany* **30** 53 54N 13 2 E
Demnate, *Morocco* **84** 31 44N 6 59W
Demonte, *Italy* **26** 44 18N 7 18 E
Demopolis, *U.S.A.* **115** 32 30N 87 48W
Dempo, Mt., *Indonesia* **56** 4 2 S 103 15 E
Demyansk, *U.S.S.R.* **36** 57 40N 32 27 E
Den Burg, *Neths.* **16** 53 3N 4 47 E
Den Chai, *Thailand* **54** 17 59N 100 4 E
Den Dungen, *Neths.* **17** 51 41N 5 22 E
Den Haag = 's-Gravenhage, *Neths.* **16** 52 7N 4 17 E
Den Ham, *Neths.* **16** 52 28N 6 30 E
Den Helder, *Neths.* **16** 52 57N 4 45 E
Den Hulst, *Neths.* **16** 52 36N 6 16 E
Den Oever, *Neths.* **16** 52 56N 5 2 E
Denain, *France* **19** 50 20N 3 22 E
Denair, *U.S.A.* **124** 37 32N 120 48W
Denau, *U.S.S.R.* **40** 38 16N 67 54 E
Denbigh, *Canada* **109** 45 8N 77 15W
Denbigh, *U.K.* **12** 53 12N 3 26W
Dendang, *Indonesia* **56** 3 7 S 107 56 E
Dender →, *Belgium* **17** 51 2N 4 6 E
Denderhoutem, *Belgium* **17** 50 53N 4 2 E
Denderleeuw, *Belgium* **17** 50 54N 4 5 E
Dendermonde, *Belgium* **17** 51 2N 4 5 E
Deneba, *Ethiopia* **89** 9 47N 39 10 E
Denekamp, *Neths.* **16** 52 22N 7 1 E
Deng Deng, *Cameroon* **94** 5 12N 13 31 E
Deng Xian, *China* **59** 32 34N 112 4 E
Dengchuan, *China* **58** 25 59N 100 3 E
Denge, *Nigeria* **91** 12 52N 5 21 E
Dengfeng, *China* **60** 34 25N 113 2 E

Dengi, *Nigeria* ...... **91** 9 25N 9 55 E
Dengkou, *China* ..... **60** 40 18N 106 55 E
Denham, *Australia* ... **79** 25 56 S 113 31 E
Denham Ra., *Australia* **72** 21 55 S 147 46 E
Denham Sd., *Australia* **79** 25 45 S 113 15 E
Denia, *Spain* .... **25** 38 49N 0 8 E
Denial B., *Australia* .. **73** 32 14 S 133 32 E
Deniliquin, *Australia* .. **74** 35 30 S 144 58 E
Denison, *Iowa, U.S.A.* **120** 42 0N 95 18W
Denison, *Tex., U.S.A.* **121** 33 50N 96 40W
Denison Plains,
Australia .... **78** 18 35 S 128 0 E
Denizli, *Turkey* ...... **46** 37 42N 29 2 E
Denman, *Australia* ... **76** 32 24 S 150 42 E
Denman Glacier,
Antarctica .... **143** 66 45 S 99 25 E
Denmark, *Australia* ... **79** 34 59 S 117 25 E
Denmark ■, *Europe* .. **11** 55 30N 9 0 E
Denmark Str., *Atl. Oc.* **144** 66 0N 30 0W
Dennison, *U.S.A.* **116** 40 21N 81 21W
Denpasar, *Indonesia* .. **56** 8 45 S 115 14 E
Denton, *Mont., U.S.A.* **122** 47 25N 109 56W
Denton, *Tex., U.S.A.* . **121** 33 12N 97 10W
D'Entrecasteaux Is.,
Papua N. G. .... **69** 9 0 S 151 0 E
D'Entrecasteaux Pt.,
Australia .... **79** 34 50 S 115 57 E
Denu, *Ghana* .... **91** 6 4N 1 8 E
Denver, *Colo., U.S.A.* **120** 39 45N 105 0W
Denver, *Ind., U.S.A.* . **119** 40 52N 86 5W
Denver, *Iowa, U.S.A.* **118** 42 40N 92 20W
Denver City, *U.S.A.* .. **121** 32 58N 102 48W
Deoband, *India* ...... **48** 29 42N 77 43 E
Deobhog, *India* ...... **50** 19 53N 82 44 E
Deogarh, *India* ...... **50** 21 32N 84 45 E
Deoghar, *India* .... **49** 24 30N 86 42 E
Deolali, *India* .... **50** 19 58N 73 50 E
Deoli = Devli, *India* .. **48** 25 50N 75 20 E
Deoria, *India* .... **49** 26 31N 83 48 E
Deosai Mts., *Pakistan* . **49** 35 40N 75 0 E
Deping, *China* .... **61** 37 25N 116 58 E
Deposit, *U.S.A.* **117** 42 5N 75 23W
Depot Springs,
Australia .... **79** 27 55 S 120 3 E
Deputatskiy, *U.S.S.R.* **41** 69 18N 139 54 E
Dêqên, *China* .... **58** 28 34N 98 51 E
Deqing, *China* .... **59** 23 8N 111 42 E
Dera Ghazi Khan,
Pakistan .... **48** 30 5N 70 43 E
Dera Ismail Khan,
Pakistan .... **48** 31 50N 70 50 E
Derbent, *U.S.S.R.* .... **38** 42 5N 48 15 E
Derby, *Australia* ..... **78** 17 18 S 123 38 E
Derby, *U.K.* **12** 52 55N 1 28W
Derby, *Conn., U.S.A.* **117** 41 20N 73 5W
Derby, *N.Y., U.S.A.* . **116** 42 40N 78 59W
Derby □, *U.K.* **12** 52 55N 1 28W
Derg →, *U.K.* **15** 54 42N 7 26W
Derg, L., *Ireland* **15** 53 0N 8 20W
Dergachi, *U.S.S.R.* ... **37** 50 9N 36 11 E
Dergholm, *Australia* .. **74** 37 24 S 141 14 E
Dernieres Isles, *U.S.A.* **121** 29 0N 90 45W
Dêrong, *China* .... **58** 28 44N 99 9 E
Derrinallum, *Australia* **74** 37 57 S 143 15 E
Derriwong, *Australia* . **76** 33 6 S 147 21 E
Derry = Londonderry,
U.K. **15** 55 0N 7 20W
Derryveagh Mts.,
Ireland **15** 55 0N 8 40W
Derudub, *Sudan* ..... **88** 17 31N 36 7 E
Derval, *France* **18** 47 40N 1 41W
Dervéni, *Greece* ...... **35** 38 8N 22 25 E
Derwent, *Canada* **111** 53 41N 110 58W
Derwent →, *Derby,*
U.K. **12** 52 53N 1 17W
Derwent →,
N. Yorks., U.K. **12** 53 45N 0 57W
Derwent Water, L.,
U.K. **12** 54 35N 3 9W
Des Moines, *Iowa,*
U.S.A. **118** 41 35N 93 37W
Des Moines, *N. Mex.,*
U.S.A. **121** 36 50N 103 51W
Des Moines →, *U.S.A.* **120** 40 23N 91 25W
Des Plaines, *U.S.A.* .. **119** 42 3N 87 52W
Des Plaines →, *U.S.A.* **119** 41 23N 88 15W
Desaguadero →,
Argentina .... **140** 34 30 S 66 46W
Desaguadero →,
Bolivia .... **136** 16 35 S 69 5W
Desbarats, *Canada* ... **108** 46 20N 83 56W
Desbiens, *Canada* **107** 48 25N 71 57W
Descanso, Pta., *Mexico* **125** 32 21N 117 3W
Descartes, *France* .... **20** 46 59N 0 42 E
Deschaillons, *Canada* . **107** 46 32N 72 7W
Deschambault, *Canada* **107** 46 39N 71 56W
Descharme →, *Canada* **111** 56 51N 109 13W
Deschênes, *Canada* ... **106** 45 23N 75 48W
Deschutes →, *U.S.A.* **122** 45 30N 121 0W
Dese, *Ethiopia* .... **89** 11 5N 39 40 E
Deseado, C., *Chile* ... **142** 52 45 S 74 42W
Desenzano del Gardo,
Italy .... **26** 45 28N 10 32 E
Deseronto, *Canada* ... **109** 44 12N 77 3W
Desert Center, *U.S.A.* **125** 33 45N 115 27W
Desert Hot Springs,
U.S.A. **125** 33 58N 116 30W
Désirade, I.,
Guadeloupe **129** 16 18N 61 3W
Deskenatlata L.,
Canada **110** 60 55N 112 3W
Desmaraisville, *Canada* **106** 49 32N 76 9W
Desméloizes, *Canada* . **106** 48 57N 79 29W
Desna →, *U.S.S.R.* .. **36** 50 33N 30 32 E
Desnătui →, *Romania* **34** 44 15N 23 27 E
Desolación, I., *Chile* .. **142** 53 0 S 74 0W
Despeñaperros, Paso,
Spain **25** 38 24N 3 30W
Despotovac, *Yugoslavia* **33** 44 6N 21 30 E
Dessau, *E. Germany* .. **30** 51 49N 12 15 E
Dessel, *Belgium* ...... **17** 51 15N 5 7 E
Dessye = Dese,
Ethiopia .... **89** 11 5N 39 40 E
D'Estrees B., *Australia* **73** 35 55 S 137 45 E
Desuri, *India* .... **48** 25 18N 73 35 E
Desvres, *France* ...... **19** 50 40N 1 48 E
Det Udom, *Thailand* . **54** 14 54N 105 5 E
Dete, *Zimb.* .... **93** 18 38 S 26 50 E
Detinja →, *Yugoslavia* **33** 43 51N 19 45 E
Detmold, *W. Germany* **30** 51 55N 8 50 E
Detour Pt., *U.S.A.* ... **114** 45 37N 86 35W
Detroit, *Mich., U.S.A.* **116** 42 23N 83 5W
Detroit, *Tex., U.S.A.* . **121** 33 40N 95 10W
Detroit Lakes, *U.S.A.* **120** 46 50N 95 50W
Deurne, *Belgium* ..... **17** 51 12N 4 24 E
Deurne, *Neths.* .... **17** 51 27N 5 49 E
Deutsche Bucht,
W. Germany .... **30** 54 0N 8 0 E
Deutschlandsberg,
Austria .... **33** 46 49N 15 14 E
Deux-Sèvres □, *France* **18** 46 35N 0 20W
Deva, *Romania* ...... **34** 45 53N 22 55 E
Devakottai, *India* .... **51** 9 55N 78 45 E
Devaprayag, *India* .... **49** 30 13N 78 35 E
Dévaványa, *Hungary* . **33** 47 2N 20 59 E
Deveci Daği, *Turkey* .. **38** 40 10N 36 0 E
Devenish, *Australia* ... **74** 36 20 S 145 54 E
Deventer, *Neths.* ..... **16** 52 15N 6 10 E
Devenyns, L., *Canada* **107** 47 5N 73 50W
Deveron →, *U.K.* **14** 57 40N 2 31W
Devgad, I., *India* ..... **51** 14 48N 74 5 E
Devgadh Bariya, *India* **48** 22 40N 73 55 E
Devil River Pk., *N.Z.* **81** 40 56 S 172 37 E
Devils Den, *U.S.A.* ... **124** 35 46N 119 58W
Devils Lake, *U.S.A.* .. **120** 48 5N 98 50W
Devils Paw, *Canada* .. **110** 58 47N 134 0W
Devil's Pt., *Sri Lanka* . **51** 9 26N 80 6 E
Devil's Pt., *Vanuatu* .. **68** 17 44 S 168 11 E
Devizes, *U.K.* **13** 51 21N 2 0W
Devli, *India* .... **48** 25 50N 75 20 E
Devnya, *Bulgaria* ..... **34** 43 13N 27 33 E
Devolii →, *Albania* .. **35** 40 57N 20 15 E
Devon, *Canada* **110** 53 24N 113 44W
Devon I., *Canada* **144** 75 10N 85 0W
Devonport, *Australia* . **72** 41 10 S 146 22 E
Devonport, *N.Z.* ..... **80** 36 49 S 174 49 E
Devonport, *U.K.* **13** 50 23N 4 11W
Devonshire □, *U.K.* .. **13** 50 50N 3 40W
Dewas, *India* .... **48** 22 59N 76 3 E
Dewetsdorp, *S. Africa* **96** 29 33 S 26 39 E
Dewsbury, *U.K.* **12** 53 42N 1 38W
Dexing, *China* .... **59** 28 46N 117 30 E
Dexter, *Mich., U.S.A.* **119** 42 20N 83 53W
Dexter, *Mo., U.S.A.* . **121** 36 50N 90 0W
Dexter, *N. Mex.,*
U.S.A. **121** 33 15N 104 25W
Dey-Dey, L., *Australia* **79** 29 12 S 131 4 E
Deyang, *China* .... **58** 31 3N 104 27 E
Deyhūk, *Iran* .... **47** 33 15N 57 30 E
Deyyer, *Iran* .... **47** 27 55N 51 55 E
Dezadeash L., *Canada* **110** 60 28N 136 58W
Dezfūl, *Iran* .... **46** 32 20N 48 30 E
Dezhneva, Mys,
U.S.S.R. **41** 66 5N 169 40W
Dezhou, *China* .... **60** 37 26N 116 18 E
Dhafra, *Oman* .... **47** 23 20N 54 0 E
Dhahaban, *Si. Arabia* . **88** 21 58N 39 3 E
Dhahira, *Oman* ...... **47** 23 40N 57 0 E
Dhahran = Aẓ Ẓahrān,
Si. Arabia .... **46** 26 10N 50 7 E
Dhaka, *Bangla.* .... **52** 23 43N 90 26 E
Dhaka □, *Bangla.* .... **52** 24 25N 90 25 E
Dhamangaon, *India* .. **50** 20 45N 78 15 E
Dhamar, *Yemen* ..... **45** 14 30N 44 20 E
Dhamási, *Greece* ..... **35** 39 43N 22 11 E
Dhampur, *India* ..... **49** 29 19N 78 33 E
Dhamtari, *India* ..... **50** 20 42N 81 35 E
Dhanbad, *India* ..... **49** 23 50N 86 30 E
Dhankuta, *Nepal* .... **49** 26 55N 87 40 E
Dhanora, *India* ..... **50** 20 20N 80 22 E
Dhar, *India* .... **48** 22 35N 75 26 E
Dharampur, *Gujarat,*
India .... **50** 20 32N 73 17 E
Dharampur, *Mad. P.,*
India .... **48** 22 13N 75 18 E
Dharamsala =
Dharmsala, *India* ... **48** 32 16N 76 23 E
Dharapuram, *India* ... **51** 10 45N 77 34 E
Dharmapuri, *India* ... **51** 12 10N 78 10 E
Dharmavaram, *India* . **51** 14 29N 77 44 E
Dharmsala, *India* .... **48** 32 16N 76 23 E
Dharwad, *India* ..... **51** 15 22N 75 15 E
Dhaulagiri, *Nepal* ... **49** 28 39N 83 28 E
Dhebar, L., *India* .... **48** 24 10N 74 0 E
Dhenkanal, *India* .... **50** 20 45N 85 35 E
Dhenoúsa, *Greece* ... **35** 37 8N 25 48 E
Dheskáti, *Greece* .... **35** 39 55N 21 49 E
Dhespotikó, *Greece* ... **35** 36 57N 24 58 E
Dhestina, *Greece* .... **35** 38 25N 22 31 E
Dhimitsána, *Greece* ... **35** 37 36N 22 3 E
Dhírfis, *Greece* ...... **35** 38 40N 23 54 E
Dhodhekánisos, *Greece* **35** 36 35N 27 0 E
Dholiana, *Greece* .... **35** 39 54N 20 32 E
Dholka, *India* .... **48** 22 44N 72 29 E
Dhoraji, *India* .... **48** 21 45N 70 37 E
Dhoxáton, *Greece* .... **35** 41 9N 24 16 E
Dhrangadhra, *India* ... **48** 22 59N 71 31 E
Dhrol, *India* .... **48** 22 33N 70 25 E
Dhubaibah, *Oman* .... **47** 23 25N 54 35 E
Dhuburi, *India* ...... **52** 26 2N 89 59 E
Dhulasar, *Bangla.* .... **52** 21 52N 90 14 E
Dhule, *India* .... **50** 20 58N 74 50 E
Dhupdhara, *India* .... **52** 26 10N 91 4 E
Di Linh, *Vietnam* ..... **55** 11 35N 108 4 E
Di Linh, Cao Nguyen,
Vietnam .... **55** 11 30N 108 0 E
Día, *Greece* .... **35** 35 26N 25 13 E
Diablo, Mt., *U.S.A.* .. **124** 37 53N 121 56W
Diablo Range, *U.S.A.* **124** 37 0N 121 5W
Diafarabé, *Mali* **90** 14 9N 4 57W
Diagonal, *U.S.A.* **118** 40 49N 94 20W
Diala, *Mali* **90** 14 10N 10 0W
Dialakoro, *Mali* **90** 12 18N 7 54W
Diallassagou, *Mali* ... **90** 13 47N 3 41W
Diamante, *Argentina* .. **140** 32 5 S 60 40W
Diamante →,
Argentina .... **140** 34 30 S 66 46W
Diamantina, *Brazil* ... **139** 18 17 S 43 40W
Diamantina →,
Australia .... **73** 26 45 S 139 10 E
Diamantino, *Brazil* ... **137** 14 30 S 56 30W
Diamond Harbour,
India .... **49** 22 11N 88 14 E
Diamond Is., *Australia* **72** 17 25 S 151 5 E
Diamond Mts., *U.S.A.* **122** 40 0N 115 58W
Diamond Springs,
U.S.A. **124** 38 42N 120 49W
Diamondville, *U.S.A.* . **122** 41 51N 110 30W
Dianbai, *China* ...... **59** 21 33N 111 0 E
Diancheng, *China* .... **59** 21 30N 111 4 E
Diano Marina, *Italy* .. **26** 43 55N 8 3 E
Dianópolis, *Brazil* ... **139** 11 38 S 46 50W
Dianra, *Ivory C.* **90** 8 45N 6 14W
Diapaga, *Burkina Faso* **91** 12 5N 1 46 E
Diapangou,
Burkina Faso ...... **91** 12 5N 0 10 E
Diapur, *Australia* .... **74** 36 19 S 141 29 E
Diariguila, *Guinea* **90** 10 35N 10 2W
Dībā, *Oman* .... **47** 25 45N 56 16 E
Dibaya, *Zaïre* .... **95** 6 30 S 22 57 E
Dibaya-Lubue, *Zaïre* . **95** 4 12 S 19 54 E
Dibbi, *Ethiopia* ...... **89** 4 10N 41 52 E
Dibble Glacier Tongue,
Antarctica .... **143** 66 8 S 134 32 E
Dibete, *Botswana* .... **96** 23 45 S 26 32 E
Dibrugarh, *India* ..... **52** 27 29N 94 55 E
Dickeyville, *U.S.A.* ... **118** 42 38N 90 36W
Dickinson, *U.S.A.* **120** 46 50N 102 48W
Dickson, *U.S.A.* **115** 36 5N 87 22W
Dickson, *U.S.S.R.* .... **40** 73 40N 80 5 E
Dickson City, *U.S.A.* . **117** 41 29N 75 40W
Dicomano, *Italy* ..... **27** 43 53N 11 30 E
Didam, *Neths.* .... **16** 51 57N 6 8 E
Didesa, W. →,
Ethiopia .... **89** 10 2N 35 32 E
Didiéni, *Mali* **90** 13 53N 8 6W
Didsbury, *Canada* **110** 51 35N 114 10W
Didwana, *India* ...... **48** 27 23N 74 36 E
Die, *France* .... **21** 44 47N 5 22 E
Diébougou,
Burkina Faso **90** 11 0N 3 15W
Diefenbaker L.,
Canada **111** 51 0N 106 55W
Diego Garcia, *Ind. Oc.* **53** 7 50 S 72 50 E
Diekirch, *Lux.* .... **17** 49 52N 6 10 E
Diélette, *France* **18** 49 33N 1 52W
Diéma, *Mali* **90** 14 32N 9 12W
Diémbéring, *Senegal* .. **90** 12 29N 16 47W
Diemen, *Neths.* ...... **16** 52 21N 4 58 E
Dien Ban, *Vietnam* ... **54** 15 53N 108 16 E
Dien Bien, *Vietnam* .. **54** 21 20N 103 0 E
Dien Khanh, *Vietnam* . **55** 12 15N 109 6 E
Diepenbeek, *Belgium* . **17** 50 54N 5 25 E
Diepenheim, *Neths.* .. **16** 52 12N 6 33 E
Diepenveen, *Neths.* ... **16** 52 18N 6 9 E
Diepholz, *W. Germany* **30** 52 37N 8 22 E
Dieppe, *France* ...... **18** 49 54N 1 4 E
Dieren, *Neths.* .... **16** 52 3N 6 6 E
Dierks, *U.S.A.* **121** 34 9N 94 0W
Diessen, *Neths.* ...... **17** 51 29N 5 10 E
Diest, *Belgium* ...... **17** 50 58N 5 4 E
Dieterich, *U.S.A.* **119** 39 4N 88 23W
Dieulefit, *France* .... **21** 44 32N 5 4 E
Dieuze, *France* ...... **19** 48 49N 6 43 E
Diever, *Neths.* ...... **16** 52 51N 6 19 E
Differdange, *Lux.* .... **17** 49 31N 5 54 E
Dig, *India* .... **48** 27 28N 77 20 E
Digba, *Zaïre* .... **92** 4 25N 25 48 E
Digboi, *India* .... **52** 27 23N 95 38 E
Digby, *Canada* **105** 44 38N 65 50W
Diggers Rest, *Australia* **74** 37 38 S 144 43 E
Digges, *Canada* **111** 58 40N 94 0W
Digges Is., *Canada* ... **103** 62 40N 77 50W
Diggora West, *Australia* **74** 36 21 S 144 32 E
Dighinala, *Bangla.* ... **52** 23 15N 92 5 E
Dighton, *U.S.A.* **120** 38 30N 100 26W
Diglur, *India* .... **50** 18 34N 77 33 E
Digne, *France* .... **21** 44 5N 6 12 E
Digoin, *France* ...... **20** 46 29N 3 58 E
Digos, *Phil.* .... **57** 6 45N 125 20 E
Digranes, *Iceland* **8** 66 4N 14 44W
Digras, *India* .... **50** 20 6N 77 45 E
Digul →, *Indonesia* .. **57** 7 7 S 138 42 E
Dijlah, Nahr →, *Asia* **46** 31 0N 47 25 E
Dijle →, *Belgium* .... **17** 50 58N 4 41 E
Dijon, *France* .... **19** 47 20N 5 0 E
Dikala, *Sudan* ...... **89** 4 45N 31 28 E
Dikkil, *Djibouti* ..... **89** 11 8N 42 20 E
Dikomu di Kai,
Botswana .... **96** 24 58 S 24 36 E
Diksmuide, *Belgium* .. **17** 51 2N 2 52 E
Dikson = Dickson,
U.S.S.R. .... **40** 73 40N 80 5 E
Dikwa, *Nigeria* ...... **91** 12 4N 13 30 E
Dila, *Ethiopia* .... **89** 6 21N 38 22 E
Dilbeek, *Belgium* .... **17** 50 51N 4 17 E
Dili, *Indonesia* ...... **57** 8 39 S 125 34 E
Dilizhan, *U.S.S.R.* ... **39** 40 46N 44 57 E
Dilkoon, *Australia* ... **77** 29 30 S 152 59 E
Dillard, *U.S.A.* **118** 37 44N 91 13W
Dillenburg,
W. Germany .... **30** 50 44N 8 17 E
Dilley, *U.S.A.* **121** 28 40N 99 12W
Dilling, *Sudan* ...... **89** 12 3N 29 35 E
Dillingen, *W. Germany* **31** 48 32N 10 29 E
Dillon, *Canada* **111** 55 56N 108 35W
Dillon, *Mont., U.S.A.* **122** 45 9N 112 36W
Dillon, *S.C., U.S.A.* .. **115** 34 26N 79 20W
Dillon →, *Canada* ... **111** 55 56N 108 56W
Dillsboro, *U.S.A.* **119** 39 1N 85 4W
Dilolo, *Zaïre* .... **95** 10 28 S 22 18 E
Dilsen, *Belgium* ..... **17** 51 2N 5 44 E
Dilston, *Australia* .... **72** 41 22 S 147 10 E
Dimapur, *India* ..... **52** 25 54N 93 45 E
Dimas, *Mexico* **126** 23 43N 106 47W
Dimashq, *Syria* ..... **46** 33 30N 36 18 E
Dimbaza, *S. Africa* ... **97** 32 50 S 27 14 E
Dimbelenge, *Zaïre* ... **95** 5 33 S 23 7 E
Dimbokro, *Ivory C.* .. **90** 6 45N 4 46W
Dimboola, *Australia* .. **74** 36 28 S 142 7 E
Dîmboviţa →,
Romania .... **34** 44 5N 26 35 E
Dîmbovnic →,
Romania .... **34** 44 28N 25 18 E
Dimbulah, *Australia* .. **72** 17 8 S 145 4 E
Dimitrovgrad, *Bulgaria* **35** 42 5N 25 35 E
Dimitrovgrad, *U.S.S.R.* **37** 54 14N 49 39 E
Dimitrovgrad,
Yugoslavia .... **33** 43 0N 22 48 E
Dimitrovo = Pernik,
Bulgaria .... **34** 42 35N 23 2 E
Dimmitt, *U.S.A.* **121** 34 36N 102 16W
Dimo, *Sudan* .... **89** 5 19N 29 10 E
Dimona, *Israel* ...... **44** 31 2N 35 1 E
Dimovo, *Bulgaria* .... **34** 43 43N 22 50 E
Dinagat, *Phil.* .... **57** 10 10N 125 40 E
Dinajpur, *Bangla.* .... **52** 25 33N 88 43 E
Dinan, *France* **18** 48 28N 2 2W
Dinant, *Belgium* ..... **17** 50 16N 4 55 E
Dinapur, *India* ...... **49** 25 38N 85 5 E
Dinar, *Turkey* ...... **46** 38 5N 30 15 E
Dinara Planina,
Yugoslavia .... **27** 44 0N 16 30 E
Dinard, *France* **18** 48 38N 2 6W
Dinaric Alps = Dinara
Planina, *Yugoslavia* . **27** 44 0N 16 30 E
Dinder, Nahr ed →,
Sudan .... **89** 14 6N 33 40 E
Dindi →, *India* ..... **51** 16 24N 78 15 E
Dindigul, *India* ...... **51** 10 25N 78 0 E
Ding Xian, *China* .... **60** 38 30N 114 59 E
Dingbian, *China* ..... **60** 37 35N 107 32 E
Dingee, *Australia* .... **74** 36 22 S 144 15 E
Dingelstädt,
E. Germany .... **30** 51 19N 10 19 E
Dinghai, *China* ...... **59** 30 1N 122 6 E
Dingle, *Ireland* **15** 52 9N 10 17W
Dingle B., *Ireland* **15** 52 3N 10 20W
Dingmans Ferry,
U.S.A. **117** 41 13N 74 55W
Dingnan, *China* ..... **59** 24 45N 115 0 E
Dingo, *Australia* ..... **72** 23 38 S 149 19 E
Dingolfing,
W. Germany .... **31** 48 38N 12 30 E
Dingtao, *China* ...... **60** 35 5N 115 35 E
Dinguiraye, *Guinea* ... **90** 11 18N 10 49W
Dingwall, *U.K.* **14** 57 36N 4 26W
Dingxi, *China* .... **60** 35 30N 104 33 E
Dingxiang, *China* .... **60** 38 30N 112 58 E
Dingyuan, *China* .... **59** 32 32N 117 41 E
Dinh, Mui, *Vietnam* .. **55** 11 22N 109 1 E
Dinh Lap, *Vietnam* .. **54** 21 33N 107 6 E
Dinhata, *India* ...... **52** 26 8N 89 27 E
Dinkel →, *Neths.* .... **16** 52 30N 6 58 E
Dinokwe, *Botswana* .. **96** 23 29 S 26 37 E
Dinosaur National
Monument, *U.S.A.* . **122** 40 30N 108 58W
Dinslaken, *W. Germany* **17** 51 34N 6 41 E
Dinsor, *Somali Rep.* .. **98** 2 24N 42 59 E
Dintel →, *Neths.* .... **17** 51 39N 4 22 E
Dinteloord, *Neths.* ... **17** 51 38N 4 22 E
Dinuba, *U.S.A.* **124** 36 31N 119 22W
Dinxperlo, *Neths.* .... **16** 51 52N 6 30 E
Dio, *Sweden* .... **11** 56 37N 14 15 E
Diósgyör, *Hungary* ... **33** 48 7N 20 43 E
Diourbel, *Senegal* **90** 14 39N 16 12W
Diphu Pass, *India* .... **52** 28 9N 97 20 E
Diplo, *Pakistan* ..... **48** 24 35N 69 35 E
Dipolog, *Phil.* .... **57** 8 36N 123 20 E
Dipşa, *Romania* ..... **34** 46 58N 24 27 E
Dipton, *N.Z.* .... **81** 45 54 S 168 22 E
Dir, *Pakistan* .... **47** 35 8N 71 59 E
Diré, *Mali* **90** 16 20N 3 25W
Dire Dawa, *Ethiopia* .. **89** 9 35N 41 45 E
Diriamba, *Nic.* **128** 11 51N 86 19W
Dirico, *Angola* ...... **95** 17 50 S 20 42 E
Dirk Hartog I.,
Australia .... **79** 25 50 S 113 5 E
Dirkou, *Niger* ...... **87** 19 1N 12 53 E
Dirranbandi, *Australia* **73** 28 33 S 148 17 E
Disa, *India* .... **48** 24 18N 72 10 E

Disa, *Sudan* **89** 12 5N 34 15 E
Disappointment, C., *U.S.A.* **122** 46 20N 124 0W
Disappointment L., *Australia* **78** 23 20 S 122 40 E
Disaster B., *Australia* **75** 37 15 S 150 0 E
Discovery B., *Australia* **74** 38 10 S 140 40 E
Disentis, *Switz.* **31** 46 42N 8 50 E
Dishna, *Egypt* **88** 26 9N 32 32 E
Disina, *Nigeria* **91** 11 35N 9 50 E
Disko, *Greenland* **144** 69 45N 53 30W
Disko Bugt, *Greenland* **144** 69 10N 52 0W
Disna, *U.S.S.R.* **36** 55 32N 28 11 E
Disna →, *U.S.S.R.* **36** 55 34N 28 12 E
Disney Reef, *Tonga* **68** 19 17 S 174 7W
Dison, *Belgium* **17** 50 37N 5 51 E
Disraëli, *Canada* **107** 45 54N 71 21W
Disteghil Sar, *Pakistan* **49** 36 20N 75 12 E
Distrito Federal □, *Brazil* **139** 15 45 S 47 45W
Distrito Federal □, *Venezuela* **134** 10 30N 66 55W
Disûq, *Egypt* **88** 31 8N 30 35 E
Ditu, *Zaïre* **95** 5 23 S 21 27 E
Diu, *India* **48** 20 45N 70 58 E
Dives →, *France* **18** 49 18N 0 7W
Dives-sur-Mer, *France* **18** 49 18N 0 8W
Divi Pt., *India* **51** 15 59N 81 9 E
Divichi, *U.S.S.R.* **39** 41 15N 48 57 E
Divide, *U.S.A.* **122** 45 48N 112 47W
Dividing Ra., *Australia* **79** 27 45 S 116 0 E
Divinópolis, *Brazil* **139** 20 10 S 44 54W
Divisões, Serra dos, *Brazil* **139** 17 0 S 51 0W
Divnoye, *U.S.S.R.* **39** 45 55N 43 21 E
Divo, *Ivory C.* **90** 5 48N 5 15W
Dīwāl Kol, *Afghan.* **48** 34 23N 67 52 E
Dix →, *U.S.A.* **119** 37 49N 84 44W
Dixie Mt., *U.S.A.* **124** 39 55N 120 16W
Dixon, *Calif., U.S.A.* **124** 38 27N 121 49W
Dixon, *Ill., U.S.A.* **118** 41 50N 89 30W
Dixon, *Iowa, U.S.A.* **118** 41 45N 90 47W
Dixon, *Mo., U.S.A.* **118** 37 59N 92 6W
Dixon, *Mont., U.S.A.* **122** 47 19N 114 25W
Dixon, *N. Mex., U.S.A.* **123** 36 15N 105 57W
Dixon Entrance, *U.S.A.* **110** 54 30N 132 0W
Dixonville, *Canada* **110** 56 32N 117 40W
Dixville, *Canada* **107** 45 4N 71 46W
Diyarbakir, *Turkey* **46** 37 55N 40 18 E
Diz Chah, *Iran* **47** 35 30N 55 30 E
Djado, *Niger* **87** 21 4N 12 14 E
Djado, Plateau du, *Niger* **87** 21 29N 12 21 E
Djakarta = Jakarta, *Indonesia* **57** 6 9 S 106 49 E
Djamâa, *Algeria* **85** 33 32N 5 59 E
Djamba, *Angola* **95** 16 45 S 13 58 E
Djambala, *Congo* **94** 2 32 S 14 30 E
Djanet, *Algeria* **85** 24 35N 9 32 E
Djaul I., *Papua N. G.* **69** 2 58 S 150 57 E
Djawa = Jawa, *Indonesia* **57** 7 0 S 110 0 E
Djebiniana, *Tunisia* **86** 35 1N 11 0 E
Djédaa, *Chad* **87** 13 31N 18 34 E
Djelfa, *Algeria* **85** 34 40N 3 15 E
Djema, *C.A.R.* **92** 6 3N 25 15 E
Djember, *Chad* **87** 10 25N 17 50 E
Djendel, *Algeria* **85** 36 15N 2 25 E
Djeneïene, *Tunisia* **86** 31 45N 10 9 E
Djenné, *Mali* **90** 14 0N 4 30W
Djenoun, Garet el, *Algeria* **85** 25 4N 5 31 E
Djerba, *Tunisia* **86** 33 52N 10 51 E
Djerid, Chott, *Tunisia* **86** 33 42N 8 30 E
Djiba, *Gabon* **94** 1 20 S 13 9 E
Djibo, *Burkina Faso* **91** 14 9N 1 35W
Djibouti, *Djibouti* **89** 11 30N 43 5 E
Djibouti ■, *Africa* **89** 12 0N 43 0 E
Djolu, *Zaïre* **92** 0 35N 22 5 E
Djougou, *Benin* **91** 9 40N 1 45 E
Djoum, *Cameroon* **94** 2 41N 12 35 E
Djourab, *Chad* **87** 16 40N 18 50 E
Djugu, *Zaïre* **92** 1 55N 30 35 E
Djúpivogur, *Iceland* **8** 64 39N 14 17W
Djursholm, *Sweden* **10** 59 25N 18 6 E
Djursland, *Denmark* **11** 56 27N 10 45 E
Dmitriev-Lgovskiy, *U.S.S.R.* **36** 52 10N 35 0 E
Dmitriya Lapteva, Proliv, *U.S.S.R.* **41** 73 0N 140 0 E
Dmitrov, *U.S.S.R.* **37** 56 25N 37 32 E
Dmitrovsk-Orlovskiy, *U.S.S.R.* **36** 52 29N 35 10 E
Dnepr →, *U.S.S.R.* **38** 46 30N 32 18 E
Dneprodzerzhinsk, *U.S.S.R.* **38** 48 32N 34 37 E
Dneprodzerzhinskoye Vdkhr., *U.S.S.R.* **38** 49 0N 34 0 E
Dnepropetrovsk, *U.S.S.R.* **38** 48 30N 35 0 E
Dneprorudnoye, *U.S.S.R.* **38** 47 21N 34 58 E
Dnestr →, *U.S.S.R.* **38** 46 18N 30 17 E
Dnestrovski = Belgorod, *U.S.S.R.* **38** 50 35N 36 35 E
Dnieper = Dnepr →, *U.S.S.R.* **38** 46 30N 32 18 E
Dniester = Dnestr →, *U.S.S.R.* **38** 46 18N 30 17 E
Dno, *U.S.S.R.* **36** 57 50N 29 58 E
Doan Hung, *Vietnam* **54** 21 30N 105 10 E
Doba, *Chad* **87** 8 40N 16 50 E
Dobbiaco, *Italy* **27** 46 44N 12 13 E
Dobbyn, *Australia* **72** 19 44 S 140 2 E
Döbeln, *E. Germany* **30** 51 7N 13 10 E
Doberai, Jazirah, *Indonesia* **57** 1 25 S 133 0 E
Dobiegniew, *Poland* **32** 52 59N 15 45 E
Doblas, *Argentina* **140** 37 5 S 64 0W
Dobo, *Indonesia* **57** 5 45 S 134 15 E
Doboj, *Yugoslavia* **33** 44 46N 18 6 E
Dobra, *Dîmbovita, Romania* **34** 44 52N 25 40 E
Dobra, *Hunedoara, Romania* **34** 45 54N 22 36 E
Dobreta-Turnu-Severin, *Romania* **34** 44 39N 22 41 E
Dobrinishta, *Bulgaria* **35** 41 49N 23 34 E
Dobrodzień, *Poland* **32** 50 45N 18 25 E
Dobropole, *U.S.S.R.* **38** 48 25N 37 2 E
Dobruja, *Romania* **34** 44 30N 28 15 E
Dobrush, *U.S.S.R.* **37** 52 28N 30 19 E
Dobtong, *Sudan* **89** 6 25N 31 40 E
Doc, Mui, *Vietnam* **54** 17 58N 106 30 E
Doce →, *Brazil* **139** 19 37 S 39 49W
Doda, *India* **49** 33 10N 75 34 E
Dodecanese = Dhodhekánisos, *Greece* **35** 36 35N 27 0 E
Dodewaard, *Neths.* **16** 51 55N 5 39 E
Dodge Center, *U.S.A.* **120** 44 1N 92 50W
Dodge City, *U.S.A.* **121** 37 42N 100 0W
Dodge L., *Canada* **111** 59 50N 105 36W
Dodgeville, *U.S.A.* **118** 42 55N 90 8W
Dodo, *Sudan* **89** 5 10N 29 57 E
Dodola, *Ethiopia* **89** 6 59N 39 11 E
Dodoma, *Tanzania* **92** 6 8 S 35 45 E
Dodoma □, *Tanzania* **92** 6 0 S 36 0 E
Dodsland, *Canada* **111** 51 50N 108 45W
Dodson, *U.S.A.* **122** 48 23N 108 16W
Doesburg, *Neths.* **16** 52 1N 6 9 E
Doetinchem, *Neths.* **16** 51 59N 6 18 E
Dog Creek, *Canada* **110** 51 35N 122 14W
Dog L., *Man., Canada* **111** 51 2N 98 31W
Dog L., *Ont., Canada* **104** 48 48N 89 30W
Dogger Bank, *N. Sea* **6** 54 50N 2 0 E
Dogliani, *Italy* **26** 44 35N 7 55 E
Dōgo, *Japan* **64** 36 15N 133 16 E
Dōgo-San, *Japan* **64** 35 2N 133 13 E
Dogondoutchi, *Niger* **91** 13 38N 4 2 E
Dogran, *Pakistan* **48** 31 48N 73 35 E
Doguéraoua, *Niger* **91** 14 0N 5 31 E
Doi, *Indonesia* **57** 2 14N 127 49 E
Doi Luang, *Thailand* **54** 18 30N 101 0 E
Doi Saket, *Thailand* **54** 18 52N 99 9 E
Doig →, *Canada* **110** 56 25N 120 40W
Dois Irmãos, Sa., *Brazil* **138** 9 0 S 42 30W
Dokka, *Norway* **9** 60 49N 10 7 E
Dokka →, *Norway* **10** 61 7N 10 0 E
Dokkum, *Neths.* **16** 53 20N 5 59 E
Dokkumer Ee →, *Neths.* **16** 53 18N 5 52 E
Dokri, *Pakistan* **48** 27 25N 68 7 E
Dol-de-Bretagne, *France* **18** 48 34N 1 47W
Doland, *U.S.A.* **120** 44 55N 98 5W
Dolbeau, *Canada* **107** 48 53N 72 18W
Dole, *France* **19** 47 7N 5 31 E
Doleib, Wadi →, *Sudan* **89** 12 10N 33 15 E
Dolgellau, *U.K.* **12** 52 44N 3 53W
Dolgelley = Dolgellau, *U.K.* **12** 52 44N 3 53W
Dolginovo, *U.S.S.R.* **36** 54 39N 27 29 E
Dolianova, *Italy* **28** 39 23N 9 11 E
Dolinskaya, *U.S.S.R.* **38** 48 6N 32 46 E
Dollart, *Neths.* **16** 53 20N 7 10 E
Dolna Banya, *Bulgaria* **34** 42 18N 23 44 E
Dolni Dŭbnik, *Bulgaria* **34** 43 24N 24 26 E
Dolo, *Ethiopia* **89** 4 11N 42 3 E
Dolo, *Italy* **27** 45 25N 12 4 E
Dolomites = Dolomiti, *Italy* **27** 46 30N 11 40 E
Dolomiti, *Italy* **27** 46 30N 11 40 E
Dolores, *Argentina* **140** 36 20 S 57 40W
Dolores, *Uruguay* **140** 33 34 S 58 15W
Dolores, *U.S.A.* **123** 37 30N 108 30W
Dolores →, *U.S.A.* **123** 38 49N 108 17W
Dolphin, C., *Falk. Is.* **142** 51 10 S 59 0W
Dolphin and Union Str., *Canada* **102** 69 5N 114 45W
Dolton, *U.S.A.* **119** 41 38N 87 36W
Dom Joaquim, *Brazil* **139** 18 57 S 43 16W
Dom Pedrito, *Brazil* **141** 31 0 S 54 40W
Dom Pedro, *Brazil* **138** 4 59 S 44 27W
Doma, *Nigeria* **91** 8 25N 8 18 E
Domasi, *Malawi* **93** 15 15 S 35 22 E
Domazlice, *Czech.* **32** 49 28N 13 0 E
Dombarovskiy, *U.S.S.R.* **40** 50 46N 59 32 E
Dombås, *Norway* **9** 62 4N 9 8 E
Dombasle-sur-Meurthe, *France* **19** 48 38N 6 21 E
Dombes, *France* **21** 46 0N 5 0 E
Dombóvár, *Hungary* **33** 46 21N 18 9 E
Domburg, *Neths.* **17** 51 34N 3 30 E
Domérat, *France* **20** 46 21N 2 32 E
Domett, *N.Z.* **81** 42 53 S 173 12 E
Domeyko, *Chile* **140** 29 0 S 71 0W
Domeyko, Cordillera, *Chile* **140** 24 30 S 69 0W
Domfront, *France* **18** 48 37N 0 40W
Dominador, *Chile* **140** 24 21 S 69 20W
Dominica ■, *W. Indies* **129** 15 20N 61 20W
Dominica Passage, *W. Indies* **129** 15 10N 61 20W
Dominican Rep. ■, *W. Indies* **129** 19 0N 70 30W
Domiongo, *Zaïre* **95** 4 37 S 21 15 E
Dömitz, *E. Germany* **30** 53 9N 11 13 E
Domme, *France* **20** 44 48N 1 12 E
Dommel →, *Neths.* **17** 51 30N 5 20 E
Domo, *Ethiopia* **98** 7 50N 47 10 E
Domodóssola, *Italy* **26** 46 6N 8 19 E
Dompaire, *France* **19** 48 14N 6 14 E
Dompierre-sur-Besbre, *France* **20** 46 31N 3 41 E
Dompim, *Ghana* **90** 5 10N 2 5W
Domrémy-la-Pucelle, *France* **19** 48 26N 5 40 E
Domsjö, *Sweden* **10** 63 16N 18 41 E
Domville, Mt., *Australia* **77** 28 1 S 151 15 E
Domvraína, *Greece* **35** 38 15N 22 59 E
Domžale, *Yugoslavia* **27** 46 9N 14 35 E
Don →, *India* **51** 16 20N 76 15 E
Don →, *England, U.K.* **12** 53 41N 0 51W
Don →, *Scotland, U.K.* **14** 57 14N 2 5W
Don →, *U.S.S.R.* **39** 47 4N 39 18 E
Don, C., *Australia* **78** 11 18 S 131 46 E
Don Benito, *Spain* **23** 38 53N 5 51W
Don Duong, *Vietnam* **55** 11 51N 108 35 E
Don Martín, Presa de, *Mexico* **126** 27 30N 100 50W
Dona Ana, *Mozam.* **93** 17 25 S 35 5 E
Donaghadee, *U.K.* **15** 54 38N 5 32W
Donald, *Australia* **74** 36 23 S 143 0 E
Donalda, *Canada* **110** 52 35N 112 34W
Donaldsonville, *U.S.A.* **121** 30 2N 91 0W
Donalsonville, *U.S.A.* **115** 31 3N 84 52W
Donau →, *Austria* **33** 48 10N 17 0 E
Donaueschingen, *W. Germany* **31** 47 57N 8 30 E
Donauwörth, *W. Germany* **31** 48 42N 10 47 E
Doncaster, *U.K.* **12** 53 31N 1 9W
Dondo, *Angola* **95** 9 45 S 14 25 E
Dondo, *Mozam.* **93** 19 33 S 34 46 E
Dondo, *Zaïre* **94** 4 11N 21 39 E
Dondo, Teluk, *Indonesia* **57** 0 29N 120 30 E
Dondra Head, *Sri Lanka* **51** 5 55N 80 40 E
Donegal, *Ireland* **15** 54 39N 8 8W
Donegal □, *Ireland* **15** 54 53N 8 0W
Donegal B., *Ireland* **15** 54 30N 8 35W
Donets →, *U.S.S.R.* **39** 47 33N 40 55 E
Donetsk, *U.S.S.R.* **38** 48 0N 37 45 E
Dong Ba Thin, *Vietnam* **55** 12 8N 109 13 E
Dong Dang, *Vietnam* **54** 21 54N 106 42 E
Dong Giam, *Vietnam* **54** 19 25N 105 31 E
Dong Ha, *Vietnam* **54** 16 55N 107 8 E
Dong Hene, *Laos* **54** 16 40N 105 18 E
Dong Hoi, *Vietnam* **54** 17 29N 106 36 E
Dong Jiang →, *China* **59** 23 6N 114 0 E
Dong Khe, *Vietnam* **54** 22 26N 106 27 E
Dong Ujimqin Qi, *China* **60** 45 32N 116 55 E
Dong Van, *Vietnam* **54** 23 16N 105 22 E
Dong Xoai, *Vietnam* **55** 11 32N 106 55 E
Donga, *Nigeria* **91** 7 45N 10 2 E
Dong'an, *China* **59** 26 23N 111 12 E
Dongara, *Australia* **79** 29 14 S 114 57 E
Dongargarh, *India* **50** 21 10N 80 40 E
Dongbei, *China* **61** 42 0N 125 0 E
Dongchuan, *China* **58** 26 8N 103 1 E
Dongen, *Neths.* **17** 51 38N 4 56 E
Donges, *France* **18** 47 18N 2 4W
Dongfang, *China* **54** 18 50N 108 33 E
Dongfeng, *China* **61** 42 40N 125 34 E
Donggala, *Indonesia* **57** 0 30 S 119 40 E
Donggan, *China* **58** 23 22N 105 9 E
Donggou, *China* **61** 39 52N 124 10 E
Dongguan, *China* **59** 22 58N 113 44 E
Dongguang, *China* **60** 37 50N 116 30 E
Donghai Dao, *China* **59** 21 0N 110 15 E
Dongjingcheng, *China* **61** 44 0N 129 10 E
Donglan, *China* **58** 24 30N 107 21 E
Dongliu, *China* **59** 30 13N 116 55 E
Dongmen, *China* **58** 22 20N 107 48 E
Dongning, *China* **61** 44 2N 131 5 E
Dongnyi, *China* **58** 28 3N 100 15 E
Dongo, *Angola* **95** 14 36 S 15 48 E
Dongola, *Sudan* **88** 19 9N 30 22 E
Dongou, *Congo* **94** 2 0N 18 5 E
Dongping, *China* **60** 35 55N 116 20 E
Dongshan, *China* **59** 23 43N 117 30 E
Dongsheng, *China* **60** 39 50N 110 0 E
Dongshi, *Taiwan* **59** 24 18N 120 49 E
Dongtai, *China* **61** 32 51N 120 21 E
Dongting Hu, *China* **59** 29 18N 112 45 E
Dongxiang, *China* **59** 28 11N 116 34 E
Dongxing, *China* **58** 21 34N 108 0 E
Dongyang, *China* **59** 29 13N 120 15 E
Dongzhi, *China* **59** 30 9N 117 0 E
Donington, C., *Australia* **73** 34 45 S 136 0 E
Doniphan, *U.S.A.* **121** 36 40N 90 50W
Donja Stubica, *Yugoslavia* **27** 45 59N 16 0 E
Donji Dušnik, *Yugoslavia* **33** 43 12N 22 5 E
Donji Miholjac, *Yugoslavia* **33** 45 45N 18 10 E
Donji Milanovac, *Yugoslavia* **33** 44 28N 22 6 E
Donji Vakuf, *Yugoslavia* **33** 44 8N 17 24 E
Donjon, Le, *France* **20** 46 22N 3 48 E
Dønna, *Norway* **8** 66 6N 12 30 E
Donna, *U.S.A.* **121** 26 12N 98 2W
Donnaconna, *Canada* **107** 46 41N 71 41W
Donnelly's Crossing, *N.Z.* **80** 35 42 S 173 38 E
Donnybrook, *Australia* **79** 33 34 S 115 48 E
Donnybrook, *S. Africa* **97** 29 59 S 29 48 E
Donora, *U.S.A.* **116** 40 11N 79 50W
Donor's Hill, *Australia* **72** 18 42 S 140 33 E
Donque, *Angola* **95** 15 28 S 14 6 E
Donskoy, *U.S.S.R.* **37** 53 55N 38 15 E
Donya Lendava, *Yugoslavia* **27** 46 35N 16 25 E
Donzère, *France* **21** 44 28N 4 43 E
Donzère-Mondragon, Barr. de, *France* **21** 44 13N 4 42 E
Donzy, *France* **19** 47 20N 3 6 E
Dooen, *Australia* **74** 36 39 S 142 16 E
Dookie, *Australia* **74** 36 20 S 145 41 E
Doon →, *U.K.* **14** 55 26N 4 41W
Doorn, *Neths.* **16** 52 2N 5 20 E
Dor, *Israel* **44** 32 37N 34 55 E
Dora, L., *Australia* **78** 22 0 S 123 0 E
Dora Báltea →, *Italy* **26** 45 11N 8 5 E
Dora Riparia →, *Italy* **26** 45 5N 7 44 E
Dorada, La, *Colombia* **134** 5 30N 74 40W
Doran L., *Canada* **111** 61 13N 108 6W
Dorat, Le, *France* **20** 46 14N 1 5 E
Dorchester, *U.K.* **13** 50 42N 2 28W
Dorchester, C., *Canada* **103** 65 27N 77 27W
Dordogne □, *France* **20** 45 5N 0 40 E
Dordogne →, *France* **20** 45 2N 0 36W
Dordrecht, *Neths.* **16** 51 48N 4 39 E
Dordrecht, *S. Africa* **96** 31 20 S 27 3 E
Dore →, *France* **20** 45 50N 3 35 E
Dore, Mts., *France* **20** 45 32N 2 50 E
Doré L., *Canada* **111** 54 46N 107 17W
Doré Lake, *Canada* **111** 54 38N 107 36W
Dores do Indaiá, *Brazil* **139** 19 27 S 45 36W
Dorfen, *W. Germany* **31** 48 16N 12 10 E
Dorgali, *Italy* **28** 40 18N 9 35 E
Dori, *Burkina Faso* **91** 14 3N 0 2W
Doring →, *S. Africa* **96** 31 54 S 18 39 E
Doringbos, *S. Africa* **96** 31 59 S 19 16 E
Dorion, *Canada* **107** 45 23N 74 3W
Dormaa-Ahenkro, *Ghana* **90** 7 15N 2 52W
Dormo, Ras, *Ethiopia* **89** 13 14N 42 35 E
Dornberg, *Yugoslavia* **27** 45 45N 13 50 E
Dornbirn, *Austria* **31** 47 25N 9 45 E
Dornes, *France* **19** 46 48N 3 18 E
Dornoch, *U.K.* **14** 57 52N 4 0W
Dornoch Firth, *U.K.* **14** 57 52N 4 0W
Dornogovĭ □, *Mongolia* **60** 44 0N 110 0 E
Doro, *Mali* **91** 16 9N 0 51W
Dorogobuzh, *U.S.S.R.* **36** 54 50N 33 18 E
Dorohoi, *Romania* **34** 47 56N 26 30 E
Döröö Nuur, *Mongolia* **62** 48 0N 93 0 E
Dorre I., *Australia* **79** 25 13 S 113 12 E
Dorrigo, *Australia* **77** 30 20 S 152 44 E
Dorris, *U.S.A.* **122** 41 59N 121 58W
Dorset, *Canada* **106** 45 14N 78 54W
Dorset, *U.S.A.* **116** 41 4N 80 40W
Dorset □, *U.K.* **13** 50 48N 2 25W
Dorsten, *W. Germany* **30** 51 40N 6 55 E
Dortmund, *W. Germany* **30** 51 32N 7 28 E
Dorum, *W. Germany* **30** 53 40N 8 33 E
Doruma, *Zaïre* **92** 4 42N 27 33 E
Dos Bahías, C., *Argentina* **142** 44 58 S 65 32W
Dos Hermanas, *Spain* **23** 37 16N 5 55W
Dos Palos, *U.S.A.* **124** 36 59N 120 37W
Dosquet, *Canada* **107** 46 28N 71 32W
Dosso, *Niger* **91** 13 0N 3 13 E
Dothan, *U.S.A.* **115** 31 10N 85 25W
Dottignies, *Belgium* **17** 50 44N 3 19 E
Doty, *U.S.A.* **124** 46 38N 123 17W
Douai, *France* **19** 50 21N 3 4 E
Douala, *Cameroon* **91** 4 0N 9 45 E
Douarnenez, *France* **18** 48 6N 4 21W
Double Island Pt., *Australia* **73** 25 56 S 153 11 E
Doubrava →, *Czech.* **32** 49 40N 15 30 E
Doubs □, *France* **19** 47 10N 6 20 E
Doubs →, *France* **19** 46 53N 5 1 E
Doubtful Sd., *N.Z.* **81** 45 20 S 166 49 E
Doubtless B., *N.Z.* **80** 34 55 S 173 26 E
Doudeville, *France* **18** 49 43N 0 47 E
Doué-la-Fontaine, *France* **18** 47 11N 0 16W
Douentza, *Mali* **90** 14 58N 2 48W
Doughboy, *Australia* **76** 35 15 S 149 38 E
Douglas, *Canada* **109** 45 31N 76 56W
Douglas, *S. Africa* **96** 29 4 S 23 46 E
Douglas, *U.K.* **12** 54 9N 4 29W
Douglas, *Alaska, U.S.A.* **110** 58 23N 134 24W
Douglas, *Ariz., U.S.A.* **123** 31 21N 109 30W
Douglas, *Ga., U.S.A.* **115** 31 32N 82 52W
Douglas, *Wyo., U.S.A.* **122** 42 45N 105 20W
Douglas Pt., *Canada* **108** 44 19N 81 37W
Douglastown, *Canada* **105** 48 46N 64 24W
Douglasville, *U.S.A.* **115** 33 46N 84 43W
Douirat, *Morocco* **84** 33 2N 4 11W
Doukáton, Ákra, *Greece* **35** 38 34N 20 30 E

Doulevant-le-Château, France 19 48 23N 4 55 E
Doullens, France 19 50 10N 2 20 E
Doumé, Cameroon 94 4 15N 13 25 E
Douna, Mali 90 13 13N 6 0W
Dounan, Taiwan 59 23 41N 120 26 E
Dounguila, Congo 94 2 53 S 11 58 E
Dounreay, U.K. 14 58 34N 3 44W
Dour, Belgium 17 50 24N 3 46 E
Dourada, Serra, Brazil 139 13 10 S 48 45W
Dourados, Brazil 141 22 9 S 54 50W
Dourados →, Brazil 141 21 58 S 54 18W
Dourdan, France 19 48 30N 2 1 E
Douro →, Europe 22 41 8N 8 40W
Douvaine, France 21 46 19N 6 16 E
Douz, Tunisia 86 33 25N 9 0 E
Douze →, France 20 43 54N 0 30W
Dove →, U.K. 12 52 51N 1 36W
Dove Creek, U.S.A. 123 37 46N 108 59W
Dover, Australia 72 43 18 S 147 2 E
Dover, U.K. 13 51 7N 1 19 E
Dover, Del., U.S.A. 114 39 10N 75 31W
Dover, Ky., U.S.A. 119 38 43N 83 52W
Dover, N.H., U.S.A. 117 43 12N 70 51W
Dover, N.J., U.S.A. 117 40 53N 74 34W
Dover, Ohio, U.S.A. 116 40 32N 81 30W
Dover, Pt., Australia 79 32 32 S 125 32 E
Dover, Str. of, Europe 18 51 0N 1 30 E
Dover-Foxcroft, U.S.A. 105 45 14N 69 14W
Dover Plains, U.S.A. 117 41 43N 73 35W
Dovey →, U.K. 13 52 32N 4 0W
Dovrefjell, Norway 10 62 15N 9 33 E
Dowa, Malawi 93 13 38 S 33 58 E
Dowagiac, U.S.A. 119 41 58N 86 8W
Dowlat Yār, Afghan. 47 34 30N 65 45 E
Dowlatābād, Iran 47 28 20N 56 40 E
Down □, U.K. 15 54 20N 6 0W
Downers Grove, U.S.A. 119 41 49N 88 1W
Downey, Calif., U.S.A. 125 42 26N 112 7W
Downey, U.S.A. 122 42 29N 112 3W
Downham Market, U.K. 13 52 36N 0 22 E
Downieville, U.S.A. 124 39 34N 120 50W
Downing, U.S.A. 118 40 29N 92 22W
Downpatrick, U.K. 15 54 20N 5 43W
Downpatrick Hd., Ireland 15 54 20N 9 21W
Dowshī, Afghan. 47 35 35N 68 43 E
Doyle, U.S.A. 124 40 2N 120 6W
Doylestown, U.S.A. 117 40 21N 75 10W
Dozois, Rés., Canada 106 47 30N 77 5W
Draa, C., Morocco 84 28 47N 11 0W
Draa, Oued →, Morocco 84 28 40N 11 10W
Drac →, France 21 45 12N 5 42 E
Drachten, Neths. 16 53 7N 6 5 E
Drăgăneşti, Romania 34 44 9N 24 32 E
Drăgăneşti-Viaşca, Romania 34 44 5N 25 33 E
Dragaš, Yugoslavia 33 42 5N 20 35 E
Drăgăsani, Romania 34 44 39N 24 17 E
Dragonera, I., Spain 24 39 35N 2 19 E
Draguignan, France 21 43 32N 6 27 E
Drain, U.S.A. 122 43 45N 123 17W
Drake, Australia 77 28 55 S 152 25 E
Drake, U.S.A. 120 47 56N 100 21W
Drake Passage, S. Ocean 143 58 0 S 68 0W
Drakensberg, S. Africa 97 31 0 S 28 0 E
Dráma, Greece 35 41 9N 24 10 E
Drammen, Norway 10 59 42N 10 12 E
Drangajökull, Iceland 8 66 9N 22 15W
Drangedal, Norway 10 59 6N 9 3 E
Dranov, Ostrov, Romania 34 44 55N 29 30 E
Dras, India 49 34 25N 75 48 E
Drau = Drava →, Yugoslavia 33 45 33N 18 55 E
Drava →, Yugoslavia 33 45 33N 18 55 E
Draveil, France 19 48 41N 2 25 E
Dravograd, Yugoslavia 27 46 36N 15 5 E
Drawa →, Poland 32 52 52N 15 59 E
Drawno, Poland 32 53 13N 15 46 E
Drayton, Canada 108 43 46N 80 40W
Drayton Plains, U.S.A. 119 42 42N 83 23W
Drayton Valley, Canada 110 53 12N 114 58W
Dreibergen, Neths. 16 52 3N 5 17 E
Drenthe □, Neths. 16 52 52N 6 40 E
Drentsche Hoofdvaart, Neths. 16 52 39N 6 4 E
Dresden, Canada 108 42 35N 82 11W
Dresden, E. Germany 30 51 2N 13 45 E
Dresden □, E. Germany 30 51 12N 14 0 E
Dreux, France 18 48 44N 1 23 E
Drexel, U.S.A. 119 39 45N 84 18W
Driel, Neths. 16 51 57N 5 49 E
Driffield, U.K. 12 54 0N 0 25W
Driftwood, U.S.A. 116 41 22N 78 9W
Driggs, U.S.A. 122 43 50N 111 8W
Drin i zi →, Albania 35 41 37N 20 28 E
Drina →, Yugoslavia 33 44 53N 19 21 E
Drincea →, Romania 34 44 20N 22 55 E
Drini →, Albania 34 42 20N 20 0 E
Drinjača →, Yugoslavia 33 44 15N 19 8 E
Drivstua, Norway 10 62 26N 9 47 E
Drniš, Yugoslavia 27 43 51N 16 10 E
Drøbak, Norway 10 59 39N 10 39 E
Drocourt, Canada 108 45 46N 80 21W
Drogheda, Ireland 15 53 45N 6 20W
Drogichin, U.S.S.R. 36 52 15N 25 8 E
Drogobych, U.S.S.R. 36 49 20N 23 30 E
Droichead Nua, Ireland 15 53 11N 6 50W
Droitwich, U.K. 13 52 16N 2 10W
Dromana, Australia 74 38 22 S 144 57 E
Drôme □, France 21 44 38N 5 15 E
Drôme →, France 21 44 46N 4 46 E
Dromedary, C., Australia 75 36 17 S 150 10 E
Dronero, Italy 26 44 29N 7 22 E
Dronfield, Australia 72 21 12 S 140 3 E
Dronne →, France 20 45 2N 0 9W
Dronning Maud Land, Antarctica 143 72 30 S 12 0 E
Dronninglund, Denmark 11 57 10N 10 19 E
Dronrijp, Neths. 16 53 11N 5 39 E
Dropt →, France 20 44 35N 0 6W
Drouin, Australia 74 38 10 S 145 53 E
Drumbo, Canada 108 43 16N 80 35W
Drumheller, Canada 110 51 25N 112 40W
Drummond, U.S.A. 122 46 40N 113 4W
Drummond I., U.S.A. 104 46 0N 83 40W
Drummond Pt., Australia 73 34 9 S 135 16 E
Drummond Ra., Australia 72 23 45 S 147 10 E
Drummondville, Canada 107 45 55N 72 25W
Drumright, U.S.A. 121 35 59N 96 38W
Drunen, Neths. 17 51 41N 5 8 E
Druskininkai, U.S.S.R. 36 54 3N 23 58 E
Drut →, U.S.S.R. 36 53 3N 30 42 E
Druten, Neths. 16 51 53N 5 36 E
Druya, U.S.S.R. 36 55 45N 27 28 E
Druzhina, U.S.S.R. 41 68 14N 145 18 E
Drvar, Yugoslavia 27 44 21N 16 23 E
Drvenik, Yugoslavia 27 43 27N 16 3 E
Dry Tortugas, U.S.A. 128 24 38N 82 55W
Dryanovo, Bulgaria 34 42 59N 25 28 E
Dryden, Canada 111 49 47N 92 50W
Dryden, U.S.A. 121 30 3N 102 3W
Drygalski I., Antarctica 143 66 0 S 92 0 E
Drysdale, Australia 74 38 11 S 144 32 E
Drysdale →, Australia 78 13 59 S 126 51 E
Drysdale I., Australia 72 11 41 S 136 0 E
Dschang, Cameroon 91 5 32N 10 3 E
Du Bois, U.S.A. 116 41 8N 78 46W
Du Quoin, U.S.A. 118 38 0N 89 10W
Duanesburg, U.S.A. 117 42 45N 74 11W
Duaringa, Australia 72 23 42 S 149 42 E
Ḍubā, Si. Arabia 46 27 10N 35 40 E
Dubai = Dubayy, U.A.E. 47 25 18N 55 20 E
Dubawnt →, Canada 111 64 33N 100 6W
Dubawnt, L., Canada 111 63 4N 101 42W
Dubayy, U.A.E. 47 25 18N 55 20 E
Dubbeldam, Neths. 16 51 47N 4 43 E
Dubbo, Australia 76 32 11 S 148 35 E
Dubele, Zaïre 92 2 56N 29 35 E
Dubica, Yugoslavia 27 45 11N 16 48 E
Dublin, Ireland 15 53 20N 6 18W
Dublin, Ga., U.S.A. 115 32 30N 82 34W
Dublin, Tex., U.S.A. 121 32 0N 98 20W
Dublin □, Ireland 15 53 24N 6 20W
Dublin B., Ireland 15 53 18N 6 5W
Dubna, R.S.F.S.R., U.S.S.R. 37 54 8N 36 59 E
Dubna, R.S.F.S.R., U.S.S.R. 37 56 44N 37 10 E
Dubno, U.S.S.R. 36 50 25N 25 45 E
Dubois, Idaho, U.S.A. 122 44 7N 112 9W
Dubois, Ind., U.S.A. 119 38 26N 86 48W
Dubossary, U.S.S.R. 38 47 15N 29 10 E
Dubossary Vdkhr., U.S.S.R. 38 47 30N 29 0 E
Dubovka, U.S.S.R. 39 49 5N 44 50 E
Dubovskoye, U.S.S.R. 39 47 28N 42 46 E
Dubrajpur, India 49 23 48N 87 25 E
Dubréka, Guinea 90 9 46N 13 31W
Dubrovitsa, U.S.S.R. 36 51 31N 26 35 E
Dubrovnik, Yugoslavia 33 42 39N 18 6 E
Dubrovskoye, U.S.S.R. 41 58 55N 111 10 E
Dubulu, Zaïre 94 4 18N 20 16 E
Dubuque, U.S.A. 118 42 30N 90 41W
Duchang, China 59 29 18N 116 12 E
Duchesne, U.S.A. 122 40 14N 110 22W
Duchess, Australia 72 21 20 S 139 50 E
Ducie I., Pac. Oc. 67 24 40 S 124 48W
Duck Cr. →, Australia 78 22 37 S 116 53 E
Duck Lake, Canada 111 52 50N 106 16W
Duck Mt. Prov. Parks, Canada 111 51 45N 101 0W
Duckwall, Mt., U.S.A. 124 37 58N 120 7W
Düdelange, Lux. 17 49 29N 6 5 E
Duderstadt, W. Germany 30 51 30N 10 15 E
Dudhnai, India 52 25 59N 90 47 E
Dudinka, U.S.S.R. 41 69 30N 86 13 E
Dudley, U.K. 13 52 30N 2 5W
Dudna →, India 50 19 17N 76 54 E
Dudo, Somali Rep. 98 9 20N 50 12 E
Dudub, Ethiopia 98 6 55N 46 43 E
Dueñas, Spain 22 41 52N 4 33W
Dueodde, Denmark 11 54 59N 15 4 E
Dueré, Brazil 139 11 20 S 49 17W
Duero → = Douro →, Europe 22 41 8N 8 40W
Duffel, Belgium 17 51 6N 4 30 E
Dufftown, U.K. 14 57 26N 3 9W
Dugger, U.S.A. 119 39 4N 87 16W
Dugi, Yugoslavia 27 44 0N 15 0 E
Dugiuma, Somali Rep. 98 1 15N 42 34 E
Dugo Selo, Yugoslavia 27 45 51N 16 18 E
Duifken Pt., Australia 72 12 33 S 141 38 E
Duisburg, W. Germany 30 51 27N 6 42 E
Duitama, Colombia 134 5 50N 73 2W
Duiveland, Neths. 17 51 38N 4 0 E
Duiwelskloof, S. Africa 97 23 42 S 30 10 E
Duke I., U.S.A. 110 54 50N 131 20W
Dukhān, Qatar 47 25 25N 50 50 E
Dukhovshchina, U.S.S.R. 36 55 15N 32 27 E
Duku, Bauchi, Nigeria 91 10 43N 10 43 E
Duku, Sokoto, Nigeria 91 11 11N 4 55 E
Dulce →, Argentina 140 30 32 S 62 33W
Dulce, G., Costa Rica 128 8 40N 83 20W
Dŭlgopol, Bulgaria 34 43 3N 27 22 E
Dulit, Banjaran, Malaysia 56 3 15N 114 30 E
Duliu, China 60 39 2N 116 55 E
Dullewala, Pakistan 48 31 50N 71 25 E
Dülmen, W. Germany 30 51 49N 7 18 E
Dulovo, Bulgaria 34 43 48N 27 9 E
Dululu, Australia 72 23 48 S 150 15 E
Duluth, U.S.A. 120 46 48N 92 10W
Dum Dum, India 49 22 39N 88 33 E
Dum Hadjer, Chad 87 13 18N 19 41 E
Dumaguete, Phil. 57 9 17N 123 15 E
Dumai, Indonesia 56 1 35N 101 28 E
Dumaran, Phil. 57 10 33N 119 50 E
Dumaresq →, Australia 77 28 40 S 150 29 E
Dumas, Ark., U.S.A. 121 33 52N 91 30W
Dumas, Tex., U.S.A. 121 35 50N 101 58W
Dumbarton, U.K. 14 55 58N 4 35W
Dumbea, N. Cal. 68 22 10 S 166 27 E
Dumbleyung, Australia 79 33 17 S 117 42 E
Dumbo, Angola 95 14 6 S 17 24 E
Dumfries, U.K. 14 55 4N 3 37W
Dumfries & Galloway □, U.K. 14 55 0N 4 0W
Dumka, India 49 24 12N 87 15 E
Dümmersee, W. Germany 30 52 30N 8 21 E
Dumoine →, Canada 106 46 13N 77 51W
Dumoine L., Canada 106 46 55N 77 55W
Dumosa, Australia 74 35 54 S 143 13 E
Dumraon, India 49 25 33N 84 8 E
Dumyât, Egypt 88 31 24N 31 48 E
Dumyât, Masabb, Egypt 88 31 28N 31 51 E
Dun Laoghaire, Ireland 15 53 17N 6 9W
Dun-le-Palestel, France 20 46 18N 1 39 E
Dun-sur-Auron, France 19 46 53N 2 33 E
Duna →, Hungary 33 45 51N 18 48 E
Dunaföldvár, Hungary 33 46 50N 18 57 E
Dunaj →, Czech. 33 47 50N 18 50 E
Dunajec →, Poland 32 50 15N 20 44 E
Dunajska Streda, Czech. 33 48 0N 17 37 E
Dunapatai, Hungary 33 46 39N 19 4 E
Dunărea →, Romania 34 45 20N 29 40 E
Dunaújváros, Hungary 33 47 0N 18 57 E
Dunav →, Yugoslavia 33 44 47N 21 20 E
Dunback, N.Z. 81 45 23 S 170 36 E
Dunbar, Australia 72 16 0 S 142 22 E
Dunbar, U.K. 14 56 0N 2 32W
Dunblane, U.K. 14 56 10N 3 58W
Duncan, Canada 110 48 45N 123 40W
Duncan, Ariz., U.S.A. 123 32 46N 109 6W
Duncan, Okla., U.S.A. 121 34 25N 98 0W
Duncan, L., Canada 104 53 29N 77 58W
Duncan L., Canada 110 62 51N 113 58W
Duncan Town, Bahamas 128 22 15N 75 45W
Duncannon, U.S.A. 116 40 23N 77 2W
Dunchurch, Canada 108 45 39N 79 51W
Dundalk, Canada 108 44 10N 80 24W
Dundalk, Ireland 15 54 1N 6 25W
Dundalk Bay, Ireland 15 53 55N 6 15W
Dundas, Canada 108 43 17N 79 59W
Dundas, L., Australia 79 32 35 S 121 50 E
Dundas I., Canada 110 54 30N 130 50W
Dundas Str., Australia 78 11 15 S 131 35 E
Dundee, Australia 77 29 33 S 151 50 E
Dundee, S. Africa 97 28 11 S 30 15 E
Dundee, U.K. 14 56 29N 3 0W
Dundee, U.S.A. 119 41 57N 83 40W
Dundgovĭ □, Mongolia 60 45 10N 106 0 E
Dundoo, Australia 73 27 40 S 144 37 E
Dundrum, U.K. 15 54 17N 5 50W
Dundrum B., U.K. 15 54 12N 5 40W
Dundwara, India 49 27 48N 79 9 E
Dunedin, N.Z. 81 45 50 S 170 33 E
Dunedin, U.S.A. 115 28 1N 82 45W
Dunedin →, Canada 110 59 30N 124 5W
Dunedoo, Australia 77 32 0 S 149 25 E
Dunfermline, U.K. 14 56 5N 3 28W
Dungannon, Canada 108 43 51N 81 36W
Dungannon, U.K. 15 54 30N 6 47W
Dungannon □, U.K. 15 54 30N 6 55W
Dungarpur, India 48 23 52N 73 45 E
Dungarvan, Ireland 15 52 6N 7 40W
Dungarvan Bay, Ireland 15 52 5N 7 35W
Dungeness, U.K. 13 50 54N 0 59 E
Dungo, L. do, Angola 95 17 15 S 19 0 E
Dungog, Australia 76 32 22 S 151 46 E
Dungowan, Australia 77 31 13 S 151 8 E
Dungu, Zaïre 92 3 40N 28 32 E
Dungunâb, Sudan 88 21 10N 37 9 E
Dungunâb, Khalij, Sudan 88 21 5N 37 12 E
Dunhinda Falls, Sri Lanka 51 7 5N 81 6 E
Dunhua, China 61 43 20N 128 14 E
Dunhuang, China 62 40 8N 94 36 E
Dunières, France 21 45 13N 4 20 E
Dunk I., Australia 72 17 59 S 146 29 E
Dunkeld, Australia 74 37 40 S 142 22 E
Dunkeld, U.K. 14 56 34N 3 36W
Dunkerque, France 19 51 2N 2 20 E
Dunkery Beacon, U.K. 13 51 15N 3 37W
Dunkirk = Dunkerque, France 19 51 2N 2 20 E
Dunkirk, U.S.A. 116 42 30N 79 18W
Dunkuj, Sudan 89 12 50N 32 49 E
Dunkwa, Central, Ghana 90 6 0N 1 47W
Dunkwa, Central, Ghana 91 5 30N 1 0W
Dunlap, U.S.A. 120 41 50N 95 36W
Dúnleary = Dun Laoghaire, Ireland 15 53 17N 6 9W
Dunmanus B., Ireland 15 51 31N 9 50W
Dunmara, Australia 72 16 42 S 133 25 E
Dunmore, U.S.A. 117 41 27N 75 38W
Dunmore Hd., Ireland 15 52 10N 10 35W
Dunmore Town, Bahamas 128 25 30N 76 39W
Dunn, U.S.A. 115 35 18N 78 36W
Dunnellon, U.S.A. 115 29 4N 82 28W
Dunnet Hd., U.K. 14 58 38N 3 22W
Dunning, U.S.A. 120 41 52N 100 4W
Dunnville, Canada 108 42 54N 79 36W
Dunolly, Australia 74 36 51 S 143 44 E
Dunoon, Australia 77 28 42 S 153 20 E
Dunoon, U.K. 14 55 57N 4 56W
Dunqul, Egypt 88 23 26N 31 37 E
Duns, U.K. 14 55 47N 2 20W
Dunseith, U.S.A. 120 48 49N 100 2W
Dunsmuir, U.S.A. 122 41 10N 122 18W
Dunstable, U.K. 13 51 53N 0 31W
Dunstan Mts., N.Z. 81 44 53 S 169 35 E
Dunster, Canada 110 53 8N 119 50W
Duntroon, N.Z. 81 44 51 S 170 40 E
Dunvegan L., Canada 111 60 8N 107 10W
Duolun, China 60 42 12N 116 28 E
Duong Dong, Vietnam 55 10 13N 103 58 E
Duparquet, Canada 106 48 30N 79 14W
Duparquet, L., Canada 106 48 28N 79 16W
Dupree, U.S.A. 120 45 4N 101 35W
Dupuy, Canada 106 48 50N 79 21W
Dupuyer, U.S.A. 122 48 11N 112 31W
Duque de Caxias, Brazil 139 22 45 S 43 19W
Duque de York, I., Chile 142 50 37 S 75 25W
Dūrā, Jordan 44 31 31N 35 1 E
Durack →, Australia 78 15 33 S 127 52 E
Durack Range, Australia 78 16 50 S 127 40 E
Durance →, France 21 43 55N 4 45 E
Durand, Ill., U.S.A. 118 42 26N 89 20W
Durand, Mich., U.S.A. 119 42 54N 83 58W
Durango, Spain 24 43 13N 2 40W
Durango, U.S.A. 123 37 16N 107 50W
Durango □, Mexico 126 25 0N 105 0W
Duranillin, Australia 79 33 30 S 116 45 E
Durant, Iowa, U.S.A. 118 41 36N 90 54W
Durant, Okla., U.S.A. 121 34 0N 96 25W
Duratón →, Spain 22 41 37N 4 7W
Durazno, Uruguay 140 33 25 S 56 31W
Durazzo = Durrësi, Albania 35 41 19N 19 28 E
Durban, France 20 42 59N 2 49 E
Durban, S. Africa 97 29 49 S 31 1 E
Durbo, Somali Rep. 98 11 37N 50 20 E
Dúrcal, Spain 23 37 0N 3 34W
Düren, W. Germany 30 50 48N 6 30 E
Durg, India 50 21 15N 81 22 E
Durgapur, India 49 23 30N 87 20 E
Durham, Canada 108 44 10N 80 49W
Durham, U.K. 12 54 47N 1 34W
Durham, Calif., U.S.A. 124 39 39N 121 48W
Durham, N.C., U.S.A. 115 36 0N 78 55W
Durham □, U.K. 12 54 42N 1 45W
Durham Downs, Australia 73 26 6 S 141 47 E
Durham Ox, Australia 74 36 6 S 143 57 E
Duri, Australia 77 31 10 S 150 51 E
Duri Mountain, Australia 77 31 12 S 150 44 E
Durmitor, Yugoslavia 33 43 10N 19 0 E
Durness, U.K. 14 58 34N 4 45W
Durrësi, Albania 35 41 19N 19 28 E
Durrie, Australia 72 25 40 S 140 15 E
Durtal, France 18 47 40N 0 18W
Duru, Zaïre 92 4 14N 28 50 E
D'Urville, Tanjung, Indonesia 57 1 28 S 137 54 E
D'Urville I., N.Z. 81 40 50 S 173 55 E
Duryea, U.S.A. 117 41 20N 75 45W
Dusa Mareb, Somali Rep. 98 5 30N 46 15 E
Dûsh, Egypt 88 24 35N 30 41 E
Dushak, U.S.S.R. 40 37 13N 60 1 E
Dushan, China 58 25 48N 107 30 E
Dushanbe, U.S.S.R. 40 38 33N 68 48 E
Dusheti, U.S.S.R. 39 42 10N 44 42 E
Dusky Sd., N.Z. 81 45 47 S 166 30 E
Dussejour, C., Australia 78 14 45 S 128 13 E
Düsseldorf, W. Germany 30 51 15N 6 46 E
Dussen, Neths. 16 51 44N 4 59 E
Dutch Harbor, U.S.A. 102 53 54N 166 35W
Dutlwe, Botswana 96 23 58 S 23 46 E
Dutsan Wai, Nigeria 91 10 50N 8 10 E
Dutton, Canada 108 42 39N 81 30W

Dutton →, Australia **72** 20 44 S 143 10 E
Duved, Sweden **10** 63 24N 12 55 E
Duvno, Yugoslavia **33** 43 42N 17 13 E
Duwādimi, Si. Arabia **46** 24 35N 44 15 E
Duyun, China **58** 26 18N 107 29 E
Duzce, Turkey **46** 40 50N 31 10 E
Duzdab = Zāhedān, Iran **47** 29 30N 60 50 E
Dvina, Sev. →, U.S.S.R. **40** 64 32N 40 30 E
Dvinsk = Daugavpils, U.S.S.R. **36** 55 53N 26 32 E
Dvor, Yugoslavia **27** 45 4N 16 22 E
Dwarka, India **48** 22 18N 69 8 E
Dwellingup, Australia **79** 32 43 S 116 4 E
Dwight, Canada **106** 45 20N 79 1W
Dwight, U.S.A. **119** 41 5N 88 25W
Dyakovskoya, U.S.S.R. **37** 60 5N 41 12 E
Dyatkovo, U.S.S.R. **36** 53 40N 34 27 E
Dyatlovo, U.S.S.R. **36** 53 28N 25 28 E
Dyer, U.S.A. **119** 37 24N 86 13W
Dyer, C., Canada **103** 66 40N 61 0W
Dyer Plateau, Antarctica **143** 70 45 S 65 30W
Dyersburg, U.S.A. **121** 36 2N 89 20W
Dyersville, U.S.A. **118** 42 29N 91 8W
Dyfed □, U.K. **13** 52 0N 4 30W
Dyje →, Czech. **32** 48 37N 16 56 E
Dyle →, Belgium **17** 50 58N 4 41 E
Dynevor Downs, Australia **73** 28 10 S 144 20 E
Dynów, Poland **32** 49 50N 22 11 E
Dysart, Canada **111** 50 57N 104 2W
Dzamin Üüd, Mongolia **60** 43 50N 111 58 E
Dzerzhinsk, Byelorussian S.S.R., U.S.S.R. **36** 53 40N 27 1 E
Dzerzhinsk, R.S.F.S.R., U.S.S.R. **37** 56 14N 43 30 E
Dzhalinda, U.S.S.R. **41** 53 26N 124 0 E
Dzhambeyty, U.S.S.R. **39** 50 16N 52 35 E
Dzhambul, U.S.S.R. **40** 42 54N 71 22 E
Dzhankoi, U.S.S.R. **38** 45 40N 34 20 E
Dzhanybek, U.S.S.R. **39** 49 25N 46 50 E
Dzhardzhan, U.S.S.R. **41** 68 10N 124 10 E
Dzhelinde, U.S.S.R. **41** 70 0N 114 20 E
Dzhetygara, U.S.S.R. **40** 52 11N 61 12 E
Dzhezkazgan, U.S.S.R. **40** 47 44N 67 40 E
Dzhikimde, U.S.S.R. **41** 59 1N 121 47 E
Dzhizak, U.S.S.R. **40** 40 6N 67 50 E
Dzhugdzur, Khrebet, U.S.S.R. **41** 57 30N 138 0 E
Dzhvari, U.S.S.R. **39** 42 42N 42 4 E
Działdowo, Poland **32** 53 15N 20 15 E
Działoszyn, Poland **32** 51 6N 18 50 E
Dzierzgoń, Poland **32** 53 58N 19 20 E
Dzierzoniów, Poland **32** 50 45N 16 39 E
Dzilam de Bravo, Mexico **127** 21 24N 88 53W
Dzioua, Algeria **85** 33 14N 5 14 E
Dzungaria = Junggar Pendi, China **62** 44 30N 86 0 E
Dzungarian Gate = Alataw Shankou, China **62** 45 5N 81 57 E
Dzuumod, Mongolia **62** 47 45N 106 58 E

E

Eabamet, L., Canada **104** 51 30N 87 46W
Eads, U.S.A. **120** 38 30N 102 46W
Eagle, Alaska, U.S.A. **102** 64 44N 141 7W
Eagle, Colo., U.S.A. **122** 39 39N 106 55W
Eagle →, Canada **105** 53 36N 57 26W
Eagle Butt, U.S.A. **120** 45 1N 101 12W
Eagle Cr. →, U.S.A. **119** 38 36N 85 4W
Eagle Grove, U.S.A. **118** 42 37N 93 53W
Eagle L., Calif., U.S.A. **122** 40 35N 120 50W
Eagle L., Maine, U.S.A. **105** 46 23N 69 22W
Eagle Lake, Canada **109** 45 8N 78 29W
Eagle Lake, U.S.A. **121** 29 35N 96 21W
Eagle Mountain, U.S.A. **125** 33 52N 115 26W
Eagle Nest, U.S.A. **123** 36 33N 105 13W
Eagle Pass, U.S.A. **121** 28 45N 100 35W
Eagle Pk., U.S.A. **124** 38 10N 119 25W
Eagle Pt., Australia **78** 16 11 S 124 23 E
Eagle River, U.S.A. **120** 45 55N 89 17W
Eagleville, U.S.A. **118** 40 28N 93 59W
Ealing, U.K. **13** 51 30N 0 19W
Earaheedy, Australia **79** 25 34 S 121 29 E
Earl Grey, Canada **111** 50 57N 104 43W
Earle, U.S.A. **121** 35 18N 90 26W
Earlimart, U.S.A. **125** 35 53N 119 16W
Earlville, U.S.A. **119** 41 35N 88 55W
Earn →, U.K. **14** 56 20N 3 19W
Earn, L., U.K. **14** 56 23N 4 14W
Earnslaw, Mt., N.Z. **81** 44 32 S 168 27 E
Earoo, Australia **79** 29 34 S 118 22 E
Earth, U.S.A. **121** 34 18N 102 30W
Easley, U.S.A. **115** 34 52N 82 35W
East Angus, Canada **107** 45 30N 71 40W
East Aurora, U.S.A. **116** 42 46N 78 38W
East B., U.S.A. **121** 29 2N 89 16W
East Beskids = Vychodné Beskydy, Europe **32** 49 30N 22 0 E
East Bluff, Mt., Australia **77** 31 53 S 150 13 E
East Brady, U.S.A. **116** 40 59N 79 36W
East Broughton Station, Canada **107** 46 14N 71 5W
East C., N.Z. **80** 37 42 S 178 35 E
East C., Papua N. G. **69** 10 13 S 150 53 E
East Chicago, U.S.A. **119** 41 40N 87 30W
East China Sea, Asia **62** 30 5N 126 0 E
East Coast Bays, N.Z. **80** 36 40 S 174 40 E
East Coulee, Canada **110** 51 23N 112 27W
East Dubuque, U.S.A. **118** 42 29N 90 39W
East Falkland, Falk. Is. **142** 51 30 S 58 30W
East Germany ■, Europe **30** 52 0N 12 0 E
East Grand Forks, U.S.A. **120** 47 55N 97 5W
East Greenwich, U.S.A. **117** 41 39N 71 27W
East Gresford, Australia **76** 32 25 S 151 31 E
East Hartford, U.S.A. **117** 41 45N 72 39W
East Helena, U.S.A. **122** 46 37N 111 58W
East Indies, Asia **56** 0 0 120 0 E
East Jordan, U.S.A. **114** 45 10N 85 7W
East Kilbride, U.K. **14** 55 46N 4 10W
East Lansing, U.S.A. **119** 42 44N 84 29W
East Liverpool, U.S.A. **116** 40 39N 80 35W
East London, S. Africa **97** 33 0 S 27 55 E
East Lynne, Australia **76** 35 35 S 150 16 E
East Main = Eastmain, Canada **104** 52 10N 78 30W
East Moline, U.S.A. **118** 41 31N 90 25W
East Orange, U.S.A. **117** 40 46N 74 13W
East Pacific Ridge, Pac. Oc. **67** 15 0 S 110 0W
East Pakistan = Bangladesh ■, Asia **52** 24 0N 90 0 E
East Palestine, U.S.A. **116** 40 50N 80 32W
East Peoria, U.S.A. **118** 40 40N 89 34W
East Pine, Canada **110** 55 48N 120 12W
East Pt., Canada **105** 46 27N 61 58W
East Point, U.S.A. **115** 33 40N 84 28W
East Providence, U.S.A. **117** 41 48N 71 22W
East Retford, U.K. **12** 53 19N 0 55W
East St. Louis, U.S.A. **118** 38 37N 90 4W
East Schelde → = Oosterschelde, Neths. **17** 51 33N 4 0 E
East Siberian Sea, U.S.S.R. **41** 73 0N 160 0 E
East Stroudsburg, U.S.A. **117** 41 1N 75 11W
East Sussex □, U.K. **13** 51 0N 0 20 E
East Tawas, U.S.A. **114** 44 17N 83 31W
East Toorale, Australia **73** 30 27 S 145 28 E
East Troy, U.S.A. **119** 42 47N 88 24W
East Walker →, U.S.A. **124** 38 52N 119 10W
Eastbourne, N.Z. **80** 41 19 S 174 55 E
Eastbourne, U.K. **13** 50 46N 0 18 E
Eastend, Canada **111** 49 32N 108 50W
Easter Islands, Pac. Oc. **67** 27 0 S 109 0W
Eastern □, Kenya **92** 0 0 38 30 E
Eastern □, Uganda **92** 1 50N 33 45 E
Eastern Cr. →, Australia **72** 20 40 S 141 35 E
Eastern Ghats, India **51** 14 0N 78 50 E
Eastern Group = Lau, Fiji **68** 17 0 S 178 30W
Eastern Group, Australia **79** 33 30 S 124 30 E
Eastern Province □, S. Leone **90** 8 15N 11 0W
Easterville, Canada **111** 53 8N 99 49W
Easthampton, U.S.A. **117** 42 15N 72 41W
Eastland, U.S.A. **121** 32 26N 98 45W
Eastleigh, U.K. **13** 50 58N 1 21W
Eastmain, Canada **104** 52 10N 78 30W
Eastmain →, Canada **104** 52 27N 78 26W
Eastman, Canada **117** 45 18N 72 19W
Eastman, Ga., U.S.A. **115** 32 13N 83 20W
Eastman, Wis., U.S.A. **118** 43 10N 91 1W
Easton, Md., U.S.A. **114** 38 47N 76 7W
Easton, Pa., U.S.A. **117** 40 41N 75 15W
Easton, Wash., U.S.A. **124** 47 14N 121 8W
Eastport, U.S.A. **105** 44 57N 67 0W
Eastsound, U.S.A. **124** 48 42N 122 55W
Eaton, Colo., U.S.A. **120** 40 35N 104 42W
Eaton, Ohio, U.S.A. **119** 39 45N 84 38W
Eaton Rapids, U.S.A. **119** 42 31N 84 39W
Eatonia, Canada **111** 51 13N 109 25W
Eatonton, U.S.A. **115** 33 22N 83 24W
Eatontown, U.S.A. **117** 40 18N 74 7W
Eatonville, Canada **107** 47 20N 69 41W
Eatonville, U.S.A. **124** 46 52N 122 16W
Eau Claire, Fr. Guiana **135** 3 30N 53 40W
Eau Claire, U.S.A. **120** 44 46N 91 30W
Eauze, France **20** 43 53N 0 7 E
Ebagoola, Australia **72** 14 15 S 143 12 E
Eban, Nigeria **91** 9 40N 4 50 E
Ebangalakata, Zaïre **94** 0 29 S 21 29 E
Ebbw Vale, U.K. **13** 51 47N 3 12W
Ebden, Australia **75** 36 10 S 147 1 E
Ebebiyín, Eq. Guin. **94** 2 9N 11 20 E
Ebeggui, Algeria **85** 26 2N 6 0 E
Ebel, Gabon **94** 0 7N 11 5 E
Ebeltoft, Denmark **9** 56 12N 10 41 E
Ebensburg, U.S.A. **116** 40 29N 78 43W
Ebensee, Austria **33** 47 48N 13 46 E
Eberbach, W. Germany **31** 49 27N 8 59 E
Eberswalde, E. Germany **30** 52 49N 13 50 E
Ebian, China **58** 29 11N 103 13 E
Ebingen, W. Germany **31** 48 13N 9 1 E
Ebino, Japan **64** 32 2N 130 48 E
Eboli, Italy **29** 40 39N 15 2 E
Ebolowa, Cameroon **91** 2 55N 11 10 E
Ebor, Australia **77** 30 22 S 152 27 E
Eboulements, Les, Canada **107** 47 28N 70 21W
Ebrach, W. Germany **31** 49 50N 10 30 E
Ébrié, Lagune, Ivory C. **90** 5 12N 4 26W
Ebro →, Spain **24** 40 43N 0 54 E
Ebro, Pantano del, Spain **22** 43 0N 3 58W
Ebstorf, W. Germany **30** 53 2N 10 23 E
Ecaussines-d' Enghien, Belgium **17** 50 35N 4 11 E
Eccleston, Australia **76** 32 14 S 151 30 E
Ech Cheliff, Algeria **85** 36 10N 1 20 E
Échelles, Les, France **21** 45 26N 5 46 E
Echeng, China **59** 30 23N 114 50 E
Echizen-Misaki, Japan **65** 35 59N 135 57 E
Echmiadzin, U.S.S.R. **39** 40 12N 44 19 E
Echo Bay, N.W.T., Canada **102** 66 5N 117 55W
Echo Bay, Ont., Canada **108** 46 29N 84 4W
Echoing →, Canada **111** 55 51N 92 5W
Échouani, L., Canada **106** 47 46N 75 42W
Echt, Neths. **17** 51 7N 5 52 E
Echternach, Lux. **17** 49 49N 6 25 E
Echuca, Australia **74** 36 10 S 144 20 E
Ecija, Spain **23** 37 30N 5 10W
Eckernförde, W. Germany **30** 54 26N 9 50 E
Eclipse Is., Australia **78** 13 54 S 126 19 E
Écommoy, France **18** 47 50N 0 17 E
Ecoporanga, Brazil **139** 18 23 S 40 50W
Écorce, L. de l', Canada **106** 47 5N 76 24W
Écos, France **19** 49 9N 1 35 E
Écouché, France **18** 48 42N 0 10W
Ecuador ■, S. Amer. **134** 2 0 S 78 0W
Écueillé, France **18** 47 5N 1 21 E
Ed, Sweden **11** 58 55N 11 55 E
Ed Dabbura, Sudan **88** 17 40N 34 15 E
Ed Dâmer, Sudan **88** 17 27N 34 0 E
Ed Debba, Sudan **88** 18 0N 30 51 E
Ed-Déffa, Egypt **88** 30 40N 26 30 E
Ed Deim, Sudan **89** 10 10N 28 20 E
Ed Dueim, Sudan **89** 14 0N 32 10 E
Edah, Australia **79** 28 16 S 117 10 E
Edam, Canada **111** 53 11N 108 46W
Edam, Neths. **16** 52 31N 5 3 E
Edapally, India **51** 11 19N 78 3 E
Eday, U.K. **14** 59 11N 2 47W
Edd, Ethiopia **89** 14 0N 41 38 E
Eddrachillis B., U.K. **14** 58 16N 5 10W
Eddystone, U.K. **13** 50 11N 4 16W
Eddystone Pt., Australia **72** 40 59 S 148 20 E
Eddyville, U.S.A. **118** 41 9N 92 38W
Ede, Neths. **16** 52 4N 5 40 E
Ede, Nigeria **91** 7 45N 4 29 E
Édea, Cameroon **91** 3 51N 10 9 E
Edegem, Belgium **17** 51 10N 4 27 E
Edehon L., Canada **111** 60 25N 97 15W
Edekel, Adrar, Algeria **85** 23 56N 6 47 E
Eden, Australia **75** 37 3 S 149 55 E
Eden, N.C., U.S.A. **115** 36 29N 79 53W
Eden, N.Y., U.S.A. **116** 42 39N 78 55W
Eden, Tex., U.S.A. **121** 31 16N 99 50W
Eden, Wyo., U.S.A. **122** 42 2N 109 27W
Eden →, U.K. **12** 54 57N 3 2W
Eden L., Canada **111** 56 38N 100 15W
Edenburg, S. Africa **96** 29 43 S 25 58 E
Edendale, N.Z. **81** 46 19 S 168 48 E
Edendale, S. Africa **97** 29 39 S 30 18 E
Edenderry, Ireland **15** 53 21N 7 3W
Edenhope, Australia **74** 37 4 S 141 19 E
Edenton, U.S.A. **115** 36 5N 76 36W
Edenville, S. Africa **97** 27 37 S 27 34 E
Eder →, W. Germany **30** 51 15N 9 25 E
Ederstausee, W. Germany **30** 51 11N 9 0 E
Edgar, U.S.A. **120** 40 25N 98 0W
Edgartown, U.S.A. **117** 41 22N 70 28W
Edge Hill, U.K. **13** 52 7N 1 28W
Edgecumbe, N.Z. **80** 37 59 S 176 47 E
Edgefield, U.S.A. **115** 33 50N 81 59W
Edgeley, U.S.A. **120** 46 27N 98 41W
Edgemont, U.S.A. **120** 43 15N 103 53W
Edgeøya, Svalbard **144** 77 45N 22 30 E
Edgeroi, Australia **77** 30 7 S 149 50 E
Edgerton, Ohio, U.S.A. **119** 41 27N 84 45W
Edgerton, Wis., U.S.A. **118** 42 50N 89 4W
Edgewood, U.S.A. **119** 38 55N 88 40W
Edhessa, Greece **35** 40 48N 22 5 E
Edievale, N.Z. **81** 45 49 S 169 22 E
Edina, Liberia **90** 6 0N 10 10W
Edina, U.S.A. **118** 40 6N 92 10W
Edinburg, Ill., U.S.A. **118** 39 39N 89 23W
Edinburg, Ind., U.S.A. **119** 39 21N 85 58W
Edinburg, Tex., U.S.A. **121** 26 22N 98 10W
Edinburgh, U.K. **14** 55 57N 3 12W
Edirne, Turkey **46** 41 40N 26 34 E
Edison, U.S.A. **124** 48 33N 122 27W
Edithburgh, Australia **73** 35 5 S 137 43 E
Edjeleh, Algeria **85** 28 38N 9 50 E
Edjudina, Australia **79** 29 48 S 122 23 E
Edmeston, U.S.A. **117** 42 42N 75 15W
Edmond, U.S.A. **121** 35 37N 97 30W
Edmonds, U.S.A. **124** 47 47N 122 22W
Edmonton, Australia **72** 17 2 S 145 46 E
Edmonton, Canada **110** 53 30N 113 30W
Edmund L., Canada **111** 54 45N 93 17W
Edmundston, Canada **105** 47 23N 68 20W
Edna, U.S.A. **121** 29 0N 96 40W
Edna Bay, U.S.A. **110** 55 55N 133 40W
Edolo, Italy **26** 46 10N 10 21 E
Edremit, Turkey **46** 39 34N 27 0 E
Edsbyn, Sweden **10** 61 23N 15 49 E
Edsel Ford Ra., Antarctica **143** 77 0 S 143 0W
Edsele, Sweden **10** 63 25N 16 32 E
Edson, Canada **110** 53 35N 116 28W
Eduardo Castex, Argentina **140** 35 50 S 64 18W
Edward →, Australia **74** 35 0 S 143 30 E
Edward, L., Africa **92** 0 25 S 29 40 E
Edward I., Canada **104** 48 22N 88 37W
Edward VII Land, Antarctica **143** 80 0 S 150 0W
Edwards, U.S.A. **125** 34 55N 117 51W
Edwards →, U.S.A. **118** 41 10N 90 59W
Edwards Plateau, U.S.A. **121** 30 30N 101 5W
Edwardsburg, U.S.A. **119** 41 48N 86 6W
Edwardsport, U.S.A. **119** 38 49N 87 15W
Edwardsville, Ill., U.S.A. **118** 38 49N 89 57W
Edwardsville, Pa., U.S.A. **117** 41 15N 75 56W
Edzo, Canada **110** 62 49N 116 4W
Eefde, Neths. **16** 52 10N 6 13 E
Eekloo, Belgium **17** 51 11N 3 33 E
Eel →, Ind., U.S.A. **119** 39 7N 86 58W
Eel →, Ind., U.S.A. **119** 40 45N 86 22W
Eelde, Neths. **16** 53 8N 6 34 E
Eem →, Neths. **16** 52 16N 5 20 E
Eems →, Neths. **16** 53 26N 6 57 E
Eems Kanaal, Neths. **16** 53 18N 6 46 E
Eenrum, Neths. **16** 53 22N 6 28 E
Eernegem, Belgium **17** 51 8N 3 2 E
Eerste Valthermond, Neths. **16** 52 53N 6 58 E
Efate, I., Vanuatu **68** 17 40 S 168 25 E
Ef'e, Nahal, Israel **44** 31 9N 35 13 E
Eferi, Algeria **85** 24 30N 9 28 E
Effingham, U.S.A. **119** 39 8N 88 30W
Eforie Sud, Romania **34** 44 1N 28 37 E
Ega →, Spain **24** 42 19N 1 55W
Égadi, Ísole, Italy **28** 37 55N 12 16 E
Eganville, Canada **109** 45 32N 77 5W
Egeland, U.S.A. **120** 48 42N 99 6W
Egenolf L., Canada **111** 59 3N 100 0W
Eger = Cheb, Czech. **32** 50 9N 12 28 E
Eger, Hungary **33** 47 53N 20 27 E
Eger →, Hungary **33** 47 38N 20 50 E
Egersund, Norway **9** 58 26N 6 1 E
Egg L., Canada **111** 55 5N 105 30W
Eggenburg, Austria **32** 48 38N 15 50 E
Eggenfelden, W. Germany **31** 48 24N 12 46 E
Egherta, Somali Rep. **98** 2 4N 43 11 E
Éghezée, Belgium **17** 50 35N 4 55 E
Eginbah, Australia **78** 20 53 S 119 47 E
Egito, Angola **95** 12 4 S 13 58 E
Égletons, France **20** 45 24N 2 3 E
Egmond-aan-Zee, Neths. **16** 52 37N 4 38 E
Egmont, C., N.Z. **80** 39 16 S 173 45 E
Egmont, Mt., N.Z. **80** 39 17 S 174 5 E
Eğridir, Turkey **46** 37 52N 30 51 E
Eğridir Gölü, Turkey **46** 37 53N 30 50 E
Egtved, Denmark **11** 55 38N 9 18 E
Éguas →, Brazil **139** 13 26 S 44 14W
Egume, Nigeria **91** 7 30N 7 14 E
Éguzon, France **20** 46 27N 1 33 E
Egvekinot, U.S.S.R. **41** 66 19N 179 50W
Egypt ■, Africa **88** 28 0N 31 0 E
Eha Amufu, Nigeria **91** 6 30N 7 46 E
Ehime □, Japan **64** 33 30N 132 40 E
Ehingen, W. Germany **31** 48 16N 9 43 E
Ehrenberg, U.S.A. **125** 33 36N 114 31W
Ehrwald, Austria **31** 47 24N 10 56 E
Eibar, Spain **24** 43 11N 2 28W
Eibergen, Neths. **16** 52 6N 6 39 E
Eichstatt, W. Germany **31** 48 53N 11 12 E
Eider →, W. Germany **30** 54 19N 8 58 E
Eidsvold, Australia **73** 25 25 S 151 12 E
Eidsvoll, Norway **9** 60 19N 11 14 E
Eifel, W. Germany **31** 50 10N 6 45 E
Eiffel Flats, Zimb. **93** 18 20 S 30 0 E
Eigg, U.K. **14** 56 54N 6 10W
Eighty Mile Beach, Australia **78** 19 30 S 120 40 E
Eil, Somali Rep. **98** 8 0N 49 50 E
Eil, L., U.K. **14** 56 50N 5 15W
Eildon, Australia **74** 37 14 S 145 55 E
Eildon, L., Australia **74** 37 10 S 146 0 E
Eileen L., Canada **111** 62 16N 107 37W
Eilenburg, E. Germany **30** 51 28N 12 38 E
Ein el Luweiqa, Sudan **89** 14 5N 33 50 E
Einasleigh, Australia **72** 18 32 S 144 5 E
Einasleigh →, Australia **72** 17 30 S 142 17 E
Einbeck, W. Germany **30** 51 48N 9 50 E
Eindhoven, Neths. **17** 51 26N 5 30 E
Einsiedeln, Switz. **31** 47 7N 8 46 E
Eire ■, Europe **15** 53 0N 8 0W
Eiríksjökull, Iceland **8** 64 46N 20 24W
Eirlandsche Gat, Neths. **16** 53 12N 4 54 E
Eirunepé, Brazil **136** 6 35 S 69 53W
Eisden, Belgium **17** 50 59N 5 42 E
Eisenach, E. Germany **30** 50 58N 10 18 E
Eisenberg, E. Germany **30** 50 59N 11 50 E
Eisenerz, Austria **33** 47 32N 14 54 E
Eisenhüttenstadt, E. Germany **30** 52 9N 14 41 E

Eisenstadt, *Austria* **33** 47 51N 16 31 E
Eiserfeld, *W. Germany* **30** 50 50N 7 59 E
Eisfeld, *E. Germany* **30** 50 25N 10 54 E
Eisleben, *E. Germany* **30** 51 31N 11 31 E
Ejby, *Denmark* **11** 55 25N 9 56 E
Eje, Sierra del, *Spain* **22** 42 24N 6 54W
Ejea de los Caballeros, *Spain* **24** 42 7N 1 9W
Ejutla, *Mexico* **127** 16 34N 96 44W
Ekalaka, *U.S.A.* **120** 45 55N 104 30W
Ekalla, *Gabon* **94** 1 27 S 14 0 E
Ekanga, *Zaïre* **94** 2 23 S 23 14 E
Ekawasaki, *Japan* **64** 33 13N 132 46 E
Ekeren, *Belgium* **17** 51 17N 4 25 E
Eket, *Nigeria* **91** 4 38N 7 56 E
Eketahuna, *N.Z.* **80** 40 38 S 175 43 E
Ekhínos, *Greece* **35** 41 16N 25 1 E
Ekibastuz, *U.S.S.R.* **40** 51 50N 75 10 E
Ekimchan, *U.S.S.R.* **41** 53 0N 133 0 E
Ekoli, *Zaïre* **92** 0 23 S 24 13 E
Eksel, *Belgium* **17** 51 9N 5 24 E
Eksjö, *Sweden* **11** 57 40N 14 58 E
Ekwan →, *Canada* **104** 53 12N 82 15W
Ekwan Pt., *Canada* **104** 53 16N 82 7W
El Aaiún, *W. Sahara* **84** 27 9N 13 12W
El Aargub, *Mauritania* **84** 23 37N 15 52W
El Aat, *Syria* **44** 32 50N 35 45 E
El Abiodh-Sidi-Cheikh, *Algeria* **85** 32 53N 0 31 E
El Adde, *Somali Rep.* **98** 2 35N 46 9 E
El Aïoun, *Morocco* **85** 34 33N 2 30W
El 'Aiyat, *Egypt* **88** 29 36N 31 15 E
El Alamein, *Egypt* **88** 30 48N 28 58 E
El Alto, *Peru* **136** 4 15 S 81 14W
El 'Arag, *Egypt* **88** 28 40N 26 20 E
El Arahal, *Spain* **23** 37 15N 5 33W
El Aricha, *Algeria* **85** 34 13N 1 10W
El Arīhā, *Jordan* **44** 31 52N 35 27 E
El Arish, *Australia* **72** 17 35 S 146 1 E
El 'Arîsh, *Egypt* **88** 31 8N 33 50 E
El Arrouch, *Algeria* **85** 36 37N 6 53 E
El Asnam = Ech Cheliff, *Algeria* **85** 36 10N 1 20 E
El Astillero, *Spain* **22** 43 24N 3 49W
El Badâri, *Egypt* **88** 27 4N 31 25 E
El Bahrein, *Egypt* **88** 28 30N 26 25 E
El Ballâs, *Egypt* **88** 26 2N 32 43 E
El Balyana, *Egypt* **88** 26 10N 32 3 E
El Banco, *Colombia* **134** 9 0N 73 58W
El Baqeir, *Sudan* **88** 18 40N 33 40 E
El Barco de Ávila, *Spain* **22** 40 21N 5 31W
El Barco de Valdeorras, *Spain* **22** 42 23N 7 0W
El Bauga, *Sudan* **88** 18 18N 33 52 E
El Baúl, *Venezuela* **134** 8 57N 68 17W
El Bawiti, *Egypt* **88** 28 25N 28 45 E
El Bayadh, *Algeria* **85** 33 40N 1 1 E
El Bierzo, *Spain* **22** 42 45N 6 30W
El Bluff, *Nic.* **128** 11 59N 83 40W
El Bolsón, *Argentina* **142** 41 55 S 71 30W
El Bonillo, *Spain* **25** 38 57N 2 35W
El Buheirat □, *Sudan* **89** 7 0N 30 0 E
El Bur, *Somali Rep.* **98** 4 40N 46 37 E
El Caín, *Argentina* **142** 41 38 S 68 19W
El Cajon, *U.S.A.* **125** 32 49N 117 0W
El Callao, *Venezuela* **135** 7 18N 61 50W
El Camp, *Spain* **24** 41 5N 1 10 E
El Campo, *U.S.A.* **121** 29 10N 96 20W
El Carmen, *Bolivia* **137** 13 40 S 63 55W
El Carmen, *Venezuela* **134** 1 16N 66 52W
El Castillo, *Spain* **23** 37 41N 6 19W
El Centro, *U.S.A.* **125** 32 50N 115 40W
El Cerro, *Bolivia* **137** 17 30 S 61 40W
El Cerro, *Spain* **23** 37 45N 6 57W
El Cocuy, *Colombia* **134** 6 25N 72 27W
El Compadre, *Mexico* **125** 32 20N 116 14W
El Corcovado, *Argentina* **142** 43 25 S 71 35W
El Coronil, *Spain* **23** 37 5N 5 38W
El Cuy, *Argentina* **142** 39 55 S 68 25W
El Cuyo, *Mexico* **127** 21 30N 87 40W
El Dab'a, *Egypt* **88** 31 0N 28 27 E
El Dambahaddo, *Somali Rep.* **98** 3 17N 46 40 E
El Deir, *Egypt* **88** 25 25N 32 20 E
El Dere, *Ethiopia* **98** 5 6N 43 5 E
El Dere, *Somali Rep.* **98** 3 50N 47 8 E
El Dere, *Somali Rep.* **98** 5 22N 46 11 E
El Descanso, *Mexico* **125** 32 12N 116 58W
El Desemboque, *Mexico* **126** 30 30N 112 57W
El Dilingat, *Egypt* **88** 30 50N 30 31 E
El Diviso, *Colombia* **134** 1 22N 78 14W
El Djem, *Tunisia* **86** 35 18N 10 42 E
El Dorado, *Ark., U.S.A.* **121** 33 10N 92 40W
El Dorado, *Kans., U.S.A.* **121** 37 55N 96 56W
El Dorado, *Venezuela* **135** 6 55N 61 37W
El Eglab, *Algeria* **84** 26 20N 4 30W
El Escorial, *Spain* **22** 40 35N 4 7W
El Eulma, *Algeria* **85** 36 9N 5 42 E
El Faiyûm, *Egypt* **88** 29 19N 30 50 E
El Fâsher, *Sudan* **89** 13 33N 25 26 E
El Fashn, *Egypt* **88** 28 50N 30 54 E
El Ferrol, *Spain* **22** 43 29N 8 15W
El Fifi, *Sudan* **89** 10 4N 25 0 E
El Fud, *Ethiopia* **98** 7 15N 42 52 E
El Fuerte, *Mexico* **126** 26 30N 108 40W
El Gal, *Somali Rep.* **98** 10 58N 50 20 E
El Gebir, *Sudan* **89** 13 40N 29 40 E
El Gedida, *Egypt* **88** 25 40N 28 30 E
El Geteina, *Sudan* **89** 14 50N 32 27 E
El Gezira □, *Sudan* **89** 15 0N 33 0 E
El Gîza, *Egypt* **88** 30 0N 31 10 E
El Goléa, *Algeria* **85** 30 30N 2 50 E
El Guettar, *Algeria* **85** 34 5N 4 38 E
El Hadeb, *W. Sahara* **84** 25 51N 13 0W
El Hadjira, *Algeria* **85** 32 36N 5 30 E
El Hagiz, *Sudan* **89** 15 15N 35 50 E
El Hajeb, *Morocco* **84** 33 43N 5 13W
El Hammam, *Egypt* **88** 30 52N 29 25 E
El Hammâmi, *Mauritania* **84** 23 3N 11 30W
El Hamurre, *Somali Rep.* **59** 7 13N 48 54 E
El Hank, *Mauritania* **84** 24 30N 7 0W
El Harrach, *Algeria* **85** 36 45N 3 5 E
El Hasian, *W. Sahara* **84** 26 20N 14 0W
El Hawata, *Sudan* **89** 13 25N 34 42 E
El Heiz, *Egypt* **88** 27 50N 28 40 E
El 'Idisât, *Egypt* **88** 25 30N 32 35 E
El Iskandarîya, *Egypt* **88** 31 0N 30 0 E
El Jadida, *Morocco* **84** 33 11N 8 17W
El Jebelein, *Sudan* **89** 12 40N 32 55 E
El Kab, *Sudan* **88** 19 27N 32 46 E
El Kala, *Algeria* **85** 36 50N 8 30 E
El Kalâa, *Morocco* **84** 32 4N 7 27W
El Kamlin, *Sudan* **89** 15 3N 33 11 E
El Kantara, *Algeria* **85** 35 14N 5 45 E
El Kantara, *Tunisia* **86** 33 45N 10 58 E
El Karaba, *Sudan* **88** 18 32N 33 41 E
El Kef, *Tunisia* **86** 36 12N 8 47 E
El Khandaq, *Sudan* **88** 18 30N 30 30 E
El Khârga, *Egypt* **88** 25 30N 30 33 E
El Khartûm, *Sudan* **89** 15 31N 32 35 E
El Khartûm □, *Sudan* **89** 16 0N 33 0 E
El Khartûm Bahrî, *Sudan* **89** 15 40N 32 31 E
El-Khroubs, *Algeria* **85** 36 10N 6 55 E
El Kseur, *Algeria* **85** 36 46N 4 49 E
El Ksiba, *Morocco* **84** 32 45N 6 1W
El Kuntilla, *Egypt* **88** 30 1N 34 45 E
El Laqâwa, *Sudan* **89** 11 25N 29 1 E
El Laqeita, *Egypt* **88** 25 50N 33 15 E
El Leiya, *Sudan* **89** 16 15N 35 28 E
El Mafâza, *Sudan* **89** 13 38N 34 30 E
El Mahalla el Kubra, *Egypt* **88** 31 0N 31 0 E
El Mahârîq, *Egypt* **88** 25 35N 30 35 E
El Mahmûdîya, *Egypt* **88** 31 10N 30 32 E
El Maitén, *Argentina* **142** 42 3 S 71 10W
El Maiz, *Algeria* **85** 28 19N 0 9W
El-Maks el-Bahari, *Egypt* **88** 24 30N 30 40 E
El Manshâh, *Egypt* **88** 26 26N 31 50 E
El Mansour, *Algeria* **85** 27 47N 0 14W
El Mansûra, *Egypt* **88** 31 0N 31 19 E
El Mantico, *Venezuela* **135** 7 38N 62 45W
El Manzala, *Egypt* **88** 31 10N 31 50 E
El Marâgha, *Egypt* **88** 26 35N 31 10 E
El Masid, *Sudan* **89** 15 15N 33 0 E
El Matariya, *Egypt* **88** 31 15N 32 0 E
El Meghaier, *Algeria* **85** 33 55N 5 58 E
El Meraguen, *Algeria* **85** 28 0N 0 7W
El Metemma, *Sudan* **89** 16 50N 33 10 E
El Miamo, *Venezuela* **135** 7 39N 61 46W
El Milagro, *Argentina* **140** 30 59 S 65 59W
El Milia, *Algeria* **85** 36 51N 6 13 E
El Minyâ, *Egypt* **88** 28 7N 30 33 E
El Molar, *Spain* **24** 40 42N 3 45W
El Mreyye, *Mauritania* **90** 18 0N 6 0W
El Obeid, *Sudan* **89** 13 8N 30 10 E
El Odaiya, *Sudan* **89** 12 8N 28 12 E
El Oro, *Mexico* **127** 19 48N 100 8W
El Oro □, *Ecuador* **134** 3 30 S 79 50W
El Oued, *Algeria* **85** 33 20N 6 58 E
El Palmar, *Bolivia* **137** 17 50 S 63 9W
El Palmar, *Venezuela* **135** 7 58N 61 53W
El Palmito, Presa, *Mexico* **126** 25 40N 105 30W
El Panadés, *Spain* **24** 41 10N 1 30 E
El Pardo, *Spain* **22** 40 31N 3 47W
El Paso, *Ill., U.S.A.* **118** 40 44N 89 1W
El Paso, *Tex., U.S.A.* **123** 31 50N 106 30W
El Paso Robles, *U.S.A.* **124** 35 38N 120 41W
El Pedernoso, *Spain* **25** 39 29N 2 45W
El Pedroso, *Spain* **23** 37 51N 5 45W
El Pobo de Dueñas, *Spain* **24** 40 46N 1 39W
El Portal, *U.S.A.* **124** 37 44N 119 49W
El Porvenir, *Mexico* **126** 31 15N 105 51W
El Prat de Llobregat, *Spain* **24** 41 18N 2 3 E
El Progreso, *Honduras* **128** 15 26N 87 51W
El Provencío, *Spain* **25** 39 23N 2 35W
El Pueblito, *Mexico* **126** 29 3N 105 4W
El Pueblo, *Canary Is.* **25** 28 36N 17 47W
El Qâhira, *Egypt* **88** 30 1N 31 14 E
El Qantara, *Egypt* **88** 30 51N 32 20 E
El Qasr, *Egypt* **88** 25 44N 28 42 E
El Quseima, *Egypt* **88** 30 40N 34 15 E
El Qusîya, *Egypt* **88** 27 29N 30 44 E
El Râshda, *Egypt* **88** 25 36N 28 57 E
El Reno, *U.S.A.* **121** 35 30N 98 0W
El Ribero, *Spain* **22** 42 30N 8 30W
El Rîdisiya, *Egypt* **88** 24 56N 32 51 E
El Rio, *U.S.A.* **125** 34 14N 119 10W
El Ronquillo, *Spain* **23** 37 44N 6 10W
El Roque, Pta., *Canary Is.* **25** 28 10N 15 25W
El Rosarito, *Mexico* **126** 28 38N 114 4W
El Rubio, *Spain* **23** 37 22N 5 0W
El Saff, *Egypt* **88** 29 34N 31 16 E
El Salto, *Mexico* **126** 23 47N 105 22W
El Salvador ■, *Cent. Amer.* **128** 13 50N 89 0W
El Sancejo, *Spain* **23** 37 4N 5 6W
El Sauce, *Nic.* **128** 13 0N 86 40W
El Shallal, *Egypt* **88** 24 0N 32 53 E
El Simbillawein, *Egypt* **88** 30 48N 31 13 E
El Sombrero, *Venezuela* **134** 9 23N 67 3W
El Suweis, *Egypt* **88** 29 58N 32 31 E
El Thamad, *Egypt* **88** 29 40N 34 28 E
El Tigre, *Venezuela* **135** 8 44N 64 15W
El Tocuyo, *Venezuela* **134** 9 47N 69 48W
El Tofo, *Chile* **140** 29 22 S 71 18W
El Tránsito, *Chile* **140** 28 52 S 70 17W
El Tûr, *Egypt* **88** 28 14N 33 36 E
El Turbio, *Argentina* **142** 51 45 S 72 5W
El Uinle, *Somali Rep.* **98** 3 4N 41 42 E
El Uqsur, *Egypt* **88** 25 41N 32 38 E
El Vado, *Spain* **24** 41 2N 3 18W
El Vallés, *Spain* **24** 41 35N 2 20 E
El Venado, *Mexico* **126** 22 56N 101 10W
El Vigía, *Venezuela* **134** 8 38N 71 39W
El Wak, *Kenya* **92** 2 49N 40 56 E
El Wak, *Somali Rep.* **98** 2 44N 41 1 E
El Waqf, *Egypt* **88** 25 45N 32 15 E
El Wâsta, *Egypt* **88** 29 19N 31 12 E
El Weguet, *Ethiopia* **89** 5 28N 42 17 E
El Wuz, *Sudan* **89** 15 0N 30 7 E
Elafónisos, *Greece* **35** 36 29N 22 56 E
Elaine, *Australia* **74** 37 44 S 144 2 E
Elamanchili, *India* **50** 17 33N 82 50 E
Elands, *Australia* **77** 31 37 S 152 20 E
Elandsvlei, *S. Africa* **96** 32 19 S 19 31 E
Élassa, *Greece* **35** 35 18N 26 21 E
Elassón, *Greece* **35** 39 53N 22 12 E
Elat, *Israel* **44** 29 30N 34 56 E
Elâzığ, *Turkey* **46** 38 37N 39 14 E
Elba, *Italy* **26** 42 48N 10 15 E
Elba, *U.S.A.* **115** 31 27N 86 4W
Elbasani, *Albania* **35** 41 9N 20 9 E
Elbe, *U.S.A.* **124** 46 45N 122 10W
Elbe →, *Europe* **30** 53 50N 9 0 E
Elberfeld, *U.S.A.* **119** 38 10N 87 27W
Elbert, Mt., *U.S.A.* **123** 39 5N 106 27W
Elberta, *U.S.A.* **114** 44 35N 86 14W
Elberton, *U.S.A.* **115** 34 7N 82 51W
Elbeuf, *France* **18** 49 17N 1 2 E
Elbidtan, *Turkey* **46** 38 13N 37 12 E
Elbing = Elbląg, *Poland* **32** 54 10N 19 25 E
Elbląg, *Poland* **32** 54 10N 19 25 E
Elbow, *Canada* **111** 51 7N 106 35W
Elbrus, *U.S.S.R.* **39** 43 21N 42 30 E
Elburg, *Neths.* **16** 52 26N 5 50 E
Elburn, *U.S.A.* **119** 41 54N 88 28W
Elburz Mts. = Alborz, Reshteh-ye Kūhhā-ye, *Iran* **47** 36 0N 52 0 E
Elche, *Spain* **25** 38 15N 0 42W
Elche de la Sierra, *Spain* **25** 38 27N 2 3W
Elcho I., *Australia* **72** 11 55 S 135 45 E
Elda, *Spain* **25** 38 29N 0 47W
Eldon, *Mo., U.S.A.* **118** 38 20N 92 38W
Eldon, *Wash., U.S.A.* **124** 47 32N 123 4W
Eldora, *U.S.A.* **118** 42 20N 93 5W
Eldorado, *Argentina* **141** 26 28 S 54 43W
Eldorado, *Ont., Canada* **109** 44 35N 77 31W
Eldorado, *Sask., Canada* **111** 59 35N 108 30W
Eldorado, *Mexico* **126** 24 20N 107 22W
Eldorado, *Ill., U.S.A.* **119** 37 50N 88 25W
Eldorado, *Tex., U.S.A.* **121** 30 52N 100 35W
Eldorado Springs, *U.S.A.* **118** 37 54N 93 59W
Eldoret, *Kenya* **92** 0 30N 35 17 E
Eldred, *U.S.A.* **116** 41 57N 78 24W
Eldridge, *U.S.A.* **118** 41 39N 90 35W
Electra, *U.S.A.* **121** 34 0N 99 0W
Elefantes →, *Mozam.* **97** 24 10 S 32 40 E
Elefantes, G., *Chile* **142** 46 28 S 73 49W
Elektrogorsk, *U.S.S.R.* **37** 55 56N 38 50 E
Elektrostal, *U.S.S.R.* **37** 55 41N 38 32 E
Elele, *Nigeria* **91** 5 5N 6 50 E
Elephant Butte Res., *U.S.A.* **123** 33 45N 107 30W
Elephant I., *Antarctica* **143** 61 0 S 55 0W
Elephant Pass, *Sri Lanka* **51** 9 35N 80 25 E
Elesbão Veloso, *Brazil* **138** 6 13 S 42 8W
Eleuthera, *Bahamas* **128** 25 0N 76 20W
Elgepiggen, *Norway* **10** 62 10N 11 21 E
Elgeyo-Marakwet □, *Kenya* **92** 0 45N 35 30 E
Elgin, *N.B., Canada* **105** 45 48N 65 10W
Elgin, *Ont., Canada* **109** 44 36N 76 13W
Elgin, *U.K.* **14** 57 39N 3 20W
Elgin, *Ill., U.S.A.* **119** 42 0N 88 20W
Elgin, *N. Dak., U.S.A.* **120** 46 24N 101 46W
Elgin, *Nebr., U.S.A.* **120** 41 58N 98 3W
Elgin, *Nev., U.S.A.* **123** 37 21N 114 20W
Elgin, *Oreg., U.S.A.* **122** 45 37N 118 0W
Elgin, *Tex., U.S.A.* **121** 30 21N 97 22W
Elgon, Mt., *Africa* **92** 1 10N 34 30 E
Eliase, *Indonesia* **57** 8 21 S 130 48 E
Elida, *U.S.A.* **121** 33 56N 103 41W
Elikón, Mt., *Greece* **35** 38 18N 22 45 E
Elim, *S. Africa* **96** 34 35 S 19 45 E
Elisabethville = Lubumbashi, *Zaïre* **93** 11 40 S 27 28 E
Eliseu Martins, *Brazil* **138** 8 13 S 43 42W
Elista, *U.S.S.R.* **39** 46 16N 44 14 E
Elizabeth, *Australia* **73** 34 42 S 138 41 E
Elizabeth, *Ill., U.S.A.* **118** 42 19N 90 13W
Elizabeth, *N.J., U.S.A.* **117** 40 37N 74 12W
Elizabeth City, *U.S.A.* **115** 36 18N 76 16W
Elizabethton, *U.S.A.* **115** 36 20N 82 13W
Elizabethtown, *Ky., U.S.A.* **114** 37 40N 85 54W
Elizabethtown, *N.Y., U.S.A.* **117** 44 13N 73 36W
Elizabethtown, *Pa., U.S.A.* **117** 40 8N 76 36W
Elizondo, *Spain* **24** 43 12N 1 30W
Elk, *Poland* **32** 53 50N 22 21 E
Elk City, *U.S.A.* **121** 35 25N 99 25W
Elk Creek, *U.S.A.* **124** 39 36N 122 32W
Elk Grove, *U.S.A.* **124** 38 25N 121 22W
Elk Island Nat. Park, *Canada* **110** 53 35N 112 59W
Elk Lake, *Canada* **106** 47 40N 80 25W
Elk Point, *Canada* **111** 53 54N 110 55W
Elk River, *Idaho, U.S.A.* **122** 46 50N 116 8W
Elk River, *Minn., U.S.A.* **120** 45 17N 93 34W
Elkader, *U.S.A.* **118** 42 51N 91 24W
Elkedra, *Australia* **72** 21 9 S 135 33 E
Elkedra →, *Australia* **72** 21 8 S 136 22 E
Elkhart, *Ind., U.S.A.* **119** 41 42N 85 55W
Elkhart, *Kans., U.S.A.* **121** 37 3N 101 54W
Elkhart →, *U.S.A.* **119** 41 41N 85 58W
Elkhorn, *Canada* **111** 49 59N 101 14W
Elkhorn, *U.S.A.* **119** 42 40N 88 33W
Elkhorn →, *U.S.A.* **120** 41 7N 98 15W
Elkhotovo, *U.S.S.R.* **39** 43 19N 44 15 E
Elkhovo, *Bulgaria* **34** 42 10N 26 40 E
Elkin, *U.S.A.* **115** 36 17N 80 50W
Elkins, *U.S.A.* **114** 38 53N 79 53W
Elko, *Canada* **110** 49 20N 115 10W
Elko, *U.S.A.* **122** 40 50N 115 50W
Ell, L., *Australia* **79** 29 13 S 127 46 E
Ellecom, *Neths.* **16** 52 2N 6 6 E
Ellef Ringnes I., *Canada* **144** 78 30N 102 2W
Ellenborough, *Australia* **77** 31 27 S 152 28 E
Ellendale, *Australia* **78** 17 56 S 124 48 E
Ellendale, *U.S.A.* **120** 46 3N 98 30W
Ellensburg, *U.S.A.* **122** 47 0N 120 30W
Ellenville, *U.S.A.* **117** 41 42N 74 23W
Ellerslie, *Australia* **74** 38 10 S 142 44 E
Ellerston, *Australia* **77** 31 49 S 151 20 E
Ellery, Mt., *Australia* **75** 37 28 S 148 47 E
Ellesmere I., *Canada* **144** 79 30N 80 0W
Ellesworth Land, *Antarctica* **143** 76 0 S 89 0W
Ellettsville, *U.S.A.* **119** 39 14N 86 38W
Ellezelles, *Belgium* **17** 50 44N 3 42 E
Ellice Is. = Tuvalu ■, *Pac. Oc.* **66** 8 0 S 178 0 E
Ellinwood, *U.S.A.* **120** 38 27N 98 37W
Elliot, *Australia* **72** 17 33 S 133 32 E
Elliot, *S. Africa* **97** 31 22 S 27 48 E
Elliot Lake, *Canada* **108** 46 25N 82 35W
Elliotdale = Xhora, *S. Africa* **97** 31 55 S 28 38 E
Ellis, *U.S.A.* **120** 39 0N 99 39W
Ellisville, *U.S.A.* **121** 31 38N 89 12W
Ellon, *U.K.* **14** 57 21N 2 5W
Ellore = Eluru, *India* **50** 16 48N 81 8 E
Ells →, *Canada* **110** 57 18N 111 40W
Ellsworth, *U.S.A.* **120** 38 47N 98 15W
Ellsworth Land, *Antarctica* **143** 76 0 S 89 0W
Ellsworth Mts., *Antarctica* **143** 78 30 S 85 0W
Ellwangen, *W. Germany* **31** 48 57N 10 9 E
Ellwood City, *U.S.A.* **116** 40 52N 80 19W
Elm, *Switz.* **31** 46 54N 9 10 E
Elma, *Canada* **111** 49 52N 95 55W
Elma, *U.S.A.* **124** 47 0N 123 30W
Elmalı, *Turkey* **46** 36 44N 29 56 E
Elmer, *U.S.A.* **118** 39 57N 92 39W
Elmhurst, *Australia* **74** 37 13 S 143 16 E
Elmhurst, *U.S.A.* **119** 41 52N 87 58W
Elmina, *Ghana* **91** 5 5N 1 21W
Elmira, *Canada* **108** 43 36N 80 33W
Elmira, *U.S.A.* **116** 42 8N 76 49W
Elmore, *Australia* **74** 36 30 S 144 37 E
Elmore, *Calif., U.S.A.* **125** 33 7N 115 49W
Elmore, *Minn., U.S.A.* **119** 41 29N 83 18W
Elmshorn, *W. Germany* **30** 53 44N 9 40 E
Elmvale, *Canada* **108** 44 35N 79 52W
Elmwood, *U.S.A.* **118** 40 47N 90 0W
Elne, *France* **20** 42 36N 2 58 E
Elnora, *U.S.A.* **119** 38 53N 87 5W
Elong Elong, *Australia* **77** 32 8 S 149 3 E
Elora, *Canada* **108** 43 41N 80 26W
Elorza, *Venezuela* **134** 7 3N 69 31W
Eloy, *U.S.A.* **123** 32 46N 111 33W
Éloyes, *France* **19** 48 6N 6 36 E
Elphin, *Canada* **109** 44 55N 76 37W
Elphinstone, *Australia* **74** 37 5 S 144 22 E
Elrose, *Canada* **111** 51 12N 108 0W
Elsas, *Canada* **104** 48 32N 82 55W
Elsie, *U.S.A.* **124** 45 52N 123 35W
Elsinore = Helsingør, *Denmark* **11** 56 2N 12 35 E
Elsinore, *U.S.A.* **123** 38 40N 112 2W
Elspe, *W. Germany* **30** 51 10N 8 1 E
Elspeet, *Neths.* **16** 52 17N 5 48 E
Elst, *Neths.* **16** 51 55N 5 51 E
Elster →, *E. Germany* **30** 51 25N 11 57 E
Elsterwerda, *E. Germany* **30** 51 27N 13 32 E
Elten, *Neths.* **16** 51 52N 6 9 E

Eltham, *Australia* **74** 37 43 S 145 12 E
Eltham, *N.Z.* **80** 39 26 S 174 19 E
Elton, *U.S.S.R.* **39** 49 5N 46 52 E
Eluanbi, *Taiwan* **59** 21 51N 120 50 E
Eluru, *India* **50** 16 48N 81 8 E
Elvas, *Portugal* **23** 38 50N 7 10W
Elven, *France* **18** 47 44N 2 36W
Elverum, *Norway* **10** 60 53N 11 34 E
Elvire →, *Australia* **78** 17 51 S 128 11 E
Elvo →, *Italy* **26** 45 23N 8 21 E
Elvran, *Norway* **10** 63 24N 11 3 E
Elwood, *Ill., U.S.A.* **119** 41 24N 88 7W
Elwood, *Ind., U.S.A.* **119** 40 20N 85 50W
Elwood, *Nebr., U.S.A.* **120** 40 38N 99 51W
Ely, *U.K.* **13** 52 24N 0 16 E
Ely, *Minn., U.S.A.* **120** 47 54N 91 52W
Ely, *Nev., U.S.A.* **122** 39 10N 114 50W
Elyashiv, *Israel* **44** 32 23N 34 55 E
Elyria, *U.S.A.* **116** 41 22N 82 8W
Elz →, *W. Germany* **31** 48 21N 7 45 E
Emådalen, *Sweden* **10** 61 20N 14 44 E
Emai, *Vanuatu* **68** 17 4 S 168 24 E
Emāmrūd, *Iran* **47** 36 30N 55 0 E
Emba, *U.S.S.R.* **40** 48 50N 58 8 E
Emba →, *U.S.S.R.* **40** 46 38N 53 14 E
Embarcación, *Argentina* **140** 23 10 S 64 0W
Embarras Portage, *Canada* **111** 58 27N 111 28W
Embarrass →, *U.S.A.* **119** 38 39N 87 37W
Embetsu, *Japan* **63** 44 44N 141 47 E
Embira →, *Brazil* **136** 7 19 S 70 15W
Embro, *Canada* **108** 43 9N 80 54W
Embrun, *France* **21** 44 34N 6 30 E
Embu, *Kenya* **92** 0 32 S 37 38 E
Embu □, *Kenya* **92** 0 30 S 37 35 E
Emden, *W. Germany* **30** 53 22N 7 12 E
'Emeq Yizre'el, *Israel* **44** 32 35N 35 12 E
Emerald, *Queens., Australia* **72** 23 32 S 148 10 E
Emerald, *Vic., Australia* **74** 37 56 S 145 29 E
Emerald Hill, *Australia* **77** 30 52 S 150 6 E
Emerson, *Canada* **111** 49 0N 97 10W
Emery, *U.S.A.* **123** 38 59N 111 17W
Emi Koussi, *Chad* **87** 20 0N 18 55 E
Emilia-Romagna □, *Italy* **26** 44 33N 10 40 E
Emilius, Mte., *Italy* **26** 45 41N 7 23 E
Eminabad, *Pakistan* **48** 32 2N 74 8 E
Eminence, *U.S.A.* **119** 38 22N 85 11W
Emlenton, *U.S.A.* **116** 41 11N 79 41W
Emlichheim, *W. Germany* **30** 52 37N 6 51 E
Emmaboda, *Sweden* **11** 56 37N 15 32 E
Emmaville, *Australia* **77** 29 26 S 151 37 E
Emme →, *Switz.* **31** 47 0N 7 42 E
Emmeloord, *Neths.* **16** 52 44N 5 46 E
Emmen, *Neths.* **16** 52 48N 6 57 E
Emmendingen, *W. Germany* **31** 48 7N 7 51 E
Emmental, *Switz.* **31** 47 0N 7 35 E
Emmer-Compascuum, *Neths.* **16** 52 49N 7 2 E
Emmerich, *W. Germany* **30** 51 50N 6 12 E
Emmet, *Australia* **72** 24 45 S 144 30 E
Emmetsburg, *U.S.A.* **118** 43 3N 94 40W
Emmett, *U.S.A.* **122** 43 51N 116 33W
Empalme, *Mexico* **126** 28 1N 110 49W
Empangeni, *S. Africa* **97** 28 50 S 31 52 E
Empedrado, *Argentina* **140** 28 0 S 58 46W
Emperor Seamount Chain, *Pac. Oc.* **66** 40 0N 170 0 E
Empoli, *Italy* **26** 43 43N 10 57 E
Emporia, *Kans., U.S.A.* **120** 38 25N 96 10W
Emporia, *Va., U.S.A.* **115** 36 41N 77 32W
Emporium, *U.S.A.* **116** 41 30N 78 17W
Empress, *Canada* **111** 50 57N 110 0W
Emptinne, *Belgium* **17** 50 19N 5 8 E
Ems →, *W. Germany* **30** 53 22N 7 15 E
Emsdale, *Canada* **106** 45 32N 79 19W
Emsdetten, *W. Germany* **30** 52 11N 7 31 E
Emu, *Australia* **74** 36 44 S 143 26 E
Emu, *China* **61** 43 40N 128 6 E
Emu Park, *Australia* **72** 23 13 S 150 50 E
Emu Vale, *Australia* **77** 28 11 S 152 15 E
En Gedi, *Israel* **44** 31 28N 35 25 E
En Gev, *Israel* **44** 32 47N 35 38 E
En Harod, *Israel* **44** 32 33N 35 22 E
'En Kerem, *Israel* **44** 31 47N 35 6 E
En Nahud, *Sudan* **89** 12 45N 28 25 E
Ena, *Japan* **65** 35 25N 137 25 E
Ena-San, *Japan* **65** 35 26N 137 36 E
Enafors, *Sweden* **10** 63 17N 12 20 E
Enambú, *Colombia* **134** 1 1N 70 17W
Enana, *Namibia* **96** 17 30 S 16 23 E
Enånger, *Sweden* **10** 61 30N 17 9 E
Enaratoli, *Indonesia* **57** 3 55 S 136 21 E
Enard B., *U.K.* **14** 58 5N 5 20W
Encantadas, Serra, *Brazil* **141** 30 40 S 53 0W
Encanto, C., *Phil.* **57** 15 45N 121 38 E
Encarnación, *Paraguay* **141** 27 15 S 55 50W
Encarnación de Diaz, *Mexico* **126** 21 30N 102 13W
Enchi, *Ghana* **90** 5 53N 2 48W
Encinal, *U.S.A.* **121** 28 3N 99 25W
Encinitas, *U.S.A.* **125** 33 3N 117 17W
Encino, *U.S.A.* **123** 34 38N 105 40W
Encontrados, *Venezuela* **134** 9 3N 72 14W
Encounter B., *Australia* **73** 35 45 S 138 45 E
Encruzilhada, *Brazil* **139** 15 31 S 40 54W
Ende, *Indonesia* **57** 8 45 S 121 40 E
Endeavour, *Canada* **111** 52 10N 102 39W
Endeavour Str., *Australia* **72** 10 45 S 142 0 E
Endelave, *Denmark* **11** 55 46N 10 18 E
Enderbury I., *Kiribati* **66** 3 8 S 171 5W
Enderby, *Canada* **110** 50 35N 119 10W
Enderby I., *Australia* **78** 20 35 S 116 30 E
Enderby Land, *Antarctica* **143** 66 0 S 53 0 E
Enderlin, *U.S.A.* **120** 46 37N 97 41W
Endicott, *N.Y., U.S.A.* **117** 42 6N 76 2W
Endicott, *Wash., U.S.A.* **122** 47 0N 117 45W
Endimari →, *Brazil* **136** 8 46 S 66 7W
Endyalgout I., *Australia* **78** 11 40 S 132 35 E
Ene →, *Peru* **136** 11 10 S 74 18W
Enewatak, *Pac. Oc.* **66** 11 30N 162 15 E
Enfida, *Tunisia* **86** 36 6N 10 28 E
Enfield, *U.K.* **13** 51 39N 0 4W
Enfield, *U.S.A.* **119** 38 6N 88 20W
Engadin, *Switz.* **31** 46 45N 10 10 E
Engaño, C., *Dom. Rep.* **129** 18 30N 68 20W
Engaño, C., *Phil.* **57** 18 35N 122 23 E
Engcobo, *S. Africa* **97** 31 37 S 28 0 E
Engelberg, *Switz.* **31** 46 48N 8 26 E
Engels, *U.S.S.R.* **37** 51 28N 46 6 E
Engemann L., *Canada* **111** 58 0N 106 55W
Enger, *Norway* **10** 60 35N 10 20 E
Enggano, *Indonesia* **56** 5 20 S 102 40 E
Enghien, *Belgium* **17** 50 37N 4 2 E
Engil, *Morocco* **84** 33 12N 4 32W
Engkilili, *Malaysia* **56** 1 3N 111 42 E
England, *U.S.A.* **121** 34 30N 91 58W
England □, *U.K.* **7** 53 0N 2 0W
Englee, *Canada* **105** 50 45N 56 5W
Englefield, *Australia* **74** 37 21 S 141 48 E
Englehart, *Canada* **106** 47 49N 79 52W
Engler L., *Canada* **111** 59 8N 106 52W
Englewood, *Colo., U.S.A.* **120** 39 40N 105 0W
Englewood, *Kans., U.S.A.* **121** 37 7N 99 59W
Englewood, *Ohio, U.S.A.* **119** 39 53N 84 18W
English, *U.S.A.* **119** 38 20N 86 28W
English →, *Canada* **111** 50 35N 93 30W
English →, *U.S.A.* **118** 41 29N 91 32W
English Bazar = Ingraj Bazar, *India* **49** 24 58N 88 10 E
English Channel, *Europe* **13** 50 0N 2 0W
English River, *Canada* **104** 49 14N 91 0W
Enid, *U.S.A.* **121** 36 26N 97 52W
Enipévs →, *Greece* **35** 39 22N 22 17 E
Enkhuizen, *Neths.* **16** 52 42N 5 17 E
Enköping, *Sweden* **10** 59 37N 17 4 E
Enle, *China* **58** 24 0N 101 9 E
Enna, *Italy* **29** 37 34N 14 15 E
Ennadai, *Canada* **111** 61 8N 100 53W
Ennadai L., *Canada* **111** 61 0N 101 0W
Ennedi, *Chad* **87** 17 15N 22 0 E
Enngonia, *Australia* **73** 29 21 S 145 50 E
Ennis, *Ireland* **15** 52 51N 8 59W
Ennis, *Mont., U.S.A.* **122** 45 20N 111 42W
Ennis, *Tex., U.S.A.* **121** 32 15N 96 40W
Enniscorthy, *Ireland* **15** 52 30N 6 35W
Enniskillen, *U.K.* **15** 54 20N 7 40W
Ennistimon, *Ireland* **15** 52 56N 9 18W
Enns →, *Austria* **33** 48 14N 14 32 E
Enontekiö, *Finland* **8** 68 23N 23 37 E
Enping, *China* **59** 22 16N 112 21 E
Enriquillo, L., *Dom. Rep.* **129** 18 20N 72 5W
Ens, *Neths.* **16** 52 38N 5 50 E
Ensay, *Australia* **75** 37 21 S 147 50 E
Enschede, *Neths.* **16** 52 13N 6 53 E
Ensenada, *Argentina* **140** 34 55 S 57 55W
Ensenada, *Mexico* **126** 31 50N 116 50W
Ensenada, La, *Chile* **142** 41 12 S 72 33W
Enshi, *China* **58** 30 18N 109 29 E
Enshū-Nada, *Japan* **65** 34 27N 137 38 E
Ensisheim, *France* **19** 47 50N 7 20 E
Entebbe, *Uganda* **92** 0 4N 32 28 E
Enter, *Neths.* **16** 52 17N 6 35 E
Enterprise, *Canada* **110** 60 47N 115 45W
Enterprise, *Oreg., U.S.A.* **122** 45 30N 117 18W
Enterprise, *Utah, U.S.A.* **123** 37 37N 113 36W
Entre Ríos, *Bolivia* **140** 21 30 S 64 25W
Entre Rios, *Bahia, Brazil* **139** 11 56 S 38 5W
Entre Rios, *Pará, Brazil* **137** 5 24 S 54 21W
Entre Ríos □, *Argentina* **140** 30 30 S 58 30W
Entrecasteaux, Pt. d', *Australia* **80** 34 50 S 115 56 E
Entrepeñas, Pantano de, *Spain* **24** 40 34N 2 42W
Enugu, *Nigeria* **91** 6 20N 7 30 E
Enugu Ezike, *Nigeria* **91** 7 0N 7 29 E
Enumclaw, *U.S.A.* **124** 47 12N 122 0W
Envermeu, *France* **18** 49 53N 1 15 E
Envigado, *Colombia* **134** 6 10N 75 35W
Envira, *Brazil* **136** 7 18 S 70 13W
Enz →, *W. Germany* **31** 49 1N 9 6 E
Enza →, *Italy* **26** 44 54N 10 31 E
Enzan, *Japan* **65** 35 42N 138 44 E
Eólie, Is., *Italy* **29** 38 30N 14 50 E
Epanomí, *Greece* **35** 40 25N 22 59 E
Epe, *Neths.* **16** 52 21N 5 59 E
Epe, *Nigeria* **91** 6 36N 3 59 E
Epéna, *Congo* **94** 1 22N 17 29 E
Épernay, *France* **19** 49 3N 3 56 E
Épernon, *France* **19** 48 35N 1 40 E
Ephesus, *Turkey* **46** 37 50N 27 33 E
Ephraim, *U.S.A.* **122** 39 21N 111 37W
Ephrata, *U.S.A.* **122** 47 20N 119 32W
Epi, *Vanuatu* **68** 16 43 S 168 15 E
Epila, *Spain* **24** 41 36N 1 17W
Épinac-les-Mines, *France* **19** 46 59N 4 31 E
Épinal, *France* **19** 48 10N 6 27 E
Epiphanie, L', *Canada* **107** 45 51N 73 29W
Epira, *Guyana* **135** 5 5N 57 20W
Eppalock, L., *Australia* **74** 36 52 S 144 34 E
Epping, *U.K.* **13** 51 42N 0 8 E
Epsom, *Australia* **74** 36 43 S 144 19 E
Epukiro, *Namibia* **96** 21 40 S 19 9 E
Equality, *U.S.A.* **119** 37 44N 88 20W
Equatorial Guinea ■, *Africa* **94** 2 0N 8 0 E
Equeipa, *Venezuela* **135** 5 22N 62 43W
Er Rahad, *Sudan* **89** 12 45N 30 32 E
Er Rif, *Morocco* **85** 35 1N 4 1W
Er Roseires, *Sudan* **89** 11 55N 34 30 E
Er Yébigué, *Chad* **87** 22 30N 17 30 E
Erandol, *India* **50** 20 56N 75 20 E
Erap, *Papua N. G.* **69** 6 37 S 146 51 E
Erāwadī Myit → = Irrawaddy →, *Burma* **52** 15 50N 95 6 E
Erba, *Italy* **26** 45 49N 9 12 E
Erba, *Sudan* **88** 19 5N 36 51 E
Ercha, *U.S.S.R.* **41** 69 45N 147 20 E
Erciyaş Daği, *Turkey* **46** 38 30N 35 30 E
Erdao Jiang →, *China* **61** 43 0N 127 0 E
Erdene, *Mongolia* **60** 44 13N 111 10 E
Erding, *W. Germany* **31** 48 18N 11 55 E
Erdre →, *France* **18** 47 13N 1 32W
Erebato →, *Venezuela* **135** 5 54N 64 16W
Erebus, Mt., *Antarctica* **143** 77 35 S 167 0 E
Erechim, *Brazil* **141** 27 35 S 52 15W
Ereğli, *Konya, Turkey* **46** 37 31N 34 4 E
Ereğli, *Zonguldak, Turkey* **46** 41 15N 31 30 E
Erei, Monti, *Italy* **29** 37 20N 14 20 E
Erembodegem, *Belgium* **17** 50 56N 4 4 E
Erenhot, *China* **60** 43 48N 111 59 E
Eresma →, *Spain* **22** 41 26N 4 45W
Erfenisdam, *S. Africa* **96** 28 30 S 26 50 E
Erfoud, *Morocco* **84** 31 30N 4 15W
Erft →, *W. Germany* **30** 51 11N 6 44 E
Erfurt, *E. Germany* **30** 50 58N 11 2 E
Erfurt □, *E. Germany* **30** 51 10N 10 30 E
Ergani, *Turkey* **46** 38 17N 39 49 E
Ergeni Vozvyshennost, *U.S.S.R.* **39** 47 0N 44 0 E
Ergli, *U.S.S.R.* **36** 56 54N 25 38 E
Eria →, *Spain* **22** 42 3N 5 44W
Eriba, *Sudan* **89** 16 40N 36 10 E
Eriboll, L., *U.K.* **14** 58 28N 4 41W
Erica, *Australia* **75** 37 59 S 146 22 E
Erica, *Neths.* **16** 52 43N 6 56 E
Érice, *Italy* **28** 38 4N 12 34 E
Erie, *Mich., U.S.A.* **119** 41 47N 83 31W
Erie, *Pa., U.S.A.* **116** 42 10N 80 7W
Erie, L., *N. Amer.* **108** 42 15N 81 0W
Erie Canal, *U.S.A.* **116** 43 15N 78 0W
Erieau, *Canada* **108** 42 16N 81 57W
Erigavo, *Somali Rep.* **98** 10 35N 47 20 E
Eriksdale, *Canada* **111** 50 52N 98 7W
Eriksslund, *Sweden* **10** 62 31N 15 54 E
Erímanthos, *Greece* **35** 37 57N 21 50 E
Erimo-misaki, *Japan* **63** 41 50N 143 15 E
Erin, *Canada* **108** 43 45N 80 7W
Erithraí, *Greece* **35** 38 13N 23 20 E
Eritrea □, *Ethiopia* **89** 14 0N 38 30 E
Erjas →, *Portugal* **23** 39 40N 7 1W
Erlangen, *W. Germany* **31** 49 35N 11 0 E
Erldunda, *Australia* **72** 25 14 S 133 12 E
Erlin, *Taiwan* **59** 23 55N 120 21 E
Ermelo, *Neths.* **16** 52 18N 5 35 E
Ermelo, *S. Africa* **97** 26 31 S 29 59 E
Ermenak, *Turkey* **46** 36 38N 33 0 E
Ermióni, *Greece* **35** 37 23N 23 15 E
Ermoúpolis = Síros, *Greece* **35** 37 28N 24 57 E
Ernakulam = Cochin, *India* **51** 9 59N 76 22 E
Erne →, *Ireland* **15** 54 30N 8 16W
Erne, Lough, *U.K.* **15** 54 26N 7 46W
Ernée, *France* **18** 48 18N 0 56W
Ernest Giles Ra., *Australia* **79** 27 0 S 123 45 E
Ernstberg, *W. Germany* **31** 50 14N 6 46 E
Erode, *India* **51** 11 24N 77 45 E
Eromanga, *Australia* **73** 26 40 S 143 11 E
Erongo, *Namibia* **96** 21 39 S 15 58 E
Erp, *Neths.* **17** 51 36N 5 37 E
Erquelinnes, *Belgium* **17** 50 19N 4 8 E
Erquy, *France* **18** 48 38N 2 29W
Erquy, C. d', *France* **18** 48 39N 2 29W
Errabiddy, *Australia* **79** 25 25 S 117 5 E
Erramala Hills, *India* **51** 15 30N 78 15 E
Errer →, *Ethiopia* **89** 7 32N 42 35 E
Errigal, Mt., *Ireland* **15** 55 2N 8 8W
Erris Hd., *Ireland* **15** 54 19N 10 0W
Erromango, *Vanuatu* **68** 18 45 S 169 5 E
Erseka, *Albania* **35** 40 22N 20 40 E
Erskine, *U.S.A.* **120** 47 37N 96 0W
Erstein, *France* **19** 48 25N 7 38 E
Ertil, *U.S.S.R.* **37** 51 55N 40 50 E
Ertvelde, *Belgium* **17** 51 11N 3 45 E
Eruwa, *Nigeria* **91** 7 33N 3 26 E
Ervy-le-Châtel, *France* **19** 48 2N 3 55 E
Erwin, *U.S.A.* **115** 36 10N 82 28W
Eryuan, *China* **58** 26 7N 99 57 E
Erzgebirge, *E. Germany* **30** 50 25N 13 0 E
Erzin, *U.S.S.R.* **41** 50 15N 95 10 E
Erzincan, *Turkey* **46** 39 46N 39 30 E
Erzurum, *Turkey* **46** 39 57N 41 15 E
Es Sahrâ' Esh Sharqîya, *Egypt* **88** 27 30N 32 30 E
Es Sînâ', *Egypt* **88** 29 0N 34 0 E
Es Sûkî, *Sudan* **89** 13 20N 33 58 E
Esa'ala, *Papua N. G.* **69** 9 45 S 150 49 E
Esambo, *Zaïre* **92** 3 48 S 23 30 E
Esan-Misaki, *Japan* **63** 41 40N 141 10 E
Esbjerg, *Denmark* **11** 55 29N 8 29 E
Escada, *Brazil* **138** 8 22 S 35 8W
Escalante, *U.S.A.* **123** 37 47N 111 37W
Escalante →, *U.S.A.* **123** 37 17N 110 53W
Escalón, *Mexico* **126** 26 46N 104 20W
Escalona, *Spain* **22** 40 9N 4 29W
Escambia →, *U.S.A.* **115** 30 32N 87 15W
Escanaba, *U.S.A.* **114** 45 44N 87 5W
Escarpé, C., *Vanuatu* **68** 20 41 S 167 13 E
Escaut →, *Belgium* **17** 51 2N 3 45 E
Esch-sur-Alzette, *Lux.* **17** 49 32N 6 0 E
Eschallens, *Switz.* **31** 46 39N 6 38 E
Eschede, *W. Germany* **30** 52 44N 10 13 E
Eschwege, *W. Germany* **30** 51 10N 10 3 E
Eschweiler, *W. Germany* **30** 50 49N 6 14 E
Escoma, *Bolivia* **136** 15 40 S 69 8W
Escondida, La, *Mexico* **126** 24 6N 99 55W
Escondido, *U.S.A.* **125** 33 9N 117 4W
Escoumins, Les, *Canada* **107** 48 21N 69 24W
Escuinapa, *Mexico* **126** 22 50N 105 50W
Escuintla, *Guatemala* **128** 14 20N 90 48W
Eséka, *Cameroon* **91** 3 41N 10 44 E
Esens, *W. Germany* **30** 53 40N 7 35 E
Esera →, *Spain* **24** 42 6N 0 15 E
Eşfahān, *Iran* **47** 33 0N 51 30 E
Esgueva →, *Spain* **22** 41 40N 4 43W
Esh Sham = Dimashq, *Syria* **46** 33 30N 36 18 E
Esh Shamâlîya □, *Sudan* **88** 19 0N 29 0 E
Eshan, *China* **58** 24 11N 102 24 E
Eshowe, *S. Africa* **97** 28 50 S 31 30 E
Eshta'ol, *Israel* **44** 31 47N 35 0 E
Esiama, *Ghana* **90** 4 56N 2 25W
Esino →, *Italy* **27** 43 39N 13 22 E
Esk →, *Dumf. & Gall., U.K.* **14** 54 58N 3 4W
Esk →, *N. Yorks., U.K.* **12** 54 27N 0 36W
Eskifjörður, *Iceland* **8** 65 3N 13 55W
Eskilstuna, *Sweden* **10** 59 22N 16 32 E
Eskimo Pt., *Canada* **111** 61 10N 94 15W
Eskişehir, *Turkey* **46** 39 50N 30 35 E
Esla →, *Spain* **22** 41 29N 6 3W
Esla, Pantano del, *Spain* **22** 41 29N 6 3W
Eslāmābād-e Gharb, *Iran* **46** 34 10N 46 30 E
Eslöv, *Sweden* **11** 55 50N 13 20 E
Esmeralda, I., *Chile* **142** 48 55 S 75 25W
Esmeralda, La, *Paraguay* **140** 22 16 S 62 33W
Esmeraldas, *Ecuador* **134** 1 0N 79 40W
Esmeraldas □, *Ecuador* **134** 0 40N 79 30W
Esmeraldas →, *Ecuador* **134** 0 58N 79 38W
Esmond, *Australia* **75** 36 5 S 146 11 E
Esneux, *Belgium* **17** 50 32N 5 33 E
Espada, Pta., *Colombia* **134** 12 5N 71 7W
Espalion, *France* **20** 44 32N 2 47 E
Espalmador, I., *Spain* **25** 38 47N 1 26 E
Espanola, *Canada* **108** 46 15N 81 46W
Espardell, I. del, *Spain* **25** 38 48N 1 29 E
Esparraguera, *Spain* **24** 41 33N 1 52 E
Esparta, *Costa Rica* **128** 9 59N 84 40W
Espejo, *Spain* **23** 37 40N 4 34W
Esperança, *Brazil* **138** 7 1 S 35 51W
Esperance, *Australia* **79** 33 45 S 121 55 E
Esperance, C., *Solomon Is.* **68** 9 15 S 159 43 E
Esperance B., *Australia* **79** 33 48 S 121 55 E
Esperantinópolis, *Brazil* **138** 4 53 S 44 53W
Esperanza, *Antarctica* **143** 65 0 S 55 0W
Esperanza, *Santa Cruz, Argentina* **142** 51 1 S 70 49W
Esperanza, *Santa Fe, Argentina* **140** 31 29 S 61 3W
Esperanza, La, *Argentina* **142** 40 26 S 68 32W
Esperanza, La, *Cuba* **128** 22 46N 83 44W
Esperanza, La, *Honduras* **128** 14 15N 88 10W
Espéraza, *France* **20** 42 56N 2 14 E
Espichel, C., *Portugal* **23** 38 22N 9 16W
Espiel, *Spain* **23** 38 11N 5 1W
Espigão, Serra do, *Brazil* **141** 26 35 S 50 30W
Espinal, *Colombia* **134** 4 9N 74 53W
Espinar, *Peru* **136** 14 51 S 71 24W
Espinazo, Sierra del = Espinhaço, Serra do, *Brazil* **139** 17 30 S 43 30W
Espinhaço, Serra do, *Brazil* **139** 17 30 S 43 30W
Espinho, *Portugal* **22** 41 1N 8 38W

Espinilho, Serra do, *Brazil* **141** 28 30 S 55 0W
Espino, *Venezuela* **134** 8 34N 66 1W
Espinosa de los Monteros, *Spain* **22** 43 5N 3 34W
Espírito Santo □, *Brazil* **139** 20 0 S 40 45W
Espíritu Santo, *Vanuatu* **68** 15 15 S 166 50 E
Espíritu Santo, B. del, *Mexico* **127** 19 15N 87 0W
Espíritu Santo, I., *Mexico* **126** 24 30N 110 23W
Espita, *Mexico* **127** 21 1N 88 19W
Esplanada, *Brazil* **139** 11 47 S 37 57W
Espluga de Francolí, *Spain* **24** 41 24N 1 7 E
Espuña, Sierra, *Spain* **25** 37 51N 1 35W
Espungabera, *Mozam.* **97** 20 29 S 32 45 E
Esquel, *Argentina* **142** 42 55 S 71 20W
Esquina, *Argentina* **140** 30 0 S 59 30W
Essaouira, *Morocco* **84** 31 32N 9 42W
Essarts, Les, *France* **18** 46 47N 1 12W
Essebie, *Zaïre* **92** 2 58N 30 40 E
Essen, *Belgium* **17** 51 28N 4 28 E
Essen, *W. Germany* **30** 51 28N 6 59 E
Essequibo □, *Guyana* **135** 7 0N 59 0W
Essequibo →, *Guyana* **135** 6 50N 58 30W
Essex, *Canada* **108** 42 10N 82 49W
Essex, *Calif., U.S.A.* **125** 34 44N 115 15W
Essex, *Ill., U.S.A.* **119** 41 11N 88 11W
Essex, *N.Y., U.S.A.* **117** 44 17N 73 21W
Essex □, *U.K.* **13** 51 48N 0 30 E
Esslingen, *W. Germany* **31** 48 43N 9 19 E
Essonne □, *France* **19** 48 30N 2 20 E
Essvik, *Sweden* **10** 62 18N 17 24 E
Estaca, Pta. del, *Spain* **22** 43 46N 7 42W
Estadilla, *Spain* **24** 42 4N 0 16 E
Estados, I. de Los, *Argentina* **142** 54 40 S 64 30W
Estagel, *France* **20** 42 47N 2 40 E
Estância, *Brazil* **138** 11 16 S 37 26W
Estancia, *U.S.A.* **123** 34 50N 106 1W
Estarreja, *Portugal* **22** 40 45N 8 35W
Estats, Pic d', *Spain* **24** 42 40N 1 24 E
Estcourt, *Canada* **107** 47 28N 69 14W
Estcourt, *S. Africa* **97** 29 0 S 29 53 E
Este, *Italy* **27** 45 12N 11 40 E
Esteban, *Spain* **22** 43 33N 6 5W
Estelí, *Nic.* **128** 13 9N 86 22W
Estella, *Spain* **24** 42 40N 2 0W
Estelline, *S. Dak., U.S.A.* **120** 44 39N 96 52W
Estelline, *Tex., U.S.A.* **121** 34 35N 100 27W
Estena →, *Spain* **23** 39 23N 4 44W
Estepa, *Spain* **23** 37 17N 4 52W
Estepona, *Spain* **23** 36 24N 5 7W
Esterhazy, *Canada* **111** 50 37N 102 5W
Esternay, *France* **19** 48 44N 3 33 E
Esterri de Aneu, *Spain* **24** 42 38N 1 5 E
Estevan, *Canada* **111** 49 10N 102 59W
Estevan Group, *Canada* **110** 53 3N 129 38W
Estherville, *U.S.A.* **120** 43 25N 94 50W
Estissac, *France* **19** 48 16N 3 48 E
Eston, *Canada* **111** 51 8N 108 40W
Estonian S.S.R. □, *U.S.S.R.* **36** 58 30N 25 30 E
Estoril, *Portugal* **23** 38 42N 9 23W
Estouk, *Mali* **91** 18 14N 1 2 E
Estrada, La, *Spain* **22** 42 43N 8 27W
Estrêla, Serra da, *Portugal* **22** 40 10N 7 45W
Estrella, *Spain* **25** 38 25N 3 35W
Estremoz, *Portugal* **23** 38 51N 7 39W
Estrondo, Serra do, *Brazil* **138** 7 20 S 48 0W
Esztergom, *Hungary* **33** 47 47N 18 44 E
Et Tîdra, *Mauritania* **90** 19 45N 16 20W
Eṭ Ṭīra, *Israel* **44** 32 14N 34 56 E
Étables-sur-Mer, *France* **18** 48 38N 2 51W
Etadunna, *Australia* **73** 28 43 S 138 38 E
Etah, *India* **49** 27 35N 78 40 E
Étain, *France* **19** 49 13N 5 38 E
Etalle, *Belgium* **17** 49 40N 5 36 E
Etamamu, *Canada* **105** 50 18N 59 59W
Étampes, *France* **19** 48 26N 2 10 E
Étang-sur-Arroux, *France* **21** 46 51N 4 11 E
Etanga, *Namibia* **96** 17 55 S 13 0 E
Étaples, *France* **19** 50 30N 1 39 E
Etawah, *India* **49** 26 48N 79 6 E
Etawah →, *U.S.A.* **115** 34 20N 84 15W
Etawney L., *Canada* **111** 57 50N 96 50W
Ete, *Nigeria* **91** 7 2N 7 28 E
Éthe, *Belgium* **17** 49 35N 5 35 E
Ethel, *U.S.A.* **124** 46 32N 122 46W
Ethel, Oued el →, *Algeria* **84** 28 31N 3 37W
Ethel Creek, *Australia* **78** 23 5 S 120 11 E
Ethelbert, *Canada* **111** 51 32N 100 25W
Ethiopia ■, *Africa* **45** 8 0N 40 0 E
Ethiopian Highlands, *Ethiopia* **82** 10 0N 37 0 E
Etive, L., *U.K.* **14** 56 30N 5 12W
Etna, *Italy* **29** 37 45N 15 0 E
Etoile, *Zaïre* **93** 11 33 S 27 30 E
Etolin I., *U.S.A.* **110** 56 5N 132 20W
Etosha Pan, *Namibia* **96** 18 40 S 16 30 E
Etoumbi, *Congo* **94** 0 1 S 14 57 E
Etowah, *U.S.A.* **115** 35 20N 84 30W
Étrépagny, *France* **19** 49 18N 1 36 E
Étretat, *France* **18** 49 42N 0 12 E
Étroits, Les, *Canada* **107** 47 24N 68 54W
Ettelbruck, *Lux.* **17** 49 51N 6 5 E
Etten, *Neths.* **17** 51 34N 4 38 E
Ettlingen, *W. Germany* **31** 48 58N 8 25 E
Ettrick Water, *U.K.* **14** 55 31N 2 55W
Etuku, *Zaïre* **92** 3 42 S 25 45 E
Etzatlán, *Mexico* **126** 20 48N 104 5W
Eu, *France* **18** 50 3N 1 26 E
Eua, *Tonga* **68** 21 22 S 174 56W
Euboea = Évvoia, *Greece* **35** 38 30N 24 0 E
Euchareena, *Australia* **76** 32 57 S 149 6 E
Euclid, *U.S.A.* **116** 41 32N 81 31W
Euclides da Cunha, *Brazil* **138** 10 31 S 39 1W
Eucumbene, *Australia* **75** 36 8 S 148 38 E
Eucumbene, L., *Australia* **75** 36 2 S 148 40 E
Eudora, *U.S.A.* **121** 33 5N 91 17W
Eufaula, *Ala., U.S.A.* **115** 31 55N 85 11W
Eufaula, *Okla., U.S.A.* **121** 35 20N 95 33W
Eufaula, L., *U.S.A.* **121** 35 15N 95 28W
Eugene, *U.S.A.* **122** 44 0N 123 8W
Eugowra, *Australia* **76** 33 22 S 148 24 E
Eulo, *Australia* **73** 28 10 S 145 3 E
Eumeralla →, *Australia* **74** 38 18 S 142 0 E
Eumungerie, *Australia* **76** 31 56 S 148 36 E
Eunice, *La., U.S.A.* **121** 30 35N 92 28W
Eunice, *N. Mex., U.S.A.* **121** 32 30N 103 10W
Eupen, *Belgium* **17** 50 37N 6 3 E
Euphrates = Furāt, Nahr al →, *Asia* **46** 31 0N 47 25 E
Eure □, *France* **18** 49 10N 1 0 E
Eure →, *France* **18** 49 18N 1 12 E
Eure-et-Loir □, *France* **18** 48 22N 1 30 E
Eureka, *Canada* **144** 80 0N 85 56W
Eureka, *Calif., U.S.A.* **122** 40 50N 124 0W
Eureka, *Ill., U.S.A.* **118** 40 43N 89 16W
Eureka, *Kans., U.S.A.* **121** 37 50N 96 20W
Eureka, *Mo., U.S.A.* **118** 38 30N 90 38W
Eureka, *Mont., U.S.A.* **122** 48 53N 115 6W
Eureka, *Nev., U.S.A.* **122** 39 32N 116 2W
Eureka, *S. Dak., U.S.A.* **120** 45 49N 99 38W
Eureka, *Utah, U.S.A.* **122** 40 0N 112 9W
Eureka, Mt., *Australia* **79** 26 35 S 121 35 E
Euroa, *Australia* **74** 36 44 S 145 35 E
Eurobodalla, *Australia* **76** 36 9 S 149 59 E
Europa, Picos de, *Spain* **22** 43 10N 4 49W
Europa, Pta. de, *Gib.* **23** 36 3N 5 21W
Europa Pt. = Europa, Pta. de, *Gib.* **23** 36 3N 5 21W
Europe **6** 50 0N 20 0 E
Europoort, *Neths.* **16** 51 57N 4 10 E
Euskirchen, *W. Germany* **30** 50 40N 6 45 E
Eustis, *U.S.A.* **115** 28 54N 81 36W
Eutin, *W. Germany* **30** 54 7N 10 38 E
Eutsuk L., *Canada* **110** 53 20N 126 45W
Eva, *Brazil* **135** 3 9 S 59 56W
Eva Downs, *Australia* **72** 18 1 S 134 52 E
Évain, *Canada* **106** 48 14N 79 8W
Eval, *Jordan* **44** 32 15N 35 15 E
Evale, *Angola* **95** 16 33 S 15 44 E
Evans, *U.S.A.* **120** 40 25N 104 43W
Evans Head, *Australia* **77** 29 7 S 153 27 E
Evans L., *Canada* **104** 50 50N 77 0W
Evans Mills, *U.S.A.* **117** 44 6N 75 48W
Evansdale, *U.S.A.* **118** 42 30N 92 17W
Evanston, *Ill., U.S.A.* **119** 42 0N 87 40W
Evanston, *Wyo., U.S.A.* **122** 41 10N 111 0W
Evansville, *Ill., U.S.A.* **118** 38 5N 89 56W
Evansville, *Ind., U.S.A.* **119** 38 0N 87 35W
Evansville, *Wis., U.S.A.* **118** 42 47N 89 18W
Évaux-les-Bains, *France* **20** 46 12N 2 29 E
Eveleth, *U.S.A.* **120** 47 29N 92 46W
Even Yahuda, *Israel* **44** 32 16N 34 53 E
Evensk, *U.S.S.R.* **41** 62 12N 159 30 E
Evenstad, *Norway* **10** 61 25N 11 7 E
Everard, L., *Australia* **73** 31 30 S 135 0 E
Everard Ras., *Australia* **79** 27 5 S 132 28 E
Evere, *Belgium* **17** 50 52N 4 25 E
Everest, Mt., *Nepal* **49** 28 5N 86 58 E
Everett, *Pa., U.S.A.* **116** 40 2N 78 24W
Everett, *Wash., U.S.A.* **124** 48 0N 122 10W
Evergem, *Belgium* **17** 51 7N 3 43 E
Everglades, *U.S.A.* **115** 26 0N 80 30W
Everglades City, *U.S.A.* **115** 25 52N 81 23W
Everglades Nat. Park., *U.S.A.* **115** 25 27N 80 53W
Evergreen, *U.S.A.* **115** 31 28N 86 55W
Everson, *U.S.A.* **122** 48 57N 122 22W
Everton, *Australia* **75** 36 25 S 146 33 E
Evesham, *U.K.* **13** 52 6N 1 57W
Évian-les-Bains, *France* **21** 46 24N 6 35 E
Evinayong, *Eq. Guin.* **94** 1 26N 10 35 E
Évinos →, *Greece* **35** 38 27N 21 40 E
Évisa, *France* **21** 42 15N 8 48 E
Évora, *Portugal* **23** 38 33N 7 57W
Évora □, *Portugal* **23** 38 33N 7 50W
Évreux, *France* **18** 49 0N 1 8 E
Évron, *France* **18** 48 10N 0 24W
Evrótas →, *Greece* **35** 36 50N 22 40 E
Évvoia, *Greece* **35** 38 30N 24 0 E
Évvoia □, *Greece* **35** 38 40N 23 40 E
Ewe, L., *U.K.* **14** 57 49N 5 38W
Ewing, *Mo., U.S.A.* **118** 40 0N 91 43W
Ewing, *Nebr., U.S.A.* **120** 42 18N 98 22W
Ewo, *Congo* **94** 0 48 S 14 45 E
Exaltación, *Bolivia* **137** 13 10 S 65 20W
Excelsior Springs, *U.S.A.* **118** 39 20N 94 10W
Excideuil, *France* **20** 45 20N 1 4 E
Exe →, *U.K.* **13** 50 38N 3 27W
Exeter, *Canada* **108** 43 21N 81 29W
Exeter, *U.K.* **13** 50 43N 3 31W
Exeter, *Calif., U.S.A.* **124** 36 17N 119 9W
Exeter, *N.H., U.S.A.* **117** 43 0N 70 58W
Exeter, *Nebr., U.S.A.* **120** 40 43N 97 30W
Exira, *U.S.A.* **118** 41 35N 94 52W
Exloo, *Neths.* **16** 52 53N 6 52 E
Exmes, *France* **18** 48 45N 0 10 E
Exmoor, *U.K.* **13** 51 10N 3 59W
Exmouth, *Australia* **78** 21 54 S 114 10 E
Exmouth, *U.K.* **13** 50 37N 3 26W
Exmouth G., *Australia* **78** 22 15 S 114 15 E
Expedition Range, *Australia* **72** 24 30 S 149 12 E
Extremadura □, *Spain* **23** 39 30N 6 5W
Exuma Sound, *Bahamas* **128** 24 30N 76 20W
Eyasi, L., *Tanzania* **92** 3 30 S 35 0 E
Eyeberry L., *Canada* **111** 63 8N 104 43W
Eyemouth, *U.K.* **14** 55 53N 2 5W
Eygurande, *France* **20** 45 40N 2 26 E
Eyjafjörður, *Iceland* **8** 66 15N 18 30W
Eymet, *France* **20** 44 40N 0 25 E
Eymoutiers, *France* **20** 45 40N 1 45 E
Eyrarbakki, *Iceland* **8** 63 52N 21 9W
Eyre, *Australia* **79** 32 15 S 126 18 E
Eyre (North), L., *Australia* **73** 28 30 S 137 20 E
Eyre (South), L., *Australia* **73** 29 18 S 137 25 E
Eyre Cr. →, *Australia* **73** 26 40 S 139 0 E
Eyre Mts., *N.Z.* **81** 45 25 S 168 25 E
Eyre Pen., *Australia* **73** 33 30 S 137 17 E
Eyzies-de-Tayac-Sireuil, Les, *France* **20** 44 56N 1 1 E
Ez Zeidab, *Sudan* **88** 17 25N 33 55 E
Ezcaray, *Spain* **24** 42 19N 3 0W
Ezmul, *Mauritania* **84** 22 15N 15 40W

F

Fabens, *U.S.A.* **123** 31 30N 106 8W
Fåborg, *Denmark* **11** 55 6N 10 15 E
Fabre, *Canada* **106** 47 12N 79 22W
Fabriano, *Italy* **27** 43 20N 12 52 E
Făcăeni, *Romania* **34** 44 32N 27 53 E
Facatativá, *Colombia* **134** 4 49N 74 22W
Fachi, *Niger* **87** 18 6N 11 34 E
Facture, *France* **20** 44 39N 0 58W
Fada, *Chad* **87** 17 13N 21 34 E
Fada-n-Gourma, *Burkina Faso* **91** 12 10N 0 30 E
Faddeyevskiy, Ostrov, *U.S.S.R.* **41** 76 0N 150 0 E
Fădilī, *Si. Arabia* **46** 26 55N 49 10 E
Fadlab, *Sudan* **88** 17 42N 34 2 E
Faenza, *Italy* **27** 44 17N 11 53 E
Fafa, *Mali* **91** 15 22N 0 48 E
Fafe, *Portugal* **22** 41 27N 8 11W
Faga, *W. Samoa* **68** 13 39 S 172 8W
Fagam, *Nigeria* **91** 11 1N 10 1 E
Fagamalo, *W. Samoa* **68** 13 25 S 172 21W
Făgăras, *Romania* **34** 45 48N 24 58 E
Făgăras, Munţii, *Romania* **34** 45 40N 24 40 E
Fågelsjö, *Sweden* **10** 61 50N 14 35 E
Fagerhult, *Sweden* **11** 57 8N 15 40 E
Fagernes, *Norway* **9** 60 59N 9 14 E
Fagersta, *Sweden* **10** 60 1N 15 46 E
Făget, *Romania* **34** 45 52N 22 10 E
Fagnano, L., *Argentina* **142** 54 30 S 68 0W
Fagnano Castello, *Italy* **29** 39 31N 16 4 E
Fagnières, *France* **19** 48 58N 4 20 E
Fahraj, *Iran* **47** 29 0N 59 0 E
Fahūd, *Oman* **47** 22 18N 56 28 E
Faillon, L., *Canada* **106** 48 21N 76 39W
Fair Hd., *U.K.* **15** 55 14N 6 10W
Fair Oaks, *U.S.A.* **124** 38 39N 121 16W
Fairbank, *U.S.A.* **123** 31 44N 110 12W
Fairbanks, *U.S.A.* **102** 64 50N 147 50W
Fairborn, *U.S.A.* **119** 39 52N 84 2W
Fairbury, *Ill., U.S.A.* **119** 40 45N 88 31W
Fairbury, *Nebr., U.S.A.* **120** 40 5N 97 5W
Fairfax, *Ohio, U.S.A.* **119** 39 5N 83 37W
Fairfax, *Okla., U.S.A.* **121** 36 37N 96 45W
Fairfield, *Australia* **76** 33 53 S 150 57 E
Fairfield, *Ala., U.S.A.* **115** 33 30N 87 0W
Fairfield, *Calif., U.S.A.* **124** 38 14N 122 1W
Fairfield, *Conn., U.S.A.* **117** 41 8N 73 16W
Fairfield, *Idaho, U.S.A.* **122** 43 21N 114 46W
Fairfield, *Ill., U.S.A.* **119** 38 20N 88 20W
Fairfield, *Iowa, U.S.A.* **118** 41 0N 91 58W
Fairfield, *Mont., U.S.A.* **122** 47 40N 112 0W
Fairfield, *Ohio, U.S.A.* **119** 39 21N 84 34W
Fairfield, *Tex., U.S.A.* **121** 31 40N 96 0W
Fairford, *Canada* **111** 51 37N 98 38W
Fairholme, *Australia* **76** 33 14 S 147 22 E
Fairhope, *U.S.A.* **115** 30 35N 87 50W
Fairlie, *N.Z.* **81** 44 5 S 170 49 E
Fairmead, *U.S.A.* **124** 37 5N 120 10W
Fairmont, *Minn., U.S.A.* **120** 43 37N 94 30W
Fairmont, *W. Va., U.S.A.* **114** 39 29N 80 10W
Fairmount, *U.S.A.* **125** 34 45N 118 26W
Fairplay, *U.S.A.* **123** 39 9N 105 40W
Fairport, *N.Y., U.S.A.* **116** 43 8N 77 29W
Fairport, *Ohio, U.S.A.* **116** 41 45N 81 17W
Fairview, *Australia* **72** 15 31 S 144 17 E
Fairview, *Canada* **110** 56 5N 118 25W
Fairview, *N. Dak., U.S.A.* **120** 47 49N 104 7W
Fairview, *Okla., U.S.A.* **121** 36 19N 98 30W
Fairview, *Utah, U.S.A.* **122** 39 50N 111 0W
Fairweather, Mt., *U.S.A.* **102** 58 55N 137 45W
Faisalabad, *Pakistan* **48** 31 30N 73 5 E
Faith, *U.S.A.* **120** 45 2N 102 4W
Faizabad, *India* **49** 26 45N 82 10 E
Faizpur, *India* **50** 21 14N 75 49 E
Fajardo, *Puerto Rico* **129** 18 20N 65 39W
Fakfak, *Indonesia* **57** 3 0 S 132 15 E
Fakobli, *Ivory C.* **90** 7 23N 7 23W
Fakse, *Denmark* **11** 55 15N 12 8 E
Fakse B., *Denmark* **11** 55 11N 12 15 E
Fakse Ladeplads, *Denmark* **11** 55 11N 12 9 E
Faku, *China* **61** 42 32N 123 21 E
Falaise, *France* **18** 48 54N 0 12W
Falaise, Mui, *Vietnam* **54** 19 6N 105 45 E
Falam, *Burma* **52** 23 0N 93 45 E
Falces, *Spain* **24** 42 24N 1 48W
Fălciu, *Romania* **34** 46 17N 28 7 E
Falcón □, *Venezuela* **134** 11 0N 69 50W
Falcon, C., *Algeria* **85** 35 50N 0 50W
Falcon Dam, *U.S.A.* **121** 26 50N 99 20W
Falconara Marittima, *Italy* **27** 43 37N 13 23 E
Falconbridge, *Canada* **108** 46 35N 80 45W
Falconer, *U.S.A.* **116** 42 7N 79 13W
Faléa, *Mali* **90** 12 16N 11 17W
Falelatai, *W. Samoa* **68** 13 55 S 171 59W
Falelima, *W. Samoa* **68** 13 32 S 172 41W
Falenki, *U.S.S.R.* **37** 58 22N 51 35 E
Faleshty, *U.S.S.R.* **38** 47 32N 27 44 E
Falfurrias, *U.S.A.* **121** 27 14N 98 8W
Falher, *Canada* **110** 55 44N 117 15W
Falkenberg, *E. Germany* **30** 51 34N 13 13 E
Falkenberg, *Sweden* **11** 56 54N 12 30 E
Falkensee, *E. Germany* **30** 52 35N 13 6 E
Falkenstein, *E. Germany* **30** 50 27N 12 24 E
Falkirk, *U.K.* **14** 56 0N 3 47W
Falkland, East, I., *Falk. Is.* **142** 51 40 S 58 30W
Falkland, West, I., *Falk. Is.* **142** 51 40 S 60 0W
Falkland Is., *Atl. Oc.* **142** 51 30 S 59 0W
Falkland Is. Dependency □, *Atl. Oc.* **143** 57 0 S 40 0W
Falkland Sd., *Falk. Is.* **142** 52 0 S 60 0W
Falköping, *Sweden* **11** 58 12N 13 33 E
Fall River, *U.S.A.* **117** 41 45N 71 5W
Fall River Mills, *U.S.A.* **122** 41 1N 121 30W
Fallbrook, *U.S.A.* **123** 33 25N 117 12W
Fallbrook, *U.S.A.* **125** 33 23N 117 15W
Fallon, *Mont., U.S.A.* **120** 46 52N 105 8W
Fallon, *Nev., U.S.A.* **122** 39 31N 118 51W
Falls City, *Nebr., U.S.A.* **120** 40 0N 95 40W
Falls City, *Oreg., U.S.A.* **122** 44 54N 123 29W
Falls Creek, *N.S.W., Australia* **76** 34 58 S 150 36 E
Falls Creek, *Vic., Australia* **75** 36 52 S 147 17 E
Falls Creek, *U.S.A.* **116** 41 8N 78 49W
Falmouth, *Jamaica* **128** 18 30N 77 40W
Falmouth, *U.K.* **13** 50 9N 5 5W
Falmouth, *U.S.A.* **119** 38 40N 84 20W
False B., *S. Africa* **96** 34 15 S 18 40 E
False Divi Pt., *India* **51** 15 43N 80 50 E
Falset, *Spain* **24** 41 7N 0 50 E
Falso, C., *Honduras* **128** 15 12N 83 21W
Falster, *Denmark* **11** 54 45N 11 55 E
Falsterbo, *Sweden* **11** 55 23N 12 50 E
Fălticeni, *Romania* **34** 47 21N 26 20 E
Falun, *Sweden* **10** 60 37N 15 37 E
Famagusta, *Cyprus* **46** 35 8N 33 55 E
Famatina, Sierra de, *Argentina* **140** 27 30 S 68 0W
Family L., *Canada* **111** 51 54N 95 27W
Famoso, *U.S.A.* **125** 35 37N 119 12W
Fan Xian, *China* **60** 35 55N 115 38 E
Fana, *Mali* **90** 13 0N 6 56W
Fandriana, *Madag.* **97** 20 14 S 47 21 E
Fang, *Thailand* **54** 19 55N 99 13 E
Fang Xian, *China* **59** 32 3N 110 40 E
Fangchang, *China* **59** 31 5N 118 4 E
Fangcheng, *Guangxi Zhuangzu, China* **58** 21 42N 108 21 E
Fangcheng, *Henan, China* **60** 33 18N 112 59 E
Fangliao, *Taiwan* **59** 22 22N 120 38 E
Fangshan, *China* **60** 38 3N 111 25 E
Fangzi, *China* **61** 36 33N 119 10 E
Fani i Madh →, *Albania* **35** 41 56N 20 16 E
Fanjiatun, *China* **61** 43 40N 125 0 E
Fannich, L., *U.K.* **14** 57 40N 5 0W
Fanny Bay, *Canada* **110** 49 37N 124 48W
Fanø, *Denmark* **11** 55 25N 8 25 E
Fano, *Italy* **27** 43 50N 13 0 E
Fanshaw, *U.S.A.* **110** 57 11N 133 30W
Fanshi, *China* **60** 39 12N 113 20 E
Fao = Al Fāw, *Iraq* **46** 30 0N 48 30 E

Faqirwali, *Pakistan* **48** 29 27N 73 0 E
Fara in Sabina, *Italy* **27** 42 13N 12 44 E
Faradje, *Zaïre* **92** 3 50N 29 45 E
Farafangana, *Madag.* **97** 22 49 S 47 50 E
Farâfra, El Wâhât el-, *Egypt* **88** 27 15N 28 20 E
Farāh, *Afghan.* **47** 32 20N 62 7 E
Farāh □, *Afghan.* **47** 32 25N 62 10 E
Farahalana, *Madag.* **97** 14 26 S 50 10 E
Faraid, Gebel, *Egypt* **88** 23 33N 35 19 E
Faramana, *Burkina Faso* **90** 11 56N 4 45W
Faranah, *Guinea* **90** 10 3N 10 45W
Farasān, Jazā'ir, *Si. Arabia* **45** 16 45N 41 55 E
Faratsiho, *Madag.* **97** 19 24 S 46 57 E
Farbarachi, *Somali Rep.* **98** 2 30N 45 30 E
Fardes →, *Spain* **25** 37 35N 3 0W
Fareara, Pte., *Tahiti* **68** 17 52 S 149 9W
Fareham, *U.K.* **13** 50 52N 1 11W
Farewell, C., *N.Z.* **81** 40 29 S 172 43 E
Farewell C. = Farvel, Kap, *Greenland* **144** 59 48N 43 55W
Farewell Spit, *N.Z.* **81** 40 35 S 173 0 E
Fargo, *U.S.A.* **120** 46 52N 96 40W
Fari'a →, *Jordan* **44** 32 12N 35 27 E
Faribault, *U.S.A.* **120** 44 15N 93 19W
Faridkot, *India* **48** 30 44N 74 45 E
Faridpur, *Bangla.* **49** 23 15N 89 55 E
Färila, *Sweden* **10** 61 48N 15 50 E
Farim, *Guinea-Biss.* **90** 12 27N 15 9W
Farīmān, *Iran* **47** 35 40N 59 49 E
Farina, *Australia* **73** 30 3 S 138 15 E
Faringe, *Sweden* **10** 59 55N 18 7 E
Farinha →, *Brazil* **138** 6 51 S 47 30W
Fariones, Pta., *Canary Is.* **25** 29 13N 13 28W
Fâriskûr, *Egypt* **88** 31 20N 31 43 E
Farmer City, *U.S.A.* **119** 40 15N 88 39W
Farmersburg, *U.S.A.* **119** 39 15N 87 23W
Farmerville, *U.S.A.* **121** 32 48N 92 23W
Farmington, *Calif., U.S.A.* **124** 37 56N 121 0W
Farmington, *Ill., U.S.A.* **118** 40 42N 90 0W
Farmington, *Iowa, U.S.A.* **118** 40 38N 91 44W
Farmington, *Mo., U.S.A.* **118** 37 47N 90 25W
Farmington, *N.H., U.S.A.* **117** 43 25N 71 7W
Farmington, *N. Mex., U.S.A.* **123** 36 45N 108 28W
Farmington, *Utah, U.S.A.* **122** 41 0N 111 12W
Farmington →, *U.S.A.* **117** 41 51N 72 38W
Farmland, *U.S.A.* **119** 40 15N 85 5W
Farmville, *U.S.A.* **114** 37 19N 78 22W
Farnborough, *U.K.* **13** 51 17N 0 46W
Farne Is., *U.K.* **12** 55 38N 1 37W
Farnham, *Canada* **117** 45 17N 72 59W
Faro, *Brazil* **135** 2 10 S 56 39W
Faro, *Portugal* **23** 37 2N 7 55W
Fårö, *Sweden* **9** 57 55N 19 5 E
Faro □, *Portugal* **23** 37 12N 8 10W
Faroe Is. = Føroyar, *Atl. Oc.* **130** 62 0N 7 0W
Farquhar, C., *Australia* **79** 23 50 S 113 36 E
Farquhar Is., *Seychelles* **53** 11 0 S 52 0 E
Farrar →, *U.K.* **14** 57 30N 4 30W
Farrars Cr. →, *Australia* **72** 25 35 S 140 43 E
Farrāshband, *Iran* **47** 28 57N 52 5 E
Farrell, *U.S.A.* **116** 41 13N 80 29W
Farrell Flat, *Australia* **73** 33 48 S 138 48 E
Farrukhabad-cum-Fatehgarh, *India* **49** 27 30N 79 32 E
Fārs □, *Iran* **47** 29 30N 55 0 E
Fársala, *Greece* **35** 39 17N 22 23 E
Farsø, *Denmark* **11** 56 46N 9 19 E
Farsund, *Norway* **9** 58 5N 6 55 E
Fartak, Râs, *Si. Arabia* **46** 28 5N 34 34 E
Fartura, Serra da, *Brazil* **141** 26 21 S 52 52W
Faru, *Nigeria* **91** 12 48N 6 12 E
Farum, *Denmark* **11** 55 49N 12 21 E
Farvel, Kap, *Greenland* **144** 59 48N 43 55W
Farwell, *U.S.A.* **121** 34 25N 103 0W
Fāryāb □, *Afghan.* **47** 36 0N 65 0 E
Fasā, *Iran* **47** 29 0N 53 39 E
Fasano, *Italy* **29** 40 50N 17 20 E
Fashoda, *Sudan* **89** 9 50N 32 2 E
Fastnet Rock, *Ireland* **15** 51 22N 9 37W
Fastov, *U.S.S.R.* **36** 50 7N 29 57 E
Fatagar, Tanjung, *Indonesia* **57** 2 46 S 131 57 E
Fatehgarh, *India* **49** 27 25N 79 35 E
Fatehpur, *Raj., India* **48** 28 0N 74 40 E
Fatehpur, *Ut. P., India* **49** 25 56N 81 13 E
Fatesh, *U.S.S.R.* **37** 52 8N 35 57 E
Fatick, *Senegal* **90** 14 19N 16 27W
Fatima, *Canada* **105** 47 24N 61 53W
Fátima, *Portugal* **23** 39 37N 8 39W
Fatoya, *Guinea* **90** 11 37N 9 10W
Faucille, Col de la, *France* **21** 46 22N 6 2 E
Faulkton, *U.S.A.* **120** 45 4N 99 8W
Faulquemont, *France* **19** 49 3N 6 36 E
Fauquembergues, *France* **19** 50 36N 2 5 E
Faure I., *Australia* **79** 25 52 S 113 50 E
Făurei, *Romania* **34** 45 6N 27 19 E
Fauresmith, *S. Africa* **96** 29 44 S 25 17 E
Fauro, *Solomon Is.* **68** 6 55 S 156 7 E
Fauske, *Norway* **8** 67 17N 15 25 E
Fauvillers, *Belgium* **17** 49 51N 5 40 E
Favara, *Italy* **28** 37 19N 13 39 E
Favignana, *Italy* **28** 37 56N 12 18 E
Favignana, I., *Italy* **28** 37 56N 12 18 E
Favourable Lake, *Canada* **104** 52 50N 93 39W
Fawn →, *Canada* **104** 55 20N 87 35W
Fawnskin, *U.S.A.* **125** 34 16N 116 56W
Faxaflói, *Iceland* **8** 64 29N 23 0W
Faya-Largeau, *Chad* **87** 17 58N 19 6 E
Fayaoué, *Vanuatu* **68** 20 38 S 166 33 E
Fayd, *Si. Arabia* **46** 27 1N 42 52 E
Fayence, *France* **21** 43 38N 6 42 E
Fayette, *Ala., U.S.A.* **115** 33 40N 87 50W
Fayette, *Iowa, U.S.A.* **118** 42 51N 91 48W
Fayette, *Mo., U.S.A.* **118** 39 10N 92 40W
Fayette, *Ohio, U.S.A.* **119** 41 40N 84 20W
Fayetteville, *Ark., U.S.A.* **121** 36 0N 94 5W
Fayetteville, *N.C., U.S.A.* **115** 35 0N 78 58W
Fayetteville, *Tenn., U.S.A.* **115** 35 8N 86 30W
Fayón, *Spain* **24** 41 15N 0 20 E
Fazenda Libongo, *Angola* **95** 8 24 S 13 24 E
Fazenda Nova, *Brazil* **139** 16 11 S 50 48W
Fazilka, *India* **48** 30 27N 74 2 E
Fazilpur, *Pakistan* **48** 29 18N 70 29 E
Fdérik, *Mauritania* **84** 22 40N 12 45W
Fé, La, *Cuba* **128** 22 2N 84 15W
Feale →, *Ireland* **15** 52 26N 9 40W
Fear, C., *U.S.A.* **115** 33 51N 78 0W
Feather →, *U.S.A.* **122** 38 47N 121 36W
Feather Falls, *U.S.A.* **124** 39 36N 121 16W
Featherston, *N.Z.* **80** 41 6 S 175 20 E
Featherstone, *Zimb.* **93** 18 42 S 30 55 E
Feathertop, Mt., *Australia* **75** 36 53 S 147 7 E
Fécamp, *France* **18** 49 45N 0 22 E
Fedala = Mohammedia, *Morocco* **84** 33 44N 7 21W
Federación, *Argentina* **140** 31 0 S 57 55W
Fedjadj, Chott el, *Tunisia* **86** 33 52N 9 14 E
Fehmarn, *E. Germany* **30** 54 26N 11 10 E
Fei Xian, *China* **61** 35 18N 117 59 E
Feijó, *Brazil* **136** 8 9 S 70 21W
Feilding, *N.Z.* **80** 40 13 S 175 35 E
Feira de Santana, *Brazil* **139** 12 15 S 38 57W
Feixiang, *China* **60** 36 30N 114 45 E
Fejø, *Denmark* **11** 54 55N 11 30 E
Felanitx, *Spain* **25** 39 28N 3 9 E
Feldberg, *E. Germany* **30** 53 20N 13 26 E
Feldberg, *W. Germany* **31** 47 51N 7 58 E
Feldkirch, *Austria* **31** 47 15N 9 37 E
Felicity, *U.S.A.* **119** 38 51N 84 6W
Felipe Carrillo Puerto, *Mexico* **127** 19 38N 88 3W
Felixlândia, *Brazil* **139** 18 47 S 44 55W
Felixstowe, *U.K.* **13** 51 58N 1 22 E
Felletin, *France* **20** 45 53N 2 11 E
Felton, *U.S.A.* **124** 37 3N 122 4W
Feltre, *Italy* **27** 46 1N 11 55 E
Femø, *Denmark* **11** 54 58N 11 53 E
Femunden, *Norway* **10** 62 10N 11 53 E
Fen He →, *China* **60** 35 36N 110 42 E
Fenelon Falls, *Canada* **109** 44 32N 78 45W
Feneroa, *Ethiopia* **89** 13 5N 39 3 E
Feng Xian, *Jiangsu, China* **60** 34 43N 116 35 E
Feng Xian, *Shaanxi, China* **60** 33 54N 106 40 E
Fengári, *Greece* **35** 40 25N 25 32 E
Fengcheng, *Jiangxi, China* **59** 28 12N 115 48 E
Fengcheng, *Liaoning, China* **61** 40 28N 124 5 E
Fengdu, *China* **58** 29 55N 107 41 E
Fengfeng, *China* **60** 36 28N 114 8 E
Fenggang, *China* **58** 27 57N 107 47 E
Fenghua, *China* **59** 29 40N 121 25 E
Fenghuang, *China* **58** 27 57N 109 29 E
Fenghuangzui, *China* **58** 33 30N 109 23 E
Fengjie, *China* **58** 31 5N 109 36 E
Fengkai, *China* **59** 23 24N 111 30 E
Fengle, *China* **59** 31 29N 112 29 E
Fengning, *China* **60** 41 10N 116 33 E
Fengqing, *China* **58** 24 38N 99 55 E
Fengqiu, *China* **60** 35 2N 114 25 E
Fengrun, *China* **61** 39 48N 118 8 E
Fengshan, *Guangxi Zhuangzu, China* **58** 24 39N 109 15 E
Fengshan, *Guangxi Zhuangzu, China* **58** 24 31N 107 3 E
Fengtai, *Anhui, China* **59** 32 50N 116 40 E
Fengtai, *Beijing, China* **60** 39 50N 116 18 E
Fengxian, *China* **59** 30 55N 121 26 E
Fengxiang, *China* **60** 34 29N 107 25 E
Fengxin, *China* **59** 28 41N 115 18 E
Fengyang, *China* **61** 32 51N 117 29 E
Fengyi, *China* **58** 25 37N 100 20 E
Fengzhen, *China* **60** 40 25N 113 2 E
Feni Is., *Papua N. G.* **69** 4 0 S 153 40 E
Fenit, *Ireland* **15** 52 17N 9 51W
Fennimore, *U.S.A.* **118** 42 58N 90 41W
Fenny, *Bangla.* **52** 22 55N 91 32 E
Feno, C. de, *France* **21** 41 58N 8 33 E
Fenoarivo Afovoany, *Madag.* **97** 18 26 S 46 34 E
Fenoarivo Atsinanana, *Madag.* **97** 17 22 S 49 25 E
Fens, The, *U.K.* **12** 52 45N 0 2 E
Fenton, *U.S.A.* **104** 42 47N 83 44W
Fenxi, *China* **60** 36 40N 111 31 E
Fenyang, *China* **60** 37 18N 111 48 E
Fenyi, *China* **59** 27 45N 114 47 E
Feodosiya, *U.S.S.R.* **38** 45 2N 35 28 E
Fer, C. de, *Algeria* **85** 37 3N 7 10 E
Ferdows, *Iran* **47** 33 58N 58 2 E
Fère, La, *France* **19** 49 39N 3 21 E
Fère-Champenoise, *France* **19** 48 45N 4 0 E
Fère-en-Tardenois, *France* **19** 49 10N 3 30 E
Ferentino, *Italy* **28** 41 42N 13 14 E
Ferfer, *Somali Rep.* **98** 5 4N 45 9 E
Fergana, *U.S.S.R.* **40** 40 23N 71 19 E
Fergus, *Canada* **108** 43 43N 80 24W
Fergus Falls, *U.S.A.* **120** 46 18N 96 7W
Ferguson, *U.S.A.* **118** 38 45N 90 18W
Fergusson I., *Papua N. G.* **69** 9 30 S 150 45 E
Fériana, *Tunisia* **86** 34 59N 8 33 E
Feričanci, *Yugoslavia* **33** 45 32N 18 0 E
Ferkane, *Algeria* **85** 34 37N 7 26 E
Ferkéssédougou, *Ivory C.* **90** 9 35N 5 6W
Ferlach, *Austria* **33** 46 32N 14 18 E
Ferland, *Canada* **104** 50 19N 88 27W
Ferlo, Vallée du, *Senegal* **90** 15 15N 14 15W
Fermanagh □, *U.K.* **15** 54 21N 7 40W
Ferme-Neuve, *Canada* **106** 46 42N 75 27W
Fermo, *Italy* **27** 43 10N 13 42 E
Fermoselle, *Spain* **22** 41 19N 6 27W
Fermoy, *Ireland* **15** 52 4N 8 18W
Fernán Nuñéz, *Spain* **23** 37 40N 4 44W
Fernández, *Argentina* **140** 27 55 S 63 50W
Fernandina Beach, *U.S.A.* **115** 30 40N 81 30W
Fernando de Noronha, *Brazil* **138** 4 0 S 33 10W
Fernando Póo = Bioko, *Eq. Guin.* **91** 3 30N 8 40 E
Fernandópolis, *Brazil* **139** 20 16 S 50 14W
Ferndale, *Calif., U.S.A.* **122** 40 37N 124 12W
Ferndale, *Wash., U.S.A.* **124** 48 51N 122 41W
Fernie, *Canada* **110** 49 30N 115 5W
Fernlees, *Australia* **72** 23 51 S 148 7 E
Fernley, *U.S.A.* **122** 39 36N 119 14W
Feroke, *India* **51** 11 9N 75 46 E
Feronia, *Canada* **108** 46 22N 79 19W
Ferozepore = Firozpur, *India* **48** 30 55N 74 40 E
Férrai, *Greece* **35** 40 53N 26 10 E
Ferrandina, *Italy* **29** 40 30N 16 28 E
Ferrara, *Italy* **27** 44 50N 11 36 E
Ferrato, C., *Italy* **28** 39 18N 9 39 E
Ferreira do Alentejo, *Portugal* **23** 38 4N 8 6W
Ferreñafe, *Peru* **136** 6 42 S 79 50W
Ferret, C., *France* **20** 44 38N 1 15W
Ferrette, *France* **19** 47 30N 7 20 E
Ferriday, *U.S.A.* **121** 31 35N 91 33W
Ferrières, *France* **19** 48 5N 2 48 E
Ferriete, *Italy* **26** 44 40N 9 30 E
Ferrol, Pen. de, *Peru* **136** 9 10 S 78 35W
Ferron, *U.S.A.* **123** 39 3N 111 3W
Ferros, *Brazil* **139** 19 14 S 43 2W
Ferryland, *Canada* **105** 47 2N 52 53W
Ferrysburg, *U.S.A.* **119** 43 5N 86 13W
Ferté-Bernard, La, *France* **18** 48 10N 0 40 E
Ferté-Macé, La, *France* **18** 48 35N 0 22W
Ferté-St.-Aubin, La, *France* **19** 47 42N 1 57 E
Ferté-sous-Jouarre, La, *France* **19** 48 56N 3 8 E
Ferté-Vidame, La, *France* **18** 48 37N 0 53 E
Fertile, *U.S.A.* **120** 47 31N 96 18W
Fertília, *Italy* **28** 40 37N 8 13 E
Fès, *Morocco* **84** 34 0N 5 0W
Feschaux, *Belgium* **17** 50 9N 4 54 E
Feshi, *Zaïre* **95** 6 8S 18 10 E
Fessenden, *U.S.A.* **120** 47 42N 99 38W
Festus, *U.S.A.* **118** 38 13N 90 24W
Feteşti, *Romania* **34** 44 22N 27 51 E
Fethiye, *Turkey* **46** 36 36N 29 10 E
Fetlar, *U.K.* **14** 60 36N 0 52W
Feuilles →, *Canada* **103** 58 47N 70 4W
Feurs, *France* **21** 45 45N 4 13 E
Feyzābād, *Afghan.* **47** 37 7N 70 33 E
Fezzan, *Libya* **82** 27 0N 15 0 E
Ffestiniog, *U.K.* **12** 52 58N 3 56W
Fiambalá, *Argentina* **140** 27 45 S 67 37W
Fianarantsoa, *Madag.* **97** 21 26 S 47 5 E
Fianarantsoa □, *Madag.* **97** 19 30 S 47 0 E
Fianga, *Cameroon* **87** 9 55N 15 9 E
Fichtelgebirge, *W. Germany* **31** 50 10N 12 0 E
Ficksburg, *S. Africa* **97** 28 51 S 27 53 E
Fidenza, *Italy* **26** 44 51N 10 3 E
Fiditi, *Nigeria* **91** 7 45N 3 53 E
Field, *Canada* **108** 46 31N 80 1W
Field →, *Australia* **72** 23 48 S 138 0 E
Field I., *Australia* **78** 12 5 S 132 23 E
Fieri, *Albania* **35** 40 43N 19 33 E
Fife □, *U.K.* **14** 56 13N 3 2W
Fife Ness, *U.K.* **14** 56 17N 2 35W
Fifield, *Australia* **76** 32 47 S 147 28 E
Fifth Cataract, *Sudan* **88** 18 22N 33 50 E
Figeac, *France* **20** 44 37N 2 2 E
Figline Valdarno, *Italy* **27** 43 37N 11 28 E
Figtree, *Zimb.* **93** 20 22 S 28 20 E
Figueira Castelo Rodrigo, *Portugal* **22** 40 57N 6 58W
Figueira da Foz, *Portugal* **22** 40 7N 8 54W
Figueiró dos Vinhos, *Portugal* **22** 39 55N 8 16W
Figueras, *Spain* **24** 42 18N 2 58 E
Figuig, *Morocco* **85** 32 5N 1 11W
Fihaonana, *Madag.* **97** 18 36 S 47 12 E
Fiherenana, *Madag.* **97** 18 29 S 48 24 E
Fiherenana →, *Madag.* **97** 23 19 S 43 37 E
Fiji ■, *Pac. Oc.* **68** 17 20 S 179 0 E
Fika, *Nigeria* **91** 11 15N 11 13 E
Filabres, Sierra de los, *Spain* **25** 37 13N 2 20W
Filadelfia, *Bolivia* **136** 11 20 S 68 46W
Filadélfia, *Brazil* **138** 7 21 S 47 30W
Filadélfia, *Italy* **29** 38 47N 16 17 E
File Axe, L., *Canada* **107** 50 18N 73 34W
Filer, *U.S.A.* **122** 42 30N 114 35W
Filey, *U.K.* **12** 54 13N 0 18W
Filiaşi, *Romania* **34** 44 32N 23 31 E
Filiátes, *Greece* **35** 39 38N 20 16 E
Filiatrá, *Greece* **35** 37 9N 21 35 E
Filicudi, *Italy* **29** 38 35N 14 33 E
Filiourí →, *Greece* **35** 41 15N 25 40 E
Filipstad, *Sweden* **10** 59 43N 14 9 E
Filisur, *Switz.* **31** 46 41N 9 40 E
Fillmore, *Canada* **111** 49 50N 103 25W
Fillmore, *Calif., U.S.A.* **125** 34 23N 118 58W
Fillmore, *Utah, U.S.A.* **123** 38 58N 112 20W
Filottrano, *Italy* **27** 43 28N 13 20 E
Fils, L. du, *Canada* **106** 46 37N 78 7W
Filyos, *Turkey* **38** 41 34N 32 4 E
Filyos →, *Turkey* **46** 41 35N 32 10 E
Finale Lígure, *Italy* **26** 44 10N 8 21 E
Finale nell' Emília, *Italy* **27** 44 50N 11 18 E
Fiñana, *Spain* **25** 37 10N 2 50W
Finch, *Canada* **106** 45 11N 75 7W
Findhorn →, *U.K.* **14** 57 38N 3 38W
Findlay, *U.S.A.* **119** 41 0N 83 41W
Fine Flower Creek, *Australia* **77** 29 24 S 152 42 E
Finger L., *Canada* **111** 53 33N 93 30W
Fíngõe, *Mozam.* **93** 14 55 S 31 50 E
Finike, *Turkey* **46** 36 21N 30 10 E
Finistère □, *France* **18** 48 20N 4 0W
Finisterre, *Spain* **22** 42 54N 9 16W
Finisterre, C., *Spain* **22** 42 50N 9 19W
Finisterre Ra., *Papua N. G.* **69** 6 0 S 146 30 E
Finke, *Australia* **72** 25 34 S 134 35 E
Finke →, *Australia* **73** 27 0 S 136 10 E
Finland ■, *Europe* **9** 63 0N 27 0 E
Finland, G. of, *Europe* **9** 60 0N 26 0 E
Finlay →, *Canada* **110** 57 0N 125 10W
Finley, *Australia* **74** 35 38 S 145 35 E
Finley, *U.S.A.* **120** 47 35N 97 50W
Finn →, *Ireland* **15** 54 50N 7 55W
Finnigan, Mt., *Australia* **72** 15 49 S 145 17 E
Finniss, C., *Australia* **73** 33 8 S 134 51 E
Finnmark fylke □, *Norway* **8** 69 30N 25 0 E
Finschhafen, *Papua N. G.* **69** 6 33 S 147 50 E
Finsteraarhorn, *Switz.* **31** 46 31N 8 10 E
Finsterwalde, *E. Germany* **30** 51 37N 13 42 E
Finsterwolde, *Neths.* **16** 53 12N 7 6 E
Fiora →, *Italy* **27** 42 20N 11 35 E
Fiordland National Park, *N.Z.* **81** 45 0 S 167 50 E
Fiorenzuola d'Arda, *Italy* **26** 44 56N 9 54 E
Fīq, *Syria* **44** 32 46N 35 41 E
Fire River, *Canada* **104** 48 47N 83 21W
Firebag →, *Canada* **111** 57 45N 111 21W
Firebaugh, *U.S.A.* **124** 36 52N 120 27W
Firedrake L., *Canada* **111** 61 25N 104 30W
Firenze, *Italy* **27** 43 47N 11 15 E
Firmi, *France* **20** 44 33N 2 19 E
Firminy, *France* **21** 45 23N 4 18 E
Firozabad, *India* **49** 27 10N 78 25 E
Firozpur, *India* **48** 30 55N 74 40 E
Fīrūzābād, *Iran* **47** 28 52N 52 35 E
Fīrūzkūh, *Iran* **47** 35 50N 52 50 E
Firvale, *Canada* **110** 52 27N 126 13W
Fish →, *Namibia* **96** 28 7 S 17 10 E
Fish →, *S. Africa* **96** 31 30 S 20 16 E
Fish Creek, *Australia* **74** 38 43 S 146 7 E
Fisher, *Australia* **79** 30 30 S 131 0 E
Fisher B., *Canada* **111** 51 35N 97 13W
Fishguard, *U.K.* **13** 51 59N 4 59W
Fishing L., *Canada* **111** 52 10N 95 24W
Fismes, *France* **19** 49 20N 3 40 E
Fitchburg, *U.S.A.* **117** 42 35N 71 47W
Fitero, *Spain* **24** 42 4N 1 52W
Fitri, L., *Chad* **87** 12 50N 17 28 E
Fitz Roy, *Argentina* **142** 47 0 S 67 0W
Fitzgerald, *Canada* **110** 59 51N 111 36W
Fitzgerald, *U.S.A.* **115** 31 45N 83 16W
Fitzmaurice →, *Australia* **78** 14 45 S 130 5 E
Fitzroy →, *Queens., Australia* **72** 23 32 S 150 52 E

Fitzroy →, W. Austral., Australia **78** 17 31 S 123 35 E
Fitzroy Crossing, Australia **78** 18 9 S 125 38 E
Fitzwilliam I., Canada **108** 45 30N 81 45W
Fiume = Rijeka, Yugoslavia **27** 45 20N 14 21 E
Fiumefreddo Brúzio, Italy **29** 39 14N 16 4 E
Five Points, U.S.A. **124** 36 26N 120 6W
Fivizzano, Italy **26** 44 12N 10 11 E
Fizi, Zaïre **92** 4 17 S 28 55 E
Fjellerup, Denmark **11** 56 29N 10 34 E
Fjerritslev, Denmark **11** 57 5N 9 15 E
Fkih ben Salah, Morocco **84** 32 32N 6 45W
Flå, Norway **10** 63 13N 10 18 E
Flagler, U.S.A. **120** 39 20N 103 4W
Flagstaff, U.S.A. **123** 35 10N 111 40W
Flaherty I., Canada **104** 56 15N 79 15W
Flåm, Norway **9** 60 50N 7 7 E
Flambeau →, U.S.A. **120** 45 18N 91 15W
Flamborough Hd., U.K. **12** 54 8N 0 4W
Flaming Gorge Dam, U.S.A. **122** 40 50N 109 46W
Flaming Gorge Res., U.S.A. **122** 41 15N 109 30W
Flamingo, Teluk, Indonesia **57** 5 30 S 138 0 E
Flanagan, U.S.A. **119** 40 53N 88 52W
Flanders = West-Vlaanderen □, Belgium **17** 51 0N 3 0 E
Flandre Occidentale □ = West-Vlaanderen □, Belgium **17** 51 0N 3 0 E
Flandre Orientale □ = Oost-Vlaanderen □, Belgium **17** 51 5N 3 50 E
Flandreau, U.S.A. **120** 44 5N 96 38W
Flanigan, U.S.A. **124** 40 10N 119 53W
Flåsjön, Sweden **8** 64 5N 15 40 E
Flat →, Canada **110** 61 33N 125 18W
Flat →, U.S.A. **119** 42 56N 85 20W
Flat River, U.S.A. **121** 37 50N 90 30W
Flat Rock, Ill., U.S.A. **119** 38 54N 87 40W
Flat Rock, Mich., U.S.A. **119** 42 4N 83 15W
Flatey, Barðastrandarsýsla, Iceland **8** 66 10N 17 52W
Flatey, Suður-þingeyjarsýsla, Iceland **8** 65 22N 22 56W
Flathead L., U.S.A. **122** 47 50N 114 0W
Flatrock →, U.S.A. **119** 38 46N 86 10W
Flattery, C., Australia **72** 14 58 S 145 21 E
Flattery, C., U.S.A. **124** 48 21N 124 43W
Flavy-le-Martel, France **19** 49 43N 3 12 E
Flaxton, U.S.A. **120** 48 52N 102 24W
Flèche, La, France **18** 47 42N 0 4W
Fleetwood, U.K. **12** 53 55N 3 1W
Flekkefjord, Norway **9** 58 18N 6 39 E
Flémalle, Belgium **17** 50 36N 5 28 E
Flemingsburg, U.S.A. **119** 38 25N 83 45W
Flemington, U.S.A. **116** 41 7N 77 28W
Flensborg Fjord, W. Germany **11** 54 50N 9 40 E
Flensburg, W. Germany **30** 54 46N 9 28 E
Flers, France **18** 48 47N 0 33W
Flesherton, Canada **108** 44 16N 80 33W
Flesko, Tanjung, Indonesia **57** 0 29N 124 30 E
Fletton, U.K. **13** 52 34N 0 13W
Fleurance, France **20** 43 52N 0 40 E
Fleurier, Switz. **31** 46 54N 6 35 E
Fleurus, Belgium **17** 50 29N 4 32 E
Flevoland □, Neths. **16** 52 30N 5 30 E
Flin Flon, Canada **111** 54 46N 101 53W
Flinders, Australia **74** 38 30 S 145 2 E
Flinders →, Australia **72** 17 36 S 140 36 E
Flinders B., Australia **79** 34 19 S 115 19 E
Flinders Group, Australia **72** 14 11 S 144 15 E
Flinders I., Australia **72** 40 0 S 148 0 E
Flinders Ranges, Australia **73** 31 30 S 138 30 E
Flinders Reefs, Australia **72** 17 37 S 148 31 E
Flint, U.K. **12** 53 15N 3 7W
Flint, U.S.A. **104** 43 5N 83 40W
Flint →, U.S.A. **115** 30 52N 84 38W
Flint I., Kiribati **67** 11 26 S 151 48W
Flinton, Australia **77** 27 55 S 149 32 E
Fliseryd, Sweden **11** 57 6N 16 15 E
Flix, Spain **24** 41 14N 0 32 E
Flixecourt, France **19** 50 0N 2 5 E
Flobecq, Belgium **17** 50 44N 3 45 E
Flodden, U.K. **12** 55 37N 2 8W
Floodwood, U.S.A. **120** 46 55N 92 55W
Flora, Norway **10** 63 27N 11 22 E
Flora, Ill., U.S.A. **114** 38 40N 88 30W
Flora, Ind., U.S.A. **119** 40 33N 86 31W
Florac, France **20** 44 20N 3 37 E
Florala, U.S.A. **115** 31 0N 86 20W
Florânia, Brazil **138** 6 8 S 36 49W
Floreffe, Belgium **17** 50 26N 4 46 E
Florence = Firenze, Italy **27** 43 47N 11 15 E
Florence, Ala., U.S.A. **115** 34 50N 87 40W
Florence, Ariz., U.S.A. **123** 33 0N 111 25W
Florence, Colo., U.S.A. **120** 38 26N 105 0W
Florence, Oreg., U.S.A. **122** 44 0N 124 3W
Florence, S.C., U.S.A. **115** 34 12N 79 44W
Florence, L., Australia **73** 28 53 S 138 9 E
Florennes, Belgium **17** 50 15N 4 35 E
Florensac, France **20** 43 23N 3 28 E
Florenville, Belgium **17** 49 40N 5 19 E
Flores, Brazil **138** 7 51 S 37 59W
Flores, Guatemala **128** 16 59N 89 50W
Flores, Indonesia **57** 8 35 S 121 0 E
Flores I., Canada **110** 49 20N 126 10W
Flores Sea, Indonesia **56** 6 30 S 124 0 E
Floresta, Brazil **138** 8 40 S 37 26W
Floresville, U.S.A. **121** 29 10N 98 10W
Floriano, Brazil **138** 6 50 S 43 0W
Florianópolis, Brazil **141** 27 30 S 48 30W
Florida, Cuba **128** 21 32N 78 14W
Florida, Uruguay **141** 34 7 S 56 10W
Florida □, U.S.A. **115** 28 30N 82 0W
Florida, Straits of, U.S.A. **128** 25 0N 80 0W
Florida B., U.S.A. **128** 25 0N 81 20W
Florida Is., Solomon Is. **68** 9 55 S 160 15 E
Florida Keys, U.S.A. **128** 25 0N 80 40W
Florídia, Italy **29** 37 6N 15 9 E
Floridsdorf, Austria **33** 48 14N 16 22 E
Flórina, Greece **35** 40 48N 21 26 E
Florissant, U.S.A. **118** 38 48N 90 20W
Florø, Norway **9** 61 35N 5 1 E
Flower Sta., Canada **106** 45 10N 76 41W
Flowerdale, Australia **74** 37 20 S 145 19 E
Flower's Cove, Canada **105** 51 14N 56 46W
Floydada, U.S.A. **121** 33 58N 101 18W
Fluk, Indonesia **57** 1 42 S 127 44 E
Flumen →, Spain **24** 41 43N 0 9W
Flumendosa →, Italy **28** 39 26N 9 38 E
Fluminimaggiore, Italy **28** 39 25N 8 30 E
Flushing = Vlissingen, Neths. **17** 51 26N 3 34 E
Flushing, U.S.A. **119** 43 4N 83 51W
Fluviá →, Spain **24** 42 12N 3 7 E
Fly →, Papua N. G. **69** 8 25 S 143 0 E
Flying Fish, C., Antarctica **143** 72 6 S 102 29W
Foa, Tonga **68** 19 45 S 174 18W
Foa, La, N. Cal. **68** 21 43 S 165 50 E
Foam Lake, Canada **111** 51 40N 103 32W
Foča, Yugoslavia **33** 43 31N 18 47 E
Focşani, Romania **34** 45 41N 27 15 E
Fogang, China **59** 23 52N 113 30 E
Foggaret el Arab, Algeria **85** 27 13N 2 49 E
Foggaret ez Zoua, Algeria **85** 27 20N 2 53 E
Fóggia, Italy **29** 41 28N 15 31 E
Foggo, Nigeria **91** 11 21N 9 57 E
Foglia →, Italy **27** 43 55N 12 54 E
Fogo, Canada **105** 49 43N 54 17W
Fogo I., Canada **105** 49 40N 54 5W
Fohnsdorf, Austria **33** 47 12N 14 40 E
Föhr, W. Germany **30** 54 40N 8 30 E
Foia, Portugal **23** 37 19N 8 37W
Foins, L. aux, Canada **106** 47 5N 78 11W
Foix, France **20** 42 58N 1 38 E
Fokino, U.S.S.R. **36** 53 30N 34 22 E
Folda, Nord-Trøndelag, Norway **8** 64 41N 10 50 E
Folda, Nordland, Norway **8** 67 38N 14 50 E
Foleyet, Canada **104** 48 15N 82 25W
Folgefonn, Norway **9** 60 3N 6 23 E
Foligno, Italy **27** 42 58N 12 40 E
Folkestone, U.K. **13** 51 5N 1 11 E
Folkston, U.S.A. **115** 30 55N 82 0W
Follett, U.S.A. **121** 36 30N 100 12W
Follette, La, U.S.A. **115** 36 23N 84 9W
Follónica, Italy **26** 42 55N 10 45 E
Follónica, G. di, Italy **26** 42 50N 10 40 E
Folsom Res., U.S.A. **124** 38 42N 121 9W
Fond-du-Lac, Canada **111** 59 19N 107 12W
Fond du Lac, U.S.A. **120** 43 46N 88 26W
Fond-du-Lac →, Canada **111** 59 17N 106 0W
Fonda, Iowa, U.S.A. **118** 42 35N 94 51W
Fonda, N.Y., U.S.A. **117** 42 57N 74 23W
Fondi, Italy **28** 41 21N 13 25 E
Fonfría, Spain **22** 41 37N 6 9W
Fongen, Norway **10** 63 11N 11 38 E
Fonni, Italy **28** 40 5N 9 16 E
Fonsagrada, Spain **22** 43 8N 7 4W
Fonseca, G. de, Cent. Amer. **128** 13 10N 87 40W
Fontaine, La, U.S.A. **119** 40 40N 85 43W
Fontaine-Française, France **19** 47 32N 5 21 E
Fontainebleau, France **19** 48 24N 2 40 E
Fontana, L., Argentina **142** 44 55 S 71 30W
Fontas →, Canada **110** 58 14N 121 48W
Fonte Boa, Brazil **134** 2 33 S 66 0W
Fontem, Cameroon **91** 5 32N 9 52 E
Fontenay-le-Comte, France **20** 46 28N 0 48W
Fontur, Iceland **8** 66 23N 14 32W
Fonuafo'ou, Tonga **68** 20 19 S 175 25W
Fonualei, Tonga **68** 18 1 S 174 19W
Fonyód, Hungary **33** 46 44N 17 33 E
Foochow = Fuzhou, China **59** 26 5N 119 16 E
Foping, China **60** 33 41N 108 0 E
Foppiano, Italy **26** 46 21N 8 24 E
Föra, Sweden **11** 57 1N 16 51 E
Forbach, France **19** 49 10N 6 52 E
Forbes, Australia **76** 33 22 S 148 0 E
Forbesganj, India **49** 26 17N 87 18 E
Forcados, Nigeria **91** 5 26N 5 26 E
Forcados →, Nigeria **91** 5 25N 5 19 E
Forcall →, Spain **24** 40 51N 0 16W
Forcalquier, France **21** 43 58N 5 47 E
Forchheim, W. Germany **31** 49 42N 11 4 E
Ford City, Calif., U.S.A. **125** 35 10N 119 27W
Ford City, Pa., U.S.A. **116** 40 47N 79 31W
Ford's Bridge, Australia **73** 29 41 S 145 29 E
Fordyce, U.S.A. **121** 33 50N 92 20W
Forécariah, Guinea **90** 9 28N 13 10W
Forel, Mt., Greenland **144** 66 52N 36 55W
Foremost, Canada **110** 49 26N 111 34W
Forenza, Italy **29** 40 50N 15 50 E
Forest, Belgium **17** 50 49N 4 20 E
Forest, Canada **108** 43 6N 82 0W
Forest, U.S.A. **121** 32 21N 89 27W
Forest City, Iowa, U.S.A. **120** 43 12N 93 39W
Forest City, N.C., U.S.A. **115** 35 23N 81 50W
Forest City, Pa., U.S.A. **117** 41 39N 75 29W
Forest Grove, U.S.A. **124** 45 31N 123 4W
Forestburg, Canada **110** 52 35N 112 1W
Foresthill, U.S.A. **124** 39 1N 120 49W
Forestier Pen., Australia **72** 43 0 S 148 0 E
Forestville, Canada **107** 48 48N 69 2W
Forestville, Calif., U.S.A. **124** 38 28N 122 54W
Forestville, Wis., U.S.A. **114** 44 41N 87 29W
Forez, Mts. du, France **20** 45 40N 3 50 E
Forfar, U.K. **14** 56 40N 2 53W
Forges-les-Eaux, France **19** 49 37N 1 30 E
Forks, U.S.A. **124** 47 56N 124 23W
Forlì, Italy **27** 44 14N 12 2 E
Forman, U.S.A. **120** 46 9N 97 43W
Formazza, Italy **26** 46 23N 8 26 E
Formby Pt., U.K. **12** 53 33N 3 7W
Formentera, Spain **25** 38 43N 1 27 E
Formentor, C. de, Spain **24** 39 58N 3 13 E
Fórmia, Italy **28** 41 15N 13 34 E
Formiga, Brazil **139** 20 27 S 45 25W
Formigine, Italy **26** 44 37N 10 51 E
Formiguères, France **20** 42 37N 2 5 E
Formosa = Taiwan ■, Asia **59** 23 30N 121 0 E
Formosa, Argentina **140** 26 15 S 58 10W
Formosa, Brazil **139** 15 32 S 47 20W
Formosa □, Argentina **140** 25 0 S 60 0W
Formosa, Serra, Brazil **137** 12 0 S 55 0W
Formosa Bay, Kenya **92** 2 40 S 40 20 E
Formoso →, Brazil **139** 10 34 S 49 56W
Fornells, Spain **24** 40 3N 4 7 E
Fornos de Algodres, Portugal **22** 40 38N 7 32W
Fornovo di Taro, Italy **26** 44 42N 10 7 E
Føroyar, Atl. Oc. **130** 62 0N 7 0W
Forres, U.K. **14** 57 37N 3 38W
Forrest, Vic., Australia **74** 38 33 S 143 47 E
Forrest, W. Austral., Australia **79** 30 51 S 128 6 E
Forrest, Mt., Australia **79** 24 48 S 127 45 E
Forrest City, U.S.A. **121** 35 0N 90 50W
Forreston, U.S.A. **118** 42 8N 89 35W
Forrières, Belgium **17** 50 8N 5 17 E
Fors, Sweden **10** 60 14N 16 20 E
Forsa, Sweden **10** 61 44N 16 55 E
Forsayth, Australia **72** 18 33 S 143 34 E
Forserum, Sweden **11** 57 42N 14 30 E
Forshaga, Sweden **10** 59 33N 13 29 E
Forskacka, Sweden **10** 60 39N 16 54 E
Forsmo, Sweden **10** 63 16N 17 11 E
Forst, E. Germany **30** 51 43N 14 37 E
Forster, Australia **77** 32 12 S 152 31 E
Forsyth, Ga., U.S.A. **115** 33 4N 83 55W
Forsyth, Mont., U.S.A. **122** 46 14N 106 37W
Forsyth I., N.Z. **81** 40 58 S 174 5 E
Forsythe, Canada **106** 48 14N 76 26W
Fort Albany, Canada **104** 52 15N 81 35W
Fort Apache, U.S.A. **123** 33 50N 110 0W
Fort Assiniboine, Canada **110** 54 20N 114 45W
Fort Atkinson, U.S.A. **119** 42 56N 88 50W
Fort Augustus, U.K. **14** 57 9N 4 40W
Fort Beaufort, S. Africa **96** 32 46 S 26 40 E
Fort Benton, U.S.A. **122** 47 50N 110 40W
Fort Bragg, U.S.A. **122** 39 28N 123 50W
Fort Bridger, U.S.A. **122** 41 22N 110 20W
Fort Chipewyan, Canada **111** 58 42N 111 8W
Fort Collins, U.S.A. **120** 40 30N 105 4W
Fort-Coulonge, Canada **106** 45 50N 76 45W
Fort Davis, U.S.A. **121** 30 38N 103 53W
Fort-de-France, Martinique **129** 14 36N 61 2W
Fort de Possel = Possel, C.A.R. **94** 5 5N 19 10 E
Fort Defiance, U.S.A. **123** 35 47N 109 4W
Fort Dodge, U.S.A. **120** 42 29N 94 10W
Fort Edward, U.S.A. **117** 43 16N 73 35W
Fort Frances, Canada **111** 48 36N 93 24W
Fort Franklin, Canada **102** 65 10N 123 30W
Fort Garland, U.S.A. **123** 37 28N 105 30W
Fort George, Canada **104** 53 50N 79 0W
Fort Good-Hope, Canada **102** 66 14N 128 40W
Fort Hancock, U.S.A. **123** 31 19N 105 56W
Fort Hertz = Putao, Burma **52** 27 28N 97 30 E
Fort Hope, Canada **104** 51 30N 88 0W
Fort Irwin, U.S.A. **125** 35 16N 116 34W
Fort Jameson = Chipata, Zambia **93** 13 38 S 32 28 E
Fort Kent, U.S.A. **105** 47 12N 68 30W
Fort Klamath, U.S.A. **122** 42 45N 122 0W
Fort Knox, U.S.A. **119** 37 54N 85 57W
Fort Lallemand, Algeria **85** 31 13N 6 17 E
Fort-Lamy = Ndjamena, Chad **87** 12 10N 14 59 E
Fort Laramie, U.S.A. **120** 42 15N 104 30W
Fort Lauderdale, U.S.A. **115** 26 10N 80 5W
Fort Leonard Wood, U.S.A. **118** 37 46N 92 11W
Fort Liard, Canada **110** 60 14N 123 30W
Fort Liberté, Haiti **129** 19 42N 71 51W
Fort Lupton, U.S.A. **120** 40 8N 104 48W
Fort Mackay, Canada **110** 57 12N 111 41W
Fort McKenzie, Canada **105** 57 20N 69 0W
Fort Macleod, Canada **110** 49 45N 113 30W
Fort MacMahon, Algeria **85** 29 43N 1 45 E
Fort McMurray, Canada **110** 56 44N 111 7W
Fort McPherson, Canada **102** 67 30N 134 55W
Fort Madison, U.S.A. **118** 40 39N 91 20W
Fort Meade, U.S.A. **115** 27 45N 81 45W
Fort Miribel, Algeria **85** 29 25N 2 55 E
Fort Morgan, U.S.A. **120** 40 10N 103 50W
Fort Myers, U.S.A. **115** 26 39N 81 51W
Fort Nelson, Canada **110** 58 50N 122 44W
Fort Nelson →, Canada **110** 59 32N 124 0W
Fort Norman, Canada **102** 64 57N 125 30W
Fort Payne, U.S.A. **115** 34 25N 85 44W
Fort Peck, U.S.A. **122** 48 1N 106 30W
Fort Peck Dam, U.S.A. **122** 48 0N 106 38W
Fort Peck L., U.S.A. **122** 47 40N 107 0W
Fort Pierce, U.S.A. **115** 27 29N 80 19W
Fort Pierre, U.S.A. **120** 44 25N 100 25W
Fort Pierre Bordes = Ti-n-Zaouatène, Algeria **85** 20 0N 2 55 E
Fort Plain, U.S.A. **117** 42 56N 74 39W
Fort Portal, Uganda **92** 0 40N 30 20 E
Fort Providence, Canada **110** 61 3N 117 40W
Fort Qu'Appelle, Canada **111** 50 45N 103 50W
Fort Recovery, U.S.A. **119** 40 25N 84 47W
Fort Resolution, Canada **110** 61 10N 113 40W
Fort Rixon, Zimb. **93** 20 2 S 29 17 E
Fort Roseberry = Mansa, Zambia **93** 11 13 S 28 55 E
Fort Ross, U.S.A. **124** 38 32N 123 13W
Fort Rousset = Owando, Congo **94** 0 29 S 15 55 E
Fort Rupert, Canada **104** 51 30N 78 40W
Fort Saint, Tunisia **86** 30 19N 9 31 E
Fort St. James, Canada **110** 54 30N 124 10W
Fort St. John, Canada **110** 56 15N 120 50W
Fort Sandeman, Pakistan **48** 31 20N 69 31 E
Fort Saskatchewan, Canada **110** 53 40N 113 15W
Fort Scott, U.S.A. **121** 37 50N 94 40W
Fort Severn, Canada **104** 56 0N 87 40W
Fort Shevchenko, U.S.S.R. **39** 43 40N 51 20 E
Fort-Sibut, C.A.R. **94** 5 46N 19 10 E
Fort Simpson, Canada **110** 61 45N 121 15W
Fort Smith, Canada **110** 60 0N 111 51W
Fort Smith, U.S.A. **121** 35 25N 94 25W
Fort Stanton, U.S.A. **123** 33 33N 105 36W
Fort Stockton, U.S.A. **121** 30 54N 102 54W
Fort Sumner, U.S.A. **121** 34 24N 104 16W
Fort Thomas, U.S.A. **119** 39 5N 84 27W
Fort Trinquet = Bir Mogrein, Mauritania **84** 25 10N 11 25W
Fort Valley, U.S.A. **115** 32 33N 83 52W
Fort Vermilion, Canada **110** 58 24N 116 0W
Fort Walton Beach, U.S.A. **115** 30 25N 86 40W
Fort Wayne, U.S.A. **119** 41 5N 85 10W
Fort William, U.K. **14** 56 48N 5 8W
Fort Worth, U.S.A. **121** 32 45N 97 25W
Fort Yates, U.S.A. **120** 46 8N 100 38W
Fort Yukon, U.S.A. **102** 66 35N 145 20W
Fortaleza, Bolivia **136** 12 6 S 66 49W
Fortaleza, Brazil **138** 3 45 S 38 35W
Forteau, Canada **105** 51 28N 56 58W
Forth, Firth of, U.K. **14** 56 5N 2 55W
Forthassa Rharbia, Algeria **85** 32 52N 1 18W
Fortín Coronel Eugenio Garay, Paraguay **137** 20 31 S 62 8W
Fortín Garrapatal, Paraguay **137** 21 27 S 61 30W
Fortín General Pando, Paraguay **137** 19 45 S 59 47W
Fortín Madrejón, Paraguay **137** 20 45 S 59 52W
Fortín Uno, Argentina **142** 38 50 S 65 18W
Fortore →, Italy **27** 41 55N 15 17 E
Fortrose, N.Z. **81** 46 38 S 168 45 E
Fortrose, U.K. **14** 57 35N 4 10W
Fortuna, Spain **25** 38 11N 1 7W
Fortuna, Calif., U.S.A. **122** 40 38N 124 8W

Fortuna, N. Dak., U.S.A. 120 48 55N 103 48W
Fortune B., Canada 105 47 30N 55 22W
Forūr, Iran 47 26 20N 54 30 E
Fos-sur-Mer, France 21 43 26N 4 56 E
Foshan, China 59 23 4N 113 5 E
Fossacesia, Italy 27 42 15N 14 30 E
Fossano, Italy 26 44 33N 7 40 E
Fosses-la-Ville, Belgium 17 50 24N 4 41 E
Fossil, U.S.A. 122 45 0N 120 9W
Fossilbrook, Australia 72 17 47 S 144 29 E
Fossombrone, Italy 27 43 41N 12 49 E
Fosston, U.S.A. 120 47 33N 95 39W
Foster, Australia 75 38 40 S 146 15 E
Foster, Canada 117 45 17N 72 30W
Foster, U.S.A. 119 38 48N 84 13W
Foster →, Canada 111 55 47N 105 49W
Fosters Ra., Australia 72 21 35 S 133 48 E
Fostoria, U.S.A. 119 41 8N 83 25W
Fotuha'a, Tonga 68 19 49 S 174 44W
Fougamou, Gabon 94 1 16 S 10 30 E
Fougères, France 18 48 21N 1 14W
Foul Pt., Sri Lanka 51 8 35N 81 18 E
Foulness I., U.K. 13 51 36N 0 55 E
Foulpointe, Madag. 97 17 41 S 49 31 E
Foum Assaka, Morocco 84 29 8N 10 24W
Foum Zguid, Morocco 84 30 2N 6 59W
Foumban, Cameroon 91 5 45N 10 50 E
Foundiougne, Senegal 90 14 5N 16 32W
Fountain, Colo., U.S.A. 120 38 42N 104 40W
Fountain, Utah, U.S.A. 122 39 41N 111 37W
Fountain Springs, U.S.A. 125 35 54N 118 51W
Fourchambault, France 19 47 0N 3 3 E
Fourchu, Canada 105 45 43N 60 17W
Fouriesburg, S. Africa 96 28 38 S 28 14 E
Fourmies, France 19 50 1N 4 2 E
Foúrnoi, Greece 35 37 36N 26 32 E
Fours, France 19 46 50N 3 42 E
Fouta Djalon, Guinea 90 11 20N 12 10W
Foux, Cap-à-, Haiti 129 19 43N 73 27W
Foveaux Str., N.Z. 81 46 42 S 168 10 E
Fowey, U.K. 13 50 20N 4 39W
Fowler, Calif., U.S.A. 124 36 41N 119 41W
Fowler, Colo., U.S.A. 120 38 10N 104 0W
Fowler, Ind., U.S.A. 119 40 37N 87 19W
Fowler, Kans., U.S.A. 121 37 28N 100 7W
Fowler, Mich., U.S.A. 119 43 0N 84 45W
Fowlers B., Australia 79 31 59 S 132 34 E
Fowlerton, U.S.A. 121 28 26N 98 50W
Fowlerville, U.S.A. 119 42 40N 84 4W
Fox →, Canada 111 56 3N 93 18W
Fox Valley, Canada 111 50 30N 109 25W
Foxe Basin, Canada 103 66 0N 77 0W
Foxe Chan., Canada 103 65 0N 80 0W
Foxe Pen., Canada 103 65 0N 76 0W
Foxen, Sweden 10 59 25N 11 55 E
Foxhol, Neths. 16 53 10N 6 43 E
Foxpark, U.S.A. 122 41 4N 106 6W
Foxton, N.Z. 80 40 29 S 175 18 E
Foyle, Lough, U.K. 15 55 6N 7 8W
Foynes, Ireland 15 52 37N 9 5W
Foz, Spain 22 43 33N 7 20W
Fóz do Cunene, Angola 95 17 15 S 11 48 E
Foz do Gregório, Brazil 136 6 47 S 70 44W
Foz do Iguaçu, Brazil 141 25 30 S 54 30W
Foz do Riosinho, Brazil 136 7 11 S 71 50W
Frackville, U.S.A. 117 40 46N 76 15W
Fraga, Spain 24 41 32N 0 21 E
Fraire, Belgium 17 50 16N 4 31 E
Frameries, Belgium 17 50 24N 3 54 E
Framingham, U.S.A. 117 42 18N 71 26W
Franca, Brazil 139 20 33 S 47 30W
Francavilla al Mare, Italy 27 42 25N 14 16 E
Francavilla Fontana, Italy 29 40 32N 17 35 E
France ■, Europe 18 47 0N 3 0 E
Frances, Australia 73 36 41 S 140 55 E
Frances →, Canada 110 60 16N 129 10W
Frances L., Canada 110 61 23N 129 30W
Francés Viejo, C., Dom. Rep. 129 19 40N 70 0W
Francesville, U.S.A. 119 40 59N 86 53W
Franceville, Gabon 94 1 40 S 13 32 E
Franche-Comté, France 19 46 50N 5 55 E
Francisco de Orellana, Ecuador 134 0 28 S 76 58W
Francisco I. Madero, Coahuila, Mexico 126 25 48N 103 18W
Francisco I. Madero, Durango, Mexico 126 24 32N 104 22W
Francisco Sá, Brazil 139 16 28 S 43 30W
Francistown, Botswana 97 21 7 S 27 33 E
Francofonte, Italy 29 37 13N 14 50 E
François, Canada 105 47 35N 56 45W
François, Martinique 129 14 38N 60 57W
François L., Canada 110 54 0N 125 30W
Francorchamps, Belgium 17 50 27N 5 57 E
Franeker, Neths. 16 53 12N 5 33 E
Frankado, Djibouti 89 12 30N 43 12 E
Frankenberg, W. Germany 30 51 3N 8 47 E
Frankenthal, W. Germany 31 49 32N 8 21 E
Frankenwald, W. Germany 31 50 18N 11 36 E
Frankford, Canada 109 44 12N 77 36W
Frankford, U.S.A. 118 39 29N 91 19W
Frankfort, S. Africa 97 27 17 S 28 30 E
Frankfort, Ind., U.S.A. 119 40 20N 86 33W
Frankfort, Kans., U.S.A. 120 39 42N 96 26W
Frankfort, Ky., U.S.A. 119 38 12N 84 52W
Frankfort, Mich., U.S.A. 114 44 38N 86 14W
Frankfort, Ohio, U.S.A. 119 39 24N 83 11W
Frankfurt □, E. Germany 30 52 30N 14 0 E
Frankfurt am Main, W. Germany 31 50 7N 8 40 E
Frankfurt an der Oder, E. Germany 30 52 20N 14 31 E
Fränkische Alb, W. Germany 31 49 20N 11 30 E
Fränkische Rezal →, W. Germany 31 49 11N 11 1 E
Fränkische Saale →, W. Germany 31 50 30N 9 42 E
Fränkische Schweiz, W. Germany 31 49 45N 11 10 E
Frankland →, Australia 79 35 0 S 116 48 E
Franklin, Ill., U.S.A. 118 39 37N 90 3W
Franklin, Ind., U.S.A. 119 39 29N 86 3W
Franklin, Ky., U.S.A. 115 36 40N 86 30W
Franklin, La., U.S.A. 121 29 45N 91 30W
Franklin, Mass., U.S.A. 117 42 4N 71 23W
Franklin, N.H., U.S.A. 117 43 28N 71 39W
Franklin, Nebr., U.S.A. 120 40 9N 98 55W
Franklin, Ohio, U.S.A. 119 39 34N 84 18W
Franklin, Pa., U.S.A. 116 41 22N 79 45W
Franklin, Tenn., U.S.A. 115 35 54N 86 53W
Franklin, Va., U.S.A. 115 36 40N 76 58W
Franklin, W. Va., U.S.A. 114 38 38N 79 21W
Franklin, L., U.S.A. 122 40 20N 115 26W
Franklin B., Canada 102 69 45N 126 0W
Franklin D. Roosevelt L., U.S.A. 122 48 30N 118 16W
Franklin I., Antarctica 143 76 10 S 168 30 E
Franklin Mts., Canada 102 65 0N 125 0W
Franklin Mts., N.Z. 81 44 55 S 167 45 E
Franklin Str., Canada 102 72 0N 96 0W
Franklinton, U.S.A. 121 30 53N 90 10W
Franklinville, U.S.A. 116 42 21N 78 28W
Franklyn Mt., N.Z. 81 42 4 S 172 42 E
Franks Peak, U.S.A. 122 43 50N 109 5W
Frankston, Australia 74 38 8 S 145 8 E
Frankton Junc., N.Z. 80 37 47 S 175 16 E
Fränsta, Sweden 10 62 30N 16 11 E
Frantsa Iosifa, Zemlya, U.S.S.R. 40 82 0N 55 0 E
Franz, Canada 104 48 25N 84 30W
Franz Josef Land = Frantsa Iosifa, Zemlya, U.S.S.R. 40 82 0N 55 0 E
Franzburg, E. Germany 30 54 9N 12 52 E
Frascati, Italy 28 41 48N 12 41 E
Fraser →, B.C., Canada 110 49 7N 123 11W
Fraser →, Nfld., Canada 105 56 39N 62 10W
Fraser, Mt., Australia 79 25 35 S 118 20 E
Fraser I., Australia 73 25 15 S 153 10 E
Fraser Lake, Canada 110 54 0N 124 50W
Fraserburg, S. Africa 96 31 55 S 21 30 E
Fraserburgh, U.K. 14 57 41N 2 0W
Fraserdale, Canada 104 49 55N 81 37W
Frasertown, N.Z. 80 38 58 S 177 28 E
Frasne, France 19 46 50N 6 10 E
Frauenfeld, Switz. 31 47 34N 8 54 E
Fray Bentos, Uruguay 140 33 10 S 58 15W
Frazier Downs, Australia 78 18 48 S 121 42 E
Frechilla, Spain 22 42 8N 4 50W
Fredericia, Denmark 11 55 34N 9 45 E
Frederick, Md., U.S.A. 114 39 25N 77 23W
Frederick, Okla., U.S.A. 121 34 22N 99 0W
Frederick, S. Dak., U.S.A. 120 45 55N 98 29W
Frederick Sd., U.S.A. 110 57 10N 134 0W
Fredericksburg, Tex., U.S.A. 121 30 17N 98 55W
Fredericksburg, Va., U.S.A. 114 38 16N 77 29W
Frederickstown, U.S.A. 121 37 35N 90 15W
Frederickton, Australia 77 31 0 S 152 53 E
Frederico I. Madero, Presa, Mexico 126 28 7N 105 40W
Fredericton, Canada 105 45 57N 66 40W
Fredericton Junc., Canada 105 45 41N 66 40W
Frederikshavn, Denmark 11 57 28N 10 31 E
Frederikssund, Denmark 11 55 50N 12 3 E
Frederiksted, Virgin Is. 129 17 43N 64 53W
Fredonia, Ariz., U.S.A. 123 36 59N 112 36W
Fredonia, Kans., U.S.A. 121 37 34N 95 50W
Fredonia, N.Y., U.S.A. 116 42 26N 79 20W
Fredrikstad, Norway 10 59 13N 10 57 E
Freeburg, U.S.A. 118 38 19N 91 56W
Freehold, U.S.A. 117 40 15N 74 18W
Freel Pk., U.S.A. 124 38 52N 119 53W
Freeland, U.S.A. 117 41 3N 75 48W
Freels, C., Canada 105 49 15N 53 30W
Freeman, Calif., U.S.A. 125 35 35N 117 53W
Freeman, Mo., U.S.A. 118 38 37N 94 30W
Freeman, S. Dak., U.S.A. 120 43 25N 97 20W
Freeport, Bahamas 128 26 30N 78 47W
Freeport, Canada 105 44 15N 66 20W
Freeport, Ill., U.S.A. 118 42 18N 89 40W
Freeport, N.Y., U.S.A. 117 40 39N 73 35W
Freeport, Tex., U.S.A. 121 28 55N 95 22W
Freetown, S. Leone 90 8 30N 13 17W
Frégate, L., Canada 104 53 15N 74 45W
Fregenal de la Sierra, Spain 23 38 10N 6 39W
Fregene, Italy 28 41 50N 12 12 E
Fregeneda, La, Spain 22 40 58N 6 54W
Fréhel, C., France 18 48 40N 2 20W
Freiberg, E. Germany 30 50 55N 13 20 E
Freibourg = Fribourg, Switz. 31 46 49N 7 9 E
Freiburg, Baden-W., W. Germany 31 48 0N 7 52 E
Freiburg, Niedersachsen, W. Germany 30 53 49N 9 17 E
Freire, Chile 142 38 54 S 72 38W
Freirina, Chile 140 28 30 S 71 10W
Freising, W. Germany 31 48 24N 11 47 E
Freistadt, Austria 32 48 30N 14 30 E
Freital, E. Germany 30 51 0N 13 40 E
Fréjus, France 21 43 25N 6 44 E
Fremantle, Australia 79 32 7 S 115 47 E
Fremont, Calif., U.S.A. 124 37 32N 122 1W
Fremont, Ind., U.S.A. 119 41 44N 84 56W
Fremont, Mich., U.S.A. 114 43 29N 85 59W
Fremont, Nebr., U.S.A. 120 41 30N 96 30W
Fremont, Ohio, U.S.A. 119 41 20N 83 5W
Fremont →, U.S.A. 123 38 15N 110 20W
Fremont, L., U.S.A. 122 43 0N 109 50W
French →, Canada 108 46 2N 80 34W
French Camp, U.S.A. 124 37 53N 121 16W
French Cr. →, U.S.A. 116 41 22N 79 50W
French Guiana ■, S. Amer. 135 4 0N 53 0W
French I., Australia 74 38 20 S 145 22 E
French Lick, U.S.A. 119 38 33N 86 37W
French Polynesia □, Pac. Oc. 67 20 0 S 145 0 E
French River, Canada 108 46 2N 80 34W
French Terr. of Afars & Issas = Djibouti ■, Africa 89 12 0N 43 0 E
Frenchburg, U.S.A. 119 37 57N 83 38W
Frenchglen, U.S.A. 122 42 48N 119 0W
Frenchman →, N. Amer. 122 48 24N 107 5W
Frenchman Butte, Canada 111 53 35N 109 38W
Frenchman Creek →, U.S.A. 120 40 13N 100 50W
Frenda, Algeria 85 35 2N 1 1 E
Fresco →, Brazil 137 7 15 S 51 30W
Freshfield, C., Antarctica 143 68 25 S 151 10 E
Fresnay-sur-Sarthe, France 18 48 17N 0 1 E
Fresnillo, Mexico 126 23 10N 103 0W
Fresno, U.S.A. 124 36 47N 119 50W
Fresno Alhandiga, Spain 22 40 42N 5 37W
Fresno Res., U.S.A. 122 48 40N 110 0W
Freudenstadt, W. Germany 31 48 27N 8 25 E
Freux, Belgium 17 49 59N 5 27 E
Frévent, France 19 50 15N 2 17 E
Frew →, Australia 72 20 0 S 135 38 E
Frewena, Australia 72 19 25 S 135 25 E
Freycinet Pen., Australia 72 42 10 S 148 25 E
Freyming-Merlebach, France 19 49 8N 6 48 E
Freyung, W. Germany 31 48 48N 13 33 E
Fria, Guinea 90 10 27N 13 38W
Fria, C., Namibia 96 18 0 S 12 0 E
Fría, La, Venezuela 134 8 13N 72 15W
Friant, U.S.A. 124 36 59N 119 43W
Frías, Argentina 140 28 40 S 65 5W
Fribourg, Switz. 31 46 49N 7 9 E
Fribourg □, Switz. 31 46 40N 7 0 E
Fridafors, Sweden 11 56 25N 14 39 E
Friday Harbor, U.S.A. 124 48 32N 123 1W
Friedberg, Bayern, W. Germany 31 48 21N 10 59 E
Friedberg, Hessen, W. Germany 31 50 21N 8 46 E
Friedland, E. Germany 30 53 40N 13 33 E
Friedrichshafen, W. Germany 31 47 39N 9 29 E
Friedrichskoog, W. Germany 30 54 1N 8 52 E
Friedrichsort, W. Germany 30 54 24N 10 11 E
Friedrichstadt, W. Germany 30 54 23N 9 6 E
Friendly Is. = Tonga ■, Pac. Oc. 68 19 50 S 174 30W
Friesack, E. Germany 30 52 43N 12 35 E
Friesche Wad, Neths. 16 53 22N 5 44 E
Friesland □, Neths. 16 53 5N 5 50 E
Friesoythe, W. Germany 30 53 1N 7 51 E
Frillesås, Sweden 11 57 20N 12 12 E
Frinnaryd, Sweden 11 57 55N 14 50 E
Frio →, U.S.A. 121 28 30N 98 10W
Friona, U.S.A. 121 34 40N 102 42W
Frisian Is., Europe 30 53 30N 6 0 E
Fristad, Sweden 11 57 50N 13 0 E
Fritch, U.S.A. 121 35 40N 101 35W
Fritsla, Sweden 11 57 33N 12 47 E
Fritzlar, W. Germany 30 51 8N 9 19 E
Friuli-Venezia Giulia □, Italy 27 46 0N 13 0 E
Frobisher B., Canada 103 62 30N 66 0W
Frobisher Bay, Canada 103 63 44N 68 31W
Frobisher L., Canada 111 56 20N 108 15W
Frogmore, Australia 76 34 15 S 148 52 E
Frohavet, Norway 8 63 50N 9 35 E
Froid, U.S.A. 120 48 20N 104 29W
Froid-Chapelle, Belgium 17 50 9N 4 19 E
Frolovo, U.S.S.R. 39 49 45N 43 40 E
Fromberg, U.S.A. 122 42 25N 108 58W
Frome, U.K. 13 51 16N 2 17W
Frome, L., Australia 73 30 45 S 139 45 E
Frome Downs, Australia 73 31 13 S 139 45 E
Frómista, Spain 22 42 16N 4 25W
Front Range, U.S.A. 122 40 0N 105 40W
Front Royal, U.S.A. 114 38 55N 78 10W
Fronteira, Portugal 23 39 3N 7 39W
Fronteiras, Brazil 138 7 5 S 40 37W
Frontera, Canary Is. 25 27 47N 17 59W
Frontera, Mexico 127 18 30N 92 40W
Frontignan, France 20 43 27N 3 45 E
Frosinone, Italy 28 41 38N 13 20 E
Frosolone, Italy 29 41 34N 14 27 E
Frostburg, U.S.A. 114 39 43N 78 57W
Frostisen, Norway 8 68 14N 17 10 E
Frouard, France 19 48 47N 6 8 E
Frövi, Sweden 10 59 28N 15 24 E
Frøya, Norway 8 63 43N 8 40 E
Fruges, France 19 50 30N 2 8 E
Frumoasa, Romania 34 46 28N 25 48 E
Frunze, U.S.S.R. 40 42 54N 74 46 E
Frutal, Brazil 139 20 0 S 49 0W
Frutigen, Switz. 31 46 35N 7 38 E
Frýdek-Místek, Czech. 32 49 40N 18 20 E
Frýdlant, Czech. 32 50 56N 15 9 E
Fryvaldov = Jeseník, Czech. 32 50 0N 17 8 E
Fu Jiang →, China 58 30 0N 106 16 E
Fu Xian, Liaoning, China 61 39 38N 121 58 E
Fu Xian, Shaanxi, China 60 36 0N 109 20 E
Fu'an, China 59 27 11N 119 36 E
Fubian, China 58 31 17N 102 22 E
Fucécchio, Italy 26 43 44N 10 51 E
Fucheng, China 60 37 50N 116 10 E
Fuchou = Fuzhou, China 59 26 5N 119 16 E
Fuchū, Hiroshima, Japan 64 34 34N 133 14 E
Fūchū, Tōkyō, Japan 65 35 40N 139 29 E
Fuchuan, China 59 24 50N 111 5 E
Fuchun Jiang →, China 59 30 5N 120 5 E
Fúcino, Conca del, Italy 27 42 1N 13 31 E
Fuding, China 59 27 20N 120 12 E
Fuencaliente, Canary Is. 25 28 28N 17 50W
Fuencaliente, Spain 23 38 25N 4 18W
Fuencaliente, Pta., Canary Is. 25 28 27N 17 51W
Fuengirola, Spain 23 36 32N 4 41W
Fuente Alamo, Albacete, Spain 25 38 44N 1 24W
Fuente Álamo, Murcia, Spain 25 37 42N 1 6W
Fuente de Cantos, Spain 23 38 15N 6 18W
Fuente de San Esteban, La, Spain 22 40 49N 6 15W
Fuente del Maestre, Spain 23 38 31N 6 28W
Fuente el Fresno, Spain 23 39 14N 3 46W
Fuente Ovejuna, Spain 23 38 15N 5 25W
Fuentes de Andalucía, Spain 23 37 28N 5 20W
Fuentes de Ebro, Spain 24 41 31N 0 38W
Fuentes de León, Spain 23 38 5N 6 32W
Fuentes de Oñoro, Spain 22 40 33N 6 52W
Fuentesaúco, Spain 22 41 15N 5 30W
Fuerte →, Mexico 126 25 50N 109 25W
Fuerte Olimpo, Paraguay 140 21 0 S 57 51W
Fuerteventura, Canary Is. 25 28 30N 14 0W
Fufeng, China 60 34 22N 108 0 E
Fugløysund, Norway 8 70 15N 20 20 E
Fugong, China 58 27 5N 98 47 E
Fugou, China 60 34 3N 114 25 E
Fugu, China 60 39 2N 111 3 E
Fuhai, China 62 47 2N 87 25 E
Fuji, Japan 65 35 9N 138 39 E
Fuji-no-miya, Japan 65 35 10N 138 40 E
Fuji-San, Japan 65 35 22N 138 44 E
Fuji-yoshida, Japan 65 35 30N 138 46 E
Fujian □, China 59 26 0N 118 0 E
Fujieda, Japan 65 34 52N 138 16 E
Fujioka, Japan 65 36 15N 139 5 E
Fujisawa, Japan 65 35 22N 139 29 E
Fukaya, Japan 65 36 12N 139 12 E
Fukien = Fujian □, China 59 26 0N 118 0 E
Fukuchiyama, Japan 65 35 19N 135 9 E
Fukue-Shima, Japan 63 32 40N 128 45 E
Fukui, Japan 65 36 0N 136 10 E
Fukui □, Japan 65 36 0N 136 12 E
Fukuma, Japan 64 33 46N 130 28 E
Fukuoka, Japan 64 33 39N 130 21 E
Fukuoka □, Japan 64 33 30N 131 0 E

Fukuroi, *Japan* .... **65** 34 45N 137 55 E
Fukushima, *Japan* .... **63** 37 44N 140 28 E
Fukuyama, *Japan* .... **64** 34 35N 133 20 E
Fulda, *W. Germany* .. **30** 50 32N 9 41 E
Fulda →, *W. Germany* **30** 51 27N 9 40 E
Fuling, *China* .... **58** 29 40N 107 20 E
Fullerton, *Calif.*,
U.S.A. **125** 33 52N 117 58W
Fullerton, *Nebr.*,
U.S.A. **120** 41 25N 98 0W
Fulongquan, *China* ... **61** 44 20N 124 42 E
Fulton, *Ill., U.S.A.* ... **118** 41 52N 90 11W
Fulton, *Ind., U.S.A.* .. **119** 40 57N 86 16W
Fulton, *Mo., U.S.A.* .. **118** 38 50N 91 55W
Fulton, *N.Y., U.S.A.* . **117** 43 20N 76 22W
Fulton, *Tenn., U.S.A.* **115** 36 31N 88 53W
Fuluälven, *Sweden* .... **10** 61 18N 13 4 E
Fulufjället, *Sweden* ... **10** 61 32N 12 41 E
Fumay, *France* .... **19** 50 0N 4 40 E
Fumel, *France* .... **20** 44 30N 0 58 E
Fumin, *China* .... **58** 25 10N 102 20 E
Funabashi, *Japan* ..... **65** 35 45N 140 0 E
Funafuti, *Pac. Oc.* .... **66** 8 30 S 179 0 E
Fundación, *Colombia* . **134** 10 31N 74 11W
Fundão, *Brazil* .... **139** 19 55 S 40 24W
Fundão, *Portugal* **22** 40 8N 7 30W
Fundy, B. of, *Canada* . **105** 45 0N 66 0W
Funing, *Hebei, China* . **61** 39 53N 119 12 E
Funing, *Jiangsu, China* **61** 33 45N 119 50 E
Funing, *Yunnan, China* **58** 23 35N 105 45 E
Funiu Shan, *China* ... **60** 33 30N 112 20 E
Funsi, *Ghana* **90** 10 21N 1 54W
Funtua, *Nigeria* ...... **91** 11 30N 7 18 E
Fuping, *Hebei, China* . **60** 38 48N 114 12 E
Fuping, *Shaanxi, China* **60** 34 42N 109 10 E
Fuqing, *China* .... **59** 25 41N 119 21 E
Fuquan, *China* .... **58** 26 40N 107 27 E
Fur, *Denmark* .... **11** 56 50N 9 0 E
Furāt, Nahr al →, *Asia* **46** 31 0N 47 25 E
Furmanov, *U.S.S.R.* .. **37** 57 10N 41 9 E
Furmanovo, *U.S.S.R.* . **39** 49 42N 49 25 E
Furnas, Reprêsa de,
Brazil .... **139** 20 50 S 45 0W
Furneaux Group,
Australia .... **72** 40 10 S 147 50 E
Furness, *U.K.* **12** 54 12N 3 10W
Fürstenau, *W. Germany* **30** 52 32N 7 40 E
Fürstenberg,
E. Germany .... **30** 53 11N 13 9 E
Fürstenfeld, *Austria* .. **33** 47 3N 16 3 E
Fürstenfeldbruck,
W. Germany .... **31** 48 10N 11 15 E
Fürstenwalde,
E. Germany .... **30** 52 20N 14 3 E
Fürth, *W. Germany* ... **31** 49 29N 11 0 E
Furth im Wald,
W. Germany .... **31** 49 19N 12 51 E
Furtwangen,
W. Germany .... **31** 48 3N 8 14 E
Furudal, *Sweden* ..... **10** 61 10N 15 11 E
Furukawa, *Japan* ..... **65** 38 34N 140 58 E
Furusund, *Sweden* .... **10** 59 40N 18 55 E
Fury and Hecla Str.,
Canada **103** 69 56N 84 0W
Fusagasuga, *Colombia* **134** 4 21N 74 22W
Fuscaldo, *Italy* .... **29** 39 25N 16 1 E
Fushan, *Shandong,*
China .... **61** 37 30N 121 15 E
Fushan, *Shanxi, China* **60** 35 58N 111 51 E
Fushun, *Liaoning,*
China .... **61** 41 50N 123 56 E
Fushun, *Sichuan, China* **58** 29 13N 104 52 E
Fusong, *China* .... **61** 42 20N 127 15 E
Füssen, *W. Germany* . **31** 47 35N 10 43 E
Fusui, *China* .... **58** 22 40N 107 56 E
Futago-Yama, *Japan* .. **64** 33 35N 131 36 E
Futrono, *Chile* .... **142** 40 8 S 72 24W
Futuna, *Wall. & F. Is.* **66** 14 25 S 178 20 E
Fuwa, *Egypt* .... **88** 31 12N 30 33 E
Fuxin, *China* .... **61** 42 5N 121 48 E
Fuyang, *Anhui, China* **60** 33 0N 115 48 E
Fuyang, *Zhejiang,*
China .... **59** 30 5N 119 57 E
Fuyang He →, *China* . **60** 38 12N 117 0 E
Fuying Dao, *China* ... **59** 26 34N 120 9 E
Fuyu, *China* .... **61** 45 12N 124 43 E
Fuyuan, *Heilongjiang,*
China .... **62** 48 20N 134 5 E
Fuyuan, *Yunnan, China* **58** 25 40N 104 16 E
Fuzhou, *China* .... **59** 26 5N 119 16 E
Fylde, *U.K.* **12** 53 50N 2 58W
Fyn, *Denmark* .... **11** 55 20N 10 30 E
Fyne, L., *U.K.* **14** 56 0N 5 20W
Fyns Amtskommune □,
Denmark .... **11** 55 15N 10 30 E
Fyresvatn, *Norway* ... **10** 59 6N 8 10 E

G

Gaanda, *Nigeria* ...... **91** 10 10N 12 27 E
Gabarin, *Nigeria* ..... **91** 11 8N 10 27 E
Gabas →, *France* **20** 43 46N 0 42W
Gabela, *Angola* ...... **95** 11 0 S 14 24 E
Gabès, *Tunisia* ...... **86** 33 53N 10 2 E
Gabès, G. de, *Tunisia* **86** 34 0N 10 30 E
Gabgaba, W. →, *Egypt* **88** 22 10N 33 5 E
Gabo I., *Australia* .... **75** 37 33 S 149 57 E
Gabon ■, *Africa* ..... **94** 0 10 S 10 0 E
Gaborone, *Botswana* . **96** 24 45 S 25 57 E
Gabriels, *U.S.A.* **117** 44 26N 74 12W
Gabro, *Ethiopia* ...... **98** 6 18N 43 16 E
Gabrovo, *Bulgaria* .... **34** 42 52N 25 19 E
Gacé, *France* .... **18** 48 49N 0 20 E
Gachsārān, *Iran* ...... **47** 30 15N 50 45 E
Gacko, *Yugoslavia* ... **33** 43 10N 18 33 E
Gadag, *India* .... **51** 15 30N 75 45 E
Gadamai, *Sudan* ..... **89** 17 11N 36 10 E
Gadap, *Pakistan* ..... **48** 25 5N 67 28 E
Gadarwara, *India* .... **49** 22 50N 78 50 E
Gadebusch,
E. Germany .... **30** 53 41N 11 6 E
Gadein, *Sudan* .... **89** 8 10N 28 45 E
Gadhada, *India* ...... **48** 22 0N 71 35 E
Gádor, Sierra de, *Spain* **25** 36 57N 2 45W
Gadsden, *Ala., U.S.A.* **115** 34 1N 86 0W
Gadsden, *Ariz., U.S.A.* **123** 32 35N 114 47W
Gadwal, *India* .... **51** 16 10N 77 50 E
Gadyach, *U.S.S.R.* ... **36** 50 21N 34 0 E
Gadzi, *C.A.R.* .... **94** 4 47N 16 42 E
Găeşti, *Romania* ..... **34** 44 48N 25 19 E
Gaeta, *Italy* .... **28** 41 12N 13 35 E
Gaeta, G. di, *Italy* .... **28** 41 0N 13 25 E
Gaffney, *U.S.A.* **115** 35 3N 81 40W
Gafsa, *Tunisia* .... **86** 34 24N 8 43 E
Gagarin, *U.S.S.R.* ... **36** 55 38N 35 0 E
Gagetown, *Canada* ... **105** 45 46N 66 10W
Gagino, *U.S.S.R.* .... **37** 55 15N 45 1 E
Gagliano del Capo,
Italy .... **29** 39 50N 18 23 E
Gagnef, *Sweden* ..... **10** 60 36N 15 5 E
Gagnoa, *Ivory C.* **90** 6 56N 5 16W
Gagnon, *Canada* **105** 51 50N 68 5W
Gagnon, L., *N.W.T.*,
Canada **111** 62 3N 110 27W
Gagnon, L., *Qué.*,
Canada **106** 46 7N 75 7W
Gagra, *U.S.S.R.* ..... **39** 43 20N 40 10 E
Gahini, *Rwanda* ..... **92** 1 50 S 30 30 E
Gahmar, *India* ...... **49** 25 27N 83 49 E
Gai Xian, *China* ..... **61** 40 22N 122 20 E
Gaibanda, *Bangla.* ... **52** 25 20N 89 36 E
Gail, *U.S.A.* **121** 32 48N 101 25W
Gail →, *Austria* ..... **33** 46 36N 13 53 E
Gaillac, *France* ...... **20** 43 54N 1 54 E
Gaillon, *France* ...... **18** 49 10N 1 20 E
Gaima, *Papua N. G.* . **69** 8 20 S 142 59 E
Gaimán, *Argentina* ... **142** 43 10 S 65 25W
Gaines, *U.S.A.* **116** 41 46N 77 35W
Gainesville, *Fla.*,
U.S.A. **115** 29 38N 82 20W
Gainesville, *Ga.*,
U.S.A. **115** 34 17N 83 47W
Gainesville, *Mo.*,
U.S.A. **121** 36 35N 92 26W
Gainesville, *Tex.*,
U.S.A. **121** 33 40N 97 10W
Gainsborough, *U.K.* .. **12** 53 23N 0 46W
Gairdner L., *Australia* **73** 31 30 S 136 0 E
Gairloch, L., *U.K.* ... **14** 57 43N 5 45W
Gakuch, *Pakistan* .... **49** 36 7N 73 45 E
Gal Laghet,
Somali Rep. .... **98** 4 9N 47 10 E
Gal Oya Res.,
Sri Lanka .... **51** 7 5N 81 30 E
Gal Tardo, *Somali Rep.* **98** 3 34N 45 58 E
Galachipa, *Bangla.* ... **52** 22 8N 90 26 E
Galah, *Australia* ..... **74** 35 4 S 142 8 E
Galán, Cerro,
Argentina .... **140** 25 55 S 66 52W
Galana →, *Kenya* .... **92** 3 9 S 40 8 E
Galangue, *Angola* .... **95** 13 42 S 16 9 E
Galangue, Serra,
Angola .... **95** 14 18 S 15 52 E
Galápagos, *Pac. Oc.* .. **67** 0 0 89 0W
Galashiels, *U.K.* **14** 55 37N 2 50W
Galatea, *N.Z.* .... **80** 38 24 S 176 45 E
Galaţi, *Romania* ..... **34** 45 27N 28 2 E
Galatina, *Italy* .... **29** 40 10N 18 10 E
Galátone, *Italy* .... **29** 40 8N 18 3 E
Galax, *U.S.A.* **115** 36 42N 80 57W
Galaxídhion, *Greece* .. **35** 38 22N 22 23 E
Galbraith, *Australia* .. **72** 16 25 S 141 30 E
Galcaio, *Somali Rep.* . **45** 6 30N 47 30 E
Galdhøpiggen, *Norway* **10** 61 38N 8 18 E
Galeana, *Mexico* **126** 24 50N 100 4W
Galela, *Indonesia* ..... **57** 1 50N 127 49 E
Galena, *U.S.A.* **118** 42 25N 90 26W
Galera, *Spain* **25** 37 45N 2 33W
Galera, Pta., *Chile* ... **142** 39 59 S 73 43W
Galera Point,
Trin. & Tob. **129** 10 8N 61 0W
Galesburg, *Ill., U.S.A.* **118** 40 57N 90 23W
Galesburg, *Mich.*,
U.S.A. **119** 42 17N 85 26W
Galeton, *U.S.A.* **116** 41 43N 77 40W
Galgasc, *Somali Rep.* . **98** 0 11N 41 38 E
Galheirão →, *Brazil* . **139** 12 23 S 45 5W
Galheiros, *Brazil* .... **139** 13 18 S 46 25W
Gali, *U.S.S.R.* .... **39** 42 37N 41 46 E
Galich, *U.S.S.R.* ..... **37** 58 23N 42 12 E
Galiche, *Bulgaria* .... **34** 43 34N 23 50 E
Galicia □, *Spain* **22** 42 43N 7 45W
Galien, *U.S.A.* **119** 41 48N 86 30W
Galilee = Hagalil,
Israel .... **44** 32 53N 35 18 E
Galilee, L., *Australia* . **72** 22 20 S 145 50 E
Galilee, Sea of = Yam
Kinneret, *Israel* .... **44** 32 45N 35 35 E
Galion, *U.S.A.* **116** 40 43N 82 48W
Galite, Is. de la,
Tunisia .... **85** 37 30N 8 59 E
Galiuro Mts., *U.S.A.* . **123** 32 40N 110 30W
Gallabat, *Sudan* ..... **89** 12 58N 36 11 E
Gallardon, *France* .... **19** 48 32N 1 42 E
Gallarte, *Italy* .... **26** 45 40N 8 48 E
Gallatin, *Mo., U.S.A.* **118** 39 55N 93 58W
Gallatin, *Tenn., U.S.A.* **115** 36 24N 86 27W
Galle, *Sri Lanka* ..... **51** 6 5N 80 10 E
Gállego →, *Spain* **24** 41 39N 0 51W
Gallegos →, *Argentina* **142** 51 35 S 69 0W
Galley Hd., *Ireland* ... **15** 51 32N 8 56W
Galliate, *Italy* .... **26** 45 27N 8 44 E
Gallinas, Pta.,
Colombia **134** 12 28N 71 40W
Gallipoli = Gelibolu,
Turkey .... **46** 40 28N 26 43 E
Gallípoli, *Italy* .... **29** 40 8N 18 0 E
Gallipolis, *U.S.A.* **114** 38 50N 82 10W
Gällivare, *Sweden* .... **8** 67 9N 20 40 E
Gallo, C., *Italy* .... **28** 38 13N 13 19 E
Gallocanta, L. de,
Spain **24** 40 58N 1 30W
Galloway, *U.K.* **14** 55 0N 4 25W
Galloway, Mull of,
U.K. **14** 54 38N 4 50W
Gallup, *U.S.A.* **123** 35 30N 108 45W
Gallur, *Spain* **24** 41 52N 1 19W
Gal'on, *Israel* .... **44** 31 38N 34 51 E
Galong, *Australia* .... **76** 34 37 S 148 34 E
Galt, *Calif., U.S.A.* .. **124** 38 15N 121 18W
Galt, *Mo., U.S.A.* **118** 40 8N 93 23W
Galtström, *Sweden* ... **10** 62 10N 17 30 E
Galtür, *Austria* ...... **31** 46 58N 10 11 E
Galty Mts., *Ireland* ... **15** 52 22N 8 10W
Galtymore, *Ireland* ... **15** 52 22N 8 12W
Galva, *U.S.A.* **118** 41 10N 90 0W
Galvarino, *Chile* ..... **142** 38 24 S 72 47W
Galve de Sorbe, *Spain* **24** 41 13N 3 10W
Galveston, *Ind., U.S.A.* **119** 40 35N 86 11W
Galveston, *Tex.*,
U.S.A. **121** 29 15N 94 48W
Galveston B., *U.S.A.* . **121** 29 30N 94 50W
Gálvez, *Argentina* .... **140** 32 0 S 61 14W
Gálvez, *Spain* **23** 39 42N 4 16W
Galway, *Ireland* **15** 53 16N 9 4W
Galway □, *Ireland* **15** 53 16N 9 3W
Galway B., *Ireland* ... **15** 53 10N 9 20W
Gam →, *Vietnam* .... **54** 21 55N 105 12 E
Gamagori, *Japan* ..... **65** 34 50N 137 14 E
Gamari, L., *Ethiopia* . **89** 11 32N 41 40 E
Gamawa, *Nigeria* .... **91** 12 10N 10 31 E
Gamba, *Angola* ...... **95** 11 42 S 17 14 E
Gambaga, *Ghana* **91** 10 30N 0 28W
Gambat, *Pakistan* .... **48** 27 17N 68 26 E
Gambela, *Ethiopia* ... **89** 8 14N 34 38 E
Gambia ■, *W. Afr.* ... **90** 13 25N 16 0W
Gambia →, *W. Afr.* .. **90** 13 28N 16 34W
Gambier, C., *Australia* **78** 11 56 S 130 57 E
Gambier Is., *Australia* **73** 35 3 S 136 30 E
Gambo, *C.A.R.* ...... **94** 4 39N 22 16 E
Gamboli, *Pakistan* .... **48** 29 53N 68 24 E
Gamboma, *Congo* .... **94** 1 55 S 15 52 E
Gamboula, *C.A.R.* ... **94** 4 8N 15 9 E
Gamerco, *U.S.A.* **123** 35 33N 108 56W
Gamlakarleby =
Kokkola, *Finland* ... **8** 63 50N 23 8 E
Gammon →, *Canada* . **111** 51 24N 95 44W
Gammouda, *Tunisia* .. **86** 35 3N 9 39 E
Gamoda-Saki, *Japan* .. **64** 33 50N 134 45 E
Gamu-Gofa □,
Ethiopia .... **89** 5 40N 36 40 E
Gan, *France* **20** 43 12N 0 27W
Gan Gan, *Argentina* .. **142** 42 30 S 68 10W
Gan Goriama, Mts.,
Cameroon .... **91** 7 44N 12 45 E
Gan Jiang →, *China* . **59** 29 15N 116 0 E
Gan Shemu'el, *Israel* . **44** 32 28N 34 56 E
Gan Yavne, *Israel* .... **44** 31 48N 34 42 E
Ganado, *Ariz., U.S.A.* **123** 35 46N 109 41W
Ganado, *Tex., U.S.A.* **121** 29 4N 96 31W
Gananoque, *Canada* .. **109** 44 20N 76 10W
Ganaveh, *Iran* .... **47** 29 35N 50 35 E
Gand = Gent, *Belgium* **17** 51 2N 3 42 E
Ganda, *Angola* ...... **95** 13 3 S 14 35 E
Gandak →, *India* .... **49** 25 39N 85 13 E
Gandava, *Pakistan* ... **48** 28 32N 67 32 E
Gander, *Canada* **105** 48 58N 54 35W
Gander L., *Canada* ... **105** 48 58N 54 35W
Ganderowe Falls,
Zimb. .... **93** 17 20 S 29 10 E
Gandesa, *Spain* ...... **24** 41 3N 0 26 E
Gandhi Sagar, *India* .. **48** 24 40N 75 40 E
Gandi, *Nigeria* ...... **91** 12 55N 5 49 E
Gandía, *Spain* **25** 38 58N 0 9W
Gandino, *Italy* .... **26** 45 50N 9 52 E
Gando, Pta., *Canary Is.* **25** 27 55N 15 22W
Gandole, *Nigeria* ..... **91** 8 28N 11 35 E
Gandu, *Brazil* .... **139** 13 45 S 39 30W
Ganedidalem = Gani,
Indonesia .... **57** 0 48 S 128 14 E
Ganetti, *Sudan* ...... **88** 18 0N 31 10 E
Ganga →, *India* ..... **49** 23 20N 90 30 E
Ganga, Mouths of the,
India .... **49** 21 30N 90 0 E
Ganganagar, *India* ... **48** 29 56N 73 56 E
Gangapur, *India* ..... **48** 26 32N 76 49 E
Gangara, *Niger* ...... **91** 14 35N 8 29 E
Gangaw, *Burma* ..... **52** 22 5N 94 5 E
Gangawati, *India* ..... **51** 15 30N 76 36 E
Gangdisê Shan, *China* **49** 31 20N 81 0 E
Ganges = Ganga →,
India .... **49** 23 20N 90 30 E
Ganges, *France* ...... **20** 43 56N 3 42 E
Gangoh, *India* .... **48** 29 46N 77 18 E
Gangtok, *India* ...... **52** 27 20N 88 37 E
Gangu, *China* .... **60** 34 40N 105 15 E
Gangyao, *China* ..... **61** 44 12N 126 37 E
Gani, *Indonesia* ..... **57** 0 48 S 128 14 E
Ganj, *India* .... **49** 27 45N 78 57 E
Gannat, *France* ...... **20** 46 7N 3 11 E
Gannett Pk., *U.S.A.* .. **122** 43 15N 109 38W
Gannvalley, *U.S.A.* ... **120** 44 3N 98 57W
Ganongga, *Solomon Is.* **68** 8 5 S 156 35 E
Ganquan, *China* ..... **60** 36 20N 109 20 E
Gänserdorf, *Austria* .. **33** 48 20N 16 43 E
Ganshui, *China* ..... **58** 28 40N 106 40 E
Gansu □, *China* ..... **60** 36 0N 104 0 E
Ganta, *Liberia* **90** 7 15N 8 59W
Gantheaume, C.,
Australia .... **73** 36 4 S 137 32 E
Gantheaume B.,
Australia .... **79** 27 40 S 114 10 E
Gantsevichi, *U.S.S.R.* . **36** 52 49N 26 30 E
Ganyem, *Indonesia* ... **57** 2 46 S 140 12 E
Ganyu, *China* .... **61** 34 50N 119 8 E
Ganyushkino, *U.S.S.R.* **39** 46 35N 49 20 E
Ganzhou, *China* ..... **59** 25 51N 114 56 E
Gao, *Mali* .... **91** 18 0N 1 0 E
Gao Xian, *China* ..... **58** 28 21N 104 32 E
Gao'an, *China* .... **59** 28 26N 115 17 E
Gaohe, *China* .... **59** 22 46N 112 57 E
Gaohebu, *China* ..... **59** 30 43N 116 49 E
Gaokeng, *China* ..... **59** 27 40N 113 58 E
Gaolan Dao, *China* ... **59** 21 55N 113 10 E
Gaoligong Shan, *China* **58** 24 45N 98 45 E
Gaomi, *China* .... **61** 36 20N 119 42 E
Gaoping, *China* ..... **60** 35 45N 112 55 E
Gaotang, *China* ..... **60** 36 50N 116 15 E
Gaoua, *Burkina Faso* . **90** 10 20N 3 8W
Gaoual, *Guinea* **90** 11 45N 13 25W
Gaoxiong, *Taiwan* .... **59** 22 38N 120 18 E
Gaoyang, *China* ..... **60** 38 40N 115 45 E
Gaoyou, *China* ...... **59** 32 47N 119 26 E
Gaoyou Hu, *China* ... **61** 32 45N 119 20 E
Gaoyuan, *China* ..... **61** 37 8N 117 58 E
Gaozhou, *China* ..... **59** 21 58N 110 50 E
Gap, *France* .... **21** 44 33N 6 5 E
Gar, *China* .... **62** 32 10N 79 58 E
Garachiné, *Panama* ... **128** 8 0N 78 12W
Garad, *Somali Rep.* .. **98** 6 57N 49 24 E
Garafia, *Canary Is.* ... **25** 28 48N 17 57W
Garah, *Australia* ..... **77** 29 5 S 149 38 E
Garajonay, *Canary Is.* **25** 28 7N 17 14W
Garanhuns, *Brazil* ... **138** 8 50 S 36 30W
Garawe, *Liberia* **90** 4 35N 8 0W
Garba Harre,
Somali Rep. .... **98** 3 19N 42 13 E
Garba Tula, *Kenya* ... **92** 0 30N 38 32 E
Garbagududu, *Ethiopia* **98** 6 12N 43 50 E
Garber, *U.S.A.* **121** 36 30N 97 36W
Garberville, *U.S.A.* ... **122** 40 11N 123 50W
Garça, *Brazil* .... **139** 22 14 S 49 37W
Garças →,
Mato Grosso, Brazil **137** 15 54 S 52 16W
Garças →,
Pernambuco, Brazil **138** 8 43 S 39 41W
Garcias, *Brazil* ...... **137** 20 34 S 52 13W
Gard, *Somali Rep.* ... **98** 9 30N 49 6 E
Gard □, *France* ..... **21** 44 2N 4 10 E
Gard →, *France* ..... **21** 43 51N 4 37 E
Garda, L. di, *Italy* ... **26** 45 40N 10 40 E
Gardanne, *France* ... **21** 43 27N 5 27 E
Garde L., *Canada* ... **111** 62 50N 106 13W
Gardelegen,
E. Germany .... **30** 52 32N 11 21 E
Garden City, *Kans.*,
U.S.A. **121** 38 0N 100 45W
Garden City, *Mo.*,
U.S.A. **118** 38 34N 94 12W
Garden City, *Tex.*,
U.S.A. **121** 31 52N 101 28W
Garden Grove, *U.S.A.* **125** 33 47N 117 55W
Gardēz, *Afghan.* ..... **47** 33 37N 69 9 E
Gardiner, *U.S.A.* **122** 45 3N 110 42W
Gardiners I., *U.S.A.* .. **117** 41 4N 72 5W
Gardner, *Ill., U.S.A.* . **119** 41 12N 88 17W
Gardner, *Mass., U.S.A.* **117** 42 35N 72 0W
Gardner Canal, *Canada* **110** 53 27N 128 8W
Gardnerville, *U.S.A.* . **124** 38 59N 119 47W
Gare Tigre, *Fr. Guiana* **135** 4 58N 53 9W
Garema, *Australia* .... **76** 33 33 S 147 56 E
Garéssio, *Italy* ...... **26** 44 12N 8 1 E
Garey, *U.S.A.* **125** 34 53N 120 19W
Garfield, *Australia* ... **74** 38 6 S 145 42 E
Garfield, *U.S.A.* **122** 47 3N 117 8W
Gargan, Mt., *France* .. **20** 45 37N 1 39 E
Gargano, Mte., *Italy* .. **29** 41 43N 15 43 E
Gargouna, *Mali* ..... **91** 15 56N 0 13 E
Garhshankar, *India* ... **48** 31 13N 76 11 E
Garibaldi Prov. Park,
Canada **110** 49 50N 122 40W
Garies, *S. Africa* .... **96** 30 32 S 17 59 E
Garigliano →, *Italy* .. **28** 41 13N 13 44 E
Garissa, *Kenya* ...... **92** 0 25 S 39 40 E
Garissa □, *Kenya* ... **92** 0 20 S 40 0 E
Garkida, *Nigeria* .... **91** 10 27N 12 36 E
Garko, *Nigeria* ...... **91** 11 45N 8 53 E
Garland, *U.S.A.* **122** 41 47N 112 10W
Garlasco, *Italy* ...... **26** 45 11N 8 55 E
Garm, *U.S.S.R.* ...... **40** 39 0N 70 20 E
Garmisch-
Partenkirchen,
W. Germany .... **31** 47 30N 11 5 E
Garmsār, *Iran* ...... **47** 35 20N 52 25 E
Garner, *U.S.A.* **118** 43 4N 93 37W
Garnett, *U.S.A.* **120** 38 18N 95 12W
Garo Hills, *India* .... **49** 25 30N 90 30 E
Garoe, *Somali Rep.* .. **98** 8 25N 48 33 E
Garonne →, *France* .. **20** 45 2N 0 36W

Garonne, Canal Latéral à la →, *France* **20** 44 15N 0 18 E
Garoua, *Cameroon* **91** 9 19N 13 21 E
Garrel, *W. Germany* **30** 52 58N 7 59 E
Garrett, *U.S.A.* **119** 41 21N 85 8W
Garrigue, *France* **20** 43 40N 4 0 E
Garrison, *Ky., U.S.A.* **119** 38 36N 83 10W
Garrison, *Mont., U.S.A.* **122** 46 30N 112 56W
Garrison, *N. Dak., U.S.A.* **120** 47 39N 101 27W
Garrison, *Tex., U.S.A.* **121** 31 50N 94 28W
Garrison Res. = Sakakawea, L., *U.S.A.* **120** 47 30N 102 0W
Garrovillas, *Spain* **23** 39 40N 6 33W
Garrucha, *Spain* **25** 37 11N 1 49W
Garry →, *U.K.* **14** 56 47N 3 47W
Garry L., *Canada* **102** 65 58N 100 18W
Garsen, *Kenya* **92** 2 20 S 40 5 E
Garson L., *Canada* **111** 56 19N 110 2W
Gartempe →, *France* **20** 46 47N 0 49 E
Gartz, *E. Germany* **30** 53 12N 14 23 E
Garu, *Ghana* **91** 10 55N 0 11W
Garub, *Namibia* **96** 26 37 S 16 0 E
Garut, *Indonesia* **57** 7 14 S 107 53 E
Garvão, *Portugal* **23** 37 42N 8 21W
Garvie Mts., *N.Z.* **81** 45 30 S 168 50 E
Garwa = Garoua, *Cameroon* **91** 9 19N 13 21 E
Garwa, *India* **49** 24 11N 83 47 E
Garwolin, *Poland* **32** 51 55N 21 38 E
Gary, *U.S.A.* **119** 41 35N 87 20W
Garz, *E. Germany* **30** 54 17N 13 21 E
Garzê, *China* **58** 31 39N 99 58 E
Garzón, *Colombia* **134** 2 10N 75 40W
Gas City, *U.S.A.* **119** 40 29N 85 36W
Gasan Kuli, *U.S.S.R.* **40** 37 40N 54 20 E
Gascogne, *France* **20** 43 45N 0 20 E
Gascogne, G. de, *Europe* **24** 44 0N 2 0W
Gasconade, *U.S.A.* **118** 38 40N 91 33W
Gasconade →, *U.S.A.* **118** 38 41N 91 33W
Gascony = Gascogne, *France* **20** 43 45N 0 20 E
Gascoyne →, *Australia* **79** 24 52 S 113 37 E
Gascoyne Junc. T.O., *Australia* **79** 25 2 S 115 17 E
Gascueña, *Spain* **24** 40 18N 2 31W
Gash, Wadi →, *Ethiopia* **89** 16 48N 35 51 E
Gashaka, *Nigeria* **91** 7 20N 11 29 E
Gasherbrum, *Pakistan* **49** 35 40N 76 40 E
Gashua, *Nigeria* **91** 12 54N 11 0 E
Gaspé, *Canada* **105** 48 52N 64 30W
Gaspé, C. de, *Canada* **105** 48 48N 64 7W
Gaspé, Pén. de, *Canada* **105** 48 45N 65 40W
Gaspésie, Parc Prov. de la, *Canada* **105** 48 55N 65 50W
Gassaway, *U.S.A.* **114** 38 42N 80 43W
Gasselte, *Neths.* **16** 52 58N 6 48 E
Gasselternijveen, *Neths.* **16** 52 59N 6 51 E
Gássino Torinese, *Italy* **26** 45 8N 7 50 E
Gassol, *Nigeria* **91** 8 34N 10 25 E
Gastonia, *U.S.A.* **115** 35 17N 81 10W
Gastoúni, *Greece* **35** 37 51N 21 15 E
Gastoúri, *Greece* **35** 39 34N 19 54 E
Gastre, *Argentina* **142** 42 20 S 69 15W
Gata, C. de, *Spain* **25** 36 41N 2 13W
Gata, Sierra de, *Spain* **22** 40 20N 6 45W
Gataga →, *Canada* **110** 58 35N 126 59W
Gătaia, *Romania* **34** 45 26N 21 30 E
Gatchina, *U.S.S.R.* **36** 59 35N 30 9 E
Gates, *U.S.A.* **116** 43 9N 77 42W
Gateshead, *U.K.* **12** 54 57N 1 37W
Gatesville, *U.S.A.* **121** 31 29N 97 45W
Gaths, *Zimb.* **93** 20 2 S 30 32 E
Gatico, *Chile* **140** 22 29 S 70 20W
Gâtinais, *France* **19** 48 5N 2 40 E
Gâtine, Hauteurs de, *France* **20** 46 35N 0 45W
Gatineau, *Canada* **106** 45 29N 75 38W
Gatineau →, *Canada* **106** 45 27N 75 42W
Gatineau, Parc de la, *Canada* **106** 45 40N 76 0W
Gattinara, *Italy* **26** 45 37N 8 22 E
Gatukai, *Solomon Is.* **68** 8 45 S 158 15 E
Gatun, L., *Panama* **128** 9 7N 79 56W
Gatyana, *S. Africa* **97** 32 16 S 28 31 E
Gau, *Fiji* **68** 18 2 S 179 18 E
Gaua, *Vanuatu* **68** 14 15 S 167 30 E
Gaucín, *Spain* **23** 36 31N 5 19W
Gauer L., *Canada* **111** 57 0N 97 50W
Gauhati, *India* **49** 26 10N 91 45 E
Gauja →, *U.S.S.R.* **36** 57 10N 24 16 E
Gaula →, *Norway* **8** 63 21N 10 14 E
Gaurain-Ramecroix, *Belgium* **17** 50 36N 3 30 E
Gausta, *Norway* **10** 59 50N 8 37 E
Gausta, Mt., *Norway* **9** 59 48N 8 40 E
Gavá, *Spain* **24** 41 18N 2 0 E
Gavarnie, *France* **20** 42 44N 0 1W
Gavāter, *Iran* **47** 25 10N 61 31 E
Gavdhopoúla, *Greece* **35** 34 56N 24 0 E
Gávdhos, *Greece* **35** 34 50N 24 5 E
Gavere, *Belgium* **17** 50 55N 3 40 E
Gavião, *Portugal* **23** 39 28N 7 56W
Gaviota, *U.S.A.* **125** 34 29N 120 13W
Gävle, *Sweden* **10** 60 40N 17 9 E
Gävleborgs län □, *Sweden* **10** 61 30N 16 15 E
Gavorrano, *Italy* **26** 42 55N 10 49 E
Gavray, *France* **18** 48 55N 1 20W
Gavrilov Yam, *U.S.S.R.* **37** 57 18N 39 49 E
Gawachab, *Namibia* **96** 27 4 S 17 55 E
Gawai, *Burma* **52** 27 56N 97 30 E
Gawilgarh Hills, *India* **50** 21 15N 76 45 E
Gawler, *Australia* **73** 34 30 S 138 42 E
Gaxun Nur, *China* **62** 42 22N 100 30 E
Gaya, *India* **49** 24 47N 85 4 E
Gaya, *Niger* **91** 11 52N 3 28 E
Gaya, *Nigeria* **91** 11 57N 9 0 E
Gaylord, *U.S.A.* **104** 45 1N 84 41W
Gayndah, *Australia* **73** 25 35 S 151 32 E
Gaysin, *U.S.S.R.* **38** 48 57N 28 25 E
Gayvoron, *U.S.S.R.* **38** 48 22N 29 52 E
Gaza, *Egypt* **44** 31 30N 34 28 E
Gaza □, *Mozam.* **97** 23 10 S 32 45 E
Gaza Strip, *Egypt* **44** 31 29N 34 25 E
Gazaoua, *Niger* **91** 13 32N 7 55 E
Gazelle Pen., *Papua N. G.* **69** 4 40 S 152 0 E
Gazi, *Zaïre* **92** 1 3N 24 30 E
Gaziantep, *Turkey* **46** 37 6N 37 23 E
Gazli, *U.S.S.R.* **40** 40 14N 63 24 E
Gbarnga, *Liberia* **90** 7 19N 9 13W
Gbekebo, *Nigeria* **91** 6 20N 4 56 E
Gboko, *Nigeria* **91** 7 17N 9 4 E
Gbongan, *Nigeria* **91** 7 28N 4 20 E
Gcuwa, *S. Africa* **97** 32 20 S 28 11 E
Gdańsk, *Poland* **32** 54 22N 18 40 E
Gdańska, Zatoka, *Poland* **32** 54 30N 19 20 E
Gdov, *U.S.S.R.* **36** 58 48N 27 55 E
Gdynia, *Poland* **32** 54 35N 18 33 E
Ge'a, *Israel* **44** 31 38N 34 37 E
Gebe, *Indonesia* **57** 0 5N 129 25 E
Gebeit Mine, *Sudan* **88** 21 3N 36 29 E
Gebel Mûsa, *Egypt* **88** 28 32N 33 59 E
Gecha, *Ethiopia* **89** 7 30N 35 18 E
Gedaref, *Sudan* **89** 14 2N 35 28 E
Gede, Tanjung, *Indonesia* **56** 6 46 S 105 12 E
Gedera, *Israel* **44** 31 49N 34 46 E
Gedinne, *Belgium* **17** 49 59N 4 56 E
Gedo, *Ethiopia* **89** 9 2N 37 25 E
Gèdre, *France* **20** 42 47N 0 2 E
Gedser, *Denmark* **11** 54 35N 11 55 E
Gedser Odde, *Denmark* **11** 54 30N 11 58 E
Geel, *Belgium* **17** 51 10N 4 59 E
Geelong, *Australia* **74** 38 10 S 144 22 E
Geelvink Chan., *Australia* **79** 28 30 S 114 0 E
Geer →, *Belgium* **17** 50 51N 5 42 E
Geestenseth, *W. Germany* **30** 53 31N 8 51 E
Geesthacht, *W. Germany* **30** 53 25N 10 20 E
Geffen, *Neths.* **16** 51 44N 5 28 E
Geidam, *Nigeria* **91** 12 57N 11 57 E
Geikie →, *Canada* **111** 57 45N 103 52W
Geili, *Sudan* **89** 16 1N 32 37 E
Geilo, *Norway* **10** 60 32N 8 14 E
Geisingen, *W. Germany* **31** 47 55N 8 37 E
Geislingen, *W. Germany* **31** 48 37N 9 51 E
Geita, *Tanzania* **92** 2 48 S 32 12 E
Geita □, *Tanzania* **92** 2 50 S 32 10 E
Gejiu, *China* **58** 23 20N 103 10 E
Gel →, *Sudan* **89** 7 5N 29 10 E
Gel River, *Sudan* **89** 7 5N 29 10 E
Gela, *Italy* **29** 37 6N 14 18 E
Gela, G. di, *Italy* **29** 37 0N 14 8 E
Geladi, *Ethiopia* **98** 6 59N 46 30 E
Gelantipy, *Australia* **75** 37 8 S 148 22 E
Gelderland □, *Neths.* **16** 52 5N 6 10 E
Geldermalsen, *Neths.* **16** 51 53N 5 17 E
Geldern, *W. Germany* **30** 51 32N 6 18 E
Geldrop, *Neths.* **17** 51 25N 5 32 E
Geleen, *Neths.* **17** 50 57N 5 49 E
Gelehun, *S. Leone* **90** 8 20N 11 40W
Gelendzhik, *U.S.S.R.* **38** 44 33N 38 10 E
Gelib, *Somali Rep.* **98** 0 29N 42 46 E
Gelibolu, *Turkey* **46** 40 28N 26 43 E
Gellibrand, *Australia* **74** 38 33 S 143 30 E
Gelnhausen, *W. Germany* **31** 50 12N 9 12 E
Gelsenkirchen, *W. Germany* **30** 51 30N 7 5 E
Gelting, *W. Germany* **30** 54 43N 9 53 E
Gemas, *Malaysia* **55** 2 37N 102 36 E
Gembloux, *Belgium* **17** 50 34N 4 43 E
Gembrook, *Australia* **74** 37 58 S 145 37 E
Gemena, *Zaïre* **94** 3 13N 19 48 E
Gemerek, *Turkey* **46** 39 15N 36 10 E
Gemert, *Neths.* **17** 51 33N 5 41 E
Gemona del Friuli, *Italy* **27** 46 16N 13 7 E
Gemsa, *Egypt* **88** 27 39N 33 35 E
Gemünden, *W. Germany* **31** 50 3N 9 43 E
Genale, *Ethiopia* **89** 6 0N 39 30 E
Genale, *Somali Rep.* **98** 1 48N 44 42 E
Genappe, *Belgium* **17** 50 37N 4 30 E
Gençay, *France* **20** 46 23N 0 23 E
Gendringen, *Neths.* **16** 51 52N 6 21 E
Gendt, *Neths.* **16** 51 53N 5 59 E
Geneina, Gebel, *Egypt* **88** 29 2N 33 55 E
Genemuiden, *Neths.* **16** 52 38N 6 2 E
General Acha, *Argentina* **140** 37 20 S 64 38W
General Alvear, *Buenos Aires, Argentina* **140** 36 0 S 60 0W
General Alvear, *Mendoza, Argentina* **140** 35 0 S 67 40W
General Artigas, *Paraguay* **140** 26 52 S 56 16W
General Belgrano, *Argentina* **140** 36 35 S 58 47W
General Cabrera, *Argentina* **140** 32 53 S 63 52W
General Carrera, L., *Chile* **142** 46 35 S 72 0W
General Cepeda, *Mexico* **126** 25 23N 101 27W
General Conesa, *Argentina* **142** 40 6 S 64 25W
General Guido, *Argentina* **140** 36 40 S 57 50W
General Juan Madariaga, *Argentina* **140** 37 0 S 57 0W
General La Madrid, *Argentina* **140** 37 17 S 61 20W
General Lorenzo Vintter, *Argentina* **142** 40 45 S 64 26W
General MacArthur, *Phil.* **57** 11 18N 125 28 E
General Martin Miguel de Güemes, *Argentina* **140** 24 50 S 65 0W
General Paz, *Argentina* **140** 27 45 S 57 36W
General Pico, *Argentina* **140** 35 45 S 63 50W
General Pinedo, *Argentina* **140** 27 15 S 61 20W
General Pinto, *Argentina* **140** 34 45 S 61 50W
General Sampaio, *Brazil* **138** 4 2 S 39 29W
General Santos, *Phil.* **57** 6 5N 125 14 E
General Toshevo, *Bulgaria* **34** 43 42N 28 6 E
General Trevino, *Mexico* **127** 26 14N 99 29W
General Trías, *Mexico* **126** 28 21N 106 22W
General Viamonte, *Argentina* **140** 35 1 S 61 3W
General Villegas, *Argentina* **140** 35 0 S 63 0W
General Vintter, L., *Argentina* **142** 43 55 S 71 40W
Genesee, *Idaho, U.S.A.* **122** 46 31N 116 59W
Genesee, *Pa., U.S.A.* **116** 41 59N 77 54W
Genesee →, *U.S.A.* **116** 43 16N 77 36W
Geneseo, *Ill., U.S.A.* **118** 41 25N 90 10W
Geneseo, *Kans., U.S.A.* **120** 38 32N 98 8W
Geneseo, *N.Y., U.S.A.* **116** 42 49N 77 49W
Geneva = Genève, *Switz.* **31** 46 12N 6 9 E
Geneva, *Ala., U.S.A.* **115** 31 2N 85 52W
Geneva, *Ill., U.S.A.* **119** 41 53N 88 18W
Geneva, *Ind., U.S.A.* **119** 40 36N 84 57W
Geneva, *N.Y., U.S.A.* **116** 42 53N 77 0W
Geneva, *Nebr., U.S.A.* **120** 40 35N 97 35W
Geneva, *Ohio, U.S.A.* **116** 41 49N 80 58W
Geneva, L. = Léman, Lac, *Switz.* **31** 46 26N 6 30 E
Geneva, L., *U.S.A.* **119** 42 38N 88 30W
Genève, *Switz.* **31** 46 12N 6 9 E
Genève □, *Switz.* **31** 46 10N 6 10 E
Gengenbach, *W. Germany* **31** 48 25N 8 0 E
Gengma, *China* **58** 23 32N 99 20 E
Genichesk, *U.S.S.R.* **38** 46 12N 34 50 E
Genil →, *Spain* **23** 37 42N 5 19W
Génissiat, Barr. de, *France* **21** 46 1N 5 48 E
Genk, *Belgium* **17** 50 58N 5 32 E
Genkai-Nada, *Japan* **64** 34 0N 130 0 E
Genlis, *France* **19** 47 11N 5 12 E
Gennargentu, Mti. del, *Italy* **28** 40 0N 9 10 E
Gennep, *Neths.* **17** 51 41N 5 59 E
Gennes, *France* **18** 47 20N 0 17W
Genoa = Génova, *Italy* **26** 44 24N 8 56 E
Genoa, *Australia* **75** 37 29 S 149 35 E
Genoa, *Ill., U.S.A.* **119** 42 6N 88 42W
Genoa, *N.Y., U.S.A.* **117** 42 40N 76 32W
Genoa, *Nebr., U.S.A.* **120** 41 31N 97 44W
Genoa, *Nev., U.S.A.* **124** 39 2N 119 50W
Genoa →, *Argentina* **142** 44 55 S 70 5W
Genoa →, *Australia* **75** 37 31 S 149 41 E
Genoa City, *U.S.A.* **119** 42 30N 88 20W
Génova, *Italy* **26** 44 24N 8 56 E
Génova, G. di, *Italy* **26** 44 0N 9 0 E
Gent, *Belgium* **17** 51 2N 3 42 E
Gentbrugge, *Belgium* **17** 51 3N 3 47 E
Genthin, *E. Germany* **30** 52 24N 12 10 E
Gentio do Ouro, *Brazil* **138** 11 25 S 42 30W
Geographe B., *Australia* **79** 33 30 S 115 15 E
Geographe Chan., *Australia* **79** 24 30 S 113 0 E
Geokchay, *U.S.S.R.* **39** 40 42N 47 43 E
Georga, Zemlya, *U.S.S.R.* **40** 80 30N 49 0 E
George, *S. Africa* **96** 33 58 S 22 29 E
George →, *Canada* **105** 58 49N 66 10W
George, L., *N.S.W., Australia* **76** 35 10 S 149 25 E
George, L., *S. Austral., Australia* **73** 37 25 S 140 0 E
George, L., *W. Austral., Australia* **78** 22 45 S 123 40 E
George, L., *Uganda* **92** 0 5N 30 10 E
George, L., *Fla., U.S.A.* **115** 29 15N 81 35W
George, L., *N.Y., U.S.A.* **117** 43 30N 73 30W
George River = Port Nouveau-Québec, *Canada* **103** 58 30N 65 59W
George Sound, *N.Z.* **81** 44 52 S 167 25 E
George Town, *Australia* **72** 41 5 S 146 49 E
George Town, *Bahamas* **128** 23 33N 75 47W
George Town, *Malaysia* **55** 5 25N 100 15 E
George V Coast, *Antarctica* **143** 69 0 S 148 0 E
George VI Sound, *Antarctica* **143** 71 0 S 68 0W
George West, *U.S.A.* **121** 28 18N 98 5W
Georgetown, *Australia* **72** 18 17 S 143 33 E
Georgetown, *Ont., Canada* **108** 43 40N 79 56W
Georgetown, *P.E.I., Canada* **105** 46 13N 62 24W
Georgetown, *Cayman Is.* **128** 19 20N 81 24W
Georgetown, *Gambia* **90** 13 30N 14 47W
Georgetown, *Guyana* **135** 6 50N 58 12W
Georgetown, *Calif., U.S.A.* **124** 38 54N 120 50W
Georgetown, *Colo., U.S.A.* **122** 39 46N 105 49W
Georgetown, *Ill., U.S.A.* **119** 39 59N 87 38W
Georgetown, *Ky., U.S.A.* **114** 38 13N 84 33W
Georgetown, *Ohio, U.S.A.* **119** 38 50N 83 50W
Georgetown, *S.C., U.S.A.* **115** 33 22N 79 15W
Georgetown, *Tex., U.S.A.* **121** 30 40N 97 45W
Georgia □, *U.S.A.* **115** 32 0N 82 0W
Georgia, Str. of, *Canada* **110** 49 25N 124 0W
Georgian B., *Canada* **108** 45 15N 81 0W
Georgian S.S.R. □, *U.S.S.R.* **39** 42 0N 43 0 E
Georgievsk, *U.S.S.R.* **39** 44 12N 43 28 E
Georgina →, *Australia* **72** 23 30 S 139 47 E
Georgina Downs, *Australia* **72** 21 10 S 137 40 E
Georgina I., *Canada* **108** 44 22N 79 17W
Georgiu-Dezh, *U.S.S.R.* **37** 51 3N 39 30 E
Gera, *E. Germany* **30** 50 53N 12 11 E
Gera □, *E. Germany* **30** 50 45N 11 45 E
Geraardsbergen, *Belgium* **17** 50 45N 3 53 E
Geral, Serra, *Bahia, Brazil* **139** 14 0 S 41 0W
Geral, Serra, *Goiás, Brazil* **138** 11 15 S 46 30W
Geral, Serra, *Sta. Catarina, Brazil* **141** 26 25 S 50 0W
Geral de Goiás, Serra, *Brazil* **139** 12 0 S 46 0W
Geral do Paranã Serra, *Brazil* **139** 15 0 S 47 30W
Gerald, *U.S.A.* **118** 38 24N 91 21W
Geraldine, *N.Z.* **81** 44 5 S 171 15 E
Geraldine, *U.S.A.* **122** 47 36N 110 18W
Geraldton, *Australia* **79** 28 48 S 114 32 E
Geraldton, *Canada* **104** 49 44N 86 59W
Gerang Gerung, *Australia* **74** 36 22 S 141 52 E
Gérardmer, *France* **19** 48 3N 6 50 E
Gerede, *Turkey* **38** 40 45N 32 10 E
Gereshk, *Afghan.* **47** 31 47N 64 35 E
Gérgal, *Spain* **25** 37 7N 2 31W
Gerik, *Malaysia* **55** 5 25N 101 0 E
Gering, *U.S.A.* **120** 41 51N 103 30W
Gerizim, *Jordan* **44** 32 13N 35 15 E
Gerlach, *U.S.A.* **122** 40 43N 119 27W
Gerlachovka, *Czech.* **32** 49 11N 20 7 E
Gerlogubi, *Ethiopia* **98** 6 53N 45 3 E
Germansen Landing, *Canada* **110** 55 43N 124 40W
Germantown, *U.S.A.* **119** 39 38N 84 22W
Germany, East ■, *Europe* **30** 52 0N 12 0 E
Germany, West ■, *Europe* **30** 52 0N 9 0 E
Germersheim, *W. Germany* **31** 49 13N 8 20 E
Germiston, *S. Africa* **97** 26 15 S 28 10 E
Gernsheim, *W. Germany* **31** 49 44N 8 29 E
Gero, *Japan* **65** 35 48N 137 14 E
Gerolstein, *W. Germany* **31** 50 12N 6 40 E
Gerolzhofen, *W. Germany* **31** 49 54N 10 21 E
Gerona, *Spain* **24** 41 58N 2 46 E
Gerona □, *Spain* **24** 42 11N 2 30 E
Gérouville, *Belgium* **17** 49 37N 5 26 E
Gerrard, *Canada* **110** 50 30N 117 17W
Gerringong, *Australia* **76** 34 46 S 150 47 E
Gers □, *France* **20** 43 35N 0 30 E
Gers →, *France* **20** 44 9N 0 39 E
Gersfeld, *W. Germany* **30** 50 27N 9 57 E
Gersoppa Falls, *India* **51** 14 12N 74 46 E
Geseke, *W. Germany* **30** 51 38N 8 29 E
Geser, *Indonesia* **57** 3 50 S 130 54 E
Gesso →, *Italy* **26** 44 24N 7 33 E

Gestro, Wabi →, Ethiopia 89 4 12N 42 2 E
Gesves, Belgium 17 50 24N 5 4 E
Getafe, Spain 22 40 18N 3 44W
Gethsémani, Canada 105 50 13N 60 40W
Gettysburg, Pa., U.S.A. 114 39 47N 77 18W
Gettysburg, S. Dak., U.S.A. 120 45 3N 99 56W
Getz Ice Shelf, Antarctica 143 75 0 S 130 0W
Geul →, Neths. 17 50 53N 5 43 E
Geurie, Australia 76 32 22 S 148 50 E
Gévaudan, France 20 44 40N 3 40 E
Gevgelija, Yugoslavia 35 41 9N 22 30 E
Gévora →, Spain 23 38 53N 6 57W
Gex, France 21 46 21N 6 3 E
Geyser, U.S.A. 122 47 17N 110 30W
Geyserville, U.S.A. 124 38 42N 122 54W
Geysir, Iceland 8 64 19N 20 18W
Ghâbat el Arab = Wang Kai, Sudan 89 9 3N 29 23 E
Ghaghara →, India 49 25 45N 84 40 E
Ghalla, Wadi el →, Sudan 89 10 25N 27 32 E
Ghallamane, Mauritania 84 23 15N 10 0W
Ghana ■, W. Afr. 91 8 0N 1 0W
Ghansor, India 49 22 39N 80 1 E
Ghanzi, Botswana 96 21 50 S 21 34 E
Ghanzi □, Botswana 96 21 50 S 21 45 E
Gharb el Istiwa'iya □, Sudan 89 5 0N 30 0 E
Gharbîya, Es Sahrâ el, Egypt 88 27 40N 26 30 E
Ghard Abû Muharik, Egypt 88 26 50N 30 0 E
Ghardaïa, Algeria 85 32 20N 3 37 E
Ghârib, G., Egypt 88 28 6N 32 54 E
Ghârib, Râs, Egypt 88 28 6N 33 18 E
Gharyān, Libya 86 32 10N 13 0 E
Gharyān □, Libya 86 30 35N 12 0 E
Ghat, Libya 86 24 59N 10 11 E
Ghatal, India 49 22 40N 87 46 E
Ghatampur, India 49 26 8N 80 13 E
Ghatere, Solomon Is. 68 7 55 S 159 0 E
Ghatprabha →, India 51 16 15N 75 20 E
Ghayl, Si. Arabia 46 21 40N 46 20 E
Ghazal, Bahr el →, Chad 87 13 0N 15 47 E
Ghazâl, Bahr el →, Sudan 89 9 31N 30 25 E
Ghazaouet, Algeria 85 35 8N 1 50W
Ghaziabad, India 48 28 42N 77 26 E
Ghazipur, India 49 25 38N 83 35 E
Ghaznī, Afghan. 47 33 30N 68 28 E
Ghaznī □, Afghan. 47 32 10N 68 20 E
Ghedi, Italy 26 45 24N 10 16 E
Ghèlinsor, Somali Rep. 98 6 28N 46 39 E
Ghent = Gent, Belgium 17 51 2N 3 42 E
Gheorghe Gheorghiu-Dej, Romania 34 46 17N 26 47 E
Gheorgheni, Romania 34 46 43N 25 41 E
Ghergani, Romania 34 44 37N 25 37 E
Gherla, Romania 34 47 0N 23 57 E
Ghilarza, Italy 28 40 8N 8 50 E
Ghisonaccia, France 21 42 1N 9 26 E
Ghisoni, France 21 42 7N 9 12 E
Ghizao, Afghan. 48 33 20N 65 44 E
Ghizar →, Pakistan 49 36 15N 73 43 E
Ghod →, India 50 18 30N 74 35 E
Ghogha, India 48 21 40N 72 20 E
Ghot Ogrein, Egypt 88 31 10N 25 20 E
Ghotaru, India 48 27 20N 70 1 E
Ghotki, Pakistan 48 28 5N 69 21 E
Ghowr □, Afghan. 47 34 0N 64 20 E
Ghudāmis, Libya 86 30 11N 9 29 E
Ghughri, India 49 22 39N 80 41 E
Ghugus, India 50 19 58N 79 12 E
Ghulam Mohammad Barrage, Pakistan 48 25 30N 68 20 E
Ghūrīān, Afghan. 47 34 17N 61 25 E
Gia Dinh, Vietnam 55 10 49N 106 42 E
Gia Lai = Pleiku, Vietnam 54 13 57N 108 0 E
Gia Nghia, Vietnam 55 12 0N 107 42 E
Gia Ngoc, Vietnam 54 14 50N 108 58 E
Gia Vuc, Vietnam 54 14 42N 108 34 E
Giamama, Somali Rep. 98 0 4N 42 44 E
Gian, Phil. 57 5 45N 125 20 E
Giannutri, Italy 26 42 16N 11 5 E
Giant Forest, U.S.A. 124 36 36N 118 43W
Giant Mts. = Krkonoše, Czech. 32 50 50N 15 35 E
Giant's Causeway, U.K. 15 55 15N 6 30W
Giarabub = Al Jaghbūb, Libya 86 29 42N 24 38 E
Giarre, Italy 29 37 44N 15 10 E
Giaveno, Italy 26 45 3N 7 20 E
Gibara, Cuba 128 21 9N 76 11W
Gibb River, Australia 78 16 26 S 126 26 E
Gibbo, Mt., Australia 75 36 38 S 147 58 E
Gibbon, U.S.A. 120 40 49N 98 45W
Gibe →, Ethiopia 89 7 20N 37 36 E
Gibellina, Italy 28 37 48N 13 0 E
Gibraléon, Spain 23 37 23N 6 58W
Gibraltar, Europe 23 36 7N 5 22W
Gibraltar, Str. of, Medit. S. 23 35 55N 5 40W
Gibson City, U.S.A. 119 40 28N 88 22W
Gibson Desert, Australia 78 24 0 S 126 0 E
Gibsonburg, U.S.A. 119 41 23N 83 19W
Gibsons, Canada 110 49 24N 123 32W
Gibsonville, U.S.A. 124 39 46N 120 54W
Giddalur, India 51 15 20N 78 57 E
Giddings, U.S.A. 121 30 11N 96 58W
Gidole, Ethiopia 89 5 40N 37 25 E
Gien, France 19 47 40N 2 36 E
Giessen, W. Germany 30 50 34N 8 40 E
Gieten, Neths. 16 53 0N 6 46 E
Gifatin, Geziret, Egypt 88 27 10N 33 50 E
Giffard, Canada 107 46 51N 71 12W
Gifford Creek, Australia 79 24 3 S 116 16 E
Gifhorn, W. Germany 30 52 29N 10 32 E
Gifu, Japan 65 35 30N 136 45 E
Gifu □, Japan 65 35 40N 137 0 E
Gigant, U.S.S.R. 39 46 28N 41 20 E
Giganta, Sa. de la, Mexico 126 25 30N 111 30W
Gigen, Bulgaria 34 43 40N 24 28 E
Gigha, U.K. 14 55 42N 5 45W
Giglei, Somali Rep. 98 5 25N 45 20 E
Giglio, Italy 26 42 20N 10 52 E
Gignac, France 20 43 39N 3 32 E
Gigüela →, Spain 25 39 8N 3 44W
Gijón, Spain 22 43 32N 5 42W
Gil Gil, Cr. →, Australia 77 30 19 S 148 42 E
Gil I., Canada 110 53 12N 129 15W
Gila →, U.S.A. 123 32 43N 114 33W
Gila Bend, U.S.A. 123 33 0N 112 46W
Gila Bend Mts., U.S.A. 123 33 15N 113 0W
Gīlān □, Iran 46 37 0N 50 0 E
Gilbert →, Australia 72 16 35 S 141 15 E
Gilbert Is., Kiribati 66 1 0N 176 0 E
Gilbert Plains, Canada 111 51 9N 100 28W
Gilbert River, Australia 72 18 9 S 142 52 E
Gilberton, Australia 72 19 16 S 143 35 E
Gilbués, Brazil 138 9 50 S 45 21W
Gilf el Kebîr, Hadabat el, Egypt 88 23 50N 25 50 E
Gilford I., Canada 110 50 40N 126 30W
Gilgai, Australia 77 29 50 S 151 9 E
Gilgandra, Australia 76 31 43 S 148 39 E
Gilgil, Kenya 92 0 30 S 36 20 E
Gilgit, India 49 35 50N 74 15 E
Gilgit →, Pakistan 49 35 44N 74 37 E
Giljeva Planina, Yugoslavia 33 43 9N 20 0 E
Gillam, Canada 111 56 20N 94 40W
Gilleleje, Denmark 11 56 8N 12 19 E
Gillen, L., Australia 79 26 11 S 124 38 E
Gilles, L., Australia 73 32 50 S 136 45 E
Gillespie, U.S.A. 118 39 7N 89 49W
Gillespies Pt., N.Z. 81 43 24 S 169 49 E
Gillette, U.S.A. 120 44 20N 105 30W
Gilliat, Australia 72 20 40 S 141 28 E
Gillingham, U.K. 13 51 23N 0 34 E
Gilly, Belgium 17 50 25N 4 29 E
Gilman, U.S.A. 119 40 46N 88 0W
Gilman City, U.S.A. 118 40 8N 93 53W
Gilmer, U.S.A. 121 32 44N 94 55W
Gilmore, Australia 76 35 20 S 148 12 E
Gilmore, L., Australia 79 32 29 S 121 37 E
Gilmour, Canada 109 44 48N 77 37W
Gilo →, Ethiopia 89 8 10N 33 15 E
Gilort →, Romania 34 44 38N 23 32 E
Gilroy, U.S.A. 124 37 1N 121 37W
Giluwe, Mt., Papua N. G. 69 6 8 S 143 52 E
Gilze, Neths. 17 51 32N 4 57 E
Gimbi, Ethiopia 89 9 3N 35 42 E
Gimigliano, Italy 29 38 58N 16 32 E
Gimli, Canada 111 50 40N 97 0W
Gimo, Sweden 10 60 11N 18 12 E
Gimone →, France 20 44 0N 1 6 E
Gimont, France 20 43 38N 0 52 E
Gimzo, Israel 44 31 56N 34 56 E
Gin →, Sri Lanka 51 6 5N 80 7 E
Gin Gin, Australia 73 25 0 S 151 58 E
Ginâh, Egypt 88 25 21N 30 30 E
Gindie, Australia 72 23 44 S 148 8 E
Gineta, La, Spain 25 39 8N 2 1W
Gingin, Australia 79 31 22 S 115 54 E
Gîngiova, Romania 34 43 54N 23 50 E
Ginir, Ethiopia 89 7 6N 40 40 E
Ginosa, Italy 29 40 35N 16 45 E
Ginzo de Limia, Spain 22 42 3N 7 47W
Giohar, Somali Rep. 98 2 48N 45 30 E
Gióia, G. di, Italy 29 38 30N 15 50 E
Gióia del Colle, Italy 29 40 49N 16 55 E
Gióia Táuro, Italy 29 38 26N 15 53 E
Gioiosa Iónica, Italy 29 38 20N 16 19 E
Gióna, Óros, Greece 35 38 38N 22 14 E
Giovi, Passo dei, Italy 26 44 33N 8 57 E
Giovinazzo, Italy 29 41 10N 16 40 E
Gir Hills, India 48 21 0N 71 0 E
Girab, India 48 26 2N 70 38 E
Giraltovce, Czech. 32 49 7N 21 32 E
Girard, Ill., U.S.A. 118 39 27N 89 48W
Girard, Kans., U.S.A. 121 37 30N 94 50W
Girard, Ohio, U.S.A. 116 41 10N 80 42W
Girard, Pa., U.S.A. 116 42 1N 80 21W
Girardot, Colombia 134 4 18N 74 48W
Girardville, Canada 107 49 0N 72 32W
Girdle Ness, U.K. 14 57 9N 2 2W
Giresun, Turkey 46 40 55N 38 30 E
Girga, Egypt 88 26 17N 31 55 E
Girgarre, Australia 74 36 18 S 145 2 E
Girgir, C., Papua N. G. 69 3 50 S 144 35 E
Giridih, India 49 24 10N 86 21 E
Girifalco, Italy 29 38 49N 16 25 E
Girilambone, Australia 73 31 16 S 146 57 E
Giro, Nigeria 91 11 7N 4 42 E
Giromagny, France 19 47 45N 6 50 E
Gironde □, France 20 44 45N 0 30W
Gironde →, France 20 45 32N 1 7W
Gironella, Spain 24 42 2N 1 53 E
Giru, Australia 72 19 30 S 147 5 E
Girvan, U.K. 14 55 15N 4 50W
Gisborne, Australia 74 37 29 S 144 36 E
Gisborne, N.Z. 80 38 39 S 178 5 E
Gisenyi, Rwanda 92 1 41 S 29 15 E
Gislaved, Sweden 11 57 19N 13 32 E
Gisors, France 19 49 15N 1 47 E
Gistel, Belgium 17 51 9N 2 59 E
Gitega, Burundi 92 3 26 S 29 56 E
Gits, Belgium 17 51 0N 3 6 E
Giuba →, Somali Rep. 98 1 30N 42 35 E
Giugliano in Campania, Italy 29 40 55N 14 12 E
Giulianova, Italy 27 42 45N 13 58 E
Giurgeni, Romania 34 44 45N 27 48 E
Giurgiu, Romania 34 43 52N 25 57 E
Giv'at Brenner, Israel 44 31 52N 34 47 E
Giv'atayim, Israel 44 32 4N 34 49 E
Give, Denmark 11 55 51N 9 13 E
Givet, France 19 50 8N 4 49 E
Givors, France 21 45 35N 4 45 E
Givry, Belgium 17 50 23N 4 2 E
Givry, France 19 46 41N 4 46 E
Giyon, Ethiopia 89 8 33N 38 1 E
Giza = El Gîza, Egypt 88 30 0N 31 10 E
Gizhiga, U.S.S.R. 41 62 3N 160 30 E
Gizhiginskaya, Guba, U.S.S.R. 41 61 0N 158 0 E
Gizo, Solomon Is. 68 8 7 S 156 50 E
Giżycko, Poland 32 54 2N 21 48 E
Gizzeria, Italy 29 38 57N 16 10 E
Gjegjan, Albania 35 41 58N 20 3 E
Gjerstad, Norway 10 58 54N 9 0 E
Gjirokastra, Albania 35 40 7N 20 10 E
Gjoa Haven, Canada 102 68 20N 96 8W
Gjøl, Denmark 11 57 4N 9 42 E
Gjøvik, Norway 10 60 47N 10 43 E
Glace Bay, Canada 105 46 11N 59 58W
Glacier B., U.S.A. 110 58 30N 136 10W
Glacier Nat. Park, Canada 110 51 15N 117 30W
Glacier Park, U.S.A. 122 48 30N 113 18W
Glacier Peak Mt., U.S.A. 122 48 7N 121 7W
Gladewater, U.S.A. 121 32 30N 94 58W
Gladstone, Queens., Australia 72 23 52 S 151 16 E
Gladstone, S. Austral., Australia 73 33 15 S 138 22 E
Gladstone, W. Austral., Australia 79 25 57 S 114 17 E
Gladstone, Canada 111 50 13N 98 57W
Gladstone, Mich., U.S.A. 114 45 52N 87 1W
Gladstone, Mo., U.S.A. 118 39 13N 94 35W
Gladwin, U.S.A. 114 43 59N 84 29W
Gladys L., Canada 110 59 50N 133 0W
Glafsfjorden, Sweden 10 59 30N 12 37 E
Gláma, Iceland 8 65 48N 23 0W
Glåma →, Norway 10 59 12N 10 57 E
Glamis, U.S.A. 125 33 0N 115 4W
Glamoč, Yugoslavia 27 44 3N 16 51 E
Glan, Sweden 11 58 37N 16 0 E
Glanerbrug, Neths. 16 52 13N 6 58 E
Glarus, Switz. 31 47 3N 9 4 E
Glasco, Kans., U.S.A. 120 39 25N 97 50W
Glasco, N.Y., U.S.A. 117 42 3N 73 57W
Glasgow, U.K. 14 55 52N 4 14W
Glasgow, Ky., U.S.A. 114 37 2N 85 55W
Glasgow, Mo., U.S.A. 118 39 14N 92 51W
Glasgow, Mont., U.S.A. 122 48 12N 106 35W
Glastonbury, U.K. 13 51 9N 2 42W
Glastonbury, U.S.A. 117 41 42N 72 27W
Glauchau, E. Germany 30 50 50N 12 33 E
Glazov, U.S.S.R. 37 58 9N 52 40 E
Gleiwitz = Gliwice, Poland 32 50 22N 18 41 E
Glen, U.S.A. 117 44 7N 71 10W
Glen Affric, U.K. 14 57 15N 5 0W
Glen Afton, N.Z. 80 37 37 S 175 4 E
Glen Alice, Australia 76 33 2 S 150 14 E
Glen Almond, Canada 106 45 42N 75 29W
Glen Canyon Dam, U.S.A. 123 37 0N 111 25W
Glen Canyon Nat. Recreation Area, U.S.A. 123 37 30N 111 0W
Glen Coe, U.K. 12 56 40N 5 0W
Glen Cove, U.S.A. 117 40 51N 73 37W
Glen Davis, Australia 76 33 5 S 150 18 E
Glen Garry, U.K. 14 57 3N 5 7W
Glen Innes, Australia 77 29 44 S 151 44 E
Glen Lyon, U.S.A. 117 41 10N 76 7W
Glen Massey, N.Z. 80 37 38 S 175 2 E
Glen Mor, U.K. 14 57 12N 4 37W
Glen Moriston, U.K. 14 57 10N 4 58W
Glen Orchy, U.K. 14 56 27N 4 52W
Glen Spean, U.K. 14 56 53N 4 40W
Glen Ullin, U.S.A. 120 46 48N 101 46W
Glen Valley, Australia 75 36 54 S 147 28 E
Glénans, Is. de, France 18 47 42N 4 0W
Glenavy, N.Z. 81 44 54 S 171 7 E
Glenbawn, L., Australia 77 32 5 S 151 0 E
Glenbrook, Australia 76 33 45 S 150 37 E
Glenburgh, Australia 79 25 26 S 116 6 E
Glenburn, Australia 74 37 27 S 145 26 E
Glencoe, Canada 108 42 45N 81 43W
Glencoe, S. Africa 97 28 11 S 30 11 E
Glencoe, U.S.A. 120 44 45N 94 10W
Glendale, Ariz., U.S.A. 123 33 40N 112 8W
Glendale, Calif., U.S.A. 125 34 7N 118 18W
Glendale, Oreg., U.S.A. 122 42 44N 123 29W
Glendale, Zimb. 93 17 22 S 31 5 E
Glendive, U.S.A. 120 47 7N 104 40W
Glendo, U.S.A. 120 42 30N 105 0W
Glenelg, Australia 73 34 58 S 138 31 E
Glenelg →, Australia 74 38 4 S 140 59 E
Glenflorrie, Australia 78 22 55 S 115 59 E
Glengarriff, Ireland 15 51 45N 9 33W
Glengarry, Australia 75 38 7 S 146 37 E
Glengyle, Australia 72 24 48 S 139 37 E
Glenham, N.Z. 81 46 26 S 168 52 E
Glenhope, N.Z. 81 41 40 S 172 39 E
Glenisla, Australia 74 37 14 S 142 12 E
Glenmaggie, Australia 75 37 54 S 146 43 E
Glenmary, Mt., N.Z. 81 44 0 S 169 55 E
Glenmora, U.S.A. 121 31 1N 92 34W
Glenmorgan, Australia 77 27 14 S 149 42 E
Glenn, U.S.A. 124 39 31N 122 1W
Glenns Ferry, U.S.A. 122 43 0N 115 15W
Glenorchy, Tas., Australia 72 42 49 S 147 18 E
Glenorchy, Vic., Australia 74 36 55 S 142 41 E
Glenore, Australia 72 17 50 S 141 12 E
Glenormiston, Australia 72 22 55 S 138 50 E
Glenreagh, Australia 77 30 2 S 153 1 E
Glenrock, U.S.A. 122 42 53N 105 55W
Glenrothes, U.K. 14 56 12N 3 11W
Glenrowan, Australia 75 36 29 S 146 13 E
Glens Falls, U.S.A. 117 43 20N 73 40W
Glenthompson, Australia 74 37 38 S 142 38 E
Glenties, Ireland 15 54 48N 8 18W
Glenville, U.S.A. 114 38 56N 80 50W
Glenwood, Alta., Canada 110 49 21N 113 31W
Glenwood, Nfld., Canada 105 49 0N 54 58W
Glenwood, Ark., U.S.A. 121 34 20N 93 30W
Glenwood, Hawaii, U.S.A. 112 19 29N 155 10W
Glenwood, Iowa, U.S.A. 120 41 7N 95 41W
Glenwood, Minn., U.S.A. 120 45 38N 95 21W
Glenwood, Wash., U.S.A. 124 46 1N 121 17W
Glenwood Sprs., U.S.A. 122 39 39N 107 21W
Glina, Yugoslavia 27 45 20N 16 6 E
Glittertind, Norway 10 61 40N 8 32 E
Gliwice, Poland 32 50 22N 18 41 E
Globe, U.S.A. 123 33 25N 110 53W
Glödnitz, Austria 33 46 53N 14 7 E
Głogów, Poland 32 51 37N 16 5 E
Gloria, La, Colombia 134 8 37N 73 48W
Glorieuses, Is., Ind. Oc. 97 11 30 S 47 20 E
Glossop, U.K. 12 53 27N 1 56W
Gloucester, Australia 77 32 0 S 151 59 E
Gloucester, U.K. 13 51 52N 2 15W
Gloucester, U.S.A. 117 42 38N 70 39W
Gloucester, C., Papua N. G. 69 5 26 S 148 21 E
Gloucester I., Australia 72 20 0 S 148 30 E
Gloucestershire □, U.K. 13 51 44N 2 10W
Gloversville, U.S.A. 117 43 5N 74 18W
Glovertown, Canada 105 48 40N 54 3W
Główno, Poland 32 51 59N 19 42 E
Głubczyce, Poland 32 50 13N 17 52 E
Glubokiy, U.S.S.R. 39 48 35N 40 25 E
Glubokoye, U.S.S.R. 36 55 10N 27 45 E
Głuchołazy, Poland 32 50 19N 17 24 E
Glücksburg, W. Germany 30 54 48N 9 34 E
Glückstadt, W. Germany 30 53 46N 9 28 E
Glukhov, U.S.S.R. 36 51 40N 33 58 E
Glussk, U.S.S.R. 36 52 53N 28 41 E
Glyngøre, Denmark 11 56 46N 8 52 E
Gmünd, Kärnten, Austria 33 46 54N 13 31 E
Gmünd, Niederösterreich, Austria 32 48 45N 15 0 E
Gnali, Gabon 94 2 34 S 11 18 E
Gnarp, Sweden 10 62 3N 17 16 E
Gnarput, L., Australia 74 38 4 S 143 24 E
Gnesta, Sweden 10 59 3N 17 17 E
Gniew, Poland 32 53 50N 18 50 E
Gniezno, Poland 32 52 30N 17 35 E
Gnoien, E. Germany 30 53 58N 12 41 E
Gnosjö, Sweden 11 57 22N 13 43 E
Gnowangerup, Australia 79 33 58 S 117 59 E
Go Cong, Vietnam 55 10 22N 106 40 E
Gō-no-ura, Japan 64 33 44N 129 40 E
Go Quao, Vietnam 55 9 43N 105 17 E
Goa, India 51 15 33N 73 59 E
Goa □, India 51 15 33N 73 59 E
Goalen Hd., Australia 75 36 33 S 150 4 E
Goalpara, India 52 26 10N 90 40 E
Goalundo Ghat, Bangla. 49 23 50N 89 47 E
Goaso, Ghana 90 6 48N 2 30W
Goat Fell, U.K. 14 55 37N 5 11W
Goba, Ethiopia 89 7 1N 39 59 E

Goba, *Mozam.* **97** 26 15 S 32 13 E
Gobabis, *Namibia* **96** 22 30 S 19 0 E
Gobernador Gregores, *Argentina* **142** 48 46 S 70 15W
Gobi, *Asia* **60** 44 0N 111 0 E
Gobichettipalayam, *India* **51** 11 31N 77 21 E
Gobles, *U.S.A.* **119** 42 22N 85 53W
Gobō, *Japan* **65** 33 53N 135 10 E
Gobo, *Sudan* **89** 5 40N 31 10 E
Goch, *W. Germany* **30** 51 40N 6 9 E
Gochas, *Namibia* **96** 24 59 S 18 55 E
Godavari →, *India* **50** 16 25N 82 18 E
Godavari Point, *India* **50** 17 0N 82 20 E
Godbout, *Canada* **105** 49 20N 67 38W
Godda, *India* **49** 24 50N 87 13 E
Goddua, *Libya* **86** 26 26N 14 19 E
Godegård, *Sweden* **11** 58 43N 15 8 E
Goderich, *Canada* **108** 43 45N 81 41W
Goderville, *France* **18** 49 38N 0 22 E
Godfrey, *U.S.A.* **118** 38 57N 90 11W
Godfreys Creek, *Australia* **76** 34 8 S 148 43 E
Godhavn, *Greenland* **144** 69 15N 53 38W
Godhra, *India* **48** 22 49N 73 40 E
Godinlave, *Somali Rep.* **98** 5 54N 46 38 E
Gödöllö, *Hungary* **33** 47 38N 19 25 E
Godoy Cruz, *Argentina* **140** 32 56 S 68 52W
Gods →, *Canada* **111** 56 22N 92 51W
Gods L., *Canada* **111** 54 40N 94 15W
Godthåb, *Greenland* **144** 64 10N 51 35W
Godwin Austen = K2, Mt., *Pakistan* **49** 35 58N 76 32 E
Goeie Hoop, Kaap die = Good Hope, C. of, *S. Africa* **96** 34 24 S 18 30 E
Goéland, L. au, *Canada* **106** 49 50N 76 48W
Goeree, *Neths.* **16** 51 50N 4 0 E
Goes, *Neths.* **17** 51 30N 3 55 E
Gogama, *Canada* **104** 47 35N 81 43W
Gogango, *Australia* **72** 23 40 S 150 2 E
Gogebic, L., *U.S.A.* **120** 46 20N 89 34W
Gogra = Ghaghara →, *India* **49** 25 45N 84 40 E
Gogriâl, *Sudan* **89** 8 30N 28 8 E
Goiana, *Brazil* **138** 7 33 S 34 59W
Goianésia, *Brazil* **139** 15 18 S 49 7W
Goiânia, *Brazil* **139** 16 43 S 49 20W
Goiás, *Brazil* **139** 15 55 S 50 10W
Goiás □, *Brazil* **138** 12 10 S 48 0W
Goiatuba, *Brazil* **139** 18 1 S 49 23W
Goio-Ere, *Brazil* **141** 24 12 S 53 1W
Goirle, *Neths.* **17** 51 31N 5 4 E
Góis, *Portugal* **22** 40 10N 8 6W
Gojam □, *Ethiopia* **89** 10 55N 36 30 E
Gojeb, Wabi →, *Ethiopia* **89** 7 12N 36 40 E
Gojō, *Japan* **65** 34 21N 135 42 E
Gojra, *Pakistan* **48** 31 10N 72 40 E
Gokak, *India* **51** 16 11N 74 52 E
Gokarannath, *India* **49** 27 57N 80 39 E
Gokarn, *India* **51** 14 33N 74 17 E
Gökçeada, *Turkey* **35** 40 10N 25 50 E
Gokurt, *Pakistan* **48** 29 40N 67 26 E
Gola, *India* **49** 28 3N 80 32 E
Golaghat, *India* **52** 26 30N 94 0 E
Golakganj, *India* **49** 26 8N 89 52 E
Golan Heights = Hagolan, *Syria* **44** 33 0N 35 45 E
Golaya Pristen, *U.S.S.R.* **38** 46 29N 32 32 E
Golchikha, *U.S.S.R.* **144** 71 45N 83 30 E
Golconda, *U.S.A.* **122** 40 58N 117 32W
Gold Beach, *U.S.A.* **122** 42 25N 124 25W
Gold Coast, *Australia* **77** 28 0 S 153 25 E
Gold Coast, *W. Afr.* **91** 4 0N 1 40W
Gold Hill, *U.S.A.* **122** 42 28N 123 2W
Goldberg, *E. Germany* **30** 53 34N 12 6 E
Golden, *Canada* **110** 51 20N 116 59W
Golden, *Colo., U.S.A.* **120** 39 42N 105 15W
Golden, *Ill., U.S.A.* **118** 40 7N 91 1W
Golden Bay, *N.Z.* **81** 40 40 S 172 50 E
Golden Gate, *U.S.A.* **122** 37 54N 122 30W
Golden Hinde, *Canada* **110** 49 40N 125 44W
Golden Lake, *Canada* **106** 45 34N 77 21W
Golden Prairie, *Canada* **111** 50 13N 109 37W
Golden Rock, *India* **51** 10 45N 78 48 E
Golden Vale, *Ireland* **15** 52 33N 8 17W
Goldendale, *U.S.A.* **122** 45 53N 120 48W
Goldfield, *U.S.A.* **123** 37 45N 117 13W
Goldfields, *Canada* **111** 59 28N 108 29W
Goldsand L., *Canada* **111** 57 2N 101 8W
Goldsboro, *U.S.A.* **115** 35 24N 77 59W
Goldsmith, *U.S.A.* **121** 32 0N 102 40W
Goldsworthy, *Australia* **78** 20 21 S 119 30 E
Goldthwaite, *U.S.A.* **121** 31 25N 98 32W
Golegã, *Portugal* **23** 39 24N 8 29W
Golęniów, *Poland* **32** 53 35N 14 50 E
Goleta, *U.S.A.* **125** 34 27N 119 50W
Golfito, *Costa Rica* **128** 8 41N 83 5W
Golfo Aranci, *Italy* **28** 41 0N 9 35 E
Goliad, *U.S.A.* **121** 28 40N 97 22W
Golija, *Yugoslavia* **33** 43 22N 20 15 E
Gollan, *Australia* **77** 32 16 S 149 5 E
Golo →, *France* **21** 42 31N 9 32 E
Golol, *Somali Rep.* **98** 3 38N 43 49 E
Golovanevsk, *U.S.S.R.* **38** 48 25N 30 30 E
Golra, *Pakistan* **48** 33 37N 72 56 E
Golspie, *Australia* **76** 34 20 S 149 42 E
Golspie, *U.K.* **14** 57 58N 3 58W
Golungo Alto, *Angola* **95** 9 8 S 14 46 E
Golyama Kamchiya →, *Bulgaria* **34** 43 10N 27 55 E
Goma, *Rwanda* **92** 2 11 S 29 18 E
Goma, *Zaïre* **92** 1 37 S 29 10 E
Gomati →, *India* **49** 25 32N 83 11 E
Gombari, *Zaïre* **92** 2 45N 29 3 E
Gombe, *Nigeria* **91** 10 19N 11 2 E
Gombe →, *Tanzania* **92** 4 38 S 31 40 E
Gombi, *Nigeria* **91** 10 12N 12 30 E
Gomel, *U.S.S.R.* **36** 52 28N 31 0 E
Gomera, *Canary Is.* **25** 28 7N 17 14W
Gómez Palacio, *Mexico* **126** 25 40N 104 0W
Gommern, *E. Germany* **30** 52 5N 11 47 E
Gomogomo, *Indonesia* **57** 6 39 S 134 43 E
Gompa = Ganta, *Liberia* **90** 7 15N 8 59W
Gonābād, *Iran* **47** 34 15N 58 45 E
Gonaïves, *Haiti* **129** 19 20N 72 42W
Gonâve, G. de la, *Haiti* **129** 19 29N 72 42W
Gonâve, I. de la, *Haiti* **129** 18 45N 73 0W
Gonbab-e Kāvūs, *Iran* **47** 37 20N 55 25 E
Gonda, *India* **49** 27 9N 81 58 E
Gondal, *India* **48** 21 58N 70 52 E
Gonder, *Ethiopia* **89** 12 39N 37 30 E
Gonder □, *Ethiopia* **89** 12 55N 37 30 E
Gondia, *India* **50** 21 23N 80 10 E
Gondola, *Mozam.* **93** 19 10 S 33 37 E
Gondomar, *Portugal* **22** 41 10N 8 35W
Gondomar, *Spain* **22** 42 7N 8 45W
Gondrecourt-le-Château, *France* **19** 48 31N 5 30 E
Gong Xian, *China* **58** 28 23N 104 47 E
Gong'an, *China* **59** 30 7N 112 12 E
Gongcheng, *China* **59** 24 50N 110 49 E
Gongga Shan, *China* **58** 29 40N 101 55 E
Gongguan, *China* **58** 21 48N 109 36 E
Gonghe, *China* **62** 36 18N 100 32 E
Gongola □, *Nigeria* **91** 8 0N 12 0 E
Gongola →, *Nigeria* **91** 9 30N 12 4 E
Gongolgon, *Australia* **73** 30 21 S 146 54 E
Gongshan, *China* **58** 27 43N 98 29 E
Gongtan, *China* **58** 28 55N 108 20 E
Goniadz, *Poland* **32** 53 30N 22 44 E
Goniri, *Nigeria* **91** 11 30N 12 15 E
Gonjo, *China* **58** 30 52N 98 17 E
Gonnesa, *Italy* **28** 39 17N 8 27 E
Gónnos, *Greece* **35** 39 52N 22 29 E
Gonnosfanadiga, *Italy* **28** 39 30N 8 39 E
Gonzales, *Calif., U.S.A.* **124** 36 35N 121 30W
Gonzales, *Tex., U.S.A.* **121** 29 30N 97 30W
González Chaves, *Argentina* **140** 38 2 S 60 5W
Goobang Creek, *Australia* **76** 33 6 S 147 10 E
Good Hope, C. of, *S. Africa* **96** 34 24 S 18 30 E
Goodenough I., *Papua N. G.* **69** 9 20 S 150 15 E
Gooderham, *Canada* **109** 44 54N 78 21W
Goodeve, *Canada* **111** 51 4N 103 10W
Gooding, *U.S.A.* **122** 43 0N 114 44W
Goodland, *U.S.A.* **120** 39 22N 101 44W
Goodnight, *U.S.A.* **121** 35 4N 101 13W
Goodooga, *Australia* **73** 29 3 S 147 28 E
Goodsoil, *Canada* **111** 54 24N 109 13W
Goodsprings, *U.S.A.* **123** 35 51N 115 30W
Goole, *U.K.* **12** 53 42N 0 52W
Goolgowi, *Australia* **74** 33 58 S 145 41 E
Gooloogong, *Australia* **76** 33 36 S 148 26 E
Goomalling, *Australia* **79** 31 15 S 116 49 E
Goombalie, *Australia* **73** 29 59 S 145 26 E
Goombungee, *Australia* **77** 27 18 S 151 51 E
Goonda, *Mozam.* **93** 19 48 S 33 57 E
Goondiwindi, *Australia* **77** 28 30 S 150 21 E
Goongarrie, *Australia* **79** 30 3 S 121 9 E
Goonumbla, *Australia* **76** 32 59 S 148 11 E
Goonyella, *Australia* **72** 21 47 S 147 58 E
Goor, *Neths.* **16** 52 13N 6 33 E
Goorambat, *Australia* **74** 36 24 S 145 56 E
Gooray, *Australia* **77** 28 25 S 150 2 E
Goose →, *Canada* **105** 53 20N 60 35W
Goose L., *U.S.A.* **122** 42 0N 120 30W
Gooty, *India* **51** 15 7N 77 41 E
Gopalganj, *Bangla.* **52** 23 1N 89 50 E
Gopalganj, *India* **49** 26 28N 84 30 E
Göppingen, *W. Germany* **31** 48 42N 9 40 E
Gor, *Spain* **25** 37 23N 2 58W
Góra, *Poland* **32** 51 40N 16 31 E
Gorakhpur, *India* **49** 26 47N 83 23 E
Gorbatov, *U.S.S.R.* **37** 56 12N 43 2 E
Gorbea, Peña, *Spain* **24** 43 1N 2 50W
Gorda, *U.S.A.* **124** 35 53N 121 26W
Gorda, Pta., *Nic.* **128** 14 20N 83 10W
Gorda, Pta., *Canary Is.* **25** 28 45N 18 0W
Gordan B., *Australia* **78** 11 35 S 130 10 E
Gordon, *S. Austral., Australia* **73** 32 7 S 138 20 E
Gordon, *Vic., Australia* **74** 37 34 S 144 6 E
Gordon, *U.S.A.* **120** 42 49N 102 12W
Gordon →, *Australia* **72** 42 27 S 145 30 E
Gordon, I., *Chile* **142** 54 55 S 69 30W
Gordon Downs, *Australia* **78** 18 48 S 128 33 E
Gordon L., *Alta., Canada* **111** 56 30N 110 25W
Gordon L., *N.W.T., Canada* **110** 63 5N 113 11W
Gordon River, *Australia* **79** 34 10 S 117 15 E
Gordonia, *S. Africa* **96** 28 13 S 21 10 E
Gordonvale, *Australia* **72** 17 5 S 145 50 E
Gore, *Australia* **77** 28 17 S 151 30 E
Goré, *Chad* **87** 7 59N 16 31 E
Gore, *Ethiopia* **89** 8 12N 35 32 E
Gore, *N.Z.* **81** 46 5 S 168 58 E
Gore Bay, *Canada* **108** 45 57N 82 28W
Gorey, *Ireland* **15** 52 41N 6 18W
Gorgān, *Iran* **47** 36 55N 54 30 E
Gorgona, *Italy* **26** 43 27N 9 52 E
Gorgona, I., *Colombia* **136** 3 0N 78 10W
Gorgora, *Ethiopia* **89** 12 15N 37 17 E
Gorham, *U.S.A.* **117** 44 23N 71 10W
Gori, *U.S.S.R.* **39** 42 0N 44 7 E
Gorin, *U.S.A.* **118** 40 22N 92 1W
Gorinchem, *Neths.* **16** 51 50N 4 59 E
Gorinhatã, *Brazil* **139** 19 15 S 49 45W
Goritsy, *U.S.S.R.* **37** 57 4N 36 43 E
Gorízia, *Italy* **27** 45 56N 13 37 E
Gorki = Gorkiy, *U.S.S.R.* **37** 56 20N 44 0 E
Gorki, *U.S.S.R.* **36** 54 17N 30 59 E
Gorkiy, *U.S.S.R.* **37** 56 20N 44 0 E
Gorkovskoye Vdkhr., *U.S.S.R.* **37** 57 2N 43 4 E
Gørlev, *Denmark* **11** 55 30N 11 15 E
Gorlice, *Poland* **32** 49 35N 21 11 E
Görlitz, *E. Germany* **30** 51 10N 14 59 E
Gorlovka, *U.S.S.R.* **38** 48 19N 38 5 E
Gorman, *Calif., U.S.A.* **125** 34 47N 118 51W
Gorman, *Tex., U.S.A.* **121** 32 15N 98 43W
Gormandale, *Australia* **75** 38 18 S 146 44 E
Gorna Dzhumayo = Blagoevgrad, *Bulgaria* **35** 42 2N 23 5 E
Gorna Oryakhovitsa, *Bulgaria* **34** 43 7N 25 40 E
Gornja Radgona, *Yugoslavia* **27** 46 40N 16 2 E
Gornja Tuzla, *Yugoslavia* **33** 44 35N 18 46 E
Gornji Grad, *Yugoslavia* **27** 46 20N 14 52 E
Gornji Milanovac, *Yugoslavia* **33** 44 0N 20 29 E
Gornji Vakuf, *Yugoslavia* **33** 43 57N 17 34 E
Gorno-Altaysk, *U.S.S.R.* **40** 51 50N 86 5 E
Gorno Slinkino, *U.S.S.R.* **40** 60 5N 70 0 E
Gornyy, *U.S.S.R.* **37** 51 50N 48 30 E
Gorodenka, *U.S.S.R.* **38** 48 41N 25 29 E
Gorodets, *U.S.S.R.* **37** 56 38N 43 28 E
Gorodishche, *R.S.F.S.R., U.S.S.R.* **37** 53 13N 45 40 E
Gorodishche, *Ukraine S.S.R., U.S.S.R.* **38** 49 17N 31 27 E
Gorodnitsa, *U.S.S.R.* **36** 50 46N 27 19 E
Gorodnya, *U.S.S.R.* **36** 51 55N 31 33 E
Gorodok, *Byelorussian S.S.R., U.S.S.R.* **36** 55 30N 30 3 E
Gorodok, *Ukraine S.S.R., U.S.S.R.* **36** 49 46N 23 32 E
Goroka, *Papua N. G.* **69** 6 7 S 145 25 E
Goroke, *Australia* **74** 36 43 S 141 29 E
Gorokhov, *U.S.S.R.* **36** 50 30N 24 45 E
Gorokhovets, *U.S.S.R.* **37** 56 13N 42 39 E
Gorom Gorom, *Burkina Faso* **91** 14 26N 0 14W
Goromonzi, *Zimb.* **93** 17 52 S 31 22 E
Gorongose →, *Mozam.* **97** 20 30 S 34 40 E
Gorongoza, *Mozam.* **93** 18 44 S 34 2 E
Gorongoza, Sa. da, *Mozam.* **93** 18 27 S 34 2 E
Gorontalo, *Indonesia* **57** 0 35N 123 5 E
Goronyo, *Nigeria* **91** 13 29N 5 39 E
Gorredijk, *Neths.* **16** 53 0N 6 3 E
Gorron, *France* **18** 48 25N 0 50W
Gorssel, *Neths.* **16** 52 12N 6 12 E
Gort, *Ireland* **15** 53 4N 8 50W
Gorumahisani, *India* **50** 22 20N 86 24 E
Gorzkowice, *Poland* **32** 51 13N 19 36 E
Gorzów Śląski, *Poland* **32** 51 3N 18 22 E
Gorzów Wielkopolski, *Poland* **32** 52 43N 15 15 E
Gose, *Japan* **65** 34 27N 135 44 E
Gosford, *Australia* **76** 33 23 S 151 18 E
Goshen, *S. Africa* **96** 25 50 S 25 0 E
Goshen, *Calif., U.S.A.* **124** 36 21N 119 25W
Goshen, *Ind., U.S.A.* **119** 41 36N 85 46W
Goshen, *N.Y., U.S.A.* **117** 41 23N 74 21W
Goslar, *W. Germany* **30** 51 55N 10 23 E
Gospič, *Yugoslavia* **27** 44 35N 15 23 E
Gosport, *U.K.* **13** 50 48N 1 8W
Gosport, *U.S.A.* **119** 39 21N 86 40W
Gosse →, *Australia* **72** 19 32 S 134 37 E
Gostivar, *Yugoslavia* **35** 41 48N 20 57 E
Gostyń, *Poland* **32** 51 50N 17 3 E
Gostynin, *Poland* **32** 52 26N 19 29 E
Göta älv →, *Sweden* **11** 57 42N 11 54 E
Göta kanal, *Sweden* **9** 58 50N 13 58 E
Göteborg, *Sweden* **11** 57 43N 11 59 E
Göteborgs och Bohus län □, *Sweden* **9** 58 30N 11 30 E
Gotemba, *Japan* **65** 35 18N 138 56 E
Götene, *Sweden* **11** 58 32N 13 30 E
Gotha, *E. Germany* **30** 50 56N 10 42 E
Gothenburg, *U.S.A.* **120** 40 58N 100 8W
Gotland, *Sweden* **11** 57 30N 18 33 E
Gotse Delchev, *Bulgaria* **35** 41 43N 23 46 E
Gotska Sandön, *Sweden* **9** 58 24N 19 15 E
Gōtsu, *Japan* **64** 35 0N 132 14 E
Göttingen, *W. Germany* **30** 51 31N 9 55 E
Gottwald, *U.S.S.R.* **38** 49 39N 36 27 E
Gottwaldov, *Czech.* **32** 49 14N 17 40 E
Goubangzi, *China* **61** 41 20N 121 52 E
Gouda, *Neths.* **16** 52 1N 4 42 E
Goudiry, *Senegal* **90** 14 15N 12 45W
Gough I., *Atl. Oc.* **4** 40 10 S 9 45W
Gouin, Rés., *Canada* **106** 48 35N 74 40W
Gouitafla, *Ivory C.* **90** 7 30N 5 53W
Goulburn, *Australia* **76** 34 44 S 149 44 E
Goulburn →, *Australia* **74** 36 6 S 144 55 E
Goulburn Is., *Australia* **72** 11 40 S 133 20 E
Goulia, *Ivory C.* **90** 10 1N 7 11W
Goulimine, *Morocco* **84** 28 56N 10 0W
Goulmina, *Morocco* **84** 31 41N 4 57W
Gounou-Gaya, *Chad* **87** 9 38N 15 31 E
Goúra, *Greece* **35** 37 56N 22 20 E
Gouraya, *Algeria* **85** 36 31N 1 56 E
Gourdon, *France* **20** 44 44N 1 23 E
Gouré, *Niger* **91** 14 0N 10 10 E
Gouri, *Chad* **87** 19 36N 19 36 E
Gourits →, *S. Africa* **96** 34 21 S 21 52 E
Gourma Rharous, *Mali* **91** 16 55N 1 50W
Gournay-en-Bray, *France* **19** 49 29N 1 44 E
Gourock Ra., *Australia* **76** 36 0 S 149 25 E
Goursi, *Burkina Faso* **90** 12 42N 2 37W
Gouvêa, *Brazil* **139** 18 27 S 43 44W
Gouverneur, *U.S.A.* **117** 44 18N 75 30W
Gouzon, *France* **20** 46 12N 2 14 E
Govan, *Canada* **111** 51 20N 105 0W
Governador Valadares, *Brazil* **139** 18 15 S 41 57W
Governor's Harbour, *Bahamas* **128** 25 10N 76 14W
Gowan Ra., *Australia* **72** 25 0 S 145 0 E
Gowanda, *U.S.A.* **116** 42 29N 78 58W
Gowd-e Zirreh, *Afghan.* **47** 29 45N 62 0 E
Gower, The, *U.K.* **13** 51 35N 4 10W
Gowna, L., *Ireland* **15** 53 52N 7 35W
Gowrie, *U.S.A.* **118** 42 17N 94 17W
Gowrie, Carse of, *U.K.* **14** 56 30N 3 10W
Goya, *Argentina* **140** 29 10 S 59 10W
Goyder Lagoon, *Australia* **73** 27 3 S 138 58 E
Goyllarisquisga, *Peru* **136** 10 31 S 76 24W
Goz Beïda, *Chad* **87** 12 10N 21 20 E
Goz Regeb, *Sudan* **89** 16 3N 35 33 E
Graaff-Reinet, *S. Africa* **96** 32 13 S 24 32 E
Grabill, *U.S.A.* **119** 41 13N 84 57W
Grabow, *E. Germany* **30** 53 17N 11 31 E
Gračac, *Yugoslavia* **27** 44 18N 15 57 E
Gračanica, *Yugoslavia* **33** 44 43N 18 18 E
Graçay, *France* **19** 47 10N 1 50 E
Grace, *U.S.A.* **122** 42 38N 111 46W
Grace, L. (North), *Australia* **79** 33 10 S 118 20 E
Grace, L. (South), *Australia* **79** 33 15 S 118 25 E
Gracefield, *Canada* **106** 46 6N 76 3W
Graceville, *U.S.A.* **120** 45 36N 96 23W
Gracias a Dios, C., *Honduras* **128** 15 0N 83 10W
Graciosa, I., *Canary Is.* **25** 29 15N 13 32W
Gradaús, *Brazil* **138** 7 43 S 51 11W
Gradaús, Serra dos, *Brazil* **138** 8 0 S 50 45W
Gradets, *Bulgaria* **34** 42 46N 26 30 E
Gradgery, *Australia* **76** 31 12 S 147 52 E
Grado, *Italy* **27** 45 40N 13 20 E
Grado, *Spain* **22** 43 23N 6 4W
Gradule, *Australia* **77** 28 32 S 149 15 E
Grady, *U.S.A.* **121** 34 52N 103 15W
Graeca, Lacul, *Romania* **34** 44 5N 26 10 E
Graénalon, L., *Iceland* **8** 64 10N 17 20W
Grafenau, *W. Germany* **31** 48 51N 13 24 E
Gräfenberg, *W. Germany* **31** 49 39N 11 15 E
Grafton, *Australia* **77** 29 38 S 152 58 E
Grafton, *Ill., U.S.A.* **118** 38 58N 90 26W
Grafton, *N. Dak., U.S.A.* **120** 48 30N 97 25W
Gragnano, *Italy* **29** 40 42N 14 30 E
Graham, *Canada* **104** 49 20N 90 30W
Graham, *N.C., U.S.A.* **115** 36 5N 79 22W
Graham, *Tex., U.S.A.* **121** 33 7N 98 38W
Graham →, *Canada* **110** 56 31N 122 17W
Graham Bell, Os., *U.S.S.R.* **40** 80 5N 70 0 E
Graham I., *Canada* **110** 53 40N 132 30W
Graham Land, *Antarctica* **143** 65 0 S 64 0W
Graham Mt., *U.S.A.* **123** 32 46N 109 58W
Grahamdale, *Canada* **111** 51 23N 98 30W
Grahamstown, *S. Africa* **96** 33 19 S 26 31 E
Graïba, *Tunisia* **86** 34 30N 10 13 E
Graide, *Belgium* **17** 49 58N 5 4 E
Graie, Alpi, *Europe* **26** 45 30N 7 10 E
Grain Coast, *W. Afr.* **90** 4 20N 10 0W
Grajaú, *Brazil* **138** 5 50 S 46 4W
Grajaú →, *Brazil* **138** 3 41 S 44 48W
Grajewo, *Poland* **32** 53 39N 22 30 E
Gramada, *Bulgaria* **34** 43 49N 22 39 E
Graman, *Australia* **77** 29 28 S 150 56 E
Gramat, *France* **20** 44 48N 1 43 E
Grammichele, *Italy* **29** 37 12N 14 37 E
Grampian □, *U.K.* **14** 57 0N 3 0W
Grampian Mts., *U.K.* **14** 56 50N 4 0W

Grampians, The, Australia **74** 37 0 S 142 20 E
Gran →, Surinam **135** 4 1N 55 30W
Gran Altiplanicie Central, Argentina **142** 49 0 S 69 30W
Gran Canaria, Canary Is. **25** 27 55N 15 35W
Gran Chaco, S. Amer. **140** 25 0 S 61 0W
Gran Paradiso, Italy **26** 45 33N 7 17 E
Gran Sabana, La, Venezuela **135** 5 30N 61 30W
Gran Sasso d'Italia, Italy **27** 42 25N 13 30 E
Granada, Nic. **128** 11 58N 86 0W
Granada, Spain **25** 37 10N 3 35W
Granada, U.S.A. **121** 38 5N 102 20W
Granada □, Spain **23** 37 18N 3 0W
Granadilla de Abona, Canary Is. **25** 28 7N 16 33W
Granard, Ireland **15** 53 47N 7 30W
Granbury, U.S.A. **121** 32 28N 97 48W
Granby, Canada **107** 45 25N 72 45W
Grand →, Canada **108** 42 51N 79 34W
Grand →, Mich., U.S.A. **119** 43 4N 86 15W
Grand →, Mo., U.S.A. **118** 39 23N 93 6W
Grand →, S. Dak., U.S.A. **120** 45 40N 100 32W
Grand Bahama, Bahamas **128** 26 40N 78 30W
Grand Bank, Canada **105** 47 6N 55 48W
Grand Bassam, Ivory C. **90** 5 10N 3 49W
Grand Bend, Canada **108** 43 19N 81 45W
Grand Béréby, Ivory C. **90** 4 38N 6 55W
Grand Blanc, U.S.A. **119** 42 56N 83 38W
Grand-Bourg, Guadeloupe **129** 15 53N 61 19W
Grand Calumet, Île du, Canada **106** 45 44N 76 41W
Grand Canal = Yun Ho →, China **61** 39 10N 117 10 E
Grand Canyon, U.S.A. **123** 36 3N 112 9W
Grand Canyon National Park, U.S.A. **123** 36 15N 112 20W
Grand Cayman, Cayman Is. **128** 19 20N 81 20W
Grand Cess, Liberia **90** 4 40N 8 12W
Grand-Combe, La, France **21** 44 13N 4 2 E
Grand Coulee, U.S.A. **122** 47 48N 119 1W
Grand Coulee Dam, U.S.A. **122** 48 0N 118 50W
Grand Erg de Bilma, Niger **87** 18 30N 14 0 E
Grand Erg Occidental, Algeria **85** 30 20N 1 0 E
Grand Erg Oriental, Algeria **85** 30 0N 6 30 E
Grand Falls, Canada **105** 48 56N 55 40W
Grand Forks, Canada **110** 49 0N 118 30W
Grand Forks, U.S.A. **120** 48 0N 97 3W
Grand-Fougeray, France **18** 47 44N 1 43W
Grand Haven, U.S.A. **119** 43 3N 86 13W
Grand I., U.S.A. **104** 46 30N 86 40W
Grand Island, U.S.A. **120** 40 59N 98 25W
Grand Isle, U.S.A. **121** 29 15N 89 58W
Grand Junction, Colo., U.S.A. **123** 39 0N 108 30W
Grand Junction, Iowa, U.S.A. **118** 42 2N 94 14W
Grand Lac Victoria, Canada **106** 47 35N 77 35W
Grand Lahou, Ivory C. **90** 5 10N 5 0W
Grand L., N.B., Canada **105** 45 57N 66 7W
Grand L., Nfld., Canada **105** 49 0N 57 30W
Grand L., Nfld., Canada **105** 53 40N 60 30W
Grand L., La., U.S.A. **121** 29 55N 92 45W
Grand L., Ohio, U.S.A. **119** 40 32N 84 25W
Grand Lake, U.S.A. **122** 40 20N 105 54W
Grand Ledge, U.S.A. **119** 42 45N 84 45W
Grand-Leez, Belgium **17** 50 35N 4 45 E
Grand-Lieu, L. de, France **18** 47 6N 1 40W
Grand-Lucé, Le, France **18** 47 52N 0 28 E
Grand Manan I., Canada **105** 44 45N 66 52W
Grand Marais, Canada **120** 47 45N 90 25W
Grand Marais, U.S.A. **104** 46 39N 85 59W
Grand-Mère, Canada **107** 46 36N 72 40W
Grand Piles, Canada **107** 46 40N 72 40W
Grand Popo, Benin **91** 6 15N 1 57 E
Grand Portage, U.S.A. **104** 47 58N 89 41W
Grand-Pressigny, Le, France **18** 46 55N 0 48 E
Grand Rapids, Canada **111** 53 12N 99 19W
Grand Rapids, Mich., U.S.A. **119** 42 57N 86 40W
Grand Rapids, Minn., U.S.A. **120** 47 15N 93 29W
Grand River, U.S.A. **118** 40 49N 93 58W
Grand St-Bernard, Col du, Switz. **31** 45 50N 7 10 E
Grand Santi, Fr. Guiana **135** 4 20N 54 24W
Grand Teton, U.S.A. **122** 43 54N 111 50W
Grand Valley, U.S.A. **122** 39 30N 108 2W
Grand View, Canada **111** 51 10N 100 42W
Grandas de Salime, Spain **22** 43 13N 6 53W
Grande →, Jujuy, Argentina **140** 24 20 S 65 2W
Grande →, Mendoza, Argentina **140** 36 52 S 69 45W
Grande →, Bolivia **137** 15 51 S 64 39W
Grande →, Bahia, Brazil **138** 11 30 S 44 30W
Grande →, Minas Gerais, Brazil **139** 20 6 S 51 4W
Grande →, Spain **25** 39 6N 0 48W
Grande →, U.S.A. **121** 25 57N 97 9W
Grande →, Venezuela **135** 8 36N 61 39W
Grande, B., Argentina **142** 50 30 S 68 20W
Grande, I., Brazil **139** 23 9 S 44 14W
Grande, La, U.S.A. **122** 45 15N 118 0W
Grande, Serra, Goiás, Brazil **138** 11 15 S 46 30W
Grande, Serra, Piauí, Brazil **138** 8 0 S 45 0W
Grande Baie, Canada **107** 48 19N 70 52W
Grande Baleine, R. de la →, Canada **104** 55 16N 77 47W
Grande Cache, Canada **110** 53 53N 119 8W
Grande de Santiago →, Mexico **126** 21 20N 105 50W
Grande-Entrée, Canada **105** 47 30N 61 40W
Grande-Motte, La, France **21** 43 23N 4 5 E
Grande Prairie, Canada **110** 55 10N 118 50W
Grande-Rivière, Canada **105** 48 26N 64 30W
Grande Sauldre →, France **19** 47 27N 2 5 E
Grande-Vallée, Canada **105** 49 14N 65 8W
Grandes-Bergeronnes, Canada **107** 48 16N 69 35W
Grandfalls, U.S.A. **121** 31 21N 102 51W
Grandoe Mines, Canada **110** 56 29N 129 54W
Grândola, Portugal **23** 38 12N 8 35W
Grandpré, France **19** 49 20N 4 50 E
Grandview, Mo., U.S.A. **118** 38 53N 94 32W
Grandview, Wash., U.S.A. **122** 46 13N 119 58W
Grandview Heights, U.S.A. **119** 39 58N 83 2W
Grandvilliers, France **19** 49 40N 1 57 E
Graneros, Chile **140** 34 5 S 70 45W
Granet, L., Canada **106** 47 47N 77 31W
Grange, La, Ga., U.S.A. **115** 33 4N 85 0W
Grange, La, Ky., U.S.A. **114** 38 20N 85 20W
Grange, La, Mo., U.S.A. **118** 40 3N 91 35W
Grange, La, Tex., U.S.A. **121** 29 54N 96 52W
Grange, La, U.S.A. **124** 37 42N 120 27W
Grangemouth, U.K. **14** 56 1N 3 43W
Granger, Wash., U.S.A. **122** 46 25N 120 5W
Granger, Wyo., U.S.A. **122** 41 35N 109 58W
Grängesberg, Sweden **10** 60 6N 15 1 E
Grangeville, U.S.A. **122** 45 57N 116 4W
Granite City, U.S.A. **118** 38 45N 90 3W
Granite Falls, U.S.A. **120** 44 45N 95 35W
Granite Mtn., U.S.A. **125** 33 5N 116 28W
Granite Peak, Australia **79** 25 40 S 121 20 E
Granite Pk., U.S.A. **122** 45 8N 109 52W
Granity, N.Z. **81** 41 39 S 171 51 E
Granja, Brazil **138** 3 7 S 40 50W
Granja de Moreruela, Spain **22** 41 48N 5 44W
Granja de Torrehermosa, Spain **23** 38 19N 5 35W
Gränna, Sweden **11** 58 1N 14 28 E
Granollers, Spain **24** 41 39N 2 18 E
Gransee, E. Germany **30** 53 0N 13 10 E
Grant, U.S.A. **120** 40 53N 101 42W
Grant, I., Australia **78** 11 10 S 132 52 E
Grant, Mt., U.S.A. **122** 38 34N 118 48W
Grant, Pt., Australia **74** 38 32 S 145 6 E
Grant City, U.S.A. **118** 40 30N 94 25W
Grant Range Mts., U.S.A. **123** 38 30N 115 30W
Grantham, Australia **77** 27 35 S 152 12 E
Grantham, U.K. **12** 52 55N 0 39W
Grantown-on-Spey, U.K. **14** 57 19N 3 36W
Grants, U.S.A. **123** 35 14N 107 51W
Grants Pass, U.S.A. **122** 42 30N 123 22W
Grantsburg, U.S.A. **120** 45 46N 92 44W
Grantsville, U.S.A. **122** 40 35N 112 32W
Granville, France **18** 48 50N 1 35W
Granville, N. Dak., U.S.A. **120** 48 18N 100 48W
Granville, N.Y., U.S.A. **114** 43 24N 73 16W
Granville, U.S.A. **118** 41 17N 89 15W
Granville L., Canada **111** 56 18N 100 30W
Granya, Australia **75** 36 8 S 147 15 E
Grao de Gandía, Spain **25** 39 0N 0 7W
Grapeland, U.S.A. **121** 31 30N 95 31W
Gras, L. de, Canada **102** 64 30N 110 30W
Graskop, S. Africa **97** 24 56 S 30 49 E
Gräsö, Sweden **10** 60 28N 18 35 E
Grass →, Canada **111** 56 3N 96 33W
Grass Range, U.S.A. **122** 47 0N 109 0W
Grass River Prov. Park, Canada **111** 54 40N 100 50W
Grass Valley, Calif., U.S.A. **124** 39 18N 121 0W
Grass Valley, Oreg., U.S.A. **122** 45 22N 120 48W
Grassano, Italy **29** 40 38N 16 17 E
Grasse, France **21** 43 38N 6 56 E
Grasset, L., Canada **106** 49 55N 78 10W
Grassmere, Australia **73** 31 24 S 142 38 E
Gratis, U.S.A. **119** 39 38N 84 32W
Gratz, U.S.A. **119** 38 28N 84 57W
Graubünden □, Switz. **31** 46 45N 9 30 E
Graulhet, France **20** 43 45N 1 59 E
Graus, Spain **24** 42 11N 0 20 E
Gravatá, Brazil **138** 8 10 S 35 29W
Grave, Neths. **16** 51 46N 5 44 E
Grave, Pte. de, France **20** 45 34N 1 4W
's-Graveland, Neths. **16** 52 15N 5 7 E
Gravelbourg, Canada **111** 49 50N 106 35W
Gravelines, France **19** 51 0N 2 10 E
's-Gravendeel, Neths. **16** 51 47N 4 37 E
's-Gravenhage, Neths. **16** 52 7N 4 17 E
Gravenhurst, Canada **106** 44 52N 79 20W
's-Gravenpolder, Neths. **17** 51 28N 3 54 E
's-Gravensande, Neths. **16** 52 0N 4 9 E
Gravesend, Australia **77** 29 35 S 150 20 E
Gravesend, U.K. **13** 51 25N 0 22 E
Gravina di Púglia, Italy **29** 40 48N 16 25 E
Gravois, Pointe-à-, Haiti **129** 18 15N 73 56W
Gravone →, France **21** 41 58N 8 45 E
Gray, France **19** 47 22N 5 35 E
Grayling, U.S.A. **104** 44 40N 84 42W
Grayling →, Canada **110** 59 21N 125 0W
Grays Harbor, U.S.A. **122** 46 55N 124 8W
Grays L., U.S.A. **122** 43 8N 111 30W
Grays River, U.S.A. **124** 46 21N 123 37W
Graysholm, Australia **77** 28 22 S 151 22 E
Grayson, Canada **111** 50 45N 102 40W
Grayville, U.S.A. **119** 38 16N 88 0W
Graz, Austria **33** 47 4N 15 27 E
Grazalema, Spain **23** 36 46N 5 23W
Greasy L., Canada **110** 62 55N 122 12W
Great Abaco I., Bahamas **128** 26 25N 77 10W
Great Australia Basin, Australia **72** 26 0 S 140 0 E
Great Australian Bight, Australia **79** 33 30 S 130 0 E
Great Bahama Bank, Bahamas **128** 23 15N 78 0W
Great Barrier I., N.Z. **80** 36 11 S 175 25 E
Great Barrier Reef, Australia **72** 18 0 S 146 50 E
Great Barrington, U.S.A. **117** 42 11N 73 22W
Great Basin, U.S.A. **122** 40 0N 116 30W
Great Bear →, Canada **102** 65 0N 124 0W
Great Bear L., Canada **102** 65 30N 120 0W
Great Bena, U.S.A. **117** 41 57N 75 45W
Great Bend, U.S.A. **120** 38 25N 98 55W
Great Blasket I., Ireland **15** 52 5N 10 30W
Great Britain, Europe **6** 54 0N 2 15W
Great Central, Canada **110** 49 20N 125 10W
Great Dividing Ra., Australia **72** 23 0 S 146 0 E
Great Duck I., Canada **108** 45 40N 82 57W
Great Exuma I., Bahamas **128** 23 30N 75 50W
Great Falls, Canada **111** 50 27N 96 1W
Great Falls, U.S.A. **122** 47 27N 111 12W
Great Fish → = Groot Vis →, S. Africa **96** 33 28 S 27 5 E
Great Guana Cay, Bahamas **128** 24 0N 76 20W
Great Harbour Deep, Canada **105** 50 25N 56 32W
Great Inagua I., Bahamas **129** 21 0N 73 20W
Great Indian Desert = Thar Desert, India **48** 28 0N 72 0 E
Great I., Canada **111** 58 53N 96 35W
Great Karoo, S. Africa **96** 31 55 S 21 0 E
Great Lake, Australia **72** 41 50 S 146 40 E
Great Orme's Head, U.K. **12** 53 20N 3 52W
Great Ouse →, U.K. **12** 52 47N 0 22 E
Great Palm I., Australia **72** 18 45 S 146 40 E
Great Papuan Plateau, Papua N. G. **69** 6 30 S 142 25 E
Great Plains, N. Amer. **100** 47 0N 105 0W
Great Ruaha →, Tanzania **92** 7 56 S 37 52 E
Great Saint Bernard P. = Grand St-Bernard, Col du, Switz. **31** 45 50N 7 10 E
Great Salt Lake, U.S.A. **122** 41 0N 112 30W
Great Salt Lake Desert, U.S.A. **122** 40 20N 113 50W
Great Salt Plains Res., U.S.A. **121** 36 40N 98 15W
Great Sandy Desert, Australia **78** 21 0 S 124 0 E
Great Scarcies →, S. Leone **90** 9 0N 13 0W
Great Sea Reef, Fiji **68** 16 15 S 179 0 E
Great Slave L., Canada **110** 61 23N 115 38W
Great Smoky Mts. Nat. Park, U.S.A. **115** 35 39N 83 30W
Great Stour = Stour →, U.K. **13** 51 15N 1 20 E
Great Victoria Desert, Australia **79** 29 30 S 126 30 E
Great Wall, China **60** 38 30N 109 30 E
Great Western, Australia **74** 37 10 S 142 50 E
Great Whernside, U.K. **12** 54 9N 1 59W
Great Yarmouth, U.K. **12** 52 40N 1 45 E
Greater Antilles, W. Indies **129** 17 40N 74 0W
Greater London □, U.K. **13** 51 30N 0 5W
Greater Manchester □, U.K. **12** 53 30N 2 15W
Greater Sunda Is., Indonesia **56** 7 0 S 112 0 E
Grebbestad, Sweden **11** 58 42N 11 15 E
Grebenka, U.S.S.R. **36** 50 9N 32 22 E
Greco, Mte., Italy **28** 41 48N 14 0 E
Gredgwin, Australia **74** 35 59 S 143 38 E
Gredos, Sierra de, Spain **22** 40 20N 5 0W
Greece, U.S.A. **116** 43 13N 77 41W
Greece ■, Europe **35** 40 0N 23 0 E
Greeley, Colo., U.S.A. **120** 40 30N 104 40W
Greeley, Nebr., U.S.A. **120** 41 36N 98 32W
Green →, Ky., U.S.A. **114** 37 54N 87 30W
Green →, Utah, U.S.A. **123** 38 11N 109 53W
Green B., U.S.A. **114** 45 0N 87 30W
Green Bay, U.S.A. **114** 44 30N 88 0W
Green C., Australia **75** 37 13 S 150 1 E
Green City, U.S.A. **118** 40 16N 92 57W
Green Cove Springs, U.S.A. **115** 29 59N 81 40W
Green Hd., Australia **79** 30 5 S 114 56 E
Green Is., Papua N. G. **69** 4 35 S 154 10 E
Green Island, N.Z. **81** 45 55 S 170 26 E
Green River, U.S.A. **123** 38 59N 110 10W
Greenbank, U.S.A. **124** 48 6N 122 34W
Greenbush, Mich., U.S.A. **116** 44 35N 83 19W
Greenbush, Minn., U.S.A. **120** 48 46N 96 10W
Greencastle, U.S.A. **119** 39 40N 86 48W
Greene, Iowa, U.S.A. **118** 42 54N 92 48W
Greene, N.Y., U.S.A. **117** 42 20N 75 45W
Greenethorpe, Australia **76** 34 0 S 148 26 E
Greenfield, Calif., U.S.A. **124** 36 19N 121 15W
Greenfield, Calif., U.S.A. **125** 35 15N 119 0W
Greenfield, Ill., U.S.A. **118** 39 21N 90 12W
Greenfield, Ind., U.S.A. **119** 39 47N 85 51W
Greenfield, Iowa, U.S.A. **118** 41 18N 94 28W
Greenfield, Mass., U.S.A. **117** 42 38N 72 38W
Greenfield, Miss., U.S.A. **121** 37 28N 93 50W
Greenfield, Ohio, U.S.A. **119** 39 21N 83 23W
Greenfield Park, Canada **117** 45 29N 73 29W
Greenland ■, N. Amer. **144** 66 0N 45 0W
Greenland Sea, Arctic **144** 73 0N 10 0W
Greenock, U.K. **14** 55 57N 4 46W
Greenore, Ireland **15** 54 2N 6 8W
Greenore Pt., Ireland **15** 52 15N 6 20W
Greenough →, Australia **79** 28 51 S 114 38 E
Greenough Pt., Canada **108** 44 58N 81 26W
Greenport, U.S.A. **117** 41 5N 72 23W
Greens Creek, Australia **74** 36 57 S 143 0 E
Greensboro, Ga., U.S.A. **115** 33 34N 83 12W
Greensboro, N.C., U.S.A. **115** 36 7N 79 46W
Greensburg, Ind., U.S.A. **119** 39 20N 85 30W
Greensburg, Kans., U.S.A. **121** 37 38N 99 20W
Greensburg, Pa., U.S.A. **116** 40 18N 79 31W
Greentown, U.S.A. **119** 40 29N 85 58W
Greenup, U.S.A. **119** 39 15N 88 10W
Greenville, Liberia **90** 5 1N 9 6W
Greenville, Ala., U.S.A. **115** 31 50N 86 37W
Greenville, Calif., U.S.A. **124** 40 8N 120 57W
Greenville, Ill., U.S.A. **118** 38 53N 89 22W
Greenville, Ind., U.S.A. **119** 38 22N 85 59W
Greenville, Maine, U.S.A. **105** 45 30N 69 32W
Greenville, Mich., U.S.A. **119** 43 12N 85 14W
Greenville, Miss., U.S.A. **121** 33 25N 91 0W
Greenville, N.C., U.S.A. **115** 35 37N 77 26W
Greenville, Ohio, U.S.A. **119** 40 5N 84 38W
Greenville, Pa., U.S.A. **116** 41 23N 80 22W
Greenville, S.C., U.S.A. **115** 34 54N 82 24W
Greenville, Tenn., U.S.A. **115** 36 13N 82 51W
Greenville, Tex., U.S.A. **121** 33 5N 96 5W
Greenwater Lake Prov. Park, Canada **111** 52 32N 103 30W

Greenwich, *U.K.* **13** 51 28N 0 0 E
Greenwich, *Conn., U.S.A.* **117** 41 1N 73 38W
Greenwich, *N.Y., U.S.A.* **117** 43 2N 73 36W
Greenwich, *Ohio, U.S.A.* **116** 41 1N 82 32W
Greenwood, *Canada* **110** 49 10N 118 40W
Greenwood, *Ind., U.S.A.* **119** 39 37N 86 7W
Greenwood, *Miss., U.S.A.* **121** 33 30N 90 4W
Greenwood, *S.C., U.S.A.* **115** 34 13N 82 13W
Greenwood, Mt., *Australia* **78** 13 48 S 130 4 E
Gregório →, *Brazil* **136** 6 50 S 70 46W
Gregory, *U.S.A.* **120** 43 14N 99 20W
Gregory →, *Australia* **72** 17 53 S 139 17 E
Gregory, L., *S. Austral., Australia* **73** 28 55 S 139 0 E
Gregory, L., *W. Austral., Australia* **79** 25 38 S 119 58 E
Gregory Downs, *Australia* **72** 18 35 S 138 45 E
Gregory Ra., *Queens., Australia* **72** 19 30 S 143 40 E
Gregory Ra., *W. Austral., Australia* **78** 21 20 S 121 12 E
Greiffenberg, *E. Germany* **30** 53 6N 13 57 E
Greifswald, *E. Germany* **30** 54 6N 13 23 E
Greifswalder Bodden, *E. Germany* **30** 54 12N 13 35 E
Greifswalder Oie, *E. Germany* **30** 54 15N 13 55 E
Grein, *Austria* **33** 48 14N 14 51 E
Greiz, *E. Germany* **30** 50 39N 12 12 E
Gremikha, *U.S.S.R.* **40** 67 50N 39 40 E
Grenå, *Denmark* **11** 56 25N 10 53 E
Grenada, *U.S.A.* **121** 33 45N 89 50W
Grenada ■, *W. Indies* **129** 12 10N 61 40W
Grenade, *France* **20** 43 47N 1 17 E
Grenadines, *W. Indies* **129** 12 40N 61 20W
Grenen, *Denmark* **11** 57 44N 10 40 E
Grenfell, *Australia* **76** 33 52 S 148 8 E
Grenfell, *Canada* **111** 50 30N 102 56W
Grenoble, *France* **21** 45 12N 5 42 E
Grenora, *U.S.A.* **120** 48 38N 103 54W
Grenville, *Australia* **74** 37 46 S 143 52 E
Grenville, *Canada* **106** 45 37N 74 36W
Grenville, C., *Australia* **72** 12 0 S 143 13 E
Grenville Chan., *Canada* **110** 53 40N 129 46W
Gréoux-les-Bains, *France* **21** 43 45N 5 52 E
Gresham, *U.S.A.* **124** 45 30N 122 25W
Gresik, *Indonesia* **57** 7 13 S 112 38 E
Grëssoney St. Jean, *Italy* **26** 45 49N 7 47 E
Greta, *Australia* **76** 32 35 S 151 24 E
Gretna Green, *U.K.* **14** 55 0N 3 3W
Grevelingen Krammer, *Neths.* **16** 51 44N 4 0 E
Greven, *W. Germany* **30** 52 7N 7 36 E
Grevená, *Greece* **35** 40 4N 21 25 E
Grevenbroich, *W. Germany* **30** 51 6N 6 32 E
Grevenmacher, *Lux.* **17** 49 41N 6 26 E
Grevesmühlen, *E. Germany* **30** 53 51N 11 10 E
Grevie, *Sweden* **11** 56 22N 12 46 E
Grevillia, *Australia* **77** 28 26 S 152 55 E
Grey →, *N.Z.* **81** 42 27 S 171 12 E
Grey, C., *Australia* **72** 13 0 S 136 35 E
Grey Range, *Australia* **73** 27 0 S 143 30 E
Grey Res., *Canada* **105** 48 20N 56 30W
Greybull, *U.S.A.* **122** 44 30N 108 3W
Greymouth, *N.Z.* **81** 42 29 S 171 13 E
Greytown, *N.Z.* **80** 41 5 S 175 29 E
Greytown, *S. Africa* **97** 29 1 S 30 36 E
Gribanovskiy, *U.S.S.R.* **37** 51 28N 41 50 E
Gribbell I., *Canada* **110** 53 23N 129 0W
Gridley, *U.S.A.* **124** 39 27N 121 47W
Griekwastad, *S. Africa* **96** 28 49 S 23 15 E
Griffin, *U.S.A.* **115** 33 17N 84 14W
Griffith, *Australia* **74** 34 18 S 146 2 E
Griffith, *Canada* **109** 45 15N 77 10W
Griffith I., *Canada* **108** 44 50N 80 55W
Grijpskerk, *Neths.* **16** 53 16N 6 18 E
Grillby, *Sweden* **10** 59 38N 17 15 E
Grimari, *C.A.R.* **94** 5 43N 20 6 E
Grimaylov, *U.S.S.R.* **36** 49 20N 26 5 E
Grimbergen, *Belgium* **17** 50 56N 4 22 E
Grimes, *U.S.A.* **124** 39 4N 121 54W
Grimma, *E. Germany* **30** 51 14N 12 44 E
Grimmen, *E. Germany* **30** 54 6N 13 2 E
Grimsby, *Canada* **108** 43 12N 79 34W
Grimsby, *U.K.* **12** 53 35N 0 5W
Grímsey, *Iceland* **8** 66 33N 18 0W
Grimshaw, *Canada* **110** 56 10N 117 40W
Grimstad, *Norway* **11** 58 22N 8 35 E
Grindelwald, *Switz.* **31** 46 38N 8 2 E
Grindsted, *Denmark* **11** 55 46N 8 55 E
Grindstone I., *Canada* **109** 44 43N 76 14W
Grindu, *Romania* **34** 44 44N 26 50 E
Grinnell, *U.S.A.* **118** 41 45N 92 43W
Griñón, *Spain* **22** 40 13N 3 51W
Grintavec, *Yugoslavia* **27** 46 22N 14 32 E
Grip, *Norway* **10** 63 16N 7 37 E
Gris-Nez, C., *France* **19** 50 52N 1 35 E
Grisolles, *France* **20** 43 49N 1 19 E
Grisons = Graubünden □, *Switz.* **31** 46 45N 9 30 E
Grisslehamn, *Sweden* **10** 60 5N 18 49 E
Grita, La, *Venezuela* **134** 8 8N 71 59W
Grivegnée, *Belgium* **17** 50 37N 5 36 E
Grmeč Planina, *Yugoslavia* **27** 44 43N 16 16 E
Groais I., *Canada* **105** 50 55N 55 35W
Groblersdal, *S. Africa* **97** 25 15 S 29 25 E
Grobming, *Austria* **33** 47 27N 13 54 E
Grodno, *U.S.S.R.* **36** 53 42N 23 52 E
Grodzisk Mázowiecki, *Poland* **32** 52 7N 20 37 E
Grodzisk Wielkopolski, *Poland* **32** 52 15N 16 22 E
Grodzyanka, *U.S.S.R.* **36** 53 31N 28 42 E
Groenlo, *Neths.* **16** 52 2N 6 37 E
Groesbeck, *U.S.A.* **121** 31 32N 96 34W
Groesbeek, *Neths.* **16** 51 47N 5 58 E
Grogan, *Australia* **76** 34 16 S 147 49 E
Groix, *France* **18** 47 38N 3 29W
Groix, I. de, *France* **18** 47 38N 3 28W
Grójec, *Poland* **32** 51 50N 20 58 E
Grolloo, *Neths.* **16** 52 56N 6 41 E
Gronau, *Niedersachsen, W. Germany* **30** 52 5N 9 47 E
Gronau, *Nordrhein-Westfalen, W. Germany* **30** 52 13N 7 2 E
Grong, *Norway* **8** 64 25N 12 8 E
Groningen, *Neths.* **16** 53 15N 6 35 E
Groningen, *Surinam* **135** 5 48N 55 28W
Groningen □, *Neths.* **16** 53 16N 6 40 E
Groninger Wad, *Neths.* **16** 53 27N 6 30 E
Grönskåra, *Sweden* **11** 57 5N 15 43 E
Gronsveld, *Neths.* **17** 50 49N 5 44 E
Groom, *U.S.A.* **121** 35 12N 100 59W
Groot →, *S. Africa* **96** 33 45 S 24 36 E
Groot Berg →, *S. Africa* **96** 32 47 S 18 8 E
Groot-Brakrivier, *S. Africa* **96** 34 2 S 22 18 E
Groot-Kei →, *S. Africa* **97** 32 41 S 28 22 E
Groot Vis →, *S. Africa* **96** 33 28 S 27 5 E
Groote Eylandt, *Australia* **72** 14 0 S 136 40 E
Grootebroek, *Neths.* **16** 52 41N 5 13 E
Grootfontein, *Namibia* **96** 19 31 S 18 6 E
Grootlaagte →, *Africa* **96** 20 55 S 21 27 E
Grootvloer, *S. Africa* **96** 30 0 S 20 40 E
Gros C., *Canada* **110** 61 59N 113 32W
Grosa, P., *Spain* **25** 39 6N 1 36 E
Grósio, *Italy* **26** 46 18N 10 17 E
Grosne →, *France* **21** 46 42N 4 56 E
Gross Glockner, *Austria* **33** 47 5N 12 40 E
Gross Ottersleben, *E. Germany* **30** 52 5N 11 33 E
Grossenbrode, *E. Germany* **30** 54 21N 11 4 E
Grossenhain, *E. Germany* **30** 51 17N 13 32 E
Grosseto, *Italy* **26** 42 45N 11 7 E
Groswater B., *Canada* **105** 54 20N 57 40W
Grote Gette →, *Neths.* **17** 50 51N 5 6 E
Grote Nete →, *Belgium* **17** 51 8N 4 34 E
Groton, *Conn., U.S.A.* **117** 41 22N 72 12W
Groton, *S. Dak., U.S.A.* **120** 45 27N 98 6W
Grottáglie, *Italy* **29** 40 32N 17 25 E
Grottaminarda, *Italy* **29** 41 5N 15 4 E
Grottammare, *Italy* **27** 42 59N 13 52 E
Grouard Mission, *Canada* **110** 55 33N 116 9W
Grouin, Pte. du, *France* **18** 48 43N 1 51W
Groundhog →, *Canada* **104** 48 45N 82 58W
Grouse Creek, *U.S.A.* **122** 41 44N 113 57W
Grouw, *Neths.* **16** 53 5N 5 51 E
Grove City, *Ohio, U.S.A.* **119** 39 53N 83 6W
Grove City, *Pa., U.S.A.* **116** 41 10N 80 5W
Groveland, *U.S.A.* **124** 37 50N 120 14W
Grover City, *U.S.A.* **125** 35 7N 120 37W
Grover Hill, *U.S.A.* **119** 41 1N 84 29W
Groveton, *N.H., U.S.A.* **117** 44 34N 71 30W
Groveton, *Tex., U.S.A.* **121** 31 5N 95 4W
Grožnjan, *Yugoslavia* **27** 45 22N 13 43 E
Groznyy, *U.S.S.R.* **39** 43 20N 45 45 E
Grubbenvorst, *Neths.* **17** 51 25N 6 9 E
Grudziądz, *Poland* **32** 53 30N 18 47 E
Gruissan, *France* **20** 43 8N 3 7 E
Grumo Áppula, *Italy* **29** 41 2N 16 43 E
Grums, *Sweden* **10** 59 22N 13 5 E
Grünberg, *W. Germany* **30** 50 37N 8 55 E
Grundy Center, *U.S.A.* **118** 42 22N 92 45W
Grundy Prov. Pk., *Canada* **108** 45 58N 80 30W
Gruver, *U.S.A.* **121** 36 19N 101 20W
Gruyères, *Switz.* **31** 46 35N 7 4 E
Gryazi, *U.S.S.R.* **37** 52 30N 39 58 E
Gryazovets, *U.S.S.R.* **37** 58 50N 40 10 E
Grycksbo, *Sweden* **10** 60 40N 15 29 E
Grythyttan, *Sweden* **10** 59 41N 14 32 E
Grytviken, *S. Georgia* **143** 53 50 S 37 10W
Gstaad, *Switz.* **31** 46 28N 7 18 E
Gua Musang, *Malaysia* **55** 4 53N 101 58 E
Guacanayabo, G. de, *Cuba* **128** 20 40N 77 20W
Guacara, *Venezuela* **134** 10 14N 67 53W
Guachípas →, *Argentina* **140** 25 40 S 65 30W
Guachiría →, *Colombia* **134** 5 27N 70 36W
Guadajoz →, *Spain* **23** 37 50N 4 51W
Guadalajara, *Mexico* **126** 20 40N 103 20W
Guadalajara, *Spain* **24** 40 37N 3 12W
Guadalajara □, *Spain* **24** 40 47N 3 0W
Guadalcanal, *Solomon Is.* **68** 9 32 S 160 12 E
Guadalcanal, *Spain* **23** 38 5N 5 52W
Guadalén →, *Spain* **23** 38 5N 3 32W
Guadales, *Argentina* **140** 34 30 S 67 55W
Guadalete →, *Spain* **23** 36 35N 6 13W
Guadalhorce →, *Spain* **23** 36 41N 4 27W
Guadalimar →, *Spain* **25** 38 5N 3 28W
Guadalmena →, *Spain* **25** 38 19N 2 56W
Guadalmez →, *Spain* **23** 38 46N 5 4W
Guadalope →, *Spain* **24** 41 15N 0 3W
Guadalquivir →, *Spain* **23** 36 47N 6 22W
Guadalupe = Guadeloupe ■, *W. Indies* **129** 16 20N 61 40W
Guadalupe, *Brazil* **138** 6 44 S 43 47W
Guadalupe, *Mexico* **125** 32 4N 116 32W
Guadalupe, *Spain* **23** 39 27N 5 17W
Guadalupe, *U.S.A.* **125** 34 59N 120 33W
Guadalupe →, *Mexico* **125** 32 6N 116 51W
Guadalupe →, *U.S.A.* **121** 28 30N 96 53W
Guadalupe, Sierra de, *Spain* **23** 39 28N 5 30W
Guadalupe Bravos, *Mexico* **126** 31 20N 106 10W
Guadalupe I., *Pac. Oc.* **67** 29 0N 118 50W
Guadalupe Pk., *U.S.A.* **123** 31 50N 105 30W
Guadalupe y Calvo, *Mexico* **126** 26 6N 106 58W
Guadarrama, Sierra de, *Spain* **22** 41 0N 4 0W
Guadeloupe ■, *W. Indies* **129** 16 20N 61 40W
Guadeloupe, La, *Canada* **107** 45 57N 70 56W
Guadeloupe Passage, *W. Indies* **129** 16 50N 62 15W
Guadiamar →, *Spain* **23** 36 55N 6 24W
Guadiana →, *Portugal* **23** 37 14N 7 22W
Guadiana Menor →, *Spain* **25** 37 56N 3 15W
Guadiaro →, *Spain* **23** 36 17N 5 17W
Guadiato →, *Spain* **23** 37 48N 5 5W
Guadiela →, *Spain* **24** 40 22N 2 49W
Guadix, *Spain* **25** 37 18N 3 11W
Guafo, Boca del, *Chile* **142** 43 35 S 74 0W
Guafo, I., *Chile* **142** 43 35 S 74 50W
Guainía □, *Colombia* **134** 2 30N 69 0W
Guainía →, *Colombia* **134** 2 1N 67 7W
Guaíra, *Brazil* **141** 24 5 S 54 10W
Guaira, La, *Venezuela* **134** 10 36N 66 56W
Guaitecas, Is., *Chile* **142** 44 0 S 74 30W
Guajará-Mirim, *Brazil* **137** 10 50 S 65 20W
Guajira □, *Colombia* **134** 11 30N 72 30W
Guajira, Pen. de la, *Colombia* **134** 12 0N 72 0W
Gualaceo, *Ecuador* **134** 2 54 S 78 47W
Gualán, *Guatemala* **128** 15 8N 89 22W
Gualdo Tadino, *Italy* **27** 43 14N 12 46 E
Gualeguay, *Argentina* **140** 33 10 S 59 14W
Gualeguaychú, *Argentina* **140** 33 3 S 59 31W
Gualicho, Salina, *Argentina* **142** 40 25 S 65 20W
Gualjaina, *Argentina* **142** 42 45 S 70 30W
Guam, *Pac. Oc.* **66** 13 27N 144 45 E
Guamá, *Brazil* **138** 1 37 S 47 29W
Guamá →, *Brazil* **138** 1 29 S 48 30W
Guamblin, I., *Chile* **142** 44 50 S 75 0W
Guaminí, *Argentina* **140** 37 1 S 62 28W
Guamote, *Ecuador* **134** 1 56 S 78 43W
Guampí, Sierra de, *Venezuela* **135** 6 0N 65 35W
Guamúchil, *Mexico* **126** 25 25N 108 3W
Guan Xian, *China* **58** 31 2N 103 38 E
Guanabacoa, *Cuba* **128** 23 8N 82 18W
Guanacaste, Cordillera del, *Costa Rica* **128** 10 40N 85 4W
Guanaceví, *Mexico* **126** 25 40N 106 0W
Guanahani = San Salvador, *Bahamas* **129** 24 0N 74 40W
Guanajay, *Cuba* **128** 22 56N 82 42W
Guanajuato, *Mexico* **126** 21 0N 101 20W
Guanajuato □, *Mexico* **126** 20 40N 101 20W
Guanambi, *Brazil* **139** 14 13 S 42 47W
Guanare, *Venezuela* **134** 8 42N 69 12W
Guanare →, *Venezuela* **134** 8 13N 67 46W
Guandacol, *Argentina* **140** 29 30 S 68 40W
Guane, *Cuba* **128** 22 10N 84 7W
Guang'an, *China* **58** 30 28N 106 35 E
Guangchang, *China* **59** 26 50N 116 21 E
Guangde, *China* **59** 30 54N 119 25 E
Guangdong □, *China* **59** 23 0N 113 0 E
Guangfeng, *China* **59** 28 20N 118 15 E
Guanghan, *China* **58** 30 58N 104 17 E
Guanghua, *China* **59** 32 22N 111 38 E
Guangji, *China* **59** 29 52N 115 30 E
Guangling, *China* **60** 39 47N 114 22 E
Guangning, *China* **59** 23 40N 112 22 E
Guangrao, *China* **61** 37 5N 118 25 E
Guangshun, *China* **58** 26 8N 106 21 E
Guangwu, *China* **60** 37 48N 105 57 E
Guangxi Zhuangzu Zizhiqu □, *China* **58** 24 0N 109 0 E
Guangyuan, *China* **58** 32 26N 105 51 E
Guangze, *China* **59** 27 30N 117 12 E
Guangzhou, *China* **59** 23 5N 113 10 E
Guanhães, *Brazil* **139** 18 47 S 42 57W
Guanipa →, *Venezuela* **135** 9 56N 62 26W
Guanling, *China* **58** 25 56N 105 35 E
Guannan, *China* **61** 34 8N 119 21 E
Guanta, *Venezuela* **135** 10 14N 64 36W
Guantánamo, *Cuba* **129** 20 10N 75 14W
Guantao, *China* **60** 36 42N 115 25 E
Guanyang, *China* **59** 25 30N 111 8 E
Guanyun, *China* **61** 34 20N 119 18 E
Guapí, *Colombia* **134** 2 36N 77 54W
Guápiles, *Costa Rica* **128** 10 10N 83 46W
Guaporé →, *Brazil* **137** 11 55 S 65 4W
Guaqui, *Bolivia* **136** 16 41 S 68 54W
Guara, Sierra de, *Spain* **24** 42 19N 0 15W
Guarabira, *Brazil* **138** 6 51 S 35 29W
Guaranda, *Ecuador* **134** 1 35 S 79 0W
Guarapari, *Brazil* **139** 20 40 S 40 30W
Guarapuava, *Brazil* **141** 25 20 S 51 30W
Guaratinguetá, *Brazil* **141** 22 49 S 45 9W
Guaratuba, *Brazil* **141** 25 53 S 48 38W
Guarda, *Portugal* **22** 40 32N 7 20W
Guarda □, *Portugal* **22** 40 40N 7 20W
Guardafui, C. = Asir, Ras, *Somali Rep.* **98** 11 55N 51 10 E
Guardamar del Segura, *Spain* **25** 38 5N 0 39W
Guardavalle, *Italy* **29** 38 31N 16 30 E
Guardia, La, *Spain* **22** 41 56N 8 52W
Guardiagrele, *Italy* **27** 42 11N 14 11 E
Guardo, *Spain* **22** 42 47N 4 50W
Guareña, *Spain* **23** 38 51N 6 6W
Guareña →, *Spain* **22** 41 29N 5 23W
Guaria □, *Paraguay* **140** 25 45 S 56 30W
Guárico □, *Venezuela* **134** 8 40N 66 35W
Guarrojo →, *Colombia* **134** 4 6N 70 42W
Guarujá, *Brazil* **141** 24 2 S 46 25W
Guarus, *Brazil* **139** 21 44 S 41 20W
Guasave, *Mexico* **126** 25 34N 108 27W
Guascama, Pta., *Colombia* **134** 2 32N 78 24W
Guasdualito, *Venezuela* **134** 7 15N 70 44W
Guasipati, *Venezuela* **135** 7 28N 61 54W
Guasopa, *Papua N. G.* **69** 9 12 S 152 56 E
Guastalla, *Italy* **26** 44 55N 10 40 E
Guatemala, *Guatemala* **128** 14 40N 90 22W
Guatemala ■, *Cent. Amer.* **128** 15 40N 90 30W
Guatire, *Venezuela* **134** 10 28N 66 32W
Guaviare →, *Colombia* **134** 4 3N 67 44W
Guaxupé, *Brazil* **141** 21 10 S 47 5W
Guayabero →, *Colombia* **134** 2 36N 72 47W
Guayama, *Puerto Rico* **129** 17 59N 66 7W
Guayaneco, Arch., *Chile* **142** 47 45 S 75 10W
Guayaquil, *Ecuador* **134** 2 15 S 79 52W
Guayaquil, G. de, *Ecuador* **134** 3 10 S 81 0W
Guayaramerín, *Bolivia* **137** 10 48 S 65 23W
Guayas →, *Ecuador* **134** 2 36 S 79 52W
Guaymas, *Mexico* **126** 27 59N 110 54W
Guazhou, *China* **59** 32 17N 119 21 E
Guba, *Zaïre* **93** 10 38 S 26 27 E
Gûbâl, Madîq, *Egypt* **88** 27 30N 34 0 E
Gubam, *Papua N. G.* **69** 8 39 S 141 53 E
Gúbbio, *Italy* **27** 43 20N 12 34 E
Gubio, *Nigeria* **91** 12 30N 12 42 E
Gubkin, *U.S.S.R.* **37** 51 17N 37 32 E
Gudalur, *India* **51** 11 30N 76 29 E
Gudata, *U.S.S.R.* **39** 43 7N 40 10 E
Gudbrandsdalen, *Norway* **9** 61 33N 10 0 E
Gudenå, *Denmark* **11** 56 27N 9 40 E
Gudermes, *U.S.S.R.* **39** 43 24N 46 5 E
Gudhjem, *Denmark* **11** 55 12N 14 58 E
Gudiña, La, *Spain* **22** 42 4N 7 8W
Gudivada, *India* **51** 16 30N 81 3 E
Gudiyattam, *India* **51** 12 57N 78 55 E
Gudur, *India* **51** 14 12N 79 55 E
Guebwiller, *France* **19** 47 55N 7 12 E
Guecho, *Spain* **24** 43 21N 2 59W
Guéguen, L., *Canada* **106** 48 6N 77 13W
Guékédou, *Guinea* **90** 8 40N 10 5W
Guelma, *Algeria* **85** 36 25N 7 29 E
Guelph, *Canada* **108** 43 35N 80 20W
Guelt es Stel, *Algeria* **85** 35 12N 3 1 E
Guelttara, *Algeria* **85** 29 23N 2 10W
Guemar, *Algeria* **85** 33 30N 6 49 E
Guéméné-Penfao, *France* **18** 47 38N 1 50W
Guéméné-sur-Scorff, *France* **18** 48 4N 3 13W
Guéné, *Benin* **91** 11 44N 3 16 E
Güepi, *Peru* **134** 0 9 S 75 10W
Guer, *France* **18** 47 54N 2 8W
Güer Aike, *Argentina* **142** 51 39 S 69 35W
Güera, La, *Mauritania* **84** 20 51N 17 0W
Guera Pk., *Chad* **87** 11 55N 18 12 E
Guérande, *France* **18** 47 20N 2 26W
Guerche-de-Bretagne, La, *France* **18** 47 57N 1 16W
Guerche-sur-l'Aubois, La, *France* **19** 46 58N 2 56 E
Guercif, *Morocco* **85** 34 14N 3 21W
Guéréda, *Chad* **87** 14 31N 22 5 E
Guéret, *France* **20** 46 11N 1 51 E
Guérigny, *France* **19** 47 6N 3 10 E
Guerneville, *U.S.A.* **124** 38 30N 123 0W
Guernica, *Spain* **24** 43 19N 2 40W
Guernsey, *U.K.* **18** 49 30N 2 35W
Guernsey, *U.S.A.* **120** 42 19N 104 45W

Guerrara, Oasis, Algeria 85 32 51N 4 22 E
Guerrara, Saoura, Algeria 85 28 5N 0 8W
Guerrero □, Mexico 127 17 30N 100 0W
Guerzim, Algeria 85 29 39N 1 40W
Gueugnon, France 21 46 36N 4 4 E
Gueydan, U.S.A. 121 30 3N 92 30W
Guglionesi, Italy 29 41 55N 14 54 E
Gui Jiang →, China 59 23 30N 111 15 E
Gui Xian, China 58 23 8N 109 35 E
Guia, Canary Is. 25 28 8N 15 38W
Guia de Isora, Canary Is. 25 28 12N 16 46W
Guia Lopes da Laguna, Brazil 141 21 26 S 56 7W
Guichi, China 59 30 39N 117 27 E
Guider, Cameroon 91 9 56N 13 57 E
Guidimouni, Niger 91 13 42N 9 31 E
Guiding, China 58 26 34N 107 11 E
Guidong, China 59 26 7N 113 57 E
Guiglo, Ivory C. 90 6 45N 7 30W
Guigues, Canada 106 47 28N 79 26W
Guijá, Mozam. 97 24 27 S 33 0 E
Guijo de Coria, Spain 22 40 6N 6 28W
Guildford, Australia 74 37 9 S 144 11 E
Guildford, U.K. 13 51 14N 0 34W
Guilford, U.S.A. 105 45 12N 69 25W
Guilin, China 59 25 18N 110 15 E
Guillaumes, France 21 44 5N 6 52 E
Guillestre, France 21 44 39N 6 40 E
Guilvinec, France 18 47 48N 4 17W
Güimar, Canary Is. 25 28 18N 16 24W
Guimarães, Brazil 138 2 9 S 44 42W
Guimarães, Portugal 22 41 28N 8 24W
Guimaras, Phil. 57 10 35N 122 37 E
Guinda, U.S.A. 124 38 50N 122 12W
Guinea ■, W. Afr. 90 10 20N 11 30W
Guinea, Gulf of, Atl. Oc. 91 3 0N 2 30 E
Guinea-Bissau ■, Africa 90 12 0N 15 0W
Güines, Cuba 128 22 50N 82 0W
Guingamp, France 18 48 34N 3 10W
Guipavas, France 18 48 26N 4 29W
Guiping, China 59 23 21N 110 2 E
Guipúzcoa □, Spain 24 43 12N 2 15W
Guir, O. →, Algeria 85 31 29N 2 17W
Guiratinga, Brazil 137 16 21 S 53 45W
Güiria, Venezuela 135 10 32N 62 18W
Guiscard, France 19 49 40N 3 1 E
Guise, France 19 49 52N 3 35 E
Guitiriz, Spain 22 43 11N 7 50W
Guiuan, Phil. 57 11 5N 125 55 E
Guixi, China 59 28 16N 117 15 E
Guiyang, Guizhou, China 58 26 32N 106 40 E
Guiyang, Hunan, China 59 25 46N 112 42 E
Guizhou □, China 58 27 0N 107 0 E
Gujan-Mestras, France 20 44 38N 1 4W
Gujarat □, India 48 23 20N 71 0 E
Gujiang, China 59 27 11N 114 47 E
Gujranwala, Pakistan 48 32 10N 74 12 E
Gujrat, Pakistan 48 32 40N 74 2 E
Gukovo, U.S.S.R. 39 48 1N 39 58 E
Gular, Australia 76 31 19 S 148 27 E
Gulargambone, Australia 76 31 20 S 148 30 E
Gulbarga, India 50 17 20N 76 50 E
Gulbene, U.S.S.R. 36 57 8N 26 52 E
Guledagudda, India 51 16 3N 75 48 E
Gulf, The, Asia 47 27 0N 50 0 E
Gulfport, U.S.A. 121 30 21N 89 3W
Gulgong, Australia 76 32 20 S 149 49 E
Gulin, China 58 28 1N 105 50 E
Gulistan, Pakistan 48 30 30N 66 35 E
Gull Lake, Canada 111 50 10N 108 29W
Gullegem, Belgium 17 50 51N 3 13 E
Gullringen, Sweden 11 57 48N 15 44 E
Gulma, Nigeria 91 12 40N 4 23 E
Gulmarg, India 49 34 3N 74 25 E
Gulpen, Neths. 17 50 49N 5 53 E
Gulshad, U.S.S.R. 40 46 45N 74 25 E
Gulsvik, Norway 10 60 24N 9 38 E
Gulu, Uganda 92 2 48N 32 17 E
Gulwe, Tanzania 92 6 30 S 36 25 E
Gulyaypole, U.S.S.R. 38 47 45N 36 21 E
Gum Lake, Australia 73 32 42 S 143 9 E
Gumal →, Pakistan 48 31 40N 71 50 E
Gumbaz, Pakistan 48 30 2N 69 0 E
Gumel, Nigeria 91 12 39N 9 22 E
Gumiel de Hizán, Spain 24 41 46N 3 41W
Gumlu, Australia 72 19 53 S 147 41 E
Gumma □, Japan 65 36 30N 138 20 E
Gummersbach, W. Germany 30 51 2N 7 32 E
Gummi, Nigeria 91 12 4N 5 9 E
Gümüsane, Turkey 46 40 30N 39 30 E
Gümüşhaciköy, Turkey 38 40 50N 35 18 E
Gumzai, Indonesia 57 5 28 S 134 42 E
Guna, India 48 24 40N 77 19 E
Guna Mt., Ethiopia 89 11 50N 37 40 E
Gunbower, Australia 74 35 59 S 144 24 E
Gundagai, Australia 76 35 3 S 148 6 E
Gundaroo, Australia 76 35 2 S 149 16 E
Gundelfingen, W. Germany 31 48 33N 10 22 E
Gundih, Indonesia 57 7 10 S 110 56 E
Gundlakamma →, India 51 15 30N 80 15 E
Gungal, Australia 76 32 17 S 150 32 E
Gungu, Zaïre 95 5 43 S 19 20 E
Gunisao →, Canada 111 53 56N 97 53W
Gunisao L., Canada 111 53 33N 96 15W
Gunnbjørn Fjeld, Greenland 144 68 45N 31 0W
Gunnedah, Australia 77 30 59 S 150 15 E
Gunning, Australia 76 34 47 S 149 14 E
Gunningbar Cr. →, Australia 76 31 14 S 147 6 E
Gunnison, Colo., U.S.A. 123 38 32N 106 56W
Gunnison, Utah, U.S.A. 122 39 11N 111 48W
Gunnison →, U.S.A. 123 39 3N 108 30W
Guntakal, India 51 15 11N 77 27 E
Guntersville, U.S.A. 115 34 18N 86 16W
Guntong, Malaysia 55 4 36N 101 3 E
Guntur, India 51 16 23N 80 30 E
Gunungapi, Indonesia 57 6 45 S 126 30 E
Gunungsitoli, Indonesia 56 1 15N 97 30 E
Gunupur, India 50 19 5N 83 50 E
Günz →, W. Germany 31 48 27N 10 16 E
Gunza, Angola 95 10 50 S 13 50 E
Günzburg, W. Germany 31 48 27N 10 16 E
Gunzenhausen, W. Germany 31 49 6N 10 45 E
Guo He →, China 61 32 59N 117 10 E
Guoyang, China 60 33 32N 116 12 E
Gupis, Pakistan 49 36 15N 73 20 E
Gura Humorului, Romania 34 47 35N 25 53 E
Gürchañ, Iran 46 34 55N 49 25 E
Gurdaspur, India 48 32 5N 75 31 E
Gurdon, U.S.A. 121 33 55N 93 10W
Gurdzhaani, U.S.S.R. 39 41 43N 45 52 E
Gurgaon, India 48 28 27N 77 1 E
Gurguéia →, Brazil 138 6 50 S 43 24W
Gurha, India 48 25 12N 71 39 E
Guri Dam, Venezuela 135 7 50N 62 52W
Gurk →, Austria 33 46 35N 14 31 E
Gurkha, Nepal 49 28 5N 84 40 E
Gurley, Australia 77 29 45 S 149 48 E
Gurnee, U.S.A. 119 42 22N 87 55W
Gurué, Mozam. 93 15 25 S 36 58 E
Gurun, Malaysia 55 5 49N 100 27 E
Gurupá, Brazil 138 1 25 S 51 35W
Gurupá, I. Grande de, Brazil 135 1 25 S 51 45W
Gurupi, Brazil 139 11 43 S 49 4W
Gurupi →, Brazil 138 1 13 S 46 6W
Gurupi, Serra do, Brazil 138 5 0 S 47 30W
Guryev, U.S.S.R. 39 47 5N 52 0 E
Gus-Khrustalnyy, U.S.S.R. 37 55 42N 40 44 E
Gusau, Nigeria 91 12 12N 6 40 E
Gusev, U.S.S.R. 36 54 35N 22 10 E
Gushan, China 61 39 50N 123 35 E
Gushi, China 59 32 11N 115 41 E
Gushiago, Ghana 91 9 55N 0 15W
Gusinje, Yugoslavia 33 42 35N 19 50 E
Gúspini, Italy 28 39 32N 8 38 E
Gusselby, Sweden 10 59 38N 15 14 E
Gustanj, Yugoslavia 27 46 36N 14 49 E
Gustine, U.S.A. 124 37 14N 121 0W
Güstrow, E. Germany 30 53 47N 12 12 E
Gusum, Sweden 11 58 16N 16 30 E
Guta = Kalárovo, Czech. 33 47 54N 18 0 E
Gütersloh, W. Germany 30 51 54N 8 25 E
Gutha, Australia 79 28 58 S 115 55 E
Guthalongra, Australia 72 19 52 S 147 50 E
Guthega Dam, Australia 75 36 20 S 148 27 E
Guthrie, U.S.A. 121 35 55N 97 30W
Guthrie Center, U.S.A. 118 41 41N 94 30W
Gutian, China 59 26 32N 118 43 E
Gutiérrez, Bolivia 137 19 25 S 63 34W
Guttenberg, U.S.A. 118 42 46N 91 10W
Guyana ■, S. Amer. 136 5 0N 59 0W
Guyang, China 60 41 0N 110 5 E
Guyenne, France 20 44 30N 0 40 E
Guymon, U.S.A. 121 36 45N 101 30W
Guyra, Australia 77 30 15 S 151 40 E
Guyuan, Hebei, China 60 41 37N 115 40 E
Guyuan, Ningxia Huizu, China 60 36 0N 106 20 E
Guzhang, China 58 28 42N 109 58 E
Guzhen, China 61 33 22N 117 18 E
Guzinozersk, U.S.S.R. 41 51 20N 106 35 E
Guzmán, L. de, Mexico 126 31 25N 107 25W
Gwa, Burma 52 17 36N 94 34 E
Gwaai, Zimb. 93 19 15 S 27 45 E
Gwabegar, Australia 77 30 31 S 149 0 E
Gwadabawa, Nigeria 91 13 28N 5 15 E
Gwādar, Pakistan 47 25 10N 62 18 E
Gwagwada, Nigeria 91 10 15N 7 15 E
Gwalia, Australia 79 28 54 S 121 20 E
Gwalior, India 48 26 12N 78 10 E
Gwanda, Zimb. 93 20 55 S 29 0 E
Gwandu, Nigeria 91 12 30N 4 41 E
Gwane, Zaïre 92 4 45N 25 48 E
Gwaram, Nigeria 91 10 15N 10 25 E
Gwarzo, Nigeria 91 12 20N 8 55 E
Gweebarra B., Ireland 15 54 52N 8 21W
Gweedore, Ireland 15 55 4N 8 15W
Gwent □, U.K. 13 51 45N 2 55W
Gweru, Zimb. 93 19 28 S 29 45 E
Gwi, Nigeria 91 9 0N 7 10 E
Gwinn, U.S.A. 114 46 15N 87 29W
Gwio Kura, Nigeria 91 12 40N 11 2 E
Gwol, Ghana 90 10 58N 1 59W
Gwoza, Nigeria 91 11 5N 13 40 E
Gwydir →, Australia 77 29 27 S 149 48 E
Gwynedd □, U.K. 12 53 0N 4 0W
Gyaring Hu, China 62 34 50N 97 40 E
Gydanskiy P-ov., U.S.S.R. 40 70 0N 78 0 E
Gympie, Australia 73 26 11 S 152 38 E
Gyobingauk, Burma 52 18 13N 95 39 E
Gyoda, Japan 65 36 10N 139 30 E
Gyoma, Hungary 33 46 56N 20 50 E
Gyöngyös, Hungary 33 47 48N 19 56 E
Györ, Hungary 33 47 41N 17 40 E
Gypsum Pt., Canada 110 61 53N 114 35W
Gypsumville, Canada 111 51 45N 98 40W
Gyttorp, Sweden 10 59 31N 14 58 E
Gyula, Hungary 33 46 38N 21 17 E
Gzhatsk = Gagarin, U.S.S.R. 36 55 38N 35 0 E

H

Ha 'Arava →, Israel 44 30 50N 35 20 E
Ha Coi, Vietnam 54 21 26N 107 46 E
Ha Dong, Vietnam 54 20 58N 105 46 E
Ha Giang, Vietnam 54 22 50N 104 59 E
Ha Tien, Vietnam 55 10 23N 104 29 E
Ha Tinh, Vietnam 54 18 20N 105 54 E
Ha Trung, Vietnam 54 20 0N 105 50 E
Haacht, Belgium 17 50 59N 4 37 E
Ha'afeva, Tonga 68 19 57 S 174 43W
Haag, W. Germany 31 48 11N 12 12 E
Haaksbergen, Neths. 16 52 9N 6 45 E
Haaltert, Belgium 17 50 55N 4 1 E
Haamstede, Neths. 17 51 42N 3 45 E
Ha'ano, Tonga 68 19 41 S 174 18W
Ha'apai Group, Tonga 68 19 47 S 174 27W
Haapamäki, Finland 8 62 18N 24 28 E
Haapsalu, U.S.S.R. 36 58 56N 23 30 E
Haarlem, Neths. 16 52 23N 4 39 E
Haast, N.Z. 81 43 51 S 169 1 E
Haast →, N.Z. 81 43 50 S 169 2 E
Haast P., N.Z. 81 44 6 S 169 21 E
Haastrecht, Neths. 16 52 0N 4 47 E
Hab Nadi Chauki, Pakistan 48 25 0N 66 50 E
Habana, La, Cuba 128 23 8N 82 22W
Habaswein, Kenya 92 1 2N 39 30 E
Habay, Canada 110 58 50N 118 44W
Habay-la-Neuve, Belgium 17 49 44N 5 38 E
Habiganj, Bangla. 52 24 24N 91 30 E
Hablingbo, Sweden 11 57 12N 18 16 E
Habo, Sweden 11 57 55N 14 6 E
Haccourt, Belgium 17 50 44N 5 40 E
Hachenburg, W. Germany 30 50 40N 7 49 E
Hachijō-Jima, Japan 65 33 5N 139 45 E
Hachinohe, Japan 63 40 30N 141 29 E
Hachiōji, Japan 65 35 40N 139 20 E
Hachy, Belgium 17 49 42N 5 41 E
Hackensack, U.S.A. 117 40 53N 74 3W
Hadali, Pakistan 48 32 16N 72 11 E
Hadarba, Ras, Sudan 88 22 4N 36 51 E
Hadd, Ras al, Oman 47 22 35N 59 50 E
Haddington, U.K. 14 55 57N 2 48W
Haddon Rig, Australia 76 31 27 S 147 52 E
Haded Plain, Somali Rep. 98 9 46N 48 2 E
Hadejia, Nigeria 91 12 30N 10 5 E
Hadejia →, Nigeria 91 12 50N 10 51 E
Haden, Australia 77 27 13 S 151 54 E
Ḥadera, Israel 44 32 27N 34 55 E
Ḥadera, N. →, Israel 44 32 28N 34 52 E
Haderslev, Denmark 11 55 15N 9 30 E
Hadhramaut = Ḥaḍramawt, S. Yemen 45 15 30N 49 30 E
Hadjeb El Aïoun, Tunisia 86 35 21N 9 32 E
Ḥaḍramawt, S. Yemen 45 15 30N 49 30 E
Hadrians Wall, U.K. 12 55 0N 2 30W
Hadsten, Denmark 11 56 19N 10 3 E
Hadsund, Denmark 11 56 44N 10 8 E
Haeju, N. Korea 61 38 3N 125 45 E
Haerhpin = Harbin, China 61 45 48N 126 40 E
Hafar al Bāţin, Si. Arabia 46 28 25N 46 0 E
Hafizabad, Pakistan 48 32 5N 73 40 E
Haflong, India 52 25 10N 93 5 E
Hafnarfjörður, Iceland 8 64 4N 21 57W
Haft-Gel, Iran 46 31 30N 49 32 E
Hafun, Ras, Somali Rep. 45 10 29N 51 30 E
Hagalil, Israel 44 32 53N 35 18 E
Hagari →, India 51 15 40N 77 0 E
Hagen, W. Germany 30 51 21N 7 29 E
Hagenow, E. Germany 30 53 25N 11 10 E
Hagerman, U.S.A. 121 33 5N 104 22W
Hagerstown, Ind., U.S.A. 119 39 55N 85 10W
Hagerstown, Md., U.S.A. 114 39 39N 77 46W
Hagersville, Canada 108 42 58N 80 3W
Hagetmau, France 20 43 39N 0 37W
Hagfors, Sweden 10 60 3N 13 45 E
Häggenås, Sweden 10 63 24N 14 55 E
Hagi, Iceland 8 65 28N 23 25W
Hagi, Japan 64 34 30N 131 22 E
Hagolan, Syria 44 33 0N 35 45 E
Hagondange-Briey, France 19 49 16N 6 11 E
Hags Hd., Ireland 15 52 57N 9 30W
Hague, C. de la, France 18 49 44N 1 56W
Hague, The = 's-Gravenhage, Neths. 16 52 7N 4 17 E
Haguenau, France 19 48 49N 7 47 E
Hai □, Tanzania 92 3 10 S 37 10 E
Hai Duong, Vietnam 54 20 56N 106 19 E
Hai'an, Guangdong, China 59 20 18N 110 11 E
Hai'an, Jiangsu, China 59 32 37N 120 27 E
Haicheng, Fujian, China 59 24 23N 117 48 E
Haicheng, Liaoning, China 61 40 50N 122 45 E
Haidar Khel, Afghan. 48 33 58N 68 38 E
Haifa = Ḥefa, Israel 44 32 46N 35 0 E
Haifeng, China 59 22 58N 115 10 E
Haig, Australia 79 30 55 S 126 10 E
Haiger, W. Germany 30 50 44N 8 12 E
Haikang, China 59 20 52N 110 8 E
Haikou, China 54 20 1N 110 16 E
Ḥā'il, Si. Arabia 46 27 28N 41 45 E
Hailakandi, India 52 24 42N 92 34 E
Hailar, China 62 49 10N 119 38 E
Hailey, U.S.A. 122 43 30N 114 15W
Haileybury, Canada 106 47 30N 79 38W
Hailin, China 61 44 37N 129 30 E
Hailing Dao, China 59 21 35N 111 47 E
Hailong, China 61 42 32N 125 40 E
Hailun, China 62 47 28N 126 50 E
Hailuoto, Finland 8 65 3N 24 45 E
Haimen, Guangdong, China 59 23 15N 116 38 E
Haimen, Jiangsu, China 59 31 52N 121 10 E
Haimen, Zhejiang, China 59 28 40N 121 24 E
Hainan Dao, China 54 19 0N 109 30 E
Hainaut □, Belgium 17 50 30N 4 0 E
Haines, U.S.A. 122 44 51N 117 59W
Haines City, U.S.A. 115 28 6N 81 35W
Haines Junction, Canada 110 60 45N 137 30W
Haining, China 59 30 28N 120 40 E
Haiphong, Vietnam 54 20 47N 106 41 E
Haiti ■, W. Indies 129 19 0N 72 30W
Haiya Junction, Sudan 88 18 20N 36 21 E
Haiyan, China 59 30 28N 120 58 E
Haiyang, China 61 36 47N 121 9 E
Haiyuan, Guangxi Zhuangzu, China 58 22 8N 107 35 E
Haiyuan, Ningxia Huizu, China 60 36 35N 105 52 E
Haizhou, China 61 34 37N 119 7 E
Haizhou Wan, China 61 34 50N 119 20 E
Haja, Indonesia 57 3 19 S 129 37 E
Hajar Bangar, Sudan 87 10 40N 22 45 E
Hajdúböszörmény, Hungary 33 47 40N 21 30 E
Hajdúszoboszló, Hungary 33 47 27N 21 22 E
Hajiganj, Bangla. 52 23 15N 90 50 E
Hajipur, India 49 25 45N 85 13 E
Hajr, Oman 47 24 0N 56 34 E
Haka, Burma 52 22 39N 93 37 E
Hakansson, Mts., Zaïre 93 8 40 S 25 45 E
Håkantorp, Sweden 11 58 18N 12 55 E
Hakataramea, N.Z. 81 44 43 S 170 30 E
Hakken-Zan, Japan 65 34 10N 135 54 E
Hakodate, Japan 63 41 45N 140 44 E
Hakota, Japan 65 36 5N 140 30 E
Haku-San, Japan 65 36 9N 136 46 E
Hakun, Burma 52 26 46N 95 42 E
Ḥalab, Syria 46 36 10N 37 15 E
Ḥalabjah, Iraq 46 35 10N 45 58 E
Halaib, Sudan 88 22 12N 36 30 E
Halanzy, Belgium 17 49 33N 5 44 E
Halberstadt, E. Germany 30 51 53N 11 2 E
Halcombe, N.Z. 80 40 8 S 175 30 E
Halcon, Mt., Phil. 57 13 0N 121 30 E
Halden, Norway 10 59 9N 11 23 E
Haldensleben, E. Germany 30 52 17N 11 30 E
Haldwani, India 49 29 31N 79 30 E
Hale, U.S.A. 118 39 36N 93 20W
Hale →, Australia 72 24 56 S 135 53 E
Haleakala Crater, U.S.A. 112 20 43N 156 12W
Halen, Belgium 17 50 57N 5 6 E
Haleyville, U.S.A. 115 34 15N 87 40W
Half Assini, Ghana 90 5 1N 2 50W
Halfmoon Bay, N.Z. 81 46 50 S 168 5 E
Halfway →, Canada 110 56 12N 121 32W
Halfway Creek, Australia 77 29 54 S 153 5 E
Ḥalḥul, Jordan 44 31 35N 35 7 E
Haliburton, Canada 109 45 3N 78 30W
Halifax, Australia 72 18 32 S 146 22 E
Halifax, Canada 105 44 38N 63 35W
Halifax, U.K. 12 53 43N 1 51W
Halifax B., Australia 72 18 50 S 147 0 E
Halifax I., Namibia 96 26 38 S 15 4 E
Halīl →, Iran 47 27 40N 58 30 E
Halin, Somali Rep. 98 9 6N 48 37 E
Hall, Australia 76 35 12 S 149 1 E
Hall, Austria 31 47 17N 11 30 E
Hall Beach, Canada 103 68 46N 81 12W
Hall Pt., Australia 78 15 40 S 124 23 E
Hallabro, Sweden 11 56 22N 15 5 E
Hallands län □, Sweden 11 56 50N 12 50 E
Hallands Väderö, Sweden 11 56 27N 12 34 E
Hallandsås, Sweden 11 56 22N 13 0 E

Halle, Belgium 17 50 44N 4 13 E
Halle, E. Germany 30 51 29N 12 0 E
Halle, W. Germany 30 52 4N 8 20 E
Halle □, E. Germany 30 51 28N 11 58 E
Hällefors, Sweden 10 59 47N 14 31 E
Hallein, Austria 33 47 40N 13 5 E
Hällekis, Sweden 11 58 38N 13 27 E
Hallett, Australia 73 33 25 S 138 55 E
Hallettsville, U.S.A. 121 29 28N 96 57W
Hällevadsholm, Sweden 11 58 35N 11 33 E
Halley Bay, Antarctica 143 75 31 S 26 36W
Hallia →, India 50 16 55N 79 20 E
Halliday, U.S.A. 120 47 20N 102 25W
Halliday L., Canada 111 61 21N 108 56W
Hallidays Point, Australia 77 32 2 S 152 32 E
Hallingdal →, Norway 9 60 34N 9 12 E
Hällnäs, Sweden 8 64 19N 19 36 E
Hallock, U.S.A. 111 48 47N 97 0W
Halls Creek, Australia 78 18 16 S 127 38 E
Halls Gap, Australia 74 37 8 S 142 34 E
Hallsberg, Sweden 10 59 5N 15 7 E
Hallstahammar, Sweden 10 59 38N 16 15 E
Hallstavik, Sweden 10 60 5N 18 37 E
Hallstead, U.S.A. 117 41 56N 75 45W
Halmahera, Indonesia 57 0 40N 128 0 E
Halmeu, Romania 34 47 57N 23 2 E
Halmstad, Sweden 11 56 41N 12 52 E
Halq el Oued, Tunisia 86 36 53N 10 18 E
Hals, Denmark 11 56 59N 10 18 E
Halsafjorden, Norway 10 63 5N 8 10 E
Hälsingborg = Helsingborg, Sweden 11 56 3N 12 42 E
Halstad, U.S.A. 120 47 21N 96 50W
Haltdalen, Norway 10 62 56N 11 8 E
Haltern, W. Germany 30 51 44N 7 10 E
Halul, Qatar 47 25 40N 52 40 E
Ham, France 19 49 45N 3 4 E
Ham Tan, Vietnam 55 10 40N 107 45 E
Ham Yen, Vietnam 54 22 4N 105 3 E
Hamab, Namibia 96 28 7 S 19 16 E
Hamad, Sudan 89 15 20N 33 32 E
Hamada, Japan 64 34 56N 132 4 E
Hamadān, Iran 46 34 52N 48 32 E
Hamadān □, Iran 46 35 0N 49 0 E
Hamadia, Algeria 85 35 28N 1 57 E
Hamāh, Syria 46 35 5N 36 40 E
Hamakita, Japan 65 34 45N 137 47 E
Hamamatsu, Japan 65 34 45N 137 45 E
Hamar, Norway 10 60 48N 11 7 E
Hamarøy, Norway 8 68 5N 15 38 E
Hamâta, Gebel, Egypt 88 24 17N 35 0 E
Hamber Prov. Park, Canada 110 52 20N 118 0W
Hamburg, Ark., U.S.A. 121 33 15N 91 47W
Hamburg, Iowa, U.S.A. 120 40 37N 95 38W
Hamburg, N.Y., U.S.A. 116 42 44N 78 50W
Hamburg, Pa., U.S.A. 117 40 33N 76 0W
Hamburg, W. Germany 30 53 32N 9 59 E
Hamburg □, W. Germany 30 53 30N 10 0 E
Ḥamḍ, W. al →, Si. Arabia 88 24 55N 36 20 E
Hamden, U.S.A. 117 41 21N 72 56W
Hame, Finland 9 61 30N 24 0 E
Hämeenlinna, Finland 8 61 0N 24 28 E
Hamélé, Ghana 90 10 56N 2 45W
Hamelin Pool, Australia 79 26 22 S 114 20 E
Hamelin Pool Bay, Australia 79 26 10 S 114 5 E
Hameln, W. Germany 30 52 7N 9 24 E
Hamer Koke, Ethiopia 89 5 15N 36 45 E
Hamersley Ra., Australia 78 22 0 S 117 45 E
Hamhung, N. Korea 61 39 54N 127 30 E
Hami, China 62 42 55N 93 25 E
Hamilton, Australia 74 37 45 S 142 2 E
Hamilton, Canada 108 43 15N 79 50W
Hamilton, N.Z. 80 37 47 S 175 19 E
Hamilton, U.K. 14 55 47N 4 2W
Hamilton, Ill., U.S.A. 118 40 24N 91 21W
Hamilton, Ind., U.S.A. 119 41 33N 84 56W
Hamilton, Mo., U.S.A. 118 39 45N 93 59W
Hamilton, Mo., U.S.A. 120 39 45N 93 59W
Hamilton, Mont., U.S.A. 122 46 20N 114 6W
Hamilton, N.Y., U.S.A. 117 42 49N 75 31W
Hamilton, Ohio, U.S.A. 119 39 20N 84 35W
Hamilton, Tex., U.S.A. 121 31 40N 98 5W
Hamilton →, Australia 72 23 30 S 139 47 E
Hamilton City, U.S.A. 124 39 45N 122 1W
Hamilton Hotel, Australia 72 22 45 S 140 40 E
Hamilton Inlet, Canada 105 54 0N 57 30W
Hamiota, Canada 111 50 11N 100 38W
Hamlet, U.S.A. 115 34 56N 79 40W
Hamley Bridge, Australia 73 34 17 S 138 35 E
Hamlin, N.Y., U.S.A. 116 43 17N 77 55W
Hamlin, Tex., U.S.A. 121 32 58N 100 8W
Hamm, W. Germany 30 51 40N 7 49 E
Hammam Bouhadjar, Algeria 85 35 23N 0 58W
Hammamet, Tunisia 86 36 24N 10 38 E
Hammamet, G. de, Tunisia 86 36 10N 10 48 E
Hammarstrand, Sweden 10 63 7N 16 20 E
Hamme, Belgium 17 51 6N 4 8 E
Hamme-Mille, Belgium 17 50 47N 4 43 E
Hammel, Denmark 11 56 16N 9 52 E
Hammelburg, W. Germany 31 50 7N 9 54 E
Hammeren, Denmark 11 55 18N 14 47 E
Hammerfest, Norway 8 70 39N 23 41 E
Hammond, Ill., U.S.A. 119 39 48N 88 36W
Hammond, Ind., U.S.A. 119 41 40N 87 30W
Hammond, La., U.S.A. 121 30 32N 90 30W
Hammonton, U.S.A. 114 39 40N 74 47W
Hamneda, Sweden 11 56 41N 13 51 E
Hamoir, Belgium 17 50 25N 5 32 E
Hamont, Belgium 17 51 15N 5 32 E
Hamoyet, Jebel, Sudan 88 17 33N 38 2 E
Hampden, N.Z. 81 45 18 S 170 50 E
Hampshire □, U.K. 13 51 3N 1 20W
Hampshire Downs, U.K. 13 51 10N 1 10W
Hampton, Australia 76 33 39 S 150 2 E
Hampton, Canada 109 43 58N 78 45W
Hampton, Ark., U.S.A. 121 33 35N 92 29W
Hampton, Iowa, U.S.A. 118 42 42N 93 12W
Hampton, N.H., U.S.A. 117 42 56N 70 48W
Hampton, S.C., U.S.A. 115 32 52N 81 2W
Hampton, Va., U.S.A. 114 37 4N 76 18W
Hampton Tableland, Australia 79 32 0 S 127 0 E
Hamrat esh Sheykh, Sudan 89 14 38N 27 55 E
Han Jiang →, China 59 23 25N 116 40 E
Han Shui →, China 60 30 35N 114 18 E
Ḥana, U.S.A. 112 20 45N 155 59W
Hanak, Si. Arabia 88 25 32N 37 0 E
Hanamaki, Japan 63 39 23N 141 7 E
Hanang, Tanzania 92 4 30 S 35 25 E
Hanau, W. Germany 31 50 8N 8 56 E
Hanbogd, Mongolia 60 43 11N 107 10 E
Hancheng, China 60 35 31N 110 25 E
Hanchuan, China 59 30 40N 113 50 E
Hancock, Mich., U.S.A. 120 47 10N 88 40W
Hancock, Minn., U.S.A. 120 45 26N 95 46W
Hancock, Pa., U.S.A. 117 41 57N 75 19W
Handa, Japan 65 34 53N 137 0 E
Handa, Somali Rep. 98 10 37N 51 2 E
Handan, China 60 36 35N 114 28 E
Handen, Sweden 10 59 12N 18 12 E
Handeni, Tanzania 92 5 25 S 38 2 E
Handeni □, Tanzania 92 5 30 S 38 0 E
Handub, Sudan 88 19 15N 37 16 E
Handwara, India 49 34 21N 74 20 E
Handzame, Belgium 17 51 2N 3 0 E
Hanegev, Israel 44 30 50N 35 0 E
Haney, Canada 110 49 12N 122 40W
Hanford, U.S.A. 124 36 23N 119 39W
Hang Chat, Thailand 54 18 20N 99 21 E
Hang Dong, Thailand 54 18 41N 98 55 E
Hangang →, S. Korea 61 37 50N 126 30 E
Hangayn Nuruu, Mongolia 62 47 30N 100 0 E
Hangchou = Hangzhou, China 59 30 18N 120 11 E
Hanggin Houqi, China 60 40 58N 107 4 E
Hanggin Qi, China 60 39 52N 108 50 E
Hangö, Finland 9 59 50N 22 57 E
Hangu, China 61 39 18N 117 53 E
Hangzhou, China 59 30 18N 120 11 E
Hangzhou Wan, China 59 30 15N 120 45 E
Hanhongor, Mongolia 60 43 55N 104 28 E
Ḥanīsh, Yemen 45 13 45N 42 46 E
Hanita, Israel 44 33 5N 35 10 E
Hanjiang, China 59 25 26N 119 6 E
Hankinson, U.S.A. 120 46 9N 96 58W
Hanko, Finland 9 59 59N 22 57 E
Hankou, China 59 30 35N 114 30 E
Hanksville, U.S.A. 123 38 19N 110 45W
Hanle, India 49 32 42N 79 4 E
Hanmer, Canada 108 46 39N 80 56W
Hanmer Springs, N.Z. 81 42 32 S 172 50 E
Hann →, Australia 78 17 26 S 126 17 E
Hann, Mt., Australia 78 15 45 S 126 0 E
Hanna, Canada 110 51 40N 111 54W
Hannaford, U.S.A. 120 47 23N 98 11W
Hannah, U.S.A. 120 48 58N 98 42W
Hannah B., Canada 104 51 40N 80 0W
Hannahs Bridge, Australia 77 31 55 S 149 41 E
Hannibal, U.S.A. 118 39 42N 91 22W
Hannik, Sudan 88 18 12N 32 20 E
Hannover, W. Germany 30 52 23N 9 43 E
Hannut, Belgium 17 50 40N 5 4 E
Hanö, Sweden 11 56 2N 14 50 E
Hanöbukten, Sweden 11 55 35N 14 30 E
Hanoi, Vietnam 54 21 5N 105 55 E
Hanover = Hannover, W. Germany 30 52 23N 9 43 E
Hanover, Canada 108 44 9N 81 2W
Hanover, S. Africa 96 31 4 S 24 29 E
Hanover, Ind., U.S.A. 119 38 43N 85 28W
Hanover, N.H., U.S.A. 117 43 43N 72 17W
Hanover, Ohio, U.S.A. 116 40 5N 82 17W
Hanover, Pa., U.S.A. 114 39 46N 76 59W
Hanover, I., Chile 142 51 0 S 74 50W
Hanpan, C., Papua N. G. 69 5 0 S 154 35 E
Hans Meyer Ra., Papua N. G. 69 4 20 S 152 55 E
Hanshou, China 59 28 56N 111 50 E
Hansi, India 48 29 10N 75 57 E
Hansjö, Sweden 10 61 10N 14 40 E
Hanson, L., Australia 73 31 0 S 136 15 E
Hanyang, China 59 30 35N 114 2 E
Hanyin, China 58 32 54N 108 28 E
Hanyū, Japan 65 36 10N 139 32 E
Hanyuan, China 58 29 21N 102 40 E
Hanzhong, China 60 33 10N 107 1 E
Hanzhuang, China 61 34 33N 117 23 E
Haora, India 49 22 37N 88 20 E
Haoxue, China 59 30 3N 112 24 E
Haparanda, Sweden 8 65 52N 24 8 E
Hapert, Neths. 17 51 22N 5 15 E
Happy, U.S.A. 121 34 47N 101 50W
Happy Camp, U.S.A. 122 41 52N 123 22W
Happy Valley-Goose Bay, Canada 105 53 15N 60 20W
Hapur, India 48 28 45N 77 45 E
Ḥaql, Si. Arabia 88 29 10N 35 0 E
Haquira, Peru 136 14 14 S 72 12W
Har, Indonesia 57 5 16 S 133 14 E
Har-Ayrag, Mongolia 60 45 47N 109 16 E
Har Hu, China 62 38 20N 97 38 E
Har Us Nuur, Mongolia 62 48 0N 92 0 E
Har Yehuda, Israel 44 31 35N 34 57 E
Ḥaraḍ, Si. Arabia 46 24 22N 49 0 E
Haraisan Plateau, Si. Arabia 46 23 0N 47 40 E
Harardera, Somali Rep. 98 4 33N 47 38 E
Harare, Zimb. 93 17 43 S 31 2 E
Harat, Ethiopia 89 16 5N 39 26 E
Harazé, Chad 87 9 57N 20 48 E
Harazé, Chad 87 14 20N 19 12 E
Harbin, China 61 45 48N 126 40 E
Harbøør, Denmark 11 56 38N 8 10 E
Harbor Beach, U.S.A. 104 43 50N 82 38W
Harbor Springs, U.S.A. 114 45 28N 85 0W
Harbour Breton, Canada 105 47 29N 55 50W
Harbour Grace, Canada 105 47 40N 53 22W
Harburg, W. Germany 30 53 27N 9 58 E
Hårby, Denmark 11 55 13N 10 7 E
Harda, India 48 22 27N 77 5 E
Hardangerfjorden, Norway 9 60 15N 6 0 E
Hardap Dam, Namibia 96 24 32 S 17 50 E
Hardegarijp, Neths. 16 53 13N 5 57 E
Harden, Australia 76 34 32 S 148 24 E
Hardenberg, Neths. 16 52 34N 6 37 E
Harderwijk, Neths. 16 52 21N 5 38 E
Hardey →, Australia 78 22 45 S 116 8 E
Hardin, Ill., U.S.A. 118 39 9N 90 37W
Hardin, Mont., U.S.A. 122 45 44N 107 35W
Harding, S. Africa 97 30 35 S 29 55 E
Harding Ra., Australia 78 16 17 S 124 55 E
Hardinsburg, U.S.A. 119 37 47N 86 28W
Hardisty, Canada 110 52 40N 111 18W
Hardman, U.S.A. 122 45 12N 119 40W
Hardoi, India 49 27 26N 80 6 E
Hardwar = Haridwar, India 48 29 58N 78 9 E
Hardwick, U.S.A. 117 44 30N 72 20W
Hardy, U.S.A. 121 36 20N 91 30W
Hardy, Pen., Chile 142 55 30 S 68 20W
Hare B., Canada 105 51 15N 55 45W
Hare Gilboa, Israel 44 32 31N 35 25 E
Hare Meron, Israel 44 32 59N 35 24 E
Harelbeke, Belgium 17 50 52N 3 20 E
Haren, Neths. 16 53 11N 6 36 E
Haren, W. Germany 30 52 47N 7 18 E
Harer, Ethiopia 89 9 20N 42 8 E
Harerge □, Ethiopia 89 7 12N 42 0 E
Hareto, Ethiopia 89 9 23N 37 6 E
Harfleur, France 18 49 30N 0 10 E
Hargeisa, Somali Rep. 98 9 30N 44 2 E
Hargraves, Australia 76 32 46 S 149 28 E
Hargshamn, Sweden 10 60 12N 18 30 E
Hari →, Indonesia 56 1 16 S 104 5 E
Haria, Canary Is. 25 29 8N 13 32W
Haricha, Hamada el, Mali 84 22 40N 3 15W
Haridwar, India 48 29 58N 78 9 E
Harihar, India 51 14 32N 75 44 E
Harima-Nada, Japan 64 34 30N 134 35 E
Haringhata →, Bangla. 52 22 0N 89 58 E
Haringvliet, Neths. 16 51 48N 4 10 E
Haripad, India 51 9 14N 76 28 E
Harīrūd, Iran 47 35 0N 61 0 E
Harīrūd →, Asia 47 37 24N 60 38 E
Harlan, Iowa, U.S.A. 120 41 37N 95 20W
Harlan, Tenn., U.S.A. 115 36 50N 83 20W
Harlech, U.K. 12 52 52N 4 7W
Harlem, U.S.A. 122 48 29N 108 47W
Harlingen, Neths. 16 53 11N 5 25 E
Harlingen, U.S.A. 121 26 20N 97 50W
Harlowton, U.S.A. 122 46 30N 109 54W
Harmånger, Sweden 10 61 55N 17 20 E
Harmil, Ethiopia 89 16 30N 40 10 E
Harney Basin, U.S.A. 122 43 30N 119 0W
Harney L., U.S.A. 122 43 0N 119 0W
Harney Pk., U.S.A. 120 43 52N 103 33W
Härnön, Sweden 10 62 36N 18 0 E
Härnösand, Sweden 10 62 38N 18 0 E
Haro, Spain 24 42 35N 2 55W
Harp L., Canada 105 55 5N 61 50W
Harpanahalli, India 51 14 47N 76 2 E
Harpe, La, U.S.A. 118 40 30N 91 0W
Harper, Liberia 90 4 25N 7 43W
Harplinge, Sweden 11 56 45N 12 45 E
Harrand, Pakistan 48 29 28N 70 3 E
Ḥarrat al Kishb, Si. Arabia 46 22 30N 40 15 E
Harrat al 'Uwairidh, Si. Arabia 46 26 50N 38 0 E
Harricana →, Canada 106 50 56N 79 32W
Harriman, U.S.A. 115 36 0N 84 35W
Harrington Harbour, Canada 105 50 31N 59 30W
Harris, U.K. 14 57 50N 6 55W
Harris, Sd. of, U.K. 14 57 44N 7 6W
Harris L., Australia 73 31 10 S 135 10 E
Harris Mts., N.Z. 81 44 49 S 168 49 E
Harris Pt., Canada 108 43 6N 82 9W
Harrisburg, Ill., U.S.A. 119 37 42N 88 30W
Harrisburg, Nebr., U.S.A. 120 41 36N 103 46W
Harrisburg, Oreg., U.S.A. 122 44 16N 123 10W
Harrisburg, Pa., U.S.A. 116 40 18N 76 52W
Harrismith, S. Africa 97 28 15 S 29 8 E
Harrison, Ark., U.S.A. 121 36 10N 93 4W
Harrison, Idaho, U.S.A. 122 47 30N 116 51W
Harrison, Nebr., U.S.A. 120 42 42N 103 52W
Harrison, C., Canada 105 54 55N 57 55W
Harrison B., U.S.A. 102 70 25N 151 30W
Harrison L., Canada 110 49 33N 121 50W
Harrisonburg, U.S.A. 114 38 28N 78 52W
Harrisonville, U.S.A. 118 38 39N 94 21W
Harriston, Canada 108 43 57N 80 53W
Harrisville, U.S.A. 116 44 40N 83 19W
Harrodsburg, Ind., U.S.A. 119 39 1N 86 33W
Harrodsburg, Ky., U.S.A. 119 37 46N 84 51W
Harrogate, U.K. 12 53 59N 1 32W
Harrow, Australia 74 37 9 S 141 35 E
Harrow, Canada 108 42 2N 82 55W
Harrow, U.K. 13 51 35N 0 15W
Harrowsmith, Canada 109 44 24N 76 40W
Harry S. Truman Res., U.S.A. 118 38 14N 93 30W
Harsefeld, W. Germany 30 53 26N 9 31 E
Harskamp, Neths. 16 52 8N 5 46 E
Harstad, Norway 8 68 48N 16 30 E
Hart, U.S.A. 114 43 42N 86 21W
Hart, L., Australia 73 31 10 S 136 25 E
Hartbees →, S. Africa 96 28 45 S 20 32 E
Hartberg, Austria 33 47 17N 15 58 E
Hartford, Conn., U.S.A. 117 41 47N 72 41W
Hartford, Ky., U.S.A. 114 37 26N 86 50W
Hartford, Mich., U.S.A. 119 42 13N 86 10W
Hartford, S. Dak., U.S.A. 120 43 40N 96 58W
Hartford, Wis., U.S.A. 120 43 18N 88 25W
Hartford City, U.S.A. 119 40 22N 85 20W
Hartland, Canada 105 46 20N 67 32W
Hartland, U.S.A. 119 43 6N 88 21W
Hartland Pt., U.K. 13 51 2N 4 32W
Hartlepool, U.K. 12 54 42N 1 11W
Hartley Bay, Canada 110 53 25N 129 15W
Hartmannberge, Namibia 96 17 0 S 13 0 E
Hartney, Canada 111 49 30N 100 35W
Harts →, S. Africa 96 28 24 S 24 17 E
Hartselle, U.S.A. 115 34 25N 86 55W
Hartshorne, U.S.A. 121 34 51N 95 30W
Hartsville, U.S.A. 115 34 23N 80 2W
Hartwell, U.S.A. 115 34 21N 82 52W
Harunabad, Pakistan 48 29 35N 73 8 E
Harur, India 51 12 3N 78 29 E
Harvard, U.S.A. 119 42 25N 88 37W
Harvey, Australia 79 33 5 S 115 54 E
Harvey, Ill., U.S.A. 119 41 40N 87 40W
Harvey, Ill., U.S.A. 119 41 36N 87 50W
Harvey, N. Dak., U.S.A. 120 47 50N 99 58W
Harwich, U.K. 13 51 56N 1 18 E
Haryana □, India 48 29 0N 76 10 E
Harz, Germany 30 51 40N 10 40 E
Harzé, Belgium 17 50 27N 5 40 E
Harzgerode, E. Germany 30 51 38N 11 8 E
Hasa, Si. Arabia 46 26 0N 49 0 E
Hasaheisa, Sudan 89 14 44N 33 20 E
Hasanpur, India 48 28 43N 78 17 E
Haselünne, W. Germany 30 52 40N 7 30 E
Hasharon, Israel 44 32 12N 34 49 E
Hashefela, Israel 44 31 30N 34 43 E
Hashima, Japan 65 35 20N 136 40 E
Hashimoto, Japan 65 34 19N 135 37 E
Håsjö, Sweden 10 63 1N 16 5 E
Haskell, Okla., U.S.A. 121 35 51N 95 40W
Haskell, Tex., U.S.A. 121 33 10N 99 45W
Haslach, W. Germany 31 48 16N 8 7 E
Hasle, Denmark 11 55 11N 14 44 E
Haslev, Denmark 11 55 18N 11 57 E
Hasparren, France 20 43 24N 1 18W
Hasselt, Belgium 17 50 56N 5 21 E
Hasselt, Neths. 16 52 36N 6 6 E
Hassene, Adrar, Algeria 85 21 0N 4 0 E
Hassfurt, W. Germany 31 50 2N 10 30 E
Hassi Berrekrem, Algeria 85 33 45N 5 16 E
Hassi bou Khelala, Algeria 85 30 17N 0 18W
Hassi Daoula, Algeria 85 33 4N 5 38 E
Hassi Djafou, Algeria 85 30 55N 3 35 E
Hassi el Abiod, Algeria 85 31 47N 3 37 E
Hassi el Biod, Algeria 85 28 30N 6 0 E
Hassi el Gassi, Algeria 85 30 52N 6 5 E
Hassi el Hadjar, Algeria 85 31 28N 4 45 E
Hassi er Rmel, Algeria 85 32 56N 3 17 E
Hassi Imoulaye, Algeria 85 29 54N 9 10 E
Hassi Inifel, Algeria 85 29 50N 3 41 E
Hassi Messaoud, Algeria 85 31 43N 6 8 E

Hassi Rhénami, *Algeria* **85** 31 50N 5 58 E
Hassi Tartrat, *Algeria* **85** 30 5N 6 28 E
Hassi Zerzour, *Morocco* **84** 30 51N 3 56W
Hastière-Lavaux, *Belgium* **17** 50 13N 4 49 E
Hastings, *Australia* **74** 38 18 S 145 12 E
Hastings, *Canada* **109** 44 18N 77 57W
Hastings, *N.Z.* **80** 39 39 S 176 52 E
Hastings, *U.K.* **13** 50 51N 0 36 E
Hastings, *Mich., U.S.A.* **119** 42 40N 85 20W
Hastings, *Minn., U.S.A.* **120** 44 41N 92 51W
Hastings, *Nebr., U.S.A.* **120** 40 34N 98 22W
Hastings →, *Australia* **77** 31 25 S 152 55 E
Hastings Ra., *Australia* **77** 31 15 S 152 14 E
Hästveda, *Sweden* **11** 56 17N 13 55 E
Hat Yai, *Thailand* **55** 7 1N 100 27 E
Hatanbulag, *Mongolia* **60** 43 8N 109 5 E
Hatano, *Japan* **65** 35 22N 139 14 E
Hatch, *U.S.A.* **123** 32 45N 107 8W
Hatches Creek, *Australia* **72** 20 56 S 135 12 E
Hatchet L., *Canada* **111** 58 36N 103 40W
Haţeg, *Romania* **34** 45 36N 22 55 E
Haţeg, Mţii., *Romania* **34** 45 25N 23 0 E
Hatert, *Neths.* **16** 51 49N 5 50 E
Hatfield P.O., *Australia* **73** 33 54 S 143 49 E
Hatgal, *Mongolia* **62** 50 26N 100 9 E
Hathras, *India* **48** 27 36N 78 6 E
Hato de Corozal, *Colombia* **134** 6 11N 71 45W
Hato Mayor, *Dom. Rep.* **129** 18 46N 69 15W
Hattah, *Australia* **74** 34 48 S 142 17 E
Hattem, *Neths.* **16** 52 28N 6 4 E
Hatteras, C., *U.S.A.* **115** 35 10N 75 30W
Hattiesburg, *U.S.A.* **121** 31 20N 89 20W
Hatvan, *Hungary* **33** 47 40N 19 45 E
Hau Bon = Cheo Reo, *Vietnam* **54** 13 25N 108 28 E
Hau Duc, *Vietnam* **54** 15 20N 108 13 E
Haubstadt, *U.S.A.* **119** 38 12N 87 34W
Haug, *Norway* **10** 60 23N 10 26 E
Haugastøl, *Norway* **10** 60 30N 7 50 E
Haugesund, *Norway* **9** 59 23N 5 13 E
Hauhungaroa Ra., *N.Z.* **80** 38 42 S 175 40 E
Haulerwijk, *Neths.* **16** 53 4N 6 20 E
Haultain →, *Canada* **111** 55 51N 106 46W
Haungpa, *Burma* **52** 25 29N 96 7 E
Hauraki Gulf, *N.Z.* **80** 36 35 S 175 5 E
Hauran, *Syria* **44** 32 50N 36 15 E
Haut Atlas, *Morocco* **84** 32 30N 5 0W
Haut-Rhin □, *France* **19** 48 0N 7 15 E
Haut Zaïre □, *Zaïre* **92** 2 20N 26 0 E
Hautah, Wahāt al, *Si. Arabia* **46** 23 40N 47 0 E
Haute-Corse □, *France* **21** 42 30N 9 30 E
Haute-Garonne □, *France* **20** 43 30N 1 30 E
Haute-Loire □, *France* **20** 45 5N 3 50 E
Haute-Marne □, *France* **19** 48 10N 5 20 E
Haute-Saône □, *France* **19** 47 45N 6 10 E
Haute-Savoie □, *France* **21** 46 0N 6 20 E
Haute-Vienne □, *France* **20** 45 50N 1 10 E
Hauterive, *Canada* **107** 49 10N 68 16W
Hautes-Alpes □, *France* **21** 44 42N 6 20 E
Hautes Fagnes, *Belgium* **17** 50 34N 6 6 E
Hautes-Pyrénées □, *France* **20** 43 0N 0 10 E
Hauteville-Lompnès, *France* **21** 45 58N 5 36 E
Hautmont, *France* **19** 50 15N 3 55 E
Hautrage, *Belgium* **17** 50 29N 3 46 E
Hauts-de-Seine □, *France* **19** 48 52N 2 15 E
Hauts Plateaux, *Algeria* **85** 35 0N 1 0 E
Hauzenberg, *W. Germany* **31** 48 39N 13 38 E
Havana = Habana, La, *Cuba* **128** 23 8N 82 22W
Havana, *U.S.A.* **118** 40 19N 90 3W
Havant, *U.K.* **13** 50 51N 0 59W
Havasu, L., *U.S.A.* **125** 34 18N 114 28W
Havdhem, *Sweden* **11** 57 10N 18 20 E
Havel →, *E. Germany* **30** 52 40N 12 1 E
Havelange, *Belgium* **17** 50 23N 5 15 E
Havelian, *Pakistan* **48** 34 2N 73 10 E
Havelock, *N.B., Canada* **105** 46 2N 65 24W
Havelock, *Ont., Canada* **109** 44 26N 77 53W
Havelock, *N.Z.* **81** 41 17 S 173 48 E
Havelte, *Neths.* **16** 52 46N 6 14 E
Haverfordwest, *U.K.* **13** 51 48N 4 59W
Haverhill, *U.S.A.* **117** 42 50N 71 2W
Haveri, *India* **51** 14 53N 75 24 E
Havering, *U.K.* **13** 51 33N 0 20 E
Haverstraw, *U.S.A.* **117** 41 12N 73 58W
Håverud, *Sweden* **11** 58 50N 12 28 E
Havilah, *Australia* **76** 32 37 S 149 45 E
Havlíčkův Brod, *Czech.* **32** 49 36N 15 33 E
Havneby, *Denmark* **11** 55 5N 8 34 E
Havre, *U.S.A.* **122** 48 34N 109 40W
Havre, Le, *France* **18** 49 30N 0 5 E
Havre-Aubert, *Canada* **105** 47 12N 61 56W
Havre-St.-Pierre, *Canada* **105** 50 18N 63 33W
Havza, *Turkey* **46** 41 0N 35 35 E
Haw →, *U.S.A.* **115** 35 36N 79 3W
Hawaii □, *U.S.A.* **112** 20 30N 157 0W
Hawaii I., *Pac. Oc.* **112** 20 0N 155 0W
Hawaiian Is., *Pac. Oc.* **112** 20 30N 156 0W
Hawaiian Ridge, *Pac. Oc.* **67** 24 0N 165 0W
Hawarden, *Canada* **111** 51 25N 106 36W
Hawarden, *U.S.A.* **120** 43 2N 96 28W
Hawea Flat, *N.Z.* **81** 44 40 S 169 19 E
Hawea Lake, *N.Z.* **81** 44 28 S 169 19 E
Hawera, *N.Z.* **80** 39 35 S 174 19 E
Hawesville, *U.S.A.* **119** 37 54N 86 45W
Hawick, *U.K.* **14** 55 25N 2 48W
Hawk Junction, *Canada* **104** 48 5N 84 38W
Hawk Point, *U.S.A.* **118** 38 58N 91 8W
Hawkdun Ra., *N.Z.* **81** 44 53 S 170 5 E
Hawke, C., *Australia* **77** 32 13 S 152 34 E
Hawke B., *N.Z.* **80** 39 25 S 177 20 E
Hawke's Bay □, *N.Z.* **80** 39 45 S 176 35 E
Hawkesbury, *Canada* **104** 45 37N 74 37W
Hawkesbury I., *Canada* **110** 53 37N 129 3W
Hawkesbury Pt., *Australia* **72** 11 55 S 134 5 E
Hawkesdale, *Australia* **74** 38 7 S 142 20 E
Hawkinsville, *U.S.A.* **115** 32 17N 83 30W
Hawkwood, *Australia* **73** 25 45 S 150 50 E
Hawley, *U.S.A.* **120** 46 58N 96 20W
Hawrān, *Syria* **44** 32 45N 36 15 E
Hawthorne, *U.S.A.* **122** 38 31N 118 37W
Hawzen, *Ethiopia* **89** 13 58N 39 28 E
Haxtun, *U.S.A.* **120** 40 40N 102 39W
Hay, *Australia* **74** 34 30 S 144 51 E
Hay →, *Australia* **72** 24 50 S 138 0 E
Hay →, *Canada* **110** 60 50N 116 26W
Hay, C., *Australia* **78** 14 5 S 129 29 E
Hay I., *Canada* **108** 44 53N 80 58W
Hay L., *Canada* **110** 58 50N 118 50W
Hay Lakes, *Canada* **110** 53 12N 113 2W
Hay-on-Wye, *U.K.* **13** 52 4N 3 9W
Hay River, *Canada* **110** 60 51N 115 44W
Hay Springs, *U.S.A.* **120** 42 40N 102 38W
Hayange, *France* **19** 49 20N 6 2 E
Hayato, *Japan* **64** 31 40N 130 43 E
Hayden, *Ariz., U.S.A.* **123** 33 2N 110 48W
Hayden, *Colo., U.S.A.* **122** 40 30N 107 22W
Haydon, *Australia* **72** 18 0 S 141 30 E
Haye-du-Puits, La, *France* **18** 49 17N 1 33W
Hayes, *U.S.A.* **120** 44 22N 101 1W
Hayes →, *Canada* **111** 57 3N 92 12W
Haynesville, *U.S.A.* **121** 33 0N 93 7W
Hays, *Canada* **110** 50 6N 111 48W
Hays, *U.S.A.* **120** 38 55N 99 25W
Haysdale, *Australia* **74** 34 54 S 143 18 E
Haystack Mountain, *Australia* **77** 28 37 S 152 30 E
Haysville, *U.S.A.* **119** 38 28N 86 55W
Hayward, *Calif., U.S.A.* **124** 37 40N 122 5W
Hayward, *Wis., U.S.A.* **120** 46 2N 91 30W
Hayward's Heath, *U.K.* **13** 51 0N 0 5W
Hazard, *U.S.A.* **114** 37 18N 83 10W
Hazaribag, *India* **49** 23 58N 85 26 E
Hazaribag Road, *India* **49** 24 12N 85 57 E
Hazebrouck, *France* **19** 50 42N 2 31 E
Hazelton, *Canada* **110** 55 20N 127 42W
Hazelton, *U.S.A.* **120** 46 30N 100 15W
Hazen, *N. Dak., U.S.A.* **120** 47 18N 101 38W
Hazen, *Nev., U.S.A.* **122** 39 37N 119 2W
Hazerswoude, *Neths.* **16** 52 5N 4 36 E
Hazlehurst, *Ga., U.S.A.* **115** 31 50N 82 35W
Hazlehurst, *Miss., U.S.A.* **121** 31 52N 90 24W
Hazleton, *Ind., U.S.A.* **119** 38 29N 87 34W
Hazleton, *Pa., U.S.A.* **117** 40 58N 76 0W
Hazlett, L., *Australia* **78** 21 30 S 128 48 E
Ḥazor, *Israel* **44** 33 2N 35 32 E
He Xian, *Anhui, China* **59** 31 45N 118 20 E
He Xian, *Guangxi Zhuangzu, China* **59** 24 27N 111 30 E
Head of Bight, *Australia* **79** 31 30 S 131 25 E
Headlands, *Zimb.* **93** 18 15 S 32 2 E
Healdsburg, *U.S.A.* **124** 38 33N 122 51W
Healdton, *U.S.A.* **121** 34 16N 97 31W
Healesville, *Australia* **74** 37 35 S 145 30 E
Heanor, *U.K.* **12** 53 1N 1 20W
Heard I., *Ind. Oc.* **53** 53 0 S 74 0 E
Hearne, *U.S.A.* **121** 30 54N 96 35W
Hearne B., *Canada* **111** 60 10N 99 10W
Hearne L., *Canada* **110** 62 20N 113 10W
Hearst, *Canada* **104** 49 40N 83 41W
Heart →, *U.S.A.* **120** 46 40N 100 51W
Heart's Content, *Canada* **105** 47 54N 53 27W
Heath →, *Bolivia* **136** 12 31 S 68 38W
Heath Mts., *N.Z.* **81** 45 39 S 167 9 E
Heath Pt., *Canada* **105** 49 8N 61 40W
Heath Steele, *Canada* **105** 47 17N 66 5W
Heathcote, *Australia* **74** 36 56 S 144 45 E
Heathmere, *Australia* **74** 38 12 S 141 35 E
Heavener, *U.S.A.* **121** 34 54N 94 36W
Hebbronville, *U.S.A.* **121** 27 20N 98 40W
Hebei □, *China* **60** 39 0N 116 0 E
Hebel, *Australia* **73** 28 58 S 147 47 E
Heber, *U.S.A.* **125** 32 44N 115 32W
Heber Springs, *U.S.A.* **121** 35 29N 91 59W
Hebert, *Canada* **111** 50 30N 107 10W
Hebgen, L., *U.S.A.* **122** 44 50N 111 15W
Hebi, *China* **60** 35 57N 114 7 E
Hebrides, *U.K.* **14** 57 30N 7 0W
Hebrides, Inner Is., *U.K.* **14** 57 20N 6 40W
Hebrides, Outer Is., *U.K.* **14** 57 30N 7 40W
Hebron = Al Khalīl, *Jordan* **44** 31 32N 35 6 E
Hebron, *Canada* **103** 58 5N 62 30W
Hebron, *N. Dak., U.S.A.* **120** 46 56N 102 2W
Hebron, *Nebr., U.S.A.* **120** 40 15N 97 33W
Heby, *Sweden* **10** 59 56N 16 53 E
Hecate Str., *Canada* **110** 53 10N 130 30W
Hechi, *China* **58** 24 40N 108 2 E
Hechingen, *W. Germany* **31** 48 20N 8 58 E
Hechtel, *Belgium* **17** 51 8N 5 22 E
Hechuan, *China* **58** 30 2N 106 12 E
Hecla, *U.S.A.* **120** 45 56N 98 8W
Hecla I., *Canada* **111** 51 10N 96 43W
Heddal, *Norway* **10** 59 36N 9 9 E
Hédé, *France* **18** 48 18N 1 49W
Hede, *Sweden* **10** 62 23N 13 30 E
Hedemora, *Sweden* **10** 60 18N 15 58 E
Hedgehope, *N.Z.* **81** 46 12 S 168 34 E
Hedley, *U.S.A.* **121** 34 53N 100 39W
Hedmark fylke □, *Norway* **10** 61 17N 11 40 E
Hedrick, *U.S.A.* **118** 41 11N 92 19W
Hedrum, *Norway* **10** 59 7N 10 5 E
Heeg, *Neths.* **16** 52 58N 5 37 E
Heegermeer, *Neths.* **16** 52 56N 5 32 E
Heemskerk, *Neths.* **16** 52 31N 4 40 E
Heemstede, *Neths.* **16** 52 22N 4 37 E
Heer, *Neths.* **17** 50 50N 5 43 E
Heerde, *Neths.* **16** 52 24N 6 2 E
's Heerenburg, *Neths.* **16** 51 53N 6 16 E
Heerenveen, *Neths.* **16** 52 57N 5 55 E
Heerhugowaard, *Neths.* **16** 52 40N 4 51 E
Heerlen, *Neths.* **17** 50 55N 6 0 E
Heers, *Belgium* **17** 50 45N 5 18 E
Heesch, *Neths.* **16** 51 44N 5 32 E
Heestert, *Belgium* **17** 50 47N 3 25 E
Heeze, *Neths.* **17** 51 23N 5 35 E
Ḥefa, *Israel* **44** 32 46N 35 0 E
Hefei, *China* **59** 31 52N 117 18 E
Hegang, *China* **62** 47 20N 130 19 E
Hegyalja, *Hungary* **33** 48 25N 21 25 E
Heichengzhen, *China* **60** 36 24N 106 3 E
Heide, *W. Germany* **30** 54 10N 9 7 E
Heidelberg, *C. Prov., S. Africa* **96** 34 6 S 20 59 E
Heidelberg, *Trans., S. Africa* **97** 26 30 S 28 23 E
Heidelberg, *W. Germany* **31** 49 23N 8 41 E
Heidenheim, *W. Germany* **31** 48 40N 10 10 E
Heigun-To, *Japan* **64** 33 47N 132 14 E
Heijing, *China* **58** 25 22N 101 44 E
Heilbron, *S. Africa* **97** 27 16 S 27 59 E
Heilbronn, *W. Germany* **31** 49 8N 9 13 E
Heiligenblut, *Austria* **33** 47 2N 12 51 E
Heiligenhafen, *W. Germany* **30** 54 21N 10 58 E
Heiligenstadt, *E. Germany* **30** 51 22N 10 9 E
Heilongjiang □, *China* **61** 48 0N 126 0 E
Heilunkiang = Heilongjiang □, *China* **61** 48 0N 126 0 E
Heino, *Neths.* **16** 52 26N 6 14 E
Heinola, *Finland* **9** 61 13N 26 2 E
Heinsch, *Belgium* **17** 49 42N 5 44 E
Heinsun, *Burma* **52** 25 52N 95 35 E
Heirnkut, *Burma* **52** 25 14N 94 44 E
Heishan, *China* **61** 41 40N 122 5 E
Heishui, *Liaoning, China* **61** 42 8N 119 30 E
Heishui, *Sichuan, China* **58** 32 4N 103 2 E
Heist, *Belgium* **17** 51 20N 3 15 E
Heist-op-den-Berg, *Belgium* **17** 51 5N 4 44 E
Hejaz = Al Ḥijāz, *Si. Arabia* **46** 26 0N 37 30 E
Hejian, *China* **60** 38 25N 116 5 E
Hejiang, *China* **58** 28 43N 105 46 E
Hejin, *China* **60** 35 35N 110 42 E
Hekelgem, *Belgium* **17** 50 55N 4 7 E
Hekimhan, *Turkey* **46** 38 50N 38 0 E
Hekinan, *Japan* **65** 34 52N 137 0 E
Hekla, *Iceland* **8** 63 56N 19 35W
Hekou, *Gansu, China* **60** 36 10N 103 28 E
Hekou, *Guangdong, China* **59** 23 13N 112 45 E
Hekou, *Yunnan, China* **62** 22 30N 103 59 E
Helagsfjället, *Sweden* **10** 62 54N 12 25 E
Helan Shan, *China* **60** 39 0N 105 55 E
Helchteren, *Belgium* **17** 51 4N 5 22 E
Helden, *Neths.* **17** 51 19N 6 0 E
Helechosa, *Spain* **23** 39 22N 4 53W
Helena, *Ark., U.S.A.* **121** 34 30N 90 35W
Helena, *Mont., U.S.A.* **122** 46 40N 112 0W
Helendale, *U.S.A.* **125** 34 44N 117 19W
Helensburgh, *Australia* **76** 34 11 S 151 1 E
Helensburgh, *U.K.* **14** 56 0N 4 44W
Helensville, *N.Z.* **80** 36 41 S 174 29 E
Ḥelez, *Israel* **44** 31 36N 34 39 E
Helgasjön, *Sweden* **11** 57 0N 14 50 E
Helgeroa, *Norway* **10** 59 0N 9 45 E
Helgoland, *W. Germany* **30** 54 10N 7 51 E
Heligoland = Helgoland, *W. Germany* **30** 54 10N 7 51 E
Heliopolis, *Egypt* **88** 30 6N 31 17 E
Hellebæk, *Denmark* **11** 56 4N 12 32 E
Hellendoorn, *Neths.* **16** 52 24N 6 27 E
Hellevoetsluis, *Neths.* **16** 51 50N 4 8 E
Hellín, *Spain* **25** 38 31N 1 40W
Helmand □, *Afghan.* **47** 31 20N 64 0 E
Helmand →, *Afghan.* **47** 31 12N 61 34 E
Helmand, Hamun, *Iran* **47** 31 15N 61 15 E
Helme →, *E. Germany* **30** 51 40N 11 20 E
Helmond, *Neths.* **17** 51 29N 5 41 E
Helmsdale, *U.K.* **14** 58 7N 3 40W
Helmstedt, *W. Germany* **30** 52 16N 11 0 E
Helnæs, *Denmark* **11** 55 9N 10 0 E
Helong, *China* **61** 42 40N 129 0 E
Helper, *U.S.A.* **122** 39 44N 110 56W
Helsingborg, *Sweden* **11** 56 3N 12 42 E
Helsinge, *Denmark* **11** 56 2N 12 12 E
Helsingfors, *Finland* **9** 60 15N 25 3 E
Helsingør, *Denmark* **11** 56 2N 12 35 E
Helsinki, *Finland* **9** 60 15N 25 3 E
Helston, *U.K.* **13** 50 7N 5 17W
Helvellyn, *U.K.* **12** 54 31N 3 1W
Helvoirt, *Neths.* **17** 51 38N 5 14 E
Helwân, *Egypt* **88** 29 50N 31 20 E
Hemavati →, *India* **51** 12 30N 76 20 E
Hemet, *U.S.A.* **125** 33 45N 116 59W
Hemingford, *U.S.A.* **120** 42 21N 103 4W
Hemmingford, *Canada* **107** 45 3N 73 35W
Hemphill, *U.S.A.* **121** 31 21N 93 49W
Hempstead, *U.S.A.* **121** 30 5N 96 5W
Hemse, *Sweden* **11** 57 15N 18 22 E
Hemsö, *Sweden* **10** 62 43N 18 5 E
Hen & Chickens Is., *N.Z.* **80** 35 58 S 174 45 E
Henan □, *China* **60** 34 0N 114 0 E
Henares →, *Spain* **24** 40 24N 3 30W
Hendaye, *France* **20** 43 23N 1 47W
Henderson, *Argentina* **140** 36 18 S 61 43W
Henderson, *Ky., U.S.A.* **119** 37 50N 87 38W
Henderson, *N.C., U.S.A.* **115** 36 20N 78 25W
Henderson, *Nev., U.S.A.* **125** 36 2N 115 0W
Henderson, *Pa., U.S.A.* **115** 35 25N 88 40W
Henderson, *Tex., U.S.A.* **121** 32 5N 94 49W
Hendersonville, *U.S.A.* **115** 35 21N 82 28W
Hendon, *Australia* **77** 28 5 S 151 50 E
Heng Xian, *China* **58** 22 40N 109 17 E
Hengcheng, *China* **60** 38 18N 106 28 E
Hengdaohezi, *China* **61** 44 52N 129 0 E
Hengelo, *Gelderland, Neths.* **16** 52 3N 6 19 E
Hengelo, *Overijssel, Neths.* **16** 52 16N 6 48 E
Hengfeng, *China* **59** 28 12N 115 48 E
Hengshan, *Hunan, China* **59** 27 16N 112 45 E
Hengshan, *Shaanxi, China* **60** 37 58N 109 5 E
Hengshui, *China* **60** 37 41N 115 40 E
Hengyang, *Hunan, China* **59** 26 52N 112 33 E
Hengyang, *Hunan, China* **59** 26 59N 112 22 E
Hénin-Beaumont, *France* **19** 50 25N 2 58 E
Henlopen, C., *U.S.A.* **114** 38 48N 75 5W
Hennan, *Sweden* **10** 62 3N 15 46 E
Hennebont, *France* **18** 47 49N 3 19W
Hennenman, *S. Africa* **96** 27 59 S 27 1 E
Hennepin, *U.S.A.* **118** 41 15N 89 21W
Hennessey, *U.S.A.* **121** 36 8N 97 53W
Hennigsdorf, *E. Germany* **30** 52 38N 13 13 E
Henrichemont, *France* **19** 47 20N 2 30 E
Henrietta, *U.S.A.* **121** 33 50N 98 15W
Henrietta, Ostrov, *U.S.S.R.* **41** 77 6N 156 30 E
Henrietta Maria C., *Canada* **104** 55 9N 82 20W
Henry, *U.S.A.* **118** 41 5N 89 20W
Henryetta, *U.S.A.* **121** 35 30N 96 0W
Henryville, *Canada* **107** 45 8N 73 11W
Hensall, *Canada* **108** 43 26N 81 30W
Hentiyn Nuruu, *Mongolia* **62** 48 30N 108 30 E
Henty, *Australia* **76** 35 30 S 147 0 E
Henzada, *Burma* **52** 17 38N 95 26 E
Hepburn Springs, *Australia* **74** 37 19 S 144 9 E
Heping, *China* **59** 24 29N 115 0 E
Heppner, *U.S.A.* **122** 45 21N 119 34W
Hepu, *China* **58** 21 40N 109 12 E
Hepworth, *Canada* **108** 44 37N 81 9W
Heqing, *China* **58** 26 37N 100 11 E
Hequ, *China* **60** 39 20N 111 15 E
Héraðsflói, *Iceland* **8** 65 42N 14 12W
Héraðsvötn →, *Iceland* **8** 65 45N 19 25W
Herald Cays, *Australia* **72** 16 58 S 149 9 E
Herāt, *Afghan.* **47** 34 20N 62 7 E
Herāt □, *Afghan.* **47** 35 0N 62 0 E
Hérault □, *France* **20** 43 34N 3 15 E
Hérault →, *France* **20** 43 17N 3 26 E
Herbault, *France* **18** 47 36N 1 8 E
Herbert →, *Australia* **72** 18 31 S 146 17 E
Herbert Downs, *Australia* **72** 23 7 S 139 9 E
Herberton, *Australia* **72** 17 20 S 145 25 E
Herbiers, Les, *France* **18** 46 52N 1 1W
Herbignac, *France* **18** 47 27N 2 18W

Herborn, *W. Germany* **30** 50 40N 8 19 E
Herby, *Poland* **32** 50 45N 18 50 E
Hercegnovi, *Yugoslavia* **33** 42 30N 18 33 E
Hercegovina = Bosna i Hercegovina □, *Yugoslavia* **33** 44 0N 18 0 E
Herculaneum, *U.S.A.* **118** 38 16N 90 23W
Herðubreið, *Iceland* **8** 65 11N 16 21W
Hereford, *U.K.* **13** 52 4N 2 42W
Hereford, *U.S.A.* **121** 34 50N 102 28W
Hereford, Mt., *Canada* **107** 45 5N 71 36W
Hereford and Worcester □, *U.K.* **13** 52 10N 2 30W
Herefoss, *Norway* **11** 58 32N 8 23 E
Herekino, *N.Z.* **80** 35 18 S 173 11 E
Herent, *Belgium* **17** 50 54N 4 40 E
Herentals, *Belgium* **17** 51 12N 4 51 E
Herenthout, *Belgium* **17** 51 8N 4 45 E
Herfølge, *Denmark* **11** 55 26N 12 9 E
Herford, *W. Germany* **30** 52 7N 8 40 E
Héricourt, *France* **19** 47 32N 6 45 E
Herington, *U.S.A.* **120** 38 43N 97 0W
Herisau, *Switz.* **31** 47 22N 9 17 E
Hérisson, *France* **20** 46 32N 2 42 E
Herjehogna, *Norway* **9** 61 43N 12 7 E
Herk →, *Belgium* **17** 50 56N 5 12 E
Herkenbosch, *Neths.* **17** 51 9N 6 4 E
Herkimer, *U.S.A.* **117** 43 0N 74 59W
Herlong, *U.S.A.* **124** 40 8N 120 8W
Herm, *Chan. Is.* **18** 49 30N 2 28W
Hermagor-Pressegger See, *Austria* **33** 46 38N 13 23 E
Herman, *U.S.A.* **120** 45 51N 96 8W
Hermann, *U.S.A.* **120** 38 40N 91 25W
Hermannsburg, *W. Germany* **30** 52 49N 10 6 E
Hermannsburg Mission, *Australia* **78** 23 57 S 132 45 E
Hermanus, *S. Africa* **96** 34 27 S 19 12 E
Herment, *France* **20** 45 45N 2 24 E
Hermidale, *Australia* **73** 31 30 S 146 42 E
Hermiston, *U.S.A.* **122** 45 50N 119 16W
Hermitage, *N.Z.* **81** 43 44 S 170 5 E
Hermitage, *U.S.A.* **118** 37 56N 93 19W
Hermite, I., *Chile* **142** 55 50 S 68 0W
Hermon, Mt. = Ash Shaykh, J., *Lebanon* **46** 33 25N 35 50 E
Hermosillo, *Mexico* **126** 29 10N 111 0W
Hernád →, *Hungary* **33** 47 56N 21 8 E
Hernandarias, *Paraguay* **141** 25 20 S 54 40W
Hernandez, *U.S.A.* **124** 36 24N 120 46W
Hernando, *Argentina* **140** 32 28 S 63 40W
Hernando, *U.S.A.* **121** 34 50N 89 59W
Herne, *Belgium* **17** 50 44N 4 2 E
Herne, *W. Germany* **17** 51 33N 7 12 E
Herne Bay, *U.K.* **13** 51 22N 1 8 E
Herning, *Denmark* **11** 56 8N 8 58 E
Heroica = Caborca, *Mexico* **126** 30 40N 112 10W
Heroica Nogales = Nogales, *Mexico* **126** 31 20N 110 56W
Heron Bay, *Canada* **104** 48 40N 86 25W
Herradura, Pta. de la, *Canary Is.* **25** 28 26N 14 8W
Hereid, *U.S.A.* **120** 45 53N 100 5W
Herrera, *Spain* **23** 37 26N 4 55W
Herrera de Alcántar, *Spain* **23** 39 39N 7 25W
Herrera de Pisuerga, *Spain* **22** 42 35N 4 20W
Herrera del Duque, *Spain* **23** 39 10N 5 3W
Herrick, *Australia* **72** 41 5 S 147 55 E
Herrin, *U.S.A.* **118** 37 50N 89 0W
Herrljunga, *Sweden* **11** 58 5N 13 1 E
Hersbruck, *W. Germany* **31** 49 30N 11 25 E
Herseaux, *Belgium* **17** 50 43N 3 15 E
Herselt, *Belgium* **17** 51 3N 4 53 E
Herstal, *Belgium* **17** 50 40N 5 38 E
Hertford, *U.K.* **13** 51 47N 0 4W
Hertford □, *U.K.* **13** 51 51N 0 5W
's-Hertogenbosch, *Neths.* **17** 51 42N 5 17 E
Hertzogville, *S. Africa* **96** 28 9 S 25 30 E
Hervás, *Spain* **22** 40 16N 5 52W
Herve, *Belgium* **17** 50 38N 5 48 E
Hervey Bay, *Australia* **72** 25 3 S 153 5 E
Herwijnen, *Neths.* **16** 51 50N 5 7 E
Herzberg, *E. Germany* **30** 51 40N 13 13 E
Herzberg, *W. Germany* **30** 51 38N 10 20 E
Herzele, *Belgium* **17** 50 53N 3 53 E
Herzliyya, *Israel* **44** 32 10N 34 50 E
Hesdin, *France* **19** 50 21N 2 0 E
Hesel, *W. Germany* **30** 53 18N 7 36 E
Heshui, *China* **60** 36 0N 108 0 E
Heshun, *China* **60** 37 22N 113 32 E
Hesperange, *Lux.* **17** 49 35N 6 10 E
Hesperia, *U.S.A.* **125** 34 25N 117 18W
Hesse = Hessen □, *W. Germany* **30** 50 40N 9 20 E
Hessen □, *W. Germany* **30** 50 40N 9 20 E
Hetch Hetchy Aqueduct, *U.S.A.* **124** 37 36N 121 25W
Hettinger, *U.S.A.* **120** 46 0N 102 38W
Hettstedt, *E. Germany* **30** 51 39N 11 30 E
Heugem, *Neths.* **17** 50 49N 5 42 E
Heule, *Belgium* **17** 50 51N 3 15 E
Heusden, *Belgium* **17** 51 2N 5 17 E
Heusden, *Neths.* **16** 51 44N 5 8 E
Hève, C. de la, *France* **18** 49 30N 0 5 E
Heverlee, *Belgium* **17** 50 52N 4 42 E
Hevron →, *Asia* **44** 31 12N 34 42 E
Hewett, C., *Canada* **103** 70 16N 67 45W
Hexham, *Australia* **74** 38 0 S 142 41 E
Hexham, *U.K.* **12** 54 58N 2 7W
Hexi, *Yunnan, China* **58** 24 9N 102 38 E
Hexi, *Zhejiang, China* **59** 27 58N 119 38 E
Hexigten Qi, *China* **61** 43 18N 117 30 E
Hexrivier, *S. Africa* **96** 33 30 S 19 35 E
Heysham, *U.K.* **12** 54 5N 2 53W
Heythuysen, *Neths.* **17** 51 15N 5 55 E
Heyuan, *China* **59** 23 39N 114 40 E
Heywood, *Australia* **74** 38 8 S 141 37 E
Heze, *China* **60** 35 14N 115 20 E
Hezhang, *China* **58** 27 8N 104 41 E
Hi-no-Misaki, *Japan* **64** 35 26N 132 38 E
Hi Vista, *U.S.A.* **125** 34 45N 117 46W
Hialeach, *U.S.A.* **115** 25 49N 80 17W
Hiawatha, *Kans., U.S.A.* **120** 39 55N 95 33W
Hiawatha, *Utah, U.S.A.* **122** 39 29N 111 1W
Hibbing, *U.S.A.* **120** 47 30N 93 0W
Hibbs B., *Australia* **72** 42 35 S 145 15 E
Hibernia Reef, *Australia* **78** 12 0 S 123 23 E
Hibiki-Nada, *Japan* **64** 34 0N 130 0 E
Hickory, *U.S.A.* **115** 35 46N 81 17W
Hicks Bay, *N.Z.* **80** 37 34 S 178 21 E
Hicks Pt., *Australia* **75** 37 49 S 149 17 E
Hicksville, *N.Y., U.S.A.* **117** 40 46N 73 30W
Hicksville, *Ohio, U.S.A.* **119** 41 18N 84 46W
Hida, *Romania* **34** 47 10N 23 19 E
Hida-Gawa →, *Japan* **65** 35 26N 137 3 E
Hida-Sammyaku, *Japan* **65** 36 30N 137 40 E
Hida-Sanchi, *Japan* **65** 36 10N 137 0 E
Hidaka, *Japan* **64** 35 30N 134 44 E
Hidalgo, *Mexico* **127** 24 15N 99 26W
Hidalgo, *U.S.A.* **119** 39 9N 88 9W
Hidalgo □, *Mexico* **127** 20 30N 99 10W
Hidalgo, Presa M., *Mexico* **126** 26 30N 108 35W
Hidalgo, Pta. del, *Canary Is.* **25** 28 33N 16 19W
Hidalgo del Parral, *Mexico* **126** 26 58N 105 40W
Hiddensee, *E. Germany* **30** 54 30N 13 6 E
Hidrolândia, *Brazil* **139** 17 0 S 49 15W
Hieflau, *Austria* **33** 47 36N 14 46 E
Hiendelaencina, *Spain* **24** 41 5N 3 0W
Hienghène, *N. Cal.* **68** 20 41 S 164 56 E
Hierro, *Canary Is.* **25** 27 44N 18 0 E
Higashi-matsuyama, *Japan* **65** 36 2N 139 25 E
Higashiōsaka, *Japan* **65** 34 40N 135 37 E
Higasi-Suidō, *Japan* **64** 34 0N 129 30 E
Higbee, *U.S.A.* **118** 39 19N 92 31W
Higgins, *U.S.A.* **121** 36 9N 100 1W
Higgins Corner, *U.S.A.* **124** 39 2N 121 5W
Higginsville, *Australia* **79** 31 42 S 121 38 E
Higginsville, *U.S.A.* **118** 39 4N 93 43W
High Atlas = Haut Atlas, *Morocco* **84** 32 30N 5 0W
High I., *Canada* **105** 56 40N 61 10W
High Island, *U.S.A.* **121** 29 32N 94 22W
High Level, *Canada* **110** 58 31N 117 8W
High Point, *U.S.A.* **115** 35 57N 79 58W
High Prairie, *Canada* **110** 55 30N 116 30W
High River, *Canada* **110** 50 30N 113 50W
High Springs, *U.S.A.* **115** 29 50N 82 40W
High Wycombe, *U.K.* **13** 51 37N 0 45W
Highbury, *Australia* **72** 16 25 S 143 9 E
Highland, *Ill., U.S.A.* **118** 38 44N 89 41W
Highland, *Ind., U.S.A.* **119** 41 33N 87 28W
Highland, *Wis., U.S.A.* **118** 43 6N 90 21W
Highland □, *U.K.* **14** 57 30N 5 0W
Highland Park, *U.S.A.* **119** 42 10N 87 50W
Highmore, *U.S.A.* **120** 44 35N 99 26W
Highrock L., *Canada* **111** 57 5N 105 32W
Higüay, *Dom. Rep.* **129** 18 37N 68 42W
Hihya, *Egypt* **88** 30 40N 31 36 E
Hiiumaa, *U.S.S.R.* **36** 58 50N 22 45 E
Híjar, *Spain* **24** 41 10N 0 27W
Ḥijārah, Ṣaḥrā' al, *Iraq* **46** 30 25N 44 30 E
Ḥijāz □, *Si. Arabia* **45** 24 0N 40 0 E
Hiji, *Japan* **64** 33 22N 131 32 E
Hijken, *Neths.* **16** 52 54N 6 30 E
Hijo = Tagum, *Phil.* **57** 7 33N 125 53 E
Hikari, *Japan* **64** 33 58N 131 58 E
Hiketa, *Japan* **64** 34 13N 134 24 E
Hiko, *U.S.A.* **124** 37 30N 115 13W
Hikone, *Japan* **65** 35 15N 136 10 E
Hilawng, *Burma* **52** 21 23N 93 48 E
Hildburghhausen, *E. Germany* **31** 50 24N 10 43 E
Hildesheim, *W. Germany* **30** 52 9N 9 55 E
Hill →, *Australia* **79** 30 23 S 115 3 E
Hill City, *Idaho, U.S.A.* **122** 43 20N 115 2W
Hill City, *Kans., U.S.A.* **120** 39 25N 99 51W
Hill City, *Minn., U.S.A.* **120** 46 57N 93 35W
Hill City, *S. Dak., U.S.A.* **120** 43 58N 103 35W
Hill End, *Australia* **75** 38 1 S 146 9 E
Hill Island L., *Canada* **111** 60 30N 109 50W
Hillared, *Sweden* **11** 57 37N 13 10 E
Hillcrest Center, *U.S.A.* **125** 35 23N 118 57W
Hillegom, *Neths.* **16** 52 18N 4 35 E
Hillerød, *Denmark* **11** 55 56N 12 19 E
Hillerstorp, *Sweden* **11** 57 20N 13 52 E
Hilli, *Bangla.* **52** 25 17N 89 1 E
Hillingdon, *U.K.* **13** 51 33N 0 29W
Hillman, *U.S.A.* **114** 45 5N 83 52W
Hillmond, *Canada* **111** 53 26N 109 41W
Hillsboro, *Ill., U.S.A.* **118** 39 9N 89 29W
Hillsboro, *Iowa, U.S.A.* **118** 40 50N 91 42W
Hillsboro, *Kans., U.S.A.* **120** 38 22N 97 10W
Hillsboro, *Mo., U.S.A.* **118** 38 14N 90 34W
Hillsboro, *N. Dak., U.S.A.* **120** 47 23N 97 9W
Hillsboro, *N.H., U.S.A.* **117** 43 8N 71 56W
Hillsboro, *N. Mex., U.S.A.* **123** 33 0N 107 35W
Hillsboro, *Ohio, U.S.A.* **119** 39 12N 83 37W
Hillsboro, *Oreg., U.S.A.* **124** 45 31N 123 0W
Hillsboro, *Tex., U.S.A.* **121** 32 0N 97 10W
Hillsborough, *Grenada* **129** 12 28N 61 28W
Hillsdale, *Mich., U.S.A.* **119** 41 55N 84 40W
Hillsdale, *N.Y., U.S.A.* **117** 42 11N 73 30W
Hillside, *Australia* **78** 21 45 S 119 23 E
Hillsport, *Canada* **104** 49 27N 85 34W
Hillston, *Australia* **73** 33 30 S 145 31 E
Hilo, *U.S.A.* **112** 19 44N 155 5W
Hilton, *U.S.A.* **116** 43 16N 77 48W
Hilton Beach, *Canada* **108** 46 15N 83 53W
Hilvarenbeek, *Neths.* **17** 51 29N 5 8 E
Hilversum, *Neths.* **16** 52 14N 5 10 E
Himachal Pradesh □, *India* **48** 31 30N 77 0 E
Himalaya, Mts., *Asia* **49** 29 0N 84 0 E
Himara, *Albania* **35** 40 8N 19 43 E
Hime-Jima, *Japan* **64** 33 43N 131 40 E
Himeji, *Japan* **64** 34 50N 134 40 E
Himi, *Japan* **65** 36 50N 137 0 E
Himmerland, *Denmark* **11** 56 45N 9 30 E
Ḥimṣ, *Syria* **46** 34 40N 36 45 E
Hinche, *Haiti* **129** 19 9N 72 1W
Hinchinbrook I., *Australia* **72** 18 20 S 146 15 E
Hinckley, *U.K.* **13** 52 33N 1 21W
Hinckley, *U.S.A.* **122** 39 18N 112 41W
Hindås, *Sweden* **11** 57 42N 12 27 E
Hindaun, *India* **48** 26 44N 77 5 E
Hindmarsh L., *Australia* **74** 36 5 S 141 55 E
Hindol, *India* **50** 20 40N 85 10 E
Hinds, *N.Z.* **81** 43 59 S 171 36 E
Hindsholm, *Denmark* **11** 55 30N 10 40 E
Hindu Bagh, *Pakistan* **48** 30 56N 67 50 E
Hindu Kush, *Asia* **47** 36 0N 71 0 E
Hindupur, *India* **51** 13 49N 77 32 E
Hines Creek, *Canada* **110** 56 20N 118 40W
Hinganghat, *India* **50** 20 30N 78 52 E
Hingeon, *Belgium* **17** 50 32N 4 59 E
Hingham, *U.S.A.* **122** 48 34N 110 29W
Hingoli, *India* **50** 19 41N 77 15 E
Hinlopenstretet, *Svalbard* **144** 79 35N 18 40 E
Hinna = Imi, *Ethiopia* **89** 6 28N 42 10 E
Hinna, *Nigeria* **91** 10 25N 11 35 E
Hino, *Japan* **65** 35 0N 136 15 E
Hinojosa del Duque, *Spain* **23** 38 30N 5 9W
Hinokage, *Japan* **64** 32 39N 131 24 E
Hinsdale, *U.S.A.* **122** 48 26N 107 2W
Hinterrhein →, *Switz.* **31** 46 40N 9 25 E
Hinton, *Canada* **110** 53 26N 117 34W
Hinton, *U.S.A.* **114** 37 40N 80 51W
Hippolytushoef, *Neths.* **16** 52 54N 4 58 E
Hirado, *Japan* **64** 33 22N 129 33 E
Hirado-Shima, *Japan* **64** 33 20N 129 30 E
Hirakarta, *Japan* **65** 34 48N 135 40 E
Hirakud, *India* **50** 21 32N 83 51 E
Hirakud Dam, *India* **50** 21 32N 83 45 E
Hirata, *Japan* **64** 35 24N 132 49 E
Hiratsuka, *Japan* **65** 35 19N 139 21 E
Hirhafok, *Algeria* **85** 23 49N 5 45 E
Hîrlău, *Romania* **34** 47 23N 27 0 E
Hiromi, *Japan* **64** 33 13N 132 36 E
Hirosaki, *Japan* **63** 40 34N 140 28 E
Hiroshima, *Japan* **64** 34 24N 132 30 E
Hiroshima □, *Japan* **64** 34 50N 133 0 E
Hiroshima-Wan, *Japan* **64** 34 5N 132 20 E
Hirsholmene, *Denmark* **11** 57 30N 10 36 E
Hirson, *France* **19** 49 55N 4 4 E
Hirşova, *Romania* **34** 44 40N 27 59 E
Hirtshals, *Denmark* **11** 57 36N 9 57 E
Hisar, *India* **48** 29 12N 75 45 E
Hispaniola, *W. Indies* **129** 19 0N 71 0W
Hita, *Japan* **64** 33 20N 130 58 E
Hitachi, *Japan* **65** 36 36N 140 39 E
Hitachiota, *Japan* **65** 36 30N 140 30 E
Hitchin, *U.K.* **13** 51 57N 0 16W
Hitoyoshi, *Japan* **64** 32 13N 130 45 E
Hitra, *Norway* **8** 63 30N 8 45 E
Hitzacker, *W. Germany* **30** 53 9N 11 1 E
Hiu, *Vanuatu* **68** 13 10 S 166 35 E
Hiuchi-Nada, *Japan* **64** 34 5N 133 20 E
Ḥiyyon, N. →, *Israel* **44** 30 25N 35 10 E
Hjalmar L., *Canada* **111** 61 33N 109 25W
Hjälmare kanal, *Sweden* **10** 59 20N 15 59 E
Hjälmaren, *Sweden* **10** 59 18N 15 40 E
Hjartdal, *Norway* **10** 59 37N 8 41 E
Hjerkinn, *Norway* **10** 62 13N 9 33 E
Hjørring, *Denmark* **11** 57 29N 9 59 E
Hjorted, *Sweden* **11** 57 37N 16 19 E
Hjortkvarn, *Sweden* **11** 58 54N 15 26 E
Hko-ut, *Burma* **52** 20 58N 98 2 E
Hkyenhpa, *Burma* **52** 27 43N 97 25 E
Hlaingbwe, *Burma* **52** 17 8N 97 50 E
Hlinsko, *Czech.* **32** 49 45N 15 54 E
Hluhluwe, *S. Africa* **97** 28 1 S 32 15 E
Hlwaze, *Burma* **52** 18 54N 96 37 E
Hńak, *Greenland* **144** 70 40N 52 10W
Ho, *Ghana* **91** 6 37N 0 27 E
Ho Chi Minh City = Phanh Bho Ho Chi Minh, *Vietnam* **55** 10 58N 106 40 E
Ho Thuong, *Vietnam* **54** 19 32N 105 48 E
Hoa Binh, *Vietnam* **54** 20 50N 105 20 E
Hoa Da, *Vietnam* **55** 11 16N 108 40 E
Hoa Hiep, *Vietnam* **55** 11 34N 105 51 E
Hoai Nhon, *Vietnam* **54** 14 28N 109 1 E
Hoare B., *Canada* **103** 65 17N 62 30W
Hobart, *Australia* **72** 42 50 S 147 21 E
Hobart, *Ind., U.S.A.* **119** 41 32N 87 15W
Hobart, *Okla., U.S.A.* **121** 35 0N 99 5W
Hobbs, *U.S.A.* **121** 32 40N 103 3W
Hobbs Coast, *Antarctica* **143** 74 50 S 131 0W
Hobo, *Colombia* **134** 2 35N 75 30W
Hoboken, *Belgium* **17** 51 11N 4 21 E
Hoboken, *U.S.A.* **117** 40 45N 74 4W
Hobro, *Denmark* **11** 56 39N 9 46 E
Hobscheid, *Lux.* **17** 49 42N 5 57 E
Hoburgen, *Sweden* **11** 56 55N 18 7 E
Hochschwab, *Austria* **33** 47 35N 15 0 E
Höchst, *W. Germany* **31** 50 6N 8 33 E
Höchstadt, *W. Germany* **31** 49 42N 10 48 E
Hockenheim, *W. Germany* **31** 49 18N 8 33 E
Hodaka-Dake, *Japan* **65** 36 17N 137 39 E
Hodgson, *Canada* **111** 51 13N 97 36W
Hódmezövásárhely, *Hungary* **33** 46 28N 20 22 E
Hodna, Chott el, *Algeria* **85** 35 30N 5 0 E
Hodna, Monts du, *Algeria* **85** 35 52N 4 42 E
Hodonín, *Czech.* **32** 48 50N 17 10 E
Hœdic, I. de, *France* **18** 47 20N 2 53W
Hoegaarden, *Belgium* **17** 50 47N 4 53 E
Hoek van Holland, *Neths.* **16** 52 0N 4 7 E
Hoeksche Waard, *Neths.* **16** 51 46N 4 25 E
Hoenderloo, *Neths.* **16** 52 7N 5 52 E
Hoensbroek, *Neths.* **17** 50 55N 5 55 E
Hoeselt, *Belgium* **17** 50 51N 5 29 E
Hoëveld, *S. Africa* **97** 26 30 S 30 0 E
Hoeven, *Neths.* **17** 51 35N 4 35 E
Hof, *Iceland* **8** 64 33N 14 40W
Hof, *W. Germany* **31** 50 18N 11 55 E
Höfðakaupstaður, *Iceland* **8** 65 50N 20 19W
Hofgeismar, *W. Germany* **30** 51 29N 9 23 E
Hofmeyr, *S. Africa* **96** 31 39 S 25 50 E
Hofors, *Sweden* **10** 60 31N 16 15 E
Hofsjökull, *Iceland* **8** 64 49N 18 48W
Hofsós, *Iceland* **8** 65 53N 19 26W
Hōfu, *Japan* **64** 34 3N 131 34 E
Hogan Group, *Australia* **72** 39 13 S 147 1 E
Hogansville, *U.S.A.* **115** 33 14N 84 50W
Hogeland, *U.S.A.* **122** 48 51N 108 40W
Hogenakai Falls, *India* **51** 12 6N 77 50 E
Högfors, *Sweden* **10** 59 58N 15 3 E
Hōgo-Kaikyō, *Japan* **64** 33 20N 131 58 E
Högsäter, *Sweden* **11** 58 38N 12 5 E
Högsby, *Sweden* **11** 57 10N 16 1 E
Högsjö, *Sweden* **10** 59 4N 15 44 E
Hogsty Reef, *Bahamas* **129** 21 41N 73 48W
Hoh →, *U.S.A.* **124** 47 45N 124 29W
Hoh Xil Shan, *China* **62** 35 0N 89 0 E
Hohe Rhön, *W. Germany* **31** 50 24N 9 58 E
Hohe Tauern, *Austria* **33** 47 11N 12 40 E
Hohe Venn, *Belgium* **17** 50 30N 6 5 E
Hohenau, *Austria* **32** 48 36N 16 55 E
Hohenems, *Austria* **31** 47 22N 9 42 E
Hohenstein-Ernstthal, *E. Germany* **30** 50 48N 12 43 E
Hohenwald, *U.S.A.* **115** 35 35N 87 30W
Hohenwestedt, *W. Germany* **30** 54 6N 9 30 E
Hohhot, *China* **60** 40 52N 111 40 E
Hohoe, *Ghana* **91** 7 8N 0 32 E
Hoi An, *Vietnam* **54** 15 30N 108 19 E
Hoi Xuan, *Vietnam* **54** 20 25N 105 9 E
Hoisington, *U.S.A.* **120** 38 33N 98 50W
Højer, *Denmark* **11** 54 58N 8 42 E
Hōjō, *Japan* **64** 33 58N 132 46 E
Hok, *Sweden* **11** 57 31N 14 16 E
Hökensås, *Sweden* **11** 58 0N 14 5 E
Hökerum, *Sweden* **11** 57 51N 13 16 E
Hokianga Harbour, *N.Z.* **80** 35 31 S 173 22 E
Hokitika, *N.Z.* **81** 42 42 S 171 0 E
Hokkaidō □, *Japan* **63** 43 30N 143 0 E
Hokksund, *Norway* **10** 59 44N 9 59 E
Hol-Hol, *Djibouti* **89** 11 20N 42 50 E
Holbæk, *Denmark* **11** 55 43N 11 43 E
Holbrook, *Australia* **76** 35 42 S 147 18 E
Holbrook, *U.S.A.* **123** 35 54N 110 10W
Holden, *Canada* **110** 53 13N 112 11W
Holden, *Mo., U.S.A.* **118** 38 43N 94 0W
Holden, *Utah, U.S.A.* **122** 39 0N 112 26W
Holdenville, *U.S.A.* **121** 35 5N 96 25W
Holderness, *U.K.* **12** 53 45N 0 5W
Holdfast, *Canada* **111** 50 58N 105 25W

Holdich, *Argentina* **142** 45 57 S 68 13W
Holdrege, *U.S.A.* **120** 40 26N 99 22W
Hole-Narsipur, *India* **51** 12 48N 76 16 E
Holgate, *U.S.A.* **119** 41 15N 84 8W
Holguín, *Cuba* **128** 20 50N 76 20W
Hollabrunn, *Austria* **32** 48 34N 16 5 E
Hollams Bird I., *Namibia* **96** 24 40 S 14 30 E
Holland, *U.S.A.* **119** 42 47N 86 7W
Hollandia = Jayapura, *Indonesia* **57** 2 28 S 140 38 E
Hollandsch Diep, *Neths.* **17** 51 41N 4 30 E
Hollandsch IJssel →, *Neths.* **16** 51 55N 4 34 E
Holleton, *Australia* **79** 31 55 S 119 0 E
Hollfeld, *W. Germany* **31** 49 56N 11 18 E
Hollick Kenyon Plateau, *Antarctica* **143** 82 0 S 110 0W
Hollidaysburg, *U.S.A.* **116** 40 26N 78 25W
Hollis, *U.S.A.* **121** 34 45N 99 55W
Hollister, *Calif., U.S.A.* **124** 36 51N 121 24W
Hollister, *Idaho, U.S.A.* **122** 42 21N 114 40W
Hollum, *Neths.* **16** 53 26N 5 38 E
Holly, *Colo., U.S.A.* **120** 38 7N 102 7W
Holly, *Mich., U.S.A.* **119** 42 48N 83 38W
Holly Hill, *U.S.A.* **115** 29 15N 81 3W
Holly Springs, *U.S.A.* **121** 34 45N 89 25W
Hollywood, *Calif., U.S.A.* **112** 34 7N 118 25W
Hollywood, *Fla., U.S.A.* **115** 26 0N 80 9W
Holm, *Sweden* **10** 62 40N 16 40 E
Holman Island, *Canada* **102** 70 42N 117 41W
Hólmavík, *Iceland* **8** 65 42N 21 40W
Holmegil, *Norway* **10** 59 10N 11 44 E
Holmes Reefs, *Australia* **72** 16 27 S 148 0 E
Holmestrand, *Norway* **10** 59 31N 10 14 E
Holmsbu, *Norway* **10** 59 32N 10 27 E
Holmsjön, *Sweden* **10** 62 26N 15 20 E
Holmsland Klit, *Denmark* **11** 56 0N 8 5 E
Holmsund, *Sweden* **8** 63 41N 20 20 E
Holon, *Israel* **44** 32 2N 34 47 E
Holroyd →, *Australia* **72** 14 10 S 141 36 E
Holstebro, *Denmark* **11** 56 22N 8 37 E
Holsworthy, *U.K.* **13** 50 48N 4 21W
Holt, *Iceland* **8** 63 33N 19 48W
Holte, *Denmark* **11** 55 50N 12 29 E
Holten, *Neths.* **16** 52 17N 6 26 E
Holton, *Canada* **105** 54 31N 57 12W
Holton, *U.S.A.* **120** 39 28N 95 44W
Holtville, *U.S.A.* **125** 32 50N 115 27W
Holwerd, *Neths.* **16** 53 22N 5 54 E
Holy Cross, *U.S.A.* **102** 62 10N 159 52W
Holy I., *England, U.K.* **12** 55 42N 1 48W
Holy I., *Wales, U.K.* **12** 53 17N 4 37W
Holyhead, *U.K.* **12** 53 18N 4 38W
Holyoke, *Colo., U.S.A.* **120** 40 39N 102 18W
Holyoke, *Mass., U.S.A.* **117** 42 14N 72 37W
Holyrood, *Canada* **105** 47 27N 53 8W
Holzkirchen, *W. Germany* **31** 47 53N 11 42 E
Holzminden, *W. Germany* **30** 51 49N 9 31 E
Homa Bay, *Kenya* **92** 0 36 S 34 30 E
Homa Bay □, *Kenya* **92** 0 50 S 34 30 E
Homalin, *Burma* **52** 24 55N 95 0 E
Homberg, *W. Germany* **30** 51 2N 9 20 E
Hombori, *Mali* **91** 15 20N 1 38W
Homburg, *W. Germany* **31** 49 19N 7 21 E
Home B., *Canada* **103** 68 40N 67 10W
Home Hill, *Australia* **72** 19 43 S 147 25 E
Home Reef, *Tonga* **68** 18 59 S 174 47W
Homedale, *U.S.A.* **122** 43 42N 116 59W
Homer, *Alaska, U.S.A.* **102** 59 40N 151 35W
Homer, *Ill., U.S.A.* **119** 40 4N 87 57W
Homer, *La., U.S.A.* **121** 32 50N 93 4W
Homer, *Mich., U.S.A.* **119** 42 9N 84 49W
Homestead, *Australia* **72** 20 20 S 145 40 E
Homestead, *Fla., U.S.A.* **115** 25 29N 80 27W
Homestead, *Oreg., U.S.A.* **122** 45 5N 116 57W
Homewood, *Calif., U.S.A.* **124** 39 4N 120 8W
Homewood, *Ill., U.S.A.* **119** 41 34N 87 40W
Hominy, *U.S.A.* **121** 36 26N 96 24W
Homnabad, *India* **50** 17 45N 77 11 E
Homoine, *Mozam.* **97** 23 55 S 35 8 E
Homoljske Planina, *Yugoslavia* **33** 44 10N 21 45 E
Homorod, *Romania* **34** 46 5N 25 15 E
Homs = Ḩimş, *Syria* **46** 34 40N 36 45 E
Hon Chong, *Vietnam* **55** 10 25N 104 30 E
Hon Me, *Vietnam* **54** 19 23N 105 56 E
Hon Quan, *Vietnam* **55** 11 40N 106 50 E
Honan = Henan □, *China* **60** 34 0N 114 0 E
Honbetsu, *Japan* **63** 43 7N 143 37 E
Honcut, *U.S.A.* **124** 39 20N 121 32W
Honda, *Colombia* **134** 5 12N 74 45W
Hondeklipbaai, *S. Africa* **96** 30 19 S 17 17 E
Hondo, *Japan* **64** 32 27N 130 12 E
Hondo, *U.S.A.* **121** 29 22N 99 6W
Hondo →, *Belize* **127** 18 25N 88 21W
Honduras ■, *Cent. Amer.* **128** 14 40N 86 30W
Honduras, G. de, *Caribbean* **128** 16 50N 87 0W
Hønefoss, *Norway* **9** 60 10N 10 18 E
Honesdale, *U.S.A.* **117** 41 34N 75 17W
Honey Harbour, *Canada* **108** 44 52N 79 49W
Honey L., *U.S.A.* **124** 40 13N 120 14W
Honfleur, *France* **18** 49 25N 0 13 E
Hong →, *Vietnam* **54** 20 17N 106 34 E
Hong Gai, *Vietnam* **54** 20 57N 107 5 E
Hong He →, *China* **60** 32 25N 115 35 E
Hong Kong ■, *Asia* **59** 22 11N 114 14 E
Hong'an, *China* **59** 31 20N 114 40 E
Honghai Wan, *China* **59** 22 40N 115 0 E
Honghu, *China* **59** 29 50N 113 30 E
Hongjiang, *China* **58** 27 7N 109 59 E
Hongliu He →, *China* **60** 38 0N 109 50 E
Hongor, *Mongolia* **60** 45 45N 112 50 E
Hongsa, *Laos* **54** 19 43N 101 20 E
Hongshui He →, *China* **58** 23 48N 109 30 E
Hongtong, *China* **60** 36 16N 111 40 E
Honguedo, Détroit d', *Canada* **105** 49 15N 64 0W
Hongya, *China* **58** 29 57N 103 22 E
Hongyuan, *China* **58** 32 51N 102 40 E
Hongze Hu, *China* **61** 33 15N 118 35 E
Honiara, *Solomon Is.* **68** 9 27 S 159 57 E
Honiton, *U.K.* **13** 50 48N 3 11W
Honjō, *Akita, Japan* **63** 39 23N 140 3 E
Honjō, *Gumma, Japan* **65** 36 14N 139 11 E
Honkawane, *Japan* **65** 35 5N 138 5 E
Honkorâb, Ras, *Egypt* **88** 24 35N 35 10 E
Honolulu, *U.S.A.* **112** 21 19N 157 52W
Honshū, *Japan* **63** 36 0N 138 0 E
Hontoria del Pinar, *Spain* **24** 41 50N 3 10W
Hood, Pt., *Australia* **79** 34 23 S 119 34 E
Hood Mt., *U.S.A.* **122** 45 24N 121 41W
Hood Pt., *Papua N. G.* **69** 10 4 S 147 45 E
Hood River, *U.S.A.* **122** 45 45N 121 31W
Hoodsport, *U.S.A.* **122** 47 24N 123 7W
Hooge, *W. Germany* **30** 54 31N 8 36 E
Hoogerheide, *Neths.* **17** 51 26N 4 20 E
Hoogeveen, *Neths.* **16** 52 44N 6 30 E
Hoogeveensche Vaart, *Neths.* **16** 52 42N 6 12 E
Hoogezand, *Neths.* **16** 53 11N 6 45 E
Hooghly → = Hughli →, *India* **49** 21 56N 88 4 E
Hooghly-Chinsura = Chunchura, *India* **49** 22 53N 88 27 E
Hoogkerk, *Neths.* **16** 53 13N 6 30 E
Hooglede, *Belgium* **17** 50 59N 3 5 E
Hoogstraten, *Belgium* **17** 51 24N 4 46 E
Hoogvliet, *Neths.* **16** 51 52N 4 21 E
Hook Hd., *Ireland* **15** 52 8N 6 57W
Hook I., *Australia* **72** 20 4 S 149 0 E
Hook of Holland = Hoek van Holland, *Neths.* **16** 52 0N 4 7 E
Hooker, *U.S.A.* **121** 36 55N 101 10W
Hooker Creek, *Australia* **78** 18 23 S 130 38 E
Hoopeston, *U.S.A.* **119** 40 30N 87 40W
Hoopstad, *S. Africa* **96** 27 50 S 25 55 E
Hoorn, *Neths.* **16** 52 38N 5 4 E
Hoover Dam, *U.S.A.* **125** 36 0N 114 45W
Hooversville, *U.S.A.* **116** 40 8N 78 57W
Hop Bottom, *U.S.A.* **117** 41 41N 75 47W
Hopà, *Turkey* **39** 41 28N 41 30 E
Hope, *Canada* **110** 49 25N 121 25W
Hope, *Ariz., U.S.A.* **125** 33 43N 113 42W
Hope, *Ark., U.S.A.* **121** 33 40N 93 36W
Hope, *Ind., U.S.A.* **119** 39 18N 85 46W
Hope, *N. Dak., U.S.A.* **120** 47 21N 97 42W
Hope, L., *Australia* **73** 28 24 S 139 18 E
Hope I., *Canada* **108** 44 55N 80 11W
Hope Pt., *U.S.A.* **102** 68 20N 166 50W
Hope Town, *Bahamas* **128** 26 35N 76 57W
Hopedale, *Canada* **105** 55 28N 60 13W
Hopefield, *S. Africa* **96** 33 3 S 18 22 E
Hopei = Hebei □, *China* **60** 39 0N 116 0 E
Hopelchén, *Mexico* **127** 19 46N 89 50W
Hopetoun, *Vic., Australia* **74** 35 42 S 142 22 E
Hopetoun, *W. Austral., Australia* **79** 33 57 S 120 7 E
Hopetown, *S. Africa* **96** 29 34 S 24 3 E
Hopin, *Burma* **52** 24 58N 96 30 E
Hopkins, *Mich., U.S.A.* **119** 42 37N 85 46W
Hopkins, *Mo., U.S.A.* **118** 40 31N 94 45W
Hopkins →, *Australia* **74** 38 25 S 142 30 E
Hopkins, L., *Australia* **78** 24 15 S 128 35 E
Hopkinsville, *U.S.A.* **115** 36 52N 87 26W
Hopland, *U.S.A.* **124** 39 0N 123 7W
Hoptrup, *Denmark* **11** 55 11N 9 28 E
Hoquiam, *U.S.A.* **124** 46 50N 123 55W
Hōrai, *Japan* **65** 34 58N 137 32 E
Horcajo de Santiago, *Spain* **24** 39 50N 3 1W
Hordaland fylke □, *Norway* **9** 60 25N 6 15 E
Horden Hills, *Australia* **78** 20 15 S 130 0 E
Hordio, *Somali Rep.* **98** 10 33N 51 6 E
Horezu, *Romania* **34** 45 6N 24 0 E
Horgen, *Switz.* **31** 47 15N 8 35 E
Horinger, *China* **60** 40 28N 111 48 E
Horlick Mts., *Antarctica* **143** 84 0 S 102 0W
Hormoz, *Iran* **47** 27 35N 55 0 E
Hormoz, Jaz. ye, *Iran* **47** 27 8N 56 28 E
Hormozgān □, *Iran* **47** 27 30N 56 0 E
Hormuz Str., *The Gulf* **47** 26 30N 56 30 E
Horn, *Ísafjarðarsýsla, Iceland* **8** 66 28N 22 28W
Horn, *Suður-Múlasýsla, Iceland* **8** 65 10N 13 31W
Horn, *Neths.* **17** 51 12N 5 57 E
Horn →, *Canada* **110** 61 30N 118 1W
Horn, Cape = Hornos, C. de, *Chile* **142** 55 50 S 67 30W
Horn Head, *Ireland* **15** 55 13N 8 0W
Horn I., *Australia* **72** 10 37 S 142 17 E
Horn I., *U.S.A.* **115** 30 17N 88 40W
Horn Mts., *Canada* **110** 62 15N 119 15W
Hornachuelos, *Spain* **23** 37 50N 5 14W
Hornavan, *Sweden* **8** 66 15N 17 30 E
Hornbæk, *Denmark* **11** 56 5N 12 26 E
Hornbeck, *U.S.A.* **121** 31 22N 93 20W
Hornbrook, *U.S.A.* **122** 41 58N 122 37W
Hornburg, *E. Germany* **30** 52 2N 10 36 E
Hornby, *N.Z.* **81** 43 33 S 172 33 E
Horncastle, *U.K.* **12** 53 13N 0 8W
Horndal, *Sweden* **10** 60 18N 16 23 E
Hornell, *U.S.A.* **116** 42 23N 77 41W
Hornell L., *Canada* **110** 62 20N 119 25W
Hornepayne, *Canada* **104** 49 14N 84 48W
Hornings Mills, *Canada* **108** 44 9N 80 12W
Hornitos, *U.S.A.* **124** 37 30N 120 14W
Hornos, C. de, *Chile* **142** 55 50 S 67 30W
Hornoy, *France* **19** 49 50N 1 54 E
Hornsby, *Australia* **76** 33 42 S 151 2 E
Hornsea, *U.K.* **12** 53 55N 0 10W
Hornslandet, *Sweden* **10** 61 35N 17 37 E
Hornslet, *Denmark* **11** 56 18N 10 19 E
Hornu, *Belgium* **17** 50 26N 3 50 E
Hörnum, *W. Germany* **30** 54 44N 8 18 E
Horqin Youyi Qianqi, *China* **61** 46 5N 122 3 E
Horqueta, *Paraguay* **140** 23 15 S 56 55W
Horqueta, La, *Venezuela* **135** 7 55N 60 20W
Horra, La, *Spain* **22** 41 44N 3 53W
Horred, *Sweden* **11** 57 22N 12 28 E
Horse Cr. →, *U.S.A.* **120** 41 57N 103 58W
Horse Is., *Canada* **105** 50 15N 55 50W
Horsefly L., *Canada* **110** 52 25N 121 0W
Horsens, *Denmark* **11** 55 52N 9 51 E
Horsens Fjord, *Denmark* **11** 55 50N 10 0 E
Horsham, *Australia* **74** 36 44 S 142 13 E
Horsham, *U.K.* **13** 51 4N 0 20W
Horst, *Neths.* **17** 51 27N 6 3 E
Horten, *Norway* **10** 59 25N 10 32 E
Hortobágy →, *Hungary* **33** 47 30N 21 6 E
Horton, *U.S.A.* **120** 39 42N 95 30W
Horton →, *Canada* **102** 69 56N 126 52W
Hörvik, *Sweden* **11** 56 2N 14 45 E
Horwood, L., *Canada* **104** 48 5N 82 20W
Hosaina, *Ethiopia* **89** 7 30N 37 47 E
Hosdurga, *India* **51** 13 49N 76 17 E
Hose, Gunung-Gunung, *Malaysia* **56** 2 5N 114 6 E
Hoshangabad, *India* **48** 22 45N 77 45 E
Hoshiarpur, *India* **48** 31 30N 75 58 E
Hosingen, *Lux.* **17** 50 1N 6 6 E
Hoskins, *Papua N. G.* **69** 5 29 S 150 27 E
Hoskinstown, *Australia* **76** 35 25 S 149 28 E
Hosmer, *U.S.A.* **120** 45 36N 99 29W
Hososhima, *Japan* **64** 32 26N 131 40 E
Hospet, *India* **51** 15 15N 76 20 E
Hospitalet de Llobregat, *Spain* **24** 41 21N 2 6 E
Hoste, I., *Chile* **142** 55 0 S 69 0W
Hostens, *France* **20** 44 30N 0 40W
Hot, *Thailand* **54** 18 8N 98 29 E
Hot Creek Ra., *U.S.A.* **122** 39 0N 116 0W
Hot Springs, *Ark., U.S.A.* **121** 34 30N 93 0W
Hot Springs, *S. Dak., U.S.A.* **120** 43 25N 103 30W
Hotagen, *Sweden* **8** 63 50N 14 30 E
Hotan, *China* **62** 37 25N 79 55 E
Hotazel, *S. Africa* **96** 27 17 S 22 58 E
Hotchkiss, *U.S.A.* **123** 38 47N 107 47W
Hotham, C., *Australia* **78** 12 2 S 131 18 E
Hotham Heights, *Australia* **75** 36 58 S 147 11 E
Hoting, *Sweden* **8** 64 8N 16 15 E
Hotte, Massif de la, *Haiti* **129** 18 30N 73 45W
Hottentotsbaai, *Namibia* **96** 26 8 S 14 59 E
Hotton, *Belgium* **17** 50 16N 5 26 E
Houailou, *N. Cal.* **68** 21 17 S 165 38 E
Houat, I. de, *France* **18** 47 24N 2 58W
Houck, *U.S.A.* **123** 35 15N 109 15W
Houdan, *France* **19** 48 48N 1 35 E
Houdeng-Goegnies, *Belgium* **17** 50 29N 4 10 E
Houei Sai, *Laos* **54** 20 18N 100 26 E
Houffalize, *Belgium* **17** 50 8N 5 48 E
Houghton, *U.S.A.* **120** 47 9N 88 39W
Houghton L., *U.S.A.* **114** 44 20N 84 40W
Houghton-le-Spring, *U.K.* **12** 54 51N 1 28W
Houhora, *N.Z.* **80** 34 49 S 173 9 E
Houille →, *Belgium* **17** 50 8N 4 50 E
Houlton, *U.S.A.* **105** 46 5N 67 50W
Houma, *U.S.A.* **121** 29 35N 90 44W
Houndé, *Burkina Faso* **90** 11 34N 3 31W
Hourtin, *France* **20** 45 11N 1 4W
Hourtin-Carcans, Étang d', *France* **20** 45 10N 1 6W
Houston, *Canada* **110** 54 25N 126 39W
Houston, *Mo., U.S.A.* **121** 37 20N 92 0W
Houston, *Tex., U.S.A.* **121** 29 50N 95 20W
Houten, *Neths.* **16** 52 2N 5 10 E
Houthalen, *Belgium* **17** 51 2N 5 23 E
Houthem, *Belgium* **17** 50 48N 2 57 E
Houthulst, *Belgium* **17** 50 59N 3 20 E
Houtman Abrolhos, *Australia* **79** 28 43 S 113 48 E
Houyet, *Belgium* **17** 50 11N 5 1 E
Hov, *Denmark* **11** 55 55N 10 15 E
Hova, *Sweden* **11** 58 53N 14 14 E
Høvåg, *Norway* **11** 58 10N 8 16 E
Hovd, *Mongolia* **62** 48 2N 91 37 E
Hove, *U.K.* **13** 50 50N 0 10W
Hovmantorp, *Sweden* **11** 56 47N 15 7 E
Hövsgöl, *Mongolia* **60** 43 37N 109 39 E
Hövsgöl Nuur, *Mongolia* **62** 51 0N 100 30 E
Hovsta, *Sweden* **10** 59 22N 15 15 E
Howakil, *Ethiopia* **89** 15 10N 40 16 E
Howar, Wadi →, *Sudan* **89** 17 30N 27 8 E
Howard, *Australia* **73** 25 16 S 152 32 E
Howard, *Kans., U.S.A.* **121** 37 30N 96 16W
Howard, *Pa., U.S.A.* **116** 41 0N 77 40W
Howard, *S. Dak., U.S.A.* **120** 44 2N 97 30W
Howard I., *Australia* **72** 12 10 S 135 24 E
Howard L., *Canada* **111** 62 15N 105 57W
Howatharra, *Australia* **79** 28 29 S 114 33 E
Howe, *U.S.A.* **122** 43 48N 113 0W
Howe, C., *Australia* **75** 37 30 S 150 0 E
Howe I., *Canada* **109** 44 16N 76 17W
Howell, *U.S.A.* **104** 42 38N 83 56W
Howes Valley, *Australia* **76** 32 51 S 150 51 E
Howick, *Canada* **117** 45 11N 73 51W
Howick, *N.Z.* **80** 36 54 S 174 56 E
Howick, *S. Africa* **97** 29 28 S 30 14 E
Howick Group, *Australia* **72** 14 20 S 145 30 E
Howitt, L., *Australia* **73** 27 40 S 138 40 E
Howley, *Canada* **105** 49 12N 57 2W
Howqua →, *Australia* **75** 37 12 S 146 29 E
Howrah = Haora, *India* **49** 22 37N 88 20 E
Howth Hd., *Ireland* **15** 53 21N 6 0W
Höxter, *W. Germany* **30** 51 45N 9 26 E
Hoy I., *U.K.* **14** 58 50N 3 15W
Hoya, *W. Germany* **30** 52 47N 9 10 E
Høyanger, *Norway* **9** 61 13N 6 4 E
Hoyerswerda, *E. Germany* **30** 51 26N 14 14 E
Hoyos, *Spain* **22** 40 9N 6 45W
Hpawlum, *Burma* **52** 27 12N 98 12 E
Hpettintha, *Burma* **52** 24 14N 95 23 E
Hpizow, *Burma* **52** 26 57N 98 24 E
Hradec Králové, *Czech.* **32** 50 15N 15 50 E
Hranice, *Czech.* **32** 49 34N 17 45 E
Hron →, *Czech.* **33** 47 49N 18 45 E
Hrubieszów, *Poland* **32** 50 49N 23 51 E
Hrvatska, *Yugoslavia* **27** 45 20N 16 0 E
Hrvatska □, *Yugoslavia* **27** 45 20N 18 0 E
Hsenwi, *Burma* **52** 23 22N 97 55 E
Hsiamen = Xiamen, *China* **59** 24 25N 118 4 E
Hsian = Xi'an, *China* **60** 34 15N 109 0 E
Hsinhailien = Lianyungang, *China* **61** 34 40N 119 11 E
Hsipaw, *Burma* **52** 22 37N 97 18 E
Hsüchou = Xuzhou, *China* **61** 34 18N 117 10 E
Htawgaw, *Burma* **52** 25 57N 98 23 E
Hu Xian, *China* **60** 34 8N 108 42 E
Hua Hin, *Thailand* **54** 12 34N 99 58 E
Hua Xian, *Henan, China* **60** 35 30N 114 30 E
Hua Xian, *Shaanxi, China* **60** 34 30N 109 48 E
Hua'an, *China* **59** 25 1N 117 32 E
Huacaya, *Bolivia* **137** 20 45 S 63 43W
Huacheng, *China* **59** 24 4N 115 37 E
Huachinera, *Mexico* **126** 30 9N 108 55W
Huacho, *Peru* **136** 11 10 S 77 35W
Huachón, *Peru* **136** 10 35 S 76 0W
Huade, *China* **60** 41 55N 113 59 E
Huadian, *China* **61** 43 0N 126 40 E
Huai He →, *China* **59** 33 0N 118 30 E
Huai Yot, *Thailand* **55** 7 45N 99 37 E
Huai'an, *Hebei, China* **60** 40 30N 114 20 E
Huai'an, *Jiangsu, China* **61** 33 30N 119 10 E
Huaide, *China* **61** 43 30N 124 40 E
Huaidezhen, *China* **61** 43 48N 124 50 E
Huaihua, *China* **58** 27 32N 109 57 E
Huaiji, *China* **59** 23 55N 112 12 E
Huainan, *China* **59** 32 38N 116 58 E
Huaining, *China* **59** 30 24N 116 40 E
Huairen, *China* **60** 39 48N 113 20 E
Huairou, *China* **60** 40 20N 116 35 E
Huaiyang, *China* **60** 33 40N 114 52 E
Huaiyuan, *Anhui, China* **61** 32 55N 117 10 E
Huaiyuan, *Guangxi Zhuangzu, China* **58** 24 31N 108 22 E
Huajianzi, *China* **61** 41 23N 125 20 E
Huajuapan de Leon, *Mexico* **127** 17 50N 97 48W
Hualapai Pk., *U.S.A.* **123** 35 8N 113 58W
Hualian, *Taiwan* **59** 23 59N 121 37 E
Huallaga →, *Peru* **136** 5 0 S 75 30W
Huallanca, *Peru* **136** 8 50 S 77 56W
Huamachuco, *Peru* **136** 7 50 S 78 5W
Huambo, *Angola* **95** 12 42 S 15 54 E
Huambo □, *Angola* **95** 13 0 S 16 0 E

Huan Jiang →, China 60 34 28N 109 0 E
Huan Xian, China 60 36 33N 107 7 E
Huancabamba, Peru 136 5 10 S 79 15W
Huancane, Peru 136 15 10 S 69 44W
Huancapi, Peru 136 13 40 S 74 0W
Huancavelica, Peru 136 12 50 S 75 5W
Huancavelica □, Peru 136 13 0 S 75 0W
Huancayo, Peru 136 12 5 S 75 12W
Huanchaca, Bolivia 136 20 15 S 66 40W
Huanchaca, Serranía de, Bolivia 137 14 30 S 60 39W
Huang Hai = Yellow Sea, China 61 35 0N 123 0 E
Huang He →, China 61 37 55N 118 50 E
Huang Xian, China 61 37 38N 120 30 E
Huangchuan, China 59 32 15N 115 10 E
Huanggang, China 59 30 29N 114 52 E
Huangling, China 60 35 34N 109 15 E
Huangliu, China 62 18 20N 108 50 E
Huanglong, China 60 35 30N 109 59 E
Huanglongtan, China 59 32 40N 110 33 E
Huangmei, China 59 30 5N 115 56 E
Huangpi, China 59 30 50N 114 22 E
Huangping, China 58 26 52N 107 54 E
Huangshi, China 59 30 10N 115 3 E
Huangsongdian, China 61 43 45N 127 25 E
Huangyan, China 59 28 38N 121 19 E
Huangyangsi, China 59 26 33N 111 39 E
Huaning, China 58 24 17N 102 56 E
Huanjiang, China 58 24 50N 108 18 E
Huanta, Peru 136 12 55 S 74 20W
Huantai, China 61 36 58N 117 56 E
Huánuco, Peru 136 9 55 S 76 15W
Huánuco □, Peru 136 9 55 S 76 14W
Huanuni, Bolivia 136 18 16 S 66 51W
Huanzo, Cordillera de, Peru 136 14 35 S 73 20W
Huaping, China 58 26 46N 101 25 E
Huaral, Peru 136 11 32 S 77 13W
Huaraz, Peru 136 9 30 S 77 32W
Huari, Peru 136 9 14 S 77 14W
Huarmey, Peru 136 10 5 S 78 5W
Huarochiri, Peru 136 12 9 S 76 15W
Huarocondo, Peru 136 13 26 S 72 14W
Huarong, China 59 29 29N 112 30 E
Huascarán, Peru 136 9 8 S 77 36W
Huascarán, Nevado, Peru 136 9 7 S 77 37W
Huasco, Chile 140 28 30 S 71 15W
Huasco →, Chile 140 28 27 S 71 13W
Huasna, U.S.A. 125 35 6N 120 24W
Huatabampo, Mexico 126 26 50N 109 50W
Huauchinango, Mexico 127 20 11N 98 3W
Huautla de Jiménez, Mexico 127 18 8N 96 51W
Huaxi, China 58 26 25N 106 40 E
Huay Namota, Mexico 126 21 56N 104 30W
Huayin, China 60 34 35N 110 5 E
Huayllay, Peru 136 11 3 S 76 21W
Huayuan, China 58 28 37N 109 29 E
Huazhou, China 59 21 33N 110 33 E
Hubbard, Iowa, U.S.A. 118 42 18N 93 18W
Hubbard, Tex., U.S.A. 121 31 50N 96 50W
Hubbart Pt., Canada 111 59 21N 94 41W
Hubei □, China 59 31 0N 112 0 E
Hubli-Dharwad = Dharwad, India 51 15 22N 75 15 E
Hückelhoven-Ratheim, W. Germany 30 51 6N 6 13 E
Huddersfield, U.K. 12 53 38N 1 49W
Hudi, Sudan 88 17 43N 34 18 E
Hudiksvall, Sweden 10 61 43N 17 10 E
Hudson, Canada 111 50 6N 92 9W
Hudson, Mass., U.S.A. 117 42 23N 71 35W
Hudson, Mich., U.S.A. 119 41 50N 84 20W
Hudson, N.Y., U.S.A. 117 42 15N 73 46W
Hudson, Wis., U.S.A. 120 44 57N 92 45W
Hudson, Wyo., U.S.A. 122 42 54N 108 37W
Hudson →, U.S.A. 117 40 42N 74 2W
Hudson Bay, Sask., Canada 111 52 51N 102 23W
Hudson Bay, Canada 103 60 0N 86 0W
Hudson Falls, U.S.A. 117 43 18N 73 34W
Hudson Mts., Antarctica 143 74 32 S 99 20W
Hudson Str., Canada 103 62 0N 70 0W
Hudson's Hope, Canada 110 56 0N 121 54W
Hudsonville, U.S.A. 119 42 52N 85 52W
Hue, Vietnam 54 16 30N 107 35 E
Huebra →, Spain 22 41 2N 6 48W
Huechucuicui, Pta., Chile 142 41 48 S 74 2W
Huedin, Romania 34 46 52N 23 2 E
Huehuetenango, Guatemala 128 15 20N 91 28W
Huejúcar, Mexico 126 22 21N 103 13W
Huelgoat, France 18 48 22N 3 46W
Huelma, Spain 25 37 39N 3 28W
Huelva, Spain 23 37 18N 6 57W
Huelva □, Spain 23 37 40N 7 0W
Huelva →, Spain 23 37 27N 6 0W
Huentelauquén, Chile 140 31 38 S 71 33W
Huércal Overa, Spain 25 37 23N 1 57W
Huerta, Sa. de la, Argentina 140 31 10 S 67 30W
Huertas, C. de las, Spain 25 38 21N 0 24W
Huerva →, Spain 24 41 39N 0 52W
Huesca, Spain 24 42 8N 0 25W
Huesca □, Spain 24 42 20N 0 1 E
Huéscar, Spain 25 37 44N 2 35W
Huetamo, Mexico 126 18 36N 100 54W
Huete, Spain 24 40 10N 2 43W
Hugh →, Australia 72 25 1 S 134 1 E
Hughenden, Australia 72 20 52 S 144 10 E
Hughes, Australia 79 30 42 S 129 31 E
Hughes, U.S.A. 102 66 0N 154 20W
Hughli →, India 49 21 56N 88 4 E
Hugo, U.S.A. 120 39 12N 103 27W
Hugoton, U.S.A. 121 37 11N 101 22W
Hui Xian, Gansu, China 60 33 50N 106 4 E
Hui Xian, Henan, China 60 35 27N 113 12 E
Hui'an, China 59 25 1N 118 43 E
Hui'anbu, China 60 37 28N 106 38 E
Huiarau Ra., N.Z. 80 38 45 S 176 55 E
Huichang, China 59 25 32N 115 45 E
Huichapán, Mexico 127 20 24N 99 40W
Huidong, China 58 26 34N 102 35 E
Huifa He →, China 61 43 0N 127 50 E
Huíla, Angola 95 15 4 S 13 32 E
Huila □, Colombia 134 2 30N 75 45W
Huila, Nevado del, Colombia 134 3 0N 76 0W
Huilai, China 59 23 0N 116 18 E
Huili, China 58 26 35N 102 17 E
Huimin, China 61 37 27N 117 28 E
Huinan, China 61 42 40N 126 2 E
Huinca Renancó, Argentina 140 34 51 S 64 22W
Huining, China 60 35 38N 105 0 E
Huinong, China 60 39 5N 106 35 E
Huiroa, N.Z. 80 39 15 S 174 30 E
Huise, Belgium 17 50 54N 3 36 E
Huishui, China 58 26 7N 106 38 E
Huisne →, France 18 47 59N 0 11 E
Huissen, Neths. 16 51 57N 5 57 E
Huiting, China 60 34 5N 116 5 E
Huitong, China 58 26 51N 109 45 E
Huixtla, Mexico 127 15 9N 92 28W
Huize, China 58 26 24N 103 15 E
Huizen, Neths. 16 52 18N 5 14 E
Huizhou, China 59 23 0N 114 23 E
Hukou, China 59 29 45N 116 21 E
Hukuntsi, Botswana 96 23 58 S 21 45 E
Hula, Ethiopia 89 6 33N 38 30 E
Hulan, China 62 46 1N 126 37 E
Ḥulayfā', Si. Arabia 46 25 58N 40 45 E
Huld, Mongolia 60 45 5N 105 30 E
Ḥulda, Israel 44 31 50N 34 51 E
Hulin He →, China 61 45 0N 122 10 E
Hull, Canada 106 45 25N 75 44W
Hull, U.K. 12 53 45N 0 20W
Hull, U.S.A. 118 39 43N 91 13W
Hull →, U.K. 12 53 43N 0 25W
Hulst, Neths. 17 51 17N 4 2 E
Hultsfred, Sweden 11 57 30N 15 52 E
Hulun Nur, China 62 49 0N 117 30 E
Humahuaca, Argentina 140 23 10 S 65 25W
Humaitá, Brazil 137 7 35 S 63 1W
Humaitá, Paraguay 140 27 2 S 58 31W
Humansdorp, S. Africa 96 34 2 S 24 46 E
Humansville, U.S.A. 118 37 48N 93 35W
Humbe, Angola 95 16 40 S 14 55 E
Humber →, U.K. 12 53 40N 0 10W
Humberside □, U.K. 12 53 50N 0 30W
Humbert River, Australia 78 16 30 S 130 45 E
Humble, U.S.A. 121 29 59N 93 18W
Humboldt, Canada 111 52 15N 105 9W
Humboldt, Iowa, U.S.A. 118 42 42N 94 15W
Humboldt, Tenn., U.S.A. 121 35 50N 88 55W
Humboldt →, U.S.A. 122 40 2N 118 31W
Humboldt Gletscher, Greenland 144 79 30N 62 0W
Humboldt Mts., N.Z. 81 44 30 S 168 15 E
Humbolt, Massif du, N. Cal. 68 21 53 S 166 25 E
Hume, Calif., U.S.A. 124 36 48N 118 54W
Hume, Kans., U.S.A. 118 38 5N 94 35W
Hume, L., Australia 75 36 0 S 147 0 E
Humenné, Czech. 32 48 55N 21 50 E
Humeston, U.S.A. 118 40 51N 93 30W
Humpata, Angola 95 15 2 S 13 24 E
Humphreys, Mt., U.S.A. 124 37 17N 118 40W
Humphreys Pk., U.S.A. 123 35 24N 111 38W
Humpolec, Czech. 32 49 31N 15 20 E
Humptulips, U.S.A. 124 47 14N 123 57W
Humula, Australia 76 35 30 S 147 46 E
Hūn, Libya 86 29 2N 16 0 E
Hun Jiang →, China 61 40 50N 125 38 E
Húnaflói, Iceland 8 65 50N 20 50W
Hunan □, China 59 27 30N 112 0 E
Hunchun, China 61 42 52N 130 28 E
Hundested, Denmark 11 55 58N 11 52 E
Hundred Mile House, Canada 110 51 38N 121 18W
Hunedoara, Romania 34 45 40N 22 50 E
Hünfeld, W. Germany 30 50 40N 9 47 E
Hung Yen, Vietnam 54 20 39N 106 4 E
Hunga, Tonga 68 18 41 S 174 7W
Hunga Ha'api, Tonga 68 20 41 S 175 7W
Hungary ■, Europe 33 47 20N 19 20 E
Hungary, Plain of, Europe 6 47 0N 20 0 E
Hungerford, Australia 73 28 58 S 144 24 E
Hŭngnam, N. Korea 61 39 49N 127 45 E
Huni Valley, Ghana 90 5 33N 1 56W
Hunsberge, Namibia 96 27 45 S 17 12 E
Hunsrück, W. Germany 31 49 30N 7 0 E
Hunstanton, U.K. 12 52 57N 0 30 E
Hunsur, India 51 12 16N 76 16 E
Hunte →, W. Germany 30 52 30N 8 19 E
Hunter, Australia 74 36 26 S 144 30 E
Hunter, N.Z. 81 44 36 S 171 2 E
Hunter, N. Dak., U.S.A. 120 47 12N 97 17W
Hunter, N.Y., U.S.A. 117 42 13N 74 13W
Hunter →, Australia 76 32 52 S 151 46 E
Hunter →, N.Z. 81 44 21 S 169 27 E
Hunter, C., Solomon Is. 68 9 48 S 159 50 E
Hunter Hills, The, N.Z. 81 44 26 S 170 46 E
Hunter I., Australia 72 40 30 S 144 45 E
Hunter I., Canada 110 51 55N 128 0W
Hunter Mts., N.Z. 81 45 43 S 167 25 E
Hunter Ra., Australia 76 32 45 S 150 15 E
Hunters Road, Zimb. 93 19 9 S 29 49 E
Hunterville, N.Z. 80 39 56 S 175 35 E
Huntingburg, U.S.A. 119 38 20N 86 58W
Huntingdon, Canada 107 45 6N 74 10W
Huntingdon, U.K. 13 52 20N 0 11W
Huntingdon, U.S.A. 116 40 28N 78 1W
Huntington, Ind., U.S.A. 119 40 52N 85 30W
Huntington, N.Y., U.S.A. 117 40 52N 73 25W
Huntington, Oreg., U.S.A. 122 44 22N 117 21W
Huntington, Utah, U.S.A. 122 39 24N 111 1W
Huntington, W. Va., U.S.A. 114 38 20N 82 30W
Huntington Beach, U.S.A. 125 33 40N 118 0W
Huntington Park, U.S.A. 123 33 58N 118 15W
Huntley, U.S.A. 119 42 10N 88 26W
Huntly, N.Z. 80 37 34 S 175 11 E
Huntly, U.K. 14 57 27N 2 48W
Huntsville, Canada 108 45 20N 79 14W
Huntsville, Ala., U.S.A. 115 34 45N 86 35W
Huntsville, Mo., U.S.A. 118 39 26N 92 33W
Huntsville, Tex., U.S.A. 121 30 45N 95 35W
Hunyani →, Zimb. 93 15 57 S 30 39 E
Hunyuan, China 60 39 42N 113 42 E
Hunza →, India 49 35 54N 74 20 E
Huo Xian, China 60 36 36N 111 42 E
Huon, G., Papua N. G. 69 7 0 S 147 30 E
Huon Pen., Papua N. G. 69 6 20 S 147 30 E
Huong Hoa, Vietnam 54 16 37N 106 45 E
Huong Khe, Vietnam 54 18 13N 105 41 E
Huonville, Australia 72 43 0 S 147 5 E
Huoqiu, China 59 32 20N 116 12 E
Huoshan, Anhui, China 59 32 28N 118 30 E
Huoshan, Anhui, China 59 31 25N 116 20 E
Huoshao Dao, Taiwan 59 22 40N 121 30 E
Hupeh □ = Hubei □, China 59 31 0N 112 0 E
Hure Qi, China 61 42 45N 121 45 E
Hurezani, Romania 34 44 49N 23 40 E
Hurghada, Egypt 88 27 15N 33 50 E
Hurley, N. Mex., U.S.A. 123 32 45N 108 7W
Hurley, Wis., U.S.A. 120 46 26N 90 10W
Huron, Calif., U.S.A. 124 36 12N 120 6W
Huron, Ohio, U.S.A. 116 41 22N 82 34W
Huron, S. Dak., U.S.A. 120 44 22N 98 12W
Huron, L., N. Amer. 108 45 0N 83 0W
Hurricane, U.S.A. 123 37 10N 113 12W
Hurso, Ethiopia 89 9 35N 41 33 E
Hurum, Norway 10 61 9N 8 46 E
Hurunui →, N.Z. 81 42 54 S 173 18 E
Hurup, Denmark 11 56 46N 8 25 E
Húsavík, Iceland 8 66 3N 17 21W
Huşi, Romania 34 46 41N 28 7 E
Huskisson, Australia 76 35 2 S 150 41 E
Huskvarna, Sweden 11 57 47N 14 15 E
Hussar, Canada 110 51 3N 112 41W
Husum, Sweden 10 63 21N 19 12 E
Husum, W. Germany 30 54 27N 9 3 E
Hutchinson, Kans., U.S.A. 121 38 3N 97 59W
Hutchinson, Minn., U.S.A. 120 44 50N 94 22W
Hutsonville, U.S.A. 119 39 6N 87 40W
Hüttental, W. Germany 30 50 52N 8 1 E
Huttig, U.S.A. 121 33 5N 92 10W
Hutton, Mt., Australia 73 25 51 S 148 20 E
Huwun, Ethiopia 89 4 23N 40 6 E
Ḥuwwārah, Jordan 44 32 9N 35 15 E
Huy, Belgium 17 50 31N 5 15 E
Hvammur, Iceland 8 65 13N 21 49W
Hvar, Yugoslavia 27 43 11N 16 28 E
Hvarski Kanal, Yugoslavia 27 43 15N 16 35 E
Hvítá, Iceland 8 64 40N 21 5W
Hvítá →, Iceland 8 64 0N 20 58W
Hvítárvatn, Iceland 8 64 37N 19 50W
Hwang Ho = Huang He →, China 61 37 55N 118 50 E
Hwange, Zimb. 93 18 18 S 26 30 E
Hwange Nat. Park, Zimb. 96 19 0 S 26 30 E
Hwekum, Burma 52 26 7N 95 22 E
Hyannis, U.S.A. 120 42 0N 101 45W
Hyargas Nuur, Mongolia 62 49 0N 93 0 E
Hybo, Sweden 10 61 49N 16 15 E
Hyde, N.Z. 81 45 18 S 170 16 E
Hyde Park, Guyana 135 6 30N 58 16W
Hyden, Australia 79 32 24 S 118 53 E
Hyderabad, India 50 17 22N 78 29 E
Hyderabad, Pakistan 48 25 23N 68 24 E
Hyères, France 21 43 8N 6 9 E
Hyères, Is. d', France 21 43 0N 6 20 E
Hyesan, N. Korea 61 41 20N 128 10 E
Hyland →, Canada 110 59 52N 128 12W
Hyland, Mt., Australia 77 30 10 S 152 27 E
Hyltebruk, Sweden 11 56 59N 13 15 E
Hymia, India 49 33 40N 78 2 E
Hyndman Pk., U.S.A. 122 43 50N 114 10W
Hyōgo □, Japan 64 35 15N 135 0 E
Hyrum, U.S.A. 122 41 35N 111 56W
Hysham, U.S.A. 122 46 21N 107 11W
Hythe, U.K. 13 51 4N 1 5 E
Hyūga, Japan 64 32 25N 131 35 E
Hyvinge = Hyvinkää, Finland 9 60 38N 24 50 E
Hyvinkää, Finland 9 60 38N 24 50 E

I

I-n-Échaï, Mali 84 20 10N 2 5W
I-n-Gall, Niger 91 16 51N 7 1 E
Iabès, Erg, Algeria 85 27 30N 2 2W
Iaco →, Brazil 136 9 3 S 68 34W
Iaçu, Brazil 139 12 45 S 40 13W
Iakora, Madag. 97 23 6 S 46 40 E
Iaşi, Romania 34 47 10N 27 40 E
Iauaretê, Colombia 134 0 36N 69 12W
Iba, Phil. 57 15 22N 120 0 E
Ibadan, Nigeria 91 7 22N 3 58 E
Ibagué, Colombia 134 4 20N 75 20W
Ibaiti, Brazil 139 23 50 S 50 10W
Iballja, Albania 34 42 12N 20 0 E
Ibăneşti, Romania 34 46 45N 24 50 E
Ibar →, Yugoslavia 33 43 43N 20 45 E
Ibara, Japan 64 34 36N 133 28 E
Ibaraki, Japan 65 34 49N 135 34 E
Ibaraki □, Japan 65 36 10N 140 10 E
Ibarra, Ecuador 134 0 21N 78 7W
Ibba, Sudan 89 4 49N 29 2 E
Ibba, Bahr el →, Sudan 89 5 30N 28 55 E
Ibbenbüren, W. Germany 30 52 16N 7 41 E
Ibembo, Zaïre 92 2 35N 23 35 E
Ibera, L., Argentina 140 28 30 S 57 9W
Iberia, U.S.A. 118 38 5N 92 18W
Iberian Peninsula, Europe 6 40 0N 5 0W
Iberville, Canada 107 45 19N 73 17W
Iberville, Lac D', Canada 104 55 55N 73 15W
Ibi, Nigeria 91 8 15N 9 44 E
Ibiá, Brazil 139 19 30 S 46 30W
Ibicaraí, Brazil 139 14 51 S 39 36W
Ibicuí, Brazil 139 14 51 S 39 59W
Ibicuy, Argentina 140 33 55 S 59 10W
Ibioapaba, Sa. da, Brazil 138 4 0 S 41 30W
Ibipetuba, Brazil 138 11 0 S 44 32W
Ibitiara, Brazil 139 12 39 S 42 13W
Ibiza, Spain 25 38 54N 1 26 E
Íblei, Monti, Italy 29 37 15N 14 45 E
Ibo, Mozam. 93 12 22 S 40 40 E
Ibonma, Indonesia 57 3 29 S 133 31 E
Ibotirama, Brazil 139 12 13 S 43 12W
Ibshawâi, Egypt 88 29 21N 30 40 E
Ibu, Indonesia 57 1 35N 127 33 E
Ibuki-Sanchi, Japan 65 35 25N 136 18 E
Iburg, W. Germany 30 52 10N 8 3 E
Ibusuki, Japan 64 31 12N 130 40 E
Icá, Peru 136 14 0 S 75 48W
Ica □, Peru 136 14 20 S 75 30W
Iça →, Brazil 136 2 55 S 67 58W
Icabarú, Venezuela 135 4 20N 61 45W
Icabarú →, Venezuela 135 4 45N 62 15W
Içana, Brazil 134 0 21N 67 19W
Içana →, Brazil 134 0 26N 67 19W
Icatu, Brazil 138 2 46 S 44 4W
Iceland ■, Atl. Oc. 8 65 0N 19 0W
Icha, U.S.S.R. 41 55 30N 156 0 E
Ich'ang = Yichang, China 59 30 40N 111 20 E
Ichchapuram, India 50 19 10N 84 40 E
Ichihara, Japan 65 35 28N 140 5 E
Ichikawa, Japan 65 35 44N 139 55 E
Ichilo →, Bolivia 137 15 57 S 64 50W
Ichinomiya, Gifu, Japan 65 35 18N 136 48 E
Ichinomiya, Kumamoto, Japan 64 32 58N 131 5 E
Ichinoseki, Japan 63 38 55N 141 8 E
Ichnya, U.S.S.R. 36 50 52N 32 24 E
Icht, Morocco 84 29 6N 8 54W
Ichtegem, Belgium 17 51 5N 3 1 E
Icó, Brazil 138 6 24 S 38 51W
Icod, Canary Is. 25 28 22N 16 43W
Icoraci, Brazil 138 1 18 S 48 28W
Icy Str., U.S.A. 110 58 20N 135 30W
Ida Grove, U.S.A. 120 42 20N 95 25W
Ida Valley, Australia 79 28 42 S 120 29 E
Idabel, U.S.A. 121 33 53N 94 50W
Idaga Hamus, Ethiopia 89 14 13N 39 48 E
Idah, Nigeria 91 7 5N 6 40 E
Idaho □, U.S.A. 122 44 10N 114 0W
Idaho City, U.S.A. 122 43 50N 115 52W
Idaho Falls, U.S.A. 122 43 30N 112 1W
Idaho Springs, U.S.A. 122 39 49N 105 30W

Idanha-a-Nova, Portugal 22 39 50N 7 15W
Idar-Oberstein, W. Germany 31 49 43N 7 19 E
Idd el Ghanam, Sudan 87 11 30N 24 19 E
Iddan, Somali Rep. 98 6 10N 48 55 E
Idehan, Libya 86 27 10N 11 30 E
Idehan Marzūq, Libya 86 24 50N 13 51 E
Idelès, Algeria 85 23 50N 5 53 E
Idfû, Egypt 88 25 0N 32 49 E
Ídhi Óros, Greece 35 35 15N 24 45 E
Ídhra, Greece 35 37 20N 23 28 E
Idi, Indonesia 56 5 2N 97 37 E
Idiofa, Zaïre 95 4 55 S 19 42 E
Idkerberget, Sweden 10 60 22N 15 15 E
Idku, Bahra el, Egypt 88 31 18N 30 18 E
Idlip, Syria 46 35 55N 36 38 E
Idna, Jordan 44 31 34N 34 58 E
Idria, U.S.A. 124 36 25N 120 41W
Idrija, Yugoslavia 27 46 0N 14 5 E
Idritsa, U.S.S.R. 36 56 25N 28 30 E
Idstein, W. Germany 31 50 13N 8 17 E
Idutywa, S. Africa 97 32 8 S 28 18 E
Ieper, Belgium 17 50 51N 2 53 E
Ierápetra, Greece 35 35 0N 25 44 E
Ierissós, Greece 35 40 22N 23 52 E
Ierzu, Italy 28 39 48N 9 32 E
Ieshima-Shotō, Japan 64 34 40N 134 32 E
Iesi, Italy 27 43 32N 13 12 E
Ifach, Punta, Spain 25 38 38N 0 5 E
Ifanadiana, Madag. 97 21 19 S 47 39 E
Ife, Nigeria 91 7 30N 4 31 E
Iférouâne, Niger 91 19 5N 8 24 E
Iffley, Australia 72 18 53 S 141 12 E
Ifni, Morocco 84 29 29N 10 12W
Ifon, Nigeria 91 6 58N 5 40 E
Iforas, Adrar des, Mali 91 19 40N 1 40 E
Ifrane, Morocco 84 33 33N 5 7W
Iga, Japan 65 34 45N 136 10 E
Iganga, Uganda 92 0 37N 33 28 E
Igara Paraná →, Colombia 134 2 9 S 71 47W
Igarapava, Brazil 139 20 3 S 47 47W
Igarapé Açu, Brazil 138 1 4 S 47 33W
Igarapé-Mirim, Brazil 138 1 59 S 48 58W
Igarka, U.S.S.R. 41 67 30N 86 33 E
Igatimi, Paraguay 141 24 5 S 55 40W
Igatpuri, India 50 19 40N 73 35 E
Igbetti, Nigeria 91 8 44N 4 8 E
Igbo-Ora, Nigeria 91 7 29N 3 15 E
Igboho, Nigeria 91 8 53N 3 50 E
Iggesund, Sweden 10 61 39N 17 10 E
Ighil Izane, Algeria 85 35 44N 0 31 E
Iglésias, Italy 28 39 19N 8 27 E
Igli, Algeria 85 30 25N 2 19W
Igloolik, Canada 103 69 20N 81 49W
Igma, Gebel el, Egypt 88 28 55N 34 0 E
Ignace, Canada 104 49 30N 91 40W
Igoshevo, U.S.S.R. 37 59 25N 42 35 E
Iguaçu →, Brazil 141 25 36 S 54 36W
Iguaçu, Cat. del, Brazil 141 25 41 S 54 26W
Iguaçu Falls = Iguaçu, Cat. del, Brazil 141 25 41 S 54 26W
Iguala, Mexico 127 18 20N 99 40W
Igualada, Spain 24 41 37N 1 37 E
Iguana Creek, Australia 75 37 46 S 147 23 E
Iguape, Brazil 139 24 43 S 47 33W
Iguassu = Iguaçu →, Brazil 141 25 36 S 54 36W
Iguatu, Brazil 138 6 20 S 39 18W
Iguéla, Gabon 94 2 0 S 9 16 E
Igunga □, Tanzania 92 4 20 S 33 45 E
Ihiala, Nigeria 91 5 51N 6 55 E
Ihosy, Madag. 97 22 24 S 46 8 E
Ihotry, L., Madag. 97 21 56 S 43 41 E
Ii, Finland 8 65 19N 25 22 E
Iida, Japan 65 35 35N 137 50 E
Iijoki →, Finland 8 65 20N 25 20 E
Iisalmi, Finland 8 63 32N 27 10 E
Iizuka, Japan 64 33 38N 130 42 E
Ijâfene, Mauritania 84 20 40N 8 0W
Ijebu-Igbo, Nigeria 91 6 56N 4 1 E
Ijebu-Ode, Nigeria 91 6 47N 3 58 E
IJmuiden, Neths. 16 52 28N 4 35 E
IJssel →, Neths. 16 52 35N 5 50 E
IJsselmeer, Neths. 16 52 45N 5 20 E
IJsselmuiden, Neths. 16 52 34N 5 57 E
IJsselstein, Neths. 16 52 1N 5 2 E
Ijuí →, Brazil 141 27 58 S 55 20W
Ijūin, Japan 64 31 37N 130 24 E
IJzendijke, Neths. 17 51 19N 3 37 E
IJzer →, Belgium 17 51 9N 2 44 E
Ikale, Nigeria 91 7 40N 5 37 E
Ikare, Nigeria 91 7 32N 5 40 E
Ikaría, Greece 35 37 35N 26 10 E
Ikast, Denmark 11 56 8N 9 10 E
Ikawa, Japan 65 35 13N 138 15 E
Ikeda, Japan 64 34 1N 133 48 E
Ikeja, Nigeria 91 6 36N 3 23 E
Ikela, Zaïre 94 1 6 S 23 6 E
Ikenge, Zaïre 94 0 8 S 18 8 E
Ikerre-Ekiti, Nigeria 91 7 25N 5 19 E
Ikhtiman, Bulgaria 34 42 27N 23 48 E
Iki, Japan 64 33 45N 129 42 E
Iki-Kaikyō, Japan 64 33 40N 129 45 E
Ikimba L., Tanzania 92 1 30 S 31 20 E
Ikire, Nigeria 91 7 23N 4 15 E
Ikitsuki-Shima, Japan 64 33 23N 129 26 E
Ikom, Nigeria 91 6 0N 8 42 E
Ikopa →, Madag. 97 16 45 S 46 40 E
Ikot Ekpene, Nigeria 91 5 12N 7 40 E
'Ikrimah, Libya 86 32 2N 23 41 E
Ikungu, Tanzania 92 1 33 S 33 42 E
Ikuno, Japan 64 35 10N 134 48 E
Ikurun, Nigeria 91 7 54N 4 40 E
Ila, Nigeria 91 8 0N 4 39 E
Ilagan, Phil. 57 17 7N 121 53 E
Īlām, Iran 46 33 0N 46 0 E
Ilam, Nepal 49 26 58N 87 58 E
Ilanskiy, U.S.S.R. 41 56 14N 96 3 E
Ilaro, Nigeria 91 6 53N 3 3 E
Iława, Poland 32 53 36N 19 34 E
Ilayangudi, India 51 9 34N 78 37 E
Ilbilbie, Australia 72 21 45 S 149 20 E
Île-à-la Crosse, Canada 111 55 27N 107 53W
Île-à-la-Crosse, Lac, Canada 111 55 40N 107 45W
Île-Bouchard, L', France 18 47 7N 0 26 E
Île-de-France, France 19 49 0N 2 20 E
Ile-Rousse, L', France 21 42 38N 8 57 E
Ilebo, Zaïre 95 4 17 S 20 55 E
Ileje □, Tanzania 93 9 30 S 33 25 E
Ilek, U.S.S.R. 40 51 32N 53 21 E
Ilek →, U.S.S.R. 40 51 30N 53 22 E
Ilero, Nigeria 91 8 0N 3 20 E
Îles, L. des, Canada 106 46 20N 75 18W
Ilesha, Kwara, Nigeria 91 8 57N 3 28 E
Ilesha, Oyo, Nigeria 91 7 37N 4 40 E
Ilford, Australia 76 33 0 S 149 52 E
Ilford, Canada 111 56 4N 95 35W
Ilfracombe, Australia 72 23 30 S 144 30 E
Ilfracombe, U.K. 13 51 13N 4 8W
Ilha Grande, Brazil 135 0 27 S 65 2W
Ilha Grande, B. da, Brazil 139 23 9 S 44 30W
Ílhavo, Portugal 22 40 33N 8 43W
Ilhéus, Brazil 139 14 49 S 39 2W
Ili →, U.S.S.R. 40 45 53N 77 10 E
Ilich, U.S.S.R. 40 40 50N 68 27 E
Iliff, U.S.A. 120 40 50N 103 3W
Iligan, Phil. 57 8 12N 124 13 E
Ilíki, L., Greece 35 38 24N 23 15 E
Iliodhrómia, Greece 35 39 12N 23 50 E
Ilion, U.S.A. 117 43 0N 75 3W
Ilirska-Bistrica, Yugoslavia 27 45 34N 14 14 E
Ilkal, India 51 15 57N 76 8 E
Ilkeston, U.K. 12 52 59N 1 19W
Illampu = Ancohuma, Nevada, Bolivia 136 16 0 S 68 50W
Illana B., Phil. 57 7 35N 123 45 E
Illapel, Chile 140 32 0 S 71 10W
'Illār, Jordan 44 32 23N 35 7 E
Ille-et-Vilaine □, France 18 48 10N 1 30W
Ille-sur-Têt, France 20 42 40N 2 38 E
Iller →, W. Germany 31 48 23N 9 58 E
Illescas, Spain 22 40 8N 3 51W
Illiers-Combray, France 18 48 18N 1 15 E
Illimani, Bolivia 136 16 30 S 67 50W
Illinois □, U.S.A. 113 40 15N 89 30W
Illinois →, U.S.A. 113 38 55N 90 28W
Illiopolis, U.S.A. 118 39 51N 89 15W
Illium = Troy, Turkey 46 39 57N 26 12 E
Illizi, Algeria 85 26 31N 8 32 E
Illora, Spain 23 37 17N 3 53W
Ilm →, E. Germany 30 51 7N 11 45 E
Ilmen, Oz., U.S.S.R. 36 58 15N 31 10 E
Ilmenau, E. Germany 30 50 41N 10 55 E
Ilo, Peru 136 17 40 S 71 20W
Ilobu, Nigeria 91 7 45N 4 25 E
Iloilo, Phil. 57 10 45N 122 33 E
Ilora, Nigeria 91 7 45N 3 50 E
Ilorin, Nigeria 91 8 30N 4 35 E
Iloulya, U.S.S.R. 39 49 15N 44 2 E
Ilovatka, U.S.S.R. 37 50 30N 45 50 E
Ilovlya →, U.S.S.R. 39 49 14N 43 54 E
Ilubabor □, Ethiopia 89 7 25N 35 0 E
Ilukste, U.S.S.R. 36 55 55N 26 20 E
Ilva Mică, Romania 34 47 17N 24 40 E
Ilwaco, U.S.A. 124 46 19N 124 3W
Ilwaki, Indonesia 57 7 55 S 126 30 E
Ilyichevsk, U.S.S.R. 38 46 10N 30 35 E
Imabari, Japan 64 34 4N 133 0 E
Imaichi, Japan 65 36 43N 139 46 E
Imaloto →, Madag. 97 23 27 S 45 13 E
Imandra, Oz., U.S.S.R. 40 67 30N 33 0 E
Imari, Japan 64 33 15N 129 52 E
Imasa, Sudan 88 18 0N 36 12 E
Imbâbah, Egypt 88 30 5N 31 12 E
Imbabura □, Ecuador 134 0 30N 78 45W
Imbaimadai, Guyana 135 5 44N 60 17W
Imbler, U.S.A. 122 45 31N 118 0W
Imdahane, Morocco 84 32 8N 7 0W
Imeni Poliny Osipenko, U.S.S.R. 41 52 30N 136 29 E
Imeri, Serra, Brazil 134 0 50N 65 25W
Imerimandroso, Madag. 97 17 26 S 48 35 E
Imesan, Mauritania 84 22 54N 15 30W
Imi, Ethiopia 89 6 28N 42 10 E
Imishly, U.S.S.R. 39 39 49N 48 4 E
Imitek, Morocco 84 29 43N 8 10W
Imlay, U.S.A. 122 40 45N 118 9W
Imlay City, U.S.A. 116 43 0N 83 2W
Immenstadt, W. Germany 31 47 34N 10 13 E
Immingham, U.K. 12 53 37N 0 12W
Immokalee, U.S.A. 115 26 25N 81 26W
Imo □, Nigeria 91 5 15N 7 20 E
Imola, Italy 27 44 20N 11 42 E
Imotski, Yugoslavia 33 43 27N 17 12 E
Imperatriz, Amazonas, Brazil 136 5 18 S 67 11W
Imperatriz, Maranhão, Brazil 138 5 30 S 47 29W
Impéria, Italy 26 43 52N 8 0 E
Imperial, Canada 111 51 21N 105 28W
Imperial, Peru 136 13 4 S 76 21W
Imperial, Calif., U.S.A. 125 32 52N 115 34W
Imperial, Nebr., U.S.A. 120 40 38N 101 39W
Imperial Beach, U.S.A. 125 32 35N 117 8W
Imperial Dam, U.S.A. 125 32 50N 114 30W
Imperial Res., U.S.A. 125 32 53N 114 28W
Imperial Valley, U.S.A. 125 32 55N 115 30W
Imperieuse Reef, Australia 78 17 36 S 118 50 E
Impfondo, Congo 94 1 40N 18 0 E
Imphal, India 52 24 48N 93 56 E
Imphy, France 20 46 55N 3 16 E
İmroz = Gökçeada, Turkey 35 40 10N 25 50 E
Imst, Austria 31 47 15N 10 44 E
Imuruan B., Phil. 57 10 40N 119 10 E
In Belbel, Algeria 85 27 55N 1 12 E
In Delimane, Mali 91 15 52N 1 31 E
In Rhar, Algeria 85 27 10N 1 59 E
In Salah, Algeria 85 27 10N 2 32 E
In Tallak, Mali 91 16 19N 3 15 E
Ina, Japan 65 35 50N 138 0 E
Ina-Bonchi, Japan 65 35 45N 137 58 E
Inajá, Brazil 138 8 54 S 37 49W
Inangahua Junc., N.Z. 81 41 52 S 171 59 E
Inanwatan, Indonesia 57 2 10 S 132 14 E
Iñapari, Peru 136 11 0 S 69 40W
Inarajan, Guam 68 13 16N 144 45 E
Inari, Finland 8 68 54N 27 5 E
Inarijärvi, Finland 8 69 0N 28 0 E
Inazawa, Japan 65 35 15N 136 47 E
Inca, Spain 24 39 43N 2 54 E
Incaguasi, Chile 140 29 12 S 71 5W
İnce-Burnu, Turkey 38 42 7N 34 56 E
Inchon, S. Korea 61 37 27N 126 40 E
Incio, Spain 22 42 39N 7 21W
Incomáti →, Mozam. 97 25 46 S 32 43 E
Incudine, L', France 21 41 50N 9 12 E
Inda Silase, Ethiopia 89 14 10N 38 15 E
Indalsälven →, Sweden 10 62 36N 17 30 E
Indaw, Burma 52 24 15N 96 5 E
Indbir, Ethiopia 89 8 7N 37 52 E
Independence, Calif., U.S.A. 124 36 51N 118 14W
Independence, Iowa, U.S.A. 118 42 27N 91 52W
Independence, Kans., U.S.A. 121 37 10N 95 43W
Independence, Ky., U.S.A. 119 38 57N 84 33W
Independence, Mo., U.S.A. 118 39 3N 94 25W
Independence, Oreg., U.S.A. 122 44 53N 123 12W
Independence Fjord, Greenland 144 82 10N 29 0W
Independence Mts., U.S.A. 122 41 30N 116 2W
Independência, Brazil 138 5 23 S 40 19W
Independencia, La, Mexico 127 16 31N 91 47W
Independenţa, Romania 34 45 25N 27 42 E
Inderborskiy, U.S.S.R. 39 48 30N 51 42 E
Index, U.S.A. 124 47 50N 121 33W
India ■, Asia 5 20 0N 78 0 E
Indian →, U.S.A. 115 27 59N 80 34W
Indian-Antarctic Ridge, Ind. Oc. 66 49 0 S 120 0 E
Indian Cabins, Canada 110 59 52N 117 40W
Indian Harbour, Canada 105 54 27N 57 13W
Indian Head, Canada 111 50 30N 103 41W
Indian Ocean 53 5 0 S 75 0 E
Indian Springs, U.S.A. 125 36 35N 115 40W
Indiana, U.S.A. 116 40 38N 79 9W
Indiana □, U.S.A. 119 40 0N 86 0W
Indianapolis, U.S.A. 119 39 42N 86 10W
Indianola, Iowa, U.S.A. 118 41 20N 93 32W
Indianola, Miss., U.S.A. 121 33 27N 90 40W
Indiapora, Brazil 139 19 57 S 50 17W
Indiga, U.S.S.R. 40 67 50N 48 50 E
Indigirka →, U.S.S.R. 41 70 48N 148 54 E
Inđija, Yugoslavia 33 45 6N 20 7 E
Indio, U.S.A. 125 33 46N 116 15W
Indispensable Strait, Solomon Is. 68 9 0 S 160 30 E
Indonesia ■, Asia 56 5 0 S 115 0 E
Indore, India 48 22 42N 75 53 E
Indramayu, Indonesia 57 6 20 S 108 19 E
Indravati →, India 50 19 20N 80 20 E
Indre □, France 19 46 50N 1 39 E
Indre →, France 18 47 16N 0 11 E
Indre-et-Loire □, France 18 47 20N 0 40 E
Indungo, Angola 95 14 48 S 16 17 E
Indus →, Pakistan 48 24 20N 67 47 E
Indus, Mouth of the, Pakistan 48 24 0N 68 0 E
Industry, U.S.A. 118 40 20N 90 36W
İnebolu, Turkey 46 41 55N 33 40 E
İnegöl, Turkey 46 40 5N 29 31 E
Inés, Mt., Argentina 142 48 30 S 69 40W
Ineu, Romania 34 46 26N 21 51 E
Inezgane, Morocco 84 30 25N 9 29W
Infantes, Spain 25 38 43N 3 1W
Infiernillo, Presa del, Mexico 126 18 9N 102 0W
Infiesto, Spain 22 43 21N 5 21W
Inganda, Zaïre 94 0 5 S 20 57 E
Ingapirca, Ecuador 134 2 38 S 78 56W
Ingebyra, Australia 75 36 39 S 148 31 E
Ingelgar, Australia 76 31 21 S 147 50 E
Ingelmunster, Belgium 17 50 56N 3 16 E
Ingende, Zaïre 94 0 12 S 18 57 E
Ingeniero Jacobacci, Argentina 142 41 20 S 69 36W
Ingenio, Canary Is. 25 27 55N 15 26W
Ingenio Santa Ana, Argentina 140 27 25 S 65 40W
Ingersoll, Canada 108 43 4N 80 55W
Ingham, Australia 72 18 43 S 146 10 E
Ingleborough, U.K. 12 54 11N 2 23W
Inglewood, Queens., Australia 77 28 25 S 151 2 E
Inglewood, Vic., Australia 74 36 29 S 143 53 E
Inglewood, N.Z. 80 39 9 S 174 14 E
Inglewood, U.S.A. 125 33 58N 118 21W
Ingólfshöfði, Iceland 8 63 48N 16 39W
Ingolstadt, W. Germany 31 48 45N 11 26 E
Ingomar, U.S.A. 122 46 35N 107 21W
Ingonish, Canada 105 46 42N 60 18W
Ingore, Guinea-Biss. 90 12 24N 15 48W
Ingraj Bazar, India 49 24 58N 88 10 E
Ingrid Christensen Coast, Antarctica 143 69 30 S 76 0 E
Ingul →, U.S.S.R. 38 46 50N 32 15 E
Ingulec, U.S.S.R. 38 47 42N 33 14 E
Ingulets →, U.S.S.R. 38 46 41N 32 48 E
Inguri →, U.S.S.R. 39 42 38N 41 35 E
Ingwavuma, S. Africa 97 27 9 S 31 59 E
Inhaca, I., Mozam. 97 26 1 S 32 57 E
Inhafenga, Mozam. 97 20 36 S 33 53 E
Inhambane, Mozam. 97 23 54 S 35 30 E
Inhambane □, Mozam. 97 22 30 S 34 20 E
Inhambupe, Brazil 139 11 47 S 38 21W
Inhaminga, Mozam. 93 18 26 S 35 0 E
Inharrime, Mozam. 97 24 30 S 35 0 E
Inharrime →, Mozam. 97 24 30 S 35 0 E
Inhuma, Brazil 138 6 40 S 41 42W
Inhumas, Brazil 139 16 22 S 49 30W
Iniesta, Spain 25 39 27N 1 45W
Ining = Yining, China 62 43 58N 81 10 E
Inini □, Fr. Guiana 135 4 0N 53 0W
Inírida →, Colombia 134 3 55N 67 52W
Inishbofin, Ireland 15 53 35N 10 12W
Inishmore, Ireland 15 53 8N 9 45W
Inishowen, Ireland 15 55 14N 7 15W
Injune, Australia 73 25 53 S 148 32 E
Inklin, Canada 110 58 56N 133 5W
Inklin →, Canada 110 58 50N 133 10W
Inkom, U.S.A. 122 42 51N 112 15W
Inle L., Burma 52 20 30N 96 58 E
Inn →, Austria 31 48 35N 13 28 E
Innamincka, Australia 73 27 44 S 140 46 E
Inner Hebrides, U.K. 14 57 0N 6 30W
Inner Mongolia = Nei Monggol Zizhiqu □, China 60 42 0N 112 0 E
Inner Sound, U.K. 14 57 30N 5 55W
Innerkip, Canada 108 43 13N 80 42W
Innerste →, W. Germany 30 52 45N 9 40 E
Innetalling I., Canada 104 56 0N 79 0W
Innisfail, Australia 72 17 33 S 146 5 E
Innisfail, Canada 110 52 0N 113 57W
Innisplain, Australia 77 28 11 S 152 54 E
In'no-shima, Japan 64 34 19N 133 10 E
Innsbruck, Austria 31 47 16N 11 23 E
Inny →, Ireland 15 53 30N 7 50W
Ino, Japan 64 33 33N 133 26 E
Inocência, Brazil 139 19 47 S 51 48W
Inongo, Zaïre 94 1 55 S 18 30 E
Inoni, Congo 94 3 4 S 15 39 E
Inoucdjouac, Canada 103 58 25N 78 15W
Inowrocław, Poland 32 52 50N 18 12 E
Inquisivi, Bolivia 136 16 50 S 67 10W
Inscription, C., Australia 79 25 29 S 112 59 E
Insein, Burma 52 16 50N 96 5 E
Însurăţei, Romania 34 44 50N 27 40 E
Intendente Alvear, Argentina 140 35 12 S 63 32W
Interior, U.S.A. 120 43 46N 101 59W
Interlaken, Switz. 31 46 41N 7 50 E
International Falls, U.S.A. 120 48 36N 93 25W
Intiyaco, Argentina 140 28 43 S 60 5W
Intutu, Peru 134 3 32 S 74 48W
Inubō-Zaki, Japan 65 35 42N 140 52 E
Inútil, B., Chile 142 53 30 S 70 15W
Inuvik, Canada 102 68 16N 133 40W
Inuyama, Japan 65 35 23N 136 56 E
Inveralochy, Australia 76 34 57 S 149 40 E
Inveraray, U.K. 14 56 13N 5 5W
Inverbervie, U.K. 14 56 50N 2 17W
Invercargill, N.Z. 81 46 24 S 168 24 E
Inverell, Australia 77 29 45 S 151 8 E
Invergordon, U.K. 14 57 41N 4 10W
Inverleigh, Australia 74 38 6 S 144 3 E
Inverloch, Australia 74 38 38 S 145 45 E
Invermere, Canada 110 50 30N 116 2W
Inverness, Canada 105 46 15N 61 19W
Inverness, U.K. 14 57 29N 4 12W
Inverness, U.S.A. 115 28 50N 82 20W
Inverurie, U.K. 14 57 15N 2 21W
Inverway, Australia 78 17 50 S 129 38 E
Investigator Group, Australia 73 34 45 S 134 20 E
Investigator Str., Australia 73 35 30 S 137 0 E
Inya, U.S.S.R. 40 50 28N 86 37 E
Inyanga, Zimb. 93 18 12 S 32 40 E

Inyangani, *Zimb.* **93** 18 5 S 32 50 E
Inyantue, *Zimb.* **93** 18 30 S 26 40 E
Inyo Mts., *U.S.A.* **123** 37 0N 118 0W
Inyokern, *U.S.A.* **125** 35 38N 117 48W
Inywa, *Burma* **52** 23 56N 96 17 E
Inza, *U.S.S.R.* **37** 53 55N 46 25 E
Inzhavino, *U.S.S.R.* **37** 52 22N 42 30 E
Ioánnina, *Greece* **35** 39 42N 20 47 E
Iola, *U.S.A.* **121** 38 0N 95 20W
Ioma, *Papua N. G.* **69** 8 19 S 147 52 E
Ion Corvin, *Romania* **34** 44 7N 27 50 E
Iona, *U.K.* **14** 56 20N 6 25W
Ione, *Calif., U.S.A.* **124** 38 20N 120 56W
Ione, *Wash., U.S.A.* **122** 48 44N 117 29W
Ionia, *U.S.A.* **119** 42 59N 85 7W
Ionian Is. = Iónioi Nísoi, *Greece* **35** 38 40N 20 0 E
Ionian Sea, *Europe* **6** 37 30N 17 30 E
Iónioi Nísoi, *Greece* **35** 38 40N 20 0 E
Iori →, *U.S.S.R.* **39** 41 3N 46 17 E
Íos, *Greece* **35** 36 41N 25 20 E
Iowa □, *U.S.A.* **120** 42 18N 93 30W
Iowa →, *U.S.A.* **118** 41 10N 91 1W
Iowa City, *U.S.A.* **118** 41 40N 91 35W
Iowa Falls, *U.S.A.* **118** 42 30N 93 15W
Ipala, *Tanzania* **92** 4 30 S 32 52 E
Ipameri, *Brazil* **139** 17 44 S 48 9W
Iparía, *Peru* **136** 9 17 S 74 29W
Ipáti, *Greece* **35** 38 52N 22 14 E
Ipatinga, *Brazil* **139** 19 32 S 42 30W
Ipatovo, *U.S.S.R.* **39** 45 45N 42 50 E
Ipel →, *Europe* **33** 48 10N 19 35 E
Ipiales, *Colombia* **134** 0 50N 77 37W
Ipiaú, *Brazil* **139** 14 8 S 39 44W
Ipin = Yibin, *China* **58** 28 45N 104 32 E
Ipirá, *Brazil* **139** 12 10 S 39 44W
Ipiranga, *Brazil* **134** 3 13 S 65 57W
Ipixuna, *Brazil* **136** 7 0 S 71 40W
Ipixuna →, *Amazonas, Brazil* **136** 7 11 S 71 51W
Ipixuna →, *Amazonas, Brazil* **137** 5 45 S 63 2W
Ipoh, *Malaysia* **55** 4 35N 101 5 E
Iporá, *Brazil* **139** 11 23 S 50 40W
Ippy, *C.A.R.* **94** 6 5N 21 7 E
Ipsárion Óros, *Greece* **35** 40 40N 24 40 E
Ipswich, *Australia* **77** 27 35 S 152 40 E
Ipswich, *U.K.* **13** 52 4N 1 9 E
Ipswich, *Mass., U.S.A.* **117** 42 40N 70 50W
Ipswich, *S. Dak., U.S.A.* **120** 45 28N 99 1W
Ipu, *Brazil* **138** 4 23 S 40 44W
Ipueiras, *Brazil* **138** 4 33 S 40 43W
Ipupiara, *Brazil* **139** 11 49 S 42 37W
Iput →, *U.S.S.R.* **36** 52 26N 31 2 E
Iquique, *Chile* **136** 20 19 S 70 5W
Iquitos, *Peru* **134** 3 45 S 73 10W
Iracoubo, *Fr. Guiana* **135** 5 30N 53 10W
Iráklia, *Greece* **35** 36 50N 25 28 E
Iráklion, *Greece* **35** 35 20N 25 12 E
Irako-Zaki, *Japan* **65** 34 35N 137 1 E
Irala, *Paraguay* **141** 25 55 S 54 35W
Iramba □, *Tanzania* **92** 4 30 S 34 30 E
Iran ■, *Asia* **47** 33 0N 53 0 E
Iran, Gunung-Gunung, *Malaysia* **56** 2 20N 114 50 E
Iranamadu Tank, *Sri Lanka* **51** 9 23N 80 29 E
Īrānshahr, *Iran* **47** 27 15N 60 40 E
Irapa, *Venezuela* **135** 10 34N 62 35W
Irapuato, *Mexico* **126** 20 40N 101 30W
Iraq ■, *Asia* **46** 33 0N 44 0 E
Irarrar, O. →, *Mali* **85** 20 0N 1 30 E
Irati, *Brazil* **141** 25 25 S 50 38W
Irbid, *Jordan* **44** 32 35N 35 48 E
Irebu, *Zaïre* **94** 0 40 S 17 46 E
Irecê, *Brazil* **138** 11 18 S 41 52W
Iregua →, *Spain* **24** 42 27N 2 24 E
Ireland ■, *Europe* **15** 53 0N 8 0W
Ireland's Eye, *Ireland* **15** 53 25N 6 4W
Irele, *Nigeria* **91** 7 40N 5 40 E
Ireng →, *Brazil* **135** 3 33N 59 51W
Iret, *U.S.S.R.* **41** 60 3N 154 20 E
Irgiz, Bolshaya →, *U.S.S.R.* **37** 52 10N 49 10 E
Irhârharene, *Algeria* **85** 27 37N 7 30 E
Irharrhar, O. →, *Algeria* **85** 28 3N 6 15 E
Irherm, *Morocco* **84** 30 7N 8 18W
Irhil Mgoun, *Morocco* **84** 31 30N 6 28W
Iri, *S. Korea* **61** 35 59N 127 0 E
Irian Jaya □, *Indonesia* **57** 4 0 S 137 0 E
Iriba, *Chad* **87** 15 7N 22 15 E
Irié, *Guinea* **90** 8 15N 9 10W
Iringa, *Tanzania* **92** 7 48 S 35 43 E
Iringa □, *Tanzania* **92** 7 48 S 35 43 E
Irinjalakuda, *India* **51** 10 21N 76 14 E
Iriona, *Honduras* **128** 15 57N 85 11W
Iriri →, *Brazil* **135** 3 52 S 52 37W
Iriri Novo →, *Brazil* **137** 8 46 S 53 22W
Irish Republic ■, *Europe* **15** 53 0N 8 0W
Irish Sea, *Europe* **12** 54 0N 5 0W
Irkineyeva, *U.S.S.R.* **41** 58 30N 96 49 E
Irkutsk, *U.S.S.R.* **41** 52 18N 104 20 E
Irma, *Canada* **111** 52 55N 111 14W
Irō-Zaki, *Japan* **65** 34 36N 138 51 E
Iroise, Mer d', *France* **18** 48 15N 4 45W
Iron Baron, *Australia* **73** 32 58 S 137 11 E
Iron Bridge, *Canada* **108** 46 17N 83 14W
Iron Gate = Portile de Fier, *Europe* **34** 44 42N 22 30 E
Iron Knob, *Australia* **73** 32 46 S 137 8 E
Iron Mountain, *U.S.A.* **114** 45 49N 88 4W
Iron River, *U.S.A.* **120** 46 6N 88 40W
Ironbridge, *U.K.* **13** 52 38N 2 29W
Irondequoit, *U.S.A.* **116** 43 13N 77 35W
Ironstone Kopje, *Botswana* **96** 25 17 S 24 5 E
Ironton, *Mo., U.S.A.* **121** 37 40N 90 40W
Ironton, *Ohio, U.S.A.* **114** 38 35N 82 40W
Ironwood, *U.S.A.* **120** 46 30N 90 10W
Iroquois, *Canada* **109** 44 51N 75 19W
Iroquois →, *U.S.A.* **119** 41 5N 87 49W
Iroquois Falls, *Canada* **106** 48 46N 80 41W
Irpen, *U.S.S.R.* **36** 50 30N 30 15 E
Irrara Cr. →, *Australia* **73** 29 35 S 145 31 E
Irrawaddy □, *Burma* **52** 17 0N 95 0 E
Irrawaddy →, *Burma* **52** 15 50N 95 6 E
Irsina, *Italy* **29** 40 45N 16 15 E
Irtysh →, *U.S.S.R.* **40** 61 4N 68 52 E
Irumu, *Zaïre* **92** 1 32N 29 53 E
Irún, *Spain* **24** 43 20N 1 52W
Irurzun, *Spain* **24** 42 55N 1 50W
Irvine, *Canada* **111** 49 57N 110 16W
Irvine, *U.K.* **14** 55 37N 4 40W
Irvine, *Calif., U.S.A.* **125** 33 41N 117 46W
Irvine, *U.S.A.* **119** 37 42N 83 58W
Irvinestown, *U.K.* **15** 54 28N 7 38W
Irvington, *U.S.A.* **119** 37 53N 86 17W
Irvona, *U.S.A.* **116** 40 46N 78 35W
Irwin →, *Australia* **79** 29 15 S 114 54 E
Irwin, Pt., *Australia* **79** 35 5 S 116 55 E
Irymple, *Australia* **74** 34 14 S 142 8 E
Is-sur-Tille, *France* **19** 47 30N 5 8 E
Isa, *Nigeria* **91** 13 14N 6 24 E
Isaac →, *Australia* **72** 22 55 S 149 20 E
Isabel, *U.S.A.* **120** 45 27N 101 22W
Isabela, I., *Mexico* **126** 21 51N 105 55W
Isabela, La, *Dom. Rep.* **129** 19 58N 71 2W
Isabella, *Phil.* **57** 6 40N 122 10 E
Isabella, Cord., *Nic.* **128** 13 30N 85 25W
Isabella Ra., *Australia* **78** 21 0 S 121 4 E
Ísafjarðardjúp, *Iceland* **8** 66 10N 23 0W
Ísafjörður, *Iceland* **8** 66 5N 23 9W
Isagarh, *India* **48** 24 48N 77 51 E
Isahaya, *Japan* **64** 32 52N 130 2 E
Isaka, *Tanzania* **92** 3 56 S 32 59 E
Isana → = Içana →, *Brazil* **134** 0 26N 67 19W
Isangi, *Zaïre* **94** 0 52N 24 10 E
Isar →, *W. Germany* **31** 48 49N 12 58 E
Isarco →, *Italy* **27** 46 57N 11 18 E
Ísari, *Greece* **35** 37 22N 22 0 E
Isbergues, *France* **19** 50 36N 2 28 E
Iscayachi, *Bolivia* **137** 21 31 S 65 3W
Íschia, *Italy* **28** 40 45N 13 51 E
Iscuandé, *Colombia* **134** 2 28N 77 59W
Isdell →, *Australia* **78** 16 27 S 124 51 E
Ise, *Japan* **65** 34 25N 136 45 E
Ise-Heiya, *Japan* **65** 34 40N 136 30 E
Ise-Wan, *Japan* **65** 34 43N 136 43 E
Isefjord, *Denmark* **11** 55 53N 11 50 E
Iseo, *Italy* **26** 45 40N 10 3 E
Iseo, L. d', *Italy* **26** 45 45N 10 3 E
Iseramagazi, *Tanzania* **92** 4 37 S 32 10 E
Isère □, *France* **21** 45 15N 5 40 E
Isère →, *France* **21** 44 59N 4 51 E
Iserlohn, *W. Germany* **30** 51 22N 7 40 E
Isérnia, *Italy* **29** 41 35N 14 12 E
Isesaki, *Japan* **65** 36 19N 139 12 E
Iseyin, *Nigeria* **91** 8 0N 3 36 E
Isherton, *Guyana* **135** 2 20N 59 25W
Ishikari-Wan, *Japan* **63** 43 25N 141 1 E
Ishikawa □, *Japan* **65** 36 30N 136 30 E
Ishim, *U.S.S.R.* **40** 56 10N 69 30 E
Ishim →, *U.S.S.R.* **40** 57 45N 71 10 E
Ishinomaki, *Japan* **63** 38 32N 141 20 E
Ishioka, *Japan* **65** 36 11N 140 16 E
Ishizuchi-Yama, *Japan* **64** 33 45N 133 6 E
Ishkuman, *Pakistan* **49** 36 30N 73 50 E
Ishpeming, *U.S.A.* **104** 46 30N 87 40W
Ishurdi, *Bangla.* **52** 24 9N 89 3 E
Isigny-sur-Mer, *France* **18** 49 19N 1 6W
Isil Kul, *U.S.S.R.* **40** 54 55N 71 16 E
Isiolo, *Kenya* **92** 0 24N 37 33 E
Isiolo □, *Kenya* **92** 2 30N 37 30 E
Isipingo Beach, *S. Africa* **97** 30 0 S 30 57 E
Isiro, *Zaïre* **92** 2 53N 27 40 E
Isisford, *Australia* **72** 24 15 S 144 21 E
İskenderun, *Turkey* **46** 36 32N 36 10 E
İskilip, *Turkey* **38** 40 50N 34 20 E
Iskŭr →, *Bulgaria* **34** 43 45N 24 25 E
Iskut →, *Canada* **110** 56 45N 131 49W
Isla →, *U.K.* **14** 56 32N 3 20W
Isla Cristina, *Spain* **23** 37 13N 7 17W
Isla Vista, *U.S.A.* **125** 34 27N 119 52W
Islamabad, *Pakistan* **48** 33 40N 73 10 E
Islamkot, *Pakistan* **48** 24 42N 70 13 E
Islampur, *India* **50** 17 2N 74 20 E
Island →, *Canada* **110** 60 25N 121 12W
Island Bend, *Australia* **75** 36 19 S 148 31 E
Island Falls, *Canada* **104** 49 35N 81 20W
Island Falls, *U.S.A.* **105** 46 0N 68 16W
Island L., *Canada* **111** 53 47N 94 25W
Island Lagoon, *Australia* **73** 31 30 S 136 40 E
Island Pt., *Australia* **79** 30 20 S 115 1 E
Island Pond, *U.S.A.* **117** 44 50N 71 50W
Islands, B. of, *Canada* **105** 49 11N 58 15W
Islands, B. of, *N.Z.* **80** 35 15 S 174 6 E
Islay, *U.K.* **14** 55 46N 6 10W
Isle →, *France* **20** 44 55N 0 15W
Isle-Adam, L', *France* **19** 49 6N 2 14 E
Isle aux Morts, *Canada* **105** 47 35N 59 0W
Isle-Jourdain, L', *Gers, France* **20** 43 36N 1 5 E
Isle-Jourdain, L', *Vienne, France* **20** 46 13N 0 31 E
Isle of Wight □, *U.K.* **13** 50 40N 1 20W
Isle Royale, *U.S.A.* **120** 48 0N 88 50W
Isle-sur-le-Doubs, L', *France* **19** 47 26N 6 34 E
Isle Verte, L', *Canada* **107** 48 1N 69 20W
Isleta, *U.S.A.* **123** 34 58N 106 46W
Isleton, *U.S.A.* **124** 38 10N 121 37W
Ismail, *U.S.S.R.* **38** 45 22N 28 46 E
Ismâ'ilîya, *Egypt* **88** 30 37N 32 18 E
Ismaning, *W. Germany* **31** 48 14N 11 41 E
Ismay, *U.S.A.* **120** 46 33N 104 44W
Isna, *Egypt* **88** 25 17N 32 30 E
Isogstalo, *India* **49** 34 15N 78 46 E
Isola del Gran Sasso d'Italia, *Italy* **27** 42 30N 13 40 E
Ísola del Liri, *Italy* **28** 41 39N 13 32 E
Ísola della Scala, *Italy* **26** 45 16N 11 0 E
Ísola di Capo Rizzuto, *Italy* **29** 38 56N 17 5 E
İsparta, *Turkey* **46** 37 47N 30 30 E
Isperikh, *Bulgaria* **34** 43 43N 26 50 E
Íspica, *Italy* **29** 36 47N 14 53 E
İspir, *Turkey* **39** 40 40N 40 50 E
Israel ■, *Asia* **44** 32 0N 34 50 E
Issano, *Guyana* **135** 5 49N 59 26W
Isseka, *Australia* **79** 28 30 S 114 35 E
Issia, *Ivory C.* **90** 6 33N 6 33W
Issoire, *France* **20** 45 32N 3 15 E
Issoudun, *Canada* **107** 46 35N 71 38W
Issoudun, *France* **19** 46 57N 2 0 E
Issyk-Kul, Ozero, *U.S.S.R.* **40** 42 25N 77 15 E
Ist, *Yugoslavia* **27** 44 17N 14 47 E
İstanbul, *Turkey* **46** 41 0N 29 0 E
Istmina, *Colombia* **134** 5 10N 76 39W
Istok, *Yugoslavia* **33** 42 45N 20 24 E
Istokpoga, L., *U.S.A.* **115** 27 22N 81 14W
Istra, *U.S.S.R.* **37** 55 55N 36 50 E
Istra, *Yugoslavia* **27** 45 10N 14 0 E
Istranca Dağları, *Turkey* **35** 41 48N 27 30 E
Istres, *France* **21** 43 31N 4 59 E
Istria = Istra, *Yugoslavia* **27** 45 10N 14 0 E
Itá, *Paraguay* **140** 25 29 S 57 21W
Itabaiana, *Paraíba, Brazil* **138** 7 18 S 35 19W
Itabaiana, *Sergipe, Brazil* **138** 10 41 S 37 37W
Itabaianinha, *Brazil* **138** 11 16 S 37 47W
Itaberaba, *Brazil* **139** 12 32 S 40 18W
Itaberaí, *Brazil* **139** 16 2 S 49 48W
Itabira, *Brazil* **139** 19 37 S 43 13W
Itabirito, *Brazil* **139** 20 15 S 43 48W
Itaboca, *Brazil* **135** 4 50 S 62 40W
Itabuna, *Brazil* **139** 14 48 S 39 16W
Itacajá, *Brazil* **138** 8 19 S 47 46W
Itacaunas →, *Brazil* **138** 5 21 S 49 8W
Itacoatiara, *Brazil* **135** 3 8 S 58 25W
Itacuaí →, *Brazil* **136** 4 20 S 70 12W
Itaguaçu, *Brazil* **139** 19 48 S 40 51W
Itaguari →, *Brazil* **139** 14 11 S 44 40W
Itaguatins, *Brazil* **138** 5 47 S 47 29W
Itaim →, *Brazil* **138** 7 2 S 42 2W
Itainópolis, *Brazil* **138** 7 24 S 41 31W
Itaipu Dam, *Brazil* **141** 25 30 S 54 30W
Itaituba, *Brazil* **135** 4 10 S 55 50W
Itajaí, *Brazil* **141** 27 50 S 48 39W
Itajubá, *Brazil* **139** 22 24 S 45 30W
Itajuípe, *Brazil* **139** 14 41 S 39 22W
Itaka, *Tanzania* **93** 8 50 S 32 49 E
Itako, *Japan* **65** 35 56N 140 33 E
Italy ■, *Europe* **7** 42 0N 13 0 E
Itamataré, *Brazil* **138** 2 16 S 46 24W
Itambacuri, *Brazil* **139** 18 1 S 41 42W
Itambé, *Brazil* **139** 15 15 S 40 37W
Itampolo, *Madag.* **97** 24 41 S 43 57 E
Itanhauã →, *Brazil* **135** 4 45 S 63 48W
Itanhém, *Brazil* **139** 17 9 S 40 20W
Itano, *Japan* **64** 34 7N 134 28 E
Itapaci, *Brazil* **139** 14 57 S 49 34W
Itapagé, *Brazil* **138** 3 41 S 39 34W
Itaparica, I. de, *Brazil* **139** 12 54 S 38 42W
Itapebi, *Brazil* **139** 15 56 S 39 32W
Itapecuru-Mirim, *Brazil* **138** 3 24 S 44 20W
Itaperuna, *Brazil* **139** 21 10 S 41 54W
Itapetinga, *Brazil* **139** 15 15 S 40 15W
Itapetininga, *Brazil* **141** 23 36 S 48 7W
Itapeva, *Brazil* **141** 23 59 S 48 59W
Itapicuru →, *Bahia, Brazil* **138** 11 47 S 37 32W
Itapicuru →, *Maranhão, Brazil* **138** 2 52 S 44 12W
Itapinima, *Brazil* **137** 5 25 S 60 44W
Itapipoca, *Brazil* **138** 3 30 S 39 35W
Itapiranga, *Brazil* **135** 2 45 S 58 1W
Itapiúna, *Brazil* **138** 4 33 S 38 57W
Itaporanga, *Brazil* **138** 7 18 S 38 0W
Itapuá □, *Paraguay* **141** 26 40 S 55 40W
Itapuranga, *Brazil* **139** 15 40 S 49 59W
Itaquari, *Brazil* **139** 20 20 S 40 25W
Itaquatiara, *Brazil* **136** 2 58 S 58 30W
Itaquí, *Brazil* **140** 29 8 S 56 30W
Itararé, *Brazil* **141** 24 6 S 49 23W
Itarsi, *India* **48** 22 36N 77 51 E
Itarumã, *Brazil* **139** 18 42 S 51 25W
Itatí, *Argentina* **140** 27 16 S 58 15W
Itatira, *Brazil* **138** 4 30 S 39 37W
Itatuba, *Brazil* **137** 5 46 S 63 20W
Itatupa, *Brazil* **135** 0 37 S 51 12W
Itaueira, *Brazil* **138** 7 36 S 43 2W
Itaueira →, *Brazil* **138** 6 41 S 42 55W
Itaúna, *Brazil* **139** 20 4 S 44 34W
Itchen →, *U.K.* **13** 50 57N 1 20W
Ite, *Peru* **136** 17 55 S 70 57W
Ithaca = Itháki, *Greece* **35** 38 25N 20 40 E
Ithaca, *U.S.A.* **117** 42 25N 76 30W
Itháki, *Greece* **35** 38 25N 20 40 E
Itinga, *Brazil* **139** 16 36 S 41 47W
Itiquira, *Brazil* **137** 17 12 S 54 7W
Itiquira →, *Brazil* **137** 17 18 S 56 44W
Itiruçu, *Brazil* **139** 13 31 S 40 9W
Itiúba, *Brazil* **138** 10 43 S 39 51W
Ito, *Japan* **65** 34 58N 139 5 E
Itomamo, L., *Canada* **107** 49 11N 70 28W
Iton →, *France* **18** 49 9N 1 12 E
Itonamas →, *Bolivia* **136** 12 28 S 64 24W
Itsa, *Egypt* **88** 29 15N 30 47 E
Itsukaichi, *Japan* **64** 34 22N 132 22 E
Itsuki, *Japan* **64** 32 24N 130 50 E
Íttiri, *Italy* **28** 40 38N 8 32 E
Itu, *Brazil* **141** 23 17 S 47 15W
Itu, *Nigeria* **91** 5 10N 7 58 E
Ituaçu, *Brazil* **139** 13 50 S 41 18W
Ituango, *Colombia* **134** 7 4N 75 45W
Ituiutaba, *Brazil* **139** 19 0 S 49 25W
Itumbiara, *Brazil* **139** 18 20 S 49 10W
Ituna, *Canada* **111** 51 10N 103 24W
Itunge Port, *Tanzania* **93** 9 40 S 33 55 E
Ituni, *Guyana* **135** 5 28N 58 15W
Itupiranga, *Brazil* **138** 5 9 S 49 20W
Iturama, *Brazil* **139** 19 44 S 50 11W
Iturbe, *Argentina* **140** 23 0 S 65 25W
Ituri →, *Zaïre* **92** 1 40N 27 1 E
Iturup, Ostrov, *U.S.S.R.* **41** 45 0N 148 0 E
Ituverava, *Brazil* **139** 20 20 S 47 47W
Ituxi →, *Brazil* **137** 7 18 S 64 51W
Ituyuro →, *Argentina* **140** 22 40 S 63 50W
Itzehoe, *W. Germany* **30** 53 56N 9 31 E
Iuka, *U.S.A.* **119** 38 37N 88 47W
Ivaí →, *Brazil* **141** 23 18 S 53 42W
Ivalo, *Finland* **8** 68 38N 27 35 E
Ivalojoki →, *Finland* **8** 68 40N 27 40 E
Ivangorod, *U.S.S.R.* **36** 59 37N 28 40 E
Ivanhoe, *N.S.W., Australia* **73** 32 56 S 144 20 E
Ivanhoe, *N. Terr., Australia* **78** 15 41 S 128 41 E
Ivanhoe, *U.S.A.* **124** 36 25N 119 13W
Ivanhoe L., *Canada* **111** 60 25N 106 30W
Ivanić Grad, *Yugoslavia* **27** 45 41N 16 25 E
Ivanjica, *Yugoslavia* **33** 43 35N 20 12 E
Ivanjšcice, *Yugoslavia* **27** 46 12N 16 13 E
Ivankoyskoye Vdkhr., *U.S.S.R.* **37** 56 37N 36 32 E
Ivano-Frankovsk, *U.S.S.R.* **36** 48 40N 24 40 E
Ivanovo, *Byelorussian S.S.R., U.S.S.R.* **36** 52 7N 25 29 E
Ivanovo, *R.S.F.S.R., U.S.S.R.* **37** 57 5N 41 0 E
Ivato, *Madag.* **97** 20 37 S 47 10 E
Ivaylovgrad, *Bulgaria* **35** 41 32N 26 8 E
Ivindo →, *Gabon* **94** 0 9 S 12 9 E
Ivinheima →, *Brazil* **141** 23 14 S 53 42W
Iviza = Ibiza, *Spain* **25** 38 54N 1 26 E
Ivohibe, *Madag.* **97** 22 31 S 46 57 E
Ivolândia, *Brazil* **139** 16 34 S 50 51W
Ivory Coast ■, *Africa* **90** 7 30N 5 0W
Ivösjön, *Sweden* **11** 56 8N 14 25 E
Ivrea, *Italy* **26** 45 30N 7 52 E
Ivugivik, *Canada* **103** 62 24N 77 55W
Iwahig, *Phil.* **56** 8 36N 117 32 E
Iwai-Jima, *Japan* **64** 33 47N 131 58 E
Iwaki, *Japan* **63** 37 3N 140 55 E
Iwakuni, *Japan* **64** 34 15N 132 8 E
Iwami, *Japan* **64** 35 32N 134 15 E
Iwamizawa, *Japan* **63** 43 12N 141 46 E
Iwanai, *Japan* **63** 42 58N 140 30 E
Iwanuma, *Japan* **63** 38 7N 140 51 E
Iwase, *Japan* **65** 36 21N 140 6 E
Iwata, *Japan* **65** 34 42N 137 51 E
Iwate-San, *Japan* **63** 39 51N 141 0 E
Iwo, *Nigeria* **91** 7 39N 4 9 E
Iwungu, *Zaïre* **95** 5 16 S 19 17 E
Ixiamas, *Bolivia* **136** 13 50 S 68 5W
Ixopo, *S. Africa* **97** 30 11 S 30 5 E
Ixtepec, *Mexico* **127** 16 32N 95 10W
Ixtlán del Río, *Mexico* **126** 21 5N 104 21W
Iyo, *Japan* **64** 33 45N 132 45 E
Iyo-mishima, *Japan* **64** 33 58N 133 30 E
Iyo-Nada, *Japan* **64** 33 40N 132 20 E
Izabal, L. de, *Guatemala* **128** 15 30N 89 10W
Izamal, *Mexico* **127** 20 56N 89 1W
Izberbash, *U.S.S.R.* **39** 42 35N 47 52 E
Izegem, *Belgium* **17** 50 55N 3 12 E
Izhevsk = Ustinov, *U.S.S.R.* **40** 56 51N 53 14 E
İzmir, *Turkey* **46** 38 25N 27 8 E
İzmit, *Turkey* **46** 40 45N 29 50 E
Iznajar, *Spain* **23** 37 15N 4 19W
Iznalloz, *Spain* **25** 37 24N 3 30W
Izobil'nyy, *U.S.S.R.* **39** 45 25N 41 44 E
Izola, *Yugoslavia* **27** 45 32N 13 39 E
Izozog, Bañados de, *Bolivia* **137** 18 48 S 62 10W
Izra, *Syria* **44** 32 51N 36 15 E
Iztochni Rodopi, *Bulgaria* **35** 41 45N 25 30 E

Izu-Hantō, Japan 65 34 45N 139 0 E
Izuhara, Japan 64 34 12N 129 17 E
Izumi, Japan 64 32 5N 130 22 E
Izumi-sano, Japan 65 34 23N 135 18 E
Izumiotsu, Japan 65 34 30N 135 24 E
Izumo, Japan 64 35 20N 132 46 E
Izyaslav, U.S.S.R. 36 50 5N 26 50 E
Izyum, U.S.S.R. 38 49 12N 37 19 E

J

J.F. Rodrigues, Brazil 138 2 55 S 50 20W
Jaba, Ethiopia 89 6 20N 35 7 E
Jaba', Jordan 44 32 20N 35 13 E
Jabal el Awlîya, Sudan 89 15 10N 32 31 E
Jabalón →, Spain 23 38 53N 4 5W
Jabalpur, India 49 23 9N 79 58 E
Jabālyah, Egypt 44 31 32N 34 27 E
Jablah, Syria 46 35 20N 36 0 E
Jablanac, Yugoslavia 27 44 42N 14 56 E
Jablonec, Czech. 32 50 43N 15 10 E
Jabłonowo, Poland 32 53 23N 19 10 E
Jaboatão, Brazil 138 8 7 S 35 1W
Jaboticabal, Brazil 141 21 15 S 48 17W
Jaburu, Brazil 137 5 30 S 64 0W
Jaca, Spain 24 42 35N 0 33W
Jacaré →, Brazil 138 10 3 S 42 13W
Jacareí, Brazil 141 23 20 S 46 0W
Jacarèzinho, Brazil 141 23 5 S 50 0W
Jaciara, Brazil 137 15 59 S 54 57W
Jacinto, Brazil 139 16 10 S 40 17W
Jaciparaná, Brazil 137 9 15 S 64 23W
Jackadgery, Australia 77 29 35 S 152 34 E
Jackman, U.S.A. 105 45 35N 70 17W
Jacksboro, U.S.A. 121 33 14N 98 15W
Jackson, Australia 73 26 39 S 149 39 E
Jackson, Ala., U.S.A. 115 31 32N 87 53W
Jackson, Calif., U.S.A. 124 38 19N 120 47W
Jackson, Ky., U.S.A. 114 37 35N 83 22W
Jackson, Mich., U.S.A. 119 42 18N 84 25W
Jackson, Minn., U.S.A. 120 43 35N 95 0W
Jackson, Miss., U.S.A. 121 32 20N 90 10W
Jackson, Mo., U.S.A. 121 37 25N 89 42W
Jackson, Ohio, U.S.A. 114 39 0N 82 40W
Jackson, Tenn., U.S.A. 115 35 40N 88 50W
Jackson, Wyo., U.S.A. 122 43 30N 110 49W
Jackson, C., N.Z. 81 40 59 S 174 20 E
Jackson, L., U.S.A. 122 43 55N 110 40W
Jackson Bay, N.Z. 81 43 58 S 168 42 E
Jackson Center, U.S.A. 119 40 27N 84 4W
Jacksons, N.Z. 81 42 46 S 171 32 E
Jacksonville, Ala., U.S.A. 115 33 49N 85 45W
Jacksonville, Calif., U.S.A. 124 37 52N 120 24W
Jacksonville, Fla., U.S.A. 115 30 15N 81 38W
Jacksonville, Ill., U.S.A. 118 39 42N 90 15W
Jacksonville, N.C., U.S.A. 115 34 50N 77 29W
Jacksonville, Oreg., U.S.A. 122 42 19N 122 56W
Jacksonville, Tex., U.S.A. 121 31 58N 95 19W
Jacksonville Beach, U.S.A. 115 30 19N 81 26W
Jacmel, Haiti 129 18 14N 72 32W
Jacob Lake, U.S.A. 123 36 45N 112 12W
Jacobabad, Pakistan 48 28 20N 68 29 E
Jacobina, Brazil 138 11 11 S 40 30W
Jacob's Well, Jordan 44 32 13N 35 13 E
Jacques-Cartier →, Canada 107 46 40N 71 45W
Jacques-Cartier, L., Canada 107 47 35N 71 13W
Jacques-Cartier, Mt., Canada 105 48 57N 66 0W
Jacqueville, Ivory C. 90 5 12N 4 25W
Jacuí →, Brazil 141 30 2 S 51 15W
Jacumba, U.S.A. 125 32 37N 116 11W
Jacundá →, Brazil 138 1 57 S 50 26W
Jade, W. Germany 30 53 22N 8 14 E
Jadebusen, W. Germany 30 53 30N 8 15 E
Jadoigne, Belgium 17 50 43N 4 52 E
Jadotville = Likasi, Zaïre 93 10 55 S 26 48 E
Jadraque, Spain 24 40 55N 2 55W
Jādū, Libya 86 32 0N 12 0 E
Jaén, Peru 136 5 25 S 78 40W
Jaén, Spain 23 37 44N 3 43W
Jaén □, Spain 23 37 50N 3 30W
Jafène, Africa 84 20 35N 5 30W
Jaffa = Tel Aviv-Yafo, Israel 44 32 4N 34 48 E
Jaffa, C., Australia 73 36 58 S 139 40 E
Jaffna, Sri Lanka 51 9 45N 80 2 E
Jagadhri, India 48 30 10N 77 20 E
Jagadishpur, India 49 25 30N 84 21 E
Jagdalpur, India 50 19 3N 82 0 E
Jagersfontein, S. Africa 96 29 44 S 25 27 E
Jagst →, W. Germany 31 49 14N 9 11 E
Jagtial, India 50 18 50N 79 0 E
Jaguaquara, Brazil 139 13 32 S 39 58W
Jaguariaíva, Brazil 141 24 10 S 49 50W
Jaguaribe, Brazil 138 5 53 S 38 37W
Jaguaribe →, Brazil 138 4 25 S 37 45W
Jaguaruana, Brazil 138 4 50 S 37 47W
Jagüey Grande, Cuba 128 22 35N 81 7W
Jagungal, Mt., Australia 76 36 8 S 148 22 E
Jahangirabad, India 48 28 19N 78 4 E
Jahrom, Iran 47 28 30N 53 31 E
Jaicós, Brazil 138 7 21 S 41 8W
Jailolo, Indonesia 57 1 5N 127 30 E
Jailolo, Selat, Indonesia 57 0 5N 129 5 E
Jaintiapur, Bangla. 52 25 8N 92 7 E
Jaipur, India 48 27 0N 75 50 E
Jajce, Yugoslavia 33 44 19N 17 17 E
Jajpur, India 50 20 53N 86 22 E
Jakarta, Indonesia 57 6 9 S 106 49 E
Jakobstad, Finland 8 63 40N 22 43 E
Jakupica, Yugoslavia 35 41 45N 21 22 E
Jal, U.S.A. 121 32 8N 103 8W
Jalalabad, Afghan. 47 34 30N 70 29 E
Jalalabad, India 49 27 41N 79 42 E
Jalalpur Jattan, Pakistan 48 32 38N 74 11 E
Jalama, U.S.A. 125 34 29N 120 29W
Jalapa, Guatemala 128 14 39N 89 59W
Jalapa Enríquez, Mexico 127 19 32N 96 55W
Jalas, Jabal al, Si. Arabia 46 27 30N 36 30 E
Jalaun, India 49 26 8N 79 25 E
Jales, Brazil 139 20 10 S 50 33W
Jaleswar, Nepal 49 26 38N 85 48 E
Jalgaon, Maharashtra, India 50 21 2N 76 31 E
Jalgaon, Maharashtra, India 50 21 0N 75 42 E
Jalhay, Belgium 17 50 33N 5 58 E
Jalingo, Nigeria 91 8 55N 11 25 E
Jalisco □, Mexico 126 20 0N 104 0W
Jalkot, Pakistan 49 35 14N 73 24 E
Jallas →, Spain 22 42 54N 9 8W
Jallumba, Australia 74 36 55 S 141 57 E
Jalna, India 50 19 48N 75 38 E
Jalón →, Spain 24 41 47N 1 4W
Jalpa, Mexico 126 21 38N 102 58W
Jalpaiguri, India 52 26 32N 88 46 E
Jalq, Iran 47 27 35N 62 46 E
Jaluit I., Pac. Oc. 66 6 0N 169 30 E
Jamaari, Nigeria 91 11 44N 9 53 E
Jamaica, U.S.A. 118 41 51N 94 18W
Jamaica ■, W. Indies 128 18 10N 77 30W
Jamalpur, Bangla. 52 24 52N 89 56 E
Jamalpur, India 49 25 18N 86 28 E
Jamalpurganj, India 49 23 2N 88 1 E
Jamanxim →, Brazil 137 4 43 S 56 18W
Jamari, Brazil 137 8 45 S 63 27W
Jamari →, Brazil 137 8 27 S 63 30W
Jambe, Indonesia 57 1 15 S 132 10 E
Jambes, Belgium 17 50 27N 4 52 E
Jambi, Indonesia 56 1 38 S 103 30 E
Jambi □, Indonesia 56 1 30 S 102 30 E
Jambusar, India 48 22 3N 72 51 E
James →, U.S.A. 120 42 52N 97 18W
James B., Canada 104 51 30N 80 0W
James Ranges, Australia 78 24 10 S 132 30 E
James Ross I., Antarctica 143 63 58 S 57 50W
Jamesport, U.S.A. 118 39 58N 93 48W
Jamestown, Australia 73 33 10 S 138 32 E
Jamestown, S. Africa 96 31 6 S 26 45 E
Jamestown, Ind., U.S.A. 119 39 56N 86 38W
Jamestown, Ky., U.S.A. 114 37 0N 85 5W
Jamestown, Mo., U.S.A. 118 38 48N 92 30W
Jamestown, N. Dak., U.S.A. 120 46 54N 98 42W
Jamestown, N.Y., U.S.A. 116 42 5N 79 18W
Jamestown, Ohio, U.S.A. 119 39 39N 83 44W
Jamestown, Pa., U.S.A. 116 41 32N 80 27W
Jamestown, Tenn., U.S.A. 115 36 25N 85 0W
Jamieson, Australia 75 37 19 S 146 9 E
Jamiltepec, Mexico 127 16 17N 97 49W
Jamkhandi, India 50 16 30N 75 15 E
Jammā'īn, Jordan 44 32 8N 35 12 E
Jammalamadugu, India 51 14 51N 78 25 E
Jammerbugt, Denmark 11 57 15N 9 20 E
Jammu, India 48 32 43N 74 54 E
Jammu & Kashmir □, India 49 34 25N 77 0 E
Jamnagar, India 48 22 30N 70 6 E
Jamner, India 50 20 45N 75 52 E
Jamoigne, Belgium 17 49 41N 5 24 E
Jampur, Pakistan 48 29 39N 70 40 E
Jamrud, Pakistan 48 33 59N 71 24 E
Jamshedpur, India 49 22 44N 86 12 E
Jamtara, India 49 23 59N 86 49 E
Jämtlands län □, Sweden 10 62 40N 13 50 E
Jamuna →, Bangla. 52 23 51N 89 45 E
Jamurki, Bangla. 52 24 9N 90 2 E
Jan Kempdorp, S. Africa 96 27 55 S 24 51 E
Jan L., Canada 111 54 56N 102 55W
Jan Mayen Is., Arctic 144 71 0N 9 0W
Janaúba, Brazil 139 15 48 S 43 19W
Janaucu, I., Brazil 138 0 30N 50 10W
Jand, Pakistan 48 33 30N 72 6 E
Janda, L. de la, Spain 23 36 15N 5 45W
Jandaia, Brazil 139 17 6 S 50 7W
Jandaq, Iran 47 34 3N 54 22 E
Jandia, Canary Is. 25 28 6N 14 21W
Jandia, Pta. de, Canary Is. 25 28 3N 14 31W
Jandiatuba →, Brazil 134 3 28 S 68 42W
Jandola, Pakistan 48 32 20N 70 9 E
Jandowae, Australia 73 26 45 S 151 7 E
Jandrain-Jandrenouilles, Belgium 17 50 40N 4 58 E
Jándula →, Spain 23 38 3N 4 6W
Jane Pk., N.Z. 81 45 15 S 168 20 E
Janesville, U.S.A. 118 42 39N 89 1W
Janga, Ghana 91 10 5N 1 0W
Jango, Brazil 137 20 27 S 55 29W
Jangoon, India 50 17 44N 79 5 E
Janhtang Ga, Burma 52 26 32N 96 38 E
Janīn, Jordan 44 32 28N 35 18 E
Janjina, Yugoslavia 33 42 58N 17 25 E
Janos, Mexico 126 30 45N 108 10W
Jánosháza, Hungary 33 47 8N 17 12 E
Janów Podlaski, Poland 32 52 11N 23 11 E
Januária, Brazil 139 15 25 S 44 25W
Janub Dârfûr □, Sudan 89 11 0N 25 0 E
Janub Kordofân □, Sudan 89 12 0N 30 0 E
Janville, France 19 48 10N 1 50 E
Janzé, France 18 47 55N 1 28W
Jaora, India 48 23 40N 75 10 E
Japan ■, Asia 63 36 0N 136 0 E
Japan, Sea of, Asia 63 40 0N 135 0 E
Japan Trench, Pac. Oc. 66 32 0N 142 0 E
Japen = Yapen, Indonesia 57 1 50 S 136 0 E
Japurá →, Brazil 134 3 8 S 64 46W
Jaque, Panama 134 7 27N 78 8W
Jara, La, U.S.A. 123 37 16N 106 0W
Jaraguá, Brazil 139 15 45 S 49 20W
Jaraguari, Brazil 137 20 9 S 54 35W
Jaraicejo, Spain 23 39 40N 5 49W
Jaraiz, Spain 22 40 4N 5 45W
Jarama →, Spain 24 40 2N 3 39W
Jaramillo, Argentina 142 47 10 S 67 7W
Jarandilla, Spain 22 40 8N 5 39W
Jaranwala, Pakistan 48 31 15N 73 26 E
Jarash, Jordan 44 32 17N 35 54 E
Jarauçu →, Brazil 135 1 48 S 52 22W
Jardas al 'Abīd, Libya 86 32 18N 20 59 E
Jardim, Brazil 140 21 28 S 56 2W
Jardín →, Spain 25 38 50N 2 10W
Jardines de la Reina, Is., Cuba 128 20 50N 78 50W
Jargalang, China 61 43 5N 122 55 E
Jargalant = Hovd, Mongolia 62 48 2N 91 37 E
Jargalant, Mongolia 62 48 2N 91 37 E
Jargeau, France 19 47 50N 2 1 E
Jari →, Brazil 135 1 9 S 51 54W
Jarmen, E. Germany 30 53 56N 13 20 E
Jarnac, France 20 45 40N 0 11W
Jarny, France 19 49 9N 5 53 E
Jarocin, Poland 32 51 59N 17 29 E
Jarosław, Poland 32 50 2N 22 42 E
Järpås, Sweden 11 58 23N 12 57 E
Järpen, Sweden 10 63 21N 13 26 E
Jarrahdale, Australia 79 32 24 S 116 5 E
Jarres, Plaine des, Laos 54 19 27N 103 10 E
Jarso, Ethiopia 89 5 15N 37 30 E
Jartai, China 60 39 45N 105 48 E
Jaru, Brazil 137 10 26 S 62 27W
Jaru →, Brazil 137 10 5 S 61 59W
Jarud Qi, China 61 44 28N 120 50 E
Jarvis, Canada 108 42 53N 80 6W
Jarvis I., Pac. Oc. 67 0 15 S 159 55W
Jarwa, India 49 27 38N 82 30 E
Jaša Tomić, Yugoslavia 33 45 26N 20 50 E
Jasin, Malaysia 55 2 20N 102 26 E
Jāsk, Iran 47 25 38N 57 45 E
Jasło, Poland 32 49 45N 21 30 E
Jason, Is., Falk. Is. 142 51 0 S 61 0W
Jasonville, U.S.A. 119 39 10N 87 13W
Jasper, Alta., Canada 110 52 55N 118 5W
Jasper, Ont., Canada 109 44 50N 75 56W
Jasper, Ont., Canada 117 44 52N 75 57W
Jasper, Ala., U.S.A. 115 33 48N 87 16W
Jasper, Fla., U.S.A. 115 30 31N 82 58W
Jasper, Ind., U.S.A. 119 38 24N 86 56W
Jasper, Minn., U.S.A. 120 43 52N 96 22W
Jasper, Tex., U.S.A. 121 30 59N 93 58W
Jasper Nat. Park, Canada 110 52 50N 118 8W
Jassy = Iaşi, Romania 34 47 10N 27 40 E
Jastrebarsko, Yugoslavia 27 45 41N 15 39 E
Jastrzębie Zdrój, Poland 32 49 57N 18 35 E
Jászárokszállás, Hungary 33 47 39N 20 1 E
Jászberény, Hungary 33 47 30N 19 55 E
Jászladány, Hungary 33 47 23N 20 10 E
Jataí, Brazil 139 17 58 S 51 48W
Jatapu →, Brazil 135 2 13 S 58 17W
Jati, Pakistan 48 24 20N 68 19 E
Jatibarang, Indonesia 57 6 28 S 108 18 E
Jatinegara, Indonesia 57 6 13 S 106 52 E
Játiva, Spain 25 39 0N 0 32W
Jatobal, Brazil 138 4 35 S 49 33W
Jatt, Israel 44 32 24N 35 2 E
Jáu, Angola 95 15 12 S 13 31 E
Jaú, Brazil 141 22 10 S 48 30W
Jaú →, Brazil 135 1 54 S 61 26W
Jauaperí →, Brazil 135 1 26 S 61 35W
Jauche, Belgium 17 50 41N 4 57 E
Jauja, Peru 136 11 45 S 75 15W
Jaunjelgava, U.S.S.R. 36 56 35N 25 0 E
Jaunpur, India 49 25 46N 82 44 E
Jauru →, Brazil 137 16 22 S 57 46W
Java = Jawa, Indonesia 57 7 0 S 110 0 E
Java Sea, Indonesia 56 4 35 S 107 15 E
Java Trench, Ind. Oc. 66 10 0 S 110 0 E
Javadi Hills, India 51 12 40N 78 40 E
Jávea, Spain 25 38 48N 0 10 E
Javhlant = Ulyasutay, Mongolia 62 47 56N 97 28 E
Javier, I., Chile 142 47 5 S 74 25W
Javla, India 50 17 18N 75 9 E
Javron, France 18 48 25N 0 25W
Jawa, Indonesia 57 7 0 S 110 0 E
Jawor, Poland 32 51 4N 16 11 E
Jaworzno, Poland 32 50 13N 19 11 E
Jay, U.S.A. 121 36 25N 94 46W
Jaya, Puncak, Indonesia 57 3 57 S 137 17 E
Jayanca, Peru 136 6 24 S 79 50W
Jayanti, India 52 26 45N 89 40 E
Jayapura, Indonesia 57 2 28 S 140 38 E
Jayawijaya, Pegunungan, Indonesia 57 5 0 S 139 0 E
Jayton, U.S.A. 121 33 17N 100 35W
Jazminal, Mexico 126 24 56N 101 25W
Jean, U.S.A. 125 35 47N 115 20W
Jean Marie River, Canada 102 61 32N 120 38W
Jean Rabel, Haiti 129 19 50N 73 5W
Jeanerette, U.S.A. 121 29 52N 91 38W
Jeannette, Ostrov, U.S.S.R. 41 76 43N 158 0 E
Jeannette, U.S.A. 116 40 20N 79 36W
Jebba, Morocco 84 35 11N 4 43W
Jebba, Nigeria 91 9 9N 4 48 E
Jebel, Bahr el →, Sudan 89 9 30N 30 25 E
Jebel Qerri, Sudan 89 16 16N 32 50 E
Jeberos, Peru 136 5 15 S 76 10W
Jedburgh, U.K. 14 55 28N 2 33W
Jedda = Jiddah, Si. Arabia 46 21 29N 39 10 E
Jędrzejów, Poland 32 50 35N 20 15 E
Jedway, Canada 110 52 17N 131 14W
Jeetze →, W. Germany 30 53 9N 11 6 E
Jefferson, Iowa, U.S.A. 118 42 3N 94 25W
Jefferson, Ohio, U.S.A. 116 41 40N 80 46W
Jefferson, Tex., U.S.A. 121 32 45N 94 23W
Jefferson, Wis., U.S.A. 119 43 0N 88 49W
Jefferson, Mt., Nev., U.S.A. 122 38 51N 117 0W
Jefferson, Mt., Oreg., U.S.A. 122 44 45N 121 50W
Jefferson City, Mo., U.S.A. 118 38 34N 92 10W
Jefferson City, Tenn., U.S.A. 115 36 8N 83 30W
Jeffersontown, U.S.A. 119 38 17N 85 44W
Jeffersonville, Ind., U.S.A. 119 38 20N 85 42W
Jeffersonville, Ohio, U.S.A. 119 39 38N 83 34W
Jega, Nigeria 91 12 15N 4 23 E
Jekabpils, U.S.S.R. 36 56 29N 25 57 E
Jelenia Góra, Poland 32 50 50N 15 45 E
Jelgava, U.S.S.R. 36 56 41N 23 49 E
Jelli, Sudan 89 5 25N 31 45 E
Jellicoe, Canada 104 49 40N 87 30W
Jemaja, Indonesia 56 3 5N 105 45 E
Jemaluang, Malaysia 55 2 16N 103 52 E
Jemappes, Belgium 17 50 27N 3 54 E
Jember, Indonesia 57 8 11 S 113 41 E
Jembongan, Malaysia 56 6 45N 117 20 E
Jemeppe, Belgium 17 50 37N 5 30 E
Jemnice, Czech. 32 49 1N 15 34 E
Jena, E. Germany 30 50 56N 11 33 E
Jena, U.S.A. 121 31 41N 92 7W
Jendouba, Tunisia 86 36 29N 8 47 E
Jenkins, U.S.A. 114 37 13N 82 41W
Jenner, U.S.A. 124 38 27N 123 7W
Jennings, La., U.S.A. 121 30 10N 92 45W
Jennings, Mo., U.S.A. 118 38 43N 90 16W
Jennings →, Canada 110 59 38N 132 5W
Jenny, Sweden 11 57 47N 16 35 E
Jenolan Caves, Australia 76 33 49 S 150 1 E
Jeparit, Australia 74 36 8 S 142 1 E
Jequié, Brazil 139 13 51 S 40 5W
Jequitaí →, Brazil 139 17 4 S 44 50W
Jequitinhonha, Brazil 139 16 30 S 41 0W
Jequitinhonha →, Brazil 139 15 51 S 38 53W
Jerada, Morocco 85 34 17N 2 10W
Jerangle, Australia 76 35 52 S 149 23 E
Jerantut, Malaysia 55 3 56N 102 22 E
Jérémie, Haiti 129 18 40N 74 10W
Jeremoabo, Brazil 138 10 4 S 38 21W
Jerez, Punta, Mexico 127 22 58N 97 40W
Jerez de García Salinas, Mexico 126 22 39N 103 0W
Jerez de la Frontera, Spain 23 36 41N 6 7W
Jerez de los Caballeros, Spain 23 38 20N 6 45W
Jericho = El Arīhā, Jordan 44 31 52N 35 27 E
Jericho, Australia 72 23 38 S 146 6 E
Jerichow, E. Germany 30 52 30N 12 2 E
Jerico Springs, U.S.A. 118 37 37N 94 1W
Jerilderie, Australia 74 35 20 S 145 41 E
Jermyn, U.S.A. 117 41 31N 75 31W
Jerome, U.S.A. 123 34 50N 112 0W
Jerrys Plains, Australia 76 32 29 S 150 53 E
Jersey, Chan. Is. 18 49 13N 2 7W

Jersey City, *U.S.A.* **117** 40 41N 74 8W
Jersey Shore, *U.S.A.* **116** 41 17N 77 18W
Jerseyville, *Australia* **77** 30 54 S 153 3 E
Jerseyville, *U.S.A.* **118** 39 5N 90 20W
Jerusalem, *Israel* **44** 31 47N 35 10 E
Jervis B., *Australia* **76** 35 8 S 150 46 E
Jervis Bay, *Australia* **76** 35 8 S 150 43 E
Jesenice, *Yugoslavia* **27** 46 28N 14 3 E
Jeseník, *Czech.* **32** 50 0N 17 8 E
Jesenké, *Czech.* **33** 48 20N 20 10 E
Jesselton = Kota Kinabalu, *Malaysia* **56** 6 0N 116 4 E
Jessnitz, *E. Germany* **30** 51 42N 12 19 E
Jessore, *Bangla.* **52** 23 10N 89 10 E
Jesup, *U.S.A.* **115** 31 36N 81 54W
Jesup, *U.S.A.* **118** 42 29N 92 4W
Jesús, *Peru* **136** 7 15 S 78 25W
Jesús Carranza, *Mexico* **127** 17 28N 95 1W
Jesús María, *Argentina* **140** 30 59 S 64 5W
Jetmore, *U.S.A.* **121** 38 10N 99 57W
Jetpur, *India* **48** 21 45N 70 10 E
Jette, *Belgium* **17** 50 53N 4 20 E
Jevnaker, *Norway* **10** 60 15N 10 26 E
Jewell, *U.S.A.* **118** 42 20N 93 39W
Jewett, *Ohio, U.S.A.* **116** 40 22N 81 2W
Jewett, *Tex., U.S.A.* **121** 31 20N 96 8W
Jewett City, *U.S.A.* **117** 41 36N 71 58W
Jeypore, *India* **50** 18 50N 82 38 E
Jeziorany, *Poland* **32** 53 58N 20 46 E
Jhajjar, *India* **48** 28 37N 76 42 E
Jhal Jhao, *Pakistan* **47** 26 20N 65 35 E
Jhalakati, *Bangla.* **52** 22 39N 90 12 E
Jhalawar, *India* **48** 24 40N 76 10 E
Jhang Maghiana, *Pakistan* **48** 31 15N 72 22 E
Jhansi, *India* **49** 25 30N 78 36 E
Jharia, *India* **49** 23 45N 86 26 E
Jharsuguda, *India* **50** 21 56N 84 5 E
Jhelum, *Pakistan* **48** 33 0N 73 45 E
Jhelum →, *Pakistan* **48** 31 20N 72 10 E
Jhunjhunu, *India* **48** 28 10N 75 30 E
Ji Xian, *Hebei, China* **60** 37 35N 115 30 E
Ji Xian, *Henan, China* **60** 35 22N 114 5 E
Ji Xian, *Shanxi, China* **60** 36 7N 110 40 E
Jia Xian, *Henan, China* **60** 33 59N 113 12 E
Jia Xian, *Shaanxi, China* **60** 38 12N 110 28 E
Jiading, *China* **59** 31 22N 121 15 E
Jiahe, *China* **59** 25 38N 112 19 E
Jiali, *Taiwan* **59** 23 12N 120 10 E
Jialing Jiang →, *China* **58** 29 30N 106 20 E
Jiamusi, *China* **62** 46 40N 130 26 E
Ji'an, *Jiangxi, China* **59** 27 6N 114 59 E
Ji'an, *Jilin, China* **61** 41 5N 126 10 E
Jianchang, *China* **61** 40 55N 120 35 E
Jianchangying, *China* **61** 40 10N 118 50 E
Jianchuan, *China* **58** 26 38N 99 55 E
Jiande, *China* **59** 29 23N 119 15 E
Jiangbei, *China* **58** 29 40N 106 34 E
Jiangcheng, *China* **58** 22 36N 101 52 E
Jiangdi, *China* **58** 26 57N 103 37 E
Jiange, *China* **58** 32 4N 105 32 E
Jiangjin, *China* **58** 29 14N 106 14 E
Jiangkou, *China* **58** 27 40N 108 49 E
Jiangle, *China* **59** 26 42N 117 23 E
Jiangling, *China* **59** 30 25N 112 12 E
Jiangmen, *China* **59** 22 32N 113 0 E
Jiangshan, *China* **59** 28 40N 118 37 E
Jiangsu □, *China* **61** 33 0N 120 0 E
Jiangxi □, *China* **59** 27 30N 116 0 E
Jiangyin, *China* **59** 31 54N 120 17 E
Jiangyong, *China* **59** 25 20N 111 22 E
Jiangyou, *China* **58** 31 44N 104 43 E
Jianhe, *China* **58** 26 37N 108 31 E
Jianli, *China* **59** 29 46N 112 56 E
Jianning, *China* **59** 26 50N 116 50 E
Jian'ou, *China* **59** 27 3N 118 17 E
Jianshi, *China* **58** 30 37N 109 38 E
Jianshui, *China* **58** 23 36N 102 43 E
Jianyang, *Fujian, China* **59** 27 20N 118 5 E
Jianyang, *Sichuan, China* **58** 30 24N 104 33 E
Jiao Xian, *China* **61** 36 18N 120 1 E
Jiaohe, *Hebei, China* **60** 38 2N 116 20 E
Jiaohe, *Jilin, China* **61** 43 40N 127 22 E
Jiaoling, *China* **59** 24 41N 116 12 E
Jiaozhou Wan, *China* **61** 36 5N 120 10 E
Jiaozuo, *China* **60** 35 16N 113 12 E
Jiashan, *China* **59** 32 46N 117 59 E
Jiawang, *China* **61** 34 28N 117 26 E
Jiaxiang, *China* **60** 35 25N 116 20 E
Jiaxing, *China* **59** 30 49N 120 45 E
Jiayi, *Taiwan* **59** 23 30N 120 24 E
Jiayu, *China* **59** 29 55N 113 55 E
Jibão, Serra do, *Brazil* **139** 14 48 S 45 0W
Jibiya, *Nigeria* **91** 13 5N 7 12 E
Jibou, *Romania* **34** 47 15N 23 17 E
Jibuti = Djibouti ■, *Africa* **89** 12 0N 43 0 E
Jicarón, I., *Panama* **128** 7 10N 81 50W
Jičín, *Czech.* **32** 50 25N 15 28 E
Jiddah, *Si. Arabia* **46** 21 29N 39 10 E
Jieshou, *China* **60** 33 18N 115 22 E
Jiexiu, *China* **60** 37 2N 111 55 E
Jieyang, *China* **59** 23 35N 116 21 E
Jifnā, *Jordan* **44** 31 58N 35 13 E
Jihlava, *Czech.* **32** 49 28N 15 35 E
Jijel, *Algeria* **85** 36 52N 5 50 E
Jijiga, *Ethiopia* **98** 9 20N 42 50 E
Jijona, *Spain* **25** 38 34N 0 30W
Jikamshi, *Nigeria* **91** 12 12N 7 45 E
Jilin, *China* **61** 43 44N 126 30 E
Jilin □, *China* **61** 44 0N 124 0 E
Jiloca →, *Spain* **24** 41 21N 1 39W
Jilong, *Taiwan* **59** 25 8N 121 42 E
Jima, *Ethiopia* **89** 7 40N 36 47 E
Jimbolia, *Romania* **34** 45 47N 20 43 E
Jimena de la Frontera, *Spain* **23** 36 27N 5 24W
Jimenbuen, *Australia* **75** 36 42 S 148 53 E
Jiménez, *Mexico* **126** 27 10N 104 54W
Jimo, *China* **61** 36 23N 120 30 E
Jin Jiang →, *China* **59** 28 24N 115 48 E
Jin Xian, *Hebei, China* **60** 38 2N 115 2 E
Jin Xian, *Liaoning, China* **61** 38 55N 121 42 E
Jinan, *China* **60** 36 38N 117 1 E
Jincheng, *China* **60** 35 29N 112 50 E
Jinchuan, *China* **58** 31 30N 102 3 E
Jind, *India* **48** 29 19N 76 22 E
Jindabyne, *Australia* **75** 36 25 S 148 35 E
Jindabyne L., *Australia* **75** 36 20 S 148 38 E
Jindrichuv Hradeç, *Czech.* **32** 49 10N 15 2 E
Jing He →, *China* **60** 34 27N 109 4 E
Jing Shan, *China* **59** 31 20N 111 35 E
Jing Xian, *Anhui, China* **59** 30 38N 118 25 E
Jing Xian, *Hunan, China* **58** 26 33N 109 40 E
Jing'an, *China* **59** 28 50N 115 17 E
Jingbian, *China* **60** 37 20N 108 30 E
Jingchuan, *China* **60** 35 20N 107 20 E
Jingde, *China* **59** 30 15N 118 27 E
Jingdezhen, *China* **59** 29 20N 117 11 E
Jingdong, *China* **58** 24 23N 100 47 E
Jingellic, *Australia* **76** 35 56 S 147 40 E
Jinggu, *China* **58** 23 35N 100 41 E
Jinghai, *China* **60** 38 55N 116 55 E
Jinghong, *China* **58** 22 0N 100 45 E
Jingjiang, *China* **59** 32 2N 120 16 E
Jingle, *China* **60** 38 20N 111 55 E
Jingmen, *China* **59** 31 0N 112 10 E
Jingning, *China* **60** 35 30N 105 43 E
Jingpo Hu, *China* **61** 43 55N 128 55 E
Jingshan, *China* **59** 31 1N 113 7 E
Jingtai, *China* **60** 37 10N 104 6 E
Jingxi, *China* **58** 23 8N 106 27 E
Jingxing, *China* **60** 38 2N 114 8 E
Jingyang, *China* **60** 34 30N 108 50 E
Jingyu, *China* **61** 42 25N 126 45 E
Jingyuan, *China* **60** 36 30N 104 40 E
Jingziguan, *China* **60** 33 15N 111 0 E
Jinhua, *China* **59** 29 8N 119 38 E
Jining, *Nei Mongol Zizhiqu, China* **60** 41 5N 113 0 E
Jining, *Shandong, China* **60** 35 22N 116 34 E
Jinja, *Uganda* **92** 0 25N 33 12 E
Jinjang, *Malaysia* **55** 3 13N 101 39 E
Jinji, *China* **60** 37 58N 106 8 E
Jinjiang, *Fujian, China* **59** 24 43N 118 33 E
Jinjiang, *Yunnan, China* **58** 26 14N 100 34 E
Jinjie, *China* **58** 23 15N 107 18 E
Jinjini, *Ghana* **90** 7 26N 3 42W
Jinkou, *China* **59** 30 20N 114 8 E
Jinmen Dao, *China* **59** 24 25N 118 25 E
Jinnah Barrage, *Pakistan* **47** 32 58N 71 33 E
Jinning, *China* **58** 24 38N 102 38 E
Jinotega, *Nic.* **128** 13 6N 85 59W
Jinotepe, *Nic.* **128** 11 50N 86 10W
Jinping, *Guizhou, China* **58** 26 41N 109 10 E
Jinping, *Yunnan, China* **58** 22 45N 103 18 E
Jinsha, *China* **58** 27 29N 106 12 E
Jinsha Jiang →, *China* **58** 28 50N 104 36 E
Jinshan, *China* **59** 30 54N 121 10 E
Jinshi, *China* **59** 29 40N 111 50 E
Jintan, *China* **59** 31 42N 119 36 E
Jinxi, *Jiangxi, China* **59** 27 56N 116 45 E
Jinxi, *Liaoning, China* **61** 40 52N 120 50 E
Jinxian, *China* **59** 28 26N 116 17 E
Jinxiang, *China* **60** 35 5N 116 22 E
Jinyun, *China* **59** 28 35N 120 5 E
Jinzhai, *China* **59** 31 40N 115 53 E
Jinzhou, *China* **61** 41 5N 121 3 E
Jiparaná →, *Brazil* **137** 8 3 S 62 52W
Jipijapa, *Ecuador* **134** 1 0 S 80 40W
Jiquilpan, *Mexico* **126** 19 57N 102 42W
Jishan, *China* **60** 35 34N 110 58 E
Jishou, *China* **58** 28 21N 109 43 E
Jishui, *China* **59** 27 12N 115 8 E
Jisr al Ḩusayn, *Jordan* **44** 31 53N 35 33 E
Jisr ash Shughūr, *Syria* **46** 35 49N 36 18 E
Jitarning, *Australia* **79** 32 48 S 117 57 E
Jitra, *Malaysia* **55** 6 16N 100 25 E
Jiu →, *Romania* **34** 43 47N 23 48 E
Jiudengkou, *China* **60** 39 56N 106 40 E
Jiujiang, *Guangdong, China* **59** 22 50N 113 0 E
Jiujiang, *Jiangxi, China* **59** 29 42N 115 58 E
Jiuling Shan, *China* **59** 28 40N 114 40 E
Jiulong, *China* **58** 28 57N 101 31 E
Jiuquan, *China* **62** 39 50N 98 20 E
Jiutai, *China* **61** 44 10N 125 50 E
Jiuxiangcheng, *China* **60** 33 12N 114 50 E
Jiuxincheng, *China* **60** 39 17N 115 59 E
Jiuyuhang, *China* **59** 30 18N 119 56 E
Jixi, *Anhui, China* **59** 30 5N 118 34 E
Jixi, *Heilongjiang, China* **61** 45 20N 130 50 E
Jiyang, *China* **61** 37 0N 117 12 E
Jīzān, *Si. Arabia* **45** 17 0N 42 20 E
Jize, *China* **60** 36 54N 114 56 E
Jizera →, *Czech.* **32** 50 10N 14 43 E
Jizō-Zaki, *Japan* **64** 35 34N 133 20 E
Joaçaba, *Brazil* **141** 27 5 S 51 31W
Joaíma, *Brazil* **139** 16 39 S 41 2W
João, *Brazil* **138** 2 46 S 50 59W
João Amaro, *Brazil* **139** 12 46 S 40 22W
João Câmara, *Brazil* **138** 5 32 S 35 48W
João Pessoa, *Brazil* **138** 7 10 S 34 52W
João Pinheiro, *Brazil* **139** 17 45 S 46 10W
Joaquim Távora, *Brazil* **139** 23 30 S 49 58W
Joaquín V. González, *Argentina* **140** 25 10 S 64 0W
Jobourg, Nez de, *France* **18** 49 41N 1 57W
Jódar, *Spain* **25** 37 50N 3 21W
Jodhpur, *India* **48** 26 23N 73 8 E
Jœuf, *France* **19** 49 12N 6 0 E
Jofane, *Mozam.* **97** 21 15 S 34 18 E
Joggins, *Canada* **105** 45 42N 64 27W
Jogjakarta = Yogyakarta, *Indonesia* **57** 7 49 S 110 22 E
Jōhana, *Japan* **65** 36 30N 136 57 E
Johannesburg, *S. Africa* **97** 26 10 S 28 2 E
Johannesburg, *U.S.A.* **125** 35 26N 117 38W
Johansfors, *Sweden* **11** 56 42N 15 32 E
Jōhen, *Japan* **64** 32 58N 132 32 E
John Day, *U.S.A.* **122** 44 25N 118 57W
John Day →, *U.S.A.* **122** 45 44N 120 39W
John H. Kerr Res., *U.S.A.* **115** 36 20N 78 30W
John o' Groats, *U.K.* **14** 58 39N 3 3W
Johnnie, *U.S.A.* **125** 36 25N 116 5W
Johnson, *U.S.A.* **121** 37 35N 101 48W
Johnson City, *Ill., U.S.A.* **118** 37 49N 88 56W
Johnson City, *N.Y., U.S.A.* **117** 42 7N 75 57W
Johnson City, *Tenn., U.S.A.* **115** 36 18N 82 21W
Johnson City, *Tex., U.S.A.* **121** 30 15N 98 24W
Johnsonburg, *U.S.A.* **116** 41 30N 78 40W
Johnsondale, *U.S.A.* **125** 35 58N 118 32W
Johnson's Crossing, *Canada* **110** 60 29N 133 18W
Johnsonville, *N.Z.* **80** 41 13 S 174 48 E
Johnston, L., *Australia* **79** 32 25 S 120 30 E
Johnston Falls = Mambilima Falls, *Zambia* **93** 10 31 S 28 45 E
Johnston I., *Pac. Oc.* **67** 17 10N 169 8W
Johnstone Str., *Canada* **110** 50 28N 126 0W
Johnstown, *N.Y., U.S.A.* **117** 43 1N 74 20W
Johnstown, *Pa., U.S.A.* **116** 40 19N 78 53W
Johor Baharu, *Malaysia* **55** 1 28N 103 46 E
Joigny, *France* **19** 47 58N 3 20 E
Joinville, *Brazil* **141** 26 15 S 48 55W
Joinville, *France* **19** 48 27N 5 10 E
Joinville I., *Antarctica* **143** 65 0 S 55 30W
Jojutla, *Mexico* **127** 18 37N 99 11W
Jokkmokk, *Sweden* **8** 66 35N 19 50 E
Jökulsá á Dal →, *Iceland* **8** 65 40N 14 16W
Jökulsá Fjöllum →, *Iceland* **8** 66 10N 16 30W
Joliet, *U.S.A.* **119** 41 30N 88 0W
Joliette, *Canada* **107** 46 3N 73 24W
Joliette, Parc. Prov. de, *Canada* **107** 46 30N 74 0W
Jolo, *Phil.* **57** 6 0N 121 0 E
Jolon, *U.S.A.* **124** 35 58N 121 9W
Jombang, *Indonesia* **57** 7 33 S 112 14 E
Jomda, *China* **58** 31 28N 98 12 E
Jome, *Indonesia* **57** 1 16 S 127 30 E
Jomfruland, *Norway* **11** 58 52N 9 36 E
Jönåker, *Sweden* **11** 58 44N 16 40 E
Jonava, *U.S.S.R.* **36** 55 8N 24 12 E
Jones Sound, *Canada* **144** 76 0N 85 0W
Jonesboro, *Ark., U.S.A.* **121** 35 50N 90 45W
Jonesboro, *Ill., U.S.A.* **121** 37 26N 89 18W
Jonesboro, *La., U.S.A.* **121** 32 15N 92 41W
Jonesburg, *U.S.A.* **118** 38 51N 91 18W
Jonesport, *U.S.A.* **105** 44 32N 67 38W
Jonesville, *Ind., U.S.A.* **119** 39 5N 85 54W
Jonesville, *Mich., U.S.A.* **119** 41 59N 84 40W
Jonglei, *Sudan* **89** 6 25N 30 50 E
Jonglei □, *Sudan* **89** 7 30N 32 30 E
Joniskis, *U.S.S.R.* **36** 56 13N 23 35 E
Jönköping, *Sweden* **11** 57 45N 14 10 E
Jönköpings län □, *Sweden* **11** 57 30N 14 30 E
Jonquière, *Canada* **107** 48 27N 71 14W
Jonsberg, *Sweden* **11** 58 30N 16 48 E
Jonsered, *Sweden* **11** 57 45N 12 10 E
Jonzac, *France* **20** 45 27N 0 28W
Joplin, *U.S.A.* **121** 37 0N 94 31W
Jordan, *U.S.A.* **122** 47 25N 106 58W
Jordan ■, *Asia* **46** 31 0N 36 0 E
Jordan →, *Asia* **46** 31 48N 35 32 E
Jordan Valley, *U.S.A.* **122** 43 0N 117 2W
Jordânia, *Brazil* **139** 15 55 S 40 11W
Jorge, C., *Chile* **142** 51 40 S 75 35W
Jorhat, *India* **52** 26 45N 94 12 E
Jorm, *Afghan.* **47** 36 50N 70 52 E
Jörn, *Sweden* **8** 65 4N 20 1 E
Jorong, *Indonesia* **56** 3 58 S 114 56 E
Jorquera →, *Chile* **140** 28 3 S 69 58W
Jos, *Nigeria* **91** 9 53N 8 51 E
José Batlle y Ordóñez, *Uruguay* **141** 33 20 S 55 10W
José de San Martín, *Argentina* **142** 44 4 S 70 26W
Joseph, *U.S.A.* **122** 45 27N 117 13W
Joseph, L., *Nfld., Canada* **105** 52 45N 65 18W
Joseph, L., *Ont., Canada* **106** 45 10N 79 44W
Joseph Bonaparte G., *Australia* **78** 14 35 S 128 50 E
Joseph City, *U.S.A.* **123** 35 0N 110 16W
Joshua Tree, *U.S.A.* **125** 34 8N 116 19W
Joshua Tree Nat. Mon., *U.S.A.* **125** 33 56N 116 5W
Josselin, *France* **18** 47 57N 2 33W
Jostedal, *Norway* **9** 61 35N 7 15 E
Jotunheimen, *Norway* **10** 61 35N 8 25 E
Jourdanton, *U.S.A.* **121** 28 54N 98 32W
Joure, *Neths.* **16** 52 58N 5 48 E
Joussard, *Canada* **110** 55 22N 115 50W
Jovellanos, *Cuba* **128** 22 40N 81 10W
Jowai, *India* **52** 25 26N 92 12 E
Jowzjān □, *Afghan.* **47** 36 10N 66 0 E
Joya, La, *Peru* **136** 16 43 S 71 52W
Joyeuse, *France* **21** 44 29N 4 16 E
Józefów, *Poland* **32** 52 10N 21 11 E
Ju Xian, *China* **61** 36 35N 118 20 E
Juan Aldama, *Mexico* **126** 24 20N 103 23W
Juan Bautista Alberdi, *Argentina* **140** 34 26 S 61 48W
Juan de Fuca Str., *Canada* **124** 48 15N 124 0W
Juan de Nova, *Ind. Oc.* **97** 17 3 S 43 45 E
Juan Fernández, Arch. de, *Pac. Oc.* **132** 33 50 S 80 0W
Juan José Castelli, *Argentina* **140** 25 27 S 60 57W
Juan L. Lacaze, *Uruguay* **140** 34 26 S 57 25W
Juanjuí, *Peru* **136** 7 10 S 76 45W
Juárez, *Argentina* **140** 37 40 S 59 43W
Juárez, *Mexico* **125** 32 20N 115 57W
Juárez, Sierra de, *Mexico* **126** 32 0N 116 0W
Juatinga, Ponta de, *Brazil* **139** 23 17 S 44 30W
Juàzeiro, *Brazil* **138** 9 30 S 40 30W
Juàzeiro do Norte, *Brazil* **138** 7 10 S 39 18W
Jubbulpore = Jabalpur, *India* **49** 23 9N 79 58 E
Jübek, *W. Germany* **30** 54 31N 9 24 E
Jubga, *U.S.S.R.* **39** 44 19N 38 48 E
Jubilee L., *Australia* **79** 29 0 S 126 50 E
Júcar →, *Spain* **25** 39 5N 0 10W
Júcaro, *Cuba* **128** 21 37N 78 51W
Juchitán, *Mexico* **127** 16 27N 95 5W
Judaea = Har Yehuda, *Israel* **44** 31 35N 34 57 E
Judenburg, *Austria* **33** 47 12N 14 38 E
Judith →, *U.S.A.* **122** 47 44N 109 38W
Judith Gap, *U.S.A.* **122** 46 40N 109 46W
Judith Pt., *U.S.A.* **117** 41 20N 71 30W
Jufari →, *Brazil* **135** 1 13 S 62 0W
Jugiong, *Australia* **76** 34 48 S 148 19 E
Jugoslavia = Yugoslavia ■, *Europe* **33** 44 0N 20 0 E
Juigalpa, *Nic.* **128** 12 6N 85 26W
Juillac, *France* **20** 45 20N 1 19 E
Juist, *W. Germany* **30** 53 40N 7 0 E
Juiz de Fora, *Brazil* **139** 21 43 S 43 19W
Jujuy □, *Argentina* **140** 23 20 S 65 40W
Julesburg, *U.S.A.* **120** 41 0N 102 20W
Juli, *Peru* **136** 16 10 S 69 25W
Julia Cr. →, *Australia* **72** 20 0 S 141 11 E
Julia Creek, *Australia* **72** 20 39 S 141 44 E
Juliaca, *Peru* **136** 15 25 S 70 10W
Julian, *U.S.A.* **125** 33 4N 116 38W
Julian Alps = Julijske Alpe, *Yugoslavia* **27** 46 15N 14 1 E
Julianakanaal, *Neths.* **17** 51 6N 5 52 E
Julianatop, *Surinam* **135** 3 40N 56 30W
Julianehåb, *Greenland* **144** 60 43N 46 0W
Jülich, *W. Germany* **30** 50 55N 6 20 E
Julijske Alpe, *Yugoslavia* **27** 46 15N 14 1 E
Julimes, *Mexico* **126** 28 25N 105 27W
Jullundur, *India* **48** 31 20N 75 40 E
Julu, *China* **60** 37 15N 115 2 E
Jumbo, *Zimb.* **93** 17 30 S 30 58 E
Jumbo Pk., *U.S.A.* **125** 36 12N 114 11W
Jumentos Cays, *Bahamas* **129** 23 0N 75 40 E
Jumet, *Belgium* **17** 50 27N 4 25 E
Jumilla, *Spain* **25** 38 28N 1 19W
Jumla, *Nepal* **49** 29 15N 82 13 E
Jumna = Yamuna →, *India* **49** 25 30N 81 53 E
Junagadh, *India* **48** 21 30N 70 30 E
Junction, *Tex., U.S.A.* **121** 30 29N 99 48W
Junction, *Utah, U.S.A.* **123** 38 10N 112 15W
Junction B., *Australia* **72** 11 52 S 133 55 E
Junction City, *Kans., U.S.A.* **120** 39 4N 96 55W
Junction City, *Oreg., U.S.A.* **122** 44 14N 123 12W
Junction Pt., *Australia* **72** 11 45 S 133 50 E
Jundah, *Australia* **72** 24 46 S 143 2 E
Jundiaí, *Brazil* **141** 24 30 S 47 0W
Juneau, *U.S.A.* **102** 58 20N 134 20W
Junee, *Australia* **76** 34 53 S 147 35 E

Jungfrau, *Switz.* **31** 46 32N 7 58 E
Junggar Pendi, *China* **62** 44 30N 86 0 E
Junglinster, *Lux.* **17** 49 43N 6 15 E
Jungshahi, *Pakistan* **48** 24 52N 67 44 E
Juniata →, *U.S.A.* **116** 40 30N 77 40W
Junín, *Argentina* **140** 34 33 S 60 57W
Junín, *Peru* **136** 11 12 S 76 0W
Junín □, *Peru* **136** 11 30 S 75 0W
Junín de los Andes, *Argentina* **142** 39 45 S 71 0W
Jūniyah, *Lebanon* **46** 33 59N 35 38 E
Junnar, *India* **50** 19 12N 73 58 E
Junquera, La, *Spain* **24** 42 25N 2 53 E
Junta, La, *U.S.A.* **121** 38 0N 103 30W
Juntura, *U.S.A.* **122** 43 44N 118 4W
Juparanã, L., *Brazil* **139** 19 16 S 40 8W
Jupiter →, *Canada* **105** 49 29N 63 37W
Juquiá, *Brazil* **139** 24 19 S 47 38W
Jur, Nahr el →, *Sudan* **89** 8 45N 29 15 E
Jura, *Europe* **19** 46 35N 6 5 E
Jura, *U.K.* **14** 56 0N 5 50W
Jura □, *France* **19** 46 47N 5 45 E
Jura, Mts., *Europe* **21** 46 40N 6 5 E
Jura, Sd. of, *U.K.* **14** 55 57N 5 45W
Jura Suisse, *Switz.* **31** 47 10N 7 0 E
Jurado, *Colombia* **134** 7 7N 77 46W
Jurilovca, *Romania* **34** 44 46N 28 52 E
Jurong, *China* **59** 31 57N 119 9 E
Juruá →, *Brazil* **134** 2 37 S 65 44W
Juruena, *Brazil* **137** 13 0 S 58 10W
Juruena →, *Brazil* **137** 7 20 S 58 3W
Juruti, *Brazil* **135** 2 9 S 56 4W
Jussey, *France* **19** 47 50N 5 55 E
Justo Daract, *Argentina* **140** 33 52 S 65 12W
Jutaí, *Brazil* **136** 5 11 S 68 54W
Jutaí →, *Brazil* **134** 2 43 S 66 57W
Jüterbog, *E. Germany* **30** 52 0N 13 6 E
Juticalpa, *Honduras* **128** 14 40N 86 12W
Jutland = Jylland, *Denmark* **11** 56 25N 9 30 E
Jutphaas, *Neths.* **16** 52 2N 5 6 E
Juventud, I. de la, *Cuba* **128** 21 40N 82 40W
Juvigny-sous-Andaine, *France* **18** 48 32N 0 30W
Juvisy-sur-Orge, *France* **19** 48 42N 2 22 E
Juwain, *Afghan.* **47** 31 45N 61 30 E
Juye, *China* **60** 35 22N 116 5 E
Juzennecourt, *France* **19** 48 10N 4 58 E
Jylland, *Denmark* **11** 56 25N 9 30 E
Jyväskylä, *Finland* **8** 62 14N 25 50 E

K

K2, Mt., *Pakistan* **49** 35 58N 76 32 E
Kaala-Gomén, *N. Cal.* **68** 20 40 S 164 25 E
Kaap die Goeie Hoop, *S. Africa* **96** 34 24 S 18 30 E
Kaap Plateau, *S. Africa* **96** 28 30 S 24 0 E
Kaapkruis, *Namibia* **96** 21 55 S 13 57 E
Kaapstad = Cape Town, *S. Africa* **96** 33 55 S 18 22 E
Kaatsheuvel, *Neths.* **17** 51 39N 5 2 E
Kabaena, *Indonesia* **57** 5 15 S 122 0 E
Kabala, *S. Leone* **90** 9 38N 11 37W
Kabale, *Uganda* **92** 1 15 S 30 0 E
Kabalo, *Zaïre* **92** 6 0 S 27 0 E
Kabambare, *Zaïre* **92** 4 41 S 27 39 E
Kabango, *Zaïre* **93** 8 35 S 28 30 E
Kabanjahe, *Indonesia* **56** 3 6N 98 30 E
Kabara, *Mali* **90** 16 40N 2 50W
Kabardinka, *U.S.S.R.* **38** 44 40N 37 57 E
Kabardino-Balkar-A.S.S.R. □, *U.S.S.R.* **39** 43 30N 43 30 E
Kabare, *Indonesia* **57** 0 4 S 130 58 E
Kabarega Falls, *Uganda* **92** 2 15N 31 30 E
Kabasalan, *Phil.* **57** 7 47N 122 44 E
Kabba, *Nigeria* **91** 7 50N 6 3 E
Kabe, *Japan* **64** 34 31N 132 31 E
Kabi, *Niger* **87** 13 30N 12 35 E
Kabin Buri, *Thailand* **54** 13 57N 101 43 E
Kabinakagami L., *Canada* **104** 48 54N 84 25W
Kabīr, Zab al →, *Iraq* **46** 36 0N 43 0 E
Kabīr Kūh, *Iran* **46** 33 0N 47 30 E
Kabkabīyah, *Sudan* **87** 13 50N 24 0 E
Kablungu, C., *Papua N. G.* **69** 6 20 S 150 1 E
Kabna, *Sudan* **88** 19 6N 32 40 E
Kabo, *C.A.R.* **94** 7 35N 18 38 E
Kabompo, *Zambia* **93** 13 36 S 24 14 E
Kabondo, *Zaïre* **93** 8 58 S 25 40 E
Kabongo, *Zaïre* **92** 7 22 S 25 33 E
Kabou, *Togo* **91** 9 28N 0 55 E
Kaboudia, Rass, *Tunisia* **86** 35 13N 11 10 E
Kabra, *Australia* **72** 23 25 S 150 25 E
Kabūd Gonbad, *Iran* **47** 37 5N 59 45 E
Kābul, *Afghan.* **47** 34 28N 69 11 E
Kābul □, *Afghan.* **47** 34 30N 69 0 E
Kabul →, *Pakistan* **48** 33 55N 72 14 E
Kabunga, *Zaïre* **92** 1 38 S 28 3 E
Kaburuang, *Indonesia* **57** 3 50N 126 30 E
Kabushiya, *Sudan* **89** 16 54N 33 41 E
Kabwe, *Zambia* **93** 14 30 S 28 29 E
Kabwum, *Papua N. G.* **69** 6 11 S 147 15 E
Kačanik, *Yugoslavia* **33** 42 13N 21 12 E
Kachanovo, *U.S.S.R.* **36** 57 25N 27 38 E
Kachchh, Gulf of, *India* **48** 22 50N 69 15 E
Kachchh, Rann of, *India* **48** 24 0N 70 0 E
Kachebera, *Zambia* **93** 13 50 S 32 50 E
Kachin □, *Burma* **52** 26 0N 97 30 E
Kachira, L., *Uganda* **92** 0 40 S 31 7 E
Kachiry, *U.S.S.R.* **40** 53 10N 75 50 E
Kachisi, *Ethiopia* **89** 9 40N 37 50 E
Kachot, *Cambodia* **55** 11 30N 103 3 E
Kackar, *Turkey* **46** 40 45N 41 10 E
Kadaingti, *Burma* **52** 17 37N 97 32 E
Kadaiyanallur, *India* **51** 9 3N 77 22 E
Kadan Kyun, *Burma* **56** 12 30N 98 20 E
Kadanai →, *Afghan.* **48** 31 22N 65 45 E
Kadarkút, *Hungary* **33** 46 13N 17 39 E
Kade, *Ghana* **91** 6 7N 0 56W
Kadi, *India* **48** 23 18N 72 23 E
Kadina, *Australia* **73** 34 0 S 137 43 E
Kadiri, *India* **51** 14 12N 78 13 E
Kadirli, *Turkey* **46** 37 23N 36 5 E
Kadiyevka = Stakhanov, *U.S.S.R.* **39** 48 35N 38 40 E
Kadoka, *U.S.A.* **120** 43 50N 101 31W
Kadom, *U.S.S.R.* **37** 54 37N 42 30 E
Kadoma, *Zimb.* **93** 18 20 S 29 52 E
Kâdugli, *Sudan* **89** 11 0N 29 45 E
Kaduna, *Nigeria* **91** 10 30N 7 21 E
Kaduna □, *Nigeria* **91** 11 0N 7 30 E
Kadungle, *Australia* **76** 32 45 S 147 36 E
Kaédi, *Mauritania* **90** 16 9N 13 28W
Kaelé, *Cameroon* **91** 10 7N 14 27 E
Kaeng Khoï, *Thailand* **54** 14 35N 101 0 E
Kaeo, *N.Z.* **80** 35 6 S 173 49 E
Kaesŏng, *N. Korea* **61** 37 58N 126 35 E
Kāf, *Si. Arabia* **46** 31 25N 37 29 E
Kafakumba, *Zaïre* **95** 9 38 S 23 46 E
Kafanchan, *Nigeria* **91** 9 40N 8 20 E
Kafareti, *Nigeria* **91** 10 25N 11 12 E
Kaffrine, *Senegal* **90** 14 8N 15 36W
Kafia Kingi, *Sudan* **94** 9 20N 24 25 E
Kafinda, *Zambia* **93** 12 32 S 30 20 E
Kafirévs, Ákra, *Greece* **35** 38 9N 24 38 E
Kafr 'Ayn, *Jordan* **44** 32 3N 35 7 E
Kafr el Dauwâr, *Egypt* **88** 31 8N 30 8 E
Kafr el Sheikh, *Egypt* **88** 31 15N 30 50 E
Kafr Kammā, *Israel* **44** 32 44N 35 26 E
Kafr Kannā, *Israel* **44** 32 45N 35 20 E
Kafr Mālik, *Jordan* **44** 32 0N 35 18 E
Kafr Mandā, *Israel* **44** 32 49N 35 15 E
Kafr Quaddūm, *Jordan* **44** 32 14N 35 7 E
Kafr Rā'ī, *Jordan* **44** 32 23N 35 9 E
Kafr Şīr, *Lebanon* **44** 33 19N 35 23 E
Kafr Yāsīf, *Israel* **44** 32 58N 35 10 E
Kafue, *Zambia* **93** 15 46 S 28 9 E
Kafue Flats, *Zambia* **93** 15 40 S 27 25 E
Kafulwe, *Zambia* **93** 9 0 S 29 1 E
Kaga, *Afghan.* **48** 34 14N 70 10 E
Kaga, *Japan* **65** 36 16N 136 15 E
Kaga Bandoro, *C.A.R.* **94** 7 0N 19 10 E
Kagan, *U.S.S.R.* **40** 39 43N 64 33 E
Kagawa □, *Japan* **64** 34 15N 134 0 E
Kagawong L., *Canada* **108** 45 54N 82 15W
Kagera □, *Tanzania* **92** 2 0 S 31 30 E
Kagera →, *Uganda* **92** 0 57 S 31 47 E
Kağizman, *Turkey* **46** 40 5N 43 10 E
Kagoshima, *Japan* **64** 31 35N 130 33 E
Kagoshima □, *Japan* **64** 31 30N 130 30 E
Kagoshima-Wan, *Japan* **64** 31 25N 130 40 E
Kagul, *U.S.S.R.* **38** 45 50N 28 15 E
Kahama, *Tanzania* **92** 4 8 S 32 30 E
Kahama □, *Tanzania* **92** 3 50 S 32 0 E
Kahang, *Malaysia* **55** 2 12N 103 32 E
Kahayan →, *Indonesia* **56** 3 40 S 114 0 E
Kahe, *Tanzania* **92** 3 30 S 37 25 E
Kahemba, *Zaïre* **95** 7 18 S 18 55 E
Kaherekoau Mts., *N.Z.* **81** 45 45 S 167 15 E
Kahil, Djebel bou, *Algeria* **85** 34 26N 4 0 E
Kahniah →, *Canada* **110** 58 15N 120 55W
Kahnūj, *Iran* **47** 27 55N 57 40 E
Kahoka, *U.S.A.* **118** 40 25N 91 42W
Kahoolawe, *U.S.A.* **112** 20 33N 156 35W
Kahramanmaras, *Turkey* **46** 37 37N 36 53 E
Kahurangi, Pt., *N.Z.* **81** 40 50 S 172 10 E
Kahuta, *Pakistan* **48** 33 35N 73 24 E
Kai, Kepulauan, *Indonesia* **57** 5 55 S 132 45 E
Kai Besar, *Indonesia* **57** 5 35 S 133 0 E
Kai-Ketil, *Indonesia* **57** 5 45 S 132 40 E
Kai Xian, *China* **58** 31 11N 108 21 E
Kaiama, *Nigeria* **91** 9 36N 4 1 E
Kaiapit, *Papua N. G.* **69** 6 18 S 146 18 E
Kaiapoi, *N.Z.* **81** 42 24 S 172 40 E
Kaibara, *Japan* **65** 35 8N 135 5 E
Kaieteur Falls, *Guyana* **135** 5 1N 59 10W
Kaifeng, *China* **60** 34 48N 114 21 E
Kaihua, *China* **59** 29 12N 118 20 E
Kaiingveld, *S. Africa* **96** 30 0 S 22 0 E
Kaikohe, *N.Z.* **80** 35 25 S 173 49 E
Kaikoura, *N.Z.* **81** 42 25 S 173 43 E
Kaikoura Pen., *N.Z.* **81** 42 25 S 173 43 E
Kaikoura Ra., *N.Z.* **81** 41 59 S 173 41 E
Kailahun, *S. Leone* **90** 8 18N 10 39W
Kailashahar, *Bangla.* **52** 24 19N 92 0 E
Kaili, *China* **58** 26 33N 107 59 E
Kailu, *China* **61** 43 38N 121 18 E
Kailua, *U.S.A.* **112** 19 39N 156 0W
Kaimana, *Indonesia* **57** 3 39 S 133 45 E
Kaimanawa Mts., *N.Z.* **80** 39 15 S 175 56 E
Kaimata, *N.Z.* **81** 42 34 S 171 28 E
Kaimganj, *India* **49** 27 33N 79 24 E
Kaimon-Dake, *Japan* **64** 31 11N 130 32 E
Kaimur Hill, *India* **49** 24 30N 82 0 E
Kainan, *Japan* **64** 34 9N 135 12 E
Kainantu, *Papua N. G.* **69** 6 18 S 145 52 E
Kaingaroa Forest, *N.Z.* **80** 38 24 S 176 30 E
Kainji Res., *Nigeria* **91** 10 1N 4 40 E
Kaipara Harbour, *N.Z.* **80** 36 25 S 174 14 E
Kaiping, *China* **59** 22 23N 112 42 E
Kaipokok B., *Canada* **105** 54 54N 59 47W
Kairana, *India* **48** 29 24N 77 15 E
Kaironi, *Indonesia* **57** 0 47 S 133 40 E
Kairouan, *Tunisia* **86** 35 45N 10 5 E
Kairuku, *Papua N. G.* **69** 8 51 S 146 35 E
Kaiserslautern, *W. Germany* **31** 49 30N 7 43 E
Kaitaia, *N.Z.* **80** 35 8 S 173 17 E
Kaitangata, *N.Z.* **81** 46 17 S 169 51 E
Kaithal, *India* **48** 29 48N 76 26 E
Kaitu →, *Pakistan* **48** 33 10N 70 30 E
Kaiwi Channel, *U.S.A.* **112** 21 13N 157 30W
Kaiyang, *China* **58** 27 4N 106 59 E
Kaiyuan, *Liaoning, China* **61** 42 28N 124 1 E
Kaiyuan, *Yunnan, China* **58** 23 40N 103 12 E
Kajaani, *Finland* **8** 64 17N 27 46 E
Kajabbi, *Australia* **72** 20 0 S 140 1 E
Kajana = Kajaani, *Finland* **8** 64 17N 27 46 E
Kajang, *Malaysia* **55** 2 59N 101 48 E
Kajiado, *Kenya* **92** 1 53 S 36 48 E
Kajiado □, *Kenya* **92** 2 0 S 36 30 E
Kajiki, *Japan* **64** 31 44N 130 40 E
Kajo Kaji, *Sudan* **89** 3 58N 31 40 E
Kaka, *Sudan* **89** 10 38N 32 10 E
Kakabeka Falls, *Canada* **104** 48 24N 89 37W
Kakamas, *S. Africa* **96** 28 45 S 20 33 E
Kakamega, *Kenya* **92** 0 20N 34 46 E
Kakamega □, *Kenya* **92** 0 20N 34 46 E
Kakamigahara, *Japan* **65** 35 28N 136 48 E
Kakanj, *Yugoslavia* **33** 44 9N 18 7 E
Kakanui Mts., *N.Z.* **81** 45 10 S 170 30 E
Kake, *Japan* **64** 34 36N 132 19 E
Kakegawa, *Japan* **65** 34 45N 138 1 E
Kakhib, *U.S.S.R.* **39** 42 28N 46 34 E
Kakhovka, *U.S.S.R.* **38** 46 40N 33 15 E
Kakhovskoye Vdkhr., *U.S.S.R.* **38** 47 5N 34 16 E
Kakinada, *India* **50** 16 57N 82 11 E
Kakisa →, *Canada* **110** 61 3N 118 10W
Kakisa L., *Canada* **110** 60 56N 117 43W
Kakogawa, *Japan* **64** 34 46N 134 51 E
Kakwa →, *Canada* **110** 54 37N 118 28W
Kala, *Nigeria* **91** 12 2N 14 40 E
Kala Oya →, *Sri Lanka* **51** 8 20N 79 45 E
Kalaa-Kebira, *Tunisia* **86** 35 59N 10 32 E
Kalabagh, *Pakistan* **48** 33 0N 71 28 E
Kalabahi, *Indonesia* **57** 8 13 S 124 31 E
Kalabáka, *Greece* **35** 39 42N 21 39 E
Kalabo, *Zambia* **95** 14 58 S 22 40 E
Kalach, *U.S.S.R.* **37** 50 22N 41 0 E
Kalach na Donu, *U.S.S.R.* **39** 48 43N 43 32 E
Kaladar, *Canada* **109** 44 37N 77 5W
Kalahari, *Africa* **96** 24 0 S 21 30 E
Kalahari Gemsbok Nat. Park, *S. Africa* **96** 25 30 S 20 30 E
Kalakamati, *Botswana* **97** 20 40 S 27 25 E
Kalakan, *U.S.S.R.* **41** 55 15N 116 45 E
K'alak'unlun Shank'ou, *Pakistan* **49** 35 33N 77 46 E
Kalam, *Pakistan* **49** 35 34N 72 30 E
Kalama, *U.S.A.* **124** 46 0N 122 55W
Kalama, *Zaïre* **92** 2 52 S 28 35 E
Kalamariá, *Greece* **35** 40 33N 22 55 E
Kalamata, *Greece* **35** 37 3N 22 10 E
Kalamazoo, *U.S.A.* **119** 42 20N 85 35W
Kalamazoo →, *U.S.A.* **119** 42 40N 86 12W
Kalamb, *India* **50** 18 3N 74 48 E
Kalambo Falls, *Tanzania* **93** 8 37 S 31 35 E
Kálamos, *Greece* **35** 38 37N 20 55 E
Kalan, *Turkey* **46** 39 7N 39 32 E
Kalannie, *Australia* **79** 30 22 S 117 5 E
Kalao, *Indonesia* **57** 7 21 S 121 0 E
Kalaotoa, *Indonesia* **57** 7 20 S 121 50 E
Kälarne, *Sweden* **10** 62 59N 16 8 E
Kalárovo, *Czech.* **33** 47 54N 18 0 E
Kalasin, *Thailand* **54** 16 26N 103 30 E
Kalat, *Pakistan* **47** 29 8N 66 31 E
Kálathos, *Greece* **35** 36 9N 28 8 E
Kalaus →, *U.S.S.R.* **39** 45 40N 44 7 E
Kalávrita, *Greece* **35** 38 3N 22 8 E
Kalaw, *Burma* **52** 20 38N 96 34 E
Kalbarri, *Australia* **79** 27 40 S 114 10 E
Kalecik, *Turkey* **38** 40 4N 33 26 E
Kalehe, *Zaïre* **92** 2 6 S 28 50 E
Kalema, *Tanzania* **92** 1 12 S 31 55 E
Kalemie, *Zaïre* **92** 5 55 S 29 9 E
Kalemyo, *Burma* **52** 23 11N 94 4 E
Kalety, *Poland* **32** 50 35N 18 52 E
Kalewa, *Burma* **52** 23 10N 94 15 E
Kálfafellsstaður, *Iceland* **8** 64 11N 15 53W
Kalgan = Zhangjiakou, *China* **60** 40 48N 114 55 E
Kalgoorlie-Boulder, *Australia* **79** 30 40 S 121 22 E
Kaliakra, Nos, *Bulgaria* **34** 43 21N 28 30 E
Kalianda, *Indonesia* **56** 5 50 S 105 45 E
Kalibo, *Phil.* **57** 11 43N 122 22 E
Kaliganj Town, *Bangla.* **49** 22 25N 89 8 E
Kalima, *Zaïre* **92** 2 33 S 26 32 E
Kalimantan, *Indonesia* **56** 0 0 114 0 E
Kalimantan Barat □, *Indonesia* **56** 0 0 110 30 E
Kalimantan Selatan □, *Indonesia* **56** 2 30 S 115 30 E
Kalimantan Tengah □, *Indonesia* **56** 2 0 S 113 30 E
Kalimantan Timur □, *Indonesia* **56** 1 30N 116 30 E
Kálimnos, *Greece* **35** 37 0N 27 0 E
Kalimpong, *India* **49** 27 4N 88 35 E
Kalinadi →, *India* **51** 14 50N 74 7 E
Kalinin, *U.S.S.R.* **37** 56 55N 35 55 E
Kaliningrad, *R.S.F.S.R., U.S.S.R.* **36** 54 42N 20 32 E
Kaliningrad, *R.S.F.S.R., U.S.S.R.* **37** 55 58N 37 54 E
Kalinkovichi, *U.S.S.R.* **36** 52 12N 29 20 E
Kalinovik, *Yugoslavia* **33** 43 31N 18 29 E
Kalipetrovo, *Bulgaria* **34** 44 5N 27 14 E
Kaliro, *Uganda* **92** 0 56N 33 30 E
Kalispell, *U.S.A.* **122** 48 10N 114 22W
Kalisz, *Poland* **32** 51 45N 18 8 E
Kaliua, *Tanzania* **92** 5 5 S 31 48 E
Kaliveli Tank, *India* **51** 12 5N 79 50 E
Kalix →, *Sweden* **8** 65 50N 23 11 E
Kalka, *India* **48** 30 46N 76 57 E
Kalkaska, *U.S.A.* **104** 44 44N 85 11W
Kalkfeld, *Namibia* **96** 20 57 S 16 14 E
Kalkfontein, *Botswana* **96** 22 4 S 20 57 E
Kalkrand, *Namibia* **96** 24 1 S 17 35 E
Kallakkurichchi, *India* **51** 11 44N 79 1 E
Kållandsö, *Sweden* **11** 58 40N 13 5 E
Kallia, *Jordan* **44** 31 46N 35 30 E
Kallidaikurichi, *India* **51** 8 38N 77 31 E
Kallinge, *Sweden* **11** 56 15N 15 18 E
Kallithéa, *Greece* **35** 37 55N 23 41 E
Kallonís, Kólpos, *Greece* **35** 39 10N 26 10 E
Kallsjön, *Sweden* **8** 63 38N 13 0 E
Kalmalo, *Nigeria* **91** 13 40N 5 20 E
Kalmar, *Sweden* **11** 56 40N 16 20 E
Kalmar län □, *Sweden* **11** 57 25N 16 0 E
Kalmar sund, *Sweden* **11** 56 40N 16 25 E
Kalmthout, *Belgium* **17** 51 23N 4 29 E
Kalmyk A.S.S.R. □, *U.S.S.R.* **39** 46 5N 46 1 E
Kalmykovo, *U.S.S.R.* **39** 49 0N 51 47 E
Kalna, *India* **49** 23 13N 88 25 E
Kalo, *Papua N. G.* **69** 10 1 S 147 48 E
Kalocsa, *Hungary* **33** 46 32N 19 0 E
Kaloko, *Zaïre* **92** 6 47 S 25 48 E
Kalol, *Gujarat, India* **48** 22 37N 73 31 E
Kalol, *Gujarat, India* **48** 23 15N 72 33 E
Kalolímnos, *Greece* **35** 37 4N 27 8 E
Kalomo, *Zambia* **93** 17 0 S 26 30 E
Kalona, *U.S.A.* **118** 41 29N 91 43W
Kalpi, *India* **49** 26 8N 79 47 E
Kalrayan Hills, *India* **51** 11 45N 78 40 E
Kalsubai, *India* **50** 19 35N 73 45 E
Kaltungo, *Nigeria* **91** 9 48N 11 19 E
Kalu, *Pakistan* **48** 25 5N 67 39 E
Kaluga, *U.S.S.R.* **37** 54 35N 36 10 E
Kalulushi, *Zambia* **93** 12 50 S 28 3 E
Kalundborg, *Denmark* **11** 55 41N 11 5 E
Kalush, *U.S.S.R.* **36** 49 3N 24 23 E
Kałuszyn, *Poland* **32** 52 13N 21 52 E
Kalutara, *Sri Lanka* **51** 6 35N 80 0 E
Kalyan, *India* **50** 20 30N 74 3 E
Kalyazin, *U.S.S.R.* **37** 57 15N 37 55 E
Kama, *Burma* **52** 19 1N 95 4 E
Kama, *Zaïre* **92** 3 30 S 27 5 E
Kama →, *U.S.S.R.* **40** 55 45N 52 0 E
Kamachumu, *Tanzania* **92** 1 37 S 31 37 E
Kamae, *Japan* **64** 32 48N 131 56 E
Kamaing, *Burma* **52** 25 26N 96 35 E
Kamaishi, *Japan* **63** 39 20N 142 0 E
Kamakura, *Japan* **65** 35 19N 139 33 E
Kamalia, *Pakistan* **48** 30 44N 72 42 E
Kamamaung, *Burma* **52** 17 21N 97 40 E
Kamandorskiye Ostrava, *U.S.S.R.* **41** 55 0N 167 0 E
Kamapanda, *Zambia* **93** 12 5 S 24 0 E
Kamaran, *Yemen* **45** 15 21N 42 35 E
Kamativi, *Zimb.* **93** 18 15 S 27 27 E
Kamba, *Nigeria* **91** 11 50N 3 45 E
Kambalda, *Australia* **79** 31 10 S 121 37 E
Kambam, *India* **51** 9 45N 77 16 E
Kambar, *Pakistan* **48** 27 37N 68 1 E
Kambia, *S. Leone* **90** 9 3N 12 53W
Kambolé, *Zambia* **93** 8 47 S 30 48 E
Kambove, *Zaïre* **93** 10 51 S 26 33 E
Kambuie, *Zaïre* **95** 6 59 S 22 19 E
Kamchatka, P-ov., *U.S.S.R.* **41** 57 0N 160 0 E
Kamen, *U.S.S.R.* **40** 53 50N 81 30 E
Kamen Kashirskiy, *U.S.S.R.* **36** 51 39N 24 56 E
Kamenets-Podolskiy, *U.S.S.R.* **38** 48 45N 26 10 E
Kamenjak, Rt., *Yugoslavia* **27** 44 47N 13 55 E
Kamenka, *R.S.F.S.R., U.S.S.R.* **37** 53 10N 44 5 E
Kamenka, *R.S.F.S.R., U.S.S.R.* **37** 50 47N 39 20 E
Kamenka, *Ukraine S.S.R., U.S.S.R.* **38** 49 3N 32 6 E
Kamenka Bugskaya, *U.S.S.R.* **36** 50 8N 24 16 E
Kamenka Dneprovskaya, *U.S.S.R.* **38** 47 29N 34 14 E

Kamenolomini, *U.S.S.R.* **39** 47 40N 40 14 E
Kamensk-Shakhtinskiy, *U.S.S.R.* **39** 48 23N 40 20 E
Kamensk Uralskiy, *U.S.S.R.* **40** 56 25N 62 2 E
Kamenskiy, *R.S.F.S.R.*, *U.S.S.R.* **37** 50 48N 45 25 E
Kamenskiy, *R.S.F.S.R.*, *U.S.S.R.* **39** 49 20N 41 15 E
Kamenskoye, *U.S.S.R.* **41** 62 45N 165 30 E
Kamenyak, *Bulgaria* **34** 43 24N 26 57 E
Kamenz, *E. Germany* **30** 51 17N 14 7 E
Kameoka, *Japan* **65** 35 0N 135 35 E
Kameyama, *Japan* **65** 34 51N 136 27 E
Kami-Jima, *Japan* **64** 32 27N 130 20 E
Kami-koshiki-Jima, *Japan* **64** 31 50N 129 52 E
Kamiah, *U.S.A.* **122** 46 12N 116 2W
Kamień Pomorski, *Poland* **32** 53 57N 14 43 E
Kamieskroon, *S. Africa* **96** 30 9 S 17 56 E
Kamiita, *Japan* **64** 34 6N 134 22 E
Kamilukuak, L., *Canada* **111** 62 22N 101 40W
Kamina, *Zaïre* **93** 8 45 S 25 0 E
Kaminak L., *Canada* **111** 62 10N 95 0W
Kamioka, *Japan* **65** 36 25N 137 15 E
Kamituga, *Zaïre* **92** 3 2 S 28 10 E
Kamloops, *Canada* **110** 50 40N 120 20W
Kamnik, *Yugoslavia* **27** 46 14N 14 37 E
Kamo, *N.Z.* **80** 35 42 S 174 20 E
Kamo, *U.S.S.R.* **39** 40 21N 45 7 E
Kamoa Mts., *Guyana* **135** 1 30N 59 0W
Kamogawa, *Japan* **65** 35 5N 140 5 E
Kamoke, *Pakistan* **48** 32 4N 74 4 E
Kamouraska, *Canada* **107** 47 34N 69 52W
Kamp →, *Austria* **33** 48 23N 15 42 E
Kampala, *Uganda* **92** 0 20N 32 30 E
Kampar, *Malaysia* **55** 4 18N 101 9 E
Kampar →, *Indonesia* **56** 0 30N 103 8 E
Kampen, *Neths.* **16** 52 33N 5 53 E
Kamperland, *Neths.* **17** 51 34N 3 43 E
Kamphaeng Phet, *Thailand* **54** 16 28N 99 30 E
Kampolombo, L., *Zambia* **93** 11 37 S 29 42 E
Kampong To, *Thailand* **55** 6 3N 101 13 E
Kampot, *Cambodia* **55** 10 36N 104 10 E
Kampsville, *U.S.A.* **118** 39 18N 90 37W
Kamptee, *India* **50** 21 9N 79 19 E
Kampti, *Burkina Faso* **90** 10 7N 3 25W
Kampuchea = Cambodia ■, *Asia* **54** 12 15N 105 0 E
Kampung →, *Indonesia* **57** 5 44 S 138 24 E
Kampung Air Putih, *Malaysia* **55** 4 15N 103 10 E
Kampung Jerangau, *Malaysia* **55** 4 50N 103 10 E
Kampung Raja, *Malaysia* **55** 5 45N 102 35 E
Kampungbaru = Tolitoli, *Indonesia* **57** 1 5N 120 50 E
Kamrau, Teluk, *Indonesia* **57** 3 30 S 133 36 E
Kamsack, *Canada* **111** 51 34N 101 54W
Kamskoye Ustye, *U.S.S.R.* **37** 55 10N 49 20 E
Kamuchawie L., *Canada* **111** 56 18N 101 59W
Kamui-Misaki, *Japan* **63** 43 20N 140 21 E
Kamyshin, *U.S.S.R.* **37** 50 10N 45 24 E
Kamyzyak, *U.S.S.R.* **39** 46 4N 48 10 E
Kan, *Burma* **52** 22 25N 94 5 E
Kanaaupscow, *Canada* **104** 54 2N 76 30W
Kanab, *U.S.A.* **123** 37 3N 112 29W
Kanab Creek, *U.S.A.* **123** 37 0N 112 40W
Kanagawa □, *Japan* **65** 35 20N 139 20 E
Kanairiktok →, *Canada* **105** 55 2N 60 18W
Kanakapura, *India* **51** 12 33N 77 28 E
Kanália, *Greece* **35** 39 30N 22 53 E
Kananga, *Zaïre* **95** 5 55 S 22 18 E
Kanarraville, *U.S.A.* **123** 37 34N 113 12W
Kanash, *U.S.S.R.* **37** 55 30N 47 32 E
Kanaskat, *U.S.A.* **124** 47 19N 121 54W
Kanata, *Canada* **109** 45 20N 75 59W
Kanawha →, *U.S.A.* **114** 38 50N 82 8W
Kanazawa, *Japan* **65** 36 30N 136 38 E
Kanbalu, *Burma* **52** 23 12N 95 31 E
Kanchanaburi, *Thailand* **54** 14 2N 99 31 E
Kanchenjunga, *Nepal* **49** 27 50N 88 10 E
Kanchipuram, *India* **51** 12 52N 79 45 E
Kanda Kanda, *Zaïre* **95** 6 52 S 23 48 E
Kandahar = Qandahār, *Afghan.* **47** 31 32N 65 30 E
Kandalaksha, *U.S.S.R.* **40** 67 9N 32 30 E
Kandangan, *Indonesia* **56** 2 50 S 115 20 E
Kandavu, *Fiji* **68** 19 0 S 178 15 E
Kandavu Passage, *Fiji* **68** 18 45 S 178 0 E
Kandep, *Papua N. G.* **69** 5 54 S 143 32 E
Kandhíla, *Greece* **35** 37 46N 22 22 E
Kandhkot, *Pakistan* **48** 28 16N 69 8 E
Kandhla, *India* **48** 29 18N 77 19 E
Kandi, *Benin* **91** 11 7N 2 55 E
Kandi, *India* **49** 23 58N 88 5 E
Kandla, *India* **48** 23 0N 70 10 E
Kandos, *Australia* **76** 32 45 S 149 58 E
Kandrian, *Papua N. G.* **69** 6 14 S 149 37 E
Kandy, *Sri Lanka* **51** 7 18N 80 43 E
Kane, *U.S.A.* **116** 41 39N 78 53W
Kane Basin, *Canada* **144** 79 1N 73 0W
Kanevskaya, *U.S.S.R.* **39** 46 3N 39 3 E
Kanfanar, *Yugoslavia* **27** 45 7N 13 50 E
Kangaba, *Mali* **90** 11 56N 8 25W
Kangar, *Malaysia* **55** 6 27N 100 12 E
Kangaroo I., *Australia* **73** 35 45 S 137 0 E
Kangaroo Mts., *Australia* **72** 23 25 S 142 0 E
Kangaroo Valley, *Australia* **76** 34 42 S 150 32 E
Kangavar, *Iran* **46** 34 40N 48 0 E
Kangding, *China* **58** 30 2N 101 57 E
Kangean, Kepulauan, *Indonesia* **56** 6 55 S 115 23 E
Kangerdlugsuak, *Greenland* **144** 68 10N 32 20W
Kanggye, *N. Korea* **61** 41 0N 126 35 E
Kangnŭng, *S. Korea* **61** 37 45N 128 54 E
Kango, *Gabon* **94** 0 11N 10 5 E
Kangoya, *Zaïre* **95** 9 55 S 22 48 E
Kangping, *China* **61** 42 43N 123 18 E
Kangpokpi, *India* **52** 25 8N 93 58 E
Kangyidaung, *Burma* **52** 16 56N 94 54 E
Kanhangad, *India* **51** 12 21N 74 58 E
Kanheri, *India* **50** 19 13N 72 50 E
Kani, *Ivory C.* **90** 8 29N 6 36W
Kaniama, *Zaïre* **92** 7 30 S 24 12 E
Kaniapiskau →, *Canada* **105** 56 40N 69 30W
Kaniapiskau L., *Canada* **105** 54 10N 69 55W
Kanin, P-ov., *U.S.S.R.* **40** 68 0N 45 0 E
Kanin Nos, Mys, *U.S.S.R.* **40** 68 45N 43 20 E
Kaniva, *Australia* **74** 36 22 S 141 18 E
Kanjiža, *Yugoslavia* **33** 46 3N 20 4 E
Kanjut Sar, *Pakistan* **49** 36 7N 75 25 E
Kankakee, *U.S.A.* **119** 41 6N 87 50W
Kankakee →, *U.S.A.* **119** 41 23N 88 16W
Kankan, *Guinea* **90** 10 23N 9 15W
Kanker, *India* **50** 20 10N 81 40 E
Kankunskiy, *U.S.S.R.* **41** 57 37N 126 8 E
Kanmuri-Yama, *Japan* **64** 34 30N 132 4 E
Kannabe, *Japan* **64** 34 32N 133 23 E
Kannapolis, *U.S.A.* **115** 35 32N 80 37W
Kannauj, *India* **49** 27 3N 79 56 E
Kano, *Nigeria* **91** 12 2N 8 30 E
Kano □, *Nigeria* **91** 11 45N 9 0 E
Kan'onji, *Japan* **64** 34 7N 133 39 E
Kanoroba, *Ivory C.* **90** 9 7N 6 8W
Kanowha, *U.S.A.* **118** 42 57N 93 47W
Kanowit, *Malaysia* **56** 2 14N 112 20 E
Kanowna, *Australia* **79** 30 32 S 121 31 E
Kanoya, *Japan* **64** 31 25N 130 50 E
Kanpetlet, *Burma* **52** 21 10N 93 59 E
Kanpur, *India* **49** 26 28N 80 20 E
Kansas, *U.S.A.* **119** 39 33N 87 56W
Kansas □, *U.S.A.* **120** 38 40N 98 0W
Kansas →, *U.S.A.* **120** 39 7N 94 36W
Kansas City, *Kans., U.S.A.* **118** 39 0N 94 40W
Kansas City, *Mo., U.S.A.* **118** 39 3N 94 30W
Kansenia, *Zaïre* **93** 10 20 S 26 0 E
Kansk, *U.S.S.R.* **41** 56 20N 95 37 E
Kansu = Gansu □, *China* **60** 36 0N 104 0 E
Kantang, *Thailand* **55** 7 25N 99 31 E
Kantché, *Niger* **91** 13 31N 8 30 E
Kanté, *Togo* **91** 9 57N 1 3 E
Kantemirovka, *U.S.S.R.* **39** 49 43N 39 55 E
Kantharalak, *Thailand* **54** 14 39N 104 39 E
Kantō □, *Japan* **65** 36 15N 139 30 E
Kantō-Heiya, *Japan* **65** 36 0N 139 30 E
Kantō-Sanchi, *Japan* **65** 35 59N 138 50 E
Kantu-long, *Burma* **52** 19 57N 97 36 E
Kanturk, *Ireland* **15** 52 10N 8 55W
Kanuma, *Japan* **65** 36 34N 139 42 E
Kanumbra, *Australia* **74** 37 3 S 145 40 E
Kanus, *Namibia* **96** 27 50 S 18 39 E
Kanye, *Botswana* **96** 25 0 S 25 28 E
Kanzenze, *Zaïre* **93** 10 30 S 25 12 E
Kanzi, Ras, *Tanzania* **92** 7 1 S 39 33 E
Kao, *Fiji* **68** 19 40 S 175 1W
Kaohsiung = Gaoxiong, *Taiwan* **59** 22 38N 120 18 E
Kaokoveld, *Namibia* **96** 19 15 S 14 30 E
Kaolack, *Senegal* **90** 14 5N 16 8W
Kaoshan, *China* **61** 44 38N 124 50 E
Kaouar, *Niger* **87** 19 5N 12 52 E
Kapadvanj, *India* **48** 23 5N 73 0 E
Kapagere, *Papua N. G.* **69** 9 46 S 147 42 E
Kapanga, *Zaïre* **95** 8 30 S 22 40 E
Kapchagai, *U.S.S.R.* **40** 43 51N 77 14 E
Kapellen, *Belgium* **17** 51 19N 4 25 E
Kapéllo, Ákra, *Greece* **35** 36 9N 23 3 E
Kapema, *Zaïre* **93** 10 45 S 28 22 E
Kapfenberg, *Austria* **33** 47 26N 15 18 E
Kapia, *Zaïre* **95** 4 17 S 19 46 E
Kapiri Mposhi, *Zambia* **93** 13 59 S 28 43 E
Kapīsā □, *Afghan.* **47** 35 0N 69 20 E
Kapiskau →, *Canada* **104** 52 47N 81 55W
Kapit, *Malaysia* **56** 2 0N 112 55 E
Kapiti I., *N.Z.* **80** 40 50 S 174 56 E
Kapka, Massif du, *Chad* **87** 15 7N 21 45 E
Kaplice, *Czech.* **32** 48 42N 14 30 E
Kapoe, *Thailand* **55** 9 34N 98 32 E
Kapoeta, *Sudan* **89** 4 50N 33 35 E
Kaponga, *N.Z.* **80** 39 29 S 174 9 E
Kapos →, *Hungary* **33** 46 44N 18 30 E
Kaposvár, *Hungary* **33** 46 25N 17 47 E
Kapowsin, *U.S.A.* **124** 46 59N 122 13W
Kappeln, *W. Germany* **30** 54 37N 9 56 E
Kapps, *Namibia* **96** 22 32 S 17 18 E
Kaprije, *Yugoslavia* **27** 43 42N 15 43 E
Kaprijke, *Belgium* **17** 51 13N 3 38 E
Kapsukas, *U.S.S.R.* **36** 54 33N 23 19 E
Kapuas →, *Indonesia* **56** 0 25 S 109 20 E
Kapuas Hulu, Pegunungan, *Malaysia* **56** 1 30N 113 30 E
Kapulo, *Zaïre* **93** 8 18 S 29 15 E
Kapunda, *Australia* **73** 34 20 S 138 56 E
Kapurthala, *India* **48** 31 23N 75 25 E
Kapuskasing, *Canada* **104** 49 25N 82 30W
Kapuskasing →, *Canada* **104** 49 49N 82 0W
Kapustin Yar, *U.S.S.R.* **39** 48 37N 45 40 E
Kaputar, Mt., *Australia* **77** 30 15 S 150 10 E
Kaputir, *Kenya* **92** 2 5N 35 28 E
Kapuvár, *Hungary* **33** 47 36N 17 1 E
Kara, *U.S.S.R.* **40** 69 10N 65 0 E
Kara Bogaz Gol, Zaliv, *U.S.S.R.* **40** 41 0N 53 30 E
Kara Kalpak A.S.S.R. □, *U.S.S.R.* **40** 43 0N 60 0 E
Kara Kum = Karakum, Peski, *U.S.S.R.* **40** 39 30N 60 0 E
Kara-Saki, *Japan* **64** 34 41N 129 30 E
Kara Sea, *U.S.S.R.* **40** 75 0N 70 0 E
Karabük, *Turkey* **38** 41 12N 32 37 E
Karaburuni, *Albania* **35** 40 25N 19 20 E
Karabutak, *U.S.S.R.* **40** 49 59N 60 14 E
Karachala, *U.S.S.R.* **39** 39 45N 48 53 E
Karachayevsk, *U.S.S.R.* **39** 43 50N 42 0 E
Karachev, *U.S.S.R.* **36** 53 10N 35 5 E
Karachi, *Pakistan* **48** 24 53N 67 0 E
Karad, *India* **50** 17 15N 74 10 E
Karadeniz Boğazı, *Turkey* **46** 41 10N 29 10 E
Karaga, *Ghana* **91** 9 58N 0 28W
Karaganda, *U.S.S.R.* **40** 49 50N 73 10 E
Karagayly, *U.S.S.R.* **40** 49 26N 76 0 E
Karaginskiy, Ostrov, *U.S.S.R.* **41** 58 45N 164 0 E
Karagwe □, *Tanzania* **92** 2 0 S 31 0 E
Karaikal, *India* **51** 10 59N 79 50 E
Karaikkudi, *India* **51** 10 0N 78 45 E
Karaitivu, I., *Sri Lanka* **51** 9 45N 79 52 E
Karaj, *Iran* **47** 35 48N 51 0 E
Karak, *Malaysia* **55** 3 25N 102 2 E
Karakas, *U.S.S.R.* **40** 48 20N 83 30 E
Karakitang, *Indonesia* **57** 3 14N 125 28 E
Karakoram Pass, *Pakistan* **49** 35 33N 77 50 E
Karakoram Ra., *Pakistan* **49** 35 30N 77 0 E
Karakum, Peski, *U.S.S.R.* **40** 39 30N 60 0 E
Karal, *Chad* **87** 12 50N 14 46 E
Karalon, *U.S.S.R.* **41** 57 5N 115 50 E
Karaman, *Turkey* **46** 37 14N 33 13 E
Karamay, *China* **62** 45 30N 84 58 E
Karambu, *Indonesia* **56** 3 53 S 116 6 E
Karamea, *N.Z.* **81** 41 14 S 172 6 E
Karamea →, *N.Z.* **81** 41 13 S 172 26 E
Karamea Bight, *N.Z.* **81** 41 22 S 171 40 E
Karamoja □, *Uganda* **92** 3 0N 34 15 E
Karamsad, *India* **48** 22 35N 72 50 E
Karanganyar, *Indonesia* **57** 7 38 S 109 37 E
Karanja, *India* **50** 20 29N 77 31 E
Karapiro, *N.Z.* **80** 37 53 S 175 32 E
Karara, *Australia* **77** 28 12 S 151 37 E
Karasburg, *Namibia* **96** 28 0 S 18 44 E
Karasino, *U.S.S.R.* **40** 66 50N 86 50 E
Karasjok, *Norway* **8** 69 27N 25 30 E
Karasuk, *U.S.S.R.* **40** 53 44N 78 2 E
Karasuyama, *Japan* **65** 36 39N 140 9 E
Karatau, *U.S.S.R.* **40** 43 10N 70 28 E
Karatau, Khrebet, *U.S.S.R.* **40** 43 30N 69 30 E
Karativu, *Sri Lanka* **51** 8 22N 79 47 E
Karatoya →, *India* **52** 24 7N 89 36 E
Karauli, *India* **48** 26 30N 77 4 E
Karawa, *Zaïre* **94** 3 18N 20 17 E
Karawanken, *Europe* **33** 46 30N 14 40 E
Karazhal, *U.S.S.R.* **40** 48 2N 70 49 E
Karbalā, *Iraq* **46** 32 36N 44 3 E
Kårböle, *Sweden* **10** 61 59N 15 22 E
Karcag, *Hungary* **33** 47 19N 20 57 E
Karcha →, *Pakistan* **49** 34 45N 76 10 E
Karda, *U.S.S.R.* **41** 55 0N 103 16 E
Kardhámila, *Greece* **35** 38 35N 26 5 E
Kardhítsa, *Greece* **35** 39 23N 21 54 E
Kärdla, *U.S.S.R.* **36** 58 50N 22 40 E
Kareeberge, *S. Africa* **96** 30 59 S 21 50 E
Kareima, *Sudan* **88** 18 30N 31 49 E
Karelian A.S.S.R. □, *U.S.S.R.* **40** 65 30N 32 30 E
Karema, *Papua N. G.* **69** 9 12 S 147 18 E
Kargānrūd, *Iran* **46** 37 55N 49 0 E
Kargasok, *U.S.S.R.* **40** 59 3N 80 53 E
Kargat, *U.S.S.R.* **40** 55 10N 80 15 E
Kargı, *Turkey* **38** 41 11N 34 30 E
Kargil, *India* **49** 34 32N 76 12 E
Karguéri, *Niger* **91** 13 27N 10 30 E
Karia ba Mohammed, *Morocco* **84** 34 22N 5 12W
Kariba, *Zimb.* **93** 16 28 S 28 50 E
Kariba Dam, *Zimb.* **93** 16 30 S 28 35 E
Kariba Gorge, *Zambia* **93** 16 30 S 28 50 E
Kariba L., *Zimb.* **93** 16 40 S 28 25 E
Karibib, *Namibia* **96** 22 0 S 15 56 E
Karimata, Kepulauan, *Indonesia* **56** 1 25 S 109 0 E
Karimata, Selat, *Indonesia* **56** 2 0 S 108 40 E
Karimnagar, *India* **50** 18 26N 79 10 E
Karimunjawa, Kepulauan, *Indonesia* **56** 5 50 S 110 30 E
Karin, *Somali Rep.* **98** 10 50N 45 52 E
Kariya, *Japan* **65** 34 58N 137 1 E
Karkal, *India* **51** 13 15N 74 56 E
Karkar I., *Papua N. G.* **69** 4 40 S 146 0 E
Karkaralinsk, *U.S.S.R.* **40** 49 26N 75 30 E
Karkinitskiy Zaliv, *U.S.S.R.* **38** 45 56N 33 0 E
Karkur, *Israel* **44** 32 29N 34 57 E
Karkur Tohl, *Egypt* **88** 22 5N 25 5 E
Karl Libknekht, *U.S.S.R.* **36** 51 40N 35 35 E
Karl-Marx-Stadt, *E. Germany* **30** 50 50N 12 55 E
Karl-Marx-Stadt □, *E. Germany* **30** 50 45N 13 0 E
Karla, L. = Voiviïs Límni, *Greece* **35** 39 30N 22 45 E
Karlobag, *Yugoslavia* **27** 44 32N 15 5 E
Karlovac, *Yugoslavia* **27** 45 31N 15 36 E
Karlovka, *U.S.S.R.* **38** 49 29N 35 8 E
Karlovy Vary, *Czech.* **32** 50 13N 12 51 E
Karlsborg, *Sweden* **11** 58 33N 14 33 E
Karlshamn, *Sweden* **11** 56 10N 14 51 E
Karlskoga, *Sweden* **10** 59 22N 14 33 E
Karlskrona, *Sweden* **11** 56 10N 15 35 E
Karlsruhe, *W. Germany* **31** 49 3N 8 23 E
Karlstad, *Sweden* **10** 59 23N 13 30 E
Karlstad, *U.S.A.* **120** 48 38N 96 30W
Karlstadt, *W. Germany* **31** 49 57N 9 46 E
Karnal, *India* **48** 29 42N 77 2 E
Karnali →, *Nepal* **49** 28 45N 81 16 E
Karnaphuli Res., *Bangla.* **52** 22 40N 92 20 E
Karnataka □, *India* **51** 13 15N 77 0 E
Karnes City, *U.S.A.* **121** 28 53N 97 53W
Karnische Alpen, *Europe* **33** 46 36N 13 0 E
Karo, *Mali* **90** 12 16N 3 18W
Karoi, *Zimb.* **93** 16 48 S 29 45 E
Karonga, *Malawi* **93** 9 57 S 33 55 E
Karoonda, *Australia* **73** 35 1 S 139 59 E
Karora, *Sudan* **88** 17 44N 38 15 E
Káros, *Greece* **35** 36 54N 25 40 E
Karousádhes, *Greece* **35** 39 47N 19 45 E
Kárpathos, *Greece* **35** 35 37N 27 10 E
Karpáthos, Stenón, *Greece* **35** 36 0N 27 30 E
Karrebæk, *Denmark* **11** 55 12N 11 39 E
Kars, *Turkey* **46** 40 40N 43 5 E
Karsakpay, *U.S.S.R.* **40** 47 55N 66 40 E
Karsha, *U.S.S.R.* **39** 49 45N 51 35 E
Karshi, *U.S.S.R.* **40** 38 53N 65 48 E
Karsiyang, *India* **49** 26 56N 88 18 E
Karst, *Yugoslavia* **27** 45 35N 14 0 E
Karsun, *U.S.S.R.* **37** 54 14N 46 57 E
Kartaly, *U.S.S.R.* **40** 53 3N 60 40 E
Kartapur, *India* **48** 31 27N 75 32 E
Karthaus, *U.S.A.* **116** 41 8N 78 9W
Kartuzy, *Poland* **32** 54 22N 18 10 E
Karuah, *Australia* **76** 32 37 S 151 56 E
Karufa, *Indonesia* **57** 3 50 S 133 20 E
Karumba, *Australia* **72** 17 31 S 140 50 E
Karumo, *Tanzania* **92** 2 25 S 32 50 E
Karumwa, *Tanzania* **92** 3 12 S 32 38 E
Karungu, *Kenya* **92** 0 50 S 34 10 E
Karup, *Denmark* **11** 56 19N 9 10 E
Karur, *India* **51** 10 59N 78 2 E
Karviná, *Czech.* **32** 49 53N 18 25 E
Karwi, *India* **49** 25 12N 80 57 E
Kasache, *Malawi* **93** 13 25 S 34 20 E
Kasai, *Japan* **64** 34 55N 134 52 E
Kasai →, *Zaïre* **95** 3 30 S 16 10 E
Kasai Occidental □, *Zaïre* **95** 6 0 S 22 0 E
Kasai Oriental □, *Zaïre* **92** 5 0 S 24 30 E
Kasaji, *Zaïre* **93** 10 25 S 23 27 E
Kasama, *Japan* **65** 36 23N 140 16 E
Kasama, *Zambia* **93** 10 16 S 31 9 E
Kasane, *Namibia* **96** 17 34 S 24 50 E
Kasanga, *Tanzania* **93** 8 30 S 31 10 E
Kasangulu, *Zaïre* **95** 4 33 S 15 15 E
Kasaoka, *Japan* **64** 34 30N 133 30 E
Kasaragod, *India* **51** 12 30N 74 58 E
Kasat, *Burma* **52** 15 56N 98 13 E
Kasba, *Bangla.* **52** 23 45N 91 2 E
Kasba L., *Canada* **111** 60 20N 102 10W
Kasba Tadla, *Morocco* **84** 32 36N 6 17W
Kaseda, *Japan* **64** 31 25N 130 19 E
Kasempa, *Zambia* **93** 13 30 S 25 44 E
Kasenga, *Zaïre* **93** 10 20 S 28 45 E
Kasese, *Uganda* **92** 0 13N 30 3 E
Kasewa, *Zambia* **93** 14 28 S 28 53 E
Kasganj, *India* **49** 27 48N 78 42 E
Kashabowie, *Canada* **104** 48 40N 90 26W
Kāshān, *Iran* **47** 34 5N 51 30 E
Kashi, *China* **62** 39 30N 76 2 E
Kashihara, *Japan* **65** 34 27N 135 46 E
Kashima, *Ibaraki, Japan* **65** 35 58N 140 38 E
Kashima, *Saga, Japan* **64** 33 7N 130 6 E
Kashima-Nada, *Japan* **65** 36 0N 140 45 E
Kashimbo, *Zaïre* **93** 11 12 S 26 19 E
Kashin, *U.S.S.R.* **37** 57 20N 37 36 E
Kashipur, *Orissa, India* **50** 19 16N 83 3 E
Kashipur, *Ut. P., India* **49** 29 15N 79 0 E
Kashira, *U.S.S.R.* **37** 54 45N 38 10 E
Kashiwa, *Japan* **65** 35 52N 139 59 E
Kashiwazaki, *Japan* **63** 37 22N 138 33 E

Kashk-e Kohneh, *Afghan.* **47** 34 55N 62 30 E
Kāshmar, *Iran* **47** 35 16N 58 26 E
Kashmir, *Asia* **49** 34 0N 76 0 E
Kashmor, *Pakistan* **48** 28 28N 69 32 E
Kashpirovka, *U.S.S.R.* **37** 53 0N 48 30 E
Kashun Noerh = Gaxun Nur, *China* **62** 42 22N 100 30 E
Kasimov, *U.S.S.R.* **37** 54 55N 41 20 E
Kasinge, *Zaïre* **92** 6 15 S 26 58 E
Kasiruta, *Indonesia* **57** 0 25 S 127 12 E
Kaskaskia →, *U.S.A.* **118** 37 58N 89 57W
Kaskattama →, *Canada* **111** 57 3N 90 4W
Kaskinen, *Finland* **8** 62 22N 21 15 E
Kaskö, *Finland* **8** 62 22N 21 15 E
Kaslo, *Canada* **110** 49 55N 116 55W
Kasmere L., *Canada* **111** 59 34N 101 10W
Kasongo, *Zaïre* **92** 4 30 S 26 33 E
Kasongo Lunda, *Zaïre* **95** 6 35 S 16 49 E
Kásos, *Greece* **35** 35 20N 26 55 E
Kasos, Stenón, *Greece* **35** 35 30N 26 30 E
Kaspi, *U.S.S.R.* **39** 41 54N 44 17 E
Kaspiysk, *U.S.S.R.* **39** 42 52N 47 40 E
Kaspiyskiy, *U.S.S.R.* **39** 45 22N 47 23 E
Kassab ed Doleib, *Sudan* **89** 13 30N 33 35 E
Kassaba, *Egypt* **88** 22 40N 29 55 E
Kassala, *Sudan* **89** 15 30N 36 0 E
Kassalâ □, *Sudan* **89** 15 20N 36 26 E
Kassel, *W. Germany* **30** 51 19N 9 32 E
Kassinger, *Sudan* **88** 18 46N 31 51 E
Kassue, *Indonesia* **57** 6 58 S 139 21 E
Kastamonu, *Turkey* **46** 41 25N 33 43 E
Kastav, *Yugoslavia* **27** 45 22N 14 20 E
Kastélli, *Greece* **35** 35 29N 23 38 E
Kastellorizon = Megiste, *Greece* **46** 36 8N 29 34 E
Kastellou, Ákra, *Greece* **35** 35 30N 27 15 E
Kasterlee, *Belgium* **17** 51 15N 4 59 E
Kastlösa, *Sweden* **11** 56 26N 16 25 E
Kastóri, *Greece* **35** 37 10N 22 17 E
Kastoría, *Greece* **35** 40 30N 21 19 E
Kastornoye, *U.S.S.R.* **37** 51 55N 38 2 E
Kástron, *Greece* **35** 39 50N 25 2 E
Kasugai, *Japan* **65** 35 12N 136 59 E
Kasukabe, *Japan* **65** 35 58N 139 49 E
Kasulu, *Tanzania* **92** 4 37 S 30 5 E
Kasulu □, *Tanzania* **92** 4 37 S 30 5 E
Kasumi, *Japan* **64** 35 38N 134 38 E
Kasumiga-Ura, *Japan* **65** 36 0N 140 25 E
Kasumkent, *U.S.S.R.* **39** 41 47N 48 15 E
Kasungu, *Malawi* **93** 13 0 S 33 29 E
Kasur, *Pakistan* **48** 31 5N 74 25 E
Kata, *U.S.S.R.* **41** 58 46N 102 40 E
Kataba, *Zambia* **93** 16 5 S 25 10 E
Katako Kombe, *Zaïre* **92** 3 25 S 24 20 E
Katákolon, *Greece* **35** 37 38N 21 19 E
Katale, *Tanzania* **92** 4 52 S 31 7 E
Katamatite, *Australia* **74** 36 6 S 145 41 E
Katanda, *Kivu, Zaïre* **92** 0 55 S 29 21 E
Katanda, *Shaba, Zaïre* **92** 7 52 S 24 13 E
Katangi, *India* **50** 21 56N 79 50 E
Katangli, *U.S.S.R.* **41** 51 42N 143 14 E
Katapakishi, *Zaïre* **95** 8 15 S 22 49 E
Katavi Swamp, *Tanzania* **92** 6 50 S 31 10 E
Katchiungo, *Angola* **95** 12 35 S 16 13 E
Kateríni, *Greece* **35** 40 18N 22 37 E
Katherîna, Gebel, *Egypt* **88** 28 30N 33 57 E
Katherine, *Australia* **78** 14 27 S 132 20 E
Kathiawar, *India* **48** 22 20N 71 0 E
Kati, *Mali* **90** 12 41N 8 4W
Katihar, *India* **49** 25 34N 87 36 E
Katima Mulilo, *Zambia* **96** 17 28 S 24 13 E
Katimbira, *Malawi* **93** 12 40 S 34 0 E
Katingan = Mendawai →, *Indonesia* **56** 3 30 S 113 0 E
Katiola, *Ivory C.* **90** 8 10N 5 10W
Katkopberg, *S. Africa* **96** 30 0 S 20 0 E
Katmandu, *Nepal* **49** 27 45N 85 20 E
Kato Akhaïa, *Greece* **35** 38 8N 21 33 E
Káto Stavros, *Greece* **35** 40 39N 23 43 E
Katol, *India* **50** 21 17N 78 38 E
Katompe, *Zaïre* **92** 6 2 S 26 23 E
Katonga →, *Uganda* **92** 0 34N 31 50 E
Katoomba, *Australia* **76** 33 41 S 150 19 E
Katowice, *Poland* **32** 50 17N 19 5 E
Katrine, L., *U.K.* **14** 56 15N 4 30W
Katrineholm, *Sweden* **10** 59 9N 16 12 E
Katsepe, *Madag.* **97** 15 45 S 46 15 E
Katsina, *Nigeria* **91** 13 0N 7 32 E
Katsina Ala →, *Nigeria* **91** 7 10N 9 20 E
Katsumoto, *Japan* **64** 33 51N 129 42 E
Katsuta, *Japan* **65** 36 25N 140 31 E
Katsuura, *Japan* **65** 35 10N 140 20 E
Katsuyama, *Japan* **65** 36 3N 136 30 E
Kattegatt, *Denmark* **11** 57 0N 11 20 E
Katumba, *Zaïre* **92** 7 40 S 25 17 E
Katunga, *Australia* **74** 35 58 S 145 28 E
Katungu, *Kenya* **92** 2 55 S 40 3 E
Katwa, *India* **49** 23 30N 88 5 E
Katwijk-aan-Zee, *Neths.* **16** 52 12N 4 24 E
Kauai, *U.S.A.* **112** 22 0N 159 30W
Kauai Chan., *U.S.A.* **112** 21 45N 158 50W
Kaub, *W. Germany* **31** 50 5N 7 46 E
Kaufbeuren, *W. Germany* **31** 47 50N 10 37 E
Kaufman, *U.S.A.* **121** 32 35N 96 20W
Kaukauna, *U.S.A.* **114** 44 20N 88 13W
Kaukauveld, *Namibia* **96** 20 0 S 20 15 E
Kaukonen, *Finland* **8** 67 31N 24 53 E
Kauliranta, *Finland* **8** 66 27N 23 41 E
Kaunas, *U.S.S.R.* **36** 54 54N 23 54 E
Kaunghein, *Burma* **52** 25 41N 95 26 E
Kaura Namoda, *Nigeria* **91** 12 37N 6 33 E
Kautokeino, *Norway* **8** 69 0N 23 4 E
Kavacha, *U.S.S.R.* **41** 60 16N 169 51 E
Kavadarci, *Yugoslavia* **35** 41 26N 22 3 E
Kavaja, *Albania* **35** 41 11N 19 33 E
Kavali, *India* **51** 14 55N 80 1 E
Kavála, *Greece* **35** 40 57N 24 28 E
Kavarna, *Bulgaria* **34** 43 26N 28 22 E
Kavieng, *Papua N. G.* **69** 2 36 S 150 51 E
Kavkaz, Bolshoi, *U.S.S.R.* **39** 42 50N 44 0 E
Kaw, *Fr. Guiana* **135** 4 30N 52 15W
Kawa, *Sudan* **89** 13 42N 32 34 E
Kawachi-Nagano, *Japan* **65** 34 28N 135 31 E
Kawagama L., *Canada* **106** 45 18N 78 45W
Kawagoe, *Japan* **65** 35 55N 139 29 E
Kawaguchi, *Japan* **65** 35 52N 139 45 E
Kawaihae, *U.S.A.* **112** 20 3N 155 50W
Kawakawa, *N.Z.* **80** 35 23 S 174 6 E
Kawambwa, *Zambia* **93** 9 48 S 29 3 E
Kawanoe, *Japan* **64** 34 1N 133 34 E
Kawarau, *N.Z.* **81** 45 3 S 168 45 E
Kawardha, *India* **49** 22 0N 81 17 E
Kawasaki, *Japan* **65** 35 35N 139 42 E
Kawau I., *N.Z.* **80** 36 25 S 174 52 E
Kawene, *Canada* **104** 48 45N 91 15W
Kawerau, *N.Z.* **80** 38 7 S 176 42 E
Kawhia Harbour, *N.Z.* **80** 38 5 S 174 51 E
Kawio, Kepulauan, *Indonesia* **57** 4 30N 125 30 E
Kawkareik, *Burma* **52** 16 33N 98 14 E
Kawlin, *Burma* **52** 23 47N 95 41 E
Kawthoolei □ = Kawthule □, *Burma* **52** 18 0N 97 30 E
Kawthule □, *Burma* **52** 18 0N 97 30 E
Kawya, *Burma* **52** 24 50N 94 58 E
Kaya, *Burkina Faso* **91** 13 4N 1 10W
Kayah □, *Burma* **52** 19 15N 97 15 E
Kayan, *Burma* **52** 16 54N 96 34 E
Kayan →, *Indonesia* **56** 2 55N 117 35 E
Kayankulam, *India* **51** 9 10N 76 33 E
Kaycee, *U.S.A.* **122** 43 45N 106 46W
Kayeli, *Indonesia* **57** 3 20 S 127 10 E
Kayenta, *U.S.A.* **123** 36 46N 110 15W
Kayes, *Congo* **95** 4 25 S 11 41 E
Kayes, *Mali* **90** 14 25N 11 30W
Kayima, *S. Leone* **90** 8 54N 11 15W
Kayl, *Lux.* **17** 49 29N 6 2 E
Kayoa, *Indonesia* **57** 0 1N 127 28 E
Kayomba, *Zambia* **93** 13 11 S 24 2 E
Kayoro, *Ghana* **91** 11 0N 1 28W
Kayrunnera, *Australia* **73** 30 40 S 142 30 E
Kaysatskoye, *U.S.S.R.* **39** 49 47N 46 49 E
Kayseri, *Turkey* **46** 38 45N 35 30 E
Kaysville, *U.S.A.* **122** 41 2N 111 58W
Kayuagung, *Indonesia* **56** 3 24 S 104 50 E
Kazachinskoye, *U.S.S.R.* **41** 56 16N 107 36 E
Kazachye, *U.S.S.R.* **41** 70 52N 135 58 E
Kazakh S.S.R. □, *U.S.S.R.* **38** 50 0N 70 0 E
Kazan, *U.S.S.R.* **37** 55 48N 49 3 E
Kazanlúk, *Bulgaria* **34** 42 38N 25 20 E
Kazanskaya, *U.S.S.R.* **39** 49 50N 41 10 E
Kazatin, *U.S.S.R.* **38** 49 45N 28 50 E
Kazbek, *U.S.S.R.* **39** 42 42N 44 30 E
Kāzerūn, *Iran* **47** 29 38N 51 40 E
Kazi Magomed, *U.S.S.R.* **39** 40 3N 49 0 E
Kazincbarcika, *Hungary* **33** 48 17N 20 36 E
Kazo, *Japan* **65** 36 7N 139 36 E
Kaztalovka, *U.S.S.R.* **39** 49 47N 48 43 E
Kazu, *Burma* **52** 25 27N 97 46 E
Kazumba, *Zaïre* **95** 6 25 S 22 5 E
Kazym →, *U.S.S.R.* **40** 63 54N 65 50 E
Kcynia, *Poland* **32** 53 0N 17 30 E
Ke-hsi Mansam, *Burma* **52** 21 56N 97 50 E
Ké-Macina, *Mali* **90** 13 58N 5 22W
Kéa, *Greece* **35** 37 35N 24 22 E
Keams Canyon, *U.S.A.* **123** 35 53N 110 9W
Kearney, *Canada* **108** 45 33N 79 13W
Kearney, *Mo., U.S.A.* **118** 39 22N 94 22W
Kearney, *Nebr., U.S.A.* **120** 40 45N 99 3W
Kébi, *Ivory C.* **90** 9 18N 6 37W
Kebili, *Tunisia* **86** 33 47N 9 0 E
Kebnekaise, *Sweden* **8** 67 53N 18 33 E
Kebri Dehar, *Ethiopia* **98** 6 45N 44 17 E
Kebumen, *Indonesia* **57** 7 42 S 109 40 E
Kecel, *Hungary* **33** 46 31N 19 16 E
Kechika →, *Canada* **110** 59 41N 127 12W
Kecskemét, *Hungary* **33** 46 57N 19 42 E
Kedada, *Ethiopia* **89** 5 25N 35 58 E
Kedainiai, *U.S.S.R.* **36** 55 15N 24 2 E
Kedgwick, *Canada* **105** 47 40N 67 20W
Kedia Hill, *Botswana* **96** 21 28 S 24 37 E
Kediri, *Indonesia* **57** 7 51 S 112 1 E
Kédougou, *Senegal* **90** 12 35N 12 10W
Kedzierzyn, *Poland* **32** 50 20N 18 12 E
Keeler, *U.S.A.* **124** 36 29N 117 52W
Keeley L., *Canada* **111** 54 54N 108 8W
Keeling Is. = Cocos Is., *Ind. Oc.* **53** 12 10 S 96 55 E
Keene, *Canada* **109** 44 15N 78 10W
Keene, *Calif., U.S.A.* **125** 35 13N 118 33W
Keene, *N.H., U.S.A.* **117** 42 57N 72 17W
Keeper Hill, *Ireland* **15** 52 46N 8 17W
Keepit Dam, *Australia* **77** 30 52 S 150 29 E
Keer-Weer, C., *Australia* **72** 14 0 S 141 32 E
Keerbergen, *Belgium* **17** 51 1N 4 38 E
Keeseville, *U.S.A.* **117** 44 29N 73 30W
Keeten Mastgat, *Neths.* **17** 51 36N 4 0 E
Keetmanshoop, *Namibia* **96** 26 35 S 18 8 E
Keewatin, *U.S.A.* **120** 47 23N 93 0W
Keewatin □, *Canada* **111** 63 20N 95 0W
Keewatin →, *Canada* **111** 56 29N 100 46W
Kefa □, *Ethiopia* **89** 6 55N 36 30 E
Kefallinía, *Greece* **35** 38 20N 20 30 E
Kefamenanu, *Indonesia* **57** 9 28 S 124 29 E
Kefar 'Eqron, *Israel* **44** 31 52N 34 49 E
Kefar Hasīdim, *Israel* **44** 32 47N 35 5 E
Kefar Nahum, *Israel* **44** 32 54N 35 34 E
Kefar Sava, *Israel* **44** 32 11N 34 54 E
Kefar Szold, *Israel* **44** 33 11N 35 39 E
Kefar Vitkin, *Israel* **44** 32 22N 34 53 E
Kefar Yehezqel, *Israel* **44** 32 34N 35 22 E
Kefar Yona, *Israel* **44** 32 20N 34 54 E
Kefar Zekharya, *Israel* **44** 31 43N 34 57 E
Kefar Zetim, *Israel* **44** 32 48N 35 27 E
Keffi, *Nigeria* **91** 8 55N 7 43 E
Keflavík, *Iceland* **8** 64 2N 22 35W
Keg River, *Canada* **110** 57 54N 117 55W
Kegalla, *Sri Lanka* **51** 7 15N 80 21 E
Kegaska, *Canada* **105** 50 9N 61 18W
Kehl, *W. Germany* **31** 48 34N 7 50 E
Keighley, *U.K.* **12** 53 52N 1 54W
Keimoes, *S. Africa* **96** 28 41 S 20 59 E
Keita, *Niger* **91** 14 46N 5 56 E
Keith, *Australia* **73** 36 6 S 140 20 E
Keith, *U.K.* **14** 57 33N 2 58W
Keith Arm, *Canada* **102** 64 20N 122 15W
Keithsburg, *U.S.A.* **118** 41 6N 90 56W
Kekri, *India* **48** 26 0N 75 10 E
Kël, *U.S.S.R.* **41** 69 30N 124 10 E
Kelamet, *Ethiopia* **89** 16 0N 38 30 E
Kelan, *China* **60** 38 43N 111 31 E
Kelang, *Malaysia* **55** 3 2N 101 26 E
Kelani Ganga →, *Sri Lanka* **51** 6 58N 79 50 E
Kelantan →, *Malaysia* **55** 6 13N 102 14 E
Kelheim, *W. Germany* **31** 48 58N 11 57 E
Kelibia, *Tunisia* **86** 36 50N 11 3 E
Kellé, *Congo* **94** 0 8 S 14 38 E
Keller, *U.S.A.* **122** 48 2N 118 44W
Kellerberrin, *Australia* **79** 31 36 S 117 38 E
Kellett C., *Canada* **144** 72 0N 126 0W
Kelleys I., *U.S.A.* **116** 41 35N 82 42W
Kellogg, *U.S.A.* **122** 47 30N 116 5W
Kelloselkä, *Finland* **8** 66 56N 28 53 E
Kells = Ceanannus Mor, *Ireland* **15** 53 42N 6 53W
Kélo, *Chad* **87** 9 10N 15 45 E
Kelowna, *Canada* **110** 49 50N 119 25W
Kelsey Bay, *Canada* **110** 50 25N 126 0W
Kelseyville, *U.S.A.* **124** 38 59N 122 50W
Kelso, *N.Z.* **81** 45 54 S 169 15 E
Kelso, *U.K.* **14** 55 36N 2 27W
Kelso, *U.S.A.* **124** 46 10N 122 57W
Keluang, *Malaysia* **55** 2 3N 103 18 E
Kelvington, *Canada* **111** 52 10N 103 30W
Kem, *U.S.S.R.* **40** 65 0N 34 38 E
Kem-Kem, *Morocco* **84** 30 40N 4 30W
Kema, *Indonesia* **57** 1 22N 125 8 E
Kemah, *Turkey* **46** 39 32N 39 5 E
Kemano, *Canada* **110** 53 35N 128 0W
Kemapyu, *Burma* **52** 18 49N 97 19 E
Kemasik, *Malaysia* **55** 4 25N 103 27 E
Kembé, *C.A.R.* **94** 4 36N 21 54 E
Kembolcha, *Ethiopia* **89** 11 2N 39 42 E
Kemerovo, *U.S.S.R.* **40** 55 20N 86 5 E
Kemi, *Finland* **8** 65 44N 24 34 E
Kemi älv = Kemijoki →, *Finland* **8** 65 47N 24 32 E
Kemijärvi, *Finland* **8** 66 43N 27 22 E
Kemijoki →, *Finland* **8** 65 47N 24 32 E
Kemmel, *Belgium* **17** 50 47N 2 50 E
Kemmerer, *U.S.A.* **122** 41 52N 110 30W
Kemp L., *U.S.A.* **121** 33 45N 99 15W
Kemp Land, *Antarctica* **143** 69 0 S 55 0 E
Kempsey, *Australia* **77** 31 1 S 152 50 E
Kempt, L., *Canada* **107** 47 25N 74 22W
Kempten, *W. Germany* **31** 47 42N 10 18 E
Kempton, *U.S.A.* **119** 40 16N 86 14W
Kemptville, *Canada* **109** 45 0N 75 38W
Kenadsa, *Algeria* **85** 31 48N 2 26W
Kendal, *Indonesia* **56** 6 56 S 110 14 E
Kendal, *U.K.* **12** 54 19N 2 44W
Kendall, *Australia* **77** 31 35 S 152 44 E
Kendall →, *Australia* **72** 14 4 S 141 35 E
Kendallville, *U.S.A.* **119** 41 25N 85 15W
Kendari, *Indonesia* **57** 3 50 S 122 30 E
Kendawangan, *Indonesia* **56** 2 32 S 110 17 E
Kende, *Nigeria* **91** 11 30N 4 12 E
Kendenup, *Australia* **79** 34 30 S 117 38 E
Kendrapara, *India* **50** 20 35N 86 30 E
Kendrew, *S. Africa* **96** 32 32 S 24 30 E
Kendrick, *U.S.A.* **122** 46 43N 116 41W
Kene Thao, *Laos* **54** 17 44N 101 10 E
Kenebri, *Australia* **77** 30 46 S 149 1 E
Kenedy, *U.S.A.* **121** 28 49N 97 51W
Kenema, *S. Leone* **90** 7 50N 11 14W
Keng Kok, *Laos* **54** 16 26N 105 12 E
Keng Tawng, *Burma* **52** 20 45N 98 18 E
Kengani, *Zaïre* **94** 2 59 S 17 36 E
Kenge, *Zaïre* **95** 4 50 S 17 4 E
Kengeja, *Tanzania* **92** 5 26 S 39 45 E
Kenhardt, *S. Africa* **96** 29 19 S 21 12 E
Kenitra, *Morocco* **84** 34 15N 6 40W
Kenli, *China* **61** 37 30N 118 20 E
Kenmare, *Ireland* **15** 51 52N 9 35W
Kenmare, *U.S.A.* **120** 48 40N 102 4W
Kenmare →, *Ireland* **15** 51 40N 10 0W
Kenmore, *Australia* **76** 34 44 S 149 45 E
Kennebec, *U.S.A.* **120** 43 56N 99 54W
Kennedy, *Zimb.* **93** 18 52 S 27 10 E
Kennedy Ra., *Australia* **79** 24 45 S 115 10 E
Kennet →, *U.K.* **13** 51 24N 0 58W
Kenneth Ra., *Australia* **79** 23 50 S 117 8 E
Kennett, *U.S.A.* **121** 36 7N 90 0W
Kennett River, *Australia* **74** 38 40 S 143 52 E
Kennewick, *U.S.A.* **122** 46 11N 119 2W
Kénogami, *Canada* **107** 48 25N 71 15W
Kenogami →, *Canada* **104** 51 6N 84 28W
Kénogami, L., *Canada* **107** 48 20N 71 23W
Kenora, *Canada* **111** 49 47N 94 29W
Kenosha, *U.S.A.* **119** 42 33N 87 48W
Kensington, *Canada* **105** 46 28N 63 34W
Kensington, *U.S.A.* **120** 39 48N 99 2W
Kensington Downs, *Australia* **72** 22 31 S 144 19 E
Kent, *Ohio, U.S.A.* **116** 41 8N 81 20W
Kent, *Oreg., U.S.A.* **122** 45 11N 120 45W
Kent, *Tex., U.S.A.* **121** 31 5N 104 12W
Kent, *Wash., U.S.A.* **124** 47 23N 122 14W
Kent □, *U.K.* **13** 51 12N 0 40 E
Kent Group, *Australia* **72** 39 30 S 147 20 E
Kent Pen., *Canada* **102** 68 30N 107 0W
Kentau, *U.S.S.R.* **40** 43 32N 68 36 E
Kentland, *U.S.A.* **119** 40 45N 87 25W
Kenton, *U.S.A.* **119** 40 40N 83 35W
Kentucky, *Australia* **77** 30 45 S 151 28 E
Kentucky □, *U.S.A.* **114** 37 20N 85 0W
Kentucky →, *U.S.A.* **119** 38 41N 85 11W
Kentucky L., *U.S.A.* **115** 36 25N 88 0W
Kentville, *Canada* **105** 45 6N 64 29W
Kentwood, *Mich., U.S.A.* **119** 30 56N 90 31W
Kentwood, *U.S.A.* **121** 31 0N 90 30W
Kenya ■, *Africa* **92** 1 0N 38 0 E
Kenya, Mt., *Kenya* **92** 0 10 S 37 18 E
Kenzou, *Cameroon* **94** 4 10N 15 2 E
Keo Neua, Deo, *Vietnam* **54** 18 23N 105 10 E
Keokuk, *U.S.A.* **118** 40 25N 91 24W
Keosauqua, *U.S.A.* **118** 40 44N 91 58W
Keota, *U.S.A.* **118** 41 22N 91 57W
Kep, *Cambodia* **55** 10 29N 104 19 E
Kep, *Vietnam* **54** 21 24N 106 16 E
Kepi, *Indonesia* **57** 6 32 S 139 19 E
Kepler Mts., *N.Z.* **81** 45 25 S 167 20 E
Kępno, *Poland* **32** 51 18N 17 58 E
Kepsut, *Turkey* **46** 39 40N 28 9 E
Kerala □, *India* **51** 11 0N 76 15 E
Keran, *Pakistan* **49** 34 35N 73 59 E
Kerang, *Australia* **74** 35 40 S 143 55 E
Keraudren, C., *Australia* **78** 19 58 S 119 45 E
Keravat, *Papua N. G.* **69** 4 17 S 152 2 E
Kerch, *U.S.S.R.* **38** 45 20N 36 20 E
Kerchenskiy Proliv, *U.S.S.R.* **38** 45 10N 36 30 E
Kerchoual, *Mali* **91** 17 12N 0 20 E
Kerem Maharal, *Israel* **44** 32 39N 34 59 E
Kerema, *Papua N. G.* **69** 7 58 S 145 50 E
Keren, *Ethiopia* **89** 15 45N 38 28 E
Kerewan, *Gambia* **90** 13 29N 16 10W
Kerguelen, *Ind. Oc.* **53** 49 15 S 69 10 E
Keri Kera, *Sudan* **89** 12 21N 32 42 E
Kericho, *Kenya* **92** 0 22 S 35 15 E
Kericho □, *Kenya* **92** 0 30 S 35 15 E
Kerikeri, *N.Z.* **80** 35 12 S 173 59 E
Kerinci, *Indonesia* **56** 1 40 S 101 15 E
Kerkdriel, *Neths.* **16** 51 47N 5 20 E
Kerkenna, Is., *Tunisia* **86** 34 48N 11 11 E
Kerki, *U.S.S.R.* **40** 37 50N 65 12 E
Kérkira, *Greece* **35** 39 38N 19 50 E
Kerkrade, *Neths.* **17** 50 53N 6 4 E
Kerma, *Sudan* **88** 19 33N 30 32 E
Kermadec Is., *Pac. Oc.* **66** 30 0 S 178 15W
Kermadec Trench, *Pac. Oc.* **66** 30 30 S 176 0W
Kermān, *Iran* **47** 30 15N 57 1 E
Kerman, *U.S.A.* **124** 36 43N 120 4W
Kermān □, *Iran* **47** 30 0N 57 0 E
Kermānshāh = Bākhtarān, *Iran* **46** 34 23N 47 0 E
Kermit, *U.S.A.* **121** 31 56N 103 3W
Kern →, *U.S.A.* **125** 35 16N 119 18W
Kernville, *U.S.A.* **125** 35 45N 118 26W
Keroh, *Malaysia* **55** 5 43N 101 1 E
Kerrabee, *Australia* **76** 32 24 S 150 19 E
Kerrobert, *Canada* **111** 51 56N 109 8W
Kerrville, *U.S.A.* **121** 30 1N 99 8W
Kerry □, *Ireland* **15** 52 7N 9 35W
Kerry Hd., *Ireland* **15** 52 26N 9 56W
Kersa, *Ethiopia* **89** 9 28N 41 48 E
Kerteminde, *Denmark* **11** 55 28N 10 39 E
Kertosono, *Indonesia* **57** 7 38 S 112 9 E
Kerulen →, *Asia* **62** 48 48N 117 0 E
Kerzaz, *Algeria* **85** 29 29N 1 37W
Kesagami →, *Canada* **104** 51 40N 79 45W
Kesagami L., *Canada* **104** 50 23N 80 15W
Keski-Suomen lääni □, *Finland* **8** 62 0N 25 30 E
Kessel, *Belgium* **17** 51 8N 4 38 E
Kessel, *Neths.* **17** 51 17N 6 3 E
Kessel-Lo, *Belgium* **17** 50 53N 4 43 E
Kestell, *S. Africa* **97** 28 17 S 28 42 E
Kestenga, *U.S.S.R.* **40** 66 0N 31 50 E
Kesteren, *Neths.* **16** 51 56N 5 34 E

Keswick, *Canada* **108** 44 15N 79 28W
Keswick, *U.K.* **12** 54 35N 3 9W
Keszthely, *Hungary* **33** 46 50N 17 15 E
Ket →, *U.S.S.R.* **40** 58 55N 81 32 E
Keta, *Ghana* **91** 5 49N 1 0 E
Ketapang, *Indonesia* **56** 1 55 S 110 0 E
Ketchikan, *U.S.A.* **102** 55 25N 131 40W
Ketchum, *U.S.A.* **122** 43 41N 114 27W
Kete Krachi, *Ghana* **91** 7 46N 0 1W
Ketef, Khalîg Umm el, *Egypt* **88** 23 40N 35 35 E
Ketelmeer, *Neths.* **16** 52 36N 5 46 E
Keti Bandar, *Pakistan* **48** 24 8N 67 27 E
Ketri, *India* **48** 28 1N 75 50 E
Kętrzyn, *Poland* **32** 54 7N 21 22 E
Kettering, *U.K.* **13** 52 24N 0 44W
Kettering, *U.S.A.* **119** 39 41N 84 10W
Kettle →, *Canada* **111** 56 40N 89 34W
Kettle Falls, *U.S.A.* **122** 48 41N 118 2W
Kettle Pt., *Canada* **108** 43 13N 82 1W
Kettleman City, *U.S.A.* **124** 36 1N 119 58W
Kevin, *U.S.A.* **122** 48 45N 111 58W
Kewanee, *U.S.A.* **118** 41 18N 89 55W
Kewanna, *U.S.A.* **119** 41 1N 86 25W
Kewaunee, *U.S.A.* **114** 44 27N 87 30W
Keweenaw B., *U.S.A.* **104** 46 56N 88 23W
Keweenaw Pen., *U.S.A.* **114** 47 30N 88 0W
Keweenaw Pt., *U.S.A.* **114** 47 26N 87 40W
Key Harbour, *Canada* **108** 45 50N 80 45W
Key West, *U.S.A.* **128** 24 33N 82 0W
Keyesport, *U.S.A.* **118** 38 45N 89 17W
Keyser, *U.S.A.* **114** 39 26N 79 0W
Keystone, *U.S.A.* **120** 43 54N 103 27W
Keytesville, *U.S.A.* **118** 39 26N 92 56W
Kezhma, *U.S.S.R.* **41** 58 59N 101 9 E
Kežmarok, *Czech.* **32** 49 10N 20 28 E
Khabarovo, *U.S.S.R.* **40** 69 30N 60 30 E
Khabarovsk, *U.S.S.R.* **41** 48 30N 135 5 E
Khābūr →, *Syria* **46** 35 0N 40 30 E
Khachmas, *U.S.S.R.* **39** 41 31N 48 42 E
Khachrod, *India* **48** 23 25N 75 20 E
Khadari, W. el →, *Sudan* **89** 10 29N 27 15 E
Khadro, *Pakistan* **48** 26 11N 68 50 E
Khadyzhensk, *U.S.S.R.* **39** 44 26N 39 32 E
Khadzhilyangar, *India* **49** 35 45N 79 20 E
Khagaria, *India* **49** 25 30N 86 32 E
Khaipur, *Bahawalpur, Pakistan* **48** 29 34N 72 17 E
Khaipur, *Hyderabad, Pakistan* **48** 27 32N 68 49 E
Khair, *India* **48** 27 57N 77 46 E
Khairabad, *India* **49** 27 33N 80 47 E
Khairagarh, *India* **49** 21 27N 81 2 E
Khakhea, *Botswana* **96** 24 48 S 23 22 E
Khalfallah, *Algeria* **85** 34 20N 0 16 E
Khalilabad, *India* **49** 26 48N 83 5 E
Khalkhāl, *Iran* **46** 37 37N 48 32 E
Khálki, *Greece* **35** 39 36N 22 30 E
Khalkís, *Greece* **35** 38 27N 23 42 E
Khalmer-Sede = Tazovskiy, *U.S.S.R.* **40** 67 30N 78 44 E
Khalmer Yu, *U.S.S.R.* **40** 67 58N 65 1 E
Khalturin, *U.S.S.R.* **37** 58 40N 48 50 E
Kham Keut, *Laos* **54** 18 15N 104 43 E
Khamaria, *India* **50** 23 10N 80 52 E
Khamas Country, *Botswana* **96** 21 45 S 26 30 E
Khambat, G. of, *India* **48** 20 45N 72 30 E
Khambhaliya, *India* **48** 22 14N 69 41 E
Khambhat, *India* **48** 22 23N 72 33 E
Khamgaon, *India* **50** 20 42N 76 37 E
Khamilonísion, *Greece* **35** 35 50N 26 15 E
Khamir, *Yemen* **45** 16 0N 44 0 E
Khammam, *India* **50** 17 11N 80 6 E
Khān Yūnis, *Egypt* **44** 31 21N 34 18 E
Khānābād, *Afghan.* **47** 36 45N 69 5 E
Khānaqīn, *Iraq* **46** 34 23N 45 25 E
Khancoban, *Australia* **76** 36 12 S 148 7 E
Khandrá, *Greece* **35** 35 3N 26 8 E
Khandwa, *India* **50** 21 49N 76 22 E
Khandyga, *U.S.S.R.* **41** 62 42N 135 35 E
Khanewal, *Pakistan* **48** 30 20N 71 55 E
Khanh Duong, *Vietnam* **54** 12 44N 108 44 E
Khaniá, *Greece* **35** 35 30N 24 4 E
Khanion Kólpos, *Greece* **35** 35 33N 23 55 E
Khanka, Ozero, *Asia* **41** 45 0N 132 24 E
Khanna, *India* **48** 30 42N 76 16 E
Khanpur, *Pakistan* **48** 28 42N 70 35 E
Khanty-Mansiysk, *U.S.S.R.* **40** 61 0N 69 0 E
Khapalu, *Pakistan* **49** 35 10N 76 20 E
Khapcheranga, *U.S.S.R.* **41** 49 42N 112 24 E
Kharagpur, *India* **49** 22 20N 87 25 E
Kharan Kalat, *Pakistan* **47** 28 34N 65 21 E
Kharānaq, *Iran* **47** 32 20N 54 45 E
Kharda, *India* **50** 18 40N 75 34 E
Khardung La, *India* **49** 34 20N 77 43 E
Khârga, El Wâhât el, *Egypt* **88** 25 10N 30 35 E
Khargon, *India* **50** 21 45N 75 40 E
Kharit, Wadi el →, *Egypt* **88** 24 26N 33 3 E
Khārk, Jazireh, *Iran* **46** 29 15N 50 28 E
Kharkov, *U.S.S.R.* **38** 49 58N 36 20 E
Kharmanli, *Bulgaria* **35** 41 55N 25 55 E
Kharovsk, *U.S.S.R.* **37** 59 56N 40 13 E
Kharsānīya, *Si. Arabia* **46** 27 10N 49 10 E
Khartoum = El Khartûm, *Sudan* **89** 15 31N 32 35 E
Khasavyurt, *U.S.S.R.* **39** 43 16N 46 40 E
Khāsh, *Iran* **47** 28 15N 61 15 E
Khashm el Girba, *Sudan* **89** 14 59N 35 58 E
Khashuri, *U.S.S.R.* **39** 41 58N 43 35 E
Khasi Hills, *India* **52** 25 30N 91 30 E
Khaskovo, *Bulgaria* **35** 41 56N 25 30 E
Khatanga, *U.S.S.R.* **41** 72 0N 102 20 E
Khatanga →, *U.S.S.R.* **41** 72 55N 106 0 E
Khatangskiy, Zaliv, *U.S.S.R.* **144** 66 0N 112 0 E
Khatauli, *India* **48** 29 17N 77 43 E
Khatyrka, *U.S.S.R.* **41** 62 3N 175 15 E
Khaybar, Harrat, *Si. Arabia* **46** 25 45N 40 0 E
Khazzân Jabal el Awliyâ, *Sudan* **89** 15 24N 32 20 E
Khe Bo, *Vietnam* **54** 19 8N 104 41 E
Khe Long, *Vietnam* **54** 21 29N 104 46 E
Khed, *Maharashtra, India* **50** 17 43N 73 27 E
Khed, *Maharashtra, India* **50** 18 51N 73 56 E
Khekra, *India* **48** 28 52N 77 20 E
Khemarak Phouminville, *Cambodia* **55** 11 37N 102 59 E
Khemelnik, *U.S.S.R.* **38** 49 33N 27 58 E
Khemis Miliana, *Algeria* **85** 36 11N 2 14 E
Khemissèt, *Morocco* **84** 33 50N 6 1W
Khemmarat, *Thailand* **54** 16 10N 105 15 E
Khenchela, *Algeria* **85** 35 28N 7 11 E
Khenifra, *Morocco* **84** 32 58N 5 46W
Kherrata, *Algeria* **85** 36 27N 5 13 E
Kherson, *U.S.S.R.* **38** 46 35N 32 35 E
Khersónisos Akrotíri, *Greece* **35** 35 30N 24 10 E
Kheta →, *U.S.S.R.* **41** 71 54N 102 6 E
Khilok, *U.S.S.R.* **41** 51 30N 110 45 E
Khimki, *U.S.S.R.* **37** 55 50N 37 20 E
Khíos, *Greece* **35** 38 27N 26 9 E
Khiuma = Hiiumaa, *U.S.S.R.* **36** 58 50N 22 45 E
Khiva, *U.S.S.R.* **40** 41 30N 60 18 E
Khīyāv, *Iran* **46** 38 30N 47 45 E
Khlong Khlung, *Thailand* **54** 16 12N 99 43 E
Khmelnitskiy, *U.S.S.R.* **36** 49 23N 27 0 E
Khmer Rep. = Cambodia ■, *Asia* **54** 12 15N 105 0 E
Khoai, Hon, *Vietnam* **55** 8 26N 104 50 E
Khojak P., *Afghan.* **47** 30 55N 66 30 E
Khok Kloi, *Thailand* **55** 8 17N 98 19 E
Khok Pho, *Thailand* **55** 6 43N 101 6 E
Khokholskiy, *U.S.S.R.* **37** 51 35N 38 40 E
Kholm, *Afghan.* **47** 36 45N 67 40 E
Kholm, *U.S.S.R.* **36** 57 10N 31 15 E
Kholmsk, *U.S.S.R.* **41** 47 40N 142 5 E
Khomas Hochland, *Namibia* **96** 22 40 S 16 0 E
Khomayn, *Iran* **46** 33 40N 50 7 E
Khon Kaen, *Thailand* **54** 16 30N 102 47 E
Khong, *Laos* **54** 14 7N 105 51 E
Khong Sedone, *Laos* **54** 15 34N 105 49 E
Khonu, *U.S.S.R.* **41** 66 30N 143 12 E
Khoper →, *U.S.S.R.* **37** 49 30N 42 20 E
Khor el 'Atash, *Sudan* **89** 13 20N 34 15 E
Khóra, *Greece* **35** 37 3N 21 42 E
Khóra Sfakion, *Greece* **35** 35 15N 24 9 E
Khorāsān □, *Iran* **47** 34 0N 58 0 E
Khorat = Nakhon Ratchasima, *Thailand* **54** 14 59N 102 12 E
Khorat, Cao Nguyen, *Thailand* **54** 15 30N 102 50 E
Khorb el Ethel, *Algeria* **84** 28 30N 6 17W
Khorixas, *Namibia* **96** 20 16 S 14 59 E
Khorog, *U.S.S.R.* **40** 37 30N 71 36 E
Khorol, *U.S.S.R.* **38** 49 48N 33 15 E
Khorramābād, *Iran* **46** 33 30N 48 25 E
Khorrāmshahr, *Iran* **46** 30 29N 48 15 E
Khotin, *U.S.S.R.* **38** 48 31N 26 27 E
Khouribga, *Morocco* **84** 32 58N 6 57W
Khowai, *Bangla.* **52** 24 5N 91 40 E
Khoyniki, *U.S.S.R.* **36** 51 54N 29 55 E
Khrami →, *U.S.S.R.* **39** 41 30N 45 0 E
Khrenovoye, *U.S.S.R.* **37** 51 4N 40 16 E
Khristianá, *Greece* **35** 36 14N 25 13 E
Khu Khan, *Thailand* **54** 14 42N 104 12 E
Khūgīānī, *Afghan.* **48** 31 28N 65 14 E
Khulna, *Bangla.* **52** 22 45N 89 34 E
Khulna □, *Bangla.* **52** 22 25N 89 35 E
Khulo, *U.S.S.R.* **39** 41 33N 42 19 E
Khumago, *Botswana* **96** 20 26 S 24 32 E
Khunzakh, *U.S.S.R.* **39** 42 35N 46 42 E
Khūr, *Iran* **47** 32 55N 58 18 E
Khurai, *India* **48** 24 3N 78 23 E
Khurayş, *Si. Arabia* **46** 24 55N 48 5 E
Khūrīyā Mūrīyā, Jazā 'ir, *Oman* **45** 17 30N 55 58 E
Khurja, *India* **48** 28 15N 77 58 E
Khushab, *Pakistan* **48** 32 20N 72 20 E
Khuzdar, *Pakistan* **48** 27 52N 66 30 E
Khūzestān □, *Iran* **46** 31 0N 49 0 E
Khvalynsk, *U.S.S.R.* **37** 52 30N 48 2 E
Khvatovka, *U.S.S.R.* **37** 52 24N 46 32 E
Khvor, *Iran* **47** 33 45N 55 0 E
Khvormūj, *Iran* **47** 28 40N 51 30 E
Khvoy, *Iran* **46** 38 35N 45 0 E
Khvoynaya, *U.S.S.R.* **36** 58 58N 34 28 E
Khyber Pass, *Afghan.* **48** 34 10N 71 8 E
Kia, *Solomon Is.* **68** 7 32 S 158 26 E
Kiabukwa, *Zaïre* **93** 8 40 S 24 48 E
Kiadho →, *India* **50** 19 37N 77 40 E
Kiama, *Australia* **76** 34 40 S 150 50 E
Kiamal, *Australia* **74** 34 58 S 142 18 E
Kiamba, *Phil.* **57** 6 2N 124 46 E
Kiambi, *Zaïre* **92** 7 15 S 28 0 E
Kiambu, *Kenya* **92** 1 8 S 36 50 E
Kiandra, *Australia* **76** 35 53 S 148 31 E
Kiangsi = Jiangxi □, *China* **59** 27 30N 116 0 E
Kiangsu = Jiangsu □, *China* **61** 33 0N 120 0 E
Kibæk, *Denmark* **11** 56 2N 8 51 E
Kibanga Port, *Uganda* **92** 0 10N 32 58 E
Kibangou, *Congo* **94** 3 26 S 12 22 E
Kibara, *Tanzania* **92** 2 8 S 33 30 E
Kibare, Mts., *Zaïre* **92** 8 25 S 27 10 E
Kibombo, *Zaïre* **92** 3 57 S 25 53 E
Kibondo, *Tanzania* **92** 3 35 S 30 45 E
Kibondo □, *Tanzania* **92** 4 0 S 30 55 E
Kibumbu, *Burundi* **92** 3 32 S 29 45 E
Kibungu, *Rwanda* **92** 2 10 S 30 32 E
Kibuye, *Burundi* **92** 3 39 S 29 59 E
Kibuye, *Rwanda* **92** 2 3 S 29 21 E
Kibwesa, *Tanzania* **92** 6 30 S 29 58 E
Kibwezi, *Kenya* **92** 2 27 S 37 57 E
Kichiga, *U.S.S.R.* **41** 59 50N 163 5 E
Kickabil, *Australia* **76** 31 50 S 148 30 E
Kicking Horse Pass, *Canada* **110** 51 28N 116 16W
Kidal, *Mali* **91** 18 26N 1 22 E
Kidderminster, *U.K.* **13** 52 24N 2 13W
Kidete, *Tanzania* **92** 6 25 S 37 17 E
Kidira, *Senegal* **90** 14 28N 12 13W
Kidnappers, C., *N.Z.* **80** 39 38 S 177 5 E
Kidston, *Australia* **72** 18 52 S 144 8 E
Kidugallo, *Tanzania* **92** 6 49 S 38 15 E
Kiel, *W. Germany* **30** 54 16N 10 8 E
Kiel Kanal = Nord-Ostsee Kanal, *W. Germany* **30** 54 15N 9 40 E
Kielce, *Poland* **32** 50 52N 20 42 E
Kieldrecht, *Belgium* **17** 51 17N 4 11 E
Kieler Bucht, *W. Germany* **30** 54 30N 10 30 E
Kien Binh, *Vietnam* **55** 9 55N 105 19 E
Kien Tan, *Vietnam* **55** 10 7N 105 17 E
Kienge, *Zaïre* **93** 10 30 S 27 30 E
Kiessé, *Niger* **91** 13 29N 4 1 E
Kieta, *Papua N. G.* **69** 6 12 S 155 36 E
Kiev = Kiyev, *U.S.S.R.* **36** 50 30N 30 28 E
Kiewa, *Australia* **75** 36 15 S 147 0 E
Kiewa →, *Australia* **75** 36 33 S 147 4 E
Kifār 'Aşyūn, *Jordan* **44** 31 39N 35 7 E
Kiffa, *Mauritania* **90** 16 37N 11 24W
Kifisiá, *Greece* **35** 38 4N 23 49 E
Kifissós →, *Greece* **35** 38 35N 23 20 E
Kifrī, *Iraq* **46** 34 45N 45 0 E
Kigali, *Rwanda* **92** 1 59 S 30 4 E
Kigarama, *Tanzania* **92** 1 1 S 31 50 E
Kigoma □, *Tanzania* **92** 5 0 S 30 0 E
Kigoma-Ujiji, *Tanzania* **92** 4 55 S 29 36 E
Kigomasha, Ras, *Tanzania* **92** 4 58 S 38 58 E
Kihee, *Australia* **73** 27 23 S 142 37 E
Kihikihi, *N.Z.* **80** 38 2 S 175 22 E
Kii-Hantō, *Japan* **65** 34 0N 135 45 E
Kii-Sanchi, *Japan* **65** 34 20N 136 0 E
Kii-Suidō, *Japan* **64** 33 40N 135 0 E
Kikinda, *Yugoslavia* **33** 45 50N 20 30 E
Kikládhes, *Greece* **35** 37 20N 24 30 E
Kikori, *Papua N. G.* **69** 7 25 S 144 15 E
Kikori →, *Papua N. G.* **69** 7 38 S 144 20 E
Kikuchi, *Japan* **64** 32 59N 130 47 E
Kikwit, *Zaïre* **95** 5 0 S 18 45 E
Kilafors, *Sweden* **10** 61 14N 16 36 E
Kilakkarai, *India* **51** 9 12N 78 47 E
Kílalki, *Greece* **35** 36 15N 27 35 E
Kilauea Crater, *U.S.A.* **112** 19 24N 155 17W
Kilcoy, *Australia* **73** 26 59 S 152 30 E
Kildare, *Ireland* **15** 53 10N 6 50W
Kildare □, *Ireland* **15** 53 10N 6 50W
Kilembe, *Zaïre* **95** 5 42 S 19 55 E
Kilgore, *U.S.A.* **121** 32 22N 94 55W
Kilifi, *Kenya* **92** 3 40 S 39 48 E
Kilifi □, *Kenya* **92** 3 30 S 39 40 E
Kilimanjaro, *Tanzania* **92** 3 7 S 37 20 E
Kilimanjaro □, *Tanzania* **92** 4 0 S 38 0 E
Kilinailau, Is., *Papua N. G.* **69** 4 45 S 155 20 E
Kilindini, *Kenya* **92** 4 4 S 39 40 E
Kilis, *Turkey* **46** 36 50N 37 10 E
Kiliya, *U.S.S.R.* **38** 45 28N 29 16 E
Kilju, *N. Korea* **61** 40 57N 129 25 E
Kilkee, *Ireland* **15** 52 41N 9 40W
Kilkenny, *Ireland* **15** 52 40N 7 17W
Kilkenny □, *Ireland* **15** 52 35N 7 15W
Kilkieran B., *Ireland* **15** 53 18N 9 45W
Kilkís, *Greece* **35** 40 58N 22 57 E
Killala, *Ireland* **15** 54 13N 9 12W
Killala B., *Ireland* **15** 54 20N 9 12W
Killaloe, *Ireland* **15** 52 48N 8 28W
Killaloe Sta., *Canada* **106** 45 33N 77 25W
Killam, *Canada* **110** 52 47N 111 51W
Killarney, *Queens., Australia* **77** 28 20 S 152 18 E
Killarney, *Vic., Australia* **74** 38 21 S 142 18 E
Killarney, *Canada* **108** 45 55N 81 30W
Killarney, *Ireland* **15** 52 2N 9 30W
Killarney, Lakes of, *Ireland* **15** 52 0N 9 30W
Killarney Prov. Park, *Canada* **108** 46 2N 81 35W
Killary Harbour, *Ireland* **15** 53 38N 9 52W
Killdeer, *Canada* **111** 49 6N 106 22W
Killdeer, *U.S.A.* **120** 47 26N 102 48W
Killeen, *U.S.A.* **121** 31 7N 97 45W
Killiecrankie, Pass of, *U.K.* **14** 56 44N 3 46W
Killin, *U.K.* **14** 56 28N 4 20W
Killíni, *Ilía, Greece* **35** 37 55N 21 8 E
Killíni, *Korinthía, Greece* **35** 37 54N 22 25 E
Killybegs, *Ireland* **15** 54 38N 8 26W
Kilmany, *Australia* **75** 38 8 S 146 55 E
Kilmar, *Canada* **106** 45 46N 74 37W
Kilmarnock, *U.K.* **14** 55 36N 4 30W
Kilmez, *U.S.S.R.* **37** 56 58N 50 55 E
Kilmez →, *U.S.S.R.* **37** 56 58N 50 28 E
Kilmore, *Australia* **74** 37 25 S 144 53 E
Kilondo, *Tanzania* **93** 9 45 S 34 20 E
Kilosa, *Tanzania* **92** 6 48 S 37 0 E
Kilosa □, *Tanzania* **92** 6 48 S 37 0 E
Kilrush, *Ireland* **15** 52 39N 9 30W
Kilsmo, *Sweden* **10** 59 6N 15 35 E
Kilwa □, *Tanzania* **93** 9 0 S 39 0 E
Kilwa Kisiwani, *Tanzania* **93** 8 58 S 39 32 E
Kilwa Kivinje, *Tanzania* **93** 8 45 S 39 25 E
Kilwa Masoko, *Tanzania* **93** 8 55 S 39 30 E
Kim, *U.S.A.* **121** 37 18N 103 20W
Kimaam, *Indonesia* **57** 7 58 S 138 53 E
Kimamba, *Tanzania* **92** 6 45 S 37 10 E
Kimba, *Australia* **73** 33 8 S 136 23 E
Kimball, *Nebr., U.S.A.* **120** 41 17N 103 40W
Kimball, *S. Dak., U.S.A.* **120** 43 47N 98 57W
Kimbe, *Papua N. G.* **69** 5 33 S 150 11 E
Kimbe B., *Papua N. G.* **69** 5 15 S 150 30 E
Kimberley, *Canada* **110** 49 40N 115 59W
Kimberley, *S. Africa* **96** 28 43 S 24 46 E
Kimberley Downs, *Australia* **78** 17 24 S 124 22 E
Kimberly, *U.S.A.* **122** 42 33N 114 25W
Kimchaek, *N. Korea* **61** 40 40N 129 10 E
Kimchŏn, *S. Korea* **61** 36 11N 128 4 E
Kími, *Greece* **35** 38 38N 24 6 E
Kímolos, *Greece* **35** 36 48N 24 37 E
Kimovsk, *U.S.S.R.* **37** 54 0N 38 29 E
Kimparana, *Mali* **90** 12 48N 5 0W
Kimry, *U.S.S.R.* **37** 56 55N 37 15 E
Kimsquit, *Canada* **110** 52 45N 126 57W
Kimstad, *Sweden* **11** 58 35N 15 58 E
Kimvula, *Zaïre* **95** 5 44 S 15 58 E
Kinabalu, *Malaysia* **56** 6 3N 116 14 E
Kínaros, *Greece* **35** 36 59N 26 15 E
Kinaskan L., *Canada* **110** 57 38N 130 8W
Kinbasket L., *Canada* **110** 52 0N 118 10W
Kincaid, *Canada* **111** 49 40N 107 0W
Kincaid, *U.S.A.* **118** 39 35N 89 25W
Kincardine, *Canada* **108** 44 10N 81 40W
Kinda, *Kasai Or., Zaïre* **93** 9 18 S 25 4 E
Kinda, *Shaba, Zaïre* **95** 4 47 S 21 48 E
Kindersley, *Canada* **111** 51 30N 109 10W
Kindia, *Guinea* **90** 10 0N 12 52W
Kindu, *Zaïre* **92** 2 55 S 25 50 E
Kinel, *U.S.S.R.* **37** 53 15N 50 40 E
Kineshma, *U.S.S.R.* **37** 57 30N 42 5 E
Kinesi, *Tanzania* **92** 1 25 S 33 50 E
King →, *Australia* **75** 36 24 S 146 23 E
King, L., *Vic., Australia* **75** 37 55 S 147 45 E
King, L., *W. Austral., Australia* **79** 33 10 S 119 35 E
King, Mt., *Australia* **72** 25 10 S 147 30 E
King City, *Calif., U.S.A.* **124** 36 11N 121 8W
King City, *Mo., U.S.A.* **118** 40 3N 94 31W
King Cr. →, *Australia* **72** 24 35 S 139 30 E
King Edward →, *Australia* **78** 14 14 S 126 35 E
King Frederick VI Land = Kong Frederik VI.s Kyst, *Greenland* **144** 63 0N 43 0W
King George B., *Falk. Is.* **142** 51 30 S 60 30W
King George I., *Antarctica* **143** 60 0 S 60 0W
King George Is., *Canada* **103** 57 20N 80 30W
King I. = Kadan Kyun, *Burma* **56** 12 30N 98 20 E
King I., *Australia* **72** 39 50 S 144 0 E
King I., *Canada* **110** 52 10N 127 40W
King Leopold Ranges, *Australia* **78** 17 30 S 125 45 E
King Sd., *Australia* **78** 16 50 S 123 20 E
King William I., *Canada* **102** 69 10N 97 25W
King William's Town, *S. Africa* **96** 32 51 S 27 22 E
Kingaroy, *Australia* **73** 26 32 S 151 51 E
Kingfisher, *U.S.A.* **121** 35 50N 97 55W
Kingisepp, *Estonia, U.S.S.R.* **36** 58 15N 22 30 E
Kingisepp, *R.S.F.S.R., U.S.S.R.* **36** 59 25N 28 40 E
Kinglake, *Australia* **74** 37 31 S 145 19 E
Kinglake West, *Australia* **74** 37 31 S 145 19 E
Kingman, *Ariz., U.S.A.* **125** 35 12N 114 2W

Kingman, *Ind., U.S.A.* **119** 39 58N 87 18W
Kingman, *Kans., U.S.A.* **121** 37 41N 98 9W
Kings →, *U.S.A.* **124** 36 10N 119 50W
Kings Canyon National Park, *U.S.A.* **124** 37 0N 118 35W
King's Lynn, *U.K.* **12** 52 45N 0 25 E
Kings Mountain, *U.S.A.* **115** 35 13N 81 20W
King's Peak, *U.S.A.* **122** 40 46N 110 27W
Kingsbridge, *U.K.* **13** 50 17N 3 46W
Kingsburg, *U.S.A.* **124** 36 35N 119 36W
Kingsbury, *U.S.A.* **119** 41 31N 86 42W
Kingscliff-Fingal, *Australia* **77** 28 16 S 153 34 E
Kingscote, *Australia* **73** 35 40 S 137 38 E
Kingscourt, *Ireland* **15** 53 55N 6 48W
Kingsey Falls, *Canada* **107** 45 51N 72 4W
Kingsley, *U.S.A.* **120** 42 37N 95 58W
Kingsport, *U.S.A.* **115** 36 33N 82 36W
Kingston, *Canada* **109** 44 14N 76 30W
Kingston, *Jamaica* **128** 18 0N 76 50W
Kingston, *N.Z.* **81** 45 20 S 168 43 E
Kingston, *Mo., U.S.A.* **118** 39 38N 94 2W
Kingston, *N.Y., U.S.A.* **117** 41 55N 74 0W
Kingston, *Pa., U.S.A.* **117** 41 19N 75 58W
Kingston, *R.I., U.S.A.* **117** 41 29N 71 30W
Kingston Pk., *U.S.A.* **125** 35 45N 115 54W
Kingston South East, *Australia* **73** 36 51 S 139 55 E
Kingston-upon-Thames, *U.K.* **13** 51 23N 0 20W
Kingstown, *Australia* **77** 30 29 S 151 6 E
Kingstown, *St. Vincent* **129** 13 10N 61 10W
Kingstree, *U.S.A.* **115** 33 40N 79 48W
Kingsville, *Canada* **108** 42 2N 82 45W
Kingsville, *U.S.A.* **121** 27 30N 97 53W
Kingussie, *U.K.* **14** 57 5N 4 2W
Kinistino, *Canada* **111** 52 57N 105 2W
Kinkala, *Congo* **95** 4 18 S 14 49 E
Kinki □, *Japan* **65** 33 30N 136 0 E
Kinleith, *N.Z.* **80** 38 20 S 175 56 E
Kinmount, *Canada* **109** 44 48N 78 45W
Kinmundy, *U.S.A.* **119** 38 46N 88 51W
Kinna, *Sweden* **11** 57 32N 12 42 E
Kinnaird, *Canada* **110** 49 17N 117 39W
Kinnairds Hd., *U.K.* **14** 57 40N 2 0W
Kinnared, *Sweden* **11** 57 2N 13 7 E
Kinneret, *Israel* **44** 32 44N 35 34 E
Kino, *Mexico* **126** 28 45N 111 59W
Kinoje →, *Canada* **104** 52 8N 81 25W
Kinomoto, *Japan* **65** 35 30N 136 13 E
Kinoni, *Uganda* **92** 0 41 S 30 28 E
Kinrooi, *Belgium* **17** 51 9N 5 45 E
Kinross, *U.K.* **14** 56 13N 3 25W
Kinsale, *Ireland* **15** 51 42N 8 31W
Kinsale, Old Hd. of, *Ireland* **15** 51 37N 8 32W
Kinshasa, *Zaïre* **95** 4 20 S 15 15 E
Kinsley, *U.S.A.* **121** 37 57N 99 30W
Kinston, *U.S.A.* **115** 35 18N 77 35W
Kintampo, *Ghana* **91** 8 5N 1 41W
Kintap, *Indonesia* **56** 3 51 S 115 13 E
Kintore Ra., *Australia* **78** 23 15 S 128 47 E
Kintyre, *U.K.* **14** 55 30N 5 35W
Kintyre, Mull of, *U.K.* **14** 55 17N 5 55W
Kinu, *Burma* **52** 22 46N 95 37 E
Kinu-Gawa →, *Japan* **65** 35 36N 139 57 E
Kinushseo →, *Canada* **104** 55 15N 83 45W
Kinuso, *Canada* **110** 55 20N 115 25W
Kinyangiri, *Tanzania* **92** 4 25 S 34 37 E
Kinzig →, *W. Germany* **31** 48 37N 7 49 E
Kinzua, *U.S.A.* **116** 41 52N 78 58W
Kinzua Dam, *U.S.A.* **116** 41 53N 79 0W
Kiosk, *Canada* **109** 46 6N 78 53W
Kiowa, *Kans., U.S.A.* **121** 37 3N 98 30W
Kiowa, *Okla., U.S.A.* **121** 34 45N 95 50W
Kipahigan L., *Canada* **111** 55 20N 101 55W
Kipanga, *Tanzania* **92** 6 15 S 35 20 E
Kiparissía, *Greece* **35** 37 15N 21 40 E
Kiparissiakós Kólpos, *Greece* **35** 37 25N 21 25 E
Kipawa, *Canada* **106** 46 47N 78 59W
Kipawa, Parc de, *Canada* **106** 47 0N 78 50W
Kipawa L., *Canada* **106** 46 50N 79 0W
Kipembawe, *Tanzania* **92** 7 38 S 33 27 E
Kipengere Ra., *Tanzania* **93** 9 12 S 34 15 E
Kipili, *Tanzania* **92** 7 28 S 30 32 E
Kipini, *Kenya* **92** 2 30 S 40 32 E
Kipling, *Canada* **111** 50 6N 102 38W
Kippure, *Ireland* **15** 53 11N 6 23W
Kipushi, *Zaïre* **93** 11 48 S 27 12 E
Kira Kira, *Solomon Is.* **68** 10 27 S 161 56 E
Kirandul, *India* **50** 18 33N 81 10 E
Kiratpur, *India* **48** 29 32N 78 12 E
Kirchhain, *W. Germany* **30** 50 49N 8 54 E
Kirchheim, *W. Germany* **31** 48 38N 9 20 E
Kirchheim-Bolanden, *W. Germany* **31** 49 40N 8 0 E
Kirensk, *U.S.S.R.* **41** 57 50N 107 55 E
Kirgella Rocks, *Australia* **79** 30 5 S 122 50 E
Kirgiz S.S.R. □, *U.S.S.R.* **40** 42 0N 75 0 E
Kiri, *Zaïre* **94** 1 29 S 19 0 E
Kiri Buru, *India* **50** 22 0N 85 0 E
Kiribati ■, *Pac. Oc.* **66** 1 0N 176 0 E
Kırıkkale, *Turkey* **46** 39 51N 33 32 E
Kirikopuni, *N.Z.* **80** 35 50 S 174 1 E
Kirillov, *U.S.S.R.* **37** 59 51N 38 14 E
Kirin = Jilin, *China* **61** 43 44N 126 30 E
Kirin □ = Jilin □, *China* **61** 44 0N 124 0 E
Kirindi →, *Sri Lanka* **51** 6 15N 81 20 E
Kirishi, *U.S.S.R.* **36** 59 28N 31 59 E
Kirishima-Yama, *Japan* **64** 31 58N 130 55 E
Kiritimati, *Kiribati* **67** 1 58N 157 27W
Kirkcaldy, *U.K.* **14** 56 7N 3 10W
Kirkcudbright, *U.K.* **14** 54 50N 4 3W
Kirkee, *India* **50** 18 34N 73 56 E
Kirkenær, *Norway* **10** 60 27N 12 3 E
Kirkenes, *Norway* **8** 69 40N 30 5 E
Kirkfield, *Canada* **109** 44 34N 78 59W
Kirkintilloch, *U.K.* **14** 55 57N 4 10W
Kirkjubæjarklaustur, *Iceland* **8** 63 47N 18 4W
Kirkland, *Ariz., U.S.A.* **123** 34 29N 112 46W
Kirkland, *Ill., U.S.A.* **119** 42 5N 88 51W
Kirkland Lake, *Canada* **104** 48 9N 80 2W
Kırklareli, *Turkey* **46** 41 44N 27 15 E
Kirklin, *U.S.A.* **119** 40 12N 86 22W
Kirkliston Ra., *N.Z.* **81** 44 25 S 170 34 E
Kirksville, *U.S.A.* **118** 40 8N 92 35W
Kirkūk, *Iraq* **46** 35 30N 44 21 E
Kirkwall, *U.K.* **14** 58 59N 2 59W
Kirkwood, *S. Africa* **96** 33 22 S 25 15 E
Kirkwood, *U.S.A.* **118** 38 35N 90 24W
Kirlampudi, *India* **50** 17 12N 82 12 E
Kirn, *W. Germany* **31** 49 46N 7 29 E
Kirov, *R.S.F.S.R., U.S.S.R.* **36** 54 3N 34 20 E
Kirov, *R.S.F.S.R., U.S.S.R.* **37** 58 35N 49 40 E
Kirovabad, *U.S.S.R.* **39** 40 45N 46 20 E
Kirovakan, *U.S.S.R.* **39** 40 48N 44 30 E
Kirovo-Chepetsk, *U.S.S.R.* **37** 58 28N 50 0 E
Kirovograd, *U.S.S.R.* **38** 48 35N 32 20 E
Kirovsk, *R.S.F.S.R., U.S.S.R.* **40** 67 48N 33 50 E
Kirovsk, *Turkmen S.S.R., U.S.S.R.* **40** 37 42N 60 23 E
Kirovsk, *Ukraine S.S.R., U.S.S.R.* **39** 48 35N 38 30 E
Kirovski, *U.S.S.R.* **39** 45 51N 48 11 E
Kirovskiy, *U.S.S.R.* **41** 54 27N 155 42 E
Kirriemuir, *U.K.* **14** 56 41N 3 0W
Kirsanov, *U.S.S.R.* **37** 52 35N 42 40 E
Kırşehir, *Turkey* **46** 39 14N 34 5 E
Kirstonia, *S. Africa* **96** 25 30 S 23 45 E
Kirtachi, *Niger* **91** 12 52N 2 30 E
Kīrteh, *Afghan.* **47** 32 15N 63 0 E
Kirthar Range, *Pakistan* **48** 27 0N 67 0 E
Kiruna, *Sweden* **8** 67 52N 20 15 E
Kirundu, *Zaïre* **92** 0 50 S 25 35 E
Kirup, *Australia* **79** 33 40 S 115 50 E
Kirya, *U.S.S.R.* **37** 55 5N 46 45 E
Kiryū, *Japan* **65** 36 24N 139 20 E
Kisa, *Sweden* **11** 58 0N 15 39 E
Kisaga, *Tanzania* **92** 4 30 S 34 23 E
Kisalaya, *Nic.* **128** 14 40N 84 3W
Kisambo, *Zaïre* **95** 6 25 S 18 14 E
Kisanga, *Zaïre* **92** 2 30N 26 35 E
Kisangani, *Zaïre* **92** 0 35N 25 15 E
Kisantu, *Zaïre* **95** 5 7 S 15 5 E
Kisar, *Indonesia* **57** 8 5 S 127 10 E
Kisaran, *Indonesia* **56** 3 0N 99 37 E
Kisarawe, *Tanzania* **92** 6 53 S 39 0 E
Kisarawe □, *Tanzania* **92** 7 3 S 39 0 E
Kisarazu, *Japan* **65** 35 23N 139 55 E
Kisbér, *Hungary* **33** 47 30N 18 0 E
Kiselevsk, *U.S.S.R.* **40** 54 5N 86 39 E
Kishanganga →, *Pakistan* **49** 34 18N 73 28 E
Kishanganj, *India* **49** 26 3N 88 14 E
Kishangarh, *India* **48** 27 50N 70 30 E
Kishi, *Nigeria* **91** 9 1N 3 52 E
Kishinev, *U.S.S.R.* **38** 47 0N 28 50 E
Kishiwada, *Japan* **65** 34 28N 135 22 E
Kishon, *Israel* **44** 32 49N 35 2 E
Kishorganj, *Bangla.* **52** 24 26N 90 40 E
Kishtwar, *India* **49** 33 20N 75 48 E
Kishwaukee →, *U.S.A.* **118** 42 12N 89 8W
Kisii, *Kenya* **92** 0 40 S 34 45 E
Kisii □, *Kenya* **92** 0 40 S 34 45 E
Kisiju, *Tanzania* **92** 7 23 S 39 19 E
Kısır, Dağ, *Turkey* **39** 41 0N 43 5 E
Kisizi, *Uganda* **92** 1 0 S 29 58 E
Kiska I., *U.S.A.* **102** 52 0N 177 30 E
Kiskatinaw →, *Canada* **110** 56 8N 120 10W
Kiskittogisu L., *Canada* **111** 54 13N 98 20W
Kiskörös, *Hungary* **33** 46 37N 19 20 E
Kiskundorozsma, *Hungary* **33** 46 16N 20 5 E
Kiskunfélegyháza, *Hungary* **33** 46 42N 19 53 E
Kiskunhalas, *Hungary* **33** 46 28N 19 37 E
Kiskunmajsa, *Hungary* **33** 46 30N 19 48 E
Kislovodsk, *U.S.S.R.* **39** 43 50N 42 45 E
Kismayu = Chisimaio, *Somali Rep.* **98** 0 22 S 42 32 E
Kiso-Gawa →, *Japan* **65** 35 20N 136 45 E
Kiso-Sammyaku, *Japan* **65** 35 45N 137 45 E
Kisofukushima, *Japan* **65** 35 52N 137 43 E
Kisoro, *Uganda* **92** 1 17 S 29 48 E
Kispest, *Hungary* **33** 47 27N 19 9 E
Kissidougou, *Guinea* **90** 9 5N 10 0W
Kissimmee, *U.S.A.* **115** 28 18N 81 22W
Kissimmee →, *U.S.A.* **115** 27 20N 80 55W
Kississing L., *Canada* **111** 55 10N 101 20W
Kistanje, *Yugoslavia* **27** 43 58N 15 55 E
Kisújszállás, *Hungary* **33** 47 12N 20 50 E
Kisuki, *Japan* **64** 35 17N 132 54 E
Kisumu, *Kenya* **92** 0 3 S 34 45 E
Kisvárda, *Hungary* **33** 48 14N 22 4 E
Kiswani, *Tanzania* **92** 4 5 S 37 57 E
Kiswere, *Tanzania* **93** 9 27 S 39 30 E
Kit Carson, *U.S.A.* **120** 38 48N 102 45W
Kita, *Mali* **90** 13 5N 9 25W
Kita-Ura, *Japan* **65** 36 0N 140 34 E
Kitab, *U.S.S.R.* **40** 39 7N 66 52 E
Kitakami-Gawa →, *Japan* **63** 38 25N 141 19 E
Kitakyūshū, *Japan* **64** 33 50N 130 50 E
Kitale, *Kenya* **92** 1 0N 35 0 E
Kitami, *Japan* **63** 43 48N 143 54 E
Kitangiri, L., *Tanzania* **92** 4 5 S 34 20 E
Kitano-Kaikyō, *Japan* **64** 34 17N 134 58 E
Kitaya, *Tanzania* **93** 10 38 S 40 8 E
Kitchener, *Australia* **79** 30 55 S 124 8 E
Kitchener, *Canada* **108** 43 27N 80 29W
Kitega = Gitega, *Burundi* **92** 3 26 S 29 56 E
Kitengo, *Zaïre* **92** 7 26 S 24 8 E
Kiteto □, *Tanzania* **92** 5 0 S 37 0 E
Kitgum, *Uganda* **92** 3 17N 32 52 E
Kíthira, *Greece* **35** 36 9N 23 0 E
Kíthnos, *Greece* **35** 37 26N 24 27 E
Kitikmeot □, *Canada* **102** 70 0N 110 0W
Kitimat, *Canada* **110** 54 3N 128 38W
Kitinen →, *Finland* **8** 67 34N 26 40 E
Kitiyab, *Sudan* **89** 17 13N 33 35 E
Kítros, *Greece* **35** 40 22N 22 34 E
Kitsuki, *Japan* **64** 33 25N 131 37 E
Kittakittaooloo, L., *Australia* **73** 28 3 S 138 14 E
Kittanning, *U.S.A.* **116** 40 49N 79 30W
Kittatinny Mts., *U.S.A.* **117** 41 0N 75 0W
Kittery, *U.S.A.* **117** 43 7N 70 42W
Kitui, *Kenya* **92** 1 17 S 38 0 E
Kitui □, *Kenya* **92** 1 30 S 38 25 E
Kitwe, *Zambia* **93** 12 54 S 28 13 E
Kitzbühel, *Austria* **31** 47 27N 12 24 E
Kitzingen, *W. Germany* **31** 49 44N 10 9 E
Kivalo, *Finland* **8** 66 18N 26 0 E
Kivarli, *India* **48** 24 33N 72 46 E
Kivu □, *Zaïre* **92** 3 10 S 27 0 E
Kivu, L., *Zaïre* **92** 1 48 S 29 0 E
Kiwai I., *Papua N. G.* **69** 8 35 S 143 30 E
Kiyev, *U.S.S.R.* **36** 50 30N 30 28 E
Kiyevskoye Vdkhr., *U.S.S.R.* **36** 51 0N 30 0 E
Kiziguru, *Rwanda* **92** 1 46 S 30 23 E
Kızıl Irmak →, *Turkey* **38** 39 15N 36 0 E
Kizil Jilga, *India* **49** 35 26N 78 50 E
Kizil Yurt, *U.S.S.R.* **39** 43 13N 46 54 E
Kızılcahamam, *Turkey* **38** 40 30N 32 30 E
Kizimkazi, *Tanzania* **92** 6 28 S 39 30 E
Kizlyar, *U.S.S.R.* **39** 43 51N 46 40 E
Kizyl-Arvat, *U.S.S.R.* **40** 38 58N 56 15 E
Kjellerup, *Denmark* **11** 56 17N 9 25 E
Kladanj, *Yugoslavia* **33** 44 14N 18 42 E
Kladno, *Czech.* **32** 50 10N 14 7 E
Kladovo, *Yugoslavia* **33** 44 36N 22 33 E
Klaeng, *Thailand* **54** 12 47N 101 39 E
Klagenfurt, *Austria* **33** 46 38N 14 20 E
Klagshamn, *Sweden* **11** 55 32N 12 53 E
Klagstorp, *Sweden* **11** 55 22N 13 23 E
Klaipeda, *U.S.S.R.* **36** 55 43N 21 10 E
Klamath →, *U.S.A.* **122** 41 40N 124 4W
Klamath Falls, *U.S.A.* **122** 42 20N 121 50W
Klamath Mts., *U.S.A.* **122** 41 20N 123 0W
Klangklang, *Burma* **52** 22 41N 93 26 E
Klanjec, *Yugoslavia* **27** 46 3N 15 45 E
Klappan →, *Canada* **110** 58 0N 129 43W
Klarälven →, *Sweden* **9** 59 23N 13 32 E
Klaten, *Indonesia* **57** 7 43 S 110 36 E
Klatovy, *Czech.* **32** 49 23N 13 18 E
Klawak, *U.S.A.* **110** 55 35N 133 0W
Klawer, *S. Africa* **96** 31 44 S 18 36 E
Klazienaveen, *Neths.* **16** 52 44N 7 0 E
Kleczew, *Poland* **32** 52 22N 18 9 E
Kleena Kleene, *Canada* **110** 52 0N 124 59W
Klein, *U.S.A.* **122** 46 26N 108 31W
Klein-Karas, *Namibia* **96** 27 33 S 18 7 E
Kleine Gette →, *Belgium* **17** 50 51N 5 6 E
Kleine Nete →, *Belgium* **17** 51 12N 4 46 E
Klekovača, *Yugoslavia* **27** 44 25N 16 32 E
Klenovec, *Czech.* **32** 48 36N 19 54 E
Klenovec, *Yugoslavia* **35** 41 32N 20 49 E
Klerksdorp, *S. Africa* **96** 26 53 S 26 38 E
Kletnya, *U.S.S.R.* **36** 53 23N 33 12 E
Kletsk, *U.S.S.R.* **36** 53 5N 26 45 E
Kletskaïa Kletskiy, *U.S.S.R.* **40** 49 20N 43 0 E
Kletskiy, *U.S.S.R.* **39** 49 20N 43 0 E
Kleve, *W. Germany* **30** 51 46N 6 10 E
Klickitat, *U.S.A.* **122** 45 50N 121 10W
Klickitat →, *U.S.A.* **124** 45 42N 121 17W
Klimovichi, *U.S.S.R.* **36** 53 36N 32 0 E
Klin, *U.S.S.R.* **37** 56 20N 36 48 E
Klinaklini →, *Canada* **110** 51 21N 125 40W
Klintsey, *U.S.S.R.* **36** 52 50N 32 10 E
Klipdale, *S. Africa* **96** 34 19 S 19 57 E
Klipplaat, *S. Africa* **96** 33 1 S 24 22 E
Klitmøller, *Denmark* **11** 57 3N 8 30 E
Kljajićevo, *Yugoslavia* **33** 45 45N 19 17 E
Ključ, *Yugoslavia* **27** 44 32N 16 48 E
Kłobuck, *Poland* **32** 50 55N 18 55 E
Kłodzko, *Poland* **32** 50 28N 16 38 E
Kloetinge, *Neths.* **17** 51 30N 3 56 E
Klondike, *Canada* **102** 64 0N 139 26W
Kloosterzande, *Neths.* **17** 51 22N 4 1 E
Klosterneuburg, *Austria* **33** 48 18N 16 19 E
Klosters, *Switz.* **31** 46 52N 9 52 E
Klötze, *E. Germany* **30** 52 38N 11 9 E
Klouto, *Togo* **91** 6 57N 0 44 E
Kluane L., *Canada* **102** 61 15N 138 40W
Kluczbork, *Poland* **32** 50 58N 18 12 E
Klundert, *Neths.* **17** 51 40N 4 32 E
Klyuchevskaya, Guba, *U.S.S.R.* **41** 55 50N 160 30 E
Knaresborough, *U.K.* **12** 54 1N 1 29W
Knee L., *Man., Canada* **111** 55 3N 94 45W
Knee L., *Sask., Canada* **111** 55 51N 107 0W
Kneïss, Is., *Tunisia* **86** 34 22N 10 18 E
Knesselare, *Belgium* **17** 51 9N 3 26 E
Knezha, *Bulgaria* **34** 43 30N 24 5 E
Knić, *Yugoslavia* **33** 43 53N 20 45 E
Knight Inlet, *Canada* **110** 50 45N 125 40W
Knighton, *U.K.* **13** 52 21N 3 2W
Knights Ferry, *U.S.A.* **124** 37 50N 120 40W
Knight's Landing, *U.S.A.* **124** 38 50N 121 43W
Knightstown, *U.S.A.* **119** 39 49N 85 32W
Knin, *Yugoslavia* **27** 44 1N 16 17 E
Knittelfeld, *Austria* **33** 47 13N 14 51 E
Knjaževac, *Yugoslavia* **33** 43 35N 22 18 E
Knob, C., *Australia* **79** 34 32 S 119 16 E
Knockmealdown Mts., *Ireland* **15** 52 16N 8 0W
Knokke, *Belgium* **17** 51 20N 3 17 E
Knowlton, *Canada* **107** 45 13N 72 31W
Knowsley, *Australia* **74** 36 50 S 144 35 E
Knox, *U.S.A.* **119** 41 18N 86 36W
Knox, C., *Canada* **110** 54 11N 133 5W
Knox City, *U.S.A.* **121** 33 26N 99 49W
Knox Coast, *Antarctica* **143** 66 30 S 108 0 E
Knoxville, *Iowa, U.S.A.* **118** 41 20N 92 55W
Knoxville, *Tenn., U.S.A.* **115** 35 58N 83 57W
Knutshø, *Norway* **10** 62 18N 9 41 E
Knysna, *S. Africa* **96** 34 2 S 23 2 E
Knyszyn, *Poland* **32** 53 20N 22 56 E
Ko Kha, *Thailand* **54** 18 11N 99 24 E
Kō-Saki, *Japan* **64** 34 5N 129 13 E
Ko Tao, *Thailand* **55** 10 6N 99 48 E
Koartac, *Canada* **103** 60 55N 69 40W
Koba, *Aru, Indonesia* **57** 6 37 S 134 37 E
Koba, *Bangka, Indonesia* **56** 2 26 S 106 14 E
Kobarid, *Yugoslavia* **27** 46 15N 13 30 E
Kobayashi, *Japan* **64** 31 56N 130 59 E
Kobdo = Hovd, *Mongolia* **62** 48 2N 91 37 E
Kobdo = Jargalant, *Mongolia* **62** 48 2N 91 37 E
Kōbe, *Japan* **65** 34 45N 135 10 E
Kobelyaki, *U.S.S.R.* **38** 49 11N 34 9 E
København, *Denmark* **11** 55 41N 12 34 E
Koblenz, *W. Germany* **31** 50 21N 7 36 E
Kobo, *Ethiopia* **89** 12 2N 39 56 E
Kobo, *Zaïre* **95** 4 54 S 17 9 E
Kobrin, *U.S.S.R.* **36** 52 15N 24 22 E
Kobroor, Kepulauan, *Indonesia* **57** 6 10 S 134 30 E
Kobuchizawa, *Japan* **65** 35 52N 138 19 E
Kobuleti, *U.S.S.R.* **39** 41 55N 41 45 E
Kobyłka, *Poland* **32** 52 21N 21 10 E
Kobylkino, *U.S.S.R.* **37** 54 8N 43 56 E
Kobylnik, *U.S.S.R.* **36** 54 58N 26 39 E
Kočani, *Yugoslavia* **35** 41 55N 22 25 E
Koceljevo, *Yugoslavia* **33** 44 28N 19 50 E
Kočevje, *Yugoslavia* **27** 45 39N 14 50 E
Koch Bihar, *India* **52** 26 22N 89 29 E
Kochas, *India* **49** 25 15N 83 56 E
Kocher →, *W. Germany* **31** 49 14N 9 12 E
Kocheya, *U.S.S.R.* **41** 52 32N 120 42 E
Kōchi, *Japan* **64** 33 30N 133 35 E
Kōchi □, *Japan* **64** 33 40N 133 30 E
Kōchi-Heiya, *Japan* **64** 33 28N 133 30 E
Kochiu = Gejiu, *China* **58** 23 20N 103 10 E
Kodaira, *Japan* **65** 35 44N 139 29 E
Koddiyar Bay, *Sri Lanka* **51** 8 33N 81 15 E
Kodiak, *U.S.A.* **102** 57 30N 152 45W
Kodiak I., *U.S.A.* **102** 57 30N 152 45W
Kodinar, *India* **48** 20 46N 70 46 E
Kodori →, *U.S.S.R.* **39** 42 47N 41 10 E
Koekelare, *Belgium* **17** 51 5N 2 59 E
Koersel, *Belgium* **17** 51 3N 5 17 E
Koes, *Namibia* **96** 26 0 S 19 15 E
Koetong, *Australia* **75** 36 10 S 147 30 E
Koffiefontein, *S. Africa* **96** 29 30 S 25 0 E
Kofiau, *Indonesia* **57** 1 11 S 129 50 E
Koforidua, *Ghana* **91** 6 3N 0 17W
Kōfu, *Japan* **65** 35 40N 138 30 E
Koga, *Japan* **65** 36 11N 139 43 E
Kogaluk →, *Canada* **105** 56 12N 61 44W
Kogan, *Australia* **77** 27 2 S 150 40 E
Kogin Baba, *Nigeria* **91** 7 55N 11 35 E
Kogota, *Japan* **63** 38 33N 141 3 E
Koh-i-Bābā, *Afghan.* **47** 34 30N 67 0 E
Koh-i-Khurd, *Afghan.* **48** 33 30N 65 59 E
Kohat, *Pakistan* **48** 33 40N 71 29 E
Kohima, *India* **52** 25 35N 94 10 E
Kohkīlūyeh va Būyer Aḥmadi □, *Iran* **47** 31 30N 50 30 E
Kohler Ra., *Antarctica* **143** 77 0 S 110 0W
Kohtla Järve, *U.S.S.R.* **36** 59 20N 27 20 E
Kohukohu, *N.Z.* **80** 35 22 S 173 38 E
Kojima, *Japan* **64** 34 30N 133 50 E
Kōjo, *Japan* **64** 34 33N 133 55 E

Kojonup, *Australia* **79** 33 48 S 117 10 E
Koka, *Sudan* **88** 20 5N 30 35 E
Kokand, *U.S.S.R.* **40** 40 30N 70 57 E
Kokanee Glacier Prov. Park, *Canada* **110** 49 47N 117 10W
Kokas, *Indonesia* **57** 2 42 S 132 26 E
Kokchetav, *U.S.S.R.* **40** 53 20N 69 25 E
Kokemäenjoki, *Finland* **9** 61 32N 21 44 E
Kokerite, *Guyana* **135** 7 12N 59 35W
Kokhma, *U.S.S.R.* **37** 56 55N 41 18 E
Kokiri, *N.Z.* **81** 42 29 S 171 25 E
Kokkola, *Finland* **8** 63 50N 23 8 E
Koko, *Nigeria* **91** 11 28N 4 29 E
Kokoda, *Papua N. G.* **69** 8 54 S 147 47 E
Kokolopozo, *Ivory C.* **90** 5 8N 6 5W
Kokomo, *U.S.A.* **119** 40 30N 86 6W
Kokonau, *Indonesia* **57** 4 43 S 136 26 E
Kokopo, *Papua N. G.* **69** 4 22 S 152 19 E
Kokoro, *Niger* **91** 14 12N 0 55 E
Koksoak →, *Canada* **103** 58 30N 68 10W
Kokstad, *S. Africa* **97** 30 32 S 29 29 E
Kokubu, *Japan* **64** 31 44N 130 46 E
Kokuora, *U.S.S.R.* **41** 71 35N 144 50 E
Kola, *Indonesia* **57** 5 35 S 134 30 E
Kola, *U.S.S.R.* **40** 68 45N 33 8 E
Kola Pen. = Kolskiy Poluostrov, *U.S.S.R.* **40** 67 30N 38 0 E
Kolachel, *India* **51** 8 10N 77 15 E
Kolahoi, *India* **49** 34 12N 75 22 E
Kolahun, *Liberia* **90** 8 15N 10 4W
Kolaka, *Indonesia* **57** 4 3 S 121 46 E
Kolar, *India* **51** 13 12N 78 15 E
Kolar Gold Fields, *India* **51** 12 58N 78 16 E
Kolari, *Finland* **8** 67 20N 23 48 E
Kolby Kås, *Denmark* **11** 55 48N 10 32 E
Kolchugino, *U.S.S.R.* **37** 56 17N 39 22 E
Kolda, *Senegal* **90** 12 55N 14 57W
Kolding, *Denmark* **11** 55 30N 9 29 E
Kole, *Zaïre* **94** 3 16 S 22 42 E
Koléa, *Algeria* **85** 36 38N 2 46 E
Kolepom = Yos Sudarso, Pulau, *Indonesia* **57** 8 0 S 138 30 E
Kolguyev, Ostrov, *U.S.S.R.* **40** 69 20N 48 30 E
Kolham, *Neths.* **16** 53 11N 6 44 E
Kolhapur, *India* **50** 16 43N 74 15 E
Kolia, *Ivory C.* **90** 9 46N 6 28W
Kolín, *Czech.* **32** 50 2N 15 9 E
Kolind, *Denmark* **11** 56 21N 10 34 E
Kölleda, *E. Germany* **30** 51 11N 11 14 E
Kollegal, *India* **51** 12 9N 77 9 E
Kolleru L., *India* **50** 16 40N 81 10 E
Kollum, *Neths.* **16** 53 17N 6 10 E
Kolmanskop, *Namibia* **96** 26 45 S 15 14 E
Köln, *W. Germany* **30** 50 56N 6 58 E
Kolo, *Poland* **32** 52 14N 18 40 E
Kołobrzeg, *Poland* **32** 54 10N 15 35 E
Kologriv, *U.S.S.R.* **37** 58 48N 44 25 E
Kolokani, *Mali* **90** 13 35N 7 45W
Kolombangara, *Solomon Is.* **68** 8 0 S 157 5 E
Kolomna, *U.S.S.R.* **37** 55 8N 38 45 E
Kolomyya, *U.S.S.R.* **38** 48 31N 25 2 E
Kolondiéba, *Mali* **90** 11 5N 6 54W
Kolonodale, *Indonesia* **57** 2 3 S 121 25 E
Koloona, *Australia* **77** 29 37 S 150 46 E
Kolosib, *India* **52** 24 15N 92 45 E
Kolpashevo, *U.S.S.R.* **40** 58 20N 83 5 E
Kolpino, *U.S.S.R.* **36** 59 44N 30 39 E
Kolpny, *U.S.S.R.* **37** 52 12N 37 10 E
Kolskiy Poluostrov, *U.S.S.R.* **40** 67 30N 38 0 E
Kolubara →, *Yugoslavia* **33** 44 35N 20 15 E
Koluszki, *Poland* **32** 51 45N 19 46 E
Kolwezi, *Zaïre* **93** 10 40 S 25 25 E
Kolyberovo, *U.S.S.R.* **37** 55 15N 38 40 E
Kolyma →, *U.S.S.R.* **41** 69 30N 161 0 E
Kolymskoye, Okhotsko, *U.S.S.R.* **41** 63 0N 157 0 E
Kôm Ombo, *Egypt* **88** 24 25N 32 52 E
Komagene, *Japan* **65** 35 44N 137 58 E
Komaki, *Japan* **65** 35 17N 136 55 E
Komárno, *Czech.* **33** 47 49N 18 5 E
Komárom, *Hungary* **33** 47 43N 18 7 E
Komarovo, *U.S.S.R.* **36** 58 38N 33 40 E
Komatipoort, *S. Africa* **97** 25 25 S 31 55 E
Komatsu, *Japan* **65** 36 25N 136 30 E
Komatsujima, *Japan* **64** 34 0N 134 35 E
Kombissiri, *Burkina Faso* **91** 12 4N 1 20W
Kombo, *Gabon* **94** 0 20 S 12 22 E
Kombori, *Burkina Faso* **90** 13 26N 3 56W
Komen, *Yugoslavia* **27** 45 49N 13 45 E
Komenda, *Ghana* **91** 5 4N 1 28W
Komi A.S.S.R. □, *U.S.S.R.* **40** 64 0N 55 0 E
Komiža, *Yugoslavia* **27** 43 3N 16 11 E
Komló, *Hungary* **33** 46 15N 18 16 E
Kommamur Canal, *India* **51** 16 0N 80 25 E
Kommunarsk, *U.S.S.R.* **39** 48 30N 38 45 E
Kommunizma, Pik, *U.S.S.R.* **47** 39 0N 72 2 E
Komodo, *Indonesia* **57** 8 37 S 119 20 E
Komoé, *Ivory C.* **90** 5 12N 3 44W
Komono, *Congo* **94** 3 10 S 13 20 E
Komoran, Pulau, *Indonesia* **57** 8 18 S 138 45 E
Komoro, *Japan* **65** 36 19N 138 26 E
Komotini, *Greece* **35** 41 9N 25 26 E
Kompasberg, *S. Africa* **96** 31 45 S 24 32 E
Kompong Bang, *Cambodia* **55** 12 24N 104 40 E
Kompong Cham, *Cambodia* **55** 12 0N 105 30 E
Kompong Chhnang, *Cambodia* **55** 12 20N 104 35 E
Kompong Chikreng, *Cambodia* **54** 13 5N 104 18 E
Kompong Kleang, *Cambodia* **54** 13 6N 104 8 E
Kompong Luong, *Cambodia* **55** 11 49N 104 48 E
Kompong Pranak, *Cambodia* **54** 13 35N 104 55 E
Kompong Som, *Cambodia* **55** 10 38N 103 30 E
Kompong Som, Chhung, *Cambodia* **55** 10 50N 103 32 E
Kompong Speu, *Cambodia* **55** 11 26N 104 32 E
Kompong Sralao, *Cambodia* **54** 14 5N 105 46 E
Kompong Thom, *Cambodia* **54** 12 35N 104 51 E
Kompong Trabeck, *Cambodia* **54** 13 6N 105 14 E
Kompong Trabeck, *Cambodia* **55** 11 9N 105 28 E
Kompong Trach, *Cambodia* **55** 11 25N 105 48 E
Kompong Tralach, *Cambodia* **55** 11 54N 104 47 E
Komrat, *U.S.S.R.* **38** 46 18N 28 40 E
Komsberg, *S. Africa* **96** 32 40 S 20 45 E
Komsomolets, Ostrov, *U.S.S.R.* **41** 80 30N 95 0 E
Komsomolsk, *R.S.F.S.R., U.S.S.R.* **37** 57 2N 40 20 E
Komsomolsk, *R.S.F.S.R., U.S.S.R.* **41** 50 30N 137 0 E
Komsomolskiy, *U.S.S.R.* **37** 53 30N 49 30 E
Konakovo, *U.S.S.R.* **37** 56 52N 36 45 E
Konarhá □, *Afghan.* **47** 35 30N 71 3 E
Konawa, *U.S.A.* **121** 34 59N 96 46W
Konch, *India* **49** 26 0N 79 10 E
Kondagaon, *India* **50** 19 35N 81 35 E
Kondakovo, *U.S.S.R.* **41** 69 36N 152 0 E
Konde, *Tanzania* **92** 4 57 S 39 45 E
Kondinin, *Australia* **79** 32 34 S 118 8 E
Kondo, *Zaïre* **95** 5 35 S 13 0 E
Kondoa, *Tanzania* **92** 4 55 S 35 50 E
Kondoa □, *Tanzania* **92** 5 0 S 36 0 E
Kondratyevo, *U.S.S.R.* **41** 57 22N 98 15 E
Konduga, *Nigeria* **91** 11 35N 13 26 E
Kondukur, *India* **51** 15 12N 79 57 E
Koné, *N. Cal.* **68** 21 4 S 164 52 E
Kong, *Ivory C.* **90** 8 54N 4 36W
Kong →, *Cambodia* **54** 13 32N 105 58 E
Kong, Koh, *Cambodia* **55** 11 20N 103 0 E
Kong Christian IX.s Land, *Greenland* **144** 68 0N 36 0W
Kong Christian X.s Land, *Greenland* **144** 74 0N 29 0W
Kong Franz Joseph Fd., *Greenland* **144** 73 20N 24 30W
Kong Frederik IX.s Land, *Greenland* **144** 67 0N 52 0W
Kong Frederik VI.s Kyst, *Greenland* **144** 63 0N 43 0W
Kong Frederik VIII.s Land, *Greenland* **144** 78 30N 26 0W
Kong Oscar Fjord, *Greenland* **144** 72 20N 24 0W
Konga, *Sweden* **11** 56 30N 15 6 E
Kongbo, *C.A.R.* **94** 4 44N 21 23 E
Kongeå, *Denmark* **11** 55 24N 9 39 E
Kongju, *S. Korea* **61** 36 30N 127 0 E
Konglu, *Burma* **52** 27 13N 97 57 E
Kongolo, *Kasai Or., Zaïre* **92** 5 26 S 24 49 E
Kongolo, *Shaba, Zaïre* **92** 5 22 S 27 0 E
Kongor, *Sudan* **89** 7 1N 31 27 E
Kongoussi, *Burkina Faso* **91** 13 19N 1 32W
Kongsberg, *Norway* **10** 59 39N 9 39 E
Kongsvinger, *Norway* **10** 60 12N 12 2 E
Kongwa, *Tanzania* **92** 6 11 S 36 26 E
Kongwak, *Australia* **74** 38 30 S 145 42 E
Koni, *Zaïre* **93** 10 40 S 27 11 E
Koni, Mts., *Zaïre* **93** 10 36 S 27 10 E
Königsberg = Kaliningrad, *U.S.S.R.* **36** 54 42N 20 32 E
Königshofen, *W. Germany* **31** 50 18N 10 29 E
Königslutter, *W. Germany* **30** 52 14N 10 50 E
Königswusterhausen, *E. Germany* **30** 52 19N 13 38 E
Konin, *Poland* **32** 52 12N 18 15 E
Kónitsa, *Greece* **35** 40 5N 20 48 E
Konjice, *Yugoslavia* **27** 46 20N 15 28 E
Konkiep, *Namibia* **96** 26 49 S 17 15 E
Konkouré →, *Guinea* **90** 9 50N 13 42W
Könnern, *E. Germany* **30** 51 40N 11 45 E
Konnur, *India* **51** 16 14N 74 49 E
Kono, *S. Leone* **90** 8 30N 11 5W
Konongo, *Ghana* **91** 6 40N 1 15W
Konos, *Papua N. G.* **69** 3 10 S 151 44 E
Konosha, *U.S.S.R.* **40** 61 0N 40 5 E
Kōnosu, *Japan* **65** 36 3N 139 31 E
Konotop, *U.S.S.R.* **36** 51 12N 33 7 E
Konqi He →, *China* **62** 40 45N 90 10 E
Końskie, *Poland* **32** 51 15N 20 23 E
Konstantinovka, *U.S.S.R.* **38** 48 32N 37 39 E
Konstantinovski, *U.S.S.R.* **39** 47 33N 41 10 E
Konstanz, *W. Germany* **31** 47 39N 9 10 E
Kontagora, *Nigeria* **91** 10 23N 5 27 E
Kontich, *Belgium* **17** 51 8N 4 26 E
Kontum, *Vietnam* **54** 14 24N 108 0 E
Kontum, Plateau du, *Vietnam* **54** 14 30N 108 0 E
Konya, *Turkey* **46** 37 52N 32 35 E
Konya Ovasi, *Turkey* **46** 38 30N 33 0 E
Konyin, *Burma* **52** 22 58N 94 42 E
Konz, *W. Germany* **31** 49 41N 6 36 E
Konza, *Kenya* **92** 1 45 S 37 7 E
Koo-wee-rup, *Australia* **74** 38 13 S 145 28 E
Kookynie, *Australia* **79** 29 17 S 121 22 E
Kooline, *Australia* **78** 22 57 S 116 20 E
Kooloonong, *Australia* **74** 34 48 S 143 10 E
Koolyanobbing, *Australia* **79** 30 48 S 119 36 E
Koondrook, *Australia* **74** 35 33 S 144 8 E
Koorawatha, *Australia* **76** 34 2 S 148 33 E
Koorda, *Australia* **79** 30 48 S 117 35 E
Kooskia, *U.S.A.* **122** 46 9N 115 59W
Kootenai →, *Canada* **122** 49 15N 117 39W
Kootenay L., *Canada* **110** 49 45N 116 50W
Kootenay Nat. Park, *Canada* **110** 51 0N 116 0W
Kootjieskolk, *S. Africa* **96** 31 15 S 20 21 E
Kopanovka, *U.S.S.R.* **39** 47 28N 46 50 E
Kopaonik Planina, *Yugoslavia* **33** 43 10N 21 50 E
Kopargaon, *India* **50** 19 51N 74 28 E
Kópavogur, *Iceland* **8** 64 6N 21 55W
Koper, *Yugoslavia* **27** 45 31N 13 44 E
Kopervik, *Norway* **9** 59 17N 5 17 E
Kopeysk, *U.S.S.R.* **40** 55 7N 61 37 E
Kopi, *Australia* **73** 33 24 S 135 40 E
Köping, *Sweden* **10** 59 31N 16 3 E
Kopiste, *Yugoslavia* **27** 42 48N 16 42 E
Köpmanholmen, *Sweden* **10** 63 10N 18 35 E
Koppal, *India* **51** 15 23N 76 5 E
Koppang, *Norway* **10** 61 34N 11 3 E
Kopparberg, *Sweden* **9** 59 52N 15 0 E
Kopparbergs län □, *Sweden* **10** 61 20N 14 15 E
Koppeh Dāgh, *Asia* **47** 38 0N 58 0 E
Kopperå, *Norway* **10** 63 24N 11 50 E
Koppies, *S. Africa* **97** 27 20 S 27 30 E
Koppom, *Sweden* **10** 59 43N 12 10 E
Koprivnica, *Yugoslavia* **27** 46 12N 16 45 E
Kopychintsy, *U.S.S.R.* **36** 49 7N 25 58 E
Kopys, *U.S.S.R.* **36** 54 20N 30 17 E
Korab, *Yugoslavia* **35** 41 44N 20 40 E
Koraput, *India* **50** 18 50N 82 40 E
Korba, *India* **49** 22 20N 82 45 E
Korbach, *W. Germany* **30** 51 17N 8 50 E
Korbu, G., *Malaysia* **55** 4 41N 101 18 E
Korça, *Albania* **35** 40 37N 20 50 E
Korce = Korça, *Albania* **35** 40 37N 20 50 E
Korčula, *Yugoslavia* **27** 42 57N 17 8 E
Korčulanski Kanal, *Yugoslavia* **27** 43 3N 16 40 E
Kordestan, *Asia* **46** 35 30N 42 0 E
Kordestān □, *Iran* **46** 36 0N 47 0 E
Korea, North ■, *Asia* **61** 40 0N 127 0 E
Korea, South ■, *Asia* **61** 36 0N 128 0 E
Korea Strait, *Asia* **61** 34 0N 129 30 E
Koregaon, *India* **50** 17 40N 74 10 E
Korenevo, *U.S.S.R.* **36** 51 27N 34 55 E
Korenovsk, *U.S.S.R.* **39** 45 30N 39 22 E
Korets, *U.S.S.R.* **36** 50 40N 27 5 E
Korgus, *Sudan* **88** 19 16N 33 29 E
Korhogo, *Ivory C.* **90** 9 29N 5 28W
Koribundu, *S. Leone* **90** 7 41N 11 46W
Korim, *Indonesia* **57** 0 58 S 136 10 E
Korinthiakós Kólpos, *Greece* **35** 38 16N 22 30 E
Kórinthos, *Greece* **35** 37 56N 22 55 E
Korioumé, *Mali* **90** 16 35N 3 0W
Kōriyama, *Japan* **63** 37 24N 140 23 E
Körmend, *Hungary* **33** 47 5N 16 35 E
Kornat, *Yugoslavia* **27** 43 50N 15 20 E
Korneshty, *U.S.S.R.* **38** 47 21N 28 1 E
Kornsjø, *Norway* **10** 58 57N 11 39 E
Kornstad, *Norway* **10** 62 59N 7 27 E
Koro, *Fiji* **68** 17 19 S 179 23 E
Koro, *Ivory C.* **90** 8 32N 7 30W
Koro, *Mali* **90** 14 1N 2 58W
Koro Sea, *Fiji* **68** 17 30 S 179 45W
Koro Toro, *Chad* **87** 16 5N 18 30 E
Koroba, *Papua N. G.* **69** 5 44 S 142 47 E
Korocha, *U.S.S.R.* **37** 50 55N 37 30 E
Korogoro Pt., *Australia* **77** 31 3 S 153 4 E
Korogwe, *Tanzania* **92** 5 5 S 38 25 E
Korogwe □, *Tanzania* **92** 5 0 S 38 20 E
Koroit, *Australia* **74** 38 18 S 142 24 E
Korong Vale, *Australia* **74** 36 22 S 143 45 E
Koronowo, *Poland* **32** 53 19N 17 55 E
Koror, *Pac. Oc.* **57** 7 20N 134 28 E
Körös →, *Hungary* **33** 46 43N 20 12 E
Korosten, *U.S.S.R.* **36** 50 57N 28 25 E
Korotoyak, *U.S.S.R.* **37** 51 1N 39 2 E
Korraraika, Helodranon' i, *Madag.* **97** 17 45 S 43 57 E
Korsakov, *U.S.S.R.* **41** 46 36N 142 42 E
Korshunovo, *U.S.S.R.* **41** 58 37N 110 10 E
Korsör, *Denmark* **9** 55 20N 11 9 E
Korsun Shevchenkovskiy, *U.S.S.R.* **38** 49 26N 31 16 E
Korsze, *Poland* **32** 54 11N 21 9 E
Kortemark, *Belgium* **17** 51 2N 3 3 E
Kortessem, *Belgium* **17** 50 52N 5 23 E
Korti, *Sudan* **88** 18 6N 31 33 E
Kortrijk, *Belgium* **17** 50 50N 3 17 E
Korumburra, *Australia* **74** 38 26 S 145 50 E
Korwai, *India* **48** 24 7N 78 5 E
Koryakskiy Khrebet, *U.S.S.R.* **41** 61 0N 171 0 E
Kos, *Greece* **35** 36 50N 27 15 E
Kosa, *Ethiopia* **89** 7 50N 36 50 E
Kosaya Gora, *U.S.S.R.* **37** 54 10N 37 30 E
Kościan, *Poland* **32** 52 5N 16 40 E
Kościerzyna, *Poland* **32** 54 8N 17 59 E
Kosciusko, *U.S.A.* **121** 33 3N 89 34W
Kosciusko, Mt., *Australia* **75** 36 27 S 148 16 E
Kosciusko I., *U.S.A.* **110** 56 0N 133 40W
Kösély →, *Hungary* **33** 47 25N 21 5 E
Kosgi, *India* **50** 16 58N 77 43 E
Kosha, *Sudan* **88** 20 50N 30 30 E
Koshigaya, *Japan* **65** 35 54N 139 48 E
K'oshih = Kashi, *China* **62** 39 30N 76 2 E
Koshiki-Rettō, *Japan* **64** 31 45N 129 49 E
Koshkonong, L., *U.S.A.* **119** 42 53N 88 58W
Kōshoku, *Japan* **65** 36 38N 138 6 E
Kosi, *India* **48** 27 48N 77 29 E
Kosi-meer, *S. Africa* **97** 27 0 S 32 50 E
Košice, *Czech.* **32** 48 42N 21 15 E
Kosjerić, *Yugoslavia* **33** 44 0N 19 55 E
Kosŏng, *N. Korea* **61** 38 40N 128 22 E
Kosovska-Mitrovica, *Yugoslavia* **33** 42 54N 20 52 E
Kostajnica, *Yugoslavia* **27** 45 17N 16 30 E
Kostanjevica, *Yugoslavia* **27** 45 51N 15 27 E
Kostelec, *Czech.* **32** 50 14N 16 35 E
Koster, *S. Africa* **96** 25 52 S 26 54 E
Kôstî, *Sudan* **89** 13 8N 32 43 E
Kostopol, *U.S.S.R.* **36** 50 51N 26 22 E
Kostroma, *U.S.S.R.* **37** 57 50N 40 58 E
Kostromskoye Vdkhr., *U.S.S.R.* **37** 57 52N 40 49 E
Kostyukovichi, *U.S.S.R.* **36** 53 20N 32 4 E
Koszalin, *Poland* **32** 54 11N 16 8 E
Köszeg, *Hungary* **33** 47 23N 16 33 E
Kot Addu, *Pakistan* **48** 30 30N 71 0 E
Kot Moman, *Pakistan* **48** 32 13N 73 0 E
Kota, *India* **48** 25 14N 75 49 E
Kota Baharu, *Malaysia* **55** 6 7N 102 14 E
Kota Belud, *Malaysia* **56** 6 21N 116 26 E
Kota Kinabalu, *Malaysia* **56** 6 0N 116 4 E
Kota Tinggi, *Malaysia* **55** 1 44N 103 53 E
Kotaagung, *Indonesia* **56** 5 38 S 104 29 E
Kotabaru, *Indonesia* **56** 3 20 S 116 20 E
Kotabumi, *Indonesia* **56** 4 49 S 104 54 E
Kotagede, *Indonesia* **57** 7 54 S 110 26 E
Kotamobagu, *Indonesia* **57** 0 57N 124 31 E
Kotaneelee →, *Canada* **110** 60 11N 123 42W
Kotawaringin, *Indonesia* **56** 2 28 S 111 27 E
Kotchandpur, *Bangla.* **52** 23 24N 89 1 E
Kotcho L., *Canada* **110** 59 7N 121 12W
Kotelnich, *U.S.S.R.* **37** 58 20N 48 10 E
Kotelnikovo, *U.S.S.R.* **39** 47 38N 43 8 E
Kotelnyy, Ostrov, *U.S.S.R.* **41** 75 10N 139 0 E
Kothagudam, *India* **50** 17 30N 80 40 E
Kothapet, *India* **50** 19 21N 79 28 E
Köthen, *E. Germany* **30** 51 44N 11 59 E
Kothi, *India* **49** 24 45N 80 40 E
Kotiro, *Pakistan* **48** 26 17N 67 13 E
Kotka, *Finland* **9** 60 28N 26 58 E
Kotlas, *U.S.S.R.* **40** 61 15N 47 0 E
Kotli, *Pakistan* **48** 33 30N 73 55 E
Kotmul, *Pakistan* **49** 35 32N 75 10 E
Kotohira, *Japan* **64** 34 11N 133 49 E
Kotonkoro, *Nigeria* **91** 11 3N 5 58 E
Kotor, *Yugoslavia* **33** 42 25N 18 47 E
Kotoriba, *Yugoslavia* **27** 46 23N 16 48 E
Kotovo, *U.S.S.R.* **37** 50 22N 44 45 E
Kotovsk, *U.S.S.R.* **38** 47 45N 29 35 E
Kotputli, *India* **48** 27 43N 76 12 E
Kotri, *Pakistan* **48** 25 22N 68 22 E
Kotri →, *India* **50** 19 15N 80 35 E
Kótronas, *Greece* **35** 36 38N 22 29 E
Kottayam, *India* **51** 9 35N 76 33 E
Kottur, *India* **51** 10 34N 76 56 E
Kotuy →, *U.S.S.R.* **41** 71 54N 102 6 E
Kotzebue, *U.S.A.* **102** 66 50N 162 40W
Kouango, *C.A.R.* **94** 5 0N 20 10 E
Koudekerke, *Neths.* **17** 51 29N 3 33 E
Koudougou, *Burkina Faso* **90** 12 10N 2 20W
Koufonísi, *Greece* **35** 34 56N 26 8 E
Kougaberge, *S. Africa* **96** 33 48 S 23 50 E
Kouibli, *Ivory C.* **90** 7 15N 7 14W
Kouilou →, *Congo* **95** 4 10 S 12 5 E
Kouki, *C.A.R.* **94** 7 22N 17 3 E
Koula Moutou, *Gabon* **94** 1 15 S 12 25 E
Koulen, *Cambodia* **54** 13 50N 104 40 E
Koulikoro, *Mali* **90** 12 40N 7 50W
Koumac, *N. Cal.* **68** 20 33 S 164 17 E
Koumala, *Australia* **72** 21 38 S 149 15 E
Koumankou, *Mali* **90** 11 58N 6 6W
Koumbia, *Burkina Faso* **90** 11 10N 3 50W
Koumbia, *Guinea* **90** 11 48N 13 29W

Koumboum, *Guinea* **90** 10 25N 13 0W
Koumpenntoum, *Senegal* **90** 13 59N 14 34W
Koumra, *Chad* **87** 8 50N 17 35 E
Koundara, *Guinea* **90** 12 29N 13 18W
Koundé, *C.A.R.* **94** 6 7N 14 38 E
Kounradskiy, *U.S.S.R.* **40** 46 59N 75 0 E
Kountze, *U.S.A.* **121** 30 20N 94 22W
Koupéla, *Burkina Faso* **91** 12 11N 0 21W
Kourizo, Passe de, *Chad* **86** 22 28N 15 27 E
Kourou, *Fr. Guiana* **135** 5 9N 52 39W
Kouroussa, *Guinea* **90** 10 45N 9 45W
Koussané, *Mali* **90** 14 53N 11 14W
Kousseri, *Cameroon* **87** 12 0N 14 55 E
Koutiala, *Mali* **90** 12 25N 5 23W
Kouto, *Ivory C.* **90** 9 53N 6 25W
Kouts, *U.S.A.* **119** 41 18N 87 2W
Kouvé, *Togo* **91** 6 25N 1 25 E
Kovačica, *Yugoslavia* **33** 45 5N 20 38 E
Kovel, *U.S.S.R.* **36** 51 10N 24 20 E
Kovilpatti, *India* **51** 9 10N 77 50 E
Kovin, *Yugoslavia* **33** 44 44N 20 59 E
Kovrov, *U.S.S.R.* **37** 56 25N 41 25 E
Kovur, *Andhra Pradesh, India* **50** 17 3N 81 39 E
Kovur, *Andhra Pradesh, India* **51** 14 30N 80 1 E
Kowkash, *Canada* **104** 50 20N 87 12W
Kowloon, *H.K.* **59** 22 20N 114 15 E
Koyabuti, *Indonesia* **57** 2 36 S 140 37 E
Kōyama, *Japan* **64** 31 20N 130 56 E
Koyuk, *U.S.A.* **102** 64 55N 161 20W
Koyukuk →, *U.S.A.* **102** 64 56N 157 30W
Koyulhisar, *Turkey* **38** 40 20N 37 52 E
Kozan, *Turkey* **46** 37 35N 35 50 E
Kozáni, *Greece* **35** 40 19N 21 47 E
Kozara, *Yugoslavia* **27** 45 0N 17 0 E
Kozarac, *Yugoslavia* **27** 44 58N 16 48 E
Kozelsk, *U.S.S.R.* **36** 54 2N 35 48 E
Kozhikode = Calicut, *India* **51** 11 15N 75 43 E
Kozje, *Yugoslavia* **27** 46 5N 15 35 E
Kozlovets, *Bulgaria* **34** 43 30N 25 20 E
Koźmin, *Poland* **32** 51 48N 17 27 E
Kozmodemyansk, *U.S.S.R.* **37** 56 20N 46 36 E
Kōzu-Shima, *Japan* **65** 34 13N 139 10 E
Kpabia, *Ghana* **91** 9 10N 0 20W
Kpalimé, *Togo* **91** 6 57N 0 44 E
Kpandae, *Ghana* **91** 8 30N 0 2W
Kpessi, *Togo* **91** 8 4N 1 16 E
Kra, Isthmus of = Kra, Kho Khot, *Thailand* **55** 10 15N 99 30 E
Kra, Kho Khot, *Thailand* **55** 10 15N 99 30 E
Kra Buri, *Thailand* **55** 10 22N 98 46 E
Krabbendijke, *Neths.* **17** 51 26N 4 7 E
Krabi, *Thailand* **55** 8 4N 98 55 E
Kragan, *Indonesia* **57** 6 43 S 111 38 E
Kragerø, *Norway* **10** 58 52N 9 25 E
Kragujevac, *Yugoslavia* **33** 44 2N 20 56 E
Krakatau = Rakata, Pulau, *Indonesia* **56** 6 10 S 105 20 E
Krakor, *Cambodia* **54** 12 32N 104 12 E
Kraków, *Poland* **32** 50 4N 19 57 E
Kraksaan, *Indonesia* **57** 7 43 S 113 23 E
Kråkstad, *Norway* **10** 59 39N 10 55 E
Kralanh, *Cambodia* **54** 13 35N 103 25 E
Králiky, *Czech.* **32** 50 6N 16 45 E
Kraljevo, *Yugoslavia* **33** 43 44N 20 41 E
Kralovice, *Czech.* **32** 49 59N 13 29 E
Kralupy, *Czech.* **32** 50 13N 14 20 E
Kramatorsk, *U.S.S.R.* **38** 48 50N 37 30 E
Krambach, *Australia* **77** 32 4 S 152 16 E
Kramfors, *Sweden* **10** 62 55N 17 48 E
Kramis, C., *Algeria* **85** 36 26N 0 45 E
Krångede, *Sweden* **10** 63 9N 16 10 E
Kranj, *Yugoslavia* **27** 46 16N 14 22 E
Kranjska Gora, *Yugoslavia* **27** 46 29N 13 48 E
Krankskop, *S. Africa* **97** 28 0 S 30 47 E
Krapina, *Yugoslavia* **27** 46 10N 15 52 E
Krapina →, *Yugoslavia* **27** 45 50N 15 50 E
Krapivna, *U.S.S.R.* **37** 53 58N 37 10 E
Krapkowice, *Poland* **32** 50 29N 17 56 E
Kraskino, *U.S.S.R.* **41** 42 44N 130 48 E
Kraslice, *Czech.* **32** 50 19N 12 31 E
Krasnaya Gorbatka, *U.S.S.R.* **37** 55 52N 41 45 E
Krasnaya Polyana, *U.S.S.R.* **39** 43 40N 40 13 E
Kraśnik, *Poland* **32** 50 55N 22 5 E
Kraśnik Fabryczny, *Poland* **32** 50 58N 22 11 E
Krasnoarmeisk, *U.S.S.R.* **38** 48 18N 37 11 E
Krasnoarmeysk, *R.S.F.S.R., U.S.S.R.* **37** 51 0N 45 42 E
Krasnoarmeysk, *R.S.F.S.R., U.S.S.R.* **39** 48 30N 44 25 E
Krasnodar, *U.S.S.R.* **39** 45 5N 39 0 E
Krasnodon, *U.S.S.R.* **39** 48 17N 39 44 E
Krasnodonetskaya, *U.S.S.R.* **39** 48 5N 40 50 E
Krasnogorskiy, *U.S.S.R.* **37** 56 10N 48 28 E
Krasnograd, *U.S.S.R.* **38** 49 27N 35 27 E
Krasnogvardeyskoye, *U.S.S.R.* **39** 45 52N 41 33 E
Krasnogvardyesk, *U.S.S.R.* **38** 45 32N 34 16 E
Krasnokutsk, *U.S.S.R.* **36** 50 10N 34 50 E
Krasnoperekopsk, *U.S.S.R.* **38** 46 0N 33 54 E
Krasnoselkupsk, *U.S.S.R.* **40** 65 20N 82 10 E
Krasnoslobodsk, *R.S.F.S.R., U.S.S.R.* **37** 54 25N 43 45 E
Krasnoslobodsk, *R.S.F.S.R., U.S.S.R.* **39** 48 42N 44 33 E
Krasnoturinsk, *U.S.S.R.* **40** 59 46N 60 12 E
Krasnoufimsk, *U.S.S.R.* **40** 56 57N 57 46 E
Krasnouralsk, *U.S.S.R.* **40** 58 21N 60 3 E
Krasnovodsk, *U.S.S.R.* **40** 40 0N 52 52 E
Krasnoyarsk, *U.S.S.R.* **41** 56 8N 93 0 E
Krasnoye = Krasnyy, *U.S.S.R.* **36** 54 25N 31 30 E
Krasnoye, *Kalmyk A.S.S.R., U.S.S.R.* **39** 46 16N 45 0 E
Krasnoye, *R.S.F.S.R., U.S.S.R.* **37** 59 15N 47 40 E
Krasnozavodsk, *U.S.S.R.* **37** 56 27N 38 25 E
Krasny Liman, *U.S.S.R.* **38** 48 58N 37 50 E
Krasny Sulin, *U.S.S.R.* **39** 47 52N 40 8 E
Krasnystaw, *Poland* **32** 50 57N 23 5 E
Krasnyy, *U.S.S.R.* **36** 54 25N 31 30 E
Krasnyy Kholm, *U.S.S.R.* **37** 58 10N 37 10 E
Krasnyy Kut, *U.S.S.R.* **37** 50 50N 47 0 E
Krasnyy Luch, *U.S.S.R.* **39** 48 13N 39 0 E
Krasnyy Profintern, *U.S.S.R.* **37** 57 45N 40 27 E
Krasnyy Yar, *Kalmyk A.S.S.R., U.S.S.R.* **39** 46 43N 48 23 E
Krasnyy Yar, *R.S.F.S.R., U.S.S.R.* **37** 53 30N 50 22 E
Krasnyy Yar, *R.S.F.S.R., U.S.S.R.* **37** 50 42N 44 45 E
Krasnyye Baki, *U.S.S.R.* **37** 57 8N 45 10 E
Krasnyyoskolskoye Vdkhr., *U.S.S.R.* **38** 49 30N 37 30 E
Kraszna →, *Hungary* **33** 48 0N 22 20 E
Kratie, *Cambodia* **54** 12 32N 106 10 E
Kratke Ra., *Papua N. G.* **69** 6 45 S 146 0 E
Krau, *Indonesia* **57** 3 19 S 140 5 E
Kravanh, Chuor Phnum, *Cambodia* **55** 12 0N 103 32 E
Krawang, *Indonesia* **57** 6 19N 107 18 E
Krefeld, *W. Germany* **30** 51 20N 6 32 E
Krémaston, Límni, *Greece* **35** 38 52N 21 30 E
Kremenchug, *U.S.S.R.* **38** 49 5N 33 25 E
Kremenchugskoye Vdkhr., *U.S.S.R.* **38** 49 20N 32 30 E
Kremenets, *U.S.S.R.* **38** 50 8N 25 43 E
Kremennaya, *U.S.S.R.* **38** 49 1N 38 10 E
Kremges = Svetlovodsk, *U.S.S.R.* **36** 49 2N 33 13 E
Kremikovtsi, *Bulgaria* **34** 42 46N 23 28 E
Kremmen, *E. Germany* **30** 52 45N 13 1 E
Kremmling, *U.S.A.* **122** 40 10N 106 30W
Krems, *Austria* **33** 48 25N 15 36 E
Kremsmünster, *Austria* **33** 48 3N 14 8 E
Kretinga, *U.S.S.R.* **36** 55 53N 21 15 E
Krettamia, *Algeria* **84** 28 47N 3 27W
Krettsy, *U.S.S.R.* **36** 58 15N 32 30 E
Kreuzberg, *W. Germany* **31** 50 22N 9 58 E
Kribi, *Cameroon* **91** 2 57N 9 56 E
Krichem, *Bulgaria* **34** 42 8N 24 28 E
Krichev, *U.S.S.R.* **36** 53 45N 31 50 E
Krim, *Yugoslavia* **27** 45 53N 14 30 E
Krimpen, *Neths.* **16** 51 55N 4 34 E
Krishna →, *India* **50** 15 57N 80 59 E
Krishnagiri, *India* **51** 12 32N 78 16 E
Krishnanagar, *India* **49** 23 24N 88 33 E
Krishnaraja Sagara, *India* **51** 12 20N 76 30 E
Kristiansand, *Norway* **9** 58 9N 8 1 E
Kristianstad, *Sweden* **11** 56 2N 14 9 E
Kristianstads län □, *Sweden* **9** 56 15N 14 0 E
Kristiansund, *Norway* **10** 63 7N 7 45 E
Kristiinankaupunki, *Finland* **8** 62 16N 21 21 E
Kristinehamn, *Sweden* **10** 59 18N 14 13 E
Kristinestad, *Finland* **8** 62 16N 21 21 E
Kríti, *Greece* **35** 35 15N 25 0 E
Kriva →, *Yugoslavia* **34** 42 5N 21 47 E
Kriva Palanka, *Yugoslavia* **34** 42 11N 22 19 E
Krivaja →, *Yugoslavia* **33** 44 27N 18 9 E
Krivoy Rog, *U.S.S.R.* **38** 47 51N 33 20 E
Križevci, *Yugoslavia* **27** 46 3N 16 32 E
Krk, *Yugoslavia* **27** 45 8N 14 40 E
Krka →, *Yugoslavia* **27** 45 50N 15 30 E
Krkonoše, *Czech.* **32** 50 50N 15 35 E
Krnov, *Czech.* **32** 50 5N 17 40 E
Krobia, *Poland* **32** 51 47N 16 59 E
Krokeaí, *Greece* **35** 36 53N 22 32 E
Krokodil →, *Mozam.* **97** 25 14 S 32 18 E
Krokom, *Sweden* **10** 63 20N 14 30 E
Krolevets, *U.S.S.R.* **36** 51 35N 33 20 E
Kroměříz, *Czech.* **32** 49 18N 17 21 E
Krommenie, *Neths.* **16** 52 30N 4 46 E
Kromy, *U.S.S.R.* **36** 52 48N 35 48 E
Kronach, *W. Germany* **31** 50 14N 11 19 E
Kronobergs län □, *Sweden* **11** 56 45N 14 30 E
Kronprins Olav Kyst, *Antarctica* **143** 69 0 S 42 0 E
Kronprinsesse Märtha Kyst, *Antarctica* **143** 73 30 S 10 0 E
Kronshtadt, *U.S.S.R.* **36** 60 5N 29 45 E
Kroonstad, *S. Africa* **96** 27 43 S 27 19 E
Kröpelin, *E. Germany* **30** 54 4N 11 48 E
Kropotkin, *R.S.F.S.R., U.S.S.R.* **39** 45 28N 40 28 E
Kropotkin, *R.S.F.S.R., U.S.S.R.* **41** 59 0N 115 30 E
Kropp, *W. Germany* **30** 54 24N 9 32 E
Krościenko, *Poland* **32** 49 29N 20 25 E
Krosno, *Poland* **32** 49 42N 21 46 E
Krosno Odrzańskie, *Poland* **32** 52 3N 15 7 E
Krotoszyn, *Poland* **32** 51 42N 17 23 E
Krško, *Yugoslavia* **27** 45 57N 15 30 E
Kruger Nat. Park, *S. Africa* **97** 23 30 S 31 40 E
Krugersdorp, *S. Africa* **97** 26 5 S 27 46 E
Kruiningen, *Neths.* **17** 51 27N 4 2 E
Kruisfontein, *S. Africa* **96** 33 59 S 24 43 E
Kruishoutem, *Belgium* **17** 50 54N 3 32 E
Kruisland, *Neths.* **17** 51 34N 4 25 E
Kruja, *Albania* **35** 41 32N 19 46 E
Krulevshchina, *U.S.S.R.* **36** 55 5N 27 45 E
Kruma, *Albania* **34** 42 14N 20 28 E
Krumbach, *W. Germany* **31** 48 15N 10 22 E
Krung Thep = Bangkok, *Thailand* **54** 13 45N 100 35 E
Krupanj, *Yugoslavia* **33** 44 25N 19 22 E
Krupinica →, *Czech.* **33** 48 15N 18 52 E
Kruševac, *Yugoslavia* **33** 43 35N 21 28 E
Kruzof I., *U.S.A.* **110** 57 10N 135 40W
Krylbo, *Sweden* **10** 60 7N 16 15 E
Krymsk Abinsk, *U.S.S.R.* **38** 44 50N 38 0 E
Krymskiy Poluostrov, *U.S.S.R.* **38** 45 0N 34 0 E
Krynica Morska, *Poland* **32** 54 23N 19 28 E
Krynki, *Poland* **32** 53 17N 23 43 E
Krzywiń, *Poland* **32** 51 58N 16 50 E
Krzyz, *Poland* **32** 52 52N 16 0 E
Ksabi, *Morocco* **84** 32 51N 4 13W
Ksar Chellala, *Algeria* **85** 35 13N 2 19 E
Ksar el Boukhari, *Algeria* **85** 35 51N 2 52 E
Ksar el Kebir, *Morocco* **84** 35 0N 6 0W
Ksar es Souk = Ar Rachidiya, *Morocco* **84** 31 58N 4 20W
Ksar Rhilane, *Tunisia* **86** 33 0N 9 39 E
Ksour, Mts. des, *Algeria* **85** 32 45N 0 30W
Kstovo, *U.S.S.R.* **37** 56 12N 44 13 E
Kuala, *Indonesia* **56** 2 55N 105 47 E
Kuala Berang, *Malaysia* **55** 5 5N 103 1 E
Kuala Dungun, *Malaysia* **55** 4 45N 103 25 E
Kuala Kangsar, *Malaysia* **55** 4 46N 100 56 E
Kuala Kelawang, *Malaysia* **55** 2 56N 102 5 E
Kuala Kerai, *Malaysia* **55** 5 30N 102 12 E
Kuala Kubu Baharu, *Malaysia* **55** 3 34N 101 39 E
Kuala Lipis, *Malaysia* **55** 4 10N 102 3 E
Kuala Lumpur, *Malaysia* **55** 3 9N 101 41 E
Kuala Nerang, *Malaysia* **55** 6 16N 100 37 E
Kuala Pilah, *Malaysia* **55** 2 45N 102 15 E
Kuala Rompin, *Malaysia* **55** 2 49N 103 29 E
Kuala Selangor, *Malaysia* **55** 3 20N 101 15 E
Kuala Trengganu, *Malaysia* **55** 5 20N 103 8 E
Kualajelai, *Indonesia* **56** 2 58 S 110 46 E
Kualakapuas, *Indonesia* **56** 2 55 S 114 20 E
Kualakurun, *Indonesia* **56** 1 10 S 113 50 E
Kualapembuang, *Indonesia* **56** 3 14 S 112 38 E
Kualasimpang, *Indonesia* **56** 4 17N 98 3 E
Kuancheng, *China* **61** 40 37N 118 30 E
Kuandang, *Indonesia* **57** 0 56N 123 1 E
Kuandian, *China* **61** 40 45N 124 45 E
Kuangchou = Guangzhou, *China* **59** 23 5N 113 10 E
Kuantan, *Malaysia* **55** 3 49N 103 20 E
Kuba, *U.S.S.R.* **39** 41 21N 48 32 E
Kuban →, *U.S.S.R.* **39** 45 20N 37 30 E
Kubenskoye, Oz., *U.S.S.R.* **37** 59 40N 39 25 E
Kuberle, *U.S.S.R.* **39** 47 0N 42 20 E
Kubokawa, *Japan* **64** 33 12N 133 8 E
Kubor, Mt., *Papua N. G.* **69** 6 10 S 144 44 E
Kubrat, *Bulgaria* **34** 43 49N 26 31 E
Kučevo, *Yugoslavia* **33** 44 30N 21 40 E
Kucha Gompa, *India* **49** 34 25N 76 56 E
Kuchaman, *India* **48** 27 13N 74 47 E
Kuchinotsu, *Japan* **64** 32 36N 130 11 E
Kucing, *Malaysia* **56** 1 33N 110 25 E
Kuçove = Qytet Stalin, *Albania* **35** 40 47N 19 57 E
Kud →, *Pakistan* **48** 26 5N 66 20 E
Kudalier →, *India* **50** 18 35N 79 48 E
Kudamatsu, *Japan* **64** 34 0N 131 52 E
Kudat, *Malaysia* **56** 6 55N 116 55 E
Kudremukh, Mt., *India* **51** 13 15N 75 20 E
Kudus, *Indonesia* **57** 6 48 S 110 51 E
Kudymkar, *U.S.S.R.* **40** 59 1N 54 39 E
Kueiyang = Guiyang, *China* **58** 26 32N 106 40 E
Kufrinjah, *Jordan* **44** 32 20N 35 41 E
Kufstein, *Austria* **31** 47 35N 12 11 E
Kugong I., *Canada* **104** 56 18N 79 50W
Kūh-e 'Alijūq, *Iran* **47** 31 30N 51 41 E
Kūh-e Dīnār, *Iran* **47** 30 40N 51 0 E
Kūh-e-Hazārām, *Iran* **47** 29 35N 57 20 E
Kūh-e-Jebāl Bārez, *Iran* **47** 29 0N 58 0 E
Kūh-e Sorkh, *Iran* **47** 35 30N 58 45 E
Kūh-e Taftān, *Iran* **47** 28 40N 61 0 E
Kūhak, *Iran* **47** 27 12N 63 10 E
Kūhhā-ye-Bashākerd, *Iran* **47** 26 45N 59 0 E
Kūhhā-ye Sabalān, *Iran* **46** 38 15N 47 45 E
Kuhnsdorf, *Austria* **33** 46 37N 14 38 E
Kūhpāyeh, *Iran* **47** 32 44N 52 20 E
Kui Buri, *Thailand* **55** 12 3N 99 52 E
Kuinre, *Neths.* **16** 52 47N 5 51 E
Kuito, *Angola* **95** 12 22 S 16 55 E
Kuji, *Japan* **63** 40 11N 141 46 E
Kujū-San, *Japan* **64** 33 5N 131 15 E
Kujukuri-Heiya, *Japan* **65** 35 45N 140 30 E
Kukawa, *Nigeria* **91** 12 58N 13 27 E
Kukerin, *Australia* **79** 33 13 S 118 0 E
Kukmor, *U.S.S.R.* **37** 56 11N 50 54 E
Kukup, *Malaysia* **55** 1 20N 103 27 E
Kukvidze, *U.S.S.R.* **37** 50 40N 43 15 E
Kula, *Yugoslavia* **33** 45 37N 19 32 E
Kula Gulf, *Solomon Is.* **68** 8 5 S 157 18 E
Kulai, *Malaysia* **55** 1 44N 103 35 E
Kulal, Mt., *Kenya* **92** 2 42N 36 57 E
Kulaly, Os., *U.S.S.R.* **39** 45 0N 50 0 E
Kulasekarappattinam, *India* **51** 8 20N 78 0 E
Kuldiga, *U.S.S.R.* **36** 56 58N 21 59 E
Kuldja = Yining, *China* **62** 43 58N 81 10 E
Kuldu, *Sudan* **89** 12 50N 28 30 E
Kulebaki, *U.S.S.R.* **37** 55 22N 42 25 E
Kulen Vakuf, *Yugoslavia* **27** 44 35N 16 2 E
Kulgam, *India* **49** 33 36N 75 2 E
Kuli, *U.S.S.R.* **39** 42 2N 47 12 E
Kulim, *Malaysia* **55** 5 22N 100 34 E
Kulin, *Australia* **79** 32 40 S 118 2 E
Kulja, *Australia* **79** 30 28 S 117 18 E
Kulm, *U.S.A.* **120** 46 22N 98 58W
Kulmbach, *W. Germany* **31** 50 6N 11 27 E
Kulsary, *U.S.S.R.* **40** 46 59N 54 1 E
Kultay, *U.S.S.R.* **39** 45 5N 51 40 E
Kulti, *India* **49** 23 43N 86 50 E
Kulumbura, *Australia* **78** 13 55 S 126 35 E
Kulunda, *U.S.S.R.* **40** 52 35N 78 57 E
Kulungar, *Afghan.* **48** 34 0N 69 2 E
Kulwin, *Australia* **74** 35 0 S 142 42 E
Kulyab, *U.S.S.R.* **40** 37 55N 69 50 E
Kum Tekei, *U.S.S.R.* **40** 43 10N 79 30 E
Kuma, *Japan* **64** 33 39N 132 54 E
Kuma →, *U.S.S.R.* **39** 44 55N 47 0 E
Kumaganum, *Nigeria* **91** 13 8N 10 38 E
Kumagaya, *Japan* **65** 36 9N 139 22 E
Kumai, *Indonesia* **56** 2 44 S 111 43 E
Kumamba, Kepulauan, *Indonesia* **57** 1 36 S 138 45 E
Kumamoto, *Japan* **64** 32 45N 130 45 E
Kumamoto □, *Japan* **64** 32 55N 130 55 E
Kumano, *Japan* **65** 33 54N 136 5 E
Kumano-Nada, *Japan* **65** 33 47N 136 20 E
Kumanovo, *Yugoslavia* **34** 42 9N 21 42 E
Kumara, *N.Z.* **81** 42 37 S 171 12 E
Kumarkhali, *Bangla.* **52** 23 51N 89 15 E
Kumarl, *Australia* **79** 32 47 S 121 33 E
Kumasi, *Ghana* **90** 6 41N 1 38W
Kumba, *Cameroon* **91** 4 36N 9 24 E
Kumbakonam, *India* **51** 10 58N 79 25 E
Kumbarilla, *Australia* **77** 27 15 S 150 55 E
Kumbo, *Cameroon* **91** 6 15N 10 36 E
Kumbukkan Oya →, *Sri Lanka* **51** 6 35N 81 40 E
Kumdok, *India* **49** 33 32N 78 10 E
Kumeny, *U.S.S.R.* **37** 58 10N 49 47 E
Kumi, *Uganda* **92** 1 30N 33 58 E
Kumla, *Sweden* **10** 59 8N 15 10 E
Kummerower See, *E. Germany* **30** 53 47N 12 52 E
Kumo, *Nigeria* **91** 10 1N 11 12 E
Kumon Bum, *Burma* **52** 26 30N 97 15 E
Kumotori-Yama, *Japan* **65** 35 51N 138 57 E
Kumta, *India* **51** 14 29N 74 25 E
Kumtorkala, *U.S.S.R.* **39** 43 2N 46 50 E
Kumusi →, *Papua N. G.* **69** 8 16 S 148 13 E
Kumylzhenskaya, *U.S.S.R.* **39** 49 51N 42 38 E
Kunama, *Australia* **76** 35 35 S 148 4 E
Kunashir, Ostrov, *U.S.S.R.* **41** 44 0N 146 0 E
Kunda, *U.S.S.R.* **36** 59 30N 26 34 E
Kundiawa, *Papua N. G.* **69** 6 2 S 145 1 E
Kundip, *Australia* **79** 33 42 S 120 10 E
Kundla, *India* **48** 21 21N 71 25 E
Kungala, *Australia* **77** 29 58 S 153 7 E

Kungälv, *Sweden* **11** 57 53N 11 59 E
Kunghit I., *Canada* **110** 52 6N 131 3W
Kungrad, *U.S.S.R.* **40** 43 6N 58 54 E
Kungsbacka, *Sweden* **11** 57 30N 12 5 E
Kungu, *Zaïre* **94** 2 47N 19 12 E
Kungur, *U.S.S.R.* **40** 57 25N 56 57 E
Kungurri, *Australia* **72** 21 3 S 148 46 E
Kungyangon, *Burma* **52** 16 27N 96 20 E
Kunhar →, *Pakistan* **49** 34 20N 73 30 E
Kunhegyes, *Hungary* **33** 47 22N 20 36 E
Kunimi-Dake, *Japan* **64** 32 33N 131 1 E
Kuningan, *Indonesia* **57** 6 59 S 108 29 E
Kunisaki, *Japan* **64** 33 33N 131 45 E
Kunlong, *Burma* **52** 23 20N 98 50 E
Kunlun Shan, *Asia* **62** 36 0N 86 30 E
Kunming, *China* **58** 25 1N 102 41 E
Kunnamkulam, *India* **51** 10 38N 76 7 E
Kunrade, *Neths.* **17** 50 53N 5 57 E
Kunsan, *S. Korea* **61** 35 59N 126 45 E
Kunshan, *China* **59** 31 22N 120 58 E
Kununurra, *Australia* **78** 15 40 S 128 50 E
Kunwarara, *Australia* **72** 22 55 S 150 9 E
Kunya-Urgench, *U.S.S.R.* **40** 42 19N 59 10 E
Künzelsau, *W. Germany* **31** 49 17N 9 41 E
Kuopio, *Finland* **8** 62 53N 27 35 E
Kuopion lääni □, *Finland* **8** 63 25N 27 10 E
Kupa →, *Yugoslavia* **27** 45 28N 16 24 E
Kupang, *Indonesia* **57** 10 19 S 123 39 E
Kupiano, *Papua N. G.* **69** 10 4 S 148 14 E
Kupres, *Yugoslavia* **33** 44 1N 17 15 E
Kupyansk, *U.S.S.R.* **38** 49 52N 37 35 E
Kupyansk-Uzlovoi, *U.S.S.R.* **38** 49 45N 37 34 E
Kuqa, *China* **62** 41 35N 82 30 E
Kur →, *Bhutan* **52** 26 50N 91 0 E
Kura →, *U.S.S.R.* **39** 39 50N 49 20 E
Kurahashi-Jima, *Japan* **64** 34 8N 132 31 E
Kuranda, *Australia* **72** 16 48 S 145 35 E
Kurashiki, *Japan* **64** 34 40N 133 50 E
Kurayoshi, *Japan* **64** 35 26N 133 50 E
Kurduvadi, *India* **50** 18 8N 75 29 E
Kŭrdzhali, *Bulgaria* **35** 41 38N 25 21 E
Kure, *Japan* **64** 34 14N 132 32 E
Kuressaare = Kingisepp, *U.S.S.R.* **36** 58 15N 22 30 E
Kurgaldzhino, *U.S.S.R.* **40** 50 35N 70 20 E
Kurgan, *U.S.S.R.* **40** 55 26N 65 18 E
Kurganinsk, *U.S.S.R.* **39** 44 54N 40 34 E
Kurgannaya = Kurganinsk, *U.S.S.R.* **39** 44 54N 40 34 E
Kuria Maria Is. = Khūrīyā Mūrīyā, Jazā'ir, *Oman* **45** 17 30N 55 58 E
Kurichchi, *India* **51** 11 36N 77 35 E
Kuridala, *Australia* **72** 21 16 S 140 29 E
Kurigram, *Bangla.* **52** 25 49N 89 39 E
Kurihashi, *Japan* **65** 36 8N 139 42 E
Kuril Is. = Kurilskiye Ostrova, *U.S.S.R.* **41** 45 0N 150 0 E
Kuril Trench, *Pac. Oc.* **66** 44 0N 153 0 E
Kurilsk, *U.S.S.R.* **41** 45 14N 147 53 E
Kurilskiye Ostrova, *U.S.S.R.* **41** 45 0N 150 0 E
Kuringen, *Belgium* **17** 50 56N 5 18 E
Kurino, *Japan* **64** 31 57N 130 43 E
Kurkur, *Egypt* **88** 23 50N 32 0 E
Kurkūrah, *Libya* **86** 31 30N 20 1 E
Kurla, *India* **50** 19 5N 72 52 E
Kurlovskiy, *U.S.S.R.* **37** 55 25N 40 40 E
Kurmuk, *Sudan* **89** 10 33N 34 21 E
Kurnool, *India* **51** 15 45N 78 0 E
Kurobe-Gawe →, *Japan* **65** 36 55N 137 25 E
Kurogi, *Japan* **64** 33 12N 130 40 E
Kurovskoye, *U.S.S.R.* **37** 55 35N 38 55 E
Kurow, *N.Z.* **81** 44 44 S 170 29 E
Kurrajong, *Australia* **76** 33 33 S 150 42 E
Kurram →, *Pakistan* **48** 32 36N 71 20 E
Kurri Kurri, *Australia* **76** 32 50 S 151 28 E
Kursavka, *U.S.S.R.* **39** 44 29N 42 32 E
Kuršenai, *U.S.S.R.* **36** 56 1N 23 3 E
Kursk, *U.S.S.R.* **37** 51 42N 36 11 E
Kuršumlija, *Yugoslavia* **33** 43 9N 21 19 E
Kuru, Bahr el →, *Sudan* **89** 8 10N 26 50 E
Kuruktag, *China* **62** 41 0N 89 0 E
Kuruman, *S. Africa* **96** 27 28 S 23 28 E
Kuruman →, *S. Africa* **96** 26 56 S 20 39 E
Kurumbul →, *Australia* **77** 28 38 S 150 35 E
Kurume, *Japan* **64** 33 15N 130 30 E
Kurunegala, *Sri Lanka* **51** 7 30N 80 23 E
Kurupukari, *Guyana* **135** 4 43N 58 37W
Kurya, *U.S.S.R.* **41** 61 15N 108 10 E
Kusatsu, *Gumma, Japan* **65** 36 37N 138 36 E
Kusatsu, *Shiga, Japan* **65** 34 58N 135 57 E
Kusawa L., *Canada* **110** 60 20N 136 13W
Kusel, *W. Germany* **31** 49 31N 7 25 E
Kushchevskaya, *U.S.S.R.* **39** 46 33N 39 35 E
Kushikino, *Japan* **64** 31 44N 130 16 E
Kushima, *Japan* **64** 31 29N 131 14 E
Kushimoto, *Japan* **65** 33 28N 135 47 E
Kushiro, *Japan* **63** 43 0N 144 25 E
Kushiro →, *Japan* **63** 42 59N 144 23 E
Kushka, *U.S.S.R.* **40** 35 20N 62 18 E
Kushol, *India* **49** 33 40N 76 36 E
Kushtia, *Bangla.* **52** 23 55N 89 5 E
Kushum →, *U.S.S.R.* **39** 49 0N 50 20 E
Kuskokwim →, *U.S.A.* **102** 60 17N 162 27W
Kuskokwim Bay, *U.S.A.* **102** 59 50N 162 56W
Kustanay, *U.S.S.R.* **40** 53 10N 63 35 E
Kusu, *Japan* **64** 33 16N 131 9 E
Kut, Ko, *Thailand* **55** 11 40N 102 35 E
Kütahya, *Turkey* **46** 39 30N 30 2 E
Kutaisi, *U.S.S.R.* **39** 42 19N 42 40 E
Kutaraja = Banda Aceh, *Indonesia* **56** 5 35N 95 20 E
Kutch, Gulf of = Kachchh, Gulf of, *India* **48** 22 50N 69 15 E
Kutch, Rann of = Kachchh, Rann of, *India* **48** 24 0N 70 0 E
Kutina, *Yugoslavia* **27** 45 29N 16 48 E
Kutiyana, *India* **48** 21 36N 70 2 E
Kutkai, *Burma* **52** 23 27N 97 56 E
Kutkashen, *U.S.S.R.* **39** 40 58N 47 47 E
Kutná Hora, *Czech.* **32** 49 57N 15 16 E
Kutno, *Poland* **32** 52 15N 19 23 E
Kuttabul, *Australia* **72** 21 5 S 148 48 E
Kutu, *Zaïre* **94** 2 40 S 18 11 E
Kutum, *Sudan* **89** 14 10N 24 40 E
Kuujjuaq, *Canada* **103** 58 6N 68 15W
Kuurne, *Belgium* **17** 50 51N 3 18 E
Kuvango, *Angola* **95** 14 28 S 16 20 E
Kuvshinovo, *U.S.S.R.* **36** 57 2N 34 11 E
Kuwait = Al Kuwayt, *Kuwait* **46** 29 30N 48 0 E
Kuwait ■, *Si. Arabia* **46** 29 30N 47 30 E
Kuwana, *Japan* **65** 35 0N 136 43 E
Kuybyshev, *R.S.F.S.R., U.S.S.R.* **37** 53 8N 50 6 E
Kuybyshev, *R.S.F.S.R., U.S.S.R.* **40** 55 27N 78 19 E
Kuybyshevo, *U.S.S.R.* **38** 47 25N 36 40 E
Kuybyshevskoye Vdkhr., *U.S.S.R.* **37** 55 2N 49 30 E
Kuye He →, *China* **60** 38 23N 110 46 E
Kūysanjaq, *Iraq* **46** 36 5N 44 38 E
Kuyumba, *U.S.S.R.* **41** 60 58N 96 59 E
Kuzey Anadolu Dağlari, *Turkey* **46** 41 30N 35 0 E
Kuzhitturai, *India* **51** 8 18N 77 11 E
Kuznetsk, *U.S.S.R.* **37** 53 12N 46 40 E
Kvænangen, *Norway* **8** 70 5N 21 15 E
Kvam, *Norway* **10** 61 40N 9 42 E
Kvareli, *U.S.S.R.* **39** 41 27N 45 47 E
Kvarner, *Yugoslavia* **27** 44 50N 14 10 E
Kvarnerič, *Yugoslavia* **27** 44 43N 14 37 E
Kvillsfors, *Sweden* **11** 57 24N 15 29 E
Kviteseid, *Norway* **10** 59 24N 8 29 E
Kwabhaca, *S. Africa* **97** 30 51 S 29 0 E
Kwadacha →, *Canada* **110** 57 28N 125 38W
Kwakhanai, *Botswana* **96** 21 39 S 21 16 E
Kwakoegron, *Surinam* **135** 5 12N 55 25W
Kwale, *Kenya* **92** 4 15 S 39 31 E
Kwale, *Nigeria* **91** 5 46N 6 26 E
Kwale □, *Kenya* **92** 4 15 S 39 10 E
KwaMashu, *S. Africa* **97** 29 45 S 30 58 E
Kwamouth, *Zaïre* **94** 3 9 S 16 12 E
Kwando →, *Africa* **95** 18 27 S 23 32 E
Kwangju, *S. Korea* **61** 35 9N 126 54 E
Kwango →, *Zaïre* **94** 3 14 S 17 22 E
Kwangsi-Chuang = Guangxi Zhuangzu Zizhiqu □, *China* **58** 24 0N 109 0 E
Kwangtung = Guangdong □, *China* **59** 23 0N 113 0 E
Kwara □, *Nigeria* **91** 8 0N 5 0 E
Kwataboahegan →, *Canada* **104** 51 9N 80 50W
Kwatisore, *Indonesia* **57** 3 18 S 134 50 E
Kweichow = Guizhou □, *China* **58** 27 0N 107 0 E
Kwekwe, *Zimb.* **93** 18 58 S 29 48 E
Kwiguk, *U.S.A.* **102** 63 45N 164 35W
Kwikila, *Papua N. G.* **69** 9 49 S 147 38 E
Kwimba □, *Tanzania* **92** 3 0 S 33 0 E
Kwinana New Town, *Australia* **79** 32 15 S 115 47 E
Kwoka, *Indonesia* **57** 0 31 S 132 27 E
Kya-in-Seikkyi, *Burma* **52** 16 2N 98 8 E
Kyabé, *Chad* **87** 9 30N 19 0 E
Kyabra Cr. →, *Australia* **73** 25 36 S 142 55 E
Kyabram, *Australia* **74** 36 19 S 145 4 E
Kyaiklat, *Burma* **52** 16 25N 95 40 E
Kyaikmaraw, *Burma* **52** 16 23N 97 44 E
Kyaikthin, *Burma* **52** 23 32N 95 40 E
Kyaikto, *Burma* **54** 17 20N 97 3 E
Kyakhta, *U.S.S.R.* **41** 50 30N 106 25 E
Kyangin, *Burma* **52** 18 20N 95 20 E
Kyaukhnyat, *Burma* **52** 18 15N 97 31 E
Kyaukse, *Burma* **52** 21 36N 96 10 E
Kyauktaw, *Burma* **52** 20 51N 92 59 E
Kyawkku, *Burma* **52** 21 48N 96 56 E
Kyburz, *U.S.A.* **124** 38 47N 120 18W
Kyeamba, *Australia* **76** 35 26 S 147 40 E
Kyeintali, *Burma* **52** 18 0N 94 29 E
Kyenjojo, *Uganda* **92** 0 40N 30 37 E
Kyidaunggan, *Burma* **52** 19 53N 96 12 E
Kyle Dam, *Zimb.* **93** 20 15 S 31 0 E
Kyle of Lochalsh, *U.K.* **14** 57 17N 5 43W
Kyll →, *W. Germany* **31** 49 48N 6 42 E
Kyllburg, *W. Germany* **31** 50 2N 6 35 E
Kyneton, *Australia* **74** 37 10 S 144 29 E
Kynuna, *Australia* **72** 21 37 S 141 55 E
Kyō-ga-Saki, *Japan* **65** 35 45N 135 15 E
Kyoga, L., *Uganda* **92** 1 35N 33 0 E
Kyogle, *Australia* **77** 28 40 S 153 0 E
Kyongju, *S. Korea* **61** 35 51N 129 14 E
Kyōto, *Japan* **65** 35 0N 135 45 E
Kyōto □, *Japan* **65** 35 15N 135 45 E
Kyren, *U.S.S.R.* **41** 51 45N 101 45 E
Kyrenia, *Cyprus* **46** 35 20N 33 20 E
Kyritz, *E. Germany* **30** 52 57N 12 25 E
Kystatyam, *U.S.S.R.* **41** 67 20N 123 10 E
Kytal Ktakh, *U.S.S.R.* **41** 65 30N 123 40 E
Kyu-hkok, *Burma* **52** 24 4N 98 4 E
Kyulyunken, *U.S.S.R.* **41** 64 10N 137 5 E
Kyunhla, *Burma* **52** 23 25N 95 15 E
Kyuquot, *Canada* **110** 50 3N 127 25W
Kyurdamir, *U.S.S.R.* **39** 40 25N 48 3 E
Kyūshū, *Japan* **64** 33 0N 131 0 E
Kyūshū □, *Japan* **64** 33 0N 131 0 E
Kyūshū-Sanchi, *Japan* **64** 32 35N 131 17 E
Kyustendil, *Bulgaria* **34** 42 16N 22 41 E
Kyusyur, *U.S.S.R.* **41** 70 39N 127 15 E
Kywong, *Australia* **75** 34 58 S 146 44 E
Kyzyl, *U.S.S.R.* **41** 51 50N 94 30 E
Kyzyl-Kiya, *U.S.S.R.* **40** 40 16N 72 8 E
Kyzylkum, Peski, *U.S.S.R.* **40** 42 30N 65 0 E
Kzyl-Orda, *U.S.S.R.* **40** 44 48N 65 28 E

L

Laaber →, *W. Germany* **31** 49 0N 12 3 E
Laage, *E. Germany* **30** 53 55N 12 21 E
Laanecoorie Res., *Australia* **74** 36 52 S 143 50 E
Laasphe, *W. Germany* **30** 50 56N 8 23 E
Laba →, *U.S.S.R.* **39** 45 11N 39 42 E
Laban, *Burma* **52** 25 52N 96 40 E
Labastide-Murat, *France* **20** 44 39N 1 33 E
Labastide-Rouairoux, *France* **20** 43 28N 2 39 E
Labbézenga, *Mali* **91** 15 2N 0 48 E
Labdah = Leptis Magna, *Libya* **86** 32 40N 14 12 E
Labe = Elbe →, *Europe* **30** 53 50N 9 0 E
Labé, *Guinea* **90** 11 24N 12 16W
Laberec →, *Czech.* **32** 48 37N 21 58 E
Laberge, L., *Canada* **110** 61 11N 135 12W
Labin, *Yugoslavia* **27** 45 5N 14 8 E
Labinsk, *U.S.S.R.* **39** 44 40N 40 48 E
Labis, *Malaysia* **55** 2 22N 103 2 E
Laboe, *W. Germany* **30** 54 25N 10 13 E
Laboka, *Gabon* **94** 0 19N 11 32 E
Labouheyre, *France* **20** 44 13N 0 55W
Laboulaye, *Argentina* **140** 34 10 S 63 30W
Labra, Peña, *Spain* **22** 43 3N 4 26W
Labrador, Coast of □, *Canada* **105** 53 20N 61 0W
Labrador City, *Canada* **105** 52 57N 66 55W
Lábrea, *Brazil* **137** 7 15 S 64 51W
Labrède, *France* **20** 44 41N 0 32W
Labrieville, *Canada* **107** 49 18N 69 34W
Labuan, Pulau, *Malaysia* **56** 5 21N 115 13 E
Labuha, *Indonesia* **57** 0 30 S 127 30 E
Labuhan, *Indonesia* **57** 6 22 S 105 50 E
Labuhanbajo, *Indonesia* **57** 8 28 S 120 1 E
Labuissière, *Belgium* **17** 50 19N 4 11 E
Labuk, Telok, *Malaysia* **56** 6 10N 117 50 E
Labutta, *Burma* **52** 16 9N 94 46 E
Labytnangi, *U.S.S.R.* **40** 66 39N 66 21 E
Lac Allard, *Canada* **105** 50 33N 63 24W
Lac-aux-Sables, *Canada* **107** 46 51N 72 24W
Lac Bouchette, *Canada* **107** 48 16N 72 11W
Lac Carré, *Canada* **107** 46 7N 74 29W
Lac-des-Écorces, *Canada* **106** 46 34N 75 22W
Lac du Flambeau, *U.S.A.* **120** 46 1N 89 51W
Lac Édouard, *Canada* **107** 47 40N 72 16W
Lac-Etchemin, *Canada* **107** 46 24N 70 30W
Lac La Biche, *Canada* **110** 54 45N 111 58W
Lac la Martre, *Canada* **102** 63 8N 117 16W
Lac-Mégantic, *Canada* **107** 45 35N 70 53W
Lac-Rémi, *Canada* **106** 46 1N 74 46W
Lac-Ste-Marie, *Canada* **106** 45 57N 75 57W
Lac Seul, Res., *Canada* **104** 50 25N 92 30W
Lac Thien, *Vietnam* **54** 12 25N 108 11 E
Lacanau, *France* **20** 44 58N 1 5W
Lacanau, Étang de, *France* **20** 44 58N 1 7W
Lacantúm →, *Mexico* **127** 16 36N 90 40W
Lacara →, *Spain* **23** 38 55N 6 25W
Lacaune, *France* **20** 43 43N 2 40 E
Lacaune, Mts. de, *France* **20** 43 43N 2 50 E
Laccadive Is. = Lakshadweep Is., *Ind. Oc.* **5** 10 0N 72 30 E
Lacepede B., *Australia* **73** 36 40 S 139 40 E
Lacepede Is., *Australia* **78** 16 55 S 122 0 E
Lacerdónia, *Mozam.* **93** 18 3 S 35 35 E
Lacey, *U.S.A.* **124** 47 7N 122 49W
Lachay, Pta., *Peru* **136** 11 17 S 77 44W
Lachen, *India* **52** 27 46N 88 36 E
Lachhmangarh, *India* **48** 27 50N 75 4 E
Lachi, *Pakistan* **48** 33 25N 71 20 E
Lachine, *Canada* **107** 45 30N 73 40W
Lachlan →, *Australia* **73** 34 22 S 143 55 E
Lachute, *Canada* **107** 45 39N 74 21W
Lackawanna, *U.S.A.* **116** 42 49N 78 50W
Lacolle, *Canada* **117** 45 5N 73 22W
Lacombe, *Canada* **110** 52 30N 113 44W
Lacon, *U.S.A.* **118** 41 2N 89 24W
Lacona, *Iowa, U.S.A.* **118** 41 11N 93 23W
Lacona, *N.Y., U.S.A.* **117** 43 37N 76 5W
Láconi, *Italy* **28** 39 54N 9 4 E
Laconia, *U.S.A.* **117** 43 32N 71 30W
Lacq, *France* **20** 43 25N 0 35W
Lacrosse, *U.S.A.* **122** 46 51N 117 58W
Ladakh Ra., *India* **49** 34 0N 78 0 E
Ladário, *Brazil* **137** 19 1 S 57 35W
Ladd, *U.S.A.* **118** 41 23N 89 13W
Laddonia, *U.S.A.* **118** 39 15N 91 39W
Ládhon →, *Greece* **35** 37 40N 21 50 E
Ladik, *Turkey* **38** 40 57N 35 58 E
Ladismith, *S. Africa* **96** 33 28 S 21 15 E
Lādīz, *Iran* **47** 28 55N 61 15 E
Ladnun, *India* **48** 27 38N 74 25 E
Ladoga, L. = Ladozhskoye Ozero, *U.S.S.R.* **40** 61 15N 30 30 E
Ladon, *France* **19** 48 0N 2 30 E
Ladozhskoye Ozero, *U.S.S.R.* **40** 61 15N 30 30 E
Ladrillero, G., *Chile* **142** 49 20 S 75 35W
Lady Grey, *S. Africa* **96** 30 43 S 27 13 E
Lady Julia Percy I., *Australia* **74** 38 25 S 142 0 E
Ladybrand, *S. Africa* **96** 29 9 S 27 29 E
Ladysmith, *Canada* **110** 49 0N 123 49W
Ladysmith, *S. Africa* **97** 28 32 S 29 46 E
Ladysmith, *U.S.A.* **120** 45 27N 91 4W
Lae, *Papua N. G.* **69** 6 40 S 147 2 E
Laem Ngop, *Thailand* **55** 12 10N 102 26 E
Laem Pho, *Thailand* **55** 6 55N 101 19 E
Læsø, *Denmark* **11** 57 15N 10 53 E
Læsø Rende, *Denmark* **11** 57 20N 10 45 E
Lafayette, *Colo., U.S.A.* **120** 40 0N 105 2W
Lafayette, *Ga., U.S.A.* **115** 34 44N 85 15W
Lafayette, *Ind., U.S.A.* **114** 40 22N 86 52W
Lafayette, *Ind., U.S.A.* **119** 40 25N 86 54W
Lafayette, *La., U.S.A.* **121** 30 18N 92 0W
Lafayette, *Tenn., U.S.A.* **115** 36 35N 86 0W
Laferte →, *Canada* **110** 61 53N 117 44W
Lafia, *Nigeria* **91** 8 30N 8 34 E
Lafiagi, *Nigeria* **91** 8 52N 5 20 E
Laflamme →, *Canada* **106** 49 17N 77 9W
Lafleche, *Canada* **111** 49 45N 106 40W
Lafon, *Sudan* **89** 5 5N 32 29 E
Laforce, *Canada* **106** 47 32N 78 44W
Laforsen, *Sweden* **10** 61 56N 15 3 E
Lagaip →, *Papua N. G.* **69** 5 4 S 142 52 E
Lagan →, *Sweden* **11** 56 56N 13 58 E
Lagan →, *U.K.* **15** 54 35N 5 55W
Lagarfljót →, *Iceland* **8** 65 40N 14 18W
Lagarto, *Brazil* **138** 10 54 S 37 41W
Lage, *Spain* **22** 43 13N 9 0W
Lage, *W. Germany* **30** 52 0N 8 47 E
Lage-Mierde, *Neths.* **17** 51 25N 5 9 E
Lågen →, *Norway* **9** 61 8N 10 25 E
Lägerdorf, *W. Germany* **30** 53 53N 9 35 E
Laggan, *Australia* **76** 34 23 S 149 31 E
Laghmān □, *Afghan.* **47** 34 20N 70 0 E
Laghouat, *Algeria* **85** 33 50N 2 59 E
Lagnieu, *France* **21** 45 55N 5 20 E
Lagny, *France* **19** 48 52N 2 44 E
Lago, *Italy* **29** 39 9N 16 8 E
Lago Posadas, *Argentina* **142** 47 30 S 71 40W
Lago Ranco, *Chile* **142** 40 19 S 72 30W
Lagôa, *Portugal* **23** 37 8N 8 27W
Lagoaça, *Portugal* **22** 41 11N 6 44W
Lagodekhi, *U.S.S.R.* **39** 41 50N 46 22 E
Lagónegro, *Italy* **29** 40 8N 15 45 E
Lagonoy Gulf, *Phil.* **57** 13 50N 123 50 E
Lagos, *Nigeria* **91** 6 25N 3 27 E
Lagos, *Portugal* **23** 37 5N 8 41W
Lagos de Moreno, *Mexico* **126** 21 21N 101 55W
Lagrange, *Australia* **78** 18 45 S 121 43 E
Lagrange, *U.S.A.* **119** 41 39N 85 25W
Lagrange B., *Australia* **78** 18 38 S 121 42 E
Laguardia, *Spain* **24** 42 33N 2 35W
Laguépie, *France* **20** 44 8N 1 57 E
Laguna, *Brazil* **141** 28 30 S 48 50W
Laguna, *U.S.A.* **123** 35 3N 107 28W
Laguna, La, *Canary Is.* **25** 28 28N 16 18W
Laguna Beach, *U.S.A.* **125** 33 31N 117 52W
Laguna de la Janda, *Spain* **23** 36 15N 5 45W
Laguna Limpia, *Argentina* **140** 26 32 S 59 45W
Laguna Madre, *U.S.A.* **127** 27 0N 97 20W
Lagunas, *Chile* **140** 21 0 S 69 45W
Lagunas, *Peru* **136** 5 10 S 75 35W
Lagunillas, *Bolivia* **137** 19 38 S 63 43W
Lahad Datu, *Malaysia* **57** 5 0N 118 20 E
Lahan Sai, *Thailand* **54** 14 25N 102 52 E
Lahanam, *Laos* **54** 16 16N 105 16 E
Laharpur, *India* **49** 27 43N 80 56 E
Lahat, *Indonesia* **56** 3 45 S 103 30 E
Lahe, *Burma* **52** 26 20N 95 26 E
Lahewa, *Indonesia* **56** 1 22N 97 12 E
Lahijan, *Iran* **46** 37 10N 50 6 E
Lahn →, *W. Germany* **31** 50 17N 7 38 E
Laholm, *Sweden* **11** 56 30N 13 2 E
Laholmsbukten, *Sweden* **11** 56 30N 12 45 E
Lahontan Res., *U.S.A.* **122** 39 28N 118 58W
Lahore, *Pakistan* **48** 31 32N 74 22 E
Lahpongsel, *Burma* **52** 27 7N 98 25 E
Lahr, *W. Germany* **31** 48 20N 7 52 E

Lahti, *Finland* **9** 60 58N 25 40 E
Lahtis = Lahti, *Finland* **9** 60 58N 25 40 E
Laï, *Chad* **87** 9 25N 16 18 E
Lai Chau, *Vietnam* **54** 22 5N 103 3 E
Lai-hka, *Burma* **52** 21 16N 97 40 E
Laiagam, *Papua N. G.* **69** 5 33 S 143 30 E
Lai'an, *China* **59** 32 28N 118 30 E
Laibin, *China* **58** 23 42N 109 14 E
Laidley, *Australia* **77** 27 39 S 152 20 E
Laifeng, *China* **59** 29 27N 109 20 E
Laignes, *France* **19** 47 50N 4 20 E
Laikipia □, *Kenya* **92** 0 30N 36 30 E
Laingsburg, *S. Africa* **96** 33 9 S 20 52 E
Lairg, *U.K.* **14** 58 1N 4 24W
Laishui, *China* **60** 39 23N 115 45 E
Laiwu, *China* **61** 36 15N 117 40 E
Laixi, *China* **61** 36 50N 120 31 E
Laiyang, *China* **61** 36 59N 120 45 E
Laiyuan, *China* **60** 39 20N 114 40 E
Laizhou Wan, *China* **61** 37 30N 119 30 E
Laja →, *Mexico* **126** 20 55N 100 46W
Lajere, *Nigeria* **91** 12 10N 11 25 E
Lajes, *Rio Grande do N., Brazil* **138** 5 41 S 36 14W
Lajes, *Sta. Catarina, Brazil* **141** 27 48 S 50 20W
Lajinha, *Brazil* **139** 20 9 S 41 37W
Lajkovac, *Yugoslavia* **33** 44 27N 20 14 E
Lajosmizse, *Hungary* **33** 47 3N 19 32 E
Lak Sao, *Laos* **54** 18 11N 104 59 E
Lakaband, *Pakistan* **48** 31 2N 69 15 E
Lakar, *Indonesia* **57** 8 15 S 128 17 E
Lakatoro, *Vanuatu* **68** 16 0 S 167 0 E
Lake Alpine, *U.S.A.* **124** 38 29N 120 0W
Lake Andes, *U.S.A.* **120** 43 10N 98 32W
Lake Anse, *U.S.A.* **114** 46 42N 88 25W
Lake Arthur, *U.S.A.* **121** 30 8N 92 40W
Lake Boga, *Australia* **74** 35 26 S 143 38 E
Lake Bolac, *Australia* **74** 37 42 S 142 49 E
Lake Cargelligo, *Australia* **73** 33 15 S 146 22 E
Lake Charles, *U.S.A.* **121** 30 15N 93 10W
Lake Charm, *Australia* **74** 35 36 S 143 46 E
Lake City, *Colo., U.S.A.* **123** 38 3N 107 27W
Lake City, *Fla., U.S.A.* **115** 30 10N 82 40W
Lake City, *Iowa, U.S.A.* **118** 42 12N 94 42W
Lake City, *Mich., U.S.A.* **114** 44 20N 85 10W
Lake City, *Minn., U.S.A.* **120** 44 28N 92 21W
Lake City, *Pa., U.S.A.* **116** 42 2N 80 20W
Lake City, *S.C., U.S.A.* **115** 33 51N 79 44W
Lake Coleridge, *N.Z.* **81** 43 17 S 171 30 E
Lake Cowal, *Australia* **76** 33 41 S 147 21 E
Lake Cullulleraine, *Australia* **74** 34 15 S 141 37 E
Lake Forest, *U.S.A.* **119** 42 15N 87 50W
Lake Geneva, *U.S.A.* **119** 42 36N 88 26W
Lake George, *U.S.A.* **117** 43 25N 73 43W
Lake Grace, *Australia* **79** 33 7 S 118 28 E
Lake Harbour, *Canada* **103** 62 50N 69 50W
Lake Havasu City, *U.S.A.* **125** 34 25N 114 29W
Lake Hughes, *U.S.A.* **125** 34 41N 118 26W
Lake Isabella, *U.S.A.* **125** 35 38N 118 28W
Lake King, *Australia* **79** 33 5 S 119 45 E
Lake Lenore, *Canada* **111** 52 24N 104 59W
Lake Louise, *Canada* **110** 51 30N 116 10W
Lake Mead Nat. Rec. Area, *U.S.A.* **125** 36 0N 114 30W
Lake Michigan Beach, *U.S.A.* **119** 42 13N 86 25W
Lake Mills, *Iowa, U.S.A.* **120** 43 23N 93 33W
Lake Mills, *Wis., U.S.A.* **119** 43 5N 88 55W
Lake Murray, *Papua N. G.* **69** 6 48 S 141 29 E
Lake Nash, *Australia* **72** 20 57 S 138 0 E
Lake Odessa, *U.S.A.* **119** 42 47N 85 8W
Lake Orion, *U.S.A.* **119** 42 47N 83 14W
Lake Providence, *U.S.A.* **121** 32 49N 91 12W
Lake River, *Canada* **104** 54 30N 82 31W
Lake St. Peter, *Canada* **109** 45 18N 78 2W
Lake Superior Prov. Park, *Canada* **104** 47 45N 84 45W
Lake Tekapo, *N.Z.* **81** 44 0 S 170 30 E
Lake Varley, *Australia* **79** 32 48 S 119 30 E
Lake Villa, *U.S.A.* **119** 42 25N 88 5W
Lake Village, *U.S.A.* **121** 33 20N 91 19W
Lake Wales, *U.S.A.* **115** 27 55N 81 32W
Lake Worth, *U.S.A.* **115** 26 36N 80 3W
Lakefield, *Canada* **109** 44 25N 78 16W
Lakeland, *U.S.A.* **115** 28 0N 82 0W
Lakemba, *Fiji* **68** 18 13 S 178 47W
Lakeport, *U.S.A.* **124** 39 1N 122 56W
Lakes Entrance, *Australia* **75** 37 50 S 148 0 E
Lakeside, *Ariz., U.S.A.* **123** 34 12N 109 59W
Lakeside, *Calif., U.S.A.* **125** 32 52N 116 55W
Lakeside, *Nebr., U.S.A.* **120** 42 5N 102 24W
Lakeview, *U.S.A.* **122** 42 15N 120 22W
Lakewood, *Colo., U.S.A.* **120** 39 44N 105 3W
Lakewood, *N.J., U.S.A.* **117** 40 5N 74 13W
Lakewood, *Ohio, U.S.A.* **116** 41 28N 81 50W
Lakewood Center, *U.S.A.* **124** 47 11N 122 32W
Lakhaniá, *Greece* **35** 35 58N 27 54 E
Lakhipur, *Assam, India* **52** 24 48N 93 0 E
Lakhipur, *Assam, India* **52** 26 2N 90 18 E
Lakhonpheng, *Laos* **54** 15 54N 105 34 E
Lakhpat, *India* **48** 23 48N 68 47 E
Laki, *Iceland* **8** 64 4N 18 14W
Lakin, *U.S.A.* **121** 37 58N 101 18W
Lakitusaki →, *Canada* **104** 54 21N 82 25W
Lakonikós Kólpos, *Greece* **35** 36 40N 22 40 E
Lakota, *Ivory C.* **90** 5 50N 5 30W
Lakota, *U.S.A.* **120** 48 0N 98 22W
Laksefjorden, *Norway* **8** 70 45N 26 50 E
Lakselv, *Norway* **8** 70 2N 24 56 E
Lakshadweep Is., *Ind. Oc.* **5** 10 0N 72 30 E
Laksham, *Bangla.* **52** 23 14N 91 8 E
Lakshmeshwar, *India* **51** 15 9N 75 28 E
Lakshmikantapur, *India* **49** 22 5N 88 20 E
Lakshmipur, *Bangla.* **52** 22 58N 90 50 E
Lakuramau, *Papua N. G.* **69** 2 54 S 151 15 E
Lal Lal, *Australia* **74** 37 38 S 144 1 E
Lala Musa, *Pakistan* **48** 32 40N 73 57 E
Lalago, *Tanzania* **92** 3 28 S 33 58 E
Lalapanzi, *Zimb.* **93** 19 20 S 30 15 E
Lalbert, *Australia* **74** 35 38 S 143 20 E
Lalbert Creek, *Australia* **74** 35 23 S 143 4 E
Lalganj, *India* **49** 25 52N 85 13 E
Lalibela, *Ethiopia* **89** 12 2N 39 2 E
Lalin, *China* **61** 45 12N 127 0 E
Lalín, *Spain* **22** 42 40N 8 5W
Lalin He →, *China* **61** 45 32N 125 40 E
Lalinde, *France* **20** 44 50N 0 44 E
Lalitpur, *India* **49** 24 42N 78 28 E
Lam, *Vietnam* **54** 21 21N 106 31 E
Lam Pao Res., *Thailand* **54** 16 50N 103 15 E
Lama Kara, *Togo* **91** 9 30N 1 15 E
Lamaipum, *Burma* **52** 25 40N 97 57 E
Lamap, *Vanuatu* **68** 16 26 S 167 43 E
Lamar, *Colo., U.S.A.* **120** 38 9N 102 35W
Lamar, *Mo., U.S.A.* **121** 37 30N 94 20W
Lamarque, *Argentina* **142** 39 24 S 65 40W
Lamas, *Peru* **136** 6 28 S 76 31W
Lamastre, *France* **21** 44 59N 4 35 E
Lamballe, *France* **18** 48 29N 2 31W
Lambaréné, *Gabon* **94** 0 41 S 10 12 E
Lambasa, *Fiji* **68** 16 30 S 179 10 E
Lambay I., *Ireland* **15** 53 30N 6 0W
Lambayeque □, *Peru* **136** 6 45 S 80 0W
Lambert, *U.S.A.* **120** 47 44N 104 39W
Lambert, C., *Papua N. G.* **69** 4 11 S 151 31 E
Lambert Glacier, *Antarctica* **143** 71 0 S 70 0 E
Lamberts Bay, *S. Africa* **96** 32 5 S 18 17 E
Lambesc, *France* **21** 43 39N 5 16 E
Lambeth, *Canada* **108** 42 54N 81 18W
Lámbia, *Greece* **35** 37 52N 21 53 E
Lambon, *Papua N. G.* **69** 4 45 S 152 48 E
Lambro →, *Italy* **26** 45 8N 9 32 E
Lambton, *Canada* **107** 45 50N 71 5W
Lame, *Nigeria* **91** 10 30N 9 20 E
Lame Deer, *U.S.A.* **122** 45 45N 106 40W
Lamego, *Portugal* **22** 41 5N 7 52W
Lamèque, *Canada* **105** 47 45N 64 38W
Lameroo, *Australia* **73** 35 19 S 140 33 E
Lamesa, *U.S.A.* **121** 32 45N 101 57W
Lamía, *Greece* **35** 38 55N 22 26 E
Lammermuir Hills, *U.K.* **14** 55 50N 2 40W
Lamon Bay, *Phil.* **57** 14 30N 122 20 E
Lamoni, *U.S.A.* **118** 40 37N 93 56W
Lamont, *Canada* **110** 53 46N 112 50W
Lamont, *Calif., U.S.A.* **125** 35 15N 118 55W
Lamont, *Iowa, U.S.A.* **118** 42 35N 91 40W
Lampa, *Peru* **136** 15 22 S 70 22W
Lampang, *Thailand* **54** 18 16N 99 32 E
Lampasas, *U.S.A.* **121** 31 5N 98 10W
Lampaul, *France* **18** 48 28N 5 7W
Lampazos de Naranjo, *Mexico* **126** 27 2N 100 32W
Lampeter, *U.K.* **13** 52 6N 4 6W
Lampione, *Medit. S.* **86** 35 33N 12 20 E
Lampman, *Canada* **111** 49 25N 102 50W
Lamprey, *Canada* **111** 58 33N 94 8W
Lampung □, *Indonesia* **56** 5 30 S 104 30 E
Lamu, *Burma* **52** 19 14N 94 10 E
Lamu, *Kenya* **92** 2 16 S 40 55 E
Lamu □, *Kenya* **92** 2 0 S 40 45 E
Lamud, *Peru* **136** 6 10 S 77 57W
Lamy, *U.S.A.* **123** 35 30N 105 58W
Lan Xian, *China* **60** 38 15N 111 35 E
Lan Yu, *Taiwan* **59** 22 5N 121 35 E
Lanai I., *U.S.A.* **112** 20 50N 156 55W
Lanak La, *India* **49** 34 27N 79 32 E
Lanaken, *Belgium* **17** 50 53N 5 39 E
Lanak'o Shank'ou = Lanak La, *India* **49** 34 27N 79 32 E
Lanao, L., *Phil.* **57** 7 52N 124 15 E
Lanark, *Canada* **106** 45 1N 76 22W
Lanark, *U.K.* **14** 55 40N 3 48W
Lancang, *China* **58** 22 36N 99 58 E
Lancang Jiang →, *China* **58** 21 40N 101 10 E
Lancashire □, *U.K.* **12** 53 40N 2 30W
Lancaster, *Canada* **106** 45 10N 74 30W
Lancaster, *U.K.* **12** 54 3N 2 48W
Lancaster, *Calif., U.S.A.* **125** 34 47N 118 8W
Lancaster, *Ky., U.S.A.* **114** 37 40N 84 40W
Lancaster, *Mo., U.S.A.* **118** 40 31N 92 32W
Lancaster, *N.H., U.S.A.* **117** 44 27N 71 33W
Lancaster, *N.Y., U.S.A.* **116** 42 53N 78 43W
Lancaster, *Pa., U.S.A.* **117** 40 4N 76 19W
Lancaster, *S.C., U.S.A.* **115** 34 45N 80 47W
Lancaster, *Wis., U.S.A.* **118** 42 48N 90 43W
Lancaster Sd., *Canada* **103** 74 13N 84 0W
Lancefield, *Australia* **74** 37 18 S 144 45 E
Lancer, *Canada* **111** 50 48N 108 53W
Lanchow = Lanzhou, *China* **60** 36 1N 103 52 E
Lanciano, *Italy* **27** 42 15N 14 22 E
Lanco, *Chile* **142** 39 24 S 72 46W
Lancones, *Peru* **136** 4 30 S 80 30W
Lancun, *China* **61** 36 25N 120 10 E
Łańcut, *Poland* **32** 50 10N 22 13 E
Landau, *Bayern, W. Germany* **31** 48 41N 12 41 E
Landau, *Rhld-Pfz., W. Germany* **31** 49 12N 8 7 E
Landeck, *Austria* **31** 47 9N 10 34 E
Landen, *Belgium* **17** 50 45N 5 3 E
Lander, *U.S.A.* **122** 42 50N 108 49W
Lander →, *Australia* **78** 22 0 S 132 0 E
Landerneau, *France* **18** 48 28N 4 17W
Landeryd, *Sweden* **11** 57 7N 13 15 E
Landes, *France* **20** 44 0N 1 0W
Landes □, *France* **20** 43 57N 0 48W
Landete, *Spain* **24** 39 56N 1 25W
Landi Kotal, *Pakistan* **48** 34 7N 71 6 E
Landivisiau, *France* **18** 48 31N 4 6W
Landor, *Australia* **79** 25 10 S 116 54 E
Landquart, *Switz.* **31** 46 58N 9 32 E
Landrecies, *France* **19** 50 7N 3 40 E
Landrienne, *Canada* **106** 48 30N 77 50W
Land's End, *U.K.* **13** 50 4N 5 43W
Landsberg, *W. Germany* **31** 48 3N 10 52 E
Landsborough Cr. →, *Australia* **72** 22 28 S 144 35 E
Landsbro, *Sweden* **11** 57 24N 14 56 E
Landshut, *W. Germany* **31** 48 31N 12 10 E
Landskrona, *Sweden* **11** 55 53N 12 50 E
Landstuhl, *W. Germany* **31** 49 25N 7 34 E
Landvetter, *Sweden* **11** 57 41N 12 17 E
Laneffe, *Belgium* **17** 50 17N 4 30 E
Lanesboro, *U.S.A.* **117** 41 57N 75 34W
Lanett, *U.S.A.* **115** 33 0N 85 15W
Lang Bay, *Canada* **110** 49 45N 124 21W
Lang Lang, *Australia* **74** 38 15 S 145 34 E
Lang Qua, *Vietnam* **54** 22 16N 104 27 E
Lang Shan, *China* **60** 41 0N 106 30 E
Lang Son, *Vietnam* **54** 21 52N 106 42 E
Lang Suan, *Thailand* **55** 9 57N 99 4 E
La'nga Co, *China* **49** 30 45N 81 15 E
Lángadhás, *Greece* **35** 40 46N 23 2 E
Langádhia, *Greece* **35** 37 43N 22 1 E
Långan →, *Sweden* **10** 63 19N 14 44 E
Langara I., *Canada* **110** 54 14N 133 1W
Langatabbetje, *Surinam* **135** 4 59N 54 28W
Langdai, *China* **58** 26 6N 105 21 E
Langdon, *U.S.A.* **120** 48 47N 98 24W
Langdorp, *Belgium* **17** 50 59N 4 52 E
Langeac, *France* **20** 45 7N 3 29 E
Langeais, *France* **18** 47 20N 0 24 E
Langeb Baraka →, *Sudan* **88** 17 28N 36 50 E
Langeberg, *S. Africa* **96** 33 55 S 21 0 E
Langeberge, *S. Africa* **96** 28 15 S 22 33 E
Langeland, *Denmark* **11** 54 56N 10 48 E
Langemark, *Belgium* **17** 50 55N 2 55 E
Langen, *W. Germany* **31** 49 59N 8 40 E
Langenburg, *Canada* **111** 50 51N 101 43W
Langeness, *W. Germany* **30** 54 34N 8 35 E
Langeoog, *W. Germany* **30** 53 44N 7 33 E
Langeskov, *Denmark* **11** 55 22N 10 35 E
Langesund, *Norway* **10** 59 0N 9 45 E
Länghem, *Sweden* **11** 57 36N 13 14 E
Langhirano, *Italy* **26** 44 39N 10 16 E
Langholm, *U.K.* **14** 55 9N 2 59W
Langjökull, *Iceland* **8** 64 39N 20 12W
Langkawi, P., *Malaysia* **55** 6 25N 99 45 E
Langklip, *S. Africa* **96** 28 12 S 20 20 E
Langkon, *Malaysia* **56** 6 30N 116 40 E
Langlade, *St- P. & M.* **105** 46 50N 56 20W
Langlois, *U.S.A.* **122** 42 54N 124 26W
Langnau, *Switz.* **31** 46 56N 7 47 E
Langogne, *France* **20** 44 43N 3 50 E
Langon, *France* **20** 44 33N 0 16W
Langøya, *Norway* **8** 68 45N 14 50 E
Langres, *France* **19** 47 52N 5 20 E
Langres, Plateau de, *France* **19** 47 45N 5 3 E
Langsa, *Indonesia* **56** 4 30N 97 57 E
Långsele, *Sweden* **10** 63 12N 17 4 E
Långshyttan, *Sweden* **10** 60 27N 16 2 E
Langtao, *Burma* **52** 27 15N 97 34 E
Langting, *India* **52** 25 31N 93 7 E
Langtry, *U.S.A.* **121** 29 50N 101 33W
Langu, *Thailand* **55** 6 53N 99 47 E
Languedoc, *France* **20** 43 58N 4 0 E
Langxi, *China* **59** 31 10N 119 12 E
Langxiangzhen, *China* **60** 39 43N 116 8 E
Langzhong, *China* **58** 31 38N 105 58 E
Lanigan, *Canada* **111** 51 51N 105 2W
Lankao, *China* **60** 34 48N 114 50 E
Lannemezan, *France* **20** 43 8N 0 23 E
Lannilis, *France* **18** 48 35N 4 32W
Lannion, *France* **18** 48 46N 3 29W
Lanoraie, *Canada* **107** 45 58N 73 13W
Lanouaille, *France* **20** 45 24N 1 9 E
Lanping, *China* **58** 26 28N 99 15 E
Lansdale, *U.S.A.* **117** 40 14N 75 18W
Lansdowne, *Australia* **77** 31 48 S 152 30 E
Lansdowne, *Canada* **109** 44 24N 76 1W
Lansdowne House, *Canada* **104** 52 14N 87 53W
Lansford, *U.S.A.* **117** 40 48N 75 55W
Lanshan, *China* **59** 25 24N 112 10 E
Lansing, *U.S.A.* **119** 42 47N 84 40W
Lanslebourg-Mont-Cenis, *France* **21** 45 17N 6 52 E
Lanta Yai, Ko, *Thailand* **55** 7 35N 99 3 E
Lantian, *China* **60** 34 11N 109 20 E
Lanus, *Argentina* **140** 34 44 S 58 27W
Lanusei, *Italy* **28** 39 53N 9 31 E
Lanxi, *China* **59** 29 13N 119 28 E
Lanzarote, *Canary Is.* **25** 29 0N 13 40W
Lanzhou, *China* **60** 36 1N 103 52 E
Lanzo Torinese, *Italy* **26** 45 16N 7 29 E
Lao →, *Italy* **29** 39 45N 15 45 E
Lao Bao, *Laos* **54** 16 35N 106 30 E
Lao Cai, *Vietnam* **54** 22 30N 103 57 E
Laoag, *Phil.* **57** 18 7N 120 34 E
Laoang, *Phil.* **57** 12 32N 125 8 E
Laoha He →, *China* **61** 43 25N 120 35 E
Laois □, *Ireland* **15** 53 0N 7 20W
Laon, *France* **19** 49 33N 3 35 E
Laona, *U.S.A.* **114** 45 32N 88 41W
Laos ■, *Asia* **54** 17 45N 105 0 E
Lapa, *Brazil* **141** 25 46 S 49 44W
Lapalisse, *France* **20** 46 15N 3 38 E
Laparan, *Phil.* **57** 6 0N 120 0 E
Lapeer, *U.S.A.* **104** 43 3N 83 20W
Lapi □, *Finland* **8** 67 0N 27 0 E
Lapland = Lappland, *Europe* **8** 68 7N 24 0 E
Laporte, *U.S.A.* **117** 41 27N 76 30W
Lapovo, *Yugoslavia* **33** 44 10N 21 2 E
Lappland, *Europe* **8** 68 7N 24 0 E
Laprida, *Argentina* **140** 37 34 S 60 45W
Laptev Sea, *U.S.S.R.* **41** 76 0N 125 0 E
Lăpuşul →, *Romania* **34** 47 25N 23 40 E
Lār, *Iran* **47** 27 40N 54 14 E
Lara, *Australia* **74** 38 2 S 144 26 E
Lara □, *Venezuela* **134** 10 10N 69 50W
Larabanga, *Ghana* **90** 9 16N 1 56W
Laracha, *Spain* **22** 43 15N 8 35W
Larache, *Morocco* **84** 35 10N 6 5W
Laragne-Montéglin, *France* **21** 44 18N 5 49 E
Laramie, *U.S.A.* **120** 41 20N 105 38W
Laramie Mts., *U.S.A.* **120** 42 0N 105 30W
Laranjeiras, *Brazil* **138** 10 48 S 37 10W
Laranjeiras do Sul, *Brazil* **141** 25 23 S 52 23W
Larantuka, *Indonesia* **57** 8 21 S 122 55 E
Larap, *Phil.* **57** 14 18N 122 39 E
Larat, *Indonesia* **57** 7 0 S 132 0 E
Laravale, *Australia* **77** 28 6 S 152 57 E
Larde, *Mozam.* **93** 16 28 S 39 43 E
Larder Lake, *Canada* **106** 48 5N 79 40W
Lárdhos, Ákra, *Greece* **35** 36 4N 28 10 E
Laredo, *Spain* **24** 43 26N 3 28W
Laredo, *U.S.A.* **121** 27 34N 99 29W
Laredo Sd., *Canada* **110** 52 30N 128 53W
Laren, *Neths.* **16** 52 16N 5 14 E
Largentière, *France* **21** 44 34N 4 18 E
Largs, *U.K.* **14** 55 48N 4 51W
Lari, *Italy* **26** 43 34N 10 35 E
Lariang, *Indonesia* **57** 1 26 S 119 17 E
Larimore, *U.S.A.* **120** 47 55N 97 35W
Larino, *Italy* **29** 41 48N 14 54 E
Lárisa, *Greece* **35** 39 49N 22 28 E
Larkana, *Pakistan* **48** 27 32N 68 18 E
Larnaca, *Cyprus* **46** 35 0N 33 35 E
Larne, *U.K.* **15** 54 52N 5 50W
Larned, *U.S.A.* **120** 38 15N 99 10W
Larochette, *Belgium* **17** 49 47N 6 13 E
Laroquebrou, *France* **20** 44 58N 2 12 E
Larrimah, *Australia* **78** 15 35 S 133 12 E
Larsen Ice Shelf, *Antarctica* **143** 67 0 S 62 0W
Larvik, *Norway* **10** 59 4N 10 0 E
Laryak, *U.S.S.R.* **40** 61 15N 80 0 E
Larzac, Causse du, *France* **20** 43 50N 3 17 E
Las Animas, *U.S.A.* **121** 38 8N 103 18W
Las Anod, *Somali Rep.* **98** 8 26N 47 19 E
Las Blancos, *Spain* **25** 37 38N 0 49W
Las Brenãs, *Argentina* **140** 27 5 S 61 7W
Las Cabezas de San Juan, *Spain* **23** 37 0N 5 58W
Las Chimeneas, *Mexico* **125** 32 8N 116 5W
Las Coloradas, *Argentina* **142** 39 34 S 70 36W
Las Cruces, *U.S.A.* **123** 32 18N 106 50W
Las Flores, *Argentina* **140** 36 10 S 59 7W
Las Heras, *Argentina* **140** 32 51 S 68 49W
Las Horquetas, *Argentina* **142** 48 14 S 71 11W
Las Khoreh, *Somali Rep.* **98** 11 10N 48 20 E
Las Lajas, *Argentina* **142** 38 30 S 70 25W
Las Lomas, *Peru* **136** 4 40 S 80 10W
Las Lomitas, *Argentina* **140** 24 43 S 60 35W
Las Marismas, *Spain* **23** 37 5N 6 20W

Las Mercedes, *Venezuela* **134** 9 7N 66 24W
Las Navas de la Concepción, *Spain* **23** 37 56N 5 30W
Las Navas de Tolosa, *Spain* **23** 38 18N 3 38W
Las Palmas, *Argentina* **140** 27 8 S 58 45W
Las Palmas, *Canary Is.* **25** 28 7N 15 26W
Las Palmas →, *Mexico* **125** 32 26N 116 54W
Las Piedras, *Uruguay* **141** 34 44 S 56 14W
Las Pipinas, *Argentina* **140** 35 30 S 57 19W
Las Plumas, *Argentina* **142** 43 40 S 67 15W
Las Rosas, *Argentina* **140** 32 30 S 61 35W
Las Tablas, *Panama* **128** 7 49N 80 14W
Las Termas, *Argentina* **140** 27 29 S 64 52W
Las Varillas, *Argentina* **140** 31 50 S 62 50W
Las Vegas, *N. Mex., U.S.A.* **123** 35 35N 105 10W
Las Vegas, *Nev., U.S.A.* **125** 36 10N 115 5W
Lascano, *Uruguay* **141** 33 35 S 54 12W
Lascelles, *Australia* **74** 35 34 S 142 34 E
Lashburn, *Canada* **111** 53 10N 109 40W
Lashio, *Burma* **52** 22 56N 97 45 E
Lashkar, *India* **48** 26 10N 78 10 E
Łasin, *Poland* **32** 53 30N 19 2 E
Laško, *Yugoslavia* **27** 46 10N 15 16 E
Lassance, *Brazil* **139** 17 54 S 44 34W
Lassay, *France* **18** 48 27N 0 30W
Lassen Pk., *U.S.A.* **122** 40 29N 121 31W
Last Mountain L., *Canada* **111** 51 5N 105 14W
Lastchance Cr. →, *U.S.A.* **124** 40 2N 121 15W
Lastoursville, *Gabon* **94** 0 55 S 12 38 E
Lastovo, *Yugoslavia* **27** 42 46N 16 55 E
Lastovski Kanal, *Yugoslavia* **27** 42 50N 17 0 E
Lat Yao, *Thailand* **54** 15 45N 99 48 E
Latacunga, *Ecuador* **134** 0 50 S 78 35W
Latakia = Al Lādhiqīyah, *Syria* **46** 35 30N 35 45 E
Latchford, *Canada* **106** 47 20N 79 50W
Late, *Tonga* **68** 18 48 S 174 39W
Laterza, *Italy* **29** 40 38N 16 47 E
Latham, *Australia* **79** 29 44 S 116 20 E
Lathen, *W. Germany* **30** 52 51N 7 21 E
Lathrop, *U.S.A.* **118** 39 33N 94 20W
Lathrop Wells, *U.S.A.* **125** 36 39N 116 24W
Latiano, *Italy* **29** 40 33N 17 43 E
Latina, *Italy* **28** 41 26N 12 53 E
Latisana, *Italy* **27** 45 47N 13 1 E
Latium = Lazio □, *Italy* **27** 42 10N 12 30 E
Laton, *U.S.A.* **124** 36 26N 119 41W
Latorica →, *Czech.* **33** 48 28N 21 50 E
Latouche Treville, C., *Australia* **78** 18 27 S 121 49 E
Latrobe, *Tas., Australia* **72** 41 14 S 146 30 E
Latrobe, *Vic., Australia* **75** 38 8 S 146 44 E
Latrobe, *U.S.A.* **116** 40 19N 79 21W
Latrónico, *Italy* **29** 40 5N 16 0 E
Latrun, *Jordan* **44** 31 50N 34 58 E
Latulipe, *Canada* **106** 47 26N 79 2W
Latur, *India* **50** 18 25N 76 40 E
Latvian S.S.R. □, *U.S.S.R.* **36** 56 50N 24 0 E
Lau, *Fiji* **68** 17 0 S 178 30W
Lauca →, *Bolivia* **136** 19 9 S 68 10W
Lauchhammer, *E. Germany* **30** 51 35N 13 48 E
Lauenburg, *W. Germany* **30** 53 23N 10 33 E
Lauffen, *W. Germany* **31** 49 4N 9 9 E
Laugarbakki, *Iceland* **8** 65 20N 20 55W
Laujar, *Spain* **25** 37 0N 2 54W
Launceston, *Australia* **72** 41 24 S 147 8 E
Launceston, *U.K.* **13** 50 38N 4 21W
Launching Race, *Australia* **74** 37 47 S 145 36 E
Laune →, *Ireland* **15** 52 5N 9 40W
Laupheim, *W. Germany* **31** 48 13N 9 53 E
Laura, *Australia* **72** 15 32 S 144 32 E
Laureana di Borrello, *Italy* **29** 38 28N 16 5 E
Laurel, *Ind., U.S.A.* **119** 39 31N 85 11W
Laurel, *Miss., U.S.A.* **121** 31 41N 89 9W
Laurel, *Mont., U.S.A.* **122** 45 46N 108 49W
Laurel Hill, *Australia* **76** 35 34 S 148 6 E
Laurencekirk, *U.K.* **14** 56 50N 2 30W
Laurens, *U.S.A.* **115** 34 32N 82 2W
Laurentian Plateau, *Canada* **103** 52 0N 70 0W
Laurentides, Parc Prov. des, *Canada* **107** 47 45N 71 15W
Lauria, *Italy* **29** 40 3N 15 50 E
Laurie L., *Canada* **111** 56 35N 101 57W
Laurier-Station, *Canada* **107** 46 32N 71 38W
Laurierville, *Canada* **107** 46 18N 71 39W
Laurieton, *Australia* **77** 31 39 S 152 48 E
Laurinburg, *U.S.A.* **115** 34 50N 79 25W
Laurium, *U.S.A.* **104** 47 14N 88 26W
Lausanne, *Switz.* **31** 46 32N 6 38 E
Laut, *Indonesia* **56** 4 45N 108 0 E
Laut Ketil, Kepulauan, *Indonesia* **56** 4 45 S 115 40 E
Lautaro, *Chile* **142** 38 31 S 72 27W
Lauterbach, *W. Germany* **30** 50 39N 9 23 E
Lauterecken, *W. Germany* **31** 49 38N 7 35 E
Lautoka, *Fiji* **68** 17 37 S 177 27 E
Lauwe, *Belgium* **17** 50 47N 3 12 E
Lauwers, *Neths.* **16** 53 32N 6 23 E
Lauwers Zee, *Neths.* **16** 53 21N 6 13 E
Lauzon, *Canada* **107** 46 48N 71 10W
Lava Hot Springs, *U.S.A.* **122** 42 38N 112 1W
Lavadores, *Spain* **22** 42 14N 8 41W
Lavagna, *Italy* **26** 44 18N 9 22 E
Laval, *Canada* **107** 45 35N 73 45W
Laval, *France* **18** 48 4N 0 48W
Lavalle, *Argentina* **140** 28 15 S 65 15W
Lavaltrie, *Canada* **107** 45 53N 73 17W
Lavandou, Le, *France* **21** 43 8N 6 22 E
Lavant Sta., *Canada* **109** 45 3N 76 42W
Lávara, *Greece* **35** 41 19N 26 22 E
Lavardac, *France* **20** 44 12N 0 20 E
Lavaur, *France* **20** 43 40N 1 49 E
Lavelanet, *France* **20** 42 57N 1 51 E
Lavello, *Italy* **29** 41 4N 15 47 E
Laverlochère, *Canada* **106** 47 26N 79 18W
Laverne, *U.S.A.* **121** 36 43N 99 58W
Lavers Hill, *Australia* **74** 38 40 S 143 25 E
Laverton, *Australia* **79** 28 44 S 122 29 E
Lavi, *Israel* **44** 32 47N 35 25 E
Lavieille, L., *Canada* **109** 45 51N 78 14W
Lavos, *Portugal* **22** 40 6N 8 49W
Lavras, *Brazil* **139** 21 20 S 45 0W
Lavre, *Portugal* **23** 38 46N 8 22W
Lavrentiya, *U.S.S.R.* **41** 65 35N 171 0W
Lávrion, *Greece* **35** 37 40N 24 4 E
Lavumisa, *Swaziland* **97** 27 20 S 31 55 E
Lawas, *Malaysia* **56** 4 55N 115 25 E
Lawele, *Indonesia* **57** 5 16 S 123 3 E
Lawksawk, *Burma* **52** 21 15N 96 52 E
Lawn Hill, *Australia* **72** 18 36 S 138 33 E
Lawra, *Ghana* **90** 10 39N 2 51W
Lawrence, *Ind., U.S.A.* **119** 39 50N 86 2W
Lawrence, *Kans., U.S.A.* **120** 39 0N 95 10W
Lawrence, *Mass., U.S.A.* **117** 42 40N 71 9W
Lawrenceburg, *Ind., U.S.A.* **119** 39 5N 84 50W
Lawrenceburg, *Ky., U.S.A.* **119** 38 2N 84 54W
Lawrenceburg, *Tenn., U.S.A.* **115** 35 12N 87 19W
Lawrenceville, *Ga., U.S.A.* **115** 33 55N 83 59W
Lawrenceville, *Ill., U.S.A.* **119** 38 44N 87 41W
Laws, *U.S.A.* **124** 37 24N 118 20W
Lawson, *U.S.A.* **118** 39 26N 94 12W
Lawton, *Mich., U.S.A.* **119** 42 10N 85 50W
Lawton, *Okla., U.S.A.* **121** 34 33N 98 25W
Lawu, *Indonesia* **57** 7 40 S 111 13 E
Laxford, L., *U.K.* **14** 58 25N 5 10W
Laylá, *Si. Arabia* **46** 22 10N 46 40 E
Layon →, *France* **18** 47 20N 0 45W
Laysan I., *Pac. Oc.* **67** 25 30N 167 0W
Laytonville, *U.S.A.* **122** 39 44N 123 29W
Laza, *Burma* **52** 26 30N 97 38 E
Lazio □, *Italy* **27** 42 10N 12 30 E
Lea →, *U.K.* **13** 51 30N 0 10W
Leach, *Cambodia* **55** 12 21N 103 46 E
Lead, *U.S.A.* **120** 44 20N 103 40W
Leader, *Canada* **111** 50 50N 109 30W
Leadhills, *U.K.* **14** 55 25N 3 47W
Leadville, *Australia* **77** 32 1 S 149 38 E
Leadville, *U.S.A.* **123** 39 17N 106 23W
Leaf →, *U.S.A.* **121** 31 0N 88 45W
Leakey, *U.S.A.* **121** 29 45N 99 45W
Lealui, *Zambia* **95** 15 10 S 23 2 E
Leamington, *Canada* **108** 42 3N 82 36W
Leamington, *U.K.* **13** 52 18N 1 32W
Leamington, *U.S.A.* **122** 39 37N 112 17W
Le'an, *China* **59** 27 22N 115 48 E
Leandro Norte Alem, *Argentina* **141** 27 34 S 55 15W
Learmonth, *Vic., Australia* **74** 37 26 S 143 44 E
Learmonth, *W. Austral., Australia* **78** 22 13 S 114 10 E
Leask, *Canada* **111** 53 5N 106 45W
Leavenworth, *Ind., U.S.A.* **119** 38 12N 86 21W
Leavenworth, *Kans., U.S.A.* **120** 39 25N 95 0W
Leavenworth, *Wash., U.S.A.* **122** 47 44N 120 37W
Leawood, *U.S.A.* **118** 38 57N 94 37W
Łeba, *Poland* **32** 54 45N 17 32 E
Lebak, *Phil.* **57** 6 32N 124 5 E
Lebam, *U.S.A.* **124** 46 34N 123 33W
Lebango, *Congo* **94** 0 39N 14 21 E
Lebanon, *Ill., U.S.A.* **118** 38 38N 89 49W
Lebanon, *Ind., U.S.A.* **119** 40 3N 86 28W
Lebanon, *Kans., U.S.A.* **120** 39 50N 98 35W
Lebanon, *Ky., U.S.A.* **114** 37 35N 85 15W
Lebanon, *Mo., U.S.A.* **118** 37 40N 92 40W
Lebanon, *Ohio, U.S.A.* **119** 39 26N 84 13W
Lebanon, *Oreg., U.S.A.* **122** 44 31N 122 57W
Lebanon, *Pa., U.S.A.* **117** 40 20N 76 28W
Lebanon, *Tenn., U.S.A.* **115** 36 15N 86 20W
Lebanon ■, *Asia* **46** 34 0N 36 0 E
Lebanon Junction, *U.S.A.* **119** 37 50N 85 44W
Lebbeke, *Belgium* **17** 51 0N 4 8 E
Lebec, *U.S.A.* **125** 34 50N 118 59W
Lebedin, *U.S.S.R.* **36** 50 35N 34 30 E
Lebedyan, *U.S.S.R.* **37** 53 0N 39 10 E
Lebel-sur-Quévillon, *Canada* **106** 49 3N 76 59W
Lebomboberge, *S. Africa* **97** 24 30 S 32 0 E
Lębork, *Poland* **32** 54 33N 17 46 E
Lebrija, *Spain* **23** 36 53N 6 5W
Lebu, *Chile* **140** 37 40 S 73 47W
Lecce, *Italy* **29** 40 20N 18 10 E
Lecco, *Italy* **26** 45 50N 9 27 E
Lecco, L. di, *Italy* **26** 45 51N 9 22 E
Lécera, *Spain* **24** 41 13N 0 43W
Lech, *Austria* **31** 47 13N 10 9 E
Lech →, *W. Germany* **31** 48 44N 10 56 E
Lechang, *China* **59** 25 10N 113 20 E
Lechtaler Alpen, *Austria* **31** 47 15N 10 30 E
Lectoure, *France* **20** 43 56N 0 38 E
Łęczyca, *Poland* **32** 52 5N 19 15 E
Ledbury, *U.K.* **13** 52 3N 2 25W
Lede, *Belgium* **17** 50 58N 3 59 E
Ledeberg, *Belgium* **17** 51 2N 3 45 E
Ledesma, *Spain* **22** 41 6N 5 59W
Ledong, *China* **54** 18 41N 109 5 E
Leduc, *Canada* **110** 53 15N 113 30W
Ledyczek, *Poland* **32** 53 33N 16 59 E
Lee, *U.S.A.* **117** 42 17N 73 18W
Lee →, *Ireland* **15** 51 50N 8 30W
Lee Vining, *U.S.A.* **124** 37 58N 119 7W
Leech L., *U.S.A.* **120** 47 9N 94 23W
Leedey, *U.S.A.* **121** 35 53N 99 24W
Leeds, *U.K.* **12** 53 48N 1 34W
Leeds, *U.S.A.* **115** 33 32N 86 30W
Leek, *Neths.* **16** 53 10N 6 24 E
Leek, *U.K.* **12** 53 7N 2 2W
Leende, *Neths.* **17** 51 21N 5 33 E
Leer, *W. Germany* **30** 53 13N 7 29 E
Leerdam, *Neths.* **16** 51 54N 5 6 E
Leersum, *Neths.* **16** 52 0N 5 26 E
Lee's Summit, *U.S.A.* **118** 38 55N 94 23W
Leesburg, *Fla., U.S.A.* **115** 28 47N 81 52W
Leesburg, *Ohio, U.S.A.* **119** 39 21N 83 33W
Leeston, *N.Z.* **81** 43 45 S 172 19 E
Leesville, *U.S.A.* **121** 31 12N 93 15W
Leeton, *Australia* **75** 34 33 S 146 23 E
Leetonia, *U.S.A.* **116** 40 53N 80 45W
Leeu Gamka, *S. Africa* **96** 32 47 S 21 59 E
Leeuwarden, *Neths.* **16** 53 15N 5 48 E
Leeuwin, C., *Australia* **79** 34 20 S 115 9 E
Leeward Is., *Atl. Oc.* **129** 16 30N 63 30W
Leeward Is., *Pac. Oc.* **67** 16 0 S 147 0W
Lefebvre, *Canada* **107** 47 12N 69 49W
Léfini, *Congo* **94** 2 55 S 15 39 E
Lefors, *U.S.A.* **121** 35 30N 100 50W
Lefroy, *Canada* **108** 44 16N 79 34W
Lefroy, L., *Australia* **79** 31 21 S 121 40 E
Legal, *Canada* **110** 53 55N 113 35W
Leganés, *Spain* **24** 40 19N 3 45W
Legazpi, *Phil.* **57** 13 10N 123 45 E
Legendre I., *Australia* **78** 20 22 S 116 55 E
Leghorn = Livorno, *Italy* **26** 43 32N 10 18 E
Legion, *Zimb.* **93** 21 25 S 28 30 E
Legionowo, *Poland* **32** 52 25N 20 50 E
Léglise, *Belgium* **17** 49 48N 5 32 E
Legnago, *Italy* **27** 45 10N 11 19 E
Legnano, *Italy* **26** 45 35N 8 55 E
Legnica, *Poland* **32** 51 12N 16 10 E
Legrad, *Yugoslavia* **27** 46 17N 16 51 E
Legume, *Australia* **77** 28 20 S 152 19 E
Leh, *India* **49** 34 9N 77 35 E
Lehi, *U.S.A.* **122** 40 20N 111 51W
Lehighton, *U.S.A.* **117** 40 50N 75 44W
Lehrte, *W. Germany* **30** 52 22N 9 58 E
Lehututu, *Botswana* **96** 23 54 S 21 55 E
Lei Shui →, *China* **59** 26 55N 112 35 E
Leiah, *Pakistan* **48** 30 58N 70 58 E
Leibnitz, *Austria* **33** 46 47N 15 34 E
Leibo, *China* **58** 28 11N 103 34 E
Leicester, *U.K.* **13** 52 39N 1 9W
Leicester □, *U.K.* **13** 52 40N 1 10W
Leichhardt →, *Australia* **72** 17 35 S 139 48 E
Leichhardt Ra., *Australia* **72** 20 46 S 147 40 E
Leiden, *Neths.* **16** 52 9N 4 30 E
Leiderdorp, *Neths.* **16** 52 9N 4 32 E
Leidschendam, *Neths.* **16** 52 5N 4 24 E
Leie →, *Belgium* **19** 51 2N 3 45 E
Leigh →, *Australia* **74** 38 18 S 144 30 E
Leignon, *Belgium* **17** 50 16N 5 7 E
Leiktho, *Burma* **52** 19 13N 96 35 E
Leine →, *W. Germany* **30** 52 20N 9 50 E
Leinster, *Australia* **79** 27 51 S 120 36 E
Leinster □, *Ireland* **15** 53 0N 7 10W
Leinster, Mt., *Ireland* **15** 52 38N 6 47W
Leipzig, *E. Germany* **30** 51 20N 12 23 E
Leipzig □, *E. Germany* **30** 51 20N 12 30 E
Leiria, *Portugal* **23** 39 46N 8 53W
Leiria □, *Portugal* **23** 39 46N 8 53W
Leisler, Mt., *Australia* **78** 23 23 S 129 20 E
Leitchville, *Australia* **74** 35 54 S 144 18 E
Leith, *U.K.* **14** 55 59N 3 10W
Leith Hill, *U.K.* **13** 51 10N 0 23W
Leitha →, *Europe* **33** 48 0N 16 35 E
Leitrim, *Ireland* **15** 54 0N 8 5W
Leitrim □, *Ireland* **15** 54 8N 8 0W
Leiyang, *China* **59** 26 27N 112 45 E
Leiza, *Spain* **24** 43 5N 1 55W
Leizhou Bandao, *China* **62** 21 0N 110 0 E
Leizhou Wan, *China* **59** 20 50N 110 20 E
Lejeune, *Canada* **107** 47 46N 68 34W
Lek →, *Neths.* **16** 51 54N 4 35 E
Leke, *Belgium* **17** 51 6N 2 54 E
Lekkerkerk, *Neths.* **16** 51 54N 4 41 E
Leksula, *Indonesia* **57** 3 46 S 126 31 E
Leland, *U.S.A.* **121** 33 25N 90 52W
Leland Lakes, *Canada* **111** 60 0N 110 59W
Leleque, *Argentina* **142** 42 28 S 71 0W
Lelu, *Burma* **52** 19 4N 95 30 E
Lelystad, *Neths.* **16** 52 30N 5 25 E
Lema, *Nigeria* **91** 12 58N 4 13 E
Léman, Lac, *Switz.* **31** 46 26N 6 30 E
Lemelerveld, *Neths.* **16** 52 26N 6 20 E
Lemera, *Zaïre* **92** 3 0 S 28 55 E
Lemfu, *Zaïre* **95** 5 18 S 15 13 E
Lemgo, *W. Germany* **30** 52 2N 8 52 E
Lemhi Ra., *U.S.A.* **122** 44 30N 113 30W
Lemieux, *Canada* **107** 46 18N 72 7W
Lemieux, L., *Canada* **106** 50 19N 74 38W
Lemmer, *Neths.* **16** 52 51N 5 43 E
Lemmon, *U.S.A.* **120** 45 59N 102 10W
Lemoine, L., *Canada* **106** 48 0N 78 0W
Lemon Grove, *U.S.A.* **125** 32 45N 117 2W
Lemoore, *U.S.A.* **124** 36 23N 119 46W
Lempdes, *France* **20** 45 22N 3 17 E
Lemsid, *W. Sahara* **84** 26 33N 13 51W
Lemvig, *Denmark* **11** 56 33N 8 20 E
Lemyethna, *Burma* **52** 17 36N 95 9 E
Lena →, *U.S.S.R.* **41** 72 52N 126 40 E
Lencloître, *France* **18** 46 50N 0 20 E
Lençóis, *Brazil* **139** 12 35 S 41 24W
Lendelede, *Belgium* **17** 50 53N 3 16 E
Lendinara, *Italy* **27** 45 4N 11 37 E
Lengerich, *W. Germany* **30** 52 12N 7 50 E
Lenggong, *Malaysia* **55** 5 6N 100 58 E
Lenggries, *W. Germany* **31** 47 41N 11 34 E
Lengua de Vaca, Pta., *Chile* **140** 30 14 S 71 38W
Lenhovda, *Sweden* **11** 57 0N 15 16 E
Lenin, *U.S.S.R.* **39** 48 20N 40 56 E
Leninabad, *U.S.S.R.* **40** 40 17N 69 37 E
Leninakan, *U.S.S.R.* **39** 40 47N 43 50 E
Leningrad, *U.S.S.R.* **36** 59 55N 30 20 E
Leningradskaya, *Antarctica* **143** 69 50 S 160 0 E
Lenino, *U.S.S.R.* **38** 45 17N 35 46 E
Leninogorsk, *U.S.S.R.* **40** 50 20N 83 30 E
Leninsk, *R.S.F.S.R., U.S.S.R.* **39** 48 40N 45 15 E
Leninsk, *R.S.F.S.R., U.S.S.R.* **39** 46 10N 43 46 E
Leninsk-Kuznetskiy, *U.S.S.R.* **40** 54 44N 86 10 E
Leninskaya Sloboda, *U.S.S.R.* **37** 56 7N 44 29 E
Leninskoye, *R.S.F.S.R., U.S.S.R.* **37** 58 23N 47 3 E
Leninskoye, *R.S.F.S.R., U.S.S.R.* **41** 47 56N 132 38 E
Lenk, *Switz.* **31** 46 27N 7 28 E
Lenmalu, *Indonesia* **57** 1 45 S 130 15 E
Lenne →, *W. Germany* **30** 51 25N 7 30 E
Lennox, I., *Chile* **142** 55 18 S 66 50W
Lennox Head, *Australia* **77** 28 46 S 153 37 E
Lennoxville, *Canada* **117** 45 22N 71 51W
Leno, *Italy* **26** 45 24N 10 14 E
Lenoir, *U.S.A.* **115** 35 55N 81 36W
Lenoir City, *U.S.A.* **115** 35 40N 84 20W
Lenora, *U.S.A.* **120** 39 39N 100 1W
Lenore L., *Canada* **111** 52 30N 104 59W
Lenox, *Iowa, U.S.A.* **118** 40 53N 94 34W
Lenox, *Mass., U.S.A.* **117** 42 20N 73 18W
Lens, *Belgium* **17** 50 33N 3 54 E
Lens, *France* **19** 50 26N 2 50 E
Lens St. Remy, *Belgium* **17** 50 39N 5 7 E
Lensk, *U.S.S.R.* **41** 60 48N 114 55 E
Lenskoye, *U.S.S.R.* **38** 45 3N 34 1 E
Lent, *Neths.* **16** 51 52N 5 52 E
Lentini, *Italy* **29** 37 18N 15 0 E
Lentvaric, *U.S.S.R.* **36** 54 39N 25 3 E
Lenwood, *U.S.A.* **125** 34 53N 117 7W
Lenzen, *E. Germany* **30** 53 6N 11 26 E
Léo, *Burkina Faso* **90** 11 3N 2 2W
Leoben, *Austria* **33** 47 22N 15 5 E
Leola, *U.S.A.* **120** 45 47N 98 58W
Leominster, *U.K.* **13** 52 15N 2 43W
Leominster, *U.S.A.* **117** 42 32N 71 45W
Léon, *France* **20** 43 53N 1 18W
León, *Mexico* **126** 21 7N 101 30W
León, *Nic.* **128** 12 20N 86 51W
León, *Spain* **22** 42 38N 5 34W
Leon, *U.S.A.* **118** 40 40N 93 40W
León □, *Spain* **22** 42 40N 5 55W
León, Montañas de, *Spain* **22** 42 30N 6 18W
Leonardtown, *U.S.A.* **114** 38 19N 76 39W
Leonforte, *Italy* **29** 37 39N 14 22 E
Leongatha, *Australia* **74** 38 30 S 145 58 E
Leonídhion, *Greece* **35** 37 9N 22 52 E
Leonora, *Australia* **79** 28 49 S 121 19 E
Leopold, *Australia* **74** 38 13 S 144 28 E
Léopold II, Lac = Mai-Ndombe, L., *Zaïre* **94** 2 0 S 18 20 E
Leopoldina, *Brazil* **139** 21 28 S 42 40W
Leopoldo Bulhões, *Brazil* **139** 16 37 S 48 46W
Leopoldsburg, *Belgium* **17** 51 7N 5 13 E
Léopoldville = Kinshasa, *Zaïre* **95** 4 20 S 15 15 E
Leoti, *U.S.A.* **120** 38 31N 101 19W
Leoville, *Canada* **111** 53 39N 107 33W
Lépa, L. do, *Angola* **95** 17 0 S 19 0 E
Lepe, *Spain* **23** 37 15N 7 12W
Lepel, *U.S.S.R.* **36** 54 50N 28 40 E
Lepikha, *U.S.S.R.* **41** 64 45N 125 55 E

Leping, *China* **59** 28 47N 117 7 E
Lepontine, Alpi, *Italy* **31** 46 22N 8 27 E
Leptis Magna, *Libya* **86** 32 40N 14 12 E
Lequeitio, *Spain* **24** 43 20N 2 32W
Lercara Friddi, *Italy* **28** 37 42N 13 36 E
Lerdo, *Mexico* **126** 25 32N 103 32W
Léré, *C.A.R.* **94** 6 46N 17 25 E
Léré, *Chad* **87** 9 39N 14 13 E
Lere, *Nigeria* **91** 9 43N 9 18 E
Leribe, *Lesotho* **97** 28 51 S 28 3 E
Lérici, *Italy* **26** 44 4N 9 58 E
Lérida, *Spain* **24** 41 37N 0 39 E
Lérida □, *Spain* **24** 42 6N 1 0 E
Lérins, Is. de, *France* **21** 43 31N 7 3 E
Lerma, *Spain* **22** 42 0N 3 47W
Léros, *Greece* **35** 37 10N 26 50 E
Lérouville, *France* **19** 48 44N 5 30 E
Lerwick, *U.K.* **14** 60 10N 1 10W
Léry, *Canada* **107** 45 21N 73 48W
Lesbos, I. = Lésvos, *Greece* **35** 39 10N 26 20 E
Leshan, *China* **58** 29 33N 103 41 E
Lésina, L. di, *Italy* **27** 41 53N 15 25 E
Lesja, *Norway* **10** 62 7N 8 51 E
Lesjaverk, *Norway* **10** 62 12N 8 34 E
Leskov I., *Antarctica* **143** 56 0 S 28 0W
Leskovac, *Yugoslavia* **33** 43 0N 21 58 E
Leslie, *Ark., U.S.A.* **121** 35 50N 92 35W
Leslie, *Mich., U.S.A.* **119** 42 27N 84 26W
Lesneven, *France* **18** 48 35N 4 20W
Lešnica, *Yugoslavia* **33** 44 39N 19 20 E
Lesnoye, *U.S.S.R.* **36** 58 15N 35 18 E
Lesotho ■, *Africa* **97** 29 40 S 28 0 E
Lesozavodsk, *U.S.S.R.* **41** 45 30N 133 29 E
Lesparre-Médoc, *France* **20** 45 18N 0 57W
Lessay, *France* **18** 49 14N 1 30W
Lesse →, *Belgium* **17** 50 15N 4 54 E
Lesser Antilles, *W. Indies* **129** 15 0N 61 0W
Lesser Slave L., *Canada* **110** 55 30N 115 25W
Lesser Sunda Is., *Indonesia* **57** 7 0 S 120 0 E
Lessines, *Belgium* **17** 50 42N 3 50 E
Lester, *U.S.A.* **124** 47 12N 121 29W
Lestock, *Canada* **111** 51 19N 103 59W
Lesuer I., *Australia* **78** 13 50 S 127 17 E
Lésvos, *Greece* **35** 39 10N 26 20 E
Leszno, *Poland* **32** 51 50N 16 30 E
Letchworth, *U.K.* **13** 51 58N 0 13W
Letea, Ostrov, *Romania* **34** 45 18N 29 20 E
Lethbridge, *Australia* **74** 37 58 S 144 6 E
Lethbridge, *Canada* **110** 49 45N 112 45W
Lethem, *Guyana* **135** 3 20N 59 50W
Leti, Kepulauan, *Indonesia* **57** 8 10 S 128 0 E
Letiahau →, *Botswana* **96** 21 16 S 24 0 E
Leticia, *Colombia* **134** 4 9 S 70 0W
Leting, *China* **61** 39 23N 118 55 E
Letjiesbos, *S. Africa* **96** 32 34 S 22 16 E
Letlhakeng, *Botswana* **96** 24 0 S 24 59 E
Letpadan, *Burma* **52** 17 45N 95 45 E
Letpan, *Burma* **52** 19 28N 94 10 E
Letterkenny, *Ireland* **15** 54 57N 7 42W
Leu, *Romania* **34** 44 10N 24 0 E
Léua, *Angola* **95** 11 34 S 20 32 E
Leucadia, *U.S.A.* **125** 33 4N 117 18W
Leucate, *France* **20** 42 56N 3 3 E
Leucate, Étang de, *France* **20** 42 50N 3 0 E
Leuk, *Switz.* **31** 46 19N 7 37 E
Leupegem, *Belgium* **17** 50 50N 3 36 E
Leuser, G., *Indonesia* **56** 3 46N 97 12 E
Leutkirch, *W. Germany* **31** 47 49N 10 1 E
Leuven, *Belgium* **17** 50 52N 4 42 E
Leuze, *Hainaut, Belgium* **17** 50 36N 3 37 E
Leuze, *Namur, Belgium* **17** 50 33N 4 54 E
Lev Tolstoy, *U.S.S.R.* **37** 53 13N 39 29 E
Levack, *Canada* **108** 46 38N 81 23W
Levádhia, *Greece* **35** 38 27N 22 54 E
Levan, *U.S.A.* **122** 39 37N 111 52W
Levanger, *Norway* **8** 63 45N 11 19 E
Levant, I. du, *France* **21** 43 3N 6 28 E
Lévanto, *Italy* **26** 44 10N 9 37 E
Levanzo, *Italy* **28** 38 0N 12 19 E
Levelland, *U.S.A.* **121** 33 38N 102 23W
Leven, *U.K.* **14** 56 12N 3 0W
Leven, L., *U.K.* **14** 56 12N 3 22W
Leven, Toraka, *Madag.* **97** 12 30 S 47 45 E
Levens, *France* **21** 43 50N 7 12 E
Leveque C., *Australia* **78** 16 20 S 123 0 E
Leverano, *Italy* **29** 40 16N 18 0 E
Leverkusen, *W. Germany* **30** 51 2N 6 59 E
Leverville, *Zaïre* **95** 4 50 S 18 44 E
Levet, *France* **19** 46 56N 2 22 E
Levice, *Czech.* **33** 48 13N 18 35 E
Levico, *Italy* **27** 46 0N 11 18 E
Levie, *France* **21** 41 40N 9 7 E
Levier, *France* **19** 46 58N 6 8 E
Levin, *N.Z.* **80** 40 37 S 175 18 E
Lévis, *Canada* **107** 46 48N 71 9W
Levis, L., *Canada* **110** 62 37N 117 58W
Levítha, *Greece* **35** 37 0N 26 28 E
Levittown, *N.Y., U.S.A.* **117** 40 41N 73 31W
Levittown, *Pa., U.S.A.* **117** 40 10N 74 51W
Lévka, *Greece* **35** 35 18N 24 3 E
Levkás, *Greece* **35** 38 40N 20 43 E
Levkôsia = Nicosia, *Cyprus* **46** 35 10N 33 25 E
Levoča, *Czech.* **32** 49 2N 20 35 E
Levroux, *France* **19** 46 59N 1 38 E
Levski, *Bulgaria* **34** 43 21N 25 10 E
Levskigrad, *Bulgaria* **34** 42 38N 24 47 E
Levuka, *Fiji* **68** 17 34 S 179 0 E
Lewe, *Burma* **52** 19 38N 96 7 E
Lewellen, *U.S.A.* **120** 41 22N 102 5W
Lewes, *U.K.* **13** 50 53N 0 2 E
Lewes, *U.S.A.* **114** 38 45N 75 8W
Lewis, *U.K.* **14** 58 10N 6 40W
Lewis →, *U.S.A.* **124** 45 51N 122 48W
Lewis, Butt of, *U.K.* **14** 58 30N 6 12W
Lewis Ra., *Australia* **78** 20 3 S 128 50 E
Lewis Ra., *U.S.A.* **122** 48 0N 113 15W
Lewisburg, *Ohio, U.S.A.* **119** 39 51N 84 33W
Lewisburg, *Pa., U.S.A.* **116** 40 57N 76 57W
Lewisburg, *Tenn., U.S.A.* **115** 35 29N 86 46W
Lewisport, *U.S.A.* **119** 37 56N 86 54W
Lewisporte, *Canada* **105** 49 15N 55 3W
Lewiston, *U.S.A.* **122** 46 25N 117 0W
Lewistown, *Ill., U.S.A.* **118** 40 24N 90 9W
Lewistown, *Mont., U.S.A.* **122** 47 0N 109 25W
Lewistown, *Pa., U.S.A.* **116** 40 37N 77 33W
Lexington, *Ill., U.S.A.* **119** 40 37N 88 47W
Lexington, *Ky., U.S.A.* **119** 38 6N 84 30W
Lexington, *Miss., U.S.A.* **121** 33 8N 90 2W
Lexington, *Mo., U.S.A.* **118** 39 7N 93 55W
Lexington, *N.C., U.S.A.* **115** 35 50N 80 13W
Lexington, *Nebr., U.S.A.* **120** 40 48N 99 45W
Lexington, *Ohio, U.S.A.* **116** 40 39N 82 35W
Lexington, *Oreg., U.S.A.* **122** 45 29N 119 46W
Lexington, *Tenn., U.S.A.* **115** 35 38N 88 25W
Lexington Park, *U.S.A.* **114** 38 16N 76 27W
Lexton, *Australia* **74** 37 16 S 143 31 E
Leyburn, *Australia* **77** 28 1 S 151 35 E
Leye, *China* **58** 24 48N 106 29 E
Leyre →, *France* **20** 44 39N 1 1W
Leyte, *Phil.* **57** 11 0N 125 0 E
Lezay, *France* **20** 46 15N 0 1 E
Lezha, *Albania* **35** 41 47N 19 42 E
Lezhi, *China* **58** 30 19N 104 58 E
Lézignan-Corbières, *France* **20** 43 13N 2 43 E
Lezoux, *France* **20** 45 49N 3 21 E
Lgov, *U.S.S.R.* **36** 51 42N 35 16 E
Lhasa, *China* **62** 29 25N 90 58 E
Lhazê, *China* **62** 29 5N 87 38 E
Lhokkruet, *Indonesia* **56** 4 55N 95 24 E
Lhokseumawe, *Indonesia* **56** 5 10N 97 10 E
Lhuntsi Dzong, *India* **52** 27 39N 91 10 E
Li, *Thailand* **54** 17 48N 98 57 E
Li Shui →, *China* **59** 29 24N 112 1 E
Li Xian, *Gansu, China* **60** 34 10N 105 5 E
Li Xian, *Hebei, China* **60** 38 30N 115 35 E
Li Xian, *Hunan, China* **59** 29 36N 111 42 E
Li Xian, *Sichuan, China* **58** 31 23N 103 13 E
Lia-Moya, *C.A.R.* **94** 6 54N 16 17 E
Liádhoi, *Greece* **35** 36 50N 26 11 E
Liamena, *Australia* **77** 31 58 S 149 22 E
Lian Xian, *China* **59** 24 51N 112 22 E
Liancheng, *China* **59** 25 42N 116 40 E
Lianga, *Phil.* **57** 8 38N 126 6 E
Liangcheng, *Nei Mongol Zizhiqu, China* **60** 40 28N 112 25 E
Liangcheng, *Shandong, China* **61** 35 32N 119 37 E
Liangdang, *China* **60** 33 56N 106 18 E
Lianghekou, *China* **58** 29 11N 108 44 E
Liangping, *China* **58** 30 38N 107 47 E
Lianhua, *China* **59** 27 3N 113 54 E
Lianjiang, *Fujian, China* **59** 26 12N 119 27 E
Lianjiang, *Guangdong, China* **59** 21 40N 110 20 E
Lianping, *China* **59** 24 26N 114 30 E
Lianshan, *China* **59** 24 38N 112 8 E
Lianshanguan, *China* **61** 40 53N 123 43 E
Lianshui, *China* **61** 33 42N 119 20 E
Lianyuan, *China* **59** 27 40N 111 38 E
Lianyungang, *China* **61** 34 40N 119 11 E
Liao He →, *China* **61** 41 0N 121 50 E
Liaocheng, *China* **60** 36 28N 115 58 E
Liaodong Bandao, *China* **61** 40 0N 122 30 E
Liaodong Wan, *China* **61** 40 20N 121 10 E
Liaoning □, *China* **61** 42 0N 122 0 E
Liaoyang, *China* **61** 41 15N 122 58 E
Liaoyuan, *China* **61** 42 58N 125 2 E
Liaozhong, *China* **61** 41 23N 122 50 E
Liapádhes, *Greece* **35** 39 42N 19 40 E
Liard →, *Canada* **110** 61 51N 121 18W
Liari, *Pakistan* **48** 25 37N 66 30 E
Líbano, *Colombia* **134** 4 55N 75 4W
Libau = Liepaja, *U.S.S.R.* **36** 56 30N 21 0 E
Libby, *U.S.A.* **122** 48 20N 115 33W
Libenge, *Zaïre* **94** 3 40N 18 55 E
Liberal, *Kans., U.S.A.* **121** 37 4N 101 0W
Liberal, *Mo., U.S.A.* **121** 37 35N 94 30W
Liberdade, *Brazil* **136** 10 5 S 70 20W
Liberdade →, *Brazil* **137** 9 40 S 52 17W
Liberec, *Czech.* **32** 50 47N 15 7 E
Liberia, *Costa Rica* **128** 10 40N 85 30W
Liberia ■, *W. Afr.* **90** 6 30N 9 30W
Libertad, *Venezuela* **134** 8 20N 69 37W
Libertad, La, *Guatemala* **128** 16 47N 90 7W
Libertad, La, *Mexico* **126** 29 55N 112 41W
Libertad, La □, *Peru* **136** 8 0 S 78 30W
Liberty, *Ind., U.S.A.* **119** 39 38N 84 56W
Liberty, *Mo., U.S.A.* **118** 39 15N 94 24W
Liberty, *Tex., U.S.A.* **121** 30 5N 94 50W
Liberty Center, *U.S.A.* **119** 41 27N 84 1W
Libertyville, *U.S.A.* **119** 42 18N 87 57W
Libibi, *Angola* **95** 14 42 S 17 44 E
Libin, *Belgium* **17** 49 59N 5 15 E
Libo, *China* **58** 25 22N 107 53 E
Libobo, Tanjung, *Indonesia* **57** 0 54 S 128 28 E
Libode, *S. Africa* **97** 31 33 S 29 2 E
Libonda, *Zambia* **95** 14 28 S 23 12 E
Libourne, *France* **20** 44 55N 0 14W
Libramont, *Belgium* **17** 49 55N 5 23 E
Libreville, *Gabon* **94** 0 25N 9 26 E
Libya ■, *N. Afr.* **86** 27 0N 17 0 E
Libyan Desert, *Africa* **82** 25 0N 25 0 E
Libyan Plateau = Ed-Déffa, *Egypt* **88** 30 40N 26 30 E
Licantén, *Chile* **140** 35 55 S 72 0W
Licata, *Italy* **28** 37 6N 13 55 E
Licheng, *China* **60** 36 28N 113 20 E
Lichfield, *U.K.* **12** 52 40N 1 50W
Lichinga, *Mozam.* **93** 13 13 S 35 11 E
Lichtaart, *Belgium* **17** 51 13N 4 55 E
Lichtenburg, *S. Africa* **96** 26 8 S 26 8 E
Lichtenfels, *W. Germany* **31** 50 7N 11 4 E
Lichtenvoorde, *Neths.* **16** 51 59N 6 34 E
Lichtervelde, *Belgium* **17** 51 2N 3 9 E
Lichuan, *Hubei, China* **58** 30 18N 108 57 E
Lichuan, *Jiangxi, China* **59** 27 18N 116 55 E
Licking, South Fork →, *U.S.A.* **119** 38 40N 84 19W
Licola, *Australia* **75** 37 39 S 146 39 E
Licosa, Punta, *Italy* **29** 40 15N 14 53 E
Lida, *U.S.A.* **123** 37 30N 117 30W
Lida, *U.S.S.R.* **36** 53 53N 25 15 E
Lidhult, *Sweden* **11** 56 50N 13 27 E
Lidingö, *Sweden* **10** 59 22N 18 8 E
Lidköping, *Sweden* **11** 58 31N 13 14 E
Lido, *Italy* **27** 45 25N 12 23 E
Lido, *Niger* **91** 12 54N 3 44 E
Lido di Roma = Óstia, Lido di, *Italy* **28** 41 43N 12 17 E
Lidzbark Warminski, *Poland* **32** 54 7N 20 34 E
Liebenwalde, *E. Germany* **30** 52 51N 13 23 E
Lieberose, *E. Germany* **30** 51 59N 14 18 E
Liechtenstein ■, *Europe* **31** 47 8N 9 35 E
Liederkerke, *Belgium* **17** 50 52N 4 5 E
Liège, *Belgium* **17** 50 38N 5 35 E
Liège □, *Belgium* **17** 50 32N 5 35 E
Liegnitz = Legnica, *Poland* **32** 51 12N 16 10 E
Liempde, *Neths.* **17** 51 35N 5 23 E
Lienart, *Zaïre* **92** 3 3N 25 31 E
Lienyünchiangshih = Lianyungang, *China* **61** 34 40N 119 11 E
Lienz, *Austria* **33** 46 50N 12 46 E
Liepaja, *U.S.S.R.* **36** 56 30N 21 0 E
Lier, *Belgium* **17** 51 7N 4 34 E
Lierneux, *Belgium* **17** 50 17N 5 47 E
Lieshout, *Neths.* **17** 51 31N 5 36 E
Liévin, *France* **19** 50 24N 2 47 E
Lièvre →, *Canada* **106** 45 31N 75 26W
Liezen, *Austria* **33** 47 34N 14 15 E
Liffey →, *Ireland* **15** 53 21N 6 20W
Lifford, *Ireland* **15** 54 50N 7 30W
Liffré, *France* **18** 48 12N 1 30W
Lifjell, *Norway* **10** 59 27N 8 45 E
Lifuka, *Tonga* **68** 19 48 S 174 21W
Lightning Ridge, *Australia* **73** 29 22 S 148 0 E
Lignano, *Italy* **27** 45 42N 13 8 E
Ligny-en-Barrois, *France* **19** 48 36N 5 20 E
Ligny-le-Châtel, *France* **19** 47 54N 3 45 E
Ligoúrion, *Greece* **35** 37 37N 23 2 E
Ligua, La, *Chile* **140** 32 30 S 71 16W
Ligueil, *France* **18** 47 2N 0 49 E
Liguria □, *Italy* **26** 44 30N 9 0 E
Ligurian Sea, *Italy* **26** 43 20N 9 0 E
Lihir Group, *Papua N. G.* **69** 3 0 S 152 35 E
Lihou Reefs and Cays, *Australia* **72** 17 25 S 151 40 E
Lihue, *U.S.A.* **112** 21 59N 159 24W
Lijiang, *China* **58** 26 55N 100 20 E
Likasi, *Zaïre* **93** 10 55 S 26 48 E
Likati, *Zaïre* **94** 3 20N 24 0 E
Likhoslavl, *U.S.S.R.* **36** 57 12N 35 30 E
Likhovski, *U.S.S.R.* **39** 48 10N 40 10 E
Likokou, *Gabon* **94** 0 12 S 12 48 E
Likoma I., *Malawi* **93** 12 3 S 34 45 E
Likumburu, *Tanzania* **93** 9 43 S 35 8 E
Liling, *China* **59** 27 42N 113 29 E
Lille, *Belgium* **17** 51 15N 4 50 E
Lille, *France* **19** 50 38N 3 3 E
Lille Bælt, *Denmark* **11** 55 20N 9 45 E
Lillebonne, *France* **18** 49 30N 0 32 E
Lillehammer, *Norway* **10** 61 8N 10 30 E
Lillers, *France* **19** 50 35N 2 28 E
Lillesand, *Norway* **11** 58 15N 8 23 E
Lilleshall, *U.K.* **13** 52 45N 2 22W
Lillestrøm, *Norway* **10** 59 58N 11 5 E
Lillian Point, Mt., *Australia* **79** 27 40 S 126 6 E
Lillimur, *Australia* **74** 36 23 S 141 11 E
Lillo, *Spain* **24** 39 45N 3 20W
Lillooet →, *Canada* **110** 49 15N 121 57W
Lilongwe, *Malawi* **93** 14 0 S 33 48 E
Liloy, *Phil.* **57** 8 4N 122 39 E
Lilydale, *Australia* **74** 37 46 S 145 20 E
Lim →, *Yugoslavia* **33** 43 0N 19 40 E
Lima, *Indonesia* **57** 3 37 S 128 4 E
Lima, *Peru* **136** 12 0 S 77 0W
Lima, *Sweden* **10** 60 55N 13 20 E
Lima, *Mont., U.S.A.* **122** 44 41N 112 38W
Lima, *Ohio, U.S.A.* **119** 40 42N 84 5W
Lima □, *Peru* **136** 12 3 S 77 3W
Lima →, *Portugal* **22** 41 41N 8 50W
Limages, *Canada* **106** 45 20N 75 16W
Liman, *U.S.S.R.* **39** 45 45N 47 12 E
Limassol, *Cyprus* **46** 34 42N 33 1 E
Limavady, *U.K.* **15** 55 3N 6 58W
Limavady □, *U.K.* **15** 55 0N 6 55W
Limay →, *Argentina* **142** 39 0 S 68 0W
Limay Mahuida, *Argentina* **140** 37 10 S 66 45W
Limbang, *Brunei* **56** 4 42N 115 6 E
Limbara, Monti, *Italy* **28** 40 50N 9 10 E
Limbdi, *India* **48** 22 34N 71 51 E
Limbe, *Cameroon* **91** 4 1N 9 10 E
Limbourg, *Belgium* **17** 50 37N 5 56 E
Limbri, *Australia* **77** 31 3 S 151 5 E
Limbueta, *Angola* **95** 12 30 S 18 42 E
Limbunya, *Australia* **78** 17 14 S 129 50 E
Limburg, *W. Germany* **31** 50 22N 8 4 E
Limburg □, *Belgium* **17** 51 2N 5 25 E
Limburg □, *Neths.* **17** 51 20N 5 55 E
Limedsforsen, *Sweden* **10** 60 52N 13 25 E
Limeira, *Brazil* **141** 22 35 S 47 28W
Limerick, *Ireland* **15** 52 40N 8 38W
Limerick □, *Ireland* **15** 52 30N 8 50W
Limestone, *U.S.A.* **116** 42 2N 78 39W
Limestone →, *Canada* **111** 56 31N 94 7W
Limevale, *Australia* **77** 28 44 S 151 12 E
Limfjorden, *Denmark* **11** 56 55N 9 0 E
Limia → = Lima →, *Portugal* **22** 41 41N 8 50W
Limmared, *Sweden* **11** 57 34N 13 20 E
Limmen, *Neths.* **16** 52 34N 4 42 E
Limmen Bight, *Australia* **72** 14 40 S 135 35 E
Limmen Bight →, *Australia* **72** 15 7 S 135 44 E
Límni, *Greece* **35** 38 43N 23 18 E
Límnos, *Greece* **35** 39 50N 25 5 E
Limoeiro, *Brazil* **138** 7 52 S 35 27W
Limoeiro do Norte, *Brazil* **138** 5 5 S 38 0W
Limoges, *Canada* **109** 45 20N 75 15W
Limoges, *France* **20** 45 50N 1 15 E
Limón, *Costa Rica* **128** 10 0N 83 2W
Limon, *U.S.A.* **120** 39 18N 103 38W
Limone Piemonte, *Italy* **26** 44 12N 7 32 E
Limousin, *France* **20** 45 30N 1 30 E
Limousin, Plateaux du, *France* **20** 45 45N 1 15 E
Limoux, *France* **20** 43 4N 2 12 E
Limpopo →, *Africa* **97** 25 5 S 33 30 E
Limuru, *Kenya* **92** 1 2 S 36 35 E
Lin Xian, *China* **60** 37 57N 110 58 E
Lin'an, *China* **59** 30 15N 119 42 E
Linares, *Chile* **140** 35 50 S 71 40W
Linares, *Colombia* **134** 1 23N 77 31W
Linares, *Mexico* **127** 24 50N 99 40W
Linares, *Spain* **25** 38 10N 3 40W
Linares □, *Chile* **140** 36 0 S 71 0W
Línas Mte., *Italy* **28** 39 25N 8 38 E
Lincang, *China* **58** 23 58N 100 1 E
Lincheng, *China* **60** 37 25N 114 30 E
Linchuan, *China* **59** 27 57N 116 15 E
Lincoln, *Argentina* **140** 34 55 S 61 30W
Lincoln, *Canada* **108** 43 10N 79 29W
Lincoln, *N.Z.* **81** 43 38 S 172 30 E
Lincoln, *U.K.* **12** 53 14N 0 32W
Lincoln, *Calif., U.S.A.* **124** 38 54N 121 17W
Lincoln, *Ill., U.S.A.* **118** 40 10N 89 20W
Lincoln, *Kans., U.S.A.* **120** 39 6N 98 9W
Lincoln, *Maine, U.S.A.* **105** 45 27N 68 29W
Lincoln, *N.H., U.S.A.* **117** 44 3N 71 40W
Lincoln, *N. Mex., U.S.A.* **123** 33 30N 105 26W
Lincoln, *Nebr., U.S.A.* **120** 40 50N 96 42W
Lincoln □, *U.K.* **12** 53 14N 0 32W
Lincoln Park, *U.S.A.* **119** 42 15N 83 11W
Lincoln Sea, *Arctic* **144** 84 0N 55 0W
Lincoln Wolds, *U.K.* **12** 53 20N 0 5W
Lincolnton, *U.S.A.* **115** 35 30N 81 15W
Lind, *U.S.A.* **122** 47 0N 118 33W
Linda, *U.S.A.* **124** 39 6N 121 34W
Lindås, *Sweden* **11** 56 38N 15 35 E
Lindau, *W. Germany* **31** 47 33N 9 41 E
Linde →, *Neths.* **16** 52 50N 5 57 E
Linden, *Guyana* **136** 6 0N 58 10W
Linden, *Calif., U.S.A.* **124** 38 1N 121 5W
Linden, *Ind., U.S.A.* **119** 40 11N 86 54W
Linden, *Mich., U.S.A.* **119** 42 49N 83 47W
Linden, *Tex., U.S.A.* **121** 33 0N 94 20W
Lindenheuvel, *Neths.* **17** 50 59N 5 48 E
Lindenhurst, *U.S.A.* **117** 40 41N 73 23W
Lindenow, *Australia* **75** 37 48 S 147 28 E
Linderöd, *Sweden* **11** 55 56N 13 47 E
Linderödsåsen, *Sweden* **11** 55 53N 13 53 E
Lindesberg, *Sweden* **10** 59 36N 15 15 E

Lindesnes, *Norway* **6** 57 58N 7 3 E
Lindi, *Tanzania* **93** 9 58 S 39 38 E
Lindi □, *Tanzania* **93** 9 40 S 38 30 E
Lindi →, *Zaïre* **92** 0 33N 25 5 E
Lindoso, *Portugal* **22** 41 52N 8 11W
Lindow, *E. Germany* **30** 52 58N 12 58 E
Lindsay, *Canada* **109** 44 22N 78 43W
Lindsay, *Calif., U.S.A.* **124** 36 14N 119 6W
Lindsay, *Okla., U.S.A.* **121** 34 51N 97 37W
Lindsborg, *U.S.A.* **120** 38 35N 97 40W
Línea de la Concepción, La, *Spain* **23** 36 15N 5 23W
Lineville, *U.S.A.* **118** 40 35N 93 31W
Linfen, *China* **60** 36 3N 111 30 E
Ling Xian, *Hunan, China* **59** 26 29N 113 48 E
Ling Xian, *Shandong, China* **60** 37 22N 116 30 E
Lingao, *China* **54** 19 56N 109 42 E
Lingayen, *Phil.* **57** 16 1N 120 14 E
Lingayen G., *Phil.* **57** 16 10N 120 15 E
Lingbi, *China* **61** 33 33N 117 33 E
Lingchuan, *Guangxi Zhuangzu, China* **59** 25 26N 110 21 E
Lingchuan, *Shanxi, China* **60** 35 45N 113 12 E
Lingen, *W. Germany* **30** 52 32N 7 21 E
Lingga, *Indonesia* **56** 0 12 S 104 37 E
Lingga, Kepulauan, *Indonesia* **56** 0 10 S 104 30 E
Linghed, *Sweden* **10** 60 48N 15 55 E
Lingle, *U.S.A.* **120** 42 10N 104 18W
Lingling, *China* **59** 26 17N 111 37 E
Lingqiu, *China* **60** 39 28N 114 22 E
Lingshan, *China* **58** 22 25N 109 18 E
Lingshi, *China* **60** 36 48N 111 48 E
Lingshou, *China* **60** 38 20N 114 20 E
Lingshui, *China* **54** 18 27N 110 0 E
Lingtai, *China* **60** 35 0N 107 40 E
Linguéré, *Senegal* **90** 15 25N 15 5W
Lingwu, *China* **60** 38 6N 106 20 E
Lingyuan, *China* **61** 41 10N 119 15 E
Lingyun, *China* **58** 25 2N 106 35 E
Linh Cam, *Vietnam* **54** 18 31N 105 31 E
Linhai, *China* **59** 28 50N 121 8 E
Linhares, *Brazil* **139** 19 25 S 40 4W
Linhe, *China* **60** 40 48N 107 20 E
Linière, *Canada* **107** 46 4N 70 32W
Linjiang, *China* **61** 41 50N 127 0 E
Linköping, *Sweden* **11** 58 28N 15 36 E
Linkou, *China* **61** 45 15N 130 18 E
Linli, *China* **59** 29 27N 111 30 E
Linlithgow, *U.K.* **14** 55 58N 3 38W
Linn, *U.S.A.* **118** 38 29N 91 51W
Linneus, *U.S.A.* **118** 39 53N 93 11W
Linnhe, L., *U.K.* **14** 56 36N 5 25W
Linosa, I., *Medit. S.* **86** 35 51N 12 50 E
Linqi, *China* **60** 35 45N 113 52 E
Linqing, *China* **60** 36 50N 115 42 E
Linqu, *China* **61** 36 25N 118 30 E
Linru, *China* **60** 34 11N 112 52 E
Lins, *Brazil* **141** 21 40 S 49 44W
Linshui, *China* **58** 30 21N 106 57 E
Lintao, *China* **60** 35 18N 103 52 E
Linth →, *Switz.* **31** 47 7N 9 7 E
Linthal, *Switz.* **31** 46 54N 9 0 E
Lintlaw, *Canada* **111** 52 4N 103 14W
Linton, *Australia* **74** 37 41 S 143 33 E
Linton, *Canada* **107** 47 15N 72 16W
Linton, *Ind., U.S.A.* **119** 39 0N 87 10W
Linton, *N. Dak., U.S.A.* **120** 46 21N 100 12W
Lintong, *China* **60** 34 20N 109 10 E
Linville, *Australia* **73** 26 50 S 152 11 E
Linwood, *Canada* **108** 43 35N 80 43W
Linwu, *China* **59** 25 19N 112 31 E
Linxi, *China* **61** 43 36N 118 2 E
Linxia, *China* **62** 35 36N 103 10 E
Linxiang, *China* **59** 29 28N 113 23 E
Linyanti →, *Africa* **96** 17 50 S 25 5 E
Linyi, *China* **61** 35 5N 118 21 E
Linz, *Austria* **33** 48 18N 14 18 E
Linz, *W. Germany* **30** 50 33N 7 18 E
Linzhenzhen, *China* **60** 36 30N 109 59 E
Linzi, *China* **61** 36 50N 118 20 E
Lion, G. du, *France* **20** 43 0N 4 0 E
Lion-d'Angers, Le, *France* **18** 47 37N 0 43W
Lioni, *Italy* **29** 40 52N 15 10 E
Lion's Den, *Zimb.* **93** 17 15 S 30 5 E
Lion's Head, *Canada* **108** 44 58N 81 15W
Liouesso, *Congo* **94** 1 2N 15 43 E
Liozno, *U.S.S.R.* **36** 55 0N 30 50 E
Lipa, *Phil.* **57** 13 57N 121 10 E
Lipali, *Mozam.* **93** 15 50 S 35 50 E
Lípari, *Italy* **29** 38 26N 14 58 E
Lípari, Is., *Italy* **29** 38 30N 14 50 E
Lipetsk, *U.S.S.R.* **37** 52 37N 39 35 E
Liping, *China* **58** 26 15N 109 7 E
Lipkany, *U.S.S.R.* **38** 48 14N 26 48 E
Lipljan, *Yugoslavia* **33** 42 31N 21 7 E
Lipno, *Poland* **32** 52 49N 19 15 E
Lipova, *Romania* **34** 46 8N 21 42 E
Lipovets, *U.S.S.R.* **38** 49 12N 29 1 E
Lippe →, *W. Germany* **30** 51 39N 6 38 E
Lippstadt, *W. Germany* **30** 51 40N 8 19 E
Lipscomb, *U.S.A.* **121** 36 16N 100 16W
Lipsko, *Poland* **32** 51 9N 21 40 E
Lipsói, *Greece* **35** 37 19N 26 50 E
Liptovsky Svaty Milkulaš, *Czech.* **32** 49 6N 19 35 E
Liptrap C., *Australia* **74** 38 50 S 145 55 E
Lipu, *China* **59** 24 30N 110 22 E
Lira, *Uganda* **92** 2 17N 32 57 E
Liri →, *Italy* **28** 41 25N 13 52 E
Liria, *Spain* **24** 39 37N 0 35W
Lisala, *Zaïre* **94** 2 12N 21 38 E
Lisboa, *Portugal* **23** 38 42N 9 10W
Lisboa □, *Portugal* **23** 39 0N 9 12W
Lisbon = Lisboa, *Portugal* **23** 38 42N 9 10W
Lisbon, *N. Dak., U.S.A.* **120** 46 30N 97 46W
Lisbon, *N.H., U.S.A.* **117** 44 13N 71 52W
Lisbon, *Ohio, U.S.A.* **116** 40 45N 80 42W
Lisburn, *U.K.* **15** 54 30N 6 9W
Lisburne, C., *U.S.A.* **102** 68 50N 166 0W
Liscannor, B., *Ireland* **15** 52 57N 9 24W
Liscia →, *Italy* **28** 41 11N 9 9 E
Lishe Jiang →, *China* **58** 24 15N 101 35 E
Lishi, *China* **60** 37 31N 111 8 E
Lishu, *China* **61** 43 20N 124 18 E
Lishui, *Jiangsu, China* **59** 31 38N 119 2 E
Lishui, *Zhejiang, China* **59** 28 28N 119 54 E
Lisianski I., *Pac. Oc.* **66** 26 2N 174 0W
Lisichansk, *U.S.S.R.* **38** 48 55N 38 30 E
Lisieux, *France* **18** 49 10N 0 12 E
Lisle-sur-Tarn, *France* **20** 43 52N 1 49 E
Lismore, *N.S.W., Australia* **77** 28 44 S 153 21 E
Lismore, *Vic., Australia* **74** 37 58 S 143 21 E
Lismore, *Ireland* **15** 52 8N 7 58W
Lisse, *Neths.* **16** 52 16N 4 33 E
List, *W. Germany* **30** 55 1N 8 26 E
Lista, *Norway* **9** 58 7N 6 39 E
Lista, *Sweden* **9** 59 19N 16 16 E
Lister, Mt., *Antarctica* **143** 78 0 S 162 0 E
Liston, *Australia* **77** 28 39 S 152 6 E
Listowel, *Canada* **108** 43 44N 80 58W
Listowel, *Ireland* **15** 52 27N 9 30W
Lit-et-Mixe, *France* **20** 44 2N 1 15W
Litang, *Guangxi Zhuangzu, China* **58** 23 12N 109 8 E
Litang, *Sichuan, China* **58** 30 1N 100 17 E
Litang, *Malaysia* **57** 5 27N 118 31 E
Litang Qu →, *China* **58** 28 4N 101 32 E
Litani →, *Lebanon* **44** 33 20N 35 14 E
Litani →, *Surinam* **46** 3 40N 54 0W
Litchfield, *Australia* **74** 36 18 S 142 52 E
Litchfield, *Calif., U.S.A.* **124** 40 24N 120 23W
Litchfield, *Conn., U.S.A.* **117** 41 44N 73 12W
Litchfield, *Ill., U.S.A.* **118** 39 10N 89 40W
Litchfield, *Minn., U.S.A.* **120** 45 5N 94 31W
Lithgow, *Australia* **76** 33 25 S 150 8 E
Líthinon, Ákra, *Greece* **35** 34 55N 24 44 E
Lithuanian S.S.R. □, *U.S.S.R.* **36** 55 30N 24 0 E
Litija, *Yugoslavia* **27** 46 3N 14 50 E
Litókhoron, *Greece* **35** 40 8N 22 34 E
Litoměřice, *Czech.* **32** 50 33N 14 10 E
Little Abaco I., *Bahamas* **128** 26 50N 77 30W
Little Barrier I., *N.Z.* **80** 36 12 S 175 8 E
Little Belt Mts., *U.S.A.* **122** 46 50N 111 0W
Little Blue →, *U.S.A.* **120** 39 41N 96 40W
Little Bushman Land, *S. Africa* **96** 29 10 S 18 10 E
Little Cadotte →, *Canada* **110** 56 41N 117 6W
Little Cayman, I., *Cayman Is.* **128** 19 41N 80 3W
Little Churchill →, *Canada* **111** 57 30N 95 22W
Little Colorado →, *U.S.A.* **123** 36 11N 111 48W
Little Current, *Canada* **108** 45 55N 82 0W
Little Current →, *Canada* **104** 50 57N 84 36W
Little Falls, *Minn., U.S.A.* **120** 45 58N 94 19W
Little Falls, *N.Y., U.S.A.* **117** 43 3N 74 50W
Little Fork →, *U.S.A.* **120** 48 31N 93 35W
Little Grand Rapids, *Canada* **111** 52 0N 95 29W
Little Humboldt →, *U.S.A.* **122** 41 0N 117 43W
Little Inagua I., *Bahamas* **129** 21 40N 73 50W
Little Karoo, *S. Africa* **96** 33 45 S 21 0 E
Little Lake, *U.S.A.* **125** 35 58N 117 58W
Little Minch, *U.K.* **14** 57 35N 6 45W
Little Missouri →, *U.S.A.* **120** 47 30N 102 25W
Little Namaqualand, *S. Africa* **96** 29 0 S 17 9 E
Little Ouse →, *U.K.* **13** 52 25N 0 50 E
Little Plain, *Australia* **77** 29 43 S 150 59 E
Little Rann, *India* **48** 23 25N 71 25 E
Little Red →, *U.S.A.* **121** 35 11N 91 27W
Little River, *N.Z.* **81** 43 45 S 172 49 E
Little Rock, *U.S.A.* **121** 34 41N 92 10W
Little Ruaha →, *Tanzania* **92** 7 57 S 37 53 E
Little Sable Pt., *U.S.A.* **114** 43 40N 86 32W
Little Sioux →, *U.S.A.* **120** 41 49N 96 4W
Little Smoky →, *Canada* **110** 54 44N 117 11W
Little Snake →, *U.S.A.* **122** 40 27N 108 26W
Little Valley, *U.S.A.* **116** 42 15N 78 48W
Little Wabash →, *U.S.A.* **119** 37 54N 88 5W
Little White →, *Canada* **108** 46 23N 83 20W
Little York, *U.S.A.* **118** 41 1N 90 45W
Littlefield, *U.S.A.* **121** 33 57N 102 17W
Littlefork, *U.S.A.* **120** 48 24N 93 35W
Littlehampton, *U.K.* **13** 50 48N 0 32W
Littleton, *U.S.A.* **117** 44 19N 71 47W
Liu He →, *China* **61** 40 55N 121 35 E
Liu Jiang →, *China* **58** 23 55N 109 30 E
Liuba, *China* **60** 33 38N 106 55 E
Liucheng, *China* **58** 24 38N 109 14 E
Liugou, *China* **61** 40 57N 118 15 E
Liuhe, *China* **61** 42 17N 125 43 E
Liuheng Dao, *China* **59** 29 40N 122 5 E
Liukang Tenggaja, *Indonesia* **57** 6 45 S 118 50 E
Liuli, *Tanzania* **93** 11 3 S 34 38 E
Liuwa Plain, *Zambia* **95** 14 20 S 22 30 E
Liuyang, *China* **59** 28 10N 113 37 E
Liuzhou, *China* **58** 24 22N 109 22 E
Liuzhuang, *China* **61** 33 12N 120 18 E
Livadherón, *Greece* **35** 40 2N 21 57 E
Livarot, *France* **18** 49 0N 0 9 E
Live Oak, *Calif., U.S.A.* **124** 39 17N 121 40W
Live Oak, *Fla., U.S.A.* **115** 30 17N 83 0W
Lively, *Canada* **108** 46 26N 81 9W
Liveringa, *Australia* **78** 18 3 S 124 10 E
Livermore, *U.S.A.* **124** 37 41N 121 47W
Livermore, Mt., *U.S.A.* **121** 30 45N 104 8W
Liverpool, *Australia* **76** 33 54 S 150 58 E
Liverpool, *Canada* **105** 44 5N 64 41W
Liverpool, *U.K.* **12** 53 25N 3 0W
Liverpool Plains, *Australia* **77** 31 15 S 150 15 E
Liverpool Ra., *Australia* **77** 31 50 S 150 30 E
Livingston, *Guatemala* **128** 15 50N 88 50W
Livingston, *Calif., U.S.A.* **124** 37 23N 120 43W
Livingston, *Mont., U.S.A.* **122** 45 40N 110 40W
Livingston, *Tex., U.S.A.* **121** 30 44N 94 54W
Livingston, *Wis., U.S.A.* **118** 42 54N 90 26W
Livingstone, *Zambia* **93** 17 46 S 25 52 E
Livingstone Memorial, *Zambia* **93** 12 20 S 30 18 E
Livingstone Mts., *N.Z.* **81** 45 15 S 168 9 E
Livingstone Mts., *Tanzania* **93** 9 40 S 34 20 E
Livingstonia, *Malawi* **93** 10 38 S 34 5 E
Livny, *U.S.S.R.* **37** 52 30N 37 30 E
Livonia, *U.S.A.* **119** 42 25N 83 23W
Livorno, *Italy* **26** 43 32N 10 18 E
Livramento, *Brazil* **141** 30 55 S 55 30W
Livramento do Brumado, *Brazil* **139** 13 39 S 41 50W
Livron-sur-Drôme, *France* **21** 44 46N 4 51 E
Liwale, *Tanzania* **93** 9 48 S 37 58 E
Liwale □, *Tanzania* **93** 9 0 S 38 0 E
Lixi, *China* **58** 26 23N 101 59 E
Liyang, *China* **59** 31 26N 119 28 E
Lizard I., *Australia* **72** 14 42 S 145 30 E
Lizard Pt., *U.K.* **13** 49 57N 5 11W
Lizarda, *Brazil* **138** 9 36 S 46 41W
Lizzano, *Italy* **29** 40 23N 17 25 E
Ljubija, *Yugoslavia* **27** 44 55N 16 35 E
Ljubljana, *Yugoslavia* **27** 46 4N 14 33 E
Ljubno, *Yugoslavia* **27** 46 25N 14 46 E
Ljubuški, *Yugoslavia* **33** 43 12N 17 34 E
Ljung, *Sweden* **11** 58 1N 13 3 E
Ljungan →, *Sweden* **10** 62 18N 17 23 E
Ljungaverk, *Sweden* **10** 62 30N 16 5 E
Ljungby, *Sweden* **11** 56 49N 13 55 E
Ljusdal, *Sweden* **10** 61 46N 16 3 E
Ljusnan →, *Sweden* **10** 61 12N 17 8 E
Ljusne, *Sweden* **10** 61 13N 17 7 E
Ljutomer, *Yugoslavia* **27** 46 31N 16 11 E
Llagostera, *Spain* **24** 41 50N 2 54 E
Llamellín, *Peru* **136** 9 0 S 76 54W
Llancanelo, Salina, *Argentina* **140** 35 40 S 69 8W
Llandeilo, *U.K.* **13** 51 53N 4 0W
Llandovery, *U.K.* **13** 51 59N 3 49W
Llandrindod Wells, *U.K.* **13** 52 15N 3 23W
Llandudno, *U.K.* **12** 53 19N 3 51W
Llanelli, *U.K.* **13** 51 41N 4 11W
Llanes, *Spain* **22** 43 25N 4 50W
Llangollen, *U.K.* **12** 52 58N 3 10W
Llangothlin, *Australia* **77** 30 7 S 151 41 E
Llanidloes, *U.K.* **13** 52 28N 3 31W
Llano, *U.S.A.* **121** 30 45N 98 41W
Llano →, *U.S.A.* **121** 30 50N 98 25W
Llano Estacado, *U.S.A.* **121** 34 0N 103 0W
Llanos, *S. Amer.* **136** 5 0N 71 35W
Llanquihue □, *Chile* **142** 41 30 S 73 0W
Llanquihue, L., *Chile* **142** 41 10 S 75 50W
Llera, *Mexico* **127** 23 19N 99 1W
Llerena, *Spain* **23** 38 17N 6 0W
Llica, *Bolivia* **136** 19 52 S 68 16W
Llico, *Chile* **140** 34 46 S 72 5W
Llobregat →, *Spain* **24** 41 19N 2 9 E
Lloret de Mar, *Spain* **24** 41 41N 2 53 E
Lloyd B., *Australia* **72** 12 45 S 143 27 E
Lloyd L., *Canada* **111** 57 22N 108 57W
Lloydminster, *Canada* **111** 53 17N 110 0W
Lluchmayor, *Spain* **25** 39 29N 2 53 E
Llullaillaco, Volcán, *S. Amer.* **140** 24 43 S 68 30W
Lo, *Belgium* **17** 50 59N 2 45 E
Lo →, *Vietnam* **54** 21 18N 105 25 E
Loa, *U.S.A.* **123** 38 18N 111 40W
Loa →, *Chile* **140** 21 26 S 70 41W
Loano, *Italy* **26** 44 8N 8 14 E
Lobatse, *Botswana* **96** 25 12 S 25 40 E
Löbau, *E. Germany* **30** 51 5N 14 42 E
Lobaye →, *C.A.R.* **94** 3 41N 18 35 E
Lobbes, *Belgium* **17** 50 21N 4 16 E
Lobenstein, *E. Germany* **30** 50 25N 11 39 E
Lobería, *Argentina* **140** 38 10 S 58 40W
Lobito, *Angola* **95** 12 18 S 13 35 E
Lobón, Canal de, *Spain* **23** 38 50N 6 55W
Lobos, *Argentina* **140** 35 10 S 59 0W
Lobos, I., *Mexico* **126** 27 15N 110 30W
Lobos, Is., *Peru* **132** 6 57 S 80 45W
Lobos, I. de, *Canary Is.* **25** 28 45N 13 50W
Lobos de Tierra, I., *Peru* **136** 6 27 S 80 52W
Loc Binh, *Vietnam* **54** 21 46N 106 54 E
Loc Ninh, *Vietnam* **55** 11 50N 106 34 E
Locarno, *Switz.* **31** 46 10N 8 47 E
Loch, *Australia* **74** 38 21 S 145 42 E
Loch Sport, *Australia* **75** 38 5 S 147 30 E
Lochaber, *U.K.* **14** 56 55N 5 0W
Lochcarron, *U.K.* **14** 57 25N 5 30W
Loche, La, *Canada* **111** 56 29N 109 26W
Lochem, *Neths.* **16** 52 9N 6 26 E
Loches, *France* **18** 47 7N 1 0 E
Lochgelly, *U.K.* **14** 56 7N 3 18W
Lochgilphead, *U.K.* **14** 56 2N 5 37W
Lochinver, *U.K.* **14** 58 9N 5 15W
Lochnagar, *Australia* **72** 23 33 S 145 38 E
Lochnagar, *U.K.* **14** 56 57N 3 14W
Lochów, *Poland* **32** 52 33N 21 42 E
Lochy →, *U.K.* **14** 56 52N 5 3W
Lock, *Australia* **73** 33 34 S 135 46 E
Lock Haven, *U.S.A.* **116** 41 7N 77 31W
Lockeford, *U.S.A.* **124** 38 10N 121 9W
Lockeport, *Canada* **105** 43 47N 65 4W
Lockerbie, *U.K.* **14** 55 7N 3 21W
Lockhart, *U.S.A.* **121** 29 55N 97 40W
Lockhart, L., *Australia* **79** 33 15 S 119 3 E
Lockington, *Australia* **74** 36 16 S 144 34 E
Lockney, *U.S.A.* **121** 34 7N 101 27W
Lockport, *Ill., U.S.A.* **119** 41 35N 88 3W
Lockport, *N.Y., U.S.A.* **116** 43 12N 78 42W
Locle, Le, *Switz.* **31** 47 3N 6 44 E
Locminé, *France* **18** 47 54N 2 51W
Locri, *Italy* **29** 38 14N 16 14 E
Locronan, *France* **18** 48 7N 4 15W
Loctudy, *France* **18** 47 50N 4 12W
Locust Cr. →, *U.S.A.* **118** 39 40N 93 17W
Lod, *Israel* **44** 31 57N 34 54 E
Loddon →, *Australia* **75** 35 31 S 143 51 E
Lodève, *France* **20** 43 44N 3 19 E
Lodge Grass, *U.S.A.* **122** 45 21N 107 20W
Lodgepole, *U.S.A.* **120** 41 12N 102 40W
Lodgepole Cr. →, *U.S.A.* **120** 41 20N 104 30W
Lodhran, *Pakistan* **48** 29 32N 71 30 E
Lodi, *Italy* **26** 45 19N 9 30 E
Lodi, *U.S.A.* **124** 38 12N 121 16W
Lodja, *Zaïre* **92** 3 30 S 23 23 E
Lodosa, *Spain* **24** 42 25N 2 4W
Lödöse, *Sweden* **11** 58 2N 12 9 E
Lodwar, *Kenya* **92** 3 10N 35 40 E
Łódź, *Poland* **32** 51 45N 19 27 E
Loei, *Thailand* **54** 17 29N 101 35 E
Loenen, *Neths.* **16** 52 7N 6 1 E
Loengo, *Zaïre* **92** 4 48 S 26 30 E
Loeriesfontein, *S. Africa* **96** 31 0 S 19 26 E
Lofoten, *Norway* **8** 68 30N 15 0 E
Lofsdalen, *Sweden* **10** 62 10N 13 20 E
Lofsen →, *Sweden* **10** 62 7N 13 57 E
Loftahammar, *Sweden* **11** 57 54N 16 41 E
Logan, *Kans., U.S.A.* **120** 39 40N 99 35W
Logan, *Ohio, U.S.A.* **114** 39 25N 82 22W
Logan, *Utah, U.S.A.* **122** 41 45N 111 50W
Logan, *W. Va., U.S.A.* **114** 37 51N 81 59W
Logan, Mt., *Canada* **102** 60 31N 140 22W
Logan Pass, *U.S.A.* **110** 48 41N 113 44W
Logandale, *U.S.A.* **125** 36 36N 114 29W
Logansport, *Ind., U.S.A.* **119** 40 45N 86 21W
Logansport, *La., U.S.A.* **121** 31 58N 93 58W
Logo, *Sudan* **89** 5 20N 30 18 E
Logone →, *Chad* **87** 12 6N 15 2 E
Logroño, *Spain* **24** 42 28N 2 27W
Logrosán, *Spain* **23** 39 20N 5 32W
Løgstør, *Denmark* **11** 56 58N 9 14 E
Loh, *Vanuatu* **68** 13 21 S 166 38 E
Lohardaga, *India* **49** 23 27N 84 45 E
Lohr, *W. Germany* **31** 50 0N 9 35 E
Lohrville, *U.S.A.* **118** 42 17N 94 33W
Loi-kaw, *Burma* **52** 19 40N 97 17 E
Loimaa, *Finland* **9** 60 50N 23 5 E
Loir →, *France* **18** 47 33N 0 32W
Loir-et-Cher □, *France* **18** 47 40N 1 20 E
Loire □, *France* **21** 45 40N 4 5 E
Loire →, *France* **18** 47 16N 2 10W
Loire-Atlantique □, *France* **18** 47 25N 1 40W
Loiret □, *France* **19** 47 55N 2 30 E
Loitz, *E. Germany* **30** 53 58N 13 8 E
Loja, *Ecuador* **136** 3 59 S 79 16W
Loja, *Spain* **23** 37 10N 4 10W
Loja □, *Ecuador* **134** 4 0 S 79 13W

Loji, Indonesia 57 1 38 S 127 28 E
Loka, Sudan 89 4 13N 31 0 E
Lokandu, Zaïre 92 2 30 S 25 45 E
Løken, Norway 10 59 48N 11 29 E
Lokeren, Belgium 17 51 6N 3 59 E
Lokhvitsa, U.S.S.R. 36 50 25N 33 18 E
Lokichokio, Kenya 92 4 19N 34 13 E
Lokitaung, Kenya 92 4 12N 35 48 E
Lokka, Finland 8 67 55N 27 35 E
Løkken, Denmark 11 57 22N 9 41 E
Løkken Verk, Norway 10 63 7N 9 43 E
Loknya, U.S.S.R. 36 56 49N 30 4 E
Lokoja, Nigeria 91 7 47N 6 45 E
Lokolama, Zaïre 94 2 35 S 19 50 E
Lokuru, Solomon Is. 68 8 20 S 157 0 E
Lol →, Sudan 89 9 13N 26 30 E
Lola, Guinea 90 7 52N 8 29W
Lola, Mt., U.S.A. 124 39 26N 120 22W
Lolibai, Gebel, Sudan 89 3 50N 33 0 E
Lolimi, Sudan 89 4 35N 34 0 E
Loliondo, Tanzania 92 2 2 S 35 39 E
Lolland, Denmark 11 54 45N 11 30 E
Lollar, W. Germany 30 50 39N 8 43 E
Lolo, U.S.A. 122 46 50N 114 8W
Lolodorf, Cameroon 91 3 16N 10 49 E
Lolowai, Vanuatu 68 15 18 S 168 0 E
Lom, Bulgaria 34 43 48N 23 12 E
Lom →, Bulgaria 34 43 45N 23 15 E
Lom Kao, Thailand 54 16 53N 101 14 E
Lom Sak, Thailand 54 16 47N 101 15 E
Loma, U.S.A. 122 47 59N 110 29W
Loma Linda, U.S.A. 125 34 3N 117 16W
Lomaloma, Fiji 68 17 17 S 178 59W
Lomami →, Zaïre 92 0 46N 24 16 E
Lomas de Zamóra, Argentina 140 34 45 S 58 25W
Lombadina, Australia 78 16 31 S 122 54 E
Lombard, U.S.A. 119 41 53N 88 1W
Lombardia □, Italy 26 45 35N 9 45 E
Lombardy = Lombardia □, Italy 26 45 35N 9 45 E
Lombe, Angola 95 9 27 S 16 13 E
Lombez, France 20 43 29N 0 55 E
Lomblen, Indonesia 57 8 30 S 123 32 E
Lombok, Indonesia 56 8 45 S 116 30 E
Lomé, Togo 91 6 9N 1 20 E
Lomela, Zaïre 94 2 19 S 23 15 E
Lomela →, Zaïre 94 0 15 S 20 40 E
Lomello, Italy 26 45 5N 8 46 E
Lometa, U.S.A. 121 31 15N 98 25W
Lomié, Cameroon 94 3 13N 13 38 E
Lomma, Sweden 11 55 43N 13 6 E
Lomme →, Belgium 17 50 8N 5 10 E
Lommel, Belgium 17 51 14N 5 19 E
Lomond, Canada 110 50 24N 112 36W
Lomond, L., U.K. 14 56 8N 4 38W
Lomonosov, U.S.S.R. 36 59 57N 29 53 E
Lomphat, Cambodia 54 13 30N 106 59 E
Lompobatang, Indonesia 57 5 24 S 119 56 E
Lompoc, U.S.A. 125 34 41N 120 32W
Lomsegga, Norway 10 61 49N 8 21 E
Łomza, Poland 32 53 10N 22 2 E
Lonavale, India 50 18 46N 73 29 E
Loncoche, Chile 142 39 20 S 72 50W
Loncopuè, Argentina 142 38 4 S 70 37W
Londa, India 51 15 30N 74 30 E
Londe-les-Maures, La, France 21 43 8N 6 14 E
Londerzeel, Belgium 17 51 0N 4 19 E
Londiani, Kenya 92 0 10 S 35 33 E
Londinières, France 18 49 50N 1 25 E
London, Canada 108 42 59N 81 15W
London, U.K. 13 51 30N 0 5W
London, Ky., U.S.A. 114 37 11N 84 5W
London, Ohio, U.S.A. 119 39 54N 83 28W
London, Greater □, U.K. 13 51 30N 0 5W
London Mills, U.S.A. 118 40 43N 90 11W
Londonderry, U.K. 15 55 0N 7 20W
Londonderry □, U.K. 15 55 0N 7 20W
Londonderry, C., Australia 78 13 45 S 126 55 E
Londonderry, I., Chile 142 55 0 S 71 0W
Londrina, Brazil 141 23 18 S 51 10W
Londuimbale, Angola 95 12 15 S 15 19 E
Lone Pine, U.S.A. 124 36 35N 118 2W
Lonely I., Canada 108 45 34N 81 28W
Long Beach, Calif., U.S.A. 125 33 46N 118 12W
Long Beach, N.Y., U.S.A. 117 40 35N 73 40W
Long Beach, Wash., U.S.A. 124 46 20N 124 1W
Long Branch, U.S.A. 117 40 19N 74 0W
Long Creek, U.S.A. 122 44 43N 119 6W
Long Eaton, U.K. 12 52 54N 1 16W
Long I., Australia 72 22 8 S 149 53 E
Long I., Bahamas 129 23 20N 75 10W
Long I., Papua N. G. 69 5 20 S 147 5 E
Long I., U.S.A. 117 40 50N 73 20W
Long I. Sd., U.S.A. 117 41 10N 73 0W
Long L., Canada 104 49 30N 86 50W
Long Lake, U.S.A. 117 43 57N 74 25W
Long Pine, U.S.A. 120 42 33N 99 41W
Long Pt., Nfld., Canada 105 48 47N 58 46W
Long Pt., Ont., Canada 108 42 35N 80 2W
Long Pt., N.Z. 81 46 34 S 169 36 E
Long Point B., Canada 108 42 40N 80 10W
Long Range Mts., Canada 105 49 30N 57 30W
Long Str. = Longa, Proliv, U.S.S.R. 144 70 0N 175 0 E
Long Thanh, Vietnam 55 10 47N 106 57 E
Long Xian, China 60 34 55N 106 55 E
Long Xuyen, Vietnam 55 10 19N 105 28 E
Longa, Angola 95 14 42 S 18 32 E
Longá, Greece 35 36 53N 21 55 E
Longa, Proliv, U.S.S.R. 144 70 0N 175 0 E
Long'an, China 58 23 10N 107 40 E
Longarone, Italy 27 46 15N 12 18 E
Longburn, N.Z. 80 40 23 S 175 35 E
Longchang, China 58 29 18N 105 15 E
Longchi, China 58 29 25N 103 24 E
Longchuan, Guangdong, China 59 24 5N 115 17 E
Longchuan, Yunnan, China 58 24 23N 97 58 E
Longde, China 60 35 30N 106 20 E
Longeau, France 19 47 47N 5 20 E
Longford, Australia 72 41 32 S 147 3 E
Longford, Ireland 15 53 43N 7 50W
Longford □, Ireland 15 53 42N 7 45W
Longguan, China 60 40 45N 115 30 E
Longhua, China 61 41 18N 117 45 E
Longhui, China 59 27 7N 111 2 E
Longido, Tanzania 92 2 43 S 36 42 E
Longiram, Indonesia 56 0 5 S 115 45 E
Longkou, Jiangxi, China 59 26 8N 115 10 E
Longkou, Shandong, China 61 37 40N 120 18 E
Longlac, Canada 104 49 45N 86 25W
Longli, China 58 26 25N 106 58 E
Longlier, Belgium 17 49 52N 5 27 E
Longlin, China 58 24 47N 105 20 E
Longling, China 58 24 37N 98 39 E
Longmen, China 59 23 40N 114 18 E
Longming, China 58 22 59N 107 7 E
Longmont, U.S.A. 120 40 10N 105 4W
Longnan, China 59 24 55N 114 47 E
Longnawan, Indonesia 56 1 51N 114 55 E
Longobucco, Italy 29 39 27N 16 37 E
Longquan, China 59 28 7N 119 10 E
Longreach, Australia 72 23 28 S 144 14 E
Longshan, China 58 29 29N 109 25 E
Longsheng, China 58 25 48N 110 0 E
Longton, Australia 72 20 58 S 145 55 E
Longtown, U.K. 13 51 58N 2 59W
Longué-Jumelles, France 18 47 22N 0 8W
Longueau, France 19 49 52N 2 21 E
Longueuil, Qué., Canada 107 45 32N 73 30W
Longueuil, Canada 117 45 32N 73 28W
Longuyon, France 19 49 27N 5 35 E
Longview, Canada 110 50 32N 114 10W
Longview, Tex., U.S.A. 121 32 30N 94 45W
Longview, Wash., U.S.A. 124 46 9N 122 58W
Longvilly, Belgium 17 50 2N 5 50 E
Longwarry, Australia 74 38 8 S 145 48 E
Longwood, Australia 74 36 48 S 145 26 E
Longwy, France 19 49 30N 5 46 E
Longxi, China 60 34 53N 104 40 E
Longyou, China 59 29 1N 119 8 E
Longzhou, China 58 22 22N 106 50 E
Lonigo, Italy 27 45 23N 11 22 E
Löningen, W. Germany 30 52 43N 7 44 E
Lonja →, Yugoslavia 27 45 30N 16 40 E
Lonkin, Burma 52 25 39N 96 22 E
Lonoke, U.S.A. 121 34 48N 91 57W
Lonquimay, Chile 142 38 26 S 71 14W
Lons-le-Saunier, France 19 46 40N 5 31 E
Lønstrup, Denmark 11 57 29N 9 47 E
Loogootee, U.S.A. 119 38 41N 86 55W
Lookout, C., Canada 104 55 18N 83 56W
Lookout, C., U.S.A. 115 34 30N 76 30W
Loolmalasin, Tanzania 92 3 0 S 35 53 E
Loon →, Alta., Canada 110 57 8N 115 3W
Loon →, Man., Canada 111 55 53N 101 59W
Loon Lake, Canada 111 54 2N 109 10W
Loon-op-Zand, Neths. 17 51 38N 5 5 E
Loongana, Australia 79 30 52 S 127 5 E
Loop Hd., Ireland 15 52 34N 9 55W
Loosduinen, Neths. 16 52 3N 4 14 E
Lop Buri, Thailand 54 14 48N 100 37 E
Lop Nor = Lop Nur, China 62 40 20N 90 10 E
Lop Nur, China 62 40 20N 90 10 E
Lopare, Yugoslavia 33 44 39N 18 46 E
Lopatin, U.S.S.R. 39 43 50N 47 35 E
Lopatina, G., U.S.S.R. 41 50 47N 143 10 E
Lopaye, Sudan 89 6 37N 33 40 E
Lopera, Spain 23 37 56N 4 14W
Lopevi, Vanuatu 68 16 30 S 168 21 E
Lopez, C., Gabon 94 0 47 S 8 40 E
Lopez I., Gabon 94 0 50 S 8 47 E
Loppersum, Neths. 16 53 20N 6 44 E
Lopphavet, Norway 8 70 27N 21 15 E
Lora →, Afghan. 47 32 0N 67 15 E
Lora, Hamun-i-, Pakistan 47 29 38N 64 58 E
Lora, La, Spain 22 42 45N 4 0W
Lora Cr. →, Australia 73 28 10 S 135 22 E
Lora del Río, Spain 23 37 39N 5 33W
Lorain, U.S.A. 116 41 28N 82 55W
Loraine, U.S.A. 118 40 9N 91 13W
Loralai, Pakistan 48 30 20N 68 41 E
Lorca, Spain 25 37 41N 1 42W
Lord Howe I., Pac. Oc. 66 31 33 S 159 6 E
Lord Howe Ridge, Pac. Oc. 66 30 0 S 162 30 E
Lordsburg, U.S.A. 123 32 22N 108 45W
Lorengau, Papua N. G. 69 2 1 S 147 15 E
Loreto, Bolivia 137 15 13 S 64 40W
Loreto, Brazil 138 7 5 S 45 10W
Loreto, Italy 27 43 26N 13 36 E
Loreto, Mexico 126 26 1N 111 21W
Loreto □, Peru 134 5 0 S 75 0W
Loreto Aprutina, Italy 27 42 24N 13 59 E
Loretteville, Canada 107 46 51N 71 21W
Lorgues, France 21 43 28N 6 22 E
Lorica, Colombia 134 9 14N 75 49W
Lorient, France 18 47 45N 3 23W
Lorimor, U.S.A. 118 41 7N 94 3W
Loristān □, Iran 46 33 20N 47 0 E
Lorn, U.K. 14 56 26N 5 10W
Lorn, Firth of, U.K. 14 56 20N 5 40W
Lorne, N.S.W., Australia 77 31 36 S 152 39 E
Lorne, Vic., Australia 74 38 33 S 143 59 E
Lörrach, W. Germany 31 47 36N 7 38 E
Lorraine, France 19 48 30N 6 0 E
Lorrainville, Canada 106 47 21N 79 23W
Los, Îles de, Guinea 90 9 30N 13 50W
Los Alamos, Calif., U.S.A. 125 34 44N 120 17W
Los Alamos, N. Mex., U.S.A. 123 35 57N 106 17W
Los Altos, U.S.A. 124 37 23N 122 7W
Los Andes, Chile 140 32 50 S 70 40W
Los Angeles, Chile 140 37 28 S 72 23W
Los Angeles, U.S.A. 125 34 0N 118 10W
Los Angeles Aqueduct, U.S.A. 125 35 25N 118 0W
Los Antiguos, Argentina 142 46 35 S 71 40W
Los Banos, U.S.A. 124 37 8N 120 56W
Los Barrios, Spain 23 36 11N 5 30W
Los Blancos, Argentina 140 23 40 S 62 30W
Los Cristianos, Canary Is. 25 28 3N 16 42W
Los Gatos, U.S.A. 124 37 14N 121 59W
Los Hermanos, Venezuela 129 11 45N 64 25W
Los Islotes, Canary Is. 25 29 4N 13 44W
Los Lagos, Chile 142 39 51 S 72 50W
Los Llanos de Aridane, Canary Is. 25 28 38N 17 54W
Los Lomas, Peru 136 4 40 S 80 10W
Los Lunas, U.S.A. 123 34 48N 106 47W
Los Menucos, Argentina 142 40 50 S 68 10W
Los Mochis, Mexico 126 25 45N 109 5W
Los Monegros, Spain 24 41 29N 0 13W
Los Monos, Argentina 142 46 1 S 69 36W
Los Olivos, U.S.A. 125 34 40N 120 7W
Los Palacios, Cuba 128 22 35N 83 15W
Los Palacios y Villafranca, Spain 23 37 10N 5 55W
Los Reyes, Mexico 126 19 34N 102 30W
Los Ríos □, Ecuador 134 1 30 S 79 25W
Los Roques, Venezuela 134 11 50N 66 45W
Los Santos de Maimona, Spain 23 38 27N 6 22W
Los Teques, Venezuela 134 10 21N 67 2W
Los Testigos, Venezuela 135 11 23N 63 6W
Los Vilos, Chile 140 32 10 S 71 30W
Los Yébenes, Spain 23 39 36N 3 55W
Losada →, Colombia 134 2 12N 73 55W
Loshkalakh, U.S.S.R. 41 62 45N 147 20 E
Lošinj, Yugoslavia 27 44 30N 14 30 E
Losser, Neths. 16 52 16N 7 1 E
Lossiemouth, U.K. 14 57 43N 3 17W
Losuia, Papua N. G. 69 8 30 S 151 4 E
Lot □, France 20 44 39N 1 40 E
Lot →, France 20 44 18N 0 20 E
Lot-et-Garonne □, France 20 44 22N 0 30 E
Lota, Chile 140 37 5 S 73 10W
Løten, Norway 10 60 51N 11 21 E
Lothair, S. Africa 97 26 22 S 30 27 E
Lothian □, U.K. 14 55 50N 3 0W
Lothiers, France 19 46 42N 1 33 E
Lotofaga, W. Samoa 68 14 1 S 171 30W
Lotschbergtunnel, Switz. 31 46 26N 7 43 E
Lottefors, Sweden 10 61 25N 16 24 E
Loubomo, Congo 94 4 9 S 12 47 E
Loudéac, France 18 48 11N 2 47W
Loudi, China 59 27 42N 111 59 E
Loudima, Congo 94 4 6 S 13 5 E
Loudon, U.S.A. 115 35 35N 84 22W
Loudonville, U.S.A. 116 40 40N 82 15W
Loudun, France 18 47 0N 0 5 E
Loué, France 18 47 59N 0 9W
Loue →, France 19 47 1N 5 28 E
Louga, Senegal 90 15 45N 16 5W
Loughborough, U.K. 12 52 46N 1 11W
Loughrea, Ireland 15 53 11N 8 33W
Loughros More B., Ireland 15 54 48N 8 30W
Louhans, France 21 46 38N 5 12 E
Louis Trichardt, S. Africa 97 23 1 S 29 43 E
Louis XIV, Pte., Canada 104 54 37N 79 45W
Louisa, U.S.A. 114 38 5N 82 40W
Louisbourg, Canada 105 45 55N 60 0W
Louisburg, U.S.A. 118 38 37N 94 41W
Louise I., Canada 110 52 55N 131 50W
Louiseville, Canada 107 46 20N 72 56W
Louisiade Arch., Papua N. G. 69 11 10 S 153 0 E
Louisiana, U.S.A. 118 39 25N 91 0W
Louisiana □, U.S.A. 121 30 50N 92 0W
Louisville, Ky., U.S.A. 119 38 15N 85 45W
Louisville, Miss., U.S.A. 121 33 7N 89 3W
Loukouo, Congo 94 3 38 S 14 39 E
Loulay, France 20 46 3N 0 30W
Loulé, Portugal 23 37 9N 8 0W
Louny, Czech. 32 50 20N 13 48 E
Loup City, U.S.A. 120 41 19N 98 57W
Loupe, La, France 18 48 29N 1 1 E
Lourdes, France 20 43 6N 0 3W
Lourdes-du-Blanc-Sablon, Canada 105 51 24N 57 12W
Lourenço, Brazil 135 2 30N 51 40W
Lourenço-Marques = Maputo, Mozam. 97 25 58 S 32 32 E
Loures, Portugal 23 38 50N 9 9W
Lourinhã, Portugal 23 39 14N 9 17W
Louroux-Béconnais, Le, France 18 47 30N 0 55W
Lousã, Portugal 22 40 7N 8 14W
Louth, Australia 73 30 30 S 145 8 E
Louth, Ireland 15 53 47N 6 33W
Louth, U.K. 12 53 23N 0 0 E
Louth □, Ireland 15 53 55N 6 30W
Louvain = Leuven, Belgium 17 50 52N 4 42 E
Louveigné, Belgium 17 50 32N 5 42 E
Louvière, La, Belgium 17 50 27N 4 10 E
Louviers, France 18 49 12N 1 10 E
Louwsburg, S. Africa 97 27 37 S 31 7 E
Lovat →, U.S.S.R. 36 58 14N 30 28 E
Love, Canada 111 53 29N 104 10W
Lovech, Bulgaria 34 43 8N 24 42 E
Loveland, Colo., U.S.A. 120 40 27N 105 4W
Loveland, Ohio, U.S.A. 119 39 16N 84 16W
Lovell, U.S.A. 122 44 51N 108 20W
Lovelock, U.S.A. 122 40 17N 118 25W
Lóvere, Italy 26 45 50N 10 4 E
Loves Park, U.S.A. 118 42 19N 89 3W
Loviisa = Lovisa, Finland 9 60 28N 26 12 E
Lovilia, U.S.A. 118 41 8N 92 55W
Loving, U.S.A. 121 32 17N 104 4W
Lovington, Ill., U.S.A. 119 39 43N 88 38W
Lovington, N. Mex., U.S.A. 121 33 0N 103 20W
Lovios, Spain 22 41 55N 8 4W
Lovisa, Finland 9 60 28N 26 12 E
Lovran, Yugoslavia 27 45 18N 14 15 E
Lövstabukten, Sweden 10 60 35N 17 45 E
Low, Canada 106 45 50N 76 0W
Low Pt., Australia 79 32 25 S 127 25 E
Lowa, Zaïre 92 1 25 S 25 47 E
Lowa →, Zaïre 92 1 24 S 25 51 E
Lowden, U.S.A. 118 41 52N 90 56W
Lowell, Ind., U.S.A. 119 41 18N 87 25W
Lowell, Mass., U.S.A. 117 42 38N 71 19W
Lower Arrow L., Canada 110 49 40N 118 5W
Lower California = Baja California, Mexico 126 31 10N 115 12W
Lower Hutt, N.Z. 80 41 10 S 174 55 E
Lower L., U.S.A. 122 41 17N 120 3W
Lower Lake, U.S.A. 124 38 56N 122 36W
Lower Post, Canada 110 59 58N 128 30W
Lower Red L., U.S.A. 120 48 0N 94 50W
Lower Saxony = Niedersachsen □, W. Germany 30 52 45N 9 0 E
Lower Tunguska = Tunguska, Nizhnyaya →, U.S.S.R. 41 65 48N 88 4 E
Lowestoft, U.K. 13 52 29N 1 44 E
Łowicz, Poland 32 52 6N 19 55 E
Lowry City, U.S.A. 118 38 7N 93 44W
Lowville, U.S.A. 117 43 48N 75 30W
Lowyar □, Afghan. 47 34 0N 69 0 E
Loxton, Australia 73 34 28 S 140 31 E
Loxton, S. Africa 96 31 30 S 22 22 E
Loyalton, U.S.A. 124 39 41N 120 14W
Loyalty Is. = Loyauté, Is., N. Cal. 68 21 0 S 167 30 E
Loyang = Luoyang, China 60 34 40N 112 26 E
Loyauté, Is., N. Cal. 68 21 0 S 167 30 E
Loyev, U.S.S.R. 36 51 56N 30 46 E
Loyoro, Uganda 92 3 22N 34 14 E
Lož, Yugoslavia 27 45 43N 14 30 E
Lozère □, France 20 44 35N 3 30 E
Loznica, Yugoslavia 33 44 32N 19 14 E
Lozovaya, U.S.S.R. 38 49 0N 36 20 E
Luachimo, Angola 95 7 23 S 20 48 E
Luacono, Angola 95 11 15 S 21 37 E
Lualaba →, Zaïre 92 0 26N 25 20 E
Luampa, Zambia 93 15 4 S 24 20 E
Lu'an, China 59 31 45N 116 29 E
Luan Chau, Vietnam 54 21 38N 103 24 E
Luan He →, China 61 39 20N 119 5 E
Luan Xian, China 61 39 40N 118 40 E
Luancheng, Guangxi Zhuangzu, China 58 22 48N 108 55 E
Luancheng, Hebei, China 60 37 53N 114 40 E
Luanda, Angola 95 8 50 S 13 15 E
Luanda □, Angola 95 9 0 S 13 10 E
Luang Prabang, Laos 54 19 52N 102 10 E
Luang Thale, Thailand 55 7 30N 100 15 E
Luangwa, Zambia 93 15 35 S 30 16 E

Luangwa →, Zambia 93 14 25 S 30 25 E
Luangwa Valley, Zambia 93 13 30 S 31 30 E
Luanne, China 61 40 55N 117 40 E
Luanping, China 61 40 53N 117 23 E
Luanshya, Zambia 93 13 3 S 28 28 E
Luapula □, Zambia 93 11 0 S 29 0 E
Luapula →, Africa 93 9 26 S 28 33 E
Luarca, Spain 22 43 32N 6 32W
Luashi, Zaïre 93 10 50 S 23 36 E
Luau, Angola 95 10 40 S 22 10 E
Lubalo, Angola 95 9 10 S 19 15 E
Lubań, Poland 32 51 5N 15 15 E
Lubana, Ozero, U.S.S.R. 36 56 45N 27 0 E
Lubang Is., Phil. 57 13 50N 120 12 E
Lubango, Angola 95 14 55 S 13 30 E
Lubartów, Poland 32 51 28N 22 42 E
Lubawa, Poland 32 53 30N 19 48 E
Lubbeek, Belgium 17 50 54N 4 50 E
Lübben, E. Germany 30 51 56N 13 54 E
Lübbenau, E. Germany 30 51 49N 13 59 E
Lubbock, U.S.A. 121 33 40N 101 53W
Lubeck, Australia 74 36 45 S 142 34 E
Lübeck, W. Germany 30 53 52N 10 41 E
Lübecker Bucht, W. Germany 30 54 3N 11 0 E
Lubefu, Zaïre 92 4 47 S 24 27 E
Lubefu →, Zaïre 92 4 10 S 23 0 E
Lubero = Luofu, Zaïre 92 0 10 S 29 15 E
Lubicon L., Canada 110 56 23N 115 56W
Lublin, Poland 32 51 12N 22 38 E
Lubliniec, Poland 32 50 43N 18 45 E
Lubny, U.S.S.R. 36 50 3N 32 58 E
Lubon, Poland 32 52 21N 16 51 E
Lubongola, Zaïre 92 2 35 S 27 50 E
Lubsko, Poland 32 51 45N 14 57 E
Lübtheen, E. Germany 30 53 18N 11 4 E
Lubuagan, Phil. 57 17 21N 121 10 E
Lubudi →, Zaïre 93 9 0 S 25 35 E
Lubuk Antu, Malaysia 56 1 3N 111 50 E
Lubuklinggau, Indonesia 56 3 15 S 102 55 E
Lubuksikaping, Indonesia 56 0 10N 100 15 E
Lubumbashi, Zaïre 93 11 40 S 27 28 E
Lubunda, Zaïre 92 5 12 S 26 41 E
Lubungu, Zambia 93 14 35 S 26 24 E
Lubutu, Zaïre 92 0 45 S 26 30 E
Luc, Le, France 21 43 23N 6 21 E
Luc An Chau, Vietnam 54 22 6N 104 43 E
Luc-en-Diois, France 21 44 36N 5 28 E
Lucala, Angola 95 9 7 S 15 58 E
Lucan, Canada 108 43 11N 81 24W
Lucca, Italy 26 43 50N 10 30 E
Luce Bay, U.K. 14 54 45N 4 48W
Lucea, Jamaica 128 18 25N 78 10W
Lucedale, U.S.A. 115 30 55N 88 34W
Lucena, Phil. 57 13 56N 121 37 E
Lucena, Spain 23 37 27N 4 31W
Lucena del Cid, Spain 24 40 9N 0 17W
Lučenec, Czech. 33 48 18N 19 42 E
Lucera, Italy 29 41 30N 15 20 E
Lucerne = Luzern, Switz. 31 47 3N 8 18 E
Lucerne, U.S.A. 124 39 6N 122 48W
Lucerne Valley, U.S.A. 125 34 27N 116 57W
Lucero, Mexico 126 30 49N 106 30W
Luceville, Canada 107 48 32N 68 22W
Luchena →, Spain 25 37 44N 1 50W
Lucheng, China 60 36 20N 113 11 E
Lucheringo →, Mozam. 93 11 43 S 36 17 E
Lüchow, W. Germany 30 52 58N 11 8 E
Luchuan, China 59 22 21N 110 12 E
Lucie →, Surinam 135 3 35N 57 38W
Lucira, Angola 95 14 0 S 12 35 E
Luckau, E. Germany 30 51 50N 13 43 E
Luckenwalde, E. Germany 30 52 5N 13 11 E
Luckey, U.S.A. 119 41 27N 83 29W
Lucknow, Australia 76 33 21 S 149 11 E
Lucknow, Canada 108 43 57N 81 31W
Lucknow, India 49 26 50N 81 0 E
Luçon, France 20 46 28N 1 10W
Lucusse, Angola 95 12 32 S 20 48 E
Lüda = Dalian, China 61 38 50N 121 40 E
Luda Kamchiya →, Bulgaria 34 43 3N 27 29 E
Ludbreg, Yugoslavia 27 46 15N 16 38 E
Lüdenscheid, W. Germany 30 51 13N 7 37 E
Lüderitz, Namibia 96 26 41 S 15 8 E
Ludewe □, Tanzania 93 10 0 S 34 50 E
Ludhiana, India 48 30 57N 75 56 E
Ludian, China 58 27 10N 103 33 E
Luding Qiao, China 58 29 53N 102 12 E
Lüdinghausen, W. Germany 30 51 46N 7 28 E
Ludington, U.S.A. 114 43 58N 86 27W
Ludlow, U.K. 13 52 23N 2 42W
Ludlow, Calif., U.S.A. 125 34 43N 116 10W
Ludlow, Vt., U.S.A. 117 43 25N 72 40W
Ludus, Romania 34 46 29N 24 5 E
Ludvika, Sweden 10 60 8N 15 14 E
Ludwigsburg, W. Germany 31 48 53N 9 11 E
Ludwigshafen, W. Germany 31 49 27N 8 27 E
Ludwigslust, E. Germany 30 53 19N 11 28 E
Ludza, U.S.S.R. 36 56 32N 27 43 E
Lue, Australia 76 32 38 S 149 50 E
Luebo, Zaïre 95 5 21 S 21 23 E
Lueki, Zaïre 92 3 20 S 25 48 E
Luena, Angola 95 12 13 S 19 51 E
Luena, Zaïre 93 9 28 S 25 43 E
Luena, Zambia 93 10 40 S 30 25 E
Luepa, Venezuela 135 5 43N 61 31W
Lüeyang, China 60 33 22N 106 10 E
Lufeng, Guangdong, China 59 22 57N 115 38 E
Lufeng, Yunnan, China 58 25 0N 102 5 E
Lufico, Angola 95 6 24 S 13 23 E
Lufira →, Zaïre 93 9 30 S 27 0 E
Lufkin, U.S.A. 121 31 25N 94 40W
Lufupa, Zaïre 93 10 37 S 24 56 E
Luga, U.S.S.R. 36 58 40N 29 55 E
Luga →, U.S.S.R. 36 59 40N 28 18 E
Lugang, Taiwan 59 24 4N 120 23 E
Lugano, Switz. 31 46 0N 8 57 E
Lugano, L. di, Switz. 31 46 0N 9 0 E
Lugansk = Voroshilovgrad, U.S.S.R. 39 48 38N 39 15 E
Lugard's Falls, Kenya 92 3 6 S 38 41 E
Lugela, Mozam. 93 16 25 S 36 43 E
Lugenda →, Mozam. 93 11 25 S 38 33 E
Lugh Ganana, Somali Rep. 98 3 48N 42 34 E
Lugnaquilla, Ireland 15 52 58N 6 28W
Lugnvik, Sweden 10 62 56N 17 55 E
Lugo, Italy 27 44 25N 11 53 E
Lugo, Spain 22 43 2N 7 35W
Lugo □, Spain 22 43 0N 7 30W
Lugoj, Romania 34 45 42N 21 57 E
Lugones, Spain 22 43 26N 5 50W
Lugovoye, U.S.S.R. 40 42 55N 72 43 E
Luhe, China 59 32 19N 118 50 E
Luhe →, W. Germany 30 53 18N 10 11 E
Luhuo, China 58 31 21N 100 48 E
Luiana, Angola 95 17 25 S 22 59 E
Luino, Italy 26 46 0N 8 42 E
Luís Correia, Brazil 138 3 0 S 41 35W
Luís Gonçalves, Brazil 138 5 37 S 50 25W
Luitpold Coast, Antarctica 143 78 30 S 32 0W
Luiza, Zaïre 95 7 40 S 22 30 E
Luizi, Zaïre 92 6 0 S 27 25 E
Luján, Argentina 140 34 45 S 59 5W
Lujiang, China 59 31 20N 117 15 E
Lukala, Zaïre 95 5 31 S 14 32 E
Lukanga Swamp, Zambia 93 14 30 S 27 40 E
Lukenie →, Zaïre 94 3 0 S 18 50 E
Lukhisaral, India 49 25 11N 86 5 E
Lŭki, Bulgaria 35 41 50N 24 43 E
Lukk, Libya 86 32 1N 24 46 E
Lukolela, Equateur, Zaïre 94 1 10 S 17 12 E
Lukolela, Kasai Or., Zaïre 92 5 23 S 24 32 E
Lukosi, Zimb. 93 18 30 S 26 30 E
Lukovit, Bulgaria 34 43 13N 24 11 E
Łuków, Poland 32 51 55N 22 23 E
Lukoyanov, U.S.S.R. 37 55 2N 44 29 E
Lule älv →, Sweden 8 65 35N 22 10 E
Luleå, Sweden 8 65 35N 22 10 E
Lüleburgaz, Turkey 46 41 23N 27 22 E
Luliang, China 58 25 0N 103 40 E
Luling, U.S.A. 121 29 45N 97 40W
Lulong, China 61 39 53N 118 51 E
Lulonga →, Zaïre 94 1 0N 18 10 E
Lulua →, Zaïre 95 4 30 S 20 30 E
Luluabourg = Kananga, Zaïre 95 5 55 S 22 18 E
Lumai, Angola 95 13 13 S 21 25 E
Lumajang, Indonesia 57 8 8 S 113 13 E
Lumbala Kaquengue, Angola 95 12 39 S 22 34 E
Lumbala N'guimbo, Angola 95 14 18 S 21 18 E
Lumberton, Miss., U.S.A. 121 31 4N 89 28W
Lumberton, N.C., U.S.A. 115 34 37N 78 59W
Lumberton, N. Mex., U.S.A. 123 36 58N 106 57W
Lumbres, France 19 50 40N 2 5 E
Lumbwa, Kenya 92 0 12 S 35 28 E
Lumding, India 52 25 46N 93 10 E
Lumi, Papua N. G. 69 3 30 S 142 2 E
Lummen, Belgium 17 50 59N 5 12 E
Lumsden, N.Z. 81 45 44 S 168 27 E
Lumut, Malaysia 55 4 13N 100 37 E
Lumut, Tg., Indonesia 56 3 50 S 105 58 E
Lunan, China 58 24 40N 103 18 E
Lunavada, India 48 23 8N 73 37 E
Lunca, Romania 34 47 22N 25 1 E
Lund, Sweden 11 55 44N 13 12 E
Lund, U.S.A. 122 38 53N 115 0W
Lunda Norte □, Angola 95 8 0 S 20 0 E
Lunda Sul □, Angola 95 10 0 S 20 0 E
Lundazi, Zambia 93 12 20 S 33 7 E
Lunde, Norway 10 59 17N 9 5 E
Lunderskov, Denmark 11 55 29N 9 19 E
Lundi →, Zimb. 93 21 43 S 32 34 E
Lundu, Malaysia 56 1 40N 109 50 E
Lundy, U.K. 13 51 10N 4 41W
Lune →, U.K. 12 54 0N 2 51W
Lüneburg, W. Germany 30 53 15N 10 23 E
Lüneburg Heath = Lüneburger Heide, W. Germany 30 53 0N 10 0 E
Lüneburger Heide, W. Germany 30 53 0N 10 0 E
Lunel, France 21 43 39N 4 9 E
Lünen, W. Germany 30 51 36N 7 31 E
Lunenburg, Canada 105 44 22N 64 18W
Lunéville, France 19 48 36N 6 30 E
Lunga →, Zambia 93 14 34 S 26 25 E
Lungi Airport, S. Leone 90 8 40N 13 17W
Lunglei, India 52 22 55N 92 45 E
Lungngo, Burma 52 21 57N 93 36 E
Luni, India 48 26 0N 73 6 E
Luni →, India 48 24 41N 71 14 E
Luninets, U.S.S.R. 36 52 15N 26 50 E
Luning, U.S.A. 122 38 30N 118 10W
Lunino, U.S.S.R. 37 53 35N 45 6 E
Lunner, Norway 10 60 19N 10 35 E
Lunsemfwa →, Zambia 93 14 54 S 30 12 E
Lunsemfwa Falls, Zambia 93 14 30 S 29 6 E
Lunteren, Neths. 16 52 5N 5 38 E
Luo He →, China 60 34 35N 110 20 E
Luocheng, China 58 24 48N 108 53 E
Luochuan, China 60 35 45N 109 26 E
Luoci, China 58 25 19N 102 18 E
Luodian, China 58 25 24N 106 43 E
Luoding, China 59 22 45N 111 40 E
Luodong, Taiwan 59 24 41N 121 46 E
Luofu, Zaïre 92 0 10 S 29 15 E
Luohe, China 60 33 32N 114 2 E
Luojiang, China 58 31 18N 104 33 E
Luonan, China 60 34 5N 110 10 E
Luoning, China 60 34 35N 111 40 E
Luoshan, China 59 32 13N 114 30 E
Luotian, China 59 30 46N 115 22 E
Luoyang, China 60 34 40N 112 26 E
Luoyuan, China 59 26 28N 119 30 E
Luozi, Zaïre 95 4 54 S 14 0 E
Luozigou, China 61 43 42N 130 18 E
Lupeni, Romania 34 45 21N 23 13 E
Lupilichi, Mozam. 93 11 47 S 35 13 E
Lupire, Angola 95 14 36 S 19 29 E
Lupoing, China 58 24 53N 104 21 E
Luquan, China 58 25 35N 102 25 E
Luque, Paraguay 140 25 19 S 57 25W
Luque, Spain 23 37 35N 4 16W
Luray, U.S.A. 114 38 39N 78 26W
Lure, France 19 47 40N 6 30 E
Luremo, Angola 95 8 30 S 17 50 E
Lurgan, U.K. 15 54 28N 6 20W
Luribay, Bolivia 136 17 6 S 67 39W
Lurin, Peru 136 12 17 S 76 52W
Lusaka, Zambia 93 15 28 S 28 16 E
Lusambo, Zaïre 92 4 58 S 23 28 E
Lusangaye, Zaïre 92 4 54 S 26 0 E
Luseland, Canada 111 52 5N 109 24W
Lushan, Henan, China 60 33 45N 112 55 E
Lushan, Sichuan, China 58 30 12N 102 52 E
Lushih, China 60 34 3N 111 3 E
Lushnja, Albania 35 40 55N 19 41 E
Lushoto, Tanzania 92 4 47 S 38 20 E
Lushoto □, Tanzania 92 4 45 S 38 20 E
Lushui, China 58 25 58N 98 44 E
Lüshun, China 61 38 45N 121 15 E
Lusignan, France 20 46 26N 0 8 E
Lusigny-sur-Barse, France 19 48 16N 4 15 E
Lusk, U.S.A. 120 42 47N 104 27W
Lussac-les-Châteaux, France 20 46 24N 0 43 E
Lussanvira, Brazil 139 20 42 S 51 7W
Luta = Dalian, China 61 38 50N 121 40 E
Lutembo, Angola 95 13 26 S 21 16 E
Luti, Solomon Is. 68 7 14 S 157 0 E
Luton, U.K. 13 51 53N 0 24W
Lutong, Malaysia 56 4 28N 114 0 E
Lutsk, U.S.S.R. 36 50 50N 25 15 E
Lutuai, Angola 95 12 41 S 20 7 E
Lützow Holmbukta, Antarctica 143 69 10 S 37 30 E
Lutzputs, S. Africa 96 28 3 S 20 40 E
Luverne, U.S.A. 120 43 35N 96 12W
Luvo, Angola 95 5 51 S 14 5 E
Luvua, Zaïre 93 8 48 S 25 17 E
Luvua →, Zaïre 92 6 50 S 27 30 E
Luwegu →, Tanzania 93 8 31 S 37 23 E
Luwuk, Indonesia 57 0 56 S 122 47 E
Luxembourg, Lux. 17 49 37N 6 9 E
Luxembourg □, Belgium 17 49 58N 5 30 E
Luxembourg ■, Europe 17 50 0N 6 0 E
Luxeuil-les-Bains, France 19 47 49N 6 24 E
Luxi, Hunan, China 59 28 20N 110 7 E
Luxi, Yunnan, China 58 24 40N 103 55 E
Luxi, Yunnan, China 58 24 27N 98 36 E
Luxor = El Uqsur, Egypt 88 25 41N 32 38 E
Luy →, France 20 43 39N 1 9W
Luy-de-Béarn →, France 20 43 39N 0 48W
Luy-de-France →, France 20 43 39N 0 48W
Luyi, China 60 33 50N 115 35 E
Luyksgestel, Neths. 17 51 17N 5 20 E
Luz-St.-Sauveur, France 20 42 53N 0 0 E
Luzern, Switz. 31 47 3N 8 18 E
Luzern □, Switz. 31 47 2N 7 55 E
Luzhai, China 58 24 29N 109 42 E
Luzhou, China 58 28 52N 105 20 E
Luziânia, Brazil 139 16 20 S 48 0W
Luzilândia, Brazil 138 3 28 S 42 22W
Luzon, Phil. 57 16 0N 121 0 E
Luzy, France 19 46 47N 3 58 E
Luzzi, Italy 29 39 28N 16 17 E
Lvov, U.S.S.R. 36 49 50N 24 0 E
Lyakhovichi, U.S.S.R. 36 53 2N 26 32 E
Lyakhovskiye, Ostrova, U.S.S.R. 41 73 40N 141 0 E
Lyaki, U.S.S.R. 39 40 34N 47 22 E
Lyal I., Canada 108 44 57N 81 24W
Lyall Mt., N.Z. 81 45 16 S 167 32 E
Lyallpur = Faisalabad, Pakistan 48 31 30N 73 5 E
Lychen, E. Germany 30 53 13N 13 20 E
Lyckeby, Sweden 11 56 12N 15 37 E
Lycksele, Sweden 8 64 38N 18 40 E
Lydda = Lod, Israel 44 31 57N 34 54 E
Lydenburg, S. Africa 97 25 10 S 30 29 E
Lyell, N.Z. 81 41 48 S 172 4 E
Lyell I., Canada 110 52 40N 131 35W
Lyell Range, N.Z. 81 41 38 S 172 20 E
Lygnern, Sweden 11 57 30N 12 15 E
Lyman, U.S.A. 122 41 24N 110 15W
Lyme Regis, U.K. 13 50 44N 2 57W
Lymington, U.K. 13 50 46N 1 32W
Lynchburg, Ohio, U.S.A. 119 39 15N 83 48W
Lynchburg, Va., U.S.A. 114 37 23N 79 10W
Lynd →, Australia 72 16 28 S 143 18 E
Lynd Ra., Australia 73 25 30 S 149 20 E
Lynden, Canada 116 43 14N 80 9W
Lynden, U.S.A. 124 48 56N 122 32W
Lyndhurst, N.S.W., Australia 76 33 41 S 149 2 E
Lyndhurst, S. Austral., Australia 73 30 15 S 138 18 E
Lyndon →, Australia 79 23 29 S 114 6 E
Lyndonville, N.Y., U.S.A. 116 43 19N 78 25W
Lyndonville, Vt., U.S.A. 117 44 32N 72 1W
Lyngdal, Norway 10 59 54N 9 32 E
Lynher Reef, Australia 78 15 27 S 121 55 E
Lynn, Ind., U.S.A. 119 40 3N 84 56W
Lynn, Mass., U.S.A. 117 42 28N 70 57W
Lynn Canal, U.S.A. 110 58 50N 135 20W
Lynn Lake, Canada 111 56 51N 101 3W
Lynnwood, U.S.A. 124 47 49N 122 19W
Lynton, U.K. 13 51 14N 3 50W
Lyntupy, U.S.S.R. 36 55 4N 26 23 E
Lynx L., Canada 111 62 25N 106 15W
Lyø, Denmark 11 55 3N 10 9 E
Lyon, France 21 45 46N 4 50 E
Lyonnais, France 21 45 45N 4 15 E
Lyons = Lyon, France 21 45 46N 4 50 E
Lyons, Australia 74 38 2 S 141 28 E
Lyons, Colo., U.S.A. 120 40 17N 105 15W
Lyons, Ga., U.S.A. 115 32 10N 82 15W
Lyons, Kans., U.S.A. 120 38 24N 98 13W
Lyons, N.Y., U.S.A. 116 43 3N 77 0W
Lyrestad, Sweden 11 58 48N 14 4 E
Lys → = Leie →, Belgium 19 51 2N 3 45 E
Lysekil, Sweden 11 58 17N 11 26 E
Lyskovo, U.S.S.R. 37 56 0N 45 3 E
Lyster, Canada 107 46 22N 71 37W
Lysvik, Sweden 10 60 1N 13 9 E
Lytle, U.S.A. 121 29 14N 98 46W
Lyttelton, N.Z. 81 43 35 S 172 44 E
Lytton, Canada 110 50 13N 121 31W
Lyuban, U.S.S.R. 36 59 16N 31 18 E
Lyubcha, U.S.S.R. 36 53 46N 26 1 E
Lyubertsy, U.S.S.R. 37 55 39N 37 50 E
Lyubim, U.S.S.R. 37 58 20N 40 39 E
Lyuboml, U.S.S.R. 36 51 11N 24 4 E
Lyubotin, U.S.S.R. 38 50 0N 36 0 E
Lyubytino, U.S.S.R. 36 58 50N 33 16 E
Lyudinovo, U.S.S.R. 36 53 52N 34 28 E

M

Ma →, Vietnam 54 19 47N 105 56 E
Mā'ad, Jordan 44 32 37N 35 36 E
Ma'alah, Si. Arabia 46 26 31N 47 20 E
Maamba, Zambia 96 17 17 S 26 28 E
Ma'ān, Jordan 46 30 12N 35 44 E
Ma'anshan, China 59 31 44N 118 29 E
Maarheeze, Neths. 17 51 19N 5 36 E
Maarianhamina, Finland 9 60 5N 19 55 E
Maarn, Neths. 16 52 3N 5 22 E
Ma'arrat un Nu'man, Syria 46 35 38N 36 40 E
Maarssen, Neths. 16 52 9N 5 2 E
Maartensdijk, Neths. 16 52 9N 5 10 E
Maas →, Neths. 16 51 45N 4 32 E
Maasbracht, Belgium 17 51 9N 5 54 E
Maasbree, Neths. 17 51 22N 6 3 E
Maasdam, Neths. 16 51 48N 4 34 E
Maasdijk, Neths. 16 51 58N 4 13 E
Maaseik, Belgium 17 51 6N 5 45 E
Maasland, Neths. 16 51 57N 4 16 E
Maasniel, Neths. 17 51 12N 6 1 E
Maassluis, Neths. 16 51 56N 4 16 E
Maastricht, Neths. 17 50 50N 5 40 E
Maave, Mozam. 97 21 4 S 34 47 E
Mabaruma, Guyana 135 8 10N 59 50W
Mabein, Burma 52 23 29N 96 37 E
Mabel L., Canada 110 50 35N 118 43W
Mabenge, Zaïre 92 4 15N 24 12 E
Maberly, Canada 109 44 50N 76 32W
Mabian, China 58 28 47N 103 37 E
Mablethorpe, U.K. 12 53 21N 0 14 E
Maboma, Zaïre 92 2 30N 28 10 E

Maboukou, *Congo* **94** 3 39 S 12 31 E
Mabrouk, *Mali* **91** 19 29N 1 15W
Mabton, *U.S.A.* **122** 46 15N 120 12W
Mabungo, *Somali Rep.* **98** 0 49N 42 35 E
Mac Bac, *Vietnam* **55** 9 46N 106 7 E
Macachín, *Argentina* **140** 37 10 S 63 43W
Macaé, *Brazil* **139** 22 20 S 41 43W
Macaíba, *Brazil* **138** 5 51 S 35 21W
Macajuba, *Brazil* **139** 12 9 S 40 22W
McAlester, *U.S.A.* **121** 34 57N 95 46W
McAllen, *U.S.A.* **121** 26 12N 98 15W
Macallister →, *Australia* **75** 38 2 S 146 59 E
Macamic, *Canada* **106** 48 45N 79 0W
Macao = Macau ■, *China* **62** 22 16N 113 35 E
Macão, *Portugal* **23** 39 35N 7 59W
Macapá, *Brazil* **138** 0 5N 51 4W
Macará, *Ecuador* **134** 4 23 S 79 57W
Macarani, *Brazil* **139** 15 33 S 40 24W
Macarena, Serranía de la, *Colombia* **134** 2 45N 73 55W
Macarthur, *Australia* **74** 38 5 S 142 0 E
McArthur →, *Australia* **72** 15 54 S 136 40 E
McArthur River, *Australia* **72** 16 27 S 136 7 E
Macas, *Ecuador* **134** 2 19 S 78 7W
Macate, *Peru* **136** 8 48 S 78 7W
Macau, *Brazil* **138** 5 0 S 36 40W
Macau ■, *China* **62** 22 16N 113 35 E
Macaúbas, *Brazil* **139** 13 2 S 42 42W
Macaya →, *Colombia* **134** 0 59N 72 20W
McBride, *Canada* **110** 53 20N 120 19W
McCall, *U.S.A.* **122** 44 55N 116 6W
McCamey, *U.S.A.* **121** 31 8N 102 15W
McCammon, *U.S.A.* **122** 42 41N 112 11W
McCauley I., *Canada* **110** 53 40N 130 15W
McCleary, *U.S.A.* **124** 47 3N 123 16W
Macclesfield, *U.K.* **12** 53 16N 2 9W
McClintock, *Canada* **111** 57 50N 94 10W
McClintock Ra., *Australia* **78** 18 44 S 127 38 E
McCloud, *U.S.A.* **122** 41 14N 122 5W
McClure, *U.S.A.* **116** 40 42N 77 20W
McClure, L., *U.S.A.* **124** 37 35N 120 16W
McClure Str., *Canada* **144** 75 0N 119 0W
McClusky, *U.S.A.* **120** 47 30N 100 31W
McComb, *U.S.A.* **121** 31 13N 90 30W
McConaughy, L., *U.S.A.* **120** 41 20N 101 40W
McCook, *U.S.A.* **120** 40 15N 100 35W
McCullough Mt., *U.S.A.* **125** 35 35N 115 13W
McCusker →, *Canada* **111** 55 32N 108 39W
McDame, *Canada* **110** 59 44N 128 59W
McDermitt, *U.S.A.* **122** 42 0N 117 45W
Macdonald →, *N.S.W., Australia* **76** 33 22 S 151 0 E
MacDonald →, *Queens., Australia* **77** 30 45 S 150 45 E
Macdonald, Mt., *Vanuatu* **68** 17 36 S 168 23 E
McDonald Is., *Ind. Oc.* **53** 53 0 S 73 0 E
Macdonald L., *Australia* **78** 23 30 S 129 0 E
Macdonnell Ranges, *Australia* **78** 23 40 S 133 0 E
McDouall Peak, *Australia* **73** 29 51 S 134 55 E
Macdougall L., *Canada* **102** 66 0N 98 27W
MacDowell L., *Canada* **104** 52 15N 92 45W
Macduff, *U.K.* **14** 57 40N 2 30W
Maceda, *Spain* **22** 42 16N 7 39W
Macedon, *Australia* **74** 37 24 S 144 35 E
Macedonia = Makedonija □, *Yugoslavia* **35** 41 53N 21 40 E
Maceió, *Brazil* **138** 9 40 S 35 41W
Maceira, *Portugal* **23** 39 41N 8 55W
Macenta, *Guinea* **90** 8 35N 9 32W
Macerata, *Italy* **27** 43 19N 13 28 E
McFarland, *U.S.A.* **125** 35 41N 119 14W
McFarlane →, *Canada* **111** 59 12N 107 58W
Macfarlane, L., *Australia* **73** 32 0 S 136 40 E
McGehee, *U.S.A.* **121** 33 40N 91 25W
McGill, *U.S.A.* **122** 39 27N 114 50W
Macgillycuddy's Reeks, *Ireland* **15** 52 2N 9 45W
MacGregor, *Canada* **111** 49 57N 98 48W
McGregor, *U.S.A.* **118** 43 0N 91 15W
McGregor →, *Canada* **110** 55 10N 122 0W
McGregor Ra., *Australia* **73** 27 0 S 142 45 E
Mach, *Pakistan* **47** 29 50N 67 20 E
Machacalis, *Brazil* **139** 17 5 S 40 45W
Machado = Jiparaná →, *Brazil* **137** 8 3 S 62 52W
Machagai, *Argentina* **140** 26 56 S 60 2W
Machakos, *Kenya* **92** 1 30 S 37 15 E
Machakos □, *Kenya* **92** 1 30 S 37 15 E
Machala, *Ecuador* **134** 3 20 S 79 57W
Machanga, *Mozam.* **97** 20 59 S 35 0 E
Machattie, L., *Australia* **72** 24 50 S 139 48 E
Machava, *Mozam.* **97** 25 54 S 32 28 E
Machece, *Mozam.* **93** 19 15 S 35 32 E
Machecoul, *France* **18** 47 0N 1 49W
Machelen, *Belgium* **17** 50 55N 4 26 E
Macheng, *China* **59** 31 12N 115 2 E
McHenry, *U.S.A.* **119** 42 21N 88 16W
Machevna, *U.S.S.R.* **41** 61 20N 172 20 E
Machezo, *Spain* **23** 39 21N 4 20W
Machias, *U.S.A.* **105** 44 40N 67 28W
Machichaco, C., *Spain* **24** 43 28N 2 47W
Machichi →, *Canada* **111** 57 3N 92 6W
Machida, *Japan* **65** 35 28N 139 23 E
Machilipatnam, *India* **51** 16 12N 81 8 E
Machine, La, *France* **19** 46 54N 3 27 E
Machiques, *Venezuela* **134** 10 4N 72 34W
Machupicchu, *Peru* **136** 13 8 S 72 30W
Machynlleth, *U.K.* **13** 52 36N 3 51W
McIlwraith Ra., *Australia* **72** 13 50 S 143 20 E
Măcin, *Romania* **34** 45 16N 28 8 E
Macina, *Mali* **90** 14 50N 5 0W
McIntosh, *U.S.A.* **120** 45 57N 101 20W
McIntosh L., *Canada* **111** 55 45N 105 0W
Macintyre →, *Australia* **77** 28 37 S 150 47 E
Macizo Galaico, *Spain* **22** 42 30N 7 30W
Mackay, *Australia* **72** 21 8 S 149 11 E
Mackay, *U.S.A.* **122** 43 58N 113 37W
MacKay →, *Canada* **110** 57 10N 111 38W
Mackay, L., *Australia* **78** 22 30 S 129 0 E
McKay Ra., *Australia* **78** 23 0 S 122 30 E
McKeesport, *U.S.A.* **116** 40 21N 79 50W
McKellar, *Canada* **108** 45 30N 79 55W
McKenna, *U.S.A.* **124** 46 56N 122 33W
Mackenzie, *Canada* **110** 55 20N 123 5W
Mackenzie, *Guyana* **135** 6 0N 58 17W
McKenzie, *U.S.A.* **115** 36 10N 88 31W
Mackenzie →, *Australia* **72** 23 38 S 149 46 E
Mackenzie →, *Canada* **102** 69 10N 134 20W
McKenzie →, *U.S.A.* **122** 44 2N 123 6W
Mackenzie City = Linden, *Guyana* **136** 6 0N 58 10W
Mackenzie Highway, *Canada* **110** 58 0N 117 15W
Mackenzie Mts., *Canada* **102** 64 0N 130 0W
Mackenzie Plains, *N.Z.* **81** 44 10 S 170 25 E
McKerrow L., *N.Z.* **81** 44 25 S 168 5 E
Mackinaw, *U.S.A.* **118** 40 32N 89 21W
Mackinaw →, *U.S.A.* **118** 40 33N 89 44W
Mackinaw City, *U.S.A.* **104** 45 47N 84 44W
McKinlay, *Australia* **72** 21 16 S 141 18 E
McKinlay →, *Australia* **72** 20 50 S 141 28 E
McKinley, Mt., *U.S.A.* **102** 63 2N 151 0W
McKinley Sea, *Arctic* **144** 84 0N 10 0W
McKinney, *U.S.A.* **121** 33 10N 96 40W
Mackinnon Road, *Kenya* **92** 3 40 S 39 1 E
Mackintosh Ra., *Australia* **79** 27 39 S 125 32 E
Macksville, *Australia* **77** 30 40 S 152 56 E
McLaughlin, *U.S.A.* **120** 45 50N 100 50W
Maclean, *Australia* **77** 29 26 S 153 16 E
McLean, *Ill., U.S.A.* **118** 40 19N 89 10W
McLean, *Tex., U.S.A.* **121** 35 15N 100 35W
McLeansboro, *U.S.A.* **119** 38 5N 88 30W
Maclear, *S. Africa* **97** 31 2 S 28 23 E
Macleay →, *Australia* **77** 30 56 S 153 0 E
McLennan, *Canada* **110** 55 42N 116 50W
MacLeod, B., *Canada* **111** 62 53N 110 0W
McLeod L., *Australia* **79** 24 9 S 113 47 E
MacLeod Lake, *Canada* **110** 54 58N 123 0W
M'Clintock Chan., *Canada* **102** 72 0N 102 0W
McLoughlin, Mt., *U.S.A.* **122** 42 10N 122 19W
McLure, *Canada* **110** 51 2N 120 13W
McMahon's Reef, *Australia* **76** 34 39 S 148 26 E
McMechen, *U.S.A.* **116** 39 57N 80 44W
McMillan L., *U.S.A.* **121** 32 40N 104 20W
McMinnville, *Oreg., U.S.A.* **122** 45 16N 123 11W
McMinnville, *Tenn., U.S.A.* **115** 35 43N 85 45W
McMorran, *Canada* **111** 51 19N 108 42W
McMurdo Sd., *Antarctica* **143** 77 0 S 170 0 E
McMurray = Fort McMurray, *Canada* **110** 56 44N 111 7W
McMurray, *U.S.A.* **124** 48 19N 122 19W
McNary, *U.S.A.* **123** 34 4N 109 53W
MacNutt, *Canada* **111** 51 5N 101 36W
Macocolo, *Angola* **95** 6 47 S 16 8 E
Macodoene, *Mozam.* **97** 23 32 S 35 5 E
Macomb, *U.S.A.* **118** 40 25N 90 40W
Macomer, *Italy* **28** 40 16N 8 48 E
Mâcon, *France* **21** 46 19N 4 50 E
Macon, *Ga., U.S.A.* **115** 32 50N 83 37W
Macon, *Ill., U.S.A.* **118** 39 43N 89 0W
Macon, *Miss., U.S.A.* **115** 33 7N 88 31W
Macon, *Mo., U.S.A.* **118** 39 40N 92 26W
Macondo, *Angola* **95** 12 37 S 23 46 E
Macossa, *Mozam.* **93** 17 55 S 33 56 E
Macoun L., *Canada* **111** 56 32N 103 40W
Macoupin Cr. →, *U.S.A.* **118** 39 11N 90 38W
Macovane, *Mozam.* **97** 21 30 S 35 0 E
McPherson, *U.S.A.* **120** 38 25N 97 40W
McPherson Pk., *U.S.A.* **125** 34 53N 119 53W
Macpherson Ra., *Australia* **77** 28 15 S 153 15 E
Macquarie, L., *Australia* **76** 33 4 S 151 36 E
Macquarie, Mt., *Australia* **76** 33 37 S 149 10 E
Macquarie Harbour, *Australia* **72** 42 15 S 145 23 E
Macquarie Is., *Pac. Oc.* **66** 54 36 S 158 55 E
MacRobertson Land, *Antarctica* **143** 71 0 S 64 0 E
Macroom, *Ireland* **15** 51 54N 8 57W
Macroy, *Australia* **78** 20 53 S 118 2 E
MacTier, *Ont., Canada* **108** 45 8N 79 47W
MacTier, *Canada* **116** 45 9N 79 46W
Macubela, *Mozam.* **93** 16 53 S 37 49 E
Macugnaga, *Italy* **26** 45 57N 7 58 E
Macuiza, *Mozam.* **93** 18 7 S 34 29 E
Macujer, *Colombia* **134** 0 24N 73 10W
Macusani, *Peru* **136** 14 4 S 70 29W
Macuse, *Mozam.* **93** 17 45 S 37 10 E
Macuspana, *Mexico* **127** 17 46N 92 36W
Macusse, *Angola* **95** 17 48 S 20 23 E
McVille, *U.S.A.* **120** 47 46N 98 11W
Madadeni, *S. Africa* **97** 27 43 S 30 3 E
Madadi, *Chad* **87** 18 28N 20 45 E
Madagali, *Nigeria* **91** 10 56N 13 33 E
Madagascar ■, *Africa* **97** 20 0 S 47 0 E
Madā'in Sālih, *Si. Arabia* **46** 26 46N 37 57 E
Madama, *Niger* **87** 22 0N 13 40 E
Madame I., *Canada* **105** 45 30N 60 58W
Madanapalle, *India* **51** 13 33N 78 28 E
Madang, *Papua N. G.* **69** 5 12 S 145 49 E
Madaoua, *Niger* **91** 14 5N 6 27 E
Madara, *Nigeria* **91** 11 45N 10 35 E
Madaripur, *Bangla.* **52** 23 19N 90 15 E
Madauk, *Burma* **52** 17 56N 96 52 E
Madawaska, *Canada* **106** 45 30N 78 0W
Madawaska →, *Canada* **109** 45 27N 76 21W
Madaya, *Burma* **52** 22 12N 96 10 E
Madbar, *Sudan* **89** 6 17N 30 45 E
Maddalena, La, *Italy* **28** 41 13N 9 25 E
Maddaloni, *Italy* **29** 41 4N 14 23 E
Made, *Neths.* **17** 51 41N 4 49 E
Madeira, *Atl. Oc.* **84** 32 50N 17 0W
Madeira, *U.S.A.* **119** 39 11N 84 22W
Madeira →, *Brazil* **135** 3 22 S 58 45W
Madeleine, Is. de la, *Canada* **105** 47 30N 61 40W
Madera, *U.S.A.* **124** 36 58N 120 1W
Madgaon, *India* **51** 15 12N 73 58 E
Madha, *India* **50** 18 0N 75 30 E
Madhubani, *India* **49** 26 21N 86 7 E
Madhumati →, *Bangla.* **52** 22 53N 89 52 E
Madhya Pradesh □, *India* **48** 21 50N 81 0 E
Madian, *China* **59** 33 0N 116 6 E
Madidi →, *Bolivia* **136** 12 32 S 66 52W
Madikeri, *India* **51** 12 30N 75 45 E
Madill, *U.S.A.* **121** 34 5N 96 49W
Madimba, *Angola* **95** 6 36 S 14 23 E
Madimba, *Zaïre* **95** 5 0 S 15 0 E
Madīnat ash Sha'b, *S. Yemen* **45** 12 50N 45 0 E
Madingou, *Congo* **94** 4 10 S 13 33 E
Madirovalo, *Madag.* **97** 16 26 S 46 32 E
Madison, *Calif., U.S.A.* **124** 38 41N 121 59W
Madison, *Fla., U.S.A.* **115** 30 29N 83 39W
Madison, *Ind., U.S.A.* **119** 38 42N 85 20W
Madison, *Mo., U.S.A.* **118** 39 28N 92 13W
Madison, *Nebr., U.S.A.* **120** 41 53N 97 25W
Madison, *Ohio, U.S.A.* **116** 41 45N 81 4W
Madison, *S. Dak., U.S.A.* **120** 44 0N 97 8W
Madison, *Wis., U.S.A.* **118** 43 5N 89 25W
Madison →, *U.S.A.* **122** 45 56N 111 30W
Madisonville, *Ky., U.S.A.* **114** 37 20N 87 30W
Madisonville, *Tex., U.S.A.* **121** 30 57N 95 55W
Madista, *Botswana* **96** 21 15 S 25 6 E
Madiun, *Indonesia* **57** 7 38 S 111 32 E
Madley, *U.K.* **13** 52 3N 2 51W
Madoc, *Canada* **109** 44 30N 77 28W
Madol, *Sudan* **89** 9 3N 27 45 E
Madon →, *France* **19** 48 36N 6 6 E
Madona, *U.S.S.R.* **36** 56 53N 26 5 E
Madonie, Le, *Italy* **28** 37 50N 13 50 E
Madras = Tamil Nadu □, *India* **51** 11 0N 77 0 E
Madras, *India* **51** 13 8N 80 19 E
Madras, *U.S.A.* **122** 44 40N 121 10W
Madre, L., *Mexico* **127** 25 0N 97 30W
Madre, L., *U.S.A.* **121** 26 0N 97 40W
Madre, Sierra, *Mexico* **127** 16 0N 93 0W
Madre, Sierra, *Phil.* **57** 17 0N 122 0 E
Madre de Dios □, *Peru* **136** 12 0 S 70 15W
Madre de Dios →, *Bolivia* **136** 10 59 S 66 8W
Madre de Dios, I., *Chile* **142** 50 20 S 75 10W
Madre del Sur, Sierra, *Mexico* **127** 17 30N 100 0W
Madre Occidental, Sierra, *Mexico* **126** 27 0N 107 0W
Madre Oriental, Sierra, *Mexico* **126** 25 0N 100 0W
Madri, *India* **48** 24 16N 73 32 E
Madrid, *Spain* **22** 40 25N 3 45W
Madrid, *U.S.A.* **118** 41 53N 93 49W
Madrid □, *Spain* **22** 40 30N 3 45W
Madridejos, *Spain* **23** 39 28N 3 33W
Madrigal de las Altas Torres, *Spain* **22** 41 5N 5 0W
Madrona, Sierra, *Spain* **23** 38 27N 4 16W
Madroñera, *Spain* **23** 39 26N 5 42W
Madu, *Sudan* **89** 14 37N 26 4 E
Madura, Selat, *Indonesia* **57** 7 30 S 113 20 E
Madura Motel, *Australia* **79** 31 55 S 127 0 E
Madurai, *India* **51** 9 55N 78 10 E
Madurantakam, *India* **51** 12 30N 79 50 E
Madzhalis, *U.S.S.R.* **39** 42 9N 47 47 E
Mae Chan, *Thailand* **54** 20 9N 99 52 E
Mae Hong Son, *Thailand* **54** 19 16N 98 1 E
Mae Khlong →, *Thailand* **54** 13 24N 100 0 E
Mae Phrik, *Thailand* **54** 17 27N 99 7 E
Mae Ramat, *Thailand* **54** 16 58N 98 31 E
Mae Rim, *Thailand* **54** 18 54N 98 57 E
Mae Sot, *Thailand* **54** 16 43N 98 34 E
Mae Suai, *Thailand* **54** 19 39N 99 33 E
Mae Tha, *Thailand* **54** 18 28N 99 8 E
Maebaru, *Japan* **64** 33 33N 130 12 E
Maebashi, *Japan* **65** 36 24N 139 4 E
Maella, *Spain* **24** 41 8N 0 7 E
Măeruş, *Romania* **34** 45 53N 25 31 E
Maesteg, *U.K.* **13** 51 36N 3 40W
Maestra, Sierra, *Cuba* **128** 20 15N 77 0W
Maestrazgo, Mts. del, *Spain* **24** 40 30N 0 25W
Maevatanana, *Madag.* **97** 16 56 S 46 49 E
Maewo, *Vanuatu* **68** 15 10 S 168 10 E
Ma'fan, *Libya* **86** 25 56N 14 29 E
Mafeking, *Canada* **111** 52 40N 101 10W
Maféré, *Ivory C.* **90** 5 30N 3 2W
Mafeteng, *Lesotho* **96** 29 51 S 27 15 E
Maffe, *Belgium* **17** 50 21N 5 19 E
Maffra, *Australia* **75** 37 53 S 146 58 E
Mafia I., *Tanzania* **92** 7 45 S 39 50 E
Mafikeng, *S. Africa* **96** 25 50 S 25 38 E
Mafra, *Brazil* **141** 26 10 S 50 0W
Mafra, *Portugal* **23** 38 55N 9 20W
Mafungabusi Plateau, *Zimb.* **93** 18 30 S 29 8 E
Magadan, *U.S.S.R.* **41** 59 38N 150 50 E
Magadi, *Kenya* **92** 1 54 S 36 19 E
Magadi, L., *Kenya* **92** 1 54 S 36 19 E
Magaliesburg, *S. Africa* **97** 26 0 S 27 32 E
Magallanes □, *Chile* **142** 52 0 S 72 0W
Magallanes, Estrecho de, *Chile* **142** 52 30 S 75 0W
Magangué, *Colombia* **134** 9 14N 74 45W
Magaria, *Niger* **91** 13 4N 9 5 E
Magburaka, *S. Leone* **90** 8 47N 12 0W
Magdalena, *Argentina* **140** 35 5 S 57 30W
Magdalena, *Bolivia* **137** 13 13 S 63 57W
Magdalena, *Malaysia* **56** 4 25N 117 55 E
Magdalena, *Mexico* **126** 30 50N 112 0W
Magdalena, *U.S.A.* **123** 34 10N 107 20W
Magdalena □, *Colombia* **134** 10 0N 74 0W
Magdalena →, *Colombia* **134** 11 6N 74 51W
Magdalena →, *Mexico* **126** 30 40N 112 25W
Magdalena, B., *Mexico* **126** 24 30N 112 10W
Magdalena, I., *Chile* **142** 44 40 S 73 0W
Magdalena, Llano de la, *Mexico* **126** 25 0N 111 30W
Magdeburg, *E. Germany* **30** 52 8N 11 36 E
Magdeburg □, *E. Germany* **30** 52 20N 11 30 E
Magdelaine Cays, *Australia* **72** 16 33 S 150 18 E
Magdi'el, *Israel* **44** 32 10N 34 54 E
Magdub, *Sudan* **89** 13 42N 25 5 E
Magee, *U.S.A.* **121** 31 53N 89 45W
Magee, I., *U.K.* **15** 54 48N 5 44W
Magelang, *Indonesia* **57** 7 29 S 110 13 E
Magellan's Str. = Magallanes, Estrecho de, *Chile* **142** 52 30 S 75 0W
Magenta, *Italy* **26** 45 28N 8 53 E
Magenta, L., *Australia* **79** 33 30 S 119 2 E
Maggia →, *Switz.* **31** 46 18N 8 36 E
Maggiorasca, Mte., *Italy* **26** 44 33N 9 29 E
Maggiore, L., *Italy* **26** 46 0N 8 35 E
Maghama, *Mauritania* **90** 15 32N 12 57W
Maghār, *Israel* **44** 32 54N 35 24 E
Magherafelt, *U.K.* **15** 54 44N 6 37W
Maghnia, *Algeria* **85** 34 50N 1 43W
Magione, *Italy* **27** 43 10N 12 12 E
Magliano in Toscana, *Italy* **27** 42 36N 11 18 E
Máglie, *Italy* **29** 40 8N 18 17 E
Magnac-Laval, *France* **20** 46 13N 1 11 E
Magnetawan, *Canada* **108** 45 40N 79 39W
Magnetic Pole (North), *Canada* **144** 77 5N 102 6W
Magnetic Pole (South), *Antarctica* **143** 65 2 S 139 4 E
Magnitogorsk, *U.S.S.R.* **40** 53 27N 59 4 E
Magnolia, *Ark., U.S.A.* **121** 33 18N 93 12W
Magnolia, *Miss., U.S.A.* **121** 31 8N 90 28W
Magnor, *Norway* **10** 59 56N 12 15 E
Magnus, Mt., *Australia* **77** 28 30 S 151 50 E
Magny-en-Vexin, *France* **19** 49 9N 1 47 E
Magog, *Canada* **107** 45 18N 72 9W
Magoro, *Uganda* **92** 1 45N 34 12 E
Magosa = Famagusta, *Cyprus* **46** 35 8N 33 55 E
Magoye, *Zambia* **93** 16 1 S 27 30 E
Magpie L., *Canada* **105** 51 0N 64 41W
Magrath, *Canada* **110** 49 25N 112 50W
Magro →, *Spain* **25** 39 11N 0 25W
Magrur, Wadi →, *Sudan* **89** 16 5N 26 30 E
Magu □, *Tanzania* **92** 2 31 S 33 28 E
Maguan, *China* **58** 23 0N 104 21 E
Maguarinho, C., *Brazil* **138** 0 15 S 48 30W
Maguse L., *Canada* **111** 61 40N 95 10W

Maguse Pt., *Canada* **111** 61 20N 93 50W
Magwe, *Burma* **52** 20 10N 95 0 E
Maha Sarakham, *Thailand* **54** 16 12N 103 16 E
Mahābād, *Iran* **46** 36 50N 45 45 E
Mahabaleshwar, *India* **50** 17 58N 73 43 E
Mahabharat Lekh, *Nepal* **49** 28 30N 82 0 E
Mahabo, *Madag.* **97** 20 23 S 44 40 E
Mahad, *India* **50** 18 6N 73 29 E
Mahaddei Uen, *Somali Rep.* **98** 2 58N 45 32 E
Mahadeo Hills, *India* **48** 22 20N 78 30 E
Mahadeopur, *India* **50** 18 48N 80 0 E
Mahagi, *Zaïre* **92** 2 20N 31 0 E
Mahaicony, *Guyana* **135** 6 36N 57 48W
Mahajamba →, *Madag.* **97** 15 33 S 47 8 E
Mahajamba, Helodranon' i, *Madag.* **97** 15 24 S 47 5 E
Mahajan, *India* **48** 28 48N 73 56 E
Mahajanga, *Madag.* **97** 15 40 S 46 25 E
Mahajanga □, *Madag.* **97** 17 0 S 47 0 E
Mahajilo →, *Madag.* **97** 19 42 S 45 22 E
Mahakam →, *Indonesia* **56** 0 35 S 117 17 E
Mahalapye, *Botswana* **96** 23 1 S 26 51 E
Maḥallāt, *Iran* **47** 33 55N 50 30 E
Mahanadi →, *India* **50** 20 20N 86 25 E
Mahanoro, *Madag.* **97** 19 54 S 48 48 E
Mahanoy City, *U.S.A.* **117** 40 48N 76 10W
Maharashtra □, *India* **50** 20 30N 75 30 E
Maharès, *Tunisia* **86** 34 32N 10 29 E
Mahari Mts., *Tanzania* **92** 6 20 S 30 0 E
Mahasolo, *Madag.* **97** 19 7 S 46 22 E
Mahaweli →, *Sri Lanka* **51** 8 30N 81 15 E
Mahaxay, *Laos* **54** 17 22N 105 12 E
Mahbes, *W. Sahara* **84** 27 10N 9 50W
Mahbubabad, *India* **50** 17 42N 80 2 E
Mahbubnagar, *India* **50** 16 45N 77 59 E
Mahdia, *Guyana* **135** 5 13N 59 8W
Mahdia, *Tunisia* **86** 35 28N 11 0 E
Mahe, *Jammu & Kashmir, India* **49** 33 10N 78 32 E
Mahé, *Pondicherry, India* **51** 11 42N 75 34 E
Mahé, *Seychelles* **53** 5 0 S 55 30 E
Mahendra Giri, *India* **51** 8 20N 77 30 E
Mahendraganj, *India* **52** 25 20N 89 45 E
Mahenge, *Tanzania* **93** 8 45 S 36 41 E
Maheno, *N.Z.* **81** 45 10 S 170 50 E
Mahesana, *India* **48** 23 39N 72 26 E
Mahia Pen., *N.Z.* **80** 39 9 S 177 55 E
Mahirija, *Morocco* **85** 34 0N 3 16W
Mahlaing, *Burma* **52** 21 6N 95 39 E
Mahmiya, *Sudan* **89** 17 12N 33 43 E
Mahmud Kot, *Pakistan* **48** 30 16N 71 0 E
Mahmudia, *Romania* **34** 45 5N 29 5 E
Mahnomen, *U.S.A.* **120** 47 22N 95 57W
Mahoba, *India* **49** 25 15N 79 55 E
Mahomet, *U.S.A.* **119** 40 12N 88 24W
Mahón, *Spain* **24** 39 53N 4 16 E
Mahone Bay, *Canada* **105** 44 30N 64 20W
Mahuta, *Nigeria* **91** 11 32N 4 58 E
Mai-Ndombe, L., *Zaïre* **94** 2 0 S 18 20 E
Mai-Sai, *Thailand* **54** 20 20N 99 55 E
Maibara, *Japan* **65** 35 19N 136 17 E
Maicao, *Colombia* **134** 11 23N 72 13W
Maicasagi →, *Canada* **106** 49 58N 76 33W
Maîche, *France* **19** 47 16N 6 48 E
Maici →, *Brazil* **137** 6 30 S 61 43W
Maicurú →, *Brazil* **135** 2 14 S 54 17W
Máida, *Italy* **29** 38 51N 16 21 E
Maidan Khula, *Afghan.* **48** 33 36N 69 50 E
Maidenhead, *U.K.* **13** 51 31N 0 42W
Maidi, *Yemen* **89** 16 20N 42 45 E
Maidstone, *Canada* **111** 53 5N 109 20W
Maidstone, *U.K.* **13** 51 16N 0 31 E
Maiduguri, *Nigeria* **91** 12 0N 13 20 E
Maignelay, *France* **19** 49 32N 2 30 E
Maigualida, Sierra, *Venezuela* **135** 5 30N 65 10W
Maigudo, *Ethiopia* **89** 7 30N 37 8 E
Maijdi, *Bangla.* **52** 22 48N 91 10 E
Maikala Ra., *India* **50** 22 0N 81 0 E
Mailly-le-Camp, *France* **19** 48 41N 4 12 E
Mailsi, *Pakistan* **48** 29 48N 72 15 E
Main →, *U.K.* **15** 54 49N 6 20W
Main →, *W. Germany* **31** 50 0N 8 18 E
Main Centre, *Canada* **111** 50 35N 107 21W
Mainburg, *W. Germany* **31** 48 37N 11 49 E
Maine, *France* **18** 48 0N 0 0 E
Maine □, *U.S.A.* **105** 45 20N 69 0W
Maine →, *Ireland* **15** 52 10N 9 40W
Maine-et-Loire □, *France* **18** 47 31N 0 30W
Maïne-Soroa, *Niger* **91** 13 13N 12 2 E
Maingkwan, *Burma* **52** 26 15N 96 37 E
Mainit, L., *Phil.* **57** 9 31N 125 30 E
Mainkaing, *Burma* **52** 24 48N 95 16 E
Mainland, *Orkney, U.K.* **14** 59 0N 3 10W
Mainland, *Shetland, U.K.* **14** 60 15N 1 22W
Mainpuri, *India* **49** 27 18N 79 4 E
Maintenon, *France* **19** 48 35N 1 35 E
Maintirano, *Madag.* **97** 18 3 S 44 1 E
Mainvault, *Belgium* **17** 50 39N 3 43 E
Mainz, *W. Germany* **31** 50 0N 8 17 E
Maipú, *Argentina* **140** 36 52 S 57 50W
Maiquetía, *Venezuela* **134** 10 36N 66 57W
Maira →, *Italy* **26** 44 49N 7 38 E
Mairabari, *India* **52** 26 30N 92 22 E
Maire, Le, Est. de, *Argentina* **142** 54 50 S 65 0W
Mairipotaba, *Brazil* **139** 17 18 S 49 28W
Maisí, *Cuba* **129** 20 17N 74 9W
Maisi, Pta. de, *Cuba* **129** 20 10N 74 10W
Maisse, *France* **19** 48 24N 2 21 E
Maissin, *Belgium* **17** 49 58N 5 10 E
Maitland, *N.S.W., Australia* **76** 32 33 S 151 36 E
Maitland, *S. Austral., Australia* **73** 34 23 S 137 40 E
Maitland →, *Canada* **116** 43 45N 81 43W
Maiyema, *Nigeria* **91** 12 5N 4 25 E
Maiyuan, *China* **59** 25 34N 117 28 E
Maiz, Is. del, *Nic.* **128** 12 15N 83 4W
Maizuru, *Japan* **65** 35 25N 135 22 E
Majagual, *Colombia* **134** 8 33N 74 38W
Majalengka, *Indonesia* **57** 6 50 S 108 13 E
Majari →, *Brazil* **135** 3 29N 60 58W
Majd el Kurūm, *Israel* **44** 32 56N 35 15 E
Majene, *Indonesia* **57** 3 38 S 118 57 E
Majes →, *Peru* **136** 16 40 S 72 44W
Maji, *Ethiopia* **89** 6 12N 35 30 E
Majiang, *China* **58** 26 28N 107 32 E
Major, *Canada* **111** 51 52N 109 37W
Majorca, I. = Mallorca, *Spain* **24** 39 30N 3 0 E
Majors Creek, *Australia* **76** 35 33 S 149 45 E
Majuriã, *Brazil* **137** 7 30 S 64 55W
Maka, *Senegal* **90** 13 40N 14 10W
Makak, *Cameroon* **91** 3 36N 11 0 E
Makakou, *Gabon* **94** 0 11 S 12 12 E
Makale, *Indonesia* **57** 3 6 S 119 51 E
Makamba, *Burundi* **92** 4 8 S 29 49 E
Makarewa, *N.Z.* **81** 46 20 S 168 21 E
Makarikari = Makgadikgadi Salt Pans, *Botswana* **96** 20 40 S 25 45 E
Makarovo, *U.S.S.R.* **41** 57 40N 107 45 E
Makarska, *Yugoslavia* **33** 43 20N 17 2 E
Makaryev, *U.S.S.R.* **37** 57 52N 43 50 E
Makasar = Ujung Pandang, *Indonesia* **57** 5 10 S 119 20 E
Makasar, Selat, *Indonesia* **57** 1 0 S 118 20 E
Makat, *U.S.S.R.* **40** 47 39N 53 19 E
Makedonija □, *Yugoslavia* **35** 41 53N 21 40 E
Makena, *U.S.A.* **112** 20 39N 156 27W
Makeni, *S. Leone* **90** 8 55N 12 5W
Makeyevka, *U.S.S.R.* **38** 48 0N 38 0 E
Makgadikgadi Salt Pans, *Botswana* **96** 20 40 S 25 45 E
Makhachkala, *U.S.S.R.* **39** 43 0N 47 30 E
Makhambet, *U.S.S.R.* **39** 47 43N 51 40 E
Makharadze, *U.S.S.R.* **39** 41 55N 42 2 E
Makian, *Indonesia* **57** 0 20N 127 20 E
Makindu, *Kenya* **92** 2 18 S 37 50 E
Makinsk, *U.S.S.R.* **40** 52 37N 70 26 E
Makkah, *Si. Arabia* **88** 21 30N 39 54 E
Makkovik, *Canada* **105** 55 10N 59 10W
Makkum, *Neths.* **16** 53 3N 5 25 E
Maklakovo, *U.S.S.R.* **41** 58 16N 92 29 E
Makó, *Hungary* **33** 46 14N 20 33 E
Makok, *Gabon* **94** 0 1 S 9 35 E
Makokou, *Gabon* **94** 0 40N 12 50 E
Makongo, *Zaïre* **92** 3 25N 26 17 E
Makoro, *Zaïre* **92** 3 10N 29 59 E
Makoua, *Congo* **94** 0 5 S 15 50 E
Makrá, *Greece* **35** 36 15N 25 54 E
Makran, *Asia* **47** 26 13N 61 30 E
Makran Coast Range, *Pakistan* **47** 25 40N 64 0 E
Makrana, *India* **48** 27 2N 74 46 E
Maksimkin Yar, *U.S.S.R.* **40** 58 42N 86 50 E
Maktar, *Tunisia* **86** 35 48N 9 12 E
Mākū, *Iran* **46** 39 15N 44 31 E
Makum, *India* **52** 27 30N 95 23 E
Makumbi, *Zaïre* **95** 5 50 S 20 43 E
Makunda, *Botswana* **96** 22 30 S 20 7 E
Makurazaki, *Japan* **64** 31 15N 130 20 E
Makurdi, *Nigeria* **91** 7 43N 8 35 E
Makwassie, *S. Africa* **96** 27 17 S 26 0 E
Mal, *India* **52** 26 51N 88 45 E
Mal B., *Ireland* **15** 52 50N 9 30W
Mal i Nemërçkës, *Albania* **35** 40 15N 20 15 E
Mal i Tomorit, *Albania* **35** 40 42N 20 11 E
Mala, *Peru* **136** 12 40 S 76 38W
Mala, Pta., *Panama* **128** 7 28N 80 2W
Mala Kapela, *Yugoslavia* **27** 44 45N 15 30 E
Malabang, *Phil.* **57** 7 36N 124 3 E
Malabar Coast, *India* **51** 11 0N 75 0 E
Malacca, Str. of, *Indonesia* **55** 3 0N 101 0 E
Malacky, *Czech.* **33** 48 27N 17 0 E
Malad City, *U.S.A.* **122** 42 10N 112 20W
Málaga, *Colombia* **134** 6 42N 72 44W
Málaga, *Spain* **23** 36 43N 4 23W
Malaga, *U.S.A.* **121** 32 12N 104 2W
Málaga □, *Spain* **23** 36 38N 4 58W
Malagarasi, *Tanzania* **92** 5 5 S 30 50 E
Malagarasi →, *Tanzania* **92** 5 12 S 29 47 E
Malagón, *Spain* **23** 39 11N 3 52W
Malagón →, *Spain* **23** 37 35N 7 29W
Malaimbandy, *Madag.* **97** 20 20 S 45 36 E
Malaita, *Pac. Oc.* **68** 9 0 S 161 0 E
Malakâl, *Sudan* **89** 9 33N 31 40 E
Malakand, *Pakistan* **48** 34 40N 71 55 E
Malakoff, *U.S.A.* **121** 32 10N 95 55W
Malam, *Chad* **87** 11 27N 20 59 E
Malamyzh, *U.S.S.R.* **41** 50 0N 136 50 E
Malang, *Indonesia* **57** 7 59 S 112 45 E
Malange, *Angola* **95** 9 36 S 16 17 E
Malange □, *Angola* **95** 9 30 S 16 0 E
Mälaren, *Sweden* **10** 59 30N 17 10 E
Malargüe, *Argentina* **140** 35 32 S 69 30W
Malartic, *Canada* **106** 48 9N 78 9W
Malartic, L., *Canada* **106** 48 15N 78 5W
Malatya, *Turkey* **46** 38 25N 38 20 E
Malau, *Vanuatu* **68** 15 0 S 166 0 E
Malawi ■, *Africa* **93** 11 55 S 34 0 E
Malawi, L., *Africa* **93** 12 30 S 34 30 E
Malay Pen., *Asia* **55** 7 25N 100 0 E
Malaya Belozërka, *U.S.S.R.* **38** 47 12N 34 56 E
Malaya Vishera, *U.S.S.R.* **36** 58 55N 32 25 E
Malaya Viska, *U.S.S.R.* **38** 48 39N 31 36 E
Malaybalay, *Phil.* **57** 8 5N 125 7 E
Malāyer, *Iran* **46** 34 19N 48 51 E
Malaysia ■, *Asia* **56** 5 0N 110 0 E
Malazgirt, *Turkey* **46** 39 10N 42 33 E
Malbaie, La, *Canada* **107** 47 40N 70 10W
Malbon, *Australia* **72** 21 5 S 140 17 E
Malbooma, *Australia* **73** 30 41 S 134 11 E
Malbork, *Poland* **32** 54 3N 19 1 E
Malca Dube, *Ethiopia* **98** 6 47N 42 4 E
Malcésine, *Italy* **26** 45 46N 10 48 E
Malchin, *E. Germany* **30** 53 43N 12 44 E
Malchow, *E. Germany* **30** 53 29N 12 25 E
Malcolm, *Australia* **79** 28 51 S 121 25 E
Malcolm, Pt., *Australia* **79** 33 48 S 123 45 E
Maldegem, *Belgium* **17** 51 14N 3 26 E
Malden, *Mass., U.S.A.* **117** 42 26N 71 5W
Malden, *Mo., U.S.A.* **121** 36 35N 90 0W
Malden I., *Kiribati* **67** 4 3 S 155 1W
Maldives ■, *Ind. Oc.* **53** 5 0N 73 0 E
Maldon, *Australia* **74** 37 0 S 144 6 E
Maldonado, *Uruguay* **141** 35 0 S 55 0W
Maldonado, Punta, *Mexico* **127** 16 19N 98 35W
Malé, *Italy* **26** 46 20N 10 55 E
Maléa, Ákra, *Greece* **35** 36 28N 23 7 E
Malebo, Pool, *Africa* **95** 4 17 S 15 20 E
Malegaon, *India* **50** 20 30N 74 38 E
Malei, *Mozam.* **93** 17 12 S 36 58 E
Malekula(Mallicolo), *Vanuatu* **68** 16 15 S 167 30 E
Malela, *Bas Zaïre, Zaïre* **95** 5 59 S 12 37 E
Malela, *Kivu, Zaïre* **92** 4 22 S 26 8 E
Malema, *Mozam.* **93** 14 57 S 37 20 E
Målerås, *Sweden* **11** 56 54N 15 34 E
Malerkotla, *India* **48** 30 32N 75 58 E
Malesherbes, *France* **19** 48 15N 2 24 E
Malestroit, *France* **18** 47 49N 2 25W
Malfa, *Italy* **29** 38 35N 14 50 E
Malgobek, *U.S.S.R.* **39** 43 30N 44 34 E
Malgomaj, *Sweden* **8** 64 40N 16 30 E
Malgrat, *Spain* **24** 41 39N 2 46 E
Malha, *Sudan* **89** 15 8N 25 10 E
Malheur →, *U.S.A.* **122** 44 3N 116 59W
Malheur L., *U.S.A.* **122** 43 19N 118 42W
Mali, *Guinea* **90** 12 10N 12 20W
Mali ■, *Africa* **91** 17 0N 3 0W
Mali Hka →, *Burma* **52** 25 42N 97 30 E
Mali Kanal, *Yugoslavia* **33** 45 36N 19 24 E
Malibu, *U.S.A.* **125** 34 2N 118 41W
Malih →, *Jordan* **44** 32 20N 35 34 E
Malik, *Indonesia* **57** 0 39 S 123 16 E
Malili, *Indonesia* **57** 2 42 S 121 6 E
Malimba, Mts., *Zaïre* **92** 7 30 S 29 30 E
Malin, *U.S.S.R.* **36** 50 46N 29 3 E
Malindi, *Kenya* **92** 3 12 S 40 5 E
Malines = Mechelen, *Belgium* **17** 51 2N 4 29 E
Maling, *Indonesia* **57** 1 0N 121 0 E
Malinyi, *Tanzania* **93** 8 56 S 36 0 E
Malipo, *China* **58** 23 7N 104 42 E
Maliqi, *Albania* **35** 40 45N 20 48 E
Malita, *Phil.* **57** 6 19N 125 39 E
Malkapur, *Maharashtra, India* **50** 20 53N 73 58 E
Malkapur, *Maharashtra, India* **50** 16 57N 76 17 E
Małkinia Górna, *Poland* **32** 52 42N 22 5 E
Malko Tŭrnovo, *Bulgaria* **35** 41 59N 27 31 E
Mallacoota Inlet, *Australia* **75** 37 34 S 149 40 E
Mallaig, *U.K.* **14** 57 0N 5 50W
Mallanganee, *Australia* **77** 28 54 S 152 44 E
Mallard, *U.S.A.* **118** 42 56N 94 41W
Mallawan, *India* **49** 27 4N 80 12 E
Mallawi, *Egypt* **88** 27 44N 30 44 E
Malleco □, *Chile* **142** 38 10 S 72 20W
Mallemort, *France* **21** 43 43N 5 11 E
Málles Venosta, *Italy* **26** 46 42N 10 32 E
Mallorca, *Spain* **24** 39 30N 3 0 E
Mallorytown, *Canada* **109** 44 29N 75 53W
Mallow, *Ireland* **15** 52 8N 8 40W
Malmbäck, *Sweden* **11** 57 34N 14 28 E
Malmberget, *Sweden* **8** 67 11N 20 40 E
Malmédy, *Belgium* **17** 50 25N 6 2 E
Malmesbury, *S. Africa* **96** 33 28 S 18 41 E
Malmö, *Sweden* **11** 55 36N 12 59 E
Malmöhus län □, *Sweden* **11** 55 45N 13 30 E
Malmsbury, *Australia* **74** 37 9 S 144 25 E
Malmslätt, *Sweden* **11** 58 27N 15 33 E
Malmyzh, *U.S.S.R.* **37** 56 31N 50 41 E
Malo, *Vanuatu* **68** 15 40 S 167 11 E
Maloarkhangelsk, *U.S.S.R.* **37** 52 28N 36 30 E
Maloca, *Brazil* **135** 0 43N 55 57W
Malolos, *Phil.* **57** 14 50N 120 49 E
Malombe L., *Malawi* **93** 14 40 S 35 15 E
Malone, *U.S.A.* **117** 44 50N 74 19W
Malong, *China* **58** 25 24N 103 34 E
Malonga, *Zaïre* **95** 10 24 S 23 10 E
Malorita, *U.S.S.R.* **36** 51 50N 24 3 E
Maloyaroslovets, *U.S.S.R.* **37** 55 2N 36 20 E
Malpartida, *Spain* **23** 39 26N 6 30W
Malpaso, *Canary Is.* **25** 27 43N 18 3W
Malpelo, *Colombia* **136** 4 3N 81 35W
Malpica, *Spain* **22** 43 19N 8 50W
Malprabha →, *India* **51** 16 20N 76 5 E
Malta, *Brazil* **138** 6 54 S 37 31W
Malta, *Idaho, U.S.A.* **122** 42 15N 113 30W
Malta, *Mont., U.S.A.* **122** 48 20N 107 55W
Malta ■, *Europe* **7** 35 50N 14 30 E
Malta Channel, *Medit. S.* **28** 36 40N 14 0 E
Maltahöhe, *Namibia* **96** 24 55 S 17 0 E
Malton, *Canada* **116** 43 42N 79 38W
Malton, *U.K.* **12** 54 9N 0 48W
Malu'a, *Solomon Is.* **68** 8 0 S 160 0 E
Maluku, *Indonesia* **57** 1 0 S 127 0 E
Maluku □, *Indonesia* **57** 3 0 S 128 0 E
Malumfashi, *Nigeria* **91** 11 48N 7 39 E
Malung, *Sweden* **10** 60 42N 13 44 E
Malvalli, *India* **51** 12 28N 77 8 E
Malvan, *India* **51** 16 2N 73 30 E
Malvern, *U.K.* **13** 52 7N 2 19W
Malvern, *U.S.A.* **121** 34 22N 92 50W
Malvern Hills, *U.K.* **13** 52 0N 2 19W
Malvik, *Norway* **10** 63 25N 10 40 E
Malvinas, Is. = Falkland Is., *Atl. Oc.* **142** 51 30 S 59 0W
Malya, *Tanzania* **92** 3 5 S 33 38 E
Malyy Lyakhovskiy, Ostrov, *U.S.S.R.* **41** 74 7N 140 36 E
Mama, *U.S.S.R.* **41** 58 18N 112 54 E
Mamadysh, *U.S.S.R.* **37** 55 44N 51 23 E
Mamahatun, *Turkey* **46** 39 50N 40 23 E
Mamaku, *N.Z.* **80** 38 5 S 176 8 E
Mamanguape, *Brazil* **138** 6 50 S 35 4W
Mamanutha Group, *Fiji* **68** 17 34 S 177 4 E
Mamarana, *Solomon Is.* **68** 7 0 S 157 0 E
Mamasa, *Indonesia* **57** 2 55 S 119 20 E
Mambasa, *Zaïre* **92** 1 22N 29 3 E
Mamberamo →, *Indonesia* **57** 2 0 S 137 50 E
Mambilima Falls, *Zambia* **93** 10 31 S 28 45 E
Mambirima, *Zaïre* **93** 11 25 S 27 33 E
Mambo, *Tanzania* **92** 4 52 S 38 22 E
Mambrui, *Kenya* **92** 3 5 S 40 5 E
Mamburao, *Phil.* **57** 13 13N 120 39 E
Mameigwess L., *Canada* **104** 52 35N 87 50W
Mamer, *Lux.* **17** 49 38N 6 2 E
Mamers, *France* **18** 48 21N 0 22 E
Mamfe, *Cameroon* **91** 5 50N 9 15 E
Mamiña, *Chile* **136** 20 5 S 69 14W
Mámmola, *Italy* **29** 38 23N 16 13 E
Mammoth, *U.S.A.* **123** 32 46N 110 43W
Mamoré →, *Bolivia* **137** 10 23 S 65 53W
Mamou, *Guinea* **90** 10 15N 12 0W
Mampatá, *Guinea-Biss.* **90** 11 54N 14 53W
Mampong, *Ghana* **91** 7 6N 1 26W
Mamuil Malal, Paso, *S. Amer.* **142** 39 35 S 71 28W
Mamuju, *Indonesia* **57** 2 41 S 118 50 E
Man, *Ivory C.* **90** 7 30N 7 40W
Man →, *India* **50** 17 31N 75 32 E
Man, I. of, *U.K.* **12** 54 15N 4 30W
Man Na, *Burma* **52** 23 27N 97 19 E
Man Tun, *Burma* **52** 23 52N 98 38 E
Mana, *Fr. Guiana* **135** 5 45N 53 55W
Mana →, *Fr. Guiana* **135** 5 45N 53 55W
Måna →, *Norway* **10** 59 55N 8 50 E
Manaar, Gulf of = Mannar, G. of, *Asia* **51** 8 30N 79 0 E
Manabí □, *Ecuador* **134** 0 40 S 80 5W
Manacacías →, *Colombia* **134** 4 23N 72 4W
Manacapuru, *Brazil* **135** 3 16 S 60 37W
Manacapuru →, *Brazil* **135** 3 18 S 60 37W
Manacor, *Spain* **24** 39 34N 3 13 E
Manado, *Indonesia* **57** 1 29N 124 51 E
Manage, *Belgium* **17** 50 31N 4 15 E
Managua, *Nic.* **128** 12 6N 86 20W
Managua, L., *Nic.* **128** 12 20N 86 30W
Manaia, *N.Z.* **80** 39 33 S 174 8 E
Manakara, *Madag.* **97** 22 8 S 48 1 E
Manakau Mt., *N.Z.* **81** 42 15 S 173 42 E
Manam I., *Papua N. G.* **69** 4 5 S 145 0 E
Manambao →, *Madag.* **97** 17 35 S 44 0 E
Manambato, *Madag.* **97** 13 43 S 49 7 E
Manambolo →, *Madag.* **97** 19 18 S 44 22 E
Manambolosy, *Madag.* **97** 16 2 S 49 40 E
Mananara, *Madag.* **97** 16 10 S 49 46 E
Mananara →, *Madag.* **97** 23 21 S 47 42 E
Manangatang, *Australia* **74** 35 5 S 142 54 E
Mananjary, *Madag.* **97** 21 13 S 48 20 E
Manantenina, *Madag.* **97** 24 17 S 47 19 E
Manaos = Manaus, *Brazil* **135** 3 0 S 60 0W

Manapire →, *Venezuela* **134** 7 42N 66 7W
Manapouri, *N.Z.* **81** 45 34 S 167 39 E
Manapouri, L., *N.Z.* **81** 45 32 S 167 32 E
Manar →, *India* **50** 18 50N 77 20 E
Manas, *China* **62** 44 17N 85 56 E
Manas, *Somali Rep.* **98** 2 57N 43 28 E
Manasir, *Si. Arabia* **47** 24 30N 51 10 E
Manaslu, Mt., *Nepal* **49** 28 33N 84 33 E
Manasquan, *U.S.A.* **117** 40 7N 74 3W
Manassa, *U.S.A.* **123** 37 12N 105 58W
Manaung, *Burma* **52** 18 45N 93 40 E
Manaus, *Brazil* **135** 3 0 S 60 0W
Manawan L., *Canada* **111** 55 24N 103 14W
Manawatu →, *N.Z.* **80** 40 28 S 175 12 E
Manay, *Phil.* **57** 7 17N 126 33 E
Mancelona, *U.S.A.* **104** 44 54N 85 5W
Mancha, La, *Spain* **25** 39 10N 2 54W
Mancha Real, *Spain* **23** 37 48N 3 39W
Manche □, *France* **18** 49 10N 1 20W
Manchester, *U.K.* **12** 53 30N 2 15W
Manchester, *Calif., U.S.A.* **124** 38 58N 123 41W
Manchester, *Conn., U.S.A.* **117** 41 47N 72 30W
Manchester, *Ga., U.S.A.* **115** 32 53N 84 32W
Manchester, *Iowa, U.S.A.* **118** 42 28N 91 27W
Manchester, *Ky., U.S.A.* **114** 37 9N 83 45W
Manchester, *Mich., U.S.A.* **119** 42 9N 84 2W
Manchester, *N.H., U.S.A.* **117** 42 58N 71 29W
Manchester, *N.Y., U.S.A.* **116** 42 56N 77 16W
Manchester, *Vt., U.S.A.* **117** 43 10N 73 5W
Manchester L., *Canada* **111** 61 28N 107 29W
Manchuria = Dongbei, *China* **61** 42 0N 125 0 E
Manciano, *Italy* **27** 42 35N 11 30 E
Mancifa, *Ethiopia* **89** 6 53N 41 50 E
Mancora, Pta., *Peru* **136** 4 9 S 81 1W
Mand →, *Iran* **47** 28 20N 52 30 E
Manda, *Chunya, Tanzania* **92** 6 51 S 32 29 E
Manda, *Ludewe, Tanzania* **93** 10 30 S 34 40 E
Mandabé, *Madag.* **97** 21 0 S 44 55 E
Mandaguari, *Brazil* **141** 23 32 S 51 42W
Mandah, *Mongolia* **60** 44 27N 108 2 E
Mandal, *Norway* **9** 58 2N 7 25 E
Mandalay, *Burma* **52** 22 0N 96 4 E
Mandale = Mandalay, *Burma* **52** 22 0N 96 4 E
Mandalgovi, *Mongolia* **60** 45 45N 106 10 E
Mandalī, *Iraq* **46** 33 43N 45 28 E
Mandan, *U.S.A.* **120** 46 50N 101 0W
Mandapeta, *India* **50** 16 47N 81 56 E
Mandar, Teluk, *Indonesia* **57** 3 35 S 119 15 E
Mandas, *Italy* **28** 39 40N 9 8 E
Mandasor = Mandsaur, *India* **48** 24 3N 75 8 E
Mandaue, *Phil.* **57** 10 20N 123 56 E
Mandelieu-la-Napoule, *France* **21** 43 34N 6 57 E
Mandera, *Kenya* **92** 3 55N 41 53 E
Mandera □, *Kenya* **92** 3 30N 41 0 E
Manderfeld, *Belgium* **17** 50 20N 6 20 E
Mandi, *India* **48** 31 39N 76 58 E
Mandimba, *Mozam.* **93** 14 20 S 35 40 E
Mandioli, *Indonesia* **57** 0 40 S 127 20 E
Mandioré, L., *S. Amer.* **137** 18 8 S 57 33W
Mandji I. = Lopez I., *Gabon* **94** 0 50 S 8 47 E
Mandla, *India* **49** 22 39N 80 30 E
Mandø, *Denmark* **11** 55 18N 8 33 E
Mandoto, *Madag.* **97** 19 34 S 46 17 E
Mandoúdhion, *Greece* **35** 38 48N 23 29 E
Mandra, *Pakistan* **48** 33 23N 73 12 E
Mandrare →, *Madag.* **97** 25 10 S 46 30 E
Mandritsara, *Madag.* **97** 15 50 S 48 49 E
Mandsaur, *India* **48** 24 3N 75 8 E
Mandurah, *Australia* **79** 32 36 S 115 48 E
Mandúria, *Italy* **29** 40 25N 17 38 E
Mandvi, *India* **48** 22 51N 69 22 E
Mandya, *India* **51** 12 30N 77 0 E
Mandzai, *Pakistan* **48** 30 55N 67 6 E
Mané, *Burkina Faso* **91** 12 59N 1 21W
Manengouba, Mts., *Cameroon* **91** 5 0N 9 50 E
Maner →, *India* **50** 18 30N 79 40 E
Maneroo, *Australia* **72** 23 22 S 143 53 E
Maneroo Cr. →, *Australia* **72** 23 21 S 143 53 E
Manfalût, *Egypt* **88** 27 20N 30 52 E
Manfred, *Australia* **73** 33 19 S 143 45 E
Manfredónia, *Italy* **29** 41 40N 15 55 E
Manfredónia, G. di, *Italy* **29** 41 30N 16 10 E
Manga, *Brazil* **139** 14 46 S 43 56W
Manga, *Burkina Faso* **91** 11 40N 1 4W
Manga, *Niger* **91** 15 0N 14 0 E
Mangabeiras, Chapada das, *Brazil* **138** 10 0 S 46 30W
Mangalagiri, *India* **51** 16 26N 80 36 E
Mangaldai, *India* **52** 26 26N 92 2 E
Mangalia, *Romania* **34** 43 50N 28 35 E
Mangalore, *Australia* **74** 36 56 S 145 10 E
Mangalore, *India* **51** 12 55N 74 47 E
Manganeses, *Spain* **22** 41 45N 5 43W
Mangaon, *India* **50** 18 15N 73 20 E
Mange, *Zaïre* **94** 0 54N 20 30 E
Manggar, *Indonesia* **56** 2 50 S 108 10 E
Manggawitu, *Indonesia* **57** 4 8 S 133 32 E
Mangin Range, *Burma* **52** 24 15N 95 45 E
Mangkalihat, Tanjung, *Indonesia* **57** 1 2N 118 59 E
Mangla Dam, *Pakistan* **49** 33 9N 73 44 E
Manglares, C., *Colombia* **134** 1 36N 79 2W
Manglaur, *India* **48** 29 44N 77 49 E
Mangnai, *China* **62** 37 52N 91 43 E
Mango, *Fiji* **68** 17 27 S 179 9W
Mango, *Togo* **91** 10 20N 0 30 E
Mangoche, *Malawi* **93** 14 25 S 35 16 E
Mangoky →, *Madag.* **97** 21 29 S 43 41 E
Mangole, *Indonesia* **57** 1 50 S 125 55 E
Mangombe, *Zaïre* **92** 1 20 S 26 48 E
Mangonui, *N.Z.* **80** 35 1 S 173 32 E
Mangoplah, *Australia* **76** 35 23 S 147 17 E
Mangualde, *Portugal* **22** 40 38N 7 48W
Mangueigne, *Chad* **87** 10 30N 21 15 E
Mangueira, L. da, *Brazil* **141** 33 0 S 52 50W
Manguéni, Hamada, *Niger* **86** 22 35N 12 40 E
Mangum, *U.S.A.* **121** 34 50N 99 30W
Mangyshlak Poluostrov, *U.S.S.R.* **39** 44 30N 52 30 E
Mangyshlakskiy Zaliv, *U.S.S.R.* **39** 44 40N 50 50 E
Manhattan, *U.S.A.* **120** 39 10N 96 40W
Manhatten, *U.S.A.* **119** 41 26N 87 59W
Manhiça, *Mozam.* **97** 25 23 S 32 49 E
Manhuaçu, *Brazil* **139** 20 15 S 42 2W
Manhumirim, *Brazil* **139** 20 22 S 41 57W
Maní, *Colombia* **134** 4 49N 72 17W
Mania →, *Madag.* **97** 19 42 S 45 22 E
Maniago, *Italy* **27** 46 11N 12 40 E
Manica, *Mozam.* **97** 18 58 S 32 59 E
Manica e Sofala □, *Mozam.* **97** 19 10 S 33 45 E
Manicaland □, *Zimb.* **93** 19 0 S 32 30 E
Manicoré, *Brazil* **137** 5 48 S 61 16W
Manicoré →, *Brazil* **137** 5 51 S 61 19W
Manicouagan →, *Canada* **107** 49 30N 68 30W
Manīfah, *Si. Arabia* **46** 27 44N 49 0 E
Manifold, *Australia* **72** 22 41 S 150 40 E
Manifold, C., *Australia* **72** 22 41 S 150 50 E
Maniganggo, *China* **58** 31 56N 99 10 E
Manigotagan, *Canada* **111** 51 6N 96 18W
Manihiki, *Cook Is.* **67** 10 24 S 161 1W
Manika, Plateau de la, *Zaïre* **93** 10 0 S 25 5 E
Manikganj, *Bangla.* **52** 23 52N 90 0 E
Manila, *Phil.* **57** 14 40N 121 3 E
Manila, *U.S.A.* **122** 41 0N 109 44W
Manila Bay, *Phil.* **57** 14 0N 120 0 E
Manildra, *Australia* **76** 33 11 S 148 41 E
Manilla, *Australia* **77** 30 45 S 150 43 E
Manimpé, *Mali* **90** 14 11N 5 28W
Manipur □, *India* **52** 25 0N 94 0 E
Manipur →, *Burma* **52** 23 45N 94 20 E
Manisa, *Turkey* **46** 38 38N 27 30 E
Manistee, *U.S.A.* **114** 44 15N 86 20W
Manistee →, *U.S.A.* **114** 44 15N 86 21W
Manistique, *U.S.A.* **114** 45 59N 86 18W
Manito, *U.S.A.* **118** 40 25N 89 47W
Manito L., *Canada* **111** 52 43N 109 43W
Manitoba □, *Canada* **111** 55 30N 97 0W
Manitoba, L., *Canada* **111** 51 0N 98 45W
Manitou, *Canada* **111** 49 15N 98 32W
Manitou Beach, *U.S.A.* **119** 41 58N 84 19W
Manitou I., *U.S.A.* **104** 47 22N 87 30W
Manitou Is., *U.S.A.* **114** 45 8N 86 0W
Manitou L., *Ont., Canada* **108** 45 51N 82 0W
Manitou L., *Qué., Canada* **105** 50 55N 65 17W
Manitou Springs, *U.S.A.* **120** 38 52N 104 55W
Manitoulin I., *Canada* **108** 45 40N 82 30W
Manitowaning, *Canada* **108** 45 46N 81 49W
Manitowoc, *U.S.A.* **114** 44 8N 87 40W
Manitsauá-Missu →, *Brazil* **137** 10 58 S 53 20W
Maniwaki, *Canada* **106** 46 23N 75 58W
Manizales, *Colombia* **134** 5 5N 75 32W
Manja, *Madag.* **97** 21 26 S 44 20 E
Manjacaze, *Mozam.* **97** 24 45 S 34 0 E
Manjakandriana, *Madag.* **97** 18 55 S 47 47 E
Manjeri, *India* **51** 11 7N 76 11 E
Manjhand, *Pakistan* **48** 25 50N 68 10 E
Manjil, *Iran* **46** 36 46N 49 30 E
Manjimup, *Australia* **79** 34 15 S 116 6 E
Manjra →, *India* **50** 18 49N 77 52 E
Mankato, *Kans., U.S.A.* **120** 39 49N 98 11W
Mankato, *Minn., U.S.A.* **120** 44 8N 93 59W
Mankayane, *Swaziland* **97** 26 40 S 31 4 E
Mankono, *Ivory C.* **90** 8 1N 6 10W
Mankota, *Canada* **111** 49 25N 107 5W
Manlay, *Mongolia* **60** 44 9N 107 0 E
Manlleu, *Spain* **24** 42 2N 2 17 E
Manly, *Australia* **76** 33 48 S 151 17 E
Manmad, *India* **50** 20 18N 74 28 E
Mann Ranges, Mts., *Australia* **79** 26 6 S 130 5 E
Manna, *Indonesia* **56** 4 25 S 102 55 E
Mannahill, *Australia* **73** 32 25 S 140 0 E
Mannar, *Sri Lanka* **51** 9 1N 79 54 E
Mannar, G. of, *Asia* **51** 8 30N 79 0 E
Mannar I., *Sri Lanka* **51** 9 5N 79 45 E
Mannargudi, *India* **51** 10 45N 79 51 E
Mannheim, *W. Germany* **31** 49 28N 8 29 E
Manning, *Canada* **110** 56 53N 117 39W
Manning, *Oreg., U.S.A.* **124** 45 45N 123 13W
Manning, *S.C., U.S.A.* **115** 33 40N 80 9W
Manning →, *Australia* **77** 31 52 S 152 43 E
Manning Prov. Park, *Canada* **110** 49 5N 120 45W
Manning Str., *Solomon Is.* **68** 7 30 S 158 0 E
Mannington, *U.S.A.* **114** 39 35N 80 25W
Mannu →, *Italy* **28** 39 15N 9 32 E
Mannu, C., *Italy* **28** 40 2N 8 24 E
Mannum, *Australia* **73** 34 50 S 139 20 E
Mannus, *Australia* **76** 35 45 S 147 55 E
Mano, *S. Leone* **90** 8 3N 12 2W
Manoa, *Bolivia* **137** 9 40 S 65 27W
Manokwari, *Indonesia* **57** 0 54 S 134 0 E
Manombo, *Madag.* **97** 22 57 S 43 28 E
Manono, *Zaïre* **92** 7 15 S 27 25 E
Manosque, *France* **21** 43 49N 5 47 E
Manotick, *Canada* **109** 45 13N 75 41W
Manouane, L., *Qué., Canada* **105** 50 45N 70 45W
Manouane, L., *Qué., Canada* **107** 47 33N 74 6W
Manouro, Pt., *Vanuatu* **68** 17 41 S 168 36 E
Manresa, *Spain* **24** 41 48N 1 50 E
Mans, Le, *France* **18** 48 0N 0 10 E
Mansa, *Gujarat, India* **48** 23 27N 72 45 E
Mansa, *Punjab, India* **48** 30 0N 75 27 E
Mansa, *Zambia* **93** 11 13 S 28 55 E
Manseau, *Canada* **107** 46 22N 72 0W
Mansehra, *Pakistan* **48** 34 20N 73 15 E
Mansel I., *Canada* **103** 62 0N 80 0W
Mansfield, *Australia* **75** 37 4 S 146 6 E
Mansfield, *U.K.* **12** 53 8N 1 12W
Mansfield, *La., U.S.A.* **121** 32 2N 93 40W
Mansfield, *Mass., U.S.A.* **117** 42 2N 71 12W
Mansfield, *Ohio, U.S.A.* **116** 40 45N 82 30W
Mansfield, *Pa., U.S.A.* **116** 41 48N 77 4W
Mansfield, *Wash., U.S.A.* **122** 47 51N 119 44W
Mansi, *Burma* **52** 24 48N 95 52 E
Mansidão, *Brazil* **138** 10 43 S 44 2W
Mansilla de las Mulas, *Spain* **22** 42 30N 5 25W
Mansle, *France* **20** 45 52N 0 12 E
Manso →, *Brazil* **139** 13 50 S 47 0W
Mansoa, *Guinea-Biss.* **90** 12 0N 15 20W
Manson, *U.S.A.* **118** 42 32N 94 32W
Manson Creek, *Canada* **110** 55 37N 124 32W
Mansoura, *Algeria* **85** 36 1N 4 31 E
Manta, *Ecuador* **134** 1 0 S 80 40W
Manta, B. de, *Ecuador* **134** 0 54 S 80 44W
Mantalingajan, Mt., *Phil.* **56** 8 55N 117 45 E
Mantare, *Tanzania* **92** 2 42 S 33 13 E
Manteca, *U.S.A.* **124** 37 50N 121 12W
Mantecal, *Venezuela* **134** 7 34N 69 17W
Mantena, *Brazil* **139** 18 47 S 40 59W
Manteno, *U.S.A.* **119** 41 15N 87 50W
Manteo, *U.S.A.* **115** 35 55N 75 41W
Mantes-la-Jolie, *France* **19** 49 0N 1 41 E
Manthani, *India* **50** 18 40N 79 35 E
Manthelan, *France* **18** 47 9N 0 47 E
Manti, *U.S.A.* **122** 39 23N 111 32W
Mantiqueira, Serra da, *Brazil* **141** 22 0 S 44 0W
Manton, *U.S.A.* **104** 44 23N 85 25W
Mantorp, *Sweden* **11** 58 21N 15 20 E
Mántova, *Italy* **26** 45 20N 10 42 E
Mänttä, *Finland* **8** 62 0N 24 40 E
Mantua = Mántova, *Italy* **26** 45 20N 10 42 E
Manturovo, *U.S.S.R.* **37** 58 30N 44 30 E
Manu, *Peru* **136** 12 10 S 70 51W
Manu →, *Peru* **136** 12 16 S 70 55W
Manua Is., *Amer. Samoa* **68** 14 13 S 169 35W
Manuae, *Cook Is.* **67** 19 30 S 159 0W
Manuel Alves →, *Brazil* **139** 11 19 S 48 28W
Manuel Alves Grande →, *Brazil* **138** 7 27 S 47 35W
Manuel Urbano, *Brazil* **136** 8 53 S 69 18W
Manui, *Indonesia* **57** 3 35 S 123 5 E
Manukau, *N.Z.* **80** 37 1 S 174 55 E
Manukau Harbour, *N.Z.* **80** 37 3 S 174 45 E
Manunui, *N.Z.* **80** 38 54 S 175 21 E
Manuripi →, *Bolivia* **136** 11 6 S 67 36W
Manus I., *Papua N. G.* **69** 2 0 S 147 0 E
Manvi, *India* **51** 15 57N 76 59 E
Manville, *U.S.A.* **120** 42 48N 104 36W
Manwath, *India* **50** 19 19N 76 32 E
Many, *U.S.A.* **121** 31 36N 93 28W
Manyara, L., *Tanzania* **92** 3 40 S 35 50 E
Manych →, *U.S.S.R.* **39** 47 15N 40 0 E
Manych-Gudilo, Oz., *U.S.S.R.* **39** 46 24N 42 38 E
Manyonga →, *Tanzania* **92** 4 10 S 34 15 E
Manyoni, *Tanzania* **92** 5 45 S 34 55 E
Manyoni □, *Tanzania* **92** 6 30 S 34 30 E
Manzai, *Pakistan* **48** 32 12N 70 15 E
Manzala, Bahra el, *Egypt* **88** 31 10N 31 56 E
Manzanares, *Spain* **25** 39 0N 3 22W
Manzaneda, Cabeza de, *Spain* **22** 42 12N 7 15W
Manzanillo, *Cuba* **128** 20 20N 77 31W
Manzanillo, *Mexico* **126** 19 0N 104 20W
Manzanillo, Pta., *Panama* **128** 9 30N 79 40W
Manzano Mts., *U.S.A.* **123** 34 30N 106 45W
Manzhouli, *China* **62** 49 35N 117 25 E
Manzini, *Swaziland* **97** 26 30 S 31 25 E
Mao, *Chad* **87** 14 4N 15 19 E
Maoke, Pegunungan, *Indonesia* **57** 3 40 S 137 30 E
Maolin, *China* **61** 43 58N 123 30 E
Maoming, *China* **59** 21 50N 110 54 E
Maowen, *China* **58** 31 41N 103 49 E
Maoxing, *China* **61** 45 28N 124 40 E
Mapam Yumco, *China* **49** 30 45N 81 28 E
Mapastepec, *Mexico* **127** 15 26N 92 54W
Mapia, Kepulauan, *Indonesia* **57** 0 50N 134 20 E
Mapimí, *Mexico* **126** 25 50N 103 50W
Mapimí, Bolsón de, *Mexico* **126** 27 30N 104 15W
Maping, *China* **59** 31 34N 113 32 E
Mapinga, *Tanzania* **92** 6 40 S 39 12 E
Mapinhane, *Mozam.* **97** 22 20 S 35 0 E
Mapire, *Venezuela* **135** 7 45N 64 42W
Maple →, *U.S.A.* **119** 42 58N 84 56W
Maple Creek, *Canada* **111** 49 55N 109 29W
Maple Valley, *U.S.A.* **124** 47 25N 122 3W
Mapleton, *U.S.A.* **122** 44 4N 123 58W
Maprik, *Papua N. G.* **69** 3 44 S 143 3 E
Mapuca, *India* **51** 15 36N 73 46 E
Mapuera →, *Brazil* **135** 1 5 S 57 2W
Maputo, *Mozam.* **97** 25 58 S 32 32 E
Maputo, B. de, *Mozam.* **97** 25 50 S 32 45 E
Maqiaohe, *China* **61** 44 40N 130 30 E
Maqnā, *Si. Arabia* **46** 28 25N 34 50 E
Maqteïr, *Mauritania* **84** 21 50N 11 40W
Maquela do Zombo, *Angola* **95** 6 0 S 15 15 E
Maquinchao, *Argentina* **142** 41 15 S 68 50W
Maquoketa, *U.S.A.* **118** 42 4N 90 40W
Mar, Serra do, *Brazil* **141** 25 30 S 49 0W
Mar Chiquita, L., *Argentina* **140** 30 40 S 62 50W
Mar del Plata, *Argentina* **140** 38 0 S 57 30W
Mar Menor, L., *Spain* **25** 37 40N 0 45W
Mara, *Guyana* **135** 6 0N 57 36W
Mara, *India* **52** 28 11N 94 14 E
Mara, *Tanzania* **92** 1 30 S 34 32 E
Mara □, *Tanzania* **92** 1 45 S 34 20 E
Maraã, *Brazil* **134** 1 52 S 65 25W
Marabá, *Brazil* **138** 5 20 S 49 5W
Maracá, I. de, *Brazil* **138** 2 10N 50 30W
Maracaibo, *Venezuela* **134** 10 40N 71 37W
Maracaibo, L. de, *Venezuela* **134** 9 40N 71 30W
Maracaju, *Brazil* **141** 21 38 S 55 9W
Maracajú, Serra de, *Brazil* **137** 23 57 S 55 1W
Maracanã, *Brazil* **138** 0 46 S 47 27W
Maracás, *Brazil* **139** 13 26 S 40 18W
Maracay, *Venezuela* **134** 10 15N 67 28W
Marādah, *Libya* **86** 29 15N 19 15 E
Maradi, *Niger* **91** 13 29N 7 20 E
Maradun, *Nigeria* **91** 12 35N 6 18 E
Marāgheh, *Iran* **46** 37 30N 46 12 E
Maragogipe, *Brazil* **139** 12 46 S 38 55W
Marāh, *Si. Arabia* **46** 25 0N 45 35 E
Marajó, B. de, *Brazil* **138** 1 0 S 48 30W
Marajó, I. de, *Brazil* **138** 1 0 S 49 30W
Maralal, *Kenya* **92** 1 0N 36 38 E
Maralinga, *Australia* **79** 30 13 S 131 32 E
Marama, *Australia* **73** 35 10 S 140 10 E
Maramasike, *Solomon Is.* **68** 9 30 S 161 25 E
Marampa, *S. Leone* **90** 8 45N 12 28W
Maran, *Malaysia* **55** 3 35N 102 45 E
Marana, *U.S.A.* **123** 32 30N 111 9W
Maranboy, *Australia* **78** 14 40 S 132 39 E
Maranchón, *Spain* **24** 41 6N 2 15W
Marand, *Iran* **46** 38 30N 45 45 E
Marang, *Malaysia* **55** 5 12N 103 13 E
Maranguape, *Brazil* **138** 3 55 S 38 50W
Maranhão = São Luís, *Brazil* **138** 2 39 S 44 15W
Maranhão □, *Brazil* **138** 5 0 S 46 0W
Marano, L. di, *Italy* **27** 45 42N 13 13 E
Maranoa →, *Australia* **73** 27 50 S 148 37 E
Marañón →, *Peru* **136** 4 30 S 73 35W
Marão, *Mozam.* **97** 24 18 S 34 2 E
Marapi →, *Brazil* **135** 0 37N 55 58W
Marari, *Brazil* **136** 5 43 S 67 47W
Mărăşeşti, *Romania* **34** 45 52N 27 14 E
Maratea, *Italy* **29** 39 59N 15 43 E
Marateca, *Portugal* **23** 38 34N 8 40W
Marathókambos, *Greece* **35** 37 43N 26 42 E
Marathon, *Australia* **72** 20 51 S 143 32 E
Marathon, *Canada* **104** 48 44N 86 23W
Marathón, *Greece* **35** 38 11N 23 58 E
Marathon, *Iowa, U.S.A.* **118** 42 52N 94 59W
Marathon, *N.Y., U.S.A.* **117** 42 25N 76 3W
Marathon, *Tex., U.S.A.* **121** 30 15N 103 15W

Maratua, *Indonesia* **57** 2 10N 118 35 E
Maraú, *Brazil* **139** 14 6 S 39 0W
Maravae, *Solomon Is.* **68** 7 54 S 156 44 E
Maravatío, *Mexico* **126** 19 51N 100 25W
Marbella, *Spain* **23** 36 30N 4 57W
Marble Bar, *Australia* **78** 21 9 S 119 44 E
Marble Falls, *U.S.A.* **121** 30 30N 98 15W
Marblehead, *U.S.A.* **117** 42 29N 70 51W
Marbleton, *Canada* **107** 45 37N 71 35W
Marburg, *W. Germany* **30** 50 49N 8 36 E
Marby, *Sweden* **10** 63 7N 14 18 E
Marcal →, *Hungary* **33** 47 41N 17 32 E
Marcapata, *Peru* **136** 13 31 S 70 52W
Marcaria, *Italy* **26** 45 7N 10 34 E
Marceline, *U.S.A.* **118** 39 43N 92 57W
March, *U.K.* **13** 52 33N 0 5 E
Marchal, *Zaïre* **95** 5 16 S 14 58 E
Marchand = Rommani, *Morocco* **84** 33 31N 6 40W
Marche, *France* **20** 46 5N 1 20 E
Marche □, *Italy* **27** 43 22N 13 10 E
Marche-en-Famenne, *Belgium* **17** 50 14N 5 19 E
Marchena, *Spain* **23** 37 18N 5 23W
Marches = Marche □, *Italy* **27** 43 22N 13 10 E
Marciana Marina, *Italy* **26** 42 44N 10 12 E
Marcianise, *Italy* **29** 41 3N 14 16 E
Marcigny, *France* **21** 46 17N 4 2 E
Marcillat-en-Combraille, *France* **20** 46 12N 2 38 E
Marcinelle, *Belgium* **17** 50 24N 4 26 E
Marck, *France* **19** 50 57N 1 57 E
Marckolsheim, *France* **19** 48 10N 7 30 E
Marcona, *Peru* **136** 15 10 S 75 0W
Marcos Juárez, *Argentina* **140** 32 42 S 62 5W
Marcus, *Pac. Oc.* **66** 24 0N 153 45 E
Marcus Necker Ridge, *Pac. Oc.* **66** 20 0N 175 0 E
Marcy Mt., *U.S.A.* **117** 44 7N 73 55W
Mardan, *Pakistan* **48** 34 20N 72 0 E
Mardie, *Australia* **78** 21 12 S 115 59 E
Mardin, *Turkey* **46** 37 20N 40 43 E
Maré, I., *N. Cal.* **68** 21 30 S 168 0 E
Marechal Deodoro, *Brazil* **138** 9 43 S 35 54W
Maree L., *U.K.* **14** 57 40N 5 30W
Mareeba, *Australia* **72** 16 59 S 145 28 E
Marek = Stanke Dimitrov, *Bulgaria* **34** 42 17N 23 9 E
Marek, *Indonesia* **57** 4 41 S 120 24 E
Maremma, *Italy* **26** 42 45N 11 15 E
Maréna, *Mali* **90** 14 0N 7 20W
Marenberg, *Yugoslavia* **27** 46 38N 15 13 E
Marengo, *U.S.A.* **118** 41 42N 92 5W
Marennes, *France* **20** 45 49N 1 7W
Marenyi, *Kenya* **92** 4 22 S 39 8 E
Marerano, *Madag.* **97** 21 23 S 44 52 E
Maréttimo, *Italy* **28** 37 58N 12 5 E
Mareuil-sur-Lay, *France* **20** 46 32N 1 14W
Marfa, *U.S.A.* **121** 30 15N 104 0W
Marganets, *U.S.S.R.* **38** 47 40N 34 40 E
Margaret Bay, *Canada* **110** 51 20N 127 35W
Margaret L., *Canada* **110** 58 56N 115 25W
Margarita, I. de, *Venezuela* **135** 11 0N 64 0W
Margarítion, *Greece* **35** 39 22N 20 26 E
Margate, *S. Africa* **97** 30 50 S 30 20 E
Margate, *U.K.* **13** 51 23N 1 24 E
Margelan, *U.S.S.R.* **40** 40 27N 71 42 E
Margeride, Mts. de la, *France* **20** 44 43N 3 38 E
Margherita, *India* **52** 27 16N 95 40 E
Margherita di Savola, *Italy* **29** 41 25N 16 5 E
Marguerite, *Canada* **110** 52 30N 122 25W
Marhoum, *Algeria* **85** 34 27N 0 11W
Mari A.S.S.R. □, *U.S.S.R.* **37** 56 30N 48 0 E
María Elena, *Chile* **140** 22 18 S 69 40W
María Grande, *Argentina* **140** 31 45 S 59 55W
Maria I., *N. Terr., Australia* **72** 14 52 S 135 45 E
Maria I., *Tas., Australia* **72** 42 35 S 148 0 E
Maria van Diemen, C., *N.Z.* **80** 34 29 S 172 40 E
Mariager, *Denmark* **11** 56 40N 10 0 E
Mariager Fjord, *Denmark* **11** 56 42N 10 19 E
Mariakani, *Kenya* **92** 3 50 S 39 27 E
Marian L., *Canada* **110** 63 0N 116 15W
Mariana Trench, *Pac. Oc.* **66** 13 0N 145 0 E
Marianao, *Cuba* **128** 23 8N 82 24W
Mariani, *India* **52** 26 39N 94 19 E
Marianna, *Ark., U.S.A.* **121** 34 48N 90 48W
Marianna, *Fla., U.S.A.* **115** 30 45N 85 15W
Mariannelund, *Sweden* **11** 57 37N 15 35 E
Mariánské Lázně, *Czech.* **32** 49 48N 12 41 E
Marias →, *U.S.A.* **122** 47 56N 110 30W
Mariato, Punta, *Panama* **128** 7 12N 80 52W
Mariazell, *Austria* **33** 47 47N 15 19 E
Ma'rib, *Yemen* **45** 15 25N 45 21 E
Maribo, *Denmark* **11** 54 48N 11 30 E
Maribor, *Yugoslavia* **27** 46 36N 15 40 E
Marico →, *Africa* **96** 23 35 S 26 57 E
Maricopa, *Ariz., U.S.A.* **123** 33 5N 112 2W
Maricopa, *Calif., U.S.A.* **125** 35 7N 119 27W
Marîdî, *Sudan* **89** 4 55N 29 25 E
Maridi, Wadi →, *Sudan* **89** 6 15N 29 21 E
Marié →, *Brazil* **134** 0 27 S 66 26W
Marie-Galante, *Guadeloupe* **129** 15 56N 61 16W
Mariecourt, *Canada* **103** 61 30N 72 0W
Mariefred, *Sweden* **10** 59 15N 17 12 E
Mariehamn, *Finland* **9** 60 5N 19 55 E
Marienberg, *E. Germany* **30** 50 40N 13 10 E
Marienberg, *Neths.* **16** 52 30N 6 35 E
Marienbourg, *Belgium* **17** 50 6N 4 31 E
Mariental, *Namibia* **96** 24 36 S 18 0 E
Marienville, *U.S.A.* **116** 41 27N 79 8W
Mariestad, *Sweden* **11** 58 43N 13 50 E
Marietta, *Ga., U.S.A.* **115** 34 0N 84 30W
Marietta, *Ohio, U.S.A.* **114** 39 27N 81 27W
Marieville, *Canada* **117** 45 26N 73 10W
Marignane, *France* **21** 43 25N 5 13 E
Mariinsk, *U.S.S.R.* **40** 56 10N 87 20 E
Mariinskiy Posad, *U.S.S.R.* **37** 56 10N 47 45 E
Marília, *Brazil* **141** 22 13 S 50 0W
Marillana, *Australia* **78** 22 37 S 119 16 E
Marimba, *Angola* **95** 8 28 S 17 8 E
Marín, *Spain* **22** 42 23N 8 42W
Marina, *U.S.A.* **124** 36 41N 121 48W
Mariña, La, *Spain* **22** 43 30N 7 40W
Marina di Cirò, *Italy* **29** 39 22N 17 8 E
Marina Plains, *Australia* **72** 14 37 S 143 57 E
Marinduque, *Phil.* **57** 13 25N 122 0 E
Marine City, *U.S.A.* **114** 42 45N 82 29W
Marinel, Le, *Zaïre* **93** 10 25 S 25 17 E
Marineo, *Italy* **28** 37 57N 13 23 E
Marinette, *U.S.A.* **114** 45 4N 87 40W
Maringá, *Brazil* **141** 23 26 S 52 2W
Marinha Grande, *Portugal* **23** 39 45N 8 56W
Marion, *Ala., U.S.A.* **115** 32 33N 87 20W
Marion, *Ill., U.S.A.* **118** 37 45N 88 55W
Marion, *Ind., U.S.A.* **119** 40 35N 85 40W
Marion, *Iowa, U.S.A.* **118** 42 2N 91 36W
Marion, *Kans., U.S.A.* **120** 38 25N 97 2W
Marion, *Mich., U.S.A.* **114** 44 7N 85 8W
Marion, *N.C., U.S.A.* **115** 35 42N 82 0W
Marion, *Ohio, U.S.A.* **119** 40 38N 83 8W
Marion, *S.C., U.S.A.* **115** 34 11N 79 22W
Marion, *Va., U.S.A.* **115** 36 51N 81 29W
Marion, L., *U.S.A.* **115** 33 30N 80 15W
Marion I., *Ind. Oc.* **53** 47 0 S 38 0 E
Maripa, *Venezuela* **135** 7 26N 65 9W
Maripasoula, *Fr. Guiana* **135** 3 40N 54 4W
Mariposa, *U.S.A.* **124** 37 31N 119 59W
Mariscal Estigarribia, *Paraguay* **140** 22 3 S 60 40W
Maritime Alps = Maritimes, Alpes, *Europe* **21** 44 10N 7 10 E
Maritimes, Alpes, *Europe* **21** 44 10N 7 10 E
Marīvān, *Iran* **46** 35 30N 46 25 E
Mariyampole = Kapsukas, *U.S.S.R.* **36** 54 33N 23 19 E
Markam, *China* **58** 29 42N 98 38 E
Markapur, *India* **51** 15 44N 79 19 E
Markaryd, *Sweden* **11** 56 28N 13 35 E
Markazī □, *Iran* **47** 35 0N 49 30 E
Markdale, *Canada* **108** 44 19N 80 39W
Marke, *Belgium* **17** 50 48N 3 14 E
Marked Tree, *U.S.A.* **121** 35 35N 90 24W
Markelsdorfer Huk, *W. Germany* **30** 54 33N 11 0 E
Marken, *Neths.* **16** 52 26N 5 12 E
Markermeer, *Neths.* **16** 52 33N 5 15 E
Market Drayton, *U.K.* **12** 52 55N 2 30W
Market Harborough, *U.K.* **13** 52 29N 0 55W
Markham, *Canada* **108** 43 52N 79 16W
Markham →, *Papua N. G.* **69** 6 41 S 147 2 E
Markham L., *Canada* **111** 62 30N 102 35W
Markham Mt., *Antarctica* **143** 83 0 S 164 0 E
Marki, *Poland* **32** 52 20N 21 2 E
Markleeville, *U.S.A.* **124** 38 44N 119 47W
Markoupoulon, *Greece* **35** 37 53N 23 57 E
Markovo, *U.S.S.R.* **41** 64 40N 169 40 E
Markoye, *Burkina Faso* **91** 14 39N 0 2 E
Marks, *U.S.S.R.* **37** 51 45N 46 50 E
Markstay, *Canada* **108** 46 29N 80 32W
Marksville, *U.S.A.* **121** 31 10N 92 2W
Markt Schwaben, *W. Germany* **31** 48 14N 11 49 E
Marktredwitz, *E. Germany* **31** 50 1N 12 2 E
Marla, *Australia* **73** 27 19 S 133 33 E
Marlbank, *Canada* **109** 44 26N 77 6W
Marlboro, *U.S.A.* **117** 42 19N 71 33W
Marlborough, *Australia* **72** 22 46 S 149 52 E
Marlborough □, *N.Z.* **81** 41 45 S 173 33 E
Marlborough Downs, *U.K.* **13** 51 25N 1 55W
Marle, *France* **19** 49 43N 3 47 E
Marlee, *Australia* **77** 31 47 S 152 20 E
Marlin, *U.S.A.* **121** 31 25N 96 50W
Marlo, *Australia* **75** 37 46 S 148 31 E
Marlow, *E. Germany* **30** 54 8N 12 34 E
Marlow, *U.S.A.* **121** 34 40N 97 58W
Marmagao, *India* **51** 15 25N 73 56 E
Marmande, *France* **20** 44 30N 0 10 E
Marmara, *Turkey* **38** 40 35N 27 38 E
Marmara, Sea of = Marmara Denizi, *Turkey* **46** 40 45N 28 15 E
Marmara Denizi, *Turkey* **46** 40 45N 28 15 E
Marmaris, *Turkey* **46** 36 50N 28 14 E
Marmarth, *U.S.A.* **120** 46 21N 103 52W
Marmelos →, *Brazil* **137** 6 6 S 61 46W
Marmion L., *Canada* **104** 48 55N 91 20W
Marmion Mt., *Australia* **79** 29 16 S 119 50 E
Marmolada, Mte., *Italy* **27** 46 25N 11 55 E
Marmolejo, *Spain* **23** 38 3N 4 13W
Marmora, *Canada* **109** 44 28N 77 41W
Marnay, *France* **19** 47 16N 5 48 E
Marne, *W. Germany* **30** 53 57N 9 1 E
Marne □, *France* **19** 48 50N 4 10 E
Marne →, *France* **19** 48 48N 2 24 E
Marnueli, *U.S.S.R.* **39** 41 30N 44 48 E
Maro, *Chad* **87** 8 30N 19 0 E
Maroa, *Venezuela* **134** 2 43N 67 33W
Maroala, *Madag.* **97** 15 23 S 47 59 E
Maroantsetra, *Madag.* **97** 15 26 S 49 44 E
Maromandia, *Madag.* **97** 14 13 S 48 5 E
Marondera, *Zimb.* **93** 18 5 S 31 42 E
Marong, *Australia* **74** 36 44 S 144 8 E
Maroni →, *Fr. Guiana* **135** 5 30N 54 0W
Maronne →, *France* **20** 45 5N 1 56 E
Maroochydore, *Australia* **73** 26 29 S 153 5 E
Maroona, *Australia* **74** 37 27 S 142 54 E
Maros →, *Hungary* **33** 46 15N 20 13 E
Marosakoa, *Madag.* **97** 15 26 S 46 38 E
Marostica, *Italy* **27** 45 44N 11 40 E
Maroua, *Cameroon* **91** 10 40N 14 20 E
Marovoay, *Madag.* **97** 16 6 S 46 39 E
Marowijne □, *Surinam* **135** 4 0N 55 0W
Marowijne →, *Surinam* **135** 5 45N 53 58W
Marquard, *S. Africa* **96** 28 40 S 27 28 E
Marqueira, *Portugal* **23** 38 41N 9 9W
Marquesas Is., *Pac. Oc.* **67** 9 30 S 140 0W
Marquette, *U.S.A.* **104** 46 30N 87 21W
Marquette, L., *Canada* **107** 48 54N 73 54W
Marquise, *France* **19** 50 50N 1 40 E
Marra, Gebel, *Sudan* **89** 7 20N 27 35 E
Marracuene, *Mozam.* **97** 25 45 S 32 35 E
Marradi, *Italy* **27** 44 5N 11 37 E
Marrakech, *Morocco* **84** 31 9N 8 0W
Marrar, *Australia* **76** 34 50 S 147 23 E
Marrawah, *Australia* **72** 40 55 S 144 42 E
Marrecas, Serra das, *Brazil* **138** 9 0 S 41 0W
Marree, *Australia* **73** 29 39 S 138 1 E
Marrilla, *Australia* **78** 22 31 S 114 25 E
Marrimane, *Mozam.* **97** 22 58 S 33 34 E
Marromeu, *Mozam.* **97** 18 15 S 36 25 E
Marroquí, Punta, *Spain* **23** 36 0N 5 37W
Marrowie Creek, *Australia* **73** 33 23 S 145 40 E
Marrubane, *Mozam.* **93** 18 0 S 37 0 E
Marrum, *Neths.* **16** 53 19N 5 48 E
Marrupa, *Mozam.* **93** 13 8 S 37 30 E
Mars, Le, *U.S.A.* **120** 43 0N 96 0W
Marsa Brega, *Libya* **86** 30 24N 19 37 E
Marsá Matrûh, *Egypt* **88** 31 19N 27 9 E
Marsá Susah, *Libya* **86** 32 52N 21 59 E
Marsabit, *Kenya* **92** 2 18N 38 0 E
Marsabit □, *Kenya* **92** 2 45N 37 45 E
Marsala, *Italy* **28** 37 48N 12 25 E
Marsciano, *Italy* **27** 42 54N 12 20 E
Marsden, *Australia* **76** 33 47 S 147 32 E
Marsdiep, *Neths.* **16** 52 58N 4 46 E
Marseillan, *France* **20** 43 23N 3 31 E
Marseille, *France* **21** 43 18N 5 23 E
Marseilles = Marseille, *France* **21** 43 18N 5 23 E
Marseilles, *U.S.A.* **119** 41 20N 88 43W
Marsh I., *U.S.A.* **121** 29 35N 91 50W
Marsh L., *U.S.A.* **120** 45 5N 96 0W
Marshall, *Liberia* **90** 6 8N 10 22W
Marshall, *Ark., U.S.A.* **121** 35 58N 92 40W
Marshall, *Ill., U.S.A.* **119** 39 23N 87 42W
Marshall, *Mich., U.S.A.* **119** 42 17N 84 59W
Marshall, *Minn., U.S.A.* **120** 44 25N 95 45W
Marshall, *Mo., U.S.A.* **118** 39 8N 93 15W
Marshall, *Tex., U.S.A.* **121** 32 29N 94 20W
Marshall →, *Australia* **72** 22 59 S 136 59 E
Marshall Is., *Pac. Oc.* **66** 9 0N 171 0 E
Marshalltown, *U.S.A.* **118** 42 5N 92 56W
Marshfield, *Mo., U.S.A.* **121** 37 20N 92 58W
Marshfield, *Wis., U.S.A.* **120** 44 42N 90 10W
Mársico Nuovo, *Italy* **29** 40 26N 15 43 E
Märsta, *Sweden* **10** 59 37N 17 52 E
Marstal, *Denmark* **11** 54 51N 10 30 E
Marstrand, *Swedbn* **11** 57 53N 11 35 E
Mart, *U.S.A.* **121** 31 34N 96 51W
Marta →, *Italy* **27** 42 14N 11 42 E
Martaban, *Burma* **52** 16 30N 97 35 E
Martaban, G. of, *Burma* **52** 16 5N 96 30 E
Martano, *Italy* **29** 40 14N 18 18 E
Martapura, *Kalimantan, Indonesia* **56** 3 22 S 114 47 E
Martapura, *Sumatera, Indonesia* **56** 4 19 S 104 22 E
Marte, *Nigeria* **91** 12 23N 13 46 E
Martel, *France* **20** 44 57N 1 37 E
Martelange, *Belgium* **17** 49 49N 5 43 E
Marten River, *Canada* **108** 46 44N 79 49W
Martensdale, *U.S.A.* **118** 41 23N 93 45W
Martés, Sierra, *Spain* **25** 39 20N 1 0W
Martha's Vineyard, *U.S.A.* **117** 41 25N 70 35W
Martigné-Ferchaud, *France* **18** 47 50N 1 20W
Martigny, *Switz.* **31** 46 6N 7 3 E
Martigues, *France* **21** 43 24N 5 4 E
Martil, *Morocco* **84** 35 36N 5 15W
Martin, *Czech.* **32** 49 6N 18 48 E
Martin, *S. Dak., U.S.A.* **120** 43 11N 101 45W
Martin, *Tenn., U.S.A.* **121** 36 23N 88 51W
Martín →, *Spain* **24** 41 18N 0 19W
Martin, L., *U.S.A.* **115** 32 45N 85 50W
Martina Franca, *Italy* **29** 40 42N 17 20 E
Martinborough, *N.Z.* **80** 41 14 S 175 29 E
Martindale, *Australia* **76** 32 27 S 150 40 E
Martinez, *U.S.A.* **124** 38 1N 122 8W
Martinho Campos, *Brazil* **139** 19 20 S 45 13W
Martinique, *W. Indies* **129** 14 40N 61 0W
Martinique Passage, *W. Indies* **129** 15 15N 61 0W
Martínon, *Greece* **35** 38 35N 23 15 E
Martinópolis, *Brazil* **141** 22 11 S 51 12W
Martins Ferry, *U.S.A.* **116** 40 5N 80 46W
Martinsburg, *Pa., U.S.A.* **116** 40 18N 78 21W
Martinsburg, *W. Va., U.S.A.* **114** 39 30N 77 57W
Martinsville, *Ill., U.S.A.* **119** 39 20N 87 53W
Martinsville, *Ind., U.S.A.* **119** 39 29N 86 23W
Martinsville, *Va., U.S.A.* **115** 36 41N 79 52W
Marton, *N.Z.* **80** 40 4 S 175 23 E
Martorell, *Spain* **24** 41 28N 1 56 E
Martos, *Spain* **23** 37 44N 3 58W
Martūbah, *Libya* **86** 32 35N 22 46 E
Martuni, *U.S.S.R.* **39** 40 9N 45 10 E
Maru, *Nigeria* **91** 12 22N 6 22 E
Marudi, *Malaysia* **56** 4 11N 114 19 E
Ma'ruf, *Afghan.* **47** 31 30N 67 6 E
Marugame, *Japan* **64** 34 15N 133 40 E
Marúggio, *Italy* **29** 40 20N 17 33 E
Marui, *Papua N. G.* **69** 4 4 S 143 2 E
Maruim, *Brazil* **138** 10 45 S 37 5W
Marulan, *Australia* **76** 34 43 S 150 3 E
Marulan South, *Australia* **76** 34 47 S 150 3 E
Marum, *Neths.* **16** 53 9N 6 16 E
Marum, Mt., *Vanuatu* **68** 16 15 S 168 7 E
Marunga, *Angola* **95** 17 28 S 20 2 E
Marungu, Mts., *Zaïre* **92** 7 30 S 30 0 E
Maruoka, *Japan* **65** 36 9N 136 16 E
Marvejols, *France* **20** 44 33N 3 19 E
Marwar, *India* **48** 25 43N 73 45 E
Mary, *U.S.S.R.* **40** 37 40N 61 50 E
Mary Frances L., *Canada* **111** 63 19N 106 13W
Mary Kathleen, *Australia* **72** 20 44 S 139 48 E
Maryborough = Port Laoise, *Ireland* **15** 53 2N 7 20W
Maryborough, *Queens., Australia* **73** 25 31 S 152 37 E
Maryborough, *Vic., Australia* **74** 37 0 S 143 44 E
Maryfield, *Canada* **111** 49 50N 101 35W
Maryland □, *U.S.A.* **114** 39 10N 76 40W
Maryland Jct., *Zimb.* **93** 17 45 S 30 31 E
Maryport, *U.K.* **12** 54 43N 3 30W
Mary's Harbour, *Canada* **105** 52 18N 55 51W
Marystown, *Canada* **105** 47 10N 55 10W
Marysvale, *U.S.A.* **123** 38 25N 112 17W
Marysville, *Australia* **74** 37 33 S 145 45 E
Marysville, *Canada* **110** 49 35N 116 0W
Marysville, *Calif., U.S.A.* **124** 39 14N 121 40W
Marysville, *Kans., U.S.A.* **120** 39 50N 96 49W
Marysville, *Mich., U.S.A.* **116** 42 55N 82 29W
Marysville, *Ohio, U.S.A.* **119** 40 15N 83 20W
Marysville, *Wash., U.S.A.* **124** 48 3N 122 11W
Maryvale, *Australia* **77** 28 4 S 152 12 E
Maryville, *Mo., U.S.A.* **118** 40 21N 94 52W
Maryville, *Tenn., U.S.A.* **115** 35 50N 84 0W
Marzo, Punta, *Colombia* **134** 6 50N 77 42W
Marzūq, *Libya* **86** 25 53N 13 57 E
Masada = Mesada, *Israel* **44** 31 20N 35 19 E
Masahunga, *Tanzania* **92** 2 6 S 33 18 E
Masai, *Malaysia* **55** 1 29N 103 55 E
Masai Steppe, *Tanzania* **92** 4 30 S 36 30 E
Masaka, *Uganda* **92** 0 21 S 31 45 E
Masalembo, Kepulauan, *Indonesia* **56** 5 35 S 114 30 E
Masalima, Kepulauan, *Indonesia* **56** 5 4 S 117 5 E
Masamba, *Indonesia* **57** 2 30 S 120 15 E
Masan, *S. Korea* **61** 35 11N 128 32 E
Masanasa, *Spain* **25** 39 25N 0 25W
Masandam, Ras, *Oman* **47** 26 30N 56 30 E
Masasi, *Tanzania* **93** 10 45 S 38 52 E

Masasi □, *Tanzania* **93** 10 45 S 38 50 E
Masaya, *Nic.* **128** 12 0N 86 7W
Masba, *Nigeria* **91** 10 35N 13 1 E
Masbate, *Phil.* **57** 12 21N 123 36 E
Mascara, *Algeria* **85** 35 26N 0 6 E
Mascarene Is., *Ind. Oc.* **53** 22 0 S 55 0 E
Mascota, *Mexico* **126** 20 30N 104 50W
Mascouche, *Canada* **107** 45 45N 73 36W
Mascoutah, *U.S.A.* **118** 38 29N 89 48W
Masela, *Indonesia* **57** 8 9 S 129 51 E
Maseru, *Lesotho* **96** 29 18 S 27 30 E
Mashaba, *Zimb.* **93** 20 2 S 30 29 E
Mashābih, *Si. Arabia* **46** 25 35N 36 30 E
Mashan, *China* **58** 23 40N 108 11 E
Masherbrum, *Pakistan* **49** 35 38N 76 18 E
Mashhad, *Iran* **47** 36 20N 59 35 E
Mashi, *Nigeria* **91** 13 0N 7 54 E
Mashiki, *Japan* **64** 32 51N 130 53 E
Mashkel, Hamun-i-, *Pakistan* **47** 28 30N 63 0 E
Mashki Chāh, *Pakistan* **47** 29 5N 62 30 E
Mashonaland Central □, *Zimb.* **97** 17 30 S 31 0 E
Mashonaland East □, *Zimb.* **97** 18 0 S 32 0 E
Mashonaland West □, *Zimb.* **97** 17 30 S 29 30 E
Mashtaga, *U.S.S.R.* **39** 40 35N 50 0 E
Masi, *Norway* **8** 69 26N 23 40 E
Masi Manimba, *Zaïre* **95** 4 40 S 17 54 E
Masindi, *Uganda* **92** 1 40N 31 43 E
Masindi Port, *Uganda* **92** 1 43N 32 2 E
Masisea, *Peru* **136** 8 35 S 74 22W
Masisi, *Zaïre* **92** 1 23 S 28 49 E
Masjed Soleyman, *Iran* **46** 31 55N 49 18 E
Mask, L., *Ireland* **15** 53 36N 9 24W
Maskelyne Is., *Vanuatu* **68** 16 32 S 167 49 E
Maski, *India* **51** 15 56N 76 46 E
Maskinongé, *Canada* **107** 46 14N 73 1W
Maslinica, *Yugoslavia* **27** 43 24N 16 13 E
Masnou, *Spain* **24** 41 28N 2 20 E
Masoala, Tanjon' i, *Madag.* **97** 15 59 S 50 13 E
Masoarivo, *Madag.* **97** 19 3 S 44 19 E
Masohi, *Indonesia* **57** 3 20 S 128 55 E
Masomeloka, *Madag.* **97** 20 17 S 48 37 E
Mason, *Mich., U.S.A.* **119** 42 35N 84 27W
Mason, *Nev., U.S.A.* **124** 38 56N 119 8W
Mason, *Ohio, U.S.A.* **119** 39 22N 84 19W
Mason, *Tex., U.S.A.* **121** 30 45N 99 15W
Mason B., *N.Z.* **81** 46 55 S 167 45 E
Mason City, *Ill., U.S.A.* **118** 40 12N 89 42W
Mason City, *Iowa, U.S.A.* **118** 43 9N 93 12W
Maspalomas, *Canary Is.* **25** 27 46N 15 35W
Maspalomas, Pta., *Canary Is.* **25** 27 43N 15 36W
Masqat, *Oman* **47** 23 37N 58 36 E
Massa, *Congo* **94** 3 45 S 15 29 E
Massa, *Italy* **26** 44 2N 10 7 E
Massa, O. →, *Morocco* **84** 30 2N 9 40W
Massa Maríttima, *Italy* **26** 43 3N 10 52 E
Massachusetts □, *U.S.A.* **117** 42 25N 72 0W
Massachusetts B., *U.S.A.* **117** 42 30N 70 0W
Massada, *Syria* **44** 33 41N 35 36 E
Massafra, *Italy* **29** 40 35N 17 8 E
Massaguet, *Chad* **87** 12 28N 15 26 E
Massakory, *Chad* **87** 13 0N 15 49 E
Massangena, *Mozam.* **97** 21 34 S 33 0 E
Massapê, *Brazil* **138** 3 31 S 40 19W
Massarosa, *Italy* **26** 43 53N 10 17 E
Massat, *France* **20** 42 53N 1 21 E
Massawa = Mitsiwa, *Ethiopia* **89** 15 35N 39 25 E
Massena, *U.S.A.* **117** 44 52N 74 55W
Massénya, *Chad* **87** 11 21N 16 9 E
Masset, *Canada* **110** 54 2N 132 10W
Massey, *Canada* **108** 46 12N 82 5W
Massiac, *France* **20** 45 15N 3 11 E
Massif Central, *France* **20** 45 30N 3 0 E
Massillon, *U.S.A.* **116** 40 47N 81 30W
Massinga, *Mozam.* **97** 23 15 S 35 22 E
Masson, *Canada* **117** 45 32N 75 25W
Masson I., *Antarctica* **143** 66 10 S 93 20 E
Massueville, *Canada* **107** 45 55N 72 56W
Mastanli = Momchilgrad, *Bulgaria* **35** 41 33N 25 23 E
Masterton, *N.Z.* **80** 40 56 S 175 39 E
Mastigouche, Parc, *Canada* **107** 46 33N 73 41W
Mástikho, Ákra, *Greece* **35** 38 10N 26 2 E
Mastuj, *Pakistan* **49** 36 20N 72 36 E
Mastung, *Pakistan* **47** 29 50N 66 56 E
Mastūrah, *Si. Arabia* **88** 23 7N 38 52 E
Masuda, *Japan* **64** 34 40N 131 51 E
Masuika, *Zaïre* **95** 7 37 S 22 32 E
Masvingo, *Zimb.* **93** 20 8 S 30 49 E
Masvingo □, *Zimb.* **93** 21 0 S 31 30 E
Maswa □, *Tanzania* **92** 3 30 S 34 0 E
Mata de São João, *Brazil* **139** 12 31 S 38 17W
Matabeleland North □, *Zimb.* **93** 19 0 S 28 0 E
Matabeleland South □, *Zimb.* **93** 21 0 S 29 0 E
Mataboor, *Indonesia* **57** 1 41 S 138 3 E
Matachel →, *Spain* **23** 38 50N 6 17W
Matachewan, *Canada* **104** 47 56N 80 39W
Matacuni →, *Venezuela* **135** 3 2N 65 16W
Matad, *Mongolia* **62** 47 11N 115 27 E
Matadi, *Zaïre* **95** 5 52 S 13 31 E
Matagalpa, *Nic.* **128** 13 0N 85 58W
Matagami, *Canada* **106** 49 45N 77 34W
Matagami, L., *Canada* **106** 49 50N 77 40W
Matagorda, *U.S.A.* **121** 28 43N 96 0W
Matagorda B., *U.S.A.* **121** 28 30N 96 15W
Matagorda I., *U.S.A.* **121** 28 10N 96 40W
Matak, P., *Indonesia* **55** 3 18N 106 16 E
Matakana, *Australia* **73** 32 59 S 145 54 E
Matala, *Angola* **95** 14 46 S 15 4 E
Matalaque, *Peru* **136** 16 26 S 70 49W
Matale, *Sri Lanka* **51** 7 30N 80 37 E
Matam, *Senegal* **90** 15 34N 13 17W
Matamata, *N.Z.* **80** 37 48 S 175 47 E
Matameye, *Niger* **91** 13 26N 8 28 E
Matamoros, *Campeche, Mexico* **127** 18 50N 90 50W
Matamoros, *Coahuila, Mexico* **126** 25 33N 103 15W
Matamoros, *Puebla, Mexico* **127** 18 2N 98 17W
Matamoros, *Tamaulipas, Mexico* **127** 25 50N 97 30W
Ma'ṭan as Sarra, *Libya* **87** 21 45N 22 0 E
Matandu →, *Tanzania* **93** 8 45 S 34 19 E
Matane, *Canada* **105** 48 50N 67 33W
Matang, *China* **58** 23 30N 104 7 E
Matankari, *Niger* **91** 13 46N 4 1 E
Matanzas, *Cuba* **128** 23 0N 81 40W
Matapan, C. = Taínaron, Ákra, *Greece* **35** 36 22N 22 27 E
Matapédia, *Canada* **105** 48 0N 66 59W
Matara, *Sri Lanka* **51** 5 58N 80 30 E
Mataram, *Indonesia* **56** 8 41 S 116 10 E
Matarani, *Peru* **136** 17 0 S 72 10W
Mataranka, *Australia* **78** 14 55 S 133 4 E
Mataró, *Spain* **24** 41 32N 2 29 E
Matarraña →, *Spain* **24** 41 14N 0 22 E
Mataso, *Vanuatu* **68** 17 14 S 168 26 E
Matata, *N.Z.* **80** 37 54 S 176 48 E
Matatiele, *S. Africa* **97** 30 20 S 28 49 E
Mataura, *N.Z.* **81** 46 11 S 168 51 E
Mataura →, *N.Z.* **81** 46 34 S 168 44 E
Matawin →, *Canada* **107** 46 54N 72 56W
Matawin, Rés., *Canada* **107** 46 46N 73 50W
Matchi-Manitou, L., *Canada* **106** 48 0N 77 4W
Mategua, *Bolivia* **137** 13 1 S 62 48W
Matehuala, *Mexico* **126** 23 40N 100 40W
Mateira, *Brazil* **139** 18 54 S 50 30W
Mateke Hills, *Zimb.* **93** 21 48 S 31 0 E
Matélica, *Italy* **27** 43 15N 13 0 E
Matera, *Italy* **29** 40 40N 16 37 E
Mátészalka, *Hungary* **33** 47 58N 22 20 E
Matetsi, *Zimb.* **93** 18 12 S 26 0 E
Mateur, *Tunisia* **86** 37 0N 9 40 E
Matfors, *Sweden* **10** 62 21N 17 2 E
Matha, *France* **20** 45 52N 0 20W
Matheson Island, *Canada* **111** 51 45N 96 56W
Mathis, *U.S.A.* **121** 28 4N 97 48W
Mathura, *India* **48** 27 30N 77 40 E
Mati, *Phil.* **57** 6 55N 126 15 E
Mati →, *Albania* **35** 41 40N 20 0 E
Matías Romero, *Mexico* **127** 16 53N 95 2W
Matibane, *Mozam.* **93** 14 49 S 40 45 E
Matima, *Botswana* **96** 20 15 S 24 26 E
Matinenda L., *Canada* **108** 46 22N 82 57W
Matlock, *U.K.* **12** 53 8N 1 32W
Matmata, *Tunisia* **86** 33 37N 9 59 E
Matna, *Sudan* **89** 13 49N 35 10 E
Mato →, *Venezuela* **135** 7 9N 65 7W
Mato, Serrania de, *Venezuela* **134** 6 25N 65 25W
Mato Grosso □, *Brazil* **137** 14 0 S 55 0W
Mato Grosso, Planalto do, *Brazil* **137** 15 0 S 55 0W
Matochkin Shar, *U.S.S.R.* **40** 73 10N 56 40 E
Matong, *Papua N. G.* **69** 5 36 S 151 50 E
Matopo Hills, *Zimb.* **93** 20 36 S 28 20 E
Matopos, *Zimb.* **93** 20 20 S 28 29 E
Matosinhos, *Portugal* **22** 41 11N 8 42W
Matour, *France* **21** 46 19N 4 29 E
Matrah, *Oman* **47** 23 37N 58 30 E
Matsena, *Nigeria* **91** 13 5N 10 5 E
Matsesta, *U.S.S.R.* **39** 43 34N 39 51 E
Matsubara, *Japan* **65** 34 33N 135 34 E
Matsudo, *Japan* **65** 35 47N 139 54 E
Matsue, *Japan* **64** 35 25N 133 10 E
Matsumae, *Japan* **63** 41 26N 140 7 E
Matsumoto, *Japan* **65** 36 15N 138 0 E
Matsusaka, *Japan* **65** 34 34N 136 32 E
Matsutō, *Japan* **65** 36 31N 136 34 E
Matsuura, *Japan* **64** 33 20N 129 49 E
Matsuyama, *Japan* **64** 33 45N 132 45 E
Matsuzaki, *Japan* **65** 34 43N 138 50 E
Mattagami →, *Canada* **104** 50 43N 81 29W
Mattancheri, *India* **51** 9 50N 76 15 E
Mattawa, *Canada* **104** 46 20N 78 45W
Mattawamkeag, *U.S.A.* **105** 45 30N 68 21W
Matterhorn, *Switz.* **31** 45 58N 7 39 E
Matteson, *U.S.A.* **119** 41 30N 87 42W
Matthew Town, *Bahamas* **129** 20 57N 73 40W
Matthews, *U.S.A.* **119** 40 23N 85 31W
Matthew's Ridge, *Guyana* **135** 7 37N 60 10W
Mattice, *Canada* **104** 49 40N 83 20W
Mattituck, *U.S.A.* **117** 40 58N 72 32W
Mattmar, *Sweden* **10** 63 18N 13 45 E
Matuba, *Mozam.* **97** 24 28 S 32 49 E
Matucana, *Peru* **136** 11 55 S 76 25W
Matuku, *Fiji* **68** 19 10 S 179 44 E
Matun, *Afghan.* **48** 33 22N 69 58 E
Maturín, *Venezuela* **135** 9 45N 63 11W
Matveyev Kurgan, *U.S.S.R.* **39** 47 35N 38 47 E
Mau, *India* **49** 25 56N 83 33 E
Mau Escarpment, *Kenya* **92** 0 40 S 36 0 E
Mau Ranipur, *India* **49** 25 16N 79 8 E
Maubeuge, *France* **19** 50 17N 3 57 E
Maubourguet, *France* **20** 43 29N 0 1 E
Maud, Pt., *Australia* **78** 23 6 S 113 45 E
Maude, *Australia* **74** 34 29 S 144 18 E
Maudheim, *Antarctica* **143** 71 5 S 11 0W
Maués, *Brazil* **135** 3 20 S 57 45W
Maui, *U.S.A.* **112** 20 45N 156 20W
Maule □, *Chile* **140** 36 5 S 72 30W
Mauléon-Licharre, *France* **20** 43 14N 0 54W
Maullín, *Chile* **142** 41 38 S 73 37W
Maulvibazar, *Bangla.* **52** 24 29N 91 42 E
Maumee, *U.S.A.* **119** 41 35N 83 40W
Maumee →, *U.S.A.* **119** 41 42N 83 28W
Maumere, *Indonesia* **57** 8 38 S 122 13 E
Maun, *Botswana* **96** 20 0 S 23 26 E
Mauna Kea, *U.S.A.* **112** 19 50N 155 28W
Mauna Loa, *U.S.A.* **112** 21 8N 157 10W
Maungatoroto, *N.Z.* **80** 36 6 S 174 23 E
Maungdow, *Burma* **52** 20 50N 92 21 E
Maupin, *U.S.A.* **122** 45 12N 121 9W
Maure-de-Bretagne, *France* **18** 47 53N 1 58W
Maurepas L., *U.S.A.* **121** 30 18N 90 35W
Maures, *France* **21** 43 15N 6 15 E
Mauriac, *France* **20** 45 13N 2 19 E
Maurice L., *Australia* **79** 29 30 S 131 0 E
Mauriceville, *N.Z.* **80** 40 45 S 175 42 E
Mauricie, Parc Nat. de la, *Canada* **107** 46 45N 73 0W
Mauritania ■, *Africa* **84** 20 50N 10 0W
Mauritius ■, *Ind. Oc.* **53** 20 0 S 57 0 E
Mauron, *France* **18** 48 9N 2 18W
Maurs, *France* **20** 44 43N 2 12 E
Mauston, *U.S.A.* **120** 43 48N 90 5W
Mauterndorf, *Austria* **33** 47 9N 13 40 E
Mauvezin, *France* **20** 43 44N 0 53 E
Mauzé-sur-le-Mignon, *France* **20** 46 12N 0 41W
Mavaca →, *Venezuela* **135** 2 31N 65 11W
Mavelikara, *India* **51** 9 14N 76 32 E
Mavinga, *Angola* **95** 15 50 S 20 21 E
Mavli, *India* **48** 24 45N 73 55 E
Mavqi'im, *Israel* **44** 31 38N 34 32 E
Mavrova, *Albania* **35** 40 26N 19 32 E
Mavuradonha Mts., *Zimb.* **93** 16 30 S 31 30 E
Mawa, *Zaïre* **92** 2 45N 26 40 E
Mawana, *India* **48** 29 6N 77 58 E
Mawand, *Pakistan* **48** 29 33N 68 38 E
Mawk Mai, *Burma* **52** 20 14N 97 37 E
Mawlaik, *Burma* **52** 23 40N 94 26 E
Mawlawkho, *Burma* **52** 17 50N 97 38 E
Mawson Base, *Antarctica* **143** 67 30 S 62 53 E
Mawson Coast, *Antarctica* **143** 68 30 S 63 0 E
Max, *U.S.A.* **120** 47 50N 101 20W
Maxcanú, *Mexico* **127** 20 40N 92 0W
Maxesibeni, *S. Africa* **97** 30 49 S 29 23 E
Maxhamish L., *Canada* **110** 59 50N 123 17W
Maxixe, *Mozam.* **97** 23 54 S 35 17 E
Maxville, *Canada* **106** 45 17N 74 51W
Maxwell, *N.Z.* **80** 39 51 S 174 49 E
Maxwell, *U.S.A.* **124** 39 17N 122 11W
Maxwelton, *Australia* **72** 20 43 S 142 41 E
May Downs, *Australia* **72** 22 38 S 148 55 E
May Pen, *Jamaica* **128** 17 58N 77 15W
May River, *Papua N. G.* **69** 4 19 S 141 58 E
Maya, *Spain* **24** 43 12N 1 29W
Maya →, *U.S.S.R.* **41** 54 31N 134 41 E
Maya Mts., *Belize* **127** 16 30N 89 0W
Mayaguana, *Bahamas* **129** 22 30N 72 44W
Mayagüez, *Puerto Rico* **129** 18 12N 67 9W
Mayahi, *Niger* **91** 13 58N 7 40 E
Mayals, *Spain* **24** 41 22N 0 30 E
Mayama, *Congo* **94** 3 51 S 14 54 E
Mayang, *China* **58** 27 53N 109 49 E
Mayarí, *Cuba* **129** 20 40N 75 41W
Mayavaram = Mayuram, *India* **51** 11 3N 79 42 E
Maybell, *U.S.A.* **122** 40 30N 108 4W
Maychew, *Ethiopia* **89** 12 50N 39 31 E
Maydena, *Australia* **72** 42 45 S 146 30 E
Mayen, *W. Germany* **31** 50 18N 7 10 E
Mayenne, *France* **18** 48 20N 0 38W
Mayenne □, *France* **18** 48 10N 0 40W
Mayenne →, *France* **18** 47 30N 0 32W
Mayer, *U.S.A.* **123** 34 28N 112 17W
Mayerthorpe, *Canada* **110** 53 57N 115 8W
Mayfield, *U.S.A.* **115** 36 45N 88 40W
Mayhill, *U.S.A.* **123** 32 58N 105 30W
Maykop, *U.S.S.R.* **39** 44 35N 40 25 E
Maymyo, *Burma* **54** 22 2N 96 28 E
Maynard, *U.S.A.* **124** 47 59N 122 55W
Maynard Hills, *Australia* **79** 28 28 S 119 49 E
Mayne →, *Australia* **72** 23 40 S 141 55 E
Maynooth, *Ireland* **15** 53 22N 6 38W
Mayo, *Canada* **102** 63 38N 135 57W
Mayo □, *Ireland* **15** 53 47N 9 7W
Mayo →, *Argentina* **142** 45 45 S 69 45W
Mayo →, *Peru* **136** 6 38 S 76 15W
Mayo L., *Canada* **102** 63 45N 135 0W
Mayoko, *Zaïre* **94** 2 18 S 12 49 E
Mayon Volcano, *Phil.* **57** 13 15N 123 41 E
Mayor I., *N.Z.* **80** 37 16 S 176 17 E
Mayorga, *Spain* **22** 42 10N 5 16W
Mayskiy, *U.S.S.R.* **39** 43 47N 44 2 E
Mayson L., *Canada* **111** 57 55N 107 10W
Maysville, *Ky., U.S.A.* **119** 38 39N 83 46W
Maysville, *Mo., U.S.A.* **118** 39 53N 94 21W
Maythalūn, *Jordan* **44** 32 21N 35 16 E
Mayu, *Indonesia* **57** 1 30N 126 30 E
Mayumba, *Gabon* **94** 3 25 S 10 39 E
Mayuram, *India* **51** 11 3N 79 42 E
Mayville, *N. Dak., U.S.A.* **120** 47 30N 97 23W
Mayville, *N.Y., U.S.A.* **116** 42 14N 79 31W
Mayya, *U.S.S.R.* **41** 61 44N 130 18 E
Mazabuka, *Zambia* **93** 15 52 S 27 44 E
Mazagán = El Jadida, *Morocco* **84** 33 11N 8 17W
Mazagão, *Brazil* **135** 0 7 S 51 16W
Mazamet, *France* **20** 43 30N 2 20 E
Mazán, *Peru* **134** 3 30 S 73 0W
Māzandarān □, *Iran* **47** 36 30N 52 0 E
Mazapil, *Mexico* **126** 24 38N 101 34W
Mazar, O. →, *Algeria* **85** 31 50N 1 36 E
Mazar-e Sharīf, *Afghan.* **47** 36 41N 67 0 E
Mazara del Vallo, *Italy* **28** 37 40N 12 34 E
Mazarredo, *Argentina* **142** 47 10 S 66 50W
Mazarrón, *Spain* **25** 37 38N 1 19W
Mazarrón, G. de, *Spain* **25** 37 27N 1 19W
Mazaruni →, *Guyana* **135** 6 25N 58 35W
Mazatán, *Mexico* **126** 29 0N 110 8W
Mazatenango, *Guatemala* **128** 14 35N 91 30W
Mazatlán, *Mexico* **126** 23 10N 106 30W
Mažeikiai, *U.S.S.R.* **36** 56 20N 22 20 E
Māzhān, *Iran* **47** 32 30N 59 0 E
Mazīnān, *Iran* **47** 36 19N 56 56 E
Mazoe, *Mozam.* **93** 16 42 S 33 7 E
Mazoe →, *Mozam.* **93** 16 20 S 33 30 E
Mazomanie, *U.S.A.* **118** 43 11N 89 48W
Mazon, *U.S.A.* **119** 41 14N 88 25W
Mazowe, *Zimb.* **93** 17 28 S 30 58 E
Mazrûb, *Sudan* **89** 14 0N 29 20 E
Mazu Dao, *China* **59** 26 10N 119 55 E
Mazurian Lakes = Mazurski, Pojezierze, *Poland* **32** 53 50N 21 0 E
Mazurski, Pojezierze, *Poland* **32** 53 50N 21 0 E
Mazzarino, *Italy* **29** 37 19N 14 12 E
Mba, *Fiji* **68** 17 33 S 177 41 E
Mbaba, *Senegal* **90** 14 59N 16 44W
Mbabane, *Swaziland* **97** 26 18 S 31 6 E
Mbagne, *Mauritania* **90** 16 6N 14 47W
M'bahiakro, *Ivory C.* **90** 7 33N 4 19W
Mbaïki, *C.A.R.* **94** 3 53N 18 1 E
Mbakana, Mt. de, *Cameroon* **94** 7 57N 15 6 E
Mbala, *Zambia* **93** 8 46 S 31 24 E
Mbale, *Uganda* **92** 1 8N 34 12 E
Mbalmayo, *Cameroon* **91** 3 33N 11 33 E
Mbamba Bay, *Tanzania* **93** 11 13 S 34 49 E
Mbandaka, *Zaïre* **94** 0 1N 18 18 E
Mbanga, *Cameroon* **91** 4 30N 9 33 E
Mbanza Congo, *Angola* **95** 6 18 S 14 16 E
Mbanza Ngungu, *Zaïre* **95** 5 12 S 14 53 E
Mbarara, *Uganda* **92** 0 35 S 30 40 E
Mbashe →, *S. Africa* **97** 32 15 S 28 54 E
Mbatto, *Ivory C.* **90** 6 28N 4 22W
Mbengga, *Fiji* **68** 18 23 S 178 8 E
Mbenkuru →, *Tanzania* **93** 9 25 S 39 50 E
Mberengwa, *Zimb.* **93** 20 29 S 29 57 E
Mberengwa N., *Zimb.* **93** 20 37 S 29 55 E
Mberubu, *Nigeria* **91** 6 10N 7 38 E
Mbesuma, *Zambia* **93** 10 0 S 32 2 E
Mbeya, *Tanzania* **93** 8 54 S 33 29 E
Mbeya □, *Tanzania* **92** 8 15 S 33 30 E
Mbigou, *Gabon* **94** 1 53 S 11 56 E
Mbinga, *Tanzania* **93** 10 50 S 35 0 E
Mbinga □, *Tanzania* **93** 10 50 S 35 0 E
Mbini □, *Eq. Guin.* **94** 1 30N 10 0 E
Mboki, *C.A.R.* **89** 5 19N 25 58 E
Mboli, *Zaïre* **94** 4 8N 23 9 E
Mboro, *Senegal* **90** 15 9N 16 54W
Mboune, *Senegal* **90** 14 42N 13 34W
Mbouoma, *Congo* **94** 0 52 S 15 4 E
Mbour, *Senegal* **90** 14 22N 16 54W
Mbout, *Mauritania* **90** 16 1N 12 38W
Mbozi □, *Tanzania* **93** 9 0 S 32 50 E
Mbrés, *C.A.R.* **94** 6 40N 19 48 E
Mbuji-Mayi, *Zaïre* **92** 6 9 S 23 40 E
Mbulu, *Tanzania* **92** 3 45 S 35 30 E
Mbulu □, *Tanzania* **92** 3 52 S 35 33 E
Mburucuyá, *Argentina* **140** 28 1 S 58 14W
Mcherrah, *Algeria* **84** 27 0N 4 30W
Mchinja, *Tanzania* **93** 9 44 S 39 45 E
Mchinji, *Malawi* **93** 13 47 S 32 58 E
Mdennah, *Mauritania* **84** 24 37N 6 0W
Mé Maoya, *N. Cal.* **68** 21 22 S 165 22 E
Mead, L., *U.S.A.* **125** 36 1N 114 44W
Meade, *U.S.A.* **121** 37 18N 100 25W
Meadow, *Australia* **79** 26 35 S 114 40 E
Meadow Lake, *Canada* **111** 54 10N 108 26W
Meadow Lake Prov. Park, *Canada* **111** 54 27N 109 0W

Meadow Valley Wash →, U.S.A. .. 125 36 39N 114 35W
Meadville, Mo., U.S.A. 118 39 47N 93 18W
Meadville, Pa., U.S.A. 116 41 39N 80 9W
Meaford, Canada 108 44 36N 80 35W
Mealhada, Portugal ... 22 40 22N 8 27W
Mealy Mts., Canada .. 105 53 10N 58 0W
Meander River, Canada 110 59 2N 117 42W
Meares, C., U.S.A. ... 122 45 37N 124 0W
Mearim →, Brazil ... 138 3 4S 44 35W
Meath □, Ireland 15 53 32N 6 40W
Meath Park, Canada .. 111 53 27N 105 22W
Meatian, Australia .... 74 35 34S 143 21 E
Meaulne, France ..... 20 46 36N 2 36 E
Meaux, France .... 19 48 58N 2 50 E
Mecanhelas, Mozam. . 93 15 12S 35 54 E
Mecaya →, Colombia 134 0 29N 75 11W
Mecca = Makkah, Si. Arabia .... 88 21 30N 39 54 E
Mecca, U.S.A. 125 33 37N 116 3W
Mechanicsburg, U.S.A. 116 40 12N 77 0W
Mechanicsville, U.S.A. 118 41 54N 91 16W
Mechanicville, U.S.A. 117 42 54N 73 41W
Mechara, Ethiopia .... 89 8 36N 40 20 E
Mechelen, Antwerpen, Belgium .... 17 51 2N 4 29 E
Mechelen, Limburg, Belgium .... 17 50 58N 5 41 E
Mecheria, Algeria 85 33 35N 0 18W
Mechernich, W. Germany .... 30 50 35N 6 39 E
Mechetinskaya, U.S.S.R. .... 39 46 45N 40 32 E
Mechra Benâbbou, Morocco 84 32 39N 7 48W
Mecitözü, Turkey .... 38 40 32N 35 17 E
Mecklenburger Bucht, E. Germany .... 30 54 20N 11 40 E
Meconta, Mozam. .... 93 14 59S 39 50 E
Meda, Australia ...... 78 17 22S 123 59 E
Meda, Portugal 22 40 57N 7 18W
Medak, India .... 50 18 1N 78 15 E
Medan, Indonesia .... 56 3 40N 98 38 E
Médanos, Argentina .. 142 38 50S 62 42W
Medanosa, Pta., Argentina 142 48 8S 66 0W
Medaryville, U.S.A. .. 119 41 4N 86 55W
Medawachchiya, Sri Lanka .... 51 8 30N 80 30 E
Medéa, Algeria ...... 85 36 12N 2 50 E
Médégué, Gabon ..... 94 0 37N 10 8 E
Medeiros Neto, Brazil 139 17 20S 40 14W
Medellín, Colombia .. 134 6 15N 75 35W
Medemblik, Neths. ... 16 52 46N 5 8 E
Médenine, Tunisia .... 86 33 21N 10 30 E
Mederdra, Mauritania . 90 17 0N 15 38W
Medford, Mass., U.S.A. 117 42 25N 71 7W
Medford, Oreg., U.S.A. 122 42 20N 122 52W
Medford, Wis., U.S.A. 120 45 9N 90 21W
Medgidia, Romania ... 34 44 15N 28 19 E
Medgun →, Australia 77 29 3S 149 24 E
Medi, Sudan .... 89 5 4N 30 42 E
Media Agua, Argentina 140 31 58S 68 25W
Media Luna, Argentina 140 34 45S 66 44W
Mediapolis, U.S.A. ... 118 41 0N 91 10W
Mediaş, Romania ..... 34 46 9N 24 22 E
Medical Lake, U.S.A. 122 47 35N 117 42W
Medicina, Italy ...... 27 44 29N 11 38 E
Medicine Bow, U.S.A. 122 41 56N 106 11W
Medicine Bow Pk., U.S.A. 122 41 21N 106 19W
Medicine Bow Ra., U.S.A. 122 41 10N 106 25W
Medicine Hat, Canada 111 50 0N 110 45W
Medicine Lake, U.S.A. 120 48 30N 104 30W
Medicine Lodge, U.S.A. 121 37 20N 98 37W
Medina = Al Madīnah, Si. Arabia .... 46 24 35N 39 52 E
Medina, Brazil 139 16 15S 41 29W
Medina, Colombia 134 4 30N 73 21W
Medina, N. Dak., U.S.A. 120 46 57N 99 20W
Medina, N.Y., U.S.A. 116 43 15N 78 27W
Medina, Ohio, U.S.A. 116 41 9N 81 50W
Medina →, U.S.A. ... 121 29 10N 98 20W
Medina de Ríoseco, Spain 22 41 53N 5 3W
Medina del Campo, Spain 22 41 18N 4 55W
Medina L., U.S.A. ... 121 29 35N 98 58W
Medina-Sidonia, Spain 23 36 28N 5 57W
Medinaceli, Spain 24 41 12N 2 30W
Medinipur, India ..... 49 22 25N 87 21 E
Mediterranean Sea, Europe .... 6 35 0N 15 0 E
Medjerda, O. →, Tunisia .... 86 37 7N 10 13 E
Medley, Canada 111 54 25N 110 16W
Médoc, France 20 45 10N 0 50W
Medora, U.S.A. 119 38 49N 86 10W
Médouneu, Gabon .... 94 0 57N 10 47 E
Medstead, Canada 111 53 19N 108 5W
Medulin, Yugoslavia .. 27 44 49N 13 55 E
Medveda, Yugoslavia . 33 42 50N 21 32 E
Medveditsa →, R.S.F.S.R., U.S.S.R. 37 49 35N 42 41 E
Medveditsa →, R.S.F.S.R., U.S.S.R. 37 57 5N 37 30 E
Medvedok, U.S.S.R. .. 37 57 20N 50 1 E
Medvezhi, Ostrava, U.S.S.R. .... 41 71 0N 161 0 E
Medvezhyegorsk, U.S.S.R. .... 40 63 0N 34 25 E
Medway →, U.K. .... 13 51 28N 0 45 E
Medyn, U.S.S.R. ..... 37 54 58N 35 52 E
Medzilaborce, Czech. . 32 49 17N 21 52 E
Meeberrie, Australia .. 79 26 57S 115 51 E
Meekatharra, Australia 79 26 32S 118 29 E
Meeker, U.S.A. 122 40 1N 107 58W
Meeniyan, Australia .. 74 38 35S 146 0 E
Meer, Belgium .... 17 51 27N 4 45 E
Meerane, E. Germany 30 50 51N 12 30 E
Meerbeke, Belgium ... 17 50 50N 4 3 E
Meerhout, Belgium ... 17 51 7N 5 4 E
Meerle, Belgium ..... 17 51 29N 4 48 E
Meerlieu, Australia ... 75 38 2S 147 24 E
Meersburg, W. Germany .... 31 47 42N 9 16 E
Meerssen, Neths. ..... 17 50 53N 5 50 E
Meerut, India .... 48 29 1N 77 42 E
Meeteetse, U.S.A. ... 122 44 10N 108 56W
Meeuwen, Belgium ... 17 51 6N 5 31 E
Mega, Ethiopia ...... 89 3 57N 38 19 E
Megálo Petalí, Greece . 35 38 0N 24 15 E
Megalópolis, Greece .. 35 37 25N 22 7 E
Meganísi, Greece ..... 35 38 39N 20 48 E
Mégantic, L., Canada . 107 45 32N 70 53W
Mégantic, Mt., Canada 107 45 28N 71 9W
Mégara, Greece ...... 35 37 58N 23 22 E
Megarine, Algeria .... 85 33 14N 6 2 E
Megève, France ...... 21 45 51N 6 37 E
Meghalaya □, India .. 52 25 50N 91 0 E
Meghezez, Mt., Ethiopia .... 89 9 18N 39 26 E
Meghna →, Bangla. .. 52 22 50N 90 50 E
Megiddo, Israel ...... 44 32 36N 35 11 E
Mégiscane →, Canada 106 48 29N 75 38W
Mégiscane, L., Canada 106 48 35N 75 55W
Megiste, Greece ...... 46 36 8N 29 34 E
Mehadia, Romania .... 34 44 56N 22 23 E
Mehaigne →, Belgium 17 50 32N 5 13 E
Mehaïguene, O. →, Algeria .... 85 32 15N 2 59 E
Meheisa, Sudan ...... 88 19 38N 32 57 E
Mehndawal, India .... 49 26 58N 83 5 E
Mehun-sur-Yèvre, France .... 19 47 10N 2 13 E
Mei Jiang →, China .. 59 24 25N 116 35 E
Mei Xian, Guangdong, China .... 59 24 16N 116 6 E
Mei Xian, Shaanxi, China .... 60 34 18N 107 55 E
Meia Ponte →, Brazil 139 18 32S 49 36W
Meicheng, China ..... 59 29 29N 119 16 E
Meichengzhen, China . 59 28 9N 111 40 E
Meichuan, China ..... 59 30 8N 115 31 E
Meiganga, Cameroon . 94 6 30N 14 25 E
Meijel, Neths. .... 17 51 21N 5 53 E
Meiktila, Burma ..... 52 20 53N 95 54 E
Meiningen, E. Germany 30 50 32N 10 25 E
Meio →, Brazil 139 13 36S 44 7W
Me'ir Shefeya, Israel .. 44 32 35N 34 58 E
Meira, Sierra de, Spain 22 43 15N 7 15W
Meiringen, Switz. ..... 31 46 43N 8 12 E
Meishan, China ...... 58 30 3N 103 23 E
Meissen, E. Germany . 30 51 10N 13 29 E
Meissner, W. Germany 30 51 13N 9 51 E
Meitan, China .... 58 27 45N 107 29 E
Mejillones, Chile 140 23 10S 70 30W
Meka, Australia ...... 79 27 25S 116 48 E
Mékambo, Gabon .... 94 1 2N 13 50 E
Mekdela, Ethiopia .... 89 11 24N 39 10 E
Mekele, Ethiopia ..... 89 13 33N 39 30 E
Mékinac, L., Canada . 107 47 3N 72 41W
Meknès, Morocco 84 33 57N 5 33W
Meko, Nigeria .... 91 7 27N 2 52 E
Mekong →, Asia .... 55 9 30N 106 15 E
Mekongga, Indonesia . 57 3 39S 121 15 E
Melagiri Hills, India .. 51 12 20N 77 30 E
Melah, Sebkhet el, Algeria 85 29 20N 1 30W
Melaka, Malaysia .... 55 2 15N 102 15 E
Melalap, Malaysia .... 56 5 10N 116 5 E
Mélambes, Greece .... 35 35 8N 24 40 E
Melanesia, Pac. Oc. .. 66 4 0S 155 0 E
Melapalaiyam, India .. 51 8 39N 77 44 E
Melbourne, Australia . 74 37 50S 145 0 E
Melbourne, Fla., U.S.A. 115 28 4N 80 35W
Melbourne, Iowa, U.S.A. 118 41 57N 93 6W
Melcher, U.S.A. 118 41 13N 93 15W
Melchor Múzquiz, Mexico 126 27 50N 101 30W
Melchor Ocampo, Mexico 126 24 52N 101 40W
Méldola, Italy .... 27 44 7N 12 3 E
Meldorf, W. Germany 30 54 5N 9 5 E
Meldrum Bay, Canada 108 45 56N 83 6W
Mêle-sur-Sarthe, Le, France .... 18 48 31N 0 22 E
Meleden, Somali Rep. 98 10 25N 49 51 E
Melegnano, Italy ..... 26 45 21N 9 20 E
Melenci, Yugoslavia .. 33 45 32N 20 20 E
Melenki, U.S.S.R. ... 37 55 20N 41 37 E
Mélèzes →, Canada .. 103 57 30N 71 0W
Melfi, Chad .... 87 11 0N 17 59 E
Melfi, Italy .... 29 41 0N 15 33 E
Melfort, Canada 111 52 50N 104 37W
Melfort, Zimb. .... 93 18 0S 31 25 E
Melgaço, Madeira 22 42 7N 8 15W
Melgar de Fernamental, Spain 22 42 27N 4 17W
Melhus, Norway ..... 10 63 17N 10 18 E
Melick, Neths. .... 17 51 10N 6 1 E
Meligalá, Greece ..... 35 37 15N 21 59 E
Melilla, Morocco 85 35 21N 2 57W
Melilot, Israel .... 44 31 22N 34 37 E
Melipilla, Chile 140 33 42S 71 15W
Melita, Canada 111 49 15N 101 0W
Mélito di Porto Salvo, Italy .... 29 37 55N 15 47 E
Melitopol, U.S.S.R. .. 38 46 50N 35 22 E
Melk, Austria .... 33 48 13N 15 20 E
Mellan-Fryken, Sweden 10 59 45N 13 10 E
Mellansel, Sweden .... 8 63 25N 18 17 E
Melle, Belgium .... 17 51 0N 3 49 E
Melle, France 20 46 14N 0 10W
Melle, W. Germany .. 30 52 12N 8 20 E
Mellégue, O. →, Tunisia .... 86 36 32N 8 51 E
Mellen, U.S.A. 120 46 19N 90 36W
Mellerud, Sweden .... 11 58 41N 12 28 E
Mellette, U.S.A. 120 45 11N 98 29W
Mellid, Spain 22 42 55N 8 1W
Mellit, Sudan .... 89 14 7N 25 34 E
Mellizo Sur, Cerro, Chile 142 48 33S 73 10W
Mellrichstadt, W. Germany .... 31 50 26N 10 19 E
Melnik, Bulgaria ..... 35 41 30N 23 25 E
Mělník, Czech. .... 32 50 22N 14 23 E
Melo, Uruguay 141 32 20S 54 10W
Melolo, Indonesia .... 57 9 53S 120 40 E
Melouprey, Cambodia 54 13 48N 105 16 E
Melovoye, U.S.S.R. .. 39 49 25N 40 5 E
Melrhir, Chott, Algeria 85 34 25N 6 24 E
Melrose, N.S.W., Australia .... 73 32 42S 146 57 E
Melrose, W. Austral., Australia .... 79 27 50S 121 15 E
Melrose, U.K. 14 53 35N 2 44W
Melrose, Iowa, U.S.A. 118 40 59N 93 3W
Melrose, N. Mex., U.S.A. 121 34 27N 103 33W
Melsele, Belgium ..... 17 51 13N 4 17 E
Melstone, U.S.A. 122 46 36N 107 50W
Melsungen, W. Germany .... 30 51 8N 9 34 E
Melton Mowbray, U.K. 12 52 46N 0 52W
Melun, France .... 19 48 32N 2 39 E
Melur, India .... 51 10 2N 78 23 E
Melut, Sudan .... 89 10 30N 32 13 E
Melville, Canada 111 50 55N 102 50W
Melville, C., Australia 72 14 11S 144 30 E
Melville, L., Canada .. 105 53 30N 60 0W
Melville B., Australia . 72 12 0S 136 45 E
Melville I., Australia .. 78 11 30S 131 0 E
Melville I., Canada ... 144 75 30N 112 0W
Melville Pen., Canada 103 68 0N 84 0W
Melvin →, Canada ... 110 59 11N 117 31W
Memaliaj, Albania .... 35 40 25N 19 58 E
Memba, Mozam. ..... 93 14 11S 40 30 E
Memboro, Indonesia .. 57 9 30S 119 30 E
Membrilla, Spain 25 38 59N 3 21W
Memel = Klaipeda, U.S.S.R. .... 36 55 43N 21 10 E
Memel, S. Africa ..... 97 27 38S 29 36 E
Memmingen, W. Germany .... 31 47 59N 10 12 E
Mempawah, Indonesia 56 0 30N 109 5 E
Memphis, Mo., U.S.A. 118 40 28N 92 10W
Memphis, Tenn., U.S.A. 121 35 7N 90 0W
Memphis, Tex., U.S.A. 121 34 45N 100 30W
Memphrémagog, L., Canada 107 45 8N 72 17W
Mena, U.S.A. 121 34 40N 94 15W
Mena →, Ethiopia ... 89 5 40N 40 50 E
Menai Strait, U.K. 12 53 14N 4 10W
Ménaka, Mali .... 91 15 59N 2 18 E
Menaldum, Neths. .... 16 53 13N 5 40 E
Menan = Chao Phraya →, Thailand 54 13 32N 100 36 E
Menangle, Australia .. 76 34 6S 150 44 E
Menarandra →, Madag. .... 97 25 17S 44 30 E
Menard, U.S.A. 121 30 57N 99 48W
Menasha, U.S.A. 114 44 13N 88 27W
Menate, Indonesia .... 56 0 12S 113 3 E
Mendawai →, Indonesia .... 56 3 30S 113 0 E
Mende, France .... 20 44 31N 3 30 E
Mendebo Mts., Ethiopia .... 89 7 0N 39 22 E
Menderes →, Turkey . 46 37 25N 28 45 E
Mendez, Mexico 127 25 7N 98 34W
Mendhar, India ...... 49 33 35N 74 10 E
Mendi, Ethiopia ...... 89 9 47N 35 4 E
Mendi, Papua N. G. ... 69 6 11S 143 39 E
Mendip Hills, U.K. ... 13 51 17N 2 40W
Mendocino, U.S.A. ... 122 39 26N 123 50W
Mendocino, C., U.S.A. 122 40 26N 124 25W
Mendocino Seascarp, Pac. Oc. 67 41 0N 140 0W
Mendon, U.S.A. 119 42 0N 85 27W
Mendooran, Australia . 77 31 50S 149 6 E
Mendota, Calif., U.S.A. 124 36 46N 120 24W
Mendota, Ill., U.S.A. . 118 41 35N 89 5W
Mendoza, Argentina .. 140 32 50S 68 52W
Mendoza □, Argentina 140 33 0S 69 0W
Mene Grande, Venezuela 134 9 49N 70 56W
Menemen, Turkey .... 46 38 34N 27 3 E
Menen, Belgium ..... 17 50 47N 3 7 E
Menéndez, L., Argentina 142 42 40S 71 51W
Menfi, Italy .... 28 37 36N 12 57 E
Mengcheng, China ... 59 33 18N 116 31 E
Mengdingjie, China ... 58 23 31N 98 58 E
Mengeš, Yugoslavia .. 27 46 24N 14 35 E
Menggala, Indonesia .. 56 4 30S 105 15 E
Menghai, China ...... 58 21 49N 100 55 E
Mengíbar, Spain 23 37 58N 3 48W
Mengjin, China ...... 60 34 55N 112 45 E
Mengla, China .... 58 21 20N 101 25 E
Menglian, China ..... 58 22 21N 99 27 E
Mengoub, Algeria 84 29 49N 5 26W
Mengshan, China .... 59 24 14N 110 55 E
Mengyin, China ...... 61 35 40N 117 58 E
Mengzhe, China ...... 58 22 2N 100 15 E
Mengzi, China .... 58 23 20N 103 22 E
Menihek L., Canada .. 105 54 0N 67 0W
Menin = Menen, Belgium .... 17 50 47N 3 7 E
Menindee, Australia .. 73 32 20S 142 25 E
Menindee, L., Australia 73 32 20S 142 25 E
Meningie, Australia ... 73 35 35S 139 0 E
Menlo Park, U.S.A. .. 124 37 27N 122 12W
Menominee, U.S.A. .. 114 45 9N 87 39W
Menominee →, U.S.A. 114 45 5N 87 36W
Menomonee Falls, U.S.A. 119 43 11N 88 7W
Menomonie, U.S.A. .. 120 44 50N 91 54W
Menongue, Angola ... 95 14 48S 17 52 E
Menorca, Spain ...... 24 40 0N 4 0 E
Mentakab, Malaysia .. 55 3 29N 102 21 E
Mentawai, Kepulauan, Indonesia .... 56 2 0S 99 0 E
Menton, France ...... 21 43 50N 7 29 E
Mentone, U.S.A. 119 41 10N 86 2W
Mentor, U.S.A. 116 41 40N 81 21W
Mentz Dam, S. Africa 96 33 10S 25 9 E
Menyamya, Papua N. G. .... 69 7 10S 145 59 E
Menzel-Bourguiba, Tunisia .... 86 37 9N 9 49 E
Menzel Chaker, Tunisia 86 35 0N 10 26 E
Menzel-Temime, Tunisia .... 86 36 46N 11 0 E
Menzies, Australia .... 79 29 40S 120 58 E
Me'ona, Israel .... 44 33 1N 35 15 E
Meoqui, Mexico 126 28 17N 105 29W
Mepaco, Mozam. .... 93 15 57S 30 48 E
Meppel, Neths. .... 114 52 42N 6 12 E
Meppen, W. Germany 30 52 41N 7 20 E
Mequinenza, Spain ... 24 41 22N 0 17 E
Mequon, U.S.A. 119 43 14N 87 59W
Mer Rouge, U.S.A. .. 121 32 47N 91 48W
Mera Lava, Vanuatu .. 68 14 25S 168 3 E
Merabéllou, Kólpos, Greece .... 35 35 10N 25 50 E
Merah North, Australia 77 30 11S 149 18 E
Merai, Papua N. G. .. 69 4 52S 152 19 E
Meramangye, L., Australia .... 79 28 25S 132 13 E
Meramec →, U.S.A. . 118 38 23N 90 54W
Meran = Merano, Italy 27 46 40N 11 10 E
Merano, Italy .... 27 46 40N 11 10 E
Merate, Italy .... 26 45 42N 9 23 E
Merauke, Indonesia .. 57 8 29S 140 24 E
Merbabu, Indonesia .. 57 7 30S 110 40 E
Merbein, Australia ... 74 34 10S 142 2 E
Merca, Somali Rep. .. 98 1 48N 44 50 E
Mercadal, Spain ...... 24 39 59N 4 5 E
Mercato Saraceno, Italy 27 43 57N 12 11 E
Merced, U.S.A. 124 37 18N 120 30W
Merced Pk., U.S.A. .. 124 37 36N 119 24W
Mercedes, Buenos Aires, Argentina 140 34 40S 59 30W
Mercedes, Corrientes, Argentina 140 29 10S 58 5W
Mercedes, San Luis, Argentina 140 33 40S 65 21W
Mercedes, Uruguay ... 140 33 12S 58 0W
Merceditas, Chile 140 28 20S 70 35W
Mercer, N.Z. .... 80 37 16S 175 5 E
Mercer, Mo., U.S.A. . 118 40 31N 93 32W
Mercer, Pa., U.S.A. .. 116 41 14N 80 13W
Merchtem, Belgium ... 17 50 58N 4 14 E
Mercier, Bolivia 136 10 42S 68 5W
Mercier, Canada 107 45 19N 73 45W
Mercury, U.S.A. 125 36 40N 115 58W
Mercy C., Canada 103 65 0N 63 30W
Merdrignac, France ... 18 48 11N 2 27W
Mere, Belgium .... 17 50 55N 3 58 E
Meredith, Australia ... 74 37 49S 144 5 E
Meredith, C., Falk. Is. 142 52 15S 60 40W
Meredith, L., U.S.A. . 121 35 30N 101 35W
Meredosia, U.S.A. ... 118 39 50N 90 34W
Meregh, Somali Rep. . 98 3 46N 47 18 E
Merelbeke, Belgium .. 17 51 0N 3 45 E
Méréville, France .... 19 48 20N 2 5 E
Merga = Nukheila, Sudan .... 88 19 1N 26 21 E
Mergenevsky, U.S.S.R. 39 49 59N 51 15 E
Mergui Arch. = Myeik Kyunzu, Burma .... 54 11 30N 97 30 E
Mérida, Mexico 127 20 9N 89 40W
Mérida, Spain 23 38 55N 6 25W
Mérida, Venezuela 134 8 24N 71 8W
Mérida □, Venezuela . 134 8 30N 71 10W
Mérida, Cord. de, Venezuela 134 9 0N 71 0W
Meriden, U.S.A. 117 41 33N 72 47W
Meridian, Calif., U.S.A. 124 39 9N 121 55W

Meridian, *Idaho, U.S.A.* **122** 43 41N 116 25W
Meridian, *Miss., U.S.A.* **115** 32 20N 88 42W
Meridian, *Tex., U.S.A.* **121** 31 55N 97 37W
Merimbula, *Australia* **75** 36 53 S 149 54 E
Mering, *W. Germany* **31** 48 15N 11 0 E
Meringur, *Australia* **74** 34 20 S 141 19 E
Merino, *Australia* **74** 37 44 S 141 35 E
Meriruma, *Brazil* **135** 1 15N 54 50W
Merkel, *U.S.A.* **121** 32 30N 100 0W
Merksem, *Belgium* **17** 51 16N 4 25 E
Merksplas, *Belgium* **17** 51 22N 4 52 E
Merlerault, Le, *France* **18** 48 41N 0 16 E
Mermaid Reef, *Australia* **78** 17 6 S 119 36 E
Mern, *Denmark* **11** 55 3N 12 3 E
Mernda, *Australia* **74** 37 36 S 145 6 E
Merowe, *Sudan* **88** 18 29N 31 46 E
Merredin, *Australia* **79** 31 28 S 118 18 E
Merrick, *U.K.* **14** 55 8N 4 30W
Merricks, *Australia* **74** 38 24 S 145 7 E
Merrickville, *Canada* **109** 44 55N 75 50W
Merrigum, *Australia* **74** 36 22 S 145 8 E
Merrill, *Oreg., U.S.A.* **122** 42 2N 121 37W
Merrill, *Wis., U.S.A.* **120** 45 11N 89 41W
Merrillville, *U.S.A.* **119** 41 29N 87 20W
Merriman, *U.S.A.* **120** 42 55N 101 42W
Merritt, *Canada* **110** 50 10N 120 45W
Merriwa, *Australia* **77** 32 6 S 150 22 E
Merriwagga, *Australia* **74** 33 47 S 145 43 E
Merry I., *Canada* **104** 55 29N 77 31W
Merrygoen, *Australia* **77** 31 51 S 149 12 E
Merryville, *U.S.A.* **121** 30 47N 93 31W
Mersa Fatma, *Ethiopia* **89** 14 57N 40 17 E
Mersch, *Lux.* **17** 49 44N 6 7 E
Merseburg, *E. Germany* **30** 51 20N 12 0 E
Mersey →, *U.K.* **12** 53 20N 2 56W
Merseyside □, *U.K.* **12** 53 25N 2 55W
Mersin, *Turkey* **46** 36 51N 34 36 E
Mersing, *Malaysia* **55** 2 25N 103 50 E
Merta, *India* **48** 26 39N 74 4 E
Mertert, *Lux.* **17** 49 43N 6 29 E
Merthyr Tydfil, *U.K.* **13** 51 45N 3 23W
Mértola, *Madeira* **23** 37 40N 7 40 E
Merton, *Australia* **74** 36 59 S 145 43 E
Mertzig, *Lux.* **17** 49 51N 6 1 E
Mertzon, *U.S.A.* **121** 31 17N 100 48W
Méru, *France* **19** 49 13N 2 8 E
Meru, *Kenya* **92** 0 3N 37 40 E
Meru, *Tanzania* **92** 3 15 S 36 46 E
Meru □, *Kenya* **92** 0 3N 37 46 E
Merville, *France* **19** 50 38N 2 38 E
Méry-sur-Seine, *France* **19** 48 31N 3 54 E
Merzifon, *Turkey* **38** 40 53N 35 32 E
Merzig, *W. Germany* **31** 49 26N 6 37 E
Merzouga, Erg Tin, *Algeria* **85** 24 0N 11 4 E
Mesa, *U.S.A.* **123** 33 20N 111 56W
Mesa, La, *Calif., U.S.A.* **125** 32 48N 117 5W
Mesa, La, *N. Mex., U.S.A.* **123** 32 6N 106 48W
Mesach Mellet, *Libya* **86** 24 30N 11 30 E
Mesada, *Israel* **44** 31 20N 35 19 E
Mesagne, *Italy* **29** 40 34N 17 48 E
Mesaras, Kólpos, *Greece* **35** 35 6N 24 47 E
Meschede, *W. Germany* **30** 51 20N 8 17 E
Mesfinto, *Ethiopia* **89** 13 20N 37 22 E
Mesgouez, L., *Canada* **104** 51 20N 75 0W
Meshchovsk, *U.S.S.R.* **36** 54 22N 35 17 E
Meshed = Mashhad, *Iran* **47** 36 20N 59 35 E
Meshoppen, *U.S.A.* **117** 41 36N 76 3W
Meshra er Req, *Sudan* **89** 8 25N 29 18 E
Mesick, *U.S.A.* **114** 44 24N 85 42W
Mesilinka →, *Canada* **110** 56 6N 124 30W
Mesilla, *U.S.A.* **123** 32 20N 106 50W
Meslay-du-Maine, *France* **18** 47 58N 0 33W
Mesocco, *Switz.* **31** 46 23N 9 12 E
Mesolóngion, *Greece* **35** 38 21N 21 28 E
Mesopotamia = Al Jazirah, *Iraq* **46** 33 30N 44 0 E
Mesoraca, *Italy* **29** 39 5N 16 47 E
Mesquite, *U.S.A.* **123** 36 47N 114 6W
Mess Cr. →, *Canada* **110** 57 55N 131 14W
Messac, *France* **18** 47 49N 1 50W
Messad, *Algeria* **85** 34 8N 3 30 E
Messalo →, *Mozam.* **93** 12 25 S 39 15 E
Méssaména, *Cameroon* **91** 3 48N 12 49 E
Messancy, *Belgium* **17** 49 36N 5 49 E
Messier, Canal, *Chile* **142** 48 20 S 74 33W
Messina, *Italy* **29** 38 10N 15 32 E
Messina, *S. Africa* **97** 22 20 S 30 0 E
Messina, Str. di, *Italy* **29** 38 5N 15 35 E
Messine, *Canada* **106** 46 14N 76 2W
Messíni, *Greece* **35** 37 4N 22 1 E
Messiniakós, Kólpos, *Greece* **35** 36 45N 22 5 E
Messkirch, *W. Germany* **31** 47 59N 9 7 E
Mesta →, *Bulgaria* **35** 41 30N 24 0 E
Mestanza, *Spain* **23** 38 35N 4 4W
Mestre, *Italy* **27** 45 30N 12 13 E
Mestre, Espigão, *Brazil* **139** 12 30 S 46 10W
Městys Zelezná Ruda, *Czech.* **32** 49 8N 13 15 E
Meta, *U.S.A.* **118** 38 19N 92 10W
Meta □, *Colombia* **134** 3 30N 73 0W
Meta →, *S. Amer.* **134** 6 12N 67 28W
Metairie, *U.S.A.* **121** 29 59N 90 9W
Metaline Falls, *U.S.A.* **122** 48 52N 117 22W
Metamora, *U.S.A.* **118** 40 47N 89 22W
Metán, *Argentina* **140** 25 30 S 65 0W
Metangula, *Mozam.* **93** 12 40 S 34 50 E
Metauro →, *Italy* **27** 43 50N 13 3 E
Metema, *Ethiopia* **89** 12 56N 36 13 E
Metengobalame, *Mozam.* **93** 14 49 S 34 30 E
Méthana, *Greece* **35** 37 35N 23 23 E
Methven, *N.Z.* **81** 43 38 S 171 40 E
Methy L., *Canada* **111** 56 28N 109 30W
Metil, *Mozam.* **93** 16 24 S 39 0 E
Metlakatla, *U.S.A.* **110** 55 10N 131 33W
Metlaoui, *Tunisia* **86** 34 24N 8 24 E
Metlika, *Yugoslavia* **27** 45 40N 15 20 E
Metropolis, *U.S.A.* **121** 37 10N 88 47W
Mettet, *Belgium* **17** 50 19N 4 41 E
Mettuppalaiyam, *India* **51** 11 18N 76 59 E
Mettur, *India* **51** 11 48N 77 47 E
Metulla, *Israel* **44** 33 17N 35 34 E
Metung, *Australia* **75** 37 54 S 147 52 E
Metz, *France* **19** 49 8N 6 10 E
Meulaboh, *Indonesia* **56** 4 11N 96 3 E
Meulan, *France* **19** 49 0N 1 55 E
Meung-sur-Loire, *France* **19** 47 50N 1 40 E
Meureudu, *Indonesia* **56** 5 19N 96 10 E
Meurthe →, *France* **19** 48 47N 6 9 E
Meurthe-et-Moselle □, *France* **19** 48 52N 6 0 E
Meuse □, *France* **19** 49 8N 5 25 E
Meuse →, *Europe* **17** 50 45N 5 41 E
Meuselwitz, *E. Germany* **30** 51 3N 12 18 E
Mexborough, *U.K.* **12** 53 29N 1 18W
Mexia, *U.S.A.* **121** 31 38N 96 32W
Mexiana, I., *Brazil* **138** 0 0 49 30W
Mexicali, *Mexico* **126** 32 40N 115 30W
México, *Mexico* **127** 19 20N 99 10W
Mexico, *Maine, U.S.A.* **117** 44 35N 70 30W
Mexico, *Mo., U.S.A.* **118** 39 10N 91 55W
México □, *Mexico* **126** 19 20N 99 10W
Mexico ■, *Cent. Amer.* **126** 25 0N 105 0W
Mexico, G. of, *Cent. Amer.* **127** 25 0N 90 0W
Meyenburg, *E. Germany* **30** 53 19N 12 15 E
Meymac, *France* **20** 45 32N 2 10 E
Meymaneh, *Afghan.* **47** 35 53N 64 38 E
Meyrargues, *France* **21** 43 38N 5 32 E
Meyrueis, *France* **20** 44 12N 3 27 E
Meyssac, *France* **20** 45 3N 1 40 E
Mezdra, *Bulgaria* **34** 43 12N 23 42 E
Mèze, *France* **20** 43 27N 3 36 E
Mezen, *U.S.S.R.* **40** 65 50N 44 20 E
Mezen →, *U.S.S.R.* **40** 66 11N 43 59 E
Mézenc, Mt., *France* **21** 44 54N 4 11 E
Mezha →, *U.S.S.R.* **36** 55 50N 31 45 E
Mézidon, *France* **18** 49 5N 0 1W
Mézilhac, *France* **21** 44 49N 4 21 E
Mézin, *France* **20** 44 4N 0 16 E
Mezöberény, *Hungary* **33** 46 49N 21 3 E
Mezökövácsháza, *Hungary* **33** 46 25N 20 57 E
Mezökövesd, *Hungary* **33** 47 49N 20 35 E
Mézos, *France* **20** 44 5N 1 10W
Mezötúr, *Hungary* **33** 47 0N 20 41 E
Mezquital, *Mexico* **126** 23 29N 104 23W
Mezzolombardo, *Italy* **26** 46 13N 11 5 E
Mgeta, *Tanzania* **93** 8 22 S 36 6 E
Mglin, *U.S.S.R.* **36** 53 2N 32 50 E
Mhlaba Hills, *Zimb.* **93** 18 30 S 30 30 E
Mhow, *India* **48** 22 33N 75 50 E
Mi-Shima, *Japan* **64** 34 46N 131 9 E
Miahuatlán, *Mexico* **127** 16 21N 96 36W
Miajadas, *Spain* **23** 39 9N 5 54W
Miallo, *Australia* **72** 16 28 S 145 22 E
Miami, *Ariz., U.S.A.* **123** 33 25N 110 54W
Miami, *Fla., U.S.A.* **115** 25 45N 80 15W
Miami, *Tex., U.S.A.* **121** 35 44N 100 38W
Miami →, *U.S.A.* **114** 39 20N 84 40W
Miami Beach, *U.S.A.* **115** 25 49N 80 6W
Miamisburg, *U.S.A.* **119** 39 40N 84 11W
Mian Xian, *China* **60** 33 10N 106 32 E
Mianchi, *China* **60** 34 48N 111 48 E
Miāndowāb, *Iran* **46** 37 0N 46 5 E
Miandrivazo, *Madag.* **97** 19 31 S 45 29 E
Mīāneh, *Iran* **46** 37 30N 47 40 E
Mianning, *China* **58** 28 32N 102 9 E
Mianwali, *Pakistan* **48** 32 38N 71 28 E
Mianyang, *Hubei, China* **59** 30 25N 113 25 E
Mianyang, *Sichuan, China* **58** 31 22N 104 47 E
Mianzhu, *China* **58** 31 22N 104 7 E
Miaoli, *Taiwan* **59** 24 37N 120 49 E
Miarinarivo, *Madag.* **97** 18 57 S 46 55 E
Miass, *U.S.S.R.* **40** 54 59N 60 6 E
Miastko, *Poland* **32** 54 0N 16 58 E
Michael, Mt., *Papua N. G.* **69** 6 27 S 145 22 E
Michelago, *Australia* **76** 35 41 S 149 11 E
Michelstadt, *W. Germany* **31** 49 40N 9 0 E
Michigan □, *U.S.A.* **113** 44 40N 85 40W
Michigan, L., *U.S.A.* **114** 44 0N 87 0W
Michigan Center, *U.S.A.* **119** 42 14N 84 20W
Michigan City, *U.S.A.* **119** 41 42N 86 56W
Michikamau L., *Canada* **105** 54 20N 63 10W
Michipicoten, *Canada* **104** 47 55N 84 55W
Michipicoten I., *Canada* **104** 47 40N 85 40W
Michoacan □, *Mexico* **126** 19 0N 102 0W
Michurin, *Bulgaria* **34** 42 9N 27 51 E
Michurinsk, *U.S.S.R.* **37** 52 58N 40 27 E
Miclere, *Australia* **72** 22 34 S 147 32 E
Mico, Pta., *Nic.* **128** 12 0N 83 30W
Micronesia, *Pac. Oc.* **66** 11 0N 160 0 E
Mid Glamorgan □, *U.K.* **13** 51 40N 3 25W
Mid-Indian Ridge, *Ind. Oc.* **66** 40 0 S 75 0 E
Mid-Oceanic Ridge, *Ind. Oc.* **66** 42 0 S 90 0 E
Midai, P., *Indonesia* **55** 3 0N 107 47 E
Midale, *Canada* **111** 49 25N 103 20W
Middagsfjället, *Sweden* **10** 63 27N 12 19 E
Middelbeers, *Neths.* **17** 51 28N 5 15 E
Middelburg, *Neths.* **17** 51 30N 3 36 E
Middelburg, *C. Prov., S. Africa* **96** 31 30 S 25 0 E
Middelburg, *Trans., S. Africa* **97** 25 49 S 29 28 E
Middelfart, *Denmark* **11** 55 30N 9 43 E
Middelharnis, *Neths.* **16** 51 46N 4 10 E
Middelkerke, *Belgium* **17** 51 11N 2 49 E
Middelrode, *Neths.* **17** 51 41N 5 26 E
Middelwit, *S. Africa* **96** 24 51 S 27 3 E
Middle →, *U.S.A.* **118** 41 26N 93 30W
Middle Alkali L., *U.S.A.* **122** 41 30N 120 3W
Middle Fork Feather →, *U.S.A.* **124** 39 35N 121 25W
Middle Loup →, *U.S.A.* **120** 41 17N 98 23W
Middle Raccoon →, *U.S.A.* **118** 41 35N 93 35W
Middleboro, *U.S.A.* **117** 41 56N 70 52W
Middleburg, *N.Y., U.S.A.* **117** 42 36N 74 19W
Middleburg, *Pa., U.S.A.* **116** 40 46N 77 5W
Middlebury, *Ind., U.S.A.* **119** 41 41N 85 42W
Middlebury, *Vt., U.S.A.* **117** 44 0N 73 9W
Middlemarch, *N.Z.* **81** 45 30 S 170 9 E
Middleport, *U.S.A.* **114** 39 0N 82 5W
Middlesboro, *U.S.A.* **115** 36 36N 83 43W
Middlesbrough, *U.K.* **12** 54 35N 1 14W
Middlesex, *Belize* **128** 17 2N 88 31W
Middlesex, *U.S.A.* **117** 40 36N 74 30W
Middleton, *Australia* **72** 22 22 S 141 32 E
Middleton, *Canada* **105** 44 57N 65 4W
Middleton, *U.S.A.* **118** 43 6N 89 30W
Middletown, *Calif., U.S.A.* **124** 38 45N 122 37W
Middletown, *Conn., U.S.A.* **117** 41 37N 72 40W
Middletown, *N.Y., U.S.A.* **117** 41 28N 74 28W
Middletown, *Ohio, U.S.A.* **119** 39 29N 84 25W
Middletown, *Pa., U.S.A.* **117** 40 12N 76 44W
Middleville, *U.S.A.* **119** 42 43N 85 28W
Midelt, *Morocco* **84** 32 46N 4 44W
Midhirst, *N.Z.* **80** 39 17 S 174 18 E
Midi, Canal du →, *France* **20** 43 45N 1 21 E
Midi d'Ossau, Pic du, *France* **20** 42 50N 0 26W
Midland, *Australia* **73** 31 54 S 115 59 E
Midland, *Canada* **108** 44 45N 79 50W
Midland, *Calif., U.S.A.* **125** 33 52N 114 48W
Midland, *Mich., U.S.A.* **104** 43 37N 84 17W
Midland, *Pa., U.S.A.* **116** 40 39N 80 27W
Midland, *Tex., U.S.A.* **121** 32 0N 102 3W
Midlands □, *Zimb.* **93** 19 40 S 29 0 E
Midleton, *Ireland* **15** 51 52N 8 12W
Midlothian, *U.S.A.* **121** 32 30N 97 0W
Midongy, Tangorombohitr' i, *Madag.* **97** 23 30 S 47 0 E
Midongy Atsimo, *Madag.* **97** 23 35 S 47 1 E
Midou →, *France* **20** 43 54N 0 30W
Midouze →, *France* **20** 43 48N 0 51W
Midu, *China* **58** 25 18N 100 30 E
Midway Is., *Pac. Oc.* **66** 28 13N 177 22W
Midway Wells, *U.S.A.* **125** 32 41N 115 7W
Midwest, *U.S.A.* **122** 43 27N 106 19W
Midwolda, *Neths.* **16** 53 12N 6 52 E
Midyat, *Turkey* **46** 37 25N 41 23 E
Mie □, *Japan* **65** 34 30N 136 10 E
Miechów, *Poland* **32** 50 21N 20 5 E
Międzychód, *Poland* **32** 52 35N 15 53 E
Międzyrzec Podlaski, *Poland* **32** 51 58N 22 45 E
Międzyrzecz, *Poland* **32** 52 26N 15 35 E
Miélan, *France* **20** 43 27N 0 19 E
Mielec, *Poland* **32** 50 15N 21 25 E
Mienga, *Angola* **95** 17 12 S 19 48 E
Miercurea Ciuc, *Romania* **34** 46 21N 25 48 E
Mieres, *Spain* **22** 43 18N 5 48W
Mierlo, *Neths.* **17** 51 27N 5 37 E
Mieso, *Ethiopia* **89** 9 15N 40 43 E
Mifflintown, *U.S.A.* **116** 40 34N 77 24W
Migdāl, *Israel* **44** 32 51N 35 30 E
Migdal Afeq, *Israel* **44** 32 5N 34 58 E
Migennes, *France* **19** 47 58N 3 31 E
Migliarino, *Italy* **27** 44 45N 11 56 E
Miguel Alemán, Presa, *Mexico* **127** 18 15N 96 40W
Miguel Alves, *Brazil* **138** 4 11 S 42 55W
Miguel Calmon, *Brazil* **138** 11 26 S 40 36W
Mihara, *Japan* **64** 34 24N 133 5 E
Mihara-Yama, *Japan* **65** 34 43N 139 23 E
Mijares →, *Spain* **24** 39 55N 0 1W
Mijas, *Spain* **23** 36 36N 4 40W
Mikese, *Tanzania* **92** 6 48 S 37 55 E
Mikha-Tskhakaya, *U.S.S.R.* **39** 42 15N 42 7 E
Mikhailovka, *U.S.S.R.* **38** 47 36N 35 16 E
Mikhaylov, *U.S.S.R.* **37** 54 14N 39 0 E
Mikhaylovgrad, *Bulgaria* **34** 43 27N 23 16 E
Mikhaylovka, *Azerbaijan, U.S.S.R.* **39** 41 31N 48 52 E
Mikhaylovka, *R.S.F.S.R., U.S.S.R.* **37** 50 3N 43 5 E
Mikhnevo, *U.S.S.R.* **37** 55 4N 37 59 E
Miki, *Hyōgo, Japan* **64** 34 48N 134 59 E
Miki, *Kagawa, Japan* **64** 34 12N 134 7 E
Mikínai, *Greece* **35** 37 43N 22 46 E
Mikkeli, *Finland* **9** 61 43N 27 15 E
Mikkeli □, *Finland* **8** 62 0N 28 0 E
Mikkwa →, *Canada* **110** 58 25N 114 46W
Mikniya, *Sudan* **89** 17 0N 33 45 E
Mikołajki, *Poland* **32** 53 49N 21 37 E
Míkonos, *Greece* **35** 37 30N 25 25 E
Mikrón Dhérion, *Greece* **35** 41 19N 26 6 E
Mikulov, *Czech.* **32** 48 48N 16 39 E
Mikumi, *Tanzania* **92** 7 26 S 37 0 E
Mikuni, *Japan* **65** 36 13N 136 9 E
Mikuni-Tōge, *Japan* **65** 36 50N 138 50 E
Mikura-Jima, *Japan* **65** 33 52N 139 36 E
Milaca, *U.S.A.* **120** 45 45N 93 40W
Milagro, *Ecuador* **134** 2 11 S 79 36W
Milan = Milano, *Italy* **26** 45 28N 9 10 E
Milan, *Ill., U.S.A.* **118** 41 27N 90 34W
Milan, *Mich., U.S.A.* **119** 42 5N 83 40W
Milan, *Mo., U.S.A.* **118** 40 10N 93 5W
Milan, *Tenn., U.S.A.* **115** 35 55N 88 45W
Milang, *Australia* **73** 32 2 S 139 10 E
Milange, *Mozam.* **93** 16 3 S 35 45 E
Milano, *Italy* **26** 45 28N 9 10 E
Milâs, *Turkey* **46** 37 20N 27 50 E
Milazzo, *Italy* **29** 38 13N 15 13 E
Milbank, *U.S.A.* **120** 45 17N 96 38W
Milden, *Canada* **111** 51 29N 107 32W
Mildmay, *Canada* **108** 44 3N 81 7W
Mildura, *Australia* **74** 34 13 S 142 9 E
Mile, *China* **58** 24 28N 103 20 E
Miléai, *Greece* **35** 39 20N 23 9 E
Miles, *Australia* **73** 26 40 S 150 9 E
Miles, *U.S.A.* **121** 31 39N 100 11W
Miles City, *U.S.A.* **120** 46 24N 105 50W
Milestone, *Canada* **111** 49 59N 104 31W
Mileto, *Italy* **29** 38 37N 16 3 E
Miletto, Mte., *Italy* **29** 41 26N 14 23 E
Mileura, *Australia* **79** 26 22 S 117 20 E
Milford, *Conn., U.S.A.* **117** 41 13N 73 4W
Milford, *Del., U.S.A.* **114** 38 52N 75 27W
Milford, *Ill., U.S.A.* **119** 40 40N 87 43W
Milford, *Mass., U.S.A.* **117** 42 8N 71 30W
Milford, *Mich., U.S.A.* **119** 42 35N 83 36W
Milford, *Pa., U.S.A.* **117** 41 20N 74 47W
Milford, *Utah, U.S.A.* **123** 38 20N 113 0W
Milford, *U.S.A.* **124** 40 10N 120 22W
Milford Haven, *U.K.* **13** 51 43N 5 2W
Milford Sd., *N.Z.* **81** 44 41 S 167 47 E
Milgun, *Australia* **79** 25 6 S 118 18 E
Milḥ, Baḩr al, *Iraq* **46** 32 40N 43 35 E
Miliana, *Aïn Salah, Algeria* **85** 27 20N 2 32 E
Miliana, *Médéa, Algeria* **85** 36 20N 2 15 E
Miling, *Australia* **79** 30 30 S 116 17 E
Militello in Val di Catánia, *Italy* **29** 37 16N 14 46 E
Milk →, *N. Amer.* **122** 48 5N 106 15W
Milk, Wadi el →, *Sudan* **88** 17 55N 30 20 E
Milk River, *Canada* **110** 49 10N 112 5W
Mill, *Neths.* **17** 51 41N 5 48 E
Mill City, *U.S.A.* **122** 44 45N 122 28W
Mill I., *Antarctica* **143** 66 0 S 101 30 E
Mill Shoals, *U.S.A.* **119** 38 15N 88 21W
Mill Valley, *U.S.A.* **124** 37 54N 122 32W
Millau, *France* **20** 44 8N 3 4 E
Millbridge, *Canada* **109** 44 41N 77 36W
Millbrook, *Canada* **109** 44 10N 78 29W
Mille, *U.S.A.* **115** 33 7N 83 15W
Mille Lacs, L., *U.S.A.* **120** 46 10N 93 30W
Mille Lacs, L. des, *Canada* **104** 48 45N 90 35W
Milledgeville, *U.S.A.* **118** 41 58N 89 46W
Millen, *U.S.A.* **115** 32 50N 81 57W
Miller, *U.S.A.* **120** 44 35N 98 59W
Millerovo, *U.S.S.R.* **39** 48 57N 40 28 E
Miller's Flat, *N.Z.* **81** 45 39 S 169 23 E
Millersburg, *Ind., U.S.A.* **119** 41 32N 85 42W
Millersburg, *Ohio, U.S.A.* **116** 40 32N 81 52W
Millersburg, *Pa., U.S.A.* **116** 40 32N 76 58W
Millerton, *N.Z.* **81** 41 39 S 171 54 E
Millerton, *U.S.A.* **117** 41 57N 73 32W
Millerton L., *U.S.A.* **124** 37 0N 119 42W
Millevaches, Plateau de, *France* **20** 45 45N 2 0 E
Millicent, *Australia* **73** 37 34 S 140 21 E
Millingen, *Neths.* **16** 51 52N 6 2 E
Millinocket, *U.S.A.* **105** 45 45N 68 45W
Millmerran, *Australia* **77** 27 53 S 151 16 E
Mills L., *Canada* **110** 61 30N 118 20W
Millsboro, *U.S.A.* **116** 40 0N 80 0W

Millthorpe, *Australia* **76** 33 26 S 149 12 E
Milltown Malbay, *Ireland* **15** 52 51N 9 25W
Millville, *U.S.A.* **114** 39 22N 75 0W
Millwood Res., *U.S.A.* **121** 33 45N 94 0W
Milly-la-Forêt, *France* **19** 48 24N 2 28 E
Milna, *Yugoslavia* **27** 43 20N 16 28 E
Milne →, *Australia* **72** 21 10 S 137 33 E
Milne Inlet, *Canada* **103** 72 30N 80 0W
Milnor, *U.S.A.* **120** 46 19N 97 29W
Milo, *Canada* **110** 50 34N 112 53W
Mílos, *Greece* **35** 36 44N 24 25 E
Miloševo, *Yugoslavia* **33** 45 42N 20 20 E
Milot, *Canada* **107** 48 54N 71 49W
Milparinka, *Australia* **73** 29 46 S 141 57 E
Milroy, *U.S.A.* **119** 39 30N 85 28W
Miltenberg, *W. Germany* **31** 49 41N 9 13 E
Milton, *Australia* **76** 35 20 S 150 27 E
Milton, *Canada* **108** 43 31N 79 53W
Milton, *N.Z.* **81** 46 7 S 169 59 E
Milton, *U.K.* **14** 57 18N 4 32W
Milton, *Calif., U.S.A.* **124** 38 3N 120 51W
Milton, *Fla., U.S.A.* **115** 30 38N 87 0W
Milton, *Iowa, U.S.A.* **118** 40 41N 92 10W
Milton, *Pa., U.S.A.* **116** 41 0N 76 53W
Milton, *Wis., U.S.A.* **119** 42 47N 88 56W
Milton-Freewater, *U.S.A.* **122** 45 57N 118 24W
Milton Keynes, *U.K.* **13** 52 3N 0 42W
Miltou, *Chad* **87** 10 14N 17 26 E
Milvale, *Australia* **76** 34 18 S 147 56 E
Milverton, *Canada* **108** 43 34N 80 55W
Milwaukee, *U.S.A.* **119** 43 9N 87 58W
Milwaukie, *U.S.A.* **124** 45 27N 122 39W
Mim, *Ghana* **90** 6 57N 2 33W
Mimizan, *France* **20** 44 12N 1 13W
Mimongo, *Gabon* **94** 1 11 S 11 36 E
Mimosa, *Australia* **76** 34 34 S 147 22 E
Mimoso, *Brazil* **139** 15 10 S 48 5W
Min Jiang →, *Fujian, China* **59** 26 0N 119 35 E
Min Jiang →, *Sichuan, China* **58** 28 45N 104 40 E
Min Xian, *China* **60** 34 25N 104 0 E
Mina, *U.S.A.* **123** 38 21N 118 9W
Mina Pirquitas, *Argentina* **140** 22 40 S 66 30W
Mīnā Su'ud, *Si. Arabia* **46** 28 45N 48 28 E
Mīnā'al Aḩmadī, *Kuwait* **46** 29 5N 48 10 E
Mīnāb, *Iran* **47** 27 10N 57 1 E
Minago →, *Canada* **111** 54 33N 98 59W
Minakami, *Japan* **65** 36 49N 138 59 E
Minaki, *Canada* **111** 49 59N 94 40W
Minakuchi, *Japan* **65** 34 58N 136 10 E
Minamata, *Japan* **64** 32 10N 130 30 E
Minas, *Uruguay* **141** 34 20 S 55 10W
Minas, Sierra de las, *Guatemala* **128** 15 9N 89 31W
Minas Basin, *Canada* **105** 45 20N 64 12W
Minas de Rio Tinto, *Spain* **23** 37 42N 6 35W
Minas de San Quintín, *Spain* **23** 38 49N 4 23W
Minas Gerais □, *Brazil* **139** 18 50 S 46 0W
Minas Novas, *Brazil* **139** 17 15 S 42 36W
Minatitlán, *Mexico* **127** 17 58N 94 35W
Minbu, *Burma* **52** 20 10N 94 52 E
Minbya, *Burma* **52** 20 22N 93 16 E
Mincio →, *Italy* **26** 45 4N 10 59 E
Mindanao, *Phil.* **57** 8 0N 125 0 E
Mindanao Sea = Bohol Sea, *Phil.* **57** 9 0N 124 0 E
Mindanao Trench, *Pac. Oc.* **57** 8 0N 128 0 E
Mindel →, *W. Germany* **31** 48 31N 10 23 E
Mindelheim, *W. Germany* **31** 48 4N 10 30 E
Mindemoya, *Canada* **108** 45 44N 82 10W
Minden, *Canada* **109** 44 55N 78 43W
Minden, *La., U.S.A.* **121** 32 40N 93 20W
Minden, *Nev., U.S.A.* **124** 38 57N 119 48W
Minden, *W. Germany* **30** 52 18N 8 45 E
Mindiptana, *Indonesia* **57** 5 55 S 140 22 E
Mindon, *Burma* **52** 19 21N 94 44 E
Mindoro, *Phil.* **57** 13 0N 121 0 E
Mindoro Strait, *Phil.* **57** 12 30N 120 30 E
Mindouli, *Congo* **95** 4 12 S 14 28 E
Mine, *Japan* **64** 34 12N 131 7 E
Minehead, *U.K.* **13** 51 12N 3 29W
Mineiros, *Brazil* **137** 17 34 S 52 34W
Mineola, *U.S.A.* **121** 32 40N 95 30W
Mineral King, *U.S.A.* **124** 36 27N 118 36W
Mineral Point, *U.S.A.* **118** 42 52N 90 11W
Mineral Wells, *U.S.A.* **121** 32 50N 98 5W
Mineralnyye Vody, *U.S.S.R.* **39** 44 2N 43 8 E
Minersville, *Pa., U.S.A.* **117** 40 11N 76 17W
Minersville, *Utah, U.S.A.* **123** 38 14N 112 58W
Minerva, *U.S.A.* **116** 40 43N 81 8W
Minervino Murge, *Italy* **29** 41 6N 16 4 E
Minetto, *U.S.A.* **117** 43 24N 76 28W
Mingan, *Canada* **105** 50 20N 64 0W
Mingechaur, *U.S.S.R.* **39** 40 45N 47 0 E
Mingechaurskoye Vdkhr., *U.S.S.R.* **39** 40 56N 47 20 E
Mingela, *Australia* **72** 19 52 S 146 38 E
Mingenew, *Australia* **79** 29 12 S 115 21 E
Mingera Cr. →, *Australia* **72** 20 38 S 137 45 E
Minggang, *China* **59** 32 24N 114 3 E
Mingin, *Burma* **52** 22 50N 94 30 E
Minglanilla, *Spain* **24** 39 34N 1 38W
Minglun, *China* **58** 25 10N 108 21 E
Mingorria, *Spain* **22** 40 45N 4 40W
Mingt'iehkaitafan = Mintaka Pass, *Pakistan* **49** 37 0N 74 58 E
Mingxi, *China* **59** 26 18N 117 12 E
Mingyuegue, *China* **61** 43 2N 128 50 E
Minhou, *China* **59** 26 0N 119 15 E
Minićevo, *Yugoslavia* **33** 43 42N 22 18 E
Minidoka, *U.S.A.* **122** 42 47N 113 34W
Minier, *U.S.A.* **118** 40 26N 89 19W
Minigwal L., *Australia* **79** 29 31 S 123 14 E
Minilya, *Australia* **79** 23 55 S 114 0 E
Minilya →, *Australia* **79** 23 45 S 114 0 E
Mininera, *Australia* **74** 37 37 S 142 58 E
Minipi, L., *Canada* **105** 52 25N 60 45W
Minj, *Papua N. G.* **69** 5 54 S 144 37 E
Mink L., *Canada* **110** 61 54N 117 40W
Minna, *Nigeria* **91** 9 37N 6 30 E
Minneapolis, *Kans., U.S.A.* **120** 39 11N 97 40W
Minneapolis, *Minn., U.S.A.* **120** 44 58N 93 20W
Minnedosa, *Canada* **111** 50 14N 99 50W
Minnesota □, *U.S.A.* **120** 46 40N 94 0W
Minnesund, *Norway* **10** 60 23N 11 14 E
Minnie Creek, *Australia* **79** 24 3 S 115 42 E
Minnitaki L., *Canada* **104** 49 57N 92 10W
Mino, *Japan* **65** 35 32N 136 55 E
Miño →, *Spain* **22** 41 52N 8 40W
Mino-Kamo, *Japan* **65** 35 23N 137 2 E
Mino-Mikawa-Kōgen, *Japan* **65** 35 10N 137 23 E
Minobu, *Japan* **65** 35 22N 138 26 E
Minobu-Sanchi, *Japan* **65** 35 14N 138 20 E
Minonk, *U.S.A.* **118** 40 54N 89 2W
Minooka, *U.S.A.* **119** 41 27N 88 16W
Minorca = Menorca, *Spain* **24** 40 0N 4 0 E
Minore, *Australia* **76** 32 14 S 148 27 E
Minot, *U.S.A.* **120** 48 10N 101 15W
Minqin, *China* **60** 38 38N 103 20 E
Minqing, *China* **59** 26 15N 118 50 E
Minquiers, Les, *Chan. Is.* **18** 48 58N 2 8W
Minsen, *W. Germany* **30** 53 43N 7 58 E
Minsk, *U.S.S.R.* **36** 53 52N 27 30 E
Mińsk Mazowiecki, *Poland* **32** 52 10N 21 33 E
Minster, *U.S.A.* **119** 40 24N 84 23W
Mintaka Pass, *Pakistan* **49** 37 0N 74 58 E
Minthami, *Burma* **52** 23 55N 94 16 E
Minto, *U.S.A.* **102** 64 55N 149 20W
Minton, *Canada* **111** 49 10N 104 35W
Mintoum, *Gabon* **94** 0 27N 12 16 E
Minturn, *U.S.A.* **122** 39 35N 106 25W
Minturno, *Italy* **28** 41 15N 13 43 E
Minûf, *Egypt* **88** 30 26N 30 52 E
Minusinsk, *U.S.S.R.* **41** 53 50N 91 20 E
Minutang, *India* **52** 28 15N 96 30 E
Minvoul, *Gabon* **94** 2 9N 12 8 E
Minya el Qamh, *Egypt* **88** 30 31N 31 21 E
Minyip, *Australia* **74** 36 29 S 142 36 E
Mionica, *Yugoslavia* **33** 44 14N 20 6 E
Miquelon, *Canada* **106** 49 25N 76 27W
Mir, *Niger* **91** 14 5N 11 59 E
Mir-Bashir, *U.S.S.R.* **39** 40 20N 46 58 E
Mira, *Italy* **27** 45 26N 12 9 E
Mira, *Portugal* **22** 40 26N 8 44W
Mira →, *Colombia* **134** 1 36N 79 1W
Mira →, *Portugal* **23** 37 43N 8 47W
Mira por vos Cay, *Bahamas* **129** 22 9N 74 30W
Mirabella Eclano, *Italy* **29** 41 3N 14 59 E
Miracema do Norte, *Brazil* **138** 9 33 S 48 24W
Mirador, *Brazil* **138** 6 22 S 44 22W
Miraflores, *Colombia* **134** 1 25N 72 13W
Miraj, *India* **50** 16 50N 74 45 E
Miram, *Australia* **72** 21 15 S 148 55 E
Miram Shah, *Pakistan* **48** 33 0N 70 2 E
Miramar, *Argentina* **140** 38 15 S 57 50W
Miramar, *Mozam.* **97** 23 50 S 35 35 E
Miramas, *France* **21** 43 33N 4 59 E
Mirambeau, *France* **20** 45 23N 0 35W
Miramichi B., *Canada* **105** 47 15N 65 0W
Miramont-de-Guyenne, *France* **20** 44 37N 0 21 E
Miranda, *Brazil* **137** 20 10 S 56 15W
Miranda □, *Venezuela* **134** 10 15N 66 25W
Miranda →, *Brazil* **137** 19 25 S 57 20W
Miranda de Ebro, *Spain* **24** 42 41N 2 57W
Miranda do Corvo, *Spain* **22** 40 6N 8 20W
Miranda do Douro, *Portugal* **22** 41 30N 6 16W
Mirande, *France* **20** 43 31N 0 25 E
Mirandela, *Portugal* **22** 41 32N 7 10W
Mirando City, *U.S.A.* **121** 27 28N 98 59W
Mirandola, *Italy* **26** 44 53N 11 2 E
Mirandópolis, *Brazil* **141** 21 9 S 51 6W
Mirango, *Malawi* **93** 13 32 S 34 58 E
Mirano, *Italy* **27** 45 29N 12 6 E
Miŕassol, *Brazil* **141** 20 46 S 49 28W
Mirbāţ, *Oman* **45** 17 0N 54 45 E
Mirboo North, *Australia* **75** 38 24 S 146 10 E
Mirear, *Egypt* **88** 23 15N 35 41 E
Mirebeau, *Côte-d'Or, France* **19** 47 25N 5 20 E
Mirebeau, *Vienne, France* **18** 46 49N 0 10 E
Mirecourt, *France* **19** 48 20N 6 10 E
Mirgorod, *U.S.S.R.* **36** 49 58N 33 37 E
Miri, *Malaysia* **56** 4 23N 113 59 E
Miriam Vale, *Australia* **72** 24 20 S 151 33 E
Mirim, L., *S. Amer.* **141** 32 45 S 52 50W
Mirimire, *Venezuela* **134** 11 10N 68 43W
Miriti, *Brazil* **137** 6 15 S 59 0W
Mirnyy, *Antarctica* **143** 66 33 S 93 1 E
Mirnyy, *U.S.S.R.* **41** 62 33N 113 53 E
Mirond L., *Canada* **111** 55 6N 102 47W
Mirpur, *Pakistan* **49** 33 32N 73 56 E
Mirpur Bibiwari, *Pakistan* **48** 28 33N 67 44 E
Mirpur Khas, *Pakistan* **48** 25 30N 69 0 E
Mirpur Sakro, *Pakistan* **48** 24 33N 67 41 E
Mirria, *Niger* **91** 13 43N 9 7 E
Mirror, *Canada* **110** 52 30N 113 7W
Mîrşani, *Romania* **34** 44 1N 23 59 E
Miryang, *S. Korea* **61** 35 31N 128 44 E
Mirzaani, *U.S.S.R.* **39** 41 24N 46 5 E
Mirzapur, *India* **49** 25 10N 82 34 E
Mirzapur-cum-Vindhyachal = Mirzapur, *India* **49** 25 10N 82 34 E
Misantla, *Mexico* **127** 19 56N 96 50W
Miscou I., *Canada* **105** 47 57N 64 31W
Mish'āb, Ra'as al, *Si. Arabia* **46** 28 15N 48 43 E
Mishagua →, *Peru* **136** 11 12 S 72 58W
Mishan, *China* **62** 45 37N 131 48 E
Mishawaka, *U.S.A.* **119** 41 40N 86 8W
Mishbih, Gebel, *Egypt* **88** 22 38N 34 44 E
Mishima, *Japan* **65** 35 10N 138 52 E
Mishmar Ayyalon, *Israel* **44** 31 52N 34 57 E
Mishmar Ha' Emeq, *Israel* **44** 32 37N 35 7 E
Mishmar Ha Negev, *Israel* **44** 31 22N 34 48 E
Mishmar Ha Yarden, *Israel* **44** 33 0N 35 36 E
Mishmi Hills, *India* **52** 29 0N 96 0 E
Misilmeri, *Italy* **28** 38 2N 13 25 E
Misima I., *Papua N. G.* **69** 10 40 S 152 45 E
Misión, *Mexico* **125** 32 6N 116 53W
Misión, La, *Mexico* **126** 32 5N 116 50W
Misión Fagnano, *Argentina* **142** 54 32 S 67 17W
Misiones □, *Argentina* **141** 27 0 S 55 0W
Misiones □, *Paraguay* **140** 27 0 S 56 0W
Miskīn, *Oman* **47** 23 44N 56 52 E
Miskitos, Cayos, *Nic.* **128** 14 26N 82 50W
Miskolc, *Hungary* **33** 48 7N 20 50 E
Misoke, *Zaïre* **92** 0 42 S 28 2 E
Misool, *Indonesia* **57** 1 52 S 130 10 E
Misrātah, *Libya* **86** 32 24N 15 3 E
Misrātah □, *Libya* **86** 29 0N 16 0 E
Misriç, *Turkey* **46** 37 55N 41 40 E
Missanabie, *Canada* **104** 48 20N 84 6W
Missão Velha, *Brazil* **138** 7 15 S 39 10W
Missinaibi →, *Canada* **104** 50 43N 81 29W
Missinaibi L., *Canada* **104** 48 23N 83 40W
Mission, *S. Dak., U.S.A.* **120** 43 21N 100 36W
Mission, *Tex., U.S.A.* **121** 26 15N 98 20W
Mission City, *Canada* **110** 49 10N 122 15W
Mission Viejo, *U.S.A.* **125** 33 41N 117 46W
Missisa L., *Canada* **104** 52 20N 85 7W
Mississagi →, *Canada* **108** 46 15N 83 9W
Mississagi Prov. Park, *Canada* **108** 46 30N 82 40W
Mississauga, *Canada* **108** 43 32N 79 35W
Mississinewa Res., *U.S.A.* **119** 40 46N 86 3W
Mississippi →, *U.S.A.* **121** 29 0N 89 15W
Mississippi, Delta of the, *U.S.A.* **121** 29 15N 90 30W
Mississippi L., *Canada* **106** 45 5N 76 10W
Mississippi Sd., *U.S.A.* **121** 30 25N 89 0W
Missoula, *U.S.A.* **122** 46 52N 114 0W
Missour, *Morocco* **84** 33 3N 4 0W
Missouri □, *U.S.A.* **120** 38 25N 92 30W
Missouri →, *U.S.A.* **120** 38 50N 90 8W
Missouri Valley, *U.S.A.* **120** 41 33N 95 53W
Mist, *U.S.A.* **124** 45 59N 123 15W
Mistake B., *Canada* **111** 62 8N 93 0W
Mistaouac, L., *Canada* **106** 49 25N 78 41W
Mistassibi →, *Canada* **107** 48 53N 72 13W
Mistassibi Nord-Est. →, *Canada* **107** 49 31N 71 56W
Mistassini, *Canada* **107** 48 53N 72 12W
Mistassini →, *Canada* **107** 48 42N 72 20W
Mistassini, Parc. Prov. de, *Canada* **107** 50 20N 74 0W
Mistassini L., *Canada* **104** 51 0N 73 30W
Mistastin L., *Canada* **105** 55 57N 63 20W
Mistatim, *Canada* **111** 52 52N 103 22W
Mistelbach, *Austria* **32** 48 34N 16 34 E
Misterbianco, *Italy* **29** 37 32N 15 0 E
Mistretta, *Italy* **29** 37 56N 14 20 E
Misty L., *Canada* **111** 58 53N 101 40W
Misugi, *Japan* **65** 34 31N 136 16 E
Misumi, *Japan* **64** 32 37N 130 27 E
Mît Ghamr, *Egypt* **88** 30 42N 31 12 E
Mitaka, *Japan* **65** 35 40N 139 33 E
Mitatib, *Sudan* **89** 15 59N 36 12 E
Mitchell, *Australia* **73** 26 29 S 147 58 E
Mitchell, *Canada* **108** 43 28N 81 12W
Mitchell, *Ind., U.S.A.* **119** 38 42N 86 25W
Mitchell, *Nebr., U.S.A.* **120** 41 58N 103 45W
Mitchell, *Oreg., U.S.A.* **122** 44 31N 120 8W
Mitchell, *S. Dak., U.S.A.* **120** 43 40N 98 0W
Mitchell →, *Queens., Australia* **72** 15 12 S 141 35 E
Mitchell →, *Vic., Australia* **75** 37 51 S 147 38 E
Mitchell, Mt., *U.S.A.* **115** 35 40N 82 20W
Mitchelstown, *Ireland* **15** 52 16N 8 18W
Mitchinamécus, Rés., *Canada* **106** 47 19N 75 9W
Mitha Tiwana, *Pakistan* **48** 32 13N 72 6 E
Mitiamo, *Australia* **74** 36 12 S 144 15 E
Mitilíni, *Grèece* **35** 39 6N 26 35 E
Mito, *Japan* **65** 36 20N 140 30 E
Mitre, *Australia* **74** 36 44 S 141 46 E
Mitsinjo, *Madag.* **97** 16 1 S 45 52 E
Mitsiwa, *Ethiopia* **89** 15 35N 39 25 E
Mitsiwa Channel, *Ethiopia* **89** 15 30N 40 0 E
Mitsukaidō, *Japan* **65** 36 1N 139 59 E
Mitta Mitta, *Australia* **75** 36 34 S 147 22 E
Mitta Mitta →, *Australia* **75** 36 14 S 147 10 E
Mittagong, *Australia* **76** 34 28 S 150 29 E
Mittelland Kanal, *W. Germany* **30** 52 23N 7 45 E
Mittenwalde, *E. Germany* **30** 52 16N 13 33 E
Mitterteich, *W. Germany* **31** 49 57N 12 15 E
Mittweida, *E. Germany* **30** 50 59N 13 0 E
Mittyack, *Australia* **74** 35 8 S 142 36 E
Mitú, *Colombia* **134** 1 8N 70 3W
Mituas, *Colombia* **134** 3 52N 68 49W
Mitumba, *Tanzania* **92** 7 8 S 31 2 E
Mitumba, Chaîne des, *Zaïre* **92** 7 0 S 27 30 E
Mitwaba, *Zaïre* **93** 8 2 S 27 17 E
Mityana, *Uganda* **92** 0 23N 32 2 E
Mitzic, *Gabon* **94** 0 45N 11 40 E
Miura, *Japan* **65** 35 12N 139 40 E
Mixteco →, *Mexico* **127** 18 11N 98 30W
Miyagi □, *Japan* **63** 38 15N 140 45 E
Miyâh, W. el →, *Egypt* **88** 25 0N 33 23 E
Miyake-Jima, *Japan* **65** 34 0N 139 30 E
Miyako, *Japan* **63** 39 40N 141 59 E
Miyakonojō, *Japan* **64** 31 40N 131 5 E
Miyanojō, *Japan* **64** 31 54N 130 27 E
Miyata, *Japan* **64** 33 49N 130 42 E
Miyazaki, *Japan* **64** 31 56N 131 30 E
Miyazaki □, *Japan* **64** 32 30N 131 30 E
Miyazu, *Japan* **65** 35 35N 135 10 E
Miyet, Bahr el = Dead Sea, *Asia* **44** 31 30N 35 30 E
Miyi, *China* **58** 26 47N 102 9 E
Miyoshi, *Japan* **64** 34 48N 132 51 E
Miyun, *China* **60** 40 28N 116 50 E
Miyun Shuiku, *China* **61** 40 30N 117 0 E
Mizal, *Si. Arabia* **46** 23 59N 45 11 E
Mizamis = Ozamis, *Phil.* **57** 8 15N 123 50 E
Mizdah, *Libya* **86** 31 30N 13 0 E
Mizen Hd., *Cork, Ireland* **15** 51 27N 9 50W
Mizen Hd., *Wicklow, Ireland* **15** 52 52N 6 4W
Mizhi, *China* **60** 37 47N 110 12 E
Mizil, *Romania* **34** 44 59N 26 29 E
Mizoram □, *India* **52** 23 30N 92 40 E
Mizpe Ramon, *Israel* **44** 30 34N 34 49 E
Mizuho, *Antarctica* **143** 70 30 S 41 0 E
Mizuho, *Japan* **65** 35 6N 135 17 E
Mizunami, *Japan* **65** 35 22N 137 15 E
Mjöbäck, *Sweden* **11** 57 28N 12 53 E
Mjölby, *Sweden* **11** 58 20N 15 10 E
Mjörn, *Sweden* **11** 57 55N 12 25 E
Mjøsa, *Norway* **10** 60 48N 11 0 E
Mkata, *Tanzania* **92** 5 45 S 38 20 E
Mkokotoni, *Tanzania* **92** 5 55 S 39 15 E
Mkomazi, *Tanzania* **92** 4 40 S 38 7 E
Mkomazi →, *S. Africa* **97** 30 12 S 30 50 E
Mkulwe, *Tanzania* **93** 8 37 S 32 20 E
Mkumbi, Ras, *Tanzania* **92** 7 38 S 39 55 E
Mkushi, *Zambia* **93** 14 25 S 29 15 E
Mkushi River, *Zambia* **93** 13 32 S 29 45 E
Mkuze, *S. Africa* **97** 27 10 S 32 0 E
Mkuze →, *S. Africa* **97** 27 45 S 32 30 E
Mladá Boleslav, *Czech.* **32** 50 27N 14 53 E
Mladenovac, *Yugoslavia* **33** 44 28N 20 44 E
Mlala Hills, *Tanzania* **92** 6 50 S 31 40 E
Mlange, *Malawi* **93** 16 2 S 35 33 E
Mlava →, *Yugoslavia* **33** 44 45N 21 13 E
Mława, *Poland* **32** 53 9N 20 25 E
Mlinište, *Yugoslavia* **27** 44 15N 16 50 E
Mljet, *Yugoslavia* **33** 42 43N 17 30 E
Młynąry, *Poland* **32** 54 12N 19 46 E
Mmabatho, *S. Africa* **96** 25 49 S 25 30 E
Mme, *Cameroon* **91** 6 18N 10 14 E
Mo i Rana, *Norway* **8** 66 15N 14 7 E
Moa, *Indonesia* **57** 8 0 S 128 0 E
Moa →, *S. Leone* **90** 6 59N 11 36W
Moab, *U.S.A.* **123** 38 40N 109 35W
Moabi, *Gabon* **94** 2 24 S 10 59 E
Moaco →, *Brazil* **136** 7 41 S 68 18W
Moała, *Fiji* **68** 18 36 S 179 53 E
Moalie Park, *Australia* **73** 29 42 S 143 3 E
Moaña, *Spain* **22** 42 18N 8 43W
Moba, *Zaïre* **92** 7 0 S 29 48 E
Mobara, *Japan* **65** 35 25N 140 18 E
Mobaye, *C.A.R.* **94** 4 25N 21 5 E
Mobayi, *Zaïre* **94** 4 15N 21 8 E

Moberly, *U.S.A.* **118** 39 25N 92 25W
Moberly →, *Canada* **110** 56 12N 120 55W
Mobile, *U.S.A.* **115** 30 41N 88 3W
Mobile B., *U.S.A.* **115** 30 30N 88 0W
Mobridge, *U.S.A.* **120** 45 31N 100 28W
Mobutu Sese Seko, L., *Africa* **92** 1 30N 31 0 E
Moc Chau, *Vietnam* **54** 20 50N 104 38 E
Moc Hoa, *Vietnam* **55** 10 46N 105 56 E
Mocaba, Sa. de, *Angola* **95** 7 12 S 15 0 E
Mocabe Kasari, *Zaïre* **93** 9 58 S 26 12 E
Mocajuba, *Brazil* **138** 2 35 S 49 30W
Moçambique, *Mozam.* **93** 15 3 S 40 42 E
Moçâmedes = Namibe, *Angola* **95** 15 7 S 12 11 E
Mocapra →, *Venezuela* **134** 7 56N 66 46W
Mocha, I., *Chile* **142** 38 22 S 73 56W
Mochudi, *Botswana* **96** 24 27 S 26 7 E
Mocimboa da Praia, *Mozam.* **93** 11 25 S 40 20 E
Möckeln, *Sweden* **11** 56 40N 14 15 E
Moclips, *U.S.A.* **124** 47 14N 124 10W
Mocoa, *Colombia* **134** 1 7N 76 35W
Mococa, *Brazil* **141** 21 28 S 47 0W
Mocorito, *Mexico* **126** 25 30N 107 53W
Moctezuma, *Mexico* **126** 29 50N 109 0W
Moctezuma →, *Mexico* **127** 21 59N 98 34W
Mocuba, *Mozam.* **93** 16 54 S 36 57 E
Mocúzari, Presa, *Mexico* **126** 27 10N 109 10W
Moda, *Burma* **52** 24 22N 96 29 E
Modane, *France* **21** 45 12N 6 40 E
Modasa, *India* **48** 23 30N 73 21 E
Modave, *Belgium* **17** 50 27N 5 18 E
Modder →, *S. Africa* **96** 29 2 S 24 37 E
Modderrivier, *S. Africa* **96** 29 2 S 24 38 E
Módena, *Italy* **26** 44 39N 10 55 E
Modena, *U.S.A.* **123** 37 55N 113 56W
Modesto, *U.S.A.* **124** 37 43N 121 0W
Módica, *Italy* **29** 36 52N 14 45 E
Modigliana, *Italy* **27** 44 9N 11 48 E
Modjamboli, *Zaïre* **94** 2 28N 22 6 E
Modo, *Sudan* **89** 5 31N 30 33 E
Modra, *Czech.* **33** 48 19N 17 20 E
Moe, *Australia* **75** 38 12 S 146 19 E
Moebase, *Mozam.* **93** 17 3 S 38 41 E
Moëlan-sur-Mer, *France* **18** 47 49N 3 38W
Moengo, *Surinam* **135** 5 45N 54 20W
Moergestel, *Neths.* **17** 51 33N 5 11 E
Moers, *W. Germany* **17** 51 27N 6 38 E
Moffat, *U.K.* **14** 55 20N 3 27W
Moga, *India* **48** 30 48N 75 8 E
Mogadishu = Muqdisho, *Somali Rep.* **98** 2 2N 45 25 E
Mogador = Essaouira, *Morocco* **84** 31 32N 9 42W
Mogadouro, *Portugal* **22** 41 22N 6 47W
Mogalakwena →, *S. Africa* **97** 22 38 S 28 40 E
Mogami →, *Japan* **63** 38 45N 140 0 E
Mogán, *Canary Is.* **25** 27 53N 15 43W
Mogaung, *Burma* **52** 25 20N 97 0 E
Møgeltønder, *Denmark* **11** 54 57N 8 48 E
Mogente, *Spain* **25** 38 52N 0 45W
Mogho, *Ethiopia* **89** 4 54N 40 16 E
Mogi das Cruzes, *Brazil* **141** 23 31 S 46 11W
Mogi-Guaçu →, *Brazil* **141** 20 53 S 48 10W
Mogi-Mirim, *Brazil* **141** 22 29 S 47 0W
Mogielnica, *Poland* **32** 51 42N 20 41 E
Mogilev, *U.S.S.R.* **36** 53 55N 30 18 E
Mogilev-Podolskiy, *U.S.S.R.* **38** 48 20N 27 40 E
Mogilno, *Poland* **32** 52 39N 17 55 E
Mogincual, *Mozam.* **93** 15 35 S 40 25 E
Mogliano Véneto, *Italy* **27** 45 33N 12 15 E
Mogo, *Australia* **76** 35 48 S 150 10 E
Mogocha, *U.S.S.R.* **41** 53 40N 119 50 E
Mogoi, *Indonesia* **57** 1 55 S 133 10 E
Mogok, *Burma* **52** 23 0N 96 40 E
Mogriguy, *Australia* **76** 32 3 S 148 40 E
Moguer, *Spain* **23** 37 15N 6 52W
Mogumber, *Australia* **79** 31 2 S 116 3 E
Mohács, *Hungary* **33** 45 58N 18 41 E
Mohaka →, *N.Z.* **80** 39 7 S 177 12 E
Mohales Hoek, *Lesotho* **96** 30 7 S 27 26 E
Mohall, *U.S.A.* **120** 48 46N 101 30W
Moḩammadābād, *Iran* **47** 37 52N 59 5 E
Mohammadia, *Algeria* **85** 35 33N 0 3 E
Mohammedia, *Morocco* **84** 33 44N 7 21W
Mohave, L., *U.S.A.* **125** 35 25N 114 36W
Mohawk →, *U.S.A.* **117** 42 47N 73 42W
Moheda, *Sweden* **11** 57 1N 14 35 E
Möhne →, *W. Germany* **30** 51 29N 7 57 E
Mohnyin, *Burma* **52** 24 47N 96 22 E
Moholm, *Sweden* **11** 58 37N 14 5 E
Mohoro, *Tanzania* **92** 8 6 S 39 8 E
Moia, *Sudan* **89** 5 3N 28 2 E
Moidart, L., *U.K.* **14** 56 47N 5 40W
Moille, La, *U.S.A.* **118** 41 32N 89 17W
Moinabad, *India* **50** 17 44N 77 16 E
Moindou, *N. Cal.* **68** 21 42 S 165 41 E
Moine, La →, *U.S.A.* **118** 39 58N 90 32W
Moineşti, *Romania* **34** 46 28N 26 31 E
Mointy, *U.S.S.R.* **40** 47 10N 73 18 E
Moira →, *Canada* **109** 44 21N 77 24W
Moirans, *France* **21** 45 20N 5 33 E
Moirans-en-Montagne, *France* **21** 46 26N 5 43 E
Moisakula, *U.S.S.R.* **36** 58 3N 25 12 E
Moisie, *Canada* **105** 50 12N 66 1W
Moisie →, *Canada* **105** 50 14N 66 5W
Moissac, *France* **20** 44 7N 1 5 E
Moïssala, *Chad* **87** 8 21N 17 46 E
Moita, *Portugal* **23** 38 38N 8 58W
Mojácar, *Spain* **25** 37 6N 1 55W
Mojados, *Spain* **22** 41 26N 4 40W
Mojave, *U.S.A.* **125** 35 8N 118 8W
Mojave Desert, *U.S.A.* **125** 35 0N 116 30W
Mojiang, *China* **58** 23 37N 101 35 E
Mojo, *Bolivia* **140** 21 48 S 65 33W
Mojo, *Ethiopia* **89** 8 35N 39 5 E
Mojokerto, *Indonesia* **57** 7 28 S 112 26 E
Mojos, Llanos de, *Bolivia* **137** 15 0 S 65 0W
Moju →, *Brazil* **138** 1 40 S 48 25W
Mokai, *N.Z.* **80** 38 32 S 175 56 E
Mokambo, *Zaïre* **93** 12 25 S 28 20 E
Mokameh, *India* **49** 25 24N 85 55 E
Mokane, *U.S.A.* **118** 38 41N 91 53W
Mokau →, *N.Z.* **80** 38 35 S 174 35 E
Mokelumne →, *U.S.A.* **124** 38 23N 121 25W
Mokelumne Hill, *U.S.A.* **124** 38 18N 120 43W
Mokhós, *Greece* **35** 35 16N 25 27 E
Mokhotlong, *Lesotho* **97** 29 22 S 29 2 E
Mokihinui →, *N.Z.* **81** 41 33 S 171 58 E
Moknine, *Tunisia* **86** 35 35N 10 58 E
Mokoan, L., *Australia* **74** 36 27 S 146 5 E
Mokpalin, *Burma* **52** 17 26N 96 53 E
Mokra Gora, *Yugoslavia* **33** 42 50N 20 30 E
Mokronog, *Yugoslavia* **27** 45 57N 15 9 E
Moksha →, *U.S.S.R.* **37** 54 45N 41 53 E
Mokshan, *U.S.S.R.* **37** 53 25N 44 35 E
Mol, *Belgium* **17** 51 11N 5 5 E
Mola, C. de la, *Spain* **24** 39 40N 4 20 E
Mola di Bari, *Italy* **29** 41 3N 17 5 E
Moláoi, *Greece* **35** 36 49N 22 56 E
Molat, *Yugoslavia* **27** 44 15N 14 50 E
Molchanovo, *U.S.S.R.* **40** 57 40N 83 50 E
Mold, *U.K.* **12** 53 10N 3 10W
Moldavia = Moldova, *Romania* **34** 46 30N 27 0 E
Moldavian S.S.R. □, *U.S.S.R.* **38** 47 0N 28 0 E
Molde, *Norway* **8** 62 45N 7 9 E
Moldova, *Romania* **34** 46 30N 27 0 E
Moldova Nouă, *Romania* **34** 44 45N 21 41 E
Moldoveanu, *Romania* **34** 45 36N 24 45 E
Mole →, *Australia* **77** 29 0 S 151 32 E
Molepolole, *Botswana* **96** 24 28 S 25 28 E
Molesworth, *N.Z.* **81** 42 5 S 173 16 E
Molfetta, *Italy* **29** 41 12N 16 35 E
Molina de Aragón, *Spain* **24** 40 46N 1 52W
Moline, *U.S.A.* **118** 41 30N 90 30W
Molinella, *Italy* **27** 44 38N 11 40 E
Molinos, *Argentina* **140** 25 28 S 66 15W
Moliro, *Zaïre* **92** 8 12 S 30 30 E
Molise □, *Italy* **27** 41 45N 14 30 E
Moliterno, *Italy* **29** 40 14N 15 50 E
Mollahat, *Bangla.* **49** 22 56N 89 48 E
Mölle, *Sweden* **11** 56 17N 12 31 E
Molledo, *Spain* **22** 43 8N 4 6W
Mollendo, *Peru* **136** 17 0 S 72 0W
Mollerin, L., *Australia* **79** 30 30 S 117 35 E
Mollerusa, *Spain* **24** 41 37N 0 54 E
Mollina, *Spain* **23** 37 8N 4 38W
Mölln, *W. Germany* **30** 53 37N 10 41 E
Mölltorp, *Sweden* **11** 58 30N 14 26 E
Mollymook, *Australia* **76** 35 21 S 150 29 E
Mölndal, *Sweden* **11** 57 40N 12 3 E
Molo, *Burma* **52** 23 22N 96 53 E
Molochansk, *U.S.S.R.* **38** 47 15N 35 35 E
Molochnaya →, *U.S.S.R.* **38** 47 0N 35 30 E
Molodechno, *U.S.S.R.* **36** 54 20N 26 50 E
Molokai, *U.S.A.* **112** 21 8N 157 0W
Moloma →, *U.S.S.R.* **37** 58 20N 48 15 E
Molong, *Australia* **76** 33 5 S 148 54 E
Molopo →, *Africa* **96** 27 30 S 20 13 E
Mólos, *Greece* **35** 38 47N 22 37 E
Molotov = Perm, *U.S.S.R.* **40** 58 0N 57 10 E
Moloundou, *Cameroon* **94** 2 8N 15 15 E
Molsheim, *France* **19** 48 33N 7 29 E
Molson L., *Canada* **111** 54 22N 96 40W
Molteno, *S. Africa* **96** 31 22 S 26 22 E
Molu, *Indonesia* **57** 6 45 S 131 40 E
Molucca Sea, *Indonesia* **57** 4 0 S 124 0 E
Moluccas = Maluku, *Indonesia* **57** 1 0 S 127 0 E
Moma, *Mozam.* **93** 16 47 S 39 4 E
Moma, *Zaïre* **92** 1 35 S 23 52 E
Mombaça, *Brazil* **138** 5 43 S 39 45W
Mombasa, *Kenya* **92** 4 2 S 39 43 E
Mombetsu, *Japan* **63** 42 27N 142 4 E
Mombil, *Burma* **52** 27 46N 98 6 E
Mombuey, *Spain* **22** 42 3N 6 20W
Momchilgrad, *Bulgaria* **35** 41 33N 25 23 E
Momence, *U.S.A.* **119** 41 10N 87 40W
Momi, *Zaïre* **92** 1 42 S 27 0 E
Momignies, *Belgium* **17** 50 2N 4 10 E
Mompós, *Colombia* **134** 9 14N 74 26W
Møn, *Denmark* **11** 54 57N 12 15 E
Mona, Canal de la, *W. Indies* **129** 18 30N 67 45W
Mona, I., *Puerto Rico* **129** 18 5N 67 54W
Mona, Pta., *Costa Rica* **128** 9 37N 82 36W
Mona, Punta, *Spain* **23** 36 43N 3 45W
Mona Quimbundo, *Angola* **95** 9 55 S 19 58 E
Monach Is., *U.K.* **14** 57 32N 7 40W
Monaco ■, *Europe* **21** 43 46N 7 23 E
Monadhliath Mts., *U.K.* **14** 57 10N 4 4W
Monagas □, *Venezuela* **135** 9 20N 63 0W
Monaghan, *Ireland* **15** 54 15N 6 58W
Monaghan □, *Ireland* **15** 54 10N 7 0W
Monahans, *U.S.A.* **121** 31 35N 102 50W
Monapo, *Mozam.* **93** 14 56 S 40 19 E
Monarch Mt., *Canada* **110** 51 55N 125 57W
Monastier-sur-Gazeille, Le, *France* **20** 44 57N 3 59 E
Monastir = Bitola, *Yugoslavia* **35** 41 5N 21 10 E
Monastir, *Tunisia* **86** 35 50N 10 49 E
Monastyriska, *U.S.S.R.* **36** 49 8N 25 14 E
Monbetsu, *Japan* **63** 44 21N 143 22 E
Moncada, *Spain* **24** 39 30N 0 24W
Moncalieri, *Italy* **26** 45 0N 7 40 E
Moncalvo, *Italy* **26** 45 3N 8 15 E
Monção, *Portugal* **22** 42 4N 8 27W
Moncarapacho, *Portugal* **23** 37 5N 7 46W
Moncayo, Sierra del, *Spain* **24** 41 48N 1 50W
Mönchengladbach, *W. Germany* **30** 51 12N 6 23 E
Monchique, *Portugal* **23** 37 19N 8 38W
Monclova, *Mexico* **126** 26 50N 101 30W
Moncontour, *France* **18** 48 22N 2 38W
Moncouche, L., *Canada* **107** 48 45N 70 42W
Moncoutant, *France* **20** 46 43N 0 35W
Moncton, *Canada* **105** 46 7N 64 51W
Mondego →, *Portugal* **22** 40 9N 8 52W
Mondego, C., *Portugal* **22** 40 11N 8 54W
Mondeodo, *Indonesia* **57** 3 34 S 122 9 E
Mondo, *Chad* **87** 13 47N 15 32 E
Mondolfo, *Italy* **27** 43 45N 13 8 E
Mondonac, L., *Canada* **107** 47 24N 73 58W
Mondoñedo, *Spain* **22** 43 25N 7 23W
Mondoví, *Italy* **26** 44 23N 7 49 E
Mondovi, *U.S.A.* **120** 44 37N 91 40W
Mondragon, *France* **21** 44 13N 4 44 E
Mondragone, *Italy* **28** 41 8N 13 52 E
Mondrain I., *Australia* **79** 34 9 S 122 14 E
Monduli □, *Tanzania* **92** 3 0 S 36 0 E
Monemvasía, *Greece* **35** 36 41N 23 3 E
Monessen, *U.S.A.* **116** 40 9N 79 50W
Monesterio, *Spain* **23** 38 6N 6 15W
Monestier-de-Clermont, *France* **21** 44 55N 5 38 E
Monêtier-les-Bains, Le, *France* **21** 44 58N 6 30 E
Monett, *U.S.A.* **121** 36 55N 93 56W
Monfalcone, *Italy* **27** 45 49N 13 32 E
Monflanquin, *France* **20** 44 32N 0 47 E
Monforte, *Portugal* **23** 39 6N 7 25W
Monforte de Lemos, *Spain* **22** 42 31N 7 33W
Mong Hta, *Burma* **52** 19 50N 98 35 E
Mong Ket, *Burma* **52** 23 8N 98 22 E
Mong Kung, *Burma* **52** 21 35N 97 35 E
Mong Kyawt, *Burma* **52** 19 56N 98 45 E
Mong Nai, *Burma* **52** 20 32N 97 46 E
Mong Ping, *Burma* **52** 21 22N 99 2 E
Mong Pu, *Burma* **52** 20 55N 98 44 E
Mong Ton, *Burma* **52** 20 17N 98 45 E
Mong Tung, *Burma* **52** 22 2N 97 41 E
Mong Yai, *Burma* **52** 22 21N 98 3 E
Monga, *Zaïre* **94** 4 12N 22 49 E
Mongalla, *Sudan* **89** 5 8N 31 42 E
Mongers, L., *Australia* **79** 29 25 S 117 5 E
Monghyr = Munger, *India* **49** 25 23N 86 30 E
Mongla, *Bangla.* **52** 22 8N 89 35 E
Mongngaw, *Burma* **52** 22 47N 96 59 E
Mongo, *Chad* **87** 12 14N 18 43 E
Mongó, *Eq. Guin.* **94** 1 52N 10 10 E
Mongolia ■, *Asia* **62** 47 0N 103 0 E
Mongomo, *Eq. Guin.* **94** 1 38N 11 19 E
Mongonu, *Nigeria* **91** 12 40N 13 32 E
Mongororo, *Chad* **87** 12 3N 22 26 E
Mongu, *Zambia* **95** 15 16 S 23 12 E
Mônguá, *Angola* **95** 16 43 S 15 20 E
Monistrol-d'Allier, *France* **20** 44 58N 3 38 E
Monistrol-sur-Loire, *France* **21** 45 17N 4 11 E
Monkey Bay, *Malawi* **93** 14 7 S 35 1 E
Monkey River, *Belize* **127** 16 22N 88 29W
Monkira, *Australia* **72** 24 46 S 140 30 E
Monkoto, *Zaïre* **94** 1 38 S 20 35 E
Monkton, *Canada* **108** 43 35N 81 5W
Monmouth, *U.K.* **13** 51 48N 2 43W
Monmouth, *U.S.A.* **118** 40 50N 90 40W
Mono, *Solomon Is.* **68** 7 20 S 155 35 E
Mono, L., *U.S.A.* **124** 38 0N 119 9W
Monolith, *U.S.A.* **125** 35 7N 118 22W
Monon, *U.S.A.* **119** 40 52N 86 53W
Monona, *Iowa, U.S.A.* **118** 43 3N 91 24W
Monona, *Wis., U.S.A.* **118** 43 4N 89 20W
Monongahela, *U.S.A.* **116** 40 12N 79 56W
Monópoli, *Italy* **29** 40 57N 17 18 E
Monor, *Hungary* **33** 47 21N 19 27 E
Monóvar, *Spain* **25** 38 28N 0 53W
Monowai, *N.Z.* **81** 45 53 S 167 31 E
Monowai, L., *N.Z.* **81** 45 53 S 167 25 E
Monqoumba, *C.A.R.* **94** 3 33N 18 40 E
Monreal del Campo, *Spain* **24** 40 47N 1 20W
Monreale, *Italy* **28** 38 6N 13 16 E
Monroe, *Ga., U.S.A.* **115** 33 47N 83 43W
Monroe, *Iowa, U.S.A.* **118** 41 31N 93 6W
Monroe, *La., U.S.A.* **121** 32 32N 92 4W
Monroe, *Mich., U.S.A.* **119** 41 55N 83 26W
Monroe, *N.C., U.S.A.* **115** 35 2N 80 37W
Monroe, *N.Y., U.S.A.* **117** 41 19N 74 11W
Monroe, *Ohio, U.S.A.* **119** 39 27N 84 22W
Monroe, *Utah, U.S.A.* **123** 38 45N 112 5W
Monroe, *Wash., U.S.A.* **124** 47 51N 121 58W
Monroe, *Wis., U.S.A.* **118** 42 38N 89 40W
Monroe, Res., *U.S.A.* **119** 39 1N 86 31W
Monroe City, *U.S.A.* **118** 39 40N 91 40W
Monroeville, *Ala., U.S.A.* **115** 31 33N 87 15W
Monroeville, *Ind., U.S.A.* **119** 40 59N 84 52W
Monroeville, *Pa., U.S.A.* **116** 40 26N 79 45W
Monrovia, *Liberia* **90** 6 18N 10 47W
Monrovia, *U.S.A.* **123** 34 7N 118 1W
Mons, *Belgium* **17** 50 27N 3 58 E
Monsaraz, *Portugal* **23** 38 28N 7 22W
Monse, *Indonesia* **57** 4 0 S 123 10 E
Monsefú, *Peru* **136** 6 52 S 79 52W
Monségur, *France* **20** 44 38N 0 4 E
Monsélice, *Italy* **27** 45 16N 11 46 E
Monster, *Neths.* **16** 52 1N 4 10 E
Mont-Carmel, *Canada* **107** 47 26N 69 52W
Mont-de-Marsan, *France* **20** 43 54N 0 31W
Mont Dore, *N. Cal.* **68** 22 16 S 166 34 E
Mont-Dore, Le, *France* **20** 45 35N 2 49 E
Mont-Joli, *Canada* **107** 48 37N 68 10W
Mont-Laurier, *Canada* **106** 46 35N 75 30W
Mont-St.-Michel, Le, *France* **18** 48 40N 1 30W
Mont-sous-Vaudrey, *France* **19** 46 58N 5 36 E
Mont-sur-Marchienne, *Belgium* **17** 50 23N 4 24 E
Mont-Tremblant, *Canada* **106** 46 13N 74 36W
Mont Tremblant Prov. Park, *Canada* **107** 46 30N 74 30W
Montabaur, *W. Germany* **30** 50 26N 7 49 E
Montagnac, *France* **20** 43 29N 3 28 E
Montagnana, *Italy* **27** 45 13N 11 29 E
Montagu, *S. Africa* **96** 33 45 S 20 8 E
Montagu I., *Antarctica* **143** 58 25 S 26 20W
Montague, *Canada* **105** 46 10N 62 39W
Montague, *U.S.A.* **122** 41 47N 122 30W
Montague, I., *Mexico* **126** 31 40N 114 56W
Montague I., *Australia* **75** 36 16 S 150 13 E
Montague I., *U.S.A.* **102** 60 0N 147 0W
Montague Ra., *Australia* **79** 27 15 S 119 30 E
Montague Sd., *Australia* **78** 14 28 S 125 20 E
Montaigu, *France* **18** 46 59N 1 18W
Montalbán, *Spain* **24** 40 50N 0 45W
Montalbano di Elicona, *Italy* **29** 38 1N 15 0 E
Montalbano Iónico, *Italy* **29** 40 17N 16 33 E
Montalbo, *Spain* **24** 39 53N 2 42W
Montalcino, *Italy* **27** 43 4N 11 30 E
Montalegre, *Portugal* **22** 41 49N 7 47W
Montalto di Castro, *Italy* **27** 42 20N 11 36 E
Montalto Uffugo, *Italy* **29** 39 25N 16 9 E
Montalvo, *U.S.A.* **125** 34 15N 119 12W
Montamarta, *Spain* **22** 41 39N 5 49W
Montaña, *Peru* **136** 6 0 S 73 0W
Montana □, *U.S.A.* **112** 47 0N 110 0W
Montaña Clara, I., *Canary Is.* **25** 29 17N 13 33W
Montánchez, *Spain* **23** 39 15N 6 8W
Montañita, *Colombia* **134** 1 22N 75 28W
Montargis, *France* **19** 47 59N 2 43 E
Montauban, *France* **20** 44 0N 1 21 E
Montauk, *U.S.A.* **117** 41 3N 71 57W
Montauk Pt., *U.S.A.* **117** 41 4N 71 52W
Montbard, *France* **19** 47 38N 4 20 E
Montbéliard, *France* **19** 47 31N 6 48 E
Montblanch, *Spain* **24** 41 23N 1 4 E
Montbrison, *France* **21** 45 36N 4 3 E
Montcalm, Pic de, *France* **20** 42 40N 1 25 E
Montceau-les-Mines, *France* **19** 46 40N 4 23 E
Montcerf, *Canada* **106** 46 32N 76 3W
Montchanin, *France* **21** 46 47N 4 30 E
Montclair, *U.S.A.* **117** 40 53N 74 13W
Montcornet, *France* **19** 49 40N 4 1 E
Montcuq, *France* **20** 44 21N 1 13 E
Montdidier, *France* **19** 49 38N 2 35 E
Monte, La, *U.S.A.* **118** 38 47N 93 27W
Monte Albán, *Mexico* **127** 17 2N 96 45W
Monte Alegre, *Brazil* **135** 2 0 S 54 0W
Monte Alegre de Goiás, *Brazil* **139** 13 14 S 47 10W
Monte Alegre de Minas, *Brazil* **139** 18 52 S 48 52W
Monte Azul, *Brazil* **139** 15 9 S 42 53W
Monte Bello Is., *Australia* **78** 20 30 S 115 45 E
Monte-Carlo, *Monaco* **21** 43 46N 7 23 E
Monte Carmelo, *Brazil* **139** 18 43 S 47 29W
Monte Caseros, *Argentina* **140** 30 10 S 57 50W
Monte Comán, *Argentina* **140** 34 40 S 67 53W
Monte Cristi, *Dom. Rep.* **129** 19 52N 71 39W

Monte Dinero, *Argentina* **142** 52 18 S 68 33W
Monte Lindo →, *Paraguay* **140** 23 56 S 57 12W
Monte Quemado, *Argentina* **140** 25 53 S 62 41W
Monte Redondo, *Portugal* **22** 39 53N 8 50W
Monte Rio, *U.S.A.* **124** 38 28N 123 0W
Monte San Giovanni, *Italy* **28** 41 39N 13 33 E
Monte San Savino, *Italy* **27** 43 20N 11 42 E
Monte Sant' Ángelo, *Italy* **29** 41 42N 15 59 E
Monte Sanţu, C. di, *Italy* **28** 40 5N 9 42 E
Monte Vista, *U.S.A.* **123** 37 40N 106 8W
Monteagudo, *Argentina* **141** 27 14 S 54 8W
Monteagudo, *Bolivia* **137** 19 49 S 63 59W
Montealegre, *Spain* **25** 38 48N 1 17W
Montebello, *Canada* **106** 45 40N 74 55W
Montebelluna, *Italy* **27** 45 47N 12 3 E
Montebourg, *France* **18** 49 30N 1 20W
Montecastrilli, *Italy* **27** 42 40N 12 30 E
Montecatini Terme, *Italy* **26** 43 55N 10 48 E
Montecito, *U.S.A.* **125** 34 26N 119 40W
Montecristi, *Ecuador* **134** 1 0 S 80 40W
Montecristo, *Italy* **26** 42 20N 10 20 E
Montefalco, *Italy* **27** 42 53N 12 38 E
Montefiascone, *Italy* **27** 42 31N 12 2 E
Montefrío, *Spain* **23** 37 20N 4 0W
Montegnée, *Belgium* **17** 50 38N 5 31 E
Montego Bay, *Jamaica* **128** 18 30N 78 0W
Montegranaro, *Italy* **27** 43 13N 13 38 E
Monteiro, *Brazil* **138** 7 48 S 37 2W
Montejicar, *Spain* **25** 37 33N 3 30W
Montejinnie, *Australia* **78** 16 40 S 131 38 E
Montelíbano, *Colombia* **134** 8 5N 75 29W
Montélimar, *France* **21** 44 33N 4 45 E
Montella, *Italy* **29** 40 50N 15 0 E
Montellano, *Spain* **23** 36 59N 5 36W
Montello, *U.S.A.* **120** 43 49N 89 21W
Montelupo Fiorentino, *Italy* **26** 43 44N 11 2 E
Montemor-o-Novo, *Portugal* **23** 38 40N 8 12W
Montemor-o-Velho, *Portugal* **22** 40 11N 8 40W
Montemorelos, *Mexico* **127** 25 11N 99 42W
Montendre, *France* **20** 45 16N 0 26W
Montenegro = Crna Gora □, *Yugoslavia* **33** 42 40N 19 20 E
Montenegro, *Brazil* **141** 29 39 S 51 29W
Montenero di Bisaccia, *Italy* **27** 42 0N 14 47 E
Montepuez, *Mozam.* **93** 13 8 S 38 59 E
Montepuez →, *Mozam.* **93** 12 32 S 40 27 E
Montepulciano, *Italy* **27** 43 5N 11 46 E
Montereale, *Italy* **27** 42 31N 13 13 E
Montereau-Fault-Yonne, *France* **19** 48 22N 2 57 E
Monterey, *Calif., U.S.A.* **124** 36 35N 121 57W
Monterey, *Ind., U.S.A.* **119** 41 11N 86 30W
Monterey B., *U.S.A.* **124** 36 50N 121 55W
Montería, *Colombia* **134** 8 46N 75 53W
Montero, *Bolivia* **137** 17 20 S 63 15W
Monteros, *Argentina* **140** 27 11 S 65 30W
Monterotondo, *Italy* **27** 42 3N 12 36 E
Monterrey, *Mexico* **126** 25 40N 100 30W
Montes Altos, *Brazil* **138** 5 50 S 47 4W
Montes Claros, *Brazil* **139** 16 30 S 43 50W
Montesano, *U.S.A.* **124** 46 58N 123 39W
Montesárchio, *Italy* **29** 41 5N 14 37 E
Montescaglioso, *Italy* **29** 40 34N 16 40 E
Montesilvano, *Italy* **27** 42 30N 14 8 E
Montevarchi, *Italy* **27** 43 30N 11 32 E
Montevideo, *Uruguay* **141** 34 50 S 56 11W
Montevideo, *U.S.A.* **120** 44 55N 95 40W
Montezuma, *Ind., U.S.A.* **119** 39 47N 87 22W
Montezuma, *Iowa, U.S.A.* **118** 41 32N 92 35W
Montfaucon, *France* **19** 49 16N 5 8 E
Montfaucon-en-Velay, *France* **21** 45 11N 4 20 E
Montfort, *France* **18** 48 9N 1 58W
Montfort, *Neths.* **17** 51 7N 5 58 E
Montfort-l'Amaury, *France* **19** 48 47N 1 49 E
Montgenèvre, *France* **21** 44 56N 6 43 E
Montgomery = Sahiwal, *Pakistan* **48** 30 45N 73 8 E
Montgomery, *U.K.* **13** 52 34N 3 9W
Montgomery, *Ala., U.S.A.* **115** 32 20N 86 20W
Montgomery, *Ill., U.S.A.* **119** 41 44N 88 21W
Montgomery, *W. Va., U.S.A.* **114** 38 9N 81 21W
Montgomery City, *U.S.A.* **118** 38 59N 91 30W
Montguyon, *France* **20** 45 12N 0 12W
Monthey, *Switz.* **31** 46 15N 6 56 E
Monticelli d'Ongina, *Italy* **26** 45 3N 9 56 E
Monticello, *Ark., U.S.A.* **121** 33 40N 91 48W
Monticello, *Fla., U.S.A.* **115** 30 35N 83 50W
Monticello, *Ill., U.S.A.* **119** 40 1N 88 34W
Monticello, *Ind., U.S.A.* **119** 40 40N 86 45W
Monticello, *Iowa, U.S.A.* **118** 42 18N 91 12W
Monticello, *Ky., U.S.A.* **115** 36 52N 84 50W
Monticello, *Minn., U.S.A.* **120** 45 17N 93 52W
Monticello, *Miss., U.S.A.* **121** 31 35N 90 8W
Monticello, *Mo., U.S.A.* **118** 40 7N 91 43W
Monticello, *N.Y., U.S.A.* **117** 41 37N 74 42W
Monticello, *Utah, U.S.A.* **123** 37 55N 109 27W
Montichiari, *Italy* **26** 45 28N 10 29 E
Montier-en-Der, *France* **19** 48 30N 4 45 E
Montignac, *France* **20** 45 4N 1 10 E
Montignies-sur-Sambre, *Belgium* **17** 50 24N 4 29 E
Montigny, *France* **19** 49 7N 6 10 E
Montigny-sur-Aube, *France* **19** 47 57N 4 45 E
Montijo, *Spain* **23** 38 52N 6 39W
Montijo, Presa de, *Spain* **23** 38 55N 6 26W
Montilla, *Spain* **23** 37 36N 4 40W
Montlhéry, *France* **19** 48 39N 2 15 E
Montluçon, *France* **20** 46 22N 2 36 E
Montmagny, *Canada* **107** 46 58N 70 34W
Montmarault, *France* **20** 46 19N 2 57 E
Montmartre, *Canada* **111** 50 14N 103 27W
Montmédy, *France* **19** 49 30N 5 20 E
Montmélian, *France* **21** 45 30N 6 4 E
Montmirail, *France* **19** 48 51N 3 30 E
Montmoreau-St.-Cybard, *France* **20** 45 23N 0 8 E
Montmorency, *Canada* **105** 46 53N 71 11W
Montmorillon, *France* **20** 46 26N 0 50 E
Montmort, *France* **19** 48 55N 3 49 E
Monto, *Australia* **72** 24 52 S 151 6 E
Montoir-sur-le-Loir, *France* **18** 47 45N 0 52 E
Montório al Vomano, *Italy* **27** 42 35N 13 38 E
Montoro, *Spain* **23** 38 1N 4 27W
Montour Falls, *U.S.A.* **116** 42 20N 76 51W
Montpelier, *Idaho, U.S.A.* **122** 42 15N 111 20W
Montpelier, *Ind., U.S.A.* **119** 40 33N 85 17W
Montpelier, *Ohio, U.S.A.* **119** 41 34N 84 40W
Montpelier, *Vt., U.S.A.* **117** 44 15N 72 38W
Montpellier, *France* **20** 43 37N 3 52 E
Montpezat-de-Quercy, *France* **20** 44 15N 1 30 E
Montpon-Ménestérol, *France* **20** 45 0N 0 11 E
Montréal, *Canada* **107** 45 31N 73 34W
Montréal, *France* **20** 43 13N 2 8 E
Montreal L., *Canada* **111** 54 20N 105 45W
Montreal Lake, *Canada* **111** 54 3N 105 46W
Montredon-Labessonnié, *France* **20** 43 45N 2 18 E
Montréjeau, *France* **20** 43 6N 0 35 E
Montrésor, *France* **18** 47 10N 1 10 E
Montreuil, *France* **19** 50 27N 1 45 E
Montreuil, L., *Canada* **106** 50 12N 77 40W
Montreuil-Bellay, *France* **18** 47 8N 0 9W
Montreux, *Switz.* **31** 46 26N 6 55 E
Montrevault, *France* **18** 47 17N 1 2W
Montrevel-en-Bresse, *France* **21** 46 21N 5 8 E
Montrichard, *France* **18** 47 20N 1 10 E
Montrose, *U.K.* **14** 56 43N 2 28W
Montrose, *Colo., U.S.A.* **123** 38 30N 107 52W
Montrose, *Pa., U.S.A.* **117** 41 50N 75 55W
Montrose, L., *U.S.A.* **118** 38 18N 93 50W
Monts, Pte. des, *Canada* **105** 49 20N 67 12W
Monts-sur-Guesnes, *France* **18** 46 55N 0 13 E
Montsalvy, *France* **20** 44 41N 2 30 E
Montsant, Sierra de, *Spain* **24** 41 17N 1 0 E
Montsauche, *France* **19** 47 13N 4 2 E
Montsech, Sierra del, *Spain* **24** 42 0N 0 45 E
Montseny, *Spain* **24** 41 55N 2 25W
Montserrat, *Spain* **24** 41 36N 1 49 E
Montserrat, *W. Indies* **129** 16 40N 62 10W
Montuenga, *Spain* **22** 41 3N 4 38W
Montuiri, *Spain* **24** 39 34N 2 59 E
Monveda, *Zaïre* **94** 2 52N 21 30 E
Monyo, *Burma* **52** 17 59N 95 30 E
Monywa, *Burma* **52** 22 7N 95 11 E
Monza, *Italy* **26** 45 35N 9 15 E
Monze, *Zambia* **93** 16 17 S 27 29 E
Monze, C., *Pakistan* **48** 24 47N 66 37 E
Monzón, *Spain* **24** 41 52N 0 10 E
Mooi River, *S. Africa* **97** 29 13 S 29 50 E
Mook, *Neths.* **16** 51 46N 5 54 E
Mo'oka, *Japan* **65** 36 26N 140 1 E
Moolawatana, *Australia* **73** 29 55 S 139 45 E
Mooliabeenee, *Australia* **79** 31 20 S 116 2 E
Mooloogool, *Australia* **79** 26 2 S 119 5 E
Moomin, Cr. →, *Australia* **77** 29 44 S 149 20 E
Moonah →, *Australia* **72** 22 3 S 138 33 E
Moonan Flat, *Australia* **77** 31 55 S 151 14 E
Moonbeam, *Canada* **104** 49 20N 82 10W
Moondarra, *Australia* **75** 38 2 S 146 30 E
Moonie, *Australia* **77** 27 46 S 150 20 E
Moonie →, *Australia* **77** 29 19 S 148 43 E
Moonta, *Australia* **73** 34 6 S 137 32 E
Moora, *Australia* **79** 30 37 S 115 58 E
Mooraberree, *Australia* **72** 25 13 S 140 54 E
Mooralla, *Australia* **74** 37 25 S 142 10 E
Moorarie, *Australia* **79** 25 56 S 117 35 E
Moorcroft, *U.S.A.* **120** 44 17N 104 58W
Moore, *Australia* **77** 30 57 S 150 52 E
Moore →, *Australia* **79** 31 22 S 115 30 E
Moore, L., *Australia* **79** 29 50 S 117 35 E
Moore Reefs, *Australia* **72** 16 0 S 149 5 E
Moorefield, *U.S.A.* **114** 39 5N 78 59W
Moores Res., *U.S.A.* **117** 44 45N 71 50W
Mooresville, *Ind., U.S.A.* **119** 39 37N 86 22W
Mooresville, *N.C., U.S.A.* **115** 35 36N 80 45W
Moorfoot Hills, *U.K.* **14** 55 44N 3 8W
Moorhead, *U.S.A.* **120** 46 51N 96 44W
Moorland, *Australia* **77** 31 46 S 152 38 E
Mooroopna, *Australia* **74** 36 25 S 145 22 E
Moorpark, *U.S.A.* **125** 34 17N 118 53W
Moorreesburg, *S. Africa* **96** 33 6 S 18 38 E
Moorslede, *Belgium* **17** 50 54N 3 4 E
Moosburg, *W. Germany* **31** 48 28N 11 57 E
Moose →, *Canada* **104** 51 20N 80 25W
Moose Creek, *Canada* **109** 45 15N 74 58W
Moose Factory, *Canada* **104** 51 16N 80 32W
Moose I., *Canada* **111** 51 42N 97 10W
Moose Jaw, *Canada* **111** 50 24N 105 30W
Moose Jaw →, *Canada* **111** 50 34N 105 18W
Moose Lake, *Canada* **111** 53 43N 100 20W
Moose Lake, *U.S.A.* **120** 46 27N 92 48W
Moose Mountain Cr. →, *Canada* **111** 49 13N 102 12W
Moose Mountain Prov. Park, *Canada* **111** 49 48N 102 25W
Moose River, *Canada* **104** 50 48N 81 17W
Moosehead L., *U.S.A.* **105** 45 34N 69 40W
Moosomin, *Canada* **111** 50 9N 101 40W
Moosonee, *Canada* **104** 51 17N 80 39W
Moosup, *U.S.A.* **117** 41 44N 71 52W
Mopeia Velha, *Mozam.* **93** 17 30 S 35 40 E
Mopipi, *Botswana* **96** 21 6 S 24 55 E
Mopoi, *C.A.R.* **92** 5 6N 26 54 E
Mopti, *Mali* **90** 14 30N 4 0W
Moqatta, *Sudan* **89** 14 38N 35 50 E
Moquegua, *Peru* **136** 17 15 S 70 46W
Moquegua □, *Peru* **136** 16 50 S 70 55W
Mór, *Hungary* **33** 47 25N 18 12 E
Móra, *Portugal* **23** 38 55N 8 10W
Mora, *Sweden* **10** 61 2N 14 38 E
Mora, *Minn., U.S.A.* **120** 45 52N 93 19W
Mora, *N. Mex., U.S.A.* **123** 35 58N 105 21W
Mora de Ebro, *Spain* **24** 41 6N 0 38 E
Mora de Rubielos, *Spain* **24** 40 15N 0 45W
Mora la Nueva, *Spain* **24** 41 7N 0 39 E
Morača →, *Yugoslavia* **33** 42 20N 19 9 E
Morada Nova, *Brazil* **138** 5 7 S 38 23W
Morada Nova de Minas, *Brazil* **139** 18 37 S 45 22W
Moradabad, *India* **49** 28 50N 78 50 E
Morafenobe, *Madag.* **97** 17 50 S 44 53 E
Morąg, *Poland* **32** 53 55N 19 56 E
Moral de Calatrava, *Spain* **25** 38 51N 3 33W
Moraleja, *Spain* **22** 40 6N 6 43W
Morales, *Colombia* **134** 2 45N 76 38W
Moramanga, *Madag.* **97** 18 56 S 48 12 E
Moran, *Kans., U.S.A.* **121** 37 53N 94 35W
Moran, *Wyo., U.S.A.* **122** 43 53N 110 37W
Moranbah, *Australia* **72** 22 1 S 148 6 E
Morangarell, *Australia* **76** 34 8 S 147 42 E
Morano Cálabro, *Italy* **29** 39 51N 16 8 E
Morant Cays, *Jamaica* **128** 17 22N 76 0W
Morant Pt., *Jamaica* **128** 17 55N 76 12W
Morar L., *U.K.* **14** 56 57N 5 40W
Moratalla, *Spain* **25** 38 14N 1 49W
Moratuwa, *Sri Lanka* **51** 6 45N 79 55 E
Morava →, *Czech.* **32** 48 10N 16 59 E
Moravia, *U.S.A.* **118** 40 50N 92 50W
Moravian Hts. = Ceskomoravská Vrchovina, *Czech.* **32** 49 30N 15 40 E
Moravica →, *Yugoslavia* **33** 43 52N 20 8 E
Moravice →, *Czech.* **32** 49 50N 17 43 E
Moraviţa, *Romania* **33** 45 17N 21 14 E
Moravská Třebová, *Czech.* **32** 49 45N 16 40 E
Morawa, *Australia* **79** 29 13 S 116 0 E
Morawhanna, *Guyana* **135** 8 30N 59 40W
Moray Firth, *U.K.* **14** 57 50N 3 30W
Morbach, *W. Germany* **31** 49 48N 7 7 E
Morbegno, *Italy* **26** 46 8N 9 34 E
Morbi, *India* **48** 22 50N 70 42 E
Morbihan □, *France* **18** 47 55N 2 50W
Morcenx, *France* **20** 44 0N 0 55W
Mordelles, *France* **18** 48 5N 1 52W
Morden, *Canada* **111** 49 15N 98 10W
Mordialloc, *Australia* **74** 38 1 S 145 6 E
Mordovian A.S.S.R. □, *U.S.S.R.* **37** 54 20N 44 30 E
Mordovo, *U.S.S.R.* **37** 52 6N 40 50 E
Møre og Romsdal fylke □, *Norway* **10** 62 30N 8 0 E
Morea, *Australia* **74** 36 45 S 141 18 E
Morea, *Greece* **6** 37 45N 22 10 E
Moreau →, *U.S.A.* **120** 45 15N 100 43W
Morecambe, *U.K.* **12** 54 5N 2 52W
Morecambe B., *U.K.* **12** 54 7N 3 0W
Moree, *Australia* **77** 29 28 S 149 54 E
Morehead, *Papua N. G.* **69** 8 41 S 141 41 E
Morehead, *U.S.A.* **119** 38 12N 83 22W
Morehead City, *U.S.A.* **115** 34 46N 76 44W
Morelia, *Mexico* **126** 19 40N 101 11W
Morella, *Australia* **72** 23 0 S 143 52 E
Morella, *Spain* **24** 40 35N 0 5W
Morelos, *Mexico* **126** 26 42N 107 40W
Morelos □, *Mexico* **127** 18 40N 99 10W
Morena, Sierra, *Spain* **23** 38 20N 4 0W
Morenci, *Ariz., U.S.A.* **123** 33 7N 109 20W
Morenci, *Mich., U.S.A.* **119** 41 43N 84 13W
Moreni, *Romania* **34** 44 59N 25 36 E
Morero, *Bolivia* **137** 11 9 S 66 15W
Moreru →, *Brazil* **137** 10 10 S 59 15W
Moresby I., *Canada* **110** 52 30N 131 40W
Morestel, *France* **21** 45 40N 5 28 E
Moret-sur-Loing, *France* **19** 48 22N 2 58 E
Moreton, *Australia* **72** 12 22 S 142 30 E
Moreton I., *Australia* **77** 27 10 S 153 25 E
Moreuil, *France* **19** 49 46N 2 30 E
Morez, *France* **21** 46 31N 6 2 E
Morgan, *Australia* **73** 34 0 S 139 35 E
Morgan, *U.S.A.* **122** 41 3N 111 44W
Morgan City, *U.S.A.* **121** 29 40N 91 15W
Morgan Hill, *U.S.A.* **124** 37 8N 121 39W
Morganfield, *U.S.A.* **114** 37 40N 87 55W
Morganton, *U.S.A.* **115** 35 46N 81 48W
Morgantown, *Ind., U.S.A.* **119** 39 22N 86 16W
Morgantown, *W. Va., U.S.A.* **114** 39 39N 79 58W
Morgat, *France* **18** 48 15N 4 32W
Morgenzon, *S. Africa* **97** 26 45 S 29 36 E
Morges, *Switz.* **31** 46 31N 6 29 E
Morhange, *France* **19** 48 55N 6 38 E
Mori, *Italy* **26** 45 51N 10 59 E
Morialmée, *Belgium* **17** 50 17N 4 35 E
Morice L., *Canada* **110** 53 50N 127 40W
Morichal, *Colombia* **134** 2 10N 70 34W
Morichal Largo →, *Venezuela* **135** 9 27N 62 25W
Moriguchi, *Japan* **65** 34 44N 135 34 E
Moriki, *Nigeria* **91** 12 52N 6 30 E
Morin-Heights, *Canada* **107** 45 54N 74 15W
Morinville, *Canada* **110** 53 49N 113 41W
Morioka, *Japan* **63** 39 45N 141 8 E
Moris, *Mexico* **126** 28 8N 108 32W
Morisset, *Australia* **76** 33 6 S 151 30 E
Morlaàs, *France* **20** 43 21N 0 18W
Morlaix, *France* **18** 48 36N 3 52W
Morlanwelz, *Belgium* **17** 50 28N 4 15 E
Mormanno, *Italy* **29** 39 53N 15 59 E
Mormant, *France* **19** 48 37N 2 52 E
Mornington, *Vic., Australia* **74** 38 15 S 145 5 E
Mornington, *W. Austral., Australia* **78** 17 31 S 126 6 E
Mornington, I., *Chile* **142** 49 50 S 75 30W
Mornington I., *Australia* **72** 16 30 S 139 30 E
Mórnos →, *Greece* **35** 38 30N 22 0 E
Moro, *Sudan* **89** 10 50N 30 9 E
Moro G., *Phil.* **57** 6 30N 123 0 E
Morobe, *Papua N. G.* **69** 7 49 S 147 38 E
Morocco, *U.S.A.* **119** 40 57N 87 27W
Morocco ■, *N. Afr.* **84** 32 0N 5 50W
Morococha, *Peru* **136** 11 40 S 76 5W
Moroga, *Solomon Is.* **68** 10 30 S 161 40 E
Morogoro, *Tanzania* **92** 6 50 S 37 40 E
Morogoro □, *Tanzania* **92** 8 0 S 37 0 E
Moroleón, *Mexico* **126** 20 8N 101 32W
Morombe, *Madag.* **97** 21 45 S 43 22 E
Moron, *Argentina* **140** 34 39 S 58 37W
Morón, *Cuba* **128** 22 8N 78 39W
Mörön →, *Mongolia* **62** 47 14N 110 37 E
Morón de Almazán, *Spain* **24** 41 29N 2 27W
Morón de la Frontera, *Spain* **23** 37 6N 5 28W
Morona →, *Peru* **134** 4 40 S 77 10W
Morona-Santiago □, *Ecuador* **134** 2 30 S 78 0W
Morondava, *Madag.* **97** 20 17 S 44 17 E
Morondo, *Ivory C.* **90** 8 57N 6 47W
Morongo Valley, *U.S.A.* **125** 34 3N 116 37W
Moronou, *Ivory C.* **90** 6 16N 4 59W
Morotai, *Indonesia* **57** 2 10N 128 30 E
Moroto, *Uganda* **92** 2 28N 34 42 E
Moroto Summit, *Kenya* **92** 2 30N 34 43 E
Morozovsk, *U.S.S.R.* **39** 48 25N 41 50 E
Morpeth, *Australia* **76** 32 44 S 151 39 E
Morpeth, *U.K.* **12** 55 11N 1 41W
Morphou, *Cyprus* **46** 35 12N 32 59 E
Morrelganj, *Bangla.* **52** 22 28N 89 51 E
Morrilton, *U.S.A.* **121** 35 10N 92 45W
Morrinhos, *Ceara, Brazil* **138** 3 14 S 40 7W
Morrinhos, *Minas Gerais, Brazil* **139** 17 45 S 49 10W
Morrinsville, *N.Z.* **80** 37 40 S 175 32 E
Morris, *Canada* **111** 49 25N 97 22W
Morris, *Ill., U.S.A.* **119** 41 20N 88 20W
Morris, *Minn., U.S.A.* **120** 45 33N 95 56W
Morris, Mt., *Australia* **79** 26 9 S 131 4 E
Morrisburg, *Canada* **109** 44 55N 75 7W

Morrison, *U.S.A.* **118** 41 47N 90 0W
Morrisonville, *U.S.A.* **118** 39 25N 89 27W
Morristown, *Ariz., U.S.A.* **123** 33 54N 112 35W
Morristown, *Ind., U.S.A.* **119** 39 40N 85 42W
Morristown, *N.J., U.S.A.* **117** 40 48N 74 30W
Morristown, *S. Dak., U.S.A.* **120** 45 57N 101 44W
Morristown, *Tenn., U.S.A.* **115** 36 18N 83 20W
Morro, Pta., *Chile* **140** 27 6 S 71 0W
Morro Bay, *U.S.A.* **124** 35 27N 120 54W
Morro del Jable, *Canary Is.* **25** 28 3N 14 23W
Morro do Chapéu, *Brazil* **139** 11 33 S 41 9W
Morro Jable, Pta. de, *Canary Is.* **25** 28 2N 14 20W
Morros, *Brazil* **138** 2 52 S 44 3W
Morrosquillo, G. de, *Colombia* **128** 9 35N 75 40W
Mörrum, *Sweden* **11** 56 12N 14 45 E
Morrumbene, *Mozam.* **97** 23 31 S 35 16 E
Mors, *Denmark* **11** 56 50N 8 45 E
Morshansk, *U.S.S.R.* **37** 53 28N 41 50 E
Mörsil, *Sweden* **10** 63 19N 13 40 E
Mortagne →, *France* **19** 48 33N 6 27 E
Mortagne-au-Perche, *France* **18** 48 31N 0 33 E
Mortagne-sur-Gironde, *France* **20** 45 28N 0 47W
Mortagne-sur-Sèvre, *France* **18** 46 59N 0 57W
Mortain, *France* **18** 48 40N 0 57W
Mortara, *Italy* **26** 45 15N 8 43 E
Mortcha, *Chad* **87** 16 0N 21 10 E
Morteau, *France* **19** 47 3N 6 35 E
Morteros, *Argentina* **140** 30 50 S 62 0W
Mortes, R. das →, *Brazil* **139** 11 45 S 50 44W
Mortlake, *Australia* **74** 38 5 S 142 50 E
Morton, *Ill., U.S.A.* **118** 40 37N 89 28W
Morton, *Tex., U.S.A.* **121** 33 39N 102 49W
Morton, *Wash., U.S.A.* **124** 46 33N 122 17W
Mortsel, *Belgium* **17** 51 11N 4 27 E
Morundah, *Australia* **75** 34 57 S 146 19 E
Moruya, *Australia* **76** 35 58 S 150 3 E
Moruya Heads, *Australia* **76** 35 55 S 150 9 E
Morvan, *France* **19** 47 5N 4 0 E
Morven, *Australia* **73** 26 22 S 147 5 E
Morven, *N.Z.* **81** 44 50 S 171 6 E
Morvern, *U.K.* **14** 56 38N 5 44W
Morwell, *Australia* **75** 38 10 S 146 22 E
Mosalsk, *U.S.S.R.* **36** 54 30N 34 55 E
Mosbach, *W. Germany* **31** 49 21N 9 9 E
Moščenice, *Yugoslavia* **27** 45 17N 14 16 E
Mosciano Sant' Ángelo, *Italy* **27** 42 42N 13 52 E
Moscos Is., *Burma* **54** 14 0N 97 30 E
Moscow = Moskva, *U.S.S.R.* **37** 55 45N 37 35 E
Moscow, *U.S.A.* **122** 46 45N 116 59W
Mosel →, *Europe* **17** 50 22N 7 36 E
Moselle = Mosel →, *Europe* **17** 50 22N 7 36 E
Moselle □, *France* **19** 48 59N 6 33 E
Moses Lake, *U.S.A.* **122** 47 9N 119 17W
Mosgiel, *N.Z.* **81** 45 53 S 170 21 E
Moshi, *Tanzania* **92** 3 22 S 37 18 E
Moshi □, *Tanzania* **92** 3 22 S 37 18 E
Moshupa, *Botswana* **96** 24 46 S 25 29 E
Mosjøen, *Norway* **8** 65 51N 13 12 E
Moskenesøya, *Norway* **8** 67 58N 13 0 E
Moskenstraumen, *Norway* **8** 67 47N 12 45 E
Moskva, *U.S.S.R.* **37** 55 45N 37 35 E
Moskva →, *U.S.S.R.* **37** 55 5N 38 51 E
Moslavačka Gora, *Yugoslavia* **27** 45 40N 16 37 E
Moso, *Vanuatu* **68** 17 30 S 168 15 E
Mosomane, *Botswana* **96** 24 2 S 26 19 E
Mosonmagyaróvár, *Hungary* **33** 47 52N 17 18 E
Mospino, *U.S.S.R.* **38** 47 52N 38 0 E
Mosquera, *Colombia* **134** 2 35N 78 24W
Mosquero, *U.S.A.* **121** 35 48N 103 57W
Mosqueruela, *Spain* **24** 40 21N 0 27W
Mosquitia, *Honduras* **128** 15 20N 84 10W
Mosquitos, G. de los, *Panama* **128** 9 15N 81 10W
Moss, *Norway* **10** 59 27N 10 40 E
Moss Vale, *Australia* **76** 34 32 S 150 25 E
Mossaka, *Congo* **94** 1 15 S 16 45 E
Mossâmedes, *Brazil* **139** 16 7 S 50 11W
Mossbank, *Canada* **111** 49 56N 105 56W
Mossburn, *N.Z.* **81** 45 41 S 168 15 E
Mosselbaai, *S. Africa* **96** 34 11 S 22 8 E
Mossendjo, *Congo* **94** 2 55 S 12 42 E
Mossgiel, *Australia* **73** 33 15 S 144 5 E
Mossman, *Australia* **72** 16 21 S 145 15 E
Mossoró, *Brazil* **138** 5 10 S 37 15W
Mossuril, *Mozam.* **93** 14 58 S 40 42 E
Mossy →, *Canada* **111** 54 5N 102 58W
Most, *Czech.* **32** 50 31N 13 38 E
Mostaganem, *Algeria* **85** 35 54N 0 5 E
Mostar, *Yugoslavia* **33** 43 22N 17 50 E
Mostardas, *Brazil* **141** 31 2 S 50 51W
Mostefa, Rass, *Tunisia* **86** 36 55N 11 3 E
Mostiska, *U.S.S.R.* **36** 49 48N 23 4 E
Mosty, *U.S.S.R.* **36** 53 27N 24 38 E
Mosul = Al Mawṣil, *Iraq* **46** 36 15N 43 5 E
Mota, *Vanuatu* **68** 13 49 S 167 42 E
Mota del Cuervo, *Spain* **24** 39 30N 2 52W
Mota del Marqués, *Spain* **22** 41 38N 5 11W
Mota Lava, *Vanuatu* **68** 13 40 S 167 40 E
Motagua →, *Guatemala* **128** 15 44N 88 14W
Motala, *Sweden* **11** 58 32N 15 1 E
Motegi, *Japan* **65** 36 32N 140 11 E
Mothe, La, Rés., *Canada* **107** 48 46N 71 9W
Mothe-Achard, La, *France* **18** 46 37N 1 40W
Motherwell, *U.K.* **14** 55 48N 4 0W
Motihari, *India* **49** 26 30N 84 55 E
Motilla del Palancar, *Spain* **24** 39 34N 1 55W
Motnik, *Yugoslavia* **27** 46 14N 14 54 E
Motocurunya, *Venezuela* **135** 4 24N 64 5W
Motovun, *Yugoslavia* **27** 45 20N 13 50 E
Motozintla de Mendoza, *Mexico* **127** 15 21N 92 14W
Motril, *Spain* **25** 36 31N 3 37W
Motru →, *Romania* **34** 44 44N 22 59 E
Mott, *U.S.A.* **120** 46 25N 102 29W
Motte, L. la, *Canada* **106** 48 20N 78 2W
Motte, La, *France* **21** 44 20N 6 3 E
Motte-Chalançon, La, *France* **21** 44 30N 5 21 E
Móttola, *Italy* **29** 40 38N 17 0 E
Motu, *N.Z.* **80** 38 18 S 177 40 E
Motueka, *N.Z.* **81** 41 7 S 173 1 E
Motul, *Mexico* **127** 21 0N 89 20W
Motupena Pt., *Papua N. G.* **69** 6 30 S 155 10 E
Mou, *N. Cal.* **68** 21 5 S 165 26 E
Mouanda, *Gabon* **94** 1 28 S 13 7 E
Mouchalagane →, *Canada* **105** 50 56N 68 41W
Mouding, *China* **58** 25 20N 101 28 E
Moudjeria, *Mauritania* **90** 17 50N 12 28W
Moudon, *Switz.* **31** 46 40N 6 49 E
Mougoundou, *Congo* **94** 2 40 S 12 41 E
Mouila, *Gabon* **94** 1 50 S 11 0 E
Mouka, *C.A.R.* **94** 7 16N 21 52 E
Moulamein, *Australia* **74** 35 3 S 144 1 E
Moule, *Guadeloupe* **129** 16 20N 61 22W
Moulins, *France* **20** 46 35N 3 19 E
Moulmein, *Burma* **52** 16 30N 97 40 E
Moulmeingyun, *Burma* **52** 16 23N 95 16 E
Moulouya, O. →, *Morocco* **85** 35 5N 2 25W
Moulton, *Iowa, U.S.A.* **118** 40 41N 92 41W
Moulton, *Tex., U.S.A.* **121** 29 35N 97 8W
Moultrie, *U.S.A.* **115** 31 11N 83 47W
Moultrie, L., *U.S.A.* **115** 33 25N 80 10W
Mound City, *Mo., U.S.A.* **120** 40 2N 95 25W
Mound City, *S. Dak., U.S.A.* **120** 45 46N 100 3W
Moúnda, Ákra, *Greece* **35** 38 5N 20 45 E
Moundou, *Chad* **87** 8 40N 16 10 E
Moundsville, *U.S.A.* **116** 39 53N 80 43W
Mounembé, *Congo* **94** 3 20 S 12 32 E
Moung, *Cambodia* **54** 12 46N 103 27 E
Moungga, *Solomon Is.* **68** 7 0 S 156 0 E
Moungoudi, *Congo* **94** 2 45 S 11 46 E
Mount Airy, *U.S.A.* **115** 36 31N 80 37W
Mount Albert, *Canada* **108** 44 8N 79 19W
Mount Alford, *Australia* **77** 28 4 S 152 35 E
Mount Amherst, *Australia* **78** 18 24 S 126 58 E
Mount Angel, *U.S.A.* **122** 45 4N 122 46W
Mount Augustus, *Australia* **79** 24 20 S 116 56 E
Mount Ayr, *U.S.A.* **118** 40 43N 94 14W
Mount Barker, *S. Austral., Australia* **73** 35 5 S 138 52 E
Mount Barker, *W. Austral., Australia* **79** 34 38 S 117 40 E
Mount Beauty, *Australia* **75** 36 47 S 147 10 E
Mount Brydges, *Canada* **108** 42 54N 81 29W
Mount Buller, *Australia* **75** 37 9 S 146 27 E
Mount Carmel, *U.S.A.* **119** 38 20N 87 48W
Mount Carroll, *U.S.A.* **118** 42 6N 89 59W
Mount Clemens, *U.S.A.* **116** 42 35N 82 50W
Mount Coolon, *Australia* **72** 21 25 S 147 25 E
Mount Darwin, *Zimb.* **93** 16 47 S 31 38 E
Mount Desert I., *U.S.A.* **105** 44 15N 68 25W
Mount Dora, *U.S.A.* **115** 28 49N 81 32W
Mount Douglas, *Australia* **72** 21 35 S 146 50 E
Mount Eden, *U.S.A.* **119** 38 3N 85 9W
Mount Edgecumbe, *U.S.A.* **110** 57 8N 135 22W
Mount Elizabeth, *Australia* **78** 16 0 S 125 50 E
Mount Emu Creek, *Australia* **74** 38 20 S 142 40 E
Mount Fletcher, *S. Africa* **97** 30 40 S 28 30 E
Mount Forest, *Canada* **108** 43 59N 80 43W
Mount Gambier, *Australia* **73** 37 50 S 140 46 E
Mount Garnet, *Australia* **72** 17 37 S 145 6 E
Mount George, *Australia* **77** 31 53 S 152 12 E
Mount Hagen, *Papua N. G.* **69** 5 52 S 144 16 E
Mount Helen, *Australia* **74** 37 38 S 143 54 E
Mount Hope, *N.S.W., Australia* **73** 32 51 S 145 51 E
Mount Hope, *S. Austral., Australia* **73** 34 7 S 135 23 E
Mount Hope, *U.S.A.* **114** 37 52N 81 9W
Mount Horeb, *U.S.A.* **118** 43 0N 89 42W
Mount Howitt, *Australia* **73** 26 31 S 142 16 E
Mount Isa, *Australia* **72** 20 42 S 139 26 E
Mount Keith, *Australia* **79** 27 15 S 120 30 E
Mount Laguna, *U.S.A.* **125** 32 52N 116 25W
Mount Larcom, *Australia* **72** 23 48 S 150 59 E
Mount Lofty Ra., *Australia* **73** 34 35 S 139 5 E
Mount Macedon, *Australia* **74** 37 23 S 144 35 E
Mount McKinley Nat. Park, *U.S.A.* **102** 64 0N 150 0W
Mount Magnet, *Australia* **79** 28 2 S 117 47 E
Mount Margaret, *Australia* **73** 26 54 S 143 21 E
Mount Martha, *Australia* **74** 38 17 S 145 1 E
Mount Maunganui, *N.Z.* **80** 37 40 S 176 14 E
Mount Molloy, *Australia* **72** 16 42 S 145 20 E
Mount Monger, *Australia* **79** 31 0 S 122 0 E
Mount Morgan, *Australia* **72** 23 40 S 150 25 E
Mount Morris, *U.S.A.* **116** 42 43N 77 50W
Mount Mulligan, *Australia* **72** 16 45 S 144 47 E
Mount Narryer, *Australia* **79** 26 30 S 115 55 E
Mount Olive, *U.S.A.* **118** 39 4N 89 44W
Mount Olivet, *U.S.A.* **119** 38 32N 84 2W
Mount Orab, *U.S.A.* **119** 39 5N 83 56W
Mount Oxide Mine, *Australia* **72** 19 30 S 139 29 E
Mount Pearl, *Canada* **105** 47 31N 52 47W
Mount Perry, *Australia* **73** 25 13 S 151 42 E
Mount Phillips, *Australia* **79** 24 25 S 116 15 E
Mount Pleasant, *Iowa, U.S.A.* **118** 40 58N 91 35W
Mount Pleasant, *Mich., U.S.A.* **104** 43 35N 84 47W
Mount Pleasant, *Pa., U.S.A.* **116** 40 9N 79 31W
Mount Pleasant, *S.C., U.S.A.* **115** 32 45N 79 48W
Mount Pleasant, *Tenn., U.S.A.* **115** 35 31N 87 11W
Mount Pleasant, *Tex., U.S.A.* **121** 33 5N 95 0W
Mount Pleasant, *Utah, U.S.A.* **122** 39 40N 111 29W
Mount Pocono, *U.S.A.* **117** 41 8N 75 21W
Mount Pulaski, *U.S.A.* **118** 40 1N 89 17W
Mount Rainier Nat. Park., *U.S.A.* **124** 46 50N 121 43W
Mount Revelstoke Nat. Park, *Canada* **110** 51 5N 118 30W
Mount Robson Prov. Park, *Canada* **110** 53 0N 119 0W
Mount Roskill, *N.Z.* **80** 36 55 S 174 45 E
Mount Sandiman, *Australia* **79** 24 25 S 115 30 E
Mount Shasta, *U.S.A.* **122** 41 20N 122 18W
Mount Signal, *U.S.A.* **125** 32 39N 115 37W
Mount Somers, *N.Z.* **81** 43 45 S 171 27 E
Mount Sterling, *Ill., U.S.A.* **118** 39 59N 90 40W
Mount Sterling, *Ky., U.S.A.* **119** 38 3N 83 57W
Mount Sterling, *Ohio, U.S.A.* **119** 39 43N 83 16W
Mount Surprise, *Australia* **72** 18 10 S 144 17 E
Mount Union, *U.S.A.* **116** 40 22N 77 51W
Mount Vernon, *Australia* **79** 24 9 S 118 2 E
Mount Vernon, *Ill., U.S.A.* **119** 38 19N 88 55W
Mount Vernon, *Ind., U.S.A.* **119** 38 17N 88 57W
Mount Vernon, *Iowa, U.S.A.* **118** 41 55N 91 23W
Mount Vernon, *N.Y., U.S.A.* **117** 40 57N 73 49W
Mount Vernon, *Ohio, U.S.A.* **116** 40 20N 82 30W
Mount Vernon, *Wash., U.S.A.* **110** 48 25N 122 20W
Mount Victoria, *Australia* **76** 33 33 S 150 16 E
Mount Washington, *U.S.A.* **119** 38 3N 85 33W
Mount Wellington, *N.Z.* **80** 36 55 S 174 52 E
Mount Zion, *U.S.A.* **119** 39 46N 88 53W
Mountain Center, *U.S.A.* **125** 33 42N 116 44W
Mountain City, *Nev., U.S.A.* **122** 41 54N 116 0W
Mountain City, *Tenn., U.S.A.* **115** 36 30N 81 50W
Mountain Grove, *U.S.A.* **121** 37 5N 92 20W
Mountain Home, *Ark., U.S.A.* **121** 36 20N 92 25W
Mountain Home, *Idaho, U.S.A.* **122** 43 11N 115 45W
Mountain Iron, *U.S.A.* **120** 47 30N 92 37W
Mountain Park, *Canada* **110** 52 50N 117 15W
Mountain Pass, *U.S.A.* **125** 35 29N 115 35W
Mountain View, *Ark., U.S.A.* **121** 35 52N 92 10W
Mountain View, *Calif., U.S.A.* **124** 37 26N 122 5W
Mountainair, *U.S.A.* **123** 34 35N 106 15W
Mountmellick, *Ireland* **15** 53 7N 7 20W
Moura, *Australia* **72** 24 35 S 149 58 E
Moura, *Brazil* **135** 1 32 S 61 38W
Moura, *Portugal* **23** 38 7N 7 30W
Mourão, *Portugal* **23** 38 22N 7 22W
Mourdi, Dépression du, *Chad* **87** 18 10N 23 0 E
Mourdiah, *Mali* **90** 14 35N 7 25W
Moure, La, *U.S.A.* **120** 46 27N 98 17W
Mourenx-Ville-Nouvelle, *France* **20** 43 22N 0 38W
Mouri, *Ghana* **91** 5 6N 1 14W
Mourilyan, *Australia* **72** 17 35 S 146 3 E
Mourmelon-le-Grand, *France* **19** 49 8N 4 22 E
Mourne →, *U.K.* **15** 54 45N 7 39W
Mourne Mts., *U.K.* **15** 54 10N 6 0W
Mouscron, *Belgium* **17** 50 45N 3 12 E
Moussoro, *Chad* **87** 13 41N 16 35 E
Moutajup, *Australia* **74** 37 40 S 142 13 E
Mouthe, *France* **19** 46 44N 6 12 E
Moutier, *Switz.* **31** 47 16N 7 21 E
Moûtiers, *France* **21** 45 29N 6 32 E
Moutong, *Indonesia* **57** 0 28N 121 13 E
Mouy, *France* **19** 49 18N 2 20 E
Mouzáki, *Greece* **35** 39 25N 21 37 E
Movas, *Mexico* **126** 28 10N 109 25W
Moville, *Ireland* **15** 55 11N 7 3W
Moweaqua, *U.S.A.* **118** 39 37N 89 1W
Moxhe, *Belgium* **17** 50 38N 5 5 E
Moxico □, *Angola* **95** 12 0 S 20 30 E
Moxotó →, *Brazil* **138** 9 19 S 38 14W
Moy →, *Ireland* **15** 54 5N 8 50W
Moyale, *Kenya* **89** 3 34N 39 4 E
Moyale, *Kenya* **92** 3 30N 39 0 E
Moyamba, *S. Leone* **90** 8 4N 12 30W
Moyen Atlas, *Morocco* **84** 33 0N 5 0W
Moyhu, *Australia* **75** 36 36 S 146 15 E
Moyle □, *U.K.* **15** 55 10N 6 15W
Moyo, *Indonesia* **56** 8 10 S 117 40 E
Moyobamba, *Peru* **136** 6 0 S 77 0W
Moyston, *Australia* **74** 37 17 S 142 45 E
Moyyero →, *U.S.S.R.* **41** 68 44N 103 42 E
Mozambique = Moçambique, *Mozam.* **93** 15 3 S 40 42 E
Mozambique ■, *Africa* **93** 19 0 S 35 0 E
Mozambique Chan., *Africa* **97** 17 30 S 42 30 E
Mozdok, *U.S.S.R.* **39** 43 45N 44 48 E
Mozhaysk, *U.S.S.R.* **37** 55 30N 36 2 E
Mozhga, *U.S.S.R.* **37** 56 26N 52 15 E
Mozirje, *Yugoslavia* **27** 46 22N 14 58 E
Mozyr, *U.S.S.R.* **36** 52 0N 29 15 E
Mpanda, *Tanzania* **92** 6 23 S 31 1 E
Mpanda □, *Tanzania* **92** 6 23 S 31 40 E
Mpésoba, *Mali* **90** 12 31N 5 39W
Mpika, *Zambia* **93** 11 51 S 31 25 E
Mpulungu, *Zambia* **93** 8 51 S 31 5 E
Mpumalanga, *S. Africa* **97** 29 50 S 30 33 E
Mpwapwa, *Tanzania* **92** 6 23 S 36 30 E
Mpwapwa □, *Tanzania* **92** 6 30 S 36 20 E
Mrągowo, *Poland* **32** 53 52N 21 18 E
Mramor, *Yugoslavia* **33** 43 20N 21 45 E
Mrimina, *Morocco* **84** 29 50N 7 9W
Mrkonjić Grad, *Yugoslavia* **33** 44 26N 17 4 E
Mrkopalj, *Yugoslavia* **27** 45 21N 14 52 E
Msab, Oued en →, *Algeria* **85** 32 25N 5 20 E
Msaken, *Tunisia* **86** 35 49N 10 33 E
Msambansovu, *Zimb.* **93** 15 50 S 30 3 E
M'sila, *Algeria* **85** 35 46N 4 30 E
Msoro, *Zambia* **93** 13 35 S 31 50 E
Msta →, *U.S.S.R.* **36** 58 25N 31 20 E
Mstislavl, *U.S.S.R.* **36** 54 0N 31 50 E
Mtama, *Tanzania* **93** 10 17 S 39 21 E
Mtilikwe →, *Zimb.* **93** 21 9 S 31 30 E
Mtsensk, *U.S.S.R.* **37** 53 25N 36 30 E
Mtskheta, *U.S.S.R.* **39** 41 52N 44 45 E
Mtubatuba, *S. Africa* **97** 28 30 S 32 8 E
Mtwara-Mikindani, *Tanzania* **93** 10 20 S 40 20 E
Mu →, *Burma* **52** 21 56N 95 38 E
Mu Gia, Deo, *Vietnam* **54** 17 40N 105 47 E
Mu Us Shamo, *China* **60** 39 0N 109 0 E
Muacandalo, *Angola* **95** 10 2 S 19 40 E
Muaná, *Brazil* **138** 1 25 S 49 15W
Muanda, *Zaïre* **95** 6 0 S 12 20 E
Muang Chiang Rai, *Thailand* **54** 19 52N 99 50 E
Muang Lamphun, *Thailand* **54** 18 40N 99 2 E

Muang Pak Beng, *Laos* **54** 19 54N 101 8 E
Muar, *Malaysia* **55** 2 3N 102 34 E
Muarabungo, *Indonesia* **56** 1 28 S 102 52 E
Muaraenim, *Indonesia* **56** 3 40 S 103 50 E
Muarajuloi, *Indonesia* **56** 0 12 S 114 3 E
Muarakaman, *Indonesia* **56** 0 2 S 116 45 E
Muaratebo, *Indonesia* **56** 1 30 S 102 26 E
Muaratembesi, *Indonesia* **56** 1 42 S 103 8 E
Muaratewe, *Indonesia* **56** 0 58 S 114 52 E
Mubarakpur, *India* **49** 26 6N 83 18 E
Mubende, *Uganda* **92** 0 33N 31 22 E
Mubi, *Nigeria* **91** 10 18N 13 16 E
Mubur, P., *Indonesia* **55** 3 20N 106 12 E
Mucajaí →, *Brazil* **135** 2 25N 60 52W
Mucajaí, Serra do, *Brazil* **135** 2 23N 61 10W
Mucari, *Angola* **95** 9 30 S 16 54 E
Muchachos, Roque de los, *Canary Is.* **25** 28 44N 17 52W
Mücheln, *E. Germany* **30** 51 18N 11 49 E
Muchinga Mts., *Zambia* **93** 11 30 S 31 30 E
Muchkapskiy, *U.S.S.R.* **37** 51 52N 42 28 E
Muck, *U.K.* **14** 56 50N 6 15W
Muckadilla, *Australia* **73** 26 35 S 148 23 E
Muco →, *Colombia* **134** 4 15N 70 21W
Mucoma, *Angola* **95** 15 18 S 13 39 E
Muconda, *Angola* **95** 10 31 S 21 15 E
Mucuim →, *Brazil* **137** 6 33 S 64 18W
Mucura, *Brazil* **135** 2 31 S 62 43W
Mucuri, *Brazil* **139** 18 0 S 39 36W
Mucurici, *Brazil* **139** 18 6 S 40 31W
Mucusso, *Angola* **95** 18 1 S 21 25 E
Muda, *Canary Is.* **25** 28 34N 13 57W
Mudan Jiang →, *China* **61** 46 20N 129 30 E
Mudanjiang, *China* **61** 44 38N 129 30 E
Mudanya, *Turkey* **38** 40 25N 28 50 E
Muddy →, *U.S.A.* **123** 38 0N 110 22W
Mudgee, *Australia* **76** 32 32 S 149 31 E
Mudgeeraba, *Australia* **78** 28 5 S 153 21 E
Mudjatik →, *Canada* **111** 56 1N 107 36W
Mudon, *Burma* **52** 16 15N 97 44 E
Mudugh □, *Somali Rep.* **98** 7 0N 47 30 E
Muecate, *Mozam.* **93** 14 55 S 39 40 E
Muêda, *Mozam.* **93** 11 36 S 39 28 E
Muela, La, *Spain* **24** 41 36N 1 7W
Mueller Ra., *Australia* **78** 18 18 S 126 46 E
Muende, *Mozam.* **93** 14 28 S 33 0 E
Muerto, Mar, *Mexico* **127** 16 10N 94 10W
Muertos, Punta de los, *Spain* **25** 36 57N 1 54W
Mufindi □, *Tanzania* **93** 8 30 S 35 20 E
Mufu Shan, *China* **59** 29 20N 114 30 E
Mufulira, *Zambia* **93** 12 32 S 28 15 E
Mufumbiro Range, *Africa* **92** 1 25 S 29 30 E
Mugardos, *Spain* **22** 43 27N 8 15W
Muge, *Portugal* **23** 39 3N 8 40W
Muge →, *Portugal* **23** 39 8N 8 44W
Múggia, *Italy* **27** 45 36N 13 47 E
Mugi, *Japan* **64** 33 40N 134 25 E
Mugia, *Spain* **22** 43 3N 9 10W
Mugila, Mts., *Zaïre* **92** 7 0 S 28 50 E
Muğla, *Turkey* **46** 37 15N 28 22 E
Műglizh, *Bulgaria* **34** 42 37N 25 32 E
Mugu, *Nepal* **49** 29 45N 82 30 E
Muhammad, Râs, *Egypt* **88** 27 44N 34 16 E
Muhammad Qol, *Sudan* **88** 20 53N 37 9 E
Muhammadabad, *India* **49** 26 4N 83 25 E
Muharraqa = Sa'ad, *Israel* **44** 31 28N 34 33 E
Muhesi →, *Tanzania* **92** 7 0 S 35 20 E
Muheza □, *Tanzania* **92** 5 0 S 39 0 E
Mühldorf, *W. Germany* **31** 48 14N 12 33 E
Mühlhausen, *E. Germany* **30** 51 12N 10 29 E
Mühlig Hofmann fjella, *Antarctica* **143** 72 30 S 5 0 E
Muhutwe, *Tanzania* **92** 1 35 S 31 45 E
Muiden, *Neths.* **16** 52 20N 5 4 E
Muine Bheag, *Ireland* **15** 52 42N 6 57W
Muiños, *Spain* **22** 41 58N 7 59W
Muir, L., *Australia* **79** 34 30 S 116 40 E
Mukachevo, *U.S.S.R.* **36** 48 27N 22 45 E
Mukah, *Malaysia* **56** 2 55N 112 5 E
Mukawwa, Geziret, *Egypt* **88** 23 55N 35 53 E
Mukdahan, *Thailand* **54** 16 32N 104 43 E
Mukden = Shenyang, *China* **61** 41 48N 123 27 E
Mukhtolovo, *U.S.S.R.* **37** 55 29N 43 15 E
Mukhtuya = Lensk, *U.S.S.R.* **41** 60 48N 114 55 E
Mukinbudin, *Australia* **79** 30 55 S 118 5 E
Mukishi, *Zaïre* **93** 8 30 S 24 44 E
Mukomuko, *Indonesia* **56** 2 30 S 101 10 E
Mukomwenze, *Zaïre* **92** 6 49 S 27 15 E
Muktsar, *India* **48** 30 30N 74 30 E
Mukur, *Afghan.* **48** 32 50N 67 42 E
Mukutawa →, *Canada* **111** 53 10N 97 24W
Mukwela, *Zambia* **93** 17 0 S 26 40 E
Mukwonago, *U.S.A.* **119** 42 52N 88 20W
Mula, *Spain* **25** 38 3N 1 33W
Mula →, *India* **50** 18 34N 74 21 E
Mulange, *Zaïre* **92** 3 40 S 27 10 E
Mulberry Grove, *U.S.A.* **118** 38 55N 89 16W
Mulchén, *Chile* **140** 37 45 S 72 20W
Mulde →, *E. Germany* **30** 51 50N 12 15 E
Muldraugh, *U.S.A.* **119** 37 56N 85 59W
Mule Creek, *U.S.A.* **120** 43 19N 104 8W
Muleba, *Tanzania* **92** 1 50 S 31 37 E
Muleba □, *Tanzania* **92** 2 0 S 31 30 E
Muleshoe, *U.S.A.* **121** 34 17N 102 42W
Mulgathing, *Australia* **73** 30 15 S 134 8 E
Mulgrave, *Canada* **105** 45 38N 61 31W
Mulgrave I., *Papua N. G.* **69** 10 5 S 142 10 E
Mulhacén, *Spain* **25** 37 4N 3 20W
Mülheim, *W. Germany* **30** 51 26N 6 53 E
Mulhouse, *France* **19** 47 40N 7 20 E
Muli, *China* **58** 27 52N 101 8 E
Mulifanua, *W. Samoa* **68** 13 50 S 171 59W
Muling, *China* **61** 44 35N 130 10 E
Mull, *U.K.* **14** 56 27N 6 0W
Mullaittvu, *Sri Lanka* **51** 9 15N 80 49 E
Mullaley, *Australia* **77** 31 5 S 149 56 E
Mullbring, *Australia* **76** 32 54 S 151 28 E
Mullen, *U.S.A.* **120** 42 5N 101 0W
Mullengudgery, *Australia* **76** 31 43 S 147 23 E
Mullens, *U.S.A.* **114** 37 34N 81 22W
Muller, Pegunungan, *Indonesia* **56** 0 30N 113 30 E
Mullet Pen., *Ireland* **15** 54 10N 10 2W
Mullewa, *Australia* **79** 28 29 S 115 30 E
Müllheim, *W. Germany* **31** 47 48N 7 37 E
Mulligan →, *Australia* **73** 26 40 S 139 0 E
Mullin, *U.S.A.* **121** 31 33N 98 38W
Mullingar, *Ireland* **15** 53 31N 7 20W
Mullins, *U.S.A.* **115** 34 12N 79 15W
Mullion Creek, *Australia* **76** 33 7 S 149 7 E
Mullsjö, *Sweden* **11** 57 56N 13 55 E
Mullumbimby, *Australia* **77** 28 30 S 153 30 E
Mulobezi, *Zambia* **93** 16 45 S 25 7 E
Mulshi L., *India* **50** 18 30N 73 48 E
Multai, *India* **50** 21 50N 78 21 E
Multan, *Pakistan* **48** 30 15N 71 36 E
Multrå, *Sweden* **10** 63 10N 17 24 E
Mulumbe, Mts., *Zaïre* **93** 8 40 S 27 30 E
Mulungushi Dam, *Zambia* **93** 14 48 S 28 48 E
Mulvane, *U.S.A.* **121** 37 30N 97 15W
Mulwad, *Sudan* **88** 18 45N 30 39 E
Mumbil, *Australia* **76** 32 41 S 149 2 E
Mumbondo, *Angola* **95** 10 9 S 14 15 E
Mumbwa, *Zambia* **93** 15 0 S 27 0 E
Mumeng, *Papua N. G.* **69** 7 1 S 146 37 E
Mummulgum, *Australia* **77** 28 50 S 152 50 E
Mumra, *U.S.S.R.* **39** 45 45N 47 41 E
Mun →, *Thailand* **54** 15 19N 105 30 E
Muna, *Indonesia* **57** 5 0 S 122 30 E
Munamagi, *U.S.S.R.* **36** 57 43N 27 4 E
Münchberg, *W. Germany* **31** 50 11N 11 48 E
Müncheberg, *E. Germany* **30** 52 30N 14 9 E
München, *W. Germany* **31** 48 8N 11 33 E
Munchen-Gladbach = Mönchengladbach, *W. Germany* **30** 51 12N 6 23 E
Muncho Lake, *Canada* **110** 59 0N 125 50W
Muncie, *U.S.A.* **119** 40 10N 85 20W
Munda, *Solomon Is.* **68** 8 20 S 157 16 E
Mundadoo, *Australia* **76** 30 48 S 147 14 E
Mundakayam, *India* **51** 9 30N 76 50 E
Mundala, *Indonesia* **57** 4 30 S 141 0 E
Mundare, *Canada* **110** 53 35N 112 20W
Munday, *U.S.A.* **121** 33 26N 99 39W
Münden, *W. Germany* **30** 51 25N 9 42 E
Mundiwindi, *Australia* **78** 23 47 S 120 9 E
Mundo →, *Spain* **25** 38 30N 2 15W
Mundo Novo, *Brazil* **139** 11 50 S 40 29W
Mundra, *India* **48** 22 54N 69 48 E
Mundrabilla, *Australia* **79** 31 52 S 127 51 E
Munducurus, *Brazil* **135** 4 47 S 58 16W
Munenga, *Angola* **95** 10 2 S 14 41 E
Munera, *Spain* **25** 39 2N 2 29W
Muneru →, *India* **51** 16 45N 80 3 E
Mungallala, *Australia* **73** 26 28 S 147 34 E
Mungallala Cr. →, *Australia* **73** 28 53 S 147 5 E
Mungana, *Australia* **72** 17 8 S 144 27 E
Mungaoli, *India* **48** 24 24N 78 7 E
Mungari, *Mozam.* **93** 17 12 S 33 30 E
Mungbere, *Zaïre* **92** 2 36N 28 28 E
Munger, *India* **49** 25 23N 86 30 E
Mungindi, *Australia* **77** 28 58 S 149 1 E
Munhango, *Angola* **95** 12 10 S 18 38 E
Munich = München, *W. Germany* **31** 48 8N 11 33 E
Munising, *U.S.A.* **104** 46 25N 86 39W
Munka-Ljungby, *Sweden* **11** 56 16N 12 58 E
Munkedal, *Sweden* **11** 58 28N 11 40 E
Munkfors, *Sweden* **10** 59 50N 13 30 E
Munku-Sardyk, *U.S.S.R.* **41** 51 45N 100 20 E
Münnerstadt, *W. Germany* **31** 50 15N 10 11 E
Munnundilla, Mt., *Australia* **76** 32 44 S 150 32 E
Muñoz Gamero, Pen., *Chile* **142** 52 30 S 73 5W
Munro, *Australia* **75** 37 56 S 147 11 E
Munroe L., *Canada* **111** 59 13N 98 35W
Munshiganj, *Bangla.* **52** 23 33N 90 32 E
Munster, *France* **19** 48 2N 7 8 E
Munster, *Niedersachsen, W. Germany* **30** 52 59N 10 5 E
Münster, *Nordrhein-Westfalen, W. Germany* **30** 51 58N 7 37 E
Munster □, *Ireland* **15** 52 20N 8 40W
Muntadgin, *Australia* **79** 31 45 S 118 33 E
Muntele Mare, *Romania* **34** 46 30N 23 12 E
Muntok, *Indonesia* **56** 2 5 S 105 10 E
Munyak, *U.S.S.R.* **40** 43 30N 59 15 E
Munyama, *Zambia* **93** 16 5 S 28 31 E
Muong Beng, *Laos* **54** 20 23N 101 46 E
Muong Boum, *Vietnam* **54** 22 24N 102 49 E
Muong Et, *Laos* **54** 20 49N 104 1 E
Muong Hai, *Laos* **54** 21 3N 101 49 E
Muong Hiem, *Laos* **54** 20 5N 103 22 E
Muong Houn, *Laos* **54** 20 8N 101 23 E
Muong Hung, *Vietnam* **54** 20 56N 103 53 E
Muong Kau, *Laos* **54** 15 6N 105 47 E
Muong Khao, *Laos* **54** 19 38N 103 32 E
Muong Khoua, *Laos* **54** 21 5N 102 31 E
Muong Liep, *Laos* **54** 18 29N 101 40 E
Muong May, *Laos* **54** 14 49N 106 56 E
Muong Ngeun, *Laos* **54** 20 36N 101 3 E
Muong Ngoi, *Laos* **54** 20 43N 102 41 E
Muong Nhie, *Vietnam* **54** 22 12N 102 28 E
Muong Nong, *Laos* **54** 16 22N 106 30 E
Muong Ou Tay, *Laos* **54** 22 7N 101 48 E
Muong Oua, *Laos* **54** 18 18N 101 20 E
Muong Peun, *Laos* **54** 20 13N 103 52 E
Muong Phalane, *Laos* **54** 16 39N 105 34 E
Muong Phieng, *Laos* **54** 19 6N 101 32 E
Muong Phine, *Laos* **54** 16 32N 106 2 E
Muong Sai, *Laos* **54** 20 42N 101 59 E
Muong Saiapoun, *Laos* **54** 18 24N 101 31 E
Muong Sen, *Vietnam* **54** 19 24N 104 8 E
Muong Sing, *Laos* **54** 21 11N 101 9 E
Muong Son, *Laos* **54** 20 27N 103 19 E
Muong Soui, *Laos* **54** 19 33N 102 52 E
Muong Va, *Laos* **54** 21 53N 102 19 E
Muong Xia, *Vietnam* **54** 20 19N 104 50 E
Muonio, *Finland* **8** 67 57N 23 40 E
Mupa, *Angola* **95** 16 5 S 15 50 E
Muping, *China* **61** 37 22N 121 36 E
Muqaddam, Wadi →, *Sudan* **88** 18 4N 31 30 E
Muqdisho, *Somali Rep.* **98** 2 2N 45 25 E
Muquequete, *Angola* **95** 14 50 S 14 16 E
Mur-de-Bretagne, *France* **18** 48 12N 3 0W
Mura →, *Yugoslavia* **27** 46 18N 16 53 E
Murallón, Cuerro, *Chile* **142** 49 48 S 73 30W
Muranda, *Rwanda* **92** 1 52 S 29 20 E
Murang'a, *Kenya* **92** 0 45 S 37 9 E
Murashi, *U.S.S.R.* **37** 59 30N 49 0 E
Murat, *France* **20** 45 7N 2 53 E
Muravera, *Italy* **28** 39 25N 9 35 E
Murça, *Portugal* **22** 41 24N 7 28W
Murchison, *Australia* **74** 36 39 S 145 14 E
Murchison, *N.Z.* **81** 41 49 S 172 21 E
Murchison →, *Australia* **79** 27 45 S 114 0 E
Murchison, Mt., *Antarctica* **143** 73 0 S 168 0 E
Murchison Falls = Kabarega Falls, *Uganda* **92** 2 15N 31 30 E
Murchison House, *Australia* **79** 27 39 S 114 14 E
Murchison Mts., *N.Z.* **81** 45 13 S 167 23 E
Murchison Ra., *Australia* **72** 20 0 S 134 10 E
Murchison Rapids, *Malawi* **93** 15 55 S 34 35 E
Murcia, *Spain* **25** 38 20N 1 10W
Murcia □, *Spain* **25** 37 50N 1 30W
Murdo, *U.S.A.* **120** 43 56N 100 43W
Murdoch Pt., *Australia* **72** 14 37 S 144 55 E
Mure, La, *France* **21** 44 55N 5 48 E
Mureş →, *Romania* **34** 46 15N 20 13 E
Mureşul = Mureş →, *Romania* **34** 46 15N 20 13 E
Muret, *France* **20** 43 30N 1 20 E
Murfatlar, *Romania* **34** 44 10N 28 26 E
Murfreesboro, *U.S.A.* **115** 35 50N 86 21W
Murg →, *W. Germany* **31** 48 55N 8 10 E
Murgab, *U.S.S.R.* **40** 38 10N 74 2 E
Murgon, *Australia* **73** 26 15 S 151 54 E
Murgoo, *Australia* **79** 27 24 S 116 28 E
Muria, *Indonesia* **57** 6 36 S 110 53 E
Muriaé, *Brazil* **139** 21 8 S 42 23W
Murias de Paredes, *Spain* **22** 42 52N 6 11W
Murici, *Brazil* **138** 9 19 S 35 56W
Muriége, *Angola* **95** 9 58 S 21 11 E
Muriel Mine, *Zimb.* **93** 17 14 S 30 40 E
Murila, *Angola* **95** 10 44 S 20 20 E
Müritz See, *E. Germany* **30** 53 25N 12 40 E
Murka, *Kenya* **92** 3 27 S 38 0 E
Murmansk, *U.S.S.R.* **40** 68 57N 33 10 E
Murmerwoude, *Neths.* **16** 53 18N 6 0 E
Murnau, *W. Germany* **31** 47 40N 11 11 E
Muro, *France* **21** 42 34N 8 54 E
Muro, *Spain* **24** 39 44N 3 3 E
Muro, C. de, *France* **21** 41 44N 8 37 E
Muro Lucano, *Italy* **29** 40 45N 15 30 E
Murom, *U.S.S.R.* **37** 55 35N 42 3 E
Muroran, *Japan* **63** 42 25N 141 0 E
Muros, *Spain* **22** 42 45N 9 5W
Muros y de Noya, Ría de, *Spain* **22** 42 45N 9 0W
Muroto, *Japan* **64** 33 18N 134 9 E
Muroto-Misaki, *Japan* **64** 33 15N 134 10 E
Murphy, *U.S.A.* **122** 43 11N 116 33W
Murphys, *U.S.A.* **124** 38 8N 120 28W
Murphysboro, *U.S.A.* **118** 37 50N 89 20W
Murrat, *Sudan* **88** 18 51N 29 33 E
Murray, *Iowa, U.S.A.* **118** 41 3N 93 57W
Murray, *Ky., U.S.A.* **115** 36 40N 88 20W
Murray, *Utah, U.S.A.* **122** 40 41N 111 58W
Murray →, *Australia* **73** 35 20 S 139 22 E
Murray →, *Canada* **110** 56 11N 120 45W
Murray, L., *Papua N. G.* **69** 7 0 S 141 35 E
Murray, L., *U.S.A.* **115** 34 8N 81 30W
Murray Bridge, *Australia* **73** 35 6 S 139 14 E
Murray Downs, *Australia* **72** 21 4 S 134 40 E
Murray Harbour, *Canada* **105** 46 0N 62 28W
Murray Seascarp, *Pac. Oc.* **67** 30 0N 135 0W
Murraysburg, *S. Africa* **96** 31 58 S 23 47 E
Murrayville, *Australia* **74** 35 16 S 141 11 E
Murrayville, *U.S.A.* **118** 39 35N 90 15W
Murree, *Pakistan* **48** 33 56N 73 28 E
Murrieta, *U.S.A.* **125** 33 33N 117 13W
Murrin Murrin, *Australia* **79** 28 58 S 121 33 E
Murringo, *Australia* **76** 34 16 S 148 32 E
Murrumbateman, *Australia* **76** 34 58 S 149 0 E
Murrumbidgee →, *Australia* **73** 34 43 S 143 12 E
Murrumburrah, *Australia* **76** 34 32 S 148 22 E
Murrurundi, *Australia* **77** 31 42 S 150 51 E
Mursala, *Indonesia* **56** 1 41N 98 28 E
Murshid, *Sudan* **88** 21 40N 31 10 E
Murshidabad, *India* **49** 24 11N 88 19 E
Murska Sobota, *Yugoslavia* **27** 46 39N 16 12 E
Murtazapur, *India* **50** 20 40N 77 25 E
Murtle L., *Canada* **110** 52 8N 119 38W
Murtoa, *Australia* **74** 36 35 S 142 28 E
Murtosa, *Portugal* **22** 40 44N 8 40W
Muru →, *Brazil* **136** 8 9 S 70 45W
Murungu, *Tanzania* **92** 4 12 S 31 10 E
Murupara, *N.Z.* **80** 38 28 S 176 42 E
Murwara, *India* **49** 23 46N 80 28 E
Murwillumbah, *Australia* **77** 28 18 S 153 27 E
Mürz →, *Austria* **33** 47 30N 15 25 E
Mürzzuschlag, *Austria* **33** 47 36N 15 41 E
Muş, *Turkey* **46** 38 45N 41 30 E
Musa, *Zaïre* **94** 2 40N 19 18 E
Musa →, *Papua N. G.* **69** 9 3 S 148 55 E
Mûsa, G., *Egypt* **88** 28 33N 33 59 E
Musa Khel, *Pakistan* **48** 30 59N 69 52 E
Mūsá Qal'eh, *Afghan.* **47** 32 20N 64 50 E
Musala, *Bulgaria* **34** 42 13N 23 37 E
Musan, *N. Korea* **61** 42 12N 129 12 E
Musangu, *Zaïre* **93** 10 28 S 23 55 E
Musasa, *Tanzania* **92** 3 25 S 31 30 E
Musashino, *Japan* **65** 35 42N 139 34 E
Musay'īd, *Qatar* **47** 25 0N 51 33 E
Muscat = Masqat, *Oman* **47** 23 37N 58 36 E
Muscat & Oman = Oman ■, *Asia* **45** 23 0N 58 0 E
Muscatine, *U.S.A.* **118** 41 25N 91 5W
Muscoda, *U.S.A.* **118** 43 11N 90 27W
Musel, *Spain* **22** 43 34N 5 42W
Musgrave Ras., *Australia* **79** 26 0 S 132 0 E
Mushie, *Zaïre* **94** 2 56 S 16 55 E
Mushin, *Nigeria* **91** 6 32N 3 21 E
Musi →, *India* **50** 16 41N 79 40 E
Musi →, *Indonesia* **56** 2 20 S 104 56 E
Muskeg →, *Canada* **110** 60 20N 123 20W
Muskegon, *U.S.A.* **119** 43 15N 86 17W
Muskegon →, *U.S.A.* **114** 43 25N 86 0W
Muskegon Hts., *U.S.A.* **119** 43 12N 86 17W
Muskogee, *U.S.A.* **121** 35 50N 95 25W
Muskoka, L., *Canada* **108** 45 0N 79 25W
Muskwa →, *Canada* **110** 58 47N 122 48W
Musmar, *Sudan* **88** 18 13N 35 40 E
Musofu, *Zambia* **93** 13 30 S 29 0 E
Musoma, *Tanzania* **92** 1 30 S 33 48 E
Musoma □, *Tanzania* **92** 1 50 S 34 30 E
Musquaro, L., *Canada* **105** 50 38N 61 5W
Musquodoboit Harbour, *Canada* **105** 44 50N 63 9W
Mussau I., *Papua N. G.* **69** 1 30 S 149 40 E
Musselburgh, *U.K.* **14** 55 57N 3 3W
Musselkanaal, *Neths.* **16** 52 57N 7 0 E
Musselshell →, *U.S.A.* **122** 47 21N 107 58W
Mussende, *Angola* **95** 10 32 S 16 5 E
Mussidan, *France* **20** 45 2N 0 22 E
Mussolo, *Angola* **95** 9 59 S 17 19 E
Mussomeli, *Italy* **28** 37 35N 13 43 E
Musson, *Belgium* **17** 49 33N 5 42 E
Mussoorie, *India* **48** 30 27N 78 6 E
Mussuco, *Angola* **95** 17 2 S 19 3 E
Mustahil, *Ethiopia* **98** 5 16N 44 45 E
Mustang, *Nepal* **49** 29 10N 83 55 E
Musters, L., *Argentina* **142** 45 20 S 69 25W
Muswellbrook, *Australia* **76** 32 16 S 150 56 E
Mût, *Egypt* **88** 25 28N 28 58 E
Mut, *Turkey* **46** 36 40N 33 28 E
Mutanda, *Mozam.* **97** 21 0 S 33 34 E
Mutanda, *Zambia* **93** 12 24 S 26 13 E
Mutaray, *U.S.S.R.* **41** 60 56N 101 0 E
Mutare, *Zimb.* **93** 18 58 S 32 38 E

Muting, *Indonesia* .... **57** 7 23 S 140 20 E
Mutoto, *Zaïre* .... **95** 5 42 S 22 42 E
Mutshatsha, *Zaïre* .... **93** 10 35 S 24 20 E
Mutsu-Wan, *Japan* ... **63** 41 5N 140 55 E
Muttaburra, *Australia* . **72** 22 38 S 144 29 E
Muttama, *Australia* ... **76** 34 46 S 148 8 E
Mutton Bird Island,
Australia .... **77** 30 18 S 153 9 E
Mutuáli, *Mozam.* ...... **93** 14 55 S 37 0 E
Mutunópolis, *Brazil* .. **139** 13 40 S 49 15W
Muvatupusha, *India* .. **51** 9 53N 76 35 E
Muxima, *Angola* ..... **95** 9 33 S 13 58 E
Muy, Le, *France* ..... **21** 43 28N 6 34 E
Muy Muy, *Nic.* **128** 12 39N 85 36W
Muya, *U.S.S.R.* ...... **41** 56 27N 115 50 E
Muyinga, *Burundi* .... **92** 3 14 S 30 33 E
Muzaffarabad, *Pakistan* **49** 34 25N 73 30 E
Muzaffargarh, *Pakistan* **48** 30 5N 71 14 E
Muzaffarnagar, *India* . **48** 29 26N 77 40 E
Muzaffarpur, *India* ... **49** 26 7N 85 23 E
Muzeze, *Angola* ...... **95** 15 3 S 17 43 E
Muzhi, *U.S.S.R.* ..... **40** 65 25N 64 40 E
Muzillac, *France* **18** 47 35N 2 30W
Muzon C., *U.S.A.* **110** 54 40N 132 40W
Muztag, *China* .... **62** 36 20N 87 28 E
Mvadhi-Ousyé, *Gabon* **94** 1 13N 13 12 E
Mvam, *Gabon* .... **94** 0 13 S 9 39 E
Mvôlô, *Sudan* .... **89** 6 2N 29 53 E
Mvuma, *Zimb.* .... **93** 19 16 S 30 30 E
Mvurwi, *Zimb.* .... **93** 17 0 S 30 57 E
Mwadui, *Tanzania* .... **92** 3 26 S 33 32 E
Mwambo, *Tanzania* .. **93** 10 30 S 40 22 E
Mwandi, *Zambia* ..... **93** 17 30 S 24 51 E
Mwanza, *Tanzania* ... **92** 2 30 S 32 58 E
Mwanza, *Zaïre* .... **92** 7 55 S 26 43 E
Mwanza, *Zambia* ..... **93** 16 58 S 24 28 E
Mwanza □, *Tanzania* . **92** 2 0 S 33 0 E
Mwaya, *Tanzania* .... **93** 9 32 S 33 55 E
Mweelrea, *Ireland* **15** 53 37N 9 48W
Mweka, *Zaïre* .... **95** 4 50 S 21 34 E
Mwendjila, *Zaïre* ..... **95** 7 12 S 18 51 E
Mwene, *Zaïre* .... **95** 6 35 S 22 27 E
Mwenezi, *Zimb.* ..... **93** 21 15 S 30 48 E
Mwenezi →, *Mozam.* **93** 22 40 S 31 50 E
Mwenga, *Zaïre* .... **92** 3 1 S 28 28 E
Mweru, L., *Zambia* .. **93** 9 0 S 28 40 E
Mweza Range, *Zimb.* .. **93** 21 0 S 30 0 E
Mwilambwe, *Zaïre* ... **92** 8 7 S 25 0 E
Mwimbi, *Tanzania* ... **93** 8 38 S 31 39 E
Mwinilunga, *Zambia* .. **93** 11 43 S 24 25 E
My Tho, *Vietnam* .... **55** 10 29N 106 23 E
Mya, O. →, *Algeria* .. **85** 30 46N 4 54 E
Myajlar, *India* .... **48** 26 15N 70 20 E
Myall, *Australia* ..... **74** 35 32 S 143 55 E
Myall →, *Australia* ... **76** 32 30 S 152 15 E
Myall, L., *Australia* ... **76** 32 30 S 152 18 E
Myanaung, *Burma* .... **52** 18 18N 95 22 E
Myaungmya, *Burma* .. **52** 16 30N 94 40 E
Mycenae = Mikínai,
Greece .... **35** 37 43N 22 46 E
Myeik Kyunzu, *Burma* **54** 11 30N 97 30 E
Myerstown, *U.S.A.* ... **117** 40 22N 76 18W
Myingyan, *Burma* .... **52** 21 30N 95 20 E
Myitkyina, *Burma* .... **52** 25 24N 97 26 E
Myittha →, *Burma* ... **52** 23 12N 94 17 E
Myjava, *Czech.* ...... **32** 48 41N 17 37 E
Mymensingh, *Bangla.* . **52** 24 45N 90 24 E
Mynydd Du, *U.K.* **13** 51 45N 3 45W
Mýrdalsjökull, *Iceland* **8** 63 40N 19 6W
Myrrhee, *Australia* ... **75** 36 46 S 146 17 E
Myrtle Beach, *U.S.A.* . **115** 33 43N 78 50W
Myrtle Creek, *U.S.A.* . **122** 43 0N 123 9W
Myrtle Point, *U.S.A.* . **122** 43 0N 124 4W
Myrtleford, *Australia* . **75** 36 34 S 146 44 E
Mysen, *Norway* ...... **10** 59 33N 11 20 E
Mysia, *Australia* ...... **74** 36 13 S 143 46 E
Myslenice, *Poland* .... **32** 49 51N 19 57 E
Myślibórz, *Poland* .... **32** 52 55N 14 50 E
Mysłowice, *Poland* ... **32** 50 15N 19 12 E
Mysore, *India* .... **51** 12 17N 76 41 E
Mysore □ =
Karnataka □, *India* . **51** 13 15N 77 0 E
Mystic, *Conn., U.S.A.* . **117** 41 21N 71 58W
Mystic, *Iowa, U.S.A.* . **118** 40 47N 92 57W
Myszków, *Poland* .... **32** 50 45N 19 22 E
Mytishchi, *U.S.S.R.* .. **37** 55 50N 37 50 E
Myton, *U.S.A.* **122** 40 10N 110 2W
Mývatn, *Iceland* **8** 65 36N 17 0W
Mzimba, *Malawi* .... **93** 11 55 S 33 39 E
Mzimkulu →, *S. Africa* **97** 30 44 S 30 28 E
Mzimvubu →,
S. Africa .... **97** 31 38 S 29 33 E
Mzuzu, *Malawi* ...... **93** 11 30 S 33 55 E

N

N' Dioum, *Senegal* ... **90** 16 31N 14 39W
Na-lang, *Burma* ...... **52** 22 42N 97 33 E
Na Noi, *Thailand* .... **54** 18 19N 100 43 E
Na Phao, *Laos* .... **54** 17 35N 105 44 E
Na Sam, *Vietnam* .... **54** 22 3N 106 37 E
Na San, *Vietnam* ..... **54** 21 12N 104 2 E
Naab →, *W. Germany* **31** 49 1N 12 2 E
Naaldwijk, *Neths.* .... **16** 51 59N 4 13 E
Na'am, *Sudan* .... **89** 9 42N 28 27 E
Na'an, *Israel* .... **44** 31 53N 34 52 E
Naantali, *Finland* ..... **9** 60 29N 22 2 E
Naarden, *Neths.* ...... **16** 52 18N 5 9 E
Naas, *Ireland* **15** 53 12N 6 40W
Nababiep, *S. Africa* .. **96** 29 36 S 17 46 E
Nabadwip = Navadwip,
India .... **49** 23 34N 88 20 E
Nabari, *Japan* .... **65** 34 37N 136 5 E
Nabawa, *Australia* .... **79** 28 30 S 114 48 E
Nabberu, L., *Australia* **79** 25 50 S 120 30 E
Nabburg, *W. Germany* **31** 49 27N 12 11 E
Nabeul, *Tunisia* ...... **86** 36 30N 10 44 E
Nabha, *India* .... **48** 30 26N 76 14 E
Nabiac, *Australia* ..... **77** 32 5 S 152 25 E
Nabire, *Indonesia* .... **57** 3 15 S 135 26 E
Nabisar, *Pakistan* ..... **48** 25 8N 69 40 E
Nabisipi →, *Canada* .. **105** 50 14N 62 13W
Nabiswera, *Uganda* .. **92** 1 27N 32 15 E
Nablus = Nābulus,
Jordan .... **44** 32 14N 35 15 E
Naboomspruit,
S. Africa .... **97** 24 32 S 28 40 E
Nābulus, *Jordan* ...... **44** 32 14N 35 15 E
Nacala-Velha, *Mozam.* **93** 14 32 S 40 34 E
Nacaome, *Honduras* .. **128** 13 31N 87 30W
Nacaroa, *Mozam.* .... **93** 14 22 S 39 56 E
Naches, *U.S.A.* **122** 46 48N 120 42W
Naches →, *U.S.A.* ... **124** 46 38N 120 31W
Nachikatsuura, *Japan* . **65** 33 33N 135 58 E
Nachingwea, *Tanzania* **93** 10 23 S 38 49 E
Nachingwea □,
Tanzania .... **93** 10 30 S 38 30 E
Nachna, *India* .... **48** 27 34N 71 41 E
Náchod, *Czech.* ...... **32** 50 25N 16 8 E
Nacimiento Res.,
U.S.A. **124** 35 46N 121 0W
Nacka, *Sweden* .... **10** 59 17N 18 12 E
Nackara, *Australia* .... **73** 32 48 S 139 12 E
Naco, *Mexico* **126** 31 20N 109 56W
Naco, *U.S.A.* **123** 31 24N 109 58W
Nacogdoches, *U.S.A.* . **121** 31 33N 94 39W
Nácori Chico, *Mexico* . **126** 29 39N 109 1W
Nacozari, *Mexico* **126** 30 24N 109 39W
Nadi, *Sudan* .... **88** 18 40N 33 41 E
Nadiad, *India* .... **48** 22 41N 72 56 E
Nădlac, *Romania* ..... **34** 46 10N 20 50 E
Nador, *Morocco* **85** 35 14N 2 58W
Nadūshan, *Iran* ...... **47** 32 2N 53 35 E
Nadvornaya, *U.S.S.R.* **38** 48 37N 24 30 E
Nadym, *U.S.S.R.* ..... **40** 65 35N 72 42 E
Nadym →, *U.S.S.R.* . **40** 66 12N 72 0 E
Næstved, *Denmark* ... **11** 55 13N 11 44 E
Nafada, *Nigeria* ...... **91** 11 8N 11 20 E
Naftshahr, *Iran* ...... **46** 34 0N 45 30 E
Nafūd ad Dahy,
Si. Arabia .... **46** 22 0N 45 0 E
Nafūsah, Jabal, *Libya* . **86** 32 12N 12 30 E
Nag Hammâdi, *Egypt* . **88** 26 2N 32 18 E
Naga, *Phil.* .... **57** 13 38N 123 15 E
Naga, Kreb en, *Africa* **84** 24 12N 6 0W
Naga-Shima,
Kagoshima, Japan .. **64** 32 10N 130 9 E
Naga-Shima,
Yamaguchi, Japan .. **64** 33 49N 132 5 E
Nagagami →, *Canada* **104** 49 40N 84 40W
Nagahama, *Ehime,*
Japan .... **64** 33 36N 132 29 E
Nagahama, *Shiga,*
Japan .... **65** 35 23N 136 16 E
Nagaland □, *India* .... **52** 26 0N 94 30 E
Nagambie, *Australia* .. **74** 36 47 S 145 10 E
Nagano, *Japan* .... **65** 36 40N 138 10 E
Nagano □, *Japan* ..... **65** 36 15N 138 0 E
Nagaoka, *Japan* ...... **63** 37 27N 138 51 E
Nagappattinam, *India* . **51** 10 46N 79 51 E
Nagar Parkar, *Pakistan* **48** 24 28N 70 46 E
Nagara →, *Japan* .... **65** 35 40N 136 43 E
Nagari Hills, *India* .... **51** 13 3N 79 45 E
Nagarjuna Sagar, *India* **51** 16 35N 79 17 E
Nagasaki, *Japan* ..... **64** 32 47N 129 50 E
Nagasaki □, *Japan* ... **64** 32 50N 129 40 E
Nagato, *Japan* .... **64** 34 19N 131 5 E
Nagaur, *India* .... **48** 27 15N 73 45 E
Nagbhir, *India* .... **50** 20 34N 79 55 E
Nagercoil, *India* ...... **51** 8 12N 77 26 E
Nagiloc, *Australia* .... **74** 34 30 S 142 22 E
Nagina, *India* .... **49** 29 30N 78 30 E
Nagīneh, *Iran* .... **47** 34 20N 57 15 E
Nagir, *Pakistan* ...... **49** 36 12N 74 42 E
Nagold, *W. Germany* . **31** 48 33N 8 43 E
Nagold →,
W. Germany .... **31** 48 52N 8 42 E
Nagoorin, *Australia* .. **72** 24 17 S 151 15 E
Nagornyy, *U.S.S.R.* .. **41** 55 58N 124 57 E
Nagorsk, *U.S.S.R.* ... **37** 59 18N 50 48 E
Nagoya, *Japan* .... **65** 35 10N 136 50 E
Nagpur, *India* .... **50** 21 8N 79 10 E
Nagua, *Dom. Rep.* ... **129** 19 23N 69 50W
Nagykanizsa, *Hungary* **33** 46 28N 17 0 E
Nagykörös, *Hungary* .. **33** 47 5N 19 48 E
Nagyléta, *Hungary* ... **33** 47 23N 21 55 E
Nahalal, *Israel* .... **44** 32 41N 35 12 E
Nahanni Butte, *Canada* **110** 61 2N 123 31W
Nahanni Nat. Park,
Canada **110** 61 15N 125 0W
Nahariyya, *Israel* ..... **44** 33 1N 35 5 E
Nahāvand, *Iran* ...... **46** 34 10N 48 22 E
Nahe →, *W. Germany* **31** 49 58N 7 57 E
Nahf, *Israel* .... **44** 32 56N 35 18 E
Nahîya, Wadi →,
Egypt .... **88** 28 55N 31 0 E
Nahlin, *Canada* **110** 58 55N 131 38W
Nahuel Huapi, L.,
Argentina .... **142** 41 0 S 71 32W
Naicá, *Mexico* **126** 27 53N 105 31W
Naicam, *Canada* **111** 52 30N 104 30W
Nā'ifah, *Si. Arabia* ... **45** 19 59N 50 46 E
Naila, *W. Germany* ... **31** 50 19N 11 43 E
Nain, *Canada* **105** 56 34N 61 40W
Nā'īn, *Iran* .... **47** 32 54N 53 0 E
Naini Tal, *India* ...... **49** 29 30N 79 30 E
Naintré, *France* ...... **18** 46 46N 0 29 E
Naipu, *Romania* ...... **34** 44 12N 25 47 E
Naira, *Indonesia* ..... **57** 4 28 S 130 0 E
Nairn, *Canada* **108** 46 20N 81 35W
Nairn, *U.K.* **14** 57 35N 3 54W
Nairobi, *Kenya* .... **92** 1 17 S 36 48 E
Naivasha, *Kenya* ..... **92** 0 40 S 36 30 E
Naivasha, L., *Kenya* .. **92** 0 48 S 36 20 E
Najac, *France* .... **20** 44 14N 1 58 E
Najafābād, *Iran* ...... **47** 32 40N 51 15 E
Najd, *Si. Arabia* ..... **46** 26 30N 42 0 E
Nájera, *Spain* **24** 42 26N 2 48W
Najerilla →, *Spain* ... **24** 42 32N 2 48W
Najibabad, *India* ..... **48** 29 40N 78 20 E
Najin, *N. Korea* ...... **61** 42 12N 130 15 E
Naka →, *Japan* ...... **65** 36 20N 140 36 E
Nakadōri-Shima, *Japan* **63** 32 57N 129 4 E
Nakalagba, *Zaïre* ..... **92** 2 50N 27 58 E
Nakama, *Japan* ...... **64** 33 56N 130 43 E
Nakaminato, *Japan* ... **65** 36 21N 140 36 E
Nakamura, *Japan* .... **64** 33 0N 133 0 E
Nakanai Mts.,
Papua N. G. .... **69** 5 40 S 151 0 E
Nakano, *Japan* ...... **65** 36 45N 138 22 E
Nakanojō, *Japan* ..... **65** 36 35N 138 51 E
Nakatsu, *Japan* ...... **64** 33 34N 131 15 E
Nakatsugawa, *Japan* .. **65** 35 29N 137 30 E
Nakfa, *Ethiopia* ...... **89** 16 40N 38 32 E
Nakhichevan
A.S.S.R. □,
U.S.S.R. .... **40** 39 14N 45 30 E
Nakhl, *Egypt* .... **88** 29 55N 33 43 E
Nakhodka, *U.S.S.R.* .. **41** 42 53N 132 54 E
Nakhon Nayok,
Thailand .... **54** 14 12N 101 13 E
Nakhon Pathom,
Thailand .... **54** 13 49N 100 3 E
Nakhon Phanom,
Thailand .... **54** 17 23N 104 43 E
Nakhon Ratchasima,
Thailand .... **54** 14 59N 102 12 E
Nakhon Sawan,
Thailand .... **54** 15 35N 100 10 E
Nakhon Si Thammarat,
Thailand .... **55** 8 29N 100 0 E
Nakhon Thai, *Thailand* **54** 17 5N 100 44 E
Nakina, *B.C., Canada* **110** 59 12N 132 52W
Nakina, *Ont., Canada* **104** 50 10N 86 40W
Nakło nad Notecią,
Poland .... **32** 53 9N 17 38 E
Nakodar, *India* .... **48** 31 8N 75 31 E
Nakskov, *Denmark* ... **11** 54 50N 11 8 E
Näkten, *Sweden* ...... **10** 62 48N 14 38 E
Naktong →, *S. Korea* **61** 35 7N 128 57 E
Nakuru, *Kenya* .... **92** 0 15 S 36 4 E
Nakuru □, *Kenya* .... **92** 0 15 S 35 5 E
Nakuru, L., *Kenya* .... **92** 0 23 S 36 5 E
Nakusp, *Canada* **110** 50 20N 117 45W
Nal →, *Pakistan* ..... **48** 25 20N 65 30 E
Nalchik, *U.S.S.R.* .... **39** 43 30N 43 33 E
Nälden, *Sweden* ...... **10** 63 21N 14 14 E
Näldsjön, *Sweden* .... **10** 63 25N 14 15 E
Nalerigu, *Ghana* **91** 10 35N 0 25W
Nalgonda, *India* ...... **50** 17 6N 79 15 E
Nalhati, *India* .... **49** 24 17N 87 52 E
Nalinnes, *Belgium* .... **17** 50 19N 4 27 E
Nallamalai Hills, *India* **51** 15 30N 78 50 E
Nalón →, *Spain* **22** 43 32N 6 4W
Nālūt, *Libya* .... **86** 31 54N 11 0 E
Nam Can, *Vietnam* ... **55** 8 46N 104 59 E
Nam Co, *China* ...... **62** 30 30N 90 45 E
Nam Dinh, *Vietnam* .. **54** 20 25N 106 5 E
Nam Du, Hon, *Vietnam* **55** 9 41N 104 21 E
Nam Ngum Dam, *Laos* **54** 18 35N 102 34 E
Nam-Phan, *Vietnam* .. **55** 10 30N 106 0 E
Nam Phong, *Thailand* . **54** 16 42N 102 52 E
Nam Tha, *Laos* ...... **54** 20 58N 101 30 E
Nam Tok, *Thailand* ... **54** 14 21N 99 4 E
Namachire, *Angola* ... **95** 11 26 S 22 43 E
Namacunde, *Angola* .. **95** 17 18 S 15 50 E
Namacurra, *Mozam.* .. **97** 17 30 S 36 50 E
Namak, Daryācheh-ye,
Iran .... **47** 34 30N 52 0 E
Namak, Kavir-e, *Iran* . **47** 34 30N 57 30 E
Namakkal, *India* ..... **51** 11 13N 78 13 E
Namaland, *Namibia* .. **96** 24 30 S 17 0 E
Namangan, *U.S.S.R.* . **40** 41 0N 71 40 E
Namapa, *Mozam.* .... **93** 13 43 S 39 50 E
Namaqualand, *S. Africa* **96** 30 0 S 17 25 E
Namasagali, *Uganda* .. **92** 1 2N 33 0 E
Namatanai,
Papua N. G. .... **69** 3 40 S 152 29 E
Namber, *Indonesia* ... **57** 1 2 S 134 49 E
Nambour, *Australia* .. **73** 26 32 S 152 58 E
Nambouwalu, *Fiji* .... **68** 17 0 S 178 45 E
Nambucca Heads,
Australia .... **77** 30 37 S 153 0 E
Namche Bazar, *Nepal* . **49** 27 51N 86 47 E
Namêche, *Belgium* ... **17** 50 28N 5 0 E
Namecunda, *Mozam.* . **93** 14 54 S 37 37 E
Nameh, *Indonesia* .... **56** 2 34N 116 21 E
Nameponda, *Mozam.* . **93** 15 50 S 39 50 E
Namerikawa, *Japan* .. **65** 36 46N 137 20 E
Nametil, *Mozam.* .... **93** 15 40 S 39 21 E
Namew L., *Canada* ... **111** 54 14N 101 56W
Namhsan, *Burma* .... **52** 22 48N 97 2 E
Namib Desert =
Namibwoestyn,
Namibia .... **96** 22 30 S 15 0 E
Namibe, *Angola* ...... **95** 15 7 S 12 11 E
Namibe □, *Angola* ... **95** 16 35 S 12 30 E
Namibia ■, *Africa* .... **96** 22 0 S 18 9 E
Namibwoestyn,
Namibia .... **96** 22 30 S 15 0 E
Namkhan, *Burma* .... **52** 23 50N 97 41 E
Namlea, *Indonesia* .... **57** 3 18 S 127 5 E
Namoi →, *Australia* .. **77** 30 12 S 149 30 E
Namous, O. en →,
Algeria **85** 31 0N 0 15W
Nampa, *U.S.A.* **122** 43 34N 116 34W
Nampula, *Mozam.* ... **93** 15 6 S 39 15 E
Namrole, *Indonesia* ... **57** 3 46 S 126 46 E
Namse Shankou, *China* **49** 30 0N 82 25 E
Namsen →, *Norway* .. **8** 64 27N 11 42 E
Namsos, *Norway* ..... **8** 64 29N 11 30 E
Namtay, *U.S.S.R.* .... **41** 62 43N 129 37 E
Namtu, *Burma* ...... **52** 23 5N 97 28 E
Namtumbo, *Tanzania* . **93** 10 30 S 36 4 E
Namu, *Canada* **110** 51 52N 127 50W
Namur, *Belgium* ..... **17** 50 27N 4 52 E
Namur, *Canada* **106** 45 54N 74 56W
Namur □, *Belgium* ... **17** 50 17N 5 0 E
Namutoni, *Namibia* .. **96** 18 49 S 16 55 E
Namwala, *Zambia* .... **93** 15 44 S 26 30 E
Namysłów, *Poland* ... **32** 51 6N 17 42 E
Nan, *Thailand* .... **54** 18 48N 100 46 E
Nan →, *Thailand* .... **54** 15 42N 100 9 E
Nan Xian, *China* ..... **59** 29 20N 112 22 E
Nana Glen, *Australia* . **77** 30 8 S 153 2 E
Nanaimo, *Canada* **110** 49 10N 124 0W
Nanam, *N. Korea* .... **61** 41 44N 129 40 E
Nanan, *China* .... **59** 24 59N 118 21 E
Nanango, *Australia* .. **73** 26 40 S 152 0 E
Nan'ao, *China* ...... **59** 23 28N 117 5 E
Nanao, *Japan* .... **63** 37 0N 137 0 E
Nanbu, *China* .... **58** 31 18N 106 3 E
Nanchang, *China* .... **59** 28 42N 115 55 E
Nancheng, *China* .... **59** 27 33N 116 35 E
Nanching = Nanjing,
China .... **62** 32 2N 118 47 E
Nanchong, *China* .... **58** 30 43N 106 2 E
Nanchuan, *China* .... **58** 29 9N 107 6 E
Nancy, *France* .... **19** 48 42N 6 12 E
Nanda Devi, *India* ... **49** 30 23N 79 59 E
Nandan, *China* ...... **58** 24 58N 107 29 E
Nandan, *Japan* ...... **64** 34 10N 134 42 E
Nanded, *India* .... **50** 19 10N 77 20 E
Nandewar Ra.,
Australia .... **77** 30 15 S 150 35 E
Nandi, *Fiji* .... **68** 17 42 S 177 20 E
Nandi □, *Kenya* ..... **92** 0 15N 35 0 E
Nandikotkur, *India* ... **51** 15 52N 78 18 E
Nandura, *India* ...... **50** 20 52N 76 25 E
Nandurbar, *India* ..... **50** 21 20N 74 15 E
Nandyal, *India* ...... **51** 15 30N 78 30 E
Nanfeng, *Guangdong,*
China .... **59** 23 45N 111 47 E
Nanfeng, *Jiangxi, China* **59** 27 12N 116 28 E
Nanga, *Australia* ..... **79** 26 7 S 113 45 E
Nanga-Eboko,
Cameroon .... **91** 4 41N 12 22 E
Nanga Parbat, *Pakistan* **49** 35 10N 74 35 E
Nangade, *Mozam.* .... **93** 11 5 S 39 36 E
Nangapinoh, *Indonesia* **56** 0 20 S 111 44 E
Nangarhár □, *Afghan.* **47** 34 20N 70 0 E
Nangatayap, *Indonesia* **56** 1 32 S 110 34 E
Nangeya Mts., *Uganda* **92** 3 30N 33 30 E
Nangis, *France* .... **19** 48 33N 3 0 E
Nangong, *China* ..... **60** 37 23N 115 22 E
Nangus, *Australia* .... **76** 35 0 S 147 52 E
Nanhua, *China* ...... **58** 25 13N 101 21 E
Nanhuang, *China* .... **61** 36 58N 121 48 E
Nanhui, *China* ...... **59** 31 5N 121 44 E
Nanjangud, *India* .... **51** 12 6N 76 43 E
Nanjeko, *Zambia* .... **93** 15 31 S 23 30 E
Nanji Shan, *China* ... **59** 27 27N 121 4 E
Nanjian, *China* ...... **58** 25 2N 100 25 E
Nanjiang, *China* ..... **58** 32 28N 106 51 E
Nanjing, *Fujian, China* **59** 24 25N 117 20 E
Nanjing, *Jiangsu, China* **62** 32 2N 118 47 E
Nanjirinji, *Tanzania* .. **93** 9 41 S 39 5 E
Nankana Sahib,
Pakistan .... **48** 31 27N 73 38 E
Nankang, *China* ..... **59** 25 40N 114 45 E
Nanking = Nanjing,
China .... **62** 32 2N 118 47 E
Nankoku, *Japan* ..... **64** 33 39N 133 44 E
Nanling, *China* ...... **59** 30 55N 118 20 E
Nanning, *China* ..... **58** 22 48N 108 20 E
Nannup, *Australia* ... **79** 33 59 S 115 48 E
Nanpan Jiang →,
China .... **58** 25 10N 106 0 E
Nanpara, *India* ...... **49** 27 52N 81 33 E
Nanpi, *China* .... **60** 38 2N 116 45 E
Nanping, *Fujian, China* **59** 26 38N 118 10 E
Nanping, *Henan, China* **59** 29 55N 112 3 E
Nanri Dao, *China* .... **59** 25 15N 119 25 E
Nanripe, *Mozam.* .... **93** 13 52 S 38 52 E
Nansei-Shotō, *Japan* .. **62** 26 0N 128 0 E
Nansen Sd., *Canada* .. **144** 81 0N 91 0W
Nansio, *Tanzania* ..... **92** 2 3 S 33 4 E
Nant, *France* .... **20** 44 1N 3 18 E
Nantes, *France* **18** 47 12N 1 33W
Nanteuil-le-Haudouin,
France .... **19** 49 9N 2 48 E
Nantiat, *France* ...... **20** 46 1N 1 11 E
Nanticoke, *U.S.A.* ... **117** 41 12N 76 1W
Nanton, *Canada* **110** 50 21N 113 46W
Nantong, *China* ..... **59** 32 1N 120 52 E
Nantua, *France* ...... **21** 46 10N 5 35 E
Nantucket I., *U.S.A.* . **100** 41 16N 70 3W
Nanuku Passage, *Fiji* . **68** 16 45 S 179 15W
Nanuque, *Brazil* ..... **139** 17 50 S 40 21W

Nanutarra, *Australia* **78** 22 32 S 115 30 E
Nanxiong, *China* **59** 25 6N 114 15 E
Nanyang, *China* **60** 33 11N 112 30 E
Nanyi Hu, *China* **59** 31 5N 119 0 E
Nan'yō, *Japan* **64** 34 3N 131 49 E
Nanyuan, *China* **60** 39 44N 116 22 E
Nanyuki, *Kenya* **92** 0 2N 37 4 E
Nanzhang, *China* **59** 31 45N 111 50 E
Náo, C. de la, *Spain* **25** 38 44N 0 14 E
Naococane L., *Canada* **105** 52 50N 70 45W
Naoetsu, *Japan* **63** 37 12N 138 10 E
Naogaon, *Bangla.* **52** 24 52N 88 52 E
Náousa, *Greece* **35** 40 42N 22 9 E
Naozhou Dao, *China* **59** 20 55N 110 20 E
Napa, *U.S.A.* **124** 38 18N 122 17W
Napa →, *U.S.A.* **124** 38 10N 122 19W
Napanee, *Canada* **109** 44 15N 77 0W
Napanoch, *U.S.A.* **117** 41 44N 74 22W
Nape, *Laos* **54** 18 18N 105 6 E
Nape Pass = Keo Neua, Deo, *Vietnam* **54** 18 23N 105 10 E
Naperville, *U.S.A.* **119** 41 46N 88 9W
Napier, *N.Z.* **80** 39 30 S 176 56 E
Napier Broome B., *Australia* **78** 14 2 S 126 37 E
Napier Downs, *Australia* **78** 17 11 S 124 36 E
Napier Pen., *Australia* **72** 12 4 S 135 43 E
Napierville, *Canada* **107** 45 11N 73 25W
Napierville □, *Canada* **107** 45 10N 73 30W
Naples = Nápoli, *Italy* **29** 40 50N 14 17 E
Naples, *U.S.A.* **115** 26 10N 81 45W
Napo, *China* **58** 23 22N 105 50 E
Napo □, *Ecuador* **134** 0 30 S 77 0W
Napo →, *Peru* **134** 3 20 S 72 40W
Napoleon, *N. Dak., U.S.A.* **120** 46 32N 99 49W
Napoleon, *Ohio, U.S.A.* **119** 41 24N 84 7W
Nápoli, *Italy* **29** 40 50N 14 17 E
Nápoli, G. di, *Italy* **29** 40 40N 14 10 E
Napopo, *Zaïre* **92** 4 15N 28 0 E
Nappa Merrie, *Australia* **73** 27 36 S 141 7 E
Nappanee, *U.S.A.* **119** 41 27N 86 0W
Naqâda, *Egypt* **88** 25 53N 32 42 E
Nara, *Japan* **65** 34 40N 135 49 E
Nara, *Mali* **90** 15 10N 7 20W
Nara □, *Japan* **65** 34 30N 136 0 E
Nara, Canal, *Pakistan* **48** 24 30N 69 20 E
Nara Visa, *U.S.A.* **121** 35 39N 103 10W
Naracoorte, *Australia* **73** 36 58 S 140 45 E
Naradhan, *Australia* **75** 33 34 S 146 17 E
Narasapur, *India* **51** 16 26N 81 40 E
Narasaropet, *India* **51** 16 14N 80 4 E
Narathiwat, *Thailand* **55** 6 30N 101 48 E
Narayanganj, *Bangla.* **52** 23 40N 90 33 E
Narayanpet, *India* **50** 16 45N 77 30 E
Narbonne, *France* **20** 43 11N 3 0 E
Narcea →, *Spain* **22** 43 33N 6 44W
Nardò, *Italy* **29** 40 10N 18 0 E
Narembeen, *Australia* **79** 32 7 S 118 24 E
Nares Stræde, *Arctic* **100** 80 0N 70 0W
Naretha, *Australia* **79** 31 0 S 124 45 E
Narew →, *Poland* **32** 52 26N 20 41 E
Nari →, *Pakistan* **48** 29 40N 68 0 E
Narindra, Helodranon' i, *Madag.* **97** 14 55 S 47 30 E
Narino □, *Colombia* **134** 1 30N 78 0W
Narita, *Japan* **65** 35 47N 140 19 E
Narmada →, *India* **48** 21 38N 72 36 E
Narnaul, *India* **48** 28 5N 76 11 E
Narni, *Italy* **27** 42 30N 12 30 E
Naro, *Ghana* **90** 10 22N 2 27W
Naro, *Italy* **28** 37 18N 13 48 E
Naro Fominsk, *U.S.S.R.* **37** 55 23N 36 43 E
Narodnaya, *U.S.S.R.* **6** 65 5N 60 0 E
Narok, *Kenya* **92** 1 55 S 35 52 E
Narok □, *Kenya* **92** 1 20 S 36 30 E
Narón, *Spain* **22** 43 32N 8 9W
Narooma, *Australia* **75** 36 14 S 150 4 E
Narowal, *Pakistan* **48** 32 6N 74 52 E
Narrabri, *Australia* **77** 30 19 S 149 46 E
Narrabri West, *Australia* **77** 30 21 S 149 46 E
Narran →, *Australia* **73** 28 37 S 148 12 E
Narrandera, *Australia* **75** 34 42 S 146 31 E
Narraway →, *Canada* **110** 55 44N 119 55W
Narrogin, *Australia* **79** 32 58 S 117 14 E
Narromine, *Australia* **76** 32 12 S 148 12 E
Narsampet, *India* **50** 17 57N 79 58 E
Narsimhapur, *India* **49** 22 54N 79 14 E
Nartkala, *U.S.S.R.* **39** 43 33N 43 51 E
Naruto, *Kantō, Japan* **64** 34 11N 134 37 E
Narutō, *Shikoku, Japan* **65** 35 36N 140 25 E
Naruto-Kaikyō, *Japan* **64** 34 14N 134 39 E
Narva, *U.S.S.R.* **36** 59 23N 28 12 E
Narva →, *U.S.S.R.* **36** 59 27N 28 2 E
Narvik, *Norway* **8** 68 28N 17 26 E
Narvskoye Vdkhr., *U.S.S.R.* **36** 59 18N 28 14 E
Narwana, *India* **48** 29 39N 76 6 E
Naryan-Mar, *U.S.S.R.* **40** 68 0N 53 0 E
Naryilco, *Australia* **73** 28 37 S 141 53 E
Narym, *U.S.S.R.* **40** 59 0N 81 30 E
Narymskoye, *U.S.S.R.* **40** 49 10N 84 15 E
Naryn, *U.S.S.R.* **40** 41 26N 75 58 E
Nasa, *Norway* **8** 66 29N 15 23 E
Nasarawa, *Nigeria* **91** 8 32N 7 41 E
Năsăud, *Romania* **34** 47 19N 24 29 E
Nasawa, *Vanuatu* **68** 15 0 S 168 0 E
Naseby, *N.Z.* **81** 45 1 S 170 10 E
Naselle, *U.S.A.* **124** 46 22N 123 49W
Naser, Buheirat en, *Egypt* **88** 23 0N 32 30 E
Nashua, *Iowa, U.S.A.* **118** 42 55N 92 34W
Nashua, *Mont., U.S.A.* **122** 48 10N 106 25W
Nashua, *N.H., U.S.A.* **117** 42 50N 71 25W
Nashville, *Ark., U.S.A.* **121** 33 56N 93 50W
Nashville, *Ga., U.S.A.* **115** 31 3N 83 15W
Nashville, *Ill., U.S.A.* **118** 38 21N 89 23W
Nashville, *Ind., U.S.A.* **119** 39 12N 86 14W
Nashville, *Mich., U.S.A.* **119** 42 36N 85 5W
Nashville, *Tenn., U.S.A.* **115** 36 12N 86 46W
Našice, *Yugoslavia* **33** 45 32N 18 4 E
Nasielsk, *Poland* **32** 52 35N 20 50 E
Nasik, *India* **50** 19 58N 73 50 E
Nasirabad, *India* **48** 26 15N 74 45 E
Naskaupi →, *Canada* **105** 53 47N 60 51W
Naso, *Italy* **29** 38 8N 14 46 E
Nass →, *Canada* **110** 55 0N 129 40W
Nassau, *Bahamas* **128** 25 0N 77 20W
Nassau, *U.S.A.* **117** 42 30N 73 34W
Nassau, B., *Chile* **142** 55 20 S 68 0W
Nasser, L. = Naser, Buheirat en, *Egypt* **88** 23 0N 32 30 E
Nasser City = Kôm Ombo, *Egypt* **88** 24 25N 32 52 E
Nassian, *Ivory C.* **90** 8 28N 3 28W
Nässjö, *Sweden* **11** 57 39N 14 42 E
Näsum, *Sweden* **11** 56 10N 14 29 E
Näsviken, *Sweden* **10** 61 46N 16 52 E
Nata, *Botswana* **96** 20 12 S 26 12 E
Natagaima, *Colombia* **134** 3 37N 75 6W
Natal, *Brazil* **138** 5 47 S 35 13W
Natal, *Canada* **110** 49 43N 114 51W
Natal, *Indonesia* **56** 0 35N 99 7 E
Natal □, *S. Africa* **97** 28 30 S 30 30 E
Natalinci, *Yugoslavia* **33** 44 15N 20 49 E
Naṭanz, *Iran* **47** 33 30N 51 55 E
Natashquan, *Canada* **105** 50 14N 61 46W
Natashquan →, *Canada* **105** 50 7N 61 50W
Natchez, *U.S.A.* **121** 31 35N 91 25W
Natchitoches, *U.S.A.* **121** 31 47N 93 4W
Natewa B., *Fiji* **68** 16 35 S 179 40 E
Nathalia, *Australia* **74** 36 1 S 145 13 E
Nathdwara, *India* **48** 24 55N 73 50 E
Natimuk, *Australia* **74** 36 42 S 142 0 E
Nation →, *Canada* **110** 55 30N 123 32W
National City, *U.S.A.* **125** 32 39N 117 7W
Natitingou, *Benin* **91** 10 20N 1 26 E
Natividad, I., *Mexico* **126** 27 50N 115 10W
Natogyi, *Burma* **52** 21 25N 95 39 E
Natoma, *U.S.A.* **120** 39 14N 99 0W
Natron, L., *Tanzania* **92** 2 20 S 36 0 E
Natrona Heights, *U.S.A.* **116** 40 39N 79 43W
Natrûn, W. el →, *Egypt* **88** 30 25N 30 13 E
Nattai River, *Australia* **76** 34 3 S 150 26 E
Natuna Besar, Kepulauan, *Indonesia* **55** 4 0N 108 15 E
Natuna Selatan, Kepulauan, *Indonesia* **55** 2 45N 109 0 E
Natural Bridge, *U.S.A.* **117** 44 5N 75 30W
Naturaliste C., *Australia* **72** 40 50 S 148 15 E
Natya, *Australia* **74** 34 57 S 143 13 E
Nau Qala, *Afghan.* **48** 34 5N 68 5 E
Naubinway, *U.S.A.* **104** 46 7N 85 27W
Naucelle, *France* **20** 44 13N 2 20 E
Nauders, *Austria* **31** 46 54N 10 30 E
Nauen, *E. Germany* **30** 52 36N 12 52 E
Naugatuck, *U.S.A.* **117** 41 28N 73 4W
Naughton, *Canada* **108** 46 24N 81 12W
Naujoji Vilnia, *U.S.S.R.* **36** 54 48N 25 27 E
Naumburg, *E. Germany* **30** 51 10N 11 48 E
Nauru ■, *Pac. Oc.* **66** 1 0 S 166 0 E
Nausori, *Fiji* **68** 18 2 S 178 32 E
Nauta, *Peru* **134** 4 31 S 73 35W
Nautla, *Mexico* **127** 20 20N 96 50W
Nauvoo, *U.S.A.* **118** 40 33N 91 23W
Nava, *Mexico* **126** 28 25N 100 46W
Nava del Rey, *Spain* **22** 41 22N 5 6W
Navacerrada, Puerto de, *Spain* **22** 40 47N 4 0W
Navadwip, *India* **49** 23 34N 88 20 E
Navahermosa, *Spain* **23** 39 41N 4 28W
Navajo Res., *U.S.A.* **123** 36 55N 107 30W
Navalcarnero, *Spain* **22** 40 17N 4 5W
Navalmoral de la Mata, *Spain* **22** 39 52N 5 33W
Navalvillar de Pela, *Spain* **23** 39 9N 5 24W
Navan = An Uaimh, *Ireland* **15** 53 39N 6 40W
Navarino, I., *Chile* **142** 55 0 S 67 40W
Navarra □, *Spain* **24** 42 40N 1 40W
Navarre, *Australia* **74** 36 53 S 143 11 E
Navarre, *U.S.A.* **116** 40 43N 81 31W
Navarrenx, *France* **20** 43 20N 0 45W
Navarro, *U.S.A.* **124** 39 10N 123 32W
Navas del Marqués, Las, *Spain* **22** 40 36N 4 20W
Navasota, *U.S.A.* **121** 30 20N 96 5W
Navassa, *W. Indies* **129** 18 30N 75 0W
Nave, *Italy* **26** 45 35N 10 17 E
Naver →, *U.K.* **14** 58 34N 4 15W
Navia, *Spain* **22** 43 35N 6 42W
Navia →, *Spain* **22** 43 15N 6 50W
Navia de Suarna, *Spain* **22** 42 58N 6 59W
Navidad, *Chile* **140** 33 57 S 71 50W
Naviti, *Fiji* **68** 17 7 S 177 15 E
Navlya, *U.S.S.R.* **36** 52 53N 34 30 E
Navoi, *U.S.S.R.* **40** 40 9N 65 22 E
Navojoa, *Mexico* **126** 27 0N 109 30W
Navolato, *Mexico* **126** 24 47N 107 42W
Návpaktos, *Greece* **35** 38 23N 21 50 E
Návplion, *Greece* **35** 37 33N 22 50 E
Navrongo, *Ghana* **91** 10 51N 1 3W
Navsari, *India* **50** 20 57N 72 59 E
Navua, *Fiji* **68** 18 6 S 178 10 E
Nawa Kot, *Pakistan* **48** 28 21N 71 24 E
Nawabganj, *Bangla.* **52** 24 35N 88 14 E
Nawabganj, *Ut. P., India* **49** 26 56N 81 14 E
Nawabganj, *Ut. P., India* **49** 28 32N 79 40 E
Nawabshah, *Pakistan* **48** 26 15N 68 25 E
Nawada, *India* **49** 24 50N 85 33 E
Nawakot, *Nepal* **49** 27 55N 85 10 E
Nawalgarh, *India* **48** 27 50N 75 15 E
Nawanshahr, *India* **49** 32 33N 74 48 E
Nawapara, *India* **50** 20 46N 82 33 E
Nawāsīf, Harrat, *Si. Arabia* **46** 21 20N 42 10 E
Nawi, *Sudan* **88** 18 32N 30 50 E
Nawng Hpa, *Burma* **52** 22 30N 98 30 E
Náxos, *Greece* **35** 37 8N 25 25 E
Nay, *France* **20** 43 10N 0 18W
Nāy Band, *Iran* **47** 27 20N 52 40 E
Naya →, *Colombia* **134** 3 13N 77 22W
Nayakhan, *U.S.S.R.* **41** 61 56N 159 0 E
Nayarit □, *Mexico* **126** 22 0N 105 0W
Nayé, *Senegal* **90** 14 28N 12 12W
Nayong, *China* **58** 26 50N 105 20 E
Nazaré, *Bahia, Brazil* **139** 13 2 S 39 0W
Nazaré, *Goiás, Brazil* **138** 6 23 S 47 40W
Nazaré, *Pará, Brazil* **137** 6 25 S 52 29W
Nazaré, *Portugal* **23** 39 36N 9 4W
Nazareth = Nazerat, *Israel* **44** 32 42N 35 17 E
Nazas, *Mexico* **126** 25 10N 104 6W
Nazas →, *Mexico* **126** 25 35N 103 25W
Naze, The, *U.K.* **13** 51 53N 1 19 E
Nazerat, *Israel* **44** 32 42N 35 17 E
Nazir Hat, *Bangla.* **52** 22 35N 91 49 E
Nazko, *Canada* **110** 53 1N 123 37W
Nazko →, *Canada* **110** 53 7N 123 34W
Nazret, *Ethiopia* **89** 8 32N 39 22 E
Nchanga, *Zambia* **93** 12 30 S 27 49 E
Ncheu, *Malawi* **93** 14 50 S 34 47 E
Ndala, *Tanzania* **92** 4 45 S 33 15 E
Ndalatando, *Angola* **95** 9 12 S 14 48 E
Ndali, *Benin* **91** 9 50N 2 46 E
Ndareda, *Tanzania* **92** 4 12 S 35 30 E
Ndélé, *C.A.R.* **61** 8 25N 20 36 E
Ndendé, *Gabon* **94** 2 22 S 11 23 E
Ndjamena, *Chad* **87** 12 10N 14 59 E
Ndjolé, *Gabon* **94** 0 10 S 10 45 E
Ndola, *Zambia* **93** 13 0 S 28 34 E
Ndoto Mts., *Kenya* **92** 2 0N 37 0 E
Ndoua, C., *N. Cal.* **68** 22 24 S 166 56 E
Nduguti, *Tanzania* **92** 4 18 S 34 41 E
Nduindui, *Vanuatu* **68** 15 24 S 167 46 E
Nea →, *Norway* **10** 63 15N 11 0 E
Néa Flippiás, *Greece* **35** 39 12N 20 53 E
Neagari, *Japan* **65** 36 26N 136 25 E
Neagh, Lough, *U.K.* **15** 54 35N 6 25W
Neah Bay, *U.S.A.* **124** 48 25N 124 40W
Neale L., *Australia* **78** 24 15 S 130 0 E
Neápolis, *Kozan, Greece* **35** 40 20N 21 24 E
Neápolis, *Lakonia, Greece* **35** 36 27N 23 8 E
Near Is., *U.S.A.* **102** 53 0N 172 0 E
Neath, *U.K.* **13** 51 39N 3 49W
Neba, I., *N. Cal.* **68** 20 9 S 163 56 E
Nebbou, *Burkina Faso* **91** 11 9N 1 51W
Nebine Cr. →, *Australia* **73** 29 27 S 146 56 E
Nebit Dag, *U.S.S.R.* **40** 39 30N 54 22 E
Nebolchy, *U.S.S.R.* **36** 59 8N 33 18 E
Nebraska □, *U.S.A.* **120** 41 30N 100 0W
Nebraska City, *U.S.A.* **120** 40 40N 95 52W
Nébrodi, Monti, *Italy* **28** 37 55N 14 50 E
Necedah, *U.S.A.* **120** 44 2N 90 7W
Nechako →, *Canada* **110** 53 30N 122 44W
Neches →, *U.S.A.* **121** 29 55N 93 52W
Neckar →, *W. Germany* **31** 49 31N 8 26 E
Necochea, *Argentina* **140** 38 30 S 58 50W
Nedelišće, *Yugoslavia* **27** 46 23N 16 22 E
Neder Rijn →, *Neths.* **16** 51 57N 6 2 E
Nederbrakel, *Belgium* **17** 50 48N 3 46 E
Nederweert, *Neths.* **17** 51 17N 5 45 E
Nédha →, *Greece* **35** 37 25N 21 45 E
Nedroma, *Algeria* **85** 35 1N 1 45W
Neede, *Neths.* **16** 52 8N 6 37 E
Needles, *U.S.A.* **125** 34 50N 114 35W
Needles, Pt., *N.Z.* **80** 36 3 S 175 25 E
Needles, The, *U.K.* **13** 50 39N 1 35W
Ñeembucú □, *Paraguay* **140** 27 0 S 58 0W
Neemuch = Nimach, *India* **48** 24 30N 74 56 E
Neenah, *U.S.A.* **114** 44 10N 88 30W
Neepawa, *Canada* **111** 50 15N 99 30W
Neer, *Neths.* **17** 51 16N 5 59 E
Neerim, *Australia* **74** 37 59 S 145 57 E
Neerim South, *Australia* **74** 38 1 S 145 58 E
Neerpelt, *Belgium* **17** 51 13N 5 26 E
Neeworra, *Australia* **77** 29 2 S 149 3 E
Nefta, *Tunisia* **86** 33 53N 7 50 E
Neftah Sidi Boubekeur, *Algeria* **85** 35 1N 0 4 E
Neftegorsk, *U.S.S.R.* **39** 44 25N 39 45 E
Negapatam = Nagappattinam, *India* **51** 10 46N 79 51 E
Negaunee, *U.S.A.* **104** 46 30N 87 36W
Negba, *Israel* **44** 31 40N 34 41 E
Negele, *Ethiopia* **89** 5 20N 39 36 E
Negev Desert = Hanegev, *Israel* **44** 30 50N 35 0 E
Negombo, *Sri Lanka* **51** 7 12N 79 50 E
Negotin, *Yugoslavia* **33** 44 16N 22 37 E
Negra, La, *Chile* **140** 23 46 S 70 18W
Negra, Peña, *Spain* **22** 42 11N 6 30W
Negra, Pta., *Mauritania* **84** 22 54N 16 18W
Negra, Pta., *Peru* **136** 6 6 S 81 10W
Negra Pt., *Phil.* **57** 18 40N 120 50 E
Negrais C., *Burma* **52** 16 0N 94 12 E
Negreira, *Spain* **22** 42 54N 8 45W
Négrine, *Algeria* **85** 34 30N 7 30 E
Negro →, *Argentina* **142** 41 2 S 62 47W
Negro →, *Bolivia* **137** 14 11 S 63 7W
Negro →, *Brazil* **135** 3 0 S 60 0W
Negro →, *Uruguay* **141** 33 24 S 58 22W
Negros, *Phil.* **57** 9 30N 122 40 E
Nehalem →, *U.S.A.* **124** 45 40N 123 56W
Nehbandān, *Iran* **47** 31 35N 60 5 E
Neheim-Hüsten, *W. Germany* **30** 51 27N 7 58 E
Nehoiaşu, *Romania* **34** 45 24N 26 20 E
Nei Monggol Zizhiqu □, *China* **60** 42 0N 112 0 E
Neiafu, *Tonga* **68** 18 39 S 173 59W
Neidpath, *Canada* **111** 50 12N 107 20W
Neihart, *U.S.A.* **122** 47 0N 110 44W
Neijiang, *China* **58** 29 35N 104 55 E
Neilrex, *Australia* **77** 31 44 S 149 20 E
Neilton, *U.S.A.* **122** 47 24N 123 52W
Neiqiu, *China* **60** 37 15N 114 30 E
Neira de Jusá, *Spain* **22** 42 53N 7 14W
Neisse →, *Europe* **30** 52 4N 14 46 E
Neiva, *Colombia* **134** 2 56N 75 18W
Neixiang, *China* **60** 33 10N 111 52 E
Nejanilini L., *Canada* **111** 59 33N 97 48W
Nejo, *Ethiopia* **89** 9 30N 35 28 E
Nekemte, *Ethiopia* **89** 9 4N 36 30 E
Nêkheb, *Egypt* **88** 25 10N 32 48 E
Neksø, *Denmark* **11** 55 4N 15 8 E
Nelas, *Portugal* **22** 40 32N 7 52W
Nelia, *Australia* **72** 20 39 S 142 12 E
Nelidovo, *U.S.S.R.* **36** 56 13N 32 49 E
Neligh, *U.S.A.* **120** 42 11N 98 2W
Nelkan, *U.S.S.R.* **41** 57 40N 136 4 E
Nelligen, *Australia* **76** 35 39 S 150 8 E
Nellikuppam, *India* **51** 11 46N 79 43 E
Nellore, *India* **51** 14 27N 79 59 E
Nelma, *U.S.S.R.* **41** 47 39N 139 0 E
Nelson, *Australia* **74** 38 3 S 141 2 E
Nelson, *Canada* **110** 49 30N 117 20W
Nelson, *N.Z.* **81** 41 18 S 173 16 E
Nelson, *U.K.* **12** 53 50N 2 14W
Nelson, *U.S.A.* **123** 35 35N 113 16W
Nelson □, *N.Z.* **81** 42 11 S 172 15 E
Nelson →, *Canada* **111** 54 33N 98 2W
Nelson, C., *Australia* **74** 38 26 S 141 32 E
Nelson, C., *Papua N. G.* **69** 9 0 S 149 20 E
Nelson, Estrecho, *Chile* **142** 51 30 S 75 0W
Nelson Bay, *Australia* **76** 32 43 S 152 9 E
Nelson Forks, *Canada* **110** 59 30N 124 0W
Nelson House, *Canada* **111** 55 47N 98 51W
Nelson L., *Canada* **111** 55 48N 100 7W
Nelspoort, *S. Africa* **96** 32 7 S 23 0 E
Nelspruit, *S. Africa* **97** 25 29 S 30 59 E
Nelungaloo, *Australia* **76** 33 7 S 148 0 E
Néma, *Mauritania* **90** 16 40N 7 15W
Neman →, *U.S.S.R.* **36** 55 25N 21 10 E
Nemeiben L., *Canada* **111** 55 20N 105 20W
Nemingha, *Australia* **77** 31 6 S 151 0 E
Nemira, *Romania* **34** 46 17N 26 19 E
Némiscachingue, L., *Canada* **106** 47 25N 74 30W
Nemours, *France* **19** 48 16N 2 40 E
Nemunas = Neman →, *U.S.S.R.* **36** 55 25N 21 10 E
Nemuro, *Japan* **63** 43 20N 145 35 E
Nemuro-Kaikyō, *Japan* **63** 43 30N 145 30 E
Nemuy, *U.S.S.R.* **41** 55 40N 136 9 E
Nen Jiang →, *China* **61** 45 28N 124 30 E
Nenagh, *Ireland* **15** 52 52N 8 11W
Nenana, *U.S.A.* **102** 64 30N 149 20W
Nenasi, *Malaysia* **55** 3 9N 103 23 E
Nendiarene, Pte., *N. Cal.* **68** 20 14 S 164 19 E
Nene →, *U.K.* **12** 52 38N 0 13 E
Nenjiang, *China* **62** 49 10N 125 10 E
Neno, *Malawi* **93** 15 25 S 34 40 E
Nenusa, Kepulauan, *Indonesia* **57** 4 45N 127 1 E
Neodesha, *U.S.A.* **121** 37 30N 95 37W
Neoga, *U.S.A.* **119** 39 19N 88 27W
Neópolis, *Brazil* **138** 10 18 S 36 35W
Neosho, *U.S.A.* **121** 36 56N 94 28W
Neosho →, *U.S.A.* **121** 35 59N 95 10W
Nepal ■, *Asia* **49** 28 0N 84 30 E
Nepalganj, *Nepal* **49** 28 5N 81 40 E
Nephi, *U.S.A.* **122** 39 43N 111 52W
Nephin, *Ireland* **15** 54 1N 9 21W
Neptune City, *U.S.A.* **117** 40 13N 74 4W
Néra →, *Romania* **34** 44 48N 21 25 E
Nérac, *France* **20** 44 8N 0 21 E
Nerang, *Australia* **77** 27 58 S 153 20 E
Nerastro, Sarīr, *Libya* **86** 24 20N 20 37 E

Nerchinsk, *U.S.S.R.* **41** 52 0N 116 39 E
Nerchinskiy Zavod, *U.S.S.R.* **41** 51 20N 119 40 E
Nereju, *Romania* **34** 45 43N 26 43 E
Nerekhta, *U.S.S.R.* **37** 57 26N 40 38 E
Néret L., *Canada* **105** 54 45N 70 44W
Neringa, *U.S.S.R.* **36** 55 30N 21 5 E
Nerja, *Spain* **23** 36 43N 3 55W
Nerl →, *U.S.S.R.* **37** 56 11N 40 34 E
Nerpio, *Spain* **25** 38 11N 2 16W
Nerriga, *Australia* **76** 35 6 S 150 6 E
Nerva, *Spain* **23** 37 42N 6 30W
Nes, *Iceland* **8** 65 53N 17 24W
Nes, *Neths.* **16** 53 26N 5 47 E
Nes Ziyyona, *Israel* **44** 31 56N 34 48 E
Nesbyen, *Norway* **10** 60 34N 9 35 E
Nesebŭr, *Bulgaria* **34** 42 41N 27 46 E
Neskaupstaður, *Iceland* **8** 65 9N 13 42W
Nesland, *Norway* **10** 59 31N 7 59 E
Neslandsvatn, *Norway* **10** 58 57N 9 10 E
Nesle, *France* **19** 49 45N 2 53 E
Nesodden, *Norway* **10** 59 48N 10 40 E
Nesque →, *France* **21** 43 59N 4 59 E
Ness, Loch, *U.K.* **14** 57 15N 4 30W
Nestaocano →, *Canada* **107** 49 38N 73 28W
Néstos →, *Greece* **35** 41 20N 24 35 E
Nesttun, *Norway* **9** 60 19N 5 21 E
Nesvizh, *U.S.S.R.* **36** 53 14N 26 38 E
Netanya, *Israel* **44** 32 20N 34 51 E
Nète →, *Belgium* **17** 51 7N 4 14 E
Nether Stowey, *U.K.* **13** 51 0N 3 10W
Netherbury, *U.K.* **13** 50 46N 2 45W
Netherby, *Australia* **74** 36 8 S 141 40 E
Netherdale, *Australia* **72** 21 10 S 148 33 E
Netherlands ■, *Europe* **16** 52 0N 5 30 E
Netherlands Antilles ■, *S. Amer.* **134** 12 15N 69 0W
Netherlands Guiana = Surinam ■, *S. Amer.* **135** 4 0N 56 0W
Neto →, *Italy* **29** 39 13N 17 8 E
Netrakona, *Bangla.* **52** 24 53N 90 47 E
Nettancourt, *France* **19** 48 51N 4 57 E
Nettilling L., *Canada* **103** 66 30N 71 0W
Nettuno, *Italy* **28** 41 29N 12 40 E
Netzahualcoyotl, Presa, *Mexico* **127** 17 10N 93 30W
Neu-Isenburg, *W. Germany* **31** 50 3N 8 42 E
Neu-Ulm, *W. Germany* **31** 48 23N 10 2 E
Neubrandenburg, *E. Germany* **30** 53 33N 13 17 E
Neubrandenburg □, *E. Germany* **30** 53 30N 13 20 E
Neubukow, *E. Germany* **30** 54 1N 11 40 E
Neuburg, *W. Germany* **31** 48 43N 11 11 E
Neuchâtel, *Switz.* **31** 47 0N 6 55 E
Neuchâtel □, *Switz.* **31** 47 0N 6 55 E
Neuchâtel, Lac de, *Switz.* **31** 46 53N 6 50 E
Neudau, *Austria* **33** 47 11N 16 6 E
Neuenhaus, *W. Germany* **30** 52 30N 6 55 E
Neuf-Brisach, *France* **19** 48 1N 7 30 E
Neufahrn, *W. Germany* **31** 48 44N 12 11 E
Neufchâteau, *Belgium* **17** 49 50N 5 25 E
Neufchâteau, *France* **19** 48 21N 5 40 E
Neufchâtel-en-Bray, *France* **18** 49 44N 1 26 E
Neufchâtel-sur-Aisne, *France* **19** 49 26N 4 1 E
Neuhaus, *E. Germany* **30** 53 16N 10 54 E
Neuillé-Pont-Pierre, *France* **18** 47 33N 0 33 E
Neuilly-St.-Front, *France* **19** 49 10N 3 15 E
Neukalen, *E. Germany* **30** 53 49N 12 48 E
Neumarkt, *W. Germany* **31** 49 16N 11 28 E
Neumarkt-Sankt Veit, *W. Germany* **31** 48 22N 12 30 E
Neumünster, *W. Germany* **30** 54 4N 9 58 E
Neung-sur-Beuvron, *France* **19** 47 30N 1 50 E
Neunkirchen, *Austria* **33** 47 43N 16 4 E
Neunkirchen, *W. Germany* **31** 49 23N 7 12 E
Neuquén, *Argentina* **142** 38 55 S 68 0W
Neuquén □, *Argentina* **140** 38 0 S 69 50W
Neuquén →, *Argentina* **142** 38 59 S 68 0W
Neuruppin, *E. Germany* **30** 52 56N 12 48 E
Neuse →, *U.S.A.* **115** 35 5N 76 30W
Neusiedler See, *Austria* **33** 47 50N 16 47 E
Neuss, *W. Germany* **17** 51 12N 6 39 E
Neussargues-Moissac, *France* **20** 45 9N 3 0 E
Neustadt, *Canada* **108** 44 5N 81 0W
Neustadt, *Gera, E. Germany* **30** 50 45N 11 43 E
Neustadt, *Potsdam, E. Germany* **30** 52 50N 12 27 E
Neustadt, *Baden-W., W. Germany* **31** 47 54N 8 13 E
Neustadt, *Bayern, W. Germany* **31** 49 42N 12 10 E
Neustadt, *Bayern, W. Germany* **31** 48 48N 11 47 E
Neustadt, *Bayern, W. Germany* **31** 49 34N 10 37 E
Neustadt, *Bayern, W. Germany* **31** 50 23N 11 0 E
Neustadt, *Hessen, W. Germany* **30** 50 51N 9 9 E
Neustadt, *Niedersachsen, W. Germany* **30** 52 30N 9 30 E
Neustadt, *Rhld-Pfz., W. Germany* **31** 49 21N 8 10 E
Neustadt, *Schleswig-Holstein, W. Germany* **30** 54 6N 10 49 E
Neustrelitz, *E. Germany* **30** 53 22N 13 4 E
Neuvic, *France* **20** 45 23N 2 16 E
Neuville, *Belgium* **17** 50 11N 4 32 E
Neuville-aux-Bois, *France* **19** 48 4N 2 3 E
Neuville-de-Poitou, *France* **20** 46 41N 0 15 E
Neuville-sur-Saône, *France* **21** 45 52N 4 51 E
Neuvy-le-Roi, *France* **18** 47 36N 0 36 E
Neuvy-St.-Sépulchre, *France* **20** 46 35N 1 48 E
Neuvy-sur-Barangeon, *France* **19** 47 20N 2 15 E
Neuwerk, *W. Germany* **30** 53 55N 8 30 E
Neuwied, *W. Germany* **30** 50 26N 7 29 E
Neva →, *U.S.S.R.* **6** 59 50N 30 30 E
Nevada, *Iowa, U.S.A.* **118** 42 1N 93 27W
Nevada, *Mo., U.S.A.* **118** 37 51N 94 22W
Nevada □, *U.S.A.* **122** 39 20N 117 0W
Nevada, Sierra, *Spain* **25** 37 3N 3 15W
Nevada, Sierra, *U.S.A.* **122** 39 0N 120 30W
Nevada City, *U.S.A.* **124** 39 20N 121 0W
Nevado, Cerro, *Argentina* **140** 35 30 S 68 32W
Nevanka, *U.S.S.R.* **41** 56 31N 98 55 E
Nevasa, *India* **50** 19 34N 75 0 E
Nevel, *U.S.S.R.* **36** 56 0N 29 55 E
Nevele, *Belgium* **17** 51 3N 3 33 E
Nevers, *France* **19** 47 0N 3 9 E
Nevertire, *Australia* **76** 31 50 S 147 44 E
Neville, *Australia* **76** 33 41 S 149 12 E
Neville, *Canada* **111** 49 58N 107 39W
Nevinnomyssk, *U.S.S.R.* **39** 44 40N 42 0 E
Nevis, *W. Indies* **129** 17 0N 62 30W
Nevrokop = Gotse Delchev, *Bulgaria* **35** 41 43N 23 46 E
Nevşehir, *Turkey* **46** 38 33N 34 40 E
New →, *Guyana* **135** 3 20N 57 37W
New Albany, *Ind., U.S.A.* **119** 38 20N 85 50W
New Albany, *Miss., U.S.A.* **121** 34 30N 89 0W
New Albany, *Pa., U.S.A.* **117** 41 35N 76 28W
New Amsterdam, *Guyana* **135** 6 15N 57 36W
New Angledool, *Australia* **73** 29 5 S 147 55 E
New Athens, *U.S.A.* **118** 38 19N 89 53W
New Bedford, *U.S.A.* **117** 41 40N 70 52W
New Berlin, *Ill., U.S.A.* **118** 39 44N 89 55W
New Berlin, *Wis., U.S.A.* **119** 42 59N 88 6W
New Bern, *U.S.A.* **115** 35 8N 77 3W
New Bethlehem, *U.S.A.* **116** 41 0N 79 22W
New Bloomfield, *U.S.A.* **116** 40 24N 77 12W
New Boston, *U.S.A.* **121** 33 27N 94 21W
New Braunfels, *U.S.A.* **121** 29 43N 98 9W
New Brighton, *N.Z.* **81** 43 29 S 172 43 E
New Brighton, *U.S.A.* **116** 40 42N 80 19W
New Britain, *Papua N. G.* **69** 5 50 S 150 20 E
New Britain, *U.S.A.* **117** 41 41N 72 47W
New Brunswick, *U.S.A.* **117** 40 30N 74 28W
New Brunswick □, *Canada* **105** 46 50N 66 30W
New Buffalo, *U.S.A.* **119** 41 47N 86 45W
New Bussa, *Nigeria* **91** 9 53N 4 31 E
New Caledonia, *Pac. Oc.* **68** 21 0 S 165 0 E
New Canton, *U.S.A.* **118** 39 37N 91 8W
New Carlisle, *Ind., U.S.A.* **119** 41 45N 86 32W
New Carlisle, *Ohio, U.S.A.* **119** 39 56N 84 2W
New Castile = Castilla La Nueva, *Spain* **23** 39 45N 3 20W
New Castle, *Ind., U.S.A.* **119** 39 55N 85 23W
New Castle, *Ky., U.S.A.* **119** 38 26N 85 10W
New Castle, *Pa., U.S.A.* **116** 41 0N 80 20W
New City, *U.S.A.* **117** 41 8N 74 0W
New Cumberland, *U.S.A.* **116** 40 30N 80 36W
New Cuyama, *U.S.A.* **125** 34 57N 119 38W
New Delhi, *India* **48** 28 37N 77 13 E
New Denver, *Canada* **110** 50 0N 117 25W
New Don Pedro Res., *U.S.A.* **124** 37 43N 120 24W
New England, *U.S.A.* **120** 46 36N 102 47W
New England Ra., *Australia* **77** 30 20 S 151 45 E
New Forest, *U.K.* **13** 50 53N 1 40W
New Franklin, *U.S.A.* **118** 39 1N 92 44W
New Georgia Is., *Solomon Is.* **68** 8 15 S 157 30 E
New Glarus, *U.S.A.* **118** 42 49N 89 38W
New Glasgow, *Canada* **105** 45 35N 62 36W
New Guinea, *Oceania* **66** 4 0 S 136 0 E
New Hamburg, *Canada* **108** 43 23N 80 42W
New Hampshire □, *U.S.A.* **117** 43 40N 71 40W
New Hampton, *U.S.A.* **118** 43 2N 92 20W
New Hanover, *Papua N. G.* **69** 2 30 S 150 10 E
New Hanover, *S. Africa* **97** 29 22 S 30 31 E
New Harmony, *U.S.A.* **119** 38 7N 87 56W
New Haven, *Conn., U.S.A.* **117** 41 20N 72 54W
New Haven, *Ill., U.S.A.* **119** 37 55N 88 8W
New Haven, *Ind., U.S.A.* **119** 41 4N 85 1W
New Haven, *Mich., U.S.A.* **116** 42 44N 82 46W
New Haven, *Mo., U.S.A.* **118** 38 37N 91 13W
New Hazelton, *Canada* **110** 55 20N 127 30W
New Hebrides = Vanuatu ■, *Pac. Oc.* **68** 15 0 S 168 0 E
New Iberia, *U.S.A.* **121** 30 2N 91 54W
New Ireland, *Papua N. G.* **69** 3 20 S 151 50 E
New Jersey □, *U.S.A.* **117** 40 30N 74 10W
New Kensington, *U.S.A.* **116** 40 36N 79 43W
New Lexington, *U.S.A.* **114** 39 40N 82 15W
New Liskeard, *Canada* **106** 47 31N 79 41W
New London, *Conn., U.S.A.* **117** 41 23N 72 8W
New London, *Iowa, U.S.A.* **118** 40 55N 91 24W
New London, *Minn., U.S.A.* **120** 45 17N 94 55W
New London, *Mo., U.S.A.* **118** 39 35N 91 24W
New London, *Ohio, U.S.A.* **116** 41 4N 82 25W
New London, *Wis., U.S.A.* **120** 44 23N 88 43W
New Madison, *U.S.A.* **119** 39 58N 84 43W
New Madrid, *U.S.A.* **121** 36 40N 89 30W
New Meadows, *U.S.A.* **122** 45 0N 116 32W
New Melones L., *U.S.A.* **124** 37 57N 120 31W
New Mexico □, *U.S.A.* **112** 34 30N 106 0W
New Miami, *U.S.A.* **119** 39 26N 84 32W
New Milford, *Conn., U.S.A.* **117** 41 35N 73 25W
New Milford, *Pa., U.S.A.* **117** 41 50N 75 45W
New Mollyan, *Australia* **77** 31 34 S 149 14 E
New Norcia, *Australia* **79** 30 57 S 116 13 E
New Norfolk, *Australia* **72** 42 46 S 147 2 E
New Orleans, *U.S.A.* **121** 30 0N 90 5W
New Palestine, *U.S.A.* **119** 39 45N 85 52W
New Paris, *U.S.A.* **119** 39 55N 84 48W
New Pekin, *U.S.A.* **119** 38 31N 86 2W
New Philadelphia, *U.S.A.* **116** 40 29N 81 25W
New Plymouth, *N.Z.* **80** 39 4 S 174 5 E
New Plymouth, *U.S.A.* **122** 43 58N 116 49W
New Providence, *Bahamas* **128** 25 25N 78 35W
New Radnor, *U.K.* **13** 52 15N 3 10W
New Richmond, *Ohio, U.S.A.* **119** 38 57N 84 17W
New Richmond, *Wis., U.S.A.* **120** 45 6N 92 34W
New Roads, *U.S.A.* **121** 30 43N 91 30W
New Rochelle, *U.S.A.* **117** 40 55N 73 46W
New Rockford, *U.S.A.* **120** 47 44N 99 7W
New Ross, *Ireland* **15** 52 24N 6 58W
New Salem, *U.S.A.* **120** 46 51N 101 25W
New Sharon, *U.S.A.* **118** 41 28N 92 39W
New Siberian Is. = Novosibirskiye Ostrava, *U.S.S.R.* **41** 75 0N 142 0 E
New Smyrna Beach, *U.S.A.* **115** 29 0N 80 50W
New South Wales □, *Australia* **73** 33 0 S 146 0 E
New Springs, *Australia* **79** 25 49 S 120 1 E
New Town, *U.S.A.* **120** 48 0N 102 30W
New Ulm, *U.S.A.* **120** 44 15N 94 30W
New Vienna, *U.S.A.* **119** 39 19N 83 42W
New Virginia, *U.S.A.* **118** 41 11N 93 44W
New Waterford, *Canada* **105** 46 13N 60 4W
New Westminster, *Canada* **110** 49 13N 122 55W
New York □, *U.S.A.* **117** 42 40N 76 0W
New York City, *U.S.A.* **117** 40 45N 74 0W
New Zealand ■, *Oceania* **81** 40 0 S 176 0 E
Newala, *Tanzania* **93** 10 58 S 39 18 E
Newala □, *Tanzania* **93** 10 46 S 39 20 E
Newark, *Del., U.S.A.* **114** 39 42N 75 45W
Newark, *N.J., U.S.A.* **117** 40 41N 74 12W
Newark, *N.Y., U.S.A.* **116** 43 2N 77 10W
Newark, *Ohio, U.S.A.* **116** 40 5N 82 24W
Newark-on-Trent, *U.K.* **12** 53 6N 0 48W
Newaygo, *U.S.A.* **114** 43 25N 85 48W
Newberg, *Mo., U.S.A.* **118** 37 55N 91 54W
Newberg, *Oreg., U.S.A.* **122** 45 22N 123 0W
Newberry, *Mich., U.S.A.* **104** 46 20N 85 32W
Newberry, *S.C., U.S.A.* **115** 34 17N 81 37W
Newberry Springs, *U.S.A.* **125** 34 50N 116 41W
Newboro L., *Canada* **109** 44 38N 76 20W
Newbridge, *Australia* **76** 33 35 S 149 22 E
Newbrook, *Canada* **110** 54 24N 112 57W
Newburgh, *Canada* **109** 44 19N 76 52W
Newburgh, *Ind., U.S.A.* **119** 37 57N 87 24W
Newburgh, *N.Y., U.S.A.* **117** 41 30N 74 1W
Newbury, *U.K.* **13** 51 24N 1 19W
Newbury, *U.S.A.* **117** 44 7N 72 6W
Newburyport, *U.S.A.* **117** 42 48N 70 50W
Newcastle, *Australia* **76** 33 0 S 151 46 E
Newcastle, *Canada* **105** 47 1N 65 38W
Newcastle, *S. Africa* **97** 27 45 S 29 58 E
Newcastle, *U.K.* **15** 54 13N 5 54W
Newcastle, *Calif., U.S.A.* **124** 38 50N 121 8W
Newcastle, *Wyo., U.S.A.* **120** 43 50N 104 12W
Newcastle Emlyn, *U.K.* **13** 52 2N 4 29W
Newcastle Ra., *Australia* **78** 15 45 S 130 15 E
Newcastle-under-Lyme, *U.K.* **12** 53 2N 2 15W
Newcastle-upon-Tyne, *U.K.* **12** 54 59N 1 37W
Newcastle Waters, *Australia* **72** 17 30 S 133 28 E
Newdegate, *Australia* **79** 33 6 S 119 0 E
Newe Etan, *Israel* **44** 32 30N 35 32 E
Newe Sha'anan, *Israel* **44** 32 47N 34 59 E
Newe Zohar, *Israel* **44** 31 9N 35 21 E
Newell, *U.S.A.* **120** 44 48N 103 25W
Newenham, C., *U.S.A.* **102** 58 40N 162 15W
Newfoundland □, *Canada* **103** 53 0N 58 0W
Newhalem, *U.S.A.* **110** 48 41N 121 16W
Newhall, *U.S.A.* **125** 34 23N 118 32W
Newham, *U.K.* **13** 51 31N 0 2 E
Newhaven, *Australia* **74** 38 32 S 145 20 E
Newhaven, *U.K.* **13** 50 47N 0 4 E
Newkirk, *U.S.A.* **121** 36 52N 97 3W
Newlyn, *Australia* **74** 37 23 S 144 0 E
Newman, *Australia* **78** 23 18 S 119 45 E
Newman, *Calif., U.S.A.* **124** 37 19N 121 1W
Newman, *Ill., U.S.A.* **119** 39 48N 87 59W
Newmarket, *Canada* **108** 44 3N 79 28W
Newmarket, *Ireland* **15** 52 13N 9 0W
Newmarket, *U.K.* **13** 52 15N 0 23 E
Newmarket, *U.S.A.* **117** 43 4N 70 57W
Newmerella, *Australia* **75** 37 45 S 148 25 E
Newnan, *U.S.A.* **115** 33 22N 84 48W
Newport, *Gwent, U.K.* **13** 51 35N 3 0W
Newport, *I. of W., U.K.* **13** 50 42N 1 18W
Newport, *Salop, U.K.* **13** 52 47N 2 22W
Newport, *Ark., U.S.A.* **121** 35 38N 91 15W
Newport, *Ind., U.S.A.* **119** 39 53N 87 26W
Newport, *Ky., U.S.A.* **119** 39 5N 84 23W
Newport, *N.H., U.S.A.* **117** 43 23N 72 8W
Newport, *Oreg., U.S.A.* **122** 44 41N 124 2W
Newport, *Pa., U.S.A.* **116** 40 28N 77 8W
Newport, *R.I., U.S.A.* **117** 41 13N 71 19W
Newport, *Tenn., U.S.A.* **115** 35 59N 83 12W
Newport, *Vt., U.S.A.* **117** 44 57N 72 17W
Newport, *Wash., U.S.A.* **122** 48 11N 117 2W
Newport Beach, *U.S.A.* **125** 33 40N 117 58W
Newport News, *U.S.A.* **114** 37 2N 76 30W
Newquay, *U.K.* **13** 50 24N 5 6W
Newry, *Australia* **75** 37 59 S 146 53 E
Newry, *U.K.* **15** 54 10N 6 20W
Newry & Mourne □, *U.K.* **15** 54 10N 6 15W
Newstead, *Australia* **74** 37 7 S 144 4 E
Newton, *Ill., U.S.A.* **119** 38 59N 88 10W
Newton, *Iowa, U.S.A.* **118** 41 40N 93 3W
Newton, *Mass., U.S.A.* **114** 42 21N 71 10W
Newton, *Mass., U.S.A.* **117** 42 21N 71 12W
Newton, *Miss., U.S.A.* **121** 32 19N 89 10W
Newton, *N.C., U.S.A.* **115** 35 42N 81 10W
Newton, *N.J., U.S.A.* **117** 41 3N 74 46W
Newton, *Tex., U.S.A.* **121** 30 54N 93 42W
Newton Abbot, *U.K.* **13** 50 32N 3 37W
Newton Boyd, *Australia* **77** 29 45 S 152 16 E
Newton Stewart, *U.K.* **14** 54 57N 4 30W
Newtonmore, *U.K.* **14** 57 4N 4 7W
Newtown, *U.K.* **13** 52 31N 3 19W
Newtown, *U.S.A.* **118** 40 22N 93 20W
Newtownabbey □, *U.K.* **15** 54 45N 6 0W
Newtownards, *U.K.* **15** 54 37N 5 40W
Newville, *U.S.A.* **116** 40 10N 77 24W
Nexon, *France* **20** 45 41N 1 11 E
Neya, *U.S.S.R.* **37** 58 21N 43 49 E
Neyrīz, *Iran* **47** 29 15N 54 19 E
Neyshābūr, *Iran* **47** 36 10N 58 50 E
Neyyattinkara, *India* **51** 8 26N 77 5 E
Nezhin, *U.S.S.R.* **36** 51 5N 31 55 E
Nezperce, *U.S.A.* **122** 46 13N 116 15W
Ngabang, *Indonesia* **56** 0 23N 109 55 E
Ngabordamlu, Tanjung, *Indonesia* **57** 6 56 S 134 11 E
N'Gage, *Angola* **95** 7 46 S 15 15 E
Ngaiphaipi, *Burma* **52** 22 14N 93 15 E
Ngambé, *Cameroon* **91** 5 48N 11 29 E
Ngami Depression, *Botswana* **96** 20 30 S 22 46 E
Ngamo, *Zimb.* **93** 19 3 S 27 32 E

Nganglong Kangri, *China* **49** 33 0N 81 0 E
Nganjuk, *Indonesia* **57** 7 32 S 111 55 E
Ngao, *Thailand* **54** 18 46N 99 59 E
Ngaoundéré, *Cameroon* **94** 7 15N 13 35 E
Ngapara, *N.Z.* **81** 44 57 S 170 46 E
Ngara, *Tanzania* **92** 2 29 S 30 40 E
Ngara □, *Tanzania* **92** 2 29 S 30 40 E
Ngaruawahia, *N.Z.* **80** 37 42 S 175 11 E
Ngatapa, *N.Z.* **80** 38 32 S 177 45 E
Ngathainggyaung, *Burma* **52** 17 24N 95 5 E
Ngauruhoe, Mt., *N.Z.* **80** 39 13 S 175 45 E
Ngawi, *Indonesia* **57** 7 24 S 111 26 E
Nggamea, *Fiji* **68** 16 46 S 179 46W
Nggela, *Solomon Is.* **68** 9 5 S 160 15 E
Nghia Lo, *Vietnam* **54** 21 33N 104 28 E
Ngidinga, *Zaïre* **95** 5 37 S 15 17 E
Ngo, *Congo* **94** 2 29 S 15 45 E
N'Gola, *Angola* **95** 14 10 S 14 30 E
Ngoma, *Malawi* **93** 13 8 S 33 45 E
Ngomahura, *Zimb.* **93** 20 26 S 30 43 E
Ngomba, *Tanzania* **93** 8 20 S 32 53 E
Ngop, *Sudan* **89** 6 17N 30 9 E
Ngoring Hu, *China* **62** 34 55N 97 5 E
Ngorkou, *Mali* **90** 15 40N 3 41W
Ngorongoro, *Tanzania* **92** 3 11 S 35 32 E
Ngouri, *Chad* **87** 13 38N 15 22 E
Ngourti, *Niger* **87** 15 19N 13 12 E
Ngozi, *Burundi* **92** 2 54 S 29 50 E
Ngudu, *Tanzania* **92** 2 58 S 33 25 E
Nguigmi, *Niger* **87** 14 20N 13 20 E
Ngukurr, *Australia* **72** 14 44 S 134 44 E
Ngunga, *Tanzania* **92** 3 37 S 33 37 E
Nguru, *Nigeria* **91** 12 56N 10 29 E
Nguru Mts., *Tanzania* **92** 6 0 S 37 30 E
Nguyen Binh, *Vietnam* **54** 22 39N 105 56 E
Nha Trang, *Vietnam* **55** 12 16N 109 10 E
Nhacoongo, *Mozam.* **97** 24 18 S 35 14 E
Nhambiquara, *Brazil* **137** 12 50 S 59 49W
Nhamundá, *Brazil* **135** 2 14 S 56 43W
Nhamundá →, *Brazil* **135** 2 12 S 56 41W
Nhangutazi, L., *Mozam.* **97** 24 0 S 34 30 E
Nhecolândia, *Brazil* **137** 19 17 S 56 58W
Nhill, *Australia* **74** 36 18 S 141 40 E
Nho Quan, *Vietnam* **54** 20 18N 105 45 E
Nhulunbuy, *Australia* **72** 12 10 S 137 20 E
Nhundo, *Angola* **95** 14 25 S 21 23 E
Nia-nia, *Zaïre* **92** 1 30N 27 40 E
Niafounké, *Mali* **90** 16 0N 4 5W
Niagara, *U.S.A.* **114** 45 45N 88 0W
Niagara Falls, *Canada* **108** 43 7N 79 5W
Niagara Falls, *U.S.A.* **116** 43 5N 79 0W
Niagara-on-the-Lake, *Canada* **108** 43 15N 79 4W
Niah, *Malaysia* **56** 3 58N 113 46 E
Niamey, *Niger* **91** 13 27N 2 6 E
Nianforando, *Guinea* **90** 9 37N 10 36W
Nianfors, *Sweden* **10** 61 36N 16 46 E
Niangala, *Australia* **77** 31 18 S 151 25 E
Niangara, *Zaïre* **92** 3 42N 27 50 E
Niangua →, *U.S.A.* **118** 38 0N 92 48W
Nias, *Indonesia* **56** 1 0N 97 30 E
Niassa □, *Mozam.* **93** 13 30 S 36 0 E
Nibbiano, *Italy* **26** 44 54N 9 20 E
Nibe, *Denmark* **11** 56 59N 9 38 E
Nicaragua ■, *Cent. Amer.* **128** 11 40N 85 30W
Nicaragua, L. de, *Nic.* **128** 12 0N 85 30W
Nicastro, *Italy* **29** 39 0N 16 18 E
Nice, *France* **21** 43 42N 7 14 E
Niceville, *U.S.A.* **115** 30 30N 86 30W
Nichinan, *Japan* **64** 31 38N 131 23 E
Nicholás, Canal, *W. Indies* **128** 23 30N 80 5W
Nicholasville, *U.S.A.* **119** 37 54N 84 31W
Nichols, *U.S.A.* **117** 42 1N 76 22W
Nicholson, *Australia* **78** 18 2 S 128 54 E
Nicholson, *U.S.A.* **117** 41 37N 75 47W
Nicholson →, *Australia* **72** 17 31 S 139 36 E
Nicholson Ra., *Australia* **79** 27 15 S 116 45 E
Nickerie □, *Surinam* **135** 4 0N 57 0W
Nickerie →, *Surinam* **135** 5 58N 57 0W
Nicobar Is., *Ind. Oc.* **53** 9 0N 93 0 E
Nicoclí, *Colombia* **134** 8 26N 76 48W
Nicola, *Canada* **110** 50 12N 120 40W
Nicolet, *Canada* **107** 46 17N 72 35W
Nicolls Town, *Bahamas* **128** 25 8N 78 0W
Nicosia, *Cyprus* **46** 35 10N 33 25 E
Nicosia, *Italy* **29** 37 45N 14 22 E
Nicótera, *Italy* **29** 38 33N 15 57 E
Nicoya, *Costa Rica* **128** 10 9N 85 27W
Nicoya, G. de, *Costa Rica* **128** 10 0N 85 0W
Nicoya, Pen. de, *Costa Rica* **128** 9 45N 85 40W
Nidd →, *U.K.* **12** 54 1N 1 32W
Nidda, *W. Germany* **30** 50 24N 9 2 E
Nidda →, *W. Germany* **31** 50 6N 8 34 E
Nidzica, *Poland* **32** 53 25N 20 28 E
Niebüll, *W. Germany* **30** 54 47N 8 49 E
Nied →, *W. Germany* **19** 49 23N 6 40 E
Niederaula, *W. Germany* **30** 50 48N 9 37 E
Niederbronn-les-Bains, *France* **19** 48 57N 7 39 E
Niedere Tauern, *Austria* **33** 47 20N 14 0 E
Niedermarsberg, *W. Germany* **30** 51 28N 8 52 E
Niedersachsen □, *W. Germany* **30** 52 45N 9 0 E
Niefang, *Eq. Guin.* **94** 1 50N 10 14 E
Niekerkshoop, *S. Africa* **96** 29 19 S 22 51 E
Niel, *Belgium* **17** 51 7N 4 20 E
Niellé, *Ivory C.* **90** 10 5N 5 38W
Niem, *C.A.R.* **94** 6 12N 15 14 E
Niemba, *Zaïre* **92** 5 58 S 28 24 E
Nienburg, *W. Germany* **30** 52 38N 9 15 E
Niers →, *W. Germany* **30** 51 35N 6 13 E
Niesky, *E. Germany* **30** 51 18N 14 48 E
Nieu Bethesda, *S. Africa* **96** 31 51 S 24 34 E
Nieuw-Amsterdam, *Neths.* **16** 52 43N 6 52 E
Nieuw Amsterdam, *Surinam* **135** 5 53N 55 5W
Nieuw Beijerland, *Neths.* **16** 51 49N 4 20 E
Nieuw-Dordrecht, *Neths.* **16** 52 45N 6 59 E
Nieuw Loosdrecht, *Neths.* **16** 52 12N 5 8 E
Nieuw Nickerie, *Surinam* **135** 6 0N 56 59W
Nieuw-Schoonebeek, *Neths.* **16** 52 39N 7 0 E
Nieuw-Vennep, *Neths.* **16** 52 16N 4 38 E
Nieuw-Vossemeer, *Neths.* **17** 51 34N 4 12 E
Nieuwe-Niedorp, *Neths.* **16** 52 44N 4 54 E
Nieuwe-Pekela, *Neths.* **16** 53 5N 6 58 E
Nieuwe-Schans, *Neths.* **16** 53 11N 7 12 E
Nieuwendijk, *Neths.* **16** 51 46N 4 55 E
Nieuwerkerken, *Belgium* **17** 50 52N 5 12 E
Nieuwkoop, *Neths.* **16** 52 9N 4 48 E
Nieuwleusen, *Neths.* **16** 52 34N 6 17 E
Nieuwnamen, *Neths.* **17** 51 18N 4 9 E
Nieuwolda, *Neths.* **16** 53 15N 6 58 E
Nieuwoudtville, *S. Africa* **96** 31 23 S 19 7 E
Nieuwpoort, *Belgium* **17** 51 8N 2 45 E
Nieuwveen, *Neths.* **16** 52 12N 4 46 E
Nieves, *Spain* **22** 42 7N 8 26W
Nieves, Pico de las, *Canary Is.* **25** 27 57N 15 35W
Nièvre □, *France* **19** 47 10N 3 40 E
Nigata, *Japan* **64** 34 13N 132 39 E
Niğde, *Turkey* **46** 38 0N 34 40 E
Nigel, *S. Africa* **97** 26 27 S 28 25 E
Niger □, *Nigeria* **91** 10 0N 5 0 E
Niger ■, *W. Afr.* **91** 17 30N 10 0 E
Niger →, *W. Afr.* **91** 5 33N 6 33 E
Nigeria ■, *W. Afr.* **91** 8 30N 8 0 E
Nightcaps, *N.Z.* **81** 45 57 S 168 2 E
Nigríta, *Greece* **35** 40 56N 23 29 E
Nihtaur, *India* **49** 29 20N 78 23 E
Nii-Jima, *Japan* **65** 34 20N 139 15 E
Niigata, *Japan* **63** 37 58N 139 0 E
Niihama, *Japan* **64** 33 55N 133 16 E
Niihau, *U.S.A.* **112** 21 55N 160 10W
Niimi, *Japan* **64** 34 59N 133 28 E
Níjar, *Spain* **25** 36 53N 2 15W
Nijkerk, *Neths.* **16** 52 13N 5 30 E
Nijlen, *Belgium* **17** 51 10N 4 40 E
Nijmegen, *Neths.* **16** 51 50N 5 52 E
Nijverdal, *Neths.* **16** 52 22N 6 28 E
Nike, *Nigeria* **91** 6 26N 7 29 E
Nikel, *U.S.S.R.* **8** 69 24N 30 12 E
Nikiniki, *Indonesia* **57** 9 49 S 124 30 E
Nikki, *Benin* **91** 9 58N 3 12 E
Nikkō, *Japan* **65** 36 45N 139 35 E
Nikolayev, *U.S.S.R.* **38** 46 58N 32 0 E
Nikolayevsk, *U.S.S.R.* **37** 50 0N 45 35 E
Nikolayevsk-na-Amur, *U.S.S.R.* **41** 53 8N 140 44 E
Nikolsk, *U.S.S.R.* **37** 59 30N 45 28 E
Nikolskoye, *U.S.S.R.* **41** 55 12N 166 0 E
Nikopol, *Bulgaria* **34** 43 43N 24 54 E
Nikopol, *U.S.S.R.* **38** 47 35N 34 25 E
Niksar, *Turkey* **38** 40 31N 37 2 E
Nīkshahr, *Iran* **47** 26 15N 60 10 E
Nikšić, *Yugoslavia* **33** 42 50N 18 57 E
Nîl, Nahr en →, *Africa* **88** 30 10N 31 6 E
Nîl el Abyad →, *Sudan* **89** 15 38N 32 31 E
Nîl el Azraq →, *Sudan* **89** 15 38N 32 31 E
Niland, *U.S.A.* **125** 33 16N 115 30W
Nile = Nîl, Nahr en →, *Africa* **88** 30 10N 31 6 E
Nile □, *Uganda* **92** 2 0N 31 30 E
Nile Delta, *Egypt* **88** 31 40N 31 0 E
Niles, *U.S.A.* **116** 41 8N 80 40W
Nilgiri Hills, *India* **51** 11 30N 76 30 E
Nilo Peçanha, *Brazil* **139** 13 37 S 39 6W
Nimach, *India* **48** 24 30N 74 56 E
Nimbahera, *India* **48** 24 37N 74 45 E
Nimbin, *Australia* **77** 28 36 S 153 13 E
Nîmes, *France* **21** 43 50N 4 23 E
Nimfaíon, Ákra-, *Greece* **35** 40 5N 24 20 E
Nimmitabel, *Australia* **75** 36 29 S 149 15 E
Nimneryskiy, *U.S.S.R.* **41** 57 50N 125 10 E
Nīmrūz □, *Afghan.* **47** 30 0N 62 0 E
Nimule, *Sudan* **89** 3 32N 32 3 E
Nin, *Yugoslavia* **27** 44 16N 15 12 E
Nīnawá, *Iraq* **46** 36 25N 43 10 E
Ninda, *Angola* **95** 14 47 S 21 24 E
Nindigully, *Australia* **73** 28 21 S 148 50 E
Ninemile, *U.S.A.* **110** 56 0N 130 7W
Ninety Mile Beach, The, *Australia* **75** 38 15 S 147 24 E
Nineveh = Nīnawá, *Iraq* **46** 36 25N 43 10 E
Ning Xian, *China* **60** 35 30N 107 58 E
Ningaloo, *Australia* **78** 22 41 S 113 41 E
Ning'an, *China* **61** 44 22N 129 20 E
Ningbo, *China* **59** 29 51N 121 28 E
Ningcheng, *China* **61** 41 32N 119 53 E
Ningde, *China* **59** 26 38N 119 23 E
Ningdu, *China* **59** 26 25N 115 59 E
Ninggang, *China* **59** 26 42N 113 55 E
Ningguo, *China* **59** 30 35N 119 0 E
Ninghai, *China* **59** 29 15N 121 27 E
Ninghua, *China* **59** 26 14N 116 45 E
Ningjin, *China* **60** 37 35N 114 57 E
Ningjing Shan, *China* **58** 30 0N 98 20 E
Ninglang, *China* **58** 27 20N 100 55 E
Ningling, *China* **60** 34 25N 115 22 E
Ningming, *China* **58** 22 8N 107 4 E
Ningnan, *China* **58** 27 5N 102 36 E
Ningpo = Ningbo, *China* **59** 29 51N 121 28 E
Ningqiang, *China* **60** 32 47N 106 15 E
Ningshan, *China* **60** 33 21N 108 21 E
Ningsia Hui A.R. = Ningxia Huizu Zizhiqu □, *China* **60** 38 0N 106 0 E
Ningwu, *China* **60** 39 0N 112 18 E
Ningxia Huizu Zizhiqu □, *China* **60** 38 0N 106 0 E
Ningxiang, *China* **59** 28 15N 112 30 E
Ningyang, *China* **60** 35 47N 116 45 E
Ningyuan, *China* **59** 25 37N 111 57 E
Ninh Binh, *Vietnam* **54** 20 15N 105 55 E
Ninh Giang, *Vietnam* **54** 20 44N 106 24 E
Ninh Hoa, *Vietnam* **54** 12 30N 109 7 E
Ninh Ma, *Vietnam* **54** 12 48N 109 21 E
Ninove, *Belgium* **17** 50 51N 4 2 E
Nioaque, *Brazil* **141** 21 5 S 55 50W
Niobrara, *U.S.A.* **120** 42 48N 97 59W
Niobrara →, *U.S.A.* **120** 42 45N 98 0W
Nioki, *Zaïre* **94** 2 47 S 17 40 E
Niono, *Mali* **90** 14 15N 6 0W
Nioro du Rip, *Senegal* **90** 13 40N 15 50W
Nioro du Sahel, *Mali* **90** 15 15N 9 30W
Niort, *France* **20** 46 19N 0 29W
Nipa, *Papua N. G.* **69** 6 9 S 143 29 E
Nipani, *India* **51** 16 20N 74 25 E
Nipawin, *Canada* **111** 53 20N 104 0W
Nipawin Prov. Park, *Canada* **111** 54 0N 104 37W
Nipigon, *Canada* **104** 49 0N 88 17W
Nipigon, L., *Canada* **104** 49 50N 88 30W
Nipin →, *Canada* **111** 55 46N 108 35W
Nipishish L., *Canada* **105** 54 12N 60 45W
Nipissing L., *Canada* **108** 46 20N 80 0W
Nipomo, *U.S.A.* **125** 35 4N 120 29W
Nipton, *U.S.A.* **125** 35 28N 115 16W
Niquelândia, *Brazil* **139** 14 33 S 48 23W
Nira →, *India* **50** 17 58N 75 8 E
Nirasaki, *Japan* **65** 35 42N 138 27 E
Nirmal, *India* **50** 19 3N 78 20 E
Nirmali, *India* **49** 26 20N 86 35 E
Niš, *Yugoslavia* **33** 43 19N 21 58 E
Nisa, *Portugal* **23** 39 30N 7 41W
Nişāb, *S. Yemen* **45** 14 25N 46 29 E
Nišava →, *Yugoslavia* **33** 43 20N 21 46 E
Niscemi, *Italy* **29** 37 8N 14 21 E
Nishi-Sonogi-Hantō, *Japan* **64** 32 55N 129 45 E
Nishinomiya, *Japan* **65** 34 45N 135 20 E
Nishio, *Japan* **65** 34 52N 137 3 E
Nishiwaki, *Japan* **64** 34 59N 134 58 E
Nísíros, *Greece* **35** 36 35N 27 12 E
Niskibi →, *Canada* **104** 56 29N 88 9W
Nispen, *Neths.* **17** 51 29N 4 28 E
Nisqually →, *U.S.A.* **124** 47 6N 122 42W
Nissafors, *Sweden* **11** 57 25N 13 37 E
Nissan →, *Sweden* **11** 56 40N 12 51 E
Nissedal, *Norway* **10** 59 10N 8 30 E
Nisser, *Norway* **10** 59 7N 8 28 E
Nissum Fjord, *Denmark* **11** 56 20N 8 11 E
Nistelrode, *Neths.* **17** 51 42N 5 34 E
Nisutlin →, *Canada* **110** 60 14N 132 34W
Nitā', *Si. Arabia* **46** 27 15N 48 35 E
Nitchequon, *Canada* **105** 53 10N 70 58W
Niterói, *Brazil* **139** 22 52 S 43 0W
Nith →, *Canada* **108** 43 12N 80 23W
Nith →, *U.K.* **14** 55 20N 3 5W
Nitra, *Czech.* **33** 48 19N 18 4 E
Nittedal, *Norway* **10** 60 1N 10 57 E
Nittendau, *W. Germany* **31** 49 12N 12 16 E
Niue I., *Cook Is.* **67** 19 2 S 169 54W
Niulan Jiang →, *China* **58** 27 30N 103 5 E
Niut, *Indonesia* **56** 0 55N 110 6 E
Niutou Shan, *China* **59** 29 5N 121 59 E
Niuzhuang, *China* **61** 40 58N 122 28 E
Nivelles, *Belgium* **17** 50 35N 4 20 E
Nivernais, *France* **19** 47 0N 3 20 E
Nixon, *U.S.A.* **121** 29 17N 97 45W
Nizam Sagar, *India* **50** 18 10N 77 58 E
Nizamabad, *India* **50** 18 45N 78 7 E
Nizamghat, *India* **52** 28 20N 95 45 E
Nizhne Kolymsk, *U.S.S.R.* **41** 68 34N 160 55 E
Nizhneangarsk, *U.S.S.R.* **41** 55 47N 109 30 E
Nizhnegorskiy, *U.S.S.R.* **38** 45 27N 34 38 E
Nizhneudinsk, *U.S.S.R.* **41** 54 54N 99 3 E
Nizhnevartovsk, *U.S.S.R.* **40** 60 56N 76 38 E
Nizhneyansk, *U.S.S.R.* **41** 71 26N 136 4 E
Nizhniy Lomov, *U.S.S.R.* **37** 53 34N 43 38 E
Nizhniy Novgorod = Gorkiy, *U.S.S.R.* **37** 56 20N 44 0 E
Nizhniy Tagil, *U.S.S.R.* **40** 57 55N 59 57 E
Nizhnyaya Tunguska →, *U.S.S.R.* **41** 64 20N 93 0 E
Nizip, *Turkey* **46** 37 5N 37 50 E
Nizké Tatry, *Czech.* **32** 48 55N 20 0 E
Nizza Monferrato, *Italy* **26** 44 46N 8 22 E
Njakwa, *Malawi* **93** 11 1 S 33 56 E
Njanji, *Zambia* **93** 14 25 S 31 46 E
Njinjo, *Tanzania* **93** 8 48 S 38 54 E
Njombe, *Tanzania* **93** 9 20 S 34 50 E
Njombe □, *Tanzania* **93** 9 20 S 34 49 E
Njombe →, *Tanzania* **92** 6 56 S 35 6 E
Nkambe, *Cameroon* **91** 6 35N 10 40 E
Nkana, *Zambia* **93** 12 50 S 28 8 E
Nkawkaw, *Ghana* **91** 6 36N 0 49W
Nkayi, *Zimb.* **93** 19 41 S 29 20 E
Nkhota Kota, *Malawi* **93** 12 56 S 34 15 E
Nkolabona, *Gabon* **94** 1 14N 11 43 E
Nkone, *Zaïre* **94** 1 2 S 22 20 E
Nkongsamba, *Cameroon* **91** 4 55N 9 55 E
Nkunga, *Zaïre* **95** 4 41 S 18 34 E
Nkurenkuru, *Namibia* **96** 17 42 S 18 32 E
Nkwanta, *Ghana* **90** 6 10N 2 10W
Noakhali = Maijdi, *Bangla.* **52** 22 48N 91 10 E
Noatak, *U.S.A.* **102** 67 32N 162 59W
Nobel, *Canada* **108** 45 25N 80 6W
Nobeoka, *Japan* **64** 32 36N 131 41 E
Nōbi-Heiya, *Japan* **65** 35 15N 136 45 E
Noble, *U.S.A.* **119** 38 42N 88 14W
Noblejas, *Spain* **24** 39 58N 3 26W
Noblesville, *U.S.A.* **119** 40 1N 85 59W
Noce →, *Italy* **26** 46 9N 11 4 E
Nocera Inferiore, *Italy* **29** 40 45N 14 37 E
Nocera Terinese, *Italy* **29** 39 2N 16 9 E
Nocera Umbra, *Italy* **27** 43 8N 12 47 E
Noci, *Italy* **29** 40 47N 17 7 E
Nockatunga, *Australia* **73** 27 42 S 142 42 E
Nocona, *U.S.A.* **121** 33 48N 97 45W
Noda, *Japan* **65** 35 56N 139 52 E
Noel, *U.S.A.* **121** 36 36N 94 29W
Noelville, *Canada* **108** 46 8N 80 26W
Nogal Valley, *Somali Rep.* **98** 8 35N 48 35 E
Nogales, *Mexico* **126** 31 20N 110 56W
Nogales, *U.S.A.* **123** 31 33N 110 56W
Nōgata, *Japan* **64** 33 48N 130 44 E
Nogent-en-Bassigny, *France* **19** 48 1N 5 20 E
Nogent-le-Rotrou, *France* **18** 48 20N 0 50 E
Nogent-sur-Seine, *France* **19** 48 30N 3 30 E
Noggerup, *Australia* **79** 33 32 S 116 5 E
Noginsk, *Moskva, U.S.S.R.* **37** 55 50N 38 25 E
Noginsk, *Sib., U.S.S.R.* **41** 64 30N 90 50 E
Nogoa →, *Australia* **72** 23 40 S 147 55 E
Nogoyá, *Argentina* **140** 32 24 S 59 48W
Nogueira de Ramuin, *Spain* **22** 42 21N 7 43W
Noguera Pallaresa →, *Spain* **24** 42 15N 1 0 E
Noguera Ribagorzana →, *Spain* **24** 41 40N 0 43 E
Nohar, *India* **48** 29 11N 74 49 E
Noire →, *Canada* **106** 45 54N 76 57W
Noire, Mt., *France* **18** 48 11N 3 40W
Noirétable, *France* **20** 45 48N 3 46 E
Noirmoutier, I. de, *France* **18** 46 58N 2 10W
Noirmoutier-en-l'Ile, *France* **18** 47 0N 2 14W
Nojane, *Botswana* **96** 23 15 S 20 14 E
Nojima-Zaki, *Japan* **65** 34 54N 139 53 E
Nok Kundi, *Pakistan* **47** 28 50N 62 45 E
Nokaneng, *Botswana* **96** 19 40 S 22 17 E
Nokhtuysk, *U.S.S.R.* **41** 60 0N 117 45 E
Nokomis, *Canada* **111** 51 35N 105 0W
Nokomis, *U.S.A.* **118** 39 18N 89 18W
Nokomis L., *Canada* **111** 57 0N 103 0W
Nokou, *Chad* **87** 14 35N 14 47 E
Nol, *Sweden* **11** 57 56N 12 5 E
Nola, *C.A.R.* **94** 3 35N 16 4 E
Nola, *Italy* **29** 40 54N 14 29 E
Nolay, *France* **19** 46 58N 4 35 E
Noli, C. di, *Italy* **26** 44 12N 8 26 E
Nolinsk, *U.S.S.R.* **37** 57 28N 49 57 E
Noma Omuramba →, *Namibia* **96** 18 52 S 20 53 E
Noma-Saki, *Japan* **64** 31 25N 130 7 E
Nomad, *Papua N. G.* **69** 6 19 S 142 13 E
Noman L., *Canada* **111** 62 15N 108 55W
Nombre de Dios, *Panama* **128** 9 34N 79 28W
Nome, *U.S.A.* **102** 64 30N 165 24W
Nominingue, *Canada* **106** 46 24N 75 2W
Nominingue, L., *Canada* **106** 46 26N 74 59W
Nomo-Zaki, *Japan* **64** 32 35N 129 44 E
Nomuka, *Tonga* **68** 20 17 S 174 48W
Nomuka Group, *Tonga* **68** 20 20 S 174 48W
Nonacho L., *Canada* **111** 61 42N 109 40W
Nonancourt, *France* **18** 48 47N 1 11 E
Nonant-le-Pin, *France* **18** 48 42N 0 12 E
Nonda, *Australia* **72** 20 40 S 142 28 E

Nong Chang, *Thailand* **54** 15 23N 99 51 E
Nong Het, *Laos* **54** 19 29N 103 59 E
Nong Khai, *Thailand* **54** 17 50N 102 46 E
Nong'an, *China* **61** 44 25N 125 5 E
Nongoma, *S. Africa* **97** 27 58 S 31 35 E
Nonoava, *Mexico* **126** 27 28N 106 44W
Nonthaburi, *Thailand* **54** 13 51N 100 34 E
Nontron, *France* **20** 45 31N 0 40 E
Nonza, *France* **21** 42 47N 9 21 E
Noojee, *Australia* **74** 37 57 S 146 1 E
Noonamah, *Australia* **78** 12 40 S 131 4 E
Noonan, *U.S.A.* **120** 48 51N 102 59W
Noondoo, *Australia* **73** 28 35 S 148 30 E
Noonkanbah, *Australia* **78** 18 30 S 124 50 E
Noorat, *Australia* **74** 38 12 S 142 55 E
Noord-Bergum, *Neths.* **16** 53 14N 6 1 E
Noord Brabant □, *Neths.* **17** 51 40N 5 0 E
Noord Holland □, *Neths.* **16** 52 30N 4 45 E
Noordbeveland, *Neths.* **17** 51 35N 3 50 E
Noordeloos, *Neths.* **16** 51 55N 4 56 E
Noordhollandsch Kanaal, *Neths.* **16** 52 55N 4 48 E
Noordhorn, *Neths.* **16** 53 16N 6 24 E
Noordoostpolder, *Neths.* **16** 52 45N 5 45 E
Noordwijk aan Zee, *Neths.* **16** 52 14N 4 26 E
Noordwijk-Binnen, *Neths.* **16** 52 14N 4 27 E
Noordwijkerhout, *Neths.* **16** 52 16N 4 30 E
Noordzee Kanaal, *Neths.* **16** 52 28N 4 35 E
Noorinbee, *Australia* **75** 37 32 S 149 10 E
Noorwolde, *Neths.* **16** 52 54N 6 8 E
Nootka, *Canada* **110** 49 38N 126 38W
Nootka I., *Canada* **110** 49 32N 126 42W
Nóqui, *Angola* **95** 5 55 S 13 30 E
Nora, *Ethiopia* **89** 16 6N 40 4 E
Nora, *Sweden* **10** 59 32N 15 2 E
Nora Springs, *U.S.A.* **118** 43 9N 93 0W
Noradjuha, *Australia* **74** 36 50 S 141 58 E
Norah Hd., *Australia* **76** 33 18 S 151 32 E
Noranda, *Canada* **106** 48 20N 79 0W
Norberg, *Sweden* **10** 60 4N 15 56 E
Norborne, *U.S.A.* **118** 39 18N 93 40W
Nórcia, *Italy* **27** 42 50N 13 5 E
Norco, *U.S.A.* **125** 33 56N 117 33W
Nord □, *France* **19** 50 15N 3 30 E
Nord-Ostsee Kanal, *W. Germany* **30** 54 15N 9 40 E
Nord-Süd Kanal, *W. Germany* **30** 53 0N 10 32 E
Nord-Trøndelag fylke □, *Norway* **8** 64 20N 12 0 E
Nordagutu, *Norway* **10** 59 25N 9 20 E
Nordaustlandet, *Svalbard* **144** 79 14N 23 0 E
Nordborg, *Denmark* **11** 55 5N 9 50 E
Nordby, *Århus, Denmark* **11** 55 58N 10 32 E
Nordby, *Ribe, Denmark* **11** 55 27N 8 24 E
Norddeich, *W. Germany* **30** 53 37N 7 10 E
Nordegg, *Canada* **110** 52 29N 116 5W
Norden, *W. Germany* **30** 53 35N 7 12 E
Nordenham, *W. Germany* **30** 53 29N 8 28 E
Norderhov, *Norway* **10** 60 7N 10 17 E
Norderney, *W. Germany* **30** 53 42N 7 15 E
Nordfriesische Inseln, *W. Germany* **30** 54 40N 8 20 E
Nordhausen, *E. Germany* **30** 51 29N 10 47 E
Nordhorn, *W. Germany* **30** 52 27N 7 4 E
Nordjyllands Amtskommune □, *Denmark* **11** 57 0N 10 0 E
Nordkapp, *Norway* **8** 71 10N 25 44 E
Nordkapp, *Svalbard* **144** 80 31N 20 0 E
Nordkinn, *Norway* **6** 71 8N 27 40 E
Nordland fylke □, *Norway* **8** 65 40N 13 0 E
Nördlingen, *W. Germany* **31** 48 50N 10 30 E
Nordrhein-Westfalen □, *W. Germany* **30** 51 45N 7 30 E
Nordstrand, *W. Germany* **30** 54 27N 8 50 E
Nordvik, *U.S.S.R.* **41** 74 2N 111 32 E
Nore, *Norway* **10** 60 10N 9 0 E
Nore →, *Ireland* **15** 52 40N 7 20W
Norefjell, *Norway* **10** 60 16N 9 29 E
Norembega, *Canada* **106** 48 59N 80 43W
Noresund, *Norway* **10** 60 11N 9 37 E
Norfolk, *Nebr., U.S.A.* **120** 42 3N 97 25W
Norfolk, *Va., U.S.A.* **114** 36 40N 76 15W
Norfolk □, *U.K.* **12** 52 39N 1 0 E
Norfolk Broads, *U.K.* **12** 52 30N 1 15 E
Norfolk I., *Pac. Oc.* **66** 28 58 S 168 3 E
Norfork Res., *U.S.A.* **121** 36 13N 92 15W
Norg, *Neths.* **16** 53 4N 6 28 E
Norilsk, *U.S.S.R.* **41** 69 20N 88 6 E
Norley, *Australia* **73** 27 45 S 143 48 E
Norma, Mt., *Australia* **72** 20 55 S 140 42 E
Normal, *U.S.A.* **118** 40 30N 89 0W
Norman, *U.S.A.* **121** 35 12N 97 30W
Norman →, *Australia* **72** 17 28 S 140 49 E
Norman Wells, *Canada* **102** 65 17N 126 51W
Normanby, *N.Z.* **80** 39 32 S 174 18 E
Normanby →, *Australia* **72** 14 23 S 144 10 E
Normanby I., *Papua N. G.* **69** 10 55 S 151 5 E
Normandie, *France* **18** 48 45N 0 10 E
Normandie, Collines de, *France* **18** 48 45N 0 45W
Normandin, *Canada* **107** 48 49N 72 31W
Normandy = Normandie, *France* **18** 48 45N 0 10 E
Normanhurst, Mt., *Australia* **79** 25 4 S 122 30 E
Normanton, *Australia* **72** 17 40 S 141 10 E
Normétal, *Canada* **106** 49 0N 79 22W
Norquay, *Canada* **111** 51 53N 102 5W
Norquinco, *Argentina* **142** 41 51 S 70 55W
Norrahammar, *Sweden* **11** 57 43N 14 7 E
Norrbotten □, *Sweden* **8** 66 30N 22 30 E
Norrby, *Sweden* **8** 64 55N 18 15 E
Nørre Åby, *Denmark* **11** 55 27N 9 52 E
Nørre Nebel, *Denmark* **11** 55 47N 8 17 E
Nørresundby, *Denmark* **11** 57 5N 9 52 E
Norris, *U.S.A.* **122** 45 40N 111 40W
Norris City, *U.S.A.* **119** 37 59N 88 20W
Norristown, *U.S.A.* **117** 40 9N 75 21W
Norrköping, *Sweden* **11** 58 37N 16 11 E
Norrland □, *Sweden* **8** 66 50N 18 0 E
Norrtälje, *Sweden* **10** 59 46N 18 42 E
Norseman, *Australia* **79** 32 8 S 121 43 E
Norsholm, *Sweden* **11** 58 31N 15 59 E
Norsk, *U.S.S.R.* **41** 52 30N 130 0 E
Norsup, *Vanuatu* **68** 16 3 S 167 24 E
Norte, Pta., *Argentina* **142** 42 5 S 63 46W
Norte, Pta. del, *Canary Is.* **25** 27 51N 17 57W
Norte de Santander □, *Colombia* **134** 8 0N 73 0W
Nortelândia, *Brazil* **137** 14 25 S 56 48W
North Adams, *U.S.A.* **117** 42 42N 73 6W
North America **100** 40 0N 100 0W
North Atlantic Ocean, *Atl. Oc.* **130** 30 0N 50 0W
North Baltimore, *U.S.A.* **119** 41 11N 83 41W
North Battleford, *Canada* **111** 52 50N 108 17W
North Bay, *Canada* **108** 46 20N 79 30W
North Belcher Is., *Canada* **104** 56 50N 79 50W
North Bend, *Canada* **110** 49 50N 121 27W
North Bend, *Oreg., U.S.A.* **122** 43 28N 124 14W
North Bend, *Pa., U.S.A.* **116** 41 20N 77 42W
North Bend, *Wash., U.S.A.* **124** 47 30N 121 47W
North Berwick, *U.K.* **14** 56 4N 2 44W
North Berwick, *U.S.A.* **117** 43 18N 70 43W
North Buganda □, *Uganda* **92** 1 0N 32 0 E
North Canadian →, *U.S.A.* **121** 35 17N 95 31W
North C., *Canada* **105** 47 2N 60 20W
North C., *N.Z.* **80** 34 23 S 173 4 E
North C., *Papua N. G.* **69** 2 32 S 150 50 E
North Caribou L., *Canada* **104** 52 50N 90 40W
North Carolina □, *U.S.A.* **115** 35 30N 80 0W
North Channel, *Canada* **108** 46 0N 83 0W
North Channel, *U.K.* **14** 55 0N 5 30W
North Chicago, *U.S.A.* **119** 42 19N 87 50W
North College Hill, *U.S.A.* **119** 39 13N 84 33W
North Dakota □, *U.S.A.* **120** 47 30N 100 0W
North Dandalup, *Australia* **79** 32 30 S 115 57 E
North Down □, *U.K.* **15** 54 40N 5 45W
North Downs, *U.K.* **13** 51 17N 0 30 E
North East, *U.S.A.* **116** 42 17N 79 50W
North East Frontier Agency = Arunachal Pradesh □, *India* **52** 28 0N 95 0 E
North East Providence Chan., *W. Indies* **128** 26 0N 76 0W
North Eastern □, *Kenya* **92** 1 30N 40 0 E
North English, *U.S.A.* **118** 41 31N 92 5W
North Esk →, *U.K.* **14** 56 44N 2 25W
North European Plain, *Europe* **6** 55 0N 20 0 E
North Fabius →, *U.S.A.* **118** 39 54N 91 28W
North Foreland, *U.K.* **13** 51 22N 1 28 E
North Fork, *U.S.A.* **124** 37 14N 119 21W
North Fork, American →, *U.S.A.* **124** 38 45N 121 8W
North Fork, Feather →, *U.S.A.* **124** 39 17N 121 38W
North Fork, Salt →, *U.S.A.* **118** 39 26N 91 53W
North Frisian Is. = Nordfriesische Inseln, *W. Germany* **30** 54 40N 8 20 E
North Gower, *Canada* **109** 45 8N 75 43W
North Hatley, *Canada* **107** 45 17N 71 58W
North Henik L., *Canada* **111** 61 45N 97 40W
North Highlands, *U.S.A.* **124** 38 40N 121 25W
North Horr, *Kenya* **92** 3 20N 37 8 E
North I., *Kenya* **92** 4 5N 36 5 E
North I., *N.Z.* **81** 38 0 S 175 0 E
North Judson, *U.S.A.* **119** 41 13N 86 46W
North Kingsville, *U.S.A.* **116** 41 53N 80 42W
North Knife →, *Canada* **111** 58 53N 94 45W
North Koel →, *India* **49** 24 45N 83 50 E
North Korea ■, *Asia* **61** 40 0N 127 0 E
North Lakhimpur, *India* **52** 27 14N 94 7 E
North Las Vegas, *U.S.A.* **125** 36 15N 115 6W
North Liberty, *U.S.A.* **119** 41 32N 86 26W
North Loup →, *U.S.A.* **120** 41 17N 98 23W
North Manchester, *U.S.A.* **119** 41 0N 85 46W
North Minch, *U.K.* **14** 58 5N 5 55W
North Nahanni →, *Canada* **110** 62 15N 123 20W
North Olmsted, *U.S.A.* **116** 41 25N 81 56W
North Ossetian A.S.S.R. □, *U.S.S.R.* **39** 43 30N 44 30 E
North Palisade, *U.S.A.* **124** 37 6N 118 32W
North Platte, *U.S.A.* **120** 41 10N 100 50W
North Platte →, *U.S.A.* **120** 41 15N 100 45W
North Pt., *Canada* **105** 47 5N 64 0W
North Pt., *Vanuatu* **68** 14 56 S 168 6 E
North Pole, *Arctic* **144** 90 0N 0 0 E
North Portal, *Canada* **111** 49 0N 102 33W
North Powder, *U.S.A.* **122** 45 2N 117 59W
North Ronaldsay, *U.K.* **14** 59 20N 2 30W
North Saskatchewan →, *Canada* **111** 53 15N 105 5W
North Sea, *Europe* **6** 56 0N 4 0 E
North Solitary I., *Australia* **77** 29 56 S 153 24 E
North Sporades = Voríai Sporádhes, *Greece* **35** 39 15N 23 30 E
North Sydney, *Canada* **105** 46 12N 60 15W
North Thompson →, *Canada* **110** 50 40N 120 20W
North Tonawanda, *U.S.A.* **116** 43 5N 78 50W
North Troy, *U.S.A.* **117** 44 59N 72 24W
North Truchas Pk., *U.S.A.* **123** 36 0N 105 30W
North Twin I., *Canada* **104** 53 20N 80 0W
North Tyne →, *U.K.* **12** 54 59N 2 7W
North Uist, *U.K.* **14** 57 40N 7 15W
North Vancouver, *Canada* **110** 49 25N 123 3W
North Vernon, *U.S.A.* **119** 39 0N 85 35W
North Wabasca L., *Canada* **110** 56 0N 113 55W
North Walsham, *U.K.* **12** 52 49N 1 22 E
North Webster, *U.S.A.* **119** 41 25N 85 48W
North West C., *Australia* **78** 21 45 S 114 9 E
North West Christmas I. Ridge, *Pac. Oc.* **67** 6 30N 165 0W
North West Frontier □, *Pakistan* **48** 34 0N 71 0 E
North West Highlands, *U.K.* **14** 57 35N 5 2W
North West Providence Channel, *W. Indies* **128** 26 0N 78 0W
North West River, *Canada* **105** 53 30N 60 10W
North West Solitary I., *Australia* **77** 30 1 S 153 16 E
North West Territories □, *Canada* **102** 67 0N 110 0W
North Western □, *Zambia* **93** 13 30 S 25 30 E
North York Moors, *U.K.* **12** 54 25N 0 50W
North Yorkshire □, *U.K.* **12** 54 15N 1 25W
Northallerton, *U.K.* **12** 54 20N 1 26W
Northam, *S. Africa* **96** 24 56 S 27 18 E
Northampton, *Australia* **79** 28 27 S 114 33 E
Northampton, *U.K.* **13** 52 14N 0 54W
Northampton, *Mass., U.S.A.* **117** 42 22N 72 31W
Northampton, *Pa., U.S.A.* **117** 40 38N 75 24W
Northampton □, *U.K.* **13** 52 16N 0 55W
Northampton Downs, *Australia* **72** 24 35 S 145 48 E
Northbridge, *U.S.A.* **117** 42 12N 71 40W
Northcliffe, *Australia* **79** 34 39 S 116 7 E
Northeim, *W. Germany* **30** 51 42N 10 0 E
Northern □, *Malawi* **93** 11 0 S 34 0 E
Northern □, *Uganda* **92** 3 5N 32 30 E
Northern □, *Zambia* **93** 10 30 S 31 0 E
Northern Circars, *India* **50** 17 30N 82 30 E
Northern Indian L., *Canada* **111** 57 20N 97 20W
Northern Ireland □, *U.K.* **15** 54 45N 7 0W
Northern Light, L., *Canada* **104** 48 15N 90 39W
Northern Marianas, *Pac. Oc.* **66** 17 0N 145 0 E
Northern Province □, *S. Leone* **90** 9 15N 11 30W
Northern Territory □, *Australia* **78** 16 0 S 133 0 E
Northfield, *U.S.A.* **120** 44 30N 93 10W
Northland □, *N.Z.* **80** 35 30 S 173 30 E
Northome, *U.S.A.* **120** 47 53N 94 15W
Northport, *Ala., U.S.A.* **115** 33 15N 87 35W
Northport, *Mich., U.S.A.* **114** 45 8N 85 39W
Northport, *Wash., U.S.A.* **122** 48 55N 117 48W
Northumberland □, *U.K.* **12** 55 12N 2 0W
Northumberland, C., *Australia* **73** 38 5 S 140 40 E
Northumberland Is., *Australia* **72** 21 30 S 149 50 E
Northumberland Str., *Canada* **105** 46 20N 64 0W
Northwich, *U.K.* **12** 53 16N 2 30W
Northwood, *Iowa, U.S.A.* **120** 43 27N 93 0W
Northwood, *N. Dak., U.S.A.* **120** 47 44N 97 30W
Norton, *U.S.A.* **120** 39 50N 99 53W
Norton, *Zimb.* **93** 17 52 S 30 40 E
Norton Sd., *U.S.A.* **102** 64 0N 164 0W
Norton Shores, *U.S.A.* **119** 43 8N 86 15W
Nortorf, *W. Germany* **30** 54 14N 9 47 E
Norwalk, *Calif., U.S.A.* **125** 33 54N 118 5W
Norwalk, *Conn., U.S.A.* **117** 41 9N 73 25W
Norwalk, *Ohio, U.S.A.* **116** 41 13N 82 38W
Norway, *U.S.A.* **114** 45 46N 87 57W
Norway ■, *Europe* **9** 63 0N 11 0 E
Norway House, *Canada* **111** 53 59N 97 50W
Norwegian Dependency □, *Antarctica* **143** 66 0 S 15 0 E
Norwegian Sea, *Atl. Oc.* **144** 66 0N 1 0 E
Norwich, *Canada* **108** 42 59N 80 36W
Norwich, *U.K.* **12** 52 38N 1 17 E
Norwich, *Conn., U.S.A.* **117** 41 33N 72 5W
Norwich, *N.Y., U.S.A.* **117** 42 32N 75 30W
Norwood, *Canada* **109** 44 23N 77 59W
Norwood, *U.S.A.* **119** 39 10N 84 27W
Noshiro, *Japan* **63** 40 12N 140 0 E
Nosok, *U.S.S.R.* **40** 70 10N 82 20 E
Nosovka, *U.S.S.R.* **36** 50 50N 31 37 E
Noşratābād, *Iran* **47** 29 55N 60 0 E
Noss Hd., *U.K.* **14** 58 29N 3 4W
Nossa Senhora da Glória, *Brazil* **138** 10 14 S 37 25W
Nossa Senhora das Dores, *Brazil* **138** 10 29 S 37 13W
Nossa Senhora do Livramento, *Brazil* **137** 15 48 S 56 22W
Nossebro, *Sweden* **11** 58 12N 12 43 E
Nossob →, *S. Africa* **96** 26 55 S 20 45 E
Nosy Boraha, *Madag.* **97** 16 50 S 49 55 E
Nosy Varika, *Madag.* **97** 20 35 S 48 32 E
Noteć →, *Poland* **32** 52 44N 15 26 E
Notigi Dam, *Canada* **111** 56 40N 99 10W
Notikewin →, *Canada* **110** 57 2N 117 38W
Notios Evvoïkos Kólpos, *Greece* **35** 38 20N 24 0 E
Noto, *Italy* **29** 36 52N 15 4 E
Noto, G. di, *Italy* **29** 36 50N 15 10 E
Notodden, *Norway* **10** 59 35N 9 17 E
Notre-Dame, *Canada* **105** 46 18N 64 46W
Notre Dame B., *Canada* **105** 49 45N 55 30W
Notre Dame de Koartac = Koartac, *Canada* **103** 60 55N 69 40W
Notre-Dame-de-la-Doré, *Canada* **107** 48 43N 72 39W
Notre-Dame-des-Bois, *Canada* **107** 45 24N 71 4W
Notre Dame d'Ivugivic = Ivugivik, *Canada* **103** 62 24N 77 55W
Notre-Dame-du-Bon-Conseil, *Canada* **107** 46 0N 72 21W
Notre Dame du Lac, *Ont., Canada* **108** 46 18N 80 11W
Notre-Dame-du-Lac, *Qué., Canada* **107** 47 36N 68 48W
Notre-Dame-du-Laus, *Canada* **106** 46 5N 75 37W
Notre-Dame-du-Nord, *Canada* **106** 47 36N 79 30W
Notre-Dame-du-Portage, *Canada* **107** 47 46N 69 37W
Notsé, *Togo* **91** 7 0N 1 17 E
Nottawasaga B., *Canada* **108** 44 35N 80 15W
Nottaway →, *Canada* **104** 51 22N 78 55W
Nøtterøy, *Norway* **10** 59 14N 10 24 E
Nottingham, *U.K.* **12** 52 57N 1 10W
Nottingham □, *U.K.* **12** 53 10N 1 0W
Nottoway →, *U.S.A.* **114** 36 33N 76 55W
Notwane →, *Botswana* **96** 23 35 S 26 58 E
Nouâdhibou, *Mauritania* **84** 20 54N 17 0W
Nouâdhibou, Ras, *Mauritania* **84** 20 50N 17 0W
Nouakchott, *Mauritania* **90** 18 9N 15 58W
Nouméa, *N. Cal.* **68** 22 17 S 166 30 E
Noupoort, *S. Africa* **96** 31 10 S 24 57 E
Nouveau Comptoir, *Canada* **104** 53 0N 78 49W
Nouvelle Calédonie = New Caledonia, *Pac. Oc.* **68** 21 0 S 165 0 E
Nouzonville, *France* **19** 49 48N 4 44 E
Nová Baňa, *Czech.* **33** 48 28N 18 39 E

Nová Bystřice, *Czech.* 32 49 2N 15 8 E
Nova Casa Nova, *Brazil* 138 9 25 S 41 5W
Nova Cruz, *Brazil* 138 6 28 S 35 25W
Nova Era, *Brazil* 139 19 45 S 43 3W
Nova Esperança, *Brazil* 141 23 8 S 52 24W
Nova Friburgo, *Brazil* 139 22 16 S 42 30W
Nova Gaia, *Angola* 95 10 10 S 17 35 E
Nova Gradiška, *Yugoslavia* 33 45 17N 17 28 E
Nova Granada, *Brazil* 139 20 30 S 49 20W
Nova Iguaçu, *Brazil* 139 22 45 S 43 28W
Nova Iorque, *Brazil* 138 7 0 S 44 5W
Nova Lamego, *Guinea-Biss.* 90 12 19N 14 11W
Nova Lima, *Brazil* 141 19 59 S 43 51W
Nova Lisboa = Huambo, *Angola* 95 12 42 S 15 54 E
Nova Lusitânia, *Mozam.* 93 19 50 S 34 34 E
Nova Mambone, *Mozam.* 97 21 0 S 35 3 E
Nova Mesto, *Yugoslavia* 27 45 47N 15 12 E
Nova Ponte, *Brazil* 139 19 8 S 47 41W
Nova Scotia □, *Canada* 105 45 10N 63 0W
Nova Sofala, *Mozam.* 97 20 7 S 34 42 E
Nova Venécia, *Brazil* 139 18 45 S 40 24W
Nova Vida, *Brazil* 137 10 11 S 62 47W
Nova Zagora, *Bulgaria* 34 42 32N 25 59 E
Noval Iorque, *Brazil* 138 6 48 S 44 0W
Novaleksandrovskaya, *U.S.S.R.* 39 45 29N 41 17 E
Novannenskiy, *U.S.S.R.* 37 50 32N 42 39 E
Novar, *Canada* 108 45 27N 79 15W
Novara, *Italy* 26 45 27N 8 36 E
Novata, *U.S.A.* 124 38 6N 122 35W
Novaya Kakhovka, *U.S.S.R.* 38 46 42N 33 27 E
Novaya Lyalya, *U.S.S.R.* 40 59 10N 60 35 E
Novaya Sibir, Ostrov, *U.S.S.R.* 41 75 10N 150 0 E
Novaya Zemlya, *U.S.S.R.* 40 75 0N 56 0 E
Novelda, *Spain* 25 38 24N 0 45W
Novellara, *Italy* 26 44 50N 10 43 E
Novelty, *U.S.A.* 118 40 1N 92 12W
Noventa Vicentina, *Italy* 27 45 18N 11 30 E
Novgorod, *U.S.S.R.* 36 58 30N 31 25 E
Novgorod-Severskiy, *U.S.S.R.* 36 52 2N 33 10 E
Novi Bečej, *Yugoslavia* 33 45 36N 20 10 E
Novi Grad, *Yugoslavia* 27 45 19N 13 33 E
Novi Krichim, *Bulgaria* 34 42 8N 24 31 E
Novi Lígure, *Italy* 26 44 45N 8 47 E
Novi Pazar, *Bulgaria* 34 43 25N 27 15 E
Novi Pazar, *Yugoslavia* 33 43 12N 20 28 E
Novi Sad, *Yugoslavia* 33 45 18N 19 52 E
Novi Vinodolski, *Yugoslavia* 27 45 10N 14 48 E
Novigrad, *Yugoslavia* 27 44 10N 15 32 E
Noville, *Belgium* 17 50 4N 5 46 E
Novinger, *U.S.A.* 118 40 14N 92 43W
Novo Acôrdo, *Brazil* 138 10 10 S 46 48W
Novo Aripuanã, *Brazil* 135 5 8 S 60 22W
Nôvo Cruzeiro, *Brazil* 139 17 29 S 41 53W
Nôvo Hamburgo, *Brazil* 141 29 37 S 51 7W
Novo Horizonte, *Brazil* 139 21 25 S 49 10W
Novo Remanso, *Brazil* 138 9 41 S 42 4W
Novo-Zavidovskiy, *U.S.S.R.* 37 56 32N 36 29 E
Novoakrainka, *U.S.S.R.* 38 48 25N 31 30 E
Novoaltaysk, *U.S.S.R.* 40 53 30N 84 0 E
Novoazovsk, *U.S.S.R.* 38 47 15N 38 4 E
Novobelitsa, *U.S.S.R.* 36 52 27N 31 2 E
Novobogatinskoye, *U.S.S.R.* 39 47 20N 51 11 E
Novocherkassk, *U.S.S.R.* 39 47 27N 40 5 E
Novodevichye, *U.S.S.R.* 37 53 37N 48 50 E
Novograd-Volynskiy, *U.S.S.R.* 36 50 34N 27 35 E
Novogrudok, *U.S.S.R.* 36 53 40N 25 50 E
Novokayakent, *U.S.S.R.* 39 42 30N 47 52 E
Novokazalinsk, *U.S.S.R.* 40 45 48N 62 6 E
Novokhopersk, *U.S.S.R.* 37 51 5N 41 39 E
Novokuybyshevsk, *U.S.S.R.* 37 53 7N 49 58 E
Novokuznetsk, *U.S.S.R.* 40 53 45N 87 10 E
Novomirgorod, *U.S.S.R.* 38 48 45N 31 33 E
Novomoskovsk, *R.S.F.S.R., U.S.S.R.* 37 54 5N 38 15 E
Novomoskovsk, *Ukraine S.S.R., U.S.S.R.* 38 48 33N 35 17 E
Novopolotsk, *U.S.S.R.* 36 55 32N 28 37 E
Novorossiysk, *U.S.S.R.* 38 44 43N 37 46 E
Novorybnoye, *U.S.S.R.* 41 72 50N 105 50 E
Novorzhev, *U.S.S.R.* 36 57 3N 29 25 E
Novoselitsa, *U.S.S.R.* 38 48 14N 26 15 E
Novoshakhtinsk, *U.S.S.R.* 39 47 46N 39 58 E
Novosibirsk, *U.S.S.R.* 40 55 0N 83 5 E
Novosibirskiye Ostrava, *U.S.S.R.* 41 75 0N 142 0 E
Novosil, *U.S.S.R.* 37 52 59N 37 2 E
Novosokolniki, *U.S.S.R.* 36 56 33N 30 5 E
Novotroitsk, *U.S.S.R.* 40 51 10N 58 15 E
Novotulskiy, *U.S.S.R.* 37 54 10N 37 43 E
Novouzensk, *U.S.S.R.* 37 50 32N 48 17 E
Novovolynsk, *U.S.S.R.* 36 50 45N 24 4 E
Novovyatsk, *U.S.S.R.* 37 58 24N 49 45 E
Novozybkov, *U.S.S.R.* 36 52 30N 32 0 E
Novska, *Yugoslavia* 33 45 19N 17 0 E
Novvy Port, *U.S.S.R.* 40 67 40N 72 30 E
Novy Bug, *U.S.S.R.* 38 47 34N 32 29 E
Nový Bydzov, *Czech.* 32 50 14N 15 29 E
Novy Dwór Mazowiecki, *Poland* 32 52 26N 20 44 E
Novyy Afon, *U.S.S.R.* 39 43 7N 40 50 E
Novyy Oskol, *U.S.S.R.* 37 50 44N 37 55 E
Now Shahr, *Iran* 47 36 40N 51 30 E
Nowa Deba, *Poland* 32 50 26N 21 41 E
Nowa Nowa, *Australia* 75 37 44 S 148 3 E
Nowa Ruda, *Poland* 32 50 35N 16 30 E
Nowa Sól, *Poland* 32 51 48N 15 44 E
Nowe, *Poland* 32 53 41N 18 44 E
Nowe Warpno, *Poland* 33 53 42N 14 18 E
Nowendoc, *Australia* 77 31 32 S 151 44 E
Nowgong, *India* 52 26 20N 92 50 E
Nowingi, *Australia* 74 34 33 S 142 15 E
Nowogard, *Poland* 32 53 41N 15 10 E
Nowogród, *Poland* 32 53 14N 21 53 E
Nowra, *Australia* 76 34 53 S 150 35 E
Nowy Korczyn, *Poland* 32 50 19N 20 48 E
Nowy Sącz, *Poland* 32 49 40N 20 41 E
Noxen, *U.S.A.* 117 41 25N 76 4W
Noxon, *U.S.A.* 122 48 0N 115 43W
Noya, *Spain* 22 42 48N 8 53W
Noyant, *France* 18 47 30N 0 6 E
Noyers, *France* 19 47 40N 4 0 E
Noyes I., *U.S.A.* 110 55 30N 133 40W
Noyon, *France* 19 49 34N 3 0 E
Noyon, *Mongolia* 60 43 2N 102 4 E
Nozay, *France* 18 47 34N 1 38W
Nsa, O. en →, *Algeria* 85 32 28N 5 24 E
Nsa, Plateau de, *Congo* 94 2 26 S 15 20 E
Nsah, *Congo* 94 2 22 S 15 19 E
Nsanje, *Malawi* 93 16 55 S 35 12 E
Nsawam, *Ghana* 91 5 50N 0 24W
Nsomba, *Zambia* 93 10 45 S 29 51 E
Nsopzup, *Burma* 52 25 51N 97 30 E
Nsukka, *Nigeria* 91 6 51N 7 29 E
Ntoum, *Gabon* 94 0 22N 9 47 E
Nu Jiang →, *China* 58 29 58N 97 25 E
Nu Shan, *China* 58 26 0N 99 20 E
Nuba Mts. = Nubah, Jibalan, *Sudan* 89 12 0N 31 0 E
Nubah, Jibalan, *Sudan* 89 12 0N 31 0 E
Nubian Desert = Nûbîya, Es Sahrâ En, *Sudan* 88 21 30N 33 30 E
Nûbîya, Es Sahrâ En, *Sudan* 88 21 30N 33 30 E
Ñuble □, *Chile* 140 37 0 S 72 0W
Nuboai, *Indonesia* 57 2 10 S 136 30 E
Nubra →, *India* 49 34 35N 77 35 E
Nueces →, *U.S.A.* 121 27 50N 97 30W
Nueima →, *Jordan* 44 31 54N 35 25 E
Nueltin L., *Canada* 111 60 30N 99 30W
Nuenen, *Neths.* 17 51 29N 5 33 E
Nueva, I., *Chile* 142 55 13 S 66 30W
Nueva Antioquia, *Colombia* 134 6 5N 69 26W
Nueva Esparta □, *Venezuela* 135 11 0N 64 0W
Nueva Gerona, *Cuba* 128 21 53N 82 49W
Nueva Imperial, *Chile* 142 38 45 S 72 58W
Nueva Palmira, *Uruguay* 140 33 52 S 58 20W
Nueva Rosita, *Mexico* 126 28 0N 101 11W
Nueva San Salvador, *El Salv.* 128 13 40N 89 18W
Nuéve de Julio, *Argentina* 140 35 30 S 61 0W
Nuevitas, *Cuba* 128 21 30N 77 20W
Nuevo, G., *Argentina* 142 43 0 S 64 30W
Nuevo Guerrero, *Mexico* 127 26 34N 99 15W
Nuevo Laredo, *Mexico* 127 27 30N 99 30W
Nuevo León □, *Mexico* 126 25 0N 100 0W
Nuevo Mundo, Cerro, *Bolivia* 136 21 55 S 66 53W
Nuevo Rocafuerte, *Ecuador* 134 0 55 S 75 27W
Nugget Pt., *N.Z.* 81 46 27 S 169 50 E
Nugrus, Gebel, *Egypt* 88 24 47N 34 35 E
Nuhaka, *N.Z.* 80 39 3 S 177 45 E
Nuits-St.-Georges, *France* 19 47 10N 4 56 E
Nukey Bluff, Mt., *Australia* 73 32 26 S 135 29 E
Nukheila, *Sudan* 88 19 1N 26 21 E
Nukiki, *Solomon Is.* 68 6 45 S 156 29 E
Nuku'alofa, *Tonga* 68 21 10 S 174 0W
Nukus, *U.S.S.R.* 40 42 20N 59 7 E
Nuland, *Neths.* 16 51 44N 5 26 E
Nulato, *U.S.A.* 102 64 40N 158 10W
Nules, *Spain* 24 39 51N 0 9W
Nullagine →, *Australia* 78 21 20 S 120 20 E
Nullarbor, *Australia* 79 31 28 S 130 55 E
Nullarbor Plain, *Australia* 79 31 10 S 129 0 E
Nullawarre, *Australia* 74 38 30 S 142 45 E
Nullawil, *Australia* 74 35 49 S 143 10 E
Numalla, L., *Australia* 73 28 43 S 144 20 E
Numan, *Nigeria* 91 9 29N 12 3 E
Numansdorp, *Neths.* 16 51 43N 4 26 E
Numata, *Japan* 65 36 45N 139 4 E
Numatinna →, *Sudan* 89 7 38N 27 20 E
Numazu, *Japan* 65 35 7N 138 51 E
Numbulwar, *Australia* 72 14 15 S 135 45 E
Numfoor, *Indonesia* 57 1 0 S 134 50 E
Numurkah, *Australia* 74 36 5 S 145 26 E
Nunaksaluk I., *Canada* 105 55 49N 60 20W
Nundle, *Australia* 77 31 29 S 151 9 E
Nuneaton, *U.K.* 13 52 32N 1 29W
Nungatta, *Australia* 75 37 11 S 149 20 E
Nungo, *Mozam.* 93 13 23 S 37 43 E
Nungwe, *Tanzania* 92 2 48 S 32 2 E
Nunivak, *U.S.A.* 102 60 0N 166 0W
Nunkun, *India* 49 33 57N 76 2 E
Nunspeet, *Neths.* 16 52 21N 5 45 E
Nuoro, *Italy* 28 40 20N 9 20 E
Nuqayy, Jabal, *Libya* 86 23 11N 19 30 E
Nuquí, *Colombia* 134 5 42N 77 17W
Nure →, *Italy* 26 45 3N 9 49 E
Nuremburg = Nürnberg, *W. Germany* 31 49 26N 11 5 E
Nuri, *Mexico* 126 28 2N 109 22W
Nurina, *Australia* 79 30 56 S 126 33 E
Nuriootpa, *Australia* 73 34 27 S 139 0 E
Nurlat, *U.S.S.R.* 37 54 29N 50 45 E
Nürnberg, *W. Germany* 31 49 26N 11 5 E
Nurran, L. = Terewah, L., *Australia* 73 29 52 S 147 35 E
Nurrari Lakes, *Australia* 79 29 1 S 130 5 E
Nurri, *Italy* 28 39 43N 9 13 E
Nusa Barung, *Indonesia* 57 8 10 S 113 30 E
Nusa Kambangan, *Indonesia* 57 7 40 S 108 10 E
Nusa Tenggara Barat □, *Indonesia* 56 8 50 S 117 30 E
Nusa Tenggara Timur □, *Indonesia* 57 9 30 S 122 0 E
Nushki, *Pakistan* 48 29 35N 66 0 E
Nutak, *Canada* 103 57 28N 61 59W
Nuth, *Neths.* 17 50 55N 5 53 E
Nutwood Downs, *Australia* 72 15 49 S 134 10 E
Nuwakot, *Nepal* 49 28 10N 83 55 E
Nuwara Eliya, *Sri Lanka* 51 6 58N 80 48 E
Nuweiba', *Egypt* 88 28 59N 34 39 E
Nuweveldberge, *S. Africa* 96 32 10 S 21 45 E
Nuyts, C., *Australia* 79 32 2 S 132 21 E
Nuyts Arch., *Australia* 73 32 35 S 133 20 E
Nuzvid, *India* 50 16 47N 80 53 E
Nxau-Nxau, *Botswana* 96 18 57 S 21 4 E
Nyaake, *Liberia* 90 4 52N 7 37W
Nyack, *U.S.A.* 117 41 5N 73 57W
Nyadal, *Sweden* 10 62 48N 17 59 E
Nyah, *Australia* 74 35 12 S 143 25 E
Nyah West, *Australia* 74 35 16 S 143 21 E
Nyahanga, *Tanzania* 92 2 20 S 33 37 E
Nyahua, *Tanzania* 92 5 25 S 33 23 E
Nyahururu, *Kenya* 92 0 2N 36 27 E
Nyainqentanglha Shan, *China* 62 30 0N 90 0 E
Nyakanazi, *Tanzania* 92 3 2 S 31 10 E
Nyakrom, *Ghana* 91 5 40N 0 50W
Nyâlâ, *Sudan* 89 12 2N 24 58 E
Nyamandhlovu, *Zimb.* 93 19 55 S 28 16 E
Nyambiti, *Tanzania* 92 2 48 S 33 27 E
Nyamwaga, *Tanzania* 92 1 27 S 34 33 E
Nyandekwa, *Tanzania* 92 3 57 S 32 32 E
Nyanding →, *Sudan* 89 8 40N 32 41 E
Nyanga →, *Gabon* 94 2 58 S 10 15 E
Nyangana, *Namibia* 96 18 0 S 20 40 E
Nyanguge, *Tanzania* 92 2 30 S 33 12 E
Nyankpala, *Ghana* 91 9 21N 0 58W
Nyanza, *Burundi* 92 4 21 S 29 36 E
Nyanza, *Rwanda* 92 2 20 S 29 42 E
Nyanza □, *Kenya* 92 0 10 S 34 15 E
Nyarling →, *Canada* 110 60 41N 113 23W
Nyarrin, *Australia* 74 35 22 S 142 43 E
Nyasa, L. = Malawi, L., *Africa* 93 12 30 S 34 30 E
Nyaunglebin, *Burma* 52 17 52N 96 42 E
Nyazura, *Zimb.* 93 18 40 S 32 16 E
Nyazwidzi →, *Zimb.* 93 20 0 S 31 17 E
Nyborg, *Denmark* 11 55 18N 10 47 E
Nybro, *Sweden* 11 56 44N 15 55 E
Nyda, *U.S.S.R.* 40 66 40N 72 58 E
Nyeri, *Kenya* 92 0 23 S 36 56 E
Nyerol, *Sudan* 89 8 41N 32 1 E
Nyhem, *Sweden* 10 62 54N 15 37 E
Nyiel, *Sudan* 89 6 9N 31 13 E
Nyinahin, *Ghana* 90 6 43N 2 3W
Nyirbátor, *Hungary* 33 47 49N 22 9 E
Nyíregyháza, *Hungary* 33 47 58N 21 47 E
Nykarleby, *Finland* 8 63 22N 22 31 E
Nykøbing, *Sjælland, Denmark* 11 55 55N 11 40 E
Nykøbing, *Storstrøm, Denmark* 11 54 56N 11 52 E
Nykøbing, *Viborg, Denmark* 11 56 48N 8 51 E
Nyköping, *Sweden* 11 58 45N 17 0 E
Nykroppa, *Sweden* 10 59 37N 14 18 E
Nykvarn, *Sweden* 10 59 11N 17 25 E
Nyland, *Sweden* 10 63 1N 17 45 E
Nylstroom, *S. Africa* 97 24 42 S 28 22 E
Nymagee, *Australia* 73 32 7 S 146 20 E
Nymboida →, *Australia* 77 29 22 S 152 32 E
Nymburk, *Czech.* 32 50 10N 15 1 E
Nynäshamn, *Sweden* 10 58 54N 17 57 E
Nyngan, *Australia* 76 31 30 S 147 8 E
Nyon, *Switz.* 31 46 23N 6 14 E
Nyong →, *Cameroon* 91 3 17N 9 54 E
Nyons, *France* 21 44 22N 5 10 E
Nyora, *Australia* 74 38 20 S 145 41 E
Nyord, *Denmark* 11 55 4N 12 13 E
Nyou, *Burkina Faso* 91 12 42N 2 1W
Nysa, *Poland* 32 50 30N 17 22 E
Nysa →, *Europe* 32 52 4N 14 46 E
Nyssa, *U.S.A.* 122 43 56N 117 2W
Nysted, *Denmark* 11 54 40N 11 44 E
Nyūgawa, *Japan* 64 33 56N 133 5 E
Nyunzu, *Zaïre* 92 5 57 S 27 58 E
Nyurba, *U.S.S.R.* 41 63 17N 118 28 E
Nzega, *Tanzania* 92 4 10 S 33 12 E
Nzega □, *Tanzania* 92 4 10 S 33 10 E
N'Zérékoré, *Guinea* 90 7 49N 8 48W
Nzeto, *Angola* 95 7 10 S 12 52 E
Nzilo, Chutes de, *Zaïre* 93 10 18 S 25 27 E
Nzubuka, *Tanzania* 92 4 45 S 32 50 E

O

Ō-Shima, *Fukuoka, Japan* 64 33 54N 130 25 E
Ō-Shima, *Nagasaki, Japan* 64 34 29N 129 33 E
Ō-Shima, *Shizuoka, Japan* 65 34 44N 139 24 E
Oacoma, *U.S.A.* 120 43 50N 99 26W
Oahe Dam, *U.S.A.* 120 44 28N 100 25W
Oahe L., *U.S.A.* 120 45 30N 100 25W
Oahu, *U.S.A.* 112 21 30N 158 0W
Oak Creek, *Colo., U.S.A.* 122 40 15N 106 59W
Oak Creek, *Wis., U.S.A.* 119 42 52N 87 55W
Oak Harb., *U.S.A.* 124 48 20N 122 38W
Oak Hill, *U.S.A.* 114 38 0N 81 7W
Oak Lawn, *U.S.A.* 119 41 43N 87 44W
Oak Park, *Ill., U.S.A.* 119 41 53N 87 47W
Oak Park, *U.S.A.* 114 41 55N 87 45W
Oak Ridge, *U.S.A.* 115 36 1N 84 12W
Oak View, *U.S.A.* 125 34 24N 119 18W
Oakbank, *Australia* 73 33 4 S 140 33 E
Oakdale, *Calif., U.S.A.* 124 37 45N 120 55W
Oakdale, *La., U.S.A.* 121 30 50N 92 38W
Oakengates, *U.K.* 12 52 42N 2 29W
Oakes, *U.S.A.* 120 46 14N 98 4W
Oakesdale, *U.S.A.* 122 47 11N 117 15W
Oakey, *Australia* 77 27 25 S 151 43 E
Oakford, *U.S.A.* 118 40 6N 89 58W
Oakham, *U.K.* 12 52 40N 0 43W
Oakhurst, *U.S.A.* 124 37 19N 119 40W
Oakland, *Calif., U.S.A.* 124 37 50N 122 18W
Oakland, *Ill., U.S.A.* 119 39 39N 88 2W
Oakland, *Oreg., U.S.A.* 122 43 23N 123 18W
Oakland City, *U.S.A.* 119 38 20N 87 20W
Oakleigh, *Australia* 74 37 54 S 145 6 E
Oakley, *Idaho, U.S.A.* 122 42 14N 113 55W
Oakley, *Kans., U.S.A.* 120 39 8N 100 51W
Oakley Creek, *Australia* 77 31 37 S 149 46 E
Oakover →, *Australia* 78 21 0 S 120 40 E
Oakridge, *U.S.A.* 122 43 47N 122 31W
Oaktown, *U.S.A.* 119 38 52N 87 27W
Oakville, *Canada* 108 43 27N 79 41W
Oakville, *U.S.A.* 124 46 50N 123 14W
Oakwood, *Australia* 77 29 38 S 151 4 E
Oakwood, *U.S.A.* 119 41 6N 84 23W
Oamaru, *N.Z.* 81 45 5 S 170 59 E
Ōamishirasato, *Japan* 65 35 31N 140 18 E
Oarai, *Japan* 65 36 21N 140 34 E
Oasis, *Calif., U.S.A.* 125 33 28N 116 6W
Oasis, *Nev., U.S.A.* 124 37 29N 117 55W
Oates Coast, *Antarctica* 143 69 0 S 160 0 E
Oatman, *U.S.A.* 125 35 1N 114 19W
Oaxaca, *Mexico* 127 17 2N 96 40W
Oaxaca □, *Mexico* 127 17 0N 97 0W
Ob →, *U.S.S.R.* 40 66 45N 69 30 E
Oba, *Canada* 104 49 4N 84 7W
Obala, *Cameroon* 91 4 9N 11 32 E
Obalski L., *Canada* 106 48 43N 77 58W
Obama, *Fukui, Japan* 65 35 30N 135 45 E
Obama, *Nagasaki, Japan* 64 32 43N 130 13 E
Obamsca, L., *Canada* 106 50 24N 78 16W
Oban, *U.K.* 14 56 25N 5 30W
Obbia, *Somali Rep.* 98 5 25N 48 30 E
Obdam, *Neths.* 16 52 41N 4 55 E
Obed, *Canada* 110 53 30N 117 10W
Obedjwan, *Canada* 106 48 40N 74 56W
Obera, *Argentina* 141 27 21 S 55 2W
Oberammergau, *W. Germany* 31 47 35N 11 3 E
Oberdrauburg, *Austria* 33 46 44N 12 58 E
Oberengadin, *Switz.* 31 46 35N 9 55 E
Oberhausen, *W. Germany* 30 51 28N 6 50 E
Oberkirch, *W. Germany* 31 48 31N 8 5 E
Oberland, *Switz.* 31 46 30N 7 30 E
Oberlin, *Kans., U.S.A.* 120 39 52N 100 31W
Oberlin, *La., U.S.A.* 121 30 42N 92 42W
Oberlin, *Ohio, U.S.A.* 116 41 15N 82 10W
Obernai, *France* 19 48 28N 7 30 E
Oberndorf, *W. Germany* 31 48 17N 8 35 E
Oberon, *Australia* 76 33 45 S 149 52 E

Oberpfälzer Wald, W. Germany 31 49 30N 12 25 E
Oberstdorf, W. Germany 31 47 25N 10 16 E
Oberting, Gabon 94 0 22 S 9 46 E
Obi, Kepulauan, Indonesia 57 1 23 S 127 45 E
Obiaruku, Nigeria 91 5 51N 6 9 E
Óbidos, Brazil 135 1 50 S 55 30W
Óbidos, Portugal 23 39 19N 9 10W
Obihiro, Japan 63 42 56N 143 12 E
Obilatu, Indonesia 57 1 25 S 127 20 E
Obilnoye, U.S.S.R. 39 47 32N 44 30 E
Obing, W. Germany 31 48 0N 12 25 E
Öbisfelde, E. Germany 30 52 27N 10 57 E
Objat, France 20 45 16N 1 24 E
Oblong, U.S.A. 119 39 0N 87 55W
Obluchye, U.S.S.R. 41 49 1N 131 4 E
Obninsk, U.S.S.R. 37 55 8N 36 37 E
Obo, C.A.R. 92 5 20N 26 32 E
Obo, Ethiopia 89 3 46N 38 52 E
Oboa, Mt., Uganda 92 1 45N 34 45 E
Obock, Djibouti 89 12 0N 43 20 E
Oborniki, Poland 32 52 39N 16 50 E
Obouya, Congo 94 0 56 S 15 43 E
Oboyan, U.S.S.R. 37 51 13N 36 37 E
Obozerskaya, U.S.S.R. 40 63 20N 40 15 E
Obrovac, Yugoslavia 27 44 11N 15 41 E
Observatory Inlet, Canada 110 55 10N 129 54W
Obshchi Syrt, U.S.S.R. 6 52 0N 53 0 E
Obskaya Guba, U.S.S.R. 40 69 0N 73 0 E
Obuasi, Ghana 91 6 17N 1 40W
Obubra, Nigeria 91 6 8N 8 20 E
Obzor, Bulgaria 34 42 50N 27 52 E
Ocala, U.S.A. 115 29 11N 82 5W
Ocamo →, Venezuela 135 2 48N 65 14W
Ocampo, Mexico 126 28 9N 108 24W
Ocaña, Colombia 134 8 15N 73 20W
Ocaña, Spain 24 39 55N 3 30W
Ocanomowoc, U.S.A. 120 43 7N 88 30W
Ocate, U.S.A. 121 36 12N 104 59W
Occidental, Cordillera, Colombia 134 5 0N 76 0W
Occidental, Cordillera, Peru 136 14 0 S 74 0W
Ocean, I. = Banaba, Kiribati 66 0 45 S 169 50 E
Ocean City, N.J., U.S.A. 114 39 18N 74 34W
Ocean City, Wash., U.S.A. 124 47 4N 124 10W
Ocean Grove, Australia 74 38 16 S 144 32 E
Ocean Park, U.S.A. 124 46 30N 124 2W
Oceano, U.S.A. 125 35 6N 120 37W
Oceanport, U.S.A. 117 40 20N 74 3W
Oceanside, U.S.A. 125 33 13N 117 26W
Ochagavia, Spain 24 42 55N 1 5W
Ochamchire, U.S.S.R. 39 42 46N 41 32 E
Ochamps, Belgium 17 49 56N 5 16 E
Ochiai, Japan 64 35 1N 133 45 E
Ochil Hills, U.K. 14 56 14N 3 40W
Ochre River, Canada 111 51 4N 99 47W
Ochsenfurt, W. Germany 31 49 38N 10 3 E
Ochsenhausen, W. Germany 31 48 4N 9 57 E
Ocilla, U.S.A. 115 31 35N 83 12W
Ockelbo, Sweden 10 60 54N 16 45 E
Ocmulgee →, U.S.A. 115 31 58N 82 33W
Ocna Sibiului, Romania 34 45 52N 24 2 E
Ocoña, Peru 136 16 26 S 73 8W
Ocoña →, Peru 136 16 28 S 73 8W
Oconee →, U.S.A. 115 31 58N 82 32W
Oconomowoc, U.S.A. 119 43 6N 88 30W
Oconto, U.S.A. 114 44 52N 87 53W
Oconto Falls, U.S.A. 114 44 52N 88 10W
Ocosingo, Mexico 127 17 10N 92 15W
Ocotal, Nic. 128 13 41N 86 31W
Ocotlán, Mexico 126 20 21N 102 42W
Ocquier, Belgium 17 50 24N 5 24 E
Ocreza →, Portugal 23 39 32N 7 50W
Octave, U.S.A. 123 34 10N 112 43W
Octeville, France 18 49 38N 1 40W
Ocumare del Tuy, Venezuela 134 10 7N 66 46W
Ocuri, Bolivia 137 18 45 S 65 50W
Oda, Ghana 91 5 50N 0 51W
Oda, Ehime, Japan 64 33 36N 132 53 E
Ōda, Shimane, Japan 64 35 11N 132 30 E
Oda, Jebel, Sudan 88 20 21N 36 39 E
Ódáðahraun, Iceland 8 65 5N 17 0W
Ödåkra, Sweden 11 56 7N 12 45 E
Odate, Japan 63 40 16N 140 34 E
Odawara, Japan 65 35 20N 139 6 E
Odda, Norway 9 60 3N 6 35 E
Odder, Denmark 11 55 58N 10 10 E
Oddur, Somali Rep. 98 4 11N 43 52 E
Ödeborg, Sweden 11 58 32N 11 58 E
Odei →, Canada 111 56 6N 96 54W
Odell, U.S.A. 119 41 0N 88 31W
Odemira, Portugal 23 37 35N 8 40W
Ödemiş, Turkey 46 38 15N 28 0 E
Odendaalsrus, S. Africa 96 27 48 S 26 45 E
Odense, Denmark 11 55 22N 10 23 E
Odenwald, W. Germany 31 49 40N 9 0 E
Oder →, W. Germany 30 53 33N 14 38 E
Oderzo, Italy 27 45 47N 12 29 E
Odessa, Canada 109 44 17N 76 43W
Odessa, Mo., U.S.A. 118 39 0N 93 57W
Odessa, Tex., U.S.A. 121 31 51N 102 23W
Odessa, Wash., U.S.A. 122 47 19N 118 35W
Odessa, U.S.S.R. 38 46 30N 30 45 E
Odiakwe, Botswana 96 20 12 S 25 17 E
Odiel →, Spain 23 37 10N 6 55W
Odienné, Ivory C. 90 9 30N 7 34W
Odintsovo, U.S.S.R. 37 55 39N 37 15 E
Odobeşti, Romania 34 45 43N 27 4 E
O'Donnell, U.S.A. 121 33 0N 101 48W
Odoorn, Neths. 16 52 51N 6 51 E
Odorheiu Secuiesc, Romania 34 46 21N 25 21 E
Odoyevo, U.S.S.R. 37 53 56N 36 42 E
Odra →, Poland 32 53 33N 14 38 E
Odra →, Spain 22 42 14N 4 17W
Odweina, Somali Rep. 98 9 25N 45 4 E
Odžaci, Yugoslavia 33 45 30N 19 17 E
Odzi, Zimb. 97 19 0 S 32 20 E
Oedelem, Belgium 17 51 10N 3 21 E
Oegstgeest, Neths. 16 52 11N 4 29 E
Oeiras, Brazil 138 7 0 S 42 8W
Oeiras, Portugal 23 38 41N 9 18W
Oelrichs, U.S.A. 120 43 11N 103 14W
Oelsnitz, E. Germany 30 50 24N 12 11 E
Oelwein, U.S.A. 120 42 41N 91 55W
Oenpelli, Australia 78 12 20 S 133 4 E
O'Fallon, U.S.A. 118 38 50N 90 43W
Ofanto →, Italy 29 41 22N 16 13 E
Offa, Nigeria 91 8 13N 4 42 E
Offaly □, Ireland 15 53 15N 7 30W
Offenbach, W. Germany 31 50 6N 8 46 E
Offenburg, W. Germany 31 48 29N 7 56 E
Offerdal, Sweden 10 63 28N 14 0 E
Officer, Australia 74 38 3 S 145 22 E
Offida, Italy 27 42 56N 13 40 E
Offranville, France 18 49 52N 1 1 E
Ofidhousa, Greece 35 36 33N 26 8 E
Ofotfjorden, Norway 8 68 27N 16 40 E
Ofu, Amer. Samoa 68 14 11 S 169 41W
Oga-Hantō, Japan 63 39 58N 139 47 E
Ogaden, Ethiopia 98 7 30N 45 30 E
Ogahalla, Canada 104 50 6N 85 51W
Ōgaki, Japan 65 35 21N 136 37 E
Ogallala, U.S.A. 120 41 12N 101 40W
Ogascanane, L., Canada 106 47 5N 78 25W
Ogbomosho, Nigeria 91 8 1N 4 11 E
Ogden, Iowa, U.S.A. 118 42 3N 94 0W
Ogden, Utah, U.S.A. 122 41 13N 112 1W
Ogdensburg, U.S.A. 117 44 40N 75 27W
Ogeechee →, U.S.A. 115 31 51N 81 6W
Ogilby, U.S.A. 125 32 49N 114 50W
Oglesby, U.S.A. 118 41 21N 89 3W
Oglio →, Italy 26 45 2N 10 39 E
Ogmore, Australia 72 22 37 S 149 35 E
Ognon →, France 19 47 16N 5 28 E
Ogoja, Nigeria 91 6 38N 8 39 E
Ogoki →, Canada 104 51 38N 85 57W
Ogoki L., Canada 104 50 50N 87 10W
Ogoki Res., Canada 104 50 45N 88 15W
Ogooué →, Gabon 94 1 0 S 9 0 E
Ōgori, Japan 64 34 6N 131 24 E
Ogosta →, Bulgaria 34 43 48N 23 55 E
Ogowe = Ogooué →, Gabon 94 1 0 S 9 0 E
Ogr = Sharafa, Sudan 89 11 59N 27 7 E
Ogrein, Sudan 88 17 55N 34 50 E
Ogulin, Yugoslavia 27 45 16N 15 16 E
Ogun □, Nigeria 91 7 0N 3 0 E
Oguni, Japan 64 33 11N 131 8 E
Oguta, Nigeria 91 5 44N 6 44 E
Ogwashi-Uku, Nigeria 91 6 15N 6 30 E
Ogwe, Nigeria 91 5 0N 7 14 E
Ohai, N.Z. 81 44 55 S 168 0 E
Ohakune, N.Z. 80 39 24 S 175 24 E
Ohanet, Algeria 85 28 44N 8 46 E
Ōhara, Japan 65 35 15N 140 23 E
Ohau, L., N.Z. 81 44 15 S 169 53 E
Ohaupo, N.Z. 80 37 56 S 175 20 E
Ohey, Belgium 17 50 26N 5 8 E
Ohio □, U.S.A. 114 40 20N 84 10W
Ohio →, U.S.A. 114 38 0N 86 0W
Ohio City, U.S.A. 119 40 46N 84 37W
Ohiwa Harbour, N.Z. 80 37 59 S 177 10 E
Ohre →, Czech. 32 50 30N 14 10 E
Ohre →, E. Germany 30 52 18N 11 47 E
Ohrid, Yugoslavia 35 41 8N 20 52 E
Ohridsko, Jezero, Yugoslavia 35 41 8N 20 52 E
Ohrigstad, S. Africa 97 24 39 S 30 36 E
Öhringen, W. Germany 31 49 11N 9 31 E
Oiapoque →, Brazil 135 4 8N 51 40W
Oikou, China 61 38 35N 117 42 E
Oil City, U.S.A. 116 41 26N 79 40W
Oil Springs, Canada 108 42 47N 82 7W
Oildale, U.S.A. 125 35 25N 119 1W
Oirschot, Neths. 17 51 30N 5 18 E
Oise □, France 19 49 28N 2 30 E
Oise →, France 19 49 0N 2 4 E
Oisterwijk, Neths. 17 51 35N 5 12 E
Ōita, Japan 64 33 14N 131 36 E
Ōita □, Japan 64 33 15N 131 30 E
Oiticica, Brazil 138 5 3 S 41 5W
Ojai, U.S.A. 125 34 28N 119 16W
Ojinaga, Mexico 126 29 34N 104 25W
Ojos del Salado, Cerro, Argentina 140 27 0 S 68 40W
Oka →, U.S.S.R. 37 56 20N 43 59 E
Okaba, Indonesia 57 8 6 S 139 42 E
Okahandja, Namibia 96 22 0 S 16 59 E
Okahukura, N.Z. 66 38 48 S 175 14 E
Okaihau, N.Z. 80 35 19 S 173 47 E
Okanagan L., Canada 110 50 0N 119 30W
Okandja, Gabon 94 0 35 S 13 45 E
Okanogan, U.S.A. 122 48 6N 119 43W
Okanogan →, U.S.A. 122 48 6N 119 43W
Okapa, Papua N. G. 69 6 38 S 145 39 E
Okaputa, Namibia 96 20 5 S 17 0 E
Okara, Pakistan 48 30 50N 73 31 E
Okarito, N.Z. 81 43 15 S 170 9 E
Okato, N.Z. 80 39 12 S 173 53 E
Okaukuejo, Namibia 96 19 10 S 16 0 E
Okavango Swamps, Botswana 96 18 45 S 22 45 E
Okawa, Japan 64 33 9N 130 21 E
Okawville, U.S.A. 118 38 26N 89 33W
Okaya, Japan 65 36 0N 138 10 E
Okayama, Japan 64 34 40N 133 54 E
Okayama □, Japan 64 35 0N 133 50 E
Okazaki, Japan 65 34 57N 137 10 E
Oke-Iho, Nigeria 91 8 1N 3 18 E
Okeechobee, U.S.A. 115 27 16N 80 46W
Okeechobee, L., U.S.A. 115 27 0N 80 50W
Okefenokee Swamp, U.S.A. 115 30 50N 82 15W
Okehampton, U.K. 13 50 44N 4 1W
Okene, Nigeria 91 7 32N 6 11 E
Oker →, W. Germany 30 52 30N 10 22 E
Okha, U.S.S.R. 41 53 40N 143 0 E
Ókhi Óros, Greece 35 38 5N 24 25 E
Okhotsk, U.S.S.R. 41 59 20N 143 10 E
Okhotsk, Sea of, Asia 41 55 0N 145 0 E
Okhotskiy Perevoz, U.S.S.R. 41 61 52N 135 35 E
Okhotsko Kolymskoye, U.S.S.R. 41 63 0N 157 0 E
Oki-no-Shima, Japan 64 32 44N 132 33 E
Oki-Shotō, Japan 64 36 5N 133 15 E
Okiep, S. Africa 96 29 39 S 17 53 E
Okigwi, Nigeria 91 5 52N 7 20 E
Okija, Nigeria 91 5 54N 6 55 E
Okitipupa, Nigeria 91 6 31N 4 50 E
Oklahoma □, U.S.A. 121 35 20N 97 30W
Oklahoma City, U.S.A. 121 35 25N 97 30W
Okmulgee, U.S.A. 121 35 38N 96 0W
Oknitsa, U.S.S.R. 38 48 25N 27 30 E
Okolo, Uganda 92 2 37N 31 8 E
Okolona, Ky., U.S.A. 119 38 8N 85 41W
Okolona, Miss., U.S.A. 121 34 0N 88 45W
Okrika, Nigeria 91 4 40N 7 10 E
Oktabrsk, U.S.S.R. 40 49 28N 57 25 E
Oktyabrsk, U.S.S.R. 37 53 11N 48 40 E
Oktyabrskiy, U.S.S.R. 36 52 38N 28 53 E
Oktyabrskoy Revolyutsii, Os., U.S.S.R. 41 79 30N 97 0 E
Oktyabrskoye = Zhovtnevoye, U.S.S.R. 38 46 54N 32 3 E
Oktyabrskoye, U.S.S.R. 40 62 28N 66 3 E
Ōkuchi, Japan 64 32 4N 130 37 E
Okulovka, U.S.S.R. 36 58 25N 33 19 E
Okuru, N.Z. 81 43 55 S 168 55 E
Okushiri-Tō, Japan 63 42 15N 139 30 E
Okuta, Nigeria 91 9 14N 3 12 E
Okwa →, Botswana 96 22 30 S 23 0 E
Ola, U.S.A. 121 35 2N 93 10W
Ólafsfjörður, Iceland 8 66 4N 18 39W
Ólafsvík, Iceland 8 64 53N 23 43W
Olancha, U.S.A. 125 36 15N 118 1W
Olancha Pk., U.S.A. 125 36 15N 118 7W
Olanchito, Honduras 128 15 30N 86 30W
Öland, Sweden 11 56 45N 16 38 E
Olargues, France 20 43 34N 2 53 E
Olary, Australia 73 32 18 S 140 19 E
Olascoaga, Argentina 140 35 15 S 60 39W
Olathe, U.S.A. 120 38 50N 94 50W
Olavarría, Argentina 140 36 55 S 60 20W
Oława, Poland 32 50 57N 17 20 E
Ólbia, Italy 28 40 55N 9 30 E
Ólbia, G. di, Italy 28 40 55N 9 35 E
Old Bahama Chan. = Bahama, Canal Viejo de, W. Indies 128 22 10N 77 30W
Old Baldy Pk. = San Antonio, Mt., U.S.A. 125 34 17N 117 38W
Old Castile = Castilla La Vieja, Spain 22 41 55N 4 0W
Old Castle, Ireland 15 53 46N 7 10W
Old Cork, Australia 72 22 57 S 141 52 E
Old Crow, Canada 102 67 30N 139 55W
Old Dale, U.S.A. 125 34 8N 115 47W
Old Dongola, Sudan 88 18 11N 30 44 E
Old Forge, N.Y., U.S.A. 117 43 43N 74 58W
Old Forge, Pa., U.S.A. 117 41 20N 75 46W
Old Fort →, Canada 111 58 36N 110 24W
Old Junee, Australia 76 34 49 S 147 31 E
Old Shinyanga, Tanzania 92 3 33 S 33 27 E
Old Speck, Mt., U.S.A. 117 44 35N 70 57W
Old Town, U.S.A. 105 45 0N 68 41W
Old Wives L., Canada 111 50 5N 106 0W
Oldbury, U.K. 13 51 38N 2 30W
Oldeani, Tanzania 92 3 22 S 35 35 E
Oldenburg, Niedersachsen, W. Germany 30 53 10N 8 10 E
Oldenburg, Schleswig-Holstein, W. Germany 30 54 16N 10 53 E
Oldenzaal, Neths. 16 52 19N 6 53 E
Oldham, U.K. 12 53 33N 2 8W
Oldman →, Canada 110 49 57N 111 42W
Olds, Canada 110 51 50N 114 10W
Olean, U.S.A. 116 42 8N 78 25W
Oléggio, Italy 26 45 36N 8 38 E
Oleiros, Portugal 22 39 56N 7 56W
Olekma →, U.S.S.R. 41 60 22N 120 42 E
Olekminsk, U.S.S.R. 41 60 25N 120 30 E
Olema, U.S.A. 124 38 3N 122 47W
Olen, Belgium 17 51 9N 4 52 E
Olenek, U.S.S.R. 41 68 28N 112 18 E
Olenek →, U.S.S.R. 41 73 0N 120 10 E
Olenino, U.S.S.R. 36 56 15N 33 30 E
Oléron, I. d', France 20 45 55N 1 15W
Oleśnica, Poland 32 51 13N 17 22 E
Olesno, Poland 32 50 51N 18 26 E
Olevsk, U.S.S.R. 36 51 12N 27 39 E
Olga, U.S.S.R. 41 43 50N 135 14 E
Olga, L., Canada 106 49 47N 77 15W
Olga, Mt., Australia 79 25 20 S 130 50 E
Olgastretet, Svalbard 144 78 35N 25 0 E
Ølgod, Denmark 11 55 49N 8 36 E
Olhão, Portugal 23 37 3N 7 48W
Olib, Yugoslavia 27 44 23N 14 44 E
Oliena, Italy 28 40 18N 9 22 E
Oliete, Spain 24 41 1N 0 41W
Olifants →, Africa 97 23 57 S 31 58 E
Olifantshoek, S. Africa 96 27 57 S 22 42 E
Ólimbos, Greece 35 35 44N 27 11 E
Ólimbos, Óros, Greece 35 40 6N 22 23 E
Olímpia, Brazil 141 20 44 S 48 54W
Olimpo □, Paraguay 140 20 30 S 58 45W
Olin, U.S.A. 118 42 0N 91 9W
Olinda, Australia 76 32 50 S 150 10 E
Olinda, Brazil 138 8 1 S 34 51W
Olindiná, Brazil 138 11 22 S 38 21W
Olite, Spain 24 42 29N 1 40W
Oliva, Argentina 140 32 0 S 63 38W
Oliva, Spain 25 38 58N 0 9W
Oliva, La, Canary Is. 25 28 36N 13 57W
Oliva, Punta del, Spain 22 43 37N 5 28W
Oliva de la Frontera, Spain 23 38 17N 6 54W
Olivares, Spain 24 39 46N 2 20W
Olive Hill, U.S.A. 119 38 18N 83 13W
Olivehurst, U.S.A. 124 39 6N 121 34W
Oliveira, Brazil 139 20 39 S 44 50W
Oliveira de Azemeis, Portugal 22 40 49N 8 29W
Oliveira dos Brejinhos, Brazil 139 12 19 S 42 54W
Olivenza, Spain 23 38 41N 7 9W
Oliver, Canada 110 49 13N 119 37W
Oliver L., Canada 111 56 56N 103 22W
Olivine Ra., N.Z. 81 44 15 S 168 30 E
Olkhovka, U.S.S.R. 39 49 48N 44 32 E
Olkusz, Poland 32 50 18N 19 33 E
Ollagüe, Chile 140 21 15 S 68 10W
Olloy, Belgium 17 50 5N 4 36 E
Olmedo, Spain 22 41 20N 4 43W
Olmos, Peru 136 5 59 S 79 46W
Olney, Ill., U.S.A. 119 38 40N 88 0W
Olney, Tex., U.S.A. 121 33 25N 98 45W
Olofström, Sweden 11 56 17N 14 32 E
Oloma, Cameroon 91 3 29N 11 19 E
Olomane →, Canada 105 50 14N 60 37W
Olombo, Congo 94 1 18 S 15 53 E
Olomouc, Czech. 32 49 38N 17 12 E
Olongapo, Phil. 57 14 50N 120 18 E
Oloron, Gave d' →, France 20 43 33N 1 5W
Oloron-Ste.-Marie, France 20 43 11N 0 38W
Olot, Spain 24 42 11N 2 30 E
Olovo, Yugoslavia 33 44 8N 18 35 E
Olovyannaya, U.S.S.R. 41 50 58N 115 35 E
Oloy →, U.S.S.R. 41 66 29N 159 29 E
Olpe, W. Germany 30 51 2N 7 50 E
Olshanka, U.S.S.R. 38 48 16N 30 58 E
Olshany, U.S.S.R. 38 50 3N 35 53 E
Olst, Neths. 16 52 20N 6 7 E
Olsztyn, Poland 32 53 48N 20 29 E
Olt →, Romania 34 43 43N 24 51 E
Olten, Switz. 31 47 21N 7 53 E
Oltenița, Romania 34 44 7N 26 42 E
Olton, U.S.A. 121 34 16N 102 7W
Oltu, Turkey 46 40 35N 41 58 E
Olvega, Spain 24 41 47N 2 0W
Olvera, Spain 23 36 55N 5 18W
Olympia, Greece 35 37 39N 21 39 E
Olympia, U.S.A. 124 47 0N 122 58W
Olympic Mts., U.S.A. 124 47 50N 123 45W
Olympic Nat. Park, U.S.A. 124 47 48N 123 30W
Olympus, Mt. = Ólimbos, Óros, Greece 35 40 6N 22 23 E
Olympus, Mt., U.S.A. 124 47 52N 123 40W
Olyphant, U.S.A. 117 41 27N 75 36W
Om →, U.S.S.R. 40 54 59N 73 22 E
Om Hajer, Ethiopia 89 14 20N 36 41 E
Om Koi, Thailand 54 17 48N 98 22 E
Ōmachi, Japan 65 36 30N 137 50 E
Omae-Zaki, Japan 65 34 36N 138 14 E
Omagh, U.K. 15 54 36N 7 20W
Omagh □, U.K. 15 54 35N 7 15W
Omaha, U.S.A. 120 41 15N 96 0W
Omak, U.S.A. 122 48 24N 119 31W
Oman ■, Asia 45 23 0N 58 0 E
Oman, G. of, Asia 47 24 30N 58 30 E
Omar Combon, Somali Rep. 98 3 10N 45 47 E
Omaruru, Namibia 96 21 26 S 16 0 E
Omaruru →, Namibia 96 22 7 S 14 15 E
Omate, Peru 136 16 45 S 71 0W

Ombai, Selat, *Indonesia* **57** 8 30 S 124 50 E
Omboué, *Gabon* **94** 1 35 S 9 15 E
Ombrone →, *Italy* **26** 42 39N 11 0 E
Omchi, *Chad* **87** 21 22N 17 53 E
Omdurmân, *Sudan* **89** 15 40N 32 28 E
Ōme, *Japan* **65** 35 47N 139 15 E
Omegna, *Italy* **26** 45 52N 8 23 E
Omemee, *Canada* **109** 44 18N 78 33W
Omeo, *Australia* **75** 37 6 S 147 36 E
Omeonga, *Zaïre* **92** 3 40 S 24 22 E
Ometepe, I. de, *Nic.* **128** 11 32N 85 35W
Ometepec, *Mexico* **127** 16 39N 98 23W
Omez, *Israel* **44** 32 22N 35 0 E
Ōmi-Shima, *Ehime, Japan* **64** 34 15N 133 0 E
Ōmi-Shima, *Yamaguchi, Japan* **64** 34 25N 131 9 E
Omihachiman, *Japan* **65** 35 7N 136 3 E
Omineca →, *Canada* **110** 56 3N 124 16W
Omiš, *Yugoslavia* **27** 43 28N 16 40 E
Omišalj, *Yugoslavia* **27** 45 13N 14 32 E
Omitara, *Namibia* **96** 22 16 S 18 2 E
Ōmiya, *Japan* **65** 35 54N 139 38 E
Omme Å →, *Denmark* **11** 55 56N 8 32 E
Ommen, *Neths.* **16** 52 31N 6 26 E
Ömnögovĭ □, *Mongolia* **60** 43 15N 104 0 E
Omo →, *Ethiopia* **89** 6 25N 36 10 E
Omolon →, *U.S.S.R.* **41** 68 42N 158 36 E
Omono-Gawa →, *Japan* **63** 39 46N 140 3 E
Omsk, *U.S.S.R.* **40** 55 0N 73 12 E
Omsukchan, *U.S.S.R.* **41** 62 32N 155 48 E
Omul, Vf., *Romania* **34** 45 27N 25 29 E
Ōmura, *Japan* **64** 32 56N 130 0 E
Omura-Wan, *Japan* **64** 32 57N 129 52 E
Omurtag, *Bulgaria* **34** 43 8N 26 26 E
Ōmuta, *Japan* **64** 33 0N 130 26 E
Omutninsk, *U.S.S.R.* **37** 58 45N 52 4 E
On, *Belgium* **17** 50 11N 5 18 E
On-Take, *Japan* **64** 31 35N 130 39 E
Oña, *Spain* **24** 42 43N 3 25W
Onaga, *U.S.A.* **120** 39 32N 96 12W
Onalaska, *U.S.A.* **120** 43 53N 91 14W
Onamia, *U.S.A.* **120** 46 4N 93 38W
Onancock, *U.S.A.* **114** 37 42N 75 49W
Onang, *Indonesia* **57** 3 2 S 118 49 E
Onaping, *Canada* **108** 46 37N 81 25W
Onaping →, *Canada* **108** 46 37N 81 18W
Onaping L., *Canada* **104** 47 3N 81 30W
Onarga, *U.S.A.* **119** 40 43N 88 1W
Onarhā, *Afghan.* **47** 35 30N 71 0 E
Onatchiway, L., *Canada* **107** 49 3N 71 5W
Oñate, *Spain* **24** 43 3N 2 25W
Onavas, *Mexico* **126** 28 28N 109 30W
Onawa, *U.S.A.* **120** 42 2N 96 2W
Onaway, *U.S.A.* **114** 45 21N 84 11W
Oncócua, *Angola* **95** 16 30 S 13 25 E
Onda, *Spain* **24** 39 55N 0 17W
Ondangua, *Namibia* **96** 17 57 S 16 4 E
Ondárroa, *Spain* **24** 43 19N 2 25W
Ondas →, *Brazil* **139** 12 8 S 45 0W
Ondava →, *Czech.* **32** 48 27N 21 48 E
Onderdijk, *Neths.* **16** 52 45N 5 8 E
Ondjiva, *Angola* **95** 16 48 S 15 50 E
Ondo, *Japan* **64** 34 11N 132 32 E
Ondo, *Nigeria* **91** 7 4N 4 47 E
Ondo □, *Nigeria* **91** 7 0N 5 0 E
Öndörhaan, *Mongolia* **62** 47 19N 110 39 E
Öndörshil, *Mongolia* **60** 45 13N 108 5 E
Öndverðarnes, *Iceland* **8** 64 52N 24 0W
Onega, *U.S.S.R.* **40** 64 0N 38 10 E
Onega →, *U.S.S.R.* **6** 63 58N 37 55 E
Onega, G. of = Onezhskaya Guba, *U.S.S.R.* **40** 64 30N 37 0 E
Onega, L. = Onezhskoye Ozero, *U.S.S.R.* **40** 62 0N 35 30 E
Onehunga, *N.Z.* **80** 36 55 S 174 48 E
Oneida, *Ill., U.S.A.* **118** 41 4N 90 13W
Oneida, *N.Y., U.S.A.* **117** 43 5N 75 40W
Oneida L., *U.S.A.* **117** 43 12N 76 0W
O'Neill, *U.S.A.* **120** 42 30N 98 38W
Onekotan, Ostrov, *U.S.S.R.* **41** 49 25N 154 45 E
Onema, *Zaïre* **92** 4 35 S 24 30 E
Oneonta, *Ala., U.S.A.* **115** 33 58N 86 29W
Oneonta, *N.Y., U.S.A.* **117** 42 26N 75 5W
Onerahi, *N.Z.* **80** 35 45 S 174 22 E
Onezhskaya Guba, *U.S.S.R.* **40** 64 30N 37 0 E
Onezhskoye Ozero, *U.S.S.R.* **40** 62 0N 35 30 E
Ongarue, *N.Z.* **80** 38 42 S 175 19 E
Ongea Levu, *Fiji* **68** 19 8 S 178 24W
Ongerup, *Australia* **79** 33 58 S 118 28 E
Ongkharak, *Thailand* **54** 14 8N 101 1 E
Ongniud Qi, *China* **61** 43 0N 118 38 E
Ongoka, *Zaïre* **92** 1 20 S 26 0 E
Ongole, *India* **51** 15 33N 80 2 E
Ongon, *Mongolia* **60** 45 41N 113 5 E
Onguren, *U.S.S.R.* **41** 53 38N 107 36 E
Onhaye, *Belgium* **17** 50 15N 4 50 E
Oni, *U.S.S.R.* **39** 42 33N 43 26 E
Onida, *U.S.A.* **120** 44 42N 100 5W
Onilahy →, *Madag.* **97** 23 34 S 43 45 E
Onitsha, *Nigeria* **91** 6 6N 6 42 E
Onmaka, *Burma* **52** 22 17N 96 41 E
Ono, *Fiji* **68** 18 55 S 178 29 E
Ono, *Fukui, Japan* **65** 35 59N 136 29 E
Ono, *Hyōgo, Japan* **64** 34 51N 134 56 E
Onoda, *Japan* **64** 34 2N 131 25 E
Onomichi, *Japan* **64** 34 25N 133 12 E
Ons, Is. d', *Spain* **22** 42 23N 8 55W
Onsala, *Sweden* **11** 57 26N 12 0 E
Onslow, *Australia* **78** 21 40 S 115 12 E
Onslow B., *U.S.A.* **115** 34 20N 77 20W
Onstwedde, *Neths.* **16** 53 2N 7 4 E
Ontake-San, *Japan* **65** 35 53N 137 29 E
Ontaneda, *Spain* **22** 43 12N 3 57W
Ontario, *Calif., U.S.A.* **125** 34 2N 117 40W
Ontario, *Oreg., U.S.A.* **122** 44 1N 117 1W
Ontario □, *Canada* **104** 52 0N 88 10W
Ontario, L., *N. Amer.* **109** 43 40N 78 0W
Onteniente, *Spain* **25** 38 50N 0 35W
Ontonagon, *U.S.A.* **120** 46 52N 89 19W
Ontur, *Spain* **25** 38 38N 1 29W
Onyx, *U.S.A.* **125** 35 41N 118 14W
Oodnadatta, *Australia* **73** 27 33 S 135 30 E
Ooldea, *Australia* **79** 30 27 S 131 50 E
Ooltgensplaat, *Neths.* **17** 51 41N 4 21 E
Oombulgurri, *Australia* **78** 15 15 S 127 45 E
Oona River, *Canada* **110** 53 57N 130 16W
Oordegem, *Belgium* **17** 50 58N 3 54 E
Oorindi, *Australia* **72** 20 40 S 141 1 E
Oost-Vlaanderen □, *Belgium* **17** 51 5N 3 50 E
Oost-Vlieland, *Neths.* **16** 53 18N 5 4 E
Oostakker, *Belgium* **17** 51 6N 3 46 E
Oostburg, *Neths.* **17** 51 19N 3 30 E
Oostduinkerke, *Belgium* **17** 51 7N 2 41 E
Oostelijk-Flevoland, *Neths.* **16** 52 31N 5 38 E
Oostende, *Belgium* **17** 51 15N 2 54 E
Oosterbeek, *Neths.* **16** 51 59N 5 51 E
Oosterdijk, *Neths.* **16** 52 44N 5 14 E
Oosterend, *Friesland, Neths.* **16** 53 24N 5 23 E
Oosterend, *Noord-Holland, Neths.* **16** 53 5N 4 52 E
Oosterhout, *Noord-Brabant, Neths.* **17** 51 53N 5 50 E
Oosterhout, *Noord-Brabant, Neths.* **17** 51 39N 4 47 E
Oosterschelde, *Neths.* **17** 51 33N 4 0 E
Oosterwolde, *Neths.* **16** 53 0N 6 17 E
Oosterzele, *Belgium* **17** 50 57N 3 48 E
Oostkamp, *Belgium* **17** 51 9N 3 14 E
Oostmalle, *Belgium* **17** 51 18N 4 44 E
Oostrozebekke, *Belgium* **17** 50 55N 3 21 E
Oostvleteven, *Belgium* **17** 50 56N 2 45 E
Oostvoorne, *Neths.* **16** 51 55N 4 5 E
Oostzaan, *Neths.* **16** 52 26N 4 52 E
Ootacamund, *India* **51** 11 30N 76 44 E
Ootha, *Australia* **76** 33 6 S 147 29 E
Ootmarsum, *Neths.* **16** 52 24N 6 54 E
Ootsa L., *Canada* **110** 53 50N 126 2W
Opala, *U.S.S.R.* **41** 51 58N 156 30 E
Opala, *Zaïre* **92** 0 40 S 24 20 E
Opanake, *Sri Lanka* **51** 6 35N 80 40 E
Opapa, *N.Z.* **80** 39 47 S 176 42 E
Opasatica, L., *Canada* **106** 48 5N 79 18W
Opasatika, *Canada* **104** 49 30N 82 50W
Opasquia, *Canada* **111** 53 16N 93 34W
Opataca, L., *Canada* **106** 50 22N 74 55W
Opatija, *Yugoslavia* **27** 45 21N 14 17 E
Opava, *Czech.* **32** 49 57N 17 58 E
Opawica, L., *Canada* **106** 49 35N 75 55W
Opeinde, *Neths.* **16** 53 8N 6 4 E
Opelousas, *U.S.A.* **121** 30 35N 92 7W
Opémisca, L., *Canada* **106** 49 56N 74 52W
Open Bay Is., *N.Z.* **81** 43 51 S 168 51 E
Opeongo L., *Canada* **109** 45 42N 78 23W
Opglabbeek, *Belgium* **17** 51 3N 5 35 E
Opheim, *U.S.A.* **122** 48 52N 106 30W
Ophir, *U.S.A.* **102** 63 10N 156 40W
Ophthalmia Ra., *Australia* **78** 23 15 S 119 30 E
Opi, *Nigeria* **91** 6 36N 7 28 E
Opinaca →, *Canada* **104** 52 15N 78 2W
Opinaca L., *Canada* **104** 52 39N 76 20W
Opiskotish, L., *Canada* **105** 53 10N 67 50W
Oploo, *Neths.* **17** 51 37N 5 52 E
Opmeer, *Neths.* **16** 52 42N 4 57 E
Opobo, *Nigeria* **91** 4 35N 7 34 E
Opochka, *U.S.S.R.* **36** 56 42N 28 45 E
Opoczno, *Poland* **32** 51 22N 20 18 E
Opole, *Poland* **32** 50 42N 17 58 E
Oporto = Porto, *Portugal* **22** 41 8N 8 40W
Opotiki, *N.Z.* **80** 38 1 S 177 19 E
Opp, *U.S.A.* **115** 31 19N 86 13W
Oppegård, *Norway* **10** 59 48N 10 48 E
Oppenheim, *W. Germany* **31** 49 50N 8 22 E
Opperdoes, *Neths.* **16** 52 45N 5 4 E
Óppido Mamertina, *Italy* **29** 38 16N 15 59 E
Oppland fylke □, *Norway* **10** 61 15N 9 40 E
Oppstad, *Norway* **10** 60 17N 11 40 E
Oprtalj, *Yugoslavia* **27** 45 23N 13 50 E
Opua, *N.Z.* **80** 35 19 S 174 9 E
Opunake, *N.Z.* **80** 39 26 S 173 52 E
Opuzen, *Yugoslavia* **33** 43 1N 17 34 E
Oquawka, *U.S.A.* **118** 40 56N 90 57W
Or, Le Mont d', *France* **19** 46 45N 6 18 E
Or Yehuda, *Israel* **44** 32 2N 34 50 E
Ora, *Israel* **44** 30 55N 35 1 E
Ora, *Italy* **27** 46 20N 11 19 E
Ora Banda, *Australia* **79** 30 20 S 121 0 E
Oracle, *U.S.A.* **123** 32 36N 110 46W
Oradea, *Romania* **34** 47 2N 21 58 E
Öræfajökull, *Iceland* **8** 64 2N 16 39W
Orahovac, *Yugoslavia* **33** 42 24N 20 40 E
Orai, *India* **49** 25 58N 79 30 E
Oraison, *France* **21** 43 55N 5 55 E
Oran, *Algeria* **85** 35 45N 0 39W
Oran, *Argentina* **140** 23 10 S 64 20W
Orange, *Australia* **76** 33 15 S 149 7 E
Orange, *France* **21** 44 8N 4 47 E
Orange, *Calif., U.S.A.* **125** 33 47N 117 51W
Orange, *Mass., U.S.A.* **117** 42 35N 72 15W
Orange, *Tex., U.S.A.* **121** 30 10N 93 50W
Orange, *Va., U.S.A.* **114** 38 17N 78 5W
Orange → = Oranje →, *S. Africa* **96** 28 41 S 16 28 E
Orange, C., *Brazil* **135** 4 20N 51 30W
Orange Cove, *U.S.A.* **124** 36 38N 119 19W
Orange Free State □, *S. Africa* **96** 28 30 S 27 0 E
Orange Grove, *U.S.A.* **121** 27 57N 97 57W
Orange Walk, *Belize* **127** 18 6N 88 33W
Orangeburg, *U.S.A.* **115** 33 35N 80 53W
Orangeville, *Canada* **108** 43 55N 80 5W
Orangeville, *U.S.A.* **118** 42 28N 89 39W
Oranienburg, *E. Germany* **30** 52 45N 13 15 E
Oranje →, *S. Africa* **96** 28 41 S 16 28 E
Oranje Vrystaat □ = Orange Free State □, *S. Africa* **96** 28 30 S 27 0 E
Oranjemund, *Namibia* **96** 28 38 S 16 29 E
Oranjerivier, *S. Africa* **96** 29 40 S 24 12 E
Or'Aquiva, *Israel* **44** 32 30N 34 54 E
Orara →, *Australia* **77** 29 45 S 152 49 E
Oras, *Phil.* **57** 12 9N 125 28 E
Orăştie, *Romania* **34** 45 50N 23 10 E
Oraşul Stalin = Braşov, *Romania* **34** 45 38N 25 35 E
Orava →, *Czech.* **32** 49 24N 19 20 E
Oravita, *Romania* **34** 45 2N 21 43 E
Orawia, *N.Z.* **81** 46 1 S 167 50 E
Oraya, La, *Peru* **136** 11 32 S 75 54W
Orb →, *France* **20** 43 15N 3 18 E
Orba →, *Italy* **26** 44 53N 8 37 E
Ørbæk, *Denmark* **11** 55 17N 10 39 E
Orbe, *Switz.* **31** 46 43N 6 32 E
Orbec, *France* **18** 49 1N 0 23 E
Orbetello, *Italy* **27** 42 26N 11 11 E
Órbigo →, *Spain* **22** 42 5N 5 42W
Orbost, *Australia* **75** 37 40 S 148 29 E
Örbyhus, *Sweden* **10** 60 15N 17 43 E
Orcadas, *Antarctica* **143** 60 44 S 44 37W
Orce, *Spain* **25** 37 44N 2 28W
Orce →, *Spain* **25** 37 44N 2 28W
Orchies, *France* **19** 50 28N 3 14 E
Orchila, I., *Venezuela* **134** 11 48N 66 10W
Orco →, *Italy* **26** 45 10N 7 52 E
Orcopampa, *Peru* **136** 15 20 S 72 23W
Orcutt, *U.S.A.* **125** 34 52N 120 27W
Ord →, *Australia* **78** 15 33 S 138 15 E
Ord, Mt., *Australia* **78** 17 20 S 125 34 E
Ordenes, *Spain* **22** 43 5N 8 29W
Orderville, *U.S.A.* **123** 37 18N 112 43W
Ordos = Mu Us Shamo, *China* **60** 39 0N 109 0 E
Ordu, *Turkey* **46** 40 55N 37 53 E
Orduña, *Álava, Spain* **24** 42 58N 2 58 E
Orduña, *Granada, Spain* **25** 37 20N 3 30W
Ordway, *U.S.A.* **120** 38 15N 103 42W
Ordzhonikidze, *N. Ossetian A.S.S.R., U.S.S.R.* **39** 43 0N 44 35 E
Ordzhonikidze, *Ukraine S.S.R., U.S.S.R.* **38** 47 39N 34 3 E
Ore, *Sweden* **10** 61 8N 15 10 E
Ore, *Zaïre* **92** 3 17N 29 30 E
Ore Mts. = Erzgebirge, *E. Germany* **30** 50 25N 13 0 E
Orealla, *Guyana* **135** 5 15N 57 23W
Orebić, *Yugoslavia* **33** 43 0N 17 11 E
Örebro, *Sweden* **10** 59 20N 15 18 E
Örebro län □, *Sweden* **10** 59 27N 15 0 E
Oregon, *Ill., U.S.A.* **118** 42 1N 89 20W
Oregon, *Ohio, U.S.A.* **119** 41 38N 83 25W
Oregon, *Wis., U.S.A.* **118** 42 56N 89 23W
Oregon □, *U.S.A.* **122** 44 0N 121 0W
Oregon City, *U.S.A.* **124** 45 21N 122 35W
Öregrund, *Sweden* **10** 60 21N 18 30 E
Öregrundsgrepen, *Sweden* **10** 60 25N 18 15 E
Orekhov, *U.S.S.R.* **38** 47 30N 35 48 E
Orekhovo-Zuyevo, *U.S.S.R.* **37** 55 50N 38 55 E
Orel, *U.S.S.R.* **37** 52 57N 36 3 E
Orel →, *U.S.S.R.* **38** 48 30N 34 54 E
Orellana, Canal de, *Spain* **23** 39 2N 6 0W
Orellana, Pantano de, *Spain* **23** 39 5N 5 10W
Orellana la Vieja, *Spain* **23** 39 1N 5 32W
Orem, *U.S.A.* **122** 40 20N 111 45W
Orenburg, *U.S.S.R.* **40** 51 45N 55 6 E
Orense, *Spain* **22** 42 19N 7 55W
Orense □, *Spain* **22** 42 15N 7 51W
Orepuki, *N.Z.* **81** 46 19 S 167 46 E
Orestiás, *Greece* **35** 41 30N 26 33 E
Øresund, *Europe* **11** 55 45N 12 45 E
Oreti →, *N.Z.* **81** 46 28 S 168 14 E
Orford Ness, *U.K.* **13** 52 6N 1 31 E
Orgañà, *Spain* **24** 42 13N 1 20 E
Organos, Pta. de los, *Canary Is.* **25** 28 12N 17 17W
Orgaz, *Spain* **23** 39 39N 3 53W
Orgeyev, *U.S.S.R.* **38** 47 24N 28 50 E
Orgon, *France* **21** 43 47N 5 3 E
Orgūn, *Afghan.* **47** 32 55N 69 12 E
Orhon Gol →, *Mongolia* **62** 50 21N 106 0 E
Ória, *Italy* **29** 40 30N 17 38 E
Orient, *Australia* **73** 28 7 S 142 50 E
Orient, *U.S.A.* **118** 41 12N 94 25W
Oriental, Cordillera, *Bolivia* **137** 17 0 S 66 0W
Oriental, Cordillera, *Colombia* **134** 6 0N 73 0W
Oriente, *Argentina* **140** 38 44 S 60 37W
Origny-Ste.-Benoîte, *France* **19** 49 50N 3 30 E
Orihuela, *Spain* **25** 38 7N 0 55W
Orihuela del Tremedal, *Spain* **24** 40 33N 1 39W
Oriku, *Albania* **35** 40 20N 19 30 E
Orillia, *Canada* **108** 44 40N 79 24W
Orinduik, *Guyana* **135** 4 40N 60 3W
Orinoco →, *Venezuela* **135** 9 15N 61 30W
Orion, *U.S.A.* **118** 41 21N 90 23W
Orissa □, *India* **50** 20 0N 84 0 E
Oristano, *Italy* **28** 39 54N 8 35 E
Oristano, G. di, *Italy* **28** 39 50N 8 22 E
Orituco →, *Venezuela* **134** 8 45N 67 27W
Orizaba, *Mexico* **127** 18 50N 97 10W
Orizona, *Brazil* **139** 17 3 S 48 18W
Orjen, *Yugoslavia* **33** 42 35N 18 34 E
Orjiva, *Spain* **25** 36 53N 3 24W
Orkanger, *Norway* **10** 63 18N 9 52 E
Örkelljunga, *Sweden* **11** 56 17N 13 17 E
Örkény, *Hungary* **33** 47 9N 19 26 E
Orkla →, *Norway* **10** 63 18N 9 51 E
Orkney, *S. Africa* **96** 26 58 S 26 40 E
Orkney □, *U.K.* **14** 59 0N 3 0W
Orkney Is., *U.K.* **14** 59 0N 3 0W
Orland, *Calif., U.S.A.* **124** 39 46N 122 12W
Orland, *Ind., U.S.A.* **119** 41 47N 85 12W
Orlando, *U.S.A.* **115** 28 30N 81 25W
Orlando, C. d', *Italy* **29** 38 10N 14 43 E
Orléanais, *France* **19** 48 0N 2 0 E
Orléans, *France* **19** 47 54N 1 52 E
Orleans, *U.S.A.* **117** 44 49N 72 10W
Orléans, I. d', *Canada* **107** 46 54N 70 58W
Orlice →, *Czech.* **32** 50 5N 16 10 E
Orlik, *U.S.S.R.* **41** 52 30N 99 55 E
Orlov, *Czech.* **32** 49 17N 20 51 E
Orlov Gay, *U.S.S.R.* **37** 50 56N 48 19 E
Ormara, *Pakistan* **47** 25 16N 64 33 E
Ormea, *Italy* **26** 44 9N 7 54 E
Ormília, *Greece* **35** 40 16N 23 39 E
Ormoc, *Phil.* **57** 11 0N 124 37 E
Ormond, *N.Z.* **80** 38 33 S 177 56 E
Ormond Beach, *U.S.A.* **115** 29 13N 81 5W
Ormondville, *N.Z.* **80** 40 5 S 176 19 E
Ormož, *Yugoslavia* **27** 46 25N 16 10 E
Ormstown, *Canada* **117** 45 8N 74 0W
Ornans, *France* **19** 47 7N 6 10 E
Orne □, *France* **18** 48 40N 0 5 E
Orne →, *France* **18** 49 18N 0 15W
Ørnhøj, *Denmark* **11** 56 13N 8 34 E
Ornö, *Sweden* **10** 59 4N 18 24 E
Örnsköldsvik, *Sweden* **10** 63 17N 18 40 E
Oro →, *Mexico* **126** 25 35N 105 2W
Oro Grande, *U.S.A.* **125** 34 36N 117 20W
Orobie, Alpi, *Italy* **26** 46 7N 10 0 E
Orocué, *Colombia* **134** 4 48N 71 20W
Orodo, *Nigeria* **91** 5 34N 7 4 E
Orogrande, *U.S.A.* **123** 32 20N 106 4W
Orol, *Spain* **22** 43 34N 7 39W
Oromocto, *Canada* **105** 45 54N 66 29W
Oron, *Nigeria* **91** 4 48N 8 14 E
Orono, *Canada* **109** 43 59N 78 37W
Oropesa, *Spain* **22** 39 57N 5 10W
Oroquieta, *Phil.* **57** 8 32N 123 44 E
Orós, *Brazil* **138** 6 15 S 38 55W
Orosei, G. di, *Italy* **28** 40 15N 9 40 E
Orosháza, *Hungary* **33** 46 32N 20 42 E
Orotava, La, *Canary Is.* **25** 28 22N 16 31W
Orote Pen., *Guam* **68** 13 26N 144 38 E
Orotukan, *U.S.S.R.* **41** 62 16N 151 42 E
Oroville, *Calif., U.S.A.* **124** 39 31N 121 30W
Oroville, *Wash., U.S.A.* **122** 48 58N 119 30W
Oroville, Res., *U.S.A.* **124** 39 33N 121 29W
Orrefors, *Sweden* **11** 56 50N 15 45 E
Orrick, *U.S.A.* **118** 39 13N 94 7W
Orroroo, *Australia* **73** 32 43 S 138 38 E
Orrville, *U.S.A.* **116** 40 50N 81 46W
Orsa, *Sweden* **10** 61 7N 14 37 E
Orsara di Púglia, *Italy* **29** 41 17N 15 16 E
Orsasjön, *Sweden* **10** 61 7N 14 37 E
Orsha, *U.S.S.R.* **36** 54 30N 30 25 E
Orsk, *U.S.S.R.* **40** 51 12N 58 34 E
Ørslev, *Denmark* **11** 55 3N 11 56 E
Orsogna, *Italy* **27** 42 13N 14 17 E
Orşova, *Romania* **34** 44 41N 22 25 E
Ørsted, *Denmark* **11** 56 30N 10 20 E
Orta, L. d', *Italy* **26** 45 48N 8 21 E
Orta Nova, *Italy* **29** 41 20N 15 40 E
Orte, *Italy* **27** 42 28N 12 23 E
Ortegal, C., *Spain* **22** 43 43N 7 52W
Orteguaza →, *Colombia* **134** 0 43N 75 16W
Orthez, *France* **20** 43 29N 0 48W
Ortho, *Belgium* **17** 50 8N 5 37 E
Ortigueira, *Spain* **22** 43 40N 7 50W
Orting, *U.S.A.* **124** 47 6N 122 12W

Ortles, *Italy* **26** 46 31N 10 33 E
Ortón →, *Bolivia* **136** 10 50 S 67 0W
Ortona, *Italy* **27** 42 21N 14 24 E
Orūmīyeh, *Iran* **46** 37 40N 45 0 E
Orūmīyeh, Daryācheh-ye, *Iran* **46** 37 50N 45 30 E
Orune, *Italy* **28** 40 25N 9 20 E
Oruro, *Bolivia* **136** 18 0 S 67 9W
Oruro□, *Bolivia* **136** 18 40 S 67 30W
Orust, *Sweden* **11** 58 10N 11 40 E
Oruzgān □, *Afghan.* **47** 33 30N 66 0 E
Orvault, *France* **18** 47 17N 1 38W
Orvieto, *Italy* **27** 42 43N 12 8 E
Orwell, *U.S.A.* **116** 41 32N 80 52W
Orwell →, *U.K.* **13** 52 2N 1 12 E
Oryakhovo, *Bulgaria* **34** 43 40N 23 57 E
Orzinuovi, *Italy* **26** 45 24N 9 55 E
Orzysz, *Poland* **32** 53 50N 21 58 E
Osa, Pen. de, *Costa Rica* **128** 8 0N 84 0W
Osage, *Iowa, U.S.A.* **120** 43 15N 92 50W
Osage, *Wyo., U.S.A.* **120** 43 59N 104 25W
Osage →, *U.S.A.* **118** 38 35N 91 57W
Osage City, *U.S.A.* **120** 38 43N 95 51W
Ōsaka, *Japan* **65** 34 40N 135 30 E
Ōsaka □, *Japan* **65** 34 30N 135 30 E
Ōsaka-Wan, *Japan* **65** 34 30N 135 18 E
Osawatomie, *U.S.A.* **120** 38 30N 94 55W
Osborne, *U.S.A.* **120** 39 30N 98 45W
Osby, *Sweden* **11** 56 23N 13 59 E
Osceola, *Ark., U.S.A.* **121** 35 40N 90 0W
Osceola, *Iowa, U.S.A.* **118** 41 0N 93 20W
Osceola, *Mo., U.S.A.* **118** 38 3N 93 42W
Oschatz, *E. Germany* **30** 51 17N 13 8 E
Oschersleben, *E. Germany* **30** 52 2N 11 13 E
Óschiri, *Italy* **28** 40 43N 9 7 E
Oscoda, *U.S.A.* **116** 44 26N 83 20W
Ösel = Saaremaa, *U.S.S.R.* **36** 58 30N 22 30 E
Osëry, *U.S.S.R.* **37** 54 52N 38 28 E
Osgood, *U.S.A.* **119** 39 8N 85 18W
Osgoode, *Canada* **109** 45 8N 75 36W
Osh, *U.S.S.R.* **40** 40 37N 72 49 E
Oshawa, *Canada* **109** 43 50N 78 50W
Oshima, *Japan* **64** 33 55N 132 14 E
Oshkosh, *Nebr., U.S.A.* **120** 41 27N 102 20W
Oshkosh, *Wis., U.S.A.* **120** 44 3N 88 35W
Oshmyany, *U.S.S.R.* **36** 54 26N 25 52 E
Oshogbo, *Nigeria* **91** 7 48N 4 37 E
Oshwe, *Zaïre* **94** 3 25 S 19 28 E
Osijek, *Yugoslavia* **33** 45 34N 18 41 E
Ósilo, *Italy* **28** 40 45N 8 41 E
Osimo, *Italy* **27** 43 28N 13 30 E
Osintorf, *U.S.S.R.* **36** 54 40N 30 39 E
Osipenko = Berdyansk, *U.S.S.R.* **38** 46 45N 36 50 E
Osipovichi, *U.S.S.R.* **36** 53 19N 28 33 E
Osizweni, *S. Africa* **97** 27 49 S 30 7 E
Oskaloosa, *U.S.A.* **118** 41 18N 92 40W
Oskarshamn, *Sweden* **11** 57 15N 16 27 E
Oskélanéo, *Canada* **106** 48 5N 75 15W
Oskol →, *U.S.S.R.* **37** 49 6N 37 25 E
Oslo, *Norway* **10** 59 55N 10 45 E
Oslob, *Phil.* **57** 9 31N 123 26 E
Oslofjorden, *Norway* **10** 59 20N 10 35 E
Osmanabad, *India* **50** 18 5N 76 10 E
Osmancık, *Turkey* **38** 40 45N 34 47 E
Osmaniye, *Turkey* **46** 37 5N 36 10 E
Ösmo, *Sweden* **10** 58 58N 17 55 E
Osnabrück, *W. Germany* **30** 52 16N 8 2 E
Osor, *Italy* **26** 44 42N 14 24 E
Osorio, *Brazil* **141** 29 53 S 50 17W
Osorno, *Chile* **142** 40 25 S 73 0W
Osorno, *Spain* **22** 42 24N 4 22W
Osorno □, *Chile* **142** 40 34 S 73 9W
Osorno, Vol., *Chile* **142** 41 0 S 72 30W
Osoyoos, *Canada* **110** 49 0N 119 30W
Ospika →, *Canada* **110** 56 20N 124 0W
Osprey Reef, *Australia* **72** 13 52 S 146 36 E
Oss, *Neths.* **16** 51 46N 5 32 E
Ossa, Mt., *Australia* **72** 41 52 S 146 3 E
Óssa, Oros, *Greece* **35** 39 47N 22 42 E
Ossa de Montiel, *Spain* **25** 38 58N 2 45W
Ossabaw I., *U.S.A.* **115** 31 45N 81 8W
Osse →, *France* **20** 44 7N 0 17 E
Ossendrecht, *Neths.* **17** 51 24N 4 20 E
Ossining, *U.S.A.* **117** 41 9N 73 50W
Ossipee, *U.S.A.* **117** 43 41N 71 9W
Ossokmanuan L., *Canada* **105** 53 25N 65 0W
Ossora, *U.S.S.R.* **41** 59 20N 163 13 E
Ostaboningue, L., *Canada* **106** 47 9N 78 53W
Ostashkov, *U.S.S.R.* **36** 57 4N 33 2 E
Oste →, *W. Germany* **30** 53 30N 9 12 E
Ostend = Oostende, *Belgium* **17** 51 15N 2 54 E
Oster, *U.S.S.R.* **36** 50 57N 30 53 E
Osterburg, *E. Germany* **30** 52 47N 11 44 E
Osterburken, *W. Germany* **31** 49 26N 9 25 E
Österbybruk, *Sweden* **10** 60 13N 17 55 E
Österbymo, *Sweden* **11** 57 49N 15 15 E
Österdalälven →, *Sweden* **9** 61 30N 13 45 E
Östergötlands län □, *Sweden* **11** 58 35N 15 45 E
Osterholz-Scharmbeck, *W. Germany* **30** 53 14N 8 48 E
Østerild, *Denmark* **11** 57 2N 8 51 E
Österkorsberga, *Sweden* **11** 57 18N 15 6 E
Östersund, *Sweden* **10** 63 10N 14 38 E
Østfold fylke □, *Norway* **10** 59 25N 11 25 E
Ostfriesische Inseln, *W. Germany* **30** 53 45N 7 15 E
Ostfriesland, *W. Germany* **30** 53 20N 7 30 E
Óstia, Lido di, *Italy* **28** 41 43N 12 17 E
Ostiglía, *Italy* **27** 45 4N 11 9 E
Ostra, *Italy* **27** 43 40N 13 5 E
Ostrava, *Czech.* **32** 49 51N 18 18 E
Ostróda, *Poland* **32** 53 42N 19 58 E
Ostrog, *U.S.S.R.* **36** 50 20N 26 30 E
Ostrogozhsk, *U.S.S.R.* **37** 50 55N 39 7 E
Ostrogróg Szamotuły, *Poland* **32** 52 37N 16 33 E
Ostrołęka, *Poland* **32** 53 4N 21 32 E
Ostrov, *Bulgaria* **34** 43 40N 24 9 E
Ostrov, *Romania* **34** 44 6N 27 24 E
Ostrov, *U.S.S.R.* **36** 57 25N 28 20 E
Ostrów Mazowiecka, *Poland* **32** 52 50N 21 51 E
Ostrów Wielkopolski, *Poland* **32** 51 36N 17 44 E
Ostrowiec-Świętokrzyski, *Poland* **32** 50 55N 21 22 E
Ostrzeszów, *Poland* **32** 51 25N 17 52 E
Ostseebad-Külungsborn, *E. Germany* **30** 54 10N 11 40 E
Ostuni, *Italy* **29** 40 44N 17 34 E
Osum →, *Bulgaria* **34** 43 40N 24 50 E
Osumi →, *Albania* **35** 40 40N 20 10 E
Ōsumi-Hantō, *Japan* **64** 31 20N 130 55 E
Ōsumi-Kaikyō, *Japan* **63** 30 55N 131 0 E
Osuna, *Spain* **23** 37 14N 5 8W
Oswego, *U.S.A.* **117** 43 29N 76 30W
Oswestry, *U.K.* **12** 52 52N 3 3W
Oświecim, *Poland* **32** 50 2N 19 11 E
Ōta, *Japan* **65** 36 18N 139 22 E
Ota-Gawa →, *Japan* **64** 34 21N 132 18 E
Otago □, *N.Z.* **81** 44 44 S 169 10 E
Otago Harb., *N.Z.* **81** 45 47 S 170 42 E
Otago Pen., *N.Z.* **81** 45 48 S 170 39 E
Otahuhu, *N.Z.* **80** 36 56 S 174 51 E
Ōtake, *Japan* **64** 34 12N 132 13 E
Ōtaki, *Japan* **65** 35 17N 140 15 E
Otaki, *N.Z.* **80** 40 45 S 175 10 E
Otane, *N.Z.* **80** 39 54 S 176 39 E
Otaru, *Japan* **63** 43 10N 141 0 E
Otaru-Wan = Ishikari-Wan, *Japan* **63** 43 25N 141 1 E
Otautau, *N.Z.* **81** 46 9 S 168 1 E
Otava →, *Czech.* **32** 49 26N 14 12 E
Otavalo, *Ecuador* **134** 0 13N 78 20W
Otavi, *Namibia* **96** 19 40 S 17 24 E
Otchinjau, *Angola* **95** 16 30 S 13 56 E
Otelec, *Romania* **34** 45 36N 20 50 E
Otero de Rey, *Spain* **22** 43 6N 7 36W
Othello, *U.S.A.* **122** 46 53N 119 8W
Othonoí, *Greece* **35** 39 52N 19 22 E
Óthris, Óros, *Greece* **35** 39 4N 22 42 E
Otira, *N.Z.* **81** 42 49 S 171 35 E
Otira Gorge, *N.Z.* **81** 42 53 S 171 33 E
Otis, *U.S.A.* **120** 40 12N 102 58W
Otjiwarongo, *Namibia* **96** 20 30 S 16 33 E
Oto Tolu Group, *Tonga* **68** 20 21 S 174 32W
Otočac, *Yugoslavia* **27** 44 53N 15 12 E
Otoineppu, *Japan* **63** 44 44N 142 16 E
Otorohanga, *N.Z.* **80** 38 12 S 175 14 E
Otoskwin →, *Canada* **104** 52 13N 88 6W
Otosquen, *Canada* **111** 53 17N 102 1W
Ōtoyo, *Japan* **64** 33 43N 133 45 E
Otranto, *Italy* **29** 40 9N 18 28 E
Otranto, C. d', *Italy* **29** 40 7N 18 30 E
Otranto, Str. of, *Italy* **29** 40 15N 18 40 E
Otse, *S. Africa* **96** 25 2 S 25 45 E
Otsego, *U.S.A.* **119** 42 27N 85 42W
Ōtsu, *Japan* **65** 35 0N 135 50 E
Ōtsuki, *Japan* **65** 35 36N 138 57 E
Otta, *Norway* **10** 61 46N 9 32 E
Ottapalam, *India* **51** 10 46N 76 23 E
Ottawa, *Canada* **109** 45 27N 75 42W
Ottawa, *Ill., U.S.A.* **119** 41 20N 88 55W
Ottawa, *Kans., U.S.A.* **120** 38 40N 95 6W
Ottawa, *Ohio, U.S.A.* **119** 41 1N 84 3W
Ottawa → = Outaouais →, *Canada* **107** 45 27N 74 8W
Ottawa Is., *Canada* **103** 59 35N 80 10W
Ottélé, *Cameroon* **91** 3 38N 11 19 E
Ottenby, *Sweden* **11** 56 15N 16 24 E
Otter L., *Canada* **111** 55 35N 104 39W
Otter Rapids, *Ont., Canada* **104** 50 11N 81 39W
Otter Rapids, *Sask., Canada* **111** 55 38N 104 44W
Otterbein, *U.S.A.* **119** 40 29N 87 6W
Otterberg, *W. Germany* **31** 49 30N 7 46 E
Otterndorf, *W. Germany* **30** 53 47N 8 52 E
Otterup, *Denmark* **11** 55 30N 10 22 E
Otterville, *Canada* **108** 42 55N 80 36W
Otterville, *U.S.A.* **118** 38 42N 93 0W
Otteys Cr. →, *Australia* **77** 28 45 S 150 33 E
Ottignies, *Belgium* **17** 50 40N 4 33 E
Otto Beit Bridge, *Zimb.* **93** 15 59 S 28 56 E
Ottosdal, *S. Africa* **96** 26 46 S 25 59 E
Ottoshoop, *S. Africa* **96** 25 45 S 25 58 E
Ottoville, *U.S.A.* **119** 40 57N 84 22W
Ottsjö, *Sweden* **10** 63 13N 13 2 E
Ottumwa, *U.S.A.* **118** 41 0N 92 25W
Otu, *Nigeria* **91** 8 14N 3 22 E
Otukpa, *Nigeria* **91** 7 9N 7 41 E
Oturkpo, *Nigeria* **91** 7 16N 8 8 E
Otway, B., *Chile* **142** 53 30 S 74 0W
Otway, C., *Australia* **74** 38 52 S 143 30 E
Otwock, *Poland* **32** 52 5N 21 20 E
Ötz, *Austria* **31** 47 13N 10 53 E
Ötz →, *Austria* **31** 47 14N 10 50 E
Ötztaler Alpen, *Austria* **31** 46 45N 11 0 E
Ou →, *Laos* **54** 20 4N 102 13 E
Ou Neua, *Laos* **54** 22 18N 101 48 E
Ouachita →, *U.S.A.* **121** 31 38N 91 49W
Ouachita, L., *U.S.A.* **121** 34 40N 93 25W
Ouachita Mts., *U.S.A.* **121** 34 50N 94 30W
Ouaco, *N. Cal.* **68** 20 50 S 164 29 E
Ouadâne, *Mauritania* **84** 20 50N 11 40W
Ouadda, *C.A.R.* **94** 8 15N 22 20 E
Ouagadougou, *Burkina Faso* **91** 12 25N 1 30W
Ouagam, *Chad* **87** 14 22N 14 42 E
Ouahigouya, *Burkina Faso* **90** 13 31N 2 25W
Ouahila, *Algeria* **84** 27 50N 5 0W
Ouahran = Oran, *Algeria* **85** 35 45N 0 39W
Oualâta, *Mauritania* **90** 17 20N 6 55W
Ouallene, *Algeria* **85** 24 41N 1 11 E
Ouanda Djallé, *C.A.R.* **94** 8 55N 22 53 E
Ouandago, *C.A.R.* **94** 7 13N 18 50 E
Ouango, *C.A.R.* **94** 4 19N 22 30 E
Ouarâne, *Mauritania* **84** 21 0N 10 30W
Ouareau, L., Rés., *Canada* **107** 46 17N 74 9W
Ouargla, *Algeria* **85** 31 59N 5 16 E
Ouarkziz, Djebel, *Algeria* **84** 28 50N 8 0W
Ouarzazate, *Morocco* **84** 30 55N 6 50W
Ouasiemsca →, *Canada* **107** 49 0N 72 30W
Ouatagouna, *Mali* **91** 15 11N 0 43 E
Ouatere, *C.A.R.* **94** 5 30N 19 8 E
Oubangi →, *Zaïre* **94** 0 30 S 17 50 E
Oubarakai, O. →, *Algeria* **85** 27 20N 9 0 E
Oubatche, *N. Cal.* **68** 20 26 S 164 39 E
Ouche →, *France* **19** 47 6N 5 16 E
Oud-Beijerland, *Neths.* **16** 51 50N 4 25 E
Oud-Gastel, *Neths.* **17** 51 35N 4 28 E
Oud Turnhout, *Belgium* **17** 51 19N 5 0 E
Ouddorp, *Neths.* **16** 51 50N 3 57 E
Oude-Pekela, *Neths.* **16** 53 6N 7 0 E
Oude Rijn →, *Neths.* **16** 52 12N 4 24 E
Oudega, *Neths.* **16** 53 8N 6 0 E
Oudenaarde, *Belgium* **17** 50 50N 3 37 E
Oudenbosch, *Neths.* **17** 51 35N 4 32 E
Oudenburg, *Belgium* **17** 51 11N 3 1 E
Ouderkerk, *Utrecht, Neths.* **16** 52 18N 4 55 E
Ouderkerk, *Zuid-Holland, Neths.* **16** 51 56N 4 38 E
Oudeschild, *Neths.* **16** 53 2N 4 50 E
Oudewater, *Neths.* **16** 52 2N 4 52 E
Oudkarspel, *Neths.* **16** 52 43N 4 49 E
Oudon, *France* **18** 47 22N 1 19W
Oudtshoorn, *S. Africa* **96** 33 35 S 22 14 E
Oued Zem, *Morocco* **84** 32 52N 6 34W
Ouégoa, *N. Cal.* **68** 20 20 S 164 26 E
Ouellé, *Ivory C.* **90** 7 26N 4 1W
Ouen, I., *N. Cal.* **68** 22 26 S 166 49 E
Ouenza, *Algeria* **85** 35 57N 8 4 E
Ouessa, *Burkina Faso* **90** 11 4N 2 47W
Ouessant, I. d', *France* **18** 48 28N 5 6W
Ouesso, *Congo* **94** 1 37N 16 5 E
Ouest, Pte., *Canada* **105** 49 52N 64 40W
Ouezzane, *Morocco* **84** 34 51N 5 35W
Ouffet, *Belgium* **17** 50 26N 5 28 E
Ouidah, *Benin* **91** 6 25N 2 0 E
Ouistreham, *France* **18** 49 17N 0 18W
Oujda, *Morocco* **85** 34 41N 1 55W
Oujeft, *Mauritania* **84** 20 2N 13 0W
Ould Yenjé, *Mauritania* **90** 15 38N 12 16W
Ouled Djellal, *Algeria* **85** 34 28N 5 2 E
Ouled Naïl, Mts. des, *Algeria* **85** 34 30N 3 30 E
Oulmès, *Morocco* **84** 33 17N 6 0W
Oulu, *Finland* **8** 65 1N 25 29 E
Oulu □, *Finland* **8** 65 10N 27 20 E
Oulujärvi, *Finland* **8** 64 25N 27 15 E
Oulujoki →, *Finland* **8** 65 1N 25 30 E
Oulx, *Italy* **26** 45 2N 6 49 E
Oum Chalouba, *Chad* **87** 15 48N 20 46 E
Oum-el-Bouaghi, *Algeria* **85** 35 55N 7 6 E
Oum el Ksi, *Algeria* **84** 29 4N 6 59W
Oum-er-Rbia, O. →, *Morocco* **84** 33 19N 8 21W
Oumè, *Ivory C.* **90** 6 21N 5 27W
Ounane, Dj., *Algeria* **85** 25 4N 7 19 E
Ounguati, *Namibia* **96** 22 0 S 15 46 E
Ounianga-Kébir, *Chad* **87** 19 4N 20 29 E
Ounianga Sérir, *Chad* **87** 18 54N 20 51 E
Our →, *Lux.* **17** 49 55N 6 5 E
Ouray, *U.S.A.* **123** 38 3N 107 40W
Ourcq →, *France* **19** 49 1N 3 1 E
Oureg, Oued el →, *Algeria* **85** 32 34N 2 10 E
Ourém, *Brazil* **138** 1 33 S 47 6W
Ouricuri, *Brazil* **138** 7 53 S 40 5W
Ourinhos, *Brazil* **141** 23 0 S 49 54W
Ourique, *Portugal* **23** 37 38N 8 16W
Ouro Fino, *Brazil* **141** 22 16 S 46 25W
Ouro Prêto, *Brazil* **141** 20 20 S 43 30W
Ouro Sogui, *Senegal* **90** 15 36N 13 19W
Oursi, *Burkina Faso* **91** 14 41N 0 27W
Ourthe →, *Belgium* **17** 50 29N 5 35 E
Ouse, *Australia* **72** 42 38 S 146 42 E
Ouse →, *E. Sussex, U.K.* **13** 50 43N 0 3 E
Ouse →, *N. Yorks., U.K.* **12** 54 3N 0 7 E
Oust, *France* **20** 42 52N 1 13 E
Oust →, *France* **18** 47 35N 2 6W
Outaouais →, *Canada* **107** 45 27N 74 8W
Outardes, *Canada* **107** 50 20N 69 10W
Outardes →, *Canada* **107** 49 24N 69 30W
Outat Oulad el Haj, *Morocco* **85** 33 22N 3 42W
Outer Hebrides, *U.K.* **14** 57 30N 7 40W
Outer I., *Canada* **105** 51 10N 58 35W
Outes, *Spain* **22** 42 52N 8 55W
Outjo, *Namibia* **96** 20 5 S 16 7 E
Outlook, *Canada* **111** 51 30N 107 0W
Outlook, *U.S.A.* **120** 48 53N 104 46W
Outreau, *France* **19** 50 40N 1 36 E
Ouvèze →, *France* **21** 43 59N 4 51 E
Ouyen, *Australia* **74** 35 1 S 142 22 E
Ouzouer-le-Marché, *France* **19** 47 54N 1 32 E
Ovada, *Italy* **26** 44 39N 8 40 E
Ovalle, *Chile* **140** 30 33 S 71 18W
Ovar, *Portugal* **22** 40 51N 8 40W
Ovejas, *Colombia* **134** 9 32N 75 14W
Ovens, *Australia* **75** 36 35 S 146 46 E
Ovens →, *Australia* **75** 36 2 S 146 12 E
Overdinkel, *Neths.* **16** 52 14N 7 2 E
Overflakkee, *Neths.* **16** 51 44N 4 10 E
Overijse, *Belgium* **17** 50 47N 4 32 E
Overijssel □, *Neths.* **16** 52 25N 6 35 E
Overijsselsch Kanaal →, *Neths.* **16** 52 31N 6 6 E
Overland, *U.S.A.* **118** 38 41N 90 23W
Overpelt, *Belgium* **17** 51 12N 5 20 E
Overton, *U.S.A.* **125** 36 32N 114 31W
Övertorneå, *Sweden* **8** 66 23N 23 38 E
Overum, *Sweden* **11** 58 0N 16 20 E
Ovid, *Colo., U.S.A.* **120** 41 0N 102 17W
Ovid, *Mich., U.S.A.* **119** 43 1N 84 22W
Ovidiopol, *U.S.S.R.* **38** 46 15N 30 30 E
Oviedo, *Spain* **22** 43 25N 5 50W
Oviedo □, *Spain* **22** 43 20N 6 0W
Oviken, *Sweden* **10** 63 0N 14 23 E
Oviksfjällen, *Sweden* **10** 63 0N 13 49 E
Övör Hangay □, *Mongolia* **60** 45 0N 102 30 E
Ovoro, *Nigeria* **91** 5 26N 7 16 E
Ovruch, *U.S.S.R.* **36** 51 25N 28 45 E
Owaka, *N.Z.* **81** 46 27 S 169 40 E
Owando, *Congo* **94** 0 29 S 15 55 E
Owase, *Japan* **65** 34 7N 136 12 E
Owatonna, *U.S.A.* **120** 44 3N 93 10W
Owbeh, *Afghan.* **47** 34 28N 63 10 E
Owego, *U.S.A.* **117** 42 6N 76 17W
Owen Falls, *Uganda* **92** 0 30N 33 5 E
Owen Mt., *N.Z.* **81** 41 35 S 172 33 E
Owen Sound, *Canada* **108** 44 35N 80 55W
Owen Stanley Range, *Papua N. G.* **69** 8 30 S 147 0 E
Owendo, *Gabon* **94** 0 17N 9 30 E
Owens →, *U.S.A.* **124** 36 32N 117 59W
Owens L., *U.S.A.* **125** 36 20N 118 0W
Owensboro, *U.S.A.* **119** 37 40N 87 5W
Owensville, *Ind., U.S.A.* **119** 38 16N 87 41W
Owensville, *Mo., U.S.A.* **118** 38 20N 91 30W
Owenton, *U.S.A.* **119** 38 32N 84 50W
Owerri, *Nigeria* **91** 5 29N 7 0 E
Owhango, *N.Z.* **80** 39 0 S 175 23 E
Owingsville, *U.S.A.* **119** 38 9N 83 46W
Owl →, *Canada* **111** 57 51N 92 44W
Owo, *Nigeria* **91** 7 10N 5 39 E
Owosso, *U.S.A.* **104** 43 0N 84 10W
Owyhee, *U.S.A.* **122** 42 0N 116 3W
Owyhee →, *U.S.A.* **122** 43 46N 117 2W
Owyhee, L., *U.S.A.* **122** 43 40N 117 16W
Ox Mts., *Ireland* **15** 54 6N 9 0W
Oxapampa, *Peru* **136** 10 33 S 75 26W
Oxberg, *Sweden* **10** 61 7N 14 11 E
Oxelösund, *Sweden* **11** 58 43N 17 15 E
Oxford, *N.Z.* **81** 43 18 S 172 11 E
Oxford, *U.K.* **13** 51 45N 1 15W
Oxford, *Iowa, U.S.A.* **118** 41 43N 91 47W
Oxford, *Mich., U.S.A.* **119** 42 49N 83 16W
Oxford, *Miss., U.S.A.* **121** 34 22N 89 30W
Oxford, *N.C., U.S.A.* **115** 36 19N 78 36W
Oxford, *Ohio, U.S.A.* **119** 39 30N 84 40W
Oxford □, *U.K.* **13** 51 45N 1 15W
Oxford L., *Canada* **111** 54 51N 95 37W
Oxley, *N.S.W., Australia* **74** 34 11 S 144 6 E
Oxley, *Vic., Australia* **75** 36 25 S 146 22 E
Oxnard, *U.S.A.* **125** 34 10N 119 14W
Oxus → = Amudarya →, *U.S.S.R.* **40** 43 40N 59 0 E
Oya, *Malaysia* **56** 2 55N 111 55 E
Oyabe, *Japan* **65** 36 47N 136 56 E
Oyama, *Japan* **65** 36 18N 139 48 E
Oyana, *Japan* **64** 32 32N 130 30 E
Oyapock →, *Fr. Guiana* **135** 4 8N 51 40W
Oyem, *Gabon* **94** 1 34N 11 31 E
Oyen, *Canada* **111** 51 22N 110 28W
Öyeren, *Norway* **10** 59 50N 11 15 E

Oykel →, *U.K.* **14** 57 55N 4 26W
Oymyakon, *U.S.S.R.* **41** 63 25N 142 44 E
Oyo, *Nigeria* **91** 7 46N 3 56 E
Oyo □, *Nigeria* **91** 8 0N 3 30 E
Oyón, *Peru* **136** 10 37 S 76 47W
Oyonnax, *France* **21** 46 16N 5 40 E
Oyster Bay, *U.S.A.* **117** 40 52N 73 32W
Ozamis, *Phil.* **57** 8 15N 123 50 E
Ozark, *Ala., U.S.A.* **115** 31 29N 85 39W
Ozark, *Ark., U.S.A.* **121** 35 30N 93 50W
Ozark, *Mo., U.S.A.* **121** 37 0N 93 15W
Ozark Plateau, *U.S.A.* **121** 37 20N 91 40W
Ozarks, L. of the, *U.S.A.* **118** 38 10N 92 40W
Ózd, *Hungary* **33** 48 14N 20 15 E
Ozette, L., *U.S.A.* **124** 48 6N 124 38W
Ozieri, *Italy* **28** 40 35N 9 0 E
Ozona, *U.S.A.* **121** 30 43N 101 11W
Ozorków, *Poland* **32** 51 57N 19 16 E
Ozu, *Ehime, Japan* **64** 33 30N 132 33 E
Ozu, *Kumamoto, Japan* **64** 32 52N 130 52 E
Ozuluama, *Mexico* **127** 21 40N 97 50W

P

P.K. le Roux Dam, *S. Africa* **96** 30 4 S 24 40 E
Pa, *Burkina Faso* **90** 11 33N 3 19W
Pa-an, *Burma* **52** 16 51N 97 40 E
Pa Mong Dam, *Thailand* **54** 18 0N 102 22 E
Paagoumène, *N. Cal.* **68** 20 29 S 164 11 E
Paal, *Belgium* **17** 51 2N 5 10 E
Paama, *Vanuatu* **68** 16 28 S 168 14 E
Paar →, *W. Germany* **31** 48 13N 10 59 E
Paarl, *S. Africa* **96** 33 45 S 18 56 E
Paatsi →, *U.S.S.R.* **8** 68 55N 29 0 E
Paauilo, *U.S.A.* **112** 20 3N 155 22W
Pab Hills, *Pakistan* **48** 26 30N 66 45 E
Pabianice, *Poland* **32** 51 40N 19 20 E
Pabna, *Bangla.* **52** 24 1N 89 18 E
Pabo, *Uganda* **92** 3 1N 32 10 E
Pacaás Novos, Serra dos, *Brazil* **137** 10 45 S 64 15W
Pacaipampa, *Peru* **136** 5 35 S 79 39W
Pacaja →, *Brazil* **138** 1 56 S 50 50W
Pacajus, *Brazil* **138** 4 10 S 38 31W
Pacaraima, Sierra, *Venezuela* **135** 4 0N 62 30W
Pacarán, *Peru* **136** 12 50 S 76 3W
Pacaraos, *Peru* **136** 11 12 S 76 42W
Pacasmayo, *Peru* **136** 7 20 S 79 35W
Pacaudière, La, *France* **20** 46 11N 3 52 E
Paceco, *Italy* **28** 37 59N 12 32 E
Pachacamac, *Peru* **136** 12 14 S 77 53W
Pachhar, *India* **48** 24 40N 77 42 E
Pachino, *Italy* **29** 36 43N 15 4 E
Pachitea →, *Peru* **136** 8 46 S 74 33W
Pachiza, *Peru* **136** 7 16 S 76 46W
Pacho, *Colombia* **134** 5 8N 74 10W
Pachora, *India* **50** 20 38N 75 29 E
Pachuca, *Mexico* **127** 20 10N 98 40W
Pacific, *Canada* **110** 54 48N 128 28W
Pacific, *U.S.A.* **118** 38 29N 90 45W
Pacific-Antarctic Basin, *Pac. Oc.* **67** 46 0 S 95 0W
Pacific-Antarctic Ridge, *Pac. Oc.* **67** 43 0 S 115 0W
Pacific Grove, *U.S.A.* **124** 36 38N 121 58W
Pacific Ocean, *Pac. Oc.* **66** 10 0N 140 0W
Pacifica, *U.S.A.* **124** 37 36N 122 30W
Pacitan, *Indonesia* **57** 8 12 S 111 7 E
Packenham, *Canada* **109** 45 22N 76 25W
Packwood, *U.S.A.* **124** 46 36N 121 40W
Pacuí →, *Brazil* **139** 16 46 S 45 1W
Padaido, Kepulauan, *Indonesia* **57** 1 5 S 138 0 E
Padang, *Indonesia* **56** 1 0 S 100 20 E
Padangpanjang, *Indonesia* **56** 0 40 S 100 20 E
Padangsidempuan, *Indonesia* **56** 1 30N 99 15 E
Padatchuang, *Burma* **52** 19 46N 94 48 E
Padauari →, *Brazil* **135** 0 15 S 64 5W
Padborg, *Denmark* **11** 54 49N 9 21 E
Padcaya, *Bolivia* **137** 21 52 S 64 48W
Paddockwood, *Canada* **111** 53 30N 105 30W
Paderborn, *W. Germany* **30** 51 42N 8 44 E
Padilla, *Bolivia* **137** 19 19 S 64 20W
Padloping Island, *Canada* **103** 67 0N 62 50W
Padma →, *Bangla.* **52** 23 22N 90 32 E
Padmanabhapuram, *India* **51** 8 16N 77 17 E
Pádova, *Italy* **27** 45 24N 11 52 E
Padra, *India* **48** 22 15N 73 7 E
Padrauna, *India* **49** 26 54N 83 59 E
Padre I., *U.S.A.* **121** 27 0N 97 20W
Padro, Mte., *France* **21** 42 28N 8 59 E
Padrón, *Spain* **22** 42 41N 8 39W
Padstow, *U.K.* **12** 50 33N 4 57W
Padua = Pádova, *Italy* **27** 45 24N 11 52 E
Paducah, *Ky., U.S.A.* **114** 37 0N 88 40W
Paducah, *Tex., U.S.A.* **121** 34 3N 100 16W
Padul, *Spain* **23** 37 1N 3 38W
Padula, *Italy* **29** 40 20N 15 40 E
Padwa, *India* **50** 18 27N 82 47 E
Paekakariki, *N.Z.* **80** 40 59 S 174 58 E
Paengaroa, *N.Z.* **80** 37 49 S 176 29 E
Paeroa, *N.Z.* **80** 37 23 S 175 41 E
Paesana, *Italy* **26** 44 40N 7 18 E
Pafúri, *Mozam.* **97** 22 28 S 31 17 E
Pag, *Yugoslavia* **27** 44 30N 14 50 E
Paga, *Ghana* **91** 11 1N 1 8W
Pagadian, *Phil.* **57** 7 55N 123 30 E
Pagai Selatan, P., *Indonesia* **56** 3 0 S 100 15 E
Pagai Utara, *Indonesia* **56** 2 35 S 100 0 E
Pagalu = Annobón, *Atl. Oc.* **83** 1 25 S 5 36 E
Pagastikós Kólpos, *Greece* **35** 39 15N 23 0 E
Pagatan, *Indonesia* **56** 3 33 S 115 59 E
Page, *Ariz., U.S.A.* **123** 36 57N 111 27W
Page, *N. Dak., U.S.A.* **120** 47 11N 97 37W
Paglieta, *Italy* **27** 42 10N 14 30 E
Pagny-sur-Moselle, *France* **19** 48 59N 6 0 E
Pago Pago, *Amer. Samoa* **68** 14 16 S 170 43W
Pagosa Springs, *U.S.A.* **123** 37 16N 107 4W
Pagwa River, *Canada* **104** 50 2N 85 14W
Pahala, *U.S.A.* **112** 19 12N 155 25W
Pahang →, *Malaysia* **55** 3 30N 103 9 E
Pahiatua, *N.Z.* **80** 40 27 S 175 50 E
Pahokee, *U.S.A.* **115** 26 50N 80 40W
Pahrump, *U.S.A.* **125** 36 15N 116 0W
Pahute Mesa, *U.S.A.* **124** 37 25N 116 50W
Pai, *Thailand* **54** 19 19N 98 27 E
Paia, *U.S.A.* **112** 20 54N 156 22W
Paicines, *U.S.A.* **124** 36 44N 121 17W
Paide, *U.S.S.R.* **36** 58 57N 25 31 E
Paignton, *U.K.* **13** 50 26N 3 33W
Paiján, *Peru* **136** 7 42 S 79 20W
Päijänne, L., *Finland* **9** 61 30N 25 30 E
Paimbœuf, *France* **18** 47 17N 2 0W
Paimpol, *France* **18** 48 48N 3 4W
Painan, *Indonesia* **56** 1 21 S 100 34 E
Painesville, *U.S.A.* **116** 41 42N 81 18W
Paint Hills = Nouveau Comptoir, *Canada* **104** 53 0N 78 49W
Paint L., *Canada* **111** 55 28N 97 57W
Paint Rock, *U.S.A.* **121** 31 30N 99 56W
Painted Desert, *U.S.A.* **123** 36 0N 111 30W
Paintsville, *U.S.A.* **114** 37 50N 82 50W
País Vasco □, *Spain* **24** 43 0N 2 30W
Paisley, *Canada* **108** 44 18N 81 16W
Paisley, *U.K.* **14** 55 51N 4 27W
Paisley, *U.S.A.* **122** 42 43N 120 40W
Païta, *N. Cal.* **68** 22 8 S 166 22 E
Paita, *Peru* **136** 5 11 S 81 9W
Paiva →, *Portugal* **22** 41 4N 8 16W
Paizhou, *China* **59** 30 12N 113 55 E
Pajares, *Spain* **22** 43 1N 5 46W
Pajares, Puerto de, *Spain* **22** 43 0N 5 46W
Pak Lay, *Laos* **54** 18 15N 101 27 E
Pak Phanang, *Thailand* **55** 8 21N 100 12 E
Pak Sane, *Laos* **54** 18 22N 103 39 E
Pak Song, *Laos* **54** 15 11N 106 14 E
Pak Suong, *Laos* **54** 19 58N 102 15 E
Pakala, *India* **51** 13 29N 79 8 E
Pakaraima Mts., *Guyana* **135** 6 0N 60 0W
Pakenham, *Australia* **74** 38 6 S 145 30 E
Pakenham, *Canada* **106** 45 18N 76 18W
Pakistan ■, *Asia* **47** 30 0N 70 0 E
Pakistan, East = Bangladesh ■, *Asia* **52** 24 0N 90 0 E
Pakkading, *Laos* **54** 18 19N 103 59 E
Pakokku, *Burma* **52** 21 20N 95 0 E
Pakpattan, *Pakistan* **48** 30 25N 73 27 E
Pakrac, *Yugoslavia* **33** 45 27N 17 12 E
Paks, *Hungary* **33** 46 38N 18 55 E
Pakse, *Laos* **54** 15 5N 105 52 E
Paktīā □, *Afghan.* **47** 33 0N 69 15 E
Pakwach, *Uganda* **92** 2 28N 31 27 E
Pala, *Chad* **87** 9 25N 15 5 E
Pala, *U.S.A.* **125** 33 22N 117 5W
Pala, *Zaïre* **92** 6 45 S 29 30 E
Palabek, *Uganda* **92** 3 22N 32 33 E
Palacios, *U.S.A.* **121** 28 44N 96 12W
Palafrugell, *Spain* **24** 41 55N 3 10 E
Palagiano, *Italy* **29** 40 35N 17 0 E
Palagonía, *Italy* **29** 37 20N 14 43 E
Palagruža, *Yugoslavia* **27** 42 24N 16 15 E
Palaiokhóra, *Greece* **35** 35 16N 23 39 E
Palais, Le, *France* **18** 47 20N 3 10W
Palakol, *India* **51** 16 31N 81 46 E
Palam, *India* **50** 19 0N 77 0 E
Palamás, *Greece* **35** 39 26N 22 4 E
Palamós, *Spain* **24** 41 50N 3 10 E
Palampur, *India* **48** 32 10N 76 30 E
Palana, *Australia* **72** 39 45 S 147 55 E
Palana, *U.S.S.R.* **41** 59 10N 159 59 E
Palanan, *Phil.* **57** 17 8N 122 29 E
Palanan Pt., *Phil.* **57** 17 17N 122 30 E
Palandri, *Pakistan* **49** 33 42N 73 40 E
Palangkaraya, *Indonesia* **56** 2 16 S 113 56 E
Palani, *India* **51** 10 30N 77 30 E
Palani Hills, *India* **51** 10 14N 77 33 E
Palanpur, *India* **48** 24 10N 72 25 E
Palapye, *Botswana* **96** 22 30 S 27 7 E
Palar →, *India* **51** 12 27N 80 13 E
Palas, *Pakistan* **49** 35 4N 73 14 E
Palatine, *U.S.A.* **119** 42 7N 88 3W
Palatka, *U.S.A.* **115** 29 40N 81 40W
Palatka, *U.S.S.R.* **41** 60 6N 150 54 E
Palawan, *Phil.* **56** 9 30N 118 30 E
Palayankottai, *India* **51** 8 45N 77 45 E
Palazzo, Pte., *France* **21** 42 28N 8 30 E
Palazzo San Gervásio, *Italy* **29** 40 53N 15 58 E
Palazzolo Acreide, *Italy* **29** 37 4N 14 54 E
Palca, *Chile* **136** 19 7 S 69 9W
Paldiski, *U.S.S.R.* **36** 59 23N 24 9 E
Palel, *India* **52** 24 27N 94 2 E
Paleleh, *Indonesia* **57** 1 10N 121 50 E
Palembang, *Indonesia* **56** 3 0 S 104 50 E
Palen Creek, *Australia* **77** 28 17 S 152 48 E
Palena →, *Chile* **142** 43 50 S 73 50W
Palena, L., *Chile* **142** 43 55 S 71 40W
Palencia, *Spain* **22** 42 1N 4 34W
Palencia □, *Spain* **22** 42 31N 4 33W
Palermo, *Colombia* **134** 2 54N 75 26W
Palermo, *Italy* **28** 38 8N 13 20 E
Palermo, *U.S.A.* **122** 39 30N 121 37W
Palestine, *Asia* **44** 32 0N 35 0 E
Palestine, *U.S.A.* **121** 31 42N 95 35W
Palestrina, *Italy* **28** 41 50N 12 52 E
Paletwa, *Burma* **52** 21 10N 92 50 E
Palghat, *India* **51** 10 46N 76 42 E
Palgrave, Mt., *Australia* **78** 23 22 S 115 58 E
Pali, *India* **48** 25 50N 73 20 E
Palinuro, C., *Italy* **29** 40 1N 15 14 E
Palisade, *U.S.A.* **120** 40 21N 101 10W
Paliseul, *Belgium* **17** 49 54N 5 8 E
Palitana, *India* **48** 21 32N 71 49 E
Palizada, *Mexico* **127** 18 18N 92 8W
Palizzi, *Italy* **29** 37 58N 15 59 E
Palk Bay, *Asia* **51** 9 30N 79 15 E
Palk Strait, *Asia* **51** 10 0N 79 45 E
Palkonda, *India* **50** 18 36N 83 48 E
Palkonda Ra., *India* **51** 13 50N 79 20 E
Palla Road = Dinokwe, *Botswana* **96** 23 29 S 26 37 E
Pallamallawa, *Australia* **77** 29 29 S 150 10 E
Pallanza = Verbánia, *Italy* **26** 45 56N 8 43 E
Pallasovka, *U.S.S.R.* **37** 50 4N 47 0 E
Palleru →, *India* **50** 16 45N 80 2 E
Pallinup, *Australia* **79** 34 0 S 117 55 E
Pallisa, *Uganda* **92** 1 12N 33 43 E
Palliser, C., *N.Z.* **80** 41 37 S 175 14 E
Palliser Bay, *N.Z.* **80** 41 26 S 175 5 E
Pallu, *India* **48** 28 59N 74 14 E
Palm Beach, *U.S.A.* **115** 26 46N 80 0W
Palm Desert, *U.S.A.* **125** 33 43N 116 22W
Palm Is., *Australia* **72** 18 40 S 146 35 E
Palm Springs, *U.S.A.* **125** 33 51N 116 35W
Palma, *Mozam.* **93** 10 46 S 40 29 E
Palma →, *Brazil* **139** 12 33 S 47 52W
Palma, B. de, *Spain* **25** 39 30N 2 39 E
Palma, La, *Canary Is.* **25** 28 40N 17 50W
Palma, La, *Panama* **128** 8 15N 78 0W
Palma, La, *Spain* **23** 37 21N 6 38W
Palma de Mallorca, *Spain* **24** 39 35N 2 39 E
Palma del Río, *Spain* **23** 37 43N 5 17W
Palma di Montechiaro, *Italy* **28** 37 12N 13 46 E
Palma Soriano, *Cuba* **128** 20 15N 76 0W
Palmahim, *Israel* **44** 31 56N 34 44 E
Palmanova, *Italy* **27** 45 54N 13 18 E
Palmares, *Brazil* **138** 8 41 S 35 28W
Palmarito, *Venezuela* **134** 7 37N 70 10W
Palmarola, *Italy* **28** 40 57N 12 50 E
Palmarolle, *Canada* **106** 48 40N 79 12W
Palmas, *Brazil* **141** 26 29 S 52 0W
Palmas, C., *Liberia* **90** 4 27N 7 46W
Pálmas, G. di, *Italy* **28** 39 0N 8 30 E
Palmas de Monte Alto, *Brazil* **139** 14 16 S 43 10W
Palmdale, *U.S.A.* **125** 34 36N 118 7W
Palmeira, *Brazil* **139** 25 25 S 50 0W
Palmeira dos Índios, *Brazil* **138** 9 25 S 36 37W
Palmeirais, *Brazil* **138** 6 0 S 43 0W
Palmeiras →, *Brazil* **139** 12 22 S 47 8W
Palmeirinhas, Pta. das, *Angola* **95** 9 2 S 12 57 E
Palmela, *Portugal* **23** 38 32N 8 57W
Palmelo, *Brazil* **139** 17 20 S 48 27W
Palmer, *U.S.A.* **102** 61 35N 149 10W
Palmer →, *Australia* **72** 15 34 S 142 26 E
Palmer Arch., *Antarctica* **143** 64 15 S 65 0W
Palmer Lake, *U.S.A.* **120** 39 10N 104 52W
Palmer Land, *Antarctica* **143** 73 0 S 60 0W
Palmerston, *Canada* **108** 43 50N 80 51W
Palmerston North, *N.Z.* **81** 40 21 S 175 39 E
Palmerton, *U.S.A.* **117** 40 47N 75 36W
Palmetto, *U.S.A.* **115** 27 33N 82 33W
Palmi, *Italy* **29** 38 21N 15 51 E
Palmira, *Argentina* **140** 32 59 S 68 34W
Palmira, *Colombia* **134** 3 32N 76 16W
Palmyra = Tudmur, *Syria* **46** 34 36N 38 15 E
Palmyra, *Ill., U.S.A.* **118** 39 26N 90 0W
Palmyra, *Mo., U.S.A.* **118** 39 45N 91 30W
Palmyra, *N.Y., U.S.A.* **116** 43 5N 77 18W
Palmyra, *Wis., U.S.A.* **119** 42 52N 88 36W
Palmyra Is., *Pac. Oc.* **67** 5 52N 162 5W
Palo Alto, *U.S.A.* **124** 37 25N 122 8W
Palo del Colle, *Italy* **29** 41 4N 16 43 E
Palo Verde, *U.S.A.* **125** 33 26N 114 45W
Paloma, La, *Chile* **140** 30 35 S 71 0W
Palombara Sabina, *Italy* **27** 42 4N 12 45 E
Palopo, *Indonesia* **57** 3 0 S 120 16 E
Palos, C. de, *Spain* **25** 37 38N 0 40W
Palos Verdes, *U.S.A.* **125** 33 48N 118 23W
Palos Verdes, Pt., *U.S.A.* **125** 33 43N 118 26W
Palouse, *U.S.A.* **122** 46 59N 117 5W
Palpa, *Peru* **136** 14 30 S 75 15W
Palparara, *Australia* **72** 24 47 S 141 28 E
Pålsboda, *Sweden* **11** 59 3N 15 22 E
Palu, *Indonesia* **57** 1 0 S 119 52 E
Palu, *Turkey* **46** 38 45N 40 0 E
Paluan, *Phil.* **57** 13 26N 120 29 E
Palwal, *India* **48** 28 8N 77 19 E
Pama, *Burkina Faso* **91** 11 19N 0 44 E
Pamanukan, *Indonesia* **57** 6 16 S 107 49 E
Pamban I., *India* **51** 9 15N 79 20 E
Pambula, *Australia* **75** 36 55 S 149 53 E
Pamekasan, *Indonesia* **57** 7 10 S 113 28 E
Pamiers, *France* **20** 43 7N 1 39 E
Pamirs, *U.S.S.R.* **40** 37 40N 73 0 E
Pamlico →, *U.S.A.* **115** 35 25N 76 30W
Pamlico Sd., *U.S.A.* **115** 35 20N 76 0W
Pampa, *U.S.A.* **121** 35 35N 100 58W
Pampa, La □, *Argentina* **140** 36 50 S 66 0W
Pampa de Agma, *Argentina* **142** 43 45 S 69 40W
Pampa de las Salinas, *Argentina* **140** 32 1 S 66 58W
Pampa Grande, *Bolivia* **137** 18 5 S 64 6W
Pampa Hermosa, *Peru* **136** 7 7 S 75 4W
Pampanua, *Indonesia* **57** 4 16 S 120 8 E
Pamparato, *Italy* **26** 44 16N 7 54 E
Pampas, *Argentina* **140** 35 0 S 63 0W
Pampas, *Peru* **136** 12 20 S 74 50W
Pampas →, *Peru* **136** 13 24 S 73 12W
Pamplona, *Colombia* **134** 7 23N 72 39W
Pamplona, *Spain* **24** 42 48N 1 38W
Pampoenpoort, *S. Africa* **96** 31 3 S 22 40 E
Pan Xian, *China* **58** 25 46N 104 38 E
Pana, *U.S.A.* **118** 39 25N 89 10W
Panaca, *U.S.A.* **123** 37 51N 114 23W
Panache, L., *Canada* **108** 46 15N 81 20W
Panagyurishte, *Bulgaria* **34** 42 30N 24 15 E
Panaitan, *Indonesia* **57** 6 36 S 105 12 E
Panaji, *India* **51** 15 25N 73 50 E
Panamá, *Panama* **128** 9 0N 79 25W
Panama ■, *Cent. Amer.* **128** 8 48N 79 55W
Panamá, G. de, *Panama* **128** 8 4N 79 20W
Panama Canal, *Panama* **128** 9 10N 79 37W
Panama City, *U.S.A.* **115** 30 10N 85 41W
Panamint Range, *U.S.A.* **125** 36 20N 117 20W
Panamint Ra., *U.S.A.* **123** 36 30N 117 20W
Panamint Springs, *U.S.A.* **125** 36 20N 117 28W
Panão, *Peru* **136** 9 55 S 75 55W
Panare, *Thailand* **55** 6 51N 101 30 E
Panarea, *Italy* **29** 38 38N 15 3 E
Panaro →, *Italy* **26** 44 55N 11 25 E
Panarukan, *Indonesia* **57** 7 42 S 113 56 E
Panay, *Phil.* **57** 11 10N 122 30 E
Panay, G., *Phil.* **57** 11 0N 122 30 E
Pancake Ra., *U.S.A.* **123** 38 30N 116 0W
Pančevo, *Yugoslavia* **33** 44 52N 20 41 E
Pancorbo, Paso, *Spain* **24** 42 32N 3 5W
Pandan, *Phil.* **57** 11 45N 122 10 E
Pandegelang, *Indonesia* **57** 6 25 S 106 0 E
Pandharpur, *India* **50** 17 41N 75 20 E
Pandhurna, *India* **50** 21 36N 78 35 E
Pandilla, *Spain* **24** 41 32N 3 43W
Pando, *Uruguay* **141** 34 44 S 56 0W
Pando □, *Bolivia* **136** 11 20 S 67 40W
Pando, L. = Hope, L., *Australia* **73** 28 24 S 139 18 E
Pandu, *Zaïre* **94** 4 59N 19 16 E
Panevezys, *U.S.S.R.* **36** 55 42N 24 25 E
Panfilov, *U.S.S.R.* **40** 44 10N 80 0 E
Panfilovo, *U.S.S.R.* **37** 50 25N 42 46 E
Panga, *Zaïre* **92** 1 52N 26 18 E
Pangala, *Congo* **94** 4 1 S 13 52 E
Pangalanes, Canal des, *Madag.* **97** 22 48 S 47 50 E
Pangani, *Tanzania* **92** 5 25 S 38 58 E
Pangani □, *Tanzania* **92** 5 25 S 39 0 E
Pangani →, *Tanzania* **92** 5 26 S 38 58 E
Pange Creek, *Australia* **76** 31 45 S 147 8 E
Pangfou = Bengbu, *China* **61** 32 58N 117 20 E
Pangil, *Zaïre* **92** 3 10 S 26 35 E
Pangkah, Tanjung, *Indonesia* **57** 6 51 S 112 33 E
Pangkai, *Burma* **52** 22 40N 98 40 E
Pangkajene, *Indonesia* **57** 4 46 S 119 34 E
Pangkalanbrandan, *Indonesia* **56** 4 1N 98 20 E
Pangkalanbuun, *Indonesia* **56** 2 41 S 111 37 E
Pangkalansusu, *Indonesia* **56** 4 2N 98 13 E
Pangkalpinang, *Indonesia* **56** 2 0 S 106 0 E
Pangkoh, *Indonesia* **56** 3 5 S 114 8 E
Pangnirtung, *Canada* **103** 66 8N 65 54W
Pangrango, *Indonesia* **57** 6 46 S 107 1 E
Pangsau Pass, *Burma* **52** 27 15N 96 10 E
Pangtara, *Burma* **52** 20 57N 96 40 E
Panguipulli, *Chile* **142** 39 38 S 72 20W
Panguitch, *U.S.A.* **123** 37 52N 112 30W
Pangutaran Group, *Phil.* **57** 6 18N 120 34 E
Panhandle, *U.S.A.* **121** 35 23N 101 23W
Pani Mines, *India* **48** 22 29N 73 50 E
Pania-Mutombo, *Zaïre* **92** 5 11 S 23 51 E
Panié, Mt., *N. Cal.* **68** 20 36 S 164 46 E
Panipat, *India* **48** 29 25N 77 2 E

Panitya, *Australia* **74** 35 15 S 141 0 E
Panjal Range, *India* **48** 32 30N 76 50 E
Panjgur, *Pakistan* **47** 27 0N 64 5 E
Panjim = Panaji, *India* **51** 15 25N 73 50 E
Panjinad Barrage, *Pakistan* **47** 29 22N 71 15 E
Panjwai, *Afghan.* **48** 31 26N 65 27 E
Pankshin, *Nigeria* **91** 9 16N 9 25 E
Panmure, *Australia* **74** 38 20 S 142 43 E
Panna, *India* **49** 24 40N 80 15 E
Panna Hills, *India* **49** 24 40N 81 15 E
Panora, *U.S.A.* **118** 41 41N 94 22W
Panorama, *Brazil* **141** 21 21 S 51 51W
Panruti, *India* **51** 11 46N 79 35 E
Panshan, *China* **61** 41 3N 122 2 E
Panshi, *China* **61** 42 58N 126 5 E
Pantar, *Indonesia* **57** 8 28 S 124 10 E
Pantelleria, *Italy* **28** 36 52N 12 0 E
Pantha, *Burma* **52** 23 55N 94 35 E
Pantin Sakan, *Burma* **52** 18 38N 97 33 E
Pantón, *Spain* **22** 42 31N 7 37W
Panton Hill, *Australia* **74** 37 39 S 145 14 E
Pánuco, *Mexico* **127** 22 0N 98 15W
Panyam, *Nigeria* **91** 9 27N 9 8 E
Panyu, *China* **59** 22 51N 113 20 E
Pao →, *Anzoátegui, Venezuela* **135** 8 6N 64 17W
Pao →, *Apure, Venezuela* **134** 8 33N 68 1W
Páola, *Italy* **29** 39 21N 16 2 E
Paola, *U.S.A.* **120** 38 36N 94 50W
Paoli, *U.S.A.* **119** 38 33N 86 28W
Paonia, *U.S.A.* **123** 38 56N 107 37W
Paoting = Baoding, *China* **60** 38 50N 115 28 E
Paot'ou = Baotou, *China* **60** 40 32N 110 2 E
Paoua, *C.A.R.* **94** 7 9N 16 20 E
Pápa, *Hungary* **33** 47 22N 17 30 E
Papagayo →, *Mexico* **127** 16 36N 99 43W
Papagayo, G. de, *Costa Rica* **128** 10 30N 85 50W
Papagni →, *India* **51** 15 35N 77 45 E
Papakura, *N.Z.* **80** 37 4 S 174 59 E
Papantla, *Mexico* **127** 20 30N 97 30W
Papar, *Malaysia* **56** 5 45N 116 0 E
Papara, *Tahiti* **68** 17 45 S 149 21W
Paparoa, *N.Z.* **81** 36 6 S 174 16 E
Paparoa Range, *N.Z.* **81** 42 5 S 171 35 E
Pápas, Ákra, *Greece* **35** 38 13N 21 20 E
Papatoetoe, *N.Z.* **80** 36 59 S 174 51 E
Papeete, *Tahiti* **68** 17 32 S 149 34W
Papenburg, *W. Germany* **30** 53 7N 7 25 E
Papenoo, *Tahiti* **68** 17 30 S 149 25W
Papetoai, *Tahiti* **68** 17 29 S 149 52W
Papien Chiang = Da →, *Vietnam* **54** 21 15N 105 20 E
Papigochic →, *Mexico* **126** 29 9N 109 40W
Papineau-Labelle, Parc Prov., *Canada* **106** 46 10N 75 15W
Papineauville, *Canada* **106** 45 37N 75 1W
Paposo, *Chile* **140** 25 0 S 70 30W
Papua, Gulf of, *Papua N. G.* **69** 9 0 S 144 50 E
Papua New Guinea ■, *Oceania* **69** 8 0 S 145 0 E
Papuča, *Yugoslavia* **27** 44 22N 15 30 E
Papudo, *Chile* **140** 32 29 S 71 27W
Papuk, *Yugoslavia* **33** 45 30N 17 30 E
Papun, *Burma* **52** 18 0N 97 30 E
Pará = Belém, *Brazil* **138** 1 20 S 48 30W
Pará □, *Brazil* **137** 3 20 S 52 0W
Pará □, *Surinam* **135** 5 20N 55 5W
Parábita, *Italy* **29** 40 3N 18 8 E
Paraburdoo, *Australia* **78** 23 14 S 117 32 E
Paracas, Pen., *Peru* **136** 13 53 S 76 20W
Paracatu, *Brazil* **139** 17 10 S 46 50W
Paracatu →, *Brazil* **139** 16 30 S 45 4W
Parachilna, *Australia* **73** 31 10 S 138 21 E
Parachinar, *Pakistan* **48** 33 55N 70 5 E
Paraćin, *Yugoslavia* **33** 43 54N 21 27 E
Paracuru, *Brazil* **138** 3 24 S 39 4W
Parada, Punta, *Peru* **136** 15 22 S 75 11W
Paradas, *Spain* **23** 37 18N 5 29W
Paradela, *Spain* **22** 42 44N 7 37W
Paradip, *India* **50** 20 15N 86 35 E
Paradis, *Canada* **106** 48 15N 76 35W
Paradise, *Calif., U.S.A.* **124** 39 46N 121 37W
Paradise, *Mont., U.S.A.* **122** 47 27N 114 17W
Paradise, *Nev., U.S.A.* **125** 36 4N 115 7W
Paradise →, *Canada* **105** 53 27N 57 19W
Paradise Valley, *U.S.A.* **122** 41 30N 117 28W
Parado, *Indonesia* **57** 8 42 S 118 30 E
Paragould, *U.S.A.* **121** 36 5N 90 30W
Paraguá →, *Bolivia* **137** 13 34 S 61 53W
Paragua →, *Venezuela* **135** 6 55N 62 55W
Paragua, La, *Venezuela* **135** 6 50N 63 20W
Paraguaçu →, *Brazil* **139** 12 45 S 38 54W
Paraguaçu Paulista, *Brazil* **141** 22 22 S 50 35W
Paraguaipoa, *Venezuela* **134** 11 21N 71 57W
Paraguaná, Pen. de, *Venezuela* **134** 12 0N 70 0W
Paraguarí, *Paraguay* **140** 25 36 S 57 0W
Paraguarí □, *Paraguay* **140** 26 0 S 57 10W
Paraguay ■, *S. Amer.* **140** 23 0 S 57 0W
Paraguay →, *Paraguay* **140** 27 18 S 58 38W
Paraíba = João Pessoa, *Brazil* **138** 7 10 S 34 52W
Paraíba □, *Brazil* **138** 7 0 S 36 0W
Paraíba do Sul →, *Brazil* **139** 21 37 S 41 3W
Parainen, *Finland* **9** 60 18N 22 18 E
Paraiso, *Mexico* **127** 18 24N 93 14W
Parakhino Paddubye, *U.S.S.R.* **36** 58 26N 33 10 E
Parakou, *Benin* **91** 9 25N 2 40 E
Paramakkudi, *India* **51** 9 31N 78 39 E
Paramaribo, *Surinam* **135** 5 50N 55 10W
Parambu, *Brazil* **138** 6 13 S 40 43W
Paramillo, Nudo del, *Colombia* **134** 7 4N 75 55W
Paramirim, *Brazil* **139** 13 26 S 42 15W
Paramirim →, *Brazil* **139** 11 34 S 43 18W
Paramithiá, *Greece* **35** 39 30N 20 35 E
Paramushir, Ostrov, *U.S.S.R.* **41** 50 24N 156 0 E
Paran →, *Israel* **44** 30 20N 35 10 E
Paraná, *Argentina* **140** 31 45 S 60 30W
Paranã, *Brazil* **139** 12 30 S 47 48W
Paraná □, *Brazil* **141** 24 30 S 51 0W
Paraná →, *Argentina* **140** 33 43 S 59 15W
Paranaguá, *Brazil* **141** 25 30 S 48 30W
Paranaíba →, *Brazil* **139** 20 6 S 51 4W
Paranapanema →, *Brazil* **141** 22 40 S 53 9W
Paranapiacaba, Serra do, *Brazil* **141** 24 31 S 48 35W
Paranavaí, *Brazil* **141** 23 4 S 52 56W
Parang, *Jolo, Phil.* **57** 5 55N 120 54 E
Parang, *Mindanao, Phil.* **57** 7 23N 124 16 E
Parangaba, *Brazil* **138** 3 45 S 38 33W
Parangippettai, *India* **51** 11 30N 79 38 E
Paraparauma, *N.Z.* **80** 40 57 S 175 3 E
Parapóla, *Greece* **35** 36 55N 23 27 E
Paraspóri, Ákra, *Greece* **35** 35 55N 27 15 E
Paratinga, *Brazil* **139** 12 40 S 43 10W
Paratoo, *Australia* **73** 32 42 S 139 40 E
Parattah, *Australia* **72** 42 22 S 147 23 E
Paraúna, *Brazil* **139** 16 55 S 50 26W
Paray-le-Monial, *France* **21** 46 27N 4 7 E
Parbati →, *India* **48** 25 50N 76 30 E
Parbatipur, *Bangla.* **52** 25 39N 88 55 E
Parbhani, *India* **50** 19 8N 76 52 E
Parchim, *E. Germany* **30** 53 25N 11 50 E
Parczew, *Poland* **32** 51 40N 22 52 E
Pardes Hanna, *Israel* **44** 32 28N 34 57 E
Pardilla, *Spain* **22** 41 33N 3 43W
Pardo →, *Bahia, Brazil* **139** 15 40 S 39 0W
Pardo →, *Mato Grosso, Brazil* **141** 21 46 S 52 9W
Pardo →, *Minas Gerais, Brazil* **139** 15 48 S 44 48W
Pardo →, *São Paulo, Brazil* **139** 20 10 S 48 38W
Pardubice, *Czech.* **32** 50 3N 15 45 E
Pare, *Indonesia* **57** 7 43 S 112 12 E
Pare □, *Tanzania* **92** 4 10 S 38 0 E
Pare Mts., *Tanzania* **92** 4 0 S 37 45 E
Parecis, Serra dos, *Brazil* **137** 13 0 S 60 0W
Paredes de Nava, *Spain* **22** 42 9N 4 42W
Parelhas, *Brazil* **138** 6 41 S 36 39W
Paren, *U.S.S.R.* **41** 62 30N 163 15 E
Parengarenga Harbour, *N.Z.* **80** 34 31 S 173 0 E
Parent, *Canada* **106** 47 55N 74 35W
Parent, L., *Canada* **106** 48 31N 77 1W
Parentis-en-Born, *France* **20** 44 21N 1 4W
Parepare, *Indonesia* **57** 4 0 S 119 40 E
Parfino, *U.S.S.R.* **36** 57 59N 31 34 E
Parham, *Canada* **109** 44 39N 76 43W
Paria, G. de, *Venezuela* **134** 10 20N 62 0W
Paria, Pen. de, *Venezuela* **135** 10 50N 62 30W
Pariaguán, *Venezuela* **135** 8 51N 64 34W
Pariaman, *Indonesia* **56** 0 47 S 100 11 E
Paricatuba, *Brazil* **135** 4 26 S 61 53W
Paricutín, Cerro, *Mexico* **126** 19 28N 102 15W
Parigi, *Java, Indonesia* **57** 7 42 S 108 29 E
Parigi, *Sulawesi, Indonesia* **57** 0 50 S 120 5 E
Parika, *Guyana* **135** 6 50N 58 20W
Parima, Serra, *Brazil* **135** 2 30N 64 0W
Parinari, *Peru* **136** 4 35 S 74 25W
Parîng, *Romania* **34** 45 20N 23 37 E
Parintins, *Brazil* **135** 2 40 S 56 50W
Paris, *Canada* **108** 43 12N 80 25W
Paris, *France* **19** 48 50N 2 20 E
Paris, *Idaho, U.S.A.* **122** 42 13N 111 30W
Paris, *Ill., U.S.A.* **119** 39 36N 87 42W
Paris, *Ky., U.S.A.* **119** 38 12N 84 12W
Paris, *Mo., U.S.A.* **118** 39 29N 92 0W
Paris, *Tenn., U.S.A.* **115** 36 20N 88 20W
Paris, *Tex., U.S.A.* **121** 33 40N 95 30W
Paris, Ville de □, *France* **19** 48 50N 2 20 E
Parish, *U.S.A.* **117** 43 24N 76 9W
Pariti, *Indonesia* **57** 10 15 S 123 45 E
Park, *U.S.A.* **124** 48 45N 122 18W
Park City, *U.S.A.* **122** 40 42N 111 35W
Park Falls, *U.S.A.* **120** 45 58N 90 27W
Park Forest, *U.S.A.* **119** 41 29N 87 40W
Park Range, *U.S.A.* **122** 40 0N 106 30W
Park Rapids, *U.S.A.* **120** 46 56N 95 0W
Park Ridge, *U.S.A.* **119** 42 2N 87 51W
Park River, *U.S.A.* **120** 48 25N 97 43W
Park Rynie, *S. Africa* **97** 30 25 S 30 45 E
Parker, *Ariz., U.S.A.* **125** 34 8N 114 16W
Parker, *S. Dak., U.S.A.* **120** 43 25N 97 7W
Parker Dam, *U.S.A.* **125** 34 13N 114 5W
Parkersburg, *Iowa, U.S.A.* **118** 42 35N 92 47W
Parkersburg, *W. Va., U.S.A.* **114** 39 18N 81 31W
Parkerview, *Canada* **111** 51 21N 103 18W
Parkes, *Australia* **76** 33 9 S 148 11 E
Parkfield, *U.S.A.* **124** 35 54N 120 26W
Parkhill, *Canada* **108** 43 15N 81 38W
Parkland, *U.S.A.* **124** 47 9N 122 26W
Parkside, *Canada* **111** 53 10N 106 33W
Parkston, *U.S.A.* **120** 43 25N 98 0W
Parksville, *Canada* **110** 49 20N 124 21W
Parkville, *Australia* **77** 31 58 S 150 53 E
Parlakimidi, *India* **50** 18 45N 84 5 E
Parli, *India* **50** 18 50N 76 35 E
Parma, *Italy* **26** 44 50N 10 20 E
Parma, *Idaho, U.S.A.* **122** 43 49N 116 59W
Parma, *Ohio, U.S.A.* **116** 41 25N 81 42W
Parma →, *Italy* **26** 44 56N 10 26 E
Parnaguá, *Brazil* **138** 10 10 S 44 38W
Parnaíba, *Piauí, Brazil* **138** 2 54 S 41 47W
Parnaíba, *São Paulo, Brazil* **137** 19 34 S 51 14W
Parnaíba →, *Brazil* **138** 3 0 S 41 50W
Parnamirim, *Brazil* **138** 8 5 S 39 34W
Parnarama, *Brazil* **138** 5 31 S 43 6W
Parnassós, *Greece* **35** 38 35N 22 30 E
Parnassus, *N.Z.* **81** 42 42 S 173 23 E
Párnis, *Greece* **35** 38 14N 23 45 E
Párnon Óros, *Greece* **35** 37 15N 22 45 E
Pärnu, *U.S.S.R.* **36** 58 28N 24 33 E
Parola, *India* **50** 20 47N 75 7 E
Paroo →, *Australia* **73** 31 28 S 143 32 E
Páros, *Greece* **35** 37 5N 25 12 E
Parowan, *U.S.A.* **123** 37 54N 112 56W
Parpaillon, *France* **21** 44 30N 6 40 E
Parral, *Chile* **140** 36 10 S 71 52W
Parramatta, *Australia* **76** 33 48 S 151 1 E
Parras, *Mexico* **126** 25 30N 102 20W
Parrett →, *U.K.* **13** 51 7N 2 58W
Parris I., *U.S.A.* **115** 32 20N 80 30W
Parrsboro, *Canada* **105** 45 30N 64 25W
Parry Is., *Canada* **144** 77 0N 110 0W
Parry Sound, *Canada* **108** 45 20N 80 0W
Parsberg, *W. Germany* **31** 49 10N 11 43 E
Parshall, *U.S.A.* **120** 47 56N 102 11W
Parsnip →, *Canada* **110** 55 10N 123 2W
Parsons, *U.S.A.* **121** 37 20N 95 17W
Parsons Ra., *Australia* **72** 13 30 S 135 15 E
Partabpur, *India* **50** 20 0N 80 42 E
Partanna, *Italy* **28** 37 43N 12 51 E
Parthenay, *France* **18** 46 38N 0 16W
Partinico, *Italy* **28** 38 3N 13 6 E
Partur, *India* **50** 19 40N 76 14 E
Paru →, *Brazil* **135** 1 33 S 52 38W
Parú →, *Venezuela* **134** 4 20N 66 27W
Paru de Oeste →, *Brazil* **135** 1 30N 56 0W
Parucito →, *Venezuela* **134** 5 18N 65 59W
Parur, *India* **51** 10 13N 76 14 E
Paruro, *Peru* **136** 13 45 S 71 50W
Parvān □, *Afghan.* **47** 35 0N 69 0 E
Parvatipuram, *India* **50** 18 50N 83 25 E
Parys, *S. Africa* **96** 26 52 S 27 29 E
Pas-de-Calais □, *France* **19** 50 30N 2 10 E
Pasadena, *Calif., U.S.A.* **125** 34 5N 118 9W
Pasadena, *Tex., U.S.A.* **121** 29 45N 95 14W
Pasaje, *Ecuador* **134** 3 23 S 79 50W
Pasaje →, *Argentina* **140** 25 39 S 63 56W
Pascagoula, *U.S.A.* **121** 30 21N 88 30W
Pascagoula →, *U.S.A.* **121** 30 21N 88 35W
Paşcani, *Romania* **34** 47 14N 26 45 E
Pasco, *U.S.A.* **122** 46 10N 119 0W
Pasco □, *Peru* **136** 10 40 S 75 0W
Pasco, Cerro de, *Peru* **136** 10 45 S 76 10W
Pasewalk, *E. Germany* **30** 53 30N 14 0 E
Pasfield L., *Canada* **111** 58 24N 105 20W
Pasha →, *U.S.S.R.* **36** 60 29N 32 55 E
Pashiwari, *Pakistan* **49** 34 40N 75 10 E
Pashmakli = Smolyan, *Bulgaria* **35** 41 36N 24 38 E
Pasighat, *India* **52** 28 4N 95 21 E
Pasing, *W. Germany* **31** 48 9N 11 27 E
Pasirian, *Indonesia* **57** 8 13 S 113 8 E
Pasley, C., *Australia* **79** 33 52 S 123 35 E
Pašman, *Yugoslavia* **27** 43 58N 15 20 E
Pasni, *Pakistan* **47** 25 15N 63 27 E
Paso Cantinela, *Mexico* **125** 32 33N 115 47W
Paso de Indios, *Argentina* **142** 43 55 S 69 0W
Paso de los Libres, *Argentina* **140** 29 44 S 57 10W
Paso de los Toros, *Uruguay* **140** 32 45 S 56 30W
Paso Flores, *Argentina* **142** 40 35 S 70 38W
Paso Robles, *U.S.A.* **123** 35 40N 120 45W
Pasorapa, *Bolivia* **137** 18 16 S 64 37W
Paspébiac, *Canada* **105** 48 3N 65 17W
Pasrur, *Pakistan* **48** 32 16N 74 43 E
Passage West, *Ireland* **15** 51 52N 8 20W
Passaic, *U.S.A.* **117** 40 50N 74 8W
Passau, *W. Germany* **31** 48 34N 13 27 E
Passendale, *Belgium* **17** 50 54N 3 2 E
Passero, C., *Italy* **29** 36 42N 15 8 E
Passo Fundo, *Brazil* **141** 28 10 S 52 20W
Passos, *Brazil* **139** 20 45 S 46 37W
Passow, *E. Germany* **30** 53 13N 14 10 E
Passy, *France* **21** 45 55N 6 41 E
Pastaza □, *Ecuador* **134** 2 0 S 77 0W
Pastaza →, *Peru* **134** 4 50 S 76 52W
Pastęk, *Poland* **32** 54 3N 19 41 E
Pasto, *Colombia* **134** 1 13N 77 17W
Pastos Bons, *Brazil* **138** 6 36 S 44 5W
Pastrana, *Spain* **24** 40 27N 2 53W
Pasuruan, *Indonesia* **57** 7 40 S 112 44 E
Patagonia, *Argentina* **142** 45 0 S 69 0W
Patagonia, *U.S.A.* **123** 31 35N 110 45W
Patan, *Gujarat, India* **50** 17 22N 73 57 E
Patan, *Maharashtra, India* **48** 23 54N 72 14 E
Patani, *Indonesia* **57** 0 20N 128 50 E
Pataudi, *India* **48** 28 18N 76 48 E
Patay, *France* **19** 48 2N 1 40 E
Patchewollock, *Australia* **74** 35 22 S 142 12 E
Patchogue, *U.S.A.* **117** 40 46N 73 1W
Patea, *N.Z.* **80** 39 45 S 174 30 E
Pategi, *Nigeria* **91** 8 50N 5 45 E
Patensie, *S. Africa* **96** 33 46 S 24 49 E
Paternò, *Italy* **29** 37 34N 14 53 E
Pateros, *U.S.A.* **122** 48 4N 119 58W
Paterson, *Australia* **76** 32 35 S 151 36 E
Paterson, *U.S.A.* **117** 40 55N 74 10W
Paterson, C., *Australia* **74** 38 41 S 145 37 E
Paterson Inlet, *N.Z.* **81** 46 56 S 168 12 E
Paterson Ra., *Australia* **78** 21 45 S 122 10 E
Paterswolde, *Neths.* **16** 53 9N 6 34 E
Pathankot, *India* **48** 32 18N 75 45 E
Patharghata, *Bangla.* **52** 22 2N 89 58 E
Pathfinder Res., *U.S.A.* **122** 42 30N 107 0W
Pathiu, *Thailand* **55** 10 42N 99 19 E
Pathum Thani, *Thailand* **54** 14 1N 100 32 E
Pati, *Indonesia* **57** 6 45 S 111 1 E
Pati Pt., *Guam* **68** 13 40N 144 50 E
Patía, *Colombia* **134** 2 4N 77 4W
Patía →, *Colombia* **134** 2 13N 78 40W
Patiala, *India* **48** 30 23N 76 26 E
Patine Kouka, *Senegal* **90** 12 45N 13 45W
Pativilca, *Peru* **136** 10 42 S 77 48W
Patkai Bum, *India* **52** 27 0N 95 30 E
Pátmos, *Greece* **35** 37 21N 26 36 E
Patna, *India* **49** 25 35N 85 12 E
Patonga, *Uganda* **92** 2 45N 33 15 E
Patos, *Brazil* **138** 6 55 S 37 16W
Patos, L. dos, *Brazil* **141** 31 20 S 51 0W
Patos de Minas, *Brazil* **139** 18 35 S 46 32W
Patquía, *Argentina* **140** 30 2 S 66 55W
Pátrai, *Greece* **35** 38 14N 21 47 E
Pátraikós, Kólpos, *Greece* **35** 38 17N 21 30 E
Patricio Lynch, I., *Chile* **142** 48 35 S 75 30W
Patrie, La, *Canada* **107** 45 24N 71 15W
Patrocínio, *Brazil* **139** 18 57 S 47 0W
Patta, *Kenya* **92** 2 10 S 41 0 E
Pattada, *Italy* **28** 40 35N 9 7 E
Pattanapuram, *India* **51** 9 6N 76 50 E
Pattani, *Thailand* **55** 6 48N 101 15 E
Patten, *U.S.A.* **105** 45 59N 68 28W
Patterson, *Calif., U.S.A.* **124** 37 30N 121 9W
Patterson, *La., U.S.A.* **121** 29 44N 91 20W
Patterson, Mt., *U.S.A.* **124** 38 29N 119 20W
Patteson, Passage, *Vanuatu* **68** 15 26 S 168 12 E
Patti, *India* **48** 31 17N 74 54 E
Patti, *Italy* **29** 38 8N 14 57 E
Pattoki, *Pakistan* **48** 31 5N 73 52 E
Patton, *U.S.A.* **116** 40 38N 78 40W
Pattonsburg, *U.S.A.* **118** 40 3N 94 8W
Pattukkattai, *India* **51** 10 25N 79 20 E
Patu, *Brazil* **138** 6 6 S 37 38W
Patuakhali, *Bangla.* **52** 22 20N 90 25 E
Patuca →, *Honduras* **128** 15 50N 84 18W
Patuca, Punta, *Honduras* **128** 15 49N 84 14W
Pâturages, *Belgium* **17** 50 25N 3 52 E
Pátzcuaro, *Mexico* **126** 19 30N 101 40W
Pau, *France* **20** 43 19N 0 25W
Pau, Gave de →, *France* **20** 43 33N 1 12W
Pau d' Arco, *Brazil* **138** 7 30 S 49 22W
Pau dos Ferros, *Brazil* **138** 6 7 S 38 10W
Paucartambo, *Peru* **136** 13 19 S 71 35W
Pauillac, *France* **20** 45 11N 0 46W
Pauini, *Brazil* **136** 7 40 S 66 58W
Pauini →, *Brazil* **135** 1 42 S 62 50W
Pauk, *Burma* **52** 21 27N 94 30 E
Paul I., *Canada* **105** 56 30N 61 20W
Paul Isnard, *Fr. Guiana* **135** 4 47N 54 1W
Paul-Sauvé, L., *Canada* **106** 50 15N 78 20W
Paulding, *U.S.A.* **119** 41 8N 84 35W
Paulhan, *France* **20** 43 33N 3 28 E
Paulis = Isiro, *Zaïre* **92** 2 53N 27 40 E
Paulista, *Brazil* **138** 7 57 S 34 53W
Paulistana, *Brazil* **138** 8 9 S 41 9W
Paullina, *U.S.A.* **120** 42 55N 95 40W
Paulo Afonso, *Brazil* **138** 9 21 S 38 15W
Paulo de Faria, *Brazil* **139** 20 2 S 49 24W
Paulpietersburg, *S. Africa* **97** 27 23 S 30 50 E
Pauls Valley, *U.S.A.* **121** 34 40N 97 17W
Pauma Valley, *U.S.A.* **125** 33 16N 116 58W
Paungde, *Burma* **52** 18 29N 95 30 E
Pauni, *India* **50** 20 48N 79 40 E
Pausa, *Peru* **136** 15 16 S 73 22W
Pauto →, *Colombia* **134** 5 9N 70 55W
Pavelets, *U.S.S.R.* **37** 53 49N 39 14 E
Pavia, *Italy* **26** 45 10N 9 10 E
Pavlikeni, *Bulgaria* **34** 43 14N 25 20 E
Pavlodar, *U.S.S.R.* **40** 52 33N 77 0 E
Pavlograd, *U.S.S.R.* **38** 48 30N 35 52 E

Pavlovo, *Gorkiy, U.S.S.R.* **37** 55 58N 43 5 E
Pavlovo, *Yakut A.S.S.R., U.S.S.R.* **41** 63 5N 115 25 E
Pavlovsk, *U.S.S.R.* **37** 50 26N 40 5 E
Pavlovskaya, *U.S.S.R.* **39** 46 17N 39 47 E
Pavlovskiy-Posad, *U.S.S.R.* **37** 55 47N 38 42 E
Pavullo nel Frignano, *Italy* **26** 44 20N 10 50 E
Pavuvu, *Solomon Is.* **68** 9 4 S 159 8 E
Paw Paw, *U.S.A.* **119** 42 13N 85 53W
Pawahku, *Burma* **52** 26 11N 98 40 E
Pawhuska, *U.S.A.* **121** 36 40N 96 25W
Pawling, *U.S.A.* **117** 41 35N 73 37W
Pawnee, *Ill., U.S.A.* **118** 39 35N 89 35W
Pawnee, *Okla., U.S.A.* **121** 36 24N 96 50W
Pawnee City, *U.S.A.* **120** 40 8N 96 10W
Pawpaw, *U.S.A.* **118** 41 41N 88 59W
Pawtucket, *U.S.A.* **117** 41 51N 71 22W
Paxoí, *Greece* **35** 39 14N 20 12 E
Paxton, *Ill., U.S.A.* **119** 40 25N 88 7W
Paxton, *Nebr., U.S.A.* **120** 41 12N 101 27W
Payakumbuh, *Indonesia* **56** 0 20 S 100 35 E
Payerne, *Switz.* **31** 46 49N 6 56 E
Payette, *U.S.A.* **122** 44 0N 117 0W
Paymogo, *Spain* **23** 37 44N 7 21W
Payne, *U.S.A.* **119** 41 5N 84 44W
Payne Bay = Bellin, *Canada* **103** 60 0N 70 0W
Payne L., *Canada* **103** 59 30N 74 30W
Paynes Find, *Australia* **79** 29 15 S 117 42 E
Paynesville, *Australia* **75** 37 55 S 147 43 E
Paynesville, *Liberia* **90** 6 20N 10 45W
Paynesville, *U.S.A.* **120** 45 21N 94 44W
Paysandú, *Uruguay* **140** 32 19 S 58 8W
Payson, *Ariz., U.S.A.* **123** 34 17N 111 15W
Payson, *Utah, U.S.A.* **122** 40 8N 111 41W
Paz →, *Guatemala* **128** 13 44N 90 10W
Paz, B. de la, *Mexico* **126** 24 15N 110 25W
Paz, La, *Entre Ríos, Argentina* **140** 30 50 S 59 45W
Paz, La, *San Luis, Argentina* **140** 33 30 S 67 20W
Paz, La, *Bolivia* **136** 16 20 S 68 10W
Paz, La, *Honduras* **128** 14 20N 87 47W
Paz, La, *Mexico* **126** 24 10N 110 20W
Paz, La □, *Bolivia* **136** 15 30 S 68 0W
Paz Centro, La, *Nic.* **128** 12 20N 86 41W
Pazar, *Turkey* **46** 41 10N 40 50 E
Pazardzhik, *Bulgaria* **34** 42 12N 24 20 E
Pazin, *Yugoslavia* **27** 45 14N 13 56 E
Pazña, *Bolivia* **136** 18 36 S 66 55W
Pčinja →, *Yugoslavia* **35** 41 50N 21 45 E
Pe Ell, *U.S.A.* **124** 46 30N 123 18W
Peabody, *U.S.A.* **117** 42 31N 70 56W
Peace →, *Canada* **110** 59 0N 111 25W
Peace Point, *Canada* **110** 59 7N 112 27W
Peace River, *Canada* **110** 56 15N 117 18W
Peach Springs, *U.S.A.* **123** 35 36N 113 30W
Peak, The, *U.K.* **12** 53 24N 1 53W
Peak Downs, *Australia* **72** 22 14 S 148 0 E
Peak Downs Mine, *Australia* **72** 22 17 S 148 11 E
Peak Hill, *N.S.W., Australia* **76** 32 47 S 148 11 E
Peak Hill, *W. Austral., Australia* **79** 25 35 S 118 43 E
Peak Range, *Australia* **72** 22 50 S 148 20 E
Peake, *Australia* **73** 35 25 S 140 0 E
Peake Cr. →, *Australia* **73** 28 2 S 136 7 E
Peale Mt., *U.S.A.* **123** 38 25N 109 12W
Pearblossom, *U.S.A.* **125** 34 30N 117 55W
Pearl, *U.S.A.* **118** 39 28N 90 38W
Pearl →, *U.S.A.* **121** 30 23N 89 45W
Pearl Banks, *Sri Lanka* **51** 8 45N 79 45 E
Pearl City, *Hawaii, U.S.A.* **112** 21 24N 158 0W
Pearl City, *Ill., U.S.A.* **118** 42 16N 89 50W
Pearsall, *U.S.A.* **121** 28 55N 99 8W
Pearse I., *Canada* **110** 54 52N 130 14W
Peary Land, *Greenland* **144** 82 40N 33 0W
Pease →, *U.S.A.* **121** 34 12N 99 7W
Pebane, *Mozam.* **93** 17 10 S 38 8 E
Pebas, *Peru* **134** 3 10 S 71 46W
Pebble, I., *Falk. Is.* **142** 51 20 S 59 40W
Pebble Beach, *U.S.A.* **124** 36 34N 121 57W
Peč, *Yugoslavia* **33** 42 40N 20 17 E
Peçanha, *Brazil* **139** 18 33 S 42 34W
Pecatonica, *U.S.A.* **118** 42 19N 89 22W
Pecatonica →, *U.S.A.* **118** 42 26N 89 17W
Péccioli, *Italy* **26** 43 32N 10 43 E
Pechea, *Romania* **34** 45 36N 27 49 E
Pechenezhin, *U.S.S.R.* **38** 48 30N 24 48 E
Pechenga, *U.S.S.R.* **40** 69 30N 31 25 E
Pechiguera, Pta., *Canary Is.* **25** 28 51N 13 53W
Pechnezhskoye Vdkhr., *U.S.S.R.* **37** 50 0N 37 10 E
Pechora →, *U.S.S.R.* **40** 68 13N 54 15 E
Pechorskaya Guba, *U.S.S.R.* **40** 68 40N 54 0 E
Pechory, *U.S.S.R.* **36** 57 48N 27 40 E
Pecica, *Romania* **34** 46 10N 21 3 E
Pečka, *Yugoslavia* **33** 44 18N 19 33 E
Pécora, C., *Italy* **28** 39 28N 8 23 E
Pecos, *U.S.A.* **121** 31 25N 103 35W
Pecos →, *U.S.A.* **121** 29 42N 102 30W
Pécs, *Hungary* **33** 46 5N 18 15 E
Peddapalli, *India* **50** 18 40N 79 24 E
Peddapuram, *India* **50** 17 6N 82 8 E
Pedder, L., *Australia* **72** 42 55 S 146 10 E
Peddie, *S. Africa* **97** 33 14 S 27 7 E
Pédernales, *Dom. Rep.* **129** 18 2N 71 44W
Pedirka, *Australia* **73** 26 40 S 135 14 E
Pedra Azul, *Brazil* **139** 16 2 S 41 17W
Pedra Grande, Recifes de, *Brazil* **139** 17 45 S 38 58W
Pedras Negras, *Brazil* **137** 12 51 S 62 54W
Pedreiras, *Brazil* **138** 4 32 S 44 40W
Pedrera, La, *Colombia* **134** 1 18 S 69 43W
Pedro Afonso, *Brazil* **138** 9 0 S 48 10W
Pedro Cays, *Jamaica* **128** 17 5N 77 48W
Pedro Chico, *Colombia* **134** 1 4N 70 25W
Pedro de Valdivia, *Chile* **140** 22 55 S 69 38W
Pedro Juan Caballero, *Paraguay* **141** 22 30 S 55 40W
Pedro Muñoz, *Spain* **25** 39 25N 2 56W
Pedrógão Grande, *Portugal* **22** 39 55N 8 9W
Peduyim, *Israel* **44** 31 20N 34 37 E
Peebinga, *Australia* **73** 34 52 S 140 57 E
Peebles, *U.K.* **14** 55 40N 3 12W
Peebles, *U.S.A.* **119** 38 57N 83 23W
Peechelba, *Australia* **75** 36 12 S 146 15 E
Peekskill, *U.S.A.* **117** 41 18N 73 57W
Peel, *Australia* **76** 33 20 S 149 38 E
Peel, *I. of Man* **12** 54 14N 4 40W
Peel →, *Australia* **77** 30 50 S 150 29 E
Peel →, *Canada* **102** 67 0N 135 0W
Peelwood, *Australia* **76** 34 7 S 149 27 E
Peene →, *E. Germany* **30** 54 9N 13 46 E
Peera Peera Poolanna L., *Australia* **73** 26 30 S 138 0 E
Peers, *Canada* **110** 53 40N 116 0W
Pegasus Bay, *N.Z.* **81** 43 20 S 173 10 E
Pegnitz, *W. Germany* **31** 49 45N 11 33 E
Pegnitz →, *W. Germany* **31** 49 29N 10 59 E
Pego, *Spain* **25** 38 51N 0 8W
Pegu, *Burma* **52** 17 20N 96 29 E
Pegu Yoma, *Burma* **52** 19 0N 96 0 E
Pehuajó, *Argentina* **140** 35 45 S 62 0W
Pei Xian, *China* **60** 34 44N 116 55 E
Peine, *Chile* **140** 23 45 S 68 8W
Peine, *W. Germany* **30** 52 19N 10 12 E
Peip'ing = Beijing, *China* **60** 39 55N 116 20 E
Peiss, *W. Germany* **31** 47 58N 11 47 E
Peissenberg, *W. Germany* **31** 47 48N 11 4 E
Peitz, *E. Germany* **30** 51 50N 14 23 E
Peixe, *Brazil* **139** 12 0 S 48 40W
Peixe →, *Brazil* **139** 21 31 S 51 58W
Peixoto de Azeredo →, *Brazil* **137** 10 6 S 55 31W
Peize, *Neths.* **16** 53 9N 6 30 E
Pek →, *Yugoslavia* **33** 44 45N 21 29 E
Pekalongan, *Indonesia* **57** 6 53 S 109 40 E
Pekan, *Malaysia* **55** 3 30N 103 25 E
Pekanbaru, *Indonesia* **56** 0 30N 101 15 E
Pekin, *U.S.A.* **118** 40 35N 89 40W
Peking = Beijing, *China* **60** 39 55N 116 20 E
Pelabuhan Kelang, *Malaysia* **55** 3 0N 101 23 E
Pelabuhan Ratu, Teluk, *Indonesia* **57** 7 5 S 106 30 E
Pelabuhanratu, *Indonesia* **57** 7 0 S 106 32 E
Pélagos, *Greece* **35** 39 17N 24 4 E
Pelaihari, *Indonesia* **56** 3 55 S 114 45 E
Pelat, Mt., *France* **21** 44 16N 6 42 E
Peleaga, *Romania* **34** 45 22N 22 55 E
Pelechuco, *Bolivia* **136** 14 48 S 69 4W
Pelée, Mt., *Martinique* **129** 14 48N 61 0W
Pelee, Pt., *Canada* **108** 41 54N 82 31W
Pelee I., *Canada* **108** 41 47N 82 40W
Pelejo, *Peru* **136** 6 10 S 75 49W
Pelekech, *Kenya* **92** 3 52N 35 8 E
Peleng, *Indonesia* **57** 1 20 S 123 30 E
Pelham, *U.S.A.* **115** 31 5N 84 6W
Pelhřimov, *Czech.* **32** 49 24N 15 12 E
Pelican L., *Canada* **111** 52 28N 100 20W
Pelican Narrows, *Canada* **111** 55 10N 102 56W
Pelican Rapids, *Canada* **111** 52 45N 100 42W
Pelkosenniemi, *Finland* **8** 67 6N 27 28 E
Pella, *S. Africa* **96** 29 1 S 19 6 E
Pella, *U.S.A.* **118** 41 30N 93 0W
Péllaro, *Italy* **29** 38 1N 15 40 E
Pelletier Sta., *Canada* **107** 47 33N 69 26W
Pellworm, *W. Germany* **30** 54 30N 8 40 E
Pelly →, *Canada* **102** 62 47N 137 19W
Pelly Bay, *Canada* **103** 68 38N 89 50W
Pelly L., *Canada* **102** 66 0N 102 0W
Peloponnese = Pelopónnisos □, *Greece* **35** 37 10N 22 0 E
Pelopónnisos □, *Greece* **35** 37 10N 22 0 E
Peloritani, Monti, *Italy* **29** 38 2N 15 25 E
Peloro, C., *Italy* **29** 38 15N 15 40 E
Pelorus Sound, *N.Z.* **81** 40 59 S 173 59 E
Pelotas, *Brazil* **141** 31 42 S 52 23W
Pelvoux, Massif de, *France* **21** 44 52N 6 20 E
Pemalang, *Indonesia* **57** 6 53 S 109 23 E
Pematangsiantar, *Indonesia* **56** 2 57N 99 5 E
Pemba, *Mozam.* **93** 12 58 S 40 30 E
Pemba, *Zambia* **93** 16 30 S 27 28 E
Pemba Channel, *Tanzania* **92** 5 0 S 39 37 E
Pemba I., *Tanzania* **92** 5 0 S 39 45 E
Pemberton, *Australia* **79** 34 30 S 116 0 E
Pemberton, *Canada* **110** 50 25N 122 50W
Pembina, *U.S.A.* **111** 48 58N 97 15W
Pembina →, *U.S.A.* **111** 49 0N 98 12W
Pembine, *U.S.A.* **114** 45 38N 87 59W
Pembino, *U.S.A.* **120** 48 58N 97 15W
Pembroke, *Canada* **109** 45 50N 77 7W
Pembroke, *U.K.* **13** 51 41N 4 57W
Pembroke, *U.S.A.* **115** 32 5N 81 32W
Pen-y-Ghent, *U.K.* **12** 54 10N 2 15W
Peña, Sierra de la, *Spain* **24** 42 32N 0 45W
Peña de Francia, Sierra de, *Spain* **22** 40 32N 6 10W
Penafiel, *Portugal* **22** 41 12N 8 17W
Peñafiel, *Spain* **22** 41 35N 4 7W
Peñaflor, *Spain* **23** 37 43N 5 21W
Peñalara, Pico, *Spain* **22** 40 51N 3 57W
Penalva, *Brazil* **138** 3 18 S 45 10W
Penamacôr, *Portugal* **22** 40 10N 7 10W
Penang = Pinang, *Malaysia* **55** 5 25N 100 15 E
Penápolis, *Brazil* **141** 21 30 S 50 0W
Peñaranda de Bracamonte, *Spain* **22** 40 53N 5 13W
Peñarroya-Pueblonuevo, *Spain* **23** 38 19N 5 16W
Peñas, C. de, *Spain* **22** 43 42N 5 52W
Penas, G. de, *Chile* **142** 47 0 S 75 0W
Peñas, Pta., *Venezuela* **135** 11 17N 62 0W
Peñas de San Pedro, *Spain* **25** 38 44N 2 0W
Peñas del Chache, *Canary Is.* **25** 29 6N 13 33W
Peñausende, *Spain* **22** 41 17N 5 52W
Pench'i = Benxi, *China* **61** 41 20N 123 48 E
Pend Oreille →, *U.S.A.* **122** 49 4N 117 37W
Pend Oreille, L., *U.S.A.* **122** 48 0N 116 30W
Pendembu, *S. Leone* **90** 9 7N 12 14W
Pendências, *Brazil* **138** 5 15 S 36 43W
Pender B., *Australia* **78** 16 45 S 122 42 E
Pendleton, *Calif., U.S.A.* **125** 33 16N 117 23W
Pendleton, *Ind., U.S.A.* **119** 40 0N 85 45W
Pendleton, *Oreg., U.S.A.* **122** 45 35N 118 50W
Penedo, *Brazil* **138** 10 15 S 36 36W
Penetanguishene, *Canada* **108** 44 50N 79 55W
Peng Xian, *China* **58** 31 4N 103 32 E
Pengalengan, *Indonesia* **57** 7 9 S 107 30 E
Penge, *Kasai Or., Zaïre* **92** 5 30 S 24 33 E
Penge, *Kivu, Zaïre* **92** 4 27 S 28 25 E
Penglai, *China* **61** 37 48N 120 42 E
Pengshui, *China* **58** 29 17N 108 12 E
Penguin, *Australia* **72** 41 8 S 146 6 E
Pengxi, *China* **58** 30 44N 105 45 E
Pengze, *China* **59** 29 52N 116 32 E
Penhalonga, *Zimb.* **93** 18 52 S 32 40 E
Peniche, *Portugal* **23** 39 19N 9 22W
Penicuik, *U.K.* **14** 55 50N 3 14W
Penida, *Indonesia* **56** 8 45 S 115 30 E
Peninsular Malaysia □, *Malaysia* **55** 4 0N 102 0 E
Peñíscola, *Spain* **24** 40 22N 0 24 E
Penitente, Serra dos, *Brazil* **138** 8 45 S 46 20W
Penmarch, *France* **18** 47 49N 4 21W
Penmarch, Pte. de, *France* **18** 47 48N 4 22W
Penn Hills, *U.S.A.* **116** 40 28N 79 52W
Penn Yan, *U.S.A.* **116** 42 39N 77 7W
Pennabilli, *Italy* **27** 43 50N 12 17 E
Pennant, *Canada* **111** 50 32N 108 14W
Penne, *Italy* **27** 42 28N 13 56 E
Penner →, *India* **51** 14 35N 80 10 E
Pennine, Alpi, *Alps* **26** 46 4N 7 30 E
Pennines, *U.K.* **12** 54 50N 2 20W
Pennington, *U.S.A.* **124** 39 15N 121 47W
Pennino, Mte., *Italy* **27** 43 6N 12 54 E
Pennsylvania □, *U.S.A.* **114** 40 50N 78 0W
Pennville, *U.S.A.* **119** 40 30N 85 9W
Penny, *Canada* **110** 53 51N 121 20W
Peno, *U.S.S.R.* **36** 57 2N 32 49 E
Penola, *Australia* **73** 37 25 S 140 21 E
Penonomé, *Panama* **128** 8 31N 80 21W
Penot, Mt., *Vanuatu* **68** 16 20 S 167 31 E
Penrhyn Is., *Cook Is.* **67** 9 0 S 158 30W
Penrith, *Australia* **76** 33 43 S 150 38 E
Penrith, *U.K.* **12** 54 40N 2 45W
Pensacola, *U.S.A.* **115** 30 30N 87 10W
Pensacola Mts., *Antarctica* **143** 84 0 S 40 0W
Pense, *Canada* **111** 50 25N 104 59W
Penshurst, *Australia* **74** 37 49 S 142 20 E
Pentecost = Pentecôte, *Vanuatu* **68** 15 42 S 168 10 E
Pentecoste, *Brazil* **138** 3 48 S 39 17W
Pentecôte, *Vanuatu* **68** 15 42 S 168 10 E
Penticton, *Canada* **110** 49 30N 119 38W
Pentland, *Australia* **72** 20 32 S 145 25 E
Pentland Firth, *U.K.* **14** 58 43N 3 10W
Pentland Hills, *U.K.* **14** 55 48N 3 25W
Penukonda, *India* **51** 14 5N 77 38 E
Penylan L., *Canada* **111** 61 50N 106 20W
Penza, *U.S.S.R.* **37** 53 15N 45 5 E
Penzance, *U.K.* **13** 50 7N 5 32W
Penzberg, *W. Germany* **31** 47 46N 11 23 E
Penzhino, *U.S.S.R.* **41** 63 30N 167 55 E
Penzhinskaya Guba, *U.S.S.R.* **41** 61 30N 163 0 E
Penzlin, *E. Germany* **30** 53 32N 13 6 E
Peoria, *Ariz., U.S.A.* **123** 33 40N 112 15W
Peoria, *Ill., U.S.A.* **118** 40 40N 89 40W
Peoria Heights, *U.S.A.* **118** 40 45N 89 35W
Peotone, *U.S.A.* **119** 41 20N 87 48W
Pepingen, *Belgium* **17** 50 46N 4 10 E
Pepinster, *Belgium* **17** 50 34N 5 47 E
Pera Hd., *Australia* **72** 12 55 S 141 37 E
Perabumilih, *Indonesia* **56** 3 27 S 104 15 E
Perakhóra, *Greece* **35** 38 2N 22 56 E
Perales de Alfambra, *Spain* **24** 40 38N 1 0W
Perales del Puerto, *Spain* **22** 40 10N 6 40W
Peralta, *Spain* **24** 42 21N 1 49W
Pérama, *Greece* **35** 35 20N 24 40 E
Percé, *Canada* **105** 48 31N 64 13W
Perche, *France* **18** 48 31N 1 1 E
Perche, Collines du, *France* **18** 48 30N 0 40 E
Percival Lakes, *Australia* **78** 21 25 S 125 0 E
Percy, *France* **18** 48 55N 1 11W
Percy, *U.S.A.* **118** 38 5N 89 41W
Percy Is., *Australia* **72** 21 39 S 150 16 E
Perdido →, *Argentina* **142** 42 55 S 67 0W
Perdido, Mte., *Spain* **20** 42 40N 0 5 E
Perdu, Mt. = Perdido, Mte., *Spain* **20** 42 40N 0 5 E
Pereira, *Colombia* **134** 4 49N 75 43W
Pereira Barreto, *Brazil* **139** 20 38 S 51 7W
Perekerten, *Australia* **74** 34 55 S 143 40 E
Perekop, *U.S.S.R.* **38** 46 10N 33 42 E
Perené →, *Peru* **136** 11 9 S 74 14W
Perenjori, *Australia* **79** 29 26 S 116 16 E
Pereslavi-Zalesskiy, *U.S.S.R.* **37** 56 45N 38 50 E
Pereyaslav Khmelnitskiy, *U.S.S.R.* **36** 50 3N 31 28 E
Pérez, I., *Mexico* **127** 22 24N 89 42W
Pergamino, *Argentina* **140** 33 52 S 60 30W
Pérgine Valsugano, *Italy* **27** 46 4N 11 15 E
Pérgola, *Italy* **27** 43 35N 12 50 E
Perham, *U.S.A.* **120** 46 36N 95 36W
Perhentian, Kepulauan, *Malaysia* **55** 5 54N 102 42 E
Periam, *Romania* **34** 46 2N 20 59 E
Péribonca →, *Canada* **107** 48 45N 72 5W
Péribonca, L., *Canada* **107** 50 1N 71 10W
Péribonka, *Canada* **107** 48 46N 72 3W
Perico, *Argentina* **140** 24 20 S 65 5W
Pericos, *Mexico* **126** 25 3N 107 42W
Périers, *France* **18** 49 11N 1 25W
Périgord, *France* **20** 45 0N 0 40 E
Périgueux, *France* **20** 45 10N 0 42 E
Perijá, Sierra de, *Colombia* **134** 9 30N 73 3W
Peristéra, *Greece* **35** 39 15N 23 58 E
Perito Moreno, *Argentina* **142** 46 36 S 70 56W
Peritoró, *Brazil* **138** 4 20 S 44 18W
Periyakulam, *India* **51** 10 5N 77 30 E
Periyar →, *India* **51** 10 15N 76 10 E
Periyar, L., *India* **51** 9 25N 77 10 E
Perković, *Yugoslavia* **27** 43 41N 16 10 E
Perlas, Arch. de las, *Panama* **128** 8 41N 79 7W
Perlas, Punta de, *Nic.* **128** 12 30N 83 30W
Perleberg, *E. Germany* **30** 53 5N 11 50 E
Perlevka, *U.S.S.R.* **37** 51 48N 38 57 E
Perm, *U.S.S.R.* **40** 58 0N 57 10 E
Pernambuco = Recife, *Brazil* **138** 8 0 S 35 0W
Pernambuco □, *Brazil* **138** 8 0 S 37 0W
Pernatty Lagoon, *Australia* **73** 31 30 S 137 12 E
Pernik, *Bulgaria* **34** 42 35N 23 2 E
Peron, C., *Australia* **79** 25 30 S 113 30 E
Peron Is., *Australia* **78** 13 9 S 130 4 E
Peron Pen., *Australia* **79** 26 0 S 113 10 E
Péronne, *France* **19** 49 55N 2 57 E
Péronnes, *Belgium* **17** 50 27N 4 9 E
Perosa Argentina, *Italy* **26** 44 57N 7 11 E
Perouse Str., La, *Asia* **66** 45 40N 142 0 E
Perow, *Canada* **110** 54 35N 126 10W
Perpendicular Pt., *Australia* **77** 31 37 S 152 52 E
Perpignan, *France* **20** 42 42N 2 53 E
Perris, *U.S.A.* **125** 33 47N 117 14W
Perros-Guirec, *France* **18** 48 49N 3 28W
Perry, *Fla., U.S.A.* **115** 30 9N 83 40W
Perry, *Ga., U.S.A.* **115** 32 25N 83 41W
Perry, *Iowa, U.S.A.* **118** 41 48N 94 5W
Perry, *Maine, U.S.A.* **115** 44 59N 67 20W
Perry, *Mich., U.S.A.* **119** 42 50N 84 13W
Perry, *Mo., U.S.A.* **118** 39 26N 91 40W
Perry, *Okla., U.S.A.* **121** 36 20N 97 20W
Perrysburg, *U.S.A.* **119** 41 34N 83 38W
Perryton, *U.S.A.* **121** 36 28N 100 48W
Perryville, *U.S.A.* **118** 37 42N 89 50W
Persberg, *Sweden* **10** 59 47N 14 15 E
Persepolis, *Iran* **47** 29 55N 52 50 E
Perseverancia, *Bolivia* **137** 14 44 S 62 48W
Persia = Iran ■, *Asia* **47** 33 0N 53 0 E
Persian Gulf = Gulf, The, *Asia* **47** 27 0N 50 0 E
Perstorp, *Sweden* **11** 56 10N 13 25 E
Perth, *Australia* **79** 31 57 S 115 52 E
Perth, *Canada* **109** 44 55N 76 15W
Perth, *U.K.* **14** 56 24N 3 27W
Perth Amboy, *U.S.A.* **117** 40 31N 74 16W

Perthus, Le, *France* **20** 42 30N 2 53 E
Perthville, *Australia* **76** 33 30 S 149 31 E
Pertuis, *France* **21** 43 42N 5 30 E
Peru, *Ill., U.S.A.* **118** 41 18N 89 12W
Peru, *Ind., U.S.A.* **119** 40 42N 86 0W
Peru ■, *S. Amer.* **134** 8 0 S 75 0W
Peru-Chile Trench, *Pac. Oc.* **67** 20 0 S 72 0W
Perúgia, *Italy* **27** 43 6N 12 24 E
Perušić, *Yugoslavia* **27** 44 40N 15 22 E
Péruwelz, *Belgium* **17** 50 31N 3 36 E
Pervomaysk, *R.S.F.S.R., U.S.S.R.* **37** 54 56N 43 58 E
Pervomaysk, *Ukraine S.S.R., U.S.S.R.* **38** 48 10N 30 46 E
Pervouralsk, *U.S.S.R.* **40** 56 55N 60 0 E
Perwez, *Belgium* **17** 50 38N 4 48 E
Pésaro, *Italy* **27** 43 55N 12 53 E
Pesca, La, *Mexico* **127** 23 46N 97 47W
Pescara, *Italy* **27** 42 28N 14 13 E
Pescara →, *Italy* **27** 42 28N 14 13 E
Peschanokopskoye, *U.S.S.R.* **39** 46 14N 41 4 E
Péscia, *Italy* **26** 43 54N 10 40 E
Pescina, *Italy* **27** 42 0N 13 39 E
Peshawar, *Pakistan* **48** 34 2N 71 37 E
Peshtigo, *U.S.A.* **114** 45 4N 87 46W
Peski, *U.S.S.R.* **37** 51 14N 42 29 E
Peskovka, *U.S.S.R.* **37** 59 23N 52 20 E
Pêso da Régua, *Portugal* **22** 41 10N 7 47W
Pesqueira, *Brazil* **138** 8 20 S 36 42W
Pessac, *France* **20** 44 48N 0 37W
Pessoux, *Belgium* **17** 50 17N 5 11 E
Pestovo, *U.S.S.R.* **36** 58 33N 35 42 E
Pestravka, *U.S.S.R.* **37** 52 28N 49 57 E
Petah Tiqwa, *Israel* **44** 32 6N 34 53 E
Petaling Jaya, *Malaysia* **55** 3 4N 101 42 E
Petaluma, *U.S.A.* **124** 38 13N 122 39W
Petange, *Lux.* **17** 49 33N 5 55 E
Petatlán, *Mexico* **126** 17 31N 101 16W
Petauke, *Zambia* **93** 14 14 S 31 20 E
Petawawa, *Canada* **109** 45 54N 77 17W
Petegem, *Belgium* **17** 50 59N 3 32 E
Petén Itzá, L., *Guatemala* **128** 16 58N 89 50W
Peter 1st, I., *Antarctica* **143** 69 0 S 91 0W
Peter Pond L., *Canada* **111** 55 55N 108 44W
Peterbell, *Canada* **104** 48 36N 83 21W
Peterborough, *Australia* **73** 32 58 S 138 51 E
Peterborough, *Canada* **109** 44 20N 78 20W
Peterborough, *U.K.* **13** 52 35N 0 14W
Peterborough, *U.S.A.* **117** 42 55N 71 59W
Peterhead, *U.K.* **14** 57 30N 1 49W
Petermann Bjerg, *Greenland* **100** 73 7N 28 25W
Peter's Mine, *Guyana* **135** 6 14N 59 20W
Petersburg, *Alaska, U.S.A.* **102** 56 50N 133 0W
Petersburg, *Ill., U.S.A.* **118** 40 1N 89 51W
Petersburg, *Ind., U.S.A.* **119** 38 30N 87 15W
Petersburg, *Va., U.S.A.* **114** 37 17N 77 26W
Petersburg, *W. Va., U.S.A.* **114** 38 59N 79 10W
Petford, *Australia* **72** 17 20 S 144 58 E
Petília Policastro, *Italy* **29** 39 7N 16 48 E
Petit Bois I., *U.S.A.* **115** 30 16N 88 25W
Petit-Cap, *Canada* **105** 49 3N 64 30W
Petit Goâve, *Haiti* **129** 18 27N 72 51W
Petit Lac Manicouagan, *Canada* **105** 51 25N 67 40W
Petit Saint Bernard, Col du, *Italy* **26** 45 40N 6 52 E
Petitcodiac, *Canada* **105** 45 57N 65 11W
Petite Baleine →, *Canada* **104** 56 0N 76 45W
Petite-Rivière, *Canada* **107** 47 20N 70 33W
Petite Saguenay, *Canada* **107** 48 15N 70 4W
Petitsikapau, L., *Canada* **105** 54 37N 66 25W
Petlad, *India* **48** 22 30N 72 45 E
Peto, *Mexico* **127** 20 10N 88 53W
Petone, *N.Z.* **80** 41 13 S 174 53 E
Petoskey, *U.S.A.* **104** 45 22N 84 57W
Petra, *Jordan* **44** 30 20N 35 22 E
Petra, *Spain* **24** 39 37N 3 6 E
Petra, Ostrova, *U.S.S.R.* **144** 76 15N 118 30 E
Petralia, *Italy* **29** 37 49N 14 4 E
Petrel, *Spain* **25** 38 30N 0 46W
Petreto-Bicchisano, *France* **21** 41 47N 8 58 E
Petrich, *Bulgaria* **35** 41 24N 23 13 E
Petrijanec, *Yugoslavia* **27** 46 23N 16 17 E
Petrikov, *U.S.S.R.* **36** 52 11N 28 29 E
Petrinja, *Yugoslavia* **27** 45 28N 16 18 E
Petrolândia, *Brazil* **138** 9 5 S 38 20W
Petrolia, *Canada* **108** 42 54N 82 9W
Petrolina, *Brazil* **138** 9 24 S 40 30W
Petropavlovsk, *U.S.S.R.* **40** 54 53N 69 13 E
Petropavlovsk-Kamchatskiy, *U.S.S.R.* **41** 53 3N 158 43 E
Petropavlovskiy = Akhtubinsk, *U.S.S.R.* **39** 48 13N 46 7 E
Petrópolis, *Brazil* **139** 22 33 S 43 9W
Petroşeni, *Romania* **34** 45 28N 23 20 E
Petroskey, *U.S.A.* **114** 45 22N 84 57W
Petrova Gora, *Yugoslavia* **27** 45 15N 15 45 E
Petrovac, *Yugoslavia* **33** 42 13N 18 57 E
Petrovsk, *U.S.S.R.* **37** 52 22N 45 19 E
Petrovsk-Zabaykalskiy, *U.S.S.R.* **41** 51 20N 108 55 E
Petrovskoye = Svetlograd, *U.S.S.R.* **39** 45 25N 42 58 E
Petrozavodsk, *U.S.S.R.* **40** 61 41N 34 20 E
Petrus Steyn, *S. Africa* **97** 27 38 S 28 8 E
Petrusburg, *S. Africa* **96** 29 4 S 25 26 E
Pettitts, *Australia* **76** 34 56 S 148 10 E
Petukhovka, *U.S.S.R.* **36** 53 42N 30 54 E
Peumo, *Chile* **140** 34 21 S 71 12W
Peureulak, *Indonesia* **56** 4 48N 97 45 E
Pevek, *U.S.S.R.* **41** 69 41N 171 19 E
Peveragno, *Italy* **26** 44 20N 7 37 E
Peyrehorade, *France* **20** 43 34N 1 7W
Peyruis, *France* **21** 44 1N 5 56 E
Pézenas, *France* **20** 43 28N 3 24 E
Pfaffenhofen, *W. Germany* **31** 48 31N 11 31 E
Pfarrkirchen, *W. Germany* **31** 48 25N 12 57 E
Pfeffenhausen, *W. Germany* **31** 48 40N 11 58 E
Pforzheim, *W. Germany* **31** 48 53N 8 43 E
Pfullendorf, *W. Germany* **31** 47 55N 9 15 E
Pfungstadt, *W. Germany* **31** 49 47N 8 36 E
Phala, *Botswana* **96** 23 45 S 26 50 E
Phalera = Phulera, *India* **48** 26 52N 75 16 E
Phalodi, *India* **48** 27 12N 72 24 E
Phalsbourg, *France* **19** 48 46N 7 15 E
Phan, *Thailand* **54** 19 28N 99 43 E
Phan Rang, *Vietnam* **55** 11 34N 109 0 E
Phan Ri = Hoa Da, *Vietnam* **55** 11 16N 108 40 E
Phan Thiet, *Vietnam* **55** 11 1N 108 9 E
Phanat Nikhom, *Thailand* **54** 13 27N 101 11 E
Phangan, Ko, *Thailand* **55** 9 45N 100 0 E
Phangnga, *Thailand* **55** 8 28N 98 30 E
Phanh Bho Ho Chi Minh, *Vietnam* **55** 10 58N 106 40 E
Phanom Sarakham, *Thailand* **54** 13 45N 101 21 E
Pharenda, *India* **49** 27 5N 83 17 E
Phatthalung, *Thailand* **55** 7 39N 100 6 E
Phayao, *Thailand* **54** 19 11N 99 55 E
Phelps, *N.Y., U.S.A.* **116** 42 57N 77 5W
Phelps, *Wis., U.S.A.* **120** 46 2N 89 2W
Phelps L., *Canada* **111** 59 15N 103 15W
Phenix City, *U.S.A.* **115** 32 30N 85 0W
Phet Buri, *Thailand* **54** 13 1N 99 55 E
Phetchabun, *Thailand* **54** 16 25N 101 8 E
Phetchabun, Thiu Khao, *Thailand* **54** 16 0N 101 20 E
Phi Phi, Ko, *Thailand* **55** 7 45N 98 46 E
Phiafay, *Laos* **54** 14 48N 106 0 E
Phibun Mangsahan, *Thailand* **54** 15 14N 105 14 E
Phichai, *Thailand* **54** 17 22N 100 10 E
Phichit, *Thailand* **54** 16 26N 100 22 E
Philadelphia, *Miss., U.S.A.* **121** 32 47N 89 5W
Philadelphia, *N.Y., U.S.A.* **117** 44 9N 75 40W
Philadelphia, *Pa., U.S.A.* **117** 40 0N 75 10W
Philip, *U.S.A.* **120** 44 4N 101 42W
Philippeville, *Belgium* **17** 50 12N 4 33 E
Philippi L., *Australia* **72** 24 20 S 138 55 E
Philippines ■, *Asia* **57** 12 0N 123 0 E
Philippolis, *S. Africa* **96** 30 15 S 25 16 E
Philippopolis = Plovdiv, *Bulgaria* **34** 42 8N 24 44 E
Philipsburg, *Canada* **107** 45 2N 73 5W
Philipsburg, *Mont., U.S.A.* **122** 46 20N 113 21W
Philipsburg, *Pa., U.S.A.* **116** 40 53N 78 10W
Philipstown, *S. Africa* **96** 30 28 S 24 30 E
Phillip, I., *Australia* **74** 38 30 S 145 12 E
Phillips, *Tex., U.S.A.* **121** 35 48N 101 17W
Phillips, *Wis., U.S.A.* **120** 45 41N 90 22W
Phillipsburg, *Kans., U.S.A.* **120** 39 48N 99 20W
Phillipsburg, *Pa., U.S.A.* **117** 40 43N 75 12W
Phillott, *Australia* **73** 27 53 S 145 50 E
Philmont, *U.S.A.* **117** 42 14N 73 37W
Philomath, *U.S.A.* **122** 44 28N 123 21W
Phimai, *Thailand* **54** 15 13N 102 30 E
Phitsanulok, *Thailand* **54** 16 50N 100 12 E
Phnom Dangrek, *Thailand* **54** 14 20N 104 0 E
Phnom Penh, *Cambodia* **55** 11 33N 104 55 E
Phoenix, *Ariz., U.S.A.* **123** 33 30N 112 10W
Phoenix, *N.Y., U.S.A.* **117** 43 13N 76 18W
Phoenix Is., *Kiribati* **66** 3 30 S 172 0W
Phoenixville, *U.S.A.* **117** 40 12N 75 29W
Phon, *Thailand* **54** 15 49N 102 36 E
Phon Tiou, *Laos* **54** 17 53N 104 37 E
Phong →, *Thailand* **54** 16 23N 102 56 E
Phong Saly, *Laos* **54** 21 42N 102 9 E
Phong Tho, *Vietnam* **54** 22 32N 103 21 E
Phonhong, *Laos* **54** 18 30N 102 25 E
Phonum, *Thailand* **55** 8 49N 98 48 E
Photharam, *Thailand* **54** 13 41N 99 51 E
Phra Chedi Sam Ong, *Thailand* **54** 15 16N 98 23 E
Phra Nakhon Si Ayutthaya, *Thailand* **54** 14 25N 100 30 E
Phra Thong, Ko, *Thailand* **55** 9 5N 98 17 E
Phrae, *Thailand* **54** 18 7N 100 9 E
Phrom Phiram, *Thailand* **54** 17 2N 100 12 E
Phu Dien, *Vietnam* **54** 18 58N 105 31 E
Phu Loi, *Laos* **54** 20 14N 103 14 E
Phu Ly, *Vietnam* **54** 20 35N 105 50 E
Phu Tho, *Vietnam* **54** 21 24N 105 13 E
Phuc Yen, *Vietnam* **54** 21 16N 105 45 E
Phuket, *Thailand* **55** 7 52N 98 22 E
Phuket, Ko, *Thailand* **55** 8 0N 98 22 E
Phulbari, *India* **52** 25 55N 90 2 E
Phulera, *India* **48** 26 52N 75 16 E
Phun Phin, *Thailand* **55** 9 7N 99 12 E
Piacá, *Brazil* **138** 7 42 S 47 18W
Piacenza, *Italy* **26** 45 2N 9 42 E
Piaçubaçu, *Brazil* **138** 10 24 S 36 25W
Piádena, *Italy* **26** 45 8N 10 22 E
Pialba, *Australia* **73** 25 20 S 152 45 E
Pian Cr. →, *Australia* **73** 30 2 S 148 12 E
Piana, *France* **21** 42 15N 8 34 E
Pianella, *Italy* **27** 42 24N 14 5 E
Piangil, *Australia* **74** 35 5 S 143 20 E
Pianoro, *Italy* **27** 44 20N 11 20 E
Pianosa, *Puglia, Italy* **27** 42 12N 15 44 E
Pianosa, *Toscana, Italy* **26** 42 36N 10 4 E
Piapot, *Canada* **111** 49 59N 109 8W
Piare →, *Italy* **27** 45 32N 12 44 E
Pias, *Portugal* **23** 38 1N 7 29W
Piaseczno, *Poland* **32** 52 5N 21 2 E
Piatã, *Brazil* **139** 13 9 S 41 48W
Piatra, *Romania* **34** 43 51N 25 9 E
Piatra Neamţ, *Romania* **34** 46 56N 26 21 E
Piauí □, *Brazil* **138** 7 0 S 43 0W
Piaui →, *Brazil* **138** 6 38 S 42 42W
Piave →, *Italy* **27** 45 32N 12 44 E
Piazza Ármerina, *Italy* **29** 37 21N 14 20 E
Pibor →, *Sudan* **89** 7 35N 33 0 E
Pibor Post, *Sudan* **89** 6 47N 33 3 E
Pica, *Chile* **136** 20 35 S 69 25W
Picardie, *France* **19** 49 50N 3 0 E
Picardie, Plaine de, *France* **19** 50 0N 2 0 E
Picardy = Picardie, *France* **19** 49 50N 3 0 E
Picayune, *U.S.A.* **121** 30 31N 89 40W
Picerno, *Italy* **29** 40 40N 15 37 E
Pichilemu, *Chile* **140** 34 22 S 72 0W
Pichincha, □, *Ecuador* **134** 0 10 S 78 40W
Pickerel L., *Canada* **104** 48 40N 91 25W
Pickle Lake, *Canada* **104** 51 30N 90 12W
Pico Truncado, *Argentina* **142** 46 40 S 68 0W
Picola, *Australia* **74** 36 0 S 145 3 E
Picos, *Brazil* **138** 7 5 S 41 28W
Picos Ancares, Sierra de, *Spain* **22** 42 51N 6 52W
Picota, *Peru* **136** 6 54 S 76 24W
Picquigny, *France* **19** 49 56N 2 10 E
Picton, *Australia* **76** 34 12 S 150 34 E
Picton, *Canada* **109** 44 1N 77 9W
Picton, *N.Z.* **81** 41 18 S 174 3 E
Picton, I., *Chile* **142** 55 2 S 66 57W
Pictou, *Canada* **105** 45 41N 62 42W
Picture Butte, *Canada* **110** 49 55N 112 45W
Picuí, *Brazil* **138** 6 31 S 36 21W
Picún Leufú, *Argentina* **142** 39 30 S 69 5W
Pidurutalagala, *Sri Lanka* **51** 7 10N 80 50 E
Piedad, La, *Mexico* **126** 20 20N 102 1W
Piedecuesta, *Colombia* **134** 6 59N 73 3W
Piedicavallo, *Italy* **26** 45 41N 7 57 E
Piedmont = Piemonte □, *Italy* **26** 45 0N 7 30 E
Piedmont, *U.S.A.* **115** 33 55N 85 39W
Piedmont Plateau, *U.S.A.* **115** 34 0N 81 30W
Piedmonte d'Alife, *Italy* **29** 41 22N 14 22 E
Piedra →, *Spain* **24** 41 18N 1 47W
Piedra del Anguila, *Argentina* **142** 40 2 S 70 4W
Piedra Lais, *Venezuela* **134** 3 10N 65 50W
Piedrabuena, *Spain* **23** 39 0N 4 10W
Piedrahita, *Spain* **22** 40 28N 5 23W
Piedras, R. de las →, *Peru* **136** 12 30 S 69 15W
Piedras Negras, *Mexico* **126** 28 35N 100 35W
Piemonte □, *Italy* **26** 45 0N 7 30 E
Pier Millan, *Australia* **74** 35 14 S 142 40 E
Pierce, *U.S.A.* **122** 46 29N 115 53W
Piercefield, *U.S.A.* **117** 44 13N 74 35W
Pierre, *U.S.A.* **120** 44 23N 100 20W
Pierre Benite, Barrage, *France* **21** 45 42N 4 49 E
Pierre-de-Bresse, *France* **21** 46 54N 5 13 E
Pierrefeu-du-Var, *France* **21** 43 13N 6 9 E
Pierrefonds, *France* **19** 49 20N 3 0 E
Pierrefontaine-les-Varans, *France* **19** 47 14N 6 32 E
Pierrefort, *France* **20** 44 55N 2 50 E
Pierrelatte, *France* **21** 44 23N 4 43 E
Pierreville, *Canada* **107** 46 4N 72 49W
Pieštany, *Czech.* **32** 48 38N 17 55 E
Piesting →, *Austria* **33** 48 6N 16 40 E
Piet Retief, *S. Africa* **97** 27 1 S 30 50 E
Pietarsaari = Jakobstad, *Finland* **8** 63 40N 22 43 E
Pietermaritzburg, *S. Africa* **97** 29 35 S 30 25 E
Pietersburg, *S. Africa* **97** 23 54 S 29 25 E
Pietraperzia, *Italy* **29** 37 26N 14 8 E
Pietrasanta, *Italy* **26** 43 57N 10 12 E
Pietrosu, *Romania* **34** 47 12N 25 8 E
Pietrosul, *Romania* **34** 47 35N 24 43 E
Pieve di Cadore, *Italy* **27** 46 25N 12 22 E
Pieve di Teco, *Italy* **26** 44 3N 7 54 E
Pievepélago, *Italy* **26** 44 12N 10 35 E
Pigádhia, *Greece* **35** 35 30N 27 12 E
Pigeon, *U.S.A.* **114** 43 50N 83 17W
Pigeon I., *India* **51** 14 2N 74 20 E
Pigeon L., *Canada* **109** 44 27N 78 30W
Piggott, *U.S.A.* **121** 36 20N 90 10W
Pigna, *Italy* **26** 43 57N 7 40 E
Pigüe, *Argentina* **140** 37 36 S 62 25W
Pihani, *India* **49** 27 36N 80 15 E
Pijnacker, *Neths.* **16** 52 1N 4 26 E
Pikalevo, *U.S.S.R.* **36** 59 37N 34 0 E
Pikedale, *Australia* **77** 28 39 S 151 38 E
Pikes Peak, *U.S.A.* **120** 38 50N 105 10W
Piketberg, *S. Africa* **96** 32 55 S 18 40 E
Pikeville, *U.S.A.* **114** 37 30N 82 30W
Pikou, *China* **61** 39 18N 122 22 E
Pikwitonei, *Canada* **111** 55 35N 97 9W
Pila, *Poland* **32** 53 10N 16 48 E
Pila, *Spain* **25** 38 16N 1 11W
Pilani, *India* **48** 28 22N 75 33 E
Pilar, *Brazil* **138** 9 36 S 35 56W
Pilar, *Paraguay* **140** 26 50 S 58 20W
Pilas Group, *Phil.* **57** 6 45N 121 35 E
Pilaya →, *Bolivia* **137** 20 55 S 64 4W
Pilbara, *Australia* **78** 21 15 S 118 16 E
Pilcomayo →, *Paraguay* **140** 25 21 S 57 42W
Pilibhit, *India* **49** 28 40N 79 50 E
Pilica →, *Poland* **32** 51 52N 21 17 E
Pilkhawa, *India* **48** 28 43N 77 42 E
Pillar Valley, *Australia* **77** 29 46 S 153 7 E
Pillaro, *Ecuador* **134** 1 10 S 78 32W
Pílos, *Greece* **35** 36 55N 21 42 E
Pilot Grove, *U.S.A.* **118** 38 53N 92 55W
Pilot Mound, *Canada* **111** 49 15N 98 54W
Pilot Point, *U.S.A.* **121** 33 26N 97 0W
Pilot Rock, *U.S.A.* **122** 45 30N 118 50W
Pilsen = Plzeň, *Czech.* **32** 49 45N 13 22 E
Pilštanj, *Yugoslavia* **27** 46 8N 15 39 E
Pima, *U.S.A.* **123** 32 54N 109 50W
Pimba, *Australia* **73** 31 18 S 136 46 E
Pimenta Bueno, *Brazil* **137** 11 35 S 61 10W
Pimentel, *Peru* **136** 6 45 S 79 55W
Pimpinio, *Australia* **74** 36 34 S 142 7 E
Pin-Blanc, L., *Canada* **106** 46 45N 78 8W
Pina, *Spain* **24** 41 29N 0 33W
Pinang, *Malaysia* **55** 5 25N 100 15 E
Pinar del Río, *Cuba* **128** 22 26N 83 40W
Pinchang, *China* **58** 31 36N 107 3 E
Pincher Creek, *Canada* **110** 49 30N 113 57W
Pinchi L., *Canada* **110** 54 38N 124 30W
Pinckneyville, *U.S.A.* **118** 38 5N 89 20W
Pîncota, *Romania* **34** 46 20N 21 45 E
Pind Dadan Khan, *Pakistan* **48** 32 36N 73 7 E
Pindar, *Australia* **79** 28 30 S 115 47 E
Pindaré →, *Brazil* **138** 3 17 S 44 47W
Pindaré Mirim, *Brazil* **138** 3 37 S 45 21W
Pindi Gheb, *Pakistan* **48** 33 14N 72 21 E
Pindiga, *Nigeria* **91** 9 58N 10 53 E
Pindobal, *Brazil* **138** 3 16 S 48 25W
Pindos Óros, *Greece* **35** 40 0N 21 0 E
Pindus Mts. = Pindos Óros, *Greece* **35** 40 0N 21 0 E
Pine, *U.S.A.* **123** 34 27N 111 30W
Pine →, *Canada* **111** 58 50N 105 38W
Pine, C., *Canada* **105** 46 37N 53 32W
Pine, La, *U.S.A.* **122** 43 40N 121 30W
Pine Bluff, *U.S.A.* **121** 34 10N 92 0W
Pine City, *U.S.A.* **120** 45 46N 93 0W
Pine Falls, *Canada* **111** 50 34N 96 11W
Pine Flat Res., *U.S.A.* **124** 36 50N 119 20W
Pine Pass, *Canada* **110** 55 25N 122 42W
Pine Point, *Canada* **110** 60 50N 114 28W
Pine Ridge, *Australia* **76** 31 10 S 147 30 E
Pine Ridge, *U.S.A.* **120** 43 0N 102 35W
Pine River, *Canada* **111** 51 45N 100 30W
Pine River, *U.S.A.* **120** 46 43N 94 24W
Pine Valley, *U.S.A.* **125** 32 50N 116 32W
Pinecrest, *U.S.A.* **124** 38 12N 120 1W
Pinedale, *U.S.A.* **124** 36 50N 119 48W
Pinega →, *U.S.S.R.* **40** 64 8N 46 54 E
Pinehill, *Australia* **72** 23 38 S 146 57 E
Pinerolo, *Italy* **26** 44 47N 7 21 E
Pineto, *Italy* **27** 42 36N 14 4 E
Pinetop, *U.S.A.* **123** 34 10N 109 57W
Pinetown, *S. Africa* **97** 29 48 S 30 54 E
Pinetree, *U.S.A.* **122** 43 42N 105 52W
Pineville, *Ky., U.S.A.* **115** 36 42N 83 42W
Pineville, *La., U.S.A.* **121** 31 22N 92 30W
Piney, *France* **19** 48 22N 4 21 E
Piney Range, *Australia* **76** 33 50 S 147 58 E
Ping →, *Thailand* **54** 15 42N 100 9 E
Pingaring, *Australia* **79** 32 40 S 118 32 E
Pingba, *China* **58** 26 23N 106 12 E
Pingchuan, *China* **58** 27 35N 101 55 E
Pingding, *China* **60** 37 47N 113 38 E
Pingdingshan, *China* **60** 33 43N 113 27 E
Pingdong, *Taiwan* **59** 22 39N 120 30 E
Pingdu, *China* **61** 36 42N 119 59 E
Pingelly, *Australia* **79** 32 32 S 117 5 E
Pingguo, *China* **58** 23 19N 107 36 E

Pinghe, *China* **59** 24 17N 117 21 E
Pinghu, *China* **59** 30 40N 121 2 E
Pingjiang, *China* **59** 28 45N 113 36 E
Pingle, *China* **59** 24 40N 110 40 E
Pingli, *China* **58** 32 27N 109 22 E
Pingliang, *China* **60** 35 35N 106 31 E
Pinglu, *China* **60** 39 31N 112 30 E
Pingluo, *China* **60** 38 52N 106 30 E
Pingnan, *Fujian, China* **59** 26 55N 119 0 E
Pingnan, *Guangxi Zhuangzu, China* **59** 23 33N 110 22 E
Pingquan, *China* **61** 41 1N 118 37 E
Pingrup, *Australia* **79** 33 32 S 118 29 E
Pingtan, *China* **59** 25 31N 119 47 E
Pingtang, *China* **58** 25 49N 107 17 E
Pingwu, *China* **60** 32 25N 104 30 E
Pingxiang, *Guangxi Zhuangzu, China* **58** 22 6N 106 46 E
Pingxiang, *Jiangxi, China* **59** 27 43N 113 48 E
Pingyao, *China* **60** 37 12N 112 10 E
Pingyi, *China* **61** 35 30N 117 35 E
Pingyin, *China* **60** 36 20N 116 25 E
Pingyuan, *Guangdong, China* **59** 24 37N 115 57 E
Pingyuan, *Shandong, China* **60** 37 10N 116 22 E
Pingyuanjie, *China* **58** 23 45N 103 48 E
Pinhal, *Brazil* **141** 22 10 S 46 46W
Pinheiro, *Brazil* **138** 2 31 S 45 5W
Pinhel, *Portugal* **22** 40 50N 7 1W
Pinhuá →, *Brazil* **137** 6 21 S 65 0W
Pini, *Indonesia* **56** 0 10N 98 40 E
Piniós →, *Ilía, Greece* **35** 37 48N 21 20 E
Piniós →, *Trikkala, Greece* **35** 39 55N 22 10 E
Pinjarra, *Australia* **79** 32 37 S 115 52 E
Pink →, *Canada* **111** 56 50N 103 50W
Pinlebu, *Burma* **52** 24 5N 95 22 E
Pinnacles, *Australia* **79** 28 12 S 120 26 E
Pinnacles, *U.S.A.* **124** 36 33N 121 19W
Pinnaroo, *Australia* **73** 35 17 S 140 53 E
Pinneberg, *W. Germany* **30** 53 39N 9 48 E
Pino Hachado, Paso, *S. Amer.* **142** 38 39 S 70 54W
Pinon Hills, *U.S.A.* **125** 34 26N 117 39W
Pinos, *Mexico* **126** 22 20N 101 40W
Pinos, Mt, *U.S.A.* **125** 34 49N 119 8W
Pinos Pt., *U.S.A.* **123** 36 38N 121 57W
Pinos Puente, *Spain* **23** 37 15N 3 45W
Pinotepa Nacional, *Mexico* **127** 16 19N 98 3W
Pinrang, *Indonesia* **57** 3 46 S 119 41 E
Pins, I. des, *N. Cal.* **68** 22 37 S 167 30 E
Pins, Pte. aux, *Canada* **108** 42 15N 81 51W
Pinsk, *U.S.S.R.* **36** 52 10N 26 1 E
Pintados, *Chile* **136** 20 35 S 69 40W
Pintumba, *Australia* **79** 31 30 S 132 12 E
Pinyang, *China* **59** 27 42N 120 31 E
Pinyug, *U.S.S.R.* **40** 60 5N 48 0 E
Pinzolo, *Italy* **26** 46 9N 10 45 E
Pio XII, *Brazil* **138** 3 53 S 45 17W
Pioche, *U.S.A.* **123** 38 0N 114 35W
Piombino, *Italy* **26** 42 54N 10 30 E
Piombino, Canale di, *Italy* **26** 42 50N 10 25 E
Pioner, Os., *U.S.S.R.* **41** 79 50N 92 0 E
Pionki, *Poland* **32** 51 29N 21 28 E
Piorini →, *Brazil* **135** 3 23 S 63 30W
Piorini, L., *Brazil* **135** 3 15 S 62 35W
Piotrków Trybunalski, *Poland* **32** 51 23N 19 43 E
Piove di Sacco, *Italy* **27** 45 18N 12 1 E
Pip, *Iran* **47** 26 45N 60 10 E
Pipar, *India* **48** 26 25N 73 31 E
Piparia, *India* **48** 22 45N 78 23 E
Pipestone, *U.S.A.* **120** 44 0N 96 20W
Pipestone →, *Canada* **104** 52 53N 89 23W
Pipestone Cr. →, *Canada* **111** 49 38N 100 15W
Pipiriki, *N.Z.* **80** 39 28 S 175 5 E
Pipmuacan, Rés., *Canada* **107** 49 45N 70 30W
Pippingarra, *Australia* **78** 20 27 S 118 42 E
Pipriac, *France* **18** 47 49N 1 58W
Piqua, *U.S.A.* **119** 40 10N 84 10W
Piquet Carneiro, *Brazil* **138** 5 48 S 39 25W
Piquiri →, *Brazil* **141** 24 3 S 54 14W
Piracanjuba, *Brazil* **139** 17 18 S 49 1W
Piracicaba, *Brazil* **141** 22 45 S 47 40W
Piracuruca, *Brazil* **138** 3 50 S 41 50W
Piræus = Piraiévs, *Greece* **35** 37 57N 23 42 E
Piraiévs, *Greece* **35** 37 57N 23 42 E
Piráino, *Italy* **29** 38 10N 14 52 E
Pirajuí, *Brazil* **141** 21 59 S 49 29W
Piran, *Yugoslavia* **27** 45 31N 13 33 E
Pirané, *Argentina* **140** 25 42 S 59 6W
Piranhas, *Brazil* **138** 9 27 S 37 46W
Pirano = Piran, *Yugoslavia* **27** 45 31N 13 33 E
Pirapemas, *Brazil* **138** 3 43 S 44 14W
Pirapora, *Brazil* **139** 17 20 S 44 56W
Piray →, *Bolivia* **137** 16 32 S 63 45W
Pires do Rio, *Brazil* **139** 17 18 S 48 17W
Pirganj, *Bangla.* **52** 25 51N 88 24 E
Pírgos, *Ilía, Greece* **35** 37 40N 21 27 E
Pírgos, *Messinia, Greece* **35** 36 50N 22 16 E
Pirgovo, *Bulgaria* **34** 43 44N 25 43 E
Piriac-sur-Mer, *France* **18** 47 22N 2 33W
Piribebuy, *Paraguay* **140** 25 26 S 57 2W
Pirin Planina, *Bulgaria* **35** 41 40N 23 30 E
Pirineos, *Spain* **24** 42 40N 1 0 E
Piripiri, *Brazil* **138** 4 15 S 41 46W
Piritu, *Venezuela* **134** 9 23N 69 12W
Pirmasens, *W. Germany* **31** 49 12N 7 30 E
Pirna, *E. Germany* **30** 50 57N 13 57 E
Pirojpur, *Bangla.* **52** 22 35N 90 1 E
Pirot, *Yugoslavia* **33** 43 9N 22 39 E
Piru, *Indonesia* **57** 3 4 S 128 12 E
Piru, *U.S.A.* **125** 34 25N 118 48W
Piryatin, *U.S.S.R.* **36** 50 15N 32 25 E
Pisa, *Italy* **26** 43 43N 10 23 E
Pisa Ra., *N.Z.* **81** 44 52 S 169 12 E
Pisac, *Peru* **136** 13 25 S 71 50W
Pisagua, *Chile* **136** 19 40 S 70 15W
Pisarovina, *Yugoslavia* **27** 45 35N 15 50 E
Pisciotta, *Italy* **29** 40 7N 15 12 E
Pisco, *Peru* **136** 13 50 S 76 12W
Písek, *Czech.* **32** 49 19N 14 10 E
Pishan, *China* **62** 37 30N 78 33 E
Pishin Lora →, *Pakistan* **48** 29 9N 64 5 E
Pising, *Indonesia* **57** 5 8 S 121 53 E
Pismo Beach, *U.S.A.* **125** 35 9N 120 38W
Pissos, *France* **20** 44 19N 0 49W
Pisticci, *Italy* **29** 40 24N 16 33 E
Pistóia, *Italy* **26** 43 57N 10 53 E
Pistol B., *Canada* **111** 62 25N 92 37W
Pisuerga →, *Spain* **22** 41 33N 4 52W
Pisz, *Poland* **32** 53 38N 21 49 E
Pitalito, *Colombia* **134** 1 51N 76 2W
Pitanga, *Brazil* **139** 24 46 S 51 44W
Pitangui, *Brazil* **139** 19 40 S 44 54W
Pitarpunga, L., *Australia* **74** 34 24 S 143 30 E
Pitcairn I., *Pac. Oc.* **67** 25 5 S 130 5W
Pite älv →, *Sweden* **8** 65 20N 21 25 E
Piteå, *Sweden* **8** 65 20N 21 25 E
Piterka, *U.S.S.R.* **37** 50 41N 47 29 E
Piteşti, *Romania* **34** 44 52N 24 54 E
Pithapuram, *India* **50** 17 10N 82 15 E
Pithara, *Australia* **79** 30 20 S 116 35 E
Píthion, *Greece* **35** 41 24N 26 40 E
Pithiviers, *France* **19** 48 10N 2 13 E
Pitigliano, *Italy* **27** 42 38N 11 40 E
Pitlochry, *U.K.* **14** 56 43N 3 43W
Pitrufquén, *Chile* **142** 38 59 S 72 39W
Pitt I., *Canada* **110** 53 30N 129 50W
Pittem, *Belgium* **17** 51 1N 3 13 E
Pittsburg, *Kans., U.S.A.* **121** 37 21N 94 43W
Pittsburg, *Tex., U.S.A.* **121** 32 59N 94 58W
Pittsburgh, *U.S.A.* **116** 40 25N 79 55W
Pittsfield, *Ill., U.S.A.* **118** 39 35N 90 46W
Pittsfield, *Mass., U.S.A.* **117** 42 28N 73 17W
Pittsfield, *N.H., U.S.A.* **117** 43 17N 71 18W
Pittston, *U.S.A.* **117** 41 19N 75 50W
Pittsworth, *Australia* **77** 27 41 S 151 37 E
Pituri →, *Australia* **72** 22 35 S 138 30 E
Piuí, *Brazil* **139** 20 28 S 45 58W
Pium, *Brazil* **138** 10 27 S 49 11W
Piura, *Peru* **136** 5 15 S 80 38W
Piura □, *Peru* **136** 5 10 S 80 0W
Pivijay, *Colombia* **134** 10 28N 74 37W
Pixley, *U.S.A.* **124** 35 58N 119 18W
Piyai, *Greece* **35** 39 17N 21 25 E
Pizarro, *Colombia* **134** 4 58N 77 22W
Pizzo, *Italy* **29** 38 44N 16 10 E
Placentia, *Canada* **105** 47 20N 54 0W
Placentia B., *Canada* **105** 47 0N 54 40W
Placerville, *U.S.A.* **124** 38 47N 120 51W
Placetas, *Cuba* **128** 22 15N 79 44W
Plain Dealing, *U.S.A.* **121** 32 56N 93 41W
Plainfield, *Ill., U.S.A.* **119** 41 37N 88 12W
Plainfield, *N.J., U.S.A.* **117** 40 37N 74 28W
Plains, *Kans., U.S.A.* **121** 37 20N 100 35W
Plains, *Mont., U.S.A.* **122** 47 27N 114 57W
Plains, *Tex., U.S.A.* **121** 33 11N 102 50W
Plainview, *Nebr., U.S.A.* **120** 42 25N 97 48W
Plainview, *Tex., U.S.A.* **121** 34 10N 101 40W
Plainville, *U.S.A.* **120** 39 18N 99 19W
Plainwell, *U.S.A.* **114** 42 28N 85 40W
Plaisance, *France* **20** 43 36N 0 3 E
Pláka, *Greece* **35** 40 0N 25 24 E
Plakhino, *U.S.S.R.* **40** 67 45N 86 5 E
Plana Cays, *Bahamas* **129** 22 38N 73 30W
Planada, *U.S.A.* **124** 37 18N 120 19W
Plancoët, *France* **18** 48 32N 2 13W
Plandište, *Yugoslavia* **33** 45 16N 21 10 E
Planeta Rica, *Colombia* **134** 8 25N 75 36W
Planina, *Slovenija, Yugoslavia* **27** 46 10N 15 20 E
Planina, *Slovenija, Yugoslavia* **27** 45 47N 14 19 E
Plankinton, *U.S.A.* **120** 43 45N 98 27W
Plano, *U.S.A.* **121** 33 0N 96 45W
Plant, La, *U.S.A.* **120** 45 11N 100 40W
Plant City, *U.S.A.* **115** 28 0N 82 8W
Plaquemine, *U.S.A.* **121** 30 20N 91 15W
Plasencia, *Spain* **22** 40 3N 6 8W
Plaški, *Yugoslavia* **27** 45 4N 15 22 E
Plassen, *Norway* **10** 61 9N 12 30 E
Plaster City, *U.S.A.* **125** 32 47N 115 51W
Plaster Rock, *Canada* **105** 46 53N 67 22W
Plata, La, *Argentina* **140** 35 0 S 57 55W
Plata, La, *Colombia* **134** 2 23N 75 53W
Plata, La, *U.S.A.* **118** 40 2N 92 29W
Plata, La, L., *Argentina* **142** 44 55 S 71 50W
Plata, Río de la, *S. Amer.* **140** 34 45 S 57 30W
Platani →, *Italy* **28** 37 23N 13 16 E
Plateau □, *Nigeria* **91** 8 0N 8 30 E
Plateau du Coteau du Missouri, *U.S.A.* **120** 47 9N 101 5W
Plato, *Colombia* **134** 9 47N 74 47W
Platte, *U.S.A.* **120** 43 28N 98 50W
Platte →, *U.S.A.* **118** 39 16N 94 50W
Platte City, *U.S.A.* **118** 39 22N 94 47W
Platteville, *Colo., U.S.A.* **120** 40 18N 104 47W
Platteville, *Wis., U.S.A.* **118** 42 44N 90 29W
Plattling, *W. Germany* **31** 48 46N 12 53 E
Plattsburg, *Miss., U.S.A.* **118** 39 34N 94 27W
Plattsburg, *N.Y., U.S.A.* **117** 44 41N 73 30W
Plattsmouth, *U.S.A.* **120** 41 0N 95 50W
Plau, *E. Germany* **30** 53 27N 12 16 E
Plauen, *E. Germany* **30** 50 29N 12 9 E
Plavinas, *U.S.S.R.* **36** 56 35N 25 46 E
Plavnica, *Yugoslavia* **33** 42 20N 19 13 E
Plavsk, *U.S.S.R.* **37** 53 40N 37 18 E
Playgreen L., *Canada* **111** 54 0N 98 15W
Pleasant Bay, *Canada* **105** 46 51N 60 48W
Pleasant Hill, *Calif., U.S.A.* **124** 37 57N 122 4W
Pleasant Hill, *Ill., U.S.A.* **118** 39 27N 90 52W
Pleasant Hill, *Mo., U.S.A.* **118** 38 48N 94 14W
Pleasant Pt., *N.Z.* **81** 44 16 S 171 9 E
Pleasanton, *U.S.A.* **121** 29 0N 98 30W
Pleasantville, *Iowa, U.S.A.* **118** 41 23N 93 18W
Pleasantville, *N.J., U.S.A.* **114** 39 25N 74 30W
Pleasure Ridge Park, *U.S.A.* **119** 38 9N 85 50W
Pléaux, *France* **20** 45 8N 2 13 E
Pleiku, *Vietnam* **54** 13 57N 108 0 E
Plélan-le-Grand, *France* **18** 48 0N 2 7W
Plémet-la-Pierre, *France* **18** 48 11N 2 36W
Pléneuf-Val-André, *France* **18** 48 35N 2 32W
Pleniţa, *Romania* **34** 44 14N 23 10 E
Plenty →, *Australia* **72** 23 25 S 136 31 E
Plenty, Bay of, *N.Z.* **80** 37 45 S 177 0 E
Plentywood, *U.S.A.* **120** 48 45N 104 35W
Plessisville, *Canada* **107** 46 14N 71 47W
Plestin-les-Grèves, *France* **18** 48 40N 3 39W
Pleszew, *Poland* **32** 51 53N 17 47 E
Pleternica, *Yugoslavia* **33** 45 17N 17 48 E
Pletipi L., *Canada* **105** 51 44N 70 6W
Pleven, *Bulgaria* **34** 43 26N 24 37 E
Plevlja, *Yugoslavia* **33** 43 21N 19 21 E
Plevna, *Canada* **109** 44 58N 76 59W
Płock, *Poland* **32** 52 32N 19 40 E
Plöcken Passo, *Italy* **27** 46 37N 12 57 E
Ploegsteert, *Belgium* **17** 50 44N 2 53 E
Ploemeur, *France* **18** 47 44N 3 26W
Ploërmel, *France* **18** 47 55N 2 26W
Ploieşti, *Romania* **34** 44 57N 26 5 E
Plombières-les-Bains, *France* **19** 47 58N 6 27 E
Plomin, *Yugoslavia* **27** 45 8N 14 10 E
Plön, *W. Germany* **30** 54 8N 10 22 E
Plöner See, *W. Germany* **30** 54 10N 10 22 E
Plonge, Lac la, *Canada* **111** 55 8N 107 20W
Płońsk, *Poland* **32** 52 37N 20 21 E
Ploty, *Poland* **32** 53 48N 15 18 E
Plouaret, *France* **18** 48 37N 3 28W
Plouay, *France* **18** 47 55N 3 21W
Ploudalmézeau, *France* **18** 48 34N 4 41W
Plougasnou, *France* **18** 48 42N 3 49W
Plouha, *France* **18** 48 41N 2 57W
Plouhinec, *France* **18** 48 0N 4 29W
Plovdiv, *Bulgaria* **34** 42 8N 24 44 E
Plum, *U.S.A.* **116** 40 29N 79 47W
Plum I., *U.S.A.* **117** 41 10N 72 12W
Plumas, *U.S.A.* **124** 39 45N 119 4W
Plummer, *U.S.A.* **122** 47 21N 116 59W
Plumtree, *Zimb.* **93** 20 27 S 27 55 E
Plunge, *U.S.S.R.* **36** 55 53N 21 59 E
Pluvigner, *France* **18** 47 46N 3 1W
Plymouth, *U.K.* **13** 50 23N 4 9W
Plymouth, *Calif., U.S.A.* **124** 38 29N 120 51W
Plymouth, *Ill., U.S.A.* **118** 40 15N 90 58W
Plymouth, *Ind., U.S.A.* **119** 41 20N 86 19W
Plymouth, *Mass., U.S.A.* **117** 41 58N 70 40W
Plymouth, *N.C., U.S.A.* **115** 35 54N 76 46W
Plymouth, *N.H., U.S.A.* **117** 43 44N 71 41W
Plymouth, *Pa., U.S.A.* **117** 41 17N 76 0W
Plymouth, *Wis., U.S.A.* **114** 43 42N 87 58W
Plymouth Sd., *U.K.* **13** 50 20N 4 10W
Plynlimon = Pumlumon Fawr, *U.K.* **13** 52 29N 3 47W
Plyussa, *U.S.S.R.* **36** 58 40N 29 20 E
Plyussa →, *U.S.S.R.* **36** 58 40N 29 0 E
Plzeň, *Czech.* **32** 49 45N 13 22 E
Pniewy, *Poland* **32** 52 31N 16 16 E
Pô, *Burkina Faso* **91** 11 14N 1 5W
Po →, *Italy* **26** 44 57N 12 4 E
Po, Foci del, *Italy* **27** 44 55N 12 30 E
Po Hai = Bo Hai, *China* **61** 39 0N 120 0 E
Pobé, *Benin* **91** 7 0N 2 56 E
Pobeda, *U.S.S.R.* **41** 65 12N 146 12 E
Pobedino, *U.S.S.R.* **41** 49 51N 142 49 E
Pobedy Pik, *U.S.S.R.* **40** 40 45N 79 58 E
Pobiedziska, *Poland* **32** 52 29N 17 11 E
Pobla de Lillet, La, *Spain* **24** 42 16N 1 59 E
Pobla de Segur, *Spain* **24** 42 15N 0 58 E
Pobladura de Valle, *Spain* **22** 42 6N 5 44W
Pocahontas, *Ark., U.S.A.* **121** 36 18N 91 0W
Pocahontas, *Ill., U.S.A.* **118** 38 50N 89 33W
Pocahontas, *Iowa, U.S.A.* **118** 42 41N 94 42W
Pocatello, *U.S.A.* **122** 42 50N 112 25W
Pocatière, La, *Canada* **107** 47 22N 70 2W
Pochep, *U.S.S.R.* **36** 52 58N 33 29 E
Pochinki, *U.S.S.R.* **37** 54 41N 44 59 E
Pochinok, *U.S.S.R.* **36** 54 28N 32 29 E
Pochutla, *Mexico* **127** 15 50N 96 31W
Poci, *Venezuela* **135** 5 57N 61 29W
Pocinhos, *Brazil* **138** 7 4 S 36 3W
Pocito Casas, *Mexico* **126** 28 32N 111 6W
Poções, *Brazil* **139** 14 31 S 40 21W
Pocomoke City, *U.S.A.* **114** 38 4N 75 32W
Poconé, *Brazil* **137** 16 15 S 56 37W
Poços de Caldas, *Brazil* **141** 21 50 S 46 33W
Poddebice, *Poland* **32** 51 54N 18 58 E
Poděbrady, *Czech.* **32** 50 9N 15 8 E
Podensac, *France* **20** 44 40N 0 22W
Podgorica = Titograd, *Yugoslavia* **33** 42 30N 19 19 E
Podkamennaya Tunguska →, *U.S.S.R.* **41** 61 50N 90 13 E
Podlapac, *Yugoslavia* **27** 44 37N 15 47 E
Podolsk, *U.S.S.R.* **37** 55 25N 37 30 E
Podor, *Senegal* **90** 16 40N 15 2W
Podravska Slatina, *Yugoslavia* **33** 45 42N 17 45 E
Podujevo, *Yugoslavia* **33** 42 54N 21 10 E
Poel, *E. Germany* **30** 54 0N 11 25 E
Pofadder, *S. Africa* **96** 29 10 S 19 22 E
Pogamasing, *Canada* **104** 46 55N 81 50W
Poggiardo, *Italy* **29** 40 3N 18 21 E
Poggibonsi, *Italy* **27** 43 27N 11 8 E
Pogoanele, *Romania* **34** 44 55N 27 0 E
Pogoso, *Zaïre* **95** 6 46 S 17 12 E
Pogradeci, *Albania* **35** 40 57N 20 37 E
Poh, *Indonesia* **57** 0 46 S 122 51 E
Pohang, *S. Korea* **61** 36 1N 129 23 E
Pohnpei, *Pac. Oc.* **66** 6 55N 158 10 E
Pohorelá, *Czech.* **32** 48 50N 20 2 E
Pohorje, *Yugoslavia* **27** 46 30N 15 20 E
Poiana Mare, *Romania* **34** 43 57N 23 5 E
Poindimié, *N. Cal.* **68** 20 56 S 165 20 E
Poinsett, C., *Antarctica* **143** 65 42 S 113 18 E
Point Danger, *Australia* **77** 28 9 S 153 30 E
Point Edward, *Canada* **108** 43 0N 82 30W
Point Lookout, Mt., *Australia* **77** 30 29 S 152 24 E
Point Pedro, *Sri Lanka* **51** 9 50N 80 15 E
Point Pelee Nat. Park, *Canada* **108** 41 57N 82 31W
Point Pleasant, *N.J., U.S.A.* **117** 40 5N 74 4W
Point Pleasant, *W. Va., U.S.A.* **114** 38 50N 82 7W
Pointe-à-la Hache, *U.S.A.* **121** 29 35N 89 55W
Pointe-à-Pitre, *Guadeloupe* **129** 16 10N 61 30W
Pointe au Baril Sta., *Canada* **108** 45 35N 80 23W
Pointe-au-Pic, *Canada* **107** 47 38N 70 9W
Pointe-aux-Outardes, *Canada* **107** 49 3N 68 26W
Pointe-aux-Trembles, *Canada* **107** 45 40N 73 30W
Pointe-Claire, *Canada* **107** 45 26N 73 50W
Pointe-Gatineau, *Canada* **109** 45 28N 75 42W
Pointe-Lebel, *Canada* **107** 49 10N 68 12W
Pointe Noire, *Congo* **95** 4 48 S 11 53 E
Poirino, *Italy* **26** 44 55N 7 50 E
Poisonbush Ra., *Australia* **78** 22 30 S 121 30 E
Poisson-Blanc, L. du, *Canada* **106** 46 0N 75 45W
Poissy, *France* **19** 48 55N 2 2 E
Poitiers, *France* **18** 46 35N 0 20 E
Poitou, *France* **20** 46 40N 0 10W
Poitou, Seuil du, *France* **20** 46 30N 0 1W
Poix de Picardie, *France* **19** 49 47N 2 0 E
Poix-Terron, *France* **19** 49 38N 4 38 E
Pojoaque Valley, *U.S.A.* **123** 35 55N 106 0W
Pokataroo, *Australia* **73** 29 30 S 148 36 E
Poko, *Sudan* **89** 5 41N 31 55 E
Poko, *Zaïre* **92** 3 7N 26 52 E
Pokrov, *U.S.S.R.* **37** 55 55N 39 7 E
Pokrovsk, *U.S.S.R.* **41** 61 29N 126 12 E
Pol, *Spain* **22** 43 9N 7 20W
Pola = Pula, *Yugoslavia* **27** 44 54N 13 57 E
Pola de Allande, *Spain* **22** 43 16N 6 37W
Pola de Gordón, La, *Spain* **22** 42 51N 5 41W
Pola de Lena, *Spain* **22** 43 10N 5 49W
Pola de Siero, *Spain* **22** 43 24N 5 39W
Pola de Somiedo, *Spain* **22** 43 5N 6 15W
Polacca, *U.S.A.* **123** 35 52N 110 25W
Polan, *Iran* **47** 25 30N 61 10 E

Poland ■, *Europe* .... **32** 52 0N 20 0 E
Polanów, *Poland* ..... **32** 54 7N 16 41 E
Polar Sub-Glacial Basin, *Antarctica* ... **143** 85 0 S 110 0 E
Polcura, *Chile* .... **140** 37 17 S 71 43W
Polden Hills, *U.K.* ... **13** 51 7N 2 50W
Polessk, *U.S.S.R.* .... **36** 54 50N 21 8 E
Polesye, *U.S.S.R.* .... **36** 52 0N 28 10 E
Polewali, *Indonesia* ... **57** 3 21 S 119 23 E
Polgar, *Hungary* ..... **33** 47 54N 21 6 E
Poli, *Cameroon* ...... **94** 8 34N 13 15 E
Políaigos, *Greece* ..... **35** 36 45N 24 38 E
Policastro, G. di, *Italy* **29** 39 55N 15 35 E
Police, *Poland* .... **32** 53 33N 14 33 E
Polignano a Mare, *Italy* **29** 41 0N 17 12 E
Poligny, *France* ...... **19** 46 50N 5 42 E
Políkhnitas, *Greece* ... **35** 39 4N 26 10 E
Polillo Is., *Phil.* ...... **57** 14 56N 122 0 E
Polístena, *Italy* .... **29** 38 25N 16 4 E
Políyiros, *Greece* ..... **35** 40 23N 23 25 E
Polk, *U.S.A.* **116** 41 22N 79 57W
Polla, *Italy* .... **29** 40 31N 15 27 E
Pollachi, *India* .... **51** 10 35N 77 0 E
Pollensa, *Spain* .... **24** 39 54N 3 1 E
Pollensa, B. de, *Spain* **24** 39 53N 3 8 E
Póllica, *Italy* .... **29** 40 13N 15 3 E
Pollino, Mte., *Italy* ... **29** 39 54N 16 13 E
Pollock, *U.S.A.* **120** 45 58N 100 18W
Polna, *U.S.S.R.* ...... **36** 58 31N 28 0 E
Polnovat, *U.S.S.R.* ... **40** 63 50N 65 54 E
Polo, *Ill., U.S.A.* **118** 41 59N 89 38W
Polo, *Mo., U.S.A.* **118** 39 33N 94 3W
Pologi, *U.S.S.R.* ..... **38** 47 29N 36 15 E
Polonnoye, *U.S.S.R.* .. **36** 50 6N 27 30 E
Polotsk, *U.S.S.R.* .... **36** 55 30N 28 50 E
Polson, *U.S.A.* **122** 47 45N 114 12W
Poltava, *U.S.S.R.* .... **38** 49 35N 34 35 E
Poltimore, *Canada* ... **106** 45 47N 75 43W
Polunochnoye, *U.S.S.R.* .... **40** 60 52N 60 25 E
Polur, *India* .... **51** 12 32N 79 11 E
Polynesia, *Pac. Oc.* ... **67** 10 0 S 162 0W
Pomarance, *Italy* ..... **26** 43 18N 10 51 E
Pomarico, *Italy* ...... **29** 40 31N 16 33 E
Pomaro, *Mexico* **126** 18 20N 103 18W
Pombal, *Brazil* .... **138** 6 45 S 37 50W
Pombal, *Portugal* **22** 39 55N 8 40W
Pómbia, *Greece* ...... **35** 35 0N 24 51 E
Pomeroy, *Ohio, U.S.A.* **114** 39 0N 82 0W
Pomeroy, *Wash., U.S.A.* **122** 46 30N 117 33W
Pomio, *Papua N. G.* .. **69** 5 32 S 151 33 E
Pomme de Terre, Res., *U.S.A.* **118** 37 54N 93 19W
Pomona, *U.S.A.* **125** 34 2N 117 49W
Pomorie, *Bulgaria* .... **34** 42 32N 27 41 E
Pomoshnaya, *U.S.S.R.* **38** 48 13N 31 36 E
Pompano Beach, *U.S.A.* **115** 26 12N 80 6W
Pompei, *Italy* .... **29** 40 45N 14 30 E
Pompey, *France* ...... **19** 48 46N 6 6 E
Pompeys Pillar, *U.S.A.* **122** 46 0N 108 0W
Ponape = Pohnpei, *Pac. Oc.* .... **66** 6 55N 158 10 E
Ponask, L., *Canada* .. **104** 54 0N 92 41W
Ponass L., *Canada* ... **111** 52 16N 103 58W
Ponca, *U.S.A.* **120** 42 38N 96 41W
Ponca City, *U.S.A.* ... **121** 36 40N 97 5W
Ponce, *Puerto Rico* ... **129** 18 1N 66 37W
Ponchatoula, *U.S.A.* .. **121** 30 27N 90 25W
Poncheville, L., *Canada* **106** 50 10N 76 55W
Poncin, *France* ...... **21** 46 6N 5 25 E
Pond, *U.S.A.* **125** 35 43N 119 20W
Pond Inlet, *Canada* ... **103** 72 40N 77 0W
Pondicherry, *India* .... **51** 11 59N 79 50 E
Pondrôme, *Belgium* .. **17** 50 6N 5 0 E
Ponds, I. of, *Canada* .. **105** 53 27N 55 52W
Ponérihouen, *N. Cal.* . **68** 21 5 S 165 24 E
Ponferrada, *Spain* **22** 42 32N 6 35W
Pongo, Wadi →, *Sudan* **89** 8 42N 27 40 E
Poniatowa, *Poland* ... **32** 51 11N 22 3 E
Ponikva, *Yugoslavia* .. **27** 46 16N 15 26 E
Ponnaiyar →, *India* .. **51** 11 50N 79 45 E
Ponnani, *India* .... **51** 10 45N 75 59 E
Ponneri, *India* .... **51** 13 20N 80 15 E
Ponnuru, *India* .... **51** 16 5N 80 34 E
Ponoi →, *U.S.S.R.* ... **40** 66 59N 41 17 E
Ponoka, *Canada* **110** 52 42N 113 40W
Ponorogo, *Indonesia* .. **57** 7 52 S 111 27 E
Pons, *France* **20** 45 35N 0 34W
Pons, *Spain* .... **24** 41 55N 1 12 E
Ponsul →, *Portugal* .. **23** 39 40N 7 31W
Pont-à-Celles, *Belgium* **17** 50 30N 4 22 E
Pont-à-Mousson, *France* **19** 48 54N 6 1 E
Pont-Audemer, *France* **18** 49 21N 0 30 E
Pont-Aven, *France* ... **18** 47 51N 3 47W
Pont Canavese, *Italy* .. **26** 45 24N 7 33 E
Pont-de-Roide, *France* **19** 47 23N 6 45 E
Pont-de-Salars, *France* **20** 44 18N 2 44 E
Pont-de-Vaux, *France* . **19** 46 26N 4 56 E
Pont-de-Veyle, *France* **21** 46 17N 4 53 E
Pont-l'Abbé, *France* .. **18** 47 52N 4 15W
Pont-l'Évêque, *France* **18** 49 18N 0 11 E
Pont-Rouge, *Canada* .. **107** 46 45N 71 42W
Pont-St.-Esprit, *France* **21** 44 16N 4 40 E
Pont-sur-Yonne, *France* **19** 48 18N 3 10 E
Ponta de Pedras, *Brazil* **138** 1 23 S 48 52W
Ponta Grossa, *Brazil* .. **141** 25 7 S 50 10W
Ponta Pora, *Brazil* .... **141** 22 20 S 55 35W
Pontacq, *France* **20** 43 11N 0 8W
Pontailler-sur-Saône, *France* .... **19** 47 13N 5 25 E
Pontal →, *Brazil* ..... **138** 9 8 S 40 12W
Pontalina, *Brazil* ..... **139** 17 31 S 49 27W
Pontarlier, *France* .... **19** 46 54N 6 20 E
Pontassieve, *Italy* ..... **27** 43 47N 11 25 E
Pontaubault, *France* .. **18** 48 40N 1 20W
Pontaumur, *France* ... **20** 45 52N 2 40 E
Pontcharra, *France* ... **21** 45 26N 6 1 E
Pontchartrain, L., *U.S.A.* **121** 30 12N 90 0W
Pontchâteau, *France* .. **18** 47 25N 2 5W
Ponte Alta, Serra do, *Brazil* .... **139** 19 42 S 47 40W
Ponte Alta do Norte, *Brazil* .... **138** 10 45 S 47 34W
Ponte Branca, *Brazil* . **137** 16 27 S 52 40W
Ponte da Barca, *Portugal* **22** 41 48N 8 25W
Ponte de Sor, *Portugal* **23** 39 17N 7 57W
Ponte dell 'Olio, *Italy* . **26** 44 52N 9 39 E
Ponte di Legno, *Italy* . **26** 46 15N 10 30 E
Ponte do Lima, *Portugal* **22** 41 46N 8 35W
Ponte do Pungué, *Mozam.* .... **93** 19 30 S 34 33 E
Ponte-Leccia, *France* . **21** 42 28N 9 13 E
Ponte Macassar, *Indonesia* .... **57** 9 30 S 123 58 E
Ponte nell' Alpi, *Italy* . **27** 46 10N 12 18 E
Ponte Nova, *Brazil* ... **139** 20 25 S 42 54W
Ponte San Martino, *Italy* .... **26** 45 36N 7 47 E
Ponte San Pietro, *Italy* **26** 45 42N 9 35 E
Pontebba, *Italy* .... **27** 46 30N 13 17 E
Pontecorvo, *Italy* ..... **28** 41 28N 13 40 E
Pontedera, *Italy* ...... **26** 43 40N 10 37 E
Pontefract, *U.K.* **12** 53 42N 1 19W
Ponteix, *Canada* **111** 49 46N 107 29W
Pontelandolfo, *Italy* ... **29** 41 17N 14 41 E
Pontevedra, *Spain* **22** 42 26N 8 40W
Pontevedra □, *Spain* .. **22** 42 25N 8 39W
Pontevedra, R. de →, *Spain* **22** 42 22N 8 45W
Pontevico, *Italy* ...... **26** 45 16N 10 6 E
Pontiac, *Ill., U.S.A.* .. **119** 40 50N 88 40W
Pontiac, *Mich., U.S.A.* **104** 42 40N 83 20W
Pontiac, Parc, *Canada* **106** 46 30N 76 30W
Pontian Kecil, *Malaysia* **55** 1 29N 103 23 E
Pontianak, *Indonesia* . **56** 0 3 S 109 15 E
Pontine Is. = Ponziane, Isole, *Italy* .... **28** 40 55N 13 0 E
Pontine Mts. = Kuzey Anadolu Dağlari, *Turkey* .... **46** 41 30N 35 0 E
Pontínia, *Italy* .... **28** 41 25N 13 2 E
Pontivy, *France* **18** 48 5N 2 58W
Pontoise, *France* ..... **19** 49 3N 2 5 E
Ponton →, *Canada* .. **110** 58 27N 116 11W
Pontorson, *France* **18** 48 34N 1 30W
Pontrémoli, *Italy* ..... **26** 44 22N 9 52 E
Pontrieux, *France* **18** 48 42N 3 10W
Ponts-de-Cé, Les, *France* **18** 47 25N 0 30W
Pontypool, *Canada* ... **109** 44 6N 78 38W
Pontypool, *U.K.* **13** 51 42N 3 1W
Pontypridd, *U.K.* **13** 51 36N 3 21W
Ponza, *Italy* .... **28** 40 55N 12 57 E
Ponziane, Isole, *Italy* . **28** 40 55N 13 0 E
Poochera, *Australia* ... **73** 32 43 S 134 51 E
Poole, *U.K.* **13** 50 42N 1 58W
Pooley I., *Canada* ... **110** 52 45N 128 15W
Poona = Pune, *India* . **50** 18 29N 73 57 E
Poonamallee, *India* ... **51** 13 3N 80 10 E
Pooncarie, *Australia* .. **73** 33 22 S 142 31 E
Poopelloe, L., *Australia* **73** 31 40 S 144 0 E
Poopó, *Bolivia* .... **136** 18 23 S 66 59W
Poopó, L. de, *Bolivia* . **136** 18 30 S 67 35W
Poor Knights Is., *N.Z.* **80** 35 29 S 174 43 E
Poowong, *Australia* ... **74** 38 21 S 145 46 E
Popanyinning, *Australia* **79** 32 40 S 117 2 E
Popayán, *Colombia* ... **134** 2 27N 76 36W
Poperinge, *Belgium* ... **17** 50 51N 2 42 E
Popigay, *U.S.S.R.* .... **41** 72 1N 110 39 E
Popilta, L., *Australia* . **73** 33 10 S 141 42 E
Popio, L., *Australia* .. **73** 33 10 S 141 52 E
Poplar, *U.S.A.* **120** 48 3N 105 9W
Poplar →, *Man., Canada* **111** 53 0N 97 19W
Poplar →, *N.W.T., Canada* **110** 61 22N 121 52W
Poplar Bluff, *U.S.A.* .. **121** 36 45N 90 22W
Poplarville, *U.S.A.* ... **121** 30 55N 89 30W
Popocatepetl, *Mexico* . **127** 19 10N 98 40W
Popokabaka, *Zaïre* ... **95** 5 41 S 16 40 E
Pópoli, *Italy* .... **27** 42 12N 13 50 E
Popondetta, *Papua N. G.* .... **69** 8 48 S 148 17 E
Popovača, *Yugoslavia* . **27** 45 30N 16 41 E
Popovo, *Bulgaria* ..... **34** 43 21N 26 18 E
Poppel, *Belgium* ..... **17** 51 27N 5 2 E
Poprád, *Czech.* ...... **32** 49 3N 20 18 E
Poprád →, *Czech.* ... **32** 49 38N 20 42 E
Poradaha, *Bangla.* .... **52** 23 51N 89 1 E
Porali →, *Pakistan* ... **48** 25 35N 66 26 E
Porangaba, *Brazil* .... **136** 8 48 S 70 36W
Porangahau, *N.Z.* .... **80** 40 17 S 176 37 E
Porangatu, *Brazil* .... **139** 13 26 S 49 10W
Porbandar, *India* ..... **48** 21 44N 69 43 E
Porce →, *Colombia* .. **134** 7 28N 74 53W
Porcher I., *Canada* ... **110** 53 50N 130 30W
Porco, *Bolivia* .... **137** 19 50 S 65 59W
Porcos →, *Brazil* .... **139** 12 42 S 45 7W
Porcuna, *Spain* **23** 37 52N 4 11W
Porcupine, *Canada* ... **106** 48 30N 81 11W
Porcupine →, *Canada* **111** 59 11N 104 46W
Porcupine →, *U.S.A.* **102** 66 35N 145 15W
Pordenone, *Italy* ..... **27** 45 58N 12 40 E
Poreč, *Yugoslavia* .... **27** 45 14N 13 36 E
Porecatu, *Brazil* ...... **139** 22 43 S 51 24W
Porepunkah, *Australia* **75** 36 42 S 146 55 E
Poretskoye, *U.S.S.R.* . **37** 55 9N 46 21 E
Pori, *Finland* .... **9** 61 29N 21 48 E
Porjus, *Sweden* .... **8** 66 57N 19 50 E
Porkhov, *U.S.S.R.* ... **36** 57 45N 29 38 E
Porkkala, *Finland* .... **9** 59 59N 24 26 E
Porlamar, *Venezuela* .. **135** 10 57N 63 51W
Porlezza, *Italy* .... **26** 46 2N 9 8 E
Porma →, *Spain* **22** 42 49N 5 28W
Pornic, *France* **18** 47 7N 2 5W
Poronaysk, *U.S.S.R.* .. **41** 49 13N 143 0 E
Póros, *Greece* .... **35** 37 30N 23 30 E
Poroshiri-Dake, *Japan* **63** 42 41N 142 52 E
Poroto Mts., *Tanzania* **93** 9 0 S 33 30 E
Porpoise B., *Antarctica* **143** 66 0 S 127 0 E
Porquerolles, I. de, *France* .... **21** 43 0N 6 13 E
Porrentruy, *Switz.* .... **31** 47 25N 7 6 E
Porreras, *Spain* ...... **24** 39 31N 3 2 E
Porretta, Passo di, *Italy* **26** 44 2N 10 56 E
Porsangen, *Norway* ... **8** 70 40N 25 40 E
Porsgrunn, *Norway* ... **10** 59 10N 9 40 E
Port Adelaide, *Australia* .... **73** 34 46 S 138 30 E
Port Alberni, *Canada* . **110** 49 14N 124 50W
Port Albert, *Australia* . **75** 38 42 S 146 42 E
Port Alfred, *Canada* .. **107** 48 18N 70 53W
Port Alfred, *S. Africa* . **96** 33 36 S 26 55 E
Port Alice, *Canada* ... **110** 50 20N 127 25W
Port Allegany, *U.S.A.* **116** 41 49N 78 17W
Port Allen, *U.S.A.* ... **121** 30 30N 91 15W
Port Alma, *Australia* .. **72** 23 38 S 150 53 E
Port Angeles, *U.S.A.* . **124** 48 7N 123 30W
Port Antonio, *Jamaica* **128** 18 10N 76 30W
Port Aransas, *U.S.A.* . **121** 27 49N 97 4W
Port Arthur = Lüshun, *China* .... **61** 38 45N 121 15 E
Port Arthur, *Australia* **72** 43 7 S 147 50 E
Port Arthur, *U.S.A.* .. **121** 30 0N 94 0W
Port au Port B., *Canada* **105** 48 40N 58 50W
Port-au-Prince, *Haiti* .. **129** 18 40N 72 20W
Port Augusta, *Australia* **73** 32 30 S 137 50 E
Port Augusta West, *Australia* .... **73** 32 29 S 137 29 E
Port Austin, *U.S.A.* .. **116** 44 3N 82 59W
Port Bell, *Uganda* .... **92** 0 18N 32 35 E
Port Bergé Vaovao, *Madag.* .... **97** 15 33 S 47 40 E
Port Blandford, *Canada* **105** 48 20N 54 10W
Port Bou, *Spain* ...... **24** 42 25N 3 9 E
Port Bouët, *Ivory C.* .. **90** 5 16N 3 57W
Port Bradshaw, *Australia* .... **72** 12 30 S 137 20 E
Port Broughton, *Australia* .... **73** 33 37 S 137 56 E
Port Burwell, *Canada* . **108** 42 40N 80 48W
Port Campbell, *Australia* .... **74** 38 37 S 143 1 E
Port Canning, *India* .. **49** 22 23N 88 40 E
Port Carling, *Canada* . **108** 45 7N 79 35W
Port-Cartier, *Canada* . **105** 50 2N 66 50W
Port Chalmers, *N.Z.* .. **81** 45 49 S 170 30 E
Port Chester, *U.S.A.* . **117** 41 0N 73 41W
Port Clements, *Canada* **110** 53 40N 132 10W
Port Clinton, *U.S.A.* .. **119** 41 30N 82 58W
Port Colborne, *Canada* **108** 42 50N 79 10W
Port Coquitlam, *Canada* **110** 49 15N 122 45W
Port Credit, *Canada* .. **108** 43 33N 79 35W
Port Curtis, *Australia* . **72** 23 57 S 151 20 E
Port Dalhousie, *Canada* **116** 43 13N 79 16W
Port Darwin, *Australia* **78** 12 24 S 130 45 E
Port Darwin, *Falk. Is.* **142** 51 50 S 59 0W
Port Davey, *Australia* . **72** 43 16 S 145 55 E
Port-de-Bouc, *France* . **21** 43 24N 4 59 E
Port-de-Paix, *Haiti* ... **129** 19 50N 72 50W
Port Dickson, *Malaysia* **55** 2 30N 101 49 E
Port Douglas, *Australia* **72** 16 30 S 145 30 E
Port Dover, *Canada* .. **108** 42 47N 80 12W
Port Edward, *Canada* . **110** 54 12N 130 10W
Port Elgin, *Canada* ... **108** 44 25N 81 25W
Port Elizabeth, *S. Africa* .... **96** 33 58 S 25 40 E
Port Ellen, *U.K.* **14** 55 38N 6 10W
Port-en-Bessin, *France* **18** 49 21N 0 45W
Port Erin, *I. of Man* .. **12** 54 5N 4 45W
Port Essington, *Australia* .... **78** 11 15 S 132 10 E
Port Etienne = Nouâdhibou, *Mauritania* **84** 20 54N 17 0W
Port Fairy, *Australia* .. **74** 38 22 S 142 12 E
Port Fitzroy, *N.Z.* .... **80** 36 8 S 175 20 E
Port Fouâd = Bûr Fuad, *Egypt* .... **88** 31 15N 32 20 E
Port Gamble, *U.S.A.* . **124** 47 51N 122 35W
Port-Gentil, *Gabon* ... **94** 0 40 S 8 50 E
Port Gibson, *U.S.A.* .. **121** 31 57N 91 0W
Port Glasgow, *U.K.* .. **14** 55 57N 4 40W
Port Harcourt, *Nigeria* **91** 4 40N 7 10 E
Port Hardy, *Canada* .. **110** 50 41N 127 30W
Port Harrison = Inoucdjouac, *Canada* **103** 58 25N 78 15W
Port Hawkesbury, *Canada* **105** 45 36N 61 22W
Port Hedland, *Australia* **78** 20 25 S 118 35 E
Port Henry, *U.S.A.* ... **117** 44 0N 73 30W
Port Hood, *Canada* ... **105** 46 0N 61 32W
Port Hope, *Canada* ... **109** 43 56N 78 20W
Port Hueneme, *U.S.A.* **125** 34 7N 119 12W
Port Huron, *U.S.A.* .. **104** 43 0N 82 28W
Port Isabel, *U.S.A.* ... **121** 26 4N 97 9W
Port Jackson, *Australia* **76** 33 50 S 151 18 E
Port Jefferson, *U.S.A.* **117** 40 58N 73 5W
Port Jervis, *U.S.A.* ... **117** 41 22N 74 42W
Port-Joinville, *France* . **18** 46 45N 2 23W
Port Katon, *U.S.S.R.* . **39** 46 52N 38 46 E
Port Kembla, *Australia* **76** 34 52 S 150 49 E
Port-la-Nouvelle, *France* .... **20** 43 1N 3 3 E
Port Laoise, *Ireland* .. **15** 53 2N 7 20W
Port Lavaca, *U.S.A.* .. **121** 28 38N 96 38W
Port-Leucate, *France* . **20** 42 53N 3 3 E
Port Lincoln, *Australia* **73** 34 42 S 135 52 E
Port Loko, *S. Leone* .. **90** 8 48N 12 46W
Port Loring, *Canada* .. **108** 45 55N 80 0W
Port Louis, *France* **18** 47 42N 3 22W
Port Louis, *Mauritius* . **53** 20 10 S 57 30 E
Port Lyautey = Kenitra, *Morocco* .. **84** 34 15N 6 40W
Port Macdonnell, *Australia* .... **73** 38 0 S 140 48 E
Port Macquarie, *Australia* .... **77** 31 25 S 152 25 E
Port Maria, *Jamaica* .. **128** 18 25N 77 5W
Port Mellon, *Canada* . **110** 49 32N 123 31W
Port-Menier, *Canada* . **105** 49 51N 64 15W
Port Morant, *Jamaica* . **128** 17 54N 76 19W
Port Moresby, *Papua N. G.* .... **69** 9 24 S 147 8 E
Port Mourant, *Guyana* **135** 6 15N 57 20W
Port Mouton, *Canada* . **105** 43 58N 64 50W
Port Musgrave, *Australia* .... **72** 11 55 S 141 50 E
Port-Navalo, *France* .. **18** 47 34N 2 54W
Port Nelson, *Canada* .. **111** 57 3N 92 36W
Port Nicholson, *N.Z.* . **80** 41 20 S 174 52 E
Port Nolloth, *S. Africa* **96** 29 17 S 16 52 E
Port Nouveau-Québec, *Canada* **103** 58 30N 65 59W
Port O'Connor, *U.S.A.* **121** 28 26N 96 24W
Port of Spain, *Trin. & Tob.* **129** 10 40N 61 31W
Port Orchard, *U.S.A.* . **124** 47 31N 122 38W
Port Orford, *U.S.A.* .. **122** 42 45N 124 28W
Port Pegasus, *N.Z.* ... **81** 47 12 S 167 41 E
Port Perry, *Canada* ... **109** 44 6N 78 56W
Port Phillip B., *Australia* .... **74** 38 10 S 144 50 E
Port Pirie, *Australia* .. **73** 33 10 S 138 1 E
Port Radium = Echo Bay, *Canada* **102** 66 5N 117 55W
Port Renfrew, *Canada* **110** 48 30N 124 20W
Port Roper, *Australia* . **72** 14 45 S 135 25 E
Port Rowan, *Canada* . **108** 42 40N 80 30W
Port Safaga = Bûr Safâga, *Egypt* ...... **88** 26 43N 33 57 E
Port Said = Bûr Sa'îd, *Egypt* .... **88** 31 16N 32 18 E
Port St. Joe, *U.S.A.* .. **115** 29 49N 85 20W
Port St. Johns, *S. Africa* .... **97** 31 38 S 29 33 E
Port-St.-Louis-du-Rhône, *France* ..... **21** 43 23N 4 49 E
Port Sanilac, *U.S.A.* .. **116** 43 26N 82 33W
Port Saunders, *Canada* **105** 50 40N 57 18W
Port Severn, *Canada* .. **108** 44 48N 79 43W
Port Shepstone, *S. Africa* .... **97** 30 44 S 30 28 E
Port Simpson, *Canada* **110** 54 30N 130 20W
Port Stanley, *Canada* . **108** 42 40N 81 10W
Port Stephens, *Australia* **76** 32 38 S 152 12 E
Port Sudan = Bûr Sûdân, *Sudan* ...... **88** 19 32N 37 9 E
Port-sur-Saône, *France* **19** 47 42N 6 2 E
Port Talbot, *U.K.* **13** 51 35N 3 48W
Port Taufîq = Bûr Taufiq, *Egypt* ...... **88** 29 54N 32 32 E
Port Townsend, *U.S.A.* **124** 48 7N 122 50W
Port-Vendres, *France* . **20** 42 32N 3 8 E
Port Wakefield, *Australia* .... **73** 34 12 S 138 10 E
Port Washington, *U.S.A.* **114** 43 25N 87 52W
Port Weld, *Malaysia* .. **55** 4 50N 100 38 E
Port Welshpool, *Australia* .... **75** 38 42 S 146 28 E
Portachuelo, *Bolivia* .. **137** 17 10 S 63 20W
Portadown, *U.K.* **15** 54 27N 6 26W
Portage, *Mich., U.S.A.* **119** 42 12N 85 35W
Portage, *U.S.A.* **120** 43 31N 89 25W
Portage →, *U.S.A.* ... **119** 41 32N 82 58W
Portage La Prairie, *Canada* **111** 49 58N 98 18W
Portageville, *U.S.A.* .. **121** 36 25N 89 40W
Portalegre, *Portugal* .. **23** 39 19N 7 25W
Portalegre □, *Portugal* **23** 39 20N 7 40W
Portales, *U.S.A.* **121** 34 12N 103 25W
Portarlington, *Australia* **74** 38 7 S 144 40 E
Portarlington, *Ireland* . **15** 53 10N 7 10W
Porte, La, *U.S.A.* **119** 41 36N 86 43W
Porte City, La, *U.S.A.* **118** 42 19N 92 12W
Porteirinha, *Brazil* .... **139** 15 44 S 43 2W
Portel, *Brazil* .... **138** 1 57 S 50 49W
Portel, *Portugal* **23** 38 19N 7 41W
Porter, *U.S.A.* **119** 41 36N 87 4W
Porter L., *N.W.T., Canada* **111** 61 41N 108 5W
Porter L., *Sask., Canada* **111** 56 20N 107 20W

Porters Retreat, Australia 76 34 2 S 149 49 E
Porterville, S. Africa 96 33 0 S 19 0 E
Porterville, U.S.A. 124 36 5N 119 0W
Porthcawl, U.K. 13 51 28N 3 42W
Porthill, U.S.A. 122 49 0N 116 30W
Portile de Fier, Europe 34 44 42N 22 30 E
Portimão, Portugal 23 37 8N 8 32W
Portland, N.S.W., Australia 76 33 20 S 150 0 E
Portland, Vic., Australia 74 38 20 S 141 35 E
Portland, Canada 109 44 42N 76 12W
Portland, Conn., U.S.A. 117 41 34N 72 39W
Portland, Ind., U.S.A. 119 40 26N 84 59W
Portland, Maine, U.S.A. 105 43 40N 70 15W
Portland, Mich., U.S.A. 119 42 52N 84 58W
Portland, Oreg., U.S.A. 124 45 35N 122 40W
Portland, Bill of, U.K. 13 50 31N 2 27W
Portland, I. of, U.K. 13 50 32N 2 25W
Portland B., Australia 74 38 15 S 141 45 E
Portland I., N.Z. 80 39 20 S 177 51 E
Portland Prom., Canada 103 58 40N 78 33W
Portneuf, Canada 107 46 43N 71 55W
Portneuf →, Canada 107 48 38N 69 5W
Portneuf, Parc Prov. de, Canada 107 47 10N 72 25W
Pôrto, Brazil 138 3 54 S 42 42W
Porto, France 21 42 16N 8 42 E
Porto, Portugal 22 41 8N 8 40W
Porto □, Portugal 22 41 8N 8 20W
Porto, G. de, France 21 42 17N 8 34 E
Pôrto Acre, Brazil 136 9 34 S 67 31W
Pôrto Alegre, Pará, Brazil 135 4 22 S 52 44W
Pôrto Alegre, Rio Grande do S., Brazil 141 30 5 S 51 10W
Porto Amboim = Gunza, Angola 95 10 50 S 13 50 E
Porto Argentera, Italy 26 44 15N 7 27 E
Porto Azzurro, Italy 26 42 46N 10 24 E
Porto Botte, Italy 28 39 3N 8 33 E
Pôrto Cajueiro, Brazil 137 11 3 S 55 53W
Porto Civitanova, Italy 27 43 19N 13 44 E
Pôrto da Fôlha, Brazil 138 9 55 S 37 17W
Pôrto de Móz, Brazil 138 1 41 S 52 13W
Pôrto de Pedras, Brazil 138 9 10 S 35 17W
Pôrto des Meinacos, Brazil 137 12 33 S 53 7W
Porto Empédocle, Italy 28 37 18N 13 30 E
Pôrto Esperança, Brazil 137 19 37 S 57 29W
Pôrto Esperidão, Brazil 137 15 51 S 58 28W
Pôrto Franco, Brazil 138 6 20 S 47 24W
Porto Garibaldi, Italy 27 44 41N 12 14 E
Pôrto Grande, Brazil 135 0 42N 51 24W
Pôrto Jofre, Brazil 137 17 20 S 56 48W
Pórto Lágo, Greece 35 40 58N 25 6 E
Porto Mendes, Brazil 141 24 30 S 54 15W
Pôrto Murtinho, Brazil 137 21 45 S 57 55W
Pôrto Nacional, Brazil 138 10 40 S 48 30W
Porto Novo, Benin 91 6 23N 2 42 E
Porto Recanati, Italy 27 43 26N 13 40 E
Porto San Giórgio, Italy 27 43 11N 13 49 E
Pôrto Santana, Brazil 135 0 3 S 51 11W
Porto Santo Stefano, Italy 26 42 26N 11 7 E
Pôrto São José, Brazil 141 22 43 S 53 10W
Pôrto Seguro, Brazil 139 16 26 S 39 5W
Porto Tolle, Italy 27 44 57N 12 20 E
Porto Tórres, Italy 28 40 50N 8 23 E
Pôrto União, Brazil 141 26 10 S 51 10W
Pôrto Válter, Brazil 136 8 15 S 72 40W
Porto-Vecchio, France 21 41 35N 9 16 E
Pôrto Velho, Brazil 137 8 46 S 63 54W
Portobelo, Panama 128 9 35N 79 42W
Portoferráio, Italy 26 42 50N 10 20 E
Portogruaro, Italy 27 45 47N 12 50 E
Portola, U.S.A. 124 39 49N 120 28W
Portomaggiore, Italy 27 44 41N 11 47 E
Portoscuso, Italy 28 39 12N 8 22 E
Portovénere, Italy 26 44 2N 9 50 E
Portovíejo, Ecuador 134 1 7 S 80 28W
Portpatrick, U.K. 14 54 50N 5 7W
Portree, U.K. 14 57 25N 6 11W
Portrush, U.K. 15 55 13N 6 40W
Portsall, France 18 48 37N 4 45W
Portsmouth, Domin. 129 15 34N 61 27W
Portsmouth, U.K. 13 50 48N 1 6W
Portsmouth, N.H., U.S.A. 117 43 5N 70 45W
Portsmouth, Ohio, U.S.A. 114 38 45N 83 0W
Portsmouth, R.I., U.S.A. 117 41 35N 71 15W
Portsmouth, Va., U.S.A. 114 36 50N 76 20W
Portsoy, U.K. 14 57 41N 2 41W
Porttipahta, Finland 8 68 5N 26 40 E
Portugal ■, Europe 22 40 0N 7 0W
Portugalete, Spain 24 43 19N 3 4W
Portuguesa □, Venezuela 134 9 10N 69 15W
Portuguese-Guinea = Guinea-Bissau ■, Africa 90 12 0N 15 0W
Portuguese Timor ■ = Timor, Indonesia 57 9 0 S 125 0 E
Portumna, Ireland 15 53 5N 8 12W
Portville, U.S.A. 116 42 3N 78 21W
Porvenir, Bolivia 136 11 10 S 68 50W
Porvenir, Chile 142 53 10 S 70 16W
Porvoo, Finland 9 60 24N 25 40 E
Porzuna, Spain 23 39 9N 4 9W
Posada →, Italy 28 40 40N 9 45 E
Posadas, Argentina 141 27 30 S 55 50W
Posadas, Spain 23 37 47N 5 11W
Poschiavo, Switz. 31 46 19N 10 4 E
Posets, Spain 24 42 39N 0 25 E
Poseyville, U.S.A. 119 38 10N 87 47W
Poshan = Boshan, China 61 36 28N 117 49 E
Posídhion, Ákra, Greece 35 39 57N 23 30 E
Poso, Indonesia 57 1 20 S 120 55 E
Posoegroenoe, Surinam 135 4 23N 55 43W
Posse, Brazil 139 14 4 S 46 18W
Possel, C.A.R. 94 5 5N 19 10 E
Possession I., Antarctica 143 72 4 S 172 0 E
Pössneck, E. Germany 30 50 42N 11 34 E
Post, U.S.A. 121 33 13N 101 21W
Post Falls, U.S.A. 122 47 46N 116 59W
Postavy, U.S.S.R. 36 55 4N 26 50 E
Poste Maurice Cortier, Algeria 85 22 14N 1 2 E
Postmasburg, S. Africa 96 28 18 S 23 5 E
Postojna, Yugoslavia 27 45 46N 14 12 E
Poston, U.S.A. 125 34 0N 114 24W
Postville, U.S.A. 118 43 5N 91 34W
Potchefstroom, S. Africa 96 26 41 S 27 7 E
Poté, Brazil 139 17 49 S 41 49W
Poteau, U.S.A. 121 35 5N 94 37W
Poteet, U.S.A. 121 29 4N 98 35W
Potelu, Lacul, Romania 34 43 44N 24 20 E
Potenza, Italy 29 40 40N 15 50 E
Potenza →, Italy 27 43 27N 13 38 E
Potenza Picena, Italy 27 43 22N 13 37 E
Poteriteri, L., N.Z. 81 46 5 S 167 10 E
Potes, Spain 22 43 15N 4 42W
Potgietersrus, S. Africa 97 24 10 S 28 55 E
Poti, U.S.S.R. 39 42 10N 41 38 E
Potiraguá, Brazil 139 15 36 S 39 53W
Potiskum, Nigeria 91 11 39N 11 2 E
Potomac →, U.S.A. 114 38 0N 76 23W
Potosí, Bolivia 137 19 38 S 65 50W
Potosi, U.S.A. 118 37 56N 90 47W
Potosí □, Bolivia 136 20 31 S 67 0W
Potosi Mt., U.S.A. 125 35 57N 115 29W
Pototan, Phil. 57 10 54N 122 38 E
Potrerillos, Chile 140 26 30 S 69 30W
Potsdam, E. Germany 30 52 23N 13 4 E
Potsdam, U.S.A. 117 44 40N 74 59W
Potsdam □, E. Germany 30 52 40N 12 50 E
Pottenstein, W. Germany 31 49 46N 11 25 E
Potter, U.S.A. 120 41 15N 103 20W
Pottery Hill = Abû Ballas, Egypt 88 24 26N 27 36 E
Pottstown, U.S.A. 117 40 17N 75 40W
Pottsville, U.S.A. 117 40 39N 76 12W
Pouancé, France 18 47 44N 1 10W
Pouce Coupé, Canada 110 55 40N 120 10W
Pouembout, N. Cal. 68 21 8 S 164 53 E
Poughkeepsie, U.S.A. 117 41 40N 73 57W
Pouilly-sur-Loire, France 19 47 17N 2 57 E
Poulaphouca Res., Ireland 15 53 8N 6 30W
Pouldu, Le, France 18 47 41N 3 36W
Poulin-de-Courval, L., Canada 107 48 52N 70 27W
Poulsbo, U.S.A. 124 47 45N 122 39W
Poum, N. Cal. 68 20 14 S 164 2 E
Poumadji, C.A.R. 94 5 56N 22 10 E
Pounga-Nganda, Gabon 94 2 58 S 10 51 E
Pourri, Mt., France 21 45 32N 6 52 E
Pouso Alegre, Mato Grosso, Brazil 137 11 46 S 57 16W
Pouso Alegre, Minas Gerais, Brazil 141 22 14 S 45 57W
Poutrincourt, L., Canada 107 49 11N 74 7W
Pouzauges, France 18 46 47N 0 50W
Povenets, U.S.S.R. 40 62 50N 34 50 E
Poverty Bay, N.Z. 80 38 43 S 178 2 E
Póvoa de Lanhosa, Portugal 22 41 33N 8 15W
Póvoa de Varzim, Portugal 22 41 25N 8 46W
Povorino, U.S.S.R. 37 51 12N 42 5 E
Powassan, Canada 108 46 5N 79 25W
Poway, U.S.A. 125 32 58N 117 2W
Powder →, U.S.A. 120 46 47N 105 12W
Powder River, U.S.A. 122 43 5N 107 0W
Powell, U.S.A. 122 44 45N 108 45W
Powell, L., U.S.A. 123 37 25N 110 45W
Powell River, Canada 110 49 50N 124 35W
Powers, Mich., U.S.A. 114 45 40N 87 32W
Powers, Oreg., U.S.A. 122 42 53N 124 2W
Powers Lake, U.S.A. 120 48 37N 102 38W
Powys □, U.K. 13 52 20N 3 20W
Poxoreu, Brazil 137 15 50 S 54 23W
Poya, N. Cal. 68 21 19 S 165 7 E
Poyang Hu, China 59 29 5N 116 20 E
Poyarkovo, U.S.S.R. 41 49 36N 128 41 E
Poza de la Sal, Spain 24 42 35N 3 31W
Poza Rica, Mexico 127 20 33N 97 27W
Požarevac, Yugoslavia 33 44 35N 21 18 E
Pozi, Taiwan 59 23 30N 120 13 E
Poznań, Poland 32 52 25N 16 55 E
Pozo, U.S.A. 125 35 20N 120 24W
Pozo Alcón, Spain 25 37 42N 2 56W
Pozo Almonte, Chile 136 20 10 S 69 50W
Pozo Colorado, Paraguay 140 23 30 S 58 45W
Pozo del Dátil, Mexico 126 30 0N 112 15W
Pozoblanco, Spain 23 38 23N 4 51W
Pozuzo, Peru 136 10 5 S 75 35W
Pozzallo, Italy 29 36 44N 14 52 E
Pozzuoli, Italy 29 40 46N 14 6 E
Pra →, Ghana 91 5 1N 1 37W
Prachin Buri, Thailand 54 14 0N 101 25 E
Prachuap Khiri Khan, Thailand 55 11 49N 99 48 E
Pradelles, France 20 44 46N 3 52 E
Pradera, Colombia 134 3 25N 76 15W
Prades, France 20 42 38N 2 23 E
Prado, Brazil 139 17 20 S 39 13W
Prado del Rey, Spain 23 36 48N 5 33W
Præstø, Denmark 11 55 8N 12 2 E
Pragersko, Yugoslavia 27 46 27N 15 42 E
Prague = Praha, Czech. 32 50 5N 14 22 E
Praha, Czech. 32 50 5N 14 22 E
Prahecq, France 20 46 19N 0 26W
Prahita →, India 50 19 0N 79 55 E
Prahova →, Romania 34 44 50N 25 50 E
Prahovo, Yugoslavia 33 44 18N 22 39 E
Praid, Romania 34 46 32N 25 10 E
Prainha, Amazonas, Brazil 137 7 10 S 60 30W
Prainha, Pará, Brazil 135 1 45 S 53 30W
Prairie, Australia 72 20 50 S 144 35 E
Prairie →, U.S.A. 121 34 30N 99 23W
Prairie City, U.S.A. 122 44 27N 118 44W
Prairie du Chien, U.S.A. 118 43 1N 91 9W
Prairie du Rocher, U.S.A. 118 38 5N 90 6W
Pramánda, Greece 35 39 32N 21 8 E
Pran Buri, Thailand 54 12 23N 99 55 E
Prang, Ghana 91 8 1N 0 56W
Prapat, Indonesia 56 2 41N 98 58 E
Prata, Brazil 139 19 25 S 48 54W
Pratapgarh, India 48 24 2N 74 40 E
Prática di Mare, Italy 28 41 40N 12 26 E
Prato, Italy 26 43 53N 11 5 E
Prátola Peligna, Italy 27 42 7N 13 51 E
Pratovécchio, Italy 27 43 44N 11 43 E
Prats-de-Mollo-la-Preste, France 20 42 25N 2 27 E
Pratt, U.S.A. 121 37 40N 98 45W
Pratten, Australia 77 28 6 S 151 48 E
Prattville, U.S.A. 115 32 30N 86 28W
Pravara →, India 50 19 35N 74 45 E
Pravdinsk, U.S.S.R. 37 56 29N 43 28 E
Pravia, Spain 22 43 30N 6 12W
Praya, Indonesia 56 8 39 S 116 17 E
Pré-en-Pail, France 18 48 28N 0 12W
Pré St. Didier, Italy 26 45 45N 7 0 E
Precordillera, Argentina 140 30 0 S 69 1W
Predáppio, Italy 27 44 7N 11 58 E
Predazzo, Italy 27 46 19N 11 37 E
Predejane, Yugoslavia 33 42 51N 22 9 E
Preeceville, Canada 111 51 57N 102 40W
Préfailles, France 18 47 9N 2 11W
Pregonero, Venezuela 134 8 1N 71 46W
Pregrada, Yugoslavia 27 46 11N 15 45 E
Preissac, L., Canada 106 48 20N 78 20W
Preko, Yugoslavia 27 44 7N 15 14 E
Prelate, Canada 111 50 51N 109 24W
Prelog, Yugoslavia 27 46 18N 16 32 E
Premer, Australia 77 31 29 S 149 56 E
Premier, Canada 110 56 4N 129 56W
Premont, U.S.A. 121 27 19N 98 8W
Premuda, Yugoslavia 27 44 20N 14 36 E
Prenjasi, Albania 35 41 6N 20 32 E
Prentice, U.S.A. 120 45 31N 90 19W
Prenzlau, E. Germany 30 53 19N 13 51 E
Prepansko Jezero, Yugoslavia 35 40 55N 21 0 E
Přerov, Czech. 32 49 28N 17 27 E
Presanella, Italy 26 46 13N 10 40 E
Prescott, Canada 109 44 45N 75 30W
Prescott, Ariz., U.S.A. 123 34 35N 112 30W
Prescott, Ark., U.S.A. 121 33 49N 93 22W
Preservation Inlet, N.Z. 81 46 8 S 166 35 E
Preševo, Yugoslavia 33 42 19N 21 39 E
Presho, U.S.A. 120 43 56N 100 4W
Presicce, Italy 29 39 53N 18 13 E
Presidencia de la Plaza, Argentina 140 27 0 S 59 50W
Presidencia Roque Saenz Peña, Argentina 140 26 45 S 60 30W
Presidente Epitácio, Brazil 139 21 56 S 52 6W
Presidente Hayes □, Paraguay 140 24 0 S 59 0W
Presidente Hermes, Brazil 137 11 17 S 61 55W
Presidente Prudente, Brazil 141 22 5 S 51 25W
Presidio, Mexico 126 29 29N 104 23W
Presidio, U.S.A. 121 29 30N 104 20W
Preslav, Bulgaria 34 43 10N 26 52 E
Prešov, Czech. 32 49 0N 21 15 E
Prespa, L. = Prepansko Jezero, Yugoslavia 35 40 55N 21 0 E
Presque Isle, U.S.A. 105 46 40N 68 0W
Prestbury, U.K. 13 51 54N 2 2W
Prestea, Ghana 90 5 22N 2 7W
Presteigne, U.K. 13 52 17N 3 0W
Presto, Bolivia 137 18 55 S 64 56W
Preston, Canada 116 43 23N 80 21W
Preston, U.K. 12 53 46N 2 42W
Preston, Idaho, U.S.A. 122 42 10N 111 55W
Preston, Iowa, U.S.A. 118 42 6N 90 24W
Preston, Minn., U.S.A. 120 43 39N 92 3W
Preston, Nev., U.S.A. 122 38 59N 115 2W
Preston, C., Australia 78 20 51 S 116 12 E
Prestonpans, U.K. 14 55 58N 3 0W
Prestwick, U.K. 14 55 30N 4 38W
Prêto →, Amazonas, Brazil 135 0 8 S 64 6W
Prêto →, Bahia, Brazil 138 11 21 S 43 52W
Prêto do Igapó-Açu →, Brazil 135 4 26 S 59 48W
Pretoria, S. Africa 97 25 44 S 28 12 E
Preuilly-sur-Claise, France 18 46 51N 0 56 E
Préveza, Greece 35 38 57N 20 47 E
Priazovskoye, U.S.S.R. 38 46 44N 35 40 E
Pribilof Is., Bering S. 144 56 0N 170 0W
Priboj, Yugoslavia 33 43 35N 19 32 E
Příbram, Czech. 32 49 41N 14 2 E
Price, U.S.A. 122 39 40N 110 48W
Price I., Canada 110 52 23N 128 41W
Prichalnaya, U.S.S.R. 39 48 57N 44 33 E
Prichard, U.S.A. 115 30 47N 88 5W
Priego, Spain 24 40 26N 2 21W
Priego de Córdoba, Spain 23 37 27N 4 12W
Priekule, U.S.S.R. 36 57 27N 21 45 E
Prien, W. Germany 31 47 52N 12 20 E
Prieska, S. Africa 96 29 40 S 22 42 E
Priest L., U.S.A. 122 48 30N 116 55W
Priest River, U.S.A. 122 48 11N 116 55W
Priest Valley, U.S.A. 124 36 10N 120 39W
Priestly, Canada 110 54 8N 125 20W
Prievidza, Czech. 32 48 46N 18 36 E
Prijedor, Yugoslavia 27 44 58N 16 41 E
Prikaspiyskaya Nizmennost, U.S.S.R. 39 47 0N 48 0 E
Prilep, Yugoslavia 35 41 21N 21 37 E
Priluki, U.S.S.R. 36 50 30N 32 24 E
Prime Seal I., Australia 72 40 3 S 147 43 E
Primeira Cruz, Brazil 138 2 30 S 43 26W
Primorsko-Akhtarsk, U.S.S.R. 38 46 2N 38 10 E
Primorskoye, U.S.S.R. 38 47 10N 37 38 E
Primrose L., Canada 111 54 55N 109 45W
Prince Albert, Canada 111 53 15N 105 50W
Prince Albert, S. Africa 96 33 12 S 22 2 E
Prince Albert Mts., Antarctica 143 76 0 S 161 30 E
Prince Albert Nat. Park, Canada 111 54 0N 106 25W
Prince Albert Pen., Canada 102 72 30N 116 0W
Prince Albert Sd., Canada 102 70 25N 115 0W
Prince Alfred C., Canada 144 74 20N 124 40W
Prince Charles I., Canada 103 67 47N 76 12W
Prince Charles Mts., Antarctica 143 72 0 S 67 0 E
Prince Edward I. □, Canada 105 46 20N 63 20W
Prince Edward Is., Ind. Oc. 53 46 35 S 38 0 E
Prince Edward Pt., Canada 109 43 56N 76 52W
Prince George, Canada 110 53 55N 122 50W
Prince of Wales, C., U.S.A. 100 65 50N 168 0W
Prince of Wales I., Canada 102 73 0N 99 0W
Prince of Wales I., U.S.A. 102 55 30N 133 0W
Prince of Wales Is., Australia 72 10 40 S 142 10 E
Prince Patrick I., Canada 144 77 0N 120 0W
Prince Regent Inlet, Canada 144 73 0N 90 0W
Prince Rupert, Canada 110 54 20N 130 20W
Princenhage, Neths. 17 51 9N 4 45 E
Princesa Isabel, Brazil 138 7 44 S 38 0W
Princess Charlotte B., Australia 72 14 25 S 144 0 E
Princess May Ranges, Australia 78 15 30 S 125 30 E
Princess Royal I., Canada 110 53 0N 128 40W
Princeton, Canada 110 49 27N 120 30W
Princeton, Calif., U.S.A. 124 39 24N 122 1W
Princeton, Ill., U.S.A. 118 41 25N 89 25W
Princeton, Ind., U.S.A. 119 38 20N 87 35W
Princeton, Ky., U.S.A. 114 37 6N 87 55W
Princeton, Mo., U.S.A. 118 40 23N 93 35W
Princeton, N.J., U.S.A. 117 40 18N 74 40W
Princeton, W. Va., U.S.A. 114 37 21N 81 8W
Princetown, Australia 74 38 41 S 143 10 E
Princeville, Canada 107 46 10N 71 53W
Princeville, U.S.A. 118 40 56N 89 46W
Principe, I. de, Atl. Oc. 94 1 37N 7 27 E
Principe Chan., Canada 110 53 28N 130 0W
Principe da Beira, Brazil 137 12 20 S 64 30W
Prineville, U.S.A. 122 44 17N 120 50W
Prins Harald Kyst, Antarctica 143 70 0 S 35 1 E

Prinsesse Astrid Kyst, *Antarctica* **143** 70 45 S 12 30 E
Prinsesse Ragnhild Kyst, *Antarctica* **143** 70 15 S 27 30 E
Prinzapolca, *Nic.* **128** 13 20N 83 35W
Prior, C., *Spain* **22** 43 34N 8 17W
Pripet = Pripyat →, *U.S.S.R.* **36** 51 20N 30 9 E
Pripet Marshes = Polesye, *U.S.S.R.* **36** 52 0N 28 10 E
Pripyat →, *U.S.S.R.* **36** 51 20N 30 9 E
Pripyat Marshes = Polesye, *U.S.S.R.* **36** 52 0N 28 10 E
Prislop, Pasul, *Romania* **34** 47 37N 25 15 E
Pristen, *U.S.S.R.* **37** 51 15N 36 44 E
Priština, *Yugoslavia* **33** 42 40N 21 13 E
Pritzwalk, *E. Germany* **30** 53 10N 12 11 E
Privas, *France* **21** 44 45N 4 37 E
Priverno, *Italy* **28** 41 29N 13 10 E
Privolzhsk, *U.S.S.R.* **37** 57 23N 41 16 E
Privolzhskaya Vozvyshennost, *U.S.S.R.* **37** 51 0N 46 0 E
Privolzhskiy, *U.S.S.R.* **37** 51 25N 46 3 E
Privolzhye, *U.S.S.R.* **37** 52 52N 48 33 E
Priyutnoye, *U.S.S.R.* **39** 46 12N 43 40 E
Prizren, *Yugoslavia* **33** 42 13N 20 45 E
Prizzi, *Italy* **28** 37 44N 13 24 E
Prnjavor, *Yugoslavia* **33** 44 52N 17 43 E
Probolinggo, *Indonesia* **57** 7 46 S 113 13 E
Procida, *Italy* **28** 40 46N 14 0 E
Proddatur, *India* **51** 14 45N 78 30 E
Proença-a-Nova, *Portugal* **23** 39 45N 7 54W
Prof. Van Blommestein Meer, *Surinam* **135** 4 45N 55 5W
Profondeville, *Belgium* **17** 50 23N 4 52 E
Progreso, *Mexico* **127** 21 20N 89 40W
Prokhladnyy, *U.S.S.R.* **39** 43 50N 44 2 E
Prokletije, *Albania* **34** 42 30N 19 45 E
Prokopyevsk, *U.S.S.R.* **40** 54 0N 86 45 E
Prokuplje, *Yugoslavia* **33** 43 16N 21 36 E
Proletarskaya, *U.S.S.R.* **39** 46 42N 41 50 E
Prome = Pyè, *Burma* **52** 18 49N 95 13 E
Prophet →, *Canada* **110** 58 48N 122 40W
Prophetstown, *U.S.A.* **118** 41 40N 89 56W
Propriá, *Brazil* **138** 10 13 S 36 51W
Propriano, *France* **21** 41 41N 8 52 E
Proserpine, *Australia* **72** 20 21 S 148 36 E
Prosser, *U.S.A.* **122** 46 11N 119 52W
Prostějov, *Czech.* **32** 49 30N 17 9 E
Proston, *Australia* **73** 26 8 S 151 32 E
Protection, *U.S.A.* **121** 37 16N 99 30W
Próti, *Greece* **35** 37 5N 21 32 E
Provadiya, *Bulgaria* **34** 43 12N 27 30 E
Proven, *Belgium* **17** 50 54N 2 40 E
Provence, *France* **21** 43 40N 5 46 E
Providence, *Ky., U.S.A.* **114** 37 25N 87 46W
Providence, *R.I., U.S.A.* **117** 41 50N 71 28W
Providence Bay, *Canada* **108** 45 41N 82 15W
Providence C., *N.Z.* **81** 45 59 S 166 29 E
Providence Mts., *U.S.A.* **123** 35 0N 115 30W
Providencia, *Ecuador* **134** 0 28 S 76 28W
Providencia, I. de, *Colombia* **128** 13 25N 81 26W
Provideniya, *U.S.S.R.* **41** 64 23N 173 18W
Provins, *France* **19** 48 33N 3 15 E
Provo, *U.S.A.* **122** 40 16N 111 37W
Provost, *Canada* **111** 52 25N 110 20W
Prozor, *Yugoslavia* **33** 43 50N 17 34 E
Prudentópolis, *Brazil* **139** 25 12 S 50 57W
Prud'homme, *Canada* **111** 52 20N 105 54W
Prudnik, *Poland* **32** 50 20N 17 38 E
Prüm, *W. Germany* **31** 50 14N 6 22 E
Pruszcz Gd., *Poland* **32** 54 17N 18 40 E
Pruszków, *Poland* **32** 52 9N 20 49 E
Prut →, *Romania* **34** 45 28N 28 10 E
Pruzhany, *U.S.S.R.* **36** 52 33N 24 28 E
Prvič, *Yugoslavia* **27** 44 55N 14 47 E
Prydz B., *Antarctica* **143** 69 0S 74 0 E
Pryor, *U.S.A.* **121** 36 17N 95 20W
Przasnysz, *Poland* **32** 53 2N 20 45 E
Przedbórz, *Poland* **32** 51 6N 19 53 E
Przemysl, *Poland* **32** 49 50N 22 45 E
Przeworsk, *Poland* **32** 50 6N 22 32 E
Przewóz, *Poland* **32** 51 28N 14 57 E
Przhevalsk, *U.S.S.R.* **40** 42 30N 78 20 E
Przysuchla, *Poland* **32** 51 22N 20 38 E
Psakhná, *Greece* **35** 38 34N 23 35 E
Psará, *Greece* **35** 38 37N 25 38 E
Psel →, *U.S.S.R.* **38** 49 5N 33 20 E
Pserimos, *Greece* **35** 36 56N 27 12 E
Pskov, *U.S.S.R.* **36** 57 50N 28 25 E
Psunj, *Yugoslavia* **33** 45 25N 17 19 E
Pszczyna, *Poland* **32** 49 59N 18 58 E
Pteleón, *Greece* **35** 39 3N 22 57 E
Ptich →, *U.S.S.R.* **36** 52 9N 28 52 E
Ptolemaís, *Greece* **35** 40 30N 21 43 E
Ptuj, *Yugoslavia* **27** 46 28N 15 50 E
Ptujska Gora, *Yugoslavia* **27** 46 23N 15 47 E
Pu Xian, *China* **60** 36 24N 111 6 E
Pua, *Thailand* **54** 19 11N 100 55 E
Puán, *Argentina* **140** 37 30 S 62 45W
Pu'an, *China* **58** 25 46N 104 57 E
Pu'apu'a, *W. Samoa* **68** 13 34 S 172 9W
Pubei, *China* **58** 22 16N 109 31 E
Pucacuro →, *Peru* **134** 3 20 S 74 58W
Pucallpa, *Peru* **136** 8 25 S 74 30W
Pucará, *Bolivia* **137** 18 43 S 64 11W
Pucará, *Peru* **136** 15 5 S 70 24W
Pucarani, *Bolivia* **136** 16 23 S 68 30W
Pucheng, *China* **59** 27 59N 118 31 E
Pučišće, *Yugoslavia* **27** 43 22N 16 43 E
Pucka, Zatoka, *Poland* **32** 54 30N 18 40 E
Puckapunyal, *Australia* **74** 37 0 S 145 3 E
Puding, *China* **58** 26 18N 105 44 E
Pudukkottai, *India* **51** 10 28N 78 47 E
Puebla, *Mexico* **127** 19 0N 98 10W
Puebla □, *Mexico* **127** 18 30N 98 0W
Puebla, La, *Spain* **24** 39 46N 3 1 E
Puebla de Alcocer, *Spain* **23** 38 59N 5 14W
Puebla de Cazalla, La, *Spain* **23** 37 10N 5 20W
Puebla de Don Fadrique, *Spain* **25** 37 58N 2 25W
Puebla de Don Rodrigo, *Spain* **23** 39 5N 4 37W
Puebla de Guzmán, *Spain* **23** 37 37N 7 15W
Puebla de los Infantes, La, *Spain* **23** 37 47N 5 24W
Puebla de Montalbán, La, *Spain* **22** 39 52N 4 22W
Puebla de Sanabria, *Spain* **22** 42 4N 6 38W
Puebla de Trives, *Spain* **22** 42 20N 7 10W
Puebla del Caramiñal, *Spain* **22** 42 37N 8 56W
Pueblo, *U.S.A.* **120** 38 20N 104 40W
Pueblo Hundido, *Chile* **140** 26 20 S 70 5W
Pueblo Nuevo, *Venezuela* **134** 8 26N 71 26W
Puelches, *Argentina* **140** 38 5 S 65 51W
Puelén, *Argentina* **140** 37 32 S 67 38W
Puente Alto, *Chile* **140** 33 32 S 70 35W
Puente del Arzobispo, *Spain* **22** 39 48N 5 10W
Puente-Genil, *Spain* **23** 37 22N 4 47W
Puente la Reina, *Spain* **24** 42 40N 1 49W
Puenteareas, *Spain* **22** 42 10N 8 28W
Puentedeume, *Spain* **22** 43 24N 8 10W
Puentes de Garcia Rodriguez, *Spain* **22** 43 27N 7 50W
Pu'er, *China* **58** 23 0N 101 15 E
Puerco →, *U.S.A.* **123** 34 22N 107 50W
Puerta, La, *Spain* **25** 38 22N 2 45W
Puerto, *Canary Is.* **25** 28 5N 17 20W
Puerto Acosta, *Bolivia* **136** 15 32 S 69 15W
Puerto Aisén, *Chile* **142** 45 27 S 73 0W
Puerto Ángel, *Mexico* **127** 15 40N 96 29W
Puerto Arista, *Mexico* **127** 15 56N 93 48W
Puerto Armuelles, *Panama* **128** 8 20N 82 51W
Puerto Ayacucho, *Venezuela* **134** 5 40N 67 35W
Puerto Barrios, *Guatemala* **128** 15 40N 88 32W
Puerto Bermejo, *Argentina* **140** 26 55 S 58 34W
Puerto Bermúdez, *Peru* **136** 10 20 S 75 0W
Puerto Bolívar, *Ecuador* **134** 3 19 S 79 55W
Puerto Cabello, *Venezuela* **134** 10 28N 68 1W
Puerto Cabezas, *Nic.* **128** 14 0N 83 30W
Puerto Cabo Gracias á Dios, *Nic.* **128** 15 0N 83 10W
Puerto Capaz = Jebba, *Morocco* **84** 35 11N 4 43W
Puerto Carreño, *Colombia* **134** 6 12N 67 22W
Puerto Castilla, *Honduras* **128** 16 0N 86 0W
Puerto Chicama, *Peru* **136** 7 45 S 79 20W
Puerto Coig, *Argentina* **142** 50 54 S 69 15W
Puerto Cortes, *Costa Rica* **128** 8 55N 84 0W
Puerto Cortés, *Honduras* **128** 15 51N 88 0W
Puerto Cumarebo, *Venezuela* **134** 11 29N 69 30W
Puerto de Gran Tarajal, *Canary Is.* **25** 28 13N 14 1W
Puerto de la Cruz, *Canary Is.* **25** 28 24N 16 32W
Puerto de Pozo Negro, *Canary Is.* **25** 28 19N 13 55W
Puerto de Santa María, *Spain* **23** 36 36N 6 13W
Puerto del Rosario, *Canary Is.* **25** 28 30N 13 52W
Puerto Deseado, *Argentina* **142** 47 55 S 66 0W
Puerto Guaraní, *Paraguay* **137** 21 18 S 57 55W
Puerto Heath, *Bolivia* **136** 12 34 S 68 39W
Puerto Huitoto, *Colombia* **134** 0 18N 74 3W
Puerto Inca, *Peru* **136** 9 22 S 74 54W
Puerto Juárez, *Mexico* **127** 21 11N 86 49W
Puerto La Cruz, *Venezuela* **135** 10 13N 64 38W
Puerto Leguízamo, *Colombia* **134** 0 12 S 74 46W
Puerto Limón, *Colombia* **134** 3 23N 73 30W
Puerto Lobos, *Argentina* **142** 42 0 S 65 3W
Puerto López, *Colombia* **134** 4 5N 72 58W
Puerto Lumbreras, *Spain* **25** 37 34N 1 48W
Puerto Madryn, *Argentina* **142** 42 48 S 65 4W
Puerto Maldonado, *Peru* **136** 12 30 S 69 10W
Puerto Manotí, *Cuba* **128** 21 22N 76 50W
Puerto Mazarrón, *Spain* **25** 37 34N 1 15W
Puerto Mercedes, *Colombia* **134** 1 11N 72 53W
Puerto Miraña, *Colombia* **134** 1 20 S 70 19W
Puerto Montt, *Chile* **142** 41 28 S 73 0W
Puerto Morelos, *Mexico* **127** 20 49N 86 52W
Puerto Nariño, *Colombia* **134** 4 56N 67 48W
Puerto Natales, *Chile* **142** 51 45 S 72 15W
Puerto Nuevo, *Colombia* **134** 5 53N 69 56W
Puerto Nutrias, *Venezuela* **134** 8 5N 69 18W
Puerto Ordaz, *Venezuela* **135** 8 16N 62 44W
Puerto Padre, *Cuba* **128** 21 13N 76 35W
Puerto Páez, *Venezuela* **134** 6 13N 67 28W
Puerto Peñasco, *Mexico* **126** 31 20N 113 33W
Puerto Pinasco, *Paraguay* **140** 22 36 S 57 50W
Puerto Pirámides, *Argentina* **142** 42 35 S 64 20W
Puerto Plata, *Dom. Rep.* **129** 19 48N 70 45W
Puerto Portillo, *Peru* **136** 9 45 S 72 42W
Puerto Princesa, *Phil.* **57** 9 46N 118 45 E
Puerto Quellón, *Chile* **142** 43 7 S 73 37W
Puerto Quepos, *Costa Rica* **128** 9 29N 84 6W
Puerto Real, *Spain* **23** 36 33N 6 12W
Puerto Rico, *Bolivia* **136** 11 5 S 67 38W
Puerto Rico ■, *W. Indies* **129** 18 15N 66 45W
Puerto Saavedra, *Chile* **142** 38 47 S 73 24W
Puerto Sastre, *Paraguay* **140** 22 2 S 57 55W
Puerto Siles, *Bolivia* **137** 12 48 S 65 5W
Puerto Suárez, *Bolivia* **137** 18 58 S 57 52W
Puerto Tejada, *Colombia* **134** 3 14N 76 24W
Puerto Umbría, *Colombia* **134** 0 52N 76 33W
Puerto Vallarta, *Mexico* **126** 20 36N 105 15W
Puerto Varas, *Chile* **142** 41 19 S 72 59W
Puerto Villazón, *Bolivia* **137** 13 32 S 61 57W
Puerto Wilches, *Colombia* **134** 7 21N 73 54W
Puertollano, *Spain* **23** 38 43N 4 7W
Puertomarin, *Spain* **22** 42 48N 7 36W
Puesto Cunambo, *Peru* **134** 2 10 S 76 0W
Pueyrredón, L., *Argentina* **142** 47 20 S 72 0W
Pugachev, *U.S.S.R.* **37** 52 0N 48 49 E
Puge, *China* **58** 27 20N 102 31 E
Puge, *Tanzania* **92** 4 45 S 33 11 E
Puget Sd., *U.S.A.* **122** 47 15N 122 30W
Puget-Théniers, *France* **21** 43 58N 6 53 E
Púglia □, *Italy* **29** 41 0N 16 30 E
Pugu, *Tanzania* **92** 6 55 S 39 4 E
Puha, *N.Z.* **80** 38 30 S 177 50 E
Pui, *Romania* **34** 45 30N 23 4 E
Puica, *Peru* **136** 15 0 S 72 33W
Puig Mayor, Mte., *Spain* **24** 39 48N 2 47 E
Puigcerdá, *Spain* **24** 42 24N 1 50 E
Puigmal, *Spain* **24** 42 23N 2 7 E
Puisaye, Collines de la, *France* **19** 47 37N 3 20 E
Puiseaux, *France* **19** 48 11N 2 30 E
Pujilí, *Ecuador* **134** 0 57 S 78 41W
Puka, *Albania* **34** 42 2N 19 53 E
Pukaki L., *N.Z.* **81** 44 4 S 170 1 E
Pukapuka, *Cook Is.* **67** 10 53 S 165 49W
Pukatawagan, *Canada* **111** 55 45N 101 20W
Pukearuhe, *N.Z.* **80** 38 55 S 174 31 E
Pukekohe, *N.Z.* **80** 37 12 S 174 55 E
Puketeraki Ra., *N.Z.* **81** 42 58 S 172 13 E
Pukeuri, *N.Z.* **81** 45 4 S 171 2 E
Pukou, *China* **59** 32 7N 118 38 E
Pula, *Italy* **28** 39 0N 9 0 E
Pula, *Yugoslavia* **27** 44 54N 13 57 E
Pulacayo, *Bolivia* **136** 20 25 S 66 41W
Pulaski, *N.Y., U.S.A.* **117** 43 32N 76 9W
Pulaski, *Tenn., U.S.A.* **115** 35 10N 87 0W
Pulaski, *Va., U.S.A.* **114** 37 4N 80 49W
Pulawy, *Poland* **32** 51 23N 21 59 E
Pulga, *U.S.A.* **124** 39 48N 121 29W
Pulgaon, *India* **50** 20 44N 78 21 E
Pulicat, L., *India* **51** 13 40N 80 15 E
Puliyangudi, *India* **51** 9 11N 77 24 E
Pullabooka, *Australia* **76** 33 44 S 147 46 E
Pullman, *U.S.A.* **122** 46 49N 117 10W
Pulog, Mt., *Phil.* **57** 16 40N 120 50 E
Púlpito do Sul, *Angola* **95** 15 46 S 12 0 E
Pultusk, *Poland* **32** 52 43N 21 6 E
Pumlumon Fawr, *U.K.* **13** 52 29N 3 47W
Puna, *Bolivia* **137** 19 45 S 65 28W
Puná, I., *Ecuador* **134** 2 55 S 80 5W
Punakha, *Bhutan* **52** 27 42N 89 52 E
Punalur, *India* **51** 9 0N 76 56 E
Punasar, *India* **48** 27 6N 73 6 E
Punata, *Bolivia* **137** 17 32 S 65 50W
Punavia, *Tahiti* **68** 17 38 S 149 36W
Punch, *India* **49** 33 48N 74 4 E
Pune, *India* **50** 18 29N 73 57 E
Pungue, Ponte de, *Mozam.* **93** 19 0 S 34 0 E
Puning, *China* **59** 23 20N 116 12 E
Punjab □, *India* **48** 31 0N 76 0 E
Punjab □, *Pakistan* **48** 30 0N 72 0 E
Puno, *Peru* **136** 15 55 S 70 3W
Punta Alta, *Argentina* **142** 38 53 S 62 4W
Punta Arenas, *Chile* **142** 53 10 S 71 0W
Punta Cardón, *Venezuela* **134** 11 38N 70 14W
Punta Coles, *Peru* **136** 17 43 S 71 23W
Punta de Bombón, *Peru* **136** 17 10 S 71 48W
Punta de Díaz, *Chile* **140** 28 0 S 70 45W
Punta de Piedras, *Venezuela* **134** 10 54N 64 6W
Punta Delgado, *Argentina* **142** 42 43 S 63 38W
Punta Gorda, *Belize* **127** 16 10N 88 45W
Punta Gorda, *U.S.A.* **115** 26 55N 82 0W
Punta Prieta, *Mexico* **126** 28 58N 114 17W
Puntabie, *Australia* **73** 32 12 S 134 13 E
Puntarenas, *Costa Rica* **128** 10 0N 84 50W
Punto Fijo, *Venezuela* **134** 11 50N 70 13W
Punxsutawney, *U.S.A.* **116** 40 56N 79 0W
Puqi, *China* **59** 29 40N 113 50 E
Puquio, *Peru* **136** 14 45 S 74 10W
Pur →, *U.S.S.R.* **40** 67 31N 77 55 E
Purace, Vol., *Colombia* **134** 2 21N 76 23W
Purari →, *Papua N. G.* **69** 7 49 S 145 0 E
Purbeck, Isle of, *U.K.* **13** 50 40N 2 5W
Purcell, *U.S.A.* **121** 35 0N 97 25W
Purchena Tetica, *Spain* **25** 37 21N 2 21W
Puri, *India* **50** 19 50N 85 58 E
Purificación, *Colombia* **134** 3 51N 74 55W
Purísima, La, *Mexico* **126** 26 10N 112 4W
Purlewaugh, *Australia* **77** 31 20 S 149 30 E
Purmerend, *Neths.* **16** 52 30N 4 58 E
Purna →, *India* **50** 19 6N 77 2 E
Purnia, *India* **49** 25 45N 87 31 E
Purnim, *Australia* **74** 38 16 S 142 36 E
Purukcahu, *Indonesia* **56** 0 35 S 114 35 E
Puruliya, *India* **49** 23 17N 86 24 E
Purus →, *Brazil* **135** 3 42 S 61 28W
Pŭrvomay, *Bulgaria* **34** 42 8N 25 17 E
Purwakarta, *Indonesia* **57** 6 35 S 107 29 E
Purwodadi, *Jawa, Indonesia* **57** 7 7 S 110 55 E
Purwodadi, *Jawa, Indonesia* **57** 7 51 S 110 0 E
Purwokerto, *Indonesia* **57** 7 25 S 109 14 E
Purworejo, *Indonesia* **57** 7 43 S 110 2 E
Pus →, *India* **50** 19 55N 77 55 E
Pusad, *India* **50** 19 56N 77 36 E
Pusan, *S. Korea* **61** 35 5N 129 0 E
Push, La, *U.S.A.* **124** 47 55N 124 38W
Pushchino, *U.S.S.R.* **41** 54 10N 158 0 E
Pushkin, *U.S.S.R.* **36** 59 45N 30 25 E
Pushkino, *R.S.F.S.R., U.S.S.R.* **37** 51 16N 47 0 E
Pushkino, *R.S.F.S.R., U.S.S.R.* **37** 56 2N 37 49 E
Püspökladány, *Hungary* **33** 47 19N 21 6 E
Pustoshka, *U.S.S.R.* **36** 56 20N 29 30 E
Putahow L., *Canada* **111** 59 54N 100 40W
Putao, *Burma* **52** 27 28N 97 30 E
Putaruru, *N.Z.* **80** 38 2 S 175 50 E
Putbus, *E. Germany* **30** 54 19N 13 29 E
Putian, *China* **59** 25 23N 119 0 E
Putignano, *Italy* **29** 40 50N 17 5 E
Putina, *Peru* **136** 14 55 S 69 55W
Puting, Tanjung, *Indonesia* **56** 3 31 S 111 46 E
Putlitz, *E. Germany* **30** 53 15N 12 3 E
Putna →, *Romania* **34** 45 42N 27 26 E
Putnam, *U.S.A.* **117** 41 55N 71 55W
Putorana, Gory, *U.S.S.R.* **41** 69 0N 95 0 E
Putorino, *N.Z.* **80** 39 4 S 177 0 E
Putre, *Chile* **136** 18 12 S 69 35W
Puttalam Lagoon, *Sri Lanka* **51** 8 15N 79 45 E
Putte, *Neths.* **17** 51 22N 4 24 E
Putten, *Neths.* **16** 52 16N 5 36 E
Puttgarden, *E. Germany* **30** 54 28N 11 15 E
Puttur, *India* **51** 12 46N 75 12 E
Putty, *Australia* **76** 32 57 S 150 42 E
Putumayo →, *S. Amer.* **134** 3 7 S 67 58W
Putuo, *China* **59** 29 56N 122 20 E
Putussibau, *Indonesia* **56** 0 50N 112 56 E
Puurs, *Belgium* **17** 51 5N 4 17 E
Puy, Le, *France* **20** 45 3N 3 52 E
Puy-de-Dôme, *France* **20** 45 46N 2 57 E
Puy-de-Dôme □, *France* **20** 45 40N 3 5 E
Puy-Guillaume, *France* **20** 45 57N 3 29 E
Puy-l'Évêque, *France* **20** 44 31N 1 9 E
Puyallup, *U.S.A.* **124** 47 10N 122 22W
Puyang, *China* **60** 35 40N 115 1 E
Puyehue, *Chile* **142** 40 40 S 72 37W
Puylaurens, *France* **20** 43 35N 2 0 E
Puyo, *Ecuador* **134** 1 28 S 77 59W
Pwani □, *Tanzania* **92** 7 0 S 39 0 E
Pweto, *Zaïre* **93** 8 25 S 28 51 E
Pwinbyu, *Burma* **52** 20 23N 94 40 E
Pwllheli, *U.K.* **12** 52 54N 4 26W
Pyalong, *Australia* **74** 37 7 S 144 51 E
Pyana →, *U.S.S.R.* **37** 55 30N 46 0 E
Pyapon, *Burma* **52** 16 20N 95 40 E
Pyasina →, *U.S.S.R.* **41** 73 30N 87 0 E
Pyatigorsk, *U.S.S.R.* **39** 44 2N 43 6 E
Pyatikhatki, *U.S.S.R.* **38** 48 28N 33 38 E
Pyaye, *Burma* **52** 19 12N 95 10 E

Pyè, *Burma* **52** 18 49N 95 13 E
Pyinbauk, *Burma* **52** 19 10N 95 12 E
Pyinmana, *Burma* **52** 19 45N 96 12 E
Pyŏngyang, *N. Korea* **61** 39 0N 125 30 E
Pyote, *U.S.A.* **121** 31 34N 103 5W
Pyramid Hill, *Australia* **74** 36 2 S 144 6 E
Pyramid L., *U.S.A.* **122** 40 0N 119 30W
Pyramid Pk., *U.S.A.* **125** 36 25N 116 37W
Pyramids, *Egypt* **88** 29 58N 31 9 E
Pyrénées, *Europe* **20** 42 45N 0 18 E
Pyrénées-Atlantiques □, *France* **20** 43 10N 0 50W
Pyrénées-Orientales □, *France* **20** 42 35N 2 26 E
Pyrzyce, *Poland* **32** 53 10N 14 55 E
Pyshchug, *U.S.S.R.* **37** 58 57N 45 47 E
Pytalovo, *U.S.S.R.* **36** 57 5N 27 55 E
Pyttegga, *Norway* **10** 62 13N 7 42 E
Pyu, *Burma* **52** 18 30N 96 28 E

Q

Qabalān, *Jordan* **44** 32 8N 35 17 E
Qabātiyah, *Jordan* **44** 32 25N 35 16 E
Qachasnek, *S. Africa* **97** 30 6 S 28 42 E
Qādib, *S. Yemen* **45** 12 37N 53 57 E
Qā'emshahr, *Iran* **47** 36 30N 52 55 E
Qagan Nur, *China* **60** 43 30N 114 55 E
Qahar Youyi Zhongqi, *China* **60** 41 12N 112 40 E
Qahremānshahr = Bākhtarān, *Iran* **46** 34 23N 47 0 E
Qaidam Pendi, *China* **62** 37 0N 95 0 E
Qala-i-Jadid, *Afghan.* **48** 31 1N 66 25 E
Qala Yangi, *Afghan.* **48** 34 20N 66 30 E
Qalāt, *Afghan.* **47** 32 15N 66 58 E
Qal'at al Akhḍar, *Si. Arabia* **46** 28 0N 37 10 E
Qal'eh-ye Now, *Afghan.* **47** 35 0N 63 5 E
Qalqīlya, *Israel* **44** 32 12N 34 58 E
Qalyûb, *Egypt* **88** 30 12N 31 11 E
Qam, *Jordan* **44** 32 36N 35 43 E
Qamar, Ghubbat al, *S. Yemen* **45** 16 20N 52 30 E
Qamdo, *China* **58** 31 15N 97 6 E
Qamruddin Karez, *Pakistan* **48** 31 45N 68 20 E
Qāna, *Lebanon* **44** 33 12N 35 17 E
Qandahār, *Afghan.* **47** 31 32N 65 30 E
Qâra, *Egypt* **88** 29 38N 26 30 E
Qara Qash →, *India* **49** 35 0N 78 30 E
Qarachuk, *Syria* **46** 37 0N 42 2 E
Qārah, *Si. Arabia* **46** 29 55N 40 3 E
Qardud, *Sudan* **89** 10 20N 29 56 E
Qarqan, *China* **62** 38 5N 85 20 E
Qarqan He →, *China* **62** 39 30N 88 30 E
Qarrasa, *Sudan* **89** 14 38N 32 5 E
Qāsim, *Syria* **44** 32 59N 36 2 E
Qaṣr Bū Hadi, *Libya* **86** 31 1N 16 45 E
Qaṣr-e Qand, *Iran* **47** 26 15N 60 45 E
Qasr Farâfra, *Egypt* **88** 27 0N 28 1 E
Qatar ■, *Asia* **47** 25 30N 51 15 E
Qattâra, *Egypt* **88** 30 12N 27 3 E
Qattâra, Munkhafed el, *Egypt* **88** 29 30N 27 30 E
Qattâra Depression = Qattâra, Munkhafed el, *Egypt* **88** 29 30N 27 30 E
Qāyen, *Iran* **47** 33 40N 59 10 E
Qazvin, *Iran* **46** 36 15N 50 0 E
Qena, *Egypt* **88** 26 10N 32 43 E
Qena, Wadi →, *Egypt* **88** 26 12N 32 44 E
Qeshm, *Iran* **47** 26 55N 56 10 E
Qezi'ot, *Israel* **44** 30 52N 34 26 E
Qi Xian, *China* **60** 34 40N 114 48 E
Qian Gorlos, *China* **61** 45 5N 124 42 E
Qian Xian, *China* **60** 34 31N 108 15 E
Qiancheng, *China* **58** 27 12N 109 50 E
Qianjiang, *Guangxi Zhuangzu, China* **58** 23 38N 108 58 E
Qianjiang, *Hubei, China* **59** 30 24N 112 55 E
Qianjiang, *Sichuan, China* **58** 29 33N 108 47 E
Qianshan, *China* **59** 30 37N 116 35 E
Qianwei, *China* **58** 29 13N 103 56 E
Qianxi, *China* **58** 27 3N 106 3 E
Qianyang, *Hunan, China* **59** 27 18N 110 10 E
Qianyang, *Shaanxi, China* **60** 34 40N 107 8 E
Qianyang, *Zhejiang, China* **59** 30 11N 119 25 E
Qiaojia, *China* **58** 26 56N 102 58 E
Qichun, *China* **59** 30 18N 115 25 E
Qidong, *Hunan, China* **59** 26 49N 112 7 E
Qidong, *Jiangsu, China* **59** 31 48N 121 38 E
Qijiang, *China* **58** 28 57N 106 35 E
Qila Safed, *Pakistan* **47** 29 0N 61 30 E
Qila Saifullāh, *Pakistan* **48** 30 45N 68 17 E
Qilian Shan, *China* **62** 38 30N 96 0 E
Qimen, *China* **59** 29 50N 117 42 E
Qin He →, *China* **60** 35 1N 113 22 E
Qin Jiang →, *China* **59** 26 15N 115 55 E
Qin Ling = Qinling Shandi, *China* **60** 33 50N 108 10 E
Qin'an, *China* **60** 34 48N 105 40 E
Qing Xian, *China* **60** 38 35N 116 45 E
Qingcheng, *China* **61** 37 15N 117 40 E
Qingdao, *China* **61** 36 5N 120 20 E
Qingfeng, *China* **60** 35 52N 115 8 E
Qinghai □, *China* **62** 36 0N 98 0 E
Qinghai Hu, *China* **62** 36 40N 100 10 E
Qinghecheng, *China* **61** 41 15N 124 30 E
Qinghemen, *China* **61** 41 48N 121 25 E
Qingjian, *China* **60** 37 8N 110 8 E
Qingjiang, *Jiangsu, China* **61** 33 30N 119 2 E
Qingjiang, *Jiangxi, China* **59** 28 4N 115 29 E
Qingliu, *China* **59** 26 11N 116 48 E
Qinglong, *China* **58** 25 49N 105 12 E
Qingping, *China* **58** 26 39N 107 47 E
Qingpu, *China* **59** 31 10N 121 6 E
Qingshui, *China* **60** 34 48N 106 8 E
Qingshuihe, *China* **60** 39 55N 111 35 E
Qingtian, *China* **59** 28 12N 120 15 E
Qingtongxia Shuiku, *China* **60** 37 50N 105 58 E
Qingxi, *China* **58** 27 8N 108 43 E
Qingxu, *China* **60** 37 34N 112 22 E
Qingyang, *Anhui, China* **59** 30 38N 117 50 E
Qingyang, *Gansu, China* **60** 36 2N 107 55 E
Qingyi Jiang →, *China* **58** 29 32N 103 44 E
Qingyuan, *Guangdong, China* **59** 23 40N 112 59 E
Qingyuan, *Liaoning, China* **61** 42 10N 124 55 E
Qingyuan, *Zhejiang, China* **59** 27 36N 119 3 E
Qingyun, *China* **61** 37 45N 117 20 E
Qingzhen, *China* **58** 26 31N 106 25 E
Qinhuangdao, *China* **61** 39 56N 119 30 E
Qinling Shandi, *China* **60** 33 50N 108 10 E
Qinshui, *China* **60** 35 40N 112 8 E
Qinyang, *China* **60** 35 7N 112 57 E
Qinyuan, *China* **60** 36 29N 112 20 E
Qinzhou, *China* **58** 21 58N 108 38 E
Qionghai, *China* **54** 19 15N 110 26 E
Qionglai, *China* **58** 30 25N 103 31 E
Qionglai Shan, *China* **58** 31 0N 102 30 E
Qiongshan, *China* **54** 19 51N 110 26 E
Qiongzhou Haixia, *China* **54** 20 10N 110 15 E
Qiqihar, *China* **62** 47 26N 124 0 E
Qiryat 'Anavim, *Israel* **44** 31 49N 35 7 E
Qiryat Ata, *Israel* **44** 32 47N 35 6 E
Qiryat Bialik, *Israel* **44** 32 50N 35 5 E
Qiryat Gat, *Israel* **44** 31 32N 34 46 E
Qiryat Ḥayyim, *Israel* **44** 32 49N 35 4 E
Qiryat Mal'akhi, *Israel* **44** 31 44N 34 44 E
Qiryat Shemona, *Israel* **44** 33 13N 35 35 E
Qiryat Yam, *Israel* **44** 32 51N 35 4 E
Qishan, *China* **60** 34 25N 107 38 E
Qishan, *Taiwan* **59** 22 52N 120 25 E
Qishon →, *Israel* **44** 32 49N 35 2 E
Qitai, *China* **62** 44 2N 89 35 E
Qiubei, *China* **58** 24 2N 104 12 E
Qixia, *China* **61** 37 17N 120 52 E
Qiyang, *China* **59** 26 35N 111 50 E
Qom, *Iran* **47** 34 40N 51 0 E
Qomsheh, *Iran* **47** 32 0N 51 55 E
Qondūz, *Afghan.* **47** 36 50N 68 50 E
Qondūz □, *Afghan.* **47** 36 50N 68 50 E
Qu Jiang →, *China* **58** 30 1N 106 24 E
Qu Xian, *Sichuan, China* **58** 30 48N 106 58 E
Qu Xian, *Zhejiang, China* **59** 28 57N 118 54 E
Quaama, *Australia* **75** 36 27 S 149 55 E
Quackenbrück, *W. Germany* **30** 52 40N 7 59 E
Quairading, *Australia* **79** 32 0 S 117 21 E
Quakertown, *U.S.A.* **117** 40 27N 75 20W
Qualeup, *Australia* **79** 33 48 S 116 48 E
Quambatook, *Australia* **74** 35 49 S 143 34 E
Quambone, *Australia* **76** 30 57 S 147 53 E
Quan Long, *Vietnam* **55** 9 7N 105 8 E
Quanan, *U.S.A.* **121** 34 20N 99 45W
Quandialla, *Australia* **76** 34 1 S 147 47 E
Quang Ngai, *Vietnam* **54** 15 13N 108 58 E
Quang Yen, *Vietnam* **54** 20 56N 106 52 E
Quannan, *China* **59** 24 45N 114 33 E
Quantock Hills, *U.K.* **13** 51 8N 3 10W
Quantong, *Australia* **74** 36 43 S 142 3 E
Quanzhou, *Fujian, China* **59** 24 55N 118 34 E
Quanzhou, *Guangxi Zhuangzu, China* **59** 25 57N 111 5 E
Quaraí, *Brazil* **140** 30 15 S 56 20W
Quarré-les-Tombes, *France* **19** 47 21N 4 0 E
Quartu Sant' Elena, *Italy* **28** 39 15N 9 10 E
Quartzsite, *U.S.A.* **125** 33 44N 114 16W
Quatsino, *Canada* **110** 50 30N 127 40W
Quatsino Sd., *Canada* **110** 50 25N 127 58W
Qubab = Mishmar Ayyalon, *Israel* **44** 31 52N 34 57 E
Qūchān, *Iran* **47** 37 10N 58 27 E
Queanbeyan, *Australia* **76** 35 17 S 149 14 E
Québec, *Canada* **107** 46 52N 71 13W
Québec □, *Canada* **105** 50 0N 70 0W
Quedlinburg, *E. Germany* **30** 51 47N 11 9 E
Queen Alexandra Ra., *Antarctica* **143** 85 0 S 170 0 E
Queen Charlotte, *Canada* **110** 53 15N 132 2W
Queen Charlotte Bay, *Falk. Is.* **142** 51 50 S 60 40W
Queen Charlotte Is., *Canada* **110** 53 20N 132 10W
Queen Charlotte Sd., *N.Z.* **81** 41 10 S 174 15 E
Queen Charlotte Str., *Canada* **110** 51 0N 128 0W
Queen City, *U.S.A.* **118** 40 25N 92 34W
Queen Elizabeth Is., *Canada* **4** 76 0N 95 0W
Queen Elizabeth Nat. Park, *Uganda* **92** 0 0 30 0 E
Queen Mary Land, *Antarctica* **143** 70 0 S 95 0 E
Queen Maud G., *Canada* **102** 68 15N 102 30W
Queen Maud Mts., *Antarctica* **143** 86 0 S 160 0W
Queens Chan., *Australia* **78** 15 0 S 129 30 E
Queenscliff, *Australia* **74** 38 16 S 144 39 E
Queensland □, *Australia* **72** 22 0 S 142 0 E
Queenstown, *Australia* **72** 42 4 S 145 35 E
Queenstown, *N.Z.* **81** 45 1 S 168 40 E
Queenstown, *S. Africa* **96** 31 52 S 26 52 E
Queets, *U.S.A.* **124** 47 32N 124 20W
Queguay Grande →, *Uruguay* **140** 32 9 S 58 9W
Queimadas, *Brazil* **138** 11 0 S 39 38W
Queiros, C., *Vanuatu* **68** 14 55 S 167 1 E
Quela, *Angola* **95** 9 10 S 16 56 E
Quelimane, *Mozam.* **93** 17 53 S 36 58 E
Quelpart = Cheju Do, *S. Korea* **61** 33 29N 126 34 E
Quemado, *N. Mex., U.S.A.* **123** 34 17N 108 28W
Quemado, *Tex., U.S.A.* **121** 28 58N 100 35W
Quemú-Quemú, *Argentina* **140** 36 3 S 63 36W
Quequén, *Argentina* **140** 38 30 S 58 30W
Querco, *Peru* **136** 13 50 S 74 52W
Querétaro, *Mexico* **126** 20 40N 100 23W
Querétaro □, *Mexico* **126** 20 30N 100 0W
Querfurt, *E. Germany* **30** 51 22N 11 33 E
Quesada, *Spain* **25** 37 51N 3 4W
Queshan, *China* **60** 32 55N 114 2 E
Quesnel, *Canada* **110** 53 0N 122 30W
Quesnel →, *Canada* **110** 52 58N 122 29W
Quesnel L., *Canada* **110** 52 30N 121 20W
Quesnoy, Le, *France* **19** 50 15N 3 38 E
Questa, *U.S.A.* **123** 36 45N 105 35W
Questembert, *France* **18** 47 40N 2 28W
Quetena, *Bolivia* **136** 22 10 S 67 25W
Quetico Prov. Park, *Canada* **104** 48 30N 91 45W
Quetrequile, *Argentina* **142** 41 33 S 69 22W
Quetta, *Pakistan* **47** 30 15N 66 55 E
Quevedo, *Ecuador* **134** 1 2 S 79 29W
Quévillon, L., *Canada* **106** 49 4N 76 57W
Quezaltenango, *Guatemala* **128** 14 50N 91 30W
Quezon City, *Phil.* **57** 14 38N 121 0 E
Qui Nhon, *Vietnam* **54** 13 40N 109 13 E
Quiaca, La, *Argentina* **140** 22 5 S 65 35W
Quibala, *Angola* **95** 10 46 S 14 59 E
Quibaxe, *Angola* **95** 8 24 S 14 27 E
Quibdo, *Colombia* **134** 5 42N 76 40W
Quiberon, *France* **18** 47 29N 3 9W
Quíbor, *Venezuela* **134** 9 56N 69 37W
Quick, *Canada* **110** 54 36N 126 54W
Quickborn, *W. Germany* **30** 53 42N 9 52 E
Quiet L., *Canada* **110** 61 5N 133 5W
Quiévrain, *Belgium* **17** 50 24N 3 41 E
Quiindy, *Paraguay* **140** 25 58 S 57 14W
Quila, *Mexico* **126** 24 23N 107 13W
Quilán, C., *Chile* **142** 43 15 S 74 30W
Quilcene, *U.S.A.* **124** 47 49N 122 53W
Quilengues, *Angola* **95** 14 12 S 14 12 E
Quilimarí, *Chile* **140** 32 5 S 71 30W
Quilino, *Argentina* **140** 30 14 S 64 29W
Quillabamba, *Peru* **136** 12 50 S 72 50W
Quillacollo, *Bolivia* **136** 17 26 S 66 17W
Quillagua, *Chile* **140** 21 40 S 69 40W
Quillaicillo, *Chile* **140** 31 17 S 71 40W
Quillan, *France* **20** 42 53N 2 10 E
Quillebeuf-sur-Seine, *France* **18** 49 28N 0 30 E
Quillota, *Chile* **140** 32 54 S 71 16W
Quilmes, *Argentina* **140** 34 43 S 58 15W
Quilon, *India* **51** 8 50N 76 38 E
Quilpie, *Australia* **73** 26 35 S 144 11 E
Quilpué, *Chile* **140** 33 5 S 71 33W
Quilua, *Mozam.* **93** 16 17 S 39 54 E
Quimbele, *Angola* **95** 6 17 S 16 41 E
Quimbonge, *Angola* **95** 8 36 S 18 30 E
Quime, *Bolivia* **136** 17 2 S 67 15W
Quimilí, *Argentina* **140** 27 40 S 62 30W
Quimper, *France* **18** 48 0N 4 9W
Quimperlé, *France* **18** 47 53N 3 33W
Quinault →, *U.S.A.* **124** 47 23N 124 18W
Quincemil, *Peru* **136** 13 15 S 70 40W
Quincy, *Calif., U.S.A.* **124** 39 56N 120 56W
Quincy, *Fla., U.S.A.* **115** 30 34N 84 34W
Quincy, *Ill., U.S.A.* **120** 39 55N 91 20W
Quincy, *Mass., U.S.A.* **117** 42 14N 71 0W
Quincy, *Wash., U.S.A.* **122** 47 22N 119 56W
Quines, *Argentina* **140** 32 13 S 65 48W
Quinga, *Mozam.* **93** 15 49 S 40 15 E
Quingey, *France* **19** 47 7N 5 52 E
Quintana de la Serena, *Spain* **23** 38 45N 5 40W
Quintana Roo □, *Mexico* **127** 19 0N 88 0W
Quintanar de la Orden, *Spain* **24** 39 36N 3 5W
Quintanar de la Sierra, *Spain* **24** 41 57N 2 55W
Quintanar del Rey, *Spain* **25** 39 21N 1 56W
Quintero, *Chile* **140** 32 45 S 71 30W
Quintin, *France* **18** 48 26N 2 56W
Quinto, *Spain* **24** 41 25N 0 32W
Quinyambie, *Australia* **73** 30 15 S 141 0 E
Quinze, L. des, *Canada* **106** 47 35N 79 5W
Quípar →, *Spain* **25** 38 15N 1 40W
Quipungo, *Angola* **95** 14 37 S 14 40 E
Quirihue, *Chile* **140** 36 15 S 72 35W
Quirimbo, *Angola* **95** 10 36 S 14 12 E
Quirindi, *Australia* **77** 31 28 S 150 40 E
Quiriquire, *Venezuela* **134** 9 59N 63 13W
Quiroga, *Spain* **22** 42 28N 7 18W
Quiruvilca, *Peru* **136** 8 1 S 78 19W
Quissac, *France* **21** 43 55N 4 0 E
Quissanga, *Mozam.* **93** 12 24 S 40 28 E
Quitapa, *Angola* **95** 10 20 S 18 19 E
Quitilipi, *Argentina* **140** 26 50 S 60 13W
Quitman, *Ga., U.S.A.* **115** 30 49N 83 35W
Quitman, *Miss., U.S.A.* **115** 32 2N 88 42W
Quitman, *Tex., U.S.A.* **121** 32 48N 95 25W
Quito, *Ecuador* **134** 0 15 S 78 35W
Quixadá, *Brazil* **138** 4 55 S 39 0W
Quixaxe, *Mozam.* **93** 15 17 S 40 4 E
Quixeramobim, *Brazil* **138** 5 12 S 39 17W
Quixinge, *Angola* **95** 9 52 S 14 23 E
Quizenga, *Angola* **95** 9 21 S 15 28 E
Qujing, *China* **58** 25 32N 103 41 E
Qul'ân, Jazâ'ir, *Egypt* **88** 24 22N 35 31 E
Qumbu, *S. Africa* **97** 31 10 S 28 48 E
Qumrān, *Jordan* **44** 31 43N 35 27 E
Quneitra, *Syria* **44** 33 7N 35 48 E
Quoin I., *Australia* **78** 14 54 S 129 32 E
Quoin Pt., *S. Africa* **96** 34 46 S 19 37 E
Quondong, *Australia* **73** 33 6 S 140 18 E
Quorn, *Australia* **73** 32 25 S 138 0 E
Qurein, *Sudan* **89** 13 30N 34 50 E
Qûs, *Egypt* **88** 25 55N 32 50 E
Quseir, *Egypt* **88** 26 7N 34 16 E
Qusrah, *Jordan* **44** 32 5N 35 20 E
Quthing, *Lesotho* **97** 30 25 S 27 36 E
Quwo, *China* **60** 35 38N 111 25 E
Quyang, *China* **60** 38 35N 114 40 E
Quynh Nhai, *Vietnam* **54** 21 49N 103 33 E
Quyon, *Canada* **106** 45 31N 76 14W
Quzi, *China* **60** 36 20N 107 20 E
Qytet Stalin, *Albania* **35** 40 47N 19 57 E

R

Ra, Ko, *Thailand* **55** 9 13N 98 16 E
Råå, *Sweden* **11** 56 0N 12 45 E
Raahe, *Finland* **8** 64 40N 24 28 E
Raalte, *Neths.* **16** 52 23N 6 16 E
Raamsdonksveer, *Neths.* **17** 51 43N 4 52 E
Ra'ananna, *Israel* **44** 32 12N 34 52 E
Raasay, *U.K.* **14** 57 25N 6 4W
Raasay, Sd. of, *U.K.* **14** 57 30N 6 8W
Rab, *Yugoslavia* **27** 44 45N 14 45 E
Raba, *Indonesia* **57** 8 36 S 118 55 E
Rába →, *Hungary* **33** 47 38N 17 38 E
Rabaçal →, *Portugal* **22** 41 30N 7 12W
Rabah, *Nigeria* **91** 13 5N 5 30 E
Rabai, *Kenya* **92** 3 50 S 39 31 E
Rabaraba, *Papua N. G.* **69** 9 58 S 149 49 E
Rabastens, *France* **20** 43 50N 1 43 E
Rabastens-de-Bigorre, *France* **20** 43 23N 0 9 E
Rabat, *Morocco* **84** 34 2N 6 48W
Rabaul, *Papua N. G.* **69** 4 24 S 152 18 E
Rabbit →, *Canada* **110** 59 41N 127 12W
Rabbit Lake, *Canada* **111** 53 8N 107 46W
Rabbitskin →, *Canada* **110** 61 47N 120 42W
Rābigh, *Si. Arabia* **46** 22 50N 39 5 E
Rabka, *Poland* **32** 49 37N 19 59 E
Rácale, *Italy* **29** 39 57N 18 6 E
Racalmuto, *Italy* **28** 37 25N 13 41 E
Racconigi, *Italy* **26** 44 47N 7 41 E
Raccoon →, *U.S.A.* **118** 41 35N 93 37W
Raccoon Cr. →, *U.S.A.* **119** 39 47N 87 23W
Race, C., *Canada* **105** 46 40N 53 5W
Rach Gia, *Vietnam* **55** 10 5N 105 5 E
Raciąż, *Poland* **32** 52 46N 20 10 E
Racibórz, *Poland* **32** 50 7N 18 18 E
Racine, *U.S.A.* **119** 42 41N 87 51W
Rackerby, *U.S.A.* **124** 39 26N 121 22W
Radama, Nosy, *Madag.* **97** 14 0 S 47 47 E
Radama, Saikanosy, *Madag.* **97** 14 16 S 47 53 E
Rădăuţi, *Romania* **34** 47 50N 25 59 E
Radbuza →, *Czech.* **32** 49 35N 13 5 E
Radcliff, *U.S.A.* **119** 37 51N 85 57W
Radeburg, *E. Germany* **30** 51 6N 13 55 E
Radeče, *Yugoslavia* **27** 46 5N 15 14 E
Radekhov, *U.S.S.R.* **37** 50 25N 24 32 E
Radford, *U.S.A.* **114** 37 8N 80 32W
Radhanpur, *India* **48** 23 50N 71 38 E

Radhwa, Jabal, *Si. Arabia* **46** 24 34N 38 18 E
Radiska →, *Yugoslavia* **35** 41 38N 20 37 E
Radisson, *Canada* **111** 52 30N 107 20W
Radium Hot Springs, *Canada* **110** 50 35N 116 2W
Radna, *Romania* **34** 46 7N 21 41 E
Radnor Forest, *U.K.* **13** 52 17N 3 10W
Radolfzell, *W. Germany* **31** 47 44N 8 58 E
Radom, *Poland* **32** 51 23N 21 12 E
Radomir, *Bulgaria* **34** 42 37N 23 4 E
Radomsko, *Poland* **32** 51 5N 19 28 E
Radomyshl, *U.S.S.R.* **36** 50 30N 29 12 E
Radoviš, *Yugoslavia* **35** 41 38N 22 28 E
Radovljica, *Yugoslavia* **27** 46 22N 14 12 E
Radstock, *U.K.* **13** 51 17N 2 25W
Radstock, C., *Australia* **73** 33 12 S 134 20 E
Răducăneni, *Romania* **34** 46 58N 27 54 E
Radviliškis, *U.S.S.R.* **36** 55 49N 23 33 E
Radville, *Canada* **111** 49 30N 104 15W
Rae, *Canada* **110** 62 50N 116 3W
Rae Bareli, *India* **49** 26 18N 81 20 E
Rae Isthmus, *Canada* **103** 66 40N 87 30W
Raeren, *Belgium* **17** 50 41N 6 7 E
Raeside, L., *Australia* **79** 29 20 S 122 0 E
Raetihi, *N.Z.* **80** 39 25 S 175 17 E
Rafaela, *Argentina* **140** 31 10 S 61 30W
Rafah, *Egypt* **88** 31 18N 34 14 E
Rafai, *C.A.R.* **92** 4 59N 23 58 E
Raffadali, *Italy* **28** 37 23N 13 29 E
Rafḩā, *Si. Arabia* **46** 29 35N 43 35 E
Rafsanjān, *Iran* **47** 30 30N 56 5 E
Raft Pt., *Australia* **78** 16 4 S 124 26 E
Ragag, *Sudan* **89** 10 59N 24 40 E
Ragged Mt., *Australia* **79** 33 27 S 123 25 E
Raglan, *Australia* **72** 23 42 S 150 49 E
Raglan, *N.Z.* **80** 37 55 S 174 55 E
Ragunda, *Sweden* **10** 63 6N 16 23 E
Ragusa, *Italy* **29** 36 56N 14 42 E
Raha, *Indonesia* **57** 4 55 S 123 0 E
Rahad, Nahr ed →, *Sudan* **89** 14 28N 33 31 E
Rahad al Bardī, *Sudan* **87** 11 20N 23 40 E
Rahaeng = Tak, *Thailand* **54** 16 52N 99 8 E
Rahden, *W. Germany* **30** 52 26N 8 36 E
Raheita, *Ethiopia* **89** 12 46N 43 4 E
Rahimyar Khan, *Pakistan* **48** 28 30N 70 25 E
Rahotu, *N.Z.* **80** 39 20 S 173 49 E
Raichur, *India* **51** 16 10N 77 20 E
Raiganj, *India* **49** 25 37N 88 10 E
Raigarh, *India* **50** 21 56N 83 25 E
Raighar, *India* **50** 19 51N 82 6 E
Raijua, *Indonesia* **57** 10 37 S 121 36 E
Railton, *Australia* **72** 41 25 S 146 28 E
Rainbow, *Australia* **74** 35 55 S 142 0 E
Rainbow Lake, *Canada* **110** 58 17N 119 23W
Rainier, *U.S.A.* **124** 46 4N 122 58W
Rainier, Mt., *U.S.A.* **124** 46 50N 121 50W
Rainy L., *Canada* **111** 48 42N 93 10W
Rainy River, *Canada* **111** 48 43N 94 29W
Raipur, *India* **50** 21 17N 81 45 E
Ra'is, *Si. Arabia* **46** 23 33N 38 43 E
Raj Nandgaon, *India* **50** 21 5N 81 5 E
Raja, Ujung, *Indonesia* **56** 3 40N 96 25 E
Raja Ampat, Kepulauan, *Indonesia* **57** 0 30 S 130 0 E
Rajahmundry, *India* **50** 17 1N 81 48 E
Rajajooseppi, *Finland* **8** 68 28N 28 29 E
Rajang →, *Malaysia* **56** 2 30N 112 0 E
Rajapalaiyam, *India* **51** 9 25N 77 35 E
Rajasthan □, *India* **48** 26 45N 73 30 E
Rajasthan Canal, *India* **48** 28 0N 72 0 E
Rajauri, *India* **49** 33 25N 74 21 E
Rajbari, *Bangla.* **52** 23 47N 89 41 E
Rajgarh, *Mad. P., India* **48** 24 2N 76 45 E
Rajgarh, *Raj., India* **48** 28 40N 75 25 E
Rajhenburg, *Yugoslavia* **27** 46 1N 15 29 E
Rajkot, *India* **48** 22 15N 70 56 E
Rajmahal Hills, *India* **49** 24 30N 87 30 E
Rajpipla, *India* **50** 21 50N 73 30 E
Rajpura, *India* **48** 30 25N 76 32 E
Rajshahi, *Bangla.* **52** 24 22N 88 39 E
Rajshahi □, *Bangla.* **49** 25 0N 89 0 E
Rakaia, *N.Z.* **81** 43 45 S 172 1 E
Rakaia →, *N.Z.* **81** 43 36 S 172 15 E
Rakan, Ra's, *Qatar* **47** 26 10N 51 20 E
Rakaposhi, *Pakistan* **49** 36 10N 74 25 E
Rakata, Pulau, *Indonesia* **56** 6 10 S 105 20 E
Rakhni, *Pakistan* **48** 30 4N 69 56 E
Rakkestad, *Norway* **10** 59 25N 11 21 E
Rakops, *Botswana* **96** 21 1 S 24 28 E
Rákospalota, *Hungary* **33** 47 30N 19 5 E
Rakov, *U.S.S.R.* **36** 53 58N 26 59 E
Rakovica, *Yugoslavia* **27** 44 59N 15 38 E
Rakovník, *Czech.* **32** 50 6N 13 42 E
Rakovski, *Bulgaria* **34** 42 21N 24 57 E
Rakvere, *U.S.S.R.* **36** 59 30N 26 25 E
Raleigh, *Australia* **77** 30 27 S 153 2 E
Raleigh, *U.S.A.* **115** 35 47N 78 39W
Raleigh B., *U.S.A.* **115** 34 50N 76 15W
Ralja, *Yugoslavia* **33** 44 33N 20 34 E
Ralls, *U.S.A.* **121** 33 40N 101 20W
Ram →, *Canada* **110** 62 1N 123 41W
Rām Allāh, *Jordan* **44** 31 55N 35 10 E
Ram Hd., *Australia* **75** 37 47 S 149 30 E
Rama, *Israel* **44** 32 56N 35 21 E
Rama, *Nic.* **128** 12 9N 84 15W
Ramacca, *Italy* **29** 37 24N 14 40 E
Ramachandrapuram, *India* **50** 16 50N 82 4 E
Ramales de la Victoria, *Spain* **24** 43 15N 3 28W
Ramalho, Serra do, *Brazil* **139** 13 45 S 44 0W
Raman, *Thailand* **55** 6 29N 101 18 E
Ramanathapuram, *India* **51** 9 25N 78 55 E
Ramanetaka, B. de, *Madag.* **97** 14 13 S 47 52 E
Ramas C., *India* **51** 15 5N 73 55 E
Ramat Gan, *Israel* **44** 32 4N 34 48 E
Ramat HaSharon, *Israel* **44** 32 7N 34 50 E
Ramatlhabama, *S. Africa* **96** 25 37 S 25 33 E
Ramban, *India* **49** 33 14N 75 12 E
Rambervillers, *France* **19** 48 20N 6 38 E
Rambi, *Fiji* **68** 16 30 S 179 59W
Rambipuji, *Indonesia* **57** 8 12 S 113 37 E
Rambla, La, *Spain* **23** 37 37N 4 45W
Rambouillet, *France* **19** 48 39N 1 50 E
Ramdurg, *India* **51** 15 58N 75 22 E
Ramea, *Canada* **105** 47 31N 57 23W
Ramechhap, *Nepal* **49** 27 25N 86 10 E
Ramelau, *Indonesia* **57** 8 55 S 126 22 E
Ramenskoye, *U.S.S.R.* **37** 55 32N 38 15 E
Ramgarh, *Bihar, India* **49** 23 40N 85 35 E
Ramgarh, *Raj., India* **48** 27 16N 75 14 E
Ramgarh, *Raj., India* **48** 27 30N 70 36 E
Rāmhormoz, *Iran* **46** 31 15N 49 35 E
Ramla, *Israel* **44** 31 55N 34 52 E
Ramlat Zalṭan, *Libya* **86** 28 30N 19 30 E
Ramlu, *Ethiopia* **89** 13 32N 41 40 E
Ramme, *Denmark* **11** 56 30N 8 11 E
Rammūn, *Jordan* **44** 31 55N 35 17 E
Ramnad = Ramanathapuram, *India* **51** 9 25N 78 55 E
Ramnagar, *India* **49** 32 47N 75 18 E
Ramnäs, *Sweden* **10** 59 46N 16 12 E
Ramon, *U.S.S.R.* **37** 51 55N 39 21 E
Ramon, Har, *Israel* **44** 30 30N 34 38 E
Ramona, *U.S.A.* **125** 33 1N 116 56W
Ramore, *Canada* **106** 48 30N 80 25W
Ramotswa, *Botswana* **96** 24 50 S 25 52 E
Rampart, *U.S.A.* **102** 65 0N 150 15W
Rampur, *H.P., India* **48** 31 26N 77 43 E
Rampur, *Mad. P., India* **48** 23 25N 73 53 E
Rampur, *Orissa, India* **50** 21 48N 83 58 E
Rampur, *Ut. P., India* **49** 28 50N 79 5 E
Rampur Hat, *India* **49** 24 10N 87 50 E
Rampura, *India* **48** 24 30N 75 27 E
Ramsel, *Belgium* **17** 51 2N 4 50 E
Ramsey, *Canada* **104** 47 25N 82 20W
Ramsey, *U.K.* **12** 54 20N 4 21W
Ramsey, *U.S.A.* **118** 39 8N 89 7W
Ramsgate, *U.K.* **13** 51 20N 1 25 E
Ramshai, *India* **52** 26 44N 88 51 E
Ramsjö, *Sweden* **10** 62 11N 15 37 E
Ramtek, *India* **50** 21 20N 79 15 E
Ramu →, *Papua N. G.* **69** 4 0 S 144 41 E
Ramvik, *Sweden* **10** 62 49N 17 51 E
Ranaghat, *India* **49** 23 15N 88 35 E
Ranahu, *Pakistan* **48** 25 55N 69 45 E
Ranau, *Malaysia* **56** 6 2N 116 40 E
Rancagua, *Chile* **140** 34 10 S 70 50W
Rance, *Belgium* **17** 50 9N 4 16 E
Rance →, *France* **18** 48 34N 1 59W
Rance, Barrage de la, *France* **18** 48 30N 2 3W
Rancharia, *Brazil* **139** 22 15 S 50 55W
Rancheria →, *Canada* **110** 60 13N 129 7W
Ranchester, *U.S.A.* **122** 44 57N 107 12W
Ranchi, *India* **49** 23 19N 85 27 E
Ranco, L., *Chile* **142** 40 15 S 72 25W
Randan, *France* **20** 46 2N 3 21 E
Randazzo, *Italy* **29** 37 53N 14 56 E
Randers, *Denmark* **11** 56 29N 10 1 E
Randers Fjord, *Denmark* **11** 56 37N 10 20 E
Randfontein, *S. Africa* **97** 26 8 S 27 45 E
Randle, *U.S.A.* **124** 46 32N 121 57W
Randolph, *Mass., U.S.A.* **117** 42 10N 71 3W
Randolph, *N.Y., U.S.A.* **116** 42 10N 78 59W
Randolph, *Utah, U.S.A.* **122** 41 43N 111 10W
Randolph, *Vt., U.S.A.* **117** 43 55N 72 39W
Randsfjord, *Norway* **10** 60 15N 10 25 E
Råne älv →, *Sweden* **8** 65 50N 22 20 E
Ranfurly, *N.Z.* **81** 45 7 S 170 6 E
Rangae, *Thailand* **55** 6 19N 101 44 E
Rangamati, *Bangla.* **52** 22 38N 92 12 E
Rangataua, *N.Z.* **80** 39 26 S 175 28 E
Rangaunu B., *N.Z.* **80** 34 51 S 173 15 E
Rångedala, *Sweden* **11** 57 47N 13 9 E
Rangeley, *U.S.A.* **117** 44 58N 70 33W
Rangely, *U.S.A.* **122** 40 3N 108 53W
Ranger, *U.S.A.* **121** 32 30N 98 42W
Rangia, *India* **52** 26 28N 91 38 E
Rangiora, *N.Z.* **81** 43 19 S 172 36 E
Rangitaiki →, *N.Z.* **80** 37 54 S 176 49 E
Rangitata →, *N.Z.* **81** 43 45 S 171 15 E
Rangitikei →, *N.Z.* **80** 40 17 S 175 15 E
Rangitoto Range, *N.Z.* **80** 38 25 S 175 35 E
Rangkasbitung, *Indonesia* **57** 6 21 S 106 15 E
Rangoon, *Burma* **52** 16 45N 96 20 E
Rangpur, *Bangla.* **52** 25 42N 89 22 E
Rangsit, *Thailand* **54** 13 59N 100 37 E
Ranibennur, *India* **51** 14 35N 75 30 E
Raniganj, *India* **49** 23 40N 87 5 E
Ranippettai, *India* **51** 12 56N 79 23 E
Ranken →, *Australia* **72** 20 31 S 137 36 E
Rankin, *Ill., U.S.A.* **119** 40 28N 87 54W
Rankin, *Tex., U.S.A.* **121** 31 16N 101 56W
Rankin Inlet, *Canada* **102** 62 30N 93 0W
Rankins Springs, *Australia* **75** 33 49 S 146 14 E
Rannoch, L., *U.K.* **14** 56 41N 4 20W
Rannoch Moor, *U.K.* **14** 56 38N 4 48W
Ranobe, Helodranon' i, *Madag.* **97** 23 3 S 43 33 E
Ranohira, *Madag.* **97** 22 29 S 45 24 E
Ranomafana, *Toamasina, Madag.* **97** 18 57 S 48 50 E
Ranomafana, *Toliara, Madag.* **97** 24 34 S 47 0 E
Ranon, *Vanuatu* **68** 16 10 S 168 7 E
Ranong, *Thailand* **55** 9 56N 98 40 E
Ransiki, *Indonesia* **57** 1 30 S 134 10 E
Ransom, *U.S.A.* **119** 41 9N 88 39W
Rantau, *Indonesia* **56** 2 56 S 115 9 E
Rantauprapat, *Indonesia* **56** 2 15N 99 50 E
Rantekombola, *Indonesia* **57** 3 15 S 119 57 E
Rantīs, *Jordan* **44** 32 4N 35 3 E
Rantoul, *U.S.A.* **119** 40 18N 88 10W
Ranum, *Denmark* **11** 56 54N 9 14 E
Raon l'Étape, *France* **19** 48 24N 6 50 E
Raoui, Erg er, *Algeria* **85** 29 0N 2 0W
Raoyang, *China* **60** 38 15N 115 45 E
Rapa Iti, *Pac. Oc.* **67** 27 35 S 144 20W
Rapallo, *Italy* **26** 44 21N 9 12 E
Rāpch, *Iran* **47** 25 40N 59 15 E
Rapid →, *Canada* **110** 59 15N 129 5W
Rapid City, *U.S.A.* **120** 44 0N 103 0W
Rapid River, *U.S.A.* **114** 45 55N 87 0W
Rapide-Blanc, *Canada* **107** 47 48N 73 2W
Rapide-Sept, *Canada* **106** 47 46N 78 19W
Rapides des Joachims, *Canada* **106** 46 13N 77 43W
Rapla, *U.S.S.R.* **36** 59 1N 24 52 E
Rappville, *Australia* **77** 29 6 S 152 57 E
Rarotonga, *Cook Is.* **67** 21 30 S 160 0W
Ra's al Khaymah, *U.A.E.* **47** 25 50N 56 5 E
Ra's al-Unuf, *Libya* **86** 30 25N 18 15 E
Ras Bânâs, *Egypt* **88** 23 57N 35 59 E
Ras Dashen, *Ethiopia* **89** 13 8N 38 26 E
Ras el Ma, *Algeria* **85** 34 26N 0 50W
Ras Mallap, *Egypt* **88** 29 18N 32 50 E
Râs Timirist, *Mauritania* **90** 19 21N 16 30W
Rasa, Punta, *Argentina* **142** 40 50 S 62 15W
Rasca, Pta. de la, *Canary Is.* **25** 27 59N 16 41W
Raseiniai, *U.S.S.R.* **36** 55 25N 23 5 E
Rashad, *Sudan* **89** 11 55N 31 0 E
Rashîd, *Egypt* **88** 31 21N 30 22 E
Rashîd, Masabb, *Egypt* **88** 31 22N 30 17 E
Rasht, *Iran* **46** 37 20N 49 40 E
Rasi Salai, *Thailand* **54** 15 20N 104 9 E
Rasipuram, *India* **51** 11 30N 78 15 E
Raška, *Yugoslavia* **33** 43 19N 20 39 E
Rason, L., *Australia* **79** 28 45 S 124 25 E
Raşova, *Romania* **34** 44 15N 27 55 E
Rasra, *India* **49** 25 50N 83 50 E
Rass el Oued, *Algeria* **85** 35 57N 5 2 E
Rasskazovo, *U.S.S.R.* **37** 52 35N 41 50 E
Rastatt, *W. Germany* **31** 48 50N 8 12 E
Rat Buri, *Thailand* **54** 13 30N 99 54 E
Rat Is., *U.S.A.* **102** 51 50N 178 15 E
Rat River, *Canada* **110** 61 7N 112 36W
Ratangarh, *India* **48** 28 5N 74 35 E
Rath, *India* **49** 25 36N 79 37 E
Rath Luirc, *Ireland* **15** 52 21N 8 40W
Rathbun Res., *U.S.A.* **118** 40 49N 92 53W
Rathdowney, *Australia* **77** 28 13 S 152 52 E
Rathdrum, *Ireland* **15** 52 57N 6 13W
Rathedaung, *Burma* **52** 20 29N 92 45 E
Rathenow, *E. Germany* **30** 52 38N 12 23 E
Rathkeale, *Ireland* **15** 52 32N 8 57W
Rathlin I., *U.K.* **15** 55 18N 6 14W
Rathlin O'Birne I., *Ireland* **15** 54 40N 8 50W
Ratibor = Racibórz, *Poland* **32** 50 7N 18 18 E
Ratlam, *India* **48** 23 20N 75 0 E
Ratnagiri, *India* **50** 16 57N 73 18 E
Ratnapura, *Sri Lanka* **51** 6 40N 80 20 E
Raton, *U.S.A.* **121** 37 0N 104 30W
Rats, R. aux →, *Canada* **107** 48 53N 72 14W
Rattaphum, *Thailand* **55** 7 8N 100 16 E
Rattray Hd., *U.K.* **14** 57 38N 1 50W
Rättvik, *Sweden* **10** 60 52N 15 7 E
Ratz, Mt., *Canada* **110** 57 23N 132 12W
Ratzeburg, *W. Germany* **30** 53 41N 10 46 E
Raub, *Malaysia* **55** 3 47N 101 52 E
Rauch, *Argentina* **140** 36 45 S 59 5W
Raufarhöfn, *Iceland* **8** 66 27N 15 57W
Raufoss, *Norway* **10** 60 44N 10 37 E
Raukumara Ra., *N.Z.* **80** 38 5 S 177 55 E
Raul Soares, *Brazil* **139** 20 5 S 42 22W
Rauland, *Norway* **10** 59 43N 8 0 E
Rauma, *Finland* **9** 61 10N 21 30 E
Rauma →, *Norway* **10** 62 34N 7 43 E
Raurkela, *India* **49** 22 14N 84 50 E
Rava Russkaya, *U.S.S.R.* **36** 50 15N 23 42 E
Ravanusa, *Italy* **28** 37 16N 13 58 E
Rāvar, *Iran* **47** 31 20N 56 51 E
Ravels, *Belgium* **17** 51 22N 5 0 E
Ravena, *U.S.A.* **117** 42 28N 73 49W
Ravenna, *Italy* **27** 44 28N 12 15 E
Ravenna, *Ky., U.S.A.* **119** 37 42N 83 55W
Ravenna, *Nebr., U.S.A.* **120** 41 3N 98 58W
Ravenna, *Ohio, U.S.A.* **116** 41 11N 81 15W
Ravensburg, *W. Germany* **31** 47 48N 9 38 E
Ravenshoe, *Australia* **72** 17 37 S 145 29 E
Ravenstein, *Neths.* **16** 51 47N 5 39 E
Ravensthorpe, *Australia* **79** 33 35 S 120 2 E
Ravenswood, *Queens., Australia* **72** 20 6 S 146 54 E
Ravenswood, *Vic., Australia* **74** 36 53 S 144 15 E
Ravenswood, *U.S.A.* **114** 38 58N 81 47W
Ravensworth, *Australia* **76** 32 26 S 151 4 E
Ravenwood, *U.S.A.* **118** 40 23N 94 41W
Ravi →, *Pakistan* **48** 30 35N 71 49 E
Ravna Gora, *Yugoslavia* **27** 45 24N 14 50 E
Rawa Mazowiecka, *Poland* **32** 51 46N 20 12 E
Rawalpindi, *Pakistan* **48** 33 38N 73 8 E
Rawāndūz, *Iraq* **46** 36 40N 44 30 E
Rawang, *Malaysia* **55** 3 20N 101 35 E
Rawdon, *Canada* **107** 46 3N 73 40W
Rawene, *N.Z.* **80** 35 25 S 173 32 E
Rawicz, *Poland* **32** 51 36N 16 52 E
Rawlinna, *Australia* **79** 30 58 S 125 28 E
Rawlins, *U.S.A.* **122** 41 50N 107 20W
Rawlinson Range, *Australia* **79** 24 40 S 128 30 E
Rawson, *Argentina* **142** 43 15 S 65 0W
Ray, *U.S.A.* **120** 48 21N 103 6W
Ray, C., *Canada* **105** 47 33N 59 15W
Rayachoti, *India* **51** 14 4N 78 50 E
Rayadurg, *India* **51** 14 40N 76 50 E
Rayagada, *India* **50** 19 15N 83 20 E
Raychikhinsk, *U.S.S.R.* **41** 49 46N 129 25 E
Raymond, *Canada* **110** 49 30N 112 35W
Raymond, *Calif., U.S.A.* **124** 37 13N 119 54W
Raymond, *Ill., U.S.A.* **118** 39 19N 89 34W
Raymond, *Wash., U.S.A.* **124** 46 45N 123 48W
Raymond Terrace, *Australia* **76** 32 45 S 151 44 E
Raymondville, *U.S.A.* **121** 26 30N 97 50W
Raymore, *Canada* **111** 51 25N 104 31W
Rayne, *U.S.A.* **121** 30 16N 92 16W
Rayón, *Mexico* **126** 29 43N 110 35W
Rayong, *Thailand* **54** 12 40N 101 20 E
Raytown, *U.S.A.* **118** 39 1N 94 28W
Rayville, *U.S.A.* **121** 32 30N 91 45W
Raywood, *Australia* **74** 36 30 S 144 15 E
Raz, Pte. du, *France* **18** 48 2N 4 47W
Ražana, *Yugoslavia* **33** 44 6N 19 55 E
Ražanj, *Yugoslavia* **33** 43 40N 21 31 E
Razdel'naya, *U.S.S.R.* **38** 46 50N 30 2 E
Razdolnoye, *U.S.S.R.* **38** 45 46N 33 29 E
Razelm, Lacul, *Romania* **34** 44 50N 29 0 E
Razgrad, *Bulgaria* **34** 43 33N 26 34 E
Razmak, *Pakistan* **48** 32 45N 69 50 E
Razole, *India* **51** 16 36N 81 48 E
Ré, I. de, *France* **20** 46 12N 1 30W
Reading, *U.K.* **13** 51 27N 0 57W
Reading, *Mich., U.S.A.* **119** 41 50N 84 45W
Reading, *Ohio, U.S.A.* **119** 39 13N 84 26W
Reading, *Pa., U.S.A.* **117** 40 20N 75 53W
Real, Cordillera, *Bolivia* **136** 17 0 S 67 10W
Realicó, *Argentina* **140** 35 0 S 64 15W
Réalmont, *France* **20** 43 48N 2 10 E
Reata, *Mexico* **126** 26 8N 101 5W
Rebais, *France* **19** 48 50N 3 10 E
Rebecca L., *Australia* **79** 30 0 S 122 15 E
Rebi, *Indonesia* **57** 6 23 S 134 7 E
Rebiana, *Libya* **86** 24 12N 22 10 E
Rebun-Tō, *Japan* **63** 45 23N 141 2 E
Recanati, *Italy* **27** 43 24N 13 32 E
Recaş, *Romania* **34** 45 46N 21 30 E
Recherche, Arch. of the, *Australia* **79** 34 15 S 122 50 E
Rechitsa, *U.S.S.R.* **36** 52 13N 30 15 E
Recht, *Belgium* **17** 50 20N 6 3 E
Recife, *Brazil* **138** 8 0 S 35 0W
Recklinghausen, *W. Germany* **17** 51 36N 7 10 E
Reconquista, *Argentina* **140** 29 10 S 59 45W
Recreio, *Brazil* **137** 8 0 S 58 25W
Recreo, *Argentina* **140** 29 25 S 65 10W
Recuay, *Peru* **136** 9 43 S 77 28W
Red → = Hong →, *Vietnam* **54** 20 17N 106 34 E
Red →, *N. Amer.* **120** 50 24N 96 48W
Red →, *U.S.A.* **121** 31 0N 91 40W
Red Bank, *U.S.A.* **117** 40 21N 74 4W
Red Bay, *Canada* **105** 51 44N 56 25W
Red Bluff, *U.S.A.* **122** 40 11N 122 11W
Red Bluff L., *U.S.A.* **121** 31 59N 103 58W
Red Bud, *U.S.A.* **118** 38 13N 90 0W
Red Cliffs, *Australia* **74** 34 19 S 142 11 E
Red Cloud, *U.S.A.* **120** 40 8N 98 33W
Red Deer, *Canada* **110** 52 20N 113 50W
Red Deer →, *Alta., Canada* **111** 50 58N 110 0W
Red Deer →, *Man., Canada* **111** 52 53N 101 1W

Red Deer L., *Canada* **111** 52 55N 101 20W
Red Indian L., *Canada* **105** 48 35N 57 0W
Red Lake, *Canada* **111** 51 3N 93 49W
Red Lake Falls, *U.S.A.* **120** 47 54N 96 15W
Red Lodge, *U.S.A.* **122** 45 10N 109 10W
Red Mountain, *U.S.A.* **125** 35 22N 117 38W
Red Oak, *U.S.A.* **120** 41 0N 95 10W
Red Range, *Australia* **77** 29 46 S 151 57 E
Red Rock, *Australia* **77** 29 59 S 153 14 E
Red Rock, *Canada* **104** 48 55N 88 15W
Red Rock, L., *U.S.A.* **118** 41 30N 93 15W
Red Rock's Pt., *Australia* **79** 32 13 S 127 32 E
Red Sea, *Asia* **45** 25 0N 36 0 E
Red Slate Mt., *U.S.A.* **124** 37 31N 118 52W
Red Sucker L., *Canada* **111** 54 9N 93 40W
Red Tower Pass = Turnu Rosu Pasul, *Romania* **34** 45 33N 24 17 E
Red Wing, *U.S.A.* **120** 44 32N 92 35W
Rédange, *Lux.* **17** 49 46N 5 52 E
Redbank, *Australia* **74** 36 56 S 143 21 E
Redbridge, *U.K.* **13** 51 35N 0 7 E
Redcar, *U.K.* **12** 54 37N 1 4W
Redcliff, *Canada* **111** 50 10N 110 50W
Redcliffe, *Australia* **77** 27 12 S 153 0 E
Redcliffe, Mt., *Australia* **79** 28 30 S 121 30 E
Reddersburg, *S. Africa* **96** 29 41 S 26 10 E
Redding, *U.S.A.* **122** 40 30N 122 25W
Redditch, *U.K.* **13** 52 18N 1 57W
Redenção, *Brazil* **138** 4 13 S 38 43W
Redesdale, *Australia* **74** 37 2 S 144 31 E
Redfield, *U.S.A.* **120** 45 0N 98 30W
Redkey, *U.S.A.* **119** 40 21N 85 9W
Redknife ➛, *Canada* **110** 61 14N 119 22W
Redlands, *U.S.A.* **125** 34 0N 117 11W
Redmond, *Australia* **79** 34 55 S 117 40 E
Redmond, *Oreg., U.S.A.* **122** 44 19N 121 11W
Redmond, *Wash., U.S.A.* **124** 47 40N 122 7W
Redon, *France* **18** 47 40N 2 6W
Redonda, *Antigua* **129** 16 58N 62 19W
Redondela, *Spain* **22** 42 15N 8 38W
Redondo, *Portugal* **23** 38 39N 7 37W
Redondo Beach, *U.S.A.* **124** 33 50N 118 23W
Redrock Pt., *Canada* **110** 62 11N 115 2W
Redruth, *U.K.* **13** 50 14N 5 14W
Redvers, *Canada* **111** 49 35N 101 40W
Redwater, *Canada* **110** 53 55N 113 6W
Redwood, *U.S.A.* **117** 44 18N 75 48W
Redwood City, *U.S.A.* **124** 37 30N 122 15W
Redwood Falls, *U.S.A.* **120** 44 30N 95 2W
Ree, L., *Ireland* **15** 53 35N 8 0W
Reed, L., *Canada* **111** 54 38N 100 30W
Reed City, *U.S.A.* **114** 43 52N 85 30W
Reeder, *U.S.A.* **120** 46 7N 102 52W
Reedley, *U.S.A.* **124** 36 36N 119 27W
Reedsburg, *U.S.A.* **120** 43 34N 90 5W
Reedsport, *U.S.A.* **122** 43 45N 124 4W
Reefton, *Australia* **74** 34 15 S 147 27 E
Reefton, *N.Z.* **81** 42 6 S 171 51 E
Reeve, L., *Australia* **75** 38 0 S 147 35 E
Reftele, *Sweden* **11** 57 11N 13 35 E
Refugio, *U.S.A.* **121** 28 18N 97 17W
Rega ➛, *Poland* **32** 54 10N 15 18 E
Regalbuto, *Italy* **29** 37 40N 14 38 E
Regavim, *Israel* **44** 32 32N 35 2 E
Regen, *W. Germany* **31** 48 58N 13 9 E
Regen ➛, *W. Germany* **31** 49 2N 12 6 E
Regeneração, *Brazil* **138** 6 15 S 42 41W
Regensburg, *W. Germany* **31** 49 1N 12 7 E
Réggio di Calábria, *Italy* **29** 38 7N 15 38 E
Réggio nell' Emilia, *Italy* **26** 44 42N 10 38 E
Regina, *Canada* **111** 50 27N 104 35W
Régina, *Fr. Guiana* **135** 4 19N 52 8W
Registro, *Brazil* **141** 24 29 S 47 49W
Reguengos de Monsaraz, *Portugal* **23** 38 25N 7 32W
Rehar ➛, *India* **49** 23 55N 82 40 E
Rehoboth, *Namibia* **96** 23 15 S 17 4 E
Rehovot, *Israel* **44** 31 54N 34 48 E
Rei-Bouba, *Cameroon* **94** 8 40N 14 15 E
Reichenbach, *E. Germany* **30** 50 36N 12 19 E
Reid, *Australia* **79** 30 49 S 128 26 E
Reid River, *Australia* **72** 19 40 S 146 48 E
Reids Flat, *Australia* **76** 34 7 S 149 0 E
Reidsville, *U.S.A.* **115** 36 21N 79 40W
Reigate, *U.K.* **13** 51 14N 0 11W
Reillo, *Spain* **24** 39 54N 1 53W
Reims, *France* **19** 49 15N 4 1 E
Reina, *Israel* **44** 32 43N 35 18 E
Reina Adelaida, Arch., *Chile* **142** 52 20 S 74 0W
Reinbeck, *U.S.A.* **118** 42 18N 92 40W
Reindeer ➛, *Canada* **111** 55 36N 103 11W
Reindeer I., *Canada* **111** 52 30N 98 0W
Reindeer L., *Canada* **111** 57 15N 102 15W
Reine, La, *Canada* **106** 48 50N 79 30W
Reinga, C., *N.Z.* **80** 34 25 S 172 43 E
Reinosa, *Spain* **22** 43 2N 4 15W
Reinosa, Paso, *Spain* **22** 42 56N 4 10W
Reitdiep, *Neths.* **16** 53 20N 6 20 E
Reitz, *S. Africa* **97** 27 48 S 28 29 E
Reivilo, *S. Africa* **96** 27 36 S 24 8 E
Rejmyre, *Sweden* **11** 58 50N 15 55 E
Reka ➛, *Yugoslavia* **27** 45 40N 14 0 E
Rekinniki, *U.S.S.R.* **41** 60 51N 163 40 E
Reliance, *Canada* **111** 63 0N 109 20W
Remad, Oued ➛, *Algeria* **85** 33 28N 1 20W
Rémalard, *France* **18** 48 26N 0 47 E
Remarkable, Mt., *Australia* **73** 32 48 S 138 10 E
Rembang, *Indonesia* **57** 6 42 S 111 21 E
Remchi, *Algeria* **85** 35 2N 1 26W
Remedios, *Colombia* **134** 7 2N 74 41W
Remedios, *Panama* **128** 8 15N 81 50W
Remeshk, *Iran* **47** 26 55N 58 50 E
Remich, *Lux.* **17** 49 32N 6 22 E
Rémigny, *Canada* **106** 47 46N 79 12W
Remington, *U.S.A.* **119** 40 45N 87 8W
Rémire, *Fr. Guiana* **135** 4 53N 52 17W
Remiremont, *France* **19** 48 0N 6 36 E
Remo, *Ethiopia* **89** 6 48N 41 20 E
Remontnoye, *U.S.S.R.* **39** 46 34N 43 37 E
Remoulins, *France* **21** 43 55N 4 35 E
Remscheid, *W. Germany* **30** 51 11N 7 12 E
Ren Xian, *China* **60** 37 8N 114 40 E
Renascença, *Brazil* **134** 3 50 S 66 21W
Rend L., *U.S.A.* **118** 38 2N 88 58W
Rende, *Italy* **29** 39 19N 16 11 E
Rendeux, *Belgium* **17** 50 14N 5 30 E
Rendína, *Greece* **35** 39 4N 21 58 E
Rendova, *Solomon Is.* **68** 8 33 S 157 17 E
Rendsburg, *W. Germany* **30** 54 18N 9 41 E
Rene, *U.S.S.R.* **41** 66 2N 179 25W
Renfrew, *Canada* **109** 45 30N 76 40W
Renfrew, *U.K.* **14** 55 52N 4 24W
Rengat, *Indonesia* **56** 0 30 S 102 45 E
Rengo, *Chile* **140** 34 24 S 70 50W
Renhua, *China* **59** 25 5N 113 40 E
Renhuai, *China* **58** 27 48N 106 24 E
Reni, *U.S.S.R.* **38** 45 28N 28 15 E
Renigunta, *India* **51** 13 38N 79 30 E
Renk, *Sudan* **89** 11 50N 32 50 E
Renkum, *Neths.* **16** 51 58N 5 43 E
Renmark, *Australia* **73** 34 11 S 140 43 E
Rennell, *Solomon Is.* **68** 11 40 S 160 10 E
Rennell Sd., *Canada* **110** 53 23N 132 35W
Renner Springs T.O., *Australia* **72** 18 20 S 133 47 E
Rennes, *France* **18** 48 7N 1 41W
Rennes, Bassin de, *France* **18** 48 0N 1 30W
Reno, *U.S.A.* **124** 39 30N 119 50W
Reno ➛, *Italy* **27** 44 37N 12 17 E
Renovo, *U.S.A.* **116** 41 20N 77 47W
Renqiu, *China* **60** 38 43N 116 5 E
Rensselaer, *Ind., U.S.A.* **119** 40 57N 87 10W
Rensselaer, *N.Y., U.S.A.* **117** 42 38N 73 41W
Rentería, *Spain* **24** 43 19N 1 54W
Renton, *U.S.A.* **124** 47 30N 122 9W
Renwick, *N.Z.* **81** 41 30 S 173 51 E
Réo, *Burkina Faso* **90** 12 28N 2 35W
Réole, La, *France* **20** 44 35N 0 1W
Reotipur, *India* **49** 25 33N 83 45 E
Repalle, *India* **51** 16 2N 80 45 E
Repentigny, *Canada* **107** 45 44N 73 28W
Republic, *Mich., U.S.A.* **104** 46 25N 87 59W
Republic, *Wash., U.S.A.* **122** 48 38N 118 42W
Republican ➛, *U.S.A.* **120** 39 3N 96 48W
Republican City, *U.S.A.* **120** 40 9N 99 20W
Republiek, *Surinam* **135** 5 30N 55 13W
Repulse B., *Antarctica* **143** 64 30 S 99 30 E
Repulse Bay, *Canada* **103** 66 30N 86 30W
Requena, *Peru* **136** 5 5 S 73 52W
Requena, *Spain* **25** 39 30N 1 4W
Resele, *Sweden* **10** 63 20N 17 5 E
Reserve, *Canada* **111** 52 28N 102 39W
Reserve, *U.S.A.* **123** 33 50N 108 54W
Resht = Rasht, *Iran* **46** 37 20N 49 40 E
Resistencia, *Argentina* **140** 27 30 S 59 0W
Reşiţa, *Romania* **34** 45 18N 21 53 E
Resolution I., *Canada* **103** 61 30N 65 0W
Resolution I., *N.Z.* **81** 45 40 S 166 40 E
Resplandes, *Brazil* **138** 6 17 S 45 13W
Resplendor, *Brazil* **139** 19 20 S 41 15W
Ressano Garcia, *Mozam.* **97** 25 25 S 32 0 E
Restinga, La, *Canary Is.* **25** 27 38N 17 59W
Reston, *Canada* **111** 49 33N 101 6W
Retalhuleu, *Guatemala* **128** 14 33N 91 46W
Reteag, *Romania* **34** 47 10N 24 0 E
Retenue, L. de, *Zaïre* **93** 11 0 S 27 0 E
Rethel, *France* **19** 49 30N 4 20 E
Rethem, *W. Germany* **30** 52 47N 9 25 E
Réthímnon, *Greece* **35** 35 18N 24 30 E
Retiche, Alpi, *Switz.* **31** 46 30N 10 0 E
Retie, *Belgium* **17** 51 16N 5 5 E
Retiers, *France* **18** 47 55N 1 23W
Retortillo, *Spain* **22** 40 48N 6 21W
Reuland, *Belgium* **17** 50 12N 6 8 E
Réunion, *Ind. Oc.* **53** 21 0 S 56 0 E
Reus, *Spain* **24** 41 10N 1 5 E
Reusel, *Neths.* **17** 51 21N 5 9 E
Reuss ➛, *Switz.* **31** 47 16N 8 24 E
Reuterstadt Stavenhagen, *E. Germany* **30** 53 41N 12 54 E
Reutlingen, *W. Germany* **31** 48 28N 9 13 E
Reutte, *Austria* **31** 47 29N 10 42 E
Reuver, *Neths.* **17** 51 17N 6 5 E
Reval = Tallinn, *U.S.S.R.* **36** 59 22N 24 48 E
Revel, *France* **20** 43 28N 2 0 E
Revelganj, *India* **49** 25 50N 84 40 E
Revelstoke, *Canada* **110** 51 0N 118 10W
Reventazón, *Peru* **136** 6 10 S 80 58W
Revigny-sur-Ornain, *France* **19** 48 49N 4 59 E
Revilla Gigedo, Is., *Pac. Oc.* **67** 18 40N 112 0W
Revillagigedo I., *U.S.A.* **110** 55 50N 131 20W
Revin, *France* **19** 49 55N 4 39 E
Revuè ➛, *Mozam.* **93** 19 50 S 34 0 E
Rewa, *India* **49** 24 33N 81 25 E
Rewa ➛, *Guyana* **135** 3 19N 58 42W
Rewari, *India* **48** 28 15N 76 40 E
Rexburg, *U.S.A.* **122** 43 55N 111 50W
Rey, Rio del ➛, *Nigeria* **91** 4 30N 8 48 E
Rey Malabo, *Eq. Guin.* **91** 3 45N 8 50 E
Reyes, *Bolivia* **136** 14 19 S 67 23W
Reyes, Pt., *U.S.A.* **124** 37 59N 123 2W
Reykjahlið, *Iceland* **8** 65 40N 16 55W
Reykjanes, *Iceland* **8** 63 48N 22 40W
Reykjavík, *Iceland* **8** 64 10N 21 57W
Reynolds, *Canada* **111** 49 40N 95 55W
Reynolds, *U.S.A.* **118** 41 20N 90 40W
Reynolds Ra., *Australia* **78** 22 30 S 133 0 E
Reynoldsville, *U.S.A.* **116** 41 5N 78 58W
Reynosa, *Mexico* **127** 26 5N 98 18W
Rezekne, *U.S.S.R.* **36** 56 30N 27 17 E
Rharis, O. ➛, *Algeria* **85** 26 0N 5 4 E
Rhayader, *U.K.* **13** 52 19N 3 30W
Rheden, *Neths.* **16** 52 0N 6 3 E
Rhein, *Canada* **111** 51 25N 102 15W
Rhein ➛, *Europe* **30** 51 52N 6 2 E
Rhein-Main-Donau-Kanal ➛, *W. Germany* **31** 49 1N 11 27 E
Rheinbach, *W. Germany* **30** 50 38N 6 54 E
Rheine, *W. Germany* **30** 52 17N 7 25 E
Rheinland-Pfalz □, *W. Germany* **31** 50 0N 7 0 E
Rheinsberg, *E. Germany* **30** 53 6N 12 52 E
Rhenen, *Neths.* **16** 51 58N 5 33 E
Rheola, *Australia* **74** 36 39 S 143 42 E
Rheriss, Oued ➛, *Morocco* **84** 30 50N 4 34W
Rheydt, *W. Germany* **30** 51 10N 6 24 E
Rhin = Rhein ➛, *Europe* **30** 51 52N 6 2 E
Rhinau, *France* **19** 48 19N 7 43 E
Rhine = Rhein ➛, *Europe* **30** 51 52N 6 2 E
Rhineland-Palatinate □ = Rheinland-Pfalz □, *W. Germany* **31** 50 0N 7 0 E
Rhinelander, *U.S.A.* **120** 45 38N 89 29W
Rhino Camp, *Uganda* **92** 3 0N 31 22 E
Rhir, Cap, *Morocco* **84** 30 38N 9 54W
Rhisnes, *Belgium* **17** 50 31N 4 48 E
Rho, *Italy* **26** 45 31N 9 2 E
Rhode Island □, *U.S.A.* **117** 41 38N 71 37W
Rhodes = Ródhos, *Greece* **35** 36 15N 28 10 E
Rhodes' Tomb, *Zimb.* **93** 20 30 S 28 30 E
Rhodesia = Zimbabwe ■, *Africa* **93** 19 0 S 30 0 E
Rhodope Mts. = Rhodopi Planina, *Bulgaria* **35** 41 40N 24 20 E
Rhodopi Planina, *Bulgaria* **35** 41 40N 24 20 E
Rhondda, *U.K.* **13** 51 39N 3 30W
Rhône □, *France* **21** 45 54N 4 35 E
Rhône ➛, *France* **21** 43 28N 4 42 E
Rhum, *U.K.* **14** 57 0N 6 20W
Rhyl, *U.K.* **12** 53 19N 3 29W
Rhymney, *U.K.* **13** 51 32N 3 7W
Ri-Aba, *Eq. Guin.* **91** 3 28N 8 40 E
Riachão, *Brazil* **138** 7 20 S 46 37W
Riacho de Santana, *Brazil* **139** 13 37 S 42 57W
Rialma, *Brazil* **139** 15 18 S 49 34W
Riang, *India* **52** 27 31N 92 56 E
Riaño, *Spain* **22** 42 59N 5 0W
Rians, *France* **21** 43 37N 5 44 E
Riansares ➛, *Spain* **24** 39 32N 3 18W
Riasi, *India* **49** 33 10N 74 50 E
Riau □, *Indonesia* **56** 0 0 102 35 E
Riau, Kepulauan, *Indonesia* **56** 0 30N 104 20 E
Riaza, *Spain* **24** 41 18N 3 30W
Riaza ➛, *Spain* **24** 41 42N 3 55W
Riba de Saelices, *Spain* **24** 40 55N 2 17W
Ribadavia, *Spain* **22** 42 17N 8 8W
Ribadeo, *Spain* **22** 43 35N 7 5W
Ribadesella, *Spain* **22** 43 30N 5 7W
Ribamar, *Brazil* **138** 2 33 S 44 3W
Ribas, *Spain* **24** 42 19N 2 15 E
Ribas do Rio Pardo, *Brazil* **137** 20 27 S 53 46W
Ribble ➛, *U.K.* **12** 54 13N 2 20W
Ribe, *Denmark* **11** 55 19N 8 44 E
Ribeauvillé, *France* **19** 48 10N 7 20 E
Ribécourt, *France* **19** 49 30N 2 55 E
Ribeira, *Spain* **22** 42 36N 8 58W
Ribeira do Pombal, *Brazil* **138** 10 50 S 38 32W
Ribeirão Prêto, *Brazil* **141** 21 10 S 47 50W
Ribeiro Gonçalves, *Brazil* **138** 7 32 S 45 14W
Ribemont, *France* **19** 49 47N 3 27 E
Ribera, *Italy* **28** 37 30N 13 13 E
Ribérac, *France* **20** 45 15N 0 20 E
Riberalta, *Bolivia* **137** 11 0 S 66 0W
Ribnica, *Yugoslavia* **27** 45 45N 14 45 E
Ribnitz-Damgarten, *E. Germany* **30** 54 14N 12 24 E
Riccarton, *N.Z.* **81** 43 32 S 172 37 E
Riccia, *Italy* **29** 41 30N 14 50 E
Riccione, *Italy* **27** 44 0N 12 39 E
Rice, *U.S.A.* **125** 34 5N 114 51W
Rice L., *Canada* **109** 44 12N 78 10W
Rice Lake, *U.S.A.* **120** 45 30N 91 42W
Riceys, Les, *France* **19** 47 59N 4 22 E
Rich, *Morocco* **84** 32 16N 4 30W
Rich, C., *Canada* **108** 44 43N 80 38W
Rich Hill, *U.S.A.* **121** 38 5N 94 22W
Richards Bay, *S. Africa* **97** 28 48 S 32 6 E
Richards L., *Canada* **111** 59 10N 107 10W
Richardson ➛, *Australia* **74** 36 40 S 142 47 E
Richardson ➛, *Canada* **111** 58 25N 111 14W
Richardson Mts., *N.Z.* **81** 44 49 S 168 34 E
Richardson Springs, *U.S.A.* **124** 39 51N 121 46W
Richardton, *U.S.A.* **120** 46 56N 102 22W
Riche, C., *Australia* **79** 34 36 S 118 47 E
Richelieu, *France* **18** 47 0N 0 20 E
Richey, *U.S.A.* **120** 47 42N 105 5W
Richfield, *Idaho, U.S.A.* **122** 43 2N 114 5W
Richfield, *Utah, U.S.A.* **123** 38 50N 112 0W
Richford, *U.S.A.* **117** 45 0N 72 40W
Richibucto, *Canada* **105** 46 42N 64 54W
Richland, *Ga., U.S.A.* **115** 32 7N 84 40W
Richland, *Iowa, U.S.A.* **118** 41 13N 92 0W
Richland, *Mo., U.S.A.* **118** 37 51N 92 26W
Richland, *Oreg., U.S.A.* **122** 44 49N 117 9W
Richland, *Wash., U.S.A.* **122** 46 15N 119 15W
Richland Center, *U.S.A.* **120** 43 21N 90 22W
Richlands, *U.S.A.* **114** 37 7N 81 49W
Richmond, *N.S.W., Australia* **76** 33 35 S 150 42 E
Richmond, *Queens., Australia* **72** 20 43 S 143 8 E
Richmond, *Ont., Canada* **109** 45 11N 75 50W
Richmond, *Qué., Canada* **107** 45 40N 72 9W
Richmond, *N.Z.* **81** 41 20 S 173 12 E
Richmond, *S. Africa* **97** 29 51 S 30 18 E
Richmond, *N. Yorks., U.K.* **12** 54 24N 1 43W
Richmond, *Surrey, U.K.* **13** 51 28N 0 18W
Richmond, *Calif., U.S.A.* **124** 37 58N 122 21W
Richmond, *Ind., U.S.A.* **119** 39 50N 84 50W
Richmond, *Ky., U.S.A.* **119** 37 40N 84 20W
Richmond, *Mich., U.S.A.* **116** 42 47N 82 45W
Richmond, *Mo., U.S.A.* **120** 39 15N 93 58W
Richmond, *Tex., U.S.A.* **121** 29 32N 95 42W
Richmond, *Utah, U.S.A.* **122** 41 55N 111 48W
Richmond, *Va., U.S.A.* **114** 37 33N 77 27W
Richmond ➛, *Australia* **77** 28 52 S 153 35 E
Richmond, Mt., *N.Z.* **81** 41 32 S 173 22 E
Richmond Hill, *Canada* **108** 43 52N 79 27W
Richmond Ra., *Australia* **77** 29 0 S 152 45 E
Richmond Ra., *N.Z.* **81** 41 32 S 173 22 E
Richton, *U.S.A.* **115** 31 23N 88 58W
Richwood, *Ohio, U.S.A.* **119** 40 26N 83 18W
Richwood, *W. Va., U.S.A.* **114** 38 17N 80 32W
Ricla, *Spain* **24** 41 31N 1 24W
Ricupe, *Angola* **95** 14 37 S 21 25 E
Riddarhyttan, *Sweden* **10** 59 49N 15 33 E
Riddell, *Australia* **74** 37 28 S 144 42 E
Ridderkerk, *Neths.* **16** 51 52N 4 35 E
Ridge Farm, *U.S.A.* **119** 39 54N 87 39W
Ridgecrest, *U.S.A.* **125** 35 37N 117 40W
Ridgedale, *Canada* **111** 53 0N 104 10W
Ridgefield, *U.S.A.* **124** 45 49N 122 45W
Ridgeland, *U.S.A.* **115** 32 30N 80 58W
Ridgelands, *Australia* **72** 23 16 S 150 17 E
Ridgetown, *Canada* **108** 42 26N 81 52W
Ridgeville, *U.S.A.* **119** 40 18N 85 2W
Ridgewood, *U.S.A.* **117** 40 59N 74 7W
Ridgway, *Ill., U.S.A.* **119** 37 48N 88 16W
Ridgway, *Pa., U.S.A.* **116** 41 25N 78 43W
Riding Mt. Nat. Park, *Canada* **111** 50 50N 100 0W
Ridley Mt., *Australia* **79** 33 12 S 122 7 E
Ried, *Austria* **33** 48 14N 13 30 E
Riedlingen, *W. Germany* **31** 48 9N 9 28 E
Riel, *Neths.* **17** 51 31N 5 1 E
Rienza ➛, *Italy* **27** 46 49N 11 47 E
Riesa, *E. Germany* **30** 51 19N 13 19 E

Riesco, I., *Chile* **142** 52 55 S 72 40W
Riesi, *Italy* **29** 37 16N 14 4 E
Riet →, *S. Africa* **96** 29 0 S 23 54 E
Rieti, *Italy* **27** 42 23N 12 50 E
Rieupeyroux, *France* **20** 44 19N 2 12 E
Riez, *France* **21** 43 49N 6 6 E
Riffe, L., *U.S.A.* **124** 46 30N 122 20W
Rifle, *U.S.A.* **122** 39 40N 107 50W
Rifstangi, *Iceland* **8** 66 32N 16 12W
Rift Valley □, *Kenya* **92** 0 20N 36 0 E
Rig Rig, *Chad* **87** 14 13N 14 25 E
Riga, *U.S.S.R.* **36** 56 53N 24 8 E
Riga, G. of = Rīgas Jūras Līcis, *U.S.S.R.* **36** 57 40N 23 45 E
Rīgas Jūras Līcis, *U.S.S.R.* **36** 57 40N 23 45 E
Rigaud, *Canada* **117** 45 29N 74 18W
Rigby, *U.S.A.* **122** 43 41N 111 58W
Rīgestān □, *Afghan.* **47** 30 15N 65 0 E
Riggins, *U.S.A.* **122** 45 29N 116 26W
Rignac, *France* **20** 44 25N 2 16 E
Rigolet, *Canada* **105** 54 10N 58 23W
Riihimäki, *Finland* **9** 60 45N 24 48 E
Riiser-Larsen-halvøya, *Antarctica* **143** 68 0 S 35 0 E
Rijau, *Nigeria* **91** 11 8N 5 17 E
Rijeka, *Yugoslavia* **27** 45 20N 14 21 E
Rijen, *Neths.* **17** 51 35N 4 55 E
Rijkevorsel, *Belgium* **17** 51 21N 4 46 E
Rijn →, *Neths.* **16** 52 12N 4 21 E
Rijnsberg, *Neths.* **16** 52 11N 4 27 E
Rijsbergen, *Neths.* **17** 51 31N 4 41 E
Rijssen, *Neths.* **16** 52 19N 6 30 E
Rijswijk, *Neths.* **16** 52 4N 4 22 E
Rike, *Ethiopia* **89** 10 50N 39 53 E
Rila Planina, *Bulgaria* **34** 42 10N 23 0 E
Riley, *U.S.A.* **122** 43 35N 119 33W
Rima →, *Nigeria* **91** 13 4N 5 10 E
Rimah, Wadi ar →, *Si. Arabia* **46** 26 5N 41 30 E
Rimavská Sobota, *Czech.* **33** 48 22N 20 2 E
Rimbey, *Canada* **110** 52 35N 114 15W
Rimbo, *Sweden* **10** 59 44N 18 21 E
Rimforsa, *Sweden* **11** 58 6N 15 43 E
Rimi, *Nigeria* **91** 12 58N 7 43 E
Rímini, *Italy* **27** 44 3N 12 33 E
Rîmnicu Sărat, *Romania* **34** 45 26N 27 3 E
Rîmnicu Vîlcea, *Romania* **34** 45 9N 24 21 E
Rimouski, *Canada* **107** 48 27N 68 30W
Rimouski →, *Canada* **107** 48 27N 68 32W
Rimouski, Parc Prov. de, *Canada* **107** 48 0N 68 15W
Rimouski-Est, *Canada* **107** 48 28N 68 31W
Rimrock, *U.S.A.* **124** 46 38N 121 10W
Rinca, *Indonesia* **57** 8 45 S 119 35 E
Rincón de Romos, *Mexico* **126** 22 14N 102 18W
Rinconada, *Argentina* **140** 22 26 S 66 10W
Ringarum, *Sweden* **11** 58 21N 16 26 E
Ringe, *Denmark* **11** 55 13N 10 28 E
Ringgold Is., *Fiji* **68** 16 15 S 179 25W
Ringim, *Nigeria* **91** 12 13N 9 10 E
Ringkøbing, *Denmark* **11** 56 5N 8 15 E
Ringling, *U.S.A.* **122** 46 16N 110 56W
Ringsaker, *Norway* **10** 60 54N 10 45 E
Ringsjön, *Sweden* **11** 55 55N 13 30 E
Ringsted, *Denmark* **11** 55 25N 11 46 E
Ringvassøy, *Norway* **8** 69 56N 19 15 E
Rinjani, *Indonesia* **56** 8 24 S 116 28 E
Rinteln, *W. Germany* **30** 52 11N 9 3 E
Río, Punta del, *Spain* **25** 36 49N 2 24W
Rio Branco, *Brazil* **136** 9 58 S 67 49W
Río Branco, *Uruguay* **141** 32 40 S 53 40W
Rio Brilhante, *Brazil* **141** 21 48 S 54 33W
Río Bueno, *Chile* **142** 40 19 S 72 58W
Río Chico, *Venezuela* **134** 10 19N 65 59W
Rio Claro, *Brazil* **141** 22 19 S 47 35W
Rio Claro, *Trin. & Tob.* **129** 10 20N 61 25W
Río Colorado, *Argentina* **142** 39 0 S 64 0W
Río Cuarto, *Argentina* **140** 33 10 S 64 25W
Rio das Pedras, *Mozam.* **97** 23 8 S 35 28 E
Rio de Contas, *Brazil* **139** 13 36 S 41 48W
Rio de Janeiro, *Brazil* **141** 23 0 S 43 12W
Rio de Janeiro □, *Brazil* **141** 22 50 S 43 0W
Rio do Prado, *Brazil* **139** 16 35 S 40 34W
Rio do Sul, *Brazil* **141** 27 13 S 49 37W
Río Gallegos, *Argentina* **142** 51 35 S 69 15W
Río Grande, *Argentina* **142** 53 50 S 67 45W
Río Grande, *Bolivia* **136** 20 51 S 67 17W
Rio Grande, *Brazil* **141** 32 0 S 52 20W
Río Grande, *Mexico* **126** 23 50N 103 2W
Río Grande, *Nic.* **128** 12 54N 83 33W
Rio Grande →, *U.S.A.* **121** 25 57N 97 9W
Rio Grande City, *U.S.A.* **121** 26 23N 98 49W
Río Grande del Norte →, *N. Amer.* **112** 26 0N 97 0W
Rio Grande do Norte □, *Brazil* **138** 5 40 S 36 0W
Rio Grande do Sul □, *Brazil* **141** 30 0 S 53 0W
Río Hato, *Panama* **128** 8 22N 80 10W
Río Lagartos, *Mexico* **127** 21 36N 88 10W
Rio Largo, *Brazil* **138** 9 28 S 35 50W
Rio Maior, *Portugal* **23** 39 19N 8 57W
Rio Marina, *Italy* **26** 42 48N 10 25 E
Río Mayo, *Argentina* **142** 45 40 S 70 15W
Río Mulatos, *Bolivia* **136** 19 40 S 66 50W
Río Muni = Mbini □, *Eq. Guin.* **94** 1 30N 10 0 E
Rio Negro, *Brazil* **141** 26 0 S 50 0W
Río Negro, *Chile* **142** 40 47 S 73 14W
Rio Negro, Pantanal do, *Brazil* **137** 19 0 S 56 0W
Rio Pardo, *Brazil* **141** 30 0 S 52 30W
Río Pico, *Argentina* **142** 44 0 S 70 22W
Rio Real, *Brazil* **139** 11 28 S 37 56W
Río Segundo, *Argentina* **140** 31 40 S 63 59W
Río Tercero, *Argentina* **140** 32 15 S 64 8W
Rio Tinto, *Brazil* **138** 6 48 S 35 5W
Rio Tinto, *Portugal* **22** 41 11N 8 34W
Rio Verde, *Brazil* **139** 17 50 S 51 0W
Río Verde, *Mexico* **127** 21 56N 99 59W
Rio Verde de Mato Grosso, *Brazil* **137** 18 56 S 54 52W
Rio Vista, *U.S.A.* **124** 38 11N 121 44W
Ríobamba, *Ecuador* **134** 1 50 S 78 45W
Ríohacha, *Colombia* **134** 11 33N 72 55W
Rioja, *Peru* **136** 6 11 S 77 5W
Rioja, La, *Argentina* **140** 29 20 S 67 0W
Rioja, La □, *Argentina* **140** 29 30 S 67 0W
Rioja, La □, *Spain* **24** 42 20N 2 20W
Riom, *France* **20** 45 54N 3 7 E
Riom-ès-Montagnes, *France* **20** 45 17N 2 39 E
Rion-des-Landes, *France* **20** 43 55N 0 56W
Rionegro, *Colombia* **134** 6 9N 75 22W
Rionero in Vúlture, *Italy* **29** 40 55N 15 40 E
Rioni →, *U.S.S.R.* **39** 42 5N 41 50 E
Rios, *Spain* **22** 41 58N 7 16W
Riosucio, *Caldas, Colombia* **134** 5 30N 75 40W
Ríosucio, *Choco, Colombia* **134** 7 27N 77 7W
Riou L., *Canada* **111** 59 7N 106 25W
Rioz, *France* **19** 47 26N 6 5 E
Riozinho →, *Brazil* **134** 2 55 S 67 7W
Riparia, Dora →, *Italy* **26** 45 7N 7 24 E
Ripatransone, *Italy* **27** 43 0N 13 45 E
Ripley, *Canada* **108** 44 4N 81 35W
Ripley, *Calif., U.S.A.* **125** 33 32N 114 39W
Ripley, *N.Y., U.S.A.* **116** 42 16N 79 44W
Ripley, *Ohio, U.S.A.* **119** 38 45N 83 51W
Ripley, *Tenn., U.S.A.* **121** 35 43N 89 34W
Ripoll, *Spain* **24** 42 15N 2 13 E
Ripon, *Canada* **106** 45 45N 75 10W
Ripon, *U.K.* **12** 54 8N 1 31W
Ripon, *Calif., U.S.A.* **124** 37 44N 121 7W
Ripon, *Wis., U.S.A.* **114** 43 51N 88 50W
Riposto, *Italy* **29** 37 44N 15 12 E
Risalpur, *Pakistan* **48** 34 3N 71 59 E
Risan, *Yugoslavia* **33** 42 32N 18 42 E
Risaralda □, *Colombia* **134** 5 0N 76 10W
Riscle, *France* **20** 43 39N 0 5W
Rishiri-Tō, *Japan* **63** 45 11N 141 15 E
Rishon le Ẕiyyon, *Israel* **44** 31 58N 34 48 E
Rishpon, *Israel* **44** 32 12N 34 49 E
Rising Sun, *U.S.A.* **119** 38 57N 84 51W
Risle →, *France* **18** 49 26N 0 23 E
Rison, *U.S.A.* **121** 33 57N 92 11W
Risør, *Norway* **11** 58 43N 9 13 E
Rissani, *Morocco* **84** 31 18N 4 12W
Riti, *Nigeria* **91** 7 57N 9 41 E
Ritidian Pt., *Guam* **68** 13 39N 144 51 E
Rittman, *U.S.A.* **116** 40 57N 81 48W
Ritzville, *U.S.A.* **122** 47 10N 118 21W
Riu, *India* **52** 28 19N 95 3 E
Riva Bella, *France* **18** 49 17N 0 18W
Riva del Garda, *Italy* **26** 45 53N 10 50 E
Rivadavia, *Buenos Aires, Argentina* **140** 35 29 S 62 59W
Rivadavia, *Mendoza, Argentina* **140** 33 13 S 68 30W
Rivadavia, *Salta, Argentina* **140** 24 5 S 62 54W
Rivadavia, *Chile* **140** 29 57 S 70 35W
Rivarolo Canavese, *Italy* **26** 45 20N 7 42 E
Rivas, *Nic.* **128** 11 30N 85 50W
Rive-de-Gier, *France* **21** 45 32N 4 37 E
River Cess, *Liberia* **90** 5 30N 9 32W
River Valley, *Canada* **108** 46 35N 80 11W
Rivera, *Uruguay* **141** 31 0 S 55 50W
Riverdale, *U.S.A.* **124** 36 26N 119 52W
Riverdsale, *S. Africa* **96** 34 7 S 21 15 E
Riverhead, *U.S.A.* **117** 40 53N 72 40W
Riverhurst, *Canada* **111** 50 55N 106 50W
Riverina, *Australia* **79** 29 45 S 120 40 E
Rivers, *Canada* **111** 50 2N 100 14W
Rivers □, *Nigeria* **91** 5 0N 6 30 E
Rivers, L. of the, *Canada* **111** 49 49N 105 44W
Rivers Inlet, *Canada* **110** 51 42N 127 15W
Riverside, *Calif., U.S.A.* **125** 34 0N 117 22W
Riverside, *Wyo., U.S.A.* **122** 41 12N 106 57W
Riversleigh, *Australia* **72** 19 5 S 138 40 E
Riverton, *Australia* **73** 34 10 S 138 46 E
Riverton, *Canada* **111** 51 1N 97 0W
Riverton, *N.Z.* **81** 46 21 S 168 0 E
Riverton, *Ill., U.S.A.* **118** 39 51N 89 33W
Riverton, *Wyo., U.S.A.* **122** 43 1N 108 27W
Riverton Heights, *U.S.A.* **124** 47 28N 122 17W
Rives, *France* **21** 45 21N 5 31 E
Rivesaltes, *France* **20** 42 47N 2 50 E
Riviera, *Europe* **26** 44 0N 8 30 E
Rivière-à-Pierre, *Canada* **107** 46 59N 72 11W
Rivière-au-Renard, *Canada* **105** 48 59N 64 23W
Rivière-aux-Rats, *Canada* **107** 47 13N 72 53W
Rivière-Bersimis, *Canada* **107** 48 56N 68 42W
Rivière-du-Loup, *Canada* **107** 47 50N 69 30W
Rivière-Ouelle, *Canada* **107** 47 26N 70 1W
Rivière-Pentecôte, *Canada* **105** 49 57N 67 1W
Rivière-Pilot, *Martinique* **129** 14 26N 60 53W
Rivière-Portneuf, *Canada* **107** 48 38N 69 6W
Rívoli, *Italy* **26** 45 3N 7 31 E
Rivoli B., *Australia* **73** 37 32 S 140 3 E
Riwaka, *N.Z.* **81** 41 5 S 172 59 E
Rixensart, *Belgium* **17** 50 43N 4 32 E
Riyadh = Ar Riyāḍ, *Si. Arabia* **46** 24 41N 46 42 E
Rize, *Turkey* **46** 41 0N 40 30 E
Rizhao, *China* **61** 35 25N 119 30 E
Rizzuto, C., *Italy* **29** 38 54N 17 5 E
Rjukan, *Norway* **10** 59 54N 8 33 E
Rô, *N. Cal.* **68** 21 23 S 167 50 E
Roa, *Norway* **10** 60 17N 10 37 E
Roa, *Spain* **22** 41 41N 3 56W
Roachdale, *U.S.A.* **119** 39 51N 86 48W
Road Town, *Virgin Is.* **129** 18 27N 64 37W
Roag, L., *U.K.* **14** 58 10N 6 55W
Roanne, *France* **21** 46 3N 4 4 E
Roanoke, *Ala., U.S.A.* **115** 33 9N 85 23W
Roanoke, *Ind., U.S.A.* **119** 40 58N 85 22W
Roanoke, *Va., U.S.A.* **114** 37 19N 79 55W
Roanoke →, *U.S.A.* **115** 35 56N 76 43W
Roanoke I., *U.S.A.* **115** 35 55N 75 40W
Roanoke Rapids, *U.S.A.* **115** 36 28N 77 42W
Roatán, *Honduras* **128** 16 18N 86 35W
Rob Roy, *Solomon Is.* **68** 7 23 S 157 36 E
Robbins I., *Australia* **72** 40 42 S 145 0 E
Robe →, *Australia* **78** 21 42 S 116 15 E
Robe →, *Ireland* **15** 53 38N 9 10W
Röbel, *E. Germany* **30** 53 24N 12 37 E
Robert Lee, *U.S.A.* **121** 31 55N 100 26W
Roberts, *Idaho, U.S.A.* **122** 43 44N 112 8W
Roberts, *Ill., U.S.A.* **119** 40 37N 88 11W
Robertsganj, *India* **49** 24 44N 83 4 E
Robertson, *Australia* **76** 34 37 S 150 36 E
Robertson, *S. Africa* **96** 33 46 S 19 50 E
Robertson I., *Antarctica* **143** 65 15 S 59 30W
Robertson Ra., *Australia* **78** 23 15 S 121 0 E
Robertsonville, *Canada* **107** 46 9N 71 13W
Robertsport, *Liberia* **90** 6 45N 11 26W
Robertstown, *Australia* **73** 33 58 S 139 5 E
Roberval, *Canada* **107** 48 32N 72 15W
Robeson Ch., *Greenland* **144** 82 0N 61 30W
Robinson, *U.S.A.* **119** 39 0N 87 44W
Robinson →, *Australia* **72** 16 3 S 137 16 E
Robinson Crusoe I., *Pac. Oc.* **67** 33 38 S 78 52W
Robinson Ranges, *Australia* **79** 25 40 S 119 0 E
Robinson River, *Australia* **72** 16 45 S 136 58 E
Robinvale, *Australia* **74** 34 40 S 142 45 E
Robla, La, *Spain* **22** 42 50N 5 41W
Roblin, *Canada* **111** 51 14N 101 21W
Roboré, *Bolivia* **137** 18 10 S 59 45W
Robson, Mt., *Canada* **110** 53 10N 119 10W
Robstown, *U.S.A.* **121** 27 47N 97 40W
Roca Partida, I., *Mexico* **126** 19 1N 112 2W
Rocas, I., *Brazil* **138** 4 0 S 34 1W
Rocca d'Aspidé, *Italy* **29** 40 27N 15 10 E
Rocca San Casciano, *Italy* **27** 44 3N 11 45 E
Roccalbegna, *Italy* **27** 42 47N 11 30 E
Roccastrada, *Italy* **27** 43 0N 11 10 E
Roccella Iónica, *Italy* **29** 38 20N 16 24 E
Rocha, *Uruguay* **141** 34 30 S 54 25W
Rochdale, *U.K.* **12** 53 36N 2 10W
Roche, La, *N. Cal.* **68** 21 26 S 168 2 E
Roche-Bernard, La, *France* **18** 47 31N 2 19W
Roche-Canillac, La, *France* **20** 45 12N 1 57 E
Roche-en-Ardenne, La, *Belgium* **17** 50 11N 5 35 E
Roche-sur-Yon, La, *France* **18** 46 40N 1 25W
Rochebaucourt, *Canada* **106** 48 41N 77 30W
Rochechouart, *France* **20** 45 50N 0 49 E
Rochedo, *Brazil* **137** 19 57 S 54 52W
Rochefort, *Belgium* **17** 50 9N 5 12 E
Rochefort, *France* **20** 45 56N 0 57W
Rochefort-en-Terre, *France* **18** 47 42N 2 22W
Rochefoucauld, La, *France* **20** 45 44N 0 24 E
Rochelle, *U.S.A.* **118** 41 55N 89 5W
Rochelle, La, *France* **20** 46 10N 1 9W
Rocher River, *Canada* **110** 61 23N 112 44W
Rocherath, *Belgium* **17** 50 26N 6 18 E
Rocheservière, *France* **18** 46 57N 1 30W
Rochester, *Australia* **74** 36 22 S 144 41 E
Rochester, *Canada* **110** 54 22N 113 27W
Rochester, *U.K.* **13** 51 22N 0 30 E
Rochester, *Ind., U.S.A.* **119** 41 5N 86 15W
Rochester, *Mich., U.S.A.* **119** 42 41N 83 8W
Rochester, *Minn., U.S.A.* **120** 44 1N 92 28W
Rochester, *N.H., U.S.A.* **117** 43 19N 70 57W
Rochester, *N.Y., U.S.A.* **116** 43 10N 77 40W
Rociana, *Spain* **23** 37 19N 6 35W
Rociu, *Romania* **34** 44 43N 25 2 E
Rock →, *Canada* **110** 60 7N 127 7W
Rock Falls, *U.S.A.* **118** 41 47N 89 41W
Rock Flat, *Australia* **75** 36 21 S 149 13 E
Rock Hill, *U.S.A.* **115** 34 55N 81 2W
Rock Island, *Canada* **107** 45 26N 73 34W
Rock Island, *U.S.A.* **118** 41 30N 90 35W
Rock Port, *U.S.A.* **120** 40 26N 95 30W
Rock Rapids, *U.S.A.* **120** 43 25N 96 10W
Rock River, *U.S.A.* **122** 41 49N 106 0W
Rock Sound, *Bahamas* **128** 24 54N 76 12W
Rock Sprs., *Mont., U.S.A.* **122** 46 55N 106 11W
Rock Sprs., *Wyo., U.S.A.* **122** 41 40N 109 10W
Rock Valley, *U.S.A.* **120** 43 10N 96 17W
Rockall, *Atl. Oc.* **6** 57 37N 13 42W
Rockanje, *Neths.* **16** 51 52N 4 4 E
Rockdale, *Tex., U.S.A.* **121** 30 40N 97 0W
Rockdale, *Wash., U.S.A.* **124** 47 22N 121 28W
Rockefeller Plateau, *Antarctica* **143** 80 0 S 140 0W
Rockford, *Ill., U.S.A.* **118** 42 20N 89 0W
Rockford, *Iowa, U.S.A.* **118** 43 3N 92 57W
Rockford, *Mich., U.S.A.* **119** 43 7N 85 34W
Rockford, *Ohio, U.S.A.* **119** 40 41N 84 39W
Rockglen, *Canada* **111** 49 11N 105 57W
Rockhampton, *Australia* **72** 23 22 S 150 32 E
Rockhampton Downs, *Australia* **72** 18 57 S 135 10 E
Rockingham, *Australia* **79** 32 15 S 115 38 E
Rockingham B., *Australia* **72** 18 5 S 146 10 E
Rockingham Forest, *U.K.* **13** 52 28N 0 42W
Rocklake, *U.S.A.* **120** 48 50N 99 13W
Rockland, *Canada* **106** 45 33N 75 17W
Rockland, *Idaho, U.S.A.* **122** 42 37N 112 57W
Rockland, *Maine, U.S.A.* **105** 44 6N 69 6W
Rockland, *Mich., U.S.A.* **120** 46 40N 89 10W
Rocklands Reservoir, *Australia* **74** 37 15 S 142 5 E
Rockley, *Australia* **76** 33 41 S 149 33 E
Rocklin, *U.S.A.* **124** 38 48N 121 14W
Rockmart, *U.S.A.* **115** 34 1N 85 2W
Rockport, *Ky., U.S.A.* **119** 37 53N 87 3W
Rockport, *Tex., U.S.A.* **121** 28 2N 97 3W
Rocksprings, *U.S.A.* **121** 30 2N 100 11W
Rockton, *Australia* **75** 37 10 S 149 18 E
Rockvale, *Australia* **77** 30 25 S 151 53 E
Rockville, *Conn., U.S.A.* **117** 41 51N 72 27W
Rockville, *Ind., U.S.A.* **119** 39 46N 87 14W
Rockville, *Md., U.S.A.* **114** 39 7N 77 10W
Rockwall, *U.S.A.* **121** 32 55N 96 30W
Rockwell City, *U.S.A.* **118** 42 20N 94 35W
Rockwood, *Canada* **108** 43 37N 80 8W
Rockwood, *U.S.A.* **115** 35 52N 84 40W
Rocky Ford, *U.S.A.* **120** 38 7N 103 45W
Rocky Fork Lake, *U.S.A.* **119** 39 12N 83 23W
Rocky Glen, *Australia* **77** 31 6 S 149 35 E
Rocky Gully, *Australia* **79** 34 30 S 116 57 E
Rocky Lane, *Canada* **110** 58 31N 116 22W
Rocky Mount, *U.S.A.* **115** 35 55N 77 48W
Rocky Mountain House, *Canada* **110** 52 22N 114 55W
Rocky Mts., *N. Amer.* **102** 55 0N 121 0W
Rocky River, *Australia* **77** 30 36 S 151 29 E
Rockyford, *Canada* **110** 51 14N 113 10W
Rocroi, *France* **19** 49 55N 4 30 E
Rod, *Pakistan* **47** 28 10N 63 5 E
Roda, La, *Albacete, Spain* **25** 39 13N 2 15W
Roda, La, *Sevilla, Spain* **23** 37 12N 4 46W
Rødberg, *Norway* **10** 60 17N 8 56 E
Rødby, *Denmark* **11** 54 41N 11 23 E
Rødbyhavn, *Denmark* **11** 54 39N 11 22 E
Roddickton, *Canada* **105** 50 51N 56 8W
Rødding, *Denmark* **11** 55 23N 9 3 E
Rødekro, *Denmark* **11** 55 4N 9 20 E
Roden, *Neths.* **16** 53 8N 6 26 E
Rødenes, *Norway* **10** 59 35N 11 34 E
Rodenkirchen, *W. Germany* **30** 53 24N 8 26 E
Roderick I., *Canada* **110** 52 38N 128 22W
Rodez, *France* **20** 44 21N 2 33 E
Rodholívas, *Greece* **35** 40 55N 24 0 E
Ródhos, *Greece* **35** 36 15N 28 10 E
Rodi Garganico, *Italy* **29** 41 55N 15 53 E
Rodna, *Romania* **34** 47 25N 24 50 E
Rodney, *Canada* **108** 42 34N 81 41W
Rodney, C., *N.Z.* **80** 36 17 S 174 50 E

Rodniki, U.S.S.R. 37 57 7N 41 47 E
Rodriguez, Ind. Oc. 53 19 45 S 63 20 E
Roe →, U.K. 15 55 10N 6 59W
Roebling, U.S.A. 117 40 7N 74 45W
Roebourne, Australia 78 20 44 S 117 9 E
Roebuck B., Australia 78 18 5 S 122 20 E
Roebuck Plains, Australia 78 17 56 S 122 28 E
Roer →, Neths. 17 51 12N 5 59 E
Roermond, Neths. 17 51 12N 6 0 E
Roes Welcome Sd., Canada 103 65 0N 87 0W
Roeselare, Belgium 17 50 57N 3 7 E
Rœulx, Belgium 17 50 31N 4 7 E
Rogachev, U.S.S.R. 36 53 8N 30 5 E
Rogagua, L., Bolivia 136 13 43 S 66 50W
Rogaland fylke □, Norway 9 59 12N 6 20 E
Rogaška Slatina, Yugoslavia 27 46 15N 15 42 E
Rogatec, Yugoslavia 27 46 15N 15 46 E
Rogatin, U.S.S.R. 36 49 24N 24 36 E
Roger, L., Canada 106 47 50N 78 59W
Rogers, U.S.A. 121 36 20N 94 5W
Rogers City, U.S.A. 104 45 25N 83 49W
Rogerson, U.S.A. 122 42 10N 114 40W
Rogersville, U.S.A. 115 36 27N 83 1W
Roggan River, Canada 104 54 25N 79 32W
Roggel, Neths. 17 51 16N 5 56 E
Roggeveldberge, S. Africa 96 32 10 S 20 10 E
Roggiano Gravina, Italy 29 39 37N 16 9 E
Rogliano, France 21 42 57N 9 30 E
Rogliano, Italy 29 39 11N 16 20 E
Rogoaguado, L., Bolivia 137 13 0 S 65 30W
Rogue →, U.S.A. 122 42 30N 124 0W
Rohan, France 18 48 4N 2 45W
Rohault, L., Canada 107 49 23N 74 20W
Rohnert Park, U.S.A. 124 38 16N 122 40W
Rohrbach-lès-Bitche, France 19 49 3N 7 15 E
Rohri, Pakistan 48 27 45N 68 51 E
Rohri Canal, Pakistan 48 26 15N 68 27 E
Rohtak, India 48 28 55N 76 43 E
Roi Et, Thailand 54 16 4N 103 40 E
Roisel, France 19 49 58N 3 6 E
Rojas, Argentina 140 34 10 S 60 45W
Rojo, C., Mexico 127 21 33N 97 20W
Rokan →, Indonesia 56 2 0N 100 50 E
Rokeby, Australia 72 13 39 S 142 40 E
Rokewood, Australia 74 37 54 S 143 44 E
Rokiskis, U.S.S.R. 36 55 55N 25 35 E
Rokitno, U.S.S.R. 36 50 57N 35 56 E
Rolândia, Brazil 141 23 18 S 51 23W
Rolde, Neths. 16 52 59N 6 39 E
Rolette, U.S.A. 120 48 42N 99 50W
Rolfe, U.S.A. 118 42 49N 94 31W
Rolla, Kans., U.S.A. 121 37 10N 101 40W
Rolla, Mo., U.S.A. 118 37 56N 91 42W
Rolla, N. Dak., U.S.A. 120 48 50N 99 36W
Rollag, Norway 10 60 2N 9 18 E
Rollands Plains, Australia 77 31 17 S 152 42 E
Rolleston, Australia 72 24 28 S 148 35 E
Rolleston, N.Z. 81 43 35 S 172 24 E
Rollet, Canada 106 47 55N 79 15W
Rolling Fork →, U.S.A. 119 38 0N 85 56W
Rollingstone, Australia 72 19 2 S 146 24 E
Rom, Sudan 89 9 54N 32 16 E
Roma, Australia 73 26 32 S 148 49 E
Roma, Italy 28 41 54N 12 30 E
Roma, Sweden 9 57 32N 18 26 E
Roman, Romania 34 46 57N 26 55 E
Roman, U.S.S.R. 41 66 4N 112 14 E
Roman-Kosh, Gora, U.S.S.R. 38 44 37N 34 15 E
Romana, La, Dom. Rep. 129 18 27N 68 57W
Romanche →, France 21 45 5N 5 43 E
Romang, Indonesia 57 7 30 S 127 20 E
Români, Egypt 88 30 59N 32 38 E
Romania ■, Europe 34 46 0N 25 0 E
Romano, Cayo, Cuba 128 22 0N 77 30W
Romano di Lombardía, Italy 26 45 32N 9 45 E
Romanovka = Bessarabka, U.S.S.R. 38 46 21N 28 58 E
Romans-sur-Isère, France 21 45 3N 5 3 E
Romanshorn, Switz. 31 47 33N 9 22 E
Romblon, Phil. 57 12 33N 122 17 E
Rombo □, Tanzania 92 3 10 S 37 30 E
Rome = Roma, Italy 28 41 54N 12 30 E
Rome, Ga., U.S.A. 115 34 20N 85 0W
Rome, N.Y., U.S.A. 117 43 14N 75 29W
Romeleåsen, Sweden 11 55 34N 13 33 E
Romenay, France 21 46 30N 5 1 E
Romerike, Norway 10 60 7N 11 10 E
Romilly-sur-Seine, France 19 48 31N 3 44 E
Romîni, Romania 34 44 59N 24 11 E
Rommani, Morocco 84 33 31N 6 40W
Romney, U.S.A. 114 39 21N 78 45W
Romney Marsh, U.K. 13 51 0N 1 0 E
Romny, U.S.S.R. 36 50 48N 33 28 E
Rømø, Denmark 11 55 10N 8 30 E
Romodan, U.S.S.R. 36 50 0N 33 15 E
Romodanovo, U.S.S.R. 37 54 26N 45 23 E
Romont, Switz. 31 46 42N 6 54 E
Romorantin-Lanthenay, France 19 47 21N 1 45 E
Romsdalen, Norway 10 62 25N 8 0 E
Romsey, Australia 74 37 21 S 144 45 E
Ron, Vietnam 54 17 53N 106 27 E
Rona, U.K. 14 57 33N 6 0W
Ronan, U.S.A. 122 47 30N 114 6W
Roncador, Cayos, Caribbean 128 13 32N 80 4W
Roncador, Serra do, Brazil 139 12 30 S 52 30W
Roncesvalles, Paso, Spain 24 43 1N 1 19W
Ronceverte, U.S.A. 114 37 45N 80 28W
Ronciglione, Italy 27 42 18N 12 12 E
Ronco →, Italy 27 44 24N 12 12 E
Ronda, Spain 23 36 46N 5 12W
Ronda, Serranía de, Spain 23 36 44N 5 3W
Rondane, Norway 10 61 57N 9 50 E
Rondeau Prov. Park, Canada 108 42 19N 81 51W
Rondón, Colombia 134 6 17N 71 6W
Rondônia, Brazil 137 10 52 S 61 57W
Rondônia □, Brazil 137 11 0 S 63 0W
Rondonópolis, Brazil 137 16 28 S 54 38W
Rong Jiang →, China 58 24 35N 109 20 E
Rong Xian, Guangxi Zhuangzu, China 59 22 50N 110 31 E
Rong Xian, Sichuan, China 58 29 23N 104 22 E
Rong'an, China 58 25 14N 109 22 E
Rongchang, China 58 29 20N 105 32 E
Ronge, L. la, Canada 111 55 6N 105 17W
Ronge, La, Canada 111 55 5N 105 20W
Rongjiang, China 58 25 57N 108 28 E
Rongotea, N.Z. 80 40 19 S 175 25 E
Rongshui, China 58 25 5N 109 12 E
Ronne Ice Shelf, Antarctica 143 78 0 S 60 0W
Ronneby, Sweden 11 56 12N 15 17 E
Ronsard, C., Australia 79 24 46 S 113 10 E
Ronse, Belgium 17 50 45N 3 35 E
Ronuro →, Brazil 137 11 56 S 53 33W
Roodepoort, S. Africa 97 26 11 S 27 54 E
Roodeschool, Neths. 16 53 25N 6 46 E
Roodhouse, U.S.A. 118 39 29N 90 24W
Roof Butte, U.S.A. 123 36 29N 109 5W
Roompot, Neths. 17 51 37N 3 44 E
Roonui, Mt., Tahiti 68 17 49 S 149 12W
Roorkee, India 48 29 52N 77 59 E
Roosendaal, Neths. 17 51 32N 4 29 E
Roosevelt, Minn., U.S.A. 120 48 51N 95 2W
Roosevelt, Utah, U.S.A. 122 40 19N 110 1W
Roosevelt →, Brazil 137 7 35 S 60 20W
Roosevelt, Mt., Canada 110 58 26N 125 20W
Roosevelt I., Antarctica 143 79 30 S 162 0W
Roosevelt Res., U.S.A. 123 33 46N 111 0W
Roper →, Australia 72 14 43 S 135 27 E
Ropesville, U.S.A. 121 33 25N 102 10W
Roque Pérez, Argentina 140 35 25 S 59 24W
Roquefort, France 20 44 2N 0 20W
Roquemaure, France 21 44 3N 4 48 E
Roquetas, Spain 24 40 50N 0 30 E
Roquevaire, France 21 43 20N 5 36 E
Roraima □, Brazil 135 2 0N 61 30W
Roraima, Mt., Venezuela 135 5 10N 60 40W
Rorketon, Canada 111 51 24N 99 35W
Røros, Norway 10 62 35N 11 23 E
Rorschach, Switz. 31 47 28N 9 30 E
Rosa, Zambia 93 9 33 S 31 15 E
Rosa, C., Algeria 85 37 0N 8 16 E
Rosa, Monte, Europe 31 45 57N 7 53 E
Rosal, Spain 22 41 57N 8 51W
Rosal de la Frontera, Spain 23 37 59N 7 13W
Rosalia, U.S.A. 122 47 14N 117 25W
Rosamond, U.S.A. 125 34 52N 118 10W
Rosans, France 21 44 24N 5 29 E
Rosario, Argentina 140 33 0 S 60 40W
Rosário, Brazil 138 3 0 S 44 15W
Rosario, Baja Calif. N., Mexico 126 30 0N 115 50W
Rosario, Sinaloa, Mexico 126 23 0N 105 52W
Rosario, Paraguay 140 24 30 S 57 35W
Rosario, Villa del, Venezuela 134 10 19N 72 19W
Rosario de la Frontera, Argentina 140 25 50 S 65 0W
Rosario de Lerma, Argentina 140 24 59 S 65 35W
Rosario del Tala, Argentina 140 32 20 S 59 10W
Rosário do Sul, Brazil 141 30 15 S 54 55W
Rosário Oeste, Brazil 137 14 50 S 56 25W
Rosarito, U.S.A. 125 32 18N 117 4W
Rosarno, Italy 29 38 29N 15 59 E
Rosas, Spain 24 42 19N 3 10 E
Roscoe, Miss., U.S.A. 118 37 58N 93 48W
Roscoe, S. Dak., U.S.A. 120 45 27N 99 20W
Roscoff, France 18 48 44N 4 0W
Roscommon, Ireland 15 53 38N 8 11W
Roscommon, U.S.A. 114 44 27N 84 35W
Roscommon □, Ireland 15 53 40N 8 15W
Roscrea, Ireland 15 52 58N 7 50W
Rose →, Australia 72 14 16 S 135 45 E
Rose Blanche, Canada 105 47 38N 58 45W
Rose Harbour, Canada 110 52 15N 131 10W
Rose Pt., Canada 110 54 11N 131 39W
Rose Valley, Canada 111 52 19N 103 49W
Roseau, Domin. 129 15 20N 61 24W
Roseau, U.S.A. 120 48 51N 95 46W
Rosebery, Tas., Australia 72 41 46 S 145 33 E
Rosebery, Vic., Australia 74 35 48 S 142 27 E
Rosebud, Australia 74 38 21 S 144 54 E
Rosebud, U.S.A. 121 31 5N 97 0W
Roseburg, U.S.A. 122 43 10N 123 20W
Rosedale, Queens., Australia 72 24 38 S 151 53 E
Rosedale, Vic., Australia 75 38 11 S 146 48 E
Rosedale, U.S.A. 121 33 51N 91 0W
Rosée, Belgium 17 50 14N 4 41 E
Roseland, U.S.A. 124 38 25N 122 43W
Rosemary, Canada 110 50 46N 112 5W
Rosemère, Canada 107 45 38N 73 48W
Rosenberg, U.S.A. 121 29 30N 95 48W
Rosendaël, France 19 51 3N 2 24 E
Rosendale, U.S.A. 118 40 4N 94 51W
Rosenheim, W. Germany 31 47 51N 12 9 E
Roseto degli Abruzzi, Italy 27 42 40N 14 2 E
Rosetown, Canada 111 51 35N 107 59W
Rosetta = Rashîd, Egypt 88 31 21N 30 22 E
Roseville, Calif., U.S.A. 124 38 46N 121 17W
Roseville, Ill., U.S.A. 118 40 44N 90 40W
Roseville, Mich., U.S.A. 119 42 30N 82 56W
Rosewood, N.S.W., Australia 76 35 38 S 147 52 E
Rosewood, N. Terr., Australia 78 16 28 S 128 58 E
Rosewood, Queens., Australia 77 27 38 S 152 36 E
Rosh Haniqra, Kefar, Israel 44 33 5N 35 5 E
Rosh Pinna, Israel 44 32 58N 35 32 E
Rosières-en-Santerre, France 19 49 49N 2 42 E
Rosignano Marittimo, Italy 26 43 23N 10 28 E
Rosignol, Guyana 135 6 15N 57 30W
Roşiori de Vede, Romania 34 44 9N 25 0 E
Rositsa, Bulgaria 34 43 57N 27 57 E
Rositsa →, Bulgaria 34 43 10N 25 30 E
Roskilde, Denmark 11 55 38N 12 3 E
Roskilde Amtskommune □, Denmark 11 55 35N 12 5 E
Roskilde Fjord, Denmark 11 55 50N 12 2 E
Roslavl, U.S.S.R. 36 53 57N 32 55 E
Roslyn, Australia 76 34 29 S 149 37 E
Rosmaninhal, Portugal 23 39 44N 7 5W
Rosmead, S. Africa 96 31 29 S 25 8 E
Røsnæs, Denmark 11 55 44N 10 55 E
Rosolini, Italy 29 36 49N 14 58 E
Rosporden, France 18 47 57N 3 50W
Ross, Australia 72 42 2 S 147 30 E
Ross, N.Z. 81 42 53 S 170 49 E
Ross Dependency □, Antarctica 143 70 0 S 170 5W
Ross I., Antarctica 143 77 30 S 168 0 E
Ross Ice Shelf, Antarctica 143 80 0 S 180 0 E
Ross L., U.S.A. 122 48 50N 121 5W
Ross on Wye, U.K. 13 51 55N 2 34W
Ross Sea, Antarctica 143 74 0 S 178 0 E
Rossan Pt., Ireland 15 54 42N 8 47W
Rossano Cálabro, Italy 29 39 36N 16 39 E
Rossburn, Canada 111 50 40N 100 49W
Rosseau, Canada 108 45 16N 79 39W
Rosseau L., Canada 108 45 10N 79 35W
Rossel, C., Vanuatu 68 20 23 S 166 36 E
Rossford, U.S.A. 119 41 36N 83 34W
Rossignol, L., Canada 104 52 43N 73 40W
Rossignol Res., Canada 105 44 12N 65 10W
Rossland, Canada 110 49 6N 117 50W
Rosslare, Ireland 15 52 17N 6 23W
Rosslau, E. Germany 30 51 52N 12 15 E
Rossmore, Canada 109 44 8N 77 23W
Rosso, Mauritania 90 16 40N 15 45W
Rossosh, U.S.S.R. 39 50 15N 39 28 E
Rossport, Canada 104 48 50N 87 30W
Rossum, Neths. 16 51 48N 5 20 E
Røssvatnet, Norway 8 65 45N 14 5 E
Rossville, Australia 72 15 48 S 145 15 E
Rossville, U.S.A. 119 40 25N 86 35W
Rosthern, Canada 111 52 40N 106 20W
Rostock, E. Germany 30 54 4N 12 9 E
Rostock □, E. Germany 30 54 10N 12 30 E
Rostov, Don, U.S.S.R. 39 47 15N 39 45 E
Rostov, Moskva, U.S.S.R. 37 57 14N 39 25 E
Rostrenen, France 18 48 14N 3 21W
Roswell, U.S.A. 121 33 26N 104 32W
Rosyth, U.K. 14 56 2N 3 26W
Rota, Spain 23 36 37N 6 20W
Rotälven →, Sweden 10 61 15N 14 3 E
Rotan, U.S.A. 121 32 52N 100 30W
Rotem, Belgium 17 51 3N 5 45 E
Rotenburg, W. Germany 30 53 6N 9 24 E
Roth, W. Germany 31 49 15N 11 6 E
Rothaargebirge, W. Germany 30 51 0N 8 20 E
Rothenburg ob der Tauber, W. Germany 31 49 21N 10 11 E
Rother →, U.K. 13 50 59N 0 40 E
Rotherham, U.K. 12 53 26N 1 21W
Rothes, U.K. 14 57 31N 3 12W
Rothesay, Canada 105 45 23N 66 0W
Rothesay, U.K. 14 55 50N 5 3W
Roti, Indonesia 57 10 50 S 123 0 E
Roto, Australia 73 33 0 S 145 30 E
Roto Aira L., N.Z. 80 39 3 S 175 45 E
Rotoehu L., N.Z. 80 38 1 S 176 32 E
Rotoiti L., N.Z. 81 41 51 S 172 49 E
Rotoma L., N.Z. 80 38 2 S 176 35 E
Rotondella, Italy 29 40 10N 16 30 E
Rotoroa, L., N.Z. 81 41 55 S 172 39 E
Rotorua, N.Z. 80 38 9 S 176 16 E
Rotorua, L., N.Z. 80 38 5 S 176 18 E
Rotselaar, Belgium 17 50 57N 4 42 E
Rott →, W. Germany 31 48 26N 13 26 E
Rottenburg, W. Germany 31 48 28N 8 56 E
Rotterdam, Neths. 16 51 55N 4 30 E
Rottnest I., Australia 79 32 0 S 115 27 E
Rottumeroog, Neths. 16 53 33N 6 34 E
Rottweil, W. Germany 31 48 9N 8 38 E
Rotuma, Fiji 66 12 25 S 177 5 E
Roubaix, France 19 50 40N 3 10 E
Rouen, France 18 49 27N 1 4 E
Rouge →, Canada 106 45 17N 74 10W
Rough Ridge, N.Z. 81 45 10 S 169 55 E
Rouillac, France 20 45 47N 0 4W
Rouleau, Canada 111 50 10N 104 56W
Round L., Canada 109 45 38N 77 30W
Round Mt., Australia 77 30 26 S 152 16 E
Round Mountain, U.S.A. 122 38 46N 117 3W
Roundup, U.S.A. 122 46 25N 108 35W
Roura, Fr. Guiana 135 4 44N 52 20W
Rousay, U.K. 14 59 10N 3 2W
Rouses Point, U.S.A. 117 44 58N 73 22W
Roussillon, Isère, France 21 45 24N 4 49 E
Roussillon, Pyrénées-Or., France 20 42 30N 2 35 E
Roussin, C., N. Cal. 68 21 20 S 167 59 E
Rouveen, Neths. 16 52 37N 6 11 E
Rouvray, L., Canada 107 49 18N 70 49W
Rouxville, S. Africa 96 30 25 S 26 50 E
Rouyn, Canada 106 48 20N 79 0W
Rovaniemi, Finland 8 66 29N 25 41 E
Rovato, Italy 26 45 34N 10 0 E
Rovenki, U.S.S.R. 39 48 5N 39 21 E
Rovereto, Italy 26 45 53N 11 3 E
Rovigo, Italy 27 45 4N 11 48 E
Rovinari, Romania 34 44 56N 23 10 E
Rovinj, Yugoslavia 27 45 5N 13 40 E
Rovira, Colombia 134 4 15N 75 20W
Rovno, U.S.S.R. 36 50 40N 26 10 E
Rovnoye, U.S.S.R. 37 50 52N 46 3 E
Rovuma →, Tanzania 93 10 29 S 40 28 E
Rowena, Australia 73 29 48 S 148 55 E
Rowes, Australia 75 37 0 S 149 6 E
Rowley Shoals, Australia 78 17 30 S 119 0 E
Roxa, Guinea-Biss. 90 11 15N 15 45W
Roxas, Phil. 57 11 36N 122 49 E
Roxboro, U.S.A. 115 36 24N 78 59W
Roxborough Downs, Australia 72 22 30 S 138 45 E
Roxburgh, N.Z. 81 45 33 S 169 19 E
Roxen, Sweden 11 58 30N 15 40 E
Roxton Falls, Canada 107 45 34N 72 31W
Roy, Mont., U.S.A. 122 47 17N 109 0W
Roy, N. Mex., U.S.A. 121 35 57N 104 8W
Roy, Le, Ill., U.S.A. 119 40 21N 88 46W
Roy, Le, Kans., U.S.A. 121 38 8N 95 35W
Roy Hill, Australia 78 22 37 S 119 58 E
Roya, Peña, Spain 24 40 25N 0 40W
Royal Center, U.S.A. 119 40 52N 86 30W
Royalla, Australia 76 35 30 S 149 9 E
Royan, France 20 45 37N 1 2W
Roye, France 19 49 42N 2 48 E
Røyken, Norway 10 59 45N 10 23 E
Rožaj, Yugoslavia 33 42 50N 20 15 E
Rozay-en-Brie, France 19 48 41N 2 58 E
Rozhishche, U.S.S.R. 36 50 54N 25 15 E
Rožňava, Czech. 32 48 37N 20 35 E
Rozoy-sur-Serre, France 19 49 40N 4 8 E
Rtishchevo, U.S.S.R. 37 55 16N 43 50 E
Rúa, Spain 22 42 24N 7 6W
Ruacaná, Angola 95 17 20 S 14 12 E
Ruahine Ra., N.Z. 80 39 55 S 176 2 E
Ruamahanga →, N.Z. 80 41 24 S 175 8 E
Ruapehu, N.Z. 80 39 17 S 175 35 E
Ruapuke I., N.Z. 81 46 46 S 168 31 E
Ruatoria, N.Z. 80 37 55 S 178 20 E
Ruaus, Wadi →, Libya 86 30 26N 15 24 E
Ruawai, N.Z. 80 36 8 S 173 59 E
Rub' al Khali, Si. Arabia 45 18 0N 48 0 E
Rubeho Mts., Tanzania 92 6 50 S 36 25 E
Rubezhnoye, U.S.S.R. 38 49 6N 38 25 E
Rubh a' Mhail, U.K. 14 55 55N 6 10W
Rubha Hunish, U.K. 14 57 42N 6 20W
Rubiataba, Brazil 139 15 8 S 49 48W
Rubicon →, U.S.A. 124 38 53N 121 4W
Rubicone →, Italy 27 44 8N 12 28 E
Rubinéia, Brazil 139 20 13 S 51 2W
Rubino, Ivory C. 90 6 4N 4 18W
Rubio, Venezuela 134 7 43N 72 22W
Rubtsovsk, U.S.S.R. 40 51 30N 81 10 E

Ruby, *Australia* **74** 38 27 S 145 55 E
Ruby, *U.S.A.* **102** 64 40N 155 35W
Ruby L., *U.S.A.* **122** 40 10N 115 28W
Ruby Mts., *U.S.A.* **122** 40 30N 115 30W
Rucava, *U.S.S.R.* **36** 56 9N 21 12 E
Rucheng, *China* **59** 25 33N 113 38 E
Rud, *Norway* **10** 60 1N 10 1 E
Ruda, *Sweden* **11** 57 6N 16 7 E
Ruda Śląska, *Poland* **32** 50 16N 18 50 E
Rudall, *Australia* **73** 33 43 S 136 17 E
Ruden, *E. Germany* **30** 54 13N 13 47 E
Rüdersdorf, *E. Germany* **30** 52 28N 13 48 E
Rudewa, *Tanzania* **93** 10 7 S 34 40 E
Rudkøbing, *Denmark* **11** 54 56N 10 41 E
Rudnik, *Yugoslavia* **33** 44 7N 20 35 E
Rudnogorsk, *U.S.S.R.* **41** 57 15N 103 42 E
Rudnya, *U.S.S.R.* **36** 54 55N 31 7 E
Rudnyy, *U.S.S.R.* **40** 52 57N 63 7 E
Rudolf, Ostrov, *U.S.S.R.* **40** 81 45N 58 30 E
Rudolstadt, *E. Germany* **30** 50 44N 11 20 E
Rudong, *China* **59** 32 20N 121 12 E
Rudozem, *Bulgaria* **35** 41 29N 24 51 E
Rudyard, *U.S.A.* **114** 46 14N 84 35W
Rue, *France* **19** 50 15N 1 40 E
Rue, La, *U.S.A.* **119** 40 35N 83 23W
Ruelle, *France* **20** 45 41N 0 14 E
Rufa'a, *Sudan* **89** 14 44N 33 22 E
Ruffec, *France* **20** 46 2N 0 12 E
Rufiji □, *Tanzania* **92** 8 0 S 38 30 E
Rufiji ➝, *Tanzania* **92** 7 50 S 39 15 E
Rufino, *Argentina* **140** 34 20 S 62 50W
Rufisque, *Senegal* **90** 14 40N 17 15W
Rufunsa, *Zambia* **93** 15 4 S 29 34 E
Rugao, *China* **59** 32 23N 120 31 E
Rugby, *Australia* **76** 34 23 S 149 0 E
Rugby, *U.K.* **13** 52 23N 1 16W
Rugby, *U.S.A.* **120** 48 21N 100 0W
Rügen, *E. Germany* **30** 54 22N 13 25 E
Rugles, *France* **18** 48 50N 0 40 E
Ruhama, *Israel* **44** 31 31N 34 43 E
Ruhea, *Bangla.* **52** 26 10N 88 25 E
Ruhengeri, *Rwanda* **92** 1 30 S 29 36 E
Ruhla, *E. Germany* **30** 50 53N 10 21 E
Ruhland, *E. Germany* **30** 51 27N 13 52 E
Ruhr ➝, *W. Germany* **30** 51 25N 6 44 E
Ruhuhu ➝, *Tanzania* **93** 10 31 S 34 34 E
Rui Barbosa, *Brazil* **139** 12 18 S 40 27W
Rui'an, *China* **59** 27 47N 120 40 E
Ruichang, *China* **59** 29 40N 115 39 E
Ruidosa, *U.S.A.* **121** 29 59N 104 39W
Ruidoso, *U.S.A.* **123** 33 19N 105 39W
Ruili, *China* **58** 24 1N 97 43 E
Ruinen, *Neths.* **16** 52 46N 6 21 E
Ruinerwold, *Neths.* **16** 52 44N 6 15 E
Ruisseau-Vert, *Canada* **107** 49 4N 68 28W
Ruiten A Kanaal ➝, *Neths.* **16** 52 54N 7 8 E
Ruk, *Pakistan* **48** 27 50N 68 42 E
Rukwa □, *Tanzania* **92** 7 0 S 31 30 E
Rukwa L., *Tanzania* **92** 8 0 S 32 20 E
Rulhieres, C., *Australia* **78** 13 56 S 127 22 E
Rulles, *Belgium* **17** 49 43N 5 32 E
Rum Cay, *Bahamas* **128** 23 40N 74 58W
Rum Jungle, *Australia* **78** 13 0 S 130 59 E
Ruma, *Yugoslavia* **33** 45 0N 19 50 E
Rumāḥ, *Si. Arabia* **46** 25 29N 47 10 E
Rumania = Romania ■, *Europe* **34** 46 0N 25 0 E
Rumbalara, *Australia* **72** 25 20 S 134 29 E
Rumbee, Mt., *Australia* **77** 29 55 S 151 35 E
Rumbêk, *Sudan* **89** 6 54N 29 37 E
Rumbeke, *Belgium* **17** 50 56N 3 10 E
Rumelange, *Lux.* **17** 49 27N 6 2 E
Rumford, *U.S.A.* **117** 44 30N 70 30W
Rumilly, *France* **21** 45 53N 5 56 E
Rumoi, *Japan* **63** 43 56N 141 39 E
Rumonge, *Burundi* **92** 3 59 S 29 26 E
Rumorosa, La, *Mexico* **125** 32 33N 116 4W
Rumsey, *Canada* **110** 51 51N 112 48W
Rumula, *Australia* **72** 16 35 S 145 20 E
Rumuruti, *Kenya* **92** 0 17N 36 32 E
Runan, *China* **60** 33 0N 114 30 E
Runanga, *N.Z.* **81** 42 25 S 171 15 E
Runcorn, *U.K.* **12** 53 20N 2 44W
Rungwa, *Tanzania* **92** 6 55 S 33 32 E
Rungwa ➝, *Tanzania* **92** 7 36 S 31 50 E
Rungwe, *Tanzania* **93** 9 11 S 33 32 E
Rungwe □, *Tanzania* **93** 9 25 S 33 32 E
Runka, *Nigeria* **91** 12 28N 7 20 E
Runn, *Sweden* **10** 60 30N 15 40 E
Ruoqiang, *China* **62** 38 55N 88 10 E
Rupa, *India* **52** 27 15N 92 21 E
Rupanyup, *Australia* **74** 36 36 S 142 40 E
Rupar, *India* **48** 31 2N 76 38 E
Rupat, *Indonesia* **56** 1 45N 101 40 E
Rupert ➝, *Canada* **104** 51 29N 78 45W
Rupert House = Fort Rupert, *Canada* **104** 51 30N 78 40W
Rupsa, *Bangla.* **52** 21 44N 89 30 E
Rupununi ➝, *Guyana* **135** 4 3N 58 35W
Rur ➝, *W. Germany* **30** 50 54N 6 24 E
Rurrenabaque, *Bolivia* **136** 14 30 S 67 32W
Rus ➝, *Spain* **25** 39 30N 2 30W
Rusambo, *Zimb.* **93** 16 30 S 32 4 E
Rusape, *Zimb.* **93** 18 35 S 32 8 E
Ruschuk = Ruse, *Bulgaria* **34** 43 48N 25 59 E
Ruse, *Bulgaria* **34** 43 48N 25 59 E
Ruşeţu, *Romania* **34** 44 57N 27 14 E
Rushan, *China* **61** 36 56N 121 30 E
Rushden, *U.K.* **13** 52 17N 0 37W
Rushford, *U.S.A.* **120** 43 48N 91 46W
Rushville, *Ill., U.S.A.* **118** 40 6N 90 35W
Rushville, *Ind., U.S.A.* **119** 39 38N 85 22W
Rushville, *Nebr., U.S.A.* **120** 42 43N 102 28W
Rushworth, *Australia* **74** 36 32 S 145 1 E
Rusken, *Sweden* **11** 57 15N 14 20 E
Russas, *Brazil* **138** 4 55 S 37 50W
Russell, *Canada* **111** 50 50N 101 20W
Russell, *N.Z.* **80** 35 16 S 174 10 E
Russell, *U.S.A.* **120** 38 56N 98 55W
Russell Is., *Solomon Is.* **68** 9 4 S 159 12 E
Russell L., *Man., Canada* **111** 56 15N 101 30W
Russell L., *N.W.T., Canada* **110** 63 5N 115 44W
Russellkonda, *India* **50** 19 57N 84 42 E
Russellville, *Ala., U.S.A.* **115** 34 30N 87 44W
Russellville, *Ark., U.S.A.* **121** 35 15N 93 8W
Russellville, *Ky., U.S.A.* **115** 36 50N 86 50W
Russi, *Italy* **27** 44 21N 12 1 E
Russian ➝, *U.S.A.* **124** 38 27N 123 8W
Russian S.F.S.R. □, *U.S.S.R.* **41** 62 0N 105 0 E
Russiaville, *U.S.A.* **119** 40 25N 86 16W
Russkaya Polyana, *U.S.S.R.* **40** 53 47N 73 53 E
Russkoye Ustie, *U.S.S.R.* **144** 71 0N 149 0 E
Rustam, *Pakistan* **48** 34 25N 72 13 E
Rustam Shahr, *Pakistan* **48** 26 58N 66 6 E
Rustavi, *U.S.S.R.* **39** 41 30N 45 0 E
Rustenburg, *S. Africa* **96** 25 41 S 27 14 E
Ruston, *U.S.A.* **121** 32 30N 92 58W
Rutana, *Burundi* **92** 3 55 S 30 0 E
Rute, *Spain* **23** 37 19N 4 23W
Ruteng, *Indonesia* **57** 8 35 S 120 30 E
Ruth, *Mich., U.S.A.* **116** 43 42N 82 45W
Ruth, *Nev., U.S.A.* **122** 39 15N 115 1W
Rutherford, *U.S.A.* **124** 38 26N 122 24W
Rutherglen, *Australia* **75** 36 5 S 146 29 E
Rutherglen, *U.K.* **14** 55 50N 4 11W
Rutigliano, *Italy* **29** 41 1N 17 0 E
Rutland Plains, *Australia* **72** 15 38 S 141 43 E
Rutledge ➝, *Canada* **111** 61 4N 112 0W
Rutledge L., *Canada* **111** 61 33N 110 47W
Rutshuru, *Zaïre* **92** 1 13 S 29 25 E
Rutter, *Canada* **108** 46 6N 80 40W
Ruurlo, *Neths.* **16** 52 5N 6 24 E
Ruvo di Púglia, *Italy* **29** 41 7N 16 27 E
Ruvu, *Tanzania* **92** 6 49 S 38 43 E
Ruvu ➝, *Tanzania* **92** 6 23 S 38 52 E
Ruvuma □, *Tanzania* **93** 10 20 S 36 0 E
Ruwenzori, *Africa* **92** 0 30N 29 55 E
Ruyigi, *Burundi* **92** 3 29 S 30 15 E
Ruyuan, *China* **59** 24 46N 113 16 E
Ruzayevka, *U.S.S.R.* **37** 54 4N 45 0 E
Ružomberok, *Czech.* **32** 49 3N 19 17 E
Rwanda ■, *Africa* **92** 2 0 S 30 0 E
Ry, *Denmark* **11** 56 5N 9 45 E
Ryakhovo, *Bulgaria* **34** 44 0N 26 18 E
Ryan, L., *U.K.* **14** 55 0N 5 2W
Ryazan, *U.S.S.R.* **37** 54 40N 39 40 E
Ryazhsk, *U.S.S.R.* **37** 53 45N 40 3 E
Rybache, *U.S.S.R.* **40** 46 40N 81 20 E
Rybinsk = Andropov, *U.S.S.R.* **37** 58 5N 38 50 E
Rybinskoye Vdkhr., *U.S.S.R.* **37** 58 30N 38 25 E
Rybnik, *Poland* **32** 50 6N 18 32 E
Rybnitsa, *U.S.S.R.* **38** 47 45N 29 0 E
Rybnoye, *U.S.S.R.* **37** 54 45N 39 30 E
Rychwał, *Poland* **32** 52 4N 18 10 E
Ryd, *Sweden* **11** 56 27N 14 42 E
Ryde, *U.K.* **13** 50 44N 1 9W
Ryderwood, *U.S.A.* **124** 46 23N 123 3W
Rydöbruk, *Sweden* **11** 56 58N 13 7 E
Rydsnäs, *Sweden* **11** 57 47N 15 9 E
Rydułtowy, *Poland* **32** 50 4N 18 23 E
Rye, *U.K.* **13** 50 57N 0 46 E
Rye ➝, *U.K.* **12** 54 12N 0 53W
Rye Park, *Australia* **76** 34 31 S 148 56 E
Rye Patch Res., *U.S.A.* **122** 40 38N 118 20W
Ryegate, *U.S.A.* **122** 46 21N 109 15W
Rylsk, *U.S.S.R.* **36** 51 36N 34 43 E
Rylstone, *Australia* **76** 32 46 S 149 58 E
Ryōhaku-Sanchi, *Japan* **65** 36 9N 136 49 E
Rypin, *Poland* **32** 53 3N 19 25 E
Ryūgasaki, *Japan* **65** 35 54N 140 11 E
Ryūkyū Is. = Nansei-Shotō, *Japan* **62** 26 0N 128 0 E
Rzeszów, *Poland* **32** 50 5N 21 58 E
Rzhev, *U.S.S.R.* **36** 56 20N 34 20 E

S

Sa, *Thailand* **54** 18 34N 100 45 E
Sa Dec, *Vietnam* **55** 10 20N 105 46 E
Sa-koi, *Burma* **52** 19 54N 97 3 E
Sa'ad, *Israel* **44** 31 28N 34 33 E
Sa'ādatābād, *Iran* **47** 30 10N 53 5 E
Saale ➝, *E. Germany* **30** 51 57N 11 56 E
Saaler Bodden, *E. Germany* **30** 54 20N 12 25 E
Saalfeld, *E. Germany* **30** 50 39N 11 21 E
Saane ➝, *Switz.* **31** 46 23N 7 18 E
Saar ➝, *Europe* **19** 49 41N 6 32 E
Saarbrücken, *W. Germany* **31** 49 15N 6 58 E
Saarburg, *W. Germany* **31** 49 36N 6 32 E
Saaremaa, *U.S.S.R.* **36** 58 30N 22 30 E
Saariselkä, *Finland* **8** 68 16N 28 15 E
Saarland □, *W. Germany* **19** 49 15N 7 0 E
Saarlouis, *W. Germany* **31** 49 19N 6 45 E
Saba, *W. Indies* **129** 17 42N 63 26W
Šabac, *Yugoslavia* **33** 44 48N 19 42 E
Sabadell, *Spain* **24** 41 28N 2 7 E
Sabae, *Japan* **65** 35 57N 136 11 E
Sabah □, *Malaysia* **56** 6 0N 117 0 E
Şabāḩ, Wadi ➝, *Si. Arabia* **46** 23 50N 48 30 E
Sabak Bernam, *Malaysia* **55** 3 46N 100 58 E
Sábana de la Mar, *Dom. Rep.* **129** 19 7N 69 24W
Sábanalarga, *Colombia* **134** 10 38N 74 55W
Sabang, *Indonesia* **56** 5 50N 95 15 E
Sabará, *Brazil* **139** 19 55 S 43 46W
Sabarania, *Indonesia* **57** 2 5 S 138 18 E
Sabari ➝, *India* **50** 17 35N 81 16 E
Sabaṣṭiyah, *Jordan* **44** 32 17N 35 12 E
Sabattis, *U.S.A.* **117** 44 6N 74 40W
Sabáudia, *Italy* **28** 41 17N 13 2 E
Sabaya, *Bolivia* **136** 19 1 S 68 23W
Sabhah, *Libya* **86** 27 9N 14 29 E
Sabhah □, *Libya* **86** 26 0N 14 0 E
Sabie, *S. Africa* **97** 25 10 S 30 48 E
Sabina, *U.S.A.* **119** 39 29N 83 38W
Sabinal, *Mexico* **126** 30 58N 107 25W
Sabinal, *U.S.A.* **121** 29 20N 99 27W
Sabinal, Punta del, *Spain* **25** 36 43N 2 44W
Sabinas, *Mexico* **126** 27 50N 101 10W
Sabinas ➝, *Mexico* **126** 27 37N 100 42W
Sabinas Hidalgo, *Mexico* **126** 26 33N 100 10W
Sabine ➝, *U.S.A.* **121** 30 0N 93 35W
Sabine L., *U.S.A.* **121** 29 50N 93 50W
Sabine Pass, *U.S.A.* **121** 29 42N 93 54W
Sabinópolis, *Brazil* **139** 18 40 S 43 6W
Sabinov, *Czech.* **32** 49 6N 21 5 E
Sabirabad, *U.S.S.R.* **39** 40 5N 48 30 E
Sabkhat Tāwurghā', *Libya* **86** 31 48N 15 30 E
Sablayan, *Phil.* **57** 12 50N 120 50 E
Sable, C., *Canada* **105** 43 29N 65 38W
Sable, C., *U.S.A.* **128** 25 13N 81 0W
Sable I., *Canada* **105** 44 0N 60 0W
Sablé-sur-Sarthe, *France* **18** 47 50N 0 20W
Sables, R. aux ➝, *Canada* **108** 46 13N 82 3W
Sables-d'Olonne, Les, *France* **20** 46 30N 1 45W
Saboeiro, *Brazil* **138** 6 32 S 39 54W
Sabolev, *U.S.S.R.* **41** 54 20N 155 30 E
Sabor ➝, *Portugal* **22** 41 10N 7 7W
Sabou, *Burkina Faso* **90** 12 1N 2 15W
Sabourin, L., *Canada* **106** 47 58N 77 41W
Sabrātah, *Libya* **86** 32 47N 12 29 E
Sabria, *Tunisia* **86** 33 22N 8 45 E
Sabrina Coast, *Antarctica* **143** 68 0 S 120 0 E
Sabugal, *Portugal* **22** 40 20N 7 5W
Sabula, *U.S.A.* **118** 42 5N 90 23W
Sabulubek, *Indonesia* **56** 1 36 S 98 40 E
Sabzevār, *Iran* **47** 36 15N 57 40 E
Sabzvārān, *Iran* **47** 28 45N 57 50 E
Sac City, *U.S.A.* **118** 42 26N 95 0W
Sacedón, *Spain* **24** 40 29N 2 41W
Sachigo ➝, *Canada* **104** 55 6N 88 58W
Sachigo, L., *Canada* **104** 53 50N 92 12W
Sachkhere, *U.S.S.R.* **39** 42 25N 43 28 E
Sacile, *Italy* **27** 45 58N 12 30 E
Sackets Harbor, *U.S.A.* **117** 43 56N 76 7W
Säckingen, *W. Germany* **31** 47 34N 7 56 E
Saco, *Maine, U.S.A.* **115** 43 30N 70 27W
Saco, *Mont., U.S.A.* **122** 48 28N 107 19W
Sacramento, *Brazil* **139** 19 53 S 47 27W
Sacramento, *U.S.A.* **124** 38 33N 121 30W
Sacramento ➝, *U.S.A.* **124** 38 3N 121 56W
Sacramento Mts., *U.S.A.* **123** 32 30N 105 30W
Sacramento Valley, *U.S.A.* **124** 39 0N 122 0W
Sacratif, C., *Spain* **25** 36 42N 3 28W
Sacré-Coeur-de-Jésus, *Canada* **107** 48 14N 69 48W
Săcueni, *Romania* **34** 47 20N 22 5 E
Sada, *Spain* **22** 43 22N 8 15W
Sada-Misaki-Hantō, *Japan* **64** 33 22N 132 1 E
Sádaba, *Spain* **24** 42 19N 1 12W
Sadani, *Tanzania* **92** 5 58 S 38 35 E
Sadao, *Thailand* **55** 6 38N 100 26 E
Sadaseopet, *India* **50** 17 38N 77 59 E
Sadd el Aali, *Egypt* **88** 23 54N 32 54 E
Saddle Mt., *U.S.A.* **124** 45 58N 123 41W
Sade, *Nigeria* **91** 11 22N 10 45 E
Sadieville, *U.S.A.* **119** 38 23N 84 32W
Sadimi, *Zaïre* **93** 9 25 S 23 32 E
Sadiya, *India* **52** 27 50N 95 40 E
Sado, *Japan* **63** 38 0N 138 25 E
Sado ➝, *Portugal* **23** 38 29N 8 55W
Sado, Shima, *Japan* **63** 38 15N 138 30 E
Sadon, *U.S.S.R.* **39** 42 52N 43 58 E
Sæby, *Denmark* **11** 57 21N 10 30 E
Saegerstown, *U.S.A.* **116** 41 42N 80 10W
Saelices, *Spain* **24** 39 55N 2 49W
Safaga, *Egypt* **88** 26 42N 34 0 E
Safata B., *W. Samoa* **68** 14 0 S 171 50W
Säffle, *Sweden* **10** 59 8N 12 55 E
Safford, *U.S.A.* **123** 32 50N 109 43W
Saffron Walden, *U.K.* **13** 52 2N 0 15 E
Safi, *Morocco* **84** 32 18N 9 20W
Safīd Kūh, *Afghan.* **47** 34 45N 63 0 E
Safonovo, *U.S.S.R.* **36** 55 4N 33 16 E
Safranbolu, *Turkey* **38** 41 15N 32 41 E
Sag Harbor, *U.S.A.* **117** 40 59N 72 17W
Sag Sag, *Papua N. G.* **69** 5 32 S 148 23 E
Saga, *Indonesia* **57** 2 40 S 132 55 E
Saga, *Kōchi, Japan* **64** 33 5N 133 6 E
Saga, *Saga, Japan* **64** 33 15N 130 16 E
Saga □, *Japan* **64** 33 15N 130 20 E
Sagaing □, *Burma* **52** 23 55N 95 56 E
Sagala, *Mali* **90** 14 9N 6 38W
Sagami-Nada, *Japan* **65** 34 58N 139 30 E
Sagami-Wan, *Japan* **65** 35 15N 139 25 E
Sagamihara, *Japan* **65** 35 33N 139 25 E
Saganoseki, *Japan* **64** 33 15N 131 53 E
Sagar, *India* **51** 14 14N 75 6 E
Sagara, *Japan* **65** 34 41N 138 12 E
Sagara, L., *Tanzania* **92** 5 20 S 31 0 E
Sagawa, *Japan* **64** 33 28N 133 11 E
Sagil, *Mongolia* **62** 50 15N 91 15 E
Saginaw, *U.S.A.* **104** 43 26N 83 55W
Saginaw B., *U.S.A.* **104** 43 50N 83 40W
Sagīr, Zab as ➝, *Iraq* **46** 35 10N 43 20 E
Sagleipie, *Liberia* **90** 7 0N 8 52W
Saglouc, *Canada* **103** 62 14N 75 38W
Sagone, *France* **21** 42 7N 8 42 E
Sagone, G. de, *France* **21** 42 4N 8 40 E
Sagra, La, *Spain* **25** 37 57N 2 35W
Sagres, *Portugal* **23** 37 0N 8 58W
Sagu, *Burma* **52** 20 13N 94 46 E
Sagua la Grande, *Cuba* **128** 22 50N 80 10W
Saguache, *U.S.A.* **123** 38 10N 106 10W
Saguenay ➝, *Canada* **107** 48 22N 71 0W
Sagunto, *Spain* **24** 39 42N 0 18W
Sahaba, *Sudan* **88** 18 57N 30 25 E
Sahagún, *Colombia* **134** 8 57N 75 27W
Sahagún, *Spain* **22** 42 18N 5 2W
Saham, *Jordan* **44** 32 42N 35 46 E
Saḩam al Jawlān, *Syria* **44** 32 45N 35 55 E
Sahand, Kūh-e, *Iran* **46** 37 44N 46 27 E
Sahara, *Africa* **82** 23 0N 5 0 E
Saharan Atlas, *Algeria* **82** 34 9N 3 29 E
Saharanpur, *India* **48** 29 58N 77 33 E
Sahasinaka, *Madag.* **97** 21 49 S 47 49 E
Sahaswan, *India* **49** 28 5N 78 45 E
Sahel, Canal du, *Mali* **90** 14 20N 6 0W
Sahibganj, *India* **49** 25 12N 87 40 E
Sahiwal, *Pakistan* **48** 30 45N 73 8 E
Sahtaneh ➝, *Canada* **110** 59 2N 122 28W
Sahuaripa, *Mexico* **126** 29 0N 109 13W
Sahuarita, *U.S.A.* **123** 31 58N 110 59W
Sahuayo, *Mexico* **126** 20 4N 102 43W
Sahy, *Czech.* **33** 48 4N 18 55 E
Sai Buri, *Thailand* **55** 6 43N 101 45 E
Sai-Cinza, *Brazil* **137** 6 17 S 57 42W
Saibai I., *Australia* **69** 9 25 S 142 40 E
Sa'id Bundas, *Sudan* **87** 8 24N 24 48 E
Saïda, *Algeria* **85** 34 50N 0 11 E
Saīdābād, *Iran* **47** 29 30N 55 45 E
Saïdia, *Morocco* **85** 35 5N 2 14W
Sa'īdiyeh, *Iran* **46** 36 20N 48 55 E
Saidor, *Papua N. G.* **69** 5 40 S 146 29 E
Saidpur, *Bangla.* **52** 25 48N 89 0 E
Saidu, *Pakistan* **49** 34 43N 72 24 E
Saignes, *France* **20** 45 20N 2 31 E
Saigō, *Japan* **64** 36 12N 133 20 E
Saigon = Phanh Bho Ho Chi Minh, *Vietnam* **55** 10 58N 106 40 E
Saih-al-Malih, *Oman* **47** 23 37N 58 31 E
Saijō, *Ehime, Japan* **64** 33 55N 133 11 E
Saijō, *Hiroshima, Japan* **64** 34 25N 132 45 E
Saiki, *Japan* **64** 32 58N 131 51 E
Saillans, *France* **21** 44 42N 5 12 E
Sailolof, *Indonesia* **57** 1 7 S 130 46 E
St. Abb's Head, *U.K.* **14** 55 55N 2 10W
St-Adalbert, *Canada* **107** 46 51N 69 53W
St. Aegyd, *Austria* **33** 47 52N 15 33 E
St.-Affrique, *France* **20** 43 57N 2 53 E
St-Agapitville, *Canada* **107** 46 34N 71 26W
St.-Agrève, *France* **21** 45 0N 4 23 E
St.-Aignan, *France* **18** 47 16N 1 22 E
St. Albans, *Australia* **76** 33 16 S 150 59 E
St. Alban's, *Canada* **105** 47 51N 55 50W
St. Albans, *U.K.* **13** 51 44N 0 19W
St. Albans, *Vt., U.S.A.* **117** 44 49N 73 7W
St. Albans, *W. Va., U.S.A.* **114** 38 21N 81 50W
St. Alban's Head, *U.K.* **13** 50 34N 2 3W
St. Albert, *Canada* **110** 53 37N 113 32W
St-Alexandre, *Canada* **107** 47 41N 69 38W
St-Alexis-des-Monts, *Canada* **107** 46 28N 73 8W
St.-Amand-en-Puisaye, *France* **19** 47 32N 3 5 E
St.-Amand-les-Eaux, *France* **19** 50 27N 3 25 E
St.-Amand-Mont-Rond, *France* **20** 46 43N 2 30 E
St.-Amarin, *France* **19** 47 54N 7 0 E
St-Ambroise, *Canada* **107** 48 33N 71 20W
St.-Amour, *France* **21** 46 26N 5 21 E
St-Anaclet, *Canada* **107** 48 29N 68 26W
St-André-Avellin, *Canada* **106** 45 43N 75 3W

St.-André-de-Cubzac, *France* **20** 44 59N 0 26W
St.-André-de-l'Eure, *France* **18** 48 54N 1 16 E
St-André-Est, *Canada* **107** 45 34N 74 20W
St.-André-les-Alpes, *France* **21** 43 58N 6 30 E
St. Andrew's, *Canada* **105** 47 45N 59 15W
St. Andrews, *N.Z.* **81** 44 33 S 171 10 E
St. Andrews, *U.K.* **14** 56 20N 2 48W
St-Anicet, *Canada* **117** 45 8N 74 22W
St. Ann B., *Canada* **105** 46 22N 60 25W
St. Anne, *U.K.* **18** 49 43N 2 11W
St. Anne, *U.S.A.* **119** 41 1N 87 43W
St. Ann's Bay, *Jamaica* **128** 18 26N 77 15W
St-Anselme, *Canada* **107** 46 37N 70 58W
St. Anthony, *Canada* **105** 51 22N 55 35W
St. Anthony, *U.S.A.* **122** 44 0N 111 40W
St-Antonin, *Canada* **107** 47 46N 69 29W
St.-Antonin-Noble-Val, *France* **20** 44 10N 1 45 E
St-Apolline, *Canada* **107** 46 48N 70 12W
St. Arnaud, *Australia* **74** 36 40 S 143 16 E
St. Arnaud Ra., *N.Z.* **81** 42 1 S 172 53 E
St. Arthur, *Canada* **105** 47 33N 67 46W
St. Asaph, *U.K.* **12** 53 15N 3 27W
St.-Astier, *France* **20** 45 8N 0 31 E
St-Aubert, *Canada* **107** 47 11N 70 13W
St.-Aubin-du-Cormier, *France* **18** 48 15N 1 26W
St-Augustin-Saguenay, *Canada* **105** 51 13N 58 38W
St. Augustine, *U.S.A.* **115** 29 52N 81 20W
St. Austell, *U.K.* **13** 50 20N 4 48W
St.-Avold, *France* **19** 49 6N 6 43 E
St-Barthélémy, *Canada* **107** 46 11N 73 8W
St.-Barthélemy, I., *W. Indies* **129** 17 50N 62 50W
St-Basile-Sud, *Canada* **107** 46 45N 71 49W
St. Bathans, *N.Z.* **81** 44 53 S 169 50 E
St. Bathan's Mt., *N.Z.* **81** 44 45 S 169 45 E
St. Bee's Hd., *U.K.* **12** 54 30N 3 38W
St.-Benoît-du-Sault, *France* **20** 46 26N 1 24 E
St. Bernard, Col du Grand, *Europe* **31** 45 53N 7 11 E
St.-Bernard, Col du Petit, *France* **21** 45 41N 6 51 E
St. Boniface, *Canada* **111** 49 53N 97 5W
St.-Bonnet, *France* **21** 44 40N 6 5 E
St.-Brévin-les-Pins, *France* **18** 47 14N 2 10W
St.-Brice-en-Coglès, *France* **18** 48 25N 1 22W
St. Bride's, *Canada* **105** 46 56N 54 10W
St. Brides B., *U.K.* **13** 51 48N 5 15W
St.-Brieuc, *France* **18** 48 30N 2 46W
St-Bruno, *Canada* **107** 48 28N 71 39W
St.-Calais, *France* **18** 47 55N 0 45 E
St-Casimir, *Canada* **107** 46 40N 72 8W
St.-Cast-le-Guildo, *France* **18** 48 37N 2 18W
St. Catharines, *Canada* **108** 43 10N 79 15W
St. Catherines I., *U.S.A.* **115** 31 35N 81 10W
St. Catherine's Pt., *U.K.* **13** 50 34N 1 18W
St.-Céré, *France* **20** 44 51N 1 54 E
St.-Cergue, *Switz.* **31** 46 27N 6 10 E
St.-Cernin, *France* **20** 45 5N 2 25 E
St-Césaire, *Canada* **107** 45 25N 73 0W
St.-Chamond, *France* **21** 45 28N 4 31 E
St. Charles, *Ill., U.S.A.* **119** 41 55N 88 21W
St. Charles, *Mo., U.S.A.* **118** 38 46N 90 30W
St.-Chély-d'Apcher, *France* **20** 44 48N 3 17 E
St.-Chinian, *France* **20** 43 25N 2 56 E
St. Christopher, *W. Indies* **129** 17 20N 62 40W
St. Christopher-Nevis ■, *W. Indies* **129** 17 20N 62 40W
St-Chrysostôme, *Canada* **107** 45 6N 73 46W
St.-Ciers-sur-Gironde, *France* **20** 45 17N 0 37W
St. Clair, *Mich., U.S.A.* **116** 42 47N 82 27W
St. Clair, *Mo., U.S.A.* **118** 38 21N 90 59W
St. Clair, *Pa., U.S.A.* **117** 40 42N 76 12W
St. Clair, L., *Canada* **108** 42 30N 82 45W
St. Clair Shores, *U.S.A.* **119** 42 30N 82 53W
St. Clairsville, *U.S.A.* **116** 40 5N 80 53W
St.-Claud, *France* **20** 45 54N 0 28 E
St. Claude, *Canada* **111** 49 40N 98 20W
St.-Claude, *France* **21** 46 22N 5 52 E
St-Clet, *Canada* **107** 45 21N 74 13W
St. Cloud, *Fla., U.S.A.* **115** 28 15N 81 15W
St. Cloud, *Minn., U.S.A.* **120** 45 30N 94 11W
St-Coeur de Marie, *Canada* **107** 48 39N 71 43W
St-Côme, *Canada* **107** 46 16N 73 47W
St. Cricq, C., *Australia* **79** 25 17 S 113 6 E
St. Croix, *Virgin Is.* **129** 17 45N 64 45W
St. Croix →, *U.S.A.* **120** 44 45N 92 50W
St. Croix Falls, *U.S.A.* **120** 45 18N 92 22W
St.-Cyr-sur-Mer, *France* **21** 43 11N 5 43 E
St-Cyrille-de-L'Islet, *Canada* **107** 47 2N 70 17W
St. David, *U.S.A.* **118** 40 30N 90 3W
St. David's, *Canada* **105** 48 12N 58 52W
St. David's, *U.K.* **13** 51 54N 5 16W
St. David's Head, *U.K.* **13** 51 55N 5 16W
St.-Denis, *France* **19** 48 56N 2 22 E
St.-Denis, *Réunion* **53** 20 52 S 55 27 E
St.-Denis-d'Orques, *France* **18** 48 2N 0 17W
St.-Dié, *France* **19** 48 17N 6 56 E
St.-Dizier, *France* **19** 48 38N 4 56 E
St-Donat-de-Montcalm, *Canada* **107** 46 19N 74 13W
St.-Égrève, *France* **21** 45 14N 5 41 E
St. Elias, Mt., *U.S.A.* **102** 60 14N 140 50W
St. Elias Mts., *Canada* **110** 60 33N 139 28W
St.-Élie, *Fr. Guiana* **135** 4 49N 53 17W
St. Elmo, *U.S.A.* **119** 39 2N 88 51W
St-Éloi, *Canada* **107** 48 2N 69 14W
St-Élouthère, *Canada* **107** 47 30N 69 15W
St.-Eloy-les-Mines, *France* **20** 46 10N 2 51 E
St.-Émilion, *France* **20** 44 53N 0 9W
St-Éphrem-de-Tring, *Canada* **107** 46 2N 70 59W
St.-Étienne, *France* **21** 45 27N 4 22 E
St.-Étienne-de-Tinée, *France* **21** 44 16N 6 56 E
St. Eugène, *Canada* **106** 45 30N 74 28W
St-Eusèbe, *Canada* **107** 47 33N 68 55W
St-Eustache, *Canada* **107** 45 33N 73 54W
St. Eustatius, *W. Indies* **129** 17 20N 63 0W
St-Fabien, *Canada* **107** 48 18N 68 52W
St-Félicien, *Canada* **107** 48 40N 72 25W
St-Félix-de-Valois, *Canada* **107** 46 10N 73 26W
St.-Florent, *France* **21** 42 41N 9 18 E
St.-Florent-sur-Cher, *France* **19** 46 59N 2 15 E
St.-Florentin, *France* **19** 48 0N 3 45 E
St.-Flour, *France* **20** 45 2N 3 6 E
St.-Fons, *France* **21** 45 42N 4 52 E
St. Francis, *U.S.A.* **120** 39 48N 101 47W
St. Francis →, *U.S.A.* **121** 34 38N 90 36W
St. Francis, C., *S. Africa* **96** 34 14 S 24 49 E
St. Francisville, *Ill., U.S.A.* **119** 38 36N 87 39W
St. Francisville, *La., U.S.A.* **121** 30 48N 91 22W
St-François, *Canada* **107** 46 48N 70 49W
St-François →, *Canada* **107** 46 7N 72 55W
St-François, L., *Qué., Canada* **107** 45 10N 74 22W
St-François, L., *Qué., Canada* **117** 45 10N 74 22W
St-François-du-Lac, *Canada* **107** 46 5N 72 50W
St-Fulgence, *Canada* **107** 48 27N 70 54W
St.-Fulgent, *France* **18** 46 50N 1 10W
St-Gabriel-de-Brandon, *Canada* **107** 46 17N 73 24W
St-Gabriel-de-Rimouski, *Canada* **107** 48 25N 68 10W
St.-Gaudens, *France* **20** 43 6N 0 44 E
St-Gédéon, *Canada* **107** 48 30N 71 46W
St-Gédéon-de-Beauce, *Canada* **107** 45 45N 70 40W
St.-Gengoux-le-National, *France* **21** 46 37N 4 40 E
St.-Geniez-d'Olt, *France* **20** 44 27N 2 58 E
St. George, *Australia* **73** 28 1 S 148 30 E
St. George, *N.B., Canada* **105** 45 11N 66 50W
St. George, *Ont., Canada* **108** 43 15N 80 15W
St. George, *S.C., U.S.A.* **115** 33 13N 80 37W
St. George, *Utah, U.S.A.* **123** 37 10N 113 35W
St. George, C., *Canada* **105** 48 30N 59 16W
St. George, C., *Papua N. G.* **69** 4 49 S 152 53 E
St. George, C., *U.S.A.* **115** 29 36N 85 2W
St. George Ra., *Australia* **78** 18 40 S 125 0 E
St-Georges, *Belgium* **17** 50 37N 5 20 E
St. George's, *Canada* **105** 48 26N 58 31W
St-Georges, *Canada* **107** 46 8N 70 40W
St.-Georges, *Fr. Guiana* **135** 4 0N 52 0W
St. George's, *Grenada* **129** 12 5N 61 43W
St. George's B., *Canada* **105** 48 24N 58 53W
St. George's Channel, *Papua N. G.* **69** 4 10 S 152 20 E
St. George's Channel, *U.K.* **15** 52 0N 6 0W
St-Georges-de-Cacouna, *Canada* **107** 47 55N 69 30W
St.-Georges-de-Didonne, *France* **20** 45 36N 1 0W
St. Georges Head, *Australia* **76** 35 12 S 150 42 E
St-Georges-Ouest, *Canada* **107** 46 7N 70 40W
St.-Gérard, *Belgium* **17** 50 21N 4 44 E
St-Gérard, *Canada* **107** 45 46N 71 25W
St.-Germain-de-Calberte, *France* **20** 44 13N 3 48 E
St-Germain-de-Grantham, *Canada* **107** 45 50N 72 34W
St.-Germain-des-Fossés, *France* **20** 46 12N 3 26 E
St.-Germain-du-Plain, *France* **19** 46 42N 4 58 E
St.-Germain-en-Laye, *France* **19** 48 54N 2 6 E
St.-Germain-Laval, *France* **21** 45 50N 4 1 E
St.-Germain-Lembron, *France* **20** 45 27N 3 14 E
St.-Gervais-d'Auvergne, *France* **20** 46 4N 2 50 E
St.-Gervais-les-Bains, *France* **21** 45 53N 6 42 E
St.-Gildas, Pte. de, *France* **18** 47 8N 2 14W
St.-Gilles, *France* **21** 43 40N 4 26 E
St.-Gilles-Croix-de-Vie, *France* **20** 46 41N 1 55W
St.-Girons, *France* **20** 42 59N 1 8 E
St. Goar, *W. Germany* **31** 50 12N 7 43 E
St. Gotthard P. = San Gottardo, Paso del, *Switz.* **31** 46 33N 8 33 E
St.-Gualtier, *France* **18** 46 39N 1 26 E
St.-Guénolé, *France* **18** 47 49N 4 23W
St-Guillaume-d'Upton, *Canada* **107** 45 53N 72 46W
St. Helena, *Atl. Oc.* **4** 15 55 S 5 44W
St. Helena, *U.S.A.* **122** 38 29N 122 30W
St Helena, Mt., *U.S.A.* **124** 38 40N 122 36W
St Helena B., *S. Africa* **96** 32 40 S 18 10 E
St. Helens, *Australia* **72** 41 20 S 148 15 E
St. Helens, *U.K.* **12** 53 28N 2 44W
St. Helens, *U.S.A.* **124** 45 55N 122 50W
St. Helens, Mt., *U.S.A.* **124** 46 12N 122 11W
St. Helier, *U.K.* **18** 49 11N 2 6W
St.-Hilaire-du-Harcouët, *France* **18** 48 35N 1 5W
St-Hilarion, *Canada* **107** 47 34N 70 24W
St-Hippolyte, *France* **19** 47 19N 6 50 E
St.-Hippolyte-du-Fort, *France* **20** 43 58N 3 52 E
St-Honoré, *Canada* **107** 48 32N 71 5W
St.-Honoré-les-Bains, *France* **19** 46 54N 3 50 E
St-Hubert, *Belgium* **17** 50 2N 5 23 E
St-Hubert-de-Témiscouata, *Canada* **107** 47 49N 69 9W
St-Hyacinthe, *Canada* **107** 45 40N 72 58W
St. Ignace, *U.S.A.* **104** 45 53N 84 43W
St. Ignace I., *Canada* **104** 48 45N 88 0W
St. Ignatius, *U.S.A.* **122** 47 19N 114 8W
St.-Imier, *Switz.* **31** 47 9N 6 58 E
St-Isidore, *Canada* **107** 45 20N 73 42W
St. Ives, *Cambs., U.K.* **13** 52 20N 0 5W
St. Ives, *Cornwall, U.K.* **13** 50 13N 5 29W
St-Jacques, *Canada* **107** 45 57N 73 34W
St.-James, *France* **18** 48 31N 1 20W
St. James, *Minn., U.S.A.* **120** 43 57N 94 40W
St. James, *Mo., U.S.A.* **118** 38 0N 91 37W
St-Jean, *Canada* **107** 45 20N 73 20W
St-Jean →, *Canada* **105** 50 17N 64 20W
St-Jean, L., *Canada* **107** 48 40N 72 0W
St. Jean Baptiste, *Canada* **111** 49 15N 97 20W
St.-Jean-d'Angély, *France* **20** 45 57N 0 31W
St.-Jean-de-Bournay, *France* **21** 45 30N 5 9 E
St-Jean-de-Dieu, *Canada* **107** 48 0N 69 3W
St.-Jean-de-Luz, *France* **20** 43 23N 1 39W
St.-Jean-de-Maurienne, *France* **21** 45 16N 6 21 E
St.-Jean-de-Monts, *France* **18** 46 47N 2 4W
St.-Jean-du-Gard, *France* **20** 44 7N 3 52 E
St.-Jean-en-Royans, *France* **21** 45 1N 5 18 E
St-Jean-Port-Joli, *Canada* **107** 47 15N 70 13W
St-Jérôme, *Qué., Canada* **107** 48 26N 71 53W
St-Jérôme, *Qué., Canada* **107** 45 47N 74 0W
St-Joachim, *Canada* **107** 47 4N 70 50W
St. Joe, *U.S.A.* **119** 41 19N 84 54W
St. John, *Canada* **105** 45 20N 66 8W
St. John, *Kans., U.S.A.* **121** 37 59N 98 45W
St. John, *N. Dak., U.S.A.* **120** 48 58N 99 40W
St. John →, *N. Amer.* **105** 45 15N 66 4W
St. John, C., *Canada* **105** 50 0N 55 32W
St. John's, *Antigua* **129** 17 6N 61 51W
St. John's, *Canada* **105** 47 35N 52 40W
St. Johns, *Ariz., U.S.A.* **123** 34 31N 109 26W
St. Johns, *Mich., U.S.A.* **119** 43 0N 84 31W
St. John's →, *U.S.A.* **115** 30 20N 81 30W
St. Johnsbury, *U.S.A.* **117** 44 25N 72 1W
St. Johnsville, *U.S.A.* **117** 43 0N 74 43W
St.-Joseph, *N. Cal.* **68** 20 27 S 166 36 E
St. Joseph, *Ill., U.S.A.* **119** 40 7N 88 2W
St. Joseph, *La., U.S.A.* **121** 31 55N 91 15W
St. Joseph, *Mich., U.S.A.* **119** 42 5N 86 30W
St. Joseph, *Mo., U.S.A.* **118** 39 46N 94 50W
St. Joseph →, *U.S.A.* **119** 42 7N 86 30W
St. Joseph, I., *Canada* **108** 46 12N 83 58W
St. Joseph, L., *Canada* **104** 51 10N 90 35W
St-Joseph-de-Beauce, *Canada* **107** 46 18N 70 53W
St-Joseph-de-la-Rivière-Bleue, *Canada* **107** 47 26N 69 3W
St-Joseph-de-Sorel, *Canada* **107** 46 2N 73 7W
St-Jovite, *Canada* **106** 46 8N 74 38W
St-Jude, *Canada* **107** 45 46N 72 59W
St.-Juéry, *France* **20** 43 57N 2 12 E
St.-Julien-Chapteuil, *France* **21** 45 2N 4 4 E
St.-Julien-du-Sault, *France* **19** 48 1N 3 17 E
St.-Julien-en-Genevois, *France* **21** 46 9N 6 5 E
St.-Junien, *France* **20** 45 53N 0 55 E
St.-Just-en-Chaussée, *France* **19** 49 30N 2 25 E
St.-Just-en-Chevalet, *France* **20** 45 55N 3 50 E
St.-Justin, *France* **20** 43 59N 0 14W
St-Justine, *Canada* **107** 46 24N 70 21W
St. Kilda, *N.Z.* **81** 45 53 S 170 31 E
St. Kitts = St. Christopher, *W. Indies* **129** 17 20N 62 40W
St. Laurent, *Canada* **111** 50 25N 97 58W
St.-Laurent, *Fr. Guiana* **135** 5 29N 54 3W
St.-Laurent-du-Pont, *France* **21** 45 23N 5 45 E
St.-Laurent-en-Grandvaux, *France* **21** 46 35N 5 58 E
St. Lawrence, *Australia* **72** 22 16 S 149 31 E
St. Lawrence, *Canada* **105** 46 54N 55 23W
St. Lawrence →, *Canada* **105** 49 30N 66 0W
St. Lawrence, Gulf of, *Canada* **105** 48 25N 62 0W
St. Lawrence I., *U.S.A.* **102** 63 0N 170 0W
St.-Léger, *Belgium* **17** 49 37N 5 39 E
St. Leonard, *Canada* **105** 47 12N 67 58W
St.-Léonard-de-Noblat, *France* **20** 45 49N 1 29 E
St-Léonard-de-Portneuf, *Canada* **107** 46 53N 71 55W
St. Lewis →, *Canada* **105** 52 26N 56 11W
St.-Lô, *France* **18** 49 7N 1 5W
St.-Louis, *Senegal* **90** 16 8N 16 27W
St. Louis, *Mich., U.S.A.* **114** 43 27N 84 38W
St. Louis, *Mo., U.S.A.* **118** 38 40N 90 12W
St. Louis →, *U.S.A.* **120** 47 15N 92 45W
St.-Loup-sur-Semouse, *France* **19** 47 53N 6 16 E
St-Luc, *Canada* **107** 45 22N 73 18W
St. Lucia ■, *W. Indies* **129** 14 0N 60 50W
St. Lucia, L., *S. Africa* **97** 28 5 S 32 30 E
St. Lucia Channel, *W. Indies* **129** 14 15N 61 0W
St-Ludger, *Canada* **107** 45 45N 70 42W
St. Lunaire-Griquet, *Canada* **105** 51 31N 55 28W
St. Maarten, *W. Indies* **129** 18 0N 63 5W
St-Magloire, *Canada* **107** 46 35N 70 17W
St.-Maixent-l'École, *France* **20** 46 24N 0 12W
St.-Malo, *France* **18** 48 39N 2 1W
St.-Malo, G. de, *France* **18** 48 50N 2 30W
St.-Mandrier-sur-Mer, *France* **21** 43 4N 5 57 E
St-Marc, *Haiti* **129** 19 10N 72 41W
St.-Marcellin, *France* **21** 45 9N 5 20 E
St.-Marcouf, Is., *France* **18** 49 30N 1 10W
St. Margaret I., *Australia* **75** 38 38 S 146 50 E
St. Maries, *U.S.A.* **122** 47 17N 116 34W
St.-Martin, I., *W. Indies* **129** 18 0N 63 0W
St.-Martin-de-Ré, *France* **20** 46 12N 1 21W
St. Martin L., *Canada* **111** 51 40N 98 30W
St.-Martin-Vésubie, *France* **21** 44 4N 7 15 E
St. Martins, *Canada* **105** 45 22N 65 34W
St. Martinsville, *U.S.A.* **121** 30 10N 91 50W
St.-Martory, *France* **20** 43 9N 0 56 E
St. Mary, Mt., *Papua N. G.* **69** 8 8 S 147 2 E
St. Mary Is., *India* **51** 13 20N 74 35 E
St. Mary Pk., *Australia* **73** 31 32 S 138 34 E
St. Marys, *N.S.W., Australia* **76** 33 44 S 150 49 E
St. Marys, *Tas., Australia* **72** 41 35 S 148 11 E
St. Marys, *Canada* **108** 43 20N 81 10W
St. Mary's, *U.K.* **13** 49 55N 6 17W
St. Marys, *Mo., U.S.A.* **118** 37 53N 89 57W
St. Marys, *Pa., U.S.A.* **116** 41 27N 78 33W
St. Mary's, C., *Canada* **105** 46 50N 54 12W
St. Mary's B., *Canada* **105** 46 50N 53 50W
St. Marys Bay, *Canada* **105** 44 25N 66 10W
St.-Mathieu, Pte. de, *France* **18** 48 20N 4 45W
St. Matthews, *U.S.A.* **119** 38 15N 85 39W
St. Matthews, I. = Zadetkyi Kyun, *Burma* **55** 10 0N 98 25 E
St. Matthias Grp., *Papua N. G.* **69** 1 30 S 150 0 E
St.-Maur-des-Fossés, *France* **19** 48 48N 2 30 E
St-Maurice →, *Canada* **107** 46 21N 72 31W
St-Maurice, Parc Prov. du, *Canada* **107** 47 5N 73 15W
St.-Médard-de-Guizières, *France* **20** 45 1N 0 4W
St.-Méen-le-Grand, *France* **18** 48 11N 2 12W

St. Meinrad, *U.S.A.* **119** 38 10N 86 49W
St. Michael's Mt., *U.K.* **13** 50 7N 5 30W
St.-Michel-de-Maurienne, *France* **21** 45 12N 6 28 E
St-Michel-des-Saints, *Canada* **107** 46 41N 73 55W
St.-Mihiel, *France* **19** 48 54N 5 32 E
St-Nazaire, *Canada* **107** 45 44N 72 37W
St.-Nazaire, *France* **18** 47 17N 2 12W
St. Neots, *U.K.* **13** 52 14N 0 16W
St.-Nicolas-de-Port, *France* **19** 48 38N 6 18 E
St-Omer, *Canada* **107** 47 3N 69 43W
St.-Omer, *France* **19** 50 45N 2 15 E
St-Ours, *Canada* **107** 45 53N 73 9W
St-Pacome, *Canada* **107** 47 24N 69 58W
St.-Palais-sur-Mer, *France* **20** 45 38N 1 5W
St-Pamphile, *Canada* **107** 46 58N 69 48W
St.-Pardoux-la-Rivière, *France* **20** 45 29N 0 45 E
St. Paris, *U.S.A.* **119** 40 8N 83 58W
St. Pascal, *Canada* **107** 47 32N 69 48W
St-Patrice, L., *Canada* **106** 46 22N 77 20W
St. Paul, *Canada* **110** 54 0N 111 17W
St. Paul, *Ind. Oc.* **53** 38 55 S 77 34 E
St. Paul, *Ind., U.S.A.* **119** 39 33N 85 38W
St. Paul, *Minn., U.S.A.* **120** 44 54N 93 5W
St. Paul, *Nebr., U.S.A.* **120** 41 15N 98 30W
St. Paul, I., *Canada* **105** 47 12N 60 9W
St.-Paul-de-Fenouillet, *France* **20** 42 48N 2 30 E
St-Paul-de-Montmigny, *Canada* **107** 46 44N 70 22W
St-Paul-du-Nord, *Canada* **107** 48 34N 69 14W
St.-Paul-lès-Dax, *France* **20** 43 44N 1 3W
St-Paulin, *Canada* **107** 46 25N 73 1W
St.-Péray, *France* **21** 44 57N 4 50 E
St.-Père-en-Retz, *France* **18** 47 11N 2 2W
St. Peter, *U.S.A.* **120** 44 21N 93 57W
St. Peter Port, *Chan. Is.* **18** 49 27N 2 31W
St. Peters, *N.S., Canada* **105** 45 40N 60 53W
St. Peters, *P.E.I., Canada* **105** 46 25N 62 35W
St. Petersburg, *U.S.A.* **115** 27 45N 82 40W
St.-Philbert-de-Grand-Lieu, *France* **18** 47 2N 1 39W
St-Philemon, *Canada* **107** 46 41N 70 27W
St-Pie, *Canada* **107** 45 30N 72 54W
St.-Pierre, *St- P. & M.* **105** 46 46N 56 12W
St. Pierre, *Seychelles* **53** 9 20 S 46 0 E
St-Pierre, L., *Qué., Canada* **107** 50 8N 68 26W
St-Pierre, L., *Qué., Canada* **107** 46 12N 72 52W
St.-Pierre-d'Oléron, *France* **20** 45 57N 1 19W
St.-Pierre-Église, *France* **18** 49 40N 1 24W
St.-Pierre-en-Port, *France* **18** 49 48N 0 30 E
St.-Pierre et Miquelon □, *St- P. & M.* **105** 46 55N 56 10W
St.-Pierre-le-Moûtier, *France* **19** 46 47N 3 7 E
St.-Pierre-sur-Dives, *France* **18** 49 2N 0 1W
St.-Pieters Leew, *Belgium* **17** 50 47N 4 16 E
St.-Pol-de-Léon, *France* **18** 48 41N 4 0W
St.-Pol-sur-Mer, *France* **19** 51 1N 2 20 E
St.-Pol-sur-Ternoise, *France* **19** 50 23N 2 20 E
St.-Pons, *France* **20** 43 30N 2 45 E
St.-Pourçain-sur-Sioule, *France* **20** 46 18N 3 18 E
St-Prime, *Canada* **107** 48 35N 72 20W
St.-Quay-Portrieux, *France* **18** 48 39N 2 51W
St.-Quentin, *France* **19** 49 50N 3 16 E
St.-Rambert-d'Albon, *France* **21** 45 17N 4 49 E
St-Raphaël, *Canada* **107** 46 48N 70 45W
St.-Raphaël, *France* **21** 43 25N 6 46 E
St-Raymond, *Canada* **107** 46 54N 71 50W
St. Regis, *U.S.A.* **122** 47 20N 115 3W
St-Rémi, *Canada* **107** 45 16N 73 37W
St.-Rémy-de-Provence, *France* **21** 43 48N 4 50 E
St.-Renan, *France* **18** 48 26N 4 37W
St-Roch, *Canada* **107** 47 18N 70 12W
St-Romuald, *Canada* **107** 46 46N 71 20W
St.-Saëns, *France* **18** 49 41N 1 16 E
St.-Sauveur-en-Puisaye, *France* **19** 47 37N 3 12 E
St.-Sauveur-le-Vicomte, *France* **18** 49 23N 1 32W
St.-Savin, *France* **20** 46 34N 0 53 E
St.-Savinien, *France* **20** 45 53N 0 42W
St-Sébastien, *Canada* **107** 45 47N 70 58W
St. Sebastien, Tanjon' i, *Madag.* **97** 12 26 S 48 44 E
St.-Seine-l'Abbaye, *France* **19** 47 26N 4 47 E
St.-Sernin-sur-Rance, *France* **20** 43 54N 2 35 E
St.-Servan-sur-Mer, *France* **18** 48 38N 2 0W
St.-Sever, *France* **20** 43 45N 0 35W
St.-Sever-Calvados, *France* **18** 48 50N 1 3W
St-Siméon, *Canada* **107** 47 51N 69 54W
St-Simon-de-Rimouski, *Canada* **107** 48 12N 69 3W
St. Stephen, *Canada* **105** 45 16N 67 17W
St.-Sulpice, *France* **20** 43 46N 1 41 E
St.-Sulpice-Laurière, *France* **20** 46 3N 1 29 E
St.-Syprien, *France* **20** 42 37N 3 2 E
St.-Thégonnec, *France* **18** 48 31N 3 57W
St. Thomas, *Canada* **108** 42 45N 81 10W
St. Thomas, *Virgin Is.* **129** 18 21N 64 55W
St-Tite, *Canada* **107** 46 45N 72 34W
St-Tite-des-Caps, *Canada* **107** 47 8N 70 47W
St.-Tropez, *France* **21** 43 17N 6 38 E
St. Troud = Sint Truiden, *Belgium* **17** 50 48N 5 10 E
St-Urbain, *Canada* **107** 47 33N 70 32W
St.-Vaast-la-Hougue, *France* **18** 49 35N 1 17W
St.-Valéry-en-Caux, *France* **18** 49 52N 0 43 E
St.-Valéry-sur-Somme, *France* **19** 50 11N 1 38 E
St.-Vallier, *France* **21** 45 11N 4 50 E
St.-Vallier-de-Thiey, *France* **21** 43 42N 6 51 E
St.-Varent, *France* **18** 46 53N 0 13W
St. Vincent, *C. Verde Is.* **130** 18 0N 26 1W
St. Vincent, *W. Indies* **129** 13 10N 61 10W
St. Vincent, G., *Australia* **73** 35 0 S 138 0 E
St. Vincent and the Grenadines ■, *W. Indies* **129** 13 0N 61 10W
St.-Vincent-de-Tyrosse, *France* **20** 43 39N 1 19W
St. Vincent Passage, *W. Indies* **129** 13 30N 61 0W
St-Vith, *Belgium* **17** 50 17N 6 9 E
St.-Yrieix-la-Perche, *France* **20** 45 31N 1 12 E
Ste-Adèle, *Canada* **107** 45 57N 74 7W
Ste.-Adresse, *France* **18** 49 31N 0 5 E
Ste-Agathe, *Canada* **107** 46 23N 71 25W
Ste-Agathe-des-Monts, *Canada* **107** 46 3N 74 17W
Ste Anne de Beaupré, *Canada* **107** 47 2N 70 58W
Ste-Anne-des-Monts, *Canada* **105** 49 8N 66 30W
Ste-Anne-du-Lac, *Canada* **106** 46 48N 75 25W
Ste-Blandine, *Canada* **107** 48 22N 68 28W
Ste-Claire, *Canada* **107** 46 36N 70 51W
Ste-Croix, *Canada* **107** 46 38N 71 44W
Ste.-Enimie, *France* **20** 44 22N 3 26 E
Ste-Famille, *Canada* **107** 46 58N 70 58W
Ste-Foy, *Canada* **107** 46 47N 71 17W
Ste.-Foy-la-Grande, *France* **20** 44 50N 0 13 E
Ste-Françoise, *Canada* **107** 48 6N 69 4W
Ste. Genevieve, *U.S.A.* **118** 37 59N 90 2W
Ste.-Hermine, *France* **20** 46 32N 1 4W
Ste.-Livrade-sur-Lot, *France* **20** 44 24N 0 36 E
Ste-Marguerite →, *Canada* **105** 50 9N 66 36W
Ste.-Marie, *Martinique* **129** 14 48N 61 1W
Ste.-Marie-aux-Mines, *France* **19** 48 15N 7 12 E
Ste-Marie de la Madeleine, *Canada* **107** 46 26N 71 0W
Ste.-Maure-de-Touraine, *France* **18** 47 7N 0 37 E
Ste.-Maxime, *France* **21** 43 19N 6 39 E
Ste.-Menehould, *France* **19** 49 5N 4 54 E
Ste.-Mère-Église, *France* **18** 49 24N 1 19W
Ste-Monique, *Canada* **107** 48 44N 71 51W
Ste-Pudentienne, *Canada* **107** 45 28N 72 40W
Ste.-Rose, *Guadeloupe* **129** 16 20N 61 45W
Ste. Rose du lac, *Canada* **111** 51 4N 99 30W
Ste-Sabine, *Canada* **107** 45 15N 73 2W
Ste-Thècle, *Canada* **107** 46 49N 72 31W
Saintes, *France* **20** 45 45N 0 37W
Saintes, I. des, *Guadeloupe* **129** 15 50N 61 35W
Stes.-Maries-de-la-Mer, *France* **21** 43 26N 4 26 E
Saintonge, *France* **20** 45 40N 0 50W
Sairecábur, Cerro, *Bolivia* **140** 22 43 S 67 54W
Sairs, L., *Canada* **106** 46 49N 78 26W
Saitama □, *Japan* **65** 36 25N 139 30 E
Saito, *Japan* **64** 32 3N 131 24 E
Sajama, *Bolivia* **136** 18 7 S 69 0W
Sajum, *India* **49** 33 20N 79 0 E
Sak →, *S. Africa* **96** 30 52 S 20 25 E
Sakai, *Japan* **65** 34 30N 135 30 E
Sakaide, *Japan* **64** 34 15N 133 50 E
Sakaiminato, *Japan* **64** 35 38N 133 11 E
Sakākah, *Si. Arabia* **46** 30 0N 40 8 E
Sakakawea, L., *U.S.A.* **120** 47 30N 102 0W
Sakami, L., *Canada* **104** 53 15N 77 0W
Sâkâne, 'Erg i-n, *Mali* **84** 20 30N 1 30W
Sakania, *Zaïre* **93** 12 43 S 28 30 E
Sakarya →, *Turkey* **38** 41 7N 30 39 E
Sakata, *Japan* **63** 38 55N 139 50 E
Sakeny →, *Madag.* **97** 20 0 S 45 25 E
Sakété, *Benin* **91** 6 40N 2 45 E
Sakhalin, *U.S.S.R.* **41** 51 0N 143 0 E
Sakhalinskiy Zaliv, *U.S.S.R.* **41** 54 0N 141 0 E
Sakhi Gopal, *India* **50** 19 58N 85 50 E
Sakhnīn, *Israel* **44** 32 52N 35 12 E
Saki, *U.S.S.R.* **38** 45 9N 33 34 E
Sakiai, *U.S.S.R.* **36** 54 59N 23 0 E
Sakon Nakhon, *Thailand* **54** 17 10N 104 9 E
Sakrand, *Pakistan* **48** 26 10N 68 15 E
Sakri, *India* **50** 21 2N 74 20 E
Sakrivier, *S. Africa* **96** 30 54 S 20 28 E
Sakskøbing, *Denmark* **11** 54 49N 11 39 E
Saku, *Japan* **65** 36 17N 138 31 E
Sakuma, *Japan* **65** 35 3N 137 49 E
Sakura, *Japan* **65** 35 43N 140 14 E
Sakurai, *Japan* **65** 34 30N 135 51 E
Sal →, *U.S.S.R.* **39** 47 31N 40 45 E
Sala, *Sweden* **10** 59 58N 16 35 E
Sala Consilina, *Italy* **29** 40 23N 15 35 E
Sala-y-Gómez, *Pac. Oc.* **67** 26 28 S 105 28W
Salaberry-de-Valleyfield, *Canada* **107** 45 15N 74 8W
Saladas, *Argentina* **140** 28 15 S 58 40W
Saladillo, *Argentina* **140** 35 40 S 59 55W
Salado →, *Buenos Aires, Argentina* **140** 35 44 S 57 22W
Salado →, *La Pampa, Argentina* **142** 37 30 S 67 0W
Salado →, *Río Negro, Argentina* **142** 41 34 S 65 3W
Salado →, *Santa Fe, Argentina* **140** 31 40 S 60 41W
Salado →, *Mexico* **126** 26 52N 99 19W
Salaga, *Ghana* **91** 8 31N 0 31W
Salala, *Liberia* **90** 6 42N 10 7W
Salala, *Sudan* **88** 21 17N 36 16 E
Salālah, *Oman* **45** 16 56N 53 59 E
Salamanca, *Chile* **140** 31 46 S 70 59W
Salamanca, *Spain* **22** 40 58N 5 39W
Salamanca, *U.S.A.* **116** 42 10N 78 42W
Salamanca □, *Spain* **22** 40 57N 5 40W
Salamina, *Colombia* **134** 5 25N 75 29W
Salamis, *Greece* **35** 37 56N 23 30 E
Salamonie, Res., *U.S.A.* **119** 40 45N 85 35W
Salar de Atacama, *Chile* **140** 23 30 S 68 25W
Salar de Uyuni, *Bolivia* **136** 20 30 S 67 45W
Sălard, *Romania* **34** 47 12N 22 3 E
Salas, *Spain* **22** 43 25N 6 15W
Salas de los Infantes, *Spain* **24** 42 2N 3 17W
Salatiga, *Indonesia* **57** 7 19 S 110 30 E
Salaverry, *Peru* **136** 8 15 S 79 0W
Salawati, *Indonesia* **57** 1 7 S 130 52 E
Salayar, *Indonesia* **57** 6 7 S 120 30 E
Salazar →, *Spain* **24** 42 40N 1 20W
Salbris, *France* **19** 47 25N 2 3 E
Salcombe, *U.K.* **13** 50 14N 3 47W
Saldaña, *Spain* **22** 42 32N 4 48W
Saldanha, *S. Africa* **96** 33 0 S 17 58 E
Saldanha B., *S. Africa* **96** 33 6 S 18 0 E
Saldus, *U.S.S.R.* **36** 56 38N 22 30 E
Sale, *Australia* **75** 38 6 S 147 6 E
Salé, *Morocco* **84** 34 3N 6 48W
Sale, *U.K.* **12** 53 26N 2 19W
Salekhard, *U.S.S.R.* **40** 66 30N 66 35 E
Salem, *India* **51** 11 40N 78 11 E
Salem, *Ill., U.S.A.* **118** 38 38N 88 57W
Salem, *Ind., U.S.A.* **119** 38 38N 86 6W
Salem, *Mass., U.S.A.* **117** 42 29N 70 53W
Salem, *Mo., U.S.A.* **121** 37 40N 91 30W
Salem, *N.J., U.S.A.* **114** 39 34N 75 29W
Salem, *Ohio, U.S.A.* **116** 40 52N 80 50W
Salem, *Oreg., U.S.A.* **122** 45 0N 123 0W
Salem, *S. Dak., U.S.A.* **120** 43 44N 97 23W
Salem, *Va., U.S.A.* **114** 37 19N 80 8W
Salemi, *Italy* **28** 37 49N 12 47 E
Salen, *Norway* **9** 64 41N 11 27 E
Salernes, *France* **21** 43 34N 6 15 E
Salerno, *Italy* **29** 40 40N 14 44 E
Salerno, G. di, *Italy* **29** 40 35N 14 45 E
Salfīt, *Jordan* **44** 32 5N 35 11 E
Salford, *U.K.* **12** 53 30N 2 17W
Salgir →, *U.S.S.R.* **38** 45 38N 35 1 E
Salgótarján, *Hungary* **33** 48 5N 19 47 E
Salgueiro, *Brazil* **138** 8 4 S 39 6W
Salies-de-Béarn, *France* **20** 43 28N 0 56W
Salin, *Burma* **52** 20 35N 94 40 E
Salina, *Italy* **29** 38 35N 14 50 E
Salina, *U.S.A.* **120** 38 50N 97 40W
Salina Cruz, *Mexico* **127** 16 10N 95 10W
Salinas, *Brazil* **139** 16 10 S 42 10W
Salinas, *Chile* **140** 23 31 S 69 29W
Salinas, *Ecuador* **134** 2 10 S 80 58W
Salinas, *U.S.A.* **124** 36 40N 121 41W
Salinas →, *Guatemala* **127** 16 28N 90 31W
Salinas →, *U.S.A.* **124** 36 45N 121 48W
Salinas, B. de, *Nic.* **128** 11 4N 85 45W
Salinas, C. de, *Spain* **25** 39 16N 3 4 E
Salinas, Pampa de las, *Argentina* **140** 31 58 S 66 42W
Salinas Ambargasta, *Argentina* **140** 29 0 S 65 0W
Salinas de Hidalgo, *Mexico* **126** 22 30N 101 40W
Salinas Grandes, *Argentina* **140** 30 0 S 65 0W
Saline →, *Ark., U.S.A.* **121** 33 10N 92 8W
Saline →, *Kans., U.S.A.* **120** 38 51N 97 30W
Salinópolis, *Brazil* **138** 0 40 S 47 20W
Salins-les-Bains, *France* **19** 46 58N 5 52 E
Salir, *Portugal* **23** 37 14N 8 2W
Salisbury = Harare, *Zimb.* **93** 17 43 S 31 2 E
Salisbury, *N.S.W., Australia* **77** 32 11 S 151 33 E
Salisbury, *S. Austral., Australia* **73** 34 46 S 138 40 E
Salisbury, *U.K.* **13** 51 4N 1 48W
Salisbury, *Md., U.S.A.* **114** 38 20N 75 38W
Salisbury, *Mo., U.S.A.* **118** 39 25N 92 48W
Salisbury, *N.C., U.S.A.* **115** 35 20N 80 29W
Salisbury Plain, *U.K.* **13** 51 13N 1 50W
Săliște, *Romania* **34** 45 45N 23 56 E
Salitre →, *Brazil* **138** 9 29 S 40 39W
Salka, *Nigeria* **91** 10 20N 4 58 E
Salle, La, *U.S.A.* **118** 41 20N 89 6W
Sallent, *Spain* **24** 41 49N 1 54 E
Salles-Curan, *France* **20** 44 11N 2 48 E
Salling, *Denmark* **11** 56 40N 8 55 E
Sallisaw, *U.S.A.* **121** 35 26N 94 45W
Sallom Junction, *Sudan* **88** 19 17N 37 6 E
Salmās, *Iran* **46** 38 11N 44 47 E
Salmerón, *Spain* **24** 40 33N 2 29W
Salmo, *Canada* **110** 49 10N 117 20W
Salmon, *U.S.A.* **122** 45 12N 113 56W
Salmon →, *Canada* **110** 54 3N 122 40W
Salmon →, *U.S.A.* **122** 45 51N 116 46W
Salmon Arm, *Canada* **110** 50 40N 119 15W
Salmon Falls, *U.S.A.* **122** 42 48N 114 59W
Salmon Gums, *Australia* **79** 32 59 S 121 38 E
Salmon Res., *Canada* **105** 48 5N 56 0W
Salmon River Mts., *U.S.A.* **122** 45 0N 114 30W
Salo, *Finland* **9** 60 22N 23 10 E
Salò, *Italy* **26** 45 37N 10 32 E
Salobreña, *Spain* **23** 36 44N 3 35W
Salome, *U.S.A.* **125** 33 51N 113 37W
Salon-de-Provence, *France* **21** 43 39N 5 6 E
Salonica = Thessaloníki, *Greece* **35** 40 38N 22 58 E
Salonta, *Romania* **34** 46 49N 21 42 E
Salop = Shropshire □, *U.K.* **13** 52 36N 2 45W
Salor →, *Spain* **23** 39 39N 7 3W
Salou, C., *Spain* **24** 41 3N 1 10 E
Salsacate, *Argentina* **140** 31 20 S 65 5W
Salses, *France* **20** 42 50N 2 55 E
Salsette I., *India* **50** 19 5N 72 50 E
Salsk, *U.S.S.R.* **39** 46 28N 41 30 E
Salso →, *Italy* **29** 37 6N 13 55 E
Salsomaggiore, *Italy* **26** 44 48N 9 59 E
Salt →, *Canada* **110** 60 0N 112 25W
Salt →, *Ariz., U.S.A.* **123** 33 23N 112 18W
Salt →, *Mo., U.S.A.* **118** 39 29N 91 5W
Salt Creek, *Australia* **73** 36 8 S 139 38 E
Salt Fork →, *U.S.A.* **121** 36 37N 97 7W
Salt Lake City, *U.S.A.* **122** 40 45N 111 58W
Salt Range, *Pakistan* **48** 32 30N 72 25 E
Salta, *Argentina* **140** 24 57 S 65 25W
Salta □, *Argentina* **140** 24 48 S 65 30W
Saltcoats, *U.K.* **14** 55 38N 4 47W
Saltee Is., *Ireland* **15** 52 7N 6 37W
Saltfjorden, *Norway* **8** 67 15N 14 10 E
Saltholm, *Denmark* **11** 55 38N 12 43 E
Salthólmavík, *Iceland* **8** 65 24N 21 57W
Saltillo, *Mexico* **126** 25 30N 100 57W
Salto, *Argentina* **140** 34 20 S 60 15W
Salto, *Uruguay* **140** 31 27 S 57 50W
Salto da Divisa, *Brazil* **139** 16 0 S 39 57W
Salton City, *U.S.A.* **125** 33 29N 115 51W
Salton Sea, *U.S.A.* **125** 33 20N 115 50W
Saltpond, *Ghana* **91** 5 15N 1 3W
Saltsjöbaden, *Sweden* **10** 59 15N 18 20 E
Saltville, *U.S.A.* **114** 36 53N 81 46W
Saluda →, *U.S.A.* **115** 34 0N 81 4W
Salûm, *Egypt* **88** 31 31N 25 7 E
Salûm, Khâlig el, *Egypt* **88** 31 30N 25 9 E
Salur, *India* **50** 18 27N 83 18 E
Salut, Is. du, *Fr. Guiana* **135** 5 15N 52 35W
Saluzzo, *Italy* **26** 44 39N 7 29 E
Salvación, B., *Chile* **142** 50 50 S 75 10W
Salvador, *Brazil* **139** 13 0 S 38 30W
Salvador, *Canada* **111** 52 10N 109 32W
Salvador, L., *U.S.A.* **121** 29 46N 90 16W
Salvaterra, *Brazil* **138** 0 46 S 48 31W
Salvaterra de Magos, *Portugal* **23** 39 1N 8 47W
Salvisa, *U.S.A.* **119** 37 54N 84 51W
Sálvora, I., *Spain* **22** 42 30N 8 58W
Salwa, *Qatar* **47** 24 45N 50 55 E
Salween →, *Burma* **52** 16 31N 97 37 E
Salyersville, *U.S.A.* **114** 37 45N 83 4W
Salza →, *Austria* **33** 47 40N 14 43 E
Salzach →, *Austria* **33** 48 12N 12 56 E
Salzburg, *Austria* **33** 47 48N 13 2 E
Salzgitter, *W. Germany* **30** 52 13N 10 22 E
Salzwedel, *E. Germany* **30** 52 50N 11 11 E
Sam, *Gabon* **94** 0 58N 11 16 E
Sam Neua, *Laos* **54** 20 29N 104 0 E
Sam Ngao, *Thailand* **54** 17 18N 99 0 E
Sam Rayburn Res., *U.S.A.* **121** 31 15N 94 20W
Sam Son, *Vietnam* **54** 19 44N 105 54 E

Sam Teu, *Laos* **54** 19 59N 104 38 E
Sama, *U.S.S.R.* **40** 60 12N 60 22 E
Sama de Langreo, *Spain* **22** 43 18N 5 40W
Samacimbo, *Angola* **95** 13 33 S 16 59 E
Samagaltai, *U.S.S.R.* **41** 50 36N 95 3 E
Samaipata, *Bolivia* **137** 18 9 S 63 52W
Samales Group, *Phil.* **57** 6 0N 122 0 E
Samalkot, *India* **50** 17 3N 82 13 E
Samâlût, *Egypt* **88** 28 20N 30 42 E
Samana, *India* **48** 30 10N 76 13 E
Samana Cay, *Bahamas* **129** 23 3N 73 45W
Samanga, *Tanzania* **93** 8 20 S 39 13 E
Samangán □, *Afghan.* **47** 36 15N 68 3 E
Samangwa, *Zaïre* **92** 4 23 S 24 10 E
Samani, *Japan* **63** 42 7N 142 56 E
Samar, *Phil.* **57** 12 0N 125 0 E
Samarai, *Papua N. G.* **69** 10 39 S 150 41 E
Samaria = Shōmrōn, *Jordan* **44** 32 15N 35 13 E
Samarinda, *Indonesia* **56** 0 30 S 117 9 E
Samarkand, *U.S.S.R.* **40** 39 40N 66 55 E
Sāmarrā, *Iraq* **46** 34 12N 43 52 E
Samastipur, *India* **49** 25 50N 85 50 E
Samatan, *France* **20** 43 29N 0 55 E
Samaúma, *Brazil* **137** 7 50 S 60 2W
Samba, *India* **49** 32 32N 75 10 E
Samba, *Zaïre* **92** 4 38 S 26 22 E
Samba Caju, *Angola* **95** 8 46 S 15 24 E
Sambaíba, *Brazil* **138** 7 8 S 45 21W
Sambalpur, *India* **50** 21 28N 84 4 E
Sambar, Tanjung, *Indonesia* **56** 2 59 S 110 19 E
Sambas, *Indonesia* **56** 1 20N 109 20 E
Sambava, *Madag.* **97** 14 16 S 50 10 E
Sambawizi, *Zimb.* **93** 18 24 S 26 13 E
Sambhal, *India* **49** 28 35N 78 37 E
Sambhar, *India* **48** 26 52N 75 6 E
Sambiase, *Italy* **29** 38 58N 16 16 E
Sambonifacio, *Italy* **26** 45 24N 11 16 E
Sambor, *Cambodia* **54** 12 46N 106 0 E
Sambor, *U.S.S.R.* **36** 49 30N 23 10 E
Sambre →, *Europe* **17** 50 27N 4 52 E
Sambuca di Sicilia, *Italy* **28** 37 39N 13 6 E
Samburu □, *Kenya* **92** 1 10N 37 0 E
Samchŏk, *S. Korea* **61** 37 30N 129 10 E
Same, *Tanzania* **92** 4 2 S 37 38 E
Samer, *France* **19** 50 38N 1 44 E
Samfya, *Zambia* **93** 11 22 S 29 31 E
Sámi, *Greece* **35** 38 15N 20 39 E
Samnū, *Libya* **86** 27 15N 14 55 E
Samo Alto, *Chile* **140** 30 22 S 71 0W
Samoan Is., *Pac. Oc.* **68** 14 0 S 171 0W
Samobor, *Yugoslavia* **27** 45 47N 15 44 E
Samoëns, *France* **21** 46 5N 6 45 E
Samokov, *Bulgaria* **34** 42 18N 23 35 E
Samoorombón, B., *Argentina* **140** 36 5 S 57 20W
Samorogouan, *Burkina Faso* **90** 11 21N 4 57W
Sámos, *Greece* **35** 37 45N 26 50 E
Samos, *Spain* **22** 42 44N 7 20W
Samoš, *Yugoslavia* **33** 45 13N 20 49 E
Samothráki, *Greece* **35** 40 28N 25 28 E
Samoylovka, *U.S.S.R.* **37** 51 12N 43 43 E
Sampa, *Ghana* **90** 8 0N 2 36W
Sampacho, *Argentina* **140** 33 20 S 64 50W
Sampang, *Indonesia* **57** 7 11 S 113 13 E
Samper de Calanda, *Spain* **24** 41 11N 0 28W
Sampit, *Indonesia* **56** 2 34 S 113 0 E
Sampit, Teluk, *Indonesia* **56** 3 5 S 113 3 E
Samra, *Si. Arabia* **46** 25 35N 41 0 E
Samrée, *Belgium* **17** 50 13N 5 39 E
Samrong, *Cambodia* **54** 14 15N 103 30 E
Samrong, *Thailand* **54** 15 10N 100 40 E
Samsø, *Denmark* **11** 55 50N 10 35 E
Samsø Bælt, *Denmark* **11** 55 45N 10 45 E
Samsun, *Turkey* **46** 41 15N 36 22 E
Samtredia, *U.S.S.R.* **39** 42 7N 42 24 E
Samui, Ko, *Thailand* **55** 9 30N 100 0 E
Samur →, *U.S.S.R.* **39** 41 53N 48 32 E
Samusole, *Zaïre* **93** 10 2 S 24 0 E
Samut Prakan, *Thailand* **54** 13 32N 100 40 E
Samut Sakhon, *Thailand* **54** 13 31N 100 13 E
Samut Songkhram →, *Thailand* **54** 13 24N 100 1 E
Samwari, *Pakistan* **48** 28 30N 66 46 E
San, *Mali* **90** 13 15N 4 57W
San →, *Cambodia* **54** 13 32N 105 57 E
San →, *Poland* **32** 50 45N 21 51 E
San Adrián, C. de, *Spain* **22** 43 21N 8 50W
San Agustín, *Colombia* **134** 1 53N 76 16W
San Agustin, C., *Phil.* **57** 6 20N 126 13 E
San Agustín de Valle Fértil, *Argentina* **140** 30 35 S 67 30W
San Ambrosio, *Pac. Oc.* **132** 26 28 S 79 53W
San Andreas, *U.S.A.* **124** 38 0N 120 39W
San Andrés, I. de, *Caribbean* **128** 12 42N 81 46W
San Andres Mts., *U.S.A.* **123** 33 0N 106 45W
San Andrés Tuxtla, *Mexico* **127** 18 30N 95 20W
San Angelo, *U.S.A.* **121** 31 30N 100 30W
San Anselmo, *U.S.A.* **124** 37 59N 122 34W
San Antonio, *Belize* **127** 16 15N 89 2W
San Antonio, *Chile* **140** 33 40 S 71 40W
San Antonio, *N. Mex., U.S.A.* **123** 33 58N 106 57W
San Antonio, *Tex., U.S.A.* **121** 29 30N 98 30W
San Antonio, *Venezuela* **134** 3 30N 66 44W
San Antonio →, *U.S.A.* **121** 28 30N 96 50W
San Antonio, C., *Argentina* **140** 36 15 S 56 40W
San Antonio, C., *Cuba* **128** 21 50N 84 57W
San Antonio, C. de, *Spain* **25** 38 48N 0 12 E
San Antonio, Mt., *U.S.A.* **125** 34 17N 117 38W
San Antonio Abad, *Spain* **25** 38 59N 1 19 E
San Antonio de los Baños, *Cuba* **128** 22 54N 82 31W
San Antonio de los Cobres, *Argentina* **140** 24 10 S 66 17W
San Antonio Oeste, *Argentina* **142** 40 40 S 65 0W
San Arcángelo, *Italy* **28** 40 14N 16 14 E
San Ardo, *U.S.A.* **124** 36 1N 120 54W
San Augustín, *Canary Is.* **25** 27 47N 15 32W
San Augustine, *U.S.A.* **121** 31 30N 94 7W
San Bartolomé, *Canary Is.* **25** 28 59N 13 37W
San Bartolomé de Tirajana, *Canary Is.* **25** 27 54N 15 34W
San Bartolomeo in Galdo, *Italy* **29** 41 23N 15 2 E
San Benedetto, *Italy* **26** 45 2N 10 57 E
San Benedetto del Tronto, *Italy* **27** 42 57N 13 52 E
San Benedicto, I., *Mexico* **126** 19 18N 110 49W
San Benito, *U.S.A.* **121** 26 5N 97 39W
San Benito →, *U.S.A.* **124** 36 53N 121 50W
San Benito Mt., *U.S.A.* **124** 36 22N 120 37W
San Bernardino, *U.S.A.* **125** 34 7N 117 18W
San Bernardino Mts., *U.S.A.* **125** 34 10N 116 45W
San Bernardino Str., *Phil.* **57** 13 0N 125 0 E
San Bernardo, *Chile* **140** 33 40 S 70 50W
San Bernardo, I. de, *Colombia* **134** 9 45N 75 50W
San Blas, *Mexico* **126** 26 4N 108 46W
San Blas, Arch. de, *Panama* **128** 9 50N 78 31W
San Blas, C., *U.S.A.* **115** 29 40N 85 12W
San Borja, *Bolivia* **136** 14 50 S 66 52W
San Buenaventura, *Bolivia* **136** 14 28 S 67 35W
San Buenaventura, *Mexico* **126** 27 5N 101 32W
San Carlos = Butuku-Luba, *Eq. Guin.* **91** 3 29N 8 33 E
San Carlos, *Argentina* **140** 33 50 S 69 0W
San Carlos, *Bolivia* **137** 17 24 S 63 45W
San Carlos, *Chile* **140** 36 10 S 72 0W
San Carlos, *Mexico* **126** 29 0N 100 54W
San Carlos, *Nic.* **128** 11 12N 84 50W
San Carlos, *Phil.* **57** 10 29N 123 25 E
San Carlos, *Uruguay* **141** 34 46 S 54 58W
San Carlos, *U.S.A.* **123** 33 24N 110 27W
San Carlos, *Amazonas, Venezuela* **134** 1 55N 67 4W
San Carlos, *Cojedes, Venezuela* **134** 9 40N 68 36W
San Carlos de Bariloche, *Argentina* **142** 41 10 S 71 25W
San Carlos de la Rápita, *Spain* **24** 40 37N 0 35 E
San Carlos del Zulia, *Venezuela* **134** 9 1N 71 55W
San Carlos L., *U.S.A.* **123** 33 15N 110 25W
San Cataldo, *Italy* **28** 37 30N 13 58 E
San Celoni, *Spain* **24** 41 42N 2 30 E
San Clemente, *Chile* **140** 35 30 S 71 29W
San Clemente, *Spain* **25** 39 24N 2 25W
San Clemente, *U.S.A.* **125** 33 29N 117 36W
San Clemente I., *U.S.A.* **125** 32 53N 118 30W
San Constanzo, *Italy* **27** 43 46N 13 5 E
San Cristóbal, *Argentina* **140** 30 20 S 61 10W
San Cristóbal, *Colombia* **134** 2 18 S 73 2W
San Cristóbal, *Dom. Rep.* **129** 18 25N 70 6W
San Cristóbal, *Solomon Is.* **68** 10 30 S 161 0 E
San Cristóbal, *Venezuela* **134** 7 46N 72 14W
San Cristóbal de las Casas, *Mexico* **127** 16 50N 92 33W
San Damiano d'Asti, *Italy* **26** 44 51N 8 4 E
San Daniele del Friuli, *Italy* **27** 46 10N 13 0 E
San Demétrio Corone, *Italy* **29** 39 34N 16 22 E
San Diego, *Calif., U.S.A.* **125** 32 43N 117 10W
San Diego, *Tex., U.S.A.* **121** 27 47N 98 15W
San Diego, C., *Argentina* **142** 54 40 S 65 10W
San Diego de la Unión, *Mexico* **126** 21 28N 100 52W
San Donà di Piave, *Italy* **27** 45 38N 12 34 E
San Elpídio a Mare, *Italy* **27** 43 16N 13 41 E
San Estanislao, *Paraguay* **140** 24 39 S 56 26W
San Esteban de Gormaz, *Spain* **24** 41 34N 3 13W
San Felice sul Panaro, *Italy* **26** 44 51N 11 9 E
San Felipe, *Chile* **140** 32 43 S 70 42W
San Felipe, *Colombia* **134** 1 55N 67 6W
San Felipe, *Mexico* **126** 31 0N 114 52W
San Felipe, *Venezuela* **134** 10 20N 68 44W
San Felipe →, *U.S.A.* **125** 33 12N 115 49W
San Feliu de Guíxols, *Spain* **24** 41 45N 3 1 E
San Feliu de Llobregat, *Spain* **24** 41 23N 2 2 E
San Félix, *Pac. Oc.* **67** 26 23 S 80 0W
San Fernando, *Chile* **140** 34 30 S 71 0W
San Fernando, *Mexico* **126** 30 0N 115 10W
San Fernando, *La Union, Phil.* **57** 16 40N 120 23 E
San Fernando, *Pampanga, Phil.* **57** 15 5N 120 37 E
San Fernando, *Spain* **23** 36 28N 6 17W
San Fernando, *Trin. & Tob.* **129** 10 20N 61 30W
San Fernando, *U.S.A.* **125** 34 15N 118 29W
San Fernando →, *Mexico* **126** 24 55N 98 10W
San Fernando de Apure, *Venezuela* **134** 7 54N 67 15W
San Fernando de Atabapo, *Venezuela* **134** 4 3N 67 42W
San Fernando di Púglia, *Italy* **29** 41 18N 16 5 E
San Francisco, *Argentina* **140** 31 30 S 62 5W
San Francisco, *Bolivia* **137** 15 16 S 65 31W
San Francisco, *U.S.A.* **124** 37 47N 122 30W
San Francisco →, *U.S.A.* **123** 32 59N 109 22W
San Francisco, Paso de, *S. Amer.* **140** 27 0 S 68 0W
San Francisco de Macorîs, *Dom. Rep.* **129** 19 19N 70 15W
San Francisco del Monte de Oro, *Argentina* **140** 32 36 S 66 8W
San Francisco del Oro, *Mexico* **126** 26 52N 105 50W
San Francisco Javier, *Spain* **25** 38 42N 1 26 E
San Francisco Solano, Pta., *Colombia* **134** 6 18N 77 29W
San Fratello, *Italy* **29** 38 1N 14 33 E
San Gabriel, *Ecuador* **134** 0 36N 77 49W
San Gavino Monreale, *Italy* **28** 39 33N 8 47 E
San Gil, *Colombia* **134** 6 33N 73 8W
San Gimignano, *Italy* **26** 43 28N 11 3 E
San Giórgio di Nogaro, *Italy* **27** 45 50N 13 13 E
San Giórgio Iónico, *Italy* **29** 40 27N 17 23 E
San Giovanni Bianco, *Italy* **26** 45 52N 9 40 E
San Giovanni in Fiore, *Italy* **29** 39 16N 16 42 E
San Giovanni in Persiceto, *Italy* **27** 44 39N 11 12 E
San Giovanni Rotondo, *Italy* **29** 41 41N 15 42 E
San Giovanni Valdarno, *Italy* **27** 43 32N 11 30 E
San Giuliano Terme, *Italy* **26** 43 45N 10 26 E
San Gorgonio Mt., *U.S.A.* **125** 34 7N 116 51W
San Gottardo, Paso del, *Switz.* **31** 46 33N 8 33 E
San Gregorio, *Uruguay* **141** 32 37 S 55 40W
San Gregorio, *U.S.A.* **124** 37 20N 122 23W
San Guiseppe Iato, *Italy* **28** 37 57N 13 11 E
San Ignacio, *Belize* **127** 17 10N 89 0W
San Ignacio, *Bolivia* **137** 16 20 S 60 55W
San Ignacio, *Mexico* **126** 27 27N 113 0W
San Ignacio, *Paraguay* **140** 26 52 S 57 3W
San Ignacio, L., *Mexico* **126** 26 50N 113 11W
San Ildefonso, C., *Phil.* **57** 16 0N 122 1 E
San Isidro, *Argentina* **140** 34 29 S 58 31W
San Jacinto, *Colombia* **134** 9 50N 75 8W
San Jacinto, *U.S.A.* **125** 33 47N 116 57W
San Javier, *Misiones, Argentina* **141** 27 55 S 55 5W
San Javier, *Santa Fe, Argentina* **140** 30 40 S 59 55W
San Javier, *Beni, Bolivia* **137** 14 34 S 64 42W
San Javier, *Santa Cruz, Bolivia* **137** 16 18 S 62 30W
San Javier, *Chile* **140** 35 40 S 71 45W
San Javier, *Spain* **25** 37 49N 0 50W
San Jerónimo, Sa. de, *Colombia* **134** 8 0N 75 50W
San Jeronimo Taviche, *Mexico* **127** 16 38N 96 32W
San Joaquín, *Bolivia* **137** 13 4 S 64 49W
San Joaquin, *U.S.A.* **124** 36 36N 120 11W
San Joaquín, *Venezuela* **134** 10 16N 67 47W
San Joaquín →, *Bolivia* **137** 13 8 S 63 41W
San Joaquin →, *U.S.A.* **124** 38 4N 121 51W
San Joaquin Valley, *U.S.A.* **124** 37 0N 120 30W
San Jorge, *Argentina* **140** 31 54 S 61 50W
San Jorge, B. de, *Mexico* **126** 31 20N 113 20W
San Jorge, G., *Argentina* **142** 46 0 S 66 0W
San Jorge, G. de, *Spain* **24** 40 50N 0 55W
San José, *Bolivia* **137** 17 53 S 60 50W
San José, *Costa Rica* **128** 10 0N 84 2W
San José, *Guatemala* **128** 14 0N 90 50W
San José, *Mexico* **126** 25 0N 110 50W
San Jose, *Luzon, Phil.* **57** 15 45N 120 55 E
San Jose, *Mindoro, Phil.* **57** 12 27N 121 4 E
San José, *Spain* **25** 38 55N 1 18 E
San Jose, *Calif., U.S.A.* **124** 37 20N 121 53W
San Jose, *Ill., U.S.A.* **118** 40 18N 89 36W
San Jose →, *U.S.A.* **123** 34 58N 106 7W
San José de Feliciano, *Argentina* **140** 30 26 S 58 46W
San José de Jáchal, *Argentina* **140** 30 15 S 68 46W
San José de Mayo, *Uruguay* **140** 34 27 S 56 40W
San José de Ocune, *Colombia* **134** 4 15N 70 20W
San José de Uchapiamonas, *Bolivia* **136** 14 13 S 68 5W
San José del Cabo, *Mexico* **126** 23 0N 109 40W
San José del Guaviare, *Colombia* **134** 2 35N 72 38W
San José do Anauá, *Brazil* **135** 0 58N 61 22W
San Juan, *Argentina* **140** 31 30 S 68 30W
San Juan, *Colombia* **134** 8 46N 76 32W
San Juan, *Mexico* **126** 21 20N 102 50W
San Juan, *Ica, Peru* **136** 15 22 S 75 7W
San Juan, *Puno, Peru* **136** 14 2 S 69 19W
San Juan, *Phil.* **57** 8 25N 126 20 E
San Juan, *Puerto Rico* **129** 18 28N 66 8W
San Juan □, *Argentina* **140** 31 9 S 69 0W
San Juan →, *Argentina* **140** 32 20 S 67 25W
San Juan →, *Bolivia* **137** 21 2 S 65 19W
San Juan →, *Colombia* **134** 4 3N 77 27W
San Juan →, *Nic.* **128** 10 56N 83 42W
San Juan →, *Calif., U.S.A.* **124** 36 14N 121 9W
San Juan →, *Utah, U.S.A.* **123** 37 20N 110 20W
San Juan →, *Venezuela* **135** 10 14N 62 38W
San Juan, C., *Eq. Guin.* **94** 1 5N 9 20 E
San Juan Bautista, *Paraguay* **140** 26 37 S 57 6W
San Juan Bautista, *Spain* **25** 39 5N 1 31 E
San Juan Bautista, *U.S.A.* **124** 36 51N 121 32W
San Juan Bautista Valle Nacional, *Mexico* **127** 17 47N 96 19W
San Juan Capistrano, *U.S.A.* **125** 33 29N 117 40W
San Juan de Guadalupe, *Mexico* **126** 24 38N 102 44W
San Juan de los Morros, *Venezuela* **134** 9 55N 67 21W
San Juan del César, *Colombia* **134** 10 46N 73 1W
San Juan del Norte, *Nic.* **128** 10 58N 83 40W
San Juan del Norte, B. de, *Nic.* **128** 11 0N 83 40W
San Juan del Puerto, *Spain* **23** 37 20N 6 50W
San Juan del Río, *Mexico* **127** 20 25N 100 0W
San Juan del Sur, *Nic.* **128** 11 20N 85 51W
San Juan I., *U.S.A.* **124** 48 32N 123 5W
San Juan Mts., *U.S.A.* **123** 38 30N 108 30W
San Julián, *Argentina* **142** 49 15 S 67 45W
San Just, Sierra de, *Spain* **24** 40 45N 0 49W
San Justo, *Argentina* **140** 30 47 S 60 30W
San Kamphaeng, *Thailand* **54** 18 45N 99 8 E
San Lázaro, C., *Mexico* **126** 24 50N 112 18W
San Lázaro, Sa., *Mexico* **126** 23 25N 110 0W
San Leandro, *U.S.A.* **124** 37 40N 122 6W
San Leonardo, *Spain* **24** 41 51N 3 5W
San Lorenzo, *Argentina* **140** 32 45 S 60 45W
San Lorenzo, *Beni, Bolivia* **137** 15 22 S 65 48W
San Lorenzo, *Tarija, Bolivia* **137** 21 26 S 64 47W
San Lorenzo, *Ecuador* **134** 1 15N 78 50W
San Lorenzo, *Paraguay* **140** 25 20 S 57 32W
San Lorenzo, *Venezuela* **134** 9 47N 71 4W
San Lorenzo →, *Mexico* **126** 24 15N 107 24W
San Lorenzo, I., *Mexico* **126** 28 35N 112 50W
San Lorenzo, I., *Peru* **136** 12 7 S 77 15W
San Lorenzo, Mt., *Argentina* **142** 47 40 S 72 20W
San Lorenzo de la Parrilla, *Spain* **24** 39 51N 2 22W

San Lorenzo de Morunys, *Spain* **24** 42 8N 1 35 E
San Lucas, *Bolivia* **137** 20 5 S 65 7W
San Lucas, *Baja Calif. S., Mexico* **126** 22 53N 109 54W
San Lucas, *Baja Calif. S., Mexico* **126** 27 10N 112 14W
San Lucas, *U.S.A.* **124** 36 8N 121 1W
San Lucas, C., *Mexico* **126** 22 50N 110 0W
San Lúcido, *Italy* **29** 39 18N 16 3 E
San Luis, *Argentina* **140** 33 20 S 66 20W
San Luis, *Cuba* **128** 22 17N 83 46W
San Luis, *Guatemala* **128** 16 14N 89 27W
San Luis, *U.S.A.* **123** 37 3N 105 26W
San Luis □, *Argentina* **140** 34 0 S 66 0W
San Luis, I., *Mexico* **126** 29 58N 114 26W
San Luis, L. de, *Bolivia* **137** 13 45 S 64 0W
San Luis, Sierra de, *Argentina* **140** 32 30 S 66 10W
San Luis de la Paz, *Mexico* **126** 21 19N 100 32W
San Luis Obispo, *U.S.A.* **125** 35 21N 120 38W
San Luis Potosí, *Mexico* **126** 22 9N 100 59W
San Luis Potosí □, *Mexico* **126** 22 10N 101 0W
San Luis Res., *U.S.A.* **124** 37 4N 121 5W
San Luis Río Colorado, *Mexico* **126** 32 29N 114 58W
San Marco Argentano, *Italy* **29** 39 34N 16 8 E
San Marco dei Cavoti, *Italy* **29** 41 20N 14 50 E
San Marco in Lámis, *Italy* **29** 41 43N 15 38 E
San Marcos, *Colombia* **134** 8 39N 75 8W
San Marcos, *Guatemala* **128** 14 59N 91 52W
San Marcos, *Mexico* **126** 27 13N 112 6W
San Marcos, *U.S.A.* **121** 29 53N 98 0W
San Marino ■, *Europe* **27** 43 56N 12 25 E
San Martin, *Antarctica* **143** 68 11 S 67 0W
San Martín, *Argentina* **140** 33 5 S 68 28W
San Martín, *Colombia* **134** 3 42N 73 42W
San Martin →, *Bolivia* **137** 13 8 S 63 43W
San Martín, L., *Argentina* **142** 48 50 S 72 50W
San Martín de los Andes, *Argentina* **142** 40 10 S 71 20W
San Martín de Valdeiglesias, *Spain* **22** 40 21N 4 24W
San Martino de Calvi, *Italy* **26** 45 57N 9 41 E
San Mateo, *Spain* **24** 40 28N 0 10 E
San Mateo, *U.S.A.* **124** 37 32N 122 19W
San Matías, *Bolivia* **137** 16 25 S 58 20W
San Matías, G., *Argentina* **142** 41 30 S 64 0W
San Miguel, *El Salv.* **128** 13 30N 88 12W
San Miguel, *Panama* **128** 8 27N 78 55W
San Miguel, *Spain* **25** 39 3N 1 26 E
San Miguel, *U.S.A.* **124** 35 45N 120 42W
San Miguel, *Venezuela* **134** 9 40N 65 11W
San Miguel →, *Bolivia* **137** 13 52 S 63 56W
San Miguel →, *S. Amer.* **134** 0 25N 76 30W
San Miguel de Huachi, *Bolivia* **136** 15 40 S 67 15W
San Miguel de Salinas, *Spain* **25** 37 59N 0 47W
San Miguel de Tucumán, *Argentina* **140** 26 50 S 65 20W
San Miguel del Monte, *Argentina* **140** 35 23 S 58 50W
San Miguel I., *U.S.A.* **125** 34 2N 120 23W
San Miniato, *Italy* **26** 43 40N 10 50 E
San Narciso, *Phil.* **57** 15 2N 120 3 E
San Nicolás, *Canary Is.* **25** 27 58N 15 47W
San Nicolás de los Arroyas, *Argentina* **140** 33 25 S 60 10W
San Nicolas I., *U.S.A.* **125** 33 16N 119 30W
San Onafre, *U.S.A.* **125** 33 22N 117 34W
San Onofre, *Colombia* **134** 9 44N 75 32W
San Pablo, *Bolivia* **140** 21 43 S 66 38W
San Paolo di Civitate, *Italy* **29** 41 44N 15 16 E
San Pedro, *Buenos Aires, Argentina* **141** 26 30 S 54 10W
San Pedro, *Jujuy, Argentina* **140** 24 12 S 64 55W
San Pedro, *Colombia* **134** 4 56N 71 53W
San-Pédro, *Ivory C.* **90** 4 50N 6 33W
San Pedro, *Mexico* **126** 23 55N 110 17W
San Pedro, *Peru* **136** 14 49 S 74 5W
San Pedro □, *Paraguay* **140** 24 0 S 57 0W
San Pedro →, *Chihuahua, Mexico* **126** 28 20N 106 10W
San Pedro →, *Michoacan, Mexico* **126** 19 23N 103 51W
San Pedro →, *Nayarit, Mexico* **126** 21 45N 105 30W
San Pedro →, *U.S.A.* **123** 33 0N 110 50W
San Pedro, Pta., *Chile* **140** 25 30 S 70 38W
San Pedro, Sierra de, *Spain* **23** 39 18N 6 40W
San Pedro Channel, *U.S.A.* **125** 33 35N 118 25W
San Pedro de Arimena, *Colombia* **134** 4 37N 71 42W
San Pedro de Atacama, *Chile* **140** 22 55 S 68 15W
San Pedro de Jujuy, *Argentina* **140** 24 12 S 64 55W
San Pedro de las Colonias, *Mexico* **126** 25 50N 102 59W
San Pedro de Lloc, *Peru* **136** 7 15 S 79 28W
San Pedro de Macorís, *Dom. Rep.* **129** 18 30N 69 18W
San Pedro del Norte, *Nic.* **128** 13 4N 84 33W
San Pedro del Paraná, *Paraguay* **140** 26 43 S 56 13W
San Pedro del Pinatar, *Spain* **25** 37 50N 0 50W
San Pedro Mártir, Sierra, *Mexico* **126** 31 0N 115 30W
San Pedro Mixtepec, *Mexico* **127** 16 2N 97 7W
San Pedro Ocampo = Melchor Ocampo, *Mexico* **126** 24 52N 101 40W
San Pedro Sula, *Honduras* **128** 15 30N 88 0W
San Pietro, I., *Italy* **28** 39 9N 8 17 E
San Pietro Vernótico, *Italy* **29** 40 28N 18 0 E
San Quintín, *Mexico* **126** 30 29N 115 57W
San Rafael, *Argentina* **140** 34 40 S 68 21W
San Rafael, *Calif., U.S.A.* **124** 37 59N 122 32W
San Rafael, *N. Mex., U.S.A.* **123** 35 6N 107 58W
San Rafael, *Venezuela* **134** 10 58N 71 46W
San Rafael Mt., *U.S.A.* **125** 34 41N 119 52W
San Rafael Mts, *U.S.A.* **125** 34 40N 119 50W
San Ramón, *Bolivia* **137** 13 17 S 64 43W
San Ramón, *Peru* **136** 11 8 S 75 20W
San Ramón de la Nueva Orán, *Argentina* **140** 23 10 S 64 20W
San Remo, *Australia* **74** 38 33 S 145 22 E
San Remo, *Italy* **26** 43 48N 7 47 E
San Román, C., *Venezuela* **134** 12 12N 70 0W
San Roque, *Argentina* **140** 28 25 S 58 45W
San Roque, *Spain* **23** 36 17N 5 21W
San Rosendo, *Chile* **140** 37 16 S 72 43W
San Saba, *U.S.A.* **121** 31 12N 98 45W
San Salvador, *Bahamas* **129** 24 0N 74 40W
San Salvador, *El Salv.* **128** 13 40N 89 10W
San Salvador de Jujuy, *Argentina* **140** 24 10 S 64 48W
San Salvador I., *Bahamas* **129** 24 0N 74 32W
San Sebastián, *Argentina* **142** 53 10 S 68 30W
San Sebastián, *Spain* **24** 43 17N 1 58W
San Sebastián, *Venezuela* **134** 9 57N 67 11W
San Sebastian de la Gomera, *Canary Is.* **25** 28 5N 17 7W
San Serverino Marche, *Italy* **27** 43 13N 13 10 E
San Simeon, *U.S.A.* **124** 35 44N 121 11W
San Simon, *U.S.A.* **123** 32 14N 109 16W
San Stéfano di Cadore, *Italy* **27** 46 34N 12 33 E
San Telmo, *Mexico* **126** 30 58N 116 6W
San Tiburcio, *Mexico* **126** 24 8N 101 32W
San Valentin, Mte., *Chile* **142** 46 30 S 73 30W
San Vicente de Alcántara, *Spain* **23** 39 22N 7 8W
San Vicente de la Barquera, *Spain* **22** 43 23N 4 29W
San Vicente del Caguán, *Colombia* **134** 2 7N 74 46W
San Vincenzo, *Italy* **26** 43 6N 10 29 E
San Vito, *Italy* **28** 39 26N 9 32 E
San Vito, C., *Italy* **28** 38 11N 12 41 E
San Vito al Tagliamento, *Italy* **27** 45 55N 12 50 E
San Vito Chietino, *Italy* **27** 42 19N 14 27 E
San Vito dei Normanni, *Italy* **29** 40 40N 17 40 E
San Yanaro, *Colombia* **134** 2 47N 69 42W
San Ygnacio, *U.S.A.* **121** 27 6N 99 24W
Saña, *Peru* **136** 6 54 S 79 36W
Sana', *Yemen* **45** 15 27N 44 12 E
Sana →, *Yugoslavia* **27** 45 3N 16 23 E
Sanaba, *Burkina Faso* **90** 12 25N 3 47W
Sanabria, La, *Spain* **22** 42 0N 6 30W
Şanāfīr, *Si. Arabia* **88** 27 56N 34 42 E
Sanaga →, *Cameroon* **91** 3 35N 9 38 E
Sanak I., *U.S.A.* **102** 53 30N 162 30W
Sanaloa, Presa, *Mexico* **126** 24 50N 107 20W
Sanana, *Indonesia* **57** 2 5 S 125 59 E
Sanand, *India* **48** 22 59N 72 25 E
Sanandaj, *Iran* **46** 35 18N 47 1 E
Sanandita, *Bolivia* **140** 21 40 S 63 45W
Sanary-sur-Mer, *France* **21** 43 7N 5 49 E
Sanawad, *India* **48** 22 11N 76 5 E
Sanbe-San, *Japan* **64** 35 6N 132 38 E
Sancergues, *France* **19** 47 10N 2 54 E
Sancerre, *France* **19** 47 20N 2 50 E
Sancerrois, Coll. du, *France* **19** 47 20N 2 40 E
Sancha He →, *China* **58** 26 48N 106 7 E
Sanchahe, *China* **61** 44 50N 126 2 E
Sánchez, *Dom. Rep.* **129** 19 15N 69 36W
Sanchor, *India* **48** 24 45N 71 55 E
Sanco Pt., *Phil.* **57** 8 15N 126 27 E
Sancoins, *France* **19** 46 47N 2 55 E
Sancti-Spíritus, *Cuba* **128** 21 52N 79 33W
Sancy, Puy de, *France* **20** 45 32N 2 50 E
Sand →, *S. Africa* **97** 22 25 S 30 5 E
Sand Creek →, *U.S.A.* **119** 39 5N 85 52W
Sand Springs, *U.S.A.* **121** 36 12N 96 5W
Sanda, *Japan* **65** 34 53N 135 14 E
Sandakan, *Malaysia* **56** 5 53N 118 4 E
Sandanski, *Bulgaria* **35** 41 35N 23 16 E
Sandaré, *Mali* **90** 14 40N 10 15W
Sanday, *U.K.* **14** 59 15N 2 30W
Sandefjord, *Norway* **10** 59 10N 10 15 E
Sanders, *Ariz., U.S.A.* **123** 35 12N 109 25W
Sanders, *Ky., U.S.A.* **119** 38 40N 84 56W
Sanderson, *U.S.A.* **121** 30 5N 102 30W
Sandfly L., *Canada* **111** 55 43N 106 6W
Sandgate, *Australia* **77** 27 18 S 153 3 E
Sandía, *Peru* **136** 14 10 S 69 30W
Sandıklı, *Turkey* **46** 38 30N 30 20 E
Sandnes, *Norway* **9** 58 50N 5 45 E
Sandness, *U.K.* **14** 60 18N 1 38W
Sandoa, *Zaïre* **95** 9 41 S 23 0 E
Sandon Bluffs, *Australia* **77** 29 41 S 153 20 E
Sandona, *Colombia* **134** 1 17N 77 28W
Sandongo, *Angola* **95** 15 30 S 21 28 E
Sandoval, *U.S.A.* **118** 38 37N 89 7W
Sandover →, *Australia* **72** 21 43 S 136 32 E
Sandpoint, *U.S.A.* **122** 48 20N 116 34W
Sandringham, *U.K.* **12** 52 50N 0 30 E
Sandslån, *Sweden* **10** 63 2N 17 49 E
Sandspit, *Canada* **110** 53 14N 131 49W
Sandstone, *Australia* **79** 27 59 S 119 16 E
Sandu, *China* **58** 26 0N 107 52 E
Sandusky, *Mich., U.S.A.* **116** 43 26N 82 50W
Sandusky, *Ohio, U.S.A.* **116** 41 25N 82 40W
Sandusky →, *U.S.A.* **119** 41 27N 83 0W
Sandvig, *Denmark* **11** 55 18N 14 48 E
Sandviken, *Sweden* **10** 60 38N 16 46 E
Sandwich, *U.S.A.* **119** 41 39N 88 37W
Sandwich, C., *Australia* **72** 18 14 S 146 18 E
Sandwich B., *Canada* **105** 53 40N 57 15W
Sandwich B., *Namibia* **96** 23 25 S 14 20 E
Sandy, *Nev., U.S.A.* **125** 35 49N 115 36W
Sandy, *Oreg., U.S.A.* **124** 45 24N 122 16W
Sandy Bight, *Australia* **79** 33 50 S 123 20 E
Sandy C., *Queens., Australia* **73** 24 42 S 153 15 E
Sandy C., *Tas., Australia* **72** 41 25 S 144 45 E
Sandy Cay, *Bahamas* **129** 23 13N 75 18W
Sandy Cr. →, *U.S.A.* **122** 41 15N 109 47W
Sandy Hollow, *Australia* **76** 32 20 S 150 32 E
Sandy L., *Canada* **104** 53 2N 93 0W
Sandy Lake, *Canada* **104** 53 0N 93 15W
Sandy Narrows, *Canada* **111** 55 5N 103 4W
Sandy Point, *Australia* **74** 38 50 S 146 6 E
Sanford, *Fla., U.S.A.* **115** 28 45N 81 20W
Sanford, *Maine, U.S.A.* **117** 43 28N 70 47W
Sanford, *N.C., U.S.A.* **115** 35 30N 79 10W
Sanford →, *Australia* **79** 27 22 S 115 53 E
Sanford Mt., *U.S.A.* **102** 62 30N 143 0W
Sang-i-Masha, *Afghan.* **48** 33 8N 67 27 E
Sanga, *Mozam.* **93** 12 22 S 35 21 E
Sanga →, *Congo* **94** 1 5 S 17 0 E
Sanga-Tolon, *U.S.S.R.* **41** 61 50N 149 40 E
Sangamner, *India* **50** 19 37N 74 15 E
Sangamon →, *U.S.A.* **118** 40 2N 90 21W
Sangar, *Afghan.* **48** 32 56N 65 30 E
Sangar, *U.S.S.R.* **41** 64 2N 127 31 E
Sangar Sarai, *Afghan.* **48** 34 27N 70 35 E
Sangasangadalam, *Indonesia* **56** 0 36 S 117 13 E
Sangay, *Ecuador* **134** 2 0 S 78 20W
Sange, *Zaïre* **92** 6 58 S 28 21 E
Sangeang, *Indonesia* **57** 8 12 S 119 6 E
Sanger, *U.S.A.* **124** 36 41N 119 35W
Sangerhausen, *E. Germany* **30** 51 28N 11 18 E
Sanggan He →, *China* **60** 38 12N 117 15 E
Sanggau, *Indonesia* **56** 0 5N 110 30 E
Sangihe, Kepulauan, *Indonesia* **57** 3 0N 126 0 E
Sangihe, P., *Indonesia* **57** 3 45N 125 30 E
Sangkapura, *Indonesia* **56** 5 52 S 112 40 E
Sangkhla, *Thailand* **54** 14 57N 98 28 E
Sangli, *India* **50** 16 55N 74 33 E
Sangmélina, *Cameroon* **91** 2 57N 12 1 E
Sangonera →, *Spain* **25** 37 59N 1 4W
Sangpang Bum, *Burma* **52** 26 30N 95 50 E
Sangre de Cristo Mts., *U.S.A.* **121** 37 0N 105 0W
Sangro →, *Italy* **27** 42 14N 14 32 E
Sangudo, *Canada* **110** 53 50N 114 54W
Sangue →, *Brazil* **137** 11 1 S 58 39W
Sangüesa, *Spain* **24** 42 37N 1 17W
Sanguinaires, Is., *France* **21** 41 51N 8 36 E
Sangzhi, *China* **59** 29 25N 110 12 E
Sanhala, *Ivory C.* **90** 10 3N 6 51W
Sanje, *Uganda* **92** 0 49 S 31 30 E
Sanjiang, *China* **58** 25 48N 109 37 E
Sankarankovil, *India* **51** 9 10N 77 35 E
Sankeshwar, *India* **51** 16 23N 74 32 E
Sankosh →, *India* **52** 26 24N 89 47 E
Sankt Blasien, *W. Germany* **31** 47 47N 8 7 E
Sankt Gallen, *Switz.* **31** 47 26N 9 22 E
Sankt Gallen □, *Switz.* **31** 47 25N 9 22 E
Sankt Ingbert, *W. Germany* **31** 49 16N 7 6 E
Sankt Moritz, *Switz.* **31** 46 30N 9 50 E
Sankt Olof, *Sweden* **11** 55 37N 14 8 E
Sankt Pölten, *Austria* **33** 48 12N 15 38 E
Sankt Valentin, *Austria* **33** 48 11N 14 33 E
Sankt Veit, *Austria* **33** 46 54N 14 22 E
Sankt Wendel, *W. Germany* **31** 49 27N 7 9 E
Sankuru →, *Zaïre* **95** 4 17 S 20 25 E
Sanlúcar de Barrameda, *Spain* **23** 36 46N 6 21W
Sanlúcar la Mayor, *Spain* **23** 37 26N 6 18W
Sanluri, *Italy* **28** 39 35N 8 55 E
Sanmaur, *Canada* **107** 47 54N 73 47W
Sanmenxia, *China* **60** 34 47N 111 12 E
Sanming, *China* **59** 26 15N 117 40 E
Sannan, *Japan* **65** 35 2N 135 1 E
Sannaspos, *S. Africa* **96** 29 6 S 26 34 E
Sannicandro Gargánico, *Italy* **29** 41 50N 15 34 E
Sannidal, *Norway* **10** 58 55N 9 15 E
Sannieshof, *S. Africa* **96** 26 30 S 25 47 E
Sano, *Japan* **65** 36 19N 139 35 E
Sanok, *Poland* **32** 49 35N 22 10 E
Sanquhar, *U.K.* **14** 55 21N 3 56W
Sansanding Dam, *Mali* **90** 13 48N 6 0W
Sansepolcro, *Italy* **27** 43 34N 12 8 E
Sansha, *China* **59** 26 58N 120 12 E
Sanshui, *China* **59** 23 10N 112 56 E
Sanski Most, *Yugoslavia* **27** 44 46N 16 40 E
Sansui, *China* **58** 26 58N 108 39 E
Santa, *Peru* **136** 8 59 S 78 40W
Sant' Ágata de Goti, *Italy* **29** 41 6N 14 30 E
Sant' Ágata di Militello, *Italy* **29** 38 2N 14 8 E
Santa Ana, *Beni, Bolivia* **137** 13 50 S 65 40W
Santa Ana, *Santa Cruz, Bolivia* **137** 18 43 S 58 44W
Santa Ana, *Santa Cruz, Bolivia* **137** 16 37 S 60 43W
Santa Ana, *Ecuador* **134** 1 16 S 80 20W
Santa Ana, *El Salv.* **128** 14 0N 89 31W
Santa Ana, *Mexico* **126** 30 31N 111 8W
Santa Ana, *U.S.A.* **125** 33 48N 117 55W
Santa Ana →, *Venezuela* **134** 9 30N 71 57W
Sant' Ángelo Lodigiano, *Italy* **26** 45 14N 9 25 E
Sant' Antíoco, *Italy* **28** 39 2N 8 30 E
Sant' Arcángelo di Romagna, *Italy* **27** 44 4N 12 26 E
Santa Bárbara, *Colombia* **134** 5 53N 75 35W
Santa Barbara, *Honduras* **128** 14 53N 88 14W
Santa Bárbara, *Mexico* **126** 26 48N 105 50W
Santa Bárbara, *Spain* **24** 40 42N 0 29 E
Santa Barbara, *U.S.A.* **125** 34 25N 119 40W
Santa Bárbara, *Venezuela* **134** 7 47N 71 10W
Santa Bárbara, Mt., *Spain* **25** 37 23N 2 50W
Santa Barbara Channel, *U.S.A.* **125** 34 20N 120 0W
Santa Barbara I., *U.S.A.* **125** 33 29N 119 2W
Santa Catalina, *Colombia* **134** 10 36N 75 17W
Santa Catalina, *Mexico* **126** 25 40N 110 50W
Santa Catalina, G. of, *U.S.A.* **125** 33 0N 118 0W
Santa Catalina I., *U.S.A.* **125** 33 20N 118 30W
Santa Catarina □, *Brazil* **141** 27 25 S 48 30W
Santa Catarina, I. de, *Brazil* **141** 27 30 S 48 40W
Santa Caterina Villarmosa, *Italy* **29** 37 37N 14 1 E
Santa Cecília, *Brazil* **141** 26 56 S 50 18W
Santa Clara, *Cuba* **128** 22 20N 80 0W
Santa Clara, *Calif., U.S.A.* **124** 37 21N 122 0W
Santa Clara, *Utah, U.S.A.* **123** 37 10N 113 38W
Santa Clara de Olimar, *Uruguay* **141** 32 50 S 54 54W
Santa Clotilde, *Peru* **134** 2 33 S 73 45W
Santa Coloma de Farners, *Spain* **24** 41 50N 2 39 E
Santa Coloma de Gramanet, *Spain* **24** 41 27N 2 13 E
Santa Comba, *Spain* **22** 43 2N 8 49W
Santa Croce Camerina, *Italy* **29** 36 50N 14 30 E
Santa Croce di Magliano, *Italy* **29** 41 43N 14 59 E
Santa Cruz, *Argentina* **142** 50 0 S 68 32W
Santa Cruz, *Bolivia* **137** 17 43 S 63 10W
Santa Cruz, *Brazil* **138** 6 13 S 36 1W
Santa Cruz, *Chile* **140** 34 38 S 71 27W
Santa Cruz, *Costa Rica* **128** 10 15N 85 35W
Santa Cruz, *Peru* **136** 5 40 S 75 56W
Santa Cruz, *Phil.* **57** 14 20N 121 24 E
Santa Cruz, *U.S.A.* **124** 36 55N 122 1W
Santa Cruz, *Venezuela* **135** 8 3N 64 27W
Santa Cruz □, *Argentina* **142** 49 0 S 70 0W
Santa Cruz □, *Bolivia* **137** 17 43 S 63 10W

Santa Cruz →, *Argentina* **142** 50 10 S 68 20W
Santa Cruz, I., *Solomon Is.* **66** 10 30 S 166 0 E
Santa Cruz Cabrália, *Brazil* **139** 16 17 S 39 2W
Santa Cruz de la Palma, *Canary Is.* **25** 28 41N 17 46W
Santa Cruz de Mudela, *Spain* **25** 38 39N 3 28W
Santa Cruz de Tenerife, *Canary Is.* **25** 28 28N 16 15W
Santa Cruz del Norte, *Cuba* **128** 23 9N 81 55W
Santa Cruz del Retamar, *Spain* **22** 40 8N 4 14W
Santa Cruz del Sur, *Cuba* **128** 20 44N 78 0W
Santa Cruz do Rio Pardo, *Brazil* **141** 22 54 S 49 37W
Santa Cruz do Sul, *Brazil* **141** 29 42 S 52 25W
Santa Cruz I., *U.S.A.* **125** 34 0N 119 45W
Santa Domingo, Cay, *Bahamas* **128** 21 25N 75 15W
Santa Elena, *Argentina* **140** 30 58 S 59 47W
Santa Elena, *Ecuador* **134** 2 16 S 80 52W
Santa Elena, C., *Costa Rica* **128** 10 54N 85 56W
Sant' Eufémia, G. di, *Italy* **29** 38 50N 16 10 E
Santa Eugenia, Pta., *Mexico* **126** 27 50N 115 5W
Santa Eulalia, *Spain* **25** 38 59N 1 32 E
Santa Fe, *Argentina* **140** 31 35 S 60 41W
Santa Fe, *Spain* **23** 37 11N 3 43W
Santa Fe, *U.S.A.* **123** 35 40N 106 0W
Santa Fé □, *Argentina* **140** 31 50 S 60 55W
Santa Filomena, *Brazil* **138** 9 6 S 45 50W
Santa Helena, *Brazil* **138** 2 14 S 45 18W
Santa Helena de Goiás, *Brazil* **139** 17 53 S 50 35W
Santa Inês, *Brazil* **139** 13 17 S 39 48W
Santa Inés, *Spain* **23** 38 32N 5 37W
Santa Inés, I., *Chile* **142** 54 0 S 73 0W
Santa Isabel = Rey Malabo, *Eq. Guin.* **91** 3 45N 8 50 E
Santa Isabel, *Argentina* **140** 36 10 S 66 54W
Santa Isabel, *Brazil* **139** 11 45 S 51 30W
Santa Isabel, *Solomon Is.* **68** 8 0 S 159 0 E
Santa Isabel, Pico, *Eq. Guin.* **91** 3 36N 8 49 E
Santa Isabel do Araguaia, *Brazil* **138** 6 7 S 48 19W
Santa Isabel do Morro, *Brazil* **139** 11 34 S 50 40W
Santa Lucía, *Corrientes, Argentina* **140** 28 58 S 59 5W
Santa Lucía, *San Juan, Argentina* **140** 31 30 S 68 30W
Santa Lucía, *Spain* **25** 37 35N 0 58W
Santa Lucía, *Uruguay* **140** 34 27 S 56 24W
Santa Lucia Range, *U.S.A.* **124** 36 0N 121 20W
Santa Magdalena, I., *Mexico* **126** 24 40N 112 15W
Santa Margarita, *Argentina* **140** 38 28 S 61 35W
Santa Margarita, *Mexico* **126** 24 30N 111 50W
Santa Margarita, *U.S.A.* **124** 35 23N 120 37W
Santa Margarita →, *U.S.A.* **125** 33 13N 117 23W
Santa Margherita, *Italy* **26** 44 20N 9 11 E
Santa María, *Argentina* **140** 26 40 S 66 0W
Santa Maria, *Brazil* **141** 29 40 S 53 48W
Santa Maria, *Spain* **24** 39 38N 2 47 E
Santa Maria, *U.S.A.* **125** 34 58N 120 29W
Santa Maria, *Zambia* **93** 11 5 S 29 58 E
Santa María →, *Mexico* **126** 31 0N 107 14W
Santa María, B. de, *Mexico* **126** 25 10N 108 40W
Santa Maria, C. de, *Portugal* **23** 36 58N 7 53W
Santa Maria Capua Vetere, *Italy* **29** 41 3N 14 15 E
Santa Maria da Vitória, *Brazil* **139** 13 24 S 44 12W
Santa María de Ipire, *Venezuela* **135** 8 49N 65 19W
Santa Maria di Leuca, C., *Italy* **29** 39 48N 18 20 E
Santa Maria do Suaçuí, *Brazil* **139** 18 12 S 42 25W
Santa Maria dos Marmelos, *Brazil* **137** 6 7 S 61 51W
Santa María la Real de Nieva, *Spain* **22** 41 4N 4 24W
Santa Marta, *Colombia* **134** 11 15N 74 13W
Santa Marta, *Spain* **23** 38 37N 6 39W
Santa Marta, Ría de, *Spain* **22** 43 44N 7 45W
Santa Marta, Sierra Nevada de, *Colombia* **134** 10 55N 73 50W
Santa Marta Grande, C., *Brazil* **141** 28 43 S 48 50W
Santa Maura = Levkás, *Greece* **35** 38 40N 20 43 E
Santa Monica, *U.S.A.* **125** 34 0N 118 30W
Santa Olalla, *Huelva, Spain* **23** 37 54N 6 14W
Santa Olalla, *Toledo, Spain* **22** 40 2N 4 25W
Santa Ona, *Solomon Is.* **68** 10 0 S 162 0 E
Sant' Onofrio, *Italy* **29** 38 42N 16 10 E
Santa Pola, *Spain* **25** 38 13N 0 35W
Santa Quitéria, *Brazil* **138** 4 20 S 40 10W
Santa Rita, *U.S.A.* **123** 32 50N 108 0W
Santa Rita, *Guarico, Venezuela* **134** 8 8N 66 16W
Santa Rita, *Zulia, Venezuela* **134** 10 32N 71 32W
Santa Rita do Araquaia, *Brazil* **137** 17 20 S 53 12W
Santa Rosa, *La Pampa, Argentina* **140** 36 40 S 64 17W
Santa Rosa, *San Luis, Argentina* **140** 32 21 S 65 10W
Santa Rosa, *Bolivia* **136** 10 36 S 67 20W
Santa Rosa, *Brazil* **141** 27 52 S 54 29W
Santa Rosa, *Colombia* **134** 3 32N 69 48W
Santa Rosa, *Ecuador* **134** 3 27 S 79 58W
Santa Rosa, *Peru* **136** 14 30 S 70 50W
Santa Rosa, *Calif., U.S.A.* **124** 38 26N 122 43W
Santa Rosa, *N. Mex., U.S.A.* **121** 34 58N 104 40W
Santa Rosa, *Venezuela* **134** 1 29N 66 55W
Santa Rosa de Cabal, *Colombia* **134** 4 52N 75 38W
Santa Rosa de Copán, *Honduras* **128** 14 47N 88 46W
Santa Rosa de Osos, *Colombia* **134** 6 39N 75 28W
Santa Rosa de Río Primero, *Argentina* **140** 31 8 S 63 20W
Santa Rosa de Viterbo, *Colombia* **134** 5 53N 72 59W
Santa Rosa del Palmar, *Bolivia* **137** 16 54 S 62 24W
Santa Rosa I., *Calif., U.S.A.* **125** 34 0N 120 6W
Santa Rosa I., *Fla., U.S.A.* **115** 30 23N 87 0W
Santa Rosa Ra., *U.S.A.* **122** 41 45N 117 30W
Santa Rosalía, *Mexico* **126** 27 20N 112 20W
Santa Sofia, *Italy* **27** 43 57N 11 55 E
Santa Sylvina, *Argentina* **140** 27 50 S 61 10W
Santa Tecla = Nueva San Salvador, *El Salv.* **128** 13 40N 89 18W
Santa Teresa, *Argentina* **140** 33 25 S 60 47W
Santa Teresa, *Brazil* **139** 19 55 S 40 36W
Santa Teresa, *Mexico* **127** 25 17N 97 51W
Santa Teresa, *Venezuela* **135** 4 43N 61 4W
Santa Teresa di Riva, *Italy* **29** 37 58N 15 21 E
Santa Teresa Gallura, *Italy* **28** 41 14N 9 12 E
Santa Vitória, *Brazil* **139** 18 50 S 50 8W
Santa Vitória do Palmar, *Brazil* **141** 33 32 S 53 25W
Santa Ynez, *U.S.A.* **125** 34 37N 120 5W
Santa Ynez →, *U.S.A.* **125** 34 37N 120 41W
Santa Ysabel, *U.S.A.* **125** 33 7N 116 40W
Santadi, *Italy* **28** 39 5N 8 42 E
Santahar, *Bangla.* **52** 24 48N 88 59 E
Santai, *China* **58** 31 5N 104 58 E
Santaluz, *Brazil* **138** 11 15 S 39 22W
Santana, *Brazil* **139** 13 2 S 44 5W
Santana, Coxilha de, *Brazil* **141** 30 50 S 55 35W
Santana do Ipanema, *Brazil* **138** 9 22 S 37 14W
Santana do Livramento, *Brazil* **141** 30 55 S 55 30W
Santanayi, *Spain* **25** 39 20N 3 5 E
Santander, *Colombia* **134** 3 1N 76 28W
Santander, *Spain* **22** 43 27N 3 51W
Santander □, *Spain* **22** 43 25N 4 0W
Santander Jiménez, *Mexico* **127** 24 11N 98 29W
Santaquin, *U.S.A.* **122** 40 0N 111 51W
Santarém, *Brazil* **135** 2 25 S 54 42W
Santarém, *Portugal* **23** 39 12N 8 42W
Santarém □, *Portugal* **23** 39 10N 8 40W
Santaren Channel, *W. Indies* **128** 24 0N 79 30W
Santee, *U.S.A.* **125** 32 50N 116 58W
Santéramo in Colle, *Italy* **29** 40 48N 16 45 E
Santerno →, *Italy* **27** 44 10N 11 38 E
Santhia, *Italy* **26** 45 20N 8 10 E
Santiago, *Bolivia* **137** 18 19 S 59 34W
Santiago, *Brazil* **141** 29 11 S 54 52W
Santiago, *Chile* **140** 33 24 S 70 40W
Santiago, *Panama* **128** 8 0N 81 0W
Santiago, *Peru* **136** 14 11 S 75 43W
Santiago □, *Chile* **140** 33 30 S 70 50W
Santiago →, *Peru* **134** 4 27 S 77 38W
Santiago, C., *Chile* **142** 50 46 S 75 27W
Santiago, Punta de, *Eq. Guin.* **91** 3 12N 8 40 E
Santiago, Serranía de, *Bolivia* **137** 18 25 S 59 25W
Santiago de Chuco, *Peru* **136** 8 9 S 78 11W
Santiago de Compostela, *Spain* **22** 42 52N 8 37W
Santiago de Cuba, *Cuba* **128** 20 0N 75 49W
Santiago de los Cabelleros, *Dom. Rep.* **129** 19 30N 70 40W
Santiago del Estero, *Argentina* **140** 27 50 S 64 15W
Santiago del Estero □, *Argentina* **140** 27 40 S 63 15W
Santiago del Teide, *Canary Is.* **25** 28 17N 16 48W
Santiago do Cacém, *Portugal* **23** 38 1N 8 42W
Santiago Ixcuintla, *Mexico* **126** 21 50N 105 11W
Santiago Papasquiaro, *Mexico* **126** 25 0N 105 20W
Santiaguillo, L. de, *Mexico* **126** 24 50N 104 50W
Santillana del Mar, *Spain* **22** 43 24N 4 6W
Santisteban del Puerto, *Spain* **25** 38 17N 3 15W
Santo, *Vanuatu* **68** 15 27 S 167 10 E
Santo →, *Peru* **136** 8 56 S 78 37W
Santo Amaro, *Brazil* **139** 12 30 S 38 43W
Santo Anastácio, *Brazil* **141** 21 58 S 51 39W
Santo André, *Brazil* **141** 23 39 S 46 29W
Santo Ângelo, *Brazil* **141** 28 15 S 54 15W
Santo Antonio, *Brazil* **137** 15 50 S 56 0W
Santo Antônio de Jesus, *Brazil* **139** 12 58 S 39 16W
Santo Antônio do Içá, *Brazil* **134** 3 5 S 67 57W
Santo Antônio do Leverger, *Brazil* **137** 15 52 S 56 5W
Santo Corazón, *Bolivia* **137** 18 0 S 58 45W
Santo Domingo, *Dom. Rep.* **129** 18 30N 69 59W
Santo Domingo, *Baja Calif. N., Mexico* **126** 30 43N 116 2W
Santo Domingo, *Baja Calif. S., Mexico* **126** 25 32N 112 2W
Santo Domingo, *Nic.* **128** 12 14N 84 59W
Santo Domingo de la Calzada, *Spain* **24** 42 26N 2 57W
Santo Domingo de los Colorados, *Ecuador* **134** 0 15 S 79 9W
Santo Stéfano di Camastro, *Italy* **29** 38 1N 14 22 E
Santo Stino di Livenza, *Italy* **27** 45 45N 12 40 E
Santo Tirso, *Portugal* **22** 41 21N 8 28W
Santo Tomás, *Mexico* **126** 31 33N 116 24W
Santo Tomás, *Peru* **136** 14 26 S 72 8W
Santo Tomé, *Argentina* **141** 28 40 S 56 5W
Santo Tomé de Guayana = Ciudad Guayana, *Venezuela* **135** 8 0N 62 30W
Santoña, *Spain* **22** 43 29N 3 27W
Santos, *Brazil* **141** 24 0 S 46 20W
Santos, Sierra de los, *Spain* **23** 38 7N 5 12W
Santos Dumont, *Brazil* **141** 22 55 S 43 10W
Santpoort, *Neths.* **16** 52 26N 4 39 E
Sānūr, *Jordan* **44** 32 22N 35 15 E
Sanvignes-les-Mines, *France* **19** 46 40N 4 18 E
San'yō, *Japan* **64** 34 2N 131 5 E
Sanyuan, *China* **60** 34 35N 108 58 E
Sanyuki-Sammyaku, *Japan* **64** 34 5N 133 0 E
Sanza Pombo, *Angola* **95** 7 18 S 15 56 E
São Anastácio, *Brazil* **141** 22 0 S 51 40W
São Bartolomeu de Messines, *Portugal* **23** 37 15N 8 17W
São Benedito, *Brazil* **138** 4 3 S 40 53W
São Bento, *Brazil* **138** 2 42 S 44 50W
São Bento do Norte, *Brazil* **138** 5 4 S 36 2W
São Bernado de Campo, *Brazil* **139** 23 45 S 46 34W
São Borja, *Brazil* **141** 28 39 S 56 0W
São Bras d'Alportel, *Portugal* **23** 37 8N 7 37W
São Caitano, *Brazil* **138** 8 21 S 36 6W
São Carlos, *Brazil* **141** 22 0 S 47 50W
São Cristóvão, *Brazil* **138** 11 1 S 37 15W
São Domingos, *Brazil* **139** 13 25 S 46 19W
São Domingos do Maranhão, *Brazil* **138** 5 42 S 44 22W
São Félix, *Brazil* **139** 11 36 S 50 39W
São Francisco, *Brazil* **139** 16 0 S 44 50W
São Francisco →, *Brazil* **138** 10 30 S 36 24W
São Francisco do Maranhão, *Brazil* **138** 6 15 S 42 52W
São Francisco do Sul, *Brazil* **141** 26 15 S 48 36W
São Gabriel, *Brazil* **141** 30 20 S 54 20W
São Gabriel da Palha, *Brazil* **139** 18 47 S 40 39W
São Gonçalo, *Brazil* **139** 22 48 S 43 5W
São Gotardo, *Brazil* **139** 19 19 S 46 3W
Sao Hill, *Tanzania* **93** 8 20 S 35 12 E
São João da Boa Vista, *Brazil* **141** 22 0 S 46 52W
São João da Pesqueira, *Portugal* **22** 41 8N 7 24W
São João da Ponte, *Brazil* **139** 15 56 S 44 1W
São João del Rei, *Brazil* **139** 21 8 S 44 15W
São João do Araguaia, *Brazil* **138** 5 23 S 48 46W
São João do Paraíso, *Brazil* **139** 15 19 S 42 1W
São João do Piauí, *Brazil* **138** 8 21 S 42 15W
São João dos Patos, *Brazil* **138** 6 30 S 43 42W
São Joaquim da Barra, *Brazil* **139** 20 35 S 47 53W
São José, B. de, *Brazil* **138** 2 38 S 44 4W
São José da Laje, *Brazil* **138** 9 1 S 36 3W
São José de Mipibu, *Brazil* **138** 6 5 S 35 15W
São José do Peixe, *Brazil* **138** 7 24 S 42 34W
São José do Rio Prêto, *Brazil* **141** 20 50 S 49 20W
São José dos Campos, *Brazil* **141** 23 7 S 45 52W
São Leopoldo, *Brazil* **141** 29 50 S 51 10W
São Lourenço, *Brazil* **139** 22 7 S 45 3W
São Lourenço →, *Brazil* **137** 17 53 S 57 27W
São Lourenço, Pantanal do, *Brazil* **137** 17 30 S 56 20W
São Luís, *Brazil* **138** 2 39 S 44 15W
São Luís do Curu, *Brazil* **138** 3 40 S 39 14W
São Luís Gonzaga, *Brazil* **141** 28 25 S 55 0W
São Marcos →, *Brazil* **139** 18 15 S 47 37W
São Marcos, B. de, *Brazil* **138** 2 0 S 44 0W
São Martinho, *Portugal* **22** 40 18N 8 8W
São Mateus, *Brazil* **139** 18 44 S 39 50W
São Mateus →, *Brazil* **139** 18 35 S 39 44W
São Miguel do Araguaia, *Brazil* **139** 13 19 S 50 13W
São Miguel dos Campos, *Brazil* **138** 9 47 S 36 5W
São Nicolau →, *Brazil* **138** 5 45 S 42 2W
São Paulo, *Brazil* **141** 23 32 S 46 37W
São Paulo □, *Brazil* **141** 22 0 S 49 0W
Sao Paulo, I., *Atl. Oc.* **4** 0 50N 31 40W
São Paulo de Olivença, *Brazil* **134** 3 27 S 68 48W
São Pedro do Sul, *Portugal* **22** 40 46N 8 4W
São Rafael, *Brazil* **138** 5 47 S 36 55W
São Raimundo das Mangabeiras, *Brazil* **138** 7 1 S 45 29W
São Raimundo Nonato, *Brazil* **138** 9 1 S 42 42W
São Romão, *Brazil* **139** 16 22 S 45 4W
São Roque, C. de, *Brazil* **138** 5 30 S 35 16W
São Sebastião, I. de, *Brazil* **141** 23 50 S 45 18W
São Sebastião do Paraíso, *Brazil* **141** 20 54 S 46 59W
São Simão, *Brazil* **139** 18 56 S 50 30W
São Teotónio, *Portugal* **23** 37 30N 8 42W
São Tomé, *Atl. Oc.* **87** 0 10N 6 39 E
São Tomé, *Brazil* **138** 5 58 S 36 4W
São Tomé, C. de, *Brazil* **139** 22 0 S 40 59W
São Tomé & Principe ■, *Africa* **95** 0 12N 6 39 E
São Vicente, *Brazil* **141** 23 57 S 46 23W
São Vicente, C. de, *Portugal* **23** 37 0N 9 0W
Saona, I., *Dom. Rep.* **129** 18 10N 68 40W
Saône →, *France* **21** 45 44N 4 50 E
Saône-et-Loire □, *France* **19** 46 30N 4 50 E
Saonek, *Indonesia* **57** 0 22 S 130 55 E
Saoura, O. →, *Algeria* **85** 29 0N 0 55W
Sapão →, *Brazil* **138** 11 1 S 45 32W
Saparua, *Indonesia* **57** 3 33 S 128 40 E
Sapé, *Brazil* **138** 7 6 S 35 13W
Sapele, *Nigeria* **91** 5 50N 5 40 E
Sapelo I., *U.S.A.* **115** 31 28N 81 15W
Sapiéntza, *Greece* **35** 36 45N 21 43 E
Sapone, *Burkina Faso* **91** 12 3N 1 35W
Saposoa, *Peru* **136** 6 55 S 76 45W
Sapozhok, *U.S.S.R.* **37** 53 59N 40 41 E
Sappemeer, *Neths.* **16** 53 10N 6 48 E
Sappho, *U.S.A.* **124** 48 4N 124 16W
Sapporo, *Japan* **63** 43 0N 141 21 E
Sapri, *Italy* **29** 40 5N 15 37 E
Sapudi, *Indonesia* **57** 7 6 S 114 20 E
Sapulpa, *U.S.A.* **121** 36 0N 96 0W
Saqqez, *Iran* **46** 36 15N 46 20 E
Sar-e Pol, *Afghan.* **47** 36 10N 66 0 E
Sar Planina, *Yugoslavia* **34** 42 10N 21 0 E
Sara, *Burkina Faso* **90** 11 40N 3 53W
Sara Buri, *Thailand* **54** 14 30N 100 55 E
Sarāb, *Iran* **46** 38 0N 47 30 E
Saragossa = Zaragoza, *Spain* **24** 41 39N 0 53W
Saraguro, *Ecuador* **134** 3 35 S 79 16W
Saraipali, *India* **50** 21 20N 82 59 E
Sarajevo, *Yugoslavia* **33** 43 52N 18 26 E
Saramacca □, *Surinam* **135** 5 0N 56 0W
Saramacca →, *Surinam* **135** 5 50N 55 55W
Saramati, *Burma* **52** 25 44N 95 2 E
Saran, G., *Indonesia* **56** 0 30 S 111 25 E
Saranac, *U.S.A.* **119** 42 56N 85 13W
Saranac Lake, *U.S.A.* **117** 44 20N 74 10W

Saranda, *Tanzania* **92** 5 45 S 34 59 E
Sarandí del Yi, *Uruguay* **141** 33 18 S 55 38W
Sarandí Grande, *Uruguay* **140** 33 44 S 56 20W
Sarangani B., *Phil.* **57** 6 0N 125 13 E
Sarangani Is., *Phil.* **57** 5 25N 125 25 E
Sarangarh, *India* **50** 21 30N 83 5 E
Saransk, *U.S.S.R.* **37** 54 10N 45 10 E
Sarapul, *U.S.S.R.* **40** 56 28N 53 48 E
Sarar Plain, *Somali Rep.* **98** 9 25N 46 17 E
Sarasota, *U.S.A.* **115** 27 20N 82 30W
Saratoga, *Calif., U.S.A.* **124** 37 16N 122 2W
Saratoga, *Wyo., U.S.A.* **122** 41 30N 106 48W
Saratoga Springs, *U.S.A.* **117** 43 5N 73 47W
Saratov, *U.S.S.R.* **37** 51 30N 46 2 E
Saravane, *Laos* **54** 15 43N 106 25 E
Sarawak □, *Malaysia* **56** 2 0N 113 0 E
Saraya, *Senegal* **90** 12 50N 11 45W
Sarbāz, *Iran* **47** 26 38N 61 19 E
Sarbīsheh, *Iran* **47** 32 30N 59 40 E
Sarca →, *Italy* **26** 45 52N 10 52 E
Sardalas, *Libya* **86** 25 50N 10 34 E
Sardarshahr, *India* **48** 28 30N 74 29 E
Sardegna, *Italy* **28** 39 57N 9 0 E
Sardhana, *India* **48** 29 9N 77 39 E
Sardina, Pta., *Canary Is.* **25** 28 9N 15 44W
Sardinata, *Colombia* **134** 8 5N 72 48W
Sardinia = Sardegna, *Italy* **28** 39 57N 9 0 E
Sardinia, *U.S.A.* **119** 39 0N 83 49W
Saréyamou, *Mali* **90** 16 7N 3 10W
Sargasso Sea, *Atl. Oc.* **130** 27 0N 72 0W
Sargent, *U.S.A.* **120** 41 42N 99 24W
Sargodha, *Pakistan* **48** 32 10N 72 40 E
Sarh, *Chad* **87** 9 5N 18 23 E
Sarhro, Djebel, *Morocco* **84** 31 6N 5 0W
Sārī, *Iran* **47** 36 30N 53 4 E
Sária, *Greece* **35** 35 54N 27 17 E
Saricumbe, *Angola* **95** 12 12 S 19 46 E
Sarida →, *Jordan* **44** 32 4N 34 45 E
Sarikamiş, *Turkey* **46** 40 22N 42 35 E
Sarikei, *Malaysia* **56** 2 8N 111 30 E
Sarina, *Australia* **72** 21 22 S 149 13 E
Sariñena, *Spain* **24** 41 47N 0 10W
Sarīr Tibasti, *Libya* **86** 22 50N 18 30 E
Sarita, *U.S.A.* **121** 27 14N 97 49W
Sariyer, *Turkey* **35** 41 10N 29 3 E
Sark, *Chan. Is.* **18** 49 25N 2 20W
Sarkad, *Hungary* **33** 46 47N 21 23 E
Sarlat-la-Canéda, *France* **20** 44 54N 1 13 E
Sarles, *U.S.A.* **120** 48 58N 99 0W
Sărmaşu, *Romania* **34** 46 45N 24 13 E
Sarmi, *Indonesia* **57** 1 49 S 138 44 E
Sarmiento, *Argentina* **142** 45 35 S 69 5W
Särna, *Sweden* **10** 61 41N 13 8 E
Sarnano, *Italy* **27** 43 2N 13 17 E
Sarnen, *Switz.* **31** 46 53N 8 13 E
Sarnia, *Canada* **108** 42 58N 82 23W
Sarno, *Italy* **29** 40 48N 14 35 E
Sarny, *U.S.S.R.* **36** 51 17N 26 40 E
Särö, *Sweden* **11** 57 31N 11 57 E
Sarolangun, *Indonesia* **56** 2 19 S 102 42 E
Saronikós Kólpos, *Greece* **35** 37 45N 23 45 E
Saronno, *Italy* **26** 45 38N 9 2 E
Sárospatak, *Hungary* **33** 48 18N 21 33 E
Sarova, *U.S.S.R.* **37** 54 55N 43 19 E
Sarpsborg, *Norway* **10** 59 16N 11 12 E
Sarracín, *Spain* **24** 42 15N 3 45W
Sarralbe, *France* **19** 49 0N 7 1 E
Sarre = Saar →, *Europe* **19** 49 41N 6 32 E
Sarre, La, *Canada* **106** 48 45N 79 15W
Sarre-Union, *France* **19** 48 57N 7 4 E
Sarrebourg, *France* **19** 48 43N 7 3 E
Sarreguemines, *France* **19** 49 5N 7 4 E
Sarriá, *Spain* **22** 42 49N 7 29W
Sarrión, *Spain* **24** 40 9N 0 49W
Sarro, *Mali* **90** 13 40N 5 15W
Sarstedt, *W. Germany* **30** 52 13N 9 50 E
Sartène, *France* **21** 41 38N 8 58 E
Sarthe □, *France* **18** 47 58N 0 10 E
Sarthe →, *France* **18** 47 33N 0 31W
Sartilly, *France* **18** 48 45N 1 28W
Sartynya, *U.S.S.R.* **40** 63 22N 63 11 E
Sárvár, *Hungary* **33** 47 15N 16 56 E
Sarvestān, *Iran* **47** 29 20N 53 10 E
Särvfjället, *Sweden* **10** 62 42N 13 30 E
Sárviz →, *Hungary* **33** 46 24N 18 41 E
Sary-Tash, *U.S.S.R.* **40** 39 44N 73 15 E
Sarych, Mys., *U.S.S.R.* **38** 44 25N 33 45 E
Saryshagan, *U.S.S.R.* **40** 46 12N 73 38 E
Sarzana, *Italy* **26** 44 5N 9 59 E
Sarzeau, *France* **18** 47 31N 2 48W
Sas van Gent, *Neths.* **17** 51 14N 3 48 E
Sasa, *Israel* **44** 33 2N 35 23 E
Sasabeneh, *Ethiopia* **98** 7 59N 44 43 E
Sasamungga, *Solomon Is.* **68** 7 0 S 156 50 E
Sasaram, *India* **49** 24 57N 84 5 E
Sasayama, *Japan* **65** 35 4N 135 13 E
Sasebo, *Japan* **64** 33 10N 129 43 E
Saseginaga, L., *Canada* **106** 47 6N 78 35W
Saser, *India* **49** 34 50N 77 50 E
Saskatchewan □, *Canada* **111** 54 40N 106 0W
Saskatchewan →, *Canada* **111** 53 37N 100 40W
Saskatoon, *Canada* **111** 52 10N 106 38W
Saskylakh, *U.S.S.R.* **41** 71 55N 114 1 E
Sasnovka, *U.S.S.R.* **37** 56 20N 51 4 E
Sasolburg, *S. Africa* **97** 26 46 S 27 49 E
Sasovo, *U.S.S.R.* **37** 54 25N 41 55 E
Sassandra, *Ivory C.* **90** 5 0N 6 8W
Sassandra →, *Ivory C.* **90** 4 58N 6 5W
Sássari, *Italy* **28** 40 44N 8 33 E
Sassenheim, *Neths.* **16** 52 14N 4 31 E
Sassnitz, *E. Germany* **30** 54 29N 13 39 E
Sasso Marconi, *Italy* **27** 44 22N 11 12 E
Sassocorvaro, *Italy* **27** 43 47N 12 30 E
Sassoferrato, *Italy* **27** 43 26N 12 51 E
Sassuolo, *Italy* **26** 44 31N 10 47 E
Sástago, *Spain* **24** 41 19N 0 21W
Sastown, *Liberia* **90** 4 45N 8 27W
Sasumua Dam, *Kenya* **92** 0 45 S 36 40 E
Sata-Misaki, *Japan* **64** 30 59N 130 40 E
Satadougou, *Mali* **90** 12 25N 11 25W
Satanta, *U.S.A.* **121** 37 30N 101 0W
Satara, *India* **50** 17 44N 73 58 E
Sataua, *W. Samoa* **68** 13 28 S 172 40W
Satilla →, *U.S.A.* **115** 30 59N 81 28W
Satipo, *Peru* **136** 11 15 S 74 25W
Satkania, *Bangla.* **52** 22 4N 92 3 E
Satkhira, *Bangla.* **52** 22 43N 89 8 E
Satmala Hills, *India* **50** 20 15N 74 40 E
Satna, *India* **49** 24 35N 80 50 E
Šator, *Yugoslavia* **27** 44 11N 16 37 E
Sátoraljaújhely, *Hungary* **33** 48 25N 21 41 E
Satpura Ra., *India* **48** 21 25N 76 10 E
Satrup, *W. Germany* **30** 54 39N 9 38 E
Satsuma-Hantō, *Japan* **64** 31 25N 130 25 E
Sattahip, *Thailand* **54** 12 41N 100 54 E
Sattenapalle, *India* **51** 16 25N 80 6 E
Satu Mare, *Romania* **34** 47 46N 22 55 E
Satui, *Indonesia* **56** 3 50 S 115 27 E
Satun, *Thailand* **55** 6 43N 100 2 E
Satupe'itea, *W. Samoa* **68** 13 45 S 172 18W
Saturnina →, *Brazil* **137** 12 15 S 58 10W
Sauce, *Argentina* **140** 30 5 S 58 46W
Sauceda, *Mexico* **126** 25 55N 101 18W
Saucillo, *Mexico* **126** 28 1N 105 17W
Sauda, *Norway* **9** 59 40N 6 20 E
Saúde, *Brazil* **138** 10 56 S 40 24W
Sauðarkrókur, *Iceland* **8** 65 45N 19 40W
Saudi Arabia ■, *Asia* **46** 26 0N 44 0 E
Sauer →, *W. Germany* **17** 49 44N 6 31 E
Saugatuck, *U.S.A.* **119** 42 40N 86 12W
Saugeen →, *Canada* **108** 44 30N 81 22W
Saugerties, *U.S.A.* **117** 42 4N 73 58W
Saugues, *France* **20** 44 58N 3 32 E
Sauherad, *Norway* **10** 59 25N 9 15 E
Saujon, *France* **20** 45 41N 0 55W
Sauk Centre, *U.S.A.* **120** 45 42N 94 56W
Sauk City, *U.S.A.* **118** 43 17N 89 43W
Sauk Rapids, *U.S.A.* **120** 45 35N 94 10W
Saül, *Fr. Guiana* **135** 3 37N 53 12W
Saulgau, *W. Germany* **31** 48 4N 9 32 E
Saulieu, *France* **19** 47 17N 4 14 E
Sault, *France* **21** 44 6N 5 24 E
Sault-au-Moulton, *Canada* **107** 48 33N 69 15W
Sault aux Cochons →, *Canada* **107** 48 44N 69 4W
Sault Ste. Marie, *Canada* **108** 46 30N 84 20W
Sault Ste. Marie, *U.S.A.* **104** 46 27N 84 22W
Saumlaki, *Indonesia* **57** 7 55 S 131 20 E
Saumur, *France* **18** 47 15N 0 5W
Saunders C., *N.Z.* **81** 45 53 S 170 45 E
Saunders I., *Antarctica* **143** 57 48 S 26 28W
Saunders Point, Mt., *Australia* **79** 27 52 S 125 38 E
Saunemin, *U.S.A.* **119** 40 54N 88 24W
Saurbær, *Borgarfjarðarsýsla, Iceland* **8** 64 24N 21 35W
Saurbær, *Eyjafjarðarsýsla, Iceland* **8** 65 27N 18 13W
Sauri, *Nigeria* **91** 11 42N 6 44 E
Saurimo, *Angola* **95** 9 40 S 20 12 E
Sausalito, *U.S.A.* **124** 37 51N 122 29W
Sautatá, *Colombia* **134** 7 50N 77 4W
Sauvage, L., *Canada* **106** 50 6N 74 30W
Sauveterre-de-Béarn, *France* **20** 43 24N 0 57W
Sauzé-Vaussais, *France* **20** 46 8N 0 8 E
Savá, *Honduras* **128** 15 32N 86 15W
Sava →, *Yugoslavia* **33** 44 50N 20 26 E
Savage, *U.S.A.* **120** 47 27N 104 20W
Savage I. = Niue I., *Cook Is.* **67** 19 2 S 169 54W
Savai'i, *W. Samoa* **68** 13 28 S 172 24W
Savalou, *Benin* **91** 7 57N 1 58 E
Savane, *Mozam.* **93** 19 37 S 35 8 E
Savanna, *U.S.A.* **118** 42 5N 90 10W
Savanna la Mar, *Jamaica* **128** 18 10N 78 10W
Savannah, *Ga., U.S.A.* **115** 32 4N 81 4W
Savannah, *Mo., U.S.A.* **118** 39 55N 94 46W
Savannah, *Tenn., U.S.A.* **115** 35 12N 88 18W
Savannah →, *U.S.A.* **115** 32 2N 80 53W
Savannakhet, *Laos* **54** 16 30N 104 49 E
Savant L., *Canada* **104** 50 16N 90 44W
Savant Lake, *Canada* **104** 50 14N 90 40W
Savantvadi, *India* **51** 15 55N 73 54 E
Savanur, *India* **51** 14 59N 75 21 E
Savda, *India* **50** 21 9N 75 56 E
Savé, *Benin* **91** 8 2N 2 29 E
Save →, *France* **20** 43 47N 1 17 E
Save →, *Mozam.* **97** 21 16 S 34 0 E
Sāveh, *Iran* **46** 35 2N 50 20 E
Savelugu, *Ghana* **91** 9 38N 0 54W
Savenay, *France* **18** 47 20N 1 55W
Saverdun, *France* **20** 43 14N 1 34 E
Saverne, *France* **19** 48 43N 7 20 E
Savigliano, *Italy* **26** 44 39N 7 40 E
Savigny-sur-Braye, *France* **18** 47 53N 0 49 E
Saviñao, *Spain* **22** 42 35N 7 38W
Savio →, *Italy* **27** 44 19N 12 20 E
Savo, *Solomon Is.* **68** 9 8 S 159 48 E
Savoie □, *France* **21** 45 26N 6 25 E
Savona, *Italy* **26** 44 19N 8 29 E
Sävsjö, *Sweden* **11** 57 20N 14 40 E
Sävsjöström, *Sweden* **11** 57 1N 15 25 E
Savusavu, *Fiji* **68** 16 34 S 179 15 E
Savusavu B., *Fiji* **68** 16 45 S 179 15 E
Sawahlunto, *Indonesia* **56** 0 40 S 100 52 E
Sawai, *Indonesia* **57** 3 0 S 129 5 E
Sawai Madhopur, *India* **48** 26 0N 76 25 E
Sawang Daen Din, *Thailand* **54** 17 28N 103 28 E
Sawankhalok, *Thailand* **54** 17 19N 99 50 E
Sawara, *Japan* **65** 35 55N 140 30 E
Sawatch Mts., *U.S.A.* **123** 38 30N 106 30W
Sawdā, Jabal as, *Libya* **86** 28 51N 15 12 E
Sawel, Mt., *U.K.* **15** 54 48N 7 5W
Sawfajjin, W. →, *Libya* **86** 31 46N 14 30 E
Sawi, *Thailand* **55** 10 14N 99 5 E
Sawmills, *Zimb.* **93** 19 30 S 28 2 E
Sawtell, *Australia* **77** 30 19 S 153 6 E
Sawu, *Indonesia* **57** 10 35 S 121 50 E
Sawu Sea, *Indonesia* **57** 9 30 S 121 50 E
Sawyerville, *Canada* **107** 45 20N 71 34W
Saxby →, *Australia* **72** 18 25 S 140 53 E
Saxony, Lower = Niedersachsen □, *W. Germany* **30** 52 45N 9 0 E
Saxton, *U.S.A.* **116** 40 12N 78 18W
Say, *Niger* **91** 13 8N 2 22 E
Saya, *Nigeria* **91** 9 30N 3 18 E
Sayabec, *Canada* **105** 48 35N 67 41W
Sayaboury, *Laos* **54** 19 15N 101 45 E
Sayán, *Peru* **136** 11 8 S 77 12W
Sayan, Vostochnyy, *U.S.S.R.* **41** 54 0N 96 0 E
Sayan, Zapadnyy, *U.S.S.R.* **41** 52 30N 94 0 E
Sayasan, *U.S.S.R.* **39** 42 56N 46 15 E
Saydā, *Lebanon* **46** 33 35N 35 25 E
Sayghān, *Afghan.* **47** 35 10N 67 55 E
Sayhan-Ovoo, *Mongolia* **60** 45 27N 103 54 E
Sayhandulaan, *Mongolia* **60** 44 40N 109 1 E
Sayḩut, *S. Yemen* **45** 15 12N 51 10 E
Saylorville Res., *U.S.A.* **118** 41 43N 93 41W
Saynshand, *Mongolia* **60** 44 55N 110 11 E
Sayō, *Japan* **64** 34 59N 134 22 E
Sayre, *Okla., U.S.A.* **121** 35 20N 99 40W
Sayre, *Pa., U.S.A.* **117** 42 0N 76 30W
Sayula, *Mexico* **126** 19 50N 103 40W
Sazin, *Pakistan* **49** 35 35N 73 30 E
Sazlika →, *Bulgaria* **35** 41 59N 25 50 E
Sbeïtla, *Tunisia* **86** 35 12N 9 7 E
Scaër, *France* **18** 48 2N 3 42W
Scafell Pikes, *U.K.* **12** 54 26N 3 14W
Scalea, *Italy* **29** 39 49N 15 47 E
Scalpay, *U.K.* **14** 57 51N 6 40W
Scandia, *Canada* **110** 50 20N 112 0W
Scandiano, *Italy* **26** 44 36N 10 40 E
Scandinavia, *Europe* **8** 64 0N 12 0 E
Scansano, *Italy* **27** 42 40N 11 20 E
Scapa Flow, *U.K.* **14** 58 52N 3 6W
Scappoose, *U.S.A.* **124** 45 45N 122 53W
Scarborough, *Trin. & Tob.* **129** 11 11N 60 42W
Scarborough, *U.K.* **12** 54 17N 0 24W
Scargill, *N.Z.* **81** 42 56 S 172 58 E
Scarsdale, *Australia* **74** 37 41 S 143 39 E
Scebeli, Wabi →, *Somali Rep.* **89** 2 0N 44 0 E
Šćedro, *Yugoslavia* **27** 43 6N 16 43 E
Scenic, *U.S.A.* **120** 43 49N 102 32W
Schaal See, *W. Germany* **30** 53 40N 10 57 E
Schaesberg, *Neths.* **17** 50 54N 6 0 E
Schaffen, *Belgium* **17** 51 0N 5 5 E
Schaffhausen □, *Switz.* **31** 47 42N 8 36 E
Schagen, *Neths.* **16** 52 49N 4 48 E
Schaijk, *Neths.* **16** 51 44N 5 38 E
Schalkhaar, *Neths.* **16** 52 17N 6 12 E
Schalkwijk, *Neths.* **16** 52 0N 5 11 E
Schanck, C., *Australia* **74** 38 30 S 144 55 E
Schärding, *Austria* **32** 48 27N 13 27 E
Scharhörn, *W. Germany* **30** 53 58N 8 24 E
Scharnitz, *Austria* **31** 47 23N 11 15 E
Scheessel, *W. Germany* **30** 53 10N 9 33 E
Schefferville, *Canada* **105** 54 48N 66 50W
Schelde →, *Belgium* **17** 51 15N 4 16 E
Schell City, *U.S.A.* **118** 38 1N 94 7W
Schell Creek Ra., *U.S.A.* **122** 39 15N 114 30W
Schenectady, *U.S.A.* **117** 42 50N 73 58W
Scherfede, *W. Germany* **30** 51 32N 9 2 E
Scherpenheuvel, *Belgium* **17** 50 58N 4 58 E
Scherpenisse, *Neths.* **17** 51 33N 4 6 E
Scherpenzeel, *Neths.* **16** 52 5N 5 30 E
Schesslitz, *W. Germany* **31** 49 59N 11 2 E
Scheveningen, *Neths.* **16** 52 6N 4 16 E
Schiedam, *Neths.* **16** 51 55N 4 25 E
Schiermonnikoog, *Neths.* **16** 53 30N 6 15 E
Schifferstadt, *W. Germany* **31** 49 22N 8 23 E
Schifflange, *Lux.* **17** 49 30N 6 1 E
Schijndel, *Neths.* **17** 51 37N 5 27 E
Schiltigheim, *France* **19** 48 35N 7 45 E
Schio, *Italy* **27** 45 42N 11 21 E
Schipbeek, *Neths.* **16** 52 14N 6 10 E
Schipluiden, *Neths.* **16** 51 59N 4 19 E
Schirmeck, *France* **19** 48 29N 7 12 E
Schlei →, *W. Germany* **30** 54 45N 9 52 E
Schleiden, *W. Germany* **30** 50 32N 6 26 E
Schleiz, *E. Germany* **30** 50 35N 11 49 E
Schleswig, *W. Germany* **30** 54 32N 9 34 E
Schleswig-Holstein □, *W. Germany* **30** 54 10N 9 40 E
Schlüchtern, *W. Germany* **31** 50 20N 9 32 E
Schmalkalden, *E. Germany* **30** 50 43N 10 28 E
Schmölin, *E. Germany* **30** 50 54N 12 22 E
Schmölln, *E. Germany* **30** 53 15N 14 6 E
Schneeberg, *Austria* **33** 47 47N 15 48 E
Schneeberg, *E. Germany* **30** 50 35N 12 39 E
Schneider, *U.S.A.* **119** 41 13N 87 28W
Schoenberg, *Belgium* **17** 50 17N 6 16 E
Schofield, *U.S.A.* **120** 44 54N 89 39W
Scholls, *U.S.A.* **124** 45 24N 122 56W
Schönberg, *E. Germany* **30** 53 50N 10 55 E
Schönberg, *W. Germany* **30** 54 23N 10 20 E
Schönebeck, *E. Germany* **30** 52 2N 11 42 E
Schongau, *W. Germany* **31** 47 49N 10 54 E
Schöningen, *W. Germany* **30** 52 8N 10 57 E
Schoolcraft, *U.S.A.* **119** 42 7N 85 38W
Schoondijke, *Neths.* **17** 51 21N 3 33 E
Schoonebeek, *Neths.* **16** 52 39N 6 52 E
Schoonhoven, *Neths.* **16** 51 57N 4 51 E
Schoorl, *Neths.* **16** 52 42N 4 42 E
Schortens, *W. Germany* **30** 53 37N 7 51 E
Schoten, *Belgium* **17** 51 16N 4 30 E
Schouten I., *Australia* **72** 42 20 S 148 20 E
Schouwen, *Neths.* **17** 51 43N 3 45 E
Schramberg, *W. Germany* **31** 48 12N 8 24 E
Schrankogl, *Austria* **31** 47 3N 11 7 E
Schreiber, *Canada* **104** 48 45N 87 20W
Schrobenhausen, *W. Germany* **31** 48 33N 11 16 E
Schruns, *Austria* **31** 47 5N 9 56 E
Schuler, *Canada* **111** 50 20N 110 6W
Schumacher, *Canada* **104** 48 30N 81 16W
Schurz, *U.S.A.* **122** 38 57N 118 48W
Schuyler, *U.S.A.* **120** 41 30N 97 3W
Schuylkill Haven, *U.S.A.* **117** 40 37N 76 11W
Schwabach, *W. Germany* **31** 49 19N 11 3 E
Schwäbisch Gmünd, *W. Germany* **31** 48 49N 9 48 E
Schwäbisch Hall, *W. Germany* **31** 49 7N 9 45 E
Schwäbische Alb, *W. Germany* **31** 48 30N 9 30 E
Schwabmünchen, *W. Germany* **31** 48 11N 10 45 E
Schwandorf, *W. Germany* **31** 49 20N 12 7 E
Schwaner, Pegunungan, *Indonesia* **56** 1 0 S 112 30 E
Schwarmstedt, *W. Germany* **30** 52 41N 9 37 E
Schwärze, *E. Germany* **30** 52 50N 13 49 E
Schwarzenberg, *E. Germany* **30** 50 31N 12 49 E
Schwarzwald, *W. Germany* **31** 48 0N 8 0 E
Schwaz, *Austria* **31** 47 20N 11 44 E
Schwedt, *E. Germany* **30** 53 4N 14 18 E
Schweinfurt, *W. Germany* **31** 50 3N 10 12 E
Schweizer-Reneke, *S. Africa* **96** 27 11 S 25 18 E
Schwerin, *E. Germany* **30** 53 37N 11 22 E
Schwerin □, *E. Germany* **30** 53 35N 11 20 E
Schweriner See, *E. Germany* **30** 53 45N 11 26 E
Schwetzingen, *W. Germany* **31** 49 22N 8 35 E
Schwyz, *Switz.* **31** 47 2N 8 39 E
Schwyz □, *Switz.* **31** 47 2N 8 39 E
Sciacca, *Italy* **28** 37 30N 13 3 E
Sciao, *Somali Rep.* **98** 3 26N 45 21 E
Scicli, *Italy* **29** 36 48N 14 41 E
Scie, La, *Canada* **105** 49 57N 55 36W
Scilla, *Italy* **29** 38 18N 15 44 E
Scilly, Isles of, *U.K.* **13** 49 55N 6 15W
Ścinawa, *Poland* **32** 51 25N 16 26 E
Scioto →, *U.S.A.* **114** 38 44N 83 0W
Scobey, *U.S.A.* **120** 48 47N 105 30W
Scone, *Australia* **77** 32 5 S 150 52 E
Scone, *U.K.* **14** 56 25N 3 26W
Scordia, *Italy* **29** 37 19N 14 50 E

Scoresbysund, *Greenland* **144** 70 20N 23 0W
Scorno, Punta dello, *Italy* **28** 41 7N 8 23 E
Scotia, *Calif., U.S.A.* **122** 40 36N 124 4W
Scotia, *N.Y., U.S.A.* **117** 42 50N 73 58W
Scotia Sea, *Antarctica* **143** 56 5 S 56 0W
Scotland, *Canada* **108** 43 1N 80 22W
Scotland, *U.S.A.* **120** 43 10N 97 45W
Scotland □, *U.K.* **14** 57 0N 4 0W
Scotland Neck, *U.S.A.* **115** 36 6N 77 32W
Scotstown, *Canada* **107** 45 32N 71 17W
Scott, *Antarctica* **143** 77 0 S 165 0 E
Scott, C., *Australia* **78** 13 30 S 129 49 E
Scott City, *U.S.A.* **120** 38 30N 100 52W
Scott Glacier, *Antarctica* **143** 66 15 S 100 5 E
Scott I., *Antarctica* **143** 67 0 S 179 0 E
Scott Inlet, *Canada* **103** 71 0N 71 0W
Scott Is., *Canada* **110** 50 48N 128 40W
Scott-Jonction, *Canada* **107** 46 30N 71 4W
Scott L., *Canada* **111** 59 55N 106 18W
Scott Reef, *Australia* **78** 14 0 S 121 50 E
Scottburgh, *S. Africa* **97** 30 15 S 30 47 E
Scottdale, *U.S.A.* **116** 40 8N 79 35W
Scottsbluff, *U.S.A.* **120** 41 55N 103 35W
Scottsboro, *U.S.A.* **115** 34 40N 86 0W
Scottsburg, *U.S.A.* **119** 38 40N 85 46W
Scottsdale, *Australia* **72** 41 9 S 147 31 E
Scottsville, *Ky., U.S.A.* **115** 36 48N 86 10W
Scottsville, *N.Y., U.S.A.* **116** 43 2N 77 47W
Scottville, *U.S.A.* **114** 43 57N 86 18W
Scranton, *Iowa, U.S.A.* **118** 42 1N 94 33W
Scranton, *Pa., U.S.A.* **117** 41 22N 75 41W
Scugog, L., *Canada* **109** 44 10N 78 55W
Scunthorpe, *U.K.* **12** 53 35N 0 38W
Scusciuban, *Somali Rep.* **98** 10 18N 50 12 E
Scutari = Üsküdar, *Turkey* **46** 41 0N 29 5 E
Sea Lake, *Australia* **74** 35 28 S 142 55 E
Seabra, *Brazil* **139** 12 25 S 41 46W
Seabrook, L., *Australia* **79** 30 55 S 119 40 E
Seaford, *Australia* **74** 38 10 S 145 11 E
Seaford, *U.S.A.* **114** 38 37N 75 36W
Seaforth, *Canada* **108** 43 35N 81 25W
Seagraves, *U.S.A.* **121** 32 56N 102 30W
Seal →, *Canada* **111** 59 4N 94 48W
Seal Cove, *Canada* **105** 49 57N 56 22W
Seal L., *Canada* **105** 54 20N 61 30W
Seal Rocks, *Australia* **76** 32 26 S 152 32 E
Sealy, *U.S.A.* **121** 29 46N 96 9W
Seaman, *U.S.A.* **119** 38 57N 83 34W
Searchlight, *U.S.A.* **125** 35 31N 114 55W
Searcy, *U.S.A.* **121** 35 15N 91 45W
Searles L., *U.S.A.* **125** 35 47N 117 17W
Seaside, *Calif., U.S.A.* **124** 36 37N 121 50W
Seaside, *Oreg., U.S.A.* **124** 45 59N 123 55W
Seaspray, *Australia* **75** 38 25 S 147 15 E
Seattle, *U.S.A.* **124** 47 41N 122 15W
Seaview Ra., *Australia* **72** 18 40 S 145 45 E
Seaward Kaikouras, Mts., *N.Z.* **81** 42 10 S 173 44 E
Sebastián Vizcaíno, B., *Mexico* **126** 28 0N 114 30W
Sebastopol = Sevastopol, *U.S.S.R.* **38** 44 35N 33 30 E
Sebastopol, *U.S.A.* **124** 38 24N 122 49W
Sebderat, *Ethiopia* **89** 15 26N 36 42 E
Sebdou, *Algeria* **85** 34 38N 1 19W
Sebewaing, *U.S.A.* **104** 43 45N 83 27W
Sebezh, *U.S.S.R.* **36** 56 14N 28 22 E
Sébi, *Mali* **90** 15 50N 4 12W
Şebinkarahisar, *Turkey* **38** 40 22N 38 28 E
Sebiş, *Romania* **34** 46 23N 22 13 E
Sebkhet Te-n-Dghâmcha, *Mauritania* **90** 18 30N 15 55W
Sebkra Azzel Mati, *Algeria* **85** 26 10N 0 43 E
Sebkra Mekerghene, *Algeria* **85** 26 21N 1 30 E
Sebnitz, *E. Germany* **30** 50 58N 14 17 E
Sebou, Oued →, *Morocco* **84** 34 16N 6 40W
Sebring, *Fla., U.S.A.* **115** 27 30N 81 26W
Sebring, *Ohio, U.S.A.* **116** 40 55N 81 2W
Sebringville, *Canada* **108** 43 24N 81 4W
Sebta = Ceuta, *Morocco* **84** 35 52N 5 18W
Sebuku, *Indonesia* **56** 3 30 S 116 25 E
Sebuku, Teluk, *Malaysia* **56** 4 0N 118 10 E
Secchia →, *Italy* **26** 44 4N 11 0 E
Sechelt, *Canada* **110** 49 25N 123 42W
Sechura, *Peru* **136** 5 39 S 80 50W
Sechura, Desierto de, *Peru* **136** 6 0 S 80 30W
Seclin, *France* **19** 50 33N 3 2 E
Secondigny, *France* **18** 46 37N 0 26W
Secretary I., *N.Z.* **81** 45 15 S 166 56 E
Secunderabad, *India* **50** 17 28N 78 30 E
Sécure →, *Bolivia* **137** 15 10 S 64 52W
Sedalia, *U.S.A.* **118** 38 40N 93 18W
Sedan, *Australia* **73** 34 34 S 139 19 E
Sedan, *France* **19** 49 43N 4 57 E
Sedan, *U.S.A.* **121** 37 10N 96 11W
Sedano, *Spain* **24** 42 43N 3 49W
Seddon, *N.Z.* **81** 41 40 S 174 7 E
Seddonville, *N.Z.* **81** 41 33 S 172 1 E
Sede Ya'aqov, *Israel* **44** 32 43N 35 7 E
Sedgewick, *Canada* **110** 52 48N 111 41W
Sedhiou, *Senegal* **90** 12 44N 15 30W
Sedičany, *Czech.* **32** 49 40N 14 25 E
Sedico, *Italy* **27** 46 8N 12 6 E
Sedley, *Canada* **111** 50 10N 104 0W
Sedom, *Israel* **44** 31 5N 35 20 E
Sedova, Pik, *U.S.S.R.* **40** 73 29N 54 58 E
Sedrata, *Algeria* **85** 36 7N 7 31 E
Sedro Woolley, *U.S.A.* **124** 48 30N 122 15W
Seduva, *U.S.S.R.* **36** 55 45N 23 45 E
Seebad Ahlbeck, *E. Germany* **30** 53 56N 14 10 E
Seehausen, *E. Germany* **30** 52 52N 11 43 E
Seeheim, *Namibia* **96** 26 50 S 17 45 E
Seekoei →, *S. Africa* **96** 30 18 S 25 1 E
Seelaw, *E. Germany* **30** 52 32N 14 22 E
Seeley's Bay, *Canada* **109** 44 29N 76 14W
Sées, *France* **18** 48 38N 0 10 E
Seesen, *W. Germany* **30** 51 53N 10 10 E
Sefadu, *S. Leone* **90** 8 35N 10 58W
Séfeto, *Mali* **90** 14 8N 9 49W
Sefrou, *Morocco* **84** 33 52N 4 52W
Sefton, *N.Z.* **81** 43 15 S 172 41 E
Sefuri-San, *Japan* **64** 33 28N 130 18 E
Sefwi Bekwai, *Ghana* **90** 6 10N 2 25W
Seg-ozero, *U.S.S.R.* **36** 63 0N 33 10 E
Segag, *Ethiopia* **98** 7 39N 42 50 E
Segamat, *Malaysia* **55** 2 30N 102 50 E
Segarcea, *Romania* **34** 44 6N 23 43 E
Segbwema, *S. Leone* **90** 8 0N 11 0W
Seget, *Indonesia* **57** 1 24 S 130 58 E
Seggueur, O. →, *Algeria* **85** 32 4N 2 4 E
Segonzac, *France* **20** 45 36N 0 14W
Segorbe, *Spain* **24** 39 50N 0 30W
Ségou, *Mali* **90** 13 30N 6 16W
Segovia = Coco →, *Cent. Amer.* **128** 15 0N 83 8W
Segovia, *Colombia* **134** 7 7N 74 42W
Segovia, *Spain* **22** 40 57N 4 10W
Segovia □, *Spain* **22** 40 55N 4 10W
Segré, *France* **18** 47 40N 0 52W
Segre →, *Spain* **24** 41 40N 0 43 E
Séguéla, *Ivory C.* **90** 7 55N 6 40W
Seguin, *U.S.A.* **121** 29 34N 97 58W
Segundo →, *Argentina* **140** 30 53 S 62 44W
Segura →, *Spain* **25** 38 6N 0 54W
Segura, Sierra de, *Spain* **25** 38 5N 2 45W
Sehitwa, *Botswana* **96** 20 30 S 22 30 E
Sehore, *India* **48** 23 10N 77 5 E
Sehwan, *Pakistan* **48** 26 28N 67 53 E
Şeica Mare, *Romania* **34** 46 1N 24 7 E
Seikpyu, *Burma* **52** 20 54N 94 48 E
Seiland, *Norway* **8** 70 25N 23 15 E
Seiling, *U.S.A.* **121** 36 10N 98 56W
Seille →, *France* **21** 46 31N 4 57 E
Seilles, *Belgium* **17** 50 30N 5 6 E
Sein, I. de, *France* **18** 48 2N 4 52W
Seinäjoki →, *Finland* **8** 62 40N 22 45 E
Seine →, *France* **18** 49 26N 0 26 E
Seine, B. de la, *France* **18** 49 40N 0 40W
Seine-et-Marne □, *France* **19** 48 45N 3 0 E
Seine-Maritime □, *France* **18** 49 40N 1 0 E
Seine-St.-Denis □, *France* **19** 48 58N 2 24 E
Seistan, *Iran* **47** 30 50N 61 0 E
Seistan, Daryācheh-ye, *Iran* **47** 31 0N 61 0 E
Sejerø, *Denmark* **11** 55 54N 11 9 E
Sejerø Bugt, *Denmark* **11** 55 53N 11 15 E
Seka, *Ethiopia* **89** 8 10N 36 52 E
Sekayu, *Indonesia* **56** 2 51 S 103 51 E
Seke, *Tanzania* **92** 3 20 S 33 31 E
Seke-Banza, *Zaïre* **95** 5 20 S 13 16 E
Sekenke, *Tanzania* **92** 4 18 S 34 11 E
Seki, *Japan* **65** 35 29N 136 55 E
Sekigahara, *Japan* **65** 35 22N 136 28 E
Sekken Veøy, *Norway* **10** 62 45N 7 30 E
Sekondi-Takoradi, *Ghana* **90** 4 58N 1 45W
Sekuma, *Botswana* **96** 24 36 S 23 50 E
Selah, *U.S.A.* **122** 46 44N 120 30W
Selama, *Malaysia* **55** 5 12N 100 42 E
Selárgius, *Italy* **28** 39 14N 9 14 E
Selaru, *Indonesia* **57** 8 9 S 131 0 E
Selb, *E. Germany* **31** 50 9N 12 9 E
Selby, *U.K.* **12** 53 47N 1 5W
Selby, *U.S.A.* **120** 45 34N 100 2W
Selca, *Yugoslavia* **27** 43 20N 16 50 E
Selden, *U.S.A.* **120** 39 33N 100 39W
Sele →, *Italy* **29** 40 27N 14 58 E
Selemdzha →, *U.S.S.R.* **41** 51 42N 128 53 E
Selenga → = Selenge Mörön →, *Asia* **62** 52 16N 106 16 E
Selenge, *Zaïre* **94** 1 58 S 18 11 E
Selenge Mörön →, *Asia* **62** 52 16N 106 16 E
Selenica, *Albania* **35** 40 33N 19 39 E
Selenter See, *W. Germany* **30** 54 19N 10 26 E
Sélestat, *France* **19** 48 16N 7 26 E
Seletan, Tg., *Indonesia* **56** 4 10 S 114 40 E
Seletin, *Romania* **34** 47 50N 25 12 E
Selfridge, *U.S.A.* **120** 46 3N 100 57W
Sélibabi, *Mauritania* **90** 15 10N 12 15W
Seliger, Oz., *U.S.S.R.* **36** 57 15N 33 0 E
Seligman, *U.S.A.* **123** 35 17N 112 56W
Şelim, *Turkey* **39** 40 30N 42 46 E
Selîma, El Wâhât el, *Sudan* **88** 21 22N 29 19 E
Selinda Spillway, *Botswana* **96** 18 35 S 23 10 E
Selinoús, *Greece* **35** 37 35N 21 37 E
Selizharovo, *U.S.S.R.* **36** 56 51N 33 27 E
Seljord, *Norway* **10** 59 30N 8 40 E
Selkirk, *Man., Canada* **111** 50 10N 96 55W
Selkirk, *Ont., Canada* **108** 42 49N 79 56W
Selkirk, *U.K.* **14** 55 33N 2 50W
Selkirk I., *Canada* **111** 53 20N 99 6W
Selkirk Mts., *Canada* **110** 51 15N 117 40W
Selles-sur-Cher, *France* **19** 47 16N 1 33 E
Sellières, *France* **19** 46 50N 5 32 E
Sells, *U.S.A.* **123** 31 57N 111 57W
Sellye, *Hungary* **33** 45 52N 17 51 E
Selma, *Ala., U.S.A.* **115** 32 30N 87 0W
Selma, *Calif., U.S.A.* **124** 36 39N 119 39W
Selma, *N.C., U.S.A.* **115** 35 32N 78 15W
Selmer, *U.S.A.* **115** 35 9N 88 36W
Selongey, *France* **19** 47 36N 5 11 E
Selowandoma Falls, *Zimb.* **93** 21 15 S 31 50 E
Selpele, *Indonesia* **57** 0 1 S 130 5 E
Selsey Bill, *U.K.* **13** 50 44N 0 47W
Seltz, *France* **19** 48 54N 8 4 E
Selu, *Indonesia* **57** 7 32 S 130 55 E
Sélune →, *France* **18** 48 38N 1 22W
Selva, *Argentina* **140** 29 50 S 62 0W
Selva, *Italy* **27** 46 33N 11 46 E
Selva, *Spain* **24** 41 13N 1 8 E
Selva, La, *Spain* **24** 42 0N 2 45 E
Selva Beach, La, *U.S.A.* **124** 36 56N 121 51W
Selvas, *Brazil* **136** 6 30 S 67 0W
Selwyn, *Australia* **72** 21 32 S 140 30 E
Selwyn L., *Canada* **111** 60 0N 104 30W
Selwyn Passage, *Vanuatu* **68** 16 3 S 168 12 E
Selwyn Ra., *Australia* **72** 21 10 S 140 0 E
Seman →, *Albania* **35** 40 45N 19 50 E
Semara, *W. Sahara* **84** 26 48N 11 41W
Semarang, *Indonesia* **57** 7 0 S 110 26 E
Semau, *Indonesia* **57** 10 13 S 123 22 E
Sembabule, *Uganda* **92** 0 4 S 31 25 E
Sembé, *Congo* **94** 1 39N 14 36 E
Sémé, *Senegal* **90** 15 4N 13 41W
Semeih, *Sudan* **89** 12 43N 30 53 E
Semenov, *U.S.S.R.* **37** 56 43N 44 30 E
Semenovka, *Ukraine S.S.R., U.S.S.R.* **36** 52 8N 32 36 E
Semenovka, *Ukraine S.S.R., U.S.S.R.* **38** 49 37N 33 10 E
Semeru, *Indonesia* **57** 8 4 S 112 55 E
Semiluki, *U.S.S.R.* **37** 51 41N 39 2 E
Seminoe Res., *U.S.A.* **122** 42 0N 107 0W
Seminole, *Okla., U.S.A.* **121** 35 15N 96 45W
Seminole, *Tex., U.S.A.* **121** 32 41N 102 38W
Semiozernoye, *U.S.S.R.* **40** 52 22N 64 8 E
Semipalatinsk, *U.S.S.R.* **40** 50 30N 80 10 E
Semirara Is., *Phil.* **57** 12 0N 121 20 E
Semisopochnoi, *U.S.A.* **102** 52 0N 179 40W
Semitau, *Indonesia* **56** 0 29N 111 57 E
Semiyarskoye, *U.S.S.R.* **40** 50 55N 78 23 E
Semmering Pass, *Austria* **33** 47 41N 15 45 E
Semnān, *Iran* **47** 35 55N 53 25 E
Semnān □, *Iran* **47** 36 0N 54 0 E
Semois →, *Europe* **17** 49 53N 4 44 E
Semporna, *Malaysia* **57** 4 30N 118 33 E
Semuda, *Indonesia* **56** 2 51 S 112 58 E
Semur-en-Auxois, *France* **19** 47 30N 4 20 E
Sena, *Bolivia* **136** 11 32 S 67 11W
Sena, *Mozam.* **93** 17 25 S 35 0 E
Sena →, *Bolivia* **136** 11 31 S 67 11W
Sena Madureira, *Brazil* **136** 9 5 S 68 45W
Senador Pompeu, *Brazil* **138** 5 40 S 39 20W
Senaja, *Malaysia* **56** 6 45N 117 3 E
Senanga, *Zambia* **96** 16 2 S 23 14 E
Senatobia, *U.S.A.* **121** 34 38N 89 57W
Sendafa, *Ethiopia* **89** 9 11N 39 3 E
Sendai, *Kagoshima, Japan* **64** 31 50N 130 20 E
Sendai, *Miyagi, Japan* **63** 38 15N 140 53 E
Sendamangalam, *India* **51** 11 17N 78 17 E
Sendenhorst, *W. Germany* **30** 51 50N 7 49 E
Sendurjana, *India* **50** 21 32N 78 17 E
Seneca, *Oreg., U.S.A.* **122** 44 10N 119 2W
Seneca, *S.C., U.S.A.* **115** 34 43N 82 59W
Seneca Falls, *U.S.A.* **117** 42 55N 76 50W
Seneca L., *U.S.A.* **116** 42 40N 76 58W
Seneffe, *Belgium* **17** 50 32N 4 16 E
Senegal ■, *W. Afr.* **90** 14 30N 14 30W
Senegal →, *W. Afr.* **90** 15 48N 16 32W
Senegambia, *Africa* **82** 12 45N 12 0W
Senekal, *S. Africa* **97** 28 20 S 27 36 E
Senftenberg, *E. Germany* **30** 51 30N 14 1 E
Senga Hill, *Zambia* **93** 9 19 S 31 11 E
Senge Khambab = Indus →, *Pakistan* **48** 24 20N 67 47 E
Sengerema □, *Tanzania* **92** 2 10 S 32 20 E
Sengiley, *U.S.S.R.* **37** 53 58N 48 46 E
Sengkang, *Indonesia* **57** 4 8 S 120 1 E
Sengua →, *Zimb.* **93** 17 7 S 28 5 E
Senguerr →, *Argentina* **142** 45 35 S 68 50W
Senhor-do-Bonfim, *Brazil* **138** 10 30 S 40 10W
Senica, *Czech.* **32** 48 41N 17 25 E
Senigállia, *Italy* **27** 43 42N 13 12 E
Seniku, *Burma* **52** 25 32N 97 48 E
Senio →, *Italy* **27** 44 35N 12 15 E
Senise, *Italy* **28** 40 6N 16 15 E
Senj, *Yugoslavia* **27** 45 0N 14 58 E
Senja, *Norway* **8** 69 25N 17 30 E
Senlis, *France* **19** 49 13N 2 35 E
Senmonorom, *Cambodia* **54** 12 27N 107 12 E
Sennâr, *Sudan* **89** 13 30N 33 35 E
Senne →, *Belgium* **17** 50 42N 4 13 E
Senneterre, *Canada* **106** 48 25N 77 15W
Senniquelle, *Liberia* **90** 7 19N 8 38W
Senno, *U.S.S.R.* **36** 54 45N 29 43 E
Sennori, *Italy* **28** 40 49N 8 36 E
Seno, *Laos* **54** 16 35N 104 50 E
Senonches, *France* **18** 48 34N 1 2 E
Senorbì, *Italy* **28** 39 33N 9 8 E
Senožeče, *Yugoslavia* **27** 45 43N 14 3 E
Sens, *France* **19** 48 11N 3 15 E
Senta, *Yugoslavia* **33** 45 55N 20 3 E
Sentery, *Zaïre* **92** 5 17 S 25 42 E
Sentinel, *U.S.A.* **123** 32 45N 113 13W
Sentolo, *Indonesia* **57** 7 55 S 110 13 E
Senya Beraku, *Ghana* **91** 5 28N 0 31W
Senye, *Eq. Guin.* **94** 1 34N 9 50 E
Seo de Urgel, *Spain* **24** 42 22N 1 23 E
Seohara, *India* **49** 29 15N 78 33 E
Seoni, *India* **49** 22 5N 79 30 E
Seoriuarayan, *India* **50** 21 45N 82 34 E
Seoul = Sŏul, *S. Korea* **61** 37 31N 126 58 E
Separation Point, *Canada* **105** 53 37N 57 25W
Sepīdān, *Iran* **47** 30 20N 52 5 E
Sepik →, *Papua N. G.* **69** 3 49 S 144 30 E
Sepone, *Laos* **54** 16 45N 106 13 E
Sept-Îles, *Canada* **105** 50 13N 66 22W
Septemvri, *Bulgaria* **34** 42 13N 24 6 E
Sepúlveda, *Spain* **22** 41 18N 3 45W
Sequeros, *Spain* **22** 40 31N 6 2W
Sequim, *U.S.A.* **124** 48 3N 123 9W
Sequoia Nat. Park, *U.S.A.* **124** 36 30N 118 30W
Serafimovich, *U.S.S.R.* **39** 49 36N 42 43 E
Seraing, *Belgium* **17** 50 35N 5 32 E
Seraja, *Indonesia* **55** 2 41N 108 35 E
Seram, *Indonesia* **57** 3 10 S 129 0 E
Seram Laut, Kepulauan, *Indonesia* **57** 4 5 S 131 25 E
Seram Sea, *Indonesia* **57** 2 30 S 128 30 E
Serang, *Indonesia* **57** 6 8 S 106 10 E
Serasan, *Indonesia* **55** 2 29N 109 4 E
Seravezza, *Italy* **26** 43 59N 10 13 E
Serbia = Srbija □, *Yugoslavia* **33** 43 30N 21 0 E
Serdo, *Ethiopia* **89** 11 56N 41 14 E
Serdobsk, *U.S.S.R.* **37** 52 28N 44 10 E
Seredka, *U.S.S.R.* **36** 58 12N 28 10 E
Seregno, *Italy* **26** 45 40N 9 12 E
Seremban, *Malaysia* **55** 2 43N 101 53 E
Serena, La, *Chile* **140** 29 55 S 71 10W
Serena, La, *Spain* **23** 38 45N 5 40W
Serengeti □, *Tanzania* **92** 2 0 S 34 30 E
Serengeti Plain, *Tanzania* **92** 2 40 S 35 0 E
Serenje, *Zambia* **93** 13 14 S 30 15 E
Sereth = Siret →, *Romania* **34** 45 24N 28 1 E
Sergach, *U.S.S.R.* **37** 55 30N 45 30 E
Serge →, *Spain* **24** 41 54N 0 50 E
Sergino, *U.S.S.R.* **40** 62 30N 65 38 E
Sergipe □, *Brazil* **138** 10 30 S 37 30W
Seria, *Brunei* **56** 4 37N 114 23 E
Serian, *Malaysia* **56** 1 10N 110 31 E
Seriate, *Italy* **26** 45 42N 9 43 E
Seribu, Kepulauan, *Indonesia* **56** 5 36 S 106 33 E
Sérifontaine, *France* **19** 49 20N 1 45 E
Sérifos, *Greece* **35** 37 9N 24 30 E
Sérignan, *France* **20** 43 17N 3 17 E
Seringapatam Reef, *Australia* **78** 13 38 S 122 5 E
Sermaize-les-Bains, *France* **19** 48 47N 4 54 E
Sermata, *Indonesia* **57** 8 15 S 128 50 E
Sérmide, *Italy* **27** 45 0N 11 17 E
Sernovodsk, *U.S.S.R.* **37** 53 54N 51 16 E
Serny Zavod, *U.S.S.R.* **40** 39 59N 58 50 E
Serón, *Spain* **25** 37 20N 2 29W
Serós, *Spain* **24** 41 27N 0 24 E
Serov, *U.S.S.R.* **40** 59 29N 60 35 E
Serowe, *Botswana* **96** 22 25 S 26 43 E
Serpa, *Madeira* **23** 37 57N 7 38 E
Serpeddi, Punta, *Italy* **28** 39 19N 9 18 E
Serpentara, *Italy* **28** 39 8N 9 38 E
Serpentine, *Australia* **79** 32 23 S 115 58 E
Serpentine Lakes, *Australia* **79** 28 30 S 129 10 E
Serpis →, *Spain* **25** 38 45N 0 9W
Serpukhov, *U.S.S.R.* **37** 54 55N 37 28 E
Serra do Navio, *Brazil* **135** 0 59N 52 3W
Serra San Bruno, *Italy* **29** 38 31N 16 23 E
Serra Talhada, *Brazil* **138** 7 59 S 38 18W
Serracapriola, *Italy* **29** 41 47N 15 12 E
Serradilla, *Spain* **22** 39 50N 6 9W
Sérrai, *Greece* **35** 41 5N 23 31 E
Serramanna, *Italy* **28** 39 26N 8 56 E
Serrat, C., *Tunisia* **86** 37 14N 9 10 E
Serre-Ponçon, L. de, *France* **21** 44 22N 6 20 E
Serres, *France* **21** 44 26N 5 43 E
Serrezuela, *Argentina* **140** 30 40 S 65 20W
Serrinha, *Brazil* **139** 11 39 S 39 0W

Serrita, *Brazil* **138** 7 56 S 39 19W
Sersale, *Italy* **29** 39 1N 16 44 E
Sertã, *Portugal* **22** 39 48N 8 6W
Sertânia, *Brazil* **138** 8 5 S 37 20W
Sertanópolis, *Brazil* **141** 23 4 S 51 2W
Sêrtar, *China* **58** 32 20N 100 41 E
Serua, *Indonesia* **57** 6 18 S 130 1 E
Serui, *Indonesia* **57** 1 53 S 136 10 E
Serule, *Botswana* **96** 21 57 S 27 20 E
Sérvia, *Greece* **35** 40 9N 21 58 E
Serviceton, *Australia* **74** 36 22 S 141 0 E
Sese Is., *Uganda* **92** 0 20 S 32 20 E
Sesepe, *Indonesia* **57** 1 30 S 127 59 E
Sesfontein, *Namibia* **96** 19 7 S 13 39 E
Sesheke, *Zambia* **96** 17 29 S 24 13 E
Sesia →, *Italy* **26** 45 5N 8 37 E
Sesimbra, *Portugal* **23** 38 28N 9 6W
Sessa, *Angola* **95** 13 56 S 20 38 E
Sessa Aurunca, *Italy* **28** 41 14N 13 55 E
Sesser, *U.S.A.* **118** 38 7N 89 3W
Sestao, *Spain* **24** 43 18N 3 0W
Sesto S. Giovanni, *Italy* **26** 45 32N 9 14 E
Sestri Levante, *Italy* **26** 44 17N 9 22 E
Sestrières, *Italy* **26** 44 58N 6 56 E
Sestrunj, *Yugoslavia* **27** 44 10N 15 0 E
Sestu, *Italy* **28** 39 18N 9 6 E
Setaka, *Japan* **64** 33 9N 130 28 E
Setana, *Japan* **63** 42 26N 139 51 E
Sète, *France* **20** 43 25N 3 42 E
Sete Lagôas, *Brazil* **139** 19 27 S 44 16W
Sétif, *Algeria* **85** 36 9N 5 26 E
Seto, *Japan* **65** 35 14N 137 6 E
Setonaikai, *Japan* **64** 34 20N 133 30 E
Setsan, *Burma* **52** 16 3N 95 23 E
Settat, *Morocco* **84** 33 0N 7 40W
Setté-Cama, *Gabon* **94** 2 32 S 9 45 E
Séttimo Tor, *Italy* **26** 45 9N 7 46 E
Setting L., *Canada* **111** 55 0N 98 38W
Settle, *U.K.* **12** 54 5N 2 18W
Settlement Pt., *Bahamas* **115** 26 40N 79 0W
Setto Calende, *Italy* **26** 45 44N 8 37 E
Setúbal, *Portugal* **23** 38 30N 8 58W
Setúbal □, *Portugal* **23** 38 25N 8 35W
Setúbal, B. de, *Portugal* **23** 38 40N 8 56W
Seugne →, *France* **20** 45 42N 0 32W
Seulimeum, *Indonesia* **56** 5 27N 95 15 E
Sevan, *U.S.S.R.* **39** 40 33N 44 56 E
Sevan, Ozero, *U.S.S.R.* **39** 40 30N 45 20 E
Sevastopol, *U.S.S.R.* **38** 44 35N 33 30 E
Seven Emu, *Australia* **72** 16 20 S 137 8 E
Seven Sisters, *Canada* **110** 54 56N 128 10W
Sevenum, *Neths.* **17** 51 25N 6 2 E
Sever →, *Spain* **23** 39 40N 7 32W
Sévérac-le-Château, *France* **20** 44 20N 3 5 E
Severn →, *Australia* **77** 29 8 S 150 59 E
Severn →, *Canada* **104** 56 2N 87 36W
Severn →, *U.K.* **13** 51 35N 2 38W
Severn L., *Canada* **104** 53 54N 90 48W
Severnaya Zemlya, *U.S.S.R.* **41** 79 0N 100 0 E
Severo-Kurilsk, *U.S.S.R.* **41** 50 40N 156 8 E
Severo-Yeniseyskiy, *U.S.S.R.* **41** 60 22N 93 1 E
Severodonetsk, *U.S.S.R.* **39** 48 58N 38 30 E
Severodvinsk, *U.S.S.R.* **40** 64 27N 39 58 E
Sevier, *U.S.A.* **123** 38 39N 112 11W
Sevier →, *U.S.A.* **123** 39 10N 113 6W
Sevier L., *U.S.A.* **122** 39 0N 113 20W
Sevilla, *Colombia* **134** 4 16N 75 57W
Sevilla, *Spain* **23** 37 23N 6 0W
Sevilla □, *Spain* **23** 37 25N 5 30W
Seville = Sevilla, *Spain* **23** 37 23N 6 0W
Sevnica, *Yugoslavia* **27** 46 2N 15 19 E
Sèvre-Nantaise →, *France* **18** 47 12N 1 33W
Sèvre-Niortaise →, *France* **20** 46 28N 0 50W
Sevsk, *U.S.S.R.* **36** 52 10N 34 30 E
Seward, *Alaska, U.S.A.* **102** 60 6N 149 26W
Seward, *Nebr., U.S.A.* **120** 40 55N 97 6W
Seward Pen., *U.S.A.* **102** 65 0N 164 0W
Sewell, *Chile* **140** 34 10 S 70 23W
Sewer, *Indonesia* **57** 5 53 S 134 40 E
Sewickley, *U.S.A.* **116** 40 33N 80 12W
Sexbierum, *Neths.* **16** 53 13N 5 29 E
Sexsmith, *Canada* **110** 55 21N 118 47W
Seychelles ■, *Ind. Oc.* **53** 5 0 S 56 0 E
Seyðisfjörður, *Iceland* **8** 65 16N 14 0W
Seym →, *U.S.S.R.* **36** 51 27N 32 34 E
Seymchan, *U.S.S.R.* **41** 62 54N 152 30 E
Seymour, *Australia* **74** 37 0 S 145 10 E
Seymour, *S. Africa* **97** 32 33 S 26 46 E
Seymour, *Conn., U.S.A.* **117** 41 23N 73 5W
Seymour, *Ind., U.S.A.* **119** 39 0N 85 50W
Seymour, *Iowa, U.S.A.* **118** 40 45N 93 7W
Seymour, *Tex., U.S.A.* **121** 33 35N 99 18W
Seymour, *Wis., U.S.A.* **114** 44 30N 88 20W
Seyne, *France* **21** 44 21N 6 22 E
Seyne, La, *France* **21** 43 7N 5 52 E
Seyssel, *France* **21** 45 57N 5 50 E
Sežana, *Yugoslavia* **27** 45 43N 13 41 E
Sézanne, *France* **19** 48 40N 3 40 E
Sezze, *Italy* **28** 41 30N 13 3 E
Sfax, *Tunisia* **86** 34 49N 10 48 E
Sfîntu Gheorghe, *Romania* **34** 45 52N 25 48 E
Sha Xi →, *China* **59** 26 35N 118 0 E
Sha Xian, *China* **59** 26 23N 117 45 E
Shaanxi □, *China* **60** 35 0N 109 0 E
Shaba □, *Zaïre* **92** 8 0 S 25 0 E
Shabunda, *Zaïre* **92** 2 40 S 27 16 E
Shache, *China* **62** 38 20N 77 10 E
Shackleton Ice Shelf, *Antarctica* **143** 66 0 S 100 0 E
Shackleton Inlet, *Antarctica* **143** 83 0 S 160 0 E
Shadi, *China* **59** 26 7N 114 47 E
Shadi, *India* **49** 33 24N 77 14 E
Shadrinsk, *U.S.S.R.* **40** 56 5N 63 32 E
Shafer, L., *U.S.A.* **119** 40 46N 86 46W
Shaffa, *Nigeria* **91** 10 30N 12 6 E
Shafter, *Calif., U.S.A.* **125** 35 32N 119 14W
Shafter, *Tex., U.S.A.* **121** 29 49N 104 18W
Shaftesbury, *U.K.* **13** 51 0N 2 12W
Shag Pt., *N.Z.* **81** 45 29 S 170 52 E
Shagamu, *Nigeria* **91** 6 51N 3 39 E
Shagram, *Pakistan* **49** 36 24N 72 20 E
Shah Bunder, *Pakistan* **48** 24 13N 67 56 E
Shahabad, *Andhra Pradesh, India* **50** 17 10N 76 54 E
Shahabad, *Punjab, India* **48** 30 10N 76 55 E
Shahabad, *Raj., India* **48** 25 15N 77 11 E
Shahabad, *Ut. P., India* **49** 27 36N 79 56 E
Shāhābād, *Iran* **47** 37 40N 56 50 E
Shahada, *India* **50** 21 33N 74 30 E
Shahadpur, *Pakistan* **48** 25 55N 68 35 E
Shahapur, *India* **51** 15 50N 74 34 E
Shahdād, *Iran* **47** 30 30N 57 40 E
Shahdād, Namakzār-e, *Iran* **47** 30 20N 58 20 E
Shahdadkot, *Pakistan* **48** 27 50N 67 55 E
Shahe, *China* **60** 37 0N 114 32 E
Shahganj, *India* **49** 26 3N 82 44 E
Shaḥḥāt, *Libya* **86** 32 48N 21 54 E
Shahjahanpur, *India* **49** 27 54N 79 57 E
Shahpur, *Karnataka, India* **50** 16 40N 76 48 E
Shahpur, *Mad. P., India* **48** 22 12N 77 58 E
Shahpur, *Pakistan* **48** 28 46N 68 27 E
Shahpura, *India* **49** 23 10N 80 45 E
Shahr Kord, *Iran* **47** 32 15N 50 55 E
Shahrig, *Pakistan* **48** 30 15N 67 40 E
Shahukou, *China* **60** 40 20N 112 18 E
Shaikhabad, *Afghan.* **48** 34 2N 68 45 E
Shajapur, *India* **48** 23 27N 76 21 E
Shakargarh, *Pakistan* **48** 32 17N 75 10 E
Shakawe, *Botswana* **96** 18 28 S 21 49 E
Shaker Heights, *U.S.A.* **116** 41 29N 81 36W
Shakhty, *U.S.S.R.* **39** 47 40N 40 16 E
Shakhunya, *U.S.S.R.* **37** 57 40N 46 46 E
Shaki, *Nigeria* **91** 8 41N 3 21 E
Shakopee, *U.S.A.* **120** 44 45N 93 30W
Shala, L., *Ethiopia* **89** 7 30N 38 30 E
Shallow Lake, *Canada* **108** 44 36N 81 5W
Shaluli Shan, *China* **58** 30 40N 99 55 E
Sham, J. ash, *Oman* **47** 23 10N 57 5 E
Shamâl Dârfûr □, *Sudan* **89** 15 0N 25 0 E
Shamâl Kordofân □, *Sudan* **89** 15 0N 30 0 E
Shamattawa, *Canada* **111** 55 51N 92 5W
Shamattawa →, *Canada* **104** 55 1N 85 23W
Shambe, *Sudan* **89** 7 8N 30 46 E
Shambu, *Ethiopia* **89** 9 32N 37 3 E
Shamgong Dzong, *Bhutan* **52** 27 13N 90 35 E
Shamīl, *Iran* **47** 27 30N 56 55 E
Shamkhor, *U.S.S.R.* **39** 40 50N 46 0 E
Shamli, *India* **48** 29 32N 77 18 E
Shammar, Jabal, *Si. Arabia* **46** 27 40N 41 0 E
Shamo = Gobi, *Asia* **60** 44 0N 111 0 E
Shamo, L., *Ethiopia* **89** 5 45N 37 30 E
Shamokin, *U.S.A.* **117** 40 47N 76 33W
Shamrock, *U.S.A.* **121** 35 15N 100 15W
Shamva, *Zimb.* **93** 17 20 S 31 32 E
Shan □, *Burma* **52** 21 30N 98 30 E
Shan Xian, *China* **60** 34 50N 116 5 E
Shanan →, *Ethiopia* **89** 8 0N 40 20 E
Shanchengzhen, *China* **61** 42 20N 125 20 E
Shandon, *U.S.A.* **124** 35 39N 120 23W
Shandong □, *China* **61** 36 0N 118 0 E
Shandong Bandao, *China* **61** 37 0N 121 0 E
Shang Xian, *China* **60** 33 50N 109 58 E
Shangalowe, *Zaïre* **93** 10 50 S 26 30 E
Shangani →, *Zimb.* **93** 18 41 S 27 10 E
Shangbancheng, *China* **61** 40 50N 118 1 E
Shangcai, *China* **59** 33 18N 114 14 E
Shangcheng, *China* **59** 31 47N 115 26 E
Shangchuan Dao, *China* **59** 21 40N 112 50 E
Shangdu, *China* **60** 41 30N 113 30 E
Shanggao, *China* **59** 28 17N 114 55 E
Shanghai, *China* **59** 31 15N 121 26 E
Shanghang, *China* **59** 25 2N 116 23 E
Shanghe, *China* **61** 37 20N 117 10 E
Shangjin, *China* **59** 33 7N 110 3 E
Shanglin, *China* **58** 23 27N 108 33 E
Shangnan, *China* **60** 33 32N 110 50 E
Shangqiu, *China* **60** 34 26N 115 36 E
Shangrao, *China* **59** 28 25N 117 59 E
Shangshui, *China* **60** 33 42N 114 35 E
Shangsi, *China* **58** 22 8N 107 58 E
Shangyou, *China* **59** 25 48N 114 32 E
Shangzhi, *China* **61** 45 22N 127 56 E
Shanhetun, *China* **61** 44 33N 127 15 E
Shani, *Nigeria* **91** 10 14N 12 2 E
Shaniko, *U.S.A.* **122** 45 0N 120 50W
Shannon, *Greenland* **144** 75 10N 18 30W
Shannon, *N.Z.* **80** 40 33 S 175 25 E
Shannon →, *Ireland* **15** 52 35N 9 30W
Shannons Flat, *Australia* **76** 35 55 S 148 58 E
Shansi = Shanxi □, *China* **60** 37 0N 112 0 E
Shantar, Ostrov Bolshoy, *U.S.S.R.* **41** 55 9N 137 40 E
Shantipur, *India* **49** 23 17N 88 25 E
Shantou, *China* **59** 23 18N 116 40 E
Shantung = Shandong □, *China* **61** 36 0N 118 0 E
Shanxi □, *China* **60** 37 0N 112 0 E
Shanyang, *China* **60** 33 31N 109 55 E
Shanyin, *China* **60** 39 25N 112 56 E
Shaoguan, *China* **59** 24 48N 113 35 E
Shaowu, *China* **59** 27 22N 117 28 E
Shaoxing, *China* **59** 30 0N 120 35 E
Shaoyang, *Hunan, China* **59** 26 59N 111 20 E
Shaoyang, *Hunan, China* **59** 27 14N 111 25 E
Shapinsay, *U.K.* **14** 59 2N 2 50W
Shaqrā', *S. Yemen* **45** 13 22N 45 44 E
Shaqra', *Si. Arabia* **46** 25 15N 45 16 E
Sharafa, *Sudan* **89** 11 59N 27 7 E
Sharavati →, *India* **51** 14 20N 74 25 E
Sharbot Lake, *Canada* **109** 44 46N 76 41W
Sharjah = Ash Shāriqah, *U.A.E.* **47** 25 23N 55 26 E
Shark B., *Australia* **79** 25 30 S 113 32 E
Sharm el Sheikh, *Egypt* **88** 27 53N 34 18 E
Sharon, *Mass., U.S.A.* **117** 42 5N 71 11W
Sharon, *Pa., U.S.A.* **116** 41 18N 80 30W
Sharon, *Wis., U.S.A.* **119** 42 30N 88 44W
Sharon, Plain of = Hasharon, *Israel* **44** 32 12N 34 49 E
Sharon Springs, *U.S.A.* **120** 38 54N 101 45W
Sharp Pt., *Australia* **72** 10 58 S 142 43 E
Sharpe L., *Canada* **111** 54 24N 93 40W
Sharpsville, *U.S.A.* **116** 41 16N 80 28W
Sharq el Istiwa'iya □, *Sudan* **89** 5 0N 33 0 E
Sharya, *U.S.S.R.* **37** 58 22N 45 20 E
Shasha, *Ethiopia* **89** 6 29N 35 59 E
Shashemene, *Ethiopia* **89** 7 13N 38 33 E
Shashi, *Botswana* **97** 21 15 S 27 27 E
Shashi, *China* **59** 30 25N 112 14 E
Shashi →, *Africa* **93** 21 14 S 29 20 E
Shasta, Mt., *U.S.A.* **122** 41 30N 122 12W
Shasta L., *U.S.A.* **122** 40 50N 122 15W
Shatsk, *U.S.S.R.* **37** 54 0N 41 45 E
Shattuck, *U.S.A.* **121** 36 17N 99 55W
Shatura, *U.S.S.R.* **37** 55 34N 39 31 E
Shaumyani, *U.S.S.R.* **39** 41 22N 41 45 E
Shaunavon, *Canada* **111** 49 35N 108 25W
Shaver Lake, *U.S.A.* **124** 37 9N 119 18W
Shaw →, *Australia* **78** 20 21 S 119 17 E
Shaw I., *Australia* **72** 20 30 S 149 2 E
Shawan, *China* **62** 44 34N 85 50 E
Shawanaga, *Canada* **108** 45 31N 80 17W
Shawano, *U.S.A.* **114** 44 45N 88 38W
Shawinigan, *Canada* **107** 46 35N 72 50W
Shawinigan Sud, *Canada* **107** 46 31N 72 45W
Shawnee, *Kans., U.S.A.* **118** 39 1N 94 43W
Shawnee, *Okla., U.S.A.* **121** 35 15N 97 0W
Shawville, *Canada* **106** 45 36N 76 30W
Shayib el Banat, Gebel, *Egypt* **88** 26 59N 33 29 E
Shchekino, *U.S.S.R.* **37** 54 1N 37 34 E
Shcherbakov = Andropov, *U.S.S.R.* **37** 58 5N 38 50 E
Shchigri, *U.S.S.R.* **37** 51 55N 36 58 E
Shchors, *U.S.S.R.* **36** 51 48N 31 56 E
Shchuchiosk, *U.S.S.R.* **40** 52 56N 70 12 E
She Xian, *Anhui, China* **59** 29 50N 118 25 E
She Xian, *Hebei, China* **60** 36 30N 113 40 E
Shea, *Guyana* **135** 2 48N 59 4W
Shebekino, *U.S.S.R.* **37** 50 28N 36 54 E
Shebele = Scebeli, Wabi →, *Somali Rep.* **89** 2 0N 44 0 E
Sheboygan, *U.S.A.* **114** 43 46N 87 45W
Shechem, *Jordan* **44** 32 13N 35 21 E
Shediac, *Canada* **105** 46 14N 64 32W
Sheelin, Lough, *Ireland* **15** 53 48N 7 20W
Sheep Haven, *Ireland* **15** 55 12N 7 55W
Sheep Hills, *Australia* **74** 36 20 S 142 33 E
Sheerness, *U.K.* **13** 51 26N 0 47 E
Sheet Harbour, *Canada* **105** 44 56N 62 31W
Shefar'am, *Israel* **44** 32 48N 35 10 E
Sheffield, *U.K.* **12** 53 23N 1 28W
Sheffield, *Ala., U.S.A.* **115** 34 45N 87 42W
Sheffield, *Ill., U.S.A.* **118** 41 21N 89 44W
Sheffield, *Iowa, U.S.A.* **118** 42 54N 93 13W
Sheffield, *Mass., U.S.A.* **117** 42 6N 73 23W
Sheffield, *Pa., U.S.A.* **116** 41 42N 79 3W
Sheffield, *Tex., U.S.A.* **121** 30 42N 101 49W
Shegaon, *India* **50** 20 48N 76 47 E
Sheguiandah, *Canada* **108** 45 54N 81 55W
Sheho, *Canada* **111** 51 35N 103 13W
Shehojele, *Ethiopia* **89** 10 40N 35 9 E
Shehong, *China* **58** 30 54N 105 18 E
Shehuen →, *Argentina* **142** 49 35 S 69 34W
Sheikhpura, *India* **49** 25 9N 85 53 E
Shek Hasan, *Ethiopia* **89** 12 5N 35 58 E
Shekhupura, *Pakistan* **48** 31 42N 73 58 E
Sheki, *U.S.S.R.* **39** 41 10N 47 5 E
Sheksna →, *U.S.S.R.* **37** 59 0N 38 30 E
Shelbina, *U.S.A.* **118** 39 47N 92 2W
Shelburn, *U.S.A.* **119** 39 10N 87 24W
Shelburne, *N.S., Canada* **105** 43 47N 65 20W
Shelburne, *Ont., Canada* **108** 44 4N 80 15W
Shelburne, *U.S.A.* **117** 44 23N 73 15W
Shelburne B., *Australia* **72** 11 50 S 142 50 E
Shelburne Falls, *U.S.A.* **117** 42 36N 72 45W
Shelby, *Mich., U.S.A.* **114** 43 34N 86 27W
Shelby, *Mont., U.S.A.* **122** 48 30N 111 52W
Shelby, *N.C., U.S.A.* **115** 35 18N 81 34W
Shelby, *Ohio, U.S.A.* **116** 40 52N 82 40W
Shelbyville, *Ill., U.S.A.* **119** 39 25N 88 45W
Shelbyville, *Ind., U.S.A.* **119** 39 30N 85 42W
Shelbyville, *Ky., U.S.A.* **119** 38 13N 85 14W
Shelbyville, *Mo., U.S.A.* **118** 39 48N 92 2W
Shelbyville, *Tenn., U.S.A.* **115** 35 30N 86 25W
Shelbyville, Res., *U.S.A.* **119** 39 26N 88 46W
Sheldon, *Iowa, U.S.A.* **120** 43 6N 95 40W
Sheldon, *Mo., U.S.A.* **118** 37 40N 94 18W
Sheldrake, *Canada* **105** 50 20N 64 51W
Shelikhova, Zaliv, *U.S.S.R.* **41** 59 30N 157 0 E
Shell Lake, *Canada* **111** 53 19N 107 2W
Shell Lakes, *Australia* **79** 29 20 S 127 30 E
Shellbrook, *Canada* **111** 53 13N 106 24W
Shellharbour, *Australia* **76** 34 31 S 150 51 E
Shelling Rocks, *Ireland* **15** 51 45N 10 35W
Shellsburg, *U.S.A.* **118** 42 6N 91 52W
Shelon →, *U.S.S.R.* **36** 58 10N 30 30 E
Shelton, *Conn., U.S.A.* **117** 41 18N 73 7W
Shelton, *Wash., U.S.A.* **124** 47 15N 123 6W
Shemakha, *U.S.S.R.* **39** 40 38N 48 37 E
Shen Xian, *China* **60** 36 15N 115 40 E
Shenandoah, *Iowa, U.S.A.* **120** 40 50N 95 25W
Shenandoah, *Pa., U.S.A.* **117** 40 49N 76 13W
Shenandoah, *Va., U.S.A.* **114** 38 30N 78 38W
Shenandoah →, *U.S.A.* **114** 39 19N 77 44W
Shenchi, *China* **60** 39 8N 112 10 E
Shencottah, *India* **51** 8 59N 77 18 E
Shendam, *Nigeria* **91** 8 49N 9 30 E
Shendî, *Sudan* **89** 16 46N 33 22 E
Shendurni, *India* **50** 20 39N 75 36 E
Sheng Xian, *China* **59** 29 35N 120 50 E
Shengfang, *China* **60** 39 3N 116 42 E
Shëngjergji, *Albania* **35** 41 17N 20 10 E
Shëngjini, *Albania* **35** 41 50N 19 35 E
Shenjingzi, *China* **61** 44 40N 124 30 E
Shenmu, *China* **60** 38 50N 110 29 E
Shennongjia, *China* **59** 31 43N 110 44 E
Shenqiu, *China* **60** 33 25N 115 5 E
Shenqiucheng, *China* **60** 33 24N 115 2 E
Shensi = Shaanxi □, *China* **60** 35 0N 109 0 E
Shenyang, *China* **61** 41 48N 123 27 E
Shepetovka, *U.S.S.R.* **36** 50 10N 27 10 E
Shephelah = Hashefela, *Israel* **44** 31 30N 34 43 E
Shepherd Is., *Vanuatu* **68** 16 55 S 168 36 E
Shepherdsville, *U.S.A.* **119** 37 59N 85 43W
Shepparton, *Australia* **74** 36 23 S 145 26 E
Shepparton East, *Australia* **74** 36 25 S 145 30 E
Sheqi, *China* **60** 33 12N 112 57 E
Sher Qila, *Pakistan* **49** 36 7N 74 2 E
Sherborne, *U.K.* **13** 50 56N 2 31W
Sherbro I., *S. Leone* **90** 7 30N 12 40W
Sherbrooke, *Canada* **107** 45 28N 71 57W
Sherda, *Chad* **87** 20 7N 16 46 E
Shereik, *Sudan* **88** 18 44N 33 47 E
Sheridan, *Ark., U.S.A.* **121** 34 20N 92 25W
Sheridan, *Ill., U.S.A.* **119** 41 32N 88 41W
Sheridan, *Ind., U.S.A.* **119** 40 8N 86 13W
Sheridan, *Iowa, U.S.A.* **118** 40 31N 94 37W
Sheridan, *Wyo., U.S.A.* **122** 44 50N 107 0W
Sherkot, *India* **49** 29 22N 78 35 E
Sherman, *U.S.A.* **121** 33 40N 96 35W
Sherpur, *Bangla.* **52** 25 0N 90 0 E
Sherridon, *Canada* **111** 55 8N 101 5W
Sherwood, *N. Dak., U.S.A.* **120** 48 59N 101 36W
Sherwood, *Ohio, U.S.A.* **119** 41 17N 84 33W
Sherwood, *Tex., U.S.A.* **121** 31 18N 100 45W
Sherwood Forest, *U.K.* **12** 53 5N 1 5W
Sheslay, *Canada* **110** 58 17N 131 52W
Sheslay →, *Canada* **110** 58 48N 132 5W
Shethanei L., *Canada* **111** 58 48N 97 50W
Shetland □, *U.K.* **14** 60 30N 1 30W
Shetland Is., *U.K.* **14** 60 30N 1 30W
Shevaroy Hills, *India* **51** 11 58N 78 12 E
Shewa □, *Ethiopia* **89** 9 33N 38 10 E
Shewa Gimira, *Ethiopia* **89** 7 4N 35 51 E
Sheyenne, *U.S.A.* **120** 47 52N 99 8W
Sheyenne →, *U.S.A.* **120** 47 5N 96 50W
Shibām, *S. Yemen* **45** 16 0N 48 36 E
Shibata, *Japan* **63** 37 57N 139 20 E
Shibetsu, *Japan* **63** 44 10N 142 23 E
Shibîn el Kôm, *Egypt* **88** 30 31N 30 55 E
Shibîn el Qanâtir, *Egypt* **88** 30 19N 31 19 E
Shibing, *China* **58** 27 2N 108 7 E

Shibogama L., *Canada* **104** 53 35N 88 15W
Shibukawa, *Japan* **65** 36 29N 139 0 E
Shibushi, *Japan* **64** 31 25N 131 8 E
Shibushi-Wan, *Japan* **64** 31 24N 131 8 E
Shicheng, *China* **59** 26 22N 116 20 E
Shidao, *China* **61** 36 50N 122 25 E
Shidian, *China* **58** 24 40N 99 5 E
Shido, *Japan* **64** 34 19N 134 10 E
Shiel, L., *U.K.* **14** 56 48N 5 32W
Shield, C., *Australia* **72** 13 20 S 136 20 E
Shiga □, *Japan* **65** 35 20N 136 0 E
Shigaib, *Sudan* **87** 15 5N 23 35 E
Shigaraki, *Japan* **65** 34 57N 136 2 E
Shigu, *China* **58** 26 51N 99 56 E
Shiguaigou, *China* **60** 40 52N 110 15 E
Shihchiachuangi = Shijiazhuang, *China* **60** 38 2N 114 28 E
Shiiba, *Japan* **64** 32 29N 131 4 E
Shijiazhuang, *China* **60** 38 2N 114 28 E
Shijiu Hu, *China* **59** 31 25N 118 50 E
Shikarpur, *India* **48** 28 17N 78 7 E
Shikarpur, *Pakistan* **48** 27 57N 68 39 E
Shikine-Jima, *Japan* **65** 34 19N 139 13 E
Shikoku, *Japan* **64** 33 30N 133 30 E
Shikoku □, *Japan* **64** 33 30N 133 30 E
Shikoku-Sanchi, *Japan* **64** 33 30N 133 30 E
Shilabo, *Ethiopia* **45** 6 22N 44 32 E
Shiliguri, *India* **52** 26 45N 88 25 E
Shilka, *U.S.S.R.* **41** 52 0N 115 55 E
Shilka →, *U.S.S.R.* **41** 53 20N 121 26 E
Shillelagh, *Ireland* **15** 52 46N 6 32W
Shillong, *India* **52** 25 35N 91 53 E
Shilo, *Jordan* **44** 32 4N 35 18 E
Shilong, *China* **59** 23 5N 113 52 E
Shilou, *China* **60** 37 0N 110 48 E
Shilovo, *U.S.S.R.* **37** 54 25N 40 57 E
Shima-Hantō, *Japan* **65** 34 22N 136 45 E
Shimabara, *Japan* **64** 32 48N 130 20 E
Shimada, *Japan* **65** 34 49N 138 10 E
Shimane □, *Japan* **64** 35 0N 132 30 E
Shimane-Hantō, *Japan* **64** 35 30N 133 0 E
Shimanovsk, *U.S.S.R.* **41** 52 15N 127 30 E
Shimen, *China* **59** 29 35N 111 20 E
Shimenjie, *China* **59** 29 29N 116 48 E
Shimian, *China* **58** 29 17N 102 23 E
Shimizu, *Japan* **65** 35 0N 138 30 E
Shimo-Jima, *Japan* **64** 32 15N 130 7 E
Shimo-Koshiki-Jima, *Japan* **64** 31 40N 129 43 E
Shimoda, *Japan* **65** 34 40N 138 57 E
Shimodate, *Japan* **65** 36 20N 139 55 E
Shimoga, *India* **51** 13 57N 75 32 E
Shimoni, *Kenya* **92** 4 38 S 39 20 E
Shimonita, *Japan* **65** 36 13N 138 47 E
Shimonoseki, *Japan* **64** 33 58N 131 0 E
Shimotsuma, *Japan* **65** 36 11N 139 58 E
Shimpuru Rapids, *Angola* **95** 17 45 S 19 55 E
Shimsha →, *India* **51** 13 15N 77 10 E
Shimsk, *U.S.S.R.* **36** 58 15N 30 50 E
Shin, L., *U.K.* **14** 58 7N 4 30W
Shin-Tone →, *Japan* **65** 35 44N 140 51 E
Shinan, *China* **58** 22 44N 109 53 E
Shinano →, *Japan* **63** 36 50N 138 30 E
Shīndand, *Afghan.* **47** 33 12N 62 8 E
Shingbwiyang, *Burma* **52** 26 41N 96 13 E
Shingleton, *U.S.A.* **104** 46 25N 86 33W
Shingū, *Japan* **65** 33 40N 135 55 E
Shinji, *Japan* **64** 35 24N 132 54 E
Shinji Ko, *Japan* **64** 35 26N 132 57 E
Shinjō, *Japan* **63** 38 46N 140 18 E
Shinkafe, *Nigeria* **91** 13 8N 6 29 E
Shinminato, *Japan* **65** 36 47N 137 4 E
Shinonoi, *Japan* **65** 36 35N 138 9 E
Shinshiro, *Japan* **65** 34 54N 137 30 E
Shinyanga, *Tanzania* **92** 3 45 S 33 27 E
Shinyanga □, *Tanzania* **92** 3 50 S 34 0 E
Shio-no-Misaki, *Japan* **65** 33 25N 135 45 E
Shiogama, *Japan* **63** 38 19N 141 1 E
Shiojiri, *Japan* **65** 36 6N 137 58 E
Ship I., *U.S.A.* **121** 30 16N 88 55W
Shipehenski Prokhod, *Bulgaria* **34** 42 45N 25 15 E
Shiping, *China* **58** 23 45N 102 23 E
Shippegan, *Canada* **105** 47 45N 64 45W
Shippensburg, *U.S.A.* **116** 40 4N 77 32W
Shiprock, *U.S.A.* **123** 36 51N 108 45W
Shiqian, *China* **58** 27 32N 108 13 E
Shiqma, N. →, *Israel* **44** 31 37N 34 30 E
Shiquan, *China* **60** 33 5N 108 15 E
Shīr Kūh, *Iran* **47** 31 39N 54 3 E
Shiragami-Misaki, *Japan* **63** 41 24N 140 12 E
Shirahama, *Japan* **65** 33 41N 135 20 E
Shirakawa, *Japan* **65** 36 17N 136 56 E
Shirane-San, *Gumma, Japan* **65** 36 48N 139 22 E
Shirane-San, *Yamanashi, Japan* **65** 35 42N 138 9 E
Shiraoi, *Japan* **63** 42 33N 141 21 E
Shīrāz, *Iran* **47** 29 42N 52 30 E
Shirbin, *Egypt* **88** 31 11N 31 32 E
Shire →, *Africa* **93** 17 42 S 35 19 E
Shirinab →, *Pakistan* **48** 30 15N 66 28 E
Shiringushi, *U.S.S.R.* **37** 53 51N 42 46 E
Shiriya-Zaki, *Japan* **63** 41 25N 141 30 E
Shirley, *U.S.A.* **119** 39 53N 85 35W
Shirol, *India* **50** 16 47N 74 41 E
Shirpur, *India* **50** 21 21N 74 57 E
Shīrvān, *Iran* **47** 37 30N 57 50 E
Shirwa, L. = Chilwa, L., *Malawi* **93** 15 15 S 35 40 E
Shishou, *China* **59** 29 38N 112 22 E
Shitai, *China* **59** 30 12N 117 25 E
Shively, *U.S.A.* **119** 38 12N 85 49W
Shivpuri, *India* **48** 25 26N 77 42 E
Shivta, *Israel* **44** 30 53N 34 40 E
Shixian, *China* **61** 43 5N 129 50 E
Shixing, *China* **59** 24 46N 114 5 E
Shiyan, *China* **59** 32 35N 110 45 E
Shiyata, *Egypt* **88** 29 25N 25 7 E
Shizhu, *China* **58** 29 58N 108 7 E
Shizong, *China* **58** 24 50N 104 0 E
Shizuishan, *China* **60** 39 15N 106 50 E
Shizuoka, *Japan* **65** 35 0N 138 24 E
Shizuoka □, *Japan* **65** 35 15N 138 40 E
Shklov, *U.S.S.R.* **36** 54 16N 30 15 E
Shkoder = Shkodra, *Albania* **34** 42 6N 19 20 E
Shkodra, *Albania* **34** 42 6N 19 20 E
Shkumbini →, *Albania* **35** 41 5N 19 50 E
Shmidt, O., *U.S.S.R.* **41** 81 0N 91 0 E
Shō-Gawa →, *Japan* **65** 36 47N 137 4 E
Shoal Cr. →, *U.S.A.* **118** 39 39N 93 35W
Shoal Lake, *Canada* **111** 50 30N 100 35W
Shoalhaven →, *Australia* **76** 34 54 S 150 42 E
Shoals, *U.S.A.* **119** 38 40N 86 47W
Shōbara, *Japan* **64** 34 51N 133 1 E
Shōdo-Shima, *Japan* **64** 34 30N 134 15 E
Shoeburyness, *U.K.* **13** 51 31N 0 49 E
Sholapur = Solapur, *India* **50** 17 43N 75 56 E
Shologontsy, *U.S.S.R.* **41** 66 13N 114 0 E
Shomera, *Israel* **44** 33 4N 35 17 E
Shōmrōn, *Jordan* **44** 32 15N 35 13 E
Shoranur, *India* **51** 10 46N 76 19 E
Shorapur, *India* **51** 16 31N 76 48 E
Shortland I., *Solomon Is.* **69** 7 0 S 155 45 E
Shoshone, *Calif., U.S.A.* **125** 35 58N 116 16W
Shoshone, *Idaho, U.S.A.* **122** 43 0N 114 27W
Shoshone L., *U.S.A.* **122** 44 30N 110 40W
Shoshone Mts., *U.S.A.* **122** 39 30N 117 30W
Shoshong, *Botswana* **96** 22 56 S 26 31 E
Shoshoni, *U.S.A.* **122** 43 13N 108 5W
Shostka, *U.S.S.R.* **36** 51 57N 33 32 E
Shou Xian, *China* **59** 32 37N 116 42 E
Shouchang, *China* **59** 29 18N 119 12 E
Shouguang, *China* **61** 37 52N 118 45 E
Shouning, *China* **59** 27 27N 119 31 E
Shouyang, *China* **60** 37 54N 113 8 E
Show Low, *U.S.A.* **123** 34 16N 110 0W
Shpola, *U.S.S.R.* **38** 49 1N 31 30 E
Shreveport, *U.S.A.* **121** 32 30N 93 50W
Shrewsbury, *U.K.* **12** 52 42N 2 45W
Shrirampur, *India* **49** 22 44N 88 21 E
Shrirangapattana, *India* **51** 12 26N 76 43 E
Shropshire □, *U.K.* **13** 52 36N 2 45W
Shuangbai, *China* **58** 24 42N 101 38 E
Shuangcheng, *China* **61** 45 20N 126 15 E
Shuangfeng, *China* **59** 27 29N 112 11 E
Shuanggou, *China* **61** 34 2N 117 30 E
Shuangjiang, *China* **58** 23 26N 99 58 E
Shuangliao, *China* **61** 43 29N 123 30 E
Shuangshanzi, *China* **61** 40 20N 119 8 E
Shuangyang, *China* **61** 43 28N 125 40 E
Shuangyashan, *China* **62** 46 28N 131 5 E
Shu'ayb, Wadi →, *Jordan* **44** 31 54N 35 38 E
Shucheng, *China* **59** 31 28N 116 57 E
Shuguri Falls, *Tanzania* **93** 8 33 S 37 22 E
Shuicheng, *China* **58** 26 38N 104 48 E
Shuiji, *China* **59** 27 13N 118 20 E
Shuiye, *China* **60** 36 7N 114 8 E
Shujalpur, *India* **48** 23 18N 76 46 E
Shukpa Kunzang, *India* **49** 34 22N 78 22 E
Shulan, *China* **61** 44 28N 127 0 E
Shule, *China* **62** 39 25N 76 3 E
Shullsburg, *U.S.A.* **118** 42 35N 90 15W
Shumagin Is., *U.S.A.* **102** 55 0N 159 0W
Shumerlya, *U.S.S.R.* **37** 55 30N 46 25 E
Shumikha, *U.S.S.R.* **40** 55 10N 63 15 E
Shunchang, *China* **59** 26 54N 117 48 E
Shunde, *China* **59** 22 42N 113 14 E
Shungay, *U.S.S.R.* **39** 48 30N 46 45 E
Shungnak, *U.S.A.* **102** 66 55N 157 10W
Shuo Xian, *China* **60** 39 20N 112 33 E
Shūr →, *Iran* **47** 28 30N 55 0 E
Shurkhua, *Burma* **52** 22 15N 93 38 E
Shurma, *U.S.S.R.* **37** 56 58N 50 21 E
Shurugwi, *Zimb.* **93** 19 40 S 30 0 E
Shūsf, *Iran* **47** 31 50N 60 5 E
Shūshtar, *Iran* **46** 32 0N 48 50 E
Shuswap L., *Canada* **110** 50 55N 119 3W
Shuwaykah, *Jordan* **44** 32 20N 35 1 E
Shuya, *U.S.S.R.* **37** 56 50N 41 28 E
Shuyang, *China* **61** 34 10N 118 42 E
Shuzenji, *Japan* **65** 34 58N 138 56 E
Shwebo, *Burma* **52** 22 30N 95 45 E
Shwegu, *Burma* **52** 24 15N 96 26 E
Shwegun, *Burma* **52** 17 9N 97 39 E
Shwenyaung, *Burma* **52** 20 46N 96 57 E
Shyok, *India* **49** 34 15N 78 12 E
Shyok →, *Pakistan* **49** 35 13N 75 53 E
Si Chon, *Thailand* **55** 9 0N 99 54 E
Si Kiang = Xi Jiang →, *China* **59** 22 5N 113 20 E
Si Prachan, *Thailand* **54** 14 37N 100 9 E
Si Racha, *Thailand* **54** 13 10N 100 48 E
Si Xian, *China* **61** 33 30N 117 50 E
Siah, *Si. Arabia* **46** 22 0N 47 0 E
Siahan Range, *Pakistan* **47** 27 30N 64 40 E
Siaksrindrapura, *Indonesia* **56** 0 51N 102 0 E
Sialkot, *Pakistan* **48** 32 32N 74 30 E
Sialsuk, *India* **52** 23 24N 92 45 E
Siam = Thailand ■, *Asia* **54** 16 0N 102 0 E
Sian = Xi'an, *China* **60** 34 15N 109 0 E
Siantan, P., *Indonesia* **55** 3 10N 106 15 E
Siàpo →, *Venezuela* **134** 2 7N 66 28W
Sīāreh, *Iran* **47** 28 5N 60 14 E
Siargao, *Phil.* **57** 9 52N 126 3 E
Siari, *Pakistan* **49** 34 55N 76 40 E
Siasi, *Phil.* **57** 5 34N 120 50 E
Siassi, *Papua N. G.* **69** 5 40 S 147 51 E
Siátista, *Greece* **35** 40 15N 21 33 E
Siau, *Indonesia* **57** 2 50N 125 25 E
Siauliai, *U.S.S.R.* **36** 55 56N 23 15 E
Siaya □, *Kenya* **92** 0 0 34 20 E
Siazan, *U.S.S.R.* **39** 41 3N 49 10 E
Sibâi, Gebel el, *Egypt* **88** 25 45N 34 10 E
Sibang, *Gabon* **94** 0 25N 9 31 E
Sibari, *Italy* **29** 39 47N 16 27 E
Sibasa, *S. Africa* **97** 22 53 S 30 33 E
Sibayi, L., *S. Africa* **97** 27 20 S 32 45 E
Šibenik, *Yugoslavia* **27** 43 48N 15 54 E
Siberia, *U.S.S.R.* **144** 60 0N 100 0 E
Siberut, *Indonesia* **56** 1 30 S 99 0 E
Sibi, *Pakistan* **48** 29 30N 67 54 E
Sibil, *Indonesia* **57** 4 59 S 140 35 E
Sibiti, *Congo* **94** 3 38 S 13 19 E
Sibiu, *Romania* **34** 45 45N 24 9 E
Sibley, *Ill., U.S.A.* **119** 40 35N 88 23W
Sibley, *Iowa, U.S.A.* **120** 43 21N 95 43W
Sibley, *La., U.S.A.* **121** 32 34N 93 16W
Sibolga, *Indonesia* **56** 1 42N 98 45 E
Sibret, *Belgium* **17** 49 58N 5 38 E
Sibsagar, *India* **52** 27 0N 94 36 E
Sibu, *Malaysia* **56** 2 18N 111 49 E
Sibuco, *Phil.* **57** 7 20N 122 10 E
Sibuguey B., *Phil.* **57** 7 50N 122 45 E
Sibutu, *Phil.* **57** 4 45N 119 30 E
Sibutu Passage, *E. Indies* **57** 4 50N 120 0 E
Sibuyan, *Phil.* **57** 12 25N 122 40 E
Sibuyan Sea, *Phil.* **57** 12 30N 122 20 E
Sicamous, *Canada* **110** 50 49N 119 0W
Sichuan □, *China* **58** 31 0N 104 0 E
Sicilia, *Italy* **29** 37 30N 14 30 E
Sicilia □, *Italy* **29** 37 30N 14 30 E
Sicilia, Canale di, *Italy* **28** 37 25N 12 30 E
Sicilian Channel = Sicilia, Canale di, *Italy* **28** 37 25N 12 30 E
Sicily = Sicilia, *Italy* **29** 37 30N 14 30 E
Sicuani, *Peru* **136** 14 21 S 71 10W
Siculiana, *Italy* **28** 37 20N 13 23 E
Sidamo □, *Ethiopia* **89** 5 0N 37 50 E
Sidaouet, *Niger* **91** 18 34N 8 3 E
Siddeburen, *Neths.* **16** 53 15N 6 52 E
Siddhapur, *India* **48** 23 56N 72 25 E
Siddipet, *India* **50** 18 0N 78 51 E
Sidell, *U.S.A.* **119** 39 55N 87 49W
Sidéradougou, *Burkina Faso* **90** 10 42N 4 12W
Siderno Marina, *Italy* **29** 38 16N 16 17 E
Sidheros, Ákra, *Greece* **35** 35 19N 26 19 E
Sidhirókastron, *Greece* **35** 41 13N 23 24 E
Sîdi Abd el Rahmân, *Egypt* **88** 30 55N 29 44 E
Sîdi Barrâni, *Egypt* **88** 31 38N 25 58 E
Sidi-bel-Abbès, *Algeria* **85** 35 13N 0 39W
Sidi Bennour, *Morocco* **84** 32 40N 8 25W
Sidi Haneish, *Egypt* **88** 31 10N 27 35 E
Sidi Kacem, *Morocco* **84** 34 11N 5 49W
Sidi Omar, *Egypt* **88** 31 24N 24 57 E
Sidi Slimane, *Morocco* **84** 34 16N 5 56W
Sidi Smaïl, *Morocco* **84** 32 50N 8 31W
Sidi 'Uzayz, *Libya* **86** 31 41N 24 55 E
Sidlaw Hills, *U.K.* **14** 56 32N 3 10W
Sidley, Mt., *Antarctica* **143** 77 2 S 126 2W
Sidmouth, *U.K.* **13** 50 40N 3 13W
Sidmouth, C., *Australia* **72** 13 25 S 143 36 E
Sidney, *Canada* **110** 48 39N 123 24W
Sidney, *Mont., U.S.A.* **120** 47 42N 104 7W
Sidney, *N.Y., U.S.A.* **117** 42 18N 75 20W
Sidney, *Nebr., U.S.A.* **120** 41 12N 103 0W
Sidney, *Ohio, U.S.A.* **119** 40 18N 84 6W
Sidoarjo, *Indonesia* **57** 7 27 S 112 43 E
Sidoktaya, *Burma* **52** 20 27N 94 15 E
Sidon = Saydā, *Lebanon* **46** 33 35N 35 25 E
Sidra, G. of = Surt, Khalīj, *Libya* **86** 31 40N 18 30 E
Siedlce, *Poland* **32** 52 10N 22 20 E
Sieg →, *W. Germany* **30** 50 46N 7 7 E
Siegburg, *W. Germany* **30** 50 48N 7 12 E
Siegen, *W. Germany* **30** 50 52N 8 2 E
Siem Pang, *Cambodia* **54** 14 7N 106 23 E
Siem Reap, *Cambodia* **54** 13 20N 103 52 E
Siena, *Italy* **27** 43 20N 11 20 E
Sieradź, *Poland* **32** 51 37N 18 41 E
Sierck-les-Bains, *France* **19** 49 26N 6 20 E
Sierpc, *Poland* **32** 52 55N 19 43 E
Sierpe, Bocas de la, *Venezuela* **134** 10 0N 61 30W
Sierra Blanca, *U.S.A.* **123** 31 11N 105 17W
Sierra Blanca Pk., *U.S.A.* **123** 33 20N 105 54W
Sierra City, *U.S.A.* **124** 39 34N 120 42W
Sierra Colorada, *Argentina* **142** 40 35 S 67 50W
Sierra de Yeguas, *Spain* **23** 37 7N 4 52W
Sierra Gorda, *Chile* **140** 22 50 S 69 15W
Sierra Grande, *Argentina* **142** 41 36 S 65 22W
Sierra Leone ■, *W. Afr.* **90** 9 0N 12 0W
Sierra Mojada, *Mexico* **126** 27 19N 103 42W
Sierraville, *U.S.A.* **124** 39 36N 120 22W
Sierre, *Switz.* **31** 46 17N 7 31 E
Sif Fatima, *Algeria* **85** 31 6N 8 41 E
Sífnos, *Greece* **35** 37 0N 24 45 E
Sifton, *Canada* **111** 51 21N 100 8W
Sifton Pass, *Canada* **110** 57 52N 126 15W
Sig, *Algeria* **85** 35 32N 0 12W
Sigdal, *Norway* **10** 60 4N 9 38 E
Sigean, *France* **20** 43 2N 2 58 E
Sighetu-Marmatiei, *Romania* **34** 47 57N 23 52 E
Sighişoara, *Romania* **34** 46 12N 24 50 E
Sigli, *Indonesia* **56** 5 25N 96 0 E
Siglufjörður, *Iceland* **8** 66 12N 18 55W
Sigmaringen, *W. Germany* **31** 48 5N 9 13 E
Signakhi, *U.S.S.R.* **39** 41 40N 45 57 E
Signal, *U.S.A.* **125** 34 30N 113 38W
Signal Pk., *U.S.A.* **125** 33 25N 114 4W
Signy I., *Antarctica* **143** 60 45 S 45 56W
Signy-l'Abbaye, *France* **19** 49 40N 4 25 E
Sigourney, *U.S.A.* **118** 41 20N 92 12W
Sigsig, *Ecuador* **134** 3 0 S 78 50W
Sigtuna, *Sweden* **10** 59 36N 17 44 E
Sigüenza, *Spain* **24** 41 3N 2 40W
Siguiri, *Guinea* **90** 11 31N 9 10W
Sigulda, *U.S.S.R.* **36** 57 10N 24 55 E
Sigurd, *U.S.A.* **123** 38 49N 112 0W
Sihanoukville = Kompong Som, *Cambodia* **55** 10 38N 103 30 E
Sihaus, *Peru* **136** 8 40 S 77 40W
Sihui, *China* **59** 23 20N 112 40 E
Si'īr, *Jordan* **44** 31 35N 35 9 E
Siirt, *Turkey* **46** 37 57N 41 55 E
Sijarira Ra., *Zimb.* **93** 17 36 S 27 45 E
Sikao, *Thailand* **55** 7 34N 99 21 E
Sikar, *India* **48** 27 33N 75 10 E
Sikasso, *Mali* **90** 11 18N 5 35W
Sikeston, *U.S.A.* **121** 36 52N 89 35W
Sikhote Alin, Khrebet, *U.S.S.R.* **41** 46 0N 136 0 E
Sikiá., *Greece* **35** 40 2N 23 56 E
Síkinos, *Greece* **35** 36 40N 25 8 E
Sikkani Chief →, *Canada* **110** 57 47N 122 15W
Sikkim □, *India* **52** 27 50N 88 30 E
Sil →, *Spain* **22** 42 27N 7 43W
Sila, La, *Italy* **29** 39 15N 16 35 E
Silacayoapan, *Mexico* **127** 17 30N 98 9W
Silandro, *Italy* **26** 46 38N 10 48 E
Sīlat az Zahr, *Jordan* **44** 32 19N 35 11 E
Silba, *Yugoslavia* **27** 44 24N 14 41 E
Silchar, *India* **52** 24 49N 92 48 E
Silcox, *Canada* **111** 57 12N 94 10W
Silenrieux, *Belgium* **17** 50 14N 4 27 E
Siler City, *U.S.A.* **115** 35 44N 79 30W
Sileru →, *India* **50** 17 49N 81 24 E
Silesia = Slask, *Poland* **32** 51 0N 16 30 E
Silet, *Algeria* **85** 22 44N 4 37 E
Silgarhi Doti, *Nepal* **49** 29 15N 81 0 E
Silghat, *India* **52** 26 35N 93 0 E
Silifke, *Turkey* **46** 36 22N 33 58 E
Siling Co, *China* **62** 31 50N 89 20 E
Silíqua, *Italy* **28** 39 20N 8 49 E
Silistra, *Bulgaria* **34** 44 6N 27 19 E
Siljan, *Sweden* **10** 60 55N 14 45 E
Silkeborg, *Denmark* **11** 56 10N 9 32 E
Sillajhuay, Cordillera, *Chile* **136** 19 46 S 68 40W
Sillé-le-Guillaume, *France* **18** 48 10N 0 8W
Sillustani, *Peru* **136** 15 50 S 70 7W
Siloam Springs, *U.S.A.* **121** 36 15N 94 31W
Silsbee, *U.S.A.* **121** 30 20N 94 8W
Silute, *U.S.S.R.* **36** 55 21N 21 33 E
Silva Porto = Kuito, *Angola* **95** 12 22 S 16 55 E
Silver City, *N. Mex., U.S.A.* **123** 32 50N 108 18W
Silver City, *Nev., U.S.A.* **122** 39 15N 119 48W
Silver Cr. →, *U.S.A.* **122** 43 16N 119 13W
Silver Creek, *U.S.A.* **116** 42 33N 79 9W
Silver Grove, *U.S.A.* **119** 39 2N 84 24W
Silver L., *U.S.A.* **124** 38 39N 120 6W
Silver Lake, *Calif., U.S.A.* **125** 35 21N 116 7W
Silver Lake, *Ind., U.S.A.* **119** 41 4N 85 53W
Silver Lake, *Oreg., U.S.A.* **122** 43 9N 121 4W
Silver Lake, *Wis., U.S.A.* **119** 42 33N 88 13W
Silver Streams, *S. Africa* **96** 28 20 S 23 33 E
Silver Water, *Canada* **108** 45 52N 82 52W
Silverspur, *Australia* **77** 28 52 S 151 17 E
Silverton, *Colo., U.S.A.* **123** 37 51N 107 45W
Silverton, *Tex., U.S.A.* **121** 34 30N 101 16W
Silves, *Portugal* **23** 37 11N 8 26W
Silvi, *Italy* **27** 42 32N 14 5 E
Silvia, *Colombia* **134** 2 37N 76 21W
Silvies →, *U.S.A.* **122** 43 22N 118 48W
Silvolde, *Neths.* **16** 51 55N 6 23 E
Silvretta Gruppe, *Switz.* **31** 46 50N 10 6 E
Silwa Bahari, *Egypt* **88** 24 45N 32 55 E

Silwād, *Jordan* **44** 31 59N 35 15 E
Silz, *Austria* **31** 47 16N 10 56 E
Sim, C., *Morocco* **84** 31 26N 9 51W
Simanggang, *Malaysia* **56** 1 15N 111 32 E
Simao, *China* **58** 22 47N 101 5 E
Simão Dias, *Brazil* **138** 10 44 S 37 49W
Simard, L., *Canada* **106** 47 40N 78 40W
Simba, *Tanzania* **92** 2 10 S 37 36 E
Simbach, *W. Germany* **31** 48 16N 13 3 E
Simbo, *Tanzania* **92** 4 51 S 29 41 E
Simcoe, *Canada* **108** 42 50N 80 20W
Simcoe, L., *Canada* **108** 44 25N 79 20W
Simenga, *U.S.S.R.* **41** 62 42N 108 25 E
Simeto →, *Italy* **29** 37 25N 15 10 E
Simeulue, *Indonesia* **56** 2 45N 95 45 E
Simferopol, *U.S.S.R.* **38** 44 55N 34 3 E
Sími, *Greece* **35** 36 35N 27 50 E
Simi Valley, *U.S.A.* **125** 34 16N 118 47W
Simikot, *Nepal* **49** 30 0N 81 50 E
Simití, *Colombia* **134** 7 58N 73 57W
Simla, *India* **48** 31 2N 77 9 E
Şimleu-Silvaniei, *Romania* **34** 47 17N 22 50 E
Simmern, *W. Germany* **31** 49 59N 7 32 E
Simmie, *Canada* **111** 49 56N 108 6W
Simmler, *U.S.A.* **125** 35 21N 119 59W
Simões, *Brazil* **138** 7 36 S 40 49W
Simojärvi, *Finland* **8** 66 5N 27 3 E
Simojoki →, *Finland* **8** 65 35N 25 1 E
Simojovel, *Mexico* **127** 17 12N 92 38W
Simonette →, *Canada* **110** 55 9N 118 15W
Simonstown, *S. Africa* **96** 34 14 S 18 26 E
Simplício Mendes, *Brazil* **138** 7 51 S 41 54W
Simplon Pass = Simplonpass, *Switz.* **31** 46 15N 8 0 E
Simplon Tunnel, *Switz.* **31** 46 15N 8 7 E
Simplonpass, *Switz.* **31** 46 15N 8 0 E
Simpson Desert, *Australia* **72** 25 0 S 137 0 E
Simrishamn, *Sweden* **11** 55 33N 14 22 E
Simunjan, *Malaysia* **56** 1 25N 110 45 E
Simushir, Ostrov, *U.S.S.R.* **41** 46 50N 152 30 E
Sina →, *India* **50** 17 30N 75 55 E
Sinabang, *Indonesia* **56** 2 30N 96 24 E
Sinadogo, *Somali Rep.* **98** 5 50N 47 0 E
Sinai = Es Sînâ', *Egypt* **88** 29 0N 34 0 E
Sinai, Mt. = Mûsa, G., *Egypt* **88** 28 33N 33 59 E
Sinaia, *Romania* **34** 45 21N 25 38 E
Sinaloa □, *Mexico* **126** 25 0N 107 30W
Sinaloa de Levya, *Mexico* **126** 25 50N 108 20W
Sinalunga, *Italy* **27** 43 12N 11 43 E
Sinan, *China* **58** 27 56N 108 13 E
Sīnāwan, *Libya* **86** 31 0N 10 37 E
Sinbaungwe, *Burma* **52** 19 43N 95 10 E
Sinbo, *Burma* **52** 24 46N 97 3 E
Sincé, *Colombia* **134** 9 15N 75 9W
Sincelejo, *Colombia* **134** 9 18N 75 24W
Sinclair, *U.S.A.* **122** 41 47N 107 10W
Sinclair Mills, *Canada* **110** 54 5N 121 40W
Sincorá, Serra do, *Brazil* **139** 13 30 S 41 0W
Sind, *Pakistan* **48** 26 0N 68 30 E
Sind □, *Pakistan* **48** 26 0N 69 0 E
Sind →, *India* **49** 34 18N 74 45 E
Sind Sagar Doab, *Pakistan* **48** 32 0N 71 30 E
Sindal, *Denmark* **11** 57 28N 10 10 E
Sindangan, *Phil.* **57** 8 10N 123 5 E
Sindangbarang, *Indonesia* **57** 7 27 S 107 1 E
Sinde, *Zambia* **93** 17 28 S 25 51 E
Sinegorski, *U.S.S.R.* **39** 48 0N 40 52 E
Sinelnikovo, *U.S.S.R.* **38** 48 25N 35 30 E
Sines, *Portugal* **23** 37 56N 8 51W
Sines, C. de, *Portugal* **23** 37 58N 8 53W
Sineu, *Spain* **24** 39 38N 3 1 E
Sinewit, Mt., *Papua N. G.* **69** 4 44 S 152 2 E
Sinfra, *Ivory C.* **90** 6 35N 5 56W
Sing Buri, *Thailand* **54** 14 53N 100 25 E
Singa, *Sudan* **89** 13 10N 33 57 E
Singanallur, *India* **51** 11 2N 77 1 E
Singapore ■, *Asia* **55** 1 17N 103 51 E
Singapore, Straits of, *Asia* **55** 1 15N 104 0 E
Singaraja, *Indonesia* **56** 8 6 S 115 10 E
Singatoka, *Fiji* **68** 18 8 S 177 30 E
Singen, *W. Germany* **31** 47 45N 8 50 E
Singida, *Tanzania* **92** 4 49 S 34 48 E
Singida □, *Tanzania* **92** 6 0 S 34 30 E
Singitikós Kólpos, *Greece* **35** 40 6N 24 0 E
Singkaling Hkamti, *Burma* **52** 26 0N 95 39 E
Singkawang, *Indonesia* **56** 1 0N 108 57 E
Singleton, *Australia* **76** 32 33 S 151 0 E
Singleton, Mt., *Australia* **79** 29 27 S 117 15 E
Singö, *Sweden* **10** 60 12N 18 45 E
Singoli, *India* **48** 25 0N 75 22 E
Singora = Songkhla, *Thailand* **55** 7 13N 100 37 E
Siniscóla, *Italy* **28** 40 35N 9 40 E
Sinj, *Yugoslavia* **27** 43 42N 16 39 E
Sinjai, *Indonesia* **57** 5 7 S 120 20 E
Sinjār, *Iraq* **46** 36 19N 41 52 E
Sinjil, *Jordan* **44** 32 3N 35 15 E
Sinkat, *Sudan* **88** 18 55N 36 49 E
Sinkiang Uighur = Xinjiang Uygur Zizhiqu □, *China* **62** 42 0N 86 0 E
Sinnai, *Italy* **28** 39 18N 9 13 E
Sinnar, *India* **50** 19 48N 74 0 E
Sinni →, *Italy* **29** 40 9N 16 42 E
Sinnuris, *Egypt* **88** 29 26N 30 31 E
Sinoe, L., *Romania* **34** 44 35N 28 50 E
Sinop, *Turkey* **38** 42 1N 35 11 E
Sinskoye, *U.S.S.R.* **41** 61 8N 126 48 E
Sint-Amandsberg, *Belgium* **17** 51 4N 3 45 E
Sint Annaland, *Neths.* **17** 51 36N 4 6 E
Sint Annaparoch, *Neths.* **16** 53 16N 5 40 E
Sint-Denijs, *Belgium* **17** 50 45N 3 23 E
Sint Eustatius, I., *Neth. Ant.* **129** 17 30N 62 59W
Sint-Genesius-Rode, *Belgium* **17** 50 45N 4 22 E
Sint-Gillis-Waas, *Belgium* **17** 51 13N 4 6 E
Sint-Huibrechts-Lille, *Belgium* **17** 51 13N 5 29 E
Sint-Katelinje-Waver, *Belgium* **17** 51 5N 4 32 E
Sint-Kruis, *Belgium* **17** 51 13N 3 15 E
Sint-Laureins, *Belgium* **17** 51 14N 3 32 E
Sint Maarten, I., *W. Indies* **129** 18 4N 63 4W
Sint-Michiels, *Belgium* **17** 51 11N 3 15 E
Sint Nicolaasga, *Neths.* **16** 52 55N 5 45 E
Sint Niklaas, *Belgium* **17** 51 10N 4 9 E
Sint Oedenrode, *Neths.* **17** 51 35N 5 29 E
Sint Pancras, *Neths.* **16** 52 40N 4 48 E
Sint Philipsland, *Neths.* **17** 51 37N 4 10 E
Sint Truiden, *Belgium* **17** 50 48N 5 10 E
Sint Willebrord, *Neths.* **17** 51 33N 4 33 E
Sîntana, *Romania* **34** 46 20N 21 30 E
Sintang, *Indonesia* **56** 0 5N 111 35 E
Sintjohannesga, *Neths.* **16** 52 55N 5 52 E
Sinton, *U.S.A.* **121** 28 1N 97 30W
Sintra, *Portugal* **23** 38 47N 9 25W
Sinugif, *Somali Rep.* **98** 8 33N 48 59 E
Sinŭiju, *N. Korea* **61** 40 5N 124 24 E
Sinyukha →, *U.S.S.R.* **38** 48 3N 30 51 E
Siocon, *Phil.* **57** 7 40N 122 10 E
Siófok, *Hungary* **33** 46 54N 18 3 E
Sioma, *Zambia* **96** 16 25 S 23 28 E
Sion, *Switz.* **31** 46 14N 7 20 E
Sioux City, *U.S.A.* **120** 42 32N 96 25W
Sioux Falls, *U.S.A.* **120** 43 35N 96 40W
Sioux Lookout, *Canada* **104** 50 10N 91 50W
Sip Song Chau Thai, *Vietnam* **54** 21 30N 103 30 E
Siping, *China* **61** 43 8N 124 21 E
Sipiwesk L., *Canada* **111** 55 5N 97 35W
Siple, *Antarctica* **143** 75 0 S 74 0 E
Sipora, *Indonesia* **56** 2 18 S 99 40 E
Siquia →, *Nic.* **128** 12 10N 84 20W
Siquijor, *Phil.* **57** 9 12N 123 35 E
Siquirres, *Costa Rica* **128** 10 6N 83 30W
Siquisique, *Venezuela* **134** 10 34N 69 42W
Sir Edward Pellew Group, *Australia* **72** 15 40 S 137 10 E
Sir Graham Moore Is., *Australia* **78** 13 53 S 126 34 E
Sira, *India* **51** 13 41N 76 49 E
Siracusa, *Italy* **29** 37 4N 15 17 E
Sirajganj, *Bangla.* **49** 24 25N 89 47 E
Sirakoro, *Mali* **90** 12 41N 9 14W
Sirasso, *Ivory C.* **90** 9 16N 6 6W
Siret, *Romania* **34** 47 55N 26 5 E
Siret →, *Romania* **34** 45 24N 28 1 E
Şiria, *Romania* **34** 46 16N 21 38 E
Sirino, Monte, *Italy* **29** 40 7N 15 50 E
Sirkali = Sirkazhi, *India* **51** 11 15N 79 41 E
Sirkazhi, *India* **51** 11 15N 79 41 E
Sírna, *Greece* **35** 36 22N 26 42 E
Sirohi, *India* **48** 24 52N 72 53 E
Sironj, *India* **48** 24 5N 77 39 E
Síros, *Greece* **35** 37 28N 24 57 E
Sirretta Pk., *U.S.A.* **125** 35 56N 118 19W
Sirsa, *India* **48** 29 33N 75 4 E
Sirsi, *India* **51** 14 40N 74 49 E
Siruela, *Spain* **23** 38 58N 5 3W
Sisak, *Yugoslavia* **27** 45 30N 16 21 E
Sisaket, *Thailand* **54** 15 8N 104 23 E
Sisante, *Spain* **25** 39 25N 2 12W
Sisargas, Is., *Spain* **22** 43 21N 8 50W
Sishen, *S. Africa* **96** 27 47 S 22 59 E
Sishui, *Henan, China* **60** 34 48N 113 15 E
Sishui, *Shandong, China* **61** 35 42N 117 18 E
Sisipuk L., *Canada* **111** 55 45N 101 50W
Sisophon, *Cambodia* **54** 13 38N 102 59 E
Sisseton, *U.S.A.* **120** 45 43N 97 3W
Sissonne, *France* **19** 49 34N 3 51 E
Sīstān va Balūchestān □, *Iran* **47** 27 0N 62 0 E
Sistema Central, *Spain* **22** 40 40N 5 55W
Sistema Iberico, *Spain* **24** 41 0N 2 10W
Sisteron, *France* **21** 44 12N 5 57 E
Sisters, *U.S.A.* **122** 44 21N 121 32W
Sitamarhi, *India* **49** 26 37N 85 30 E
Sitapur, *India* **49** 27 38N 80 45 E
Siteki, *Swaziland* **97** 26 32 S 31 58 E
Sitges, *Spain* **24** 41 17N 1 47 E
Sitía, *Greece* **35** 35 13N 26 6 E
Sítio da Abadia, *Brazil* **139** 14 48 S 46 16W
Sitka, *U.S.A.* **102** 57 9N 135 20W
Sitoti, *Botswana* **96** 23 15 S 23 40 E
Sitra, *Egypt* **88** 28 40N 26 53 E
Sittang →, *Burma* **52** 17 10N 96 58 E
Sittard, *Neths.* **17** 51 0N 5 52 E
Sittaung, *Burma* **52** 24 10N 94 35 E
Sittensen, *W. Germany* **30** 53 17N 9 32 E
Sittona, *Ethiopia* **89** 14 25N 37 23 E
Sittwe, *Burma* **52** 20 18N 92 45 E
Situbondo, *Indonesia* **57** 7 45 S 114 0 E
Siuna, *Nic.* **128** 13 37N 84 45W
Siuri, *India* **49** 23 50N 87 34 E
Sivaganga, *India* **51** 9 50N 78 28 E
Sivagiri, *India* **51** 9 16N 77 26 E
Sivakasi, *India* **51** 9 24N 77 47 E
Sivana, *India* **48** 28 37N 78 6 E
Sīvand, *Iran* **47** 30 5N 52 55 E
Sivas, *Turkey* **46** 39 43N 36 58 E
Siverek, *Turkey* **46** 37 50N 39 19 E
Sivrihisar, *Turkey* **46** 39 30N 31 35 E
Sivry, *Belgium* **17** 50 10N 4 12 E
Sīwa, *Egypt* **88** 29 11N 25 31 E
Sīwa, El Wâhât es, *Egypt* **88** 29 10N 25 30 E
Siwalik Range, *Nepal* **49** 28 0N 83 0 E
Siwan, *India* **49** 26 13N 84 21 E
Siyâl, Jazâ'ir, *Egypt* **88** 22 49N 36 12 E
Sizewell, *U.K.* **13** 52 13N 1 38 E
Siziwang Qi, *China* **60** 41 25N 111 40 E
Sjælland, *Denmark* **11** 55 30N 11 30 E
Sjællands Odde, *Denmark* **11** 56 0N 11 15 E
Själevad, *Sweden* **10** 63 18N 18 36 E
Sjenica, *Yugoslavia* **33** 43 16N 20 0 E
Sjoa, *Norway* **10** 61 41N 9 33 E
Sjöbo, *Sweden* **11** 55 37N 13 45 E
Sjösa, *Sweden* **11** 58 47N 17 4 E
Sjumen = Šumen, *Bulgaria* **34** 43 18N 26 55 E
Skadovsk, *U.S.S.R.* **38** 46 17N 32 52 E
Skagafjörður, *Iceland* **8** 65 54N 19 35W
Skagastølstindane, *Norway* **9** 61 28N 7 52 E
Skagen, *Denmark* **11** 57 43N 10 35 E
Skagen, *Norway* **9** 68 37N 14 27 E
Skagern, *Sweden* **10** 59 0N 14 20 E
Skagerrak, *Denmark* **11** 57 30N 9 0 E
Skagit →, *U.S.A.* **124** 48 20N 122 25W
Skagway, *U.S.A.* **102** 59 23N 135 20W
Skaidi, *Norway* **8** 70 26N 24 30 E
Skala Podolskaya, *U.S.S.R.* **38** 48 50N 26 15 E
Skalat, *U.S.S.R.* **36** 49 23N 25 55 E
Skalni Dol = Kamenyak, *Bulgaria* **34** 43 24N 26 57 E
Skals, *Denmark* **11** 56 34N 9 24 E
Skanderborg, *Denmark* **11** 56 2N 9 55 E
Skänninge, *Sweden* **11** 58 24N 15 5 E
Skanör, *Sweden* **11** 55 24N 12 50 E
Skara, *Sweden* **11** 58 25N 13 30 E
Skaraborgs län □, *Sweden* **11** 58 20N 13 30 E
Skardu, *Pakistan* **49** 35 20N 75 44 E
Skarrild, *Denmark* **11** 55 58N 8 53 E
Skarzysko Kamienna, *Poland* **32** 51 7N 20 52 E
Skattungbyn, *Sweden* **10** 61 10N 14 56 E
Skebokvarn, *Sweden* **10** 59 7N 16 45 E
Skeena →, *Canada* **110** 54 9N 130 5W
Skeena Mts., *Canada* **110** 56 40N 128 30W
Skegness, *U.K.* **12** 53 9N 0 20 E
Skeldon, *Guyana* **135** 5 55N 57 20W
Skellefte älv →, *Sweden* **8** 64 45N 21 10 E
Skellefteå, *Sweden* **8** 64 45N 20 58 E
Skelleftehamn, *Sweden* **8** 64 47N 20 59 E
Skender Vakuf, *Yugoslavia* **33** 44 29N 17 22 E
Skene, *Sweden* **11** 57 30N 12 37 E
Skenes Creek, *Australia* **74** 38 43 S 143 43 E
Skerries, The, *U.K.* **12** 53 27N 4 40W
Skhoinoúsa, *Greece* **35** 36 53N 25 31 E
Ski, *Norway* **10** 59 43N 10 52 E
Skíathos, *Greece* **35** 39 12N 23 30 E
Skibbereen, *Ireland* **15** 51 33N 9 16W
Skiddaw, *U.K.* **12** 54 39N 3 9W
Skien, *Norway* **10** 59 12N 9 35 E
Skierniewice, *Poland* **32** 51 58N 20 10 E
Skikda, *Algeria* **85** 36 50N 6 58 E
Skillett Fork, Little Wabash →, *U.S.A.* **119** 38 6N 88 9W
Skillingaryd, *Sweden* **11** 57 27N 14 5 E
Skillinge, *Sweden* **11** 55 30N 14 16 E
Skillingmark, *Sweden* **10** 59 48N 12 1 E
Skinári, Ákra, *Greece* **35** 37 56N 20 40 E
Skipton, *Australia* **74** 37 39 S 143 40 E
Skipton, *U.K.* **12** 53 57N 2 1W
Skirmish Pt., *Australia* **72** 11 59 S 134 17 E
Skíros, *Greece* **35** 38 55N 24 34 E
Skivarp, *Sweden* **11** 55 26N 13 34 E
Skive, *Denmark* **11** 56 33N 9 2 E
Skjálfandafljót →, *Iceland* **8** 65 59N 17 25W
Skjálfandi, *Iceland* **8** 66 5N 17 30W
Skjeberg, *Norway* **10** 59 12N 11 12 E
Skjern, *Denmark* **11** 55 57N 8 30 E
Škofja Loka, *Yugoslavia* **27** 46 9N 14 19 E
Skoghall, *Sweden* **10** 59 20N 13 30 E
Skokie, *U.S.A.* **119** 42 3N 87 45W
Skole, *U.S.S.R.* **36** 49 3N 23 30 E
Skópelos, *Greece* **35** 39 9N 23 47 E
Skopin, *U.S.S.R.* **37** 53 55N 39 32 E
Skopje, *Yugoslavia* **35** 42 1N 21 32 E
Skórcz, *Poland* **32** 53 47N 18 30 E
Skövde, *Sweden* **9** 58 15N 13 59 E
Skovorodino, *U.S.S.R.* **41** 54 0N 125 0 E
Skowhegan, *U.S.A.* **105** 44 49N 69 40W
Skownan, *Canada* **111** 51 58N 99 35W
Skradin, *Yugoslavia* **27** 43 52N 15 53 E
Skreanäs, *Sweden* **11** 56 52N 12 35 E
Skudeneshavn, *Norway* **9** 59 10N 5 10 E
Skull, *Ireland* **15** 51 32N 9 40W
Skultorp, *Sweden* **11** 58 24N 13 51 E
Skunk →, *U.S.A.* **118** 40 42N 91 7W
Skuodas, *U.S.S.R.* **36** 56 21N 21 45 E
Skurup, *Sweden* **11** 55 28N 13 30 E
Skutskär, *Sweden* **11** 60 37N 17 25 E
Skvira, *U.S.S.R.* **38** 49 44N 29 40 E
Skwierzyna, *Poland* **32** 52 33N 15 30 E
Skye, *U.K.* **14** 57 15N 6 10W
Skykomish, *U.S.A.* **122** 47 43N 121 16W
Skyros = Skíros, *Greece* **35** 38 55N 24 34 E
Slagelse, *Denmark* **11** 55 23N 11 19 E
Slagharen, *Neths.* **16** 52 37N 6 34 E
Slamet, *Indonesia* **56** 7 16 S 109 8 E
Slaney →, *Ireland* **15** 52 52N 6 45W
Slangerup, *Denmark* **11** 55 50N 12 11 E
Slano, *Yugoslavia* **33** 42 48N 17 53 E
Slantsy, *U.S.S.R.* **36** 59 7N 28 5 E
Ślązk, *Poland* **32** 51 0N 16 30 E
Slate Is., *Canada* **104** 48 40N 87 0W
Slater, *U.S.A.* **118** 39 13N 93 4W
Slatina, *Romania* **34** 44 28N 24 22 E
Slaton, *U.S.A.* **121** 33 27N 101 38W
Slave →, *Canada* **110** 61 18N 113 39W
Slave Coast, *W. Afr.* **91** 6 0N 2 30 E
Slave Lake, *Canada* **110** 55 17N 114 43W
Slave Pt., *Canada* **110** 61 11N 115 56W
Slavgorod, *U.S.S.R.* **40** 53 1N 78 37 E
Slavnoye, *U.S.S.R.* **36** 54 24N 29 15 E
Slavonska Požega, *Yugoslavia* **33** 45 20N 17 40 E
Slavonski Brod, *Yugoslavia* **33** 45 11N 18 0 E
Slavuta, *U.S.S.R.* **36** 50 15N 27 2 E
Slavyansk, *U.S.S.R.* **38** 48 55N 37 36 E
Slavyansk-na-Kubani, *U.S.S.R.* **38** 45 15N 38 11 E
Sławno, *Poland* **32** 54 20N 16 41 E
Sławoborze, *Poland* **32** 53 55N 15 42 E
Sleaford, *U.K.* **12** 53 0N 0 22W
Sleaford B., *Australia* **73** 34 55 S 135 45 E
Sleat, Sd. of, *U.K.* **14** 57 5N 5 47W
Sleeper Is., *Canada* **103** 58 30N 81 0W
Sleepy Eye, *U.S.A.* **120** 44 15N 94 45W
Sleidinge, *Belgium* **17** 51 8N 3 41 E
Sleman, *Indonesia* **57** 7 40 S 110 20 E
Slemon L., *Canada* **110** 63 13N 116 4W
Slidell, *U.S.A.* **121** 30 20N 89 48W
Sliedrecht, *Neths.* **16** 51 50N 4 45 E
Slieve Aughty, *Ireland* **15** 53 4N 8 30W
Slieve Bloom, *Ireland* **15** 53 4N 7 40W
Slieve Donard, *U.K.* **15** 54 10N 5 57W
Slieve Gullion, *U.K.* **15** 54 8N 6 26W
Slieve Mish, *Ireland* **15** 52 12N 9 50W
Slievenamon, *Ireland* **15** 52 25N 7 37W
Sligo, *Ireland* **15** 54 17N 8 28W
Sligo □, *Ireland* **15** 54 10N 8 35W
Sligo B., *Ireland* **15** 54 20N 8 40W
Slijpe, *Belgium* **17** 51 9N 2 51 E
Slikkerveer, *Neths.* **16** 51 53N 4 36 E
Slite, *Sweden* **11** 57 42N 18 48 E
Sliven, *Bulgaria* **34** 42 42N 26 19 E
Slivnitsa, *Bulgaria* **34** 42 50N 23 0 E
Sljeme, *Yugoslavia* **27** 45 57N 15 58 E
Sloan, *U.S.A.* **125** 35 57N 115 13W
Sloansville, *U.S.A.* **117** 42 45N 74 22W
Slobodskoy, *U.S.S.R.* **37** 58 40N 50 6 E
Slobozia, *Romania* **34** 44 34N 27 23 E
Slocan, *Canada* **110** 49 48N 117 28W
Slochteren, *Neths.* **16** 53 12N 6 48 E
Slöinge, *Sweden* **11** 56 51N 12 42 E
Slonim, *U.S.S.R.* **36** 53 4N 25 19 E
Slotermeer, *Neths.* **16** 52 55N 5 38 E
Slough, *U.K.* **13** 51 30N 0 35W
Sloughhouse, *U.S.A.* **124** 38 26N 121 12W
Slovakian Ore Mts. = Slovenské Rudohorie, *Czech.* **32** 48 45N 20 0 E
Slovenia = Slovenija □, *Yugoslavia* **27** 45 58N 14 30 E
Slovenija □, *Yugoslavia* **27** 45 58N 14 30 E
Slovenj Gradec, *Yugoslavia* **27** 46 31N 15 5 E
Slovenska Bistrica, *Yugoslavia* **27** 46 24N 15 35 E
Slovenské Rudohorie, *Czech.* **32** 48 45N 20 0 E
Słubice, *Poland* **32** 52 22N 14 35 E
Sluch →, *U.S.S.R.* **36** 51 37N 26 38 E
Sluis, *Neths.* **17** 51 18N 3 23 E
Slunj, *Yugoslavia* **27** 45 6N 15 33 E
Słupca, *Poland* **32** 52 15N 17 52 E
Słupsk, *Poland* **32** 54 30N 17 3 E
Slurry, *S. Africa* **96** 25 49 S 25 42 E
Slutsk, *U.S.S.R.* **36** 53 2N 27 31 E
Slyne Hd., *Ireland* **15** 53 25N 10 10W
Slyudyanka, *U.S.S.R.* **41** 51 40N 103 40 E
Smålandsfarvandet, *Denmark* **11** 55 10N 11 20 E
Smålandsstenar, *Sweden* **11** 57 10N 13 25 E
Small Nggela, *Solomon Is.* **68** 9 0 S 160 0 E
Smalltree L., *Canada* **111** 61 0N 105 0W
Smarje, *Yugoslavia* **27** 46 15N 15 34 E

Smartt Syndicate Dam, *S. Africa* **96** 30 45 S 23 10 E
Smartville, *U.S.A.* **124** 39 13N 121 18W
Smeaton, *Canada* **111** 53 30N 104 49W
Smederevo, *Yugoslavia* **33** 44 40N 20 57 E
Smederevska Palanka, *Yugoslavia* **33** 44 22N 20 58 E
Smela, *U.S.S.R.* **38** 49 15N 31 58 E
Smethport, *U.S.A.* **116** 41 50N 78 28W
Smidovich, *U.S.S.R.* **41** 48 36N 133 49 E
Smilde, *Neths.* **16** 52 58N 6 28 E
Smiley, *Canada* **111** 51 38N 109 29W
Smith, *Canada* **110** 55 10N 114 0W
Smith →, *Canada* **110** 59 34N 126 30W
Smith Arm, *Canada* **102** 66 15N 123 0W
Smith Center, *U.S.A.* **120** 39 50N 98 50W
Smith Sund, *Greenland* **144** 78 30N 74 0W
Smithburne →, *Australia* **72** 17 3 S 140 57 E
Smithers, *Canada* **110** 54 45N 127 10W
Smithfield, *S. Africa* **97** 30 9 S 26 30 E
Smithfield, *N.C., U.S.A.* **115** 35 31N 78 16W
Smithfield, *Utah, U.S.A.* **122** 41 50N 111 50W
Smiths Falls, *Canada* **109** 44 55N 76 0W
Smithton, *Australia* **72** 40 53 S 145 6 E
Smithtown, *Australia* **77** 30 58 S 152 48 E
Smithville, *Canada* **108** 43 6N 79 33W
Smithville, *Mo., U.S.A.* **118** 39 23N 94 35W
Smithville, *Tex., U.S.A.* **121** 30 2N 97 12W
Smoky →, *Canada* **110** 56 10N 117 21W
Smoky Bay, *Australia* **73** 32 22 S 134 13 E
Smoky Cape, *Australia* **77** 30 55 S 153 5 E
Smoky Falls, *Canada* **104** 50 4N 82 10W
Smoky Hill →, *U.S.A.* **120** 39 3N 96 48W
Smoky Lake, *Canada* **110** 54 10N 112 30W
Smøla, *Norway* **10** 63 23N 8 3 E
Smolensk, *U.S.S.R.* **36** 54 45N 32 0 E
Smolikas, Óros, *Greece* **35** 40 9N 20 58 E
Smolník, *Czech.* **32** 48 43N 20 44 E
Smolyan, *Bulgaria* **35** 41 36N 24 38 E
Smooth Rock Falls, *Canada* **104** 49 17N 81 37W
Smoothstone L., *Canada* **111** 54 40N 106 50W
Smorgon, *U.S.S.R.* **36** 54 20N 26 24 E
Smyadovo, *Bulgaria* **34** 43 2N 27 1 E
Smyrna = İzmir, *Turkey* **46** 38 25N 27 8 E
Snaefell, *U.K.* **12** 54 18N 4 26W
Snæfellsjökull, *Iceland* **8** 64 49N 23 46W
Snake →, *U.S.A.* **122** 46 12N 119 2W
Snake I., *Australia* **75** 38 47 S 146 33 E
Snake L., *Canada* **111** 55 32N 106 35W
Snake Ra., *U.S.A.* **122** 39 0N 114 30W
Snake River Plain, *U.S.A.* **122** 43 13N 113 0W
Snake Valley, *Australia* **74** 37 37 S 143 35 E
Snapper Point, *Australia* **77** 35 34 S 150 23 E
Snarum, *Norway* **10** 60 1N 9 54 E
Snedsted, *Denmark* **11** 56 55N 8 32 E
Sneek, *Neths.* **16** 53 2N 5 40 E
Sneeker-meer, *Neths.* **16** 53 2N 5 45 E
Sneeuberge, *S. Africa* **96** 31 46 S 24 20 E
Snejbjerg, *Denmark* **11** 56 8N 8 54 E
Snelling, *U.S.A.* **124** 37 31N 120 26W
Snezhnoye, *U.S.S.R.* **39** 48 0N 38 58 E
Snežnik, *Yugoslavia* **27** 45 36N 14 35 E
Snigirevka, *U.S.S.R.* **38** 47 2N 32 49 E
Snizort, L., *U.K.* **14** 57 33N 6 28W
Snøhetta, *Norway* **10** 62 19N 9 16 E
Snohomish, *U.S.A.* **124** 47 53N 122 6W
Snoul, *Cambodia* **55** 12 4N 106 26 E
Snow Hill, *U.S.A.* **114** 38 10N 75 21W
Snow Lake, *Canada* **111** 54 52N 100 3W
Snow Mt., *U.S.A.* **124** 39 22N 122 44W
Snowbird L., *Canada* **111** 60 45N 103 0W
Snowdon, *U.K.* **12** 53 4N 4 8W
Snowdrift, *Canada* **111** 62 24N 110 44W
Snowdrift →, *Canada* **111** 62 24N 110 44W
Snowflake, *U.S.A.* **123** 34 30N 110 4W
Snowshoe Pk., *U.S.A.* **122** 48 13N 115 41W
Snowtown, *Australia* **73** 33 46 S 138 14 E
Snowville, *U.S.A.* **122** 41 59N 112 47W
Snowy →, *Australia* **75** 37 46 S 148 30 E
Snowy Mts., *Australia* **75** 36 30 S 148 20 E
Snug Corner, *Bahamas* **129** 22 33N 73 52W
Snyatyn, *U.S.S.R.* **38** 48 30N 25 50 E
Snyder, *Okla., U.S.A.* **121** 34 40N 99 0W
Snyder, *Tex., U.S.A.* **121** 32 45N 100 57W
Soacha, *Colombia* **134** 4 35N 74 13W
Soahanina, *Madag.* **97** 18 42 S 44 13 E
Soalala, *Madag.* **97** 16 6 S 45 20 E
Soan →, *Pakistan* **48** 33 1N 71 44 E
Soanierana-Ivongo, *Madag.* **97** 16 55 S 49 35 E
Soap Lake, *U.S.A.* **122** 47 23N 119 31W
Sobat, Nahr →, *Sudan* **89** 9 22N 31 33 E
Sobhapur, *India* **48** 22 47N 78 17 E
Sobinka, *U.S.S.R.* **37** 56 0N 40 0 E
Sobo-Yama, *Japan* **62** 32 51N 131 22 E
Sobótka, *Poland* **32** 50 54N 16 44 E
Sobrado, *Spain* **22** 43 2N 8 2W
Sobral, *Brazil* **138** 3 50 S 40 20W
Sobreira Formosa, *Portugal* **23** 39 46N 7 51W
Soc Giang, *Vietnam* **54** 22 54N 106 1 E
Soc Trang, *Vietnam* **55** 9 37N 105 50 E
Soča →, *Europe* **27** 46 20N 13 40 E
Sochaczew, *Poland* **32** 52 15N 20 13 E
Soch'e = Shache, *China* **62** 38 20N 77 10 E
Sochi, *U.S.S.R.* **39** 43 35N 39 40 E
Société, Is. de la, *Pac. Oc.* **67** 17 0 S 151 0W
Society Is. = Société, Is. de la, *Pac. Oc.* **67** 17 0 S 151 0W
Socompa, Portezuelo de, *Chile* **140** 24 27 S 68 18W
Socorro, *Colombia* **134** 6 29N 73 16W
Socorro, *U.S.A.* **123** 34 4N 106 54W
Socorro, I., *Mexico* **126** 18 45N 110 58W
Socotra, *Ind. Oc.* **45** 12 30N 54 0 E
Socúellmos, *Spain* **25** 39 16N 2 47W
Soda L., *U.S.A.* **123** 35 7N 116 2W
Soda Plains, *India* **49** 35 30N 79 0 E
Soda Springs, *U.S.A.* **122** 42 40N 111 40W
Söderfors, *Sweden* **10** 60 23N 17 25 E
Söderhamn, *Sweden* **10** 61 18N 17 10 E
Söderköping, *Sweden* **10** 58 31N 16 20 E
Södermanlands län □, *Sweden* **10** 59 10N 16 30 E
Södertälje, *Sweden* **10** 59 12N 17 39 E
Sodiri, *Sudan* **89** 14 27N 29 0 E
Sodo, *Ethiopia* **89** 7 0N 37 41 E
Södra Vi, *Sweden* **11** 57 45N 15 45 E
Sodražica, *Yugoslavia* **27** 45 45N 14 39 E
Sodus, *U.S.A.* **116** 43 13N 77 5W
Soekmekaar, *S. Africa* **97** 23 30 S 29 55 E
Soest, *Neths.* **16** 52 9N 5 19 E
Soest, *W. Germany* **30** 51 34N 8 7 E
Soestdijk, *Neths.* **16** 52 11N 5 17 E
Sofádhes, *Greece* **35** 39 20N 22 4 E
Sofala, *Australia* **76** 33 4 S 149 43 E
Sofara, *Mali* **90** 13 59N 4 9W
Sofia = Sofiya, *Bulgaria* **34** 42 45N 23 20 E
Sofia →, *Madag.* **97** 15 27 S 47 23 E
Sofievka, *U.S.S.R.* **38** 48 6N 33 55 E
Sofiiski, *U.S.S.R.* **41** 52 15N 133 59 E
Sofikón, *Greece* **35** 37 47N 23 3 E
Sofiya, *Bulgaria* **34** 42 45N 23 20 E
Sogakofe, *Ghana* **91** 6 2N 0 39 E
Sogamoso, *Colombia* **134** 5 43N 72 56W
Sögel, *W. Germany* **30** 52 50N 7 32 E
Sogeri, *Papua N. G.* **69** 9 26 S 147 35 E
Sogn og Fjordane fylke □, *Norway* **9** 61 40N 6 0 E
Sogndalsfjøra, *Norway* **9** 61 14N 7 5 E
Sognefjorden, *Norway* **9** 61 10N 5 50 E
Sohâg, *Egypt* **88** 26 33N 31 43 E
Sohano, *Papua N. G.* **69** 5 22 S 154 37 E
Soignies, *Belgium* **17** 50 35N 4 5 E
Soira, Mt., *Ethiopia* **89** 14 45N 39 30 E
Soissons, *France* **19** 49 25N 3 19 E
Sōja, *Japan* **64** 34 40N 133 45 E
Sojat, *India* **48** 25 55N 73 45 E
Sok →, *U.S.S.R.* **37** 53 24N 50 8 E
Sokal, *U.S.S.R.* **36** 50 31N 24 15 E
Söke, *Turkey* **46** 37 48N 27 28 E
Sokelo, *Zaïre* **93** 9 55 S 24 36 E
Sokki, Oued In →, *Algeria* **85** 29 30N 3 42 E
Sokna, *Norway* **10** 60 16N 9 50 E
Soknedal, *Norway* **10** 62 57N 10 13 E
Soko Banja, *Yugoslavia* **33** 43 40N 21 51 E
Sokodé, *Togo* **91** 9 0N 1 11 E
Sokol, *U.S.S.R.* **37** 59 30N 40 5 E
Sokółka, *Poland* **32** 53 25N 23 30 E
Sokolo, *Mali* **90** 14 53N 6 8W
Sokołów Małpolski, *Poland* **32** 50 12N 22 7 E
Sokołów Podlaski, *Poland* **32** 52 25N 22 15 E
Sokoto, *Nigeria* **91** 13 2N 5 16 E
Sokoto □, *Nigeria* **91** 12 30N 5 0 E
Sokoto →, *Nigeria* **91** 11 20N 4 10 E
Sol Iletsk, *U.S.S.R.* **40** 51 10N 55 0 E
Solai, *Kenya* **92** 0 2N 36 12 E
Solana, La, *Spain* **25** 38 59N 3 14W
Solano, *Phil.* **57** 16 31N 121 15 E
Solapur, *India* **50** 17 43N 75 56 E
Solares, *Spain* **22** 43 23N 3 43W
Solberga, *Sweden* **11** 57 45N 14 43 E
Solec Kujawski, *Poland* **32** 53 5N 18 14 E
Soledad, *Colombia* **134** 10 55N 74 46W
Soledad, *U.S.A.* **124** 36 27N 121 16W
Soledad, *Venezuela* **135** 8 10N 63 34W
Solent, The, *U.K.* **13** 50 45N 1 25W
Solenzara, *France* **21** 41 53N 9 23 E
Solesmes, *France* **19** 50 10N 3 30 E
Solfonn, *Norway* **9** 60 2N 6 57 E
Soligalich, *U.S.S.R.* **37** 59 5N 42 10 E
Soligorsk, *U.S.S.R.* **36** 52 51N 27 27 E
Solikamsk, *U.S.S.R.* **40** 59 38N 56 50 E
Solila, *Madag.* **97** 21 25 S 46 37 E
Solimões → = Amazonas →, *S. Amer.* **135** 0 5 S 50 0W
Solingen, *W. Germany* **17** 51 10N 7 4 E
Sollebrunn, *Sweden* **11** 58 8N 12 32 E
Sollefteå, *Sweden* **10** 63 12N 17 20 E
Sollentuna, *Sweden* **10** 59 26N 17 56 E
Sóller, *Spain* **24** 39 46N 2 43 E
Solling, *W. Germany* **30** 51 44N 9 36 E
Solna, *Sweden* **10** 59 22N 18 1 E
Solnechnogorsk, *U.S.S.R.* **37** 56 10N 36 57 E
Sologne, *France* **19** 47 40N 1 45 E
Solok, *Indonesia* **56** 0 45 S 100 40 E
Sololá, *Guatemala* **128** 14 49N 91 10 E
Solomon, N. Fork →, *U.S.A.* **120** 39 29N 98 26W
Solomon, S. Fork →, *U.S.A.* **120** 39 25N 99 12W
Solomon Is. ■, *Pac. Oc.* **68** 6 0 S 155 0 E
Solomon Sea, *Papua N. G.* **69** 7 0 S 150 0 E
Solomon's Pools = Birak Sulaymān, *Jordan* **44** 31 42N 35 7 E
Solon, *China* **62** 46 32N 121 10 E
Solon Springs, *U.S.A.* **120** 46 19N 91 47W
Solonópole, *Brazil* **138** 5 44 S 39 1W
Solor, *Indonesia* **57** 8 27 S 123 0 E
Solotcha, *U.S.S.R.* **37** 54 48N 39 53 E
Solothurn, *Switz.* **31** 47 13N 7 32 E
Solothurn □, *Switz.* **31** 47 18N 7 40 E
Solsona, *Spain* **24** 42 0N 1 31 E
Solta, *Yugoslavia* **27** 43 24N 16 15 E
Solṭānābād, *Iran* **47** 36 29N 58 5 E
Soltau, *W. Germany* **30** 52 59N 9 50 E
Soltsy, *U.S.S.R.* **36** 58 10N 30 30 E
Solunska Glava, *Yugoslavia* **35** 41 44N 21 31 E
Solvang, *U.S.A.* **125** 34 36N 120 8W
Solvay, *U.S.A.* **117** 43 5N 76 17W
Sölvesborg, *Sweden* **11** 56 5N 14 35 E
Solway Firth, *U.K.* **12** 54 45N 3 38W
Solwezi, *Zambia* **93** 12 11 S 26 21 E
Somali Rep. ■, *Africa* **98** 7 0N 47 0 E
Sombe Dzong, *Bhutan* **52** 27 13N 89 8 E
Sombernon, *France* **19** 47 20N 4 40 E
Sombor, *Yugoslavia* **33** 45 46N 19 9 E
Sombra, *Canada* **108** 42 43N 82 29W
Sombrerete, *Mexico* **126** 23 40N 103 40W
Sombrero, *Anguilla* **129** 18 37N 63 30W
Someren, *Neths.* **17** 51 23N 5 42 E
Somers, *U.S.A.* **122** 48 4N 114 18W
Somerset, *Canada* **111** 49 25N 98 39W
Somerset, *Colo., U.S.A.* **123** 38 55N 107 30W
Somerset, *Ky., U.S.A.* **114** 37 5N 84 40W
Somerset, *Mass., U.S.A.* **117** 41 45N 71 10W
Somerset, *Pa., U.S.A.* **116** 40 1N 79 4W
Somerset □, *U.K.* **13** 51 9N 3 0W
Somerset East, *S. Africa* **96** 32 42 S 25 35 E
Somerset I., *Canada* **102** 73 30N 93 0W
Somerset West, *S. Africa* **96** 34 8 S 18 50 E
Somerton, *Australia* **77** 30 55 S 150 38 E
Somerton, *U.S.A.* **123** 32 35N 114 47W
Somerville, *Australia* **74** 38 14 S 145 11 E
Somerville, *U.S.A.* **117** 40 34N 74 36W
Someş →, *Romania* **34** 47 49N 22 43 E
Someşul Mare →, *Romania* **34** 47 18N 24 30 E
Somma Lombardo, *Italy* **26** 45 41N 8 42 E
Somma Vesuviana, *Italy* **29** 40 52N 14 23 E
Sommariva, *Australia* **73** 26 24 S 146 36 E
Sommatino, *Italy* **28** 37 20N 14 0 E
Somme □, *France* **19** 50 0N 2 20 E
Somme →, *France* **19** 50 11N 1 38 E
Somme, B. de la, *France* **18** 50 14N 1 33 E
Sommelsdijk, *Neths.* **16** 51 46N 4 9 E
Sommen, *Jönköping, Sweden* **11** 58 12N 15 0 E
Sommen, *Östergötland, Sweden* **11** 58 0N 15 15 E
Sommepy-Tahure, *France* **19** 49 15N 4 31 E
Sömmerda, *E. Germany* **30** 51 10N 11 8 E
Sommesous, *France* **19** 48 44N 4 12 E
Sommières, *France* **21** 43 47N 4 6 E
Somosomo Str., *Fiji* **68** 16 0 S 180 0 E
Somoto, *Nic.* **128** 13 28N 86 37W
Sompolno, *Poland* **32** 52 26N 18 30 E
Somport, Paso, *Spain* **24** 42 48N 0 31W
Somport, Puerto de, *Spain* **24** 42 48N 0 31W
Somuncurá, Meseta de, *Argentina* **142** 41 30 S 67 0W
Son, *Neths.* **17** 51 31N 5 30 E
Son, *Norway* **10** 59 32N 10 42 E
Son, *Spain* **22** 42 43N 8 58W
Son Ha, *Vietnam* **54** 15 3N 108 34 E
Son Hoa, *Vietnam* **54** 13 2N 108 58 E
Son La, *Vietnam* **54** 21 20N 103 50 E
Son Tay, *Vietnam* **54** 21 8N 105 30 E
Soná, *Panama* **128** 8 0N 81 20W
Sonamarg, *India* **49** 34 18N 75 21 E
Sonamukhi, *India* **49** 23 18N 87 27 E
Sonamura, *India* **52** 23 29N 91 15 E
Soncino, *Italy* **26** 45 24N 9 52 E
Sondag →, *S. Africa* **96** 33 44 S 25 51 E
Sóndalo, *Italy* **26** 46 20N 10 20 E
Sondar, *India* **49** 33 28N 75 56 E
Sønder Omme, *Denmark* **11** 55 50N 8 54 E
Sønder Ternby, *Denmark* **11** 57 31N 9 58 E
Sønderborg, *Denmark* **11** 54 55N 9 49 E
Sønderjyllands Amtskommune □, *Denmark* **11** 55 10N 9 10 E
Sondershausen, *E. Germany* **30** 51 22N 10 50 E
Sóndrio, *Italy* **26** 46 10N 9 53 E
Sone, *Mozam.* **93** 17 23 S 34 55 E
Sonepur, *India* **50** 20 55N 83 50 E
Song, *Thailand* **54** 18 28N 100 11 E
Song Cau, *Vietnam* **54** 13 27N 109 18 E
Song Xian, *China* **60** 34 12N 112 8 E
Songea, *Tanzania* **93** 10 40 S 35 40 E
Songea □, *Tanzania* **93** 10 30 S 36 0 E
Songeons, *France* **19** 49 32N 1 50 E
Songhua Hu, *China* **61** 43 35N 126 50 E
Songhua Jiang →, *China* **61** 47 45N 132 30 E
Songjiang, *China* **59** 31 1N 121 12 E
Songkan, *China* **58** 28 35N 106 52 E
Songkhla, *Thailand* **55** 7 13N 100 37 E
Songming, *China* **58** 25 12N 103 2 E
Songo, *Angola* **95** 7 22 S 14 51 E
Songololo, *Zaïre* **95** 5 42 S 14 2 E
Songpan, *China* **58** 32 40N 103 30 E
Songtao, *China* **58** 28 11N 109 10 E
Songwe, *Zaïre* **92** 3 20 S 26 16 E
Songwe →, *Africa* **93** 9 44 S 33 58 E
Songxi, *China* **59** 27 31N 118 44 E
Songzi, *China* **59** 30 12N 111 45 E
Sonid Youqi, *China* **61** 42 45N 112 48 E
Sonipat, *India* **48** 29 0N 77 5 E
Sonkovo, *U.S.S.R.* **37** 57 50N 37 5 E
Sonmiani, *Pakistan* **48** 25 25N 66 40 E
Sonnino, *Italy* **28** 41 25N 13 13 E
Sono →, *Goiás, Brazil* **138** 9 58 S 48 11W
Sono →, *Minas Gerais, Brazil* **139** 17 2 S 45 32W
Sonobe, *Japan* **65** 35 6N 135 28 E
Sonora, *Calif., U.S.A.* **124** 37 59N 120 27W
Sonora, *Tex., U.S.A.* **121** 30 33N 100 37W
Sonora □, *Mexico* **126** 29 0N 111 0W
Sonora →, *Mexico* **126** 28 50N 111 33W
Sonora Desert, *U.S.A.* **125** 33 40N 114 15W
Sonoyta, *Mexico* **126** 31 51N 112 50W
Sonsonate, *El Salv.* **128** 13 43N 89 44W
Sonthofen, *W. Germany* **31** 47 31N 10 16 E
Soochow = Suzhou, *China* **59** 31 19N 120 38 E
Sop Hao, *Laos* **54** 20 33N 104 27 E
Sop Prap, *Thailand* **54** 17 53N 99 20 E
Sopachuy, *Bolivia* **137** 19 29 S 64 31W
Sopi, *Indonesia* **57** 2 34N 128 28 E
Sopo, Nahr →, *Sudan* **89** 8 40N 26 30 E
Sopot, *Poland* **32** 54 27N 18 31 E
Sopotnica, *Yugoslavia* **35** 41 23N 21 13 E
Sopron, *Hungary* **33** 47 45N 16 32 E
Sop's Arm, *Canada* **105** 49 46N 56 56W
Sopur, *India* **49** 34 18N 74 27 E
Sør-Rondane, *Antarctica* **143** 72 0 S 25 0 E
Sør-Trøndelag fylke □, *Norway* **10** 63 0N 10 0 E
Sora, *Italy* **28** 41 45N 13 36 E
Sorada, *India* **50** 19 45N 84 26 E
Sorah, *Pakistan* **48** 27 13N 68 56 E
Söråker, *Sweden* **10** 62 30N 17 32 E
Sorano, *Italy* **27** 42 40N 11 42 E
Sorata, *Bolivia* **136** 15 50 S 68 40W
Sorbas, *Spain* **25** 37 6N 2 7W
Sorel, *Canada* **107** 46 0N 73 10W
Sorento, *Australia* **74** 38 22 S 144 47 E
Sorento, *U.S.A.* **118** 39 0N 89 34W
Soreq, N. →, *Israel* **44** 31 57N 34 43 E
Soresina, *Italy* **26** 45 17N 9 51 E
Sorgono, *Italy* **28** 40 1N 9 6 E
Sorgues, *France* **21** 44 1N 4 53 E
Soria, *Spain* **24** 41 43N 2 32W
Soria □, *Spain* **24** 41 46N 2 28W
Soriano, *Uruguay* **140** 33 24 S 58 19W
Soriano nel Cimino, *Italy* **27** 42 25N 12 14 E
Sorkh, Kuh-e, *Iran* **47** 35 40N 58 30 E
Sorø, *Denmark* **11** 55 26N 11 32 E
Soro, *Guinea* **90** 10 9N 9 48W
Sorocaba, *Brazil* **141** 23 31 S 47 27W
Soroki, *U.S.S.R.* **38** 48 8N 28 12 E
Soron, *India* **49** 27 55N 78 45 E
Sorong, *Indonesia* **57** 0 55 S 131 15 E
Soroti, *Uganda* **92** 1 43N 33 35 E
Sørøya, *Norway* **8** 70 40N 22 30 E
Sørøysundet, *Norway* **8** 70 25N 23 0 E
Sorraia →, *Portugal* **23** 38 55N 8 53W
Sorrento, *Italy* **29** 40 38N 14 23 E
Sorsele, *Sweden* **8** 65 31N 17 30 E
Sorso, *Italy* **28** 40 50N 8 34 E
Sorsogon, *Phil.* **57** 13 0N 124 0 E
Sortino, *Italy* **29** 37 9N 15 1 E
Sorvizhi, *U.S.S.R.* **37** 57 52N 48 32 E
Sos, *Spain* **24** 42 30N 1 13W
Soscumica, L., *Canada* **106** 50 15N 77 27W
Sosna →, *U.S.S.R.* **37** 52 42N 38 55 E
Sosnovka, *R.S.F.S.R., U.S.S.R.* **37** 53 13N 41 24 E
Sosnovka, *R.S.F.S.R., U.S.S.R.* **41** 54 9N 109 35 E
Sosnowiec, *Poland* **32** 50 20N 19 10 E
Sospel, *France* **21** 43 52N 7 27 E
Sostanj, *Yugoslavia* **27** 46 23N 15 4 E
Soto la Marina →, *Mexico* **127** 23 40N 97 40W
Soto y Amío, *Spain* **22** 42 46N 5 53W
Sotteville-lès-Rouen, *France* **18** 49 24N 1 5 E
Sotuta, *Mexico* **127** 20 29N 89 43W
Souanké, *Congo* **94** 2 10N 14 3 E
Soucy, *Canada* **106** 48 10N 75 30W
Soufflay, *Congo* **94** 2 1N 14 54 E
Sougne-Remouchamps, *Belgium* **17** 50 29N 5 42 E
Souillac, *France* **20** 44 53N 1 29 E
Souk-Ahras, *Algeria* **85** 36 23N 7 57 E

Souk el Arba du Rharb, *Morocco* **84** 34 43N 5 59W
Soukhouma, *Laos* **54** 14 38N 105 48 E
Sŏul, *S. Korea* **61** 37 31N 126 58 E
Soulac-sur-Mer, *France* **20** 45 30N 1 7W
Soultz-sous-Forêts, *France* **19** 48 57N 7 52 E
Soumagne, *Belgium* **17** 50 37N 5 44 E
Sound, The, *Denmark* **9** 56 7N 12 30 E
Soúnion, Ákra, *Greece* **35** 37 37N 24 1 E
Sour el Ghozlane, *Algeria* **85** 36 10N 3 45 E
Sources, Mt. aux, *Lesotho* **97** 28 45 S 28 50 E
Sourdeval, *France* **18** 48 43N 0 55W
Soure, *Brazil* **138** 0 35 S 48 30W
Soure, *Portugal* **22** 40 4N 8 38W
Souris, *Man., Canada* **111** 49 40N 100 20W
Souris, *P.E.I., Canada* **105** 46 21N 62 15W
Souris →, *Canada* **120** 49 40N 99 34W
Sousa, *Brazil* **138** 6 45 S 38 10W
Sousel, *Brazil* **138** 2 38 S 52 29W
Sousel, *Portugal* **23** 38 57N 7 40W
Souss, O. →, *Morocco* **84** 30 27N 9 31W
Sousse, *Tunisia* **86** 35 50N 10 38 E
Soustons, *France* **20** 43 45N 1 19W
Souterraine, La, *France* **20** 46 15N 1 30 E
South Africa, Rep. of ■, *Africa* **96** 32 0 S 23 0 E
South America **132** 10 0 S 60 0W
South Atlantic Ocean **131** 20 0 S 10 0W
South Aulatsivik I., *Canada* **105** 56 45N 61 30W
South Australia □, *Australia* **73** 32 0 S 139 0 E
South Baldy, Mt., *U.S.A.* **123** 34 6N 107 27W
South Baymouth, *Canada* **108** 45 33N 82 1W
South Beloit, *U.S.A.* **118** 42 29N 89 2W
South Bend, *Ind., U.S.A.* **119** 41 38N 86 20W
South Bend, *Wash., U.S.A.* **124** 46 44N 123 52W
South Boston, *U.S.A.* **115** 36 42N 78 58W
South Branch, *Canada* **105** 47 55N 59 2W
South Brook, *Canada* **105** 49 26N 56 5W
South Buganda □, *Uganda* **92** 0 15 S 31 30 E
South Carolina □, *U.S.A.* **115** 33 45N 81 0W
South Charleston, *U.S.A.* **114** 38 20N 81 40W
South China Sea, *Asia* **66** 10 0N 113 0 E
South Dakota □, *U.S.A.* **120** 45 0N 100 0W
South Downs, *U.K.* **13** 50 53N 0 10W
South East C., *Australia* **72** 43 40 S 146 50 E
South-East Indian Rise, *Ind. Oc.* **66** 43 0 S 80 0 E
South East Is., *Australia* **79** 34 17 S 123 30 E
South Esk →, *U.K.* **14** 56 44N 3 3W
South Foreland, *U.K.* **13** 51 7N 1 23 E
South Fork →, *U.S.A.* **122** 47 54N 113 15W
South Fork, American →, *U.S.A.* **124** 38 45N 121 5W
South Fork, Feather →, *U.S.A.* **124** 39 17N 121 36W
South Georgia, *Antarctica* **143** 54 30 S 37 0W
South Glamorgan □, *U.K.* **13** 51 30N 3 20W
South Grand →, *U.S.A.* **118** 38 17N 93 55W
South Haven, *U.S.A.* **119** 42 22N 86 20W
South Henik, L., *Canada* **111** 61 30N 97 30W
South Honshu Ridge, *Pac. Oc.* **66** 23 0N 143 0 E
South Horr, *Kenya* **92** 2 12N 36 56 E
South I., *Kenya* **92** 2 35N 36 35 E
South I., *N.Z.* **81** 44 0 S 170 0 E
South Invercargill, *N.Z.* **81** 46 26 S 168 23 E
South Knife →, *Canada* **111** 58 55N 94 37W
South Korea ■, *Asia* **61** 36 0N 128 0 E
South Lake Tahoe, *U.S.A.* **124** 38 57N 120 2W
South Loup →, *U.S.A.* **120** 41 4N 98 40W
South Lyon, *U.S.A.* **119** 42 28N 83 39W
South Magnetic Pole, *Antarctica* **143** 65 2 S 139 4 E
South Milwaukee, *U.S.A.* **119** 42 50N 87 52W
South Molton, *U.K.* **13** 51 1N 3 50W
South Nahanni →, *Canada* **110** 61 3N 123 21W
South Nation →, *Canada* **109** 45 34N 75 6W
South Negril Pt., *Jamaica* **128** 18 14N 78 30W
South Orkney Is., *Antarctica* **143** 63 0 S 45 0W
South Pass, *U.S.A.* **122** 42 20N 108 58W
South Pekin, *U.S.A.* **118** 40 30N 89 39W
South Pines, *U.S.A.* **115** 35 10N 79 25W
South Pittsburg, *U.S.A.* **115** 35 1N 85 42W
South Platte →, *U.S.A.* **120** 41 7N 100 42W
South Pole, *Antarctica* **143** 90 0 S 0 0 E
South Porcupine, *Canada* **104** 48 30N 81 12W
South River, *Canada* **108** 45 52N 79 23W
South River, *U.S.A.* **117** 40 27N 74 23W
South Ronaldsay, *U.K.* **14** 58 46N 2 58W
South Sandwich Is., *Antarctica* **143** 57 0 S 27 0W
South Saskatchewan →, *Canada* **111** 53 15N 105 5W
South Seal →, *Canada* **111** 58 48N 98 8W
South Shetland Is., *Antarctica* **143** 62 0 S 59 0W
South Shields, *U.K.* **12** 54 59N 1 26W
South Sioux City, *U.S.A.* **120** 42 30N 96 24W
South Solitary I., *Australia* **77** 30 12 S 153 16 E
South Taranaki Bight, *N.Z.* **80** 39 40 S 174 5 E
South Thompson →, *Canada* **110** 50 40N 120 20W
South Twin I., *Canada* **104** 53 7N 79 52W
South Tyne →, *U.K.* **12** 54 46N 2 25W
South Uist, *U.K.* **14** 57 20N 7 15W
South Wayne, *U.S.A.* **118** 42 34N 89 53W
South West Africa = Namibia ■, *Africa* **96** 22 0 S 18 9 E
South West C., *Australia* **72** 43 34 S 146 3 E
South West Rocks, *Australia* **77** 30 52 S 153 3 E
South Whitley, *U.S.A.* **119** 41 5N 85 38W
South Yemen ■, *Asia* **45** 15 0N 48 0 E
South Yorkshire □, *U.K.* **12** 53 30N 1 20W
Southampton, *Canada* **108** 44 30N 81 25W
Southampton, *U.K.* **13** 50 54N 1 23W
Southampton, *U.S.A.* **117** 40 54N 72 22W
Southampton I., *Canada* **103** 64 30N 84 0W
Southbridge, *N.Z.* **81** 43 48 S 172 16 E
Southbridge, *U.S.A.* **117** 42 4N 72 2W
Southeast Pacific Basin, *Pac. Oc.* **67** 16 30 S 92 0W
Southend, *Canada* **111** 56 19N 103 22W
Southend-on-Sea, *U.K.* **13** 51 32N 0 42 E
Southern □, *Malawi* **93** 15 0 S 35 0 E
Southern □, *S. Leone* **90** 8 0N 12 30W
Southern □, *Zambia* **93** 16 20 S 26 20 E
Southern Alps, *N.Z.* **81** 43 41 S 170 11 E
Southern Cross, *Australia* **79** 31 12 S 119 15 E
Southern Hills, *Australia* **79** 32 15 S 122 40 E
Southern Indian L., *Canada* **111** 57 10N 98 30W
Southern Ocean, *Antarctica* **143** 62 0 S 60 0 E
Southern Uplands, *U.K.* **14** 55 30N 3 3W
Southfield, *U.S.A.* **119** 42 29N 83 17W
Southington, *U.S.A.* **117** 41 37N 72 53W
Southland □, *N.Z.* **81** 45 51 S 168 13 E
Southold, *U.S.A.* **117** 41 4N 72 26W
Southport, *Australia* **77** 27 58 S 153 25 E
Southport, *U.K.* **12** 53 38N 3 1W
Southport, *U.S.A.* **115** 33 55N 78 0W
Southwestern Pacific Basin, *Pac. Oc.* **66** 42 0 S 170 0W
Southwold, *U.K.* **13** 52 19N 1 41 E
Soutpansberg, *S. Africa* **97** 23 0 S 29 30 E
Souvigny, *France* **20** 46 33N 3 10 E
Sovetsk, *Lithuania, U.S.S.R.* **36** 55 6N 21 50 E
Sovetsk, *R.S.F.S.R., U.S.S.R.* **37** 57 38N 48 53 E
Sovetskaya Gavan, *U.S.S.R.* **41** 48 50N 140 0 E
Sovicille, *Italy* **27** 43 16N 11 12 E
Soviet Union = Union of Soviet Socialist Republics ■, *Eurasia* **41** 60 0N 100 0 E
Sovra, *Yugoslavia* **33** 42 44N 17 34 E
Soweto, *S. Africa* **97** 26 14 S 27 54 E
Sōya-Kaikyō = Perouse Str., La, *Asia* **66** 45 40N 142 0 E
Sōya-Misaki, *Japan* **63** 45 30N 142 0 E
Soyo, *Angola* **95** 6 13 S 12 20 E
Sozh →, *U.S.S.R.* **36** 51 57N 30 48 E
Sozopol, *Bulgaria* **34** 42 23N 27 42 E
Spa, *Belgium* **17** 50 29N 5 53 E
Spain ■, *Europe* **7** 40 0N 5 0W
Spakenburg, *Neths.* **16** 52 15N 5 22 E
Spalding, *Australia* **73** 33 30 S 138 37 E
Spalding, *U.K.* **12** 52 47N 0 9W
Spalding, *U.S.A.* **120** 41 45N 98 27W
Spangler, *U.S.A.* **116** 40 39N 78 48W
Spaniard's Bay, *Canada* **105** 47 38N 53 20W
Spanish, *Canada* **108** 46 12N 82 20W
Spanish →, *Canada* **108** 46 11N 82 19W
Spanish Fork, *U.S.A.* **122** 40 10N 111 37W
Spanish Town, *Jamaica* **128** 18 0N 76 57W
Sparks, *U.S.A.* **124** 39 30N 119 45W
Sparta = Spárti, *Greece* **35** 37 5N 22 25 E
Sparta, *Ga., U.S.A.* **115** 33 18N 82 59W
Sparta, *Ill., U.S.A.* **118** 38 7N 89 42W
Sparta, *Mich., U.S.A.* **119** 43 10N 85 42W
Sparta, *Wis., U.S.A.* **120** 43 55N 90 47W
Spartanburg, *U.S.A.* **115** 35 0N 82 0W
Spartansburg, *U.S.A.* **116** 41 48N 79 43W
Spartel, C., *Morocco* **84** 35 47N 5 56W
Spárti, *Greece* **35** 37 5N 22 25 E
Spartivento, C., *Calabria, Italy* **29** 37 56N 16 4 E
Spartivento, C., *Sard., Italy* **28** 38 52N 8 50 E
Spas-Demensk, *U.S.S.R.* **36** 54 20N 34 0 E
Spas-Klepiki, *U.S.S.R.* **37** 55 10N 40 10 E
Spassk-Dalniy, *U.S.S.R.* **41** 44 40N 132 48 E
Spassk-Ryazanskiy, *U.S.S.R.* **37** 54 24N 40 25 E
Spátha, Akra, *Greece* **35** 35 42N 23 43 E
Spatsizi →, *Canada* **110** 57 42N 128 7W
Spearfish, *U.S.A.* **120** 44 32N 103 52W
Spearman, *U.S.A.* **121** 36 15N 101 10W
Speed, *Australia* **74** 35 21 S 142 27 E
Speedway, *U.S.A.* **119** 39 47N 86 15W
Speers, *Canada* **111** 52 43N 107 34W
Speightstown, *Barbados* **129** 13 15N 59 39W
Speke Gulf, *Tanzania* **92** 2 20 S 32 50 E
Spekholzerheide, *Neths.* **17** 50 51N 6 2 E
Spence Bay, *Canada* **102** 69 32N 93 32W
Spencer, *Idaho, U.S.A.* **122** 44 18N 112 8W
Spencer, *Ind., U.S.A.* **119** 39 17N 86 46W
Spencer, *Iowa, U.S.A.* **120** 43 5N 95 19W
Spencer, *N.Y., U.S.A.* **117** 42 14N 76 30W
Spencer, *Nebr., U.S.A.* **120** 42 52N 98 43W
Spencer, *W. Va., U.S.A.* **114** 38 47N 81 24W
Spencer, C., *Australia* **73** 35 20 S 136 53 E
Spencer B., *Namibia* **96** 25 30 S 14 47 E
Spencer G., *Australia* **73** 34 0 S 137 20 E
Spencerville, *Canada* **109** 44 51N 75 33W
Spencerville, *U.S.A.* **119** 40 43N 84 21W
Spences Bridge, *Canada* **110** 50 25N 121 20W
Spenser Mts., *N.Z.* **81** 42 15 S 172 45 E
Sperkhiós →, *Greece* **35** 38 57N 22 3 E
Sperrin Mts., *U.K.* **15** 54 50N 7 0W
Spessart, *W. Germany* **31** 50 10N 9 20 E
Spétsai, *Greece* **35** 37 15N 23 10 E
Spey →, *U.K.* **14** 57 26N 3 25W
Speyer, *W. Germany* **31** 49 19N 8 26 E
Speyer →, *W. Germany* **31** 49 19N 8 27 E
Spézia, La, *Italy* **26** 44 8N 9 50 E
Spezzano Albanese, *Italy* **29** 39 41N 16 19 E
Spickard, *U.S.A.* **118** 40 14N 93 36W
Spiekeroog, *W. Germany* **30** 53 45N 7 42 E
Spielfeld, *Austria* **27** 46 43N 15 38 E
Spiez, *Switz.* **31** 46 40N 7 40 E
Spijk, *Neths.* **16** 53 24N 6 50 E
Spijkenisse, *Neths.* **16** 51 51N 4 20 E
Spilimbergo, *Italy* **27** 46 7N 12 53 E
Spin Baldak = Qala-i-Jadid, *Afghan.* **48** 31 1N 66 25 E
Spinazzola, *Italy* **29** 40 58N 16 5 E
Spirit Lake, *Idaho, U.S.A.* **122** 47 56N 116 56W
Spirit Lake, *Wash., U.S.A.* **124** 46 15N 122 9W
Spirit River, *Canada* **110** 55 45N 118 50W
Spiritwood, *Canada* **111** 53 24N 107 33W
Spišská Nová Ves, *Czech.* **32** 48 58N 20 34 E
Spithead, *U.K.* **13** 50 43N 1 5W
Spittal, *Austria* **33** 46 48N 13 31 E
Spitzbergen = Svalbard, *Arctic* **144** 78 0N 17 0 E
Split, *Yugoslavia* **27** 43 31N 16 26 E
Split L., *Canada* **111** 56 8N 96 15W
Splitski Kanal, *Yugoslavia* **27** 43 31N 16 20 E
Splügenpass, *Switz.* **31** 46 30N 9 20 E
Spofford, *U.S.A.* **121** 29 10N 100 27W
Spokane, *U.S.A.* **122** 47 45N 117 25W
Spoleto, *Italy* **27** 42 46N 12 47 E
Spoon →, *U.S.A.* **118** 40 19N 90 4W
Spooner, *U.S.A.* **120** 45 49N 91 51W
Sporyy Navolok, Mys, *U.S.S.R.* **40** 75 50N 68 40 E
Spragge, *Canada* **108** 46 15N 82 40W
Sprague, *U.S.A.* **122** 47 18N 117 59W
Sprague River, *U.S.A.* **122** 42 28N 121 31W
Spratly, I., *S. China Sea* **56** 8 20N 112 0 E
Spray, *U.S.A.* **122** 44 50N 119 46W
Spree →, *E. Germany* **30** 52 32N 13 13 E
Spremberg, *E. Germany* **30** 51 33N 14 21 E
Sprimont, *Belgium* **17** 50 30N 5 40 E
Spring City, *U.S.A.* **122** 39 31N 111 28W
Spring Garden, *U.S.A.* **124** 39 52N 120 47W
Spring Green, *U.S.A.* **118** 43 11N 90 4W
Spring Hill, *Australia* **76** 33 23 S 149 9 E
Spring Mts., *U.S.A.* **123** 36 20N 115 43W
Spring Ridge, *Australia* **77** 32 15 S 149 21 E
Spring Valley, *Calif., U.S.A.* **125** 32 45N 117 0W
Spring Valley, *Ill., U.S.A.* **118** 41 20N 89 14W
Spring Valley, *Minn., U.S.A.* **120** 43 40N 92 23W
Springbok, *S. Africa* **96** 29 42 S 17 54 E
Springdale, *Canada* **105** 49 30N 56 6W
Springdale, *Ark., U.S.A.* **121** 36 10N 94 5W
Springdale, *Wash., U.S.A.* **122** 48 1N 117 50W
Springe, *W. Germany* **30** 52 12N 9 35 E
Springer, *U.S.A.* **121** 36 22N 104 36W
Springerville, *U.S.A.* **123** 34 10N 109 16W
Springfield, *Canada* **108** 42 50N 80 56W
Springfield, *N.Z.* **81** 43 19 S 171 56 E
Springfield, *Colo., U.S.A.* **121** 37 26N 102 40W
Springfield, *Ill., U.S.A.* **118** 39 48N 89 40W
Springfield, *Ky., U.S.A.* **119** 37 41N 85 13W
Springfield, *Mass., U.S.A.* **117** 42 8N 72 37W
Springfield, *Mo., U.S.A.* **121** 37 15N 93 20W
Springfield, *Ohio, U.S.A.* **119** 39 58N 83 48W
Springfield, *Oreg., U.S.A.* **122** 44 2N 123 0W
Springfield, *Tenn., U.S.A.* **115** 36 35N 86 55W
Springfield, *Vt., U.S.A.* **117** 43 20N 72 30W
Springfield, L., *U.S.A.* **118** 39 46N 89 36W
Springfontein, *S. Africa* **96** 30 15 S 25 40 E
Springhill, *Canada* **105** 45 40N 64 4W
Springhouse, *Canada* **110** 51 56N 122 7W
Springhurst, *Australia* **75** 36 10 S 146 31 E
Springs, *S. Africa* **97** 26 13 S 28 25 E
Springsure, *Australia* **72** 24 8 S 148 6 E
Springvale, *Queens., Australia* **72** 23 33 S 140 42 E
Springvale, *W. Austral., Australia* **78** 17 48 S 127 41 E
Springvale, *U.S.A.* **117** 43 28N 70 48W
Springville, *Calif., U.S.A.* **124** 36 8N 118 49W
Springville, *N.Y., U.S.A.* **116** 42 31N 78 41W
Springville, *Utah, U.S.A.* **122** 40 14N 111 35W
Springwater, *Canada* **111** 51 58N 108 23W
Springwood, *Australia* **76** 33 41 S 150 33 E
Spruce-Creek, *U.S.A.* **116** 40 36N 78 9W
Sprucedale, *Canada* **108** 45 29N 79 28W
Spur, *U.S.A.* **121** 33 28N 100 50W
Spurgeon, *U.S.A.* **119** 38 14N 87 15W
Spurn Hd., *U.K.* **12** 53 34N 0 8 E
Spuž, *Yugoslavia* **34** 42 32N 19 10 E
Spuzzum, *Canada* **110** 49 37N 121 23W
Squam L., *U.S.A.* **117** 43 45N 71 32W
Squamish, *Canada* **110** 49 45N 123 10W
Square Islands, *Canada* **105** 52 47N 55 47W
Squatec, *Canada* **107** 47 53N 68 43W
Squillace, G. di, *Italy* **29** 38 43N 16 35 E
Squinzano, *Italy* **29** 40 27N 18 1 E
Squires, Mt., *Australia* **79** 26 14 S 127 28 E
Sragen, *Indonesia* **57** 7 26 S 111 2 E
Srbac, *Yugoslavia* **33** 45 7N 17 30 E
Srbija □, *Yugoslavia* **33** 43 30N 21 0 E
Srbobran, *Yugoslavia* **33** 45 32N 19 48 E
Sre Khtum, *Cambodia* **55** 12 10N 106 52 E
Sre Umbell, *Cambodia* **55** 11 8N 103 46 E
Srebrnica, *Yugoslavia* **33** 44 10N 19 18 E
Sredinnyy Khrebet, *U.S.S.R.* **41** 57 0N 160 0 E
Sredinnyy Ra. = Sredinnyy Khrebet, *U.S.S.R.* **41** 57 0N 160 0 E
Središče, *Yugoslavia* **27** 46 24N 16 17 E
Sredna Gora, *Bulgaria* **34** 42 40N 24 20 E
Sredne Tambovskoye, *U.S.S.R.* **41** 50 55N 137 45 E
Srednekolymsk, *U.S.S.R.* **41** 67 27N 153 40 E
Srednevilyuysk, *U.S.S.R.* **41** 63 50N 123 5 E
Śrem, *Poland* **32** 52 6N 17 2 E
Sremska Mitrovica, *Yugoslavia* **33** 44 59N 19 33 E
Srepok →, *Cambodia* **54** 13 33N 106 16 E
Sretensk, *U.S.S.R.* **41** 52 10N 117 40 E
Sri Kalahasti, *India* **51** 13 45N 79 44 E
Sri Lanka ■, *Asia* **51** 7 30N 80 50 E
Sriharikota, I., *India* **51** 13 40N 80 20 E
Srikakulam, *India* **50** 18 14N 83 58 E
Srinagar, *India* **49** 34 5N 74 50 E
Sripur, *Bangla.* **52** 24 14N 90 30 E
Srirangam, *India* **51** 10 54N 78 42 E
Srivardhan, *India* **50** 18 4N 73 3 E
Srivilliputtur, *India* **51** 9 31N 77 40 E
Środa Wielkopolski, *Poland* **32** 52 15N 17 19 E
Srpska Itabej, *Yugoslavia* **33** 45 35N 20 44 E
Staaten →, *Australia* **72** 16 24 S 141 17 E
Staberhuk, *E. Germany* **30** 54 23N 11 18 E
Stabroek, *Belgium* **17** 51 20N 4 22 E
Stad Delden, *Neths.* **16** 52 16N 6 43 E
Stade, *W. Germany* **30** 53 35N 9 31 E
Staden, *Belgium* **17** 50 59N 3 1 E
Staðarhólskirkja, *Iceland* **8** 65 23N 21 58W
Städjan, *Sweden* **10** 61 56N 12 52 E
Stadlandet, *Norway* **8** 62 10N 5 10 E
Stadskanaal, *Neths.* **16** 53 4N 6 55 E
Stadthagen, *W. Germany* **30** 52 20N 9 14 E
Stadtlohn, *W. Germany* **30** 52 0N 6 52 E
Stadtroda, *E. Germany* **30** 50 51N 11 44 E
Stafafell, *Iceland* **8** 64 25N 14 52W
Staffa, *U.K.* **14** 56 26N 6 21W
Stafford, *U.K.* **12** 52 49N 2 9W
Stafford, *U.S.A.* **121** 38 0N 98 35W
Stafford □, *U.K.* **12** 52 53N 2 10W
Stafford Springs, *U.S.A.* **117** 41 58N 72 20W
Stagnone, *Italy* **28** 37 50N 12 28 E

Staines, *U.K.* 13 51 26N 0 30W
Stakhanov, *U.S.S.R.* 39 48 35N 38 40 E
Stalingrad = Volgograd, *U.S.S.R.* 39 48 40N 44 25 E
Staliniri = Tskhinvali, *U.S.S.R.* 39 42 14N 44 1 E
Stalino = Donetsk, *U.S.S.R.* 38 48 0N 37 45 E
Stalinogorsk = Novomoskovsk, *U.S.S.R.* 37 54 5N 38 15 E
Stalowa Wola, *Poland* 32 50 34N 22 3 E
Stalybridge, *U.K.* 12 53 29N 2 4W
Stamford, *Australia* 72 21 15 S 143 46 E
Stamford, *U.K.* 13 52 39N 0 29W
Stamford, *Conn., U.S.A.* 117 41 5N 73 30W
Stamford, *Tex., U.S.A.* 121 32 58N 99 50W
Stamping Ground, *U.S.A.* 119 38 16N 84 41W
Stamps, *U.S.A.* 121 33 22N 93 30W
Stanberry, *U.S.A.* 120 40 12N 94 32W
Stančevo = Kalipetrovo, *Bulgaria* 34 44 5N 27 14 E
Standerton, *S. Africa* 97 26 55 S 29 7 E
Standish, *U.S.A.* 114 43 58N 83 57W
Stanford, *U.S.A.* 122 47 11N 110 10W
Stange, *Norway* 10 60 43N 11 5 E
Stanger, *S. Africa* 97 29 27 S 31 14 E
Stanhope, *Australia* 74 36 27 S 144 59 E
Stanhope, *U.S.A.* 118 42 17N 93 48W
Stanislaus →, *U.S.A.* 124 37 40N 121 15W
Stanislav = Ivano-Frankovsk, *U.S.S.R.* 36 48 40N 24 40 E
Stanke Dimitrov, *Bulgaria* 34 42 17N 23 9 E
Stanley, *Australia* 72 40 46 S 145 19 E
Stanley, *N.B., Canada* 105 46 20N 66 44W
Stanley, *Sask., Canada* 111 55 24N 104 22W
Stanley, *Falk. Is.* 142 51 40 S 59 51W
Stanley, *Idaho, U.S.A.* 122 44 10N 114 59W
Stanley, *N. Dak., U.S.A.* 120 48 20N 102 23W
Stanley, *N.Y., U.S.A.* 116 42 48N 77 6W
Stanley, *Wis., U.S.A.* 120 44 57N 91 0W
Stanley Res., *India* 51 11 50N 77 40 E
Stannifer, *Australia* 77 29 52 S 151 14 E
Stanovoy Khrebet, *U.S.S.R.* 41 55 0N 130 0 E
Stanovoy Ra. = Stanovoy Khrebet, *U.S.S.R.* 41 55 0N 130 0 E
Stansmore Ra., *Australia* 78 21 23 S 128 33 E
Stanthorpe, *Australia* 77 28 36 S 151 59 E
Stanton, *U.S.A.* 121 32 8N 101 45W
Stanwell Park, *Australia* 76 34 13 S 150 58 E
Stanwood, *U.S.A.* 124 48 15N 122 23W
Staphorst, *Neths.* 16 52 39N 6 12 E
Staples, *U.S.A.* 120 46 21N 94 48W
Stapleton, *U.S.A.* 120 41 30N 100 31W
Star City, *Canada* 111 52 50N 104 20W
Stara-minskaya, *U.S.S.R.* 39 46 33N 39 0 E
Stara Moravica, *Yugoslavia* 33 45 50N 19 30 E
Stara Planina, *Bulgaria* 34 43 15N 23 0 E
Stara Zagora, *Bulgaria* 34 42 26N 25 39 E
Starachowice, *Poland* 32 51 3N 21 2 E
Starashcherbinovskaya, *U.S.S.R.* 39 46 40N 38 53 E
Staraya Russa, *U.S.S.R.* 36 57 58N 31 23 E
Starbuck I., *Kiribati* 67 5 37 S 155 55W
Stargard Szczeciński, *Poland* 32 53 20N 15 0 E
Stari Trg, *Yugoslavia* 27 45 29N 15 7 E
Staritsa, *U.S.S.R.* 36 56 33N 35 0 E
Starke, *U.S.A.* 115 30 0N 82 10W
Starkville, *Colo., U.S.A.* 121 37 10N 104 31W
Starkville, *Miss., U.S.A.* 115 33 26N 88 48W
Starnberg, *W. Germany* 31 48 0N 11 20 E
Starnberger See, *W. Germany* 31 47 55N 11 20 E
Starobelsk, *U.S.S.R.* 39 49 16N 39 0 E
Starodub, *U.S.S.R.* 36 52 30N 32 50 E
Starogard, *Poland* 32 53 59N 18 30 E
Starokonstantinov, *U.S.S.R.* 38 49 48N 27 10 E
Start Pt., *U.K.* 13 50 13N 3 38W
Staryy Biryuzyak, *U.S.S.R.* 39 44 46N 46 50 E
Staryy Chartoriysk, *U.S.S.R.* 36 51 15N 25 54 E
Staryy Kheydzhan, *U.S.S.R.* 41 60 0N 144 50 E
Staryy Krym, *U.S.S.R.* 38 45 3N 35 8 E
Staryy Oskol, *U.S.S.R.* 37 51 19N 37 55 E
Stassfurt, *E. Germany* 30 51 51N 11 34 E
State Center, *U.S.A.* 118 42 1N 93 10W
State College, *U.S.A.* 116 40 47N 77 1W
Stateline, *U.S.A.* 124 38 57N 119 56W
Staten, I. = Estados, I. de Los, *Argentina* 142 54 40 S 64 30W
Staten I., *U.S.A.* 117 40 35N 74 10W
Statesboro, *U.S.A.* 115 32 26N 81 46W
Statesville, *U.S.A.* 115 35 48N 80 51W
Stauffer, *U.S.A.* 125 34 45N 119 3W
Staunton, *Ill., U.S.A.* 118 39 0N 89 49W
Staunton, *Va., U.S.A.* 114 38 7N 79 4W
Stavanger, *Norway* 9 58 57N 5 40 E
Staveley, *N.Z.* 81 43 40 S 171 32 E
Stavelot, *Belgium* 17 50 23N 5 55 E
Stavenisse, *Neths.* 17 51 35N 4 1 E
Staveren, *Neths.* 16 52 53N 5 22 E
Stavern, *Norway* 10 59 0N 10 1 E
Stavre, *Sweden* 10 62 51N 15 19 E
Stavropol, *U.S.S.R.* 39 45 5N 42 0 E
Stavroúpolis, *Greece* 35 41 12N 24 45 E
Stawell, *Australia* 74 37 5 S 142 47 E
Stawell →, *Australia* 72 20 20 S 142 55 E
Stawiszyn, *Poland* 32 51 56N 18 4 E
Stayner, *Canada* 108 44 25N 80 5W
Steamboat Springs, *U.S.A.* 122 40 30N 106 50W
Steele, *U.S.A.* 120 46 56N 99 52W
Steelton, *U.S.A.* 116 40 17N 76 50W
Steelville, *U.S.A.* 118 37 57N 91 21W
Steen River, *Canada* 110 59 40N 117 12W
Steenbergen, *Neths.* 17 51 35N 4 19 E
Steenkool = Bintuni, *Indonesia* 57 2 7 S 133 32 E
Steenvoorde, *France* 19 50 48N 2 33 E
Steenwijk, *Neths.* 16 52 47N 6 7 E
Steep Pt., *Australia* 79 26 8 S 113 8 E
Steep Rock, *Canada* 111 51 30N 98 48W
Ştefăneşti, *Romania* 34 47 44N 27 15 E
Stefanie L. = Chew Bahir, *Ethiopia* 89 4 40N 36 50 E
Stefansson Bay, *Antarctica* 143 67 20 S 59 8 E
Stege, *Denmark* 11 55 0N 12 18 E
Steiermark □, *Austria* 33 47 26N 15 0 E
Steigerwald, *W. Germany* 31 49 45N 10 30 E
Steilacoom, *U.S.A.* 124 47 10N 122 36W
Stein, *Neths.* 17 50 58N 5 45 E
Steinbach, *Canada* 111 49 32N 96 40W
Steinfort, *Lux.* 17 49 39N 5 55 E
Steinheim, *W. Germany* 30 51 50N 9 6 E
Steinhuder Meer, *W. Germany* 30 52 48N 9 20 E
Steinkjer, *Norway* 8 63 59N 11 31 E
Steinkopf, *S. Africa* 96 29 18 S 17 43 E
Stekene, *Belgium* 17 51 12N 4 2 E
Stellarton, *Canada* 105 45 32N 62 30W
Stellenbosch, *S. Africa* 96 33 58 S 18 50 E
Stellendam, *Neths.* 16 51 49N 4 1 E
Stemshaug, *Norway* 10 63 19N 8 44 E
Stendal, *E. Germany* 30 52 36N 11 50 E
Stene, *Belgium* 17 51 12N 2 56 E
Stensele, *Sweden* 8 65 3N 17 8 E
Stenstorp, *Sweden* 11 58 17N 13 45 E
Stephan, *U.S.A.* 120 48 30N 96 53W
Stephens Creek, *Australia* 73 31 50 S 141 30 E
Stephens I., *Canada* 110 54 10N 130 45W
Stephens I., *N.Z.* 81 40 40 S 174 1 E
Stephenville, *Canada* 105 48 31N 58 35W
Stephenville, *U.S.A.* 121 32 12N 98 12W
Stepnica, *Poland* 32 53 38N 14 36 E
Stepnoi = Elista, *U.S.S.R.* 39 46 16N 44 14 E
Stepnyak, *U.S.S.R.* 40 52 50N 70 50 E
Steppe, *Asia* 42 50 0N 50 0 E
Sterkstroom, *S. Africa* 96 31 32 S 26 32 E
Sterling, *Colo., U.S.A.* 120 40 40N 103 15W
Sterling, *Ill., U.S.A.* 118 41 45N 89 45W
Sterling, *Kans., U.S.A.* 120 38 17N 98 13W
Sterling City, *U.S.A.* 121 31 50N 100 59W
Sterling Heights, *U.S.A.* 119 42 35N 83 0W
Sterling Run, *U.S.A.* 116 41 25N 78 12W
Sterlitamak, *U.S.S.R.* 40 53 40N 56 0 E
Sternberg, *E. Germany* 30 53 42N 11 48 E
Šternberk, *Czech.* 32 49 45N 17 15 E
Stettin = Szczecin, *Poland* 32 53 27N 14 27 E
Stettiner Haff, *E. Germany* 30 53 50N 14 25 E
Stettler, *Canada* 110 52 19N 112 40W
Steubenville, *U.S.A.* 116 40 21N 80 39W
Stevens Port, *U.S.A.* 120 44 32N 89 34W
Stevenson, *U.S.A.* 124 45 42N 121 53W
Stevenson L., *Canada* 111 53 55N 96 0W
Stevns Klint, *Denmark* 11 55 17N 12 28 E
Steward, *U.S.A.* 118 41 51N 89 1W
Stewardson, *U.S.A.* 119 39 16N 88 38W
Stewart, *B.C., Canada* 110 55 56N 129 57W
Stewart, *N.W.T., Canada* 102 63 19N 139 26W
Stewart, *U.S.A.* 124 39 5N 119 46W
Stewart, C., *Australia* 72 11 57 S 134 56 E
Stewart, I., *Chile* 142 54 50 S 71 15W
Stewart I., *N.Z.* 81 46 58 S 167 54 E
Stewarts Point, *U.S.A.* 124 38 39N 123 20W
Stewartsville, *U.S.A.* 118 39 45N 94 30W
Stewiacke, *Canada* 105 45 9N 63 22W
Steynsburg, *S. Africa* 96 31 15 S 25 49 E
Steyr, *Austria* 33 48 3N 14 25 E
Steytlerville, *S. Africa* 96 33 17 S 24 19 E
Stia, *Italy* 27 43 48N 11 41 E
Stiens, *Neths.* 16 53 16N 5 46 E
Stigler, *U.S.A.* 121 35 19N 95 6W
Stigliano, *Italy* 29 40 24N 16 13 E
Stigsnæs, *Denmark* 11 55 13N 11 18 E
Stigtomta, *Sweden* 11 58 47N 16 48 E
Stikine →, *Canada* 102 56 40N 132 30W
Stilfontein, *S. Africa* 96 26 51 S 26 50 E
Stilís, *Greece* 35 38 55N 22 47 E
Stillwater, *N.Z.* 81 42 27 S 171 20 E
Stillwater, *Minn., U.S.A.* 120 45 3N 92 47W
Stillwater, *N.Y., U.S.A.* 117 42 55N 73 41W
Stillwater, *Okla., U.S.A.* 121 36 5N 97 3W
Stillwater Ra., *U.S.A.* 122 39 45N 118 6W
Stilwell, *U.S.A.* 121 35 52N 94 36W
Štip, *Yugoslavia* 35 41 42N 22 10 E
Stíra, *Greece* 35 38 9N 24 14 E
Stirling, *Australia* 72 17 12 S 141 35 E
Stirling, *Alta., Canada* 110 49 30N 112 30W
Stirling, *Ont., Canada* 109 44 18N 77 33W
Stirling, *N.Z.* 81 46 14 S 169 49 E
Stirling, *U.K.* 14 56 7N 3 57W
Stirling Ra., *Australia* 79 34 23 S 118 0 E
Stittsville, *Canada* 106 45 15N 75 55W
Stockach, *W. Germany* 31 47 51N 9 1 E
Stockaryd, *Sweden* 11 57 19N 14 36 E
Stockbridge, *U.S.A.* 119 42 27N 84 11W
Stockerau, *Austria* 33 48 24N 16 12 E
Stockett, *U.S.A.* 122 47 23N 111 7W
Stockholm, *Sweden* 10 59 20N 18 3 E
Stockholms län □, *Sweden* 10 59 30N 18 20 E
Stockinbingal, *Australia* 76 34 30 S 147 53 E
Stockport, *U.K.* 12 53 25N 2 11W
Stockton, *Australia* 76 32 50 S 151 47 E
Stockton, *Calif., U.S.A.* 124 38 0N 121 20W
Stockton, *Ill., U.S.A.* 118 42 21N 90 1W
Stockton, *Kans., U.S.A.* 120 39 30N 99 20W
Stockton, *Mo., U.S.A.* 118 37 40N 93 48W
Stockton-on-Tees, *U.K.* 12 54 34N 1 20W
Stockvik, *Sweden* 10 62 17N 17 23 E
Stöde, *Sweden* 10 62 28N 16 35 E
Stogovo, *Yugoslavia* 35 41 31N 20 38 E
Stoke, *N.Z.* 81 41 19 S 173 14 E
Stoke-on-Trent, *U.K.* 12 53 1N 2 11W
Stokes Bay, *Canada* 108 45 0N 81 28W
Stokes Pt., *Australia* 72 40 10 S 143 56 E
Stokes Ra., *Australia* 78 15 50 S 130 50 E
Stokkseyri, *Iceland* 8 63 50N 21 2W
Stokksnes, *Iceland* 8 64 14N 14 58W
Stolac, *Yugoslavia* 33 43 8N 17 59 E
Stolberg, *W. Germany* 30 50 48N 6 13 E
Stolbovaya, *R.S.F.S.R., U.S.S.R.* 37 55 10N 37 32 E
Stolbovaya, *R.S.F.S.R., U.S.S.R.* 41 64 50N 153 50 E
Stolbovoy, Ostrov, *U.S.S.R.* 41 56 44N 163 14 E
Stolbtsy, *U.S.S.R.* 36 53 30N 26 43 E
Stolin, *U.S.S.R.* 36 51 53N 26 50 E
Stolwijk, *Neths.* 16 51 59N 4 47 E
Ston, *Yugoslavia* 33 42 51N 17 43 E
Stoneham, *Canada* 107 47 0N 71 22W
Stonehaven, *U.K.* 14 56 58N 2 11W
Stonehenge, *Australia* 72 24 22 S 143 17 E
Stonewall, *Canada* 111 50 10N 97 19W
Stoney Creek, *Canada* 108 43 14N 79 45W
Stonington, *U.S.A.* 118 39 44N 89 12W
Stony L., *Man., Canada* 111 58 51N 98 40W
Stony L., *Ont., Canada* 109 44 30N 78 0W
Stony Rapids, *Canada* 111 59 16N 105 50W
Stony Tunguska = Tunguska, Podkamennaya →, *U.S.S.R.* 41 61 36N 90 18 E
Stonyford, *U.S.A.* 124 39 23N 122 33W
Stopnica, *Poland* 32 50 27N 20 57 E
Stora Gla, *Sweden* 10 59 30N 12 30 E
Stora Karlsö, *Sweden* 11 57 17N 17 59 E
Stora Lulevatten, *Sweden* 8 67 10N 19 30 E
Stora Sjöfallet, *Sweden* 8 67 29N 18 40 E
Storavan, *Sweden* 8 65 45N 18 10 E
Store Bælt, *Denmark* 11 55 20N 11 0 E
Store Creek, *Australia* 76 32 54 S 149 6 E
Store Heddinge, *Denmark* 11 55 18N 12 23 E
Støren, *Norway* 10 63 3N 10 18 E
Storm B., *Australia* 72 43 10 S 147 30 E
Storm Lake, *U.S.A.* 120 42 35N 95 11W
Stormberge, *S. Africa* 96 31 16 S 26 17 E
Stormsrivier, *S. Africa* 96 33 59 S 23 52 E
Stornoway, *U.K.* 14 58 12N 6 23W
Storozhinets, *U.S.S.R.* 38 48 14N 25 45 E
Storsjö, *Sweden* 10 62 49N 13 5 E
Storsjøen, *Hedmark, Norway* 10 60 20N 11 40 E
Storsjøen, *Hedmark, Norway* 10 61 30N 11 14 E
Storsjön, *Gävleborg, Sweden* 10 60 35N 16 45 E
Storsjön, *Jämtland, Sweden* 10 62 50N 13 8 E
Storstrøms Amt. □, *Denmark* 11 54 50N 11 45 E
Storuman, *Sweden* 8 65 5N 17 10 E
Storvik, *Sweden* 10 60 35N 16 33 E
Story City, *U.S.A.* 118 42 11N 93 36W
Stouffville, *Canada* 108 43 58N 79 15W
Stoughton, *Canada* 111 49 40N 103 0W
Stoughton, *U.S.A.* 118 42 55N 88 59W
Stour →, *Dorset, U.K.* 13 50 48N 2 7W
Stour →, *Hereford & Worcs., U.K.* 13 52 25N 2 13W
Stour →, *Kent, U.K.* 13 51 15N 1 20 E
Stour →, *Suffolk, U.K.* 13 51 55N 1 5 E
Stourbridge, *U.K.* 13 52 28N 2 8W
Stout, L., *Canada* 111 52 0N 94 40W
Stove Pipe Wells Village, *U.S.A.* 125 36 35N 117 11W
Stowmarket, *U.K.* 13 52 11N 1 0 E
Strabane, *U.K.* 15 54 50N 7 28W
Strabane □, *U.K.* 15 54 45N 7 25W
Stracin, *Yugoslavia* 34 42 13N 22 2 E
Stradella, *Italy* 26 45 4N 9 20 E
Strahan, *Australia* 72 42 9 S 145 20 E
Strakonice, *Czech.* 32 49 15N 13 53 E
Straldzha, *Bulgaria* 34 42 35N 26 40 E
Stralsund, *E. Germany* 30 54 17N 13 5 E
Strand, *S. Africa* 96 34 9 S 18 48 E
Strangford, L., *U.K.* 15 54 30N 5 37W
Strängnäs, *Sweden* 10 59 23N 17 2 E
Strangsville, *U.S.A.* 116 41 19N 81 50W
Stranraer, *U.K.* 14 54 54N 5 0W
Strasbourg, *Canada* 111 51 4N 104 55W
Strasbourg, *France* 19 48 35N 7 42 E
Strasburg, *E. Germany* 30 53 30N 13 44 E
Strasburg, *U.S.A.* 120 46 12N 100 9W
Strassen, *Lux.* 17 49 37N 6 4 E
Stratford, *N.S.W., Australia* 77 32 7 S 151 55 E
Stratford, *Vic., Australia* 75 37 59 S 147 7 E
Stratford, *Canada* 108 43 23N 81 0W
Stratford, *N.Z.* 80 39 20 S 174 19 E
Stratford, *Calif., U.S.A.* 124 36 10N 119 49W
Stratford, *Conn., U.S.A.* 117 41 13N 73 8W
Stratford, *Tex., U.S.A.* 121 36 20N 102 3W
Stratford-on-Avon, *U.K.* 13 52 12N 1 42W
Strath Spey, *U.K.* 14 57 15N 3 40W
Strathalbyn, *Australia* 73 35 13 S 138 53 E
Strathclyde □, *U.K.* 14 56 0N 4 50W
Strathcona Prov. Park, *Canada* 110 49 38N 125 40W
Strathmerton, *Australia* 74 35 54 S 145 30 E
Strathmore, *Australia* 72 17 50 S 142 35 E
Strathmore, *Canada* 110 51 5N 113 18W
Strathmore, *U.K.* 14 56 40N 3 4W
Strathmore, *U.S.A.* 124 36 9N 119 4W
Strathnaver, *Canada* 110 53 20N 122 33W
Strathpeffer, *U.K.* 14 57 35N 4 32W
Strathroy, *Canada* 108 42 58N 81 38W
Strathy Pt., *U.K.* 14 58 35N 4 0W
Stratton, *U.K.* 12 51 41N 1 45W
Stratton, *U.S.A.* 120 39 20N 102 36W
Straubing, *W. Germany* 31 48 53N 12 35 E
Straumnes, *Iceland* 8 66 26N 23 8W
Strausberg, *E. Germany* 30 52 40N 13 52 E
Strawberry Point, *U.S.A.* 118 42 41N 91 32W
Strawberry Res., *U.S.A.* 122 40 10N 111 7W
Strawn, *U.S.A.* 121 32 36N 98 30W
Strážnice, *Czech.* 32 48 54N 17 19 E
Streaky B., *Australia* 73 32 51 S 134 18 E
Streaky Bay, *Australia* 73 32 48 S 134 13 E
Streatham, *Australia* 74 37 43 S 143 5 E
Streator, *U.S.A.* 119 41 9N 88 52W
Streé, *Belgium* 17 50 17N 4 18 E
Streeter, *U.S.A.* 120 46 39N 99 21W
Streetsville, *Canada* 108 43 35N 79 42W
Strehaia, *Romania* 34 44 37N 23 10 E
Strelcha, *Bulgaria* 34 42 25N 24 19 E
Strelka, *U.S.S.R.* 41 58 5N 93 3 E
Streng →, *Cambodia* 54 13 12N 103 37 E
Strésa, *Italy* 26 45 52N 8 28 E
Strezhevoy, *U.S.S.R.* 40 60 42N 77 34 E
Stříbro, *Czech.* 32 49 44N 13 0 E
Strickland →, *Papua N. G.* 69 7 35 S 141 36 E
Strijen, *Neths.* 16 51 45N 4 33 E
Strimón →, *Greece* 35 40 46N 23 51 E
Strimonikós Kólpos, *Greece* 35 40 33N 24 0 E
Stroeder, *Argentina* 142 40 12 S 62 37W
Strofádhes, *Greece* 35 37 15N 21 0 E
Strömbacka, *Sweden* 10 61 58N 16 44 E
Strómboli, *Italy* 29 38 48N 15 12 E
Stromeferry, *U.K.* 14 57 20N 5 33W
Stromness, *U.K.* 14 58 58N 3 18W
Ströms vattudal, *Sweden* 8 64 15N 14 55 E
Strömsnäsbruk, *Sweden* 11 56 35N 13 45 E
Strömstad, *Sweden* 10 58 55N 11 15 E
Strömsund, *Sweden* 8 63 51N 15 33 E
Stronghurst, *U.S.A.* 118 40 45N 90 55W
Stróngoli, *Italy* 29 39 16N 17 2 E
Stronsay, *U.K.* 14 59 8N 2 38W
Stronsburg, *U.S.A.* 120 41 7N 97 36W
Stroud, *Australia* 76 32 25 S 152 0 E
Stroud, *Canada* 108 44 19N 79 37W
Stroud, *U.K.* 13 51 44N 2 12W
Stroud Road, *Australia* 77 32 18 S 151 57 E
Stroudsberg, *U.S.A.* 117 40 59N 75 15W
Struer, *Denmark* 11 56 30N 8 35 E
Struga, *Yugoslavia* 35 41 13N 20 44 E
Strugi Krasnyye, *U.S.S.R.* 36 58 21N 29 1 E
Strumica, *Yugoslavia* 35 41 28N 22 41 E
Strumica →, *Europe* 35 41 20N 23 22 E
Struthers, *Canada* 104 48 41N 85 51W
Struthers, *U.S.A.* 116 41 6N 80 38W
Stryi, *U.S.S.R.* 36 49 16N 23 48 E
Stryker, *U.S.A.* 122 48 40N 114 44W
Strzegom, *Poland* 32 50 58N 16 20 E
Strzelce Krajeńskie, *Poland* 32 52 52N 15 33 E
Strzelecki Cr. →, *Australia* 73 29 37 S 139 59 E
Strzelin, *Poland* 32 50 46N 17 2 E
Strzelno, *Poland* 32 52 35N 18 9 E

Strzyżów, *Poland* ..... **32** 49 52N 21 47 E
Stuart, *Fla., U.S.A.* .. **115** 27 11N 80 12W
Stuart, *Iowa, U.S.A.* .. **118** 41 30N 94 19W
Stuart, *Nebr., U.S.A.* . **120** 42 39N 99 8W
Stuart →, *Canada* **110** 54 0N 123 35W
Stuart L., *Canada* **110** 54 30N 124 30W
Stuart Mts., *N.Z.* .... **81** 45 2 S 167 39 E
Stuart Range, *Australia* **73** 29 10 S 134 56 E
Stuart Town, *Australia* **76** 32 44 S 149 4 E
Stubbekøbing, *Denmark* .... **11** 54 53N 12 9 E
Studholme Junc., *N.Z.* **81** 44 42 S 171 9 E
Stugun, *Sweden* ...... **10** 63 10N 15 40 E
Stühlingen, *W. Germany* .... **31** 47 44N 8 26 E
Stull, L., *Canada* **104** 54 24N 92 34W
Stung Treng, *Cambodia* **13** 31N 105 58 E
Stupart →, *Canada* .. **111** 56 0N 93 25W
Stupino, *U.S.S.R.* .... **37** 54 57N 38 2 E
Sturgeon →, *Canada* . **108** 46 35N 80 11W
Sturgeon B., *Canada* . **111** 52 0N 97 50W
Sturgeon Bay, *U.S.A.* .. **114** 44 52N 87 20W
Sturgeon Falls, *Canada* **108** 46 25N 79 57W
Sturgeon L., *Alta., Canada* **110** 55 6N 117 32W
Sturgeon L., *Ont., Canada* **104** 50 0N 90 45W
Sturgeon L., *Ont., Canada* **109** 44 28N 78 43W
Sturgis, *Mich., U.S.A.* **119** 41 50N 85 25W
Sturgis, *S. Dak., U.S.A.* **120** 44 25N 103 30W
Sturkö, *Sweden* ...... **11** 56 5N 15 42 E
Sturt Cr. →, *Australia* **78** 19 8 S 127 50 E
Sturt Creek, *Australia* . **78** 19 12 S 128 8 E
Stutterheim, *S. Africa* . **96** 32 33 S 27 28 E
Stuttgart, *U.S.A.* **121** 34 30N 91 33W
Stuttgart, *W. Germany* **31** 48 46N 9 10 E
Stuyvesant, *U.S.A.* ... **117** 42 23N 73 45W
Stykkishólmur, *Iceland* **8** 65 2N 22 40W
Styr →, *U.S.S.R.* .... **36** 52 7N 26 35 E
Styria = Steiermark □, *Austria* .... **33** 47 26N 15 0 E
Su-no-Saki, *Japan* .... **65** 34 58N 139 45 E
Su Xian, *China* ...... **60** 33 41N 116 59 E
Suakin, *Sudan* .... **88** 19 8N 37 20 E
Suapure →, *Venezuela* **134** 6 48N 67 1W
Suaqui, *Mexico* **126** 29 12N 109 41W
Suatá →, *Venezuela* .. **135** 7 52N 65 22W
Subang, *Indonesia* .... **57** 6 34 S 107 45 E
Subansiri →, *India* ... **52** 26 48N 93 50 E
Subi, *Indonesia* ...... **55** 2 58N 108 50 E
Subiaco, *Italy* .... **27** 41 56N 13 5 E
Subotica, *Yugoslavia* .. **33** 46 6N 19 49 E
Success, *Canada* **111** 50 28N 108 6W
Suceava, *Romania* .... **34** 47 38N 26 16 E
Suceava →, *Romania* . **34** 47 38N 26 16 E
Sucha-Beskidzka, *Poland* .... **32** 49 44N 19 35 E
Suchan, *Poland* ...... **32** 53 18N 15 18 E
Suchitoto, *El Salv.* ... **128** 13 56N 89 0W
Suchou = Suzhou, *China* .... **59** 31 19N 120 38 E
Süchow = Xuzhou, *China* .... **61** 34 18N 117 10 E
Suchowola, *Poland* ... **32** 53 33N 23 3 E
Sucio →, *Colombia* .. **134** 7 27N 77 7W
Suck →, *Ireland* **15** 53 17N 8 18W
Suckling, Mt., *Papua N. G.* .... **69** 9 49 S 148 53 E
Sucre, *Bolivia* .... **137** 19 0 S 65 15W
Sucre, *Colombia* **134** 8 49N 74 44W
Sucre □, *Colombia* ... **134** 8 50N 75 40W
Sucre □, *Venezuela* ... **135** 10 25N 63 30W
Sucuaro, *Colombia* ... **134** 4 34N 68 50W
Sućuraj, *Yugoslavia* ... **27** 43 10N 17 8 E
Sucuriju, *Brazil* **138** 1 39N 49 57W
Sucuriú →, *Brazil* ... **137** 20 47 S 51 38W
Sud, Pte., *Canada* **105** 49 3N 62 14W
Sud-Ouest, Pte. du, *Canada* **105** 49 23N 63 36W
Suda →, *U.S.S.R.* ... **37** 59 0N 37 40 E
Sudair, *Si. Arabia* ... **46** 26 0N 45 0 E
Sudak, *U.S.S.R.* ..... **38** 44 51N 34 57 E
Sudan, *U.S.A.* **121** 34 4N 102 32W
Sudan ■, *Africa* ..... **89** 15 0N 30 0 E
Suday, *U.S.S.R.* ..... **37** 59 0N 43 0 E
Sudbury, *Canada* **108** 46 30N 81 0W
Sudbury, *U.K.* .... **13** 52 2N 0 44 E
Sûdd, *Sudan* .... **89** 8 20N 30 0 E
Suddie, *Guyana* **135** 7 8N 58 29W
Süderbrarup, *W. Germany* .... **30** 54 38N 9 47 E
Süderlügum, *W. Germany* .... **30** 54 50N 8 55 E
Süderoog-Sand, *W. Germany* .... **30** 54 27N 8 30 E
Sudetan Mts. = Sudety, *Europe* .... **32** 50 20N 16 45 E
Sudety, *Europe* ...... **32** 50 20N 16 45 E
Sudi, *Tanzania* .... **93** 10 11 S 39 57 E
Sudirman, Pegunungan, *Indonesia* .... **57** 4 30 S 137 0 E
Sudogda, *U.S.S.R.* ... **37** 55 55N 40 50 E
Sudr, *Egypt* .... **88** 29 40N 32 42 E
Sudzha, *U.S.S.R.* ..... **36** 51 14N 35 17 E
Sueca, *Spain* **25** 39 12N 0 21W
Suedala, *Sweden* ..... **11** 55 30N 13 15 E
Sueur, Le, *U.S.A.* **120** 44 25N 93 52W
Suez = El Suweis, *Egypt* .... **88** 29 58N 32 31 E
Suez, G. of = Suweis, Khalîg el, *Egypt* .... **88** 28 40N 33 0 E
Suez Canal = Suweis, Qanâl es, *Egypt* .... **88** 31 0N 32 20 E
Sūf, *Jordan* .... **44** 32 19N 35 49 E
Suffield, *Canada* **111** 50 12N 111 10W
Suffolk, *U.S.A.* **114** 36 47N 76 33W
Suffolk □, *U.K.* ...... **13** 52 16N 1 0 E
Suga no-Sen, *Japan* ... **64** 35 25N 134 25 E
Sugar →, *Ill., U.S.A.* **118** 42 25N 89 15W
Sugar →, *Ind., U.S.A.* **119** 39 50N 87 23W
Sugar City, *U.S.A.* ... **120** 38 18N 103 38W
Sugar Cr. →, *U.S.A.* . **118** 40 12N 89 41W
Sugluk = Saglouc, *Canada* **103** 62 14N 75 38W
Sugny, *Belgium* ...... **17** 49 49N 4 54 E
Suhaia, L., *Romania* .. **34** 43 45N 25 15 E
Suhār, *Oman* .... **47** 24 20N 56 40 E
Sühbaatar, *Mongolia* .. **62** 50 17N 106 10 E
Sühbaatar □, *Mongolia* **60** 45 30N 114 0 E
Suhl, *E. Germany* .... **30** 50 35N 10 40 E
Suhl □, *E. Germany* .. **30** 50 37N 10 43 E
Sui Xian, *Henan, China* **59** 31 42N 113 24 E
Sui Xian, *Henan, China* **60** 34 25N 115 2 E
Suiá Missu →, *Brazil* . **137** 11 13 S 53 15W
Suichang, *China* ...... **59** 28 29N 119 15 E
Suichuan, *China* ...... **59** 26 20N 114 32 E
Suide, *China* .... **60** 37 30N 110 12 E
Suifenhe, *China* ...... **61** 44 25N 131 10 E
Suihua, *China* .... **62** 46 32N 126 55 E
Suijiang, *China* ...... **58** 28 40N 103 59 E
Suining, *Hunan, China* **59** 26 35N 110 10 E
Suining, *Jiangsu, China* **61** 33 56N 117 58 E
Suining, *Sichuan, China* **58** 30 26N 105 35 E
Suiping, *China* .... **60** 33 10N 113 59 E
Suippes, *France* ...... **19** 49 8N 4 30 E
Suir →, *Ireland* **15** 52 15N 7 10W
Suita, *Japan* .... **65** 34 45N 135 32 E
Suixi, *China* .... **59** 21 19N 110 18 E
Suiyang, *Guizhou, China* .... **58** 27 58N 107 18 E
Suiyang, *Heilongjiang, China* .... **61** 44 30N 130 56 E
Suizhong, *China* ...... **61** 40 21N 120 20 E
Sujangarh, *India* ..... **48** 27 42N 74 31 E
Sukabumi, *Indonesia* .. **57** 6 56 S 106 50 E
Sukadana, *Kalimantan, Indonesia* .... **56** 1 10 S 110 0 E
Sukadana, *Sumatera, Indonesia* .... **56** 5 5 S 105 33 E
Sukaraja, *Indonesia* ... **56** 2 28 S 110 25 E
Sukarnapura = Jayapura, *Indonesia* **57** 2 28 S 140 38 E
Sukhinichi, *U.S.S.R.* .. **36** 54 8N 35 10 E
Sukhona →, *U.S.S.R.* **40** 60 30N 45 0 E
Sukhothai, *Thailand* .. **54** 17 1N 99 49 E
Sukhumi, *U.S.S.R.* ... **39** 43 0N 41 0 E
Sukkur, *Pakistan* ..... **48** 27 42N 68 54 E
Sukkur Barrage, *Pakistan* .... **48** 27 40N 68 50 E
Sukma, *India* .... **50** 18 24N 81 45 E
Sukumo, *Japan* ...... **64** 32 56N 132 44 E
Sukunka →, *Canada* . **110** 55 45N 121 15W
Sul, Canal do, *Brazil* . **138** 0 10 S 48 30W
Sula →, *U.S.S.R.* .... **36** 49 40N 32 41 E
Sula, Kepulauan, *Indonesia* .... **57** 1 45 S 125 0 E
Sulaco →, *Honduras* . **128** 15 2N 87 44W
Sulaiman Range, *Pakistan* .... **48** 30 30N 69 50 E
Sulak →, *U.S.S.R.* ... **39** 43 20N 47 34 E
Sulam Tsor, *Israel* .... **44** 33 4N 35 6 E
Sulawesi □, *Indonesia* **57** 2 0 S 120 0 E
Sulechów, *Poland* ..... **32** 52 5N 15 40 E
Sulejów, *Poland* ...... **32** 51 26N 19 53 E
Sulima, *S. Leone* **90** 6 58N 11 32W
Sulina, *Romania* ..... **34** 45 10N 29 40 E
Sulingen, *W. Germany* **30** 52 41N 8 47 E
Sulitälma, *Sweden* .... **8** 67 17N 17 28 E
Sulitjelma, *Norway* ... **8** 67 9N 16 3 E
Sullana, *Peru* .... **136** 4 52 S 80 39W
Sullivan, *Canada* **106** 48 7N 77 50W
Sullivan, *Ill., U.S.A.* .. **119** 39 40N 88 40W
Sullivan, *Ind., U.S.A.* .. **119** 39 5N 87 26W
Sullivan, *Mo., U.S.A.* .. **118** 38 10N 91 10W
Sullivan Bay, *Canada* . **110** 50 55N 126 50W
Sully, *U.S.A.* **118** 41 34N 92 50W
Sully-sur-Loire, *France* **19** 47 45N 2 20 E
Sulmona, *Italy* .... **27** 42 3N 13 55 E
Sulphur, *La., U.S.A.* .. **121** 30 13N 93 22W
Sulphur, *Okla., U.S.A.* **121** 34 35N 97 0W
Sulphur Pt., *Canada* .. **110** 60 56N 114 48W
Sulphur Springs, *U.S.A.* **121** 33 5N 95 36W
Sulphur Springs Draw →, *U.S.A.* .. **121** 32 12N 101 36W
Sulsul, *Ethiopia* ...... **98** 5 5N 44 50 E
Sultan, *Canada* **104** 47 36N 82 47W
Sultan, *U.S.A.* **124** 47 51N 121 49W
Sultanpur, *India* ..... **49** 26 18N 82 4 E
Sulu Arch., *Phil.* ..... **57** 6 0N 121 0 E
Sulu Sea, *E. Indies* .... **57** 8 0N 120 0 E
Sululta, *Ethiopia* .... **89** 9 10N 38 43 E
Suluq, *Libya* .... **86** 31 44N 20 14 E
Sulzbach, *W. Germany* **31** 49 18N 7 4 E
Sulzbach-Rosenberg, *W. Germany* .... **31** 49 30N 11 46 E
Sulzberger Ice Shelf, *Antarctica* .... **143** 78 0 S 150 0 E
Sumalata, *Indonesia* .. **57** 1 0N 122 31 E
Sumampa, *Argentina* .. **140** 29 25 S 63 29W
Sumatera □, *Indonesia* **56** 0 40N 100 20 E
Sumatra = Sumatera □, *Indonesia* .... **56** 0 40N 100 20 E
Sumatra, *U.S.A.* **122** 46 38N 107 31W
Sumba, *Indonesia* .... **57** 9 45 S 119 35 E
Sumba, Selat, *Indonesia* **57** 9 0 S 118 40 E
Sumbawa, *Indonesia* .. **56** 8 26 S 117 30 E
Sumbawa Besar, *Indonesia* .... **56** 8 30 S 117 26 E
Sumbawanga □, *Tanzania* .... **92** 8 0 S 31 30 E
Sumbe, *Angola* ...... **95** 11 10 S 13 48 E
Sumburgh Hd., *U.K.* . **14** 59 52N 1 17W
Sumdo, *India* .... **49** 35 6N 78 41 E
Sumé, *Brazil* .... **138** 7 39 S 36 55W
Sumedang, *Indonesia* . **57** 6 52 S 107 55 E
Šumen, *Bulgaria* ..... **34** 43 18N 26 55 E
Sumenep, *Indonesia* .. **57** 7 1 S 113 52 E
Sumgait, *U.S.S.R.* .... **39** 40 34N 49 38 E
Sumisu-Jima, *Japan* ... **65** 31 27N 140 3 E
Summer L., *U.S.A.* ... **122** 42 50N 120 50W
Summerland, *Canada* . **110** 49 32N 119 41W
Summerside, *Canada* . **105** 46 24N 63 47W
Summerville, *Ga., U.S.A.* **115** 34 30N 85 20W
Summerville, *S.C., U.S.A.* **115** 33 2N 80 11W
Summit Lake, *Canada* **110** 54 20N 122 40W
Summit Pk., *U.S.A.* .. **123** 37 20N 106 48W
Sumner, *N.Z.* .... **81** 43 35 S 172 48 E
Sumner, *Ill., U.S.A.* .. **119** 38 42N 87 53W
Sumner, *Iowa, U.S.A.* **118** 42 49N 92 7W
Sumner, *Wash., U.S.A.* **124** 47 12N 122 14W
Sumner L., *N.Z.* ..... **81** 42 42 S 172 15 E
Sumoto, *Japan* .... **64** 34 21N 134 54 E
Sumprabum, *Burma* .. **52** 26 33N 97 36 E
Sumter, *U.S.A.* **115** 33 55N 80 22W
Sumy, *U.S.S.R.* ...... **36** 50 57N 34 50 E
Sun City, *Ariz., U.S.A.* **123** 33 41N 112 16W
Sun City, *Calif., U.S.A.* **125** 33 41N 117 11W
Sun Prairie, *U.S.A.* ... **118** 43 11N 89 13W
Sunart, L., *U.K.* **14** 56 42N 5 43W
Sunburst, *U.S.A.* **122** 48 56N 111 59W
Sunbury, *Australia* .... **74** 37 35 S 144 44 E
Sunbury, *U.S.A.* **117** 40 50N 76 46W
Sunchales, *Argentina* .. **140** 30 58 S 61 35W
Suncho Corral, *Argentina* .... **140** 27 55 S 63 27W
Sunchon, *S. Korea* ... **61** 34 52N 127 31 E
Suncook, *U.S.A.* **117** 43 8N 71 27W
Sunda, Selat, *Indonesia* **56** 6 20 S 105 30 E
Sunda Is., *Indonesia* .. **66** 5 0 S 105 0 E
Sundance, *U.S.A.* **120** 44 27N 104 27W
Sundarbans, The, *Asia* **52** 22 0N 89 0 E
Sundargarh, *India* .... **50** 22 4N 84 5 E
Sunday I., *Australia* .. **75** 38 43 S 146 38 E
Sundays = Sondag →, *S. Africa* .... **96** 33 44 S 25 51 E
Sundbyberg, *Sweden* .. **10** 59 22N 17 58 E
Sunderland, *Canada* .. **109** 44 16N 79 4W
Sunderland, *U.K.* **12** 54 54N 1 22W
Sundre, *Canada* **110** 51 49N 114 38W
Sundridge, *Canada* ... **108** 45 45N 79 25W
Sunds, *Denmark* ..... **11** 56 13N 9 1 E
Sundsjö, *Sweden* ..... **10** 62 59N 15 9 E
Sundsvall, *Sweden* .... **10** 62 23N 17 17 E
Sung Hei, *Vietnam* ... **55** 10 20N 106 2 E
Sungai Kolok, *Thailand* **55** 6 2N 101 58 E
Sungai Lembing, *Malaysia* .... **55** 3 55N 103 3 E
Sungai Patani, *Malaysia* **55** 5 37N 100 30 E
Sungaigerong, *Indonesia* .... **56** 2 59 S 104 52 E
Sungailiat, *Indonesia* .. **56** 1 51 S 106 8 E
Sungaipakning, *Indonesia* .... **56** 1 19N 102 0 E
Sungaipenuh, *Indonesia* **56** 2 1 S 101 20 E
Sungaitiram, *Indonesia* **56** 0 45 S 117 8 E
Sungari = Songhua Jiang →, *China* .... **61** 47 45N 132 30 E
Sungguminasa, *Indonesia* .... **57** 5 17 S 119 30 E
Sunghua Chiang = Songhua Jiang →, *China* .... **61** 47 45N 132 30 E
Sungikai, *Sudan* ...... **89** 12 20N 29 51 E
Sungurlu, *Turkey* ..... **38** 40 12N 34 21 E
Sunja, *Yugoslavia* .... **27** 45 21N 16 35 E
Sunne, *Sweden* .... **10** 59 52N 13 5 E
Sunnyside, *Utah, U.S.A.* **122** 39 34N 110 24W
Sunnyside, *Wash., U.S.A.* **122** 46 24N 120 2W
Sunnyvale, *U.S.A.* ... **124** 37 23N 122 2W
Sunray, *U.S.A.* **121** 36 1N 101 47W
Sunshine, *Australia* ... **74** 37 48 S 144 52 E
Suntar, *U.S.S.R.* ..... **41** 62 15N 117 30 E
Sunyani, *Ghana* **90** 7 21N 2 22W
Suō-Nada, *Japan* ..... **64** 33 50N 131 30 E
Supai, *U.S.A.* **123** 36 14N 112 44W
Supamo →, *Venezuela* **135** 6 48N 61 50W
Supaul, *India* .... **49** 26 10N 86 40 E
Supe, *Peru* .... **136** 11 0 S 77 30W
Superior, *Ariz., U.S.A.* **123** 33 19N 111 9W
Superior, *Mont., U.S.A.* **122** 47 15N 114 57W
Superior, *Nebr., U.S.A.* **120** 40 3N 98 2W
Superior, *Wis., U.S.A.* **120** 46 45N 92 5W
Superior, L., *N. Amer.* **113** 47 40N 87 0W
Supetar, *Yugoslavia* .. **27** 43 25N 16 32 E
Suphan Buri, *Thailand* **54** 14 14N 100 10 E
Suphan Daği, *Turkey* . **46** 38 54N 42 48 E
Supriori, Kepulauan, *Indonesia* .... **57** 1 0 S 136 0 E
Suq al Jum'ah, *Libya* . **86** 32 58N 13 12 E
Suqian, *China* .... **61** 33 54N 118 8 E
Sūr, *Lebanon* .... **44** 33 19N 35 16 E
Sūr, *Oman* .... **47** 22 34N 59 32 E
Sur, Pt., *U.S.A.* **124** 36 18N 121 54W
Sura →, *U.S.S.R.* .... **37** 56 6N 46 0 E
Surab, *Pakistan* ...... **48** 28 25N 66 15 E
Surabaja = Surabaya, *Indonesia* .... **57** 7 17 S 112 45 E
Surabaya, *Indonesia* .. **57** 7 17 S 112 45 E
Surahammar, *Sweden* . **10** 59 43N 16 13 E
Suraia, *Romania* ..... **34** 45 40N 27 25 E
Surakarta, *Indonesia* .. **57** 7 35 S 110 48 E
Surakhany, *U.S.S.R.* .. **39** 40 25N 50 1 E
Surandai, *India* ...... **51** 8 58N 77 26 E
Surat, *Australia* ...... **77** 27 10 S 149 6 E
Surat, *India* .... **50** 21 12N 72 55 E
Surat Thani, *Thailand* . **55** 9 6N 99 20 E
Suratgarh, *India* ..... **48** 29 18N 73 55 E
Surazh, *Byelorussian S.S.R., U.S.S.R.* .... **36** 55 25N 30 44 E
Surazh, *R.S.F.S.R., U.S.S.R.* .... **36** 53 5N 32 27 E
Surduc Pasul, *Romania* **34** 45 21N 23 23 E
Surdulica, *Yugoslavia* . **33** 42 41N 22 11 E
Sûre = Sauer →, *W. Germany* .... **17** 49 44N 6 31 E
Surendranagar, *India* . **48** 22 45N 71 40 E
Surf, *U.S.A.* **125** 34 41N 120 36W
Surfers Paradise, *Australia* .... **77** 28 0 S 153 25 E
Surgères, *France* **20** 46 7N 0 47W
Surgut, *U.S.S.R.* ..... **40** 61 14N 73 20 E
Surhuisterveen, *Neths.* **16** 53 11N 6 10 E
Suriapet, *India* .... **50** 17 10N 79 40 E
Şūrīf, *Jordan* .... **44** 31 40N 35 4 E
Surigao, *Phil.* .... **57** 9 47N 125 29 E
Surin, *Thailand* ...... **54** 14 50N 103 34 E
Surin Nua, Ko, *Thailand* .... **55** 9 30N 97 55 E
Surinam ■, *S. Amer.* . **135** 4 0N 56 0W
Suriname □, *Surinam* **135** 5 30N 55 0W
Suriname →, *Surinam* **135** 5 50N 55 15W
Surmene, *Turkey* ..... **39** 41 0N 40 1 E
Surovikino, *U.S.S.R.* . **39** 48 32N 42 55 E
Surprise, L., *Canada* .. **106** 49 20N 74 55W
Surprise L., *Canada* ... **110** 59 40N 133 15W
Surrey □, *U.K.* **13** 51 16N 0 30W
Sursee, *Switz.* .... **31** 47 11N 8 6 E
Sursk, *U.S.S.R.* ...... **37** 53 3N 45 40 E
Surt, *Libya* .... **86** 31 11N 16 39 E
Surt, Al Hammadah al, *Libya* .... **86** 30 0N 17 50 E
Surt, Khalīj, *Libya* ... **86** 31 40N 18 30 E
Surtsey, *Iceland* **8** 63 20N 20 30W
Surubim, *Brazil* ...... **138** 7 50 S 35 45W
Surud Ad, *Somali Rep.* **98** 10 42N 47 9 E
Suruga-Wan, *Japan* ... **65** 34 45N 138 30 E
Surumu →, *Brazil* ... **135** 3 22N 60 19W
Susa, *Italy* .... **26** 45 8N 7 3 E
Suså →, *Denmark* ... **11** 55 20N 11 42 E
Sušac, *Yugoslavia* .... **27** 42 46N 16 30 E
Susak, *Yugoslavia* .... **27** 44 30N 14 18 E
Susaki, *Japan* .... **64** 33 22N 133 17 E
Sūsangerd, *Iran* ...... **46** 31 35N 48 6 E
Susanino, *U.S.S.R.* ... **41** 52 50N 140 14 E
Susanville, *U.S.A.* **122** 40 28N 120 40W
Susong, *China* .... **59** 30 10N 116 5 E
Susquehanna →, *U.S.A.* **117** 39 33N 76 5W
Susquehanna Depot, *U.S.A.* **117** 41 55N 75 36W
Susques, *Argentina* ... **140** 23 35 S 66 25W
Sussex, *Canada* **105** 45 45N 65 37W
Sussex, *U.S.A.* **117** 41 12N 74 38W
Sussex, E. □, *U.K.* ... **13** 51 0N 0 20 E
Sussex, W. □, *U.K.* .. **13** 51 0N 0 30W
Susteren, *Neths.* ..... **17** 51 4N 5 51 E
Sustut →, *Canada* ... **110** 56 20N 127 30W
Susubona, *Solomon Is.* **68** 8 19 S 159 27 E
Susuman, *U.S.S.R.* ... **41** 62 47N 148 10 E
Susunu, *Indonesia* .... **57** 3 20 S 133 25 E
Sutherland, *Australia* . **76** 34 2 S 151 4 E
Sutherland, *S. Africa* . **96** 32 24 S 20 40 E
Sutherland, *U.S.A.* ... **120** 41 12N 101 11W
Sutherland Falls, *N.Z.* **81** 44 48 S 167 46 E
Sutherlin, *U.S.A.* **122** 43 28N 123 16W
Sutivan, *Yugoslavia* .. **27** 43 23N 16 30 E
Sutlej →, *Pakistan* ... **48** 29 23N 71 3 E
Sutter, *U.S.A.* **124** 39 10N 121 45W
Sutter Creek, *U.S.A.* . **124** 38 24N 120 48W
Sutton, *Australia* ..... **76** 35 10 S 149 15 E
Sutton, *Ont., Canada* . **108** 44 18N 79 22W
Sutton, *Qué., Canada* . **107** 45 6N 72 37W
Sutton, *N.Z.* .... **81** 45 34 S 170 8 E
Sutton, *U.S.A.* **120** 40 40N 97 50W
Sutton →, *Canada* ... **104** 55 15N 83 45W
Sutton-in-Ashfield, *U.K.* **12** 53 7N 1 20W
Suttor →, *Australia* .. **72** 21 36 S 147 2 E
Su'u, *Solomon Is.* ..... **68** 9 11 S 160 56 E
Suva, *Fiji* .... **68** 18 6 S 178 30 E
Suva Reka, *Yugoslavia* **33** 42 21N 20 50 E
Suvo Rudište, *Yugoslavia* .... **33** 43 17N 20 49 E
Suvorov, *U.S.S.R.* .... **37** 54 7N 36 30 E
Suvorov Is. = Suwarrow Is., *Cook Is.* .... **67** 15 0 S 163 0W
Suwa, *Japan* .... **65** 36 2N 138 8 E
Suwa-Ko, *Japan* ...... **65** 36 3N 138 5 E
Suwałki, *Poland* ...... **32** 54 8N 22 59 E
Suwannaphum, *Thailand* .... **54** 15 33N 103 47 E
Suwannee →, *U.S.A.* **115** 29 18N 83 9W

Suwanose-Jima, *Japan* **63** 29 38N 129 43 E
Suwarrow Is., *Cook Is.* **67** 15 0 S 163 0W
Suweis, Khalîg el, *Egypt* **88** 28 40N 33 0 E
Suweis, Qanâl es, *Egypt* **88** 31 0N 32 20 E
Suwŏn, *S. Korea* **61** 37 17N 127 1 E
Suzaka, *Japan* **65** 36 39N 138 19 E
Suzdal, *U.S.S.R.* **37** 56 29N 40 26 E
Suze-sur-Sarthe, La, *France* **18** 47 53N 0 2 E
Suzhou, *China* **59** 31 19N 120 38 E
Suzu-Misaki, *Japan* **63** 37 31N 137 21 E
Suzuka, *Japan* **65** 34 55N 136 36 E
Suzuka-Sam, *Japan* **65** 35 5N 136 30 E
Suzzara, *Italy* **26** 45 0N 10 45 E
Svalbard, *Arctic* **144** 78 0N 17 0 E
Svalbarð, *Iceland* **8** 66 12N 15 43W
Svalöv, *Sweden* **11** 55 57N 13 8 E
Svanvik, *Norway* **8** 69 25N 30 3 E
Svappavaara, *Sweden* **8** 67 40N 21 3 E
Svarstad, *Norway* **10** 59 27N 9 56 E
Svartisen, *Norway* **8** 66 40N 13 50 E
Svartvik, *Sweden* **10** 62 19N 17 24 E
Svatovo, *U.S.S.R.* **38** 49 35N 38 11 E
Svay Chek, *Cambodia* **54** 13 48N 102 58 E
Svay Rieng, *Cambodia* **55** 11 5N 105 48 E
Svealand □, *Sweden* **9** 59 55N 15 0 E
Sveg, *Sweden* **9** 62 2N 14 21 E
Svendborg, *Denmark* **11** 55 4N 10 35 E
Svene, *Norway* **10** 59 45N 9 31 E
Svenljunga, *Sweden* **11** 57 29N 13 5 E
Svenstrup, *Denmark* **11** 56 58N 9 50 E
Sverdlovsk, *R.S.F.S.R., U.S.S.R.* **40** 56 50N 60 30 E
Sverdlovsk, *Ukraine S.S.R., U.S.S.R.* **39** 48 5N 39 37 E
Sverdrup Is., *Canada* **144** 79 0N 97 0W
Svetac, *Yugoslavia* **27** 43 3N 15 43 E
Sveti Ivan Zelina, *Yugoslavia* **27** 45 57N 16 16 E
Sveti Jurij, *Yugoslavia* **27** 46 14N 15 24 E
Sveti Lenart, *Yugoslavia* **27** 46 36N 15 48 E
Sveti Nikole, *Yugoslavia* **35** 41 51N 21 56 E
Sveti Trojica, *Yugoslavia* **27** 46 37N 15 50 E
Svetlogorsk, *U.S.S.R.* **36** 52 38N 29 46 E
Svetlograd, *U.S.S.R.* **39** 45 25N 42 58 E
Svetlovodsk, *U.S.S.R.* **36** 49 2N 33 13 E
Svetozarevo, *Yugoslavia* **33** 44 5N 21 15 E
Svidník, *Czech.* **32** 49 20N 21 37 E
Svilaja Pl., *Yugoslavia* **27** 43 49N 16 31 E
Svilengrad, *Bulgaria* **35** 41 49N 26 12 E
Svir →, *U.S.S.R.* **6** 60 30N 32 48 E
Svishtov, *Bulgaria* **34** 43 36N 25 23 E
Svisloch, *U.S.S.R.* **36** 53 3N 24 2 E
Svitava →, *Czech.* **32** 49 30N 16 37 E
Svitavy, *Czech.* **32** 49 47N 16 28 E
Svobodnyy, *U.S.S.R.* **41** 51 20N 128 0 E
Svolvær, *Norway* **8** 68 15N 14 34 E
Svratka →, *Czech.* **32** 49 11N 16 38 E
Svrljig, *Yugoslavia* **33** 43 25N 22 6 E
Swa, *Burma* **52** 19 15N 96 17 E
Swa Tende, *Zaïre* **95** 7 9 S 17 7 E
Swabian Alps = Schwäbische Alb, *W. Germany* **31** 48 30N 9 30 E
Swainsboro, *U.S.A.* **115** 32 38N 82 22W
Swakopmund, *Namibia* **96** 22 37 S 14 30 E
Swale →, *U.K.* **12** 54 5N 1 20W
Swalmen, *Neths.* **17** 51 13N 6 2 E
Swan Hill, *Australia* **74** 35 20 S 143 33 E
Swan Hills, *Canada* **110** 54 42N 115 24W
Swan Is., *W. Indies* **128** 17 22N 83 57W
Swan L., *Canada* **111** 52 30N 100 40W
Swan Reach, *Australia* **75** 37 49 S 147 53 E
Swan River, *Canada* **111** 52 10N 101 16W
Swanage, *U.K.* **13** 50 36N 1 59W
Swanpool, *Australia* **74** 36 44 S 146 2 E
Swansea, *Australia* **76** 33 3 S 151 35 E
Swansea, *U.K.* **13** 51 37N 3 57W
Swar →, *Pakistan* **49** 34 40N 72 5 E
Swartberge, *S. Africa* **96** 33 20 S 22 0 E
Swartmodder, *S. Africa* **96** 28 1 S 20 32 E
Swartruggens, *S. Africa* **96** 25 39 S 26 42 E
Swarzędz, *Poland* **32** 52 25N 17 4 E
Swastika, *Canada* **106** 48 7N 80 6W
Swatow = Shantou, *China* **59** 23 18N 116 40 E
Swaziland ■, *Africa* **97** 26 30 S 31 30 E
Sweden ■, *Europe* **8** 57 0N 15 0 E
Swedru, *Ghana* **91** 5 32N 0 41W
Sweet Home, *U.S.A.* **122** 44 26N 122 25W
Sweet Springs, *U.S.A.* **118** 38 58N 93 25W
Sweetwater, *Nev., U.S.A.* **124** 38 27N 119 9W
Sweetwater, *Tex., U.S.A.* **121** 32 30N 100 28W
Sweetwater →, *U.S.A.* **122** 42 31N 107 2W
Swellendam, *S. Africa* **96** 34 1 S 20 26 E
Świdnica, *Poland* **32** 50 50N 16 30 E
Świdnik, *Poland* **32** 51 13N 22 39 E
Świdwin, *Poland* **32** 53 47N 15 49 E
Świebodzin, *Poland* **32** 52 15N 15 31 E
Świecie, *Poland* **32** 53 25N 18 30 E
Świętokrzyskie, Góry, *Poland* **32** 51 0N 20 30 E
Swift Current, *Canada* **111** 50 20N 107 45W
Swiftcurrent →, *Canada* **111** 50 38N 107 44W
Swifts Creek, *Australia* **75** 37 17 S 147 44 E
Swilly, L., *Ireland* **15** 55 12N 7 35W
Swindle, I., *Canada* **110** 52 30N 128 35W
Swindon, *U.K.* **13** 51 33N 1 47W
Swinemünde = Świnoujście, *Poland* **32** 53 54N 14 16 E
Świnoujście, *Poland* **32** 53 54N 14 16 E
Switzerland ■, *Europe* **31** 46 30N 8 0 E
Swords, *Ireland* **15** 53 27N 6 15W
Syasstroy, *U.S.S.R.* **36** 60 5N 32 15 E
Sychevka, *U.S.S.R.* **36** 55 59N 34 16 E
Sydenham →, *Canada* **108** 42 33N 82 25W
Sydney, *Australia* **76** 33 53 S 151 10 E
Sydney, *Canada* **105** 46 7N 60 7W
Sydney Mines, *Canada* **105** 46 18N 60 15W
Sydprøven, *Greenland* **144** 60 30N 45 35W
Sydra G. of = Surt, Khalīj, *Libya* **86** 31 40N 18 30 E
Syke, *W. Germany* **30** 52 55N 8 50 E
Syktyvkar, *U.S.S.R.* **40** 61 45N 50 40 E
Sylacauga, *U.S.A.* **115** 33 10N 86 15W
Sylarna, *Sweden* **8** 63 2N 12 13 E
Sylhet, *Bangla.* **52** 24 54N 91 52 E
Sylt, *W. Germany* **30** 54 50N 8 20 E
Sylvan Lake, *Canada* **110** 52 20N 114 3W
Sylvania, *Ga., U.S.A.* **115** 32 45N 81 37W
Sylvania, *Ohio, U.S.A.* **119** 41 43N 83 42W
Sylvester, *U.S.A.* **115** 31 31N 83 50W
Sym, *U.S.S.R.* **40** 60 20N 88 18 E
Symón, *Mexico* **126** 24 42N 102 35W
Synnott Ra., *Australia* **78** 16 30 S 125 20 E
Syracuse, *Ind., U.S.A.* **119** 41 28N 85 47W
Syracuse, *Kans., U.S.A.* **121** 38 0N 101 46W
Syracuse, *N.Y., U.S.A.* **117** 43 4N 76 11W
Syrdarya →, *U.S.S.R.* **40** 46 3N 61 0 E
Syria ■, *Asia* **46** 35 0N 38 0 E
Syriam, *Burma* **52** 16 44N 96 19 E
Syrian Desert, *Asia* **42** 31 0N 40 0 E
Syul'dzhyukyor, *U.S.S.R.* **41** 63 14N 113 32 E
Syzran, *U.S.S.R.* **37** 53 12N 48 30 E
Szaraz →, *Hungary* **33** 46 28N 20 44 E
Szarvas, *Hungary* **33** 46 50N 20 38 E
Szczebrzeszyn, *Poland* **32** 50 42N 22 59 E
Szczecin, *Poland* **32** 53 27N 14 27 E
Szczecinek, *Poland* **32** 53 43N 16 41 E
Szczekocimy, *Poland* **32** 50 38N 19 48 E
Szczytno, *Poland* **32** 53 33N 21 0 E
Szechwan = Sichuan □, *China* **58** 31 0N 104 0 E
Szeged, *Hungary* **33** 46 16N 20 10 E
Szeghalom, *Hungary* **33** 47 1N 21 10 E
Székesfehérvár, *Hungary* **33** 47 15N 18 25 E
Szekszárd, *Hungary* **33** 46 22N 18 42 E
Szendrö, *Hungary* **33** 48 24N 20 41 E
Szentendre, *Hungary* **33** 47 39N 19 4 E
Szentes, *Hungary* **33** 46 39N 20 21 E
Szentgotthárd, *Hungary* **33** 46 58N 16 19 E
Szentlörinc, *Hungary* **33** 46 3N 18 1 E
Szigetvár, *Hungary* **33** 46 3N 17 46 E
Szolnok, *Hungary* **33** 47 10N 20 15 E
Szombathely, *Hungary* **33** 47 14N 16 38 E
Szprotawa, *Poland* **32** 51 33N 15 35 E
Szydłowiec, *Poland* **32** 51 15N 20 51 E
Szypliszki, *Poland* **32** 54 17N 23 2 E

T

't Harde, *Neths.* **16** 52 24N 5 54 E
't Zandt, *Neths.* **16** 53 22N 6 46 E
Ta Khli Khok, *Thailand* **54** 15 18N 100 20 E
Ta Lai, *Vietnam* **55** 11 24N 107 23 E
Tabacal, *Argentina* **140** 23 15 S 64 15W
Tabaco, *Phil.* **57** 13 22N 123 44 E
Tabagné, *Ivory C.* **90** 7 59N 3 4W
Ţābah, *Si. Arabia* **46** 26 55N 42 38 E
Tabajara, *Brazil* **137** 8 56 S 62 8W
Tabalos, *Peru* **136** 6 26 S 76 37W
Tabar Is., *Papua N. G.* **69** 2 50 S 152 0 E
Tabarca, I. de, *Spain* **25** 38 17N 0 30W
Tabarka, *Tunisia* **86** 36 56N 8 46 E
Ţabas, *Khorāsān, Iran* **47** 32 48N 60 12 E
Ţabas, *Khorāsān, Iran* **47** 33 35N 56 55 E
Tabasará, Serranía de, *Panama* **128** 8 35N 81 40W
Tabasco □, *Mexico* **127** 17 45N 93 30W
Tabatinga, Serra da, *Brazil* **138** 10 30 S 44 0W
Tabayin, *Burma* **52** 22 42N 95 20 E
Tabelbala, Kahal de, *Algeria* **85** 28 47N 2 0W
Taber, *Canada* **110** 49 47N 112 8W
Tabernas, *Spain* **25** 37 4N 2 26W
Tabernes de Valldigna, *Spain* **25** 39 5N 0 13W
Tabi, *Angola* **95** 8 10 S 13 18 E
Tabira, *Brazil* **138** 7 35 S 37 33W
Tablas, *Phil.* **57** 12 25N 122 2 E
Table B. = Tafelbaai, *S. Africa* **96** 33 35 S 18 25 E
Table B., *Canada* **105** 53 40N 56 25W
Table Grove, *U.S.A.* **118** 40 20N 90 27W
Table Mt., *S. Africa* **96** 34 0 S 18 22 E
Table Top, Mt., *Australia* **72** 23 24 S 147 11 E
Tableland, *Australia* **78** 17 16 S 126 51 E
Tábor, *Czech.* **32** 49 25N 14 39 E
Tabor, *Israel* **44** 32 42N 35 24 E
Tabora, *Tanzania* **92** 5 2 S 32 50 E
Tabora □, *Tanzania* **92** 5 0 S 33 0 E
Tabou, *Ivory C.* **90** 4 30N 7 20W
Tabrīz, *Iran* **46** 38 7N 46 20 E
Tabuenca, *Spain* **24** 41 42N 1 33W
Tabūk, *Si. Arabia* **46** 28 23N 36 36 E
Tabulam, *Australia* **77** 28 53 S 152 35 E
Tabwemasana, Mt., *Vanuatu* **68** 15 20 S 166 44 E
Tacámbaro de Codallos, *Mexico* **126** 19 14N 101 28W
Tacheng, *China* **62** 46 40N 82 58 E
Tachibana-Wan, *Japan* **64** 32 45N 130 7 E
Tachikawa, *Japan* **65** 35 42N 139 25 E
Tach'ing Shan = Daqing Shan, *China* **60** 40 40N 111 0 E
Táchira □, *Venezuela* **134** 8 7N 72 15W
Tácina →, *Italy* **29** 38 57N 16 55 E
Tacloban, *Phil.* **57** 11 15N 124 58 E
Tacna, *Peru* **136** 18 0 S 70 20W
Tacna □, *Peru* **136** 17 40 S 70 20W
Tacoma, *U.S.A.* **124** 47 15N 122 30W
Tacuarembó, *Uruguay* **141** 31 45 S 56 0W
Tacutu →, *Brazil* **135** 3 1N 60 29W
Tademaït, Plateau du, *Algeria* **85** 28 30N 2 30 E
Tadent, O. →, *Algeria* **85** 22 25N 6 40 E
Tadine, *N. Cal.* **68** 21 33 S 167 52 E
Tadjerdjeri, O. →, *Algeria* **85** 26 0N 8 0W
Tadjerouna, *Algeria* **85** 33 31N 2 3 E
Tadjettaret, O. →, *Algeria* **85** 21 20N 7 22 E
Tadjmout, *Oasis, Algeria* **85** 33 52N 2 30 E
Tadjmout, *Saoura, Algeria* **85** 25 37N 3 48 E
Tadjoura, *Djibouti* **89** 11 50N 42 55 E
Tadjoura, Golfe de, *Djibouti* **89** 11 50N 43 0 E
Tadmor, *N.Z.* **81** 41 27 S 172 45 E
Tadotsu, *Japan* **64** 34 16N 133 45 E
Tadoule, L., *Canada* **111** 58 36N 98 20W
Tadoussac, *Canada* **107** 48 11N 69 42W
Tadzhik S.S.R. □, *U.S.S.R.* **40** 35 30N 70 0 E
Taegu, *S. Korea* **61** 35 50N 128 37 E
Taejŏn, *S. Korea* **61** 36 20N 127 28 E
Tafalla, *Spain* **24** 42 30N 1 41W
Tafar, *Sudan* **89** 6 52N 28 15 E
Ţafas, *Syria* **44** 32 44N 36 5 E
Tafassasset, O. →, *Algeria* **85** 22 0N 9 57 E
Tafelbaai, *S. Africa* **96** 33 35 S 18 25 E
Tafelney, C., *Morocco* **84** 31 3N 9 51W
Tafermaar, *Indonesia* **57** 6 47 S 134 10 E
Taffermit, *Morocco* **84** 29 37N 9 15W
Tafí Viejo, *Argentina* **140** 26 43 S 65 17W
Tafiré, *Ivory C.* **90** 9 4N 5 4W
Tafnidilt, *Morocco* **84** 28 47N 10 58W
Tafraoute, *Morocco* **84** 29 50N 8 58W
Taft, *Phil.* **57** 11 57N 125 30 E
Taft, *Calif., U.S.A.* **125** 35 9N 119 28W
Taft, *Tex., U.S.A.* **121** 27 58N 97 23W
Taga, *W. Samoa* **68** 13 46 S 172 28W
Taga Dzong, *Bhutan* **52** 27 5N 89 55 E
Taganrog, *U.S.S.R.* **39** 47 12N 38 50 E
Taganrogskiy Zaliv, *U.S.S.R.* **38** 47 0N 38 30 E
Tagânt, *Mauritania* **90** 18 20N 11 0W
Tagap Ga, *Burma* **52** 26 56N 96 13 E
Tagbilaran, *Phil.* **57** 9 39N 123 51 E
Tage, *Papua N. G.* **69** 6 19 S 143 20 E
Taggerty, *Australia* **74** 37 21 S 145 43 E
Tággia, *Italy* **26** 43 52N 7 50 E
Taghrīfat, *Libya* **86** 29 5N 17 26 E
Taghzout, *Morocco* **84** 33 30N 4 49W
Tagish, *Canada* **110** 60 19N 134 16W
Tagish L., *Canada* **102** 60 10N 134 20W
Tagliacozzo, *Italy* **27** 42 4N 13 13 E
Tagliamento →, *Italy* **27** 45 38N 13 5 E
Táglio di Po, *Italy* **27** 45 0N 12 12 E
Tagna, *Colombia* **134** 2 24 S 70 37W
Tagomago, I. de, *Spain* **25** 39 2N 1 39 E
Tagua, La, *Colombia* **134** 0 3N 74 40W
Taguatinga, *Brazil* **139** 12 16 S 42 26W
Tagula, *Papua N. G.* **69** 11 22 S 153 15 E
Tagula I., *Papua N. G.* **69** 11 30 S 153 30 E
Tagum, *Phil.* **57** 7 33N 125 53 E
Tagus → = Tejo →, *Europe* **23** 38 40N 9 24W
Tahakopa, *N.Z.* **81** 46 30 S 169 23 E
Tahala, *Morocco* **84** 34 0N 4 28W
Tahan, Gunong, *Malaysia* **55** 4 34N 102 17 E
Tahara, *Japan* **65** 34 40N 137 16 E
Tahat, *Algeria* **85** 23 18N 5 33 E
Tāherī, *Iran* **47** 27 43N 52 20 E
Tahiti, *Pac. Oc.* **68** 17 37 S 149 27W
Tahoe, L., *U.S.A.* **124** 39 0N 120 9W
Tahoe City, *U.S.A.* **124** 39 12N 120 9W
Taholah, *U.S.A.* **124** 47 21N 124 17W
Tahora, *N.Z.* **80** 39 2 S 174 49 E
Tahoua, *Niger* **91** 14 57N 5 16 E
Tahta, *Egypt* **88** 26 44N 31 32 E
Tahuamanu →, *Bolivia* **136** 11 6 S 67 36W
Tahulandang, *Indonesia* **57** 2 27N 125 23 E
Tahuna, *Indonesia* **57** 3 38N 125 30 E
Taï, *Ivory C.* **90** 5 55N 7 30W
Tai Hu, *China* **62** 31 5N 120 10 E
Tai Shan, *China* **61** 36 25N 117 20 E
Tai Xian, *China* **59** 32 30N 120 7 E
Tai'an, *China* **61** 36 12N 117 8 E
Taiarapu, Presq. de, *Tahiti* **68** 17 47 S 149 14W
Taibei, *Taiwan* **59** 25 4N 121 29 E
Taibique, *Canary Is.* **25** 27 42N 17 58W
Taibus Qi, *China* **60** 41 54N 115 22 E
T'aichung = Taizhong, *Taiwan* **59** 24 12N 120 35 E
Taidong, *Taiwan* **59** 22 43N 121 9 E
Taieri →, *N.Z.* **81** 46 3 S 170 12 E
Taiga Madema, *Libya* **86** 23 46N 15 25 E
Taigu, *China* **60** 37 28N 112 30 E
Taihang Shan, *China* **60** 36 0N 113 30 E
Taihape, *N.Z.* **80** 39 41 S 175 48 E
Taihe, *Anhui, China* **60** 33 20N 115 42 E
Taihe, *Jiangxi, China* **59** 26 47N 114 52 E
Taihu, *China* **59** 30 22N 116 20 E
Taijiang, *China* **58** 26 39N 108 21 E
Taikang, *China* **60** 34 5N 114 50 E
Taikkyi, *Burma* **52** 17 20N 96 0 E
Tailem Bend, *Australia* **73** 35 12 S 139 29 E
Tailfingen, *W. Germany* **31** 48 15N 9 1 E
Taimyr = Taymyr, Poluostrov, *U.S.S.R.* **41** 75 0N 100 0 E
Taimyr, Oz., *U.S.S.R.* **41** 74 20N 102 0 E
Tain, *U.K.* **14** 57 49N 4 4W
Tainan, *Taiwan* **59** 23 17N 120 18 E
Taínaron, Ákra, *Greece* **35** 36 22N 22 27 E
Tainggyo, *Burma* **52** 17 49N 94 29 E
Taining, *China* **59** 26 54N 117 9 E
Taintignies, *Belgium* **17** 50 33N 3 22 E
Taiobeiras, *Brazil* **139** 15 49 S 42 14W
T'aipei = Taibei, *Taiwan* **59** 25 4N 121 29 E
Taiping, *China* **59** 30 15N 118 6 E
Taiping, *Malaysia* **55** 4 51N 100 44 E
Taipingzhen, *China* **60** 33 35N 111 42 E
Taipu, *Brazil* **138** 5 37 S 35 36W
Taisha, *Japan* **64** 35 24N 132 40 E
Taishan, *China* **59** 22 14N 112 41 E
Taishun, *China* **59** 27 30N 119 42 E
Taita □, *Kenya* **92** 4 0 S 38 30 E
Taita Hills, *Kenya* **92** 3 25 S 38 15 E
Taitao, C., *Chile* **142** 45 53 S 75 5W
Taitao, Pen. de, *Chile* **142** 46 30 S 75 0W
Taivalkoski, *Finland* **8** 65 33N 28 12 E
Taiwan ■, *Asia* **59** 23 30N 121 0 E
Taiwan Shan, *Taiwan* **59** 23 40N 121 20 E
Taixing, *China* **59** 32 11N 120 0 E
Taïyetos Óros, *Greece* **35** 37 0N 22 23 E
Taiyib →, *Jordan* **44** 31 55N 35 17 E
Taiyiba, *Israel* **44** 32 36N 35 27 E
Taiyuan, *China* **60** 37 52N 112 33 E
Taizhong, *Taiwan* **59** 24 12N 120 35 E
Taizhou, *China* **59** 32 28N 119 55 E
Taizhou Liedao, *China* **59** 28 30N 121 55 E
Ta'izz, *Yemen* **45** 13 35N 44 2 E
Tajapuru, Furo do, *Brazil* **138** 1 50 S 50 25W
Tajarḥī, *Libya* **86** 24 21N 14 28 E
Tajima, *Japan* **63** 37 19N 139 8 E
Tajimi, *Japan* **65** 35 19N 137 8 E
Tajo → = Tejo →, *Europe* **23** 38 40N 9 24W
Tājūrā, *Libya* **86** 32 51N 13 21 E
Tak, *Thailand* **54** 16 52N 99 8 E
Takachiho, *Japan* **64** 32 42N 131 18 E
Takada, *Japan* **63** 37 7N 138 15 E
Takahashi, *Japan* **64** 34 51N 133 39 E
Takaka, *N.Z.* **81** 40 51 S 172 50 E
Takamatsu, *Japan* **64** 34 20N 134 5 E
Takanabe, *Japan* **64** 32 8N 131 30 E
Takaoka, *Japan* **65** 36 47N 137 0 E
Takapau, *N.Z.* **80** 40 2 S 176 21 E
Takapuna, *N.Z.* **80** 36 47 S 174 47 E
Takasago, *Japan* **64** 34 45N 134 48 E
Takasaki, *Japan* **65** 36 20N 139 0 E
Takase, *Japan* **64** 34 7N 133 48 E
Takataka, *Solomon Is.* **68** 9 17 S 161 14 E
Takatsuki, *Japan* **65** 34 51N 135 37 E
Takaungu, *Kenya* **92** 3 38 S 39 52 E
Takawa, *Japan* **64** 33 38N 130 51 E
Takayama, *Japan* **65** 36 18N 137 11 E
Takayama-Bonchi, *Japan* **65** 36 0N 137 18 E
Takefu, *Japan* **65** 35 50N 136 10 E
Takehara, *Japan* **64** 34 21N 132 55 E
Takengon, *Indonesia* **56** 4 45N 96 50 E
Takeo, *Cambodia* **55** 10 59N 104 47 E
Takeo, *Japan* **64** 33 12N 130 1 E
Tåkern, *Sweden* **11** 58 22N 14 45 E
Tākestān, *Iran* **46** 36 0N 49 40 E
Taketa, *Japan* **64** 32 58N 131 24 E
Takh, *India* **49** 33 6N 77 32 E
Takhār □, *Afghan.* **47** 36 40N 70 0 E
Takhman, *Cambodia* **55** 11 29N 104 57 E
Taki, *Papua N. G.* **69** 6 29 S 155 52 E
Takla L., *Canada* **110** 55 15N 125 45W
Takla Landing, *Canada* **110** 55 30N 125 50W
Takla Makan = Taklimakan Shamo, *China* **62** 38 0N 83 0 E
Taklimakan Shamo, *China* **62** 38 0N 83 0 E
Taku, *Japan* **64** 33 18N 130 3 E
Taku →, *Canada* **110** 58 30N 133 50W
Takum, *Nigeria* **91** 7 18N 9 36 E
Takuma, *Japan* **64** 34 13N 133 40 E
Takundi, *Zaïre* **95** 4 45 S 16 34 E
Takutu →, *Guyana* **135** 3 1N 60 29W
Tala, *Uruguay* **141** 34 21 S 55 46W
Talagante, *Chile* **140** 33 40 S 70 50W
Talaïnt, *Morocco* **84** 29 41N 9 40W
Talak, *Niger* **91** 18 0N 5 0 E

Talamanca, Cordillera de, *Cent. Amer.* **128** 9 20N 83 20W
Talara, *Peru* **136** 4 38 S 81 18W
Talas, *U.S.S.R.* **40** 42 30N 72 13 E
Talasea, *Papua N. G.* **69** 5 20 S 150 2 E
Talata Mafara, *Nigeria* **91** 12 38N 6 4 E
Talaud, Kepulauan, *Indonesia* **57** 4 30N 127 10 E
Talavera de la Reina, *Spain* **22** 39 55N 4 46W
Talawana, *Australia* **78** 22 51 S 121 9 E
Talawgyi, *Burma* **52** 25 4N 97 19 E
Talayan, *Phil.* **57** 6 52N 124 24 E
Talbert, Sillon de, *France* **18** 48 53N 3 5W
Talbingo Dam, *Australia* **76** 35 40 S 148 20 E
Talbor, *Australia* **74** 37 10 S 143 44 E
Talbot, C., *Australia* **78** 13 48 S 126 43 E
Talbragar →, *Australia* **76** 32 12 S 148 37 E
Talca, *Chile* **140** 35 28 S 71 40W
Talca □, *Chile* **140** 35 20 S 71 46W
Talcahuano, *Chile* **140** 36 40 S 73 10W
Talcher, *India* **50** 21 0N 85 18 E
Talcho, *Niger* **91** 14 44N 3 28 E
Taldy Kurgan, *U.S.S.R.* **40** 45 10N 78 45 E
Ţalesh, Kūhhā-ye, *Iran* **46** 39 0N 48 30 E
Talfīt, *Jordan* **44** 32 5N 35 17 E
Talguharai, *Sudan* **88** 18 19N 35 56 E
Tali Post, *Sudan* **89** 5 55N 30 44 E
Taliabu, *Indonesia* **57** 1 45 S 125 0 E
Talibon, *Phil.* **57** 10 9N 124 20 E
Talibong, Ko, *Thailand* **55** 7 15N 99 23 E
Talihina, *U.S.A.* **121** 34 45N 95 1W
Talikota, *India* **51** 16 29N 76 17 E
Taliwang, *Indonesia* **56** 8 50 S 116 55 E
Talkeetna, *U.S.A.* **102** 62 20N 150 9W
Tall, *Jordan* **44** 33 0N 35 6 E
Tall 'Afar, *Iraq* **46** 36 22N 42 27 E
Tall 'Asūr, *Jordan* **44** 31 59N 35 17 E
Talla, *Egypt* **88** 28 5N 30 43 E
Talladega, *U.S.A.* **115** 33 28N 86 2W
Tallahassee, *U.S.A.* **115** 30 25N 84 15W
Tallangatta, *Australia* **75** 36 15 S 147 19 E
Tallarook, *Australia* **74** 37 5 S 145 6 E
Tallawang, *Australia* **77** 32 12 S 149 28 E
Tällberg, *Sweden* **10** 60 51N 15 2 E
Tallering Pk., *Australia* **79** 28 6 S 115 37 E
Tallinn, *U.S.S.R.* **36** 59 22N 24 48 E
Tallulah, *U.S.A.* **121** 32 25N 91 12W
Ţallūzā, *Jordan* **44** 32 17N 35 18 E
Talmalmo, *Australia* **76** 35 55 S 147 29 E
Talmest, *Morocco* **84** 31 48N 9 21W
Talmont, *France* **20** 46 27N 1 37W
Talnoye, *U.S.S.R.* **38** 48 50N 30 44 E
Taloda, *India* **50** 21 34N 74 11 E
Talodi, *Sudan* **89** 10 35N 30 22 E
Talovaya, *U.S.S.R.* **37** 51 6N 40 45 E
Talpa de Allende, *Mexico* **126** 20 23N 104 51W
Talsi, *U.S.S.R.* **36** 57 10N 22 30 E
Talsinnt, *Morocco* **85** 32 33N 3 27W
Taltal, *Chile* **140** 25 23 S 70 33W
Taltson →, *Canada* **110** 61 24N 112 46W
Talwood, *Australia* **77** 28 29 S 149 29 E
Talyawalka Cr. →, *Australia* **73** 32 28 S 142 22 E
Tam Chau, *Vietnam* **55** 10 48N 105 12 E
Tam Ky, *Vietnam* **54** 15 34N 108 29 E
Tam Quan, *Vietnam* **54** 14 35N 109 3 E
Tama, *U.S.A.* **118** 41 56N 92 37W
Tamala, *Australia* **79** 26 42 S 113 47 E
Tamalameque, *Colombia* **134** 8 52N 73 49W
Tamale, *Ghana* **91** 9 22N 0 50W
Taman, *U.S.S.R.* **38** 45 14N 36 41 E
Tamana, *Japan* **64** 32 58N 130 32 E
Tamanar, *Morocco* **84** 31 1N 9 46W
Tamano, *Japan* **64** 34 29N 133 59 E
Tamanrasset, *Algeria* **85** 22 50N 5 30 E
Tamanrasset, O. →, *Algeria* **85** 22 0N 2 0 E
Tamanthi, *Burma* **52** 25 19N 95 17 E
Tamaqua, *U.S.A.* **117** 40 46N 75 58W
Tamar →, *U.K.* **13** 50 33N 4 15W
Támara, *Colombia* **134** 5 50N 72 10W
Tamarang, *Australia* **77** 31 27 S 150 5 E
Tamarite de Litera, *Spain* **24** 41 52N 0 25 E
Tamaroa, *U.S.A.* **118** 38 8N 89 14W
Tamashima, *Japan* **64** 34 32N 133 40 E
Tamaské, *Niger* **91** 14 49N 5 43 E
Tamaulipas □, *Mexico* **127** 24 0N 99 0W
Tamaulipas, Sierra de, *Mexico* **127** 23 30N 98 20W
Tamazula, *Mexico* **126** 24 55N 106 58W
Tamazunchale, *Mexico* **127** 21 16N 98 47W
Tamba-Dabatou, *Guinea* **90** 11 50N 10 40W
Tambacounda, *Senegal* **90** 13 45N 13 40W
Tambar Springs, *Australia* **77** 31 20 S 149 51 E
Tambelan, Kepulauan, *Indonesia* **56** 1 0N 107 30 E
Tambellup, *Australia* **79** 34 4 S 117 37 E
Tambo, *Australia* **72** 24 54 S 146 14 E
Tambo, *Peru* **136** 12 57 S 74 1W
Tambo →, *Australia* **75** 37 50 S 147 50 E
Tambo →, *Peru* **136** 10 42 S 73 47W
Tambo de Mora, *Peru* **136** 13 30 S 76 8W
Tambobamba, *Peru* **136** 13 54 S 72 8W
Tambohorano, *Madag.* **97** 17 30 S 43 58 E
Tambopata →, *Peru* **136** 13 21 S 69 36W
Tambora, *Indonesia* **56** 8 12 S 118 5 E
Tamboritha, Mt., *Australia* **75** 37 31 S 146 40 E
Tambov, *U.S.S.R.* **37** 52 45N 41 28 E
Tambre →, *Spain* **22** 42 49N 8 53W
Tambuku, *Indonesia* **57** 7 8 S 113 40 E
Tamburâ, *Sudan* **89** 5 40N 27 25 E
Tâmchekket, *Mauritania* **90** 17 25N 10 40W
Tame, *Colombia* **134** 6 28N 71 44W
Tamega →, *Portugal* **22** 41 5N 8 21W
Tamelelt, *Morocco* **84** 31 50N 7 32W
Tamenglong, *India* **52** 25 0N 93 35 E
Tamerza, *Tunisia* **86** 34 23N 7 58 E
Tamiahua, L. de, *Mexico* **127** 21 30N 97 30W
Tamil Nadu □, *India* **51** 11 0N 77 0 E
Tamines, *Belgium* **17** 50 26N 4 36 E
Tamis →, *Yugoslavia* **34** 44 51N 20 39 E
Tamluk, *India* **49** 22 18N 87 58 E
Tammerfors = Tampere, *Finland* **9** 61 30N 23 50 E
Tammisaari, *Finland* **9** 60 0N 23 26 E
Ţammūn, *Jordan* **44** 32 18N 35 23 E
Tämnaren, *Sweden* **10** 60 10N 17 25 E
Tamo Abu, Pegunungan, *Malaysia* **56** 3 10N 115 0 E
Tampa, *U.S.A.* **115** 27 57N 82 38W
Tampa B., *U.S.A.* **115** 27 40N 82 40W
Tampere, *Finland* **9** 61 30N 23 50 E
Tampico, *Mexico* **127** 22 20N 97 50W
Tampico, *U.S.A.* **118** 41 38N 89 47W
Tampin, *Malaysia* **55** 2 28N 102 13 E
Tamri, *Morocco* **84** 30 49N 9 50W
Tamrida = Qādib, *S. Yemen* **45** 12 37N 53 57 E
Tamsalu, *U.S.S.R.* **36** 59 11N 26 8 E
Tamuja →, *Spain* **23** 39 38N 6 29W
Tamworth, *Australia* **77** 31 7 S 150 58 E
Tamworth, *Canada* **109** 44 29N 77 0W
Tamworth, *U.K.* **13** 52 38N 1 41W
Tan An, *Vietnam* **55** 10 32N 106 25 E
Tan-tan, *Morocco* **84** 28 29N 11 1W
Tana, *Norway* **8** 70 26N 28 14 E
Tana →, *Kenya* **92** 2 32 S 40 31 E
Tana →, *Norway* **8** 70 30N 28 23 E
Tana, L., *Ethiopia* **89** 13 5N 37 30 E
Tana River, *Kenya* **92** 2 0 S 39 30 E
Tanabe, *Japan* **65** 33 44N 135 22 E
Tanabi, *Brazil* **139** 20 37 S 49 37W
Tanafjorden, *Norway* **8** 70 45N 28 25 E
Tanaga, Pta., *Canary Is.* **25** 27 42N 18 10W
Tanagro →, *Italy* **29** 40 35N 15 25 E
Tanahbala, *Indonesia* **56** 0 30 S 98 30 E
Tanahgrogot, *Indonesia* **56** 1 55 S 116 15 E
Tanahjampea, *Indonesia* **57** 7 10 S 120 35 E
Tanahmasa, *Indonesia* **56** 0 12 S 98 39 E
Tanahmerah, *Indonesia* **57** 6 5 S 140 16 E
Tanami, *Australia* **78** 19 59 S 129 43 E
Tanami Desert, *Australia* **78** 18 50 S 132 0 E
Tanana, *U.S.A.* **102** 65 10N 152 15W
Tanana →, *U.S.A.* **102** 65 9N 151 55W
Tananarive = Antananarivo, *Madag.* **97** 18 55 S 47 31 E
Tanannt, *Morocco* **84** 31 54N 6 56W
Tánaro →, *Italy* **26** 45 1N 8 47 E
Tanaunella, *Italy* **28** 40 42N 9 45 E
Tanba-Sanchi, *Japan* **65** 35 7N 135 48 E
Tancarville, *France* **18** 49 29N 0 28 E
Tancheng, *China* **61** 34 25N 118 20 E
Tanchŏn, *N. Korea* **61** 40 27N 128 54 E
Tanda, *Ut. P., India* **49** 26 33N 82 35 E
Tanda, *Ut. P., India* **49** 28 57N 78 56 E
Tanda, *Ivory C.* **90** 7 48N 3 10W
Tandag, *Phil.* **57** 9 4N 126 9 E
Tandaia, *Tanzania* **93** 9 25 S 34 15 E
Tăndărei, *Romania* **34** 44 39N 27 40 E
Tandaué, *Angola* **95** 16 58 S 18 5 E
Tandil, *Argentina* **140** 37 15 S 59 6W
Tandil, Sa. del, *Argentina* **140** 37 30 S 59 0W
Tandlianwala, *Pakistan* **48** 31 3N 73 9 E
Tando Adam, *Pakistan* **48** 25 45N 68 40 E
Tandou L., *Australia* **73** 32 40 S 142 5 E
Tandsbyn, *Sweden* **10** 63 0N 14 45 E
Tandur, *India* **50** 19 11N 79 30 E
Tane-ga-Shima, *Japan* **63** 30 30N 131 0 E
Taneatua, *N.Z.* **80** 38 4 S 177 1 E
Tanen Tong Dan, *Burma* **54** 16 30N 98 30 E
Tanezrouft, *Algeria* **85** 23 9N 0 11 E
Tang, Koh, *Cambodia* **55** 10 16N 103 7 E
Tang Krasang, *Cambodia* **54** 12 34N 105 3 E
Tanga, *Tanzania* **92** 5 5 S 39 2 E
Tanga □, *Tanzania* **92** 5 20 S 38 0 E
Tanga Is., *Papua N. G.* **69** 3 20 S 153 15 E
Tangail, *Bangla.* **52** 24 15N 89 55 E
Tanganyika, L., *Africa* **92** 6 40 S 30 0 E
Tanger, *Morocco* **84** 35 50N 5 49W
Tangerang, *Indonesia* **57** 6 11 S 106 37 E
Tangerhütte, *E. Germany* **30** 52 26N 11 50 E
Tangermünde, *E. Germany* **30** 52 32N 11 57 E
Tanggu, *China* **61** 39 2N 117 40 E
Tanggula Shan, *China* **62** 32 40N 92 10 E
Tanghe, *China* **60** 32 47N 112 50 E
Tangier = Tanger, *Morocco* **84** 35 50N 5 49W
Tangorin P.O., *Australia* **72** 21 47 S 144 12 E
Tangshan, *China* **61** 39 38N 118 10 E
Tangtou, *China* **61** 35 28N 118 30 E
Tanguiéta, *Benin* **91** 10 35N 1 21 E
Tangxi, *China* **59** 29 3N 119 25 E
Tangyan He →, *China* **58** 28 54N 108 19 E
Tanimbar, Kepulauan, *Indonesia* **57** 7 30 S 131 30 E
Taninges, *France* **21** 46 7N 6 36 E
Taniyama, *Japan* **64** 31 31N 130 31 E
Tanjay, *Phil.* **57** 9 30N 123 5 E
Tanjong Malim, *Malaysia* **55** 3 42N 101 31 E
Tanjore = Thanjavur, *India* **51** 10 48N 79 12 E
Tanjung, *Indonesia* **56** 2 10 S 115 25 E
Tanjungbalai, *Indonesia* **56** 2 55N 99 44 E
Tanjungbatu, *Indonesia* **56** 2 23N 118 3 E
Tanjungkarang Telukbetung, *Indonesia* **56** 5 20 S 105 10 E
Tanjungpandan, *Indonesia* **56** 2 43 S 107 38 E
Tanjungpinang, *Indonesia* **56** 1 5N 104 30 E
Tanjungpriok, *Indonesia* **57** 6 8 S 106 55 E
Tanjungredeb, *Indonesia* **56** 2 9N 117 29 E
Tanjungselor, *Indonesia* **56** 2 55N 117 25 E
Tank, *Pakistan* **48** 32 14N 70 25 E
Tanna, *Vanuatu* **68** 19 30 S 169 20 E
Tänndalen, *Sweden* **10** 62 33N 12 18 E
Tannis Bugt, *Denmark* **11** 57 40N 10 15 E
Tannu-Ola, *U.S.S.R.* **41** 51 0N 94 0 E
Tano →, *Ghana* **90** 5 7N 2 56W
Tanout, *Niger* **91** 14 50N 8 55 E
Tanquinho, *Brazil* **139** 11 58 S 39 6W
Tanta, *Egypt* **88** 30 45N 30 57 E
Tantangara Res., *Australia* **76** 35 45 S 148 38 E
Tantoyuca, *Mexico* **127** 21 21N 98 10W
Tantung = Dandong, *China* **61** 40 10N 124 20 E
Tantūra = Dor, *Israel* **44** 32 37N 34 55 E
Tanuku, *India* **50** 16 45N 81 44 E
Tanumshede, *Sweden* **11** 58 42N 11 20 E
Tanunda, *Australia* **73** 34 30 S 139 0 E
Tanur, *India* **51** 11 1N 75 52 E
Tanus, *France* **20** 44 8N 2 19 E
Tanzania ■, *Africa* **92** 6 0 S 34 0 E
Tanzawa-Sanchi, *Japan* **65** 35 27N 139 0 E
Tanzilla →, *Canada* **110** 58 8N 130 43W
Tao Ko, *Thailand* **55** 10 5N 99 52 E
Tao'an, *China* **61** 45 22N 122 40 E
Tao'er He →, *China* **61** 45 45N 124 5 E
Taohua Dao, *China* **59** 29 50N 122 20 E
Taolanaro, *Madag.* **97** 25 2 S 47 0 E
Taole, *China* **60** 38 48N 106 40 E
Taormina, *Italy* **29** 37 52N 15 16 E
Taos, *U.S.A.* **123** 36 28N 105 35W
Taoudenni, *Mali* **84** 22 40N 3 55W
Taoudrart, Adrar, *Algeria* **85** 24 25N 2 24 E
Taounate, *Morocco* **84** 34 25N 4 41W
Taourirt, *Algeria* **85** 26 37N 0 20 E
Taourirt, *Morocco* **85** 34 25N 2 53W
Taouz, *Morocco* **84** 30 53N 4 0W
Taoyuan, *China* **59** 28 55N 111 16 E
Taoyuan, *Taiwan* **59** 25 0N 121 13 E
Tapa, *U.S.S.R.* **36** 59 15N 25 50 E
Tapa Shan = Daba Shan, *China* **58** 32 0N 109 0 E
Tapachula, *Mexico* **127** 14 54N 92 17W
Tapah, *Malaysia* **55** 4 12N 101 15 E
Tapajós →, *Brazil* **135** 2 24 S 54 41W
Tapaktuan, *Indonesia* **56** 3 15N 97 10 E
Tapanahoni →, *Surinam* **135** 4 20N 54 25W
Tapanui, *N.Z.* **81** 45 56 S 169 18 E
Tapauá, *Brazil* **137** 5 40 S 64 20W
Tapauá →, *Brazil* **137** 5 40 S 64 21W
Tapeta, *Liberia* **90** 6 29N 8 52W
Taphan Hin, *Thailand* **54** 16 13N 100 26 E
Tapi →, *India* **50** 21 8N 72 41 E
Tapia, *Spain* **22** 43 34N 6 56W
Tapini, *Papua N. G.* **69** 8 19 S 147 0 E
Tápiószele, *Hungary* **33** 47 25N 19 55 E
Tapiraí, *Brazil* **139** 19 52 S 46 1W
Tapirapé →, *Brazil* **138** 10 41 S 50 38W
Tapirapecó, Serra, *Venezuela* **135** 1 10N 65 0W
Tapirapuã, *Brazil* **137** 14 51 S 57 45W
Tapoeripa, *Surinam* **135** 5 22N 56 34W
Tapolca, *Hungary* **33** 46 53N 17 29 E
Tappahannock, *U.S.A.* **114** 37 56N 76 50W
Tapuaenuku, Mt., *N.Z.* **81** 42 0 S 173 39 E
Tapul Group, *Phil.* **57** 5 35N 120 50 E
Tapun, *India* **52** 27 35N 96 22 E
Tapurucuará, *Brazil* **135** 0 24 S 65 2W
Taquara, *Brazil* **141** 29 36 S 50 46W
Taquari →, *Brazil* **137** 19 15 S 57 17W
Taquaritinga, *Brazil* **139** 21 24 S 48 30W
Tara, *Australia* **77** 27 17 S 150 31 E
Tara, *Canada* **108** 44 28N 81 9W
Tara, *Japan* **64** 33 2N 130 11 E
Tara, *U.S.S.R.* **40** 56 55N 74 24 E
Tara, *Zambia* **93** 16 58 S 26 45 E
Tara →, *U.S.S.R.* **40** 56 42N 74 36 E
Tara-Dake, *Japan* **64** 32 58N 130 6 E
Tarabagatay, Khrebet, *U.S.S.R.* **40** 48 0N 83 0 E
Tarabuco, *Bolivia* **137** 19 10 S 64 57W
Tarābulus, *Lebanon* **46** 34 31N 35 50 E
Tarābulus, *Libya* **86** 32 49N 13 7 E
Taradale, *N.Z.* **80** 39 33 S 176 53 E
Tarago, *Australia* **76** 35 6 S 149 39 E
Tarahouahout, *Algeria* **85** 22 41N 5 59 E
Tarajalejo, *Canary Is.* **25** 28 12N 14 7W
Tarakan, *Indonesia* **56** 3 20N 117 35 E
Tarakit, Mt., *Kenya* **92** 2 2N 35 10 E
Taralga, *Australia* **76** 34 26 S 149 52 E
Taramakau →, *N.Z.* **81** 42 34 S 171 8 E
Tarana, *Australia* **76** 33 31 S 149 52 E
Taranagar, *India* **48** 28 43N 74 50 E
Taranaki □, *N.Z.* **80** 39 5 S 174 51 E
Tarancón, *Spain* **24** 40 1N 3 1W
Taranga, *India* **48** 23 56N 72 43 E
Taranga Hill, *India* **48** 24 0N 72 40 E
Táranto, *Italy* **29** 40 30N 17 11 E
Táranto, G. di, *Italy* **29** 40 0N 17 15 E
Tarapacá, *Colombia* **134** 2 56 S 69 46W
Tarapacá □, *Chile* **140** 20 45 S 69 30W
Tarapoto, *Peru* **136** 6 30 S 76 20W
Taraquá, *Brazil* **134** 0 6N 68 28W
Tarare, *France* **21** 45 54N 4 26 E
Tararua Range, *N.Z.* **80** 40 45 S 175 25 E
Tarasag, *Vanuatu* **68** 14 13 S 167 35 E
Tarascon, *France* **21** 43 48N 4 39 E
Tarascon-sur-Ariège, *France* **20** 42 50N 1 36 E
Tarashcha, *U.S.S.R.* **38** 49 30N 30 31 E
Tarata, *Peru* **136** 17 27 S 70 2W
Tarauacá, *Brazil* **136** 8 6 S 70 48W
Tarauacá →, *Brazil* **136** 6 42 S 69 48W
Taravo →, *France* **21** 41 42N 8 49 E
Tarawera, *N.Z.* **80** 39 2 S 176 36 E
Tarawera L., *N.Z.* **80** 38 13 S 176 27 E
Tarawera Mt., *N.Z.* **80** 38 14 S 176 32 E
Tarazona, *Spain* **24** 41 55N 1 43W
Tarazona de la Mancha, *Spain* **25** 39 16N 1 55W
Tarbat Ness, *U.K.* **14** 57 52N 3 48W
Tarbela Dam, *Pakistan* **48** 34 8N 72 52 E
Tarbert, *Strathclyde, U.K.* **14** 55 55N 5 25W
Tarbert, *W. Isles, U.K.* **14** 57 54N 6 49W
Tarbes, *France* **20** 43 15N 0 3 E
Tarboro, *U.S.A.* **115** 35 55N 77 30W
Tarbrax, *Australia* **72** 21 7 S 142 26 E
Tarbū, *Libya* **86** 26 0N 15 5 E
Tarcento, *Italy* **27** 46 12N 13 12 E
Tarcoola, *Australia* **73** 30 44 S 134 36 E
Tarcoon, *Australia* **73** 30 15 S 146 43 E
Tarcutta, *Australia* **76** 35 16 S 147 44 E
Tardets-Sorholus, *France* **20** 43 8N 0 52W
Tardoire →, *France* **20** 45 52N 0 14 E
Taree, *Australia* **77** 31 50 S 152 30 E
Tarentaise, *France* **21** 45 30N 6 35 E
Tarf, Ras, *Morocco* **84** 35 40N 5 11W
Tarfa, Wadi el →, *Egypt* **88** 28 25N 30 50 E
Tarfaya, *Morocco* **84** 27 55N 12 55W
Targon, *France* **20** 44 44N 0 16W
Targuist, *Morocco* **84** 34 59N 4 14W
Tarhbalt, *Morocco* **84** 30 39N 5 20W
Tarhit, *Algeria* **85** 30 58N 2 0W
Tarhūnah, *Libya* **86** 32 27N 13 36 E
Tari, *Papua N. G.* **69** 5 54 S 142 59 E
Táriba, *Venezuela* **134** 7 49N 72 13W
Tarifa, *Spain* **23** 36 1N 5 36W
Tarija, *Bolivia* **140** 21 30 S 64 40W
Tarija □, *Bolivia* **140** 21 30 S 63 30W
Tariku →, *Indonesia* **57** 2 55 S 138 26 E
Tarim →, *China* **62** 39 30N 88 30 E
Tarim Basin = Tarim Pendi, *China* **62** 40 0N 84 0 E
Tarim Pendi, *China* **62** 40 0N 84 0 E
Tarime □, *Tanzania* **92** 1 15 S 34 0 E
Taritatu →, *Indonesia* **57** 2 54 S 138 27 E
Tarka →, *S. Africa* **96** 32 10 S 26 0 E
Tarkastad, *S. Africa* **96** 32 0 S 26 16 E
Tarkhankut, Mys, *U.S.S.R.* **38** 45 25N 32 30 E
Tarko Sale, *U.S.S.R.* **40** 64 55N 77 50 E
Tarkwa, *Ghana* **90** 5 20N 2 0W
Tarlac, *Phil.* **57** 15 29N 120 35 E
Tarlton Downs, *Australia* **72** 22 40 S 136 45 E
Tarm, *Denmark* **11** 55 56N 8 31 E
Tarma, *Peru* **136** 11 25 S 75 45W
Tarn □, *France* **20** 43 49N 2 8 E
Tarn →, *France* **20** 44 5N 1 6 E
Tarn-et-Garonne □, *France* **20** 44 8N 1 20 E
Tarna →, *Hungary* **33** 47 31N 19 59 E
Tarnagulla, *Australia* **74** 36 45 S 143 49 E
Tårnby, *Denmark* **11** 55 37N 12 36 E
Tarnobrzeg, *Poland* **32** 50 35N 21 41 E
Tarnów, *Poland* **32** 50 3N 21 0 E
Táro →, *Italy* **26** 45 0N 10 15 E
Taroom, *Australia* **73** 25 36 S 149 48 E
Taroudannt, *Morocco* **84** 30 30N 8 52W
Tarp, *W. Germany* **30** 54 40N 9 25 E
Tarpon Springs, *U.S.A.* **115** 28 8N 82 42W
Tarquínia, *Italy* **27** 42 15N 11 45 E
Tarqūmiyah, *Jordan* **44** 31 35N 35 1 E
Tarragona, *Spain* **24** 41 5N 1 17 E
Tarragona □, *Spain* **24** 41 0N 1 0 E
Tarrasa, *Spain* **24** 41 34N 2 1 E
Tárrega, *Spain* **24** 41 39N 1 9 E
Tarrington, *Australia* **74** 37 46 S 142 7 E

Tarrytown, *U.S.A.* **117** 41 5N 73 52W
Tarshiha = Me'ona, *Israel* **44** 33 1N 35 15 E
Tarso Emissi, *Chad* **87** 21 27N 18 36 E
Tarso Ourari, *Chad* **87** 21 27N 17 27 E
Tarsus, *Turkey* **46** 36 58N 34 55 E
Tartagal, *Argentina* **140** 22 30 S 63 50W
Tartas, *France* **20** 43 50N 0 49W
Tartu, *U.S.S.R.* **36** 58 20N 26 44 E
Ṭarṭūs, *Syria* **46** 34 55N 35 55 E
Tarumirim, *Brazil* **139** 19 16 S 41 59W
Tarumizu, *Japan* **64** 31 29N 130 42 E
Tarussa, *U.S.S.R.* **37** 54 44N 37 10 E
Tarutao, Ko, *Thailand* **55** 6 33N 99 40 E
Tarutung, *Indonesia* **56** 2 0N 98 54 E
Tarvisio, *Italy* **27** 46 31N 13 35 E
Tarz Ulli, *Libya* **86** 25 32N 10 8 E
Tasahku, *Burma* **52** 27 33N 97 52 E
Tasāwah, *Libya* **86** 26 0N 13 30 E
Taschereau, *Canada* **106** 48 40N 78 40W
Taseko →, *Canada* **110** 52 8N 123 45W
Tasgaon, *India* **50** 17 2N 74 39 E
Tash-Kumyr, *U.S.S.R.* **40** 41 40N 72 10 E
Tashauz, *U.S.S.R.* **40** 41 49N 59 58 E
Tashi Chho Dzong = Thimphu, *Bhutan* **52** 27 31N 89 45 E
Tashkent, *U.S.S.R.* **40** 41 20N 69 10 E
Tashtagol, *U.S.S.R.* **40** 52 47N 87 53 E
Tasikmalaya, *Indonesia* **57** 7 18 S 108 12 E
Tåsjön, *Sweden* **8** 64 15N 16 0 E
Taskan, *U.S.S.R.* **41** 62 59N 150 20 E
Taskopru, *Turkey* **46** 41 30N 34 15 E
Tasman →, *N.Z.* **81** 43 48 S 170 8 E
Tasman, Mt., *N.Z.* **81** 43 34 S 170 12 E
Tasman B., *N.Z.* **81** 40 59 S 173 25 E
Tasman Mts., *N.Z.* **81** 41 3 S 172 25 E
Tasman Pen., *Australia* **72** 43 10 S 148 0 E
Tasman Sea, *Pac. Oc.* **66** 36 0 S 160 0 E
Tasmania □, *Australia* **72** 42 0 S 146 30 E
Tăşnad, *Romania* **34** 47 30N 22 33 E
Tassil Tin-Rerhoh, *Algeria* **85** 20 5N 3 55 E
Tassili n-Ajjer, *Algeria* **85** 25 47N 8 1 E
Tassili-Oua-n-Ahaggar, *Algeria* **85** 20 41N 5 30 E
Tasu Sd., *Canada* **110** 52 47N 132 2W
Tata, *Morocco* **84** 29 46N 7 56W
Tatabánya, *Hungary* **33** 47 32N 18 25 E
Tatahouine, *Tunisia* **86** 32 57N 10 29 E
Tatar A.S.S.R. □, *U.S.S.R.* **40** 55 30N 51 30 E
Tatarbunary, *U.S.S.R.* **38** 45 50N 29 39 E
Tatarsk, *U.S.S.R.* **40** 55 14N 76 0 E
Tatebayashi, *Japan* **65** 36 15N 139 32 E
Tateshina-Yama, *Japan* **65** 36 8N 138 11 E
Tateyama, *Japan* **65** 35 0N 139 50 E
Tatham, *Australia* **77** 28 56 S 153 9 E
Tathlina L., *Canada* **110** 60 33N 117 39W
Tathra, *Australia* **75** 36 44 S 149 59 E
Tatinnai L., *Canada* **111** 60 55N 97 40W
Tatnam, C., *Canada* **111** 57 16N 91 0W
Tatong, *Australia* **75** 36 43 S 146 9 E
Tatra = Tatry, *Czech.* **32** 49 20N 20 0 E
Tatry, *Czech.* **32** 49 20N 20 0 E
Tatsuno, *Japan* **64** 34 52N 134 33 E
Tatta, *Pakistan* **48** 24 42N 67 55 E
Tatuī, *Brazil* **141** 23 25 S 47 53W
Tatum, *U.S.A.* **121** 33 16N 103 16W
Tat'ung = Datong, *China* **60** 40 6N 113 18 E
Tatura, *Australia* **74** 36 29 S 145 16 E
Tatvan, *Turkey* **46** 38 31N 42 15 E
Tau, *Amer. Samoa* **68** 14 15 S 169 30W
Tauá, *Brazil* **138** 6 1 S 40 26W
Taubaté, *Brazil* **141** 23 0 S 45 36W
Tauberbischofsheim, *W. Germany* **31** 49 37N 9 40 E
Taucha, *E. Germany* **30** 51 22N 12 31 E
Taufikia, *Sudan* **89** 9 24N 31 37 E
Taumarunui, *N.Z.* **80** 38 53 S 175 15 E
Taumaturgo, *Brazil* **136** 8 54 S 72 51W
Taung, *S. Africa* **96** 27 33 S 24 47 E
Taungdwingyi, *Burma* **52** 20 1N 95 40 E
Taunggyi, *Burma* **52** 20 50N 97 0 E
Taungtha, *Burma* **52** 21 12N 95 25 E
Taungup, *Burma* **52** 18 51N 94 14 E
Taungup Pass, *Burma* **52** 18 40N 94 45 E
Taunsa Barrage, *Pakistan* **48** 30 42N 70 50 E
Taunton, *U.K.* **13** 51 1N 3 7W
Taunton, *U.S.A.* **117** 41 54N 71 6W
Taunus, *W. Germany* **31** 50 15N 8 20 E
Taupo, *N.Z.* **80** 38 41 S 176 7 E
Taupo, L., *N.Z.* **80** 38 46 S 175 55 E
Taurage, *U.S.S.R.* **36** 55 14N 22 16 E
Tauranga, *N.Z.* **80** 37 42 S 176 11 E
Tauranga Harb., *N.Z.* **80** 37 30 S 176 5 E
Tauri →, *Papua N. G.* **69** 8 8 S 146 8 E
Taurianova, *Italy* **29** 38 22N 16 1 E
Taurus Mts. = Toros Dağlari, *Turkey* **46** 37 0N 35 0 E
Tauste, *Spain* **24** 41 58N 1 18W
Tautira, *Tahiti* **68** 17 44 S 149 9W
Tauz, *U.S.S.R.* **39** 41 0N 45 40 E
Tavaar, *Somali Rep.* **98** 3 6N 46 1 E
Tavda, *U.S.S.R.* **40** 58 7N 65 8 E
Tavda →, *U.S.S.R.* **40** 59 20N 63 28 E
Taverny, *France* **19** 49 2N 2 13 E
Taveta, *Tanzania* **92** 3 23 S 37 37 E
Taveuni, *Fiji* **68** 16 51 S 179 58W
Tavignano →, *France* **21** 42 7N 9 33 E
Tavira, *Portugal* **23** 37 8N 7 40W
Tavistock, *Canada* **108** 43 19N 80 50W
Tavistock, *U.K.* **13** 50 33N 4 9W
Tavolara, *Italy* **28** 40 55N 9 40 E
Távora →, *Portugal* **22** 41 8N 7 35W
Tavoy, *Burma* **54** 14 2N 98 12 E
Tavua, *Fiji* **68** 17 37 S 177 5 E
Taw →, *U.K.* **13** 51 4N 4 11W
Tawas City, *U.S.A.* **104** 44 16N 83 31W
Tawau, *Malaysia* **56** 4 20N 117 55 E
Tawitawi, *Phil.* **57** 5 10N 120 0 E
Tawngche, *Burma* **52** 26 34N 95 38 E
Tawonga, *Australia* **75** 36 41 S 147 8 E
Tāwurgha', *Libya* **86** 32 1N 15 2 E
Taxila, *Pakistan* **48** 33 42N 72 52 E
Tay →, *U.K.* **14** 56 37N 3 38W
Tay, Firth of, *U.K.* **14** 56 25N 3 8W
Tay, L., *Australia* **79** 32 55 S 120 48 E
Tay, L., *U.K.* **14** 56 30N 4 10W
Tay Ninh, *Vietnam* **55** 11 20N 106 5 E
Tayabamba, *Peru* **136** 8 15 S 77 16W
Taylakovy, *U.S.S.R.* **40** 59 13N 74 0 E
Taylor, *Canada* **110** 56 13N 120 40W
Taylor, *Mich., U.S.A.* **119** 42 14N 83 16W
Taylor, *Nebr., U.S.A.* **120** 41 46N 99 23W
Taylor, *Pa., U.S.A.* **117** 41 23N 75 43W
Taylor, *Tex., U.S.A.* **121** 30 30N 97 30W
Taylor, Mt., *N.Z.* **81** 43 30 S 171 20 E
Taylor Mt., *U.S.A.* **123** 35 16N 107 36W
Taylors Arm, *Australia* **77** 30 45 S 152 45 E
Taylorsville, *U.S.A.* **119** 38 2N 85 21W
Taylorville, *U.S.A.* **118** 39 32N 89 20W
Taymā, *Si. Arabia* **46** 27 35N 38 45 E
Taymyr, Poluostrov, *U.S.S.R.* **41** 75 0N 100 0 E
Tayport, *U.K.* **14** 56 27N 2 52W
Ṭayr Zibnā, *Lebanon* **44** 33 14N 35 23 E
Tayshet, *U.S.S.R.* **41** 55 58N 98 1 E
Tayside □, *U.K.* **14** 56 25N 3 30W
Taytay, *Phil.* **57** 10 45N 119 30 E
Taz →, *U.S.S.R.* **40** 67 32N 78 40 E
Taza, *Morocco* **84** 34 16N 4 6W
Taze, *Burma* **52** 22 57N 95 24 E
Tazenakht, *Morocco* **84** 30 35N 7 12W
Tazerbo, *Libya* **86** 25 45N 21 0 E
Tazin L., *Canada* **111** 59 44N 108 42W
Tazoult, *Algeria* **85** 35 29N 6 11 E
Tazovskiy, *U.S.S.R.* **40** 67 30N 78 44 E
Tbilisi, *U.S.S.R.* **39** 41 43N 44 50 E
Tchad = Chad ■, *Africa* **87** 15 0N 17 15 E
Tchad, L., *Chad* **87** 13 30N 14 30 E
Tchaourou, *Benin* **91** 8 58N 2 40 E
Tch'eng-tou = Chengdu, *China* **58** 30 38N 104 2 E
Tchentlo L., *Canada* **110** 55 15N 125 0W
Tchibanga, *Gabon* **94** 2 45 S 11 0 E
Tchien, *Liberia* **90** 5 59N 8 15W
Tchikala-Tcholohanga, *Angola* **95** 12 38 S 16 3 E
Tchin Tabaraden, *Niger* **91** 15 58N 5 56 E
Tchingou, Massif de, *N. Cal.* **68** 20 54 S 165 0 E
Tcholliré, *Cameroon* **94** 8 24N 14 10 E
Tch'ong-k'ing = Chongqing, *China* **58** 29 35N 106 25 E
Tczew, *Poland* **32** 54 8N 18 50 E
Te Anau, L., *N.Z.* **81** 45 15 S 167 45 E
Te Araroa, *N.Z.* **80** 37 39 S 178 25 E
Te Aroha, *N.Z.* **80** 37 32 S 175 44 E
Te Awamutu, *N.Z.* **80** 38 1 S 175 20 E
Te Kaha, *N.Z.* **80** 37 44 S 177 52 E
Te Karaka, *N.Z.* **80** 38 26 S 177 53 E
Te Kauwhata, *N.Z.* **80** 37 25 S 175 9 E
Te Kopuru, *N.Z.* **80** 36 2 S 173 56 E
Te Kuiti, *N.Z.* **80** 38 20 S 175 11 E
Te Puke, *N.Z.* **80** 37 46 S 176 22 E
Te Waewae B., *N.Z.* **81** 46 13 S 167 33 E
Tea →, *Brazil* **134** 0 30 S 65 9W
Tea Gardens, *Australia* **76** 32 38 S 152 10 E
Tea Tree, *Australia* **72** 22 5 S 133 22 E
Teague, *U.S.A.* **121** 31 40N 96 20W
Teano, *Italy* **29** 41 15N 14 1 E
Teapa, *Mexico* **127** 18 35N 92 56W
Teba, *Spain* **23** 36 59N 4 55W
Tebakang, *Malaysia* **56** 1 6N 110 30 E
Teberda, *U.S.S.R.* **39** 43 30N 41 46 E
Tébessa, *Algeria* **85** 35 22N 8 8 E
Tebicuary →, *Paraguay* **140** 26 36 S 58 16W
Tebingtinggi, *Indonesia* **56** 3 20N 99 9 E
Tébourba, *Tunisia* **86** 36 49N 9 51 E
Téboursouk, *Tunisia* **86** 36 29N 9 10 E
Tebulos, *U.S.S.R.* **39** 42 36N 45 17 E
Tecate, *Mexico* **126** 32 34N 116 38W
Tech →, *France* **20** 42 36N 3 3 E
Techiman, *Ghana* **90** 7 35N 1 58W
Tecka, *Argentina* **142** 43 29 S 70 48W
Tecomán, *Mexico* **126** 18 55N 103 53W
Tecopa, *U.S.A.* **125** 35 51N 116 14W
Tecoripa, *Mexico* **126** 28 37N 109 57W
Tecuala, *Mexico* **126** 22 23N 105 27W
Tecuci, *Romania* **34** 45 51N 27 27 E
Tecumseh, *Canada* **108** 42 19N 82 54W
Tecumseh, *U.S.A.* **119** 42 1N 83 59W
Ted, *Somali Rep.* **98** 4 24N 43 55 E
Teddywaddy, *Australia* **74** 36 12 S 143 21 E
Tedzhen, *U.S.S.R.* **40** 37 23N 60 31 E
Tee Lake, *Canada* **106** 46 40N 79 0W
Tees →, *U.K.* **12** 54 36N 1 25W
Teesdale, *Australia* **74** 38 2 S 144 2 E
Teesside, *U.K.* **12** 54 37N 1 13W
Teeswater, *Canada* **108** 43 59N 81 17W
Tefé, *Brazil* **135** 3 25 S 64 50W
Tefé →, *Brazil* **135** 3 35 S 64 47W
Tegal, *Indonesia* **57** 6 52 S 109 8 E
Tegelen, *Neths.* **17** 51 20N 6 9 E
Tegernsee, *W. Germany* **31** 47 43N 11 46 E
Teggiano, *Italy* **29** 40 24N 15 32 E
Teghra, *India* **49** 25 30N 85 34 E
Tegid, L. = Bala, L., *U.K.* **12** 52 53N 3 38W
Tegina, *Nigeria* **91** 10 5N 6 11 E
Tegua, *Vanuatu* **68** 13 15 S 166 37 E
Tegucigalpa, *Honduras* **128** 14 5N 87 14W
Tehachapi, *U.S.A.* **125** 35 11N 118 29W
Tehachapi Mts., *U.S.A.* **125** 35 0N 118 40W
Tehamiyam, *Sudan* **88** 18 20N 36 32 E
Tehilla, *Sudan* **88** 17 42N 36 6 E
Téhini, *Ivory C.* **90** 9 39N 3 40W
Tehrān, *Iran* **47** 35 44N 51 30 E
Tehuacán, *Mexico* **127** 18 30N 97 30W
Tehuantepec, *Mexico* **127** 16 21N 95 13W
Tehuantepec, G. de, *Mexico* **127** 15 50N 95 0W
Tehuantepec, Istmo de, *Mexico* **127** 17 0N 94 30W
Teide, *Canary Is.* **25** 28 15N 16 38W
Teifi →, *U.K.* **13** 52 4N 4 14W
Teign →, *U.K.* **13** 50 41N 3 42W
Teignmouth, *U.K.* **13** 50 33N 3 30W
Teil, Le, *France* **21** 44 33N 4 40 E
Teilleul, Le, *France* **18** 48 32N 0 53W
Teixeira, *Brazil* **138** 7 13 S 37 15W
Teixeira Pinto, *Guinea-Biss.* **90** 12 3N 16 0W
Tejo →, *Europe* **23** 38 40N 9 24W
Tejon Pass, *U.S.A.* **125** 34 49N 118 53W
Tekamah, *U.S.A.* **120** 41 48N 96 22W
Tekapo, L., *N.Z.* **81** 43 53 S 170 33 E
Tekax, *Mexico* **127** 20 11N 89 18W
Tekeli, *U.S.S.R.* **40** 44 50N 79 0 E
Tekeze →, *Ethiopia* **89** 14 20N 35 50 E
Tekija, *Yugoslavia* **33** 44 42N 22 26 E
Tekirdağ, *Turkey* **46** 40 58N 27 30 E
Tekkali, *India* **50** 18 37N 84 15 E
Tekoa, *U.S.A.* **122** 47 19N 117 4W
Tekouiât, O. →, *Algeria* **85** 22 25N 2 35 E
Tel Adashim, *Israel* **44** 32 30N 35 17 E
Tel Aviv-Yafo, *Israel* **44** 32 4N 34 48 E
Tel Lakhish, *Israel* **44** 31 34N 34 51 E
Tel Megiddo, *Israel* **44** 32 35N 35 11 E
Tel Mond, *Israel* **44** 32 15N 34 56 E
Tela, *Honduras* **128** 15 40N 87 28W
Télagh, *Algeria* **85** 34 51N 0 32W
Telanaipura = Jambi, *Indonesia* **56** 1 38 S 103 30 E
Telavi, *U.S.S.R.* **39** 42 0N 45 30 E
Telde, *Canary Is.* **25** 27 59N 15 25W
Telefomin, *Papua N. G.* **69** 5 10 S 141 31 E
Telegraph Cr. →, *Canada* **110** 58 0N 131 10W
Telegraph Point, *Australia* **77** 31 20 S 152 49 E
Telekhany, *U.S.S.R.* **36** 52 30N 25 46 E
Telemark fylke □, *Norway* **10** 59 25N 8 30 E
Telén, *Argentina* **140** 36 15 S 65 31W
Teleño, *Spain* **22** 42 23N 6 22W
Teleorman →, *Romania* **34** 44 15N 25 20 E
Teles Pires →, *Brazil* **137** 7 21 S 58 3W
Telescope Peak, *U.S.A.* **125** 36 6N 117 7W
Teletaye, *Mali* **91** 16 31N 1 30 E
Telford, *U.K.* **12** 52 42N 2 31W
Telfs, *Austria* **31** 47 19N 11 4 E
Telgte, *W. Germany* **30** 51 59N 7 46 E
Télimélé, *Guinea* **90** 10 54N 13 2W
Telkwa, *Canada* **110** 54 41N 127 5W
Tell City, *U.S.A.* **119** 38 0N 86 44W
Tellicherry, *India* **51** 11 45N 75 30 E
Tellin, *Belgium* **17** 50 5N 5 13 E
Telluride, *U.S.A.* **123** 37 58N 107 48W
Teloloapán, *Mexico* **127** 18 21N 99 51W
Telpos Iz, *U.S.S.R.* **6** 63 35N 57 30 E
Telsen, *Argentina* **142** 42 30 S 66 50W
Telšiai, *U.S.S.R.* **36** 55 59N 22 14 E
Teltow, *E. Germany* **30** 52 24N 13 15 E
Teluk Anson, *Malaysia* **55** 4 3N 101 0 E
Teluk Betung = Tanjungkarang Telukbetung, *Indonesia* **56** 5 20 S 105 10 E
Teluk Intan = Teluk Anson, *Malaysia* **55** 4 3N 101 0 E
Telukbutun, *Indonesia* **55** 4 13N 108 12 E
Telukdalem, *Indonesia* **56** 0 33N 97 50 E
Tema, *Ghana* **91** 5 41N 0 0 E
Temanggung, *Indonesia* **57** 7 18 S 110 10 E
Temapache, *Mexico* **127** 21 4N 97 38W
Temax, *Mexico* **127** 21 10N 88 50W
Temba, *S. Africa* **97** 25 20 S 28 17 E
Tembe, *Zaïre* **92** 0 16 S 28 14 E
Temblador, *Venezuela* **135** 8 59N 62 44W
Tembleque, *Spain* **24** 39 41N 3 30W
Temblor Ra., *U.S.A.* **125** 35 30N 120 0W
Teme →, *U.K.* **13** 52 23N 2 15W
Temecula, *U.S.A.* **125** 33 26N 117 6W
Temerloh, *Malaysia* **55** 3 27N 102 25 E
Temir, *U.S.S.R.* **40** 49 21N 57 3 E
Temirtau, *Kazakh S.S.R., U.S.S.R.* **40** 50 5N 72 56 E
Temirtau, *R.S.F.S.R., U.S.S.R.* **40** 53 10N 87 30 E
Témiscaming, *Canada* **106** 46 44N 79 5W
Témiscamingue, L., *Canada* **106** 47 10N 79 25W
Temma, *Australia* **72** 41 12 S 144 48 E
Temnikov, *U.S.S.R.* **37** 54 40N 43 11 E
Temo →, *Italy* **28** 40 20N 8 30 E
Temora, *Australia* **76** 34 30 S 147 30 E
Temosachic, *Mexico* **126** 28 58N 107 50W
Tempe, *U.S.A.* **123** 33 26N 111 59W
Tempe Downs, *Australia* **78** 24 22 S 132 24 E
Témpio Pausania, *Italy* **28** 40 53N 9 6 E
Tempiute, *U.S.A.* **124** 37 39N 115 38W
Temple, *U.S.A.* **121** 31 5N 97 22W
Temple B., *Australia* **72** 12 15 S 143 3 E
Templemore, *Ireland* **15** 52 48N 7 50W
Templeton, *U.S.A.* **124** 35 33N 120 42W
Templeton →, *Australia* **72** 21 0 S 138 40 E
Templeuve, *Belgium* **17** 50 39N 3 17 E
Templin, *E. Germany* **30** 53 8N 13 31 E
Tempoal, *Mexico* **127** 21 31N 98 23W
Temryuk, *U.S.S.R.* **38** 45 15N 37 24 E
Temse, *Belgium* **17** 51 7N 4 13 E
Temska →, *Yugoslavia* **33** 43 17N 22 33 E
Temuco, *Chile* **142** 38 45 S 72 40W
Temuka, *N.Z.* **81** 44 14 S 171 17 E
Ten Boer, *Neths.* **16** 53 16N 6 42 E
Tena, *Ecuador* **134** 0 59 S 77 49W
Tenabo, *Mexico* **127** 20 2N 90 12W
Tenaha, *U.S.A.* **121** 31 57N 94 25W
Tenali, *India* **51** 16 15N 80 35 E
Tenancingo, *Mexico* **127** 19 0N 99 33W
Tenango, *Mexico* **127** 19 7N 99 33W
Tenasserim, *Burma* **55** 12 6N 99 3 E
Tenasserim □, *Burma* **54** 14 0N 98 30 E
Tenay, *France* **21** 45 55N 5 31 E
Tenby, *U.K.* **13** 51 40N 4 42W
Tenda, Col di, *France* **21** 44 7N 7 36 E
Tendaho, *Ethiopia* **89** 11 48N 40 54 E
Tende, *France* **21** 44 5N 7 35 E
Tendelti, *Sudan* **89** 13 1N 31 55 E
Tendjedi, Adrar, *Algeria* **85** 23 41N 7 32 E
Tendrara, *Morocco* **85** 33 3N 1 58W
Teneida, *Egypt* **88** 25 30N 29 19 E
Tenente Marques →, *Brazil* **137** 11 10 S 59 56W
Ténéré, *Niger* **91** 19 0N 10 30 E
Ténéré, Erg du, *Niger* **87** 17 35N 10 55 E
Tenerife, *Canary Is.* **25** 28 15N 16 35W
Tenerife, Pico, *Canary Is.* **25** 27 43N 18 1W
Ténès, *Algeria* **85** 36 31N 1 14 E
Teng Xian, *Guangxi Zhuangzu, China* **59** 23 21N 110 56 E
Teng Xian, *Shandong, China* **61** 35 5N 117 10 E
Tengah □, *Indonesia* **57** 2 0 S 122 0 E
Tengah Kepulauan, *Indonesia* **56** 7 5 S 118 15 E
Tengchong, *China* **58** 25 0N 98 28 E
Tengchowfu = Penglai, *China* **61** 37 48N 120 42 E
Tenggara □, *Indonesia* **57** 3 0 S 122 0 E
Tenggarong, *Indonesia* **56** 0 24 S 116 58 E
Tenggol, P., *Malaysia* **55** 4 48N 103 41 E
Tengiz, Ozero, *U.S.S.R.* **40** 50 30N 69 0 E
Tenino, *U.S.A.* **124** 46 51N 122 51W
Tenkasi, *India* **51** 8 55N 77 20 E
Tenke, *Shaba, Zaïre* **93** 11 22 S 26 40 E
Tenke, *Shaba, Zaïre* **93** 10 32 S 26 7 E
Tenkodogo, *Burkina Faso* **91** 11 54N 0 19W
Tenna →, *Italy* **27** 43 12N 13 47 E
Tennant Creek, *Australia* **72** 19 30 S 134 15 E
Tennessee □, *U.S.A.* **113** 36 0N 86 30W
Tennessee →, *U.S.A.* **114** 37 4N 88 34W
Tenneville, *Belgium* **17** 50 6N 5 32 E
Tennille, *U.S.A.* **115** 32 58N 82 50W
Tennsift, Oued →, *Morocco* **84** 32 3N 9 28W
Tennyson, *U.S.A.* **119** 38 5N 87 7W
Teno, Pta. de, *Canary Is.* **25** 28 21N 16 55W
Tenom, *Malaysia* **56** 5 4N 115 57 E
Tenosique, *Mexico* **127** 17 30N 91 24W
Tenri, *Japan* **65** 34 39N 135 49 E
Tenryū, *Japan* **65** 34 52N 137 49 E
Tenryū-Gawa →, *Japan* **65** 35 39N 137 48 E
Tent L., *Canada* **111** 62 25N 107 54W
Tenterfield, *Australia* **77** 29 0 S 152 0 E
Teófilo Otoni, *Brazil* **139** 17 50 S 41 30W
Teotihuacán, *Mexico* **127** 19 44N 98 50W
Tepa, *Indonesia* **57** 7 52 S 129 31 E
Tepalcatepec →, *Mexico* **126** 18 35N 101 59W
Tepehuanes, *Mexico* **126** 25 21N 105 44W
Tepequem, Serra, *Brazil* **135** 3 45N 61 45W
Tepetongo, *Mexico* **126** 22 28N 103 9W
Tepic, *Mexico* **126** 21 30N 104 54W
Tepoca, C., *Mexico* **126** 30 20N 112 25W
Tequila, *Mexico* **126** 20 54N 103 47W
Ter →, *Spain* **24** 42 0N 3 12 E
Ter Apel, *Neths.* **16** 52 53N 7 5 E
Téra, *Niger* **91** 14 0N 0 45 E
Tera →, *Spain* **24** 41 54N 5 44W
Teraina, I., *Kiribati* **67** 4 43N 160 25W
Téramo, *Italy* **27** 42 40N 13 40 E

Terang, *Australia* **74** 38 15 S 142 55 E
Terawhiti, C., *N.Z.* **80** 41 16 S 174 38 E
Terazit, Massif de, *Niger* **87** 20 2N 8 30 E
Terborg, *Neths.* **16** 51 56N 6 22 E
Tercero →, *Argentina* **140** 32 58 S 61 47W
Terdal, *India* **50** 16 33N 75 3 E
Terebovlya, *U.S.S.R.* **36** 49 18N 25 44 E
Terek →, *U.S.S.R.* **39** 44 0N 47 30 E
Terenos, *Brazil* **137** 20 26 S 54 50W
Tereshka →, *U.S.S.R.* **37** 51 48N 46 26 E
Teresina, *Brazil* **138** 5 9 S 42 45W
Teresinha, *Brazil* **135** 0 58N 52 2W
Terewah, L., *Australia* **73** 29 52 S 147 35 E
Terges →, *Portugal* **23** 37 49N 7 41W
Tergnier, *France* **19** 49 40N 3 17 E
Terhazza, *Mali* **84** 23 38N 5 22W
Terheijden, *Neths.* **17** 51 38N 4 45 E
Teridgerie, *Australia* **76** 30 53 S 148 50 E
Teridgerie Cr. →, *Australia* **73** 30 25 S 148 50 E
Terlizzi, *Italy* **29** 41 8N 16 32 E
Terme, *Turkey* **38** 41 11N 37 0 E
Termeil, *Australia* **76** 35 30 S 150 22 E
Termez, *U.S.S.R.* **40** 37 15N 67 15 E
Términi Imerese, *Italy* **28** 37 58N 13 42 E
Términos, L. de, *Mexico* **127** 18 35N 91 30W
Térmoli, *Italy* **27** 42 0N 15 0 E
Ternate, *Indonesia* **57** 0 45N 127 25 E
Terneuzen, *Neths.* **17** 51 20N 3 50 E
Terney, *U.S.S.R.* **41** 45 3N 136 37 E
Terni, *Italy* **27** 42 34N 12 38 E
Ternitz, *Austria* **33** 47 43N 16 2 E
Ternopol, *U.S.S.R.* **36** 49 30N 25 40 E
Terowie, *Australia* **76** 32 27 S 147 52 E
Terra Bella, *U.S.A.* **125** 35 58N 119 3W
Terra Nova B., *Antarctica* **143** 74 50 S 164 40 E
Terrace, *Canada* **110** 54 30N 128 35W
Terrace Bay, *Canada* **104** 48 47N 87 5W
Terracina, *Italy* **28** 41 17N 13 12 E
Terralba, *Italy* **28** 39 42N 8 38 E
Terranova = Ólbia, *Italy* **28** 40 55N 9 30 E
Terranuova Bracciolini, *Italy* **27** 43 31N 11 35 E
Terrasini Favarotta, *Italy* **28** 38 10N 13 4 E
Terrasson-la-Villedieu, *France* **20** 45 8N 1 18 E
Terre Haute, *U.S.A.* **119** 39 28N 87 24W
Terrebonne, *Canada* **107** 45 42N 73 38W
Terrebonne B., *U.S.A.* **121** 29 15N 90 28W
Terrecht, *Mali* **85** 20 10N 0 10W
Terrell, *U.S.A.* **121** 32 44N 96 19W
Terrenceville, *Canada* **105** 47 40N 54 44W
Terrick Terrick, *Australia* **72** 24 44 S 145 5 E
Territoire de Belfort □, *France* **19** 47 40N 6 55 E
Terry, *U.S.A.* **120** 46 47N 105 20W
Terry Hie Hie, *Australia* **77** 29 47 S 150 10 E
Terschelling, *Neths.* **16** 53 25N 5 20 E
Terter →, *U.S.S.R.* **39** 40 35N 47 22 E
Teruel, *Spain* **24** 40 22N 1 8W
Teruel □, *Spain* **24** 40 48N 1 0W
Tervel, *Bulgaria* **34** 43 45N 27 28 E
Tervola, *Finland* **8** 66 6N 24 49 E
Teryaweyna L., *Australia* **73** 32 18 S 143 22 E
Tešanj, *Yugoslavia* **33** 44 38N 17 59 E
Teseney, *Ethiopia* **89** 15 5N 36 42 E
Tesha →, *U.S.S.R.* **37** 55 38N 42 9 E
Teshio, *Japan* **63** 44 53N 141 44 E
Teshio-Gawa →, *Japan* **63** 44 53N 141 45 E
Tesiyn Gol →, *Mongolia* **62** 50 40N 93 20 E
Teslin, *Canada* **102** 60 10N 132 43W
Teslin →, *Canada* **110** 61 34N 134 35W
Teslin L., *Canada* **110** 60 15N 132 57W
Tesouro, *Brazil* **137** 16 4 S 53 34W
Tessalit, *Mali* **91** 20 12N 1 0 E
Tessaoua, *Niger* **91** 13 47N 7 56 E
Tessenderlo, *Belgium* **17** 51 4N 5 5 E
Tessin, *E. Germany* **30** 54 2N 12 28 E
Tessit, *Mali* **91** 15 13N 0 18 E
Test →, *U.K.* **13** 51 7N 1 30W
Testa del Gargano, *Italy* **29** 41 50N 16 10 E
Teste, La, *France* **20** 44 37N 1 8W
Têt →, *France* **20** 42 44N 3 2 E
Tetachuck L., *Canada* **110** 53 18N 125 55W
Tetas, Pta., *Chile* **140** 23 31 S 70 38W
Tete, *Mozam.* **93** 16 13 S 33 33 E
Tete □, *Mozam.* **93** 15 15 S 32 40 E
Tetepari, I., *Solomon Is.* **68** 8 45 S 157 35 E
Teterev →, *U.S.S.R.* **36** 51 1N 30 5 E
Teteringen, *Neths.* **17** 51 37N 4 49 E
Teterow, *E. Germany* **30** 53 45N 12 34 E
Teteven, *Bulgaria* **34** 42 58N 24 17 E
Tethul →, *Canada* **110** 60 35N 112 12W
Tetiyev, *U.S.S.R.* **38** 49 22N 29 38 E
Teton →, *U.S.A.* **122** 47 58N 111 0W
Tétouan, *Morocco* **84** 35 35N 5 21W
Tetovo, *Yugoslavia* **34** 42 1N 21 2 E
Tetuán = Tétouan, *Morocco* **84** 35 35N 5 21W
Tetyushi, *U.S.S.R.* **37** 54 55N 48 49 E
Teuco →, *Argentina* **140** 25 35 S 60 11W
Teulada, *Italy* **28** 38 59N 8 47 E
Teulon, *Canada* **111** 50 23N 97 16W
Teun, *Indonesia* **57** 6 59 S 129 8 E
Teutoburger Wald, *W. Germany* **30** 52 5N 8 20 E
Tevere →, *Italy* **27** 41 44N 12 14 E
Teverya, *Israel* **44** 32 47N 35 32 E
Teviot →, *U.K.* **14** 55 21N 2 51W
Tewantin, *Australia* **73** 26 27 S 153 3 E
Tewkesbury, *U.K.* **13** 51 59N 2 8W
Texada I., *Canada* **110** 49 40N 124 25W
Texarkana, *Ark., U.S.A.* **121** 33 25N 94 0W
Texarkana, *Tex., U.S.A.* **121** 33 25N 94 3W
Texas, *Australia* **77** 28 49 S 151 9 E
Texas □, *U.S.A.* **121** 31 40N 98 30W
Texas City, *U.S.A.* **121** 29 20N 94 55W
Texel, *Neths.* **16** 53 5N 4 50 E
Texhoma, *U.S.A.* **121** 36 32N 101 47W
Texline, *U.S.A.* **121** 36 26N 103 0W
Texoma L., *U.S.A.* **121** 34 0N 96 38W
Teykovo, *U.S.S.R.* **37** 56 55N 40 30 E
Teyvareh, *Afghan.* **47** 33 30N 64 24 E
Teza →, *U.S.S.R.* **37** 56 32N 41 53 E
Tezin, *Afghan.* **48** 34 24N 69 30 E
Teziutlán, *Mexico* **127** 19 50N 97 22W
Tezpur, *India* **52** 26 40N 92 45 E
Tezzeron L., *Canada* **110** 54 43N 124 30W
Tha-anne →, *Canada* **111** 60 31N 94 37W
Tha Deua, *Laos* **54** 17 57N 102 53 E
Tha Deua, *Laos* **54** 19 26N 101 50 E
Tha Pla, *Thailand* **54** 17 48N 100 32 E
Tha Rua, *Thailand* **54** 14 34N 100 44 E
Tha Sala, *Thailand* **55** 8 40N 99 56 E
Tha Song Yang, *Thailand* **54** 17 34N 97 55 E
Thaba Nchu, *S. Africa* **96** 29 17 S 26 52 E
Thaba Putsoa, *Lesotho* **97** 29 45 S 28 0 E
Thabana Ntlenyana, *Lesotho* **97** 29 30 S 29 16 E
Thabazimbi, *S. Africa* **97** 24 40 S 27 21 E
Thabeikkyin, *Burma* **52** 22 53N 95 59 E
Thai Binh, *Vietnam* **54** 20 35N 106 1 E
Thai Hoa, *Vietnam* **54** 19 20N 105 20 E
Thai Muang, *Thailand* **55** 8 24N 98 16 E
Thai Nguyen, *Vietnam* **54** 21 35N 105 55 E
Thailand ■, *Asia* **54** 16 0N 102 0 E
Thailand, G. of, *Asia* **55** 11 30N 101 0 E
Thakhek, *Laos* **54** 17 25N 104 45 E
Thakurgaon, *Bangla.* **52** 26 2N 88 34 E
Thal, *Pakistan* **48** 33 28N 70 33 E
Thal Desert, *Pakistan* **48** 31 10N 71 30 E
Thala, *Tunisia* **86** 35 35N 8 40 E
Thalabarivat, *Cambodia* **54** 13 33N 105 57 E
Thallon, *Australia* **73** 28 39 S 148 49 E
Thalwil, *Switz.* **31** 47 17N 8 35 E
Thame →, *U.K.* **13** 51 35N 1 8W
Thames, *N.Z.* **80** 37 7 S 175 34 E
Thames →, *Canada* **108** 42 20N 82 25W
Thames →, *U.K.* **13** 51 30N 0 35 E
Thames →, *U.S.A.* **117** 41 18N 72 9W
Thames, Firth of, *N.Z.* **80** 37 0 S 175 25 E
Thamesford, *Canada* **108** 43 4N 81 0W
Thamesville, *Canada* **108** 42 33N 81 59W
Thāmit, W. →, *Libya* **86** 30 51N 16 14 E
Than Uyen, *Vietnam* **54** 22 0N 103 54 E
Thanbyuzayat, *Burma* **52** 15 58N 97 44 E
Thane, *India* **50** 19 12N 72 59 E
Thanesar, *India* **48** 30 1N 76 52 E
Thanet, I. of, *U.K.* **13** 51 21N 1 20 E
Thangoo, *Australia* **78** 18 10 S 122 22 E
Thangool, *Australia* **72** 24 38 S 150 42 E
Thanh Hoa, *Vietnam* **54** 19 48N 105 46 E
Thanh Hung, *Vietnam* **55** 9 55N 105 43 E
Thanh Pho Ho Chi Minh = Phanh Bho Ho Chi Minh, *Vietnam* **55** 10 58N 106 40 E
Thanh Thuy, *Vietnam* **54** 22 55N 104 51 E
Thanjavur, *India* **51** 10 48N 79 12 E
Thann, *France* **19** 47 48N 7 5 E
Thaon-les-Vosges, *France* **19** 48 15N 6 24 E
Thap Sakae, *Thailand* **55** 11 30N 99 37 E
Thap Than, *Thailand* **54** 15 27N 99 54 E
Thar Desert, *India* **48** 28 0N 72 0 E
Tharad, *India* **48** 24 30N 71 44 E
Thargomindah, *Australia* **73** 27 58 S 143 46 E
Tharrawaddy, *Burma* **52** 17 38N 95 48 E
Tharrawaw, *Burma* **52** 17 41N 95 28 E
Tharwa, *Australia* **76** 35 31 S 149 4 E
Thásos, *Greece* **35** 40 40N 24 40 E
That Khe, *Vietnam* **54** 22 16N 106 28 E
Thatcher, *Ariz., U.S.A.* **123** 32 54N 109 46W
Thatcher, *Colo., U.S.A.* **121** 37 38N 104 6W
Thaton, *Burma* **52** 16 55N 97 22 E
Thau, Bassin de, *France* **20** 43 23N 3 36 E
Thaungdut, *Burma* **52** 24 30N 94 40 E
Thayer, *U.S.A.* **121** 36 34N 91 34W
Thayetmyo, *Burma* **52** 19 20N 95 10 E
The Alberga →, *Australia* **73** 27 6 S 135 33 E
The Bight, *Bahamas* **129** 24 19N 75 24W
The Blue Mt., *Australia* **77** 30 50 S 151 41 E
The Dalles, *U.S.A.* **122** 45 40N 121 11W
The English Company's Is., *Australia* **72** 11 50 S 136 32 E
The Entrance, *Australia* **76** 33 21 S 151 30 E
The Frome →, *Australia* **73** 29 8 S 137 54 E
The Grenadines, Is., *W. Indies* **129** 12 40N 61 20W
The Hague = 's-Gravenhage, *Neths.* **16** 52 7N 4 17 E
The Hamilton →, *Australia* **73** 26 40 S 135 19 E
The Lynd, *Australia* **72** 19 12 S 144 20 E
The Macumba →, *Australia* **73** 27 52 S 137 12 E
The Neales →, *Australia* **73** 28 8 S 136 47 E
The Oaks, *Australia* **76** 34 3 S 150 34 E
The Officer →, *Australia* **79** 27 46 S 132 30 E
The Pas, *Canada* **111** 53 45N 101 15W
The Range, *Zimb.* **93** 19 2 S 31 2 E
The Rock, *Australia* **76** 35 15 S 147 2 E
The Salt Lake, *Australia* **73** 30 6 S 142 8 E
The Stevenson →, *Australia* **73** 27 6 S 135 33 E
The Warburton →, *Australia* **73** 28 4 S 137 28 E
Thebes = Thívai, *Greece* **35** 38 19N 23 19 E
Thebes, *Egypt* **88** 25 40N 32 35 E
Thedford, *Canada* **108** 43 9N 81 51W
Thedford, *U.S.A.* **120** 41 59N 100 31W
Theebine, *Australia* **73** 25 57 S 152 34 E
Theil, Le, *France* **18** 48 16N 0 42 E
Thekulthili L., *Canada* **111** 61 3N 110 0W
Thelon →, *Canada* **111** 62 35N 104 3W
Thénezay, *France* **18** 46 44N 0 2W
Thenia, *Algeria* **85** 36 44N 3 33 E
Thenon, *France* **20** 45 9N 1 4 E
Theodore, *Australia* **72** 24 55 S 150 3 E
Thepha, *Thailand* **55** 6 52N 100 58 E
Thérain →, *France* **19** 49 15N 2 27 E
Theresa, *U.S.A.* **117** 44 13N 75 50W
Thermaïkos Kólpos, *Greece* **35** 40 15N 22 45 E
Thermopolis, *U.S.A.* **122** 43 35N 108 10W
Thermopylae P., *Greece* **35** 38 48N 22 35 E
Thessalía □, *Greece* **35** 39 30N 22 0 E
Thessalon, *Canada* **108** 46 20N 83 30W
Thessaloníki, *Greece* **35** 40 38N 22 58 E
Thessaloniki, Gulf of = Thermaïkos Kólpos, *Greece* **35** 40 15N 22 45 E
Thessaly = Thessalía □, *Greece* **35** 39 30N 22 0 E
Thetford, *U.K.* **13** 52 25N 0 44 E
Thetford Mines, *Canada* **107** 46 8N 71 18W
Theun →, *Laos* **54** 18 19N 104 0 E
Theunissen, *S. Africa* **96** 28 26 S 26 43 E
Theux, *Belgium* **17** 50 32N 5 49 E
Thevenard, *Australia* **73** 32 9 S 133 38 E
Thiámis →, *Greece* **35** 39 15N 20 6 E
Thiberville, *France* **18** 49 8N 0 27 E
Thibodaux, *U.S.A.* **121** 29 48N 90 49W
Thicket Portage, *Canada* **111** 55 19N 97 42W
Thief River Falls, *U.S.A.* **120** 48 15N 96 48W
Thiel Mts., *Antarctica* **143** 85 15 S 91 0W
Thiene, *Italy* **27** 45 42N 11 29 E
Thiérache, *France* **19** 49 51N 3 45 E
Thiers, *France* **20** 45 52N 3 33 E
Thies, *Senegal* **90** 14 50N 16 51W
Thiet, *Sudan* **89** 7 37N 28 49 E
Thika, *Kenya* **92** 1 1 S 37 5 E
Thille-Boubacar, *Senegal* **90** 16 31N 15 5W
Thillot, Le, *France* **19** 47 53N 6 46 E
Thimphu, *Bhutan* **52** 27 31N 89 45 E
þingvallavatn, *Iceland* **8** 64 11N 21 9W
Thio, *N. Cal.* **68** 21 37 S 166 14 E
Thionville, *France* **19** 49 20N 6 10 E
Thíra, *Greece* **35** 36 23N 25 27 E
Thirasía, *Greece* **35** 36 26N 25 21 E
Thirlmere, *Australia* **76** 34 11 S 150 35 E
Thirsk, *U.K.* **12** 54 15N 1 20W
Thiruvarur, *India* **51** 10 46N 79 38 E
Thisted, *Denmark* **9** 56 58N 8 40 E
Thistle I., *Australia* **73** 35 0 S 136 8 E
Thitgy, *Burma* **52** 18 15N 96 13 E
Thithia, *Fiji* **68** 17 45 S 179 18W
Thitpokpin, *Burma* **52** 19 24N 95 58 E
Thívai, *Greece* **35** 38 19N 23 19 E
Thiviers, *France* **20** 45 25N 0 54 E
Thizy, *France* **21** 46 2N 4 18 E
þjórsá →, *Iceland* **8** 63 47N 20 48W
Thlewiaza →, *Man., Canada* **111** 59 43N 100 5W
Thlewiaza →, *N.W.T., Canada* **111** 60 29N 94 40W
Thmar Puok, *Cambodia* **54** 13 57N 103 4 E
Tho Vinh, *Vietnam* **54** 19 16N 105 42 E
Thoa →, *Canada* **111** 60 31N 109 47W
Thoen, *Thailand* **54** 17 43N 99 12 E
Thoeng, *Thailand* **54** 19 41N 100 12 E
Thoissey, *France* **21** 46 12N 4 48 E
Tholdi, *Pakistan* **49** 35 5N 76 6 E
Tholen, *Neths.* **17** 51 32N 4 13 E
Thomas, *Okla., U.S.A.* **121** 35 48N 98 48W
Thomas, *W. Va., U.S.A.* **114** 39 10N 79 30W
Thomas, L., *Australia* **73** 26 4 S 137 58 E
Thomas Hill Res., *U.S.A.* **118** 39 34N 92 39W
Thomaston, *U.S.A.* **115** 32 54N 84 20W
Thomasville, *Ala., U.S.A.* **115** 31 55N 87 42W
Thomasville, *Ga., U.S.A.* **115** 30 50N 84 0W
Thomasville, *N.C., U.S.A.* **115** 35 55N 80 4W
Thommen, *Belgium* **17** 50 14N 6 5 E
Thompson, *Canada* **111** 55 45N 97 52W
Thompson, *U.S.A.* **123** 39 0N 109 50W
Thompson →, *Canada* **110** 50 15N 121 24W
Thompson →, *U.S.A.* **120** 39 46N 93 37W
Thompson Falls, *U.S.A.* **122** 47 37N 115 20W
Thompson Landing, *Canada* **111** 62 56N 110 40W
Thompson Pk., *U.S.A.* **122** 41 0N 123 3W
Thomson, *U.S.A.* **118** 41 58N 90 6W
Thomson →, *Queens., Australia* **72** 25 11 S 142 53 E
Thomson →, *Vic., Australia* **75** 36 52 S 141 4 E
Thomson's Falls = Nyahururu, *Kenya* **92** 0 2N 36 27 E
Thon Buri, *Thailand* **55** 13 43N 100 29 E
Thônes, *France* **21** 45 54N 6 18 E
Thongwa, *Burma* **52** 16 45N 96 33 E
Thonon-les-Bains, *France* **21** 46 22N 6 29 E
Thonze, *Burma* **52** 17 38N 95 47 E
Thorez, *U.S.S.R.* **39** 48 4N 38 34 E
þórisvatn, *Iceland* **8** 64 20N 18 55W
þorlákshöfn, *Iceland* **8** 63 51N 21 22W
Thornaby on Tees, *U.K.* **12** 54 36N 1 19W
Thornbury, *Canada* **108** 44 34N 80 26W
Thornbury, *N.Z.* **81** 46 17 S 168 9 E
Thornton, *U.S.A.* **118** 42 57N 93 23W
Thornton-Beresfield, *Australia* **76** 32 50 S 151 40 E
Thorntown, *U.S.A.* **119** 40 8N 86 36W
Thorold, *Canada* **108** 43 7N 79 12W
Thorpedale, *Australia* **75** 38 19 S 146 13 E
þórshöfn, *Iceland* **8** 66 12N 15 20W
Thouarcé, *France* **18** 47 17N 0 30W
Thouars, *France* **18** 46 58N 0 15W
Thouin, C., *Australia* **78** 20 20 S 118 10 E
Thousand Oaks, *U.S.A.* **125** 34 10N 118 50W
Thrakikón Pélagos, *Greece* **35** 40 30N 25 0 E
Thredbo Village, *Australia* **75** 36 31 S 148 20 E
Three Forks, *U.S.A.* **122** 45 55N 111 32W
Three Hills, *Canada* **110** 51 43N 113 15W
Three Hummock I., *Australia* **72** 40 25 S 144 55 E
Three Lakes, *U.S.A.* **120** 45 48N 89 10W
Three Oaks, *U.S.A.* **119** 41 48N 86 36W
Three Points, C., *Ghana* **90** 4 42N 2 6W
Three Rivers, *Australia* **79** 25 10 S 119 5 E
Three Rivers, *Calif., U.S.A.* **124** 36 26N 118 54W
Three Rivers, *Mich., U.S.A.* **119** 41 57N 85 38W
Three Rivers, *Tex., U.S.A.* **121** 28 30N 98 10W
Three Sisters, Mt., *U.S.A.* **122** 44 10N 121 46W
Three Sisters Is., *Solomon Is.* **68** 10 10 S 161 57 E
Throssell, L., *Australia* **79** 27 33 S 124 10 E
Throssell Ra., *Australia* **78** 22 3 S 121 43 E
Thuan Hoa, *Vietnam* **55** 8 58N 105 30 E
Thubun Lakes, *Canada* **111** 61 30N 112 0W
Thuddungra, *Australia* **76** 34 8 S 148 8 E
Thueyts, *France* **21** 44 41N 4 9 E
Thuillies, *Belgium* **17** 50 18N 4 20 E
Thuin, *Belgium* **17** 50 20N 4 17 E
Thuir, *France* **20** 42 38N 2 45 E
Thule, *Antarctica* **143** 59 27 S 27 19W
Thule, *Greenland* **144** 77 40N 69 0W
Thun, *Switz.* **31** 46 45N 7 38 E
Thundelarra, *Australia* **79** 28 53 S 117 7 E
Thunder B., *U.S.A.* **116** 45 0N 83 20W
Thunder Bay, *Canada* **104** 48 20N 89 15W
Thunersee, *Switz.* **31** 46 43N 7 39 E
Thung Song, *Thailand* **55** 8 10N 99 40 E
Thunkar, *Bhutan* **52** 27 55N 91 0 E
Thuong Tra, *Vietnam* **54** 16 2N 107 42 E
Thur →, *Switz.* **31** 47 32N 9 10 E
Thurgau □, *Switz.* **31** 47 34N 9 10 E
Thüringer Wald, *E. Germany* **30** 50 35N 11 0 E
Thurles, *Ireland* **15** 52 40N 7 53W
Thurloo Downs, *Australia* **73** 29 15 S 143 30 E
Thurn P., *Austria* **31** 47 20N 12 25 E
Thursday I., *Australia* **72** 10 30 S 142 3 E
Thurso, *Canada* **106** 45 36N 75 15W
Thurso, *U.K.* **14** 58 34N 3 31W
Thurston I., *Antarctica* **143** 72 0 S 100 0W
Thury-Harcourt, *France* **18** 48 59N 0 30W
Thutade L., *Canada* **110** 57 0N 126 55W
Thuy, Le, *Vietnam* **54** 17 14N 106 49 E
Thyborøn, *Denmark* **11** 56 42N 8 12 E
Thylungra, *Australia* **73** 26 4 S 143 28 E
Thyolo, *Malawi* **93** 16 7 S 35 5 E
Thysville = Mbanza Ngungu, *Zaïre* **95** 5 12 S 14 53 E
Ti-n-Barraouene, O. →, *Africa* **91** 18 40N 4 5 E
Ti-n-Medjerdam, O. →, *Algeria* **85** 25 45N 1 30 E

Ti-n-Tarabine, O. →, *Algeria* **85** 21 0N 7 25 E
Ti-n-Toumma, *Niger* **87** 16 4N 12 40 E
Ti-n-Zaouatène, *Algeria* **85** 20 0N 2 55 E
Tia, *Australia* **77** 31 10 S 150 34 E
Tiahuanacu, *Bolivia* **136** 16 33 S 68 42W
Tian Shan, *China* **62** 43 0N 84 0 E
Tianchang, *China* **59** 32 40N 119 0 E
Tiandong, *China* **58** 23 36N 107 8 E
Tian'e, *China* **58** 25 1N 107 9 E
Tianguá, *Brazil* **138** 3 44 S 40 59W
Tianhe, *China* **58** 24 48N 108 40 E
Tianjin, *China* **61** 39 8N 117 10 E
Tiankoura, *Burkina Faso* **90** 10 47N 3 17W
Tianlin, *China* **58** 24 21N 106 12 E
Tianmen, *China* **59** 30 39N 113 9 E
Tianquan, *China* **58** 30 7N 102 43 E
Tianshui, *China* **60** 34 32N 105 40 E
Tiantai, *China* **59** 29 10N 121 2 E
Tianyang, *China* **58** 23 42N 106 53 E
Tianzhen, *China* **60** 40 24N 114 5 E
Tianzhu, *China* **58** 26 54N 109 11 E
Tianzhuangtai, *China* **61** 40 43N 122 5 E
Tiaret, *Algeria* **85** 35 20N 1 21 E
Tiassalé, *Ivory C.* **90** 5 58N 4 57W
Ti'avea, *W. Samoa* **68** 13 57 S 171 24W
Tibagi, *Brazil* **141** 24 30 S 50 24W
Tibagi →, *Brazil* **141** 22 47 S 51 1W
Tibati, *Cameroon* **91** 6 22N 12 30 E
Tiber = Tevere →, *Italy* **27** 41 44N 12 14 E
Tiber Res., *U.S.A.* **122** 48 20N 111 15W
Tiberias = Teverya, *Israel* **44** 32 47N 35 32 E
Tiberias, L. = Yam Kinneret, *Israel* **44** 32 45N 35 35 E
Tibesti, *Chad* **87** 21 0N 17 30 E
Tibet = Xizang □, *China* **62** 32 0N 88 0 E
Tibiri, *Niger* **91** 13 34N 7 4 E
Ţibleş, *Romania* **34** 47 32N 24 15 E
Tibnīn, *Lebanon* **44** 33 12N 35 24 E
Tibooburra, *Australia* **73** 29 26 S 142 1 E
Tibro, *Sweden* **11** 58 28N 14 10 E
Tibugá, G. de, *Colombia* **134** 5 45N 77 20W
Tiburón, *Mexico* **126** 29 0N 112 30W
Tichborne, *Australia* **76** 33 12 S 148 8 E
Tîchît, *Mauritania* **90** 18 21N 9 29W
Tichla, *Mauritania* **84** 21 36N 14 58W
Ticho, *Ethiopia* **89** 7 50N 39 32 E
Ticino □, *Switz.* **31** 46 20N 8 45 E
Ticino →, *Italy* **26** 45 9N 9 14 E
Ticonderoga, *U.S.A.* **117** 43 50N 73 28W
Ticul, *Mexico* **127** 20 20N 89 31W
Tidaholm, *Sweden* **11** 58 12N 13 55 E
Tiddim, *Burma* **52** 23 28N 93 45 E
Tideridjaouine, Adrar, *Algeria* **85** 23 0N 2 15 E
Tidikelt, *Algeria* **85** 26 58N 1 30 E
Tidjikja, *Mauritania* **90** 18 29N 11 35W
Tidore, *Indonesia* **57** 0 40N 127 25 E
Tiébissou, *Ivory C.* **90** 7 9N 5 10W
Tiéboro, *Chad* **87** 21 20N 17 7 E
Tiel, *Neths.* **16** 51 53N 5 26 E
Tiel, *Senegal* **90** 14 55N 15 5W
Tieling, *China* **61** 42 20N 123 55 E
Tielt, *Belgium* **17** 51 0N 3 20 E
Tien Shan, *Asia* **47** 42 0N 80 0 E
Tien-tsin = Tianjin, *China* **61** 39 8N 117 10 E
Tien Yen, *Vietnam* **54** 21 20N 107 24 E
T'ienching = Tianjin, *China* **61** 39 8N 117 10 E
Tienen, *Belgium* **17** 50 48N 4 57 E
Tiénigbé, *Ivory C.* **90** 8 11N 5 43W
Tientsin = Tianjin, *China* **61** 39 8N 117 10 E
Tierp, *Sweden* **10** 60 20N 17 30 E
Tierra Amarilla, *Chile* **140** 27 28 S 70 18W
Tierra Amarilla, *U.S.A.* **123** 36 42N 106 33W
Tierra Colorada, *Mexico* **127** 17 10N 99 35W
Tierra de Barros, *Spain* **23** 38 40N 6 30W
Tierra de Campos, *Spain* **22** 42 10N 4 50W
Tierra del Fuego □, *Argentina* **142** 54 0 S 67 45W
Tierra del Fuego, I. Gr. de, *Argentina* **142** 54 0 S 69 0W
Tierralta, *Colombia* **134** 8 11N 76 4W
Tiétar →, *Spain* **22** 39 50N 6 1W
Tieté →, *Brazil* **141** 20 40 S 51 35W
Tieyon, *Australia* **73** 26 12 S 133 52 E
Tifarati, *W. Sahara* **84** 26 9N 10 33W
Tiffin, *U.S.A.* **119** 41 8N 83 10W
Tiffin →, *U.S.A.* **119** 41 20N 84 24W
Tiflèt, *Morocco* **84** 33 54N 6 20W
Tiflis = Tbilisi, *U.S.S.R.* **39** 41 43N 44 50 E
Tifrah, *Israel* **44** 31 19N 34 42 E
Tifton, *U.S.A.* **115** 31 28N 83 32W
Tifu, *Indonesia* **57** 3 39 S 126 24 E
Tiga, I., *N. Cal.* **68** 21 7 S 167 49 E
Tigil, *U.S.S.R.* **41** 57 49N 158 40 E
Tignish, *Canada* **105** 46 58N 64 2W
Tigray □, *Ethiopia* **89** 13 35N 39 15 E
Tigre →, *Peru* **136** 4 30 S 74 10W
Tigre →, *Venezuela* **135** 9 20N 62 30W
Tigris = Dijlah, Nahr →, *Asia* **46** 31 0N 47 25 E
Tiguentourine, *Algeria* **85** 27 52N 9 8 E
Tigyaing, *Burma* **52** 23 45N 96 10 E
Tigzerte, O. →, *Morocco* **84** 28 10N 9 37W
Tîh, Gebel el, *Egypt* **88** 29 32N 33 26 E
Tihodaine, Dunes de, *Algeria* **85** 25 15N 7 15 E
Tijesno, *Yugoslavia* **27** 43 48N 15 39 E
Tījī, *Libya* **86** 32 0N 11 18 E
Tijuana, *Mexico* **126** 32 30N 117 10W
Tikal, *Guatemala* **128** 17 13N 89 24W
Tikamgarh, *India* **49** 24 44N 78 50 E
Tikhoretsk, *U.S.S.R.* **39** 45 56N 40 5 E
Tikhvin, *U.S.S.R.* **36** 59 35N 33 30 E
Tikkadouine, Adrar, *Algeria* **85** 24 28N 1 30 E
Tiko, *Cameroon* **91** 4 4N 9 20 E
Tikrīt, *Iraq* **46** 34 35N 43 37 E
Tiksi, *U.S.S.R.* **41** 71 40N 128 45 E
Tilamuta, *Indonesia* **57** 0 32N 122 23 E
Tilburg, *Neths.* **17** 51 31N 5 6 E
Tilbury, *Canada* **108** 42 17N 82 23W
Tilbury, *U.K.* **13** 51 27N 0 24 E
Tilcara, *Argentina* **140** 23 36 S 65 23W
Tilden, *Nebr., U.S.A.* **120** 42 3N 97 45W
Tilden, *Tex., U.S.A.* **121** 28 28N 98 33W
Tilemses, *Niger* **91** 15 37N 4 44 E
Tilemsi, Vallée du, *Mali* **91** 17 42N 0 15 E
Tilhar, *India* **49** 28 0N 79 45 E
Tilia, O. →, *Algeria* **85** 27 32N 0 55 E
Tilichiki, *U.S.S.R.* **41** 60 27N 166 5 E
Tiligul →, *U.S.S.R.* **38** 47 4N 30 57 E
Tililane, *Algeria* **85** 27 49N 0 6W
Tilin, *Burma* **52** 21 41N 94 6 E
Till →, *U.K.* **12** 55 35N 2 3W
Tillabéri, *Niger* **91** 14 28N 1 28 E
Tillamook, *U.S.A.* **122** 45 29N 123 55W
Tillberga, *Sweden* **10** 59 52N 16 39 E
Tillia, *Niger* **91** 16 8N 4 47 E
Tillsonburg, *Canada* **108** 42 53N 80 44W
Tílos, *Greece* **35** 36 27N 27 27 E
Tilpa, *Australia* **73** 30 57 S 144 24 E
Tilrhemt, *Algeria* **85** 33 9N 3 22 E
Tilsit = Sovetsk, *U.S.S.R.* **36** 55 6N 21 50 E
Tilt →, *U.K.* **14** 56 50N 3 50W
Tilton, *U.S.A.* **117** 43 25N 71 36W
Timagami L., *Canada* **106** 47 0N 80 10W
Timaru, *N.Z.* **81** 44 23 S 171 14 E
Timashevsk, *U.S.S.R.* **39** 45 35N 39 0 E
Timau, *Italy* **27** 46 35N 13 0 E
Timau, *Kenya* **92** 0 4N 37 15 E
Timbaúba, *Brazil* **138** 7 31 S 35 19W
Timbedgha, *Mauritania* **90** 16 17N 8 16W
Timber Lake, *U.S.A.* **120** 45 29N 101 6W
Timber Mt., *U.S.A.* **124** 37 6N 116 28W
Timbío, *Colombia* **134** 2 20N 76 40W
Timbiqui, *Colombia* **134** 2 46N 77 42W
Timboon, *Australia* **74** 38 30 S 142 58 E
Timboram, L., *Australia* **74** 35 19 S 143 3 E
Timbuktu = Tombouctou, *Mali* **90** 16 50N 3 0W
Timellouline, *Algeria* **85** 29 22N 8 55 E
Timétrine Montagnes, *Mali* **91** 19 25N 1 0W
Timfristós, Óros, *Greece* **35** 38 57N 21 50 E
Timhadit, *Morocco* **84** 33 15N 5 4W
Tîmia, *Niger* **91** 18 4N 8 40 E
Timimoun, *Algeria* **85** 29 14N 0 16 E
Timiş → = Tamis →, *Yugoslavia* **34** 44 51N 20 39 E
Timişoara, *Romania* **34** 45 43N 21 15 E
Timmins, *Canada* **104** 48 28N 81 25W
Timok →, *Yugoslavia* **33** 44 10N 22 40 E
Timon, *Brazil* **138** 5 8 S 42 52W
Timor, *Australia* **77** 31 46 S 151 5 E
Timor, *Indonesia* **57** 9 0 S 125 0 E
Timor □, *Indonesia* **57** 9 0 S 125 0 E
Timor Sea, *Ind. Oc.* **78** 10 0 S 127 0 E
Tin Alkoum, *Algeria* **85** 24 42N 10 17 E
Tin Gornai, *Mali* **91** 16 38N 0 38W
Tin Mt., *U.S.A.* **124** 36 54N 117 28W
Tîna, Khalîg el, *Egypt* **88** 31 20N 32 42 E
Tinaca Pt., *Phil.* **57** 5 30N 125 25 E
Tinaco, *Venezuela* **134** 9 42N 68 26W
Tinafak, O. →, *Algeria* **85** 27 10N 7 0 E
Tinajo, *Canary Is.* **25** 29 4N 13 42W
Tinaquillo, *Venezuela* **134** 9 55N 68 18W
Tinca, *Romania* **34** 46 46N 21 58 E
Tinchebray, *France* **18** 48 47N 0 45W
Tindivanam, *India* **51** 12 15N 79 41 E
Tindouf, *Algeria* **84** 27 42N 8 10W
Tinée →, *France* **21** 43 55N 7 11 E
Tineo, *Spain* **22** 43 21N 6 27W
Tinerhir, *Morocco* **84** 31 29N 5 31W
Tinfouchi, *Algeria* **84** 28 52N 5 49W
Ting Jiang →, *China* **59** 24 45N 116 35 E
Tinggi, Pulau, *Malaysia* **55** 2 18N 104 7 E
Tingha, *Australia* **77** 29 56 S 151 14 E
Tingkawk Sakan, *Burma* **52** 26 4N 96 44 E
Tinglev, *Denmark* **11** 54 57N 9 13 E
Tingo Maria, *Peru* **136** 9 10 S 75 54W
Tingsryd, *Sweden* **11** 56 31N 15 0 E
Tinh Bien, *Vietnam* **55** 10 36N 104 57 E
Tinharé, I. de, *Brazil* **139** 13 30 S 38 58W
Tinkurrin, *Australia* **79** 32 59 S 117 46 E
Tinnevelly = Tirunelveli, *India* **51** 8 45N 77 45 E
Tinnoset, *Norway* **10** 59 55N 9 3 E
Tinnsjø, *Norway* **10** 59 55N 8 54 E
Tinogasta, *Argentina* **140** 28 5 S 67 32W
Tínos, *Greece* **35** 37 33N 25 8 E
Tiñoso, C., *Spain* **25** 37 32N 1 6W
Tinsukia, *India* **52** 27 29N 95 20 E
Tinta, *Peru* **136** 14 3 S 71 20W
Tintaldra, *Australia* **75** 36 2 S 147 55 E
Tintigny, *Belgium* **17** 49 41N 5 31 E
Tintina, *Argentina* **140** 27 2 S 62 45W
Tintinara, *Australia* **73** 35 48 S 140 2 E
Tinto →, *Spain* **23** 37 12N 6 55W
Tinui, *N.Z.* **80** 40 52 S 176 5 E
Tinwald, *N.Z.* **81** 43 55 S 171 43 E
Tioga, *U.S.A.* **116** 41 54N 77 9W
Tioman, Pulau, *Malaysia* **55** 2 50N 104 10 E
Tione di Trento, *Italy* **26** 46 3N 10 44 E
Tionesta, *U.S.A.* **116** 41 29N 79 28W
Tior, *Sudan* **89** 6 26N 31 11 E
Tioulilin, *Algeria* **85** 27 1N 0 2W
Tipp City, *U.S.A.* **119** 39 58N 84 11W
Tippecanoe →, *U.S.A.* **119** 40 31N 86 47W
Tipperary, *Ireland* **15** 52 28N 8 10W
Tipperary □, *Ireland* **15** 52 37N 7 55W
Tipton, *U.K.* **13** 52 32N 2 4W
Tipton, *Calif., U.S.A.* **124** 36 3N 119 19W
Tipton, *Ind., U.S.A.* **119** 40 17N 86 0W
Tipton, *Iowa, U.S.A.* **118** 41 45N 91 12W
Tipton, *Mo., U.S.A.* **118** 38 41N 92 48W
Tipton, Mt., *U.S.A.* **125** 35 32N 114 16W
Tiptonville, *U.S.A.* **121** 36 22N 89 30W
Tiptur, *India* **51** 13 15N 76 26 E
Tiquié →, *Brazil* **134** 0 5N 68 25W
Tiracambu, Serra do, *Brazil* **138** 3 15 S 46 30W
Tīrān, *Iran* **47** 32 45N 51 8 E
Tīrân, *Si. Arabia* **88** 27 57N 34 32 E
Tirana, *Albania* **35** 41 18N 19 49 E
Tiranë = Tirana, *Albania* **35** 41 18N 19 49 E
Tirano, *Italy* **26** 46 13N 10 11 E
Tiraspol, *U.S.S.R.* **38** 46 55N 29 35 E
Tirat Karmel, *Israel* **44** 32 46N 34 58 E
Tirat Yehuda, *Israel* **44** 32 1N 34 56 E
Tirat Ẕevi, *Israel* **44** 32 26N 35 31 E
Tiratimine, *Algeria* **85** 25 56N 3 37 E
Tirdout, *Mali* **91** 16 7N 1 5W
Tire, *Turkey* **46** 38 5N 27 50 E
Tirebolu, *Turkey* **46** 40 58N 38 45 E
Tiree, *U.K.* **14** 56 31N 6 55W
Tîrgovişte, *Romania* **34** 44 55N 25 27 E
Tîrgu Frumos, *Romania* **34** 47 12N 27 2 E
Tîrgu-Jiu, *Romania* **34** 45 5N 23 19 E
Tîrgu Mureş, *Romania* **34** 46 31N 24 38 E
Tîrgu Neamţ, *Romania* **34** 47 12N 26 25 E
Tîrgu Ocna, *Romania* **34** 46 16N 26 39 E
Tîrgu Secuiesc, *Romania* **34** 46 0N 26 10 E
Tirich Mir, *Pakistan* **47** 36 15N 71 55 E
Tiriola, *Italy* **29** 38 57N 16 32 E
Tiririca, Serra da, *Brazil* **139** 17 6 S 47 6W
Tiris, *W. Sahara* **84** 23 10N 13 20W
Tirna →, *India* **50** 18 4N 76 57 E
Tîrnava Mare →, *Romania* **34** 46 15N 24 30 E
Tîrnava Mică →, *Romania* **34** 46 17N 24 30 E
Tîrnăveni, *Romania* **34** 46 19N 24 13 E
Tírnavos, *Greece* **35** 39 45N 22 18 E
Tirodi, *India* **50** 21 40N 79 44 E
Tiros, *Brazil* **139** 19 0 S 45 58W
Tirschenreuth, *W. Germany* **31** 49 51N 12 20 E
Tirso →, *Italy* **28** 39 52N 8 33 E
Tirso, L. del, *Italy* **28** 40 8N 8 56 E
Tirua, Pt., *N.Z.* **80** 38 25 S 174 40 E
Tiruchchendur, *India* **51** 8 30N 78 11 E
Tiruchchirappalli, *India* **51** 10 45N 78 45 E
Tiruchengodu, *India* **51** 11 23N 77 56 E
Tirumangalam, *India* **51** 9 49N 77 58 E
Tirunelveli, *India* **51** 8 45N 77 45 E
Tirupati, *India* **51** 13 39N 79 25 E
Tiruppattur, *India* **51** 12 30N 78 30 E
Tiruppur, *India* **51** 11 5N 77 22 E
Tirutturaippundi, *India* **51** 10 32N 79 41 E
Tiruvadaimarudur, *India* **51** 11 2N 79 27 E
Tiruvallar, *India* **51** 13 9N 79 57 E
Tiruvannamalai, *India* **51** 12 15N 79 5 E
Tiruvettipuram, *India* **51** 12 39N 79 33 E
Tiruvottiyur, *India* **51** 13 10N 80 22 E
Tisa →, *Yugoslavia* **33** 45 15N 20 17 E
Tisdale, *Canada* **111** 52 50N 104 0W
Tishomingo, *U.S.A.* **121** 34 14N 96 38W
Tisjön, *Sweden* **10** 60 56N 13 0 E
Tisnaren, *Sweden* **10** 58 58N 15 56 E
Tisovec, *Czech.* **32** 48 41N 19 56 E
Tissemsilt, *Algeria* **85** 35 35N 1 50 E
Tissint, *Morocco* **84** 29 57N 7 16W
Tissø, *Denmark* **11** 55 35N 11 18 E
Tista →, *India* **52** 25 23N 89 43 E
Tisza →, *Hungary* **33** 46 8N 20 2 E
Tiszafüred, *Hungary* **33** 47 38N 20 50 E
Tiszavasvári, *Hungary* **33** 47 58N 21 18 E
Tit, *Ahaggar, Algeria* **85** 23 0N 5 10 E
Tit, *Tademait, Algeria* **85** 27 0N 1 29 E
Tit-Ary, *U.S.S.R.* **41** 71 55N 127 2 E
Titaguas, *Spain* **24** 39 53N 1 6W
Titahi Bay, *N.Z.* **80** 41 6 S 174 50 E
Titel, *Yugoslavia* **33** 45 10N 20 18 E
Tithwal, *Pakistan* **49** 34 21N 73 50 E
Titicaca, L., *S. Amer.* **136** 15 30 S 69 30W
Titiwa, *Nigeria* **91** 12 14N 12 53 E
Titlagarh, *India* **50** 20 15N 83 11 E
Titograd, *Yugoslavia* **33** 42 30N 19 19 E
Titov Veles, *Yugoslavia* **35** 41 46N 21 47 E
Titova Korenica, *Yugoslavia* **27** 44 45N 15 41 E
Titovo Užice, *Yugoslavia* **33** 43 55N 19 50 E
Titule, *Zaïre* **92** 3 15N 25 31 E
Titumate, *Colombia* **134** 8 19N 77 5W
Titusville, *Fla., U.S.A.* **115** 28 37N 80 49W
Titusville, *Pa., U.S.A.* **116** 41 35N 79 39W
Tivaouane, *Senegal* **90** 14 56N 16 45W
Tiveden, *Sweden* **11** 58 50N 14 30 E
Tiverton, *Canada* **108** 44 16N 81 32W
Tiverton, *U.K.* **13** 50 54N 3 30W
Tívoli, *Italy* **27** 41 58N 12 45 E
Tiwī, *Oman* **47** 22 45N 59 12 E
Tiyo, *Ethiopia* **89** 14 41N 40 15 E
Tizga, *Morocco* **84** 32 1N 5 9W
Ti'zi N'Isli, *Morocco* **84** 32 28N 5 47W
Tizi-Ouzou, *Algeria* **85** 36 42N 4 3 E
Tizimín, *Mexico* **127** 21 0N 88 1W
Tiznados →, *Venezuela* **134** 8 16N 67 47W
Tiznit, *Morocco* **84** 29 48N 9 45W
Tjeggelvas, *Sweden* **8** 66 37N 17 45 E
Tjeukemeer, *Neths.* **16** 52 53N 5 48 E
Tjirebon = Cirebon, *Indonesia* **57** 6 45 S 108 32 E
Tjøme, *Norway* **10** 59 8N 10 26 E
Tjonger Kanaal, *Neths.* **16** 52 52N 5 52 E
Tjörn, *Sweden* **11** 58 0N 11 35 E
Tkibuli, *U.S.S.R.* **39** 42 26N 43 0 E
Tkvarcheli, *U.S.S.R.* **39** 42 47N 41 42 E
Tlacotalpan, *Mexico* **127** 18 37N 95 40W
Tlahualilo, *Mexico* **126** 26 20N 103 30W
Tlaquepaque, *Mexico* **126** 20 39N 103 19W
Tlaxcala, *Mexico* **127** 19 20N 98 14W
Tlaxcala □, *Mexico* **127** 19 30N 98 20W
Tlaxiaco, *Mexico* **127** 17 18N 97 40W
Tlell, *Canada* **110** 53 34N 131 56W
Tlemcen, *Algeria* **85** 34 52N 1 21W
Tleta Sidi Bouguedra, *Morocco* **84** 32 16N 9 59W
Tlumach, *U.S.S.R.* **38** 48 51N 25 0 E
Tlyarata, *U.S.S.R.* **39** 42 9N 46 26 E
Tmassah, *Libya* **86** 26 19N 15 51 E
Tnine d'Anglou, *Morocco* **84** 29 50N 9 50W
To Bong, *Vietnam* **54** 12 45N 109 16 E
To-Shima, *Japan* **65** 34 31N 139 17 E
Toad →, *Canada* **110** 59 25N 124 57W
Toamasina, *Madag.* **97** 18 10 S 49 25 E
Toamasina □, *Madag.* **97** 18 0 S 49 0 E
Toay, *Argentina* **140** 36 43 S 64 38W
Toba, *Japan* **65** 34 30N 136 51 E
Toba Kakar, *Pakistan* **48** 31 30N 69 0 E
Toba Tek Singh, *Pakistan* **48** 30 55N 72 25 E
Tobago, *W. Indies* **129** 11 10N 60 30W
Tobarra, *Spain* **25** 38 37N 1 44W
Tobelo, *Indonesia* **57** 1 45N 127 56 E
Tobermorey, *Australia* **72** 22 12 S 138 0 E
Tobermory, *Canada* **108** 45 12N 81 40W
Tobermory, *U.K.* **14** 56 37N 6 4W
Tobin, *U.S.A.* **124** 39 55N 121 19W
Tobin, L., *Australia* **78** 21 45 S 125 49 E
Tobin L., *Canada* **111** 53 35N 103 30W
Toboali, *Indonesia* **56** 3 0 S 106 25 E
Tobol, *U.S.S.R.* **40** 52 40N 62 39 E
Tobol →, *U.S.S.R.* **40** 58 10N 68 12 E
Toboli, *Indonesia* **57** 0 38 S 120 5 E
Tobolsk, *U.S.S.R.* **40** 58 15N 68 10 E
Tobruk = Tubruq, *Libya* **86** 32 7N 23 55 E
Tobyhanna, *U.S.A.* **117** 41 10N 75 25W
Tocache Nuevo, *Peru* **136** 8 9 S 76 26W
Tocantínia, *Brazil* **138** 9 33 S 48 22W
Tocantinópolis, *Brazil* **138** 6 20 S 47 25W
Tocantins →, *Brazil* **138** 1 45 S 49 10W
Toccoa, *U.S.A.* **115** 34 32N 83 17W
Toce →, *Italy* **26** 45 56N 8 29 E
Tochigi, *Japan* **65** 36 25N 139 45 E
Tochigi □, *Japan* **65** 36 45N 139 45 E
Tocina, *Spain* **23** 37 37N 5 44W
Tocopilla, *Chile* **140** 22 5 S 70 10W
Tocumwal, *Australia* **74** 35 51 S 145 31 E
Tocuyo →, *Venezuela* **134** 11 3N 68 23W
Tocuyo de la Costa, *Venezuela* **134** 11 2N 68 23W
Todd →, *Australia* **72** 24 52 S 135 48 E
Todeli, *Indonesia* **57** 1 38 S 124 34 E
Todenyang, *Kenya* **92** 4 35N 35 56 E
Todi, *Italy* **27** 42 47N 12 24 E
Todos los Santos, B. de, *Brazil* **139** 12 48 S 38 38W
Todos Santos, *Mexico* **126** 23 27N 110 13W
Todtnau, *W. Germany* **31** 47 50N 7 56 E
Toecé, *Burkina Faso* **91** 11 50N 1 16W
Toetoes B., *N.Z.* **81** 46 42 S 168 41 E
Tofield, *Canada* **110** 53 25N 112 40W
Tofino, *Canada* **110** 49 11N 125 55W
Töfsingdalens nationalpark, *Sweden* **10** 62 15N 12 44 E
Toftlund, *Denmark* **11** 55 11N 9 2 E
Tofua, *Tonga* **68** 19 45 S 175 5W
Toga, *Vanuatu* **68** 13 26 S 166 42 E
Tōgane, *Japan* **65** 35 33N 140 22 E
Togba, *Mauritania* **90** 17 26N 10 12W
Togbo, *C.A.R.* **94** 6 0N 17 27 E
Togian, Kepulauan, *Indonesia* **57** 0 20 S 121 50 E
Togliatti, *U.S.S.R.* **37** 53 32N 49 24 E
Togo ■, *W. Afr.* **91** 8 30N 1 35 E

Togtoh, China 60 40 15N 111 10 E
Toi, Japan 65 34 54N 138 47 E
Toinya, Sudan 89 6 17N 29 46 E
Tojo, Indonesia 57 1 20 S 121 15 E
Tōjō, Japan 64 34 53N 133 16 E
Toka, Guyana 135 3 58N 59 17W
Tokaanu, N.Z. 80 38 58 S 175 46 E
Tokachi-Gawa →, Japan 63 42 44N 143 42 E
Tokai, Japan 65 35 2N 136 55 E
Tokaj, Hungary 33 48 8N 21 27 E
Tokala, Indonesia 57 1 30 S 121 40 E
Tokanui, N.Z. 81 46 34 S 168 56 E
Tokar, Sudan 88 18 27N 37 56 E
Tokara Kaikyō, Japan 63 30 0N 130 0 E
Tokarahi, N.Z. 81 44 56 S 170 39 E
Tokat, Turkey 46 40 22N 36 35 E
Tokeland, U.S.A. 124 46 42N 123 59W
Tokelau Is., Pac. Oc. 66 9 0 S 171 45W
Toki, Japan 65 35 18N 137 8 E
Tokmak, U.S.S.R. 40 42 49N 75 15 E
Toko Ra., Australia 72 23 5 S 138 20 E
Tokomaru Bay, N.Z. 80 38 8 S 178 22 E
Tokoname, Japan 65 34 53N 136 51 E
Tokoroa, N.Z. 80 38 13 S 175 50 E
Tokorozawa, Japan 65 35 47N 139 28 E
Toku, Tonga 68 18 10 S 174 11W
Tokuji, Japan 64 34 11N 131 42 E
Tokushima, Japan 64 34 4N 134 34 E
Tokushima □, Japan 64 34 15N 134 0 E
Tokuyama, Japan 64 34 3N 131 50 E
Tōkyō, Japan 65 35 45N 139 45 E
Tōkyō □, Japan 65 35 40N 139 30 E
Tōkyō-Wan, Japan 65 35 25N 139 47 E
Tolbukhin, Bulgaria 34 43 37N 27 49 E
Toledo, Spain 22 39 50N 4 2W
Toledo, Ill., U.S.A. 119 39 16N 88 15W
Toledo, Iowa, U.S.A. 118 42 0N 92 35W
Toledo, Ohio, U.S.A. 119 41 37N 83 33W
Toledo, Oreg., U.S.A. 122 44 40N 123 59W
Toledo, Wash., U.S.A. 122 46 29N 122 51W
Toledo, Montes de, Spain 23 39 33N 4 20W
Tolentino, Italy 27 43 12N 13 17 E
Tolga, Algeria 85 34 40N 5 22 E
Tolga, Norway 10 62 26N 11 1 E
Toliara, Madag. 97 23 21 S 43 40 E
Toliara □, Madag. 97 21 0 S 45 0 E
Tolima □, Colombia 134 3 45N 75 15W
Tolima, Vol., Colombia 134 4 40N 75 19W
Tolitoli, Indonesia 57 1 5N 120 50 E
Tolkamer, Neths. 16 51 52N 6 6 E
Tollarp, Sweden 11 55 55N 13 58 E
Tolleson, U.S.A. 123 33 29N 112 10W
Tollhouse, U.S.A. 124 37 1N 119 24W
Tolmachevo, U.S.S.R. 36 58 56N 29 51 E
Tolmezzo, Italy 27 46 23N 13 0 E
Tolmin, Yugoslavia 27 46 11N 13 45 E
Tolo, Zaïre 94 2 55 S 18 34 E
Tolo, Teluk, Indonesia 57 2 20 S 122 10 E
Tolochin, U.S.S.R. 36 54 25N 29 42 E
Tolono, U.S.A. 119 39 59N 88 16W
Tolosa, Spain 24 43 8N 2 5W
Tolox, Spain 23 36 41N 4 54W
Toltén, Chile 142 39 13 S 74 14W
Toluca, Mexico 127 19 20N 99 40W
Tom Burke, S. Africa 97 23 5 S 28 0 E
Tom Price, Australia 78 22 40 S 117 48 E
Tomah, U.S.A. 120 43 59N 90 30W
Tomahawk, U.S.A. 120 45 28N 89 40W
Tomakomai, Japan 63 42 38N 141 36 E
Tomales, U.S.A. 124 38 15N 122 53W
Tomales B., U.S.A. 124 38 15N 123 58W
Tomanlivi, Fiji 68 17 37 S 178 1 E
Tomar, Portugal 23 39 36N 8 25W
Tomás Barrón, Bolivia 136 17 35 S 67 31W
Tomaszów Mazowiecki, Poland 32 51 30N 19 57 E
Tomatlán, Mexico 126 19 56N 105 15W
Tombador, Serra do, Brazil 137 12 0 S 58 0W
Tombé, Sudan 89 5 53N 31 40 E
Tombigbee →, U.S.A. 115 31 4N 87 58W
Tombôco, Angola 95 6 48 S 13 18 E
Tombong, Australia 75 36 54 S 148 56 E
Tombouctou, Mali 90 16 50N 3 0W
Tombstone, U.S.A. 123 31 40N 110 4W
Tombua, Angola 95 15 55 S 11 55 E
Tomé, Chile 140 36 36 S 72 57W
Tomé-Açu, Brazil 138 2 25 S 48 9W
Tomelilla, Sweden 11 55 33N 13 58 E
Tomelloso, Spain 25 39 10N 3 2W
Tomiko L., Canada 108 46 32N 79 49W
Tomingley, Australia 76 32 6 S 148 16 E
Tomini, Indonesia 57 0 30N 120 30 E
Tomini, Teluk, Indonesia 57 0 10 S 122 0 E
Tominian, Mali 90 13 17N 4 35W
Tomiño, Spain 22 41 59N 8 46W
Tomioka, Japan 65 37 20N 141 0 E
Tomkinson Ranges, Australia 79 26 11 S 129 5 E
Tommot, U.S.S.R. 41 59 4N 126 20 E
Tomnavoulin, U.K. 14 57 19N 3 18W
Tomnop Ta Suos, Cambodia 55 11 20N 104 15 E
Tomo, Colombia 134 2 38N 67 32W
Tomo, Japan 64 34 23N 133 23 E
Tomo →, Colombia 134 5 20N 67 48W
Tomobe, Japan 65 36 20N 140 20 E
Toms Place, U.S.A. 124 37 34N 118 41W
Toms River, U.S.A. 117 39 59N 74 12W
Tomsk, U.S.S.R. 40 56 30N 85 5 E
Tomtabacken, Sweden 11 57 30N 14 30 E
Tonalá, Mexico 127 16 8N 93 41W
Tonale, Passo del, Italy 26 46 15N 10 34 E
Tonalea, U.S.A. 123 36 17N 110 58W
Tonami, Japan 65 36 40N 136 58 E
Tonantins, Brazil 134 2 45 S 67 45W
Tonasket, U.S.A. 122 48 45N 119 30W
Tonate, Fr. Guiana 135 5 0N 52 28W
Tonawanda, U.S.A. 116 43 0N 78 54W
Tonbridge, U.K. 13 51 12N 0 18 E
Tondano, Indonesia 57 1 35N 124 54 E
Tondela, Portugal 22 40 31N 8 5W
Tønder, Denmark 11 54 58N 8 50 E
Tondi, India 51 9 45N 79 4 E
Tondi Kiwindi, Niger 91 14 28N 2 2 E
Tondibi, Mali 91 16 39N 0 14W
Tonekābon, Iran 47 36 45N 51 12 E
Tong Xian, China 60 39 55N 116 35 E
Tonga ■, Pac. Oc. 68 19 50 S 174 30W
Tonga Trench, Pac. Oc. 66 18 0 S 175 0W
Tongaat, S. Africa 97 29 33 S 31 9 E
Tongala, Australia 74 36 14 S 144 56 E
Tong'an, China 59 24 37N 118 8 E
Tongareva, Cook Is. 67 9 0 S 158 0W
Tongatapu, Tonga 68 21 10 S 174 0W
Tongatapu Group, Tonga 68 21 0 S 175 0W
Tongbai, China 59 32 20N 113 23 E
Tongcheng, Anhui, China 59 31 4N 116 56 E
Tongcheng, Hubei, China 59 29 15N 113 50 E
Tongchuan, China 60 35 6N 109 3 E
Tongdao, China 58 26 10N 109 42 E
Tongeren, Belgium 17 50 47N 5 28 E
Tonggu, China 59 28 31N 114 20 E
Tongguan, China 60 34 40N 110 25 E
Tonghai, China 58 24 10N 102 53 E
Tonghua, China 61 41 42N 125 58 E
Tongjiang, Heilongjiang, China 62 47 40N 132 27 E
Tongjiang, Sichuan, China 58 31 58N 107 11 E
Tongking, G. of = Tonkin, G. of, Asia 54 20 0N 108 0 E
Tongliang, China 58 29 50N 106 3 E
Tongliao, China 61 43 38N 122 18 E
Tongling, China 59 30 55N 117 48 E
Tonglu, China 59 29 45N 119 37 E
Tongnan, China 58 30 9N 105 50 E
Tongoa, Vanuatu 68 16 54 S 168 34 E
Tongobory, Madag. 97 23 32 S 44 20 E
Tongoy, Chile 140 30 16 S 71 31W
Tongren, China 58 27 43N 109 11 E
Tongres = Tongeren, Belgium 17 50 47N 5 28 E
Tongsa Dzong, Bhutan 52 27 31N 90 31 E
Tongue, U.K. 14 58 29N 4 25W
Tongue →, U.S.A. 120 46 24N 105 52W
Tongwei, China 60 35 0N 105 5 E
Tongxin, China 60 36 59N 105 58 E
Tongyu, China 61 44 45N 123 4 E
Tongzi, China 58 28 9N 106 49 E
Tonica, U.S.A. 118 41 13N 89 4W
Tonj, Sudan 89 7 20N 28 44 E
Tonk, India 48 26 6N 75 54 E
Tonkawa, U.S.A. 121 36 44N 97 22W
Tonkin = Bac Phan, Vietnam 54 22 0N 105 0 E
Tonkin, G. of, Asia 54 20 0N 108 0 E
Tonlé Sap, Cambodia 54 13 0N 104 0 E
Tonnay-Charente, France 20 45 56N 0 55W
Tonneins, France 20 44 23N 0 19 E
Tonnerre, France 19 47 51N 3 59 E
Tönning, W. Germany 30 54 18N 8 57 E
Tonopah, U.S.A. 123 38 4N 117 12W
Tonoshō, Japan 64 34 29N 134 11 E
Tonosí, Panama 128 7 20N 80 20W
Tønsberg, Norway 10 59 19N 10 25 E
Tonumea, Tonga 68 20 30 S 174 30W
Tonzang, Burma 52 23 36N 93 42 E
Tonzi, Burma 52 24 39N 94 57 E
Toobeah, Australia 77 28 25 S 149 54 E
Tooele, U.S.A. 122 40 30N 112 20W
Toogong, Australia 76 33 19 S 148 38 E
Toolleen, Australia 74 36 45 S 144 42 E
Toolondo, Australia 74 36 58 S 141 58 E
Tooloom, Australia 77 28 36 S 152 27 E
Tooma, Australia 76 35 57 S 148 3 E
Toompine, Australia 73 27 15 S 144 19 E
Toongi, Australia 76 32 28 S 148 30 E
Toonpan, Australia 72 19 28 S 146 48 E
Toonumbar, Australia 77 28 34 S 152 46 E
Toora, Australia 75 38 39 S 146 23 E
Toora-Khem, U.S.S.R. 41 52 28N 96 17 E
Tooradin, Australia 74 38 13 S 145 23 E
Tooraweenah, Australia 76 31 26 S 148 52 E
Toowoomba, Australia 77 27 32 S 151 56 E
Topalu, Romania 34 44 31N 28 3 E
Topaz, U.S.A. 124 38 41N 119 30W
Topeka, U.S.A. 120 39 3N 95 40W
Topki, U.S.S.R. 40 55 20N 85 35 E
Topl'a →, Czech. 32 48 45N 21 45 E
Topley, Canada 110 54 49N 126 18W
Toplica →, Yugoslavia 33 43 15N 21 49 E
Toplița, Romania 34 46 55N 25 20 E
Topocalma, Pta., Chile 140 34 10 S 72 2W
Topock, U.S.A. 125 34 46N 114 29W
Topola, Yugoslavia 33 44 17N 20 41 E
Topolčany, Czech. 32 48 35N 18 12 E
Topoli, U.S.S.R. 39 47 59N 51 38 E
Topolnitsa →, Bulgaria 34 42 11N 24 18 E
Topolobampo, Mexico 126 25 40N 109 4W
Topolovgrad, Bulgaria 34 42 5N 26 20 E
Toppenish, U.S.A. 122 46 27N 120 16W
Topusko, Yugoslavia 27 45 18N 15 59 E
Toquepala, Peru 136 17 24 S 70 25W
Torá, Spain 24 41 49N 1 25 E
Tora Kit, Sudan 89 11 2N 32 36 E
Toraka Vestale, Madag. 97 16 20 S 43 58 E
Torata, Peru 136 17 23 S 70 1W
Torbat-e Heydārīyeh, Iran 47 35 15N 59 12 E
Torbat-e Jām, Iran 47 35 16N 60 35 E
Torbay, Canada 105 47 40N 52 42W
Torbay, U.K. 13 50 26N 3 31W
Torbreck, Mt., Australia 74 37 23 S 145 58 E
Tørdal, Norway 10 59 10N 8 45 E
Tordesillas, Spain 22 41 30N 5 0W
Tordoya, Spain 22 43 6N 8 36W
Töreboda, Sweden 11 58 41N 14 7 E
Torey, U.S.S.R. 41 50 33N 104 50 E
Torfajökull, Iceland 8 63 54N 19 0W
Torgau, E. Germany 30 51 32N 13 0 E
Torgelow, E. Germany 30 53 40N 13 59 E
Torhout, Belgium 17 51 5N 3 7 E
Tori, Ethiopia 89 7 53N 33 35 E
Torigni-sur-Vire, France 18 49 3N 0 58W
Torija, Spain 24 40 44N 3 2W
Torin, Mexico 126 27 33N 110 15W
Toriñana, C., Spain 22 43 3N 9 17W
Torino, Italy 26 45 4N 7 40 E
Torit, Sudan 89 4 27N 32 31 E
Torkovichi, U.S.S.R. 36 58 51N 30 21 E
Tormes →, Spain 22 41 18N 6 29W
Tornado Mt., Canada 110 49 55N 114 40W
Torne älv →, Sweden 8 65 50N 24 12 E
Torneå = Tornio, Finland 8 65 50N 24 12 E
Torneträsk, Sweden 8 68 24N 19 15 E
Tornio, Finland 8 65 50N 24 12 E
Tornionjoki →, Finland 8 65 50N 24 12 E
Tornquist, Argentina 140 38 8 S 62 15W
Toro, Spain 22 41 35N 5 24W
Torö, Sweden 11 58 48N 17 50 E
Toro, Cerro del, Chile 140 29 10 S 69 50W
Toro Pk., U.S.A. 125 33 34N 116 24W
Törökszentmiklós, Hungary 33 47 11N 20 27 E
Toroníos Kólpos, Greece 35 40 5N 23 30 E
Toronto, Australia 76 33 0 S 151 30 E
Toronto, Canada 108 43 39N 79 20W
Toronto, U.S.A. 116 40 27N 80 36W
Toropets, U.S.S.R. 36 56 30N 31 40 E
Tororo, Uganda 92 0 45N 34 12 E
Toros Dağlari, Turkey 46 37 0N 35 0 E
Torotoro, Bolivia 137 18 7 S 65 46W
Torowie, Australia 73 33 8 S 138 55 E
Torpshammar, Sweden 10 62 29N 16 20 E
Torquay, Australia 74 38 20 S 144 19 E
Torquay, Canada 111 49 9N 103 30W
Torquay, U.K. 13 50 27N 3 31W
Torquemada, Spain 22 42 2N 4 19W
Torralba de Calatrava, Spain 23 39 1N 3 44W
Torrance, U.S.A. 125 33 50N 118 19W
Torrão, Portugal 23 38 16N 8 11W
Torre Annunziata, Italy 29 40 45N 14 26 E
Tôrre de Moncorvo, Portugal 22 41 12N 7 8W
Torre del Greco, Italy 29 40 47N 14 22 E
Torre del Mar, Spain 23 36 44N 4 6W
Torre-Pacheco, Spain 25 37 44N 0 57W
Torre Pellice, Italy 26 44 49N 7 13 E
Torreblanca, Spain 24 40 14N 0 12 E
Torrecampo, Spain 23 38 29N 4 41W
Torrecilla en Cameros, Spain 24 42 15N 2 38W
Torredembarra, Spain 24 41 9N 1 24 E
Torredonjimeno, Spain 23 37 46N 3 57W
Torrejoncillo, Spain 22 39 54N 6 28W
Torrelaguna, Spain 24 40 50N 3 38W
Torrelavega, Spain 22 43 20N 4 5W
Torremaggiore, Italy 29 41 42N 15 17 E
Torremolinos, Spain 23 36 38N 4 30W
Torrens, L., Australia 73 31 0 S 137 50 E
Torrens Cr. →, Australia 72 22 23 S 145 9 E
Torrens Creek, Australia 72 20 48 S 145 3 E
Torrente, Spain 25 39 27N 0 28W
Torrenueva, Spain 25 38 38N 3 22W
Torreón, Mexico 126 25 33N 103 25W
Torreperogil, Spain 25 38 2N 3 17W
Torres, Mexico 126 28 46N 110 47W
Torres, Is., Vanuatu 68 13 15 S 166 37 E
Torres Novas, Portugal 23 39 27N 8 33W
Torres Strait, Australia 69 9 50 S 142 20 E
Torres Vedras, Portugal 23 39 5N 9 15W
Torrevieja, Spain 25 37 59N 0 42W
Torrey, U.S.A. 123 38 18N 111 25W
Torridge →, U.K. 13 50 51N 4 10W
Torridon, L., U.K. 14 57 35N 5 50W
Torrijos, Spain 22 39 59N 4 18W
Torrington, Australia 77 29 19 S 151 44 E
Torrington, Conn., U.S.A. 117 41 50N 73 9W
Torrington, Wyo., U.S.A. 120 42 5N 104 8W
Torroella de Montgri, Spain 24 42 2N 3 8 E
Torrox, Spain 23 36 46N 3 57W
Torsås, Sweden 11 56 24N 16 0 E
Torsby, Sweden 10 60 7N 13 0 E
Torsö, Sweden 11 58 48N 13 45 E
Tortola, Virgin Is. 129 18 19N 65 0W
Tórtoles de Esgueva, Spain 22 41 49N 4 2W
Tortona, Italy 26 44 53N 8 54 E
Tortoreto, Italy 27 42 50N 13 55 E
Tortorici, Italy 29 38 2N 14 48 E
Tortosa, Spain 24 40 49N 0 31 E
Tortosa, C., Spain 24 40 41N 0 52 E
Tortosendo, Portugal 22 40 15N 7 31W
Tortue, I. de la, Haiti 129 20 5N 72 57W
Tortuga, La, Venezuela 129 11 0N 65 22W
Torūd, Iran 47 35 25N 55 5 E
Toruń, Poland 32 53 0N 18 39 E
Torup, Denmark 11 57 5N 9 5 E
Torup, Sweden 11 56 57N 13 5 E
Tory I., Ireland 15 55 17N 8 12W
Torysa →, Czech. 32 48 39N 21 21 E
Torzhok, U.S.S.R. 36 57 5N 34 55 E
Tosa, Japan 64 33 24N 133 23 E
Tosa-Shimizu, Japan 64 32 52N 132 58 E
Tosa-Wan, Japan 64 33 15N 133 30 E
Tosa-yamada, Japan 64 33 36N 133 38 E
Toscana, Italy 26 43 30N 11 5 E
Toscano, Arcipelago, Italy 26 42 30N 10 30 E
Tosno, U.S.S.R. 36 59 38N 30 46 E
Tossa, Spain 24 41 43N 2 56 E
Tostado, Argentina 140 29 15 S 61 50W
Tostaree, Australia 75 37 44 S 148 10 E
Tostedt, W. Germany 30 53 17N 9 42 E
Tostón, Pta. de, Canary Is. 25 28 42N 14 2W
Tosu, Japan 64 33 22N 130 31 E
Tosya, Turkey 46 41 1N 34 2 E
Totana, Spain 25 37 45N 1 30W
Toten, Norway 10 60 37N 10 53 E
Toteng, Botswana 96 20 22 S 22 58 E
Tôtes, France 18 49 41N 1 3 E
Tótkomlós, Hungary 33 46 24N 20 45 E
Totma, U.S.S.R. 37 60 0N 42 40 E
Totnes, U.K. 13 50 26N 3 41W
Totness, Surinam 135 5 53N 56 19W
Totonicapán, Guatemala 128 14 58N 91 12W
Totora, Bolivia 137 17 42 S 65 9W
Totoya, I., Fiji 68 18 57 S 179 50W
Totten Glacier, Antarctica 143 66 45 S 116 10 E
Tottenham, Australia 76 32 14 S 147 21 E
Tottenham, Canada 108 44 1N 79 49W
Tottori, Japan 64 35 30N 134 15 E
Tottori □, Japan 64 35 30N 134 12 E
Touat, Algeria 85 27 27N 0 30 E
Touba, Ivory C. 90 8 22N 7 40W
Toubkal, Djebel, Morocco 84 31 0N 8 0W
Toucy, France 19 47 44N 3 15 E
Tougan, Burkina Faso 90 13 11N 2 58W
Touggourt, Algeria 85 33 6N 6 4 E
Tougué, Guinea 90 11 25N 11 50W
Touho, N. Cal. 68 20 47 S 165 14 E
Toukley, Australia 76 33 14 S 151 31 E
Toukmatine, Algeria 85 24 49N 7 11 E
Toul, France 19 48 40N 5 53 E
Toulepleu, Ivory C. 90 6 32N 8 24W
Toulon, France 21 43 10N 5 55 E
Toulon, U.S.A. 118 41 6N 89 52W
Toulouse, France 20 43 37N 1 27 E
Toummo, Niger 86 22 45N 14 8 E
Toummo Dhoba, Niger 86 22 30N 14 31 E
Toumodi, Ivory C. 90 6 32N 5 4W
Tounassine, Hamada, Algeria 84 28 48N 5 0W
Toungoo, Burma 52 19 0N 96 30 E
Touques →, France 18 49 22N 0 8 E
Touquet-Paris-Plage, Le, France 19 50 30N 1 36 E
Tour-du-Pin, La, France 21 45 33N 5 27 E
Touraine, France 18 47 20N 0 30 E
Tourane = Da Nang, Vietnam 54 16 4N 108 13 E
Tourcoing, France 19 50 42N 3 10 E
Tourine, Mauritania 84 22 23N 11 50W
Tournai, Belgium 17 50 35N 3 25 E
Tournan-en-Brie, France 19 48 44N 2 46 E
Tournay, France 20 43 13N 0 13 E
Tournon, France 21 45 4N 4 50 E
Tournon-St.-Martin, France 18 46 45N 0 58 E
Tournus, France 21 46 35N 4 54 E
Touros, Brazil 138 5 12 S 35 28W
Tours, France 18 47 22N 0 40 E
Touside, Pic, Chad 87 21 1N 16 29 E
Touwsrivier, S. Africa 96 33 20 S 20 2 E
Tovar, Venezuela 134 8 20N 71 46W
Tovarkovskiy, U.S.S.R. 37 53 40N 38 14 E
Tovdal, Norway 11 58 47N 8 10 E
Tovdalselva →, Norway 11 58 15N 8 5 E
Towamba, Australia 75 37 6 S 149 43 E
Towanda, Ill., U.S.A. 119 40 36N 88 53W
Towanda, N.Y., U.S.A. 117 41 46N 76 30W
Tower, U.S.A. 120 47 49N 92 17W
Towerhill Cr. →, Australia 72 22 28 S 144 35 E
Towner, U.S.A. 120 48 25N 100 26W
Townsend, U.S.A. 122 46 25N 111 32W

Townsend Mt., Australia 75 36 25 S 148 16 E
Townshend I., Australia 72 22 10 S 150 31 E
Townsville, Australia 72 19 15 S 146 45 E
Towong, Australia 75 36 8 S 147 59 E
Towson, U.S.A. 114 39 26N 76 34W
Toyah, U.S.A. 121 31 20N 103 48W
Toyahvale, U.S.A. 121 30 58N 103 45W
Toyama, Japan 65 36 40N 137 15 E
Toyama □, Japan 65 36 45N 137 30 E
Toyama-Wan, Japan 63 37 0N 137 30 E
Tōyō, Japan 64 33 26N 134 16 E
Toyohashi, Japan 65 34 45N 137 25 E
Toyokawa, Japan 65 34 48N 137 27 E
Toyonaka, Japan 65 34 50N 135 28 E
Toyooka, Japan 64 35 35N 134 48 E
Toyota, Japan 65 35 3N 137 7 E
Toyoura, Japan 64 34 6N 130 57 E
Tozeur, Tunisia 86 33 56N 8 8 E
Tra On, Vietnam 55 9 58N 105 55 E
Trabancos →, Spain 22 41 36N 5 15W
Traben Trarbach, W. Germany 31 49 57N 7 7 E
Trabzon, Turkey 46 41 0N 39 45 E
Tracadie, Canada 105 47 30N 64 55W
Tracy, Canada 107 46 1N 73 9W
Tracy, Calif., U.S.A. 124 37 46N 121 27W
Tracy, Minn., U.S.A. 120 44 12N 95 38W
Tradate, Italy 26 45 43N 8 54 E
Traer, U.S.A. 118 42 12N 92 28W
Trafalgar, Australia 75 38 14 S 146 12 E
Trafalgar, C., Spain 22 36 10N 6 2W
Trāghān, Libya 86 26 0N 14 30 E
Tragowel, Australia 74 35 50 S 144 0 E
Traiguén, Chile 142 38 15 S 72 41W
Trail, Canada 110 49 5N 117 40W
Trainor L., Canada 110 60 24N 120 17W
Traíra →, Brazil 134 1 4 S 69 26W
Tralee, Ireland 15 52 16N 9 42W
Tralee B., Ireland 15 52 17N 9 55W
Tramore, Ireland 15 52 10N 7 10W
Tran Ninh, Cao Nguyen, Laos 54 19 30N 103 10 E
Tranås, Sweden 11 58 3N 14 59 E
Trancas, Argentina 140 26 11 S 65 20W
Tranche-sur-Mer, La, France 18 46 20N 1 27W
Trancoso, Portugal 22 40 49N 7 21W
Tranebjerg, Denmark 11 55 51N 10 36 E
Tranemo, Sweden 11 57 30N 13 20 E
Trang, Thailand 55 7 33N 99 38 E
Trangahy, Madag. 97 19 7 S 44 31 E
Trangan, Indonesia 57 6 40 S 134 20 E
Trangie, Australia 76 32 4 S 148 0 E
Trångsviken, Sweden 10 63 19N 14 0 E
Trani, Italy 29 41 17N 16 24 E
Tranoroa, Madag. 97 24 42 S 45 4 E
Tranquebar, India 51 11 1N 79 54 E
Tranqueras, Uruguay 141 31 13 S 55 45W
Trans Nzoia □, Kenya 92 1 0N 35 0 E
Transantarctic Mts., Antarctica 143 85 0 S 170 0W
Transcaucasia = Zakavkazye, U.S.S.R. 39 42 0N 44 0 E
Transcona, Canada 111 49 55N 97 0W
Transilvania, Romania 34 46 19N 25 0 E
Transkei □, S. Africa 97 32 15 S 28 15 E
Transtrand, Sweden 10 61 6N 13 20 E
Transvaal □, S. Africa 96 25 0 S 29 0 E
Transylvania = Transilvania, Romania 34 46 19N 25 0 E
Transylvanian Alps, Romania 6 45 30N 25 0 E
Trápani, Italy 28 38 1N 12 30 E
Trapper Peak, U.S.A. 122 45 56N 114 29W
Traralgon, Australia 75 38 12 S 146 34 E
Traryd, Sweden 11 56 35N 13 45 E
Trarza □, Mauritania 90 17 30N 15 0W
Trás-os-Montes, Angola 95 10 17 S 19 5 E
Trasacco, Italy 27 41 58N 13 30 E
Trăscău, Munţii, Romania 34 46 14N 23 14 E
Trasimeno, L., Italy 27 43 10N 12 5 E
Trat, Thailand 55 12 14N 102 33 E
Traun, Austria 33 48 14N 14 15 E
Traunstein, W. Germany 31 47 52N 12 40 E
Tråvad, Sweden 11 58 15N 13 5 E
Traveller's L., Australia 73 33 20 S 142 0 E
Travemünde, W. Germany 30 53 58N 10 52 E
Travers, Mt., N.Z. 81 42 1 S 172 45 E
Traverse City, U.S.A. 114 44 45N 85 39W
Travnik, Yugoslavia 33 44 17N 17 39 E
Trawalla, Australia 74 37 25 S 143 28 E
Trayning, Australia 79 31 7 S 117 16 E
Trazo, Spain 22 43 0N 8 30W
Trbovlje, Yugoslavia 27 46 12N 15 5 E
Treasury Is., Solomon Is. 68 7 22 S 155 37 E
Trébbia →, Italy 26 45 4N 9 41 E
Trebel →, E. Germany 30 53 55N 13 1 E
Trebinje, Yugoslavia 33 42 44N 18 22 E
Trebisacce, Italy 29 39 52N 16 32 E
Trebišnica →, Yugoslavia 33 42 47N 18 8 E
Trebišov, Czech. 32 48 38N 21 41 E
Trebižat →, Yugoslavia 33 43 15N 17 30 E
Trebnje, Yugoslavia 27 45 54N 15 1 E
Třeboň, Czech. 32 48 59N 14 48 E
Trebujena, Spain 23 36 52N 6 11W
Trecate, Italy 26 45 26N 8 42 E
Tredegar, U.K. 13 51 47N 3 16W
Tregaron, U.K. 13 52 14N 3 56W
Trégastel-Plage, France 18 48 49N 3 31W
Tregnago, Italy 27 45 31N 11 10 E
Tregrosse Is., Australia 72 17 41 S 150 43 E
Tréguier, France 18 48 47N 3 16W
Trégunc, France 18 47 51N 3 51W
Treherne, Canada 111 49 38N 98 42W
Tréia, Italy 27 43 20N 13 20 E
Treignac, France 20 45 32N 1 48 E
Treinta y Tres, Uruguay 141 33 16 S 54 17W
Treis, W. Germany 31 50 9N 7 19 E
Trekveld, S. Africa 96 30 35 S 19 45 E
Trelde Næs, Denmark 11 55 38N 9 53 E
Trelew, Argentina 142 43 10 S 65 20W
Trélissac, France 20 45 11N 0 47 E
Trelleborg, Sweden 11 55 20N 13 10 E
Trélon, France 19 50 5N 4 6 E
Tremblade, La, France 20 45 46N 1 8W
Tremblant, Mt., Canada 106 46 16N 74 35W
Tremiti, Italy 27 42 8N 15 30 E
Tremonton, U.S.A. 122 41 45N 112 10W
Tremp, Spain 24 42 10N 0 52 E
Trenche →, Canada 107 47 46N 72 53W
Trenčín, Czech. 32 48 52N 18 4 E
Trenggalek, Indonesia 57 8 3 S 111 43 E
Trenque Lauquen, Argentina 140 36 5 S 62 45W
Trent →, Canada 109 44 6N 77 34W
Trent →, U.K. 12 53 33N 0 44W
Trente et un Milles, L. des, Canada 106 46 12N 75 49W
Trentham, Australia 74 37 23 S 144 21 E
Trentino-Alto Adige □, Italy 26 46 30N 11 0 E
Trento, Italy 26 46 5N 11 8 E
Trenton, Canada 109 44 10N 77 34W
Trenton, Mich., U.S.A. 119 42 8N 83 11W
Trenton, Mo., U.S.A. 118 40 5N 93 37W
Trenton, N.J., U.S.A. 117 40 15N 74 41W
Trenton, Nebr., U.S.A. 120 40 14N 101 4W
Trenton, Tenn., U.S.A. 121 35 58N 88 57W
Trepassey, Canada 105 46 43N 53 25W
Tréport, Le, France 18 50 3N 1 20 E
Trepuzzi, Italy 29 40 26N 18 4 E
Tres Arroyos, Argentina 140 38 26 S 60 20W
Três Corações, Brazil 141 21 44 S 45 15W
Três Lagoas, Brazil 139 20 50 S 51 43W
Tres Lagos →, Argentina 142 49 35 S 71 25W
Tres Marías, Mexico 126 21 25N 106 28W
Três Marias, Reprêsa, Brazil 139 18 12 S 45 15W
Tres Montes, C., Chile 142 46 50 S 75 30W
Tres Pinos, U.S.A. 124 36 48N 121 19W
Três Pontas, Brazil 139 21 23 S 45 29W
Tres Puentes, Chile 140 27 50 S 70 15W
Tres Puntas, C., Argentina 142 47 0 S 66 0W
Três Rios, Brazil 139 22 6 S 43 15W
Tres Valles, Mexico 127 18 15N 96 8W
Treska →, Yugoslavia 35 42 0N 21 20 E
Trespaderne, Spain 24 42 47N 3 24W
Trets, France 21 43 27N 5 41 E
Treuchtlingen, W. Germany 31 48 58N 10 55 E
Treuenbrietzen, E. Germany 30 52 6N 12 51 E
Treungen, Norway 9 59 1N 8 31 E
Trêve, L. la, Canada 106 49 56N 75 30W
Treviglio, Italy 26 45 31N 9 35 E
Trevinca, Peña, Spain 22 42 15N 6 46W
Treviso, Italy 27 45 40N 12 15 E
Trévoux, France 21 45 57N 4 47 E
Treysa, W. Germany 30 50 55N 9 12 E
Trgovište, Yugoslavia 33 42 20N 22 10 E
Triabunna, Australia 72 42 30 S 147 55 E
Trial B., Australia 77 30 48 S 153 2 E
Triang, Malaysia 55 3 15N 102 26 E
Triaucourt-en-Argonne, France 19 48 59N 5 2 E
Tribsees, E. Germany 30 54 4N 12 46 E
Tribulation, C., Australia 72 16 5 S 145 29 E
Tribune, U.S.A. 120 38 30N 101 45W
Tricárico, Italy 29 40 37N 16 9 E
Tricase, Italy 29 39 56N 18 20 E
Trichinopoly = Tiruchchirappalli, India 51 10 45N 78 45 E
Trichur, India 51 10 30N 76 18 E
Trida, Australia 73 33 1 S 145 1 E
Trier, W. Germany 31 49 45N 6 37 E
Trieste, Italy 27 45 39N 13 45 E
Trieste, G. di, Italy 27 45 37N 13 40 E
Trieux →, France 18 48 43N 3 9W
Triggiano, Italy 29 41 4N 16 58 E
Triglav, Yugoslavia 27 46 21N 13 50 E
Trigno →, Italy 27 42 4N 14 48 E
Trigueros, Spain 23 37 24N 6 50W
Trikhonis, Límni, Greece 35 38 34N 21 30 E
Tríkkala, Greece 35 39 34N 21 47 E
Trikora, Puncak, Indonesia 57 4 15 S 138 45 E
Trilj, Yugoslavia 27 43 38N 16 42 E
Trillo, Spain 24 40 42N 2 35W
Trim, Ireland 15 53 34N 6 48W
Trincomalee, Sri Lanka 51 8 38N 81 15 E
Trindade, Brazil 139 16 40 S 49 30W
Trindade, I., Atl. Oc. 4 20 20 S 29 50W
Tring-Jonction, Canada 107 46 16N 70 59W
Trinidad, Bolivia 137 14 46 S 64 50W
Trinidad, Colombia 134 5 25N 71 40W
Trinidad, Cuba 128 21 48N 80 0W
Trinidad, Uruguay 140 33 30 S 56 50W
Trinidad, U.S.A. 121 37 15N 104 30W
Trinidad, W. Indies 129 10 30N 61 15W
Trinidad →, Mexico 127 17 49N 95 9W
Trinidad, G., Chile 142 49 55 S 75 25W
Trinidad, I., Argentina 142 39 10 S 62 0W
Trinidad & Tobago ■, W. Indies 129 10 30N 61 20W
Trinitápoli, Italy 29 41 22N 16 5 E
Trinity, Canada 105 48 59N 53 55W
Trinity, U.S.A. 121 30 59N 95 25W
Trinity →, Calif., U.S.A. 122 41 11N 123 42W
Trinity →, Tex., U.S.A. 121 30 30N 95 0W
Trinity B., Canada 105 48 20N 53 10W
Trinity Mts., U.S.A. 122 40 20N 118 50W
Trinkitat, Sudan 88 18 45N 37 51 E
Trino, Italy 26 45 10N 8 18 E
Trion, U.S.A. 115 34 35N 85 18W
Trionto, C., Italy 29 39 38N 16 47 E
Triora, Italy 26 44 0N 7 46 E
Tripoli = Tarābulus, Lebanon 46 34 31N 35 50 E
Tripoli = Tarābulus, Libya 86 32 49N 13 7 E
Tripoli, U.S.A. 118 42 49N 92 16W
Tripp, U.S.A. 120 43 16N 97 58W
Tripura □, India 52 24 0N 92 0 E
Trischen, W. Germany 30 54 3N 8 32 E
Tristan da Cunha, Atl. Oc. 4 37 6 S 12 20W
Trivandrum, India 51 8 41N 77 0 E
Trivento, Italy 29 41 48N 14 31 E
Trnava, Czech. 33 48 23N 17 35 E
Trobriand Is., Papua N. G. 69 8 30 S 151 0 E
Trochu, Canada 110 51 50N 113 13W
Trodely I., Canada 104 52 15N 79 26W
Trogir, Yugoslavia 27 43 32N 16 15 E
Troglav, Yugoslavia 27 43 56N 16 36 E
Trøgstad, Norway 10 59 37N 11 16 E
Tróia, Italy 29 41 22N 15 19 E
Troilus, L., Canada 104 50 50N 74 35W
Troina, Italy 29 37 47N 14 34 E
Trois Fourches, Cap des, Morocco 85 35 26N 2 58W
Trois-Pistoles, Canada 107 48 5N 69 10W
Trois-Rivières, Canada 107 46 25N 72 34W
Troisvierges, Belgium 17 50 8N 6 0 E
Troitsk, U.S.S.R. 40 54 10N 61 35 E
Troitsko Pechorsk, U.S.S.R. 40 62 40N 56 10 E
Trölladyngja, Iceland 8 64 54N 17 16W
Trollhättan, Sweden 11 58 17N 12 20 E
Trollheimen, Norway 10 62 46N 9 1 E
Trombetas →, Brazil 135 1 55 S 55 35W
Tromelin I., Ind. Oc. 53 15 52 S 54 25 E
Troms fylke □, Norway 8 68 56N 19 0 E
Tromsø, Norway 8 69 40N 18 56 E
Trona, U.S.A. 125 35 46N 117 23W
Tronador, Argentina 142 41 10 S 71 50W
Trondheim, Norway 10 63 36N 10 25 E
Trondheimsfjorden, Norway 8 63 35N 10 30 E
Trönninge, Sweden 11 56 37N 12 51 E
Trönö, Sweden 10 61 22N 16 54 E
Tronto →, Italy 27 42 54N 13 55 E
Troon, U.K. 14 55 33N 4 40W
Tropea, Italy 29 38 40N 15 53 E
Tropic, U.S.A. 123 37 36N 112 4W
Tropoja, Albania 34 42 23N 20 10 E
Trossachs, The, U.K. 14 56 14N 4 24W
Trostan, U.K. 15 55 4N 6 10W
Trostberg, W. Germany 31 48 2N 12 33 E
Trostyanets, U.S.S.R. 36 50 33N 34 59 E
Trotternish, U.K. 14 57 32N 6 15W
Troup, U.S.A. 121 32 10N 95 3W
Trout →, Canada 110 61 19N 119 51W
Trout Creek, Canada 108 45 59N 79 22W
Trout L., N.W.T., Canada 110 60 40N 121 14W
Trout L., Ont., Canada 111 51 20N 93 15W
Trout Lake, Mich., U.S.A. 104 46 10N 85 2W
Trout Lake, Wash., U.S.A. 124 46 0N 121 32W
Trout River, Canada 105 49 29N 58 8W
Trouville-sur-Mer, France 18 49 21N 0 5 E
Trowbridge, U.K. 13 51 18N 2 12W
Troy, Turkey 46 39 57N 26 12 E
Troy, Ala., U.S.A. 115 31 50N 85 58W
Troy, Idaho, U.S.A. 122 46 44N 116 46W
Troy, Ill., U.S.A. 118 38 44N 89 54W
Troy, Ind., U.S.A. 119 38 0N 86 48W
Troy, Kans., U.S.A. 120 39 47N 95 2W
Troy, Mich., U.S.A. 119 42 37N 83 9W
Troy, Mo., U.S.A. 118 38 56N 90 59W
Troy, Mont., U.S.A. 122 48 30N 115 58W
Troy, N.Y., U.S.A. 117 42 45N 73 39W
Troy, Ohio, U.S.A. 119 40 0N 84 10W
Troyan, Bulgaria 34 42 57N 24 43 E
Troyes, France 19 48 19N 4 3 E
Trpanj, Yugoslavia 33 43 1N 17 15 E
Trstena, Czech. 32 49 21N 19 37 E
Trstenik, Yugoslavia 33 43 36N 21 0 E
Trubchevsk, U.S.S.R. 36 52 33N 33 47 E
Trucial States = United Arab Emirates ■, Asia 47 23 50N 54 0 E
Truckee, U.S.A. 124 39 20N 120 11W
Truite, L. à la, Canada 106 47 20N 78 20W
Trujillo, Colombia 134 4 10N 76 19W
Trujillo, Honduras 128 16 0N 86 0W
Trujillo, Peru 136 8 6 S 79 0W
Trujillo, Spain 23 39 28N 5 55W
Trujillo, U.S.A. 121 35 34N 104 44W
Trujillo, Venezuela 134 9 22N 70 38W
Trujillo □, Venezuela 134 9 25N 70 30W
Truk, Pac. Oc. 66 7 25N 151 46 E
Trumann, U.S.A. 121 35 42N 90 32W
Trumbull, Mt., U.S.A. 123 36 25N 113 8W
Trun, France 18 48 50N 0 2 E
Trundle, Australia 76 32 53 S 147 35 E
Trung-Phan, Vietnam 54 16 0N 108 0 E
Truro, Canada 105 45 21N 63 14W
Truro, U.K. 13 50 17N 5 2W
Truslove, Australia 79 33 20 S 121 45 E
Trustrup, Denmark 11 56 20N 10 46 E
Truth or Consequences, U.S.A. 123 33 9N 107 16W
Trutnov, Czech. 32 50 37N 15 54 E
Truyère →, France 20 44 38N 2 34 E
Tryavna, Bulgaria 34 42 54N 25 25 E
Tryon, U.S.A. 115 35 15N 82 16W
Tryonville, U.S.A. 116 41 42N 79 48W
Trzcianka, Poland 32 53 3N 16 25 E
Trzebiatów, Poland 32 54 3N 15 18 E
Trzebiez, Poland 32 53 38N 14 31 E
Trzebinia-Siersza, Poland 32 50 11N 19 18 E
Trzebnica, Poland 32 51 20N 17 1 E
Tržič, Yugoslavia 27 46 22N 14 18 E
Tsageri, U.S.S.R. 39 42 39N 42 46 E
Tsaratanana, Madag. 97 16 47 S 47 39 E
Tsaratanana, Mt. de, Madag. 97 14 0 S 49 0 E
Tsarevo = Michurin, Bulgaria 34 42 9N 27 51 E
Tsarichanka, U.S.S.R. 38 48 55N 34 30 E
Tsau, Botswana 96 20 8 S 22 22 E
Tsebrikovo, U.S.S.R. 38 47 9N 30 10 E
Tselinograd, U.S.S.R. 40 51 10N 71 30 E
Tsetserleg, Mongolia 62 47 36N 101 32 E
Tshabong, Botswana 96 26 2 S 22 29 E
Tshane, Botswana 96 24 5 S 21 54 E
Tshela, Zaïre 95 4 57 S 13 4 E
Tshesebe, Botswana 97 21 51 S 27 32 E
Tshibeke, Zaïre 92 2 40 S 28 35 E
Tshibinda, Zaïre 92 2 23 S 28 43 E
Tshikapa, Zaïre 95 6 28 S 20 48 E
Tshilenge, Zaïre 92 6 17 S 23 48 E
Tshinsenda, Zaïre 93 12 20 S 28 0 E
Tshofa, Zaïre 92 5 13 S 25 16 E
Tshwane, Botswana 96 22 24 S 22 1 E
Tsigara, Botswana 96 20 22 S 25 54 E
Tsihombe, Madag. 97 25 18 S 45 29 E
Tsimlyansk, U.S.S.R. 39 47 40N 42 6 E
Tsimlyanskoye Vdkhr., U.S.S.R. 39 48 0N 43 0 E
Tsinan = Jinan, China 60 36 38N 117 1 E
Tsineng, S. Africa 96 27 5 S 23 5 E
Tsinghai = Qinghai □, China 62 36 0N 98 0 E
Tsingtao = Qingdao, China 61 36 5N 120 20 E
Tsinjomitondraka, Madag. 97 15 40 S 47 8 E
Tsiroanomandidy, Madag. 97 18 46 S 46 2 E
Tsivilsk, U.S.S.R. 37 55 50N 47 25 E
Tsivory, Madag. 97 24 4 S 46 5 E
Tskhinvali, U.S.S.R. 39 42 14N 44 1 E
Tsna →, U.S.S.R. 37 54 55N 41 58 E
Tso Moriri, L., India 49 32 50N 78 20 E
Tsodilo Hill, Botswana 96 18 49 S 21 43 E
Tsogttsetsiy, Mongolia 60 43 43N 105 35 E
Tsolo, S. Africa 97 31 18 S 28 37 E
Tsomo, S. Africa 97 32 0 S 27 42 E
Tsu, Japan 65 34 45N 136 25 E
Tsu L., Canada 110 60 40N 111 52W
Tsuchiura, Japan 65 36 5N 140 15 E
Tsugaru-Kaikyō, Japan 63 41 35N 141 0 E
Tsukumi, Japan 64 33 4N 131 52 E
Tsukushi-Sanchi, Japan 64 33 25N 130 30 E
Tsumeb, Namibia 96 19 9 S 17 44 E
Tsumis, Namibia 96 23 39 S 17 29 E
Tsuna, Japan 64 34 28N 134 56 E
Tsuno-Shima, Japan 64 34 21N 130 52 E
Tsuru, Japan 65 35 31N 138 57 E
Tsuruga, Japan 65 35 45N 136 2 E
Tsuruga-Wan, Japan 65 35 50N 136 3 E
Tsurugi, Japan 65 36 29N 136 37 E
Tsurugi-San, Japan 64 33 51N 134 6 E
Tsurumi-Saki, Japan 64 32 56N 132 5 E
Tsuruoka, Japan 63 38 44N 139 50 E
Tsurusaki, Japan 64 33 14N 131 41 E
Tsushima, Gifu, Japan 65 35 10N 136 43 E
Tsushima, Nagasaki, Japan 64 34 20N 129 20 E
Tsvetkovo, U.S.S.R. 38 49 8N 31 33 E
Tu →, Burma 52 21 50N 96 15 E
Tua →, Portugal 22 41 13N 7 26W
Tuai, N.Z. 80 38 47 S 177 10 E
Tuakau, N.Z. 80 37 16 S 174 59 E
Tual, Indonesia 57 5 38 S 132 44 E
Tuam, Ireland 15 53 30N 8 50W
Tuamarina, N.Z. 81 41 25 S 173 59 E
Tuamotu Arch., Pac. Oc. 67 17 0 S 144 0W

Tuamotu Ridge, *Pac. Oc.* .... 67 20 0 S 138 0W
Tuanfeng, *China* ..... 59 30 38N 114 52 E
Tuanxi, *China* .... 58 27 28N 107 8 E
Tuao, *Phil.* .... 57 17 55N 122 22 E
Tuapse, *U.S.S.R.* ..... 39 44 5N 39 10 E
Tuatapere, *N.Z.* ..... 81 46 8 S 167 41 E
Tuba City, *U.S.A.* 123 36 8N 111 18W
Tuban, *Indonesia* ..... 57 6 54 S 112 3 E
Tubarão, *Brazil* ...... 141 28 30 S 49 0W
Tūbās, *Jordan* .... 44 32 20N 35 22 E
Tubau, *Malaysia* ..... 56 3 10N 113 40 E
Tubbergen, *Neths.* .... 16 52 24N 6 48 E
Tübingen, *W. Germany* 31 48 31N 9 4 E
Tubize, *Belgium* ...... 17 50 42N 4 13 E
Tubruq, *Libya* .... 86 32 7N 23 55 E
Tubuaeran I., *Pac. Oc.* 67 3 51N 159 22W
Tubuai Is., *Pac. Oc.* .. 67 25 0 S 150 0W
Tuc Trung, *Vietnam* .. 55 11 1N 107 12 E
Tucacas, *Venezuela* ... 134 10 48N 68 19W
Tucano, *Brazil* .... 138 10 58 S 38 48W
Tuchang, *Taiwan* ..... 59 24 59N 121 30 E
Tuchodi →, *Canada* .. 110 58 17N 123 42W
Tuchola, *Poland* ..... 32 53 33N 17 52 E
Tucson, *U.S.A.* 123 32 14N 110 59W
Tucumán □, *Argentina* 140 26 48 S 66 2W
Tucumcari, *U.S.A.* ... 121 35 12N 103 45W
Tucunaré, *Brazil* ..... 137 5 18 S 55 51W
Tucupido, *Venezuela* .. 134 9 17N 65 47W
Tucupita, *Venezuela* .. 135 9 2N 62 3W
Tucuruí, *Brazil* .... 138 3 42 S 49 44W
Tudela, *Spain* 24 42 4N 1 39W
Tudela de Duero, *Spain* 22 41 37N 4 39W
Tudmur, *Syria* .... 46 34 36N 38 15 E
Tudor, L., *Canada* ... 105 55 50N 65 25W
Tudora, *Romania* .... 34 47 31N 26 45 E
Tuella →, *Portugal* ... 22 41 30N 7 12W
Tuen, *Australia* ...... 73 28 33 S 145 37 E
Tuena, *Australia* ..... 76 34 1 S 149 19 E
Tueré →, *Brazil* ..... 138 2 48 S 50 59W
Tufi, *Papua N. G.* .... 69 9 8 S 149 19 E
Tugela →, *S. Africa* .. 97 29 14 S 31 30 E
Tuggerah, L., *Australia* 76 33 18 S 151 30 E
Tuguegarao, *Phil.* .... 57 17 35N 121 42 E
Tugur, *U.S.S.R.* ...... 41 53 44N 136 45 E
Tuineje, *Canary Is.* ... 25 28 19N 14 3W
Tukangbesi, Kepulauan, *Indonesia* 57 6 0 S 124 0 E
Tukarak I., *Canada* ... 104 56 15N 78 45W
Tûkh, *Egypt* .... 88 30 21N 31 12 E
Tukobo, *Ghana* 90 5 1N 2 47W
Tūkrah, *Libya* .... 86 32 30N 20 37 E
Tuktoyaktuk, *Canada* . 102 69 27N 133 2W
Tukums, *U.S.S.R.* .... 36 57 2N 23 10 E
Tukuyu, *Tanzania* .... 93 9 17 S 33 35 E
Tula, *Hidalgo, Mexico* 127 20 0N 99 20W
Tula, *Tamaulipas, Mexico* 127 23 0N 99 40W
Tula, *Nigeria* .... 91 9 51N 11 27 E
Tula, *U.S.S.R.* .... 37 54 13N 37 38 E
Tulak, *Afghan.* .... 42 33 55N 63 40 E
Tulancingo, *Mexico* ... 127 20 5N 99 22W
Tulare, *U.S.A.* 124 36 15N 119 26W
Tulare Lake Bed, *U.S.A.* 124 36 0N 119 48W
Tularosa, *U.S.A.* 123 33 4N 106 1W
Tulbagh, *S. Africa* ... 96 33 16 S 19 6 E
Tulcán, *Ecuador* 134 0 48N 77 43W
Tulcea, *Romania* ..... 34 45 13N 28 46 E
Tulchin, *U.S.S.R.* .... 38 48 41N 28 49 E
Tulemalu L., *Canada* . 111 62 58N 99 25W
Tuli, *Indonesia* .... 57 1 24 S 122 26 E
Tuli, *Zimb.* .... 93 21 58 S 29 13 E
Tulia, *U.S.A.* 121 34 35N 101 44W
Ţulkarm, *Jordan* ..... 44 32 19N 35 2 E
Tullahoma, *U.S.A.* 115 35 23N 86 12W
Tullamore, *Australia* .. 76 32 39 S 147 36 E
Tullamore, *Ireland* ... 15 53 17N 7 30W
Tulle, *France* .... 20 45 16N 1 46 E
Tullibigeal, *Australia* .. 73 33 25 S 146 44 E
Tullins, *France* .... 21 45 18N 5 29 E
Tulln, *Austria* .... 33 48 20N 16 4 E
Tullow, *Ireland* 15 52 48N 6 45W
Tullus, *Sudan* .... 89 11 7N 24 31 E
Tully, *Australia* ...... 72 17 56 S 145 55 E
Ţulmaythah, *Libya* ... 86 32 40N 20 55 E
Tulmur, *Australia* .... 72 22 40 S 142 20 E
Tulnici, *Romania* ..... 34 45 51N 26 38 E
Tulovo, *Bulgaria* ..... 34 42 33N 25 32 E
Tulsa, *U.S.A.* 121 36 10N 96 0W
Tulsequah, *Canada* ... 110 58 39N 133 35W
Tulu Milki, *Ethiopia* .. 89 9 55N 38 20 E
Tulu Welel, *Ethiopia* . 89 8 56N 34 47 E
Tulua, *Colombia* 134 4 6N 76 11W
Tulun, *U.S.S.R.* ..... 41 54 32N 100 35 E
Tulungagung, *Indonesia* 56 8 5 S 111 54 E
Tum, *Indonesia* ...... 57 3 36 S 130 21 E
Tuma, *U.S.S.R.* ...... 37 55 10N 40 30 E
Tuma →, *Nic.* 128 13 6N 84 35W
Tumaco, *Colombia* ... 134 1 50N 78 45W
Tumaco, Ensenada, *Colombia* 134 1 55N 78 45W
Tumatumari, *Guyana* . 135 5 20N 58 55W
Tumba, *Sweden* ...... 10 59 12N 17 48 E
Tumba, L., *Zaïre* ..... 94 0 50 S 18 0 E
Tumbarumba, *Australia* 76 35 44 S 148 0 E
Tumbaya, *Argentina* .. 140 23 50 S 65 26W
Túmbes, *Peru* .... 136 3 37 S 80 27W
Tumbes □, *Peru* ..... 136 3 50 S 80 30W
Tumblong, *Australia* .. 76 35 6 S 148 1 E
Tumbulgum, *Australia* 77 28 17 S 153 27 E
Tumbwe, *Zaïre* ...... 93 11 25 S 27 15 E
Tumby Bay, *Australia* . 73 34 21 S 136 8 E
Tumd Youqi, *China* .. 60 40 30N 110 30 E
Tumen, *China* .... 61 43 0N 129 50 E
Tumen Jiang →, *China* 61 42 20N 130 35 E
Tumeremo, *Venezuela* 135 7 18N 61 30W
Tumiritinga, *Brazil* ... 139 18 58 S 41 38W
Tumkur, *India* .... 51 13 18N 77 6 E
Tummel, L., *U.K.* 14 56 43N 3 55W
Tump, *Pakistan* ...... 47 26 7N 62 16 E
Tumpat, *Malaysia* .... 55 6 11N 102 10 E
Tumsar, *India* .... 50 21 26N 79 45 E
Tumu, *Ghana* 90 10 56N 1 56W
Tumucumaque, Serra, *Brazil* 135 2 0N 55 0W
Tumupasa, *Bolivia* ... 136 14 9 S 67 55W
Tumut, *Australia* ..... 76 35 16 S 148 13 E
Tumwater, *U.S.A.* 122 47 0N 122 58W
Tunas de Zaza, *Cuba* . 128 21 39N 79 34W
Tunbridge Wells, *U.K.* 13 51 7N 0 16 E
Tuncurry, *Australia* ... 77 32 17 S 152 29 E
Tunduru, *Tanzania* ... 93 11 8 S 37 25 E
Tunduru □, *Tanzania* . 93 11 5 S 37 22 E
Tundzha →, *Bulgaria* 35 41 40N 26 35 E
Tunga →, *India* ..... 51 15 0N 75 50 E
Tunga Pass, *India* .... 52 29 0N 94 14 E
Tungabhadra →, *India* 51 15 57N 78 15 E
Tungabhadra Dam, *India* .... 51 15 0N 75 50 E
Tungamah, *Australia* .. 74 36 10 S 145 54 E
Tungaru, *Sudan* ...... 89 10 9N 30 52 E
Tungi, *Bangla.* .... 52 23 53N 90 24 E
Tungla, *Nic.* 128 13 24N 84 21W
Tungnafellsjökull, *Iceland* 8 64 45N 17 55W
Tungsten, *Canada* 110 61 57N 128 16W
Tungurahua □, *Ecuador* .... 134 1 15 S 78 35W
Tunguska, Nizhnyaya →, *U.S.S.R.* .... 41 65 48N 88 4 E
Tunguska, Podkamennaya →, *U.S.S.R.* .... 41 61 36N 90 18 E
Tuni, *India* .... 50 17 22N 82 36 E
Tunia, *Colombia* 134 2 41N 76 31W
Tunica, *U.S.A.* 121 34 43N 90 23W
Tunis, *Tunisia* .... 86 36 50N 10 11 E
Tunis, Golfe de, *Tunisia* .... 86 37 0N 10 30 E
Tunisia ■, *Africa* ..... 86 33 30N 9 10 E
Tunja, *Colombia* 134 5 33N 73 25W
Tunkhannock, *U.S.A.* . 117 41 32N 75 46W
Tunliu, *China* .... 60 36 13N 112 52 E
Tunnsjøen, *Norway* ... 8 64 45N 13 25 E
Tunungayualok I., *Canada* 105 56 0N 61 0W
Tunuyán, *Argentina* .. 140 33 35 S 69 0W
Tunuyán →, *Argentina* 140 33 33 S 67 30W
Tunxi, *China* .... 59 29 42N 118 25 E
Tuo Jiang →, *China* .. 58 28 50N 105 35 E
Tuolumne, *U.S.A.* 124 37 59N 120 16W
Tuolumne →, *U.S.A.* . 124 37 36N 121 13W
Tuoy-Khaya, *U.S.S.R.* 41 62 32N 111 25 E
Tupã, *Brazil* .... 141 21 57 S 50 28W
Tupaciguara, *Brazil* ... 139 18 35 S 48 42W
Tupelo, *U.S.A.* 115 34 15N 88 42W
Tupik, *R.S.F.S.R., U.S.S.R.* .... 36 55 42N 33 22 E
Tupik, *R.S.F.S.R., U.S.S.R.* .... 41 54 26N 119 57 E
Tupinambaranas, *Brazil* 135 3 0 S 58 0W
Tupirama, *Brazil* ..... 138 8 58 S 48 12W
Tupiratins, *Brazil* .... 138 8 23 S 48 8W
Tupiza, *Bolivia* ...... 140 21 30 S 65 40W
Tupman, *U.S.A.* 125 35 18N 119 21W
Tupper, *Canada* 110 55 32N 120 1W
Tupper Lake, *U.S.A.* . 117 44 18N 74 30W
Tupungato, Cerro, *S. Amer.* .... 140 33 15 S 69 50W
Tuquan, *China* .... 61 45 18N 121 38 E
Tuque, La, *Canada* ... 107 47 30N 72 50W
Túquerres, *Colombia* . 134 1 5N 77 37W
Tura, *India* .... 52 25 30N 90 16 E
Tura, *U.S.S.R.* .... 41 64 20N 100 17 E
Turabah, *Si. Arabia* .. 46 28 20N 43 15 E
Turagua, Serranía, *Venezuela* 135 7 20N 64 35W
Turaiyur, *India* ...... 51 11 9N 78 38 E
Turakina, *N.Z.* ...... 80 40 3 S 175 16 E
Turakirae Hd., *N.Z.* .. 80 41 26 S 174 56 E
Tūrān, *Iran* .... 47 35 39N 56 42 E
Turan, *U.S.S.R.* ...... 41 51 55N 95 0 E
Turayf, *Si. Arabia* ... 46 31 41N 38 39 E
Turégano, *Spain* 22 41 9N 4 1W
Turek, *Poland* .... 32 52 3N 18 30 E
Turen, *Venezuela* 134 9 17N 69 6W
Turfan = Turpan, *China* .... 62 43 58N 89 10 E
Turfan Depression = Turpan Hami, *China* 62 42 40N 89 25 E
Turgeon →, *Canada* . 106 50 0N 78 56W
Turgeon, L., *Canada* . 106 49 2N 79 4W
Tŭrgovishte, *Bulgaria* . 34 43 17N 26 38 E
Turgutlu, *Turkey* ..... 46 38 30N 27 48 E
Turhal, *Turkey* ...... 38 40 24N 36 5 E
Turia →, *Spain* 25 39 27N 0 19W
Turiaçu, *Brazil* ...... 138 1 40 S 45 19W
Turiaçu →, *Brazil* ... 138 1 36 S 45 19W
Turin = Torino, *Italy* . 26 45 4N 7 40 E
Turin, *Canada* 110 49 58N 112 31W
Turka, *U.S.S.R.* ...... 36 49 10N 23 2 E
Turkana □, *Kenya* ... 92 3 0N 35 30 E
Turkana, L., *Africa* ... 92 3 30N 36 5 E
Turkestan, *U.S.S.R.* .. 40 43 17N 68 16 E
Túrkeve, *Hungary* .... 33 47 6N 20 44 E
Turkey ■, *Eurasia* ... 46 39 0N 36 0 E
Turkey →, *U.S.A.* ... 118 42 43N 91 2W
Turkey Creek, *Australia* 78 17 2 S 128 12 E
Turki, *U.S.S.R.* ...... 37 52 0N 43 15 E
Turkmen S.S.R. □, *U.S.S.R.* .... 40 39 0N 59 0 E
Turks Is., *W. Indies* .. 129 21 20N 71 20W
Turks Island Passage, *W. Indies* 129 21 30N 71 30W
Turku, *Finland* .... 9 60 30N 22 19 E
Turkwe →, *Kenya* ... 92 3 6N 36 6 E
Turlock, *U.S.A.* 124 37 30N 120 55W
Turnagain →, *Canada* 110 59 12N 127 35W
Turnagain, C., *N.Z.* .. 80 40 28 S 176 38 E
Turneffe Is., *Belize* ... 127 17 20N 87 50W
Turner, *Australia* ..... 78 17 52 S 128 16 E
Turner, *U.S.A.* 122 48 52N 108 25W
Turner Pt., *Australia* .. 72 11 47 S 133 32 E
Turner Valley, *Canada* 110 50 40N 114 17W
Turners Falls, *U.S.A.* . 117 42 36N 72 34W
Turnhout, *Belgium* ... 17 51 19N 4 57 E
Turnor L., *Canada* ... 111 56 35N 108 35W
Tŭrnovo, *Bulgaria* .... 34 43 5N 25 41 E
Turnu Măgurele, *Romania* .... 34 43 46N 24 56 E
Turnu Rosu Pasul, *Romania* .... 34 45 33N 24 17 E
Turon, *U.S.A.* 121 37 48N 98 27W
Tuross Head, *Australia* 76 36 3 S 150 8 E
Turpan, *China* .... 62 43 58N 89 10 E
Turpan Hami, *China* .. 62 42 40N 89 25 E
Turriff, *U.K.* 14 57 32N 2 28W
Tursha, *U.S.S.R.* ..... 37 56 55N 47 36 E
Tursi, *Italy* .... 29 40 15N 16 27 E
Turtle Hd. I., *Australia* 72 10 56 S 142 37 E
Turtle L., *Canada* 111 53 36N 108 38W
Turtle Lake, *N. Dak., U.S.A.* 120 47 30N 100 55W
Turtle Lake, *Wis., U.S.A.* 120 45 22N 92 10W
Turtleford, *Canada* ... 111 53 23N 108 57W
Turua, *N.Z.* .... 80 37 14 S 175 35 E
Turukhansk, *U.S.S.R.* 41 65 21N 88 5 E
Turun ja Porin lääni □, *Finland* .... 9 60 27N 22 15 E
Turzovka, *Czech.* .... 32 49 25N 18 35 E
Tuscaloosa, *U.S.A.* ... 115 33 13N 87 31W
Tuscánia, *Italy* .... 27 42 25N 11 53 E
Tuscany = Toscana, *Italy* .... 26 43 30N 11 5 E
Tuscola, *Ill., U.S.A.* .. 119 39 48N 88 15W
Tuscola, *Tex., U.S.A.* . 121 32 15N 99 48W
Tuscumbia, *Ala., U.S.A.* 115 34 42N 87 42W
Tuscumbia, *Mo., U.S.A.* 118 38 14N 92 28W
Tuskar Rock, *Ireland* . 15 52 12N 6 10W
Tuskegee, *U.S.A.* 115 32 24N 85 39W
Tustna, *Norway* ...... 10 63 10N 8 5 E
Tutayev, *U.S.S.R.* .... 37 57 53N 39 32 E
Tuticorin, *India* ...... 51 8 50N 78 12 E
Tutin, *Yugoslavia* .... 33 43 0N 20 20 E
Tutóia, *Brazil* .... 138 2 45 S 42 20W
Tutong, *Brunei* .... 56 4 47N 114 40 E
Tutova →, *Romania* . 34 46 20N 27 30 E
Tutrakan, *Bulgaria* ... 34 44 2N 26 40 E
Tutshi L., *Canada* 110 59 56N 134 30W
Tuttle, *U.S.A.* 120 47 9N 100 0W
Tuttlingen, *W. Germany* .... 31 47 59N 8 50 E
Tutuala, *Indonesia* .... 57 8 25 S 127 15 E
Tutuila, *Amer. Samoa* 68 14 19 S 170 50W
Tutuko Mt., *N.Z.* .... 81 44 35 S 168 1 E
Tututepec, *Mexico* ... 127 16 9N 97 38W
Tutye, *Australia* ..... 74 35 12 S 141 29 E
Tuva A.S.S.R. □, *U.S.S.R.* .... 41 51 30N 95 0 E
Tuvalu ■, *Pac. Oc.* ... 66 8 0 S 178 0 E
Tuvutha, *Fiji* .... 68 17 40 S 178 48W
Tuxpan, *Mexico* 127 20 58N 97 23W
Tuxtla Gutiérrez, *Mexico* 127 16 50N 93 10W
Tuy, *Spain* 22 42 3N 8 39W
Tuy An, *Vietnam* ..... 54 13 17N 109 16 E
Tuy Duc, *Vietnam* .... 55 12 15N 107 27 E
Tuy Hoa, *Vietnam* .... 54 13 5N 109 10 E
Tuy Phong, *Vietnam* .. 55 11 14N 108 43 E
Tuya L., *Canada* 110 59 7N 130 35W
Tuyen Hoa, *Vietnam* .. 54 17 50N 106 10 E
Tuyen Quang, *Vietnam* 54 21 50N 105 10 E
Tuz Gölü, *Turkey* .... 46 38 45N 33 30 E
Ţūz Khurmātū, *Iraq* .. 46 34 56N 44 38 E
Tuzla, *Yugoslavia* .... 33 44 34N 18 41 E
Tuzlov →, *U.S.S.R.* .. 39 47 28N 39 45 E
Tvååker, *Sweden* ..... 11 57 4N 12 25 E
Tvedestrand, *Norway* . 11 58 38N 8 58 E
Tvŭrditsa, *Bulgaria* ... 34 42 42N 25 53 E
Twain, *U.S.A.* 124 40 1N 121 3W
Twain Harte, *U.S.A.* . 124 38 2N 120 14W
Tweed, *Canada* 109 44 29N 77 19W
Tweed →, *U.K.* 14 55 42N 2 10W
Tweed Heads, *Australia* 77 28 10 S 153 31 E
Tweedsmuir Prov. Park, *Canada* 110 53 0N 126 20W
Twello, *Neths.* .... 16 52 14N 6 6 E
Twentynine Palms, *U.S.A.* 125 34 10N 116 4W
Twillingate, *Canada* .. 105 49 42N 54 45W
Twin Bridges, *U.S.A.* . 122 45 33N 112 23W
Twin Falls, *U.S.A.* ... 122 42 30N 114 30W
Twin Valley, *U.S.A.* .. 120 47 18N 96 15W
Twinnge, *Burma* ..... 52 23 10N 96 2 E
Twisp, *U.S.A.* 122 48 21N 120 5W
Twistringen, *W. Germany* .... 30 52 48N 8 38 E
Two Harbors, *U.S.A.* . 120 47 1N 91 40W
Two Hills, *Canada* ... 110 53 43N 111 52W
Two Rivers, *U.S.A.* .. 114 44 10N 87 31W
Two Thumbs Ra., *N.Z.* 81 43 45 S 170 44 E
Twofold B., *Australia* . 75 37 8 S 149 59 E
Tyabb, *Australia* ..... 74 38 16 S 145 11 E
Tyagong, *Australia* ... 76 34 4 S 148 15 E
Tyalgum, *Australia* ... 77 28 22 S 153 10 E
Tychy, *Poland* .... 32 50 9N 18 59 E
Tykocin, *Poland* ..... 32 53 13N 22 46 E
Tyldal, *Norway* ...... 10 62 8N 10 48 E
Tyler, *Minn., U.S.A.* . 120 44 18N 96 8W
Tyler, *Tex., U.S.A.* ... 121 32 18N 95 18W
Týn nad Vltavou, *Czech.* .... 32 49 13N 14 26 E
Tynda, *U.S.S.R.* ..... 41 55 10N 124 43 E
Tyne →, *U.K.* 12 54 58N 1 28W
Tyne & Wear □, *U.K.* 12 54 55N 1 35W
Tynemouth, *U.K.* 12 55 1N 1 27W
Tynong, *Australia* .... 74 38 5 S 145 38 E
Tynset, *Norway* ...... 10 62 17N 10 47 E
Tyre = Sūr, *Lebanon* . 44 33 19N 35 16 E
Tyrendarra, *Australia* . 74 38 12 S 141 50 E
Tyrifjorden, *Norway* .. 10 60 2N 10 8 E
Tyringe, *Sweden* ..... 11 56 9N 13 35 E
Tyringham, *Australia* . 77 30 15 S 152 35 E
Tyristrand, *Norway* ... 10 60 5N 10 5 E
Tyrnyauz, *U.S.S.R.* .... 39 43 21N 42 45 E
Tyrone, *U.S.A.* 116 40 39N 78 10W
Tyrrell →, *Australia* .. 74 35 26 S 142 51 E
Tyrrell, L., *Australia* .. 74 35 20 S 142 50 E
Tyrrell Arm, *Canada* . 111 62 27N 97 30W
Tyrrell L., *Canada* ... 111 63 7N 105 27W
Tyrrhenian Sea, *Europe* 28 40 0N 12 30 E
Tysfjorden, *Norway* .. 8 68 7N 16 25 E
Tystberga, *Sweden* .... 11 58 51N 17 15 E
Tyub Karagan, M., *U.S.S.R.* .... 39 44 40N 50 19 E
Tyuleniy, *U.S.S.R.* ... 39 44 28N 47 30 E
Tyumen, *U.S.S.R.* .... 40 57 11N 65 29 E
Tywi →, *U.K.* 13 51 48N 4 20W
Tywyn, *U.K.* 13 52 36N 4 5W
Tzaneen, *S. Africa* ... 97 23 47 S 30 9 E
Tzermíadhes Neápolis, *Greece* .... 35 35 11N 25 29 E
Tzoumérka, Óros, *Greece* .... 35 39 30N 21 26 E
Tzukong = Zigong, *China* .... 58 29 15N 104 48 E
Tzummarum, *Neths.* .. 16 53 14N 5 32 E

U

U Taphao, *Thailand* .. 54 12 35N 101 0 E
Uacalla Iero, *Somali Rep.* .... 98 1 48N 42 38 E
Uachadi, Sierra, *Venezuela* 135 4 54N 65 18W
Uainambi, *Colombia* .. 134 1 43N 69 51W
Uanda, *Australia* ..... 72 21 37 S 144 55 E
Uanle Uen, *Somali Rep.* .... 98 2 37N 44 54 E
Uarbry, *Australia* ..... 77 32 3 S 149 49 E
Uarsciek, *Somali Rep.* 98 2 28N 45 55 E
Uascen, *Somali Rep.* .. 98 4 11N 43 13 E
Uasin □, *Kenya* ..... 92 0 30N 35 20 E
Uato-Udo, *Indonesia* . 57 9 7 S 125 36 E
Uatumã →, *Brazil* ... 135 2 26 S 57 37W
Uauá, *Brazil* .... 138 9 50 S 39 28W
Uaupés, *Brazil* .... 134 0 8 S 67 5W
Uaupés →, *Brazil* ... 134 0 2N 67 16W
Uaxactún, *Guatemala* . 128 17 25N 89 29W
Ubá, *Brazil* .... 141 21 8 S 43 0W
Ubaitaba, *Brazil* ..... 139 14 18 S 39 20W
Ubangi = Oubangi →, *Zaïre* .... 94 0 30 S 17 50 E
Ubaté, *Colombia* 134 5 19N 73 49W
Ubauro, *Pakistan* ..... 48 28 15N 69 45 E
Ubaye →, *France* .... 21 44 28N 6 18 E
Ube, *Japan* .... 64 33 56N 131 15 E
Ubeda, *Spain* 25 38 3N 3 23W
Uberaba, *Brazil* ...... 139 19 50 S 47 55W
Uberaba, L., *Brazil* ... 137 17 30 S 57 50W
Uberlândia, *Brazil* .... 139 19 0 S 48 20W
Überlingen, *W. Germany* .... 31 47 46N 9 10 E
Ubiaja, *Nigeria* ...... 91 6 41N 6 22 E
Ubolratna Phong, L., *Thailand* .... 54 16 45N 102 30 E
Ubombo, *S. Africa* ... 97 27 31 S 32 4 E
Ubon Ratchathani, *Thailand* .... 54 15 15N 104 50 E
Ubondo, *Zaïre* .... 92 0 55 S 25 42 E
Ubort →, *U.S.S.R.* .. 36 52 6N 28 30 E
Ubrique, *Spain* 23 36 41N 5 27W
Ubuna, *Solomon Is.* .. 68 10 11 S 161 21 E
Ubundu, *Zaïre* .... 92 0 22 S 25 30 E
Ucayali →, *Peru* ..... 136 4 30 S 73 30W
Uccle, *Belgium* ...... 17 50 48N 4 22 E
Uchi Lake, *Canada* ... 111 51 5N 92 35W
Uchiko, *Japan* .... 64 33 33N 132 39 E
Uchiura-Wan, *Japan* .. 63 42 25N 140 40 E
Uchiza, *Peru* .... 136 8 25 S 76 20W
Uchte, *W. Germany* ... 30 52 29N 8 52 E
Uchur →, *U.S.S.R.* .. 41 58 48N 130 35 E
Ucluelet, *Canada* 110 48 57N 125 32W
Ucuriş, *Romania* ..... 34 46 41N 21 58 E

Uda →, *U.S.S.R.* **41** 54 42N 135 14 E
Udaipur, *India* **48** 24 36N 73 44 E
Udaipur Garhi, *Nepal* **49** 27 0N 86 35 E
Udbina, *Yugoslavia* **27** 44 31N 15 47 E
Uddeholm, *Sweden* **10** 60 1N 13 38 E
Uddel, *Neths.* **16** 52 15N 5 48 E
Uddevalla, *Sweden* **11** 58 21N 11 55 E
Uddjaur, *Sweden* **8** 65 25N 21 15 E
Uden, *Neths.* **17** 51 40N 5 37 E
Udgir, *India* **50** 18 25N 77 5 E
Udhampur, *India* **49** 33 0N 75 5 E
Udi, *Nigeria* **91** 6 17N 7 21 E
Údine, *Italy* **27** 46 5N 13 10 E
Udmurt A.S.S.R. □, *U.S.S.R.* **40** 57 30N 52 30 E
Udon Thani, *Thailand* **54** 17 29N 102 46 E
Udumalaippettai, *India* **51** 10 35N 77 15 E
Udupi, *India* **51** 13 25N 74 42 E
Udvoy Balkan, *Bulgaria* **34** 42 50N 26 50 E
Udzungwa Range, *Tanzania* **93** 9 30 S 35 10 E
Ueckermünde, *E. Germany* **30** 53 45N 14 1 E
Ueda, *Japan* **65** 36 24N 138 16 E
Uedineniya, Os., *U.S.S.R.* **144** 78 0N 85 0 E
Uel Scimbirro, *Somali Rep.* **98** 2 23N 44 14 E
Uele →, *Zaïre* **94** 3 45N 24 45 E
Uelen, *U.S.S.R.* **41** 66 10N 170 0W
Uelzen, *W. Germany* **30** 53 0N 10 33 E
Ueno, *Japan* **65** 34 45N 136 8 E
Ufa, *U.S.S.R.* **40** 54 45N 55 55 E
Uffenheim, *W. Germany* **31** 49 32N 10 15 E
Ugab →, *Namibia* **96** 20 55 S 13 30 E
Ugalla →, *Tanzania* **92** 5 8 S 30 42 E
Uganda ■, *Africa* **92** 2 0N 32 0 E
Ugchelen, *Neths.* **16** 52 11N 5 56 E
Ugento, *Italy* **29** 39 55N 18 10 E
Ugep, *Nigeria* **91** 5 53N 8 2 E
Ugi, *Fiji* **68** 10 14 S 161 44 E
Ugie, *S. Africa* **97** 31 10 S 28 13 E
Ugijar, *Spain* **25** 36 58N 3 7W
Ugine, *France* **21** 45 45N 6 25 E
Uglegorsk, *U.S.S.R.* **41** 49 5N 142 2 E
Uglich, *U.S.S.R.* **37** 57 33N 38 20 E
Ugljane, *Yugoslavia* **27** 43 35N 16 46 E
Ugolyak, *U.S.S.R.* **41** 64 33N 120 30 E
Ugra →, *U.S.S.R.* **36** 54 30N 36 7 E
Ugŭrchin, *Bulgaria* **34** 43 6N 24 26 E
Uh →, *Czech.* **33** 48 7N 21 25 E
Uherske Hradiště, *Czech.* **32** 49 4N 17 30 E
Uhrichsville, *U.S.A.* **116** 40 23N 81 22W
Uíge, *Angola* **95** 7 30 S 14 40 E
Uige □, *Angola* **95** 7 0 S 16 0 E
Uiha, *Tonga* **68** 19 54 S 174 25W
Uijŏngbu, *S. Korea* **61** 37 48N 127 0 E
Ŭiju, *N. Korea* **61** 40 15N 124 35 E
Uinta Mts., *U.S.A.* **122** 40 45N 110 30W
Uitenhage, *S. Africa* **96** 33 40 S 25 28 E
Uitgeest, *Neths.* **16** 52 32N 4 43 E
Uithoorn, *Neths.* **16** 52 14N 4 50 E
Uithuizen, *Neths.* **16** 53 24N 6 41 E
Uitkerke, *Belgium* **17** 51 18N 3 9 E
Újfehértó, *Hungary* **33** 47 49N 21 41 E
Ujhani, *India* **49** 28 0N 79 6 E
Uji, *Japan* **65** 34 53N 135 48 E
Ujjain, *India* **48** 23 9N 75 43 E
Újpest, *Hungary* **33** 47 32N 19 6 E
Újszász, *Hungary* **33** 47 19N 20 7 E
Ujung Pandang, *Indonesia* **57** 5 10 S 119 20 E
Uka, *U.S.S.R.* **41** 57 50N 162 0 E
Ukara I., *Tanzania* **92** 1 50 S 33 0 E
Ukerewe □, *Tanzania* **92** 2 0 S 32 30 E
Ukerewe I., *Tanzania* **92** 2 0 S 33 0 E
Ukholovo, *U.S.S.R.* **37** 53 47N 40 30 E
Ukhrul, *India* **52** 25 10N 94 25 E
Ukhta, *U.S.S.R.* **40** 63 55N 54 0 E
Uki, *Australia* **77** 28 26 S 153 20 E
Ukiah, *U.S.A.* **124** 39 10N 123 9W
Ukki Fort, *India* **49** 33 28N 76 54 E
Ukmerge, *U.S.S.R.* **36** 55 15N 24 45 E
Ukrainian S.S.R. □, *U.S.S.R.* **38** 49 0N 32 0 E
Uku, *Angola* **95** 11 24 S 14 22 E
Ukwi, *Botswana* **96** 23 29 S 20 30 E
Ulaanbaatar, *Mongolia* **62** 47 55N 106 53 E
Ulaangom, *Mongolia* **62** 50 0N 92 10 E
Ulamambri, *Australia* **77** 31 19 S 149 23 E
Ulamba, *Zaïre* **93** 9 3 S 23 38 E
Ulan, *Australia* **77** 32 16 S 149 46 E
Ulan Bator = Ulaanbaatar, *Mongolia* **62** 47 55N 106 53 E
Ulan Ude, *U.S.S.R.* **41** 51 45N 107 40 E
Ulanga □, *Tanzania* **93** 8 40 S 36 50 E
Ulanów, *Poland* **32** 50 30N 22 16 E
Ulawa, *Solomon Is.* **68** 9 46 S 161 57 E
Ulaya, *Morogoro, Tanzania* **92** 7 3 S 36 55 E
Ulaya, *Tabora, Tanzania* **92** 4 25 S 33 30 E
Ulcinj, *Yugoslavia* **35** 41 58N 19 10 E
Ulco, *S. Africa* **96** 28 21 S 24 15 E
Ulfborg, *Denmark* **11** 56 16N 8 20 E
Ulft, *Neths.* **16** 51 53N 6 23 E
Ulhasnagar, *India* **50** 19 15N 73 10 E
Ulinda, *Australia* **77** 31 35 S 149 30 E
Uljma, *Yugoslavia* **33** 45 2N 21 10 E
Ulla →, *Spain* **22** 42 39N 8 44W
Ulladulla, *Australia* **76** 35 21 S 150 29 E
Ullånger, *Sweden* **10** 62 58N 18 10 E
Ullapool, *U.K.* **14** 57 54N 5 10W
Ullared, *Sweden* **11** 57 8N 12 42 E
Ulldecona, *Spain* **24** 40 36N 0 20 E
Ullswater, *U.K.* **12** 54 35N 2 52W
Ullung-do, *S. Korea* **61** 37 30N 130 30 E
Ulm, *W. Germany* **31** 48 23N 10 0 E
Ulmarra, *Australia* **77** 29 37 S 153 4 E
Ulmeni, *Romania* **34** 45 4N 26 40 E
Ulong, *Australia* **77** 30 14 S 152 54 E
Ulonguè, *Mozam.* **93** 14 37 S 34 19 E
Ulricehamn, *Sweden* **11** 57 46N 13 26 E
Ulrum, *Neths.* **16** 53 22N 6 20 E
Ulsberg, *Norway* **10** 62 45N 9 59 E
Ulster □, *U.K.* **15** 54 35N 6 30W
Ultima, *Australia* **74** 35 30 S 143 18 E
Ulubaria, *India* **49** 22 31N 88 4 E
Uluguru Mts., *Tanzania* **92** 7 15 S 37 40 E
Ulungur →, *China* **62** 47 1N 87 24 E
Ulutau, *U.S.S.R.* **40** 48 39N 67 1 E
Ulvenhout, *Neths.* **17** 51 33N 4 48 E
Ulverston, *U.K.* **12** 54 13N 3 7W
Ulverstone, *Australia* **72** 41 11 S 146 11 E
Ulya, *U.S.S.R.* **41** 59 10N 142 0 E
Ulyanovsk, *U.S.S.R.* **37** 54 20N 48 25 E
Ulyasutay, *Mongolia* **62** 47 56N 97 28 E
Ulysses, *U.S.A.* **121** 37 39N 101 25W
Umag, *Yugoslavia* **27** 45 26N 13 31 E
Umala, *Bolivia* **136** 17 25 S 68 5W
Uman, *U.S.S.R.* **38** 48 40N 30 12 E
Umarkhed, *India* **50** 19 37N 77 46 E
Umatac, *Guam* **68** 13 18N 144 39 E
Umatilla, *U.S.A.* **122** 45 58N 119 17W
Umba, *U.S.S.R.* **40** 66 50N 34 20 E
Umbertide, *Italy* **27** 43 18N 12 20 E
Umboi I., *Papua N. G.* **69** 5 40 S 148 0 E
Umbrella Mts., *N.Z.* **81** 45 35 S 169 5 E
Umbria □, *Italy* **27** 42 53N 12 30 E
Ume älv →, *Sweden* **8** 63 45N 20 20 E
Umeå, *Sweden* **8** 63 45N 20 20 E
Umera, *Indonesia* **57** 0 12 S 129 37 E
Umfuli →, *Zimb.* **93** 17 30 S 29 23 E
Umgusa, *Zimb.* **93** 19 29 S 27 52 E
Umi, *Japan* **64** 33 34N 130 30 E
Umka, *Yugoslavia* **33** 44 40N 20 19 E
Umkomaas, *S. Africa* **97** 30 13 S 30 48 E
Umm al Arānib, *Libya* **86** 26 10N 14 43 E
Umm al Qaywayn, *U.A.E.* **47** 25 30N 55 35 E
Umm Arda, *Sudan* **89** 15 17N 32 31 E
Umm Bel, *Sudan* **89** 13 35N 28 0 E
Umm Dubban, *Sudan* **89** 15 23N 32 52 E
Umm el Fahm, *Israel* **44** 32 31N 35 9 E
Umm Koweika, *Sudan* **89** 13 10N 32 16 E
Umm Lajj, *Si. Arabia* **46** 25 0N 37 23 E
Umm Merwa, *Sudan* **88** 18 4N 32 30 E
Umm Qays, *Jordan* **44** 32 40N 35 41 E
Umm Ruwaba, *Sudan* **89** 12 50N 31 20 E
Umm Sidr, *Sudan* **89** 14 29N 25 10 E
Ummanz, *E. Germany* **30** 54 29N 13 9 E
Umnak, *U.S.A.* **102** 53 20N 168 20W
Umniati →, *Zimb.* **93** 16 49 S 28 45 E
Umpqua →, *U.S.A.* **122** 43 42N 124 3W
Umpulo, *Angola* **95** 12 38 S 17 42 E
Umred, *India* **50** 20 51N 79 18 E
Umreth, *India* **48** 22 41N 73 4 E
Umshandige Dam, *Zimb.* **93** 20 10 S 30 40 E
Umtata, *S. Africa* **97** 31 36 S 28 49 E
Umuahia, *Nigeria* **91** 5 33N 7 29 E
Umuarama, *Brazil* **141** 23 45 S 53 20W
Umvukwe Ra., *Zimb.* **93** 16 45 S 30 45 E
Umzimvubu = Port St. Johns, *S. Africa* **97** 31 38 S 29 33 E
Umzingwane →, *Zimb.* **93** 22 12 S 29 56 E
Umzinto, *S. Africa* **97** 30 15 S 30 45 E
Una, *India* **48** 20 46N 71 8 E
Una →, *Yugoslavia* **27** 45 16N 16 55 E
Unac →, *Yugoslavia* **27** 44 30N 16 9 E
Unadilla, *U.S.A.* **117** 42 20N 75 17W
Unalaska, *U.S.A.* **102** 53 40N 166 40W
Unanderra, *Australia* **76** 34 27 S 150 49 E
Uncastillo, *Spain* **24** 42 21N 1 8W
Uncía, *Bolivia* **136** 18 25 S 66 40W
Uncompahgre Pk., *U.S.A.* **123** 38 5N 107 32W
Unden, *Sweden* **11** 58 45N 14 25 E
Undera, *Australia* **74** 36 18 S 145 13 E
Underberg, *S. Africa* **97** 29 50 S 29 22 E
Underbool, *Australia* **74** 35 10 S 141 51 E
Undersaker, *Sweden* **10** 63 19N 13 21 E
Undersvik, *Sweden* **10** 61 36N 16 20 E
Undu Pt., *Fiji* **68** 16 8 S 179 57W
Unecha, *U.S.S.R.* **36** 52 50N 32 37 E
Uneiuxi →, *Brazil* **134** 0 37 S 65 34W
Ungarie, *Australia* **75** 33 38 S 146 56 E
Ungarra, *Australia* **73** 34 12 S 136 2 E
Ungava B., *Canada* **103** 59 30N 67 30W
Ungava Pen., *Canada* **103** 60 0N 74 0W
Ungeny, *U.S.S.R.* **38** 47 11N 27 51 E
Unggi, *N. Korea* **61** 42 16N 130 28 E
Ungwatiri, *Sudan* **89** 16 52N 36 10 E
Uni, *U.S.S.R.* **37** 56 44N 51 47 E
União da Vitória, *Brazil* **141** 26 13 S 51 5W
União dos Palmares, *Brazil* **138** 9 10 S 36 2W
Unije, *Yugoslavia* **27** 44 40N 14 15 E
Unimak, *U.S.A.* **102** 55 0N 164 0W
Unimak Pass., *U.S.A.* **102** 53 30N 165 15W
Unini →, *Brazil* **135** 1 41 S 61 31W
Union, *Miss., U.S.A.* **121** 32 34N 89 14W
Union, *Mo., U.S.A.* **118** 38 25N 91 0W
Union, *S.C., U.S.A.* **115** 34 43N 81 39W
Unión, La, *Chile* **142** 40 10 S 73 0W
Unión, La, *Colombia* **134** 1 35N 77 5W
Unión, La, *El Salv.* **128** 13 20N 87 50W
Unión, La, *Mexico* **126** 17 58N 101 49W
Unión, La, *Peru* **136** 9 43 S 76 45W
Unión, La, *Spain* **25** 37 38N 0 53W
Union, Mt., *U.S.A.* **123** 34 34N 112 21W
Union City, *Calif., U.S.A.* **124** 37 36N 122 1W
Union City, *N.J., U.S.A.* **117** 40 47N 74 5W
Union City, *Pa., U.S.A.* **116** 41 53N 79 50W
Union City, *Tenn., U.S.A.* **121** 36 25N 89 0W
Union Gap, *U.S.A.* **122** 46 38N 120 29W
Union Grove, *U.S.A.* **119** 42 41N 88 3W
Union of Soviet Socialist Republics ■, *Eurasia* **41** 60 0N 100 0 E
Union Springs, *U.S.A.* **115** 32 9N 85 44W
Union Star, *U.S.A.* **118** 39 59N 94 36W
Uniondale, *S. Africa* **96** 33 39 S 23 7 E
Uniontown, *Ky., U.S.A.* **119** 37 47N 87 56W
Uniontown, *Pa., U.S.A.* **114** 39 54N 79 45W
Unionville, *U.S.A.* **118** 40 29N 93 1W
United Arab Emirates ■, *Asia* **47** 23 50N 54 0 E
United Kingdom ■, *Europe* **7** 55 0N 3 0W
United States of America ■, *N. Amer.* **113** 37 0N 96 0W
United States Trust Terr. of the Pacific Is. □, *Pac. Oc.* **66** 10 0N 160 0 E
Unity, *Canada* **111** 52 30N 109 5W
Universales, Mtes., *Spain* **24** 40 18N 1 33W
University City, *U.S.A.* **118** 38 40N 90 20W
Unjha, *India* **48** 23 46N 72 24 E
Unnao, *India* **49** 26 35N 80 30 E
Uno, Ilha, *Guinea-Biss.* **90** 11 15N 16 13W
Unst, *U.K.* **14** 60 50N 0 55W
Unstrut →, *E. Germany* **30** 51 10N 11 48 E
Unuk →, *Canada* **110** 56 5N 131 3W
Unumgar, *Australia* **77** 28 25 S 152 47 E
Ünye, *Turkey* **38** 41 5N 37 15 E
Unzen-Dake, *Japan* **64** 32 45N 130 17 E
Unzha, *U.S.S.R.* **37** 58 0N 44 0 E
Unzha →, *U.S.S.R.* **37** 57 30N 43 40 E
Uozu, *Japan* **65** 36 48N 137 24 E
Upa →, *Czech.* **32** 50 35N 16 15 E
Upata, *Venezuela* **135** 8 1N 62 24W
Upemba, L., *Zaïre* **93** 8 30 S 26 20 E
Upernavik, *Greenland* **144** 72 49N 56 20W
Upington, *S. Africa* **96** 28 25 S 21 15 E
Upleta, *India* **48** 21 46N 70 16 E
Upolu, *W. Samoa* **68** 13 58 S 172 0W
Upper Alkali Lake, *U.S.A.* **122** 41 47N 120 8W
Upper Arlington, *U.S.A.* **119** 40 0N 83 4W
Upper Arrow L., *Canada* **110** 50 30N 117 50W
Upper Foster L., *Canada* **111** 56 47N 105 20W
Upper Horton, *Australia* **77** 30 6 S 150 26 E
Upper Hutt, *N.Z.* **80** 41 8 S 175 5 E
Upper Juba □, *Somali Rep.* **98** 3 0N 43 0 E
Upper Klamath L., *U.S.A.* **122** 42 16N 121 55W
Upper L. Erne, *U.K.* **15** 54 14N 7 22W
Upper Lake, *U.S.A.* **124** 39 10N 122 55W
Upper Manilla, *Australia* **77** 30 38 S 150 40 E
Upper Musquodoboit, *Canada* **105** 45 10N 62 58W
Upper Red L., *U.S.A.* **120** 48 0N 95 0W
Upper Rouchel, *Australia* **77** 32 6 S 151 5 E
Upper Sandusky, *U.S.A.* **119** 40 50N 83 17W
Upper Sheikh, *Somali Rep.* **98** 9 56N 45 13 E
Upper Taimyr →, *U.S.S.R.* **41** 74 15N 99 48 E
Upper Volta = Burkina Faso ■, *Africa* **90** 12 0N 1 0W
Upphärad, *Sweden* **11** 58 9N 12 19 E
Uppsala, *Sweden* **10** 59 53N 17 38 E
Uppsala län □, *Sweden* **10** 60 0N 17 30 E
Upshi, *India* **49** 33 48N 77 52 E
Upstart, C., *Australia* **72** 19 41 S 147 45 E
Upton, *Canada* **107** 45 39N 72 41W
Upton, *U.S.A.* **120** 44 8N 104 35W
Ur, *Iraq* **46** 30 55N 46 25 E
Urabá, G. de, *Colombia* **134** 8 25N 76 53W
Uracara, *Brazil* **136** 2 20 S 57 50W
Urach, *W. Germany* **31** 48 29N 9 25 E
Urad Qianqi, *China* **60** 40 40N 108 30 E
Uraga-Suidō, *Japan* **65** 35 13N 139 45 E
Urakawa, *Japan* **63** 42 9N 142 47 E
Ural →, *U.S.S.R.* **40** 47 0N 51 48 E
Ural, Mt., *Australia* **73** 33 21 S 146 12 E
Ural Mts. = Uralskie Gory, *U.S.S.R.* **40** 60 0N 59 0 E
Uralla, *Australia* **77** 30 37 S 151 29 E
Uralsk, *U.S.S.R.* **40** 51 20N 51 20 E
Uralskie Gory, *U.S.S.R.* **40** 60 0N 59 0 E
Urambo, *Tanzania* **92** 5 4 S 32 0 E
Urambo □, *Tanzania* **92** 5 0 S 32 0 E
Urandangi, *Australia* **72** 21 32 S 138 14 E
Uranium City, *Canada* **111** 59 34N 108 37W
Uranquinty, *Australia* **76** 35 10 S 147 12 E
Uraricaá →, *Brazil* **135** 3 20N 61 56W
Uraricuera →, *Brazil* **135** 3 2N 60 30W
Uravakonda, *India* **51** 14 57N 77 12 E
Urawa, *Japan* **65** 35 50N 139 40 E
Uray, *U.S.S.R.* **40** 60 5N 65 15 E
Urbana, *Ill., U.S.A.* **119** 40 7N 88 12W
Urbana, *Mo., U.S.A.* **118** 37 51N 93 10W
Urbana, *Ohio, U.S.A.* **119** 40 9N 83 44W
Urbana, La, *Venezuela* **134** 7 8N 66 56W
Urbandale, *U.S.A.* **118** 41 38N 93 43W
Urbánia, *Italy* **27** 43 40N 12 31 E
Urbano Santos, *Brazil* **138** 3 12 S 43 23W
Urbel →, *Spain* **24** 42 21N 3 40W
Urbenville, *Australia* **77** 28 29 S 152 34 E
Urbino, *Italy* **27** 43 43N 12 38 E
Urbión, Picos de, *Spain* **24** 42 1N 2 52W
Urcos, *Peru* **136** 13 40 S 71 38W
Urda, *Spain* **23** 39 25N 3 43W
Urda, *U.S.S.R.* **39** 48 52N 47 23 E
Urdinarrain, *Argentina* **140** 32 37 S 58 52W
Urdos, *France* **20** 42 51N 0 35W
Urdzhar, *U.S.S.R.* **40** 47 5N 81 38 E
Ure →, *U.K.* **12** 54 20N 1 25W
Uren, *U.S.S.R.* **37** 57 35N 45 55 E
Urengoy, *U.S.S.R.* **40** 65 58N 28 25 E
Ureparapara, *Vanuatu* **68** 13 32 S 167 20 E
Ures, *Mexico* **126** 29 30N 110 30W
Ureshino, *Japan* **64** 33 6N 129 59 E
Urfa, *Turkey* **46** 37 12N 38 50 E
Urfahr, *Austria* **33** 48 19N 14 17 E
Urgench, *U.S.S.R.* **40** 41 40N 60 41 E
Uri, *India* **49** 34 8N 74 2 E
Uri □, *Switz.* **31** 46 43N 8 35 E
Uribante →, *Venezuela* **134** 7 25N 71 50W
Uribe, *Colombia* **134** 3 13N 74 24W
Uribia, *Colombia* **134** 11 43N 72 16W
Urim, *Israel* **44** 31 18N 34 32 E
Uriondo, *Bolivia* **140** 21 41 S 64 41W
Urique, *Mexico* **126** 27 13N 107 55W
Urique →, *Mexico* **126** 26 29N 107 58W
Urk, *Neths.* **16** 52 39N 5 36 E
Urla, *Turkey* **46** 38 20N 26 47 E
Urlati, *Romania* **34** 44 59N 26 15 E
Urmia = Orūmīyeh, *Iran* **46** 37 40N 45 0 E
Urmia, L. = Orūmīyeh, Daryācheh-ye, *Iran* **46** 37 50N 45 30 E
Uroševac, *Yugoslavia* **33** 42 23N 21 10 E
Urrao, *Colombia* **134** 6 20N 76 11W
Urshult, *Sweden* **11** 56 31N 14 50 E
Ursus, *Poland* **32** 52 12N 20 53 E
Uruaçu, *Brazil* **139** 14 30 S 49 10W
Uruana, *Brazil* **139** 15 30 S 49 41W
Uruapan, *Mexico* **126** 19 30N 102 0W
Uruará →, *Brazil* **135** 2 6 S 53 38W
Urubamba, *Peru* **136** 13 20 S 72 10W
Urubamba →, *Peru* **136** 10 43 S 73 48W
Urubaxi →, *Brazil* **135** 0 31 S 64 50W
Urubu →, *Brazil* **135** 2 55 S 58 25W
Uruçara, *Brazil* **135** 2 32 S 57 45W
Uruçuí, *Brazil* **138** 7 20 S 44 28W
Uruçuí, Serra do, *Brazil* **138** 9 0 S 44 45W
Uruçuí Prêto →, *Brazil* **138** 7 20 S 44 38W
Urucuia →, *Brazil* **139** 16 8 S 45 5W
Urucurituba, *Brazil* **135** 2 41 S 57 40W
Uruguai →, *Brazil* **141** 26 0 S 53 30W
Uruguaiana, *Brazil* **140** 29 50 S 57 0W
Uruguay ■, *S. Amer.* **140** 32 30 S 56 30W
Uruguay →, *S. Amer.* **140** 34 12 S 58 18W
Urumchi = Ürümqi, *China* **62** 43 45N 87 45 E
Ürümqi, *China* **62** 43 45N 87 45 E
Urunga, *Australia* **77** 30 31 S 153 1 E
Urup →, *U.S.S.R.* **39** 46 0N 41 10 E
Urup, Os., *U.S.S.R.* **41** 46 0N 151 0 E
Urutaí, *Brazil* **139** 17 28 S 48 12W
Uryung-Khaya, *U.S.S.R.* **41** 72 48N 113 23 E
Uryupinsk, *U.S.S.R.* **37** 50 45N 41 58 E
Urzhum, *U.S.S.R.* **37** 57 10N 49 56 E
Urziceni, *Romania* **34** 44 40N 26 42 E
Usa, *Japan* **64** 33 31N 131 21 E
Uşak, *Turkey* **46** 38 43N 29 28 E
Usakos, *Namibia* **96** 21 54 S 15 31 E
Usborne, Mt., *Falk. Is.* **142** 51 42 S 58 50W
Ušće, *Yugoslavia* **33** 43 30N 20 39 E
Usedom, *E. Germany* **30** 53 50N 13 55 E
'Usfān, *Si. Arabia* **88** 21 58N 39 27 E
Ush-Tobe, *U.S.S.R.* **40** 45 16N 78 0 E
Ushakova, O., *U.S.S.R.* **144** 82 0N 80 0 E
Ushant = Ouessant, I. d', *France* **18** 48 28N 5 6W
Ushashi, *Tanzania* **92** 1 59 S 33 57 E
Ushat, *Sudan* **89** 7 59N 29 28 E
Ushibuka, *Japan* **64** 32 11N 130 1 E
Ushuaia, *Argentina* **142** 54 50 S 68 23W
Ushumun, *U.S.S.R.* **41** 52 47N 126 32 E
Usk →, *U.K.* **13** 51 37N 2 56W
Üsküdar, *Turkey* **46** 41 0N 29 5 E

Uslar, W. Germany 30 51 39N 9 39 E
Usman, U.S.S.R. 37 52 5N 39 48 E
Usoke, Tanzania 92 5 8 S 32 24 E
Usolye Sibirskoye, U.S.S.R. 41 52 48N 103 40 E
Usoro, Nigeria 91 5 33N 6 11 E
Uspallata, P. de, Argentina 140 32 37 S 69 22W
Uspenskiy, U.S.S.R. 40 48 41N 72 43 E
Usquert, Neths. 16 53 24N 6 36 E
Ussel, France 20 45 32N 2 18 E
Ussuriysk, U.S.S.R. 41 43 48N 131 59 E
Ust-Aldan = Batamay, U.S.S.R. 41 63 30N 129 15 E
Ust Amginskoye = Khandyga, U.S.S.R. 41 62 42N 135 35 E
Ust-Bolsheretsk, U.S.S.R. 41 52 50N 156 15 E
Ust Buzulukskaya, U.S.S.R. 37 50 8N 42 11 E
Ust chaun, U.S.S.R. 41 68 47N 170 30 E
Ust-Donetskiy, U.S.S.R. 39 47 35N 40 55 E
Ust'-Ilga, U.S.S.R. 41 55 5N 104 55 E
Ust Ilimpeya = Yukti, U.S.S.R. 41 63 26N 105 42 E
Ust-Ilimsk, U.S.S.R. 41 58 3N 102 39 E
Ust Ishim, U.S.S.R. 40 57 45N 71 10 E
Ust-Kamchatsk, U.S.S.R. 41 56 10N 162 28 E
Ust-Kamenogorsk, U.S.S.R. 40 50 0N 82 36 E
Ust-Karenga, U.S.S.R. 41 54 25N 116 30 E
Ust Khayryuzova, U.S.S.R. 41 57 15N 156 45 E
Ust-Kut, U.S.S.R. 41 56 50N 105 42 E
Ust Kuyga, U.S.S.R. 41 70 1N 135 43 E
Ust-Labinsk, U.S.S.R. 39 45 15N 39 41 E
Ust Luga, U.S.S.R. 36 59 35N 28 20 E
Ust Maya, U.S.S.R. 41 60 30N 134 28 E
Ust-Mil, U.S.S.R. 41 59 40N 133 11 E
Ust-Nera, U.S.S.R. 41 64 35N 143 15 E
Ust-Nyukzha, U.S.S.R. 41 56 34N 121 37 E
Ust Olenek, U.S.S.R. 41 73 0N 119 48 E
Ust-Omchug, U.S.S.R. 41 61 9N 149 38 E
Ust Port, U.S.S.R. 40 69 40N 84 26 E
Ust Tsilma, U.S.S.R. 40 65 25N 52 0 E
Ust-Tungir, U.S.S.R. 41 55 25N 120 36 E
Ust Urt = Ustyurt, Plato, U.S.S.R. 40 44 0N 55 0 E
Ust Vorkuta, U.S.S.R. 40 67 24N 64 0 E
Ustaoset, Norway 10 60 30N 8 2 E
Ustaritz, France 20 43 24N 1 27W
Uste, U.S.S.R. 37 59 35N 39 40 E
Ústí nad Labem, Czech. 32 50 41N 14 3 E
Ústí nad Orlicí, Czech. 32 49 58N 16 24 E
Ustica, Italy 28 38 42N 13 10 E
Ustinov, U.S.S.R. 40 56 51N 53 14 E
Ustka, Poland 32 54 35N 16 55 E
Ustrzyki Dolne, Poland 32 49 27N 22 40 E
Ustye, U.S.S.R. 41 57 46N 94 37 E
Ustyurt, Plato, U.S.S.R. 40 44 0N 55 0 E
Ustyuzhna, U.S.S.R. 37 58 50N 36 32 E
Usu, China 62 44 27N 84 40 E
Usuki, Japan 64 33 8N 131 49 E
Usulután, El Salv. 128 13 25N 88 28W
Usumacinta →, Mexico 127 17 0N 91 0W
Usumbura = Bujumbura, Burundi 92 3 16 S 29 18 E
Usure, Tanzania 92 4 40 S 34 22 E
Uta, Indonesia 57 4 33 S 136 0 E
'Uta Vava'u, Tonga 68 18 36 S 174 0W
Utah □, U.S.A. 122 39 30N 111 30W
Utah, L., U.S.A. 122 40 10N 111 58W
Ute Cr. →, U.S.A. 121 35 21N 103 45W
Utena, U.S.S.R. 36 55 27N 25 40 E
Ütersen, W. Germany 30 53 40N 9 40 E
Utete, Tanzania 92 8 0 S 38 45 E
Uthai Thani, Thailand 54 15 22N 100 3 E
Uthal, Pakistan 48 25 44N 66 40 E
Utiariti, Brazil 137 13 0 S 58 10W
Utica, N.Y., U.S.A. 117 43 5N 75 18W
Utica, Ohio, U.S.A. 116 40 13N 82 26W
Utiel, Spain 24 39 37N 1 11W
Utik L., Canada 111 55 15N 96 0W
Utikuma L., Canada 110 55 50N 115 30W
Utinga, Brazil 139 12 6 S 41 5W
Uto, Japan 64 32 41N 130 40 E
Utrecht, Neths. 16 52 5N 5 8 E
Utrecht, S. Africa 97 27 38 S 30 20 E
Utrecht □, Neths. 16 52 6N 5 7 E
Utrera, Spain 23 37 12N 5 48W
Utsjoki, Finland 8 69 51N 26 59 E
Utsunomiya, Japan 65 36 30N 139 50 E
Uttar Pradesh □, India 49 27 0N 80 0 E
Uttaradit, Thailand 54 17 36N 100 5 E
Uttoxeter, U.K. 12 52 53N 1 50W
Ütze, W. Germany 30 52 28N 10 11 E
Uudenmaan lääni □, Finland 9 60 25N 25 0 E
Uusikaarlepyy, Finland 8 63 32N 22 31 E
Uusikaupunki, Finland 9 60 47N 21 25 E
Uva, U.S.S.R. 37 56 59N 52 13 E
Uvá →, Colombia 134 3 41N 70 3W
Uvalde, U.S.A. 121 29 15N 99 48W
Uvarovo, U.S.S.R. 37 51 59N 42 14 E
Uvat, U.S.S.R. 40 59 5N 68 50 E
Uvéa, I., Vanuatu 68 20 30 S 166 35 E
Uvinza, Tanzania 92 5 5 S 30 24 E
Uvira, Zaïre 92 3 22 S 29 3 E
Uvs Nuur, Mongolia 62 50 20N 92 30 E
Uwa, Japan 64 33 22N 132 31 E
Uwajima, Japan 64 33 10N 132 35 E
Uweinat, Jebel, Sudan 88 21 54N 24 58 E
Uxbridge, Canada 108 44 6N 79 7W
Uxin Qi, China 60 38 50N 109 5 E
Uxmal, Mexico 127 20 22N 89 46W
Uyandi, U.S.S.R. 41 69 19N 141 0 E
Uyo, Nigeria 91 5 1N 7 53 E
Uyu →, Burma 52 24 51N 94 57 E
Uyuni, Bolivia 136 20 28 S 66 47W
Uzbek S.S.R. □, U.S.S.R. 40 41 30N 65 0 E
Uzen, Bol. →, U.S.S.R. 37 50 0N 49 30 E
Uzen, Mal. →, U.S.S.R. 37 50 0N 48 30 E
Uzerche, France 20 45 25N 1 34 E
Uzès, France 21 44 1N 4 26 E
Uzh →, U.S.S.R. 36 51 15N 30 12 E
Uzhgorod, U.S.S.R. 36 48 36N 22 18 E
Uzlovaya, U.S.S.R. 37 54 0N 38 5 E
Uzunköprü, Turkey 35 41 16N 26 43 E

V

Vaal →, S. Africa 96 29 4 S 23 38 E
Vaal Dam, S. Africa 97 27 0 S 28 14 E
Vaals, Neths. 17 50 46N 6 1 E
Vaalwater, S. Africa 97 24 15 S 28 8 E
Vaasa, Finland 8 63 6N 21 38 E
Vaasan lääni □, Finland 8 63 2N 22 50 E
Vaassen, Neths. 16 52 17N 5 58 E
Vabre, France 20 43 42N 2 24 E
Vác, Hungary 33 47 49N 19 10 E
Vacaria, Brazil 141 28 31 S 50 52W
Vacaville, U.S.A. 124 38 21N 122 0W
Vaccarès, Étang de, France 21 43 32N 4 34 E
Vach →, U.S.S.R. 40 60 45N 76 45 E
Vache, I.-à-, Haiti 129 18 2N 73 35W
Väddö, Sweden 10 59 55N 18 50 E
Vadnagar, India 48 23 47N 72 40 E
Vado Ligure, Italy 26 44 16N 8 26 E
Vadodara, India 48 22 20N 73 10 E
Vadsø, Norway 8 70 3N 29 50 E
Vadstena, Sweden 11 58 28N 14 54 E
Vaduz, Liech. 31 47 8N 9 31 E
Værøy, Norway 8 67 40N 12 40 E
Vagnhärad, Sweden 10 58 57N 17 33 E
Vagos, Portugal 22 40 33N 8 42W
Váh →, Czech. 33 47 55N 18 0 E
Vahsel B., Antarctica 143 75 0 S 35 0W
Vaigach, U.S.S.R. 40 70 10N 59 0 E
Vaigai →, India 51 9 15N 79 10 E
Vaiges, France 18 48 2N 0 30W
Vaihingen, W. Germany 31 48 55N 8 58 E
Vaijapur, India 50 19 58N 74 45 E
Vaikam, India 51 9 45N 76 25 E
Vailly-sur-Aisne, France 19 49 24N 3 31 E
Vaippar →, India 51 9 0N 78 25 E
Vaison-la-Romaine, France 21 44 14N 5 4 E
Vaitogi, Amer. Samoa 68 14 21 S 170 44W
Vajpur, India 50 21 24N 73 17 E
Val-Alain, Canada 107 46 24N 71 45W
Val-Barrette, Canada 106 46 30N 75 21W
Val Caron, Canada 108 46 37N 81 1W
Val-d'Ajol, Le, France 19 47 55N 6 30 E
Val-de-Marne □, France 19 48 45N 2 28 E
Val-des-Bois, Canada 106 45 54N 75 35W
Val-d'Oise □, France 19 49 5N 2 10 E
Val d'Or, Canada 106 48 7N 77 47W
Val Marie, Canada 111 49 15N 107 45W
Valadares, Portugal 22 41 5N 8 38W
Valahia, Romania 34 44 35N 25 0 E
Valais □, Switz. 31 46 12N 7 45 E
Valandovo, Yugoslavia 35 41 19N 22 34 E
Valcheta, Argentina 142 40 40 S 66 8W
Valcourt, Canada 107 45 29N 72 18W
Valdagno, Italy 27 45 38N 11 18 E
Valday, U.S.S.R. 36 57 58N 33 9 E
Valdayskaya Vozvyshennost, U.S.S.R. 36 57 0N 33 30 E
Valdeazogues →, Spain 23 38 45N 4 55W
Valdemarsvik, Sweden 11 58 14N 16 40 E
Valdepeñas, Ciudad Real, Spain 23 38 43N 3 25W
Valdepeñas, Jaén, Spain 23 37 33N 3 47W
Valderaduey →, Spain 22 41 31N 5 42W
Valderrobres, Spain 24 40 53N 0 9 E
Valdés, Pen., Argentina 142 42 30 S 63 45W
Valdez, Ecuador 134 1 15N 79 0W
Valdez, U.S.A. 102 61 14N 146 17W
Valdivia, Chile 142 39 50 S 73 14W
Valdivia, Colombia 134 7 11N 75 27W
Valdivia □, Chile 142 40 0 S 73 0W
Valdobbiádene, Italy 27 45 53N 12 0 E
Valdosta, U.S.A. 115 30 50N 83 20W
Valdoviño, Spain 22 43 36N 8 8W
Valdres, Norway 10 60 55N 9 28 E
Vale, U.S.A. 122 44 0N 117 15W
Vale, U.S.S.R. 39 41 30N 42 58 E
Valea lui Mihai, Romania 34 47 32N 22 11 E
Valença, Brazil 139 13 20 S 39 5W
Valença, Portugal 22 42 1N 8 34W
Valença do Piauí, Brazil 138 6 20 S 41 45W
Valençay, France 19 47 9N 1 34 E
Valence, Drôme, France 21 44 57N 4 54 E
Valence, Tarn-et-Garonne, France 20 44 6N 0 53 E
Valencia, Spain 25 39 27N 0 23W
Valencia, Venezuela 134 10 11N 68 0W
Valencia □, Spain 25 39 20N 0 40W
Valencia, Albufera de, Spain 25 39 20N 0 27W
Valencia, G. de, Spain 25 39 30N 0 20 E
Valencia de Alcántara, Spain 23 39 25N 7 14W
Valencia de Don Juan, Spain 22 42 17N 5 31W
Valencia del Ventoso, Spain 23 38 15N 6 29W
Valenciennes, France 19 50 20N 3 34 E
Valensole, France 21 43 50N 5 59 E
Valentia Harbour, Ireland 15 51 56N 10 17W
Valentia I., Ireland 15 51 54N 10 22W
Valentim, Sa. do, Brazil 138 6 0 S 43 30W
Valentine, Nebr., U.S.A. 120 42 50N 100 35W
Valentine, Tex., U.S.A. 121 30 36N 104 28W
Valenza, Italy 26 45 2N 8 39 E
Valera, Venezuela 134 9 19N 70 37W
Valga, U.S.S.R. 36 57 44N 26 0 E
Valguarnera Caropepe, Italy 29 37 30N 14 22 E
Valier, U.S.A. 122 48 25N 112 9W
Valinco, G. de, France 21 41 40N 8 52 E
Valjevo, Yugoslavia 33 44 18N 19 53 E
Valkeakoski, Finland 9 61 16N 24 2 E
Valkenburg, Neths. 17 50 52N 5 50 E
Valkenswaard, Neths. 17 51 21N 5 29 E
Vall de Uxó, Spain 24 39 49N 0 15W
Valla, Sweden 10 59 2N 16 20 E
Valladolid, Mexico 127 20 40N 88 11W
Valladolid, Spain 22 41 38N 4 43W
Valladolid □, Spain 22 41 38N 4 43W
Vallata, Italy 29 41 3N 15 16 E
Valldemosa, Spain 24 39 43N 2 37 E
Valle d'Aosta □, Italy 26 45 45N 7 22 E
Valle de Arán, Spain 24 42 50N 0 55 E
Valle de Cabuérniga, Spain 22 43 14N 4 18W
Valle de la Pascua, Venezuela 134 9 13N 66 0W
Valle de las Palmas, Mexico 125 32 20N 116 43W
Valle de Santiago, Mexico 126 20 25N 101 15W
Valle de Suchil, Mexico 126 23 38N 103 55W
Valle de Zaragoza, Mexico 126 27 28N 105 49W
Valle del Cauca □, Colombia 134 3 45N 76 30W
Valle Fértil, Sierra del, Argentina 140 30 20 S 68 0W
Valle Hermoso, Mexico 127 25 35N 97 40W
Vallecas, Spain 22 40 23N 3 41W
Valledupar, Colombia 134 10 29N 73 15W
Vallée-Jonction, Canada 107 46 22N 70 55W
Vallehermoso, Canary Is. 25 28 10N 17 15W
Vallejo, U.S.A. 124 38 12N 122 15W
Vallenar, Chile 140 28 30 S 70 50W
Valleraugue, France 20 44 6N 3 39 E
Vallet, France 18 47 10N 1 15W
Valletta, Malta 86 35 54N 14 30 E
Valley Center, U.S.A. 125 33 13N 117 2W
Valley City, U.S.A. 120 46 57N 98 0W
Valley Falls, U.S.A. 122 42 33N 120 16W
Valley Park, U.S.A. 118 38 33N 90 29W
Valley Springs, U.S.A. 124 38 11N 120 50W
Valley Station, U.S.A. 119 38 10N 85 50W
Valley Wells, U.S.A. 125 35 27N 115 46W
Valleyview, Canada 110 55 5N 117 17W
Valli di Comácchio, Italy 27 44 40N 12 15 E
Vallimanca, Arroyo, Argentina 140 35 40 S 59 10W
Vallo della Lucánia, Italy 29 40 14N 15 16 E
Vallon-Pont-d'Arc, France 21 44 24N 4 24 E
Vallorbe, Switz. 31 46 42N 6 20 E
Valls, Spain 24 41 18N 1 15 E
Vallsta, Sweden 10 61 31N 16 22 E
Valmaseda, Spain 24 43 11N 3 12W
Valmeyer, U.S.A. 118 38 18N 90 19W
Valmiera, U.S.S.R. 36 57 37N 25 29 E
Valmont, France 18 49 45N 0 30 E
Valmontone, Italy 28 41 48N 12 55 E
Valmy, France 19 49 5N 4 45 E
Valnera, Mte., Spain 24 43 9N 3 40W
Valognes, France 18 49 30N 1 28W
Valona = Vlóra, Albania 35 40 32N 19 28 E
Valongo, Portugal 22 41 8N 8 30W
Valpaços, Portugal 22 41 36N 7 17W
Valparaíso, Chile 140 33 2 S 71 40W
Valparaíso, Mexico 126 22 50N 103 32W
Valparaiso, U.S.A. 119 41 27N 87 2W
Valparaíso □, Chile 140 33 2 S 71 40W
Valpovo, Yugoslavia 33 45 39N 18 25 E
Valréas, France 21 44 24N 5 0 E
Vals, Switz. 31 46 39N 9 11 E
Vals →, S. Africa 96 27 23 S 26 30 E
Vals, Tanjung, Indonesia 57 8 26 S 137 25 E
Vals-les-Bains, France 21 44 42N 4 24 E
Valsad, India 50 20 40N 72 58 E
Valskog, Sweden 10 59 27N 15 57 E
Válta, Greece 35 40 3N 23 25 E
Valtellina, Italy 26 46 9N 9 55 E
Valuyki, U.S.S.R. 37 50 10N 38 5 E
Valverde, Canary Is. 25 27 48N 17 55W
Valverde del Camino, Spain 23 37 35N 6 47W
Valverde del Fresno, Spain 22 40 15N 6 51W
Vama, Romania 34 47 34N 25 42 E
Vámos, Greece 35 35 24N 24 13 E
Vamsadhara →, India 50 18 21N 84 8 E
Van, Turkey 46 38 30N 43 20 E
Van, L. = Van Gölü, Turkey 46 38 30N 43 0 E
Van Alstyne, U.S.A. 121 33 25N 96 36W
Van Bruyssel, Canada 107 47 56N 72 9W
Van Buren, Canada 105 47 10N 67 55W
Van Buren, Ark., U.S.A. 121 35 28N 94 18W
Van Buren, Maine, U.S.A. 115 47 10N 68 1W
Van Buren, Mo., U.S.A. 121 37 0N 91 0W
Van Canh, Vietnam 54 13 37N 109 0 E
Van Diemen, C., N. Terr., Australia 78 11 9 S 130 24 E
Van Diemen, C., Queens., Australia 72 16 30 S 139 46 E
Van Diemen G., Australia 78 11 45 S 132 0 E
Van Gölü, Turkey 46 38 30N 43 0 E
Van Horn, U.S.A. 121 31 3N 104 55W
Van Horne, U.S.A. 118 42 1N 92 4W
Van Ninh, Vietnam 54 12 42N 109 14 E
Van Reenen P., S. Africa 97 28 22 S 29 27 E
Van Rees, Pegunungan, Indonesia 57 2 35 S 138 15 E
Van Tassell, U.S.A. 120 42 40N 104 3W
Van Tivu, India 51 8 51N 78 15 E
Van Wert, U.S.A. 119 40 52N 84 31W
Van Yen, Vietnam 54 21 4N 104 42 E
Vanavara, U.S.S.R. 41 60 22N 102 16 E
Vanceburg, U.S.A. 119 38 36N 83 19W
Vancouver, Canada 110 49 15N 123 10W
Vancouver, U.S.A. 124 45 44N 122 41W
Vancouver, C., Australia 79 35 2 S 118 11 E
Vancouver I., Canada 110 49 50N 126 0W
Vandalia, Ill., U.S.A. 118 38 57N 89 4W
Vandalia, Mo., U.S.A. 118 39 18N 91 30W
Vandalia, Ohio, U.S.A. 119 39 54N 84 12W
Vandavasi, India 51 12 30N 79 30 E
Vandeloos Bay, Sri Lanka 51 8 0N 81 45 E
Vandenburg, U.S.A. 125 34 35N 120 33W
Vanderbijlpark, S. Africa 97 26 42 S 27 54 E
Vandergrift, U.S.A. 116 40 36N 79 33W
Vanderhoof, Canada 110 54 0N 124 0W
Vanderlin I., Australia 72 15 44 S 137 2 E
Vandry, Canada 107 47 52N 73 34W
Vandyke, Australia 72 24 10 S 147 51 E
Vänern, Sweden 11 58 47N 13 30 E
Vänersborg, Sweden 11 58 26N 12 19 E
Vang Vieng, Laos 54 18 58N 102 32 E
Vanga, Kenya 92 4 35 S 39 12 E
Vangaindrano, Madag. 97 23 21 S 47 36 E
Vanguard, Canada 111 49 55N 107 20W
Vangunu, Solomon Is. 68 8 40 S 158 5 E
Vanier, Canada 109 45 27N 75 40W
Vanimo, Papua N. G. 69 2 42 S 141 21 E
Vanivilasa Sagara, India 51 13 45N 76 30 E
Vaniyambadi, India 51 12 46N 78 44 E
Vankarem, U.S.S.R. 41 67 51N 175 50 E
Vankleek Hill, Canada 109 45 32N 74 40W
Vanna, Norway 8 70 6N 19 50 E
Vännäs, Sweden 8 63 58N 19 48 E
Vannes, France 18 47 40N 2 47W
Vanoise, Massif de la, France 21 45 25N 6 40 E
Vanrhynsdorp, S. Africa 96 31 36 S 18 44 E
Vanrook, Australia 72 16 57 S 141 57 E
Vans, Les, France 21 44 25N 4 7 E
Vansbro, Sweden 10 60 32N 14 15 E
Vansittart B., Australia 78 14 3 S 126 17 E
Vanthli, India 48 21 28N 70 25 E
Vanua Levu, Fiji 68 16 33 S 179 15 E
Vanua Mbalavu, Fiji 68 17 40 S 178 57W
Vanuatu ■, Pac. Oc. 68 15 0 S 168 0 E
Vanwyksvlei, S. Africa 96 30 18 S 21 49 E
Vanzylsrus, S. Africa 96 26 52 S 22 4 E
Vapnyarka, U.S.S.R. 38 48 32N 28 45 E
Var □, France 21 43 27N 6 18 E
Var →, France 21 43 39N 7 12 E
Vara, Sweden 11 58 16N 12 55 E
Varada →, India 51 15 0N 75 40 E
Varades, France 18 47 25N 1 1W
Varaita →, Italy 26 44 49N 7 36 E
Varallo, Italy 26 45 50N 8 13 E
Varanasi, India 49 25 22N 83 0 E
Varangerfjorden, Norway 8 70 3N 29 25 E

Varaždin, Yugoslavia 27 46 20N 16 20 E
Varazze, Italy 26 44 21N 8 36 E
Varberg, Sweden 11 57 6N 12 20 E
Vardak □, Afghan. 47 34 0N 68 0 E
Vardar → = Axiós →, Greece 35 40 57N 22 35 E
Varde, Denmark 11 55 38N 8 29 E
Varde Å, Denmark 11 55 35N 8 19 E
Varel, W. Germany 30 53 23N 8 9 E
Varella, Mui, Vietnam 54 12 54N 109 26 E
Varena, U.S.S.R. 36 54 12N 24 30 E
Varennes-sur-Allier, France 20 46 19N 3 24 E
Vareš, Yugoslavia 33 44 12N 18 23 E
Varese, Italy 26 45 49N 8 50 E
Varese Lígure, Italy 26 44 22N 9 33 E
Vårgårda, Sweden 11 58 2N 12 49 E
Vargem Bonita, Brazil 139 20 20 S 46 22W
Vargem Grande, Brazil 138 3 33 S 43 56W
Varginha, Brazil 141 21 33 S 45 25W
Vargön, Sweden 11 58 22N 12 20 E
Variadero, U.S.A. 121 35 43N 104 17W
Varillas, Chile 140 24 0 S 70 10W
Väring, Sweden 11 58 30N 14 0 E
Värmeln, Sweden 10 59 35N 12 54 E
Värmlands län □, Sweden 10 60 0N 13 20 E
Varna, Bulgaria 34 43 13N 27 56 E
Varna, U.S.A. 118 41 2N 89 14W
Varna →, India 50 16 48N 74 32 E
Värnamo, Sweden 11 57 10N 14 3 E
Värö, Sweden 11 57 16N 12 11 E
Vars, Canada 106 45 21N 75 21W
Varsseveld, Neths. 16 51 56N 6 29 E
Varvarin, Yugoslavia 33 43 43N 21 20 E
Varzaneh, Iran 47 32 25N 52 40 E
Várzea Alegre, Brazil 138 6 47 S 39 17W
Várzea da Palma, Brazil 139 17 36 S 44 44W
Várzea Grande, Brazil 137 15 39 S 56 8W
Varzi, Italy 26 44 50N 9 12 E
Varzo, Italy 26 46 12N 8 15 E
Varzy, France 19 47 22N 3 20 E
Vasa, Finland 8 63 6N 21 38 E
Vasa Barris →, Brazil 138 11 10 S 37 10W
Vascão →, Portugal 23 37 31N 7 31W
Vaşcău, Romania 34 46 28N 22 30 E
Vascongadas □, Spain 24 42 50N 2 45W
Väse, Sweden 10 59 23N 13 52 E
Vasht = Khāsh, Iran 47 28 15N 61 15 E
Vasilevichi, U.S.S.R. 36 52 15N 29 50 E
Vasilikón, Greece 35 38 25N 23 40 E
Vasilkov, U.S.S.R. 36 50 7N 30 15 E
Vaslui, Romania 34 46 38N 27 42 E
Väsman, Sweden 10 60 9N 15 5 E
Vassar, Canada 111 49 10N 95 55W
Vassar, U.S.A. 114 43 23N 83 33W
Västerås, Sweden 10 59 37N 16 38 E
Västerbottens län □, Sweden 8 64 58N 18 0 E
Västernorrlands län □, Sweden 10 63 30N 17 30 E
Västervik, Sweden 11 57 43N 16 43 E
Västmanlands län □, Sweden 10 59 45N 16 20 E
Vasto, Italy 27 42 8N 14 40 E
Vasvár, Hungary 33 47 3N 16 47 E
Vatan, France 19 47 4N 1 50 E
Vaté = Efate, I., Vanuatu 68 17 40 S 168 25 E
Vathí, Greece 35 37 46N 27 1 E
Váthia, Greece 35 36 29N 22 29 E
Vatican City ■, Italy 27 41 54N 12 27 E
Vaticano, C., Italy 28 38 40N 15 48 E
Vatnajökull, Iceland 8 64 30N 16 48W
Vatnås, Norway 10 59 58N 9 37 E
Vatneyri, Iceland 8 65 35N 24 0W
Vatoloha, Mt., Madag. 97 17 52 S 47 48 E
Vatomandry, Madag. 97 19 20 S 48 59 E
Vatra-Dornei, Romania 34 47 22N 25 22 E
Vättern, Sweden 11 58 25N 14 30 E
Vatulele, Fiji 68 18 33 S 177 37 E
Vaucluse □, France 21 43 50N 5 20 E
Vaucouleurs, France 19 48 37N 5 40 E
Vaud □, Switz. 31 46 35N 6 30 E
Vaughn, Mont., U.S.A. 122 47 37N 111 36W
Vaughn, N. Mex., U.S.A. 123 34 37N 105 12W
Vaupe □, Colombia 134 1 0N 71 0W
Vaupés → = Uaupés →, Brazil 134 0 2N 67 16W
Vauvert, France 21 43 42N 4 17 E
Vauxhall, Canada 110 50 5N 112 9W
Vavoua, Ivory C. 90 7 23N 6 29W
Vaxholm, Sweden 10 59 25N 18 20 E
Växjö, Sweden 11 56 52N 14 50 E
Vaygach, Ostrov, U.S.S.R. 40 70 0N 60 0 E
Veadeiros, Brazil 139 14 7 S 47 31W
Vechta, W. Germany 30 52 47N 8 18 E
Vechte →, Neths. 30 52 34N 6 6 E
Vecilla, La, Spain 22 42 51N 5 27W
Vecsés, Hungary 33 47 26N 19 19 E
Vedaranniyam, India 51 10 25N 79 50 E
Veddige, Sweden 11 57 17N 12 20 E
Vedea →, Romania 34 43 53N 25 59 E
Vedia, Argentina 140 34 30 S 61 31W
Vedra, I. del, Spain 25 38 52N 1 12 E
Vedrin, Belgium 17 50 30N 4 52 E
Veendam, Neths. 16 53 5N 6 52 E
Veenendaal, Neths. 16 52 2N 5 34 E
Veerle, Belgium 17 51 4N 4 59 E
Vefsna →, Norway 8 65 48N 13 10 E
Vega, Norway 8 65 40N 11 55 E
Vega, U.S.A. 121 35 18N 102 26W
Vega, La, Dom. Rep. 129 19 20N 70 30W
Vega, La, Peru 136 10 41 S 77 44W
Vegadeo, Spain 22 43 27N 7 4W
Vegafjorden, Norway 8 65 37N 12 0 E
Vegesack, W. Germany 30 53 10N 8 38 E
Veghel, Neths. 17 51 37N 5 32 E
Vegorritis, Límni, Greece 35 40 45N 21 45 E
Vegreville, Canada 110 53 30N 112 5W
Vegusdal, Norway 11 58 32N 8 10 E
Veii, Italy 27 42 0N 12 24 E
Vejen, Denmark 11 55 30N 9 9 E
Vejer de la Frontera, Spain 23 36 15N 5 59W
Vejle, Denmark 11 55 43N 9 30 E
Vejle Fjord, Denmark 11 55 40N 9 50 E
Vela, La, Venezuela 134 11 27N 69 34W
Vela Luka, Yugoslavia 27 42 59N 16 44 E
Velanai I., Sri Lanka 51 9 45N 79 45 E
Velas, C., Costa Rica 128 10 21N 85 52W
Velasco, Sierra de, Argentina 140 29 20 S 67 10W
Velay, Mts. du, France 20 45 0N 3 40 E
Velddrif, S. Africa 96 32 42 S 18 11 E
Veldegem, Belgium 17 51 7N 3 10 E
Velden, Neths. 17 51 25N 6 10 E
Veldhoven, Neths. 17 51 24N 5 25 E
Velebit Planina, Yugoslavia 27 44 50N 15 20 E
Velebitski Kanal, Yugoslavia 27 44 45N 14 55 E
Veleka →, Bulgaria 34 42 4N 27 58 E
Velenje, Yugoslavia 27 46 23N 15 8 E
Velestínon, Greece 35 39 23N 22 43 E
Veleta, La, Spain 23 37 1N 3 22W
Vélez, Colombia 134 6 1N 73 41W
Vélez Blanco, Spain 25 37 41N 2 5W
Vélez Málaga, Spain 23 36 48N 4 5W
Vélez Rubio, Spain 25 37 41N 2 5W
Velhas →, Brazil 139 17 13 S 44 49W
Velika, Yugoslavia 33 45 27N 17 40 E
Velika Gorica, Yugoslavia 27 45 44N 16 5 E
Velika Kapela, Yugoslavia 27 45 10N 15 5 E
Velika Kladuša, Yugoslavia 27 45 11N 15 48 E
Velika Morava →, Yugoslavia 33 44 43N 21 3 E
Velikaya →, U.S.S.R. 36 57 48N 28 20 E
Velikaya Lepetikha, U.S.S.R. 38 47 2N 33 58 E
Velike Lašče, Yugoslavia 27 45 49N 14 45 E
Velikiye Luki, U.S.S.R. 36 56 25N 30 32 E
Velikonda Range, India 51 14 45N 79 10 E
Velikoye, Oz., U.S.S.R. 37 55 15N 40 10 E
Velingrad, Bulgaria 35 42 4N 23 58 E
Velino, Mte., Italy 27 42 10N 13 20 E
Velizh, U.S.S.R. 36 55 36N 31 11 E
Velke Meziřici, Czech. 32 49 21N 16 1 E
Vella G., Solomon Is. 68 8 0 S 156 50 E
Vella Lavella, Solomon Is. 68 7 45 S 156 40 E
Vellar →, India 51 11 30N 79 36 E
Velletri, Italy 28 41 43N 12 43 E
Vellinge, Sweden 11 55 29N 13 0 E
Vellore, India 51 12 57N 79 10 E
Velp, Neths. 16 52 0N 5 59 E
Velsen-Noord, Neths. 16 52 27N 4 40 E
Velten, E. Germany 30 52 40N 13 11 E
Veluwe Meer, Neths. 16 52 24N 5 44 E
Velva, U.S.A. 120 48 6N 100 56W
Vembanad L., India 51 9 36N 76 15 E
Veme, Norway 10 60 14N 10 7 E
Ven, Sweden 11 55 55N 12 45 E
Vena, Sweden 11 57 31N 16 0 E
Venaco, France 21 42 14N 9 11 E
Venado Tuerto, Argentina 140 33 50 S 62 0W
Venafro, Italy 29 41 28N 14 3 E
Venarey-les-Laumes, France 19 47 32N 4 26 E
Venaria, Italy 26 45 6N 7 39 E
Venčane, Yugoslavia 33 44 24N 20 28 E
Vence, France 21 43 43N 7 6 E
Venda □, S. Africa 97 22 40 S 30 35 E
Vendas Novas, Portugal 23 38 39N 8 27W
Vendée □, France 18 46 50N 1 35W
Vendée →, France 18 46 20N 1 10W
Vendéen, Bocage, France 20 46 40N 1 20W
Vendeuvre-sur-Barse, France 19 48 14N 4 28 E
Vendôme, France 18 47 47N 1 3 E
Vendrell, Spain 24 41 10N 1 30 E
Vendsyssel, Denmark 11 57 22N 10 0 E
Véneta, L., Italy 27 45 23N 12 25 E
Véneto □, Italy 27 45 40N 12 0 E
Venev, U.S.S.R. 37 54 22N 38 17 E
Venézia, Italy 27 45 27N 12 20 E
Venézia, G. di, Italy 27 45 20N 13 0 E
Venezuela ■, S. Amer. 134 8 0N 66 0W
Venezuela, G. de, Venezuela 134 11 30N 71 0W
Vengurla, India 51 15 53N 73 45 E
Vengurla Rocks, India 51 15 55N 73 22 E
Venice = Venézia, Italy 27 45 27N 12 20 E
Venkatagiri, India 51 14 0N 79 35 E
Venkatapuram, India 50 18 20N 80 30 E
Venlo, Neths. 17 51 22N 6 11 E
Venosta, Canada 106 45 52N 76 1W
Venraij, Neths. 17 51 31N 6 0 E
Vent, Is. du, Pac. Oc. 68 17 30 S 149 30W
Venta, La, Mexico 127 18 8N 94 3W
Venta de Cardeña, Spain 23 38 16N 4 20W
Venta de San Rafael, Spain 22 40 42N 4 12W
Ventana, Punta de la, Mexico 126 24 4N 109 48W
Ventana, Sa. de la, Argentina 140 38 0 S 62 30W
Ventersburg, S. Africa 96 28 7 S 27 9 E
Venterstad, S. Africa 96 30 47 S 25 48 E
Ventimíglia, Italy 26 43 50N 7 39 E
Ventnor, U.K. 13 50 35N 1 12W
Ventotene, Italy 28 40 48N 13 25 E
Ventoux, Mt., France 21 44 10N 5 17 E
Ventspils, U.S.S.R. 36 57 25N 21 32 E
Ventuarí →, Venezuela 134 3 58N 67 2W
Ventucopa, U.S.A. 125 34 50N 119 29W
Ventura, U.S.A. 125 34 16N 119 18W
Ventura, La, Mexico 126 24 38N 100 54W
Venturosa, La, Colombia 134 6 8N 68 48W
Venus B., Australia 74 38 40 S 145 42 E
Vera, Argentina 140 29 30 S 60 20W
Vera, Spain 25 37 15N 1 51W
Veracruz, Mexico 127 19 10N 96 10W
Veracruz □, Mexico 127 19 0N 96 15W
Veraval, India 48 20 53N 70 27 E
Verbánia, Italy 26 45 56N 8 43 E
Verbicaro, Italy 29 39 46N 15 54 E
Vercelli, Italy 26 45 19N 8 25 E
Verchères, Canada 107 45 47N 73 21W
Verchovchevo, U.S.S.R. 38 48 32N 34 10 E
Verdalsøra, Norway 8 63 48N 11 30 E
Verde →, Argentina 142 41 56 S 65 5W
Verde →, Goiás, Brazil 139 19 11 S 50 44W
Verde →, Goiás, Brazil 139 18 1 S 50 14W
Verde →, Mato Grosso, Brazil 137 21 25 S 52 20W
Verde →, Mato Grosso, Brazil 137 11 54 S 55 48W
Verde →, Chihuahua, Mexico 126 26 29N 107 58W
Verde →, Oaxaca, Mexico 127 15 59N 97 50W
Verde →, Veracruz, Mexico 126 21 10N 102 50W
Verde →, Paraguay 140 23 9 S 57 37W
Verde, Cay, Bahamas 128 23 0N 75 5W
Verde Grande →, Brazil 139 16 13 S 43 49W
Verde Pequeno →, Brazil 139 14 48 S 43 31W
Verden, W. Germany 30 52 58N 9 18 E
Verdi, U.S.A. 124 39 31N 119 59W
Verdigre, U.S.A. 120 42 38N 98 0W
Verdon →, France 21 43 43N 5 46 E
Verdon-sur-Mer, Le, France 20 45 33N 1 4W
Verdun, France 19 49 9N 5 24 E
Verdun-sur-le-Doubs, France 19 46 54N 5 2 E
Vereeniging, S. Africa 97 26 38 S 27 57 E
Vérendrye, Parc Prov. de la, Canada 106 47 20N 76 40W
Verga, C., Guinea 90 10 30N 14 10W
Vergato, Italy 26 44 18N 11 8 E
Vergemont, Australia 72 23 33 S 143 1 E
Vergemont Cr. →, Australia 72 24 16 S 143 16 E
Vergennes, U.S.A. 117 44 9N 73 15W
Vergt, France 20 45 2N 0 43 E
Verín, Spain 22 41 57N 7 27W
Veriña, Spain 22 43 32N 5 43W
Verkhnedvinsk, U.S.S.R. 36 55 45N 27 58 E
Verkhnevilyuysk, U.S.S.R. 41 63 27N 120 18 E
Verkhneye Kalinino, U.S.S.R. 41 59 54N 108 8 E
Verkhniy Baskunchak, U.S.S.R. 39 48 14N 46 44 E
Verkhovye, U.S.S.R. 37 52 55N 37 15 E
Verkhoyansk, U.S.S.R. 41 67 35N 133 25 E
Verkhoyansk Ra. = Verkhoyanskiy Khrebet, U.S.S.R. 41 66 0N 129 0 E
Verkhoyanskiy Khrebet, U.S.S.R. 41 66 0N 129 0 E
Verlo, Canada 111 50 19N 108 35W
Verma, Norway 10 62 21N 8 3 E
Vermenton, France 19 47 40N 3 42 E
Vermilion, Canada 111 53 20N 110 50W
Vermilion →, Alta., Canada 111 53 22N 110 51W
Vermilion →, Qué., Canada 107 47 38N 72 56W
Vermilion →, Ill., U.S.A. 118 41 19N 89 5W
Vermilion →, Ind., U.S.A. 119 39 57N 87 27W
Vermilion, B., U.S.A. 121 29 45N 91 55W
Vermilion Bay, Canada 111 49 51N 93 34W
Vermilion Chutes, Canada 110 58 22N 114 51W
Vermilion L., U.S.A. 120 47 53N 92 25W
Vermillion, U.S.A. 120 42 50N 96 56W
Vermont, U.S.A. 118 40 18N 90 26W
Vermont □, U.S.A. 117 43 40N 72 50W
Vernal, U.S.A. 122 40 28N 109 35W
Vernalis, U.S.A. 124 37 36N 121 17W
Verner, Canada 108 46 25N 80 8W
Verneuil-sur-Avre, France 18 48 45N 0 55 E
Verneukpan, S. Africa 96 30 0 S 21 0 E
Vernon, Canada 110 50 20N 119 15W
Vernon, France 18 49 5N 1 30 E
Vernon, Ill., U.S.A. 118 38 48N 89 5W
Vernon, Ind., U.S.A. 119 38 59N 85 36W
Vernon, Tex., U.S.A. 121 34 10N 99 20W
Vernonia, U.S.A. 124 45 52N 123 11W
Vero Beach, U.S.A. 115 27 39N 80 23W
Véroia, Greece 35 40 34N 22 12 E
Verolanuova, Italy 26 45 20N 10 5 E
Véroli, Italy 28 41 43N 13 24 E
Verona, Canada 109 44 29N 76 42W
Verona, Italy 26 45 27N 11 0 E
Verona, U.S.A. 118 42 59N 89 32W
Veropol, U.S.S.R. 41 65 15N 168 40 E
Versailles, France 19 48 48N 2 8 E
Versailles, Ill., U.S.A. 118 39 53N 90 39W
Versailles, Ind., U.S.A. 119 39 4N 85 15W
Versailles, Ky., U.S.A. 119 38 3N 84 44W
Versailles, Mo., U.S.A. 118 38 26N 92 51W
Versailles, Ohio, U.S.A. 119 40 13N 84 29W
Versalles, Bolivia 137 12 44 S 63 18W
Vert, C., Senegal 90 14 45N 17 30W
Verte, I., Canada 107 48 2N 69 26W
Vertou, France 18 47 10N 1 28W
Vertus, France 19 48 54N 4 0 E
Verulam, S. Africa 97 29 38 S 31 2 E
Verviers, Belgium 17 50 37N 5 52 E
Vervins, France 19 49 50N 3 53 E
Verzej, Yugoslavia 27 46 34N 16 13 E
Vescavoto, France 21 42 30N 9 27 E
Vesdre →, Belgium 17 50 36N 6 0 E
Veselí nad Lužnicí, Czech. 32 49 12N 14 43 E
Veselovskoye Vdkhr., U.S.S.R. 39 47 0N 41 0 E
Veshenskaya, U.S.S.R. 39 49 35N 41 44 E
Vesle →, France 19 49 23N 3 28 E
Vesoul, France 19 47 40N 6 11 E
Vessigebro, Sweden 11 56 58N 12 40 E
Vest-Agder fylke □, Norway 9 58 30N 7 15 E
Vesta, Costa Rica 128 9 43N 83 3W
Vesterålen, Norway 8 68 45N 15 0 E
Vestersche Veld, Neths. 16 52 52N 6 9 E
Vestfjorden, Norway 8 67 55N 14 0 E
Vestfold fylke □, Norway 9 59 15N 10 0 E
Vestmannaeyjar, Iceland 8 63 27N 20 15W
Vestmarka, Norway 10 59 56N 11 59 E
Vestone, Italy 26 45 40N 10 25 E
Vestsjællands Amtskommune □, Denmark 11 55 30N 11 20 E
Vestspitsbergen, Svalbard 144 78 40N 17 0 E
Vestvågøy, Norway 8 68 18N 13 50 E
Vesuvio, Italy 29 40 50N 14 22 E
Vesuvius, Mt. = Vesuvio, Italy 29 40 50N 14 22 E
Vesyegonsk, U.S.S.R. 37 58 40N 37 16 E
Veszprém, Hungary 33 47 8N 17 57 E
Vésztö, Hungary 33 46 55N 21 16 E
Vetapalem, India 51 15 47N 80 18 E
Vetlanda, Sweden 11 57 24N 15 3 E
Vetluga, U.S.S.R. 37 57 53N 45 45 E
Vetlugu →, U.S.S.R. 40 56 18N 46 24 E
Vetluzhskiy, U.S.S.R. 37 57 17N 45 12 E
Vetovo, Bulgaria 34 43 42N 26 16 E
Vetralia, Italy 27 42 20N 12 2 E
Vettore, Monte, Italy 27 42 49N 13 16 E
Veurne, Belgium 17 51 5N 2 40 E
Vevay, U.S.A. 119 38 45N 85 4W
Vevey, Switz. 31 46 28N 6 51 E
Veynes, France 21 44 32N 5 49 E
Veys, Iran 46 31 30N 49 0 E
Vézelise, France 19 48 30N 6 5 E
Vézère →, France 20 44 53N 0 53 E
Vi Thanh, Vietnam 55 9 42N 105 26 E
Viacha, Bolivia 136 16 39 S 68 18W
Viadana, Italy 26 44 55N 10 30 E
Viamão, Brazil 141 30 5 S 51 0W
Viana, Brazil 138 3 13 S 45 0W
Viana, Spain 24 42 31N 2 22W
Viana del Bollo, Spain 22 42 11N 7 6W
Viana do Alentejo, Portugal 23 38 17N 7 59W
Viana do Castelo, Portugal 22 41 42N 8 50W
Vianden, Belgium 17 49 56N 6 12 E
Vianen, Neths. 16 51 59N 5 5 E
Vianna do Castelo □, Portugal 22 41 50N 8 30W
Vianópolis, Brazil 139 16 40 S 48 35W
Viar →, Spain 23 37 36N 5 50W
Viaréggio, Italy 26 43 52N 10 13 E
Viaur →, France 20 44 8N 1 58 E
Vibank, Canada 111 50 20N 103 56W
Vibo Valéntia, Italy 29 38 40N 16 5 E
Viborg, Denmark 11 56 27N 9 23 E
Vibraye, France 18 48 3N 0 44 E
Vic-en-Bigorre, France 20 43 24N 0 3 E
Vic-Fézensac, France 20 43 47N 0 19 E

Vic-sur-Cère, France 20 44 59N 2 38 E
Vicenza, Italy 27 45 32N 11 31 E
Vich, Spain 24 41 58N 2 19 E
Vichada □, Colombia 134 5 0N 69 30W
Vichada →, Colombia 134 4 55N 67 50W
Vichuga, U.S.S.R. 37 57 12N 41 55 E
Vichy, France 20 46 9N 3 26 E
Vicksburg, Ariz., U.S.A. 125 33 45N 113 45W
Vicksburg, Mich., U.S.A. 119 42 10N 85 30W
Vicksburg, Miss., U.S.A. 121 32 22N 90 56W
Vico, L. di, Italy 27 42 20N 12 10 E
Vico del Gargaro, Italy 29 41 54N 15 57 E
Viçosa, Brazil 138 9 28 S 36 14W
Viçosa do Ceará, Brazil 138 3 34 S 41 5W
Victor, India 48 21 0N 71 30 E
Victor, Colo., U.S.A. 120 38 43N 105 7W
Victor, N.Y., U.S.A. 116 42 58N 77 24W
Victor Emanuel Ra., Papua N. G. 69 5 20 S 142 15 E
Victor Harbor, Australia 73 35 30 S 138 37 E
Victoria, Argentina 140 32 40 S 60 10W
Victoria, Canada 110 48 30N 123 25W
Victoria, Chile 142 38 13 S 72 20W
Victoria, Guinea 90 10 50N 14 32W
Victoria, Malaysia 56 5 20N 115 14 E
Victoria, Seychelles 53 5 0 S 55 40 E
Victoria, Ill., U.S.A. 118 41 2N 90 6W
Victoria, Kans., U.S.A. 120 38 52N 99 8W
Victoria, Tex., U.S.A. 121 28 50N 97 0W
Victoria →, Australia 78 15 10 S 129 40 E
Victoria, Grand L., Canada 106 47 31N 77 30W
Victoria, L., Africa 92 1 0 S 33 0 E
Victoria, L., N.S.W., Australia 73 33 57 S 141 15 E
Victoria, L., Vic., Australia 75 38 2 S 147 34 E
Victoria, La, Venezuela 134 10 14N 67 20W
Victoria, Mt., Burma 52 21 15N 93 55 E
Victoria, Mt., Papua N. G. 69 8 55 S 147 32 E
Victoria Beach, Canada 111 50 40N 96 35W
Victoria de Durango, Mexico 126 24 3N 104 39W
Victoria de las Tunas, Cuba 128 20 58N 76 59W
Victoria Falls, Zimb. 93 17 58 S 25 52 E
Victoria Harbour, Canada 108 44 45N 79 45W
Victoria I., Canada 102 71 0N 111 0W
Victoria Ld., Antarctica 143 75 0 S 160 0 E
Victoria Nile →, Uganda 92 2 14N 31 26 E
Victoria Ra., N.Z. 81 42 12 S 172 7 E
Victoria Res., Canada 105 48 20N 57 27W
Victoria River Downs, Australia 78 16 25 S 131 0 E
Victoria West, S. Africa 96 31 25 S 23 4 E
Victoriaville, Canada 107 46 4N 71 56W
Victorica, Argentina 140 36 20 S 65 30W
Victorville, U.S.A. 125 34 32N 117 18W
Vicuña, Chile 140 30 0 S 70 50W
Vicuña Mackenna, Argentina 140 33 53 S 64 25W
Vidal, U.S.A. 125 34 7N 114 31W
Vidal Junction, U.S.A. 125 34 11N 114 34W
Vidalia, U.S.A. 115 32 13N 82 25W
Vidauban, France 21 43 25N 6 27 E
Vidigueira, Portugal 23 38 12N 7 48W
Vidin, Bulgaria 34 43 59N 22 50 E
Vidio, C., Spain 22 43 35N 6 14W
Vidisha, India 48 23 28N 77 53 E
Vidöstern, Sweden 11 57 5N 14 0 E
Vidzy, U.S.S.R. 36 55 23N 26 37 E
Viechtach, W. Germany 31 49 5N 12 53 E
Viedma, Argentina 142 40 50 S 63 0W
Viedma, L., Argentina 142 49 30 S 72 30W
Vieira, Portugal 22 41 38N 8 8W
Viella, Spain 24 42 43N 0 44 E
Vielsalm, Belgium 17 50 17N 5 54 E
Vienenburg, W. Germany 30 51 57N 10 35 E
Vieng Pou Kha, Laos 54 20 41N 101 4 E
Vienna = Wien, Austria 33 48 12N 16 22 E
Vienna, Canada 108 42 41N 80 48W
Vienna, Ill., U.S.A. 121 37 29N 88 54W
Vienna, Mo., U.S.A. 118 38 11N 91 57W
Vienne, France 21 45 31N 4 53 E
Vienne □, France 20 46 30N 0 42 E
Vienne →, France 18 47 13N 0 5 E
Vientiane, Laos 54 17 58N 102 36 E
Vientos, Paso de los, Caribbean 129 20 0N 74 0W
Vierlingsbeek, Neths. 17 51 36N 6 1 E
Viersen, W. Germany 30 51 15N 6 23 E
Vierwaldstättersee, Switz. 31 47 0N 8 30 E
Vierzon, France 19 47 13N 2 5 E
Vieste, Italy 28 41 52N 16 14 E
Vietnam ■, Asia 54 19 0N 106 0 E
Vieux-Boucau-les-Bains, France 20 43 48N 1 23W
Vif, France 21 45 5N 5 41 E
Vigan, Phil. 57 17 35N 120 28 E
Vigan, Le, France 20 43 59N 3 36 E
Vigévano, Italy 26 45 18N 8 50 E
Vigia, Brazil 138 0 50 S 48 5W
Vigía Chico, Mexico 127 19 46N 87 35W
Vignemale, Pic du, France 20 42 47N 0 10W
Vigneulles-lès-Hattonchâtel, France 19 48 59N 5 43 E
Vignola, Italy 26 44 29N 11 0 E
Vigo, Spain 22 42 12N 8 41W
Vigo, Ría de, Spain 22 42 15N 8 45W
Vihiers, France 18 47 10N 0 30W
Vijayadurg, India 50 16 30N 73 25 E
Vijayawada, India 51 16 31N 80 39 E
Vijfhuizen, Neths. 16 52 22N 4 41 E
Viken, Sweden 11 58 39N 14 20 E
Viking, Canada 110 53 7N 111 50W
Vikna, Norway 8 64 55N 10 58 E
Vikramasingapuram, India 51 8 40N 76 47 E
Viksjö, Sweden 10 62 45N 17 26 E
Vikulovo, U.S.S.R. 40 56 50N 70 40 E
Vila, Vanuatu 68 17 44 S 168 19 E
Vila da Maganja, Mozam. 93 17 18 S 37 30 E
Vila de João Belo = Xai-Xai, Mozam. 97 25 6 S 33 31 E
Vila de Manica, Mozam. 93 18 58 S 32 59 E
Vila de Rei, Portugal 23 39 41N 8 9W
Vila do Bispo, Portugal 23 37 5N 8 53W
Vila do Chibuto, Mozam. 97 24 40 S 33 33 E
Vila do Conde, Portugal 22 41 21N 8 45W
Vila Franca de Xira, Portugal 23 38 57N 8 59W
Vila Gamito, Mozam. 93 14 12 S 33 0 E
Vila Gomes da Costa, Mozam. 97 24 20 S 33 37 E
Vila Machado, Mozam. 93 19 15 S 34 14 E
Vila Mouzinho, Mozam. 93 14 48 S 34 25 E
Vila Nova de Foscôa, Portugal 22 41 5N 7 9W
Vila Nova de Ourém, Portugal 23 39 40N 8 35W
Vila Novo de Gaia, Portugal 22 41 4N 8 40W
Vila Pouca de Aguiar, Portugal 22 41 30N 7 38W
Vila Real, Portugal 22 41 17N 7 48W
Vila Real de Santo António, Portugal 23 37 10N 7 28W
Vila Vasco da Gama, Mozam. 93 14 54 S 32 14 E
Vila Velha, Amapá, Brazil 135 3 13N 51 13W
Vila Velha, Espirito Santo, Brazil 139 20 20 S 40 17W
Vila Viçosa, Portugal 23 38 45N 7 27W
Vilaboa, Spain 22 42 21N 8 39W
Vilaine →, France 18 47 30N 2 27W
Vilanandro, Tanjona, Madag. 97 16 11 S 44 27 E
Vilanculos, Mozam. 97 22 1 S 35 17 E
Vilar Formosa, Portugal 22 40 38N 6 45W
Vilareal □, Portugal 22 41 36N 7 35W
Vilaseca-Salou, Spain 24 41 7N 1 9 E
Vilcabamba, Cordillera, Peru 136 13 0 S 73 0W
Vilcanchos, Peru 136 13 40 S 74 25W
Vileyka, U.S.S.R. 36 54 30N 26 53 E
Vilhelmina, Sweden 8 64 35N 16 39 E
Vilhena, Brazil 137 12 40 S 60 5W
Viliga, U.S.S.R. 41 61 36N 156 56 E
Viliya →, U.S.S.R. 36 55 54N 23 53 E
Viljandi, U.S.S.R. 36 58 28N 25 30 E
Vilkovo, U.S.S.R. 38 45 28N 29 32 E
Villa Abecia, Bolivia 140 21 0 S 68 18W
Villa Ahumada, Mexico 126 30 38N 106 30W
Villa Ana, Argentina 140 28 28 S 59 40W
Villa Ángela, Argentina 140 27 34 S 60 45W
Villa Bella, Bolivia 137 10 25 S 65 22W
Villa Bens = Tarfaya, Morocco 84 27 55N 12 55W
Villa Cañás, Argentina 140 34 0 S 61 35W
Villa Cisneros = Dakhla, Mauritania 84 23 50N 15 53W
Villa Colón, Argentina 140 31 38 S 68 20W
Villa Constitución, Argentina 140 33 15 S 60 20W
Villa de Cura, Venezuela 134 10 2N 67 29W
Villa de María, Argentina 140 29 55 S 63 43W
Villa del Rosario, Venezuela 134 10 19N 72 19W
Villa Dolores, Argentina 140 31 58 S 65 15W
Villa Frontera, Mexico 126 26 56N 101 27W
Villa Grove, U.S.A. 119 39 52N 88 10W
Villa Guillermina, Argentina 140 28 15 S 59 29W
Villa Hayes, Paraguay 140 25 0 S 57 20W
Villa Iris, Argentina 140 38 12 S 63 12W
Villa Juárez, Mexico 126 27 37N 100 44W
Villa María, Argentina 140 32 20 S 63 10W
Villa Mazán, Argentina 140 28 40 S 66 30W
Villa Minozzo, Italy 26 44 21N 10 30 E
Villa Montes, Bolivia 140 21 10 S 63 30W
Villa Ocampo, Argentina 140 28 30 S 59 20W
Villa Ocampo, Mexico 126 26 29N 105 30W
Villa Ojo de Agua, Argentina 140 29 30 S 63 44W
Villa San Giovanni, Italy 29 38 13N 15 38 E
Villa San José, Argentina 140 32 12 S 58 15W
Villa San Martín, Argentina 140 28 15 S 64 9W
Villa Santina, Italy 27 46 25N 12 55 E
Villa Unión, Mexico 126 23 12N 106 14W
Villablino, Spain 22 42 57N 6 19W
Villacañas, Spain 24 39 38N 3 20W
Villacarlos, Spain 24 39 53N 4 17 E
Villacarriedo, Spain 24 43 14N 3 48W
Villacarrillo, Spain 25 38 7N 3 3W
Villacastín, Spain 22 40 46N 4 25W
Villach, Austria 33 46 37N 13 51 E
Villaciado, Italy 28 39 27N 8 45 E
Villada, Spain 22 42 15N 4 59W
Villadiego, Spain 22 42 31N 4 1W
Villadóssola, Italy 26 46 4N 8 16 E
Villafeliche, Spain 24 41 10N 1 30W
Villafranca, Spain 24 42 17N 1 46W
Villafranca de los Barros, Spain 23 38 35N 6 18W
Villafranca de los Caballeros, Spain 25 39 26N 3 21W
Villafranca del Bierzo, Spain 22 42 38N 6 50W
Villafranca del Cid, Spain 24 40 26N 0 16W
Villafranca del Panadés, Spain 24 41 21N 1 40 E
Villafranca di Verona, Italy 26 45 20N 10 51 E
Villagarcía de Arosa, Spain 22 42 34N 8 46W
Villagrán, Mexico 127 24 29N 99 29W
Villaguay, Argentina 140 32 0 S 59 0W
Villaharta, Spain 23 38 9N 4 54W
Villahermosa, Mexico 127 18 0N 92 50W
Villahermosa, Spain 25 38 46N 2 52W
Villaines-la-Juhel, France 18 48 21N 0 20W
Villajoyosa, Spain 25 38 30N 0 12W
Villalba, Spain 22 43 26N 7 40W
Villalba de Guardo, Spain 22 42 42N 4 49W
Villalcampo, Pantano de, Spain 22 41 31N 6 0W
Villalón de Campos, Spain 22 42 5N 5 4W
Villalpando, Spain 22 41 51N 5 25W
Villaluenga, Spain 22 40 2N 3 54W
Villamanán, Spain 22 42 19N 5 35W
Villamartín, Spain 23 36 52N 5 38W
Villamayor, Spain 24 39 50N 2 59W
Villamblard, France 20 45 2N 0 32 E
Villanova Monteleone, Italy 28 40 30N 8 28 E
Villanueva, Colombia 134 10 37N 72 59W
Villanueva, U.S.A. 123 35 16N 105 23W
Villanueva de Castellón, Spain 25 39 5N 0 31W
Villanueva de Córdoba, Spain 23 38 20N 4 38W
Villanueva de la Fuente, Spain 25 38 42N 2 42W
Villanueva de la Serena, Spain 23 38 59N 5 50W
Villanueva de la Sierra, Spain 22 40 12N 6 24W
Villanueva de los Castillejos, Spain 23 37 30N 7 15W
Villanueva del Arzobispo, Spain 25 38 10N 3 0W
Villanueva del Duque, Spain 23 38 20N 5 0W
Villanueva del Fresno, Spain 23 38 23N 7 10W
Villanueva y Geltrú, Spain 24 41 13N 1 40 E
Villaodrid, Spain 22 43 20N 7 11W
Villaputzu, Italy 28 39 28N 9 33 E
Villar del Arzobispo, Spain 24 39 44N 0 50W
Villar del Rey, Spain 23 39 7N 6 50W
Villarcayo, Spain 24 42 56N 3 34W
Villard-Bonnot, France 21 45 14N 5 53 E
Villard-de-Lans, France 21 45 3N 5 33 E
Villarino de los Aires, Spain 22 41 18N 6 23W
Villarosa, Italy 29 37 36N 14 9 E
Villarramiel, Spain 22 42 2N 4 55W
Villarreal, Spain 24 39 55N 0 3W
Villarrica, Chile 142 39 15 S 72 15W
Villarrica, Paraguay 140 25 40 S 56 30W
Villarrobledo, Spain 25 39 18N 2 36W
Villarroya de la Sierra, Spain 24 41 27N 1 46W
Villarrubia de los Ojos, Spain 25 39 14N 3 36W
Villars-les-Dombes, France 21 46 0N 5 3 E
Villarta de San Juan, Spain 25 39 15N 3 25W
Villasayas, Spain 24 41 24N 2 39W
Villaseca de los Gamitos, Spain 22 41 2N 6 7W
Villastar, Spain 24 40 17N 1 9W
Villatobas, Spain 24 39 54N 3 20W
Villavicencio, Argentina 140 32 28 S 69 0W
Villavicencio, Colombia 134 4 9N 73 37W
Villaviciosa, Spain 22 43 32N 5 27W
Villazón, Bolivia 140 22 0 S 65 35W
Ville-Marie, Canada 106 47 20N 79 30W
Ville Platte, U.S.A. 121 30 45N 92 17W
Villebon, L., Canada 106 47 58N 77 17W
Villedieu-les-Poêlles, France 18 48 50N 1 13W
Villefort, France 20 44 28N 3 56 E
Villefranche-de-Lauragais, France 20 43 25N 1 44 E
Villefranche-de-Rouergue, France 20 44 21N 2 2 E
Villefranche-du-Périgord, France 20 44 38N 1 5 E
Villefranche-sur-Cher, France 19 47 18N 1 46 E
Villefranche-sur-Saône, France 21 45 59N 4 43 E
Villegrande, Bolivia 137 18 30 S 64 10W
Villel, Spain 24 40 14N 1 12W
Villemaur-sur-Vanne, France 19 48 15N 3 44 E
Villemontel, Canada 106 48 38N 78 22W
Villemur-sur-Tarn, France 20 43 51N 1 31 E
Villena, Spain 25 38 39N 0 52W
Villenauxe-la-Grande, France 19 48 35N 3 33 E
Villenave-d'Ornon, France 20 44 46N 0 33W
Villeneuve, Italy 26 45 40N 7 10 E
Villeneuve-l'Archevêque, France 19 48 14N 3 32 E
Villeneuve-lès-Avignon, France 21 43 58N 4 49 E
Villeneuve-St.-Georges, France 19 48 44N 2 28 E
Villeneuve-sur-Allier, France 20 46 40N 3 13 E
Villeneuve-sur-Lot, France 20 44 24N 0 42 E
Villeréal, France 20 44 38N 0 45 E
Villers-Bocage, France 18 49 3N 0 40W
Villers-Bretonneux, France 19 49 50N 2 30 E
Villers-Cotterêts, France 19 49 15N 3 4 E
Villers-le-Bouillet, Belgium 17 50 34N 5 15 E
Villers-le-Gambon, Belgium 17 50 11N 4 37 E
Villers-sur-Mer, France 18 49 21N 0 2W
Villersexel, France 19 47 33N 6 26 E
Villerupt, France 19 49 28N 5 55 E
Villerville, France 18 49 26N 0 5 E
Villiers, S. Africa 97 27 2 S 28 36 E
Villingen, W. Germany 31 48 4N 8 28 E
Villingen-Schwenningen, W. Germany 31 48 3N 8 29 E
Villisca, U.S.A. 118 40 55N 94 59W
Villupuram, India 51 11 59N 79 31 E
Vilna, Canada 110 54 7N 111 55W
Vilnius, U.S.S.R. 36 54 38N 25 19 E
Vils, Austria 31 47 33N 10 37 E
Vils →, W. Germany 31 48 38N 13 11 E
Vilsbiburg, W. Germany 31 48 27N 12 23 E
Vilshofen, W. Germany 31 48 38N 13 11 E
Vilskutskogo, Proliv, U.S.S.R. 41 78 0N 103 0 E
Vilusi, Yugoslavia 33 42 44N 18 34 E
Vilvoorde, Belgium 17 50 56N 4 26 E
Vilyuy →, U.S.S.R. 41 64 24N 126 26 E
Vilyuysk, U.S.S.R. 41 63 40N 121 35 E
Vimercate, Italy 26 45 38N 9 25 E
Vimiosa, Portugal 22 41 35N 6 31W
Vimmerby, Sweden 11 57 40N 15 55 E
Vimoutiers, France 18 48 57N 0 10 E
Vimperk, Czech. 32 49 3N 13 46 E
Viña del Mar, Chile 140 33 0 S 71 30W
Vinaroz, Spain 24 40 30N 0 27 E
Vincennes, U.S.A. 119 38 42N 87 29W
Vincent, U.S.A. 125 34 33N 118 11W
Vinces, Ecuador 134 1 32 S 79 45W
Vinchina, Argentina 140 28 45 S 68 15W
Vindel älven →, Sweden 8 63 55N 19 50 E
Vindeln, Sweden 8 64 12N 19 43 E
Vinderup, Denmark 11 56 29N 8 45 E
Vindhya Ra., India 48 22 50N 77 0 E
Vine Grove, U.S.A. 119 37 49N 85 59W
Vineland, U.S.A. 114 39 30N 75 0W
Vinga, Romania 34 46 0N 21 14 E
Vingnes, Norway 10 61 7N 10 26 E
Vinh, Vietnam 54 18 45N 105 38 E
Vinh Linh, Vietnam 54 17 4N 107 2 E
Vinh Long, Vietnam 55 10 16N 105 57 E
Vinh Yen, Vietnam 54 21 21N 105 35 E
Vinhais, Portugal 22 41 50N 7 0W
Vinica, Hrvatska, Yugoslavia 27 46 20N 16 9 E
Vinica, Slovenija, Yugoslavia 27 45 28N 15 16 E
Vinita, U.S.A. 121 36 40N 95 12W
Vinkeveen, Neths. 16 52 13N 4 56 E
Vinkovci, Yugoslavia 33 45 19N 18 48 E
Vinnitsa, U.S.S.R. 38 49 15N 28 30 E
Vinson Massif, Antarctica 143 78 35 S 85 25W
Vinstra, Norway 10 61 37N 9 44 E
Vinton, Calif., U.S.A. 124 39 48N 120 10W
Vinton, Iowa, U.S.A. 118 42 8N 92 1W
Vinton, La., U.S.A. 121 30 13N 93 35W
Vinţu de Jos, Romania 34 46 0N 23 30 E

Viöl, *W. Germany* **30** 54 32N 9 12 E
Viola, *U.S.A.* **118** 41 12N 90 35W
Violet Town, *Australia* **74** 36 38 S 145 42 E
Vipava, *Yugoslavia* **27** 45 51N 13 58 E
Vipiteno, *Italy* **27** 46 55N 11 25 E
Viqueque, *Indonesia* **57** 8 52 S 126 23 E
Vir, *Yugoslavia* **27** 44 17N 15 3 E
Virac, *Phil.* **57** 13 30N 124 20 E
Virachei, *Cambodia* **54** 13 59N 106 49 E
Virago Sd., *Canada* **110** 54 0N 132 30W
Virajpet = Virarajendrapet, *India* **51** 12 10N 75 50 E
Viramgam, *India* **48** 23 5N 72 0 E
Viranşehir, *Turkey* **46** 37 13N 39 45 E
Virarajendrapet, *India* **51** 12 10N 75 50 E
Viravanallur, *India* **51** 8 40N 77 30 E
Virden, *Canada* **111** 49 50N 100 56W
Virden, *U.S.A.* **118** 39 30N 89 46W
Vire, *France* **18** 48 50N 0 53W
Vire →, *France* **18** 49 20N 1 7W
Virgem da Lapa, *Brazil* **139** 16 49 S 42 21W
Vírgenes, C., *Argentina* **142** 52 19 S 68 21W
Virgin →, *Canada* **111** 57 2N 108 17W
Virgin →, *U.S.A.* **123** 36 50N 114 10W
Virgin Gorda, *Virgin Is.* **129** 18 30N 64 26W
Virgin Is., *W. Indies* **129** 18 40N 64 30W
Virginia, *S. Africa* **96** 28 8 S 26 55 E
Virginia, *Ill., U.S.A.* **118** 39 57N 90 13W
Virginia, *Minn., U.S.A.* **120** 47 30N 92 32W
Virginia □, *U.S.A.* **114** 37 45N 78 0W
Virginia Beach, *U.S.A.* **114** 36 54N 75 58W
Virginia City, *Mont., U.S.A.* **122** 45 18N 111 58W
Virginia City, *Nev., U.S.A.* **124** 39 19N 119 39W
Virginia Falls, *Canada* **110** 61 38N 125 42W
Virginiatown, *Canada* **106** 48 9N 79 36W
Virieu-le-Grand, *France* **21** 45 51N 5 39 E
Viroqua, *U.S.A.* **120** 43 33N 90 57W
Virovitica, *Yugoslavia* **33** 45 51N 17 21 E
Virserum, *Sweden* **11** 57 20N 15 35 E
Virton, *Belgium* **17** 49 35N 5 32 E
Virtsu, *U.S.S.R.* **36** 58 32N 23 33 E
Virú, *Peru* **136** 8 25 S 78 45W
Virudunagar, *India* **51** 9 30N 78 0 E
Vis, *Yugoslavia* **27** 43 0N 16 10 E
Vis Kanal, *Yugoslavia* **27** 43 4N 16 5 E
Visale, *Solomon Is.* **68** 9 15 S 159 42 E
Visalia, *U.S.A.* **124** 36 25N 119 18W
Visayan Sea, *Phil.* **57** 11 30N 123 30 E
Visby, *Sweden* **11** 57 37N 18 18 E
Viscount Melville Sd., *Canada* **144** 74 10N 108 0W
Visé, *Belgium* **17** 50 44N 5 41 E
Višegrad, *Yugoslavia* **33** 43 47N 19 17 E
Viseu, *Brazil* **138** 1 10 S 46 5W
Viseu, *Portugal* **22** 40 40N 7 55W
Viseu □, *Portugal* **22** 40 40N 7 55W
Vişeu de Sus, *Romania* **34** 47 45N 24 25 E
Vishakhapatnam, *India* **50** 17 45N 83 20 E
Visingsö, *Sweden* **11** 58 2N 14 20 E
Viskafors, *Sweden* **11** 57 37N 12 50 E
Vislanda, *Sweden* **11** 56 46N 14 30 E
Visnagar, *India* **48** 23 45N 72 32 E
Višnja Gora, *Yugoslavia* **27** 45 58N 14 45 E
Viso, Mte., *Italy* **26** 44 38N 7 5 E
Viso del Marqués, *Spain* **25** 38 32N 3 34W
Visoko, *Yugoslavia* **33** 43 58N 18 10 E
Visokoi I., *Antarctica* **143** 56 43 S 27 15W
Visp, *Switz.* **31** 46 17N 7 52 E
Visselhövede, *W. Germany* **30** 52 59N 9 36 E
Vista, *U.S.A.* **125** 33 12N 117 14W
Vistula = Wisła →, *Poland* **32** 54 22N 18 55 E
Vit →, *Bulgaria* **34** 43 30N 24 30 E
Vitanje, *Yugoslavia* **27** 46 25N 15 18 E
Vitebsk, *U.S.S.R.* **36** 55 10N 30 15 E
Viterbo, *Italy* **27** 42 25N 12 8 E
Viti Levu, *Fiji* **68** 17 30 S 177 30 E
Vitiaz Str., *Papua N. G.* **69** 5 40 S 147 10 E
Vitigudino, *Spain* **22** 41 1N 6 26W
Vitim, *U.S.S.R.* **41** 59 28N 112 35 E
Vitim →, *U.S.S.R.* **41** 59 26N 112 34 E
Vitória, *Brazil* **139** 20 20 S 40 22W
Vitoria, *Spain* **24** 42 50N 2 41W
Vitória da Conquista, *Brazil* **139** 14 51 S 40 51W
Vitória de São Antão, *Brazil* **138** 8 10 S 35 20W
Vitorino Friere, *Brazil* **138** 4 4 S 45 10W
Vitré, *France* **18** 48 8N 1 12W
Vitry-le-François, *France* **19** 48 43N 4 33 E
Vitsi, Óros, *Greece* **35** 40 40N 21 25 E
Vitteaux, *France* **19** 47 24N 4 30 E
Vittel, *France* **19** 48 12N 5 57 E
Vittória, *Italy* **29** 36 58N 14 30 E
Vittório Véneto, *Italy* **27** 45 59N 12 18 E
Vitu Is., *Papua N. G.* **69** 4 50 S 149 25 E
Vivario, *France* **21** 42 10N 9 11 E
Vivegnis, *Belgium* **17** 50 42N 5 39 E
Viver, *Spain* **24** 39 55N 0 36W
Vivero, *Spain* **22** 43 39N 7 38W
Viviers, *France* **21** 44 30N 4 40 E
Vivonne, *France* **20** 46 25N 0 15 E
Vizcaíno, Desierto de, *Mexico* **126** 27 40N 113 50W
Vizcaíno, Sierra, *Mexico* **126** 27 30N 114 0W
Vizcaya □, *Spain* **24** 43 15N 2 45W
Vizianagaram, *India* **50** 18 6N 83 30 E
Vizille, *France* **21** 45 5N 5 46 E
Viziñada, *Yugoslavia* **27** 45 20N 13 46 E
Viziru, *Romania* **34** 45 0N 27 43 E
Vizovice, *Czech.* **32** 49 12N 17 56 E
Vizzini, *Italy* **29** 37 9N 14 43 E
Vlaardingen, *Neths.* **16** 51 55N 4 21 E
Vlădeasa, *Romania* **34** 46 47N 22 50 E
Vladimir, *U.S.S.R.* **37** 56 15N 40 30 E
Vladimir Volynskiy, *U.S.S.R.* **36** 50 50N 24 18 E
Vladimirovac, *Yugoslavia* **33** 45 1N 20 53 E
Vladimirovka, *R.S.F.S.R., U.S.S.R.* **39** 48 27N 46 10 E
Vladimirovka, *R.S.F.S.R., U.S.S.R.* **39** 44 45N 44 41 E
Vladislavovka, *U.S.S.R.* **38** 45 15N 35 15 E
Vladivostok, *U.S.S.R.* **41** 43 10N 131 53 E
Vlamertinge, *Belgium* **17** 50 51N 2 49 E
Vlasenica, *Yugoslavia* **33** 44 11N 18 59 E
Vlasinsko Jezero, *Yugoslavia* **33** 42 44N 22 22 E
Vleuten, *Neths.* **16** 52 6N 5 1 E
Vlieland, *Neths.* **16** 53 16N 4 55 E
Vliestroom, *Neths.* **16** 53 19N 5 8 E
Vlijmen, *Neths.* **17** 51 42N 5 14 E
Vlissingen, *Neths.* **17** 51 26N 3 34 E
Vlóra, *Albania* **35** 40 32N 19 28 E
Vlorës, Gjiri i, *Albania* **35** 40 29N 19 27 E
Vltava →, *Czech.* **32** 50 21N 14 30 E
Vo Dat, *Vietnam* **55** 11 9N 107 31 E
Vobarno, *Italy* **26** 45 38N 10 30 E
Voćin, *Yugoslavia* **33** 45 37N 17 33 E
Vodice, *Yugoslavia* **27** 43 47N 15 47 E
Vodnjan, *Yugoslavia* **27** 44 59N 13 52 E
Vogelkop = Doberai, Jazirah, *Indonesia* **57** 1 25 S 133 0 E
Vogelsberg, *W. Germany* **30** 50 37N 9 15 E
Voghera, *Italy* **26** 44 59N 9 1 E
Voh, *N. Cal.* **68** 20 58 S 164 42 E
Vohibinany, *Madag.* **97** 18 49 S 49 4 E
Vohimarina, *Madag.* **97** 13 25 S 50 0 E
Vohimena, Tanjon' i, *Madag.* **97** 25 36 S 45 8 E
Vohipeno, *Madag.* **97** 22 22 S 47 51 E
Voi, *Kenya* **92** 3 25 S 38 32 E
Void, *France* **19** 48 40N 5 36 E
Voiron, *France* **21** 45 22N 5 35 E
Voisey B., *Canada* **105** 56 15N 61 50W
Voitsberg, *Austria* **33** 47 3N 15 9 E
Voiviïs Límni, *Greece* **35** 39 30N 22 45 E
Vojens, *Denmark* **11** 55 16N 9 18 E
Vojmsjön, *Sweden* **8** 64 55N 16 40 E
Vojnik, *Italy* **26** 46 18N 15 19 E
Vojnió, *Yugoslavia* **27** 45 19N 15 43 E
Vokhma, *U.S.S.R.* **37** 59 0N 46 45 E
Vokhma →, *U.S.S.R.* **37** 56 20N 46 20 E
Vokhtoga, *U.S.S.R.* **37** 58 46N 41 8 E
Volborg, *U.S.A.* **120** 45 50N 105 44W
Volcano Is., *Pac. Oc.* **66** 25 0N 141 0 E
Volchansk, *U.S.S.R.* **37** 50 17N 36 58 E
Volchayevka, *U.S.S.R.* **41** 48 40N 134 30 E
Volchya →, *U.S.S.R.* **38** 48 0N 37 0 E
Volda, *Norway* **8** 62 9N 6 5 E
Volendam, *Neths.* **16** 52 30N 5 4 E
Volga, *U.S.S.R.* **37** 57 58N 38 16 E
Volga →, *U.S.S.R.* **39** 48 30N 46 0 E
Volga Hts. = Privolzhskaya Vozvyshennost, *U.S.S.R.* **37** 51 0N 46 0 E
Volgodonsk, *U.S.S.R.* **39** 47 33N 42 5 E
Volgograd, *U.S.S.R.* **39** 48 40N 44 25 E
Volgogradskoye Vdkhr., *U.S.S.R.* **37** 50 0N 45 20 E
Volgorechensk, *U.S.S.R.* **37** 57 28N 41 14 E
Volkach, *W. Germany* **31** 49 52N 10 14 E
Volkerak, *Neths.* **17** 51 39N 4 18 E
Volkhov, *U.S.S.R.* **36** 59 55N 32 15 E
Volkhov →, *U.S.S.R.* **36** 60 8N 32 20 E
Völklingen, *W. Germany* **31** 49 15N 6 50 E
Volkovysk, *U.S.S.R.* **36** 53 9N 24 30 E
Volksrust, *S. Africa* **97** 27 24 S 29 53 E
Vollenhove, *Neths.* **16** 52 40N 5 58 E
Vol'n'ansk, *U.S.S.R.* **38** 47 55N 35 29 E
Volnovakha, *U.S.S.R.* **38** 47 35N 37 30 E
Volochanka, *U.S.S.R.* **41** 71 0N 94 28 E
Volodarsk, *U.S.S.R.* **37** 56 12N 43 15 E
Vologda, *U.S.S.R.* **37** 59 10N 40 0 E
Volokolamsk, *U.S.S.R.* **37** 56 5N 35 57 E
Volokonovka, *U.S.S.R.* **37** 50 33N 37 52 E
Vólos, *Greece* **35** 39 24N 22 59 E
Volosovo, *U.S.S.R.* **36** 59 27N 29 32 E
Volozhin, *U.S.S.R.* **36** 54 3N 26 30 E
Volsk, *U.S.S.R.* **37** 52 5N 47 22 E
Volta →, *Ghana* **91** 5 46N 0 41 E
Volta, L., *Ghana* **91** 7 30N 0 15 E
Volta Blanche = White Volta →, *Ghana* **91** 9 10N 1 15W
Volta Redonda, *Brazil* **141** 22 31 S 44 5W
Voltaire, C., *Australia* **78** 14 16 S 125 35 E
Volterra, *Italy* **26** 43 24N 10 50 E
Voltri, *Italy* **26** 44 25N 8 43 E
Volturara Áppula, *Italy* **29** 41 30N 15 2 E
Volturno →, *Italy* **29** 41 1N 13 55 E
Volubilis, *Morocco* **84** 34 2N 5 33W
Volvo, *Australia* **73** 31 41 S 143 57 E
Volzhsk, *U.S.S.R.* **37** 55 57N 48 23 E
Volzhskiy, *U.S.S.R.* **39** 48 56N 44 46 E
Vondrozo, *Madag.* **97** 22 49 S 47 20 E
Voorburg, *Neths.* **16** 52 5N 4 24 E
Voorne Putten, *Neths.* **16** 51 52N 4 10 E
Voorst, *Neths.* **16** 52 10N 6 8 E
Voorthuizen, *Neths.* **16** 52 11N 5 36 E
Vopnafjörður, *Iceland* **8** 65 45N 14 40W
Vóras Óros, *Greece* **35** 40 57N 21 45 E
Vorbasse, *Denmark* **11** 55 39N 9 6 E
Vorden, *Neths.* **16** 52 6N 6 19 E
Vorderrhein →, *Switz.* **31** 46 49N 9 25 E
Vordingborg, *Denmark* **11** 55 0N 11 54 E
Voreppe, *France* **21** 45 18N 5 39 E
Voríai Sporádhes, *Greece* **35** 39 15N 23 30 E
Vórios Evvoïkos Kólpos, *Greece* **35** 38 45N 23 15 E
Vorkuta, *U.S.S.R.* **40** 67 48N 64 20 E
Vorma →, *Norway* **10** 60 9N 11 27 E
Vorona →, *U.S.S.R.* **37** 51 22N 42 3 E
Voronezh, *R.S.F.S.R., U.S.S.R.* **37** 51 40N 39 10 E
Voronezh, *Ukraine S.S.R., U.S.S.R.* **36** 51 47N 33 28 E
Voronezh →, *U.S.S.R.* **37** 51 56N 37 17 E
Vorontsovo-Aleksandrovskoye = Zelenokumsk, *U.S.S.R.* **39** 44 24N 43 53 E
Voroshilovgrad, *U.S.S.R.* **39** 48 38N 39 15 E
Vorovskoye, *U.S.S.R.* **41** 54 30N 155 50 E
Vorselaar, *Belgium* **17** 51 12N 4 46 E
Vorskla →, *U.S.S.R.* **38** 48 50N 34 10 E
Võru, *U.S.S.R.* **36** 57 48N 26 54 E
Vorupør, *Denmark* **11** 56 58N 8 22 E
Vosges, *France* **19** 48 20N 7 10 E
Vosges □, *France* **19** 48 12N 6 20 E
Voskopoja, *Albania* **35** 40 40N 20 33 E
Voskresensk, *U.S.S.R.* **37** 55 19N 38 43 E
Voskresenskoye, *U.S.S.R.* **37** 56 51N 45 30 E
Voss, *Norway* **9** 60 38N 6 26 E
Vosselaar, *Belgium* **17** 51 19N 4 52 E
Vostochnyy Sayan, *U.S.S.R.* **41** 54 0N 96 0 E
Vostok I., *Kiribati* **67** 10 5 S 152 23W
Vouga →, *Portugal* **22** 40 41N 8 40W
Vouillé, *France* **18** 46 38N 0 10 E
Voulou, *C.A.R.* **94** 8 33N 22 36 E
Voulte-sur-Rhône, La, *France* **21** 44 48N 4 46 E
Vouvray, *France* **18** 47 25N 0 48 E
Voúxa, Ákra, *Greece* **35** 35 37N 23 32 E
Vouzela, *Portugal* **22** 40 43N 8 7W
Vouziers, *France* **19** 49 22N 4 40 E
Voves, *France* **19** 48 15N 1 38 E
Voxna, *Sweden* **10** 61 20N 15 40 E
Vozhgaly, *U.S.S.R.* **37** 58 9N 50 11 E
Voznesenka, *U.S.S.R.* **41** 56 40N 95 3 E
Voznesensk, *U.S.S.R.* **38** 47 35N 31 21 E
Voznesenye, *U.S.S.R.* **40** 61 0N 35 45 E
Vrådal, *Norway* **10** 59 20N 8 25 E
Vrakhnéïka, *Greece* **35** 38 10N 21 40 E
Vrancei, Munţii, *Romania* **34** 46 0N 26 30 E
Vrangelya, Ostrov, *U.S.S.R.* **41** 71 0N 180 0 E
Vranica, *Yugoslavia* **33** 43 55N 17 50 E
Vranje, *Yugoslavia* **33** 42 34N 21 54 E
Vransko, *Yugoslavia* **27** 46 17N 14 58 E
Vratsa, *Bulgaria* **34** 43 13N 23 30 E
Vrbas, *Yugoslavia* **33** 45 40N 19 40 E
Vrbas →, *Yugoslavia* **33** 45 8N 17 29 E
Vrbnik, *Yugoslavia* **27** 45 4N 14 40 E
Vrbovec, *Yugoslavia* **27** 45 53N 16 28 E
Vrbovsko, *Yugoslavia* **27** 45 24N 15 5 E
Vrchlabí, *Czech.* **32** 50 38N 15 37 E
Vrede, *S. Africa* **97** 27 24 S 29 6 E
Vredefort, *S. Africa* **96** 27 0 S 27 22 E
Vredenburg, *S. Africa* **96** 32 56 S 18 0 E
Vredendal, *S. Africa* **96** 31 41 S 18 35 E
Vreeswijk, *Neths.* **16** 52 1N 5 6 E
Vrena, *Sweden* **11** 58 54N 16 41 E
Vrgorac, *Yugoslavia* **33** 43 12N 17 20 E
Vrhnika, *Yugoslavia* **27** 45 58N 14 15 E
Vriddhachalam, *India* **51** 11 30N 79 20 E
Vridi, *Ivory C.* **90** 5 15N 4 3W
Vries, *Neths.* **16** 53 5N 6 35 E
Vriezenveen, *Neths.* **16** 52 25N 6 38 E
Vrindavan, *India* **48** 27 37N 77 40 E
Vrnograč, *Yugoslavia* **27** 45 10N 15 57 E
Vroomshoop, *Neths.* **16** 52 27N 6 34 E
Vršac, *Yugoslavia* **33** 45 8N 21 18 E
Vrsacki Kanal, *Yugoslavia* **33** 45 15N 21 0 E
Vryburg, *S. Africa* **96** 26 55 S 24 45 E
Vryheid, *S. Africa* **97** 27 45 S 30 47 E
Vsetín, *Czech.* **32** 49 20N 18 0 E
Vu Liet, *Vietnam* **54** 18 43N 105 23 E
Vucha →, *Bulgaria* **35** 42 10N 24 26 E
Vught, *Neths.* **17** 51 38N 5 20 E
Vukovar, *Yugoslavia* **33** 45 21N 18 59 E
Vulcan, *Canada* **110** 50 25N 113 15W
Vulcan, *U.S.A.* **114** 45 46N 87 51W
Vulcano, *Italy* **29** 38 25N 14 58 E
Vŭlchedruma, *Bulgaria* **34** 43 42N 23 27 E
Vulci, *Italy* **27** 42 23N 11 37 E
Vulkaneshty, *U.S.S.R.* **38** 45 35N 28 30 E
Vunduzi →, *Mozam.* **93** 18 56 S 34 1 E
Vung Tau, *Vietnam* **55** 10 21N 107 4 E
Vunisea, *Fiji* **68** 19 3 S 178 10 E
Vŭrbitsa, *Bulgaria* **34** 42 59N 26 40 E
Vuyyuru, *India* **51** 16 28N 80 50 E
Vyara, *India* **50** 21 8N 73 28 E
Vyasniki, *U.S.S.R.* **37** 56 10N 42 10 E
Vyatka →, *U.S.S.R.* **37** 56 30N 51 0 E
Vyatskiye Polyany, *U.S.S.R.* **37** 56 5N 51 0 E
Vyazemskiy, *U.S.S.R.* **41** 47 32N 134 45 E
Vyazma, *U.S.S.R.* **36** 55 10N 34 15 E
Vyborg, *U.S.S.R.* **40** 60 43N 28 47 E
Vychegda →, *U.S.S.R.* **40** 61 18N 46 36 E
Vychodné Beskydy, *Europe* **32** 49 30N 22 0 E
Vyksa, *U.S.S.R.* **37** 55 19N 42 11 E
Vypin, *India* **51** 10 10N 76 15 E
Vyrnwy, L., *U.K.* **12** 52 48N 3 30W
Vyshniy Volochek, *U.S.S.R.* **36** 57 30N 34 30 E
Vyškov, *Czech.* **32** 49 17N 17 0 E
Vysoké Mýto, *Czech.* **32** 49 58N 16 10 E
Vysokovsk, *U.S.S.R.* **37** 56 22N 36 30 E
Vysotsk, *U.S.S.R.* **36** 51 43N 26 32 E

W

W.A.C. Bennett Dam, *Canada* **110** 56 2N 122 6W
Wa, *Ghana* **90** 10 7N 2 25W
Waal →, *Neths.* **16** 51 59N 4 30 E
Waalwijk, *Neths.* **17** 51 42N 5 4 E
Waarschoot, *Belgium* **17** 51 10N 3 36 E
Waasmunster, *Belgium* **17** 51 6N 4 5 E
Wabag, *Papua N. G.* **69** 5 32 S 143 40 E
Wabakimi L., *Canada* **104** 50 38N 89 45W
Wabana, *Canada* **105** 47 40N 53 0W
Wabano →, *Canada* **107** 48 20N 74 3W
Wabao, C., *N. Cal.* **68** 21 35 S 167 53 E
Wabasca, *Canada* **110** 55 57N 113 56W
Wabash, *U.S.A.* **119** 40 48N 85 46W
Wabash →, *U.S.A.* **114** 37 46N 88 2W
Wabawng, *Burma* **52** 26 20N 97 25 E
Wabeno, *U.S.A.* **114** 45 25N 88 40W
Wabi →, *Ethiopia* **89** 7 45N 40 50 E
Wabigoon L., *Canada* **111** 49 44N 92 44W
Wabowden, *Canada* **111** 54 55N 98 38W
Wąbrzeźno, *Poland* **32** 53 16N 18 57 E
Wabu Hu, *China* **59** 32 20N 116 50 E
Wabuk Pt., *Canada* **104** 55 20N 85 5W
Wabush, *Canada* **105** 52 55N 66 52W
Wabuska, *U.S.A.* **122** 39 9N 119 13W
Wachtebeke, *Belgium* **17** 51 11N 3 52 E
Wächtersbach, *W. Germany* **31** 50 16N 9 18 E
Waco, *U.S.A.* **121** 31 33N 97 5W
Waconichi, L., *Canada* **107** 50 8N 74 0W
Wad Ban Naqa, *Sudan* **89** 16 32N 33 9 E
Wad Banda, *Sudan* **89** 13 10N 27 56 E
Wad el Haddad, *Sudan* **89** 13 50N 33 30 E
Wad en Nau, *Sudan* **89** 14 10N 33 34 E
Wad Hamid, *Sudan* **89** 16 30N 32 45 E
Wâd Medanî, *Sudan* **89** 14 28N 33 30 E
Wad Thana, *Pakistan* **48** 27 22N 66 23 E
Wadayama, *Japan* **64** 35 19N 134 52 E
Waddān, *Libya* **86** 29 9N 16 10 E
Waddān, Jabal, *Libya* **86** 29 0N 16 15 E
Waddeneilanden, *Neths.* **16** 53 25N 5 10 E
Waddenzee, *Neths.* **16** 53 6N 5 10 E
Wadderin Hill, *Australia* **79** 32 0 S 118 25 E
Waddington, *U.S.A.* **117** 44 51N 75 12W
Waddington, Mt., *Canada* **110** 51 23N 125 15W
Waddinxveen, *Neths.* **16** 52 2N 4 40 E
Waddy Pt., *Australia* **73** 24 58 S 153 21 E
Wadena, *Canada* **111** 51 57N 103 47W
Wadena, *U.S.A.* **120** 46 25N 95 8W
Wädenswil, *Switz.* **31** 47 14N 8 40 E
Wadesboro, *U.S.A.* **115** 35 2N 80 2W
Wadhams, *Canada* **110** 51 30N 127 30W
Wādī ash Shāţi', *Libya* **86** 27 30N 15 0 E
Wādī Banī Walīd, *Libya* **86** 31 49N 14 0 E
Wadi Gemâl, *Egypt* **88** 24 35N 35 10 E
Wadi Halfa, *Sudan* **88** 21 53N 31 19 E
Wadian, *China* **59** 32 42N 112 29 E
Wadowice, *Poland* **32** 49 52N 19 30 E
Wadsworth, *U.S.A.* **122** 39 38N 119 22W
Wafrah, *Si. Arabia* **46** 28 33N 47 56 E
Wagenberg, *Neths.* **17** 51 40N 4 46 E
Wageningen, *Neths.* **16** 51 58N 5 40 E
Wageningen, *Surinam* **135** 5 50N 56 50W
Wager B., *Canada* **103** 65 26N 88 40W
Wager Bay, *Canada* **103** 65 56N 90 49W
Wagga Wagga, *Australia* **76** 35 7 S 147 24 E
Waghete, *Indonesia* **57** 4 10 S 135 50 E
Wagin, *Australia* **79** 33 17 S 117 25 E
Wagina, *Solomon Is.* **68** 7 25 S 157 47 E
Wagon Mound, *U.S.A.* **121** 36 1N 104 44W
Wagoner, *U.S.A.* **121** 36 0N 95 20W
Wagrowiec, *Poland* **32** 52 48N 17 11 E
Wah, *Pakistan* **48** 33 45N 72 40 E
Wahai, *Indonesia* **57** 2 48 S 129 35 E
Wahgunyah, *Australia* **75** 35 57 S 146 25 E
Wahiawa, *U.S.A.* **112** 21 30N 158 2W
Wahnai, *Afghan.* **48** 32 40N 65 50 E
Wahoo, *U.S.A.* **120** 41 15N 96 35W

Wahpeton, *U.S.A.* . . . **120** 46 20N 96 35W
Wahpool, L., *Australia* **74** 35 18 S 142 58 E
Wai, *India* . . . . **50** 17 56N 73 57 E
Wai, Koh, *Cambodia* . **55** 9 55N 102 55 E
Waiai →, *N.Z.* . . . . . . **81** 46 12 S 167 38 E
Waiau, *N.Z.* . . . . **81** 42 39 S 173 5 E
Waiau →, *N.Z.* . . . . . . **81** 42 47 S 173 22 E
Waiawe Ganga →,
Sri Lanka . . . . **51** 6 15N 81 0 E
Waibeem, *Indonesia* . . **57** 0 30 S 132 59 E
Waiblingen,
W. Germany . . . . **31** 48 49N 9 20 E
Waidhofen,
Niederösterreich,
Austria . . . . **32** 48 49N 15 17 E
Waidhofen,
Niederösterreich,
Austria . . . . **33** 47 57N 14 46 E
Waigeo, *Indonesia* . . . . **57** 0 20 S 130 40 E
Waihao →, *N.Z.* . . . . **81** 44 52 S 171 11 E
Waihao Downs, *N.Z.* . **81** 44 48 S 170 55 E
Waiheke Islands, *N.Z.* **80** 36 48 S 175 6 E
Waihi, *N.Z.* . . . . **80** 37 23 S 175 52 E
Waihola, *N.Z.* . . . . **81** 46 1 S 170 8 E
Waihola L., *N.Z.* . . . . **81** 45 59 S 170 8 E
Waihou →, *N.Z.* . . . . **81** 37 15 S 175 40 E
Waika, *Zaïre* . . . . **92** 2 22 S 25 42 E
Waikabubak, *Indonesia* **57** 9 45 S 119 25 E
Waikaia, *N.Z.* . . . . **81** 45 44 S 168 51 E
Waikaka, *N.Z.* . . . . **81** 45 55 S 169 1 E
Waikare, L., *N.Z.* . . . . **80** 37 26 S 175 13 E
Waikaremoana, *N.Z.* . **80** 38 42 S 177 12 E
Waikaremoana L.,
N.Z. . . . . **80** 38 49 S 177 9 E
Waikari, *N.Z.* . . . . **81** 42 58 S 172 41 E
Waikato →, *N.Z.* . . . . **80** 37 23 S 174 43 E
Waikerie, *Australia* . . . **73** 34 9 S 140 0 E
Waikiekie, *N.Z.* . . . . . . **80** 35 57 S 174 16 E
Waikokopu, *N.Z.* . . . . **80** 39 3 S 177 52 E
Waikouaiti, *N.Z.* . . . . . **81** 45 36 S 170 41 E
Waimangaroa, *N.Z.* . . **81** 41 43 S 171 46 E
Waimarie, *N.Z.* . . . . . . **81** 41 35 S 171 58 E
Waimate, *N.Z.* . . . . **81** 44 45 S 171 3 E
Waimea Plain, *N.Z.* . . **81** 45 55 S 168 35 E
Waimes, *Belgium* . . . . . **17** 50 25N 6 7 E
Wainganga →, *India* . **50** 18 50N 79 55 E
Waingapu, *Indonesia* . **57** 9 35 S 120 11 E
Waingmaw, *Burma* . . . **52** 25 21N 97 26 E
Waini →, *Guyana* . . . **135** 8 20N 59 50W
Wainuiomata, *N.Z.* . . . **80** 41 17 S 174 56 E
Wainwright, *Canada* . . **111** 52 50N 110 50W
Wainwright, *U.S.A.* . . **102** 70 39N 160 1W
Waiotapu, *N.Z.* . . . . . . **80** 38 21 S 176 25 E
Waiouru, *N.Z.* . . . . **80** 39 28 S 175 41 E
Waipahi, *N.Z.* . . . . **81** 46 6 S 169 15 E
Waipapa Pt., *N.Z.* . . . **81** 46 40 S 168 51 E
Waipara, *N.Z.* . . . . **81** 43 3 S 172 46 E
Waipawa, *N.Z.* . . . . . . **80** 39 56 S 176 38 E
Waipiro, *N.Z.* . . . . **80** 38 2 S 178 22 E
Waipu, *N.Z.* . . . . **80** 35 59 S 174 29 E
Waipukurau, *N.Z.* . . . . **80** 40 1 S 176 33 E
Wairakei, *N.Z.* . . . . . . **80** 38 37 S 176 6 E
Wairarapa, L., *N.Z.* . . **80** 41 14 S 175 15 E
Wairau →, *N.Z.* . . . . **81** 41 32 S 174 7 E
Wairio, *N.Z.* . . . . **81** 45 59 S 168 3 E
Wairoa, *N.Z.* . . . . **80** 39 3 S 177 25 E
Wairoa →, *N.Z.* . . . . **80** 36 5 S 173 59 E
Waitaha, *N.Z.* . . . . **81** 43 0 S 170 45 E
Waitaki →, *N.Z.* . . . . **81** 44 56 S 171 7 E
Waitaki Plains, *N.Z.* . . **81** 44 22 S 170 0 E
Waitara, *N.Z.* . . . . **80** 38 59 S 174 15 E
Waitchie, *Australia* . . . **74** 35 22 S 143 8 E
Waitoa, *N.Z.* . . . . **80** 37 37 S 175 35 E
Waitotara, *N.Z.* . . . . . . **80** 39 49 S 174 44 E
Waitsburg, *U.S.A.* **122** 46 15N 118 0W
Waiuku, *N.Z.* . . . . **80** 37 15 S 174 45 E
Waiyevo, *Fiji* . . . . **68** 16 48 S 179 59W
Wajima, *Japan* . . . . **63** 37 30N 137 0 E
Wajir, *Kenya* . . . . **92** 1 42N 40 5 E
Wajir □, *Kenya* . . . . . . **92** 1 42N 40 20 E
Waka, *Zaïre* . . . . **94** 1 1N 20 13 E
Wakarusa, *U.S.A.* **119** 41 32N 86 1W
Wakasa, *Japan* . . . . **64** 35 20N 134 24 E
Wakasa-Wan, *Japan* . . **65** 35 40N 135 30 E
Wakatipu, L., *N.Z.* . . . **81** 45 5 S 168 33 E
Wakaw, *Canada* **111** 52 39N 105 44W
Wakayama, *Japan* . . . . **65** 34 15N 135 15 E
Wakayama-ken □,
Japan . . . . **65** 33 50N 135 30 E
Wake, *Japan* . . . . **64** 34 48N 134 8 E
Wake Forest, *U.S.A.* . . **115** 35 58N 78 30W
Wake I., *Pac. Oc.* . . . . **66** 19 18N 166 36 E
Wakefield, *Canada* . . . **106** 45 38N 75 56W
Wakefield, *N.Z.* . . . . . **81** 41 24 S 173 5 E
Wakefield, *U.K.* **12** 53 41N 1 31W
Wakefield, *Mass.,*
U.S.A. **117** 42 30N 71 3W
Wakefield, *Mich.,*
U.S.A. **120** 46 28N 89 53W
Wakema, *Burma* . . . . . **52** 16 30N 95 11 E
Wakkanai, *Japan* . . . . . **63** 45 28N 141 35 E
Wakkerstroom,
S. Africa . . . . **97** 27 24 S 30 10 E
Wakomata L., *Canada* **108** 46 34N 83 22W
Wakool, *Australia* . . . . **74** 35 28 S 144 23 E
Wakool →, *Australia* . **74** 35 5 S 143 33 E
Wakre, *Indonesia* . . . . **57** 0 19 S 131 5 E
Waku, *Papua N. G.* . . **69** 6 5 S 149 9 E
Wakuach L., *Canada* . **105** 55 34N 67 32W
Walamba, *Zambia* . . . . **93** 13 30 S 28 42 E
Wałbrzych, *Poland* . . . **32** 50 45N 16 18 E
Walbury Hill, *U.K.* . . . **13** 51 22N 1 28W
Walcha, *Australia* . . . . **77** 30 55 S 151 31 E
Walcha Road, *Australia* **77** 30 55 S 151 24 E
Walcheren, *Neths.* . . . . **17** 51 30N 3 35 E
Walcott, *U.S.A.* **122** 41 50N 106 55W
Wałcz, *Poland* . . . . **32** 53 17N 16 27 E
Wald, *Switz.* . . . . **31** 47 17N 8 56 E
Waldbröl, *W. Germany* **30** 50 52N 7 36 E
Waldburg Ra.,
Australia . . . . **79** 24 40 S 117 35 E
Waldeck, *W. Germany* **30** 51 12N 9 4 E
Walden, *Colo., U.S.A.* **122** 40 47N 106 20W
Walden, *N.Y., U.S.A.* **117** 41 32N 74 13W
Waldport, *U.S.A.* **122** 44 30N 124 2W
Waldron, *U.S.A.* **121** 34 52N 94 4W
Waldshut, *W. Germany* **31** 47 37N 8 12 E
Walembele, *Ghana* . . . **90** 10 30N 1 58W
Walensee, *Switz.* . . . . . **31** 47 7N 9 13 E
Wales □, *U.K.* **13** 52 30N 3 30W
Walewale, *Ghana* **91** 10 21N 0 50W
Walgett, *Australia* . . . . **73** 30 0 S 148 5 E
Walgreen Coast,
Antarctica . . . . **143** 75 15 S 105 0W
Walhalla, *Australia* . . . **75** 37 56 S 146 29 E
Walhalla, *U.S.A.* **111** 48 55N 97 55W
Walkaway, *Australia* . . **79** 28 59 S 114 48 E
Walker, *Minn., U.S.A.* **120** 47 4N 94 35W
Walker, *Mo., U.S.A.* . **118** 37 54N 94 14W
Walker L., *Man.,*
Canada **111** 54 42N 95 57W
Walker L., *Qué.,*
Canada **105** 50 20N 67 11W
Walker L., *U.S.A.* . . . **122** 38 56N 118 46W
Walkerston, *Australia* . **72** 21 11 S 149 8 E
Walkerton, *Canada* . . . **108** 44 10N 81 10W
Walkerton, *U.S.A.* . . . **119** 41 28N 86 29W
Walkerville, *Australia* . **74** 38 52 S 146 0 E
Wall, *U.S.A.* **120** 44 0N 102 14W
Walla Walla, *U.S.A.* . . **122** 46 3N 118 25W
Wallabadah, *N.S.W.,*
Australia . . . . **77** 31 31 S 150 49 E
Wallabadah, *Queens.,*
Australia . . . . **72** 17 57 S 142 15 E
Wallace, *Idaho, U.S.A.* **122** 47 30N 116 0W
Wallace, *N.C., U.S.A.* **115** 34 44N 77 59W
Wallace, *Nebr., U.S.A.* **120** 40 51N 101 12W
Wallaceburg, *Canada* . **108** 42 34N 82 23W
Wallacetown, *N.Z.* . . . **81** 46 21 S 168 19 E
Wallachia = Valahia,
Romania . . . . **34** 44 35N 25 0 E
Wallacia, *Australia* . . . **76** 33 50 S 150 39 E
Wallal, *Australia* . . . . . **73** 26 32 S 146 7 E
Wallal Downs,
Australia . . . . **78** 19 47 S 120 40 E
Wallambin, L.,
Australia . . . . **79** 30 57 S 117 35 E
Wallan, *Australia* . . . . . **74** 37 26 S 144 59 E
Wallangarra, *Australia* **77** 28 56 S 151 58 E
Wallangra, *Australia* . . **77** 29 15 S 150 54 E
Wallaroo, *Australia* . . . **73** 33 56 S 137 39 E
Wallasey, *U.K.* **12** 53 26N 3 2W
Walldürn, *W. Germany* **31** 49 34N 9 23 E
Wallendbeen, *Australia* **76** 34 31 S 148 11 E
Wallerawang, *Australia* **76** 33 25 S 150 4 E
Wallhallow, *Australia* . **72** 17 50 S 135 50 E
Wallingford, *U.K.* **12** 51 40N 1 15W
Wallingford, *U.S.A.* . . **117** 41 27N 72 50W
Wallis, L., *Australia* . . **77** 32 15 S 152 28 E
Wallis & Futuna,
Pac. Oc. . . . . **66** 13 18 S 176 10W
Wallowa, *U.S.A.* **122** 45 40N 117 35W
Wallowa, Mts., *U.S.A.* **122** 45 20N 117 30W
Wallsend, *Australia* . . . **76** 32 55 S 151 40 E
Wallsend, *U.K.* **12** 54 59N 1 30W
Wallula, *U.S.A.* **122** 46 3N 118 59W
Wallumbilla, *Australia* **73** 26 33 S 149 9 E
Walmsley, L., *Canada* **111** 63 25N 108 36W
Walney, Isle of, *U.K.* . **12** 54 5N 3 15W
Walnut, *U.S.A.* **118** 41 33N 89 36W
Walnut Creek, *U.S.A.* **124** 37 54N 122 4W
Walnut Ridge, *U.S.A.* **121** 36 7N 90 58W
Walpeup, *Australia* . . . **74** 35 7 S 142 2 E
Walsall, *U.K.* **13** 52 36N 1 59W
Walsenburg, *U.S.A.* . . . **121** 37 42N 104 45W
Walsh, *U.S.A.* **121** 37 28N 102 15W
Walsh →, *Australia* . . **72** 16 31 S 143 42 E
Walsh P.O., *Australia* . **72** 16 40 S 144 0 E
Walshoutem, *Belgium* . **17** 50 43N 5 4 E
Walsrode, *W. Germany* **30** 52 51N 9 37 E
Waltair, *India* . . . . **50** 17 44N 83 23 E
Walterboro, *U.S.A.* . . . **115** 32 53N 80 40W
Walters, *U.S.A.* **121** 34 25N 98 20W
Waltershausen,
E. Germany . . . . **30** 50 53N 10 33 E
Waltham, *U.S.A.* **117** 42 22N 71 12W
Waltham Sta., *Canada* **106** 45 57N 76 57W
Waltman, *U.S.A.* **122** 43 8N 107 15W
Walton, *Ky., U.S.A.* . . **119** 38 52N 84 37W
Walton, *N.Y., U.S.A.* **117** 42 12N 75 9W
Waltonville, *U.S.A.* . . **118** 38 13N 89 2W
Walu, *Burma* . . . . **52** 26 28N 98 2 E
Walvisbaai, *S. Africa* . **96** 23 0 S 14 28 E
Walwa, *Australia* . . . . . **75** 35 59 S 147 44 E
Wamba, *Kenya* . . . . . . **92** 0 58N 37 19 E
Wamba, *Zaïre* . . . . **92** 2 10N 27 57 E
Wambelong, Mt.,
Australia . . . . **76** 31 19 S 148 54 E
Wamego, *U.S.A.* **120** 39 14N 96 22W
Wamena, *Indonesia* . . . **57** 4 4 S 138 57 E
Wamsasi, *Indonesia* . . **57** 3 27 S 126 7 E
Wan Hat, *Burma* . . . . . **52** 20 14N 97 53 E
Wan Kinghao, *Burma* . **52** 21 34N 98 17 E
Wan Lai-kam, *Burma* . **52** 21 21N 98 22 E
Wan Tup, *Burma* . . . . . **52** 21 13N 98 42 E
Wan Xian, *China* . . . . . **60** 38 47N 115 7 E
Wana, *Pakistan* . . . . . . **48** 32 20N 69 32 E
Wanaaring, *Australia* . **73** 29 38 S 144 9 E
Wanaka L., *N.Z.* . . . . . **81** 44 33 S 169 7 E
Wan'an, *China* . . . . **59** 26 26N 114 49 E
Wanapiri, *Indonesia* . . **57** 4 30 S 135 59 E
Wanapitei →, *Canada* **108** 46 2N 80 51W
Wanapitei L., *Canada* **108** 46 45N 80 40W
Wanbi, *Australia* . . . . . **73** 34 46 S 140 17 E
Wandaik, *Guyana* **135** 4 27N 59 35W
Wandanian, *Australia* . **76** 35 6 S 150 30 E
Wanderer, *Zimb.* . . . . . **93** 19 36 S 30 1 E
Wandoan, *Australia* . . **73** 26 5 S 149 55 E
Wandong, *Australia* . . **74** 37 21 S 145 2 E
Wandre, *Belgium* . . . . . **17** 50 40N 5 39 E
Wanfercée-Baulet,
Belgium . . . . **17** 50 28N 4 35 E
Wanfu, *China* . . . . **61** 40 8N 122 38 E
Wang →, *Thailand* . . . **54** 17 8N 99 2 E
Wang Kai, *Sudan* . . . . **89** 9 3N 29 23 E
Wang Noi, *Thailand* . . **54** 14 13N 100 44 E
Wang Saphung,
Thailand . . . . **54** 17 18N 101 46 E
Wang Thong, *Thailand* **54** 16 50N 100 26 E
Wanga, *Zaïre* . . . . **92** 2 58N 29 12 E
Wangal, *Indonesia* . . . . **57** 6 8 S 134 9 E
Wanganella, *Australia* . **74** 35 6 S 144 49 E
Wanganui, *N.Z.* . . . . . . **80** 39 56 S 175 3 E
Wanganui →, *N.I.,*
N.Z. . . . . **80** 39 55 S 175 4 E
Wanganui →, *S.I.,*
N.Z. . . . . **81** 43 3 S 170 26 E
Wangaratta, *Australia* . **75** 36 21 S 146 19 E
Wangcang, *China* . . . . **58** 32 18N 106 20 E
Wangdu, *China* . . . . . . **60** 38 40N 115 7 E
Wangdu Phodrang,
Bhutan . . . . **52** 27 28N 89 54 E
Wangerooge,
W. Germany . . . . **30** 53 47N 7 52 E
Wangi, *Kenya* . . . . **92** 1 58 S 40 58 E
Wangiwangi, *Indonesia* **57** 5 22 S 123 37 E
Wangjiang, *China* . . . . **59** 30 10N 116 42 E
Wangmo, *China* . . . . . . **58** 25 11N 106 5 E
Wangqing, *China* . . . . . **61** 43 12N 129 42 E
Wankaner, *India* . . . . . **48** 22 35N 71 0 E
Wanless, *Canada* **111** 54 11N 101 21W
Wannian, *China* . . . . . . **59** 28 42N 117 4 E
Wannon →, *Australia* **74** 37 38 S 141 25 E
Wanon Niwat, *Thailand* **54** 17 38N 103 46 E
Wanquan, *China* . . . . . **60** 40 50N 114 40 E
Wanrong, *China* . . . . . **60** 35 25N 110 50 E
Wanshan, *China* . . . . . **58** 27 30N 109 12 E
Wanshengchang, *China* **58** 28 57N 106 53 E
Wanssum, *Neths.* . . . . . **17** 51 32N 6 5 E
Wanstead, *N.Z.* . . . . . . **80** 40 8 S 176 30 E
Wantabadgery,
Australia . . . . **76** 35 0 S 147 43 E
Wanxian, *China* . . . . . . **58** 30 42N 108 20 E
Wanyin, *Burma* . . . . . . **52** 20 23N 97 15 E
Wanyuan, *China* . . . . . **58** 32 4N 108 3 E
Wanzai, *China* . . . . **59** 28 7N 114 30 E
Wanze, *Belgium* . . . . . . **17** 50 32N 5 13 E
Wapakoneta, *U.S.A.* . . **119** 40 35N 84 10W
Wapato, *U.S.A.* **122** 46 30N 120 25W
Wapawekka L., *Canada* **111** 54 55N 104 40W
Wapello, *U.S.A.* **118** 41 11N 91 11W
Wapikopa L., *Canada* **104** 52 56N 87 53W
Wappingers Falls,
U.S.A. **117** 41 35N 73 56W
Wapsipinicon →,
U.S.A. **118** 41 44N 90 19W
Warabi, *Japan* . . . . **65** 35 49N 139 41 E
Waranga Res.,
Australia . . . . **74** 36 32 S 145 5 E
Warangal, *India* . . . . . . **50** 17 58N 79 35 E
Waratah, *Australia* . . . **72** 41 30 S 145 30 E
Waratah B., *Australia* . **74** 38 54 S 146 5 E
Warburg, *W. Germany* **30** 51 29N 9 10 E
Warburton, *Vic.,*
Australia . . . . **74** 37 47 S 145 42 E
Warburton,
W. Austral., Australia **79** 26 8 S 126 35 E
Warburton Ra.,
Australia . . . . **79** 25 55 S 126 28 E
Ward, *N.Z.* . . . . **81** 41 49 S 174 11 E
Ward →, *Australia* . . . **73** 26 28 S 146 6 E
Ward Cove, *U.S.A.* . . **110** 55 25N 132 43W
Ward Hunt, C.,
Papua N. G. . . . . **69** 8 2 S 148 10 E
Ward Hunt Str.,
Papua N. G. . . . . **69** 9 30 S 150 0 E
Ward Mt., *U.S.A.* **124** 37 12N 118 54W
Wardell, *Australia* . . . . **77** 28 54 S 153 31 E
Warden, *S. Africa* . . . . **97** 27 50 S 29 0 E
Warden Head,
Australia . . . . **77** 35 22 S 150 29 E
Wardha, *India* . . . . **50** 20 45N 78 39 E
Wardlow, *Canada* **110** 50 56N 111 31W
Wards River, *Australia* **77** 32 11 S 151 56 E
Ware, *Canada* **110** 57 26N 125 41W
Ware, *U.S.A.* **117** 42 16N 72 15W
Waregem, *Belgium* . . . **17** 50 53N 3 27 E
Wareham, *U.S.A.* **117** 41 45N 70 44W
Waremme, *Belgium* . . **17** 50 43N 5 15 E
Waren, *E. Germany* . . **30** 53 30N 12 41 E
Warendorf,
W. Germany . . . . **30** 51 57N 8 0 E
Warialda, *Australia* . . . **77** 29 29 S 150 33 E
Wariap, *Indonesia* . . . . **57** 1 30 S 134 5 E
Warin Chamrap,
Thailand . . . . **54** 15 12N 104 53 E
Warkopi, *Indonesia* . . . **57** 1 12 S 134 9 E
Warkworth, *N.Z.* . . . . **80** 36 24 S 174 41 E
Warley, *U.K.* **13** 52 30N 2 0W
Warm Springs, *U.S.A.* **123** 38 16N 116 32W
Warman, *Canada* **111** 52 19N 106 30W
Warmbad, *Namibia* . . . **96** 28 25 S 18 42 E
Warmbad, *S. Africa* . . **97** 24 51 S 28 19 E
Warmenhuizen, *Neths.* **16** 52 43N 4 44 E
Warmeriville, *France* . **19** 49 20N 4 13 E
Warmond, *Neths.* . . . . **16** 52 12N 4 30 E
Warnambool Downs,
Australia . . . . **72** 22 48 S 142 52 E
Warnemünde,
E. Germany . . . . **30** 54 9N 12 5 E
Warner, *Canada* **110** 49 17N 112 12W
Warner Mts., *U.S.A.* . **122** 41 30N 120 20W
Warner Robins, *U.S.A.* **115** 32 41N 83 36W
Warnes, *Bolivia* . . . . . . **137** 17 30 S 63 10W
Warneton, *Belgium* . . . **17** 50 45N 2 57 E
Warning, Mt., *Australia* **77** 28 24 S 153 16 E
Warnow →,
E. Germany . . . . **30** 54 6N 12 9 E
Warnsveld, *Neths.* . . . . **16** 52 8N 6 14 E
Waroona, *Australia* . . . **79** 32 50 S 115 58 E
Warora, *India* . . . . **50** 20 14N 79 1 E
Warragul, *Australia* . . . **74** 38 10 S 145 58 E
Warrawagine, *Australia* **78** 20 51 S 120 42 E
Warrego →, *Australia* **73** 30 24 S 145 21 E
Warrego Ra., *Australia* **72** 24 58 S 146 0 E
Warren, *Australia* . . . . **76** 31 42 S 147 51 E
Warren, *Canada* **108** 46 27N 80 18W
Warren, *Ark., U.S.A.* . **121** 33 35N 92 3W
Warren, *Ill., U.S.A.* . . **118** 42 30N 89 59W
Warren, *Mich., U.S.A.* **119** 42 31N 83 2W
Warren, *Minn., U.S.A.* **120** 48 12N 96 46W
Warren, *Ohio, U.S.A.* **116** 41 18N 80 52W
Warren, *Pa., U.S.A.* . . **116** 41 52N 79 10W
Warrenpoint, *U.K.* . . . **15** 54 7N 6 15W
Warrensburg, *Ill.,*
U.S.A. **118** 39 56N 89 4W
Warrensburg, *Mo.,*
U.S.A. **120** 38 45N 93 45W
Warrenton, *S. Africa* . **96** 28 9 S 24 47 E
Warrenton, *Mo.,*
U.S.A. **118** 38 49N 91 9W
Warrenton, *Oreg.,*
U.S.A. **124** 46 11N 123 59W
Warrenville, *Australia* . **73** 25 48 S 147 22 E
Warri, *Nigeria* . . . . **91** 5 30N 5 41 E
Warrina, *Australia* . . . . **73** 28 12 S 135 50 E
Warrington, *N.Z.* . . . . **81** 45 43 S 170 35 E
Warrington, *U.K.* **12** 53 25N 2 38W
Warrington, *U.S.A.* . . **115** 30 22N 87 16W
Warrnambool, *Australia* **74** 38 25 S 142 30 E
Warroad, *U.S.A.* **120** 48 54N 95 19W
Warsa, *Indonesia* . . . . . **57** 0 47 S 135 55 E
Warsaw = Warszawa,
Poland . . . . **32** 52 13N 21 0 E
Warsaw, *Ill., U.S.A.* . . **118** 40 22N 91 26W
Warsaw, *Ind., U.S.A.* . **119** 41 14N 85 50W
Warsaw, *Ky., U.S.A.* . . **119** 38 47N 84 54W
Warsaw, *Mo., U.S.A.* . **118** 38 15N 93 23W
Warsaw, *N.Y., U.S.A.* **116** 42 46N 78 10W
Warsaw, *Ohio, U.S.A.* **116** 40 20N 82 0W
Warstein, *W. Germany* **30** 51 26N 8 20 E
Warszawa, *Poland* . . . . **32** 52 13N 21 0 E
Warta →, *Poland* . . . . **32** 52 35N 14 39 E
Warthe = Warta →,
Poland . . . . **32** 52 35N 14 39 E
Waru, *Indonesia* . . . . . **57** 3 30 S 130 36 E
Warud, *India* . . . . **50** 21 30N 78 16 E
Warwick, *Australia* . . . **77** 28 10 S 152 1 E
Warwick, *U.K.* **13** 52 17N 1 36W
Warwick, *U.S.A.* **117** 41 43N 71 25W
Warwick □, *U.K.* **13** 52 20N 1 30W
Wasaga Beach, *Canada* **108** 44 31N 80 1W
Wasatch Ra., *U.S.A.* . **122** 40 30N 111 15W
Wasbank, *S. Africa* . . **97** 28 15 S 30 9 E
Wasco, *Calif., U.S.A.* . **125** 35 37N 119 16W
Wasco, *Oreg., U.S.A.* **122** 45 36N 120 46W
Waseca, *U.S.A.* **120** 44 3N 93 31W
Wasekamio L., *Canada* **111** 56 45N 108 45W
Wash, The, *U.K.* . . . . . **12** 52 58N 0 20 E
Washago, *Canada* **108** 44 45N 79 20W
Washburn, *Ill., U.S.A.* **118** 40 55N 89 17W
Washburn, *N. Dak.,*
U.S.A. **120** 47 17N 101 0W
Washburn, *Wis.,*
U.S.A. **120** 46 38N 90 55W
Washim, *India* . . . . **50** 20 3N 77 0 E
Washington, *D.C.,*
U.S.A. **114** 38 52N 77 0W
Washington, *Ga.,*
U.S.A. **115** 33 45N 82 45W
Washington, *Ind.,*
U.S.A. **119** 38 40N 87 8W
Washington, *Iowa,*
U.S.A. **118** 41 20N 91 45W
Washington, *Mo.,*
U.S.A. **118** 38 35N 91 1W
Washington, *N.C.,*
U.S.A. **115** 35 35N 77 1W
Washington, *N.J.,*
U.S.A. **117** 40 45N 74 59W
Washington, *Pa.,*
U.S.A. **116** 40 10N 80 20W
Washington, *Utah,*
U.S.A. **123** 37 10N 113 30W
Washington □, *U.S.A.* **122** 47 45N 120 30W
Washington, Mt.,
U.S.A. **117** 44 15N 71 18W
Washington Court
House, *U.S.A.* **119** 39 34N 83 26W
Washington I., *U.S.A.* **114** 45 24N 86 54W
Washougal, *U.S.A.* . . . **124** 45 35N 122 21W
Wasian, *Indonesia* . . . . **57** 1 47 S 133 19 E

Wasior, Indonesia 57 2 43 S 134 30 E
Waskaiowaka, L., Canada 111 56 33N 96 23W
Waskesiu Lake, Canada 111 53 55N 106 5W
Wasmes, Belgium 17 50 25N 3 50 E
Waspik, Neths. 17 51 41N 4 57 E
Wassenaar, Neths. 16 52 8N 4 24 E
Wasserburg, W. Germany 31 48 4N 12 15 E
Wasserkuppe, W. Germany 30 50 30N 9 56 E
Wassy, France 19 48 30N 4 58 E
Waswanipi, Canada 106 49 40N 76 29W
Waswanipi →, Canada 106 49 40N 76 25W
Waswanipi, L., Canada 106 49 35N 76 40W
Watangpone, Indonesia 57 4 29 S 120 25 E
Watchem, Australia 74 36 9 S 142 52 E
Water Park Pt., Australia 72 22 56 S 150 47 E
Water Valley, U.S.A. 121 34 9N 89 38W
Waterberge, S. Africa 97 24 10 S 28 0 E
Waterbury, Conn., U.S.A. 117 41 32N 73 0W
Waterbury, Vt., U.S.A. 117 44 22N 72 44W
Waterbury L., Canada 111 58 10N 104 22W
Waterdown, Canada 108 43 20N 79 53W
Waterford, Australia 77 27 42 S 153 9 E
Waterford, Canada 108 42 56N 80 17W
Waterford, Ireland 15 52 16N 7 8W
Waterford, Calif., U.S.A. 124 37 38N 120 46W
Waterford, Wis., U.S.A. 119 42 46N 88 13W
Waterford □, Ireland 15 52 10N 7 40W
Waterford Harb., Ireland 15 52 10N 6 58W
Waterhen L., Man., Canada 111 52 10N 99 40W
Waterhen L., Sask., Canada 111 54 28N 108 25W
Wateringen, Neths. 16 52 2N 4 16 E
Waterloo, Belgium 17 50 43N 4 25 E
Waterloo, Ont., Canada 108 43 30N 80 32W
Waterloo, Qué., Canada 117 45 22N 72 32W
Waterloo, S. Leone 90 8 26N 13 8W
Waterloo, Ill., U.S.A. 118 38 22N 90 6W
Waterloo, Ind., U.S.A. 119 41 24N 85 2W
Waterloo, Iowa, U.S.A. 118 42 27N 92 20W
Waterloo, N.Y., U.S.A. 116 42 54N 76 53W
Waterloo, Wis., U.S.A. 118 43 11N 88 59W
Waterman, U.S.A. 119 41 46N 88 47W
Watermeal-Boitsford, Belgium 17 50 48N 4 25 E
Watersmeet, U.S.A. 120 46 15N 89 12W
Waterton Glacier Int. Peace Park, U.S.A. 122 48 35N 113 40W
Watertown, Conn., U.S.A. 117 41 36N 73 7W
Watertown, N.Y., U.S.A. 117 43 58N 75 57W
Watertown, S. Dak., U.S.A. 120 44 57N 97 5W
Watertown, Wis., U.S.A. 119 43 15N 88 45W
Waterval-Boven, S. Africa 97 25 40 S 30 18 E
Waterville, Canada 117 45 16N 71 54W
Waterville, Maine, U.S.A. 105 44 35N 69 40W
Waterville, N.Y., U.S.A. 117 42 56N 75 23W
Waterville, Pa., U.S.A. 116 41 19N 77 21W
Waterville, Wash., U.S.A. 122 47 38N 120 1W
Watervliet, Belgium 17 51 17N 3 38 E
Watervliet, Mich., U.S.A. 119 42 11N 86 18W
Watervliet, N.Y., U.S.A. 117 42 46N 73 43W
Wates, Indonesia 57 7 51 S 110 10 E
Watford, Canada 108 42 57N 81 53W
Watford, U.K. 13 51 38N 0 23W
Watford City, U.S.A. 120 47 50N 103 23W
Wathaman →, Canada 111 57 16N 102 59W
Watheroo, Australia 79 30 15 S 116 0 E
Wating, China 60 35 40N 106 38 E
Watkins Glen, U.S.A. 116 42 25N 76 55W
Watling I. = San Salvador, Bahamas 129 24 0N 74 40W
Watonga, U.S.A. 121 35 51N 98 24W
Watou, Belgium 17 50 51N 2 38 E
Watrous, Canada 111 51 40N 105 25W
Watrous, U.S.A. 121 35 50N 104 55W
Watsa, Zaïre 92 3 4N 29 30 E
Watseka, U.S.A. 119 40 45N 87 45W
Watson, Australia 79 30 29 S 131 31 E
Watson, Canada 111 52 10N 104 30W
Watson Lake, Canada 102 60 6N 128 49W
Watsonville, U.S.A. 124 36 55N 121 49W
Wattiwarriganna Cr. →, Australia 73 28 57 S 136 10 E
Wattle Flat, Australia 76 33 8 S 149 43 E
Wattwil, Switz. 31 47 18N 9 6 E
Watuata = Batuata, Indonesia 57 6 12 S 122 42 E
Watubela, Kepulauan, Indonesia 57 4 28 S 131 35 E
Wau, Papua N. G. 69 7 21 S 146 47 E
Waubach, Neths. 17 50 55N 6 3 E
Waubamik, Canada 108 45 27N 80 1W
Waubaushene, Canada 108 44 45N 79 42W
Waubay, U.S.A. 120 45 22N 97 17W
Waubra, Australia 74 37 21 S 143 39 E
Wauchope, Australia 77 31 28 S 152 45 E
Wauchula, U.S.A. 115 27 35N 81 50W
Waugh, Canada 111 49 40N 95 11W
Waukegan, U.S.A. 119 42 22N 87 54W
Waukesha, U.S.A. 119 43 0N 88 15W
Waukon, U.S.A. 120 43 14N 91 33W
Wauneta, U.S.A. 120 40 27N 101 25W
Waupaca, U.S.A. 120 44 22N 89 8W
Waupun, U.S.A. 120 43 38N 88 44W
Waurika, U.S.A. 121 34 12N 98 0W
Wausau, U.S.A. 120 44 57N 89 40W
Wauseon, U.S.A. 119 41 33N 84 8W
Wautoma, U.S.A. 120 44 3N 89 20W
Wauwatosa, U.S.A. 119 43 6N 87 59W
Wave Hill, Australia 78 17 32 S 131 0 E
Waveland, U.S.A. 119 39 53N 87 3W
Waveney →, U.K. 13 52 24N 1 20 E
Waverley, N.Z. 80 39 46 S 174 37 E
Waverly, Ill., U.S.A. 118 39 36N 89 57W
Waverly, Iowa, U.S.A. 118 42 40N 92 30W
Waverly, Mo., U.S.A. 118 39 13N 93 31W
Waverly, N.Y., U.S.A. 117 42 0N 76 33W
Wavre, Belgium 17 50 43N 4 38 E
Wavreille, Belgium 17 50 7N 5 15 E
Wâw, Sudan 89 7 45N 28 1 E
Wāw al Kabīr, Libya 86 25 20N 16 43 E
Wāw an Nāmūs, Libya 86 24 55N 17 46 E
Wawa, Canada 104 47 59N 84 47W
Wawa, Nigeria 91 9 54N 4 27 E
Wawa, Sudan 88 20 30N 30 22 E
Wawagosic →, Canada 106 49 58N 79 6W
Wawanesa, Canada 111 49 36N 99 40W
Wawasee, L., U.S.A. 119 41 24N 85 42W
Wawoi →, Papua N. G. 69 7 48 S 143 16 E
Wawona, U.S.A. 124 37 32N 119 39W
Waxahachie, U.S.A. 121 32 22N 96 53W
Waxweiler, W. Germany 31 50 6N 6 22 E
Way, L., Australia 79 26 45 S 120 16 E
Wayabula Rau, Indonesia 57 2 29N 128 17 E
Wayagamac, L., Canada 107 47 21N 72 39W
Wayatinah, Australia 72 42 19 S 146 27 E
Waycross, U.S.A. 115 31 12N 82 25W
Wayi, Sudan 89 5 8N 30 10 E
Wayland, U.S.A. 119 42 40N 85 39W
Wayne, Nebr., U.S.A. 120 42 16N 97 0W
Wayne, W. Va., U.S.A. 114 38 15N 82 27W
Wayne City, U.S.A. 119 38 21N 88 35W
Waynesboro, Ga., U.S.A. 115 33 6N 82 1W
Waynesboro, Miss., U.S.A. 115 31 40N 88 39W
Waynesboro, Pa., U.S.A. 114 39 46N 77 32W
Waynesboro, Va., U.S.A. 114 38 4N 78 57W
Waynesburg, U.S.A. 114 39 54N 80 12W
Waynesville, Kans., U.S.A. 118 37 50N 92 12W
Waynesville, N.C., U.S.A. 115 35 31N 83 0W
Waynesville, Ohio, U.S.A. 119 39 32N 84 5W
Waynoka, U.S.A. 121 36 38N 98 53W
Wāzin, Libya 86 31 58N 10 40 E
Wazirabad, Pakistan 48 32 30N 74 8 E
We, Indonesia 56 5 51N 95 18 E
Weald, The, U.K. 13 51 7N 0 9 E
Wear →, U.K. 12 54 55N 1 22W
Weatherford, Okla., U.S.A. 121 35 30N 98 45W
Weatherford, Tex., U.S.A. 121 32 45N 97 48W
Weaubleau, U.S.A. 118 37 54N 93 32W
Weaverville, U.S.A. 122 40 44N 122 56W
Webb City, U.S.A. 121 37 9N 94 30W
Webbwood, Canada 108 46 16N 81 52W
Weber, N.Z. 80 40 24 S 176 20 E
Webo = Nyaake, Liberia 90 4 52N 7 37W
Webster, Mass., U.S.A. 117 42 4N 71 54W
Webster, N.Y., U.S.A. 116 43 11N 77 27W
Webster, S. Dak., U.S.A. 120 45 24N 97 33W
Webster, Wis., U.S.A. 120 45 53N 92 25W
Webster City, U.S.A. 118 42 30N 93 50W
Webster Green, U.S.A. 120 38 38N 90 20W
Webster Springs, U.S.A. 114 38 30N 80 25W
Weda, Indonesia 57 0 21N 127 50 E
Weda, Teluk, Indonesia 57 0 30N 127 50 E
Weddell I., Falk. Is. 142 51 50 S 61 0W
Weddell Sea, Antarctica 143 72 30 S 40 0W
Wedderburn, Australia 74 36 26 S 143 33 E
Wedgeport, Canada 105 43 44N 65 59W
Wedza, Zimb. 93 18 40 S 31 33 E
Wee Jasper, Australia 76 35 8 S 148 40 E
Wee Waa, Australia 77 30 11 S 149 26 E
Weed, U.S.A. 122 41 29N 122 22W
Weed Heights, U.S.A. 124 38 59N 119 13W
Weedon-Centre, Canada 107 45 42N 71 27W
Weedsport, U.S.A. 117 43 3N 76 35W
Weedville, U.S.A. 116 41 17N 78 28W
Weemelah, Australia 77 29 2 S 149 15 E
Weenen, S. Africa 97 28 48 S 30 7 E
Weener, W. Germany 30 53 10N 7 23 E
Weert, Neths. 17 51 15N 5 43 E
Weesp, Neths. 16 52 18N 5 2 E
Weetaliba, Australia 77 31 35 S 149 39 E
Wegliniec, Poland 32 51 18N 15 10 E
Węgorzewo, Poland 32 54 13N 21 43 E
Węgrów, Poland 32 52 24N 22 0 E
Wehl, Neths. 16 51 58N 6 13 E
Wei He →, Hebei, China 60 36 10N 115 45 E
Wei He →, Shaanxi, China 60 34 38N 110 15 E
Weichang, China 61 41 58N 117 49 E
Weichuan, China 60 34 20N 113 59 E
Weida, E. Germany 30 50 47N 12 3 E
Weiden, W. Germany 31 49 40N 12 10 E
Weifang, China 61 36 44N 119 7 E
Weihai, China 61 37 30N 122 6 E
Weilburg, W. Germany 30 50 28N 8 17 E
Weilheim, W. Germany 31 47 50N 11 9 E
Weimar, E. Germany 30 51 0N 11 20 E
Weinan, China 60 34 31N 109 29 E
Weingarten, W. Germany 31 47 49N 9 39 E
Weinheim, W. Germany 31 49 33N 8 40 E
Weining, China 58 26 50N 104 17 E
Weipa, Australia 72 12 40 S 141 50 E
Weir →, Australia 77 28 20 S 149 50 E
Weir →, Canada 111 56 54N 93 21W
Weir River, Canada 111 56 49N 94 6W
Weirton, U.S.A. 116 40 23N 80 35W
Weiser, U.S.A. 122 44 10N 117 0W
Weishan, Shandong, China 61 34 47N 117 5 E
Weishan, Yunnan, China 58 25 12N 100 20 E
Weissenburg, W. Germany 31 49 2N 10 58 E
Weissenfels, E. Germany 30 51 11N 12 0 E
Weisswasser, E. Germany 30 51 30N 14 36 E
Weiswampach, Belgium 17 50 8N 6 5 E
Weixi, China 58 27 10N 99 10 E
Weixin, China 58 27 48N 105 3 E
Weiyuan, China 60 35 7N 104 10 E
Weiz, Austria 33 47 13N 15 39 E
Weizhou Dao, China 58 21 0N 109 5 E
Wejherowo, Poland 32 54 35N 18 12 E
Wekusko L., Canada 111 54 40N 99 50W
Welbourn Hill, Australia 73 27 21 S 134 6 E
Welch, U.S.A. 114 37 29N 81 36W
Weldya, Ethiopia 89 11 50N 39 34 E
Welega □, Ethiopia 89 9 25N 34 20 E
Welkenraedt, Belgium 17 50 39N 5 58 E
Welkite, Ethiopia 89 8 15N 37 42 E
Welkom, S. Africa 96 28 0 S 26 46 E
Welland, Canada 108 43 0N 79 15W
Welland →, U.K. 12 52 43N 0 10W
Wellen, Belgium 17 50 50N 5 21 E
Wellesley Is., Australia 72 16 42 S 139 30 E
Wellin, Belgium 17 50 5N 5 6 E
Wellingborough, U.K. 13 52 18N 0 41W
Wellington, Australia 76 32 35 S 148 59 E
Wellington, Canada 109 43 57N 77 20W
Wellington, N.Z. 80 41 19 S 174 46 E
Wellington, S. Africa 96 33 38 S 19 1 E
Wellington, Salop, U.K. 12 52 42N 2 31W
Wellington, Somerset, U.K. 13 50 58N 3 13W
Wellington, Colo., U.S.A. 120 40 43N 105 0W
Wellington, Kans., U.S.A. 121 37 15N 97 25W
Wellington, Mo., U.S.A. 118 39 8N 93 59W
Wellington, Nev., U.S.A. 124 38 47N 119 28W
Wellington, Ohio, U.S.A. 116 41 9N 82 12W
Wellington, Tex., U.S.A. 121 34 55N 100 13W
Wellington □, N.Z. 81 40 8 S 175 36 E
Wellington, C., Australia 75 39 4 S 146 29 E
Wellington, I., Chile 142 49 30 S 75 0W
Wellington, L., Australia 75 38 6 S 147 20 E
Wells, Norfolk, U.K. 12 52 57N 0 51 E
Wells, Somerset, U.K. 13 51 12N 2 39W
Wells, Maine, U.S.A. 117 43 18N 70 35W
Wells, Minn., U.S.A. 120 43 44N 93 45W
Wells, Nev., U.S.A. 122 41 8N 115 0W
Wells Gray Prov. Park, Canada 110 52 30N 120 15W
Wells L., Australia 79 26 44 S 123 15 E
Wells River, U.S.A. 117 44 9N 72 4W
Wellsboro, U.S.A. 116 41 45N 77 20W
Wellsburg, U.S.A. 116 40 15N 80 36W
Wellsford, N.Z. 80 36 16 S 174 32 E
Wellsville, Mo., U.S.A. 118 39 4N 91 30W
Wellsville, N.Y., U.S.A. 116 42 9N 77 53W
Wellsville, Ohio, U.S.A. 116 40 36N 80 40W
Wellsville, Utah, U.S.A. 122 41 35N 111 59W
Wellton, U.S.A. 123 32 39N 114 6W
Welmel, Wabi →, Ethiopia 89 5 38N 40 47 E
Welo, Somali Rep. 98 9 25N 48 55 E
Welo □, Ethiopia 89 11 50N 39 48 E
Wels, Austria 33 48 9N 14 1 E
Welshpool, Australia 75 38 42 S 146 26 E
Welshpool, U.K. 13 52 40N 3 9W
Wem, U.K. 12 52 52N 2 45W
Wembere →, Tanzania 92 4 10 S 34 15 E
Wemmel, Belgium 17 50 55N 4 18 E
Wen Xian, Gansu, China 60 32 43N 104 36 E
Wen Xian, Henan, China 60 34 55N 113 5 E
Wenatchee, U.S.A. 122 47 30N 120 17W
Wenchang, China 54 19 38N 110 42 E
Wencheng, China 59 27 46N 120 4 E
Wenchi, Ghana 90 7 46N 2 8W
Wenchow = Wenzhou, China 59 28 0N 120 38 E
Wenchuan, China 58 31 22N 103 35 E
Wendell, U.S.A. 122 42 50N 114 42W
Wendeng, China 61 37 15N 122 5 E
Wendesi, Indonesia 57 2 30 S 134 17 E
Wendo, Ethiopia 89 6 40N 38 27 E
Wendon, U.S.A. 125 33 49N 113 33W
Wendover, U.S.A. 122 40 49N 114 1W
Wenduine, Belgium 17 51 18N 3 5 E
Weng'an, China 58 27 5N 107 25 E
Wengcheng, China 59 24 22N 113 50 E
Wengyuan, China 59 24 20N 114 9 E
Wenjiang, China 58 30 44N 103 55 E
Wenling, China 59 28 21N 121 20 E
Wenlock →, Australia 72 12 2 S 141 55 E
Wenona, U.S.A. 118 41 3N 89 3W
Wenshan, China 58 23 20N 104 18 E
Wenshang, China 60 35 45N 116 30 E
Wenshui, Guizhou, China 58 28 27N 106 28 E
Wenshui, Shanxi, China 60 37 26N 112 1 E
Wensu, China 62 41 15N 80 10 E
Wentworth, Australia 74 34 2 S 141 54 E
Wentzville, U.S.A. 118 38 49N 90 51W
Wenut, Indonesia 57 3 11 S 133 19 E
Wenxi, China 60 35 20N 111 10 E
Wenzhou, China 59 28 0N 120 38 E
Weott, U.S.A. 122 40 19N 123 56W
Wepener, S. Africa 96 29 42 S 27 3 E
Werbomont, Belgium 17 50 23N 5 41 E
Werda, Botswana 96 25 24 S 23 15 E
Werdau, E. Germany 30 50 45N 12 20 E
Werder, E. Germany 30 52 23N 12 56 E
Werder, Ethiopia 98 6 58N 45 1 E
Werdohl, W. Germany 30 51 15N 7 47 E
Weri, Indonesia 57 3 10 S 132 38 E
Werkendam, Neths. 16 51 50N 4 53 E
Werne, W. Germany 30 51 38N 7 38 E
Werneck, W. Germany 31 49 59N 10 6 E
Wernigerode, E. Germany 30 51 49N 10 45 E
Werombi, Australia 76 33 58 S 150 34 E
Werra →, W. Germany 30 51 26N 9 39 E
Werribee, Australia 74 37 54 S 144 40 E
Werribee →, Australia 74 37 51 S 144 37 E
Werrimull, Australia 74 34 25 S 141 38 E
Werris Creek, Australia 77 31 18 S 150 38 E
Wersar, Indonesia 57 1 30 S 131 55 E
Wertach →, W. Germany 31 48 24N 10 53 E
Wertheim, W. Germany 31 49 44N 9 32 E
Wertingen, W. Germany 31 48 33N 10 41 E
Wervershoof, Neths. 16 52 44N 5 10 E
Wervik, Belgium 17 50 47N 3 3 E
Wesel, W. Germany 30 51 39N 6 34 E
Weser →, W. Germany 30 53 33N 8 30 E
Wesiri, Indonesia 57 7 30 S 126 30 E
Weslemkoon L., Canada 109 45 2N 77 25W
Wesley Vale, U.S.A. 123 35 3N 106 2W
Wesleyville, Canada 105 49 8N 53 36W
Wesleyville, U.S.A. 116 42 9N 80 1W
Wessel, C., Australia 72 10 59 S 136 46 E
Wessel Is., Australia 72 11 10 S 136 45 E
Wesselburen, W. Germany 30 54 11N 8 53 E
Wessem, Neths. 17 51 11N 5 49 E
Wessington, U.S.A. 120 44 30N 98 40W
Wessington Springs, U.S.A. 120 44 10N 98 35W
West, U.S.A. 121 31 50N 97 5W
West Allis, U.S.A. 119 43 1N 87 0W
West B., U.S.A. 121 29 5N 89 27W
West Baines →, Australia 78 15 38 S 129 59 E
West Bend, U.S.A. 114 43 25N 88 10W
West Bengal □, India 49 23 0N 88 0 E
West Branch, U.S.A. 104 44 16N 84 13W
West Bromwich, U.K. 13 52 32N 2 1W
West Cape Howe, Australia 79 35 8 S 117 36 E
West Carrollton, U.S.A. 119 39 40N 84 17W
West Chazy, U.S.A. 117 44 49N 73 28W
West Chester, U.S.A. 114 39 58N 75 36W
West Chicago, U.S.A. 119 41 53N 88 12W
West Columbia, U.S.A. 121 29 10N 95 38W
West Covina, U.S.A. 125 34 4N 117 54W
West Des Moines, U.S.A. 118 41 30N 93 45W
West End, Bahamas 128 26 41N 78 58W
West Falkland, Falk. Is. 142 51 40 S 60 0W
West Frankfurt, U.S.A. 118 37 56N 89 0W
West Germany ■, Europe 30 52 0N 9 0 E
West Glamorgan □, U.K. 13 51 40N 3 55W
West Hartford, U.S.A. 117 41 45N 72 45W

West Haven, *U.S.A.* **117** 41 18N 72 57W
West Helena, *U.S.A.* **121** 34 30N 90 40W
West Ice Shelf, *Antarctica* **143** 67 0 S 85 0 E
West Indies, *Cent. Amer.* **129** 15 0N 70 0W
West Lafayette, *U.S.A.* **119** 40 27N 86 55W
West Liberty, *Iowa, U.S.A.* **118** 41 34N 91 16W
West Liberty, *Ky., U.S.A.* **119** 37 55N 83 16W
West Liberty, *Ohio, U.S.A.* **119** 40 15N 83 45W
West Lorne, *Canada* **108** 42 36N 81 36W
West Lunga →, *Zambia* **93** 13 6 S 24 39 E
West Manchester, *U.S.A.* **119** 39 55N 84 38W
West Memphis, *U.S.A.* **121** 35 5N 90 11W
West Midlands □, *U.K.* **13** 52 30N 1 55W
West Mifflin, *U.S.A.* **116** 40 22N 79 52W
West Milton, *U.S.A.* **119** 39 58N 84 20W
West Monroe, *U.S.A.* **121** 32 32N 92 7W
West Moors, *U.K.* **12** 50 49N 1 50W
West Newton, *U.S.A.* **116** 40 14N 79 46W
West Nicholson, *Zimb.* **93** 21 2 S 29 20 E
West Palm Beach, *U.S.A.* **115** 26 44N 80 3W
West Plains, *U.S.A.* **121** 36 45N 91 50W
West Pt., *Australia* **73** 35 1 S 135 56 E
West Point, *Ga., U.S.A.* **115** 32 54N 85 10W
West Point, *Ill., U.S.A.* **118** 40 15N 91 11W
West Point, *Iowa, U.S.A.* **118** 40 43N 91 27W
West Point, *Ky., U.S.A.* **119** 37 59N 85 57W
West Point, *Miss., U.S.A.* **115** 33 36N 88 38W
West Point, *Nebr., U.S.A.* **120** 41 50N 96 43W
West Point, *Va., U.S.A.* **114** 37 35N 76 47W
West Pokot □, *Kenya* **92** 1 30N 35 15 E
West Road →, *Canada* **110** 53 18N 122 53W
West Rutland, *U.S.A.* **117** 43 38N 73 0W
West Salem, *U.S.A.* **119** 38 31N 88 1W
West Schelde → = Westerschelde →, *Neths.* **17** 51 25N 3 25 E
West Seneca, *U.S.A.* **116** 42 51N 78 48W
West Siberian Plain, *U.S.S.R.* **42** 62 0N 75 0 E
West Sussex □, *U.K.* **13** 50 55N 0 30W
West Terre Haute, *U.S.A.* **119** 39 27N 87 27W
West-Terschelling, *Neths.* **16** 53 22N 5 13 E
West Union, *Iowa, U.S.A.* **118** 42 57N 91 49W
West Union, *Ohio, U.S.A.* **119** 38 48N 83 33W
West Unity, *U.S.A.* **119** 41 35N 84 26W
West Virginia □, *U.S.A.* **114** 39 0N 81 0W
West-Vlaanderen □, *Belgium* **17** 51 0N 3 0 E
West Walker →, *U.S.A.* **124** 38 54N 119 9W
West Wyalong, *Australia* **76** 33 56 S 147 10 E
West Yellowstone, *U.S.A.* **122** 44 47N 111 4W
West Yorkshire □, *U.K.* **12** 53 45N 1 40W
Westall Pt., *Australia* **73** 32 55 S 134 4 E
Westbrook, *Maine, U.S.A.* **115** 43 40N 70 22W
Westbrook, *Tex., U.S.A.* **121** 32 25N 101 0W
Westbury, *Australia* **72** 41 30 S 146 51 E
Westby, *U.S.A.* **120** 48 52N 104 3W
Westend, *U.S.A.* **125** 35 42N 117 24W
Westerbork, *Neths.* **16** 52 51N 6 37 E
Westerland, *W. Germany* **30** 54 51N 8 20 E
Western □, *Kenya* **92** 0 30N 34 30 E
Western □, *Uganda* **92** 1 45N 31 30 E
Western □, *Zambia* **93** 15 15 S 24 30 E
Western Australia □, *Australia* **79** 25 0 S 118 0 E
Western Duck I., *Canada* **108** 45 45N 83 0W
Western Ghats, *India* **51** 14 0N 75 0 E
Western Isles □, *U.K.* **14** 57 30N 7 10W
Western Sahara ■, *Africa* **84** 25 0N 13 0W
Western Samoa ■, *Pac. Oc.* **68** 14 0 S 172 0W
Westernport, *U.S.A.* **114** 39 30N 79 5W
Westerschelde →, *Neths.* **17** 51 25N 3 25 E
Westerstede, *W. Germany* **30** 53 15N 7 55 E
Westervoort, *Neths.* **16** 51 58N 5 59 E
Westerwald, *W. Germany* **30** 50 39N 8 0 E
Westfield, *Ill., U.S.A.* **119** 39 27N 88 0W
Westfield, *Ind., U.S.A.* **119** 40 2N 86 8W
Westfield, *Mass., U.S.A.* **117** 42 9N 72 49W
Westfield, *N.Y., U.S.A.* **116** 42 20N 79 38W
Westfield, *Pa., U.S.A.* **116** 41 54N 77 32W
Westgat, *Neths.* **17** 51 39N 3 44 E
Westhope, *U.S.A.* **120** 48 55N 101 0W
Westkapelle, *Belgium* **17** 51 19N 3 19 E
Westkapelle, *Neths.* **17** 51 31N 3 28 E
Westland, *U.S.A.* **119** 42 15N 83 20W
Westland □, *N.Z.* **81** 43 33 S 169 59 E
Westland Bight, *N.Z.* **81** 42 55 S 170 5 E
Westlock, *Canada* **110** 54 9N 113 55W
Westmalle, *Belgium* **17** 51 18N 4 42 E
Westmeath □, *Ireland* **15** 53 30N 7 30W
Westmere, *Australia* **74** 37 42 S 142 58 E
Westminster, *U.S.A.* **114** 39 34N 77 1W
Westmorland, *U.S.A.* **123** 33 2N 115 42W
Weston, *Malaysia* **56** 5 10N 115 35 E
Weston, *Ohio, U.S.A.* **119** 41 21N 83 47W
Weston, *Oreg., U.S.A.* **122** 45 50N 118 30W
Weston, *W. Va., U.S.A.* **114** 39 3N 80 29W
Weston I., *Canada* **104** 52 33N 79 36W
Weston-super-Mare, *U.K.* **13** 51 20N 2 59W
Westphalia, *U.S.A.* **118** 38 26N 92 0W
Westport, *Canada* **109** 44 40N 76 25W
Westport, *Ireland* **15** 53 44N 9 31W
Westport, *N.Z.* **81** 41 46 S 171 37 E
Westport, *Ind., U.S.A.* **119** 39 11N 85 34W
Westport, *Oreg., U.S.A.* **124** 46 10N 123 23W
Westport, *Wash., U.S.A.* **122** 46 48N 124 4W
Westray, *Canada* **111** 53 36N 101 24W
Westray, *U.K.* **14** 59 18N 3 0W
Westree, *Canada* **104** 47 26N 81 34W
Westville, *Calif., U.S.A.* **124** 39 8N 120 42W
Westville, *Ill., U.S.A.* **119** 40 3N 87 36W
Westville, *Ind., U.S.A.* **119** 41 35N 86 55W
Westville, *Okla., U.S.A.* **121** 36 0N 94 33W
Westwood, *U.S.A.* **122** 40 26N 121 0W
Wetar, *Indonesia* **57** 7 30 S 126 30 E
Wetaskiwin, *Canada* **110** 52 55N 113 24W
Wethersfield, *U.S.A.* **117** 41 43N 72 40W
Wetlet, *Burma* **52** 22 20N 95 53 E
Wetteren, *Belgium* **17** 51 0N 3 52 E
Wetzlar, *W. Germany* **30** 50 33N 8 30 E
Wevelgem, *Belgium* **17** 50 49N 3 12 E
Wewak, *Papua N. G.* **69** 3 38 S 143 41 E
Wewaka, *U.S.A.* **121** 35 10N 96 35W
Wexford, *Ireland* **15** 52 20N 6 28W
Wexford □, *Ireland* **15** 52 20N 6 25W
Wexford Harbour, *Ireland* **15** 52 20N 6 25W
Weyburn, *Canada* **111** 49 40N 103 50W
Weyburn L., *Canada* **110** 63 0N 117 59W
Weyer, *Austria* **33** 47 51N 14 40 E
Weyib →, *Ethiopia* **89** 7 15N 40 15 E
Weymouth, *Canada* **105** 44 30N 66 1W
Weymouth, *U.K.* **13** 50 36N 2 28W
Weymouth, *U.S.A.* **117** 42 13N 70 53W
Weymouth, C., *Australia* **72** 12 37 S 143 27 E
Wezemaal, *Belgium* **17** 50 57N 4 45 E
Wezep, *Neths.* **16** 52 28N 6 0 E
Whakamaru, *N.Z.* **80** 38 23 S 175 50 E
Whakatane, *N.Z.* **80** 37 57 S 177 1 E
Whalan Cr. →, *Australia* **77** 29 5 S 149 1 E
Whale →, *Canada* **105** 58 15N 67 40W
Whale Cove, *Canada* **102** 62 11N 92 36W
Whales, B. of, *Antarctica* **143** 78 0 S 165 0W
Whalsay, *U.K.* **14** 60 22N 1 0W
Whangamata, *N.Z.* **80** 37 12 S 175 53 E
Whangamomona, *N.Z.* **80** 39 8 S 174 44 E
Whangarei, *N.Z.* **80** 35 43 S 174 21 E
Whangarei Harbour, *N.Z.* **80** 35 45 S 174 28 E
Whangaroa Harb., *N.Z.* **80** 35 4 S 173 46 E
Wharanui, *N.Z.* **81** 41 55 S 174 6 E
Wharfe →, *U.K.* **12** 53 55N 1 30W
Wharfedale, *U.K.* **12** 54 7N 2 4W
Wharton, *N.J., U.S.A.* **117** 40 53N 74 36W
Wharton, *Pa., U.S.A.* **116** 41 31N 78 1W
Wharton, *Tex., U.S.A.* **121** 29 20N 96 6W
Whataroa, *N.Z.* **81** 43 18 S 170 24 E
Whataroa →, *N.Z.* **81** 43 7 S 170 16 E
Wheatfield, *U.S.A.* **119** 41 13N 87 4W
Wheatland, *Calif., U.S.A.* **124** 39 1N 121 25W
Wheatland, *Ind., U.S.A.* **119** 38 40N 87 19W
Wheatland, *Wyo., U.S.A.* **120** 42 4N 104 58W
Wheatley, *Canada* **108** 42 6N 82 27W
Wheaton, *Ill., U.S.A.* **119** 41 52N 88 6W
Wheaton, *Minn., U.S.A.* **120** 45 50N 96 29W
Wheelbarrow Pk., *U.S.A.* **124** 37 26N 116 5W
Wheeler, *Oreg., U.S.A.* **122** 45 50N 123 57W
Wheeler, *Tex., U.S.A.* **121** 35 29N 100 15W
Wheeler →, *Canada* **111** 57 25N 105 30W
Wheeler Pk., *N. Mex., U.S.A.* **123** 36 34N 105 25W
Wheeler Pk., *Nev., U.S.A.* **123** 38 57N 114 15W
Wheeler Ridge, *U.S.A.* **125** 35 0N 118 57W
Wheeling, *U.S.A.* **116** 40 2N 80 41W
Whernside, *U.K.* **12** 54 14N 2 24W
Wherrol Flat, *Australia* **77** 31 46 S 152 15 E
Whetstone, *Australia* **77** 28 30 S 150 56 E
Whidbey I., *U.S.A.* **110** 48 15N 122 40W
Whiporie, *Australia* **77** 29 18 S 152 58 E
Whiskey Gap, *Canada* **110** 49 0N 113 3W
Whiskey Jack L., *Canada* **111** 58 23N 101 55W
Whistleduck Cr. →, *Australia* **72** 20 15 S 135 18 E
Whitby, *Canada* **109** 43 52N 78 56W
Whitby, *U.K.* **12** 54 29N 0 37W
White →, *Ark., U.S.A.* **121** 33 53N 91 3W
White →, *Colo., U.S.A.* **122** 40 8N 109 41W
White →, *Ind., U.S.A.* **119** 38 25N 87 45W
White →, *S. Dak., U.S.A.* **120** 43 45N 99 30W
White →, *Wash., U.S.A.* **124** 47 12N 122 15W
White, East Fork →, *U.S.A.* **119** 38 33N 87 14W
White B., *Canada* **105** 50 0N 56 35W
White Bear Res., *Canada* **105** 48 10N 57 5W
White Bird, *U.S.A.* **122** 45 46N 116 21W
White Butte, *U.S.A.* **120** 46 23N 103 19W
White City, *U.S.A.* **120** 38 50N 96 45W
White Cliffs, *Australia* **73** 30 50 S 143 10 E
White Deer, *U.S.A.* **121** 35 30N 101 8W
White Hall, *U.S.A.* **118** 39 25N 90 27W
White Haven, *U.S.A.* **117** 41 3N 75 47W
White I., *N.Z.* **80** 37 30 S 177 13 E
White L., *Canada* **106** 45 18N 76 31W
White L., *U.S.A.* **121** 29 45N 92 30W
White Mts., *Calif., U.S.A.* **124** 37 30N 118 15W
White Mts., *N.H., U.S.A.* **117** 44 15N 71 15W
White Nile = Nîl el Abyad →, *Sudan* **89** 15 38N 32 31 E
White Nile Dam = Khazzân Jabal el Awliyâ, *Sudan* **89** 15 24N 32 20 E
White Otter L., *Canada* **104** 49 5N 91 55W
White Pass, *Canada* **102** 59 40N 135 3W
White Pass, *U.S.A.* **124** 46 38N 121 24W
White Pigeon, *U.S.A.* **119** 41 48N 85 39W
White Plains, *U.S.A.* **117** 41 2N 73 44W
White River, *Canada* **104** 48 35N 85 20W
White River, *S. Africa* **97** 25 20 S 31 0 E
White River, *U.S.A.* **120** 43 34N 100 45W
White Russia = Byelorussian S.S.R. □, *U.S.S.R.* **36** 53 30N 27 0 E
White Sea = Beloye More, *U.S.S.R.* **40** 66 30N 38 0 E
White Sulphur Springs, *Mont., U.S.A.* **122** 46 35N 110 54W
White Sulphur Springs, *W. Va., U.S.A.* **114** 37 50N 80 16W
White Swan, *U.S.A.* **124** 46 23N 120 44W
White Volta →, *Ghana* **91** 9 10N 1 15W
Whitecliffs, *N.Z.* **81** 43 26 S 171 55 E
Whitecourt, *Canada* **110** 54 10N 115 45W
Whiteface, *U.S.A.* **121** 33 35N 102 40W
Whitefield, *U.S.A.* **117** 44 23N 71 37W
Whitefish, *Canada* **108** 46 23N 81 19W
Whitefish, *U.S.A.* **122** 48 25N 114 22W
Whitefish Bay, *U.S.A.* **119** 43 23N 87 54W
Whitefish Falls, *Canada* **108** 46 7N 81 44W
Whitefish L., *Canada* **111** 62 41N 106 48W
Whitefish Pt., *U.S.A.* **114** 46 45N 85 0W
Whitegull, L., *Canada* **105** 55 27N 64 17W
Whitehall, *Mich., U.S.A.* **114** 43 21N 86 20W
Whitehall, *Mont., U.S.A.* **122** 45 52N 112 4W
Whitehall, *N.Y., U.S.A.* **117** 43 32N 73 28W
Whitehall, *Wis., U.S.A.* **120** 44 20N 91 19W
Whitehaven, *U.K.* **12** 54 33N 3 35W
Whitehorse, *Canada* **102** 60 43N 135 3W
Whitehorse, Vale of, *U.K.* **13** 51 37N 1 30W
Whiteman, *U.S.A.* **118** 38 45N 93 40W
Whiteman Ra., *Papua N. G.* **69** 5 55 S 150 0 E
Whitemark, *Australia* **72** 40 7 S 148 3 E
Whitemouth, *Canada* **111** 49 57N 95 58W
Whiteplains, *Liberia* **90** 6 28N 10 40W
Whitesands, *Vanuatu* **68** 19 28 S 169 25 E
Whitesboro, *N.Y., U.S.A.* **117** 43 8N 75 20W
Whitesboro, *Tex., U.S.A.* **121** 33 40N 96 58W
Whiteshell Prov. Park, *Canada* **111** 50 0N 95 40W
Whiteside, *U.S.A.* **118** 39 12N 91 2W
Whiteside, Canal, *Chile* **142** 53 55 S 70 15W
Whitetail, *U.S.A.* **120** 48 54N 105 15W
Whiteville, *U.S.A.* **115** 34 20N 78 40W
Whitewater, *U.S.A.* **119** 42 50N 88 45W
Whitewater Baldy, Mt., *U.S.A.* **123** 33 20N 108 44W
Whitewater L., *Canada* **104** 50 50N 89 10W
Whitewood, *Australia* **72** 21 28 S 143 30 E
Whitewood, *Canada* **111** 50 20N 102 20W
Whitfield, *Australia* **75** 36 42 S 146 24 E
Whithorn, *U.K.* **14** 54 44N 4 25W
Whitianga, *N.Z.* **80** 36 47 S 175 41 E
Whiting, *U.S.A.* **119** 41 41N 87 29W
Whitman, *U.S.A.* **117** 42 4N 70 55W
Whitmire, *U.S.A.* **115** 34 33N 81 40W
Whitney, *Canada* **106** 45 31N 78 14W
Whitney, Mt., *U.S.A.* **124** 36 35N 118 14W
Whitney Point, *U.S.A.* **117** 42 19N 75 59W
Whitstable, *U.K.* **13** 51 21N 1 2 E
Whitsunday I., *Australia* **72** 20 15 S 149 4 E
Whittemore, *U.S.A.* **118** 43 4N 94 26W
Whittier, *Alaska, U.S.A.* **102** 60 46N 148 48W
Whittier, *Calif., U.S.A.* **125** 33 58N 118 3W
Whittlesea, *Australia* **74** 37 27 S 145 9 E
Whitwell, *U.S.A.* **115** 35 15N 85 30W
Wholdaia L., *Canada* **111** 60 43N 104 20W
Whorouly, *Australia* **75** 36 31 S 146 35 E
Whyalla, *Australia* **73** 33 2 S 137 30 E
Whyjonta, *Australia* **73** 29 41 S 142 28 E
Wiangaree, *Australia* **77** 28 30 S 152 59 E
Wiarton, *Canada* **108** 44 40N 81 10W
Wiawso, *Ghana* **90** 6 10N 2 25W
Wibaux, *U.S.A.* **120** 47 0N 104 13W
Wichabai, *Guyana* **135** 2 57N 59 35W
Wichian Buri, *Thailand* **54** 15 39N 101 7 E
Wichita, *U.S.A.* **121** 37 40N 97 20W
Wichita Falls, *U.S.A.* **121** 33 57N 98 30W
Wick, *U.K.* **14** 58 26N 3 5W
Wicked Pt., *Canada* **109** 43 52N 77 15W
Wickenburg, *U.S.A.* **123** 33 58N 112 45W
Wickepin, *Australia* **79** 32 50 S 117 30 E
Wickham, *Canada* **107** 45 45N 72 30W
Wickham, C., *Australia* **72** 39 35 S 143 57 E
Wickliffe, *U.S.A.* **116** 41 36N 81 29W
Wicklow, *Ireland* **15** 53 0N 6 2W
Wicklow □, *Ireland* **15** 52 59N 6 25W
Wicklow Hd., *Ireland* **15** 52 59N 6 3W
Wicklow Mts., *Ireland* **15** 53 0N 6 30W
Widgiemooltha, *Australia* **79** 31 30 S 121 34 E
Widnes, *U.K.* **12** 53 22N 2 44W
Wiedenbrück, *W. Germany* **30** 51 52N 8 15 E
Wiek, *E. Germany* **30** 54 37N 13 17 E
Wielbark, *Poland* **32** 53 24N 20 55 E
Wieliczka, *Poland* **32** 50 0N 20 5 E
Wieluń, *Poland* **32** 51 15N 18 34 E
Wien, *Austria* **33** 48 12N 16 22 E
Wiener Neustadt, *Austria* **33** 47 49N 16 16 E
Wieprz →, *Koszalin, Poland* **32** 54 26N 16 35 E
Wieprz →, *Lublin, Poland* **32** 51 34N 21 49 E
Wierden, *Neths.* **16** 52 22N 6 35 E
Wiers, *Belgium* **17** 50 30N 3 32 E
Wiesbaden, *W. Germany* **31** 50 7N 8 17 E
Wiesental, *W. Germany* **31** 49 15N 8 30 E
Wigan, *U.K.* **12** 53 33N 2 38W
Wiggins, *Colo., U.S.A.* **120** 40 16N 104 3W
Wiggins, *Miss., U.S.A.* **121** 30 53N 89 9W
Wight, I. of, *U.K.* **13** 50 40N 1 20W
Wigtown, *U.K.* **14** 54 52N 4 27W
Wigtown B., *U.K.* **14** 54 46N 4 15W
Wijchen, *Neths.* **16** 51 48N 5 44 E
Wijhe, *Neths.* **16** 52 23N 6 8 E
Wijk bij Duurstede, *Neths.* **16** 51 59N 5 21 E
Wikwemikong, *Canada* **108** 45 48N 81 43W
Wil, *Switz.* **31** 47 28N 9 3 E
Wilber, *U.S.A.* **120** 40 34N 96 59W
Wilberforce, *Canada* **106** 45 2N 78 13W
Wilberforce, C., *Australia* **72** 11 54 S 136 35 E
Wilburton, *U.S.A.* **121** 34 55N 95 15W
Wilcannia, *Australia* **73** 31 30 S 143 26 E
Wilcox, *U.S.A.* **116** 41 34N 78 43W
Wildbad, *W. Germany* **31** 48 44N 8 32 E
Wildcat Creek →, *U.S.A.* **119** 40 28N 86 48W
Wildervank, *Neths.* **16** 53 5N 6 52 E
Wildeshausen, *W. Germany* **30** 52 54N 8 25 E
Wildrose, *Calif., U.S.A.* **125** 36 14N 117 11W
Wildrose, *N. Dak., U.S.A.* **120** 48 36N 103 11W
Wildspitze, *Austria* **31** 46 53N 10 53 E
Wildwood, *U.S.A.* **114** 38 59N 74 46W
Wilge →, *S. Africa* **97** 27 3 S 28 20 E
Wilhelm II Coast, *Antarctica* **143** 68 0 S 90 0 E
Wilhelm Mt., *Papua N. G.* **69** 5 50 S 145 1 E
Wilhelm-Pieck-Stadt Guben, *E. Germany* **30** 51 59N 14 48 E
Wilhelmina, Geb., *Surinam* **135** 3 50N 56 30W
Wilhelmina Kanaal, *Neths.* **17** 51 36N 5 6 E
Wilhelmsburg, *Austria* **33** 48 6N 15 36 E
Wilhelmsburg, *W. Germany* **30** 53 28N 10 1 E
Wilhelmshaven, *W. Germany* **30** 53 30N 8 9 E
Wilhelmstal, *Namibia* **96** 21 58 S 16 21 E
Wilkes Barre, *U.S.A.* **117** 41 15N 75 52W
Wilkes Land, *Antarctica* **143** 69 0 S 120 0 E
Wilkes Sub-Glacial Basin, *Antarctica* **143** 75 0 S 130 0 E
Wilkesboro, *U.S.A.* **115** 36 10N 81 9W
Wilkie, *Canada* **111** 52 27N 108 42W
Wilkinsburg, *U.S.A.* **116** 40 26N 79 50W
Wilkinson Lakes, *Australia* **79** 29 40 S 132 39 E
Willamina, *U.S.A.* **122** 45 9N 123 32W

Willandra Billabong Creek →, *Australia* **73** 33 22 S 145 52 E
Willapa, B., *U.S.A.* .. **122** 46 44N 124 0W
Willapa Hills, *U.S.A.* .. **124** 46 35N 123 25W
Willard, *N. Mex., U.S.A.* **123** 34 35N 106 1W
Willard, *Utah, U.S.A.* **122** 41 28N 112 1W
Willaura, *Australia* ... **74** 37 31 S 142 45 E
Willcox, *U.S.A.* **123** 32 13N 109 53W
Willebroek, *Belgium* .. **17** 51 4N 4 22 E
Willemstad, *Neth. Ant.* **129** 12 5N 69 0W
Willeroo, *Australia* ... **78** 15 14 S 131 37 E
William →, *Canada* .. **111** 59 8N 109 19W
William, Mt., *Australia* **74** 37 17 S 142 35 E
William Creek, *Australia* .... **73** 28 58 S 136 22 E
Williambury, *Australia* **79** 23 45 S 115 12 E
Williams, *Australia* ... **79** 33 2 S 116 52 E
Williams, *Ariz., U.S.A.* **123** 35 16N 112 11W
Williams, *Calif., U.S.A.* **124** 39 9N 122 9W
Williams Lake, *Canada* **110** 52 10N 122 10W
Williamsburg, *Ky., U.S.A.* **115** 36 45N 84 10W
Williamsburg, *Pa., U.S.A.* **116** 40 27N 78 14W
Williamsburg, *Va., U.S.A.* **114** 37 17N 76 44W
Williamsfield, *U.S.A.* . **118** 40 55N 90 1W
Williamson, *N.Y., U.S.A.* **116** 43 14N 77 15W
Williamson, *W. Va., U.S.A.* **114** 37 46N 82 17W
Williamsport, *Ind., U.S.A.* **119** 40 17N 87 17W
Williamsport, *Pa., U.S.A.* **116** 41 18N 77 1W
Williamston, *Mich., U.S.A.* **119** 42 41N 84 17W
Williamston, *S.C., U.S.A.* **115** 35 50N 77 5W
Williamstown, *Australia* **74** 37 51 S 144 52 E
Williamstown, *Ky., U.S.A.* **119** 38 38N 84 34W
Williamstown, *Mass., U.S.A.* **117** 42 41N 73 12W
Williamstown, *N.Y., U.S.A.* **117** 43 25N 75 54W
Williamsville, *Ill., U.S.A.* **118** 39 57N 89 33W
Williamsville, *Mo., U.S.A.* **121** 37 0N 90 33W
Williamtown, *Australia* **76** 32 48 S 151 50 E
Willimantic, *U.S.A.* .. **117** 41 45N 72 12W
Willis Group, *Australia* **72** 16 18 S 150 0 E
Willisburg, *U.S.A.* **119** 37 49N 85 8W
Williston, *S. Africa* ... **96** 31 20 S 20 53 E
Williston, *Fla., U.S.A.* **115** 29 25N 82 28W
Williston, *N. Dak., U.S.A.* **120** 48 10N 103 35W
Williston L., *Canada* .. **110** 56 0N 124 0W
Willits, *U.S.A.* **122** 39 28N 123 17W
Willmar, *U.S.A.* **120** 45 5N 95 0W
Willoughby, *U.S.A.* ... **116** 41 38N 81 26W
Willow Bunch, *Canada* **111** 49 20N 105 35W
Willow L., *Canada* ... **110** 62 10N 119 8W
Willow Lake, *U.S.A.* .. **120** 44 40N 97 40W
Willow Springs, *U.S.A.* **121** 37 0N 92 0W
Willow Tree, *Australia* **77** 31 40 S 150 45 E
Willow Wall, The, *China* .... **61** 42 10N 122 0 E
Willowlake →, *Canada* **110** 62 42N 123 8W
Willowmore, *S. Africa* **96** 33 15 S 23 30 E
Willows, *Australia* .... **72** 23 39 S 147 25 E
Willows, *U.S.A.* **124** 39 30N 122 10W
Willowvale = Gatyana, *S. Africa* .... **97** 32 16 S 28 31 E
Wills, L., *Australia* ... **78** 21 25 S 128 51 E
Wills Cr. →, *Australia* **72** 22 43 S 140 2 E
Wills Point, *U.S.A.* ... **121** 32 42N 95 57W
Willunga, *Australia* ... **73** 35 15 S 138 30 E
Wilmette, *U.S.A.* **114** 42 6N 87 44W
Wilmington, *Australia* . **73** 32 39 S 138 7 E
Wilmington, *Del., U.S.A.* **114** 39 45N 75 32W
Wilmington, *Ill., U.S.A.* **119** 41 19N 88 10W
Wilmington, *N.C., U.S.A.* **115** 34 14N 77 54W
Wilmington, *Ohio, U.S.A.* **119** 39 27N 83 50W
Wilpena Cr. →, *Australia* .... **73** 31 25 S 139 29 E
Wilrijk, *Belgium* ..... **17** 51 9N 4 22 E
Wilsall, *U.S.A.* **122** 45 59N 110 40W
Wilson, *U.S.A.* **115** 35 44N 77 54W
Wilson →, *Queens., Australia* .... **73** 27 38 S 141 24 E
Wilson →, *W. Austral., Australia* .... **78** 16 48 S 128 16 E
Wilson Bluff, *Australia* **79** 31 41 S 129 0 E
Wilson Str., *Solomon Is.* .... **68** 8 0 S 156 39 E
Wilsons Promontory, *Australia* .... **75** 38 55 S 146 25 E
Wilster, *W. Germany* . **30** 53 55N 9 23 E
Wilton, *U.K.* **13** 51 5N 1 52W
Wilton, *U.S.A.* **120** 47 12N 100 47W
Wilton →, *Australia* .. **72** 14 45 S 134 33 E
Wiltshire □, *U.K.* **13** 51 20N 2 0W
Wiltz, *Lux.* .... **17** 49 57N 5 55 E
Wiluna, *Australia* ..... **79** 26 36 S 120 14 E
Wimereux, *France* .... **19** 50 45N 1 37 E
Wimmera, *Australia* .. **74** 36 30 S 142 0 E
Wimmera →, *Australia* **74** 36 8 S 141 56 E
Winam G., *Kenya* .... **92** 0 20 S 34 15 E
Winamac, *U.S.A.* **119** 41 3N 86 36W
Winburg, *S. Africa* ... **96** 28 30 S 27 2 E
Winchelsea, *Australia* . **74** 38 10 S 144 1 E
Winchendon, *U.S.A.* . **117** 42 40N 72 3W
Winchester, *Canada* .. **109** 45 6N 75 21W
Winchester, *N.Z.* ..... **81** 44 11 S 171 17 E
Winchester, *U.K.* **13** 51 4N 1 19W
Winchester, *Conn., U.S.A.* **117** 41 53N 73 9W
Winchester, *Idaho, U.S.A.* **122** 46 11N 116 32W
Winchester, *Ill., U.S.A.* **118** 39 38N 90 27W
Winchester, *Ind., U.S.A.* **119** 40 10N 84 56W
Winchester, *Ky., U.S.A.* **119** 38 0N 84 8W
Winchester, *N.H., U.S.A.* **117** 42 47N 72 22W
Winchester, *Nev., U.S.A.* **125** 36 6N 115 10W
Winchester, *Ohio, U.S.A.* **119** 38 57N 83 40W
Winchester, *Tenn., U.S.A.* **115** 35 11N 86 8W
Winchester, *Va., U.S.A.* **114** 39 14N 78 8W
Wind →, *U.S.A.* **122** 43 8N 108 12W
Wind Pt., *U.S.A.* **119** 42 47N 87 46W
Wind River Range, *U.S.A.* **122** 43 0N 109 30W
Windber, *U.S.A.* **116** 40 14N 78 50W
Windermere, L., *U.K.* **12** 54 20N 2 57W
Windeyer, *Australia* .. **76** 32 46 S 149 32 E
Windfall, *Canada* **110** 54 12N 116 13W
Windfall, *U.S.A.* **119** 40 22N 85 57W
Windflower L., *Canada* **110** 62 52N 118 30W
Windhoek, *Namibia* .. **96** 22 35 S 17 4 E
Windigo →, *Canada* . **107** 47 46N 73 19W
Windom, *U.S.A.* **120** 43 48N 95 3W
Windorah, *Australia* .. **72** 25 24 S 142 36 E
Window Rock, *U.S.A.* **123** 35 47N 109 4W
Windrush →, *U.K.* ... **13** 51 48N 1 35W
Windsor, *Australia* ... **76** 33 37 S 150 50 E
Windsor, *N.S., Canada* **105** 44 59N 64 5W
Windsor, *Nfld., Canada* **105** 48 57N 55 40W
Windsor, *Ont., Canada* **108** 42 18N 83 0W
Windsor, *Qué., Canada* **107** 45 34N 72 0W
Windsor, *N.Z.* .... **81** 44 59 S 170 49 E
Windsor, *U.K.* **13** 51 28N 0 36W
Windsor, *Colo., U.S.A.* **120** 40 33N 104 45W
Windsor, *Conn., U.S.A.* **117** 41 50N 72 40W
Windsor, *Ill., U.S.A.* . **119** 39 26N 88 36W
Windsor, *Mo., U.S.A.* **118** 38 32N 93 31W
Windsor, *N.Y., U.S.A.* **117** 42 5N 75 37W
Windsor, *Vt., U.S.A.* . **117** 43 30N 72 25W
Windsorton, *S. Africa* . **96** 28 16 S 24 44 E
Windward Is., *Pac. Oc.* **67** 18 0 S 149 0W
Windward Is., *W. Indies* **129** 13 0N 63 0W
Windward Passage = Vientos, Paso de los, *Caribbean* **129** 20 0N 74 0W
Windy L., *Canada* **111** 60 20N 100 2W
Winefred L., *Canada* . **111** 55 30N 110 30W
Winejok, *Sudan* ...... **89** 9 1N 27 30 E
Winfield, *Ill., U.S.A.* . **118** 41 5N 91 30W
Winfield, *Kans., U.S.A.* **121** 37 15N 97 0W
Winfield, *Mo., U.S.A.* **118** 39 0N 90 44W
Wingate Mts., *Australia* **78** 14 25 S 130 40 E
Wingello, *Australia* ... **76** 34 42 S 150 10 E
Wingen, *Australia* .... **77** 31 54 S 150 54 E
Wingene, *Belgium* .... **17** 51 3N 3 17 E
Wingham, *Australia* .. **77** 31 48 S 152 22 E
Wingham, *Canada* **108** 43 55N 81 20W
Winifred, *U.S.A.* **122** 47 30N 109 28W
Winisk, *Canada* **104** 55 20N 85 15W
Winisk →, *Canada* ... **104** 55 17N 85 5W
Winisk L., *Canada* ... **104** 52 55N 87 22W
Wink, *U.S.A.* **121** 31 49N 103 9W
Winkler, *Canada* **111** 49 10N 97 56W
Winlock, *U.S.A.* **124** 46 29N 122 56W
Winneba, *Ghana* **91** 5 25N 0 36W
Winnebago, *Ill., U.S.A.* **118** 42 15N 89 18W
Winnebago, *Minn., U.S.A.* **120** 43 43N 94 8W
Winnebago L., *U.S.A.* **114** 44 0N 88 20W
Winnecke Cr. →, *Australia* .... **78** 18 35 S 131 34 E
Winnemucca, *U.S.A.* . **122** 41 0N 117 45W
Winnemucca, L., *U.S.A.* **122** 40 25N 119 21W
Winner, *U.S.A.* **120** 43 23N 99 52W
Winnett, *U.S.A.* **122** 47 2N 108 21W
Winnfield, *U.S.A.* ... **121** 31 57N 92 38W
Winnibigoshish L., *U.S.A.* **120** 47 25N 94 12W
Winning, *Australia* ... **78** 23 9 S 114 30 E
Winnipeg, *Canada* **111** 49 54N 97 9W
Winnipeg →, *Canada* **111** 50 38N 96 19W
Winnipeg, L., *Canada* **111** 52 0N 97 0W
Winnipeg Beach, *Canada* **111** 50 30N 96 58W
Winnipegosis, *Canada* **111** 51 39N 99 55W
Winnipegosis L., *Canada* **111** 52 30N 100 0W
Winnipesaukee, L., *U.S.A.* **117** 43 38N 71 21W
Winnsboro, *La., U.S.A.* **121** 32 10N 91 41W
Winnsboro, *S.C., U.S.A.* **115** 34 23N 81 5W
Winnsboro, *Tex., U.S.A.* **121** 32 56N 95 15W
Winokapau, L., *Canada* **105** 53 15N 62 50W
Winona, *Miss., U.S.A.* **121** 33 30N 89 42W
Winona, *Wis., U.S.A.* **120** 44 2N 91 39W
Winooski, *U.S.A.* **117** 44 31N 73 11W
Winschoten, *Neths.* ... **16** 53 9N 7 3 E
Winsen, *W. Germany* . **30** 53 21N 10 11 E
Winslow, *Ariz., U.S.A.* **123** 35 2N 110 41W
Winslow, *Ind., U.S.A.* **119** 38 23N 87 13W
Winslow, *Wash., U.S.A.* **124** 47 37N 122 31W
Winsted, *U.S.A.* **117** 41 55N 73 5W
Winston-Salem, *U.S.A.* **115** 36 7N 80 15W
Winsum, *Neths.* ...... **16** 53 20N 6 32 E
Winter Garden, *U.S.A.* **115** 28 33N 81 35W
Winter Haven, *U.S.A.* **115** 28 0N 81 42W
Winter Park, *U.S.A.* .. **115** 28 34N 81 19W
Winterberg, *W. Germany* ...... **30** 51 12N 8 30 E
Winterhaven, *U.S.A.* . **125** 32 47N 114 39W
Winters, *Calif., U.S.A.* **124** 38 32N 121 58W
Winters, *Tex., U.S.A.* **121** 31 58N 99 58W
Winterset, *U.S.A.* **118** 41 18N 94 0W
Wintersville, *U.S.A.* .. **116** 40 22N 80 38W
Winterswijk, *Neths.* .. **16** 51 58N 6 43 E
Winterthur, *Switz.* .... **31** 47 30N 8 44 E
Winthrop, *Minn., U.S.A.* **120** 44 31N 94 25W
Winthrop, *Wash., U.S.A.* **122** 48 27N 120 6W
Winton, *Queens., Australia* .... **72** 22 24 S 143 3 E
Winton, *Vic., Australia* **74** 36 32 S 146 7 E
Winton, *N.Z.* .... **81** 46 8 S 168 20 E
Winton, *U.S.A.* **115** 36 25N 76 58W
Winton Swamp, *Australia* .... **74** 36 27 S 146 5 E
Wintzenheim, *France* . **19** 48 4N 7 17 E
Wipper →, *E. Germany* ...... **30** 51 17N 11 10 E
Wirral, *U.K.* **12** 53 25N 3 0W
Wirrinya, *Australia* ... **76** 33 39 S 147 48 E
Wirrulla, *Australia* .... **73** 32 24 S 134 31 E
Wisbech, *U.K.* .... **12** 52 39N 0 10 E
Wisconsin □, *U.S.A.* . **120** 44 30N 90 0W
Wisconsin →, *U.S.A.* **120** 43 0N 91 15W
Wisconsin Dells, *U.S.A.* **120** 43 38N 89 45W
Wisconsin Rapids, *U.S.A.* **120** 44 25N 89 50W
Wisdom, *U.S.A.* **122** 45 37N 113 27W
Wisemans Ferry, *Australia* .... **76** 33 22 S 150 59 E
Wishaw, *U.K.* **14** 55 46N 3 55W
Wishek, *U.S.A.* **120** 46 20N 99 35W
Wisła, *Poland* .... **32** 49 38N 18 53 E
Wisła →, *Poland* .... **32** 54 22N 18 55 E
Wisłok →, *Poland* ... **32** 50 13N 22 32 E
Wisłoka →, *Poland* .. **32** 50 27N 21 23 E
Wismar, *E. Germany* . **30** 53 53N 11 23 E
Wismar, *Guyana* **135** 5 59N 58 18W
Wisner, *U.S.A.* **120** 42 0N 96 46W
Wissant, *France* ...... **19** 50 52N 1 40 E
Wissembourg, *France* . **19** 49 2N 7 57 E
Wissenkerke, *Neths.* .. **17** 51 35N 3 45 E
Witbank, *S. Africa* ... **97** 25 51 S 29 14 E
Witdraai, *S. Africa* ... **96** 26 58 S 20 48 E
Witham →, *U.K.* **12** 53 3N 0 8W
Withernsea, *U.K.* .... **12** 53 43N 0 2 E
Witmarsum, *Neths.* ... **16** 53 6N 5 28 E
Witney, *U.K.* **13** 51 47N 1 29W
Witnossob →, *Namibia* **96** 26 55 S 20 37 E
Wittdün, *W. Germany* **30** 54 38N 8 23 E
Witten, *W. Germany* . **17** 51 26N 7 19 E
Wittenberg, *E. Germany* ...... **30** 51 51N 12 39 E
Wittenberge, *E. Germany* ...... **30** 53 0N 11 44 E
Wittenburg, *E. Germany* ...... **30** 53 30N 11 4 E
Wittenoom, *Australia* . **78** 22 15 S 118 20 E
Wittingen, *W. Germany* **30** 52 43N 10 43 E
Wittlich, *W. Germany* **31** 50 0N 6 54 E
Wittmund, *W. Germany* **30** 53 39N 7 45 E
Wittow, *E. Germany* . **30** 54 37N 13 21 E
Wittstock, *E. Germany* **30** 53 10N 12 30 E
Witzenhausen, *Germany* .... **30** 51 60N 9 46 E
Wlingi, *Indonesia* .... **57** 8 5 S 112 25 E
Włocławek, *Poland* ... **32** 52 40N 19 3 E
Włodawa, *Poland* .... **32** 51 33N 23 31 E
Włoszczowa, *Poland* .. **32** 50 50N 19 55 E
Woburn, *U.S.A.* **117** 42 31N 71 7W
Wodian, *China* ...... **60** 32 50N 112 35 E
Wodonga, *Australia* .. **75** 36 5 S 146 50 E
Woerden, *Neths.* ..... **16** 52 5N 4 54 E
Woerth, *France* ...... **19** 48 57N 7 45 E
Woëvre, *France* ...... **19** 49 15N 5 45 E
Wognum, *Neths.* ..... **16** 52 40N 5 1 E
Woinbogoin, *China* ... **58** 32 51N 98 39 E
Wokam, *Indonesia* ... **57** 5 45 S 134 28 E
Wokha, *India* .... **52** 26 6N 94 16 E
Wolbrom, *Poland* .... **32** 50 24N 19 45 E
Wolcottville, *U.S.A.* .. **119** 41 32N 85 22W
Woldegk, *E. Germany* **30** 53 27N 13 35 E
Wolf →, *Canada* **110** 60 17N 132 33W
Wolf Creek, *U.S.A.* ... **122** 47 1N 112 2W
Wolf L., *Canada* **110** 60 24N 131 40W
Wolf Point, *U.S.A.* ... **120** 48 6N 105 40W
Wolfe I., *Canada* **109** 44 7N 76 20W
Wolfenbüttel, *W. Germany* ...... **30** 52 10N 10 33 E
Wolfheze, *Neths.* .... **16** 52 0N 5 48 E
Wolfsberg, *Austria* ... **33** 46 50N 14 52 E
Wolfsburg, *W. Germany* ...... **30** 52 27N 10 49 E
Wolgast, *E. Germany* . **30** 54 3N 13 46 E
Wolhusen, *Switz.* ..... **31** 47 4N 8 4 E
Wolin, *Poland* .... **32** 53 50N 14 37 E
Wollar, *Australia* ..... **76** 32 20 S 149 56 E
Wollaston, Is., *Chile* .. **142** 55 40 S 67 30W
Wollaston L., *Canada* . **111** 58 7N 103 10W
Wollaston Pen., *Canada* **102** 69 30N 115 0W
Wollogorang, *Australia* **72** 17 13 S 137 57 E
Wollombi, *Australia* .. **76** 32 56 S 151 8 E
Wollomombi, *Australia* **77** 30 30 S 152 4 E
Wollondilly →, *Australia* .... **76** 34 12 S 150 18 E
Wollongong, *Australia* **76** 34 25 S 150 54 E
Wolmaransstad, *S. Africa* .... **96** 27 12 S 25 59 E
Wolmirstedt, *E. Germany* ...... **30** 52 15N 11 35 E
Wolseley, *Australia* ... **73** 36 23 S 140 54 E
Wolseley, *Canada* **111** 50 25N 103 15W
Wolseley, *S. Africa* ... **96** 33 26 S 19 7 E
Wolstenholme, C., *Canada* **100** 62 35N 77 30W
Wolstenholme Fjord, *Canada* **144** 76 0N 70 0W
Wolsztyn, *Poland* .... **32** 52 8N 16 5 E
Wolumla, *Australia* ... **75** 36 51 S 149 50 E
Wolvega, *Neths.* ..... **16** 52 52N 6 0 E
Wolverhampton, *U.K.* **13** 52 35N 2 6W
Wombat, *Australia* ... **76** 34 24 S 148 16 E
Wombeyan Caves, *Australia* .... **76** 34 17 S 149 59 E
Wommels, *Neths.* .... **16** 53 6N 5 36 E
Wonarah, *Australia* ... **72** 19 55 S 136 20 E
Wonboyn, *Australia* .. **75** 37 15 S 149 55 E
Wonck, *Belgium* ..... **17** 50 46N 5 38 E
Wondai, *Australia* .... **73** 26 20 S 151 49 E
Wondalga, *Australia* .. **76** 35 24 S 148 8 E
Wondelgem, *Belgium* . **17** 51 5N 3 44 E
Wonder Gorge, *Zambia* **93** 14 40 S 29 0 E
Wongalarroo L., *Australia* .... **73** 31 32 S 144 0 E
Wongan Hills, *Australia* **79** 30 51 S 116 37 E
Wongarbon, *Australia* . **76** 32 20 S 148 45 E
Wongawol, *Australia* .. **79** 26 5 S 121 55 E
Wongungarra →, *Australia* .... **75** 37 12 S 147 3 E
Wŏnju, *S. Korea* ..... **61** 37 22N 127 58 E
Wonnangatta →, *Australia* .... **75** 37 32 S 147 15 E
Wonosari, *Indonesia* .. **57** 7 58 S 110 36 E
Wŏnsan, *N. Korea* ... **61** 39 11N 127 27 E
Wonthaggi, *Australia* . **74** 38 37 S 145 37 E
Wonwron, *Australia* .. **75** 38 27 S 146 45 E
Woocalla, *Australia* ... **73** 31 42 S 137 12 E
Wood Buffalo Nat. Park, *Canada* **110** 59 0N 113 41W
Wood Is., *Australia* ... **78** 16 24 S 123 19 E
Wood L., *Canada* **111** 55 17N 103 17W
Wood Lake, *U.S.A.* .. **120** 42 38N 100 14W
Wood River, *U.S.A.* .. **118** 38 52N 90 5W
Woodah I., *Australia* . **72** 13 27 S 136 10 E
Woodanilling, *Australia* **79** 33 31 S 117 24 E
Woodbridge, *Canada* . **108** 43 47N 79 36W
Woodburn, *Australia* . **77** 29 6 S 153 23 E
Woodenbong, *Australia* **77** 28 24 S 152 39 E
Woodend, *Australia* .. **74** 37 20 S 144 33 E
Woodfords, *U.S.A.* ... **124** 38 47N 119 50W
Woodgreen, *Australia* . **72** 22 26 S 134 12 E
Woodlake, *U.S.A.* **124** 36 25N 119 6W
Woodland, *U.S.A.* **124** 38 40N 121 50W
Woodlands, *Australia* . **79** 24 46 S 118 8 E
Woodlark I., *Papua N. G.* .... **69** 9 10 S 152 50 E
Woodpecker, *Canada* . **110** 53 30N 122 40W
Woodridge, *Canada* .. **111** 49 20N 96 9W
Woodroffe, Mt., *Australia* .... **79** 26 20 S 131 45 E
Woodruff, *Ariz., U.S.A.* **123** 34 51N 110 1W
Woodruff, *Utah, U.S.A.* **122** 41 30N 111 4W
Woods, L., *Australia* . **72** 17 50 S 133 30 E
Woods, L., *Canada* ... **105** 54 30N 65 13W
Woods, L. of the, *Canada* **111** 49 15N 94 45W
Woods Point, *Australia* **75** 37 32 S 146 16 E
Woods Reef, *Australia* **77** 30 22 S 150 45 E
Woodside, *Australia* .. **73** 38 31 S 146 52 E
Woodstock, *N.S.W., Australia* .... **76** 33 45 S 148 53 E
Woodstock, *Queens., Australia* .... **72** 19 35 S 146 50 E
Woodstock, *W. Austral., Australia* **78** 21 41 S 118 57 E
Woodstock, *N.B., Canada* **105** 46 11N 67 37W
Woodstock, *Ont., Canada* **108** 43 10N 80 45W
Woodstock, *U.K.* **13** 51 51N 1 20W
Woodstock, *Ill., U.S.A.* **119** 42 17N 88 30W
Woodstock, *Vt., U.S.A.* **117** 43 37N 72 31W
Woodsville, *U.S.A.* ... **117** 44 10N 72 0W
Woodville, *N.Z.* ..... **80** 40 20 S 175 53 E
Woodville, *Ohio, U.S.A.* **119** 41 27N 83 22W
Woodville, *Tex., U.S.A.* **121** 30 45N 94 25W

Woodward, *U.S.A.* **121** 36 24N 99 28W
Woody, *U.S.A.* **125** 35 42N 118 50W
Woody Head, *Australia* **77** 29 22 S 153 22 E
Woolamai, C., *Australia* **74** 38 30 S 145 23 E
Woolbrook, *Australia* **77** 30 56 S 151 25 E
Woolgoolga, *Australia* **77** 30 6 S 153 11 E
Wooli, *Australia* **77** 29 52 S 153 17 E
Woolsthorpe, *Australia* **74** 38 11 S 142 26 E
Woomargama, *Australia* **76** 35 50 S 147 15 E
Woombye, *Australia* **73** 26 40 S 152 55 E
Woomelang, *Australia* **74** 35 37 S 142 40 E
Woomera, *Australia* **73** 31 30 S 137 10 E
Woonona, *Australia* **76** 34 21 S 150 54 E
Woonsocket, *R.I., U.S.A.* **117** 42 0N 71 30W
Woonsocket, *S. Dak., U.S.A.* **120** 44 5N 98 15W
Wooragee, *Australia* **75** 36 16 S 146 44 E
Wooramel, *Australia* **79** 25 45 S 114 17 E
Wooramel →, *Australia* **79** 25 47 S 114 10 E
Woori Yallock, *Australia* **74** 37 47 S 145 32 E
Woorinen, *Australia* **74** 35 14 S 143 27 E
Wooroloo, *Australia* **79** 31 48 S 116 18 E
Wooster, *U.S.A.* **116** 40 48N 81 55W
Wootton, *Australia* **77** 32 17 S 152 18 E
Worcester, *S. Africa* **96** 33 39 S 19 27 E
Worcester, *U.K.* **13** 52 12N 2 12W
Worcester, *Mass., U.S.A.* **117** 42 14N 71 49W
Worcester, *N.Y., U.S.A.* **117** 42 35N 74 45W
Worden, *U.S.A.* **118** 38 56N 89 50W
Wörgl, *Austria* **31** 47 29N 12 3 E
Workington, *U.K.* **12** 54 39N 3 34W
Worksop, *U.K.* **12** 53 19N 1 9W
Workum, *Neths.* **16** 52 59N 5 26 E
Worland, *U.S.A.* **122** 44 0N 107 59W
Wormerveer, *Neths.* **16** 52 30N 4 46 E
Wormhoudt, *France* **19** 50 52N 2 28 E
Worms, *W. Germany* **31** 49 37N 8 21 E
Wörth, *W. Germany* **31** 49 1N 12 24 E
Wortham, *U.S.A.* **121** 31 48N 96 27W
Wörther See, *Austria* **33** 46 37N 14 10 E
Worthing, *U.K.* **13** 50 49N 0 21W
Worthington, *Ind., U.S.A.* **119** 39 7N 86 59W
Worthington, *Minn., U.S.A.* **120** 43 35N 95 36W
Worthington, *Ohio, U.S.A.* **119** 40 5N 83 1W
Wosi, *Indonesia* **57** 0 15 S 128 0 E
Wottonville, *Canada* **107** 45 44N 71 48W
Wou-han = Wuhan, *China* **59** 30 31N 114 18 E
Woubrugge, *Neths.* **16** 52 10N 4 39 E
Woudenberg, *Neths.* **16** 52 5N 5 25 E
Woudsend, *Neths.* **16** 52 56N 5 38 E
Wour, *Chad* **87** 21 14N 16 0 E
Wouw, *Neths.* **17** 51 31N 4 23 E
Wowoni, *Indonesia* **57** 4 5 S 123 5 E
Woy Woy, *Australia* **76** 33 30 S 151 19 E
Wrangel I., *U.S.S.R.* **42** 71 0N 180 0 E
Wrangell, *U.S.A.* **102** 56 30N 132 25W
Wrangell, I., *U.S.A.* **110** 56 20N 132 10W
Wrangell Mts., *U.S.A.* **102** 61 40N 143 30W
Wrath, C., *U.K.* **14** 58 38N 5 0W
Wray, *U.S.A.* **120** 40 8N 102 18W
Wrekin, The, *U.K.* **12** 52 41N 2 35W
Wrens, *U.S.A.* **115** 33 13N 82 23W
Wrexham, *U.K.* **12** 53 5N 3 0W
Wriezen, *E. Germany* **30** 52 43N 14 9 E
Wright, *Canada* **110** 51 52N 121 40W
Wright, *Phil.* **57** 11 42N 125 2 E
Wrightson, Mt., *U.S.A.* **123** 31 43N 110 56W
Wrightwood, *U.S.A.* **125** 34 21N 117 38W
Wrigley, *Canada* **102** 63 16N 123 37W
Wrocław, *Poland* **32** 51 5N 17 5 E
Września, *Poland* **32** 52 21N 17 36 E
Wschowa, *Poland* **32** 51 48N 16 20 E
Wu Jiang →, *China* **58** 29 40N 107 20 E
Wu'an, *China* **60** 36 40N 114 15 E
Wubin, *Australia* **79** 30 6 S 116 37 E
Wubu, *China* **60** 37 28N 110 42 E
Wuchang, *China* **61** 44 55N 127 5 E
Wucheng, *China* **60** 37 12N 116 20 E
Wuchuan, *Guangdong, China* **59** 21 33N 110 43 E
Wuchuan, *Guizhou, China* **58** 28 25N 108 3 E
Wuchuan, *Nei Mongol Zizhiqu, China* **60** 41 5N 111 28 E
Wudi, *China* **61** 37 40N 117 35 E
Wuding, *China* **58** 25 24N 102 21 E
Wuding He →, *China* **60** 37 2N 110 23 E
Wudu, *China* **60** 33 22N 104 54 E
Wufeng, *China* **59** 30 12N 110 42 E
Wugang, *China* **59** 26 44N 110 35 E
Wugong Shan, *China* **59** 27 30N 114 0 E
Wuhan, *China* **59** 30 31N 114 18 E
Wuhe, *China* **61** 33 10N 117 50 E
Wuhsi = Wuxi, *China* **59** 31 33N 120 18 E
Wuhu, *China* **59** 31 22N 118 21 E
Wujiang, *China* **59** 31 10N 120 38 E
Wukari, *Nigeria* **91** 7 51N 9 42 E
Wulajie, *China* **61** 44 6N 126 33 E
Wulanbulang, *China* **60** 41 5N 110 55 E
Wulehe, *Ghana* **91** 8 39N 0 0 E
Wulian, *China* **61** 35 40N 119 12 E
Wuliang Shan, *China* **58** 24 30N 100 40 E
Wuliaru, *Indonesia* **57** 7 27 S 131 0 E
Wulumuchi = Ürümqi, *China* **62** 43 45N 87 45 E
Wum, *Cameroon* **91** 6 24N 10 2 E
Wuming, *China* **58** 23 12N 108 18 E
Wunghnu, *Australia* **74** 36 9 S 145 27 E
Wuning, *China* **59** 29 17N 115 5 E
Wunnummin L., *Canada* **104** 52 55N 89 10W
Wunsiedel, *W. Germany* **31** 50 2N 12 0 E
Wunstorf, *W. Germany* **30** 52 26N 9 29 E
Wuntho, *Burma* **52** 23 55N 95 45 E
Wuping, *China* **59** 25 5N 116 5 E
Wuppertal, *S. Africa* **96** 32 13 S 19 12 E
Wuppertal, *W. Germany* **30** 51 15N 7 8 E
Wuqing, *China* **61** 39 23N 117 4 E
Wurung, *Australia* **72** 19 13 S 140 38 E
Würzburg, *W. Germany* **31** 49 46N 9 55 E
Wurzen, *E. Germany* **30** 51 21N 12 45 E
Wushan, *Gansu, China* **60** 34 43N 104 53 E
Wushan, *Sichuan, China* **58** 31 7N 109 54 E
Wustrow, *E. Germany* **30** 54 4N 11 33 E
Wutach →, *W. Germany* **31** 47 37N 8 15 E
Wutai, *China* **60** 38 40N 113 12 E
Wuting = Huimin, *China* **61** 37 27N 117 28 E
Wutong, *China* **59** 25 24N 110 4 E
Wutonghaolai, *China* **61** 42 50N 120 5 E
Wutongqiao, *China* **58** 29 22N 103 50 E
Wuustwezel, *Belgium* **17** 51 23N 4 36 E
Wuwei, *Anhui, China* **59** 31 18N 117 54 E
Wuwei, *Gansu, China* **62** 37 57N 102 34 E
Wuxi, *Jiangsu, China* **59** 31 33N 120 18 E
Wuxi, *Sichuan, China* **58** 31 23N 109 35 E
Wuxiang, *China* **60** 36 49N 112 50 E
Wuxing, *China* **59** 30 51N 120 8 E
Wuxuan, *China* **58** 23 34N 109 38 E
Wuyang, *China* **60** 33 25N 113 35 E
Wuyi, *Hebei, China* **60** 37 46N 115 56 E
Wuyi, *Zhejiang, China* **59** 28 52N 119 50 E
Wuyi Shan, *China* **59** 27 0N 117 0 E
Wuyo, *Nigeria* **91** 10 23N 11 50 E
Wuyuan, *Jiangxi, China* **59** 29 15N 117 50 E
Wuyuan, *Nei Mongol Zizhiqu, China* **60** 41 2N 108 20 E
Wuzhai, *China* **60** 38 54N 111 48 E
Wuzhi Shan, *China* **54** 18 45N 109 45 E
Wuzhong, *China* **60** 38 2N 106 12 E
Wuzhou, *China* **59** 23 30N 111 18 E
Wyaaba Cr. →, *Australia* **72** 16 27 S 141 35 E
Wyaga, *Australia* **77** 28 11 S 150 37 E
Wyalkatchem, *Australia* **79** 31 8 S 117 22 E
Wyalusing, *U.S.A.* **117** 41 40N 76 16W
Wyan, *Australia* **77** 29 5 S 152 52 E
Wyandotte, *U.S.A.* **119** 42 14N 83 13W
Wyandra, *Australia* **73** 27 12 S 145 56 E
Wyangala Res., *Australia* **76** 33 54 S 149 0 E
Wyara, L., *Australia* **73** 28 42 S 144 14 E
Wycheproof, *Australia* **74** 36 0 S 143 17 E
Wye →, *U.K.* **13** 51 36N 2 40W
Wyemandoo, Mt., *Australia* **79** 28 28 S 118 29 E
Wyk, *W. Germany* **30** 54 41N 8 33 E
Wymondham, *U.K.* **13** 52 45N 0 42W
Wymore, *U.S.A.* **120** 40 10N 96 40W
Wynbring, *Australia* **73** 30 33 S 133 32 E
Wyndham, *N.S.W., Australia* **75** 36 55 S 149 39 E
Wyndham, *W. Austral., Australia* **78** 15 33 S 128 3 E
Wyndham, *N.Z.* **81** 46 20 S 168 51 E
Wyndmere, *U.S.A.* **120** 46 23N 97 7W
Wynne, *U.S.A.* **121** 35 15N 90 50W
Wynnum, *Australia* **77** 27 27 S 153 9 E
Wynyard, *Australia* **72** 41 5 S 145 44 E
Wynyard, *Canada* **111** 51 45N 104 10W
Wyola, L., *Australia* **79** 29 8 S 130 17 E
Wyoming, *Canada* **108** 42 57N 82 7W
Wyoming, *Ill., U.S.A.* **118** 41 4N 89 47W
Wyoming, *Iowa, U.S.A.* **118** 42 4N 91 0W
Wyoming, *Mich., U.S.A.* **119** 42 53N 85 42W
Wyoming □, *U.S.A.* **112** 42 48N 109 0W
Wyong, *Australia* **76** 33 14 S 151 24 E
Wyszków, *Poland* **32** 52 36N 21 25 E
Wyszogród, *Poland* **32** 52 23N 20 9 E
Wytheville, *U.S.A.* **114** 37 0N 81 3W

X

Xa-Muteba, *Angola* **95** 9 34 S 17 50 E
Xai-Xai, *Mozam.* **97** 25 6 S 33 31 E
Xainza, *China* **62** 30 58N 88 35 E
Xambioá, *Brazil* **138** 6 25 S 48 40W
Xangongo, *Angola* **95** 16 45 S 15 5 E
Xanten, *W. Germany* **30** 51 40N 6 27 E
Xánthi, *Greece* **35** 41 10N 24 58 E
Xapuri, *Brazil* **136** 10 35 S 68 35W
Xar Moron He →, *China* **61** 43 25N 120 35 E
Xau, L., *Botswana* **96** 21 15 S 24 44 E
Xavantina, *Brazil* **141** 21 15 S 52 48W
Xenia, *Ill., U.S.A.* **119** 38 38N 88 38W
Xenia, *Ohio, U.S.A.* **119** 39 42N 83 57W
Xhora, *S. Africa* **97** 31 55 S 28 38 E
Xhumo, *Botswana* **96** 21 7 S 24 35 E
Xi Jiang →, *China* **59** 22 5N 113 20 E
Xi Xian, *Henan, China* **59** 32 20N 114 43 E
Xi Xian, *Shanxi, China* **60** 36 41N 110 58 E
Xia Xian, *China* **60** 35 8N 111 12 E
Xiachengzi, *China* **61** 44 40N 130 18 E
Xiachuan Dao, *China* **59** 21 40N 112 40 E
Xiaguan, *China* **58** 25 32N 100 16 E
Xiajiang, *China* **59** 27 30N 115 10 E
Xiajin, *China* **60** 36 56N 116 0 E
Xiamen, *China* **59** 24 25N 118 4 E
Xi'an, *China* **60** 34 15N 109 0 E
Xian Xian, *China* **60** 38 12N 116 6 E
Xianfeng, *China* **59** 29 40N 109 8 E
Xiang Jiang →, *China* **59** 28 55N 112 50 E
Xiangcheng, *Henan, China* **60** 33 29N 114 52 E
Xiangcheng, *Henan, China* **60** 33 50N 113 27 E
Xiangcheng, *Sichuan, China* **58** 28 53N 99 47 E
Xiangdu, *China* **58** 23 13N 106 58 E
Xiangfan, *China* **59** 32 2N 112 8 E
Xianghuang Qi, *China* **60** 42 2N 113 50 E
Xiangning, *China* **60** 35 58N 110 50 E
Xiangquan, *China* **60** 36 30N 113 1 E
Xiangshan, *China* **59** 29 29N 121 51 E
Xiangshui, *China* **61** 34 12N 119 33 E
Xiangtan, *China* **59** 27 51N 112 54 E
Xiangxiang, *China* **59** 27 43N 112 28 E
Xiangyang, *China* **59** 32 1N 112 8 E
Xiangyin, *China* **59** 28 38N 112 54 E
Xiangyun, *China* **58** 25 34N 100 35 E
Xiangzhou, *China* **58** 23 58N 109 40 E
Xianju, *China* **59** 28 51N 120 44 E
Xianning, *China* **59** 29 51N 114 16 E
Xianshui He →, *China* **58** 30 10N 100 59 E
Xianyang, *China* **60** 34 20N 108 40 E
Xianyou, *China* **59** 25 22N 118 38 E
Xiao Hinggan Ling, *China* **62** 49 0N 127 0 E
Xiao Xian, *China* **60** 34 15N 116 55 E
Xiaofeng, *China* **59** 30 35N 119 32 E
Xiaogan, *China* **59** 30 52N 113 55 E
Xiaojin, *China* **58** 30 59N 102 21 E
Xiaolan, *China* **59** 22 38N 113 13 E
Xiaoshan, *China* **59** 30 12N 120 18 E
Xiaoyi, *China* **60** 37 8N 111 48 E
Xiapu, *China* **59** 26 54N 119 59 E
Xiawa, *China* **61** 42 35N 120 38 E
Xiayi, *China* **60** 34 15N 116 10 E
Xichang, *China* **58** 27 51N 102 19 E
Xichong, *China* **58** 30 57N 105 54 E
Xichuan, *China* **60** 33 0N 111 30 E
Xiemahe, *China* **59** 31 38N 111 12 E
Xieng Khouang, *Laos* **54** 19 17N 103 25 E
Xifei He →, *China* **60** 32 45N 116 40 E
Xifeng, *Guizhou, China* **58** 27 7N 106 42 E
Xifeng, *Liaoning, China* **61** 42 42N 124 45 E
Xifengzhen, *China* **60** 35 40N 107 40 E
Xigazê, *China* **62** 29 5N 88 45 E
Xihe, *China* **60** 34 2N 105 20 E
Xihua, *China* **60** 33 45N 114 30 E
Xiliao He →, *China* **61** 43 32N 123 35 E
Xilin, *China* **58** 24 30N 105 6 E
Xilókastron, *Greece* **35** 38 4N 22 43 E
Xin Jiang →, *China* **59** 28 45N 116 35 E
Xin Xian, *China* **60** 38 22N 112 46 E
Xinavane, *Mozam.* **97** 25 2 S 32 47 E
Xinbin, *China* **61** 41 40N 125 2 E
Xincai, *China* **59** 32 43N 114 58 E
Xinchang, *China* **59** 29 28N 120 52 E
Xincheng, *Guangxi Zhuangzu, China* **58** 24 5N 108 39 E
Xincheng, *Jiangxi, China* **59** 26 48N 114 6 E
Xinfeng, *Guangdong, China* **59** 24 5N 114 16 E
Xinfeng, *Jiangxi, China* **59** 27 7N 116 11 E
Xinfeng, *Jiangxi, China* **59** 25 27N 114 58 E
Xing Xian, *China* **60** 38 27N 111 7 E
Xing'an, *Guangxi Zhuangzu, China* **59** 25 38N 110 40 E
Xingan, *Jiangxi, China* **59** 27 46N 115 20 E
Xingcheng, *China* **61** 40 40N 120 45 E
Xingguo, *China* **59** 26 21N 115 21 E
Xinghe, *China* **60** 40 55N 113 55 E
Xinghua, *China* **61** 32 58N 119 48 E
Xinghua Wan, *China* **59** 25 15N 119 20 E
Xinglong, *China* **61** 40 25N 117 30 E
Xingning, *China* **59** 24 3N 115 42 E
Xingping, *China* **60** 34 20N 108 28 E
Xingren, *China* **58** 25 24N 105 11 E
Xingshan, *China* **59** 31 15N 110 45 E
Xingtai, *China* **60** 37 3N 114 32 E
Xingu →, *Brazil* **135** 1 30 S 51 53W
Xingyang, *China* **60** 34 45N 112 52 E
Xinhe, *China* **60** 37 30N 115 15 E
Xinhua, *China* **59** 27 42N 111 13 E
Xinhuang, *China* **58** 27 21N 109 12 E
Xinhui, *China* **59** 22 25N 113 0 E
Xining, *China* **62** 36 34N 101 40 E
Xinjiang, *China* **60** 35 34N 111 11 E
Xinjiang Uygur Zizhiqu □, *China* **62** 42 0N 86 0 E
Xinjie, *China* **58** 26 48N 101 15 E
Xinjin, *Liaoning, China* **61** 39 25N 121 58 E
Xinjin, *Sichuan, China* **58** 30 24N 103 47 E
Xinkai He →, *China* **61** 43 32N 123 35 E
Xinle, *China* **60** 38 25N 114 40 E
Xinlitun, *China* **61** 42 0N 122 8 E
Xinlong, *China* **58** 30 57N 100 12 E
Xinmin, *China* **61** 41 59N 122 50 E
Xinning, *China* **59** 26 28N 110 50 E
Xinping, *China* **58** 24 5N 101 59 E
Xinshao, *China* **59** 27 21N 111 26 E
Xintai, *China* **61** 35 55N 117 45 E
Xintian, *China* **59** 25 55N 112 13 E
Xinxiang, *China* **60** 35 18N 113 50 E
Xinxing, *China* **59** 22 35N 112 15 E
Xinyang, *China* **59** 32 6N 114 3 E
Xinye, *China* **59** 32 30N 112 21 E
Xinyi, *China* **59** 22 25N 111 0 E
Xinyu, *China* **59** 27 49N 114 58 E
Xinzhan, *China* **61** 43 50N 127 18 E
Xinzheng, *China* **60** 34 20N 113 45 E
Xinzhou, *China* **59** 30 50N 114 48 E
Xinzhu, *Taiwan* **59** 24 49N 120 57 E
Xiong Xian, *China* **60** 38 59N 116 8 E
Xiongyuecheng, *China* **61** 40 12N 122 5 E
Xiping, *Henan, China* **60** 33 22N 114 0 E
Xiping, *Henan, China* **60** 33 25N 111 8 E
Xiping, *Zhejiang, China* **59** 28 16N 119 29 E
Xique-Xique, *Brazil* **138** 10 50 S 42 40W
Xiruá →, *Brazil* **136** 6 3 S 67 50W
Xishui, *China* **59** 30 30N 115 15 E
Xituozhen, *China* **58** 30 22N 108 11 E
Xiuning, *China* **59** 29 45N 118 10 E
Xiuren, *China* **59** 24 27N 110 12 E
Xiushan, *China* **58** 28 25N 108 57 E
Xiushui, *China* **59** 29 2N 114 33 E
Xiuwen, *China* **58** 26 49N 106 32 E
Xiuyan, *China* **61** 40 18N 123 11 E
Xixabangma Feng, *China* **49** 28 20N 85 40 E
Xixia, *China* **60** 33 25N 111 29 E
Xixiang, *China* **60** 33 0N 107 44 E
Xiyang, *China* **60** 37 38N 113 38 E
Xizang □, *China* **62** 32 0N 88 0 E
Xu Jiang →, *China* **59** 28 0N 116 25 E
Xuan Loc, *Vietnam* **55** 10 56N 107 14 E
Xuancheng, *China* **59** 30 56N 118 43 E
Xuan'en, *China* **59** 30 0N 109 30 E
Xuanhan, *China* **58** 31 18N 107 38 E
Xuanhua, *China* **60** 40 40N 115 2 E
Xuchang, *China* **60** 34 2N 113 48 E
Xuefeng Shan, *China* **59** 27 5N 110 35 E
Xuejiaping, *China* **59** 31 39N 110 16 E
Xun Jiang →, *China* **59** 23 35N 111 30 E
Xun Xian, *China* **60** 35 42N 114 33 E
Xundian, *China* **58** 25 36N 103 15 E
Xunwu, *China* **59** 24 54N 115 37 E
Xunyang, *China* **60** 32 48N 109 22 E
Xunyi, *China* **60** 35 8N 108 20 E
Xupu, *China* **59** 27 53N 110 32 E
Xushui, *China* **60** 39 2N 115 40 E
Xuwen, *China* **59** 20 20N 110 10 E
Xuyen Moc, *Vietnam* **55** 10 34N 107 25 E
Xuyong, *China* **58** 28 10N 105 22 E
Xuzhou, *China* **61** 34 18N 117 10 E

Y

Ya 'Bad, *Jordan* **44** 32 27N 35 10 E
Ya Xian, *China* **54** 18 14N 109 29 E
Yaamba, *Australia* **72** 23 8 S 150 22 E
Ya'an, *China* **58** 29 58N 103 5 E
Yaapeet, *Australia* **74** 35 45 S 142 3 E
Yabassi, *Cameroon* **91** 4 30N 9 57 E
Yabba North, *Australia* **74** 36 13 S 145 42 E
Yabelo, *Ethiopia* **89** 4 50N 38 8 E
Yablonovy Khrebet, *U.S.S.R.* **41** 53 0N 114 0 E
Yablonovy Ra. = Yablonovy Khrebet, *U.S.S.R.* **41** 53 0N 114 0 E
Yabrai Shan, *China* **60** 39 40N 103 0 E
Yackandandah, *Australia* **75** 36 18 S 146 52 E
Yacuiba, *Bolivia* **140** 22 0 S 63 43W
Yacuma →, *Bolivia* **137** 13 38 S 65 23W
Yadgir, *India* **50** 16 45N 77 5 E
Yadkin →, *U.S.A.* **115** 35 23N 80 3W
Yadrin, *U.S.S.R.* **37** 55 57N 46 12 E
Yagaba, *Ghana* **91** 10 14N 1 20W
Yagodnoye, *U.S.S.R.* **41** 62 33N 149 40 E
Yagoua, *Cameroon* **94** 10 20N 15 13 E
Yaguas →, *Peru* **134** 2 45 S 70 10W
Yagur, *Israel* **44** 32 45N 35 4 E
Yaha, *Thailand* **55** 6 29N 101 8 E
Yahila, *Zaïre* **92** 0 13N 24 28 E
Yahk, *Canada* **110** 49 6N 116 10W
Yahuma, *Zaïre* **94** 1 0N 23 10 E
Yaiza, *Canary Is.* **25** 28 57N 13 46W
Yaizu, *Japan* **65** 34 52N 138 20 E
Yajiang, *China* **58** 30 2N 100 57 E
Yajua, *Nigeria* **91** 11 27N 12 49 E
Yakage, *Japan* **64** 34 37N 133 35 E
Yakamba, *Zaïre* **94** 2 42N 19 38 E
Yakima, *U.S.A.* **122** 46 42N 120 30W
Yakima →, *U.S.A.* **122** 47 0N 120 30W
Yako, *Burkina Faso* **90** 12 59N 2 15W
Yakoma, *Zaïre* **94** 4 5N 22 27 E
Yakoruda, *Bulgaria* **35** 42 1N 23 39 E
Yakut A.S.S.R. □, *U.S.S.R.* **41** 62 0N 130 0 E
Yakutat, *U.S.A.* **102** 59 29N 139 44W

Yakutsk, *U.S.S.R.* **41** 62 5N 129 50 E
Yala, *Thailand* **55** 6 33N 101 18 E
Yalbalgo, *Australia* **79** 25 10 S 114 45 E
Yalboroo, *Australia* **72** 20 50 S 148 40 E
Yale, *U.S.A.* **116** 43 9N 82 47W
Yalgoo, *Australia* **79** 28 16 S 116 39 E
Yali, *Zaïre* **94** 0 4N 21 3 E
Yaligimba, *Zaïre* **94** 2 13N 22 56 E
Yalinga, *C.A.R.* **94** 6 33N 23 10 E
Yalkubul, Punta, *Mexico* **127** 21 32N 88 37W
Yalleroi, *Australia* **72** 24 3 S 145 42 E
Yalobusha →, *U.S.A.* **121** 33 30N 90 12W
Yaloke, *C.A.R.* **94** 5 19N 17 5 E
Yalong Jiang →, *China* **58** 26 40N 101 55 E
Yalpukh, Oz., *U.S.S.R.* **34** 45 30N 28 41 E
Yalta, *U.S.S.R.* **38** 44 30N 34 10 E
Yalu Jiang →, *China* **61** 40 0N 124 22 E
Yalutorovsk, *U.S.S.R.* **40** 56 41N 66 12 E
Yam Ha Melaḥ = Dead Sea, *Asia* **44** 31 30N 35 30 E
Yam Kinneret, *Israel* **44** 32 45N 35 35 E
Yamada, *Japan* **64** 33 33N 130 49 E
Yamaga, *Japan* **64** 33 1N 130 41 E
Yamagata, *Japan* **63** 38 15N 140 15 E
Yamagawa, *Japan* **64** 31 12N 130 39 E
Yamaguchi, *Japan* **64** 34 10N 131 32 E
Yamaguchi □, *Japan* **64** 34 20N 131 40 E
Yamal, Poluostrov, *U.S.S.R.* **40** 71 0N 70 0 E
Yamanaka, *Japan* **65** 36 15N 136 22 E
Yamanashi □, *Japan* **65** 35 40N 138 40 E
Yamantau, *U.S.S.R.* **40** 54 20N 57 40 E
Yamaska, *Canada* **107** 46 0N 72 55W
Yamato, *Japan* **65** 35 27N 139 25 E
Yamatotakada, *Japan* **65** 34 31N 135 45 E
Yamazaki, *Japan* **64** 35 0N 134 32 E
Yamba, *N.S.W., Australia* **77** 29 26 S 153 23 E
Yamba, *S. Austral., Australia* **73** 34 10 S 140 52 E
Yambah, *Australia* **72** 23 10 S 133 50 E
Yambarran Ra., *Australia* **78** 15 10 S 130 25 E
Yambata, *Zaïre* **94** 2 26N 21 58 E
Yâmbiô, *Sudan* **89** 4 35N 28 16 E
Yambol, *Bulgaria* **34** 42 30N 26 36 E
Yambuk, *Australia* **74** 38 18 S 142 5 E
Yamdena, *Indonesia* **57** 7 45 S 131 20 E
Yame, *Japan* **64** 33 13N 130 35 E
Yamethin, *Burma* **52** 20 29N 96 18 E
Yamil, *Nigeria* **91** 12 53N 8 4 E
Yamma-Yamma, L., *Australia* **73** 26 16 S 141 20 E
Yamoussoukro, *Ivory C.* **90** 6 49N 5 17W
Yampa →, *U.S.A.* **122** 40 37N 108 59W
Yampi Sd., *Australia* **78** 16 8 S 123 38 E
Yampol, *U.S.S.R.* **38** 48 15N 28 15 E
Yamrat, *Nigeria* **91** 10 11N 9 55 E
Yamrukchal, *Bulgaria* **34** 42 44N 24 52 E
Yamuna →, *India* **49** 25 30N 81 53 E
Yamzho Yumco, *China* **62** 28 48N 90 35 E
Yan, *Nigeria* **91** 10 5N 12 11 E
Yan →, *Sri Lanka* **51** 9 0N 81 10 E
Yana →, *U.S.S.R.* **41** 71 30N 136 0 E
Yanac, *Australia* **74** 36 8 S 141 25 E
Yanagawa, *Japan* **64** 33 10N 130 24 E
Yanahara, *Japan* **64** 34 58N 134 2 E
Yanai, *Japan* **64** 33 58N 132 7 E
Yanam, *India* **50** 16 47N 82 15 E
Yan'an, *China* **60** 36 35N 109 26 E
Yanbian, *China* **58** 26 47N 101 31 E
Yanbu 'al Baḥr, *Si. Arabia* **46** 24 0N 38 5 E
Yancannia, *Australia* **73** 30 12 S 142 35 E
Yanchang, *China* **60** 36 43N 110 1 E
Yancheng, *Henan, China* **60** 33 35N 114 0 E
Yancheng, *Jiangsu, China* **61** 33 23N 120 8 E
Yanchi, *China* **60** 37 48N 107 20 E
Yanchuan, *China* **60** 36 51N 110 10 E
Yanco Cr. →, *Australia* **73** 35 14 S 145 35 E
Yandal, *Australia* **79** 27 35 S 121 10 E
Yandanooka, *Australia* **79** 29 18 S 115 29 E
Yandaran, *Australia* **72** 24 43 S 152 6 E
Yandé, I., *N. Cal.* **68** 20 3 S 163 49 E
Yandina, *Solomon Is.* **68** 9 7 S 159 13 E
Yandja, *Zaïre* **94** 1 41 S 17 43 E
Yandongi, *Zaïre* **94** 2 51N 22 16 E
Yandoon, *Burma* **52** 17 0N 95 40 E
Yanfeng, *China* **58** 25 52N 101 8 E
Yanfolila, *Mali* **90** 11 11N 8 9W
Yang Xian, *China* **60** 33 15N 107 30 E
Yangambi, *Zaïre* **92** 0 47N 24 20 E
Yangbi, *China* **58** 25 41N 99 58 E
Yangcheng, *China* **60** 35 28N 112 22 E
Yangch'ü = Taiyuan, *China* **60** 37 52N 112 33 E
Yangchun, *China* **59** 22 11N 111 48 E
Yanggao, *China* **60** 40 21N 113 55 E
Yanggu, *China* **60** 36 8N 115 43 E
Yangi-Yer, *U.S.S.R.* **40** 40 17N 68 48 E
Yangjiang, *China* **59** 21 50N 110 59 E
Yangliuqing, *China* **61** 39 2N 117 5 E
Yangping, *China* **59** 31 12N 111 25 E
Yangpingguan, *China* **60** 32 58N 106 5 E
Yangquan, *China* **60** 37 58N 113 31 E
Yangshan, *China* **59** 24 30N 112 40 E
Yangshuo, *China* **59** 24 48N 110 29 E
Yangtze Kiang = Chang Jiang →, *China* **59** 31 48N 121 10 E
Yangxin, *China* **59** 29 50N 115 12 E
Yangyuan, *China* **60** 40 1N 114 10 E
Yangzhou, *China* **59** 32 21N 119 26 E
Yanhe, *China* **58** 28 31N 108 29 E
Yanji, *China* **61** 42 59N 129 30 E
Yanjin, *China* **58** 28 5N 104 18 E
Yanjing, *China* **58** 29 7N 98 33 E
Yankton, *U.S.A.* **120** 42 55N 97 25W
Yanna, *Australia* **73** 26 58 S 146 0 E
Yanonge, *Zaïre* **92** 0 35N 24 38 E
Yanqi, *China* **62** 42 5N 86 35 E
Yanqing, *China* **60** 40 30N 115 58 E
Yanshan, *Hebei, China* **61** 38 4N 117 22 E
Yanshan, *Jiangxi, China* **59** 28 15N 117 41 E
Yanshan, *Yunnan, China* **58** 23 35N 104 20 E
Yanshou, *China* **61** 45 28N 128 22 E
Yantabulla, *Australia* **73** 29 21 S 145 0 E
Yantai, *China* **61** 37 34N 121 22 E
Yanting, *China* **58** 31 11N 105 24 E
Yantra →, *Bulgaria* **34** 43 40N 25 37 E
Yanwa, *China* **58** 27 35N 98 55 E
Yanyuan, *China* **58** 27 25N 101 30 E
Yanzhou, *China* **60** 35 35N 116 49 E
Yao, *Chad* **87** 12 56N 17 33 E
Yao, *Japan* **65** 34 32N 135 36 E
Yao Xian, *China* **60** 34 55N 108 59 E
Yao Yai, Ko, *Thailand* **55** 8 0N 98 35 E
Yao'an, *China* **58** 25 31N 101 18 E
Yaodu, *China* **58** 32 45N 105 22 E
Yaoundé, *Cameroon* **91** 3 50N 11 35 E
Yaowan, *China* **61** 34 15N 118 3 E
Yap Is., *Pac. Oc.* **66** 9 30N 138 10 E
Yapen, *Indonesia* **57** 1 50 S 136 0 E
Yapen, Selat, *Indonesia* **57** 1 20 S 136 10 E
Yappar →, *Australia* **72** 18 22 S 141 16 E
Yaqui →, *Mexico* **126** 27 37N 110 39W
Yar, *U.S.S.R.* **37** 58 14N 52 5 E
Yar-Sale, *U.S.S.R.* **40** 66 50N 70 50 E
Yaracuy □, *Venezuela* **134** 10 20N 68 45W
Yaracuy →, *Venezuela* **134** 10 33N 68 15W
Yaraka, *Australia* **72** 24 53 S 144 3 E
Yarangüme, *Turkey* **46** 37 35N 29 8 E
Yaransk, *U.S.S.R.* **37** 57 22N 47 49 E
Yaratishky, *U.S.S.R.* **36** 54 3N 26 0 E
Yardea P.O., *Australia* **73** 32 23 S 135 32 E
Yare →, *U.K.* **13** 52 36N 1 28 E
Yarensk, *U.S.S.R.* **40** 61 10N 49 8 E
Yarí →, *Colombia* **134** 0 20 S 72 20W
Yaritagua, *Venezuela* **134** 10 5N 69 8W
Yarkand = Shache, *China* **62** 38 20N 77 10 E
Yarker, *Canada* **109** 44 23N 76 46W
Yarkhun →, *Pakistan* **49** 36 17N 72 30 E
Yarmouth, *Canada* **105** 43 50N 66 7W
Yarmūk →, *Syria* **44** 32 42N 35 40 E
Yaroslavl, *U.S.S.R.* **37** 57 35N 39 55 E
Yarra →, *Australia* **74** 37 50 S 144 53 E
Yarra Glen, *Australia* **74** 37 40 S 145 22 E
Yarra Yarra Lakes, *Australia* **79** 29 40 S 115 45 E
Yarrabandai, *Australia* **76** 33 6 S 147 36 E
Yarraden, *Australia* **72** 14 17 S 143 15 E
Yarragon, *Australia* **74** 38 12 S 146 4 E
Yarraloola, *Australia* **78** 21 33 S 115 52 E
Yarram, *Australia* **75** 38 29 S 146 9 E
Yarraman, *Australia* **73** 26 50 S 152 0 E
Yarranvale, *Australia* **73** 26 50 S 145 20 E
Yarras, *Australia* **77** 31 25 S 152 20 E
Yarrawonga, *Australia* **74** 36 0 S 146 0 E
Yarrill Cr. →, *Australia* **77** 28 20 S 150 8 E
Yarrowmere, *Australia* **72** 21 27 S 145 53 E
Yarrowyck, *Australia* **77** 30 27 S 151 20 E
Yarto, *Australia* **74** 35 28 S 142 16 E
Yartsevo, *R.S.F.S.R., U.S.S.R.* **36** 55 6N 32 43 E
Yartsevo, *R.S.F.S.R., U.S.S.R.* **41** 60 20N 90 0 E
Yarumal, *Colombia* **134** 6 58N 75 24W
Yasawa, *Fiji* **68** 16 47 S 177 31 E
Yasawa Group, *Fiji* **68** 17 0 S 177 23 E
Yaselda →, *U.S.S.R.* **36** 52 7N 26 28 E
Yashi, *Nigeria* **91** 12 23N 7 54 E
Yashiro-Jima, *Japan* **64** 33 55N 132 15 E
Yasin, *Pakistan* **49** 36 24N 73 23 E
Yasinovataya, *U.S.S.R.* **38** 48 7N 37 57 E
Yasinski, L., *Canada* **104** 53 16N 77 35W
Yasothon, *Thailand* **54** 15 50N 104 10 E
Yass, *Australia* **76** 34 49 S 148 54 E
Yasugi, *Japan* **64** 35 26N 133 15 E
Yas'ur, *Israel* **44** 32 54N 35 10 E
Yata →, *Bolivia* **137** 10 29 S 65 26W
Yates Center, *U.S.A.* **121** 37 53N 95 45W
Yates Pt., *N.Z.* **81** 44 29 S 167 49 E
Yathkyed L., *Canada* **111** 62 40N 98 0W
Yatsuo, *Japan* **65** 36 34N 137 8 E
Yatsushiro, *Japan* **64** 32 30N 130 40 E
Yatsushiro-Kai, *Japan* **64** 32 30N 130 25 E
Yatta Plateau, *Kenya* **92** 2 0 S 38 0 E
Yaṭṭah, *Jordan* **44** 31 27N 35 6 E
Yauca, *Peru* **136** 15 39 S 74 35W
Yauya, *Peru* **136** 8 59 S 77 17W
Yauyos, *Peru* **136** 12 19 S 75 50W
Yaval, *India* **50** 21 10N 75 42 E
Yavari →, *Peru* **136** 4 21 S 70 2W
Yavatmal, *India* **50** 20 20N 78 15 E
Yavne, *Israel* **44** 31 52N 34 45 E
Yavorov, *U.S.S.R.* **36** 49 55N 23 20 E
Yawatahama, *Japan* **64** 33 27N 132 24 E
Yawri B., *S. Leone* **90** 8 22N 13 0W
Yaxi, *China* **58** 27 33N 106 41 E
Yazagyo, *Burma* **52** 23 30N 94 6 E
Yazd, *Iran* **47** 31 55N 54 27 E
Yazd □, *Iran* **47** 32 0N 55 0 E
Yazdān, *Iran* **47** 33 30N 60 50 E
Yazoo →, *U.S.A.* **121** 32 35N 90 50W
Yazoo City, *U.S.A.* **121** 32 48N 90 28W
Yding Skovhøj, *Denmark* **9** 55 59N 9 46 E
Ye Xian, *Henan, China* **60** 33 35N 113 25 E
Ye Xian, *Shandong, China* **61** 37 8N 119 57 E
Yea, *Australia* **74** 37 14 S 145 26 E
Yea →, *Australia* **74** 37 18 S 145 28 E
Yealering, *Australia* **79** 32 36 S 117 36 E
Yearinan, *Australia* **77** 31 10 S 149 11 E
Yebbi-Souma, *Chad* **87** 21 7N 17 54 E
Yecla, *Spain* **25** 38 35N 1 5W
Yécora, *Mexico* **126** 28 20N 108 58W
Yedashe, *Burma* **52** 19 10N 96 20 E
Yedintsy, *U.S.S.R.* **38** 48 9N 27 18 E
Yeeda, *Australia* **78** 17 31 S 123 38 E
Yeelanna, *Australia* **73** 34 9 S 135 45 E
Yefremov, *U.S.S.R.* **37** 53 8N 38 3 E
Yegorlyk →, *U.S.S.R.* **39** 46 33N 41 40 E
Yegorlykskaya, *U.S.S.R.* **39** 46 35N 40 35 E
Yegoryevsk, *U.S.S.R.* **37** 55 27N 38 55 E
Yegros, *Paraguay* **140** 26 20 S 56 25W
Yehuda, Midbar, *Israel* **44** 31 35N 35 15 E
Yei, *Sudan* **89** 4 9N 30 40 E
Yei, Nahr →, *Sudan* **89** 6 15N 30 13 E
Yekumbe, *Zaïre* **94** 1 2 S 23 27 E
Yelan, *U.S.S.R.* **37** 50 55N 43 43 E
Yelan-Kolenovski, *U.S.S.R.* **37** 51 16N 41 4 E
Yelandur, *India* **51** 12 6N 77 0 E
Yelanskoye, *U.S.S.R.* **41** 61 25N 128 0 E
Yelarbon, *Australia* **77** 28 33 S 150 38 E
Yelatma, *U.S.S.R.* **37** 55 0N 41 45 E
Yelcho, L., *Chile* **142** 43 18 S 72 18W
Yelets, *U.S.S.R.* **37** 52 40N 38 30 E
Yélimané, *Mali* **90** 15 9N 10 34W
Yell, *U.K.* **14** 60 35N 1 5W
Yell Sd., *U.K.* **14** 60 33N 1 15W
Yellamanchilli = Elamanchili, *India* **50** 17 33N 82 50 E
Yellow Sea, *China* **61** 35 0N 123 0 E
Yellowhead P., *Canada* **110** 52 53N 118 25W
Yellowknife, *Canada* **110** 62 27N 114 29W
Yellowknife →, *Canada* **102** 62 31N 114 19W
Yellowstone →, *U.S.A.* **120** 47 58N 103 59W
Yellowstone L., *U.S.A.* **122** 44 30N 110 20W
Yellowstone National Park, *U.S.A.* **122** 44 35N 110 0W
Yellowtail Res., *U.S.A.* **122** 45 6N 108 8W
Yelnya, *U.S.S.R.* **36** 54 35N 33 15 E
Yelsk, *U.S.S.R.* **36** 51 50N 29 10 E
Yelta, *Australia* **74** 34 8 S 141 59 E
Yelvertoft, *Australia* **72** 20 13 S 138 45 E
Yelwa, *Nigeria* **91** 10 49N 4 41 E
Yembongo, *Zaïre* **94** 3 12N 19 2 E
Yemen ■, *Asia* **45** 15 0N 44 0 E
Yen Bai, *Vietnam* **54** 21 42N 104 52 E
Yenakiyevo, *U.S.S.R.* **38** 48 15N 38 15 E
Yenangyaung, *Burma* **52** 20 30N 95 0 E
Yenanma, *Burma* **52** 19 46N 94 49 E
Yenda, *Australia* **75** 34 13 S 146 14 E
Yendéré, *Ivory C.* **90** 10 12N 4 59W
Yendi, *Ghana* **91** 9 29N 0 1W
Yengo, *Congo* **94** 0 22N 15 29 E
Yenisaía, *Greece* **35** 41 1N 24 57 E
Yenisey →, *U.S.S.R.* **40** 71 50N 82 40 E
Yeniseysk, *U.S.S.R.* **41** 58 27N 92 13 E
Yeniseyskiy Zaliv, *U.S.S.R.* **40** 72 20N 81 0 E
Yenne, *France* **21** 45 43N 5 44 E
Yenotayevka, *U.S.S.R.* **39** 47 15N 47 0 E
Yenyuka, *U.S.S.R.* **41** 57 57N 121 15 E
Yeo, L., *Australia* **79** 28 0 S 124 30 E
Yeola, *India* **50** 20 0N 74 30 E
Yeoval, *Australia* **76** 32 47 S 148 9 E
Yeovil, *U.K.* **13** 50 57N 2 38W
Yepes, *Spain* **24** 39 55N 3 39W
Yeppoon, *Australia* **72** 23 5 S 150 47 E
Yeráki, *Greece* **35** 37 0N 22 42 E
Yerbent, *U.S.S.R.* **40** 39 30N 58 50 E
Yerbogachen, *U.S.S.R.* **41** 61 16N 108 0 E
Yerevan, *U.S.S.R.* **39** 40 10N 44 31 E
Yerilla, *Australia* **79** 29 24 S 121 47 E
Yerla →, *India* **50** 16 50N 74 30 E
Yermak, *U.S.S.R.* **40** 52 2N 76 55 E
Yermakovo, *U.S.S.R.* **41** 52 25N 126 20 E
Yermo, *U.S.A.* **125** 34 58N 116 50W
Yerofey Pavlovich, *U.S.S.R.* **41** 54 0N 122 0 E
Yerseke, *Neths.* **17** 51 29N 4 3 E
Yershov, *U.S.S.R.* **37** 51 22N 48 16 E
Yerunaja, Cerro, *Peru* **136** 10 16 S 76 55W
Yerushalayim, *Israel* **44** 31 47N 35 10 E
Yerville, *France* **18** 49 40N 0 53 E
Yes Tor, *U.K.* **13** 50 41N 3 59W
Yesagyo, *Burma* **52** 21 38N 95 14 E
Yesnogorsk, *U.S.S.R.* **37** 54 32N 37 38 E
Yeso, *U.S.A.* **121** 34 29N 104 37W
Yessentuki, *U.S.S.R.* **39** 44 0N 42 53 E
Yessey, *U.S.S.R.* **41** 68 29N 102 10 E
Yeste, *Spain* **25** 38 22N 2 19W
Yetman, *Australia* **77** 28 56 S 150 48 E
Yeu, I. d', *France* **18** 46 42N 2 20W
Yevlakh, *U.S.S.R.* **39** 40 39N 47 7 E
Yevpatoriya, *U.S.S.R.* **38** 45 15N 33 20 E
Yevstratovskiy, *U.S.S.R.* **37** 50 11N 39 45 E
Yeya →, *U.S.S.R.* **39** 46 40N 38 40 E
Yeysk, *U.S.S.R.* **38** 46 40N 38 12 E
Yezd = Yazd, *Iran* **47** 31 55N 54 27 E
Yhati, *Paraguay* **140** 25 45 S 56 35W
Yhú, *Paraguay* **141** 25 0 S 56 0W
Yi →, *Uruguay* **140** 33 7 S 57 8W
Yi He →, *China* **61** 34 10N 118 8 E
Yi Xian, *Anhui, China* **59** 29 55N 117 57 E
Yi Xian, *Hebei, China* **60** 39 20N 115 30 E
Yi Xian, *Liaoning, China* **61** 41 30N 121 22 E
Yialí, *Greece* **35** 36 41N 27 11 E
Yi'allaq, G., *Egypt* **88** 30 21N 33 31 E
Yiáltra, *Greece* **35** 38 51N 22 59 E
Yiannitsa, *Greece* **35** 40 46N 22 24 E
Yibin, *China* **58** 28 45N 104 32 E
Yichang, *China* **59** 30 40N 111 20 E
Yicheng, *Henan, China* **59** 31 41N 112 12 E
Yicheng, *Shanxi, China* **60** 35 42N 111 40 E
Yichuan, *China* **60** 36 2N 110 10 E
Yichun, *Heilongjiang, China* **62** 47 44N 128 52 E
Yichun, *Jiangxi, China* **59** 27 48N 114 22 E
Yidu, *Hubei, China* **59** 30 25N 111 27 E
Yidu, *Shandong, China* **61** 36 43N 118 28 E
Yidun, *China* **58** 30 22N 99 21 E
Yihuang, *China* **59** 27 30N 116 12 E
Yijun, *China* **60** 35 28N 109 8 E
Yilan, *Taiwan* **59** 24 51N 121 44 E
Yiliang, *Yunnan, China* **58** 27 38N 104 2 E
Yiliang, *Yunnan, China* **58** 24 56N 103 11 E
Yilong, *China* **58** 31 34N 106 23 E
Yimen, *China* **58** 24 40N 102 10 E
Yimianpo, *China* **61** 45 7N 128 2 E
Yinchuan, *China* **60** 38 30N 106 15 E
Yindarlgooda, L., *Australia* **79** 30 40 S 121 52 E
Ying He →, *China* **60** 32 30N 116 30 E
Ying Xian, *China* **60** 39 32N 113 10 E
Yingcheng, *China* **59** 30 56N 113 35 E
Yingde, *China* **59** 24 10N 113 25 E
Yingjiang, *China* **58** 24 41N 97 55 E
Yingjing, *China* **58** 29 41N 102 52 E
Yingkou, *China* **61** 40 37N 122 18 E
Yingshan, *Henan, China* **59** 31 35N 113 50 E
Yingshan, *Hubei, China* **59** 30 41N 115 32 E
Yingshan, *Sichuan, China* **58** 31 4N 106 35 E
Yingshang, *China* **59** 32 38N 116 12 E
Yingtan, *China* **62** 28 12N 117 0 E
Yining, *China* **62** 43 58N 81 10 E
Yinjiang, *China* **58** 28 1N 108 21 E
Yinnar, *Australia* **75** 38 19 S 146 20 E
Yinnietharra, *Australia* **79** 24 39 S 116 12 E
Yioúra, *Greece* **35** 39 23N 24 10 E
Yipinglang, *China* **58** 25 10N 101 52 E
Yirga Alem, *Ethiopia* **89** 6 48N 38 22 E
Yishan, *China* **58** 24 28N 108 38 E
Yishui, *China* **61** 35 47N 118 30 E
Yíthion, *Greece* **35** 36 46N 22 34 E
Yitiaoshan, *China* **60** 37 5N 104 2 E
Yitong, *China* **61** 43 13N 125 20 E
Yiwu, *China* **59** 29 20N 120 3 E
Yixing, *China* **59** 31 21N 119 48 E
Yiyang, *Henan, China* **60** 34 27N 112 10 E
Yiyang, *Hunan, China* **59** 28 35N 112 18 E
Yiyang, *Jiangxi, China* **59** 28 22N 117 20 E
Yizhang, *China* **59** 25 27N 112 57 E
Yizheng, *China* **59** 32 18N 119 10 E
Yizre'el, *Israel* **44** 32 34N 35 19 E
Ylitornio, *Finland* **8** 66 19N 23 39 E
Ylivieska, *Finland* **8** 64 4N 24 28 E
Yngaren, *Sweden* **11** 58 50N 16 35 E
Ynykchanskiy, *U.S.S.R.* **41** 60 15N 137 35 E
Yoakum, *U.S.A.* **121** 29 20N 97 20W
Yobuko, *Japan* **64** 33 32N 129 54 E
Yog Pt., *Phil.* **57** 14 6N 124 12 E
Yogan, *Togo* **91** 6 23N 1 30 E
Yogyakarta, *Indonesia* **57** 7 49 S 110 22 E
Yoho Nat. Park, *Canada* **110** 51 25N 116 30W
Yojoa, L. de, *Honduras* **128** 14 53N 88 0W
Yokadouma, *Cameroon* **94** 3 26N 14 55 E
Yōkaichiba, *Japan* **65** 35 42N 140 33 E
Yokkaichi, *Japan* **65** 35 0N 136 38 E
Yoko, *Cameroon* **91** 5 32N 12 20 E
Yokohama, *Japan* **65** 35 27N 139 28 E
Yokosuka, *Japan* **65** 35 20N 139 40 E
Yokote, *Japan* **63** 39 20N 140 30 E
Yola, *Nigeria* **91** 9 10N 12 29 E
Yolaina, Cordillera de, *Nic.* **128** 11 30N 84 0W
Yolombo, *Zaïre* **94** 1 36 S 23 12 E
Yombi, *Gabon* **94** 1 26 S 10 37 E
Yonago, *Japan* **64** 35 25N 133 19 E
Yoneshiro →, *Japan* **63** 40 15N 140 15 E
Yonezawa, *Japan* **63** 37 57N 140 4 E
Yong Peng, *Malaysia* **55** 2 0N 103 3 E
Yong Sata, *Thailand* **55** 7 8N 99 41 E
Yong'an, *China* **59** 25 59N 117 25 E
Yongcheng, *China* **60** 33 55N 116 20 E
Yongchuan, *China* **58** 29 17N 105 55 E
Yongchun, *China* **59** 25 16N 118 20 E
Yongdeng, *China* **60** 36 38N 103 25 E
Yongding, *China* **59** 24 43N 116 45 E
Yongfeng, *China* **59** 27 20N 115 22 E
Yongfu, *China* **58** 24 59N 109 59 E
Yonghe, *China* **60** 36 46N 110 38 E

Yongji, China 60 34 52N 110 28 E
Yongkang, Yunnan, China 58 24 9N 99 20 E
Yongkang, Zhejiang, China 59 28 55N 120 2 E
Yongnian, China 60 36 47N 114 29 E
Yongning, Guangxi Zhuangzu, China 58 22 44N 108 28 E
Yongning, Ningxia Huizu, China 60 38 15N 106 14 E
Yongping, China 58 25 27N 99 38 E
Yongqing, China 60 39 25N 116 28 E
Yongren, China 58 26 4N 101 40 E
Yongshan, China 58 28 11N 103 35 E
Yongsheng, China 58 26 38N 100 46 E
Yongshun, China 58 29 2N 109 51 E
Yongtai, China 59 25 49N 118 58 E
Yongxin, China 59 26 58N 114 15 E
Yongxing, China 59 26 9N 113 8 E
Yongxiu, China 59 29 2N 115 42 E
Yonibana, S. Leone 90 8 30N 12 19W
Yonkers, U.S.A. 117 40 57N 73 51W
Yonne □, France 19 47 50N 3 40 E
Yonne →, France 19 48 23N 2 58 E
Yoqne'am, Israel 44 32 40N 35 6 E
York, Australia 79 31 52 S 116 47 E
York, U.K. 12 53 58N 1 7W
York, Ala., U.S.A. 115 32 30N 88 18W
York, Nebr., U.S.A. 120 40 55N 97 35W
York, Pa., U.S.A. 114 39 57N 76 43W
York, C., Australia 72 10 42 S 142 31 E
York, Kap, Greenland 144 75 55N 66 25W
York Sd., Australia 78 15 0 S 125 5 E
Yorke Pen., Australia 73 34 50 S 137 40 E
Yorkshire Wolds, U.K. 12 54 0N 0 30W
Yorkton, Canada 111 51 11N 102 28W
Yorktown, U.S.A. 121 29 0N 97 29W
Yorkville, Calif., U.S.A. 124 38 52N 123 13W
Yorkville, Ill., U.S.A. 119 41 38N 88 27W
Yornup, Australia 79 34 2 S 116 10 E
Yoro, Honduras 128 15 9N 87 7W
Yos Sudarso, Pulau, Indonesia 57 8 0 S 138 30 E
Yosemite National Park, U.S.A. 124 38 0N 119 30W
Yosemite Village, U.S.A. 124 37 45N 119 35W
Yoshii, Japan 64 33 16N 129 46 E
Yoshimatsu, Japan 64 32 0N 130 47 E
Yoshkar Ola, U.S.S.R. 37 56 38N 47 55 E
Yŏsu, S. Korea 61 34 47N 127 45 E
Yotala, Bolivia 137 19 10 S 65 17W
Yotvata, Israel 44 29 55N 35 2 E
You Jiang →, China 62 23 22N 110 3 E
You Xian, China 59 27 1N 113 17 E
Youanmi, Australia 79 28 37 S 118 49 E
Youbou, Canada 110 48 53N 124 13W
Youghal, Ireland 15 51 58N 7 51W
Youghal B., Ireland 15 51 55N 7 50W
Youkounkoun, Guinea 90 12 35N 13 11W
Young, Australia 76 34 19 S 148 18 E
Young, Canada 111 51 47N 105 45W
Young, Uruguay 140 32 44 S 57 36W
Young Ra., N.Z. 81 44 10 S 169 30 E
Younghusband, L., Australia 73 30 50 S 136 5 E
Younghusband Pen., Australia 73 36 0 S 139 25 E
Youngstown, Canada 111 51 35N 111 10W
Youngstown, N.Y., U.S.A. 116 43 16N 79 2W
Youngstown, Ohio, U.S.A. 116 41 7N 80 41W
Youngsville, U.S.A. 116 41 51N 79 21W
Youssoufia, Morocco 84 32 16N 8 31W
Youxi, China 59 26 10N 118 13 E
Youyang, China 58 28 47N 108 42 E
Youyu, China 60 40 10N 112 20 E
Yoweragabbie, Australia 79 28 14 S 117 39 E
Yowrie, Australia 75 36 17 S 149 46 E
Yozgat, Turkey 46 39 51N 34 47 E
Ypané →, Paraguay 140 23 29 S 57 19W
Yport, France 18 49 45N 0 15 E
Ypres = Ieper, Belgium 17 50 51N 2 53 E
Ypsilanti, U.S.A. 104 42 18N 83 40W
Yreka, U.S.A. 122 41 44N 122 40W
Ysabel Chan., Papua N. G. 69 2 0 S 150 0 E
Ysleta, U.S.A. 123 31 45N 106 24W
Yssingeaux, France 21 45 9N 4 8 E
Ystad, Sweden 11 55 26N 13 50 E
Ythan →, U.K. 14 57 26N 2 12W
Ytterhogdal, Sweden 10 62 12N 14 56 E
Ytyk-Kel, U.S.S.R. 41 62 30N 133 45 E
Yu Shan, Taiwan 59 23 30N 120 58 E
Yu Xian, Hebei, China 60 39 50N 114 35 E
Yu Xian, Henan, China 60 34 10N 113 28 E
Yu Xian, Shanxi, China 60 38 5N 113 20 E
Yuan Jiang →, Hunan, China 59 28 55N 111 50 E
Yuan Jiang →, Yunnan, China 58 22 20N 103 59 E
Yuan'an, China 59 31 3N 111 34 E
Yuanjiang, Hunan, China 59 28 47N 112 21 E
Yuanjiang, Yunnan, China 58 23 32N 102 0 E
Yuanli, Taiwan 59 24 29N 120 39 E
Yuanlin, Taiwan 59 23 58N 120 30 E
Yuanling, China 59 28 29N 110 22 E
Yuanmou, China 58 25 42N 101 53 E
Yuanqu, China 60 35 18N 111 40 E
Yuanyang, Henan, China 60 35 3N 113 58 E
Yuanyang, Yunnan, China 58 23 10N 102 43 E
Yuat →, Papua N. G. 69 4 10 S 143 52 E
Yuba →, U.S.A. 124 39 8N 121 36W
Yuba City, U.S.A. 124 39 12N 121 37W
Yūbari, Japan 63 43 4N 141 59 E
Yūbetsu, Japan 63 43 13N 144 5 E
Yucatán □, Mexico 127 21 30N 86 30W
Yucatán, Canal de, Caribbean 128 22 0N 86 30W
Yucatan Str. = Yucatán, Canal de, Caribbean 128 22 0N 86 30W
Yucca, U.S.A. 125 34 56N 114 6W
Yucca Valley, U.S.A. 125 34 8N 116 30W
Yucheng, China 60 36 55N 116 32 E
Yuci, China 60 37 42N 112 46 E
Yudino, R.S.F.S.R., U.S.S.R. 37 55 51N 48 55 E
Yudino, R.S.F.S.R., U.S.S.R. 40 55 10N 67 55 E
Yudu, China 59 25 59N 115 30 E
Yuendumu, Australia 78 22 16 S 131 49 E
Yueqing, China 59 28 9N 120 59 E
Yueqing Wan, China 59 28 5N 121 20 E
Yuexi, Anhui, China 59 30 50N 116 20 E
Yuexi, Sichuan, China 58 28 37N 102 26 E
Yueyang, China 59 29 21N 113 5 E
Yufu-Dake, Japan 64 33 17N 131 33 E
Yugan, China 59 28 43N 116 37 E
Yugoslavia ■, Europe 33 44 0N 20 0 E
Yuhuan, China 59 28 9N 121 12 E
Yujiang, China 59 28 10N 116 43 E
Yukhnov, U.S.S.R. 36 54 44N 35 15 E
Yūki, Japan 65 36 18N 139 53 E
Yukon →, N. Amer. 102 65 30N 150 0W
Yukon Territory □, Canada 102 63 0N 135 0W
Yukti, U.S.S.R. 41 63 26N 105 42 E
Yukuhashi, Japan 64 33 44N 130 59 E
Yule →, Australia 78 20 41 S 118 17 E
Yuli, Nigeria 91 9 44N 10 12 E
Yulin, Guangxi Zhuangzu, China 59 22 40N 110 8 E
Yulin, Shaanxi, China 60 38 20N 109 30 E
Yuma, Ariz., U.S.A. 125 32 45N 114 37W
Yuma, Colo., U.S.A. 120 40 10N 102 43W
Yuma, B. de, Dom. Rep. 129 18 20N 68 35W
Yumbe, Uganda 92 3 28N 31 15 E
Yumbi, Zaïre 92 1 12 S 26 15 E
Yumbo, Colombia 134 3 35N 76 28W
Yumen, China 62 39 50N 97 30 E
Yun Ho →, China 61 39 10N 117 10 E
Yun Xian, Hubei, China 59 32 50N 110 46 E
Yun Xian, Yunnan, China 58 24 27N 100 8 E
Yuna, Australia 79 28 20 S 115 0 E
Yunan, China 59 23 12N 111 30 E
Yuncheng, Henan, China 60 35 36N 115 57 E
Yuncheng, Shanxi, China 60 35 2N 111 0 E
Yunfu, China 59 22 50N 112 0 E
Yungas, Bolivia 137 17 0 S 66 0W
Yungay, Chile 140 37 10 S 72 5W
Yungay, Peru 136 9 2 S 77 45W
Yunhe, China 59 28 8N 119 33 E
Yunlin, Taiwan 59 23 42N 120 30 E
Yunling, China 58 27 0N 99 20 E
Yunlong, China 58 25 57N 99 13 E
Yunmeng, China 59 31 2N 113 43 E
Yunnan □, China 58 25 0N 102 0 E
Yunomae, Japan 64 32 12N 130 59 E
Yunotso, Japan 64 35 5N 132 21 E
Yunquera de Henares, Spain 24 40 47N 3 11W
Yunta, Australia 73 32 34 S 139 36 E
Yunxi, China 60 33 0N 110 22 E
Yunxiao, China 59 23 59N 117 18 E
Yunyang, China 58 30 58N 108 54 E
Yuping, China 58 27 13N 108 56 E
Yupukarri, Guyana 135 3 45N 59 20W
Yuqing, China 58 27 13N 107 53 E
Yur, U.S.S.R. 41 59 52N 137 41 E
Yuraraba, Australia 77 28 20 S 151 25 E
Yurgao, U.S.S.R. 40 55 42N 84 51 E
Yuribei, U.S.S.R. 40 71 8N 76 58 E
Yurimaguas, Peru 136 5 55 S 76 7W
Yurya, U.S.S.R. 37 59 1N 49 13 E
Yuryev-Polskiy, U.S.S.R. 37 56 30N 39 40 E
Yuryevets, U.S.S.R. 37 57 25N 43 2 E
Yuscarán, Honduras 128 13 58N 86 45W
Yushanzhen, China 58 29 28N 108 22 E
Yushe, China 60 37 4N 112 58 E
Yushu, Jilin, China 61 44 43N 126 38 E
Yushu, Qinghai, China 62 33 5N 96 55 E
Yutai, China 60 35 0N 116 45 E
Yutian, China 61 39 53N 117 45 E
Yuxi, China 58 24 30N 102 35 E
Yuyao, China 59 30 3N 121 10 E
Yuzha, U.S.S.R. 37 56 34N 42 1 E
Yuzhno-Sakhalinsk, U.S.S.R. 41 46 58N 142 45 E
Yvelines □, France 19 48 40N 1 45 E
Yverdon, Switz. 31 46 47N 6 39 E
Yvetot, France 18 49 37N 0 44 E

Z

Zaamslag, Neths. 17 51 19N 3 55 E
Zaan →, Neths. 16 52 25N 4 52 E
Zaandam, Neths. 16 52 26N 4 49 E
Zab, Monts du, Algeria 85 34 55N 5 0 E
Žabalj, Yugoslavia 33 45 21N 20 5 E
Žabari, Yugoslavia 33 44 22N 21 15 E
Zabarjad, Egypt 88 23 40N 36 12 E
Zabaykalskiy, U.S.S.R. 41 49 40N 117 25 E
Zabid, Yemen 45 14 0N 43 10 E
Ząbkowice Śląskie, Poland 32 50 35N 16 50 E
Zabłudów, Poland 32 53 0N 23 19 E
Zābol, Iran 47 31 0N 61 32 E
Zābol □, Afghan. 47 32 0N 67 0 E
Zābolī, Iran 47 27 10N 61 35 E
Zabré, Burkina Faso 91 11 12N 0 36W
Zabrze, Poland 32 50 18N 18 50 E
Zacapa, Guatemala 128 14 59N 89 31W
Zacapu, Mexico 126 19 50N 101 43W
Zacatecas, Mexico 126 22 49N 102 34W
Zacatecas □, Mexico 126 23 30N 103 0W
Zacatecoluca, El Salv. 128 13 29N 88 51W
Zacoalco, Mexico 126 20 14N 103 33W
Zacualtipán, Mexico 127 20 39N 98 36W
Zadar, Yugoslavia 27 44 8N 15 14 E
Zadawa, Nigeria 91 11 33N 10 19 E
Zadetkyi Kyun, Burma 55 10 0N 98 25 E
Zadonsk, U.S.S.R. 37 52 25N 38 56 E
Zafra, Spain 23 38 26N 6 30W
Zafriya, Israel 44 31 59N 34 51 E
Żagań, Poland 32 51 39N 15 22 E
Zagazig, Egypt 88 30 40N 31 30 E
Zaghouan, Tunisia 86 36 23N 10 10 E
Zaglivérion, Greece 35 40 36N 23 15 E
Zaglou, Algeria 85 27 17N 0 3W
Zagnanado, Benin 91 7 18N 2 28 E
Zagorá, Greece 35 39 27N 23 6 E
Zagora, Morocco 84 30 22N 5 51W
Zagorsk, U.S.S.R. 37 56 20N 38 10 E
Zagreb, Yugoslavia 27 45 50N 16 0 E
Zāgros, Kuhhā-ye, Iran 47 33 45N 47 0 E
Zaguinaso, Ivory C. 90 10 1N 6 14W
Zāhedān, Iran 47 29 30N 60 50 E
Zahirabad, India 50 17 43N 77 37 E
Zahlah, Lebanon 46 33 52N 35 50 E
Zahna, E. Germany 30 51 54N 12 47 E
Zahrez Chergui, Algeria 85 35 0N 3 30 E
Zahrez Rharbi, Algeria 85 34 50N 2 55 E
Zaire □, Angola 95 7 0 S 14 0 E
Zaïre ■, Africa 95 3 0 S 23 0 E
Zaïre →, Africa 94 6 4 S 12 24 E
Zaječar, Yugoslavia 33 43 53N 22 18 E
Zakamensk, U.S.S.R. 41 50 23N 103 17 E
Zakani, Zaïre 94 2 33N 23 16 E
Zakataly, U.S.S.R. 39 41 38N 46 35 E
Zakavkazye, U.S.S.R. 39 42 0N 44 0 E
Zākhū, Iraq 46 37 10N 42 50 E
Zákinthos, Greece 35 37 47N 20 57 E
Zakopane, Poland 32 49 18N 19 57 E
Zala, Angola 95 7 52 S 13 42 E
Zala →, Hungary 33 46 43N 17 16 E
Zalaegerszeg, Hungary 33 46 53N 16 47 E
Zalalövö, Hungary 33 46 51N 16 35 E
Zalamea de la Serena, Spain 23 38 40N 5 38W
Zalamea la Real, Spain 23 37 41N 6 38W
Zalazna, U.S.S.R. 37 58 39N 52 31 E
Žalec, Yugoslavia 27 46 16N 15 10 E
Zaleshchiki, U.S.S.R. 38 48 45N 25 45 E
Zalingei, Sudan 87 12 51N 23 29 E
Zaltan, Jabal, Libya 86 28 46N 19 45 E
Zaltbommel, Neths. 16 51 48N 5 15 E
Zambeke, Zaïre 92 2 8N 25 17 E
Zambeze →, Africa 93 18 35 S 36 20 E
Zambezi = Zambeze →, Africa 93 18 35 S 36 20 E
Zambezi, Zambia 95 13 30 S 23 15 E
Zambezia □, Mozam. 93 16 15 S 37 30 E
Zambia ■, Africa 93 15 0 S 28 0 E
Zamboanga, Phil. 57 6 59N 122 3 E
Zambrano, Colombia 134 9 45N 74 49W
Zambrów, Poland 32 52 59N 22 14 E
Zametchino, U.S.S.R. 37 53 30N 42 30 E
Zamora, Ecuador 134 4 4 S 78 58W
Zamora, Mexico 126 20 0N 102 21W
Zamora, Spain 22 41 30N 5 45W
Zamora □, Spain 22 41 30N 5 46W
Zamora-Chinchipe □, Ecuador 134 4 15 S 78 50W
Zamość, Poland 32 50 43N 23 15 E
Zamuro, Sierra del, Venezuela 135 4 0N 62 30W
Zamzam, W. →, Libya 86 31 0N 14 30 E
Zan, Ghana 91 9 26N 0 17W
Zanaga, Congo 94 2 48 S 13 48 E
Záncara →, Spain 25 39 18N 3 18W
Zandijk, Neths. 16 52 28N 4 49 E
Zandvoort, Neths. 16 52 22N 4 32 E
Zanesville, U.S.A. 116 39 56N 82 0W
Zangue →, Mozam. 93 17 50 S 35 21 E
Zanjan, Iran 46 36 40N 48 35 E
Zanjān □, Iran 46 37 20N 49 30 E
Zannone, Italy 28 40 58N 13 2 E
Zante = Zákinthos, Greece 35 37 47N 20 57 E
Zanthus, Australia 79 31 2 S 123 34 E
Zanzibar, Tanzania 92 6 12 S 39 12 E
Zanzūr, Libya 86 32 55N 13 1 E
Zaouiet El-Kala = Bordj Omar Driss, Algeria 85 28 10N 6 40 E
Zaouiet Reggane, Algeria 85 26 32N 0 3 E
Zaoyang, China 59 32 10N 112 45 E
Zaozhuang, China 61 34 50N 117 35 E
Zapadna Morava →, Yugoslavia 33 43 38N 21 30 E
Zapadnaya Dvina, U.S.S.R. 36 56 15N 32 3 E
Zapadnaya Dvina →, U.S.S.R. 36 57 4N 24 3 E
Západné Beskydy, Europe 32 49 30N 19 0 E
Zapala, Argentina 142 39 0 S 70 5W
Zapaleri, Cerro, Bolivia 140 22 49 S 67 11W
Zapata, U.S.A. 121 26 56N 99 17W
Zapatón →, Spain 23 39 0N 6 49W
Zapiga, Chile 136 19 40 S 69 55W
Zapodnyy Sayan, U.S.S.R. 41 52 30N 94 0 E
Zaporozhye, U.S.S.R. 38 47 50N 35 10 E
Zapponeta, Italy 29 41 27N 15 57 E
Zara, Turkey 46 39 58N 37 43 E
Zaragoza, Colombia 134 7 30N 74 52W
Zaragoza, Coahuila, Mexico 126 28 30N 101 0W
Zaragoza, Nuevo León, Mexico 127 24 0N 99 46W
Zaragoza, Spain 24 41 39N 0 53W
Zaragoza □, Spain 24 41 35N 1 0W
Zarand, Iran 47 30 46N 56 34 E
Zărandului, Munţii, Romania 34 46 14N 22 7 E
Zaranj, Afghan. 47 30 55N 61 55 E
Zarasai, U.S.S.R. 36 55 40N 26 20 E
Zarate, Argentina 140 34 7 S 59 0W
Zaraysk, U.S.S.R. 37 54 48N 38 53 E
Zaraza, Venezuela 135 9 21N 65 19W
Zarembo I., U.S.A. 110 56 20N 132 50W
Zaria, Nigeria 91 11 0N 7 40 E
Zarqā' →, Jordan 44 32 10N 35 37 E
Zaruma, Ecuador 134 3 40 S 79 38W
Żary, Poland 32 51 37N 15 10 E
Zarza, La, Spain 23 37 42N 6 51W
Zarza de Alange, Spain 23 38 49N 6 13W
Zarza de Granadilla, Spain 22 40 14N 6 3W
Zarzaïtine, Algeria 85 28 15N 9 34 E
Zarzal, Colombia 134 4 24N 76 4W
Zarzis, Tunisia 86 33 31N 11 2 E
Zas, Spain 22 43 4N 8 53W
Zashiversk, U.S.S.R. 41 67 25N 142 40 E
Zaskar →, India 49 34 13N 77 20 E
Zaskar Mountains, India 49 33 15N 77 30 E
Zastron, S. Africa 96 30 18 S 27 7 E
Zavāreh, Iran 47 33 29N 52 28 E
Zaventem, Belgium 17 50 53N 4 28 E
Zavetnoye, U.S.S.R. 39 47 13N 43 50 E
Zavidovići, Yugoslavia 33 44 27N 18 13 E
Zavitinsk, U.S.S.R. 41 50 10N 129 20 E
Zavodovski, Antarctica 143 56 0 S 27 45W
Zavolzhsk, U.S.S.R. 37 57 30N 42 10 E
Zavolzhye, U.S.S.R. 37 56 37N 43 26 E
Zawiercie, Poland 32 50 30N 19 24 E
Zāwiyat al Bayḍā, Libya 86 32 30N 21 40 E
Zāwiyat Masūs, Libya 86 31 35N 21 1 E
Zawyet Shammâs, Egypt 88 31 30N 26 37 E
Zâwyet Um el Rakham, Egypt 88 31 18N 27 1 E
Zâwyet Ungeîla, Egypt 88 31 23N 26 42 E
Zāyandeh →, Iran 47 32 35N 52 0 E
Zayarsk, U.S.S.R. 41 56 12N 102 55 E
Zaysan, U.S.S.R. 40 47 28N 84 52 E
Zaysan, Oz., U.S.S.R. 40 48 0N 83 0 E
Zaytā, Jordan 44 32 23N 35 2 E
Zayü, China 58 28 48N 97 27 E
Zāzamt, W. →, Libya 86 30 29N 14 30 E
Zazir, O. →, Algeria 85 22 0N 5 40 E
Zbarazh, U.S.S.R. 36 49 43N 25 44 E
Zbąszyń, Poland 32 52 14N 15 56 E
Zblewo, Poland 32 53 56N 18 19 E
Zdolbunov, U.S.S.R. 36 50 30N 26 15 E
Ždrelo, Yugoslavia 33 44 16N 21 28 E
Zduńska Wola, Poland 32 51 37N 18 59 E
Zearing, U.S.A. 118 42 10N 93 20W
Zeballos, Canada 110 49 59N 126 50W
Zebediela, S. Africa 97 24 20 S 29 17 E
Zedelgem, Belgium 17 51 8N 3 8 E
Zeebrugge, Belgium 17 51 19N 3 12 E
Zeehan, Australia 72 41 52 S 145 25 E
Zeeland, Neths. 17 51 41N 5 40 E
Zeeland, U.S.A. 119 42 49N 86 1W
Zeeland □, Neths. 17 51 30N 3 50 E
Ze'elim, Israel 44 31 13N 34 32 E
Ze'elim, Nahr →, Israel 44 31 21N 35 24 E
Zeelst, Neths. 17 51 25N 5 25 E
Zeerust, S. Africa 96 25 31 S 26 4 E
Zefat, Israel 44 32 58N 35 29 E
Zegdou, Algeria 84 29 51N 4 45W
Zege, Ethiopia 89 11 43N 37 18 E
Zegelsem, Belgium 17 50 49N 3 43 E
Zégoua, Mali 90 10 32N 5 35W
Zehdenick, E. Germany 30 52 59N 13 20 E
Zeigler, U.S.A. 118 37 55N 89 5W
Zeil, Mt., Australia 78 23 30 S 132 23 E
Zeila, Somali Rep. 98 11 21N 43 30 E
Zeist, Neths. 16 52 5N 5 15 E
Zeitz, E. Germany 30 51 3N 12 9 E
Zele, Belgium 17 51 4N 4 2 E
Zelee, C., Solomon Is. 68 9 44 S 161 34 E

Zelenodolsk, *U.S.S.R.* **37** 55 55N 48 30 E
Zelenograd, *U.S.S.R.* **36** 56 1N 37 12 E
Zelenogradsk, *U.S.S.R.* **36** 54 53N 20 29 E
Zelenokumsk, *U.S.S.R.* **39** 44 24N 43 53 E
Zelënyy, *U.S.S.R.* **39** 48 6N 50 45 E
Zelhem, *Neths.* **16** 52 0N 6 21 E
Zell, *Baden-W., W. Germany* **31** 47 42N 7 50 E
Zell, *Rhld-Pfz., W. Germany* **31** 50 2N 7 11 E
Zell am See, *Austria* **33** 47 19N 12 47 E
Zella Mehlis, *E. Germany* **30** 50 40N 10 41 E
Zelzate, *Belgium* **17** 51 13N 3 47 E
Zembra, I., *Tunisia* **86** 37 5N 10 56 E
Zémio, *C.A.R.* **92** 5 2N 25 5 E
Zemlya Frantsa Iosifa, *Arctic* **144** 81 0N 55 0 E
Zemmora, *Algeria* **85** 35 44N 0 51 E
Zemmur, *W. Sahara* **84** 25 5N 12 0W
Zemoul, O. →, *Algeria* **84** 29 15N 7 0W
Zemst, *Belgium* **17** 50 59N 4 28 E
Zemun, *Yugoslavia* **33** 44 51N 20 25 E
Zengbe, *Cameroon* **91** 5 46N 13 4 E
Zengcheng, *China* **59** 23 13N 113 52 E
Zenica, *Yugoslavia* **33** 44 10N 17 57 E
Zenina, *Algeria* **85** 34 30N 2 37 E
Zentsūji, *Japan* **64** 34 14N 133 47 E
Zenza do Itombe, *Angola* **95** 9 16S 14 13 E
Žepče, *Yugoslavia* **33** 44 28N 18 2 E
Zeraf, Bahr ez →, *Sudan* **89** 9 42N 30 52 E
Zerbst, *E. Germany* **30** 51 59N 12 8 E
Zermatt, *Switz.* **31** 46 2N 7 46 E
Zernez, *Switz.* **31** 46 42N 10 7 E
Zernograd, *U.S.S.R.* **39** 46 52N 40 19 E
Zerqani, *Albania* **35** 41 30N 20 20 E
Zestafoni, *U.S.S.R.* **39** 42 6N 43 0 E
Zetel, *W. Germany* **30** 53 25N 7 57 E
Zetten, *Neths.* **16** 51 56N 5 44 E
Zeulenroda, *E. Germany* **30** 50 39N 12 0 E
Zeven, *W. Germany* **30** 53 17N 9 19 E
Zevenaar, *Neths.* **16** 51 56N 6 5 E
Zevenbergen, *Neths.* **17** 51 38N 4 37 E
Zévio, *Italy* **26** 45 23N 11 10 E
Zeya, *U.S.S.R.* **41** 53 48N 127 14 E
Zeya →, *U.S.S.R.* **41** 53 13N 127 35 E
Zêzere →, *Portugal* **23** 39 28N 8 20W
Zgierz, *Poland* **32** 51 50N 19 27 E
Zgorzelec, *Poland* **32** 51 10N 15 0 E
Zhabinka, *U.S.S.R.* **36** 52 13N 24 2 E
Zhailma, *U.S.S.R.* **40** 51 37N 61 33 E
Zhangbei, *China* **60** 41 10N 114 45 E
Zhangguangcai Ling, *China* **61** 45 0N 129 0 E
Zhanghua, *Taiwan* **59** 24 6N 120 29 E
Zhangjiakou, *China* **60** 40 48N 114 55 E
Zhangping, *China* **59** 25 17N 117 23 E
Zhangpu, *China* **59** 24 8N 117 35 E
Zhangwu, *China* **61** 42 43N 123 52 E
Zhangye, *China* **62** 38 50N 100 23 E
Zhangzhou, *China* **59** 24 30N 117 35 E
Zhanhua, *China* **61** 37 40N 118 8 E
Zhanjiang, *China* **59** 21 15N 110 20 E
Zhanyi, *China* **58** 25 38N 103 48 E
Zhanyu, *China* **61** 44 30N 122 30 E
Zhao Xian, *China* **60** 37 43N 114 45 E
Zhao'an, *China* **59** 23 41N 117 10 E
Zhaocheng, *China* **60** 36 22N 111 38 E
Zhaojue, *China* **58** 28 1N 102 49 E
Zhaoping, *China* **59** 24 11N 110 48 E
Zhaoqing, *China* **59** 23 0N 112 20 E
Zhaotong, *China* **58** 27 20N 103 44 E
Zhaoyuan, *Heilongjiang, China* **61** 45 27N 125 0 E
Zhaoyuan, *Shandong, China* **61** 37 20N 120 23 E
Zharkovskiy, *U.S.S.R.* **36** 55 56N 32 19 E
Zhashkov, *U.S.S.R.* **38** 49 15N 30 5 E
Zhashui, *China* **60** 33 40N 109 8 E
Zhdanov, *U.S.S.R.* **38** 47 5N 37 31 E
Zhecheng, *China* **60** 34 7N 115 20 E
Zhegao, *China* **59** 31 46N 117 45 E
Zhejiang □, *China* **59** 29 0N 120 0 E
Zheleznogorsk, *U.S.S.R.* **36** 52 22N 35 23 E
Zheleznogorsk-Ilimskiy, *U.S.S.R.* **41** 56 34N 104 8 E
Zheltyye Vody, *U.S.S.R.* **38** 48 21N 33 31 E
Zhen'an, *China* **60** 33 27N 109 9 E
Zhenfeng, *China* **58** 25 22N 105 40 E
Zheng'an, *China* **58** 28 32N 107 27 E
Zhengding, *China* **60** 38 8N 114 32 E
Zhenghe, *China* **59** 27 20N 118 50 E
Zhengyang, *China* **59** 32 37N 114 22 E
Zhengyangguan, *China* **59** 32 30N 116 29 E
Zhengzhou, *China* **60** 34 45N 113 34 E
Zhenhai, *China* **59** 29 59N 121 42 E
Zhenjiang, *China* **59** 32 11N 119 26 E
Zhenlai, *China* **61** 45 50N 123 5 E
Zhenning, *China* **58** 26 4N 105 45 E
Zhenping, *Henan, China* **60** 33 10N 112 16 E
Zhenping, *Shaanxi, China* **58** 31 59N 109 31 E
Zhenxiong, *China* **58** 27 27N 104 50 E
Zhenyuan, *Gansu, China* **60** 35 35N 107 30 E
Zhenyuan, *Guizhou, China* **58** 27 4N 108 21 E
Zherdevka, *U.S.S.R.* **37** 51 56N 41 29 E
Zherong, *China* **59** 27 15N 119 52 E
Zhidan, *China* **60** 36 48N 108 48 E
Zhigansk, *U.S.S.R.* **41** 66 48N 123 27 E
Zhigulevsk, *U.S.S.R.* **37** 53 28N 49 30 E
Zhijiang, *Hubei, China* **59** 30 28N 111 45 E
Zhijiang, *Hunan, China* **58** 27 27N 109 42 E
Zhijin, *China* **58** 26 37N 105 45 E
Zhirnovsk, *U.S.S.R.* **37** 50 57N 44 49 E
Zhitomir, *U.S.S.R.* **36** 50 20N 28 40 E
Zhizdra, *U.S.S.R.* **36** 53 45N 34 40 E
Zhlobin, *U.S.S.R.* **36** 52 55N 30 0 E
Zhmerinka, *U.S.S.R.* **38** 49 2N 28 2 E
Zhodino, *U.S.S.R.* **36** 54 5N 28 17 E
Zhokhova, Ostrov, *U.S.S.R.* **41** 76 4N 152 40 E
Zhong Xian, *China* **58** 30 21N 108 1 E
Zhongdian, *China* **58** 27 48N 99 42 E
Zhongdong, *China* **58** 22 48N 107 47 E
Zhongdu, *China* **58** 24 40N 109 40 E
Zhongning, *China* **60** 37 29N 105 40 E
Zhongshan, *Guangdong, China* **59** 22 26N 113 20 E
Zhongshan, *Guangxi Zhuangzu, China* **59** 24 29N 111 18 E
Zhongtiao Shan, *China* **60** 35 0N 111 10 E
Zhongwei, *China* **60** 37 30N 105 12 E
Zhongxiang, *China* **59** 31 12N 112 34 E
Zhongyang, *China* **60** 37 20N 111 11 E
Zhoucun, *China* **61** 36 47N 117 48 E
Zhouning, *China* **59** 27 12N 119 20 E
Zhoushan Dao, *China* **59** 28 5N 122 10 E
Zhouzhi, *China* **60** 34 10N 108 12 E
Zhovtnevoye, *U.S.S.R.* **38** 46 54N 32 3 E
Zhuanghe, *China* **61** 39 40N 123 0 E
Zhucheng, *China* **61** 36 0N 119 27 E
Zhugqu, *China* **60** 33 40N 104 30 E
Zhuhai, *China* **59** 22 15N 113 30 E
Zhuji, *China* **59** 29 40N 120 10 E
Zhukovka, *U.S.S.R.* **36** 53 35N 33 50 E
Zhumadian, *China* **60** 32 59N 114 2 E
Zhuo Xian, *China* **60** 39 28N 115 58 E
Zhuolu, *China* **60** 40 20N 115 12 E
Zhuozi, *China* **60** 41 0N 112 25 E
Zhupanovo, *U.S.S.R.* **41** 53 40N 159 52 E
Zhushan, *China* **59** 32 15N 110 13 E
Zhuxi, *China* **59** 32 25N 109 40 E
Zhuzhou, *China* **59** 27 49N 113 12 E
Zi Shui →, *China* **59** 28 40N 112 40 E
Ziarat, *Pakistan* **48** 30 25N 67 49 E
Zibo, *China* **61** 36 47N 118 3 E
Zichang, *China* **60** 37 18N 109 40 E
Zichem, *Belgium* **17** 51 2N 4 59 E
Zielona Góra, *Poland* **32** 51 57N 15 31 E
Zierikzee, *Neths.* **17** 51 40N 3 55 E
Ziesar, *E. Germany* **30** 52 16N 12 19 E
Zifta, *Egypt* **88** 30 43N 31 14 E
Zigey, *Chad* **87** 14 43N 15 50 E
Zigong, *China* **58** 29 15N 104 48 E
Zigui, *China* **59** 31 0N 110 40 E
Ziguinchor, *Senegal* **90** 12 35N 16 20W
Zihuatanejo, *Mexico* **126** 17 38N 101 33W
Zijin, *China* **59** 23 33N 115 8 E
Zikhron Ya'Aqov, *Israel* **44** 32 34N 34 56 E
Zile, *Turkey* **46** 40 15N 35 52 E
Žilina, *Czech.* **32** 49 12N 18 42 E
Zillah, *Libya* **86** 28 30N 17 33 E
Zillertaler Alpen, *Austria* **31** 47 6N 11 45 E
Zima, *U.S.S.R.* **41** 54 0N 102 5 E
Zimane, Adrar in, *Algeria* **85** 22 10N 4 30 E
Zimapán, *Mexico* **127** 20 54N 99 20W
Zimba, *Zambia* **93** 17 20S 26 11 E
Zimbabwe, *Zimb.* **93** 20 16S 30 54 E
Zimbabwe ■, *Africa* **93** 19 0S 30 0 E
Zimovniki, *U.S.S.R.* **39** 47 10N 42 25 E
Zinder, *Niger* **91** 13 48N 9 0 E
Zinga, *Tanzania* **93** 9 16S 38 49 E
Zingem, *Belgium* **17** 50 54N 3 40 E
Zingst, *E. Germany* **30** 54 24N 12 45 E
Ziniaré, *Burkina Faso* **91** 12 35N 1 18W
Zinkgruvan, *Sweden* **11** 58 50N 15 6 E
Zinnowitz, *E. Germany* **30** 54 5N 13 54 E
Zion, *U.S.A.* **119** 42 27N 87 50W
Zion Nat. Park, *U.S.A.* **123** 37 25N 112 50W
Zionsville, *U.S.A.* **119** 39 57N 86 16W
Zipaquirá, *Colombia* **134** 5 0N 74 0W
Zippori, *Israel* **44** 32 45N 35 16 E
Zirc, *Hungary* **33** 47 17N 17 42 E
Žiri, *Yugoslavia* **27** 46 5N 14 5 E
Žirje, *Yugoslavia* **27** 43 39N 15 42 E
Zirl, *Austria* **31** 47 17N 11 14 E
Zitácuaro, *Mexico* **126** 19 28N 100 21W
Zitava →, *Czech.* **33** 48 14N 18 21 E
Zittau, *E. Germany* **30** 50 54N 14 47 E
Zitundo, *Mozam.* **97** 26 48S 32 47 E
Živinice, *Yugoslavia* **33** 44 27N 18 36 E
Ziway, L., *Ethiopia* **89** 8 0N 38 50 E
Zixi, *China* **59** 27 45N 117 4 E
Zixing, *China* **59** 25 59N 113 21 E
Ziyang, *Shaanxi, China* **60** 32 32N 108 31 E
Ziyang, *Sichuan, China* **58** 30 6N 104 40 E
Ziyun, *China* **58** 25 45N 106 5 E
Ziz, Oued →, *Morocco* **84** 31 40N 4 15W
Zizhixian, *China* **59** 25 0N 111 47 E
Zizhong, *China* **58** 29 48N 104 47 E
Zlarin, *Yugoslavia* **27** 43 42N 15 49 E
Zlatar, *Yugoslavia* **27** 46 5N 16 3 E
Zlataritsa, *Bulgaria* **34** 43 2N 25 55 E
Zlatitsa, *Bulgaria* **34** 42 41N 24 7 E
Zlatograd, *Bulgaria* **35** 41 22N 25 7 E
Zlatoust, *U.S.S.R.* **40** 55 10N 59 40 E
Zletovo, *Yugoslavia* **35** 41 59N 22 17 E
Zlin = Gottwaldov, *Czech.* **32** 49 14N 17 40 E
Zlītan, *Libya* **86** 32 32N 14 35 E
Złocieniec, *Poland* **32** 53 30N 16 1 E
Złoczew, *Poland* **32** 51 24N 18 35 E
Złotoryja, *Poland* **32** 51 8N 15 55 E
Złotów, *Poland* **32** 53 22N 17 2 E
Zmeinogorsk, *U.S.S.R.* **40** 51 10N 82 13 E
Żmigród, *Poland* **32** 51 28N 16 53 E
Znamenka, *U.S.S.R.* **38** 48 45N 32 30 E
Znamensk, *U.S.S.R.* **36** 54 37N 21 17 E
Żnin, *Poland* **32** 52 51N 17 44 E
Znojmo, *Czech.* **32** 48 50N 16 2 E
Zoar, *S. Africa* **96** 33 30S 21 26 E
Zobia, *Zaïre* **92** 3 0N 25 59 E
Zoetermeer, *Neths.* **16** 52 3N 4 30 E
Zogang, *China* **58** 29 55N 97 42 E
Zogno, *Italy* **26** 45 49N 9 41 E
Zogqên, *China* **58** 32 13N 98 47 E
Zolder, *Belgium* **17** 51 1N 5 19 E
Zolochev, *U.S.S.R.* **36** 49 45N 24 51 E
Zolotonosha, *U.S.S.R.* **38** 49 39N 32 5 E
Zomba, *Malawi* **93** 15 22S 35 19 E
Zomergem, *Belgium* **17** 51 7N 3 33 E
Zongo, *Zaïre* **94** 4 20N 18 35 E
Zonguldak, *Turkey* **38** 41 28N 31 50 E
Zonhoven, *Belgium* **17** 50 59N 5 23 E
Zonza, *France* **21** 41 45N 9 11 E
Zorgo, *Burkina Faso* **91** 12 15N 0 35W
Zorita, *Spain* **23** 39 17N 5 39W
Zorritos, *Peru* **136** 3 43S 80 40W
Zorzor, *Liberia* **90** 7 46N 9 28W
Zossen, *E. Germany* **30** 52 13N 13 28 E
Zottegem, *Belgium* **17** 50 52N 3 48 E
Zou Xiang, *China* **60** 35 30N 116 58 E
Zouar, *Chad* **87** 20 30N 16 32 E
Zouérate, *Mauritania* **84** 22 44N 12 21W
Zousfana, O. →, *Algeria* **85** 31 28N 2 17W
Zoushan Dao, *China* **59** 30 5N 122 10 E
Zoutkamp, *Neths.* **16** 53 20N 6 18 E
Zrenjanin, *Yugoslavia* **33** 45 22N 20 23 E
Zuarungu, *Ghana* **91** 10 49N 0 46W
Zuba, *Nigeria* **91** 9 11N 7 12 E
Zubayr, *Yemen* **89** 15 3N 42 10 E
Zubia, *Spain* **23** 37 8N 3 33W
Zubtsov, *U.S.S.R.* **36** 56 10N 34 34 E
Zudáñez, *Bolivia* **137** 19 6S 64 44W
Zuénoula, *Ivory C.* **90** 7 34N 6 3W
Zuera, *Spain* **24** 41 51N 0 49W
Zuetina, *Libya* **86** 30 58N 20 7 E
Zufar, *Oman* **45** 17 40N 54 0 E
Zug, *Switz.* **31** 47 10N 8 31 E
Zugdidi, *U.S.S.R.* **39** 42 30N 41 55 E
Zugersee, *Switz.* **31** 47 7N 8 35 E
Zugspitze, *W. Germany* **31** 47 25N 10 59 E
Zuid-Holland □, *Neths.* **16** 52 0N 4 35 E
Zuidbeveland, *Neths.* **17** 51 30N 3 50 E
Zuidbroek, *Neths.* **16** 53 10N 6 52 E
Zuidelijk-Flevoland, *Neths.* **16** 52 22N 5 22 E
Zuidhorn, *Neths.* **16** 53 15N 6 23 E
Zuidlaarder meer, *Neths.* **16** 53 8N 6 42 E
Zuidlaren, *Neths.* **16** 53 6N 6 42 E
Zuidwolde, *Neths.* **16** 52 40N 6 26 E
Zújar, *Spain* **25** 37 34N 2 50W
Zújar →, *Spain* **23** 39 1N 5 47W
Zújar, Pantano del, *Spain* **23** 38 55N 5 35W
Zula, *Ethiopia* **89** 15 17N 39 40 E
Zulia □, *Venezuela* **134** 10 0N 72 10W
Zulpich, *W. Germany* **30** 50 41N 6 38 E
Zumaya, *Spain* **24** 43 19N 2 15W
Zumbo, *Mozam.* **93** 15 35S 30 26 E
Zummo, *Nigeria* **91** 9 51N 12 59 E
Zumpango, *Mexico* **127** 19 48N 99 6W
Zundert, *Neths.* **17** 51 28N 4 39 E
Zungeru, *Nigeria* **91** 9 48N 6 8 E
Zunhua, *China* **61** 40 18N 117 58 E
Zuni, *U.S.A.* **123** 35 7N 108 57W
Zunyi, *China* **58** 27 42N 106 53 E
Zuoquan, *China* **60** 37 5N 113 22 E
Zuozhou, *China* **58** 22 42N 107 27 E
Županja, *Yugoslavia* **33** 45 4N 18 43 E
Zurich, *Canada* **108** 43 26N 81 37W
Zürich, *Switz.* **31** 47 22N 8 32 E
Zürich □, *Switz.* **31** 47 26N 8 40 E
Zürichsee, *Switz.* **31** 47 18N 8 40 E
Zuromin, *Poland* **32** 53 4N 19 51 E
Zuru, *Nigeria* **91** 11 20N 5 11 E
Žut, *Yugoslavia* **27** 43 52N 15 17 E
Zutendaal, *Belgium* **17** 50 56N 5 35 E
Zutphen, *Neths.* **16** 52 9N 6 12 E
Zuwārah, *Libya* **86** 32 58N 12 1 E
Zuyevka, *U.S.S.R.* **37** 58 27N 51 10 E
Žužemberk, *Yugoslavia* **27** 45 52N 14 56 E
Zvenigorodka, *U.S.S.R.* **38** 49 4N 30 56 E
Zverinogolovskoye, *U.S.S.R.* **40** 54 23N 64 40 E
Zvezdets, *Bulgaria* **34** 42 6N 27 26 E
Zvishavane, *Zimb.* **93** 20 17S 30 2 E
Zvolen, *Czech.* **32** 48 33N 19 10 E
Zvonce, *Yugoslavia* **33** 42 57N 22 34 E
Zvornik, *Yugoslavia* **33** 44 26N 19 7 E
Zwaag, *Neths.* **16** 52 40N 5 4 E
Zwanenburg, *Neths.* **16** 52 23N 4 45 E
Zwarte Meer, *Neths.* **16** 52 38N 5 57 E
Zwarte Waler, *Neths.* **16** 52 39N 6 1 E
Zwartemeer, *Neths.* **16** 52 43N 7 2 E
Zwartsluis, *Neths.* **16** 52 39N 6 4 E
Zwedru = Tchien, *Liberia* **90** 5 59N 8 15W
Zweibrücken, *W. Germany* **31** 49 15N 7 20 E
Zwenkau, *E. Germany* **30** 51 13N 12 19 E
Zwevegem, *Belgium* **17** 50 48N 3 20 E
Zwickau, *E. Germany* **30** 50 43N 12 30 E
Zwiesel, *W. Germany* **31** 49 1N 13 14 E
Zwijnaarde, *Belgium* **17** 51 0N 3 43 E
Zwijndrecht, *Belgium* **17** 51 13N 4 20 E
Zwijndrecht, *Neths.* **16** 51 50N 4 39 E
Zwischenahn, *W. Germany* **30** 53 12N 8 1 E
Zwolle, *Neths.* **16** 52 31N 6 6 E
Zwolle, *U.S.A.* **121** 31 38N 93 38W
Zymoetz →, *Canada* **110** 54 33N 128 31W
Żyrardów, *Poland* **32** 52 3N 20 28 E
Zyrya, *U.S.S.R.* **39** 40 20N 50 15 E
Zyryanka, *U.S.S.R.* **41** 65 45N 150 51 E
Zyryanovsk, *U.S.S.R.* **40** 49 43N 84 20 E

See inside front cover for detailed coverage of Canada.
150°
135°
120°
105°
90°
75°
60°
45°
30°
15°
0°
102–103
110–111
104–105
116–117
118–119
122–123
124–125
120–121
114–115
126–127
128–129
134–135
136–137
138–139
140–141
142
8
14
15
12–13
16–17
18–19
20–21
22–23
24–25
84–85
90–91
Arctic Circle
Tropic of Cancer
Equator
Tropic of Capricorn
ATLANTIC
OCEAN
130–131
PACIFIC OCEAN
66–67
The page numbers refer to the World map section.